HEPPLE AND MATTHEWS'

TORT
CASES AND MATERIALS

SIXTH EDITION

By

MARTIN MATTHEWS
JONATHAN MORGAN
COLM O'CINNEIDE

Consultant editors

SIR BOB HEPPLE QC
DAVID HOWARTH MP

OXFORD
UNIVERSITY PRESS

OXFORD
UNIVERSITY PRESS

Great Clarendon Street, Oxford OX2 6DP

Oxford University Press is a department of the University of Oxford.
It furthers the University's objective of excellence in research, scholarship,
and education by publishing worldwide in

Oxford New York

Auckland Cape Town Dar es Salaam Hong Kong Karachi
Kuala Lumpur Madrid Melbourne Mexico City Nairobi
New Delhi Shanghai Taipei Toronto

With offices in

Argentina Austria Brazil Chile Czech Republic France Greece
Guatemala Hungary Italy Japan Poland Portugal Singapore
South Korea Switzerland Thailand Turkey Ukraine Vietnam

Oxford is a registered trade mark of Oxford University Press
in the UK and in certain other countries

Published in the United States
by Oxford University Press Inc., New York

British Library Cataloguing in Publication Data

Data available

Library of Congress Cataloging in Publication Data

Matthews, M. H. (Martin Hubie)
  Hepple & Matthews' tort cases and materials / By Martin Matthews, Jonathan Morgan, Colm
O'Cinneide ; Consultant editors Bob Hepple, David Howarth.—6th ed.
    p. cm.
  Rev. ed. of : Hepple, Howarth and Matthews' tort / by D.R. Howarth and
J.A. O'Sullivan. 5th ed. 2000.
  ISBN 978-0-19-920384-0
  1. Torts—Great Britain—Digests.   2. Law reports, digests, etc.—Great Britain.   I. Morgan,
Jonathan.   II. O'Cinneide, Colm.   III. Howarth, David, 1958- Hepple, Howarth and Matthews'
tort.   IV. Title.   V. Title: Hepple and Matthews' tort cases and materials.
  KD1949.M375 2008
346.4103—dc22   2008034303

Typeset by Newgen Imaging Systems (P) Ltd., Chennai, India
Printed in Great Britain
on acid-free paper by
Ashford Colour Press Ltd, Gosport, Hampshire

ISBN 978-0-19-920384-0

10 9 8 7 6 5 4 3 2 1

PREFACE

Tort continues to be a particularly dynamic and fast-moving department of the law. In the eight years since the last edition of this book, tort law's development has continued apace, above all under the influence of the Human Rights Act 1998, which came into force just as that fifth edition was published. The current edition attempts to take stock of those developments, although the student of the law can in particular expect further consideration of the impact of the ECHR upon the common law in the years to come.

Tort law has also changed rapidly in areas as yet untouched by the human rights revolution. For example, the law on causation has been considered by the House of Lords on a number of occasions since 2000, especially as regards to asbestos-related diseases. It is not an everyday occurrence to hear questions raised at Prime Minister's Question Time about a negligence case, but the House of Lords' majority decision in *Barker v Corus (UK) plc* [2006] 3 All ER 785, [2006] UKHL 20 (p. 358, post) proved so controversial that Parliament moved swiftly to reverse it (with retrospective effect) in what became s. 3 of the Compensation Act 2006 (p. 324, post). The media has also made much of the 'compensation culture', which has received judicial notice in cases such as *Tomlinson v Congleton Borough Council* [2003] 3 All ER 1122, [2003] UKHL 47 (p. 574, post). Whether the alleged tidal wave of compensation claims represents empirical reality or simply a self-sustaining public perception is, however, less clear.

The authors are extremely grateful for the contributions of the consultant editors, Sir Bob Hepple QC, and David Howarth MP, and would also like to thank Sarah Viner, Gareth Malna, and all at OUP for their guidance, efficiency, and support. Martin Matthews would also like to thank Alex Cook for assistance with proof-reading, while Colm O'Cinneide would like to thank Catriona Mace for her patience.

The book attempts to state the law as at it stood on 8 May 2008, although we have been able to insert some reference to later developments at proof stage including an Appendix which summarises the proposals made in the *Law Commission Consultation paper No. 187, Administrative Redress: Public Bodies and the Citizen,* published on July 3rd 2008.

M. H. Matthews
Jonathan Morgan
Colm O'Cinneide
Oxford, Cambridge, and London
July 8th 2008

CONTENTS

PART ONE   PRINCIPLES AND POLICY OF NEGLIGENCE

PART TWO   SPECIFIC DUTIES AND INTERESTS

PART THREE   LOSS DISTRIBUTION

ACKNOWLEDGMENTS

The publishers and authors wish to thank the following for permission to reprint material from the sources indicated. The publishers would also be pleased to hear from those copyright holders from whom permission has been sought but not yet received.

Professor P. S. Atiyah: *Vicarious Liability in the Law of Torts* (1967); and with Professor Peter Cane: *Accidents, Compensations and the Law*, 6th edn. (1999).

AXA Insurance UK plc, for permission to use the specimen defamation insurance policy of the former Guardian Royal Exchange Insurance Group (which was acquired by AXA in 1999).

Butterworths (Australia): Australian Law Reports: *Todorovic v Waller* (1981) 37 ALR 481.

Cambridge University Press: T. Weir: *Cambridge Law Journal*, 1998, p. 243.

Clarendon Press: Professor Donald Harris, *Compensation and Support for Illness and Injury* (Oxford, 1984), pp. 317–21; 321–323, 327–8; Professor Hazel Genn, *Hard Bargaining: Out of Court Settlement in Personal Injury Actions* (Oxford, 1987), pp. 13–15, 163–169.

Commission of the European Communities: R. Freeman, S. Thomson and J. Meltzer; Lovells LLP: Lovells, *Product Liability in the European Union: A Report for the European Commission*, MARKT/2001/11/D, http://ec.europa.eu/enterprise/regulation/goods/docs/liability/studies/lovells-study_en.pdf

Federal Communications Law Journal for D. Vick and L. Macpherson (1997) 49 *Federal Communications L.J.* 621.

Hansard: Minutes of Evidence to the Select Committee on Home Affairs, Tuesday 17 March 1998.

Hart Publishing: Professor Hazel Genn, *Paths to Justice: What People Do and Think About Going to Law* (1999), pp. 317–321, 161–162; Professor Richard Lewis, 'Tort Law in Practice: Appearance and Reality in Reforming Periodical Payments of Damages', in J. Neyers, E. Chamberlain and S. Pitel (eds.), *Emerging Issues in Tort Law* (2007), pp. 487–492.

The Controller of Her Majesty's Stationery Office: Extracts from official reports Cmnd. 5012; Cmnd. 7054; Cm. 394; Cm. 1102; Law Commission No. 21; Law Commission Consultation Paper No. 140; Law Commission Consultation Paper No. 144; Law Commission Consultation Paper No. 147; Law Commission Consultation Paper No. 160; Law Commission Consultation Paper No 187; Law Commission Discussion Paper, *Monetary Remedies in Public Law*: Pearson Committee Report, para. 1643; Lord Chancellor's Department, Civil Justice Review Consultation Paper; Criminal Injuries Compensation Authority: Notes on the Scheme 2001.

Incorporated Council of Law Reporting for England and Wales: *The Law Reports; The Weekly Law Reports*: with particular reference to the following cases: *McKennitt v Ash* [2007] 3 WLR 194; *Gleaner Co Ltd v Abrahams* [2004] 1 AC 628; *Burstein v Times Newspapers Ltd* [2001] 1 WLR 579; *A (a child) v Ministry of Defence* [2005] QB 183.

The Law Book Co. Ltd.: Professor John G. Fleming: *The Law of Torts*, 9th edn. (1998)

LBC Information Services for D. Howarth (2000) 8 *Tort L Rev* 85.

Lloyds of London Press Ltd.: *Lloyd's Law Reports*, 1971, vol. 2, pp. 411, 412; 1998, vol. 2, p 97; 1998, vol. 2, p. 262; 1999, vol. 2, p. 1.

Professor M. A. Millner: *Negligence in Modern Law* (1967).

Motor Insurers' Bureau: *Notes* and *Frequently Asked Questions* concerning the MIB agreement, from the website www.mib.org.uk;

Oxford University Press: Professor Donald Harris et al.: *Compensation and Support for Illness and Injury* © Social Science Research Council, 1984, pp. 317–323, 327; Professor Hazel Genn: *Hard Bargaining* © Economic and Social Research Council, 1987, pp. 11–13, 163–169.

Reed Elsevier (UK) Limited, trading as LexisNexis, for all statutory material and for the following cases as reported in the All England Law Reports, the All England Reporter and the Butterworths Human Rights Cases: *D v East Berkshire Community Health NHS Trust* [2005] 2 All ER 443; *Brooks v Metropolitan Police Commissioner* [2005] 2 All ER 489; *Gorringe v Calderdale Metropolitan Borough Council* [2004] 2 All ER 326; *McFarlane v Tayside Health Board* [1999] 4 All ER 961; *Rees v Darlington Memorial Hospital NHS Trust* [2003] 4 All ER 987; *Customs and Excise Commissioners v Barclays Bank plc* [2006] 4 All ER 256; *Hatton v Sutherland* [2002] 2 All ER 1; *Fairchild v Glenhaven Funeral Services Ltd* [2002] 3 All ER 305; *Barker v Corus (UK) Ltd* [2006] 3 All ER 785; *Gregg v Scott* [2005] 4 All ER 812; *Chester v Afshar* [2004] 4 All ER 587; *Lamb v London Borough of Camden* [1981] 2 All ER 408; *Lagdon v O'Connor* [2004] 1 All ER 277; *Vellino v Chief Constable of Greater Manchester* [2002] 3 All ER 78; *Severn Water Ltd v Barnes* [2004] All ER (D) 179 (May) ([2004] EWCA Civ 570); *Kuddus v Chief Constable of Leicestershire Constabulary* [2001] 3 All ER 193; *Heil v Rankin* [2000] 3 All ER 138; *Tomlinson v Congleton Borough Council* [003] 3 All ER 1122; *A v National Blood Authority* [001] 3 All ER 289; *Mirvahedy v Henley* 2003] 2 All ER 401; *Cullen v Chief Constable of the Royal Ulster Constabulary* [2004] 2 All ER 237; *Wainwright v Home Office* [2003] 4 All ER 969; *Marcic v Thames Water Utilities* [2004] 1 All ER 135; *Transco Plc v Stockport Metropolitan Borough Council* [2004] 1 All ER 589; *Revenue and Customs Commissioners v Total Network SL* [2008] 2 All ER 413; *OBG Ltd v Allan* [2007] 4 All ER 545; *Standard Chartered Bank v Pakistan National Shipping Corp (No 2)* [2003] 1 All ER 173; *Jameel v Wall Street Journal Europe Sprl* [2006] 4 All ER 1279; *Hulton & Co v Jones* [1908–10] All ER Rep 29; *Bunt v Tilley* [2006] 3 All ER 336; *Tse Wai Chun v Cheng* (2000) 10 BHRC 525; *Kiam v MGN Ltd* [2002] 2 All ER 219; *Greene v Associated Newspapers Ltd* [2005] 1 All ER 30; *Douglas and others v Hello! Ltd* [2001] 2 All ER 289; *Campbell v Mirror Group Newspapers Ltd* [2004] 2 All ER 995; *Douglas and others v Hello! Ltd (No 3)* [2005] 4 All ER 128; *Dubai Aluminium Co Ltd v Salaam* [2003] 1 All ER 97; *Lister v Hesley Hall Ltd* [2001] 2 All ER 769; *Fytche v Wincanton Logistics plc* [2004] 4 All ER 221; *Heaton v Axa Equity and Law Life Assurance Society plc* [2002] 2 All ER 961; *Stovin v Wise* [1996] 3 All ER 801; *Capital & Counties Plc v Hampshire County Council* [1997] 2 All ER 865. All are reproduced by permission of Reed Elsevier (UK) Limited, trading as LexisNexis.

Scottish Council of Law Reporting: *Session Cases.*

Stevens and Sons Ltd.: Professor Jane Stapleton; Professor Glanville Williams: *Law Quarterly Review*, 1988, vol. 104, pp. 392–393, 404, 405; 1961, vol. 77, p. 196.

Sweet & Maxwell Ltd. and editors: *Salmond and Heuston on Torts*, 21st edn, pp. 40, 144, 443; *Winfield and Jolowicz on Tort*, 13th edn, p. 157; *HL v UK* (2005) 40 EHRR 32 [89]-[91]; *CC v AB* [2007] Entertainment and Media Law Reports 11 [25]-[30].

Times Publishing Co. Ltd: *Times Law Reports.*

Wiley-Blackwell Publishing: Modern Law Review Ltd.: Mr. A. Evans, Estate O. Kahn-Freund. Dr. P. M. North, Mr. P. J. Pace, Mr. D. M. A. Strachan, Professor J. Stapleton, Professor Glanville Williams, Professor R. Lewis and Mr. D. Howarth MP: *Modern Law Review*, 1982, vol. 45, p. 331; 1951, vol. 14, pp. 505–506; 1966, vol. 29, p. 31; 1977, vol. 40, pp. 141, 151–153; 1970, vol. 33, 386, p. 391; 1995, vol. 58, 820 at pp. 821–823, 843–45; 1960 vol. 23, p. 233; 2006, vol. 69, 419, pp. 422–5; 2005, vol. 68, 195, pp. 231–2.

Professor Glanville Williams: 'Two Cases of False Imprisonment', in *Law, Justice and Equity* (1967), chapter 5, p. 51; and (1951) 4 *Current LP*, p. 137.

TABLE OF CASES

Page numbers printed in **bold** indicate where the facts of the case are set out in part or full.

TABLE OF STATUTES

Page numbers printed in **bold** type indicate where the Statute is set out in part or full.

TABLE OF ABBREVIATIONS

Atiyah—Atiyah's Accidents, Compensation and the Law, 6th edn by P. Cane (London, Butterworths, 1999)

Carty—An Analysis of the Economic Torts by H. Carty (Oxford, 2001)

Clerk & Lindsell—Clerk & Lindsell on Torts, 19th edn, general editors A. M. Dugdale and M. A.Jones (London, Sweet & Maxwell, 2006)

Conaghan and Mansell—The Wrongs of Tort by J. Conaghan and W. Mansell, 2nd edn (London, Pluto Press, 1999)

Fleming—The Law of Torts by J. Fleming, 9th edn (Sydney, LBC Information Services, 1998)

Glanville Williams—Joint Torts and Contributory Negligence, by G. L. Williams (London, Stevens, 1951)

Harris et al—Compensation and Support for Illness and Injury by D. Harris *et al.*, Oxford Socio-Legal Studies (Oxford, Clarendon Press, 1984)

Harris, Remedies—Remedies in Contract and Tort by D. Harris, D. Campbell, and R. Halson, 2nd edn (London, Butterworths, 2002)

Howarth –Textbook on Tort by D. Howarth (London, Butterworths, 1995)

Markesinis and Deakin—Markesinis and Deakin's Tort Law by S. Deakin, A. Johnston, and B. Markesinis, 6th edn (Oxford, Clarendon Press, 2007)

Pearson Commission—Report of the Royal Commission on Civil Liability and Compensation for Personal Injury Cmnd. 7054 (London, HMSO, 1978)

Salmond & Heuston—Salmond and Heuston on the Law of Torts, by R.F.V. Heuston and R.A. Buckley, 21st edn (London, Sweet & Maxwell, 1996)

Smith & Hogan—Smith and Hogan, Criminal Law, by D. Ormerod, 11th edn (London, Butterworths, 2005)

Steele—Tort Law Text, Cases and Materials by J. Steele (Oxford, Oxford University Press, 2007)

Stevens—Torts and Rights by R. Stevens (Oxford, Oxford University Press, 2007)

Street—Street on Torts, by J. Murphy, 12th edn (Oxford, Oxford University Press, 2007)

Williams & Hepple—Foundations of the Law of Tort by Glanville Williams and B.A.Hepple, 2nd edn (London, Butterworths, 1984)

Winfield & Jolowicz—Winfield & Jolowicz on Tort, by W.V.H. Rogers, 17th edn (London, Sweet & Maxwell, 2006)

INTRODUCTION

I have gathered a posie of other men's flowers and nothing but the thread that binds them is my own.

MONTAIGNE

The materials in this book are concerned with the protection against extra-contractual harm afforded by the English common law and statutory extensions of the common law. The primary task of the law of tort is to define the circumstances in which a person whose interests have been harmed by another may seek compensation. Scots law, more accurately than English law, calls this branch of the law reparation. The name given to it by most civil law systems is delict which, like the old Norman French word 'tort', simply means a wrong.

But tort actions have any number of other functions. They can sometimes be used as an alternative to the law of contract where a person has relied on a promise (e.g. to do work carefully) or to supplement the law of contract (e.g. where lying induces a person to make a contract). Torts relating to wrongful interference with goods are useful appendages to property law and restitution. An award of damages for tort may have an admonitory effect; an injunction granted to stop a threatened or continuing tort (e.g. nuisance, or inducing breach of contract) may act as a specific deterrent. Tort law may also be used as a vehicle for determining rights. Disputed possession of land may be tested through an action for trespass; the misappropriation of chattels is peculiarly dealt with in English law through the tort of conversion, which is primarily concerned with questions of title, although the ultimate remedy is to compensate the owner for his loss. Important questions of civil liberty and human rights may be tested by an action for nominal damages (e.g. trespass to the person; trespass to land; or trespass to goods, such as the seizure of a passport).

These various functions of the law of tort make it particularly difficult to present a rational or logical classification of the subject. The lawyer in a civil law system does not face exactly this problem, largely because questions of title to property are not dealt with through the law of delict, but by means of the vindicatory action of the owner, that is, as a part of property law. Infringements of the citizen's constitutional rights (rather than liberties) are a part of a relatively distinct body of public law. Even in the uncodified hybrid systems (like Roman-Dutch law and Scots law) there is a body of general principle, traceable to the Roman law of Justinian as received in medieval Europe, which gives the law of delict an inner coherence and unity. This is a quality which the English law of tort still lacks, although several attempts have been made by writers and judges to lay down certain general propositions. Of these attempts, Pollock and Winfield's suggested principle that the infliction of harm is tortious unless justified and Lord Atkin's famous principle of a duty of care to one's neighbours stand out as landmarks. In the 1970s there were judicial attempts to make the 'neighbour' principle apply in all situations unless there was a policy justification for excluding it, an attempt at definition which fell to the re-introduction of a 'proximity' requirement in the

1980s. More recently, the courts have propounded the idea that there should potentially be liability, regardless of 'lack of proximity', whenever the defendant has 'assumed responsibility' for the relevant aspect of the claimant's welfare. These attempts to find a single unifying principle have often raised yet more questions, for example, what conduct is 'justified', who is my 'neighbour' to whom a duty of care is owed, what should judicial 'policy' be in regard to matters such as liability for omissions or for economic loss, and what counts as an 'assumption of responsibility' when the defendant claims subjectively to have done no such thing? These further questions often lead to the modification or abandonment of the general principle, especially if it is unclear to judges precisely where the general principle is leading. In these frequent periods of retrenchment the courts often resort to narrowing techniques of interpretation, such as insisting that the law expand 'incrementally' or 'by analogy with existing categories'.

The really striking and all-important development has been the emergence of negligence and its subsequent octopus-like spread into the waters once occupied by older torts such as trespass and defamation and its constant interaction with contract law. The struggle to establish new duty-situations in negligence has revealed both the flexible, open-ended nature of the tort and the objections to letting it apply in all situations without modification or limitation (e.g. in regard to the liability of public authorities, psychiatric damage, and pure economic loss).

Nevertheless, the imperial progress of negligence—dare we call it 'neglomania'—is at least partly the result of the simplicity and moral attractiveness of its basic principle, which is, in the words of a television commercial advertising legal assistance for accident victims, 'where there's blame, there's a claim'. Negligence is liability for *fault*. It requires those who have injured others by acting badly to compensate those whom they have injured. The concept of fault in use in negligence is admittedly largely an objective one—it is faulty to have acted in a way in which a reasonable person would not have acted at the time—so that it is much wider in scope than conscious wrongdoing. The main complications arise, however, when one asks more probing questions. The most fundamental question of all is under what circumstances should people be allowed to cause harm by acting in an objectively faulty way—in which, for example, the law should only interfere when the conduct was intentionally wrong, or in which the law should not interfere at all. This is the question of the 'existence' of a 'duty of care' (chap. 2). For historical and procedural reasons, this question has often been conflated with other questions, such as whether it is even remotely plausible to say that the defendant was at fault (e.g. if no harm was foreseeable at all at the time by a reasonable person), and whether someone else is so much more clearly responsible for the harm than the defendant that the defendant's acts should count as too remote (the 'proximity' issue). Even when separated from those other questions, a large number of considerations are brought into play in deciding the 'duty' question—including whether the form of loss deserves to be protected at all (chap. 3 and chap. 4), whether the law should be so intrusive as to condemn those who merely fail to help fellow citizens already in trouble, and whether the defendant deserves special protection (e.g. because it is a branch of government; see chap. 3).

The duty question is far from the only complexity in negligence—issues of the standards of care required (e.g. should there be special requirements placed on professionals (chap. 5)), the need to show factual causation of the damage and then legal causation (should the damage be ascribed to the fault of the defendant in the light of the other causes of the damage) (chap. 6), and also to specify the loss (chap. 8) take on great significance. Such complications are only to be expected when a moral principle, such as the fault principle, no matter how simple in appearance, is translated into legal terms.

On the other hand, several objections have been raised against the fault principle itself, both by those who advocate liability without fault ('strict' liability) and those who advocate no liability. These objections usually complain that in reality the tort of negligence does not require the wrongdoers to pay, but instead, other people end up paying. Critics point, for example, to vicarious liability, the doctrine that often obliges employers to pay compensation for the torts of their employees (chap. 18) and insurance (chap. 20). Other objections amount to claiming that the legal standard for fault counts as fault acts or omissions that are too trivial to have any moral force.

It would be a mistake, however, to overstate these objections. Vicarious liability, for example, is an attempt, perhaps too crude at times, to attribute responsibility to organisations rather than individuals. In an age of organisations, to fail to define the circumstances in which blame can be attributed to organisations would be to allow much faulty behaviour to go untouched by the law. In addition, vicarious liability gives organisations incentives to reduce the risk of harm. As for insurance, it is often forgotten that, in respect of small compensation payments, insurance is merely a form of deferred payment, since the insurance company will recover the payment in the form of future increased premiums. As the costs of collecting and processing information fall, it may become more worthwhile for insurance companies to individualise premiums. Insurance may only act to spread the loss beyond the insured defendant to all the defendant's fellow customers of the insurance company when the amount of compensation is very large and unlikely to be recovered in the defendant's premiums. Even then, the increased premiums may act as a partial deterrent.

Furthermore, the justification for the fault principle goes beyond giving a reason why faulty defendants should pay compensation but non-faulty defendants should not pay. It also includes the point that *claimants* have no legitimate expectation of receiving compensation from others for their misfortunes unless someone else was at fault. Complaints about whether the compensation really moves from a faulty party attacks only the first point, not the second.

Objections based on the content of the fault standard—whether it is right to count momentary inadvertence as fault, for example—are important, but they depend on the specific content of the law, on what the law counts as reasonable and unreasonable conduct. These questions are particularly acute in the field of professional negligence. The loud lobbies calling, for example, for the medical profession or the National Health Service to be given protection from negligence claims should be seen in the light of the standards, arguably extremely favourable to professionals, set by the law and in the light of the scheme to be established under the NHS Redress Act 2006, noted p. 168, post. Further questions have to be asked by those wishing to understand the aims and future of tort law, such as, what is the effect of granting or denying the claimant compensation, as the case may be, what other sources of compensation are available to her, how is this loss absorbed, either by the group to which the claimant (e.g. houseowners) or the defendant (e.g. motorists or employers or manufacturers) belongs, or by taxpayers, and how is the spreading of that loss administered (e.g. through private insurance or a form of social security)? It means taking into account the reality of insurance and the various other methods of compensation which exist. These questions are taken up in the chapters which follow on damages (chap. 8) and loss distribution (chaps. 18–20).

If, as was suggested earlier, the primary function of tort law is to define the circumstances in which a court should order compensation for harm, a central question is what are the main interests which may be harmed? A textbook which aims to set out these interests in detail might contain a number of divisions such as (i) interests in personal security; (ii) interests in one's own property (here distinguishing land and chattels); (iii) interests in another's life (e.g. a bread-winner or employee); (iv) interests in another's property (e.g. a car hirer's interest in the car she has hired); (v) interests of a purely economic nature (e.g. loss of production through a strike, competition by a rival trader); (vi) interests in reputation (protected by the torts of libel and slander); and (vii) interests in privacy (a nascent interest only partially protected by some existing actions, see chap. 17). A sourcebook, in the existing state of English law, cannot make these detailed classifications for the simple reason that several of these interests are discussed interchangeably in many of the cases. This is particularly true of interests in persons and property (Lord Atkin's 'duty' test clearly applies to both). The limited acceptance by the judiciary of duty-situations in the case of negligent interference with pure economic interests (chap. 4) cannot realistically be explained in terms of the absence of foresight. The question is sometimes confused by calling this 'pecuniary' loss and saying that there is no obvious or intrinsic reason why this should be differently treated from other kinds of loss. Of course, all compensation is 'pecuniary' in the sense that the harm to the interest affected must be translated into money terms. The real distinction is between the different *interests* which the law seeks to protect, and not between the money terms in which those interests are compensated for harm.

The interests which the law protects are neither static nor rigidly defined. The law even now is an amalgam of rules and principles developed at different times for different purposes. When agriculture was the dominant economic activity, it was interests in land, the predominant economic asset, which were regarded as meriting the greatest degree of protection. They were vindicated through the writ of trespass. So important were the interests in land that very little attention was paid to the quality of the defendant's behaviour. Unless they were not masters of their own volition, they were liable for the act of trespass irrespective of their mental state or the consequences. The need to restore law and order after the ruinous Barons' Wars meant that trespass to the person (particularly assault and battery) and trespass to goods were used as devices to suppress feuding. These wrongs also did not rest on any notion of fault, although, as Winfield showed, liability was never absolute. Reputation was another interest which received early protection, on the basis of strict liability; here the social need was to provide a legal alternative to duelling.

The rise of industrial activity, with the consequent proliferation of dangerous machinery, railways, road traffic, and polluting activities, brought other interests to the fore. Interests in personal security became more salient. The interests of entrepreneurs often ran counter to those of the people whom their activities hurt: their workers, the consumers of their products, travellers on their railways, and so on. A balance was struck by the judges: there was to be no liability without fault. This principle was not established overnight or without exceptions; indeed, it was only in 1959 that it was finally established that the claimant in a personal injuries case must prove fault and there are still exceptional situations in which liability for personal injuries is strict, such as where a lamp overhanging a highway falls on a passerby (public nuisance), dangerous escapes from land and damage by certain classes of animal. Secondly, an important class of claimants, that is employees, were denied compensation from their employers when they were injured by the fault of fellow-employees. This doctrine of common employment, judicially recognised in 1837, was qualified by statute in 1880 and by-passed by the Workmen's Compensation Acts after 1897, but it remained a part of the law until scrapped by Parliament in 1948. In the changed political, economic, and social climate at the end of the nineteenth century, the judiciary found ways around the doctrine, for example by creating torts out of industrial safety legislation to which the doctrine did not apply and by expanding the concept of personal 'non-delegable' duties owed by an employer to his employees. But the fault principle rose to its zenith in the twentieth century as a limitation on the protection of physical interests, in particular interests in personal security.

As the core of economic activity shifts yet again, with the rise of services which deal mainly with the production, distribution, and use of information, tort law has yet again had to make judgments about the degree of protection those who make losses from the use of information should have from those who produce and distribute it. This new reality is impinging on the law concerning negligently caused pure economic loss, defamation, and privacy, among others. The emerging rule is that the fault principle will govern these relations, but frequently subject to contract-like restrictions such as the requirement that the defendant 'assumed responsibility'.

This emphasis on negligence is reflected in Part I of this sourcebook. Part II deals with a number of specific duties and interests, relating to defective premises (chap. 9), defective products (chap. 10), personal security (chap. 13), and land (chap. 14), all of which have been greatly influenced by the fault principle, as have statutory torts (chap. 12). A distinctive feature of several of the torts relating to interference with trade or business (chap. 15) and with interests in reputation (chap. 16) and to the abuse of power is that three parties are usually involved. There is a claimant (C) who has suffered damage, an intermediary (X) who has been the vehicle through which that loss has been inflicted on C, and a defendant (D) who is alleged to be responsible. The loss arises not from an infringement of personal security or tangible property, but from an interference with C's relations with X. That is why these are sometimes called *relational* interests. Examples are D's inducement of X to break his contract with C or intentionally causing loss to C by the use of some 'unlawful means' involving X (e.g. threatening X with violence or some other wrong if he does not break off relations with C). Relational interests are also considered in Part I in cases where D interferes with C's interest in the life of X, by tortiously killing X, and where D harms C's economic interests by negligently damaging X's property. The protection of relational interests at all is controversial, since claimants can often be seen as the authors of their own misfortune in having created the relevant relationship themselves, or else as trying, by claiming compensation, to put themselves into a better position than their previous dependence. Where these objections do not apply, it is usually easier to establish liability.

Reputation might, if one preferred, be classed as an aspect of personal security, but it is a relational interest in English law because liability depends on publication to a third party: the claimant's esteem in the eyes of others and not his or her own injured feelings is at stake. The relationships concerned are, however, usually far from voluntary. The tort of defamation might be considered from another angle as an aspect of English civil liberty, since the essential task of the court (within a complex set of technical rules) is to balance reputation against free speech. Liberty and autonomy of the person are also protected through the torts collectively grouped together under the category of trespass to the person (chap. 13). Indeed, until recently, tort law served as perhaps the primary mechanism in English law for protecting civil liberties and personal autonomy. However, the Human Rights Act 1998 (HRA) now supplements and in places expands the protection offered to individual rights in English law. The HRA will often provide a remedy against abuses of rights stemming from the acts or omissions of public authorities which may parallel or go beyond that offered in tort law. In addition, the 'horizontal effect' of the HRA may require the courts to develop existing causes of actions even where a private party is the defendant in tort to ensure that the UK remains in conformity with its obligations under the European Convention on Human Rights (ECHR). The HRA has already had a significant influence in this area of the law, as it has had throughout English law in general, and the interaction of tort law and the HRA promises to remain a fruitful source of new developments in the years ahead.

The rules and concepts through which tort law seeks to balance the claimant's interest against the defendant's claim for freedom of action have been essentially judge-made in the area of torts to physical interests. Where statutes have intervened it has principally been to reform areas where the case-by-case development of principles has led to anomalous or socially undesirable results. Examples are the continuation of claims by and against the estates of deceased persons (1934), the establishment of a general right of contribution between tortfeasors (1935, revised in 1978), the replacement of the 'all or nothing rule' with a rule of comparative fault where the claimant has contributed to his damage (1945), the reform of the complex rules about an occupier's duty to those who enter his land with permission (1957), and to trespassers (1984), the reform of the law relating to liability for damage caused by animals (1971) and for defective premises (1972) and defective products (1987), the provision of a remedy to children born with a disability attributable to a prenatal injury (1976), and the minor reforms of the assessment of damages for personal injury (1982). (The Human Rights Act, of course, represents another significant legislative intervention, although the motive force for its passing was rather different from that lying behind the legislation just mentioned.) However, legislative intervention has been of overwhelming importance for the so-called 'economic torts' (chap. 15). The relatively short heyday of *laissez-faire* economic liberalism, which some economic historians date from abolition of the Corn Laws in 1846 to the ending of free trade in 1931, was reflected in deliberate Parliamentary abstention from economic regulation. Where the judges appeared to be following a different policy, as in the development of torts of conspiracy and inducing breach of contract in the context of trade disputes, Parliament intervened to protect economic liberties. In the new era of state regulation particularly since World War II, however, the common law of torts to economic interests was replaced by a statutory law of tort in some fields. Monopolies and restrictive practices in the business market are controlled by complex legislation justiciable before specialist institutions, and by the rules of the European Union. Misappropriation of ideas and other intellectual property is regulated by a specialised body of patents, trade marks, and copyright legislation. The judges have an important function in interpreting these and other statutes, but their unique role as creators of tort law in some spheres continues. The new specialised bodies of law, while in theory a part of the law of tort, are in practice best studied in the context of subjects such as labour law, monopolies and restrictive practices, and intellectual property.

The economic and sociological reality is that losses are typically not simply shifted, but are *spread or distributed*. Part III of this sourcebook is concerned with some of the legal devices for loss distribution. Vicarious liability (chap. 18) is largely judge-made law, but the rules for contribution between tortfeasors (chap. 19) are statutory. They mean that the defendant who pays may be able to recover from other tortfeasors on the basis of comparative fault. But the most significant modern influence towards loss distribution is the practice of liability insurance. When victims of industrial accidents became entitled, under the Workmen's Compensation Act 1897, to claim compensation from employers regardless of fault, employers looked to liability insurance to cover themselves; the cost of premiums was widely spread by employers, being reflected (at least in theory) in the price of products and the wages paid to workers. The risks of tort liability created by the driving of motor vehicles gave another major impetus to liability insurance. When it became clear that this insurance was beneficial not only to potential tortfeasors, but also to their victims, Parliament intervened, first in 1930, to make it compulsory. Employers' liability insurance has been compulsory since 1972. This kind of loss distribution has been described by Professor John Fleming as 'vertical', in contrast to the 'horizontal' spreading of losses, by making collateral sources of compensation available to the claimant. In the United Kingdom, social security benefits (and also criminal injuries compensation) are the most important of these collateral sources.

The practical objections to the present combination of systems are manifold. For example, it is argued that courts are congested (although this has not been a problem recently); that litigation is a 'lottery' because of the uncertainty produced by the vagaries of the fault rules and the difficulties of reconstructing, usually years after the event, the minute details of 'negligent' conduct upon which liability is made to turn; that the assessment of damages, and in particular the calculation of lump sums, means that some claimants get too much and many get too little or nothing at all (although the impact of the new system of periodical payments will have to be borne in mind here); that the insurers and lawyers engaged in the 'injury industry' cream off as administrative costs money which could be more efficiently distributed among accident victims (although these claims often ignore the costs of running any other system or the increased numbers of injuries which would ensue if there were no tort system at all); that there are legal gaps in insurance protection (although nearly all of these are now covered by an arrangement between the Motor Insurers' Bureau and the government, see chap. 20), so far as motor insurance is concerned; and that the excessive concentration on compensation claims results in little time being devoted to the problems of accident prevention and rehabilitation of accident victims. The prospects of far-reaching reform, such as that initiated in New Zealand (see chap. 20), are now probably dim, not only because of financial objections but also because of the growing recognition of the part tort law can play in calling to account those who otherwise might escape accountability because of their political or economic influence. Nevertheless, it should be recognised that compensation is not itself an 'aim' of tort law. Tort law says when compensation ought to be paid and when it ought not to be paid. That means that the law is aiming as much at *not* ordering compensation as ordering it. The very existence of tort law therefore means that some injured people will not be compensated. Those who say that tort law somehow fails when the injured go uncompensated have set tort law an impossible test, a test it is bound by its nature to fail. The question remains, however, how much help we want to give on some different basis to those who have been injured but who do not have a tort claim.

Reform proposals are clustering around the co-ordination of social security, insurance, and other forms of assistance (for example, from within the victim's family) with those of tort law: to avoid unjustified duplication of compensation and to rationalise the distribution of losses. Attention should be paid, however, not just to payments from injurer to injured but also from injurer to third party providers of services to the injured. One important theme of recent legislation, for example, has been the 'clawback', a mechanism under which the injurer compensates the third party (usually the state) for the value of services rendered to the injured and, where relevant, the value of those services is deducted from the sum the injurer has to pay the injured.

The student who works his or her way through the pages which follow is likely to be left with a sense of unease. Tort law changes very fast, with fundamental alterations in doctrine always on the cards, legislative intervention, albeit usually of a limited kind, far from unlikely, and some commentators even calling for large parts of the law to be abolished. This, then, is one of those times in legal and social history when the student has to live through the process of profound controversy which may lead to future change. A most important lesson of tort law is the one that Shelley wrote of Man: 'Naught may endure but mutability.'

PRINCIPLES AND POLICY OF NEGLIGENCE

PART ONE

PRINCIPLES
AND POLICY OF
NEGLIGENCE

CHAPTER ONE

AN ACTION FOR DAMAGES IN PERSPECTIVE

The purpose of this chapter is to give the student a bird's eye view of an action for damages before beginning a detailed study of the technical rules. The consolidated actions which have been used for this purpose suggest a number of fundamental questions about the aims and functions of the law of tort. These questions are raised as the basis for a preliminary discussion of issues which will recur throughout this sourcebook. Some reading has been suggested. The student will want to return to these writings at the end of the course and may by then also be equipped to read some of the materials and the proposals to reform tort law which are collected in the further reading, p. 1171, post. Although the events in the case to which we will refer occurred more than 20 years ago, it remains useful as a point of reference to consider the role played by tort, raising, as it does, issues concerning the range of potential defendants, who pays compensation, and also allowing some consideration as to the potential impact on tort of the Human Rights Act 1998.

1 THE BRADFORD FOOTBALL FIRE

(a) The background

On 11 May 1985 Bradford City Football Club, having gained promotion to the Second Division of the Football League, was playing a match at the Bradford City ground, Valley Parade, Bradford, which should have been a celebratory occasion. However, during the match a fire of 'horrifying proportions and severity' occurred, spreading through the main stand within a period of not more than five minutes. This account is taken from the judgment in the action *Susan Fletcher and Martin Lee Fletcher v Bradford City AFC (1983) Ltd*, Leeds, 23rd February 1987, and information provided by the claimants' solicitors: see too A. MacDonald (1987) 137 NLJ 481.

The stand, which had a seating capacity of 2,119, was full of spectators. Fifty-six persons who had been occupying seats in the stand lost their lives and many others were seriously injured. The grandstand had been built around 1909 by the Bradford City Association Football Club (1908) Ltd (the 'old club'). In 1983 that company had become insolvent and was wound up. The ground, including the stand, was taken over by a new club, the Bradford City Association Football Club (1983) Ltd. The stand was built on a hillside which sloped upwards from the level of the pitch at an angle of about 15 degrees. The seating consisted of a staggered timber framework bearing footboards and square wooden seats nailed onto continuous planking. The footboards consisted of two parallel close boarded planks. Shrinkage and usage over time had caused gaps to open between these planks. Each row of seats was raised above the row in front. There was a gap under each seat which was closed off by a sloping board called a kick board, but some of the kick boards had become dislodged or damaged and where this happened there was an open gap into a continuous void nine inches or more deep which extended under the whole of the floor of that part of the stand.

An investigation by a senior forensic scientist immediately after the fire revealed that large quantities of inflammable rubbish had accumulated in the void. That the debris had accumulated over a long period was shown by the discovery in the void of a pre-decimal price tag (placing the sale before February 1971) and a copy of a local newspaper dated 1968. The scientist concluded that the fire must have been caused by a lighted match or a burning cigarette or some burning tobacco falling through a gap or hole in the floor. The combination of an upward sloping bed of inflammable debris overlaid by the staggered wooden structure was an 'ideal situation for flames to spread rapidly up the slope as they did'.

(b) The actions

In August 1985, Mrs Susan Fletcher, the widow of John Fletcher, who died in the fire, commenced an action claiming damages, as administratrix, on behalf of his estate and under the Fatal Accidents Acts for the benefit of his dependants. She also sued as mother and next friend of her minor son, Martin Fletcher, who claimed damages in respect of his injuries sustained in the fire. Their action was against the Bradford City Association Football Club (1983) Ltd (the first defendants). These plaintiffs (now called claimants) alleged that the fire, the death of John Fletcher, and the injuries to Martin were caused by the negligence of the Club.

The Club denied negligence, and alleged that the death and injuries were caused by the negligence and/or breach of statutory duty of the Health and Safety Executive and/or the West Yorkshire Metropolitan County Council. The Executive is a statutory body, whose duty, as defined by s. 18 of the Health and Safety at Work etc. Act 1974, is to make adequate arrangements for the enforcement of the safety provisions of that Act. The County Council was the fire authority on whom certain duties were imposed by the Fire Precautions Act 1971 in respect of premises within its area. (This Act is no longer in force: for the position today see the Regulatory Reform (Fire Safety) Order 2005, SI 2005/1541.) The County Council was also the local authority which had powers and duties under the Safety of Sports Grounds Act 1975 to ensure safety at sports grounds and which was alleged by the Club to have been negligent and/or in breach of duty in respect of two quite distinct functions. The Club issued 'third party' notices (now replaced by what are called Part 20 claims under the Civil Procedure Rules (CPR)) against the Executive and County Council claiming an indemnity against the claimants' claim and costs or a contribution. Third party notices enable a defendant to claim that a person who is not a party to the proceedings should be responsible in whole or in part for any damages the defendant may have to pay to the claimant. This has the effect that the issues between the defendant and the third party can be determined in the proceedings between the claimant and the defendant. The Executive and County Council were then joined by the claimants as second and third defendants respectively in the action, thus enabling the claimants to obtain judgment in the same action against whichever parties were held liable.

In accordance with pre-trial directions, the action was consolidated with that of a serving police officer, David Britton, who was injured in the course of rescuing spectators in the blazing stand. The actions were tried, on the issue whether or not the defendants were liable, by Sir Joseph Cantley, sitting as a deputy High Court Judge, in Leeds over 11 working days in November 1986 and he gave judgment on 23 February 1987.

(c) Judgment

SIR JOSEPH CANTLEY: ...

There is no dispute as to the cause of the fire. It was caused accidentally by a lighted match or a burning cigarette or some burning tobacco falling through a gap or hole in the floor. ... There it ignited inflammable debris which lay in large quantities under the wooden floor. ... This accumulation of inflammable rubbish was not recent. It had built up over the years. ... This was a fire hazard of long standing.

[His Lordship found that build-up of combustible materials was visible even on a casual inspection and that the Club had notice of the existence of the hazard of fire following a visit in September 1980 by an inspector of the Health and Safety Executive and in July 1984 by an engineer employed by the County Council.] ...

In his final submission to me [counsel for the first defendants] conceded that the club was at fault in not finding a way to clear the void of inflammable material. They could ... have done so with assistance from the City Council. It was a proper and I think inevitable concession. However the duty of the club at common law and under the Occupiers' Liability Act 1957 goes beyond finding a way to make the stand safe. If an occupier has a stand which he uses for the accommodation of 2,000 spectators of all ages and conditions and he knows or ought to know that the state of affairs in the stand is such that there is a real and constant risk of a fire starting and developing under them he cannot be absolved from his duty towards them by establishing that he is not able to find or not able to afford a way of removing that danger from the stand. He must not expose spectators to the danger even if it means that he must take the stand entirely out of use. ...

The omission of the club to take any action to deal with this dangerous situation of which it had notice and knowledge and of which it should have been aware without notice from outside parties is enough in itself to establish the claim of the plaintiffs against the first defendant. It is only right that I should say that I think it would be unfair to conclude that [the Chairman, the vice-Chairman], the board of directors or any of them were intentionally and callously indifferent to the safety of spectators using the stand. They were at fault, but the fault was that no one in authority seem ever to have properly appreciated the real gravity of this fire hazard and consequently no one gave it the attention it certainly ought to have received. The board had many other problems to contend with. The new club had taken over a distinctly ramshackle set of premises. The main stand needed a new roof. The terraces were in disrepair to an extent which could be regarded as dangerous. Almost everything needed attention. [The Chairman] told me that it was obvious in 1983 that no repairs had been done in the previous 10 years. In addition the new club was immediately and chronically short of money. ... They had to avoid all expenditure which did not seem to them to be immediately necessary. ...

[His Lordship went on to find that there were precautions which if they had been taken would have prevented all or at least most of the deaths and injuries which occurred. These included the provision of accessible and sufficient exits and an evacuation system for operation in emergencies. In these and other respects his Lordship referred to the 'Guide to Safety at Sports Grounds', an official publication of 1976 popularly called the 'Green Guide'.] In case I am misunderstood I should make it clear that I am not using the Green Guide as if it were law. It has no legal force. It is expressed to be a voluntary code devised for improving spectators' safety at football grounds to provide a reasonable degree of safety. It is recognised in the code itself that the problem of crowd safety in football grounds is complex and further complicated by the rampant pestilence of hooliganism. ...

I respectfully agree with the conclusion in Popplewell J.'s interim report [Committee of Inquiry into Crowd Safety and Control at Sports Grounds, Home Office] that this tragedy with its appalling number of injuries was caused by the devastating effects of a rapidly developing fire and by the available exits being insufficient to enable the spectators to escape. For both these causes the first defendant must be held responsible.

The Health and Safety Executive

I turn now to the case alleged against the Health and Safety Executive. It is a statutory public body exercising its relevant functions under the Health and Safety at Work etc. Act 1974...

Like most statutes relating to public authorities the Health and Safety at Work etc. Act 1974 contains areas of discretion.... [His Lordship then considered the relevant provisions of the Act of 1974. He noted that in relation to fire risks there was an overlap between the powers of the Executive and the powers of the fire authority under the Fire Precautions Act 1971 and the powers of the local author- ity under the Safety of Sports Grounds Act 1975. The Executive had recognised this was so and had, in 1978, issued a memorandum of advice to their inspectors stating that the Executive would only be responsible for the manner in which undertakings were conducted. It also indicated the primary responsibility for fire risks should reside with the fire authority. In September 1980 an inspector had visited the ground and noted the litter in the void, advising that it should be removed and the void blanked off. He went on to advise the club of the Green Guide.] ... In evidence [the inspector] told me that he thought that the presence of this rubbish was a hazard which came within s. 3 of the 1974 Act because it was reasonably practicable for the club to deal with it. ... [He] told me that he did not regard this rubbish as a matter of serious concern to be reported to the fire authority. Had he so regarded it he would have reported it. He told me that at the time he thought it inconceivable that the fire bri- gade did not inspect the club and he was anxious not to tread on the toes of the authority which was primarily concerned with fire matters. With hindsight of course it seems obvious that [the inspector's] assessment of the gravity of this risk was wrong and that it ought to have been reported to the fire authority. ... Although he might at the time have made further investigation and inquiry which would have altered the opinion he formed I certainly do not feel justified in holding that he made his decision irresponsibly or otherwise than in good faith. [His Lordship found that there had been a number of other visits by the same inspector and others, but the question of the litter was never raised again. The risks of an emergency in the stand were raised in 1981 and the club was advised to consider their evacu- ation procedures. His Lordship considered some of the pleaded allegations against the Executive and rejected them all.] ... Having seen and heard [the inspector] I do not consider myself justified in holding that he acted so carelessly and unreasonably that he acted in abuse or excess of his power ... I have come to the conclusion that the action against the second defendant must fail. ... [But note that today a public authority acting under statutory powers or duties can be liable in negligence even though its powers have not been exceeded: see pp.88–109, post].

West Yorkshire Metropolitan County Council

The third defendant was the fire authority for the purposes of the Fire Precautions Act 1971. It was also the local authority for the purposes of the Safety of Sports Grounds Act 1975. [His Lordship found that as the club was in the Third Division and had not been 'designated' by the Secretary of State no safety certificate was required under the Act of 1975. The fire authority had the power, but were under no statutory duty to inspect the premises of the club—but see note 1, p. 20, post. However, his Lordship found that in July 1984 an engineering member of a safety team set up by the local authority had noticed that litter lay in the voids. A letter was subsequently sent to the club on 19th July 1984 pointing out the fire hazard. A copy of the letter was sent to the deputy fire prevention officer but there was no evidence whether that letter was received or considered by him. The club was not again visited or mentioned at meetings of the fire and public protection committee of the authority. No one thought to follow up the letter.] ... My conclusion is that either the letter was not considered at all, or that an irresponsible decision was made without proper consideration. In either case it was not a valid exercise of discretion and was negligent. If it was an exercise of discretion at all it was to quote Lord Reid [in *Home Office v Dorset Yacht Co Ltd* [1970] AC at p. 1031] 'exercised so carelessly or unreasonably that it was no exercise of the discretion which Parliament conferred'.

[Counsel] on behalf of the County Council conceded very properly in my opinion, that on common law principles there was a sufficient relationship between the County Council and members of the public to establish a prima facie duty of care by the Council towards members of the public. The declared object of the Fire Precautions Act 1971 is the protection of persons from fire risks and under section 18 it was the duty of the Council, as fire authority, to enforce its provisions....The Safety of Sports Grounds Act 1975 is...specifically directed to the safety of spectators at sports grounds....

[Counsel] submitted that the death of Mr Fletcher and the injuries of Martin Fletcher and Sergeant Britton were too remote a consequence of any negligence attributable to the Council because the continuing negligence of the Football Club is what is called a 'novus actus interveniens' breaking the chain of causation....The primary duty was, of course, that of the club and the County Council's function was only a supervisory one; but one which was a supervisory one in the interests of the public. They embarked on it but left it unfinished. It was at all times foreseeable to a competent fire officer, or I would have thought, to any intelligent person, that if the club did not take proper action before the season started a fire might start at any time during the season, as in fact it did. If the proper, and in my view obvious, action had been taken by the fire prevention department, as it should have been, they would have exercised their powers of inspection and discovered the nature of the void and a sufficient indication of the extent of the inflammable deposit to realise that [the letter of 19 July]...referred to a quite alarming danger. They could, of course, have threatened or even taken action under section 10 of either of the statutes, but that would probably have been unnecessary. It might even have been sufficient, in the case of this club, to have told the club firmly, without making an inspection at once, that this danger must not be allowed to continue into the next season and that compulsory powers would have to be used if it was not dealt with before the season began....

In my view the continuing negligence of the club and their continued inaction or indifference of the County Council through its various departments and officers after it had been alerted to the existence of the danger, were concurrent causes of this disaster, and I hold both of them to be liable in damages to the plaintiffs.

There only remains the apportionment of responsibility between the first and third defendants. As I have already stated, the primary duty was on the club and the functions of the County Council were supervisory and its liability is for negligent breach of a common law duty arising out of the way in which they dealt with or ignored their statutory powers. That duty was not a duty to the club but a duty to the spectators and other persons in the stand. However, the responsibility of the club is, in my view, very much greater and I apportion responsibility between the two defendants as to two-thirds on the first defendant and one-third on the third defendant.

NOTE

For consideration of how various changes in the law might have affected the position of the Health and Safety Executive and the West Yorkshire County Council today, see note 1, p. 20, post.

(d) The compensation

The claimants, together with a group of about 200 other claimants represented by the same solicitors, subsequently received lump sums by way of damages. The amounts were negotiated by their solicitors with the insurers of the Club and the Council. The solicitors took the opinion of leading counsel on a specimen cross-section of cases reflecting the types of injury sustained. By far the greatest number of cases were burn injuries and these were sub-divided into categories. Based on counsel's figures and the solicitors' assessments, settlements were negotiated with the defendants' insurers. The amounts have not been disclosed.

No account was taken of payments made to them by the Bradford Disaster Appeal Fund, which was set up as a discretionary trust soon after the tragedy. The Trust distributed about £4 million, raised by public donations, to the dependants of the 56 who died and to the 300 who suffered injuries. Ninety-five per cent of these payments were made within ten months of the tragedy, that is, nearly a year before the judgment in the negligence actions. The amounts paid to individuals and the criteria used for the distribution of the Fund have not been disclosed. Assessment was undertaken by a team comprising a burns specialist, a psychiatric specialist, and a claims assessor.

2 POINTS FOR DISCUSSION

(a) The claimants

QUESTION

Who makes tort claims and gets tort damages?

■ Paths to Justice: What People Do and Think About Going to Law.
Hazel Genn (Hart Publishing, Oxford, 1999), pp. 126, 161–162

About eight per cent of the surveyed population reported having had one or more injury or health problems in the last five years that resulted from an accident, or from poor working conditions and which necessitated a visit to a doctor or hospital…

…In about 13% of cases included in the main survey where respondents had suffered accidental injury or work-related ill-health that required medical treatment, no action was taken to seek any compensation or other remedy. This was the largest proportion of respondents taking no action of any problem type. Among those accident and ill-health victims who took some action to obtain redress, only a very small proportion tried to handle the problem themselves without first taking some advice (about 14%). However, of the small number who did take some action without advice, about one in three said that they had succeeded in settling the claim by agreement with the other side.

In a further third of the cases (35%) an agreement had been reached between the parties to settle the claim after receiving advice (about 6% apparently after the issue of court proceedings). A relatively small proportion of personal injury and work-related ill health cases were concluded on the basis of a court decision (5%), although at the time of the interview another three per cent of respondents who had suffered an injury or ill health were waiting for a court hearing…

In about 47% of all injury and work-related ill-health cases the respondent had failed to reach any kind of agreement with the other side. In about 8% of these cases the respondent said that the problem had somehow resolved itself, but in almost half of these cases this was because the respondent had abandoned their claim…

NOTES

1. The above extract, from a wide-ranging survey of how people deal with problems that could end in the civil courts, confirms earlier evidence that a significant number of victims of accidents and ill health take no action to seek compensation or any other

remedy, or abandon their claim. Where action is taken, only a small proportion are actually tried in the courts. The majority are settled by negotiation and agreement.

2. The extract, post, from the report of a survey carried out during 1976 and 1977 for the Oxford Centre for Socio-Legal Studies, showed that only about 12 per cent of accidental injuries attracted tort compensation. This report, and other studies, identify a number of factors which inhibit the use of the law of tort. Among these are:

(a) ignorance of the law, and lack of knowledge as to where to find an expert in personal injury litigation;

(b) lack of precision in the concept of negligence leading to uncertainty;

(c) problems about providing evidence of fault;

(d) delays in the legal process (although this is thought to have become less of a problem in recent years); and

(e) lack of resources to cover the costs of litigation.

These and other pressures deter accident victims from going to law and result in premature and inadequate settlements (see further H. Genn, *Hard Bargaining: Out of Court Settlement in Personal Injury Actions* (Oxford, 1987)). The problems are even more acute for the victims of 'man-made' diseases who face special difficulties in proving that the defendant's fault caused their illness, and, because of the gradual onset and latency of many diseases, in bringing their claims within the usual three-year period allowed by the Limitation Acts (see generally J. Stapleton, *Disease and the Compensation Debate* (Oxford, 1986)).

More generally see also the recent study by R. Lewis, A. Morris, and K. Oliphant (2006) 14 *Torts LJ* 158, referred to at p. 28, post, who note, looking back to the 1970s, that there has been an 'approximately three-fold rise in total claims numbers over 30 years', an increase which suggests an enhanced claims-consciousness compared with the Harris et al. study conducted in 1976–7: this point should be kept in mind throughout this section.

■ Compensation and Support for Illness and Injury

Donald Harris et al. Oxford Socio-Legal Studies (Clarendon Press: Oxford, 1984), pp. 317–321

The survey showed that only a small minority of all accident victims initiate legal claims and obtain damages for the losses they have suffered....For all types of accident taken together, the figure is 12 per cent of cases, but there are important differences in the success rates between different categories of accident. While fewer than one in three of road accident victims, and one in five of work accident victims obtained damages, fewer than one in fifty of all other types of accident victims obtained damages, despite the fact that this represented the largest category of accidents suffered by victims in the sample. Although the chances of obtaining damages were very high once there had been contact with a solicitor about the possibility of making a claim, the vast majority of victims either never considered the question of claiming compensation, or if they did so, failed to take any positive steps to make a definite claim.

Elderly victims and young victims appeared on the whole to be reluctant to claim damages, irrespective of the type of accident suffered, and, for elderly victims at least, irrespective of the degree of residual disability suffered as a result of the accident. Women suffering work accidents claimed less often than men suffering work accidents, although for road and other accidents the proportions were similar. In general, accident victims in full- or part-time employment were considerably more likely to claim damages than those not in employment. Contrary to our expectations, accident victims in lower status socio-economic groups were proportionately *more* likely to obtain damages than victims in professional or managerial groups. The seriousness of injury in both physical terms and the amount of time taken off work was not consistently associated with the likelihood that damages would be obtained, underlining the fact that the tort system is based on the cause of accidents rather than on the consequences. . . .

The actual operation of the damages system . . . produced relatively low amounts for our sample: a mean of £1,135, but a median of only £500. Many pressures on claimants led them to accept amounts which heavily discounted the full award which a court would make. There may be a discount for each risk or uncertainty facing the claimant: the risks that his evidence might not prove fault on the part of the defendant, that he himself might be found partly at fault (contributory negligence), or that the medical reports on his prognosis might be wrong; the uncertainties about whether he could bear the further delay and expense of waiting for a court hearing, and about how much a judge would award for his injuries. The cumulative effect of all these uncertainties was that nearly all claimants agreed to compromise their cases in out-of-court settlements for sums much lower than 'full' legal liability would justify. Every uncertainty and risk is a negotiating weapon in the hands of the insurance company; a particularly powerful weapon is an allegation of contributory negligence, as was shown by solicitors' reports that it was taken into account in nearly half the settlements. The pressures to settle meant that very few cases (five out of 1,177, or 0.4 per cent) actually reached the stage of a contested hearing in court, although formal court proceedings were commenced in about 40 per cent of the claims ultimately settled. . . .

Delay is an inescapable part of the present tort system. In the survey, the average delay between the date of the accident and the actual receipt of damages was a little over nineteen months; nearly all successful claimants had returned to work before receiving damages. Solicitors had advised delay in 40 per cent of the claims, in order to wait until medical treatment was complete or until the medical condition of the claimant had stabilised. Several trends are clear from the data—the delay is likely to be longer, the longer the victim is off work, and the greater the degree of his residual disability. The data also indicated that the longer the delay before a lawyer is consulted, the worse the chance of obtaining damages: the difficulties of collecting evidence increase with the delay. . . .

Our data showed that it was not victims' attributions of fault which motivated them to make a damages claim. . . . Fault was not always seen as appropriate grounds for compensation, nor was it necessarily seen as a precondition if a claim was to be made. In only half those cases where the victim took steps to initiate a claim for damages had he also attributed fault to the person against whom the claim would be made. Only about half of those who said their accident was someone else's fault said they had at any time thought that that person should compensate them. Moreover, the pattern of responses for different types of accidents suggested that even in those cases where attributions of fault did coincide with the initiation of a claim, the attribution of fault was a justification rather than a reason for the claim, and that, without the prospect of a possible damages award, fault might have been attributed quite differently, if at all. The question of fault was certainly not unimportant to the victims. In particular, holding someone to blame was clearly seen as threatening to a relationship. However, the factors determining whether or not fault was attributed to someone else, and if so how, were extremely complex, and included many factors beside the causes and circumstances of the accident. Rather than the law reflecting the ordinary man's view of fault and liability, the victims' attributions of fault and liability reflected legal norms and the likelihood of a successful damages claim. The findings also confirmed that the attribution of fault in the context of a particular damages claim is very much a function of that context. It cannot be assumed that the type of attribution of fault generated by the tort system will be appropriate also for purposes of deterrence or accident prevention, where it may be far more effective to focus on quite different causal factors.

NOTES

1.   An earlier, but less comprehensive, survey carried out in 1974 for the Pearson Commission (vol. 2, chap. 18) found that only about 6.5 per cent of all injuries attracted tort compensation, and gave broadly similar reasons to those above. The Pearson

Commission (vol. 1, para. 83) estimated that the operating costs of the tort system amounted to about 87 per cent of tort compensation payments, while the costs of the social security system were only 11 per cent of social security benefits (para. 261). The Oxford study (ante) found that the average cost of settling claims ranged from 15 per cent of damages obtained in larger claims, to 29 per cent of damages in smaller claims. The Report of the Review Body on Civil Justice (Cm. 394, 1988), para. 427 found that county court personal injury cases were particularly expensive for successful claimants: claimants' costs alone amounted to more than 50 per cent of compensation in 85 per cent of cases, compared to nearly 50 per cent of cases in the High Court.

2.   An analysis of costs undertaken for Lord Woolf's inquiry *Access to Justice: Final Report* (Lord Chancellor's Department, 1996, Annex III), on the basis of a sample of bills submitted for taxation to the Supreme Court Taxing Office during the period 1990–5, revealed a lack of proportionality between costs and the value of the claim. When costs were expressed as a percentage of the value of the claim, median costs among the lowest value claims (under £12,500) consistently represented more than 100 per cent of the claim value. In personal injury cases, costs were 135 per cent of claims less than £12,500 and 41 per cent of claims between £12,500 and £25,000. In medical negligence cases these percentages were 137 per cent and 57 per cent, respectively. See further the view of the National Audit Office, to be found in the report *Making Amends* (2003, Department of Health) and dealing with NHS cases, that 'the legal and administrative costs of settling claims exceed the money actually paid to the victim in the majority of claims under £45,000 and take up an even higher proportion of smaller claims'. In recent years it is thought that costs have, if anything, increased.

3.   An analysis of case duration for Lord Woolf's inquiry (op cit., Annex III, para. 21), measured from the date of first instruction to the date of conclusion, showed that medical negligence cases lasted longest on average (65 months), followed by personal injury cases (56 months), and professional negligence cases (41 months). The average delay between instructions and issue of proceedings in medical negligence cases was 21 months, and in personal injury cases it was 17 months (para. 27). In personal injury cases, the more straightforward the case, the longer the period between instruction and the issue of proceedings (para. 32). When the successful party had legal aid, the delay between instruction and conclusion of claim were longer: a 20 per cent increase in the length of personal injury cases, and a 25 per cent increase in medical negligence cases (para. 29). Among the explanations for this may be the administrative time taken in obtaining legal aid, the possibility that legal aid work is given a low priority, or that legal aid cases are run harder and further than might otherwise be the case because there is no risk of costs for the party with legal aid (para. 40). Note, however, that today legal aid is only available in personal injury claims in clinical negligence cases. It is believed that in recent years the time from the issue of proceedings to final disposition has in general come down.

(b) The defendants

QUESTION

The directors of the Club, and the officers of the County Council, were found to have been negligent. Why was it that the claimants sued the corporations which they served, rather than the individuals? See further chap. 18, post.

NOTES

1.   The Bradford City Association Football Club (1983) Ltd and the Council are corporate bodies which were insured. These features are relevant to financial responsibility: if a task of tort law is to compensate the victim, how does it ensure that the defendant can pay?

It was the insurers of the Club and the Council which defended the proceedings in their insureds' names and dealt with the settlement negotiations. The right to do so arose under the terms of insurance contracts. Such insurance is not as a matter of law compulsory in the case of football clubs, but it is in respect of employers' liability (p. 1146, post), and road traffic accidents (p. 1142, post). As to the claimant's rights if the defendant becomes insolvent, see p. 1149, post, or if the defendant fails to insure where this is compulsory, see p. 1150, post. See generally, *Atiyah*, chap. 9 and 10.

2.   In the Bradford case about 200 claimants were able to pool resources and to instruct two firms of solicitors who coordinated the actions and were able to bargain on an equal footing with the insurers. The position may be different where there is a single claimant: see the extract from Genn, op cit., set out at p. 1152, post.

(c) The cause of action

QUESTION

What did the claimants have to prove in order to succeed against (1) the Club; (2) the Health and Safety Executive; (3) the County Council?

NOTES

1.   Of special interest in Sir Joseph Cantley's judgment are his findings that (1) the Club was liable for 'fault' even though the directors had not been 'intentionally or callously indifferent', and the Club was impecunious; (2) the Health and Safety Executive (HSE) was not liable even though 'with hindsight ... the [inspector's] assessment of the gravity of the risk was wrong and ... it ought to have been reported to the fire authority'; and (3) the County Council was held liable for 'continued inaction or indifference' which amounted to a concurrent 'cause' of the fire and injuries.

How would this case be decided today? It would appear that potentially the action against the HSE might be easier today but that any action against the appropriate successor body to the County Council (which was abolished in 1986) would fail. In the action against the HSE, Sir Joseph Cantley required it to be shown that the official had acted outside his powers before there could be a negligence action. This would no longer be required; however, there can still be problems if the question of whether there was negligence raises what are called non-justiciable matters (matters which the courts do not believe are appropriate for them to resolve) such as questions concerning the allocation of scarce resources. Furthermore, the courts can be concerned that the imposition of negligence liability is not inconsistent with the relevant statutory framework. As against the appropriate successor body to the West Yorkshire Metropolitan County Council, note that, as mentioned ante, the Fire Precaution Act 1971 is no longer in force. Today, however, any stand at a sporting venue with cover for more than

500 people has to have a safety certificate issued by the local authority: this is laid down by the Fire Safety and Safety of Sports Ground Act 1987, within which the Bradford stand would presumably have fallen, but the Act was not in existence at the time of the events in the *Bradford* case. Note the following two sections of the 1987 Act.

34(1) It shall be the duty of every local authority to enforce within their area the provisions of this Part [of this Act] and for that purpose to arrange for the periodical inspection of sports grounds at which there are regulated stands . . .

37 Except in so far as this Part otherwise expressly provides, and subject to section 18 of the Interpretation Act 1978 (offences under two or more laws), the provisions of this Part shall not be construed as—

(a) conferring a right of action in any civil proceedings (other than proceedings for the recovery of a fine) in respect of any contravention of this Part or of any of the terms or conditions of a safety certificate thereunder; or

(b) affecting any requirement or restriction imposed by or under any other enactment whether contained in a public general Act or in a local or private Act; or

(c) derogating from any right of action or other remedy (whether civil or criminal) in proceedings instituted otherwise than under this Part.

Section 37 puts aside any possibilities of any attempt to base an action on s. 34. On the action for breach of statutory duty, see chap. 12, post. Furthermore, it will be seen at pp. 100–117, post that even in the absence of a provision such as s. 37, a public body under the current law will not be liable for an omission to exercise a statutory power per se; a claimant would have to prove a relationship between the claimant and the public body such as an assumption of responsibility and reliance.

2. It will be seen from the materials in this book that public bodies are quite often defendants in tort actions. They have attractions from a claimant's point of view. They tend not to go out of existence—or if they do, are likely to have a successor body which takes over their responsibilities—and also will usually be worth suing. Since October 2000 there has been another important possible basis for claiming compensation from public bodies, namely the Human Rights Act 1998 (HRA), although the HRA is not a 'tort statute' (*R (Greenfield) v Secretary of State for Home Affairs* [2005] 2 All ER 240, [2005] UKHL 14).

Section 7 of the HRA permits individuals to bring an action alleging a breach of European Convention rights against bodies that come within s. 6 of the Act, i.e. 'core public authorities' or bodies performing 'functions of a public nature'. However, if the alleged violation of rights has stemmed from actions or omissions done in the course of giving effect to an Act of the UK Parliament, then the courts will only be able to grant a remedy if the Act of Parliament in question can be interpreted in a manner that is 'compatible with the under-lying thrust of the legislation' (Lord Nicholls in *Ghaidan v Godin-Mendoza* [2004] 3 All ER 411, at [33]) so as to give effect to the ECHR rights of the victim. If this cannot be done, the courts may only under s. 4 HRA make a declaration of incompatibility, stating that the relevant Act of Parliament appears to be incompatible with the ECHR. This has no legal effect, although it may result in Parliament changing the law.

In contrast, if a body does not fall within the scope of s. 6 of the HRA, then an alleged victim of a breach of Convention rights cannot seek a remedy under the Act directly against that private body. Nevertheless, the HRA may still be of use to an aggrieved claimant in such circumstances. The HRA has been recognised by the English courts as having 'indirect horizontal effect': as courts are 'public authorities' for the purposes of s. 6 of the HRA, they are under an obligation within the constraints of their constitutional role to apply legislation, statutory instruments, or the common law in litigation between two private parties in a manner that ensures that an individual's Convention rights are not breached (see *Campbell v MGN Ltd (No 2)* [2005] 4 All ER 793, [2005] UKHL 61. Alternatively, a claimant may be able to bring an action against a public authority on the basis that, by failing to protect him or her against the abuse of his rights by a private body, that public authority failed to adhere to its 'positive obligations' to ensure the adequate protection of Convention rights under the ECHR.

The HRA can permit a claimant to bring an action directly against a public body in circumstances where a claim in tort may not be available. At times it also enables parallel claims to be brought in tort and under the HRA. In addition, the HRA has indirectly influenced the development of the common law of tort in a variety of ways, which are examined at various points of this book: see in particular the question of it having an effect on the imposition of a common law duty of care upon public authorities (see pp. 52–57, post), and the recent evolution of a cause of action for breach of privacy (chap. 17, post). In all of these ways, the HRA has exercised a considerable influence on the recent evolution of tort, which shows no signs of dissipating in the years ahead.

If the Bradford fire were to take place now, the claimants in all likelihood would bring parallel claims in tort and under the HRA against the Health and Safety Executive and the appropriate contemporary successor body to the County Council. Both these bodies would appear to come squarely within the definition of public authority contained in s. 6 of the HRA. Therefore, if the claimants could show that either or both authorities had discharged their duties in a manner that violated the claimants' Convention rights or the rights of the deceased, then liability might be imposed under the HRA which would complement any liability imposed under tort. In this scenario, the question would be whether the public authority defendants had violated the right to life of the deceased (as protected by Article 2 of the ECHR) and the right to family life of the claimants themselves (as protected by Article 8 of the ECHR).

The circumstances in which a failure by a public authority to take positive steps to protect a person's right to life will constitute a violation of Article 2 will usually involve a failure of procedural justice, such as when a public authority fails to ensure a proper investigation of a killing (see e.g. *R (Amin) v Secretary of State for the Home Department* [2003] 4 All ER 1264, [2003] UKHL 51). However, there may be circumstances where a failure to take the required steps to ensure the safety of the victim may also generate liability under Article 2 (and also under Article 8, as a result of the loss inflicted upon the family of the deceased). In *Osman v UK* (1998) 29 EHRR 245, noted p. 48, post, the European Court of Human Rights stated at [115]–[116] that a breach of Article 2 could arise if '[a]uthorities knew or ought to have known of the existence of a real and immediate risk to the life of an identified individual and that they failed to take measures within the scope of their powers....which judged reasonably might have been expected to avoid that risk'.

In *Savage v South Essex Partnership NHS Foundation Trust* [2007] EWCA Civ 1375, the deceased had been detained in a mental hospital, which, after several unsuccessful attempts, she managed to leave, whereupon she travelled to a nearby train station and threw herself under a train. The Court of Appeal took the approach that the Convention jurisprudence indicated that treatment resembling 'gross negligence' might be required before a health authority would be ordinarily liable under Article 2 of the ECHR for a failure to take reasonable care of a patient. However, where the deceased was involuntarily detained or imprisoned, or in a similar situation of dependence upon the state, then a less demanding standard would be applied. Sir Anthony Clarke MR, giving the judgment of the court, took the view at [35] that a breach of Article 2 could be established in such a situation where the public authority 'at the material time…knew or ought to have known of the existence of a real and immediate risk to the life of [the deceased]…and that it failed to take measures within the scope of their powers which, judged reasonably, might have been expected to avoid that risk'. At the time of writing, this judgment has been appealed to the House of Lords. However, the potential relevance of *Savage* to the circumstances of the Bradford fire if it had occurred today should be apparent. Were the football fans a 'vulnerable group'? Could either the HSE or the County Council be said to have fallen foul of the HRA? The presence of this alternative form of remedy should not be neglected in analysing the scope and extent of liability under tort today.

In general, the monetary compensation that is obtained for a breach of the HRA may often be more limited than that obtainable in a similar case for a breach of duty of care in negligence. The principles that govern the award of damages under the ECHR are often regarded as opaque in nature (see Law Commission Report, Law Com No. 266, *Damages Under the Human Rights Act 1998* Cm 4853). Section 8 of the HRA makes the award of damages under the Act discretionary, and unlike the case in tort, they are not available as of right. In addition, s. 8 establishes that the purpose of any award of damages under the HRA is to provide 'just satisfaction' for the violation of the claimant's rights. This guiding purpose of affording 'just satisfaction' has been largely interpreted by the English courts as entailing the use of monetary compensation as a secondary or 'less prominent' mechanism for vindicating the rights of the claimant, with declaratory relief being treated as the primary mechanism for affording redress.

In *Greenfield* Lord Bingham emphasised that damage awards under the HRA were distinct in nature, role, and purpose from damage awards in tort, and indicated that domestic courts should follow the European Court of Human Rights in adopting a restrained approach in determining the quantum of damages under the HRA. Note, however, that relatively substantial compensation awards may be available in some limited circumstances under the HRA: see in particular *Van Colle v Chief Constable of Hertfordshire Police* [2007] 3 All ER 122, [2007] EWCA Civ 325, where a failure by the police to take the necessary steps to protect the right to life of the deceased victim was held to have violated Article 2 of the ECHR and to justify an overall compensation award of £25,000. (At the time of writing, this decision is on appeal to the House of Lords.)

(d) Sources of compensation

QUESTIONS

1.   What are the main sources of compensation for victims of accident and 'man-made' disease? Consider in particular (a) social security benefits (p. 1156, post); (b) criminal injuries compensation (p. 1158, post); (c) 'personal' (sometimes called loss or 'first

party') insurance (p. 1136, post); (d) occupational and statutory sick pay (p. 1156, post); and (e) disaster funds and other donations.

2.   To what extent is 'double compensation' or 'overcompensation' possible? (For the deductions which may be made from common law damages, see p. 533, post.)

NOTES

1.   In the settlements in the *Bradford* case private insurance was disregarded, as were the substantial payments received before the trial from the highly successful disaster appeal (see ante). In the larger claims social security benefits were taken into account (see p. 1156, post).

2.   According to the Report of the Review Body on Civil Justice, para. 391 some 1.8m new claimants obtain social security payments each year; 1m obtain occupational sick pay; and 250,000 benefit from personal insurance, while only 340,000 victims make claims in tort on the basis of negligence or breach of statutory duty. Ninety-nine per cent of all tort claims are settled without going to trial.

■ Compensation and Support for Illness and Injury

Donald Harris et al. Oxford Socio-Legal Studies (Clarendon Press: Oxford, 1984), pp. 321–323, 327

The main financial support for victims in the survey came from social security…; but only four out of ten actually received some benefit (averaging £731 up to the time of the interview, but with some future entitlement to benefits which could be worth thousands of pounds)….About a third of the social security beneficiaries in the survey had to rely on means-tested supplementary benefits, which fact indicates that, for many victims of illness and injury, minimum income levels are not being maintained by the social security benefits specifically designed for illness and injury. A third of the beneficiaries received the long-term invalidity benefits, and a fifth the short-term sickness benefit. In practice entitlement to social security benefit depends largely on previous work status. Nearly three-quarters of those in full-time work before the illness or injury received some benefit but fewer than one in five of other victims received any benefit. This goes some way to explain the fact that many more men than women received support from the social security system.

Data from the survey suggest that difficulties in the administration of social security arise from two factors—the complexity of the criteria for entitlement to some benefits (e.g. means-tested supplementary benefit) and the need for special medical examinations for some benefits (e.g. attendance allowance).

Only seven of the twenty-one victims of criminal injury in our sample obtained an award from the Criminal Injuries Compensation Board….One person applied for an award but was refused for reasons which were not clear in the account given by the victim. Those people who did not apply were either confused about the regulations regarding awards (for example, they might have thought that it was only possible to apply if the identity of the offender was known) or did not think that they would have been entitled to compensation because the injury was caused in a domestic dispute or in a fight between acquaintances. The criminal injuries reported were generally of a serious nature and in some cases caused long periods off work. The amounts awarded were quite small (mean £245, median £207) and most claims were made direct by the victim to the Board rather than through a solicitor.

Although occupational sick pay is obviously confined to employees, it is an important form of support for those who have lost earnings as the result of illness or injury….Our data showed that official statistics on membership of sick pay schemes (to the effect that about 80 per cent of full-time workers are covered) are not a reliable guide to actual receipts of sick pay. In the survey, of those who had held their employment for less than six months, only 25 per cent obtained some sick pay; for those with six months but less than two years' service, 49 per cent obtained some; and for those with more than five years; service, 62 per cent obtained some. The mean total amount of sick pay received was £248; a typical recipient was someone absent for up to twenty-six weeks being paid £20 to £30 per week. When added to social security benefits, these amounts can provide total compensation equal to full pay for the whole or part of the period of absence, but the longer the absence, the less likely that sick pay will continue to be received: only a relatively small amount of sick pay was received for absences beyond six months.

Our data indicated that private, first-party insurance is an insignificant proportion of present support for illness and injury.... Only 14 per cent of people in the survey held a policy of this type, and they were mainly work and road accident victims (who were also those most likely to obtain some damages). Fewer than half those with policies received a payment, and the mean amount was only £81.

The survey data on social care...showed that, on average, illness has more serious medical conse-quences than accidents: those who are ill are more likely to be in hospital for more than a week, and to use the services of general practitioners; they are also more likely to suffer residual disabilities.... The same holds for local authority and community health services: illness victims (particularly the elderly) make nearly three times as much use of these services as do accident victims.... On the basis of service use, therefore, the 'needs' of illness victims would appear to be greater than those of accident victims, yet the tort system in practice benefits only the latter group.

More than half the victims in the survey received informal care and support from family, relatives or neighbours.... This assistance often continued on a daily basis for more than six months and came largely from family members: it was not dependent on the age of the victim, nor the cause of his incapacity. Informal support is given without payment, and often in addition to, rather than instead of, local authority support.

A comparison of the different combinations of support received by the various categories of victims showed that those who obtain damages (almost exclusively work and road accident victims) are more likely than other victims to receive in addition some social security support, and slightly more likely to receive some private insurance payment....

In practice, compensation under the damages system is virtually confined to accident cases. Illness caused by the fault of another person can rarely be proved: out of the 1882 cases where damages were paid in the survey, only two were for illness—both were claims against employers, one for pneumo-coniosis suffered by a miner, and one for poisoning from asbestos dust suffered by a factory worker. In a similar way, benefits under the industrial injuries scheme are concentrated almost entirely on accident cases: only one in fifty of the injury benefits commencing in 1976–7 (the year nearest to our survey period) were for diseases prescribed under the scheme (*Social Security Statistics 1977*, Table 20.50). It should be noted, however, that the preference shown by existing compensation systems is not for accident cases in general, but rather for restricted categories of accidents—injuries suffered at work, on the roads, by criminal violence, or through service with the Armed Forces.... Our survey data indi-cate that although those injured in other categories of accident form the vast majority of accident victims...only one in fifty of them obtains any payment of damages....

NOTE

For the current text of the Criminal Injuries Compensation Scheme see pp. 1158–1166, post, and for a brief guide to the current social welfare benefits, pp. 1156–1158, post. It is suggested that while the details of these schemes have undergone many changes since the date of the Harris study, the general points made in the extract remain valid: i.e. the modernised CICS and benefits regimes have unfortunately retained the complexity which Harris et al. found to be an obstacle to claiming compensation, notoriously so in the new tax credits system (p. 1157, post).

(e) The aims of the law of tort

QUESTIONS

To what extent does the judgment in the *Bradford* case:
(a)   deter clubs and supervisory authorities from allowing or continuing similar dangerous hazards in future?
(b)   relieve the suffering of individual victims by spreading their losses through liability insurance or the price mechanism?
(c)   satisfy the principle of justice that one who has been damaged by the fault of another ought to be compensated by that other?

NOTES

1.   The argument for tort law as a deterrent assumes that, without tort liability, people would put their selfish interests ahead of the safety of others. Compare this with Sir Joseph Cantley's observation that it might have been sufficient simply to have told the Club that 'this danger must not be allowed to continue'. It is often argued that other social mechanisms, such as regulatory agencies, are more effective means than tort law for making people act reasonably, despite the failures of agencies like the fire authority in the *Bradford* case. Since the Bradford tragedy, regulation to prevent similar occurrences has been strengthened by the Fire Safety and Safety of Places of Sport Act 1987 (see note 1, pp. 20–21, ante), and in respect of responsibility for fire precautions in general a different regime now operates: see the Regulatory Reform (Fire Safety) Order 2005, SI 2005/1541).

Generally on deterrence theories see *Williams & Hepple*, pp. 138–142; Gl. Williams (1951) 4 CLP 137; *Atiyah*, pp. 424–458; *Harris et al.*, pp. 139–163; P. A. Bell and J. O'Connell, *Accidental Justice: the Dilemmas of Tort Law* (New Haven and London, 1997), pp. 68–100; P. Cane, *The Anatomy of Tort Law* (Oxford, 1997) pp. 217–225.

2.   Compensation is usually seen as the principal goal of tort law. This springs from a natural compassion for victims of accident and disease but rests on the dubious assumptions that tort defendants are the best loss-spreaders, that the forensic and out-of-court mechanisms for determining fault and assessing damages are capable of delivering compensation to most victims, and that other means of compensation (such as social security) are inadequate.

For the arguments for and against compensation theories, see *Williams & Hepple*, pp. 24–30, 78–86, 206–208; *Atiyah*, pp. 411–419; *Conaghan and Mansell*, pp. 105–123.

3.   The corrective justice theory of tort law, looked at from the point of view of the victim, is sometimes called the principle of 'ethical compensation', and from the offender's viewpoint, 'ethical retribution': see Gl. Williams (1951) 4 CLP at p. 140ff. Whatever the attractions of doing justice between two individuals, in practice the amount that claimants recover is likely to be far less than they 'deserve' and the amount an uninsured defendant might have to pay is far greater that he or she 'deserves' to pay for momentary inattention or 'negligence'.

See *Williams & Hepple*, pp. 136–137; *Atiyah*, pp. 419–423; R. A. Posner in *Foundations of Tort Law* (ed. S. Levmore) (New York and London, 1994), pp. 59–66.

3 CIVIL JUSTICE REFORMS AND FUNDING OF CIVIL ACTIONS

NOTE

Since the *Bradford Football Fire* case and many other English cases included in this book were decided there have been profound changes in the civil justice system, and the way in which civil actions are funded. The procedural reforms result from two reports by Lord Woolf: *Access to Justice: Interim Report* (Lord Chancellor's Department, 1995), and *Access to Justice, Final Report* (Lord Chancellor's Department, 1996). The changes in procedure are embodied in the Civil Procedure Rules 1998 (CPR), which came into force on 27 April 1999. Other changes result from the Access to Justice Act 1969, one of which relates to the funding of civil actions. The Legal Services Commission has established a publicly funded Community Legal Service, providing information, advice, and assistance, and manages a fund replacing the present system of civil legal aid. The Legal Services Commission will make contracts with all kinds of providers in order to deliver information and legal services.

Most personal injury actions are likely to be funded by conditional fees, which were introduced under the Courts and Legal Services Act 1990, s. 58, and to which changes have been made by the Access to Justice Act 1999, s. 27. Under a conditional fee agreement (CFA), the lawyer agrees not to charge a fee if the case is lost, in return for a higher fee than normal if it is won. The client or lawyer can take out insurance to cover the risk of losing and having to pay the other side's costs. In a successful case, the other party will usually be ordered to pay most of the lawyer's normal fees and it is possible for the winning party to recover the success fee and any insurance premium from the losing party, although the success fee cannot be more than 100 per cent of the normal fee. P. Fenn et al., *The Funding of Personal Injury Litigation* (2006, Department of Constitutional Affairs) find that for non-clinical personal injuries, where legal aid is no longer available, CFAs are now the 'predominant' means for financing claims.

The House of Lords considered the recoverability of success fees and 'after the event' (ATE) insurance premiums in *Callery v Gray* [2002] 3 All ER 417, [2002] UKHL 28. A majority of their Lordships held that the Court of Appeal was in a better position to regulate civil procedure matters (including costs). However, several of their Lordships expressed unease about the new regime for funding litigation. Lord Nicholls, at [12]–[13], was concerned that excessive costs were being incurred by claimants, since the defendant bears those costs if the claimant wins, whereas the claimant pays no fees (and the ATE insurance pays the defendant's fees) if the claim fails. Thus as Lord Bingham stated at [5], 'the practical result is to transfer the entire cost of funding this kind of litigation to the liability insurers of unsuccessful defendants (and defendants who settle the claims made against them) and thus, indirectly, to the wider public who pay premiums to insure themselves against liability to pay compensation for causing personal injury'.

In the report *Making Amends* (2003, Department of Health), analysing negligence claims against the National Health Service, the Chief Medical Officer considered that CFAs may have led to an increase in the NHS compensation bill, but the evidence was 'inconclusive'. However, contrary to the Chief Medical Officer's finding that 'there has so far been little take up of CFAs and insurance-backed products in the field of clinical negligence', the comprehensive study of Fenn et al., first published in 2005, shows that the funding of clinical negligence claims is divided equally between legal aid, CFAs, and other sources (i.e. private hourly fees). However, CFAs seem here to be highly selective, mostly associated with 'relatively high value but relatively low risk clinical negligence claims' (suggesting that solicitors are particularly cautious about taking such cases on a conditional fee basis, given that causation and liability difficulties render clinical claims 'notoriously difficult to win').

R. Lewis, A. Morris, and K. Oliphant (2006) 14 *TLJ* 158 consider an array of data on levels of compensation with wide statistical bases, emanating from government and the insurance industry. They conclude that 'contrary to popular belief', CFAs (and advertising by personal injury lawyers) have made no difference to the frequency of claims. There is little evidence that a 'nothing to lose' attitude has fostered litigiousness on the part of claimants, as the number of claims has been 'relatively stable since at least 1997–1998' (the first year in which reliable data are available from the government's Compensation Recovery Unit). More generally, the authors conclude that the increase in the total compensation bill in recent years is attributable to higher compensation per claim, rather than higher numbers of claims. However, looking back further (to the 1970s), there has been an 'approximately three-fold rise in total claims numbers over 30 years', an increase which suggests an enhanced claims-consciousness compared with the Harris et al. study conducted in 1976–7 (p. 17, ante). The survey of Lewis et al., firmly grounded in reliable statistics, should be kept in mind when consideration is given to the 'compensation culture'. On the 'compensation culture' debate, see further p. 293, post and K. Williams (2005) 25 LS 499.

CHAPTER TWO

THE DUTY OF CARE

The tort of negligence has been the subject of varying classifications. It is sometimes said that it involves a duty of care, a breach of that duty, and damage caused to the claimant by that breach, and following that breakdown of the tort, it is the duty of care concept with which this chapter is concerned.

The traditional point at which to commence a consideration of the duty of care is the broad 'neighbour principle' enunciated by Lord Atkin in *M'Alister (or Donoghue) v Stevenson* [1932] AC 562 (p. 32, post) in which he attempted to rationalise and develop the earlier case law. The principle works fairly well when applied to negligent interference with physical interests. Indeed, in *Home Office v Dorset Yacht Co Ltd* [1970] AC 1004, [1970] 2 All ER 294 (p. 71, post) Lord Reid went so far as to say 'the time has come when we can and should say that it ought to apply unless there is some justification or valid explanation for its exclusion'; and there was a similar approach in *Anns v Merton London Borough Council* [1978] AC 728, [1977] 2 All ER 492. However, recent years have witnessed a shift away from any general principle and a retreat to a more individual and compartmentalised approach: see, for example, *Caparo Industries plc v Dickman* [1990] 2 AC 605, [1990] 1 All ER 568 (p. 37, post), although the use in, for example, *Henderson v Merrett Syndicates Ltd* [1995] 2 AC 145, [1994] 3 All ER 506 (p. 232, post) of the broad principle derived from *Hedley Byrne & Co Ltd v Heller & Partners Ltd* [1964] AC 465, [1963] 2 All ER 575 (p. 207, post) should be noted.

It has been generally recognised that concepts such as 'duty', 'remoteness', 'causation', and 'negligence' (in the sense of breach of duty) have been interchangeably used as mechanisms to control liability; at times the ambiguity inherent in the notion of 'foreseeability' has been stretched to provide a sole determinant of liability, but its very ambiguity and the realisation that defendants are not always made responsible for foreseeable harm have revitalised other verbal mechanisms. Nevertheless, as *Atiyah* states (at p. 69), 'the main function of the concept of the duty of care is to define the boundaries of liability for damage caused by negligent conduct by reference to what are commonly called "policy considerations"'. It will, though, be seen (p. 157, post) that there has been a tendency in recent times for the courts to deny that they may consider 'public policy', as opposed to 'legal policy'.

Over the years a significant distinction has been drawn between what is variously called 'financial' or 'pecuniary' or 'economic' loss, on the one hand, and physical damage, on the other hand. At times the validity of this distinction has been questioned and the complexity of the issues involved merits a separate chapter for discussion of the scope of the protection of a person's economic interests. Pragmatic objections, which have been raised to the extension of the 'neighbour principle' to the question of recovery of damages for economic loss, have not been raised to the same extent in regard to the kinds of conduct—such as omissions and control of the conduct of others—which may give rise to a duty of care. These are discussed in this chapter. Particular problems have been experienced with negligence liability where public authorities' discretionary powers are involved, with the question of recovery for psychiatric illness and with various issues concerning the birth of children: these merit a separate chapter and thus the consideration of the duty of care will span three chapters.

The use of the concept of 'duty-situations' has become so deeply entrenched in judicial thinking that the academic controversies about whether it is a necessary element in the tort of negligence now seem somewhat strange (but W. W. Buckland (1935) 51 LQR 637 still repays reading; see also the views expressed more recently by D. Howarth [1991] CLJ 58; cf. J. Stapleton, (1995) 111 LQR 301 at 303–304; B. Hepple (1997) 50 CLP 69). However, its potential abolition was discussed, but rejected, by Lord Nicholls in *D v East Berkshire Community Health NHS Trust* [2005] 2 All ER 443, [2005] UKHL 23 at [92]–[94] (p. 52, post). The duty concept is certainly still capable of provoking discussion. N.J. McBride (2004) 24 Oxf LJS 417 argues that the duty element has a real existence; cf. the view in *Atiyah*, p. 69 that to 'say that a person owes a duty of care in a particular situation means (and means only) that the person will be liable for causing damage by negligence in that situation' (and see further ibid, note 7). McBride argues that there are many duties of care: duty is a relational concept (i.e. arising out of the particular relationship of the parties), but Howarth (2006) 26 Oxf JLS 449 has argued for one all-embracing duty of care, albeit with certain immunities. (The evolution of the Restatement (3d) of Torts also gave rise to discussion of duty in the USA: see, for example, D. Owen (2001) 54 Vand L Rev 767.) Whatever the position on the matters raised ante, the rapid growth of technology and new situations of danger mean that the judiciary will always have to deal with the unexpected. It is this which gives to the duty of care cases a special importance for understanding the judicial process.

1 GENERAL PRINCIPLES

■ Donoghue (or M'Alister) v Stevenson
House of Lords [1932] All ER Rep 1

Appeal from an interlocutor of the Second Division of the Court of Session in Scotland.

On 26 August 1928, the appellant, a shop assistant, drank a bottle of ginger-beer manufactured by the respondent, which a friend had ordered on her behalf from a retailer in a shop at Paisley and given to her. She stated that the shopkeeper, who supplied the ginger-beer, opened the bottle, which she said was sealed with a metal cap and was made of dark opaque glass, and poured some of its contents into a tumbler which contained some ice cream, and that she drank some of the contents of the tumbler, that her friend then lifted the bottle and was pouring the remainder of the contents into the tumbler, when a snail which had been in the bottle floated out in a state of decomposition. As a result, the appellant alleged, she had contracted a serious illness, and she claimed from the respondent damages for negligence. She alleged that the respondent, as the manufacturer of an article intended for consumption and contained in a receptacle which prevented inspection, owed a duty to her as consumer of the article to take care that there was no noxious element in the article, that he neglected such duty, and that he was, consequently, liable for any damage caused by such neglect. The case then came before the Lord Ordinary, who rejected the plea in law of the respondent and allowed the parties a proof of their averments, but on a reclaiming note the Second Division (the Lord Justice Clerk, Lord Ormidale and Lord Anderson; Lord Hunter dissenting) recalled the interlocutor of the Lord Ordinary and dismissed the action. On appeal to the House of Lords:

LORD ATKIN: . . .

The sole question for determination in this case is legal: Do the averments made by the pursuer in her pleading, if true, disclose a cause of action? I need not re-state the particular facts. The question is whether the manufacturer of an article of drink sold by him to a distributor in circumstances which prevent the distributor or the ultimate purchaser or consumer from discovering by inspection any defect is under any legal duty to the ultimate purchaser or consumer to take reasonable care that the article is free from defect likely to cause injury to health. I do not think a more important problem has occupied your Lordships in your judicial capacity, important both because of its bearing on public health and because of the practical test which it applies to the system of law under which it arises. The case has to be determined in accordance with Scots law, but it has been a matter of agreement between the experienced counsel who argued this case, and it appears to be the basis of the judgments of the learned judges of the Court of Session, that for the purposes of determining this problem the law of Scotland and the law of England are the same. I speak with little authority on this point, but my own research, such as it is, satisfies me that the principles of the law of Scotland on such a question as the present are identical with those of English law, and I discuss the issue on that footing. The law of both countries appears to be that in order to support an action for damages for negligence the complainant has to show that he has been injured by the breach of a duty owed to him in the circumstances by the defendant to take reasonable care to avoid such injury. In the present case we are not concerned with the breach of the duty; if a duty exists, that would be a question of fact which is sufficiently averred and for the present purposes must be assumed. We are solely concerned with the question whether as a matter of law in the circumstances alleged the defender owed any duty to the pursuer to take care.

It is remarkable how difficult it is to find in the English authorities statements of general application defining the relations between parties that give rise to the duty. The courts are concerned with the particular relations which come before them in actual litigation, and it is sufficient to say whether the duty exists in those circumstances. The result is that the courts have been engaged upon an elaborate classification of duties as they exist in respect of property, whether real or personal, with further divisions as to ownership, occupation or control, and distinctions based on the particular relations of the one side or the other, whether manufacturer, salesman or landlord, customer, tenant, stranger, and so on. In this way it can be ascertained at any time whether the law recognises a duty, but only where the case can be referred to some particular species which has been examined and classified. And yet the duty which is common to all the cases where liability is established must logically be based upon some element common to the cases where it is found to exist. To exist[1] a complete logical definition of the general principle is probably to go beyond the function of the judge, for, the more general the definition, the more likely it is to omit essentials or introduce non-essentials. The attempt was made by Lord Esher in *Heaven v Pender*[2] . . . As framed it was demonstrably too wide, though it appears to me, if properly limited, to be capable of affording a valuable practical guide.

At present I content myself with pointing out that in English law there must be and is some general conception of relations giving rise to a duty of care, of which the particular cases found in the books are but instances. The liability for negligence, whether you style it such or treat it as in other systems as a species of 'culpa', is no doubt based upon a general public sentiment of moral wrongdoing for which the offender must pay. But acts or omissions which any moral code would censure cannot in a practical world be treated so as to give a right to every person injured by them to demand relief. In this way rules of law arise which limit the range of complainants and the extent of their remedy. The rule that you are

---

[1] This word does not appear in the Law Reports, [1932] AC 562 at 580, but is replaced by the word 'seek'.
[2] (1883) 11 QBD 503.

to love your neighbour becomes in law: You must not injure your neighbour, and the lawyers' question: Who is my neighbour? receives a restricted reply. You must take reasonable care to avoid acts or omissions which you can reasonably foresee would be likely to injure your neighbour. Who then, in law, is my neighbour? The answer seems to be persons who are so closely and directly affected by my act that I ought reasonably to have them in contemplation as being so affected when I am directing my mind to the acts or omissions which are called in question. This appears to me to be the doctrine of *Heaven v Pender*[2] as laid down by Lord Esher when it is limited by the notion of proximity introduced by Lord Esher himself and A. L. Smith LJ in *Le Lievre v Gould*.[3] Lord Esher MR says ([1893] 1 QB at p. 497):

> 'That case established that, under certain circumstances, one man may owe a duty to another, even though there is no contract between them. If one man is near to another, or is near to the property of another, a duty lies upon him not to do that which may cause a personal injury to that other, or may injure his property.'

So A. L. Smith LJ says ([1893] 1 QB at p. 504):

> 'The decision of *Heaven v Pender*[2] was founded upon the principle that a duty to take due care did arise when the person or property of one was in such proximity to the person or property of another that, if due care was not taken damage might be done by the one to the other.'

I think that this sufficiently states the truth if proximity be not confined to mere physical proximity, but be used, as I think it was intended, to extend to such close and direct relations that the act complained of directly affects a person whom the person alleged to be bound to take care would know would be directly affected by his careless act. That this is the sense in which nearness or 'proximity' was intended by Lord Esher is obvious from his own illustration in *Heaven v Pender*[2] (11 QBD at p. 510) of the application of his doctrine to the sale of goods.

> 'This [i.e., the rule he has just formulated] includes the case of goods, & c., supplied to be used immediately by a particular person or persons, or one of a class of persons, where it would be obvious to the person supplying, if he thought, that the goods would in all probability be used at once by such persons before a reasonable opportunity for discovering any defect which might exist, and where the thing supplied would be of such a nature that a neglect of ordinary care or skill as to its condition or the manner of supplying it would probably cause danger to the person or property of the person for whose use it was supplied, and who was about to use it. It would exclude a case in which the goods are supplied under circumstances in which it would be a chance by whom they would be used, or whether they would be used or not, or whether they would be used before there would probably be means of observing any defect, or where the goods would be of such a nature that a want of care or skill as to their condition or the manner of supplying them would not probably produce danger of injury to person or property.'

I draw particular attention to the fact that Lord Esher emphasises the necessity of goods having to be 'used immediately' and 'used at once before a reasonable opportunity of inspection'. This is obviously to exclude the possibility of goods having their condition altered by lapse of time, and to call attention to the proximate relationship, which may be too remote where inspection even by the person using, certainly by an intermediate person, may reasonably be interposed. With this necessary qualification of proximate relationship, as explained in *Le Lievre v Gould*,[4] I think the judgment of Lord Esher expresses the law of England. Without the qualification, I think that the majority of the court in *Heaven v Pender*[5] was justified in thinking that the principle was expressed in too general terms. There will, no doubt, arise cases where it will be difficult to determine whether the contemplated relationship is so close that the duty arises but in the class of case now before the court I cannot conceive any difficulty to arise.

³ [1893] 1 QB 491.   ⁴ [1893] 1 QB 491.   ⁵ (1883) 11 QBD 503.

A manufacturer puts up an article of food in a container which he knows will be opened by the actual consumer. There can be no inspection by any purchaser and no reasonable preliminary inspection by the consumer. Negligently in the course of preparation he allows the contents to be mixed with poison. It is said that the law of England and Scotland is that the poisoned consumer has no remedy against the negligent manufacturer. If this were the result of the authorities, I should consider the result a grave defect in the law and so contrary to principle that I should hesitate long before following any decision to that effect which had not the authority of this House. . . . There are other instances than of articles of food and drink where goods are sold intended to be used immediately by the consumer, such as many forms of goods sold for cleaning purposes, when the same liability must exist. The doctrine supported by the decision below would not only deny a remedy to the consumer who was injured by consuming bottled beer or chocolates poisoned by the negligence of the manufacturer, but also to the user of what should be a harmless proprietary medicine, an ointment, a soap, a cleaning fluid or cleaning powder. I confine myself to articles of common household use, where everyone, including the manufacturer, knows that the articles will be used by persons other than the actual ultimate purchaser—namely, by members of his family and his servants, and, in some cases, his guests. I do not think so ill of our jurisprudence as to suppose that its principles are so remote from the ordinary needs of civilised society and the ordinary claims which it makes upon its members as to deny a legal remedy where there is so obviously a social wrong.

It will be found, I think, on examination, that there is no case in which the circumstances have been such as I have just suggested where the liability has been negatived. There are numerous cases where the relations were much more remote where the duty has been held not to exist. There are also dicta in such cases which go further than was necessary for the determination of the particular issues, which have caused the difficulty experienced by the courts below. I venture to say that in the branch of the law which deals with civil wrongs, dependent in England, at any rate, entirely upon the application by judges of general principles also formulated by judges, it is of particular importance to guard against the danger of stating propositions of law in wider terms than is necessary, lest essential factors be omitted in the wider survey and the inherent adaptability of English law be unduly restricted. For this reason it is very necessary, in considering reported cases in the law of torts, that the actual decision alone should carry authority, proper weight, of course, being given to the dicta of the judges. . . .

I do not find it necessary to discuss at length the cases dealing with duties where a thing is dangerous, or, in the narrower category, belongs to a class of things which are dangerous in themselves. I regard the distinction as an unnatural one so far as it is used to serve as a logical differentiation by which to distinguish the existence or non-existence of a legal right. In this respect I agree with what was said by Scrutton LJ in *Hodge & Sons v Anglo-American Oil Co*[6] (12 Ll L Rep at p. 187), a case which was ultimately decided on a question of fact:

> 'Personally, I do not understand the difference between a thing dangerous in itself as poison and a thing not dangerous as a class, but by negligent construction dangerous as a particular thing. The latter, if anything, seems the more dangerous of the two; it is a wolf in sheep's clothing instead of an obvious wolf.'

The nature of the thing may very well call for different degrees of care, and the person dealing with it may well contemplate persons as being within the sphere of his duty to take care who would not be sufficiently proximate with less dangerous goods, so that not only the degree of care but the range of persons to whom a duty is owed may be extended. But they all illustrate the general principle. . . .

If your Lordships accept the view that the appellant's pleading discloses a relevant cause of action, you will be affirming the proposition that by Scots and English law alike a manufacturer of products which he sells in such a form as to show that he intends them to reach the ultimate consumer in the

---

[6] (1922) 12 Ll L Rep 183.

form in which they left him, with no reasonable possibility of intermediate examination, and with the knowledge that the absence of reasonable care in the preparation or putting up of the products will result in injury to the consumer's life or property, owes a duty to the consumer to take that reasonable care.

It is a proposition that I venture to say no one in Scotland or England who was not a lawyer would for one moment doubt. It will be an advantage to make it clear that the law in this matter, as in most others, is in accordance with sound common sense. I think that this appeal should be allowed.

LORD MACMILLAN: . . .

The law takes no cognizance of carelessness in the abstract. It concerns itself with carelessness only where there is a duty to take care and where failure in that duty has caused damage. In such circumstances carelessness assumes the legal quality of negligence and entails the consequences in law of negligence. What then are the circumstances which give rise to this duty to take care? In the daily contacts of social and business life human beings are thrown into or place themselves in an infinite variety of relationships with their fellows, and the law can refer only to the standards of the reasonable man in order to determine whether any particular relationship gives rise to a duty to take care as between those who stand in that relationship to each other. The grounds of action may be as various and manifold as human errancy, and the conception of legal responsibility may develop in adaptation to altering social conditions and standards. The criterion of judgment must adjust and adapt itself to the changing circumstances of life. The categories of negligence are never closed. The cardinal principle of liability is that the party complained of should owe to the party complaining a duty to take care and that the party complaining should be able to prove that he has suffered damage in consequence of a breach of that duty. Where there is room for diversity of view is in determining what circumstances will establish such a relationship between the parties as to give rise on the one side to a duty to take care and on the other side to a right to have care taken.

To descend from these generalities to the circumstances of the present case I do not think that any reasonable man or any twelve reasonable men would hesitate to hold that if the appellant establishes her allegations the respondent has exhibited carelessness in the conduct of his business. For a manufacturer of aerated water to store his empty bottles in a place where snails can get access to them and to fill his bottles without taking any adequate precautions by inspection or otherwise to ensure that they contain no deleterious foreign matter may reasonably be characterised as carelessness without applying too exacting a standard. But, as I have pointed out, it is not enough to prove the respondent to be careless in his process of manufacture. The question is: Does he owe a duty to take care, and to whom does he owe that duty? I have no hesitation in affirming that a person who for gain engages in the business of manufacturing articles of food and drink intended for consumption by members of the public in the form in which he issues them is under a duty to take care in the manufacture of these articles. That duty, in my opinion, he owes to those whom he intends to consume his products. He manufactures his commodities for human consumption; he intends and contemplates that they shall be consumed. By reason of that very fact he places himself in a relationship with all the potential consumers of his commodities, and that relationship, which he assumes and desires for his own ends, imposes upon him a duty to take care to avoid injuring them. He owes them a duty not to convert by his own carelessness an article which he issues to them as wholesome and innocent into an article which is dangerous to life and health.

. . . It must always be a question of circumstances whether the carelessness amounts to negligence and whether the injury is not too remote from the carelessness. I can readily conceive that where a manufacturer has parted with his product and it has passed into other hands it may well be exposed to vicissitudes which may render it defective or noxious and for which the manufacturer could not in any view be held to be to blame. It may be a good general rule to regard responsibility as ceasing when control ceases. So also where between the manufacturer and the user there is interposed a party who has the means and opportunity of examining the manufacturer's product before he reissues it to the actual user. But where, as in the present case, the article of consumption is so prepared as to be intended to reach the consumer in the condition in which it leaves the manufacturer and the manufacturer takes steps to ensure this by sealing or otherwise closing the container, so that the contents cannot be tampered with, I regard his control as remaining effective until the article reaches the consumer and the container is opened by him. The intervention of any exterior agency is intended to be excluded, and was in fact in the present case excluded....

...I am...of opinion that this appeal should be allowed, the judgment of the Second Division of the Court of Session reversed, and the judgment of the Lord Ordinary restored.

[LORD THANKERTON delivered a speech in favour of allowing the appeal. LORD BUCKMASTER and LORD TOMLIN delivered speeches in favour of dismissing the appeal.]

Appeal allowed.

QUESTIONS

1. It has been said that this case exploded the 'privity of contract fallacy'. What does this mean?
2. What policy reasons might there have been for the existence of this 'fallacy'?
3. What is the ratio decidendi of the case? (See R. F. V. Heuston (1957) 20 MLR 1 at 5–9.)

NOTES

1. Whether a snail was present in the ginger-beer bottle was never judicially determined. (See e.g. (1955) 71 LQR 472; G. Lewis, *Lord Atkin* (London, 1983), pp. 52–53. For more background to the case see Lewis, op cit., p. 51 et seq; M. R. Taylor (1983) 17 UBCL Rev 59; A. M. Linden ibid. 67; A. Rodger (1988) 41 Current LP 1 and (1992) 108 LQR 236; J. D. Gordon 111, (1999) 115 LQR 183; W. W. McBryde in *Obligations in Context: Essays in Honour of Professor D. M. Walker*, edited by A. J. Gamble, (Edinburgh, 1990), p. 13.)
2. This case has been important in the general development of the tort of negligence, as well as the more specific area of liability for products. This latter point is dealt with in chap. 10, post, where it will be seen that there is now a statutory strict liability regime for defective products (although the tort of negligence co-exists with it).
3. In *Deyong v Shenburn* [1946] KB 227, [1946] 1 All ER 226 Du Parcq LJ stated (at p. 229):

   It is not true to say that wherever a man finds himself in such a position that unless he does a certain act another person may suffer, or that if he does something another person will suffer, then it is his duty in the one case to be careful to do the act and in the other case to be careful not to do the act. Any such proposition is much too wide. One has to find that there has been a breach of a duty which the law recognises, and to see what the law recognises one can only look at the decisions of the courts.

   For example, in *Stephens v Anglian Water Authority* [1987] 3 All ER 379, [1987] 1 WLR 1381, noted by J. G. Fleming (1988) 104 LQR 183, the Court of Appeal regarded itself as bound by the authorities to conclude that no duty of care is owed by a landowner in abstracting percolating water under his land where such abstraction causes subsidence to another's land.

   The result of the inquiry into the precedents, which Du Parcq LJ required in *Deyong v Shenburn*, ante, may, of course, be that there is no answer, or at least no clear, binding answer. The judges will then have a choice whether to accept that the foreseeable harm in question should be compensated or not (i.e. to say that there is or is not a duty of care). This is the question to which we must now turn.

■ Governors of the Peabody Donation Fund v Sir Lindsay Parkinson & Co Ltd

House of Lords [1984] 3 All ER 529

LORD KEITH OF KINKEL: . . .

Lord Atkin's famous enunciation of the general principles on which the law of negligence is founded, in *Donoghue v Stevenson* [1932] AC 562 at 580, [1932] All ER Rep 1 at 11, has long been recognised as not intended to afford a comprehensive definition, to the effect that every situation which is capable of falling within the terms of the utterance and which results in loss automatically affords a remedy in damages. Lord Reid said in *Home Office v Dorset Yacht Co Ltd* [1970] 2 All ER 294 at 297–298, [1970] AC 1004 at 1027:

> 'It is not to be treated as if it were a statutory definition. It will require qualification in new circumstances. But I think that the time has come when we can and should say that it ought to apply unless there is some justification or valid explanation for its exclusion. For example, causing economic loss is a different matter; for one thing it is often caused by deliberate action. Competition involves traders being entitled to damage their rivals' interests by promoting their own, and there is a long chapter of the law determining in what circumstances owners of land can, and in what circumstances they may not, use their proprietary rights so as to injure their neighbours. But where negligence is involved the tendency has been to apply principles analogous to those stated by Lord Atkin (cf *Hedley Bryne & Co Ltd v Heller & Partners Ltd* [1963] 2 All ER 575, [1964] AC 465). And when a person has done nothing to put himself in any relationship with another person in distress or with his property mere accidental propinquity does not require him to go to that person's assistance. There may be a moral duty to do so, but it is not practicable to make it a legal duty.'

Lord Wilberforce spoke on similar lines in *Anns v Merton London Borough* [1977] 2 All ER 492 at 498, [1978] AC 728 at 751–752:

> 'Through the trilogy of cases in this House, *Donoghue v Stevenson* [1932] AC 562, [1932] All ER Rep 1; *Hedley Bryne & Co Ltd v Heller & Partners Ltd* [1963] 2 All ER 575, [1964] AC 465, and *Home Office v Dorset Yacht Co Ltd* [1970] 2 All ER 294, [1970] AC 1004, the position has now been reached that in order to establish that a duty of care arises in a particular situation, it is not necessary to bring the facts of that situation within those of previous situations in which a duty of care has been held to exist. Rather the question has to be approached in two stages. First one has to ask whether, as between the alleged wrongdoer and the person who has suffered damage there is a sufficient relationship of proximity or neighbourhood such that, in the reasonable contemplation of the former, carelessness on his part may be likely to cause damage to the latter, in which case a prima facie duty of care arises. Secondly, if the first question is answered affirmatively, it is necessary to consider whether there are any considerations which ought to negative, or to reduce or limit the scope of the duty or the class of person to whom it is owed or the damages to which a breach of it may give rise (see the *Dorset Yacht* case [1970] 2 All ER 294 at 297–298, [1970] AC 1004 at 1027 per Lord Reid).'

There has been a tendency in some recent cases to treat these passages as being themselves of a definitive character. This is a temptation which should be resisted. The true question in each case is whether the particular defendant owed to the particular plaintiff a duty of care having the scope which is contended for, and whether he was in breach of that duty with consequent loss to the plaintiff. A relationship of proximity in Lord Atkin's sense must exist before any duty of care can arise, but the scope of the duty must depend on all the circumstances of the case. In *Home Office v Dorset Yacht Co Ltd* [1970] 2 All ER 294 at 307–308, [1970] AC 1004 at 1038–1039 Lord Morris, after observing that at the conclusion of his speech in *Donoghue v Stevenson* [1932] AC 562 at 599, [1932] All ER Rep 1 at 20 Lord Atkin said that it was advantageous if the law 'is in accordance with sound common sense' and expressing the view that a special relation existed between the prison officers and the yacht company which gave rise to a duty on the former to control their charges so as to prevent them doing damage, continued:

> 'Apart from this I would conclude that in the situation stipulated in the present case it would not only be fair and reasonable that a duty of care should exist but that it would be contrary to the fitness of things were it not so. I doubt whether it is necessary to say, in cases where the court is asked whether in a particular situation a duty existed, that the court is called on to make a decision as to policy. Policy need not be invoked where reasons and good sense will at once point the way. If the test whether in some particular situation a duty of care arises may in some cases have to be whether it is fair and reasonable that it should so arise the court must not shrink from being the arbiter. As Lord Radcliffe said in his speech in *Davis Contractors Ltd v Fareham Urban District Council* [1956] 2 All ER 145 at 160, [1956] AC 696 at 728, the court is "the spokesman of the fair and reasonable man".'

So in determining whether or not a duty of care of particular scope was incumbent on a defendant it is material to take into consideration whether it is just and reasonable that it should be so. . . .

[LORD SCARMAN, LORD BRIDGE OF HARWICH, LORD BRANDON OF OAKBROOK, and LORD TEMPLEMAN agreed with LORD KEITH OF KINKEL's speech.]

QUESTIONS

1.   How do the comments of Lord Reid in *Dorset Yacht* and of Lord Wilberforce in *Anns* (both of which are quoted in the extract above) affect Lord Atkin's 'neighbour principle'? Do they expand it or restrict it?
2.   Does *Peabody* restrict the comments of Lord Reid and Lord Wilberforce? If so, how?
3.   Consider the extract (set out in *Peabody*) from Lord Morris' speech in the *Dorset Yacht* case. How do 'policy' and 'reasons and good sense' differ?

NOTE

Lord Wilberforce's two-stage test in *Anns*, which is set out in *Peabody*, ante, was for some time cited with approval in the subsequent case law. Writing in 1984, *Williams & Hepple*, p. 102, saw its significance as lying in the shift of the 'neighbour principle' 'from being an argument to support new areas of liability, if there were policy considerations in favour of doing so, into a principle that would apply unless there was a policy justification for excluding it. The onus of argument shifted, with "policy" operating only as a long-stop where the logical application of the factual test of reasonable foreseeability would lead to obviously undesirable social or financial consequences.' *Peabody*, however, marked something of a turning-point, and the downgrading of the importance of the *Anns* two-stage test continued until the test was replaced.

■ Caparo Industries plc v Dickman
House of Lords [1990] 1 All ER 568

Caparo Industries plc owned shares in a public company, F Ltd. In reliance on the audited accounts prepared by the defendants, Touche Ross & Co, Caparo purchased more shares in F Ltd and later purchased the entire share capital in the company. The audited accounts showed that F Ltd was profitable, but in fact the company was making a loss, having been defrauded by its directors. Caparo commenced proceedings against the auditors, alleging that they had been negligent in auditing the accounts. On the trial of a preliminary issue as to whether the auditors owed Caparo a duty of care, as potential investors in F Ltd, the claim was struck out by the judge at first instance and this was confirmed by the Court of Appeal. On appeal to the House of Lords, Caparo's appeal was dismissed.

LORD BRIDGE OF HARWICH:...

In determining the existence and scope of the duty of care which one person may owe to another in the infinitely varied circumstances of human relationships there has for long been a tension between two different approaches. Traditionally the law finds the existence of the duty in different specific situations each exhibiting its own particular characteristics. In this way the law has identified a wide variety of duty situations, all falling within the ambit of the tort of negligence, but sufficiently distinct to require separate definition of the essential ingredients by which the existence of the duty is to be recognised. Commenting on the outcome of this traditional approach, Lord Atkin, in his seminal speech in *Donoghue v Stevenson* [1932] AC 562 at 579–580, [1932] All ER Rep 1 at 11, observed:

> 'The result is that the Courts have been engaged upon an elaborate classification of duties as they exist in respect of property, whether real or personal, with further divisions as to ownership, occupation or control, and distinctions based on the particular relations of the one side or the other, whether manufacturer, salesman or landlord, customer, tenant, stranger, and so on. In this way it can be ascertained at any time whether the law recognizes a duty, but only where the case can be referred to some particular species which has been examined and classified. And yet the duty which is common to all the cases where liability is established must logically be based upon some element common to the cases where it is found to exist.'

It is this last sentence which signifies the introduction of the more modern approach of seeking a single general principle which may be applied in all circumstances to determine the existence of a duty of care. Yet Lord Atkin himself sounds the appropriate note of caution by adding:

> 'To seek a complete logical definition of the general principle is probably to go beyond the function of the judge, for the more general the definition the more likely it is to omit essentials or to introduce non-essentials.'

...The most comprehensive attempt to articulate a single general principle is reached in the well-known passage from the speech of Lord Wilberforce in *Anns v Merton London Borough* [1977] 2 All ER 492 at 498, [1978] AC 728 at 751–752...

But since *Anns's* case a series of decisions of the Privy Council and of your Lordships' House, notably in judgments and speeches delivered by Lord Keith, have emphasised the inability of any single general principle to provide a practical test which can be applied to every situation to determine whether a duty of care is owed and, if so, what is its scope: see *Peabody Donation Fund v Sir Lindsay Parkinson & Co Ltd* [1984] 3 All ER 529 at 533–534, [1985] AC 210 at 239–241, *Yuen Kun-yeu v A-G of Hong Kong* [1987] 2 All ER 705 at 709–712, [1988] AC 175 at 190–194, *Rowling v Takaro Properties Ltd* [1988] 1 All ER 163 at 172, [1988] AC 473 at 501 and *Hill v Chief Constable of West Yorkshire* [1988] 2 All ER 238 at 241, [1989] AC 53 at 60. What emerges is that, in addition to the foreseeability of damage, necessary ingredients in any situation giving rise to a duty of care are that there should exist between the party owing the duty and the party to whom it is owed a relationship characterised by the law as one of 'proximity' or 'neighbourhood' and that the situation should be one in which the court considers it fair, just and reasonable that the law should impose a duty of a given scope on the one party for the benefit of the other. But it is implicit in the passages referred to that the concepts of proximity and fairness embodied in these additional ingredients are not susceptible of any such precise definition as would be necessary to give them utility as practical tests, but amount in effect to little more than convenient labels to attach to the features of different specific situations which, on a detailed examination of all the circumstances, the law recognises pragmatically as giving rise to a duty of care of a given scope. Whilst recognising, of course, the importance of the underlying general principles common to the whole field of negligence, I think the law has now moved in the direction of attaching greater significance to the more traditional categorisation of distinct and recognisable situations as guides to the existence, the scope and the limits of the varied duties of care which the law imposes. We must now, I think, recognise the wisdom of the words of Brennan J in the High Court of Australia in *Sutherland Shire Council v Heyman* (1985) 60 ALR 1 at 43–44, where he said:

> 'It is preferable in my view, that the law should develop novel categories of negligence incrementally and by analogy with established categories, rather than by a massive extension of a prima facie duty of care restrained only by indefinable "considerations which ought to negative, or to reduce or limit the scope of the duty or the class of person to whom it is owed".'

One of the most important distinctions always to be observed lies in the law's essentially different approach to the different kinds of damage which one party may have suffered in consequence of the act or omissions of another. It is one thing to owe a duty of care to avoid causing injury to the person or property of others. It is quite another to avoid causing others to suffer purely economic loss....

...It is never sufficient to ask simply whether A owes B a duty of care. It is always necessary to determine the scope of the duty by reference to the kind of damage from which A must take care to save B harmless:

> 'The question is always whether the defendant was under a duty to avoid or prevent that damage, but the actual nature of the damage suffered is relevant to the existence and extent of any duty to avoid or prevent it.'

(See *Sutherland Shire Council v Heyman* (1985) 60 ALR 1 at 48 per Brennan J.)...

LORD ROSKILL:...
I agree with your Lordships that it has now to be accepted that there is no simple formula or touchstone to which recourse can be had in order to provide in every case a ready answer to the questions whether, given certain facts, the law will or will not impose liability for negligence or, in cases where such liability can be shown to exist, determine the extent of that liability. Phrases such as 'foreseeability', 'proximity', 'neighbourhood', 'just and reasonable', 'fairness', 'voluntary acceptance of risk' or 'voluntary assumption of responsibility' will be found used from time to time in the different cases. But, as your Lordships have said, such phrases are not precise definitions. At best they are but labels or phrases descriptive of the very different factual situations which can exist in particular cases and which must be carefully examined in each case before it can be pragmatically determined whether a duty of care exists and, if so, what is the scope and extent of that duty. If this conclusion involves a return to the traditional categorisation of cases as pointing to the existence and scope of any duty of care, as my noble and learned friend Lord Bridge, suggests, I think this is infinitely preferable to recourse to somewhat wide generalisations which leave their practical application matters of difficulty and uncertainty. This conclusion finds strong support from the judgment of Brennan J in the High Court of Australia in the passage cited by my noble and learned friends (see *Sutherland Shire Council v Heyman* (1985) 60 ALR 1 at 43–44)....

LORD OLIVER OF AYLMERTON:...
[I]t is now clear from a series of decisions in this House that, at least so far as concerns the law of the United Kingdom, the duty of care in tort depends not solely on the existence of the essential ingredient of the foreseeability of damage to the plaintiff but on its coincidence with a further ingredient to which has been attached the label 'proximity' and which was described by Lord Atkin in the course of his speech in *Donoghue v Stevenson* [1932] AC 562 at 581, [1932] All ER Rep 1 at 12 as—

> 'such close and direct relations that the act complained of directly affects a person whom the person alleged to be bound to take care would know would be directly affected by his careless act.'

It must be remembered, however, that Lord Atkin was using these words in the context of loss caused by physical damage where the existence of the nexus between the careless defendant and the injured plaintiff can rarely give rise to any difficulty. To adopt the words of Bingham LJ in the instant case ([1989] 1 All ER 798 at 808, [1989] QB 653 at 686):

> 'It is enough that the plaintiff chances to be (out of the whole world) the person with whom the defendant collided or who purchased the offending ginger beer.'

The extension of the concept of negligence since the decision of this House in *Hedley Byrne & Co Ltd v Heller & Partners Ltd* [1963] 2 All ER 575, [1964] AC 465 to cover cases of pure economic loss not resulting from physical damage has given rise to a considerable...difficulty of definition. The opportunities for the infliction of pecuniary loss from the imperfect performance of everyday tasks on the proper performance of which people rely for regulating their affairs are illimitable and the effects are far reaching. A defective bottle of ginger beer may injure a single consumer but the damage stops there. A single statement may be repeated endlessly with or without the permission of its author and may be relied on in a different way by many different people. Thus the postulate of a simple duty to avoid any harm that is, with hindsight, reasonably capable of being foreseen becomes untenable without the imposition of some intelligible limits to keep the law of negligence within the bounds of common sense and practicality. Those limits have been found by the requirement of what has been called a 'relationship of proximity' between plaintiff and defendant and by the imposition of a further requirement that the attachment of liability for harm which has occurred be 'just and reasonable'. But, although the cases in which the courts have imposed or withheld liability are capable of an approximate categorisation, one looks in vain for some common denominator by which the existence of the essential relationship can be tested. Indeed, it is difficult to resist a conclusion that what have been treated as three separate requirements are, at least in most cases, in fact merely facets of the same thing, for in some cases the degree of foreseeability is such that it is from that alone that the requisite proximity can be deduced, whilst in others the absence of that essential relationship can most rationally be attributed simply to the court's view that it would not be fair and reasonable to hold the defendant responsible. 'Proximity' is, no doubt, a convenient expression so long as it is realised that it is no more than a label which embraces not a definable concept but merely a description of circumstances from which, pragmatically, the courts conclude that a duty of care exists.

There are, of course, cases where, in any ordinary meaning of the words, a relationship of proximity (in the literal sense of 'closeness') exists but where the law, whilst recognising the fact of the relationship, nevertheless denies a remedy to the injured party on the ground of public policy....*Hill v Chief Constable of West Yorkshire* [1988] 2 All ER 238, [1989] AC 53 [was such a case], so far as concerns the alternative ground of that decision. But such cases do nothing to assist in the identification of those features from which the law will deduce the essential relationship on which liability depends and, for my part, I think that it has to be recognised that to search for any single formula which will serve as a general test of liability is to pursue a will-o'-the wisp. The fact is that once one discards, as it is now clear that one must, the concept of foreseeability of harm as the single exclusive test, even a prima facie test, of the existence of the duty of care, the attempt to state some general principle which will determine liability in an infinite variety of circumstances serves not to clarify the law but merely to bedevil its development in a way which corresponds with practicality and common sense...

Perhaps...the most that can be attempted is a broad categorisation of the decided cases according to the type of situation in which liability has been established in the past in order to found an argument by analogy....

QUESTION

Why do you think there has been this retreat from the *Anns* two-stage test? (Consider *Rowling v Takaro Properties Ltd* [1988] AC 473 at 501; R. Kidner, (1987) 7 LS 319 at 326–327; D. Howarth, [1991] CLJ 58; K. Stanton, (1992) 45 Current LP 83 at 99–105.)

NOTES

1. On the approach to the duty of care in *Anns* and the later case law, see further *Murphy v Brentwood District Council* [1991] 1 AC 398, [1990] 2 All ER 908 (p. 183, post). For discussion of *Caparo* in the context of economic loss, see pp. 224–232, post.

2. Lord Hoffmann commented in *Stovin v Wise* [1996] 3 All ER 801 (on which, see further p. 110, post) on the significance of the difference between the *Anns* approach and the sort of incremental approach to be found, for example, in *Caparo*. He said ([1996] 3 All ER at p. 824):

   Lord Wilberforce, who gave the leading speech [in *Anns*], first stated the well-known two-stage test for the existence of a duty of care. This involves starting with a prima facie assumption that a duty of care exists if it is reasonably foreseeable that carelessness may cause damage and then asking whether there are any considerations which ought to 'negative, or to reduce or limit the scope of the duty or the class of person to whom it is owed or the damages to which a breach of it may arise'. Subsequent decisions in this House and the Privy Council have preferred to approach the question the other way round, starting with situations in which a duty has been held to exist and then asking whether there are considerations of analogy, policy, fairness and justice for extending it to cover a new situation (see e.g. *Caparo Industries plc v Dickman* [1990] 1 All ER 568 at 573–574, [1990] 2 AC 605 at 617–618 per Lord Bridge of Harwich). It can be said that, provided that the considerations of policy etc are properly analysed, it should not matter whether one starts from one end or the other. On the other hand the assumption from which one starts makes a great deal of difference if the analysis is wrong. The trend of authorities has been to discourage the assumption that anyone who suffers loss is prima facie entitled to compensation from a person (preferably insured or a public authority) whose act or omission can be said to have caused it. The default position is that he is not.

   His Lordship returned to this point about the current default position (extra-judicially) in his Foreword to *Stevens*, but added that the 'grounds upon which it may be reversed remain obscure', a point to which we will return.

3. On 'incrementalism' see further L. Dolding and R. Mullender, (1996) 47 NILQ 12; K. Stanton, *Torts in the Nineties*, edited by N. J. Mullany, (Sydney, 1997), chap. 2. The relationship between incrementalism and the three-fold *Caparo* tests is not an easy one, as was acknowledged by Buxton LJ in *Islington London Borough Council v University College London Hospital NHS Trust* [2006] PIQR P3, [2005] EWCA Civ 596, at [25], noted p. 256, post. His Lordship went on to say that he regarded incrementalism as a 'check or guide to the application of the *Caparo* tests' and that if a case only incrementally extended an established category, then this was 'a good indication that [the] claim met the *Caparo* requirements'. This seems consistent with guidance on the role of the 'incremental approach' that can now be found in *Customs & Excise Commissioners v Barclays Bank plc* [2006] 4 All ER 256; [2006] UKHL 28 (p. 259, post) where Lord Bingham stated (at [7]):

   ...I incline to agree with the view expressed by the Messrs Mitchell in their article...('Negligence Liability for Pure Economic Loss' (2005) 121 LQR 194, 199) that the incremental test is of little value as a test in itself, and is only helpful when used in combination with a test or principle which identifies the legally significant features of a situation. The closer the facts of the case in issue to those of a case in which a duty of care has been held to exist, the readier a court will be, on the approach of Brennan J adopted in *Caparo Industries plc v Dickman*, to find that there has been an assumption of responsibility or that the proximity and policy conditions of the threefold test are satisfied. The converse is also true.

In the same case Lord Mance expressed the view (at [84] and [93]):

Incrementalism [in *Caparo*] was viewed as a corollary of the rejection, now uncontroversial, of any generalised liability for negligently caused economic loss, rather than as necessarily inconsistent with the development of novel categories of negligence. Having said that, caution and analogical reasoning are generally valuable accompaniments to judicial activity...

...[T]here is no single common denominator, even in cases of economic loss, by which liability may be determined. The threefold test of foreseeability, proximity and fairness, justice and reasonableness provides a convenient general framework although it operates at so high a level of abstraction. Incrementalism operates as an important cross-check on any other approach.

The other side of the incremental development coin was mentioned by the Court of Appeal in *M v Commissioner of Police for the Metropolis* [2007] EWCA Civ 1361, namely that if the novel case is very close to a situation where a duty of care has previously been rejected, it will be particularly difficult for a claimant to succeed on the duty issue.

4.   The three factors listed in *Caparo* for making the incremental analogy from existing precedent to a novel factual situation are foresight, proximity, and whether the imposition of a duty of care would be fair, just, and reasonable. There can be some overlap between these factors. For example, foresight of personal injury may in itself constitute the necessary proximity and be a powerful element in deciding that a duty of care is indeed fair, just, and reasonable. Lord Hoffmann in *Sutradhar v Natural Environment Research Council* [2006] 4 All ER 490 at [32] described the 'porous' nature of the boundaries as 'probably none the worse for that'. The 'proximity' and 'fair, just and reasonable' requirements will be considered in more detail in this and the following chapters. By way of brief introduction, it is important to see the requirements in context.

5.   So far as proximity is concerned, D. Howarth Tort LRev 85 [2000] comments:

Much trouble in negligence law comes from taking judges too literally and from not noticing the context of their pronouncements. A stray remark in a case on particular facts is not necessarily a general rule. Telling the difference between the two is often difficult, but when considering a rule excluding or limiting liability one can often simply apply it to a situation of clear liability, a carelessly caused road accident for example, and ask whether it still makes sense. If it does not make sense, the rule is particular, not general.

Take, for example, the alleged rule that negligence requires 'proximity of relationship'. Applying that rule to a road accident case, one sees immediately that it cannot be a general rule. Must road accident victims prove that they had a prior relationship with the person who hit them? Clearly not. But if one observes the context in which remarks about 'proximity of relationship' arise, cases such as *Hill v Chief Constable of West Yorkshire* [1989] AC 53, it quickly emerges that the rule has a particular scope. It is a way of evading the Hart and Honoré third party intervention rule—that free, informed and deliberate interventions by third parties exploiting the situation created by the defendant's carelessness break the chain of causation [see further p. 394, post]. Where there is no such intervention, or some variation on it, no need to consider 'relationships' arises.

Thus proximity is generally a relevant requirement in cases where the defendant has merely omitted to act or has failed to prevent harm caused by a third party. As such, the requirement will be considered in more detail at p. 400, post. The same observation, reached by slightly different reasoning, was made by Lord Oliver in *Caparo* (p. 40, ante), who indicated that mere foresight can constitute the element of proximity in cases of direct physical damage. As Howarth observes above, this can be contrasted with a case such as *Hill v Chief Constable of West Yorkshire* [1989] AC 53, [1988] 2 All ER 238 (p. 46, post), where the allegation related to harm caused by a third party and where the claim failed, partly because of a lack of proximity. (See also *Smith v Littlewoods Organisation Ltd* [1987] AC 241, [1987] 1 All ER 710, p. 78, post.) On lack of proximity note also *Sutradhar v Natural Environment Research Council* [2006] 4 All ER 490, [2006] UKHL 33, which involved a case by a Bangladeshi resident for personal injury brought against the Natural Environment Research Council claiming negligence in issuing a geological report which allegedly induced the health authorities in Bangladesh not to take steps to ensure that drinking water was not contaminated by arsenic. The House of Lords was of the view that there was clearly insufficient proximity to establish the existence of a duty of care under the *Caparo* test.

6.   So far as the 'fair, just and reasonable' category is concerned, this is a convenient label for numerous issues, including those of policy, relevant to whether there should or should not be negligence liability in a given situation. Although Lord Phillips MR in *Watson v British Boxing Board of Control Ltd* [2001] QB 1134, [2001] EWCA Civ 2116 at [86] acknowledged that 'it is difficult, or perhaps impossible, to avoid a degree of subjectivity' when considering this category, he counselled that 'the approach must be to apply established principles and standards'.

Occasionally, the courts have suggested that this third category is not a distinct one in its own right: see, for example, the views of Lord Nicholls in *Stovin v Wise* [1996] 3 All ER 801at 808 that 'Proximity is convenient shorthand for a relationship between two parties that makes it fair and reasonable that one should owe the other a duty of care. This is only another way of saying that, when assessing the requirements of fairness and reasonableness regard must be had to the relationship of the parties.' However, the more common approach is to regard the two requirements as conceptually separate, so that the court will, where appropriate, decide that it would not be fair, just, and reasonable that there should be a duty of care, even though the court was of the view that proximity existed. Consider, in the context of property damage, *Norwich City Council v Harvey* [1989] 1 All ER 1180, [1989] 1 WLR 828; cf. *British Telecommunications plc v James Thompson & Sons (Engineers) Ltd* [1999] 2 All ER 241, [1999] 1 WLR 9, and for a recent example in the context of an economic loss claim, see *Jain v Trent Strategic Health Authority* [2007] EWCA Civ 1361. Further attention might also be paid at this point to *Marc Rich & Co AG v Bishop Rock Marine Co Ltd* [1996] 2 AC 211, [1995] 3 All ER 307, noted by T. K. Feng (1996) 112 LQR 209 and P. Cane [1995] LMCLQ 433, which raised a preliminary issue as to whether a surveyor employed by a classification society owed a duty of care to the owners of cargo on a ship he surveyed. Although for the purposes of the case it was assumed that physical damage to property was involved, the case is discussed in more detail at p. 204, post, when the protection of economic interests is under discussion (for reasons which will become apparent at that point). A majority of the House of Lords (Lord Lloyd dissenting) denied the existence of a duty of care, and the case provides an example of its rejection on the 'fair, just and reasonable ground' even though the House was prepared to assume (though not decide) that the proximity requirement had been met. Other examples will be found throughout this and the next two chapters.

On the relationship of proximity and fair, just, and reasonable, consider Witting's view (2005) 25 Oxf JLS 33 at 34:

It is preferable that duty determinations be made primarily by reference to proximity, rather than by reference to policy criteria because proximity factors focus upon structural features that relate the parties one to the other, while courts ordinarily utilise policy considerations to examine the acceptability of liability rules upon parties other than those presently in dispute. Often, policy considerations are inadequate decision making criteria because courts are unable properly to ascertain how future parties will react to the recognition of different liability rules and because of the normative contestability of the policies. Greater consistency in decision making is likely to be achieved by way of legal reasoning based upon tests for proximity than on the basis of policy deliberation.

7.   It should be mentioned that the House of Lords in the *Marc Rich* case, noted ante, accepted that all three of the *Caparo* criteria are relevant in all cases, irrespective of the type of damage involved; nevertheless, Lord Steyn in his majority speech did specifically accept the view expressed in the Court of Appeal by Saville LJ ([1994] 3 All ER 686 at 692–693) that there would be a duty of care in most cases where physical injury was directly inflicted by carelessness. In *Palmer v Tees Health Authority* [2000] PIQR P1 the Court of Appeal was faced with an argument that foresight of injury was sufficient in a case of personal injury, relying on the passage from the speech of Lord Oliver in *Caparo* mentioned above, and another passage from the speech of Lord Steyn in *Marc Rich*, but concluded that neither Lord Oliver nor Lord Steyn had intended to cover a case where the harm was caused by the conscious and voluntary act of a third party.

As has been mentioned already in the context of proximity, there is no need to re-evaluate well-established duty-situations (the paradigm being the case of the negligent driver causing a road accident) in the light of the three requirements for a duty of care in a novel factual situation. See also the view of Hobhouse LJ in *Perrett v Collins* [1998] 2 Lloyd's Rep 255 that where a case fits into an established category, it is not necessary to consider the 'fair, just-and reasonable' category: *Marc Rich* had not intended to disturb existing categories and principles concerning personal injury.

8.   *Perrett* concerned the issue of a certificate that an aircraft was fit to fly and, therefore, involved statements leading to physical damage: it might be noted that this was the allegation in several other cases mentioned in this set of notes: see *Sutradhar*, *Marc Rich*, and *Watson v British Boxing Board of Control Ltd* [2001] QB 1134, [2001] EWCA Civ 2116. As will be seen from comments in *Hedley Byrne & Co Ltd v Heller and Partners Ltd* [1964] AC 465, [1963] 2 All ER 575 (p. 207, ante), statements can be more problematic for the law than acts (difficult though that distinction can be to draw), and this may be the case even though physical damage is involved.

For Hobhouse LJ in *Perrett* the 'established category'—see the previous note—was as follows ([1998] 2 Lloyd's Rep at p. 262):

Where the plaintiff belongs to a class which either is or ought to be within the contemplation of the defendant and the defendant by reason of his involvement in an activity which gives him a measure of control over and responsibility for a situation which, if dangerous, will be liable to injure the plaintiff, the defendant is liable if as a result of his unreasonable lack of care he causes a situation to exist which does in fact cause the plaintiff injury.

Compare Swinton Thomas LJ's judgment, who did consider the 'fair, just and reasonable' category. Buxton LJ thought this was a case of direct physical injury, but was prepared to consider the 'fair, just and reasonable' category if he was wrong in so classifying the case. Nevertheless, when considering such matters, the fact that personal injuries were involved was a significant factor and one that Buxton LJ described as 'deeply embedded in the law of negligence' ([1998] 2 Lloyd's Rep at p. 275).

These differences in *Perrett* were noted in *Watson*, where the question in issue concerned whether the defendant body owed a duty of care to boxers in relation to safety at boxing events under their rules. The Court of Appeal's view of the general position from the case law (including *Perrett*) was that where A advises B as to action to be taken which will directly and foreseeably affect the safety or well-being of C, a situation of sufficient proximity exists to found a duty of care on the part of A towards C, although acknowledging that the actual existence of the duty will depend on the facts of the case (also involving the 'fair, just and reasonable' ground). On the particular facts of the *Watson* case, a duty of care was established. On this topic in general, see C. Witting, *Liability for Negligent Misstatements* (Oxford, 2004), chap. 5.

9.   The *Caparo* tripartite test is widely used in novel cases. However, it is not the only terminology which the courts use when resolving this issue and such differing terminology will be found in cases in this and following chapters. It was stated by Brooke LJ in *Parkinson v St James and Seacroft University Hospital NHS Trust* [2001] 3 All ER 97, [2001] EWCA Civ 530 at [27] that there was not one 'correct' test, but he adopted the words of Sir Brian Neill in *Bank of Credit and Commerce International (Overseas) Ltd v Price Waterhouse (No 2)* [1998] PNLR 564 at 586, who stated that 'if the facts are properly analysed and the policy considerations are correctly evaluated, the several approaches will yield the same result'. Compare the view of Lord Hoffmann set out in note 2 ante, and note that in the *Barclays* case the House of Lords was prepared to consider liability under the *Caparo* test even if a case did not fit the voluntary assumption of responsibility test. This latter test provides an example of the differing terminology, and it is used in particular in cases concerning pure economic loss, although not the exclusive test in that area, as the *Barclays* case shows. Would a judge who thought that there had been an assumption of responsibility be likely to decide that the three factors in *Caparo* had not been met? In *Henderson v Merrett Syndicates Ltd* [1995] 2 AC 145, [1994] 3 All ER 306, (p. 232, post) Lord Goff stated that if the former test was satisfied, then there was no need to consider the 'fair, just and reasonable' limb of *Caparo*, a view that has found support in later case law. However, in *Welton v North Cornwall District Council* [1997] 1 WLR 570 it was accepted that if a case involved statutory powers or duties, these would have to be examined to see if they were inconsistent with the duty of care argued for; note furthermore the view of Laws LJ in *Hibbert Pownall & Newton (a firm) v Whitehead* [2008] EWCA Civ 285 at [31] that *Caparo*'s reasoning is 'over-arching' and 'covers every instance of duty of care in tort, because the triple requirement of "fair, just and reasonable" constitutes a necessary condition for the duty's imposition in any circumstances'.

Another phrase that has been used in the debate whether a duty of care is owed is 'distributive justice': see *McFarlane v Tayside Health Board* [2000] 2 AC 59, [1999] 4 All ER 961 (p. 153, post), where Lord Steyn would, if necessary, have placed the distributive justice issue in that case under the 'fair, just and reasonable' label; *White v Chief Constable of the South Yorkshire Police* [1999] 2 AC 455, [1999] 1 All ER 1, (p. 137, post). 'Distributive justice' appears to be contrasted with 'corrective justice' but in *Lee v Taunton and Somerset NHS Trust* [2001] 1 FLR 419 at 426 Toulson J thought that it would an 'oversimplification' to interpret Lord Steyn as intending them to be 'rival' concepts. Do you agree? In giving the 8th John Maurice Kelly Memorial Lecture, *Perspectives of Corrective and Distributive Justice in Tort Law*, Lord Steyn did state (at p. 6) that tort's primary aim is the 'the pursuit of corrective justice'. Note further Crennan J's discussion in *Harriton v Stephens* (2006) 226 CLR 52 at [271]–[275]: in particular, at [274] she states that 'in emphasising "corrective justice", even as added to by his notion of "distributive justice", Aristotle left unexplored the dependence of "correction" on the prior establishment of principles', referring to J. M. Finnis *Natural Law and Natural Rights* (Oxford, 1980), pp. 178–179 (and see A. Beever, *Rediscovering the Law of Negligence* (2007), pp. 59–61).

10. How much guidance do the *Caparo* labels give in any particular novel case? Although one can acknowledge that, as Kirby J stated in an Australian case, *Perre v Apand Pty Ltd* (1999) 164 ALR 606 at 684, labels 'help to steer the mind through the task in hand'—a view approved by Lord Walker in the *Barclays* case—more guidance may still be needed. As Lord Hoffmann stated in *Barclays* (at [35]):

   > There is a tendency, which has been remarked upon by many judges, for phrases like 'proximate', 'fair, just and reasonable' and 'assumption of responsibility' to be used as slogans rather than practical guides to whether a duty should exist or not. These phrases are often illuminating but discrimination is needed to identify the factual situations in which they provide useful guidance.

   See also the speech of Lord Mance, who argued (at [83]) that the *Caparo* tests among others 'operate at a high level of abstraction. What matters is how and by reference to what lower-level factors they are interpreted in practice.' Note also the view of Lord Rodger, who at [53] stated:

   > Part of the function of appeal courts is to try to assist judges and practitioners by boiling down a mass of case law and distilling some shorter statement of the applicable law. The temptation to try to identify some compact underlying rule which can then be applied to solve all future cases is obvious. . . . But the unhappy experience with the rule so elegantly formulated by Lord Wilberforce in *Anns v London Borough of Merton* [1977] 2 All ER 492 at 498–499, [1978] AC 728 at 751–752, suggests that appellate judges should follow the philosopher's advice to 'Seek simplicity, and distrust it'.

11. The rest of this chapter will provide illustrations of some of the substantive arguments used by the courts in deciding whether or not there is proximity, and whether a duty of care would be fair, just, and reasonable. Both issues arose in the following case.

■ Hill v Chief Constable of West Yorkshire
House of Lords [1988] 2 All ER 238

This was an action on behalf of the estate of a murder victim. The allegations in the statement of claim were that murders and attempted murders had previously been committed by the murderer (and they were set out), that it was reasonable to infer that the same person had committed these offences, that it was foreseeable he would commit further offences of the same nature if not caught, and that the police owed a duty of care to catch him so as to protect potential future victims. The House of Lords held that there was insufficient proximity for a duty to exist (see p. 78, post), but also considered the question of public policy.

LORD KEITH OF KINKEL . . .

[T]here is another reason why an action for damages in negligence should not lie against the police in circumstances such as those of the present case, and that is public policy. In *Yuen Kun-yeu v A-G of Hong Kong* [1987] 2 All ER 705 at 712, [1988] AC 175 at 193, I expressed the view that the category of cases where the second stage of Lord Wilberforce's two-stage test in *Anns v Merton London Borough* [1977] 2 All ER 492 at 498, [1978] AC 728 at 752 might fall to be applied was a limited one, one example of that category being *Rondel v Worsley* [1967] 3 All ER 993, [1969] 1 AC 191. Application of that second stage is, however, capable of constituting a separate and independent ground for holding that the existence of liability in negligence should not be entertained. Potential existence of such liability may in many instances be in the general public interest, as tending towards the observance of a higher standard of care in the carrying on of various different types of activity. I do not, however, consider that this can be said of police activities. The general sense of public duty which motivates police forces is unlikely to be appreciably reinforced by the imposition of such liability so far as concerns their function in the investigation and suppression of crime. From time to time they make mistakes in the exercise of that function, but it is not to be doubted that they apply their best endeavours to the performance of it. In some instances the imposition of liability may lead to the exercise of a function being carried on in a detrimentally defensive frame of mind. The possibility of this happening in relation to the investigative operations of the police cannot be excluded. Further, it would be reasonable to expect that if potential liability were to be imposed it would be not uncommon for actions to be raised against police forces on the ground that they had failed to catch some criminal as soon as they might have done, with the result that he went on to commit further crimes. While some such actions might involve allegations of a simple and straightforward types of failure, for example that a police officer negligently tripped and fell while pursuing a burglar, others would be likely to enter deeply into the general nature of a police investigation, as indeed the present action would seek to do. The manner of conduct of such an investigation must necessarily involve a variety of decisions to be made on matters of policy and discretion, for example as to which particular line of inquiry is most advantageously to be pursued and what is the most advantageous way to deploy the available resources. Many such decisions would not be regarded by the courts as appropriate to be called in question, yet elaborate investigation of the facts might be necessary to ascertain whether or not this was so. A great deal of police time, trouble and expense might be expected to have to be put into the preparation of the defence to the action and the attendance of witnesses at the trial. The result would be a significant diversion of police manpower and attention from their most important function, that of the suppression of crime. Closed investigations would require to be reopened and retraversed, not with the object of bringing any criminal to justice but to ascertain whether or not they had been competently conducted. I therefore consider that Glidewell LJ, in his judgment in the Court of Appeal in the present case, was right to take the view that the police were immune from an action of this kind....

[LORD BRANDON OF OAKBROOK, LORD OLIVER OF AYLMERTON, and LORD GOFF OF CHIEVELEY agreed with LORD KEITH's speech. LORD TEMPLEMAN delivered a speech in which he was also against allowing the action.]

QUESTIONS

1. To what extent might, for example, the medical profession make similar policy arguments against the duty of care which they undoubtedly owe to their patients?
2. Where in the *Caparo* tripartite structure would you place the sort of considerations in the extract ante (and see *Smith v Chief Constable of Sussex Police* [2008] EWCA Civ 39 at [34])?

NOTES

1. There were several attempts to sue the police in the years after *Hill*. Note for example, *Calveley v Chief Constable of the Merseyside Police* [1989] AC 1228, [1989] 1 All ER 1025, where the House of Lords denied that the police investigating a possible crime owed a duty of care to a suspect (cf. the recent Supreme Court of Canada decision in *Hill v Hamilton-Wentworth Regional Police Services Board* (2007) 285 DLR (4th) 620, noted by E. Chamberlain (2008) 124 LQR 205); and see *Elguzouli-Daf v Metropolitan Police Comr* [1995] QB 335, [1995] 1 All ER 833, where it was held that the Crown Prosecution Service does not owe a duty of care to those it prosecutes (unless there is an assumption of responsibility to a particular defendant). From the other cases, attention might be drawn to *Alexandrou v Oxford* [1993] 4 All ER 328 (where the Court of Appeal decided, on ground of lack of proximity, that the police did not owe a duty of care on receipt of an emergency call) and in particular, *Osman v Ferguson* ibid 344, noted by M. Tregilgas-Davey (1993) 56 MLR 732 and J. Steele and D. S. Cowan [1994] PL 4. In *Osman* no duty of care was held to be owed. Here it was alleged the second claimant and his father had been shot by someone against whom the police should previously have taken action.

On the other hand, see the later case of *Swinney v Chief Constable of the Northumbria Police* [1997] QB 464, [1996] 3 All ER 449, where it was accepted that there might be some public policy considerations which could outweigh the factors set out in *Hill*. In *Swinney* it was regarded as arguable that the public interest in preserving the confidentiality of informers was capable of doing so, and that there could be a duty of care in relation to the storage of such confidential information; and in *Swinney v Chief Constable of the Northumbria Police (No 2)* (1999) *Times*, 25 May the police were held to owe a duty of care to avoid unnecessary disclosure to the public of the information given in confidence to them by the claimant in the course of a murder investigation (although on the facts the court held that the duty of care had not been breached). The important case of *Brooks v Metropolitan Police Commissioner* [2005] 2 All ER 489, [2005] UKHL 24, from which the next extract is taken (post), will continue this debate, but events between *Hill* and *Brooks* and which involved the ECHR should first be set out.

2.   The possibility of policy arguments being overridden was crucial to the judgment of the European Court of Human Rights when the *Osman* case reached that body (*Osman v United Kingdom* (2000) 29 EHRR 245). In *Osman*, the Court of Appeal by a majority had decided that there was a sufficiently proximate relationship, but had struck out the action under the 'fair, just and reasonable' criterion, relying on the *Hill* ground for rejecting the duty of care. This striking out was held by the European Court (ECtHR) to contravene Article 6.1 of the European Convention of Human Rights (entitlement to a fair hearing by a tribunal in determining a person's civil rights and obligations) in that the automatic exclusion of police liability without consideration of any countervailing policy factors was a disproportionate restriction on the right of access to the court granted by that Article. It is important to underline, however, that the European Court did accept the legitimacy of the aim behind the *Hill* ruling; the contravention of Article 6.1 arose from the European Court's view that in *Osman* contrary policy arguments had not been weighed against them in the particular case. The factors involved in the *Hill* ruling remain relevant considerations.

The *Osman* case proved to be controversial in England: see, for example, the views of Lord Browne-Wilkinson in *Barrett v Enfield London Borough Council* [2001] 2 AC 550 at 558–560; Hoffman (1999) 62 MLR 159 at 162–164, and the position has been altered by later cases in the ECtHR. In *TP v United Kingdom* (2002) 34 EHRR 42 and *Z v United Kingdom* (2002) 34 EHRR 97, the ECtHR accepted that rejection of a case on the ground that it was not 'fair, just and reasonable' that there should be a duty of care was not a breach of Article 6: the claimant had had access to a court to argue the case before it was struck out, although as A. Davies (2001) 117 LQR 521 at 524 points out, 'courts will have to examine claimants' policy arguments "properly and fairly" (*Z* at [101]) if they are not to fall foul of Article 6'.

■ Brooks v Metropolitan Police Commissioner
House of Lords [2005] 2 All ER 489

This litigation arose out of the well-known and tragic Stephen Lawrence case. The claimant had also been attacked and abused, but, unlike Stephen Lawrence, he survived and was a key witness.

LORD STEYN: . . .

[14] The agreed issues before the House are as follows. (1) Whether, on the pleaded facts, there are no reasonable grounds for the claim that there was sufficient proximity between the

Commissioner and/or those for whom he is vicariously responsible, on the one hand, and Mr Brooks, on the other, to give rise to the following duties of care: (a) to take reasonable steps to assess whether Mr Brooks was a victim of crime and then to accord him reasonably appropriate protection, support, assistance and treatment if he was so assessed (the first surviving duty); (b) to take reasonable steps to afford Mr Brooks the protection, assistance and support commonly afforded to a key eye witness to a serious crime of violence (the second surviving duty); (c) to afford reasonable weight to the account given by Mr Brooks and to act upon that account accordingly (the third surviving duty). (2) Whether there are no reasonable grounds for the claim that it is fair, just and reasonable to hold that the Commissioner and/or those for whom he is vicariously responsible owed to Mr Brooks the duties of care set out above.

. . .

[16] First, I accept that in these proceedings it must be assumed without equivocation that each and every one of the allegations of fact in the pleading under consideration could conceivably be established at trial. In particular the matter must be considered on the basis that Mr Brooks has suffered personal injury (in the form of an exacerbation of or aggravation of the PTSD that was induced by the racist attack itself) in consequence of the negligence of the officers and that injury of this type was reasonably foreseeable. Secondly, counsel for Mr Brooks cautioned the House about the danger of trying to resolve complex questions of law on an application to strike out a pleading. He emphasised particularly the undesirability of embarking on a strike-out application in the face of a developing state of a particular branch of law. He referred to what Lord Slynn of Hadley said in *Waters v Comr of Police of the Metropolis* [2000] 4 All ER 934 at 941, [2000] ICR 1064 at 1071:

> 'It is very important to bear in mind what was said in *X and ors (minors) v Bedfordshire CC, M (a minor) v Newham London BC, E (a minor) v Dorset CC* [1995] 3 All ER 353, [1995] 2 AC 633, in *Barrett v Enfield London BC* [1999] 3 All ER 193, [2001] 2 AC 550 and in *W v Essex CC* [2000] 2 All ER 237, [2001] 2 AC 592 as to the need for caution in striking out on the basis of assumed fact in an area where the law is developing as it is in negligence in relation to public authorities if not specifically in relation to the police.'

These observations are important and will have to be carefully considered.

. . .

[18] Counsel for Mr Brooks did not in any way challenge the decision in *Hill*'s case but submitted that it does not stand in the way of his arguments. His central submission was that the police owe a duty of care not to cause by positive acts or omissions harm to victims of serious crime, or witnesses to serious crime, with whom they have contact. He said that the first, second and third pleaded duties of care were concrete manifestations of this general duty.

[Having referred to *Hill* and stated that as an alternative ground for the decision the passage on policy (whch can be found at p. 46, ante) is part of the ratio decidendi, LORD STEYN referred to other case law and continued:]

[27] Since the decision in *Hill*'s case there have been developments which affect the reasoning of that decision in part. In *Hill*'s case the House relied on the barrister's immunity enunciated in *Rondel v Worsley* [1967] 3 All ER 993, [1969] 1 AC 191. That immunity no longer exists: see *Arthur JS Hall & Co (a firm) v Simons, Barratt v Ansell (t/a Woolf Seddon (a firm)), Harris v Scholfield Roberts & Hill (a firm)* [2000] 3 All ER 673, [2002] 1 AC 615. More fundamentally since the decision of the European Court of Human Rights in *Z v UK* (2001) 34 EHRR 97 at 138 (para 100), it would be best for the principle in *Hill*'s case to be reformulated in terms of the absence of a duty of care rather than a blanket immunity.

[28] With hindsight not every observation in *Hill*'s case can now be supported. Lord Keith observed ([1988] 2 All ER 238 at 243, [1989] AC 53 at 63): 'From time to time [the police] make mistakes in the exercise of that function, but it is not to be doubted that they apply their best endeavours to the performance of it.' Nowadays, a more sceptical approach to the carrying out of all public functions is necessary.

[29] Counsel for the Commissioner concedes that cases of assumption of responsibility under the extended *Hedley Byrne* doctrine fall outside the *Hill* principle. In such cases there is no need to embark

on an inquiry whether it is 'fair, just and reasonable' to impose liability for economic loss: see *Williams v Natural Life Health Foods Ltd* [1998] 2 All ER 577, [1998] 1 WLR 830.

[30] But the core principle of *Hill*'s case has remained unchallenged in our domestic jurisprudence and in European jurisprudence for many years. If a case such as ... *Hill*'s case, arose for decision today I have no doubt that it would be decided in the same way. ... A retreat from the principle in *Hill*'s case would have detrimental effects for law enforcement. Whilst focusing on investigating crime, and the arrest of suspects, police officers would in practice be required to ensure that in every contact with a potential witness or a potential victim time and resources were deployed to avoid the risk of causing harm or offence. Such legal duties would tend to inhibit a robust approach in assessing a person as a possible suspect, witness or victim. By placing general duties of care on the police to victims and witnesses the police's ability to perform their public functions in the interests of the community, fearlessly and with despatch, would be impeded. It would, as was recognised in *Hill*'s case, be bound to lead to an unduly defensive approach in combating crime.

[31] It is true, of course, that the application of the *Hill* principle will sometimes leave citizens, who are entitled to feel aggrieved by negligent conduct of the police, without a private law remedy for psychiatric harm. But domestic legal policy, and the Human Rights Act 1998, sometimes compel this result. ... Unfortunately, when other specific torts and the [Race Relations Act 1976] (as amended) are inapplicable, an aggrieved citizen may in cases such as those under consideration have to be content with pursuing a complaint under the constantly improved police complaints procedure: see the Police Reform Act 2002, the Police (Conduct) Regulations 2004 and Police (Complaints and Misconduct) Regulations 2004, SI 2004/643. For all these reasons, I am satisfied that the decision in *Hill*'s case must stand. ...

[33] That brings me to the three critical alleged duties of care before the House. It is realistic and fair to pose the question whether the three surviving duties of care can arguably be said to be untouched by the core principle in *Hill*'s case. In my view the three alleged duties are undoubtedly inextricably bound up with the police function of investigating crime which is covered by the principle in *Hill*'s case. For example, the second duty of care is to 'take reasonable steps to afford [Mr Brooks] the protection, assistance and support commonly afforded to a key eye witness to a serious crime of violence'. It is quite impossible to separate this alleged duty from the police function of investigating crime. The same is, however, true of the other two pleaded duties. If the core principle in *Hill*'s case stands, as it must, these pleaded duties of care cannot survive.

[34] It is unnecessary in this case to try to imagine cases of outrageous negligence by the police, unprotected by specific torts, which could fall beyond the reach of the *Hill* principle. It would be unwise to try to predict accurately what unusual cases could conceivably arise. I certainly do not say that they could not arise. But such exceptional cases on the margins of the *Hill* principle will have to be considered and determined if and when they occur.

[35] Making full allowance for the fact that this is a strike-out application, and that the law regarding the liability of the police in tort is not set in stone, I am satisfied that the three duties of care put forward in this case are conclusively ruled out by the principle in *Hill*'s case, as restated, and must be struck out. ...

[36] I would allow the appeal of the Commissioner.

[LORD BINGHAM OF CORNHILL delivered a speech in favour of dismissing the appeal, as did LORD NICHOLLS OF BIRKENHEAD, who agreed with the speeches of LORD BINGHAM and LORD STEYN. LORD RODGER OF EARLSFERRY delivered a speech in which he agreed with LORD STEYN and LORD BROWN OF EATON-UNDER-HEYWOOD agreed with LORD STEYN.]

NOTES

1.   The greater flexibility which can be seen in the extract ante is also reflected in the following comment of Lord Nicholls in *Brooks* (at [6]):

Like Lord Bingham and Lord Steyn ... I am not to be taken as indorsing the full width of all the observations in *Hill*. ... There may be exceptional cases where the circumstances compel the conclusion that the absence of a remedy sounding in damages would be an affront to the principles which underlie the common law. Then the decision in *Hill's* case should not stand in the way of granting an appropriate remedy.

2. Lord Steyn refers (at [16]) to strike out applications. Under r. 3.4(2)(a) of the Civil Procedure Rules (CPR) there is a power for the court to strike out a statement of case that in its opinion discloses no reasonable ground for the action, reflecting a similar rule in the old Rules of the Supreme Court (RSC), although with the difference that evidence can now be received under the CPR application. The ECtHR's ruling in *Osman* (see p. 48, ante) caused some uncertainty in relation to the exercise of the striking out of power for a while. However, in *Kent v Griffiths* [2001] QB 36, [2000] 2 All ER 474 Lord Woolf MR stated at [38]:

> In so far as *Osman's* case underlined the dangers of a blanket approach so much the better. However, it would be wrong for the *Osman* decision to be taken as a signal that, even when the legal position is clear and an investigation of the facts would provide no assistance, the courts should be reluctant to dismiss cases which have no real prospect of success. Courts are now encouraged, where an issue or issues can be identified which will resolve or help to resolve litigation, to take that issue or those issues at an early stage of the proceedings so as to achieve expedition and save expense. There is no question of any contravention of art 6 of the ECHR in so doing. Defendants as well as claimants are entitled to a fair trial and it is an important part of the case management function to bring proceedings to an end as expeditiously as possible. Although a strike-out may appear to be a summary remedy, it is in fact indistinguishable from deciding a case on a preliminary point of law.

See further *M v Commissioner of Police of the Metropolis* [2007] EWCA Civ 1361, where the Court of Appeal express the opinion that Lord Browne-Wilkinson's views in the *Barrett* case, indirectly referred it at [16] ante, should not be regarded as 'too prescriptive' and also point to the number of important negligence cases that have indeed involved such proceedings.

There is now another procedure available to defendants which they could not use under the old RSC regime, namely an application for summary judgment. On the relationship of these two procedures, see *S v Gloucestershire County Council* [2001] Fam 313, [2000] 3 All ER 34, and note *Sutradhar v National Environment Research Council* [2006] 4 All ER 390, [2006] UKHL 33, where Lord Hoffmann stated (at [3]):

> Under CPR 24.2 the court has power to give summary judgment against a claimant if it considers that (a) he 'has no real prospect of succeeding on the claim … and (b) there is no other compelling reason why the case or issue should be disposed of at a trial'. This is a broader power than existed under the old rules, when a claim could be struck out only on the grounds that the pleading disclosed no cause of action (the old demurrer, on which no evidence was admissible) or that the claim was frivolous, vexatious and an abuse of the process of the court.

His Lordship then proceeded to say that the question was whether there was a reasonable prospect of success at the trial on the assumption that all the allegations of primary fact were true and also making allowance for the chance of further facts appearing via discovery or at the later trial.

3. There has been further case law in the Court of Appeal since *Brooks* concerning the positon of the police. In *M v Commissioner of Police of the Metropolis*, it was decided that the police owed no duty of care to a complainant to prosecute an alleged wrongdoer, although accepting that in appropriate circumstances assumption of responsibility and reliance could create a duty of care. The *M* case was a strike-out application, as was *Smith v Chief Constable of Sussex Police* [2008] EWCA Civ 39, but in the latter case

the result was different. The alleged facts involved injury to the claimant from an attack by someone whose prior death threats to the claimant had been reported to the police. In Sedley LJ's opinion a duty of care could be owed if, for example, 'someone's life or safety has been so firmly placed in the hands of the police as to make it incumbent on them to take at least elementary steps to protect it'. He continued that 'if the facts upon which [the action] is founded are established, the claimant was both a key witness to a serious offence and the potential victim', and all the members of the Court of Appeal were agreed that the claim was not bound to fail and should not be struck out.

4.   The impact of the ECHR and the Human Rights Act on the tort of negligence has been seen in the section ante. In *Jain v Trent Strategic Health Authority* [2007] EWCA Civ 1186 Arden LJ thought the Human Rights Act had 'encourage[d] courts to identify more specific policy factors and to consider the interests of the individual affected by the decision-making by the public authority'. The *Smith* case, mentioned in the previous note, also involved discussion of this issue. Actions can be brought against the state where police activity, or inactivity, is alleged to have infringed the rights safeguarded by the ECHR, for example the right to life in Article 2, and this could provide a route around the restrictive approach in negligence. In *Van Colle v Chief Constable of the Hertfordshire Police* [2007] 3 All ER 122, [2007] EWCA Civ 325, noted by J. R. Spencer [2008] CLJ 15, a prosecution witness was murdered before the criminal trial. The Court of Appeal acknowledged the difficulty of an action in the tort of negligence, but a breach of Article 2 was found and damages were awarded: see *Van Colle* at [100]–[129] as to the measure of damages. *Van Colle* was mentioned by all three members of the Court of Appeal in *Smith*. Rimer LJ (at [45]) thought it 'odd' that English law could display 'two parallel, but potentially inconsistent, approaches to the same factual situation' and, speaking of the argument that the positive obligations under Article 2 should have a 'relevant impact' upon the development of negligence, expressed the opinion:

… it is arguable that they should, on the basis that where a common law duty covers the same ground as a Convention right, it shouild so far as practicable, develop in harmony with it; if so, the common law may well require a re-visiting of the *Hill* policy considerations, at least in the context of cases raising considerations of the right to life.

For Pill LJ there was a strong argument that negligence should develop in the light of the ECHR. In his view (at [55]) Article 2 rights should be absorbed into the negligence action and a 'claim in negligence should, on appropriate facts, have regard to the duties imposed and standards required by Article 2 of the Convention which … includes safeguards for the police'. Cf. *Lawrence v Pembrokeshire County Council* [2007] 1 WLR 2991, [2007] EWCA Civ 446, noted p. 57, ante. (Both *Van Colle* and *Smith* are currently under appeal.) The indirect influence of the ECHR can also be seen in the litigation which is the concern of the next extract, although it is particularly concerned with the problem of a conflict of interests.

■ D v East Berkshire Community Health NHS Trust
House of Lords [2005] 2 All ER 443

This case involved the question whether medical professionals as well as a local authority owed a duty of care to the child and to the child's parents in cases of suspected child abuse. It will be seen at p. 94, post that the local authority's liability had been denied by the House of Lords in *X v Bedfordshire County Council* [1995] 2 AC 633, [1995] 3 All ER 353 on the fair, just, and reasonable limb of the *Caparo* test. This was not followed in the Court of Appeal in *D* [2003] 4 All ER 796, [2003] EWCA Civ 1151 (despite it involving the overturning of a House of Lords case) on the basis of the Human Rights Act 1998, even though, because of the timing of the events in question, it did not apply to this case. The Court of Appeal's view, basically, was that as there could now be an action for, and consequent investigation of, an alleged breach of ECHR rights (in particular in this context, Articles 3 and 8), allowing a negligence action would not significantly affect the defendant's activities adversely. (This treatment of a House of Lords case was approved by the House in *Kay* v *Lambeth London Borough Council* [2006] 4 All ER 128, [2006] UKHL 10 on what was seen as the exceptional position in the *D* case, but not regarded as normally open to a lower court.) The Court of Appeal decided that a duty of care could be owed to the child, but not to the child's parents. On appeal to the House of Lords:

LORD NICHOLLS OF BIRKENHEAD....

[52] My Lords, it must be every parent's nightmare to be suspected of deliberately injuring his or her own child. In the three cases before your Lordships' House doctors suspected a child had been the subject of non-accidental injury by a parent or, in one case, false reporting carrying a future risk of non-accidental injury. In each case after further investigation it turned out this was not so. In each case the parent then brought proceedings against the hospital trust and, in one instance, the doctor personally claiming damages for negligence in the clinical investigation, diagnosis and reporting of the child's condition.

[53] The primary question before the House is whether doctors and, vicariously or directly, health trusts are liable in damages to a parent in such a case. Hand-in-hand with this is a parallel question concerning the liability of a local authority in respect of its investigation of suspected child abuse.

[54] None of these cases has proceeded beyond the pleadings stage.

. . .

[70] There are two cardinal features in these cases. One feature is that a parent was suspected of having deliberately harmed his or her own child or having fabricated the child's medical condition. The other feature, which is to be assumed, is that the ensuing investigation by the doctors was con-ducted negligently. In consequence, the suspected parent's family life was disrupted, to greater or lesser extent, and the suspected parent suffered psychiatric injury.

[71] It is the combination of these features which creates the difficult problem now before the House. In the ordinary course the interests of parent and child are congruent. This is not so where a parent wilfully harms his child. Then the parent is knowingly acting directly contrary to his parental responsibilities and to the best interests of his child. So the liability of doctors and social workers in these cases calls into consideration two countervailing interests, each of high social importance: the need to safeguard children from abuse by their own parents, and the need to protect parents from unnecessary interference with their family life.

[72] The first of these interests involves protection of children as the victims of crime. Child abuse is criminal conduct of a particularly reprehensible character: children are highly vulnerable members of society. Child abuse is also a form of criminal conduct peculiarly hard to combat, because its existence is difficult to discover. Babies and young children are unable to complain, older children too frightened. If the source of the abuse is a parent, the child is at risk from his primary and natural protector within the privacy of his home. This both increases the risk of abuse and means that investigation necessitates intrusion into highly sensitive areas of family life, with the added complication that the parent who is responsible for the abuse will give a false account of the child's history.

[73] The other, countervailing interest is the deep interest of the parent in his or her family life. Society sets much store by family life. Family life is to be guarded jealously. This is reflected in art 8 of the European Convention for the Protection of Human Rights and Fundamental Freedoms 1950 (as set out in Sch 1 to the Human Rights Act 1998). Interference with family life requires cogent justification, for the sake of children and parents alike. So public authorities should, so far as possible, co-operate with the parents when making decisions about their children. Public authorities should disclose matters

relied upon by them as justifying interference with family life. Parents should be involved in the decision-making process to whatever extent is appropriate to protect their interests adequately.

[74] The question raised by these appeals is how these countervailing interests are best balanced when a parent is wrongly suspected of having abused his child. Public confidence in the child protection system can only be maintained if a proper balance is struck, avoiding unnecessary intrusion in families while protecting children at risk of significant harm

[75] ...[T]he starting point is to note that in each of the three cases before the House the doctors acted properly in considering whether the claimant parents had deliberately inflicted injury on the child in question. The doctors were entitled, indeed bound, to consider this possibility. Further, having become suspicious, the doctors rightly communicated their suspicions to the statutory services responsible for child protection. This is the essential next step in child protection...

[76] In each case the suspected parent was eventually cleared of suspicion. In one case this was after ten days, in the other cases after much longer periods. The second point to note therefore is that, essentially, the parents' complaints relate to the periods for which they remained under suspicion.... [T]he essence of the claims is that health professionals responsible for protecting a child victim owe a person suspected of having committed a crime against the child a duty to investigate their suspicions, a duty sounding in damages if they act in good faith but carelessly.

[77] Stated in this broad form, this is a surprising proposition. In this area of the law, concerned with the reporting and investigation of suspected crime, the balancing point between the public interest and the interest of a suspected individual has long been the presence or absence of good faith. Good faith is required but not more. A report, made to the appropriate authorities, that a person has or may have committed a crime attracts qualified privilege. A false statement (malicious falsehood) attracts a remedy if made maliciously. Misfeasance in public office calls for an element of bad faith or recklessness. Malice is an essential ingredient of causes of action for the misuse of criminal or civil proceedings. In *Calveley v Chief Constable of the Merseyside Police* [1989] 1 All ER 1025 at 1030, [1989] AC 1228 at 1238, Lord Bridge of Harwich observed that 'where no action for malicious prosecution would lie, it would be strange indeed if an acquitted defendant could recover damages for negligent investigation'. This must be equally true of a person who has been suspected but not prosecuted.

[78] This background accords ill with the submission that those responsible for the protection of a child against criminal conduct owe suspected perpetrators the duty suggested. The existence of such a duty would fundamentally alter the balance in this area of the law. It would mean that if a parent suspected that a babysitter or a teacher at a nursery or school might have been responsible for abusing her child, and the parent took the child to a general practitioner or consultant, the doctor would owe a duty of care to the suspect. The law of negligence has of course developed much in recent years, reflecting the higher standards increasingly expected in many areas of life. But there seems no warrant for such a fundamental shift in the long established balance in this area of the law....

INTERFERENCE WITH FAMILY LIFE

...

[85] ...Ultimately the factor which persuades me that, at common law, interference with family life does not justify according a suspected parent a higher level of protection than other suspected perpetrators is the factor conveniently labelled 'conflict of interest'. A doctor is obliged to act in the best interests of his patient. In these cases the child is his patient. The doctor is charged with the protection of the child, not with the protection of the parent. The best interests of a child and his parent normally march hand-in-hand. But when considering whether something does not feel 'quite right', a doctor must be able to act single-mindedly in the interests of the child. He ought not to have at the back of his mind an awareness that if his doubts about intentional injury or sexual abuse prove unfounded he may be exposed to claims by a distressed parent.

[86] This is not to suggest doctors or other health professionals would be consciously swayed by this consideration. These professionals are surely made of sterner stuff. Doctors often owe duties to more than one person; for instance, a doctor may owe duties to his employer as well as his patient. But the

seriousness of child abuse as a social problem demands that health professionals, acting in good faith in what they believe are the best interests of the child, should not be subject to potentially conflicting duties when deciding whether a child may have been abused, or when deciding whether their doubts should be communicated to others, or when deciding what further investigatory or protective steps should be taken. The duty they owe to the child in making these decisions should not be clouded by imposing a conflicting duty in favour of parents or others suspected of having abused the child.

[87] This is not to say that the parents' interests should be disregarded or that the parents should be kept in the dark. The decisions being made by the health professionals closely affect the parents as well as the child. Health professionals are of course fully aware of this. They are also mindful of the importance of involving the parents in the decision-making process as fully as is compatible with the child's best interests. But it is quite a step from this to saying that the health professionals personally owe a suspected parent a duty sounding in damages.

[88] The claimants sought to meet this 'conflict of interest' point by noting that the suggested duty owed to parents has the same content as the duty owed to the child: to exercise due skill and care in investigating the possibility of abuse. This response is not adequate. The time when the presence or absence of a conflict of interest matters is when the doctor is carrying out his investigation. At that time the doctor does not know whether there has been abuse by the parent. But he knows that when he is considering this possibility the interests of parent and child are diametrically opposed. The interests of the child are that the doctor should report any suspicions he may have and that he should carry out further investigation in consultation with other child care professionals. The interests of the parent do not favour either of these steps. This difference of interest in the outcome is an unsatisfactory basis for imposing a duty of care on a doctor in favour of a parent....

[90] For these reasons I am not persuaded that the common law should recognise the duty propounded by Mr Langstaff. In principle the appropriate level of protection for a parent suspected of abusing his child is that clinical and other investigations must be conducted in good faith. This affords suspected parents a similar level of protection to that afforded generally to persons suspected of committing crimes.

[91] This should be the general rule, where the relationship between doctor and parent is confined to the fact that the parent is father or mother of the doctor's patient. There may, exceptionally, be circumstances where this is not so. Different considerations may apply then. But there is nothing of this sort in any of these three cases.

[92] A wider approach has...been canvassed. The suggestion has been made that, in effect, the common law should jettison the concept of duty of care as a universal prerequisite to liability in negligence. Instead the standard of care should be 'modulated' to accommodate the complexities arising in fields such as social workers dealing with children at risk of abuse: Fairgrieve, Andenas and Bell *Tort Liability of Public Authorities in Comparative Perspective* (2002) p 485. The contours of liability should be traced in other ways.

[93] For some years it has been all too evident that identifying the parameters of an expanding law of negligence is proving difficult, especially in fields involving the discharge of statutory functions by public authorities. So this radical suggestion is not without attraction. This approach would be analogous to that adopted when considering breaches of human rights under the European Convention. Sometimes in human rights cases the identity of the defendant, whether the state in claims under the convention or a public authority in claims under the Human Rights Act 1998, makes it appropriate for an international or domestic court to look backwards over everything which happened. In deciding whether overall the end result was acceptable the court makes a value judgment based on more flexible notions than the common law standard of reasonableness and does so freed from the legal rigidity of a duty of care.

[94] This approach, as I say, is not without attraction. It is peculiarly appropriate in the field of human rights. But I have reservations about attempts to transplant this approach wholesale into the domestic law of negligence in cases where, as here, no claim is made for breach of a convention right. Apart from anything else, such an attempt would be likely to lead to a lengthy and unnecessary period of

uncertainty in an important area of the law. It would lead to uncertainty because there are types of cases where a person's acts or omissions do not render him liable in negligence for another's loss even though this loss may be foreseeable.... Abandonment of the concept of a duty of care in English law, unless replaced by a control mechanism which recognises this limitation, is unlikely to clarify the law. That control mechanism has yet to be identified and introducing this protracted period of uncertainty is unnecessary, because claims may now be brought directly against public authorities in respect of breaches of convention rights.

LORD RODGER OF EARLSFERRY:...

[100] Harm which constitutes a wrong' in the contemplation of the law must, of course, be remedied. But the world is full of harm for which the law furnishes no remedy. For instance, a trader owes no duty of care to avoid injuring his rivals by destroying their long-established businesses. If he does so and, as a result, one of his competitors descends into a clinical depression and his family are reduced to penury, in the eyes of the law they suffer no wrong and the law will provide no redress—because competition is regarded as operating to the overall good of the economy and society. A young man whose fiancée deserts him for his best friend may become clinically depressed as a result, but in the circumstances the fiancée owes him no duty of care to avoid causing this suffering. So he too will have no right to damages for his illness. The same goes for a middle-aged woman whose husband runs off with a younger woman. Experience suggests that such intimate matters are best left to the individuals themselves. However badly one of them may have treated the other, the law does not get involved in awarding damages.

[101] Other relationships are also important. We may have children, parents, grandparents, brothers, sisters, uncles and aunts—not to mention friends, colleagues, employees and employers—who play an essential part in our lives and contribute to our happiness and prosperity. We share in their successes, but are also affected by anything bad which happens to them. So it is—and always has been—readily foreseeable that if a defendant injures or kills someone, his act is likely to affect not only the victim but many others besides. To varying degrees, these others can plausibly claim to have suffered real harm as a result of the defendant's act. For the most part, however, the policy of the law is to concentrate on compensating the victim for the effects of his injuries while doing little or nothing for the others. In technical language, the defendants owe a duty of care to the victim but not to the third parties, who therefore suffer no legal wrong....

[105] For the most part, then, the settled policy of the law is opposed to granting remedies to third parties for the effects of injuries to other people.

[LORD BINGHAM OF CORNHILL delivered a speech in favour of allowing the appeal. LORD BROWN OF EATON-UNDER-HEYWOOD delivered a speech in favour of dismissing the appeal and LORD STEYN agreed with the speeches of LORD NICHOLLS, LORD RODGER, and LORD BROWN.]

Appeal dismissed.

NOTES

1.   For later discussion in the Court of Appeal of the question of a duty of care in this situation, see *D v Bury Metropolitan Borough Council* [2006] 1 WLR 917, [2006] EWCA Civ 1. The passage extracted above asserts the continued vitality of the duty concept in this area, despite certain case law which will be dealt with at pp. 95–106, post being seen as something of a shift from duty to breach: see P. Craig and D. Fairgrieve, [1999] PL 626. See also *Lawrence v Pembrokeshire County Council* [2007] 1 WLR 2991, [2007] EWCA Civ 446 at [48]–[50]. On this question of 'shift' see further S. Bailey (2006) 26 LS 155 and note the views of B. Markesinis and J Fedtke, [2007] PL 299, who present empirical evidence from Germany to argue against fears based on the economic consequences of a shift to resolving cases through the mechanism of breach rather than

duty. Contrast with the view of Lord Nicholls the opinion of Lord Bingham at [49] in his dissenting speech in the same case:

It would seem clear that the appellants' claim would not be summarily dismissed in France, where recovery depends on showing gross fault: see Markesinis, Auby, Coester-Waltjen and Deakin *Tortious Liability of Statutory Bodies* (1999) pp 15–20; Fairgrieve 'Child Welfare and State Liability in France' in Fairgrieve and Green *Child Abuse Tort Claims against Public Bodies: A Comparative Law View* (2004) pp 179–197, Fairgrieve 'Beyond Illegality: Liability for Fault in English and French Law' in *State Liability in Tort* (2003) ch 4. Nor would they be summarily dismissed in Germany where, it is said, some of the policy considerations which influenced the House in *X (minors) v Bedfordshire CC* were considered by those who framed para 839 of the BGB and were rejected many years ago: see *Markesinis* pp 58–71; Martina Künnecke 'National Report on Germany' in *Fairgrieve and Green* pp 199–207. Yet in neither of those countries have the courts been flooded with claims. If, as some respected academic authorities suggested, *Barrett's* case shifted the emphasis of the English courts from consideration of duty to consideration of breach (see Craig and Fairgrieve '*Barrett*, Negligence and Discretionary Powers' [1999] PL 626, Fairgrieve *State Liability in Tort* (2003) p 84, para 2.1.2.7), I would for my part regard that shift as welcome, since the concept of duty has proved itself a somewhat blunt instrument for dividing claims which ought reasonably to lead to recovery from claims which ought not. But I should make it plain that if breach rather than duty were to be the touchstone of recovery, no breach could be proved without showing a very clear departure from ordinary standards of skill and care. It should be no easier to succeed here than in France or Germany.

2. The potential action for breach of convention rights referred to by Lord Nicholls is that under the Human Rights Act 1998, where public authorities can be sued if they infringe a person's rights as set out in the Act. Damages are, however, not always available, merely 'just satisfaction' which may or may not require the award of damages (though cf. Article 5(5) of the ECHR), and the 1998 Act has been described as 'not a tort statute' (*R (Greenfield) v Secretary of State for the Home Department* [2005] 2 All ER 240, [2005] UKHL 14 at [19]). The timing of the events in *D v East Berkshire* was such that the Human Rights Act 1998 was not applicable. It was later argued on behalf of a parent that the coming into force of the Act made a difference, with reliance being placed on Article 8 of the ECHR (right to family life), but this was unsuccessful in the *Lawrence* case. Auld LJ thought that this Article 'with its wholly different legal construct of engaging liability without reference to a duty of care, complements [the law of negligence] in facilitating a similar protection through mechanism for justification'. Cf. the discussion in note 4, p. 52, ante. In the context of a different tort, note *W v Westminster City Council (Note)* [2005] 4 All ER 96, where it was stated that an action based on Article 8 could succeed even if a defamation action was defeated by qualified privilege.

3. Several of the cases which have been discussed in the preceding pages have involved public bodies. The specific topic of suing public bodies in negligence will be considered further in chap. 3, post, and see further the Appendix.

4. It will have been seen in *D v East Berkshire* that a possible conflict of interest can be a powerful factor militating against a duty of care being owed to a particular person. See further *Jain v Trent Strategic Health Authority* [2008] QB 246, [2007] EWCA Civ 1186. *Howarth*, pp. 165–167 identifies nine arguments that have been put forward (not always successfully) in an attempt to dissuade a court from finding that a duty of care would be fair, just, and reasonable. These include: that liability would only lead to an increase in expense and inconvenience without altering the defendant's conduct; that the courts should not, via the imposition of liability, become involved in important

matters of political policy, especially those concerning public expenditure, which should be left to other organs of government; that imposing a duty of care would undermine or evade some other legal rule or procedure; that the law should not recognise the type of harm suffered by the claimant because it is, for example, too trivial; and that the public benefits so greatly from the defendant's activities that these should be allowed to continue whatever the cost in terms of harm caused. See further J. Stapleton in *The Law of Obligations*, edited by P. Cane and J. Stapleton, (Oxford, 1998), p. 59, but see the views of C.R. Witting (2005) 25 Oxf JLS 33.

5.   One of the arguments referred to ante is the undesirability of allowing an action in negligence when this would undermine or evade some other legal rule. This is seen, for example, in *Murphy v Brentwood District Council* [1991] 1 AC 398, [1990] 2 All ER 908 (p. 183, post), where the House of Lords declined to recognise a duty of care in circumstances which fell outside the regime for liability enacted by Parliament in the Defective Premises Act 1972. However, on occasion the courts take the opposite view, deciding that liability in negligence would not conflict with another legal rule. A notable example is found in the following extract:

■ Spring v Guardian Assurance plc
House of Lords [1994] 3 All ER 129

The plaintiff was employed as a sales director by the defendant life assurance company. He lost his job with the defendant and attempted to obtain alternative employment, selling insurance policies for another company. That company sought a reference from the defendant, which described the plaintiff in damning terms as being 'dishonest' and 'a man of little or no integrity'. In consequence, the plaintiff was unable to obtain alternative employment. In fact, the allegations in the reference were unwarranted. The plaintiff claimed damages for the loss caused to him by the reference. The plaintiff's claim in negligence was successful at first instance, but the Court of Appeal allowed the defendant's appeal, holding that the giver of a reference owed no duty of care in negligence to the person who was the subject of the reference either in giving or compiling the reference or in obtaining the information on which it was based, and that his only remedy lay in defamation (which would in any event be defeated by the defence of qualified privilege). On the plaintiff's appeal to the House of Lords:

LORD GOFF OF CHIEVELEY:...
[His Lordship first decided that, subject to issues of policy, the giver of an employment reference should owe a duty of care to the subject of the reference under the principles derived from *Hedley Byrne & Co v Heller & Partners* [1964] AC 465, [1963] 2 All ER 575, (on which see further p. 242, post). He then continued]...

If so, whether such a duty will nevertheless be negatived because it would, if recognised, pro tanto undermine the policy underlying the defence of qualified privilege in the law of defamation
   I think it desirable that I should first of all identify the nature of this policy objection. As I understand it, the objection is as follows. First of all, reference is made to the description of the policy underlying the defence of qualified privilege given by Lord Diplock in *Horrocks v Lowe* [1974] 1 All ER 662 at 669–670, [1975] AC 135 at 149, in the course of which he said:

'The public interest that the law should provide an effective means whereby a man can vindicate his reputation against calumny, has nevertheless to be accommodated to the competing public interest in permitting men to communicate frankly and freely with one another about matters with respect to which the law recognises that they have a duty to perform or an interest to protect in doing so. What is published in good faith on matters of these kinds is published on a privileged occasion. It is not actionable even though it be defamatory and turns out to be untrue.'

Second, it is suggested that the policy which underlies the defence of qualified privilege, viz that in the relevant circumstances men should be permitted to communicate frankly and freely with one another about all relevant matters, prevents the recognition of a duty of care owed by the giver of the reference to the subject of the reference. In this connection, reliance is placed in particular upon decisions of the Court of Appeal of New Zealand in *Bell-Booth Group Ltd v A-G* [1989] 3 NZLR 148 and *South Pacific Manufacturing Co Ltd v New Zealand Security Consultants and Investigations Ltd, Mortensen v Laing* [1992] 2 NZLR 282. In the *Bell-Booth* case Cooke P said (at 156):

'The common law rules, and their statutory modifications, regarding defamation and injurious falsehood represent compromises gradually worked out by the Courts over the years, with some legislative adjustments, between competing values. Personal reputation and freedom to trade on the one hand have to be balanced against freedom to speak or criticise on the other. In the result the present rules are in broad terms well-known and reasonably clear. To an action for defamation truth is an absolute defence. Privilege, where applicable, is in a few areas an absolute but in most a qualified defence. Fair comment is a qualified defence subject to rather different rules. In injurious falsehood, on the other hand, the plaintiff has the burden of proving both falsity and malice. These evolved compromises may not draw the lines in places that will always be found generally acceptable in the community. Some argue, for instance, for greater media freedom or licence; statutory changes have been recommended but not enacted. It is a controversial area. The important point for present purposes is that the law as to injury to reputation and freedom of speech is a field of its own.'

Now I for my part accept that, as stated by Hallett J in *Foaminol Laboratories Ltd v British Artid Plastics Ltd* [1941] 2 All ER 393 at 399, 'a claim for mere loss of reputation is the proper subject of an action for defamation, and cannot ordinarily be sustained by means of any other form of action...' Furthermore, it is (with respect) understandable that, in the *Bell-Booth* case the New Zealand Court of Appeal should have rejected a claim in negligence against the New Zealand Ministry of Agriculture and Fisheries in respect of an alleged failure to inform the plaintiffs of the results of certain trials of a product of the plaintiffs, or to consult them about the presentation of the results, as a result of which trials the product was truthfully described as 'ineffective' in a television broadcast; or that in the *South Pacific Manufacturing* and *Mortensen* cases the same court should have rejected claims in negligence against fire-loss investigators, whose reports to insurers (by whom they were instructed) should have resulted in the rejection of claims by parties whose premises had been damaged by fire and, in one case, a prosecution for arson. In neither case was any question of assumption of responsibility to the plaintiffs before the court.

By way of contrast, in the English case of *Lawton v BOC Transhield Ltd* [1987] 2 All ER 608, [1987] ICR 7 Tudor Evans J held that an employer owed a duty of care to a former employee in respect of the preparation of a reference for him. However, on the facts of the case he held that there was no breach of duty; and in any event he gave no consideration to the impact of the law of defamation upon his decision that a duty was owed by the employer.

In these circumstances it is, I consider, necessary to approach the question as a matter of principle. Since, for the reasons I have given, it is my opinion that in cases such as the present the duty of care arises by reason of an assumption of responsibility by the employer to the employee in respect of the relevant reference, I can see no good reason why the duty to exercise due skill and care which rests upon the employer should be negatived because, if the plaintiff were instead to bring an action for damage to his reputation, he would be met by the defence of qualified privilege which could only be defeated by proof of malice. It is not to be forgotten that the *Hedley Byrne* duty arises where there is a relationship which is, broadly speaking, either contractual or equivalent to contract. In these circumstances, I cannot see that principles of the law of defamation are of any relevance.

It is true that recognition of a duty of care to an employee in cases such as the present, based on the *Hedley Bryne* principle, may have some inhibiting effect on the manner in which references are expressed, in the sense that it may discourage employers from expressing views such as those which are encouraged by r. 3.5(2) of the Lautro rules [the code of conduct of the insurance industry's self-regulatory body, requiring reference to make 'full and frank disclosure of all relevant matters…']. For my part, however, I suspect that such an inhibition exists in any event. Employers may well, like many people, be unwilling to indulge in unnecessary criticism of their employees: hence the perceived necessity for r. 3.5(2). In all the circumstances, I do not think that we may fear too many ill effects from the recognition of the duty. The vast majority of employers will continue, as before, to provide careful references. But those who, as in the present case, fail to achieve that standard, will have to compensate their employees or former employees who suffer damage in consequence. Justice, in my opinion, requires that this should be done; and I, for my part, cannot see any reason in policy why that justice should be denied.

For these reasons I would allow the appeal; but I would nevertheless remit the matter to the Court of Appeal to consider the issue of the extent to which the damage suffered by the plaintiff was caused by the breach of duty of the defendants.

LORD LOWRY:…

The defendants have two main arguments. The first is that to confer on the plaintiff a cause of action in negligence would distort and subvert the law of defamation in cases where the defence relied on is one of qualified privilege, that is, where, on an occasion when he has either a duty to communicate information or a legitimate interest of his own to protect, the defendant in good faith and without malice defames the plaintiff. I believe that the answer to this argument is that a person owes a general duty, subject to the principles governing the law of defamation and to the relationship, if any, between the defamer and the defamed, not to defame any other person, whereas a liability based on negligent mis-statement can exist only if (1) damage is foreseeable (and damage occurs) and (2) there is such proximity between the maker and the subject of the mis-statement as will impose a duty of care on the former for the protection of the latter. The existence of that foreseeability and that proximity between the plaintiff and the defendant is a justification, not for *extending* the liability for *defamation* by dispensing with the need for malice, but for bringing into play a *different* principle of liability according to which, in a restricted class of situations, a plaintiff can rely on *negligence* as the ingredient of the defendant's conduct which is essential to the existence of that liability. I consider that in the instant case damage stemming from the defendants' careless mis-statement when giving a reference *was* foreseeable and that the proximity between the defendants and the plaintiff imposed a duty of care on the former for the protection of the latter.

The defendants' second argument (which, in order that it may prevail, must be made to stand independently on its own feet) is that, even if one concedes foreseeability and proximity and even if it would otherwise be just and reasonable for the plaintiff to recover under the head of negligence, *public policy dictates* that the person who has been the subject of a negligent mis-statement shall not recover. The argument is grounded on the proposition that the maker of the mis-statement, provided he has acted in good faith, must, even if he has been negligent, be free to express his views in the kind of situation (including the giving of any reference) which is contemplated by the doctrine of qualified privilege which is part of the law of defamation.

This argument falls to be considered on the assumption that, but for the overriding effect of public policy, a plaintiff who is in the necessary proximate relation to a defendant will be entitled to succeed in negligence if he proves his case. To assess the validity of the argument entails not the resolution of a point of law but a balancing of moral and practical arguments. This exercise could no doubt produce different answers but, for my own part, I come down decisively on the side of the plaintiff.

On the one hand looms the probability, often amounting to a certainty, of damage to the individual, which in some cases will be serious and may indeed be irreparable. The entire future prosperity and happiness of someone who is the subject of a damaging reference which is given carelessly but in perfectly good faith may be irretrievably blighted. Against this prospect is set the possibility that some referees will be deterred from giving frank references or indeed any references. Placing full reliance here on the penetrating observations of my noble and learned friend Lord Woolf, I am inclined to view this possibility as a spectre conjured up by the defendants to frighten your Lordships into submission. I also believe that the courts in general and your Lordships' House in particular ought to think very carefully before resorting to public policy considerations which will defeat a claim that ex hypoethesi is a perfectly good cause of action. It has been said that public policy should be invoked only in clear cases in which the potential harm to the public is incontestable, that whether the anticipated harm to the public will be likely to occur must be determined on tangible grounds instead of on mere generalities and that the burden of proof lies on those who assert that the court should not enforce a liability which prima facie exists. Even if one should put the matter in a more neutral way, I would say that public policy ought not to be invoked if the arguments are evenly balanced: in such a situation the ordinary rule of law, once established, should prevail.

In marshalling my thoughts on public policy I have drawn freely upon the argument in *Rondel v Worsley* [1969] 1 AC 191 at 203 of Louis Blom-Cooper whose submissions, although not rewarded with success in that appeal, strike me as particularly appropriate in the context of the present case....

For these reasons, and for the reasons in regard to negligence given by my noble and learned friends, I would allow this appeal....

[LORD SLYNN OF HADLEY and LORD WOOLF delivered speeches in favour of allowing the appeal. LORD KEITH OF KINKEL delivered a speech in favour of dismissing the appeal.]

Appeal allowed.

NOTES

1. For further consideration of the issues raised in *Spring*, see chap. 4, post.

2. In *D v East Berkshire Community Health NHS Trust* [2005] 2 All ER 443, [2005] UKHL 23 (p. 52, ante), Lord Brown, noting that there would be a defence of qualified privilege to any defamation action brought to protect the parent's reputation and that this defence would not be defeated by mere negligence, saw the basis of this as the need for candour in communications. Although he accepted that this did not stop a duty of care being established in *Spring*, he referred to the importance of the employer/employee relationship to the decision. Note also that when *D* was in the Court of Appeal [2003] 4 All ER 796, [2003] EWCA Civ 1151, the Court of Appeal stated at [102] that it was not possible to bypass a defence such as qualified privilege 'by advancing a claim in defamation in the guise of a claim for negligence'. How does this differ from an argument based on there being an alternative remedy, such as an appeal (on which see p. 109, post)?

3. It is not only where the overlapping relationship is between negligence and another tort where problems may occur. The relationship between negligence and contract has also caused much discussion, particularly in relation to cases of pure economic loss, and this issue will be revisited later when recovery for such loss is dealt with (chap. 4, post).

4. At the time when the validity of blanket immunities in the light of the European Convention of Human Rights was under discussion in the light of the *Osman* decision, noted p. 48, ante, the House of Lords rejected another traditional immunity, which was formerly accorded to advocates, examining in detail and rejecting a number of policy arguments traditionally cited in support of the immunity.

■ Arthur J S Hall & Co. (a firm) v Simons
House of Lords [2000] 3 All ER 673

LORD STEYN: ...
My Lords, there are three appeals before the House from orders of the Court of Appeal in a building case and in two cases involving family proceedings. Clients raised claims in negligence

against firms of solicitors. In response the solicitors relied on the immunity of advocates from suits in negligence. In all three cases judges at first instance ruled that the claims against the solicitors were unsustainable. The circumstances of these cases and the disposals are set out in the judgment of the Court of Appeal ([1999] 3 WLR 873) given by Lord Bingham of Cornhill CJ. In effect the Court of Appeal ruled in all three cases presently before the House that the claims were wrongly struck out. The solicitors now appeal. The results of the appeals are of great importance to the parties. But transcending the importance of the specific issues arising on the appeals there are two fundamental general questions, namely: (1) ought the current immunity of an advocate in respect of and relating to conduct of legal proceedings as enunciated by the House in *Rondel v Worsley* [1967] 3 All ER 993, [1969] 1 AC 191, and explained in *Saif Ali v Sydney Mitchell & Co (a firm) (P, third party)* [1978] 3 All ER 1033, [1980] AC 198, to be maintained in England; and (2) what is or ought to be the proper scope in England of the general principle barring a collateral attack in a civil action on the decision of a criminal court as enunciated in *Hunter v Chief Constable of West Midlands* [1981] 3 All ER 727, [1982] AC 529...

The existing immunity of barristers

For more than two centuries barristers have enjoyed an immunity from actions in negligence. The reasons for this immunity were various.... In *Hedley Bryne & Co Ltd v Heller & Partners Ltd* [1963] 2 All ER 575, [1964] AC 465 the rule was established that irrespective of contract, if someone possessed of a special skill undertakes to apply that skill for the assistance of another person who relies upon such skill, a duty of care will arise (see [1963] 2 All ER 575 at 594, [1964] AC 465 at 502–503). The fact that the barrister did not enter into a contract with his solicitor or client ceased to be a ground of justification for the immunity. Nevertheless, in a unanimous decision the House in *Rondel v Worsley* [1967] 3 All ER 993 at 998, [1969] 1 AC 191 at 227 upheld the ancient immunity on considerations of 'public policy [which are] not immutable' (per Lord Reid). It is worth recalling that in that case the appellant had obtained the services of the respondent to defend him on a dock brief, and alleged that the respondent had been negligent in the conduct of his defence. It is undoubtedly right, as counsel for the solicitors submitted and nobody disputed, that the principal ground of the decision is the overriding duty of a barrister to the court. The House thought that the existence of liability in negligence, and indeed the very possibility of making assertions of liability against a barrister, might tend to undermine the willingness of barristers to carry out their duties to the court. Lord Morris of Borth-y-Gest ([1967] 3 All ER 993 at 1013, [1969] 1 AC 191 at 251) encapsulated the core idea by saying: 'It would be a retrograde development if an advocate were under pressure unwarrantably to subordinate his duty to the court to his duty to the client.' Other members of the appellate committee expressed similar views (see [1967] 3 All ER 993 at 1000, 1027–1028, 1034, 1041, [1969] 1 AC 191 at 231, 272–273, 283, 293 per Lord Reid, Lord Pearce, Lord Upjohn and Lord Pearson respectively). This factor is the pivot on which in 1967 the existence of the immunity hinged. But for it the case would probably have been decided differently. There were however supporting reasons. Perhaps the most important of these was the undesirability of relitigating issues already decided (see [1967] 3 All ER 993 at 1000–1001, 1012–1013, [1969] 1 AC 191 at 230, 249–250 per Lord Reid and Lord Morris respectively)....

Eleven years later in the *Saif Ali* case the House revisited this topic. On this occasion the immunity established in *Rondel v Worsley* was not challenged and was not directly in issue. The existence of the debate on the merits of the immunity was not re-opened. The terrain of the debate centred on the scope of the immunity....

The next development was the introduction by statute of a power enabling the court to make wasted costs orders against legal practitioners: see s. 51 of the Supreme Court Act 1981 as substituted by s. 4 of the Courts and Legal Services Act 1990. Not surprisingly barristers are occasionally guilty of wholly unjustifiable conduct which occasions a waste of expenditure. The Bar argued that because of the immunity of barristers no such orders ought in principle to be made against barristers. The Court of Appeal ruled to the contrary: *Ridehalgh v Horsefield* [1994] 3 All ER 848, [1994] Ch 205. And that decision was accepted by the Bar. It operates satisfactorily. It has not been detrimental to the functioning of the court system or indeed the interests of the bar....

It is now possible to take stock of the arguments for and against the immunity....

[Having rejected the idea that the 'cab-rank' rule or any analogy with the immunity enjoyed by other participants in court proceedings were in themselves sufficient to justify any immunity for barristers, LORD STEYN continued:] The third factor is the public policy against relitigating a decision of a court of competent jurisdiction. This factor cannot support an immunity extending to cases where there was no verdict by the jury or decision by the court. It cannot arguably justify the immunity in its present width. The major question arises in regard to criminal trials which have resulted in a verdict by a jury or a decision by the court. Prosecuting counsel owes no duty of care to a defendant: *Elguzouli-Daf v Comr of Police of the Metropolis* [1995] 1 All ER 833, [1995] QB 335. The position of defence counsel must however be considered. Unless debarred from doing so, defendants convicted after a full and fair trial who failed to appeal successfully, will from time to time attempt to challenge their convictions by suing advocates who appeared for them. This is the paradigm of an abusive challenge. It is a principal focus of the principle in *Hunter*'s case. Public policy requires a defendant, who seeks to challenge his conviction, to do so directly by seeking to appeal his conviction. In this regard the creation of the Criminal Cases Review Commission was a notable step forward. Recently in *R v Secretary of State for the Home Dept, ex p Simms* [1999] 3 All ER 400 at 409, [1999] 3 WLR 328 at 338, there was uncontroverted evidence before the House that the commission is seriously under-resourced and under-funded. Incoming cases apparently have to wait two years before they are assigned to a case worker. This is a depressing picture. The answer is that the functioning of the Commission must be improved. But I have no doubt that the principle underlying *Hunter*'s case must be maintained as a matter of high public policy. In *Hunter*'s case the House did not, however, 'lay down an inflexible rule to be applied willy-nilly to all cases which might arguably be said to be within it' (see *Smith v Linskills (a firm)* [1996] 2 All ER 353 at 358, [1996] 1 WLR 763 at 769 per Bingham MR (now Lord Bingham of Cornhill). It is, however, prima facie an abuse to initiate a collateral civil challenge to a criminal conviction. Ordinarily therefore a collateral civil challenge to a criminal conviction will be struck out as an abuse of process. On the other hand, if the convicted person has succeeded in having his conviction set aside on any ground, an action against a barrister in negligence will no longer be barred by the particular public policy identified in *Hunter*'s case. But, in such a case, the civil action in negligence against the barrister may nevertheless be struck out as unsustainable under the new flexible Civil Procedure Rules 1998; CPR 3.4(2)(a) and 24.2. If *Hunter*'s case is interpreted and applied in this way, the principal force of the fear of oblique challenges to criminal convictions disappears. Relying on my experience of the criminal justice system as a presiding judge on the Northern Circuit and as a member of the Court of Appeal (Criminal Division), I do not share intuitive judgments that the public policy against relitigation still requires the immunity to be maintained in criminal cases. That leaves collateral challenges to civil decisions. The principles of res judicata, issue estoppel and abuse of process as understood in private law should be adequate to cope with this risk. It would not ordinarily be necessary to rely on the *Hunter* principle in the civil context but I would accept that the policy underlying it should still stand guard against unforeseen gaps. In my judgment a barrister's immunity is not needed to deal with collateral attacks on criminal and civil decisions. The public interest is satisfactorily protected by independent principles and powers of the court.

The critical factor is, however, the duty of a barrister to the court. It also applies to every person who exercises rights of audience before any court, or who exercises rights to conduct litigation before a court: see ss. 27(2A) and 28(2A) of the 1990 Act as inserted by s. 42 of the Access to Justice Act 1999. It is essential that nothing should be done which might undermine the overriding duty of an advocate to the court. The question is however whether the immunity is needed to ensure that barristers will respect their duty to the court. The view of the House in 1967 was that assertions of negligence would tend to erode this duty. In the world of today there are substantial grounds for questioning this ground of public policy. In 1967 the House considered that for reasons of public policy barristers must be accorded a special status. Nowadays a comparison with other professionals is important. Thus doctors have duties not only to their patients but also to an ethical code. Doctors are sometimes faced with a tension between these duties. Concrete examples of such conflicting duties are given by Ian Kennedy

Treat Me Right, Essays in Medical Law and Ethics (1988). A topical instance is the case where an Aids infected patient asks a consultant not to reveal his condition to the patient's wife, general practitioner and other healthcare officials. Such decisions may easily be as difficult as those facing barristers. And nobody argues that doctors should have an immunity from suits in negligence. I regard the Canadian empirically tested experience as the most relevant. It tends to demonstrate that the fears that the possibility of actions in negligence against barristers would tend to undermine the public interest are unnecessarily pessimistic.

There would be benefits to be gained from the ending of immunity. First, and most importantly, it will bring to an end an anomalous exception to the basic premise that there should be a remedy for a wrong. There is no reason to fear a flood of negligence suits against barristers. The mere doing of his duty to the court by the advocate to the detriment of his client could never be called negligent. Indeed if the advocate's conduct was bona fide dictated by his perception of his duty to the court there would be no possibility of the court holding him to be negligent. Moreover, when such claims are made courts will take into account the difficult decisions faced daily by barristers working in demanding situations to tight timetables...[I]t will not be easy to establish negligence against a barrister. The courts can be trusted to differentiate between errors of judgment and true negligence. In any event, a plaintiff who claims that poor advocacy resulted in an unfavourable outcome will face the very great obstacle of showing that a better standard of advocacy would have resulted in a more favourable outcome. Unmeritorious claims against barristers will be struck out. The new CPR have made it easier to dispose summarily of such claims: CPR 3.4(2)(a) and 24.2. The only argument that remains is that the fear of unfounded actions might have a negative effect on the conduct of advocates. This is a most flimsy foundation, unsupported by empirical evidence, for the immunity. Secondly, it must be borne in mind that one of the functions of tort law is to set external standards of behaviour for the benefit of the public. And it would be right to say that while standards at the Bar are generally high, in some respects there is room for improvement. An exposure of isolated acts of incompetence at the Bar will strengthen rather than weaken the legal system. Thirdly, and most importantly, public confidence in the legal system is not enhanced by the existence of the immunity. The appearance is created that the law singles out its own for protection no matter how flagrant the breach of the barrister. The world has changed since 1967. The practise of law has become more commercialised: barristers may now advertise. They may now enter into contracts for legal services with their professional clients. They are now obliged to carry insurance. On the other hand, today we live in a consumerist society in which people have a much greater awareness of their rights. If they have suffered a wrong as a result of the provision of negligent professional services, they expect to have the right to claim redress. It tends to erode confidence in the legal system if advocates, alone among professional men, are immune from liability for negligence. It is also noteworthy that there is no obligation on the barrister (or for that matter the solicitor advocate) to inform a client at the inception of the relationship that he is not liable in negligence, and in practice the client is never so informed. Given that the resort to litigation is often one of the most important decisions in the life of the client, it has to be said that this is not a satisfactory position. Moreover, conduct covered by the immunity is beyond the remit of the Legal Services Ombudsman: s. 22(7)(b) of the 1990 Act. In combination these factors reinforce the already strong case for ending the immunity.

My Lords, one is intensely aware that *Rondel v Worsley* was a carefully reasoned and unanimous decision of the House. On the other hand, it is now clear that when the balance is struck between competing factors it is no longer in the public interest that the immunity in favour of barristers should remain. I am far from saying that *Rondel v Worsley* was wrongly decided. But on the information now available and developments since *Rondel v Worsley* I am satisfied that in today's world that decision no longer correctly reflects public policy. The basis of the immunity of barristers has gone. And exactly the same reasoning applies to solicitor advocates. There are differences between the two branches of the profession but not of a character to differentiate materially between them in respect of the issue before the House. I would treat them in the same way.

That brings me to the argument that the ending of the immunity, if it is to be undertaken, is a matter for Parliament....

It would certainly be the easy route for the House to say 'let us leave it to Parliament'. On balance my view is that it would be an abdication of our responsibilities with the unfortunate consequence of plunging both branches of the legal profession in England into a state of uncertainty over a prolonged period. That would be a disservice to the public interest. On the other hand, if the decision is made to end the immunity now, both branches of the profession will know where they stand. They ought to find it relatively easy to amend their rules where necessary and to adjust their already existing insurance arrangements in so far as that may be necessary.

My Lords, the cards are now heavily stacked against maintaining the immunity of advocates. I would rule that there is no longer any such immunity in criminal and civil cases. In doing so I am quite confident that the legal profession does not need the immunity.

[LORD BROWNE-WILKINSON, LORD HOFFMANN, and LORD MILLETT delivered speeches agreeing with LORD STEYN that advocates no longer enjoy immunity from suit in respect of their conduct of civil or criminal proceedings. LORD HOPE OF CRAIGHEAD, LORD HUTTON, and LORD HOBHOUSE OF WOODBOROUGH dissented on the issue of criminal proceedings only.]

Appeal allowed.

NOTES

1. The High Court of Australia has taken a different view of the position: see *D'Orta-Ekenaike v Victoria Legal Aid* (2005) 214 ALR 92, noted by P. Cane (2005) 13 *TLJ* 93. The basis for this decision was the High Court's view of the need for finality in judicial decision-making. One of the grounds for distinguishing *Hall v Simons* was what was perceived to be the 'significant effect' of the influence of the imminent application of Article 6 of the European Convention of Human Rights in English law by the Human Rights Act 1998, although Article 6 of the ECHR and the *Osman* decision were not the main basis for the House of Lords' decision. On the position in Scotland, see G. Gordon (2007) 70 MLR 471 commenting on *Wright v Paton Farrell* 2006 SLT 259. Although seeing 'some force' in the concerns over relitigation, the arguments against immunity were found by the New Zealand Court of Appeal to outweigh those favouring protection in civil cases (*Lai v Chamberlain* [2005] 3 NZLR 291, noted by R. Tobin (2006) 14 *TLJ* 24: the position in relation to criminal cases was not decided as it had not been argued in the case). On relitigation, note the following view of Lord Hoffmann, after having discussed relitigation in general in *Hall v Simons* [2000] 3 All ER at p. 703):

    My Lords, [this] discussion shows, first, that not all relitigation of the same issue will be manifestly unfair to a party or bring the administration of justice into disrepute, and secondly, that when relitigation is for one or other of these reasons an abuse, the court has power to strike it out. This makes it very difficult to use the possibility of relitigation as a reason for giving lawyers immunity against all actions for negligence in the conduct of litigation, whether such proceedings would be an abuse of process or not. It is burning down the house to roast the pig; using a broad-spectrum remedy when a more specific remedy without side effects can handle the problem equally well.

2. It will have been noted that Lord Steyn in *Hall v Simons* did not determine that the decision in *Rondel v Worsley* was wrong at the time it was reached. The normal retroactivity of judicial decisions was, therefore, modified in this particular case and this can become an issue in relation to the running of the limitation period: see *Awoyomi v Radford* [2008] 3 WLR 34, [2007] EWHC 1671 (QB). It was, however, still retroactive to an extent (the case did not require a precise date to be fixed), and Lloyd Jones J in *Awoyomi* rejected the argument that the House of Lords had intended *Hall v Simons* to be prospective in its effects. It was recently clearly stated in *In re Spectrum Plus Ltd* [2005]

4 All ER 209, [2005] UKHL 41 that prospective decisions are possible in English law in very exceptional circumstances. How might this affect decisions on the existence of a duty of care?

3. For a study of the effects of this immunity, see J. Hill (1986) 6 Oxf JLS 183.

2 PURE OMISSIONS

■ Stovin v Wise (Norfolk County Council, third party)

House of Lords [1996] 3 All ER 801

For further discussion of this case, see p. 110, post. Note that two of the other members of the House of Lords sitting in this case agreed with Lord Hoffmann's speech.

LORD HOFFMANN: . . .

Omissions, like economic loss, are notoriously a category of conduct in which Lord Atkin's generalisation in *Donoghue v Stevenson* offers limited help. In the High Court of Australia in *Hargrave v Goldman* (1963) 110 CLR 40 at 65–66 Windeyer J drew attention to the irony in Lord Atkin's allusion ([1932] AC 562 at 580, [1932] All ER Rep 1 at 11), in formulating his 'neighbour' test, to the parable of the Good Samaritan:

> 'The priest and the Levite, when they saw the wounded man by the road, passed by on the other side. He obviously was a person whom they had in contemplation and who was closely and directly affected by their action. Yet the common law does not require a man to act as the Samaritan did.'

A similar point was made by Lord Diplock in *Home Office v Dorset Yacht Co Ltd* [1970] 2 All ER 294 at 325, [1970] AC 1004 at 1060. There are sound reasons why omissions require different treatment from positive conduct. It is one thing for the law to say that a person who undertakes some activity shall take reasonable care not to cause damage to others. It is another thing for the law to require that a person who is doing nothing in particular shall take steps to prevent another from suffering harm from the acts of third parties . . . or natural causes. One can put the matter in political, moral or economic terms. In political terms it is less of an invasion of an individual's freedom for the law to require him to consider the safety of others in his actions than to impose upon him a duty to rescue or protect. A moral version of this point may be called the 'Why pick on me?' argument. A duty to prevent harm to others or to render assistance to a person in danger or distress may apply to a large and indeterminate class of people who happen to be able to do something. Why should one be held liable rather than another? In economic terms, the efficient allocation of resources usually requires an activity should bear its own costs. If it benefits from being able to impose some of its costs on other people (what economists call 'externalities') the market is distorted because the activity appears cheaper than it really is. So liability to pay compensation for loss caused by negligent conduct acts as a deterrent against increasing the cost of the activity to the community and reduces externalities. But there is no similar justification for requiring a person who is not doing anything to spend money on behalf of someone else. Except in special cases (such as marine salvage) English law does not reward someone who voluntarily confers a benefit on another. So there must be some special reason why he should have to put his hand in his pocket.

In *Hargrave v Goldman* (1963) 110 CLR 40 at 66 Windeyer J said:

> 'The trend of judicial development of the law of negligence has been . . . to found a duty of care either in some task undertaken, or in the ownership, occupation or use of land or chattels.'

There may be a duty to act if one has undertaken to do so or induced a person to rely upon one doing so. Or the ownership or occupation of land may give rise to a duty to take positive steps for the benefit of those who come upon the land and sometimes for the benefit of neighbours. In *Hargrave v Goldman* the High Court of Australia held that the owner and occupier of a 600-acre grazing property in Western Australia had a duty to take reasonable steps to extinguish a fire, which had been started by lightning striking a tree on his land, so as to prevent it from spreading to his neighbour's land. This is a case in which the limited class of persons who owe the duty (neighbours) is easily identified and the political, moral and economic arguments which I have mentioned are countered by the fact that the duties are mutual. One cannot tell where the lightning may strike and it is therefore both fair and efficient to impose upon each landowner a duty to have regard to the interests of his neighbour. In giving the advice of the Privy Council affirming the decision (*Goldman v Hargrave* [1966] 2 All ER 989, [1967] 1 AC 645) Lord Wilberforce underlined the exceptional nature of the liability when he pointed out that the question of whether the landowner had acted reasonably should be judged by reference to the resources he actually had at his disposal and not by some general or objective standard. This is quite different from the duty owed by a person who undertakes a positive activity which carries the risk of causing damage to others. If he does not have the resources to take such steps as are objectively reasonable to prevent such damage, he should not undertake that activity at all....

NOTES

1. On *Goldman v Hargrave* [1967] 1 AC 645, [1966] 2 All ER 989 which is discussed in this extract, see chap. 14, post, and on the position of public bodies in relation to omissions, with which *Stovin v Wise* was directly concerned, see p. 110 post.

2. The passage extracted from *Stovin v Wise* discusses why the law should be chary of imposing liability for omissions, and for comment on the view in *Stovin* see K. Williams (2001) 21 Oxf JLS 393 at 397–400 and J. Kortman, *Altruism in Private Law* (Oxford, 2005), chap. 3. See further *Atiyah*, pp. 73–75, where possible reasons are put forward, including the more burdensome nature of affirmative obligations, the idea that the defendant has not identified himself in the way in which affirmative conduct leading to damage identifies a person and causal arguments, in that the defendant may merely have failed to prevent harm occurring. For criticism of these views, however, see *Atiyah*, pp. 75–77 and for further discussion of policy factors, see J. G. Logie [1989] CLJ 115 at 117–120.

3. The 'fundamental distinction' that tort law draws between acts and omissions was acknowledged in *Banque Keyser Ullman SA v Skandia (UK) Insurance Co Ltd* [1990] 1 QB 665, [1989] 2 All ER 952, when that case was in the Court of Appeal, where reference was made to the view of Lord Goff in *Smith v Littlewoods Organisation Ltd* [1987] AC 241 at 271 (p. 82, post), to that of Lord Keith in *Yuen Kun Yeu v A-G of Hong Kong* [1988] AC 175 at 192 and to that of Lord Bridge in *Curran v Northern Ireland Co-Ownership Housing Association Ltd* [1987] AC 718 at 724. In the Court of Appeal in *Banque Keyser* it was further stated (at p. 798) that the reluctance of the courts to render pure omissions actionable in tort 'applies, perhaps even more so, when the omission is a failure to prevent economic harm'.

4. On occasions, however, the law will impose a duty to act and failure to act can involve liability; see *Fleming*, pp. 162–172. One situation is that the law may impose liability on those who fail to control others when there is a sufficient relationship of control over another person. So for example, those caring for children, such as parents and schools, owe a duty to protect the child from injuring him- or herself: see *Barnes v Hampshire County Council* [1969] 3 All ER 746, [1969] 1 WLR 1563, where a child aged five was injured when hit by a lorry on a busy road a short distance from her school. The court found that she had been let out of school five minutes early, and that if she had been let

out at the official time, her mother would have been there to meet her. Consequently, the education authority was liable to the child.

5.   It should be noted that the existence of an affirmative duty of care can be uncontroversial and the result will depend on whether there has been a breach of that duty (on which see further chap. 5, post). In *Surtees v Kingston-Upon-Thames Borough Council* [1991] 2 FLR 559 negligence was unsuccessfully alleged against a foster parent in an action for injuries to a two-year-old child's left foot caused by contact with hot water while she was in foster care. The child's foot had been scalded when she was briefly left unattended by the foster parent. The existence of a duty on the part of the foster parent (whose position was equated with that of a parent) was relatively uncontroversial and was treated as turning merely on the question of reasonable foreseeability of injury on the facts. However, the Court of Appeal decided that the foster parent was not in breach of this duty. As Sir Nicholas Browne-Wilkinson V-C explained: 'We should be slow to characterise as negligent the care which ordinary loving and careful mothers are able to give to individual children, given the rough-and-tumble of home life' (see further chap. 5).

At another point in *Surtees*, Sir Nicholas Browne-Wilkinson said that 'there are very real public policy considerations to be taken into account if the conflicts inherent in legal proceedings are to be brought into family relationships'. On this basis, is there a case for not allowing any action by a child against its parents (by denying the existence of a duty of care), or at least for restricting recovery to those cases where the parent is actually insured or (so as not to discriminate against a child with less prudent parents) to those situations where there is compulsory insurance? Note that in the Court of Appeal in *Barrett v Enfield London Borough Council* [1997] 3 All ER 171 at 178 Lord Woolf MR, while accepting that a parent could be liable to his or her child for negligent driving, thought it totally wrong that there should be liability on parents making decisions concerning their child's future. See further the view of Lord Slynn when *Barrett* reached the House of Lords [1999] 3 All ER 193 at 212–213 (p. 95, post), and that of Lord Hutton ibid., 226, who specifically agreed that a child should not be able to sue its parents for erroneous decisions concerning its upbringing (but distinguished the position of a local authority with a statutory duty to take a child into care or make arrangements concerning the child's future). There has been debate as to whether there is a general duty of care on parents towards their children or whether it only arises in particular circumstances: see C. McIvor, *Third Party Liability in Tort* (2006), pp. 21–24; L. Hoyano and C. Keenan, *Child Abuse* (Oxford, 2007), pp. 271–274. On the problems of litigation within the family, see further *Greatorex v Greatorex* [2000] 4 All ER 769, [2000] 1 WLR 1970, noted p. 131, post).

6.   Examples of liability for omissions can be found in *Barnett v Chelsea and Kensington Hospital Management Committee* [1969] 1 QB 428, [1968] 1 All ER 1068 (p. 344, post) and in the law relating to occupiers' liability. See further *Kirkham v Chief Constable of the Greater Manchester Police* [1990] 2 QB 283 [1990] 3 All ER 246, where liability was established when the police, who were aware of the suicidal tendencies of the claimant's husband, had not passed this information on to the prison authorities when he was remanded in custody by a magistrates' court. Lloyd LJ accepted that there could be liability for an omission where a claimant had relied on an assumption of responsibility to him by the defendant. In *Kirkham* Lloyd LJ found an assumption of responsibility by the police to relay to the prison authorities, upon the transfer of the claimant's husband from police custody to them, information potentially relevant to his well-being and

he inferred that there had been reliance by him on that assumption of responsibility (see also *Reeves v Metropolitan Police Comr* [2000] 1 AC 360, [1999] 3 All ER 897, p. 392, post; *Orange v Chief Constable of West Yorkshire Police* [2002] QB 347, [2001] EWCA Civ 611). On assumption of responsibility, consider further *Bishara v Sheffield Teaching Hospital NHS Trust* [2007] EWCA Civ 353 where, having referred to *Barrett v Ministry of Defence* [1995] 3 All ER 87, noted post, the court stated that 'assumption of responsibility is simply one of the ways in which the necessary proximity may arise'.

Note the point in *Fleming*, p. 167, that even where there is no close personal relationship, 'a duty may be found in justifiable reliance on a more general assumption of protective care'. He cites cases on the liability of railways for accidents on level crossings such as *Smith v South Eastern Rly Co* [1896] 1 QB 178 (reliance by person crossing railway track on practice of defendant's servant signalling to approaching trains), though he also mentions the argument that misfeasance may be involved here.

7.   What other situations should give rise to an affirmative duty to protect others? Might the licensee of a public house be liable to a customer who, as a result of the consumption of alcoholic drink on the premises, was knocked over by a car on a busy road or fell over a nearby cliff? Consider *Munro v Porthkerry Park Holiday Estates Ltd* [1984] LS Gaz R 1368, but see *Joy v Newell (t/a The Copper Room)* [2000] NI 91. In *Barrett v Ministry of Defence*, it was held that no duty of care was owed to a serviceman on a base to prevent him from becoming unconscious through drink but that thereafter, on the facts, there had been an assumption of responsibility to him (and see *Watson v British Boxing Board of Control Ltd* [2001] QB 1134 at [49]–[53], [2001] EWCA Civ 2116). Note also *Jebson v Ministry of Defence* [2000] 1 WLR 2055, [2000] EWCA Civ 1 which shows that where transport is provided for a night out during which it is foreseeable that there could be drinking, a duty of care can be imposed to establish supervision (here in the back of the lorry in which people were travelling on their return from the night out). In *Griffiths v Brown and Lindsay* [1999] PIQR P131 the duty of care owed by a taxi driver in stopping at a place where the passenger could safely leave the cab was held not to be altered by the fact that the passenger had been drinking.

Generally on the subject of this note, see McIvor, op cit., pp. 74–80; E. Chamberlain [2004] Common Law World Review 103; and J. Fulbrook [2007] JPIL 220. (For discussion in the High Court of Australia, see *Cole v South Tweed Heads Rugby League Football* Club (2004) 217 CLR 469, on which see G.Orr and G. Dale (2005) 13 TLJ 103.) What about a social host? See Chamberlain op cit., though note the later Supreme Court of Canada decision in *Childs v Desormeaux* (2006) 266 DLR (4th) 257.

8.   For further consideration of assumption of responsibility, reliance, and liability for omissions, see *Henderson v Merrett Syndicates Ltd* [1995] 2 AC 145, [1994] 3 All ER 506 (p. 232, post). Here, the House of Lords indicated the broad principle of assumption of responsibility; derived from *Hedley Bryne & Co Ltd v Heller & Partners Ltd* [1964] AC 465, [1963] 2 All ER 575 (p. 207, post), could encompass liability for omissions, on which consider further *White v Jones* [1995] 2 AC 207, [1994] 1 All ER 691 (p. 243, post).

9.   *Stovin v Wise* also makes it clear—see in particular the reference to the parable of the Good Samaritan—that there is generally no liability at common law on a person who fails to attempt a rescue. What if a person does attempt a rescue but fails to effect it? In *Capital and Counties plc v Hampshire County Council* [1997] QB 1004, [1997] 2 All ER 865, the Court of Appeal (at p. 885) thought that it was 'not clear why a rescuer who is not under an obligation to attempt a rescue should assume a duty to be careful in effecting a rescue merely by undertaking the attempt' and that it 'would be strange if such

a person were liable to the dependants of a drowning man who but for his carelessness he would have saved, but without the attempt would have drowned anyway'. Indeed, reference was made to this having been decided in *Horsley v Maclaren, The Ogopogo* [1971] 2 Lloyd's Rep 410, to it being consistent with *East Suffolk Rivers Catchment Board v Kent* [1941] AC 74, [1940] 4 All ER 527, and to it being the effect of *Alexandrou v Oxford* [1993] 4 All ER 328, noted p. 47, ante.

The Ogopogo merits further attention here as it raises the question of the potential liability of one rescuer *to another rescuer*. In this case Matthews fell by accident from Maclaren's boat (on which he was a guest) into a lake. Maclaren manoeuvred the boat whilst rescue attempts were unsuccessfully made, and, after some minutes, Horsley, another guest, dived into the water in an attempt to rescue Matthews. Matthews' body, in fact, was never found, and Horsley also died. Ritchie J, delivering the majority judgment of the Supreme Court of Canada, held that there was a duty on Maclaren 'in his capacity as a host and as the owner and operator of the *Ogopogo*, to do the best he could to effect the rescue of one of his guests who had accidentally fallen overboard'. (Laskin J (with Hall J concurring) delivered a dissenting judgment, but on this point was prepared to find that Maclaren had a duty to take reasonable care for his guests' safety, and his obligation extended to 'rescue from perils of the sea where this is consistent with his duty to see to the safety of his other passengers and with concern for his own safety'.) Ritchie J went on to say (at p. 412):

In the present case a situation of peril was created when Matthews fell overboard, but it was not created by any fault on the part of Maclaren, and before Maclaren can be found to have been in any way responsible for Horsley's death, it must be found that there was such negligence in his method of rescue as to place Matthews in an apparent position of increased danger subsequent to and distinct from the danger to which he had been initially exposed by his accidental fall. In other words, any duty owing to Horsley must stem from the fact that a new situation of peril was created by Maclaren's negligence which induced Horsley to act as he did.

Ritchie J, however, held that Maclaren had, in fact, not been negligent. In this situation, should there be a requirement of increased danger 'distinct from' the initial danger? Should a first rescuer, who was not under an existing duty to rescue, be liable to a second rescuer who only attempts a rescue because of the first rescuer's careless efforts? For discussion of these and other issues, see E. R. Alexander (1972) XXII Univ Tor LJ 98. *The Ogopogo* is also discussed by W. Binchy (1974) 25 NILQ 147. On the liability of the rescue services, see note 5, p. 116, post.

3 PROXIMITY AND FAILURE TO PREVENT HARM

NOTE

As has been seen, the general rule in English law is that there is no liability for pure omissions. However, as the exceptions to that general rule already discussed show, the fact that the parties were in a prior relationship may be enough to import an affirmative duty to act to prevent harm. It is in this context that the requirement of 'proximity' for the establishment of a duty of care has a meaningful role to play. The first case extracted is very significant, being the first occasion on which the House of Lords allowed an action against a defendant for failing to prevent deliberate harm caused by a third party. The action was allowed to succeed because, in today's language, of the high degree of proximity between the defendant and the wrongdoer, and between the defendant and the claimants.

■ Home Office v Dorset Yacht Co Ltd
House of Lords [1970] 2 All ER 294

This was an appeal by the Home Office from the order of the Court of Appeal (Lord Denning MR and Edmund Davies and Phillimore LJJ) dated 10 March 1969 and reported, [1969] 2 All ER 564, dismissing the appeal of the Home Office from a judgment of Thesiger J dated 19 December 1968, who decided a preliminary issue on a point of law in favour of the respondents, the Dorset Yacht Co Ltd. The facts are set out in the opinion of Lord Reid.

LORD REID: . . .
My Lords, on 21 September 1962, a party of borstal trainees were working on Brownsea Island in Poole Harbour under the supervision and control of three borstal officers. During that night seven of them escaped and went aboard a yacht which they found nearby. They set this yacht in motion and collided with the respondents' yacht which was moored in the vicinity. Then they boarded the respondents' yacht. Much damage was done to this yacht by the collision and some by the subsequent conduct of these trainees. The respondents sued the appellant, the Home Office, for the amount of this damage.

The case comes before your Lordships on a preliminary issue whether the Home Office or these borstal officers owed any duty of care to the respondents capable of giving rise to a liability in damages. So it must be assumed that the respondents can prove all that they could prove on the pleadings if the case goes to trial. The question then is whether on that assumption the Home Office would be liable in damages. It is admitted that the Home Office would be vicariously liable if an action would lie against any of these borstal officers.

The facts which I think we must assume are that this party of trainees was in the lawful custody of the governor of the Portland Borstal Institution and was sent by him to Brownsea Island on a training exercise in the custody and under the control of the three officers with instructions to keep them in custody and under control. But in breach of their instructions these officers simply went to bed leaving the trainees to their own devices. If they had obeyed their instructions they could and would have prevented these trainees from escaping. They would therefore be guilty of the disciplinary offences of contributing by carelessness or neglect to the escape of a prisoner and to the occurrence of loss, damage or injury to any person or property. All the escaping trainees had criminal records and five of them had a record of previous escapes from borstal institutions. The three officers knew or ought to have known that these trainees would probably try to escape during the night, would take some vessel to make good their escape and would probably cause damage to it or some other vessel. There were numerous vessels moored in the harbour, and the trainees could readily board one of them. So it was a likely consequence of their neglect of duty that the respondents' yacht would suffer damage.

The case for the Home Office is that under no circumstances can borstal officers owe any duty to any member of the public to take care to prevent trainees under their control or supervision from injuring him or his property. If that is the law then enquiry into the facts of this case would be a waste of time and money because whatever the facts may be the respondents must lose. That case is based on three main arguments. First, it is said that there is virtually no authority for imposing a duty of this kind. Secondly, it is said that no person can be liable for a wrong done by another who is of full age and capacity and who is not the servant or acting on behalf of that person. And thirdly, it is said that public policy (or the policy of the relevant legislation) requires that these officers should be immune from any such liability.

[In rejecting the first argument for denying a duty of care (in a passage of which part has been set out at p. 36, ante), LORD REID concluded that there was 'nothing to prevent our approaching the present case with Lord Atkin's principles [in *M'Alister* (or *Donoghue*) *v Stevenson* [1932] AC 562 at 580] in mind': on the role of Lord Atkin's approach today, see pp. 36–46, ante. LORD REID continued:] Even so it is said that the respondents must fail because there is a general principle that no person can be responsible for the acts of another who is not his servant or acting on his behalf. But here the ground of liability is not responsibility for the acts of the escaping trainees; it is liability for damage caused by the carelessness of these officers in the knowledge that their carelessness would probably result in the trainees causing damage of this kind. So the question is really one of remoteness of damage. . . .

[Having quoted passages from the judgments in *The Oropesa*,[7] *Haynes v Harwood*[8] and *Scott's Trustees v Moss*,[9] he continued:] These cases show that, where human action forms one of the links between the original wrongdoing of the defendant and the loss suffered by the plaintiff, that action must at least have been something very likely to happen if it is not to be regarded as novus actus interveniens breaking the chain of causation. I do not think that a mere foreseeable possibility is or should be sufficient, for then the intervening human action can more properly be regarded as a new cause than as a consequence of the original wrongdoing. But if the intervening action was likely to happen I do not think it can matter whether that action was innocent or tortious or criminal. Unfortunately tortious or criminal action by a third party is often the 'very kind of thing' which is likely to happen as a result of the wrongful or careless act of the defendant. And in the present case, on the facts which we must assume at this stage, I think that the taking of a boat by the escaping trainees and their unskilful navigation leading to damage to another vessel were the very kind of thing that these borstal officers ought to have seen to be likely.

There was an attempt to draw a distinction between loss caused to the plaintiff by failure to control an adult of full capacity and loss caused by failure to control a child or mental defective. As regards causation, no doubt it is easier to infer novus actus interveniens in the case of an adult but that seems to me to be the only distinction. In the present case on the assumed facts there would in my view be no novus actus when the trainees damaged the respondents' property and I would therefore hold that damage to have been caused by the borstal officers' negligence.

If the carelessness of the borstal officers was the cause of the respondents' loss what justification is there for holding that they had no duty to take care? The first argument was that their right and power to control the trainees was purely statutory and that any duty to exercise that right and power was only a statutory duty owed to the Crown. I would agree but there is very good authority for the proposition that, if a person performs a statutory duty carelessly so that he causes damage to a member of the public which would not have happened if he had performed his duty properly, he may be liable. In *Geddis v Proprietors of Bann Reservoir*[10] Lord Blackburn said:

'For I take it, without citing cases, that it is now thoroughly well established that no action will lie for doing that which the legislature has authorised, if it be done without negligence, although it does occasion damage to anyone; but an action does lie for doing that which the legislature has authorised, if it be done negligently.'

The reason for that is, I think, that Parliament deems it to be in the public interest that things otherwise unjustifiable should be done, and that those who do such things with due care should be immune from liability to persons who may suffer thereby. But Parliament cannot reasonably be supposed to have licensed those who do such things to act negligently in disregard of the interests of others so as to cause them needless damage.

Where Parliament confers a discretion the position is not the same. Then there may, and almost certainly will, be errors of judgment in exercising such a discretion and Parliament cannot have intended

---

[7] [1943] P 32 at 37, [1943] 1 All ER 211 at 214.
[8] [1935] 1 KB 146 at 156, [1934] All ER Rep 103 at 107.
[9] (1889) 17 R 32 at 36 and 37.   [10] (1878) 3 App Cas 430 at 455, 456.

that members of the public should be entitled to sue in respect of such errors. But there must come a stage when the discretion is exercised so carelessly or unreasonably that there has been no real exercise of the discretion which Parliament has conferred. The person purporting to exercise his discretion has acted in abuse or excess of his power. Parliament cannot be supposed to have granted immunity to persons who do that. The present case does not raise that issue because no discretion was given to these borstal officers. They were given orders which they negligently failed to carry out....

...[T]he responsible authorities must weigh on the one hand the public interest of protecting neighbours and their property from the depredations of escaping trainees and on the other hand the public interest of promoting rehabilitation. Obviously there is much room here for differences of opinion and errors of judgment. In my view there can be no liability if the discretion is exercised with due care. There could only be liability if the person entrusted with discretion either unreasonably failed to carry out his duty to consider the matter or reached a conclusion so unreasonable as again to show failure to do his duty....

It was suggested that a decision against the Home Office would have very far reaching effects; it was indeed suggested in the Court of Appeal[11] that it would make the Home Office liable for the loss occasioned by a burglary committed by a trainee on parole or a prisoner permitted to go out to attend a funeral. But there are two reasons why in the vast majority of cases that would not be so. In the first place it would have to be shown that the decision to allow any such release was so unreasonable that it could not be regarded a real exercise of discretion by the responsible officer who authorised the release. And secondly it would have to be shown that the commission of the offence was the natural and probable, as distinct from merely a foreseeable, result of the release—that there was no novus actus interveniens....I think the fears of the Home Office are unfounded; I cannot believe that negligence or dereliction of duty is widespread among prison or borstal officers.

Finally, I must deal with public policy. It is argued that it would be contrary to public policy to hold the Home Office or its officers liable to a member of the public for this carelessness—or indeed any failure of duty on their part. The basic question is who shall bear the loss caused by that carelessness—the innocent respondents or the Home Office who are vicariously liable for the conduct of their careless officers? I do not think that the argument for the Home Office can be put better than it was put by the Court of Appeals of New York in *Williams v New York State*:[12]

> '...public policy also requires that the State be not held liable. To hold otherwise would impose a heavy responsibility upon the State, or dissuade the wardens and principal keepers of our prison system from continued experimentation with "minimum security" work details—which provide a means for encouraging better-risk prisoners to exercise their senses of responsibility and honor and so prepare themselves for their eventual return to society. Since 1917, the Legislature has expressly provided for out-of-prison work, Correction law, §182, and its intention should be respected without fostering the reluctance of prison officials to assign eligible men to minimum security work, lest they thereby give rise to costly claims against the State, or indeed inducing the State itself to terminate this "salutary procedure" looking towards rehabilitation.'

It may be that public servants of the State of New York are so apprehensive, easily dissuaded from doing their duty, and intent on preserving public funds from costly claims, that they could be influenced in this way. But my experience leads me to believe that Her Majesty's servants are made of sterner stuff. So I have no hesitation in rejecting this argument. I can see no good ground in public policy for giving this immunity to a government department. I would dismiss this appeal.

LORD PEARSON:...

It may be artificial and unhelpful to consider the question as to the existence of a duty of care in isolation from the elements of breach of duty and damage. The actual damage alleged to have been suffered by the respondents may be an example of a kind or range of potential damage which

---

[11] [1969] 2 QB 412, [1969] 2 All ER 564.　　[12] 127 NE (2d) 545 (1955) at 550.

was foreseeable, and if the act or omission by which the damage was caused is identifiable, it may put one on the trail of a possible duty of care of which the act or omission would be a breach. In short, it may be illuminating to start with the damage and work back through the cause of it to the possible duty which may have been broken. . . .

What would be the nature of the duty of care owed by the Home Office to the respondents if it existed? In my opinion, the Home Office did not owe to the respondents any general duty to keep the borstal boys in detention. If the Home Office had, in the exercise of its discretion, released some of these boys, taking them on shore and putting them on trains or buses with tickets to their homes, there would have been no prospect of damage to the respondents as boatowners and the respondents would not have been concerned and would have had nothing to complain of. Again the boys might have escaped in such a way that no damage could be caused to the respondents as boat owners; for instance, they might have escaped by swimming ashore or by going ashore in a boat belonging to or hired by the borstal authorities or by having their friends bring a rescue boat from outside and carry them off to a refuge in the Isle of Wight of Portsmouth or elsewhere. On the other hand the boys might interfere with the boats from motives of curiosity and desire for amusement without having any intention to escape from borstal detention. The essential feature of this case is not the 'escape' (whatever that may have amounted to) but the interference with the boats. The duty of care would be simply a duty to take reasonable care to prevent such interference. The duty would not be broken merely by the Home Office's failure to prevent an escape from borstal detention or from borstal train-ing. Performance of the duty might incidentally involve an element of physical detention, if interference with the boats by some particular boy could not be prevented by any other means. But if some other means—such as supervision, keeping watch, dissuasion or deterrence—would suffice, physical deten-tion would not be required for performance of the duty.

Can such a duty be held to exist on the facts alleged here? On this question there is no judicial authority except the one decision in the Ipswich county court in *Greenwell v Prison Comrs*.[13] In this situ-ation it seems permissible, indeed almost inevitable, that one should revert to the statement of basic principle by Lord Atkin in *M'Alister* (or *Donoghue*) *v Stevenson*[14]. . . . It seems to me that prima facie, in the situation which arose in this case according to the allegations, the respondents as boat owners were in law 'neighbours' of the Home Office and so there was a duty of care owing by the Home Office to the respondents. It is true that the *M'Alister* (or *Donoghue*) *v Stevenson*[14] principle as stated in the passage which has been cited is a basic and general but not universal principle and does not in law apply to all the situations which are covered by the wide words of the passage. To some extent the deci-sion in this case must be a matter of impression and instinctive judgment as to what is fair and just. It seems to me that this case ought to, and does, come within the *M'Alister* (or *Donoghue*) *v Stevenson*[14] principle unless there is some sufficient reason for not applying the principle to this case. Therefore, one has to consider the suggested reasons for not applying the principle here.[15]

Proximity or remoteness. As there is no evidence, one can only judge from the allegations in the state-ment of claim. It seems clear that there was sufficient proximity; there was geographical proximity and it was foreseeable that the damage was likely to occur unless some care was taken to prevent it. In other cases a difficult problem may arise as to how widely the 'neighbourhood' extends, but no such problem faces the respondents in this case.

Act of third party. In *Weld-Blundell v Stephens*[16] Lord Sumner said:

'In general (apart from special contracts and relations and the maxim respondent superior), even though A is in fault, he is not responsible for injury to C which B, a stranger to him, deliberately chooses to do.'

---

[13] (1951) 101 L Jo 486.   [14] [1932] AC 562 at 580, [1932] All ER Rep 1 at 11.
[15] [But on the approach to the duty of care today, see pp. 36–46, ante.]
[16] [1920] AC 956 at 986, [1920] All ER Rep 32 at 47.

In *Smith v Leurs*[17] Dixon J said:

> '...apart from vicarious responsibility, one man may be responsible to another for the harm done
> to the latter by a third person; he may be responsible on the ground that the act of the third person
> could not have taken place but for his own fault or breach of duty. There is more than one descrip-
> tion of duty the breach of which may produce this consequence. For instance, it may be a duty of
> care in reference to things involving special danger. It may even be a duty of care with reference to
> the control of actions or conduct of the third person. It is, however, exceptional to find in the law a
> duty to control anothers' actions to prevent harm to strangers. The general rule is that one man is
> under no duty of controlling another to prevent his doing damage to a third. There are, however,
> special relations which are the source of a duty of this nature. It appears now to be recognised that
> it is incumbent upon a parent who maintains control over a young child to take reasonable care so
> to exercise that control as to avoid conduct on his part exposing the person or property of others to
> unreasonable danger. Parental control, where it exists, must be exercised with due care to prevent
> the child inflicting intentional damage on others or causing damage by conduct involving unreason-
> able risk of injury to others.'

In my opinion, this case falls under the exception and not the rule, because there was a special relation.
The borstal boys were under the control of the Home Office's officers, and control imports responsibility. The boy's interference with the boats appears to have been a direct result of the Home Office's
officers' failure to exercise proper control and supervision. Problems may arise in other cases as to the
responsibility of the Home Office's officers for acts done by borstal boys when they have completed
their escape from control and are fully at large and acting independently. No such problem faces the
respondents in this case.

Statutory duty. Not only with respect to the detention of borstal boys but also with respect to the
discipline, supervision and control of them the Home office's officers were acting in pursuance of
statutory duties. These statutory duties were owed to the Crown and not to private individuals such as
the respondents. The respondents, however, do not base their claim on breach of statutory duty. The
existence of statutory duties does not exclude liability at common law for negligence in the performance of the statutory duties....Be it assumed that the Home Office's officers were acting in pursuance
of statutory powers (or statutory duties which must include powers) in bringing the borstal boys to
Brownsea Island to work there under the supervision and control of the Home Office's officers. No
complaint could be made of the Home Office's officers doing that. But in doing that they had a duty to
the respondents as 'neighbours' to make proper exercise of the powers of supervision and control for
the purpose of preventing damage to the respondents as 'neighbours'.

Public policy. It is said, and in the absence of evidence I assume (and perhaps it is common knowledge
and can be judicially noticed) that one method of borstal training, which is employed in relation to
boys who may be able to respond to it, is to give them a considerable measure of freedom, initiative
and independence in order that they may develop their self-reliance and sense of responsibility. This
method, at any rate when it is intensively applied, must diminish the amount of supervision and control
which can be exercised over the borstal boys by the Home Office's officers, and there is then a risk,
which is not wholly avoidable, that some of the boys will escape and may in the course of escaping or
after escaping do injury to persons or damage to property. There is no evidence to show whether or
not this method was being employed, intensively or at all, in the present case. But supposing that it
was, I am of opinion that it would affect only the content or standard and not the existence of the duty
of care. It may be that when the method is being intensively employed there is not very much that the
Home Office's officers can do for the protection of the neighbours and their property. But it does not
follow that they have no duty to do anything at all for this purpose. They should exercise such care for

---

[17]   (1945) 70 CLR 256 at 261, 262.

the protection of the neighbours and their property as is consistent with the due carrying out of the borstal system of training. The needs of the borstal system, important as they no doubt are, should not be treated as so paramount and all-important as to require or justify complete absence of care for the safety of the neighbours and their property and complete immunity from any liability for anything that the neighbours may suffer.

...I would say that the Home office owed no duty to the respondents with regard to the detention of the borstal boys (except perhaps incidentally as an element in supervision and control) nor with regard to the treatment or employment of them, but the Home Office did owe to the respondents a duty of care, capable of giving rise to a liability in damages, with respect to the manner in which the borstal boys were disciplined, controlled and supervised.

I would dismiss the appeal.

LORD DIPLOCK:...

In the present appeal...the conduct of the Home Office which is called in question differs from the kind of conduct discussed in *M'Alister* (or *Donoghue*) *v Stevenson*[18] in at least two special characteristics. First, the actual damage sustained by the respondents was the direct consequence of a tortious act done with conscious volition by a third party responsible in law for his own acts and this act was interposed between the act of the Home Office complained of and the sustension of damage by the respondents. Secondly, there are two separate 'neighbour relationships' of the Home Office involved, a relationship with the respondents and a relationship with the third party. These are capable of giving rise to conflicting duties of care. This appeal, therefore, also[19] raises the lawyer's question 'Am I my brother's keeper'? A question which may also[19] receive a restricted reply.

I start, therefore, with an examination [of] the previous cases in which both or one of these special characteristics are present....

[Having discussed various authorities, he continued: From the previous decision of the English courts...it is possible to arrive by induction at an established proposition of law as respects one of those special-relations: viz. A is responsible for damage caused to the person or property of B by the tortious act of C (a person responsible in law for his own acts) where the relationship between A and C has the characteristics: (1) that A has the legal right to detain C in penal custody and to control his act while in custody; (2) that A is actually exercising his legal right of custody of C at the time of C's tortious act; and (3) that A if he had taken reasonable care in the exercise of his right of custody could have prevented C from doing the tortious act which caused damage to the person or property of B; and where also the relationship between A and B has the characteristics; (4) that at the time of C's tortious act A has the legal right to control the situation of B or his property as respects physical proximity to C; and (5) that A can reasonably foresee that B is likely to sustain damage to his person or property if A does not take reasonable care to prevent C from doing tortious acts of the kind which he did.

On the facts which your Lordships are required to assume for the purposes of the present appeal the relationship between the Home Office, A, and the borstal trainees, C, did possess characteristics (1) and (3) but did not possess characteristic (2); while the relationship between the Home Office, A, and the respondents, B, did possess characteristic (5) but did not possess characteristic (4). What your Lordships have to decide as respects each of the relationships is whether the missing characteristic is essential to the existence of the duty or whether the facts assumed for the purposes of this appeal disclose some other characteristic which if substituted for that which is missing would produce a new proposition of law which *ought* to be true.

...To give rise to a duty on the part of the custodian owed to a member of the public to take reasonable care to prevent a borstal trainee from escaping from his custody before completion of the trainee's sentence there should be some relationship between the custodian and the person to whom the duty

---

[18] [1932] AC 562, [1932] All ER Rep 1.

[19] The word 'also' would appear to be a reference to Lord Atkin's speech in *M'Alister (or Donoghue) v Stevenson* [1932] AC 562 at 580 (p. 32, ante), where Lord Atkin mentions the lawyer's question as to who is my neighbour which, he says, receives a restricted reply.

is owed which exposes that person to a particular risk of damage in consequence of that escape which is different in its incidence from the general risk of damage from criminal acts of others which he shares with all members of the public.

What distinguishes a borstal trainee who has escaped from one who has been duly released from custody, is his liability to recapture, and the distinctive added risk which is a reasonably foreseeable consequence of a failure to exercise due care in preventing him from escaping is the likelihood that in order to elude pursuit immediately on the discovery of his absence the escaping trainee may steal or appropriate and damage property which is situated in the vicinity of the place of detention from which he has escaped.

So long as Parliament is content to leave the general risk of damage from criminal acts to lie where it falls without any remedy except against the criminal himself, the courts would be exceeding their limited function in developing the common law to meet changing conditions if they were to recognise a duty of care to prevent criminals escaping from penal custody owed to a wider category of members of the public than those whose property was exposed to an exceptional added risk by the adoption of a custodial system for young offenders which increased the likelihood of their escape unless due care was taken by those responsible for their custody.

I should therefore hold that my duty of a borstal officer to use reasonable care to prevent a borstal trainee from escaping from his custody was owed only to persons whom he could reasonably foresee had property situate in the vicinity of the place of detention of the detainee which the detainee was likely to steal or to appropriate and damage in the course of eluding immediate pursuit and recapture. Whether or not any person fell within this category would depend on the facts of the particular case including the previous criminal and escaping record of the individual trainee concerned and the nature of the place from which he escaped. . . .

In the present appeal the place from which the trainees escaped was an island from which the only means of escape would presumably be a boat accessible from the shore of the island. There is thus material, fit for consideration at the trial, for holding that the respondents, as the owners of a boat moored off the island, fell within the category of persons to whom a duty of care to prevent the escape of the trainees was owed by the officers responsible for their custody. . . .

[LORD MORRIS OF BORTH-Y-GEST delivered a speech in favour of dismissing the appeal. VISCOUNT DILHORNE delivered a speech in favour of allowing the appeal.]

Appeal dismissed.

NOTES

1. Borstal institutions were abolished by the Criminal Justice Act 1982.
2. Lord Reid's treatment of novus actus interveniens has been criticised in recent times and must be considered in the light of later cases: see pp. 400–405, post. At this stage, it is merely worth pausing to note that the result in *Dorset Yacht* cannot be justified by reference to 'foreseeability' alone. After all, it is considerably *more* foreseeable that borstal boys will go on a crime spree once they have made good their escape, than that they will cause damage to a yacht in the process of escaping (when one might expect them to be extra careful). Yet the House of Lords decided that the Home Office is only liable for the acts of the boys in the immediate course of their escape.
3. On the question of actions in negligence against public authorities, see chap. 3 and Appendix, and note especially the comments on the *Dorset Yacht* case in *X (Minors) v Bedfordshire County Council* [1995] 2 AC 633, [1995] 3 All ER 353 (p. 88, post) and in *Barrett v Enfield Borough Council* [2001] 2 AC 550, [1999] 3 All ER 193 (p. 95, post).
4. P. S. Atiyah, *The Damages Lottery* (Oxford, 1997), p. 132 notes that this action was brought by the claimant's insurance company against the Home Office, which in

accordance with normal government practice was not insured. He continues that '[w]hat the claim was really about was whether yacht owners and yacht club members or taxpayers should cover the damage done to yachts in circumstances of this sort'.

5.   Compare the *Dorset Yacht* case with *Smith v Scott* [1973] Ch 314, [1972] 3 All ER 645. In this case the Scott family had been placed in a house by the London Borough of Lewisham. The Scotts' behaviour was found by Pennycuick V-C to have been 'altogether intolerable both in respect of physical damage and of noise', and the Smiths, who lived in an adjoining house, moved out. Several points were argued for the claimant (Mr Smith) in this unsuccessful action against the borough, but it might be noted at this stage that the court held that the borough owed no duty of care to the neighbours in this situation, i.e. in the selection of a tenant. Particular reference was made to Lord Reid's speech in *Home Office v Dorset Yacht Co Ltd* [1970] AC 1004 at 1027, where he mentioned the 'long chapter of the law' governing the use by a landowner of his proprietary rights. Pennycuick V-C declined to alter the law by the introduction of a duty of care, although he acknowledged that the position could well have been different if this had been an area of the law which was being brought to the court's attention for the first time. See further *O'Leary v London Borough of Islington* (1983) 9 HLR 83.

6.   *Dorset Yacht* was distinguished in *Hill v Chief Constable of West Yorkshire* [1989] AC 53, [1988] 2 All ER 238, which raised the question whether the police owed a duty of care to individual members of the public who might be injured by criminals. (For more details of the case see p. 46, ante where the question of public policy in relation to such a claim was considered.) Distinguishing features were (a) the criminal was never in the police's custody; and (b) the victim was one of a very large number of females potentially at risk; on this latter point a contrast was drawn with a special risk to those whose yachts were moored off Brownsea Island in the *Dorset Yacht* case—and see Lord Diplock's speech in that case (p. 77, ante), which was cited in *Hill*. The requisite proximity was therefore lacking in *Hill*. See also *Palmer v Tees Health Authority* [2000] PIQR P1 where, rejecting proximity in a case in which it was alleged that the defendant was liable for a third party's acts, Stuart-Smith LJ claimed that it was essential for there to be a relationship between the victim and the defendant. For Pill LJ, however, the identifiability of the victim was only a factor to be taken into account.

7.   On the position of the police, see further pp. 46–52, ante.

8.   The liability of parents or schools to children in their care was discussed at pp. 67–68, ante, but such bodies might also be liable for failure to control such a child when, as a result, the child causes injury to a third party. In *Carmarthenshire County Council v Lewis* [1955] AC 549, [1955] 1 All ER 565, for example, a four-year-old child strayed out of an infants' school playground and ran into a busy road, causing the death of a lorry driver who swerved to avoid him. The House of Lords decided that the school authority owed a duty of care to the lorry driver. See generally on this topic, C. McIvor, *Third Party Liability in Tort*, pp. 24–34. Note that parents are not vicariously liable for the torts of their children—should they be?

■ Smith v Littlewoods Organisation Ltd (Chief Constable, Fife Constabulary, third party)

House of Lords [1987] 1 All ER 710

Littlewoods bought a cinema in Dunfermline. Their intention was to demolish the cinema and build a supermarket on the site. During a period when the cinema was empty and when none of Littlewoods' employees or contractors were in attendance, a fire was deliberately started by children (or teenagers) and the fire spread to and damaged the appellants' buildings. The appellants' actions succeeded before the Lord Ordinary, but this was reversed by the First Division of the Inner House of the Court of Session, 1986 SLT 272. There were then appeals to the House of Lords.

LORD GRIFFITHS: . . .
My Lords, I regard these appeals as turning on the evaluation and application of the particular facts of this case to a well-established duty and standard of care. . . .

The duty of care owed by Littlewoods was to take reasonable care that the condition of the premises they occupied was not a source of danger to neighbouring property.

[Having decided that the appeals should be dismissed, LORD GRIFFITHS added:] I doubt myself if any search will reveal a touchstone that can be applied as a universal test to decide when an occupier is to be held liable for a danger created on his property by the act of a trespasser for whom he is not responsible. I agree that mere foreseeability of damage is certainly not a sufficient basis to found liability. But with this warning I doubt that more can be done than to leave it to the good sense of the judges to apply realistic standards in conformity with generally accepted patterns of behaviour to determine whether in the particular circumstances of a given case there has been a breach of duty sounding in negligence.

LORD MACKAY OF CLASHFERN: . . .
The claims are based on the allegation that Littlewoods, as owners and occupiers of the Regal Cinema, had a duty to take reasonable care for the safety of premises adjoining, that they knew or ought to have known that a disused cinema would be a ready target for vandals, and that they knew or ought to have known that their cinema was, in fact, the subject of extensive vandalism and that if they did not take steps to prevent the entry of vandals they would cause damage not only to their own property, whether by fire or otherwise, but further such fire might spread and cause damage to adjoining properties. In the circumstances, it was claimed that Littlewoods had a duty to take reasonable care to keep and maintain the premises lockfast, to cause frequent and regular inspection to be made and to lock and board up any doors and windows found to be open or smashed and to employ a caretaker to watch over the premises and to prevent the entry of vandals. In the course of the hearing before your Lordships counsel for the appellants accepted that, in the light of the evidence, the only precaution that was likely to be effective in preventing the entry of vandals was to arrange for a 24-hour watch to be maintained on the premises. Littlewoods, while accepting that as owners and occupiers of the premises they had a duty to take reasonable care for the safety of premises adjoining, strenuously denied that they owed the duties on which these claims are founded.

. . . The judges of the First Division unanimously concluded that . . . in the circumstances it had not been shown that it was reasonably to be foreseen by Littlewoods that if they took no steps to discourage widespread use of the cinema by youngsters, including vandals, one or more of them, or some other intruder, would be likely deliberately to set fire to the building or deliberately to set such a fire in such a place as would be likely to engulf the building.

. . . [I]t has to be borne in mind that the damage to the neighbouring properties, on which the claims against Littlewoods are founded, is damage by fire or otherwise resulting from vandalism in Littlewoods' premises. A duty of care to prevent this damage is the only duty alleged to be incumbent on Littlewoods relevant to this case. From this it follows that, unless Littlewoods were bound reasonably to anticipate and guard against this danger, they had no duty of care, relevant to this case, requiring them to inspect their premises. Unless, therefore, Littlewoods, on taking control of these premises without any knowledge of the subsequent history of the property after they assumed control, ought reasonably to have anticipated that they would be set on fire and thus or otherwise create a substantial risk of damage to neighbouring properties if they did not take precautions, the claims must fail. . . . In my opinion, their Lordships of the First Division applied their minds to the correct question. In my opinion, the question whether, in all the circumstances described in evidence, a reasonable person in the position of Littlewoods was bound to anticipate as probable, if he took no action to keep these premises lockfast, that, in a comparatively short time before the premises were demolished, they would be set on fire with consequent risk to the neighbouring properties is a matter for the judges of fact to determine. Once it has been determined on the correct basis, an appeal court should be slow to interfere with the determination: see, for example, Lord Thankerton in *Glasgow Corp v Muir* [1943] 2 All ER 44 at 47, [1943] AC 448 at 454 and Lord Porter in *Bolton v Stone* [1951] 1 All ER 1078 at 1082, [1951] AC 850 at 860.

The cases to which counsel for the appellants drew attention in his argument, and s 78 of the [Criminal Justice (Scotland) Act 1980], illustrate that a consequence of this kind, if premises are left unoccupied, is a possibility, but the extent to which such an occurrence is probable must depend on the circumstances of the particular case. While no doubt in this case, as the judges in the courts below have found, it was probable that children and young persons might attempt to break into the vacated cinema, this by no means establishes that it was a probable consequence of its being vacated with no steps being taken to maintain it lockfast that it would be set on fire with consequent risk of damage to neighbouring properties. A telling point in favour of Littlewoods is that, although Littlewoods' particulars were shown on a board prominently displayed at the front of the premises, no one made any protest to them about the state of the premises, or indicated to them any concern that, unless they took some action, neighbouring premises were at risk....

This is sufficient for the disposal of this appeal but in view of the general importance of some of the matters raised in the parties' submissions it is right that I should add some observations on these.

First, counsel for the appellants urged us to say that the ordinary principle to be deduced from Lord Atkin's speech in *Donoghue v Stevenson* should apply to cases where the damage in question was caused by human agency. It is plain from the authorities that the fact that the damage, on which a claim is founded, was caused by a human agent quite independent of the person against whom a claim in negligence is made does not, of itself, preclude success of the claim, since breach of duty on the part of the person against whom the claim is made may also have played a part in causing the damage.

[Having quoted the passage concerning human action and novus actus interveniens from Lord Reid's speech in the *Dorset Yacht* case [1970] AC 1004 at 1030 (p. 72, ante), LORD MACKAY continued:]...It has to be borne in mind that Lord Reid was demonstrating only that the submission with which he was dealing was incorrect. If a person can be responsible for damage caused by acts of another who is not his servant or acting on his behalf that sufficed to answer the question that Lord Reid had before him in the respondent's favour. It was accordingly not critical whether the test was foreseeability of that damage as likely or very likely. At the stage at which Lord Reid used the phrase 'very likely' he was giving his view on what the two cases he had cited showed. In the first of these, the phrase used is 'the very kind of thing which is likely to happen' (see [1935] 1 KB 146 at 156, [1934] All ER Rep 103 at 107 per Greer LJ) and, in the second, the consequence that was being considered was described in the passage quoted from the Lord President (Inglis) as 'the natural and almost inevitable consequence' of the defender's action which was the foundation of the claim (see 17 R (Ct of Sess) 32 at 36). When Lord Reid turns to state his own position, he does so on the basis that the intervening action was likely to happen....

It is true, as has been pointed out by Oliver LJ in *Lamb v Camden London Borough* [1981] 2 All ER 408 at 418, [1981] QB 625 at 642, that human conduct is particularly unpredictable and that every society will have a sprinkling of people who behave most abnormally. The result of this consideration, in my opinion, is that, where the only possible source of the type of damage or injury which is in question is agency of a human being for whom the person against whom the claim is made has no responsibility, it may not be easy to find that as a reasonable person he was bound to anticipate that type of damage as a consequence of his act or omission. The more unpredictable the conduct in question, the less easy to affirm that any particular result from it is probable and in many circumstances the only way in which a judge could properly be persuaded to come to the conclusion that the result was not only possible but reasonably foreseeable as probable would be to convince him that, in the circumstances, it was highly likely. In this type of case a finding that the reasonable man should have anticipated the consequence of human action as just probable may not be a very frequent option. Unless the judge can be satisfied that the result of the human action is highly probable or very likely he may have to conclude that all that the reasonable man could say was that it was a mere possibility. Unless the needle that measures the probability of a particular result flowing from the conduct of a human agent is near the top of the scale it may be hard to conclude that it has risen sufficiently from the bottom to create the duty reasonably to foresee it.

In summary I conclude, in agreement with both counsel, that what the reasonable man is bound to foresee in a case involving injury or damage by independent human agency, just as in cases where such agency plays no part, is the probable consequences of his own act or omission, but that, in such a case, a clear basis will be required on which to assert that the injury or damage is more than a mere possibility....

Cases of theft where the thief uses a neighbour's premises to gain access to the premises of the owner of the stolen goods are, in my opinion, in an important respect different from cases of fire such as that with which your Lordships are concerned in the present appeal. In the case of fire, a hazard is created on the first occupier's premises and it is that hazard which operating from the first occupier's premises creates danger to the neighbouring properties.... [E]ven though that hazard is created by the act of a trespasser on the first premises the occupier of these premises, once he knows of the physical facts giving rise to the hazard, has a duty to take reasonable care to prevent the hazard causing damage to neighbouring properties. In the ordinary case of theft where the thief uses the first proprietor's property only as an access to the property of the person from whom the stolen property is taken there is no similar hazard on the first proprietor's land which causes the damage to the neighbouring property. Success of the theft depends very much on its mode and occasion being unexpected. The only danger consists in the thief or thieves who, having passed from trespassing on the first proprietor's property, go on to trespass on his neighbour's. There is also a sense in which neighbouring proprietors can, independently, take action to protect themselves against theft in a way that is not possible with fire. Once the fire had taken hold on Littlewoods' buildings, St Paul's proprietors[20] could not be expected to take effective steps to prevent sparks being showered over on their property....

Where the question is whether or not the duty to take a particular precaution is incumbent on a defendant, the probability of the risk emerging is not the only consideration, as was pointed out by Lord Reid giving the opinion of the Board in *The Wagon Mound (No 2), Overseas Tankship (UK) Ltd v Miller Steamship Co Pty Ltd* [1966] 2 All ER 709 at 718, [1967] 1 AC 617 at 642–643 in reference to *Bolton v Stone* [1951] 1 All ER 1078, [1951] AC 850.

[His Lordship proceeded to cite from the opinions of the Privy Council in *The Wagon Mound (No 2)* and in *Goldman v Hargrave* [1966] 2 All ER 989, [1967] 1 AC 645, and continued:] My Lords, I think it is well to remember as Lord Radcliffe pointed out in *Bolton v Stone* [1951] 1 All ER 1078 at 1087, [1951] AC 850 at 868–869:

> '...a breach of duty has taken place if [the facts] show the appellants guilty of a failure to take reasonable care to prevent the accident. One may phrase it [as] "reasonable care" or "ordinary care" or "proper care"—all these phrases are to be found in decisions of authority—but the fact remains that, unless there has been something which a reasonable man would blame as falling beneath the standard of conduct that he would set for himself and require of his neighbour, there has been no breach of legal duty...'

This is the fundamental principle and in my opinion various factors will be taken into account by the reasonable man in considering cases involving fire on the one hand and theft on the other, but since this is the principle the precise weight to be given to these factors in any particular case will depend on the circumstances and rigid distinctions cannot be made between one type of hazard and another. I consider that much must depend on what the evidence shows is done by ordinary people in like circumstances to those in which the claim of breach of duty arises.

In my view, if the test of the standard of the reasonable man is applied to the steps an occupier of property must take to protect neighbouring properties from the hazard of fire arising on his property

---

[20] St Paul's Church was damaged by the fire and had to be demolished.

on further consideration of policy arises that should lessen the responsibility of the occupier in a case such as this....

In my opinion, these appeals should be refused....

LORD GOFF OF CHIEVELEY:...

My Lords, the Lord President (Lord Emslie)[1] founded his judgment on the proposition that the defenders, who were both owners and occupiers of the cinema, were under a general duty to take reasonable care for the safety of premises in the neighbourhood.

Now if this proposition is understood as relating to a general duty to take reasonable care *not to cause damage* to premises in the neighbourhood (as I believe that the Lord President intended it to be understood) then it is unexceptionable. But it must not be overlooked that a problem arises when the pursuer is seeking to hold the defender responsible for having failed to *prevent* a third party from causing damage to the pursuer or his property by the third party's own deliberate wrongdoing. In such a case, it is not possible to invoke a general duty of care; for it is well recognised that there is no *general* duty of care to prevent third parties from causing such damage. The point is expressed very clearly in Hart and Honoré *Causation in the Law* (2nd edn, 1985) p. 196, where the authors state:

> 'The law might acknowledge a general principle that, whenever the harmful conduct of another is reasonable foreseeable, it is our duty to take precautions against it...But, up to now, no legal system has gone so far as this...'

The same point is made in Fleming *The Law of Torts* (6th edn, 1983) p. 200, where it is said: '...there is certainly no *general* duty to protect others against theft or loss.' (Fleming's emphasis.)

I wish to add that no such general duty exists even between those who are neighbours in the sense of being occupiers of adjoining premises. There is no general duty on a householder that he should act as a watchdog, or that his house should act as a bastion, to protect his neighbour's house.

Why does the law not recognise a general duty of care to prevent others from suffering loss or damage caused by the deliberate wrongdoing of third parties? The fundamental reason is that the common law does not impose liability for what are called pure omissions...... I think it important that we should realise that problems like that in the present case are unlikely to be solved by a simple abandonment of the common law's present strict approach to liability for pure omissions.

[A] statement of principle, which has been much quoted, is the observation of Lord Sumner in *Weld-Blundell v Stephens* [1920] AC 956 at 986, [1920] All ER Rep 32 at 47:

> 'In general...even though A. is in fault, he is not responsible for injury to C. which B., a stranger to him, deliberately chooses to do.'

This dictum may be read as expressing the general idea that the voluntary act of another, independent of the defender's fault, is regarded as a novus actus interveniens which, to use the old metaphor, 'breaks the chain of causation'. But it also expresses a general perception that we ought not to be held responsible in law for the deliberate wrongdoing of others. Of course, if a duty of care is imposed to guard against deliberate wrongdoing by others, it can hardly be said that the harmful effects of such wrongdoing are not caused by such breach of duty. We are therefore thrown back to the duty of care. But one thing is clear, and that is that liability in negligence for harm caused by the deliberate wrongdoing of others cannot be founded simply on foreseeability that the pursuer will suffer loss or damage by reason of such wrongdoing. There is no such general principle. We have therefore to identify the circumstances in which such liability may be imposed.

That there are special circumstances in which a defender may be held responsible in law for injuries suffered by the pursuer through a third party's deliberate wrongdoing is not in doubt. For example, a duty of care may arise from a relationship between the parties which gives rise to an imposition of assumption of responsibility on or by the defenders, as in *Stansbie v Troman* [1948] 1 All ER 599, [1948]

---

[1] In the First Division of the Inner House of the Court of Session.

2 KB 48, where such responsibility was held to arise from a contract. In that case a decorator, left alone on the premises by the householder's wife, was held liable when he went out leaving the door on the latch and a thief entered the house and stole property. Such responsibility might well be held to exist in other cases where there is no contract, as for example where a person left alone in a house has entered as a licensee of the occupier. Again, the defender may be vicariously liable for the third party's act; or he may be held liable as an occupier to a visitor on his land. Again, as appears from the dictum of Dixon J in *Smith v Leurs* (1945) 70 CLR 256 at 262, a duty may arise from a special relationship between the defender and the third party, by virtue of which the defender is responsible for controlling the third party: see, for example, *Home Office v Dorset Yacht Co Ltd*. More pertinently, in a case between adjoining occupiers of land, there may be liability in nuisance if one occupier causes or permits persons to g[a]ther on his land, and they impair his neighbour's enjoyment of his land. Indeed, even if such persons come onto his land as trespassers, the occupier may, if they constitute a nuisance, be under an affirmative duty to abate the nuisance. As I pointed out in *P Perl (Exporters) Ltd v Camden London BC* [1983] 3 All ER 161 at 172, [1984] QB 342 at 359, there may well be other cases.

These are all special cases. But there is a more general circumstance in which a defender may be held liable in negligence to the pursuer, although the immediate cause of the damage suffered by the pursuer is the deliberate wrongdoing of another. This may occur where the defender negligently causes or permits to be created a source of danger, and it is reasonably foreseeable that third parties may interfere with it and, sparking off the danger, thereby cause damage to persons in the position of the pursuer. The classic example of such a case is, perhaps, *Haynes v Harwood* [1935] 1 KB 146, [1934] All ER Rep 103 . . .

Haynes v Harwood was a case concerned with the creation of a source of danger in a public place. We are concerned in the present case with an allegation that the defenders should be held liable for the consequences of deliberate wrongdoing by others who were trespassers on the defenders' property. In such a case it may be said that the defenders are entitled to use their property as their own and so should not be held liable if, for example, trespassers interfere with dangerous things on their land. But this is, I consider, too sweeping a proposition. It is well established that an occupier of land may be liable to a trespasser who has suffered injury on his land; though in *British Rlys Board v Herrington* [1972] 1 All ER 749, [1972] AC 877[2], in which the nature and scope of such liability was reconsidered by your Lordships' House, the standard of care so imposed on occupiers was drawn narrowly so as to take proper account of the rights of occupiers to enjoy the use of their land. It is, in my opinion, consistent with the existence of such liability that an occupier who negligently causes or permits a source of danger to be created on his land, and can reasonably foresee that third parties may trespass on his land and, interfering with the source of danger, may spark it off, thereby causing damage to the person or property of those in the vicinity, should be held liable to such a person for damage so caused to him. . . .

There is another basis on which a defender may be held liable for damage to neighbouring property caused by a fire started on his (the defender's) property by the deliberate wrongdoing of a third party. This arises where he has knowledge or means of knowledge that a third party has created or is creating a risk of fire, or indeed has started a fire, on his premises, and then fails to take such steps as are reasonably open to him (in the limited sense explained by Lord Wilberforce in *Goldman v Hargrave* [1966] 2 All ER 989 at 995–996, [1967] 1 AC 645 at 663–664) to prevent any such fire from damaging neighbouring property . . .

Turning to the facts of the present case, I cannot see that the defenders should be held liable under either of these two possible heads of liability. First, I do not consider that the empty cinema could properly be described as an unusual danger in the nature of a fire hazard. . . .

Nor can I see that the defenders should be held liable for having failed to take reasonable steps to abate a fire risk created by third parties on their property without their fault. If there was any such fire risk, they had no means of knowing that it existed. . . .

---

[2] See now the Occupiers' Liability Act 1984, p. 587, post.

[LORD GOFF then moved on to consider the question of whether there could be liability where a thief gained access to one person's premises from another's property, and continued:] For my part, I do not think that liability can be imposed on an occupier of property in negligence simply because it can be said that it is reasonably foreseeable, or even (having regard, for example, to some particular temptation to thieves in adjacent premises) that it is highly likely, that if he fails to keep his property lockfast a thief may gain access to his property and thence to the adjacent premises. So to hold must presuppose that the occupier of property is under a general duty to *prevent* thieves from entering his property to gain access to neighbouring property, where there is a sufficient degree of foresight that this may occur. But there is no general duty to *prevent* third parties from causing damage to others, even though there is a high degree of foresight that they may do so. The practical effect is that everybody has to take such steps as he thinks fit to protect his own property, whether house or flat or shop, against thieves. He is able to take his own precautions; and, in deciding what precautions to take, he can and should take into account the fact that, in the ordinary course of life, adjacent property is likely to be from time to time unoccupied (often obviously so, and sometimes for a considerable period of time) and is also likely from time to time not to be lockfast. He has to form his own judgment as to the precautions which he should take, having regard to all the circumstances of the case, including (if it be the case) the fact that his premises are a jeweller's shop which offers a special temptation to thieves. I must confess that I do not find this practical result objectionable. . . .

The present case is, of course, concerned with entry not by thieves but by vandals. Here the point can be made that, whereas an occupier of property can take precautions against thieves, he cannot (apart from insuring his property and its contents) take effective precautions against physical damage caused to his property by a vandal who has gained access to adjacent property and has there created a source of danger which has resulted in damage to his property by, for example, fire or escaping water. Even so, the same difficulty arises. Suppose, taking the example I have given of the family going away on holiday and leaving their front door unlocked, it was not a thief but a vandal who took advantage of that fact; and that the vandal, in wrecking the flat, caused damage to the plumbing which resulted in a water leak and consequent damage to the shop below. Are the occupiers of the flat to be held liable in negligence for such damage? I do not think so, even though it may be well known that vandalism is prevalent in the neighbourhood. The reason is the same, that there is no general duty to *prevent* third parties from causing damage to others, even though there is a high degree of foresight that this may occur. In the example I have given, it cannot be said that the occupiers of the flat have caused or permitted the creation of a source of danger (as in *Haynes v Harwood* [1935] 1 KB 146, [1934] All ER Rep 103 . . .) which they ought to have guarded against; nor of course were there any special circumstances giving rise to a duty of care. The practical effect is that it is the owner of the damaged premises (or, in the vast majority of cases, his insurers) who is left with a worthless claim against the vandal, rather than the occupier of the property which the vandal entered (or his insurers), a conclusion which I find less objectionable than one which may throw an unreasonable burden on ordinary householders. For these reasons, I consider that both *Lamb v Camden London Borough* [1981] 2 All ER 408, [1981] QB 625 and *King v Liverpool City Council* [1986] 3 All ER 544, [1986] 1 WLR 890 were rightly decided; but I feel bound to say, with all respect, that the principle propounded by Lord Wylie in *Evans v Glasgow DC* 1978 SLT 17 at 19, viz that there is—

'a general duty on owners or occupiers of property . . . to take reasonable care to see that it [is] proof against the kind of vandalism which was calculated to affect adjoining property,'

is, in my opinion, too wide.

I wish to emphasise that I do not think that the problem in these cases can be solved simply through the mechanism of foreseeability. When a duty *is* cast on a person to take precautions against the wrongdoing of third parties, the ordinary standard of foreseeability applies; and so the possibility of such wrongdoing does not have to be very great before liability is imposed. I do not myself subscribe to the opinion that liability for the wrongdoing of others is limited because of the unpredictability of human conduct. So, for example, in *Haynes v Harwood* [1935] 1 KB 146, [1934] All ER Rep 103, liability was imposed although it cannot have been at all likely that a small boy would throw a stone at the horses left unattended in the public road, and in *Stansbie v Troman* [1948] 1 All ER 599, [1948] 2 KB 48 liability was imposed although it cannot have been at all likely that a thief would take advantage of the fact that the defendant left the door on the latch while he was out. Per contra, there is at present no general duty at common law to prevent persons from harming others by their deliberate wrongdoing, however foreseeable such harm may be if the defender does not take steps to prevent it.

Of course, if persons trespass on the defender's property and the defender either knows or has the means of knowing that they are doing so and that in doing so they constitute a danger to neighbouring property, then the defender may be under an affirmative duty to take reasonable steps to exclude them, in the limited sense explained by Lord Wilberforce in *Goldman v Hargrave* [1966] 2 All ER 989 at 995–996, [1967] 1 AC 645 at 663–664, but that is another matter. I incline to the opinion that this duty arises from the fact that the defender, as occupier, is in exclusive control of the premises on which the danger has arisen.

In preparing this opinion, I have given careful consideration to the question whether *P Perl (Exporters) Ltd v Camden London BC* [1983] 3 All ER 161, [1984] QB 342, in which I myself was a member of the Court of Appeal, was correctly decided. I have come to the conclusion that it was, though on rereading it I do not think that my own judgment was very well expressed. But I remain of the opinion that to impose a general duty on occupiers to take reasonable care to prevent others from entering their property would impose an unreasonable burden on ordinary householders and an unreasonable curb on the ordinary enjoyment of their property; and I am also of the opinion that to do so would be contrary to principle. It is very tempting to try to solve all problems of negligence by reference to an all-embracing criterion of foreseeability, thereby effectively reducing all decisions in this field to questions of fact. But this comfortable solution is, alas, not open to us. The law has to accommodate all the untidy complexity of life; and there are circumstances where considerations of practical justice impel us to reject a general imposition of liability for foreseeable damage. An example of this phenomenon is to be found in cases of pure economic loss . . . As the present case shows, another example of this phenomenon is to be found in cases where the plaintiff has suffered damage through the deliberate wrongdoing of a third party; and it is not surprising that once again we should find the courts seeking to identify specific situations in which liability can properly be imposed. Problems such as these are solved in Scotland, as in England, by means of the mechanism of the duty of care . . .

For these reasons I would dismiss these appeals.

[LORD KEITH OF KINKEL agreed with LORD MACKAY OF CLASHFERN and LORD GOFF OF CHIEVELEY. LORD BRANDON OF OAKBROOK delivered a speech in favour of dismissing the appeals.]

Appeals dismissed.

QUESTIONS

1. Is Lord Griffiths' approach more similar to that of Lord Mackay or that of Lord Goff?
2. How is Lord Mackay's speech to be squared with the approach to when a duty of care will be imposed in *Caparo Industries plc v Dickman* [1990] 2 HC 605, [1990] 1 All ER 568 (p. 37, ante)?

NOTES

1. Lord Brandon decided that Littlewoods owed the appellants a general duty of care to see that its property was not and did not become a source of danger to the neighbouring buildings. However, this did not in his view include a specific duty to take reasonable care to stop young people gaining unlawful access to the property and unlawfully setting fire to it because this was not reasonably foreseeable. D. Howarth, [1991] CLJ 58

at 72 argues that this concept of a specific duty is an example of a confusion between duty and breach, and see Howarth, op cit., pp. 72–81 more generally on *Smith v Littlewoods* (and two other cases) and the question of the separation of duty and breach. For further discussion of *Smith v Littlewoods* see B. S. Markesinis, (1989) 105 LQR 104. Arguing that Lords Brandon, Griffiths, and Mackay did not rule out liability on the basis of any general rule of no duty in this situation but decided it on its facts, he goes on to speculate as to the potential impact of these speeches in opening up liability in the situation where one person fails to stop another harming himself: see op cit., pp. 119–124.

2.   The question of the liability for the acts of third parties can arise in discussion of causation and remoteness of damage as well as duty, and will be further considered at that stage. The two issues are of course interrelated. As Oliver LJ pointed out in *P Perl (Exporters) Ltd v Camden London Borough Council* [1984] QB 342 at 353, if there is a duty of care to stop a third party causing damage, then it is difficult to see how damage caused in breach of that duty can be too remote. See further *King v Liverpool City Council* [1986] 3 All ER 544 at 552–553, and for Lord Mackay's comments on that case, see [1987] AC 241 at 266–267.

3.   When considering cases such as *Smith v Littlewoods*, bear in mind that property owners can normally be expected to insure against damage to their property, but note Markesinis's point (op cit., p. 111) that it may be difficult to obtain insurance against fire (or theft) in some inner city areas. (On the relevance of property insurance in the context of another tort, see p. 1139, post.)

4.   *Smith v Littlewoods* on its facts was concerned with damage to the appellants' property caused by fire but the situation where thieves gain access to a claimant's property from the defendant's premises was also discussed. In the earlier case of *P Perl (Exporters) Ltd v Camden London Borough Council* [1984] QB 342, [1983] 3 All ER 161 the defendant council owned adjoining premises, one (No. 144) being divided into flats and the other (No. 142) being let to the claimant, which used its basement to store clothing. The evidence showed that, for example, there was no lock on the front door of No. 144 at the relevant time. Thieves entered an unoccupied basement flat in No. 144, knocked a hole in the common wall between the basement flat in No. 144 and the basement in No. 142, and more than 700 garments were stolen from the latter basement. The Court of Appeal decided that the defendant council was not liable. Mere foreseeability of harm was regarded as insufficient to establish a duty of care. In *Smith v Littlewoods* [1987] AC at pp. 263–266 Lord Mackay justified the decision on the basis that the mode of entry onto the claimant's premises was only a foreseeable possibility: cf. Lord Goff's speech. Lord Mackay did also state that if a proprietor came upon a thief on his premises boring a hole into a neighbour's property, then the proprietor would have to take reasonable steps to stop him endeavouring to effect entry in this way.

5.   *Smith v Littlewoods* was cited in *Topp v London Country Bus (South West Ltd)* [1993] 3 All ER 448, [1993] 1 WLR 976, noted by J. G. Fleming (1994) 110 LQR 187, in which a woman had been knocked down and killed by a minibus that had been stolen by joyriders. It was held that the owners of the minibus, which was left unattended, unlocked, and with the ignition key in it for some hours in a lay-by near a public house, did not owe her a duty of care to take precautions against the wrongful acts of third parties. See further *Denton v United Omnibus Co Ltd* (1986) Times, 6 May, a case which the Court of Appeal in *Topp* did not think could be validly distinguished from the case before them and which is also discussed by Fleming op cit. *Topp* is considered by D. Howarth, (1994) 14 LS 88. Howarth points out the court's reliance in *Topp* on Lord Goff's speech

in *Smith v Littlewoods* (i.e. the general idea his Lordship derived from *Weld-Blundell v Stephens* [1920] AC 956 at 986, set out p. 82, *ante*), rather than Lord Mackay's speech, which it is said was endorsed by a majority of the House of Lords. Apart from the argument that Lord Mackay's general comments on this area of the law were *obiter* (see May J at first instance in *Topp* [1993] 3 All ER at p. 455), something which Howarth acknowledges, it might also be questioned how far the views of Lords Brandon and Griffiths can be applied in a case such as *Topp*. Do they go beyond the circumstances they set out concerning occupiers of land?

For discussion of the possible injustice to claimants and defendants from adoption of either Lord Mackay's or Lord Goff's approach, bearing in mind in the former case the fact that a tortfeasor will have to pay all the damages if the third party cannot be found or is not worth suing, see Howarth, op cit., who finds a possible compromise solution in the idea of proportionate liability. For further discussion of the issues in *Smith v Littlewoods* and *Topp*, see J. Stapleton (1995) 111 LQR 301 at 311–317.

6.   For further discussion of *Dorset Yacht* and *Smith v Littlewoods*, see *Attorney-General for the British Virgin Islands v Hartwell* [2004] 1 WLR 1273, [2004] UKPC 12, but the case was not really an omissions case. On *Hartwell*, see further note 4, p. 1094, *post*.

CHAPTER THREE

DUTY OF CARE: SPECIAL PROBLEMS

In this chapter, some of the specific situations in which the courts have to apply the general duty of care principles already discussed will be considered in more detail (save insofar as they concern the recovery of pure economic loss, which is considered in chap. 4). Duty of care problems generally arise either because of the nature of the parties involved (as in cases against public bodies) or because a form of loss has been suffered which differs from the paradigm case of negligently inflicted personal injury (such as cases of psychiatric harm and those where the complaint is the conception of an unwanted child). This chapter will illustrate the unique difficulties presented by problems of this kind.

1 LIABILITY OF PUBLIC AUTHORITIES

■ X (Minors) v Bedfordshire County Council
House of Lords [1995] 3 All ER 353

LORD BROWNE-WILKINSON: . . .

My lords, in each of these five appeals the plaintiffs by their statements of claim allege they have been injured by public authorities in the carrying out of functions imposed upon them by statute. The defendants have applied to strike out the claims on the grounds that they disclose no cause of action. In the first group of appeals (the *Bedfordshire* and *Newham* cases), the allegations are that the public authorities negligently carried out, or failed to carry out, statutory duties imposed on them for the purpose of protecting children from child abuse. In the second group (the *Dorset, Hampshire* and *Bromley* cases), the plaintiffs allege that the local authorities failed to carry out duties imposed upon them as education authorities by the Education Acts 1944 to 1981 in relation to children with special educational needs.

Although each case is different, all of them raise in one form or another the difficult and important question to what extent authorities charged with statutory duties are liable in damages to individuals injured by the authorities' failure properly to perform such duties. Such liability may be alleged to arise in a number of different ways: it can be based on breach of statutory duty simpliciter, on the failure to carry out the statutory duty without due care or on a breach of a common law duty of care. In considering the decided cases, and consequently the argument submitted on these appeals, it is not always clear which basis of liability is under consideration. I therefore propose, before turning to the individual appeals, to attempt a more general analysis of the problems raised in this field so far as they affect these cases.

GENERAL APPROACH

Introductory—public law and private law
The question is whether, if Parliament has imposed a statutory duty on an authority to carry out a particular function, a plaintiff who has suffered damage in consequence of the authority's performance or non-performance of that function has a right of action in damages against the authority. It is important to distinguish such actions to recover damages, based on a private law cause of action, from actions in public law to enforce the due performance of statutory duties, now brought by way of judicial review. The breach of a public law right by itself gives rise to no claim for damages. A claim for damages must be based on a private law cause of action. The distinction is important because a number of earlier cases (particularly in the field of education) were concerned with the enforcement by declaration and injunction of what would now be called public law duties. They were relied on in argument as authorities supporting the plaintiffs' claim for damages in this case...

Private law claims for damages can be classified into four different categories, viz: (A) actions for breach of statutory duty simpliciter (i.e. irrespective of carelessness); (B) actions based solely on the careless performance of a statutory duty in the absence of any other common law right of action; (C) actions based on a common law duty of care arising either from the imposition of the statutory duty or from the performance of it; and (D) misfeasance in public office, i.e. the failure to exercise, or the exercise of, statutory powers either with the intention to injure the plaintiff or in the knowledge that the conduct is unlawful.

Category (D) is not in issue in this case. I will consider each of the other categories but I must make it clear that I am not attempting any general statement of the applicable law: rather, I am seeking to set out a logical approach to the wide ranging arguments advanced in these appeals.

[Having considered the action for breach of statutory duty in a passage, which is set out p. 673, post, Lord BROWNE-WILKINSON continued:]

(B) *The careless performance of a statutory duty—no common law duty of care*
This category comprises those cases in which the plaintiff alleges (i) the statutory duty and (ii) the 'negligent' breach of that duty but does not allege that the defendant was under a common law duty of care to the plaintiff. It is the use of the word 'negligent' in this context which gives rise to confusion: it is sometimes used to connote mere carelessness (there being no common law duty of care) and sometimes to import the concept of a common law duty of care. In my judgment it is important in considering the authorities to distinguish between the two concepts: as will appear, in my view the careless performance of a statutory duty does not in itself give rise to any cause of action in the absence of either a statutory right of action (category (A) above) or a common law duty of care (category (C) below).

Much of the difficulty can be traced back to the confusion between the ability to rely on a statutory provision as a defence and the ability to rely on it as founding a cause of action. The source of the confusion is to be found in the dictum of Lord Blackburn in *Geddis v Proprietors of Bann Reservoir* (1878) 3 App Cas 430 at 455–456:

'For I take it, without citing cases, that is now thoroughly well established that no action will lie for doing that which the legislature has authorized, if it be done without negligence, although it does occasion damage to anyone; but an action does lie for doing that which the legislature has authorized, if it be done negligently. And I think that if by a reasonable exercise of the powers, either given by statute to the promoters, or which they have at common law, the damage could be prevented it is, within this rule, "negligence" not to make such reasonable exercise of their powers.'

This dictum, divorced from its context, suggests that the careless performance of a statutory duty in itself gives rise to a cause of action for damages. But it has to be read in context.

[His lordship discussed the *Geddis* case and several other authorities and continued:] If Lord Blackburn's dictum in *Geddis v Proprietors of Bann Reservoir* merely refers to the circumstances in which statutory authority can be used as a defence it raises no problems.

In my judgment *Geddis v Proprietors of Bann Reservoir* is best treated as a decision that the careless exercise by the defendant of a statutory duty or power provides no defence to a claim by the plaintiff based on a free-standing common law cause of action. It was so treated by Lord Wilberforce in *Allen v Gulf Oil Refining Ltd* [1981] 1 All ER 353 at 356, [1981] AC 1001 at 1011:...

[LORD BROWNE-WILKINSON then considered the decision of the House of Lords in *Home Office v Dorset Yacht Co Ltd* [1970] 2 All ER 294, [1970] AC 1004 (p.71, ante) and continued:]

Dorset Yacht is not a case which establishes that a cause of action for damages can be based on the mere 'negligent' exercise of statutory powers. It is a case founded on common law duties of care and the circumstances in which a defence of statutory authority can succeed.

In my judgment the correct view is that in order to found a cause of action flowing from the careless exercise of statutory powers or duties, the plaintiff has to show that the circumstances are such as to raise a duty of care at common law. The mere assertion of the careless exercise of a statutory power or duty is not sufficient.

(C) The common law duty of care

In this category, the claim alleges either that a statutory duty gives rise to a common law duty of care owed to the plaintiff by the defendant to do or refrain from doing a particular act, or (more often) that in the course of carrying out a statutory duty the defendant has brought about such a relationship between himself and the plaintiff as to give rise to a duty of care at common law. A further variant is a claim by the plaintiff that, whether or not the authority is itself under a duty of care to the plaintiff, its servant in the course of performing the statutory function was under a common law duty of care for breach of which the authority is vicariously liable.

Mr Munby QC, in his reply in the *Newham* case, invited your Lordships to lay down the general principles applicable in determining the circumstances in which the law would impose a common law duty of care arising from the exercise of statutory powers or duties. I have no doubt that, if possible, this would be most desirable. But I have found it quite impossible either to detect such principle in the wide range of authorities and academic writings to which we were referred or to devise any such principle de novo. The truth of the matter is that statutory duties now exist over such a wide range of diverse activities and take so many different forms that no one principle is capable of being formulated applicable to all cases. However, in my view it is possible in considering the problems raised by these particular appeals to identify certain points which are of significance.

(1) Co-existence of statutory duty and common law duty of care

It is clear that a common law duty of care may arise in the performance of statutory functions. But a broad distinction has to be drawn between: (a) cases in which it is alleged that the authority owes a duty of care in the manner in which it exercises a statutory discretion; and (b) cases in which a duty of care is alleged to arise from the manner in which the statutory duty has been implemented in practice.

An example of (a) in the educational field would be a decision whether or not to exercise a statutory discretion to close a school, being a decision which necessarily involves the exercise of a discretion. An example of (b) would be the actual running of a school pursuant to the statutory duties. In such latter case a common law duty to take reasonable care for the physical safety of the pupils will arise. The fact that the school is being run pursuant to a statutory duty is not necessarily incompatible with a common law duty of care arising from the proximate relationship between a school and the pupils it has agreed to accept. The distinction is between (a) taking care in exercising a statutory discretion whether or not to do an act and (b) having decided to do that act, taking care in the manner in which you do it.

(2) Discretion, justiciability and the policy/operational test
(a) Discretion

Most statutes which impose a statutory duty on local authorities confer on the authority a discretion as to the extent to which, and the methods by which, such statutory duty is to be performed. It is clear both in principle and from the decided cases that the local authority cannot be liable in damages for doing that which Parliament has authorised. Therefore if the decisions complained of fall within the ambit of such statutory discretion they cannot be actionable in common law. However, if the decision complained of is so unreasonable that it falls outside the ambit of the discretion conferred upon the local authority, there is no a priori reason for excluding all common law liability.

That this is the law is established by the decision in the *Dorset Yacht* case and by that part of the decision in *Anns v Merton London Borough* [1977] 2 All ER 492, [1978] AC 728 which, so far as I am aware, has largely escaped criticism in later decisions....

... [I]n seeking to establish that a local authority is liable at common law for negligence in the exercise of a discretion conferred by statute, the first requirement is to show that the decision was outside the ambit of the discretion altogether: if it was not, a local authority cannot itself be in breach of any duty of care owed to the plaintiff.

In deciding whether or not this requirement is satisfied, the court has to assess the relevant factors taken into account by the authority in exercising the discretion. Since what are under consideration are discretionary powers conferred on public bodies for public purposes the relevant factors will often include policy matters, for example social policy, the allocation of finite financial resources between the different calls made upon them or (as in the *Dorset Yacht* case) the balance between pursuing desirable social aims as against the risk to the public inherent in so doing. It is established that the courts cannot enter upon the assessment of such 'policy' matters. The difficulty is to identify in any particular case whether or not the decision in question is a 'policy' decision.

(b) Justiciability and the policy/operational dichotomy

In English law the first attempt to lay down the principles applicable in deciding whether or not a decision was one of policy was made by Lord Wilberforce in *Anns v Merton London Borough* [1977] 2 All ER 492 at 500, [1978] AC 728 at 754:

> 'Most, indeed probably all, statutes relating to public authorities or public bodies, contain in them a large area of policy. The courts call this "discretion", meaning that the decision is one for the authority or body to make, and not for the courts. Many statutes, also, prescribe or at least pre-suppose the practical execution of policy decisions: a convenient description of this is to say that in addition to the area of policy or discretion, there is an operational area. Although this distinction between the policy area and the operational area is convenient, and illuminating, it is probably a distinction of degree; many "operational" powers or duties have in them some element of "discretion". It can safely be said that the more "operational" a power or duty may be, the easier it is to superimpose on it a common law duty of care.'

As Lord Wilberforce appreciated, this approach did not provide a hard and fast test as to those matters which were open to the court's decision.

[His Lordship then referred to a passage (which will be found later in this section) in *Rowling v Takaro Properties Ltd* [1988] AC 473, [1988] 1 All ER 16 on this distinction and continued:]

From these authorities I understand the applicable principles to be as follows. Where Parliament has conferred a statutory discretion on a public authority, it is for that authority, not for the courts, to exercise the discretion: nothing which the authority does within the ambit of the discretion can be actionable at common law. If the decision complained of falls outside the statutory discretion, it *can* (but not necessarily will) give rise to common law liability. However, if the factors relevant to the exercise of the discretion include matters of policy, the court cannot adjudicate on such policy matters and therefore cannot reach the conclusion that the decision was outside the ambit of the statutory discretion. Therefore a common law duty of care in relation to the taking of decisions involving policy matters cannot exist.

(3) *If justiciable, the ordinary principles of negligence apply*

If the plaintiff's complaint alleges carelessness, not in the taking of a discretionary decision to do some act, but in the practical manner in which that act has been performed (e.g. the running of a school) the question whether or not there is a common law duty of care falls to be decided by applying the usual principles, i.e. those laid down in *Caparo Industries plc v Dickman* [1990] 1 All ER 568 at 573–574, [1990] 2 AC 605 at 617–618. Was the damage to the plaintiff reasonably foreseeable? Was the relationship between the plaintiff and the defendant sufficiently proximate? It is just and reasonable to impose a duty of care? See *Rowling v Takaro Properties Ltd* and *Hill v Chief Constable of West Yorkshire* [1988] 2 All ER 238, [1989] AC 53.

However, the question whether there is such a common law duty and if so its ambit, must be profoundly influenced by the statutory framework within which the acts complained of were done. The position is directly analogous to that in which a tortious duty of care owed by A to C can arise out of the performance by A of a contract between A and B. In *Henderson v Merrett Syndicates Ltd* [1994] 3 All ER 506, [1994] 3 WLR 761 your Lordships held that A (the managing agent) who had contracted with B (the members' agent) to render certain services for C (the names) came under a duty of care to C in the performance of those services. It is clear that any tortious duty of care owed to C in those circumstances could not be inconsistent with the duty owed in contact by A to B. Similarly, in my judgment, a common law duty of care cannot be imposed on a statutory duty if the observance of such common law duty of care would be inconsistent with, or have a tendency to discourage, the due performance by the local authority of its statutory duties.

(4) Direct liability and vicarious liability

In certain of the appeals before the House, the local authorities are alleged to be under a direct duty of care to the plaintiff not only in relation to the exercise of a statutory discretion but also in relation to the operational way in which they performed that duty.

This allegation of a direct duty of care owed by the authority to the plaintiff is to be contrasted with those claims which are based on the vicarious liability of the local authority for the negligence of its servants, i.e. for the breach of a duty of care owed by the servant to the plaintiff, the authority itself not being under any relevant duty of care to the plaintiff. Thus, in the *Newham* case the plaintiffs' claim is wholly based on allegations that two professionals, a social worker and a psychiatrist, individually owed professional duties of care to the plaintiff for the breach of which the authorities as their employers are vicariously liable. It is not alleged that the authorities were themselves under a duty of care to the plaintiff.

This distinction between direct and vicarious liability can be important since the authority may not be under a direct duty of care at all or the extent of the duty of care owed directly by the authority to the plaintiff may well differ from that owed by a professional to a patient. However, it is important not to lose sight of the fact that, even in the absence of a claim based on vicarious liability, an authority under a direct duty of care to the plaintiff will be liable for the negligent acts or omissions of its servant which constitute a breach of that direct duty. The authority can only act through its servants.

[LORD BROWNE-WILKINSON then proceeded to decide whether any of the claims should be struck out. Some reference to the later part of his speech will be found in note 4, p. 94, post.]

[LORD LANE and LORD ACKNER agreed with LORD BROWNE-WILKINSON. LORD JAUNCEY OF TULLICHETTLE delivered a speech in which he agreed with LORD BROWNE-WILKINSON. LORD NOLAN delivered a speech in which he agreed generally with LORD BROWNE-WILKINSON, but disagreed with him on one point which is not relevant to this extract.]

QUESTIONS

1. Should public authorities be in a special position with regard to negligence actions? Consider C. Harlow (1980) 43 MLR 241 (discussing the position before *X v Bedfordshire*, of course) and also see P. P. Craig, *Administrative Law* 6th edn (London, 2008), paras 29-004–29-020, S. H. Bailey and M. J. Bowman [1986] CLJ 430 and [2000] CLJ 85.

2. What do you understand by Lord Browne-Wilkinson's reference to a 'free standing common law cause of action'? (See D. Brodie (1998) 18 LS 1.)

NOTES

1. *X v Bedfordshire* is noted by P. Cane (1996) 112 LQR 13; D. Fleming [1996] CLJ 29; J. Lowry and D. Oughton (1996) 4 Tort L Rev 12. See further the articles by C. J. Hilson and W. V. H. Rogers (1995) 3 TLJ 221 and J. Wright (1998) 18 OJLS 1, and see P. Cane, *Administrative Law* 4th edn (Oxford, 2004), pp. 274–282. Two of the consolidated appeals were taken to the European Court of Human Rights: see *Z v United Kingdom* (2002) 34 EHRR 97, noted p. 48, ante, and *TP and KM v United Kingdom* (2002) 34 EHRR 42. In these two cases, no breach of Article 6 was found, but in the former case there was held to be a breach of Article 3 (prohibition on inhuman and degrading treatment), where adequate measures had not been taken to protect the claimant children, and in the latter case there was held to be a breach of Article 8 (family life) when a child was removed from home. In both cases there had been a breach of Article 13 (need for effective national remedy for breach of an ECHR right) and compensation was awarded.

   For general discussion of suing public authorities for negligence, see C. Booth and D. Squires, *The Negligence Liability of Public Authorities* (Oxford, 2006), and note the Law Commission's 2004 Consultation Paper, *Monetary Remedies in Public Law*, on which see R. Bagshaw (2006) 26 LS 4. (see farther the Appendix.)

2. It is clear that Lord Browne-Wilkinson considered that an extra hurdle is faced by those bringing a negligence claim against a public authority carrying out a statutory function, in addition to the usual requirement that a duty of care should exist under the *Caparo* principles. The reason is a concern that the common law courts should not usurp the sovereignty of Parliament by deciding that a public body is liable for acting in a manner authorised by Parliament. This explains Lord Browne-Wilkinson's insistence that a public body can only be liable in negligence if acting utterly unreasonably and therefore *ultra vires*. A related concern is the sense that certain matters, particularly involving political decisions about the allocation of resources, are inherently unsuitable for judicial determination—in short, they are matters for politicians, not judges. (This is what Lord Browne-Wilkinson meant by 'policy' matters, when that term is contrasted with 'operational' matters, and should not be confused with the references to policy relevant to deciding whether a duty of care would be fair, just, and reasonable.) Unfortunately, there has been disagreement amongst judges as to what this initial 'filter' should be and, as will be seen in the next two extracts, cases since *X v Bedfordshire* have departed to an extent from Lord Browne-Wilkinson's approach. Accordingly, a detailed discussion of this issue will be postponed until after the next two case extracts.

3. On the question of the statutory framework affecting consideration of a duty of care, to which Lord Browne-Wilkinson referred to in *X v Bedfordshire*, see further *Yuen Kun Yeu v A-G Hong Kong* [1988] AC 175, [1987] 2 All ER 705. Here it was decided that the Commissioner of Deposit-taking Companies in Hong Kong did not owe a duty to members of the public who might be minded to deposit their money in companies registered by the Commissioner to exercise reasonable care to see that they did not suffer loss through the companies being carried on by their managers in a fraudulent or improvident fashion. The Privy Council decided the case on a 'no proximity' basis. The decisive factors in this connection appear to have been that (a) the Commissioner had no power to control the day-to-day activities of those who allegedly caused the loss; and (b) the Commissioner had not voluntarily assumed any responsibility to investors, and

reliance by them on the fact of registration as a guarantee of the soundness of a particular company would be neither reasonable nor justifiable, nor should the Commissioner reasonably be expected to know of such reliance if it existed. As *Yuen Kun Yeu* shows, the fact that one of the purposes of the statutory power is the protection of the group to which the claimant belongs does not necessarily mean that there will be a duty of care. *Yun Kun Yeu* is one of several cases discussed in this section which involve statutory regulatory powers. In *Davis v Radcliffe* it was pointed out ([1990] 2 All ER at p. 541) that the emphasis on the broader public interest which is involved in the characteristic task of modern regulatory agencies 'militates strongly against the imposition of a duty of care being imposed on such an agency in favour of any particular section of the public'. Note also *Lam v Brennan and Torbay Borough Council* [1997] PNLR P488 (no duty of care on a planning authority in respect of the exercise or non-exercise of the grant or refusal of planning permission under s. 29 of the Town and Country Planning Act 1971 or in relation to the enforcement powers in respect of statutory nuisances). Cf. *Perrett v Collins* [1998] 2 Lloyd's Rep 255, noted p. 442, ante. On the question of the statutory framework, see also notes 6 and 7. p. 109, post and *Gorringe v Calderdale Metropolitan Borough Council* [2004] 2 All ER 326, [2004] UKHL 15 (p. 111, post).

4.   After the extract from *X v Bedfordshire*, which has been set out ante, Lord Browne-Wilkinson moved on to consider in detail the question whether there might be a duty of care in the various cases before the House of Lords. Some points from that consideration, at least from the argument that there was a direct duty of care on the authorities in relation to suspected child abuse, might be highlighted here. In *X v Bedfordshire*, where it was argued there was a duty of care to protect children in relation to whom the council had received a report of neglect or ill-treatment, which was alleged to have happened in the case, his Lordship did not think that it was just or reasonable that there should be a direct duty of care. Among the factors leading to that conclusion were that such a duty would cut across the system of statutory protection for children at risk which involved the participation of various bodies; the danger of inducing local authorities to adopt a defensive approach to their duties; that there were statutory procedures under which grievances could be investigated; and, bearing in mind the approach in *Caparo Industries plc v Dickman* [1990] 2 AC 605, [1990] 1 All ER 568 (p. 37, ante) of proceeding incrementally and by analogy to decided cases, that the nearest analogies were cases in which a duty of care had been denied (*Hill v Chief Constable of West Yorkshire* [1989] AC 53, [1988] 2 All ER 238 (p. 46, ante) and the *Yuen Kun Yeu* case). In Lord Browne-Wilkinson's opinion ([1995] 3 All ER at p. 382) the 'courts should proceed with great care before holding liable in negligence those who have been charged by Parliament with the task of protecting society from the wrongdoings of others'.

Since *X v Bedfordshire*, a number of the reasons suggested by Lord Browne-Wilkinson as to why a duty of care would not be fair, just, and reasonable have been treated with some scepticism by commentators (see, for example, S. H. Bailey and M. J. Bowman [2000] CLJ 85). The courts, too, have not endorsed everything said in *X v Bedfordshire*. For example, the question of liability inducing an overcautious approach was considered in *Barrett v Enfield London Borough Council* (p. 95, post). Lord Slynn, with whose speech Lords Nolan and Steyn agreed, approved the following view expressed by Evans LJ in the Court of Appeal in *Barrett* [1997] 3 All ER 171 at 181:

I would agree that what is said to be a "policy" consideration, namely that imposing a duty of care might lead to defensive conduct on the part of the person concerned and might require him to spend more time and resources on keeping full records or otherwise providing self-justification, if called upon to do so, should normally be a factor of little, if any, weight. If the conduct in question is of a kind which can be measured against the standards of the reasonable man, placed as the defendant was, then I do not see why the law in the public interest should not require those standards to be observed.

See too the speech of Lord Hutton [1993] 3 All ER 193 at 228; his Lordship would not give the 'defensive approach' factor great weight in the circumstances of the *Barrett* case, and agreed (perhaps more generally and, if so, more significantly) with the last sentence quoted from Evans LJ's judgment. In *Phelps v Hillingdon London Borough Council* [2001] 2 AC 619, [2000] 4 All ER 504 (p. 992, post) Lord Clyde was able to distinguish a number of the policy concerns from *X v Bedfordshire* as having no application on the facts of *Phelps* itself. Furthermore, on the particular point of a duty of care being owed to a child suspected of being the victim of abuse, it has become clear from *D v East Berkshire Community Health NHS Trust* [2005] 2 All ER 443, [2005] UKHL 23 (p. 52, ante) that such a duty of care can be owed, although not to the parent, a view confirmed after the entry into force of, and consequent potential influence of, the Human Rights Act 1998 in *Lawrence v Pembrokeshire County Council* [2007] 1 WLR 2991, [2007] EWCA Civ 446: see further note 2, p. 57, ante.

5. Lord Browne-Wilkinson expressly left open the possibility of claims by children claiming that their special educational needs had not been met, where such claims were brought on the basis of vicarious liability on the part of a public authority for the negligence of individual employees, refusing to strike out such actions. Recently, as will be seen in the extract set out at p. 99, post, the House of Lords in *Phelps v Hillingdon London Borough Council* [2001] 2 AC 619, [2000] 4 All ER 504 has found in favour of the claimants in 'vicarious liability' cases of this kind. For further discussion, see *B v Reading Borough Council* [2007] EWCA Civ 1313 at [28]–[37]. See also *Carty v London Borough of Croydon* [2005] 2 All ER 517, [2005] EWCA Civ 19.

■ Barrett v Enfield London Borough Council
House of Lords [1999] 3 All ER 193

The appellant (claimant) alleged that, while still an infant, he was mistreated by his mother and was, as a result, placed under the care of the respondent (defendant). The appellant alleged (inter alia) that the respondent owed (and had breached) a common law duty of care in the practical implementation of its obligations under various statutes concerning the protection and welfare of children. The common law duty was said to include a duty to act *in loco parentis* and to provide the appellant with the standard of care which could be expected of a reasonable parent. The appellant alleged that this duty had been breached by the respondent's failures (inter alia) to consider whether he could be placed with his half-sister on a long-term basis; have regard to his health and hygiene; find a proper home for him (he was accommodated with various foster parents and in children's homes but was not adopted); properly manage his meetings with his mother after 11 years of separation; and to provide him with appropriate psychiatric treatment. The appellant alleged that, if these breaches of duty had not occurred, then he would not 'on the balance of probabilities have left the care of the Local Authority as a young man of eighteen years with no family or attachments whatsoever, who had developed a psychiatric illness causing him to self-harm and who had been involved in criminal activities'. The Court of Appeal struck out the appellant's claim; he appealed to the House of Lords.

LORD SLYNN OF HADLEY: . . .

[Having quoted passages from Lord Reid's speech in *Home Office v Dorset Yacht Co Ltd* [1970] AC 1004 at 1031, referred to Lord Diplock's speech in the same case and quoted from Lord Wilberforce's speech in *Anns v Merton London Borough Council* [1978] AC 728 at 755, continued:]

On this basis, if an authority acts wholly within its discretion—i.e. it is doing what Parliament has said it can do, even if it has to choose between several alternatives open to it, then there can be no liability in negligence. It is only if a plaintiff can show that what has been done is outside the discretion and the power, then he can go on to show the authority was negligent. But if that stage is reached, the authority is not exercising a statutory power, but purporting to do so and the statute is no defence.

This, however, does not in my view mean that if an element of discretion is involved in an act being done subject to the exercise of the overriding statutory power, common law negligence is necessarily ruled out. Acts may be done pursuant and subsequent to the exercise of a discretion where a duty of care may exist—as has often been said even knocking a nail into a piece of wood involves the exercise of some choice or discretion and yet there may be a duty of care in the way it is done. Whether there is an element of discretion to do the act is thus not a complete test leading to the result that, if there is, a claim against an authority for what it actually does or fails to do must necessarily be ruled out.

Another distinction which is sometimes drawn between decisions as to 'policy' and as to 'operational acts' sounds more promising. A pure policy decision where Parliament has entrusted the decision to a public authority is not something which a court would normally be expected to review in a claim in negligence. But again this is not an absolute test. Policy and operational acts are closely linked and the decision to do an operational act may easily involve and flow from a policy decision. Conversely, the policy is affected by the result of the operational act (see *R v Chief Constable of Sussex, ex p International Trader's Ferry Ltd* [1999] 1 All ER 129, [1998] 3 WLR 1260).

Where a statutory power is given to a local authority and damage is caused by what it does pursuant to that power, the ultimate question is whether the particular issue is justiciable or whether the court should accept that it has no role to play. The two tests (discretion and policy/operational) to which I have referred are guides in deciding that question. The greater the element of policy involved, the wider the area of discretion accorded, the more likely it is that the matter is not justiciable so that no action in negligence can be brought. It is true that Lord Reid and Lord Diplock in *Home Office v Dorset Yacht Co Ltd* accepted that before a claim can be brought in negligence, the plaintiffs must show that the authority is behaving so unreasonably that it is not in truth exercising the real discretion given to it. But the passage I have cited was, as I read it, obiter, since Lord Reid made it clear that the case did not concern such a claim, but rather was a claim that Borstal officers had been negligent when they had disobeyed orders given to them. Moreover, I share Lord Browne-Wilkinson's reluctance to introduce the concepts of administrative law into the law of negligence, as Lord Diplock appears to have done. But in any case I do not read what either Lord Reid or Lord Wilberforce in *Anns'* case (and in particular Lord Reid) said as to the need to show that there has been an abuse of power before a claim can be brought in negligence in the exercise of a statutory discretion as meaning that an action can never be brought in negligence where an act has been done pursuant to the exercise of the discretion. A claim of negligence in the taking of a decision to exercise a statutory discretion is likely to be barred, unless it is wholly unreasonable so as not to be a real exercise of the discretion, or if it involves the making of a policy decision involving the balancing of different public interests; acts done pursuant to the lawful exercise of the discretion can, however, in my view be subject to a duty of care, even if some element of discretion is involved. Thus accepting that a decision to take a child into care pursuant to a statutory power is not justiciable, it does not in my view follow that, having taken a child into care, an authority cannot be liable for what it or its employees do in relation to the child without it being shown that they have acted in excess of power. It may amount to an excess of power, but that is not in my opinion the test to be adopted: the test is whether the conditions in *Caparo Industries plc v Dickman* [1990] 1 All ER 568, [1990] 2 AC 605 have been satisfied.

In *Rowling v Takaro Properties Ltd* [1988] 1 All ER 163 at 172, [1988] AC 473 at 501 Lord Keith of Kinkel, said in giving the opinion of the Privy Council in relation to the policy/operational test:

> 'They incline to the opinion, expressed in the literature, that this distinction does not provide a touchstone of liability, but rather is expressive of the need to exclude altogether those cases in which the decision under attack is of such a kind that a question whether it has been made negligently is unsuitable for judicial resolution, of which notable examples are discretionary decisions on the allocation of scarce resources or the distribution of risks (see especially the discussion in Craig *Administrative Law* (1983) pp 534–538). If this is right, classification of the relevant decision as a policy or planning decision in this sense may exclude liability; but a conclusion that it does not fall within that category does not, in their Lordships' opinion, mean that a duty of care will necessarily exist.'

Both in deciding whether particular issues are justiciable and whether if a duty of care is owed, it has been broken, the court must have regard to the statutory context and to the nature of the tasks involved. The mere fact that something has gone wrong or that a mistake has been made, or that someone has been inefficient does not mean that there was a duty to be careful or that such duty has been broken. Much of what has to be done in this area involves the balancing of delicate and difficult factors and courts should not be too ready to find in these situations that there has been negligence by staff who largely are skilled and dedicated.

Yet although in my view the staff are entitled to rely mutatis mutandis on the principle stated in *Bolam v Friern Hospital Management Committee* [1957] 2 All ER 118, [1957] 1 WLR 582,[1] the jurisdiction to consider whether there is a duty of care in respect of their acts and whether it has been broken is there. I do not see how the interests of the child can be sufficiently protected otherwise. . . .

In the present case, the allegations which I have summarised are largely directed to the way in which the powers of the local authority were *exercised*. It is arguable (and that is all we are concerned with in this case at this stage) that if some of the allegations are made out, a duty of care was owed and was broken. Others involve the exercise of a discretion which the court may consider to be not justiciable—e.g. whether it was right to arrange adoption at all, though the question of whether adoption was ever considered and if not, why not, may be a matter for investigation in a claim of negligence. I do not think it right in this case to go through each allegation in detail to assess the chances of it being justiciable. The claim is of an on-going failure of duty and must be seen as a whole. I do not think that it is the right approach to look only at each detailed allegation and to ask whether that in itself could have caused the injury. That must be done but it is appropriate also to consider whether the cumulative effect of the allegations, if true, could have caused the injury.

Nor do I accept that because the court should be slow to hold that a child can sue its parents for negligent decisions in its upbringing that the same should apply necessarily to all acts of a local authority. The latter has to take decisions which parents never or rarely have to take (e.g. as to adoption or as to an appropriate foster parent or institution). In any case, in respect of some matters, parents do have an actionable duty of care.

On the basis that *X and ors (minors) v Bedfordshire CC* does not conclude the present case in my view it is arguable that at least in respect of some matters alleged both individually and cumulatively a duty of care was owed and was broken.

[LORD SLYNN then proceeded to decide that the claim should not be struck out on the ground that causation could not be established, taking the view that it was a matter that required investigation at the trial.]

LORD HUTTON: . . .

I consider that subsequent decisions have shown that the underlying principle to be derived from the passages in the judgments of Lord Reid and Lord Diplock in *Home Office v Dorset Yacht Co Ltd* relating

---

[1] This concerns the question of breach of duty: see chap. 5.

to negligence in the exercise of a statutory discretion is that the courts will not permit a claim for negligence to be brought where a decision on the existence of negligence would involve the courts in considering matters of policy raising issues which they are ill-equipped and ill-suited to assess and on which Parliament could not have intended that the courts would substitute their views for the views of ministers or officials.

[His Lordship then quoted passages from Lord Wilberforce's speech in *Anns v Merton London Borough Council* [1978] AC 728 at 754, from the Privy Council's opinion in *Rowling v Takaro Properties Ltd* [1988] AC 473 at 501, from *Lonhro plc v Tebbit* [1991] 4 All ER 973 at 981 and from *Stovin v Wise* [1996] AC 923 at 928, and continued:]

…[T]hese judgments lead me to the provisional view that the fact that the decision which is challenged was made within the ambit of a statutory discretion and is capable of being described as a policy decision is not in itself a reason why it should be held that no claim for negligence can be brought in respect of it. As I read it this is what is said by the Privy Council in its judgment in *Rowling v Takaro Properties Ltd* [1988] 1 All ER 163 at 172, [1988] AC 473 at 501. It is only where the decision involves the weighing of competing public interests or is dictated by considerations which the courts are not fitted to assess that the courts will hold that the issue is non-justiciable on the ground that the decision was made in the exercise of a statutory discretion….

…I do not think that the speech of Lord Browne-Wilkinson in *X and ors (minors) v Bedfordshire CC* precludes a ruling in the present case that although the decisions of the defendant were within the ambit of its statutory discretion, nevertheless those decisions did not involve the balancing of the type of policy considerations which renders the decisions non-justiciable….

In *X and ors (minors) v Bedfordshire CC* [1995] 3 All ER 353 at 369, [1995] 2 AC 633 at 736 Lord Browne-Wilkinson said: 'For myself, I do not believe that it is either helpful or necessary to introduce public law concepts as to the validity of a decision into the question of liability at common law for negligence.'

I am in agreement with this view and I consider that where a plaintiff claims damages for personal injuries which he alleges have been caused by decisions negligently taken in the exercise of a statutory discretion, and provided that the decisions do not involve issues of policy which the courts are ill-equipped to adjudicate upon, it is preferable for the courts to decide the validity of the plaintiff's claim by applying directly the common law concept of negligence than by applying as a preliminary test the public law concept of *Wednesbury* unreasonableness (see *Associated Provincial Picture Houses Ltd v Wednesbury Corp* [1947] 2 All ER 680, [1948] 1 KB 223) to determine if the decision fell outside the ambit of the statutory discretion. I further consider that in each case the court's resolution of the question whether the decision or decisions taken by the defendant in exercise of the statutory discretion are unsuitable for judicial determination will require, as Lord Keith stated in *Rowling v Takaro Properties Ltd* [1988] 1 All ER 163 at 172, [1988] AC 473 at 501, a careful analysis and weighing of the relevant circumstances….

At this early stage in the present case it is not clear in my opinion that if the action proceeds to trial the judge will be required to weigh policy factors which the court is not equipped to decide. It is not known at this stage what factors the defendant and its officials and social workers did take into account in making decisions relating to the plaintiff and in planning his future. It may be that no matters of policy involving the balancing of competing public interests or the allocation of limited financial resources were involved in the decision and it may be that at a trial the judge, in the words of Mason J in *Sutherland Shire Council v Heyman* (1985) 157 CLR 424 at 469, would be called upon—

> 'to apply a standard of care to action or inaction that is merely the product of administrative direction, expert or professional opinion, technical standards or general standards of reasonableness.'

Therefore I would not strike out the action at this stage on the ground that it gives rise to issues which are non-justiciable. If it does appear at the trial that the case gives rise to an issue which relates to a matter of policy such as the balancing of competing public interests, then the judge can at that stage rule out the issue as being non-justiciable.

[LORD HUTTON then proceeded to consider the 'fair, just and reasonable' ground on which the Court of Appeal in this case had also held that the action should be struck out. His Lordship found that *X v Bedfordshire* [1995] 2 AC 633, [1995] 3 All ER 353 on which see note 4, p. 94, ante, was distinguishable, and took the view that the case should not be struck out on this ground, nor on the ground of causation. His Lordship continued:]

The standard of care
Although I would allow this appeal for the reasons which I have given and would permit the action to proceed to trial, I wish to emphasise that the considerations relied on by the defendant on the issue of justiciability will be of relevance and important when the trial judge comes to consider the question whether the plaintiff has established a breach of the duty to take reasonable care. The standard of care in negligence must be related to the nature of the duty to be performed and to the circumstances in which the defendant has to carry it out. Therefore the standard of care to be required of the defendant in this case in order to establish negligence at common law will have to be determined against the background that it is given discretions to exercise by statute in a sphere involving difficult decisions in relation to the welfare of children. Accordingly when the decisions taken by a local authority in respect of a child in its care are alleged to constitute negligence at common law, the trial judge, bearing in mind the room for differences of opinion as to the best course to adopt in a difficult field and that the discretion is to be exercised by the authority and its social workers and not by the court, must be satisfied that the conduct complained of went beyond mere errors of judgment in the exercise of a discretion and constituted conduct which can be regarded as negligent.

I would allow the appeal.

[LORD BROWNE-WILKINSON delivered a speech in favour of allowing the appeal. LORD NOLAN and LORD STEYN agreed with the speeches of LORD BROWNE-WILKINSON, LORD SLYNN OF HADLEY, and LORD HUTTON.]

Appeal allowed.

■ Phelps v Hillingdon London Borough Council
House of Lords [2000] 4 All ER 504

LORD SLYNN OF HADLEY: . . .
My Lords, the appeals in these four cases were heard together. They all raise questions as to the liability of a local education authority for what is said to have been a failure, either by the local authority or by employees for whom the local authority was vicariously liable, in the provision of appropriate educational services for children at school.

[His Lordship summarised the facts in the cases and the issues of law involved, concluding first that the relevant statutory duties did not give rise to a cause of action for damages for breach of statutory duty and concluded:] . . . it does not seem to me that it can be said that Parliament intended that there should be a remedy by way of damages for breach of statutory duty in respect of the matters complained of here.

The common law
It does not follow that the local authority can never be liable in common law negligence for damage resulting from acts done in the course of the performance of a statutory duty by the authority or by its servants or agents. This House decided in *Barrett v Enfield London BC* [1999] 3 All ER 193, [1999] 3 WLR 79 that the fact that acts which are claimed to be negligent are carried out within the ambit of a statutory discretion is not in itself a reason why it should be held that no claim for negligence can be brought in respect of them. It is only where what is done has involved the weighing of competing public interests or has been dictated by considerations on which Parliament could not have intended that the courts would substitute their views for the views of ministers or officials that the courts will hold that the issue is non-justiciable on the ground that the decision was made in the exercise of a statutory

discretion. In Pamela's case there is no such ground for holding that her claim is non-justiciable and therefore the question to be determined is whether the damage relied on is foreseeable and proximate and whether it is just and reasonable to recognise a duty of care (*Caparo Industries plc v Dickman* [1990] 1 All ER 568 at 573–574, [1990] 2 AC 605, at 617–618). If a duty of care would exist where advice was given other than pursuant to the exercise of statutory powers, such duty of care is not excluded because the advice is given pursuant to the exercise of statutory powers. This is particularly important where other remedies laid down by the statute (e.g. an appeals review procedure) do not in themselves provide sufficient redress for loss which has already been caused.

Where, as in Pamela's case, a person is employed by a local education authority to carry out professional services as part of the fulfilment of the authority's statutory duty, it has to be asked whether there is any overriding reason in principle why (a) that person should not owe a duty of care (the first question) and (b) why, if the duty of care is broken by that person, the authority as employer or principal should not be vicariously liable (the second question).

I accept that, as was said in *X (minors) v Bedfordshire CC*, there may be cases where to recognise such as vicarious liability on the part of the authority may so interfere with the performance of the local education authority's duties that it would be wrong to recognise any liability on the part of the authority. It must, however, be for the local authority to establish that: it is not to be presumed and I anticipate that the circumstances where it could be established would be exceptional.

As to the first question, it is long and well-established, now elementary, that persons exercising a particular skill or profession may owe a duty of care in the performance to people who it can be foreseen will be injured if due skill and care are not exercised, and if injury or damage can be shown to have been caused by the lack of care. Such duty does not depend on the existence of any contractual relationship between the person causing and the person suffering the damage. A doctor, an accountant and an engineer are plainly such a person. So in my view is an educational psychologist or psychiatrist a teacher including a teacher in a specialised area, such as a teacher concerned with children having special educational needs. So maybe an education officer performing the functions of a local education authority in regard to children with special educational needs. There is no more justification for a blanket immunity in their cases than there was in *Capital & Counties plc v Hampshire CC*...[1997] 2 All ER 865, [1997] QB 1004.

I fully agree with what was said by Lord Browne-Wilkinson in *X (minors) v Bedfordshire CC* [1995] 3 All ER 353 at 395, [1995] 2 AC 633 at 766 that a head teacher owes 'a duty of care to exercise the reasonable skills of a headmaster in relation to such [sc. a child's] educational needs; and a special advisory teacher brought in to advise on the educational needs of a specific pupil, particularly if he knows that his advice will be communicated to the pupil's parents, 'owes a duty to the child to exercise the skill and care of a reasonable advisory teacher'. A similar duty on specific facts may arise for others engaged in the educational process, e.g. an educational psychologist being part of the local authority's team to provide the necessary services. The fact that the educational psychologist owes a duty to the authority to exercise skill and care in the performance of his contract of employment does not mean that no duty of care can be or is owed to the child. Nor does the fact that the educational psychologist is called in in pursuance of the performance of the local authority's statutory duties mean that no duty of care is owed by him, if in exercising his profession he would otherwise have a duty of care.

That, however, is only the beginning of the enquiry. It must still be shown that the educational psychologist is acting in relation to a particular child in a situation where the law recognises a duty of care. A casual remark, an isolated act may occur in a situation where there is no sufficient nexus between the two persons for a duty of care to exist. But where an educational psychologist is specifically called in to advise in relation to the assessment and future provision for a specific child, and it is clear that the parents acting for the child and the teachers will follow that advice, *prima facie* a duty of care arises. It is sometimes said that there has to be an assumption of responsibility by the person concerned. That phrase can be misleading in that it can suggest that the professional person must knowingly and deliberately accept responsibility. It is, however, clear that the test is an objective one (*Henderson v Merrett Syndicates Ltd* [1994] 3 All ER 506 at 521, [1995] 2 AC 145, 181). The phrase means simply that the law recognises that there is a duty of care. It is not so much that responsibility is assumed as that it is recognised or imposed by the law. The question is thus whether in the particular circumstances the necessary nexus has been shown.

The result of a failure by an educational psychologist to take care may be that the child suffers emotional or psychological harm, perhaps even physical harm. There can be no doubt that if foreseeability and causation are established, psychological injury may constitute damage for the purpose of the common law. But so in my view can a failure to diagnose a congenital condition and to take appropriate action as a result of which failure a child's level of achievement is reduced, which leads to loss of employment and wages. Questions as to causation and as to the quantum of damage, particularly if actions are brought long after the event, may be very difficult, but there is no reason in principle to rule out such claims.

As to the second question, if a breach of the duty of care to the child by such an employee is established, *prima facie* a local or education authority is vicariously liable for the negligence of its employee. If the educational psychologist does have a duty of care on the facts is it to be held that it is not just and reasonable that the local education authority should be vicariously liable if there is a breach of that duty? Are there reasons of public policy why the courts should not recognise such a liability? I am very conscious of the need to be cautious in recognising such a duty of care where so much is discretionary in these as in other areas of social policy. As has been said, it is obviously important that those engaged in the provision of educational services under the statutes should not be hampered by the imposition of such a vicarious liability. I do not, however, see that to recognise the existence of the duties necessarily leads or is likely to lead to that result. The recognition of the duty of care does not of itself impose unreasonably high standards. The courts have long recognised that there is no negligence if a doctor 'exercises the ordinary skill of an ordinary competent man exercising that particular art'.

> 'A doctor is not guilty of negligence if he has acted in accordance with a practice accepted as proper by a responsible body of medical men skilled in that particular art. . . . Putting it the other way round, a doctor is not negligent, if he is acting in accordance with such a practice, merely because there is a body of opinion that takes a contrary view.' (See *Bolam v Friern Hospital Management Committee* [1957] 2 All ER 118 at 122, [1957] 1 WLR 582 at 587 *per* McNair, J.).

The difficulties of the tasks involved and of the circumstances under which people have to work in this area must also be borne fully in mind. The professionalism, dedication and standards of those engaged in the provision of educational services are such that cases of liability for negligence will be exceptional. But though claims should not be encouraged once the Courts should not find negligence too readily, the fact that some claims may be without foundation or exaggerated does not mean that valid claims should necessarily be excluded.

The House has been referred to a number of decisions of the United States Courts in some of which it has been held that a local education authority did not owe an actionable duty of care. But the legislative and administrative provisions and the approach of the courts in those cases are different and there is not complete unanimity. I do not consider that these cases assist in the determination of the present problem.

The duty in this case on the basis, therefore, that an educational psychologist may owe a duty of care in performing duties on behalf of the local education authority, was the Judge justified in finding that there was a duty here and that there was a breach?

[His Lordship examined the facts, concluding that the educational psychologist owed a duty to Pamela, that she was in breach of it, and agreeing with the trial judge that the educational psychologist's breach of duty caused damage to Pamela capable of forming a claim in negligence.]

Pamela thus succeeds on the basis of vicarious liability of the local authority. I do not consider that the case of direct liability on the part of Hillingdon is made out, nor indeed was necessary. Your Lordships have, however, been asked to consider whether such a claim can exist and such a question is relevant in the case of Jarvis.

Direct liability

In *X (minors) v Bedfordshire CC* [1995] 3 All ER 353 at 392, [1995] 2 AC 633 at 762, LORD BROWNE-WILKINSON said:

> 'For these reasons I reach the conclusion that an educational authority owes no common law duty
> of care in the exercise of the powers and discretions relating to children with special educational
> needs specifically conferred on them by the Act of 1981'.

It seems to me that if he had not thought that the service of psychological advice was offered to the public (which in fact in the present case it was not), but was 'merely part and parcel of the system established by the defendant authority for the discharge of its statutory duties under the Act of 1981' (page 763C), he would have accepted that there was no duty of care in respect of an educational psychologist in the present case.

I do not rule out the possibility of a direct claim in all situations where a local authority is exercising its powers. If it exercises its discretion by deciding to set up a particular scheme pursuant to a policy which it has lawfully adopted, there is no, or at least there is unlikely to be any, common law duty of care. If, however, it then, for example, appoints to carry out the duties in regard to children with special educational needs a psychologist or other professionals who at the outset transparently are neither qualified nor competent to carry out the duties, the position is different. That may be an unlikely scenario, but if it happens, I do not see why as a matter of principle a claim at common law in negligence should never be possible. Over-use of the distinction between policy and operational matters so as respectively to limit or create liability has been criticised, but there is some validity in the distinction. Just as the individual social worker in *Barrett v Enfield London Borough Council* (supra) could be 'negligent in an operational manner' (Lord Woolf, MR [1998] QB 367 at page 378, my speech [1999] 3 WLR 79, 97E), so it seems to me that the local education authority could in some circumstances owe a duty of care and be negligent in the performance of it. The fact that the parents have their own duties under Section 36 of the Act of 1944 and that consultation and appeal procedures exist (of which the parents may or may not be informed) does not seem to me to lead to the conclusion that a duty of care does not or should not exist.

Since the authority can only act through its employees or agents, and if they are negligent vicarious liability will arise, it may rarely be necessary to invoke a claim for direct liability. After the argument in these cases, I do not, however, accept the absolute statement that an education authority 'owes no common law duty of care... in the exercise of the powers... relating to children with special educational needs' under the Act of 1981. That issue, however, as I have said does not fall for decision in Pamela's case.

I would accordingly allow the appeal and restore the order of Garland, J.

[His Lordship then proceeded to apply the same principles to the other cases in the appeal.]

LORD CLYDE: . . .

In principle it is not immediately easy to see why the law should not admit the possibility of a duty of care upon professional employees of an education authority. Indeed the decision in *E (A Minor) v Dorset CC.*, reported with *X and ors (minors) v Bedfordshire CC*. . . [1995] 3 All ER 353, [1995] 2 AC 633, directly supports the existence of such a duty of care upon an educational psychologist. As Lord Browne-Wilkinson observed 'Psychologists hold themselves out as having special skills and they are, in my judgment, like any other professional bound both to possess such skills and to exercise them carefully' (see [1995] 3 All ER 353 at 393, [1995] 2 AC 633 at 763). In principle the same view should apply to any professional member of the staff of an education authority. Where a child privately consults an educational psychologist there should be a duty on the latter to exercise due professional care in the giving of advice. While a basis for a claim might be found in contract in such a case, by way even of an implied term of an obligation to take reasonable care, it would be curious if it could not be found also in tort. If in the private arena an educational psychologist culpably erred in the diagnosis which he or she made of the cause of a child's disability and the child suffered some consequential loss or injury, there would seem to be no reason why a liability in damages should not follow. It would be surprising if the same was not also to be possible where the advice is given by one employed by an education authority. One consideration which influenced the Court of Appeal ([1999] 1 All ER 421, [1999] 1 WLR 500 in their holding in *Phelps* that there was no duty of care was the fear that by admitting a vicarious claim the immunity which local education authorities may enjoy against direct claims could readily be circumvented. But it has to be noticed that one consideration which weighed with Lord Browne-Wilkinson in excluding a direct claim in *E (a minor) v Dorset CC* was that a vicarious liability would be available. As he observed:

> '...in almost every case which could give rise to a claim for the negligent exercise of the statutory discretions, it is probable that...there will be an alternative remedy by way of a claim against the authority on the grounds of their vicarious liability for the negligent advice on the basis of which they exercise their discretion...' (See [1995] 3 All ER 353 at 392, [1995] 2 AC 633 at 762.)

But it is contended that such persons are under no such duty. Two issues then arise, one general and one particular. The question whether the defendant in any claim for damages on the ground of negligence owes a duty of care to the claimant can be answered in the negative on the basis that on grounds of fairness the law will not recognise a duty of care between such parties. There was no duty because there cannot be a duty. It is only if the law admits the possibility of such a duty that the next question can arise: whether in the circumstances of the particular case a duty did exist between the particular parties. Whether a duty can exist and whether a duty does exist are different kinds of questions and it seems to me that the law gives different kinds of answers to them. The former may be resolved by considerations of policy, and in particular whether it is fair, just and reasonable to admit such a duty. The latter requires a consideration of the facts of the case and may be susceptible to different answers in different circumstances. Of course common kinds of relationship, like that of employer and employee acting within the course of an employment, may so often satisfy the test of proximity that categories of cases can be identified where a duty will arise with little if any further investigation or analysis. But the requirements of proximity and foreseeability form the basis on which the existence of the duty may rest in any particular circumstances.

[LORD CLYDE proceeded to discuss the approach to the duty of care in general and then dealt with the question of policy:]...It does not seem to me that there is any wider interest of the law which would require that no remedy in damages be available. I am not persuaded that the recognition of a liability upon employees of the education authority for damages for negligence in education would lead to a flood of claims, or even vexatious claims, which would overwhelm the school authorities, nor that it would add burdens and distractions to the already intensive life of teachers. Nor should it inspire some peculiarly defensive attitude in the performance of their professional responsibilities. On the contrary it may have the healthy effect of securing that high standards are sought and secured. If it is thought that there would only be a few claims and for that reason the duty should not be recognised, the answer must be that if there are only a few claims there is the less reason to refuse to allow them to be entertained. As regards the need for this remedy, even if there are alternative procedures by which some form of redress might be obtained, such as resort to judicial review, or to an ombudsman, or the adoption of such statutory procedures as are open to parents, which might achieve some correction of the situation for the future, it may only be through a claim for damages at common law that compensation for the damage done to the child may be secured for the past as well as the future.

Any fear of a flood of claims may be countered by the consideration that in order to get off the ground the claimant must be able to demonstrate that the standard of care fell short of that set by the *Bolam v Friern Hospital Management Committee* [1957] 2 All ER 118, [1957] 1 WLR 582 test. That is deliberately and properly a high standard in recognition of the difficult nature of some decisions which those to whom the test applies require to make and of the room for genuine differences of view on the propriety of one course of action as against another. In the field of educational matters there may well exist distinct but respectable opinions upon matters of method and practice, and it may be difficult to substantiate a case of fault against the background of a variety of professional practices. In cases of a failure to diagnose a particular disability from which a child may be suffering there may well be considerable difficulties in the making of the diagnosis which may render proof of negligence hazardous.

Not only may there be difficulties in establishing negligence in relation to the making of professional judgments in particular circumstances or the exercise of a professional choice in particular cases, but there may well be practical difficulties in the adequacy of records or of recollection about the details regarding the educational progress and achievements of a particular child which may be highly relevant to the claim which is brought. But that there may be such difficulty is no reason for excluding deserving cases. There may also be severe difficulty in establishing a causal connection between the alleged negligence and the alleged loss and in the assessment of any damages. But these possible difficulties should not be allowed to stand in the way of the presentation of a proper claim, nor should justice be altogether denied on the ground that a claim is of a complex nature. That any claims which are made may require a large number of witnesses, a consideration which weighed with the Court of Appeal, and involve considerable time and cost, are again practical considerations which should not be allowed to justify a total exclusion of an otherwise legitimate claim. While I recognise that the general view in the jurisprudence of the United States of America is adverse to the admission of a liability upon teachers for negligence upon general grounds of policy, I am not persuaded that a corresponding view should be taken in this country.

The present claims all arise in the public sector where there is a very obvious statutory context. The education authorities are creatures of statute and operate to a considerable extent under the provisions of the Education Acts. The question arises whether the common law duty can or cannot stand in the face of the statutory context. But while no common law can stand in contradiction of some statutory provision, . . . the existence of a statutory background against which the professionals are exercising their particular skills should not inhibit the existence of a common law duty of care. The provisions of the Education Act 1981 sought to secure that appropriate education would be available for children with special educational needs. The procedures contained in the Act include various rights for the parents, for example the provisions for consultation in section 3, for notification under section 5(3), in relation to assessments under sections 6(1) and 9, and for discussion and for appeal in relation to the making of statements under sections 7 and 8. Such provisions plainly reflect the interest which the parents are recognised to have in the child's education. What is envisaged is not some adversarial relationship between the authority and the parents, but rather a partnership between them aimed at securing the interests of the child's education. Indeed in paragraph 6 of the Circular 1/83 by the Department of Education and Science the process of assessment was seen as a 'partnership between teachers, other professionals, and parents, in a joint endeavour to discover and understand the nature of the difficulties and needs of individual children'. However at least in the case of *Phelps* the procedures and systems contained in the statutory provisions were not directly in issue. In *Phelps* what was alleged to have gone wrong was a failure to diagnose the existence of a dyslexia. The psychologist was not carrying out any particular function under the statute. There is no statutory provision in the case which is inconsistent with the existence of a duty of care on the part of an educational psychiatrist.

A distinction may be suggested between on the one hand matters of policy or discretion and on the other hand matters of an operational or administrative character. But this kind of classification does not appear to provide any absolute test for determining whether the case is one which allows or excludes a duty of care. The classification may provide some guide towards identifying some kinds of case where a duty of care may be thought to be inappropriate. Where a statutory authority has to make a choice between various courses of action, all of which are within its powers, and the choice involves a weighing of resources and the establishment of priorities, it will in general be inappropriate that someone injured through the particular decision which the authority has made should have a remedy in damages. But it was recognised by Lord Browne-Wilkinson in *X (minors) v Bedfordshire CC* [1955] 3 All ER 353, [1995] 2 AC 633 at 738 that even in matters of a discretionary character the authority may be liable in damages if its decision falls without the ambit of the discretion, as where the action taken is so totally unreasonable as to amount to an abuse of the discretion. Beyond that, as Lord Keith of Kinkel observed in *Rowling v Takaro Properties Ltd* [1988] 1 All ER 163 at 172, [1988] AC 473 at 501:

> '...classification of the relevant decision as a policy or planning decision in this sense may exclude liability; but a conclusion that it does not fall within that category does not, in their Lordships' opinion, mean that a duty of care will necessarily exist'.

Another circumstance which may give rise to difficulty in the present context is that there may be a multi-disciplinary unit concerned in the giving of the advice. But that is a practical problem which cannot constitute a legal bar on a claim. Even where such a situation exists it should be possible to disentangle the relevant parts played by particular individuals and identify where the alleged negligence occurred. The problem may not of course be significant for a plaintiff if a claim can lie directly against the authority, as in *Barrett v Enfield London BC* [1997] 3 All ER 371, [1998] QB 367. Certainly the view of the commission in *Z v UK*, [2000] 2 FCR 245 at 272 in para. 114 of their report took the view that the multi-disciplinary aspect of child protection work 'may provide a factual complexity to cases but cannot by itself provide a justification for excluding liability from a body found to have acted negligently'. At least in the present cases there is no difficulty in identifying the advice given by each of the professional persons involved, and in particular in identifying that it was particularly within the area of expertise of the educational psychologist to make the diagnosis.

I turn now from matters of policy to matters of proximity and foreseeability. One question which arises here is whether the advice was being given to the education authority for their guidance, and not to the child nor the parents. Circumstances may of course occur where it can be shown that although the parents had some involvement with the decision making process the advice given was not intended to be acted upon by them nor was reliance expected to be placed by them on it. The distinction noted by Lord Browne-Wilkinson in *X (minors) v Bedfordshire CC* [1955] 3 All ER 353 at 393, [1995] 2 AC 633 at 763–764 is drawn between education cases and child abuse cases. In the former case it may more readily be concluded that the involvement of the parents is both consistent with and supports the conclusion that a duty of care existed through them to the child. In the latter, despite the general intention that all the interested parties should work together, the opportunity for conflict between the parents and the professional advisers may be far greater than in the educational context. But that is not the situation in the present case where all shared the same intention to secure the proper education for the child concerned. Where a professional person is employed by one person to advise him, it is a question of circumstances whether there will also be a duty owed to other persons. Examples may be found in the cases of a doctor examining a patient for insurance purposes or a surveyor acting for a prospective mortgagee.

The view was taken by Stuart-Smith LJ ([[1999] 1 All ER 421 at 437, [1999] 1 WLR 500 at 517) in the Court of Appeal in *Phelps* that the defendants' psychology service was not a service to the public:

> 'It was set up and used by the defendants to advise them and their other employees on the discharge of their statutory functions in teaching the plaintiff. It is quite different from, for example, a health authority setting up a clinic where people can come to see doctors and nurses for treatment. In such a case there would be a direct relationship of doctor and patient, and an assumption of responsibility to treat him or her.'

But it seems to me that while that analysis may be strictly correct, it is not inconsistent with the conclusion that the psychologist was in the circumstances in *Phelps* also advising the plaintiff through her parents. I consider that the judge was right to observe that 'it does not accord with reality or common sense to regard her as owing a duty only to the defendants'. On the evidence he was certainly entitled to reach the conclusion that the psychologist also owed a duty to the plaintiff through her parents. In the particular circumstances of the case of *Phelps* it appears perfectly clear that the plaintiff and her parents were going to and did rely upon the advice. Miss Melling, who is blamed by the plaintiff, discussed the contents of her report with Mr and Mrs Phelps. While the educational psychiatrist was advising the teachers, the parents were also recipients of the substance of the advice. The judge found that the Special Needs Co-ordinators and the head teacher all expected information to be passed to the parents and the fundamental elements of that advice would derive from Miss Melling. Indeed the respondent's own consultation document 'Learning Together' of November–December 1990 stresses the support which the educational psychologist may give to a parent and the involvement educational psychologists will have with the family as well as the teachers. Nor can it be seriously doubted that the plaintiff was in a sufficient proximity to the defendant. The statutory context to which I have already referred shows very clearly that the parent is to be involved in the identification of the appropriate forms of education for the child and even if the statutory provisions are not immediately relevant that is at the least consistent with the child through her parents being in a close relationship with the education authority.

So far as the case of *Phelps* is concerned I have reached the view that there was a duty on the educational psychologist to exercise due care to the appellant. Two areas of the case have caused me some hesitation, namely, whether the plaintiff had in fact established professional negligence on the part of the psychologist and whether the causal link had been proved between the alleged negligence and the loss which was claimed. I have however been persuaded that both of these hurdles have been surmounted on the facts and that the judge was entitled to reach the conclusion which he did.

The appellant claims a direct liability on the authority as well as a vicarious liability. But there is no necessity to explore that aspect of the matter in the case of *Phelps* which can succeed upon the basis of a vicarious liability. With regard to the other cases where the issue is still open, careful consideration would require to be given to the view expressed by Lord Browne-Wilkinson in *X (minors) v Bedfordshire CC* [1955] 3 All ER 353 at 391–392, [1995] 2 AC 633 at 761–762, along with the further qualification which he added in *Barrett v Enfield London BC* [1999] 3 All ER 193 at 197, [1999] 3 WLR 79 at 83. But it may be open to argument that a prohibition upon a direct liability should not be a matter of absolute exclusion. Where the parents of a child have participated in the decision under attack it may well be difficult to allow a claim that the decision was negligently taken. But the case might be different if the parents did not take a hand in the making of the decision. It may be that few cases would arise of direct claims, but it might not seem that justice is being served if on that account the door of the court should be closed. The point may be open to further argument but it would be inappropriate to embark upon that chapter without any inquiry into the facts. I am certainly not prepared to deny the possibility that such a duty may exist. A comparable point was raised in *Cassidy v Ministry of Health* [1951] 1 All ER 574, [1951] 2 KB 343 and some academic support for the proposition can be found in Montgomery 'Suing Hospitals Direct' (1987) 137 New LJ 573, referred to in *Clerk and Lindsell on Torts* (17th edn, 1995) p 455 (para. 8–63). Given the room for argument on the point in the present context it seems to me that this is pre-eminently a point to be resolved after trial when the facts have been explored....

[LORD NICHOLLS OF BIRKENHEAD delivered a speech in which he 'broadly' agreed with the speeches of LORD SLYNN OF HADLEY and LORD CLYDE. LORD JAUNCEY OF TULLICHETTLE and LORD LLOYD OF BERWICK agreed with all three of these speeches. LORD MILLETT delivered a speech in which he expressed a 'large measure of agreement' with the speeches of LORD SLYNN OF HADLEY and LORD CLYDE.]

QUESTIONS

1.   What type of injury is involved in a case of failure to diagnose dyslexia? Is it personal injury? (See *Adams v Bracknell Forest Borough Council* [2004] 3 All ER 897, [2004] UKHL 89; cf. *Skipper v Calderdale Metropolitan Borough Council* [2007] EWCA Civ 238.)

2.   Where do these last two cases leave the comment in *Davis v Radcliffe* [1990] 2 All ER 536, [1990] 1 WLR 821 set out in note 8, p. 94, ante?

NOTES

1. As has already been mentioned (note 2, p. 93, ante), the ordinary principles used to establish a duty of care are not the only considerations when a public authority is alleged to have acted negligently in the exercise of statutory powers and duties. Claimants face the additional hurdle of establishing that the authority's action is an appropriate matter for challenge in a private law claim at all, although, as the previous extracts show, there has been disagreement amongst the courts as to the precise nature of that hurdle. For Lord Browne-Wilkinson in *X v Bedfordshire*, the initial hurdle was essentially a public law test of ultra vires: 'if the decisions complained of fall within the ambit of such statutory discretion they cannot be actionable in common law. However, if the decision complained of is so unreasonable that it falls outside the ambit of the discretion conferred upon the local authority, there is no a priori reason for excluding all common law liability.' This is despite Lord Browne-Wilkinson's own view in *X v Bedfordshire* that he did not 'believe that it is either helpful or necessary to introduce public law concepts as to the validity of a decision into the question of liability at common law for negligence', since there is no question that he tied the issue of actionability in negligence to the issue of whether a discretion was exercised ultra vires.

2. Lord Hutton in *Barrett* (with whose speech Lord Nolan and Lord Steyn agreed) rejected the use of public law concepts as a pre-condition of liability in negligence. For him, the fact that a decision was within the ambit of a discretion did not necessarily exclude the possibility of liability in negligence. What counted instead was whether a non-justiciable issue was involved (see note 4, post). In part, this is a reaction against some of the difficulties of importing public law concepts into the negligence cases. For example, although detailed consideration of the concept of abuse of discretion is a matter for courses on Administrative Law, it is worth noting briefly that total unreasonableness is not the only ground on which a discretion can be abused. For example, if a body reaches a decision having taken into account an 'irrelevant consideration', it will also have acted ultra vires; and see Cane (1996) 112 LQR at pp. 16–17. In short, one difficulty is that the test of being outside the ambit of a discretion as a precondition for actionability does not satisfactorily explain why only one of the different ways in which a decision can be outside discretion allows the possibility of liability in negligence. Lord Slynn in *Barrett* (with whose speech Lord Nolan and Lord Steyn also agreed) was a little more cautious than Lord Hutton in his departure from *X v Bedfordshire*, but he did draw attention to a further difficulty with Lord Browne-Wilkinson's approach, namely its suggestion that all exercises of discretion will not be actionable in negligence unless utterly unreasonable. Lord Slynn did not accept that 'if an element of discretion is involved in an act being done subject to the exercise of the overriding statutory power, common law negligence is necessarily ruled out. Acts may be done pursuant to and subsequent to the exercise of a discretion where a duty of care may exist—as has often been said even knocking a nail into a piece of wood involves the exercise of some choice or discretion and yet there may be a duty of care in the way it is done.'

3. One tool that has been used in dealing with the problem raised by discretionary powers is the policy/operational distinction, to which references are found in the preceding extracts. This distinction was first found in the United States (on which see P. P. Craig, (1978) 94 LQR 428 at 442–447), but was adopted in English law in *Anns v Merton London Borough Council* [1978] AC 728, [1977] 2 All ER 492. The gist of this distinction is that decisions of political policy are matters for the public authority itself,

not the courts, so that, for example, a claimant could not sue in negligence if he or she suffered greater injury because of a political decision to save money by closing the nearest casualty department. However, once a decision has been taken, the 'operational' manner in which it is implemented 'on the ground' may very well be the subject of negligence actions. For an example of a case where it was held a duty of care could be owed in the administrative implementation of immigration decisions, see *R (A) v Secretary of State for the Home Department* [2004] EWHC 1585 (Admin). There are certainly difficulties with retaining a rigid demarcation between policy and operational matters, which led to academic criticism of the efficacy of the distinction: see S. H. Bailey and M. J. Bowman, [1986] CLJ 430 at 437–439. Since *Anns*, the courts have also rejected a clearcut distinction between policy and operational matters. However, Lord Browne-Wilkinson in *X v Bedfordshire* made use of a similar version of policy, in that he would not allow a claimant to argue for total unreasonableness in a case involving matters of policy.

4.   It is clear from *Barrett, Phelps,* and subsequent cases that the policy/operational distinction, though problematic, has at its root the key to this area, namely the need to exclude from the ambit of negligence liability any challenge to political decisions of policy, principally involving decisions as to the allocation of limited resources, which the courts are ill-suited to consider. For example, the Privy Council in *Rowling v Takaro Properties Ltd* [1988] AC 473, [1988] 1 All ER 163 accepted that the policy/operational distinction essentially concerned the need to exclude non-justiciable political issues. It may be that the policy/operational label has a tendency to obscure this fundamental question, in which case the more explicit approach in *Barrett* and *Phelps* to isolating non-justiciable seems more helpful. On this approach, the fact that a discretion was involved, and indeed the fact that the discretion was exercised intra vires, will not necessarily rule out a duty of care per se, unless non justiciable issues were involved. However, that is not to say that it is irrelevant that, for example, a discretion was exercised reasonably and thus intra vires—such issues will remain extremely relevant, albeit when considering whether the authority *breached* its duty of care: see, for example, the last paragraph from Lord Hutton's speech in *Barrett*. It should be noted that some commentators, notably S. H. Bailey and M. J. Bowman [2000] CLJ 85, reject the need for any additional test, of non-justiciability or otherwise, in cases involving public authorities, arguing that the ordinary principles of negligence liability (the need to establish a duty of care, fault, and causation) provide sufficient protection for such defendants.

5.   The role of 'discretion' and of 'unreasonableness' in the case law after *Barrett* and *Phelps* has revealed some difference of emphasis. In *A v Essex County Council* [2004] 1 WLR 1881, [2003] EWCA Civ 1848 Hale LJ (giving the Court of Appeal's judgment) thought (at [33]) that potentially there were still three matters to be considered, although acknowledging a degree of overlap between them: these factors were justiciability (coupled in this first category with the statutory framework issue—see note 3, p. 93, ante); second, whether 'it involves the exercise of a statutory discretion which only gives rise to liability in tort if it is so unreasonable that it falls outside the ambit of the discretion'; and third the *Caparo* 'fair, just and reasonable' test. In *Carty v Croydon London Borough Council* [2005] 2 All ER 517, [2005] EWCA Civ 19 Dyson LJ pointed to the ambiguity of meaning associated with the word 'discretion' and thought it better to focus on the substance of the decision, rather than whether it contained any discretionary element. Although acknowledging that a 'totally unreasonable' decision may

be needed for there to be a breach of duty in the case of a decision that was close to the non-justiciable end of the spectrum, his Lordship thought there was 'much to be said' for an approach that only involved two stages, namely justiciability and the three-fold *Caparo* test. On the other hand, in *Jain v Trent Strategic Health Authority* [2008] QB 246, [2007] EWCA Civ 1186 Arden LJ (with whose judgment Wilson LJ agreed) regarded Hale LJ's approach in *A* as a 'helpful statement' and stated (at [62]:

> The first at least of these lines of enquiry has assumed less importance as the law has evolved in recent years. As the judgment of the Court of Appeal in [*D v East Berkshire Community Health NHS Trust* [2003] 4 All ER 796, [2003] EWCA Civ 1151] demonstrates, following the [Human Rights Act 1998], courts now have to consider questions of social policy with which they were not previously concerned. From this, in my judgment, it is possible to conclude that courts will hold that fewer matters are now non-justiciable on the grounds that they involve policy issues. The second line of enquiry also as it seems to me reflects a concern about justiciability. Moreover, we have also seen from *Barrett* that the courts are now reluctant to introduce administrative law concepts into the law of negligence, and that would seem to be the result if in any case the court were to conclude that there should be liability only if the act was actually outside the statutory discretion. In the circumstances, I conclude that the first two lines of enquiry in the statement by Hale LJ in *Essex* are not likely in future to be as important or to have the same weight as the third line of enquiry.

6. Public bodies can be liable in suitable circumstances for negligent advice or under the broader principle of assumption of responsibility put forward in *Henderson v Merrett Syndicates* [1995] 2 AC 145, [1994] 3 All ER 506 (p. 232, post). When that case is studied, it will be seen that Lord Goff thought that if a case fitted within that broader principle, it should be unnecessary for the court to devote any further time to the question whether it is 'fair, just and reasonable' for there to be a duty of care, a view that has met with approval in later case law. However, in *Welton v North Cornwall District Council* [1997] 1 WLR 570 it was accepted that where a case involved statutory powers or duties, then these would have to be considered to see if they were inconsistent with the existence of the duty of care argued for. (In relation to *Welton* note further the comments in *Harris v Evans* [1998] 3 All ER 522, [1998] 1 WLR 1285, and see the note by R. Mullender (1999) 62 MLR 425.) See further Lord Browne-Wilkinson (p. 92, ante) in the *Bedfordshire* case: it would seem from a later part of his speech that he ties this factor (i.e. the statutory framework) in with the 'fair, just and reasonable' label. On the other hand, in *Rowley v Secretary of State for Department of Work and Pensions* [2007] 1 WLR 2861, [2007] EWCA Civ 598 the Court of Appeal stated (at [61]):

> It may be said that this is better considered as a free-standing question, rather than as an aspect of the third limb of the *Caparo* test. In *A v Essex County Council* [2003] EWCA Civ 1848, [2004] 1 WLR 1881 at para 33, Hale LJ considered the question whether to impose a common law duty of care would be inconsistent with the statutory framework as an aspect of justiciability, rather than as an aspect of the third limb of the *Caparo* test But she acknowledged that "the considerations relevant to each of these issues overlap and it is not always possible to draw hard and fast lines between them". Perhaps the classifiication does not matter. The important point is that the duty of care must not be inconsistent with the presumed intention of Parliament.

7. On the statutory framework and the duty of care, see note 3, p. 93, ante. This framework may provide an appeal or other alternative remedies, which might militate against the existence of a duty of care. Consider the view of Lord Browne-Wilkinson in *X v Bedfordshire*, set out in note 4, p. 94, ante, and that of Lord Clyde in *Phelps* (p. 103, ante), though cf. *Newall v Ministry of Defence* [2002] EWHC 1006 (QB) at [60].

(It should, however, be noted that this debate can occur in the case of private bodies as well.) In *Jones v Department of Employment* [1989] QB 1, [1988] 1 All ER 725, which was concerned with public bodies, Glidewell LJ stated (at p. 736), with the approval of the other members of the Court of Appeal, that 'it is a general principle that if a government department or officer, charged with the making of decisions whether certain payments should be made, is subject to a statutory right of appeal against his decisions, he owes no duty of care in private law'. However, in *Rowley* the Court of Appeal was of the view that this general principle should be treated with 'some caution': this was because of comments in the later case law to the effect that a duty of care on a public body might not be negated by the existence of an alternative remedy. (See, for example, Lord Clyde's view in *Phelps*, p. 103, ante.) *Rowley* concerned the Child Support Act 1991, and one argument alleged that the defendant owed a duty of care in exercising his functions under the 1991 Act in relation to the assessment, collection, and enforcement of the obligation to pay child support maintenance. The Act provided an appeal against the refusal to make an assessment or against the amount of any such assessment, as well as the possibility for the recovery of interest on arrears in certain circumstances; further-more, there was the existence of judicial review if the Child Support Agency did not collect or enforce arrears of maintenance. In this context, the argument for a duty of care was unsuccessful, with the Court of Appeal taking the view that the imposition of a duty of care would be inconsistent with the statutory scheme, even though acknow-ledging that in some cases losses would not be recovered in the absence of a duty of care. More generally, Dyson LJ (with the agreement of Keene and Waller LJ) was of the opinion (at [73]):

I accept, of course, that the mere fact that there is an alternative remedy is not necessarily a reason for denying the existence of a common law duty of care. It is important to see how comprehensive a remedy is provided and to consider it in the context of the statutory scheme as a whole. Ultimately, what has to be decided is whether, having regard to the purpose of the legislation, Parliament is to be taken as having intended that there should be a right to damages for negligence. The more comprehensive the remedy provided by Parliament, the less likely it is that Parliament is to be taken as having had that intention.

In this context does it matter if the question is whether Parliament intended there to be a negligence action or if it is whether Parliament had excluded such an action? (Cf. note 2, p. 114, post in the discussion of *Gorringe v Calderdale Metropolitan Borough Council* [2004] 2 All ER 326, [2004] UKHL 15.)

8.   The duty of care of care concept can be a particularly difficult hurdle to surmount in the case of omissions: see the extract from Lord Hoffmann's speech in *Stovin v Wise* [1996] AC 923, [1996] 3 All ER 80 (p. 66, ante). As that case concerned the position of a public body, its precise facts now merit more attention. Stovin was seriously injured when his motor cycle collided with a car negligently driven by Wise. The accident happened at a particular junction which the county council, the highway authority, knew to be dangerous because the view was restricted by a bank on adjoining land. The council offered to pay for removing the bank if the land owner agreed, but did not exercise its statutory power under s. 79 of the Highways Act 1980 to require the landowner to remove it. Stovin's claim against Wise was settled, but Wise claimed a contribution from the county council, claiming, inter alia, that it had been negligent in failing to take reasonable steps to reduce the danger at the junction. The House of Lords (by a majority) dismissed the case against the council. The essence of the major-ity's reasoning will be seen in the next extract. While hostile to the idea of a duty of care

being imposed in the case of a failure to exercise statutory powers, Lord Hoffmann did contemplate there being a duty of care if it had been irrational not to exercise the power and if the policy of the statute required the award of compensation. *Stovin v Wise* was decided before *Barrett* and *Phelps*, and Lord Hutton in *Barrett* regarded *Stovin* as only applicable to cases of omissions to exercise statutory powers. The issue of the liability of public authorities for omissions returned to the House of Lords in the case from which the next extract is taken.

■ Gorringe v Calderdale Metropolitan Borough Council
House of Lords [2004] 2 All ER 326

LORD HOFFMANN:

[7] My Lords, on 15 July 1996, on a country road in Yorkshire, Mrs Denise Gorringe drove her car head-on into a bus. It was hidden behind a sharp crest in the road until just before she reached the top. When she first caught sight of it, a curve on the far side may have given her the impression that it was actually on her side of the road. At any rate, she slammed on the brakes and at 50 miles an hour the wheels locked and the car skidded into the path of the bus. Mrs Gorringe suffered brain injuries severely affecting various bodily functions including speech and movement.

[8] On the face of it, the accident was her own fault. It was certainly not the fault of the bus driver. He was driving with proper care when Mrs Gorringe skidded into him. But she claims in these proceedings that it was the fault of the local authority, the Calderdale Metropolitan Borough Council (the council). She says that the council caused the accident by failing to give her proper warning of the danger involved in driving fast when you could not see what was coming. In particular, the council should have painted the word 'SLOW' on the road surface at some point before the crest. There had been such a marking in the past, but it disappeared, probably when the road was mended seven or eight years before.

. . .

[18] . . . [Counsel for Mrs Gorringe] Mr Wingate-Saul submits that a common law duty has been created by (or 'in parallel' with) s 39(2) and (3) of the Road Traffic Act 1988:

'(2) Each local authority must prepare and carry out a programme of measures designed to promote road safety . . .

(3) Without prejudice to the generality of subsection (2) above, in pursuance of their duty under that subsection each local authority—(a) must carry out studies into accidents arising out of the use of vehicles on roads . . . within their area, (b) must, in the light of those studies, take such measures as appear to the authority to be appropriate to prevent such accidents, including the dissemination of information and advice relating to the use of roads, the giving of practical training to road users or any class or description of road users, the construction, improvement, maintenance or repair of roads for which they are the highway authority . . . and other measures taken in the exercise of their powers for controlling, protecting or assisting the movement of traffic on roads . . .'

[19] These provisions, with their repeated use of the word 'must', impose statutory duties. But they are typical public law duties expressed in the widest and most general terms: compare s 1(1) of the National Health Service Act 1977: 'It is the Secretary of State's duty to continue the promotion . . . of a comprehensive health service . . .' No one suggests that such duties are enforceable by a private individual in an action for breach of statutory duty. They are enforceable, so far as they are justiciable at all, only in proceedings for judicial review.

[20] Nevertheless, Mr Wingate-Saul submits that s 39 casts a common law shadow and creates a duty to users of the highway to take reasonable steps to carry out the necessary studies and take the appropriate measures. At any rate, their conduct in compliance with these duties must not be such as can be described as 'wholly unreasonable'. The judge found that it was unreasonable for the council

not to have painted a warning sign on the road and Potter LJ thought that he was entitled to come to this conclusion.

[21] The effect of statutory powers and duties on the common law liability of a highway author-ity was considered by this House in *Stovin v Wise (Norfolk CC, third party)* [1996] 3 All ER 801, [1996] AC 923....

[22] ...I pointed out in my speech [in *Stovin*] that the council had done nothing which, apart from statute, would have attracted a common law duty of care. It had done nothing at all. The only basis on which it was a candidate for liability was that Parliament had entrusted it with general responsibility for the highways and given it the power to improve them and take other measures for the safety of their users.

[23] Since the existence of these statutory powers is the only basis upon which a common law duty was claimed to exist, it seemed to me relevant to ask whether, in conferring such powers, Parliament could be taken to have intended to create such a duty. If a statute actually imposes a duty, it is well set-tled that the question of whether it was intended to give rise to a private right of action depends upon the construction of the statute (see *Hague v Deputy Governor of Parkhurst Prison, Weldon v Home Office* [1991] 3 All ER 733 at 741, 748–752, [1992] 1 AC 58 at 159, 168–171). If the statute does not create a private right of action, it would be, to say the least, unusual if the mere existence of the statu-tory duty could generate a common law duty of care.

[24] For example, in *O'Rourke v Camden London BC* [1997] 3 All ER 23, [1998] AC 188 a homeless person sued for damages on the ground that the council had failed in its statutory duty to provide him with accommodation. The action was struck out on the ground that the statute did not create a private law right of action....

[25] In the absence of a right to sue for breach of the statutory duty itself, it would in my opinion have been absurd to hold that the council was nevertheless under a common law duty to take reason-able care to provide accommodation for homeless persons whom it could reasonably foresee would otherwise be reduced to sleeping rough. (Compare *Stovin v Wise* [1996] 3 All ER 801 at 827–828, [1996] AC 923 at 952–953.) And the argument would in my opinion have been even weaker if the council, instead of being under a duty to provide accommodation, merely had a power to do so.

[26] This was the reasoning by which the majority in *Stovin v Wise* came to the conclusion that the council owed no duty to road users which could in any circumstances have required it to improve the intersection. But misunderstanding seems to have arisen because the majority judgment goes on to discuss, in the alternative, what the nature of such a duty might have been if there had been one. It suggests that it would have given rise to liability only if it would have been irrational in a public law sense not to exercise the statutory power to do the work. And it deals with this alternative argument by concluding that, on the facts, there had been no breach even of such a duty. The suggestion that there might exceptionally be a case in which a breach of a public law duty could found a private law right of action has proved controversial and it may have been ill-advised to speculate upon such matters.

...

[32] [Having referred to *Larner v Sollihull Metropolitan Borough Council* [2001] LGR 255 in which *Stovin v Wise* had been cited and in which Lord Woolf MR had said, in respect of s 39(2) of the Road Traffic Act 1988, that exceptionally a common law duty of care might arise, LORD HOFFMANN continued:] Speaking for myself, I find it difficult to imagine a case in which a common law duty can be founded simply upon the failure (however irrational) to provide some benefit which a public authority has power (or a public law duty) to provide. For example, the majority reasoning in *Stovin v Wise* was applied in *Capital and Counties plc v Hampshire CC* [1997] 2 All ER 865, [1997] QB 1004 to fire authorities, which have a general public law duty to make provision for efficient fire-fighting services (see s 1 of the Fire Services Act 1947). The Court of Appeal held, in my view correctly, that this did not create a common law duty. Stuart-Smith LJ (giving the judgment of the Court of Appeal) said:

'In our judgment the fire brigade are not under a common law duty to answer the call for help, and are not under a duty to take care to do so. If therefore they fail to turn up or fail to turn up in time because they have carelessly misunderstood the message, got lost on the way or run into a tree, they are not liable.' (See [1997] 2 All ER 865 at 878, [1997] QB 1004 at 1030.)

[33] The Court of Appeal in *Larner's* case went on to hold that on the facts there had been no breach of duty. But the consequences of the door which it left open can be seen in the present case. The council was obliged to give discovery of documents relating to its accident studies undertaken pursuant to s 39(3)(a), the decision-making process by which it decided what measures in the light of such studies were appropriate and the steps which had been taken to implement such measures. It was heavily criticised by the judge for the lateness and insufficiency of such discovery. The trial lasted six days, during which the council called a number of its officers as witnesses and was criticised for not calling enough. The simple facts which I have summarised at the beginning of this speech seem to have disappeared from view in the enthusiasm for a hostile judicial inquiry into the council's administration. If s 39 continues to provoke investigations of this nature, much of the road safety budget will be consumed in the cost of litigation. . . .

[38] My Lords, I must make it clear that this appeal is concerned only with an attempt to impose upon a local authority a common law duty to act based solely on the existence of a broad public law duty. We are not concerned with cases in which public authorities have actually done acts or entered into relationships or undertaken responsibilities which give rise to a common law duty of care. In such cases the fact that the public authority acted pursuant to a statutory power or public duty does not necessarily negative the existence of a duty. A hospital trust provides medical treatment pursuant to the public law duty in the National Health Service Act 1977, but the existence of its common law duty is based simply upon its acceptance of a professional relationship with the patient no different from that which would be accepted by a doctor in private practice. The duty rests upon a solid, orthodox common law foundation and the question is not whether it is created by the statute but whether the terms of the statute (for example, in requiring a particular thing to be done or conferring a discretion) are sufficient to exclude it. The law in this respect has been well established since *Geddis v Proprietors of Bann Reservoir* (1878) 3 App Cas 430. . . .

[40] [Thus] in *Phelps v Hillingdon London BC* [2000] 4 All ER 504, [2001] 2 AC 619 . . . the House held that the duty of care did not depend upon the statute. It arose because the psychologist had impliedly undertaken to exercise proper professional skill in diagnosis, in the same way as a doctor provided by the National Heath Service. The fact that the doctor-patient relationship was brought into being pursuant to public law duties was irrelevant except so far as the statute provided a defence. The House decided that no such defence had been established. . . .

[44] My Lords, in this case the council is not alleged to have done anything to give rise to a duty of care. The complaint is that it did nothing. Section 39 is the sole ground upon which it is alleged to have had a common law duty to act. In my opinion the statute could not have created such a duty. The action must therefore fail. For these reasons and those of my noble and learned friends Lord Scott of Foscote, Lord Rodger of Earlsferry and Lord Brown of Eaton-under-Heywood, I would dismiss the appeal.

LORD SCOTT OF FOSCOTE: [71] . . .

In my opinion, if a statutory duty does not give rise to a private right to sue cannot create a duty of care that would not have been owed at common law if the statute were not there. If the policy of the statute is not consistent with the creation of a statutory liability to pay compensation for damage caused by a breach of the statutory duty, the same policy would, in my opinion, exclude the use of the statutory duty in order to create a common law duty of care that would be broken by a failure to perform the statutory duty. I would respectfully accept Lord Browne-Wilkinson's comment in *X v Bedfordshire CC* [1995] 3 All ER 353 at 371, [1995] 2 AC 633 at 739 that—

> 'the question whether there is such a common law duty and if so its ambit, must be profoundly influenced by the statutory framework within which the acts complained of were done.'

But that comment cannot be applied to a case where the defendant has done nothing at all to create the duty of care and all that is relied on to create it is the existence of the statutory duty. In short, I do not accept that a common law duty of care can grow parasitically out of a statutory duty not intended to be owed to individuals. . . .

[73] There are, of course, many situations in which a public authority with public duties has a relationship with a member of the public that justifies imposing on the public authority a private law duty of care towards that person. And the steps required to be taken to discharge that private law duty of care may be steps comprehended within the public duties. *Barrett v Enfield LBC* [1999] 3 All ER 193, [2001] 2 AC 550 and *Phelps v Hillingdon London BC* [2000] 4 All ER 504, [2001] 2 AC 619 are examples. But the council in the present case had no relationship with Mrs Gorringe that it did not have with every other motorist driving on the stretch of road in question. . . .

[LORD STEYN delivered a speech in favour of dismissing the appeal. LORD RODGER OF EARLSFERRY and LORD BROWN OF EATON-UNDER-HEYWOOD delivered speeches in favour of dismissing the appeal, in which they agreed with each other's speeches, as well as those of LORD HOFFMANN and LORD SCOTT.]

Appeal dismissed.

QUESTION

Should public authorities be under the same liability for omissions as a private person or can an argument be made that they should be under a greater liability or, conversely, a lesser liability?

NOTES

1. *Gorringe* is noted by D. Howarth [2004] CLJ 546 and J. Morgan (2005) 121 LQR 43. The *O'Rourke* case to which Lord Hoffmann refers in the extract can be found at p. 675, post.

2. Although Lord Steyn did agree that the appeal should be dismissed in *Gorringe*, he does seem more open to the possibility of actions in this area than his brethren. In addition to referring to the effect (which he clearly regarded as a liberalising one) of the reasoning to be found in *Barrett* and *Phelps* on Lord Hoffmann's suggested exceptional duty situations in *Stovin v Wise*, one important point made by Lord Steyn was that the courts must be careful to keep clear a 'principled distinction' between actions for breach of statutory duty and those in the context of a statutory power or duty but grounded in the tort of negligence: whereas in the former the question is whether the legislature has created a cause of action, in the case of the latter it is whether the legislature has excluded the action in negligence. On the action for breach of statutory duty, see chap. 12, post. Do you think Lord Hoffmann paid sufficient attention to this distinction in *Gorringe*? Lord Scott (at [71]) seems to be even more hostile to a negligence action than Lord Hoffmann, and see *Davies v Secretary of State for Justice* [2008] EWHC 397 (Admin).

3. The basis of Lord Hoffmann's reasoning in *Stovin v Wise* and *Gorringe* can be found at [23]–[25] of the extract from *Gorringe*. In relation to [23] bear in mind that when the separate tort of breach of statutory duty is considered (chap. 12), it will be seen that the search for parliamentary intention is an artificial and complex process: this is not perhaps an ideal basis on which to reach conclusions about the position of common law negligence. Furthermore, a statutory duty may be strict and the fact that the legislature is not thought to have created a private cause of action for a breach simpliciter does not necessarily mean that it would have been opposed to an action in the tort

of negligence for a careless breach. Lord Hoffmann then (see [25] in the extract ante) seeks to strengthen his argument by referring to the fact that a mere power rather than a duty has been created; but it might be asked whether in general Parliament's choice of mandatory or permissive language was really influenced by the question of common law compensation. (See Craig *Administrative Law*, para 29–018, who regards it as 'overly formalistic to draw a radical division' between instances of powers and duties, stressing that many duties contain some discretion, and conversely that it is generally assumed by Parliament that statutory powers will be exercised.) Indeed, Lord Hoffmann in *Stovin v Wise* did acknowledge that the choice of language might be because the subject matter precluded a duty from being sufficiently precisely stated.

4.   There is a sense in which cases like *Barrett* and *Phelps* can be regarded as omission cases insofar as they involved allegations of failure to confer benefits. In distinguishing *Barrett*, Lord Hoffmann (at [40] in the extract ante) refers to the idea of undertaking responsibilities. His Lordship also had a similar explanation for the decision in *Phelps*. Lord Brown agreed with Lord Hoffmann's approach to these cases, although had an additional ground for distinguishing them from the case in hand. Note also the comments of Lord Scott (at [73] in the extract ante). Following on from *Stovin v Wise* and *Gorringe*, the Court of Appeal has suggested the following synthesis of the latter decision in *Sandhar v Department of Transport, Environment and the Regions* [2004] EWCA Civ 1440, [2005] 1 WLR 1362, a case concerning an allegation of failure to salt a road by a highway authority. It was stated at [37]:

Although statutory duties or powers which do not give rise to a private law right of action may constitute part of the relevant factual background, the existence of those duties or powers cannot reinforce parasitically the existence of a common law duty of care in the public authority. In short, unless a statute on its proper construction provides a private law right of action or conversely unless the statute excludes it, the existence of a common law duty of care depends on unvarnished common law principles.

The source for these 'unvarnished comon law principles' in cases of indirectly caused physical harm and cases of economic loss was thought to be *Caparo Industries Plc v Dickman* [1990] 2 AC 605, [1990] 1 All ER 568 (p. 37, ante) and *Henderson v Merrett Syndicates Ltd* [1995] 2 AC 145, [1994] 3 All ER 506 (p. 232, post), with reliance playing an important role. The court also indicated, relying on *Barrett* and *Phelps,* that the necessary assumption of responsibility for a duty of care to exist 'normally requires a particular relationship with an individual or individuals'. See further *Neil Martin Ltd v Commissioners of Her Majesty's Revenue and Customs* [2007] EWCA Civ 1041, where it was held that the defendant, in performing a statutory duty to issue a particular certificate, did not owe a duty of care to deal with the application with reasonable speed, but that on the facts one particular act of one of its employees had gone so far as to involve an assumption of responsibility to the applicant for the certificate.

Another case worthy of consideration in this context is *Rice v Secretary of State for Trade and Industry* [2007] PIQR P23, [2007] EWCA Civ 289. Here the defendant was the successor to the liabilities of the National Dock Labour Board (NDLB). Although there were close similarities with a contract of employment, the NDLB did not always have an employer/employee relationship with the registered dock workers whom it allocated to particular work for others in the dock. The case concerned workers' exposure to asbestos dust during some of the work allocated to them. The NDLB had owed a statutory duty to make satisfactory provision for the workers' health, a duty which covered the jobs in question. Pointing out that the statutory duty was not a target duty which was owed for the benefit of all the public, May LJ (with whom Keane and Smith LJJ agreed) regarded this as a case where 'the policy of the statute can only be seen as enabling a relationship such that the law should impose a common law duty of care'. Importantly in the light of *Gorringe*, his Lordship thought a private employer in the position of the NDLB would also have owed a duty of care. Cf. *Newton-Sealey v Armor Group Services Ltd* [2008] EWHC 233 (QB).

5.   It will have been seen that at one point in his speech in *Gorringe* Lord Hoffmann referred to the position of the fire authorities, as established by the Court of Appeal in *Capital and Counties plc v Hampshire County Council* [1997] QB 1004, [1997] 2 All ER 865, in which three cases were consolidated. In the *Hampshire* case itself a fire officer had negligently turned off an automatic sprinkler system; in *John Munroe (Acrylics) Ltd v London Fire Brigade and Civil Defence Authority* [1997] 2 All ER 865 it was alleged that there had been negligence in failing to ensure that there was no risk of fire on leaving an area to which the brigade had been called after an explosion had caused burning debris to be scattered over a wide area; and in *Church of Jesus Christ of Latter Day Saints (GB) v West Yorkshire Fire and Civil Defence Authority* [1997] QB 1004 it was alleged that there had been a failure on the part of the fire authority to take reasonable steps to see that there was an adequate supply of water at a fire. Any duty of care in the second and third cases was rejected on the ground of lack of proximity. The court did accept, however, that where a rescue service created the danger which caused the damage in suit, a duty of care could be owed, and for this purpose was prepared to equate a substantial increase in an existing risk with the creation of a new risk: there was, therefore a duty of care in the *Hampshire* case (and on a causation point in this case, see note 4, p. 347, post).

Consider also cases on the police referred to at pp. 46–52, ante. The position of the police was discussed in *Capital and Counties*, which followed *Alexandrou v Oxford* [1993] 4 All ER 328, where the Court of Appeal had denied, on the ground of lack of proximity, that the police owed a duty of care consequent upon the receipt of an emergency call, and see the later decision in *Costello v Chief Constable of the Northumbria Police* [1999] 1 All ER 550 (no duty of care owed, other than in exceptional circumstances, by one police officer to rescue another). It has also been decided that a similar approach to that adopted in *Capital and Counties* should apply in the case of the coastguard: *OLL Ltd v Secretary of State for Transport* [1997] 3 All ER 897, which refers to two pre-*Capital & Counties* suits against the coastguard. For discussion of the liability of emergency services, see R. Bagshaw [1999] LMCLQ 71, and for an investigation into the effects of *Capital and Counties* on fire authorities, see J. Hartshorne, N. Smith and R. Everton (2000) 63 MLR 502. For discussion of insurance in the *Capital and Counties* case, see further notes 1 and 2, post.

After Bagshaw's article was written, the position of the ambulance service reached the Court of Appeal in *Kent v Griffiths (No 3)* [2001] QB 36, [2000] 2 All ER 474 involving a claim for damages for the ambulance service's inexplicable delay in sending an ambulance to transport the claimant to hospital: the London Ambulance Service's appeal against the award of damages against them by Turner J was dismissed. Lord Woolf (with whom the other members of the Court of Appeal agreed) found that proximity existed, reiterating the reasoning from the earlier Court of Appeal decision in the same case refusing to strike out the claim (*Kent v London Ambulance Services* [1999] Lloyd's Rep Med 58) that the ambulance service fell into a different category from other rescue services: the primary duty of the other rescue services was to protect the public at large, whereas that of the ambulance service was more closely akin to the service provided by NHS hospitals. His Lordship further held that the claim did not involve a non-justiciable challenge to a policy decision such as the allocation of resources. Significantly, Lord Woolf MR placed no emphasis on the 'reliance' reasoning adopted in the earlier unsuccessful strike-out application, thereby avoiding the unedifying prospect of a duty of care being owed to those with access to alternative transport, but not, for example, to an elderly person living alone. Does the argument that, unlike the ambulance service, the other rescue services owe conflicting duties to the public at large apply with equal force to all the other rescue services? What about the coastguard service? In *Kent* Lord Woolf, distinguishing *Stovin v Wise*, regarded the case in hand as 'one in which it would have been irrational not to have accepted the request to provide an ambulance', so that there was in effect 'a public law duty to act'. For criticism of this reasoning from a public law perspective, see T. Hickman [2000] CLJ 432. In any event, can this reasoning withstand the later decision in *Gorringe*? Nevertheless, the *Sandhar* case would suggest that the result in *Kent v Griffiths* is correct since the Court of Appeal in that case regarded its rationalisation of the law as consistent with *Kent, Capital & Counties* and the *OLL* case (as well as *Watson v British Boxing Board of Control Ltd* [2001] QB 1134, [2000] EWCA Civ 2116, noted p. 44, ante). On the effects of *Kent v Griffiths*, see K. Williams, [2007] Med L Rev 153, who concludes (at 174) that '*Kent* has not generated an unmanageably large or costly tranche of novel rescue claims that are difficult to defend'.

2 PSYCHIATRIC HARM

Claimants who suffer psychiatric harm have always been treated somewhat warily by the courts, particularly where such harm is not consequent on some physical injury (such as a blow to the head). Even the common legal label for this sort of harm—'nervous shock'—is not an entirely neutral (or accurate) one. Particular concerns in the past have been the danger of fraudulent claims, the prospect of widespread, indeterminate liability, and the suspicion that nervous reactions were somehow the fault of the character of the victim. The courts may find themselves concerned with difficult questions of medical causation, and the legal and medical professions have not always seen eye to eye on the problems involved in cases of this kind (see J. Harvard (1956) 19 MLR 478). Lord Bridge in *McLoughlin v O'Brian* [1983] 1 AC 410 at 433 refers to the suspicious attitude on the part of earlier generations of judges towards psychiatry, although, as he goes on to acknowledge, attitudes are changing. Lord Lloyd makes a similar observation in *Page v Smith* [1995] 2 All ER 736 at 758 (p. 132, post), referring to the importance of the law not being seen to 'limp too far behind' advances in medical science.

The cases in the twentieth century revealed in general an expansion of the area of liability for psychiatric harm; indeed, at one time after the decision in *McLoughlin v O'Brian* [1983] 1 AC 410, [1982] 2 All ER 298 the question arose as to whether the law might have reached the position that reasonable foreseeability was both a necessary and a sufficient condition for liability. This was clearly shown not to be the case by *Alcock v Chief Constable of South Yorkshire Police* [1992] 1 AC 310, [1991] 4 All ER 907 (p. 120 post). Furthermore, although the Law Commission (*Liability for Psychiatric Illness*, Law Com No. 249, 1998) proposed some liberalisation of the current law, it did not go as far as suggesting that the normal principles of negligence liability should apply to all cases of psychiatric harm.

As will be seen, the most problematic area for the law concerns cases where the claimant suffers psychiatric harm as a result of what happens, or what they fear has happened, to a third party. It is important to note that mere shock, grief, or mental distress are not compensated in the tort of negligence: a recognised psychiatric illness is required. It should also be noted that, by virtue of the Fatal Accidents Act, damages for bereavement can be obtained by a limited category of people (see p. 280, post).

The following short extract introduces some of the perceived difficulties with claims for psychiatric harm and the policies at work in this area (for the facts and further extracts from this case, see p. 120, post):

■ White v Chief Constable of South Yorkshire
House of Lords [1999] 1 All ER 1

LORD STEYN: . . .
Policy Considerations and Psychiatric Harm
Policy considerations have undoubtedly played a role in shaping the law governing recovery for pure psychiatric harm. The common law imposes different rules for the recovery of compensation for physical injury and psychiatric harm. Thus it is settled law that bystanders at tragic events, even if they suffer foreseeable psychiatric harm, are not entitled to recover damages: *Alcock v Chief Constable of the South Yorkshire Police* [1991] 4 All ER 907, [1992] 1 AC 310. The courts have regarded the policy reasons against admitting such claims as compelling.

It seems to me useful to ask why such different rules have been created for the recovery of the two kinds of damage. In his *Casebook on Tort* (7th edn, 1992) p. 88 Weir gives the following account:

> '. . . there is equally no doubt that the public. . . draws a distinction between the neurotic and the cripple, between the man who loses his concentration and the man who loses his leg. It is widely felt that being frightened is less than being struck, that trauma to the mind is less than lesion to the body. Many people would consequently say that the duty to avoid injury to strangers is greater than the duty not to upset them. The law has reflected this distinction as one would expect, not only by refusing damages for grief altogether, but by granting recovery for other psychical harm only late and grudgingly, and then only in very clear cases. In tort, clear means close—close to the victim, close to the accident, close to the defendant.'

I do not doubt that public perception has played a substantial role in the development of this branch of the law. But nowadays we must accept the medical reality that psychiatric harm may be more serious than physical harm. It is therefore necessary to consider whether there are other objective policy considerations which may justify different rules for the recovery of compensation for physical injury and psychiatric harm. And in my view it would be insufficient to proceed on the basis that there are unspecified policy considerations at stake. If, as I believe, there are such policy considerations it is necessary to explain what the policy considerations are so that the validity of my assumptions can be critically examined by others.

My impression is that there are at least four distinctive features of claims for psychiatric harm which in combination may account for the differential treatment. Firstly, there is the complexity of drawing the line between acute grief and psychiatric harm: see Hedley 'Nervous shock: wider still and wider' [1997] CLJ 254. The symptoms may be the same. but there is greater diagnostic uncertainty in psychiatric injury cases than in physical injury cases. The classification of emotional injury is often controversial. In order to establish psychiatric harm expert evidence is required. That involves the calling of consultant psychiatrists on both sides. It is a costly and time-consuming exercise. If claims for psychiatric harm were to be treated as generally on a par with physical injury it would have implications for the administration of justice. On its own this factor may not be entitled to great weight and may not outweigh the considerations of justice supporting genuine claims in respect of pure psychiatric injury. Secondly, there is the effect of the expansion of the availability of compensation on potential claimants who have witnessed gruesome events. I do not have in mind fraudulent or bogus claims. In general it ought to be possible for the administration of justice to expose such claims. But I do have in mind the *unconscious* effect of the prospect of compensation on potential claimants. Where there is generally no prospect of recovery, such as in the case of injuries sustained in sport, psychiatric harm appears not to obtrude often. On the other hand, in the case of industrial accidents, where there is often a prospect of recovery of compensation, psychiatric harm is repeatedly encountered and often endures until the process of claiming compensation comes to an end: see *James v Woodall Duckham Construction Co Ltd* [1969] 2 All ER 794, [1969] 1 WLR 903. The litigation is sometimes an unconscious disincentive to rehabilitation. It is true that this factor is already present in cases of physical injuries with concomitant mental suffering. But it may play a larger role in cases of pure psychiatric harm, particularly if the categories of potential recovery are enlarged. For my part this factor cannot be dismissed.

The third factor is important. The abolition or a relaxation of the special rules governing the recovery of damages for psychiatric harm would greatly increase the class of persons who can recover damages in tort. It is true that compensation is routinely awarded for psychiatric harm where the plaintiff has suffered some physical harm. It is also well established that psychiatric harm resulting from the apprehension of physical harm is enough: *Page v Smith* [1995] 2 All ER 736, [1996] AC 155. These two principles are not surprising. Inbuilt in such situations are restrictions on the classes of plaintiff who can sue: the requirement of the infliction of some physical injury or apprehension of it introduces an element of immediacy which restricts the category of potential plaintiffs. But in cases of pure psychiatric harm there is potentially a wide class of plaintiffs involved. Fourthly, the imposition of liability for pure psychiatric harm in a wide range of situations may result in a burden of liability on defendants which may be disproportionate to tortious conduct involving perhaps momentary lapses of concentration, e.g. in a motor car accident.

The wide scope of potential liability for pure psychiatric harm is not only illustrated by the rather unique events of Hillsborough but also by accidents involving trains, coaches and buses, and the everyday occurrence of serious collisions of vehicles all of which may result in gruesome scenes. In such cases there may be many claims for psychiatric harm by those who have witnessed and in some ways assisted at the scenes of the tragic events. Moreover, protagonists of very wide theories of liability for pure psychiatric loss have suggested that 'workplace claims loom large as the next growth area of psychiatric injury law', the paradigm case being no doubt a workman who has witnessed a tragic accident to an employee: Mullany and Handford 'Hillsborough replayed' (1998) 113 LQR 410 at 415.

QUESTION

Does Lord Steyn's fourth policy concern (the risk of a disproportionate burden on defendants following what may only have been a momentary lapse of concentration) have any special relevance to cases of psychiatric harm, or is it applicable in the law of negligence generally? (On Lord Steyn's policy factors, see further paras 85–87 of the Department of Constitutional Affairs' Consultation Paper, *The Law of Damages*, CP 9/07.)

NOTES

1. Compare with Lord Steyn's reference to litigation sometimes being an 'unconscious disincentive to rehabilitation', the view of Teff, [1998] CLJ at pp. 95–100 who (at p. 99) argues that '[t]hough the litigation process may affect prognosis, as one factor in the reinforcement and maintenance of psychiatric disorder, most modern research

attaches greater significance to considerations such as personality, environmental factors, employment prospects, and, critically, the time when psychological management of symptoms commences'.

2.   Lord Steyn makes reference in the above extract to different rules applicable to claimants who suffer psychiatric harm resulting from the apprehension of physical harm to themselves. This refers to the distinction generally drawn in this area of the law between 'primary victims' and 'secondary victims', with which the next case extracts are concerned.

■ Alcock v Chief Constable of South Yorkshire
House of Lords [1991] 4 All ER 907

LORD KEITH OF KINKEL:...

My Lords, the litigation with which these appeals are concerned arose out of the disaster at Hillsborough Stadium, Sheffield, which occurred on 15 April 1989. On that day a football match was arranged to be played at the stadium between the Liverpool and the Nottingham Forest football clubs. It was a semi-final of the FA Cup. The South Yorkshire police force, which was responsible for crowd control at the match, allowed an excessively large number of intending spectators to enter the ground at the Leppings Lane end, an area reserved for Liverpool supporters. They crammed into pens 3 and 4, below the West Stand, and in the resulting crush 95 people were killed and over 400 physically injured. Scenes from the ground were broadcast live on television from time to time during the course of the disaster, and recordings were broadcast later. The Chief Constable of South Yorkshire has admitted liability in negligence in respect of the deaths and physical injuries. Sixteen separate actions were brought against him by persons none of whom was present in the area where the disaster occurred, although four of them were elsewhere in the ground. All of them were connected in various ways with persons who were in that area, being related to such persons or, in one case, being a fiancé. In most cases the person with whom the plaintiff was concerned was killed, in other cases that person was injured, and in one case turned out to be uninjured. All the plaintiffs claim damages for nervous shock resulting in psychiatric illness which they allege was caused by the experiences inflicted on them by the disaster.

The actions came on for trial before Hidden J on 19 June 1990, and he gave judgment on 31 July 1990 (see [1991] 1 All ER 353, [1991] 2 WLR 814). That judgment was concerned with the question whether the defendant owed a duty of care in relation to nervous shock to any, and if so to which, of the plaintiffs. The defendant admitted that if he owed such a duty to any plaintiff, and if that plaintiff could show causation, then the defendant was in breach of duty and liable in damages to that plaintiff. For the purposes of his judgment Hidden J assumed in the case of each plaintiff that causation was established, leaving that matter to be dealt with, if necessary, in further proceedings. In the result, he found in favour of ten out of the sixteen plaintiffs before him and against six of them. The defendant appealed to the Court of Appeal in the cases of nine out of the ten successful plaintiffs, and the six unsuccessful plaintiffs also appealed to that court. On 3 May 1991 the Court of Appeal (Parker, Stocker and Nolan LJJ) gave judgment allowing the defendant's appeals in the cases of the nine formerly successful plaintiffs and rejecting the appeals of the six unsuccessful ones (see [1991] 3 All ER 88). Ten only of these fifteen plaintiffs now appeal to your Lordships' House, with leave granted in the Court of Appeal....

The question of liability in negligence for what is commonly, if inaccurately, described as 'nervous shock' has only twice been considered by this House, in *Hay (or Bourhill) v Young* [1942] 2 All ER 396, [1943] AC 92 and in *McLoughlin v O'Brian* [1982] 2 All ER 298, [1983] 1 AC 410. In the latter case the plaintiff, after learning of a motor accident involving her husband and three of her children about two hours after it had happened, went to the hospital where they had been taken. There she was told that one of the children had been killed, and saw her husband and the other two in a distressed condition and bearing on their persons the immediate effects of the accident. She claimed to have suffered psychiatric illness as a result of her experience, and at the trial of her action of damages against those responsible for the accident this was assumed to be the fact. This House, reversing the Court of Appeal (see [1981] 1 All ER 809, [1981] QB 599), held that she was entitled to recover damages. The leading speech was delivered by Lord Wilberforce. Having set out the position so far reached in the decided cases on nervous shock ([1982] 2 All ER 298 at 301–302, [1983] 1 AC 410 at 418–419), he expressed the opinion that foreseeability did not of itself and automatically give rise to a duty of care owed to a person or class of persons and that considerations of policy entered into the conclusion that such a duty existed. He then considered the arguments on policy which had led the Court of Appeal to reject the plaintiff's claim, and concluded that they were not of great force. He continued ([1982] 2 All ER 298 at 304–305, [1983] 1 AC 410 at 421–423):

'But these discounts accepted, there remains, in my opinion, just because "shock" in its nature is capable of affecting so wide a range of people, a real need for the law to place some limitation on the extent of admissible claims. It is necessary to consider three elements inherent in any claim: the class of persons whose claims should be recognised; the proximity of such persons to the accident; and the means by which the shock is caused. As regards the class of persons, the possible range is between the closest of family ties, of parent and child, or husband and wife, and the ordinary bystander. Existing law recognises the claims of the first; it denies that of the second, either on the basis that such persons must be assumed to be possessed of fortitude sufficient to enable them to endure the calamities of modern life or that defendants cannot be expected to compensate the world at large. In my opinion, these positions are justifiable, and since the present case falls within the first class it is strictly unnecessary to say more. I think, however, that it should follow that other cases involving less close relationships must be very carefully scrutinised. I cannot say that they should never be admitted. The closer the tie (not merely in relationship, but in care) the greater the claim for consideration. The claim, in any case, has to be judged in the light of the other factors, such as proximity to the scene in time and place, and the nature of the accident. As regards proximity to the accident, it is obvious that this must be close in both time and space. It is after all, the fact and consequence of the defendant's negligence that must be proved to have caused the "nervous shock". Experience has shown that to insist on direct and immediate sight or hearing would be impractical and unjust and that under what may be called the "aftermath" doctrine, one who, from close proximity comes very soon on the scene, should not be excluded . . . Finally, and by way of reinforcement of "aftermath" cases, I would accept, by analogy with "rescue" situations, that a person of whom it could be said that one could expect nothing else than that he or she would come immediately to the scene (normally a parent or a spouse) could be regarded as being within the scope of foresight and duty. Where there is not immediate presence, account must be taken of the possibility of alterations in the circumstances, for which the defendant should not be responsible. Subject only to these qualifications, I think that a strict test of proximity by sight or hearing should be applied by the courts. Lastly, as regards communication, there is no case in which the law has compensated shock brought about by communication by a third party. In *Hambrook v Stokes Bros* [1925] 1 KB 141, [1924] All ER Rep 110, indeed, it was said that liability would not arise in such a case, and this is surely right. It was so decided in *Abramzik v Brenner* (1967) 65 DLR (2d) 651. The shock must come through sight or hearing of the event or of its immediate aftermath. Whether some equivalent of sight or hearing, e.g. through simultaneous television, would suffice may have to be considered.'

Lord Bridge of Harwich, with whom Lord Scarman agreed (see [1982] 2 All ER 298 at 310, [1983] 1 AC 410 at 429), appears to have rested his finding of liability simply on the test of reasonable foreseeability of psychiatric illness affecting the plaintiff as a result of the consequences of the road accident (see [1982] 2 All ER 298 at 317–320, [1983] 1 AC 410 at 439–443). Lord Edmund-Davies and Lord Russell of Killowen both considered the policy arguments which had led the Court of Appeal to dismiss the plaintiff's claim to be unsound (see [1982] 2 All ER 298 at 309, 310, [1983] 1 AC 410 at 428, 429). Neither speech contained anything inconsistent with that of Lord Wilberforce.

It was argued for the appellants in the present case that reasonable foreseeability of the risk of injury to them in the particular form of psychiatric illness was all that was required to bring home liability to the respondent. In the ordinary case of direct physical injury suffered in an accident at work or elsewhere, reasonable foreseeability of the risk is indeed the only test that need be applied to determine liability. But injury by psychiatric illness is more subtle, as Lord Macmillan observed in *Bourhill v Young* [1942] 2 All ER 396 at 402, [1943] AC 92 at 103. In the present type of case it is a secondary sort of injury brought about by the infliction of physical injury, or the risk of physical injury, upon another person. That can affect those closely connected with that person in various ways. One way is by subjecting a close relative to the stress and strain of caring for the injured person over a prolonged period, but psychiatric illness due to such stress and strain has not so far been treated as founding a claim in damages. So I am of the opinion that in addition to reasonable foreseeability liability for injury in the particular form of psychiatric illness must depend in addition upon a requisite relationship of proximity between the claimant and the party said to owe the duty. Lord Atkin in *M'Alister (or Donoghue) v Stevenson* [1932] AC 562 at 580, [1932] All ER Rep 1 at 11 described those to whom a duty of care is owed as being—

> 'persons who are so closely and directly affected by my act that I ought reasonably to have them in contemplation as being so affected when I am directing my mind to the acts or omissions which are called in question.'

The concept of a person being closely and directly affected has been conveniently labelled 'proximity', and this concept has been applied in certain categories of cases, particularly those concerned with pure economic loss, to limit and control the consequences as regards liability which would follow if reasonable foreseeability were the sole criterion.

As regards the class of persons to whom a duty may be owed to take reasonable care to avoid inflicting psychiatric illness through nervous shock sustained by reason of physical injury or peril to another, I think it sufficient that reasonable foreseeability should be the guide. I would not seek to limit the class by reference to particular relationships such as husband and wife or parent and child. The kinds of relationship which may involve close ties of love and affection are numerous, and it is the existence of such ties which leads to mental disturbance when the loved one suffers a catastrophe. They may be present in family relationships or those of close friendship, and may be stronger in the case of engaged couples than in that of persons who have been married to each other for many years. It is common knowledge that such ties exist, and reasonably foreseeable that those bound by them may in certain circumstances be at real risk of psychiatric illness if the loved one is injured or put in peril. The closeness of the tie would, however, require to be proved by a plaintiff, though no doubt being capable of being presumed in appropriate cases. The case of a bystander unconnected with the victims of an accident is difficult. Psychiatric injury to him would not ordinarily, in my view, be within the range of reasonable foreseeability, but could not perhaps be entirely excluded from it if the circumstances of a catastrophe occurring very close to him were particularly horrific.

In the case of those within the sphere of reasonable foreseeability the proximity factors mentioned by Lord Wilberforce in *McLoughlin v O'Brian* [1982] 2 All ER 298 at 304, [1983] 1 AC 410 at 422, must, however, be taken into account in judging whether a duty of care exists. The first of these is proximity of the plaintiff to the accident in time and space. For this purpose the accident is to be taken to include its immediate aftermath, which in *McLoughlin*'s case was held to cover the scene at the hospital which was experienced by the plaintiff some two hours after the accident. In *Jaensch v Coffey* (1984) 54 ALR 417 the plaintiff saw her injured husband at the hospital to which he had been taken in severe pain before and between his undergoing a series of emergency operations, and the next day stayed with him in the intensive care unit and thought he was going to die.

She was held entitled to recover damages for the psychiatric illness she suffered as a result. Deane J said (at 462–463):

'...the aftermath of the accident extended to the hospital to which the injured person was taken and persisted for so long as he remained in the state produced by the accident up to and including immediate post-accident treatment...Her psychiatric injuries were the result of the impact upon her of the facts of the accident itself and its aftermath while she was present at the aftermath of the accident at the hospital.'

As regards the means by which the shock is suffered, Lord Wilberforce said in *McLoughlin*'s case [1982] 2 All ER 298 at 305, [1983] 1 AC 410 at 423 that it must come through sight or hearing of the event or of its immediate aftermath. He also said that it was surely right that the law should not compensate shock brought about by communication by a third party....

Of the present appellants two, Brian Harrison and Robert Alcock, were present at the Hillsborough ground, both of them in the West Stand, from which they witnessed the scenes in pens 3 and 4. Brian Harrison lost two brothers, while Robert Alcock lost a brother-in-law and identified the body at the mortuary at midnight. In neither of these cases was there any evidence of particularly close ties of love or affection with the brothers or brother-in-law. In my opinion the mere fact of the particular relationship was insufficient to place the plaintiff within the class of persons to whom a duty of care could be owed by the defendant as being foreseeably at risk of psychiatric illness by reason of injury or peril to the individuals concerned. The same is true of other plaintiffs who were not present at the ground and who lost brothers, or in one case a grandson. I would, however, place in the category of members to which risk of psychiatric illness was reasonably foreseeable Mr and Mrs Copoc, whose son was killed, and Alexandra Penk who lost her fiancé. In each of these cases the closest ties of love and affection fall to be presumed from the fact of the particular relationship, and there is no suggestion of anything which might tend to rebut that presumption. These three all watched scenes from Hillsborough on television, but none of these depicted suffering of recognisable individuals, such being excluded by the broadcasting code of ethics, a position known to the defendant. In my opinion the viewing of these scenes cannot be equiparated with the viewer being within 'sight or hearing of the event or of its immediate aftermath', to use the words of Lord Wilberforce in *McLoughlin v O'Brian* [1982] 2 All ER 298 at 305, [1983] 1 AC 410 at 423, nor can the scenes reasonably be regarded as giving rise to shock, in the sense of a sudden assault on the nervous system. They were capable of giving rise to anxiety for the safety of relatives known or believed to be present in the area affected by the crush and undoubtedly did so, but that is very different from seeing the fate of the relative or his condition shortly after the event. The viewing of the television scenes did not create the necessary degree of proximity.

My Lords, for these reasons I would dismiss each of these appeals.

LORD OLIVER OF AYLMERTON: ...

There is, to begin with, nothing unusual or peculiar in the recognition by the law that compensatable injury may be caused just as much by a direct assault upon the mind or the nervous system as by direct physical contact with the body. This is no more than the natural and inevitable result of the growing appreciation by modern medical science of recognisable causal connections between shock to the nervous system and physical or psychiatric illness. Cases in which damages are claimed for directly inflicted injuries of this nature may present greater difficulties of proof but they are not, in their essential elements, any different from cases where the damages claimed arise from direct physical injury and they present no very difficult problems of analysis where the plaintiff has himself been directly involved in the accident from which the injury is said to arise. In such a case he can be properly said to be the primary victim of the defendant's negligence and the fact that the injury which he sustains is inflicted through the medium of an assault on the nerves or senses does not serve to differentiate the case, except possibly in the degree of evidentiary difficulty, from a case of direct physical injury.

It is customary to classify cases in which damages are claimed for injury occasioned in this way under a single generic label as cases of 'liability for nervous shock'. This may be convenient but in fact the label is misleading if and to the extent that it is assumed to lead to a conclusion that they have more in common than the factual similarity of the medium through which the injury is sustained—that of an assault upon the nervous system of the plaintiff through witnessing or taking part in an event—and that they will, on account of this factor, provide a single common test for the circumstances which give rise to a duty of care. Broadly they divide into two categories, that is to say those cases in which the injured plaintiff was involved, either mediately or immediately, as a participant, and those in which the plaintiff was no more than the passive and unwilling witness of injury caused to others. In the context of the instant appeals the cases of the former type are not particularly helpful, except to the extent that they yield a number of illuminating dicta, for they illustrate only a directness of relationship (and thus a duty) which is almost self-evident from a mere recital of the facts. . . .

Thus, *Dulieu v White & Sons* [1901] 2 KB 669, [1900–3] All ER Rep 353, where the plaintiff was naturally and obviously put in fear for her own safety when a runaway vehicle broke through the front of the public house where she was employed, is, at any rate to modern eyes, a tolerably obvious case. Had she sustained bodily injury from the incursion there could never have been the slightest doubt about the defendant's liability and the fact that what brought about the injury was not an actual contact but the imminent threat to her personally posed by the defendant's negligence could make no difference to the result. As the person directly threatened, she was quite clearly in a sufficiently direct and proximate relationship with him. The principal interest of the case lies in the view expressed by Kennedy J, apparently following an earlier unreported decision of Wright J, *Smith v Johnson & Co* (January 1897), that illness caused by fear for the safety of anyone other than the plaintiff herself was not capable of grounding liability—a view clearly now unsustainable in the light of subsequent authority. . . .

Into the [former] category, as it seems to me, fall the so-called 'rescue cases'. It is well established that the defendant owes a duty of care not only to those who are directly threatened or injured by his careless acts but also to those who, as a result, are induced to go to their rescue and suffer injury in so doing. The fact that the injury suffered is psychiatric and is caused by the impact on the mind of becoming involved in personal danger or in scenes of horror and destruction makes no difference. 'Danger invites rescue. The cry of distress is the summons to relief . . . the act, whether impulsive or deliberate, is the child of the occasion' (see *Wagner v International Rly Co* (1921) 232 NY 176 at 180–181 per Cardozo J). So in *Chadwick v British Transport Commission* [1967] 2 All ER 945, [1967] 1 WLR 912 the plaintiff recovered damages for the psychiatric illness caused to her deceased husband through the traumatic effects of his gallantry and self-sacrifice in rescuing and comforting victims of the Lewisham railway disaster.

These are all cases where the plaintiff has, to a greater or lesser degree, been personally involved in the incident out of which the action arises, either through the direct threat of bodily injury to himself or in coming to the aid of others injured or threatened. Into the same category, I believe, fall those cases such as *Dooley v Cammell Laird & Co Ltd* [1951] 1 Lloyd's Rep 271, *Galt v British Railways Board* (1983) 133 NLJ 870 and *Wigg v British Railways Board* (1986) 136 NLJ 446 where the negligent act of the defendant has put the plaintiff in the position of being, or of thinking that he is about to be or has been, the involuntary cause of another's death or injury and the illness complained of stems from the shock to the plaintiff of the consciousness of this supposed fact. The fact that the defendant's negligent conduct has foreseeably put the plaintiff in the position of being an unwilling participant in the event establishes of itself a sufficiently proximate relationship between them and the principal question is whether, in the circumstances, injury of that type to that plaintiff was or was not reasonably foreseeable.

In those cases in which, as in the instant appeals, the injury complained of is attributable to the grief and distress of witnessing the misfortune of another person in an event by which the plaintiff is not personally threatened or in which he is not directly involved as an actor, the analysis becomes more complex. The infliction of injury on an individual, whether through carelessness or deliberation, necessarily produces consequences beyond those to the immediate victim. Inevitably the impact of the event and its aftermath, whether immediate or prolonged, is going to be felt in greater or lesser degree by those with whom the victim is connected whether by ties of affection, of blood relationship, of duty or simply of business. In many cases those persons may suffer not only injured feelings or inconvenience but adverse financial consequences as, for instance, by the need to care for the victim or the interruption or non-performance of his contractual obligations to third parties. Nevertheless…the common law has, in general, declined to entertain claims for such consequential injuries from third parties save possibly where loss has arisen from the necessary performance of a legal duty imposed on such party by the injury to the victim….

The failure of the law in general to compensate for injuries sustained by persons unconnected with the event precipitated by a defendant's negligence must necessarily import the lack of any legal duty owed by the defendant to such persons. That cannot, I think, be attributable to some arbitrary but unenunciated rule of 'policy' which draws a line as the outer boundary of the area of duty. Nor can it rationally be made to rest upon such injury being without the area of reasonable foreseeability. It must, as it seems to me, be attributable simply to the fact that such persons are not, in contemplation of law, in a relationship of sufficient proximity to or directness with the tortfeasor as to give rise to a duty of care, though no doubt 'policy', if that is the right word, or perhaps more properly, the impracticability or unreasonableness of entertaining claims to the ultimate limits of the consequences of human activity, necessarily plays a part in the court's perception of what is sufficiently proximate.

What is more difficult to account for is why, when the law in general declines to extend the area of compensation to those whose injury arises only from the circumstances of their relationship to the primary victim, an exception has arisen in those cases in which the event of injury to the primary victim has been actually witnessed by the plaintiff and the injury claimed is established as stemming from that fact. That such an exception exists is now too well established to be called in question. What is less clear, however, is the ambit of the duty in such cases or, to put it another way, what is the essential characteristic of such cases that marks them off from those cases of injury to uninvolved persons in which the law denies any remedy for injury of precisely the same sort.

Although it is convenient to describe the plaintiff in such a case as a 'secondary' victim, that description must not be permitted to obscure the absolute essentiality of establishing a duty owed by the defendant directly to him—a duty which depends not only upon the reasonable foreseeability of damage of the type which has in fact occurred to the particular plaintiff but also upon the proximity or directness of the relationship between the plaintiff and the defendant. The difficulty lies in identifying the features which, as between two persons who may suffer effectively identical psychiatric symptoms as a result of the impression left upon them by an accident, establish in the case of one who was present at or near the scene of the accident a duty in the defendant which does not exist in the case of one who was not. The answer cannot, I think, [lie] in the greater foreseeability of the sort of damage which the plaintiff has suffered. The traumatic effect on, for instance, a mother on the death of her child is as readily foreseeable in a case where the circumstances are described to her by an eye witness at the inquest as it is in a case where she learns of it at a hospital immediately after the event. Nor can it be the mere suddenness or unexpectedness of the event, for the news brought by a policeman hours after the event may be as sudden and unexpected to the recipient as the occurrence of the event is to the spectator present at the scene. The answer has, as it seems to me, to be found in the existence of a combination of circumstances from which the necessary degree of 'proximity' between the plaintiff and the defendant can be deduced. And, in the end, it has to be accepted that the concept of 'proximity' is an artificial one which depends more upon the court's perception of what is the reasonable area for the imposition of liability than upon any logical process of analogical deduction.

The common features of all the reported cases of this type decided in this country prior to the decision of Hidden J in the instant case ([1991] 1 All ER 353, [1991] 2 WLR 814) and in which the plaintiff succeeded in establishing liability are, first, that in each case there was a marital or parental relationship between the plaintiff and the primary victim, secondly, that the injury for which damages were claimed arose from the sudden and unexpected shock to the plaintiff's nervous system, thirdly, that the plaintiff in each case was either personally present at the scene of the accident or was in the more or less immediate vicinity and witnessed the aftermath shortly afterwards and, fourthly, that the injury suffered arose from witnessing the death of, extreme danger to, or injury and discomfort suffered by the primary victim. Lastly, in each case there was not only an element of physical proximity to the event but a close temporal connection between the event and the plaintiff's perception of it combined with a close relationship of affection between the plaintiff and the primary victim. It must, I think, be from these elements that the essential requirement of proximity is to be deduced, to which has to be added the reasonable foreseeability on the part of the defendant that in that combination of circumstances there was a real risk of injury of the type sustained by the particular plaintiff as a result of his or her concern for the primary victim. There may, indeed, be no primary 'victim' in fact. It is, for instance, readily conceivable that a parent may suffer injury, whether physical or psychiatric, as a result of witnessing a negligent act which places his or her child in extreme jeopardy but from which, in the event, the child escapes unharmed....

...[T]here is in many cases, as for instance cases of direct physical injury in a highway accident, an almost necessary coalescence of the twin elements of foreseeability and proximity, the one flowing from the other. But where such convergence is not self-evident, the question of proximity requires separate consideration. In deciding it the court has reference to no defined criteria and the decision necessarily reflects to some extent the court's concept of what policy—or perhaps common sense—requires.

My Lords, speaking for myself, I see no logic and no virtue in seeking to lay down as a matter of 'policy' categories of relationship within which claims may succeed and without which they are doomed to failure to limine. So rigid an approach would, I think, work great injustice and cannot be rationally justified. Obviously a claim for damages for psychiatric injury by a remote relative of the primary victim will factually require most cautious scrutiny and faces considerable evidentiary difficulties. Equally obviously, the foreseeability of such injury to such a person will be more difficult to establish than similar injury to a spouse or parent of the primary victim. But these are factual difficulties and I can see no logic and no policy reason for excluding claims by more remote relatives. Suppose, for instance, that the primary victim has lived with the plaintiff for 40 years, both being under the belief that they are lawfully married. Does she suffer less shock or grief because it is subsequently discovered that their marriage was invalid? The source of the shock and distress in all these cases is the affectionate relationship which existed between the plaintiff and the victim and the traumatic effect of the negligence is equally foreseeable, given that relationship, however the relationship arises. Equally, I would not exclude the possibility envisaged by my noble and learned friend Lord Ackner of a successful claim, given circumstances of such horror as would be likely to traumatise even the most phlegmatic spectator, by a mere bystander. That is not, of course, to say that the closeness of the relationship between plaintiff and primary victim is irrelevant, for the likelihood or unlikelihood of a person in that relationship suffering shock of the degree claimed from the event must be a most material factor to be taken into account in determining whether that consequence was reasonably foreseeable. In general, for instance, it might be supposed that the likelihood of trauma of such a degree as to cause psychiatric illness would be less in the case of a friend or a brother-in-law than in that of a parent or fiancé.

But in every case the underlying and essential postulate is a relationship of proximity between plaintiff and defendant and it is this, as it seems to me, which must be the determining factor in the instant appeals. No case prior to the hearing before Hidden J ([1991] 1 All ER 353, [1991] 2 WLR 814) from which these appeals arise has countenanced an award of damages for injuries suffered where there was not at the time of the event a degree of physical propinquity between the plaintiff and the event caused by the defendant's breach of duty to the primary victim nor where the shock sustained by the plaintiff was not either contemporaneous with the event or separated from it by a relatively short interval of time. The necessary element of proximity between plaintiff and defendant is furnished, at least in part, by both physical and temporal propinquity and also by the sudden and direct visual impression on the plaintiff's mind of actually witnessing the event or its immediate aftermath. To use Lord Wilberforce's words in *McLoughlin's* case [1982] 2 All ER 298 at 304–305, [1983] 1 AC 410 at 422–423:

> 'As regards proximity to the accident, it is obvious that this must be close in both time and space . . . The shock must come through sight or hearing of the event or of its immediate aftermath.'

Grief, sorrow, deprivation and the necessary for caring for loved ones who have suffered injury or misfortune must, I think, be considered as ordinary and inevitable incidents of life which, regardness of individual susceptibilities, must be sustained without compensation. It would be inaccurate and hurtful to suggest that grief is made any the less real or deprivation more tolerable by a more gradual realisation, but to extend liability to cover injury in such cases would be to extend the law in a direction for which there is no pressing policy need and in which there is no logical stopping point. In my opinion, the necessary proximity cannot be said to exist where the elements of immediacy, closeness of time and space, and direct visual or aural perception are absent. I would agree with the view expressed by Nolan LJ[2] that there may well be circumstances where the element of visual perception may be provided by witnessing the actual injury to the primary victim on simultaneous television, but that is not the case in any of the instant appeals and I agree with my noble and learned friend Lord Keith of Kinkel that, for the reasons which he gives, the televised images seen by the various appellants cannot be equiparated with 'sight or hearing of the event'. Nor did they provide the degree of immediacy required to sustain a claim for damages for nervous shock....

Whilst, therefore, I cannot, for the reasons which I have sought to explain, accept [the] submission that it is for your Lordships to lay down, on grounds of public policy, an arbitrary requirement of the existence of a particular blood or marital relationship as a precondition of liability, I equally believe that further pragmatic extensions of the accepted concepts of what constitutes proximity must be approached with the greatest caution. *McLoughlin v O'Brian* was a case which itself represented an extension not, as I think, wholly free from difficulty and any further widening of the area of potential liability to cater for the expanded and expanding range of the media of communication ought, in my view, to be undertaken rather by Parliament, with full opportunity for public debate and representation, then by the process of judicial extrapolation.

...I too would dismiss the appeals....

I would only add that I cannot, for my part, regard the present state of the law as either entirely satisfactory or as logically defensible. If there exists a sufficient degree of proximity to sustain a claim for damages for nervous shock, why it may justifiably be asked, does not that proximity also support that perhaps more easily foreseeable loss which the plaintiff may suffer as a direct result of the death or injury from which the shock arises. That it does not is, I think, clear from *Hinz v Berry* [1970] 1 All ER 1074 esp at 1076–1077, [1970] 2 QB 40 esp at 44 per Lord Pearson. But the reason why it does not has, I think, to be found not in logic but in policy. Whilst not dissenting from the case-by-case approach advocated by Lord Bridge in *McLoughlin*'s case, the ultimate boundaries within which claims for damages in such cases can be entertained must I think depend in the end upon considerations of policy. For example, in his illuminating judgment in *Jaensch v Coffey* (1984) 54 ALR 417 Deane J expressed the view that no claim could be entertained as a matter of law in a case where the primary victim is the negligent defendant himself and the shock to the plaintiff arises from witnessing the victim's self-inflicted injury. The question does not, fortunately, fall to be determined in the instant case, but I suspect that an English court would be likely to take a similar view. But if that be so, the limitation must be based upon policy rather than upon logic from the suffering and shock of a wife or mother at witnessing the death of her husband or son is just as immediate, just as great and just as foreseeable whether the accident be due to the victim's own or to another's negligence and if the claim is based, as it must be, on the combination of proximity and foreseeability, there is certainly no logical reason why a remedy should be denied in such a case. Indeed, Mr Hytner QC, for the appellants, has boldly claimed that it should not be. Take, for instance, the case of a mother who suffers shock and psychiatric injury through witnessing the death of her son when he negligently walks in front of an oncoming motor car. If liability is to be denied in such a case such denial can only be because the policy of the law forbids such a claim, for it is difficult to visualise a greater proximity or a greater degree of foreseeability. Moreover, I can visualise great difficulty arising, if this be the law, where the accident, though not solely caused by the primary

---

[2] In the Court of Appeal.

victim has been materially contributed to by his negligence. If, for instance, the primary victim is himself 75% responsible for the accident, it would be a curious and wholly unfair situation if the plaintiff were enabled to recover damages for his or her traumatic injury from the person responsible only in a minor degree whilst he in turn remained unable to recover any contribution from the person primarily responsible since the latter's negligence vis-à-vis the plaintiff would not even have been tortious.

Policy considerations such as this could, I cannot help feeling, be much better accommodated if the rights of persons injured in this way were to be enshrined in and limited by legislation as they have been in … Australian statute law.…

[LORD ACKNER and LORD JAUNCEY OF TULLICHETTLE delivered speeches in favour of dismissing the appeals. LORD LOWRY agreed that the appeals should be dismissed.]

Appeals dismissed.

QUESTIONS

1. What is the essence of the distinction drawn in Lord Oliver's speech between 'primary' and 'secondary' victims?

2. *Alcock* indicates that there is no liability if the claimant hears of the injury after the event. Should the person who breaks bad but true news insensitively be liable in negligence? (See N. J. Mullany and P. R. Handford, *Tort Liability for Psychiatric Damage*, 2nd edn by P. R. Handford (Sydney, 2006), paras. 26.160–26.280). Should the case be any different if the bad news is incorrect and the defendant was careless in that respect? (See Mullany and Handford, op cit., paras. 26.50–26.150, and (on both situations raised in this question) C. Witting, *Liability for Negligent Misstatements* (Oxford, 2004), paras. 6.10–6.29.)

NOTES

1. For notes on *Alcock* see S. Hedley [1992] CLJ 16; B. Lynch (1992) 108 LQR 367 and K. J. Nasir (1992) 55 MLR 705, and see further H. Teff, (1992) 12 Oxf JLS 440; M. Davie (1992) 43 NILQ 237. Consider also J. Murphy, (1995) 15 LS 415, and for a general treatment of the question of liability for nervous shock, see Mullany and Handford, op cit. In 1998 the topic was also discussed by the Law Commission in its report entitled *Liability for Psychiatric Illness* (Law Com No. 249), noted by H. Teff (1998) 61 MLR 840. The Law Commission's views will be mentioned at various points in this section. They still merit attention even though for some time now there does not seem to have been much prospect of Parliament implementing the proposals; indeed, in chapter 3 of a recent Department of Constitutional Affairs Consultation Paper (*The Law of Damages*, CP 9/07), it is stated that the Government prefers to see any development of liability in this area through case law. The Law Commission's proposals involved a mixture of statutory duties of care co-existing (where they do not overlap) with the common law duty of care. Note, in particular, at this point the Commission's view that there should be legislation to remove the requirement of proximity in terms of time and space and the 'own unaided senses' rule (paras. 6.10–6.18). On the other hand, it was proposed (paras. 6.24–6.35) to keep the condition that there be a close tie of love and affection and that a fixed list of relationships where such a tie is irrebuttably presumed to exist should be laid down by statute. This would include brothers and sisters as well as the parent, spouse, and child, and would also include a co-habitant who was defined as 'a person

who, although not married to the immediate victim, had lived with him or her as man or wife (or, if of the same gender, in the equivalent relationship) for a period of at least two years'. It would of course be open to a claimant to prove the relevant tie even if not within one of these relationships. It has been provisionally estimated (in Annex B to the Department of Constitutional Affairs 2007 Consultation Paper) that implementation of the Law Commission's proposals would jointly cost insurers and the NHS £270,000,000 per annum (and an additional £468,000,000 if made retrospective).

For further argument in favour of a more liberal view than that to be found in *Alcock*, see H. Teff, [1998] CLJ 91. Mullany and Handford, op cit. also favour a more liberal view; compare J. Stapleton in *The Frontiers of Liability*, vol ii, edited by P. B. H. Birks, (1994), pp. 94–96, but see N. J. Mullany in *Torts in the Nineties*, edited by N. J. Mullany, (1997), pp. 101–114. See also the Scottish Law Commission's Report in 2004 (*Damages for Psychiatric Injury*, Scot Law Com No 196), noted by D. Nolan, (2005) 68 MLR 983. Some discussion of academics' views will be found in *White v Chief Constable of the South Yorkshire Police* [1999] 2 AC 455, [1999] 1 All ER 1 (p. 137, post).

2.   In later litigation damages for nervous shock were awarded to the half-brother of a person who died in the Hillsborough disaster. The claimant and his half-brother, who had been in different stands at the ground, were found by the judge to have been part of a close-knit family and the claimant was held to have met all the criteria laid down for recovery in *Alcock*: see *The Times*, 12 December 1996, p. 9. For further litigation arising from the tragic events of Hillsborough, see *Hicks v Chief Constable of the South Yorkshire Police* [1992] 2 All ER 65, noted p. 516 and p. 559, post and *White v Chief Constable of the South Yorkshire Police* [1999] 2 AC 455, [1999] 1 All ER 1 (p. 137, post).

3.   As has already been mentioned, damages will not be awarded for mere mental distress on its own. Cf. C. Hilson (1998) 6 Tort L Rev 37 at 53–54. However, where there has been actionable physical injury, damages can be awarded for associated grief and distress, and what counts as physical injury for this purpose is not always as simple as it might seem. *Rothwell v Chemical & Insulating Co Ltd* [2007] 4 All ER 1047, [2007] UKHL 39 concerned cases in which the claimants had been subjected to exposure to asbestos and had developed pleural plaques (thickening of the membrane around the lungs). The House of Lords held that this did not qualify as physical injury: it did not hurt, it could not be seen and although indicating exposure to asbestos, did not in itself make it any more likely that an asbestos–related disease would be suffered. Damages for anxiety and distress were, therefore, not recoverable. (For another aspect of this case, see note 4, p. 135, post.) On the other hand, a psychiatric illness which may be actionable because of the circumstances in which it comes about (e.g. witnessing the death of a near relative) may be in part brought about by a greater than average reaction to grief. According to Evans LJ in *Vernon v Bosley* [1997] 1 All ER 577 there is no discount for this. Note further that a distinction between a recognisable psychiatric illness and mental distress is, for the psychiatric profession, a matter of degree (see the Law Commission, op cit., paras. 3.27–3.29 and 3.33). In *White* Lord Hoffmann ([1999] 1 All ER at p. 40) said of the distinction between a recognised psychiatric illness and fear, anxiety, or grief:

Current medical opinion suggests that this may be a somewhat arbitrary distinction; the limits of normal reaction to stressful events are wide and debatable, while feelings of terror and grief may have as devastating an effect upon people's lives as the 'pain and suffering' consequent upon physical injury for which damages are regularly awarded.

Cf. Teff, [1998] CLJ at p. 103; (1998) 61 MLR at p. 851.

4.   The extracts from *Alcock* indicate that in the view of Lords Keith and Oliver (and see also Lord Ackner, [1991] 4 All ER at p. 919) in certain circumstances a mere bystander who suffered nervous shock might be able to recover damages. These dicta were cited in *McFarlane v E E Caledonia Ltd* [1994] 2 All ER 1, noted by K. F. Tan (1995) 111 LQR 48, but, perhaps surprisingly, the possibility of recovery by a bystander was not accepted by the Court of Appeal. In this case the claimant was on a vessel that went to assist the Piper Alpha oil rig, on which there had been an explosion leading to a fire. For the purposes of the trial the case proceeded on the assumption that the defendants, who were the owners and operators of the rig, were liable in negligence to those killed or injured on the oil rig and that the claimant's nervous shock was causally related to this. One argument for the claimant was that he should recover because he had witnessed a horrendous event. However, Stuart-Smith LJ (with whose judgment McCowan and Ralph Gibson LJJ agreed) thought that to extend recovery beyond those with the relevant ties of love and affection would be to base liability purely on the reasonable foreseeability test which *Alcock* had not accepted as the sole criterion of liability; furthermore, he envisaged practical difficulties because of the subjectivity of people's responses to horrific events. His Lordship concluded (at p. 14):

> In my judgment both as a matter of principle and policy the court should not extend the duty to those who are mere bystanders or witnesses of horrific events unless there is a sufficient degree of proximity, which requires both nearness in time and place and a close relationship of love and affection between plaintiff and victim.

It is interesting to note that Stuart-Smith LJ's judgment was described by Lord Lloyd as 'illuminating' in *Page v Smith* [1995] 2 All ER 736 at 760 (p. 132, post), and it met with support from Lord Steyn in *White v Chief Constable of the South Yorkshire Police* [1999] 1 All ER at p. 32 (p. 137, post), and from Rose and Henry LJJ when *White* was in the Court of Appeal, sub nom *Frost v Chief Constable of the South Yorkshire Police* [1997] 1 All ER at pp. 550 and 562 respectively, though cf. Judge LJ at p. 573. On the question of bystanders see further D. Oughton and J. Lowry (1995) 46 NILQ 18; Mullany and Handford, op cit., paras. 7.370–7.460, and note that the Law Commission, op cit., paras. 7.11–7.16 thought that the question of recovery by bystanders should be left to judicial development.

5.   On the idea that for there to be a successful claim in nervous shock there must be a 'sudden assault on the nervous system' (*Alcock*, per Lord Keith) or a 'sudden appreciation by sight or sound of a horrifying event' (*Alcock* [1994] 4 All ER at p. 918 per Lord Ackner), see further *Sion v Hampstead Health Authority* [1994] 5 Med LR 170. However, Peter Gibson LJ (with Waite LJ agreeing) did point out that the breach of duty did not necessarily have to give rise to a sudden or violent event: what was vital was the 'sudden awareness, violently agitating the mind, of what is occurring or has occurred'. The example he gave was where the body of someone who had been negligently killed by the wrong medicine having been administered, was discovered by a close relative who had come to visit them in hospital. This example was mentioned in *North Glamorgan NHS Trust v Walters* [2003] PIQR P16, [2002] EWCA Civ 1792, where a period of 36 hours lasting from a child's epileptic fit to its death in its mother's arms was, on the facts of the case, regarded as one 'horrifying event', and the mother's nervous shock was not the result of the cumulative effect of 'gradual assaults on the mind'; cf. *White v Lidl UK GmbH* [2005] EWHC 871 (QB). On the 'suddenness' criterion, see further *Tredget and Tredget v Bexley Health Authority* [1994] 5 Med LR 178; *Taylorson v Shieldness Produce Ltd* [1994] PIQR P329, and the criticism by H. Teff (1996) 4 Tort L Rev 44; cf. *White v*

Chief Constable of the South Yorkshire Police when that case was in the Court of Appeal, [1997] 1 All ER at p. 556 per Henry LJ. The Law Commission (op cit., paras. 5.28–5.33) recommended that there should be legislation to remove the requirement that the psychiatric illness be induced by shock, and the 'sudden shock' concept has been rejected by the Australian High Court as a necessary element of the cause of action (*Tame v New South Wales* (2002) 211 CLR 317). On this requirement generally, see Mullany and Handford, op cit., chap. 10.

6. In relation to the adoption of the 'unaided senses' rule, note the point made by H. Teff (1983) 99 LQR 100 at 107 that 'there is medical support for the view that, in some circumstances, hearing of the loss of a loved one in an accident could prompt an even stronger reaction than seeing it, given the human mind's propensity for constructing an image of the event even more gruesome than the reality'. See also Teff (1992) 12 Oxf JLS at p. 442 and his point—(1983) 99 LQR at p. 104—that from a medical viewpoint the critical factor in determining whether a person suffers a recognisable psychiatric illness 'is almost invariably the nature of his relationship with the victim'. On the causes of psychiatric illness, see *Jaensch v Coffey* (1984) 155 CLR 549 at 600–601. For the Law Commission's discussion of medical opinion in respect of psychiatric illness, see Part III of its report and see further Mullany and Handford, op cit., chap. 3.

7. It will have been seen that witnessing the aftermath of an incident may suffice to satisfy the *Alcock* criteria. As was said by Haynes J in the Australian High Court in *Tame* at [270] aftermath is not a term of art. For examples of cases falling within the aftermath doctrine, see the speech of Lord Keith in *Alcock* (p. 122, ante). See further *W v Essex County Council* [2000] 2 All ER 237, [2001] 2 AC 592 (p. 147, post) and *Galli-Atkinson v Seghal* [2003] Lloyds Rep Med 285, [2003] EWCA Civ 697 (visit to mortuary part of the aftermath on the facts of this case). Could a visit to the mortuary solely for the purpose of identifying a body be part of the aftermath? (Consider Lord Jauncey's view in *Alcock* [1991] 4 All ER 907 at p. 937 and *Galli-Atkinson* at [38].)

8. Lord Oliver in Alcock (p. 127, ante) suggests that there would be no liability where the defendant negligently endangers himself thereby causing nervous shock to those who otherwise fit the criteria for recovery established in the case law (and see Lord Ackner's speech [1991] 4 All ER at pp. 917–918). The Law Commission, op cit., paras 5.34–5.43 had been in favour of allowing the possibility of recovery when the defendant has injured himself, but, recognising the restriction this would place on self-determination, also recommended that the court should be able to deny a duty of care where it was not just and reasonable to impose one because of the defendant's exercise of a choice to put himself or herself in danger (e.g. participating in a dangerous sport). The issue came up squarely for decision in *Greatorex v Greatorex* [2000] 4 All ER 769, [2000] 1 WLR 1970, where Cazalet J accepted that there was no binding authority on the point, but took the view that the weight of Commonwealth authority was against a duty of care being owed by a person who negligently injured himself to someone who suffered nervous shock from witnessing the event (though see Mullany and Handford, op cit., chap. 17). His Lordship went on to decide that on policy grounds no duty of care was owed, even if the claimant fulfilled the *Alcock* criteria for secondary victims to recover. One factor was the restriction on a person's freedom of action that any such duty would impose; however, of more weight for the judge was the fact that the *Alcock* criteria meant that a claimant would normally be a member of the same family as the defendant, and that claims in such a situation with the potential for claims of contributory negligence could harm family relations. In Cazalet J's opinion, the policy arguments outweighed the

unfairness to a joint tortfeasor to which Lord Oliver had pointed in *Alcock*. Any solution was thought to require legislative intervention. Compare s. 1(7) of the Congenital Disabilities (Civil Liability) Act 1976, p. 149, post. See further the comparative law insights on this area provided by B.S. Markesinis [2002] CLJ 386. As Cazalet J acknowledged, however, it must be realised that actions between family members in cases of physical damage are generally allowed and note also that a rescuer who suffers physical injury can sue the person who carelessly puts himself in peril.

■ Page v Smith

House of Lords [1995] 2 All ER 736

The plaintiff, who had been driving his car at about 30 mph, was involved in a collision with another car. The two cars involved suffered considerable damage but the plaintiff was not physically injured. The accident did, however, in the trial judge's view, cause in the plaintiff a recurrence of myalagic encephalomyelitis (ME, sometimes referred to as CFS), which he had previously experienced in a mild form and sporadically, but which was not permanent and of 'chronic intensity'. On the causation issue, see further note 1, p. 135, post. The trial judge (Otton J) awarded the plaintiff damages, but this was reversed by the Court of Appeal, [1994] 4 All ER 522. There was a further appeal to the House of Lords.

LORD LLOYD OF BERWICK: ...

In [*Bourhill v Young* [1942] 2 All ER 396, [1943] AC 92; *McLoughlin v O'Brian* [1982] 2 All ER 298, [1983] 1 AC 410; and *Alcock v Chief Constable of the South Yorkshire Police* [1991] 4 All ER 907, [1992] 1 AC 310.] the plaintiff was the secondary victim of the defendant's negligence. He or she was in the position of a spectator or bystander. In the present case, by contrast, the plaintiff was a participant. He was himself directly involved in the accident, and well within the range of foreseeable physical injury. He was the primary victim. This is thus the first occasion on which your Lordships have had to decide whether, in such a case, the foreseeability of physical injury is enough to enable the plaintiff to recover damaged for nervous shock.

The factual distinction between primary and secondary victims of an accident is obvious of long-standing. . . .

[LORD LLOYD referred, inter alia, to Lord Oliver's speech in *Alcock* (p. 120, ante) and continued by stating that '[t]hough the distinction between primary and secondary victims is a factual one, it has, as will be seen, important legal consequences' and that therefore 'the classification of all nervous shock cases under the same head may be misleading'. His Lordship then referred to the facts and continued:]

Otton J [stated]:

'Once it is established that CFS exists and that a relapse or recrudescence can be triggered by the trauma of an accident and that nervous shock was suffered by the plaintiff who is actually involved in the accident, it becomes a foreseeable consequence. The nervous shock cases relied on by Mr Priest, in my judgment, have no relevance. The plaintiff was not a spectator of the accident who suffered shock from what he witnessed happening to another. He was directly involved and suffered the shock directly on experiencing the accident. The remoteness argument, therefore, must be rejected.'

Since physical injury to the plaintiff was clearly foreseeable, although it did not in the event occur, the judge did not consider, as a separate question, whether the defendant should have foreseen injury by nervous shock.

When the case got to the Court of Appeal ([1994] 4 All ER 522), the approach became more complicated.

[LORD LLOYD then pointed out that the Court of Appeal in this case had required there to be reasonable foresight of nervous shock to the plaintiff, and continued:]

I must say at once that I prefer the simplicity of the judge's approach.... Foreseeability of psychiatric injury remains a crucial ingredient when the plaintiff is the secondary victim, for the very reason that the secondary victim is almost always outside the area of physical impact, and therefore outside the range of foreseeable physical injury. But where the plaintiff is the primary victim of the defendant's negligence, the nervous shock cases, by which I mean the cases following on from *Bourhill v Young*, are not in point. Since the defendant was admittedly under a duty of care not to cause the plaintiff foreseeable physical injury, it was unnecessary to ask whether he was under a separate duty of care not to cause foreseeable psychiatric injury.

Apart from its simplicity, Otton J's approach has other attractions. As medical science advances, it is important that the law should not be seen to limp too far behind: ...

In an age when medical knowledge is expanding fast, and psychiatric knowledge with it, it would not be sensible to commit the law to a distinction between physical and psychiatric injury, which may already seem somewhat artificial, and may soon be altogether outmoded. Nothing will be gained by treating them as different 'kinds' of personal injury, so as to require the application of different tests in law.

My noble and learned friend, Lord Keith of Kinkel, has drawn attention to an observation of Lord Wright in *Bourhill v Young* [1942] 2 All ER 396 at 405, [1943] AC 92 at 110 that in nervous shock cases the circumstances of the accident or event must be viewed ex post facto. There are similar observations by Lord Wilberforce and Lord Bridge in *McLoughlin v O'Brian* [1982] 2 All ER 298 at 303 and 312, [1983] 1 AC 410 at 420 and 432. This makes sense, as Lord Keith points out, where the plaintiff is a secondary victim. For if you do not know the outcome of the accident or event, it is impossible to say whether the defendant should have foreseen injury by shock. It is necessary to take account of what happened in order to apply the test of reasonable foreseeability at all. But it makes no sense in the case of a primary victim. Liability for physical injury depends on what was reasonably foreseeable by the defendant before the event. It could not be right that a negligent defendant should escape liability for psychiatric injury just because, though serious physical injury was foreseeable, it did not in fact transpire. Such a result in the case of a primary victim is neither necessary, logical nor just. To introduce hindsight into the trial of an ordinary running-down action would do the law no service.

Are there any disadvantages in taking the simple approach adopted by Otton J? It may be said that it would open the door too wide, and encourage bogus claims. As for opening the door, this is a very important consideration in claims by secondary victims. It is for this reason that the courts have, as a matter of policy, rightly insisted on a number of control mechanisms. Otherwise, a negligent defendant might find himself being made liable to all the world. Thus in the case of secondary victims, foreseeability of injury by shock is not enough. The law also requires a degree of proximity: see *Alcock* [1991] 4 All ER 907 at 914, [1992] 1 AC 310 at 396 per Lord Keith, and the illuminating judgment of Stuart-Smith LJ in *McFarlane v EE Caledonia Ltd* [1994] 2 All ER 1 at 14. This means not only proximity to the event in time and space, but also proximity of relationship between the primary victim and the secondary victim. A further control mechanism is that the secondary victim will only recover damages for nervous shock if the defendant should have foreseen injury by shock to a person or normal fortitude or 'ordinary phlegm'.

None of these mechanisms are required in the case of a primary victim. Since liability depends on foreseeability of physical injury, there could be no question of the defendant finding himself liable to all the world. Proximity of relationship cannot arise, and proximity in time and space goes without saying.

Nor in the case of a primary victim is it appropriate to ask whether he is a person of 'ordinary phlegm'. In the case of physical injury there is no such requirement. The negligent defendant, or more usually his insurer, takes his victim as he finds him. The same should apply in the case of psychiatric injury. There is no difference in principle, as Geoffrey Lane J pointed out in *Malcolm v Broadhurst* [[1970] 3 All ER 508], between an eggshell skull and an eggshell personality. Since the number of potential claimants is limited by the nature of the case, there is no need to impose any further limit by reference to a person of ordinary phlegm. Nor can I see any justification for doing so.

As for bogus claims, it is sometimes said that if the law were such as I believe it to be, the plaintiff would be able to recover damages for a fright. This is not so. Shock by itself is not the subject of compensation, any more than fear or grief or any other human emotion occasioned by the defendant's negligent conduct. It is only when shock is followed by recognisable psychiatric illness that the defendant may be held liable.

There is another limiting factor. Before a defendant can be held liable for psychiatric injury suffered by a primary victim, he must at least have foreseen the risk of physical injury. . . .

So I do not foresee any great increase in unmeritorious claims. . . .

My provisional conclusion, therefore, is that Otton J's approach was correct. The test in every case ought to be whether the defendant can reasonably foresee that his conduct will expose the plaintiff to risk of personal injury. If so, then he comes under a duty of care to that plaintiff. If a working definition of 'personal injury' is needed, it can be found in s. 38(1) of the Limitation Act 1980: ' "Personal injuries" includes any disease and any impairment of a person's physical or mental condition . . .' There are numerous other statutory definitions to the same effect. In the case of a secondary victim, the question will usually turn on whether the foreseeable injury is psychiatric, for the reasons already explained. In the case of a primary victim the question will almost always turn on whether the foreseeable injury is physical. But it is the same test in both cases, with different applications. There is no justification for regarding physical and psychiatric injury as different 'kinds' of injury. Once it is established that the defendant is under a duty of care to avoid causing personal injury to the plaintiff, it matters not whether the injury in fact sustained is physical, psychiatric or both. The utility of a single test is most apparent in those cases such as *Schneider v Eisovitch* [1960] 1 All ER 169, [1960] 2 QB 430, *Malcolm v Broadhurst* and *Brice v Brown* [1984] 1 All ER 997, where the plaintiff is both primary and secondary victim of the same accident.

Applying that test in the present case, it was enough to ask whether the defendant should have reasonably foreseen that the plaintiff might suffer physical injury as a result of the defendant's negligence, so as to bring him within the range of the defendant's duty of care. It was unnecessary to ask, as a separate question, whether the defendant should reasonably have foreseen injury by shock; and it is irrelevant that the plaintiff did not, in fact, suffer any external physical injury.

The authorities
I turn now to the authorities. . . .

[His Lordship then proceeded to survey various authorities: see note 3 post. At the end of his speech he stated:]

In conclusion, the following propositions can be supported.

(1) In cases involving nervous shock, it is essential to distinguish between the primary victim and secondary victims.

(2) In claims by secondary victims the law insists on certain control mechanisms, in order as a matter of policy to limit the number of potential claimants. Thus, the defendant will not be liable unless psychiatric injury is foreseeable in a person of normal fortitude. These control mechanisms have no place where the plaintiff is the primary victim.

(3) In claims by secondary victims, it may be legitimate to use hindsight in order to be able to apply the test of reasonable foreseeability at all. Hindsight, however, has no part to play where the plaintiff is the primary victim.

(4) Subject to the above qualifications, the approach in all cases should be the same, namely, whether the defendant can reasonably foresee that his conduct will expose the plaintiff to the risk of personal injury, whether physical or psychiatric. If the answer is yes, then the duty of care is established, even though physical injury does not, in fact, occur. There is no justification for regarding physical and psychiatric injury as different 'kinds of damage'.

(5) A defendant who is under a duty of care to the plaintiff, whether as primary or secondary vic- tim, is not liable for damages for nervous shock unless the shock results in some recognised psychiatric illness. It is no answer that the plaintiff was predisposed to psychiatric illness. Nor is it relevant that the illness takes a rare form or is of unusual severity. The defendant must take his victim as he finds him. . . .

In the result, I would restore the judgment of Otton J, but subject to one last caveat. One of the grounds of appeal from Otton J's judgment was that his finding on causation was against the weight of the evidence. Ralph Gibson LJ upheld this ground of appeal, but it was left open by Farquharson and Hoffmann LJJ. Unless, therefore, the claim can now be settled, the case will have to go back to the Court of Appeal for a finding on this issue. . . .

[LORD BROWNE-WILKINSON and LORD ACKNER delivered speeches in which they agreed with LORD LLOYD OF BERWICK's speech. LORD KEITH OF KINKEL and LORD JAUNCEY OF TULLICHETTLE delivered speeches in favour of dismissing the appeal.]

Appeal allowed.

QUESTION

Does the 'sudden shock' requirement (see note 5, p. 130, ante) apply in the case of primary victims (see Teff (1996) 4 Tort L Rev at p. 57)?

NOTES

1. When the case went back to the Court of Appeal (*Page v Smith (No 2)* [1996] 3 All ER 272, [1996] 1 WLR 855), Otton J's finding on causation was upheld.
2. *Page v Smith* is noted by C. A. Hopkins [1995] CLJ 491; F. A. Trindade (1996) 112 LQR 221; W. V. H. Rogers (1995) 3 *TLJ* 149. It was also discussed by the Law Commission (op cit., paras. 5.11–5.16), who did not propose to overrule the view that it was unnecessary to foresee nervous shock when physical injury to the claimant was reasonably foresee- able; cf. the views of the Scottish Law Commission.
3. Prior to *Page v Smith*, support could be found in the case law for the view that nervous shock had to be foreseeable before there could be liability. However, in Lord Lloyd's opinion in *Page v Smith* these dicta 'are to be found in cases where the plaintiff was the secondary victim' and were, in his view, based on a misunderstanding of a comment of Denning LJ in *King v Phillips* [1953] 1 QB 429 at 441. For reference to criticism of *Page v Smith*, see Lord Goff's speech in *White* [1999] 1 All ER at pp. 15–16 and see also the next note.
4. Fear of the chance that physical harm might occur in the future as a result of a defend- ant's tortious act may induce psychiatric illness before—and indeed whether or not— the physical harm actually occurs. For discussion, see generally Mullany and Handford, op cit., chap. 27, discussing, inter alia, *Group B Plaintiffs v Medical Research Council* (1997) 41 BMLR 157, on which see J. O'Sullivan (1999) 15 PN 96. Whether such a situ- ation can be encompassed within the *Page v Smith* doctrine arose for decision in the House of Lords in *Rothwell v Chemical & Insulating Co Ltd* [2007] 4 All ER 1047, [2007] UKHL 39. The litigation concerned cases in which the claimants had been subjected to exposure to asbestos and had developed pleural plaques (thickening of the membrane around the lungs). The House of Lords held that this did not qualify as physical injury.

However, the presence of pleural plaques did indicate exposure to asbestos and the risk of illness in the future, and in one of the cases before the House the claimant had suffered from a psychiatric illness as a consequence of being so informed after an x-ray many years after the exposure. The claimant had been negligently exposed to the risk of physical illness by the defendant and consequently endeavoured to avail himself of the facts of the *Page v Smith* doctrine. This was, however, unsuccessful as that case was distinguished on two linked grounds: these were that any future illness would not be the immediate result of the exposure and also that it came about as the result of information received after the x-ray. Cf. *Simmons v British Steel plc* [2004] ICR 585, [2004] UKHL 20, though note the comments of Lord Mance in *Rothwell* at [104].

Nevertheless, some comments were made in *Rothwell* about the status of *Page v Smith*. Although Lord Hoffmann did not think the House should depart from it when confined to a foreseeable event which has caused physical harm, Lords Hope and Mance raised doubts about the decision. The former referred to the argument that psychiatric injury itself should have to be reasonably foreseeable as 'attractive', but did not need to decide the matter. Lord Mance, seeing force in some of the criticisms that had been raised, left open its correctness for decision on another occasion; indeed, his Lordship maintained this position, along with Lord Neuberger, in the later case of *Corr v IBC Vehicles Ltd* [2008] 2 All ER 943, [2008] UKHL 13, noted p. 400, post, although Lord Walker referred to it as providing a 'much simpler' test for judges in this area.

5. Can a claimant recover damages for nervous shock suffered as a result of witnessing damage to their property? Since this may only involve physical damage to property, it would appear not to be caught by the ruling in *Page v Smith*. The question was raised (before *Page*) in *Attia v British Gas plc* [1988] QB 304, [1987] 3 All ER 455, where the defendants admitted that their employees had negligently caused a fire at the claimant's house. The claimant alleged that she had suffered nervous shock by virtue of seeing her home and its contents on fire, but did not allege that she feared for anyone else's safety. The preliminary issue raised was whether such a claim could, as a matter of law, successfully be made. The Court of Appeal thought it could. Dillon LJ's judgment laid stress on the fact that in relation to the damage to the house and its contents a duty was already owed to the claimant not to start a fire; problems of proximity were thereby avoided. Woolf LJ also placed emphasis on a duty of care already being owed to the claimant. In addition to the position concerning property damage, he pointed out that the claimant would have been owed a duty of care in relation to physical injuries if she had been injured when she had entered her house (as she had in fact done) to telephone the fire brigade; in his view there was no policy reason for treating the two types of injury differently. Bingham LJ agreed that the claim should not be struck out as a matter of law, but seemed less influenced by a duty of care already being owed to the claimant. Is there any reason to deny liability where property damage leads to foreseeable nervous shock to a person to whom a duty is not otherwise owed (e.g. a worshipper who is not physically endangered but who witnesses the destruction of an article of extreme religious importance)? The Law Commission, op cit., paras. 7.24–7.31, did not necessarily wish to rule out recovery for psychiatric illness suffered consequent on property damage, and was content to leave it to judicial development. See generally Mullany and Handford, op cit., chap. 25.

The *Attia* case shows that the question of liability for nervous shock can be treated as an issue of remoteness of damage (see chap. 6, post), rather than at the level of duty (as in, for example, *Alcock*). In *Attia* the existence of a duty to the claimant led Dillon and

Woolf LJJ to treat the nervous shock issue as one of remoteness; Bingham LJ acknowledged that the matter could be decided at the level of duty but preferred to treat it as one of remoteness. For criticism of Bingham LJ's approach, see R. Kidner (1989) LS 1 at 5–6. Can the approach in *Attia* be reconciled with the denial of liability in *Alcock* to those of the claimants who were spectators elsewhere in the stadium, to whom, presumably, the police owed a duty of care in respect of physical harm?

6. On *Page v Smith* and the 'thin skull' rule (i.e. the rule that you take your victim as you find him), see note 3, p. 416, post.

7. According to the decision in *Page v Smith* the classification of a victim as either primary or secondary is of great importance, but discussion of this matter will be postponed until the next case extract is considered as the matter was revisited by the House of Lords.

■ White v Chief Constable of the South Yorkshire Police

House of Lords [1999] 1 All ER 1

This case, like *Alcock v Chief Constable of the South Yorkshire Police* [1992] 1 AC 310, [1991] 4 All ER 907, arose from the tragic events at Hillsborough. Here the plaintiffs were police officers who had been on duty at Hillsborough on the day in question and who were claiming damages for nervous shock. They were not physically endangered, nor had they believed that they were, but they were all involved in the aftermath of the tragedy, for example in the attempted resuscitation of victims or carrying the dead and injured. Waller J (1995) Times, 3 July dismissed the actions, sub nom *Frost v Chief Constable of the South Yorkshire Police*, but in the Court of Appeal, [1997] 1 All ER 540, all but one of the appeals were allowed. On appeal to the House of Lords by the defendants:

LORD STEYN: . . .

[His Lordship considered the policy considerations set out p. 118, ante, and continued:]

The police officers' claims

In the present case, the police officers were more than mere bystanders. They were all on duty at the stadium. They were all involved in assisting in the course of their duties in the aftermath of the terrible events. And they have suffered debilitating psychiatric harm. The police officers therefore argue, and are entitled to argue, that the law ought to provide compensation for the wrong which caused them harm. This argument cannot be lightly dismissed. But I am persuaded that a recognition of their claims would substantially expand the existing categories in which compensation can be recovered for pure psychiatric harm. Moreover, as the majority in the Court of Appeal was uncomfortably aware, the awarding of damages to these police officers sits uneasily with the denial of the claims of bereaved relatives by the decision of the House of Lords in *Alcock v Chief Constable of the South Yorkshire Police* [1991] 4 All ER 907, [1992] 1 AC 310. The decision of the Court of Appeal has introduced an imbalance in the law of tort which might perplex the man on the Underground. Since the answer may be that there should be compensation in all these categories I must pursue the matter further.

[Having set out in outline the development of, and commented on, the case law up to *Page v Smith*, LORD STEYN continued:]

The decision of the House of Lords in *Page v Smith* [1995] 2 All ER 736, [1996] AC 155 was the next important development in this branch of the law. The plaintiff was directly involved in a motor car accident. He was within the range of potential physical injury. As a result of the accident he suffered from chronic fatigue syndrome. In this context Lord Lloyd of Berwick adopted a distinction between primary and secondary victims: Lord Ackner and Lord Browne-Wilkinson agreed. Lord Lloyd said that a plaintiff who had been within the range of foreseeable injury was a primary victim. Mr Page fulfilled this requirement and could in principle recover compensation for psychiatric loss. In my view it follows that all other victims, who suffer pure psychiatric harm, are secondary victims and must satisfy the control mechanisms laid down in *Alcock*'s case. There has been criticism of this classification: see Teff 'Liability for negligently inflicted psychiatric harm: justifications and boundaries' [1998] CLJ 91 at 93. But, if the narrow formulation by Lord Lloyd of Berwick of who may be a primary victim is kept in mind, this classification ought not to produce inconsistent results. In any event, the decision of the House of Lords in *Page v Smith* was plainly intended, in the context of pure psychiatric harm, to narrow the range of potential secondary victims. The reasoning of Lord Lloyd and the Law Lords who agreed with him was based on concerns about an ever-widening circle of plaintiffs.

[LORD STEYN then proceeded to reject recovery based on arguments as to the police officers' employment position or that they were rescuers. His Lordship continued:]

Thus far and no further

My Lords, the law on the recovery of compensation for pure psychiatric harm is a patchwork quilt of distinctions which are difficult to justify. There are two theoretical solutions. The first is to wipe out recovery in tort for pure psychiatric injury. The case for such a course has been argued by Professor Stapleton.[3] But that would be contrary to precedent and, in any event, highly controversial. Only Parliament could take such a step. The second solution is to abolish all the special limiting rules applicable to psychiatric harm. That appears to be the course advocated by Mullany and Handford *Tort Liability for Psychiatric Damage: The Law of Nervous Shock* (1993). They would allow claims for pure psychiatric damage by mere bystanders: see 'Hillsborough replayed' (1998) 113 LQR 410 at 415. Precedent rules out this course and, in any event there are cogent policy considerations against such a bold innovation. In my view the only sensible general strategy for the courts is to say thus far and no further. The only prudent course is to treat the pragmatic categories as reflected in authoritative decisions such as *Alcock*'s case and *Page v Smith* as settled for the time being but by and large to leave any expansion or development in this corner of the law to Parliament. In reality there are no refined analytical tools which will enable the courts to draw lines by way of compromise solution in a way which is coherent and morally defensible. It must be left to Parliament to undertake the task of radical law reform.

Conclusion

My Lords, I am in substantial agreement with the reasons given by Waller J for dismissing the claims of the police officers. In my judgment the Court of Appeal erred in reversing Waller J in respect of the claims under consideration. For these reasons, as well as the reasons given by Lord Hoffmann, I would allow the appeals.

LORD HOFFMANN [having discussed the earlier case law, continued:] In order to give due weight to the earlier decisions, particularly at first instance, it is necessary to have regard to their historical context. They cannot simply be laid out flat and pieced together to form a timeless mosaic of legal rules. Some contained the embryonic forms of later developments; others are based on theories of liability which had respectable support at the time but have since been left stranded by the shifting tides.

The position which the law has reached as a result of *Alcock*'s case has not won universal approval. The control mechanisms have been criticised as drawing distinctions which the ordinary man would find hard to understand. Professor Jane Stapleton has said that a mother who suffers psychiatric injury after finding her child's mangled body in a mortuary 'might wonder why the law rules her child's blood too dry to found an action': see *The Frontiers of Liability* ed Birks, (1994) vol 2, p. 84. Equally, the spectacle of a plaintiff, who has, ex hypothesi, suffered psychiatric illness in consequence of his brother's death or injury, being cross-examined on the closeness of their ties of love and affection and then perhaps contradicted by the evidence of a private investigator, might not be to everyone's taste: see the Law Commission report on *Liability for Psychiatric Illness* (Law Com No 249) (1998) para 6.24.

---

[3] In *The Frontiers of Liability* vol ii edited by P. Birks, (1994) pp. 94–96.

Academic writers have made contradictory but equally radical suggestions for reform. Mullany and Handford, in their excellent book *Tort Liability for Psychiatric Damage: The Law of Nervous Shock* (1993), advocate getting rid of the control mechanisms and, in the light of advances in psychiatric knowledge, equating psychiatric injury to physical injury. Professor Jane Stapleton, on the other hand, would abolish recovery for psychiatric injury together...see the article to which I have already referred.

The appeal of these two opposing proposals rather depends upon where one starts from. If one starts from the proposition that in principle the law of torts is there to give legal force to an Aristotelian system of corrective justice, then there is obviously no valid distinction to be drawn between physical and psychiatric injury. On this view, the control mechanisms merely reflect a vulgar scepticism about the reality of psychiatric injury or a belief that it is less worthy of compensation than physical injury: therein the patient must minister to himself. On the other hand, if one starts from the imperfect reality of the way the law of torts actually works, in which the vast majority of cases of injury and disability, both physical and psychiatric, go uncompensated because the persons (if any) who caused the damage were not negligent (a question which often involves very fine distinctions), or because the plaintiff lacks the evidence or the resources to prove to a court that they were negligent, or because the potential defendants happen to have no money, then questions of distributive justice tend to intrude themselves. Why should X receive generous compensation for his injury when Y receives nothing? Is the administration of so arbitrary and imperfect a system of compensation worth the very considerable cost? On this view, a uniform refusal to provide compensation for psychiatric injury adds little to the existing stock of anomaly in the law of torts and at least provides a rule which is easy to understand and cheap to administer.

The Law Commission in its recent report on *Liability for Psychiatric Illness* inclines somewhat to the Mullany and Handford point of view by recommending that the condition of close ties of love and affection for secondary victims be retained in a modified form but that the other two be abolished. The reason given for retention of any control mechanism was that: 'a review of the medical literature has led us to believe that the adoption of a simple foreseeability test would or could result in a significant increase in the number of claims which, at least at this point in time, would be unacceptable.'

I shall in due course return to this concept of unacceptability and try to analyse what it means. But I shall not enter further into the merits of the various proposals for reform because neither of the radical solutions, or indeed the Law Commission solution, is open to your Lordships. It is too late to go back on the control mechanisms as stated in *Alcock*'s case [1991] 4 All ER 907, [1992] 1 AC 310. Until there is legislative change, the courts must live with them and any judicial developments must take them into account.

The control mechanisms were plainly never intended to apply to all cases of psychiatric injury. They contemplate that the injury has been caused in consequence of death or injury suffered (or apprehended to have been suffered or as likely to be suffered) by someone else. In *Page v Smith* [1995] 2 All ER 736 at 755, [1996] AC 155 at 184 Lord Lloyd of Berwick described such a plaintiff as a 'secondary victim' who was 'in the position of a spectator or bystander'. He described the plaintiff in that case (who had suffered psychiatric injury in consequence of being involved in a minor motor accident) as a 'primary victim' who was 'directly involved in the accident and well within the range of foreseeable physical injury'. The issue in *Page v Smith* was whether it is sufficient that a primary victim who, in consequence of a foreseeable accident, has suffered psychiatric injury, should have been within the range of foreseeable physical injury or whether it must have been foreseeable, in the light of the circumstances of the accident as it actually happened, that he would suffer psychiatric illness. A majority of your Lordships held that foreseeability of physical injury was enough to found a claim for any psychiatric injury which the accident caused.

This question does not arise in the present case, but the classification into primary and secondary victims has been debated at length. The plaintiffs say that they were primary victims because they were not 'spectators or bystanders'. The defendants say that the plaintiffs were secondary victims because they were not 'within the range of foreseeble physical injury'. Both arguments have some support from the speeches in *Page v Smith*, which did not have the present question in mind. Essentially, however . . . the plaintiffs draw two distinctions between their position and that of spectators or bystanders. The first is that they had a relationship analogous to employment with the chief constable. Although constitutionally a constable holds an office rather than being employed, there is no dispute that his chief constable owes him the same duty of care which he would to an employee. The plaintiffs say that they were therefore owed a special duty which required the chief constable and those for whom he was vicariously liable to take reasonable care not to expose them to unnecessary risk of injury, whether physical or psychiatric. Secondly, the plaintiffs (and in this respect there is no difference between the police and many others in the crowd that day) did more than stand by and look. They actively rendered assistance and should be equated to 'rescuers,' who, it was said, always qualify as primary victims.

My Lords, I shall consider first the claim to primary status by virtue of the employment relationship. Mr Hytner QC, for the plaintiffs, said that prima facie an employer's duty required him to take reasonable steps to safeguard his employees from unnecessary risk of harm. The word 'unnecessary' must be stressed because obviously a policeman takes the risk of injury which is an unavoidable part of his duty. But there is no reason why he should be exposed to injuries which reasonable care could prevent. Why, in this context, should psychiatric injury should be treated differently from physical injury? He referred to *Walker v Northumberland CC* [1995] 1 All ER 737 where an employee recovered damages for a mental breakdown, held to have been foreseeably caused by the stress and pressure of his work as a social services officer. This, he said, showed that no distinction could be made.

I think, my Lords, that this argument really assumes what it needs to prove. The liability of an employer to his employees for negligence, either direct or vicarious, is not a separate tort with its own rules. It is an aspect of the general law of negligence. The relationship of employer and employee establishes the employee as a person to whom the employer owes a duty of care. But this tells one nothing about the circumstances in which he will be liable for a particular type of injury. For this one must look to the general law concerning the type of injury which has been suffered. It would not be suggested that the employment relationship entitles the employee to recover damages in tort (I put aside contractual liability, which obviously raises different questions) for economic loss which would not ordinarily be recoverable in negligence. The employer is not, for example, under a duty in tort to take reasonable care not to do something which would cause the employee purely financial loss, e.g. by reducing his opportunities to earn bonuses. The same must surely be true of psychiatric injury. There must be a reason why, if the employee would otherwise have been regarded as a secondary victim, the employment relationship should require him to be treated as a primary one. The employee in *Walker v Northumberland CC* was in no sense a secondary victim. His mental breakdown was caused by the strain of doing the work which his employer had required him to do.

Should the employment relationship be a reason for allowing an employee to recover damages for psychiatric injury in circumstances in which he would otherwise be a secondary victim and not satisfy the *Alcock* control mechanisms? I think, my Lords, that the question vividly illustrates the dangers inherent in applying the traditional incrementalism of the common law to this part of the law of torts. If one starts from the employer's liability in respect of physical injury, it seems an easy step, even rather forward-looking, to extend liability on the same grounds to psychiatric injury. It makes the law seem more attuned to advanced medical thinking by eliminating (or not introducing) a distinction which rests upon uneasy empirical foundations. It is important, however to have regard, not only to how the proposed extension of liability can be aligned with cases in which liability exists, but also to the situations in which damages are not recoverable. If one then steps back and looks at the rules of liability for psychiatric injury as a whole, in their relationship with each other, the smoothing of the fabric at one point has produced an ugly ruck at another. In their application to other secondary victims, the *Alcock* control mechanisms stand obstinately in the way of rationalisation and the effect is to produce striking anomalies. Why should the policemen, simply by virtue of the employment analogy and irrespective of what they actually did, be treated different from first-aid workers or ambulance men? . . .

In principle . . . I do not think it would be fair to give police officers the right to a larger claim merely because the disaster was caused by the negligence of other policemen. In the circumstances in which the injuries were caused, I do not think that this is a relevant distinction and if it were to be given effect, the law would not be treating like cases alike. I must therefore consider whether the authorities require a contrary conclusion. And in examining them, it is important to bear in mind, as I said earlier, that they are not contemporaneous statements of the law but represent legal thinking at different points in half a century of uneven development.

[Having referred to *Dooley v Cammell Laird & Co Ltd* [1951] 1 Lloyd's Rep 271, *Galt v British Railways Board* (1983) 133 NLJ 870, *Wigg v British Railways Board* (1986) Times, 4 February, and *Mount Isa Mines v Pusey* (1970) 125 CLR 383, LORD HOFFMANN continued:]

In *Alcock's* case itself, Lord Oliver of Aylmerton attempted an ex post facto rationalisation of the three English cases by saying that in each, the plaintiff had been put in a position in which he was, or thought he was about to be or had been, the immediate instrument of death or injury to another. In *Wigg's* case, for example, the plaintiff was the driver of a train which had caused the death of a passenger by moving off when he was trying to board. The driver had started because the guard, for whom the employer was vicariously liable, had negligently given the signal. This is an elegant, not to say ingenious, explanation, which owes nothing to the actual reasoning (so far as we have it) in any of the cases. And there may be grounds for treating such a rare category of case as exceptional and exempt from the *Alcock* control mechanisms. I do not need to express a view because none of the plaintiffs in this case come within it. In *Robertson v Forth Road Bridge Joint Board, Rough v Forth Road Bridge Joint Board* 1996 SLT 263 Lord Hope adopted Lord Oliver's explanation of the English cases and rejected a claim for psychiatric injury by employees who had witnessed the death of a fellow employee in the course of being engaged on the same work. I respectfully agree with the reasoning of my noble and learned friend, which I regard as a rejection of the employment relationship as in itself a sufficient basis for liability.

The second way in which the plaintiffs put their case is that they were not 'bystanders or spectators' but participants in the sense that they actually did things to help. They submit that there is an analogy between their position and that of a 'rescuer', who, on the basis of the decision of Waller J in *Chadwick v British Transport Commission* [1967] 2 All ER 945, [1967] 1 WLR 912, is said to be treated as a primary victim, exempt from the control mechanisms.

In *Chadwick's* case, the plaintiff suffered psychiatric injury as a result of his experiences in assisting the victims of a railway accident. He spent 12 hours crawling in the wreckage, helping people to extricate themselves and given pain killing injections to the injured. Waller J ([1967] 2 All ER 945 at 952, [1967] 1 WLR 912 at 921) said that it was foreseeable that 'somebody might try and rescue passengers and suffer injury in the process'. The defendants therefore owed a duty of care to the plaintiff. He went on to say that it did not matter that the injury suffered was psychiatric rather than physical but in any event 'shock was foreseeable and...rescue was foreseeable'. Thus the judge's reasoning is based purely upon the foreseeability of psychiatric injury in the same way as in other cases of that time. And I think there can be no doubt that if foreseeability was the only question, the judge's conclusion was unexceptionable.

References to the authorities to rescuers sometimes give the impression that they are a category of persons who would not qualify for compensation under the strict rules of the law of negligence but receive special treatment on grounds of humanity and as a reward for altruism. A florid passage by Cardozo J in *Wagner v International Rly Co* (1921) 232 NY 176 at 180 is frequently quoted. If rescuers formed a specially privileged category of plaintiff, one would expect that the rule would give rise to a definitional problem about who counted as a rescuer and so qualified for special treatment. In fact, as one can see from the absence of any such problem in the cases, rescuers can be accommodated without difficulty in the general principles of the law of negligence. There are two questions which may arise. The first is whether injury to the rescuer was foreseeable. There is usually no difficulty in holding that if it was foreseeable that someone would be put in danger, it was also foreseeable that someone would go to look for him or try to rescue him or otherwise help him in his distress. The second question is whether the voluntary act of the rescuer, searcher or helper in putting himself in peril negatives the causal connection between the original negligent conduct and his injury. Again, the courts have had equally little difficulty in holding that such a person, acting out of a sense of moral obligation, does not make the free choice which would be necessary to eliminate the causal effect of the defendant's conduct. In the same way, its causal effect is not negatived by an unsuccessful attempt of the person in peril, whose freedom of choice has been limited by the position into which the defendant has put him, to extricate himself from danger: see *Lord v Pacific Steam Navigation Co Ltd, The Oropesa* [1943] 1 All ER 211, [1943] P 32.

The cases on rescuers are therefore quite simple illustrations of the application of general principles of foreseeability and causation to particular facts. There is no authority which decides that a rescuer is in any special position in relation to liability for psychiatric injury. And it is no criticism of the excellent judgment of Waller J in *Chadwick*'s case to say that such a question obviously never entered his head. Questions of such nicety did not arise until the *Alcock* control mechanisms had been enunciated.

There does not seem to me to be any logical reason why the normal treatment of rescuers on the issues of foreseeability and causation should lead to the conclusion that, for the purpose of liability for psychiatric injury, they should be given special treatment as primary victims when they were not within the range of foreseeable physical injury and their psychiatric injury was caused by witnessing or participating in the aftermath of accidents which caused death or injury to others. It would of course be possible to create such a rule by an ex post facto rationalisation of *Chadwick*'s case. In both *McLoughlin v O'Brian* [1982] 2 All ER 298, [1983] 1 AC 410 and in *Alcock v Chief Constable of the South Yorkshire Police* [1991] 4 All ER 907, [1992] 1 AC 310, members of the House referred to *Chadwick*'s case with approval. But I do not think that too much should be read into these remarks. In neither case was it argued that the plaintiffs were entitled to succeed as rescuers and anything said about the duty to rescuers was therefore necessarily obiter. If one is looking for an ex post facto rationalisation of *Chadwick*'s case, I think that the most satisfactory is that offered in the Court of Appeal in *McLoughlin v O'Brian* [1981] 1 All ER 809 at 827, [1981] QB 599 at 622 by my noble and learned friend Lord Griffiths, who had been the successful counsel for Mr Chadwick. He said: 'Mr Chadwick might have been injured by a wrecked carriage collapsing on him as he worked among the injured. A duty of care is owed to a rescuer in such circumstances...' If Mr Chadwick was, as Lord Griffiths said, within the range of foreseeable physical injury, then the case is no more than an illustration of the principle applied by the House in *Page v Smith* [1995] 2 All ER 736, [1996] AC 155, namely that such a person can recover even if the injury he actually suffers is not physical but psychiatric. And in addition (unlike *Page v Smith*) Waller J made a finding that psychiatric injury was also foreseeable.

Should then your Lordships take the incremental step of extending liability for psychiatric injury to 'rescuers' (a class which would now require definition) who give assistance at or after some disaster without coming within the range of foreseeable physical injury? It may be said that this would encourage people to offer assistance. The category of secondary victims would be confined to 'spectators and bystanders' who take no part in dealing with the incident or its aftermath. On the authorities, as it seems to me, your Lordships are free to take such a step.

In my opinion there are two reasons why your Lordships should not do so. The less important reason is the definitional problem to which I have alluded. The concept of a rescuer as someone who puts himself in danger of physical injury is easy to understand. But once this notion is extended to include others who give assistance, the line between them and bystanders becomes difficult to draw with any precision. For example, one of the plaintiffs in... *Alcock*'s case, a Mr O'Dell, went to look for his nephew. 'He searched among the bodies... and assisted those who staggered out from the terraces' (see [1991] 3 All ER 88 at 94, [1992] 1 AC 310 at 354). He did not contend that his case was different from those of the other relatives and it was also dismissed. Should he have put himself forward as a rescuer?

But the more important reason for not extending the law is that in my opinion the result would be quite unacceptable. I have used this word on a number of occasions and the time has come to explain what I mean. I do not mean that the burden of claims would be too great for the insurance market or the public funds, the two main sources for the payment of damages in tort. The Law Commission may have had this in mind when they said that removal of all the control mechanism would lead to an 'unacceptable' increase in claims, since they described it as a 'floodgates' argument. These are questions on which it is difficult to offer any concrete evidence and I am simply not in a position to form a view one way or the other. I am therefore willing to accept that, viewed against the total sums paid as damages for personal injury, the increase resulting from an extension of liability to helpers would be modest. But I think that such an extension would be unacceptable to the ordinary person because (though he might not put it this way) it would offend against his notions of distributive justice. He would think it unfair between one class of claimants and another, at best not treating like cases alike and, at worst, favouring the less deserving against the more deserving. He would think it wrong that policemen, even as part of a general class of persons who rendered assistance, should have the right to compensation for psychiatric injury out of public funds while the bereaved relatives are sent away with nothing.

To some extent this opinion would be based upon notions which the law would not accept. Many people feel that the statutory £7,500[4] (see s. 1A of the Fatal Accidents Act 1976) is an inadequate payment to someone like Mr Hicks, who lost his two daughters in such horrifying circumstances. And on the other side of the comparison, there is the view that policemen must expect to encounter harrowing experiences in the course of their duties and that their conditions of employment provide for ill-health pensions and injury pensions if they suffer injuries, physical or psychiatric, which result in their having to leave the force before normal retirement age. There may be other reasons also, from which I do not exclude ignorance about the nature of mental illness, but, all in all, I have no doubt that most people would regard it as wrong to award compensation for psychiatric injury to the professionals and deny compensation for similar injury to the relatives.

It may be said that the common law should not pay attention to these feelings about the relative merits of different classes of claimants. It should stick to principle and not concern itself with distributive justice. An extension of liability to rescuers and helpers would be a modest incremental development in the common law tradition and, as between these plaintiffs and these defendants, produce a just result. My Lords, I disagree. It seems to me that in this area of the law, the search for principle was called off in *Alcock v Chief Constable of the South Yorkshire Police* [1991] 4 All ER 907, [1992] 1 AC 310. No one can pretend that the existing law, which your Lordships have to accept, is founded upon principle. I agree with Professor Jane Stapleton's remark (see *The Frontiers of Liability* ed Birks (1994) vol 2, p 87) that 'once the law has taken a wrong turning or otherwise fallen into an unsatisfactory internal state in relation to a particular cause of action, incrementalism cannot provide the answer'. Consequently your Lordships are now engaged, not in the bold development of principle, but in a practical attempt, under adverse conditions, to preserve the general perception of the law as system of rules which is fair between one citizen and another.

I should say in passing that I do not suggest that someone should be unable to recover for injury caused by negligence, in circumstances in which he would normally be entitled to sue, merely because his occupation required him to run the risk of such injury. Such a rule, called 'the foreman's rule' obtains in some of the United States but was rejected by your Lordships' House in *Ogwo v Taylor* [1987] 3 All ER 961, [1988] AC 431. This would be too great an affront to the idealised model of the law of torts as a system of corrective justice between equals. But the question here is rather different. It is not whether a policeman should be disqualified in circumstances in which he would ordinarily have a right of action, but whether there should be liability to rescuers and helpers as a class. And in considering whether liability for psychiatric injury should be extended to such a class, I think it is legitimate to take into account the fact that, in the nature of things, many of its members will be from occupations in which they are trained and required to run such risks and which provide for appropriate benefits if they should suffer such injuries.

Naturally I feel great sympathy for the plaintiffs' claims, as I do for all those whose lives were blighted by that day at Hillsborough. But I think that fairness demands that your Lordships should reject them. I have also read in draft the speech of my noble and learned friend Lord Steyn and agree with his

---

[4] Damages for bereavement: see p. 285, post. The amount is now £11,800.

reasons for taking the same course, which seem to me substantially the same as my own. I would therefore allow these appeals and dismiss the actions.

[LORD BROWNE-WILKINSON agreed with LORD STEYN and LORD HOFFMANN. LORD GRIFFITHS delivered a speech in
favour of allowing the appeals in the case of those police officers who relied on their employment position, but in favour of dismissing the appeals in the case of those officers who were rescuers. LORD GOFF
OF CHIEVELEY delivered a speech in favour of dismissing the appeals.]

Appeals allowed.

NOTES

1.   *White* is noted by S. Todd (1999) 115 LQR 345; W. V. H. Rogers (1999) 7 *TLJ* 23; and
     L. Lomax and S. Treece (1999) 7 Tort L Rev 207.
2.   As will be seen in other chapters, rescuers who suffer injury whilst effecting a rescue
     are generally accorded favourable treatment in the law of negligence (so, for example,
     a rescue attempt is unlikely to be classed as a novus actus interveniens, p. 391, post,
     nor is the defence of volenti likely to apply, p. 391, post). It was in relation to the pos-
     ition of rescuers that Lord Griffiths disagreed with the majority in *White*. His Lordship
     would have allowed rescuers (as opposed to those who merely treated the victims
     once they had been rescued) to recover if psychiatric illness was reasonably foresee-
     able, even though physical injury was not. Lord Goff in his dissenting speech would
     have classified rescuers as primary victims, referring to Lord Oliver's speech in *Alcock*.
     Nevertheless, the majority view in *White* is that unless a rescuer is physically endan-
     gered or reasonably believes that such is the case, he or she does not count as a primary
     victim and must meet the criteria laid down in *Alcock*. The majority was, therefore,
     obliged to distinguish the case of *Chadwick v British Transport Commission* [1967] 2
     All ER 945, [1967] 1 WLR 912, a case in which a rescuer (who assisted the victims of
     the Lewisham train disaster) recovered damages for psychiatric harm which was not
     triggered by fear for his own safety, but by the horror of what he had experienced. The
     basis on which this case was distinguished was less than satisfactory. Lord Steyn, for
     example ([1999] 1 All ER at 38), relied on a throw-away remark made by the judge in
     Chadwick that 'there was clearly an element of personal danger in what Mr Chadwick
     was doing'. Bizarrely, he interpreted this as support for the proposition that, to count
     as a primary victim, a rescuer must be in actual or apprehended danger, but went on to
     state that, '[i]n order to recover compensation for pure psychiatric harm as rescuer it is
     not necessary to establish that his psychiatric condition was *caused* by the perception
     of personal danger'. Is this a rational way to distinguish *Chadwick*? Would it have been
     preferable to distinguish between amateur rescuers (like Mr Chadwick) and profes-
     sional rescuers (like the police) who are trained and paid to run the risks of this kind of
     psychiatric trauma? Note, however, that, as Lord Hoffmann mentioned in *White*, there
     is no 'fireman's rule', as in some parts of the USA, barring professional rescuers from
     suing: see *Ogwo v Taylor* [1988] AC 431, [1987] 3 All ER 691.
3.   As the previous three case extracts show, the courts have not been consistent about the
     precise classifications of primary and secondary victims, and the definitions appear to
     have evolved. According to Lord Keith in *Alcock*, secondary victims were characterised
     as those whose injury is 'brought about by the infliction of physical injury, or the risk
     of physical injury, upon another person' (in other words, defined solely by the 'rela-
     tional' nature of the injury): note also that Lord Oliver in *Alcock* drew a participant/
     non-participant distinction. In *Page v Smith*, Lord Lloyd defined primary victims as

those 'directly involved...and well within the range of foreseeable physical injury', while the majority in *White* held that a primary victim is one who is physically endangered or reasonably fears for his or her physical safety. Lord Hoffmann in *White* seemed to espouse this view when dealing with the position of rescuers (p. 142, ante), but note his reference, when discussing the case of employees, to the possibility of recovery by those with a particular involvement in the events leading to the death or injury of another (such as *Dooley v Cammell Laird* [1951] 1 Lloyd's Rep 271). The Law Commission, op cit., paras. 7.5–7.8, favoured recovery for this group, though contrast *Hunter v British Coal Corporation* [1999] QB 140, [1998] 2 All ER 97, decided before *White*. See further *Salter v UB Frozen & Chilled Foods Ltd* [2003] Scot CS 212 (no need for an active participant to feel any sense of blame for the accident); *Gregg v Ashbrae Ltd* [2005] NIQB 37. Nevertheless, Lord Hoffmann in *White* (cf. *Salter*) does not say that if such a claim were permitted, a claimant in that position would be classified as a primary victim, merely that they might be able to sue without meeting the control mechanisms in *Alcock* (described in *Tame* (2002) 211 CLR 317 at [257] by Hayne J as 'nearness, hearness and dearness').

Note that there may be an issue as to the precise event or accident in relation to which the primary/secondary classification is drawn: see *Cullin v London Fire and Civil Defence Authority* [1999] PIQR P314, in which it was said that the question should be approached broadly, although note also that a decision on what is the precise event in question can also be important even when the claimant is clearly a secondary victim (*White v Lidl UK GmbH* [2005] EWHC 871 (QB)).

4.   On the duty owed by an employer to an employee in general, see chap. 18, p. 1101, post. In *White* it will have been seen that Lord Hoffmann referred to *Walker v Northumberland County Council* [1995] 1 All ER 737, dealing with the issue of an employee suffering psychiatric illness from stress at work; his Lordship did not regard such a claimant as a secondary victim. In one sense such a claimant is the primary victim as there is no intermediary victim, but under the 'risk of physical injury' definition in the preceding note, he or she is not in that category. The key question is, perhaps, whether the *Alcock* criteria have to be met. As O'Sullivan (1999) 15 PN 96 at 100 writes (relying on P. Cane, *The Anatomy of Tort Law* (Oxford, 1997), p. 69):

Despite its nomenclature, one way to regard the primary victim category is merely a standard application of the general law of negligence, so that the 'primary' label imports no special treatment but is merely used to mark the contrast with the truly exceptional category of secondary victims (which call for special treatment because of the relational nature of the plaintiff's claim).

This view obviously extends the notion of 'primary' from that in *Page v Smith*: indeed, it can be asked whether the law would be more coherent if it recognised just one category calling for special treatment, that of secondary victims (defined in the relational sense), leaving all other cases of psychiatric harm to be treated according to the ordinary principles of the law of negligence. After all, most of the policy concerns mentioned at the beginning of this section apply only to secondary victims. For example, in *Butchart v Home Office* [2006] 1 WLR 1155, [2006] EWCA Civ 239 at [15], the *Alcock* criteria were described as 'the control mechanisms in cases involving injury caused by the witnessing of the death of or serious injury to another, where the primary duty is to that other', whereas in *Butchart* (which was not a case of that sort) it is said (at [17] that 'the real question...is whether or not the relationship between the defendant and the claimant gave rise to a duty of care which encompassed a duty to take reasonable steps to avoid psychiatric harm'. Consider further P. Handford (2007) 27 LS 26. *Butchart* (in which a duty of care was found) involved the question of liability for psychiatric illness suffered by the claimant prisoner as a result of his treatment by the prison authorities; reference was also made in *Butchart* to such a duty existing between a solicitor and client (*McLoughlin v Jones* [2002] 1 QB 1312, [2001] EWCA Civ 1743) and to the stress at work cases. On this view, of course, the claimants in *White*, insofar as they based their action in the circumstances of that case on the employment relationship, were properly classed as subject to the *Alcock* criteria. Cases like *Walker* are different, however, and guidance as to how the courts should approach them can be found in the next extract, after which the classification question will be revisited.

■ Hatton v Sutherland

Court of Appeal [2002] 2 All ER 1

HALE LJ [delivering the judgment of the Court of Appeal]:...

[43] From the above discussion, the following practical propositions emerge. (1) There are no special control mechanisms applying to claims for psychiatric (or physical) illness or injury arising from the stress of doing the work the employee is required to do...The ordinary principles of employer's liability apply...(2) The threshold question is whether this kind of harm to this particular employee was reasonably foreseeable...: this has two components (a) an injury to health (as distinct from occupational stress) which (b) is attributable to stress at work (as distinct from other factors)...(3) Foreseeability depends upon what the employer knows (or ought reasonably to know) about the individual employee. Because of the nature of mental disorder, it is harder to foresee than physical injury, but may be easier to foresee in a known individual than in the population at large.... An employer is usually entitled to assume that the employee can withstand the normal pressures of the job unless he knows of some particular problem or vulnerability...(4) The test is the same whatever the employment: there are no occupations which should be regarded as intrinsically dangerous to mental health...(5) Factors likely to be relevant in answering the threshold question include: (a) The nature and extent of the work done by the employee...Is the workload much more than is normal for the particular job? Is the work particularly intellectually or emotionally demanding for this employee? Are demands being made of this employee unreasonable when compared with the demands made of others in the same or comparable jobs? Or are there signs that others doing this job are suffering harmful levels of stress? Is there an abnormal level of sickness or absenteeism in the same job or the same department? (b) Signs from the employee of impending harm to health...Has he a particular problem or vulnerability? Has he already suffered from illness attributable to stress at work? Have there recently been frequent or prolonged absences which are uncharacteristic of him? Is there reason to think that these are attributable to stress at work, for example because of complaints or warnings from him or others? (6) The employer is generally entitled to take what he is told by his employee at face value, unless he has good reason to think to the contrary. He does not generally have to make searching inquiries of the employee or seek permission to make further inquiries of his medical advisers...(7) To trigger a duty to take steps, the indications of impending harm to health arising from stress at work must be plain enough for any reasonable employer to realise that he should do something about it...

[The Court of Appeal's list of 'practical propositions' then moved on to issues of breach of duty, causation and assessment of damages: see p. 319 post on breach.]

NOTES

1. The Court of Appeal in *Hatton* dealt with four conjoined appeals. In one of these cases (*Barber v Somerset County Council* [2004] 2 All ER 385, [2004] UKHL 13) there was an appeal to the House of Lords. The appeal was successful, but the propositions (above)

laid down by the Court of Appeal met with approval, as they have done in later case law. On difficulties concerning remoteness of damage that might arise, see *Pratley v Surrey County Council* [2004] ICR 159, [2003] EWCA Civ 1067, noted p. 421, post.

2. As pointed out by Brooke LJ in *Leach v Chief Constable of Gloucestershire Constabulary* [1999] 1 All ER 215, [1999] 1 WLR 1421, stress at work cases can be classified along with various other situations where recovery may be allowed for psychiatric illness even though the defendant has neither physically injured anyone nor put anyone at risk of such injury. Brooke LJ also cites the case of a person to whom bad news is broken carelessly, leading to nervous shock on the part of the recipient of the information. In this situation it is uncertain whether in English law at the moment a duty of care is owed by the disseminator of the information (see Question 2, p. 128, ante), but it is suggested that whether or not such a duty does exist is to be answered along the lines of the test outlined in *Butchart*, ante. The same could be said for the case that was alleged in *Leach,* where the claimant asserted she had suffered a psychiatric illness as a result of attending the police interviews with Frederick West who was being questioned about several murders. The claimant had been present as an 'appropriate adult' as required under the relevant Code of Practice. It was decided that no duty of care was owed to the claimant in respect of inviting her to carry out the task, but that it was arguable that there could be a duty of care to provide counselling. See further *N v Agrawal* [1999] PNLR 939 and *In re Organ Retention Group Litigation* [2005] QB 506, [2004] EWHC 644 (QB). In the latter case a duty of care in relation to counselling parents concerning post-mortems conducted on their children was held to encompass liability for nervous shock based on the existence of a doctor/patient relationship with the parent. Another case placed in the category set out above by Brooke LJ is *Attia v British Gas plc* [1988] QB 304, [1987] 3 All ER 455, on which see note 5, p. 136, ante. Might it be argued that the *Alcock* criteria could in fact be applied here without too much adaptation? This leaves the 'involuntary participant' cases looking for a home, but perhaps the *Alcock* criteria are appropriate here, subject to the loving relationship criterion for foreseeability being relaxed. The involvement of the claimant might be thought to make psychiatric illness reasonably foreseeable in a similar way to the existence of a loving relationship.

3. Even if the primary/secondary victim distinction is still going to figure to some extent, the rigidity of the distinction may be subject to relaxation, as the next extract reveals.

■ W v Essex County Council
House of Lords [2000] 2 All ER 237

The adult claimants volunteered to foster an adolescent into their family home, but made it clear to the social services department of the local authority that they were not prepared to foster anyone known or suspected of being a sexual abuser. However, the social services department placed a boy 'G' with the family, despite knowing that he had committed acts of sexual abuse in the past. In the following weeks, G committed serious acts of sexual abuse against the claimants' four young children. The Court of Appeal in *W v Essex County Council* [1998] 3 All ER 111 refused to strike out the children's claims against the local authority, but struck out the claims of the parents on the grounds that they were secondary victims and did not fulfil the requirements laid down in *Alcock*. On appeal to the House of Lords, the parents' claims were reinstated.

LORD SLYNN: [after reviewing the earlier case law and considering the defendants' arguments, his Lordship continued . . .] On the other hand it is right to recall that in *McLoughlin*'s case [1982] 2 All ER 298 at 310, [1983] 1 AC 410 at 430, Lord Scarman recognised the need for flexibility in dealing with new situations not clearly covered by existing decisions; that in *Page v Smith* [1995] 2 All ER 736 at 768, [1996] AC 155 at 197 Lord Lloyd of Berwick said that once it was accepted that the defendant could foresee that his conduct would expose the claimant to personal injury 'There is no justification for regarding physical and psychiatric injury as different "kinds of damage" '; that in this still developing area the courts must proceed incrementally (see *Caparo Industries plc v Dickman* [1990] 1 All ER 568, [1990] 2 AC 605).

On a strike out application it is not necessary to decide whether the parents' claim must or should succeed if the facts they allege are proved. On the contrary, it would be wrong to express any view on that matter. The question is whether if the facts are proved they must fail. It is not enough to recognise, as I do recognise at this stage, that the parents may have difficulties in establishing their claim.

On the other hand, it seems to me impossible to say that the psychiatric injury they claim is outside the range of psychiatric injury which the law recognises. Prima facie pleaded it is more than 'acute grief'. . . . Nor do I find it possible to say that a person of reasonable fortitude would be bound to take in his or her stride being told of the sexual abuse of his or her young children when that person had even innocently brought together the abuser and the abused. A judge might find on a full investigation of the circumstances that they might. I do not feel sufficiently informed on the detailed facts at this stage to rule it out.

This, however, is only the beginning. Is it clear beyond reasonable doubt that the parents cannot satisfy the necessary criteria as 'primary' or 'secondary' victims? As to being primary victims it is beyond doubt that they were not physically injured by the abuse and on the present allegations it does not seem reasonably foreseeable that there was risk of sexual abuse of the parents. But the categorisation of those claiming to be included as primary or secondary victims is not as I read the cases finally closed. It is a concept still to be developed in different factual situations. Lord Goff of Chieveley (dissenting) in *White*'s case [1999] 1 All ER 1 at 13–14, [1999] 2 AC 455 at 472 said that Lord Oliver 'did not attempt any definition of this category [ie of primary victims], but simply referred to a number of examples'. In *Robertson v Forth Road Bridge Joint Board* 1996 SLT 263 at 269 Lord President (Hope) said 'Nor is there any basis in the evidence for attributing this illness to a belief that they had been the unwitting cause of Smith's death'. That seems to recognise that if there had been such a basis a claim might have been arguable (see also the discussion in *Young v Charles Church (Southern) Ltd* (1997) 39 BMLR 146, as to whether the claimant there was a primary or a secondary victim).

I do not consider that any of the cases to which your Lordships have been referred conclusively shows that, if the psychiatric injury suffered by the parents flows from a feeling that they brought the abuser and the abused together or that they have a feeling of responsibility that they did not detect earlier what was happening, they are prevented from being primary victims. Indeed, in *Alcock*'s case [1991] 4 All ER 907 at 924, [1992] 1 AC 310 at 408 Lord Oliver said:

> 'The fact that the defendant's negligent conduct has foreseeably put the plaintiff in the position of being an unwilling participant in the event establishes of itself a sufficiently proximate relationship between them and the principal question is whether, in the circumstances, injury of that type to that plaintiff was or was not reasonably foreseeable.'

Reference has been made to the 'rescue' cases but these do not seem to be necessarily relevant: the plaintiffs here are in no sense claiming as rescuers.

Whilst I accept that there has to be some temporal and spatial limitation on the persons who can claim to be secondary victims, very much for the reasons given by Lord Steyn in *White*'s case, it seems to me that the concept of 'the immediate aftermath' of the incident has to be assessed in the particular factual situation. I am not persuaded that in a situation like the present the parents must come across the abuser or the abused 'immediately' after the sexual incident has terminated. All the incidents here happened in the period of four weeks before the parents learned of them. It might well be that if the matter were investigated in depth a judge would think that the temporal and spatial limitations were not satisfied. On the other hand he might find that the flexibility to which Lord Scarman referred indicated that they were.

If this were, on the authorities, a clear-cut case I would not hesitate to strike it out. However I wholly agree with the decision of Hooper J and the majority of the Court of Appeal as to the children's claim and I have come to the conclusion that the parents' claim cannot be said to be so certainly or clearly bad that they should be barred from pursuing it to trial. I stress to the parents that I am not giving any indication either way as to the outcome of the case but, win or lose, if they wish to pursue the claim they should not be barred from doing so. I would allow the appeal.

[LORD STEYN, LORD HOPE, LORD HOBHOUSE, and LORD MILLETT agreed with the speech delivered by LORD SLYNN.]

Appeal allowed.

NOTE

We have seen that *White* was against any major changes in the law in this area by the courts, and extra-judicially (in the 8th John Maurice Kelly Memorial lecture, 2001), Lord Steyn thought that 'the distinctions based on a crude perception of immediacy and physical contact are likely to continue to exert a dominant influence on the English law of tort', whilst not denying that the law could develop. The plea for flexibility in *W v Essex County Council* is evidence that the law is indeed developing and is likely to continue to develop. See further note 4, p. 145, ante and *French v Chief Constable of Sussex Police* [2006] EWCA Civ 312 (no 'magic' in the primary victim/secondary victim classification), and the Government's recent indication (see note 1, p. 128, ante) that legislation is not envisaged may perhaps provide a catalyst.

3 WRONGFUL CONCEPTION, WRONGFUL BIRTH, AND THE UNBORN CHILD

■ The Congenital Disabilities (Civil Liability) Act 1976[5]

1. Civil liability to child born disabled.—(1) If a child is born disabled as the result of such an occurrence before its birth as is mentioned in subsection (2) below, and a person (other than the child's own mother) is under this section answerable to the child in respect of the occurrence, the child's disabilities are to be regarded as damage resulting from the wrongful act of that person and actionable accordingly at the suit of the child.

(2) An occurrence to which this section applies is one which—

(a) affected either parent of the child in his or her ability to have a normal, healthy child; or

(b) affected the mother during her pregnancy, or affected her or the child in the course of its birth, so that the child is born with disabilities which would not otherwise have been present.

(3) Subject to the following subsections, a person (here referred to as 'the defendant') is answerable to the child if he was liable in tort to the parent or would, if sued in due time, have been so; and it is no answer that there could not have been such liability because the parent suffered no actionable injury, if there was a breach of legal duty which, accompanied by injury, would have given rise to the liability.

(4) In the case of an occurrence preceding the time of conception, the defendant is not answerable to the child if at that time either or both of the parents knew the risk of their child being born disabled

---

[5] For amendments to this Act dealing with infertility treatments, see s. 44 of the Human Fertilisation and Embryology Act 1990 and see also s. 35 of that Act.

(that is to say, the particular risk created by the occurrence); but should it be the child's father who is the defendant, this subsection does not apply if he knew of the risk and the mother did not.

(5) The defendant is not answerable to the child, for anything he did or omitted to do when responsible in a professional capacity for treating or advising the parent, if he took reasonable care having due regard to then received professional opinion applicable to the particular class of case; but this does not mean that he is answerable only because he departed from received opinion.

(6) Liability to the child under this section may be treated as having been excluded or limited by contract made with the parent affected, to the same extent and subject to the same restrictions as liability in the parent's own case; and a contract term which could have been set up by the defendant in an action by the parent, so as to exclude or limit his liability to him or her, operates in the defendant's favour to the same, but no greater, extent in an action under this section by the child.

(7) If in the child's action under this section it is shown that the parent affected shared the responsibility for the child being born disabled, the damages are to be reduced to such extent as the court thinks just and equitable having regard to the extent of the parent's responsibility.

. . .

2. Liability of woman driving when pregnant.—A woman driving a motor vehicle when she knows (or ought reasonably to know) herself to be pregnant is to be regarded as being under the same duty to take care for the safety of her unborn child as the law imposes on her with respect to the safety of other people; and if in consequence of her breach of that duty her child is born with disabilities which would not otherwise have been present, those disabilities are to be regarded as damage resulting from her wrongful act and actionable accordingly at the suit of the child.

4. Interpretation and other supplementary provisions.—(1) References in this Act to a child being born disabled or with disabilities are to its being born with any deformity, disease or abnormality, including predisposition (whether or not susceptible of immediate prognosis) to physical or mental defect in the future.

(2) In this Act—

    (a) 'born' means born alive (the moment of a child's birth being when it first has a life separate from its mother), and 'birth' has a corresponding meaning; and

    (b) 'motor vehicle' means a mechanically propelled vehicle intended or adapted for use on roads. . . .

(3) Liability to a child under section 1 . . . or 2 of this Act is to be regarded—

    (a) as respects all its incidents and any matters arising or to arise out of it; and

    (b) subject to any contrary context or intention, for the purpose of construing references in enactments and documents to personal or bodily injuries and cognate matters,

as liability for personal injuries sustained by the child immediately after its birth.

(5) This Act applies in respect of births after (but not before) its passing, and in respect of any such birth it replaces any law in force before its passing, whereby a person could be liable to a child in respect of disabilities with which it might be born; but in section 1(3) of this Act the expression 'liable in tort' does not include any reference to liability by virtue of this Act, or to liability by virtue of any such law.

. . .

5. Crown application.—This Act binds the Crown.

QUESTIONS

1.   Why should the mother have an immunity from liability which is not possessed by the father?

2. Why should a mother be liable in the circumstances set out in s. 2 of the Act, but not otherwise?

NOTES

1. Before this Act was passed, no English court had decided whether at common law the child injured whilst 'en ventre sa mere' could successfully maintain an action for damages after birth if he or she could establish negligence, although it was later decided, in *Burton v Islington Health Authority* [1993] QB 204, [1992] 3 All ER 833, that such a claim was permissible at common law. As will have been seen, in the case of births occurring after 22 July 1976 (the date of the passing of the Congenital Disabilities (Civil Liability) Act 1976), the Act replaces any action that existed at common law (s. 4(5)).
2. In relation to s. 1(6) of the Act, note the restriction imposed by the Unfair Contract Terms Act 1977 (p. 402, post).
3. Note that a posthumous child may claim under the Fatal Accidents Act 1976 (p. 280, post). (*The George and Richard* (1871) LR 3 A&E 466); thus a child born financially disabled may be compensated. For a statutory provision dealing with compensation for the child who is severely disabled as a result of a vaccination against particular diseases given in certain circumstances to that child's mother before the child's birth, see s. 1 of the Vaccine Damage Payments Act 1979, as amended; note, however, the conditions of entitlement set out in s. 2 of that Act, and in particular the age requirement in s. 2(1)(c).
4. Section 3 of the Congenital Disabilities (Civil Liability) Act 1976, which is concerned with the operation of the Nuclear Installations Act 1965, is summarised at p. 668, post.
5. For the effect of s. 1 of the 1976 Act in relation to the Consumer Protection Act 1987 (strict liability for defective products), see s. 6(3) of the latter Act (p. 632, post).

■ Civil Liability for Pre-Natal Injuries
P. J. Pace (1977) 40 MLR 141 at 151–153

The Act requires that the child should be born alive disabled or with disabilities. According to section 4(1) this means that the child must be born with 'any deformity, disease or abnormality, including predisposition (whether or not susceptible of immediate prognosis) to physical or mental defect in the future.' This obviously limits the operation of the Act to damage which is capable of being assessed in pecuniary terms, so that the courts will not be faced with the novel situation in the American case of *Williams v State of New York*.[6] There an illegitimate child was born to her mentally deficient mother as a result of a sexual assault upon her mother, then a mental patient in a State institution. The plaintiff alleged that the State had been negligent in failing to provide proper supervision and protection for her mother, and that this alleged negligence had caused her (the plaintiff) to bear the stigma of illegitimacy and to be prejudiced in her property rights. The court dismissed the claim because it found it impossible to decide whether non-existence was preferable to existence as an illegitimate child. Such a disability would not fall within the definition of 'disability' proposed by the Act. The Law Commission disapproved of the approach in *Williams* and differentiated between the situation in which, e.g. the child's disability was caused by syphilitic intercourse when an action would lie, and the situation where, e.g. negligent treatment of a pregnant woman prevented spontaneous abortion,[7] when no action

---

[6] 18 NY 2d 481 (1966). The Act would presumably cover injuries causing traumatic nymphomania; see *Gloria Sykes v San Francisco Municipal Rly* 11 Med Sci & Law 51 (1971).

[7] See *Gleitman v Cosgrove* 49 NJ 22 (1967).

would lie. This difference is attributable, according to the Law Commission, to the fact that, in the latter case only, logic dictates that the child's claim must be based on the contention that he would have been better off had the spontaneous abortion succeeded and he had never been born. To guard against the possibility of so-called 'wrongful life' actions, section 1(2)(b) states that an action lies only where, but for the conduct giving rise to the disabled birth, the child would have been born normal—not that it would not have been born at all. There is, however, a difficulty in not treating the former case as a 'wrongful life' claim. As Tedeschi has pointed out:[8]

> 'How could the Manhattan hospital have prevented the unlawful birth and the mental heredity of Christian Williams without preventing her conception as well? And even assuming, for the sake of argument, that it could have been possible to create that life without those adverse circumstances— the fact remains that a single act had been committed, an act on which the plaintiff relied as her cause of action without it being open artificially to a split so as to advance the plaintiff's case.'

Pre-conception fault

Although it is a considerable extension of the existing Commonwealth and American authorities, the Act provides that pre-conception occurrences may found a cause of action. This situation could arise where negligent X-ray treatment or defective birth-control substances affected a parent's reproductive system to such an extent that the child subsequently conceived was born disabled.[9] The child has no right of action if at the time of the occurrence either parent knew of the risk of the child being born disabled, though this does not apply if the father is the defendant or where the occurrence is coincident with or *post* conception. This poses problems since 'new embryological data…purport to indicate that conception is a "process" overtime, rather than an event.'[10] Apart from this difficulty, the point has been made[11] that to allow recovery for pre-conception negligence would be to recognise a legal interest in *not* being conceived. If this analysis is correct then English law will recognise the validity of 'wrongful life' actions and, indeed, Tedeschi would argue that pre-conception negligence does give rise to a 'wrongful life' action:

> 'When a person fathers a child and infects it with a disease by one and the same act, then either the semen was already infected when it came into contact with the ovum, so that the new entity created is diseased from its conception (and this is the true meaning of congenital disease), or the single act results in paternity and in the infection of the mother, which will be transmitted from her to the infant. In the first case it is obvious that there was only one alternative to the new being, either not to exist or to exist with the disease. But in the second case as well no separation can be made between the act of the parent causing paternity and that causing the infection, as we are faced with a single act.

The Law Commission, favouring an action in such circumstances, approached the situation on the basis that, if a child has a legal right to begin life with a sound mind and body, and this is the effect of the proposed legislation, there is a correlative duty on its parents and others to avoid producing conception where the circumstances are likely to result in birth of a disabled child. In other words, the remedy is sought not for being born but 'for compensation for the disability resulting from the sexual intercourse.' It should also be noted that in pre-conception cases compensation would not, without the help of the fiction provided by the Act, fulfil the function, as in other areas of tort, of restoring, as far as money can, the status quo. The fiction is contained in section 4(3) which states that 'Liability

[8]   I. Tedeschi, 'On tort liability for "wrongful life"' [1966] Israel LR 513, 531.

[9]   Edwards, 'The Problem of Compensation for Antenatal Injuries' (1973) 246 *Nature* 54, 55, draws attention to the lack of clear evidence of a causal link between pre-conception damage to gametic cells and post-natal injury.

[10]   *Roe v Wade* 35 L Ed 2d 147, 93 S Ct (1973) per Blackmun J at p. 181.

[11]   'The Impact of Medical Knowledge on the Law Relating to Pre-Natal Injuries' (1962) 110 University of Pennsylvania Law Review 554, 584, n.

under this Act is to be regarded…as liability for personal injuries sustained by the child immediately after its birth.'

NOTES

1. This article discusses other aspects of the Congenital Disabilities (Civil Liability) Act 1976, on which see also K. M. Stanton (1976) 6 Fam Law 206; P. F. Cane (1977) 51 ALJ 704; J.M. Eekelaar and R. W. M. Dingwall [1984] JSWL 258.
2. The Pearson Commission agreed with the Law Commission that there should be no cause of action for damages for 'wrongful life' (para. 1486), and in *McKay v Essex Area Health Authority* [1982] QB 1166, [1982] 2 All ER 771 the Court of Appeal accepted (obiter) that s. 1(2)(b) of the 1976 Act did indeed achieve that goal (though note the points in Pace's article (ante)). In the *McKay* case the birth in question occurred before 22 July 1976 and so the matter was governed by the common law which the Court of Appeal decided did not allow such an action. *McKay* is noted by G. Robertson (1982) 45 MLR 697 and T. Weir [1982] CLJ 225. See further H. Teff (1985) 34 ICLQ 423; J. E. S. Fortin [1981] JSWL 306; R. Lee in *Birthrights*, edited by R. Lee and D. Morgan, (London, 1989), chap. 10; A. Morris and S. Saintier (2003) 11 Med L Rev 167. For a recent survey of the position in various jurisdictions, see *Harriton v Stephens* (2006) 226 CLR 52, noted by K.A. Warner (2007) 123 LQR 209, where the High Court of Australia was against allowing such claims (and see note 4, p. 164, post.)
3. As Robertson points out, the position of a child denied an action for 'wrongful life' can be ameliorated if the parents have an action for 'wrongful birth'.

■ McFarlane v Tayside Health Board

House of Lords [1999] 4 All ER 961

LORD STEYN:…

My Lords, a surgeon wrongly and negligently advised a husband and wife that a vasectomy had rendered the husband infertile. Acting on his advice they ceased to take contraceptive precautions. The wife became pregnant and gave birth to a healthy child. The question is what damages, if any, the parents are in principle entitled to recover.

It may be helpful to state at the outset the nature and shape of the case before the House. First, a distinction must be made between two types of claims which can arise from the failure of a sterilisation procedure, resulting in the birth of a child. There is the action (if permitted) for 'wrongful life' brought by a disadvantaged or disabled child for damage to himself arising from the fact of his birth. The present case does not fall within this category. It is what in the literature is called an action for 'wrongful birth.' It is an action by parents of an unwanted child for damage resulting *to them* from the birth of the child. Secondly, the claim before the House is framed in delict [i.e. in tort]. Counsel cited observations to the effect that it is immaterial whether such an action is brought in contract or in delict. The correctness of this assumption may depend on the nature of the term of the contract alleged to have been breached. Usually, since a contract of services is involved, it may be an obligation to take reasonable care. On the other hand, the term may be expressed more stringently and may amount to a warranty of an outcome. It is unnecessary in the present case to consider whether different considerations may arise in such cases. My views are confined to claims in delict. Thirdly, the claim is brought under the extended *Hedley Byrne* principle (*Hedley Byrne & Co Ltd v Heller & Partners Ltd* [1963] 2 All ER 575, [1964] AC 465) as explained in *Henderson v Merrett Syndicates Ltd*…[1994] 3 All ER 566, [1995] 2 AC 145 and *Williams v Natural Life Health Foods Ltd* [1998] 2 All ER 577, [1998] 1 WLR 830 that is, it is based on an assumption of responsibility by the doctor who gave the negligent advice.…

The unwanted child
In 1989 Mr and Mrs McFarlane already had four children. They decided to move to a bigger house. They needed a larger mortgage. In order to meet the increased financial commitments Mrs McFarlane returned to work. They further decided not to have any more children and that Mr McFarlane would undergo a vasectomy operation. On 16 October 1989 a consultant surgeon performed the operation on Mr McFarlane at a hospital for which Tayside Health Board is responsible. The operation was carried out without complication. One of the risks of a vasectomy operation is spontaneous recanalisation of the divided vas. For this reason Mr and Mrs McFarlane were advised to adopt contraceptive precautions until sperm samples had been analysed. In January and February 1990 that was done. On 23 March 1990 the consultant surgeon wrote to Mr McFarlane saying "your sperm counts are now negative and you may dispense with contraceptive precautions." Mr and Mrs McFarlane acted on this advice. Nevertheless in September 1991 Mrs McFarlane became pregnant. On 6 May 1992 Mrs McFarlane gave birth to a healthy daughter, Catherine. Mr and Mrs McFarlane love their daughter and care for her as an integral part of the family.

The legal proceedings in Scotland
The parents sued the Tayside Health Board in delict. The claim is divided into two parts. First, Mrs McFarlane claimed a sum of £10,000 in respect of pain, suffering and distress resulting from the unwanted pregnancy. Secondly, Mr and Mrs McFarlane claimed a sum of £100,000 in respect of the financial cost of bringing up Catherine.

The issues
The statement of facts and issues summarised the questions to be considered as follows. (i) Are the pursuers entitled to damages? (ii) Is the second pursuer entitled to claim solatium? (iii) Are the pursuers entitled to claim for the financial consequences of pregnancy and the birth of the child? (iv) Is a claim for the financial consequences of the pregnancy and birth excluded as being for pure economic loss? (v) Does public policy exclude the pursuers' claims for damages in whole or in part? (vi) Does the fact that the pursuers now have, as a result of the alleged negligence, a live healthy child, disentitle them to damages in whole or in part? These issues overlap. Different considerations apply to the two heads of claim and it will be necessary to consider them separately. It will be convenient first to consider the claim of the parents for the total cost of bringing up Catherine and then to consider the smaller claim of Mrs McFarlane for a solatium for pain, suffering and distress resulting from her pregnancy. It is common ground that in regard to the sustainability in law of the two heads of claim there are no material differences between the law of Scotland and the law of England.

The cost of bringing up Catherine
It will be convenient to examine first the line of English cases on which the Inner House founded its decision that the cost of bringing up Catharine is a sustainable claim.

[Having referred to *Udale v Bloomsbury Health Authority* [1983]2 All ER 522, [1983] 1 WLR 1098, *Thake v Maurice* [1984] 2 All ER 513, [1986] QB 644 and *Emeh v Kensington and Chelsea and Westminster Area Health Authority* [1984] 3 All ER 1044, [1985] QB 1012, LORD STEYN continued:] Here the father's part of the claim for the cost of bringing up the unwanted child is undoubtedly a claim for pure economic loss. Realistically, despite the pregnancy and child birth, the mother's part of the claim is also for pure economic loss. In any event, in respect of the claim for the costs of bringing up the unwanted child, it would be absurd to distinguish between the claims of the father and the mother. This feature of the claim is important. The common law has a great capacity for growth but the development of a new ground of liability, or a new head of such liability, for the recovery of economic loss must be justified by cogent reasons.

...In the present case your Lordships have had the advantage of considering [the] issue in the light of far more analytical and comprehensive arguments from both counsel than were put before the Court of Appeal in *Emeh's* case. Counsel took your Lordships on a valuable tour d'horizon of comparative jurisprudence. Claims by parents for the cost of bringing up an unwanted but healthy child as opposed to more limited claims by the mother in respect of pain, suffering and distress associated with the pregnancy have proved controversial in foreign jurisdictions: ... [LORD STEYN considered the position in various other jurisdictions and continued:] From this comparative survey I deduce that claims by parents for full compensation for the financial consequences of the birth of a healthy child have sometimes been allowed. It may be that the major theme in such cases is that one is simply dealing with an ordinary tort case in which there are no factors negativing liability in delict. Considerations of corrective justice as between the negligent surgeon and the parents were dominant in such decisions. In an overview one would have to say that more often such claims are not allowed. The grounds for decision are diverse. Sometimes it is said that there was no personal injury, a lack of foreseeability of the costs of bringing up the child, no causative link between the breach of duty and the birth of a healthy child, or no loss since the joys of having a healthy child always outweigh the financial losses. Sometimes the idea that the couple could have avoided the financial cost of bringing up the unwanted child by abortion or adoption has influenced decisions. Policy considerations undoubtedly played a role in decisions denying a remedy for the cost of bringing up an unwanted child. My Lords, the discipline of comparative law does not aim at a poll of the solutions adopted in different countries. It has the different and inestimable value of sharpening our focus on the weight of competing considerations. And it reminds us that the law is part of the world of competing ideas markedly influenced by cultural differences. Thus Fleming has demonstrated that it may be of relevance, depending on the context, to know whether the particular state has an effective social security safety net: see *Fleming, The American Tort Process* (1988) pp 26–27.

I will now eliminate the grounds upon which I would not decide against the parents' claim for compensation for financial loss arising from the child's birth. Counsel for the health board rightly did not argue that it is a factor against the claim that the parents should have resorted to abortion or adoption. I cannot conceive of any circumstances in which the autonomous decision of the parents not to resort to even a lawful abortion could be questioned. For similar reasons the parents' decision not to have the child adopted was plainly natural and commendable. It is difficult to envisage any circumstances in which it would be right to challenge such a decision of the parents. The starting point is the right of parents to make decisions on family planning and, if those plans fail, their right to care for an initially unwanted child. The law does and must respect these decisions of parents which are so closely tied to their basic freedoms and rights of personal autonomy.

Counsel for the health authority argued as his primary submission that the whole claim should fail because the natural processes of conception and childbirth cannot in law amount to personal injury. This is a view taken in some jurisdictions. On the other hand, it is inconsistent with many other decisions, notably where limited recovery of compensation for pain, suffering and distress is allowed. I would not follow this path. After all, the hypothesis is that the negligence of the surgeon caused the physical consequences of pain and suffering associated with pregnancy and childbirth. And every pregnancy involves substantial discomfort and pain. I would therefore reject the argument of the health authority on this point. In the alternative counsel argued that, if money spent on Catherine is regarded as a detriment to her parents, it is outweighed by the many and undisputed benefits which they have derived and will derive from Catherine. While this factor is relevant in an assessment of the justice of the parents' claim I do not regard such a 'set-off' as the correct legal analysis of the position.

It is possible to view the case simply from the perspective of corrective justice. It requires somebody who has harmed another without justification to indemnify the other. On this approach the parents' claim for the cost of bringing up Catherine must succeed. But one may also approach the case from the vantage point of distributive justice. It requires a focus on the just distribution of burdens and losses among members of a society. If the matter is approached in this way, it may become relevant to ask of the commuters on the Underground the following question: Should the parents of an unwanted but healthy child be able to sue the doctor or hospital for compensation equivalent to the cost of bringing up the child for the years of his or her minority, i e until about 18 years? My Lords, I have not consulted my fellow travellers on the London Underground but I am firmly of the view that an overwhelming number of ordinary men and women would answer the question with an emphatic No. And the reason for such a response would be an inarticulate premise as to what is morally acceptable and what is not. Like Ognall J in *Jones v Berkshire Area Health Authority* (2 July 1986, unreported) they will have in mind that many couples cannot have children and others have the sorrow and burden of looking after a disabled child. The realisation that compensation for financial loss in respect of the upbringing of a child would necessarily have to discriminate between rich and poor would, surely appear unseemly to them. It would also worry them that parents may be put in a position of arguing in court that the unwanted child, which they accepted and care for, is more trouble than it is worth. Instinctively, the traveller on the Underground would consider that the law of tort has no business to provide legal remedies consequent upon the birth of a healthy child, which all of us regard as a valuable and good thing.

My Lords, to explain decisions denying a remedy for the cost of bringing up an unwanted child by saying that there is no loss, no foreseeable loss, no causative link or no ground for reasonable restitution is to resort to unrealistic and formalistic propositions which mask the real reasons for the decisions. And judges ought to strive to give the real reasons for their decision. It is my firm conviction that where courts of law have denied a remedy for the cost of bringing up an unwanted child the real reasons have been grounds of distributive justice. That is of course, a moral theory. It may be objected that the House must act like a court of law and not like a court of morals. That would only be partly right. The court must apply positive law. But judges' sense of the moral answer to a question, or the justice of the case, has been one of the great shaping forces of the common law. What may count in a situation of difficulty and uncertainty is not the subjective view of the judge but what he reasonably believes that the ordinary citizen would regard as right. . . . The truth is that tort law is a mosaic in which the principles of corrective justice and distributive justice are interwoven. And in situations of uncertainty and difficulty a choice sometimes has to be made between the two approaches.

In my view it is legitimate in the present case to take into account considerations of distributive justice. That does not mean that I would decide the case on grounds of public policy. On the contrary, I would avoid those quick sands. Relying on principles of distributive justice I am persuaded that our tort law does not permit parents of a healthy unwanted child to claim the costs of bringing up the child from a health authority or a doctor. If it were necessary to do so. I would say that the claim does not satisfy the requirement of being fair, just and reasonable.

This conclusion is reinforced by an argument of coherence. There is no support in Scotland and England for a claim by a disadvantaged child for damage to him arising from his birth: see *McKay v Essex Area Health Authority* [1982] 2 All ER 771, [1982] QB 1166. Given this position, which also prevails in Australia, *Trindade and Cane, The Law of Torts in Australia* (2nd edn, 1993) p 434, observe: '. . . it might seem inconsistent to allow a claim by the parents while that of the child, whether healthy or disabled, is rejected. Surely the parents' claim is equally repugnant to ideas of the sanctity and value of human life and rests, like that of the child, on a comparison between a situation where a human being exists and one where it does not.' In my view this reasoning is sound. Coherence and rationality demand that the claim by the parents should also be rejected.

Two supplementary points remain to be mentioned. First, I have taken into account that the claim in the present case is based on an assumption of responsibility by the doctor who gave negligent advice. But in regard to the sustainability of a claim for the cost of bringing up the child it ought not to make any difference whether the claim is based on negligence simpliciter or on the extended *Hedley Byrne* principle. After all, the latter is simply the rationalisation adopted by the common law to provide a remedy for the recovery of economic loss for a species of negligently performed services: see *Williams v Natural Life Health Foods Ltd* [1988] 2 All ER 577 at 581, [1998] 1 WLR 830, 834. Secondly, counsel for the health board was inclined to concede that in the case of an unwanted child who was born seriously disabled the rule may have to be different. There may be force in this concession but it does not arise in the present appeal and it ought to await decision where the focus is on such cases.

I would hold that the Inner House erred in ruling that Mr and Mrs McFarlane are entitled in principle to recover the costs of bringing up Catherine.

The claim for pain, suffering and distress

The claim for a solatium simply alleges that Mrs McFarlane became pregnant and had to undergo a pregnancy and confinement and the pain and distress of giving birth to the child. It will be recalled that I have already rejected the argument that Mrs McFarlane suffered no personal injury. The considerations of distributive justice which militated against the claim for the cost of bringing up Catherine do not apply to the claim for a solatium. The constituent elements of a claim in delict are present. There is nothing objectionable to allowing such a claim. And such limited recovery is supported by a great deal of authority worldwide. I would uphold it. The pleadings also allege that the wife gave up work during the later stages of her pregnancy. Counsel for the health authority concedes that if a claim for limited recovery is allowed such an ancillary claim would also be sustainable. This consequential relief is within the spirit of the limited recovery principle and I would endorse it.

For the reasons I have given I would uphold the decision of the Inner House on this part of the claim.

The disposal of the appeal

I would allow the appeal on the cost of bringing up Catherine and dismiss the appeal on the claim for a solatium by Mrs McFarlane.

[LORD SLYNN OF HADLEY, LORD HOPE OF CRAIGHEAD, and LORD CLYDE delivered speeches in favour of allowing the mother's claim for damages for the pain and inconvenience of pregnancy, but of rejecting the claim for damages for the birth of Catherine. LORD MILLETT delivered a speech in favour of dismissing both claims (though see note 2 post).]

QUESTIONS

1. How did *McFarlane* differ from (a) a claim under the Congenital Disabilities (Civil Liability) Act 1976; and (b) a claim for 'wrongful life'?

2. In *Parkinson v St James and Seacroft University Hospital NHS Trust* [2002] QB 206, [2001] 3 All ER 97 at [46] Brooke LJ distinguished what he termed 'failed sterilisation' cases—later in *Groom v Selby* [2002] PIQR P18, [2002] EWCA Civ 1522, calling them 'wrongful conception' cases (such as *McFarlane*)—from 'wrongful birth' cases (where e.g. a doctor has failed to detect that the mother has contracted rubella during the pregnancy) on the ground that in the latter the parents have lost the opportunity to terminate the pregnancy. He went on to say (at [48]) that the policy issues are different in 'wrongful birth' cases. What do you think he meant by this? See *Groom v Selby* at [19]; cf. Hale LJ at [28].

3. Lord Steyn decided that there should be no recovery for the costs of bringing up an unwanted child in part on the basis of principles of 'distributive justice' or 'legal policy', but is adamant that his decision has nothing to do with public policy. Can such a distinction be maintained? Should a judge decide a case of this kind without, for example, some express consideration of the effect on a publicly funded health service of liability for medical procedures designed to facilitate 'lifestyle' choices, rather than to treat or prevent illness? See generally on this point R. Bagshaw (2000) 30 Student Law Review 67–68. In *Rees v Darlington Memorial Hospital NHS Trust* [2004] 1 AC 309, [2003] 4 All ER 987, Lord Millett distinguishing 'legal policy' from 'public policy', stated (at [105]) that the award of damages in *McFarlane* would not have been against public policy. Do you agree with this terminology?

NOTES

1.   *McFarlane* is noted by T. Weir [2000] CLJ 241.

2.   Other Law Lords in *McFarlane* adopted slightly different reasoning when rejecting the claim for damages for the birth of Catherine. Lord Slynn stressed that the loss in question was economic loss and that it would not be fair, just, and reasonable to recognise a duty of care in this regard, since 'the doctor does not assume responsibility for these economic losses'. Lord Hope, like Lord Steyn, said that it would not be fair, just, and reasonable for parents to be able to obtain damages for the costs of bringing up a child, whilst leaving out of account the 'incalculable' benefits of having a child. Lord Clyde, on the other hand, did not regard the relevant issue as turning on the existence or non-existence of a duty of care, but instead as an aspect of the principle of compensatory damages, which he described as one of 'reasonable restitution'. Although Lord Millett (unlike the other Law Lords) would have dismissed the claim for the pain and inconvenience of the pregnancy, it should be noted that he would have compensated the parents' lost autonomy (i.e. to limit the number of children they had) and suggested that a trial judge could award up to £5,000 for this loss. This idea became important when the issue returned to the House of Lords: see the next case extract from *Rees v Darlington Memorial Hospital NHS Trust*.

3.   A majority of the House of Lords left open the question of whether any different result would be appropriate where the birth of a handicapped child was involved: see e.g. Lord Steyn's speech, ante. This issue did arise for decision in *Parkinson v St James and Seacroft University Hospital NHS Trust* [2002] QB 206, [2001] 3 All ER 97, where the Court of Appeal held that the *extra* costs of bringing up a disabled child were recoverable, a decision which was followed in *Groom v Selby* [2002] PIQR P18, [2002] EWCA Civ 1522. In *Parkinson* Brooke LJ thought that logic and justice dictated this outcome. Hale LJ (and note that the third member of the court agreed with both judgments) referred to the 'deemed equilibrium' of benefits and burdens in the case of the birth of a healthy child; a disabled child was deemed to bring the same benefits, but the costs were clearly increased and therefore the extra costs associated with the disability should be recoverable. Hale LJ repeated this theory when the *Rees* case was in the Court of Appeal [2003] QB 20, [2002] 2 All ER 127. However, it was not accepted by the other members of the Court of Appeal and when *Rees* reached the House of Lords, Lord Steyn, Lord Hope, Lord Hutton, and Lord Millett disapproved of the 'deemed equilibrium' interpretation of *McFarlane*, regarding the decision there as based on the impossibility of carrying out the calculation. In *Parkinson* Hale LJ did not decide whether the father, as opposed to the mother, could make the sort of claim allowed in *Parkinson*. The point was also left open in *Hibbert Pownall & Newton (a firm) v Whitehead* [2008] EWCA Civ 285 with Laws LJ at [51] pointing to various difficulties with such a claim. Should it be allowed?

■ Rees v Darlington Memorial Hospital NHS Trust

House of Lords [2003] 4 All ER 987

LORD BINGHAM OF CORNHILL: . . .

[1] My Lords, in *McFarlane v Tayside Health Board* [1999] 4 All ER 961, [2000] 2 AC 59 a husband and wife, themselves healthy and normal, sought to recover as damages the cost of bringing up a healthy and normal child born to the wife, following allegedly negligent advice on the effect of a vasectomy

performed on the husband. Differing from the Inner House of the Court of Session (1998 SLT 307), the House unanimously rejected this claim. A factual variant of that case reached the Court of Appeal in *Parkinson v St James and Seacroft University Hospital NHS Trust* [2001] EWCA Civ 530, [2001] 3 All ER 97, [2002] QB 266: the mother, who had undergone a negligently-performed sterilisation operation, conceived and bore a child who was born with severe disabilities. Following *McFarlane*'s case, the Court of Appeal held that the mother could not recover the whole cost of bringing up the child; but it held that she could recover the additional costs she would incur so far as they would be attributable to the child's disabilities. There was no appeal from that decision. The present case raises a further factual variant of *McFarlane*'s case. The claimant in these proceedings (Ms Rees) suffers a severe and progressive visual disability, such that she felt unable to discharge the ordinary duties of a mother, and for that reason wished to be sterilised. She made her wishes known to a consultant employed by the appellant NHS Trust, who carried out a sterilisation operation but did so negligently, and the claimant conceived and bore a son. The child is normal and healthy but the claimant's disability remains. She claimed as damages the cost of rearing the child. The Court of Appeal (Robert Walker and Hale LJJ, Waller LJ dissenting) held that she was entitled to recover the additional costs she would incur so far as they would be attributable to her disability: [2002] EWCA Civ 88, [2002] 2 All ER 177, [2003] QB 20. The appellant NHS Trust now challenges that decision as inconsistent with *McFarlane*'s case. The claimant seeks to uphold the decision, but also claims the whole cost of bringing up the child, inviting the House to reconsider its decision in *McFarlane*'s case....

[3] It is convenient to begin by considering *McFarlane*'s case. In that case there were, as it seems to me, broadly three solutions which the House could have adopted to the problem then before it. (I can, for present purposes, omit two of the solutions which Kirby J listed in para 138 of his judgment in [*Cattanach v Melchior* [2003] HCA 38] but gratefully adopt his formulation of the remaining three, while altering their order). They were the following. (1) That full damages against the tortfeasor for the cost of rearing the child may be allowed, subject to the ordinary limitations of reasonable foreseeability and remoteness, with no discount for joys, benefits and support, leaving restrictions upon such recovery to such limitations as may be enacted by a Parliament with authority to do so. (2) That damages may be recovered in full for the reasonable costs of rearing an unplanned child to the age when that child might be expected to be economically self-reliant, whether the child is 'healthy' or 'disabled' or 'impaired' but with a deduction from the amount of such damages for the joy and benefits received, and the potential economic support derived, from the child. (3) That no damages may be recovered where the child is born healthy and without disability or impairment....

[6] The five members of the House who gave judgment in *McFarlane*'s case adopted different approaches and gave different reasons for adopting the third solution listed in [3], above. But it seems to me clear that all of them were moved to adopt it for reasons of policy (legal, not public, policy). This is not a criticism.... The policy considerations underpinning the judgments of the House were, as I read them, an unwillingness to regard a child (even if unwanted) as a financial liability and nothing else, a recognition that the rewards which parenthood (even if involuntary) may or may not bring cannot be quantified and a sense that to award potentially very large sums of damages to the parents of a normal and healthy child against a National Health Service always in need of funds to meet pressing demands would rightly offend the community's sense of how public resources should be allocated. Kirby J was surely right to suggest (in his judgment in *Cattanach v Melchior* [2003] HCA 38 (at para 178)) that:

> 'Concern to protect the viability of the National Health Service at a time of multiple demands upon it might indeed help to explain the invocation in the House of Lords in *McFarlane* of the notion of "distributive justice".'

It is indeed hard to think that, if the House had adopted the first solution discussed above, its decision would have long survived the first award to well-to-do parents of the estimated cost of providing private education, presents, clothing and foreign holidays for an unwanted child (even if at no more expensive a level than the parents had provided for earlier, wanted, children) against a National Health

Service found to be responsible, by its negligence, for the birth of the child. In favouring the third solution, holding the damages claimed to be irrecoverable, the House allied itself with the great majority
of state courts in the United States and relied on arguments now strongly supported by the dissenting
judgments of Gleeson CJ, Hayne and Heydon JJ in *Melchior's* case.

[7] I am of the clear opinion, for reasons more fully given by my noble and learned friends, that it
would be wholly contrary to the practice of the House to disturb its unanimous decision in *McFarlane's*
case given as recently as four years ago, even if a differently-constituted committee were to conclude
that a different solution should have been adopted. It would reflect no credit on the administration
of the law if a line of English authority were to be disapproved in 1999 and reinstated in 2003 with
no reason for the change beyond a change in the balance of judicial opinion. I am not in any event
persuaded that the arguments which the House rejected in 1999 should now be accepted, or that the
policy considerations which (as I think) drove the decision have lost their potency. Subject to one gloss,
therefore, which I regard as important, I would affirm and adhere to the decision in *McFarlane's* case.

[8] My concern is this. Even accepting that an unwanted child cannot be regarded as a financial
liability and nothing else and that any attempt to weigh the costs of bringing up a child against the
intangible rewards of parenthood is unacceptably speculative, the fact remains that the parent of a
child born following a negligently-performed vasectomy or sterilisation, or negligent advice on the
effect of such a procedure, is the victim of a legal wrong. The members of the House who gave judgment in *McFarlane's* case recognised this by holding, in each case, that some award should be made
to Mrs McFarlane (although Lord Millett based this on a ground which differed from that of the other
members and he would have made a joint award to Mr and Mrs McFarlane). I can accept and support
a rule of legal policy which precludes recovery of the full cost of bringing up a child in the situation
postulated, but I question the fairness of a rule which denies the victim of a legal wrong any recompense at all beyond an award immediately related to the unwanted pregnancy and birth. The spectre
of well-to-do parents plundering the National Health Service should not blind one to other realities:
that of the single mother with young children, struggling to make ends meet and counting the days
until her children are of an age to enable her to work more hours and so enable the family to live a less
straitened existence; the mother whose burning ambition is to put domestic chores so far as possible
behind her and embark on a new career or resume an old one. Examples can be multiplied. To speak
of losing the freedom to limit the size of one's family is to mask the real loss suffered in a situation
of this kind. This is that a parent, particularly (even today) the mother, has been denied, through the
negligence of another, the opportunity to live her life in the way that she wished and planned. I do not
think that an award immediately relating to the unwanted pregnancy and birth gives adequate recognition of or does justice to that loss. I would accordingly support the suggestion favoured by Lord Millett
in *McFarlane's* case ([1999] 4 All ER 961 at 158, [2000] 2 AC 59 at 114) that in all cases such as these
there be a conventional award to mark the injury and loss, although I would favour a greater figure
than the £5,000 he suggested (I have in mind a conventional figure of £15,000) and I would add this
to the award for the pregnancy and birth. This solution is in my opinion consistent with the ruling and
rationale of *McFarlane's* case. The conventional award would not be, and would not be intended to be,
compensatory. It would not be the product of calculation. But it would not be a nominal, let alone a
derisory, award. It would afford some measure of recognition of the wrong done. And it would afford
a more ample measure of justice than the pure *McFarlane's* case rule.

[9] I would for my part apply this rule also, without differentiation, to cases in which either the child
or the parent is (or claims to be) disabled. (1) While I have every sympathy with the Court of Appeal's
view that Mrs Parkinson should be compensated, it is arguably anomalous that the defendant's liability
should be related to a disability which the doctor's negligence did not cause and not to the birth which
it did. (2) The rule favoured by the Court of Appeal majority in the present case inevitably gives rise to
anomalies such as those highlighted by Waller LJ in paras [53]–[54] of his dissenting judgment. (3) It is
undesirable that parents, in order to recover compensation, should be encouraged to portray either
their children or themselves as disabled. There is force in the points made by Kirby J in paras 163–166
of his judgment in *Melchior's* case. (4) In a state such as ours, which seeks to make public provision for

the consequences of disability, the quantification of additional costs attributable to disability, whether of the parent or the child, is a task of acute difficulty. This is highlighted by the inability of the claimant in this appeal to give any realistic indication of the additional costs she seeks to recover.

[10] I would accordingly allow the appeal, set aside the orders of the Court of Appeal and of the deputy judge, and order that judgment be entered for the claimant for £15,000. . . .

LORD MILLETT. . . .

[109] In a lecture to the Personal Injury Bar Association's Annual Conference in 2003 Sir Roger Toulson, Chairman of the Law Commission, described the ratio of *McFarlane*'s case as follows:

> 'Although at a detailed level there are therefore significant differences between the judgments, at a broader level two features dominate them. These are, first, the incalculability in monetary terms of the benefits to the parents of the birth of a healthy child; and, secondly, a sense that for the parents to recover the costs of bringing up a healthy child ran counter to the values which they held and which they believed that society at large could be expected to hold.'

[110] I agree with this analysis, which accurately represents my own reasoning and, I believe, that of other members of the Committee. . . .

[112] *McFarlane*'s case decides that the costs of bringing up a normal, healthy child must be taken to be outweighed by the incalculable blessings which such a child brings to his or her parents and do not sound in damages. *Parkinson*'s case decides that the additional costs of bringing up a disabled child are recoverable in damages. It may be that strict logic demands a different answer. A disabled child is not 'worth' less than a healthy one. The blessings of his or her birth are no less incalculable. Society must equally 'regard the balance as beneficial'. But the law does not develop by strict logic; and most people would instinctively feel that there was a difference, even if they had difficulty in articulating it. Told that a friend has given birth to a normal, healthy baby, we would express relief as well as joy. Told that she had given birth to a seriously disabled child, most of us would feel (though not express) sympathy for the parents. Our joy at the birth would not be unalloyed; it would be tinged with sorrow for the child's disability. Speaking for myself, I would not find it morally offensive to reflect this difference in an award of compensation. But it is not necessary for the disposal of the present appeal to reach any conclusion whether *Parkinson*'s case was rightly decided, and I would wish to keep the point open. It would in any case be necessary to limit the compensation to the *additional* costs attributable to the child's disability; and this may prove difficult to achieve without introducing nice distinctions and unacceptable refinements of a kind which tend to bring the law into disrepute. . . . I would not for my part wish to distinguish between the various motives which the parties might have for desiring to avoid a pregnancy.

[113] However that may be, the decision of the Court of Appeal in the present case is not a legitimate extension of *Parkinson*'s case, but an illegitimate gloss on *McFarlane*'s case. The conventional approach to damages would allow the costs of bringing up a healthy child, but only so far as they were reasonable. Costs which are incurred unreasonably are not recoverable. So what *McFarlane*'s case decides is that the costs of bringing up a healthy child, even though reasonably incurred, are not recoverable.

[114] Such costs are infinitely variable. . . . But *McFarlane*'s case teaches that none of these costs are recoverable in the case of a healthy child, however reasonably they may be incurred. In principle, the same must be true of the disabled parent. To the extent that her disability has any effect, it increases the amount of the costs which she reasonably incurs in bringing up the child, costs which are nevertheless not recoverable. . . .

[118] Disability is a misfortune, and it is the mark of a civilised society that it should provide financial assistance to the disabled. The United Kingdom discharges this responsibility by payment of disability allowance. But this is the responsibility of the state and is properly funded by general taxation. It is not the responsibility of the private citizen whose conduct has neither caused nor contributed to the disability. *McFarlane*'s case teaches that the costs of bringing up a healthy child by an unimpaired parent do not sound in damages. Whatever we may say to the contrary, an award of the 'extra' costs which are attributable to the fact that the parent is disabled is an award of damages for the disability.

[119] It is accepted that care must be taken not to award damages for the parent's disability. An immediate difficulty is that the costs which are attributable to the parent's disability cannot be disentangled from those which are attributable to the birth of the child. If the parent is unable through disability to look after her healthy child, she must employ someone to do so. How are those costs to be characterised? They must be due at least in part to the birth of the child, and in part to the parent's disability. It is impossible to separate the two elements. They are not different components of the cost, but a single cost with composite causes.

[120] But even if they could be separately identified it would not help, for in principle no part of the costs is recoverable. This is what marks the difference between the present case and *Parkinson*'s case. Where it is the child who is disabled the costs are attributable either to the birth of the child or to the fact that the child is disabled. The former are not recoverable; the latter are. Where it is the mother who is disabled they are attributable either to the birth of the child or to the fact that the mother is disabled. There is no third possibility. To the extent that they are due to the birth of the child *McFarlane*'s case precludes recovery and to the extent that they are not due to the birth of the child, the causal link with the wrong is broken and the defendants are not liable for them in any case. The fact that the mother is disabled aggravates the financial consequences of the birth of a healthy child, and the birth of a healthy child aggravates the financial consequences of the mother's disability. The former is the defendants' responsibility but does not sound in damages and the latter is not the responsibility of the defendants at all.

[121] In my opinion, principle mandates the rejection of the parent's claim. But in this case principle also marches with justice. The decision of the majority of the Court of Appeal is destructive of the concept of distributive justice. It renders the law incoherent and is bound to lead to artificial and indefensible distinctions being drawn as the courts struggle to draw a principled line between costs which are recoverable and those which are not....

[Having approved the comments of Waller LJ on this point made when *Rees* was in the Court of Appeal (at [53]), his Lordship continued:]

[122] ...In my opinion, principle, common justice and the coherence of the law alike demand that the line be drawn between those costs which are referable to the characteristics of the child and those which are referable to the characteristics of the parent. I agree with Waller LJ [in the Court of Appeal in *Rees*] that ordinary people would think it unfair that a disabled person should recover the costs of looking after a healthy child when a person not suffering from disability who through no fault of her own was no better able to look after such a child could not. I can identify no legal principle by which such a distinction could be defended....

LORD SCOTT OF FOSCOTE [having decided that the *McFarlane* principle covered the claim in this case, continued:]

[145] The question how the *McFarlane* principle should be applied to a case in which the mother is healthy but the child is born with a disability is not one which needs to be resolved on this appeal. In my opinion, however, a distinction may need to be drawn between a case where the avoidance of the birth of a child with a disability is the very reason why the parent or parents sought the medical treatment or services to avoid conception that, in the event, were negligently provided and a case where the medical treatment or services were sought simply to avoid conception. *Parkinson*'s case was a case in the latter category. In such a case, where the parents have had no particular reason to fear that if a child is born to them it will suffer from a disability, I do not think there is any sufficient basis for treating the expenses occasioned by the disability as falling outside the principles underlying *McFarlane*'s case. The striking of the balance between the burden of rearing the disabled child and the benefit to the parents of the child as a member of their family seems to me as invidious and impossible as in the case of the child born without any disability.

[146] Moreover, the immediate cause of the extra expenses is the child's disability, not the doctor's negligence. In *Emeh v Kensington and Chelsea and Westminster Area Health Authority* [1984] 3 All ER 1044, [1985] QB 1012 evidence was given to the effect that the chance of a baby being born with a congenital abnormality was between one in 200 and one in 400 (see [1984] 3 All ER 1044

at 1049, [1985] QB 1012 at 1019 per Waller LJ). Waller LJ's reference to this statistic was cited by Brooke LJ in *Parkinson*'s case in support of his conclusion that the birth of a child with abnormalities was a reasonably foreseeable consequence of the negligent failure to carry out a sterilisation operation successfully.

[147] My Lords, I have some doubts about this conclusion. The possibility that a child may be born with a congenital abnormality is plainly present to some degree in the case of every pregnancy. But is that a sufficient reason for holding the negligent doctor liable for the extra costs, attributable to the abnormality, of rearing the child? In my opinion it is not. Foreseeability of a one in 200 to 400 chance does not seem to me, by itself, enough to make it reasonable to impose on the negligent doctor liability for these costs. It might be otherwise in a case where there had been particular reason to fear that if a child were conceived and born it might suffer from some inherited disability. And, particularly, it might be otherwise in a case where the very purpose of the sterilisation operation had been to protect against that fear. But on the facts of *Parkinson*'s case I do not think the Court of Appeal's conclusion was consistent with *McFarlane*'s case. . . .

[LORD NICHOLLS OF BIRKENHEAD delivered a speech in favour of allowing the appeal and expressly agreed with LORD BINGHAM's speech. LORD MILLETT and LORD SCOTT OF FOSCOTE agreed with the award of £15,000 suggested by LORD BINGHAM. LORD STEYN, LORD HOPE OF CRAIGHEAD, and LORD HUTTON delivered speeches in favour of dismissing the appeal.]

QUESTIONS

1. What is the basis for the award of £15,000 (and see note 3, post)?
2. The three dissenting Lords agreed with the decision in *Parkinson*. Has it survived *Rees* (and see *Farraj v Kings Healthcare Trust NHS Trust* [2006] PIQR P29, [2006] EWHC 1228 (QB) at [39])? Should the motive for the desire not to have a child be relevant?

NOTES

1. *Rees* is noted by A. Pedain [2004] CLJ 19 and P. Cane (2004) 120 LQR 189.
2. As will have been seen, there were seven members of the House of Lords sitting in *Rees* as *McFarlane* was under challenge. Six of their Lordships expressly approved the decision in *McFarlane*, but in any event the general view was that even if it had been wrongly decided, it would not be appropriate to overturn it.
3. The 'gloss' on *McFarlane*, constituted by the award of £15,000 for lost autonomy, is a particularly interesting feature of *Rees*. Lord Steyn and Lord Hope (who would have allowed the claim for the extra costs of the child's upbringing caused by the mothers disability) disapproved of this award. As mentioned in note 2, p. 158, ante, Lord Millett in *McFarlane* had favoured an award of up to £5,000 on this basis. In *Rees* Lord Steyn, who had, of course, been a member of the House in *McFarlane*, stated that although the majority in that case had not discussed the point, it should not be assumed that it had not been considered; furthermore, he expressed the view that he, Lord Hope, Lord Slynn, and Lord Clyde had found it 'unacceptable' and that it was, therefore, against the majority view in *McFarlane*. On the other hand, in *Rees* Lord Millett did not think *McFarlane* had ruled on his suggestion either way and thought that its adoption would not involve any departure from that decision and (as seen ante in the case extract) Lord Bingham thought such an award was consistent with *McFarlane*.

Is the award based on a right? Lord Bingham does not use this term, but Lord Millett stated at [123]:

I still regard the proper outcome in all these cases is to award the parents a modest conventional sum by way of general damages, not for the birth of the child, but for the denial of an important aspect of their personal autonomy, viz the right to limit the size of their family. This is an important aspect of human dignity, which is increasingly being regarded as an important human right which should be protected by law. The loss of this right is not an abstract or theoretical one. As my noble and learned friend Lord Bingham of Cornhill has pointed out, the parents have lost the opportunity to live their lives in the way that they wished and planned to do. The loss of this opportunity, whether characterised as a right or a freedom, is a proper subject for compensation by way of damages.

Lord Hope, however, (at [70]), thought that this analysis begged many questions. It should also be borne in mind that the Court of Appeal in *Greenfield v Irwin* [2001] 1 WLR 1279, [2001] EWCA Civ 113 had previously decided that the ruling in *McFarlane* was not a breach of Article 8 of the European Convention of Human Rights (which deals with the right to family life). In arguing against the award of £15,000, Lord Steyn noted that the depth of consideration of the issue had been affected in *McFarlane* as it was only raised in oral argument at the hearing before the House of Lords, and continued (at [46]):

...I regard the idea of a conventional award in the present case as contrary to principle. It is a novel procedure for judges to create such a remedy. There are limits to permissible creativity for judges. In my view the majority have strayed into forbidden territory. It is also a backdoor evasion of the legal policy enunciated in *McFarlane*'s case. If such a rule is to be created it must be done by Parliament. The fact is, however, that it would be a hugely controversial legislative measure. It may well be that the Law Commissions and Parliament ought in any event, to consider the impact of the creation of a power to make a conventional award in the cases under consideration for the coherence of the tort system.

See further Lord Hope's speech at [71]–[77] for his arguments against the award.

4.   In *Cattanach v Melchior* (2003) 215 CLR 1, which is noted by P. Cane (2004) 120 LQR 23, and referred to by Lord Bingham in the extract above, the High Court of Australia by a majority took a different view to that adopted in *McFarlane*. However, in *Harriton v Stephens* (2006) 226 CLR 52, any action by the mother for 'wrongful birth' had been lost as a result of the limitation period, but this did not lead the court to allow a 'wrongful life' action. It would be more than an incremental development from a 'wrongful birth' case. See also *Waller v James* (2006) 226 CLR 136. Note further that legislation has affected the position in Australia since the decision in *Cattenach v Melchior*: for references see *Harriton* at [277].

CHAPTER FOUR

PURE ECONOMIC LOSS

The law of tort protects wealth. Wealth is made up of all those things which can be used or exchanged. The 'things' may be tangible, such as land and goods, or they may be intangible such as debts, patents, and copyrights. Wealth may include rights under a contract as well as the expectation of pecuniary advantage from a business transaction or employment relationship, or the capital of a company or the investments in a fund managed by trustees. In a broad sense, all of these are 'economic interests'.

The *kind* of damage recoverable in the tort of negligence is usually said to be limited in the main to those 'economic' losses which are consequent upon some harm to the claimant's person or to his or her property. In the case of personal injury this includes loss of earning capacity and expenses, such as the value of services provided by others to the injured claimant (p. 510, post). Where property is destroyed by the defendant's tort, the normal measure of damages is the value of the property at the time of destruction or, where it is damaged, the cost of repair. There may also be other recoverable losses, such as the loss of profits on property used in the course of a business.

However, there has been reluctance to protect other kinds of economic interest through the mechanism of tort. Proponents of 'rights-based' theories of tort law suggest that the infliction of economic loss in itself does not violate the rights of a claimant: there is no entitlement in ordinary circumstances in a society which is based at least partially on free-market principles to be free from economic loss (see *Stevens*, pp. 20–21). Alternatively, policy grounds have been invoked to explain this concern with over-extending protection for economic loss, in particular the familiar 'floodgates' argument—the fear of 'liability for an indeterminate amount to an indeterminate class' (*Ultramares Corporation v Touche* 174 NE 441 (1931) at 444, per Cardozo J): the concern exists that permitting wide-ranging recovery for economic loss might expose defendants to liability of an uncertain, fluctuating, and uncontainable scope. The reluctance to permit recovery for economic loss has also been justified as necessary to maintain the doctrinal integrity of private law (e.g. the view that negligence law should not circumvent the rule in contract law that third party beneficiaries may not sue on a contract).

The argument has also been made that economic loss is intrinsically less serious than other forms of damage, and therefore there is a less pressing need to permit recovery for this form of loss (see T. Weir, *Tort Law* (OUP, 2002) 42–43). However, above all, the reluctance of the common law to permit economic loss appears to be rooted in the morality of a market economy. It is self-evident that harm caused by free trade and competition should not be actionable in an economy based on competitive markets. But beyond that, it is usually thought to be right for businesses to bear the risk of economic losses not only which they contract to bear but also which they could plausibly have shifted by contract to others.

The common law's prejudice against recovery for economic loss should be seen as a general reluctance to permit such recovery, rather than a hard and fast doctrinal rule. Some commentators even suggest that the inability to recover certain forms of economic loss is best explained by the absence of proximity requirements such as 'directness' in many cases where such loss is present, rather than by the presence or absence of a distinct type of economic loss (e.g. A. Kramer (2003) 11 *TLR* 70 at 84–85 and 90–100). Instead of speaking of a general rule against recovery for pure economic loss, it may be more precise to describe English common law as identifying certain types or 'pockets' of negligently inflicted economic loss, which in ordinary circumstances will not give rise to recovery. Alternatively, the contrary could be argued: Stevens has suggested that the circumstances which give rise to economic loss will usually not involve any infringement of the rights or entitlements of others, and so the 'ocean of non-liability' for economic loss should be seen as broken only by 'isolated islands' of liability (see *Stevens*, p. 21).

Whichever conceptual approach is adopted, cases in the late nineteenth century established that two important forms of economic loss in particular should not be recoverable when caused by negligence. *Cattle v Stockton Waterworks* (1875) LR 10 QB 453, [1874–80] All ER Rep 220 (p. 170, post) decided that there should be no action where the defendant negligently interfered with a pre-existing contract between the claimant and a third party to the disadvantage of the claimant—the 'relational loss' suffered by the claimant as a result of the damage caused to the property of the third party could not be recovered. *Derry v Peek* (1889) 14 App Cas 337, [1886-90] All ER Rep 1 (p. 172, post) decided that there should also be no action where the defendant negligently caused the claimant to enter into a losing contract with a third party, for example by providing the claimant with inaccurate information. Note that in both cases the claimant has entered into a voluntary arrangement with a third party and as a consequence suffers harm. The difference between the cases is that in *Cattle* the claimant has already entered into the relationship when the defendant intervenes, whereas in *Derry* the claimant enters into the losing relationship after (and as a result of) the defendant's intervention.

In both types of case there was existing authority that such losses were in principle recoverable, but the courts were able to distinguish the older cases, such as *Lumley v Gye* (1853) 2 E & B 216, [1843–1860] All ER Rep 208 (p. 891, post) and *Pasley v Freeman* (1789) 3 Term Rep 51, [1775–1802] All ER Rep 31 by saying that the defendant in those cases had harmed the claimant intentionally or recklessly. This distinction between intentionally and negligently caused pure economic loss still exists. The intentional economic torts, the descendants of *Lumley v Gye*, are dealt with below in chap. 15. However, it can be questioned whether the distinction between intentional and negligent pure economic loss makes much inherent sense (see D. Howarth, 'The Future of the Intentional Torts', in *The Classification of Obligations* (Oxford 1997), edited by P. Birks).

The rule in *Derry v Peek* always seemed the less justifiable of the two. The rule in *Cattle v Stockton* flows naturally from the view that those who have contracted to bear certain risks have obtained advantages under that contract in exchange for bearing those risks and should therefore not be allowed to shift the risk to others. It is more difficult to say that a person who has been misled in entering into a new relationship, as in *Derry*, has volunteered to bear the risk. Conceivably those who are experts in a field might be considered to take the risk that the information they use is inaccurate or misleading, because they are also experts in judging the credibility of evidence relevant to their field, but where it is reasonable for the claimant to rely on the information supplied by the defendant, the claimant is not a real volunteer.

Derry also seems weaker than *Cattle* because of the different relationship in the two cases between the claimant and the defendant. In *Derry*, claimant and defendant come together voluntarily and the claimant does something—enters into the contract with the third party—that the defendant would have envisaged at the time of the interaction between them. In *Cattle* there is no voluntary relationship between the parties and the claimant is not doing anything that would have been envisaged or intended by the defendant. In other words there is a 'contractal-style' argument for liability in *Derry* that does not apply to the defendant in *Cattle*, where a reciprocal relationship of reliance and dependence does not exist to the same degree (see D. Harris and C. Veljanovski, 'Liability for Economic Loss in Tort' in *The Law of Tort: Policies and Trends in Liability for Damage to Property and Economic Loss*, edited by M. Furmston (Duckworth, 1986)).

Eventually, in *Hedley Byrne & Co Ltd v Heller & Partners Ltd* [1964] AC 465, [1963] 2 All ER 575 (p. 207, post), the House of Lords removed the earlier restrictions on liability for careless information and advice causing economic loss. But their Lordships were cautious, being unwilling to apply Lord Atkin's 'neighbour' principle (p. 29, ante) to its fullest possible extent. They limited the boundaries of the new duty of care not to cause loss by negligent information or advice in a variety of ways. One restriction was that the claimant should have acted reasonably in relying on the defendant's advice. Another suggestion proposed by Lord Devlin was that the claimant and defendant should have had a relationship 'equivalent to contract', in the sense of a pre-existing general relationship such as banker and customer or solicitor and client or arising out of the specific circumstances of the transaction. Yet another, which began as a way of explaining 'equivalent to contract' but which has now taken on a life of its own, is that the defendant must have 'assumed responsibility' for the claimant's economic welfare.

The interaction of these various restrictions on liability under *Hedley Byrne* has produced a large, intricate but by now well-developed case law. However, the courts have found particular difficulty with cases in which the defendant allegedly produced the misleading information for purposes other than those for which the claimant used it (see *Caparo Industries plc v Dickman* [1990] 2 AC 605, [1990] 1 All ER 568 (p. 224, post) and *Smith v Eric S Bush* [1990] 1 AC 831, [1989] 2 All ER 514 (p. 218, post) and cases in which the claimant is sufficiently expert to be plausibly considered to have come to an independent decision about how to act, even though the information supplied by the defendant was inaccurate (see *South Australia Asset Management Corpn v York Montague* [1997] AC 191, [1996] 3 All ER 365 (p. 271, post)).

The rule in *Cattle v Stockton* has fared better than the rule in *Derry v Peek*. During the early 1980s there was a short period in which it appeared that *Cattle v Stockton* was about to be abrogated. In *Junior Books v Veitchi* [1983] 1 AC 520, [1982] 3 All ER 201, using the freedom to reshape negligence law the House of Lords gave itself in *Anns v Merton London Borough Council* [1978] AC 728, [1977] 2 All ER 492, the Law Lords suddenly allowed a claim against a sub-contractor whose alleged careless work had caused extra expense to a customer of the general contractor. *Junior Books* seemed to contradict some of the most fundamental arguments against pure economic loss. For example, it tended to undermine the third party beneficiary rule in contract law and it allowed recovery by a claimant who could have protected itself against the loss by including appropriate terms in the contract with a third party. The decision in *Anns* seemed itself to be at variance with the *Cattle v Stockton* approach in what it classified as constituting pure economic loss.

Almost at once a reaction set in. *Junior Books* was distinguished and 'confined to its own facts'. (It is sometimes now classified as a special instance where the 'assumption of responsibility' test was satisfied: see the comments of Lord Keith in *Murphy v Brentwood District Council* [1991] 1 AC 398, 466). More significantly, in two landmark cases, *The Mineral Transporter* [1986] AC 1, [1985] 2 All ER 935 and *The Aliakmon* [1986] AC 785, [1986] 2 All ER 145 (p. 176, post), the Law Lords restored the authority of *Cattle v Stockton*. Subsequently, the decision in *Anns* was reversed in the important decision of *Murphy v Brentwood District Council* [1991] 1 AC 398, [1990] 2 All ER 908. These cases confirmed the distinction implicit in *Cattle* between property damage, which is recoverable, and 'pure' economic loss, which is generally not recoverable. Property damage means harm to the possessory or proprietary interests of the claimant. Pure economic loss means harm to non-possessory interests, such as interests under contracts, and includes a reduction in value of property, goods, and chattels due to inherent defects which are 'introduced' before a claimant acquires possessory title.

The *Cattle* principle has reasserted itself in a wide range of cases. The risks of a failed investment, or of a failure to take out insurance, or of not taking adequate precautions to protect one's interests when renegotiating a contract, or of leasing premises, or of buying products which are worth less than one reasonably expected, or of having one's business interrupted by a cut in the electricity supply were all seen as risks inherent in business. More controversially, similar considerations influenced cases in which the claimants were not businesses but were, for example, employees, rugby-playing schoolboys, 'ordinary' house purchasers, and ordinary tenants and consumers.

But the 'assumption of responsibility' approach adopted in *Hedley Byrne* was applied in a series of very important decisions in the 1990s, which have again substantially eroded the scope of the general non-recovery rule laid down in *Cattle*. In *Henderson v Merrett Syndicates Ltd* [1995] 2 AC 145, [1994] 3 All ER 306 (p. 232, post), Lord Goff said that the 'assumption of responsibility' theory of *Hedley Byrne* could produce liability not only in the *Derry v Peek* situation but also where the defendants' negligence affected the profitability of pre-existing contracts between the claimants and third parties. And in *White v Jones* [1995] 2 AC 207, [1995] 1 All ER 691 (p. 243, post), the House of Lords, with Lord Goff again using the 'assumption of responsibility' theory, allowed a claim by the beneficiaries of a will which the defendant firm of solicitors had negligently failed to alter. Here there was no reliance, reasonable or otherwise, acted upon by the claimants[1] and no misleading information causing them to enter into a losing deal. One possible interpretation of *White* is that the defendant firm caused the claimants' pre-existing relationship with a third party, here the testator, to be less lucrative than the claimants expected. To allow recovery in *White* is therefore to grant a remedy to claimants with an even weaker case than that of the claimants in *Cattle*, because the claimants did not have even a contractual interest in their legacies, let alone a possessory or proprietary interest.

The overall picture is therefore complex. However, in recent years, a degree of stability has crept into the case law after the turbulence of the 1980s and 1990s. The assumption of responsibility theory, itself once treated with strong scepticism by the House of Lords (*Smith v Eric S Bush* [1990] 1 AC 831, [1989] 2 All ER 514 (p. 218, post)), appears to have been transformed from a descriptive account of the *Hedley Byrne* exception into a well-established doctrinal test (albeit one with very uncertain and blurred edges) that eats to some extent into the scope of the *Cattle v Stockton* rule. But exactly how one determines whether there has been such an 'objective' assumption of responsibility is still the subject of debate. There also appear to be other circumstances where the *Caparo* three-pronged test, which imposes a duty of care where the damage in question is 'reasonably forseeable', sufficient 'proximity'

---

[1] (1866) LR 1 Exch 265; affd (1868) LR 3 HL 330.

exists between the parties, and it is 'fair, just and reasonable' to do so, will allow recovery for pure economic loss in *Cattle*-style situations, where an analogy can be drawn with existing situations where recovery is permitted. The relationship between the circumstances where the 'assumption of responsibility' test will be deemed to be satisfied and the other circumstances where the *Caparo* test will be applied directly to impose a duty of care in respect of pure economic loss is still uncertain. The judgment of the House of Lords in *Customs and Excise Commissioners v Barclays Bank Plc* [2006] 4 All ER 256, [2006] UKHL 28 (p. 259, post) has gone some way towards clarifying the law. However, the development of doctrine in this area remains a work in progress. (Note that this broad concept of assumption of responsibility seems to have migrated into the spheres of physical loss and property damage: see e.g. *Phelps v London Borough of Hillingdon* [2001] 2 AC 619, [2000] 4 All ER 504, p. 99, ante).

It is therefore important for students to have some idea of the arguments that repeatedly are called upon in different contexts either to oppose the imposition of liability for pure economic loss or to support it. Much of the reasoning offered by courts to justify a refusal to impose liability for economic loss begins and ends with the crude 'floodgates' argument. However, judges have used a wide range of rather more subtle and interesting arguments, including arguments about the nature of valuable information—imposing liability for negligent statements resulting in economic loss may result in a reluctance to share economically useful information, to the detriment of society's interest in a free-flow of such information (see W. Bishop, (1980) 96 LQR 360)—and arguments about incentives—restricting recovery for pure economic loss encourages the use of alternative mechanisms to protect against loss, such as contractual mechanisms, as discussed above. It could be argued that the policy arguments supporting the general rule against recovery for pure economic loss may be less compelling than is often assumed. French law, for example, appears to operate quite happily without any presumption against recovery for pure economic loss. Nevertheless, the common law's prejudice against economic loss, irrespective of the exact nature of its underlying rationale, appears well-established and broadly accepted.

Given the objections that exist to recovery for economic loss, students should ask themselves whether these objections deserve to be overcome by arguments that recovery for pure economic loss should be permitted in circumstances where an 'assumption of responsibility' or some other special relationship exists. At first glance, such arguments are very attractive: they appear to answer the demands of justice by permitting recovery against defendants who behaved in a negligent manner when they knew or should have known that the claimants were relying or depending upon them. Some of the considerations that supposedly militate against recovery for pure economic loss are also apparently less pressing in such cases. For example, it is usually thought that the assumption of responsibility argument meets the 'floodgates' argument by restricting the number of potential claimants to those for whom the defendant assumes responsibility. But there are nevertheless real problems with how the exceptions to the general non-recovery rule are defined. If the existence of an 'assumption of responsibility' is not determined by what went through the defendant's head (i.e. is not defined as existing just when the defendant voluntarily agreed to assume responsibility) but instead is based upon an objective judgment by the court about the appropriateness of liability, then the phrase 'assumption of responsibility' may add nothing to why any particular extent of liability should count as 'too much'. Using the phrase 'assumption of responsibility', or the alternative steps of referring to the existence of 'special relationships' which are 'akin to contract' or based on 'mutuality', may just be a form of verbal shorthand, which may obscure more than it clarifies.

Another important question is whether 'assumption of responsibility' explains the circumstances under which the relational nature of the losses can be ignored. Prima facie, the argument is a good one. If C loses because A has harmed B, with whom C has a relationship, C should be able to sue A if A has 'assumed responsibility' for C's relationship with B. But, yet again, the problem is with how one tells whether A has assumed responsibility, what that may consist of, and in which other circumstances liability for pure economic loss will be imposed under the general *Caparo* test, as discussed above. The exceptions to the non-recovery rules in the context of pure economic loss have proved difficult to define. The area of economic loss remains prone to conceptual uncertainty.

Note Stapleton's argument that the courts should engage in explicit consideration of policy factors in determining when a duty of care should be imposed in respect of pure economic loss, rather than relying upon the application of 'a priori pockets of case law': J. Stapleton, (1991) 107 LQR 249. This predates the recent development of 'assumption of responsibility' analysis, but do Stapleton's arguments for explicit engagement with policy considerations remain valid today? Alternatively, does this involve a premature abandonment of the search for a firm conceptual foundation for the complex and uncertain economic loss case?

1. THE ORIGINS OF THE RULE AGAINST THE RECOVERY OF NEGLIGENTLY CAUSED ECONOMIC LOSS

■ Cattle v Stockton Waterworks Co
Court of Queen's Bench [1874–80] All ER Rep 220

The defendants in this case were a waterworks company, who had laid down and subsequently maintained one of their main pipes along and under a turnpike road. A Mr Knight was owner of the soil on both sides of the turnpike road, at a spot where the natural surface of the ground formed a valley, which the turnpike road crossed on an artificial embankment. Mr Knight wished to have a tunnel under the road to connect both parts of his property and, after obtaining the necessary consent from the relevant public authorities, hired the claimant, Mr Cattle, to dig a tunnel through the road embankment in return for a fixed lump sum. Unknown to any of the parties to the action, one of the defendant's pipes was defective and had leaked water, which had become pooled in the soil of the embankment. When the claimant, Mr Cattle, dug into the embankment, the water build-up obstructed the progress of his work. The defendants were informed of the problem, but for some time neglected to take any action. When the leaking pipe was eventually repaired, Mr Cattle completed the work but had been delayed and put to extra expense, and therefore brought a claim for recovery against the defendants.

BLACKBURN J: . . .
This was an action tried before my Brother Amphlett B., at Leeds, when the plaintiff had a verdict for £26, subject to leave to move to enter a nonsuit. . .

On the argument before my Brothers Mellor and Lush and myself, the plaintiff's counsel contended that, according to the doctrine laid down in *Fletcher v Rylands*,[1] the defendants were under an obligation to keep in the water in their pipes, and therefore that it was not necessary to prove negligence in fact, in the defendants; but that, at all events, negligence was clearly shown from the time they had notice of the mischief in not taking immediate steps to repair it.

The defendants' counsel contended that the doctrine of *Fletcher v Rylands* did not apply to a case like the present, where the defendants were authorised by statute to make and maintain the pipe; and that the damages were assessed on the supposition that the defendants were liable for the damage during the whole time, and consequently, if the plaintiff was entitled to recover only for a part, there should be a new trial to ascertain the quantum. If it were necessary to decide these questions, we should require further time to consider, as we are not as yet quite agreed on the principle of law applicable to such a case. But there is another point on which we are agreed that the rule must be absolute to enter a nonsuit.

Assuming for the present what we purposely leave undecided, that Knight, if himself doing the work, might have maintained an action in his own name for this damage and even assuming that he might, under the circumstances that exist, have maintained the action in his own name, and recovered the amount as trustee for the plaintiff, on the ground that he would have had to bear this loss if the plaintiff had not by his contract indemnified him against it, the question arises can the plaintiff sue in his own name for the loss which he has sustained, in consequence of the damage which the defendants have done to the property of Knight, causing the plaintiff to lose money under his contract? We think he cannot.

In the present case the objection is technical and against the merits, and we should be glad to avoid giving it effect. But if we did so we should establish an authority for saying that in such a case as that of *Fletcher v Rylands*, the defendant would be liable, not only to an action by the owner of the drowned mine, and by such of his workmen as had their tools or clothes destroyed, but also to an action by every workman and person employed in the mine, who in consequence of its stoppage made less wages than he would otherwise have done. Many similar cases to which this would apply might be suggested. It may be said that it is just that all such persons should have compensation for such a loss, and that if the law does not give them redress it is imperfect. Perhaps it may be so. But, as was pointed by COLERIDGE J, in *Lumley v Gye*,[2] courts of justice should not 'allow themselves, in the pursuit of perfectly complete remedies for all wrongful acts, to transgress the bounds which our law, in a wise consciousness, as I conceive, of its limited powers, has imposed on itself, of redressing only the proximate and direct consequences of wrongful acts.' In this we quite agree. No authority in favour of the plaintiff's right to sue was cited, and as far as our knowledge goes, there was none that could have been cited.

The two cases which go further in allowing a right of action to one injured in consequence of a breach of a contract with a third person, or of a breach of duty to a third person, are *Langridge v Levy*[3] and *Lumley v Gye*. In *Langridge v Levy*, the plaintiff was a son whose hand was shattered by the bursting of a gun which had been sold to the father for his (the son's) use with a false and fraudulent representation that it was a safe one. But the court below and the court in error both carefully point out . . . as the ground of their judgment, that:

> 'as there was fraud and damage, the result of that fraud, not from an act remote and consequential, but one contemplated by the defendant at the time as one of its results, the party guilty of the fraud is responsible to the party injured.'[4]

In *Lumley v Gye* the majority of the court held that an action would lie for maliciously procuring a third person to break her contract with the plaintiff. But all three of the judges who gave judgment for the plaintiff relied upon malicious intention. It would be a waste of time to do more than refer to the elaborate judgments in that case for the law and authorities on this branch of the law.

In the present case there is no pretence for saying that the defendants were malicious or had any intention to injure anyone. They were at most guilty of a neglect of duty, which occasioned injury to the property of Knight, but which did not injure any property of the plaintiff. The plaintiff's claim is to recover the damage which he has sustained by his contract with Knight becoming less profitable; or,

---

[2] (1853) 2 E & B 216 at 252; 22 LJ QB 463 at 479.
[3] (1837) 2 M & W 519; affirmed in error, (1838) 4 M & W 337.   [4] 2 M & W at 532; 4 M & W at 338.

it may be a losing contract, in consequence of this injury to Knight's property. We think this does not give him any right of action.

Rule absolute.

QUESTION

Could Mr Knight have sued for damage to his property? What would his loss have been?

NOTES

1. The claimant agreed to do the work 'for a lump sum'. That meant that if he had miscalculated the cost of carrying out the job, he could not go back to Mr Knight to ask for more. He had accepted the risk of increases in cost. Cf. the more complex contractual arrangements in *The Aliakmon* p. 176, post, where the same point applies.
2. Blackburn J cites Coleridge J in *Lumley v Gye*. In that case a claimant successfully sued a defendant who had induced a singer to break her contract with the claimant and to work instead for the defendant (see p. 891, post). Blackburn J does not say, although lawyers reading his judgment at the time would surely have been aware, that Coleridge J dissented in *Lumley v Gye*. Coleridge J considered that the damage in *Lumley* was too remote. The claimant knew that there was a risk that the singer might breach her contract. His proper action lay against her. The contract made him vulnerable precisely to what happened, and it was up to him to make sure that he had sufficient protection both in the contract itself and by making other arrangements.
3. 'Proximity' and 'directness' are important concepts in *Cattle*. Why is the claimant's case not proximate or direct? Note that the claimant's difficulties arise partly out of his own decision to accept a lump sum contract.
4. Blackburn J's remark that deciding for the claimant would mean that workmen in *Fletcher v Rylands* (see p. 828, post) could have sued for lost wages might be taken to suggest a 'floodgates' argument—that there should not be too much liability for the courts or defendants to cope with. But is that what he really means? At the time many workers could be dismissed at a moment's notice and most had no contractual right to be paid if, for whatever reason, there was no work available for them. Does Blackburn J mean instead that it would be surprising for such workers to be in a better position against the defendant than against their own employer? That is, the workmen are the wrong claimants. If they could sue the defendant, they would recover more than they were entitled to expect under the deals they had made with their employer. The right claimant is their employer. The workmen's entitlement depends on their contractual relationship with their employer.

■ Derry v Peek

House of Lords [1886–90] All ER Rep 1

The Plymouth, Devonport and District Tramways Co Ltd was authorised by statute to make certain tramways. The statute provided that the tramways might be moved by animal power and, with the Board of Trade's consent, by steam or mechanical power. The defendants, directors of the company, issued a prospectus containing the following paragraph:

One great feature of this undertaking, to which considerable importance should be attached, is, that by the special Act of Parliament obtained, the company has the right to use steam or mechanical motive power instead of horses, and it is fully expected that by means of this a considerable saving will result in the working expenses of the line, as compared with other tramways worked by horses.

The plaintiff, relying on these representations, obtained shares in the company. The Board of Trade subsequently refused its consent to the use of steam or mechanical power except on certain portions of the tramways. The company was wound up, and the plaintiff brought an action against the appellants claiming damages for fraudulent misrepresentation.

Stirling J dismissed the action. The Court of Appeal, which held that negligence was sufficient to support liability, reversed this decision. The House of Lords reversed the decision of the Court of Appeal.

LORD BRAMWELL:...

I am of opinion that this judgment should be reversed. I am glad to come to this conclusion, for, as far as my judgment goes, it exonerates five men of good character and conduct from a charge of fraud, which, with all submission, I think wholly unfounded—a charge supported on such materials as to make all character precarious...

...I think we need not trouble ourselves about 'legal fraud,' nor whether it is a good or bad expression; because I hold that actual fraud must be proved in this case to make the defendants liable....

[Stirling J at first instance] makes an excellent remark, that:

'mercantile men dealing with matters of business would be the first to cry out if I extended the notion of deceit into what is honestly done in the belief that those things would come about, and when they did not come about, make them liable in an action of fraud.'...

COTTON LJ [in the court below] says...:

'There is a duty cast upon a director who makes that statement to take care that there are no statements in it which in fact are false; to take care that he has reasonable grounds for the material statements which are contained in that document [prospectus], which he intends should be acted on by others. And although in my opinion it is not necessary there should be what I should call fraud, there must be a departure from duty, and he has violated the right which those who received the statements have to have true statements only made to them.'

This seems to be a most formidable matter. I agree there is some such duty. I agree that not only directors in prospectuses, but all persons in all dealings, should tell the truth. If they do not, they furnish evidence of fraud; they subject themselves to have the contract rescinded. But to say that there is 'a right to have true statements only made,' I cannot agree, and I think it would be much to be regretted if there was any such right. Mercantile men, as STIRLING J says, would indeed cry out. No qualification is stated. If this is law, the statement may be reasonably believed to be true by him who makes it, but, if untrue, there is to be a cause of action; and that although he may have refused a warranty. I hope not. There is a duty to tell the truth; but it is a duty of imperfect obligation. It is a duty for non-observance of which the law gives no remedy if there is no fraud....

I think, with all respect, that in all the judgments there is, I must say it, a confusion of unreasonableness of belief as evidence of dishonesty, and unreasonableness of belief as of itself a ground of action....I think it is most undesirable that actions should be maintainable in respect of statements, made unreasonably perhaps, but honestly. I think it would be disastrous if there was 'a right to have true statements only made.' This case is an example. I think that in this kind of case, as in some others, courts of equity have made the mistake of disregarding a valuable general principle in the desire to effect what is, or is thought to be, justice in a particular instance. It might, perhaps, be desirable to enact that in prospectuses of public companies there should be a warranty of the truth of all statements except where it was expressly said there was no warranty. The objection is to exceptional legislation, and to the danger of driving respectable and responsible men from being promoters, and of substituting for them those who are neither. In this particular case I hold that, unless fraud in the defendants could be shown, the action is not maintainable....

LORD HERSCHELL:...

'To make a statement careless whether it be true or false, and, therefore, without any real belief in its truth, appears to me to be an essentially different thing from making, through want of care, a false statement which is nevertheless honestly believed to be true. And it is surely conceivable that a man may believe that what he states is the fact, though he has been so wanting in care that the court may think that there were no sufficient grounds to warrant his belief.

I shall have to consider hereafter whether the want of reasonable ground for believing the statement made is sufficient to support an action of deceit. I am only concerned for the moment to point out that it does not follow that it is so because there is authority for saying that a statement made recklessly, without caring whether it be true or false, affords sufficient foundation for such an action....

...I think those who put before the public a prospectus to induce them to embark their money in a commercial enterprise ought to be vigilant to see that it contains such representations only as are in strict accordance with fact, and I should be very unwilling to give any countenance to the contrary idea. I think there is much to be said for the view that this moral duty ought to some extent to be converted into a legal obligation, and that the want of reasonable care to see that statements, made under such circumstances, are true should be made an actionable wrong. But this is not a matter fit for discussion on the present occasion. If it is to be done, the legislature must intervene....It ought not, I think, to be done by straining the law, and holding that to be fraudulent which the tribunal feels cannot properly be so described. I think mischief is likely to result from blurring the distinction between carelessness and fraud, and equally holding a man fraudulent whether his acts can or cannot be justly so designated....

[LORD HALSBURY LC, LORD WATSON, and LORD FITZGERALD delivered speeches in favour of allowing the appeal.]

QUESTION

Would it be fair to say that Lords Bramwell and Herschell decide for the defendants because they both think that accusations of 'fraud' and 'deceit' should be confined to defendants who deserve to lose their reputations for honesty? Does this case necessarily rule out suing such defendants for 'negligence'?

NOTES

1. Parliament agreed more with Lord Herschell than with Lord Bramwell about the desirability of liability for careless statements in prospectuses. As a result of this decision, the Directors Liability Act 1890 imposed certain statutory obligations on persons issuing a prospectus. These are now contained in Part VI of and Schedule 9 to the Financial Services and Markets Act 2000, and the Prospectus Regulations 2005, which implemented the EU Prospectus Directive (2003/71/EC).

2. For the development of the tort of deceit see p. 939, post: the decision by the House of Lords in *Derry v Peek* marks the point at which deceit became recognised as a distinct tort, separate from other forms of liability for economic loss.

3. The law with regard to misrepresentation and the rescission of contracts has changed dramatically since *Derry v Peek*. The Misrepresentation Act 1967 ended the strict separation between representations that become contractual promises ('warranties')

enforceable in contract law and those which did not. It also allowed a remedy in damages when there is no breach of contract and no fraud where the court decides that it would be equitable to award damages instead of rescinding the contract.

■ The Misrepresentation Act 1967

2. Damages for misrepresentation—(1) Where a person has entered into a contract after a misrepresentation has been made to him by another party thereto and as a result thereof he has suffered loss, then, if the person making the misrepresentation would be liable to damages in respect thereof had the misrepresentation been made fraudulently, that person shall be so liable notwithstanding that the misrepresentation was not made fraudulently, unless he proves that he had reasonable ground to believe and did believe up to the time the contract was made that the facts represented were true.

(2) Where a person has entered into a contract after a misrepresentation has been made to him otherwise than fraudulently, and he would be entitled, by reason of the misrepresentation, to rescind the contract, if it is claimed, in any proceedings arising out of the contract, that the contract ought to be or has been rescinded the court or arbitrator may declare the contract subsisting and award damages in lieu of rescission, if of opinion that it would be equitable to do so, having regard to the nature of the misrepresentation and the loss that would be caused by it if the contract were upheld, as well as to the loss that rescission would cause to the other party.

(3) Damages may be awarded against a person under subsection (2) of this section whether or not he is liable to damages under subsection (1) thereof, but where he is so liable any award under the said subsection (2) shall be taken into account in assessing his liability under the said subsection (1).

NOTE

Section 2(1) of the Misrepresentation Act 1967 creates a statutory tort which extends the tort of deceit. It enables a party who was induced by the defendant to enter into a contract with him by means of a false representation to recover damages for resulting loss without proving fraud. It is more favourable to the representee than the common law action for careless statements (p. 207, post) because (a) there is no need to prove a 'special relationship' or 'assumption of responsibility' such as to justify the imposition of a duty of care; and (b) the burden of proof on the representor to show that he had reasonable grounds to believe the facts represented to be true is not easily discharged: *Howard Marine and Dredging Co Ltd v A Ogden & Sons (Excavations) Ltd* [1978] QB 574 at 592–593, 596 and 601 (during negotiations for hire of barges, the owner's representative honestly misstated their deadweight capacity in reliance on wrong information in Lloyd's register; the correct figure was available in shipping documents in the owner's possession: held burden not discharged). However, where the representation was made by someone not a party to the subsequent contract, the representee will have to rely on the tort of negligence. On the sort of misrepresentation which is within s. 2(1) of the 1967 Act, see *Banque Keyser Ullmann SA v Skandia (UK) Insurance Co Ltd* [1990] 1 QB 665 at 790, when that case was in the Court of Appeal.

2 WHAT IS PURE ECONOMIC LOSS?

Cattle v Stockton and *Derry v Peek* have been interpreted as establishing the existence of a general prejudice against recovery for negligently inflicted pure economic loss in the common law. (Although, as discussed above, it remains a contested point as to whether such a general presumption of non-recovery exists, as distinct from a series of specific 'pockets' where recovery for economic loss is precluded or limited to special circumstances.) In contrast, economic loss such as loss of earnings, medical costs, and so on that flow from, or are consequential upon, negligently inflicted damage to property or to the person are recoverable. Distinguishing between what constitutes pure economic loss and what is consequential economic loss may be difficult. There are many forms of pure economic loss that are instantly recognisable as such: loss of profit from financial transactions, loss of benefit from testators, depreciation of the value of assets, and so on. However, there are other forms of loss that are not so instantly identifiable as pure economic loss, as they are linked to forms of physical damage. Disentangling what constitutes pure economic loss in such circumstances can present the courts with tricky conceptual challenges.

■ Leigh and Sillavan Ltd v Aliakmon Shipping Co Ltd, The Aliakmon
House of Lords [1986] 2 All ER 145

In this case, the appellant buyers agreed to buy from Kinsho-Mataichi Corp (the sellers) a quantity of steel coils (the goods) to be shipped from Korea to Immingham on 'cost & freight terms' ('c & f terms'—a then-standard form of shipping contract). The price of the goods was to be paid by a 180-day bill of exchange to be indorsed by the buyers' bank in return for a bill of lading relating to the goods: in other words, the sellers on tendering the bill of lading for the goods would receive payment via the appellant buyers' bank. The buyers intended to finance the transaction by making a contract for the resale of the goods to sub-buyers before the bill of lading was tendered by the sellers. The buyers later found themselves unable to make the contract for the resale of the goods which they had intended to make. As a result, the buyers and the sellers agreed to vary the terms of the contract. As interpreted by the Court of Appeal, this meant that the sellers, despite delivery of the bill of lading to the buyers, retained the right to dispose of the goods covered by this bill, i.e. the sellers retained a possessory title over the godds until they were paid by the buyers. While the buyers were to present the bill of lading to the ship at Immingham and take delivery of the goods there, they were to only do so as agents for the sellers, and the goods were to be stored in a covered warehouse to the sole order of the sellers. On arrival of the ship at Immingham the buyers duly carried out the terms of the revised contract of sale. However, on arrival, the goods were found to be in a damaged condition. Staughton J at first instance found that a substantial part of this damage had been caused by improper stowage of the goods by the agents of the respondent shipping company.

If the buyers had completed the c & f contract in the manner intended, they would have been entitled to sue the shipowners for the damage to the goods in contract under the bill of lading, and no question of any separate duty of care in tort would have arisen. Under the varied contract, however, the risk of damage had already passed to the buyers on shipment not because of the original c & f terms, but because, owing to the sellers' reservation of the right of disposal of the goods in the revised contract, the property in the goods did not pass to the buyers at the required time to allow them to bring a contractual action against the respondent shipping company under the hill of lading. As a result, the appellant buyers attempted to establish a separate claim against the shipowners founded in the tort of negligence, but were ultimately unsuccessful in the House of Lords.

LORD BRANDON OF OAKBROOK: ...
My Lords, this appeal arises in an action in the Commercial Court in which the appellants, who were the c & f buyers of goods carried in the respondents' ship, the Aliakmon, claim damages against the latter for damage done to such goods at a time when the risk, but not yet the

legal property in them, had passed to the appellants. The main question to be determined is whether, in the circumstances just stated, the respondents (the shipowners) owed a duty of care in tort to the appellants (the buyers) in respect of the carriage of such goods; and, if so, whether and to what extent such duty was qualified by the terms of the bill of lading under which the goods were carried.

The buyers' claim was put forward originally in both contract and tort. Staughton J at first instance gave judgment for the buyers on their claim in contract, so making it unnecessary for him to reach a decision on their further claim in tort (see [1983] 1 Lloyd's Rep 203). However, on appeal by the shipowners to the Court of Appeal (Sir John Donaldson MR, Oliver and Robert Goff LJJ), that court set aside the judgment of Staughton J and dismissed the buyers' claims in both contract and tort (see [1985] 2 All ER 44, [1985] QB 350). Sir John Donaldson MR and Oliver LJ rejected the claim in tort on the ground that the shipowners did not at the material time owe any duty of care to the buyers. Robert Goff LJ rejected the claim in tort on the ground that, although the shipowners owed a duty of care to the buyers, they had not, on the facts, committed any breach of that duty...

My Lords, there is a long line of authority for a principle of law that, in order to enable a person to claim in negligence for loss caused to him by reason of loss of or damage to property, he must have had either the legal ownership of or a possessory title to the property concerned at the time when the loss or damage occurred, and it is not enough for him to have only had contractual rights in relation to such property which have been adversely affected by the loss of or damage to it...

[His Lordship then considered each of the five grounds on which counsel for the buyers relied. First, he held that the fact that a buyer under a cif or c & f contract was the prospective legal owner of the goods was not a material distinction from the other non-recovery cases in which the plaintiffs were not persons who had contracted to buy the property. Secondly, he held that even if an equitable property in the goods could be created or passed under the contract of sale (of which he was 'extremely doubt-ful'), an equitable owner not in possession has no right to sue without joining the legal owner as a party to the action. Thirdly, he decided that there was nothing in what Lord Wilberforce said in *Anns v Merton London Borough Council* [1978] AC 728 at 751–752 about the role of policy in negativing a prima facie duty of care, which would compel a departure from the line of authorities against recovery, and went on to say:]

...Counsel for the buyers said, rightly in my view, that the policy reason for excluding a duty of care in cases like [*Candlewood Navigation Corpn Ltd v Mitsui OSK Lines Ltd*] *The Mineral Transporter* [[1986] AC 1, [1985] 2 All ER 935] and what I earlier called the other non-recovery cases was to avoid the open-ing of the floodgates so as to expose a person guilty of want of care to unlimited liability to an indefinite number of other persons whose contractual rights have been adversely affected by such want of care. Counsel for the buyers went on to argue that recognition by the law of a duty of care owed by ship-owners to a cif or c & f buyer, to whom the risk, but not yet the property in the goods carried in such shipowners' ship has passed, would not of itself open any floodgates of the kind described. It would, he said, only create a strictly limited exception to the general rule, based on the circumstance that the considerations of policy on which that general rule was founded did not apply to that particular case. I do not accept that argument. If an exception to the general rule were to be made in the field of car-riage by sea, it would no doubt have to be extended to the field of carriage by land, and I do not think that it is possible to say that no undue increase in the scope of a person's liability for want of care would follow. In any event, where a general rule, which is simple to understand and easy to apply, has been established by a long line of authority over many years, I do not think that the law should allow special pleading in a particular case within the general rule to detract from its application. If such detraction were to be permitted in one particular case, it would lead to attempts to have it permitted in a variety of other particular cases, and the result would be that the certainty, which the application of the gen-eral rule presently provides, would be seriously undermined. Yet certainty of the law is of the utmost importance, especially but by no means only, in commercial matters. I therefore think that the general rule, reaffirmed as it has been so recently by the Privy Council in *The Mineral Transporter*, ought to apply to a case like the present one, and that there is nothing in what Lord Wilberforce said in the *Anns* case which would compel a different conclusion...

Ground 4: the requirements of a rational system of law

My Lords, under this head counsel for the buyers submitted that any rational system of law ought to provide a remedy for persons who suffered the kind of loss which the buyers suffered in the present case, with the clear implication that, if your Lordships' House were to hold that the remedy for which he contended was not available, it would be lending its authority to an irrational feature of English law. I do not agree with this submission for, as I shall endeavour to show, English law does, in all normal cases, provide a fair and adequate remedy for loss of or damage to goods the subject matter of a cif or c & f contract, and the buyers in this case could easily, if properly advised at the time when they agreed to the variation of the original c & f contract, have secured to themselves the benefit of such a remedy.

As I indicated earlier, under the usual cif or c & f contract the bill of lading issued in respect of the goods is indorsed and delivered by the seller to the buyer against payment by the buyer of the price. When that happens, the property in the goods passes from the sellers to the buyers on or by reason of such indorsement, and the buyer is entitled, by virtue of s 1 of the Bills of Lading Act 1855, to sue the shipowner for loss of or damage to the goods on the contract contained in the bill of lading. The remedy so available to the buyer is adequate and fair to both parties, and there is no need for any parallel or alternative remedy in tort for negligence. In the present case, as I also indicated earlier, the variation of the original c & f contract agreed between the sellers and the buyers produced a hybrid contract of an extremely unusual character. It was extremely unusual in that what had originally been an ordinary c & f contract became, in effect, a sale ex warehouse at Immingham, but the risk in the goods during their carriage by sea remained with the buyers as if the sale had still been on a c & f basis. In this situation the persons who had a right to sue the shipowners for loss of or damage to the goods on the contract contained in the bill of lading were the sellers, and the buyers, if properly advised, should have made it a further term of the variation that the sellers should either exercise this right for their account (see *The Albazero* [1976] 3 All ER 129, [1977] AC 774) or assign such right to them to exercise for themselves. If either of these two precautions had been taken, the law would have provided the buyers with a fair and adequate remedy for their loss.

These considerations show, in my opinion, not that there is some lacuna in English law relating to these matters, but only that the buyers, when they agreed to the variation of the original contract of sale, did not take the steps to protect themselves which, if properly advised, they should have done. To put the matter quite simply the buyers, by the variation to which they agreed, were depriving themselves of the right of suit under s 1 of the Bills of Lading Act 1855 which they would otherwise have had, and commercial good sense required that they should obtain the benefit of an equivalent right in one or other of the two different ways which I have suggested.

Ground 5: the judgment of Robert Goff LJ

My Lords, after a full examination of numerous authorities relating to the law of negligence Goff LJ said[5] ([1985] 2 All ER 44 at 77, [1985] QB 350 at 399):

> 'In my judgment, there is no good reason in principle or in policy, why the c & f buyer should not have...a direct cause of action. The factors which I have already listed point strongly towards liability. I am particularly influenced by the fact that the loss in question is of a character which will ordinarily fall on the goods' owner, who will have a good claim against the shipowner, but in a case such as the present the loss may, in practical terms, fall on the buyer. It seems to me that the policy reasons pointing towards a direct right of action by the buyer against the shipowner in a case of this kind outweigh the policy reasons which generally preclude recovery for purely economic loss. There is here no question of any wide or indeterminate liability being imposed on wrongdoers; on the contrary, the shipowner is simply held liable to the buyer in damages for loss for which he would ordinarily be liable to the goods' owner. There is a recognised principle underlying the imposition of liability, which can be called 'the principle of transferred loss'. Furthermore, that principle can be formulated. For the purposes of the present case, I would formulate it in the following deliberately

---

[5] In the Court of Appeal in this case.

narrow terms, while recognising that it may require modification in the light of experience. Where A owes a duty of care in tort not to cause physical damage to B's property, and commits a breach of that duty in circumstances in which the loss of or physical damage to the property will ordinarily fall on B but (as is reasonably foreseeable by A) such loss or damage, by reason of a contractual relationship between B and C, falls on C, then C will be entitled, subject to the terms of any contract restricting A's liability to B, to bring an action in tort against A in respect of such loss or damage to the extent that it falls on him, C. To that proposition there must be exceptions. In particular, there must, for the reasons I have given, be an exception in the case of contracts of insurance. I have also attempted so to draw the principle as to exclude the case of the time charterer who remains liable for hire for the chartered ship while under repair following collision damage, though this could if necessary be treated as another exception having regard to the present state of the authorities.'

With the greatest possible respect to Robert Goff LJ, the principle of transferred loss which he there enunciated, however useful in dealing with special factual situations it may be in theory, is not only not supported by authority, but is on the contrary inconsistent with it. Even if it were necessary to introduce such a principle in order to fill a genuine lacuna in the law, I should myself, perhaps because I am more faint hearted than Robert Goff LJ, be reluctant to do so. As I have tried to show earlier, however, there is in truth no such lacuna in the law which requires to be filled. Neither Sir John Donaldson MR nor Oliver LJ was prepared to accept the introduction of such a principle and I find myself entirely in agreement with their unwillingness to do so . . .

[LORD KEITH OF KINKEL, LORD BRIGHTMAN, LORD GRIFFITHS, and LORD ACKNER all agreed that the appeal should be dismissed for the reasons given by LORD BRANDON OF OAKBROOK.]

Appeal dismissed.

QUESTION

Why was this a case of pure economic loss? Notice that the damage was physical (rust and crushing). But who owned (or, to be more accurate, had a possessory interest in) the steel coils when they were damaged?

NOTES

1. Note the reference to the argument of Goff LJ in the Court of Appeal that the loss was recoverable on the basis of a principle of 'transferred loss', which was rejected by the House of Lords. What would the result of *Cattle v Stockton Waterworks* have been if Goff LJ's principle of 'transferred loss' had been the law? Is it important at all for the court in *Cattle* whether the existence of the contract between Knight and Cattle was 'foreseeable'? Lord Goff, as he later became, responded to Lord Brandon's rejection of his transferred loss doctrine in *White v Jones* [1995] 1 All ER 691 at 705–707:

   I wish next to refer to another German doctrine known as *Drittschadens-liquidation*, which is available in cases of transferred loss (*Schadensverlagerung*). In these cases, as a leading English comparatist has explained:

   " . . . the person who has suffered the loss has no remedy while the person who has the remedy has suffered no loss. If such a situation is left unchallenged, the defaulting party may never face the consequences of his negligent conduct; his insurer may receive an unexpected (and undeserved) windfall; and the person on whom the loss has fallen may be left without any redress." (See Markesinis, *The German Law of Torts : A Comparative Introduction* (1994, 3rd edn) p 56.)

Under this doctrine, to take one example, the defendant, A, typically a carrier, may be held liable to the seller of goods, B, for the loss suffered by the buyer, C, to whom the risk but not the property in the goods has passed. In such circumstances the seller is held to have a contractual claim against the carrier in respect of the damage suffered by the buyer. This claim can be pursued by the seller against the carrier; but it can also be assigned by him to the buyer. If, exceptionally, the seller refuses either to exercise his right for the benefit of the buyer or to assign his claim to him, the seller can be compelled to make the assignment (see Professor Lorenz in *Essays in Memory of Professor F H Lawson* (1986) pp 86, 89–90), Markesinis (ed) in *The Gradual Convergence* (1994) pp 65, 88–89, 92–93 and Professor Hein Kötz in (1990) 10 Tel Aviv Univ Studies in Law 195 at 209). Professor Lorenz (*Essays* p 89) has stated that it is at least arguable that the idea of *Drittschadensliquidation* might be 'extended so as to cover' such cases as the *Testamentfall* case, an observation which is consistent with the view expressed by the German Supreme Court that the two doctrines may overlap (see BGH 19 January 1977, NJW 1977, 2073 = VersR 1977, 638, translated in Markesinis, *German Law of Torts* p. 293). At all events both doctrines have the effect of extending to the plaintiff the benefit of what is, in substance, a contractual cause of action; though, at least as seen through English eyes, this result is achieved not by orthodox contractual reasoning, but by the contractual remedy being made available by law in order to achieve practical justice.

Transferred loss in English law

I can deal with this topic briefly. The problem of transferred loss has arisen in particular in maritime law, when a buyer of goods seeks to enforce against a shipowner a remedy in tort in respect of loss of or damage to goods at his risk when neither the rights under the contract nor the property in the goods has passed to him (see *Leigh & Sillavan Ltd v Aliakmon Shipping Co Ltd, The Aliakmon* [1985] 2 All ER 44 at 77, [1985] QB 350 at 399 per Robert Goff LJ and [1986] 2 All ER 145 at 157, [1986] AC 785 at 820 per Lord Brandon). In cases such as these (with all respect to the view expressed by Lord Brandon [1986] 2 All ER 145 at 156, [1986] AC 785 at 819) there was a serious lacuna in the law, as was revealed when all relevant interests in the City of London called for reform to make a remedy available to the buyers who under the existing law were without a direct remedy against the shipowners. The problem was solved, as a matter of urgency, by the Carriage of Goods by Sea Act 1992, I myself having the honour of introducing the Bill into your Lordships' House (acting in its legislative capacity) on behalf of the Law Commission. The solution adopted by the Act was to extend the rights of suit available under s 1 of the Bills of Lading Act 1855 (there restricted to cases where the property in the goods had passed upon or by reason of the consignment or endorsement of the relevant bill of lading) to all holders of bills of lading (and indeed other documents): see s 2(1) of the 1992 Act. Here is a sweeping statutory reform, powered by the needs of commerce, which has the effect of enlarging the circumstances in which contractual rights may be transferred by virtue of the transfer of certain documents. For present purposes, however, an important consequence is the solution in this context of a problem of transferred loss, the lacuna being filled by statute rather than by the common law.

As Lord Goff appears to concede in the last sentence of the extract, the common law in the wake of the decision of the House of Lords in *The Aliakmon* does not appear to contain a principle of transferred loss: hence the need for the specific amending legislation to which he refers. German law contains a general rule against recovery for pure economic loss, but has adopted broad concepts of privity of contract and third party recovery to circumvent some of the constraints of this general non-recovery rule. However, English common law has been slow to draw upon German doctrine to extend the scope of recovery for economic loss. We will return to this theme later in this chapter: however, for criticism of this reluctance to make use of comparative material, see *Markesinis and Deakin*, 166–167.

2. Note that the Canadian Supreme Court was prepared to adopt a form of 'trans-ferred loss' analysis within a tort framework in *National Railway Steamship Co Ltd v Norsk Pacific* (1992) 91 DLR (4th) 289): see in particular the interesting judgment of McLachlin J, as well as the dissenting opinion of La Forest J.

3. Goff LJ said in *The Aliakmon* that the reason the law generally refuses to allow recovery for negligently caused pure economic loss is the fear of opening up 'wide or indeter-minate liability'. Lord Brandon also took a similar view. But the loss in *Cattle* was said to be too remote, even though it was very unlikely that very many people other than Knight would be affected by the defendant's carelessness. Is the fear of wide or indeter-minate liability (the 'floodgates' argument) the driving force behind *Cattle*? Concerns about permitting recovery in situations where there is a lack of proximity or 'direct-ness' between the economic loss suffered and the acts of a defendant may be a greater motivating force behind the common law's reluctance to permit recovery for pure eco-nomic loss than the oft-quoted fear of 'indeterminate liability'.

4. Goff LJ also remarked in *The Aliakmon* in the Court of Appeal [1985] 2 All ER 44 at 73 that 'the philosophy of the market place presumes that it is lawful to gain profit by causing others economic loss'. But can a single rigid rule which bars all recovery by non-owners in all circumstances achieve the multiple economic objectives that the law is sometimes required to meet, e.g. (a) deterrence, i.e. making potential defendants (in this case the shipowners) act more carefully and thereby reduce the total cost of acci-dents; (b) optimal risk allocation, i.e. imposing liability on the party best able to avoid or minimise the loss and to insure against the risk of loss; and (c) control of default by the potentially negligent party, i.e. imposing liability on the party with the great-est incentive to monitor the relevant conduct? Might not a better approach be to treat the 'philosophy of the market place' point primarily as going to the question of breach rather than to the question of duty? (See *Howarth*, pp. 309–310).

5. The arrangements in *The Aliakmon* were negotiated by the parties. In the Court of Appeal, Sir John Donaldson MR made the following analysis ([1985] 2 All ER at p. 53):

> The relationship between buyer and seller on the one hand and cargo-owner and shipowner on the other are quite distinct. In each case the parties seek to establish an economic balance, but there is no reason why it should be the same balance. The buyer may well be able to obtain the goods more cheaply if he undertakes not to hold the seller liable if the goods are lost or dam-aged after shipment and before they are delivered to him and to pay the price in any event. The shipowner may well charge a lower freight if, in return, he is to enjoy the protection of exceptions and limitations on his liability. Indeed he may be unwilling to accept the goods for carriage at all, if to do so will involve him in assuming any more extended duty of care or more extended liability for breach of that duty.

This reflects the *Cattle v Stockton Waterworks* view that where the parties have vol-untarily negotiated the terms of their relationship on the basis of a clear legal rule which bars the non-owner from recovery, it must be presumed that as far as they are concerned this represents what is in their mutual interests: see generally, Harris and Veljanovski, op cit., pp. 45–57. But was the non-recovery rule really so clear to the par-ties in *The Aliakmon*? Is it realistic to presume that parties intended their contractual arrangements to govern all the forms of loss that might result from the relationship? Is it realistic for the common law to prefer that parties allocate risks and liability for pure economic loss via contract in *Cattle v Stockton*-style circumstances in general, and to operate on the presumption that this has occurred?

6.   P has a right over some property that will disappear if D fails to give notice to subsequent purchasers of the land. P has no contract with D and D has never owned the land. D negligently fails to give the necessary notice and P's property right disappears. Is this property damage? Even if there is no physical damage to property as such, some of P's property rights have, in a sense, been destroyed. Or is it damage to the equivalent of a contractual right to obtain property, as in *The Aliakmon*, in which case it will constitute pure economic loss and therefore be non-recoverable? See *Ministry of Housing and Local Government v Sharp* [1970] 2 QB 223, [1970] 1 All ER 1009, where a clerk in a local land registry carelessly stated that a particular land interest was free of charges: the land was subsequently sold without notice of the existence of a charge in favour of the claimant, who was therefore deprived of its benefit. The Court of Appeal appeared to assume that this loss constituted pure economic loss, before moving on to find that liability could nevertheless attach to the defendants in the circumstances on the basis that the 'neighbour' principle cited by Lord Atkin in *Donoghue v Stevenson* (see p. 30, ante) was satisfied. However, it could be argued that the loss in question was damage to tangible property rights and not just to a contractual right to obtain a benefit.

7.   The decision in *The Aliakmon* confirmed the well-established common law rule that, in the words of Lord Brandon, 'in order to enable a person to claim in negligence for loss caused to him by reason of loss of or damage to property, he must have had either the legal ownership of or a possessory title to the property concerned at the time when the loss or damage occurred, and it is not enough for him to have only had contractual rights in relation to such property which have been adversely affected by the loss of or damage to it…'. This means, as occurred in *The Aliakmon*, that if a person purchases or obtains property or goods which have been previously damaged before they acquired the possessory interest, any reduction in the value or quality of this property caused by this damage will constitute pure economic loss from the perspective of tort law.

8.   This has important implications. For example, if a manufacturer negligently puts into circulation a chattel which contains a defect, damage to persons or property caused by this chattel may be recoverable: see *Donoghue v Sevenson* [1932] AC 562 (p. 30, ante). However, the cost of repairing or replacing the defective chattel itself will not be ordinarily recoverable, because the defect to the chattel constitutes a reduction in its value or quality, and therefore is classified as pure economic loss: see *Murphy v Brentwood District Council* [1991] 1 AC 398, [1990] 2 All ER 908 (p. 183, post). Just as the steel coils in *The Aliakmon* were damaged and rendered defective prior to coming into the possession of the claimant in that case, so too are defects 'built into' a product prior to its circulation classified as damage caused before a possessory interest was acquired by a potential claimant: when these defective goods are subsequently acquired, their loss in value is classed as pure economic loss, whereas any 'external' loss they cause to persons or property is not.

9.   However, drawing the line between pure economic loss caused by inherent defects in property or goods and 'external' loss caused by defective property or goods to persons or other property may at times be difficult. (See for further comprehensive discussion of this, p. 183, post.) It certainly has caused considerable problems for the English courts in deciding whether defects in dwellings constitute pure economic loss or property damage. For some time, it had been assumed that if a builder built a house with a hidden defect which was discovered only after the house had been sold on from the original purchaser of the property from the builder, so that the house turned out to be worth much less than the second or subsequent purchasers paid for it, the loss was

not purely economic if the defect could potentially pose some danger to the health or safety of occupants. In *Anns v Merton Borough Council* [1978] AC 728, [1977] 2 All ER 492, Lord Wilberforce had characterised such damage as 'material physical damage' to the property: consequently, recovery was possible for repair costs incurred as a result of defective foundations causing cracking in the walls of houses. Doubt was subsequently cast on this classification in *D & F Estates Ltd v Church Commissioners for England* [1989] AC 177, [1988] 2 All ER 992, where the House of Lords accepted that loss incurred as a result of defects in structures should be treated as pure economic loss, in line with the conventional approach in common law. As a result, defective plastering work was classified as unrecoverable pure economic loss.

10. In *D&F*, Lord Bridge suggested that the decision in *Anns* could be explained on the basis that, in 'complex structures' such as dwellings, if a defect in one part of the structure caused damage to another part of the structure, that damage could be classified as 'external' property damage. However, in *Murphy v Brentwood District Council* [1991] 1 AC 398, [1990] 2 All ER 908, the House of Lords put paid to such theories, with the seven-member panel overruling the earlier decision in *Anns*. Lord Keith of Kinkel said bluntly ([1990] 2 All ER at p. 919): 'In my opinion it must now be recognised that, although the damage in *Anns* was characterised as physical damage by Lord Wilberforce, it was purely economic loss.' Lord Bridge also abandoned his 'complex structure' analysis, on the basis that the different parts of a dwelling were so interdependent that any defect in part of a structure was a defect in the whole, and therefore counted as pure economic loss. See also the decision of the Court of Appeal in *Warner v Basildon Development Corpn* (1990) 6 Const LJ 146, and the discussion at p. 194, post.

11. Even if the defect in a dwelling could be characterised as 'damage' to the building, the claimant had no property interest in the building at the time the defect was introduced. Claimants had succeeded before *Murphy* because it was thought that the problem could be glossed over by saying that the claimant had a property interest at the time the defect was discovered (or became reasonably discoverable): this assumption seemed to underlie the decision in *Anns*. But the essential point is that the claimant's loss arises, as in *Cattle v Stockton Waterworks* and *The Aliakmon*, because of the terms of the contract between the claimant and a third party, in this case the intermediate seller of the house. As is customary in house sales, the buyer accepted the risk of hidden defects not specifically mentioned in the contract of sale. The risk was therefore transferred to the second buyer of the property, who could not bring an action for 'damage' caused before the possessory interest was acquired in the property.

■ Murphy v Brentwood District Council
House of Lords [1991] 2 All ER 908

In 1970 the plaintiff purchased one of a pair of newly built semi-detached houses from a construction company. The houses were built over filled ground on concrete raft foundations. The design had been submitted to the defendant council for approval under building regulations. The council had sought the advice of independent consulting engineers, who recommended the approval of the plans. In 1981 serious cracks appeared and it was discovered that as a result of defective design the concrete raft had cracked and become distorted so causing differential settlement and cracks in some walls and the fracturing of a gas pipe and soil pipe. The plaintiff sold the house subject to defects for £35,000 less than its value in sound condition. He brought an action against the council claiming damages on the grounds that they were liable for the consultant engineer's negligence.

The trial judge (1988) 13 Con LR 96, found that the council's consultant engineers had been negligent in approving the design, and that there was an imminent danger to the health and safety of the occupants of the house. He awarded damages of £38,777, being the loss on the sale of the house and expenses.

The Court of Appeal, [1990] 2 All ER 269, upheld this judgment on the basis of the decision of the House of Lords in *Anns v Merton London Borough Council* [1978] AC 728, [1977] 2 All ER 492 and held that the council owed a duty of care to the plaintiff to see that the house was properly built so as to avoid injury to the safety and health of those who lived in it. The Court of Appeal decided that the council were in breach of this duty in approving the plans for a defective raft foundation.

The council appealed to the House of Lords, who allowed the appeal.

LORD KEITH OF KINKEL: . . .

Before your Lordships' House it was argued on behalf of the council that *Anns* was wrongly decided and should be departed from under the practice statement of 26 July 1966 (see *Note* [1966] 3 All ER 77, [1966] 1 WLR 1234). The speeches of Lord Bridge and Lord Oliver in *D & F Estates Ltd v Church Comrs for England* [1988] 2 All ER 992, [1989] AC 177 contain some passages expressing doubts as to the extent to which the decision in *Anns* is capable of being reconciled with pre-existing principle. It is therefore appropriate to subject the decision to careful reconsideration.

As is well known, it was held in *Anns* that a local authority might be liable in negligence to long lessees occupying maisonettes built on inadequate foundations not complying with relevant building regulations, on the ground of failure by the authority to discover by inspection the inadequacy of the foundations before they were covered over. The proceedings arose out of the trial of a preliminary issue whether or not the plaintiffs had any cause of action against the local authority, and the damages claimed by them were not specified in the pleadings. It appeared, however, that such damages would include the cost of repairing cracks in the structure and of underpinning the foundations of the block of maisonettes . . .

In *Anns* the House of Lords approved, subject to explanation, the decision of the Court of Appeal in *Dutton v Bognor Regis United Building Co Ltd* [1972] 1 All ER 462, [1972] 1 QB 373. In that case Lord Denning MR said ([1972] 1 All ER 462 at 474, [1972] 1 QB 373 at 396):

> 'Counsel for the Council submitted that the liability of the council would, in any case, be limited to those who suffered bodily harm; and did not extend to those who only suffered economic loss. He suggested, therefore, that although the council might be liable if the ceiling fell down and injured a visitor, they would not be liable simply because the house was diminished in value . . . I cannot accept this submission. The damage done here was not solely economic loss. It was physical damage to the house. If counsel's submission were right, it would mean that, if the inspector negligently passes the house as properly built and it collapses and injures a person, the council are liable; but, if the owner discovers the defect in time to repair it—and he does repair it—the council are not liable. That is an impossible distinction. They are liable in either case. I would say the same about the manufacturer of an article. If he makes it negligently, with a latent defect (so that it breaks to pieces and injures someone), he is undoubtedly liable. Suppose that the defect is discovered in time to prevent the injury. Surely he is liable for the cost of repair.'

The jump which is here made from liability under the *Donoghue v Stevenson* principle for damage to person or property caused by a latent defect in a carelessly manufactured article to liability for the cost of rectifying a defect in such an article which is *ex hypothesi* no longer latent is difficult to accept. As Stamp LJ recognised in the same case, there is no liability in tort on a manufacturer towards the purchaser from a retailer of an article which turns out to be useless or valueless through defects due to careless manufacture (see [1972] 1 All ER 426 at 489–490 [1972] 1 QB 373 at 414–415). The loss is economic. It is difficult to draw a distinction in principle between an article which is useless or valueless and one which suffers from a defect which would render it dangerous in use but which is discovered by the purchaser in time to avert any possibility of injury. The purchaser may incur expense in putting right the defect, or, more probably, discard the article. In either case the loss is purely economic. Stamp LJ appears to have taken the view that in the case of a house the builder would not be liable to a purchaser where the defect was discovered in time to prevent injury but that a local authority which had failed to discover the defect by careful inspection during the course of construction was so liable…

Consideration of the nature of the loss suffered in this category of cases is closely tied up with the question of when the cause of action arises. Lord Wilberforce in *Anns v Merton London Borough* [1977] 2 All ER 492 at 505, [1978] AC 728 at 760 regarded it as arising when the state of the building is such that there is present an imminent danger to the health or safety of persons occupying it. That state of affairs may exist when there is no actual physical damage to the building itself, though Lord Wilberforce had earlier referred to the relevant damage being material physical damage. So his meaning may have been that there must be a concurrence of material physical damage and also present or imminent danger to the health or safety of occupants. On that view there would be no cause of action where the building had suffered no damage (or possibly, having regard to the word 'material', only very slight damage) but a structural survey had revealed an underlying defect, presenting imminent danger. Such a discovery would inevitably cause a fall in the value of the building, resulting in economic loss to the owner. That such is the nature of the loss is made clear in cases where the owner abandons the building as incapable of being put in a safe condition (as in *Butty*'s case) or where he chooses to sell it at the lower value rather than undertake remedial works. In *Pirelli General Cable Works Ltd v Oscar Faber & Partners (a firm)* [1983] 1 All ER 65, [1983] 2 AC 1 it was held that the cause of action in tort against consulting engineers who had negligently approved a defective design for a chimney arose when damage to the chimney caused by the defective design first occurred, not when the damage was discovered or with reasonable diligence might have been discovered. The defendants there had in relation to the design been in contractual relations with the plaintiffs, but it was common ground that a claim in contract was time-barred. If the plaintiffs had happened to discover the defect before any damage had occurred there would seem to be no good reason for holding that they would not have had a cause of action in tort at that stage, without having to wait until some damage had occurred. They would have suffered economic loss through having a defective chimney on which they required to expend money for the purpose of removing the defect. It would seem that in a case such as the *Pirelli General Cable Works* case, where the tortious liability arose out of a contractual relationship with professional people, the duty extended to take reasonable care not to cause economic loss to the client by the advice given. The plaintiffs built the chimney as they did in reliance on that advice. The case would accordingly fall within the principle of *Hedley Byrne & Co Ltd v Heller & Partners Ltd* [1963] 2 All ER 575, [1964] AC 465. I regard *Junior Books Ltd v Veitchi Co Ltd* [1982] 3 All ER 201, [1983] 1 AC 520 as being an application of that principle.

In my opinion it must now be recognised that, although the damage in *Anns* was characterised as physical damage by Lord Wilberforce, it was purely economic loss. ..[LORD KEITH then proceeded to set out the similar approach adopted in the judgment of Deane J in the decision of the High Court of Australia in *Sutherland Shire Council v Heyman* (1985) 60 ALR 1, with which he expressed himself to be in complete agreement. His Lordship continued:]

It being recognised that the nature of the loss held to be recoverable in *Anns* was pure economic loss, the next point for examination is whether the avoidance of loss of that nature fell within the scope of any duty of care owed to the plaintiffs by the local authority. On the basis of the law as it stood at the time of the decision the answer to that question must be in the negative. The right to recover for pure economic loss, not flowing from physical injury, did not then extend beyond the situation where the loss had been sustained through reliance on negligence misstatements, as in *Hedley Byrne*…

The existence of a duty of that nature should not, in my opinion, be affirmed without a careful examination of the implications of such affirmation. To start with, if such a duty is incumbent on the local authority, a similar duty must necessarily be incumbent also on the builder of the house. If the builder of the house is to be so subject, there can be no grounds in logic or in principle for not extending liability on like grounds to the manufacturer of a chattel. That would open on an exceedingly wide field of claims, involving the introduction of something in the nature of a transmissible warranty of quality. The purchaser of an article who discovered that it suffered from a dangerous defect before that defect had caused any damage would be entitled to recover from the manufacturer the cost of rectifying the defect, and, presumably, if the article was not capable of economic repair, the amount of loss sustained through discarding it. Then it would be open to question whether there should not also be a right to recovery where the defect renders the article not dangerous but merely useless. The economic loss in either case would be the same. There would also be a problem where the defect causes the destruction of the article itself, without causing any personal injury or damage to other property. A similar problem could arise, if the *Anns* principle is to be treated as confined to real property, where a building collapses when unoccupied....

In *D & F Estates Ltd v Church Comrs for England* [1988] 2 All ER 992, [1989] AC 177 both Lord Bridge and Lord Oliver expressed themselves as having difficulty in reconciling the decision in *Anns* with pre-existing principle and as being uncertain as to the nature and scope of such new principle as it introduced. Lord Bridge suggested that in the case of a complex structure such as a building one element of the structure might be regarded for *Donoghue v Stevenson* purposes as distinct from another element, so that damage to one part of the structure caused by a hidden defect in another part might qualify to be treated as damage to 'other property' (see [1988] 2 All ER 992 at 1006, [1989] AC 177 at 206). I think that it would be unrealistic to take this view as regards a building the whole of which had been erected and equipped by the same contractor. In that situation the whole package provided by the contractor would, in my opinion, fall to be regarded as one unit rendered unsound as such by a defect in the particular part. On the other hand, where, for example, the electric wiring had been installed by a sub-contractor and due to a defect caused by lack of care a fire occurred which destroyed the building, it might not be stretching ordinary principles too far to hold the electrical sub-contractor liable for the damage....But, even if Lord Bridge's theory were to be held acceptable, it would not seem to extend to the founding of liability on a local authority, considering that the purposes of the 1936 Act are concerned with averting danger to health and safety, not danger or damage to property. Further, it would not cover the situation which might arise through discovery, before any damage had occurred, of a defect likely to give rise to damage in the future.

Liability under the *Anns* decision is postulated on the existence of as present or imminent danger to health or safety. But, considering that the loss involved in incurring expenditure to avert the danger is pure economic loss, there would seem to be no logic in confining the remedy to cases where such danger exists. There is likewise no logic confining it to cases where some damage (perhaps comparatively slight) has been caused to the building, but refusing it where the existence of the danger has come to light in some other way, for example through a structural survey which happens to have been carried out, or where the danger inherent in some particular component or material has been revealed through failure in some other building. Then there is the question whether the remedy is available where the defect is rectified, not in order to avert danger to an inhabitant occupier himself, but in order to enable an occupier, who may be a corporation, to continue to occupy the building through its employees without putting those employees at risk.

In my opinion it is clear that *Anns* did not proceed on any basis of established principle, but introduced a new species of liability governed by a principle indeterminate in character but having the potentiality of covering a wide range of situations, involving chattels as well as real property, in which it had never hitherto been thought that the law of negligence had any proper place...

In my opinion there can be no doubt that *Anns* has for long been widely regarded as an unsatisfactory decision. In relation to the scope of the duty owed by a local authority it proceeded on what must, with due respect to its source, be regarded as a somewhat superficial examination of principle and there has been extreme difficulty, highlighted most recently by the speeches in the *D & F Estates* case, in ascertaining on exactly what basis of principle it did proceed. I think it must now be recognised that it did not proceed on any basis of principle at all, but constituted a remarkable example of judicial legislation. It has engendered a vast spate of litigation, and each of the cases in the field which have reached this House has been distinguished. Others have been distinguished in the Court of Appeal. The result has been to keep the effect of the decision within reasonable bounds, but that has been achieved only by applying strictly the words of Lord Wilberforce and by refusing to accept the logical implications of the decision itself. These logical implications show that the case properly considered has potentiality for collision with long-established principles regarding liability in the tort of negligence for economic loss. There can be no doubt that to depart from the decision would re-establish a degree of certainty in this field of law which it has done a remarkable amount to upset...

It must, of course, be kept in mind that the decision has stood for some 13 years. On the other hand, it is not a decision of the type that is to a significant extent taken into account by citizens or indeed local authorities in ordering their affairs. No doubt its existence results in local authorities having to pay increased insurance premiums, but to be relieved of that necessity would be to their advantage, not to their detriment. To overrule it is unlikely to result in significantly increased insurance premiums for householders. It is perhaps of some significance that most litigation involving the decision consists in contests between insurance companies, as is largely the position in the present case. The decision is capable of being regarded as affording a measure of justice, but as against that the impossibility of finding any coherent and logically based doctrine behind it is calculated to put the law of negligence into a state of confusion defying rational analysis. It is also material that *Anns* has the effect of imposing on builders generally a liability going far beyond that which Parliament thought fit to impose on house builders alone by the Defective Premises Act 1972, a statute very material to the policy of the decision but not adverted to in it. There is much to be said for the view that in what is essentially a consumer protection field, as was observed by Lord Bridge in *D & F Estates Ltd v Church Comrs for England* [1988] 2 All ER 992 at 1007, [1989] AC 177 at 207, the precise extent and limits of the liabilities which in the public interest should be imposed on builders and local authorities are best left to the legislature.

My Lords, I would hold that *Anns* was wrongly decided as regards the scope of any private law duty of care resting on local authorities in relation to their function of taking steps to secure compliance with building byelaws or regulations and should be departed from. It follows that *Dutton v Bognor Regis United Building Co Ltd* [1972] 1 All ER 462, [1972] 1 QB 373 should be overruled, as should all cases subsequent to *Anns* which were decided in reliance on it...

LORD BRIDGE OF HARWICH:...
My Lords, the speech of my noble and learned friend Lord Keith addresses comprehensively all the issues on which the outcome of this appeal depends. I find myself in full agreement with it...

Dangerous defects and defects of quality
If a manufacturer negligently puts into circulation a chattel containing a latent defect which renders it dangerous to persons or property, the manufacturer, on the well-known principles established by *Donoghue v Stevenson* [1932] AC 562, [1932] All ER Rep, will be liable in tort for injury to persons or damage to property which the chattel causes. But if a manufacturer produces and sells a chattel which is merely defective in quality, even to the extent that it is valueless for the purpose for which it is intended, the manufacturer's liability at common law arises only under and by reference to the terms of any contract to which he is a party in relation to the chattel; the common law does not impose on him any liability in tort to persons to whom he owes no duty in contract but who, having acquired the chattel, suffer economic loss because the chattel is defective in quality. If a dangerous defect in a chattel is discovered before it causes any personal injury or damage to property, because the danger is now known and the chattel cannot be safely used unless the defect is repaired, the defect becomes merely a defect in quality. The chattel is either capable of repair at economic cost or it is worthless and must be scrapped. In either case the loss sustained by the owner or hirer of the chattel is purely economic. It is recoverable against any party who owes the loser a relevant contractual duty. But it is not recoverable

in tort in the absence of a special relationship of proximity imposing on the tortfeasor a duty of care to safeguard the plaintiff from economic loss. There is no such special relationship between the manufacturer of a chattel and a remote owner or hirer.

I believe that these principles are equally applicable to buildings. If a builder erects a structure containing a latent defect which renders it dangerous to persons or property, he will be liable in tort for injury to persons or damage to property resulting from the dangerous defect. But, if the defect becomes apparent before any injury or damage has been caused, the loss sustained by the building owner is purely economic. If the defect can be repaired at economic cost, that is the measure of the loss. If the building cannot be repaired, it may have to be abandoned as unfit for occupation and therefore valueless. These economic losses are recoverable if they flow from breach of a relevant contractual duty, but, here again, in the absence of a special relationship of proximity they are not recoverable in tort. The only qualification I would make to this is that, if a building stands so close to the boundary of the building owner's land that after discovery of the dangerous defect it remains a potential source of injury to persons or property on neighbouring land or on the highway, the building owner ought, in principle, to be entitled to recover in tort from the negligent builder the cost of obviating the danger, whether by repair or by demolition, so far as that cost is necessarily incurred in order to protect himself from potential liability to third parties. . . .

The complex structure theory
In my speech in the *D & F Estates* case [1988] 2 All ER 992 at 1006–1007, [1989] AC 177 at 206–207 I mooted the possibility that in complex structures or complex chattels one part of a structure or chattel might, when it caused damage to another part of the same structure or chattel, be regarded in the law of tort as having caused damage to 'other property' for the purpose of the application of *Donoghue v Stevenson* principles. I expressed no opinion as to the validity of this theory, but put it forward for consideration as a possible ground on which the facts considered in *Anns* might be distinguishable from the facts which had to be considered in *D & F Estates* itself. I shall call this for convenience 'the complex structure theory' and it is, so far as I can see, only if and to the extent that this theory can be affirmed and applied that there can be any escape from the conclusions I have indicated above under the rubric 'Dangerous defects and defects of quality'.

The complex structure theory has, so far as I know, never been subjected to express and detailed examination in any English authority. . . .

. . . The reality is that the structural elements in any building form a single indivisible unit of which the different parts are essentially interdependent. To the extent that there is any defect in one part of the structure it must to a greater or lesser degree necessarily affect all other parts of the structure. Therefore any defect in the structure is a defect in the quality of the whole and it is quite artificial, in order to impose a legal liability which the law would not otherwise impose, to treat a defect in an integral structure, so far as it weakens the structure, as a dangerous defect liable to cause damage to 'other property'.

A critical distinction must be drawn here between some part of a complex structure which is said to be a 'danger' only because it does not perform its proper function in sustaining the other parts and some distinct item incorporated in the structure which positively malfunctions so as to inflict positive damage on the structure in which it is incorporated. Thus, if a defective central heating boiler explodes and damages a house or a defective electrical installation malfunctions and sets the house on fire, I see no reason to doubt that the owner of the house, if he can prove that the damage was due to the negligence of the boiler manufacturer in the one case or the electrical contractor in the other, can recover damages in tort on *Donoghue v Stevenson* principles. But the position in law is entirely different where, by reason of the inadequacy of the foundations of the building to support the weight of the superstructure, differential settlement and consequent cracking occurs. Here, once the first cracks appear, the structure as a whole is seen to be defective and the nature of the defect is known. Even if, contrary to my view, the initial damage could be regarded as damage to other property caused by a latent defect, once the defect is known the situation of the building owner is analogous to that of the car owner who discovers that the car has faulty brakes.[6] He may have a house which, until repairs are effected, is unfit for habitation, but, subject to the reservation I have expressed with respect to ruinous buildings at or near the boundary of the owner's property, the building no longer represents a source of danger and as it deteriorates will only damage itself.

For these reasons the complex structure theory offers no escape from the conclusion that damage to a house itself which is attributable to a defect in the structure of the house is not recoverable in tort on *Donoghue v Stevenson* principles, but represents purely economic loss which is only recoverable in contract or in tort by reason of some special relationship of proximity which imposes on the tortfeasor a duty of care to protect against economic loss.

The relative positions of the builder and the local authority

I have so far been considering the potential liability of a builder for negligent defects in the structure of a building to persons to whom he owes no contractual duty. Since the relevant statutory function of the local authority is directed to no other purpose than securing compliance with building byelaws or regulations by the builder, I agree with the view expressed in *Anns* and by the majority of the Court of Appeal in *Dutton*[7] that a negligent performance of that function can attract no greater liability than attaches to the negligence of the builder whose fault was the primary tort giving rise to any relevant damage. I am content for present purposes to assume, though I am by no means satisfied that the assumption is correct, that where the local authority, as in this case or in *Dutton*, has in fact approved the defective plans or inspected the defective foundations and negligently failed to discover the defect, its potential liability in tort is coextensive with that of the builder...

Imminent danger to health or safety

A necessary element in the building owner's cause of action against the negligent local authority, which does not appear to have been contemplated in *Dutton* but which, it is said in *Anns*, must be present before the cause of action accrues, is that the state of the building is such that there is present or imminent danger to the health or safety of persons occupying it. Correspondingly the damages recoverable are said to include the amount of expenditure necessary to restore the building to a condition in which it is no longer such a danger, but presumably not any further expenditure incurred in any merely qualitative restoration. I find these features of the *Anns* doctrine very difficult to understand. The theoretical difficulty of reconciling this aspect of the doctrine with previously accepted legal principle was pointed out by Lord Oliver in *D & F Estates* [1988] 2 All ER 992 at 1011, [1989] AC 177 at 212–213. But apart from this there are, as it appears to me, two insuperable difficulties arising from the requirement of imminent danger to health or safety as an ingredient of the cause of action which lead to quite irrational and capricious consequences in the application of the *Anns* doctrine. The first difficulty will arise where the relevant defect in the building, when it is first discovered, is not a present or imminent danger to health or safety. What is the owner to do if he is advised that the building will gradually deteriorate, if not repaired, and will in due course become a danger to health and safety, but that the longer he waits to effect repairs the greater the cost will be? Must he spend £1,000 now on the necessary repairs with no redress against the local authority? Or is he entitled to wait until the building has so far deteriorated that he has a cause of action and then to recover from the local authority the £5,000 which the necessary repairs are now going to cost? I can find no answer to this conundrum. A second difficulty will arise where the latent defect is not discovered until it causes the sudden and total collapse of the building, which occurs when the building is temporarily unoccupied and causes no damage to property except to the building itself. The building is now no longer capable of occupation and hence cannot be a danger

---

6 Lord Bridge had earlier stated ([1990] 2 All ER at p. 927):
   'If I buy a secondhand car and find it to be faulty, it can make no difference to the manufacturer's liability in tort whether the fault is in the brakes or in the engine, ie whether the car will not stop or will not start. In either case the car is useless until repaired. The manufacturer is no more liable in tort for the cost of the repairs in the one case than in the other.'

7 *Dutton v Bognor Regis Urban District Council* [1972] 1 QB 373, [1972] 1 All ER 462.

to health and safety. It seems a very strange result that the building owner should be without remedy in this situation if he would have been able to recover from the local authority the full cost of repairing the building if only the defect had been discovered before the building fell down.

Liability for economic loss

All these considerations lead inevitably to the conclusion that a building owner can only recover the cost of repairing a defective building on the ground of the authority's negligence in performing its statutory function of approving plans or inspecting buildings in the course of construction if the scope of the authority's duty of care is wide enough to embrace purely economic loss. The House has already held in *D & F Estates* that a builder, in the absence of any contractual duty or of a special relationship of proximity introducing the *Hedley Byrne* principle of reliance, owes no duty of care in tort in respect of the quality of his work. As I pointed out in *D & F Estates*, to hold that the builder owed such a duty of care to any person acquiring an interest in the product of the builder's work would be to impose on him the obligations of an indefinitely transmissible warranty of quality.

By s. 1 of the Defective Premises Act 1972 Parliament has in fact imposed on builders and others undertaking work in the provision of dwellings the obligation of a transmissible warranty of the quality of their work and of the fitness for habitation of the completed dwelling. But, besides being limited to dwellings, liability under that Act is subject to a limitation period of six years from the completion of the work and to the exclusion provided for by s. 2. It would be remarkable to find that similar obligations in the nature of a transmissible warranty of quality, applicable to buildings of every kind and subject to no such limitations or exclusions as are imposed by the 1972 Act, could be derived from the builder's common law duty of care or from the duty imposed by building byelaws or regulations. In *Anns* Lord Wilberforce expressed the opinion that a builder could be held liable for a breach of statutory duty in respect of buildings which do not comply with the byelaws. But he cannot, I think, have meant that the statutory obligation to build in conformity with the byelaws by itself gives rise to obligations in the nature of transmissible warranties of quality. If he did mean that, I must respectfully disagree. I find it impossible to suppose that anything less than clear express language such as is used in s. 1 of the 1972 Act would suffice to impose such a statutory obligation.

As I have already said, since the function of a local authority in approving plans or inspecting buildings in the course of construction is directed to ensuring that the builder complies with building byelaws or regulations, I cannot see how, in principle, the scope of the liability of the authority for a negligent failure to ensure compliance can exceed that of the liability of the builder for his negligent failure to comply.

There may, of course, be situations where, even in the absence of contract, there is a special relationship of proximity between builder and building owner which is sufficiently akin to contract to introduce the element of reliance so that the scope of the duty of care owed by the builder to the owner is wide enough to embrace purely economic loss. The decision in *Junior Books Ltd v Veitchi Co Ltd* [1982] 3 All ER 201, [1983] 1 AC 520 can, I believe, only be understood on this basis.

In *Sutherland Shire Council v Heyman* (1985) 60 ALR 1 the critical role of the reliance principle as an element in the cause of action which the plaintiff sought to establish is the subject of close examination, particularly in the judgment of Mason J. The central theme of his judgment, and a subordinate theme in the judgments of Brennan and Deane JJ, who together with Mason J formed the majority rejecting the *Anns* doctrine, is that a duty of care of a scope sufficient to make authority liable for damage of the kind suffered can only be based on the principle of reliance and that there is nothing in the ordinary relationship of a local authority, as statutory supervisor of building operations, and the purchaser of a defective building capable of giving rise to such a duty. I agree with these judgments. It cannot, I think, be suggested, nor do I understand *Anns*...to be in fact suggesting, that the approval of plans or the inspection of a building in the course of construction by the local authority in performance of their statutory function and a subsequent purchase of the building by the plaintiff are circumstances in themselves sufficient to introduce the principle of reliance which is the foundation of a duty of care of the kind identified in *Hedley Byrne*.

In *Dutton* [1972] 1 All ER 462 at 475, [1972] 1 QB 373 at 397–398 Lord Denning MR said:

'...Mrs Dutton has suffered a grievous loss. The house fell down without any fault of hers. She is in no position herself to bear the loss. Who ought in justice to bear it? I should think those who were responsible. Who are they? In the first place, the builder was responsible. It was he who laid the foundations so badly that the house fell down. In the second place, the council's inspector was responsible. It was his job to examine the foundations to see if they would take the load of the house. He failed to do it properly. In the third place, the council should answer for his failure. They were entrusted by Parliament with the task of seeing that houses were properly built. They received public funds for the purpose. The very object was to protect purchasers and occupiers of houses. Yet, they failed to protect them. Their shoulders are broad enough to bear the loss.'

These may be cogent reasons of social policy for imposing liability on the authority. But the shoulders of a public authority are only 'broad enough to bear the loss' because they are financed by the public at large. It is pre-eminently for the legislature to decide whether these policy reasons should be accepted as sufficient for imposing on the public the burden of providing compensation for private financial losses. If they do so decide, it is not difficult for them to say so...

LORD OLIVER OF AYLMERTON:...
My Lords, I have had the advantage of reading in draft the speeches prepared by my noble and learned friends Lord Keith and Lord Bridge. For the reasons which they have given I too would allow this appeal...

...[D]espite the categorisation of the damage as 'material, physical damage' (see *Anns* [1977] 2 All ER 492 at 595, [1978] AC 728 at 759 per Lord Wilberforce), it is, I think, incontestable on analysis that what the plaintiffs suffered was pure pecuniary loss and nothing more. If one asks, 'What were the damages to be awarded *for*?' clearly they were not to be awarded for injury to the health or person of the plaintiffs, for they had suffered none. But equally clearly, although the 'damage' was described, both in the Court of Appeal in *Dutton* and in this House in *Anns*, as physical or material damage, this simply does not withstand analysis. To begin with, it makes no sort of sense to accord a remedy where the defective nature of the structure has manifested itself by some physical symptom, such as a crack or a fractured pipe, but to deny it where the defect has been brought to light by, for instance, a structural survey in connection with a proposed sale. Moreover, the imminent danger to health or safety which was said to be the essential ground of the action was not the result of the physical manifestations which had appeared but of the inherently defective nature of the structure which they revealed. They were merely the outward signs of a deterioration resulting from the inherently defective condition with which the building had been brought into being from its inception and cannot properly be described as damage caused to the building in any accepted use of the word 'damage'.

In the speech of Lord Bridge and in my own speech in *D & F Estates Ltd v Church Comrs for England* [1988] 2 All ER 992, [1989] AC 177 there was canvassed what has been called 'the complex structure theory'. This has been rightly criticised by academic writers, although I confess that I thought that both Lord Bridge and I had made it clear that it was a theory which was not embraced with any enthusiasm but was advanced as the only logically possible explanation of the categorisation of the damage in *Anns* as 'material, physical damage'. Lord Bridge has, in the course of his speech in the present case, amply demonstrated the artificiality of the theory and, for the reasons which he has given, it must be rejected as a viable explanation of the underlying basis for the decision in *Anns*. However that decision is analysed, therefore, it is in the end inescapable that the only damage for which compensation was to be awarded and which formed the essential foundation of the action was pecuniary loss and nothing more. The injury which the plaintiff suffers in such a case is that his consciousness of the possible injury to his own health or safety or that of others puts him in a position in which, in order to enable him either to go on living in the property or to exploit its financial potentiality without that risk, whether substantial or insubstantial, he has to expend money in making good the defects which have now become patent....

It does not, of course, at all follow as a matter of necessity from the mere fact that the only damage suffered by a plaintiff in an action for the tort of negligence is pecuniary or 'economic' that his claim is bound to fail. . . .

The critical question, as was pointed out in the analysis of Brennan J in his judgment in *Sutherland Shire Council v Heyman* (1985) 60 ALR 1, is not the nature of the damage in itself, whether physical or pecuniary, but whether the scope of the duty of care in the circumstances of the case is such as to embrace damage of the kind which the plaintiff claims to have sustained (see *Caparo Industries plc v Dickman* [1990] 1 All ER 568, [1990] 2 WLR 358). The essential question which has to be asked in every case, given that damage which is the essential ingredient of the action has occurred, is whether the relationship between the plaintiff and the defendant is such, or, to use the favoured expression, whether it is of sufficient 'proximity', that it imposes on the latter a duty to take care to avoid or prevent that loss which has in fact been sustained. . . .

[Having referred to the need to place some limits on the extent of liability for foreseeable pure economic loss, LORD OLIVER continued:] I frankly doubt whether, in searching for such limits, the categorisation of the damage as 'material', 'physical', 'pecuniary' or 'economic' provides a particularly useful contribution. Where it does, I think, serve a useful purpose is in identifying those cases in which it is necessary to search for and find something more than the mere reasonably foreseeability of damage which has occurred as providing the degree of 'proximity' necessary to support the action . . . The infliction of physical injury to the person or property of another universally requires to be justified. The causing of economic loss does not. If it is to be categorised as wrongful it is necessary to find some factor beyond the mere occurrence of the loss and the fact that its occurrence could be foreseen. Thus the categorisation of damage as economic serves at least the useful purpose of indicating that something more is required and it is one of the unfortunate features of *Anns* that it resulted initially in this essential distinction being lost sight of.

. . . [Proximity] is an expression which persistently defies definition, but my difficulty in rationalising the basis of *Dutton* and *Anns* is and has always been not so much in defining it as in discerning the circumstances from which it could have been derived. For reasons which I have endeavoured to explain, the starting-point in seeking to rationalise these decisions must, as it seems to me, be to establish the basis of the liability of the person who is the direct and immediate cause of the plaintiff's loss. Anyone, whether he be a professional builder or a do-it-yourself enthusiast, who builds or alters a semi-permanent structure must be taken to contemplate that at some time in the future it will, whether by purchase, gift or inheritance, come to be occupied by another person and that if it is defectively built or altered it may fall down and injure that person or his property or may put him in a position in which, if he wishes to occupy it safely or comfortably, he will have to expend money on rectifying the defect. The case of physical injury to the owner or his licensees or to his or their property presents no difficulty. He who was responsible for the defect (and it will be convenient to refer to him compendiously as 'the builder') is, by the reasonable foreseeability of that injury, in a proximate 'neighbour' relationship with the injured person on ordinary *Donoghue v Stevenson* principles. But, when no such injury has occurred and when the defect has been discovered and is therefore no longer latent, whence arises that relationship of proximity required to fix him with responsibility for putting right the defect? Foresight alone is not enough, but from what else can the relationship be derived? Apart from contract, the manufacturer of a chattel assumes no responsibility to a third party into whose hands it has come for the cost of putting it into a state in which it can safely continue to be used for the purpose for which it was intended. *Anns*, of course, does not go so far as to hold the builder liable for every latent defect which depreciates the value of the property but limits the recovery, and thus the duty, to the cost of putting it into a state in which it is no longer an imminent threat to the health or safety of the occupant. But it is difficult to see any logical basis for such a distinction. If there is no relationship of proximity such as to create a duty to avoid pecuniary loss resulting from the plaintiff's perception of non-dangerous defects, on what principle can such a duty arise at the moment when the defect is perceived to be an imminent danger to health? Take the case of an owner-occupier who has inherited the property from a derivative purchaser. He suffers, in fact, no 'loss' save that the property for which he paid nothing is less valuable to him by the amount which it will cost him to repair it if he wishes to continue to live in it. If one assumes the parallel case of one who has come into possession of a defective chattel, for instance a yacht, which may be a danger if it is used without being repaired, it is impossible to see on what principle such a person, simply because the chattel has become dangerous, could recover the cost of repair from the original manufacturer. . . .

My Lords, for the reasons which I endeavoured to state in the course of my speech in *D & F Estates Ltd v Church Comrs for England* [1988] 2 All ER 992, [1989] AC 177 and which are expounded in more felicitous terms both in the speeches of my noble and learned friends in the instant case and in that of Lord Keith in *Dept of the Environment v Thomas Bates & Son Ltd* [1990] 2 All ER 943, I have found it impossible to reconcile the liability of the builder propounded in *Anns* with any previously accepted principles of the tort of negligence and I am able to see no circumstances from which there can be deduced a relationship of proximity such as to render the builder liable in tort for pure pecuniary damage sustained by a derivative owner with whom he has no contractual or other relationship. Whether, as suggested in the speech of my noble and learned friend Lord Bridge, he could be held responsible for the cost necessarily incurred by a building owner in protecting himself from potential liability to third parties is a question on which I prefer to reserve my opinion until the case arises, although I am not at the moment convinced of the basis for making such a distinction . . .

For the reasons which I have endeavoured to express I do not think that *Anns* can be regarded as consistent with [the] general principles [of the English law of civil wrongs]. Nor do I think that it can properly be left to stand as a peculiar doctrine applicable simply to defective buildings, for I do not think that its logical consequences can be contained within so confined a compass. It may be said that to hold local authorities liable in damages for failure effectively to perform their regulatory functions serves a useful social purpose by providing what is, in effect, an insurance fund from which those who are unfortunate enough to have acquired defective premises can recover part at least of the expense to which they have been put or the loss of value which they have sustained. One cannot but have sympathy with such a view, although I am not sure that I see why the burden should fall on the community at large rather than be left to be covered by private insurance. But, in any event, like my noble and learned friends, I think that the achievement of beneficial social purposes by the creation of entirely new liabilities is a matter which properly falls within the province of the legislature and within that province alone. At the date when *Anns* was decided the Defective Premises Act 1972, enacted after a most careful consideration by the Law Commission, had shown clearly the limits within which Parliament had thought it right to superimpose additional liabilities on those previously existing at common law and it is one of the curious features of the case that no mention even of the existence of this important measure, let alone of its provisions, and in particular the provision regarding the accrual of the cause of action, appears in any of the speeches or in the reported summary in the Law Reports of the argument of counsel.

There may be very sound social and political reasons for imposing on local authorities the burden of acting, in effect, as insurers that buildings erected in their areas have been properly constructed in accordance with the relevant building regulations. Statute may so provide. It has not done so and I do not, for my part, think that it is right for the courts not simply to expand existing principles but to create at large new principles in order to fulfil a social need in an area of consumer protection which has already been perceived by the legislature but for which, presumably advisedly, it has not thought it necessary to provide.

LORD JAUNCEY OF TULLICHETTLE: . . .

My Lords, I agree with the views of my noble and learned friend Lord Bridge in this appeal that to apply the complex structure theory to a house so that each part of the entire structure is treated as a separate piece of property is quite unrealistic. A builder who builds a house from foundations upwards is creating a single integrated unit of which the individual components are interdependent. To treat the foundations as a piece of property separate from the walls or the floors is a wholly artificial exercise. If the foundations are inadequate the whole house is affected. Furthermore, if the complex structure theory is tenable there is no reason in principle why it should not also be applied to chattels consisting of integrated parts such as a ship or a piece of machinery. The consequence of such an application would be far reaching. It seems to me that the only context for the complex structure theory in the case of a building would be where one integral component of the structure was built by a separate contractor and where a defect in such a component had caused damage to other parts of the structure, e.g. a steel frame erected by a specialist contractor which failed to give adequate support to floors or walls. Defects in such ancillary equipment as central heating boilers or electrical installations would be subject to the normal *Donoghue v Stevenson* principle if such defects gave rise to damage to other parts of the building....

Appeal Allowed.

NOTES

1. In *Murphy*, after determining that the loss in question was best classified as pure economic loss, the House of Lords proceeded to hold that no exception to the general rule of non-recovery in cases of pure economic loss should be recognised where a local authority had failed to ensure that a builder had constructed a dwelling in accordance with local bye-laws. In a case heard together with *Murphy, Department of the Environment v Thomas Bates and Son Ltd* [1991] 1 AC 499, [1990] 2 All ER 943, the House of Lords also held that a builder owned no duty to subsequent buyers in respect of the pure economic loss sustained as a result of defects in dwellings. (For further discussion, see p. 597, post.)

2. Lord Oliver in his decision in *Murphy* expressed particular concern about the lack of proximity between those responsible for the original defects and subsequent buyers of the dwellings affected, and also about the potential for indeterminate liability for an indefinite duration to be imposed upon builders and local authorities. He noted that 'it does not at all follow as a matter of necessity from the mere fact that the only damage suffered by a claimant in an action for the tort of negligence is pecuniary or "economic" that his claim is bound to fail'. However, Lord Oliver concluded that these concerns were sufficient to justify the application of the general presumption that 'something more' was required than mere forseeability for liability to attach in cases of pure economic loss. In contrast, Lord Keith and Lord Bridge placed more emphasis on maintaining the clarity and consistency of the rule that defects in property and chattels constituted non-recoverable pure economic loss (unless recovery is possible under the *Hedley Byrne* principle: see p. 207, post). However, Lord Keith also proceeded to set out wider policy reasons for the exclusion of liability in such cases. Steele has argued that the speeches in *Murphy* 'do not set out...a *general* exclusionary rule for recovery of pure economic loss' (Steele, p. 359). Do you agree?

3. The House of Lords was influenced in its decision as to whether to overrule *Anns* by its view of the relationship of the courts and the legislature in this field and in particular by the existence of the Defective Premises Act 1972. (See note 5, p. 607, post.)

4. While the 'complex structures' theory was decisively rejected in *Murphy*, Lords Keith, Bridge, and Jauncey suggested that in certain circumstances, if a defect in an independent and ancillary part of a dwelling caused damage to another element of the dwelling, then standard liability for property damage under *Donoghue v Stevenson* may apply. Lords Bridge and Jauncey gave the example of a defective central heating boiler exploding, or of an electrical installation malfunctioning, and suggested that recovery for fire damage to the house could be recoverable in such cases. Lord Keith seemed to be open to such a possibility, except that he considered that liability could only attach where the defective 'independent' parts had been installed by sub-contractors. Lord Jauncey

went furthest in suggesting that if 'one integral component of the structure was built by a separate contractor and where a defect in such a component had caused damage to other parts of the structure', this loss was recoverable: he used the example of a steel frame installed by a sub-contractor which failed to support the floors or walls of the structure.

However, the lack of precision in these suggestions and the conceptual difficulty of identifying 'separate' parts of a building have resulted in judicial reluctance to develop these dicta. In *Jacobs v Morton and Partners* (1994) 72 BLR 92, Recorder Rupert Jackson QC interpreted *Murphy* as having retained the 'complex structure' theory in English law, referring to the remarks by Lords Keith, Bridge, and Jauncey above. However, in *Bellefield Computer Services Ltd v E Turner & Sons Ltd* [2000] BLR 97, the Court of Appeal felt bound (if not without reservations) to follow *Murphy* in rejecting a claim for damage to a building caused by a builder's failure to construct an effective fire-break, as this part of the overall construction could not be separated out from the building as a whole. For discussion of this decision, see Duncan Wallace (2000) 116 LQR 530. See also *Bacardi-Martini Beverages Ltd v Thomas Hardy Packaging Ltd* [2002] 2 Lloyd's Rep 279, [2002] EWCA Civ 549, where the Court of Appeal held that the activities of the first defendant in mixing carbon dioxide with the claimant's property created a new product which was defective from the moment of its creation: as such, the loss sustained constituted pure economic loss in line with *Murphy*. Similarly, in *Tunnel Refineries Ltd v Bryan Donkin Company* [1998] CILL 1392, Recorder Peter Susman QC cast doubt on the decision in *Jacobs v Morton and Partners* and concluded that in the wake of *Murphy*, there was no 'complex chattel' theory recognised in English law: a defect in a component part of a machine which caused damage to another part of the machine was treated as an inherent defect in the machine itself, and therefore the loss in question was purely economic.

Note that in *Nitrigin Eireann Teoranta v Inco Alloys Ltd* [1992] 1 All ER 854, [1992] 1 WLR 498, a factory owner sued for damage caused by an explosion resulting from negligently manufactured tubing associated with a furnace. It was conceded by counsel for the manufacturer that the defective tubing caused damage to other property. In *Tunnel Refineries Ltd v Bryan Donkin Company*, Recorder Peter Susman QC at [29] took the view that there was no clear indication in the report that the concession was based upon acceptance that the damaged tubing could be treated as separate from the furnace and therefore was an example of a 'complex chattel': the concession may have been based on the damage caused by the defective tubing to the factory building. In *Hamble Fisheries Ltd v L Gardner & Sons Ltd (The 'Rebecca Elaine')* [1999] 2 Lloyd's Rep 1 (p. 620, post), where defective pistons were installed as part of the engine of a fishing boat, the Court of Appeal accepted that the engine as a whole constituted a defective product, with the result that the resulting damage in question was treated as pure economic loss.

5. However, there may be situations where such a form of 'independent component' analysis may have some merit. What if the original builder a few years later negligently installed a new electric wiring system which causes damage to the building? Alternatively, if flats in one building are in different ownership, would the flats count as different property for the purpose under consideration here? (Consider *Lindenberg v Canning* (1992) 62 BLR 147 at 161.) See also the discussion in *Aswan Engineering v Lupdine* [1987] 1 All ER 135, [1987] 1 WLR 1 of whether a distinction could be made between stored material and the means of storage, and whether damage to the former

caused by defects in the latter would qualify as property damage (as Lloyd LJ maintained) or pure economic loss. Lloyd LJ's approach in *Aswan Engineering* was subsequently doubted by Mance J in *The Orjula* [1995] Lloyd's Rep 395 at p. 401. However, in *Bacardi-Martini Beverages Ltd v Thomas Hardy Packaging Ltd*, Mance LJ (as he had become) at [18] considered that there could be 'borderline cases' of the type suggested by Lords Keith, Bridge, and Jauncey in *Murphy*, while again casting doubt on the applicability of *Aswan Engineering* post-*Murphy*. (See further p. 195, ante.)

6.   A distinction was drawn in the judgments in *Murphy* between 'latent' and 'patent' defects. A builder is under a duty of care in respect of *personal or property* damage caused by latent damage, i.e. by defects in the property which are not detected and eventually cause damage to persons or other property. If a defect however is 'patent', i.e. once a defect is discovered or ought to have been reasonably discoverable, then the judgment of Lord Keith made clear that any expense incurred by the owner of the house in putting this defect right constituted pure economic loss. It seems questionable that a home owner cannot recover for dangerous 'patent' defects which pose a real risk to persons or property, when that defect has been caused by the negligence of others. (It is also worth bearing in mind that home owners may not have the resources to remedy a patent defect.) Nicholls VC in *Targett v Torfaen Borough Council* [1992] 3 All ER 27 at 37 appeared to suggest that there may be circumstances where it may be reasonable for a home owner not to remove a patent defect. See also the decision of the Court of Appeal in *Baxall Securities Ltd v Sheard Walshaw Partnership* [2002] PNLR 24, [2002] EWCA Civ 9, at [54] (See p. 603, post.)

7.   Some uncertainty has persisted in the case law as to when a 'latent' defect became 'patent', and in particular when a claimant ought to have become aware of the existence of a defect, thereby rendering any economic loss incurred as a result of that defect non-recoverable. In *Baxall Securities Ltd v Sheard Walshaw Partnership*, the Court of Appeal took the view that a defect would be deemed to be patent if it was reasonable for the claimant to inspect the property and that inspection would have uncovered the defect, or where there were reasonable grounds for the claimant to carry out an inspection in his own interests that would have revealed the defect, if the inspection was done with reasonable skill. However, the Court of Appeal in *Pearson Education Ltd v Charter Partnership Ltd* [2007] All ER (D) 262, [2007] EWCA Civ 130 expressed considerable doubts about the reasoning applied in *Baxall*. Nevertheless, applying the *Baxall* test, it was held that discovery of a defect by a third party who had not informed the claimants of its existence did not render the latent defect patent. As a result, the architects who had designed an inadequate drainage system for a storage warehouse were liable for the property damage to the contents of the warehouse caused by this latent defect: the fact that an earlier flood had occurred of which a previous leaseholder and the insurer for the damaged property were aware did not render the defect patent. (See p. 607, post.)

Note that in *Nitrigin Eireann Teoranta v Inco Alloys Ltd* [1992] 1 All ER 854, [1992] 1 WLR 498, noted by A. McGee (1992) 108 LQR 364, the assumed facts for the purposes of the trial of a preliminary issue were that the claimants had made a reasonable but unsuccessful investigation of the cause of a crack in a pipe, but the steps they took to deal with the crack did not prevent a later crack and burst in the pipe. This damaged other property belonging to the claimants. May J did not consider that the discovery of the earlier crack in the pipe meant that the later physical damage had to be classified as economic loss. However, if the claimant should have discovered the defect on the occasion of the first crack, he thought that the claimant could sue for physical damage but that contributory negligence would reduce or extinguish the claim.

8. Note that Lord Bridge in *Murphy* indicated that he considered that an action could lie against a builder for 'preventive damages' in the case of a building near to the highway or a neighbour's property decisions. (See note 1, p. 597, post.)

9. As we will see later in this chapter, a negligent surveyor may be liable to a purchaser of a house for economic loss, as an assumption of responsibility to the purchaser may exist: see *Smith v Eric S Bush* [1990] 1 AC 831, [1989] 2 All ER 514 (p. 218, post). However, post-*Murphy*, a negligent builder will generally not be liable. Is this distinction justifiable? For discussion of this, see J. Stapleton, (1991) 107 LQR 249 at pp. 278–280; cf. (1995) 111 LQR 301 at 335–337. Deakin, Johnston, and Markesinis are very critical of this differential treatment: see *Markesinis and Deakin*, p. 184. However, the key distinguishing factor between the *Murphy/Bates* line of authority and *Smith v Bush* is that in *Murphy* and *Bates*, the claimants were not the original purchasers of the property from the builders, but had been the second or later buyers: this meant that they could be described as coming squarely within the *Cattle v Stockton* rule, whereby no recovery is possible for economic loss arising from property damage that occurred when the property was in another's possession, whereas in *Smith v Bush*, a close relationship of dependence could be said to exist between purchasers and the negligent surveyor which is not ordinarily present between a builder and later purchasers of the building. It was emphasised in *Holding & Management (Solitaire) Ltd v Ideal Homes North West Ltd* [2005] PNLR 16, [2004] EWHC 2408 that a key element in *Murphy* was the fact that the defect was not caused while the property was in the possession of the subsequent possessors and that, in the absence of a special assumption of responsibility, no special relationship would exist between builders and subsequent buyers that would justify abandoning the *Cattle v Stockton* rule.

10. *Murphy* and *Bates* have been the target of some sharp criticism, in particular for the alleged neglect in these decisions of the reality that many house purchasers lack bargaining power to protect themselves adequately via warranties and other contractual mechanisms against the cost of addressing serious structural defects: see R. O'Dair (1991) 54 MLR 561, Grubb and Mullis, [1991] Conv 225.

Commonwealth jurisdictions have in general been reluctant to follow *Murphy*. For example, see the Canadian decision of *Winnipeg Condominium Corpn No 36 v Bird Construction Co Ltd* (1995) 121 DLR (4th) 193, noted by L. C. H. Hoyano (1995) 58 MLR 887, where it was held that a building owner could sue a contractor to recover the cost of making safe a dangerous defect in a building. The Canadian courts have retained an approach similar to that adopted in *Anns* and consequently tend to permit a wider range of recovery for pure economic loss. For an analysis of the 'categorisation' approach of the Canadian courts in this area, see P. Giliker (2005) 25 *Legal Studies* 49. In *Invercargill City Council v Hamlin* [1996] AC 624, [1996] 1 All ER 756, the Privy Council held the New Zealand Court of Appeal were justified in departing from *Murphy* and holding a local authority liable for negligent inspection of defective foundations of a house causing economic loss. (See p. 599, post.) This decision was based upon social conditions in New Zealand: can *Murphy* be said to reflect social conditions in England and Wales? Is the inability of often cash-strapped and heavily mortgaged home buyers in England and Wales to recover the costs of serious defects from negligent builders defensible as a matter of policy (as distinct from being defensible within the parameters of precedent-based common law reasoning, as *Murphy* arguably is)?

Note that the New Zealand Court of Appeal subsequently distinguished *Invercargill City Council v Hamlin* in holding that local authorities owed no duty of care to owners of commercial premises: see *Rolls-Royce New Zealand Ltd v Carter Holt Harvey Ltd* [2005] 1 NZLR 324 (CA); *Three Meade Street Ltd v Rotorua District Council* [2005] 1 NZLR 504.

In Australia, the High Court of Australia took the position in *Bryan v Maloney* (1995) 128 ALR 163 that a subsequent purchaser could sue a builder for economic loss (specifically the diminution in value when a latent defect became manifest); however, *Bryan* was distinguished and a more restrictive approach to recovery was adopted in *Woolcock Street Investments v CDG* (2004) 216 CLR 515, where the High Court refused to extend liability for building defects to commercial premises. In Singapore, contrast *RSP Architects Planners & Engineers (Raglan Squire & Partners FE) v Management Corporation Strata Title Plan No 1075* [1999] 2 SLR 449 with the later, more restrictive, decision of *Man B&W Diesel S E Asia Pte v PT Bumi International Tankers* [2004] 2 SLR 300.

11. The decision in *Murphy* has confirmed that a duty of care in tort will generally not be imposed upon contractors, sub-contractors, and others in respect of inherent defects to property, goods and chattels, unless a 'latent' defect causes property or personal loss. Decisions to the contrary which predated *Murphy* were re-interpreted in the judgment of Lord Keith as involving a *Hedley Byrne* style 'assumption of responsibility', convincingly so in the case of *Pirelli General Cable Works Ltd v Oscar Faber & Partners (a firm)* [1983] 2 AC 1, [1983] 1 All ER 65, perhaps less so in the case of *Junior Books Ltd v Veitchi Co Ltd* [1983] 1 AC 520, [1982] 3 All ER 201 (noted p. 240, post). In overruling *Anns*, the decision in *Murphy* marked a significant shift towards a much more incremental and cautious approach to the imposition of liability in negligence.

12. The decision in *Murphy* continues to generate a certain amount of confused case law. In *Payne v John Setchell Ltd* (1995) 73 Con. L.R. 1, *Murphy* was interpreted as precluding on policy grounds the possibility of any recovery by any purchaser of the costs of repairing a defect from builders, in the absence of a specific contractual term imposing liability. This decision was not followed in *Tesco Stores Ltd v Costain Construction Ltd* [2003] EWHC 1487 (TCC), where it was held that the immediate purchaser had a cause of action, on the basis that the construction company which built the defective shopping centre in question could in the circumstances could be said to have assumed responsibility to the purchaser (*Henderson v Merritt* was applied: see p. 232, post). See also *Storey v Charles Church Developments Ltd* (1995) 73 Con. L.R. 1. As noted above, no such assumption of responsibility was held to exist between the builder and a subsequent purchaser in *Holding & Management (Solitaire) Ltd v Ideal Homes North West Ltd* [2005] PNLR 16, [2004] EWHC 2408 and *Murphy* was therefore applied to preclude liability. For the complex question of when the English courts will consider the economic loss in *Murphy*-style cases to begin to accrue (if that loss is recoverable) for the purpose of limitation periods, see *New Islington and Hackney Housing v Pollard Thomas and Edwards Ltd* [2001] BLR 74; *London Borough of Lewisham v MR Ltd* [2003] BLR 504; and *Abbott v Gannon & Smith Ltd* [2005] PNLR 30, [2005] EWCA Civ 198. See also p. 609, post.

13. Notwithstanding the criticisms of the decision in *Murphy* not to impose liability for negligent construction resulting in defects in dwellings, the analysis of the House of Lords to the effect that the type of loss at issue was pure economic loss has been widely accepted. It constituted a clear restatement of the decision in *The Aliakmon*. Given that, to what extent can the following case, often taken to represent a clear statement of the

distinction between pure and consequential economic loss, stand in the light of *The Aliakmon* and *Murphy v Brentwood District Council?*

■ Spartan Steel and Alloys Ltd v Martin & Co (Contractors) Ltd
Court of Appeal [1972] 3 All ER 557

LORD DENNING MR: ...

The plaintiffs, Spartan Steel & Alloys Ltd, have a factory in Birmingham where they manufacture stainless steel. The factory obtains its electricity by a direct cable from a power station of the Midlands Electricity Board.

In June 1969 contractors called Martin & Co (Contractors) Ltd, the defendants, were doing work on a road about a quarter of a mile away. They were going to dig up the road with a big power-driven excavating shovel. They made enquiries about the place of the cables, mains and so forth, under the road. They were given plans showing them. But unfortunately their men did not take reasonable care. The shovel damaged the cable which supplied electricity to the plaintiffs' works. The electricity board shut down the power whilst they mended the cable.

The factory was at that time working continuously for 24 hours all round the clock. The electric power was shut off at 7.40 pm on 12 June 1969, and was off for 14-1/2 hours until it was restored at 10.00 am on 13 June 1969. This was all through the night and a couple of hours more. But, as this factory was doing night work, it suffered loss. At the time when the power was shut off, there was an arc furnace in which metal was being melted in order to be converted into ingots. Electric power was needed throughout in order to maintain the temperature and melt the metal. When the power failed, there was a danger that the metal might solidify in the furnace and do damage to the lining of the furnace. So the plaintiffs used oxygen to melt the material and poured it from a tap out of the furnace. But this meant that the melted material was of much less value. The physical damage was assessed at £368. In addition, if that particular melt had been properly completed, the plaintiffs would have made a profit on it of £400. Furthermore, during those 14-1/2 hours, when the power was cut off, the plaintiffs would have been able to put four more melts through the furnace; and, by being unable to do so, they lost a profit of £1,767.

The plaintiffs claim all those sums as damages against the defendants for negligence. No evidence was given at the trial, because the defendants admitted that they had been negligent. The contest was solely on the amount of damages. The defendants take their stand on the recent decision in this court of *SCM (United Kingdom) Ltd v W.J. Whittall & Son Ltd*. They admit that they are liable for the £368 physical damages. They did not greatly dispute that they are also liable for the £400 loss of profit on the first melt, because that was truly consequently on the physical damages and thus covered by *SCM v Whittall*. But they deny that they are liable for the £1,767 for the other four melts. They say that was economic loss for which they are not liable. The judge rejected their contention and held them liable for all the loss. The defendants appeal to this court. ...

At bottom I think the question of recovering economic loss is one of policy. Whenever the courts draw a line to mark out the bounds of *duty*, they do it as a matter of policy so as to limit the responsibility of the defendant. Whenever the courts set bounds to the *damages* recoverable—saying that they are, or are not, too remote—they do it as matter of policy so as to limit the liability of the defendant.

In many of the cases where economic loss has been held not to be recoverable, it has been put on the ground that the defendant was under no *duty* to the plaintiff. Thus where a person is injured in a road accident by the negligence of another, the negligent driver owes a duty to the injured man himself, but he owes no duty to the servant of the injured man: see *Best v Samuel Fox & Co Ltd*;[8] nor to the master of the injured man: *Inland Revenue Comrs v Hambrook*;[9] nor to anyone else who suffers loss because

---

[8] [1952] AC 716 at 731, [1952] 2 All ER 394 at 398.
[9] [1956] 2 QB 641 at 660, [1956] 3 All ER 338 at 339, 340.

he had a contract with the injured man: see *Simpson & Co v Thomson*;[10] nor indeed to anyone who only suffers economic loss on account of the accident: see *Kirkham v Boughey*.[11] Likewise, when property is damaged by the negligence of another, the negligent tortfeasor owes a duty to the owner or possessor of the chattel, but not to one who suffers loss only because he had a contract entitling him to use the chattel or giving him a right to receive it at some later date: see *Elliot Steam Tug Co v Shipping Controller*[12] and *Margarine Union GmbH v Cambay Prince Steamship Co Ltd*.[13]

In other cases, however, the defendant seems clearly to have been under a duty to the plaintiff, but the economic loss has not been recovered because it is too remote. Take the illustration given by Blackburn J in *Cattle v Stockton Waterworks Co*[14] when water escapes from a reservoir and floods a coalmine where many men are working; those who had their tools or clothes destroyed could recover, but those who only lost their wages could not. Similarly, when the defendants' ship negligently sank a ship which was being towed by a tug, the owner of the tug lost his remuneration, but he could not recover it from the negligent ship although the same duty (of navigation with reasonable care) was owed to both tug and tow: see *Société Remorquage à Hélice v Bennetts*.[15] In such cases if the plaintiff or his property had been physically injured, he would have recovered; but, as he only suffered economic loss, he is held not entitled to recover. This is, I should think, because the loss is regarded by the law as too remote: see *King v Phillips*.[16]

On the other hand, in the cases where economic loss by itself has been held to be recoverable, it is plain that there was a duty to the plaintiff and the loss was not too remote. Such as when one ship negligently runs down another ship, and damages it, with the result that the cargo has to be discharged and reloaded. The negligent ship was already under a duty to the cargo-owners; and they can recover the cost of discharging and reloading it, as it is not too remote: see *Morrison Steamship Co Ltd v Steamship Greystoke Castle*.[17] Likewise, when a banker negligently gives a reference to one who acts on it, the duty is plain and the damage is not too remote: see *Hedley Byrne & Co Ltd v Heller & Partners Ltd*.[18]

The more I think about these cases, the more difficult I find it to put each into its proper pigeon-hole. Sometimes I say: 'There was no duty.' In others I say: 'The damage was too remote.' So much so that I think the time has come to discard those tests which have proved so elusive. It seems to me better to consider the particular relationship in hand, and see whether or not, as a matter of policy, economic loss should be recoverable. Thus in *Weller & Co v Foot and Mouth Disease Research Institute*[19] it was plain that the loss suffered by the auctioneers was not recoverable, no matter whether it is put on the ground that there was no duty or that the damage was too remote. Again, in *Electrochrome Ltd v Welsh Plastics Ltd*,[20] it is plain that the economic loss suffered by the plaintiffs' factory (due to the damage to the fire hydrant) was not recoverable, whether because there was no duty or that it was too remote.

So I turn to the relationship in the present case. It is of common occurrence. The parties concerned are the electricity board who are under a statutory duty to maintain supplies of electricity in their district; the inhabitants of the district, including this factory, who are entitled by statute to a continuous supply of electricity for their use; and the contractors who dig up the road. Similar relationships occur with other statutory bodies, such as gas and water undertakings. The cable may be damaged by the negligence of the statutory undertaker, or by the negligence of the contractor, or by accident without any negligence by anyone; and the power may have to be cut off whilst the cable is repaired. Or the power may be cut off owing to a short-circuit in the power house; and so forth. If the cutting off of

---

[10] (1877) 3 App Cas 279 at 289.   [11] [1958] 2 QB 338 at 341, [1957] 3 All ER 153 at 155.

[12] [1922] 1 KB 127 at 139.   [13] [1969] 1 QB 219 at 251, 252, [1967] 3 All ER 775 at 794.

[14] (1875) LR 10 QB 453 at 457, [1874-80] All ER Rep 220 at 223.   [15] [1911] 1 KB 243 at 248.

[16] [1953] 1 QB 429 at 439, 440, [1953] 1 All ER 617 at 622.

[17] [1947] AC 265, [1946] 2 All ER 696.   [18] [1964] AC 465, [1963] 2 All ER 575.

[19] [1966] 1 QB 569, [1965] 3 All ER 560.   [20] [1968] 2 All ER 205.

the supply causes economic loss to the consumers, should it as matter of policy be recoverable? And against whom?

The first consideration is the position of the statutory undertakers. If the board do not keep up the voltage or pressure of electricity, gas or water—or, likewise, if they shut it off for repairs—and thereby cause economic loss to their consumers, they are not liable in damages, not even if the cause of it is due to their own negligence. The only remedy (which is hardly ever pursued) is to prosecute the board before the justices. Such is the result of many cases, starting with a water board: *Atkinson v Newcastle and Gateshead Waterworks Co;*[1] going on to a gas board: *Clegg, Parkinson & Co v Earby Gas Co;*[2] and then to an electricity company: *Stevens v Aldershot Gas, Water and District Lighting Co.*[3] In those cases the courts, looking at the legislative enactments, held that Parliament did not intend to expose the board to liability for damages to the inhabitants en masse: see what Lord Cairns LC said[4] and Wills J.[5] No distinction was made between economic loss and physical damage; and taken at their face value the reasoning would mean that the board was not liable for physical damage either. But there is another group of cases which go to show that, if the board, by their negligence in the conduct of their supply, cause direct physical damage to person or property, the cases seem to show that they are liable: see *Milnes v Huddersfield Corpn*[6] per Lord Blackburn; *Midwood & Co Ltd v Manchester Corpn;*[7] *Heard v Brymbo Steel Co Ltd*[8] and *Hartley v Mayoh & Co.*[9] But one thing is clear, the board have never been held liable for economic loss only. If such be the policy of the legislature in regard to electricity boards, it would seem right for the common law to adopt a similar policy in regard to contractors. If the electricity boards are not liable for economic loss due to negligence which results in the cutting off of the supply, nor should a contractor be liable.

The second consideration is the nature of the hazard, namely, the cutting of the supply of electricity. This is a hazard which we all run. It may be due to a short circuit, to a flash of lightning, to a tree falling on the wires, to an accidental cutting of the cable, or even to the negligence of someone or other. And when it does happen, it affects a multitude of persons; not as a rule by way of physical damage to them or their property, but by putting them to inconvenience, and sometimes to economic loss. The supply is usually restored in a few hours, so the economic loss is not very large. Such a hazard is regarded by most people as a thing they must put up with—without seeking compensation from anyone. Some there are who install a stand-by system. Others seek refuge by taking out an insurance policy against breakdown in the supply. But most people are content to take the risk on themselves. When the supply is cut off, they do not go running round to their solicitor. They do not try to find out whether it was anyone's fault. They just put up with it. They try to make up the economic loss by doing more work next day. This is a healthy attitude which the law should encourage.

The third consideration is this. If claims for economic loss were permitted for this particular hazard, there would be no end of claims. Some might be genuine, but many might be inflated, or even false. A machine might not have been in use anyway, but it would be easy to put it down to the cut in supply. It would be well-nigh impossible to check the claims. If there was economic loss on one day, did the applicant do his best to mitigate it by working harder next day? And so forth. Rather than expose claimants to such temptation and defendants to such hard labour—on comparatively small claims—it is better to disallow economic loss altogether, at any rate when it stands alone, independent of any physical damage.

The fourth consideration is that, in such a hazard as this, the risk of economic loss should be suffered by the whole community who suffer the losses—usually many but comparatively small losses—rather than on the one pair of shoulders, that is, on the contractor on whom the total of them, all added together, might be very heavy.

---

[1] (1877) 2 Ex D 441, [1874-80] All ER Rep 757.   [2] [1896] 1 QB 592.   [3] (1932) 102 LJKB 12.
[4] In *Atkinson v Newcastle and Gateshead Waterworks Co* (1877) 2 Ex D at p. 445.
[5] In *Clegg, Parkinson & Co v Earby Gas Co* [1896] 1 QB at p. 595.   [6] (1886) 11 App Cas 511 at 530.
[7] [1905] 2 KB 597.   [8] [1947] KB 692.   [9] [1954] 1 QB 383, [1954] 1 All ER 375.

The fifth consideration is that the law provides for deserving cases. If the defendant is guilty of negligence which cuts off the electricity supply and causes actual physical damage to person or property, that physical damage can be recovered; see *Baker v Crow Carrying Co Ltd*[10] referred to by Buckley LJ in *SCM v Whittall*,[11] and also any economic loss truly consequential on the material damage: see *British Celanese Ltd v A H Hunt (Capacitors) Ltd*[12] and *SCM v Whittall*.[13] Such cases will be comparatively few. They will be readily capable of proof and will be easily checked. They should be and are admitted.

These considerations lead me to the conclusion that the plaintiffs should recover for the physical damage to the one melt (£368), and the loss of profit on that melt consequent thereon (£400); but not for the loss of profit on the four melts (£1,767), because that was economic loss independent of the physical damage. I would, therefore, allow the appeal and reduce the damages to £768.

EDMUND-DAVIES LJ [dissenting on the question of the pure economic loss]: . . .
For my part, I cannot see why the £400 loss of profit here sustained should be recoverable and not the £1,767. It is common ground that both types of loss were equally foreseeable and equally direct consequences of the defendants' admitted negligence, and the only distinction drawn is that the former figure represents the profit loss as a result of the physical damage done to the material in the furnace at the time when the power was cut off. But what has that purely fortuitous fact to do with legal principle? In my judgment, nothing. . . .

Having considered the intrinsic nature of the problem presented in this appeal, and having consulted the relevant authorities, my conclusion . . . is that an action lies in negligence for damages in respect of purely economic loss, provided that it was a reasonably foreseeable and direct consequence of failure in a duty of care. The application of such a rule can undoubtedly give rise to difficulties in certain sets of circumstances, but so can the suggested rule that economic loss may be recovered *provided* it is directly consequential on physical damage. Many alarming situations were conjured up in the course of counsel's arguments before us. In their way, they were reminiscent of those formerly advanced against awarding damages for nervous shock; for example, the risk of fictitious claims and expensive litigation, the difficulty of disproving the alleged cause and effect, and the impossibility of expressing such a claim in financial terms. But I suspect that they . . . would for the most part be resolved either on the ground that no duty of care was owed to the injured party or that the damages sued for were irrecoverable *not* because they were simply financial but because they were too remote. . . .

[LAWTON LJ delivered a judgment in favour of allowing the appeal and reducing the damages to £768.]

Appeal allowed.

QUESTION

Can you see any connection between the reasons Lord Denning gives for restricting recovery for pure economic loss and the decision he comes to in *Spartan Steel*? Is this a case of 'indeterminate liability', capable of generating 'no end of claims'? Stevens suggests that none of the arguments offered by Lord Denning justifies the eventual outcome: see *Stevens*, p. 25.

NOTES

1. *Spartan Steel* can be seen as a case that yet again illustrates that there may be no rigid doctrine of non-recoverability for pure economic loss—Lord Denning explicitly turns to policy considerations to determine whether a duty exists in this case. The Court

---

[10] (1 February 1960, unreported).   [11] [1971] 1 QB at p. 356, [1970] 3 All ER at p. 261.
[12] [1969] 2 All ER 1252, [1969] 1 WLR 959.   [13] [1971] 1 QB 337, [1970] 3 All ER 245.

of Appeal took the view in *Spartan Steel* that the loss of profit represented by the loss of the four melts was caused by damage to the property of a third party (in this case, the electricity company), and thus therefore constituted pure economic loss, which was unrecoverable in the circumstances. At first sight, *Spartan* Steel appears to be a straightforward application of the *Cattle v Stockton* rule.

2. However, it could be queried in what sense was the loss of the opportunity to process the four melts in *Spartan Steel* 'purely' economic? The headnote claims that *Spartan Steel* follows *Cattle v Stockton* in disallowing compensation for economic losses unconnected with physical damage. But there was physical damage to property in *Cattle*. There was simply no damage to the *claimant's* property. In *Spartan Steel* the defendants' negligence interfered with two sorts of property belonging to the claimants—their materials and their machinery—and both sorts of interference were also arguably 'physical', depending on how one defines that term. The metal had to be damaged to salvage it (cf. *Blue Circle Industries plc v Ministry of Defence* [1999] Ch 289, [1998] 3 All ER 385), and the machine did not work because it had been deprived of electricity, which is as much physical interference as removing petrol from the engine of a car. Therefore, it could be argued that physical damage was caused to both the metal and the arc furnace, and therefore the consequential financial loss stemming from the 'physical' damage to the arc furnace could be recoverable.

3. The question should perhaps have been how to value these losses. To a business the value of property or capital assets is the revenue it can generate. Businesses only sell their materials, machinery, or other capital assets if their revenue-generating value falls below their resale or scrap value (this happens, for example, when the business invests in more efficient machinery and intends no longer to use the old machinery). Should the court value property as the business values it or should it count only the scrap or resale values? The majority view in *Spartan Steel*, as Edmund-Davies LJ points out in his dissent, takes the former view for the materials and the latter view for the machinery. Plainly the machine's scrap or resale value would not have been affected much by the incident. But the value of the machine to the claimants, its capacity to generate revenue for the business, was affected. Should this 'damage' be classed as pure economic loss, or physical damage to property? *Spartan Steel* could be seen as a case where policy considerations influenced not only whether a duty of care was held to exist, but also the definition of the type of loss at issue. (For an argument that permitting recovery of 'pure economic loss' is economically efficient if the case involves 'impairment loss' (i.e. interference with use of an income-earning asset) or lack of liability would lead to inefficient investment in spare capacity, see G.D. Mattiacci and H. Schäfer, (2007) 27 International Review of Law and Economics 8.)

4. In contrast, *Weller & Co v Foot & Mouth Disease Research Institute* [1966] 1 QB 569, [1965] 3 All ER 560 is a more straightforward case of pure economic loss. Here the assumed facts were that foot and mouth disease virus escaped from the defendant's premises and infected cattle on neighbouring land, prompting the authorities to close Guildford and Farnham markets. The claimant cattle auctioneers suffered a loss of business because of this closure. It was further assumed that this loss was foreseeable and that the escape of the virus was caused by the defendant's negligence. Widgery J held that a duty of care was owed to the owners of the cattle in the neighbourhood but not to the claimants, who had no proprietary interest in anything which might conceivably be damaged by the virus if it escaped and therefore had only suffered a loss of profit from damage to the property interests of others. Harris and Veljanovski, op cit., pp. 64–67, point out that '[t]he negligent act of the defendant did not directly affect [the

auctioneers'] production activities, but only led to a change in the market for their services—a fall in demand, which was similar to falls caused by other fluctuations in the market resulting from non-negligent or political factors'. They argue that it was sufficient from the point of view of deterrence for the defendant to have to compensate the farmers. The auctioneers (whose fees could reflect the risks they took) would not suffer any permanent loss in the demand for their services. Harris and Veljanovski also argue that if the defendant had to compensate the auctioneers (and logically others whose markets were affected) they would be exposed to crushing liability which would halt or limit their research activities—but note that the 'crushing liability' argument is a two-edged sword. What if the claimant will go out of business unless it receives compensation?

5. The House of Lords in *Esso Petroleum Co Ltd v Hall Russell & Co Ltd* [1989] AC 643, [1989] 1 All ER 37 said that it is not enough that a claimant who has suffered economic loss has also sustained damage to his own property. The economic loss must be consequent upon, and not merely additional to, the damage to his property.

6. An insurer of someone else's property may not sue a tortfeasor who destroys the property. But, having satisfied the claim, the insurer may be subrogated to the owner's rights and so entitled to sue *in the owner's name*: *Simpson v Thomson* (1877) 3 App Cas 279. For critical comment see T. Weir [1989] LMCLQ 1, and B. Hepple, All ER Rev 1989, p. 329. This can be seen as an exception to the *Cattle v Stockton* rule of no recovery for economic loss incurred through damage to the property of others. Note too the provisions of the Fatal Accidents Act 1976, (p. 280 post), and the Civil Liability (Contribution) Act 1978, (p. 1122 post).

7. This again shows that there is no rigid rule of non-recovery for pure economic loss in the common law. In addition, the following case shows that many of the policy considerations that are cited to justify the common law's reluctance to impose liability for pure economic loss may also be relevant at times in cases of property damage: it is important to realise that sharp distinctions between economic and property loss may be difficult to draw.

■ Marc Rich & Co AG v Bishop Rock Marine Co Ltd, The Nicholas H
House of Lords [1995] 3 All ER 307

The defendant classification society, the function of which was to decide whether ships were seaworthy for insurance purposes, gave way to pressure from the owner of a temporarily repaired ship to be allowed to put to sea. The ship sank, and the claimant's cargo, worth more than $6 million, was completely lost. The terms of the plaintiff's contract with the shipowner were regulated by international agreements (including the 'Hague-Visby Rules'), according to which the shipowner's liability was restricted to $0.5 million. The claimant attempted unsuccessfully to recover the rest of the value of the cargo from the classification society.

LORD STEYN: . . .
(c) The bill of lading contracts
The first and principal ground of the decision of Saville LJ [in the Court of Appeal] was the impact of the terms of the bill of lading contracts. He said ([1994] 3 All ER 686 at 695–696, [1994] 1 WLR 1071 at 1080):

'The Hague Rules (and their successor the Hague Visby Rules (which are scheduled to the Carriage of Goods by Sea Act 1971)) form an internationally recognised code adjusting the rights and duties existing between shipowners and those shipping goods under bills of lading. As Donaldson MR said in *Leigh & Sillavan Ltd v Aliakmon Shipping Co Ltd, The Aliakmon* [1985] 2 All ER 44 at 54, [1985] QB 350 at 368 the rules create an intricate blend of responsibilities and liabilities, rights and immunities, limitations on the amount of damages recoverable, time bars, evidential provisions, indemnities and liberties, all in relation to the carriage of goods under bills of lading. The proposition advanced by Mr Gross would add an identical or virtually identical duty owed by the classification society to that owed by the shipowners, but without any of these balancing factors, which are internationally recognised and accepted. I do not regard that as a just, fair or reasonable proposition.'

SAVILLE LJ ended this part of his judgment by explicitly stating ([1994] 3 All ER 686 at 697, [1994] 1 WLR 1071 at 1081):

'The question is not whether the classification society is covered by the rules, but whether in all the circumstances it is just, fair and reasonable to require them to shoulder a duty which by the rules primarily lies on the shipowners, without the benefits of those rules or other international conventions.'

That question Saville LJ (and, by adoption, Balcombe LJ) answered in the negative. And Mann LJ was in substantial agreement on this point.

It was the principal task of counsel for the cargo owners to try to dismantle the reasoning of Saville LJ. He pointed out that Saville LJ apparently assumed that the limitation of the claim of cargo owners against the shipowners arose under the Hague Rules. In truth the limitation arose by reason of tonnage limitation as already explained. This is not a point of substance. Tonnage limitation is a part of the international code which governs the claims under consideration. It is as relevant as any limitation under the Hague Rules.

Moving on to more substantial matters, counsel for the cargo owners submitted that the allocation of risks in the Hague Rules between shipowners and the owners of cargo is irrelevant to the question whether NKK owed a duty of care to the owners of the cargo. He said the bill of lading contract on Hague Rules terms, and the international character of those rules, is only a piece of history, which explains the positions in which NKK and the owners of the cargo found themselves. In the course of these submissions Mr Gross referred your Lordships to a valuable article by P F Cane 'The Liability of Classification Societies' [1994] LMCLQ 363. Mr Cane observed trenchantly (at 373):

'But why should an allocation of risks between shipowners and cargo owners be enforced as between cargo owners and classification societies? Whatever good reasons there may be to do so, the mere existence of the Hague Rules is surely not one of them.'

That is a cogent argument against the reasoning of the Court of Appeal. There is, however, a further dimension of the problem that must be considered.

The dealings between shipowners and cargo owners are based on a contractual structure, the Hague Rules, and tonnage limitation, on which the insurance of international trade depends: see Dr Malcolm Clarke 'Misdelivery and Time Bars' [1990] LMCLQ 314. Underlying it is the system of double or overlapping insurance of cargo. Cargo owners take out direct insurance in respect of the cargo. Shipowners take out liability risks insurance in respect of breaches of their duties of care in respect of the cargo. The insurance system is structured on the basis that the potential liability of shipowners to cargo owners is limited under the Hague Rules and by virtue of tonnage limitation provisions. And insurance premiums payable by owners obviously reflect such limitations on the shipowners' exposure.

If a duty of care by classification societies to cargo owners is recognised in this case, it must have a substantial impact on international trade. In his article Mr Cane described the likely effect of imposing such duty of care as follows ([1994] LMCLQ 363 at 375):

'Societies would be forced to buy appropriate liability insurance unless they could bargain with shipowners for an indemnity. To the extent that societies were successful in securing indemnities from shipowners in respect of loss suffered by cargo owners, the limitation of the liability of shipowners to cargo owners under the Hague(-Visby) Rules would effectively be destroyed. Shipowners would need to increase their insurance cover in respect of losses suffered by cargo owners; but at the same time, cargo owners would still need to insure against losses above the Hague-Visby recovery limit which did not result from actionable negligence on the part of a classification society. At least if classification societies are immune from non-contractual liability, they can confidently go without insurance in respect of third-party losses, leaving third parties to insure themselves in respect of losses for which they could not recover from shipowners.'

Counsel for the cargo owners challenged this analysis. On instructions he said that classification societies already carry liability risks insurance. That is no doubt right since classification societies do not have a blanket immunity from all tortious liability. On the other hand, if a duty of care is held to exist in this case, the potential exposure of classification societies to claims by cargo owners will be large. That greater exposure is likely to lead to an increase in the cost to classification societies of obtaining appropriate liability risks insurance. Given their role in maritime trade classification societies are likely to seek to pass on the higher cost to owners. Moreover, it is readily predictable that classification societies will require owners to give appropriate indemnities. Ultimately, shipowners will pay.

The result of a recognition of a duty of care in this case will be to enable cargo owners, or rather their insurers, to disturb the balance created by the Hague Rules and Hague Visby Rules as well as by tonnage limitation provisions, by enabling cargo owners to recover in tort against a peripheral party to the prejudice of the protection of shipowners under the existing system. For these reasons I would hold that the international trade system tends to militate against the recognition of the claim in tort put forward by the cargo owners against the classification society.

NOTES

1. *The Nicholas H* concerns property damage, not pure economic loss. But it is of interest here because the majority of the House of Lords suggests that some of the reasons for restricting the recovery of pure economic loss might also apply to property damage. This once again shows that the common law does not necessarily recognise a clear distinction between pure economic loss and property loss: considerations of proximity and policy may be relevant in determining whether a duty of care exists for both types of loss.

2. Would it be so bad to rearrange the allocation of risk under the Hague-Visby rules? Since insurance follows risk, if classification societies or ship owners had to insure against greater liability, the cost of the cargo owners' insurance would fall, which might result in lower overall costs. In addition, in his dissent in *The Nicholas H*, Lord Lloyd says that the court should have taken more seriously the concern in the shipping industry at the time about sub-standard classification societies. Lord Steyn's approach appears to pay no attention to the question of deterrence. Is the use of policy considerations here convincing? Should courts give considerable weight to insurance considerations in deciding such a case (see p. 1135, post)? See also J. Morgan, (2004) 67 MLR 384.

3. Saville LJ, in a passage endorsed by Lord Steyn, said that property damage cases are just as suitable as pure economic cases to be scrutinised for whether there is proximity and whether it is just, fair, and reasonable to impose a duty of care. The *Cattle v Stockton* denial of recovery to claimants who have brought about their own misfortune by making deals of a particular kind is capable of expansion to cover some property damage cases. Might one say, for example, that a claimant who decided, voluntarily, to acquire unusually valuable and sensitive objects has made himself particularly vulnerable to any subsequent damage to those objects? See D. Howarth in *Civil Liability for Pure Economic Loss*, edited by E. Banakas (London, 1996). However, in *Perrett v Collins* [1998] 2 Lloyd's

Rep 255, Hobhouse LJ rejected an argument that Lord Steyn meant to upset the existing categories of liability for *personal* injury (see further note 7, p. 44, ante).

4.   In *Norwich City Council v Harvey* [1989] 1 All ER 1180, [1989] 1 WLR 828 sub-contractors negligently set fire to a building belonging to the claimant. The contract between the claimants and the main contractor excluded liability for fire damage, but there was no direct contract between the claimant and the sub-contractor. The Court of Appeal nevertheless held that the exclusion clause prevented any duty arising between the sub-contractors and the claimant. See also *British Telecommunications plc v James Thomson & Sons (Engineers) Ltd* [1999] 2 All ER 241, [1999] 1 WLR 9, where a duty of care was held to exist between client and sub-contractor where the sub-contractor had damaged the client's property, because, although the main contract between the client and the general contractor specified that the client should take out insurance against the relevant damage, and although the main contract specified that the client's insurer would have no right to proceed against certain other types of sub-contractor, the absence of a provision excluding the insurer from pursuing the particular sub-contractor who caused the damage was an argument in favour of imposing a duty of care, not an argument against imposing one. In both cases, a similar approach was adopted as in the *Nicholas H*.

5.   Is it possible to re-assess *Spartan Steel* in the light of *The Nicholas H*? Might one say that, even if one classifies *Spartan Steel* as a property damage case, it is important to preserve the effect of the existing contractual arrangements between the electricity supplier and the claimant, just as in *The Nicholas H*? Notice that Lord Denning says that since the claimants could not sue the electricity company, they should not be allowed to sue these defendants either. The relationship between the claimants and the electricity company in *Spartan Steel* is, admittedly, not fully voluntary, but, because some of its provisions are compulsory, neither are relationships governed by the Hague-Visby rules. One can, however, choose a line of business not covered by the Hague-Visby rules, whereas it is very difficult to find a business that does not need electricity.

6.   These cases show the complexity of defining pure economic loss and separating out this form of loss from other forms of damage. In general, as demonstrated in *The Aliakmon*, *Murphy* and *Spartan Steel*, the classification of loss as purely economic in nature will generally result in the courts refusing to impose a duty of care upon the parties alleged to have caused that loss. However, the seminal decision by the House of Lords in *Hedley Byrne & Co Ltd v Heller & Partners Ltd* [1964] AC 465, [1963] 2 All ER 575 and the subsequent application of this precedent in a series of key cases has resulted in a gradual erosion of the scope of the rule of non-recovery for pure economic loss.

3 THE *HEDLEY BYRNE* EXCEPTION

■ Hedley Byrne & Co Ltd v Heller & Partners Ltd
House of Lords [1964] AC 465, [1963] 2 All ER 575

The plaintiff advertising agents booked advertising on television and in newspapers on behalf of a customer, Easipower Ltd, on terms which meant that the plaintiffs became personally liable. Becoming doubtful of Easipower's financial position they asked their bankers,

National Provincial, to obtain a report from the defendants, merchant bankers with whom Easipower Ltd had an account. The defendants telephoned to say that they believed Easipower 'to be respectably constituted and considered good for its normal business engagements' and that 'the company would not undertake any commitments they were unable to fulfil'. Three months later, a further inquiry was made by letter asking whether Easipower were 'trustworthy...to the extent of £100,000 per annum'. The defendants replied, in a letter headed 'Confidential. For your private use and without responsibility on the part of this bank or its officials', that Easipower was a '... [r]espectably constituted company, considered good for its ordinary business engagements. Your figures are larger than we are accustomed to see.' The plaintiffs relied on these statements and as a result they lost £17,661 18s 6d, when Easipower went into liquidation. McNair J held that the defendants were negligent but that they owed no duty of care to the plaintiffs. The Court of Appeal likewise held that there was no duty of care. The House of Lords affirmed the judgment on different grounds.

LORD REID:...
Apart altogether from authority I would think that the law must treat negligent words differently from negligent acts. The law ought so far as possible to reflect the standards of the reasonable man, and that is what *M'Alister (or Donoghue) v Stevenson*[14] sets out to do. The most obvious difference between negligent words and negligent acts is this. Quite careful people often express definite opinions on social or informal occasions, even when they see that others are likely to be influenced by them; and they often do that without taking that care which they would take if asked for their opinion professionally, or in a business connexion. The appellants agree that there can be no duty of care on such occasions, and we were referred to American and South African authorities where that is recognised, although their law appears to have gone much further than ours has yet done. But it is at least unusual casually to put into circulation negligently-made articles which are dangerous. A man might give a friend a negligently-prepared bottle of home-made wine and his friend's guests might drink it with dire results; but it is by no means clear that those guests would have no action against the negligent manufacturer. Another obvious difference is that a negligently-made article will only cause one accident, and so it is not very difficult to find the necessary degree of proximity or neighbourhood between the negligent manufacturer and the person injured. But words can be broadcast with or without the consent or the foresight of the speaker or writer. It would be one thing to say that the speaker owes a duty to a limited class, but it would be going very far to say that he owes a duty to every ultimate 'consumer' who acts on those words to his detriment. It would be no use to say that a speaker or writer owes a duty, but can disclaim responsibility if he wants to. He, like the manufacturer, could make it part of a contract that he is not to be liable for his negligence: but that contract would not protect him in a question with a third party at least if the third party was unaware of it.

So it seems to me that there is good sense behind our present law that in general an innocent but negligent misrepresentation gives no cause of action. There must be something more than the mere misstatement.... [After considering earlier authorities, including a statement by Lord Haldane in *Robinson v Bank of Scotland*[15]]:... He speaks of other special relationships and I can see no logical stopping place short of all those relationships where it is plain that the party seeking information or advice was trusting the other to exercise such a degree of care as the circumstances required, where it was reasonable for him to do that, and where the other gave the information or advice when he knew or ought to have known that the inquirer was relying on him. I say 'ought to have known' because in questions of negligence we now apply the objective standard of what the reasonable man would have done.

A reasonable man, knowing that he was being trusted or that his skill and judgment were being relied on, would, I think, have three courses open to him. He could keep silent or decline to give the information or advice sought: or he could give an answer with a clear qualification that he accepted no responsibility for it or that it was given without that reflection or inquiry which a careful answer

---

[14] [1932] AC 562, [1932] All ER Rep 1.   [15] 1916 SC (HL) 154 at 157.

would require: or he could simply answer without any such qualification. If he chooses to adopt the last course he must, I think, be held to have accepted some responsibility for his answer being given carefully, or to have accepted a relationship with the inquirer which requires him to exercise such care as the circumstances require....

What the appellants complain of is not negligence in the ordinary sense of carelessness, but rather misjudgment in that Mr Heller, while honestly seeking to give a fair assessment, in fact made a statement which gave a false and misleading impression of his customer's credit. It appears that bankers now commonly give references with regard to their customers as part of their business. I do not know how far their customers generally permit them to disclose their affairs, but even with permission it cannot always be easy for a banker to reconcile his duty to his customer with his desire to give a fairly balanced reply to an inquiry; and inquirers can hardly expect a full and objective statement of opinion or accurate factual information such as skilled men would be expected to give in reply to other kinds of inquiry. So it seems to me to be unusually difficult to determine just what duty, beyond a duty to be honest, a banker would be held to have undertaken if he gave a reply without an adequate disclaimer of responsibility or other warning....

Here, however, the appellants' bank, who were their agents in making the enquiry, began by saying that 'they wanted to know in confidence and without responsibility on our part', i.e. on the part of the respondents. So I cannot see how the appellants can now be entitled to disregard that and maintain that the respondents did incur a responsibility to them.

The appellants founded on a number of cases in contract where very clear words were required to exclude the duty of care which would otherwise have flowed from the contract. To that argument there are, I think, two answers. In the case of a contract it is necessary to exclude liability for negligence, but in this case the question is whether an undertaking to assume a duty to take care can be inferred; and that is a very different matter. Secondly, even in cases of contract general words may be sufficient if there was no other kind of liability to be excluded except liability for negligence: the general rule is that a party is not exempted from liability for negligence 'unless adequate words are used' per SCRUTTON LJ in *Rutter v Palmer*.[16] It being admitted that there was here a duty to give an honest reply, I do not see what further liability there could be to exclude except liability for negligence: there being no contract there was no question of warranty.

I am therefore of opinion that it is clear that the respondents never undertook any duty to exercise care in giving their replies. The appellants cannot succeed unless there was such a duty and therefore in my judgment this appeal must be dismissed.

LORD MORRIS OF BORTH-Y-GEST:...

My lords, it seems to me that if A assumes a responsibility to B to tender him deliberate advice there could be a liability if the advice is negligently given. I say 'could be' because the ordinary courtesies and exchanges of life would become impossible if it were sought to attach legal obligation to every kindly and friendly act. But the principle of the matter would not appear to be in doubt....

My lords, I consider that...it should now be regarded as settled that if someone possessed of a special skill undertakes, quite irrespective of contract, to apply that skill for the assistance of another person who relies on such skill, a duty of care will arise. The fact that the service is to be given by means of, or by the instrumentality of, words can make no difference. Furthermore, if, in a sphere in which a person is so placed that others could reasonably rely on his judgment or his skill or on his ability to make careful inquiry, a person takes it on himself to give information or advice to, or allows his information or advice to be passed on to, another person who, as he knows or should know, will place reliance on it, then a duty of care will arise.

...I approach the case on the footing that the bank knew that what they said would in fact be passed on to some unnamed person who was a customer of National Provincial Bank, Ltd. The fact that it was said that 'they', i.e. National Provincial Bank, Ltd, 'wanted to know' does not prevent this

---

[16] [1922] 2 KB 87 at 92; cf. [1922] All ER Rep 367 at 370.

conclusion. In these circumstances I think that some duty towards the unnamed person, whoever it was, was owed by the bank. There was a duty of honesty. The great question, however, is whether there was a duty of care. The bank need not have answered the inquiry from National Provincial Bank Ltd. It appears, however, that it is a matter of banking convenience or courtesy and presumably of mutual business advantage that inquiries as between banks will be answered. The fact that it is most unlikely that the bank would have answered a direct inquiry from Hedleys does not affect the question as to what the bank must have known as to the use that would be made of any answer that they gave but it cannot be left out of account in considering what it was that the bank undertook to do. It does not seem to me that they undertook before answering an inquiry to expend time or trouble 'in searching records, studying documents, weighing and comparing the favourable and unfavourable features and producing a well-balanced and well-worded report.' (I quote the words of Pearson LJ).[17] Nor does it seem to me that the inquiring bank (nor therefore their customer) would expect such a process.... There was in the present case no contemplation of receiving anything like a formal and detailed report such as might be given by some concern charged with the duty (probably for reward) of making all proper and relevant inquiries concerning the nature, scope and extent of a company's activities and of obtaining and marshalling all available evidence as to its credit, efficiency, standing and business reputation. There is much to be said, therefore, for the view that if a banker gives a reference in the form of a brief expression of opinion in regard to credit-worthiness he does not accept, and there is not expected from him, any higher duty than that of giving an honest answer. I need not, however, seek to deal with this aspect of the matter which perhaps cannot be covered by any statement of general application, because in my judgment the bank in the present case, by the words which they employed, effectively disclaimed any assumption of a duty of care. They stated that they only responded to the inquiry on the basis that their reply was without responsibility. If the inquirers chose to receive and act upon the reply they cannot disregard the definite terms upon which it was given. They cannot accept a reply given with a stipulation and then reject the stipulation. Furthermore, within accepted principles (as illustrated in *Rutter v Palmer*[18]) the words employed were apt to exclude any liability for negligence....

LORD DEVLIN: ...

A simple distinction between negligence in word and negligence in deed might leave the law defective but at least it would be intelligible. This is not, however, the distinction that is drawn in counsel for the respondents' argument and it is one which would be unworkable. A defendant who is given a car to overhaul and repair if necessary is liable to the injured driver (a) if he overhauls it and repairs it negligently and tells the driver that it is safe when it is not; (b) if he overhauls it and negligently finds it not to be in need of repair and tells the driver that it is safe when it is not; and (c) if he negligently omits to overhaul it at all and tells the driver that it is safe when it is not. It would be absurd in any of these cases to argue that the proximate cause of the driver's injury was not what the defendant did or failed to do but his negligent statement on the faith of which the driver drove the car and for which he could not recover. In this type of case where if there were a contract there would undoubtedly be a duty of service, it is not practicable to distinguish between the inspection or examination, the acts done or omitted to be done, and the advice or information given....

In my opinion the appellants in their argument tried to press *M'Alister* (or *Donoghue*) *v Stevenson*[19] too hard. They asked whether the principle of proximity should not apply as well to words as to deeds. I think that it should, but as it is only a general conception it does not yet get them very far. Then they take the specific proposition laid down by *Donoghue v Stevenson* and try to apply it literally to a certificate or a banker's reference. That will not do, for a general conception cannot be applied to pieces of paper in the same way as to articles of commerce, or to writers in the same way as to manufacturers. An inquiry into the possibilities of intermediate examination of a certificate will not be fruitful. The real value of *Donoghue v Stevenson* to the argument in this case is that it shows how the

---

[17] [1962] 1 QB at 414, [1961] All ER at 902, letter E.
[18] [1922] 2 KB 87, [1922] All ER Rep 367.   [19] [1932] AC 562, [1932] All ER Rep 1.

law can be developed to solve particular problems. Is the relationship between the parties in this case such that it can be brought within a category giving rise to a special duty? As always in English law the first step in such an inquiry is to see how far the authorities have gone, for new categories in the law do not spring into existence overnight.

It would be surprising if the sort of problem that is created by the facts of this case had never until recently arisen in English law. As a problem it is a by-product of the doctrine of consideration. If the respondents had made a nominal charge for the reference, the problem would not exist. If it were possible in English law to construct a contract without consideration, the problem would move at once out of the first and general phase into the particular; and the question would be, not whether on the facts of the case there was a special relationship, but whether on the facts of the case there was a contract.

The respondents in this case cannot deny that they were performing a service. Their sheet anchor is that they were performing it gratuitously and therefore no liability for its performance can arise. My lords, in my opinion this is not the law. A promise given without consideration to perform a service cannot be enforced as a contract by the promisee; but if the service is in fact performed and done negligently, the promisee can recover in an action in tort. This is the foundation of the liability of a gratuitous bailee. In the famous case of *Coggs v Bernard*,[20] where the defendant had charge of brandy belonging to the plaintiff and had spilt a quantity of it, there was a motion in arrest of judgment 'for that it was not alleged in the declaration that the defendant was a common porter, nor averred that he had anything for his pains'. The declaration was held to be good notwithstanding that there was not any consideration laid. Gould J said:

'The reason of the action is, the particular trust reposed in the defendant, to which he has concurred by his assumption, and in the executing which he has miscarried by his neglect.'

This proposition is not limited to the law of bailment. In *Skelton v London & North Western Rly Co.*[1] Willes J applied it generally to the law of negligence. He said:[2]

'Actionable negligence must consist in the breach of some duty ... if a person undertakes to perform a voluntary act, he is liable if he performs it improperly, but not if he neglects to perform it. Such is the result of the decision in the case of *Coggs v Bernard*.'

Likewise in *Banbury v Bank of Montreal*,[3] where the bank had advised a customer on his investments, Lord Finlay LC said:[4] 'He is under no obligation to advise, but if he takes upon himself to do so, he will incur liability if he does so negligently.'

[His Lordship cited several more cases, including those in which the courts had considered what counted as consideration in contract law, and continued:]

My lords, I have cited these instances so as to show that in one way or another the law has ensured that in this type of case a just result has been reached. But I think that today the result can and should be achieved by the application of the law of negligence and that it is unnecessary and undesirable to construct an artificial consideration. I agree with Sir Frederick Pollock's note on the case of *De la Bere v Pearson, Ltd*[5] where he wrote in *Pollock on Contract* (13th edn) 140 (note 31) that 'the cause of action is better regarded as arising from default in the performance of a voluntary undertaking independent of contract'.

My lords, it is true that this principle of law has not yet been clearly applied to a case where the service which the defendant undertakes to perform is or includes the obtaining and imparting of information. But I cannot see why it should not be: and if it had not been thought erroneously that *Derry v Peek*[6] negatived any liability for negligent statements, I think that by now it probably would have been. It cannot matter whether the information consists of fact or of opinion or is a mixture of both, nor

---

[20] (1703) 2 Ld Raym 909.   [1] (1867) LR 2 CP 631.   [2] (1867) LR 2 CP at p. 636.
[3] [1918] AC 626, [1918-19] All ER Rep 1.   [4] [1918] AC at 654.
[5] [1908] 1 KB 280, [1904-7] All ER Rep 755.   [6] (1889) 14 App Cas 337.

whether it was obtained as a result of special inquiries or comes direct from facts already in the defendant's possession or from his general store of professional knowledge. One cannot, as I have already endeavoured to show, distinguish in this respect between a duty to inquire and a duty to state.

I think, therefore, that there is ample authority to justify your lordships in saying now that the categories of special relationships, which may give rise to a duty to take care in word as well as deed, are not limited to contractual relationships or to relationships of fiduciary duty, but include also relationships which in the words of Lord Shaw in *Nocton v Lord Ashburton*[7] are 'equivalent to contract' that is, where there is an assumption of responsibility in circumstances in which, but for the absence of consideration, there would be a contract. Where there is an express undertaking, an express warranty as distinct from mere representation, there can be little difficulty. The difficulty arises in discerning those cases in which the undertaking is to be implied. In this respect the absence of consideration is not irrelevant. Payment for information or advice is very good evidence that it is being relied on and that the informer or adviser knows that it is. Where there is no consideration, it will be necessary to exercise greater care in distinguishing between social and professional relationships and between those which are of a contractual character and those which are not. It may often be material to consider whether the adviser is acting purely out of good nature or whether he is getting his reward in some indirect form. The service that a bank performs in giving a reference is not done simply out of a desire to assist commerce. It would discourage the customers of the bank if their deals fell through because the bank had refused to testify to their credit when it was good.

I have had the advantage of reading all the opinions prepared by your lordships and of studying the terms which your lordships have framed by way of definition of the sort of relationship which gives rise to a responsibility towards those who act on information or advice and so creates a duty of care towards them. I do not understand any of your lordships to hold that it is a responsibility imposed by law on certain types of persons or in certain sorts of situations. It is a responsibility that is voluntarily accepted or undertaken either generally where a general relationship, such as that of solicitor and client or banker and customer, is created, or specifically in relation to a particular transaction. In the present case the appellants were not, as in *Woods v Martins Bank, Ltd*[8] the customers or potential customers of the bank. Responsibility can attach only to the single act, i.e., the giving of the reference, and only if the doing of that act implied a voluntary undertaking to assume responsibility. This is a point of great importance because it is, as I understand it, the foundation for the ground on which in the end the House dismisses the appeal. I do not think it possible to formulate with exactitude all the conditions under which the law will in a specific case imply a voluntary undertaking, any more than it is possible to formulate those in which the law will imply a contract. But in so far as your lordships describe the circumstances in which an implication will ordinarily be drawn, I am prepared to adopt any one of your lordships' statements as showing the general rule; and I pay the same respect to the statement by DENNING LJ in his dissenting judgment in *Candler v Crane, Christmas & Co*[9] about the circumstances in which he says a duty to use care in making a statement exists....

I shall therefore content myself with the proposition that wherever there is a relationship equivalent to contract there is a duty of care. Such a relationship may be either general or particular....

I regard this proposition as an application of the general conception of proximity. Cases may arise in the future in which a new and wider proposition, quite independent of any notion of contract, will be needed....

On the facts of the present case counsel for the respondents...submits, first, that it ought not to be inferred that the respondents knew that National Provincial Bank Ltd were asking for the reference for the use of a customer. If the respondents did know that, then counsel submits that they did not intend that the reference itself should be communicated to the customer; it was intended only as material upon which the customer's bank could advise the customer on its own responsibility. I should consider

---

[7] [1914] AC at 972, [1914-15] All ER Rep at 62.   [8] [1959] 1 QB 55, [1958] 3 All ER 166.
[9] [1951] 2 KB 164 at 179, [1951] 1 All ER 426 at 433.

it necessary to examine these contentions were it not for the general disclaimer of responsibility which appears to me in any event to be conclusive. I agree entirely with the reasoning and conclusion on this point of my noble and learned friend LORD REID. A man cannot be said voluntarily to be undertaking a responsibility if at the very moment when he is said to be accepting it he declares that in fact he is not. The problem of reconciling words of exemption with the existence of a duty arises only when a party is claiming exemption from a responsibility which he has already undertaken or which he is contracting to undertake. For this reason alone, I would dismiss the appeal.

[LORD HODSON and LORD PEARCE delivered speeches in favour of dismissing the appeal.]

Appeal dismissed.

QUESTION

How can this case be distinguished from *Derry v Peek* (p. 172, ante)? What difference in principle can there be between negligently misleading someone into making an investment and negligently misleading someone into extending credit? On the other hand, can this case be distinguished from *Cattle v Stockton Waterworks* (p. 170, ante)? To what extent are the claimants in *Hedley Byrne* the authors of their own misfortune? Should one treat a person who is acting on false information as acting as voluntarily as the claimant in *Cattle* when he accepted the fixed-price contract? Or is there greater vulnerability or dependence in the former case than in the latter?

NOTES

1. The duty of care recognised to exist in *Hedley Byrne* was described differently in the different speeches of their Lordships (a tendency that persists to this day in this area of tort law). In very general terms, their Lordships considered that a duty of care would exist where a defendant had assumed responsibility for the provision of information and reasonable reliance had been placed upon that information by the claimant, resulting in economic loss. By recognising the existence of such a duty, the decision in *Hedley Byrne* opened up considerable new scope for the recovery of pure economic loss: if the duty applied, then a defendant could be liable for otherwise non-recoverable economic loss. The *Derry v Peek* rule of non-recovery was, in effect, undermined.

2. According to the majority of the Privy Council in *Mutual Life & Citizens' Assurance Co Ltd v Evatt* [1971] AC 793, [1971] 1 All ER 150, the duty recognised in *Hedley Byrne* was limited to professional advisers (such as accountants, investment advice businesses, valuers, analysts, surveyors, architects, and solicitors). But according to the minority opinion of Lord Reid and Lord Morris ([1971] 1 All ER at 163) 'when an enquirer consults a businessman in the course of his business and makes it plain to him that he is seeking considered advice and intends to act upon it in a particular way, any reasonable businessman would realise that, if he chooses to give advice without any warning or qualification, he is putting himself under a moral obligation to take some care... [and that it is] within the principles established by the *Hedley Byrne* case to regard his action in giving such advice as creating a special relationship between him and the enquirer and to translate his moral obligation into a legal obligation to take such care as is reasonable in the whole circumstances'. The English courts have preferred the minority opinion: see *Esso Petroleum Co Ltd v Mardon* [1976] QB 801, [1976] 2 All ER 5, and *Howard Marine and Dredging Co Ltd v A Ogden & Sons (Excavations) Ltd* [1978]

QB 574, [1978] 2 All ER 1134. The majority position in *Evatt* seems to be clearly incompatible with Lord Devlin's view in *Hedley Bryne* that it is 'not... possible to formulate with exactitude all the conditions under which the law will in a specific case imply a voluntary undertaking'.

3. Before *Hedley Byrne* there could be liability in damages for careless misstatements causing economic loss only if there was a contractual duty to take care (which might be artificially devised as in *De la Bere v Pearson Ltd* [1908] 1 KB 280) or a fiduciary relationship between the parties (e.g. solicitor and client, as in *Nocton v Lord Ashburton* [1914] AC 932; banker and customer). But, as the speeches show, their Lordships were not willing to apply Lord Atkin's neighbour principle (p. 30, ante) literally, which would have meant opening the door for liability to be imposed on every person who negligently inflicts reasonably foreseeable pure economic loss. Instead, the scope of liability was confined to where the defendant had assumed responsibility for the provision of information and a relationship of reliance and dependency existed between the claimant and the defendant. The objections of their Lordships to adopting Lord Aitken's principle to its fullest extent were as follows:

(a) The representation might be made in circumstances in which no reasonable person in the position of the claimant would take it seriously, for example at a party or while shopping (see Lord Denning M.R. *Howard Marine and Dredging Co Ltd v A Ogden & Sons (Excavations) Ltd* [1978] QB 574, [1978] 2 All ER 1134). This explains their Lordship's requirement for some element of reasonable reliance on the part of the claimant and a clear assumption of responsibility on the part of the defendant. One strict view is that there should be liability for advice only where the claimant made it clear that he was seeking *considered* advice of a professional nature, and intended to act upon it in a specific way (per Lord Reid and Lord Morris in their dissenting opinion in the Privy Council decision in *Mutual Life and Citizens' Assurance Co Ltd v Evatt* [1971] AC 793 at 812).

However, in *Chaudhry v Prabhakar* [1988] 3 All ER 718, [1989] 1 WLR 29 the Court of Appeal was prepared to countenance duties of care between friends giving and receiving advice about such things as the fitness of a second-hand car. The claimant asked a close family friend, who claimed to know about motor cars, to look out for a suitable second-hand car for her to buy. She specifically asked him to find out if the car had been involved in an accident. Despite some fairly obvious signs that it had been damaged, he highly recommended a car being sold by a panel beater. A few months later it became apparent that it had been involved in a very bad accident, had been poorly repaired, and was unroadworthy. Counsel for the friend conceded that, as a gratuitous agent, a duty of care was owed, but argued that the relevant standard of care was subjective—to take such care towards his principal as he would towards his own affairs. All three members of the Court of Appeal rejected this view. The appropriate standard is an objective one—to take such care as is reasonable in all the circumstances. May LJ doubted whether counsel's concession of the existence of a duty of care had been rightly made. To impose a duty on a family friend in these circumstances would he thought 'make social regulations [sic] and responsibilities between friends unnecessarily hazardous' (at 725). Stuart-Smith LJ, on the other hand, said that 'the fact that principal and agent are friends does not in my judgment affect the existence of the duty of care, although conceivably it may be a relevant circumstance in considering the degree or standard of care' (at 721; cf. Stocker LJ at 723.). An alternative approach would be to accept that there should be a duty of care in such cases but to limit it by contributory negligence.

(b) As long ago as *Pasley v Freeman* (1789) 3 Term Rep 51 (p. 939, post), the courts sought to distinguish situations in which the claimant was in as good a position to judge the truth of the representation as the defendant and those in which the defendant was in a much better position to know. Where the former was the case, there was no liability even for deceit. But as for the latter, as Lord Kenyon CJ said, 'There are many situations in life, and particularly in the commercial world, where a man cannot by any diligence inform himself of the degree of credit which ought to be given to the persons with whom he deals; in which case he must apply to those whose sources of intelligence enable them to give that information. The law of prudence leads him to apply to them, and the law of morality ought to induce them to give the information required.' In *Hedley Byrne* this concern comes out as the defendant should be 'a person … so placed that others could reasonably rely on his judgment or his skill or on his ability to make careful inquiry'. Again, this requirement was imposed by their Lordships to restrict the scope of the duty. The fundamental point is that people should normally take responsibility for the consequences of their own decisions. The defendant should take responsibility only where the decision was within the defendant's sphere of knowledge and outside the claimant's. However, the question is how to tell the difference and distinguish these two spheres.

One recent approach to this problem is to distinguish between cases in which the defendant supplies 'information' and the claimant makes the decision, and cases in which the defendant offers 'advice' on which the claimant acts (*South Australia Asset Management Corpn v York Montague Ltd* [1997] AC 191, [1996] 3 All ER 365, p. 271 post). It is not clear, however, whether this approach does more than put new labels on the problem. Note also that the courts, since *Hedley Byrne*, have often been unwilling to draw any distinction between representations, statements of fact, opinions, and advice: see *Midland Bank Trust Co Ltd v Hett, Stubbs and Kemp (a firm)* [1979] Ch 384, [1978] 3 All ER 571; *Ross v Caunters* [1980] Ch 297, [1979] 3 All ER 580. However, as Shaw LJ pointed out in *Howard Marine and Dredging Co Ltd v A Ogden & Sons (Excavations) Ltd* [1978] QB 574 at 600–601, where the claimant *asks* the defendant for a specific *fact*, which the claimant has no direct means of ascertaining, this may go to show 'the gravity of the inquiry or the importance and influence attached to the answer'. Conversely if the defendant told the claimant that he was giving his opinion without checking his files or without doing any research, there would presumably be no liability (see A. Honoré (1965) 8 JSPTL (NS) 284 at 290–291; R. Stevens (1964) 27 MLR 121).

Much may depend on how costly it would have been for either the claimant or the defendant to obtain accurate information, the relative position of the two parties, the degree of reliance and dependency of the claimant upon the defendant, and on what each party expects of the other. Consider, for example, *Esso Petroleum Co Ltd v Mardon* [1976] QB 801, [1976] 2 All ER 5. Esso's representative induced the claimant to enter into a tenancy contract of an Esso petrol filling station by an honest but negligent misrepresentation that the consumption of petrol would reach 200,000 gallons in the third year of operations. The consumption never got anywhere near this figure and the claimant (Mardon) lost all the capital he had put into the station. The facts took place before s. 2(1) of the Misrepresentation Act 1967 came into force. The Court of Appeal held that *Hedley Byrne* could be used to impose liability for pre-contractual statements. The claimant in this case was largely reliant upon Esso to provide him with the necessary information, which Esso had undertaken to supply. Also, as Bishop puts it in (1980) 96 LQR 360 at 371, '[a]lmost certainly the cost of care to Esso was less than the cost of error to Mardon so that a rule making Esso liable is likely to minimise transaction costs. Furthermore, parties probably expect care in cases of this kind . . . .'

(c) The faulty information might spread from person to person, causing losses to large numbers of people, despite the best efforts of the defendant and without the defendant being able to restrict his or her liability for it. In *Hedley Byrne*, this factor was cited as justifying the restriction in scope of the duty to where there had been some element of direct communication to the claimant. In Lord Reid's words, [1963] 2 All ER at 581, the information

'can be broadcast with or without the consent or the foresight of the speaker or writer. It would be one thing to say that the speaker owes a duty to a limited class, but it would be going very far to say that he owes a duty to every ultimate "consumer" who acts on those words to his detriment. It would be no use to say that a speaker or writer owes a duty, but can disclaim responsibility if he wants to. He, like the manufacturer, could make it part of a contract that he is not to be liable for his negligence: but that contract would not protect him in a question with a third party at least if the third party was unaware of it.'

(d) This fear is reminiscent of Cardozo CJ's warning in *Ultramares Corpn v Touche* 255 NY 170 (1931) against liability 'in an indeterminate amount for an indeterminate time to an indeterminate class'. But why is this a problem? Such liability can arise in the context of personal or property damage: for example, consider the current wave of asbestos-related litigation. Lord Bridge in *Caparo Industries plc v Dickman* [1990] 2 AC 605 at 621 offers another explanation. He says that to allow the claimant to win in such cases would be to 'confer on the world a quite unwarranted entitlement to appropriate for their own purposes the benefit of the expert knowledge or professional expertise attributed to the maker of the statement'. This argument can be restated in economic terms: the problem is that information is a valuable resource but unlike other valuable resources it is very difficult to prevent those who have not paid for it benefiting from it. If this happens, then people may put less effort into producing information than its value would justify, which would have negative economic consequences for society at large. Imposing legal liability for misleading information obtained otherwise than through a reasonably close and direct relationship would make the problem worse and act as a disincentive to the free circulation of information; see Bishop, op cit., and *Howarth* pp. 316–18. However, in practice, the *Hedley Byrne* doctrine does extend beyond cases in which the defendant supplies information directly to the claimant or to the claimant's agent; see *Smith v Eric S Bush* and *Morgan Crucible Co plc v Hill Samuel & Co Ltd* [1991] Ch 295, [1991] 1 All ER 148 (p. 218, post). But in such cases the claimant has to 'know or inferentially know' (Lord Oliver in *Caparo*) that the information would be communicated to the claimant, or at least to a member of an identifiable class of possible claimants, and that the information is required for a specific purpose. In addition, it must be likely that the claimant would rely on the information for the specific purpose. Such a requirement maintains the need for some element of proximity in the relationship between claimant and defendant, which is necessary before liability can arise in the wake of *Caparo*.

4.   What about a negligent misrepresentation made *after* the formation of contract? Say that A has contracted to provide B with a burglar alarm system. After a burglary at another customer's premises, A negligently assures B that the system performs properly, but in fact it does not, so causing loss to B. Should this be classified as coming with the duty of care recognised in *Hedley Byrne*, or as a matter that solely goes to the question of whether A is conforming to his contractual obligations? In *J Nunes Diamonds Ltd v Dominion Electric Protection Co* (1972) 26 DLR (3d) 699, the Supreme Court of Canada held (by a narrow majority) on these facts that there was no duty of care, on the ground, among others, that liability in tort could be based only on a tort unconnected with performance of the contract. Would an English court reach the same conclusion? The position is perhaps unclear. The existence of a contract is no longer thought to be a bar to tort liability (*Henderson v Merrett Syndicates Ltd* [1995] 2 AC 145, [1994] 3 All ER 506 (p. 232, post), but in most contexts the courts are keen to keep the content of any tort duties in line with the parties' contractual duties (see *White v Chief Constable of South Yorkshire* [1999] 2 AC 445, [1999] 1 All ER 1, p. 243, ante).

5.   Occasionally a duty of care concerning information or advice may be denied on explicit policy grounds. Judges have a wide immunity from suit (*Sirros v Moore* [1975] QB 118, [1974] 3 All ER 776), 'otherwise no man but a beggar, or a fool, would be a judge' (Stair, *Institutions*, Bk 4, tit. 1, s. 5, quoted by Lord Fraser in *Arenson v Casson Beckman Rutley & Co* [1977] AC 405 at 440). For much the same reason, arbitrators are said to be immune from actions for negligence, although in *Arenson's* case Lord Kilbrandon and Lord Fraser expressed some doubt about this exception, and Lord Salmon said that it ought not apply in all cases. A surveyor appointed to determine rent under a rent review clause in a lease has been held to be acting merely as an 'expert' and therefore not to enjoy the arbitrator's immunity: *Palacath Ltd v Flanagan* [1985] 2 All ER 161; *N v C* [1998] 1 FLR 63. Barristers and solicitor-advocates were until recently accorded the special privilege of immunity from actions for negligence in the conduct and management of litigation. The immunity was removed by the House of Lords in *Arthur J S Hall & Co v Simons* [2002] 1 AC 615, [2000] 3 All ER 673 (p. 61, ante). Attempts to re-litigate issues by means of such actions are liable, however, to be struck out as an abuse of process. For a discussion of the relationship between *Hedley Byrne* liability and qualified privilege, see *Spring v Guardian Assurance plc* [1995] 2 AC 296, [1994] 3 All ER 129 (p. 58, ante, and p. 242, post).

4 THE BASIS AND DEVELOPMENT OF THE *HEDLEY BYRNE* EXCEPTION

Although there are common elements in their Lordships' speeches in *Hedley Byrne*, it is plain that they do not agree about the underlying justification of the decision. For Lord Reid, the difficulty in the claimant's case is that harm caused by faulty information has special features not shared with harm caused by physical impact, a difficulty which can be met by imposing special conditions on liability in information cases—namely that it has to be plain that the claimant was relying on the defendant to exercise reasonable care, that it was reasonable for the claimant to rely, and that the defendant knew or ought to have known that the claimant was relying. For Lord Reid, therefore, the problem is about the proper reach of the tort of negligence. For Lord Morris and Lord Devlin the difficulty in the claimant's case is rather that there is no contract between claimant and defendant. For them the problem is the boundary between tort and contract. Lord Morris says that the difficulty does not arise where the defendant has 'assumed responsibility' by offering to perform a service for the claimant using special skills. The protection of the law extends to those whom the defendant knows or ought to know might rely on that performance. Lord Devlin says that the difficulty does not arise where the relationship between the parties, although not technically contractual, is 'equivalent to contract', where there is an assumption of responsibility albeit without technical consideration. The question of the proper basis of *Hedley Byrne* has been for some time a persistent problem for the courts. After considerable uncertainty, the existence of an 'assumption of responsibility' on the part of a defendant towards a claimant has emerged as a key factor. If such an assumption of responsibility has occurred, then this will in general be treated as justifying the imposition of liability for economic loss. However, what exactly constitutes such an 'assumption of responsibility' is not always clear, nor is its relationship to the wider *Caparo* test for determining whether a duty of care should be imposed. In addition, it seemed for some time that the assumption of responsibility test had been rejected or sidelined as a basis for what is often referred to as '*Hedley Byrne* liability'.

■ Smith v Eric S Bush; Harris v Wyre Forest District Council
House of Lords [1989] 2 All ER 514

In the first of these cases (in which the appeals were heard together), Mrs Smith (the respondent) applied to the Abbey National Building Society for a mortgage to enable her to purchase a house. The Society instructed Eric S Bush (the appellants), an independent firm of surveyors and valuers, to prepare a written valuation report so as to ensure that there would be adequate security for the loan. Mrs Smith paid the Society the standard inspection fee, and signed an application form which stated that she would be provided with a copy of the report and also contained a disclaimer saying that neither the Society nor the surveyor warranted that the report and the valuation would be accurate and that the report would be supplied without any assumption of responsibility. The copy of the report which she received contained a similar disclaimer. In sole reliance on the report, which said that no essential repairs were necessary, she purchased the house. The surveyors, who knew that the report would be shown to the purchaser, were found to be negligent in failing to discover and report a structural defect in one of the chimneys. As a result of this defect one of the chimney flues collapsed, eighteen months after the purchase, crashing through the bedroom ceiling and causing considerable damage. The trial judge held the surveyors liable. The Court of Appeal, [1987] 3 All ER 179, affirmed this decision. The surveyors appealed to the House of Lords, which affirmed the decision of the Court of Appeal.

In the second case, Mr and Mrs Harris (the appellants) applied to a local council for a mortgage. The council instructed one of their own employees, Mr Lee, to carry out the survey. The mortgage application form stated that the valuation was confidential and was intended solely for the information of the council, and that no responsibility whatsoever was implied or accepted for the value or condition of the property. The council's employee valued the house at the asking price of £9,450, and the council offered to advance Mr and Mrs Harris 90 per cent of that sum subject to some minor repairs being done to the house. The report was not made available to Mr and Mrs Harris, but they assumed that the house was worth at least the amount of the valuation and that the surveyor had found no serious defects. They purchased the house for £9,000. When they tried to resell it, three years later, a new survey revealed that the house was subject to settlement, was virtually unsaleable, and could be repaired, if at all, at a cost more than the purchase price. The trial judge, [1987] 1 EGLR 231, awarded damages for negligence against the council, but the Court of Appeal, [1988] 1 All ER 691, reversed this decision on the ground that the disclaimer notice excluded liability. The House of Lords reversed the Court of Appeal's decision.

LORD TEMPLEMAN: . . .

My Lords, these appeals involve consideration of three questions. The first question is whether a valuer instructed by a building society or other mortgagee to value a house, knowing that his valuation will probably be relied on by the prospective purchaser and mortgagor of the house, owes to the purchaser in tort a duty to exercise reasonable skill and care in carrying out the valuation unless the valuer disclaims liability. If so, the second question is whether a disclaimer of liability by or on behalf of the valuer is a notice which purports to exclude liability for negligence within the Unfair Contract Terms Act 1977 and is, therefore, ineffective unless it satisfies the requirement of reasonableness. If so, the third question is whether, in the absence of special circumstances, it is fair and reasonable for the valuer to rely on the notice excluding liability . . . .

[In relation to the first question, his Lordship referred to the speech of Lord Devlin in the *Hedley Byrne* case, and said:] In the present appeals the relationship between the valuer and the purchaser is 'akin to contract'. The valuer knows that the consideration which he receives derives from the purchaser and is passed on by the mortgagee, and the valuer also knows that the valuation will determine whether or not the purchaser buys the house . . . .

In general, I am of the opinion that in the absence of a disclaimer of liability the valuer who values a house for the purpose of a mortgage, knowing that the mortgagee will rely and the mortgagor will probably rely on the valuation, knowing that the purchaser mortgagor has in effect paid for the valuation, is under a duty to exercise reasonable skill and care and that duty is owed to both parties to the mortgage for which the valuation is made. Indeed, in both the appeals now under consideration the existence of such a dual duty is tacitly accepted and acknowledged because notices excluding liability for breach of the duty owed to the purchaser were drafted by the mortgagee and imposed on the purchaser. In these circumstances it is necessary to consider the second question which arises in these appeals, namely whether the disclaimers of liability are notices which fall within the Unfair Contract Terms Act 1977.

In *Harris v Wyre Forest DC* the Court of Appeal (Kerr, Nourse LJJ and Caufield J) accepted an argument that the 1977 Act did not apply because the council by their express disclaimer refused to obtain a valuation save on terms that the valuer would not be under any obligation to Mr and Mrs Harris to take reasonable care or exercise reasonable skill. The council did not exclude liability for negligence but excluded negligence so that the valuer and the council never came under a duty of care to Mr and Mrs Harris and could not be guilty of negligence. This construction would not give effect to the manifest intention of the 1977 Act but would emasculate the Act. The construction would provide no control over standard form exclusion clauses which individual members of the public are obliged to accept. A party to a contract or a tortfeasor could opt out of the 1977 Act by declining, in the words of Nourse LJ, to recognise 'their own answerability to the plaintiffs' (see [1988] 1 All ER 691 at 697, [1988] QB 835 at 845). Caulfield J said that the Act 'can only be relevant where there is on the facts a potential liability' (see [1988] 1 All ER 691 at 704, [1988] QB 835 at 850). But no one intends to commit a tort and therefore any notice which excludes liability is a notice which excludes a potential liability. Kerr LJ sought to confine the Act to 'situations where the existence of a duty of care is not open to doubt' or where there is 'an inescapable duty of care' (see [1988] 1 All ER 691 at 702, [1988] QB 835 at 853). I can find nothing in the 1977 Act or in the general law to identify or support this distinction. In the result the Court of Appeal held that the Act does not apply to 'negligent misstatements where a disclaimer has prevented a duty of care from coming into existence' (see [1988] 1 All ER 691 at 699-700, [1988] QB 835 at 848 per Nourse LJ). My Lords, this confuses the valuer's report with the work which the valuer carries out in order to make his report. The valuer owed a duty to exercise reasonable skill and care in his inspection and valuation. If he had been careful in his work, he would not have made a 'negligent misstatement' in his report.

Section 11(3) of the 1977 Act provides that, in considering whether it is fair and reasonable to allow reliance on a notice which excludes liability in tort, account must be taken of 'all the circumstances obtaining when the liability arose or (but for the notice) would have arisen'. Section 13(1) of the Act prevents the exclusion of any right or remedy and (to that extent) s 2 also prevents the exclusion of liability 'by reference to . . . notices which exclude . . . the relevant obligation or duty'. Nourse LJ dismissed s 11(3) as 'peripheral' and made no comment on s 13(1). In my opinion both these provisions support the view that the 1977 Act requires that all exclusion notices which would in common law provide a defence to an action for negligence must satisfy the requirement of reasonableness.

The answer to the second question involved in these appeals is that the disclaimer of liability made by the council on its own behalf in *Harris's* case and by the Abbey National on behalf of the appellant surveyors in *Smith's* case constitute notices which fall within the 1977 Act and must satisfy the requirement of reasonableness.

[His Lordship went on to decide the third question in relation to each exclusion clause and held that it was not 'fair and reasonable' to allow reliance on each clause.]

LORD GRIFFITHS: . . .

Counsel for the council and Mr Lee drew attention to the doubts expressed about the correctness of this decision by Kerr LJ in the course of his judgment in the Court of Appeal, and submitted, on the authority of *Hedley Byrne & Co Ltd v Heller & Partners Ltd* [1963] 2 All ER 575, [1964] AC 465, that it was essential to found liability for a negligent misstatement that there had been 'a voluntary assumption of responsibility' on the part of the person giving the advice. I do not accept this submission and I do not think that voluntary assumption of responsibility is a helpful or realistic test for liability. It is true that reference is made in a number of the speeches in the *Hedley Byrne* case to the assumption of responsibility as a test of liability but it must be remembered that those speeches were made in the context of a case in which the central issue was whether a duty of care could arise when there had been an express disclaimer of responsibility for the accuracy of the advice. Obviously, if an adviser expressly assumes responsibility for his advice, a duty of care will arise, but such is extremely unlikely in the ordinary course of events. The House of Lords approved a duty of care being imposed on the facts in *Cann v Willson* (1888) 39 Ch D 39 and in *Candler v Crane Christmas & Co* [1951] 1 All ER 426, [1951] 2 KB 164. But, if the surveyor in *Cann v Willson* or the accountant in *Candler v Crane Christmas & Co* had actually been asked if he was voluntarily assuming responsibility for his advice to the mortgagee or the purchaser of the shares, I have little doubt he would have replied: 'Certainly not. My responsibility is limited to the person who employs me.' The phrase 'assumption of responsibility' can only have any real meaning if it is understood as referring to the circumstances in which the law will deem the maker of the statement to have assumed responsibility to the person who acts on the advice.

In *Ministry of Housing and Local Government v Sharp* [1970] 1 All ER 1009, [1970] 2 QB 223 both Lord Denning MR and Salmon LJ rejected the argument that a voluntary assumption of responsibility was the sole criterion for imposing a duty of care for the negligent preparation of a search certificate in the local land charges register.

The essential distinction between the present case and the situation being considered in the *Hedley Byrne* case and in the two earlier cases is that in those cases the advice was being given with the intention of persuading the recipient to act on it. In the present case the purpose of providing the report is to advise the mortgagee but it is given in circumstances in which it is highly probable that the purchaser will in fact act on its contents, although that was not the primary purpose of the report. I have had considerable doubts whether it is wise to increase the scope of the duty for negligent advice beyond the person directly intended by the giver of the advice to act on it to those whom he knows may do so. Certainly in the field of the law of mortgagor and mortgagee there is authority that points in the other direction . . . .

[His Lordship considered these cases. He then concluded that *Yianni v Edwin Evans & Sons* [1982] QB 438, [1981] 3 All ER 592, in which Park J held that in the circumstances of the case a valuer and surveyor employed by a building society to inspect and value a house owed a duty of care to the purchaser who had applied to the building society for a loan, was correctly decided. He continued:] I have already given my view that the voluntary assumption of responsibility is unlikely to be a helpful or realistic test in most cases. I therefore return to the question in what circumstances should the law deem those who give advice to have assumed responsibility to the person who acts on the advice or, in other words, in what circumstances should a duty of care be owed by the adviser to those who act on his advice? I would answer: only if it is foreseeable that if the advice is negligent the recipient is likely to suffer damage, that there is a sufficiently proximate relationship between the parties and that it is just and reasonable to impose the liability. In the case of a surveyor valuing a small house for a building society or local authority, the application of these three criteria leads to the conclusion that he owes a duty of care to the purchaser. If the valuation is negligent and is relied on damage in the form of economic loss to the purchaser is obviously foreseeable. The necessary proximity arises from the surveyor's know-ledge that the overwhelming probability is that the purchaser will rely on his valuation, the evidence was that surveyors knew that approximately 90% of purchasers did so, and the fact that the surveyor only obtains the work because the purchaser is willing to pay his fee. It is just and reasonable that the duty should be imposed for the advice is given in a professional as opposed to a social context and liability for breach of the duty will be limited both as to its extent and amount. The extent of the liability is limited to the purchaser of the house: I would not extend it to subsequent purchasers. The amount of the liability cannot be very great because it relates to a modest house. There is no question here of creating a liability of indeterminate amount to an indeterminate class. I would certainly wish to stress, that in cases where the advice has not been given for the specific purpose of the recipient acting on it, it should only be in cases when the adviser knows that there is a high degree of probability that some other identifiable person will act on the advice that a duty of care should be imposed. It would impose an intolerable burden on those who give advice in a professional or commercial context if they were to owe a duty not only to those to whom they give the advice but to any other person who might choose to act on it.

I accept that the mere fact of a contract between mortgagor and mortgagee will not of itself in all cases be sufficient to found a duty of care. But I do not accept the view of the Court of Appeal in *Curran v Northern Ireland Co-ownership Housing Association Ltd* (1986) 8 NIJB 1 that a mortgagee who accepts a fee to obtain a valuation of a small house owes no duty of care to the mortgagor in the selec-tion of the valuer to whom he entrusts the work. In my opinion, the mortgagee in such a case, knowing that the mortgagor will rely on the valuation, owes a duty to the mortgagor to take reasonable care to employ a reasonably competent valuer. Provided he does this the mortgagee will not be held liable for the negligence of the independent valuer who acts as an independent contractor....

[LORD JAUNCEY OF TULLICHETTLE delivered a speech in favour of dismissing the appeal in the first case and allowing the appeal in the second case. LORD KEITH OF KINKEL and LORD BRANDON OF OAKBROOK agreed with all the speeches.]

QUESTION

Lord Griffiths explicitly rejects 'assumption of responsibility' as the explanation of *Hedley Byrne*. What does Lord Templeman think of 'assumption of responsibility'? Although Lord Templeman refers to Lord Devlin's 'equivalent to contract' theory, does he consider 'assump-tion of responsibility' to be an element of it?

NOTES

1. Lord Griffiths, in effect, updates Lord Reid's approach to *Hedley Byrne*. His starting point is whether it is permissible to extend the protection of negligence law to cases of

negligent information. Lord Griffiths anticipates the approach of the House of Lords in *Caparo Industries v Dickman* [1990] 2 AC 605, [1990] 1 All ER 568 (p. 37, ante and p. 224, post) to such questions. He asks whether the harm was reasonably foreseeable, whether there was 'proximity', and whether it would be just, fair, and reasonable to impose liability. What are the objections to liability considered by Lord Griffiths? Does his three-part test deal with them adequately?

2. Lord Griffiths says that where the advice has been given other than for the specific purpose of the recipient there should be no liability unless 'the adviser knows that there is a high degree of probability that some other identifiable person will act on the advice that a duty of care should be imposed'. Notice also the overlap between this and his exposition of why there is proximity in the case before him. Is the concept of proximity well-defined here? Notice that there are two other important factual causes of the harm to the claimant—the fact that the building society passed on the valuation to the claimant and the fact that the claimant acted on the valuation. Would either of these events count as breaking the chain of causation? Is the claimant the author of his own misfortune? Is he at least contributorily negligent (see generally M. Harwood (1987) 50 MLR 588). Is the position different if the lender is the claimant? Should the valuation then count not as 'advice' but only as 'information' which the claimant uses to make up its own mind about how much to lend taking into account all the surrounding factors? The House of Lords seemed to think so in *South Australia Asset Management Corpn v York Montague Ltd* [1997] AC 191, [1996] 3 All ER 365 (p. 271, post).

3. From December 2007, by virtue of Part V of the Housing Act 2004 and the Home Information Packs Regulations 2007, SI 2007/992 and 2007/1667, sellers have to obtain surveys on their houses as part of completing the compulsory Home Information Packs (HIPs) which they must provide to potential buyers. Given that the cost of these surveys will be borne by the seller, and that HIPs surveys will be available to all potential buyers, when might it be fair, just, and reasonable for the eventual buyer of a property to be able to maintain an action in tort against a surveyor who has prepared a HIPs survey? If a buyer commissions their own survey of the property in question, might this break any chain of causation, even if a duty of care exists to the buyer on the part of the surveyor providing a HIPs survey? Again, the decision in *South Australia Asset Management Corpn v York Montague Ltd* would appear to limit liability in this situation (see p. 271, post).

4. *South Australia Asset Management Corpn v York Montague Ltd* is also the leading case on remoteness of damage and the measure of damages in *Hedley Byrne* situations. See also *Platform Home Loans Ltd v Oyston Shipways* [2000] 2 AC 190, [1999] 1 All ER 833, (p. 277, post). See in addition *Aneco Reinsurance Underwriting Ltd v Johnson & Higgins Ltd* [2001] 2 All ER (Comm) 929, [2001] UKHL 51.

5. The position established in *Smith v Bush* in respect of surveyors is different where the claimant has an adversarial relationship with the professional concerned, for example lawyers representing the other side in a dispute. The position is summarised thus by Lord Goff in *White v Jones* [1995] 1 All ER 691 at 698–699:

First, the general rule is well established that a solicitor acting on behalf of a client owes a duty of care only to his client. The relationship between a solicitor and his client is nearly always contractual, and the scope of the solicitor's duties will be set by the terms of his retainer; but a duty of care owed by a solicitor to his client will arise concurrently in contract and in tort (see *Midland Bank Trust Co Ltd v Hett, Stubbs & Kemp (a firm)* [1978] 3 All ER 571, [1979] Ch 384, recently approved by your Lordships' House in *Henderson v Merrett Syndicates Ltd* [1995] 2 AC 145, [1994] 3 All ER 506). But, when a solicitor is performing his duties to his client, he will generally owe no duty of care to third parties. Accordingly, as Nicholls V-C pointed out in the present case, a solicitor acting for a seller of land does not generally owe a duty of care to the buyer: see *Gran Gelato Ltd v Richcliff (Group) Ltd* [1992] 1 All ER 865, [1992] Ch 560. Nor, as a general rule, does a solicitor acting for a party in adversarial litigation owe a duty of care to that party's opponent: see *Al-Kandari v J R Brown & Co (a firm)* [1988] 1 All ER 833 at 836, [1988] QB 665 at 672 per Lord Donaldson MR. Further, it has been held that a solicitor advising a client about a proposed dealing with his property in his lifetime owes no duty of care to a prospective beneficiary under the client's then will who may be prejudicially affected: see *Clarke v Bruce Lance & Co (a firm)* [1988] 1 All ER 364, [1988] 1 WLR 881.

The Court of Appeal reached similar conclusions in *West Wiltshire District Council v Garland* [1995] Ch 297, [1995] 2 All ER 17, in which district auditors, despite being subject to duties in favour of the council whose accounts they were auditing and of the electors of the district, were held to owe no duty to the council's officers about whom they made critical reports. It was important that the auditors should be free of the threat of civil action when carrying out their central function of protecting the council.

Note, however, that in *Al-Kandari v J R Brown & Co* [1988] QB 665, [1988] 1 All ER 833 the Court of Appeal did, exceptionally, declare there to have been a duty of care. The solicitor had stepped outside his role as his client's representative and had given an undertaking (embodied in a consent order in matrimonial proceedings) as to the custody of his client's passport. By so doing he had assumed a duty to the other party to litigation (his client's wife) to take reasonable care not to allow the passport to come into his own client's hands. Somehow the passport did get into the client's hands. He had his wife kidnapped and abducted their children to Kuwait, using the passport to do so. The children were never recovered. There was held to be a breach of the assumed duty of care. The Court of Appeal (reversing the trial judge on this point) found that the damages for physical illness and psychiatric illness suffered by the wife were a natural and probable consequence of the breach of duty and not too remote. See also *Dean v Allin & Watts* [2001] 2 Lloyd's Rep 249, [2001] EWCA Civ 758, where in the particular circumstances of that case a solicitor was found to have assumed a duty of care in tort to a lender, even though the solicitor's client was the borrower.

6. The Court of Appeal in *Merrett v Babb* [2001] QB 1174, [2001] EWCA Civ 214 applied *Smith v Bush* and imposed liability upon a surveyor who was employed by a valuation firm: the fact that the surveyor was an employee rather than an independent contractor was held to be irrelevant to the question of whether the surveyor owed a duty of care to the house buyers. The Court of Appeal distinguished this case from the decision of the House of Lords in *Williams v Natural Life Health Foods Ltd* [1998] 2 All ER 577, [1998] UKHL 17, where it was held that it was necessary for a director of a company to have personally assumed responsibility towards the claimant before the duty of care owed by the company in respect of the pure economic loss sustained by the claimant would also extend to the director (see p. 258, post). In giving the main judgment of the Court, May LJ at [44–45] considered that the nature of the activity performed by the surveyor and his personal performance of the valuation at issue meant that the defendant surveyor in *Merrett v Babb* could be deemed to have assumed personal responsibility towards the claimants, even in the absence of 'direct dealing…between the valuer and the purchaser'. As the employing firm had gone bankrupt and its liability insurance had been discontinued, this meant that the liability fell on the surveyor personally.

7.	The decision in *Merrett v Babb* is also notable for its analysis of the relationship between the judgments in *Smith v Bush*, in particular Lord Griffith's rejection of the 'assumption of responsibility' concept, and the subsequent importance given to this concept in the later case law. May LJ suggested that these approaches could be reconciled on the basis that the 'assumption of responsibility' test should be regarded as essentially merging with and having no real independent existence from the general test as to whether a duty of care existed, as set out in the seminal case of *Caparo v Dickman* [1990] 2 AC 605, [1990] 1 All ER 568. Some doubt may have been cast over this approach by the House of Lords in *Customs and Excise Commissioners v Barclays Bank Plc* [2006] 4 All ER 265, [2006] UKHL 28: see p. 259, post.

■ Caparo Industries plc v Dickman

House of Lords [1990] 1 All ER 568

For the facts see p. 37, ante

LORD BRIDGE OF HARWICH: ...

[After considering the general approach to the duty of care, set out p. 41, ante, his Lordship continued:] The damage which may be caused by the negligently spoken or written word will normally be confined to economic loss sustained by those who rely on the accuracy of the information or advice they receive as a basis for action. The question what, if any, duty is owed by the maker of a statement to exercise due care to ensure its accuracy arises typically in relation to statements made by a person in the exercise of his calling or profession. In advising the client who employs him the professional man owes a duty to exercise that standard of skill and care appropriate to his professional status and will be liable both in contract and in tort for all losses which his client may suffer by reason of any breach of that duty. But the possibility of any duty of care being owed to third parties with whom the professional man was in no contractual relationship was for long denied because of the wrong turning taken by the law in *Le Lievre v Gould* [1893] 1 QB 491 in overruling *Cann v Willson* (1888) 39 Ch D 39. In *Candler v Crane Christmas & Co* [1951] 1 All ER 426, [1951] 2 KB 164 Denning LJ, in his dissenting judgment, made a valiant attempt to correct the error. But it was not until the decision of this House in *Hedley Byrne & Co Ltd v Heller & Partners Ltd* [1963] 2 All ER 575, [1964] AC 465 that the law was once more set on the right path.

[His Lordship reviewed the subsequent authorities and continued:] The salient feature of all these cases is that the defendant giving advice or information was fully aware of the nature of the transaction which the plaintiff had in contemplation, knew that the advice or information would be communicated to him directly or indirectly and knew that it was very likely that the plaintiff would rely on that advice or information in deciding whether or not to engage in the transaction in contemplation. In these circumstances the defendant could clearly be expected, subject always to the effect of any disclaimer of responsibility, specifically to anticipate that the plaintiff would rely on the advice or information given by the defendant for the very purpose for which he did in the event rely on it. So also the plaintiff, subject again to the effect of any disclaimer, would in that situation reasonably suppose that he was entitled to rely on the advice or information communicated to him for the very purpose for which he required it. The situation is entirely different where a statement is put into more or less general circulation and may foreseeably be relied on by strangers to the maker of the statement for any one of a variety of different purposes which the maker of the statement has no specific reason to anticipate. To hold the maker of the statement to be under a duty of care in respect of the accuracy of the statement to all and sundry for any purpose for which they may choose to rely on it is not only to subject him, in the classic words of Cardozo CJ, to 'liability in an indeterminate amount for an indeterminate time to an indeterminate class' (see *Ultramares Corpn v Touche* (1931) 255 NY 170 at 179), it is also to confer on the world at large a quite unwarranted entitlement to appropriate for their own purposes the benefit of the expert knowledge or professional expertise attributed to the maker of the statement. Hence, looking only at the circumstances of these decided cases where a duty of care in respect of negligent statements has been held to exist, I should expect to find that the 'limit or control mechanism ... imposed on the liability of a wrongdoer towards those who have suffered economic damage in consequence of his negligence' (see the *Candlewood* case [1985] 2 All ER 935 at 945, [1986] AC 1 at 25) rested on the necessity to prove in this category of the tort of negligence, as an essential ingredient of the 'proximity' between the plaintiff and the defendant, that the defendant knew that his statement would be communicated to the plaintiff, either as an individual or as a member of an identifiable class, specifically in connection with a particular transaction or transactions of a particular kind (e.g. in a prospectus inviting invest-ment) and that the plaintiff would be very likely to rely on it for the purpose of deciding whether or not to enter on that transaction or on a transaction of that kind. ...

[His Lordship reviewed other authorities, and then considered the position of auditors in relation to the shareholders of a public limited company arising from the provisions of the Companies Act 1985.]

No doubt these provisions establish a relationship between the auditors and the shareholders of a company on which the shareholder is entitled to rely for the protection of his interest. But the crucial question concerns the extent of the shareholder's interest which the auditor has a duty to protect. The shareholders of a company have a collective interest in the company's proper management and in so far as a negligent failure of the auditor to report accurately on the state of the company's finances deprives the shareholders of the opportunity to exercise their powers in general meeting to call the directors to book and to ensure that errors in management are corrected, the shareholders ought to be entitled to a remedy. But in practice no problem arises in this regard since the interest of the share-holders in the proper management of the company's affairs is indistinguishable from the interest of the company itself and any loss suffered by the shareholders, e.g. by the negligent failure of the auditor to discover and expose a misappropriation of funds by a director of the company, will be recouped by a claim against the auditor in the name of the company, not by individual shareholders.

I find it difficult to visualise a situation arising in the real world in which the individual shareholder could claim to have sustained a loss in respect of his existing shareholding referable to the negligence of the auditor which could not be recouped by the company. But on this part of the case your Lordships were much pressed with the argument that such a loss might occur by a negligent undervaluation of the company's assets in the auditor's report relied on by the individual shareholder in deciding to sell his shares at an undervalue. The argument then runs thus. The shareholder, qua shareholder, is entitled to rely on the auditor's report as the basis of his investment decision to sell his existing shareholding. If he sells at an undervalue he is entitled to recover the loss from the auditor. There can be no distinction in law between the shareholder's investment decision to sell the shares he has or to buy additional shares. It follows, therefore, that the scope of the duty of care owed to him by the auditor extends to cover any loss sustained consequent on the purchase of additional shares in reliance on the auditor's negligent report.

I believe this argument to be fallacious. Assuming without deciding that a claim by a shareholder to recover a loss suffered by selling his shares at an undervalue attributable to an undervaluation of the company's assets in the auditor's report could be sustained at all, it would not be by reason of any reliance by the shareholder on the auditor's report in deciding to sell: the loss would be referable to the depreciatory effect of the report on the market value of the shares before ever the decision of the shareholder to sell was taken. A claim to recoup a loss alleged to flow from the purchase of overvalued shares, on the other hand, can only be sustained on the basis of the purchaser's reliance on the report. The specious equation of 'investment decisions' to sell or to buy as giving rise to parallel claims thus appears to me to be untenable. Moreover, the loss in the case of the sale would be of a loss of part of the value of the shareholder's existing holding, which, assuming a duty of care owed to individual shareholders, it might sensibly lie within the scope of the auditor's duty to protect. A loss, on the other hand, resulting from the purchase of additional shares would result from a wholly independent transac-tion having no connection with the existing shareholding.

I believe it is this last distinction which is of critical importance and which demonstrates the unsound-ness of the conclusion reached by the majority of the Court of Appeal. It is never sufficient to ask simply whether A owes B a duty of care. It is always necessary to determine the scope of the duty by reference to the kind of damage from which A must take care to save B harmless:

> 'The question is always whether the defendant was under a duty to avoid or prevent that damage, but the actual nature of the damage suffered is relevant to the existence and extent of any duty to avoid or prevent it.'

See *Sutherland Shire Council v Heyman* (1985) 60 ALR 1 at 48 per Brennan J.

Assuming for the purpose of the argument that the relationship between the auditor of a company and individual shareholders is of sufficient proximity to give rise to a duty of care, I do not understand how the scope of that duty can possibly extend beyond the protection of any individual shareholder from losses in the value of the shares which he holds. As a purchaser of additional shares in reliance on the auditor's report, he stands in no different position from any other investing member of the public to whom the auditor owes no duty.

I would allow the appeal and dismiss the cross-appeal.

LORD OLIVER OF AYLMERTON: . . .

[After considering the general approach to the duty of care, set out on p. 39, ante, his Lordship said:] What can be deduced from the *Hedley Byrne* case . . . is that the necessary relationship between the maker of a statement or giver of advice (the adviser) and the recipient who acts in reliance on it (the advisee) may typically be held to exist where (1) the advice is required for a purpose, whether particularly specified or generally described, which is made known, either actually or inferentially, to the adviser at the time when the advice is given, (2) the adviser knows, either actually or inferentially, that his advice will be communicated to the advisee, either specifically or as a member of an ascertainable class, in order that it should be used by the advisee for that purpose, (3) it is known, either actually or inferentially, that the advice so communicated is likely to be acted on by the advisee for that purpose without independent inquiry and (4) it is so acted on by the advisee to his detriment. That is not, of course, to suggest that these conditions are either conclusive or exclusive, but merely that the actual decision in the case does not warrant any broader propositions. . . .

My Lords, no decision of this House has gone further than *Smith v Eric S Bush*, but your Lordships are asked by Caparo to widen the area of responsibility even beyond the limits to which it was extended by the Court of Appeal in this case and to find a relationship of proximity between the adviser and third parties to whose attention the advice may come in circumstances in which the reliance said to have given rise to the loss is strictly unrelated either to the intended recipient or to the purpose for which the advice was required. My Lords, I discern no pressing reason of policy which would require such an extension and there seems to me to be powerful reasons against it. As Lord Reid observed in the course of his speech in the *Hedley Byrne* case [1963] 2 All ER 575 at 581, [1964] AC 465 at 483, words can be broadcast with or without the consent or foresight of the speaker or writer; and in his speech in the same case Lord Pearce drew attention to the necessity for the imposition of some discernible limits to liability in such cases. . . .

In seeking to ascertain whether there should be imposed on the adviser a duty to avoid the occurrence of the kind of damage which the advisee claims to have suffered it is not, I think, sufficient to ask simply whether there existed a 'closeness' between them in the sense that the advisee had a legal entitlement to receive the information on the basis of which he has acted or in the sense that the information was intended to serve his interest or to protect him. One must, I think, go further and ask, in what capacity was his interest to be served and from what was he intended to be protected? A company's annual accounts are capable of being utilised for a number of purposes and if one thinks about it it is entirely foreseeable that they may be so employed. But many of such purposes have absolutely no connection with the recipient's status or capacity, whether as a shareholder, voting or non-voting, or as a debenture-holder. Before it can be concluded that the duty is imposed to protect the recipient against harm which he suffers by reason of the particular use that he chooses to make of the information which he receives, one must, I think, first ascertain the purpose for which the information is required to be given. Indeed, the paradigmatic *Donoghue v Stevenson* case of a manufactured article requires, as an essential ingredient of liability, that the article has been used by the consumer in the manner in which it was intended to be used (see *Grant v Australian Knitting Mills Ltd* [1936] AC 85 at 104, [1935] All ER Rep 209 at 217 and *Junior Books Ltd v Veitchi Co Ltd* [1982] 3 All ER 201 at 216, 218, [1983] 1 AC 520 at 549, 552). I entirely follow that if the conclusion is reached that the very purpose of providing the information is to serve as the basis for making investment decisions or giving investment advice, it is not difficult then to conclude also that the duty imposed on the adviser extends to protecting the recipient against loss occasioned by an unfortunate investment decision which is based on carelessly inaccurate information....

...I do not believe and I see no grounds for believing that, in enacting the statutory provisions, Parliament had in mind the provision of information for the assistance of purchasers of shares or debentures in the market, whether they be already the holders of shares or other securities or persons having no previous proprietary interest in the company. It is unnecessary to decide the point on this appeal, but I can see more force in the contention that one purpose of providing the statutory information might be to enable the recipient to exercise whatever rights he has in relation to his proprietary interest by virtue of which he receives it, by way, for instance of disposing of that interest. I can, however, see no ground for supposing that the legislature was intending to foster a market for the existing holders of shares or debentures by providing information for the purpose of enabling them to acquire such securities from other holders who might be minded to sell....

In my judgment, accordingly, the purpose for which the auditors' certificate is made and published is that of providing those entitled to receive the report with information to enable them to exercise in conjunction those powers which their respective proprietary interests confer on them and not for the purposes of individual speculation with a view to profit. The same considerations as limit the existence of a duty of care also, in my judgment, limit the scope of the duty and I agree with O'Connor LJ that the duty of care is one owed to the shareholders as a body and not to individual shareholders.

To widen the scope of the duty to include loss caused to an individual by reliance on the accounts for a purpose for which they were not supplied and were not intended would be to extend it beyond the limits which are so far deducible from the decisions of this House. It is not, as I think, an extension which either logic requires or policy dictates and I, for my part, am not prepared to follow the majority of the Court of Appeal in making it. In relation to the purchase of shares of other shareholders in a company, whether in the open market or as a result of an offer made to all or a majority of the existing shareholders, I can see no sensible distinction, so far as a duty of care is concerned, between a potential purchaser who is, vis-à-vis the company, a total outsider and one who is already the holder of one or more shares. I accordingly agree with what has already fallen from my noble and learned friend Lord Bridge, and I, too, would allow the appeal and dismiss the cross-appeal.

[LORD ROSKILL and LORD JAUNCEY OF TULLICHETTLE delivered speeches in favour of allowing the appeal and dismissing the cross-appeal. LORD ACKNER agreed with all the speeches.]

Appeal allowed; cross-appeal dismissed.

QUESTION

What view of *Hedley Byrne* do these judges take? Is it the view that *Hedley Byrne* concerns the boundary between contract and tort, or the view that the particular problems of harm caused by faulty information require special conditions to be imposed on the use of the tort of negligence? Is it fair to say that *Caparo* could be read as a footnote to Lord Griffiths's speech in *Smith v Eric Bush* (p. 218, ante)? What is the difference between what Lord Griffiths says and what the *Caparo* judges say about what the defendant has to know as to the purpose to which the claimant puts the information?

NOTES

1.   It is crucial to their Lordships' reasoning that the statutory provisions concerning the audit of companies were not intended to protect potential investors, but only to aid existing shareholders in holding directors to account. This argument was always of doubtful historical validity (see D. Howarth, [1991] CLJ 58), and it is unclear what interest existing shareholders have in the rule that the company's accounts must be available to the general public at Companies House. The interests of existing shareholders can be secured by a rule entitling merely the shareholders themselves to audited accounts. For general criticisms of the view taken in *Caparo* of the purposes of the annual audit, see *Markesinis and Deakin*, pp. 166–168. Percival has described the view taken in *Caparo* of the annual audit as 'an artificial interpretation, which takes no account of commercial reality': see M. Percival, (1991) 54 MLR 739 at 742.

2.   Subsequent to the facts of *Caparo*, company law changed in a way that suggests that the *Caparo* view of the purpose of the audit requirement should also change. Under the Companies Acts 1985 and 1989, and now the Companies Act 2006, Part 16, Ch. 1, small and medium-sized companies are allowed to opt for a very light regulatory regime concerning the accounts they must file with Companies House. For example, small companies need file only a simplified balance sheet and need not file profit and loss accounts at all. But any company with the power lawfully to offer its securities to the public, that is any company seeking to attract outside investors, may not take advantage of any of the provisions allowing the filing of abbreviated accounts. Under existing company law, therefore, one of the purposes of the requirements to file audited accounts with Companies House must be to provide information to prospective investors. Should this change in purpose underlying the statutory auditing requirements be reflected in a shift of approach in imposing a duty of care in *Caparo*-style scenarios? See also *Law Society v KPMG Peat Marwick* [2000] 4 All ER 540, [2000] 1 WLR 1921, where the Court of Appeal held that the defendants owed a duty of care to the claimants in respect of a report on the accounts of a firm of solicitors. Even though the report was paid for by the firm of solicitors, it was prepared for the purpose of enabling the Law Society to exercise its regulatory powers as trustee of the Solicitors' Compensation Fund. As a result, the Court held that the defendants owed a duty of care to the Law Society.

3.   In *James McNaughton Paper Group Ltd v Hicks Anderson & Co* [1991] 2 QB 113, [1991] 1 All ER 134 the Court of Appeal held that accountants who had prepared, at short notice, draft accounts of a client company for the company's chairman owed no duty of care to a bidder who took over the company after having inspected those accounts. Neill LJ identified a number of (overlapping) matters likely to be of importance in determining whether a duty exists: (a) the purpose for which the statement was made; (b) the purpose for which the statement was communicated; (c) the relationship between the adviser, the advisee, and any relevant third party; (d) the size of any class to which the advisee belonged; (e) the state of knowledge of the adviser; and (f) reliance by the advisee. (The test for 'reliance' suggested by Stephenson LJ in *JEB Fasteners Ltd v Marks Bloom & Co (a firm)* [1983] 1 All ER 583 at 589 is whether the statement plays a 'real and substantial part, though not by itself a decisive part, in inducing a plaintiff to act'.) The approach adopted by Neill LJ was subsequently applied by Royce J in *West Bromwich Albion Football Club Ltd v El-Safty* [2006] All ER (D) 123 (Oct), [2005] EWHC 2866, with the Court of Appeal subsequently confirming Royce J's decision, albeit adopting a different analysis based upon the nature of the relationships at issue and a classification

of the case as one involving the provision of services, not advice: [2007] PIQR P7, [2006] EWCA Civ 1299.

In *Morgan Crucible Co plc v Hill Samuel & Co Ltd* [1991] Ch 295, [1991] 1 All ER 148, the Court of Appeal at last found a case in which a duty of care arose, on the basis that statements in question had been made with the clear purpose of influencing the conduct of an identified bidder. This case, and its relationship with *Caparo*, were analysed by Glidewell LJ in the subsequent case *Galoo Ltd (in liq) v Bright Grahame Murray (a firm)* [1994] 1 All ER 16, [1994] 1 WLR 1360:

> The distinction between the set of facts which it was held in *Morgan Crucible* would suffice to establish a duty of care owed by auditors from those facts which it was held in *Caparo* would not have this effect is inevitably a fine one. In my judgment that distinction may be expressed as follows. Mere foreseeability that a potential bidder may rely on the audited accounts does not impose on the auditor a duty of care to the bidder, but if the auditor is expressly made aware that a particular identified bidder will rely on the audited accounts or other statements approved by the auditor, and intends that the bidder should so rely, the auditor will be under a duty of care to the bidder for the breach of which he may be liable.

Notice how the idea of 'purpose', which was emphasised by the Court of Appeal in *Morgan Crucible* and present in Glidewell LJ's exposition of the relevant legal principles in *Galoo*, disappears from his final statement of the distinction between *Caparo* and *Morgan Crucible*. In the end, knowledge of *who* the claimant is will suffice to establish knowledge of the claimant's purpose.

4. What if the defendant intends that all those who come into contact with the information should rely on it? Can the defendant say that the claimants form too large a class to count as 'identifiable', or does the defendant's intention to influence the world at large nullify any argument based on the identity of the claimant? One can see this question as a way of asking whether the 'floodgates' argument can stand alone, or whether, as seems more reasonable, it stands for a judgment about how far the defendant should be held liable given the defendant's own intentions. In *Possfund Custodian Trustee Ltd v Diamond* [1996] 2 All ER 774, [1996] 1 WLR 1351 Lightman J had to decide whether investors in the 'after-market' for a company floated on the Unlisted Securities Market could sue on the basis of misleading information in the company's prospectus. Investors in the 'after-market' are those who buy shares in a new company not directly from the company or its merchant bank but so soon after the flotation that the only available financial information about the company is still that contained in its prospectus. Lightman J decided that these investors had an arguable case even if they could show only that the defendants intended all such investors to rely on the prospectus, rather than that the defendants knew who these investors would be.

5. For an argument that in auditor liability cases the emphasis should not be on what the auditor knew about the transaction but on the precise objective standards of care applicable to professionals, see J. J. Ganuza and F. Gomez, (2007) 27 International Review of Law and Economics 95.

6. Do surveyors have reason to be aggrieved by the contrast between the outcome of *Smith v Eric S Bush* and the outcome of *Caparo*? After all, surveyors' valuation of property is no easier a task than auditors' valuation of companies. Hoffmann J at first instance in *Morgan Crucible* gave the following explanation [1990] 3 All ER 330 at 385:

> First, Mr Smith had paid for the survey; although he had no contract with the surveyor, the relationship was, as Lord Templeman said 'akin to contract'. Economically there was no distinction. Caparo Industries plc, on the other hand, had not paid for the audit. Secondly, the typical

plaintiff in a *Smith v Bush*-type case is a person of modest means and making the most expensive purchase of his or her life. He is very unlikely to be insured against the manifestation of inherent defects. The surveyor can protect himself relatively easily by insurance. The take-over bidder, on the other hand, is an entrepreneur taking high risks for high rewards and while some accountants may be able to take out sufficient insurance, others may not. Furthermore, the take-over bidder is a limited liability company and the accountants are individuals for whom, save so far as they are covered by insurance, liability would mean personal ruin. Third, the imposition of liability on surveyors would probably not greatly increase their insurance costs and push up the cost of surveys because the typical buyer who relies on a building society survey is buying a relatively modest house. Take-overs on the Stock Exchange involve huge amounts and the effects on accountants' insurance and fees are unpredictable.

Is this convincing? This reasoning is rooted in policy, rather than in a clear conceptual analysis of the distinctions between the two situations. It is not clear why the identity of who pays for the survey should be a relevant factor in this context. Who pays for a survey is merely a matter of the building societies' billing practices. They could easily waive the fee and recover the money in other ways. Buyers have no influence over the choice, and thus the quality, of the surveyor: there is very little in the way of obvious proximity between the surveyor and a buyer.

On the insurance point, what is the difference between accountants and surveyors? If the problem is the relative importance of the purchase to the claimant, should rich house buyers be excluded from suing surveyors and should poor investors be allowed to sue auditors? And as for the effects of imposing liability on insurance rates, audit firms can easily pass the cost onto their clients because audit is a legal requirement. The only difference would be that competent audit firms would be able to charge less than their incompetent competitors and would gain more business.

Hoffmann J (as he was then) may be correct in identifying the more vulnerable status of many home buyers as an important consideration (even if this concern was perhaps not so evident in *Murphy*). However, the general policy factors he invokes would ideally be supported by an analytical distinction that does not appear to be meaningfully developed as yet.

It could be argued that a distinction can be made between *Caparo* and *Smith* on the basis that the former case denied recovery on the basis that the purpose for which the audit was undertaken had no link to the transaction at issue, while the survey in *Smith* was closely linked to a particular transaction. However, it is uncertain whether this distinction is particularly convincing or clear-cut. In 'survey' cases such as *Smith* and *Merrett v Babb*, the courts appear willing to accept the existence of a sufficiently proximate link between the survey and a particular transaction, which may not necessarily reflect the exact purpose for which the survey was conducted, or the specific beneficiaries the surveyor may have had in mind at the time of conducting the survey.

There is an economic argument in favour of liability for surveyors and against liability for auditors, based on the idea, already discussed, that tort law should encourage the flow of accurate and socially useful information (see *Howarth*, pp. 316–318 and Bishop p. 203, ante). Imposing liability on surveyors should ensure the circulation of better quality information that might not otherwise be put into circulation: in contrast, imposing liability upon auditors could encourage greater defensiveness and restraint in the production in audit accounts of socially useful information intended for a wide audience. However, the professional requirements of accounting bodies already impose a regulatory framework upon the provision of audited accounts: does the *Caparo* exemption from liability make much of a difference in freeing up information flow?

7. In *Coulthard v Neville Russell (a firm)* [1998] 1 BCLC 143 company directors alleged that the company's auditors had negligently failed to warn them that certain loan transactions in which they were engaged were illegal and left them open to disqualification as directors. The Court of Appeal dismissed an application to strike out the action. Chadwick LJ commented ([1998] 1 BCLC at 155):

    In my view the liability of professional advisers, including auditors, for failure to provide accurate information or correct advice can, truly, be said to be in a state of transition or development. As the House of Lords has pointed out, repeatedly, this is an area in which the law is developing pragmatically and incrementally. It is pre-eminently an area in which the legal result is sensitive to the facts. I am very far from persuaded that the claim in the present case is bound to fail whatever, within the reasonable confines of the pleaded case, the facts turn out to be. That is not to be taken as an expression of view that the claim will succeed; only as an expression of view that this is not one of those plain and obvious cases in which it could be right to deny the plaintiffs the opportunity to attempt to establish their claim at a trial.

    However, in the personal injury case of *Sutradhar v Natural Environment Research Council* [2006] 4 All ER 490, [2006] UKHL 60, the House of Lords indicated the courts should be prepared to strike out claims based on the alleged existence of a *Hedley Byrne*-style assumption of responsibility where such claims were hopeless or doomed to fail. This case involved a claim by a Bangladeshi resident for personal injury brought against the Natural Environment Research Council ("NERC") for negligence in issuing a geological report which allegedly induced the health authorities in Bangladesh not to take steps to ensure that drinking water was not contaminated by arsenic. The House of Lords was of the view that there was clearly insufficient proximity to establish the existence of a duty of care under the *Caparo* test, and additional problems existed with showing causation and other elements of the claim. As such, it was an appropriate case to be struck out under the Civil Procedure Rules. This may indicate a greater judicial willingness to regard the evolution of liability under *Hedley Byrne* and associated precedents as sufficiently developed to justify a more robust attitude to cases lacking any realistic chance of success. (See further p. 43, ante.)

8. In *Goodwill v British Pregnancy Advisory Service* [1996] 2 All ER 161, [1996] 1 WLR 1397 the defendants negligently advised a man that a vasectomy operation they had arranged to be performed on him would make him permanently infertile and that he would never need to use contraception again. The man repeated the advice to his subsequent sexual partners, including the claimant. The claimant, although correctly advised by her own doctor that vasectomies were not necessarily 100 per cent successful, ceased taking other contraceptive measures and consequently became pregnant. She sued the defendants for the financial losses she incurred as a result of having to bring up a daughter. The Court of Appeal accepted that the defendant would have owed a duty to the man's wife at the time of the operation, but denied a remedy to the claimant. They decided that the claimant could not establish Lord Oliver's third condition in *Caparo*, that it must be 'known, either actually or inferentially, that the advice so communicated is likely to be acted on by the advisee for that purpose without independent inquiry'. The underlying point is that the defendants were entitled to expect that subsequent partners would ask their own doctor for advice before ceasing to take other contraceptive measures. As long as they received adequate advice, any subsequent events were their own responsibility. Cf. the distinction between 'advice' and 'information' in *South Australia Asset Management Corpn v York Montague Ltd* (p. 271, post). (Thorpe LJ added several other points, including that he thought there

was no reliance and that the range of possible claimants was too large. Also, the possible number of claimants point not only appears to be a crude, unsupported floodgates argument; it is also open to the objection that it is unfair to use the *potential* as opposed to the *likely* number of claimants.) On this topic, see now *McFarlane v Tayside Health Board* [2000] 2 AC 59, [1999] 4 All ER 961 (p. 153, ante), where permitting recovery for the economic loss incurred by the birth of the child was rejected as incompatible with the 'far, just and reasonable' leg of the *Caparo* test. Compare also *Parkinson v St James and Seacroft University Hospital NHS Trust* [2001] 3 All ER 97, [2001] EWCA Civ 530 (noted p. 157, ante), and the subsequent House of Lords decision in *Rees v Darlington Memorial Hospital NHS Trust* [2003] 4 All ER 987, [2003] UKHL 52 (p. 157, ante).

9. For some time, *Hedley Byrne* was widely understood as establishing a duty of care in respect of negligent statements or the negligent provision of information resulting in economic loss. The position with regards to the negligent performance of services was less clear. However, the House of Lords in *Henderson v Merrett Syndicates Ltd* [1995] 2 AC 145, [1994] 3 All ER 506 confirmed that liability could be imposed in respect of the negligent performance of services, and that the approach set out in *Hedley Byrne* was not confined to the negligent provision of information. The decision in *Henderson* also marks the significant return to prominence of the 'assumption of responsibility' test, which now looms large in the field of economic loss, as well as in other contexts (see e.g. *Phelps v Hillingdon Borough Council* [2001] 2 AC 619, [2000] 4 All ER 504, p. 99, ante).

■ Henderson v Merrett Syndicates Ltd
House of Lords [1994] 3 All ER 506

The plaintiffs were Lloyd's 'names', investors in the Lloyd's insurance market. They were members of syndicates managed by the defendant underwriting agents. The plaintiffs were either 'direct names', where the relevant syndicate was managed by the members' agents themselves, or 'indirect names', where the members' agents placed names with syndicates managed by other agents and entered into sub-agency agreements with the managing agents of those syndicates. It was accepted that there was an implied term in the agreements that the agents would exercise due care and skill. The plaintiffs sued the defendants, alleging that the defendants had been negligent in the conduct and management of the plaintiffs' syndicates. The plaintiffs needed, for limitation purposes, to establish a duty of care in tort in addition to any contractual duty that might be owed by the defendants. The judge found in favour of the plaintiffs on all the issues. The defendants appealed to the Court of Appeal, which dismissed the appeal. The defendants appealed to the House of Lords.

LORD GOFF: . . .
(1) *Introduction*
. . . The first issue . . . is concerned with the question whether managing agents, which were not also members' agents, owed to indirect names a duty of care in tort to carry out their underwriting functions with reasonable care and skill. The second issue is concerned with the question whether managing agents, which were also members' agents, owed such a duty to direct names.

The first of these issues, relating to indirect names, arises in both the Merrett appeals and the Feltrim appeals. However the issue in the Merrett appeals arises in the context of the pre-1985 byelaw forms of agency and sub-agency agreements, whereas that in the Feltrim appeals does so in the context of the forms of agreement prescribed under the 1985 byelaw. The second of these issues, relating to direct names, arises only in the Merrett appeals, in the context of the pre-1985 byelaw forms.

It is desirable that I should at once identify the reasons why names in the Merrett and Feltrim actions are seeking to establish that there is a duty of care owed to them by managing agents in tort. First, the direct names in the Merrett actions seek to hold the managing agents concurrently liable in contract and in tort. Where, as in the case of direct names, the agents are combined agents, there can be no doubt that there is a contract between the names and the agents, acting as managing agents, in respect of the underwriting carried out by the managing agents on behalf of the names as members of the syndicate or syndicates under their management, the only question being as to the scope of the managing agents' contractual responsibility in this respect. Even so, in the Merrett actions, names are concerned to establish the existence of a concurrent duty of care in tort, if only because there is a limitation issue in one of the actions, in which names wish therefore to be able to take advantage of the more favourable date for the accrual of the cause of action in tort, as opposed to that in contract. Second, the indirect names in both the Merrett and the Feltrim actions are seeking to establish the existence of a duty of care on the part of the managing agents in tort, no doubt primarily to establish a direct liability to them by the managing agents, but also, in the case of the Merrett actions, to take advantage of the more advantageous position on limitation. Your Lordships were informed that there is no limitation issue in the Feltrim actions.

I turn next to the forms of agreement which provide the contractual context for these issues. I have already recorded that, so far as the pre-1985 byelaw forms are concerned, no form was prescribed, but those in use were substantially similar if not identical, and that specimen forms of agency and sub-agency agreement were agreed for the purposes of these preliminary issues and are scheduled to the judgment of Saville J.

[His Lordship then set out the terms of the agreements and continued:] In the result, in neither the specimen agreements nor the agreements prescribed by the 1985 byelaw is there any express provision imposing on the agent a duty to exercise care and skill in the exercise of the relevant functions under the agreement; but I understand it not to be in dispute that a term to that effect must be implied into the agreements. It is against that background that the question falls to be considered whether a like obligation rested upon the managing agents in tort, so that the managing agents which were also members' agents owed such a duty of care in tort to direct names, with the effect that the direct names had alternative remedies, in contract and tort, against the managing agents; and whether managing agents which were not also members' agents owed such a duty of care in tort to indirect names, so that the indirect names had a remedy in tort against the managing agents, notwithstanding the existence of a contractual structure embracing indirect names, members' agents and managing agents, under which such a duty was owed in contract by the managing agents to the members' agents, and by the members' agents to the indirect names. . . .

Saville J resolved all these issues in favour of the names. He held that a duty of care was owed by managing agents in tort both to direct names and to indirect names, and that the existence of such a duty of care was not excluded by reason of the relevant contractual regime, whether under the pre-1985 specimen agreements, or under the forms of agreement prescribed by the 1985 byelaw. In particular, he held that the absolute discretion conferred on the agent under cl 6(a) of the pre-1985 byelaw specimen agency agreement, and delegated to the managing agent under cll 5 and 6 of the related sub-agency agreement, did not exclude any such duty of care. On all these points Saville J's decision was, as I have recorded, affirmed by the Court of Appeal.

(2) *The argument of the managing agents*

The main argument advanced by the managing agents against the existence of a duty of care in tort was that the imposition of such a duty upon them was inconsistent with the contractual relationship between the parties. In the case of direct names, where there was a direct contract between the names and the managing agents, the argument was that the contract legislated exclusively for the relationship between the parties, and that a parallel duty of care in tort was therefore excluded by the contract. In the case of indirect names, reliance was placed on the fact that there had been brought into existence a contractual chain, between name and members' agent, and between members' agent and managing agent; and it was said that, by structuring their contractual relationship in this way, the indirect names and the managing agents had deliberately excluded any direct responsibility, including any tortious duty of care, to the indirect names by the managing agents. In particular, the argument ran, it was as a result not permissible for the names to pray in aid, for limitation purposes, the more favourable time for accrual of a cause of action in tort. To do so, submitted the managing agents, would deprive them of their contractual expectations, and would avoid the policy of Parliament that there are different limitation regimes for contract and tort.

Such was the main argument advanced on behalf of the managing agents. Moreover, as appears from my summary of it, the argument is not precisely the same in the case of direct names and indirect names respectively. However, in any event, I think it desirable first to consider the principle upon which a duty of care in tort may in the present context be imposed upon the managing agents, assuming that to impose such a duty would not be inconsistent with the relevant contractual relationship. In considering this principle, I bear in mind in particular the separate submission of the managing agents that no such duty should be imposed, because the loss claimed by the names is purely economic loss. However the identification of the principle is, in my opinion, relevant to the broader question of the impact of the relevant contract or contracts.

(3) *The governing principle*

Even so, I can take this fairly shortly. I turn immediately to the decision of this House in *Hedley Byrne & Co Ltd v Heller & Partners Ltd* [1963] 2 All ER 575, [1964] AC 465. There, as is of course well known, the question arose whether bankers could be held liable in tort in respect of the gratuitous provision of a negligently favourable reference for one of their customers, when they knew or ought to have known that the plaintiff would rely on their skill and judgment in furnishing the reference, and the plaintiff in fact relied upon it and in consequence suffered financial loss. Your Lordships' House held that, in principle, an action would lie in such circumstances in tort; but that, in the particular case, a duty of care was negatived by a disclaimer of responsibility under cover of which the reference was supplied.

The case has always been regarded as important in that it established that, in certain circumstances, a duty of care may exist in respect of words as well as deeds, and further that liability may arise in negligence in respect of pure economic loss which is not parasitic upon physical damage. But, perhaps more important for the future development of the law, and certainly more relevant for the purposes of the present case, is the principle upon which the decision was founded. The governing principles are perhaps now perceived to be most clearly stated in the speeches of Lord Morris of Borth-y-Gest (with whom Lord Hodson agreed) and of Lord Devlin.

[His Lordship then quoted substantially the same passages from the speeches of Lords Morris and Devlin as those quoted at p. 210, ante and continued.] From these statements, and from their application in *Hedley Byrne*, we can derive some understanding of the breadth of the principle underlying the case. We can see that it rests upon a relationship between the parties, which may be general or specific to the particular transaction, and which may or may not be contractual in nature. All of their Lordships spoke in terms of one party having assumed or undertaken a responsibility towards the other. On this point, Lord Devlin spoke in particularly clear terms in both passages from his speech which I have quoted above. Further, Lord Morris spoke of that party being possessed of a 'special skill' which he undertakes to 'apply for the assistance of another who relies upon such skill'. But the facts of *Hedley Byrne* itself, which was concerned with the liability of a banker to the recipient for negligence in the provision of a reference gratuitously supplied, show that the concept of a 'special skill' must be understood broadly, certainly broadly enough to include special knowledge. Again, though *Hedley Byrne* was concerned with the provision of information and advice, the example given by Lord Devlin of the relationship between solicitor and client, and his and Lord Morris's statements of principle, show that the principle extends beyond the provision of information and advice to include the performance of other services. It follows, of course, that although, in the case of the provision of information and advice, reliance upon it by the other party will be necessary to establish a cause of action (because otherwise the negligence will have no causative effect), nevertheless there may be other circumstances in which there will be the necessary reliance to give rise to the application of the principle. In particular, as cases concerned with solicitor and client demonstrate, where the plaintiff entrusts the defendant with the conduct of his affairs, in general or in particular, he may be held to have relied on the defendant to exercise due skill and care in such conduct.

In subsequent cases concerned with liability under the *Hedley Byrne* principle in respect of negligent mis-statements, the question has frequently arisen whether the plaintiff falls within the category of persons to whom the maker of the statement owes a duty of care. In seeking to contain that category of persons within reasonable bounds, there has been some tendency on the part of the courts to criticise the concept of 'assumption of responsibility' as being 'unlikely to be a helpful or realistic test in most cases' (see *Smith v Eric S Bush (a firm)*, *Harris v Wyre Forest DC* [1989] 2 All ER 514 at 536, [1990] 1 AC 831 at 864–865 per Lord Griffiths; and see also *Caparo Industries plc v Dickman* [1990] 1 All ER 568 at 582–583, [1990] 2 AC 605 at 628 per Lord Roskill). However, at least in cases such as the present, in which the same problem does not arise, there seems to be no reason why recourse should not be had to the concept, which appears after all to have been adopted, in one form or another, by all of their Lordships in *Hedley Byrne & Co Ltd v Heller & Partners Ltd* [1963] 2 All ER 575 at 581, 583, 588, 610–611, 612, 616, [1964] AC 465 at 483, 486, 487, 494, 529, 531, 538, per Lord Reid, Lord Morris (with whom Lord Hodson agreed), Lord Devlin and Lord Pearce. Furthermore, especially in a context concerned with a liability which may arise under a contract or in a situation 'equivalent to contract', it must be expected that an objective test will be applied when asking the question whether, in a particular case, responsibility should be held to have been assumed by the defendant to the plaintiff: see *Caparo Industries plc v Dickman* [1990] 1 All ER 568 at 588–589, [1990] 2 AC 605 at 637 per Lord Oliver of Aylmerton. In addition, the concept provides its own explanation why there is no problem in cases of this kind about liability for pure economic loss; for if a person assumes responsibility to another in respect of certain services, there is no reason why he should not be liable in damages for that other in respect of economic loss which flows from the negligent performance of those services. It follows that, once the case is identified as falling within the *Hedley Byrne* principle, there should be no need to embark upon any further inquiry whether it is 'fair, just and reasonable' to impose liability for economic loss—a point which is, I consider, of some importance in the present case. The concept indicates too that in some circumstances, for example where the undertaking to furnish the relevant service is given on an informal occasion, there may be no assumption of responsibility; and likewise that an assumption of responsibility may be negatived by an appropriate disclaimer. I wish to add in parenthesis that, as Oliver J recognised in *Midland Bank Trust Co Ltd v Hett Stubbs & Kemp (a firm)* [1978] 3 All ER 571 at 595, [1979] Ch 384 at 416 (a case concerned with concurrent liability of solicitors in tort and contract, to which I will have to refer in a moment), an assumption of responsibility by, for example, a professional man may give rise to liability in respect of negligent omissions as much as negligent acts of commission, as for example when a solicitor assumes responsibility for business on behalf of his client and omits to take a certain step, such as the service of a document, which falls within the responsibility so assumed by him.

(4) The application of the principle to managing agents at Lloyd's
Since it has been submitted on behalf of the managing agents that no liability should attach to them in negligence in the present case because the only damage suffered by the names consists of pure economic loss, the question arises whether the principle in *Hedley Byrne* is capable of applying in the case of underwriting agents at Lloyd's who are managing agents. Like Saville J and the Court of Appeal, I have no difficulty in concluding that the principle is indeed capable of such application. The principle has been expressly applied to a number of different categories of person who perform services of a professional or quasi-professional nature, such as bankers (in *Hedley Byrne* itself); solicitors (as foreshadowed by Lord Devlin in *Hedley Byrne*, and as held in the leading case of *Midland Bank Trust Co Ltd v Hett Stubbs & Kemp (a firm)* [1978] 3 All ER 571, [1979] Ch 384, and other cases in which that authority has been followed); surveyors and valuers (as in *Smith v Eric S Bush (a firm)*, *Harris v Wyre Forest DC* [1989] 2 All ER 514, [1990] 1 AC 831); and accountants (as in *Caparo Industries plc v Dickman* [1990] 1 All ER 568, [1990] 2 AC 605). Another category of persons to whom the principle has been applied, and on which particular reliance was placed by the names in the courts below and in argument before your Lordships, is insurance brokers. As Phillips J pointed out in *Youell v Bland Welch & Co Ltd (The 'Superhulls*

Cover' Case) (No 2) [1990] 2 Lloyd's Rep 431 at 459, it has been accepted, since before 1964, that an insurance broker owes a duty of care in negligence towards his client, whether the broker is bound by contract or not. Furthermore, in *Punjab National Bank v de Boinville* [1992] 3 All ER 104, [1992] 1 WLR 1138 it was held by the Court of Appeal, affirming the decision of Hobhouse J, that a duty of care was owed by an insurance broker not only to his client but also to a specific person whom he knew was to become an assignee of the policy. For my part I can see no reason why a duty of care should not likewise be owed by managing agents at Lloyd's to a name who is a member of a syndicate under the management of the agents. Indeed, as Saville J and the Court of Appeal both thought, the relationship between name and managing agent appears to provide a classic example of the type of relationship to which the principle in *Hedley Byrne* applies. In so saying, I put on one side the question of the impact, if any, upon the relationship of the contractual context in which it is set. But, that apart, there is in my opinion plainly an assumption of responsibility in the relevant sense by the managing agents towards the names in their syndicates. The managing agents have accepted the names as members of a syndi-cate under their management. They obviously hold themselves out as possessing a special expertise to advise the names on the suitability of risks to be underwritten; and on the circumstances in which, and the extent to which, reinsurance should be taken out and claims should be settled. The names, as the managing agents well knew, placed implicit reliance on that expertise, in that they gave authority to the managing agents to bind them to contracts of insurance and reinsurance and to the settlement of claims. I can see no escape from the conclusion that, in these circumstances, prima facie a duty of care is owed in tort by the managing agents to such names. To me, it does not matter if one proceeds by way of analogy from the categories of relationship already recognised as falling within the principle in *Hedley Byrne* or by a straight application of the principle stated in the *Hedley Byrne* case itself. On either basis the conclusion is, in my opinion, clear. Furthermore, since the duty rests on the principle in *Hedley Byrne*, no problem arises from the fact that the loss suffered by the names is pure economic loss....

[His Lordship then dealt with the question of whether there could be concurrent liabilities in tort and contract, concluding that there was no rule that excluded a tort action merely because a contract action might have been possible had the plaintiffs sued in time. He concluded:] [F]or the present pur-poses...in the present case liability can, and in my opinion should, be founded squarely on the principle established in *Hedley Byrne* itself, from which it follows that an assumption of responsibility coupled with the concomitant reliance may give rise to a tortious duty of care irrespective of whether there is a contractual relationship between the parties, and in consequence, unless his contract precludes him from doing so, the plaintiff, who has available to him concurrent remedies in contract and tort, may choose that remedy which appears to him to be the most advantageous....

(7) Application of the above principles in the present case
...I turn to the indirect names....It is...submitted on behalf of the managing agents that the indirect names and the managing agents, as parties to the chain of contracts contained in the relevant agency and sub-agency agreements, must be taken to have thereby structured their relationship so as to exclude any duty of care owed directly by the managing agents to the indirect names in tort.

In essence the argument must be that, because the managing agents have, with the consent of the indirect names, assumed responsibility in respect of the relevant activities to another party, i.e. the members' agents, under a sub-agency agreement, it would be inconsistent to hold that they have also assumed responsibility in respect of the same activities to the indirect names. I for my part cannot see why in principle a party should not assume responsibility to more than one person in respect of the same activity. Let it be assumed (unlikely though it may be) that, in the present case, the managing agents were in a contractual relationship not only with the members' agents under a sub-agency agreement but also directly with the relevant names, under both of which they assumed responsibility for the same activities. I can see no reason in principle why the two duties of care so arising should not be capable of co-existing....

I wish, however, to add that I strongly suspect that the situation which arises in the present case is most unusual; and that in many cases in which a contractual chain comparable to that in the present case is constructed it may well prove to be inconsistent with an assumption of responsibility which has the effect of, so to speak, short-circuiting the contractual structure so put in place by the parties. It cannot therefore be inferred from the present case that other sub-agents will be held directly liable to the agent's principal in tort. Let me take the analogy of the common case of an ordinary building contract, under which main contractors contract with the building owner for the construction of the relevant building, and the main contractor sub-contracts with sub-contractors or suppliers (often nominated by the building owner) for the performance of work or the supply of materials in accordance with standards and subject to terms established in the sub-contract. I put on one side cases in which the sub-contractor causes physical damage to property of the building owner, where the claim does not depend on an assumption of responsibility by the sub-contractor to the building owner; though the sub-contractor may be protected from liability by a contractual exemption clause authorised by the building owner. But if the sub-contracted work or materials do not in the result conform to the required standard, it will not ordinarily be open to the building owner to sue the sub-contractor or supplier direct under the *Hedley Byrne* principle, claiming damages from him on the basis that he has been negligent in relation to the performance of his functions. For there is generally no assumption of responsibility by the sub-contractor or supplier direct to the building owner, the parties having so structured their relationship that it is inconsistent with any such assumption of responsibility. This was the conclusion of the Court of Appeal in *Simaan General Contracting Co v Pilkington Glass Ltd (No 2)* [1988] 1 All ER 791 at 803, [1988] QB 758 at 781. As Bingham LJ put it:

> 'I do not, however, see any basis on which [the nominated suppliers] could be said to have assumed a direct responsibility for the quality of the goods to [the building owners]; such a responsibility is, I think, inconsistent with the structure of the contract the parties have chosen to make.'

It is true that, in this connection, some difficulty has been created by the decision of your Lordships' House in *Junior Books Ltd v Veitchi Co Ltd* [1982] 3 All ER 201, [1983] 1 AC 520. In my opinion, however, it is unnecessary for your Lordships to reconsider that decision for the purposes of the present appeal. Here however I can see no inconsistency between the assumption of responsibility by the managing agents to the indirect names, and that which arises under the sub-agency agreement between the managing agents and the members' agents, whether viewed in isolation or as part of the contractual chain stretching back to and so including the indirect names. For these reasons, I can see no reason why the indirect names should not be free to pursue their remedy against the managing agents in tort under the *Hedley Byrne* principle.

[His Lordship then found that the issue of a fiduciary duty did not arise in the Merrett and Feltrim appeals and agreed with the trial judge and the Court of Appeal both on certain questions of construction concerning the agreements between the names and the members' agents and on an issue concerning whether the 1985 rules or the 1984 rules applied in the Merrett case. He then continued:]

Conclusion
For these reasons, I would answer all the questions in the same manner as Saville J and the Court of Appeal, and I would dismiss the appeals of the members' agents and the managing agents with costs.

[LORD KEITH OF KINKEL, LORD MUSTILL, and LORD NOLAN agreed with LORD GOFF OF CHIEVELEY. LORD BROWNE-WILKINSON delivered a speech in favour dismissing the appeal but also agreed with LORD GOFF.]

NOTES

1. In *Williams v Natural Life Health Foods Ltd* [1998] 2 All ER 577 at 581, Lord Steyn attempted to summarise the significance of *Henderson v Merrett* in these terms:

   'First, in *Henderson*'s case it was settled that the assumption of responsibility principle enunciated in *the Hedley Byrne* case is not confined to statements but may apply to any assumption of responsibility for the provision of services. The extended *Hedley Byrne* principle is the rationalisation or technique adopted by English law to provide a remedy for the recovery of damages in respect of economic loss caused by the negligent performance of services. Secondly, it was established that once a case is identified as falling within the extended *Hedley Byrne* principle, there is no need to embark on any further inquiry whether it is 'fair, just and reasonable' to impose liability for economic loss (see [1994] 3 All ER 506 at 521, [1995] 2 AC 145 at 181). Thirdly, and applying *Hedley Byrne*, it was made clear that—

"reliance upon [the assumption of responsibility] by the other party will be necessary to establish a cause of action (because otherwise the negligence will have no causative effect)...(See [1994] 3 All ER 506 at 520, [1995] 2 AC 145 at 180.)"

Fourthly, it was held that the existence of a contractual duty of care between the parties does not preclude the concurrence of a tort duty in the same respect.'

Lord Steyn's third point may have to be read in the light of *White v Jones* (p. 243, post). Reliance might not be necessary where other means exist of showing causation.

2.   Lord Goff emphasises the speeches of Lords Morris and Devlin in *Hedley Byrne*. For them, as for Lord Goff, the key point about *Hedley Byrne* is that it deals with the boundary between contract and tort. Contract law allows the recovery of pure economic loss. Indeed, one might say that the protection of claimants from pure economic loss is its main function. But the justification for such protection is that the defendant undertook to provide it in the formation of the contract. Tort law does not provide such protection, according to Lord Goff, unless there is a similar undertaking, whether or not it amounts to a contract recognised by contract law. Note that where the courts allow such a tort law action, to the extent that contract law would not by itself have protected the claimant, the courts are undermining those contract law doctrines that prevent recovery. See B. Markesinis (1987) 103 LQR 354.

3.   *Henderson v Merrett* marks a triumphant reassertion of the 'assumption of responsibility' theory. How does Lord Goff deal with the objections to that theory made by Lord Griffiths in *Smith v Eric Bush*? Is Lord Goff's explanation of *Smith* convincing? Was Lord Griffiths' concern to limit the number of possible claimants? Or was it to undermine the view there could be no liability for pure economic loss at all unless there had been an assumption of responsibility?

Lord Goff's concession that 'assumption of responsibility' is to be judged 'objectively' is capable of two interpretations. It might mean that the court decides whether the defendant should count as having assumed responsibility in the light of all the circumstances and whether it is fair and reasonable to impose liability. If so, it is open to the criticism that it adds nothing to the discussion at large of whether it is fair, just, or reasonable that the court should impose a duty of care. It would, just like the phrase 'fair, just and reasonable' itself, merely signify a conclusion, rather than stand for a substantive reason for deciding the case one way or the other. See e.g. K. Barker (1993) 109 LQR 461, (2006) 26 OJLS 289; B. Hepple (1997) 50 CLP 67. Lord Steyn rejected this interpretation in *Williams v Natural Life Health Foods Ltd*, but Lord Slynn in *Phelps v London Borough of Hillingdon* [2001] 2AC 619, [2000] 4 All ER 504 at 518 says straightforwardly, 'The phrase means simply that the law recognises that there is a duty of care. It is not so much that responsibility is assumed as that it is recognised or imposed by the law.'

The other interpretation of 'objective' is that which is used in contract law, where normally the subjective intentions of the parties is irrelevant: intention is judged 'objectively', that is, as it would reasonably appear to the other party.

How would a reasonable person in the position of the claimant in *Hedley Byrne* have understood the assumed responsibilities of the defendant? What about a reasonable person in the position of the claimants in *Henderson*?

As for which of these interpretations is correct, see *White v Jones* (p. 243, post), where the House of Lords adopted the objective approach in analysing the relationship between the parties. However, a further question can be asked: what is the defendant undertaking responsibility for when deemed to have assumed responsibility towards the claimant? The protection of the claimant's economic interests? Or the competent carrying out of the defendant's own tasks? To what extent should the subjective intention of the parties be taken into account in determining what responsibility a defendant has assumed?

4.   Lord Goff spends much of his speech discussing the effect of the contractual context on tort liability. In the 1980s and early 1990s courts were generally unwilling to allow actions in tort to be superimposed on actions in contract; see e.g. *Tai Hing Cotton Mill Ltd v Liu Chong Hing Bank Ltd* [1986] AC 80, [1985] 2 All ER 947; *Greater Nottingham Co-operative Society Ltd v Cementation Piling and Foundations Ltd* [1989] QB 71, [1988] 2 All ER 971; and *Reid v Rush & Tompkins Group plc* [1989] 3 All ER 228, [1990] 1 WLR 202. Lord Goff now interprets this unwillingness not as reflecting a general objection to the confusion of tort and contract but as an aspect of the assumption of responsibility theory. The existence of a contract did not mean that there was any bar per se to recovery in tort. (Similar reasoning was deployed by Oliver J in *Midland Bank Trust Co v Hett, Stubbs and Kemp* [1979] Ch 384, [1978] 3 All ER 571. See also now *Riyad Bank v Ahli United Bank (UK) plc* [2006] 2 All ER (Comm) 777, [2006] EWCA Civ 780.) However, if the contracts to which the claimant was a party imply that the claimant accepted that the defendant did not assume responsibility towards the claimant, there would be in general no tort action. The contractual context or structure is said to be inconsistent with the possibility of a tort action. Also, in *Henderson*, Lord Browne-Wilkinson emphasised that the contractual arrangements of the parties would 'modify and shape' their tortious duties ([1995] 2 AC 145 at 206): the underlying contract should be taken as moulding any applicable tort duties of care.

For an earlier example of this approach in action, see *Pacific Associates Inc v Baxter* [1990] 1 QB 993, [1989] 2 All ER 159, where the claimant contractors complained of negligence by the defendant engineers which, the claimants claimed, prevented them from claiming £45 million in compensation from their clients. The engineers had a contract with the clients to investigate and give opinions on disputes between the client and the contractors. The contractors' contract with the clients required the contractors to submit claims to the defendant engineers. There was, however, no contract between the contractors and the engineers. The Court of Appeal refused to allow an action in tort by the contractors against the engineers because the contract between the contractors and the clients contained clauses which (a) exempted the engineers from personal responsibility, and (b) required the parties to submit any disagreements with the engineers' decisions to arbitration.

But there are doubts about whether all these 1980s cases so readily fit Lord Goff's explanation, or the decision in *Henderson*. In *Simaan General Contracting Co v Pilkington Glass Ltd (No 2)* [1988] QB 758, [1988] 1 All ER 791 the claimant contractor sued, in tort, the supplier of a sub-contractor for supplying sub-standard goods (namely glass for a building that was the wrong colour). The only special feature of the contractual context was that the claimant contractor had no choice in the matter of who would supply the glass. Under its own contract with its client it was required to choose the defendant. The Court of Appeal said that this lack of choice meant that there was no 'real reliance' by the claimant and therefore tort liability would be inconsistent with the contractual structure in question. But how does lack of choice in the choice of supplier imply acceptance that there will be no recourse for sub-standard performance by that supplier? Should the courts be so ready to interpret contractual provisions as closing off tortuous remedies? How can the courts infer that the parties intended that their contractual arrangements should be a definitive statement of all their rights and obligations? (On this point, see S. Hedley [1995] CLJ 27.) More important, how does the situation of the contractor in *Simaan* differ from the situation of the indirect names in *Henderson v Merrett*? Did they have any choice in the matter of to whom their agents sub-contracted their responsibilities?

Notice also that the main reason the claimants in *Henderson* wanted to establish that they had actions in tort as well as actions in contract was that the limitation rules were more favourable to the claimant in tort. In crude terms, time runs from the breach in contract but only from the occurrence of the damage in tort. But with regard to the direct names, could it be argued that by choosing to structure their relationship by a contract, the parties had chosen to adopt the contract rules for limitation? As a matter of principle, if liability to the indirect names under *Hedley Byrne* rests on the notion that the relationship between the parties was close to contract, which limitation rules should apply? There may be greater tension between the scope of tort remedies in the wake of *Henderson* and the specific contractual arrangements that parties may agree in different circumstances than either Lord Browne-Wilkinson or Lord Goff were prepared to acknowledge in *Henderson*. (See S. Whittaker (1997) 17 LS 169.)

5.   In *Junior Books v Veitchi* [1983] 1 AC 520, [1982] 3 All ER 201, the House of Lords applied the expansive approach to determining when a duty of care existed established in *Anns v Merton London Borough Council* [1978] AC 728, [1977] 2 All ER 492, and permitted a claim against a sub-contractor whose alleged careless work had caused extra expense to a customer of the general contractor. Subsequently, in *D & F Estates Ltd v Church Commissioners for England* [1989] 1 AC 177, [1988] 2 All ER 992, Lord Bridge indicated that *Junior Books* was 'so far dependent upon the unique, albeit non-contractual, relationship between the pursuer and the defender in that case and the unique scope of the duty of care owed by the defender to the pursuer arising from that relationship that the decision cannot be regarded as laying down any principle of general application in the law of tort or delict' ([1989] 1 AC 177 at 202). In *Murphy v Brentwood District Council* [1991] 1 AC 398 at 466, Lord Keith indicated that *Junior Books* could perhaps be reclassified as an application of *Hedley Byrne* reasoning. An attempt to reconstruct *Junior Books* can be attempted using the judgment in *Henderson*, on the basis that an assumption of responsibility existed on the part of the sub-contractor to exercise due care in the performance of services. However, imposing a duty of care in such circumstances may not be compatible with Lord Goff's emphasis in *Henderson* on the need for tort liability not to undermine an agreed contractual allocation of responsibilities and liabilites. In the Scottish case of *Realstone Ltd v J & E Shepherd* [2008] ScotCS CSOH_31 (21 February 2008), Lord Hodge noted (at [22]) 'there is a concern that the general law should not impose duties which would cut across the detailed contractual provisions which parties in a contractual chain have put in place to govern their liability *inter se*. The risk of introducing uncertainty into complex commercial transactions justifies the retreat from *Junior Books*.' (See further p. 198, ante.)

However, again the question should be asked whether *Henderson* itself does not also 'cut across' a contractual framework to some extent. Note that architects, designers, and builders have been held liable where an assumption of responsibility existed, even where an underlying contract was in place: see *Storey v Charles Church Developments Ltd* (1995) 73 Con. L.R. 1 and *Tesco Stores v Costain Construction Ltd* [2003] EWHC 1487 (TCC). It is increasingly apparent that 'mere' contractual relations will not establish the existence of an assumption of responsibility: some additional element of 'taking on' special responsibility or a relationship of dependence and extra reliance is required for liability to accrue.

It should also be noted that Lord Hodge in his judgment in *Realstone Ltd v J & E Shepherd* emphasises the risk of introducing uncertainty into complex *commercial* transactions. It appears that the courts may be more willing to recognise the existence of an assumption of responsibility in cases where vulnerable consumers cannot adequately protect themselves via the contractual route: e.g. *Smith v Bush* [1990] 1 AC 831, [1989] 2 All ER 514 (p. 218, ante); *White v Jones* [1995] 2 AC 207, [1995] 1 All ER 691 (p. 243, post). *Henderson* could be seen as involving a similar relationship of vulnerable dependence upon the skill of the agents concerned, notwithstanding its commercial context.

6.   In *Biffa Waste Services Ltd v Maschinenfabrik Ernst Hese GmbH* [2008] EWHC 6 (TCC) (11 January 2008), Ramsey J at [169] attempted to set out the principles applicable to the interaction of tort and contract in this context:

'(1) …a duty of care in tort can exist in parallel with or in addition to any contractual duties between the parties. The duty will depend on general principles of foreseeability and proximity and such other requirements applicable to the nature of the particular duty.

(2) …in the case of liability in tort both for pure economic loss in accordance with the principle in *Hedley Byrne* and for loss arising from personal injury or damage to property, the terms of any relevant contract between the parties or authorised by a party will be relevant to the existence, scope and extent of a duty of care.

(3) The appropriate question in considering the impact of any relevant contractual terms is the same whether the case involves an assumption of responsibility for *Hedley Byrne* liability or whether it relates to what is just, fair and reasonable when imposing liability in tort for personal injury or physical damage to property.

(4) The test is whether the parties having so structured their relationship that it is inconsistent with any such assumption of responsibility or with it being fair, just and reasonable to impose liability. In particular, a duty of care should not be permitted to circumvent or escape a contractual exclusion or limitation of liability for the act or omission that would constitute the tort.'

7.   As Lord Steyn pointed out in *Williams v Natural Life Health Foods*, *Henderson* makes clear that the *Hedley Byrne* exception to the rule that pure economic loss is not recoverable in negligence reaches beyond cases of negligent mis-statement into cases of the negligent carrying out of a service. It also shows that the fact that the defendant is accused of omitting to act, rather than acting badly, is of no particular importance. But it is not safe to assume that it follows that it is now straightforward to establish liability where the defendant is accused of negligently keeping silent. In *Banque Financière de la Cité SA v Westgate Insurance Co Ltd* [1991] 2 AC 249, [1990] 2 All ER 947 (the *Keyser Ullman* case), the claimant banks claimed that a failure by an employee of the defendants to disclose the existence of fraudulent behaviour had resulted in extra financial losses. The Court of Appeal decided that there was no duty of care in tort because such a duty would

undermine the rule in contract law that there is usually no liability in damages arising out of non-disclosure in pre-contractual negotiations. Slade LJ, speaking for the Court, did, however, say that there was no absolute bar to *Hedley Byrne* liability for silence, 'but subject to the all important proviso that there has been on the facts a voluntary assumption of responsibility in the relevant sense and reliance on that assumption'. He added, 'These features may be much more difficult to infer in a case of mere silence than in a case of misrepresentation.' (See further *Hamble Fisheries Ltd v L Gardner & Sons Ltd (The 'Rebecca Elaine')* [1999] 2 Lloyd's Rep 1, p. 620, post.) On appeal in the *Keyser Ullman* case, the House of Lords decided that the failure to disclose in this case could not amount to a breach of duty, even if there was a duty: the failure to disclose would have made no difference to the claimant's position. On the duty point itself, the Law Lords came to no conclusion. However, Lord Templeman considered that the defendants' silence did not amount to a relevant misrepresentation and the claimants had not relied on that silence in any case, while Lord Jauncey reserved his position on the duty question, but added 'it is clear that the scope of any such duty would not extend to the disclosure of facts which are not material to the risk insured'.

8.　In *Spring v Guardian Assurance plc* [1995] 2 AC 296, [1994] 3 All ER 129 (p. 58, ante), the House of Lords allowed a claim for negligence by a claimant who had been unable to find employment because his former employer, who was required to provide a reference under the rules of the relevant regulatory body, had carelessly sent an inaccurate reference. The majority took different approaches to justify this conclusion. Lord Woolf applied the broad *Caparo* test and concluded that sufficient proximity existed due to the nature of the employer–employee relationship that had previously existed between the claimant and the defendant. He considered that in the circumstances it was appropriate for the courts to apply 'a measured extension to the ambit of the law of negligence': the provision of a reference could be considered to be analogous to the provision of information in *Hedley Byrne*. In contrast, Lord Goff considered that the case could be resolved by the direct application of the approach established in *Hedley Byrne*, on the basis that the defendant had assumed responsibility to exercise due care in providing the reference for the claimant. He stated that '[w]here the plaintiff entrusts the defendant with the conduct of his affairs, in general or in particular, the defendant may be held to have assumed responsibility to the plaintiff, and the plaintiff to have relied on the defendant to exercise due skill and care, in respect of such conduct': [1992] 2 AC 296 at 318.

　　This seemed to involve a considerable expansion of the concept of assumption of responsibility as, unlike the case in *Hedley Byrne*, there was no representation or voluntary undertaking to exercise skill made by the defendant to the claimant, nor was there actual reliance by the claimant. Lord Keith dissented on this basis, considering that these factors took the case outside of the ambit of *Hedley Byrne*. Indeed, counsel for the claimant had not developed an argument based on *Hedley Byrne*, presumably on the basis that it was considered not to be applicable. However, Lord Goff considered that an assumption of responsibility could be regarded as having risen in the circumstances, thereby applying an objective analysis and treating a relationship of dependence as capable of generating an assumption of responsibility. Note that Lord Brown in *D v East Berkshire Community Health NHS Trust* [2005] 2 All ER 443 at 487, suggested that the decision in *Spring* should be understood as based on (and implicitly confined to) the special relationship between the employer and the employee: see p. 61, ante.

9.　Lord Goff's approach in *Spring* paved the way for the further development of the 'assumption of responsibility' test in *Henderson*. However, the objective approach to this test adopted by Lord Goff means that this concept now appeared to capture a wider range of relationships than those that involve a voluntary assumption of responsibility to a specific claimant, who in turn acts in reliance upon that undertaking. Such a voluntary assumption of responsibility, as delineated by Lord Devlin in *Hedley Byrne*, may be sufficient to establish a duty of care, but now does not appear to be always a necessary requirement for such a duty to exist. It appears as if a duty of care can now be imposed in additional circumstances, such as where there is an element of dependence in the relationship at issue, or where the defendant is in a position to exercise power in a manner that impacts on the claimant. (See N.J. McBride and A. Hughes (1995) 15 LS 376.) (Note that this broad concept of assumption of responsibility seems to have migrated into the spheres of physical loss and property damage: see e.g. *Phelps v London Borough of Hillingdon* [2001] 2 AC 619, [2000] 4 All ER 504, p. 99, ante.)

■ White v Jones
House of Lords [1995] 1 All ER 691

The plaintiffs were the daughters of a 78-year-old man who had employed the defendants' solicitors to draw up his will. As a result of a family dispute, on the father's instructions, the defendants designed the will so that it cut the daughters out of the estate. The dispute was, however, settled and the father asked the defendants to change the will to include £9,000 legacies for the plaintiffs. The defendants failed to carry out the father's instructions, in the process failing to keep several appointments with him. Several months later, with the original will still unchanged, the father died. The family was unable to agree to modify the will and the daughters, deprived of their legacies, sued the defendants in negligence. Turner J dismissed the claim, distinguishing *Ross v Caunters (a firm)* [1980] Ch 297, [1979] 3 All ER 580, in which Megarry V-C decided that solicitors could be held liable to a disappointed beneficiary of a will where, because of the solicitors' negligence, the will was completely invalid. The Court of Appeal, [1993] 3 All ER 481, reversed. The House of Lords, by a majority of 3–2, affirmed the judgment of the Court of Appeal in favour of the plaintiffs.

LORD GOFF OF CHIEVELEY:...
I turn to the principal issue which arises on the appeal, which is whether in the circumstances of cases such as *Ross v Caunters* and the present case the testator's solicitors are liable to the disappointed beneficiary. As I have already stated, the question is one which has been much discussed, not only in this country and other common law countries, but also in some civil law countries, notably Germany. There can be no doubt that *Ross v Caunters* has been generally welcomed by academic writers...Furthermore, it does not appear to have been the subject of adverse comment in the higher courts in this country, though it has not been approved except by the Court of Appeal in the present case. Indeed, as far as I am aware, *Ross v Caunters* has created no serious problems in practice since it was decided nearly 15 years ago....

The conceptual difficulties
Even so, it has been recognised on all hands that *Ross v Caunters* raises difficulties of a conceptual nature, and that as a result it is not altogether easy to accommodate the decision within the ordinary principles of our law of obligations....
   They are as follows.
   (1) First, the general rule is well established that a solicitor acting on behalf of a client owes a duty of care only to his client. The relationship between a solicitor and his client is nearly always contractual, and the scope of the solicitor's duties will be set by the terms of his retainer; but a duty of care owed by a solicitor to his client will arise concurrently in contract and in tort (see *Midland Bank Trust Co Ltd v*

Hett, Stubbs & Kemp (a firm) [1978] 3 All ER 571, [1979] Ch 384, recently approved by your Lordships' House in *Henderson v Merrett Syndicates Ltd* [1994] 3 All ER 506, [1994] 3 WLR 761). But, when a solicitor is performing his duties to his client, he will generally owe no duty of care to third parties. Accordingly, as Nicholls V-C pointed out in the present case, a solicitor acting for a seller of land does not generally owe a duty of care to the buyer: see *Gran Gelato Ltd v Richcliff (Group) Ltd* [1992] 1 All ER 865, [1992] Ch 560. Nor, as a general rule, does a solicitor acting for a party in adversarial litigation owe a duty of care to that party's opponent: see *Al-Kandari v J R Brown & Co (a firm)* [1988] 1 All ER 833 at 836, [1988] QB 665 at 672 per Lord Donaldson MR. Further, it has been held that a solicitor advising a client about a proposed dealing with his property in his lifetime owes no duty of care to a prospective beneficiary under the client's then will who may be prejudicially affected: see *Clarke v Bruce Lance & Co (a firm)* [1988] 1 All ER 364, [1988] 1 WLR 881.

As I have said, the scope of the solicitor's duties to his client are set by the terms of his retainer; and as a result it has been said that the content of his duties is entirely within the control of his client. The solicitor can, in theory at least, protect himself by the introduction of terms into his contract with his client; but, it is objected, he could not similarly protect himself against any third party to whom he might be held responsible, where there is no contract between him and the third party.

In these circumstances, it is said, there can be no liability of the solicitor to a beneficiary under a will who has been disappointed by reason of negligent failure by the solicitor to give effect to the testator's intention. There can be no liability in contract, because there is no contract between the solicitor and the disappointed beneficiary. Nor could there be liability in tort, because in the performance of his duties to his client a solicitor owes no duty of care in tort to a third party such as a disappointed beneficiary under his client's will.

(2) A further reason is given which is said to reinforce the conclusion that no duty of care is owed by the solicitor to the beneficiary in tort. Here, it is suggested, is one of those situations in which a plaintiff is entitled to damages if, and only if, he can establish a breach of contract by the defendant. First, the plaintiff's claim is one for purely financial loss; and as a general rule, apart from cases of assumption of responsibility arising under the principle in *Hedley Byrne & Co Ltd v Heller & Partners Ltd* [1963] 2 All ER 575, [1964] AC 465, no action will lie in respect of such loss in the tort of negligence. Furthermore, in particular, no claim will lie in tort for damages in respect of a mere loss of an expectation, as opposed to damages in respect of damage to an existing right or interest of the plaintiff. Such a claim falls within the exclusive zone of contractual liability; and it is contrary to principle that the law of tort should be allowed to invade that zone. Of course, Parliament can create exceptions to that principle by extending contractual rights to persons who are not parties to a contract, as was done, for example, in the Bills of Lading Act 1855 and the Carriage of Goods by Sea Act 1992. But as a matter of principle a step of this kind cannot be taken by the courts, though they can redefine the boundaries of the exclusive zone, as they did in *Donoghue v Stevenson* [1932] AC 562, [1932] All ER Rep 1.

The present case, it is suggested, falls within that exclusive zone. Here, it is impossible to frame the suggested duty except by reference to the contract between the solicitor and the testator—a contract to which the disappointed beneficiary is not a party, and from which, therefore, he can derive no rights. Second, the loss suffered by the disappointed beneficiary is not in reality a loss at all; it is, more accurately, a failure to obtain a benefit. All that has happened is that what is sometimes called a spes succesionis has failed to come to fruition. As a result, he has not become better off; but he is not made worse off. A claim in respect of such a loss of expectation falls, it is said, clearly within the exclusive zone of contractual liability.

(3) A third, and distinct, objection is that, if liability in tort was recognised in cases such as *Ross v Caunters*, it would be impossible to place any sensible bounds to cases in which such recovery was allowed. In particular, the same liability should logically be imposed in cases where an inter vivos transaction was ineffective, and the defect was not discovered until the donor was no longer able to repair it. Furthermore, liability could not logically be restricted to cases where a specific named beneficiary was disappointed, but would inevitably have to be extended to cases in which wide, even indeterminate, classes of persons could be said to have been adversely affected.

(4) Other miscellaneous objections were taken, though in my opinion they were without substance. In particular—(a) Since the testator himself owes no duty to the beneficiary, it would be illogical to impose any such duty on his solicitor. I myself cannot however see any force in this objection. (b) To enable the disappointed beneficiary to recover from the solicitor would have the undesirable, and indeed fortuitous, effect of substantially increasing the size of the testator's estate—even of doubling it in size; because it would not be possible to recover any part of the estate which had lawfully devolved upon others by an unrevoked will or on an intestacy, even though that was not in fact the testator's intention. I cannot however see what impact this has on the disappointed beneficiary's remedy. It simply reflects the fact that those who received the testator's estate, either under an unrevoked will or on an intestacy, were lucky enough to receive a windfall...

(5) There is however another objection of a conceptual nature, which was not adumbrated in argument before the Appellate Committee. In the present case, unlike *Ross v Caunters* itself, there was no act of the defendant solicitor which could be characterised as negligent. All that happened was that the solicitor did nothing at all for a period of time, with the result that the testator died before his new testamentary intentions could be implemented in place of the old. As a general rule, however, there is no liability in tortious negligence for an omission, unless the defendant is under some pre-existing duty. Once again, therefore, the question arises how liability can arise in the present case in the absence of a contract....

[After describing as obiter dicta remarks made by the House of Lords in *Robertson v Fleming* (1861) 4 Macq 167, which clearly supported the defendants' case, LORD GOFF continued:]

The impulse to do practical justice
Before addressing the legal questions which lie at the heart of the present case, it is, I consider, desirable to identify the reasons of justice which prompt judges and academic writers to conclude, like Megarry V-C in *Ross v Caunters*, that a duty should be owed by the testator's solicitor to a disappointed beneficiary. The principal reasons are, I believe, as follows.

(1) In the forefront stands the extraordinary fact that, if such a duty is not recognised, the only persons who might have a valid claim (ie the testator and his estate) have suffered no loss, and the only person who has suffered a loss (ie the disappointed beneficiary) has no claim: see *Ross v Caunters* [1979] 3 All ER 580 at 583, [1980] Ch 297 at 303 per Megarry V-C. It can therefore be said that, if the solicitor owes no duty to the intended beneficiaries, there is a lacuna in the law which needs to be filled. This I regard as being a point of cardinal importance in the present case.

(2) The injustice of denying such a remedy is reinforced if one considers the importance of legacies in a society which recognises (subject only to the incidence of inheritance tax, and statutory requirements for provision for near relatives) the right of citizens to leave their assets to whom they please, and in which, as a result, legacies can be of great importance to individual citizens, providing very often the only opportunity for a citizen to acquire a significant capital sum; or to inherit a house, so providing a secure roof over the heads of himself and his family; or to make special provision for his or her old age...

(3) There is a sense in which the solicitors' profession cannot complain if such a liability may be imposed upon their members. If one of them has been negligent in such a way as to defeat his client's testamentary intentions, he must regard himself as very lucky indeed if the effect of the law is that he is not liable to pay damages in the ordinary way. It can involve no injustice to render him subject to such a liability, even if the damages are payable not to his client's estate for distribution to the disappointed beneficiary (which might have been the preferred solution) but direct to the disappointed beneficiary.

(4) That such a conclusion is required as a matter of justice is reinforced by consideration of the role played by solicitors in society. The point was well made by Cooke J in *Gartside v Sheffield Young & Ellis* [1983] NZLR 37 at 43, when he observed:

'To deny an effective remedy in a plain case would seem to imply a refusal to acknowledge the solicitor's professional role in the community. In practice the public relies on solicitors (or statutory officers with similar functions) to prepare effective wills.'

The question therefore arises whether it is possible to give effect in law to the strong impulse for practical justice which is the fruit of the foregoing considerations. For this to be achieved, I respectfully agree with Nicholls V-C when he said that the court will have to fashion 'an effective remedy for the solicitor's breach of his professional duty to his client' in such a way as to repair the injustice to the disappointed beneficiary (see [1993] 3 All ER 481 at 489, [1993] 3 WLR 730 at 739).

Ross v Caunters and the conceptual problems
In *Ross v Caunters* Megarry V-C approached the problem as one arising under the ordinary principles of the tort of negligence. He found himself faced with two principal objections to the plaintiff's claim. The first, founded mainly upon the decision of the Court of Appeal in *Groom v Crocker* [1938] 2 All ER 394, [1939] 1 KB 194, was that a solicitor could not be liable in negligence in respect of his professional work to anyone except his client, his liability to his client arising only in contract and not in tort. This proposition Megarry V-C rejected without difficulty, relying primarily upon the judgment of Oliver J in *Midland Bank Trust Co Ltd v Hett, Stubbs & Kemp* [1978] 3 All ER 571, [1979] Ch 384 (recently approved by this House in *Henderson v Merrett Syndicates Ltd* [1994] 3 All ER 506, [1994] 3 WLR 761). The second, and more fundamental, argument was that, apart from cases falling within the principle established in *Hedley Byrne* no action lay in the tort of negligence for pure economic loss. This argument Megarry V-C approached following the path traced by Lord Wilberforce in *Anns v Merton London Borough* [1977] 2 All ER 492 at 498–499, [1978] AC 728 at 751–752; and on that basis, relying in particular on *Ministry of Housing and Local Government v Sharp* [1970] 1 All ER 1009, [1970] 2 QB 223 (which he regarded as conclusive of the point before him), he held that here liability could properly be imposed in negligence for pure economic loss, his preferred basis being by direct application of *Donoghue v Stevenson* [1932] itself.

It will at once be seen that some of the conceptual problems raised by the appellants in argument before the Appellate Committee were not raised in *Ross v Caunters*. Others which were raised plainly did not loom so large in argument as they have done in the present case . . . They have to be faced; and it is immediately apparent that they raise the question whether the claim properly falls within the law of contract or the law of tort. This is because, although the plaintiffs' claim has been advanced, and indeed held by the Court of Appeal to lie, in the tort of negligence, nevertheless the response of the appellants has been that the claim, if properly analysed, must necessarily have contractual features which cannot ordinarily exist in the case of an ordinary tortious claim. Here I refer not only to the fact that the claim is one for damages for pure economic loss, but also to the need for the defendant solicitor to be entitled to invoke as against the disappointed beneficiary any terms of the contract with his client which may limit or exclude his liability; to the fact that the damages claimed are for the loss of an expectation; and also to the fact (not adverted to below) that the claim in the present case can be said to arise from a pure omission, and as such will not (apart from special circumstances) give rise to a claim in tortious negligence. Faced with points such as these, the strict lawyer may well react by saying that the present claim can lie only in contract, and is not therefore open to a disappointed beneficiary as against the testator's solicitor . . .

It must not be forgotten however that a solicitor who undertakes to perform services for his client may be liable to his client for failure to exercise due care and skill in relation to the performance of those services not only in contract, but also in negligence under the principle in *Hedley Byrne v Heller* (see *Midland Bank Trust Co Ltd v Hett, Stubbs & Kemp* [1978] 3 All ER 571, [1979] Ch 384) on the basis of assumption of responsibility by the solicitor towards his client. Even so there is great difficulty in holding, on ordinary principles, that the solicitor has assumed any responsibility towards an intended beneficiary under a will which he has undertaken to prepare on behalf of his client but which, through his negligence, has failed to take effect in accordance with his client's instructions. The relevant work is plainly performed by the solicitor for his client; but, in the absence of special circumstances, it cannot be said to have been undertaken for the intended beneficiary. Certainly, again in the absence of special circumstances, there will have been no reliance by the intended beneficiary on the exercise by the solicitor of due care and skill; indeed, the intended beneficiary may not even have been aware that the solicitor was engaged on such a task, or that his position might be affected...From this it would appear to follow that the real reason for concern in cases such as the present lies in the extraordinary fact that, if a duty owed by the testator's solicitor to the disappointed beneficiary is not recognised, the only person who may have a valid claim has suffered no loss, and the only person who has suffered a loss has no claim. This is a point to which I will return later in this opinion, when I shall give further consideration to the application of the *Hedley Byrne* principle in circumstances such as those in the present case.

[LORD GOFF then referred to German law, especially to doctrines allowing third parties to claim the benefit of contracts and to the doctrine of transferred loss—see p. 179, ante. He continued:]

A contractual approach
It may be suggested that, in cases such as the present, the simplest course would be to solve the problem by making available to the disappointed beneficiary, by some means or another, the benefit of the contractual rights (such as they are) of the testator or his estate against the negligent solicitor, as is for example done under the German principle of Vertrag mit Schutzwirkung für Dritte. Indeed that course has been urged upon us by Professor Markesinis in 'An Expanding Tort Law' (1987) 103 LQR 354 at 396–397, echoing a view expressed by Professor Fleming in *'Comparative Law of Torts'* (1986) 4 OJLS 235 at 241. Attractive though this solution is, there is unfortunately a serious difficulty in its way. The doctrine of consideration still forms part of our law of contract, as does the doctrine of privity of contract which is considered to exclude the recognition of a jus quaesitum tertio. To proceed as Professor Markesinis has suggested may be acceptable in German law, but in this country could be open to criticism as an illegitimate circumvention of these long-established doctrines...

[LORD GOFF then discussed how alternative forms of contractual remedies were not of use in this case. He continued:]

The tortious solution
I therefore return to the law of tort for a solution to the problem. For the reasons I have already given, an ordinary action in tortious negligence on the lines proposed by Megarry V-C in *Ross v Caunters* [1979] 3 All ER 580, [1980] Ch 297 must, with the greatest respect, be regarded as inappropriate, because it does not meet any of the conceptual problems which have been raised. Furthermore, for the reasons I have previously given, the *Hedley Byrne* principle cannot, in the absence of special circumstances, give rise on ordinary principles to an assumption of responsibility by the testator's solicitor towards an intended beneficiary. Even so, it seems to me that it is open to your Lordships' House, as in *Linden Gardens Trust Ltd v Lenesta Sludge Disposals Ltd* [1993] 3 All ER 417, [1994] 1 AC 85, to fashion a remedy to fill a lacuna in the law and so prevent the injustice which would otherwise occur on the facts of cases such as the present...In my opinion, therefore, your Lordships' House should in cases such as these extend to the intended beneficiary a remedy under the *Hedley Byrne* principle by holding that the assumption of responsibility by the solicitor towards his client should be held in law to extend to the intended beneficiary who (as the solicitor can reasonably foresee) may, as a result of the solicitor's negligence, be deprived of his intended legacy in circumstances in which neither the testator nor his estate will have a remedy against the solicitor. Such liability will not of course arise in cases in which the defect in the will comes to light before the death of the testator, and the testator either leaves the will as it is or otherwise continues to exclude the previously intended beneficiary from the relevant benefit. I only wish to add that, with the benefit of experience during the 15 years in which *Ross v Caunters* has been regularly applied, we can say with some confidence that a direct remedy by the intended beneficiary against the solicitor appears to create no problems in practice. That is therefore the solution which I would recommend to your Lordships...

As I see it, not only does this conclusion produce practical justice as far as all parties are concerned, but it also has the following beneficial consequences.

(1) There is no unacceptable circumvention of established principles of the law of contract.
(2) No problem arises by reason of the loss being of a purely economic character.

(3) Such assumption of responsibility will of course be subject to any term of the contract between the solicitor and the testator which may exclude or restrict the solicitor's liability to the testator under the principle in *Hedley Byrne*. It is true that such a term would be most unlikely to exist in practice; but as a matter of principle it is right that this largely theoretical question should be addressed.

(4) Since the *Hedley Byrne* principle is founded upon an assumption of responsibility, the solicitor may be liable for negligent omissions as well as negligent acts of commission: see *Midland Bank Trust Co Ltd v Hett, Stubbs & Kemp* [1978] 3 All ER 571 at 595, [1979] Ch 384 at 416 per Oliver J, and my own speech in *Henderson v Merrett Syndicates Ltd* [1994] 3 All ER 506 at 521, [1994] 3 WLR 761 at 777. This conclusion provides justification for the decision of the Court of Appeal to reverse the decision of Turner J in the present case, although this point was not in fact raised below or before your Lordships.

(5) I do not consider that damages for loss of an expectation are excluded in cases of negligence arising under the principle in *Hedley Byrne*, simply because the cause of action is classified as tortious. Such damages may in principle be recoverable in cases of contractual negligence; and I cannot see that, for present purposes, any relevant distinction can be drawn between the two forms of action. In particular, an expectation loss may well occur in cases where a professional man, such as a solicitor, has assumed responsibility for the affairs of another; and I for my part can see no reason in principle why the professional man should not, in an appropriate case, be liable for such loss under the *Hedley Byrne* principle.

In the result, all the conceptual problems, including those which so troubled Lush and Murphy JJ in *Seale v Perry* [1982] VR 193, can be seen to fade innocuously away. Let me emphasise that I can see no injustice in imposing liability upon a negligent solicitor in a case such as the present where, in the absence of a remedy in this form, neither the testator's estate nor the disappointed beneficiary will have a claim for the loss caused by his negligence. This is the injustice which, in my opinion, the judges of this country should address by recognising that cases such as these call for an appropriate remedy, and that the common law is not so sterile as to be incapable of supplying that remedy when it is required.

Unlimited claims

I come finally to the objection that, if liability is recognised in a case such as the present, it will be impossible to place any sensible limits to cases in which recovery is allowed. Before your Lordships, as before the Court of Appeal, Mr Matheson conjured up the spectre of solicitors being liable to an indeterminate class, including persons unborn at the date of the testator's death. I must confess that my reaction to this kind of argument was very similar to that of Cooke J in *Gartside v Sheffield Young & Ellis* [1983] NZLR 37 at 44, when he said that he was not 'persuaded that we should decide a fairly straightforward case against the dictates of justice because of foreseeable troubles in more difficult cases'. We are concerned here with a liability which is imposed by law to do practical justice in a particular type of case. There must be boundaries to the availability of a remedy in such cases; but these will have to be worked out in the future, as practical problems come before the courts. In the present case Nicholls V-C observed that, in cases of this kind, liability is not to an indeterminate class, but to the particular beneficiary or beneficiaries whom the client intended to benefit through the particular will. I respectfully agree, and I also agree with him that the ordinary case is one in which the intended beneficiaries are a small number of identified people. If by any chance a more complicated case should arise to test the precise boundaries of the principle in cases of this kind, that problem can await solution when such a case comes forward for decision.

Conclusion

For these reasons I would dismiss the appeal with costs.

LORD BROWNE-WILKINSON: . . .

My Lords, I have read the speech of my noble and learned friend, Lord Goff of Chieveley, and agree with him that this appeal should be dismissed. In particular, I agree that your Lordships should hold that the defendant solicitors were under a duty of care to the plaintiffs arising from an extension of the principle of assumption of responsibility explored in *Hedley Byrne & Co Ltd v Heller & Partners Ltd* [1963] 2 All ER 575, [1964] AC 465. In my view, although the present case is not directly covered by the decided cases, it is legitimate to extend the law to the limited extent proposed using the incremental approach by way of analogy advocated in *Caparo Industries plc v Dickman* [1990] 1 All ER 568, [1990] 2 AC 605. To explain my reasons requires me to attempt an analysis of what is meant by 'assumption of responsibility' in the law of negligence. To avoid misunderstanding I must emphasise that I am considering only whether some duty of care exists, not with the extent of that duty which will vary according to the circumstances.

Far from that concept having been invented by your Lordships' House in *Hedley Byrne*, its genesis is to be found in *Nocton v Lord Ashburton* [1914] AC 932, [1914–15] All ER Rep 45. It is impossible to analyse what is meant by 'assumption of responsibility' or 'the *Hedley Byrne* principle' without first having regard to *Nocton's* case. In that case, the plaintiff, Lord Ashburton, had relied on advice by his solicitor, Nocton, in relation to certain lending transactions. The determination of the case was bedeviled by questions of pleading. The trial judge and the Court of Appeal took the view that on the pleadings the plaintiff could only succeed if he proved fraud. In their view Lord Ashburton could not succeed in negligence since it had not been pleaded. This House (whilst rejecting the finding of fraud against Nocton) held that the pleadings sufficiently alleged a fiduciary duty owed to Lord Ashburton by Nocton as his solicitor and held that Nocton had breached that fiduciary duty by giving negligent advice. In rejecting the notion that *Derry v Peek* (1889) 14 App Cas 337, 58 LJ Ch 864 precluded a finding of such liability, Viscount Haldane LC said ([1914] AC 932 at 948, [1914–15] All ER Rep 45 at 50):

> 'Although liability for negligence in word has in material respects been developed in our law differently from liability for negligence in act, it is none the less true that a man may come under a special duty to exercise care in giving information or advice. I should accordingly be sorry to be thought to lend countenance to the idea that recent decisions have been intended to stereotype the cases in which people can be held to have assumed such a special duty. Whether such a duty has been assumed must depend on the relationship of the parties, and it is at least certain that there are a good many cases in which that relationship may be properly treated as giving rise to a special duty of care in statement.'

. . . In my judgment, there are three points relevant to the present case which should be gathered from *Nocton's* case. First, there can be special relationships between the parties which give rise to the law treating the defendant as having assumed a duty to be careful in circumstances where, apart from such relationship, no duty of care would exist. Second, a fiduciary relationship is one of those special relationships. Third, a fiduciary relationship is not the only such special relationship: other relationships may be held to give rise to the same duty . . .

. . . [I]n my judgment *Nocton's* case demonstrates that there is at least one special relationship giving rise to the imposition of a duty of care that is dependent neither upon mutuality of dealing nor upon actual reliance by the plaintiff on the defendants actions.

I turn then to consider *Hedley Byrne v Heller*. In that case this House had to consider the circumstances in which there could be liability for negligent misstatement in the absence of either a contract or a fiduciary relationship between the parties. The first, and for present purposes perhaps the most important, point is that there is nothing in *Hedley Byrne* to cast doubt on the decision in *Nocton's* case. On the contrary, each of their Lordships treated *Nocton's* case as their starting point and asked the question: in the absence of any contractual or fiduciary duty, what circumstances give rise to a special relationship between the plaintiff and the defendant sufficient to justify the imposition of the duty of care in the making of statements?' The House was seeking to define a further special relationship in addition to, not in substitution for, fiduciary relationships: see [1963] 2 All ER 575 at 583, 594, 599, 606, 617, [1964] AC 465 at 486, 502, 511, 523, 539 per Lord Reid, Lord Morris, Lord Hodson, Lord Devlin and Lord Pearce respectively.

Second, since this House was concerned with cases of negligent misstatement or advice, it was inevitable that any test laid down required both that the plaintiff should rely on the statement or advice and that the defendant could reasonably foresee that he would do so. In the case of claims based on negligent statements (as opposed to negligent actions) the plaintiff will have no cause of action at all unless he can show damage and he can only have suffered damage if he has relied on the negligent statement. Nor will a defendant be shown to have satisfied the requirement that he should foresee damage to the plaintiff unless he foresees such reliance by the plaintiff as to give rise to the damage. Therefore, although reliance by the plaintiff is an essential ingredient in a case based on negligent misstatement or advice, it does not follow that in all cases based on negligent action or inaction by the defendant it is necessary in order to demonstrate a special relationship that the plaintiff has in fact relied on the defendant or the defendant has foreseen such reliance. If in such a case careless conduct can be foreseen as likely to cause and does in fact cause damage to the plaintiff that should be sufficient to found liability.

Third, it is clear that the basis on which (apart from the disclaimer) the majority would have held the bank liable for negligently giving the reference was that, were it not for the disclaimer, the bank would have assumed responsibility for such reference. Although there are passages in the speeches which may point the other way, the reasoning of the majority in my judgment points clearly to the fact that the crucial element was that, by choosing to answer the inquiry, the bank had assumed to act, and thereby created the special relationship on which the necessary duty of care was founded...

Just as in the case of fiduciary duties, the assumption of responsibility referred to is the defendants' assumption of responsibility for the task, not the assumption of legal liability. Even in cases of ad hoc relationships, it is the undertaking to answer the question posed which creates the relationship. If the responsibility for the task is assumed by the defendant he thereby creates a special relationship between himself and the plaintiff in relation to which the law (not the defendant) attaches a duty to carry out carefully the task so assumed. If this be the right view, it does much to allay the doubts about the utility of the concept of assumption of responsibility voiced by Lord Griffiths in *Smith v Eric S Bush (a firm), Harris v Wyre Forest DC* [1989] 2 All ER 514 at 534, [1990] 1 AC 831 at 862 and by Lord Roskill in *Caparo Industries plc v Dickman* [1990] 1 All ER 568 at 582, [1990] 2 AC 605 at 628: see also Barker 'Unreliable Assumptions in the Modern Law of Negligence' (1993) 109 LQR 461. As I read those judicial criticisms they proceed on the footing that the phrase 'assumption of responsibility' refers to the defendant having assumed legal responsibility. I doubt whether the same criticisms would have been directed at the phrase if the words had been understood, as I think they should be, as referring to a conscious assumption of responsibility for the task rather than a conscious assumption of legal liability to the plaintiff for its careful performance. Certainly, the decision in both cases is consistent with the view I take.

In *Henderson v Merrett Syndicates Ltd* [1994] 3 All ER 506, [1994] 3 WLR 761 your Lordships recently applied the concept of assumption of liability to cases where the defendants (the managing agents) had pursuant to a contract with a third party (the members' agents) undertaken the management of the underwriting affairs of the plaintiffs. For the present purposes the case is important for two reasons. First, it shows (if it was previously in doubt) that the principle of a special relationship arising from the assumption of responsibility is as applicable to a case of negligent acts giving rise to pure economic loss as it is to negligent statement. Second, it demonstrates that the fact that the defendant assumed to act in the plaintiffs' affairs pursuant to a contract with a third party is not necessarily incompatible with the finding that, by so acting, the defendant also entered into a special relationship with the plaintiff with whom he had no contract. (I should add that I agree with my noble and learned friend, Lord Mustill, that this factor should not lead to the conclusion that a duty of care will necessarily be found to exist even where there is a contractual chain of obligations designed by the parties to regulate their dealings).

Let me now seek to bring together these various strands so far as is necessary for the purposes of this case: I am not purporting to give any comprehensive statement of this aspect of the law. The law of England does not impose any general duty of care to avoid negligent misstatements or to avoid causing pure economic loss even if economic damage to the plaintiff was foreseeable. However, such a duty of care will arise if there is a special relationship between the parties. Although the categories of cases in which such a special relationship can be held to exist are not closed, as yet only two categories have been identified, viz (1) where there is a fiduciary relationship and (2) where the defendant has voluntarily answered a question or tenders skilled advice or services in circumstances where he knows or ought to know that an identified plaintiff will rely on his answers or advice. In both these categories the special relationship is created by the defendant voluntarily assuming to act in the matter by involving himself in the plaintiff's affairs or by choosing to speak. If he does so assume to act or speak he is said to have assumed responsibility for carrying through the matter he has entered upon. In the words of Lord Reid in *Hedley Byrne v Heller* [1963] 2 All ER 575 at 583, [1964] AC 465 at 486, he has 'accepted a relationship…which requires him to exercise such care as the circumstances require,' ie although the extent of the duty will vary from category to category, some duty of care arises from the special relationship. Such relationship can arise even though the defendant has acted in the plaintiff's affairs pursuant to a contract with a third party…

The solicitor who accepts instructions to draw a will knows that the future economic welfare of the intended beneficiary is dependent upon his careful execution of the task. It is true that the intended beneficiary (being ignorant of the instructions) may not rely on the particular solicitor's actions. But, as I have sought to demonstrate, in the case of a duty of care flowing from a fiduciary relationship liability is not dependent upon actual reliance by the plaintiff on the defendant's actions but on the fact that, as the fiduciary is well aware, the plaintiff's economic well-being is dependent upon the proper discharge by the fiduciary of his duty. Second, the solicitor by accepting the instructions has entered upon, and therefore assumed responsibility for, the task of procuring the execution of a skilfully drawn will knowing that the beneficiary is wholly dependent upon his carefully carrying out his function. That assumption of responsibility for the task is a feature of both the two categories of special relationship so far identified in the authorities. It is not to the point that the solicitor only entered on the task pursuant to a contract with the third party (ie the testator). There are therefore present many of the features which in the other categories of special relationship have been treated as sufficient to create a special relationship to which the law attaches a duty of care. In my judgment the analogy is close.

Moreover, there are more general factors which indicate that it is fair, just and reasonable to impose liability on the solicitor. Save in the case of those rash testators who make their own wills, the proper transmission of property from one generation to the next is dependent upon the due discharge by solicitors of their duties. Although in any particular case it may not be possible to demonstrate that the intended beneficiary relied upon the solicitor, society as a whole does rely on solicitors to carry out their will-making functions carefully. To my mind it would be unacceptable if, because of some technical rules of law, the wishes and expectations of testators and beneficiaries generally could be defeated by the negligent actions of solicitors without there being any redress. It is only just that the intended beneficiary should be able to recover the benefits which he would otherwise have received…

In all the circumstances, I would hold that by accepting instructions to draw a will, a solicitor does come into a special relationship with those intended to benefit under it in consequence of which the law imposes a duty to the intended beneficiary to act with due expedition and care in relation to the task on which he has entered. For these and the other reasons given by my noble and learned friend, Lord Goff of Chieveley, I would dismiss the appeal.

LORD MUSTILL [DISSENTING]: . . .
I will proceed at once to explain why I have felt it difficult to join company with those who, judges and commentators alike, have almost unanimously found it too plain to need elaboration that the plaintiffs' claims ought to succeed, if only an intellectually sustainable means can be found; and also that the proper route to such a conclusion passes through the law of tort. The soundness of these assumptions must, I believe, be confronted at the start, because they dominate the landscape within which the whole inquiry takes place.

The first assumption, which comes to this, that there must be something wrong with the law if the plaintiffs do not succeed, itself embodies two distinct propositions—that the plaintiffs' disappointment should be relieved by an award of money and that the money should, if the law permits, come from the solicitor. I am sceptical on both counts. I do not of course ascribe to those who support the plaintiffs' claim that the contemporary perception that all financial and other misfortunes suffered by one person should be put right at the expense of someone else. Nobody argues for this. Even under the most supportive of legal regimes there must be many situations in which the well-founded expectations of a potential beneficiary are defeated by an untoward turn of events and yet he or she is left without recourse...

As I understand your Lordships' opinions only one feature of existing law is relied upon as the starting point for a new principle wide enough to yield an affirmative answer to the question just posed: namely *Hedley Byrne* itself...In *Hedley Byrne* the plaintiffs asked the defendants to do something; the defendants did it, and did so imperfectly. Here, leaving aside the special facts of this appeal, and concentrating on the general case of the disappointed beneficiary, the complaint is that the solicitor did not do something which the beneficiary never asked him to do. It is therefore necessary to determine the ratio which underlies the decision in *Hedley Byrne*. This ground has only recently been covered by this House in *Henderson v Merrett Syndicates Ltd* [1994] 3 All ER 506, [1994] 3 WLR 761, but the context there was so different from the present that it is prudent to start with *Hedley Byrne* itself. In my judgment it is possible to detect within the speeches four themes, which I will label 'mutuality', 'special relationship', 'reliance' and 'undertaking of responsibility'...

I believe that the element of what I have called mutuality was central to the decision. I think it clear from the passage quoted above (a passage in which Lord Devlin summed up not only his own opinion but also his understanding of those expressed by the other members of the House) that the legal responsibility accepted or undertaken by the person in question was one where the acceptance or undertaking was a reflection of the relationship in question. On the facts of *Hedley Byrne* this relationship was bilateral, being created on the one hand by the acts of the plaintiffs in first asking for a reference in circumstances which showed that the bankers' skill and care would be relied upon and then subsequently relying on it; and on the other hand by the bankers' compliance with the request. What conclusion the House would have reached if the element of mutuality had been absent if, for example, the defendants had for some reason despatched the reference spontaneously, without prior request cannot be ascertained from the speeches, but even if a claim had been upheld the reasoning must, I believe, have been fundamentally different.

Two further aspects of the decision call for mention. First, the use of the word 'undertaking'. There is a degree of ambiguity about this. In context however I think it clear that the word was not used in the sense of taking on or tackling a job. The passages quoted show that the defendants were held liable because the relationship was such as to show that they took upon themselves a legal duty to give with reasonable care whatever reference they chose to furnish.

Secondly, there was the element of reliance, to which great attention has been directed in the present case. This element was of course crucial to the success of the claim in *Hedley Byrne*; for without reliance there could be no damage, and without damage there could be no cause of action in negligence. But, so far as the duty of care was concerned, the reliance merely consummated the relationship already initiated by the plaintiffs' request and the defendants' response. To my mind therefore *Hedley Byrne* says nothing, one way or the other, about reliance or the anticipation of reliance as either necessary or sufficient for the recognition of a duty of care differently conceived.

I turn now to *Henderson v Merrett Syndicates Ltd* [1994] 3 All ER 506, [1994] 3 WLR 761...[this] case fell squarely within the concept of the undertaking of legal responsibility for careful and diligent performance in the context of a mutual relationship which in my opinion was the essence of the decision in *Hedley Byrne*.

Can the principles thus formulated and applied be sufficient in themselves to yield a duty of care owed to an intended beneficiary? The proposition may conveniently be tested by reference to a will intended to be executed in favour of a charity. It often happens that the charity will not only have no knowledge of the testator's intention, but will never even have heard of the testator and his solicitor. In such a situation I can find no trace of a special relationship such as was contemplated by *Hedley Byrne*, and which actually existed in the two leading cases. The charity does nothing. It neither invites the solicitor to prepare the will, nor determines its conduct on the assumption that it will be skilfully and diligently prepared. There is no mutual relationship…For these reasons therefore I conclude that the judgment in favour of the plaintiffs cannot be sustained by the direct application of the existing authorities. There still remains however the question whether a new rule should be devised to encompass the present situation. This could happen in either of two ways. First, the court might start with an established principle, and by the incremental process recognised and adopted in cases from *Caparo Industries plc v Dickman* onwards extend the law to encompass the new situation. Secondly, the court might proceed directly to the recognition of a duty, without using any of the existing law as a starting-point.

Taking these methods in turn, it is plain that *Hedley Byrne* and *Henderson* together represent the only solid basis for an accretive process which could yield a recovery to disappointed beneficiaries. Even though the elements of request and reliance conspicuous in those two cases are absent from the situation now under review it is no great step, so the argument would run, to build upon the crucial fact, common to all the cases, that the defendant undertook the task in question; and to treat *Hedley Byrne*, *Henderson* and the present as being fundamentally the same. Whilst acknowledging the attractions of this proposition I am unable to accept it, for it is not to my mind the application of *Hedley Byrne* by enlargement—in consimili casu, as it were—but the enunciation of something quite different…

For the reasons stated, I would allow the appeal.

[LORD NOLAN delivered a speech in which he agreed with both LORD GOFF OF CHIEVELEY and LORD BROWNE-WILKINSON, adding that it was important that the solicitors acted as 'family solicitors' for the benefit of the whole family. LORD KEITH OF KINKEL delivered a speech in favour of allowing the appeal in which he agreed with LORD MUSTILL.]

Appeal dismissed.

NOTES

1. It is important to understand the different approaches adopted in the judgments in *White v Jones*. Lord Goff was of the opinion that the 'ordinary principles' applied under the standard 'assumption of responsibility' analysis adopted in *Hedley Byrne* and other cases could not provide a remedy in this type of case, as there was an insufficiently close relationship of reliance and dependence. However, he considered that the justice of the case required that an assumption of responsibility be held 'at law' to exist, given the inability of contractual routes to offer a remedy. Lord Mustill in his dissenting opinion appeared to take a similar view that there was no assumption of responsibility within the scope of how that concept had been hitherto defined in the case law: however, he differed from Lord Goff's analysis in his view that there was insufficient 'mutuality' to justify the imposition of a duty of care. Lord Browne-Wilkinson considered that the scope of the existing *Hedley Byrne* principles (which he described as originating the earlier judgment in *Nocton v Lord Ashburton* [1914] AC 932, [1914–15] All ER Rep 45) *were* sufficient to enable the courts to find that a duty of care existed in this case.

2. Is Lord Browne-Wilkinson's approach developed with sufficient precision to identify who will come within a 'special relationship' for the purpose of imposing liability for economic loss? Is Lord Mustill correct to point to the lack of sufficient 'mutuality' in this case between the solicitor and the thwarted beneficiaries? Does Lord Goff consider that the standard 'assumption of responsibility' analysis does not cover this type of claim? J. Murphy [1996] CLJ 43 suggests that it would be appropriate to treat *White v Jones* as based on the application of the general *Caparo* test: sufficient forseeability, proximity, and 'fair, just and reasonable' policy considerations existed to justify the imposition of a duty of care. (See also the decision of the Australian High Court in *Hill*

v Van Erp (1997) 71 ALJR 487.) Does this explanation work? Does Lord Goff's finding that an 'assumption of responsibility' should be held to exist at law unnecessarily complicate a straightforward application of *Caparo*? For criticism of the use of a tort remedy in *White*, see T. Weir (1995) 111 LQR 357. The 'problem' at issue in *White v Jones* could be addressed by changing the law of probate, or even by establishing restitutionary remedies against 'unintended legatees'. Why rely on a remedy in tort?

3.   A key difference of opinion between Lord Browne-Wilkinson and Lord Mustill concerns what the defendant must have undertaken responsibility for. Lord Mustill insists that *Hedley Byrne* requires the defendant to have undertaken a legal duty to take care of the claimant. Lord Browne-Wilkinson says that it is sufficient for the defendant to have undertaken to carry out carefully some task requiring skill and care. Lord Browne-Wilkinson's notion would have far-reaching effects. It might, for example, retrieve the decision in *Ministry of Housing and Local Government v Sharp* [1970] 2 QB 223, [1970] 1 All ER 1009, noted p. 182, ante, which appears to reflect pre-*Caparo* analysis and lack any significant element of a voluntary assumption of responsibility. But does Lord Browne-Wilkinson intend to say that anyone can sue who might have benefited if the defendant had carried out the task properly? Should *Caparo*-style limitations apply on who can sue?

4.   One striking feature of *White v Jones* is that there was liability based on *Hedley Byrne* even though there was no discernible element of reliance (except to Lord Nolan, who thought that reliance was demonstrated merely by the daughters' knowledge of attempts to change the will). Even Lord Mustill agrees in his dissent that reliance forms no necessary part of the inquiry into whether there should be a duty under *Hedley Byrne*. Reliance, especially foreseeable and reasonable reliance, can certainly be relevant to whether the court should say that the defendant assumed responsibility, but its absence does not appear to be fatal (see further *Spring v Guardian Assurance*, p. 242, ante, and also *Hamble Fisheries Ltd v L Gardner & Sons Ltd (The 'Rebecca Elaine')* [1999] 2 Lloyd's Rep 1 (p. 620, post)). This again confirms that the 'assumption of responsibility' analysis as applied by the courts has moved considerably from the relatively limited scope of this concept first articulated in *Hedley Byrne*. Note, however, that reliance, especially 'reasonable reliance', may often be relevant to other elements of the negligence claim. It will be relevant in determining whether a breach of the duty of care has taken place, since if the claimant relies unexpectedly, the defendant can argue that a reasonable person in the position of the claimant at the time would have estimated the risk of harm as so low that it would not have been worthwhile to take more care. It will also be relevant to remoteness, or legal cause, since unreasonable reliance might amount to a break in the chain of causation. It may also still be required for the 'assumption of responsibility' test to be satisfied in certain circumstances: see *Williams v Natural Life Health Foods* [1998] 2 All ER 577, although there is some ambiguity in this judgment as to whether reliance is required before a duty of care will be imposed, or whether it is required to establish causation.

5.   Lord Mustill, perhaps inconsistently with his view on reliance, insists that the majority is wrong to ignore the importance of mutuality under *Hedley Byrne*. By mutuality he means that both claimant and defendant must have actively participated in the transaction from which liability arose. Apart from authority, why should this be so? One frequently advanced argument is that without mutuality it is difficult to measure the value each side puts on their expectation (see e.g. Lord Brandon's dissent in *Junior Books Ltd*

v Veitchi Ltd [1983] 1 AC 520, [1982] 3 All ER 201). But this argument does not work in *White* since the value of the legacies is clear. Perhaps a better point is to draw an analogy, as Lord Mustill does, with the non-enforcement of promises of a gift. Without mutuality, it might be argued, there is no evidence that the transfer of the property from one person to the other is welfare-enhancing for the two people taken together, unlike a voluntary trade in which each person gives up something in exchange for something which that person considers more valuable. On the other hand, might there not be an argument that if testators know that beneficiaries might not get the legacies intended for them because of negligence by lawyers, they will make inter vivos transfers instead? Such transfers will presumably be less convenient and less congenial for the testators, otherwise such gifts would have been their first choice. The rule in *White* at least counteracts such a welfare loss by testators.

'Mutuality' can of course also be seen as another verbal formula used to describe the circumstances where a sufficient pre-existing relationship exists between a sufficiently defined group of persons to justify the imposition of liability for economic loss. Lord Mustill may perhaps in *White v Jones* be attempting to give this term more substance and analytical content than it was ever intended to bear when used in *Hedley Byrne*.

6.   The decision in *White* has been applied to a relatively narrow range of circumstances. It has been extended to financial institutions offering will-making services: see *Esterhuizen v Allied Dunbar Plc* [1998] 2 FLR 668. In *Gorham v British Telecommunications Plc* [2000] 4 All ER 867, [2000] EWCA Civ 234, *White* was extended to impose liability upon a financial adviser in respect of financial loss to dependants of the deceased which stemmed from negligent advice on pensions given to the deceased. Where the estate itself has suffered loss, and therefore can sue, the beneficiaries nevertheless still have an action, as established in *Carr-Glynn v Frearsons (a firm)* [1999] Ch 326, [1998] 4 All ER 225. In this case, the defendant solicitors said that it would be unfair to force them to pay twice for the same mistake. They also said that the real reason for the decision in *White* was that otherwise there would be a 'lacuna' in the law: where the estate can sue there is no such lacuna and therefore they argued that no liability should attach. This argument was rejected by the Court of Appeal, which held that the lacuna remedied in *White* concerned the absence of a remedy for the disappointed benficiaries, which a right of action vested in the estate would not fill. (But see now *Alfred McAlpine Construction Ltd v Panatown Ltd* [2001] 1 AC 518, [2000] 4 All ER 97, noted p. 257, post.)

However, if alternative remedies of a practical and feasible nature are available to disappointed beneficiaries in a *White*-style situation, then a duty of care may not be imposed: see *Walker v Geo Medlicott & Son* [1999] *Horsfall v Haywards* [1999] 1 FLR 1182. Also, a solicitor will not usually be liable in situations where the intent of the deceased to confer a benefit on a particular person was uncertain (see *Clark v Bruce, Lance* [1988] 1 WLR 881), or where errors in an *inter vivos* transaction were remediable before the death of the deceased (see *Hemmens v Wilson Browne* [1995] Ch 223, [1993] 4 All ER 826, as well as the discussion in *Hughes v Richards (t/a Colin Richards & Co)* [2004] EWCA Civ 266 at [26–28]).

7.   Also, attempts to extend *White* beyond the testamentary context have met with limited success. For example, see *Goodwill v British Pregnancy Advisory Service* [1996] 2 All ER 161, [1996] 1 WLR 1397, noted p. 231 ante, where an argument that the defendant was employed to confer a benefit upon a class of which the claimant mother was a member was rejected. In *West Bromwich Albion Football Club Ltd v El-Safty* [2007] PIQR P7, [2006] EWCA Civ 1299, West Bromwich Albion Football Club brought a claim against

a surgeon for the negligent performance of an operation on a player, which resulted in the club being deprived of his services and therefore incurring financial loss. The Court of Appeal held that there was no relationship of sufficient proximity between the club and the surgeon to incur liability: an attempt to use *White v Jones* and *Gorham v BT* to argue for the existence of concurrent duties of care both to the patients of the surgeon and to the club was rejected, on the basis that there was little or no connection between the club and the surgeon beyond their employment of the injured player. The Court of Appeal also emphasised that the 'dominant relationship' at stake was that of a doctor and patient: there was a risk of an actual conflict of interest arising in this case if a duty was imposed, on the basis that the doctor's duty to his patient could conflict with any duty to safeguard the financial interest of the club in the player.

Similarly, in *Kapfunde v Abbey National Plc* [1999] ICR 1, [1998] EWCA Civ 535, the Court of Appeal refused to impose a duty of care upon a doctor retained by Abbey National to assess the medical fitness of job applicants, whose allegedly negligent advice had resulted in the rejection of the claimant's job application. The Court of Appeal held that insufficient proximity existed between the claimant and the doctor, and neither *Spring v Guardian Assurance* or *White v Jones* should be interpreted as establishing the existence of a duty of care in these circumstances.

See also *Islington v UCL Hospital NHS Trust* [2006] PIQR P3, [2005] EWCA Civ 596, where a local authority sued a hospital for the cost it had incurred making care provision for a former patient who had suffered a stroke as a result of negligent advice on the part of the hospital. The Court of Appeal held that it would not be 'fair, just and reasonable' to impose a duty of care in the circumstances, given the complex framework of statutory duties and public authority responsibilities involved. Buxton LJ at [29] emphasised that *White v Jones* involved a relationship that was very close to contract, and suggested that outside of such quasi-contractual circumstances, 'the potential for incremental development of *White v Jones* is very limited'.

8. Lord Goff appears to suggest that there might be a future case which would be suitable for the reconsideration of contract doctrines as fundamental as consideration and the third party beneficiary rule. The Law Commission's Consultation Paper, *Privity of Contract: Contracts for the Benefit of Third Parties*, Law Com. No. 242, Cm 3329 (1996) called for reform of the third party beneficiary rule (while indicating that it welcomed the *White* decision as providing a necessary remedy in a specific context), as did Steyn LJ (see *Darlington Borough Council v Wiltshier Northern Ltd* [1995] 3 All ER 895, [1995] 1 WLR 68). The result was limited legislative intervention in the form of the Contracts (Rights of Third Parties) Act 1999, the main provisions of which are:

1. (1) …a person who is not a party to a contract (a 'third party') may in his own right enforce a term of the contract if-
   (a) the contract expressly provides that he may, or
   (b) …the term purports to confer a benefit on him.
   (2) Subsection (1)(b) does not apply if on a proper construction of the contract it appears that the parties did not intend the term to be enforceable by the third party.

Would the Act have conferred any rights on the claimants in *White*? Did the contract between the father and the defendants 'purport to confer a benefit' on the claimants? Does it matter that the contract did not 'purport' to confer a benefit, but merely had the effect of conferring a benefit? In any case, does s. 1(2) apply?

Does the existence of the Act now preclude any further judicial intervention? See *Alfred McAlpine Construction Ltd v Panatown Ltd* [2001] 1 AC 518, [2000] 4 All ER 97, in which Lord Goff says that at the very least the existence of the Act does not preclude the development of new remedies for the promisee.

9.   *Alfred McAlpine Construction Ltd v Panatown Ltd* took up further the question of the position of the promisee in contracts where, because the promisee has no rights in the subject matter of the contract, it can be argued that the promisee suffers no loss from any breach of contract and should be entitled to only nominal damages. In *McAlpine*, a majority of the House of Lords held, or was prepared to assume, that Lord Griffiths was correct in *Linden Gardens* [1993] 3 All ER 417 to say that the promisee in such circumstances is entitled to substantial damages on the basis that the promisee has not received the performance promised in the contract. Two other members of the Court are prepared to countenance such a result only if the promisee has paid or is intending to pay for corrective measures. The result of this particular case, however, turned on the decision by one of the majority on the point of principle (Lord Browne-Wilkinson) to agree with the minority that even if the principle applies, it is subject to an exception that if the third party itself has substantive rights against the promisor, the promisee's rights fail.

What is the effect of *McAlpine* on *White*? One possibility is to say that since the third parties in *White* are entitled to substantial damages from the promisor, albeit in tort rather than in contract, the majority position in *McAlpine* means that the promisee, the father's estate in *White*, is still entitled to nothing more than nominal damages, with the result that *White* should remain intact. But another possibility is to argue that *McAlpine* means that the father's estate now has a right to substantial damages in contract, so that there is no longer a 'lacuna' in the law that needs to be filled by establishing a right in tort for the daughters. But note that the 'lacuna' is now taken to be the fact that the daughters have no remedy for their loss of expectation, not merely that the solicitors have no incentive to do their job (*Carr-Glynn v Frearsons*). This means that the attractiveness of the second argument will depend on the resolution of a point much debated in *McAlpine* but ultimately left undecided by it, namely whether the promisee has to hand over to the third party any substantive damages to which it is entitled. If there is such a duty, and it applies in the circumstances of *White*, the lacuna is filled and the need for the tort remedy has disappeared. But if not, the need to fill the lacuna remains.

10. The decision in *McAlpine* potentially opens up new avenues for obtaining contractual remedies in situations where the restrictive privity of contract doctrine of the common law has traditionally precluded recovery. This may induce a reorientation towards contractual remedies and away from reliance on *Hedley Byrne* principles, as well as further relaxation of the privity rules: see *Markesinis and Deakin*, pp. 175–77. It remains to be seen whether this has any significant impact on the evolution of tort law.

11. The decision in *White v Jones* resulted in considerable uncertainty shrouding the status of the 'assumption of responsibility' test. It was apparent that the sequence of decisions in *Spring*, *Henderson*, and *White* had established that this test was objective in nature. However, this left the nature of the test uncertain: if an 'assumption of responsibility' could be imputed to a defendant, as Lord Goff appeared to suggest in his judgment in *White*, then did the test have any real content? Or was it just a shorthand description for the circumstances where the application of the general *Caparo* test for the existence of a duty of care would result in such a duty being imposed in the context of pure economic loss?

12. Several different approaches to this test began to develop in the case law. One approach was to regard the 'assumption of responsibility' test as essentially another form of words

for the application of the standard *Caparo* analysis. Thus, in *Merrett v Babb* [2001] QB 1174, [2001] EWCA Civ 214, noted at p. 223, ante, the Court of Appeal treated the 'assumption of responsibility test' as another way of articulating the *Caparo* requirements, referring to the comment by Lord Slynn in *Phelps v Hillingdon London Borough Council* [2001] 2 AC 619, [2000] 4 All ER 504 that '[assumption of responsibility] means simply that the law recognizes that there is a duty of care. It is not so much that responsibility is assumed as that it is recognised or imposed by law.'

13. Another approach was to treat the 'assumption of responsibility' test as a special and distinct test, which if satisfied would result in the imposition of a duty of care in circumstances where such liability might not otherwise be imposed. In *Williams v Natural Life Health Foods* [1998] 2 All ER 577, [1998] UKHL 17, Lord Steyn, delivering the judgment of the House of Lords, adopted what Barker has described as a 'strong' version of the 'assumption of responsibility' approach, which he describes as requiring that the defendant had 'impliedly agreed to be legally responsible for the claimant's economic welfare, in circumstances falling only marginally short of contract': see K. Barker, (2006) 26 Oxf JLS 289 at 290.

In *Williams*, Lord Steyn took the view that once a case has been identified as involving an 'assumption of responsibility' in line with what he described as the 'extended *Hedley Byrne* principle', a duty of care would be imposed: there was no further need to apply the 'fair, just and reasonable' stage of the *Caparo* analysis. (See p. 237, ante.) However, Lord Steyn also stated that 'reliance upon [the assumption of responsibility] by the other party will be necessary to establish a cause of action (because otherwise the negligence will have no causative effect)....'. *Smith v Bush* and *White v Jones* were described as 'decided on special facts', and explained away on the basis that '[c]oherence must sometime yield to practical justice'. Applying this approach, their Lordships held that a company director had assumed no *personal* responsibility to the claimants in respect of their pure economic loss, although the company in question (which had subsequently been wound up) would have owed a duty of care.

Williams is sometimes explained as a decision turning on the particular facts of the case and the distinction that their Lordships were eager to emphasise between the position vis-à-vis the claimants of the company and the defendant director. However, Lord Steyn's analysis of the 'assumption of responsibility' approach is not confined to the specific relationship at issue, but instead is clearly couched in general terms. Therefore, in *Williams*, the House of Lords treated the 'assumption of responsibility' test as distinct from the *Caparo* duty of care test, and as only being satisfied where a defendant has clearly assumed personal responsibility to the claimant in a context where reasonable reliance can be said to exist.

In contrast, Lord Goff could be seen as applying a weaker and less demanding version of this test in *Spring* and *Henderson*, as Lord Browne-Wilkinson clearly did in *Henderson* and *White*. As discussed above, there are significant differences in approach between the two judges, illustrated by their judgments in *White*. Both nevertheless appear to regard the 'assumption of responsibility' test as a separate and distinct approach from the application of the standard *Caparo* test, with Lord Goff emphasising in *Henderson* and *Spring* that if the 'assumption of responsibility' test was satisfied, then there was no need for the court to take into account policy factors as is usual in the *Caparo* test (see *Henderson* [1995] 2 AC 145 at 181). That much is in common with the approach of Lord Steyn in *Williams*. However, Lord Browne-Wilkinson's interpretation of the scope of the 'assumption of responsibility' test appears in particular to be much more concerned with the existence of a relationship of power and dependence, and much less concerned with the existence of an assumption of personal responsibility, than is Lord Steyn's approach in *Williams*. Lord Goff's approach also appears to be less concerned with the existence of reliance.

14. Yet another approach emerged in the Court of Appeal decision in *Bank of Credit and Commerce International (Overseas) Ltd v Price Waterhouse* [1998] BCC 617, where Sir Brian Neill applied three separate approaches in determining whether a duty of care existed. The assumption of responsibility test, the standard *Caparo* test, and a third 'incremental' test were all separately applied, with the 'incremental' test examining whether the circumstances at issue in this case were analogous to other situations where a duty of care in respect of pure economic loss was applied. The Court of Appeal appeared to consider that all three approaches should yield the same result.

15. This 'composite' approach, also adopted by the Court of Appeal in *Customs and Excise Commissioners v Barclays Bank* [2005] 3 All ER 852 and by Lightman J. in *Dean v Allin & Watts* [2001] 2 Lloyd's Rep 249, [2001] EWCA Civ 758 at [33], has been subject to some harsh academic criticism. To begin with, the 'incremental' analysis appears to be part of the standard *Caparo* approach. In addition, the assumption that all the different tests should produce the same result seemed very questionable. This composite approach was described as a 'catalogue of possibilities, not a statement of principle' (C. Mitchell and P. Mitchell (2005) 121 LQR 194 at 199), while Barker has argued this approach lacks coherence (K. Barker (2006) 26 Oxf JLS 289). Note that the composite test can be defended on the basis that each of the three approaches can be seen as suitable lenses for determining whether sufficient proximity exists for the imposition of liability: if all three indicate the existence of sufficient proximity, then a duty of care can be said to arise. However, this approach involves an acceptance that each of the three separate tests is essentially descriptive and has little or no analytic content: Barker argues that if this is the case, then it is better to apply the *Caparo* test directly and cut out the use of superfluous concepts.

16. The decision of the House of Lords in *Customs and Excise Commissioners v Barclays Bank plc* [2006] 4 All ER 256, [2006] UKHL 28 has, however, seen a little more clarity introduced to this composite approach, while appearing to also confirm that the 'acceptance of responsibility' test has a distinct and particular substantive content of its own.

■ Customs and Excise Commissioners v Barclays Bank plc
House of Lords [2006] 4 All ER 256

The claimant Commissioners obtained freezing orders ('Mareva injunctions') in respect of outstanding value added tax against two companies, both of which held current accounts with the defendant bank. The orders specifically prohibited disposal of or dealing with assets up to a stated amount, including in particular any money in specified accounts at the bank. The bank was served with copies of the orders. Several hours later, the bank authorised payments to be made out of the companies' respective accounts. The claimants claimed damages against the bank in the amount of the sums paid out in breach of the injunctions, alleging that the bank had been negligent in permitting the payments to be made after being notified of the freezing orders. The bank denied that it owed any duty of care to the claimants to prevent the payments and that question was ordered to be tried as a preliminary issue. Colman J held that the bank did not owe a duty of care to the claimants but the Court of Appeal [2005] 3 All ER 852 reversed his decision. The bank appealed.

LORD BINGHAM OF CORNHILL:...

[1] My Lords, the important question raised by this appeal is whether a bank, notified by a third party of a freezing injunction granted to the third party against one of the bank's customers, affecting an account held by the customer with the bank, owes a duty to the third party to take reasonable care to comply with the terms of the injunction

...

[4] The parties were agreed that the authorities disclose three tests which have been used in deciding whether a defendant sued as causing pure economic loss to a claimant owed him a duty of care in tort. The first is whether the defendant assumed responsibility for what he said and did vis-à-vis the claimant, or is to be treated by the law as having done so. The second is commonly known as the threefold test: whether loss to the claimant was a reasonably foreseeable consequence of what the defendant did or failed to do; whether the relationship between the parties was one of sufficient proximity; and whether in all the circumstances it is fair, just and reasonable to impose a duty of care on the defendant towards the claimant (what Kirby J in *Perre v Apand Pty Ltd* (1999) 164 ALR 606 at 676, (1999) 198 CLR 180 at 275 (para 259), succinctly labelled 'policy'). Third is the incremental test, based on the observation of Brennan J in *Sutherland Shire Council v Heyman* (1985) 60 ALR 1 at 43–44, (1985) 157 CLR 424 at 481, approved by Lord Bridge of Harwich in *Caparo Industries plc v Dickman* [1990] 1 All ER 568 at 576, [1990] 2 AC 605 at 618, that:

> 'It is preferable in my view, that the law should develop novel categories of negligence incrementally and by analogy with established categories, rather than by a massive extension of a prima facie duty of care restrained only by indefinable "considerations which ought to negative, or to reduce or limit the scope of the duty or the class of person to whom it is owed".'

Mr Brindle QC for the bank contended that the assumption of responsibility test was most appropriately applied to this case, and that if applied it showed that the bank owed no duty of care to the commissioners on the present facts. But if it was appropriate to apply either of the other tests the same result was achieved. Mr Sales for the commissioners submitted that the threefold test was appropriate here, and that if applied it showed that a duty of care was owed. But if it was appropriate to apply either of the other tests they showed the same thing. In support of their competing submissions counsel made detailed reference to the leading authorities...These authorities yield many valuable insights, but they contain statements which cannot readily be reconciled. I intend no discourtesy to counsel in declining to embark on yet another exegesis of these well-known texts. I content myself at this stage with five general observations. First, there are cases in which one party can accurately be said to have assumed responsibility for what is said or done to another, the paradigm situation being a relationship having all the indicia of contract save consideration. *Hedley Byrne & Co Ltd v Heller & Partners Ltd* would, but for the express disclaimer, have been such a case. *White v Jones* and *Henderson v Merrett Syndicates Ltd*, although the relationship was more remote, can be seen as analogous. Thus, like Colman J (whose methodology was commended by Paul Mitchell and Charles Mitchell, 'Negligence Liability for Pure Economic Loss' (2005) 121 LQR 194, 199), I think it is correct to regard an assumption of responsibility as a sufficient but not a necessary condition of liability, a first test which, if answered positively, may obviate the need for further inquiry. If answered negatively, further consideration is called for.

[5] Secondly, however, it is clear that the assumption of responsibility test is to be applied objectively (see *Henderson v Merrett Syndicates Ltd* [1994] 3 All ER 506 at 521, [1995] 2 AC 145 at 181) and is not answered by consideration of what the defendant thought or intended...Lord Oliver of Aylmerton, in *Caparo Industries plc v Dickman* [1990] 1 All ER 568 at 589, [1990] 2 AC 605 at 637, thought 'voluntary assumption of responsibility'—

> 'a convenient phrase but it is clear that it was not intended to be a test for the existence of the duty for, on analysis, it means no more than that the act of the defendant in making the statement or tendering the advice was voluntary and that the law attributes to it an assumption of responsibility

if the statement or advice is inaccurate and is acted on. It tells us nothing about the circumstances from which such attribution arises.'...

The problem here is, as I see it, that the further this test is removed from the actions and intentions of the actual defendant, and the more notional the assumption of responsibility becomes, the less difference there is between this test and the threefold test.

[6] Thirdly, the threefold test itself provides no straightforward answer to the vexed question whether or not, in a novel situation, a party owes a duty of care...

[7] Fourthly, I incline to agree with the view expressed by the Messrs Mitchell in their article cited above ('Negligence Liability for Pure Economic Loss' (2005) 121 LQR 194, 199) that the incremental test is of little value as a test in itself, and is only helpful when used in combination with a test or principle which identifies the legally significant features of a situation. The closer the facts of the case in issue to those of a case in which a duty of care has been held to exist, the readier a court will be, on the approach of Brennan J adopted in *Caparo Industries plc v Dickman*, to find that there has been an assumption of responsibility or that the proximity and policy conditions of the threefold test are satisfied. The converse is also true.

[8] Fifthly, it seems to me that the outcomes (or majority outcomes) of the leading cases cited above are in every or almost every instance sensible and just, irrespective of the test applied to achieve that outcome. This is not to disparage the value of and need for a test of liability in tortious negligence, which any law of tort must propound if it is not to become a morass of single instances. But it does in my opinion concentrate attention on the detailed circumstances of the particular case and the particular relationship between the parties in the context of their legal and factual situation as a whole...

[LORD BINGHAM proceeded to analyse the nature of the freezing orders at issue and the consequences of a breach of these orders. He then continued:]

[12] There was discussion in argument whether the relationship of the commissioners and the bank as a notified party, was adverse or antagonistic, like that of opposing parties to litigation. The commissioners contended that it was not. The bank carried on banking business, and it is now a routine feature of such business that freezing injunctions are notified to it and are given effect. The substantial relief the commissioners were seeking was against the bank's customers, not it. The bank answered that this analysis did not fully reflect the reality of the situation...

[13] ...[T]he commissioners are right that they were not claiming substantive relief against the bank as a claimant seeks it against a defendant. But I think the bank is right to say that that is not the whole story, for three main reasons. First, the effect of notification of the order is to override the ordinary contractual duties which govern the relationship of banker and customer. This is not something of which a bank can complain or of which the bank does complain. A bank's relationship with its customers is subject to the law of the land, which provides for the grant of freezing injunctions. But the effect is none the less to oblige the bank to act in a way which but for the order would be a gross breach of contract. Such a situation must necessarily be very unwelcome to any bank which values its relationship with its customer. Secondly, the order exposes the bank to the risk that its employees may be imprisoned, the bank fined and its assets sequestrated. Of course, this is only a risk if the bank breaches the order in a sufficiently culpable way. But it is not a risk which exists independently of the order, and not a risk to which anyone would wish to be exposed. Thirdly, I think that the notice informing a bank of its right to set aside or discharge the order, addressed to both the customer and to the notified party, recognises its potentially prejudicial nature. If an order were neutral in its effect on the notified party, there would be no need to inform it of its right to vary or discharge it. While, therefore, the relationship of the commissioners and the bank was not, on notification of the order, that of hostile litigating parties, I think the bank is right to describe the relationship as adverse.

[14] I do not think that the notion of assumption of responsibility, even on an objective approach, can aptly be applied to the situation which arose between the commissioners and the bank on notification to it of the orders. Of course [the bank] was bound by law to comply. But it had no choice. It did not assume any responsibility towards the commissioners as the giver of references in *Hedley Byrne & Co*

Ltd v Heller & Partners Ltd (but for the disclaimer) and *Spring v Guardian Assurance plc*, the valuers in *Smith v Eric S Bush*, the solicitors in *White v Jones* and the agents in *Henderson v Merrett Syndicates Ltd* may plausibly be said to have done towards the recipient or subject of the references, the purchasers, the beneficiaries and the Lloyd's Names...Nor do I think that the commissioners can be said in any meaningful sense to have relied on the bank. The commissioners, having obtained their orders and notified them to the bank, were no doubt confident that the bank would act promptly and effectively to comply. But reliance in the law is usually taken to mean that if A had not relied on B he would have acted differently. Here the commissioners could not have acted differently, since they had availed them-selves of the only remedy which the law provided. Mr Sales [counsel for the Commissioners] suggested, although only as a fall-back argument, that the relationship between the commissioners and the bank was, in Lord Shaw's words adopted by Lord Devlin in *Hedley Byrne & Co Ltd v Heller & Partners Ltd* [1963] 2 All ER 575 at 610, [1964] AC 465 at 529, 'equivalent to contract'. But the essence of any con-tract is voluntariness, and the bank's position was wholly involuntary.

[15] It is common ground that the foreseeability element of the threefold test is satisfied here. The bank obviously appreciated that, since risk of dissipation has to be shown to obtain a freezing injunc-tion, the commissioners were liable to suffer loss if the injunction were not given effect. It was not con-tended otherwise. The concept of proximity in the context of pure economic loss is notoriously elusive. But it seems to me that the parties were proximate only in the sense that one served a court order on the other and that other appreciated the risk of loss to the first party if it was not obeyed. I think it is the third, policy, ingredient of the threefold test which must be determinative...

[16] In urging that a duty of care should be imposed on the bank the commissioners submitted that the orders were made by the court and notified to the bank to protect their interests; that recognition of a duty would in practical terms impose no new or burdensome obligation on the bank; that the rule of public policy which has first claim on the loyalty of the law is that wrongs should be remedied (see *X (minors) v Bedfordshire CC, M (a minor) v Newham London BC, E (a minor) v Dorset CC* [1995] 3 All ER 353 at 380, [1995] 2 AC 633 at 663, 749); that, since there are no facts here which would found a claim for effective redress in contempt, the commissioners will otherwise be left without any remedy; that a duty of care to the commissioners would not be inconsistent with the bank's duty to the court; and that there would, in such a case, be no indeterminacy as to those to whom the duty would be owed. These are formidable arguments and I am not surprised that the Court of Appeal accepted them. But I have difficulty in doing so, for six main and closely associated reasons.

[17] ...[T]he Mareva jurisdiction has developed as one exercised by court order enforceable only by the court's power to punish those who break its orders. The documentation issued by the court does not hint at the existence of any other remedy. This regime makes perfect sense on the assumption that the only duty owed by a notified party is to the court.

[18] Secondly, it cannot be suggested that the customer owes a duty to the party which obtains an order, since they are opposing parties in litigation and no duty is owed by a litigating party to its opponent...

[19] It is clear, thirdly, that a duty of care in tort may co-exist with a similar duty in contract or a statutory duty, and I would accept in principle that a tortious duty of care to the commissioners could co-exist with a duty of compliance owed to the court. But I know of no instance in which a non-consensual court order, without more, has been held to give rise to a duty of care owed to the party obtaining the order, or a *Norwich Pharmacal* order (see *Norwich Pharmacal Co v Comrs of Customs and Excise* [1973] 2 All ER 943, [1974] AC 133), or a witness summons, in any case where economic loss is a foreseeable consequence of breach. It would seem that the commissioners' argument involves a radical innovation.

[20] Fourthly, it is a notable feature of this appeal that the commissioners adduce no comparative jurisprudence to support their argument...

[21] Fifthly, the cases relied on by the commissioners as providing the closest analogy with the present case do not in my opinion, on examination, reveal any real similarity

...

[23] Lastly, it seems to me in the final analysis unjust and unreasonable that the bank should, on being notified of an order which it had no opportunity to resist, become exposed to a liability which was in this case for a few million pounds only, but might in another case be for very much more. For this exposure it had not been in any way rewarded, its only protection being the commissioners' undertaking to make good (if ordered to do so) any loss which the order might cause it, protection scarcely consistent with a duty of care owed to the commissioners but in any event valueless in a situation such as this.

[24] I would allow the appeal and dismiss the commissioners' claim with costs in the House and below.

LORD HOFFMANN: . . .

[35] There is a tendency, which has been remarked upon by many judges, for phrases like 'proximate', 'fair, just and reasonable' and 'assumption of responsibility' to be used as slogans rather than practical guides to whether a duty should exist or not. These phrases are often illuminating but discrimination is needed to identify the factual situations in which they provide useful guidance. For example, in a case in which A provides information to C which he knows will be relied upon by D, it is useful to ask whether A assumed responsibility to D (see *Hedley Byrne & Co Ltd v Heller & Partners Ltd* [1963] 2 All ER 575, [1964] AC 465; *Smith v Eric S Bush (a firm), Harris v Wyre Forest DC* [1989] 2 All ER 514, [1990] 1 AC 831). Likewise, in a case in which A provides information on behalf of B to C for the purpose of being relied upon by C, it is useful to ask whether A assumed responsibility to C for the information or was only discharging his duty to B (see *Williams v Natural Life Health Foods Ltd* [1998] 2 All ER 577, [1998] 1 WLR 830). Or in a case in which A provided information to B for the purpose of enabling him to make one kind of decision, it may be useful to ask whether he assumed responsibility for its use for a different kind of decision (see *Caparo Industries plc v Dickman* [1990] 1 All ER 568, [1990] 2 AC 605). In these cases in which the loss has been caused by the claimant's reliance on information provided by the defendant, it is critical to decide whether the defendant (rather than someone else) assumed responsibility for the accuracy of the information to the claimant (rather than to someone else) or for its use by the claimant for one purpose (rather than another). The answer does not depend upon what the defendant intended but, as in the case of contractual liability, upon what would reasonably be inferred from his conduct against the background of all the circumstances of the case. The purpose of the inquiry is to establish whether there was, in relation to the loss in question, the necessary relationship (or 'proximity') between the parties and, as Lord Goff of Chieveley pointed out in *Henderson v Merrett Syndicates Ltd* [1994] 3 All ER 506 at 521, [1995] 2 AC 145 at 181, the existence of that relationship and the foreseeability of economic loss will make it unnecessary to undertake any further inquiry into whether it would be fair, just and reasonable to impose liability. In truth, the case is one in which, but for the alleged absence of the necessary relationship, there would be no dispute that a duty to take care existed and the relationship is what makes it fair, just and reasonable to impose the duty.

[36] It is equally true to say that a sufficient relationship will be held to exist when it is fair, just and reasonable to do so. Because the question of whether a defendant has assumed responsibility is a legal inference to be drawn from his conduct against the background of all the circumstances of the case, it is by no means a simple question of fact. Questions of fairness and policy will enter into the decision and it may be more useful to try to identify these questions than simply to bandy terms like 'assumption of responsibility' and 'fair, just and reasonable'. In *Morgan Crucible Co plc v Hill Samuel Bank Ltd* [1990] 3 All ER 330 at 333–335, sub nom *Morgan Crucible Co plc v Hill Samuel & Co Ltd* [1991] Ch 295 at 300–303 I tried to identify some of these considerations in order to encourage the evolution of lower-level principles which could be more useful than the high abstractions commonly used in such debates.

[37] In *Henderson v Merrett Syndicates Ltd* itself, the House used the concept of assumption of responsibility in a situation which did not involve reliance upon information but where, once again, the issue was whether the necessary relationship between claimant and defendant existed. The issues in

that case were whether the managing agents of a Lloyd's syndicate owed a duty of care in respect of their underwriting to Names with whom they had no contractual relationship and whether they owed a separate duty in tort to Names with whom they did have a contractual relationship. In fact, the arguments in *Henderson v Merrett Syndicates Ltd* were a re-run of *Donoghue v Stevenson* in a claim for economic loss. In that case, as it seems to me, the use of the concept of assumption of responsibility, while perfectly legitimate, was less illuminating. The question was not whether the defendant had assumed responsibility for the accuracy of a particular statement but a much more general responsibility for the consequences of their conduct of the underwriting. To say that the managing agents assumed a responsibility to the Names to take care not to accept unreasonable risks is little different from saying that a manufacturer of ginger beer assumes a responsibility to consumers to take care to keep snails out of his bottles.

[38] Even in this context, however, the notion of assumption of responsibility serves a different, weaker, but nevertheless useful purpose in drawing attention to the fact that a duty of care is ordinarily generated by something which the defendant has decided to *do*: giving a reference, supplying a report, managing a syndicate, making ginger beer. It does not much matter why he decided to do it; it may be that he thought it would be profitable or it may be that he was providing a service pursuant to some statutory duty, as in *Phelps v London Borough of Hillingdon, Anderton v Clwyd CC, Jarvis v Hampshire CC, Re G (a minor)* [2000] 4 All ER 504, [2001] 2 AC 619 and *Ministry of Housing and Local Government v Sharp* [1970] 1 All ER 1009, [1970] 2 QB 223. In the present case, however, the duty is not alleged to arise from anything which the bank was doing. It is true that the bank was carrying on the business of banking, handling money on behalf of its customers. But that is not alleged to have been either necessary or sufficient to generate the duty in this case. Not necessary, because if such a duty is created by notice of the freezing order, it must apply to anyone who has possession or control of the defendant's assets: the garage holding his car, the stockbroker nominee company holding his shares, his grandmother holding a drawer-full of his bank notes. On being given notice of the order, they would all be under an obligation to take reasonable care to ensure that the defendant did not get his hands on the assets. Not sufficient, because there is no suggestion that, apart from the freezing order, the bank in carrying on its ordinary business would be under any duty to protect the position of the commissioners.

[39] There is, in my opinion, a compelling analogy with the general principle that, for the reasons which I discussed in *Stovin v Wise* [1996] 3 All ER 801 at 818–820, [1996] AC 923 at 943–944, the law of negligence does not impose liability for mere omissions. It is true that the complaint is that the bank did something: it paid away the money. But the payment is alleged to be the breach of the duty and not the conduct which generated the duty. The duty was generated ab extra, by service of the order. The question of whether the order can have generated a duty of care is comparable with the question of whether a statutory duty can generate a common law duty of care. The answer is that it cannot (see *Gorringe v Calderdale Metropolitan BC* [2004] UKHL 15, [2004] 2 All ER 326, [2004] 1 WLR 1057). The statute either creates a statutory duty or it does not. (That is not to say, as I have already mentioned, that conduct undertaken pursuant to a statutory duty cannot generate a duty of care in the same way as the same conduct undertaken voluntarily.) But you cannot derive a common law duty of care directly from a statutory duty. Likewise, as it seems to me, you cannot derive one from an order of court. The order carries its own remedies and its reach does not extend any further.

[40] Colman J relied upon the fact that the advisers of one party to litigation owe no duty to the other party and for this purpose treated a party's bank as being in much the same position as his lawyers (see [2004] EWHC 122 (Comm), [2004] 2 All ER 789, [2004] 1 WLR 2027). For my part I prefer to place no particular weight upon this factor. The freezing order suspended the bank's duty to its client and compliance would therefore have created no conflict of interest. The Court of Appeal relied upon the fact that the order provided for payment to the bank of its reasonable costs incurred as a result of this order. I do not regard this as a material factor either. It is one thing to have to do some paper work and another to be put on risk for millions of pounds.

[41] I would therefore allow the appeal and restore the judgment of Colman J.

LORD RODGER OF EARLSFERRY:...

[51] Part of the function of appeal courts is to try to assist judges and practitioners by boiling down a mass of case law and distilling some shorter statement of the applicable law. The temptation to try to identify some compact underlying rule which can then be applied to solve all future cases is obvious. Mr Brindle submitted that in this area the House had identified such a rule in the need to find that the defendant had voluntarily assumed responsibility. But the unhappy experience with the rule so elegantly formulated by Lord Wilberforce in *Anns v London Borough of Merton* [1977] 2 All ER 492 at 498–499, [1978] AC 728 at 751–752, suggests that appellate judges should follow the philosopher's advice to 'Seek simplicity, and distrust it'.

[52] Therefore it is not surprising that there are cases in the books—notably *Ministry of Housing and Local Government v Sharp* [1970] 1 All ER 1009, [1970] 2 QB 223, approved by Lord Slynn of Hadley in *Spring v Guardian Assurance plc* [1994] 3 All ER 129 at 158–159, [1995] 2 AC 296 at 332—which do not readily yield to analysis in terms of a voluntary assumption of responsibility, but where liability has none the less been held to exist. I see no reason to treat these cases as exceptions to some over-arching rule that there must be a voluntary assumption of responsibility before the law recognises a duty of care. Such a rule would inevitably lead to the concept of voluntary assumption of responsibility being stretched beyond its natural limits—which would in the long run undermine the very real value of the concept as a criterion of liability in the many cases where it is an appropriate guide...any event, as the words which I have quoted from his speech in *Henderson v Merrett Syndicates Ltd* make clear, Lord Goff himself recognised that, although it may be decisive in many situations, the presence or absence of a voluntary assumption of responsibility does not necessarily provide the answer in all cases...

[60] The courts make quite extensive use of freezing orders. So, in practice, banks like Barclays can be expected to have in place a system for freezing accounts when they are notified of an order—and to take care when they have to operate the system. But, of itself, this does not mean that if they fail to take care they are liable to the applicant who obtained the order. For instance, as I pointed out in *Brooks v Metropolitan Police Comr* [2005] UKHL 24 at [38], [2005] 2 All ER 489 at [38], [2005] 1 WLR 1495, a prosecutor is under a professional and ethical duty to take care in preparing and presenting the case against a defendant whom he is prosecuting. If he fails to take the necessary care, any conviction may be unsafe and he himself may be subject to some disciplinary sanction. Nevertheless, the prosecutor does not assume a responsibility to the defendant to act carefully and owes him no duty of care in the law of tort (see *Elguzouli-Daf v Metropolitan Police Comr, McBrearty v Ministry of Defence* [1995] 1 All ER 833 at 842, [1995] QB 335 at 349 per Steyn LJ).

[61] In most cases the third party will be a bank or similar institution. But sometimes a private individual who happens, for example, to be looking after the addressee's car will be startled to receive notification of a freezing order. This puts him in essentially the same position as a bank which is notified of an order. Usually, he will do his best to respect the order and to hold on to the car. Should the law add to his burdens, however, by exposing him to an uninsured liability in damages if he fails to take the care which is ultimately considered to be reasonable and the addressee makes off with the car?

[62] Punishment for contempt of court is the remedy which the law provides for the addressee's failure to comply with an injunction such as a freezing order. Liability is strict and so he may be guilty of contempt even where he did not deliberately flout the order, the degree of his fault being relevant in determining the appropriate punishment (see *A-G v Times Newspapers Ltd* [1991] 2 All ER 398 at 415, [1992] 1 AC 191 at 217 per Lord Oliver of Aylmerton).

[63] By contrast, a third party who is notified of an injunction is guilty of contempt of court only if he knowingly takes a step which will frustrate the court's purpose in granting the order. So a bank will be in contempt only if it knowingly fails to freeze a customer's account and pays away sums in the account after being notified of an order. [Counsel for the Revenue Commissioners] argued that this was not a sufficient sanction: the law of tort could usefully supplement the law of contempt by imposing on the bank a duty of care in favour of the party who obtained the freezing order. I would reject that argument.

[64] The policy of the law is that a third party, such as a bank, which is notified of a freezing order, must not knowingly undermine the court's purpose in granting the order. If this is all that the court which makes the order can demand, it would be inconsistent to hold that, by reason of the selfsame notification, the applicant could simultaneously demand a higher standard of performance from the bank—and then claim damages for the bank's failure to achieve it. Notification imposes a duty on the bank to respect the order of the court; it does not of itself generate a duty of care to the applicant. And here the commissioners can point to nothing more than the order and Barclays' negligent failure to respond to it.

...

[66] ...Having regard to all these circumstances, in my view, not only is there not the necessary proximity between the applicant and a third party, such as a bank, who is notified of a freezing order, but it would not be fair, just and reasonable to hold that the third party owes a duty of care to the applicant.

LORD WALKER OF GESTINGTHORPE:...

[73] I would add a footnote in relation to the notion of 'voluntary assumption of responsibility'. So far as the modern law is concerned, this expression seems to be traceable mainly to the speeches of Lord Reid and Lord Devlin in *Hedley Byrne & Co Ltd v Heller & Partners Ltd* [1963] 2 All ER 575 at 583, [1964] AC 465 at 486 ('held to have accepted some responsibility') and [1963] 2 All ER 575 at 611, [1964] AC 465 at 529 ('a voluntary undertaking to assume responsibility'). Earlier in his speech Lord Devlin had referred ([1963] 2 All ER 575 at 608, [1964] AC 465 at 526) to early authority going back as far as *Coggs v Bernard* (1703) 2 Ld Raym 909, 91 ER 25...The old cases show liability being imposed *despite* the defendant's conduct having been (in one or both senses) voluntary. As the law has developed (and in the field of pure economic loss) liability is imposed *because of* the voluntary assumption of responsibility. But in the modern context the word 'voluntary' is being used, it seems to me, with the connotation of 'conscious', 'considered' or 'deliberate'. That appears, for instance, in *White v Jones* [1995] 1 All ER 691, [1995] 2 AC 207, both in the speech of Lord Browne-Wilkinson ([1995] 1 All ER 691 at 716, [1995] 2 AC 207 at 274) and in the dissenting speech of Lord Mustill ([1995] 1 All ER 691 at 729, [1995] 2 AC 207 at 286–287). That is particularly important in considering whether the defendant has undertaken responsibility for economic loss towards anyone other than the person or persons with whom he is in an obviously proximate relationship. In such cases the voluntary assumption of responsibility towards others, judged objectively, may provide the necessary proximity.

[75] ...If this issue affected only banks, I would be slow to conclude that there could never be liability for carelessly failing to comply with a freezing order. Banks are already subject to strict regulation and potential sanctions in connection with money-laundering and similar activities. They are enjoined to know their customers. They become liable for breach of fiduciary duty if they shut their eyes to dishonest dealings by their customers...

[76] I am also rather disinclined to put much weight on the litigation context. A bank whose customer is a party to litigation may occasionally be joined as a party to the litigation, either for the purposes of a freezing order or in the pursuit of a proprietary remedy. But that is unusual, and it did not happen in this case. The bank's duty to its customer was overridden and suspended by the freezing order. Its position was a neutral position.

[77] However, Mr Sales, appearing for the commissioners, realistically acknowledged that if in these circumstances a duty of care is to be imposed on a bank, it must also be imposed on any other person affected by notice of a freezing order. In many cases that would produce unfair, unjust and unreasonable results. I too would allow this appeal and make the order which Lord Bingham proposes.

LORD MANCE:...

[82] The conceptual basis on which courts decide whether a duty of care exists in particular circumstances has been repeatedly examined. Three broad approaches have been suggested, involving consideration (a) whether there has been an assumption of responsibility, (b) whether a threefold test of

foreseeability, proximity and 'fairness, justice and reasonableness' has been satisfied or (c) whether the alleged duty would be 'incremental' to previous cases. Mr Michael Brindle QC for the bank argues that in cases of economic loss the only relevant question is whether there has been an 'assumption of responsibility'. Mr Philip Sales for the commissioners submits that the primary approach should be through the threefold test of foreseeability, proximity and 'fairness, justice and reasonableness' and that assumption of responsibility and incrementalism are no more than potentially relevant factors under that test.

[83] All three approaches may often (though not inevitably) lead to the same result. Assumption of responsibility is on any view a core area of liability for economic loss. But all three tests operate at a high level of abstraction. What matters is how and by reference to what lower-level factors are interpreted in practice, see eg *Caparo Industries plc v Dickman* [1990] 1 All ER 568 at 573–574, [1990] 2 AC 605 at 617–618 per Lord Bridge of Harwich and [1990] 1 All ER 568 at 585, [1990] 2 AC 605 at 633 per Lord Oliver of Aylmerton.

[84] As to incrementalism, I note that the House's support for this approach in *Caparo Industries plc v Dickman* was given with reference to a passage in Brennan J's judgment in *Sutherland Shire Council v Heyman* (1985) 60 ALR 1 at 43–44, (1985) 157 CLR 424 at 481, where he was rejecting the House's approach in *Anns v London Borough of Merton* [1977] 2 All ER 492, [1978] AC 728, from which the House itself resiled a year after *Caparo Industries plc v Dickman* in *Murphy v Brentwood DC* [1990] 2 All ER 908, [1991] 1 AC 398. Brennan J said of *Anns v London Borough of Merton*:

> 'I am unable to accept that approach. It is preferable, in my view, that the law should develop novel categories of negligence incrementally and by analogy with established categories, rather than by a massive extension of a prima facie duty of care restrained only by indefinable "considerations which ought to negative, or to reduce or limit the scope of the duty or the class of person to whom it is owed".'

Incrementalism was therefore viewed as a corollary of the rejection, now uncontroversial, of any generalised liability for negligently caused economic loss, rather than as necessarily inconsistent with the development of novel categories of negligence. Having said that, caution and analogical reasoning are generally valuable accompaniments to judicial activity, and this is particularly true in the present area...

[86] In *Hedley Byrne & Co Ltd v Heller & Partners Ltd* the concept was one of assumption of responsibility by the defendant towards the claimant. Lord Devlin's contractual analogy also indicates, and Mr Brindle accepts, that whether there has been an assumption of responsibility is to be assessed objectively: see *Henderson v Merrett Syndicates Ltd* [1994] 3 All ER 506 at 521, [1995] 2 AC 145 at 181 per Lord Goff, with whose speech all other members of the House agreed. Similarly, an assumption of responsibility may arise from the provision not merely of information or advice, but also of services: see [1994] 3 All ER 506 at 520, [1995] 2 AC 145 at 180 per Lord Goff.

[87] However, it has been said on a number of occasions that it is artificial or unhelpful to insist on fitting all claims for breach of a duty of care to avoid economic loss within the conception of assumption of responsibility, and there are several cases involving economic loss where the threefold test and incrementalism have been preferred...

[93] This review of authority confirms that there is no single common denominator, even in cases of economic loss, by which liability may be determined. The threefold test of foreseeability, proximity and fairness, justice and reasonableness provides a convenient general framework although it operates at so high a level of abstraction. Assumption of responsibility is particularly useful as a concept in the two core categories of case identified by Lord Browne-Wilkinson in *White v Jones* [1995] 1 All ER 691 at 716–717, [1995] 2 AC 207 at 274, when it may effectively subsume all aspects of the threefold approach. But if all that is meant by voluntary assumption of responsibility is the voluntary assumption of responsibility for a task, rather than of liability towards the defendant, then questions of foreseeability, proximity and fairness, reasonableness and justice may be very relevant. In *White v Jones* itself

there was no doubt that the solicitor had voluntarily undertaken responsibility for a task, but it was the very fact that he had done so for the testator, not the disappointed beneficiary, that gave rise to the stark division of opinion in the House. Incrementalism operates as an important cross-check on any other approach.

[94] The present cannot be regarded as a case of assumption of responsibility. The involuntary nature of the bank's involvement with the commissioners makes it impossible to regard the situation as one 'akin to contract'; it is also difficult in any meaningful sense to speak of the bank as having voluntarily assumed responsibility even for the task in relation to which it was allegedly negligent, let alone responsibility towards the commissioners for the task. In a very general sense any bank, indeed anyone carrying on any activity during the course of which they might have cause to hold the monies or possessions of another, might be said to accept the risk that a third party might obtain a freezing order in respect of such monies or possessions. But that is to assign to the concept of voluntary assumption of responsibility so wide a meaning as to deprive it of effective utility.

[95] Mr Brindle thus submits that no duty of care on the bank can be recognised because the bank did not voluntarily undertake responsibility even for the task which it is now alleged negligently to have executed. But Mr Sales can point to cases where a duty of care has been recognised even though the defendant cannot realistically be said to have voluntarily undertaken the relevant task. Instances may be found in *Ministry of Housing and Local Government v Sharp* [1970] 1 All ER 1009, [1970] 2 QB 223, *Spring v Guardian Assurance plc* [1994] 3 All ER 129, [1995] 2 AC 296 and *Phelps v London Borough of Hillingdon* [2000] 4 All ER 504, [2001] 2 AC 619...

[LORD MANCE went on to conclude that the *Caparo* test for imposing a duty of care was not satisfied in the circumstaces.]

Appeal allowed.

QUESTIONS

Do their Lordships share a common view of the contours of the assumption of responsibility test? To what extent do each of their Lordships classify the following decisions as involving an assumption of responsibility: *Spring v Guardian Assurance plc* [1995] 2 AC 296, [1994] 3 All ER 129 (p. 58, ante, and noted at p. 242, ante); *Ministry of Housing and Local Government v Sharp* [1970] 2 QB 223, [1970] 1 All ER 1009, noted at p. 182, ante; *Henderson v Merrett Syndicates Ltd* [1995] 2 AC 145, [1994] 3 All ER 506 (p. 232, ante)?

NOTES

1.   All their Lordships adopt a broadly similar approach. All five appeared to suggest the key underlying issue in economic loss claims was whether the *Caparo* test for the existence of duty of care was satisfied in any given case. All the speeches place considerable emphasis on the absence of hard and fast rules in this context and the need for context-sensitive analysis. See the similar approach adopted in *Gray v Fire Alarm Fabrication Services Ltd* [2007] ICR 247, [2006] EWCA Civ 1496. However, is this ultimately very helpful to lower courts? Is there a danger in encouraging excessive reliance on the broad-brush *Caparo* approach in an area such as economic loss? See the Scottish case of *Realstone Ltd v J & E Shepherd* [2008] ScotCS CSOH 31 (21 February 2008), where Lord Hodge suggests a need for courts to exercise caution in applying the *Caparo* test in the economic loss context. Their Lordships in *Barclays* express a distrust of 'high abstractions,' in the words of Lord Hoffmann, but perhaps leave the

current state of the law very dependent upon the abstractions of the *Caparo* test. Lord Mance suggests at [93] that '[i]ncrementalism operates as an important cross-check' to the application of the *Caparo* analysis: however, given the diversity of much of the case law, it is not clear even post-*Barclays* that existing cases always prove particularly useful in guiding the evolution of the jurisprudence.

2. The five speeches in *Barclays* appear to take the view that if a voluntary assumption of responsibility exists, then this will satisfy the *Caparo* requirements, in particular by providing the 'necessary proximity' as Lord Walker phrases it, at [73]. Similarly, Lord Mance suggests at [93] that the assumption of responsibility test may 'effectively subsume all aspects of the threefold approach'. If such an assumption of responsibility does exist, then the judgments in *Barclays* indicate that this is sufficient in itself to establish the existence of a duty of care. The judgments in *Barclays* appear to depart from the approach taken by the Court of Appeal in *Merrett v Babb* [2001] QB 1174, [2001] EWCA Civ 214, whereby the assumption of responsibility test is essentially merged within the wider *Caparo* analysis: instead 'assumption of responsibility' is retained as a distinct test, which if satisfied will give rise to liability.

3. Their Lordships in general define 'assumption of responsibility' in the 'strong' sense of an active 'taking on' of responsibility in a 'conscious, considered, or deliberate' manner (per Lord Walker at [73]). Lord Bingham indicates at [4] that 'the paradigm situation being a relationship having all the indicia of contract save consideration', returns to the language of Lord Devlin in *Hedley Byrne*. Therefore, for the most part, 'assumption of responsibility' is being interpreted in a strong sense, as requiring a voluntary and active act and reasonable reliance upon that deliberate taking on of responsibility. For an application of this approach, see *Rowley v Secretary of State for the Department of Work and Pensions* [2007] 1 WLR 2861, [2007] EWCA Civ 598, where the Court of Appeal took the view that the exercise of professional skill and judgement on the part of the caseworkers of the Child Support Agency with the intention of benefiting the claimant was not sufficient to give rise to a voluntary assumption of responsibility.

4. However, there are some underlying divergences in approach between their Lordships in defining the circumstances when this test is satisfied and when the language of assumption of responsibility should be used. Lord Rodger suggests that confining the use of the term 'assumption of responsibility' to where an active taking on of responsibility exists would be useful. In contrast, Lord Hoffmann is happier to use 'assumption of responsibility' in a broader categorical sense, capable in his view of having both a 'strong' and a 'weak' interpretation, with the term being used in the latter sense to indicate that the *Caparo* requirements for liability are satisfied. In addition, Lord Bingham appears to treat cases such as *Spring, Henderson,* and *White v Jones* as involving a deliberate taking on of responsibility, while Lord Rodger and Lord Hoffmann appear to treat *Spring* as falling outside this category, with Lord Hoffmann also appearing to consider *Henderson* as outside this 'strong' category of assumption of responsibility.

5. Further difficulties exist. All five speeches appear to take the well-established view that the assumption of responsibility test is objective in nature. However, at times, the emphasis on the defendant 'deliberately' taking on responsibility appears to open up the possibility of the subjective intention of the defendant becoming relevant. Note that in the subsequent case of *Man Nutzfahrzeuge AG v Freightliner Ltd* [2007] EWCA Civ 910, Chadwick LJ at [56] cited Lord Hoffmann's approach in *Barclays*, but placed considerable emphasis on what the defendant would have reasonably thought was being undertaken: '[t]o hold that the auditors assumed responsibility for the use which

a dishonest employee of the audited company might make of the accounts in the context of the parent company's negotiations for the sale of the company would, I think, be to impose on them a liability greater than they could reasonably have thought they were undertaking'.

6.   Therefore, *Barclays* does not completely clarify when 'assumption of responsibility' will exist, even if it does establish that where such an assumption exists, then that will be sufficient to ground liability. Nevertheless, it does clearly establish that if such an assumption of responsibility does not exist, liability may also nevertheless be imposed under the standard *Caparo* approach: in other words, a voluntary assumption of responsibility is a 'sufficient but not a necessary condition of liability' (Lord Bingham at [4]). The two tests are therefore distinguished: a defendant may not be liable under the assumption of responsibility analysis, but could be under the *Caparo* test. This appears to involve a departure from the approach taken by the Court of Appeal in *Bank of Credit and Commerce International (Overseas) Ltd v Price Waterhouse* [1998] BCC 617 and in *Barclays* itself, whereby a defendant would be liable if both the assumption of responsibility and *Caparo* tests are satisfied: the use in both of these judgments of a third test, the 'incremental' analysis, is correctly classified by their Lordships as an aspect of the *Caparo* test.

7.   The defendants in *Barclays* were held not to have satisfied the *Caparo* test, and therefore were under no duty of care to prevent the economic loss occurring to the Revenue Commissioners. How convincing do you find the reasoning supporting this conclusion in the various judgments? Lord Bingham placed particular emphasis on why the nature of the relationship between a bank and its customers made the imposition of a duty of care inappropriate. However, Lord Walker took the view that he would have been happy for a duty of care to be imposed upon banks, save for the absence of any factor that could distinguish banks from others in similar situations. Could it be argued that a bank should be treated as being in a special position, both *vis-à-vis* its customers and the Revenue Commissioners? If so, might the special position of a bank justify the imposition of a duty of care in the public interest? Note that Peter Gibson LJ in the Court of Appeal at [63] had considered the arguments that their Lordships subsequently favoured not to be 'cogent'.

8.   Lord Hoffmann placed considerable emphasis on the fact that this case involved an omission by the bank, rather than an active commitment to a course of action. However, is this a meaningful distinction in this context? Is there any real distinction to be made between freezing an account and permitting withdrawal? As is often the case with omission/commission distinctions, much depends upon how you describe the activity of the defendant.

9.   *Barclays* was applied in the fascinating case of *Calvert v William Hill Credit Ltd* [2008] EWHC 454 (Ch). In this case, a serial gambler brought a claim in negligence for the economic loss he sustained following the failure of a bookmaker to take steps to prevent him from accessing their gambling facilities, despite an undertaking by that bookmaker that the gambler would be prohibited from using their facilities for a specified period. In his judgment, Briggs J rightly described this case as 'a journey to the outermost reaches of the tort of negligence, to the realm of the truly exceptional'. This case involved difficult and complex issues relating to the interaction of public policy and individual responsibility. From the perspective of economic loss, Briggs J took a nuanced approach. He considered that the bookmakers, despite drawing up a 'social responsibility policy' and accompanying set of procedures which made provision for

assistance to be given to problem gamblers, would not usually be deemed to incur liability for making gambling facilities available to known gambling addicts under either the assumption of responsibility test or the wider *Caparo* analysis. However, Briggs J proceeded to find that a specific assumption of responsibility had taken place in this case. The bookmakers had entered into a 'self-exclusion agreement' with the individual claimant, which they had not taken the necessary steps to implement. They had thereby consciously and deliberately entered into a voluntary assumption of responsibility within the 'strong' sense used by the House of Lords in *Barclays*, and the claimant had placed reasonable reliance upon this assumption being implemented. Nevertheless, as the claimant was a 'pathological gambler', it could not be demonstrated that the breach of the self-exclusion agreement had caused the claimant's eventual losses.

10. In Australia, in *Perre v Apand Pty Ltd* (1999) 164 ALR 606, the High Court of Australia placed emphasis on the existence of a relationship of vulnerability and dependence in deciding whether to impose a duty of care in respect of economic loss: see C. Witting, (2002) 118 LQR 214. Might greater guidance by the superior courts on the policy considerations to be taken into account in determining when the *Caparo* test is satisfied in the economic loss context be useful? See J. Stapleton (1991) 107 LQR 249. For an example of public policy reasoning playing a direct role in determining whether a duty of care should be imposed in respect of economic loss, see *Harris v Evans* [1998] EWCA Civ 709, [1998] 3 All ER 523. In this case the Court of Appeal refused to impose liability on a health and safety inspector in respect of statements in respect of the claimant's bungee jumping operation, on the basis that imposing such a duty would be detrimental to the aims of the healthy and safety legislation by potentially engendering an excessively cautious approach on the part of safety inspectors.

5 THE MEASURE OF DAMAGES UNDER *HEDLEY BYRNE*: THE 'SCOPE' OF THE DUTY

■ South Australia Asset Management Corpn v York Montague Ltd
House of Lords [1996] 3 All ER 365

LORD HOFFMANN: . . .

My Lords, the three appeals before the House raise a common question of principle. What is the extent of the liability of a valuer who has provided a lender with a negligent overvaluation of the property offered as security for the loan? The facts have two common features. The first is that if the lender had known the true value of the property, he would not have lent. The second is that a fall in the property market after the date of the valuation greatly increased the loss which the lender eventually suffered.

The Court of Appeal (*Banque Bruxelles Lambert SA v Eagle Star Insurance Co. Ltd.*, [1995] 2 All ER 769), [1995] QB 375 decided that in a case in which the lender would not otherwise have lent (which they called a 'no-transaction' case), he is entitled to recover the difference between the sum which he lent, together with a reasonable rate of interest, and the net sum which he actually got back. The valuer bears the whole risk of a transaction which, but for his negligence, would not have happened. He is therefore liable for all the loss attributable to a fall in the market. They distinguished what they called a 'successful transaction' case, in which the evidence shows that if the lender had been correctly advised, he would still have lent a lesser sum on the same security. In such a case, the lender can recover only the difference between what he has actually lost and what he would have lost if he had lent the lesser amount. Since the fall in the property market is a common element in both the actual and the hypothetical calculations, it does not increase the valuer's liability.

The valuers appeal. They say that a valuer provides an estimate of the value of the property at the date of the valuation. He does not undertake the role of a prophet. It is unfair that merely because for one reason or other the lender would not otherwise have lent, the valuer should be saddled with the whole risk of the transaction, including a subsequent fall in the value of the property.

Much of the discussion, both in the judgment of the Court of Appeal and in argument at the Bar, has assumed that the case is about the correct measure of damages for the loss which the lender has suffered. . . .

I think that this was the wrong place to begin. Before one can consider the principle on which one should calculate the damages to which a plaintiff is entitled as compensation for loss, it is necessary to decide for what kind of loss he is entitled to compensation. A correct description of the loss for which the valuer is liable must precede any consideration of the measure of damages. For this purpose it is better to begin at the beginning and consider the lender's cause of action.

The lender sues on a contract under which the valuer, in return for a fee, undertakes to provide him with certain information. Precisely what information he has to provide depends, of course, upon the terms of the individual contract. There is some dispute on this point in respect of two of the appeals, to which I shall have to return. But there is one common element which everyone accepts. In each case the valuer was required to provide an estimate of the price which the property might reasonably be expected to fetch if sold in the open market at the date of the valuation.

There is again agreement on the purpose for which the information was provided. It was to form part of the material on which the lender was to decide whether, and if so how much, he would lend. The valuation tells the lender how much, at current values, he is likely to recover if he has to resort to his security. This enables him to decide what margin, if any, an advance of a given amount will allow for: a fall in the market; reasonably foreseeable variance from the figure put forward by the valuer (a valuation is an estimate of the most probable figure which the property will fetch, not a prediction that it will fetch precisely that figure); accidental damage to the property and any other of the contingencies which may happen. The valuer will know that if he overestimates the value of the property, the lender's margin for all these purposes will be correspondingly less.

On the other hand, the valuer will not ordinarily be privy to the other considerations which the lender may take into account, such as how much money he has available, how much the borrower needs to borrow, the strength of his covenant, the attraction of the rate of interest, or the other personal or commercial considerations which may induce the lender to lend.

Because the valuer will appreciate that his valuation, though not the only consideration which would influence the lender, is likely to be a very important one, the law implies into the contract a term that the valuer will exercise reasonable care and skill. The relationship between the parties also gives rise to a concurrent duty in tort (see *Henderson v Merrett Syndicates Ltd, Arbuthnot v Feltrim Underwriting Agencies Ltd, Deeny v Gouda Walker Ltd (in liq)* [1994] 3 All ER 506, [1995] 2 AC 145.) But the scope of the duty in tort is the same as in contract.

A duty of care such as the valuer owes does not, however, exist in the abstract. A plaintiff who sues for breach of a duty imposed by the law (whether in contract or tort or under statute) must do more than prove that the defendant has failed to comply. He must show that the duty was owed to him and that it was a duty in respect of the kind of loss which he has suffered. . . . In the present case, there is no dispute that the duty was owed to the lenders. The real question in this case is the kind of loss in respect of which the duty was owed.

How is the scope of the duty determined? In the case of a statutory duty, the question is answered by deducing the purpose of the duty from the language and context of the statute (see *Gorris v Scott* (1874) LR 9 Ex Ch 125). In the case of tort, it will similarly depend upon the purpose of the rule imposing the duty. Most of the judgments in *Caparo*[10] are occupied in examining the Companies Act 1985 to ascertain the purpose of the auditor's duty to take care that the statutory accounts comply with the Act... The scope of the duty, in the sense of the consequences for which the valuer is responsible, is that which the law regards as best giving effect to the express obligations assumed by the valuer: neither cutting them down so that the lender obtains less than he was reasonably entitled to expect, nor extending them so as to impose on the valuer a liability greater than he could reasonably have thought he was undertaking.

What therefore should be the extent of the valuer's liability? The Court of Appeal said that he should be liable for the loss which would not have occurred if he had given the correct advice. The lender having, in reliance on the valuation, embarked upon a transaction which he would not otherwise have undertaken, the valuer should bear all the risks of that transaction, subject only to the limitation that the damage should have been within the reasonable contemplation of the parties.

There is no reason in principle why the law should not penalise wrongful conduct by shifting on to the wrongdoer the whole risk of consequences which would not have happened but for the wrongful act. Hart and Honoré in *Causation in the Law*, 2nd ed. (1985) p 120 say that it would, for example, be perfectly intelligible to have a rule by which an unlicenced driver was responsible for all the consequences of his having driven, even if they were unconnected with his not having a licence. One might adopt such a rule in the interests of deterring unlicenced driving. But that is not the normal rule. One may compare, for example, *Western Steamship Co Ltd v NV Koninklijk Rotterdamsche Lloyd, The Empire Jamaica* [1955] 3 All ER 60 at 61, [1955] P 259 at 264, in which a collision was caused by a 'blunder in seamanship of...a somewhat serious and startling character' by an uncertificated second mate. Although the owners knew that the mate was not certificated and it was certainly the case that the collision would not have happened if he had not been employed, it was held in limitation proceedings that the damage took place without the employers' 'actual fault or privity' because the mate was in fact experienced and (subject to this one aberration) competent. The collision was not, therefore, attributable to his not having a certificate. The owners were not treated as responsible for all the consequences of having employed an uncertificated mate, but only for the consequences of his having been uncertificated.

Rules which make the wrongdoer liable for all the consequences of his wrongful conduct are exceptional and need to be justified by some special policy. Normally the law limits liability to those consequences which are attributable to that which made the act wrongful. In the case of liability in negligence for providing inaccurate information, this would mean liability for the consequences of the information being inaccurate.

I can illustrate the difference between the ordinary principle and that adopted by the Court of Appeal by an example. A mountaineer about to undertake a difficult climb is concerned about the fitness of his knee. He goes to a doctor who negligently makes a superficial examination and pronounces the knee fit. The climber goes on the expedition, which he would not have undertaken if the doctor had told him the true state of his knee. He suffers an injury which is an entirely foreseeable consequence of mountaineering but has nothing to do with his knee.

On the Court of Appeal's principle, the doctor is responsible for the injury suffered by the mountaineer because it is damage which would not have occurred if he had been given correct information about his knee. He would not have gone on the expedition and would have suffered no injury. On what I have suggested is the more usual principle, the doctor is not liable. The injury has not been caused by the doctor's bad advice, because it would have occurred even if the advice had been correct.

The Court of Appeal summarily rejected the application of the latter principle to the present case, saying ([1995] 2 All ER 769 at 840, [1995] QB 375 at 404):

'The complaint made and upheld against the valuers in these cases is...not that they were wrong. A professional opinion may be wrong without being negligent. The complaint in each case is that the valuer expressed an opinion that the land was worth more than any careful and competent valuer would have advised.'

---

[10] [1990] 2 AC 605, [1990] 1 All ER 568.

I find this reasoning unsatisfactory. It seems to be saying that the valuer's liability should be restricted to the consequences of the valuation being wrong if he had warranted that it was correct, but not if he had only promised to use reasonable care to see that it was correct. There are, of course, differences between the measure of damages for breach of warranty and for injury caused by negligence, to which I shall return. In the case of liability for providing inaccurate information, however, it would seem paradoxical that the liability of a person who warranted the accuracy of the information should be less than that of a person who gave no such warranty but failed to take reasonable care.

Your Lordships might, I would suggest, think that there was something wrong with a principle which, in the example which I have given, produced the result that the doctor was liable. What is the reason for this feeling? I think that the Court of Appeal's principle offends common sense because it makes the doctor responsible for consequences which, though in general terms foreseeable, do not appear to have a sufficient causal connection with the subject matter of the duty. The doctor was asked for information on only one of the considerations which might affect the safety of the mountaineer on the expedition. There seems no reason of policy which requires that the negligence of the doctor should require the transfer to him of all the foreseeable risks of the expedition.

I think that one can to some extent generalise the principle upon which this response depends. It is that a person under a duty to take reasonable care to provide information on which someone else will decide upon a course of action is, if negligent, not generally regarded as responsible for all the consequences of that course of action. He is responsible only for the consequences of the information being wrong. A duty of care which imposes upon the informant responsibility for losses which would have occurred even if the information which he gave had been correct is not in my view fair and reasonable as between the parties. It is therefore inappropriate either as an implied term of a contract or as a tortious duty arising from the relationship between them.

The principle thus stated distinguishes between a duty to *provide information* for the purpose of enabling someone else to decide upon a course of action and a duty to *advise* someone as to what course of action he should take. If the duty is to advise whether or not a course of action should be taken, the adviser must take reasonable care to consider all the potential consequences of that course of action. If he is negligent, he will therefore be responsible for all the foreseeable loss which is a consequence of that course of action having been taken. If his duty is only to supply information, he must take reasonable care to ensure that the information is correct and if he is negligent, will be responsible for all the foreseeable consequences of the information being wrong.

[LORD HOFFMANN discussed *Banque Financière de la Cité SA v Westgate Insurance Co Ltd* [1990] 2 All ER 947, [1991] 2 AC 249 (noted p. 241, ante) and then continued:]

...The principle that a person providing information upon which another will rely in choosing a course of action is responsible only for the consequences of the information being wrong is not without exceptions. This is not the occasion upon which to attempt a list, but fraud is commonly thought to be one....

The measure of damages in an action for breach of a duty to take care to provide accurate information must also be distinguished from the measure of damages for breach of a warranty that the information is accurate. In the case of breach of a duty of care, the measure of damages is the loss attributable to the inaccuracy of the information which the plaintiff has suffered by reason of having entered into the transaction on the assumption that the information was correct. One therefore compares the loss he has actually suffered, with what his position would have been if he had not entered into the transaction and asks what element of this loss is attributable to the inaccuracy of the information. In the case of a warranty, one compares the plaintiff's position as a result of entering into the transaction with what it would have been if the information had been accurate. Both measures are concerned with the consequences of the inaccuracy of the information, but the tort measure is the extent to which the plaintiff is worse off because the information was wrong, whereas the warranty measure is the extent to which he would have been better off if the information had been right....

The other cases cited by the Court of Appeal and counsel for the respondent plaintiffs fall into two categories. The first comprises those cases concerned with the calculation of the loss which the plaintiff has suffered in consequence of having entered into the transaction. They do not address the question of the extent to which that loss is within the scope of the defendant's duty of care. The calculation of loss must, of course, involve comparing what the plaintiff has lost as a result of making the loan with what his position would have been if he had not made it. If, for example, the lender would have lost the same money on some other transaction, then the valuer's negligence has caused him no loss. Likewise, if he has substantially overvalued the property, so that the lender stands to make a loss if he has to sell the security at current values, but a rise in the property market enables him to realise enough to pay off the whole loan, the lender has suffered no loss. But the question of whether the lender has suffered a loss is not the same as the question of how one defines the kind of loss which falls within the scope of the duty of care. The Court of Appeal justified its view on the latter question by an appeal to symmetry: 'if the market moves upwards, the valuer reaps the benefit; if it moves downwards, he stands the loss.' (see [1995] 2 All ER 769 at 856, [1995] QB 375 at 421). This seems to me to confuse the two questions. If the market moves upwards, it reduces or eliminates the loss which the lender would otherwise have suffered. If it moves downwards, it may result in more loss than is attributable to the valuer's error. There is no contradiction in the asymmetry. A plaintiff has to prove both that he has suffered loss and that the loss fell within the scope of the duty. The fact that he cannot recover for loss which he has not suffered does not entitle him to an award of damages for loss which he has suffered, but which does not fall within the scope of the valuer's duty of care.

The distinction between the 'no-transaction' and 'successful transaction' cases is, of course, quite irrelevant to the scope of the duty of care. In either case, the valuer is responsible for the loss suffered by the lender in consequence of having lent upon an inaccurate valuation. When it comes to calculating the lender's loss, however, the distinction has a certain pragmatic truth. I say this only because, in practice, the alternative transaction which a defendant is most likely to be able to establish is that the lender would have lent a lesser amount to the same borrower on the same security. If this was not the case, it will not ordinarily be easy for the valuer to prove what else the lender would have done with his money. But in principle there is no reason why the valuer should not be entitled to prove that the lender has suffered no loss, because he would have used his money in some altogether different, but equally disastrous venture. Likewise the lender is entitled to prove that, even though he would not have lent to that borrower on that security, he would have done something more advantageous than keep his money on deposit: a possibility contemplated by Lord Lowry in *Swingcastle Ltd v Alastair Gibson (a firm)* [1991] 2 All ER 353 at 365, [1991] 2 AC 223 at 239. Every transaction induced by a negligent valuation is a 'no-transaction' case in the sense that ex hypothesi the transaction which actually happened would not have happened. A 'successful transaction' in the sense in which that expression is used by the Court of Appeal (meaning a disastrous transaction which would have been somewhat less disastrous if the lender had known the true value of the property) is only the most common example of a case in which the court finds that, on the balance of probability, some other transaction would have happened instead. The distinction is not based on any principle and should, in my view, be abandoned. The second category of cases relied upon by the plaintiffs concerns the question of whether the plaintiff's voluntary action in attempting to extricate himself from some financial predicament in which the defendant has landed him negatives the causal connection between the defendant's breach of duty and the subsequent loss. These cases are not concerned with the scope of the defendant's duty of care. They are all cases in which the reasonably foreseeable consequences of the plaintiff's predicament are plainly within the scope of the duty. The question is rather whether the loss can be said to be a consequence of the plaintiff being placed in that predicament. The principle which they apply is that a plaintiff's reasonable attempt to cope with the consequences of the defendant's breach of duty does not negative the causal connection between that breach of duty and the ultimate loss. This is the principle of which, in the sphere of physical damage, *Lord v Pacific Steam Navigation Co Ltd, The Oropesa* [1943] 1 All ER 211, [1943] P 32 is perhaps the best-known example. . . .

I turn now to the various theories suggested by the appellant defendants for defining the extent of the valuer's liability. One was described as the 'cushion theory' and involved calculating what the plaintiff would have lost if he had made a loan of the same proportion of the true value of the property as his loan bore to the amount of the valuation. The advantage claimed for this theory was that it allowed the lender to claim loss caused by a fall in the market, but only to the extent of the proportionate margin or 'cushion' which he had intended to allow himself. But this theory allows the damages to vary according to a decision which the lender made for a different purpose, namely, in deciding how much he should lend on the value reported to him. There seems no justification for deeming him, in the teeth of the evidence, to have been willing to lend the same proportion on a lower valuation.

An alternative theory was that the lender should be entitled to recover the whole of his loss, subject to a 'cap' limiting his recovery to the amount of the overvaluation. This theory will ordinarily produce the same result as the requirement that loss should be a consequence of the valuation being wrong, because the usual such consequence is that the lender makes an advance which he thinks is secured to a correspondingly greater extent. But I would not wish to exclude the possibility that other kinds of loss may flow from the valuation being wrong and in any case, as Mr Sumption QC said on behalf of the defendants York Montague Ltd, it seems odd to start by choosing the wrong measure of damages (the whole loss) and then correct the error by imposing a cap. The appearance of a cap is actually the result of the plaintiff having to satisfy two separate requirements: first, to prove that he has suffered loss, and, secondly, to establish that the loss fell within the scope of the duty he was owed.

[LORD HOFFMANN rejected submissions by the defendants attempting to restrict the damages to the losses as they would have been valued at the time of the breach and to the amount of loss that would have been suffered not given the defendants' valuation but given the highest valuation that would not have counted as negligent. He continued:] I turn now to the facts of the three cases. In *South Australia Asset Management Corpn v York Montague Ltd*, the lenders on 3 August 1990 advanced £11m. on a property valued at £15m. May J found that the actual value at the time was £5m. On 5 August 1994 the property was sold for £2,477,000. May J quantified the loss at £9,753,927.99 and deducted 25% for the plaintiff's contributory negligence. The consequence of the valuation being wrong was that the plaintiff had 10m. less security than they thought. If they had had this margin, they would have suffered no loss. The whole loss was therefore within the scope of the defendants' duty. It follows that the appeal must be dismissed. £75m on the security of a property valued by the defendants at £2.5m. The judge found that the correct value was between £1.8m and £1.85m. It was sold in February 1992 for £950,000. Gage J quantified the lenders' loss (including unpaid interest) at £1,309,876.46 and awarded this sum as damages.

In my view the damages should have been limited to the consequences of the valuation being wrong, which were that the lender had £700,000 or £650,000 less security than he thought. The plaintiffs say that the situation produced by the overvaluation was not merely that they had less security, but also that there was a greater risk of default. But the valuer was not asked to advise on the risk of default, which would depend upon a number of matters outside his knowledge, including the personal resources of the borrower. The greater risk of default, if such there was, is only another reason why the lender, if he had known the true facts, would not have entered into the particular transaction. But that does not affect the scope of the valuer's duty.

I would therefore allow the appeal and reduce the damages to the difference between the valuation and the correct value. If the parties cannot agree whether on the valuation date the property was worth £1.8m. or £1.85m. or some intermediate figure on the date of valuation, the question will have to be remitted to the trial judge for decision on the basis of the evidence called at the trial.

In *Nykredit Mortgage Bank plc v Edward Erdman Group Ltd* the lenders on 12 March 1990 advanced £2.45m on the security of a property valued by the defendants at £3.5m. The correct value was said by Judge Byrt QC sitting as a judge of the Queen's Bench Division to be £2m or at most £2.375m. The price obtained on a sale by auction in February 1993 was £345,000. The judge quantified the loss (including unpaid interest) at £3,058,555.52 and gave judgment for the plaintiffs in this sum....

I would, therefore, allow the appeal and substitute for the judge's award of damages a figure equal to the difference between £3.5m and the true value of the property at the date of valuation. The judge appears to have been inclined to fix the latter figure at £2m. The reference to £2.35m was based upon a concession made by plaintiffs' counsel on the basis that, for the purposes of calculating the damages according to the principle adopted by the Court of Appeal, it did not matter one way or the other. However, if the parties cannot agree upon the figure, it will also have to be remitted to the judge for determination on the evidence adduced at the trial.

[LORD GOFF OF CHIEVELEY, LORD JAUNCEY OF TULLICHETTLE, LORD SLYNN OF HADLEY, and LORD NICHOLLS OF BIRKENHEAD agreed with LORD HOFFMANN's speech.]

NOTES

1. The main point of contention in *SAAMCO*, as this case is sometimes known, is how to identify the loss for which the defendants' breach of duty is responsible. Lord Hoffmann essentially argues that the scope of recovery should be determined by the 'scope' of the duty of care at issue. More specifically, in this case, Lord Hoffmann applies this general rule to determine that the relevant loss here is the 'loss of coverage'. 'Coverage' is the amount by which the value of the security for a loan exceeds the amount of the loan. It is a kind of safety margin. Lord Hoffmann argues that if, as in *SAAMCO* itself, the lender lends £11 million on the security of a building the lender thinks is worth £15 million, but which is in reality worth only £5 million, the lender has 'lost coverage' of £10 million. Lord Hoffmann is saying (and he makes this even clearer in the subsequent case *Nykredit Mortgage Bank v Edward Erdman Group Ltd (No 2)* [1998] 1 All ER 305, [1997] 1 WLR 1627) that this loss of coverage is the real loss attributable to the defendant giving false information and not the 'transaction' or 'basic' or 'whole' loss—the amount by which the lender is out of pocket as a result of the deal. The 'scope' of the defendant's duty was to take care to avoid exposing the claimant to this loss of coverage.

    But does this approach take into account the reality of the situation? The lender's purpose is to have sufficient security in case the borrower defaults on the loan. If the security turns out to be worth more than the outstanding value of the loan, the lender has successfully secured the loan regardless of whether the original valuation was right or wrong. If the building in *SAAMCO* had turned out to be worth only £11 million, the lender would have recovered all of its money, but would have 'lost coverage' of £4 million. Lord Hoffmann goes on to say that in such circumstances the lender could not sue because it must show that it has 'suffered loss'. But is this entirely satisfactory? Lord Hoffmann claims that it is wrong to start with 'the whole loss'. How can he then use the lack of any such loss to justify denying the claimant a remedy?

    The latent difficulties in Lord Hoffmann's position became clear in *Platform Home Loans Ltd v Oyston Shipways Ltd* [2000] 2AC 190, [1999] 1 All ER 833, on which see D. Howarth [2000] Tort L. Rev. 85. The claimant lent £1.05 million on a property valued by the defendant at £1.5 million but in fact worth only £435,000. The defendant said that there was contributory negligence because the claimant had not checked the borrowers' capacity to repay the loan. The claimant said that, in the light of Lord Hoffmann's speech in *SAAMCO*, since the relevant loss was the 'loss of coverage' and nothing that the claimant had done had affected the degree of that loss, contributory negligence was irrelevant. But the House of Lords decided that contributory negligence should be deducted from the 'whole loss' and the resulting sum should be compared with the 'loss of coverage', declaring that courts should award the lower of the 'loss of coverage' and the discounted 'whole loss'. Lord Millett said that the claimant's argument against being required to contribute failed because 'the £500,000 is merely the amount of the overvaluation. The damage which the appellant suffered as a result of the transaction which they entered into in consequence of the overvaluation is not £500,000 but £611,748.' Lord Millett does not advert to the obvious point that such a charactersation stands in clear contradiction to Lord Hoffmann's position in *SAAMCO*. Lord Hobhouse attempted a different explanation, referring to *Froom v Butcher* [1976] QB 286, [1975] 3 All ER 520, where the Court of Appeal said that in contributory negligence, contributing to the damage was crucial, not contributing to the accident that caused the injury (see p. 435, post). Thus, not wearing a seat belt could constitute contributory negligence in a road accident case, even though it had no influence on whether the accident happened. It is, however, difficult to see how Lord Hobhouse's point works. As Howarth op cit. says, 'In *Froom* there was only one plausible way of characterising the loss, namely the consequences of the plaintiff's injuries. In *Platform Homes,* either the transaction loss or the valuation loss was the relevant loss. In *SAAMCO* and *Nykredit,* the House of Lords insisted that the transaction loss itself was outside the scope of the applicable duty of care. The question should surely be whether the claimant contributed to the valuation loss.'

2.   Lord Hoffmann uses the important example of the doctor and the mountaineer. The doctor wrongly advises the mountaineer that his knee is sound. The mountaineer consequently goes on his expedition and is injured in an unrelated accident. Lord Hoffmann assumes that the doctor would not be liable because the accident would have happened even if the knee really had been sound. Why? One possible explanation is there is no link between faulty diagnosis and avalanches. But is the injury such a coincidence? If doctors constantly err on the side of telling mountaineers that they are fit when they are not—as opposed to telling them that they are unfit when they are fit—what effect will this have on the number of mountaineers who are injured over time? If mountains are more dangerous than most places, one can argue that the false negative (saying that there is no injury when there is) produces more risk than the false positive (saying there is an injury when there is not), even if the injuries themselves are irrelevant to the other events which produce the accidents. We would not say that the doctor is liable if, as a result of a false positive, the mountaineer decides to stay at home and he is then struck by a meteorite. This is because there is no reason to suppose that the mountaineer was any more at risk from the meteorite at home than on the mountain, but the same point does not apply to the false negative if mountains are inherently more risky places. See G. Calabresi (1975) 43 U Chi LR 69.

3.   Is it helpful to describe the central question in *SAAMCO* as one of 'the scope of the duty'? Lord Hoffmann might be accused of running several issues together. First, there is factual causation—what would have happened had the defendant acted properly? Answering this question requires a degree of clarity about what exactly the defendant should have done instead. Second, there is legal causation (or 'remoteness')—should the court allow the defendant to escape liability because of the nature of the other causes of the loss (see chap. 6, post)? Third, there is the question of why there should be exceptions to the rule that pure economic loss should not be recoverable in negligence. Is this too much for one concept to bear? Note that writing extra-judicially, Lord Hoffmann has subsequently recast *SAAMCO* as turning primarily on causation analysis: see (2005) 121 LQR 592.

4.   Space prevents further analysis of the *SAAMCO* decision. However, the reader is referred in particular to the following academic criticism: J. Stapleton (1997) 113 LQR 1 and (2006) 122 LQR 426; J. O'Sullivan [1997] CLJ 19; Howarth, op cit.

5. *SAAMCO* continues to be applied to determine the measure of damages under *Hedley Byrne*, notwithstanding the criticism it has attracted. However, the courts have struggled at times with the application of the *SAAMCO* approach. For example, in the professional negligence context, Chadwick J's application of *SAAMCO* in *Bristol & West Building Society v Fancy &* Jackson [1997] 4 All ER 582, where the scope of recovery was defined by reference to the consequences flowing from the information in question being wrong, has been very influential: however, as noted by C. Kinsky (2006) 22(2) PN 86, this analysis appears to depart from that of Lord Hoffmann in *SAAMCO*, where the extent to which the faulty information potentially exposed the claimant to loss was the key criterion. It remains to be seen whether *SAAMCO* retains its current authority: nevertheless, for now, it remains an important touchstone.

6. For an example of a case where *SAAMCO* was not applied and the defendant was made liable for the whole of the foreseeable loss suffered by the claimant, on the basis that the defendant was not under a duty to provide specific information but rather to advise generally, see *Aneco Reinsurance Underwriting Ltd v Johnson & Higgins Ltd* [2001] 2 All ER (Comm) 929, [2001] UKHL 51.

6 FATAL ACCIDENTS—AN EXAMPLE OF RECOVERING PURE ECONOMIC LOSS UNDER STATUTE

■ Admiralty Commissioners v Steamship Amerika (Owners). The Amerika
House of Lords [1916-17] All ER Rep 177

A submarine sank due to the negligent navigation of the respondents' steamship. All but one of the crew were drowned. The Commissioners of Admiralty brought this action to recover the damage they had sustained. This included the capitalised amount of pensions payable by them to relatives of the deceased.

The House of Lords dismissed an appeal from a decision of the Court of Appeal which had disallowed this as an item of damages. Their Lordships held that (1) the payments had been made on compassionate grounds; since a person may not increase his claim for damages by a voluntary act, the payments were not recoverable from the tortfeasor; (2) the rule in *Baker v Bolton* (set out in Lord Sumner's speech, post) applied.

LORD SUMNER: . . .
This appeal has been brought principally to test the rule in *Baker v Bolton*,[11] that 'in a civil court the death of a human being cannot be complained of as an injury', a rule which has long been treated as universally applicable at common law. Some attempt was made to contest it only in its application to the case of master and servant. I will discuss both the narrower and the wider proposition, but it is clear that the action was not brought for the loss to a master of the services of his employee, but for the respondents' bad navigation, which sank the Crown's submarine, and the item of damage now in dispute, namely, pensions and allowances to dependants of seamen who were drowned, was claimed merely as one of the natural consequences of the tort, which consisted in sinking the ship. . . .

---

[11] (1808) 1 Camp 493 per Lord Ellenborough.

Never during the many centuries that have passed since reports of the decisions of English courts first began has the recovery of damages for the death of a human being as a civil injury been recorded. Since LORD ELLENBOROUGH's time the contrary has been uniformly decided by the Court of Exchequer and by the Court of Appeal. In addition to the weight of LORD ELLENBOROUGH's name (no mean authority even when sitting at nisi prius in spite of LORD CAMPBELL's sneer), the rule has been definitely asserted by LORD SELBORNE (*Clarke v. Carfin Coal Co* [1891] AC at p. 414), LORD BOWEN (*The Vera Cruz (No 2)* 9 PD at p. 101), and LORD ALVERSTONE and LORD GORELL (*Clark v. London General Omnibus Co., Ltd.* [[1906] 2 KB 648]). It has been accepted as the rule of the common law by the Supreme Court of the Dominion of Canada (*Re The Garland, Monaghan v. Horn* [(1881) 7 SCR 409]), and the Supreme Court of the United States of America (*The Corsair* [145 US 335 (1892)]). That the rule has also received statutory recognition appears to me to be abundantly plain. I agree that the preamble to s. 1 of the Fatal Accidents Act, 1846, should be read as applying to the particular defect in the existing law, which it was passed to remedy, namely, the disadvantageous position of widows and children, and not to the limited rights of masters and employers though only Bramwell B.'s intrepid individualism could dismiss it as a 'loose recital in an incorrectly drawn section of a statute, on which the courts had to put a meaning from what it did not rather than what it did say' (*Osborn (Osborne) v Gillett* LR 8 Exch. at p. 95). Still I think that the view taken by the legislature in 1846 is clear.... It provided a new cause of action and did not merely regulate or enlarge an old one. It excluded Scotland from its operation because a sufficient remedy already existed there, when in England none existed at all. So much seems to me to be indubitable. It did not deal with the case of master and servant as such, presumably because the legislature found nothing in the common law rule in this regard which called for reconsideration....

[EARL LOREBURN LC and LORD PARKER OF WADDINGTON delivered speeches to the same effect.]

■ Hansard's Parliamentary Debates, Third Series, House of Lords, 24 April 1846, cols. 967-968

LORD CAMPBELL (moving the second reading of the Death By Accident Compensation Bill [which, when enacted, became popularly known as Lord Campbell's Act, and was given the title the Fatal Accidents Act by the Short Titles Act 1896])...
said that he had a great respect for the common law; but still he felt that there could be no doubt that some of its doctrines were not applicable to the present state of society. One of these doctrines was that the life of a man was so valuable that they could not put any estimate upon it in case of a death by accident; and, therefore, if a man had his leg broken, on account of negligence on the part of coach-proprietors or of a railway company, he had his remedy in a court of justice; but if the negligence were still grosser, and if a life were destroyed, there was no remedy whatever....

NOTE

For a critique of the historical reasoning in *The Amerika*, see W. S. Holdsworth, *History of English Law*, vol. iii, pp. 331-336 and Appendix viii, pp. 676–677.

■ The Fatal Accidents Act 1976

1. Right of action for wrongful act causing death[12]
(1) If death is caused by any wrongful act, neglect or default which is such as would (if death had not ensued) have entitled the person injured to maintain an action and recover damages in respect thereof, the person who would have been liable if death had not ensued shall be liable to an action for damages, notwithstanding the death of the person injured.

[12] Amended by s. 83 of the Civil Partnership Act 2004.

(2) Subject to section 1A(2) below, every such action shall be for the benefit of the dependants of the person ('the deceased') whose death has been so caused.

(3) In this Act 'dependant' means

(a)   the wife or husband or former wife or husband of the deceased;

(aa) the civil partner or former civil partner of the deceased;

(b)   any person who

(i)   was living with the deceased in the same household immediately before the date of the death; and

(ii) had been living with the deceased in the same household for at least two years before that date; and

(iii) was living during the whole of that period as the husband or wife or civil partner of the deceased;

(c)   any parent or other ascendant of the deceased;

(d)   any person who was treated by the deceased as his parent;

(e)   any child or other descendant of the deceased;

(f)   any person (not being a child of the deceased) who, in the case of any marriage to which the deceased was at any time a party, was treated by the deceased as a child of the family in relation to that marriage;

(fa) any person (not being a child of the deceased) who, in the case of any civil partnership in which the deceased was at any time a civil partner, was treated by the deceased as a child of the family in relation to that civil partnership;

(g)   any person who is, or is the issue of, a brother, sister, uncle or aunt of the deceased.

(4) The reference to the former wife or husband of the deceased in subsection (3)(a) above includes a reference to a person whose marriage to the deceased has been annulled or declared void as well as a person whose marriage to the deceased has been dissolved.

(4A) The reference to the former civil partner of the deceased in subsection (3)(aa) above includes a reference to a person whose civil partnership with the deceased has been annulled as well as a person whose civil partnership with the deceased has been dissolved.

(5) In deducing any relationship for the purposes of subsection (3) above

(a)   any relationship by marriage or civil partnership shall be treated as a relationship by consanguinity, any relationship of the half blood as a relationship of the whole blood, and the stepchild of any person as his child, and

(b)   an illegitimate person shall be treated as the legitimate child of his mother and reputed father.

(6) Any reference in this Act to injury includes any disease and any impairment of a person's physical or mental condition.

1A. Bereavement

(1) An action under this Act may consist of or include a claim for damages for bereavement.

(2) A claim for damages for bereavement shall only be for the benefit

(a) of the wife or husband or civil partner of the deceased; and

(a) where the deceased was a minor or a civil partner who was never married

(i)   of his parents, if he was legitimate; and

(ii) of his mother, if he was illegitimate.

(3) Subject to subsection (5) below, the sum to be awarded as damages under this section shall be [£11,800].

(4) Where there is a claim for damages under this section for the benefit of both the parents of the deceased, the sum awarded shall be divided equally between them (subject to any deduction falling to be made in respect of costs not recovered from the defendant).

(5) The Lord Chancellor may by order made by statutory instrument, subject to annulment in pursuance of a resolution of either House of Parliament, amend this section by varying the sum for the time being specified in subsection (3) above.

2. Persons entitled to bring the action

(1) The action shall be brought by and in the name of the executor or administrator of the deceased.

(2) If

(a) there is no executor or administrator of the deceased, or

(b) no action is brought within six months after the death by and in the name of an executor or administrator of the deceased,

the action may be brought by and in the name of all or any of the persons for whose benefit an executor or administrator could have brought it.

(3) Not more than one action shall lie for and in respect of the same subject matter of complaint.

(4) The plaintiff in the action shall be required to deliver to the defendant or his solicitor full particulars of the persons for whom and on whose behalf the action is brought and of the nature of the claim in respect of which damages are sought to be recovered.

3. Assessment of damages

(1) In the action such damages, other than damages for bereavement, may be awarded as are proportioned to the injury resulting from the death to the dependants respectively.

(2) After deducting the costs not recovered from the defendant any amount recovered otherwise than as damages for bereavement shall be divided among the dependants in such shares as may be directed.

(3) In an action under this Act where there fall to be assessed damages payable to a widow in respect of the death of her husband there shall not be taken into account the re-marriage of the widow or her prospects of re-marriage.

(4) In an action under this Act where there fall to be assessed damages payable to a person who is a dependant by virtue of section 1(3)(b) above in respect of the death of the person with whom the dependant was living as husband or wife or civil partner there shall be taken into account (together with any other matter that appears to the court to be relevant to the action) the fact that the dependant had no enforceable right to financial support by the deceased as a result of their living together.

(5) If the dependants have incurred funeral expenses in respect of the deceased, damages may be awarded in respect of those expenses.

(6) Money paid into court in satisfaction of a cause of action under this Act may be in one sum without specifying any person's share.

4. Assessment of damages: disregard of benefits

In assessing damages in respect of a person's death in an action under this Act, benefits which have accrued or will or may accrue to any person from his estate or otherwise as a result of his death shall be disregarded.[13]

5. Contributory negligence

Where any person dies as the result partly of his own fault and partly of the fault of any other person or persons, and accordingly if an action were brought for the benefit of the estate under the Law Reform (Miscellaneous Provisions) Act 1934 the damages recoverable would be reduced under section 1(1) of the Law Reform (Contributory Negligence) Act 1945, any damages recoverable in an action...[14] under this Act shall be reduced to a proportionate extent.

---

[13]   Sections 1–4 were substituted by s. 3 of the Administration of Justice Act 1982.

[14]   Words deleted by s. 4(2) of the Administration of Justice Act 1982.

NOTES

1. The Fatal Accidents Act (Lord Campbell's Act) was first passed in 1846. The present Act, consolidating earlier legislation, was itself amended in important respects by the Administration of Justice Act 1982 in the light of recommendations by the Law Commission (Law Com. No. 56) and the Pearson Commission (vol. 1, paras. 399–477 and 537–539).

    One of the changes made in 1976 was that benefits derived from the deceased's estate are now disregarded in the assessment of damages (s. 4). This section has to be read in conjunction with the Law Reform (Miscellaneous Provisions) Act 1934 (see p. 558, post), which allows some aspects of actions for personal injury to survive the death of the victim and to be pursued for the benefit of the victim's estate. Section 1(5) of the 1934 Act says that the rights conferred by the 1934 Act for the benefit of the estates of deceased persons 'shall be in addition to and not in derogation of any rights conferred on the dependants of deceased persons by the Fatal Accidents Acts...'.

    S. M. Waddams (1984) 47 MLR 437 argues that the dual system of recovery by the estate under the 1934 Act and by the dependants under the Fatal Accidents Act leads to undue complication and the constant danger of anomaly. Waddams recommends that the right of the estate to claim for the 'lost years' (see p. 524, post) should be restored and the Fatal Accidents Act abolished. All recovery would then occur through the estate. The Law Commission, however, in its Consultation Paper No. 148 *Claims for Wrongful Death* (1997) and in its final report Law Com. No. 263 *Claims for Wrongful Death* (1999), says that the Fatal Accidents Act should be retained. (This conclusion was accepted without debate by the Department of Constitutional Affairs in its Consultation Paper (CP 9/07), *The Law of Damages*, at p. 12.) The Law Commission argues that the Waddams's proposal would leave many dependants to the vagaries of the law on intestacy. It would also stop dependants claiming compensation for loss of non-pecuniary support. Also, restoration of the lost years claim of the estate would provide a windfall for the estates of people without dependants. On the other hand, operating through the estate reflects the reality that the degree of support is rarely a matter of duty alone and is often a matter of the deceased's choice. The Fatal Accidents Act transforms voluntary support into certainty. Moreover, it is potentially a major defect in the law, from the point of view of providing appropriate incentives, that at present the lives of people without dependants are valued so cheaply. Note that in *Thompson v Arnold* [2008] PIQR P1, [2007] EWHC 1875 (QB), Langstaff J considered that the focus of the 1976 Act was on ensuring that a defendant would not escape paying damages for which he would, but for the death which he had caused, have been liable: the right conferred on dependants by the 1976 Act was thus a special right conferred by statute and not a more general right to sue for loss or mental distress following the death of the deceased.

2. Section 1(1) '...*would (if death had not ensued) have entitled the person injured to maintain an action*'. The dependants have no right of action if the deceased himself could not have sued during his lifetime. However, if the deceased had initiated a claim before his death in respect of the wrongful act that ultimately lead to his death, the cause of action under the 1976 Act is a separate claim that is initiated with his death and is not just an amendment or extension of the original claim: see *Reader v Molesworths Bright Clegg Solicitors* [2007] 3 All ER 107, [2007] EWCA Civ 169. (The deceased's cause of action would be transmitted to his estate pursuant to the Law Reform

(Miscellaneous Provisions) Act 1934: see p. 558, post. Note that the deceased's claim would be governed by ss. 11 and 14 of the Limitation Act 1980, which requires that a claim has to be brought within three years of the wrongful act, or where the claim related to a progressive disease, within three years of the date on which the claimant knew or ought reasonably to have known of the claim: see p. 17, post. However, the cause of action under the 1976 Act is governed by s. 12 of the Limitation Act, which provides that the claim can be brought within three years of the date of the death in question. (As a result, the separate actions may have separate limitation periods, marking the claims as distinct, as accepted by the Court of Appeal in *Reader v Molesworths Bright Clegg Solicitors*.) However, where the deceased had pursued a claim for a wrongful act that resulted in his death to judgment or settled a claim before his death, then his dependants had no cause of action under the 1976 Act, as the dependants would already had received compensation for the wrongful act resulting in the deceased's death: see *Thompson v Arnold* [2008] PIQR P1, [2007] EWHC 1875 (QB). Note that by virtue of s. 3 of the Damages Act 1996, an award of provisional damages shall not operate as a bar to an action in respect of that person's death under the 1976 Act: any part of such damages that was intended to compensate the deceased for pecuniary loss in a period which in the event falls after his death shall be taken into account in assessing the amount of any loss of support suffered by a dependent bringing an action under the 1976 Act.

In *Corr v IBC Vehicles Ltd* [2008] 2 All ER 943, [2008] UKHL 13, noted at p. 289, post, the House of Lords held that the loss attributable to a suicide of a husband could be recovered by his surviving wife, where the suicide resulted from a breach of a duty of care on the part of the defendant to refrain from exposing the deceased person to damage to his mental health and well-being (see p. 289, post, for the discussion in this judgment as to whether the deceased's suicide could qualify as 'fault' and therefore constitute contributory negligence for the purpose of s. 5 of the 1976 Act). The defences of volenti non fit injuria, contributory negligence and illegality might avail a defendant who killed the deceased during a criminal affray instigated by the deceased for the purpose of harming the defendant: see *Murphy v Culhane* [1977] QB 94, [1976] 3 All ER 533, but note the reservations about whether contributory negligence could ever be a defence open to a defendant who had intended to harm the claimant expressed by Lord Rodger in *Standard Chartered Bank v Pakistan National Shipping Corpn* [2003] 1 All ER 173, [2002] UKHL 43, at [45]. The dependants may be barred from bringing an action under the Act if the support they were afforded before the death of the deceased emanated from the proceeds of crime: *Burns v Edman* [1970] 2 QB 541, [1970] 1 All ER 886. (Note that it may be questioned whether this rule would apply to all types of criminal transactions.) Similarly, the courts will ignore the deceased's earnings from the underground economy where the deceased, to the knowledge of the claimant, was defrauding the social security and tax systems by not declaring his income. (See *Hunter v Butler* [1996] RTR 396.)

3. *Section 1(2)–(5): classes of dependants.* Although the action must be brought by and in the name of the executor or administrator of the deceased (s. 2), it exists for the benefit of those classes of dependants set out in the Act. Among the most important additions by the Administration of Justice Act 1982 were the former wife or husband of the deceased (s. 1(3)(a)) and the so-called 'common law spouse' (s. 1(3)(b)), but in assessing damages payable to the latter, account must be taken of the fact that the dependant

has no enforceable right to financial support (s. 3(4)). In *Shepherd v Post Office* (1995) *Times*, 15 June, the Court of Appeal held that a remarried divorced woman who later returned to her first husband could count as a former wife for the purposes of the Act. This meant that she did not have to show that she had been living with the first husband in the same household for at least two years prior to his death. Section 83 of the Civil Partnership Act 2004 has also added civil partners to the recognised class of dependants set out in the Act.

The 1976 Act creates an exception to the common law rule in *Baker v Bolton* (1808) 1 Camp. 493, so no classes other than those named may sue. As a result, there can be no claim based on simple friendship and no claim by the 'step-children' of a 'common-law spouse' or homosexual partner who has not entered into a civil partnership, even if dependency on the deceased exists in practice. Therefore, in *Kotke v Saffarini* [2005] PIQR P26, [2005] EWCA Civ 221, a claimant was unable to obtain compensation for the death of her partner, despite the fact that the relationship had lasted some years and they had a child together, as she had not been living with the deceased in the same household for two years before his death. The Law Commission (Law Com. No. 263, para. 3.46) proposes an addition to the list of dependants in the Act in the form of a catch-all residual provision in favour of anyone who 'was being wholly or partly maintained by the deceased immediately before the death or who would, but for the death, have been so maintained at a time beginning after the death'. This proposal would allow the law to develop directly in line with social developments and would remove arguably surplus moral judgements from the law. However, the problem with such a general 'injury' clause (which would, for example, allow recovery by anyone who has lost the reasonable expectation of a non-business benefit, roughly the current test for the *extent* of claimable damages) is that it would bring within the Act's protection even people who were not really *dependent* on the deceased—and the amelioration of dependency is the reason for allowing the Act to evade the normal rules against recovery of pure economic loss. On the other hand, the Law Commission also rejects replacing the current list in the Act with a test allowing any dependant to claim, since that would mean that people who are currently in a position to claim for losses of reasonable expectation of benefits solely because they are on the list would have to prove their *dependency*, which might not be the same thing. There was therefore an inherent tension in the Law Commission's proposals between emphasising dependency as a central requirement for recovery but also expanding the Act's scope to cover individuals who were not actually dependent upon the deceased but who would have so become had the death not occurred. The Department for Constitutional Affairs in its consultation paper, *The Law of Damages* CP 9/07, at pp. 13–14, has proposed the insertion into the 1976 Act of a general dependency clause similar to that proposed by the Law Commission, but suggests that this should be confined to any person who was being wholly or partly maintained by the deceased immediately before the death: in contrast, the Commission's proposal to extend this to those who would have become dependent but for the death has been rejected, on the basis that it is too openended and serves no significant purpose.

4. *Section 1A: bereavement.* The purpose of the bereavement payment is to compensate for grief and sorrow and for the loss, in the words of s. 1(4) of the Damages (Scotland) Act 1976, of 'such non-patrimonial benefit as the relative might have been expected to derive from the deceased's society and guidance if he had not died'. The Law

Commission recommends putting statements into the statute to this effect. (Law Com. No. 263, para. 6.7). The DCA Consultation Paper expressed some scepticism as to the usefulness of such a statement: see CP 9/07, pp. 24–25.

The Law Commission recommends extending eligibility for bereavement payments to include the deceased's spouse, children of any age (including adoptive children), parents (including adoptive parents), siblings (including adoptive siblings), fiancé(e), or cohabitee (whether in a heterosexual or homosexual relationship) of at least two years' standing (Law Com. No. 263, para. 6.31). The DCA Consultation Paper has made similar proposals, except within the general categories identified by the Law Commission it suggests limiting recovery to unmarried fathers who have parental responsibility, cohabitees who have lived together for not less than two years immediately prior to the accident, and children under the age of 18. It also suggests that bereavement payments should not be available for siblings or fiancé(e)s.

Finally, the Law Commission recommends an initial uprating of the award to £10,000 and thereafter subsequently index-linking it (Law Com. No. 263, paras. 6.41 and 6.43). It also recommends, however, that awards should be limited to three times the specified amount for any one incident (Law Com. No. 263, para. 6.51). The DCA Consultation Paper has made similar proposals with, however, some significant modifications, including the rejection of a cap on awards in favour of fixed sums for different categories of claimant, with only spouses, civil partners, or cohabitees entitled to the full £10,000 plus award.

Note that entitlement to a bereavement award does not survive the death of the bereaved person (Law Reform (Miscellaneous Provisions) Act 1934, s. 1(1A)).

5. *Section 3: assessment of damages.* The method of assessing damages under the Fatal Accidents Act was enunciated by Lord Wright in *Davies v Powell Duffryn Associated Collieries Ltd* [1942] AC 601, [1942] 1 All ER 657:

> The starting point is the amount of wages which the deceased was earning, the ascertainment of which to some extent may depend on the regularity of his employment. Then there is an estimate of how much was required or expected for his own personal and living expenses. The balance will give a datum or base figure which will generally be turned into a lump sum by taking a certain number of years' purchase. That sum, however, has to be taxed down by having due regard to uncertainties.

In other words, the annual value of the lost expected benefit is estimated (this is called the multiplicand) and is multiplied by a figure related to how long the benefit would have lasted (the multiplier). In *Graham v Dodds* [1983] 2 All ER 953, [1983] 1 WLR 808, the House of Lords held that this multiplier is to be calculated from the date of death rather than the date of the trial of the action, otherwise 'the longer the trial of the dependants' claims could be delayed the more they would eventually recover' (per Lord Bridge at p. 958). *Graham* was followed by the Court of Appeal in *Fletcher (Executrix of the estate of Carl Fletcher (deceased)) v A Train & Sons Ltd* [2008] EWCA Civ 413, where the court confirmed that the multiplier had to be selected once and for all as at the date of the death. (Note the Court of Appeal in *Fletcher* also confirmed that the House of Lords in *Cookson v Knowles* [1979] AC 556, [1978] 2 All ER 604 had established that no interest should be awarded in respect of damages for post-trial losses awarded for loss of dependency in a fatal accidents claim: this part of a damages award under the Act constituted compensation for future loss, and therefore the award of interest was inappropriate.)

Graham was distinguished in *Corbett v Barking, Havering and Brentwood Health Authority* [1991] 2 QB 408, [1991] 1 All ER 498, where the Court of Appeal said that *Graham* applied only to the question of how long the deceased was likely to have provided support. It did not apply to the other relevant question, which is the length of time the dependant would require support. The multiplier depends on the lower of these two figures. The Law Commission (Law Com. No. 263), although recognising that *Corbett* improves the *Graham* rule, calls the resulting method of calculation 'irrational' and 'unduly complex' (para 4.13).

The degree of dependency is a matter of fact. Except under s. 3(4) it does not matter whether the deceased had a legal right to the future income. Factual expectation, even loss of a chance, is enough (see *Davies v Taylor* [1974] AC 207, [1972] 3 All ER 836). If the deceased and the dependant were in receipt of state benefits before the accident and the dependant is still in receipt of state benefits after the accident, the question for the court is whether the dependant is any worse off as a result of the accident. Benefits such as housing benefit will usually be unaffected and, in the case of other benefits, even though the type of benefit payable might change, the dependant suffers no loss if the total amount of benefit paid by the state after the accident is the same as before: *Hunter v Butler* [1996] RTR 396, as explained in *Cox v Hockenhull* [1999] 3 All ER 577, [2000] 1 WLR 750. There is no principle that state benefits as a source of income are to be treated differently from any other source of income (see *Cox v Hockenhull* per Stuart-Smith LJ), but some of the ordinary presumptions about apportionment will not necessarily apply in benefit cases. For example, it is usually supposed, in the absence of evidence to the contrary, that a person would use up only a third of his or her income on him- or herself, and that therefore two thirds of the income was devoted to support of dependants. But where major household expenditures are dealt with by benefit, e.g. the rent by housing benefit, courts will often be justified in assuming that a higher proportion than a third of any remaining income from benefits was devoted to the personal use of the deceased (see *Cox v Hockenhull*).

In addition to compensation for lost financial support (the 'disbursement dependency') there might also be a claim for lost services and emotional support (the 'services dependency'): see *Cresswell v Eaton* [1991] 1 All ER 484, [1991] 1 WLR 1113. This type of claim is typically brought by children when they have lost a parent, but is also claimed in respect of spouses (see e.g. *Cox v Hockenhull*). The court will start with an estimate of the money value of the services based on the market cost of employing an equivalent carer and then make adjustments for the quality, quantity, and probable duration of the lost care.

6.   *Section 3(3)* contains provisions formerly in s. 4(1) of the Law Reform (Miscellaneous Provisions) Act 1971 because Parliament agreed with Phillimore J in *Buckley v John Allen and Ford (Oxford) Ltd* [1967] 2 QB 637 at 644, that it was distasteful for a judge to have to put a money value upon a widow's chances of remarriage. The resulting legislation contains what the Pearson Commission (vol. I, para. 411) described as 'the manifest absurdity of awarding damages for a loss which is known to have ceased'. The Law Commission now recommends repealing the section on the basis that, in an era when both men and women take paid work, the mere prospects of remarriage should not count in any case (except in the case of an engagement to be married, and even then only on the basis of clear evidence of intent), but that the fact of remarriage (or an equivalent relationship) should be taken into account. The DCA in its Consultation

Paper CP 9/07 has recommended that s. 3(4) of the FAA would be repealed and replaced by a provision to the effect that the prospect of breakdown in a cohabiting relationship between the deceased and his or her partner would not be taken into account when assessing damages under the 1976 Act, unless the relationship was in the course of being terminated.

7.   *Section 3(5)* establishes a claim for funeral expenses. The Law Commission's Consultation Paper wondered whether, since everyone will have to have a funeral at some time, the amount should be subject to a discount, and also asked whether there should be statutory recognition of different cultural traditions with regard to funerals. But the final paper (Law Com. No. 263, para. 3.50) recommends no change. The former reform was regarded by consultees as somewhat mean-spirited and the latter reform as unnecessary. The DCA Consultation Paper has taken a similar view, and has also agreed with the Commission that pecuniary losses resulting from the death other than funeral expenses should not be recoverable. Note that in *Jones v Royal Devon & Exeter NHS Foundation Trust* [2008] EWHC 558 (QB), King J held that the cost of a wake was not recoverable under s. 3(5).

8.   *Section 4* applies not only to financial benefits accruing to the claimant as a result of the victim's death (insurance moneys, for example) but also to service benefits: see *Stanley v Saddique* [1992] QB 1, [1991] 1 All ER 529. Benefits provided for the children of the deceased by a parent who had not hitherto played an active role in their support will also be disregarded under s. 4: see *H v S* [2003] QB 965, [2002] EWCA Civ 792. It was suggested in *Hayden v Hayden* [1992] 4 All ER 681, [1992] 1 WLR 986 that where the benefits flow from the tortfeasor, for example where a father, responsible for the death of his own wife, steps in to take on enhanced parenting responsibilities, the value of those services is deducted from the award representing the loss of the mother's services to the children. However, in *R v Criminal Injuries Compensation Board, ex p Kavanagh* [1998] 2 FLR 1071, it was made clear that *Hayden* applies only to a situation where the parental services are provided by the tortfeasor: see also *ATH v MS* [2002] EWCA Civ 792. Subsequently, in *Arnup v MW White Ltd* [2007] EWHC 601, Judge Seymour QC held that there was no justification for treating the provision of services or money by a tortfeasor to a dependant in some special manner for the purpose of the 1976 Act. However, on appeal, the Court of Appeal [2008] EWCA Civ 447 took the view that s. 4 covered all benefits obtained by the dependant as a result of the death and not only those benefits which could be said to have directly resulted from the death in question.

In *Jameson v Central Electricity Generating Board* [2000] 1 AC 455, [1999] 1 All ER 193, the House of Lords avoided a potential problem that, since amounts received under the deceased's will are to be disregarded, if the deceased settled a claim against one defendant and then died, a dependant might be able to proceed for full dependency from another defendant without having to deduct any amount received under the will. The House of Lords said that, even for concurrent tortfeasors, a full and final settlement with one defendant bars claims against the other defendants. It is not clear that this rule is beneficial, and since their Lordships made clear that much would depend on the terms of the settlement, so that the rule is not an invariable one, the problem is bound to recur. To illustrate this, see now *Heaton v Axa Equity & Law Assurance Society Plc* [2002] 2 All ER 961, [2002] UKHL 15, where compromise settlements were not held in the circumstances to represent full compensation for loss or to exhaust all claims for compensation: *Jameson* was interpreted as not establishing a general rule (see pp. 1113–1121, post).

The Law Commission saw too many anomalies in the effects of s. 4, especially in comparison with the general rules on collateral benefits (see p. 533, post). It comments abolishing this sweeping exemption and replacing it with provisions to bring Fatal Accidents law into line with the general law (Law Com. No. 263, para. 5.39).

9. *Section 5* allows a reduction of damages if the deceased was contributorily negligent. What if the *dependant* was partly responsible for the breadwinner's death? In *Mulholland v McCrea* [1961] NI 135 the deceased was a passenger in a car driven by her husband. The husband was partly responsible for the accident. He claimed as personal representative under the Fatal Accidents Acts and under the Northern Irish Law Reform (Miscellaneous Provisions) Act 1937 (which corresponds to the English Act of 1934). The Northern Irish Court of Appeal held by a majority that the amount awarded to the husband as dependant should be reduced having regard to his share in the responsibility for his wife's death. However, the negligence of one dependant cannot affect the claim of another dependant. In *Dodds v Dodds* [1978] QB 543, [1978] 2 All ER 539, the deceased was killed wholly as a result of his wife's negligence. It was conceded that she had no claim as a dependant, but this did not affect her son's claim as a dependant against her (in effect against the insurers standing behind her). The Law Commission (Law Com. No. 263, para. 6.63) recommends making clear that contributory negligence on the part of the bereaved will also reduce the bereavement award. In *Corr v IBC Vehicles Ltd* [2008] 2 All ER 943, [2008] UKHL 13, the majority of the House of Lords considered that there could be a reduction in damages under s. 5 of the 1976 Act for the loss attributable to a suicide of a husband, even where the impairment to the mental wellbeing of the husband which resulted in his suicide resulted from a breach of a duty of care on the part of the defendant. Their Lordships adopted the position that Lords Scott, Mance, and Neuberger considered that it would be inconsistent with the principle of respect of personal autonomy for 100 per cent recovery to be awarded in such circumstances: Lord Mance at [51] emphasised that an 'impairment' should not be taken as wholly denying autonomy and freedom of choice to the deceased and reducing them to the status of an 'automaton': see also the opinion of Lord Scott at [31] and that of Lord Neuberger at [57–70]. In contrast, Lords Bingham and Walker considered that in the circumstances no blame or element of 'fault' should be attached to the deceased and therefore no reduction in damages should be ordered, on the basis that the suicide was the result of the injury to his mental wellbeing which arose from the employer's breach of his duty to prevent causing this form of harm to the deceased. Lord Walker argued that this approach did not require denying the personal autonomy of the deceased: '[s]uicide was his decision, but it came from his feelings of worthlessness and hopelessness, which were the result of his depression, which was in turn the result of his accident' ([43]).

10. Note that in *Bubbins v UK* (2005) 41 EHRR 458, the European Court of Human Rights ruled that the inability of non-dependants to obtain non-pecuniary damages under the Fatal Accidents Act 1976 if a person had been killed unlawfully by agents of the State contrary to Article 2 of the ECHR meant that an appropriate remedy for the violation of the Convention right was not available in English law, as required by Article 13 of the ECHR. In addition, in *Cachia v Faluyi* [2002] 1 All ER 192, [2001] EWCA Civ 998, the

Court of Appeal interpreted s. 2(3) of the 1976 Act in conformity with Article 6 of the ECHR to find that the issuing of a writ in a claim under the 1976 Act which was not subsequently served on the defendant did not preclude the bringing of a new action some years later. However, note that in *Thompson v Arnold* [2008] PIQR P1, [2007] EWHC 1875 (QB), Langstaff J. rejected the argument that the provisions of Articles 6 and 8 of the ECHR required that the 1976 Act should be interpreted as permitting claims to be brought by dependants in respect of a wrongful act resulting in death where the deceased had settled her claim before her death.

CHAPTER FIVE
BREACH OF DUTY

The tort of negligence, as its very name implies, requires fault to be proved against the defendant. If there is a duty of care imposed upon the defendant, the claimant must prove, inter alia, that the defendant acted, or omitted to act, negligently. This is sometimes called the 'negligence issue', and it is with this issue that the materials in this chapter are concerned. The courts are not consistent in their terminology, however, and not infrequently the word 'duty' is used in relation to this issue (e.g. *Haley v London Electricity Board* [1965] AC 778, [1964] 3 All ER 185, p. 314, post). The student must therefore be alive to the sense in which the judges use this concept (see D. Howarth [1991] CLJ 58, at pp. 72–81). The standard of care which is formulated is that of the 'reasonable man', who now is becoming the 'reasonable person': while the 'reasonable man' was intended to be no different from the 'reasonable woman', some commentators have questioned whether this was or is the case (see M. Moran, *Rethinking the Reasonable Person* (Oxford, 2003)). However, it is important to realise that irrespective of his or her gender, the 'reasonable person' is a fictional character, the reference to whom is a thin disguise for the value judgement of the defendant's conduct which is made by the judge; nevertheless, as has been pointed out (M. A. Millner (1976) 92 LQR 131, at 133), 'by and large there is a substantial measure of objectivity in the assessment of prudent and sensible behaviour, reflecting the behavioural norms of the time, and place, even though it be filtered... through the judge's personal experience' (cf. J. Conaghan and W. Mansell, *The Wrongs of Tort* 2nd edn (London, 1998), pp. 52–60). Although in general the courts will hold negligent anyone who has fallen below the standard of the reasonable man (but see the heading 'Infants', p. 311, post), the amount of care and skill required of the defendant may be greater than that which could be expected of the ordinary man in the street (e.g. where he is a member of a trade or profession or holds himself out as possessing a particular skill, p. 303, post). The cases reveal the factors which the courts take into account in deciding whether a person has been negligent. This is essentially a balancing process, where various factors such as the nature of the activity in question, the costs of risk avoidance, the likelihood of harm arising from the activity in question, and the extent of the harm that may be caused are all taken into account. Demonstrating that a defendant has been negligent may be a difficult task for the claimant, on whom rests the burden to show on the balance of probabilities that the defendant was at fault. His case may founder for lack of witnesses—the victim of a 'hit-and-run' driver is the most obvious but not the only example. Thus the practical problem of proving negligence, even though the claimant may be assisted in certain cases by the maxim res ipsa loquitur or by statute (p. 336, post), should not be underestimated.

For an appraisal of the fault principle generally in the law of tort, see *Atiyah*, chap. 7 and *The Damages Lottery* (Oxford, 1997) pp. 33–35. See further T. Honoré (1988) 104 LQR 530; *Harris* et al., chap. 4. Judicial dissatisfaction with the requirement of fault can be found in *Ashcroft v Mersey Regional Health Authority* [1983] 2 All ER 245 (medical treatment) and *Snelling v Whitehead* (1975) Times, 31 July (road accident). In the latter case, for example, in which a seriously injured child failed to recover damages because the defendant driver was not proved to have been negligent, Lord Wilberforce felt that the case was one 'which should attract automatic compensation regardless of any question of fault'. The Pearson Commission considered both these areas in 1972. For its views on road accidents, see vol. 1, chap. 18 of the Report. In relation to medical injuries (discussed in vol. 1, chap. 24), the Commission concluded that a no-fault scheme should not be introduced for medical accidents (para. 1370) (though it favoured strict liability to volunteers for medical research or clinical trials who suffer severe damage (para. 1341)). (Note that the NHS Redress Act 2006 has now established an enabling framework whereby redress schemes can be set up to provide claimants with compensation outside of the normal court structures in limited circumstances for loss resulting from negligent primary health care: see p. 1168, post.)

There is an extensive economic literature dealing with the merits and demerits of fault as opposed to strict liability. See especially R. Cooter and T. Ulen, *Law and Economics* 5th edn (Harlow, 2007) chaps. 8 and 9; R. Posner (1972) 1 J. Legal Studies 29; S. Shavell (1980) 9 J. Legal Studies 1. The literature assumes that, under a fault regime, the court attempts to set a standard which treats as unreasonable any failure to take precautions which would have been justified in terms of the cost and benefits of that precaution. A fault regime, therefore, exonerates defendants even if they could have prevented the harm, if they could only have done so at a cost to themselves or to others which would have seemed excessive in the light of the chances of the accident occurring and the degree of harm if it did occur. The starting point for the analysis is that if the court sets the standard correctly, in terms of the assessment of the costs and benefits of taking further precautions, the law will act as an incentive to take the socially optimal level of precaution. But there are a number of well-known difficulties with fault. First, the total number of accidents depends not just on how careful people are but also on how often they engage in risky activities. Potential injurers might meet the correct standard every time they engage in the activity, and so escape liability, but if they engage in it often enough, some low probability accidents will happen anyway. Fault regimes are therefore said not to provide efficient incentives for injurer 'activity levels'. Second, what happens if the court has a tendency to set the standard wrongly? The trouble with fault is that a court error in the direction of setting the standard too high is very costly to a defendant who has followed the correct standard, whereas a court error setting the standard too low brings such a defendant no benefit. Thus, the prospect of court error, even if it is random error—sometimes too high, sometimes too low—will have a tendency to make potential defendants overcautious. Third, fault standards are inherently expensive to set.

On the other hand, strict liability or 'no-fault' standards have their own well-known set of objections. Under strict liability, unless there is a contributory negligence rule (the application of which brings back many of the problems of fault) there is no incentive at all for victims to look after themselves—not much of a problem in personal injury cases, perhaps, but a big problem in property damage and economic loss cases. Moreover, strict liability has no effect on *victim* activity levels, even if there is a contributory negligence defence. Second, under strict liability the precise level of damages has greater economic effect. Under fault, the incentive effect comes from the all-or-nothing nature of the judgment. If one keeps to the standard, there is nothing to pay, which is always cheaper, even with insurance, than having to pay compensation. But under strict liability, the injurer always pays. The question is how much. If compensation levels do not fully reflect the harm suffered by the victim, strict liability will tend to provide inadequate incentives. Thus the main lesson to be drawn from economic analysis is not that one rule is always superior to the other but that different rules suit different kinds of case. It remains to be seen how any redress schemes introduced under the NHS Redress Act 2006 operate in practice in the specific context of primary health care.

It should also be noted that there has been in recent years a growing scepticism about the ability of tort law to provide fair and cost-effective compensation. This has also been accompanied by concerns about the perceived growth of a 'compensation culture', which is conceptualised as involving a growing degree of dependence upon (and sometimes manipulation of) tort remedies to compensate for individual losses, with a concomitant increase in the costs inflicted upon businesses and employers, greater risk-adverse behaviour on the part of public and private bodies, and a decrease in reliance upon personal responsibility. While the Better Regulation Task Force in its 2005 report, *Better Routes to Redress*, concluded that the existence of this 'compensation culture' was largely a myth, the Task Force nevertheless concluded that the perception that such a culture existed was encouraging greater risk-adverse behaviour. In its response, the government adopted a similar analysis: see http://www.dca.gov.uk/majrep/bettertaskforce/better-task-force.pdf (last accessed 9th April 2008). See also the report published by the House of Commons Constitutional Affairs Committee, HC 754-I, 2005–06, *Compensation Culture*: see also K. Williams (2005) 25 LS 499, and R. Lewis, A. Morris and K. Oliphant (2006) 14(2) *TLJ* 158.

These policy concerns have resulted in the introduction of s. 1 of the Compensation Act 2006, a curious provision which is apparently intended to provide reassurance that the standard of care expected from defendants in respect of negligence liability is not excessive, while not changing the existing common law approach. In other words, s. 1 of the 2006 Act appears to be rhetorical reassurance, masquerading as legislative reform. However, it remains to be seen whether its provisions will have a tangible impact upon how standard of care analysis is applied in the context of negligence.

Just as the legislature has responded to the tide of concern about the perceived 'compensation culture', so too the courts appear to be anxious to encourage a greater emphasis on individual responsibility. Spigelman AC (Chief Justice of New South Wales) has spoken of a significant change in expectations within Australian society, which in turn has been reflected in a shift in emphasis away from awarding compensation towards striking an 'appropriate balance between personal responsibility for one's own conduct and social expectations of proper compensation and care': see (2006) 14 *TLR* 5. For a discussion of the limits on the extent to which law can provide compensation for the individual and a reiteration of the 'individualist' values of the common law, see the leading judgment by Lord Hoffmann in *Tomlinson v Congleton Borough Council* [2003] 3 All ER 1122, [2003] UKHL 47 (p. 573 post), in particular at [4] and [47]. See also *Hampstead Heath Winter Swimming Club v Corporation of London* [2005] EWHC 713. It remains to be seen how this new emphasis on individual responsibility will impact in the medium- to long-term on the application of standard of care analysis before the courts.

1 THE REASONABLE PERSON

(a) The average standard

■ Glasgow Corporation v Muir
House of Lords [1943] 2 All ER 44

A church party, desiring accommodation where they could eat their tea, obtained permission for 12s 6d to use the tea room in a mansion house belonging to the appellants. They had to carry their tea urn to the mansion house, and the route to the tea room then lay along a passageway, the width of which narrowed from five feet to three feet three inches. There were some children from another party buying sweets and ices at a counter at the beginning of this passage and, just after McDonald (a church officer) and Taylor, who were carrying the urn, had turned down the passage, the church officer let go of one handle of the urn, and the scalding tea that escaped injured six children. The action brought on their behalf was grounded on the alleged negligence of Mrs Alexander (the manageress), who had given the permission to use the tea room. The First Division of the Court of Session reversed the dismissal of the action by the Lord Ordinary. On appeal to the House of Lords:

LORD MACMILLAN:...

My Lords, the degree of care for the safety of others which the law requires human beings to observe in the conduct of their affairs varies according to the circumstances. There is no absolute standard, but it may be said generally that the degree of care required varies directly with the risk involved. Those who engage in operations inherently dangerous must take precautions which are not required of persons engaged in the ordinary routine of daily life. It is no doubt true that in every act which an individual performs there is present a potentiality of injury to others. All things are possible and, indeed, it has become proverbial that the unexpected always happens. But while the precept *alterum non laedere* requires us to abstain from intentionally injuring others, it does not impose liability for every injury which our conduct may occasion. In Scotland, at any rate, it has never been a maxim of the law that a man acts at his peril. Legal liability is limited to those consequences of our acts which a reasonable man of ordinary intelligence and experience so acting would have in contemplation....

The standard of foresight of the reasonable man is in one sense an impersonal test. It eliminates the personal equation and is independent of the idiosyncrasies of the particular person whose conduct is in question. Some persons are by nature unduly timorous and imagine every path beset with lions; others, of more robust temperament, fail to foresee or nonchalantly disregard even the most obvious dangers. The reasonable man is presumed to be free both from over-apprehension and from over-confidence. But there is a sense in which the standard of care of the reasonable man involves in its application a subjective element. It is still left to the judge to decide what in the circumstances of the particular case the reasonable man would have had in contemplation and what accordingly the party sought to be made liable ought to have foreseen. Here there is room for diversity of view, as, indeed, is well illustrated in the present case. What to one judge may seem far-fetched may seem to another both natural and probable.

...The question, as I see it, is whether Mrs Alexander, when she was asked to allow a tea urn to be brought into the premises under her charge, ought to have had in mind that it would require to be carried through a narrow passage in which there were a number of children and that there would be a risk of the contents of the urn being spilt and scalding some of the children. If as a reasonable person she ought to have had these considerations in mind, was it her duty to require that she should be informed of the arrival of the urn and, before allowing it to be carried through the narrow passage, to clear all the children out of it, in case they might be splashed with scalding water?

The urn was an ordinary medium-sized cylindrical vessel of about 15 ins. diameter and about 16 ins. in height, made of light sheet metal with a fitting lid, which was closed. It had a handle at each side. Its capacity was about 9 gallons, but it was only a third or a half full.[1] It was not in itself an inherently dangerous thing and could be carried quite safely and easily by two persons exercising ordinary care. A caterer, called as a witness on behalf of the pursuers, who had large experience of the use of such urns, said that he had never had a mishap with an urn while it was being carried. The urn was in charge of two responsible persons, McDonald, the church officer, and the lad Taylor, who carried it between them. When they entered the passage-way they called out to the children there congregated to keep out of the way and the children drew back to let them pass. Taylor who held the front handle had safely passed the children when, for some unexplained reason, McDonald loosened hold of the other handle, the urn tilted over and some of its contents were spilt, scalding several of the children who were standing by. The urn was not upset but came to the ground on its base.

In my opinion, Mrs Alexander had no reason to anticipate that such an event would happen as a consequence of granting permission for a tea urn to be carried through the passage-way where the children were congregated, and consequently there was no duty incumbent on her to take precautions against the occurrence of such an event. I think that she was entitled to assume that the urn would be in charge of responsible persons (as it was) who would have regard for the safety of the children in the passage (as they did have regard) and that the urn would be carried with ordinary care, in which case its transit would occasion no danger to bystanders. The pursuers have left quite unexplained the actual cause of the accident. The immediate cause was not the carrying of the urn through the passage, but McDonald's losing grip of his handle. How he came to do so is entirely a matter of speculation. He may have stumbled or he may have suffered a temporary muscular failure. We do not know and the pursuers have not chosen to enlighten us by calling McDonald as a witness. Yet it is argued that Mrs Alexander ought to have foreseen the possibility, nay, the reasonable probability of an occurrence the nature of which is unascertained. Suppose that McDonald let go his handle through carelessness. Was Mrs Alexander bound to foresee this as reasonably probable and to take precautions against the possible consequences? I do not think so. The only ground on which the view of the majority of the judges of the first division can be justified is that Mrs Alexander ought to have foreseen that some accidental injury might happen to the children in the passage if she allowed an urn containing hot tea to be carried through the passage and ought, therefore, to have cleared out the children entirely during its transit, which Lord Moncrieff describes as 'the only effective step'. With all respect I think that this would impose upon Mrs Alexander a degree of care higher than the law exacts. . . . As, in my opinion, no negligence has been established I agree with what I understand to be the view of all your Lordships that the appeal should be allowed and the judgment of the Lord Ordinary restored.

[LORD WRIGHT, LORD CLAUSON, LORD THANKERTON, and LORD ROMER delivered speeches in favour of allowing the appeal.]

Appeal allowed.

NOTES

1. In *Hall v Brooklands Auto-Racing Club* [1932] All ER Rep 208 at 217, Greer LJ said that the reasonable member of the public 'is sometimes described as 'the man in the street', or 'the man in the Clapham omnibus'. Lord Radcliffe described this commuting personage as the 'anthropomorphic conception of justice': *Davis Contractors Ltd v Fareham Urban District Council* [1956] AC 686 at 728. More recently, Lord Steyn in *McFarlane v Tayside Health Board* [1999] 4 All ER 961 at 977 (p. 153, ante) adopted the perspective of 'commuters on the London Underground' in determining whether a duty of care should be imposed in a 'wrongful conception' case. However, note that

---

[1] Lord Thankerton thought it was no more than two-thirds full.

the 'man in the Clapham omnibus' has traditionally been called upon as a reference point in determining whether a breach of duty has occurred: Lord Steyn is introducing a questionable innovation in making use of the commuter perspective to determine the existence of a duty of care in the first place.

2.   *Glasgow Corporation v Muir* in fact concerned injury to children, a topic which was referred to at p. 68, ante, where the question of parental liability was considered. It will be recalled that, in *Surtees v Kingston-Upon-Thames Borough Council* [1991] 2 FLR 559, Sir Nicholas Browne-Wilkinson V-C expressed the view that the courts should be 'slow to characterise as negligent' the care given by parents to children, pointing to the 'very real public policy considerations to be taken into account if the conflicts inherent in legal proceedings are to be brought into family relationships'.

(b) Foreseeability and the standard of care

■ Bolton v Stone
House of Lords [1951] 1 All ER 1078

A cricket club had played cricket on their ground since about 1864. The respondent, Miss Stone, who was standing on the road outside her house, was hit by a cricket ball which had been straight-driven by a batsman playing for a visiting team. She was nearly one hundred yards from where the ball was struck. The ball cleared a fence which was approximately seventy-eight yards from the striker of the ball, the fence being seven feet high and, in fact, the slope of the ground meant that the top of the fence was seventeen feet above the level of the pitch. A witness with a house nearer the ground that that of Miss Stone, said that cricket balls had hit his house or gone into his yard five or six times in the preceding few years. There was other evidence that the hit was an exceptional one, and that—as was accepted by the trial judge (Oliver J)—it was a rare occurrence for the ball to go over the fence during a match. The respondent sued the committee and members of the club, the appellants here, for damages for negligence and nuisance. Oliver J, [1949] 1 All ER 237, dismissed both claims, but the Court of Appeal, [1949] 2 All ER 851, held the appellants liable in negligence. On appeal to the House of Lords:

LORD OAKSEY:....
Cricket has been played for about ninety years on the ground in question and no ball has been proved to have struck anyone on the highways near the ground until the respondent was struck, nor has there been any complaint to the appellants. In such circumstances was it the duty of the appellants, who are the committee of the club, to take some special precautions other than those they did take to prevent such an accident as happened? The standard of care in the law of negligence is the standard of an ordinarily careful man, but, in my opinion, an ordinarily careful man does not take precautions against every foreseeable risk. He can, of course, foresee the possibility of many risks, but life would be almost impossible if he were to attempt to take precautions against every risk which he can foresee. He takes precautions against risks which are reasonably likely to happen. Many foreseeable risks are extremely unlikely to happen and cannot be guarded against except by almost complete isolation. The ordinarily prudent owner of a dog does not keep his dog always on a lead on a country highway for fear it may cause injury to a passing motor cyclist, nor does the ordinarily prudent pedestrian avoid the use of the highway for fear of skidding motor cars. It may very well be that after this accident the ordinarily prudent committee man of a similar cricket ground would take some further precaution, but that is not to say that he would have taken a similar precaution before the accident....

LORD REID: My Lords, it was readily foreseeable that an accident such as befell the respondent might possibly occur during one of the appellants' cricket matches. Balls had been driven into the public road from time to time, and it was obvious that if a person happened to be where a ball fell that person would receive injuries which might or might not be serious. On the other hand, it was plain that the chance of that happening was small. The exact number of times a ball has been driven into the road is not known, but it is not proved that this has happened more than about six times in about thirty years. If I assume that it has happened on the average once in three seasons I shall be doing no injustice to the respondent's case. Then there has to be considered the chance of a person being hit by a ball falling in the road. The road appears to be an ordinary side road giving access to a number of private houses, and there is no evidence to suggest that the traffic on this road is other than what one might expect on such a road. On the whole of that part of the road where a ball could fall there would often be nobody and seldom any great number of people. It follows that the chances of a person ever being struck even in a long period of years was very small.

This case, therefore, raises sharply the question what is the nature and extent of the duty of a person who promotes on his land operations which may cause damage to persons on an adjoining highway. Is it that he must not carry out or permit an operation which he knows or ought to know clearly can cause such damage, however improbable that result may be, or is it that he is only bound to take into account the possibility of such damage if such damage is a likely or probable consequence of what he does or permits, or if the risk of damage is such that a reasonable man, careful of the safety of his neighbour, would regard that risk as material? I do not know of any case where this question has had to be decided or even where it has been fully discussed. Of course there are many cases in which somewhat similar questions have arisen, but, generally speaking, if injury to another person from the defendants' acts is reasonably foreseeable the chance that injury will result is substantial and it does not matter in which way the duty is stated. In such cases I do not think that much assistance is to be got from analysing the language which a judge has used. More assistance is to be got from cases where judges have clearly chosen their language with care in setting out a principle, but even so, statements of the law must be read in light of the facts of the particular case. Nevertheless, making all allowances for this, I do find at least a tendency to base duty rather on the likelihood of damage to others than on its foreseeability alone. . . . I think that reasonable men do, in fact, take into account the degree of risk and do not act on a bare possibility as they would if the risk were more substantial. . . .

Counsel for the respondent in the present case had to put his case so high as to say that, at least as soon as one ball had been driven into the road in the ordinary course of a match, the appellants could and should have realised that that might happen again, and that, if it did, someone might be injured, and that that was enough to put on the appellants a duty to take steps to prevent such an occurrence. If the true test is foreseeability alone I think that must be so. Once a ball has been driven on to a road without there being anything extraordinary to account for the fact, there is clearly a risk that another will follow and if it does there is clearly a chance, small though it may be, that somebody may be injured. On the theory that it is foreseeability alone that matters it would be irrelevant to consider how often a ball might be expected to land in the road and it would not matter whether the road was the busiest street or the quietest country lane. The only difference between these cases is in the degree of risk. It would take a good deal to make me believe that the law has departed too far from the standards which guide ordinary careful people in ordinary life. In the crowded conditions of modern life even the most careful person cannot avoid creating some risks and accepting others. What a man must not do, and what I think a careful man tries not to do, is to create a risk which is substantial. Of course, there are numerous cases where special circumstances require that a higher standard shall be observed and where that is recognised by the law, but I do not think that this case comes within any such special category. . . . In my judgment, the test to be applied here is whether the risk of damage to a person on the road was so small that a reasonable man in the position of the appellants, considering the matter from the point of view of safety, would have thought it right to refrain from taking steps to prevent the danger. In considering the matter I think that it would be right to take into account, not only how remote is the chance that a person might be struck, but also how serious the consequences are likely to be if a person is struck, but I do not think that it would be right to take into account the difficulty of remedial measures. If cricket cannot be played on a ground without creating a substantial risk, then it should not be played there at all. I think that this is in substance the test which Oliver J applied in this case. He considered whether the appellants' ground was large enough to be safe for all practical purposes and held that it was. This is a question, not of law, but of fact and degree. It is not an easy question, and it is one on which opinions may well differ. I can only say that, having given the whole matter repeated and anxious consideration, I find myself unable to decide this question in favour of the respondent. I think, however, that this case is not far from the borderline. If this appeal is allowed, that does not, in my judgment, mean that in every case where cricket has been played on a ground for a number of years without accident or complaint those who organise matches there are safe to go on in reliance on past immunity. I would have reached a different conclusion if I had thought that the risk here had been other than extremely small because I do not think that a reasonable man, considering the matter from the point of view of safety, would or should disregard any risk unless it is extremely small.

This case was also argued as a case of nuisance, but counsel for the respondent admitted that he could not succeed on that ground if the case on negligence failed. I, therefore, find it unnecessary to deal with the question of nuisance and I reserve my opinion as to what constitutes nuisance in cases of this character. In my judgment, the appeal should be allowed.

LORD RADCLIFFE: . . . It seems to me that a reasonable man, taking account of the chances against an accident happening, would not have felt himself called on either to abandon the use of the ground for cricket or to increase the height of his surrounding fences. He would have done what the appellants did. In other words, he would have done nothing. . . .

I agree with the others of your Lordships that, if the respondent cannot succeed in negligence, she cannot succeed on any other head of claim.

[LORD PORTER and LORD NORMAND delivered speeches in favour of allowing the appeal.]

Appeal allowed.

QUESTION

Would the appellants have been liable if Miss Stone had been one of a large procession which, to their knowledge, was assembling in the road outside?

NOTES

1.   On the relevance of the difficulty and cost of remedial measures, compare Lord Reid's views in this case with those in the next case, *The Wagon Mound (No 2)* and see also *Latimer v AEC Ltd* [1953] AC 643, [1953] 2 All ER 449 (p. 320, post). The Court of Appeal in *Shine v London Borough of Tower Hamlets* [2006] All ER (D) 79 (Jan), [2006] EWCA Civ 852 took the view that *Bolton v Stone* should not be interpreted as establishing that the costs of prevention had to be accorded considerable weight when balanced against the likely severity of an injury or the risk of that injury occurring: Buxton LJ at [25] stated that '[i]n *Bolton v Stone*, the House [of Lords] indicated that there had to be a balance between the likely severity of the accident and the cost of putting it right . . . Although the case is authority for the general principle that there should be a balance, it goes no further than that.'

2.   Compare with *Bolton v Stone* the decision relating to liability in negligence in *Miller v Jackson* [1977] QB 966, [1977] 3 All ER 338. (As in *Bolton v Stone* the question of nuisance was also raised in this case, and on this point see chap. 14.) In *Miller v Jackson* a housing

estate had been built next to a cricket ground and the claimants, Mr and Mrs Miller who owned one of the houses on the estate, sued the chairman and secretary of the club on their own behalf and on behalf of the other members of the club. Between 1972 and 1974 cricket balls had on a number of occasions gone on to the claimants' property, causing some property damage, though no personal injury. In 1975 the height of the fence between the ground and the estate was increased so it stood nearly fifteen feet high, the maximum height possible because of the wind. Nevertheless, cricket balls were still hit over the fence. According to the club's count, balls had gone over the fence six times in the 1975 season and on eight or nine occasions in the 1976 season, and according to the claimants some of these balls had come on to their property. In the opinion of the majority of the Court of Appeal the 'risk of injury to persons and property is so great that on each occasion when a ball comes over the fence and causes damage to the claimants, the defendants are guilty of negligence' ([1977] 3 All ER at p. 348). See further *Hilder v Associated Portland Cement Manufacturers Ltd* [1961] 3 All ER 709, [1961] 1 WLR 1434.

■ The Wagon Mound (No 2), Overseas Tankship (UK) Ltd v The Miller Steamship Co Pty Ltd
Judicial Committee of the Privy Council [1966] 2 All ER 709

LORD REID: . . .

This is an appeal from a judgment of Walsh J,[2] dated 10 October 1963, in the Supreme Court of New South Wales (Commercial Causes) by which he awarded to the respondents sums of £80,000 and £1,000 in respect of damage from fire sustained by their vessels, Corrimal and Audrey D, on 1 November 1951. These vessels were then at Sheerlegs Wharf, Morts Bay, in Sydney Harbour undergoing repairs. The appellant was charterer by demise of a vessel, the Wagon Mound, which in the early hours of 30 October 1951, had been taking in bunkering oil from Caltex Wharf not far from Sheerlegs Wharf. By reason of carelessness of the Wagon Mound engineers a large quantity of this oil overflowed from the Wagon Mound on to the surface of the water. Some hours later much of the oil had drifted to and accumulated round Sheerlegs Wharf and the respondents' vessels. About 2 p.m. on 1 November this oil was set alight: the fire spread rapidly and caused extensive damage to the wharf and to the respondents' vessels.

An action was raised against the present appellant by the owners of Sheerlegs Wharf on the ground of negligence. On appeal to the Board it was held that the plaintiffs were not entitled to recover on the ground that it was not foreseeable that such oil on the surface of the water could be set alight (*Overseas Tankship (UK) Ltd v Morts Dock and Engineering Co Ltd*).[3] Their lordships will refer to this case as the *Wagon Mound (No. 1)*. The issue of nuisance was also raised but their lordships did not deal with it: they remitted this issue to the Supreme Court and their lordships now understand that the matter was not pursued there in that case.

In the present case the respondents sue alternatively in nuisance and in negligence. Walsh J[4] had found in their favour in nuisance but against them in negligence. Before their lordships the appellant appeals against his decision on nuisance and the respondents appeal against his decision on negligence. Their lordships are indebted to that learned judge for the full and careful survey of the evidence which is set out in his judgment.[5] Few of his findings of fact have been attacked, and their lordships do not find it necessary to set out or deal with the evidence at any length; but it is desirable to give some explanation of how the fire started before setting out the learned judge's findings.

² [1963] 1 Lloyd's Rep 402.   ³ [1961] AC 388, [1961] 1 All ER 404.
⁴ [1963] 1 Lloyd's Rep 402.   ⁵ [1963] 1 Lloyd's Rep at pp. 406–408.

In the course of repairing the respondents' vessels the Morts Dock Co, the owners of Sheerlegs Wharf, were carrying out oxy-acetylene welding and cutting. This work was apt to cause pieces or drops of hot metal to fly off and fall in the sea. So when their manager arrived on the morning of 30 October and saw the thick scum of oil round the Wharf, he was apprehensive of fire danger and he stopped the work while he took advice. He consulted the manager of Caltex Wharf and, after some further consultation, he was assured that he was safe to proceed: so he did so, and the repair work was carried on normally until the fire broke out on 1 November. Oil of this character with a flash point of 170°F is extremely difficult to ignite in the open; but we now know that that is not impossible. There is no certainty about how this oil was set alight, but the most probable explanation, accepted by Walsh J, is that there was floating in the oil-covered water some object supporting a piece of inflammable material, and that a hot piece of metal fell on it when it burned for a sufficient time to ignite the surrounding oil.

The findings of the learned trial judge are as follows:[6]

'(i)   Reasonable people in the position of the officers of the Wagon Mound would regard furnace oil as very difficult to ignite on water.

'(ii)   Their personal experience would probably have been that this had very rarely happened.

'(iii)   If they had given attention to the risk of fire from the spillage, they would have regarded it as a possibility, but one which could become an actuality only in very exceptional circumstances.

'(iv)   They would have considered the chances of the required exceptional circumstances happening whilst the oil remained spread on the harbour waters, as being remote.

'(v)   I find that the occurrence of damage to [the respondents'] property as a result of the spillage, was not reasonably foreseeable by those for whose acts [the appellant] would be responsible.

'(vi)   I find that the spillage of oil was brought about by the careless conduct of persons for whose acts [the appellant] would be responsible.

'(vii)   I find that the spillage of oil was a cause of damage to the property of each of [the respondents].

'(viii)   Having regard to those findings, and because of finding (v), I hold that the claim of each of [the respondents] framed in negligence fails.' . . .

It is now necessary to turn to the respondents' submission that the trial judge was wrong in holding that damage from fire was not reasonably foreseeable. In *Wagon Mound (No. 1)*[7] the finding on which the Board proceeded was that of the trial judge:

'. . . [the appellants] did not know and could not reasonably be expected to have known that [the oil] was capable of being set afire when spread on water.'

In the present case the evidence led was substantially different from the evidence led in *Wagon Mound (No. 1)*[8] and the findings of Walsh J[9] are significantly different. That is not due to there having been any failure by the plaintiffs in *Wagon Mound (No. 1)*[8] in preparing and presenting their case. The plaintiffs there were no doubt embarrassed by a difficulty which does not affect the present plaintiffs. The outbreak of the fire was consequent on the act of the manager of the plaintiffs in *Wagon Mound (No. 1)*[8] in resuming oxy-acetylene welding and cutting while the wharf was surrounded by this oil. So if the plaintiffs in the former case had set out to prove that it was foreseeable by the engineers of the Wagon Mound that this oil could be set alight, they might have had difficulty in parrying the reply that then this must also have been foreseeable by their manager. Then there would have been contributory negligence and at that time contributory negligence was a complete defence in New South Wales.

---

[6] [1963] 1 Lloyd's Rep at p. 426.   [7] [1961] AC at p. 413, [1961] 1 All ER at p. 407.
[8] [1961] AC 388, [1961] 1 All ER 404.   [9] [1963] 1 Lloyd's Rep 402.

The crucial finding of Walsh J[10] in this case is in finding (v): that the damage was 'not reasonably foreseeable by those for whose acts the defendant would be responsible.' That is not a primary finding of fact but an inference from the other findings, and it is clear from the learned judge's judgment that in drawing this inference he was to a large extent influenced by his view of the law. The vital parts of the findings of fact which have already been set out in full are (i) that the officers of the Wagon Mound 'would regard furnace oil as very difficult to ignite on water'—not that they would regard this as impossible: (ii) that their experience would probably have been 'that this had very rarely happened'— not that they would never have heard of a case where it had happened, and (iii) that they would have regarded it as a 'possibility, but one which could become an actuality only in very exceptional circumstances'—not, as in *Wagon Mound (No. 1)*,[8] that they could not reasonably be expected to have known that this oil was capable of being set afire when spread on water. The question which must now be determined is whether these differences between the findings in the two cases do or do not lead to different results in law.

In *Wagon Mound (No. 1)*[8] the Board were not concerned with degrees of foreseeability because the finding was that the fire was not foreseeable at all. So Viscount Simonds[11] had no cause to amplify the statement that the 'essential factor in determining liability is whether the damage is of such a kind as the reasonable man should have foreseen'. Here the findings show, however, that some risk of fire would have been present to the mind of a reasonable man in the shoes of the ship's chief engineer. So the first question must be what is the precise meaning to be attached in this context to the words 'foreseeable' and 'reasonably foreseeable'.

Before *Bolton v Stone*[12] the cases had fallen into two classes: (i) those where, before the event, the risk of its happening would have been regarded as unreal either because the event would have been thought to be physically impossible or because the possibility of its happening would have been regarded as so fantastic or far-fetched that no reasonable man would have paid any attention to it—'a mere possibility which would never occur to the mind of a reasonable man' (per Lord Dunedin in *Fardon v Harcourt-Rivington*[13])—or (ii) those where there was a real and substantial risk or chance that something like the event which happens might occur and then the reasonable man would have taken the steps necessary to eliminate the risk.

Bolton v Stone[14] posed a new problem. There a member of a visiting team drove a cricket ball out of the ground on to an unfrequented adjacent public road and it struck and severely injured a lady who happened to be standing in the road. That it might happen that a ball would be driven on to this road could not have been said to be a fantastic or far-fetched possibility: according to the evidence it had happened about six times in twenty-eight years. Moreover it could not have been said to be a far-fetched or fantastic possibility that such a ball would strike someone in the road: people did pass along the road from time to time. So it could not have been said that, on any ordinary meaning of the words, the fact that a ball might strike a person in the road was not foreseeable or reasonably foreseeable. It was plainly foreseeable; but the chance of its happening in the foreseeable future was infinitesimal. A mathematician given the data could have worked out that it was only likely to happen once in so many thousand years. The House of Lords held that the risk was so small that in the circumstances a reasonable man would have been justified in disregarding it and taking no steps to eliminate it.

It does not follow that, no matter what the circumstances may be, it is justifiable to neglect a risk of such a small magnitude. A reasonable man would only neglect such a risk if he had some valid reason for doing so: e.g. that it would involve considerable expense to eliminate the risk. He would weigh the risk against the difficulty of eliminating it. If the activity which caused the injury to Miss Stone had been an unlawful activity there can be little doubt but that *Bolton v Stone*[14] would have been decided differently. In their lordships' judgment *Bolton v Stone*[14] did not alter the general principle that a person

---

[10] [1963] 1 Lloyd's Rep at p. 426.   [11] [1961] AC at p. 426, [1961] 1 All ER at p. 415.
[12] [1951] AC 850, [1951] 1 All ER 1078.   [13] [1932] All ER Rep 81 at 83.
[14] [1951] AC 850, [1951] 1 All ER 1078.

must be regarded as negligent if he does not take steps to eliminate a risk which he knows or ought to know is a real risk and not a mere possibility which would never influence the mind of a reasonable man. What that decision did was to recognise and give effect to the qualification that it is justifiable not to take steps to eliminate a real risk if it is small and if the circumstances are such that a reasonable man, careful of the safety of his neighbour, would think it right to neglect it.

In the present case there was no justification whatever for discharging the oil into Sydney Harbour. Not only was it an offence to do so, but also it involved considerable loss financially. If the ship's engineer had thought about the matter there could have been no question of balancing the advantages and disadvantages. From every point of view it was both his duty and his interest to stop the discharge immediately.

It follows that in their lordships' view the only question is whether a reasonable man having the knowledge and experience to be expected of the chief engineer of the Wagon Mound would have known that there was a real risk of the oil on the water catching fire in some way: if it did, serious damage to ships or other property was not only foreseeable but very likely. Their lordships do not dissent from the view of the trial judge that the possibilities of damage[15] 'must be significant enough in a practical sense to require a reasonable man to guard against them', but they think that he may have misdirected himself in saying[16]

> 'there does seem to be a real practical difficulty, assuming that some risk of fire damage was foreseeable, but not a high one, in making a factual judgment as to whether this risk was sufficient to attract liability if damage should occur.'

In this difficult chapter of the law decisions are not infrequently taken to apply to circumstances far removed from the facts which give rise to them, and it would seem that here too much reliance has been placed on some observations in *Bolton v Stone*[17] and similar observations in other cases.

In their lordships' view a properly qualified and alert chief engineer would have realised there was a real risk here, and they do not understand Walsh J to deny that; but he appears to have held that, if a real risk can properly be described as remote, it must then be held to be not reasonably foreseeable. That is a possible interpretation of some of the authorities; but this is still an open question and on principle their lordships cannot accept this view. If a real risk is one which would occur to the mind of a reasonable man in the position of the defendant's servant and which he would not brush aside as far-fetched, and if the criterion is to be what that reasonable man would have done in the circumstances, then surely he would not neglect such a risk if action to eliminate it presented no difficulty, involved no disadvantage and required no expense.

In the present case the evidence shows that the discharge of so much oil on to the water must have taken a considerable time, and a vigilant ship's engineer would have noticed the discharge at an early stage. The findings show that he ought to have known that it is possible to ignite this kind of oil on water, and that the ship's engineer probably ought to have known that this had in fact happened before. The most that can be said to justify inaction is that he would have known that this could only happen in very exceptional circumstances; but that does not mean that a reasonable man would dismiss such risk from his mind and do nothing when it was so easy to prevent it. If it is clear that the reasonable man would have realised or foreseen and prevented the risk, then it must follow that the appellants are liable in damages. The learned judge found this a difficult case: he said that this matter is[18] 'one on which different minds would come to different conclusions'. Taking a rather different view of the law from that of the learned judge, their lordships must hold that the respondents are entitled to succeed on this issue....

Appeal and cross-appeal allowed.

---

15 [1963] 1 Lloyd's Rep at p. 411.   16 [1963] 1 Lloyd's Rep at p. 413.
17 [1951] AC 850, [1951] 1 All ER 1078.   18 [1963] 1 Lloyd's Rep at p. 424.

NOTE

The Wagon Mound (No 1) [1961] AC 388, [1961] 1 All ER 404 (p. 408, post) is the leading authority on remoteness of damage in negligence. A given set of facts may give rise to claims in the torts of nuisance and negligence, and nuisance itself can be subdivided into public and private nuisance (see chap. 14). There are important differences between these torts, but, in the sphere of remoteness of damage, *The Wagon Mound (No 2)* (in a part of the judgment which has been omitted at this stage) establishes that in nuisance, as in the tort of negligence, there must be foreseeability of the kind of damage suffered before the defendant will be held liable for that particular item of damage. (See p. 802, post where the Privy Council's judgment on this aspect of the case is set out.) Foreseeability plays a large and varied role in the tort of negligence. Not only is it relevant to breach of duty (which is under consideration at this point) and remoteness of damage (as has just been mentioned), but it is also relevant to the question whether a duty is owed to this particular claimant (p. 37, post). It is important that the different uses of the foreseeability doctrine should be appreciated, and discussion of this point can be found in an article by R. W. M. Dias [1967] CLJ 62.

(c) Special skill

■ Philips v William Whiteley Ltd
King's Bench Division [1938] 1 All ER 566

The plaintiff went to the defendants' jewellery department to arrange for her ears to be pierced to enable her to wear earrings. The defendants did not have any member of their own staff who did this job, but arranged for Mr Couzens, an employee of another firm, to pierce the ears. Approximately twelve or thirteen days after the piercing she felt pain in her neck. An abscess developed which had to be operated on and the operation left a small scar. It appeared that Mr Couzens had performed over one thousand ear piercings and nothing of this nature had happened on any other occasion. The plaintiff claimed damages, alleging negligence against Mr Couzens, the defendants' agent.

GODDARD J: . . .
In this case, the first thing that I have to consider is the standard of care demanded from Mr Couzens—or, I should say, from Whiteleys, because Whiteleys were the people who undertook to do the piercing. It is not easy in any case to lay down a particular canon or standard by which the care can be judged, but, while it is admitted here, and admitted on all hands, that Mr Couzens did not use the same precautions of procuring an aseptic condition of his instruments as a doctor or a surgeon would use, I do not think that he could be called upon to use that degree of care. Whiteleys have to see that whoever they employ for the operation uses the standard of care and skill that may be expected from a jeweller, and, of course, if the operation is negligently performed—if, for instance, a wholly unsuitable instrument were used, so that the ear was badly torn, or something of that sort happened—undoubtedly they would be liable. So, too, if they did not take that degree of care to see that the instruments were clean which one would expect a person of the training and the standing of a jeweller to use. To say, however, that a jeweller warrants or undertakes that he will use instruments which have the degree of surgical cleanliness that a surgeon brings about when he is going to perform a serious operation, or indeed any operation, is, I think, putting the matter too high. The doctors all seem to agree in this case that, if a lady went to a surgeon for the piercing of her ears, he would render his instruments sterile. After all, however, aseptic surgery is a thing of very modern growth. As anybody who has read the life of Lord Lister or the history of medicine in the last fifty or sixty years knows, it is not so many

years ago that the best surgeon in the land knew nothing about even antiseptic surgery. Then antiseptic surgery was introduced, and that was followed by aseptic surgery. I do not think that a jeweller holds himself out as a surgeon or professes that he is going to conduct the operation of piercing a lady's ears by means of aseptic surgery, about which it is not to be supposed that he knows anything.

If a person wants to ensure that the operation of piercing her ears is going to be carried out with that proportion of skill and so forth that a Fellow of the Royal College of Surgeons would use, she must go to a surgeon. If she goes to a jeweller, she must expect that he will carry it out in the way that one would expect a jeweller to carry it out. One would expect that he would wash his instruments. One would expect that he would take some means of disinfecting his instrument, just in the same way as one knows that the ordinary layman, when he is going to use a needle to prick a blister or prick a little gathering on a finger, generally takes the precaution to put the needle in a flame, as I think Mr Couzens did. I accept the evidence of Mr Couzens as to what he says he did on this occasion—how he put his instrument in a flame before he left his shop, and how he washed his hands, and so forth. I think that he did. I see no reason to suppose that he is not telling me the absolute truth when he says what he did, and, as Dr Pritchard, who holds the very high qualification of a Fellow of the Royal College of Physicians, said, for all practical purposes that is enough. That is to say, for the ordinary every-day matters that would be regarded as enough. It is not a degree of surgical cleanliness, which is a very different thing from ordinary cleanliness. It is not the cleanliness which a doctor would insist upon, because, as I say, Mr Couzens is not a doctor. He was known not to be a doctor. One does not go to a jeweller to get one's ears attended to if one requires to have a doctor in attendance to do it. If one wants a doctor in attendance, one goes to his consulting room or one has him come to see one. I do not see any ground here for holding that Mr Couzens was negligent in the way in which he performed this operation. It might be better, and I think that it probably would, if he boiled his instrument beforehand at his place, or if he took a spirit lamp with him and boiled his instrument at the time, but in view of the medical evidence, the evidence of Dr Pritchard, which I accept, I see no ground for holding that Mr Couzens departed from the standard of care which you would expect that a man of his position and his training, being what he held himself out to be, was required to possess. Therefore, the charge of negligence fails.

Even if I am wrong in that, and even if another court were to take the view that a person who undertakes to pierce an ear is bound, although he holds himself out to be more than a jeweller, to take all the precautions that a trained surgeon would take, I am quite unable, on the evidence, to find that the abscess from which Mrs Philips suffered was due to any action of Mr Couzens. . . .

Judgment for the defendants

QUESTIONS

1.   What is the standard of care of a first aid volunteer? (See G. Ll. H. Griffiths (1990) 53 MLR 255.)
2.   Should the standard of care in a prison hospital match that of a psychiatric hospital outside prison? (See *Knight v Home Office* [1990] 3 All ER 237.) What about a prison hospital matching the standard of ante-natal care elsewhere? (See *Brooks v Home Office* (1999) 48 BMLR 109.)

NOTES

1.   In relation to the position of skilled defendants, see the oft-quoted test in *Bolam v Friern Hospital Management Committee* [1957] 2 All ER 118, [1957] 1 WLR 582, noted p. 326, post, that 'the test is the standard of the ordinary skilled man exercising and professing to have that special skill'. Note that a person who holds himself out as possessing a

particular skill or specialism will be judged by reference to the objective standard of a reasonably competent person exercising that specific skill or specialism: see *Shakoor v Situ (t/a Eternal Health Co)* [2000] 4 All ER 181, where a practitioner of Chinese herbal medicine was held to the standard of an ordinarily skilled practitioner in that particular field. (Note also that in *Shakoor*, the ordinary skilled practitioner was treated as adhering to standard UK practice in that field.) In *Vowles v Evans* [2003] 1 WLR 1607, [2003] EWCA Civ 318, a rugby union referee who had undertaken an intensive refereeing course and been listed as suitable for refereeing higher-quality games was held to the standard of care that should be expected from a referee with his qualifications, even if the type of game in question was periodically refereed by less qualified individuals and he had volunteered to serve as referee for this particular game: the standard of care that was applied by the Court of Appeal in assessing his actions was that to be expected from a specialist of his training and experience.

2. The following warning delivered by Denning LJ in *Roe v Minister of Health* [1954] 2 QB 66, [1954] 2 All ER 131 should be borne in mind. He said (at p. 137):

> It is so easy to be wise after the event and to condemn as negligence that which was only a misadventure. We ought always to be on our guard against it, especially in cases against hospitals and doctors. Medical science has conferred great benefits on mankind, but these benefits are attended by considerable risks. Every surgical operation is attended by risks. We cannot take the benefits without taking the risks. Every advance in technique is also attended by risks. Doctors, like the rest of us, have to learn by experience; and experience often teaches in a hard way. Something goes wrong and shows up a weakness, and then it is put right. ... We must not look at the 1947 accident with 1954 spectacles.

On the position of medical practitioners, see further *Whitehouse v Jordan* [1981] 1 All ER 267, [1981] 1 WLR 246; *Maynard v West Midlands Regional Area Health Authority* [1985] 1 All ER 635, [1984] 1 WLR 634; *Sidaway v Board of Governors of the Bethlem Royal Hospital and the Maudsley Hospital* [1985] AC 871, [1985] 1 All ER 643 (p. 329, post); *Bolitho v City and Hackney Health Authority* [1998] AC 232, [1997] 4 All ER 771 (p. 326, post). Note that *Bolitho* established the important principle that the final determination of what was to be considered reasonable skilled practice in the medical field lies with the courts, who before accepting that a particular standard medical practice is reasonable have to be satisfied that the standard professional practice in question rests on a 'logical basis' and is 'defensible': see Lord Browne-Wilkinson, [1998] AC 232, at 241–242. Nevertheless, it should be noted that Lord Browne-Wilkinson in the same case also noted that 'it will very seldom be right for a judge to reach the conclusion that views genuinely held by a competent medical expert are unreasonable' [1998] AC 232, at 243. See p. 328, post.

3. When will a person be defined as a professional, so as to benefit from the *Bolam* test? In *M v Newham London Borough Council* [1995] 2 AC 633 at 666, Sir Thomas Bingham MR said:

> Those who engage professionally in social work bring to their task skill and expertise, the product partly of training and partly of experience, which ordinary uninstructed members of the public are bound to lack. I have no doubt that they should be regarded as members of a skilled profession. Their task is one of immense difficulty, and frequently they are exposed to unjust criticism; but both those things may, to a greater or lesser extent, be said of other professionals also.

These observations were approved by Lord Slynn in *Barrett v Enfield London Borough Council* [2001] 2 AC 550, [1999] 3 All ER 193 (p. 95, ante) and applied by the Court of

Appeal in *Carty v Croydon London Borough Council* [2005] 2 All ER 517, [2005] EWCA Civ 19 to distinguish between local authority education officers, who were deemed to be exercising professional skills, and 'ordinary' civil servants. In *Adams v Rhymney Valley District Council* [2000] 39 EG 144, the majority of the Court of Appeal took the view that the *Bolam* test applied to the exercise of professional skills even where a defendant exercising these skills lacked the relevant professional qualification and where there was an absence of evidence that close consideration had been given to the application of these skills in the relevant context. (However, note Sedley LJ's dissent in this case.)

4.   In *Luxmoore-May v Messenger May Baverstock (a firm)* [1990] 1 All ER 1067, at 1075–1076, the *Bolam* approach to setting (and controlling) the standards of care to be expected from members of the medical profession was applied in the context of a firm of provincial auctioneers and valuers. A similar approach was adopted towards the standard of care expected from social care workers, educational psychologists, and education officers working in the public sector, who are classified as professions exercising specialist skills: see *Phelps v Hillingdon London Borough Council* [2001] 2 AC 619, [2000] 4 All ER 504 (p. 99, ante). Note that outside of the medical context, some decisions evidence a certain reluctance to permitting defendants to argue that they acted reasonably in following generally established practice in their field of expertise: see *Lloyds Bank v Savory* [1933] AC 201; *Edward Wong Finance Co Ltd v Johnson Stokes & Master* [1984] AC 296. However, in *Carty v Croydon London Borough Council*, the Court of Appeal took the view that the existence of negligence should not be easily inferred where standard professional practice and procedures have been followed. Similarly, in *Architects of Wine Ltd v Barclays Bank Plc* [2007] EWCA Civ 239, the Court of Appeal considered that current banking practice was highly relevant to determining the standard of care to be applied to bankers exercising their specialist skills: *Lloyds Bank v Savory* was distinguished.

5.   There may of course be specialities within a particular profession. In *Maynard West Midlands Regional Area Health Authority* [1985] 1 All ER 635 it was stated (at p. 638) that 'a doctor who professes to exercise a special skill must exercise the ordinary skill of his speciality', and see *Sidaway* [1985] AC 871, [1985] 1 All ER 643, and also *Wilsher v Essex Area Health Authority* [1987] QB 730, [1986] 3 All ER 801, noted p. 311, post. Is the position of someone who is more knowledgeable than other professionals within his field affected by this greater knowledge? In *Wimpey Construction UK Ltd v D V Poole* [1984] 2 Lloyd's Rep 499, Webster J stated that:

The second gloss which [counsel for the claimant] sought to put upon the [reasonable man] test was that it is the duty of a professional man to exercise reasonable skill and care in the light of his actual knowledge and that the question whether he exercised reasonable care cannot be answered by reference to a lesser degree of knowledge than he had, on the grounds that the ordinary competent practitioner would only have had that lesser degree of knowledge. I accept [this] submission; but I do not regard it as a gloss upon the test of negligence as applied to a professional man. As it seems to me that test is only to be applied where the professional man causes damage because he lacks some knowledge or awareness. The test establishes the degree of knowledge or awareness which he ought to have in that context. Where, however, a professional man has knowledge, and acts or fails to act in way which, having that knowledge he ought reasonably to foresee would cause damage, then, if the other aspects of duty are present, he would be liable in negligence by virtue of the direct application of Lord Atkins' original test in *Donoghue v Stevenson*.

This statement was applied by Kirkham J in *Sandhu Menswear Company Ltd v Woolworths Plc* [2006] EWHC 1299 (TCC). On the position within the solicitors' profession, see the views expressed in *Duchess of Argyll v Beuselinck* [1972] 2 Lloyd's

Rep 172, at 183, and the decision in *Matrix-Securities Ltd v Theodore Goddard* [1998] PNLR 290. Note also Sir John Donaldson MR's dicta in *Condon v Basi* [1985] 2 All ER 453, at 454, that 'there will of course be a higher degree of care required of a player in a First Division football match than of a player in a local league football match'. See however A. H. Hudson's comments (1986) 102 LQR 11 at 12 on this dicta and the need for professionals pushing the boundary of their profession's skills to have the chance to fail. See also the reservations expressed as to Sir John Donaldson's view by C. Gearty [1985] CLJ 371 and by Drake J in the unreported case of *Elliott v Saunders* in 1994, which are set out by E. Grayson (1994) NLJ 1094. Can any guidance on this question be adopted from the approach of the Court of Appeal in *Smolden v Whitworth & Nolan* [1997] PIQR P133 at P139 and in *Vowles v Evans*? Note that this issue of whether 'superior' professionals should be held to a superior level of care can usually be circumvented on the basis that the professional in question will be held to the standard of care that he held himself out as exercising when engaging to undertake a task.

6.   Where professional skill is not being exercised, then the *Bolam* test will not be applied and the standard approach set out in *Bolton v Stone* and *The Wagon Mound (No. 2)* will be applied. The Court of Appeal took this view in *Gold v Haringey Health Authority* [1988] 1 QB 481: see also *J.D. Williams v Michael Hyde & Associates Ltd* [2000] Lloyd's Rep PN 823; *Royal Brompton Hospital National Health Service Trust v Hammond* [2002] EWHC 2037 (TCC). Note also the dissenting opinion by Sedley LJ in *Adams v Rhymney Valley District Council* (2000) 39 EG 144.

■ Nettleship v Weston
Court of Appeal [1971] 3 All ER 581

The plaintiff agreed to teach the defendant to drive in the defendant's husband's car after he had been correctly told, in response to a remark of his about the insurance position, that he was covered as a passenger by the fully comprehensive insurance if there was an accident. During the third lesson he in fact assisted her by moving the gear lever, applying the hand brake and occasionally helping with the steering. In the course of that lesson, they made a slow left turn after having stopped at a halt sign. However, the defendant did not straighten out the wheel and panicked. Although the plaintiff got hold of the hand brake with one hand and tried to get hold of the steering wheel with the other hand so as to correct it, the car hit a lamp standard. The plaintiff's left knee-cap was broken and he appealed against the dismissal of his claim for damages from the defendant who had been convicted of driving without due care and attention.

MEGAW LJ: . . .
The important question of principle which arises is whether, because of Mr Nettleship's knowledge that Mrs Weston was not an experienced driver, the standard of care which was owed to him by her was lower than would otherwise have been the case.

In *Insurance Comr v Joyce*,[19] Dixon J stated persuasively the view that there is, or may be, a 'particular relation' between the driver of a vehicle and his passenger resulting in a variation of the standard of duty owed by the driver. . . . He summarised the same principle in these words:[20]

'It appears to me that the circumstances in which the defendant accepts the plaintiff as a passenger and in which the plaintiff accepts the accommodation in the conveyance should determine the measure of duty . . .'

---

[19] (1948) 77 CLR 39 at 56, 60.   [20] (1948) 77 CLR at p. 59.

Theoretically, the principle as thus expounded is attractive. But, with very great respect, I venture to think that the theoretical attraction should yield to practical considerations.

As I see it, if this doctrine of varying standards were to be accepted as part of the law on these facts, it could not logically be confined to the duty of care owed by learner-drivers. There is no reason, in logic, why it should not operate in a much wider sphere. The disadvantages of the resulting unpredictability, uncertainty and, indeed, impossibility of arriving at fair and consistent decisions outweigh the advantages. The certainty of a general standard is preferable to the vagaries of a fluctuating standard.

As a first example of what is involved, consider the converse case: the standard of care (including skill) owed not by the driver to the passenger, but by the passenger-instructor to the learner-driver. Surely the same principle of varying standards, if it is a good principle, must be available also to the passenger, if he is sued by the driver for alleged breach of the duty of care in supervising the learner-driver. On this doctrine, the standard of care, or skill, owed by the instructor, vis-à-vis the driver, may vary according to the knowledge which the learner-driver had, at some moment of time, as to the skill and experience of the particular instructor. Indeed, if logic is to prevail, it would not necessarily be the knowledge of the driver which would be the criterion. It would be the expectation which the driver reasonably entertained of the instructor's skill and experience, if that reasonable expectation were greater than the actuality. Thus, if the learner-driver knew that the instructor had never tried his hand previously even at amateur instructing, or if, as may be the present case, the driver knew that the instructor's experience was confined to two cases of amateur instructing some years previously, there would, under this doctrine, surely be a lower standard than if the driver knew or reasonably supposed that the instructor was a professional or that he had had substantial experience in the recent past. But what that standard would be, and how it would or should be assessed, I know not. For one has thus cut oneself adrift from the standard of the competent and experienced instructor, which up to now the law has required without regard to the particular personal skill, experience, physical characteristics or temperament of the individual instructor, and without regard to a third party's knowledge or assessment of those qualities or characteristics.

Again, when one considers the requisite standard of care of the learner-driver, if this doctrine were to apply, would not logic irresistibly demand that there should be something more than a mere, single, conventional, standard applicable to anyone who falls into the category of learner-driver, i.e. of anyone who has not yet qualified for (or perhaps obtained) a full licence? That standard itself would necessarily vary over a wide range, not merely with the actual progress of the learner, but also with the passenger's knowledge of that progress; or, rather, if the passenger has in fact over-estimated the driver's progress, it would vary with the passenger's reasonable assessment of that progress at the relevant time. The relevant time would not necessarily be the moment of the accident.

The question, what is the relevant time? would itself have to be resolved by reference to some principle. The instructor's reasonable assessment of the skill and competence of the driver (and also the driver's assessment of the instructor's skill and competence) might alter drastically between the start of the first lesson and the start of a later lesson, or even in the course of one particular spell of driving. I suppose the principle would have to be that the relevant time is the last moment when the plaintiff (whether instructor or driver) could reasonably have refused to continue as passenger or driver in the light of his then knowledge. That factor in itself would introduce yet another element of difficulty, uncertainty and, I believe, serious anomaly. I for my part, with all respect, do not think that our legal process could successfully or satisfactorily cope with the task of fairly assessing, or applying to the facts of a particular case, such varying standards, depending on such complex and elusive factors, including the assessment by the court, not merely of a particular person's actual skill or experience, but also of another person's knowledge or assessment of that skill or experience at a particular moment of time.

Again, if the principle of varying standards is to be accepted, why should it operate, in the field of driving motor vehicles, only up to the stage of the driver qualifying for a full licence? And why should it be limited to the quality of inexperience? If the passenger knows that his driver suffers from some relevant defect, physical or temperamental, which could reasonably be expected to affect the quality of his driving, why should not the same doctrine of varying standards apply? Dixon J thought it should apply. Logically there can be no distinction. If the passenger knows that his driver, though holding a full driving licence, is blind in one eye or has the habit of taking corners too fast, and if an accident happens which is attributable wholly or partly to that physical or that temperamental defect, why should not some lower standard apply vis-à-vis the fully informed passenger, if standards are to vary? Why should the doctrine, if it be part of the law, be limited to cases involving the driving of motor cars? Suppose that to the knowledge of the patient a young surgeon, whom the patient has chosen to operate on him, has only just qualified. If the operation goes wrong because of the surgeon's inexperience, is there a defence on the basis that the standard of skill and care was lower than the standard of a competent and experienced surgeon? Does the young, newly-qualified, solicitor owe a lower standard of skill and care, when the client chooses to instruct him with knowledge of his inexperience?

True, these last two examples may fall within the sphere of contract; and a contract may have express terms which deal with the question, or it may have implied terms. But in relationships such as are involved in this case, I see no good reason why a different term should be implied where there is a contract from the term which the law should attach where there is, or may be, no contract. Of course, there may be a difference—not because of any technical distinction between cases which fall within the law of tort and those which fall within the law of contract—but because the very factor or factors which create the contractual relationship may be relevant on the question of the implication of terms. ....

In my judgment, in cases such as the present it is preferable that there should be a reasonably certain and reasonably ascertainable standard of care, even if on occasion that may appear to work hardly against an inexperienced driver, or his insurers. The standard of care required by the law is the standard of the competent and experienced driver; and this is so, as defining the driver's duty towards a passenger who knows of his experience, as much as towards a member of the public outside the car; and as much in civil as in criminal proceedings.

It is not a valid argument against such a principle that it attributes tortious liability to one who may not be morally blameworthy. For tortious liability has in many cases ceased to be based on moral blameworthiness. For example, there is no doubt whatever that if Mrs Weston had knocked down a pedestrian on the pavement when the accident occurred, she would have been liable to the pedestrian. Yet so far as any moral blame is concerned, no different considerations would apply in respect of the pedestrian from those which apply in respect of Mr Nettleship....

[LORD DENNING MR adopted the view that the standard of care did not vary—it was that of the skilled, experienced and careful driver. SALMON LJ thought that the standard of care could vary, but that on the facts of this case the standard of the ordinary driver should be applied. LORD DENNING MR and SALMON LJ (MEGAW LJ dissenting on this point) accepted the apportionment of responsibility which had been made by the trial judge, and damages were reduced by one-half because of the plaintiff's contributory negligence.]

Appeal allowed.

QUESTION

Does the learner driver hold himself out as possessing the skill and experience required by this case in the light of the fact that 'L' plates must be displayed on the car? Why do the courts require him to attain the standard of 'the competent and experienced driver'?

NOTES

1. The judgments in *Nettleship v Weston* also discuss the defence of volenti non fit injuria. (See p. 449, post.)

2. In *Cook v Cook* (1986) 68 ALR 353, noted by S. Todd (1989) 105 LQR 24, the High Court of Australia was unconvinced by Megaw LJ's arguments in *Nettleship v Weston* concerning the practical disadvantages which he saw as arising from the adoption of Dixon J's approach in *Insurance Comr v Joyce* (1948) 77 CLR 39: see (1987) 68 ALR at pp. 359–360. Whilst accepting that normally the standard applicable to a driver would be that of the experienced and competent driver, in their view (at pp. 360–361) 'when special and exceptional circumstances clearly transform the relationship between a particular driver and a particular passenger into a special or different class or category of relationship ... the case will be one in which the duty of care owed by the particular driver to the particular passenger will be either expanded or confined by reference to the objective standard of skill or care which is reasonably to be expected of a driver to a passenger in the category of a case where that special or different relationship exists'. An example given of a lower standard of care was that owed by a pupil receiving his first driving lesson to a professional driving instructor. On the sort of issue raised in *Cook v Cook* (and indeed more generally in relation to this chapter), see R. Kidner (1991) 11 LS 1. However, note that the decision in *Cook v Cook* has subsequently been distinguished and confined to a narrow range of circumstances by the High Court of Australia: see *Joslyn v Berryman* (2003) 198 ALR 137.

3. It is perhaps worth underlining at this point that the relevant standard is one of reasonable care in all the circumstances. Thus when a police officer is driving a car in pursuit of another car the 'stressful circumstances' are to be taken into account: see *Marshall v Osmond* [1983] QB 1034, [1983] 2 All ER 225, in which the Court of Appeal held that there had been an error of judgment by the officer but that he had not been negligent. See also *Vowles v Evans* [2003] 1 WLR 1607, [2003] EWCA Civ 318, where the circumstances of the rugby game in which a referee took the relevant decisions at issue were taken into account. Also, note *Caldwell v Maguire*, [2002] PIQR P45, [2001] EWCA Civ 1054 where Tuckey LJ emphasised at [23] that 'there will be no liability for errors of judgment, oversights or lapses of which any participant might be guilty in the context of a fast-moving contest. Something more serious is required.'

4. When damage is suffered in the course of activity into which the claimant has entered voluntarily, the standard of care applied will also reflect the expectations and assumptions of a reasonable person participating in that activity. See *Blake v Galloway* [2004] 3 All ER 315, [2004] EWCA Civ 814, where the Court of Appeal took the view that where a defendant caused an injury to a claimant in the course of horseplay in which they were both participating, which was based upon some tacitly agreed shared understandings, the defendant would only be in breach of the duty of care owed by him to the claimant if his conduct amounted to recklessness or a very high degree of carelessness. See also *Condon v Basi* [1985] 2 All ER 453; *Caldwell v Maguire* [2002] PIQR P45, [2001] EWCA Civ 1054; *Wooldridge v Sumner* [1963] 2 QB 43, [1962] 2 All ER 978.

5. If a driver was in a state of automatism at the relevant time so that his actions were totally beyond his control, then he will not be liable to an injured person. Furthermore, if there is some impairment of consciousness of which the driver is unaware, he will not be liable if he has met the standard of a reasonably competent driver who was unaware of the fact or the possibility that he was subject to a condition adversely affecting his ability to drive: *Mansfield v Weetabix Ltd* [1998] 1 WLR 1263.

6. Should the fact that a junior hospital doctor is involved in the process of learning and acquiring experience in particular areas while actually performing his duties in those areas affect the standard of care? This point was raised in *Wilsher v Essex Area Health Authority* [1987] QB 730, [1986] 3 All ER 801, where Sir Nicolas Browne-Wilkinson V-C was of the opinion that, as liability was based on personal fault, then the standard should be that of a doctor with the qualifications and experience of the particular defendant. However, the majority view in the Court of Appeal was more objective. In particular, Mustill LJ saw the test as being the degree of care that could reasonably be required not from someone of the defendant's rank but from a holder of the defendant's post. (This matter was not discussed when the case went to the House of Lords, [1988] AC 1074, [1988] 1 All ER 871.) In a different context note *Smolden v Whitworth & Nolan* [1997] PIQR P133 at P139, where the Court of Appeal preferred the view that the level of skill required of a rugby referee was related to the function he was performing rather than his grade (although it did not matter on the facts of the case). However, on this particular point, see now *Vowles v Evans* [2003] 1 WLR 1607, [2003] EWCA Civ 318.

7. Even where odd jobs are done around the house, the courts are prepared to demand a certain level of skill from a defendant householder. In *Wells v Cooper* [1958] 2 QB 265, [1958] 2 All ER 527 where the defendant had fixed a handle to a door, it was held that he must keep to the standard of a reasonably competent carpenter.

(d) Infants

■ Mullins v Richards
Court of Appeal [1998] 1 All ER 920

HUTCHISON LJ (GIVING THE FIRST JUDGMENT AT THE INVITATION OF BUTLER-SLOSS LJ): ...
On 29 February 1988 at Perry Beeches Secondary School in Birmingham two 15-year-old schoolgirls, Teresa Jane Mullin and Heidi Richards, who were friends and were sitting side by side at their desk, were engaged in playing around, hitting each other's white plastic 30 cm rulers as though in a play sword fight, when one or other of the rulers snapped and a fragment of plastic entered Teresa's right eye with the very unhappy result that she lost all useful sight in that eye, something that must be a source, I am sure, of great distress to her and her family.

Teresa brought proceedings against Heidi and the Birmingham City Council, who were the education authority, alleging negligence. . . . My summary [of the facts] reflects the learned judge's unchallenged findings of fact as well as the case pleaded by Heidi in her defence. The judge dismissed the claim against the authority, holding that the mathematics teacher, Miss Osborne, whose class was coming to an end when the mishap occurred, had not been guilty of negligence and the plaintiff does not appeal against that decision. . . . However, the judge . . . concluded that [Teresa and Heidi] had [each] been guilty of negligence, that Teresa's injury was the foreseeable result and that, accordingly, her claim against Heidi succeeded subject to a reduction of 50% for contributory negligence.

From that decision Heidi now appeals to this court. . . .

So far as negligence is concerned, the relevant principles are well settled and I do not understand there to be any real difference between the views of counsel for the parties to this appeal. I would sum- marise the principles that govern liability in negligence in a case such as the present as follows. In order to succeed the plaintiff must show that the defendant did an act which it was reasonably foreseeable would cause injury to the plaintiff, that the relationship between the plaintiff and the defendant was such as to give rise to a duty of care, and that the act was one which caused injury to the plaintiff. In the present case, as it seems to me, no difficulty arose as to the second and third requirements because

Teresa and Heidi were plainly in a sufficiently proximate relationship to give rise to a duty of care and the causation of the injury is not an issue. The argument centres on foreseeability. The test of foreseeability is an objective one; but the fact that the first defendant was at the time a 15-year-old schoolgirl is not irrelevant. The question for the judge is not whether the actions of the defendant were such as an ordinarily prudent and reasonable adult in the defendant's situation would have realised gave rise to a risk of injury, it is whether an ordinarily prudent and reasonable 15-year-old schoolgirl in the defendant's situation would have realised as much. In that connection both counsel referred us to, and relied upon, the Australian decision in *McHale v Watson* (1966) 115 CLR 199 esp at 213–214 in the judgment of Kitto J. I cite a portion of the passage I have referred to, all of which was cited to us by Mr Lee on behalf of the appellant, and which Mr Stephens has adopted as epitomising the correct approach:

> 'The standard of care being objective, it is no answer for him [that is a child], any more than it is for an adult, to say that the harm he caused was due to his being abnormally slow-witted, quick-tempered, absent-minded or inexperienced. But it does not follow that he cannot rely in his defence upon a limitation upon the capacity for foresight or prudence, not as being personal to himself, but as being characteristic of humanity at his stage of development and in that sense normal. By doing so he appeals to a standard of ordinariness, to an objective and not a subjective standard.'

Mr Stephens also cited to us a passage in the judgment of Owen J (at 234):

> '... the standard by which his conduct is to be measured is not that to be expected of a reasonable adult but that reasonably to be expected of a child of the same age, intelligence and experience.'

I venture to question the word 'intelligence' in that sentence, but I understand Owen J to be making the same point essentially as was made by Kitto J. It is perhaps also material to have in mind the words of Salmon LJ in *Gough v Thorne* [1966] 3 All ER 398 at 400, [1966] 1 WLR 1387 at 1391, which is cited also by Mr Stephens, where he said:

> 'The question as to whether the plaintiff can be said to have been guilty of contributory negligence depends on whether any ordinary child of 13½ can be expected to have done any more than this child did. I say "any ordinary child". I do not mean a paragon of prudence, nor do I mean a scatter-brained child; but the ordinary girl of 13½.'

I need say no more about that principle as to the way in which age affects the assessment of negligence because counsel are agreed upon it and, despite the fact that we have been told that there has been a good deal of controversy in other jurisdictions and that there is no direct authority in this jurisdiction, the approach in *McHale v Watson* seems to me to have the advantage of obvious, indeed irrefutable, logic....

Applying those principles to the facts of the present case the central question to which this appeal gives rise is whether on the facts found by the judge and in the light of the evidence before him he was entitled to conclude that an ordinary, reasonable 15-year-old schoolgirl in the first defendant's position would have appreciated that by participating to the extent that she did in a play fight, involving the use of plastic rulers as though they were swords, gave rise to a risk of injury to the plaintiff of the same general kind as she sustained. In that connection I emphasise that a mere possibility is not enough as passages in the well-known case of *Bolton v Stone* [1951] 1 All ER 1078, [1951] AC 850, to which Mr Lee[1] helpfully referred us, make clear....at 1080, 1081 [1951] AC 850 at 857.

[Having considered the matter further, his Lordship concluded that there was 'no justification for attributing to the participants the foresight of any significant risk of the likelihood of injury' and rejected the view that either schoolgirl had been negligent.]

[SIR JOHN VINELOTT and BUTLER-SLOSS LJ delivered judgments in favour of allowing the appeal and in which they agreed with HUTCHISON LJ's judgment, and BUTLER-SLOSS LJ also agreed with SIR JOHN VINELOTT's judgment.]

Appeal allowed.

---

[1] Counsel for Heidi Richards.

QUESTIONS

1. In the light of Hutchison LJ's conclusion on the question of foresight, do you agree that a duty of care was owed on the facts of this case?
2. In the light of *Nettleship v Weston* [1971] 2 QB 691, [1971] 3 All ER 581 (p. 307, ante), what standard of skill and care would be required of a person aged seventeen who is driving a car? Would his age be taken into account?
3. Is there also a separate category of old age pensioners? (Compare *Daly v Liverpool Corpn* [1939] 2 All ER 142.)

NOTES

1. Prior to *Mullins v Richards* there had been a surprising dearth of direct English authority on the standard of care expected of infants though see, for example, *Watkins v Birmingham City Council* (1975) 126 NLJ 442. It may be, as McTiernan ACJ pointed out in *McHale v Watson* (1965–66) 115 CLR 199 at 204, that a child is not in general worth suing. As a result, the claimant who has been injured by a child's act might on occasion sue not the child but one of its parents (or the appropriate school authority) alleging negligence on their part, e.g. in not properly supervising the child's use of a firearm—see *Donaldson v McNiven* [1952] 2 All ER 691 (father found not negligent).
2. In *Mullins v Richards*, Butler-Sloss LJ referred with approval to a passage from Kitto J's judgment in *McHale v Watson* (1965–66) 115 CLR 199 at 213 containing, inter alia, the opinion that 'tribunals of fact may well give effect to different views as to the age at which normal adult foresight and prudence are reasonably to be expected in relation to particular sets of circumstances'. Compare *Williams v Humphrey* (1975) Times, 20 February, noted p. 724, post (injury suffered at a swimming pool: defendant who was nearly sixteen years old to be judged by the standard of an adult) with *Foskett v Mistry* [1984] RTR 1, where in the context of contributory negligence in a case in which the claimant had run out into the road, it was thought 'to be putting it a little too high to equate a sixteen and a half year old with a fully grown adult with respect to road safety'.
3. For consideration of contributory negligence and children, see p. 443, post.

2 APPLICATION OF THE STANDARD OF CARE

(a) The likelihood of the occurrence of injury

■ Bolton v Stone
p. 296, ante

■ The Wagon Mound (No 2)
p. 299, ante

■ Haley v London Electricity Board

House of Lords [1964] 3 All ER 185

The respondents had, under statutory power, made an excavation in the pavement. One of the precautions which they took was to leave, at one end of this excavation, a punner (a heavy weight attached to a long handle). The weighted end was on the pavement and the other end of the handle was lodged two feet high in some railings, so the handle was sloping between these two points. The appellant, who often walked along this stretch of the pavement to reach a bus stop, was blind but could avoid ordinary obstacles by the use of his white stick. He used the stick correctly, but missed the punner handle and tripped over it. When he fell, he banged his head on the pavement and as a result became deaf. The Court of Appeal, [1963] 3 All ER 1003, dismissed an appeal from the judgment of Marshall J, who had dismissed the appellant's action for damages. On appeal to the House of Lords:

LORD REID: . . . .

The trial judge held that what the respondents' men did gave adequate warning to ordinary people with good sight, and I am not disposed to disagree with that. . . .

On the other hand, if it was the duty of the respondents to have in mind the needs of blind or infirm pedestrians, I think that what they did was quite insufficient. Indeed the evidence shows that an obstacle attached to a heavy weight and only nine inches above the ground may well escape detection by a blind man's stick and is for him a trap rather than a warning. So the question for your lordships' decision is the nature and extend of the duty owed to pedestrians by persons who carry out operations on a city pavement. The respondents argue that they were only bound to have in mind or to safeguard ordinary able-bodied people and were under no obligation to give particular consideration to the blind or infirm. If that is right, it means that a blind or infirm person, who goes out alone goes at his peril. He may meet obstacles which are a danger to him, but not to those with good sight, because no one is under any obligation to remove or protect them; and if such an obstacle causes him injury he must suffer the damage in silence.

I could understand the respondents' contention if it was based on an argument that it was not reasonably foreseeable that a blind person might pass along that pavement on that day; or that, although foreseeable, the chance of a blind man coming there was so small and the difficulty of affording protection to him so great that it would have been in the circumstances unreasonable to afford that protection. Those are well recognised grounds of defence; but in my judgment neither is open to the respondents in this case.

In deciding what is reasonably foreseeable one must have regard to common knowledge. We are all accustomed to meeting blind people walking alone with their white sticks on city pavements. No doubt there are many places open to the public where for one reason or another one would be surprised to see a blind person walking alone, but a city pavement is not one of them; and a residential street cannot be different from any other. The blind people whom we meet must live somewhere, and most of them probably left their homes unaccompanied. It may seem surprising that blind people can avoid ordinary obstacles so well as they do, but we must take account of the facts. There is evidence in this case about the number of blind people in London and it appears from government publications that the proportion in the whole country is near one in five hundred. By no means all are sufficiently skilled or confident to venture out alone, but the number who habitually do so must be very large. I find it quite impossible to say that it is not reasonably foreseeable that a blind person may pass along a particular pavement on a particular day.

No question can arise in this case of any great difficulty in affording adequate protection for the blind. In considering what is adequate protection against one must have regard to common knowledge. One is entitled to expect of a blind person a high degree of skill and care because none but the most foolhardy would venture to go out alone without having that skill and exercising that care. We know that in fact blind people do safely avoid all ordinary obstacles on pavements; there can be no question of padding lamp posts as was suggested in one case.[2] A moment's reflection, however, shows that a low obstacle in an unusual place is a grave danger: on the other hand it is clear from the evidence in this case and also I think from common knowledge that quite a light fence some two feet high is an adequate warning. There would have been no difficulty in providing such a fence here. The evidence is that the Post Office always provide one, and that the respondents have similar fences which are often used. Indeed the evidence suggests that the only reason why there was no fence here was that the accident occurred before the necessary fences had arrived. So, if the respondents are to succeed, it can only be on the ground that there was no duty to do more than safeguard ordinary able-bodied people. . . .

I can see no justification for laying down any hard and fast rule limiting the classes of persons for whom those interfering with a pavement must make provision. It is said that it is impossible to tell what precautions will be adequate to protect all kinds of infirm pedestrians or that taking such precautions would be unreasonably difficult or expensive. I think that such fears are exaggerated, and it is worth recollecting that when the courts sought to lay down specific rules as to the duties of occupiers the law became so unsatisfactory that Parliament had to step in and pass the Occupiers Liability Act 1957. It appears to me that the ordinary principles of the common law must apply in streets as well as elsewhere, and that fundamentally they depend on what a reasonable man, careful of his neighbour's safety, would do having the knowledge which a reasonable man in the position of the defendant must be deemed to have. I agree with the statement of law at the end of the speech of Lord Sumner in *Glasgow Corpn v Taylor*[3]—

> 'a measure of care appropriate to the inability or disability of those who are immature or feeble in mind or body is due from others who know of, or ought to anticipate, the presence of such persons within the scope and hazard of their own operations.'

I would therefore allow this appeal. The assessment of damages has been deferred and the case must be remitted for such assessment.

LORD MORTON OF HENRYTON: . . .

There is no dispute as to the facts, and only two questions arise for decision—first, what is the duty owed by those who engage on operations on the pavement of a highway and, secondly, was that duty discharged in the present case.

My lords, I would answer the first question as follows. It is their duty to take reasonable care not to act in a way likely to endanger other persons who may reasonably be expected to walk along the pavement. That duty is owed to blind persons if the operators foresee or ought to have foreseen that blind persons may walk along the pavement and is in no way different from the duty owed to persons with sight, though the carrying out of the duty may involve extra precautions in the case of blind pedestrians. I think that everyone living in greater London must have seen blind persons walking slowly along on the pavement and waving a white stick in front of them, so as to touch any obstruction which may be in their way, and I think that the respondents' workmen ought to have foreseen that a blind person might well come along the pavement in question.

I have not found it easy to answer the second question, but I have come to the conclusion that the workmen failed adequately to discharge the duty which I have stated, though I would accept the finding of the learned trial judge that 'what the [respondents] did was adequate to give reasonable and proper warning to normal pedestrians'. . . .

I would allow the appeal. Counsel for the respondents submitted that a decision against them would have very far-reaching consequences and would make it necessary for persons working in any public place to take elaborate and extreme precautions to prevent blind persons from suffering injury. My lords, I do not think that the consequences would be so serious as counsel suggests, bearing in mind, first, that there are many places to which one would not reasonably expect a blind person to go unaccompanied and, secondly, that workmen are entitled to assume that such a person will take responsible

---

[2] See *M'Kibbin v Glasgow City Corpn* 1920 SC 590 at 598.
[3] [1922] 1 AC 44 at 67, [1921] All ER Rep 1 at 13.

care to protect himself, for example by using a stick in order to ascertain if there is anything in his way and by stopping if his stick touches any object.

[LORD EVERSHED, LORD HODSON, and LORD GUEST delivered speeches in favour of allowing the appeal.]

Appeal allowed.

NOTE

In addition to the protection that the decision in *Haley* affords to blind persons, s. 1 of the Disabled Persons Act 1981 requires a highway authority, local authority or anyone exercising statutory power to carry out work on a highway to have regard to the needs of disabled or blind persons where the work may impede their mobility. In particular, the needs of blind persons to have openings in the street properly protected must be taken into account. See also the duty to promote equality of opportunities for persons with disabilities imposed upon public authorities by s. 4 of the Disability Discrimination Act 2005, which inserted a new s. 49A into the Disability Discrimination Act 1995.

(b) The gravity of the injury which may be suffered

■ Paris v Stepney Borough Council
House of Lords [1951] 1 All ER 42

LORD SIMONDS: . . .
My Lords, this is an appeal from an order of the Court of Appeal[4] setting aside a judgment of Lynskey J, in favour of the appellant for £5,250 damages and costs. On 13 May 1942, the appellant entered the service of the respondents as a garage hand in their cleansing department. He was then for all practical purposes blind in his left eye, having suffered serious injury in May 1941, as the result of enemy action, but this fact was not known to the respondents at that time. On or about 19 July 1946, he was medically examined with a view to his becoming a member of the permanent staff and joining the superannuation scheme, and on 22 July 1946, the medical officer reported to a Mr Boden, the respondents' public cleansing officer, that the appellant was not fit on account of his disablement to join the superannuation scheme. On 16 May 1947, he was given two weeks' notice expiring on 30 May 1947, to terminate his employment. I will assume that at this date the respondents had notice of his physical disability, including the blindness of his left eye. On 28 May 1947, the accident occurred which gave rise to the present action. The appellant was engaged in dismantling the chassis of a gulley cleaner, a type of vehicle generally used by local authorities for the cleansing and flushing of street gulleys. The vehicle had been raised about four and a half feet from the garage floor by means of a ramp. The appellant had to remove a U-bolt holding the springs of an axle, and, to release it, he hit the U-bolt with a steel hammer. As the result of his doing so a piece of metal flew off and entered his right eye with the disastrous consequence that he lost the sight of it altogether. On 8 August 1947, he commenced his action against the respondents claiming damages for their negligence and breach of statutory duty. The respondents put in a defence denying negligence and raising an alternative plea of contributory negligence which has not been pursued. Nor has the appellant pursued his claim for breach of statutory duty. The single question is whether the appellant proved the negligence of the respondents, a question answered in the affirmative by Lynskey J, in the negative by the Court of Appeal.

What, then, was the negligence alleged by the appellant and denied by the respondents? It was that it was the duty of the respondents to supply the appellant with suitable goggles for the protection of

---

[4] [1950] 1 KB 320, [1949] 2 All ER 843.

his eyes which he was engaged in such work and to require him to use them....I will say at once that I do not dissent from the view that an employer owes a particular duty to each of his employees. His liability in tort arises from his failure to take reasonable care in regard to the particular employee and it is clear that, if so, all the circumstances relevant to that employee must be taken into consideration. I see no valid reason for excluding as irrelevant the gravity of the damage which the employee will suffer if an accident occurs, and with great respect to the judgments of the Court of Appeal I cannot accept the view, neatly summarised by Asquith LJ ([1949] 2 All ER 845), that the greater risk of injury is, but the risk of greater injury is not, a relevant circumstance. I find no authority for such a proposition nor does it appear to me to be founded on any logical principle....

LORD MORTON OF HENRYTON:...
My Lords, it cannot be doubted that there are occupations in which the possibility of an accident occurring to any workman is extremely remote, while there are other occupations in which there is constant risk of accident to the workmen. Similarly, there are occupations in which, if an accident occurs, it is likely to be of a trivial nature, while there are other occupations in which, if an accident occurs, the result to the workman may well be fatal. Whether one is considering the likelihood of an accident occurring, or the gravity of the consequences if an accident happens, there is in each case a gradually ascending scale between the two extremes which I have already mentioned. In considering generally the precautions which an employer ought to take for the protection of his workmen it must, in my view, be right to take into account both elements, the likelihood of an accident happening and the gravity of the consequences. I take as an example two occupations in which the risk of an accident taking place is exactly equal. If an accident does occur in the one occupation, the consequences to the workman will be comparatively trivial; if an accident occurs in the other occupation the consequences to the workman will be death or mutilation. Can it be said that the precautions which it is the duty of an employer to take for the safety of his workmen are exactly the same in each of these occupations? My Lords, that is not my view. I think that the more serious the damage which will happen if an accident occurs, the more thorough are the precautions which an employer must take. If I am right as to this general principle, I think it follows logically that if A and B, who are engaged on the same work, run precisely the same risk of an accident happening, but if the results of an accident will be more serious to A than to B, precautions which are adequate in the case of B may not be adequate in the case of A, and it is a duty of the employer to take such additional precautions for the safety of A as may be reasonable. The duty to take reasonable precautions against injury is one which is owed by the employer to every individual workman.

   In the present case it is submitted by counsel for the appellant that, although the appellant ran no greater risk of injury than the other workmen engaged in the maintenance work, he ran a risk of greater injury. Counsel points out that an accident to one eye might transform the appellant into a blind man, but not so serious as the results have been to the appellant. My Lords, the Court of Appeal thought that the one-eyed condition of the appellant, known to his employers, was wholly irrelevant in determining the question whether the employer did or did not take reasonable precautions to avoid an accident of this kind. I do not agree. Applying the general principle which I have endeavoured to state, I agree with your Lordships and with Lynskey J, that the condition of the appellant was a relevant fact to be taken into account....

[LORD OAKSEY, LORD MACDERMOTT, and LORD NORMAND delivered speeches to a similar effect on this point. However, on the facts of the case, it was only by a majority (LORD SIMONDS and LORD MORTON OF HENRYTON dissenting) that the judgment of LYNSKEY J on liability was restored.]

Appeal allowed.

NOTES

1. In *Withers v Perry Chain Co Ltd* [1961] 3 All ER 676, [1961] 1 WLR 1314, the claimant had had an attack of dermatitis from a reaction to grease used in her job. When she

returned to work, the defendants put her on work which in their opinion was the best available for her in the circumstances, but she suffered further attacks and sued her employers, alleging negligence in employing her on work which they ought to have known could cause (or exacerbate) dermatitis. Sellers LJ stated (at p. 680) that the duty of the defendants 'was to take all reasonable care for the plaintiff in the employment in which she was engaged, including, of course, a duty to have regard to the fact that she had had dermatitis previously', but it was held that no breach of duty had been established in the case. Devlin LJ said (also at p. 680):

> It may be also (on the principle of *Paris v Stepney Borough Council*) that when the susceptibility of an employee to dermatitis is known there is a duty on the employer to take extra or special precautions to protect such an employee. But it is not suggested that there were any extra or special precautions here which could have been taken.

In particular, the Court of Appeal ruled that the employer had not been negligent in refusing the employee permission to resume her work even though there was a risk that she would develop full-blown dermatitis. Devlin LJ said that '...there is no legal duty upon an employer to prevent an adult employee from doing work which he or she is willing to do...The relationship between employer and employee is not that of a schoolmaster and pupil' ([1961] 3 All ER 676 at 680). This '*Withers* principle' was approved by the Court of Appeal in *Hatton v Sutherland* [2002] 2 All ER 1 and by Lord Rodger in the House of Lords decision in *Barber v Somerset County* Council [2004] 2 All ER 385 at [30] (see note 3, post). However, in *Coxall v Goodyear Great Britain Ltd* [2003] 1 WLR 536, [2002] EWCA Civ 1010, the Court of Appeal considered that while the *Withers* principle 'was no less effective today than when it was first adumbrated' (Simon Brown LJ, [28]), there may be circumstances where the nature and magnitude of the risk might entail that an employer would be negligent in permitting an employee to undertake a particular form of work, even if the employee consented to run the risk in question.

2.   In *Walker v Northumberland County Council* [1995] 1 All ER 737, a social worker working for the defendant council sued the council in negligence in respect of two nervous breakdowns he had suffered as a result of intolerable stress and an excessive workload at work. Colman J held that the defendant was not liable in respect of the first nervous breakdown, since prior to that breakdown it was not reasonably foreseeable that the claimant's workload would give rise to a material risk of mental illness—there was nothing at that stage to indicate that he was any more susceptible than any other employee. However, the defendant was at fault in respect of the second nervous breakdown, since, on his return to work after the first breakdown, both the likelihood of another breakdown and its potential severity were known to be greater than for the average employee. Colman J concluded ([1995] 1 All ER 737 at 759) that, 'Having regard to the reasonably foreseeable size of the risk of repetition of Mr Walker's illness if his duties were not alleviated by effective additional assistance and to the reasonably foreseeable gravity of the mental breakdown which might result if nothing were done', the defendant was in breach of duty.

3.   This general approach was endorsed in the important decisions of the Court of Appeal in *Hatton v Sutherland* [2002] 2 All ER 1, [2002] EWCA Civ 76 and the subsequent House of Lords determination in *Barber v Somerset County Council* [2004] 2 All ER 385, [2004] UKHL 13, which established the guiding principles that should apply in

determining when employers have been negligent in situations where employees have suffered stress-related psychiatric illnesses. In *Hatton v Sutherland* Hale LJ set out a series of 'practical propositions' applicable in cases where an employee alleges that an employer's negligence resulted in psychiatric illness arising from stress. On the question of when an employer would be held to have breached his duty of care, she took the following approach ([2002] 2 All ER 1 at 15–16):

■ Hatton v Sutherland
Court of Appeal [2002] 2 All ER 1

HALE LJ:

[33] It is essential, therefore, once the risk of harm to health from stresses in the workplace is foreseeable, to consider whether and in what respect the employer has broken that duty. There may be a temptation, having concluded that some harm was foreseeable and that harm of that kind has taken place, to go on to conclude that the employer was in breach of his duty of care in failing to prevent that harm (and that that breach of duty caused the harm). But *in every case it is necessary to consider what the employer not only could but should have done.* We are not here concerned with such comparatively simple things as gloves, goggles, earmuffs or non-slip flooring. Many steps might be suggested: giving the employee a sabbatical; transferring him to other work; redistributing the work; giving him some extra help for a while; arranging treatment or counselling; providing buddying or mentoring schemes to encourage confidence; and much more. But in all of these suggestions it will be necessary to consider how reasonable it is to expect the employer to do this, either in general or in particular: *the size and scope of its operation will be relevant to this, as will its resources, whether in the public or private sector, and the other demands placed upon it. Among those other demands are the interests of other employees in the workplace.* It may not be reasonable to expect the employer to rearrange the work for the sake of one employee in a way which prejudices the others. As we have already said, an employer who tries to balance all these interests by offering confidential help to employees who fear that they may be suffering harmful levels of stress is unlikely to be found in breach of duty: except where he has been placing totally unreasonable demands upon an individual in circumstances where the risk of harm was clear.

[34] Moreover, *the employer can only reasonably be expected to take steps which are likely to do some good.* This is a matter on which the court is likely to require expert evidence. In many of these cases it will be very hard to know what would have done some let alone enough good. In some cases the only effective way of safeguarding the employee would be to dismiss or demote him. There may be no other work at the same level of pay which it is reasonable to expect the employer to offer him. *In principle the law should not be saying to an employer that it is his duty to sack an employee who wants to go on working for him for the employer's own good* . . .

NOTE

While reversing the finding of the Court of Appeal in the specific case at issue (Lord Scott dissenting on this issue), the House of Lords in *Barber v Somerset County Council* [2004] 2 All ER 385, [2004] UKHL 13 endorsed this approach in general terms, while emphasising that this guidance should not be treated as having statutory force. (Note Lord Scott's view in his dissenting opinion that appellate courts should be prepared to review the standard of care analysis applied by first instance courts and to review their consequent findings of facts if necessary: [2004] 2 All ER 385 at [12]–[15].)

(c) The cost and practicability of measures necessary to overcome the risk

■ Latimer v AEC Ltd
House of Lords [1953] 2 All ER 449

The respondents' large factory was flooded by an unusually heavy rainstorm and the water mixed with an oily liquid usually collected in channels in the floor. This mixture when it drained away left a film, making the surface very slippery. Sawdust was then spread on the floor but there was insufficient to cover all the area, even though the respondents had had enough there to meet any situation they could have been expected to foresee. The appellant, who was working in the factory on the night shift, slipped on a part of the floor which had not had sawdust applied to it, and a barrel, which he was putting on to a trolley, rolled on to and injured his ankle. Pilcher J, [1952] 1 All ER 443, gave judgment for the appellant against the respondents in negligence, but the Court of Appeal, [1952] 1 All ER 1302, reversed this decision. On appeal to the House of Lords:

LORD TUCKER: . . .

In the present case, the respondents were faced with an unprecedented situation following a phenomenal rain storm. They set forty men to work on cleaning up the factory when the flood subsided and used all the available supply of sawdust, which was approximately three tons. The judge has found that they took every step which could reasonably have been taken to deal with the conditions which prevailed before the night shift came on duty, and he has negatived every specific allegation of negligence as pleaded, but he has held the respondents liable because they did not close down the factory, or the part of the factory where the accident occurred, before the commencement of the night shift. I do not question that such a drastic step may be required on the part of a reasonably prudent employer if the peril to his employees is sufficiently grave, and to this extent it must always be a question of degree, but, in my view, there was no evidence in the present case which could justify a finding of negligence for failure on the part of the respondents to take this step. This question was never canvassed in evidence, or was sufficient evidence given as to the condition of the factory as a whole to enable a satisfactory conclusion to be reached. The learned judge seems to have accepted the reasoning of counsel for the appellant to the effect that the floor was slippery, that slipperiness is a potential danger, that the respondents must be taken to have been aware of this, that in the circumstances nothing could have been done to remedy the slipperiness, that the respondents allowed work to proceed, that an accident due to slipperiness occurred, and that the respondents are, therefore, liable.

This is not the correct approach. The problem is perfectly simple. The only question was: Has it been proved that the floor was so slippery that, remedial steps not being possible, a reasonably prudent employer would have closed down the factory rather than allow his employees to run the risks involved in continuing work? The learned judge does not seem to me to have posed this question to himself, nor was there sufficient evidence before him to have justified an affirmative answer. The absence of any evidence that anyone in the factory during the afternoon or night shift, other than the appellant, slipped, or experienced any difficulty, or that any complaint was made by or on behalf of the workers, all points to the conclusion that the danger was, in fact, not such as to impose on a reasonable employer the obligation placed on the respondents by the trial judge. I agree that the appeal be dismissed.

[On the question of common law negligence, LORD REID agreed with LORD TUCKER and LORD PORTER, LORD OAKSEY, and LORD ASQUITH OF BISHOPSTONE delivered speeches in favour of dismissing the appeal. A claim for breach of statutory duty was rejected.]

Appeal dismissed.

NOTE

1. Although the standard of care is certainly an objective one, in *Walker v Northumberland County Council* [1995] 1 All ER 737, noted p. 318, ante, Colman J stated (at p. 751) that the resources and facilities at the defendant's disposal had to be taken into account when considering the practicability of remedial measures. However, it should be remembered that the defendant in that case was a public authority (on which see further chap. 3) and Colman J went on to emphasise this point. He said (at p. 759), 'there can be no basis for treating the public body differently *in principle* from any other commercial employer, although there would have to be taken into account considerations such as budgetary constraints and perhaps lack of flexibility of decision-taking which might not arise with a commercial employer'. This approach was approved by Hale LJ in *Sussex Ambulance NHS Trust v King* [2002] ICR 1413, [2002] EWCA Civ 953, at [23] (note at p. 322, post). In *Barber v Somerset County Council* [2004] 2 All ER 385, Lord Rodger at [24] considered that government education and funding policies, as well as pay and working conditions fixed through national negotiations between education authorities and trade unions, could be 'relevant factors' in assessing whether a breach of duty had occurred.

2. To what extent should it be relevant to the issue of breach of duty when a public body is sued that 'resources available for the public service are limited and that the allocation of resources is a matter for Parliament' (*Knight v Home Office* [1990] 3 All ER 237 at 243)? (Consider M. A. Jones, *Medical Negligence* 3rd edn (London, 2007), pp. 345–354; A. Grubb, *Principles of Medical Law* 2nd edn (Oxford, 2004), pp. 541–542.) Note also Pill LJ's comments in *Knight* about the potential problems of a 'resources' defence. See also *Sussex Ambulance NHS Trust v King*, noted at p. 322, post.

(d) The purpose of the defendant's acts

■ Daborn v Bath Tramways Motor Co Ltd and T. Smithey
Court of Appeal [1946] 2 All ER 333

The plaintiff was driving an ambulance with a left-hand drive. A notice on the back of the vehicle stated 'Caution—Left hand drive—No signals'. The ambulance was shut in at the back, but, by using a mirror on the left hand side, the plaintiff could see vehicles some yards behind her. She gave evidence that she signalled with her left hand that she was going to make a right turn. However, as the ambulance was turning right, it was hit by a bus, and the plaintiff suffered grave injuries when she was thrown out of the ambulance as a result of the collision. In an unsuccessful appeal by the defendants from a decision of Croom-Johnson J awarding the plaintiff damages, it was argued that the plaintiff had been negligent.

ASQUITH LJ: . . .

In determining whether a party is negligent, the standard of reasonable care is that which is reasonably to be demanded in the circumstances. A relevant circumstance to take into account may be the importance of the end to be served by behaving in this way or in that. As has often been pointed out, if all the trains in this country were restricted to a speed of 5 miles an hour, there would be fewer accidents, but our national life would be intolerably slowed down. The purpose to be served, if sufficiently important, justifies the assumption of abnormal risk. The relevance of this applied to the present case is this: during the war which was, at the material time, in progress, it was necessary for many highly important operations to be carried out by means of motor vehicles with left-hand drives, no others being available.

So far as this was the case, it was impossible for the drivers of such cars to give the warning signals which could otherwise be properly demanded of them. Meanwhile, it was essential that the ambulance service should be maintained. It seems to me, in those circumstances, it would be demanding too high and an unreasonable standard of care from the drivers of such cars to say to them: 'Either you must give signals which the structure of your vehicle renders impossible or you must not drive at all.' It was urged by counsel for the defendants that these alternatives were not exhaustive, since the driver of such a car should, before executing a turn, stop his car, move to the right-hand seat and look backwards to see if another car was attempting to overtake him and then start up again. Counsel for the plaintiff has satisfied me that such a procedure, besides involving possible delay, might be wholly ineffective. I think the plaintiff did all that in the circumstances could reasonably be required to do if you include in those circumstances, as I think you should: (i) the necessity in time of national emergency of employing all transport resources which were available, and (ii) the inherent limitations and incapacities of this particular form of transport. In considering whether reasonable care has been observed, one must balance the risk against the consequences of not assuming that risk, and in the present instance this calculation seems to me to work out in favour of the plaintiff. I agree... that this appeal should be dismissed.

[MORTON and TUCKER LJJ delivered judgments in favour of dismissing the appeal.]

NOTES

1. Attention might also be paid to *Watt v Hertfordshire County Council* [1954] 2 All ER 368, [1954] 1 WLR 835, where the claimant, a fireman, was in a team called out to an emergency. A jack was to be taken out as the call said that a woman was trapped under a heavy vehicle a few hundred yards away. There was a vehicle specially fitted to carry this jack, which weighed two or three hundredweight, but it was out on other service, and so the jack was lifted on to a lorry. Unfortunately the driver had to brake suddenly, and the claimant was injured when the jack, which stood on four small wheels, moved and caught his leg. It was held that the defendants, his employers, had not been negligent. Saving life and limb, Denning LJ said, justified a considerable risk being taken. He went on to state (at p. 371) that 'I quite agree that fire engines, ambulances and doctors' cars should not shoot past the traffic lights when they show a red light. That is because the risk is too great to warrant the incurring of the danger.' Would this view still prevail if the driver of a fire engine, seeing a man ahead of him in dire peril from a fire, had looked both ways before crossing the red light, but had collided with a car which had just come round a bend? (On an ambulance crossing a red light, see further *Griffith v Mersey Regional Ambulance* [1998] PIQR P34.)

2. In *Sussex Ambulance NHS Trust v King* [2002] ICR 1413, [2002] EWCA Civ 953, the claimant, an ambulance technician employed by the defendants, was injured while carrying a patient downstairs. In allowing the appeal against an award in favour of the claimant at first instance, Hale LJ emphasised that the risk of the activity and the potential harm to the claimant had to be balanced with other relevant considerations, such as the resource constraints on the defendants, in the sense of the difficulty that existed in accessing appropriate equipment quickly, and the demands imposed by their obligations towards their patients. While acknowledging Denning LJ's comments in *Watts*, she also noted that the ambulance services were under an obligation to respond to call-outs, and this had to be factored in the assessment of the standard of care. Buxton LJ agreed, but also commented on the approach adopted in *Watts*, at [44]–[46]:

   I agree that our case was not one of emergency in the extreme sense deployed in *Watt*, but it was a case where something had to be done, and to be done with reasonable despatch... Within the context of the available equipment there could be no criticism of the service for not doing what it could have done, because no other equipment was on the market. The case is in that respect stronger than *Watt*, where suitable equipment was available and in the possession of each brigade but, it was held reasonably, not provided to every station. It should also be emphasised that the problem facing the service in our case is not one of lack of *resources*. If that were the defence, it would be vulnerable to the criticism deployed by, for instance, Pill J in *Knight v Home Office* [1990] 3 All ER 237, and further explained in *Clerk & Lindsell*, § 7–182. Rather, the problem is the *impossibility* of performing the public duty in a way that reasonably ensures the safety of the men. That, in my view, brings the case well within the jurisprudence of *Watt*. . . .It is not open to this court, and certainly not open to it on the evidence in this case, to go behind *Watt*. The balance required by *Watt*, and for the reasons stated in that case, therefore has to come down against liability. But in another case, possibly in a higher tribunal, that conclusion might call for reassessment. . .

3. In *United States v Carroll Towing Co Inc* 159 F 2d 169 (1947) Learned Hand J set out a formula for deciding on negligence that encapsulates factors which have just been covered in Parts (A)–(D) ante. He stated (at p. 173) that 'if the probability be called P; the injury, L; and the burden, B; liability depends upon whether B is less than L multiplied by P: i.e., whether B < PL'. For discussion of this formula as part of the economic analysis of law see e.g. R. A. Posner (1972) 1 J Leg Stud 29 esp. at 32–33; *Tort Law: Cases and Economic Analysis* (Boston, 1982), esp. chap. 1; C. Veljanovski, *The Economics of Law: An Introductory Text* (London, 1990), pp. 64–72; Conaghan and Mansell, op cit, pp. 60–62; G. Keating (1996) 48 Stanford LR 311. However, for criticism of Richard Posner's analysis of *United States v Carroll Towing Co Inc* and the argument that the 'Learned Hand test' does not reflect the practice of US courts, see R. Wright, (2003) 4 Theoretical Inquiries in Law 145; B. Zipursky, (2007) 48 William and Mary LR 1999. For a restructuring of the Learned Hand test, see A. M. Feldman and J. Kim (2005) 7 Am Law Econ Rev 523. From your reading of the cases in this chapter, does the 'Learned Hand' formula reflect the approach of English courts? For a useful economic analysis suggesting that the standard of care required should be adjusted in different contexts to reflect the likelihood of different types of error, see B. Bhole (2007) 27 International Review of Law and Economics 154.

■ The Compensation Act 2006

1 Deterrent effect of potential liability
A court considering a claim in negligence or breach of statutory duty may, in determining whether the defendant should have taken particular steps to meet a standard of care (whether by taking precautions against a risk or otherwise), have regard to whether a requirement to take those steps might—

   (a) prevent a desirable activity from being undertaken at all, to a particular extent or in a particular way, or

   (b) discourage persons from undertaking functions in connection with a desirable activity.

QUESTIONS

1. Does s. 1 of the 2006 Act add anything to the existing common law position? Compare the approach taken by the Court of Appeal in *Daborn* (p. 321, ante), and the provisions of this section. Also compare s. 1 with the approach adopted by the House of Lords

in *Tomlinson v Congleton Borough Council* [2003] 3 All ER 1122, [2003] UKHL 47 (p. 573 post). See also *Hampstead Heath Winter Swimming Club v Corporation of London* [2005] EWHC 713. Will anything be gained by the insertion of s. 1 of the 2006 Act into law?

2.   What is a 'desirable activity'? Presumably providing an ambulance service or swimming ponds will qualify, but what about playing cricket? Could the defendants in *Latimer v AEC Ltd* [1953] 2 All ER 449 (p. 320, ante) have claimed that they were engaged in a 'desirable activity'?

NOTE

For the background to the 2006 Act, see p. 293, ante. The Explanatory Notes produced to accompany the Act (available at http://www.opsi.gov.uk/Acts/acts2006/en/ukpgaen_20060029_en_1) explain its purpose as follows:

> 10. This provision is intended to contribute to improving awareness of this aspect of the law; providing reassurance to the people and organisations who are concerned about possible litigation; and to ensuring that normal activities are not prevented because of the fear of litigation and excessively risk-averse behaviour.
>
> 11. This provision is not concerned with and does not alter the standard of care, nor the circumstances in which a duty to take that care will be owed. It is solely concerned with the court's assessment of what constitutes reasonable care in the case before it...

On this account of the intended impact of s. 1, it is not intended to change how the courts set about defining the required standard of care, but it is supposed a) to reassure the public, and b) to assist courts in assessing what constitutes reasonable care in a specific case. For criticism of the Act, see the comments made by David Howarth M.P., 447 H.C. Debs. (6th Series), cols. 488–491. See also K. Williams (2005) 155 *NLJ* 1938, and see further [2006] JPIL 347.

(e) Common practice

■ Morton v William Dixon Ltd
Court of Session 1909 SC 807

LORD DUNEDIN: ...
Where the negligence of the employer consists of what I may call a fault of omission, I think it is absolutely necessary that the proof of that fault of omission should be one of two kinds, either—to shew that the thing which he did not do was a thing which was commonly done by other persons in the like circumstances, or—to shew that it was a thing which was so obviously wanted that it would be folly in anyone to neglect to provide it. ...

NOTES

1.   This passage from Lord Dunedin's judgment has been cited and interpreted in several cases, on which see *Salmond & Heuston*, pp. 236–237, who state that the word 'folly' 'really...means no more than "imprudent" or "unreasonable"'.

2.   It should be noted, however, that a defendant can be held to have been negligent, even though there is evidence that he acted in accordance with common practice. (See e.g. *Cavanagh v Ulster Weaving Co Ltd* [1960] AC 145, [1959] 2 All ER 745;

J. Holyoak (1990) 10 LS 201.) On the other hand, a defendant is not necessarily negligent if he does not adopt a common practice. In *Brown v Rolls Royce Ltd* [1960] 1 All ER 577, [1960] 1 WLR 210, among the facts found by the court below (the Court of Session) were that the appellant contracted industrial dermatitis from contact with oil in his work, that, although there were ample washing facilities, barrier cream was not supplied by his employers (on the advice of their medical officer who was not at fault), and that its value in relation to dermatitis was the subject of strong differences of opinion amongst the medical profession. In addition, it had been found that barrier cream was commonly supplied by employers to men doing the sort of work in which the appellant was involved, but that it was not proved that it would stop them, or would probably have stopped him, contracting dermatitis. The House of Lords held that the employers were not at fault in failing to supply barrier cream. Lord Keith of Avonholm said (at p. 581):

A common practice in like circumstances not followed by an employer may no doubt be a weighty circumstance to be considered by judge or jury in deciding whether failure to comply with this practice, taken along with all the other material circumstances in the case, yields an inference of negligence on the part of the employers.

However, he added that the 'ultimate test is lack of reasonable care for the safety of the workman in all the circumstances of the case'. Note also Lord Denning's speech in which he stated (at p. 582):

If defenders do not follow the usual precautions, it raises a prima facie case against them in this sense, that it is evidence from which negligence *may* be inferred, but not in the sense that it *must* be inferred unless the contrary is proved. At the end of the day, the court has to ask itself whether the defenders were negligent or not.

3. Further consideration was given to the effect of a general practice in the context of employers' liability by Swanwick J in *Stokes v Guest, Keen and Nettlefold (Bolts and Nuts) Ltd* [1968] 1 WLR 1776. After referring to several authorities relating to employers' duty to workmen, he deduced the following principles (at p. 1783):

... that the overall test is still the conduct of the reasonable and prudent employer, taking positive thought for the safety of his workers in the light of what he knows or ought to know; where there is a recognised and general practice which has been followed for a substantial period in similar circumstances without mishap, he is entitled to follow it, unless in the light of common sense or newer knowledge it is clearly bad; but, where there is developing knowledge, he must keep reasonably abreast of it and not be too slow to apply it; and where he has in fact greater than average knowledge of the risks, he may be thereby obliged to take more than the average or standard precautions.

Is the last part of the quotation an encouragement to ignorance?

Swanwick J's principles were adopted (though added to) by Mustill J in *Thompson v Smiths Shiprepairers (North Shields) Ltd* [1984] QB 405, [1984] 1 All ER 881. He pointed out that there may be a situation where a particular practice is regularly followed in an industry but *not* 'without mishap'; the risk may have been 'an inescapable feature of the industry' and, if so, the employer is not liable (though in certain circumstances there will be a duty to warn (see *White v Holbrook Precision Castings Ltd* [1985] IRLR 215 at 218)). Mustill J went on to point out (at p. 889) that common practice in an industry is relevant (though not conclusive) on the issue of negligence, not only when the negligence is said to be constituted by a failure to take known precautions, 'but also where the omission involves an absence of initiative in seeking out knowledge of facts which are not in themselves obvious'. Although the employer 'must keep up to date ... the court must be slow to blame him for not ploughing a lone furrow'. Note that the majority of the House of Lords in *Barber v Somerset County* Council [2004] 2 All ER 385, [2004] UKHL 13 re-affirmed Swanwick J's approach in *Stokes* and applied it in the context of employee claims relating to psychiatric loss resulting from workplace-induced stress.

4. Adherence to good professional practice involves keeping abreast (within reasonable limits) of developments in the field and evolving standards, as well as applying accepted professional norms when developing experimental treatment: see *Hepworth v Kerr* [1995] 6 Med LR 139. If an event is sufficiently rare for there to be no common professional practices in respect of it to be considered by the court, the Court of Appeal considered in *AB v Tameside & Glossop Health Authority* [1997] PNLR 140 at 154–155, that the standard principles applied in determining whether a breach of duty of care had taken place outside of the *Bolam* context would be applied. What is the position when there are conflicting views as to the proper practice to adopt? In *Bolam v Friern Hospital Management Committee* [1957] 2 All ER 118, [1957] 1 WLR 582 McNair J, directing the jury, told them that a doctor was not negligent if he adopted a practice which a responsible body of skilled medical men accepted as proper, and that this was unaffected by the mere fact that there was a contrary body of opinion. This view has been approved in later cases (see e.g. *Maynard v West Midlands Regional Health Authority* [1985] 1 All ER 635, [1984] 1 WLR 634, where Lord Scarman referred to a practice accepted as proper by a responsible body of medical opinion) and it has been decided that the responsible body of medical opinion need not be substantial (*De Freitas v O'Brien and Connolly* [1995] 6 Med LR 108 and see the comment by M. Khan and M. Robson (1995) 11 PN 121). Moreover it was acknowledged in *Gold v Haringey Health Authority* [1988] QB 481, [1987] 2 All ER 888 that this view is not confined to the medical profession but applies to 'any other profession or calling which requires special skill, knowledge or experience'.

5. As has been mentioned earlier (p. 305, ante), courts can (exceptionally) find adherence to an accepted practice to be negligent. There had, however, been debate whether this was indeed the case with the medical profession and this is the concern of the next case extract.

■ Bolitho (administratix of the estate of Bolitho (decd)) v City and Hackney Health Authority
House of Lords [1997] 4 All ER 771

It was in the context of an issue of causation that this case raised the point mentioned in the last note. Causation will be discussed in chap. 6, and for the purposes of this extract it is not necessary to delve into the facts of the case.

LORD BROWNE-WILKINSON: . . .
The locus classicus of the test for the standard of care required of a doctor or any other person professing some skill or competence is the direction to the jury given by McNair J in *Bolam v Friern Hospital Management Committee* [1957] 2 All ER 118 at 122, [1957] 1 WLR 583 at 587:

> 'I myself would prefer to put it this way: a doctor is not guilty of negligence if he has acted in accordance with a practice accepted as proper by a responsible body of medical men skilled in that particular art . . . Putting it the other way round, a doctor is not negligent, if he is acting in accordance with such a practice, merely because there is a body of opinion that takes a contrary view.'

. . .

My Lords, I agree with [leading counsel for the appellant's] submissions to the extent that, in my view, the court is not bound to hold that a defendant doctor escapes liability for negligent treatment or diagnosis just because he leads evidence from a number of medical experts who are genuinely of opinion that the defendant's treatment or diagnosis accorded with sound medical practice. In *Bolam's* case [1957] 2 All ER 118 at 122, [1957] 1 WLR 583 at 587 McNair J stated that the defendant had to have acted in accordance with the practice accepted as proper by a '*responsible* body of medical men' (my emphasis). Later he referred to 'a standard of practice recognised as proper by a competent *reasonable* body of opinion' (see [1957] 2 All ER 118 and 122, [1957] 1 WLR 583 at 588; my emphasis). Again, in *Maynard v West Midlands Regional Health Authority* [1985] 1 All ER 635 at 639, Lord Scarman refers to a 'respectable' body of professional opinion. The use of these adjectives—responsible, reasonable and respectable—all show that the court has to be satisfied that the exponents of the body of opinion relied on can demonstrate that such opinion has a logical basis. In particular, in cases involving, as they so often do, the weighing of risks against benefits, the judge before accepting a body of opinion as being responsible, reasonable or respectable, will need to be satisfied that, in forming their views, the experts have directed their minds to the question of comparative risks and benefits and have reached a defensible conclusion on the matter.

There are decisions which demonstrate that the judge is entitled to approach expert professional opinion on this basis. For example, in *Hucks v Cole* (1968) (1993) 4 Med LR 393, a doctor failed to treat with penicillin a patient who was suffering from septic places on her skin though he knew them to contain organisms capable of leading to puerperal fever. A number of distinguished doctors gave evidence that they would not, in the circumstances, have treated with penicillin. The Court of Appeal found the defendant to have been negligent. Sachs LJ said (at 397):

'When the evidence shows that a lacuna in professional practice exists by which risks of grave danger are knowingly taken, then, however small the risks, the court must anxiously examine that lacuna—particularly if the risks can be easily and inexpensively avoided. If the court finds, on an analysis of the reasons given for not taking those precautions that, in the light of current professional knowledge, there is no proper basis for the lacuna, and that it is definitely not reasonable that those risks should have been taken, its function is to state that fact and where necessary to state that it constitutes negligence. In such a case the practice will no doubt thereafter be altered to the benefit of patients. On such occasions the fact that other practitioners would have done the same thing as the defendant practitioner is a very weighty matter to be put on the scales on his behalf; but it is not, as Mr Webster readily conceded, conclusive. The court must be vigilant to see whether the reasons given for putting a patient at risk are valid in the light of any well-known advance in medical knowledge, or whether they stem from a residual adherence to out-of-date ideas ...'

Again, in *Edward Wong Finance Co Ltd v Johnson Stokes & Master (a firm)* [1984] AC 296, [1984] 2 WLR 1, the defendant's solicitors had conducted the completion of a mortgage transaction in 'Hong Kong style' rather than in the old-fashioned English style. Completion in Hong Kong style provides for money to be paid over against an undertaking by the solicitors for the borrowers subsequently to hand over the executed documents. This practice opened the gateway through which a dishonest solicitor for the borrower absconded with the loan money without providing the security documents for such loan. The Privy Council held that even though completion in Hong Kong style was almost universally adopted in Hong Kong and was therefore in accordance with a body of professional opinion there, the defendant's solicitors were liable for negligence because there was an obvious risk which could have been guarded against. Thus, the body of professional opinion, though almost universally held, was not reasonable or responsible.

These decisions demonstrate that in cases of diagnosis and treatment there are cases where, despite a body of professional opinion sanctioning the defendant's conduct, the defendant can properly be held liable for negligence (I am not here considering questions of disclosure of risk). In my judgment that is because, in some cases, it cannot be demonstrated to the judge's satisfaction that the body of opinion relied on is reasonable or responsible. In the vast majority of cases the fact that distinguished experts in the field are of a particular opinion will demonstrate the reasonableness of that opinion. In particular, where there are questions of assessment of the relative risks and benefits of adopting a particular medical practice, a reasonable view necessarily presupposes that the relative risks and benefits have been weighed by the experts in forming their opinions. But if, in a rare case, it can be demonstrated that the professional opinion is not capable of withstanding logical analysis, the judge is entitled to hold that the body of opinion is not reasonable or responsible.

I emphasise that, in my view, it will very seldom be right for a judge to reach the conclusion that views genuinely held by a competent medical expert are unreasonable. The assessment of medical risks and benefits is a matter of clinical judgment which a judge would not normally be able to make without expert evidence. As . . . Lord Scarman makes clear [in *Maynard*'s case] it would be wrong to allow such assessment to deteriorate into seeking to persuade the judge to prefer one of two views both of which are capable of being logically supported. It is only where a judge can be satisfied that the body of expert opinion cannot be logically supported at all that such opinion will not provide the bench mark by reference to which the defendant's conduct falls to be assessed.

[His Lordship then concluded that this was plainly not 'one of those rare cases'.]

[LORD SLYNN OF HADLEY delivered a speech in which he agreed with LORD BROWNE-WILKINSON's analysis of the question to be decided in this sort of case and of the correct approach in law to them. LORD NOLAN, LORD HOFFMANN, and LORD CLYDE agreed with LORD BROWNE-WILKINSON's speech.]

QUESTION

To what extent does *Bolitho* allow the courts to question clinical judgments? (See H. Teff (1998) 18 Oxf JLS 473 at 479–481).

NOTES

1. *Bolitho* is noted by J. Keown [1998] CLJ 248 and A. Grubb (1998) 6 Med L Rev 380. (See further Teff, op cit.)
2. One of the most significant passages in *Bolitho* is Lord Browne-Wilkinson's discussion of the need for professional opinion to withstand 'logical analysis'. His Lordship stated that, 'where there are questions of assessment of the relative risks and benefits of adopting a particular medical practice, a reasonable view necessarily presupposes that the relative risks and benefits have been weighed by experts in forming their opinions. But if, in a rare case, it can be demonstrated that the professional opinion is not capable of withstanding logical analysis, the judge is entitled to hold that the body of opinion is not reasonable or responsible.' The key to understanding this passage is to realise that this reference to logic is not merely an issue about consistency and coherence; it is also about making sure that the professionals use the law's method for judging reasonableness (namely the weighing of risks and benefits). In other words, even if the court thinks that it cannot make judgments about the substance of what the experts say, it can at least insist on a legally approved method of supporting their conclusions, one which forces them to take their patients' (or, indeed, clients') interests into account.
3. *Bolitho* was applied by the Court of Appeal in *Marriott v West Midlands Health Authority* [1999] Lloyd's Rep Med 23, noted by M. Jones (1999) 15 PN 117. Here, most unusually, the Court of Appeal refused to overturn the trial judge's conclusion that a general practitioner had not acted in accordance with a logical, responsible body of medical opinion, notwithstanding the evidence of the general practitioner's expert witnesses. See also *AB & Ors v Leeds Teaching Hospital NHS Trust* [2005] Lloyds Rep

Med 1, [2004] EWHC 644, where Gage J ruled that an established medical practice of not informing the parents of deceased children that the organs of the children were removed and retained after post-mortem examination was not an objectively justified practice. It should also be noted that in *Penney v East Kent Health Authority* [2000] Lloyd's Rep Med 41, [1999] EWCA Civ 3005, the Court of Appeal stated that the *Bolam/Bolitho* approach is not applicable to questions of *fact* that have to be resolved, even where there is conflicting expert evidence on such a question. See also *Conway v Cardiff and Vale NHS* Trust [2004] EWHC 1841. In *Gouldsmith v Mid Staffordshire General Hospitals NHS Trust* [2007] EWCA Civ 397 (see note 2, p. 346, post), the majority of the Court of Appeal also considered that the *Bolam/Bolitho* test should not be applied in determining the factual causation question of what 'would have happened' if a patient had been referred to a specialist hospital.

4.   It will be seen from *Sidaway v Bethlem Royal Hospital Governors* [1985] AC 871, [1985] 1 All ER 643 that there is a duty of care on the medical profession in respect of the disclosure of risks. Note that Lord Browne-Wilkinson put this aspect of a doctor's responsibility to one side in *Bolitho* (p. 326, ante). The extent to which an approach like that in *Bolitho* already applied in *Sidaway* is no easy matter and will be addressed in note 2, p. 334, post. *Sidaway* is concerned with the issue whether the 'responsible body of medical opinion' test should be applied, not only to diagnosis and treatment, but also to the amount of information a medical practitioner must give to a patient as to the risks involved in a course of treatment.

■ Sidaway v Bethlem Royal Hospital Governors
House of Lords [1985] 1 All ER 643

This was an appeal from the Court of Appeal, [1984] 1 All ER 1018, which had dismissed an appeal from a decision of Skinner J, who had dismissed the appellant's action.

LORD BRIDGE OF HARWICH: . . .
The appellant underwent at the hospital for which the first respondents are the responsible authority an operation on her cervical vertebrae performed by a neuro-surgeon, since deceased, whose executors are the second respondents. The nature of the operation was such that, however skilfully performed, it involved a risk of damage to the nerve root at the site of the operation or to the spinal cord. The trial judge described that risk as 'best expressed to a layman as a 1% or 2% risk of ill-effects ranging from the mild to the catastrophic'. The appellant in fact suffered, without negligence on the surgeon's part in the performance of the operation, a degree of damage to the spinal cord of which the effects, if not catastrophic, were certainly severe. Damages have been agreed, subject to liability, in the sum of £67,500 . . .

There was a difference of opinion between the neuro-surgeons called as expert witnesses whether they themselves would, in the circumstances, have warned the appellant specifically of the risk of damage to the spinal cord. But the one expert witness called for the appellant agreed readily and without reservation that the deceased surgeon, in omitting any such warning, would have been following a practice accepted as proper by a responsible body of competent neuro-surgeons.

Broadly, a doctor's professional functions may be divided into three phases: diagnosis, advice and treatment. In performing his functions of diagnosis and treatment, the standard by which English law measures the doctor's duty of care to his patient is not open to doubt. 'The test is the standard of the ordinary skilled man exercising and professing to have that special skill.' These are the words of McNair J in *Bolam v Friern Hospital Management Committee* [1957] 2 All ER 118 at 121, [1957] 1 WLR 582 at 586, approved by this House in *Whitehouse v Jordan* [1981] 1 All ER 267 at 277, [1981] 1 WLR 246 at 258 per Lord Edmund-Davies and in *Maynard v West Midlands Regional Health*

Authority [1985] 1 All ER 635 per Lord Scarman. The test is conveniently referred to as the *Bolam* test. In *Maynard*'s case Lord Scarman, with whose speech the other four members of the Appellate Committee agreed, further cited with approval the words of the Lord President (Clyde) in *Hunter v Hanley* 1955 SLT 213 at 217:

> 'In the realm of diagnosis and treatment there is ample scope for genuine difference of opinion and one man clearly is not negligent merely because his conclusion differs from that of other professional men … The true test for establishing negligence in diagnosis or treatment on the part of a doctor is whether he has been proved to be guilty of such failure as no doctor of ordinary skill would be guilty of if acting with ordinary care. …'

The language of the *Bolam* test clearly requires a different degree of skill from a specialist in his own special field than from a general practitioner. In the field of neuro-surgery it would be necessary to substitute for the Lord President's phrase 'no doctor of ordinary skill', the phrase 'no neuro-surgeon of ordinary skill'. All this is elementary and, in the light of the two recent decisions of this House referred to, firmly established law.

The important question which this appeal raises is whether the law imposes any, and if so what, different criterion as the measure of the medical man's duty of care to his patient when giving advice with respect to a proposed course of treatment. It is clearly right to recognise that a conscious adult patient of sound mind is entitled to decide for himself whether or not he will submit to a particular course of treatment proposed by the doctor, most significantly surgical treatment under general anaesthesia. This entitlement is the foundation of the doctrine of 'informed consent' which has led in certain American jurisdictions to decisions and, in the Supreme Court of Canada, to dicta on which the appellant relies, which would oust the *Bolam* test and substitute an 'objective' test of a doctor's duty to advise the patient of the advantages and disadvantages of undergoing the treatment proposed and more particularly to advise the patient of the risks involved.

There are, it appears to me, at least theoretically, two extreme positions which could be taken. It could be argued that, if the patient's consent is to be fully informed, the doctor must specifically warn him of *all* risks involved in the treatment offered, unless he has some sound clinical reason not to do so. Logically, this would seem to be the extreme to which a truly objective criterion of the doctor's duty would lead. Yet this position finds no support from any authority to which we have been referred in any jurisdiction. It seems to be generally accepted that there is no need to warn of the risks inherent in all surgery under general anaesthesia. This is variously explained on the ground that the patient may be expected to be aware of such risks or that they are relatively remote. If the law is to impose on the medical profession a duty to warn of risks to secure 'informed consent' independently of accepted medical opinion of what is appropriate, neither of these explanations for confining the duty to special as opposed to general surgical risks seems to me wholly convincing.

At the other extreme it could be argued that, once the doctor has decided what treatment is, on balance of advantages and disadvantages, in a patient's best interest, he should not alarm the patient by volunteering a warning of any risk involved, however grave and substantial, unless specifically asked by the patient. I cannot believe that contemporary medical opinion would support this view, which would effectively exclude the patient's right to decide in the very type of case where it is most important that he should be in a position to exercise that right and, perhaps even more significantly, to seek a second opinion whether he should submit himself to the significant risk which has been drawn to his attention. I should perhaps add at this point, although the issue does not strictly arise in this appeal, that, when questioned specifically by a patient of apparently sound mind about risks involved in a particular treatment proposed, the doctor's duty must, in my opinion, be to answer both truthfully and as fully as the questioner requires.

The decision mainly relied on to establish a criterion of the doctor's duty to disclose the risks inherent in a proposed treatment which is prescribed by the law and can be applied independently of any medical opinion or practice is that of the District of Columbia Circuit Court of Appeals in *Canterbury v*

Spence 464 F 2d 772 (1972). The judgment of the court (Wright, Leventhal and Robinson JJ), delivered by Robinson J, expounds the view that an objective criterion of what is a sufficient disclosure of risk is necessary to ensure that the patient is enabled to make an intelligent decision and cannot be left to be determined by the doctors. He said (at 784):

'Respect for the patient's right of self-determination on particular therapy demands a standard set by law for physicians rather than one which physicians may or may not impose upon themselves.'

In an attempt to define the objective criterion it is said (at 787) that—

'the issue on non-disclosure must be approached from the viewpoint of the reasonableness of the physician's divulgence in terms of what he knows or should know to be the patient's informational needs.'

A risk is required to be disclosed—

'when a reasonable person, in what the physician knows or should know to be the patient's position, would be likely to attach significance to the risk or cluster of risks in deciding whether or not to forego the proposed therapy.'

The judgment adds (at 788): 'Whenever non-disclosure of particular risk information is open to debate by reasonable-minded men, the issue is for the finder of facts.'

The court naturally recognises exceptions from the duty laid down in the case of an unconscious patient, an immediate emergency or a case where the doctor can establish that disclosure would be harmful to the patient.

Expert medical evidence will be needed to indicate the nature and extent of the risks and benefits involved in the treatment (and presumably of any alternative course). But the court affirms (at 792): 'Experts are unnecessary to a showing of the materiality of a risk to a patient's decision on treatment, or to the reasonably, expectable effect of risk disclosure on the decision.' In English law, if this doctrine were adopted, expert medical opinion whether a particular risk should or should not have been disclosed would presumably be inadmissible in evidence.

I recognise the logical force of the *Canterbury* doctrine, proceeding from the premise that the patient's right to make his own decision must at all costs be safeguarded against the kind of medical paternalism which assumes that 'doctor knows best'. But, with all respect, I regard the doctrine as quite impractical in application for three principal reasons. First, it gives insufficient weight to the realities of the doctor/patient relationship. A very wide variety of factors must enter into a doctor's clinical judgment not only as to what treatment is appropriate for a particular patient, but also as to how best to communicate to the patient the significant factors necessary to enable the patient to make an informed decision whether to undergo the treatment. The doctor cannot set out to educate the patient to his own standard of medical knowledge of all the relevant factors involved. He may take the view, certainly with some patients, that the very fact of his volunteering, without being asked, information of some remote risk involved in the treatment proposed, even though he describes it as remote, may lead to that risk assuming an undue significance in the patient's calculations. Second, it would seem to be quite unrealistic in any medical negligence action to confine the expert medical evidence to an explanation of the primary medical factors involved and to deny the court the benefit of evidence of medical opinion and practice on the particular issue of disclosure which is under consideration. Third, the objective test which *Canterbury* propounds seems to me to be so imprecise as to be almost meaningless. If it is to be left to individual judges to decide for themselves what 'a reasonable person in the patient's position' would consider a risk of sufficient significance that he should be told about it, the outcome of litigation in this field is likely to be quite unpredictable . . .

Having rejected the *Canterbury* doctrine as a solution to the problem of safeguarding the patient's right to decide whether he will undergo a particular treatment advised by his doctor, the question remains whether that right is sufficiently safeguarded by the application of the *Bolam* test without qualification to the determination of the question what risks inherent in a proposed treatment should be disclosed. The case against a simple application of the *Bolam* test is cogently stated by Laskin CJC, giving the judgment of the Supreme Court of Canada in *Reibl v Hughes* (1980) 114 DLR (3d) 1 at 13:

> 'To allow expert medical evidence to determine what risks are material and, hence, should be disclosed and, correlatively, what risks are not material is to hand over to the medical profession the entire question of the scope of the duty of disclosure, including the question whether there has been a breach of that duty. Expert medical evidence is, of course, relevant to findings as to the risks that reside in or are a result of recommended surgery or other treatment. It will also have a bearing on their materiality but this is not a question that is to be concluded on the basis of the expert medical evidence alone. The issue under consideration is a different issue from that involved where the question is whether the doctor carried out his professional activities by applicable professional standards. What is under consideration here is the patient's right to know what risks are involved in undergoing or foregoing certain surgery or other treatment.'

I fully appreciate the force of this reasoning, but can only accept it subject to the important qualification that a decision what degree of disclosure of risks is best calculated to assist a particular patient to make a rational choice whether or not to undergo a particular treatment must primarily be a matter of clinical judgment. It would follow from this that the issue whether non-disclosure in a particular case should be condemned as a breach of the doctor's duty of care is an issue to be decided primarily on the basis of expert medical evidence, applying the *Bolam* test. But I do not see that this approach involves the necessity 'to hand over to the medical profession the entire question of the scope of the duty of disclosure, including the question whether there has been a breach of that duty'. Of course, if there is a conflict of evidence whether a responsible body of medical opinion approves of non-disclosure in a particular case, the judge will have to resolve that conflict. But, even in a case where, as here, no expert witness in the relevant medical field condemns the non-disclosure as being in conflict with accepted and responsible medical practice, I am of opinion that the judge might in certain circumstances come to the conclusion that disclosure of a particular risk was so obviously necessary to an informed choice on the part of the patient that no reasonably prudent medical man would fail to make it. The kind of case I have in mind would be an operation involving a substantial risk of grave adverse consequences, as for example the 10% risk of a stroke from the operation which was the subject of the Canadian case of *Reibl v Hughes* (1980) 114 DLR (3d) 1. In such a case, in the absence of some cogent clinical reason why the patient should not be informed, a doctor, recognising and respecting his patient's right of decision, could hardly fail to appreciate the necessity for an appropriate warning.

In the instant case I can see no reasonable ground on which the judge could properly reject the conclusion to which the unchallenged medical evidence led in the application of the *Bolam* test. The trial judge's assessment of the risk at 1% or 2% covered both nerve root and spinal cord damage and covered a spectrum of possible ill-effects 'ranging from the mild to the catastrophic'. In so far as it is possible and appropriate to measure such risks in percentage terms (some of the expert medical witnesses called expressed a marked and understandable reluctance to do so), the risk of damage to the spinal cord of such severity as the appellant in fact suffered was, it would appear, certainly less than 1%. But there is no yardstick either in the judge's findings or in the evidence to measure what fraction of 1% that risk represented. In these circumstances, the appellant's expert witness's agreed that the non-disclosure of neuro-surgical opinion afforded the respondents a complete defence to the appellant's claim.

I would dismiss the appeal.

LORD SCARMAN:...

I am satisfied, for reasons which I shall develop, that the trial judge and the Court of Appeal erred in law in holding that, in a case where the alleged negligence is a failure to warn the patient of a risk inherent in the treatment proposed, the *Bolam* test, (see *Bolam v Friern Hospital Management Committee* [1957] 2 All ER 118, [1957] 1 WLR 582)...is to be applied. In my view the question whether or not the omission to warn constitutes a breach of the doctor's duty of care towards his patient is to be determined not exclusively by reference to the current state of responsible and competent professional opinion and practice at the time, though both are, of course, relevant consideration[s], but by the court's view whether the doctor in advising his patient gave the consideration which the law requires him to give to the right of the patient to make up her own mind in the light of the relevant information whether or not she will accept the treatment which he proposes. This being my view of the law, I have tested the facts found by the trial judge by what I believe to be the correct legal criterion. In my view the appellant has failed to prove that Mr Falconer was in breach of the duty of care which he owed to her in omitting to disclose the risk which the trial judge found as a fact he did not disclose to her.

...[W]as [the judge in *Bolam*] correct in treating the 'standard of competent professional opinion' as the criterion in determining whether a doctor is under a duty to warn his patient of the risk, or risks, inherent in the treatment which he recommends? Skinner J and the Court of Appeal have in the instant case held that [he] was correct. Bristow J adopted the same criterion in *Chatterton v Gerson* [1981] 1 All ER 257, [1981] QB 432. The implications of this view of the law are disturbing. It leaves the determination of a legal duty to the judgment of doctors. Responsible medical judgment may, indeed, provide the law with an acceptable standard in determining whether a doctor in diagnosis or treatment has complied with his duty. But is it right that medical judgment should determine whether there exists a duty to warn of risk and its scope? It would be a strange conclusion if the courts should be led to conclude that our law, which undoubtedly recognises a right in the patient to decide whether he will accept or reject the treatment proposed, should permit the doctors to determine whether and in what circumstances a duty arises requiring the doctor to warn his patient of the risks inherent in the treatment which he proposes.

The right of 'self-determination', the description applied by some to what is no more and no less than the right of a patient to determine for himself whether he will or will not accept the doctor's advice, is vividly illustrated where the treatment recommended is surgery. A doctor who operates without the consent of his patient is, save in cases of emergency or mental disability, guilty of the civil wrong of trespass to the person; he is also guilty of the criminal offence of assault. The existence of the patient's right to make his own decision, which may be seen as a basic human right protected by the common law, is the reason why a doctrine embodying a right of the patient to be informed of the risks of surgical treatment has been developed in some jurisdictions in the United States of America and has found favour with the Supreme Court of Canada. Known as the 'doctrine of informed consent', it amounts to this: where there is a 'real' or a 'material' risk inherent in the proposed operation (however competently and skilfully performed) the question whether and to what extent a patient should be warned before he gives his consent is to be answered not by reference to medical practice but by accepting as a matter of law that, subject to all proper exceptions (of which the court, not the profession, is the judge), a patient has a right to be informed of the risks inherent in the treatment which is proposed. The profession, it is said, should not be judge in its own cause; or, less emotively but more correctly, the courts should not allow medical opinion as to what is best for the patient to override the patient's right to decide for himself whether he will submit to the treatment offered him....

...In a medical negligence case where the issue is as to the advice and information given to the patient as to the treatment proposed, the available options and the risk, the court is concerned primarily with a patient's right. The doctor's duty arises from his patient's rights. If one considers the scope of the doctor's duty by beginning with the right of the patient to make his own decision whether he will or will not undergo the treatment proposed, the right to be informed of significant risk and the doctor's corresponding duty are easy to understand, for the proper implementation of the right requires that the doctor be under a duty to inform his patient of the material risks inherent in the treatment. And it is plainly right that a doctor may avoid liability for failure to warn of a material risk if he can show that he reasonably believed that communication to the patient of the existence of the risk would be detrimental to the health (including, of course, the mental health) of his patient....

My conclusion as to the law is therefore this. To the extent that I have indicated, I think that English law must recognise a duty of the doctor to warn his patient of risk inherent in the treatment which he is proposing; and especially so if the treatment be surgery. The critical limitation is that the duty is confined to material risk. The test of materiality is whether in the circumstances of the particular case, the court is satisfied that a reasonable person in the patient's position would be likely to attach significance to the risk. Even if the risk be material, the doctor will not be liable if on a reasonable assessment of his patient's condition he takes the view that a warning would be detrimental to his patient's health....

[LORD SCARMAN proceeded to apply these principles to the specific facts in question and would have allowed the appeal.]

[LORD KEITH OF KINKEL agreed with LORD BRIDGE OF HARWICH. LORD DIPLOCK, and LORD TEMPLEMAN delivered speeches in favour of dismissing the appeal.]

Appeal dismissed.

NOTES

1. Lord Diplock in *Sidaway* did not think any distinction should be made between cases concerning the amount of information a medical practitioner should reveal and other aspects of a practitioner's duty. He mentioned that 'the criterion of the duty of care owed by a doctor to his patient is whether he has acted in accordance with a practice accepted as proper by a body of responsible and skilled medical opinion' and acknowledged that there might be several such practices in relation to a particular matter. However, he underlined at a later stage that the court must be satisfied by expert evidence that the body of medical opinion is a responsible one.

2. The 'responsible body of medical opinion' test is a synonym for the *Bolam* test. I. Kennedy, *Treat Me Right* (Oxford, 1988), pp. 193–212 (and see P. D. G. Skegg, *Law, Ethics and Medicine* (Oxford, 1988), p. 263) argues that the decision in *Sidaway* is best understood as cutting free the issue of informed consent from the control of the *Bolam* test. Kennedy views Lord Diplock alone as applying the *Bolam* test, and is unhappy with the view taken in *Gold v Haringey Health Authority* [1988] QB 481, [1987] 2 All ER 888 that the House of Lords in *Sidaway* applied the *Bolam* test: see Kennedy, op cit., pp. 210–212. See further A. Grubb [1988] CLJ 12 and in *Medicine, Ethics and the Law*, edited by M. D. A. Freeman, (London, 1988), pp. 133–139 and note his reference (at p. 139) to the unreported case in 1987 of *Palmer v Eadie*. But is Lord Bridge's opinion (with which Lord Keith agreed) really any different from that of Lord Diplock? Is Lord Diplock leaving the decision to the medical profession in all cases, especially given his reservation that a body of medical opinion supporting limited disclosure in a particular circumstance may need to be responsible?

    Nevertheless, *Sidaway* is generally interpreted as applying the *Bolam* test to the provision of advice to a patient on the risks associated with a medical procedure: see Lord Hope's comments in *Chester v Afshar* [2004] 4 All ER 587, [2004] UKHL 1 at [53] (see p. 383, post). See also *Deriche v Ealing Hospital NHS Trust* [2003] EWHC 3104 (QB). In *Gold v Haringey Health Authority* [1988] QB 481, [1987] 2 All ER 888, the Court of Appeal rejected the idea that the *Bolam* test would not apply to advice on non-therapeutic matters. Such a distinction was thought to go against the 'thrust' of the majority view in *Sidaway*, particular attention being paid to Lord Diplock's speech. In *Pearce v United Bristol Healthcare NHS Trust* [1999] PIQR P53, the Court of Appeal also regarded Lord Diplock's speech as applying the *Bolam* test to the giving of advice and as adopting the same approach as that of Lord Bridge (with whom Lord Keith concurred). Note also *Powell v Boldaz* [1998] Lloyd's Rep Med 116 at 124–125.

One area where it was thought that the *Bolam* test did not apply was where a patient specifically asked for advice on a particular matter: see e.g. Lord Bridge's speech, p. 330, ante. However, in *Blyth v Bloomsbury Health Authority* [1993] 4 Med LR. 151, Kerr LJ was of the opinion that the *Bolam* test applied to the same extent to the provision of information in response to a general inquiry as in the case where no inquiry was made and (obiter) was unconvinced that it was irrelevant even if a specific inquiry was made. Consider also Neill LJ's opinion that the *Bolam* test applied 'as a general proposition' in relation to the amount of information to be provided when the patient had asked questions. However, in *Pearce v United Bristol Healthcare NHS Trust* [1999] PIQR at P54, the view expressed by Lord Bridge in *Sidaway* that an honest answer must be given to a specific request for information was repeated by Lord Woolf, who emphasised that if there was a significant risk which would influence the judgment of a patient, then the normal course of action would be for the doctor to inform the patient of that risk. In *Chester v Afshar*, at [15], Lord Steyn approved the approach adopted in *Pearce*. In *Wyatt v Curtis* [2003] EWCA Civ 1779, Sedley LJ applied the approach taken in *Pearce*, stating at [15] that an obligation to disclose arose where substantial risks were attached to a medical procedure, 'irrespective of the *Bolam* threshold'.

3. As disclosure in the interests of informed consent becomes more common in standard medical practice, *Sidaway* has become less of an obstacle to claimants bringing claims in respect of alleged failures to inform of risks contingent upon medical procedures. Furthermore, the approach in *Bolitho*, which is essentially an interpretation of the *Bolam* test, applies to cases on the giving of advice, as held by Lord Woolf in *Pearce* .(Furthermore, it might be mentioned that before *Bolitho* was decided, Morland J in *Smith v Tunbridge Wells Health Authority* [1994] 5 Med LR 334 at 339, noted by J. Keown [1995] CLJ 30 at 31–32, stated that although some surgeons may not have been warning of a particular risk at the relevant date, 'that omission was neither reasonable nor responsible'.) However, the legal position remains less than satisfactory, even with acceptance of Lord Woolf's interpretation of *Sidaway* in *Pearce*: as Sedley LJ commented in *Wyatt v Curtis*, at [19] 'there is arguably something unreal about placing the onus of asking upon a patient who may not know that there is anything to ask about'. Nevertheless, a shift in the approach of the English courts towards a greater emphasis on 'informed consent' can be clearly detected. In *Chester v Afshar*, Lord Hope at [54]–[55] emphasised the passages in the opinions in *Sidaway* which acknowledged the rights of patients to be informed of risk, and placed considerable importance on the right of a patient to make the final decision, which in his view imposed a duty on doctors to inform patients of special disadvantages and dangers linked with a procedure. Lord Steyn took a similar view at [16]. See also *Khalid (A Child) v Barnet & Chase Farm Hospital NHS Trust* [2007] EWHC 644 (QB).

4. The High Court of Australia has preferred an approach similar to that of Lord Scarman in *Sidaway* on this matter (*Rogers v Whitaker* (1992) 109 ALR 625, noted by J. Keown [1994] CLJ 16 and F. A. Trindade (1993) 109 LQR 352) and see further K. Tickner (1995) 15 Oxf JLS 109.

5. For an empirical study of the effect in Canada of the adoption by that country's Supreme Court of the 'informed consent' doctrine (*Reibl v Hughes* (1980) 114 DLR (3d) 1), see G. Robertson (1990) 70 Can Bar Rev 423. Proving causation could be a problem for a claimant; on the Canadian law see A. N. Dugdale (1986) 2 PN 108; Robertson, op cit.; *Smith v Arndt* (1997) 148 DLR (4th) 48, noted by T. Honoré (1998) 114 LQR 52.

6. The Human Rights Act 1998 imposes certain requirements upon public health authorities in respect of the care and treatment of patients, and requires respect for autonomy rights: see *R(N) v Dr M* [2002] EWCA Civ 1789; *R (B) v Dr SS* [2005] EWHC 86 (Admin).

3 AIDS IN DISCHARGING THE BURDEN OF PROOF

(a) Statute

■ The Civil Evidence Act 1968

11. Convictions as evidence in civil proceedings.—(1) In any civil proceedings the fact that a person has been convicted of an offence by or before any court in the United Kingdom or by a court-martial there or elsewhere shall (subject to subsection (3) below) be admissible in evidence for the purpose of proving, where to do so is relevant to any issue in those proceedings, that he committed that offence, whether he was so convicted upon a plea of guilty or otherwise and whether or not he is a party to the civil proceedings; but no conviction other than a subsisting one shall be admissible in evidence by virtue of this section.

(2) In any civil proceedings in which by virtue of this section a person is proved to have been convicted of an offence by or before any court in the United Kingdom or by a court-martial there or elsewhere –

(a) he shall be taken to have committed that offence unless the contrary is proved; and

(b) without prejudice to the reception of any other admissible evidence for the purpose of identifying the facts on which the conviction was based, the contents of any document which is admissible as evidence of the conviction, and the contents of the information, complaint, indictment or charge-sheet on which the person in question was convicted, shall be admissible in evidence for that purpose.

(3) Nothing in this section shall prejudice the operation of section 13 of this Act or any other enactment whereby a conviction or a finding of fact in any criminal proceedings is for the purposes of any other proceedings made conclusive evidence of any fact.

NOTES

1. For discussion of this provision, see *Cross and Tapper on Evidence* 11th edn by C. Tapper (Oxford, 2007), pp. 119–122.
2. Another way in which statute might help a claimant discharge the burden of proof should be noted. Although a breach of statutory duty can constitute a tort in its own right (see chap. 12), nevertheless a breach of statutory duty can also be evidence of negligence. On the other hand, it might be noted here that compliance with a legislative standard can be evidence that the defendant has not been negligent, although it does not necessarily rule out a contrary finding (*Bux v Slough Metals Ltd* [1974] 1 All ER 262, [1973] 1 WLR 1358, noted p. 671, post; cf. *Budden v BP Oil Ltd and Shell Oil Ltd* [1980] JPL 586, on which see R. B. Macrory [1981] JPL 258).

3. See also s. 2 of the Compensation Act 2006: 'An apology, an offer of treatment or other redress, shall not of itself amount to an admission of negligence or breach of statutory duty.' Why do you think this provision was inserted in the 2006 Act? Does it effect any alteration in the existing legal position? See *X v London Borough of Hounslow* [2008] EWHC 1168 [125].
4. Note that s. 2 provides that an apology or other offer of redress shall not 'by itself' amount to an admission of negligence. Does this mean that an apology can constitute evidence of negligence in combination with other factors? Would a claimant ever realistically rely upon an apology alone to mount a claim?

(b) Common law—res ipsa loquitur

■ Scott v London and St Katherine Docks Co
Court of Exchequer Chamber [1861–73] All ER Rep 246

The plaintiff by his declaration alleged that the defendants were possessed of certain docks, and warehouses therein, that the plaintiff was lawfully therein, that the defendants by their servants were lowering bags of sugar by means of a crane or hoist, and that by the negligence of the defendants' servants a bag of sugar fell upon the plaintiff and injured him. The defendants denied liability. At the trial before Martin B and a special jury, the plaintiff, who was the only witness called, gave evidence relative to the accident, and stated that he was a Custom House officer of twenty six years' standing; that on 19 January 1864, the occasion in question, he was at the defendants' docks, and had performed his duty at the East Quay there as a superintendent of the weighing of goods; that he was directed by Mr Lilley, his superior officer, to go from the East Quay to the Spirit Quay, which he proceeded to do, having to pass the warehouses in his way. Not being able to find Lilley, he inquired of a workman where he was, and was told he was in a warehouse, which was pointed out to him, and, in passing from the doorway of one warehouse to the other, he was felled to the ground by the falling upon him of six bags of sugar which were being lowered to the ground from the upper part of the warehouse by means of a crane or jigger hoist. The plaintiff said that he had no warning, and there was no fence or barrier to show persons that the place was dangerous, and nobody called out to him to stop him from going through the door or under the hoist. He also said that instantly before the bags fell he 'heard the rattling of a chain overhead'. No other evidence being given, the learned judge proposed to nonsuit the plaintiff for want of evidence showing negligence in defendants, but on the plaintiff's resisting that course, with a view to a bill of exceptions, his Lordship directed the jury to find a verdict for the defendants. A rule was subsequently obtained to set that verdict aside, and for a new trial, on the ground that there was evidence of negligence by the defendants' servants, which rule after argument was made absolute by the Court of Exchequer, on the authority of *Byrne v Boadle*[5] (dubitante Pollock CB, and dissentiente Martin B, on the authority of *Hammack v White*[6]), and against that decision the defendants now appealed.

ERLE CJ:...
The majority of the court have come to the following conclusion. There must be reasonable evidence of negligence, but, where the thing is shown to be under the management of the defendant, or his servants, and the accident is such as, in the ordinary course of things, does not happen if those who have

---

[5] (1863) 2 H & C 722.   [6] (1862) 11 CBNS 588.

the management of the machinery use proper care, it affords reasonable evidence, in the absence of explanation by the defendant, that the accident arose from want of care. We all assent to the principle laid down in the cases cited for the defendants; but the judgment turns upon the construction to be put on the judge's notes. As my brother Mellor and myself read those notes, we cannot find that reasonable evidence in the present case of the want of care which seems apparent to the rest of the court. The judgment of the court below is, therefore, affirmed, and the case must go down to a new trial, when the real effect of the evidence will, in all probability, be more correctly ascertained.

Appeal dismissed.

NOTES

1. It is reported at (1865–6) 13 LT (NS) 148 at 149 that at the second trial there was a verdict for the defendants.

2. In *Barkway v South Wales Transport Co Ltd* [1950] AC 185n, [1950] 1 All ER 392, Lord Porter referred to Erle CJ's exposition of the doctrine (ante) and stated (at pp. 394–395):

   The doctrine is dependant on the absence of explanation, and, although it is the duty of the defendants, if they desire to protect themselves, to give an adequate explanation of the cause of the accident, yet, if the facts are sufficiently known, the question ceases to be one where the facts speak for themselves, and the solution is to be found by determining whether, on the facts as established, negligence is to be inferred or not.

3. The maxim res ipsa loquitur has been raised in the sphere of the protection of economic interests. In *Stafford v Conti Commodity Services Ltd* [1981] 1 All ER 691, where the defendants were a company of brokers dealing on the commodities futures market, the case for its application was that only ten out of forty-six transactions in an eight-month period had been profitable. Reference was made to Erle CJ's classic statement of the doctrine (ante), and the defendants contended that the maxim was inapplicable. One argument concerned the requirement that the loss be such as would not in the ordinary course of things happen if due care was taken. This, it was argued, was not satisfied in the case of transactions on the commodities market, a point seemingly accepted by Mocatta J, since he thought that in such a volatile area negligence could not be established by res ipsa loquitur, but would require 'exceedingly strong evidence from expert brokers in relation to individual transactions'. See further *Merrill Lynch Futures Inc v York House Trading Ltd* (1984) Times, 24 May, where Griffiths LJ stopped short of saying there could never be circumstances from which an inference of negligence could be drawn, but agreed with Mocatta J's view which has been quoted in the latter part of the previous sentence.

4. For discussion of res ipsa loquitur in the context of products liability, see pp. 617–618, post. See in particular *Carroll v Fearon* [1998] PIQR P146, where the Court of Appeal applied res ipsa loquitur to a *Donoghue v Stevenson* case of a defective, exploding tyre. The court expressed the view that res ipsa loquitur is a matter of commonsense inference, and should not be subjected to detailed analysis based on case law.

■ Henderson v Henry E Jenkins & Sons
House of Lords [1969] 3 All ER 756

The hydraulic brakes of a lorry suddenly failed whilst it was descending a hill and it collided with two vehicles and killed the appellant's husband. The reason for the failure was a hole in a corroded part of the brake pipe. Although part of the pipe could be seen whilst it remained on the lorry, the part which in fact was badly corroded could not have been inspected without the pipe being removed. The evidence showed that it was unusual for there to be complete and sudden failure of brakes from corrosion. The respondents pleaded that the brake failure resulted 'from a latent defect...which occurred without any fault on the part of the [respondents and the driver] and the existence of which was not discoverable by the exercise of reasonable care by them'. They argued that ordinary practice only required that the visible parts of the pipe be regularly inspected (which they had done), and it was established that neither the Ministry of Transport nor the manufacturers advised that the pipes be removed for inspection. The appellant's action for damages against the respondents and the driver was dismissed by Nield J. She appealed to the Court of Appeal, [1969] 1 All ER 401, against the dismissal of the action against the respondents and, after that appeal had been dismissed, she appealed to the House of Lords.

LORD REID [having earlier referred to the evidence of the respondents' 'leading expert' who, in response to a question, had agreed that the pipe 'was subjected to some unusual treatment from outside', continued:]

If there were nothing in the evidence to indicate a probability that something unusual must have happened to this lorry to cause the very unusual type of brake failure which the learned trial judge has held in fact occurred here, then undoubtedly the respondents would have proved that they had exercised all proper care in this case. But if the evidence indicates a likelihood that something unusual has occurred to cause a break-down, then I do not see how the owner can say that he has exercised all proper care unless he can prove that he neither knew nor ought to have known of any such occurrence. For if he did know of it he would have been bound to take adequate steps to prevent any resulting break-down. It may well be that it would be sufficient for him to prove that he had a proper system for drivers reporting all unusual occurrences and that none had been reported to him.

...It may be that they [the respondents] could have proved that, so far as they knew or could have discovered by reasonable enquiry, nothing unusual ever happened to it which could have led to this corrosion. Or it may be that they did know of something but did not realise the possible danger resulting from it although they ought to have done so. We do not know. They had to prove that in all the circumstances which they knew or ought to have known that they took all proper steps to avoid danger. In my opinion they have failed to do that, and I am therefore of opinion that this appeal should be allowed. Damages have been agreed to be £5,700.

LORD PEARSON:...

My Lords, in my opinion, the decision in this appeal turns on what is sometimes called 'the evidential burden of proof', which is to be distinguished from the formal (or legal or technical) burden of proof....For the purposes of the present case the distinction can be simply stated in this way. In an action for negligence the plaintiff must allege, and has the burden of proving, that the accident was caused by negligence on the part of the defendants. That is the issue throughout the trial, and in giving judgment at the end of the trial the judge has to decide whether he is satisfied on a balance of probabilities that the accident was caused by negligence on the part of the defendants, and if he is not so satisfied the plaintiff's action fails. The formal burden of proof does not shift. But if in the course of the trial there is proved a set of facts which raises a prima facie inference that the accident was caused by negligence on the part of the defendants, the issue will be decided in the plaintiff's favour unless the defendants by their evidence provide some answer which is adequate to displace the prima facie inference. In this situation there is said to be an evidential burden of proof resting on the defendants. I have some doubts whether it is strictly correct to use the expression 'burden of proof' with this meaning, as there is a risk of it being confused with the formal burden of proof, but it is a familiar and convenient usage....

...The respondents and the driver were, by this plea [of latent defect], alleging and, therefore, admitting that the accident was caused by a sudden brake failure resulting from corrosion of the brake fluid pipe, and were assuming an evidential burden of proving that the corrosion occurred without any fault on their part and that its existence was not discoverable by the exercise of reasonable care by them.

That was the effect of the pleading of the respondents and the driver, but in any case the physical facts of the case raise a strong prima facie inference that the respondents and the driver[7] were at fault and that their fault was a cause of the accident....

[Having referred to the facts of the case, he continued:] From these facts it seems to me clear, as a prima facie inference, that the accident must have been due to default of the respondents in respect of inspection or maintenance or both. Unless they had a satisfactory answer, sufficient to displace the inference, they should have been held liable.

The respondents' answer was that they had followed a practice of relying solely on visual inspection of the pipes, and that this was a general and proper practice. The learned judge's finding was that 'it is plainly the custom in the ordinary course of things not to remove these fluid pipes.' This may be a general and proper practice for an ordinary case in which there are no special circumstances increasing the risk. But I think the respondents' answer should not have been accepted without evidence from the respondents sufficiently showing that this was an ordinary case without special circumstances increasing the risk.

...The respondents might perhaps have been able to show by evidence that the lorry had not been used in any way, or involved in any incident, that would cause abnormal corrosion or require special inspection or treatment, or at any rate that they neither knew nor ought to have known of any such use or incident. But they did not call any such evidence. Their answer was incomplete. They did not displace the inference, arising from the physical facts of the case, that the accident must have been due to their default in respect of inspection or maintenance or both.

While fully accepting the learned judge's findings of primary fact, I am of the opinion that he drew a wrong conclusion in holding that the accident was not caused by negligence of the respondents. I would allow the appeal.

[LORD DONOVAN delivered a speech in favour of allowing the appeal. LORD GUEST and VISCOUNT DILHORNE delivered speeches in favour of dismissing the appeal.]

Appeal allowed.

QUESTION

There is no express mention of res ipsa loquitur in the speeches in this case. Is it, nevertheless, correctly classified under this heading?

NOTE

The particular issue that these extracts are concerned with is the effect that a successful invocation of res ipsa loquitur produces, a matter on which there has been some doubt. The two speeches ante reflect different approaches. On the *Henderson* case see generally P. S. Atiyah (1972) 33 MLR 337, which article also discussed *Colvilles Ltd v Devine* [1969] 2 All ER 53, [1969] 1 WLR 475. In this case Lord Guest stated (at p. 57) that if res ipsa loquitur applied, the appellants in that case were 'absolved if they can give a reasonable explanation of the accident and show this explanation was consistent with no lack of care on their part'. See also Lord Upjohn at p. 58; cf. Lord Donovan also at p. 58. In *Henderson* Lord Donovan took a similar view to that of Lord Reid (i.e. that the burden of disproving negligence lay

---

[7] But note that there was no appeal from the dismissal of the action against the driver.

on the defendants) and Atiyah argues that, in their dissenting speeches in that case, both Lord Guest and Viscount Dilhorne 'seem to have accepted that the defendants had the burden of disproving negligence, but both held that the defendants had in fact discharged the burden'. However, it is Lord Pearson's approach in *Henderson* that has received approval in the later cases.

■ Lloyde v West Midlands Gas Board
Court of Appeal [1971] 2 All ER 1240

MEGAW LJ: . . .
I doubt whether it is right to describe res ipsa loquitur as a 'doctrine'. I think it is no more than an exotic, though convenient, phrase to describe what is in essence no more than a common sense approach, not limited by technical rules, to the assessment of the effect of evidence in certain circumstances. It means that a plaintiff prima facie establishes negligence where: (i) it is not possible for him to prove precisely what was the relevant act or omission which set in train the events leading to the accident; but (ii) on the evidence as it stands at the relevant time it is more likely than not that the effective cause of the accident was *some* act or omission of the defendant or of someone for whom the defendant is responsible, which act or omission constitutes a failure to take proper care for the plaintiff's safety.

I have used the words 'evidence as it stands at the relevant time'. I think this can most conveniently be taken as being at the close of the plaintiff's case. On the assumption that a submission of no case is then made, would the evidence, as it then stands, enable the plaintiff to succeed because, although the precise cause of the accident cannot be established, the proper inference on balance of probability is that that cause, whatever it may have been, involved a failure by the defendant to take due care for the plaintiff's safety? If so, res ipsa loquitur. If not, the plaintiff fails. Of course, if the defendant does not make a submission of no case, the question still falls to be tested by the same criterion, but evidence for the defendant, given thereafter, may rebut the inference. The res, which previously spoke for itself, may be silenced, or its voice may, on the whole of the evidence, become too weak or muted. . . .

NOTES

1. Megaw LJ's approach in this case met with approval in *Turner v Mansfield Corpn* (1975) 119 Sol Jo 629. See also the Privy Council's view in *Ng Chun Pui v Lee Chuen Tat* [1988] RTR 298, where this passage from Megaw LJ's judgment and the bulk of the first paragraph in the extract from Lord Pearson's speech in *Henderson v Henry E Jenkins & Sons* (p. 339, ante) were adopted 'as most clearly expressing the true meaning and effect of the so-called doctrine of res ipsa loquitur'. Furthermore, they are described in *Ratcliffe v Plymouth & Torbay Health Authority* [1998] PIQR P170 at P178 (a decision which reviews the doctrine in the context of medical negligence cases) as 'authoritative expositions of the operation of the maxim'. See further *Widdowson v Newgate Meat Corpn and Scullion and Enaas* [1998] PIQR P138 and *Bergin v David Wickes Television Ltd* [1994] PIQR P167. In *Drake v Harbour* [2008] EWCA Civ 25, Longmore LJ again referred with approval to Megaw LJ's approach in *Lloyde*, suggesting at [20] that 'it is wrong to describe the maxim as a doctrine. Rather it is a guide on the question whether the claimant had raised a case to answer or whether her case should fail regardless of any evidence called by the defendant.'

2. The view (for which there was some support in the earlier case law—e.g. Lord Reid's speech in *Henderson v Jenkins*, ante) that the burden of proof is formally shifted to the defendant once res ipsa loquitur is applicable, is not being followed today. Note

also that res ipsa loquitur will only be of use to a claimant when the happening of the event actually serves as evidence of the existence of negligence: see *Fryer v Pearson* (2000) Times, 4 April. (Note May LJ's comments in this decision about 'unhelpful Latin phrases'.)

3. More fundamentally, it has been said in Canada (by the Supreme Court in *Fontaine v Insurance Corpn of British Columbia* (1998) 156 DLR (4th) 577 at 585, noted by M. McInnes (1998) 114 LQR 547), that it 'would appear that the law would be better served if the maxim was treated as expired and no longer used as a separate component in negligence actions'. However, contrast the High Court of Australia's decision in *Schellenberg v Tunnel Holdings* (2000) 74 ALJR 743. For criticism of the uncertainty surrounding the use of the maxim, see C. Witting (2001) 117 LQR 392.

4. For an example of the importance of res ipsa loquitur and its operation in practice, see *Ward v Tesco Stores Ltd* [1976] 1 All ER 219. In applying res ipsa loquitur here, Lawton LJ appears to be equating 'proper care' on the part of the defendants with ensuring that the floors of the supermarket were kept clean and spillages were dealt with immediately. This, in the view of one commentator on the case (C. Manchester (1979) 93 LQR 13 at 14), 'seems to be imposing an extremely high duty of care on the defendants, one which, in effect, is almost tantamount to strict liability'. On the question of the strictness of the liability in *Ward v Tesco Stores*, see also *Howarth*, p. 87, who sees the case as an example of the use of res ipsa loquitur 'to create strict liability out of the material of the fault regime'. Note that the High Court of Australia took a different line in a somewhat similar case (*Dulhunty v J B Young Ltd* (1975) 7 ALR 409) decided shortly before *Ward v Tesco Stores Ltd*: see (1977) 93 LQR 486 for commentary.

5. On the importance of the use of res ipsa loquitur, see *Ratcliffe v Plymouth & Torbay Health Authority* [1998] PIQR P170, 188–189, where Hobhouse LJ stated that res ipsa loquitur's 'essential role... is to enable the plaintiff who is not in possession of all the material facts to be able to plead an allegation of negligence in an acceptable form and to force the defendant to respond to it at the peril of having a finding of negligence made against the defendant if the defendant does not make an adequate response'. Consider further *Howarth*, p. 87. In essence, res ipsa loquitur is a potential aid to the claimant in discharging the burden of proof, which may be of great use in specific circumstances.

CHAPTER SIX

CAUSATION AND REMOTENESS OF DAMAGE

This topic is relevant to all torts, although most of the decided cases are on the tort of negligence. A connection must be shown between the defendant's breach of duty and the damage suffered by the claimant. The language used by writers and judges to describe this problem is perplexing. For example, it is said that a defendant is not liable unless he 'caused' the damage; on the other hand, it is said that he is not liable for all the damage he has 'caused'. Adjectives such as 'legal', 'proximate', or 'remote' do little to unravel the mysteries of this topic.

The courts are involved in various inquiries. One is the question of 'cause-and-effect'. This is sometimes called 'factual causation', and is said to depend upon notions of the physical sequence of events. The 'but for' test—the defendant's breach of duty is a cause of the damage if it is shown on the balance of probabilities that damage would not have occurred *but for* it—is widely applied, but does not solve all problems, particularly where there are multiple causes (p. 348, post). Furthermore, at the next stage when the courts have to select among the operative factual causes, they do not view causation in the same way as a scientist or meta-physician, but in the manner of the 'man in the street' (per Lord Wright in *Yorkshire Dale Steamship Co Ltd v Minister of War Transport, the Coxwold* [1942] AC 691 at 706), though see note 2, p. 387, post.

The courts must decide how far the defendant should be held liable for the consequences of his breach of duty. A single act of negligence, for example, may lead to disastrous consequences, bearing heavily on the defendant. Some practical and reasonable limitation has to be placed on loss-shifting. In the tort of negligence, the courts have moved towards the formulation that the kind of harm to his claimant must be foreseeable (*The Wagon Mound* [1961] AC 388, [1961] 1 All ER 404, p. 408, post). However, the earlier 'direct consequences' test (*Re Polemis* [1921] 3 KB 560, p. 406, post) is still relevant, since the *Wagon Mound* test has very little bearing on the question of whether an event subsequent to the defendant's negligence 'breaks the chain of causation'. It is clear from cases such as *McKew v Holland and Hannen and Cubitts (Scotland) Ltd* [1969] 3 All ER 1621 (p. 389, post), *Lamb v Camden London Borough Council* [1981] QB 625, [1981] 2 All ER 408 (p. 401, post), and *The Sivand* [1998] 2 Lloyd's Rep 97 that the two issues (*Wagon Mound* foreseeability and the chain of causation) are conceptually separate.

1 FACTUAL CAUSATION

■ Barnett v Chelsea and Kensington Hospital Management Committee
Queen's Bench Division [1968] 1 All ER 1068

The plaintiff's husband, after drinking some tea, experienced persisting vomiting for a three-hour period. Along with two other men who had also drunk the tea and who were in a similar condition, he went to the casualty department of a hospital. A nurse (against whom no complaint was made) contacted Dr Banerjee by telephone, telling him that the three men were complaining of vomiting after drinking tea. The doctor, who was himself tired and unwell, sent a message to them through the nurse to the effect that they should go home to bed and call their own doctors (with the exception of one of the men who had to have an X-ray on account of a separate incident). Some time later, the plaintiff's husband died from arsenical poisoning, and the coroner's verdict was one of murder by a person or persons unknown.

NEILD J [having found that 'the defendants [the Hospital Management Committee] were negligent and in breach of their duty in that they or their servants or agents did not see and did not examine and did not admit and did not treat the deceased', continued:] . . .

It remains to consider whether it is shown that the deceased's death was caused by the negligence or whether, as the defendants have said, the deceased must have died in any event. In his concluding submission counsel for the plaintiff submitted that Dr Banerjee should have examined the deceased, and, had he done so, he would have caused tests to be made which would have indicated the treatment required and that, since the defendants were at fault in these respects, therefore the onus of proof passed to the defendants to show that the appropriate treatment would have failed, and authorities were cited to me. I find myself unable to accept this argument and I am of the view that the onus of proof remains on the plaintiff, and I have in mind (without quoting it) the decision quoted by counsel for the defendants in *Bonnington Castings Ltd v Wardlaw*.[1] However, were it otherwise and the onus did pass to the defendants, then I would find that they have discharged it, as I would proceed to show.

There has been put before me a timetable which, I think, is of much importance. The deceased attended at the casualty department at 8.5 or 8.10 am. If Dr Banerjee had got up and dressed and come to see the three men and examined them and decided to admit them, the deceased . . . could not have been in bed in a ward before 11 am. I accept Dr Goulding's evidence that an intravenous drip would not have been set up before 12 noon, and if potassium loss was suspected it could not have been discovered until 12.30. Dr Lockett, dealing with this, said 'If [the deceased] had not been treated until after 12 noon the chances of survival were not good'.

Without going in detail into the considerable volume of technical evidence which has been put before me, it seems to me to be the case that when death results from arsenical poisoning it is brought about by two conditions; on the one hand dehydration and on the other disturbance of the enzyme processes. If the principal condition is one of enzyme disturbance—as I am of the view that it was here—then the only method of treatment which is likely to succeed is the use of the specific or antidote which is commonly called BAL. Dr Goulding said this in the course of his evidence:

'The only way to deal with this is to use the specific BAL. I see no reasonable prospect of the deceased being given BAL before the time at which he died,'

and at a later point in his evidence:

'I feel that even if fluid loss had been discovered death would have been caused by the enzyme disturbance. Death might have occurred later.'

---

[1] [1956] AC 613, [1956] 1 All ER 615.

I regard that evidence as very moderate, and that it might be a true assessment of the situation to say that there was no chance of BAL being administered before the death of the deceased.

For these reasons, I find that the plaintiff has failed to establish, on the grounds of probability, that the defendants' negligence caused the death of the deceased.

Judgment for the defendants.

NOTE

1. This case is often mentioned by writers in discussion of the 'but-for' test which has been defined at p. 343, ante. Consider further, for example, *Robinson v Post Office* [1974] 2 All ER 737, [1974] 1 WLR 1176 and see *The Empire Jamaica* [1957] AC 386, [1956] 3 All ER 144, which was mentioned by Lord Hoffmann in *South Australia Asset Management Corpn v York Montague Ltd* [1996] 3 All ER 365 at 371 (p. 273, ante). The 'but-for' test needs to be kept in mind throughout this section although, as will be seen, it can cause difficulty.

2. A material contribution to the injury will suffice, although on the ambiguity of this term, see J Stapleton (2003) 119 LQR 388 at 394–395. In *Bonnington Castings Ltd v Wardlaw* [1956] AC 613, [1956] 1 All ER 615 the claimant sustained pneumoconiosis as a result of inhaling silica dust at work. This disease was caused by the cumulative effect of the dust, some of which had arisen from a non-tortious source and some from a tortious one. The House of Lords held that it was sufficient that the tortious dust had made a material contribution (i.e. not a *de minimis* one) to the disease. It should be noted that in *Bonnington Castings* Lord Keith thought that the natural inference was that, absent the cumulative effect of the dust, the claimant would not have developed the disease at the time he did or perhaps not at all, although speaking of the fact that the law accepts material contribution to the injury as sufficient, Lord Rodger in *Fairchild v Glenhaven Funeral Services Ltd* [2002] 3 All ER 305, [2002] UKHL 22 at [129] expressed the view that the 'law is not applying the causa sine qua non or "but-for" test of causation'. A particular objection raised by J. Stapleton (1984) 104 LQR 389 to *Bonnington Castings* is that the defendant is paying for some damage that has not been shown on the balance of probabilities that they have caused. She continues (at pp. 404–405):

    [Allowing the pursuer in . . . *Bonnington Castings*] to recover for the *entire* injury, not just for the portion of that injury which he had proved to have been caused by the defender's fault . . . is tantamount to allowing the gist of the claim to be formulated in terms of the entire outcome while the causation requirement which the [claimant] is asked to satisfy is limited to only a portion of that gist damage. This non-coincidence of gist damage and the damage in respect of which the causal issue is formulated means that a [claimant] is also able to recover for that part of the overall injury to which he has been unable on the balance of probabilities to show any causal connection. Thus, even though the form of the causal issue in these cases may now be seen as the orthodox one, the outcome still represents an abandonment of the traditional rule that the defendant should only pay for past injuries which he has been shown on the balance of probabilities to have caused. It over-internalises costs to the defendant and over-deters his conduct.

    A further, related complication of the problem of factual causation was considered in *Holtby v Brigham & Cowan (Hull) Ltd* [2000] 3 All ER 421, noted by S. Hedley [2000] CLJ 435. Here the claimant was exposed to asbestos dust for most of his working life. For approximately half the relevant period, he was employed by the defendant, and for the rest of the time he was employed by other employers, doing similar work. He developed asbestosis and sued the defendant in negligence and for breach of statutory duty. The trial judge found the defendant liable, but held that the asbestosis would have been less severe if the claimant had only sustained exposure to asbestos whilst working for the defendant. The judge accordingly reduced the claimant's damages by 25 per cent to reflect the fact that the defendant was not solely responsible for all the damage. The claimant appealed, claiming that having proved that the defendant's conduct had made a material contribution to his disease, the defendant was liable for the total damage (but with the possibility of claiming a contribution from anyone else responsible for the damage, on which statutory claim see p. 1122, post). The Court of Appeal rejected this argument. Stuart-Smith LJ (with whose judgment Mummery LJ agreed) held ([2000] 3 All ER at p. 428) that 'the onus of proving causation is on the claimant; it does not shift to the defendant. He will be entitled to succeed if he can prove that the defendant's tortious conduct made a material contribution to his disability. But strictly speaking the defendant is liable only to the extent of that contribution. However, if the point is never raised or argued by the defendant, the claimant will succeed in full as in the *Bonnington* case...'. See further *Thompson v Smiths Shiprepairers (North Shields) Ltd* [1984] [1984] QB 405, 1 All ER 881; *Allen v British Rail Engineering Ltd* [2001] ICR 942 at [20] and more generally A. Porat and A. Stein (2003) 23 Oxf JLS 667, although note that this article was written before the important case of *Barker v Corus (UK) Ltd* [2006] 3 All ER 785, [2006] UKHL 20 (p. 357, post) was decided. Do you prefer the basis of distinction relied on by Clarke LJ in *Holtby*, namely that there is a difference between 'indivisible' causes of the same injury and cases like *Holtby* where the injury is caused by 'sequential' exposure to causes that are not truly indivisible? See further Question 5, p. 363, post. Consider further *Rahman v Arearose Ltd* [2001] QB 351, noted by T. Weir [2001] CLJ 237, raising questions concerning concurrent tortfeasors (on which see chap. 19). Such tortfeasors are each responsible for all the damage concurrently caused.

3. On the difficulties of the 'but-for' test and factual causation, see the discussion in *March v E & M H Stramare Pty Ltd* (1990–1) 171 CLR 506, commented on by N. J. Mullany (1992) 12 Oxf JLS 431, and the extract from Strachan's article, p. 376, post. An example from the medical world is provided by a case which has previously been considered on the question of the standard of care: *Bolitho v City and Hackney Health Authority* [1998] AC 232, [1997] 4 All ER 771 (p. 326, ante). Here there had been a breach of duty in the circumstances by a doctor not attending a patient (or arranging for some other suitable person to do so). The causation question that then arose was whether if this breach had not occurred, a particular method of treatment (intubation) would have been administered in time to prevent the cardiac arrest suffered by the patient. On the facts the trial judge accepted it would not have been, but that was not the end of the matter (cf. a case such as *Gouldsmith v Mid Staffordshire General Hospitals NHS Trust* [2007] EWCA Civ 397). The courts in *Bolitho* then addressed the question (which was the issue considered at p. 326, ante) whether it would have been a breach of duty not to administer intubation. On this issue it was held that it would not have been and the case failed on that ground. Suppose, however, that the issue of any later negligence had been decided differently. Could a defendant in this situation still argue that the causal link between the first breach of duty (concerning attendance) and the cardiac arrest was lacking (i.e. that on the facts found by the judge the cardiac arrest would still have happened)? The House of Lords thought not, accepting as correct the defendants' concession that they could not raise their own breach of duty (if it had been established) in this way. In a different case (*Joyce v Merton Sutton and Wandsworth Health Authority* (1995) 27 BMLR 124) Hobhouse LJ had stated (at p. 156) that a claimant proves his case

by establishing that his injuries would not have occurred if proper care had continued to be taken and this view was adopted by the House of Lords in *Bolitho*. For general comment see A. Grubb [1998] Med LR 380 at 384–386.

4. As the previous note shows, confusion often results from considering other ways in which the defendant might have breached the duty of care. Such considerations are irrelevant. When the but-for question is spelled out in full, this becomes clear. It is: 'Would the harm still have happened if, instead of acting the way he did, the defendant acted in a way which did not amount to a breach of duty?' In other words, the comparison is between what the defendant actually did and what he should have done; there is simply no place for comparing other courses of action which might also have constituted breaches of duty. One consequence of this is that causal problems tend to dissolve if the standard of care is set at a higher level.

The same sort of problem can arise in reverse. It is futile for the defendant to try to exonerate himself by pointing to other ways in which he might still have caused the same harm *without* being in breach of duty. The fire brigade tried, unsuccessfully, to use this sort of argument in *Capital and Counties plc v Hampshire County Council* [1997] QB 1004, [1997] 2 All ER 865, noted p. 116, ante). The fire brigade arrived to fight a fire at the claimant's premises but instead, bizarrely, switched off the automatic sprinkler system. As will have been seen, the Court of Appeal held that, in general, fire brigades were only liable where they made harm worse, but were under no duty of care to act to put out fires. On this basis, the Hampshire fire brigade tried to rely on the trial judge's finding that he was 'unable to say whether or not, on balance of probabilities, if the fire brigade had done nothing and the sprinklers had been left on the building would have burned down completely'. The Court of Appeal did not accept this argument. Stuart Smith LJ stated ([1997] 2 All ER at p. 882):

Having negligently turned off the sprinklers which were at that stage containing the fire, the defendants by their positive act exacerbated the fire so that it spread rapidly. The question is thus one of causation and has to be tested with the benefit of hindsight by comparing what would have happened if the sprinklers had been left on with what in fact happened. This is what the judge did. He was correct to compare one hypothetical situation with one real eventuality, rather than two hypothetical situations. It is not to be supposed that having arrived on the fire ground the fire brigade would simply have sat on their hands.

5. Factual causation problems have surfaced in several House of Lords cases over the years. In *McGhee v National Coal Board* [1972] 3 All ER 1008, [1973] 1WLR 1 the pursuer, who was employed at a brickworks, contracted a skin disease (dermatitis) as a result of his work, but the exact causes of this disease were not well-known to medical science. Brick dust would accumulate on the pursuer's skin, and the defender was in breach of duty in not providing adequate washing facilities before the pursuer left work. However, the pursuer could not prove on the balance of probabilities that the fact of cycling home unwashed was the cause of his skin disease, i.e. that but-for the defender's breach of duty he would not have sustained dermatitis. It merely increased the risk of sustaining the disease. Nevertheless, the House of Lords was prepared in the circumstances to equate materially increasing the risk of the disease with materially contributing to it. The case was controversial, and for general discussion see E.J. Weinrib (1975) 38 MLR 518. Some years later *McGhee* came under scrutiny in the House of Lords in *Wilsher v Essex Area Health Authority* [1988] 1 All ER 871, [1988] AC 1074. In this case the claimant, who was born almost three months prematurely, sustained retrolental fibroplasia (RLF), which caused him to be totally blind in one eye

and to suffer from seriously impaired vision in the other. His claim was that the RLF was caused by an excess of oxygen tension in his blood in the early weeks after birth and that this was due to negligence in the management of his oxygen supply. In the Court of Appeal, [1986] 3 All ER 801, a finding of negligence was upheld against a registrar for failure to notice from an X-ray that a catheter, used to measure the partial pressure of oxygen (PO_2), had been misplaced (i.e. put in a vein rather than an artery). In this situation it would give a misleading reading and this led to the administration of too much oxygen. This finding of negligence was not challenged in the House of Lords, where the question of causation was in issue, since there were four non-negligent other possible causes of the claimant's RLF. Lord Bridge (with whose speech his brethren agreed) thought that *McGhee* did not establish any new principle and was merely an example of a robust approach to the primary facts leading to an inference that the defender's negligence had materially contributed to the dermatitis. However, it will be seen (p. 351, post) that this passage in *Wilsher* in which his view is expressed was disapproved in a later House of Lords case. On the evidence in *Wilsher* a sufficient causal link had not been shown in the House of Lords' opinion, and the case was sent back for retrial as to whether the negligence for which the defendant was responsible caused or materially contributed to the RLF. However, as will be seen shortly, *McGhee* has been reinterpreted and rehabilitated by the House of Lords in recent years, albeit without overturning the decision in *Wilsher*.

■ Fairchild v Glenhaven Funeral Services Ltd
House of Lords [2002] 3 All ER 305

LORD BINGHAM OF CORNHILL: . . .

[2] The essential question underlying the appeals may be accurately expressed in this way. If (1) C was employed at different times and for differing periods by both A and B, and (2) A and B were both subject to a duty to take reasonable care or to take all practicable measures to prevent C inhaling asbestos dust because of the known risk that asbestos dust (if inhaled) might cause a mesothelioma, and (3) both A and B were in breach of that duty in relation to C during the periods of C's employment by each of them with the result that during both periods C inhaled excessive quantities of asbestos dust, and (4) C is found to be suffering from a mesothelioma, and (5) any cause of C's mesothelioma other than the inhalation of asbestos dust at work can be effectively discounted, but (6) C cannot (because of the current limits of human science) prove, on the balance of probabilities, that his mesothelioma was the result of his inhaling asbestos dust during his employment by A or during his employment by B or during his employment by A and B taken together, is C entitled to recover damages against either A or B or against both A and B? To this question (not formulated in these terms) the Court of Appeal (Brooke, Latham and Kay LJJ), in a reserved judgment of the court ([2001] EWCA Civ 1881, [2002] 1 WLR 1052), gave a negative answer. It did so because, applying the conventional 'but for' test of tortious liability, it could not be held that C had proved against A that his mesothelioma would probably not have occurred but for the breach of duty by A, nor against B that his mesothelioma would probably not have occurred but for the breach of duty by B, nor against A and B that his mesothelioma would probably not have occurred but for the breach of duty by both A and B together. So C failed against both A and B. The crucial issue on appeal is whether, in the special circumstances of such a case, principle, authority or policy requires or justifies a modified approach to proof of causation.

[3] It is common ground that in each of the three cases under appeal conditions numbered (1) to (5) above effectively obtained. During his working life the late Mr Fairchild worked for an employer (whose successor was wrongly identified as the first-named defendant) who carried out sub-contract work for

the Leeds City Council in the early 1960s and may have built packing cases for the transportation of industrial ovens lined with asbestos. He also worked for a builder, in whose employment he cut asbestos sheeting both to repair various roofs and while renovating a factory for Waddingtons plc. In the course of his work Mr Fairchild inhaled substantial quantities of asbestos dust containing asbestos fibre which caused him to suffer a mesothelioma of the pleura, from which he died on 18 September 1996 at the age of 60. Waddingtons plc accepted at trial that it had exposed Mr Fairchild to the inhalation of asbestos fibres by a breach of the duty owed to him under s 63 of the Factories Act 1961. (Waddingtons plc was not an employer, but nothing turns on this distinction with the other cases.) It thereby admitted that he had been exposed to a substantial quantity of dust or had been exposed to dust to such an extent as was likely to be injurious to him. After the death of Mr Fairchild his widow brought this action, originally against three defendants (not including the builder). She discontinued proceedings against the first-named defendant, and on 1 February 2001 Curtis J dismissed her claim against Waddingtons plc and the Leeds City Council. The Court of Appeal dismissed her appeal against that decision in the judgment already referred to, finding it unnecessary (because of its decision on causation) to reach a final decision on all aspects of her common law claim against the Leeds City Council. She challenges that causation decision on appeal to the House.

[Having described the facts of the other two cases involved in this appeal, his Lordship continued:]

[7] From about the 1960s, it became widely known that exposure to asbestos dust and fibres could give rise not only to asbestosis and other pulmonary diseases, but also to the risk of developing a mesothelioma. This is a malignant tumour, usually of the pleura, sometimes of the peritoneum. In the absence of occupational exposure to asbestos dust it is a very rare tumour indeed, afflicting no more than about one person in a million per year. But the incidence of the tumour among those occupationally exposed to asbestos dust is about 1,000 times greater than in the general population, and there are some 1,500 cases reported annually. It is a condition which may be latent for many years, usually for 30–40 years or more; development of the condition may take as short a period as ten years, but it is thought that that is the period which elapses between the mutation of the first cell and the manifestation of symptoms of the condition. It is invariably fatal, and death usually occurs within one to two years of the condition being diagnosed. The mechanism by which a normal mesothelial cell is transformed into a mesothelioma cell is not known. It is believed by the best medical opinion to involve a multi-stage process, in which six or seven genetic changes occur in a normal cell to render it malignant. Asbestos acts in at least one of those stages and may (but this is uncertain) act in more than one. It is not known what level of exposure to asbestos dust and fibre can be tolerated without significant risk of developing a mesothelioma, but it is known that those living in urban environments (although without occupational exposure) inhale large numbers of asbestos fibres without developing a mesothelioma. It is accepted that the risk of developing a mesothelioma increases in proportion to the quantity of asbestos dust and fibres inhaled: the greater the quantity of dust and fibre inhaled, the greater the risk. But the condition may be caused by a single fibre, or a few fibres, or many fibres: medical opinion holds none of these possibilities to be more probable than any other, and the condition once caused is not aggravated by further exposure. So if C is employed successively by A and B and is exposed to asbestos dust and fibres during each employment and develops a mesothelioma, the very strong probability is that this will have been caused by inhalation of asbestos dust containing fibres. But C could have inhaled a single fibre giving rise to his condition during employment by A, in which case his exposure by B will have had no effect on his condition; or he could have inhaled a single fibre giving rise to his condition during his employment by B, in which case his exposure by A will have had no effect on his condition; or he could have inhaled fibres during his employment by A and B which together gave rise to his condition; but medical science cannot support the suggestion that any of these possibilities is to be regarded as more probable than any other. There is no way of identifying, even on a balance of probabilities, the source of the fibre or fibres which initiated the genetic process which culminated in the malignant tumour. It is on this rock of uncertainty, reflecting the point to which medical science has so far advanced, that the three claims were rejected by the Court of Appeal and by two of the three trial judges.

Principle

[8] In a personal injury action based on negligence or breach of statutory duty the claimant seeks to establish a breach by the defendant of a duty owed to the claimant, which has caused him damage. For the purposes of analysis, and for the purpose of pleading, proving and resolving the claim, lawyers find it convenient to break the claim into its constituent elements: the duty, the breach, the damage and the causal connection between the breach and the damage. In the generality of personal injury actions, it is of course true that the claimant is required to discharge the burden of showing that the breach of which he complains caused the damage for which he claims and to do so by showing that but for the breach he would not have suffered the damage.

[9] The issue in these appeals does not concern the general validity and applicability of that requirement, which is not in question, but is whether in special circumstances such as those in these cases there should be any variation or relaxation of it. The overall object of tort law is to define cases in which the law may justly hold one party liable to compensate another. Are these such cases? A and B owed C a duty to protect C against a risk of a particular and very serious kind. They failed to perform that duty. As a result the risk eventuated and C suffered the very harm against which it was the duty of A and B to protect him. Had there been only one tortfeasor, C would have been entitled to recover, but because the duty owed to him was broken by two tortfeasors and not only one, he is held to be entitled to recover against neither, because of his inability to prove what is scientifically unprovable. If the mechanical application of generally accepted rules leads to such a result, there must be room to question the appropriateness of such an approach in such a case. . . .

[13] I do not . . . consider that the House is acting contrary to principle in reviewing the applicability of the conventional test of causation to cases such as the present. Indeed, it would seem to me contrary to principle to insist on application of a rule which appeared, if it did, to yield unfair results. And I think it salutary to bear in mind Lord Mansfield's aphorism in *Blatch v Archer* (1774) 1 Cowp 63 at 65, 98 ER 969 at 970 quoted with approval by the Supreme Court of Canada in *Snell v Farrell*:

> 'It is certainly a maxim that all evidence is to be weighed according to the proof which it was in the power of one side to have produced, and in the power of the other to have contradicted.'

[LORD BINGHAM then discussed various authorities, including the *McGhee* case, and continued:]

[21] This detailed review of *McGhee*'s case permits certain conclusions to be drawn. First, the House was deciding a question of law. Lord Reid expressly said so ([1972] 3 All ER 1008 at 1009, [1973] 1 WLR 1 at 3). The other opinions, save perhaps that of Lord Kilbrandon, cannot be read as decisions of fact or as orthodox applications of settled law. Secondly, the question of law was whether, on the facts of the case as found, a pursuer who could not show that the defender's breach had probably caused the damage of which he complained could nonetheless succeed. Thirdly, it was not open to the House to draw a factual inference that the breach probably had caused the damage: such an inference was expressly contradicted by the medical experts on both sides; and once that evidence had been given the crux of the argument before the Lord Ordinary and the First Division and the House was whether, since the pursuer could not prove that the breach had probably made a material contribution to his contracting dermatitis, it was enough to show that the breach had increased the risk of his contracting it. Fourthly, it was expressly held by three members of the House ([1972] 3 All ER 1008 at 1011, 1014, 1018, [1973] 1 WLR 1 at 5, 8, 12–13 per Lord Reid, Lord Simon and Lord Salmon respectively) that in the circumstances no distinction was to be drawn between making a material contribution to causing the disease and materially increasing the risk of the pursuer contracting it. Thus the proposition expressly rejected by the Lord Ordinary, the Lord President and Lord Migdale was expressly accepted by a majority of the House and must be taken to represent the ratio of the decision, closely tied though it was to the special facts on which it was based. Fifthly, recognising that the pursuer faced an insuperable problem of proof if the orthodox test of causation was applied, but regarding the case as one in which justice demanded a remedy for the pursuer, a majority of the House adapted the orthodox test to meet the particular case. The authority is of obvious importance in the present appeal since the

medical evidence left open the possibility, as Lord Reid pointed out ([1972] 3 All ER 1008 at 1010, [1973] 1 WLR 1 at 4) that the pursuer's dermatitis could have begun with a single abrasion, which might have been caused when he was cycling home, but might equally have been caused when he was working in the brick kiln; in the latter event, the failure to provide showers would have made no difference. In *McGhee*'s case, however, unlike the present appeals, the case was not complicated by the existence of additional or alternative wrongdoers.

[22] In *Wilsher v Essex Area Health Authority* [1988] 1 All ER 871, [1988] AC 1074…the House was right to allow the defendants' appeal…. It is one thing to treat an increase of risk as equivalent to the making of a material contribution where a single noxious agent is involved, but quite another where any one of a number of noxious agents may equally probably have caused the damage. But much difficulty is caused by the following passage in Lord Bridge's opinion in which, having cited the opinions of all members of the House in *McGhee*'s case, he said:

'The conclusion I draw from these passages is that *McGhee v National Coal Board* laid down no new principle of law whatever. On the contrary, it affirmed the principle that the onus of proving causation lies on the pursuer or plaintiff. Adopting a robust and pragmatic approach to the undisputed primary facts of the case, the majority concluded that it was a legitimate inference of fact that the defenders' negligence had materially contributed to the pursuer's injury. The decision, in my opinion, is of no greater significance than that and the attempt to extract from it some esoteric principle which in some way modifies, as a matter of law, the nature of the burden of proof of causation which a plaintiff or pursuer must discharge once he has established a relevant breach of duty is a fruitless one.' (See [1988] 1 All ER 871 at 881–882, [1988] AC 1074 at 1090.)

This is a passage to which the Court of Appeal ([2002] 1 WLR 1052 at [103]) very properly gave weight, and in argument on these appeals counsel for the respondents strongly relied on it as authority for their major contention that a claimant can only succeed if he proves on the balance of probabilities that the default of the particular defendant had caused the damage of which he complains. As is apparent from the conclusions expressed in [21], above, I cannot for my part accept this passage in Lord Bridge's opinion as accurately reflecting the effect of what the House, or a majority of the House, decided in *McGhee*'s case, which remains sound authority. I am bound to conclude that this passage should no longer be treated as authoritative.

[LORD BINGHAM then went on to consider the way other legal systems had dealt with the problem and continued:]

[32] This survey shows, as would be expected, that though the problem underlying cases such as the present is universal the response to it is not. Hence the plethora of decisions given in different factual contexts. Hence also the intensity of academic discussion, exemplified by the articles of the late Professor Fleming ('Probabilistic Causation in Tort Law' 68 Canadian Bar Review, No 4, December 1989, 661) and Professor Robertson ('The Common Sense of Cause in Fact' (1996–1997) 75 Tex L Rev 1765). In some jurisdictions, it appears, the plaintiff would fail altogether on causation grounds, as the Court of Appeal held that the present appellants did. Italy, South Africa and Switzerland may be examples (see *Unification of Tort Law: Causation* (2000) pp 90, 102 and 120). But it appears that in most of the jurisdictions considered the problem of attribution would not, on facts such as those of the present cases, be a fatal objection to a plaintiff's claim. Whether by treating an increase in risk as equivalent to a material contribution, or by putting a burden on the defendant, or by enlarging the ordinary approach to acting in concert, or on more general grounds influenced by policy considerations, most jurisdictions would, it seems, afford a remedy to the plaintiff. Development of the law in this country cannot of course depend on a head-count of decisions and codes adopted in other countries around the world, often against a background of different rules and traditions. The law must be developed coherently, in accordance with principle, so as to serve, even-handedly, the ends of justice. If, however, a decision is given in this country which offends one's basic sense of justice, and if consideration of international sources suggests that a different and more acceptable decision would be given in

most other jurisdictions, whatever their legal tradition, this must prompt anxious review of the decision in question. In a shrinking world (in which the employees of asbestos companies may work for those companies in any one or more of several countries) there must be some virtue in uniformity of outcome whatever the diversity of approach in reaching that outcome.

Policy

[33] The present appeals raise an obvious and inescapable clash of policy considerations. On the one hand are the considerations powerfully put by the Court of Appeal ([2002] 1 WLR 1052 at [103]) which considered the claimants' argument to be not only illogical but—

> 'also susceptible of unjust results. It may impose liability for the whole of an insidious disease on an employer with whom the claimant was employed for quite a short time in a long working life, when the claimant is wholly unable to prove on the balance of probabilities that that period of employment had any causative relationship with the inception of the disease. This is far too weighty an edifice to build on the slender foundations of *McGhee v National Coal Board*, and Lord Bridge has told us in *Wilsher v Essex Area Health Authority* that *McGhee* established no new principle of law at all. If we were to accede to the claimants' arguments, we would be distorting the law to accommodate the exigencies of a very hard case. We would be yielding to a contention that all those who have suffered injury after being exposed to a risk of that injury from which someone else should have protected them should be able to recover compensation even when they are quite unable to prove who was the culprit. In a quite different context Lord Steyn has recently said in [*White v Chief Constable of the South Yorkshire Police* [1999] 1 All ER 1 at 30, [1999] 2 AC 455 at 491] that our tort system sometimes results in imperfect justice, but it is the best the common law can do.'

The Court of Appeal had in mind that in [three cases Lord Bingham had previously referred to (in an omitted passage) and in *McGhee*] there was only one employer involved. Thus there was a risk that the defendant might be held liable for acts for which he should not be held legally liable but no risk that he would be held liable for damage which (whether legally liable or not) he had not caused. The crux of cases such as the present, if the appellants' argument is upheld, is that an employer may be held liable for damage he has not caused. The risk is the greater where all the employers potentially liable are not before the court. This is so on the facts of each of the three appeals before the House, and is always likely to be so given the long latency of this condition and the likelihood that some employers potentially liable will have gone out of business or disappeared during that period. It can properly be said to be unjust to impose liability on a party who has not been shown, even on a balance of probabilities, to have caused the damage complained of. On the other hand, there is a strong policy argument in favour of compensating those who have suffered grave harm, at the expense of their employers who owed them a duty to protect them against that very harm and failed to do so, when the harm can only have been caused by breach of that duty and when science does not permit the victim accurately to attribute, as between several employers, the precise responsibility for the harm he has suffered. I am of opinion that such injustice as may be involved in imposing liability on a duty-breaking employer in these circumstances is heavily outweighed by the injustice of denying redress to a victim. Were the law otherwise, an employer exposing his employee to asbestos dust could obtain complete immunity against mesothelioma (but not asbestosis) claims by employing only those who had previously been exposed to excessive quantities of asbestos dust. Such a result would reflect no credit on the law. It seems to me, as it did to Lord Wilberforce in *McGhee*'s case [1972] 3 All ER 1008 at 1013, [1973] 1 WLR 1 at 7, that—

> 'the employers should be liable for an injury, squarely within the risk which they created and that they, not the pursuer, should suffer the consequence of the impossibility, foreseeably inherent in the nature of his injury, of segregating the precise consequence of their default.'

Conclusion

[34] To the question posed in [2], above, I would answer that where conditions (1)–(6) are satisfied C is entitled to recover against both A and B. That conclusion is in my opinion consistent with principle, and

also with authority (properly understood). Where those conditions are satisfied, it seems to me just and in accordance with common sense to treat the conduct of A and B in exposing C to a risk to which he should not have been exposed as making a material contribution to the contracting by C of a condition against which it was the duty of A and B to protect him. I consider that this conclusion is fortified by the wider jurisprudence reviewed above. Policy considerations weigh in favour of such a conclusion. It is a conclusion which follows even if either A or B is not before the court. It was not suggested in argument that C's entitlement against either A or B should be for any sum less than the full compensation to which C is entitled, although A and B could of course seek contribution against each other or any other employer liable in respect of the same damage in the ordinary way. No argument on apportionment was addressed to the House. I would in conclusion emphasise that my opinion is directed to cases in which each of the conditions specified in (1)–(6) of [2], above is satisfied and to no other case. It would be unrealistic to suppose that the principle here affirmed will not over time be the subject of incremental and analogical development. Cases seeking to develop the principle must be decided when and as they arise. For the present, I think it unwise to decide more than is necessary to resolve these three appeals which, for all the foregoing reasons, I concluded should be allowed.

[35] For reasons given above, I cannot accept the view (considered in the opinion of my noble and learned friend Lord Hutton) that the decision in *McGhee*'s case was based on the drawing of a factual inference. Nor, in my opinion, was the decision based on the drawing of a legal inference. Whether, in certain limited and specific circumstances, a legal inference is drawn or a different legal approach is taken to the proof of causation, may not make very much practical difference. But Lord Wilberforce, in one of the passages of his opinion in *McGhee*'s case…, wisely deprecated resort to fictions and it seems to me preferable, in the interests of transparency, that the courts' response to the special problem presented by cases such as these should be stated explicitly. I prefer to recognise that the ordinary approach to proof of causation is varied than to resort to the drawing of legal inferences inconsistent with the proven facts.

LORD HOFFMANN: . . .

[60] The problem in this appeal is to formulate a just and fair rule. Clearly the rule must be based upon principle. However deserving the claimants may be, your Lordships are not exercising a discretion to adapt causal requirements to the individual case. That does not mean, however, that it must be a principle so broad that it takes no account of significant differences which affect whether it is fair and just to impose liability.

[61] What are the significant features of the present case? First, we are dealing with a duty specifically intended to protect employees against being unnecessarily exposed to the risk of (among other things) a particular disease. Secondly, the duty is one intended to create a civil right to compensation for injury relevantly connected with its breach. Thirdly, it is established that the greater the exposure to asbestos, the greater the risk of contracting that disease. Fourthly, except in the case in which there has been only one significant exposure to asbestos, medical science cannot prove whose asbestos is more likely than not to have produced the cell mutation which caused the disease. Fifthly, the employee has contracted the disease against which he should have been protected.

[62] In these circumstances, a rule requiring proof of a link between the defendant's asbestos and the claimant's disease would, with the arbitrary exception of single-employer cases, empty the duty of content. If liability depends upon proof that the conduct of the defendant was a necessary condition of the injury, it cannot effectively exist. It is however open to your Lordships to formulate a different causal requirement in this class of case. The Court of Appeal was in my opinion wrong to say that in the absence of a proven link between the defendant's asbestos and the disease, there was no 'causative relationship' whatever between the defendant's conduct and the disease. It depends entirely upon the level at which the causal relationship is described. To say, for example, that the cause of Mr Matthews' [one of the other claimants] cancer was his significant exposure to asbestos during two employments over a period of eight years, without being able to identify the day upon which he inhaled the fatal fibre, is a meaningful causal statement. The medical evidence shows that it is the only kind of causal

statement about the disease which, in the present state of knowledge, a scientist would regard as possible. There is no a priori reason, no rule of logic, which prevents the law from treating it as sufficient to satisfy the causal requirements of the law of negligence. The question is whether your Lordships think such a rule would be just and reasonable and whether the class of cases to which it applies can be sufficiently clearly defined.

[63] So the question of principle is this: in cases which exhibit the five features I have mentioned, which rule would be more in accordance with justice and the policy of common law and statute to protect employees against the risk of contracting asbestos-related diseases? One which makes an employer in breach of his duty liable for the claimant's injury because he created a significant risk to his health, despite the fact that the physical cause of the injury *may* have been created by someone else? Or a rule which means that unless he was subjected to risk by the breach of duty of a single employer, the employee can never have a remedy? My Lords, as between the employer in breach of duty and the employee who has lost his life in consequence of a period of exposure to risk to which that employer has contributed, I think it would be both inconsistent with the policy of the law imposing the duty and morally wrong for your Lordships to impose causal requirements which exclude liability.

[64] My Lords, I turn from principle to authority. The case which most closely resembles the present is *McGhee v National Coal Board* [1972] 3 All ER 1008, [1973] 1 WLR 1, which my noble and learned friend Lord Bingham of Cornhill has analysed in some detail. There too, the employer was under a duty (to provide washing facilities) specifically intended to protect employees against being unnecessarily exposed to the risk of (among other things) a particular disease, namely dermatitis. Secondly, the duty was one intended to create a civil right to compensation for injury relevantly connected with its breach. Thirdly, it was established that the longer the workman exerted himself while particles of dust adhered to his skin, the greater was the risk of his contracting dermatitis. Fourthly, the mechanism by which dust caused the disease was unknown, so that medical science was unable to prove whether the particular dust abrasions which caused the dermatitis were more likely than not to have occurred before or after the dust would have been removed if washing facilities had been provided. All that could be said was that the absence of facilities added materially to the risk that he would contract the disease. Fifthly, the employee contracted the disease against which he should have been protected.

[65] My Lords, in these circumstances, which in my opinion reproduce the essential features of the present case, the House decided that materially increasing the risk that the disease would occur was sufficient to satisfy the causal requirements for liability.... [W]hen some members of the House said that in the circumstances there was no distinction between materially increasing the risk of disease and materially contributing to the disease, what I think they meant was that, in the particular circumstances, a breach of duty which materially increased the risk should be treated *as if* it had materially contributed to the disease. I would respectfully prefer not resort to legal fictions and to say that the House treated a material increase in risk as sufficient in the circumstances to satisfy the causal requirements for liability. That this was the effect of the decision seems to me inescapable.

[66] The grounds upon which the House was willing to formulate a special causal requirements rule in *McGhee*'s case seem to me equally applicable in this case....

[67] I therefore regard *McGhee*'s case as a powerful support for saying that when the five factors I have mentioned are present, the law should treat a material increase in risk as sufficient to satisfy the causal requirements for liability....

[LORD HOFFMANN then pointed out that the five factors to which he had referred were not present in *Wilsher* and continued:]

[70] I...think that *Wilsher*'s case was correctly decided. The appellants have not made any submission to the contrary. But the grounds upon which *McGhee*'s case was distinguished are unsatisfactory....

[73] The question is how narrowly the principle developed in *McGhee*'s case and applied in this case should be confined. In my opinion, caution is advisable.... I would suggest that the rule now laid down by the House should be limited to cases which have the five features I have described.

[74] That does not mean that the principle is not capable of development and application in new situations....For present purposes, the *McGhee* principle is sufficient. I would therefore allow the appeals.

LORD RODGER OF EARLSFERRY:...

[151] Although counsel for the respondents accepted that, if reinstated, the principle in *McGhee*'s case would govern the present appeals and would mean that the appeals would have to be allowed, it is worth noticing why that should be so.

[152] The parallels between the cases are striking. In *McGhee*'s case the defenders had negligently failed to provide showers to remove sweat and dust; in these cases the defendants had negligently failed to provide protection from asbestos dust. In *McGhee*'s case, by removing the sweat and dust, the showers would have been intended to guard the workmen against suffering skin diseases such as dermatitis; here the protection against inhaling asbestos dust would have been intended to guard the workmen against suffering asbestos-related illnesses such as mesothelioma. In *McGhee*'s case the failure to provide the showers materially increased the risk of the pursuer developing dermatitis; in these cases the failure to protect against inhaling asbestos dust materially increased the risk of the claimants developing mesothelioma. In *McGhee*'s case the pursuer developed dermatitis due to the presence of dust and sweat on his skin, while in these cases the claimants developed mesothelioma due to inhaling asbestos dust. In *McGhee*'s case it was not possible in the state of medical knowledge for the pursuer to prove in the usual way whether the dermatitis started because of a single abrasion or because of multiple abrasions. Here in the state of medical knowledge it is not possible for the claimants to prove whether the mesothelioma started from the effect of a single fibre or from the effect of multiple fibres. In *McGhee*'s case it was simply not possible for the pursuer to prove that his dermatitis was caused by an accumulation of abrasions; similarly, here it is simply not possible for the claimants to prove that their mesothelioma was caused by an accumulation of asbestos fibres. In *McGhee*'s case it was not possible for the pursuer to prove that the hypothetical single abrasion had been caused at a time after he should have had a shower and was cycling home. Here it is not possible for the claimants to prove that the hypothetical single fibre had been inhaled while they were working with any particular employer and especially while they were working with any of the defendants.

[153] In one respect, of course, the cases diverge. In *McGhee*'s case the only possible source of the dust and sweat was the National Coal Board's kiln and the only possible wrongdoers were the coal board. Here, by contrast, the defendants are simply some among a number of employers who negligently exposed the claimants to asbestos dust. The Court of Appeal ([2002] 1 WLR 1052 at [104]) attached some importance to this distinction. On closer inspection, however, the distinction does not appear to be material for present purposes. The important point is that in both cases the state of scientific knowledge makes it impossible for the victim to prove on the balance of probabilities that his injury was caused by the defenders' or defendants' wrongdoing rather than by events of a similar nature which would not constitute wrongdoing on their part. Therefore, if the principle applies to permit the pursuer to recover in *McGhee*'s case, it should similarly apply to allow the claimants to recover in these cases. Indeed, on one view the principle is easier to apply in the present cases than in *McGhee*'s case since it is not disputed that the men developed mesothelioma as a result of a tort by one of their employers. The claimants thus have all the necessary elements for a successful claim except, it is argued, proof of causation. In *McGhee*'s case, on the other hand, it was possible that the pursuer's dermatitis had been prompted purely by his exposure to dust in the kiln and by his exertions there, for which the employers would not have been liable in delict. So, application of the principle was crucial to connect the pursuer's illness not just with the defenders' legal wrong but with any legal wrong at all. In that sense these cases are a fortiori *McGhee*'s case.

[154] The decision in *McGhee*'s case undoubtedly involved a development of the law relating to causation....

[155] As counsel for the defendants submitted, the principle in *McGhee*'s case involves an element of rough justice, since it is possible that a defendant may be found liable when, if science permitted the

matter to be clarified completely, it would turn out that the defendant's wrongdoing did not in fact lead to the men's illness. That consideration weighed with the Court of Appeal ([2002] 1 WLR 1052 at [103]). It must be faced squarely. The opposing potential injustice to claimants should also be addressed squarely. If defendants are not held liable in such circumstances, then claimants have no claim, even though, similarly, if the matter could be clarified completely, it might turn out that the defendants were indeed the authors of the men's illness. Other considerations colour the picture. The men did nothing wrong, whereas all the defendants wrongly exposed them to the risk of developing a fatal cancer, a risk that has eventuated in these cases. At best, it was only good luck if any particular defendant's negligence did not trigger the victim's mesothelioma. The defendants, in effect, say that it is because they are all wrongdoers that the claimants have no case. In other words: the greater the risk that the men have run at the hands of successive negligent employers, the smaller the claimants' chances of obtaining damages. In these circumstances, one might think, in dubio the law should favour the claimants. Moreover, in *McGhee*'s case the House did nothing more than set the requirement of proof at the highest that the pursuer could possibly attain—hardly a relaxation in any real sense. He had proved all that he could and had established that the defenders' wrongdoing had put him at risk of the very kind of injury which befell him. To require more would have been to say that he could never recover for his injury—unless he achieved the impossible. Finally, as was recognised in *McGhee* ([1972] 3 All ER 1008 at 1015, 1018, [1973] 1 WLR 1 at 9, 12 per Lord Simon and Lord Salmon respectively), if the law did indeed impose a standard of proof that no pursuer could ever satisfy, then, so far as the civil law is concerned, employers could with impunity negligently expose their workmen to the risk of dermatitis—or, far worse, of mesothelioma. The substantive duty of care would be emptied of all practical content so far as victims are concerned. In my view considerations of these kinds justified the House in developing the approach of Viscount Simonds and Lord Cohen in *Nicholson*'s case [[1957] 1 All ER 776, [1957] 1 WLR 613] to fashion and apply the principle in *McGhee*'s case. A fortiori they justify the application of that principle in the present case where the risk to the men was so much worse.

[156] I derive support for that conclusion from what has been done in other legal systems. In the course of the hearing counsel for both sides referred to authorities from a number of different jurisdictions. It would be impossible to do justice to all of them in this opinion. Broadly speaking, they appear to me to demonstrate two things: first, that other systems have identified the need to adopt special rules or principles to cope with situations where the claimant cannot establish which of a number of wrongdoers actually caused his injury; secondly, that there are considerable divergences of view and indeed uncertainty as to the proper area within which any such special rules or principles should apply....

[LORD RODGER then referred to the position in other legal systems, including Roman law, and continued:]

[168] At the very least, the cross-check with these systems suggests that it is not necessarily the hallmark of a civilised and sophisticated legal system that it treats cases where strict proof of causation is impossible in exactly the same way as cases where such proof is possible. As I have tried to show, there are obvious policy reasons why, in certain cases at least, a different approach is preferable in English law too. The present are among such cases. Following the approach in *McGhee*'s case I accordingly hold that, by proving that the defendants individually materially increased the risk that the men would develop mesothelioma due to inhaling asbestos fibres, the claimants are taken in law to have proved that the defendants materially contributed to their illness.

[169] While that is sufficient for the decision of the appeals, Mr Stewart urged that, if minded to apply some version of the principle in *McGhee*'s case, the House should define its scope. He pointed out that the speeches in *McGhee*'s case had left doubt as to the scope of the principle that the House had been applying and the decision of the Court of Appeal in *Wilsher*'s case had shown only too clearly that it could be extended too far. It is indeed plain that, as Lord Nicholls of Birkenhead has observed, considerable restraint is called for in using the principle. Identifying, at an abstract level, the defining characteristics of the cases where it is, none the less, proper to apply the principle is far from easy. The common law naturally and traditionally shies away from such generalisations especially in a developing

area of the law. But, having regard to the cases cited by counsel and also, in particular, to the cases and textbooks on the German law referred to in van Gerven *Tort Law*, pp 444–447 and 459–461, I would tentatively suggest that certain conditions are necessary, but may not always be sufficient, for applying the principle. All the criteria are satisfied in the present cases.

[170] First, the principle is designed to resolve the difficulty that arises where it is inherently impossible for the claimant to prove exactly how his injury was caused. It applies, therefore, where the claimant has proved all that he possibly can, but the causal link could only ever be established by scientific investigation and the current state of the relevant science leaves it uncertain exactly how the injury was caused and, so, who caused it. *McGhee*'s case and the present cases are examples. Secondly, part of the underlying rationale of the principle is that the defendant's wrongdoing has materially increased the risk that the claimant will suffer injury. It is therefore essential not just that the defendant's conduct created a material risk of injury to a class of persons but that it actually created a material risk of injury to the claimant himself. Thirdly, it follows that the defendant's conduct must have been capable of causing the claimant's injury. Fourthly, the claimant must prove that his injury was caused by the eventuation of the kind of risk created by the defendant's wrongdoing. In *McGhee*'s case, for instance, the risk created by the defenders' failure was that the pursuer would develop dermatitis due to brick dust on his skin and he proved that he had developed dermatitis due to brick dust on his skin. By contrast, the principle does not apply where the claimant has merely proved that his injury could have been caused by a number of different events, only one of which is the eventuation of the risk created by the defendant's wrongful act or omission. *Wilsher*'s case is an example. Fifthly, this will usually mean that the claimant must prove that his injury was caused, if not by exactly the same agency as was involved in the defendant's wrongdoing, at least by an agency that operated in substantially the same way. A possible example would be where a workman suffered injury from exposure to dusts coming from two sources, the dusts being particles of different substances each of which, however, could have caused his injury in the same way. Without having heard detailed argument on the point, I incline to the view that the principle was properly applied by the Court of Appeal in *Fitzgerald v Lane* [1987] 2 All ER 455, [1987] QB 781. Sixthly, the principle applies where the other possible source of the claimant's injury is a similar wrongful act or omission of another person, but it can also apply where, as in *McGhee*'s case, the other possible source of the injury is a similar, but lawful, act or omission of the same defendant. I reserve my opinion as to whether the principle applies where the other possible source of injury is a similar but lawful act or omission of someone else or a natural occurrence.

[171] For these reasons I was in favour of allowing the appeals and of making the appropriate orders in each of the cases.

[LORD NICHOLLS OF BIRKENHEAD and LORD HUTTON delivered speeches in favour of allowing the appeals.]

Appeals allowed.

NOTE

Comments on the current position will be postponed until after the extract from the next case, which interprets *Fairchild*, but for notes on and discussion of *Fairchild* before the later developments, see T. Weir [2002] CLJ 519; J. Morgan (2003) 66 MLR 277 ; J. Stapleton (2002) 10 *TLJ* 276.

■ Barker v Corus (UK) Ltd

House of Lords [2006] 3 All ER 785

LORD HOFFMANN:...

My Lords:...

[2] These three appeals raise two important questions which were left undecided in *Fairchild v Glenhaven Funeral Services Ltd*. First, what are the limits of the exception? In *Fairchild v Glenhaven*

Funeral Services Ltd the causal agent (asbestos dust) was the same in every case, the claimants had all been exposed in the course of employment, all the exposures which might have caused the disease involved breaches of duty by employers or occupiers and although it was likely that only one breach of duty had been causative, science could not establish which one it was. Must all these factors be present? Secondly, what is the extent of liability? Is any defendant who is liable under the exception deemed to have caused the disease? On orthodox principles, all defendants who have actually caused the damage are jointly and severally liable. Or is the damage caused by a defendant in a *Fairchild* case the creation of a risk that the claimant will contract the disease? In that case, each defendant will be liable only for his aliquot contribution to the total risk of the claimant contracting the disease—a risk which is known to have materialised.

The three cases
[3] Both of these questions are raised by the appeal in *Barker v Corus (UK) Ltd*. Mr Barker died of asbestos-related mesothelioma on 14 June 1996. During his working career he had three material exposures to asbestos. The first was for six weeks in 1958 while working for a company called Graessers Ltd. The second was between April and October 1962, while working for John Summers Ltd (now Corus (UK) Ltd (Corus)). The third was for at least three short periods between 1968 and 1975, while working as a self-employed plasterer. The first two exposures were in consequence of breaches of duty by the employers and the last is agreed to have involved a failure by Mr Barker to take reasonable care for his own safety. Thus, unlike the facts of *Fairchild v Glenhaven Funeral Services Ltd*, not all the exposures which could have caused the disease involved breaches of duty to the claimant or were within the control of a defendant. The first question is whether this takes the case outside the *Fairchild* exception. If it does not, the second question is whether Corus is liable for all the damage suffered by Mr Barker's estate and dependants or only for its aliquot contribution to the materialised risk that he would contract mesothelioma. Moses J decided that the case was within the *Fairchild* exception and that Corus was liable jointly and severally with Graessers Ltd, but subject to a 20% reduction for Mr Barker's contributory negligence while he was self-employed. As Graessers Ltd is insolvent and without any identified insurer, Corus is unable to recover any contribution. The Court of Appeal ((Kay, Keene and Wall LJJ) agreed with the judge on both points: see *Barker v Saint-Gobain Pipelines plc* [2004] EWCA Civ 545, [2005] 3 All ER 661.

[4] In the other two appeals, all the exposures to asbestos were in breach of duties owed by employers or occupiers and there was no dispute that the cases fell within the *Fairchild* exception. The only question was whether liability was joint and several or only several....

The limits of Fairchild V Glenhaven Funeral Services Ltd
[5] My Lords, the opinions of all of your Lordships who heard *Fairchild v Glenhaven Funeral Services Ltd* expressed concern, in varying degrees, that the new exception should not be allowed to swallow up the rule. It is only natural that, the dyke having been breached, the pressure of a sea of claimants should try to enlarge the gap.... But each member of the Committee in *Fairchild v Glenhaven Funeral Services Ltd* [2002] 3 All ER 305, [2003] 1 AC 32 stated the limits of what he thought the case was deciding in slightly different terms....

[11] The assistance which can be derived from these various formulations is limited. No one expressly adverted to the case in which the claimant was himself responsible for a significant exposure. Lord Bingham's formulation requires that all possible sources of asbestos should have involved breaches of duty to the claimant; Lord Rodger allowed for a non-tortious exposure by a defendant who was also responsible for a tortious exposure but reserved his position on any other non-tortious exposure. The most that can be said of the others is that they did not formulate the issue in terms which excluded the possibility of liability when there had been non-tortious exposures. On the other hand, no one thought that the formulations in *Fairchild* were the last word on the scope of the exception....Lord Bingham said, at [34]:

'It would be unrealistic to suppose that the principle here affirmed will not over time be the subject of incremental and analogical development. Cases seeking to develop the principle must be decided when and as they arise....'

Now such cases have arisen.

The reinterpretation of Mcghee v National Coal Board

[12] Given that neither of the issues which I have identified arose or was argued in *Fairchild v Glenhaven Funeral Services Ltd,* counsel on both sides very sensibly did not place great weight upon a close textual analysis of the way their Lordships formulated the exception. Perhaps more profitable is an examination of what the House said about its earlier decision in *McGhee v National Coal Board* [1972] 3 All ER 1008, [1973] 1 WLR 1. The facts of this case are too well known to need detailed repetition....

[13] The House treated *McGhee v National Coal Board* as an application avant la lettre of the *Fairchild* exception. This came as a surprise to some commentators (see, for example, Tony Weir, 'Making it More Likely v Making it Happen' [2002] CLJ 519) because Lord Bridge of Harwich, speaking for the House in *Wilsher v Essex Area Health Authority* [1988] 1 All ER 871 at 881, [1988] AC 1074, at 1090, had said that *McGhee v National Coal Board* demonstrated no more than a 'robust and pragmatic' (ie in the teeth of the evidence) inference from the primary facts. In *Fairchild v Glenhaven Funeral Services Ltd,* however, only Lord Hutton was willing to accept this interpretation. *McGhee v National Coal Board* must therefore be accepted as an approved application of the *Fairchild* exception.

[14] For present purposes, the importance of *McGhee v National Coal Board* is that it was a case in which there had been two possible causes of the pursuer's dermatitis: the brick dust which adhered to his skin while he was working in the brick kilns and the dust which continued to adhere to his skin while he was on his way home. Both risks had been created by his work for the Coal Board but the exposure while working in the kilns was not alleged to involve any breach of duty. The only breach was the failure to provide showers so that he could wash off the dust before cycling home. So one source of risk was tortious but the other was not. The House decided that the *Fairchild* exception allowed him to recover damages although he could not prove that the persistence of dust after he had left work was more likely to have caused the dermatitis than its original presence on his body while he was working.

[15] It was in order to accommodate this case that Lord Rodger in *Fairchild v Glenhaven Funeral Services Ltd* accepted (at [170]) that the exception could apply 'where, as in *McGhee's* case, the other possible source of the injury is a similar, but lawful, act or omission of the same defendant'. Likewise, Mr Stuart-Smith QC, who appeared for the appellants, did not insist that all sources of risk should have been tortious. He allowed for what he called the '*McGhee* extension' where the risk was created by a similar but lawful act or omission of the same defendant or another tortfeasor.

[16] It seems to me, however, as it did to Moses J, that once one accepts that the exception can operate even though not all the potential causes of damage were tortious, there is no logic in requiring that a non-tortious source of risk should have been created by someone who was also a tortfeasor....

[17] It should not...matter whether the person who caused the non-tortious exposure happened also to have caused a tortious exposure. The purpose of the *Fairchild* exception is to provide a cause of action against a defendant who has materially increased the risk that the claimant will suffer damage and may have caused that damage, but cannot be proved to have done so because it is impossible to show, on a balance of probability, that some other exposure to the same risk may not have caused it instead. For this purpose, it should be irrelevant whether the other exposure was tortious or non-tortious, by natural causes or human agency or by the claimant himself. These distinctions may be relevant to whether and to whom responsibility can also be attributed, but from the point of view of satisfying the requirement of a sufficient causal link between the defendant's conduct and the claimant's injury, they should not matter. On this point I am therefore in agreement with Moses J and the Court of Appeal.

DISTINGUISHING *WILSHER V ESSEX AREA HEALTH AUTHORITY*

[18] If the *Fairchild* exception does not require that all the potential causes of the injury should be tortious, what are the conditions which mark out its limits? For this purpose, it is necessary to examine the way in which the House distinguished *Wilsher v Essex Area Health Authority* [1988] 1 All ER 871, [1988] AC 1074.

[Having discussed this question, LORD HOFFMANN continued:]

[24] ...In my opinion it is an essential condition for the operation of the exception that the impossibility of proving that the defendant caused the damage arises out of the existence of another potential causative agent which operated in the same way. It may have been different in some causally irrelevant respect, as in Lord Rodger's example of the different kinds of dust, but the mechanism by which it caused the damage, whatever it was, must have been the same. So, for example, I do not think that the exception applies when the claimant suffers lung cancer which may have been caused by exposure to asbestos or some other carcinogenic matter but may also have been caused by smoking and it cannot be proved which is more likely to have been the causative agent.

Apportionment

[25] The second issue arising in all three appeals is whether under the *Fairchild* exception a defendant is liable, jointly and severally with any other defendants, for all the damage consequent upon the contraction of mesothelioma by the claimant or whether he is liable only for an aliquot share, apportioned according to the share of the risk created by his breach of duty....

[31] My Lords, [the first of these views] would be unanswerable if the House of Lords in *Fairchild v Glenhaven Funeral Services Ltd* had proceeded upon the fiction that a defendant who had created a material risk of mesothelioma was deemed to have caused or materially contributed to the contraction of the disease. The disease is undoubtedly an indivisible injury.... But only Lord Hutton and Lord Rodger adopted this approach. The other members of the House made it clear that the creation of a material risk of mesothelioma was sufficient for liability....

Creating a risk as damage

[35] Consistency of approach would suggest that if the basis of liability is the wrongful creation of a risk or chance of causing the disease, the damage which the defendant should be regarded as having caused is the creation of such a risk or chance. If that is the right way to characterize the damage, then it does not matter that the disease as such would be indivisible damage. Chances are infinitely divisible and different people can be separately responsible to a greater or lesser degree for the chances of an event happening, in the way that a person who buys a whole book of tickets in a raffle has a separate and larger chance of winning the prize than a person who has bought a single ticket.

[36] Treating the creation of the risk as the damage caused by the defendant would involve having to quantify the likelihood that the damage (which is known to have materialised) was caused by that particular defendant. It will then be possible to determine the share of the damage which should be attributable to him. The quantification of chances is by no means unusual in the courts. For example, in quantifying the damage caused by an indivisible injury, such as a fractured limb, it may be necessary to quantify the chances of future complications. Sometimes the law treats the loss of a chance of a favourable outcome as compensatable damage in itself. The likelihood that the favourable outcome would have happened must then be quantified: see, for example, *Chaplin v Hicks* [1911] 2 KB 786 and *Kitchen v Royal Air Force Association* [1958] 2 All ER 241, [1958] 1 WLR 563. [37] These are of course cases in which there is uncertainty as to what will be, or would have been, the outcome of a known event; for example, the consequences of a fractured ankle, a beauty contest or a lawsuit. The present case involves uncertainty as to the cause of a known outcome, namely, the mesothelioma. But in principle I can see no reason why the courts cannot quantify the chances of X having been the cause of Y just as well as the chance of Y being the outcome of X....

Fairness

[40] So far I have been concerned to demonstrate that characterising the damage as the risk of contracting mesothelioma would be in accordance with the basis upon which liability is imposed

and would not be inconsistent with the concept of damage in the law of torts. In the end, however, the important question is whether such a characterisation would be fair. The *Fairchild* exception was created because the alternative of leaving the claimant with no remedy was thought to be unfair. But does fairness require that he should recover in full from any defendant liable under the exception? . . .

[43] In my opinion, the attribution of liability according to the relative degree of contribution to the chance of the disease being contracted would smooth the roughness of the justice which a rule of joint and several liability creates. The defendant was a wrongdoer, it is true, and should not be allowed to escape liability altogether, but he should not be liable for more than the damage which he caused and, since this is a case in which science can deal only in probabilities, the law should accept that position and attribute liability according to probabilities. The justification for the joint and several liability rule is that if you caused harm, there is no reason why your liability should be reduced because someone else also caused the same harm. But when liability is exceptionally imposed because you may have caused harm, the same considerations do not apply and fairness suggests that if more than one person may have been responsible, liability should be divided according to the probability that one or other caused the harm . . . .

Joint tortfeasors and contributary negligence

[46] The effect of the Civil Liability (Contribution) Act 1978 is that if each defendant is treated as having caused the mesothelioma as an indivisible injury and pays the damages in full, he will be able to recover contribution to the extent that he has paid more than his fair share of the responsibility from such other tortfeasors as are traceable and solvent. But he will in effect be a guarantor of the liability of those who are not traceable or solvent and, as time passes, the number of these will grow larger. Experience in the United States, where, for reasons which I need not examine, the DES rule of several liability has not been applied to indivisible injuries caused by asbestos, suggests that liability will progressively be imposed upon parties who may have had a very small share in exposing the claimant to risk but still happen to be traceable and solvent or insured: see Jane Stapleton, 'Two causal fictions at the heart of US asbestos doctrine', (2006) 122 LQR 189. That would, as I have said, not be unfair in cases in which they did actually cause the injury. It is however unfair in cases in which there is merely a relatively small chance that they did so.

[47] Similarly, if the defendant is deemed to have caused the mesothelioma but the claimant, like Mr Barker, was himself responsible for a significant period of exposure, the court may find that he did not take adequate care for his own safety or was in breach of safety regulations and, as Moses J did in the *Barker* case, reduce the damages for contributory negligence. On the other hand, if liability is several, there is no question of contributory negligence any more than of contribution. A defendant is liable for the risk of disease which he himself has created and not for the risks created by others, whether they are defendants, persons not before the court or the claimant himself.

Quantification

[48] Although the *Fairchild* exception treats the risk of contracting mesothelioma as the damage, it applies only when the disease has actually been contracted. . . .

[49] In the *Barker* case I would therefore allow the appeal, but only to the extent of setting aside the award of damages against Corus and remitting the case to the High Court to re-determine the damages by reference to the proportion of the risk attributable to the breach of duty by John Summers Ltd. . . .

LORD RODGER OF EARLSFERRY: . . .

[71] My Lords, I accept of course that the problem in *Fairchild v Glenhaven Funeral Services Ltd* can be analysed as Lord Hoffmann now proposes, and indeed had already suggested in *Gregg v Scott* [the next case extracted]. But that is quite different from saying that the House actually chose to analyse it that way. By adopting the proposed analysis your Lordships are not so much reinterpreting as rewriting the key decisions in *McGhee v National Coal Board* [1972] 3 All ER 1008, 1973] 1 WLR 1 and *Fairchild v Glenhaven Funeral Services Ltd.* . . .

[80] Lord Hoffmann suggests that in *Fairchild*...the majority did not proceed on the basis that a defendant who had created a material risk of mesothelioma was deemed to have caused or materially contributed to the contraction of the disease....

[83] Given the terms of Lord Bingham's speech, with which I agreed, and given the terms of my own speech, it respectfully appears to me to be impossible to say that in *Fairchild*...the majority of the House decided the case simply on the basis that the creation of a material risk of mesothelioma 'would suffice' for liability. That is to ignore the further stage in the reasoning—derived fair and square from the reasoning of the majority in *McGhee v National Coal Board*—that in cases of this kind there is, in Lord Bingham's words..., 'no distinction' between making a material contribution to causing the disease and materially increasing the risk of the victim contracting it. When that stage was included, by proving that the defendants had materially increased the risk of the victim contracting mesothelioma, the plaintiffs had proved that the defendants had made a material contribution to causing the disease and were accordingly liable for causing it. Reading the speeches as though they were saying something different is unlikely to make an already difficult topic any easier.

[84] In his speech today Lord Hoffmann says (at [35] above):

> 'Consistency of approach would suggest that if the basis of liability is the wrongful creation of a risk or chance of causing the disease, the damage which the defendant should be regarded as having caused is the creation of such a risk or chance.'

That may well be so if the dominant aim is to secure internal consistency between the basis of liability and the nature of the damage. But the reasoning in *McGhee*...and *Fairchild*.... indicates that the House was primarily concerned to maintain a consistency of approach with the main body of law on personal injuries. Under that law victims recover damages because the defendants' wrongful act has materially contributed to them becoming ill, not because it has created a risk that they will become ill. By reasoning as they did, the members of the House minimised the disruption to this long-settled aspect of the law.

[85] The new analysis which the House is adopting will tend to maximise the inconsistencies in the law by turning the *Fairchild* exception into an enclave where a number of rules apply which have been rejected for use elsewhere in the law of personal injuries....

[86] Why...is the House spontaneously embarking upon this adventure of redefining the nature of the damage suffered by the victims? The majority are not just on a mission to tidy up the reasoning in *McGhee National Coal Board* and *Fairchild v Glenhaven Funeral Services Ltd*. Their aim is to open the way to making each defendant severally liable for a share of the damages, rather than liable in solidum for the whole of the damages. This is said to be a preferable, fairer, solution when the defendants are found liable for creating the risk of illness rather than for causing it....

[101] If the defendants' liability under the *Fairchild* exception had been in solidum, in my view the potential injustice to a defendant in applying the exception in a case where the victim was solely responsible for a material exposure to asbestos dust would have been too great. On that basis I would have favoured applying the normal rule for proof of causation. The majority conclusion is, however, that a defendant's liability is to be several only. This involves such a major reduction in the scope of the defendants' liability that, on that basis, I too would conclude that the balance of potential injustices favours applying the *Fairchild* exception.

[102] For these reasons, in respectful disagreement with your Lordships, I would have dismissed the defendants' appeals on the question of apportionment. But, having regard to the majority conclusion that the defendants' liability is to be several, I would dismiss the appeal by Corus in the *Barker* case and hold them liable on the basis of the *Fairchild* exception.

LORD WALKER OF GESTINGTHORPE:...

[117] The injustice recognised in *Fairchild v Glenhaven Funeral Services Ltd*, of denying a claimant any remedy in a situation in which his (or the deceased's) fatal disease *must* have been caused by a breach of duty on the part of at least one of two or more employers loses some of its edge if the disease

might have been caused by the claimant's (or the deceased's) own fault or...by exposure to asbestos...which did not involve any breach of duty by an employer or occupier, and without contributory negligence on the part of the claimant (or the deceased). In that sort of situation the possible injustice to the defendant assumes more importance. Nevertheless, if your Lordships accept that the right way forward is to limit a defendant's liability by reference to its own contribution to the risk, the balance of fairness is still clearly, to my mind, in favour of applying the *Fairchild* principle where less than 100% of the risk has been caused by employers or occupiers guilty of breaches of duty....

BARONESS HALE OF RICHMOND:...

[128] ...If the damage could have been suffered during a period of non-tortious exposure, it is suggested that the tortious exposers should escape liability altogether. There is considerable logic in this. One way of explaining *Fairchild v Glenhaven Funeral Services Ltd* is that all were in breach of duty and one of them must be guilty, so that it made sense that all should be liable. That rationale does not apply, or certainly not with the same force, if there are other non-tortious causers in the frame. But if the tortious exposers are only liable in proportion to their own contribution to the claimant's overall exposure to the risk of harm, then the problem does not arise. The victim's own behaviour is only relevant if he fails to take reasonable care for his own safety during a period of tortuous exposure by a defendant....

[LORD SCOTT OF FOSCOTE delivered a speech in which he agreed with LORD HOFFMANN's speech, as did LORD WALKER. In her speech, BARONESS HALE also agreed with lord HOFFMANN's speech, but did agree with LORD RODGER that 'the damage which is the "gist" of these actions is the mesothelomia and its physical and financial consequences...not the risk of contracting the disease'.]

Appeals allowed.

QUESTIONS

1. What do you think is the 'gist' of the damage in *Barker*?
2. What effect does *Barker* have on *McGhee*?
3. Does *Barker* help to avoid the danger of over-internalisation of costs referred to by Stapleton (note 2, p. 345, *ante*) when discussing *Bonnington Castings Ltd v Wardlaw* [1956] AC 613, [1956] 1 All ER 615?
4. Can the *Fairchild/ Barker* principle apply to cases where factories by discharging radiation or chemicals increase the general risk of a fairly common cancer in the area around them? (See A. Kramer (2006) 122 LQR 547 at 552.)
5. In *Novartis Grimsby Ltd v Cookson* [2007] EWCA Civ 1261 at [72] Smith LJ (with whose judgment the other members of the Court of Appeal agreed) raised the question whether 'the principle in *Bonnington* [applies] only to "divisible" conditions where the various exposures contribute to the severity of the disease' or whether it also applies 'to cases in which the various exposures contribute only to the risk that the disease will develop'. How would you answer this question?

NOTES

1. *Barker* is noted by J.M. Scherpe [2006] CLJ 487 and Kramer *op cit*. It is also discussed (along with other cases) by L Khoury (2008) 124 LQR 103, who finds a parallel in Lord Hoffmann's reasoning with the approach of French courts, although acknowledging there are differences (see *ibid*, pp. 121–130). In Khoury's opinion (*ibid*, p. 121) the limitations on the approach in *Barker* 'are based on the fear of increasing uncertainty in

the law, the reluctance to establish new generalised tort principles, and the desire to maintain the authority of *Wilsher*'.

2.   A *de minimis* increase in the risk will not suffice to fall within the *Fairchild/Barker* principle, but any material increase will: *Rolls Royce Industrial Power (India) Ltd v Cox* [2007] EWCA Civ 1189, which also points out, following *Brett v University of Reading* [2007] EWCA Civ 88, that the principle still requires there to be proof of a breach of duty.

3.   In *Novartis Grimsby Ltd v Cookson* [2007] EWCA Civ 1261 the trial judge found that occupational exposure to chemicals and smoking cigarettes had both involved a risk of bladder cancer which the claimant had suffered, but that the former amounted to 70 per cent to 75 per cent of the overall risk. On this basis, the Court of Appeal took the view that, applying the 'but-for' test, the occupational exposure was the cause of the cancer and that the *Fairchild/Barker* principle did not need to be invoked. In the light of this view, if the occupational exposure had been less than a 51 per cent portion of the overall risk, would it have been fair to have allowed the *Fairchild/Barker* principle to apply? Consider Baroness Hale's speech in *Gregg v Scott* [2005] 4 All ER 812, [2005] UKHL 2 (p. 373, post). If the principle had in theory applied, Lord Hoffmann's opinion in *Barker* ([24] in the extract ante) about exposure to asbestos and smoking would not seem to have ruled out its operation since in this case the risk from the occupational exposure and the risk from smoking would act in the same way and would, therefore, be similar agents.

4.   In *Fitzgerald v Lane* [1987] QB 781, [1987] 2 All ER 455 the claimant was badly injured in a road accident. While walking briskly across a pelican crossing which had the red light showing against him, he was struck by D1's car, propelled onto its bonnet, into its windscreen, and then onto the road where he was struck by D2's car. Both D1 and D2 were found to have been negligent and the claimant was found to have been contributorily negligent. The trial judge took the view that there were three equally possible causes for the partial tetraplegia which the claimant had sustained: the impact with the windscreen, the impact with the ground, and D2's car striking the claimant. The case was decided by the Court of Appeal before even *Wilsher* had reached the House of Lords, and, relying on a principle formulated by Mustill LJ when *Wilsher* was in the Court of Appeal ([1987] QB 730 at 771–772) but which was later disapproved on the appeal to the House of Lords, a causal link was found to have been established between D2's negligence and the tetraplegia. How would this case be decided today? (See Lord Rodger's opinion in *Fairchild* (p. 357, ante) and consider *Clough v First Choice Holidays and Flights Ltd* [2006] EWCA Civ 15 at [40], a pre-*Barker* decision. (*Fitzgerald v Lane* did in fact later go to the House of Lords, [1989] AC 328, [1988] 2 All ER 961, noted pp. 446 and 1125, post, but this causation issue was not discussed.)

5.   The House of Lords decision in *Barker* produced some concern that claimants would not receive damages for all their losses. The risk of any defendants' insolvency in effect now shifted to the claimant. At the time of the decision in *Barker*, the Compensation Act 2006 was proceeding through Parliament and the opportunity was taken to add in a new section (s. 3).

■ The Compensation Act 2006

3 Mesothelioma: damages

(1) This section applies where—

   (a) a person ("the responsible person") has negligently or in breach of statutory duty caused or permitted another person ("the victim") to be exposed to asbestos,

(b) the victim has contracted mesothelioma as a result of exposure to asbestos,

(c) because of the nature of mesothelioma and the state of medical science, it is not possible to determine with certainty whether it was the exposure mentioned in paragraph (a) or another exposure which caused the victim to become ill, and

(d) the responsible person is liable in tort, by virtue of the exposure mentioned in paragraph (a), in connection with damage caused to the victim by the disease (whether by reason of having materially increased a risk or for any other reason).

(2) The responsible person shall be liable—

(a) in respect of the whole of the damage caused to the victim by the disease (irrespective of whether the victim was also exposed to asbestos—

(i) other than by the responsible person, whether or not in circumstances in which another person has liability in tort, or

(ii) by the responsible person in circumstances in which he has no liability in tort), and

(b) jointly and severally with any other responsible person.

(3) Subsection (2) does not prevent—

(a) one responsible person from claiming a contribution from another, or

(b) a finding of contributory negligence.

(4) In determining the extent of contributions of different responsible persons in accordance with subsection (3)(a), a court shall have regard to the relative lengths of the periods of exposure for which each was responsible; but this subsection shall not apply—

(a) if or to the extent that responsible persons agree to apportion responsibility amongst themselves on some other basis, or

(b) if or to the extent that the court thinks that another basis for determining contributions is more appropriate in the circumstances of a particular case.

(5) In subsection (1) the reference to causing or permitting a person to be exposed to asbestos includes a reference to failing to protect a person from exposure to asbestos.

(7) The Treasury may make regulations about the provision of compensation to a responsible person where—

(a) he claims, or would claim, a contribution from another responsible person in accordance with subsection (3)(a), but

(b) he is unable or likely to be unable to obtain the contribution, because an insurer of the other responsible person is unable or likely to be unable to satisfy the claim for a contribution.

. . .

(10) In subsections (7). . .—

(a) a reference to a responsible person includes a reference to an insurer of a responsible person. . .

16 Commencement

. . .

(3) Section 3 shall be treated as always having had effect.

QUESTIONS

1. How far does s. 3 affect a case like *McGhee*?

2. How far does s. 3 affect *Barker*? Suppose A suffers from mesothelioma as a result of tortious exposure to asbestos due to the fault of B and C and a further non-tortious exposure, all the exposures being for a similar period. The overall loss is assessed at £X. How much would B and C pay to A (a) under *Barker*, and (b) after s. 3 was passed if

both are solvent? What would the position be in both situations if B is insolvent? How far would the previous situations be altered if A was negligent in relation to the third non-tortious exposure?

NOTES

1.   On the general subject of contribution between tortfeasors, see chap. 19 post.
2.   There is a potential problem with this Parliamentary interference with *Barker* consequent on the fact that it only deals with part of the ruling and leaves alone that part which applies *Fairchild* to cases where there was a non-tortious exposure. As David Howarth MP asked in the debate on the Compensation Bill (449 H.C. Debs (6th Series) col. 42) ' Is not there a danger that the law will go back to its state before Barker if the new law is passed?'. It will have been seen that there was a concern in *Barker* for the increased unfairness to the defendants in the situation in that case, a concern which was alleviated by the decision about the amount of damage for which any one defendant would be liable. The latter has now been changed for mesothelioma cases by s. 3. Might the House of Lords have decided *Barker* differently if there would have been joint and several liability for all the loss? Does this mean that it is today arguable that *in a mesothelioma case* the House of Lords will distinguish or overrule *Barker*, or can it be argued that Parliament has sanctioned any unfairness to defendants that the combination of *Barker* and s. 3 might be thought to produce?
3.   As seen in note 4, p. 347, ante, problems of factual causation can sometimes disappear if a different notion of 'breach' is adopted. The same effect can be achieved if the notion of the claimant's 'damage' is adjusted. This is shown in *Barker*. On the other hand, as that case should also show, there are limits to the situations in which the courts are prepared to allow this, and the following extract represents an unsuccessful attempt to avoid the difficulty of proving factual causation by alleging that the defendant's fault caused the loss of a chance of a favourable outcome.

■ Gregg v Scott

House of Lords [2005] 4 All ER 812

LORD NICHOLLS OF BIRKENHEAD [dissenting]: . . .

[5] . . . I must mention the salient facts of this appeal. . . . At the risk of over-simplification they can be summarised as follows. The defendant Dr Scott negligently diagnosed as innocuous a lump under the left arm of the claimant Mr Malcolm Gregg when in fact it was cancerous (non-Hodgkin's lymphoma). This led to nine months' delay in Mr Gregg receiving treatment. During this period his condition deteriorated by the disease spreading elsewhere. The deterioration in Mr Gregg's condition reduced his prospects of disease-free survival for ten years from 42%, when he first consulted Dr Scott, to 25% at the date of the trial. The judge found that, if treated promptly, Mr Gregg's initial treatment would probably have achieved remission without an immediate need for high dose chemotherapy. Prompt treatment would, at least initially, have prevented the cancer spreading to the left pectoral region.

[6] However, the judge found also that, although Mr Gregg's condition deteriorated and in consequence his prospects were reduced in this way, a better outcome was never a probability. It was not possible to conclude on the balance of probability that, in the absence of the negligence, Mr Gregg's medical condition would have been better or that he would have avoided any particular treatment. Before the negligence Mr Gregg had a less than evens chance (45%) of avoiding the deterioration in his condition which ultimately occurred. The delay did not extinguish this chance but reduced it by roughly half. The judge assessed this reduction at 20%. That was the extent to which the negligence reduced

Mr Gregg's prospects of avoiding the deterioration in his condition which ultimately occurred. The facts can be found more fully stated in the judgments of the Court of Appeal ([2002] EWCA Civ 1471, (2003) 71 BMLR 16) and in the speech of my noble and learned friend Lord Phillips of Worth Matravers.

[7] On these findings the trial judge, Judge Inglis, dismissed the claim. He considered he was driven to this conclusion by the reasoning of your Lordships' House in *Hotson v East Berkshire Area Health Authority* [1987] 2 All ER 909, [1987] AC 750. The Court of Appeal by a majority (Simon Brown and Mance LJJ, Latham LJ dissenting) dismissed Mr Gregg's appeal.

Past facts and future prospects
[8] In order to set the question now before the House in its legal perspective I must next say something about the common law approach to proof of actionable damage, that is, damage which the law regards as founding a claim for compensation. It is trite law that in the ordinary way a claimant must prove the facts giving rise to a cause of action against the defendant. Where the claim is based on negligence the facts to be proved include those constituting actionable damage as well as those giving rise to the existence of a duty of care and its breach.

[9] In the normal way proof of the facts constituting actionable damage calls for proof of the claimant's present position and proof of what would have been the claimant's position in the absence of the defendant's wrongful act or omission. As to what constitutes proof, traditionally the common law has drawn a distinction between proof of past facts and proof of future prospects. A happening in the past either occurred or it did not. Whether an event happened in the past is a matter to be established in civil cases on the balance of probability. If an event probably happened no discount is made for the possibility it did not. Proof of future possibilities is approached differently. Whether an event will happen in the future calls for an assessment of the likelihood of that event happening, because no one knows for certain what will happen in the future.

[10] This distinction between past and future is applied also when deciding what would have happened in the past or future but for a past happening such as the defendant's negligent act. What would have happened in the past but for something which happened in the past is, at least generally, a question decided by the courts on the all-or-nothing basis of the balance of probability. On this the authorities are not altogether consistent, but this seems to be the generally accepted practice. In contrast, what would have happened in the future but for something which happened in the past calls for an assessment of likelihood. . . .

[13] This sharp distinction between past events and future possibilities is open to criticism. Whether an event occurred in the past can be every bit as uncertain as whether an event is likely to occur in the future. But by and large this established distinction works well enough. It has a comfortable simplicity which accords with everyday experience of the difference between knowing what happened in the past and forecasting what may happen in the future.

[14] In practice the distinction is least satisfactory when applied to hypothetical events (what would have happened had the wrong not been committed). The theory underpinning the all-or-nothing approach to proof of past facts appears to be that a past fact either happened or it did not and the law should proceed on the same footing. But the underlying certainty, that a past fact happened or it did not, is absent from hypothetical facts. By definition hypothetical events did not happen in the past, nor will they happen in the future. They are based on false assumptions. The defendant's wrong precluded them from ever materialising.

Loss of an opportunity or chance as actionable damage
[15] It is perhaps not surprising therefore that it is principally in the field of hypothetical past events that difficulties have arisen in practice. Sometimes, whether a claimant has suffered actionable damage cannot fairly be decided on an all-or-nothing basis by reference to what, on balance of probability, would have happened but for the defendant's negligence. Sometimes this would be too crude an approach. What would have happened in the absence of the defendant's negligence is altogether too uncertain for the all-or-nothing approach to be satisfactory. In some cases what the claimant lost by the negligence was the opportunity or chance to achieve a desired result whose achievement was outside

his control and inherently uncertain. The defendant's wrong consisted of depriving the claimant of a chance he would otherwise have had to achieve a desired outcome.

[16] Then, the greater the uncertainty surrounding the desired future outcome, the less attractive it becomes to define the claimant's loss by whether or not, on balance of probability, he would have achieved the desired outcome but for the defendant's negligence. This definition of the claimant's loss becomes increasingly unattractive because, as the uncertainty of outcome increases, this way of defining the claimant's loss accords ever less closely with what in practice the claimant had and what in practice he lost by the defendant's negligence.

[17] In order to achieve a just result in such cases the law defines the claimant's actionable damage more narrowly by reference to the *opportunity* the claimant lost, rather than by reference to the loss of the desired *outcome* which was never within his control. In adopting this approach the law does not depart from the principle that the claimant must prove actionable damage on the balance of probability. The law adheres to this principle but defines actionable damage in different, more appropriate terms. The law treats the claimant's loss of his opportunity or chance as itself actionable damage. The claimant must prove this loss on balance of probability. The court will then measure this loss as best it may. The chance is to be ignored if it was merely speculative, but evaluated if it was substantial: see *Davies v Taylor* [1972] 3 All ER 836 at 838, [1974] AC 207 at 212, per Lord Reid.

[18] Some familiar examples will suffice. A woman who was wrongly deprived of the chance of being one of the winners in a beauty competition was awarded damages for loss of a chance. The court did not attempt to decide on balance of probability the hypothetical past event of what would have happened if the claimant had been duly notified of her interview: *Chaplin v Hicks* [1911] 2 KB 786, [1911–13] All ER Rep 224. When a solicitor's failure to issue a writ in time deprived a claimant of the opportunity to pursue court proceedings damages were not assessed on an all-or-nothing basis by reference to what probably would have been the outcome if the proceedings had been commenced in time. The court assessed what would have been the claimant's prospects of success in the proceedings which the solicitor's negligence prevented him from pursuing: *Kitchen v Royal Air Forces Association* [1958] 2 All ER 241, [1958] 1 WLR 563. When an employer negligently supplied an inaccurate character reference, the employee did not need to prove that, but for the negligence, he would probably have been given the new job. The employee only had to prove he lost a reasonable chance of employment, which the court would evaluate: *Spring v Guardian Assurance plc* [1994] 3 All ER 129 at 154, [1995] 2 AC 296 at 327.

[19] In *Allied Maples Group Ltd v Simmons & Simmons (a firm)* [1995] 4 All ER 907, [1995] 1 WLR 1602 a solicitor's negligence deprived the claimant of an opportunity to negotiate a better bargain. The Court of Appeal applied the 'loss of chance' approach. Stuart-Smith LJ ([1995] 4 All ER 907 at 915, [1995] 1 WLR 1602 at 1611) regarded the case as one of those where 'the plaintiff's loss depends on the hypothetical action of a third party, either in addition to action by the plaintiff ... or independently of it'. It is clear that Stuart-Smith LJ did not intend this to be a precise or exhaustive statement of the circumstances where loss of a chance may constitute actionable damage and his observation should not be so understood.

Medical negligence

[20] Against this background I turn to the primary question raised by this appeal: how should the loss suffered by a patient in Mr Gregg's position be identified? The defendant says 'loss' is confined to an *outcome* which is shown, on balance of probability, to be worse than it otherwise would have been. Mr Gregg must prove that, on balance of probability, his medical condition after the negligence was worse than it would have been in the absence of the negligence. Mr Gregg says his 'loss' includes proved diminution in the *prospects* of a favourable outcome. Dr Scott's negligence deprived him of a worthwhile chance that his medical condition would not have deteriorated as it did. . . .

Identifying a lost chance in medical negligence cases

[34] I come next to a further twist in the story. It concerns an additional complication. It is a difficult part of this appeal. With 'loss of chance' cases such as *Chaplin v Hicks* [1911] 2 KB 786, [1911–13] All ER Rep 224 identifying the 'chance' the claimant lost is straightforward enough. . . .

[35] The position with medical negligence claims is different. The patient's actual condition at the time of the negligence will often be determinative of the answer to the crucially important hypothetical question of what would have been the claimant's position in the absence of the negligence. *Hotson v East Berkshire Area Health Authority* [1987] 2 All ER 909, [1987] AC 750 is an instance of this. The relevant factual question concerning Stephen Hotson's condition immediately prior to the negligence was whether his fall from the tree had left sufficient blood vessels intact to keep his left femoral epiphysis alive. The answer to this question of actual fact ipso facto provided the answer to the vital hypothetical question: would avascular necrosis have been avoided if Stephen Hotson's leg had been treated promptly? The answer to the first question necessarily provided the answer to the second question, because the second question is no more than a mirror image of the first. Built into the formulation of the first question was the answer to the second question.

[36] This is not always so. Many cases are not so straightforward. Sometimes it is not possible to frame factual questions about a patient's condition which are (a) susceptible of sure answer and also (b) determinative of the outcome for the patient. As already noted, limitations on scientific and medical knowledge do not always permit this to be done. There are too many uncertainties involved in this field.

[37] The present case is a good example. Identifying the nature and extent of Mr Gregg's cancer at the time of the mistaken diagnosis (the first question), so far as this could be achieved with reasonable certainty, did not provide a simple answer to what would have been the outcome had he been treated promptly (the second question). There were several possible outcomes. Recourse to past experience in other cases, that is statistics, personalised so far as possible, was the best that could be done. These statistics expressed the various possible outcomes in percentage terms of likelihood....

[41] ...The question in the present, 'Gregg' type of case concerns how the law should proceed when, a patient's condition at the time of the negligence having been duly identified on the balance of probability with as much particularity as is reasonably possible, medical opinion is unable to say with a reasonable degree of certainty what the outcome would have been if the negligence had not occurred.

[42] In principle, the answer to this question is clear and compelling. In such cases, as in the economic 'loss of chance' cases, the law should recognise the manifestly unsatisfactory consequences which would follow from adopting an all-or-nothing balance of probability approach as the answer to this question. The law should recognise that Mr Gregg's prospects of recovery had he been treated promptly, expressed in percentage terms of likelihood, represent the reality of his position so far as medical knowledge is concerned. The law should be exceedingly slow to disregard medical reality in the context of a legal duty whose very aim is to protect medical reality. In these cases a doctor's duty to act in the best interests of his patient involves maximising the patient's recovery prospects, and doing so whether the patient's prospects are good or not so good. In the event of a breach of this duty the law must fashion a matching and meaningful remedy. A patient should have an appropriate remedy when he loses the very thing it was the doctor's duty to protect. To this end the law should recognise the existence and loss of poor and indifferent prospects as well as those more favourable.

[43] Application of the all-or-nothing balance of probability approach in the 'Gregg' type of cases would not achieve this object. In such cases the law should therefore put aside this approach when considering what would have happened had there been no negligence. It cannot be right to adopt a procedure having the effect that, in law, a patient's prospects of recovery are treated as non-existent whenever they exist but fall short of 50%. If the law were to proceed in this way it would deserve to be likened to the proverbial ass. Where a patient's condition is attended with such uncertainty that medical opinion assesses the patient's recovery prospects in percentage terms, the law should do likewise. The law should not, by adopting the all-or-nothing balance of probability approach, assume certainty where none in truth exists: see Deane J in *Commonwealth of Australia v Amann Aviation Pty Ltd* (1991) 104 ALR 1 at 42, (1991) 174 CLR 64 at 124. The difference between good and poor prospects is a matter going to the amount of compensation fairly payable, not to liability to make

payment at all. As Dore J said *Herskovits v Group Health Cooperative of Puget Sound* (1983) 664 P 2d 474 at 477:

> 'To decide otherwise would be a blanket release from liability for doctors and hospitals any time there was less than a 50 % chance of survival, regardless of how flagrant the negligence.'

[44] The way ahead must surely be to recognise that where a patient is suffering from illness or injury and his prospects of recovery are attended with a significant degree of medical uncertainty, and he suffers a significant diminution of his prospects of recovery by reason of medical negligence whether of diagnosis or treatment, that diminution constitutes actionable damage. This is so whether the patient's prospects immediately before the negligence exceeded or fell short of 50%. 'Medical uncertainty' is uncertainty inherent in the patient's condition, uncertainty which medical opinion cannot resolve. This is to be contrasted with uncertainties arising solely from differences of view expressed by witnesses. Evidential uncertainties of this character should be resolved in the usual way.

[45] This approach would represent a development of the law. So be it. If the common law is to retain its legitimacy it must remain capable of development. It must recognise the great advances made in medical knowledge and skills. It must recognise also the medical uncertainties which still exist. The law must strive to achieve a result which is fair to both parties in present-day conditions. The common law's ability to develop in this way is its proudest boast....

LORD HOFFMANN:...

[64] The question which has given rise to this appeal is whether Dr Scott's negligence caused injury to Mr Gregg.... The expert witnesses treated a cure as meaning survival for more than ten years.... What the delay [did], according to the experts, was to reduce the chances of survival for more than ten years... from 42% to 25%....

Loss of chance

[72] [One] submission was that reduction in the prospect of a favourable outcome ("loss of a chance") should be a recoverable head of damage. There are certainly cases in which it is. *Chaplin v Hicks* [1911] 2 KB 786, [19911–13] All ER Rep 224 is a well-known example. The question is whether the principle of that case can apply to a case of clinical negligence such as this.

[73] The answer can be derived from three cases in the House of Lords: *Hotson v East Berkshire Area Health Authority* [1987] 2 All ER 909, [1987] AC 750, *Wilsher v Essex Area Health Authority* [1988] 1 All ER 871, [1988] AC 1074, and *Fairchild v Glenhaven Funeral Services Ltd* [2002] 3 All ER 305, [2003] 1 AC 32

[74] In *Hotson's* case the claimant was a boy who broke his hip when he fell out of a tree. The hospital negligently failed to diagnose the fracture for five days. The hip joint was irreparably damaged by the loss of blood supply to its cartilage. The judge found that the rupture of the blood vessels caused by the fall had probably made the damage inevitable but there was a 25% chance that enough had remained intact to save the joint if the fracture had been diagnosed at the time. He and the Court of Appeal awarded the claimant damages for loss of the 25% chance of a favourable outcome.

[75] The House of Lords unanimously reversed this decision. They said that the claimant had not lost a chance because, on the finding of fact, nothing could have been done to save the joint. The outcome had been determined by what happened when he fell out of the tree. Either he had enough surviving blood vessels or he did not. That question had to be decided on a balance of probability and had been decided adversely to the claimant....

[78] [Having referred to *Wilsher* and *Fairchild*, his Lordship continued:] [The] rule [in *Fairchild*] was restrictively defined in terms which make it inapplicable in this case.

[79] What these cases show is that, as Helen Reece points out in an illuminating article ('Losses of Chances in the Law' (1996) 59 MLR 188) the law regards the world as in principle bound by laws of causality. Everything has a determinate cause, even if we do not know what it is. The blood-starved hip joint in *Hotson's* case, the blindness in *Wilsher's* case, the mesothelioma in *Fairchild's* case; each had its

cause and it was for the plaintiff to prove that it was an act or omission for which the defendant was responsible. The narrow terms of the exception made to this principle in *Fairchild's* case only serves to emphasise the strength of the rule. The fact that proof is rendered difficult or impossible because no examination was made at the time, as in *Hotson's* case, or because medical science cannot provide the answer, as in *Wilsher's* case, makes no difference. There is no inherent uncertainty about what caused something to happen in the past or about whether something which happened in the past will cause something to happen in the future. Everything is determined by causality. What we lack is knowledge and the law deals with lack of knowledge by the concept of the burden of proof.

[80] Similarly in the present case, the progress of Mr Gregg's disease had a determinate cause. It may have been inherent in his genetic make-up at the time when he saw Mr Scott, as Hotson's fate was determined by what happened to his thigh when he fell out of the tree. Or it may, as Mance LJ suggests, have been affected by subsequent events and behaviour for which Dr Scott was not responsible. Medical science does not enable us to say. But the outcome was not random; it was governed by laws of causality and, in the absence of a special rule as in *Fairchild's* case, inability to establish that delay in diagnosis caused the reduction in expectation in life cannot be remedied by treating the outcome as having been somehow indeterminate . . .

[82] One striking exception to the assumption that everything is determined by impersonal laws of causality is the actions of human beings. The law treats human beings as having free will and the ability to choose between different courses of action, however strong may be the reasons for them to choose one course rather than another. This may provide part of the explanation for why in some cases damages are awarded for the loss of a chance of gaining an advantage or avoiding a disadvantage which depends upon the independent action of another person: see *Allied Maples Group Ltd v Simmons & Simmons* [1995] 4 All ER 907, [1995] 1 WLR 1602 and the cases there cited.

[83] But the true basis of these cases is a good deal more complex. The fact that one cannot prove as a matter of necessary causation that someone would have done something is no reason why one should not prove that he was more likely than not to have done it. So, for example, the law distinguishes between cases in which the outcome depends upon what the claimant himself (*McWilliams v Sir William Arrol & Co*[1962] 1 All ER 623, [1962] 1 WLR 295) or someone for whom the defendant is responsible (*Bolitho v City and Hackney Health Authority* [1997] 4 All ER 771, [1998] AC 232) would have done, and cases in which it depends upon what some third party would have done. In the first class of cases the claimant must prove on a balance of probability that he or the defendant would have acted so as to produce a favourable outcome. In the latter class, he may recover for loss of the chance that the third party would have so acted. This apparently arbitrary distinction obviously rests on grounds of policy. In addition, most of the cases in which there has been recovery for loss of a chance have involved financial loss, where the chance can itself plausibly be characterised as an item of property, like a lottery ticket. It is however unnecessary to discuss these decisions because they obviously do not cover the present case. . . .

[Having rejected various control mechanisms, LORD HOFFMANN continued:]

[90] . . . But a wholesale adoption of possible rather than probable causation as the criterion of liability would be so radical a change in our law as to amount to a legislative act. It would have enormous consequences for insurance companies and the National Health Service. In company with my noble and learned friends Lord Phillips of Worth Matravers and Baroness Hale of Richmond, I think that any such change should be left to Parliament. . . .

LORD HOPE OF CRAIGHEAD [dissenting]: . . .

[117] The key to the decision in this case lies, I think, in the way in which the appellant's cause of action is identified. The description of it as a claim for the loss of a chance is invited by the approach which the pleader has taken to the issue of damages. The description is apt in cases where the claim is for an economic loss or the loss of something to which the claimant has a right, such as in *Chaplin v Hicks* [1911] 2 KB 786, [1911–13] All ER Rep 224 and *Kitchen v Royal Air Forces Association* [1958] 2 All ER 241, [1958] 1 WLR 563. But that is not what this claim is about. It is, in essence, a claim for the loss and

damage caused by the enlargement of the tumour due to the delay in diagnosis. It is for the loss and damage caused, in other words, by a physical injury which the appellant would not have suffered but for the doctor's negligence. The fact that there was a physical injury has been proved on a balance of probabilities. So too has the fact that, in addition to pain and suffering, it caused a reduction in the prospects of a successful outcome. I would hold that, where these factors are present, the way is open for losses which are consequential on the physical injury to be claimed too. I do not think that those consequences of the physical injury should be treated as if they were the product of a separate cause of action from the pain and suffering. I see the reduction in the prospects of a successful outcome as one element among several in the claim for which there is a single cause—the enlargement of the tumour. This was a physical injury, the avoidance or minimisation of which was within the scope of the doctor's duty of care when the appellant consulted him....

Conclusion

[121] I would hold therefore that the significant reduction in the prospects of a successful outcome which the negligence caused is a loss for which the appellant is entitled to be compensated. If it is necessary to prove that this loss was caused by a physical injury, the enlargement of the tumour which the negligence caused was such an injury. But I agree with Lord Nicholls that the fact that the appellant was already suffering from illness at the date of the doctor's negligence from which he had at that date significant prospects of recovery provides him with a cause of action for the reduction in those prospects that resulted from the negligence. I also agree with him that what has to be valued is what the appellant has lost, and that the principle on which that loss must be calculated is the same irrespective of whether the prospects were better or less than 50%....

LORD PHILLIPS OF WORTH MATRAVERS [having examined the evidence in detail, his Lordship, continued:]...

[170] My Lords, these reflections on the present case demonstrate, so it seems to me, that the exercise of assessing the loss of a chance in clinical negligence cases is not an easy one. Deductions cannot safely be drawn from statistics without expert assistance. I am all too well aware that I have drawn a number of deductions from the evidence in this case without expert assistance and that these are at odds with those that have been drawn by others. Even if some of my deductions can be shown to be unsound, I hope that I have demonstrated that analysis of the evidence in this case is no easy task. In contrast, the task of determining the effect of Dr Scott's negligence on a balance of probabilities was very much easier. It is always likely to be much easier to resolve issues of causation on balance of probabilities than to identify in terms of percentage the effect that clinical negligence had on the chances of a favourable outcome. This reality is a policy factor that weighs against the introduction into this area of a right to compensation for the loss of a chance. A robust test which produces rough justice may be preferable to a test that on occasion will be difficult, if not impossible, to apply with confidence in practice....

[190] The complications of this case have persuaded me that it is not a suitable vehicle for introducing into the law of clinical negligence the right to recover damages for the loss of a chance of a cure. Awarding damages for the reduction of the prospect of a cure, when the long term result of treatment is still uncertain, is not a satisfactory exercise. Where medical treatment has resulted in an adverse outcome and negligence has increased the chance of that outcome, there may be a case for permitting a recovery of damages that is proportionate to the increase in the chance of the adverse outcome. That is not a case that has been made out on the present appeal. I would uphold the conventional approach to causation that was applied by [the trial judge].

Conclusion

[191] The judge concluded, on the data before him, that on balance of probabilities the delay in commencing Mr Gregg's treatment that was attributable to Dr Scott's negligence had not affected the course of his illness or his prospects of survival, which had never been as good as even. The data have now changed and Mr Gregg's prospects of survival, despite the delay in commencing his treatment, seem good. The delay may well, however, have meant that his path to what seems a likely cure has

involved more intrusive treatment, and more pain, suffering and distress than would have been experienced had treatment commenced promptly. Those acting for Mr Gregg have, however, not sought to reopen the facts but have relied on the facts as found by the judge. On those facts I agree with Lord Hoffmann and Baroness Hale that this appeal must be dismissed.

BARONESS HALE OF RICHMOND: . . .

[223] Until now, the gist of the action for personal injuries has been damage to the person. My negligence probably caused the loss of your leg: I pay you the full value of the loss of the leg (say £100,000). My negligence probably did not cause the loss of your leg. I do not pay you anything. Compare the loss of a chance approach: my negligence probably caused a reduction in the chance of your keeping that leg: I pay you the value of the loss of your leg, discounted by the chance that it would have happened anyway. If the chance of saving the leg was very good, say 90%, the claimant still gets only 90% of his damages, say £90,000. But if the chance of saving the leg was comparatively poor, say 20%, the claimant still gets £20,000. So the claimant ends up with less than full compensation even though his chances of a more favourable outcome were good. And the defendant ends up paying substantial sums even though the outcome is one for which by definition he cannot be shown to be responsible.

[224] Almost any claim for loss of an outcome could be reformulated as a claim for loss of a chance of that outcome. The implications of retaining them both as alternatives would be substantial. That is, the claimant still has the prospect of 100% recovery if he can show that it is more likely than not that the doctor's negligence caused the adverse outcome. But if he cannot show that, he also has the prospect of lesser recovery for loss of a chance. If . . . it would in practice always be tempting to conclude that the doctor's negligence had affected his chances to some extent, the claimant would almost always get something. It would be a 'heads you lose everything, tails I win something' situation. But why should the defendant not also be able to redefine the gist of the action if it suits him better?

[225] The appellant in this case accepts that the proportionate recovery effect must cut both ways. If the claim is characterised as loss of a chance, those with a better than evens chance would still only get a proportion of the full value of their claim. But I do not think that he accepts that the same would apply in cases where the claim is characterised as loss of an outcome. In that case there is no basis for calculating the odds. If the two are alternatives available in every case, the defendant will almost always be liable for something. He will have lost the benefit of the 50% chance that causation cannot be proved. But if the two approaches cannot sensibly live together, the claimants who currently obtain full recovery on an adverse outcome basis might in future only achieve a proportionate recovery. This would surely be a case of two steps forward, three steps back for the great majority of straightforward personal injury cases. In either event, the expert evidence would have to be far more complex than it is at present. Negotiations and trials would be a great deal more difficult. Recovery would be much less predictable both for claimants and for defendants' liability insurers. There is no reason in principle why the change in approach should be limited to medical negligence. Whether or not the policy choice is between retaining the present definition of personal injury in outcome terms and redefining it in loss of opportunity terms, introducing the latter would cause far more problems in the general run of personal injury claims than the policy benefits are worth.

[226] Much of the discussion in the cases and literature has centred round cases where the adverse outcome has already happened. The patient has lost his leg. Did the doctor's negligence cause him to lose the leg? If not, did it reduce the chances of saving the leg? But in this case the most serious of the adverse outcomes has not yet happened, and (it is to be hoped) may never happen. The approach to causation should be the same for both past and future events. What, if anything, has the doctor's negligence caused in this case? We certainly do not know whether it has caused this outcome, because happily Mr Gregg has survived each of the significant milestones along the way. Can we even say that it reduced the chances of a successful outcome, given that Mr Gregg has turned out to be one of the successful minority at each milestone? This is quite different from the situation in *Hotson's* case, where the avascular necrosis had already happened. . . . Mr Gregg faced a risk of an adverse outcome which happily has not so far materialised, serious though the effects of his illness, treatment and prognosis

have been. The complexities of attempting to introduce liability for the loss of a chance of a more favourable outcome in personal injury claims have driven me, not without regret, to conclude that it should not be done....

Appeal dismissed.

QUESTIONS

1.   What was the gist of the damage here?
2.   Why did the claim fail?
3.   Do Lord Hoffmann and Baroness Hale agree on how *Gregg v Scott* relates to *Hotson*? (See further on the treatment of *Hotson,* E. Peel (2005) 121 LQR 364 at 366–367, who points out that the two dissenting speeches (as well as Mance LJ in the Court of Appeal) share Baroness Hale's view.)
4.   If the point left open by Lord Phillips was in future decided in a claimant's favour, could it or should it be confined to medical cases?

NOTES

1.   *Gregg v Scott* is noted by J. Morgan [2005] LMCLQ 281; J. R. Spencer [2005] CLJ 282; E. Peel op cit., and also discussed by L. Khoury, *Uncertain Causation in Medical Liability* (2006), pp. 101–104 and (in part) (2008) 124 LQR 103, and see *Uncertain Causation,* pp. 117–140 on the loss of a chance doctrine.
2.   As Lord Hoffmann makes clear, the law does not always rule out recovery for loss of a chance in negligence actions. Several are mentioned in the extract from *Gregg v Scott,* and the subsequent case of *Barker* provides another example: for further examples where lost chances were quantified, see *Davies v Taylor* [1974] AC 207, [1972] 3 All ER 836, and *Doyle v Wallace* [1998] PIQR Q146. Prior to *Gregg v Scott,* the Court of Appeal had rationalised this area somewhat in *Allied Maples Group Ltd v Simmons & Simmons (a firm)* [1995] 4 All ER 907, [1995] 1 WLR 1602, noted by T. Church [1996] CLJ 187 and discussed in the extract from *Gregg v Scott.* Here, a firm of solicitors advising the claimants, who were negotiating to take over the assets of the vendor group of companies, negligently failed to spot that a standard clause protecting the claimants' position had not been included in the draft take-over agreement, or to advise as to the effect of such an omission. Consequently, the agreement was executed without the clause, and the claimants subsequently lost money. At the trial of a preliminary issue, the trial judge held that, on the balance of probabilities, there was a real and not a mere speculative chance that, if the defendants had given proper advice to the claimants, the claimants would have successfully renegotiated with the vendor to obtain proper protection. The defendants appealed, arguing that the claimants could not prove that, but for the defendants' fault, the claimants would not have suffered loss. In other words, they could not prove that, on the balance of probabilities, the vendor would have conceded the point and agreed to include the relevant protective clause in the take-over agreement. The Court of Appeal rejected this argument, holding that where the claimant's loss depends on the hypothetical action of a third party, the claimant need only show a real or substantial chance, rather than a speculative one, that the loss would have been avoided. The precise degree of the chance is then taken into account in the quantification of the damage. This approach has subsequently been applied in many

later cases involving negligent professional advice. Should the court take account of factors relevant to the hypothetical action but which happened after the hypothetical action would have been decided? Consider *Hibbert Pownall & Newton (a firm) v Whitehead* [2008] EWCA Civ 285.

There is certainly a difference between the sorts of lost chances involved in *Allied Maples* and in *Gregg v Scott*. In *Gregg v Scott* the claimant's lost chance was of avoiding a physical injury (mesothelioma), whereas in *Allied Maples* the harm was pure economic loss. In this context note that, for example, in *Spring v Guardian Assurance plc* [1995] 2 AC 296, [1994] 3 All ER 129 (p. 58, ante) Lord Lowry held that the claimant would only have to prove the loss of a reasonable chance of employment, which would then be evaluated by the court (a passage which was expressly approved in *Allied Maples*). However, does the distinction between the type of loss explain the contrasting results in *Gregg v Scott* and *Allied Maples,* bearing in mind that both *Fairchild* and *Barker* involved physical injury? How would you answer the question posed by J. Stapleton (2003) 119 LQR 388 at 403 as to the position if, in a case like *Bolitho v City and Hackney Health Authority* [1998] AC 232, [1997] 4 All ER 771 (p. 326, ante, and see especially note 3, p. 346, ante), 'the evidence was that had [the doctor] attended the patient and ordered a procedure by a third party (e.g. an x-ray) that would have avoided the injury, there was only a 20 per cent chance that the third party would have carried out the procedure?'. See also Khoury, *Uncertain Causation in Medical Liability*, p. 101.

Another explanation of the distinction is that, where harm is dependent on the hypothetical actions of a third party, it is never possible to prove what would have happened, since human beings have free will and free will does not obey the laws of physics (unlike, for example, human hip joints). So it is possible (with sufficiently advanced medical evidence) to be certain whether a physical condition would have developed, but impossible to do anything more than speculate about what a human being would have decided to do, had the defendant not been at fault. It just so happens that cases involving the hypothetical actions of third parties tend, on the whole, to involve economic loss.

This explanation raises the problem of cases such as *McWilliams v Sir William Arrol & Co Ltd* [1962] 1 All ER 623, [1962] 1 WLR 295. Here an employee of the defendant fell to his death while working as a steel erector: no safety harness had been provided by the defendant. The employee's widow sued the defendant, alleging negligence and breach of statutory duty in failing to provide a harness, and succeeded in establishing both forms of fault. However, her claim failed on the basis of but-for causation. The evidence established overwhelmingly that the deceased never wore safety harnesses and the court held that, even if a harness had been provided on the occasion of his death, he would not have worn it. In other words, the widow had been unable to prove on the balance of probabilities that, but for the fault of the defendant, Mr McWilliams would not have died. Here, the harm was dependent on the hypothetical actions of the claimant, not a third party. Is there any justification for treating the hypothetical action of a third party differently from the hypothetical action of the claimant? Of course, on the facts of *McWilliams*, the chance of Mr McWilliams acting 'out of character' on the day of his death was so slim as to fail the 'real and substantial chance' test in *Allied Maples* anyway, but what of a case where the claimant wore a safety harness roughly 40 per cent of the time?

Might it be at all relevant that amongst the early 'hypothetical action by third party' cases (a) *Chaplin v Hicks* [1911] 2 KB 786 has often been seen as a contract case, and (b) *Kitchen v Royal Air Forces Association* [1958] 2 All ER 241, [1958] 1 All ER 563 concerned the prospects of litigation, a matter which judges may feel well-qualified to assess?

On *Allied Maples* see further J. Stapleton (2003) 119 LQR 388 at 404–411 and see the discussion by Lord Hoffmann at [82] –[83] in the extract ante (and note the view of Maurice Kay LJ in *Gouldsmith v Mid Staffordshire General Hospitals NHS Trust* [2007] EWCA Civ 397 at [50]). How far would Lord Hoffmann agree with the views expressed in this note? (See further Lord Nicholls' speech in *Gregg v Scott* at [15]–[19] and that of Baroness Hale at [218]–[220].) There are signs that *Gregg v Scott* may lead to an attack on loss of a chance being recovered in the *Allied v Maples* sort of case: see *Phillips & Co (A Firm) v Whatley* [2007] PNLR 27, [2007] UKPC 28 at [2].

3. A separate problem of factual causation is discussed in the following passage by D. M. A. Strachan (1970) 33 MLR 386 at 391 (footnotes omitted):

> The "but-for" test, though attractive and serviceable because of its basic simplicity, is incapable of dealing with all questions of factual causation. In certain situations common sense demands that a person be held responsible for a certain injury although that injury would have occurred without his participation. It is in situations where there are two independent factors, each being sufficient to produce the injury, that the test proves unsatisfactory. Such factors may operate either concurrently or successively. They operate concurrently if two independent fires, both negligently started, converge on a house and demolish it. Short shrift should be given to the contention that the damage is not caused by one, since another set of circumstances existed which would have caused the damage independently. The logical conclusion, if such a contention were to succeed, would be that the house-owner would be left with no redress since neither fire could be said to have caused the loss.…
>
> The problem becomes more convoluted when the independent factors, each of which is sufficient to produce the injury, are successive rather than concurrent.

■ Baker v Willoughby

House of Lords [1969] 3 All ER 1528

The appellant, when crossing a road, had been knocked down by the respondent's car and his left leg and ankle were injured, the ankle becoming stiff. Apart from suffering pain, he lost those 'amenities of life' which are dependent on the ability to move freely and his earning capacity was reduced. The House of Lords restored the trial judge's apportionment of 75 per cent responsibility on the respondent motorist for the accident. After the accident but before the trial of the action, the appellant was involved in several different sorts of employment. One day he was sorting scrap metal when he was shot by one of two men who had unsuccessfully demanded money from him. His left leg was so badly affected by the shot that its amputation was necessary and the substitution of an artificial limb for what had been a stiff leg increased his disability. On the question of the effect on the respondent's liability of the second injury:

LORD REID:…
The appellant argues that the loss which he suffered from the car accident has not been diminished by his second injury. He still suffers from reduced capacity to earn although these[2] may have

---

[2] [I.e. these losses.]

been to some extent increased. And he will suffer these losses for as long as he would have done because it is not said that the second injury curtained his expectation of life.[3] The respondent on the other hand argues that the second injury removed the very limb from which the earlier disability had stemmed, and that therefore no loss suffered thereafter can be attributed to the respondent's negligence. He says that the second injury submerged or obliterated the effect of the first and that all loss thereafter must be attributed to the second injury. The trial judge[4] rejected this argument which he said was more ingenious than attractive. But it was accepted by the Court of Appeal.[5]

The respondent's argument was succinctly put to your Lordships by his counsel. He could not run before the second injury; he cannot run now. But the cause is now quite different. The former cause was an injured leg but now he has no leg and the former cause can no longer operate. His counsel was inclined to agree that if the first injury had caused some neurosis or other mental disability, that disability might be regarded as still flowing from the first accident; even if it had been increased by the second accident the respondent might still have to pay for that part which he caused. I agree with that and I think that any distinction between a neurosis and a physical injury depends on a wrong view of what is the proper subject for compensation. A man is not compensated for the physical injury; he is compensated for the loss which he suffers as a result of that injury. His loss is not in having a stiff leg; it is in his inability to lead a full life, his inability to enjoy those amenities which depend on freedom of movement and his inability to earn as much as he used to earn or could have earned if there had been no accident. In this case the second injury did not diminish any of these. So why should it be regarded as having obliterated or superseded them?

If it were the case that in the eye of the law an effect could only have one cause then the respondent might be right. It is always necessary to prove that any loss for which damages can be given was caused by the defendant's negligent act. But it is commonplace that the law regards many events as having two causes; that happens whenever there is contributory negligence, for then the law says that the injury was caused both by the negligence of the defendant and by the negligence of the plaintiff. And generally it does not matter which negligence occurred first in point of time.

I see no reason why the appellant's present disability cannot be regarded as having two causes, and if authority be needed for this I find it in *Harwood v Wyken Colliery Co*[6]....

[Having discussed various other cases, LORD REID continued:] These cases exemplify the general rule that a wrongdoer must take the plaintiff (or his property) as he finds him: that may be to his advantage or disadvantage. In the present case the robber is not responsible or liable for the damage caused by the respondent; he would only have to pay for additional loss to the appellant by reason of his now having an artificial limb instead of a stiff leg....

If...later injury suffered before the date of the trial either reduces the disabilities from the injury for which the defendant is liable, or shortens the period during which they will be suffered by the plaintiff then the defendant will have to pay less damages. But if the later injuries merely become a concurrent cause of the disabilities caused by the injury inflicted by the defendant, then in my view they cannot diminish the damages....

Finally, I must advert to the pain suffered and to be suffered by the appellant as a result of the car accident. If the result of the amputation was that the appellant suffered no more pain thereafter, then he could not claim for pain after the amputation which he would never suffer. But the facts with regard to this are not clear, the amount awarded for pain subsequent to the date of the amputation was probably only a small part of the £1,600 damages and counsel for the respondent did not make a point of this. So in these circumstances we can neglect this matter....

LORD PEARSON:...

There is a plausible argument for the respondent on the following lines. The original accident, for which the respondent is liable, inflicted on the appellant a permanently injured left ankle, which caused pain

---

[3] [Compare *Pickett v British Rail Engineering Ltd* [1980] AC 136, [1979] 1 All ER 774 (p. 522, post).]
[4] [1969] 1 QB 38, [1968] 2 All ER 236.   [5] [1969] 2 All ER 549, [1969] 2 WLR 489.
[6] [1913] 2 KB 158.

from time to time, diminished his mobility and so reduced his earning capacity, and was likely to lead to severe arthritis. The proper figure of damages for those consequences of the accident, as assessed by the judge before making his apportionment, was £1,600. That was the proper figure for those consequences if they were likely to endure for a normal period and run a normal course. But the supervening event, when the robbers shot the appellant in his left leg, necessitated an amputation of the left leg above the knee. The consequences of the original accident therefore have ceased. He no longer suffers pain in his left ankle, because there no longer is a left ankle. He will never have the arthritis. There is no longer any loss of mobility through stiffness or weakness of the left ankle, because it is no longer there. The injury to the left ankle, resulting from the original accident, is not still operating as one of two concurrent causes both producing discomfort and disability. It is not operating at all nor causing anything. The present state of disablement, with the stump and the artificial leg on the left side, was caused wholly by the supervening event and not at all by the original accident. Thus the consequences of the original accident have been submerged and obliterated by the greater consequences of the supervening event.

That is the argument, and it is formidable. But it must not be allowed to succeed, because it produces manifest injustice. The supervening event has not made the appellant less lame nor less disabled nor less deprived of amenities. It has not shortened the period over which he will be suffering. It has made him more lame, more disabled, more deprived of amenities. He should not have less damages through being worse off than might have been expected.

The nature of the injustice becomes apparent if the supervening event is treated as a tort (as indeed it was) and if one envisages the appellant suing the robbers who shot him. They would be entitled, as the saying is, to 'take the plaintiff as they find him'. (*Performance Cars Ltd v Abraham.*[7]) They have not injured and disabled a previously fit and able-bodied man. They have only made an already lame and disabled man more lame and more disabled. Take, for example, the reduction of earnings. The original accident reduced his earnings from £x per week to £y per week, and the supervening event further reduced them from £y per week to £z per week. If the respondent's argument is correct, there is, as counsel for the appellant has pointed out, a gap. The appellant recovers from the respondent the £x-y not for the whole period of the remainder of his working life, but only for the short period up to the date of the supervening event. The robbers are liable only for the £y-z from the date of the supervening event onwards. In the Court of Appeal[8] an ingenious attempt was made to fill the gap by holding that the damages recoverable from the later tortfeasors (the robbers) would include a novel head of damage, viz., the diminution of the appellant's damages recoverable from the original tortfeasor (the respondent). I doubt whether that would be an admissible head of damage; it looks too remote. In any case it would not help the appellant, if the later tortfeasors could not be found or were indigent and uninsured. These later tortfeasors cannot have been insured in respect of the robbery which they committed.

I think a solution of the theoretical problem can be found in cases such as this by taking a comprehensive and unitary view of the damage caused by the original accident. Itemisation of the damages by dividing them into heads and sub-heads is often convenient, but is not essential. In the end judgment is given for a single lump sum of damages and not for a total of items set out under heads and sub-heads. The original accident caused what may be called a 'devaluation' of the plaintiff, in the sense that it produced a general reduction of his capacity to do things, to earn money and to enjoy life. For that devaluation the original tortfeasor should be and remain responsible to the full extent, unless before the assessment of the damages something has happened which either diminishes the devaluation (e.g. if there is an unexpected recovery from some of the adverse effects of the accident) or by shortening the expectation of life diminishes the period over which the plaintiff will suffer from the devaluation. If the supervening event is a tort, the second tortfeasor should be responsible for the additional devaluation caused by him....

[LORD GUEST, VISCOUNT DILHORNE, and LORD DONOVAN concurred with LORD REID.]

Appeal allowed.

---

[7] [1962] 1 QB 33, [1961] 3 All ER 413.   [8] [1969] 2 All ER 549, [1969] 2 WLR 489.

NOTE

In *Performance Cars Ltd v Abraham* [1962] 1 QB 33, [1961] 3 All ER 413, which is referred to in *Baker v Willoughby*, the defendant, whose car had collided with the claimant's Rolls-Royce causing damage to its wing and bumper, accepted responsibility for the accident. The damage to the wing necessitated a respray of the lower part of the car. A fortnight before, this same Rolls-Royce had been in a collision caused by the fault of another person and the damages in that case included the cost of a respray which had not yet been carried out. Nothing had been recovered under that judgment and the claim against the defendant in the present case included the cost of a respray. This was held by the Court of Appeal to be irrecoverable from this defendant. The second collision had not caused the need for a respray: such a need already existed. *Performance Cars* was said still to be good law by the Court of Appeal in *Halsey v Milton Keynes General NHS Trust* [2004] 4 All ER 920, [2004] EWCA Civ 576.

■ Jobling v Associated Dairies Ltd
House of Lords [1981] 2 All ER 752

In 1973 the appellant injured his back at work, an injury for which the respondents were held liable, and this injury led to his earning capacity being reduced by 50 per cent. However, in 1976 (before the trial of the action) the appellant was rendered totally unfit for work by the onset of a condition known as spondylotic myelopathy, a disease of the spine. This condition had developed after the original accident and was in no way connected with it. Reeve J decided, on the basis of *Baker v Willoughby*, that he had to ignore the later condition in assessing damages, but the Court of Appeal disagreed, [1980] 3 All ER 769. On appeal to the House of Lords:

LORD WILBERFORCE: . . .
In an attempt to solve the present case, and similar cases of successive causes of incapacity according to some legal principle, a number of arguments have been invoked.

1. Causation arguments. The unsatisfactory character of these is demonstrated by the case of *Baker v Willoughby* [1970] AC 467, [1969] 3 All ER 1528. I think that it can now been seen that Lord Reid's theory of concurrent causes even if workable on the particular facts of *Baker v Willoughby* (where successive injuries were sustained by the same limb) is as a general solution not supported by the authority he invokes (*Harwood v Wyken Colliery Co* [1913] 2 KB 158) or workable in other cases. . . .

2. The 'vicissitudes' argument. This is that since, according to accepted doctrine, allowance, and if necessary some discount, has to be made in assessing loss of future earnings for the normal contingencies of life, amongst which 'illness' is normally enumerated, so, if one of these contingencies becomes actual before the date of trial, this actuality must be taken into account. Reliance is here placed on the apophthegm 'the court should not speculate when it knows'. This argument has a good deal of attraction. But it has its difficulties: it raises at once the question whether a discount is to be made on account of all possible 'vicissitudes' or only on account of 'non-culpable' vicissitudes (i.e. such that if they occur there will be no cause of action against anyone, the theory being that the prospect of being injured by a tort is not a normally foreseeable vicissitude) or only on account of 'culpable' vicissitudes (such as per contra). And if this distinction is to be made how is the court to act when a discounted vicissitude happens before trial? Must it attempt to decide whether there was culpability or not? And how is it to do this if, as is likely, the alleged culprit is not before it?

This actual distinction between 'culpable' and 'non-culpable' events was made, with supporting argument, in the Alberta case of *Penner v Mitchell* [1978] 5 WWR 328. One may add to it the rider that, as pointed out by Dickson J in the Supreme Court of Canada in *Andrews v Grand & Toy Alberta Ltd* (1978) 83 DLR (3d) 452 at 470, there are in modern society many public and private schemes which cushion the individual against adverse circumstances. One then has to ask whether a discount should be made in respect of (a) such cases or (b) cases where there is no such cushion. There is indeed in the 'vicissitude' argument some degree of circularity, since a discount in respect of possible events would only be fair if the actual event, discounted as possible, were to be taken into account when happening. But the whole question is whether it should be. One might just as well argue from what happens in 'actual' cases to what should happen in discountable cases.

In spite of these difficulties, the 'vicissitude' argument is capable in some, perhaps many, cases of providing a workable and reasonably just rule, and I would certainly not discountenance its use, either in the present case or in others.

The fact, however, is that to attempt a solution of these and similar problems, where there are successive causes of incapacity in some degree, on classical lines ('the object of damages for tort is to place the plaintiff in as good a position as if etc'; 'the defendant must compensate for the loss caused by his wrongful act, no more'; 'the defendant must take the plaintiff as he finds him etc') is, in many cases, no longer possible. We do not live in a world governed by the pure common law and its logical rules. We live in a mixed world where a man is protected against injury and misfortune by a whole web of rules and dispositions, with a number of timid legislative interventions. To attempt to compensate him on the basis of selected rules without regard to the whole must lead either to logical inconsistencies or to over- or under-compensation. As my noble and learned friend Lord Edmund-Davies has pointed out, no account was taken in *Baker v Willoughby* of the very real possibility that the plaintiff might obtain compensation from the Criminal Injuries Compensation Board. if he did in fact obtain this compensation he would, on the ultimate decision, be over-compensated.

In the present case, and in other industrial cases, there seems to me no justification for disregarding the fact that the injured man's employer is insured (indeed since 1972 compulsorily insured) against liability to his employees. The state has decided, in other words, on a spreading of risk. There seems to me no more justification for disregarding the fact that the plaintiff (presumably; we have not been told otherwise), is entitled to sickness and invalidity benefit in respect of his myelopathy, the amount of which may depend on his contribution record, which in turn may have been affected by his accident. So we have no means of knowing whether the plaintiff would be over-compensated if he were, in addition, to receive the assessed damages from his employer, or whether he would be under-compensated if left to his benefit. It is not easy to accept a solution by which a partially incapacitated man becomes worse off in terms of damages and benefit through a greater degree of incapacity. Many other ingredients, of weight in either direction, may enter into individual cases. Without any satisfaction I draw from this the conclusion that no general, logical or universally fair rules can be stated which will cover, in a manner consistent with justice, cases of supervening events, whether due to tortious, partially tortious, non-culpable or wholly accidental events. The courts can only deal with each case as best they can in a manner so as to provide just and sufficient but not excessive compensation, taking all factors into account. I think that this is what *Baker v Willoughby* did, and indeed that Lord Pearson reached his decision in this way; the rationalisation of the decision, as to which I at least have doubts, need and should not be applied to other cases. In the present case the Court of Appeal reached the unanswerable conclusion that to apply *Baker v Willoughby* to the facts of the present case would produce an unjust result, and I am willing to accept the corollary that justice, so far as it can be perceived, lies the other way and that the supervening myelopathy should not be disregarded. If rationalisation is needed, I am willing to accept the 'vicissitudes' argument as the best available. I should be more firmly convinced of the merits of the conclusion if the whole pattern of benefits had been considered, in however general a way. The result of the present case may be lacking in precision and rational justification, but so long as we are content to live in a mansion of so many different architectures this is inevitable.

I would dismiss the appeal.

LORD KEITH OF KINKEL: . . .

Counsel for the appellant sought to draw a distinction between the case where the plaintiff, at the time of the tortious injury, is already suffering from a latent undetected condition which later develops into a disabling illness and the case where the inception of the illness occurs wholly at a later date. In the former case, so it was maintained, the illness would properly fall to be taken into account in diminution of damages, on the principle that the tortfeasor takes his victim as he finds him, but in the latter case it would not. There is no trace of the suggested distinction in any of the authorities, and in my opinion it is unsound and apt to lead to great practical difficulties, providing ample scope for disputation among medical men. What would be the position, it might be asked, of an individual having a constitutional weakness making him specially prone to illness generally, or as hereditary tendency to some specific disease?

I am...of opinion that the majority in *Baker v Willoughby* were mistaken in approaching the problems common to the case of a supervening tortious act and to that of supervening illness wholly from the point of view of causation. While it is logically correct to say that in both cases the original tort and the supervening event may be concurrent causes of incapacity, that does not necessarily, in my view, provide the correct solution. In the case of supervening illness, it is appropriate to keep in view that this is one of the ordinary vicissitudes of life, and when one is comparing the situation resulting from the accident with the situation, had there been no accident, to recognise that the illness would have overtaken the plaintiff in any event, so that it cannot be disregarded in arriving at proper compensation, and no more than proper compensation.

Additional considerations come into play when dealing with the problems arising where the plaintiff has suffered injuries from two or more successive and independent tortious acts. In that situation it is necessary to secure that the plaintiff is fully compensated for the aggregate effects of all his injuries. As Lord Pearson noted in *Baker v Willoughby* [1970] AC 467 at 495, [1969] 3 All ER 1528 at 1535 it would clearly be unjust to reduce the damages awarded for the first tort because of the occurrence of the second tort, damages for which are to be assessed on the basis that the plaintiff is already partially incapacitated. I do not consider it necessary to formulate any precise juristic basis for dealing with this situation differently from the case of supervening illness. It might be said that a supervening tort is not one of the ordinary vicissitudes of life, or that it is too remote a possibility to be taken into account, or that it can properly be disregarded because it carries its own remedy. None of these formulations, however, is entirely satisfactory. The fact remains that the principle of full compensation requires that a just and practical solution should be found. In the event that damages against two successive tortfeasors fall to be assessed at the same time, it would be highly unreasonable if the aggregate of both awards were less than the total loss suffered by the plaintiff. The computation should start from an assessment of that total loss. The award against the second tortfeasor cannot in fairness to him fail to recognise that the plaintiff whom he injured was already to some extent incapacitated. In order that the plaintiff may be fully compensated, it becomes necessary to deduct the award so calculated from the assessment of the plaintiff's total loss and award the balance against the first tortfeasor. If that be a correct approach, it follows that, in proceedings against the first tortfeasor alone, the occurrence of the second tort cannot be successfully relied on by the defendant as reducing the damages which he must pay. That, in substance, was the result of the decision in *Baker v Willoughby*, where the supervening event was a tortious act, and to that extent the decision was, in my view, correct.

Before leaving the case, it is right to face up to the fact that, if a non-tortious supervening event is to have the effect of reducing damages but a subsequent tortious act is not, there may in some cases be difficulty in ascertaining whether the event in question is or is not of a tortious character, particularly in the absence of the alleged tortfeasor. Possible questions of contributory negligence may cause additional complications. Such difficulties are real, but are not sufficient, in my view, to warrant the conclusion that the distinction between tortious and non-tortious supervening events should not be accepted. The court must simply do its best to arrive at a just assessment of damages in a pragmatical way in the light of the whole circumstances of the case.

My Lords, for these reasons I would dismiss the appeal.

LORD BRIDGE OF HARWICH:...

The vicissitudes principle itself, it seems to me, stems from the fundamental proposition of law that the object of every award of damages for monetary loss is to put the party wronged so far as possible in the same position, no better and no worse, as he would be in if he had not suffered the wrong in respect of which he claims. To assume that an injured plaintiff, if not injured, would have continued to earn his full wages for a full working life, is very probably to over-compensate him. To apply a discount in respect of possible future loss of earnings arising from independent ca[u]ses may be to under-compensate him. When confronted by future uncertainty, the court assesses the prospects and strikes a balance between these opposite dangers as best it can. But, when the supervening illness or injury which is the independent cause of loss of earning capacity has manifested itself before trial, the vent has demonstrated that, even if the plaintiff had never sustained the tortious injury, his earnings would now be reduced or extinguished. To hold the tortfeasor, in this situation, liable to pay damages for a notional continuing loss of earnings attributable to the tortious injury is to put the plaintiff in a better position than he would be in if he had never suffered the tortious injury. Put more shortly, applying well-established principles for the assessment of damages at common law, when a plaintiff injured by the defendant's tort is wholly incapacitated from earning by supervening illness or accidental injury, the law will no longer treat the tort as a continuing cause of any loss of earning capacity. . . .

[LORD EDMUND-DAVIES and LORD RUSSELL OF KILLOWEN delivered speeches in favour of dismissing the appeal.]

Appeal dismissed.

NOTES

1. All their Lordships in *Jobling* criticised Lord Reid's reliance in *Baker v Willoughby* (p. 377, ante) on *Harwood v Wyken Colliery Co* [1913] 2 KB 158, which concerned the old Workmen's Compensation Scheme. However, note A. Evans' argument—(1982) 45 MLR 329 at 331—that this criticism was 'not so much in his use of that decision to found a causation argument but in his failure to recognise the inadequacies of caus-ation arguments on their own and, in particular, to take account of the "vicissitudes" argument which Hamilton LJ in *Harwood* had clearly recognised as pertaining in a tor-tious context'. (Cf. *Bushby v Morris* (1978–80) 28 ALR 611 at 616.) The actual decision in *Baker v Willoughby* was not challenged by counsel for the respondents in *Jobling* and it was not reversed by the House of Lords. In addition to the views of Lord Wilberforce and Lord Keith set out ante, Lord Edmund-Davies thought it possible for the deci-sion in *Baker v Willoughby* to be accepted 'on its own facts', although he was wor-ried by a couple of features of the decision (see [1981] 2 All ER at p. 759). Lord Russell 'was not prepared to state disagreement' with the decision in *Baker v Willoughby*, but Lord Bridge was not willing to go even this far. Given the approach of the respondents' counsel mentioned ante, Lord Bridge was content to leave open the current status of the decision. In *Rahman v Arearose Ltd* [2001] QB 351 at [32] Laws LJ stated that he saw 'no inconsistency whatever between the two decisions', and in *Halsey v Milton Keynes General NHS Trust* [2004] 4 All ER 920, [2004] EWCA Civ 576 at [66] the Court of Appeal thought that the exception to the but-for principle evidenced in *Baker v Willoughby* should be regarded as justified by the principle of full compensation.

2. Lord Wilberforce said that although no account was taken in *Baker v Willoughby* of the chance that the claimant might be awarded compensation by the Criminal Injuries Compensation Board, he thought there was a 'very real possibility' that he would be. Lord Wilberforce concluded that, if this happened, the claimant would be over-compensated. On the other hand, the first tortfeasor in *Baker v Willoughby* did not have to pay for the additional disability resulting from the shooting. How, therefore, could the claimant have been over-compensated?

3. One of Lord Keith's suggestions for reconciling *Baker v Willoughby* with *Jobling*—that a supervening tort is not one of the ordinary vicissitudes of life—met with some support

from Lord Russell who was 'prepared to suggest' that physical damage from such an event would not be a 'relevant vicissitude'. Compare the approach of Lord Wilberforce and Lord Bridge set out ante.

To distinguish the situation in *Baker v Willoughby* is one thing, but the question of the justification for such a distinction must also be considered. It does seem unfair to allow a person such as the claimant in *Baker v Willoughby* to be worse off because he has been the victim of two torts rather than of one; and of course the decision obviates that result. See further J. Stapleton (2003) 119 LQR 388 at 412–413. However, it should be borne in mind that, as Lord Wilberforce made clear in *Jobling*, tort is not the only system of compensation. See T. Hervey (1981) 97 LQR 210 at 211–212 who, in commenting on the Court of Appeal's decision in *Jobling*, points out that an injured person can suffer, not just from 'falling between' two tortfeasors (which *Baker v Willoughby* does manage to avoid), but also from 'falling between' tort and another compensation system. In the light of this should a distinction be drawn between tortious and non-tortious supervening events?

4. What is the position if the court thinks there is a chance that a tortiously inflicted injury would have occurred in the future and affected the claimant's ability to work if the original tort had not already stopped him from working? In *Heil v Rankin* [2001] PIQR Q3, which involved a claim by a policeman, the Court of Appeal thought this possibility should be taken into account as a relevant 'vicissitude', which should lead to a reduction of damages. The approach in *Baker* was regarded as appropriate for cases where there would otherwise not be full compensation, whereas to ignore the chance in *Heil* would in the Court of Appeal's view lead to over-compensation. It might further be argued that the chance would in reality only be present if the claimant kept on working, which he was not going to do: the potential second tort would only occur if the first tort had not occurred and therefore there would not be a situation in which a second tortfeasor could use the 'but-for' argument with the consequences that *Baker* was concerned to avoid. Cf. *Winfield & Jolowicz* who argue (at pp. 278–279) that 'from an intuitive point of view it looks odd to ignore what we know has happened and take into account what might have happened'.

5. Reverting to the basic but-for' test, consider the following situation. It has been seen (p. 329, ante) that a doctor may be in breach of a duty of care in not advising a patient of even a small risk associated with some proposed operation. Is there any problem with the application of the 'but-for' test in a case where the warning was not given and the risk eventuated despite the operation being carried out with reasonable care if the evidence is either that the patient would have had the operation even if warned or would never have had the operation if warned? In the light of this, consider the next extract.

■ Chester v Afshar
House of Lords [2004] 4 All ER 587

LORD STEYN:
[11] My Lords, the facts of this case can be simplified. The claimant suffered from low back pain. A neurosurgeon advised her to undergo an elective lumbar surgical procedure. The procedure entails a 1%–2% chance of serious neurological damage arising from the operation. The claimant was entitled to be informed of this fact. In breach of the common law duty of care the surgeon failed to inform the claimant of the risk. The claimant reluctantly agreed to the operation. Three days after her consultation with the surgeon the claimant underwent the surgery. The claimant sustained serious neurological

damage. In the result the very injury about which she should have been warned occurred. The surgeon had not been negligent in performing the operation: he did not increase the risks inherent in the surgery. On the other hand, if the claimant had been warned she would not have agreed to the operation. Instead she would have sought further advice on alternatives. The judge found that if the claimant had been properly warned the operation would not have taken place when it did, if at all. The judge was unable to find whether if the claimant had been duly warned she would with the benefit of further medical advice have given or refused consent to surgery. What is clear is that if she had agreed to surgery at a subsequent date, the risk attendant upon it would have been the same, ie 1%–2%. It is therefore improbable that she would have sustained neurological damage.

[12] On these facts the judge found that the claimant had established a causal link between the breach and the injury she had sustained and held that the defendant was liable in damages. In a detailed and careful judgment the Court of Appeal (Hale LJ, Sir Christopher Slade and Sir Denis Henry ([2002] EWCA Civ 724, [2002] 3 All ER 552, [2003] QB 356)) upheld the conclusion of the judge.

[13] Counsel for the surgeon submitted that it is contrary to general principles of tort law to award damages when a defendant's wrong has not been proved to have increased the claimant's exposure to risk. He argued that in order to establish causation in a case of a surgeon's failure to warn a patient of a significant risk of injury, the patient must prove both that she would not have consented to run the relevant risk then and there, and that she would not, ultimately, have consented to run the relevant risk. The only qualification was the case where a claimant could prove an accelerated onset of injury. That the claimant could not do on the facts of the case. On analysis it was an all or nothing case. Counsel said that the injury that the claimant sustained was just a coincidence, a piece of abominable bad luck, like lightning striking a person. This was a powerful argument and persuasively presented.

[14] The legal context requires consideration of a number of other relevant factors. First, the nature of the correlative rights and duties of the patient and surgeon must be kept in mind. The starting point is that every individual of adult years and sound mind has a right to decide what may or may not be done with his or her body. Individuals have a right to make important medical decisions affecting their lives for themselves: they have the right to make decisions which doctors regard as ill advised. Surgery performed without the informed consent of the patient is unlawful. The court is the final arbiter of what constitutes informed consent. Usually, informed consent will presuppose a general warning by the surgeon of a significant risk of the surgery.

[15] In the case before the House a single cause of action is under consideration, viz the tort of negligence. . . .

[16] A surgeon owes a legal duty to a patient to warn him or her in general terms of possible serious risks involved in the procedure. The only qualification is that there may be wholly exceptional cases where objectively in the best interests of the patient the surgeon may be excused from giving a warning. This is, however, irrelevant in the present case. In modern law medical paternalism no longer rules and a patient has a prima facie right to be informed by a surgeon of a small, but well established, risk of serious injury as a result of surgery.

[17] Secondly, not all rights are equally important. But a patient's right to an appropriate warning from a surgeon when faced with surgery ought normatively to be regarded as an important right which must be given effective protection whenever possible.

[18] Thirdly, in the context of attributing legal responsibility, it is necessary to identify precisely the protected legal interests at stake. A rule requiring a doctor to abstain from performing an operation without the informed consent of a patient serves two purposes. It tends to avoid the occurrence of the particular physical injury the risk of which a patient is not prepared to accept. It also ensures that due respect is given to the autonomy and dignity of each patient. . . .

[19] Fourthly, it is a distinctive feature of the present case that but for the surgeon's negligent failure to warn the claimant of the small risk of serious injury the actual injury would not have occurred when it did and the chance of it occurring on a subsequent occasion was very small. It could therefore be said that the breach of the surgeon resulted in the very injury about which the claimant was entitled to be warned.

[20] These factors must be considered in combination. But they must also be weighed against the undesirability of departing from established principles of causation, except for good reasons. The collision of competing ideas poses a difficult question of law.

[21] That such problems do not necessarily have a single right answer is illustrated by the judgment of the Australian High Court in *Chappel v Hart* (1999) 2 LRC 341, (1998) 72 ALJR 1344. A surgeon failed to warn a patient of a small risk of an operation. She underwent the operation. In the result the very injury of which she should have been warned took place. As in the present case the position was that the patient would not have had the operation at the time and place when she did. If the patient had the operation on a subsequent occasion, the outcome would probably have been uneventful. On these facts the court decided by a majority of three (Gaudron, Gummow and Kirby JJ) to two (McHugh and Hayne JJ) that the patient was entitled to recover substantial damages from the surgeon for the physical injuries suffered as a result of the operation performed on her. The judgments are illuminating. For my part I found the dissenting judgment of McHugh J particularly powerful, and rightly counsel for the surgeon relied heavily on it. *Chappel v Hart* mirrors the issues and arguments in the present case. It will not serve any useful purpose to cite at length from the judgments. I also do not think a process of counting heads in a case such as *Chappel v Hart* is a particularly helpful exercise in regard to the issue before the House. At the very least, however, this Australian case reveals two fundamentally different approaches, the one favouring firm adherence to traditionalist causation techniques and the other a greater emphasis on policy and corrective justice.

[22] The House was referred to a valuable body of academic literature which discusses problems such as arose in *Chappel v Hart*, and in the present case, in some detail. Not surprisingly, the authors approach the matter from slightly different angles. It is, however, fair to say that there is general support for the majority decision in *Chappel v Hart*, and for the view which prevailed in the Court of Appeal in the present case (see Cane 'A Warning about Causation' (1999) 115 LQR 21; Grubb 'Clinical Negligence: Informed Consent and Causation' (2002) 10 Med LRev 322; Honoré 'Medical non-disclosure, causation and risk: *Chappel v Hart*' (1999) 7 Torts Law Journal 1; Jones ' "But for" causation in actions for non-disclosure of risk' (2002) 18 PN 192; Stapleton 'Cause-in-Fact and the Scope of Liability for Consequences' (2003) 119 LQR 388; Stauch 'Taking the Consequences for Failure to Warn of Medical Risks' (2000) 63 MLR 261)). The case note by the co-author of the seminal treatise on causation is particularly interesting. Professor Honoré said:

> '. . . does it follow that Mrs Hart should not recover? Or is this a case where courts are entitled to see to it that justice is done despite the absence of causal connection? I think it is the latter and for the following reason. The duty of a surgeon to warn of the dangers inherent in an operation is intended to help minimise the risk to the patient. But it is also intended to enable the patient to make an informed choice whether to undergo the treatment recommended and, if so, at whose hands and when. Dr Chappel violated Mrs Hart's right to choose for herself, even if he did not increase the risk to her. Judges should vindicate rights that have been violated if they can do so consistently with the authority of statutes and decided cases. In this case the High Court did just this, in effect by making Dr Chappel, when he operated on Mrs Hart, strictly liable for any injury he might cause of the type against which he should have warned her. For Dr Chappel *did* cause the harm that Mrs Hart suffered, though not by the advice he failed to give her. He did so by operating on her and, though he operated with due care, he slit open her oesophagus with disastrous consequences. Morally he was responsible for the outcome of what he did . . . All the High Court has therefore done is to give legal sanction to an underlying moral responsibility for causing injury of the very sort against the risk of which the defendant should have warned her. Do the courts have power in certain cases to override causal considerations in order to vindicate a plaintiff's rights? I believe they do though the right must be exercised with great caution.' (See (1999) 7 Torts Law Journal 1 at 8.)

In my view Professor Honoré was right to face up to the fact that *Chappel v Hart*—and therefore the present case—cannot neatly be accommodated within conventional causation principles. But he was also right to say that policy and corrective justice pull powerfully in favour of vindicating the patient's right to know.

[23] It is true that there is no direct English authority permitting a modification of the approach to the proof of causation in a case such as the present. On the other hand, there is the analogy of *Fairchild v Glenhaven Funeral Services Ltd*...[2002] UKHL 22, [2002] 3 All ER 305, [2003] 1 AC 32 [p. 348, ante] which reveals a principled approach to such a problem....At the very least *Fairchild's* case shows that where justice and policy *demand* it a modification of causation principles is not beyond the wit of a modern court.

[24] Standing back from the detailed arguments, I have come to the conclusion that, as a result of the surgeon's failure to warn the patient, she cannot be said to have given informed consent to the surgery in the full legal sense. Her right of autonomy and dignity can and ought to be vindicated by a narrow and modest departure from traditional causation principles.

[25] On a broader basis I am glad to have arrived at the conclusion that the claimant is entitled in law to succeed. This result is in accord with one of the most basic aspirations of the law, namely to right wrongs. Moreover, the decision announced by the House today reflects the reasonable expectations of the public in contemporary society....

[27] For these reasons as well as the reasons given by my noble and learned friends Lord Hope of Craighead and Lord Walker of Gestingthorpe I would dimiss the appeal.

[LORD BINGHAM OF CORNHILL and LORD HOFFMANN delivered speeches in favour of allowing the appeal. LORD HOPE OF CRAIGHEAD and LORD WALKER OF GESTINGHOPE delivered speeches in favour of dismissing the appeal and in which they agreed with LORD STEYN's speech.]

Appeal dismissed.

NOTES

1. *Chester v Afshar* is noted by K. Amarthalingam [2005] CLJ 32 and R. Stevens (2005) 121 LQR 189; and see J. Stapleton (2006) 122 LQR 426.
2. The attitude of the Court of Appeal in two later cases (*White v Paul Davidson & Taylor* [2003] EWCA Civ 1511; *Beary v Pall Mall Investments (a firm)* [2005] EWCA Civ 415) has been that the approach to causation in *Chester* should be confined to cases of failure to warn in medical cases. However, did *Chester* need any moderation to the rules of factual causation to get through that stage of the inquiry? The dissenting Law Lords (Lord Bingham and Lord Hoffmann) thought that factual causation was lacking. Do you agree? What answer do you obtain if the 'but-for' test is applied? Does it matter at this stage of the inquiry if the material risk is not *increased* by the failure to warn? It can be argued that the issue whether the damage was sufficiently causally connected to the failure to warn only really raised issues of selection amongst the operative factual causes, which is the concern of the next section. See generally Stapleton (2006) 122 LQR 426.

2 SELECTION AMONG OPERATIVE FACTUAL CAUSES

■ Stapley v Gypsum Mines Ltd
House of Lords [1953] 2 All ER 478

LORD ASQUITH OF BISHOPSTONE:...
Courts of law must accept the fact that the philosophic doctrine of causation and the juridical doctrine of responsibility for the consequences of a negligent act are not congruent. To a philosopher—a term

which I use in no disparaging sense, for what is a philosopher but one who, inter alia, reasons severely and with precision?—to a philosopher, the whole legal doctrine of responsibility must seem anomalous. To him, if event C could not occur unless each of two previous events—A and B—had preceded it, it would be unmeaning to say that A was more responsible for the occurrence of C than was B, or that B was more responsible for its occurrence than was A. The whole modern doctrine of contributory negligence, however, proceeds on the contrary assumption. If not, there would be no question of apportionment. But the fission between law and strict logic goes deeper than that. For I am persuaded that it is still part of the law of this country that two causes may both be necessary preconditions of a particular result—damage to X—yet the one may, if the facts justify that conclusion, be treated as the real, substantial, direct or effective cause, and the other dismissed as at best a causa sine qua non and ignored for purposes of legal liability. . . .

NOTES

1. It will have been seen that Lord Asquith used the phrase causa sine qua non in this extract, which approximates to passing the 'but-for' test. This Latin tag is often contrasted with another, namely causa causans, the search for which is the concern of the present section. However, the degree of help which such phrases give should not be overestimated. As Laws LJ stated in *Rahman v Arearose Ltd* [2001] QB 351 at [32]–[33]:

    The law has dug no deeper in the philosophical thickets of causation than to distinguish between a causa sine qua non and a causa causans. The latter is an empty tautology. The former proves everything, and therefore nothing: if A kills B by stabbing him, the birth of either of them 30 years before is as much a causa sine qua non of the death as is the wielding of the knife. So the law makes appeal to the notion of *proximate* cause; but how proximate does it have to be? As a concept it tells one nothing. So in all these cases the real question is, What is the damage for which the defendant under consideration should be held *responsible*.

2. In *Stapley* (in an extract which is set out at p. 433, post, dealing with contributory negligence) Lord Reid stated that causation was established by the application of the court's common sense to the facts of any particular case. This point was discussed and followed in the High Court of Australia in *March v E & M H Stramare Pty Ltd* (1990–91) 171 CLR 506, commented on by N. J. Mullany (1992) 12 Ox JLS 431, where it was acknowledged that value judgments and policy decisions came into the decision (and again in an Australian context see also *Chappell v Hart* (1998) 156 ALR 517). *March* was one of the Australian decisions followed in the Court of Appeal in *Galoo Ltd v Bright Grahame Murray (a firm)* [1995] 1 All ER 16, [1994] 1 WLR 1360, noted by J. O'Sullivan [1995] CLJ 25, where, considering contract cases and tort cases analogous to breach of contract, the 'common sense' approach to causation was followed.

    However, recourse to vague notions of common sense cannot on its own solve problems of this kind. As the Court of Appeal said in *Young v Purdy* [1997] PNLR 130, the test of judicial common sense is an 'unsure guide' to questions of causation. So from time to time the courts articulate a more principled approach. In *The Sivand* [1998] 2 Lloyd's Rep 97, Evans LJ stated (at p. 102):

    The reference to common sense must be accompanied by a reminder that this is not a subjective test, which would be an unreliable guide. It implies a full knowledge of the material facts and that the question is answered in accordance with the thinking process of a normal person. The reference to "material" facts means that some mental process of selection is required. It is not enough, in my judgment, to specify common sense standards without identifying the reasoning involved.

In *Fairchild v Glenhaven Funeral Services Ltd* [2002] 3 All ER 305 (and see *Empress Car Co (Abertillery) Ltd v National Rivers Authority* [1999] 2 AC 22, [1998] 1 All ER 481 and (2005) 121 LQR 592), Lord Hoffmann stated:

[53] Then there is the role of common sense. Of course the causal requirements for liability are normally framed in accordance with common sense. But there is sometimes a tendency to appeal to common sense in order to avoid having to explain one's reasons. It suggests that causal requirements are a matter of incommunicable judicial instinct. I do not think that this is right. It should be possible to give reasons why one form of causal relationship will do in one situation but not in another.

[54] In my opinion, the essential point is that the causal requirements are just as much part of the legal conditions for liability as the rules which prescribe the kind of conduct which attracts liability or the rules which limit the scope of that liability. If I may repeat what I have said on another occasion, one is never simply liable, one is always liable for something—to make compensation for damage, the nature and extent of which is delimited by the law. The rules which delimit what one is liable for may consist of causal requirements or may be rules unrelated to causation, such as the foreseebility requirements in the rule in *Hadley v Baxendale* (1854) 9 Exch 341. But in either case they are rules of law, part and parcel of the conditions of liability. Once it is appreciated that the rules laying down causal requirements are not autonomous expressions of some form of logic or judicial instinct but creatures of the law, part of the conditions of liability, it is possible to explain their content on the grounds of fairness and justice in exactly the same way as the other conditions of liability.

3.   The most significant problem of attribution of responsibility when there are successive causes is to determine when a subsequent act has sufficient causative potency to exonerate the original tortfeasor from responsibility for the ensuing harm. In legal jargon, does the intervening act 'break the chain of causation' from the original tort? A highly influential academic treatment of this issue is found in *Causation in the Law* by H. L. A. Hart and T. Honoré, 2nd edn (Oxford, 1985). Hart and Honoré's definition of intervening acts which break the chain of causation, thereby exonerating the original tortfeasor, is cited with approval by Lord Hoffmann in *Reeves v Metropolitan Police Comr* [1999] 3 All ER 897 at 902 (p. 394, post) and should be borne in mind throughout this section.

4.   The traditional approach to the question of whether the act of a third party broke the chain of causation was to ask, as a question of fact, whether the intervening act was so out of the ordinary that the defendant's original responsibility 'paled into insignificance'. This is the gist of the Hart and Honoré definition of a new cause and is seen, for example, in *The Oropesa* [1943] P 32. Two ships collided, as a result of the defendant's negligence. Despite bad weather conditions, the master of one of the ships set off in a lifeboat with several crew members, to confer with the other ship's master. The lifeboat capsized and some of the crew drowned. The claimants (the parents of one of the deceased crew members) sued the defendant, who retorted that the master's act of launching the lifeboat was a novus actus interveniens. The Court of Appeal rejected this argument, holding that the master's decision to launch the lifeboat was a reasonable one in the circumstances. In the course of his judgment, Lord Wright said:

To break the chain of causation it must be shown that there is something which I will call ultroneous, something unwarrantable, a new cause which disturbs the sequence of events, something which can be described as either unreasonable or extraneous or extrinsic. I doubt whether the law can be stated more precisely than that.

However, the decision of the Privy Council in *The Wagon Mound (No 1)* [1961] AC 388, [1961] 1 All ER 404 appeared to adopt a different approach, based entirely on foreseeability (see p. 408, post, where the separate question of the foreseeability of the type of harm is considered). The search for breaks in the chain of causation was criticised as leading 'nowhere but the neverending and insoluble problems of causation' (p. 409, post). Foreseeability would in future provide the answer, with the Privy Council suggesting (obiter) that the defendant should be liable even if there was an 'intervening cause', as long as that cause was foreseeable. Thus the foreseeability of the intervention appeared to have been elevated to decisive status, rather than merely being one of the factors a court should take into account as suggested by *The Oropesa* approach. In the years that followed, however, it became clear that the courts were not prepared to concede quite such a large role to foreseeablity, whether the intervening act was that of the claimant or of a third party or a natural event.

(i) Acts of the claimant

■ McKew v Holland and Hannen and Cubitts (Scotland) Ltd
Second Division of the Court of Session, and the House of Lords [1969] 3 All ER 1621

The appellant was slightly injured as a result of the fault of the respondents and one consequence was that for a short time thereafter he occasionally lost control of his left leg. Shortly after sustaining these injuries, the appellant, along with his wife, child, and brother-in-law, went to inspect a flat to which access was provided by a steep flight of stairs with no handrail. Having inspected the flat, he was about to go down the stairs with his child, ahead of his wife and brother-in-law. According to his evidence, his left leg gave way, he thrust the child back and, to avoid going down head first, he threw himself and landed mainly on his right leg. His ankle was broken, and the question was whether the appellant could recover for the damage caused by this accident. The claim failed before the Lord Ordinary and the Court of Session. The following passage from the opinion of the Lord Justice-Clerk in the Court of Session received approval in the House of Lords:

THE LORD JUSTICE-CLERK: . . .
It may well be that, in the situation in which he [the appellant] thought he was placed and with, apparently, an immediate choice to be made between two evils, the [appellant] was not unreasonable in jumping as he did. In my opinion, however, the chain of causation had already been broken. On his own evidence, his left leg had 'gone away' from him on several occasions before the second accident, both in the street and in his house. Yet, with this knowledge and experience, he set out to descend a flight of stairs without a stick or other support and without the assistance, which was available, of his wife or brother-in-law. I cannot regard this as a reasonable act and it was, in my opinion, an intervening act which broke the chain of causation. But for the first accident and the resulting weakness of the left leg the second accident would, no doubt, not have happened. The latter was indirectly connected with the former, but it was not the result of it, except possibly in some remote and indirect way, and a fortiori it was not the natural and direct or probable result of it, in whatever sense these words be used. . . .
    [On appeal to the House of Lords:]

LORD REID: . . .
In my view the law is clear. If a man is injured in such a way that his leg may give way at any moment he must act reasonably and carefully. It is quite possible that in spite of all reasonable care his leg may give way in circumstances such that as a result he sustains further injury. Then that second

injury was caused by his disability which in turn was caused by the defender's fault. But if the injured man acts unreasonably he cannot hold the defender liable for injury caused by his own unreasonable conduct. His unreasonable conduct is novus actus interveniens. The chain of causation has been broken and what follows must be regarded as caused by his own conduct and not by the defender's fault or the disability caused by it. Or one may say that unreasonable conduct of the pursuer and what follows from it is not the natural and probable result of the original fault of the defender or of the ensuing disability. I do not think that foreseeability comes into this. A defender is not liable for a consequence of a kind which is not foreseeable. But it does not follow that he is liable for every consequence which a reasonable man could foresee. What can be foreseen depends almost entirely on the facts of the case, and it is often easy to foresee unreasonable conduct or some other novus actus interveniens as being quite likely. But that does not mean that the defender must pay for damage caused by the novus actus. It only leads to trouble...if one tries to graft on to the concept of foreseeability some rule of law to the effect that a wrongdoer is not bound to foresee something which in fact he could readily foresee as quite likely to happen. For it is not at all unlikely or unforeseeable that an active man who has suffered such a disability will take some quite unreasonable risk. But if he does he cannot hold the defender liable for the consequences.

So in my view the question here is whether the second accident was caused by the appellant doing something unreasonable. It was argued that the wrongdoer must take his victim as he finds him and that that applies not only to a thin skull[9] but also to his intelligence. But I shall not deal with that argument because there is nothing in the evidence to suggest that the appellant is abnormally stupid. This case can be dealt with equally well by asking whether the appellant did something which a moment's reflection would have shown him was an unreasonable thing to do.

He knew that this left leg was liable to give way suddenly and without warning. He knew that this stair was steep and that there was no handrail. He must have realised, if he had given the matter a moment's thought, that he could only safely descend the stair if he either went extremely slowly and carefully so that he could sit down if his leg gave way, or waited for the assistance of his wife and brother-in-law. But he chose to descend in such a way that when his leg gave way he could not stop himself. I agree with what the Lord Justice-Clerk says at the end of his opinion and I think that this is sufficient to require this appeal to be dismissed.

But I think it right to say a word about the argument that the fact that the appellant made to jump when he felt himself falling is conclusive against him. When his leg gave way the appellant was in a very difficult situation. He had to decide what to do in a fraction of a second. He may have come to a wrong decision; he probably did. But if the chain of causation had not been broken before this by his putting himself in a position where he might be confronted with an emergency, I do not think that he would put himself out of court by acting wrongly in the emergency unless his action was so utterly unreasonable that even on the spur of the moment no ordinary man would have been so foolish as to do what he did. In an emergency it is natural to try to do something to save oneself and I do not think that his trying to jump in this emergency was so wrong that it could be said to be...more than an error of judgment. But for the reasons already given I would dismiss this appeal.

[LORD HODSON and VISCOUNT DILHORNE concurred with LORD REID. LORD GUEST delivered a speech in favour of dismissing the appeal, and LORD UPJOHN concurred generally.]

Appeal dismissed.

QUESTION

Why did Mr McKew's claim for damages for his broken right ankle fail altogether on the grounds of causation, rather than merely being reduced on account of his contributory

---

[9] [See p. 412, post.]

negligence? Contrast *March v E & M H Stramare Pty Ltd* (1990–91) 171 CLR 506. On contributory negligence generally, see chap. 7.

NOTES

1. *McKew* concerned the question of whether the claimant's own action amounted to a novus actus interveniens, exonerating the defendant from responsibility for the claimant's broken right ankle (even though the defendant's initial negligence was undoubtedly a 'but-for' cause of that injury). *Wieland v Cyril Lord Carpets Ltd* [1969] 3 All ER 1006 is a case dealing with a similar problem, but one in which the court came to a different decision. The first accident was caused by the defendant's negligence. Two days after the accident, the claimant, who wore bifocal spectacles, returned to hospital and her neck was fitted with a surgical collar. The position of her neck in the collar 'deprived her of her usual ability to adjust herself automatically to the bi-focals'. After leaving the hospital, the claimant was in a nervous state as a result of the accident and her visit to the doctor, and this, coupled with the problem which the bifocal spectacles now presented, meant that the claimant was somewhat unsteady. She went to her son's office to ask him to take her home. He accompanied her down the stairs in the office building, but, on nearing the foot of the stairs, the claimant fell and injured her ankles. Eveleigh J held that the fall and the consequent injury were caused by the defendant's negligence in the first accident. The claimant's skill in descending stairs whilst wearing the bifocal spectacles had been impaired, resulting in the fall. Unlike Mr McKew, Mrs Wieland did not act unreasonably in attempting to descend the stairs.

2. On the question of whether a claimant's action breaks the chain of causation, see further Lord Hoffmann's comments in *South Australia Asset Management Corpn v York Montague* [1996] 3 All ER 365 at 376–377 (pp. 273–274, ante) and see note 2, p. 278, ante.

3. Rescuers who are injured in the course of attempting a rescue are rarely regarded as the cause of their own injuries, despite the fact that their intervention is deliberate and voluntary, unless the reaction of the rescuer is grossly foolish and disproportionate in the circumstances. See, for example, *Baker v T E Hopkins & Son Ltd* [1959] 3 All ER 225, [1959] 1 WLR 966, where a doctor was overcome by carbon-monoxide fumes and killed whilst attempting to rescue workmen in a well which was being cleaned using a petrol driven pump. The defendant attempted to argue that Dr Baker's decision to descend into the well was a novus actus interveniens, but this was rejected by the Court of Appeal. As Morris LJ said, 'these submissions are wholly unsustainable once it is held that the company were negligent in creating a situation of great danger and further in failing to ensure that their servants would not be exposed to it. There is happily in all men of good will an urge to save those who are in peril. Those who put men in peril can hardly be heard to say that they never thought that rescue might be attempted or be heard to say that the rescue attempt was not caused by the creation of the peril.' See also *Haynes v Harwood* [1935] 1 KB 146; *Videan v British Transport Commission* [1963] 2 QB 650, [1963] 2 All ER 860. The same applies where the defendant negligently endangers himself, so that a rescuer comes to his aid and is injured: see *Harrison v British Railways Board* [1981] 3 All ER 679. On the question of whether a kidney donor can recover damages from the person liable in tort for the loss of the donee's kidney, consider *Urbanski v Patel* (1978) 84 DLR (3d) 650, noted by J. R. Spencer [1979] CLJ 45; G. Robertson (1980) 96 LQR 19; cf. *Sirianni v Anna* 285 NYS (2d) 709 (1967).

4.   The question of whether a failure to have an abortion or arrange adoption of a child could constitute a novus actus interveniens in a 'wrongful birth' action was not argued in *McFarlane v Tayside Health Board* [2000] 2 AC 59, [1999] 4 All ER 961 (p. 153, ante) but, if it had been argued, would not have met with the House of Lords' approval. For example, Lord Steyn said (at [1999] 4 All ER at 976), 'I cannot conceive of any circumstances in which the autonomous decision of the parents not to resort to even a lawful abortion could be questioned. For similar reasons the parents' decision not to have the child adopted was plainly natural and commendable. It is difficult to envisage any circumstances in which it would be right to challenge such a decision of the parents.'

5.   Suicide by the claimant might be thought to be a paradigm example of conduct which will amount to a novus actus interveniens, but this is not always the case. It is relatively straightforward to conclude that the suicide should not break the chain of causation where the claimant was not of sound mind at the time of the suicide. See *Kirkham v Chief Constable of the Greater Manchester Police* [1989] 3 All ER 882, where a man hanged himself in police custody, while mentally unbalanced, and was able to do so because the police had negligently failed to activate the protective 'suicide watch' procedure. His suicide was held not to amount to a novus actus interveniens and his widow's action against the police succeeded. (The Court of Appeal affirmed the decision on other grounds [1990] 2 QB 283, [1990] 3 All ER 246.) However, the House of Lords has more recently held (by a majority) that suicide by a person of sound mind in custody does not amount to a novus actus interveniens:

■ Reeves v Metropolitan Police Commissioner
House of Lords [1999] 3 All ER 897

LORD HOFFMANN: . . .

My Lords, on 23 March 1990 Martin Lynch hanged himself in his cell in Kentish Town police station. He had been remanded in custody on charges of credit fraud and was also under investigation for handling stolen vehicles. He had made two previous attempts at suicide. One had been in a cell at Clerkenwell Magistrates' Court three months earlier. The second was in a cell at Brent Magistrates' Court that very morning. On each occasion he had tried to strangle himself with his belt. After the first incident, the police noted on his record that he was a suicide risk. When he was brought back to Kentish Town police station after the second incident, he was seen by a doctor. She found no other evidence of mental disturbance but gave instructions that, as a suicide risk, he should be frequently observed. An hour later, at 1.57 pm, a policeman looked through the open wicket hatch in his cell door and saw that he was lying on his bed. A few minutes later he used his shirt as a ligature to hang himself by pushing it through the wicket hatch and securing it to the door. He was found by another policeman at 2.05 pm. Despite attempts at resuscitation, he died a week later.

The police and prison service have long been aware that prisoners are more than usually likely to attempt suicide or self-injury. In 1994 the Director of Prisons issued an Instruction to Governors (IG 1/1994), which said: 'The care of prisoners who are at risk of suicide and self-harm is one of the Prison Service's most vital tasks.' The risk of suicide is particularly high among prisoners on remand facing a new environment and an uncertain future. Between 1972 and 1982, 45% of suicides in prisons were remand prisoners, although they made up only 10–15% of the prison population (report by Helen Grindrod QC and Gabriel Black 'Suicides at Leeds Prison: An enquiry into the deaths of five teenagers during 1988/89' (Howard League for Penal Reform (1989) p. 5). As long ago as 1968 the Home Office sent a circular to chief constables (Home Office circular 92/1968 (police cells)) drawing attention to the need to ensure that fittings in cells should not provide an opportunity for the prisoner to do himself injury. Paragraph 4 said:

'...where cell doors are fitted with a drop-down service hatch, the hatch should not be left open when the cell is occupied by a prisoner. With the hatch open it would be possible for a person inside the cell to secure a ligature on the handle of the hatch.'

Mr Lynch did not use the handle. He fastened his shirt through the spyhole above the hatch. But he was able to do so because the hatch had been left open.

The plaintiff in this action is Mrs Sheila Reeves, who had lived with Mr Lynch for some years and had a child by him. She sues the Commissioner of Police of the Metropolis under the Fatal Accidents Act 1976 for negligently causing Mr Lynch's death. The trial judge (Judge White) found that having regard to the fact that the police knew that Mr Lynch was a suicide risk, they owed him a duty to take reasonable care to prevent him from committing suicide while being held in custody. He also found that the police had been negligent and in breach of this duty by failing to shut the wicket hatch after he had been put in the cell. There has been no appeal against these two findings.

The judge found, however, that the breach of duty by the police did not cause Mr Lynch's death. He was of sound mind and his judgment was not impaired. The sole cause of his death was therefore his deliberate act in killing himself. The judge thought that this result could be expressed in Latin either by the maxim volenti non fit injuria (Mr Lynch had consented to the injury he received) or by saying that his suicide was a novus actus interveniens. He also gave the commissioner leave to amend the defence to raise an alternative plea of contributory negligence. On the assumption that the death had been caused partly by the fault of the commissioner and partly by the fault of Mr Lynch, he assessed the responsibility of Mr Lynch in accordance with s 1(1) of the Law Reform (Contributory Negligence) Act 1945 at 100%. The judge was also inclined, without deciding the point, to think that the plaintiff's claim should fail on grounds of public policy in accordance with the maxim ex turpi causa non oritur actio. He held that if the action had succeeded, he would have assessed the damages at £8,690.

Mrs Reeves appealed to the Court of Appeal ([1998] 2 All ER 381, [1999] QB 169). By a majority, the appeal was allowed. Lord Bingham of Cornhill CJ and Buxton LJ said that, as the police did not deny that they owed Mr Lynch a duty to take reasonable care to prevent him from committing suicide or that their breach of duty had enabled him to commit suicide, they could not say that their breach of duty was not a cause of his death. 'So to hold,' said Lord Bingham CJ ([1998] 2 All ER 381 at 403–404, [1999] QB 169 at 196) 'would be to deprive the duty of meaningful content.' Morritt LJ dissented, saying that a deliberate act of suicide by a person of sound mind must negative the causal connection between acts which merely created the opportunity and the subsequent death.

On contributory negligence, there was no clear majority view. Buxton LJ...thought that the concept really had no application. Lord Bingham CJ said it did, and would have held the commissioner and Mr Lynch responsible in equal shares. Morritt LJ agreed in principle that contributory negligence could apply but said that the judge was right to assess Mr Lynch's responsibility at 100%. In order to have some majority judgment on the point, Lord Bingham CJ, while adhering to the view that Mr Lynch's fault contributed to his death, agreed to assess his share of responsibility at 0%. So the plaintiff recovered the damages in the full amount of £8,690 assessed by the judge.

The commissioner appeals to your Lordships' House. Mr Pannick QC argued two points on his behalf. The first was the question of causation: was the breach of duty by the police a cause of Mr Lynch's death? The way he put the answer was to say that the deliberate act of suicide, while of sound mind, was a novus actus interveniens which negatived the causal connection between the breach of duty and the death. He said at first that he was going to argue the application of the maxim volenti non fit injuria as a separate point. But when it came down to it, he accepted that if the breach of duty was a cause of the death, he could not succeed on volenti non fit injuria. I think that is right. In the present case, volenti non fit injuria can only mean that Mr Lynch voluntarily caused his own death to the exclusion of any causal effect on the part of what was done by the police. So I think it all comes to the same thing: was the breach of duty by the police a cause of the death?

The other point argued by Mr Pannick was contributory negligence. The question of public policy or ex turpi causa non oritur actio, which had not found favour with any member of the Court of Appeal, was not pursued.

On the first question, Mr Pannick relied upon the general principle stated in Hart and Honoré *Causation in the Law* (2nd edn, 1985) p. 136: '... *the free, deliberate and informed act or omission of a human being, intended to exploit the situation created by defendant, negatives causal connection.*' (Authors' emphasis). However, as *Hart and Honoré* pp. 194–204 also point out there is an exception to this undoubted rule in the case in which the law imposes a duty to guard against loss caused by the free, deliberate and informed act of a human being. It would make nonsense of the existence of such a duty if the law were to hold that the occurrence of the very act which ought to have been prevented negatived causal connection between the breach of duty and the loss. This principle has been recently considered by your Lordships' House in *Empress Car Co (Abertillery) Ltd v National Rivers Authority* [1998] 1 All ER 481, [1998] 2 WLR 350. In that case, examples are given of cases in which liability has been imposed for causing events which were the immediate consequence of the deliberate acts of third parties but which the defendant had a duty to prevent or take reasonable care to prevent.

Mr Pannick accepted this principle when the deliberate act was that of a third party. But he said that it was different when it was the act of the plaintiff himself. Deliberately inflicting damage on oneself had to be an act which negatived causal connection with anything which had gone before.

This argument is based upon the sound intuition that there is a difference between protecting people against harm caused to them by third parties and protecting them against harm which they inflict upon themselves. It reflects the individualist philosophy of the common law. People of full age and sound understanding must look after themselves and take responsibility for their actions. This philosophy expresses itself in the fact that duties to safeguard from harm deliberately caused by others are unusual and a duty to protect a person of full understanding from causing harm to himself is very rare indeed. But, once it is admitted that this is the rare case in which such a duty is owed, it seems to me self-contradictory to say that the breach could not have been a cause of the harm because the victim caused it to himself.

Morritt LJ drew a distinction between a prisoner who was of sound mind and one who was not. He said that when a prisoner was of sound mind, 'I find it hard to see how there is any material increase in the risk in any causative sense' (see [1998] 2 All ER 381 at 398, [1999] QB 169 at 190). In *Kirkham v Chief Constable of the Greater Manchester Police* [1990] 3 All ER 246 at 259, [1990] 2 QB 283 at 289–290 Lloyd LJ said much the same. It seems to me, however, they were really saying that the police should not owe a person of sound mind a duty to take reasonable care to prevent him from committing suicide. If he wants to take his life, that is his business. He is a responsible human being and should accept the intended consequences of his acts without blaming anyone else. Volenti non fit injuria. The police might owe a general moral duty not to provide any prisoner with a means of committing suicide, whether he is of sound mind or not. Such a duty might even be enforceable by disciplinary measures. But the police did not owe Mr Lynch, a person of sound mind, a duty of care so as to enable him or his widow to bring an action in damages for its breach.

My Lords, I can understand this argument, although I do not agree with it. It is not, however, the position taken by the commissioner. He accepts that he owed a duty of care to Mr Lynch to take reasonable care to prevent him from committing suicide. Mr Lynch could not rely on a duty owed to some other hypothetical prisoner who was of unsound mind. The commissioner does not seek to withdraw this concession on the ground that Mr Lynch has been found to have been of sound mind. For my part, I think that the commissioner is right not to make this distinction. The difference between being of sound and unsound mind, while appealing to lawyers who like clear-cut rules, seems to me inadequate to deal with the complexities of human psychology in the context of the stresses caused by imprisonment. The duty, as I have said, is a very unusual one, arising from the complete control which the police or prison authorities have over the prisoner, combined with the special danger of people in prison taking their own lives.

Mr Pannick also suggested that the principle of human autonomy might be infringed by holding the commissioner liable. Autonomy means that every individual is sovereign over himself and cannot be denied the right to certain kinds of behaviour, even if intended to cause his own death. On this principle, if Mr Lynch had decided to go on hunger strike, the police would not have been entitled to administer forcible feeding. But autonomy does not mean that he would have been entitled to demand to be given poison, or that the police would not have been entitled to control his environment in non-invasive ways calculated to make suicide more difficult. If this would not infringe the principle of autonomy, it cannot be infringed by the police being under a duty to take such steps. In any case, this argument really goes to the existence of the duty which the commissioner admits rather than to the question of causation.

The decision of the majority of the Court of Appeal is supported by the Commonwealth and United States authority to which we were referred: see in particular *Pallister v Waikato Hospital Board* [1975] 2 NZLR 725, *Funk v Clapp* (1986) 68 DLR (4th) 229 and *Hickey v Zezulka, Hickey v Michigan State University* (1992) 487 NW 2d 106....

[LORD HOFFMANN went on to consider the question of contributory negligence, on which see p. 426, post.]

LORD JAUNCEY OF TULLICHETTLE: ...

Novus actus interveniens
Mr Pannick submitted that the deceased's death was caused not by the negligence of the police officers but by the voluntary act of the deceased while of sound mind. This act broke the chain of causation between the commissioner's breach of duty and the death. He referred to *Kirkham v Chief Constable of the Greater Manchester Police* [1990] 3 All ER 246, [1990] 2 QB 283 and in particular to the following observations of Lloyd LJ ([1990] 3 All ER 246 at 250, [1990] 2 QB 283 at 290):

'So I would be inclined to hold that where a man of sound mind commits suicide, his estate would be unable to maintain an action against the hospital or prison authorities, as the case might be. Volenti non fit injuria would provide them with a complete defence.'

Lloyd LJ then pointed out that the plaintiff was not of sound mind. Mr Pannick went on to develop his argument by referring to the fundamental principle of the autonomy of each individual and his or her right of self-determination as expounded in *St George's Healthcare NHS Trust v S, R v Collins, ex p S* [1998] 3 All ER 673 at 685, [1999] Fam 26 at 44. If it is unlawful forcibly to administer food or medicine to a patient against his will because of his right of self-determination it must follow that an adult of sound mind who chooses to take his own life must bear the whole responsibility for his act.

My Lords, I consider that this argument is flawed. In *Clerk and Lindsell on Torts* (17th edn, 1995) p. 54, para. 2–24 it states:

'...if a particular consequence of the defendant's wrongdoing is attributable to some independent act or event which supersedes the effect of the initial tortious conduct, the defendant's responsibilities may not extend to the consequences of the supervening act or event.'

It goes on to state that the novus actus interveniens 'must constitute an event of such impact that it rightly obliterates the wrongdoing of the defendant'. The reference to an independent act superseding the effect of the tortious conduct must, in my view, relate to an act which was outwith the contemplated scope of events to which the duty of care was directed. Where such a duty is specifically directed at the prevention of the occurrence of a certain event I cannot see how it can be said that the occurrence of that event amounts to an independent act breaking the chain of causation from the breach of duty, even although it may be unusual for one person to come under a duty to prevent another person deliberately inflicting harm on himself. It is the very thing at which the duty was directed: see

Stansbie v Troman [1948] 1 All ER 599 at 600–601, [1948] 2 KB 48 at 51–52 per Tucker LJ. In *Kirkham v Chief Constable of the Greater Manchester Police* [1990] 3 All ER 246 at 254, [1990] 2 QB 283 at 295 Farquharson LJ rejected the defence of volenti non fit injuria as 'inappropriate where the act of the deceased relied on is the very act which the duty cast on the defendant required him to prevent.' These observations are equally apposite to the defence of novus actus interveniens in the present case. In *Pallister v Waikato Hospital Board* [1975] 2 NZLR 725 at 742 Woodhouse J in a dissenting judgment put the matter most succinctly: 'The concept of a novus actus interveniens does not embrace foreseeable acts in respect of which the duty of care has specifically arisen.' It follows that the observations of Lloyd LJ in *Kirkham v Chief Constable of the Greater Manchester Police* [1990] 3 All ER 246 at 250, [1990] 2 QB 283 at 290 cannot apply to a case in which there exists a duty of care on a custodier to prevent a man with known suicidal tendencies from committing suicide.

The individual's right of self-determination is irrelevant here for two reasons. In the first place it is not a defence to a breach of duty but rather an argument against the existence of a duty at all. If an individual can do to his own body what he wills, whether by positive act or neglect then there can be no duty on anyone else to prevent his so doing. In this case, however, it is accepted that the commissioner owed a duty of care to the deceased. In the second place the cases in which the principle has been recognised and to which your Lordships have been referred were cases in which prevention of injury to health or death would have involved an unlawful physical invasion of the individual's rights. In this case performance of the duty of care by closing the flap would have involved no invasion of any rights of the deceased.

...

My Lords, I have no doubt that given the admitted breach of duty of care the defence of novus actus interveniens cannot assist the commissioner. The deceased's suicide was the precise event to which the duty was directed and as an actus it was accordingly neither novus nor interveniens.

LORD HOBHOUSE OF WOODBOROUGH:...

The plaintiff's cause of action arises out of the death of her former husband, Mr Lynch. She is to be taken as having sued under both the Fatal Accidents Act 1976 and the Law Reform (Miscellaneous Provisions) Act 1934. Under s 1(1) of each of these Acts, the plaintiff is not entitled to assert any cause of action which the deceased could not have asserted if he had survived and the defendant can rely upon the defences he would have had against the deceased (see also s 5 of the 1976 Act). This needs to be stressed at the outset since there are indications in the judgments of both Buxton LJ and Lord Bingham CJ in the Court of Appeal in the present case that they were influenced by the fact that the action was being brought for the benefit, not of the deceased, but of his relatives. But it is fundamental that it is the deceased's cause of action (if any) which is being sued on. For the purposes of my discussion of causation it is both convenient and right to treat the deceased as the plaintiff. The principles of law to be applied are those which relate to the assessment of the conduct of a plaintiff as the cause of his own loss.

The starting point in the present case is the acceptance that the defendant owed Mr Lynch a duty of care. As Lord Bingham CJ put it ([1998] 2 All ER 381 at 403, [1999] QB 169 at 196):

'...the defendant by his officers at Kentish Town police station owed the deceased a duty to take reasonable care to ensure that he was not afforded an opportunity to take his own life.'

(This duty is an application of the more general duty to take reasonable care of a person in one's custody: see *Hague v Deputy Governor of Parkhurst Prison, Weldon v Home Office* [1991] 3 All ER 733, [1992] 1 AC 58.) Lord Bingham CJ emphasised that the duty was a duty to take reasonable care and not to guarantee that a fatality did not occur. He then went on to say in two similar passages ([1998] 2 All ER 381 at 403–404, [1999] QB 169 at 196–197):

'Since an act of self-destruction by the deceased was the very risk against which the defendant was bound in law to take reasonable precautions, I cannot see how that act can be regarded as a novus actus. So to hold would be to deprive the duty of meaningful content. This was, after all, the very thing against which the defendant was duty-bound to take precautions. It can make no difference that the deceased was mentally "normal" (assuming he was), since it is not suggested that the defendant's duty was owed only to the abnormal. The suicide of the deceased cannot in my view be regarded as breaking the chain of causation…If the defendant owed the deceased a duty of care despite the fact that the deceased was of sound mind, then it again seems to me to empty that duty of meaningful content if any claim based on breach of the duty is inevitably defeated by a defence of volenti.'

I would draw attention to three features of these two passages. The first is that Lord Bingham CJ apparently does not accept that any conduct of the suicide would be capable of constituting the sole legal cause of his death. The second is the peculiarity of the present case that the deceased was held by the trial judge to have been of sound mind in contrast with the finding which had been made in *Kirkham v Chief Constable of the Greater Manchester Police* [1990] 3 All ER 246, [1990] 2 QB 283, and had formed the basis of the Court of Appeal's decision in that case. The third is the use of metaphors and Latin tags which I will suggest have outlived their usefulness and now only serve to cause confusion (a view expressed by Lord Sumner as long ago as 1915: see *British Columbia Electric Rly Co Ltd v Loach* [1916] 1 AC 719 at 727–728).

My Lords, in relation to the first feature, let me take two hypothetical situations, neither unduly fanciful. Suppose that the detainee is a political agitator whose primary motivation is to further a political cause. Such persons are liable to see self-destruction, in circumstances which they hope will attract as much publicity and media attention as possible, as an appropriate means of advancing their political cause. Can such a person, having taken advantage of a careless oversight by the police and carried out his purpose, vicariously bring an action against the police and recover damages from them? Or suppose a detainee who and whose family are in serious financial difficulties and who, knowing what the Court of Appeal decided in the present case, says to himself 'the best way for me to help those I love is to commit suicide' and then carries out that purpose by taking advantage of a careless oversight. As Mr Pannick QC said in argument, he might even leave a suicide note for his wife telling her this. In cases such as these it would be surprising if the courts were to say that, notwithstanding the determinative, rational and deliberate choice of the deceased, that choice had not become the only legally relevant cause of the death. It would also in my judgment be contrary to principle. It certainly would be contrary to principle to resort to the function of saying that he was guilty of 100% contributory negligence: if the responsibility for his death was his alone, the principled answer is to say that the sole legal cause was his own voluntary choice. Yet, if such a case were hereafter to come before a court, that court, on the basis of the majority decision of the Court of Appeal, would be bound to award the plaintiff damages.

I give these examples to illustrate the need to identify a dividing line unless one is to say that even in such cases the deliberate voluntary choice of the deceased, the quasi-plaintiff, can never break the chain of causation. The view accepted by the majority of the Court of Appeal reduces all such questions to an examination of the scope of the duty of care or remoteness (which in the context of the law of negligence is effectively the same thing: see *Overseas Tankship (UK) Ltd v Morts Dock and Engineering Co Ltd* [1961] 1 All ER 404, [1961] AC 388). The reason why this is contrary to principle is that it is a basic rule of English law that a plaintiff cannot complain of the consequences of *his own* fully voluntary conduct—his own '*free, deliberate and informed*' act: see Hart and Honoré *Causation in the Law* (2nd edn, 1985) p. 136 (authors' emphasis). This principle, overlooked by the plaintiff, is to be found in a variety of guises in most branches of the law. In the law of tort it overlaps with other principles and invites recourse to expressions (usually Latin maxims) not all of which have a consistent usage.

…The reasoning of Buxton LJ [in the Court of Appeal] was similar [to that of Lord Bingham CJ] but went rather further. He gave a number of grounds for rejecting the causation/volens argument. He held that the defence was inconsistent with the duty which contemplated and was directed to the very act of suicide; he adopted the alternative ground of Farquharson LJ in *Kirkham*'s case [1990] 3 All

ER 246 at 254, [1990] 2 QB 283 at 295: '...the defence is inappropriate where the act of the deceased relied on is the very act which the duty cast on the defendant required him to prevent.'

This is a mistaken analysis. The act of the deceased relied upon as providing the defence is not the act of suicide: it is the voluntary choice which precedes the act of suicide. His second ground involves a similar error; he suggests that the claim could never succeed and the duty is owed to those who are of sound mind as well as to those who are not. The defence does not affect or negative the duty of care. It presupposes the existence of such a duty and that it has been broken in a factually relevant way. Where, as in *Kirkham*'s case and the New Zealand case *Pallister v Waikato Hospital Board* [1975] 2 NZLR 725, the deceased was not of sound mind at the relevant time, the defence will fail. As everyone accepts, the cases where the defence will succeed will be exceptional. But this is not a reason for denying the defence when exceptionally such a case occurs....

[In discussing causation and remoteness in general, LORD HOBHOUSE addressed the question of a plaintiff's responsibility for the matter in relation to which the action was being brought:]

A number of principles are involved. First there is the fundamental principle of human autonomy. Where a natural person is not under any disability, that person has a right to choose his own fate. He is constrained in so far as his choice may affect others, society or the body politic. But, so far as he himself alone is concerned, he is entitled to choose. The choice to commit suicide is such a choice. A corollary of this principle is, subject to the important qualification to which I will refer, the principle that a person may not complain of the consequences of his own choices. This both reflects coherent legal principle and conforms to the accepted use of the word cause: the person's choice becomes, so far as he is concerned, the cause. The autonomy of the individual human confers the right and the responsibility.

To qualify as an autonomous choice, the choice made must be free and unconstrained—i.e. voluntary, deliberate and informed. If the plaintiff is under a disability, either through lack of mental capacity or lack of excess of age, the plaintiff will lack autonomy and will not have made a free and unconstrained choice. Child plaintiffs come into this category. Both as a matter of causation and the attribution of responsibility, their conduct does not (without more) remove the responsibility of the defendant or transfer the responsibility to the child plaintiff: see *Yachuk v Oliver Blais Co Ltd* [1949] 2 All ER 150, [1949] AC 386. Similarly, plaintiffs suffering from a temporary or a more serious loss of mental capacity (see *Kirkham v Chief Constable of the Greater Manchester Police* [1990] 3 All ER 246, [1990] 2 QB 283, *Pallister v Waikato Hospital Board* [1975] 2 NZLR 725 and *Pigney v Pointers Transport Services Ltd* [1957] 2 All ER 807, [1957] 1 WLR 1121), will not have made the requisite free and unconstrained choice. Where the plaintiff's lack of mental capacity has been caused by the defendant's breach of duty, the entitlement to recover is all the stronger. On the same basis choices made under constraint of circumstances, such as those made by rescuers or persons placed in immediate danger, will not carry with them the consequence that the choice was the sole cause of the subsequent injury to the plaintiff nor will it result in his bearing the sole responsibility for his injury: see *Haynes v Harwood* [1935] 1 KB 146, [1934] All ER Rep 103: cf *Cutler v United Dairies (London) Ltd* [1933] 2 KB 297, [1933] All ER Rep 594. The same applies if the plaintiff's choice was vitiated by misinformation or lack of information. In the context of employment, the question of the reality of the employee's assent and his acceptance of risk has been the subject of many decisions; perhaps the most illuminating discussion for present purposes is to be found in *Imperial Chemical Industrial Ltd v Shatwell* [1964] 2 All ER 999 esp at 1008–1009, [1965] AC 656 esp at 680–681 per Lord Hodson where he stresses that the plaintiff's conduct cannot be described as voluntary unless he truly had a free choice. (The case also, like *Stapley v Gypsum Mines Ltd* [1953] 2 All ER 478, [1953] AC 663, illustrates the distinction between lack of care for one's own safety and the true acceptance of risk.) These qualifications are fundamental and are the basis of the decisions where a plaintiff has been held entitled still to sue notwithstanding his having made a choice which led to the event of which he complains.

The simplest way in which to express the relevant principles, both the basic principle of autonomy and the qualification, is in terms of causation. Both as a matter of the ordinary use of language and as a matter of law it is correct to say that the plaintiff's voluntary choice was *the* cause of his loss. Another partial expression of this principle is the maxim volenti non fit injuria. This maxim, originating from a rather different Roman law context, is a notorious source of confusion: see *Dann v Hamilton* [1939] All ER 59, [1939] 1 KB 509. In intentional torts it means consent by the plaintiff to the act which would otherwise be the tort. In the law of negligence it means the acceptance variously of the risk created by the defendant's negligence or of the risk of the defendant's negligence. In such cases it is probably best confined to cases where it can be said that the plaintiff has expressly or impliedly agreed to exempt the defendant from the duty of care which he would otherwise have owed (*Nettleship v Weston* [1971] 3 All ER 581, [1971] 2 QB 691), a formulation which, it will be appreciated, immediately brings the maxim into potential conflict with s 2 of the Unfair Contract Terms Act 1977. It will also be appreciated that so interpreted the maxim would only have an artificial application to the facts of the present case. The suggestion that Mr Lynch was agreeing to exempt the police authority from anything is both objectionable and wholly unrealistic. (It may be that this consideration understandably coloured counsel's presentation of the defendant's case.)

But, my Lords, if the question raised by Mr Lynch's conduct is seen as a question of causation, these artificialities fall away. If Mr Lynch, knowing that the police officers had put him in a cell with a defective door and had failed to close the hatch, then voluntarily and deliberately, in full possession of his faculties, made the rational choice to commit suicide, principle and language say that it was his choice which was the cause of his subsequent death. He was not, on the judge's findings, acting under any disability or compulsion. He made a free choice: he is responsible for the consequence of that choice....

[LORD HOPE OF CRAIGHEAD delivered a speech agreeing with LORD HOFFMANN and LORD JAUNCEY OF TULLICHETTLE that the deceased's act of suicide did not amount to a *novus actus interveniens*. LORD MACKAY OF CLASHFERN agreed with the speeches of LORD HOFFMANN and LORD HOPE.]

QUESTIONS

1. Was the concession made by counsel for the police authority that a duty of care was owed to Mr Lynch correctly made? Or should the police authority have argued that there was only a duty to take reasonable steps to prevent suicide by mentally ill prisoners?
2. Does Lord Hoffmann's doubt about the validity of the distinction between being of sound and unsound mind 'in the context of the stresses caused by imprisonment' mean that no one in police custody can be regarded as fully responsible for his or her actions? What implications might this have for other areas of the law?

NOTES

1. The treatment in *Reeves* of the defence of contributory negligence is considered in chap. 7, p. 426, post.
2. The reasoning adopted by the majority of both the Court of Appeal and the House of Lords in *Reeves* that, once it is shown that a defendant owes a duty of care to guard against a particular sort of conduct or harm, the occurrence of that conduct or harm cannot be regarded as a novus actus interveniens, was cogently criticised by T. Weir [1998] CLJ 241, commenting on the Court of Appeal's judgment. Weir states (at pp. 242–243):

   The function of the duty concept at common law is to conduce to an apparent rationalisation of a decision, reached on other grounds, that a defendant must—or need not—pay for harm suffered by the plaintiff as a relevant result of relevantly unreasonable conduct on the part of the defendant: it does not by itself determine what consequences are relevant. "Duty" is an operator, not a real number. To say that the police are under a duty to take care of those in their charge (and whose autonomy is to that extent restricted) can rightly mean only that if a detainee is injured it is appropriate to inquire into the conduct of the defendant and ask, *inter alia*, whether it was a relevant cause of the injury. For an appeal judge to say, and keep repeating, that the finding of such a duty precludes any question as to causation or any other reason why the party injured should not recover full damages is nothing short of dotty. Courts are supposed to answer questions, not beg them.

3. The House of Lords was called upon to decide another suicide case, albeit with rather different facts, in *Corr v IBC Vehicles Ltd* [2008] 2 All ER 943, [2008] UKHL 13. Here the defendant's negligence had caused a head injury which led to the victim (Mr Corr) suffering from severe depression, which in turn led him to commit suicide nearly six years after the original accident. At the time of his suicide, Corr did appreciate what he was doing but his capacity to make rational decisions was impaired by the depression. The House of Lords held that the chain of causation remained intact whether or not the suicide was foreseeable (a matter on which there was some difference of opinion). Lord Bingham distinguished a Canadian case (*Wright v Davidson* (1992) 88 DLR (4th) 698) on the ground of the 'lack of a disabling mental illness' there. Another point to note is that at [17] Lord Bingham, referring to some comments of Lord Rodger in *Simmons v British Steel plc* [2004] ICR 585, [2004] UKHL 20 at [67], accepted a theoretical distinction between a case of novus actus and one involving unreasonable conduct on the part of the claimant, but concluded that his reasons for denying there had been a novus actus in the case in hand meant that an unreasonableness argument concerning causation must also fail, since the suicide had been 'induced' by the defendant's negligence. Lord Hoffman's argument in *Reeves* for a more flexible treatment outside the criminal law of the question of mental impairment in prison cases is reflected (more generally) in *Corr*. On *Corr* see further *Gray v Thames Trains Ltd* [2008] EWCA Civ, 713.

    On the question of contributory negligence in relation to this case, see note 2, p. 426, post.

(ii) Acts of third parties

■ Home Office v Dorset Yacht Co Ltd
p. 72, ante

NOTES

1. The speech of Lord Reid is the one that is particularly important in this context. However, Sir R. Cooke [1978] CLJ 288 at 294–295 argues that the other members of the House of Lords in the *Dorset Yacht* case did not take 'the same line as a matter of principle', and he points out that Lord Reid did not regard the resumption of welding, which might be regarded as intervening human conduct, as 'of any particular significance' in *The Wagon Mound (No. 2)* [1967] 1 AC 617, [1966] 2 All ER 709 (p. 299, ante and p. 802, post). The author of this article, sitting as a member of the New Zealand Court of Appeal, expressed similar views in *Taupo Borough Council v Birnie* [1978] 2 NZLR 397 at 410–411.

2. The problem in *Dorset Yacht*, of deliberate intervening conduct on the part of third parties, has been a persistent problem for the courts since *The Wagon Mound (No. 1)*,

since it is perfectly clear that, in certain cases, deliberate conduct by a third party might be perfectly foreseeable, and yet should undoubtedly count as an intervening cause.

■ Lamb v London Borough of Camden
Court of Appeal [1981] 2 All ER 408

Contractors employed by the defendant local authority broke into a water main whilst replacing a sewer near to the plaintiff's house. The owner (Mrs Lamb) was in the USA at the time and had let her house to a tenant. The water that came out of the broken main affected the foundations of the house, rendering it unsafe for habitation, and thus the tenant moved out of the premises. Having arrived back in England Mrs Lamb put her furniture in store because of the extent of the repairs necessary to the house and then returned to the USA. Thereafter squatters moved into the house but they left after proceedings to evict them had been started. Boards were then put up in an effort to secure the house but squatters got in again and after the gas and electricity services were cut off, they burnt panelling which they had pulled off the walls. They also took other things in the house. There was a claim for compensation (including the cost of damage done by the squatters) and the defendant council admitted liability for nuisance (on which see chap. 14, post). The damages were assessed by an official referee, who thought that squatting was a reasonably foreseeable risk but that it was not likely. Applying Lord Reid's speech in the *Dorset Yacht* case, he held that the damage caused by the squatters was too remote, and an appeal was taken from this decision to the Court of Appeal. The judgments in the Court of Appeal refer to *The Wagon Mound* [1961] AC 388, [1961] 1 All ER 404 (p. 468, post) and *The Wagon Mound (No 2)* [1967] 1 AC 617, [1966] 2 All ER 709 (p. 299, ante and p. 802, post). These cases will be considered later, but basically establish that in both negligence and nuisance the kind of damage must be reasonably foreseeable.

LORD DENNING MR [having criticised Lord Reid's test in the *Dorset Yacht* case (p. 72, ante) as including too much and as difficult to reconcile with *Stansbie v Troman* [1948] 2 KB 48, [1948] 1 All ER 599 and *The Wagon Mound* and *The Wagon Mound (No 2)*:] If Lord Reid's test is wrong, what is the alternative test? Logically, I suppose that liability and compensation should go hand in hand. If reasonable foresight is the criterion in negligence, so also it should be in remoteness of damage. That was the test for which counsel for Mrs Lamb contended....

To my mind that alternative test is also not acceptable. It would extend the range of compensation far too widely.... Take...the illustration I took from the *Dorset Yacht* case of the criminal who escapes (owing to the negligence of the prison staff) and breaks into people's houses. Although it could reasonably be foreseen, the Home Office are not liable for his depredations....

The truth
The truth is that all these three, duty, remoteness and causation, are all devices by which the courts limit the range of liability for negligence or nuisance. As I said recently in *Compania Financiera Soleada SA v Hamoor Tanker Corpn Inc, The Borag* [1981] 1 All ER 856 at 861, [1981] 1 WLR 274 at 281: '...it is not every consequence of a wrongful act which is the subject of compensation. The law has to draw a line somewhere.'

Sometimes it is done by limiting the range of the persons to whom duty is owed. Sometimes it is done by saying that there is a break in the chain of causation. At other times it is done by saying that the consequence is too remote to be a head of damage. All these devices are useful in their way. But ultimately it is a question of policy for the judges to decide....

Looking at the question as one of policy, I ask myself: whose job was it to do something to keep out the squatters? And, if they got in, to evict them? To my mind the answer is clear. It was the job of the owner of the house, Mrs Lamb, through her agents....

On broader grounds of policy, I would add this: the criminal acts here, malicious damage and theft, are usually covered by insurance. By this means the risk of loss is spread throughout the community. It does not fall too heavily on one pair of shoulders alone. The insurers take the premium to cover just this sort of risk and should not be allowed, by subrogation, to pass it on to others.... It is commonplace nowadays for the courts, when considering policy, to take insurance into account....

So here, it seems to me, that, if Mrs Lamb was insured against damage to the house and theft, the insurers should pay the loss. If she was not insured, that is her misfortune.

Taking all these policy matters into account, I think the council are not liable for the acts of these squatters.

I would dismiss this appeal.

OLIVER LJ [having quoted from Lord Reid's speech in the *Dorset Yacht* case concerning intervening human action:]

The views which Lord Reid there expressed are not reflected in the speeches of the others of their Lordships in the case, and were, I think, obiter, since there was no scope for argument on the assumed facts that the damage which occurred was not the very thing that was likely to happen. But, obiter or no, Lord Reid's opinion must be at least of the very highest persuasive authority. For my part, however, I very much doubt whether he was, in what he said regarding the likelihood of the act of a third party, intending to bring back into the test of remoteness some further philosophical consideration of nexus or direct or indirect causation. As it seems to me, all that Lord Reid was saying was this, that, where as a matter of fact the consequence which the court is considering is one which results from, or would not have occurred but for, the intervention of some independent human agency over which the tortfeasor has no control it has to approach the problem of what could be reasonably foreseen by the tortfeasor, and thus of the damage for which he is responsible, with particular care. The immediate cause is known: it is the independent human agency; and one has therefore to ask: on what basis can the act of that person be attributed back to the tortfeasor? It may be because the tortfeasor is responsible for his actions or because the third party act which has precipitated the damage is the very thing that the tortfeasor is employed to prevent. But what is the position in the absence of some such consideration? Few things are less certainly predictable than human behaviour, and if one is asked whether in any given situation a human being may behave idiotically, irrationally or even criminally the answer must always be that that is a possibility, for every society has its proportion of idiots and criminals. It cannot be said that you cannot foresee the possibility that people will do stupid or criminal acts, because people are constantly doing stupid or criminal acts. But the question is not what is foreseeable merely as a possibility but what would the reasonable man actually foresee if he thought about it, and all that Lord Reid seems to me to be saying is that the hypothetical reasonable man in the position of the tortfeasor cannot be said to foresee the behaviour of another person unless that behaviour is such as would, viewed objectively, be very likely to occur....

Now if this is right, it does raise a difficulty over the official referee's finding. If the likelihood of human behaviour is an element in reasonable foreseeability the official referee's disposition to say that the invasion of squatters was reasonably foreseeable is inconsistent with his actual finding of fact that squatting was unlikely, and that is the only actual finding. What I think, with respect, he was doing in this passage of his judgment was confusing 'foreseeable' with 'reasonably foreseeable'. That indeed would be consistent with the passage from Lord Reid's speech on which he was relying as stating the principle. Lord Reid said in terms that foreseeability 'as a possibility' was not sufficient and I think that what the official referee has done is to treat that as meaning, in the context, *reasonable* foreseeability as a possibility'. In the context in which, as I think, Lord Reid was using the expression 'as a possibility' (that is to say, as meaning '*only* a bare possibility and no more') that seems to me to be a contradiction in terms, and for the reasons which I have endeavoured to explain it was not what Lord Reid intended and it was not what he said. The critical finding here is, to my mind, that the incursion of squatters was in fact unlikely.

Given this finding, it seems to me that, accepting Lord Reid's test as correct (which counsel for the plaintiff challenges), it must be fatal to the plaintiff's contentions on this appeal, because it constitutes in effect a finding that the damage claimed is not such as could be reasonably foreseen. And that, indeed, seems to me to accord with the common sense of the matter....

I should perhaps add that I do not dissent from the view of Lord Denning MR that the test expressed by Lord Reid (with, as I think, the intention of restricting the ambit of the duty in tort) was incorrect, in that it was not exhaustive and did not go far enough in that direction. To apply a straight test of foreseeability or likelihood to hypothetical circumstances which could arise in relation to the acts of independent third parties in the case of, for instance, carelessness on the part of servants of the Home Office does, as Lord Denning MR points out, produce some astonishing results. Suppose that as a result of the carelessness of a prison officer a prisoner escapes and commits a crime of the same type as that for which he is in custody a fortnight later and 400 miles away from the place at which he escaped. Is it any less foreseeable that he will do so than that he will steal his rail fare from a house adjoining the prison? And is the Home Office to be liable without limit until the prisoner is apprehended? Does it make any difference if he is, at the date of his escape, on remand or due for parole? Happily, such hypothetical questions do not, on the view that I take, have to be answered in the instant case, but whether or not it is right to regard questions of remoteness according to some flexible test of the policy of the law from time to time (on which I prefer at the moment to express no view) I concur with Lord Denning MR in regarding the straight test of foreseeability, at least in cases where the acts of independent third parties are concerned, as one which can, unless subjected to some further limitation, produce results which extend the ambit of liability beyond all reason. Speaking for myself, I would respectfully regard Lord Reid's test as a workable and sensible one, subject only to this, that I think that he may perhaps have understated the *degree* of likelihood required before the law can or should attribute the free act of a responsible third person to the tortfeasor. Such attribution cannot, as I think, rationally be made simply on the basis of some geographical or temporal proximity, and even `likelihood' is a somewhat uncertain touchstone. It may be that some more stringent standard is required. There may, for instance, be circumstances in which the court would require a degree of likelihood amounting almost to inevitability before it fixes a defendant with responsibility for the act of a third party over whom he has and can have no control. On the official referee's finding, however, that does not arise here, and the problem can be left for a case in which it directly arises.

WATKINS LJ: ...

I feel bound to say with respect that what Lord Reid said in the *Dorset Yacht* case does nothing to simplify the task of deciding for or against remoteness, especially where the fresh damage complained of has been caused by the intervening act of a third party. It may be that in respect of such an act he is to be understood as saying, without using his remarkable and usual clarity of expression, that damage is inevitably too remote unless it can reasonably be foreseen as likely to occur. If that be so, it could be said that he was not intending to depart from the *Wagon Mound* test save in cases involving intervening human action to which he would apply a rather stricter than usual test by placing acts which are *not likely to occur* within the realm of remoteness .

... [The decision in *McKew v Holland & Hannen & Cubitts (Scotland) Ltd* [1969] 3 All ER 1621 (p. 389, ante)] has in some quarters been criticised on the basis that it would have been more in accordance with principle to have treated the plaintiff's unreasonable conduct as contributory negligence. I do not agree. I prefer to regard the decision in *McKew* as a good example of a determination to bring realistic consideration to bear on the question of fresh damage arising from an event or act occurring subsequently to the initial negligent act in the context of remoteness of damage.

It seems to me that if the sole and exclusive test of remoteness is whether the fresh damage has arisen from an event or act which is reasonably foreseeable, or reasonably foreseeable as a possibility, or likely or quite likely to occur, absurd, even bizarre, results might ensue in actions for damages for negligence. Why, if this test were to be rigidly applied to the facts in the *Dorset Yacht* case, one can envisage the Home Office being found liable for the damage caused by an escaped borstal boy committing a burglary in John o'Groats. This would plainly be a ludicrous conclusion.

I do not think that words such as, among others, 'possibility', 'likely' or 'quite likely' assist in the application of the test of reasonable foreseeability. If the crisply stated test which emanates from *The Wagon Mound (No. 2)* is to be festooned with additional words supposedly there for the purpose of amplification or qualification, an understandable application of it will become impossible.

In my view the *Wagon Mound* test should always be applied without any of the gloss which is from time to time being applied to it.

But when so applied it cannot in all circumstances in which it arises conclude consideration of the question of remoteness, although in the vast majority of cases it will be adequate for this purpose. In other cases, the present one being an example of these in my opinion, further consideration is necessary, always providing, of course, a plaintiff survives the test of reasonable foreseeability.

This is because the very features of an event or act for which damages are claimed themselves suggest that the event or act is not on any practical view of it remotely in any way connected with the original act of negligence. These features will include such matters as the nature of the event or act, the time it occurred, the place where it occurred, the identity of the perpetrator and his intentions, and responsibility, if any, for taking measures to avoid the occurrence and matters of public policy.

A robust and sensible approach to this very important area of the study of remoteness will more often than not produce, I think, an instinctive feeling that the event or act being weighed in the balance is too remote to sound in damages for the plaintiff. I do not pretend that in all cases the answer will come easily to the inquirer. But that the question must be asked and answered in all these cases I have no doubt.

To return to the present case, I have the instinctive feeling that the squatters' damage is too remote. I could not possibly come to any other conclusion, although on the primary facts I, too, would regard that damage or something like it as reasonably foreseeable in these times.

We are here dealing with unreasonable conduct of an outrageous kind. It is notorious that squatters will take the opportunity of entering and occupying any house, whether it be damaged or not, which is found to be unoccupied for more than a very temporary duration. In my opinion this kind of antisocial and criminal behaviour provides a glaring example of an act which inevitably, or almost so, is too remote to cause a defendant to pay damages for the consequences of it.

Accordingly, I would hold that the damage caused by the squatters in the present case is too remote to be recovered from these defendants....

Appeal dismissed.

NOTES

1. Lord Reid's speech in *Dorset Yacht* attempted to reconcile the difficulty of applying *The Wagon Mound (No 1)* to intervening human conduct by considering different degrees of foreseeability. However, is it meaningful to think in terms of degrees of foreseeability? Surely an event is either foreseeable or it is not? It is, of course, perfectly rational to talk of degrees of likelihood, but the two concepts are not the same. Lord Reid's views were quoted without any qualification in *Paterson Zochonis & Co Ltd v Merfaken Packaging Ltd* [1986] 3 All ER 522. For further discussion and attempted reconciliation of Lord Reid's speech and of the various approaches in *Lamb*, see *Ward v Cannock Chase District Council* [1986] Ch 546, [1985] 3 All ER 537, and also the speech of Lord Mackay in *Smith v Littlewoods Organisation Ltd* [1987] AC 241, [1987] 1 All ER 710 (p. 78, ante).

2. For other examples of cases dealing with the novus actus doctrine, see *Rouse v Squires* [1973] QB 889, [1973] 2 All ER 903, where intervening negligent driving by a third party did not break the chain of causation from the defendant's original negligence. Cairns LJ explained that:

   If a driver so negligently manages his vehicle as to cause it to obstruct the highway and constitute a danger to other road users, including those who are driving too fast or not keeping a proper lookout, but not those who deliberately or recklessly drive into the obstruction, then the first driver's negligence may be held to have contributed to the causation of an accident of which the immediate cause was the negligent driving of the vehicle which because of the presence of the obstruction collides with it or with some other vehicle or some other person.

Reckless driving by the defendant in *Wright v Lodge* [1993] 4 All ER 299 was sufficient to break the chain of causation and exonerate the claimant for responsibility for her own careless conduct.

In *Knightley v Johns* [1982] 1 All ER 851, [1982] 1 WLR 349 Johns negligently overturned his car near the exit of a tunnel carrying one-way traffic. The police inspector in charge, who had forgotten to close the tunnel, ordered the claimant, PC Knightley, to ride on his motorcycle the wrong way along the tunnel, against the flow of traffic, to close the entrance. In doing so, the claimant, who was not negligent, collided with an oncoming car (whose driver was not negligent). The Court of Appeal held that the police inspector had been negligent in not closing the tunnel and in ordering or allowing the claimant to do so by a dangerous manoeuvre and that there had been a new cause interrupting the sequence of events between Johns' negligence and the claimant's accident. Accordingly, the police inspector (and the Chief Constable) were liable to the claimant but Johns was not. Stephenson LJ (with whose judgment Dunn LJ and Sir David Cairns agreed) stated (at p. 865) that in assessing the sequence of events to see if the chain of causation remained intact:

> ....[I]t is helpful but not decisive to consider which of these events were deliberate choices to do positive acts and which were mere omissions or failures to act; which acts and omissions were innocent mistakes or miscalculations and which were negligent having regard to the pressures and the gravity of the emergency and the need to act quickly. Negligent conduct is more likely to break the chain of causation than conduct which is not; positive acts will more easily constitute new causes than inaction. Mistakes and mischances are to be expected when human beings, however well trained, have to cope with a crisis; what exactly they will be cannot be predicted, but if those which occur are natural the wrongdoer cannot, I think, escape responsibility for them and their consequences simply by calling them improbable or unforeseeable. He must accept the risk of some unexpected mischances...

3. Conaghan and Mansell, *The Wrongs of Tort*, pp. 71–72 argue that 'the judges simply do not know how to justify drawing the line on recovery where they do' and continue:

    > They only know that they are comfortable drawing the line at that point. Watkins LJ's 'instinctive feeling' [in *Lamb*] or Staughton LJ's invocation of common sense in *Wright v Lodge* [[1993] 4 All ER 299] (where the Court of Appeal were required to allocate responsibility in a motorway pile-up) expresses an intuitive sense among judges that to hold a person liable for the acts of another is essentially unjust and to be avoided. Individual responsibility requires that we are responsible for our own activities but not those of others. Moreover judges are often suspicious of attempts to bypass a tortfeasor in order to reach for a "deeper pocket", a common enough feature of suits involving intervening actors. It is precisely because the actor immediately responsible for the harm (the vandal, the borstal boy) is not worth suing that the plaintiff seeks to recover from someone else further along the chain of causation. There is a sense that such actors are less "at fault" (even though they have been clearly negligent) because there is a greater distance between them and the harm done.

    Conaghan and Mansell go on to criticise this approach, which they regard as one which 'fundamentally misrepresents the nature of social activity'. Their standpoint is an ideological one, criticising the law for 'conceiving of human activity in individual rather than social terms'. But is it not inherent in a system of tort liability that it deals with individual responsibility?

4. A further effect of the confusion introduced into this area by *The Wagon Mound (No 1)* is the emergence of the importance of 'proximity' in the formulation of a duty of care (see chap. 2). A number of the issues raised under the rubric of proximity are essentially the same as those traditionally considered as issues of intervening cause.

    See, for example in *Topp v London Country Bus (South West)* [1993] 3 All ER 448, the facts of which were given at p. 86, ante. Rather than focus on the question of whether the deliberate conduct of the joyriders broke the chain of causation between the defendant's fault and Mrs Topp's death, May J treated the case as turning on whether the defendant owed Mrs Topp a duty of care, concluding that no such duty was owed. The case did not fall within the small category of cases (such as *Haynes v Harwood* [1935] 1 KB 146) where a person is liable for negligently causing or permitting a source of danger to be created in circumstances where it was reasonably foreseeable that a third party might set off the danger. A similar 'duty' analysis was adopted in the Court of Appeal, where the claim failed both because of lack of proximity and because the imposition of a duty of care would not be fair, just, and reasonable. This result, perfectly consistent with the Hart and Honoré approach to causation, would be difficult to justify in *Wagon Mound* terms, since the intervention of joyriders is certainly foreseeable of facts of this kind (indeed, might well be regarded as 'highly likely' on Lord Reid's approach in *Dorset Yacht*).

    The reasoning here (as in the 'proximity' discussion in *Hill v Chief Constable of West Yorkshire Police* [1989] AC 53, [1988] 2 All ER 238, noted p. 78, ante, where once again the third party intervention was foreseeable) is essentially that there are no good reasons to allow an exception to the general rule that deliberate third party intervention breaks the chain of causation. In contrast, there were good reasons for allowing an exception, and thus recognising proximity, in, for example, *Swinney v Chief Constable of Northumbria Police* [1997] QB 464, [1996] 3 All ER 449, noted p. 48, ante, the key factor being the defendant's undertaking, and subsequent breach, of confidentiality towards the claimant. See further *Howarth*, pp. 114–119. Do questions of this kind become any easier to answer by phrasing them as pure questions of law ('Is there a duty of care?'), rather than as mixed questions of fact and law ('Did the defendant's fault cause the harm?')?

5. As stated in the introduction to this chapter, the correct approach to legal causation is to regard questions of intervening cause, and the *Wagon Mound* question of the foreseeability of the type of harm suffered, as two entirely separate issues. The second issue (namely the foreseeability of the type of harm) is considered in the following sections.

3 FORESEEABILITY OF THE KIND OF DAMAGE

■ Re Polemis and Furness, Withy & Co Ltd
Court of Appeal [1921] All ER Rep 40

The charterers of a ship carried in it a cargo which included benzine or petrol in cases. Whilst the vessel was being unloaded at Casablanca, a plank fell into the hold, and there was an explosion, leading to a fire which destroyed the ship. The owners alleged that negligence on the part of the charterers' servants caused the loss of the ship, and one of the charterers' arguments was that the damage was too remote. The following findings of fact were made by the arbitrators:

> (a) That the ship was lost by fire. (b) That the fire arose from a spark igniting petrol vapour in the hold. (c) That the spark was caused by the falling board coming into contact with some substance in the hold. (d) That the fall of the board was caused by the negligence of the Arabs (other than the winchman) engaged in the work of discharging. (e) That the said Arabs were employed by the charterers or their agents the Cie Transatlantique on behalf of the charterers, and that the said Arabs were the servants of the charterers. (f) That the causing of the spark could not reasonably have been anticipated from the falling of the board, though some damage to the ship might reasonably have been anticipated. (g) There was no evidence before us that the Arabs chosen were known or likely to be negligent. (h) That the damages sustained by the owners through the said accident amount to the sum of £196,165 1s 11d. . . .

Sankey J affirmed the award. The charterers appealed.

BANKES LJ: . . .

In the present case the arbitrators have found as a fact that the falling of the plank was due to the negligence of the defendants' servants. The fire appears to me to have been directly caused by the falling of the plank. In these circumstances I consider that it is immaterial that the causing of the spark by the falling of the plank could not have been reasonably anticipated. The charterers' junior counsel sought to draw a distinction between the anticipation of the extent of damage resulting from a negligent act, and the anticipation of the type of damage resulting from such an act. He admitted that it could not lie in the mouth of a person whose negligent act had caused damage to say that he could not reasonably have foreseen the extent of the damage, but he contended that the negligent person was entitled to rely upon the fact that he could not reasonably have anticipated the type of damage which resulted from his negligent act. I do not think that the distinction can be admitted. Given the breach of duty which constitutes the negligence, and given the damage as a direct result of that negligence, the anticipations of the person whose negligent act has produced the damage appear to me to be irrelevant. I consider that the damages claimed are not too remote. . . .

WARRINGTON LJ: . . .

The presence or absence of reasonable anticipation of damage determines the legal quality of the act as negligent or innocent. If it be thus determined to be negligent, then the question whether particular damages are recoverable depends only on the answer to the question whether they are the direct consequence of the act. . . . In the present case it is clear that the act causing the plank to fall was in law a negligent act, because some damage to the ship might reasonably be anticipated. If this is so then the charterers are liable for the actual loss, that being on the findings of the arbitrators the direct result of the falling board: see per Lord Sumner in *Weld-Blundell v Stephens*[10] ([1920] AC at p. 983). On the whole, in my opinion, the appeal must be dismissed with costs.

SCRUTTON LJ: . . .

To determine whether an act is negligent, it is relevant to determine whether any reasonable person would foresee that the act would cause damage; if he would not, the act is not negligent. But if the act would or might probably cause damage, the fact that the damage it in fact causes is not the exact kind of damage one would expect is immaterial, so long as the damage is in fact caused sufficiently directly by the negligent act, and not by the operation of independent causes having no connection with the negligent act, except that they could not avoid its results. Once the act is negligent, the fact that its exact operation was not foreseen is immaterial. . . . In the present case it was negligent in discharging cargo to knock down the planks of the temporary staging, for they might easily cause some damage either to workmen, or cargo, or the ship. The fact that they did directly produce an unexpected result, a spark in an atmosphere of petrol vapour which caused a fire, does not relieve the person who was

---

[10] [1920] AC 956.

negligent from the damage which his negligent act directly caused. For these reasons the experienced arbitrators and the judge appealed from came, in my opinion, to a correct decision, and the appeal must be dismissed with costs.

Appeal dismissed.

QUESTION

Polemis has been severely criticised in later cases, but is there anything wrong with the result? On whom should the loss fall—the innocent claimant, or the defendant who is at fault, whose fault caused the loss, and where there are no intervening causes between his fault and the loss? On *Polemis* see R. W. M. Dias [1962] CLJ 178 and M. Davies (1982) 45 MLR 534.

■ Overseas Tankship (UK) Ltd v Morts Dock and Engineering Co Ltd, The Wagon Mound

Judicial Committee of the Privy Council [1961] 1 All ER 404

The appellants were charterers of the SS *Wagon Mound,* which was taking on bunkering oil at the Caltex wharf in Sydney harbour. As a result of the appellants' servants' carelessness, some of the oil spilt into the bay, spreading over a large part of it, and, in particular, there was a thick concentration of the oil near to the respondents' wharf (the Sheerlegs Wharf). The respondents' workmen had been using electric and oxy-acetylene welding equipment, and, on becoming aware of the situation, their works manager prohibited any welding or burning until further orders. After making further enquiry, he took the view that their operations could be continued with safety, and he gave the appropriate instructions, but in addition ordered all safety precautions to be taken to prevent inflammable material getting into the oil from the wharf. About two days later the oil caught fire because, the trial judge found, molten metal had fallen from the wharf and set fire to some cotton waste or rag floating in the oil on a piece of débris. The wharf also caught fire and was damaged, as was some equipment on the wharf, and the respondents claimed damages. The trial judge found that the appellants 'did not know, and could not reasonably be expected to have known, that [the oil] was capable of being set afire when spread on water', [1958] 1 Lloyd's Rep at p. 582, and also that some damage was caused to the respondents as a direct result of the spilling of the oil, namely the oil congealing on the slipways of their wharf, although no compensation was claimed for this damage. The Full Court of the Supreme Court of New South Wales dismissed an appeal from Kinsella J, who held the appellants liable, and there was a further appeal to the Judicial Committee of the Privy Council.

VISCOUNT SIMONDS:....It is inevitable that first consideration should be given to *Re Polemis and Furness, Withy & Co Ltd,*[11] which will henceforward be referred to as *Polemis.* For it was avowedly in deference to that decision and to decisions of the Court of Appeal that followed it that the full court was constrained to decide the present case in favour of the respondents....

There can be no doubt that the decision of the Court of Appeal in *Polemis*[11] plainly asserts that, if the defendant is guilty of negligence, he is responsible for all the consequences, whether reasonably foreseeable or not. The generality of the proposition is, perhaps, qualified by the fact that each of the lords justices refers to the outbreak of fire as the direct result of the negligent act. There is thus introduced the conception that the negligent actor is not responsible for consequences which are not 'direct', whatever that may mean....

---

[11] [1921] 3 KB 560, [1921] All ER Rep 40.

[Having referred to several authorities decided after *Re Polemis*,[11] he continued:] Enough has been said to show that the authority of *Polemis*[11] has been severely shaken, though lip-service has from time to time been paid to it. In their Lordships' opinion, it should no longer be regarded as good law. It is not probable that many cases will for that reason have a different result, though it is hoped that the law will be thereby simplified, and that, in some cases at least, palpable injustice will be avoided. For it does not seem consonant with current ideas of justice or morality that, for an act of negligence, however slight or venial, which results in some trivial foreseeable damage, the actor should be liable for all consequences, however unforeseeable and however grave, so long as they can be said to be 'direct'. It is a principle of civil liability, subject only to qualifications which have no present relevance, that a man must be considered to be responsible for the probable consequences of his act. To demand more of him is too harsh a rule, to demand less is to ignore that civilised order requires the observance of a minimum standard of behaviour. This concept, applied to the slowly developing law of negligence, has led to a great variety of expressions which can, as it appears to their Lordships, be harmonised with little difficulty with the single exception of the so-called rule in *Polemis*.[11] For, if it is asked why a man should be responsible for the natural or necessary or probable consequences of his act (or any other similar description of them), the answer is that it is not because they are natural or necessary or probable, but because, since they have this quality, it is judged, by the standard of the reasonable man, that he ought to have foreseen them. Thus it is that, over and over again, it has happened that, in different judgments in the same case and sometimes in a single judgment, liability for a consequence has been imposed on the ground that it was reasonably foreseeable, or alternatively on the ground that it was natural or necessary or probable. The two grounds have been treated as coterminous, and so they largely are. But, where they are not, the question arises to which the wrong answer was given in *Polemis*.[12] For, if some limitation must be imposed on the consequences for which the negligent actor is to be held responsible—and all are agreed that some limitation there must be—why should that test (reasonable foreseeability) be rejected which, since he is judged by what the reasonable man ought to foresee, corresponds with the common conscience of mankind, and a test (the 'direct' consequence) be substituted which leads to nowhere but the never ending and insoluble problems of causation. 'The lawyer' said Sir Frederick Pollock 'cannot afford to adventure himself with philosophers in the logical and metaphysical controversies that beset the idea of cause.' Yet this is just what he has most unfortunately done and must continue to do if the rule in *Polemis*[11] is to prevail. A conspicuous example occurs when the actor seeks to escape liability on the ground that the 'chain of causation' is broken by a 'nova causa' or 'novus actus interveniens'.

The validity of a rule or principle can sometimes be tested by observing it in operation. Let the rule in *Polemis*[12] be tested in this way. In *The Edison*,[12] the appellants, whose vessel had been fouled by the respondents, claimed damages under various heads. The respondents were admittedly at fault; therefore, said the appellants, invoking the rule in *Polemis*,[13] they were responsible for all damage whether reasonably foreseeable or not. Here was the opportunity to deny the rule or to place it secure on its pedestal. But the House of Lords took neither course; on the contrary, it distinguished *Polemis*[14] on the ground that, in that case, the injuries suffered were the 'immediate physical consequences' of the negligent act. It is not easy to understand why a distinction should be drawn between 'immediate physical' and other consequences, nor where the line is to be drawn. It was, perhaps, this difficulty which led Denning LJ in *Roe v Ministry of Health*[13] to say that foreseeability is only disregarded when the negligence is the immediate or *precipitating* cause of the damage. This new word may well have been thought as good a word as another for revealing or disguising the fact that he sought loyally to enforce an unworkable rule. In the same connexion may be mentioned the conclusion to which the full court finally came in the present case. Applying the rule in *Polemis*[11] and holding, therefore, that the unforeseeability of the damage by fire afforded no defence, they went on to consider the remaining question. Was it a 'direct' consequence? On this, Manning J said:

> 'Notwithstanding that, if regard is had separately to each individual occurrence in the chain of events that led to this fire, each occurrence was improbable and, in one sense, improbability was

---

[12] [1933] AC 449, [1933] All ER Rep 144.
[13] [1954] 2 QB 66 at 85, [1954] 2 All ER 131 at 138.

heaped upon improbability, I cannot escape from the conclusion that if the ordinary man in the street had been asked, as a matter of common sense, without any detailed analysis of the circumstances, to state the cause of the fire at Morts Dock, he would unhesitatingly have assigned such cause to spillage of oil by the appellants' employees.'

Perhaps he would, and probably he would have added 'I never should have thought it possible.' But, with great respect to the full court, this is surely irrelevant, or, if it is relevant, only serves to show that the *Polemis* rule[11] works in a very strange way. After the event even a fool is wise. Yet it is not the hindsight of a fool, but it is the foresight of the reasonable man which alone can determine responsibility. The *Polemis* rule,[11] by substituting 'direct' for 'reasonably foreseeable' consequence, leads to a conclusion equally illogical and unjust.

At an early stage in this judgment, their Lordships intimated that they would deal with the proposition which can best be stated by reference to the well-known dictum of Lord Sumner:[14] This, however, goes to culpability, not to compensation.' It is with the greatest respect to that very learned judge and to those who have echoed his words that their Lordships find themselves bound to state their view that this proposition is fundamentally false.

It is, no doubt, proper when considering tortious liability for negligence to analyse its elements and to say that the plaintiff must prove a duty owed to him by the defendant, a breach of that duty by the defendant, and consequent damage. But there can be no liability until the damage has been done. It is not the act but the consequences on which tortious liability is founded. Just as (as it has been said) there is no such thing as negligence in the air, so there is no such thing as liability in the air. Suppose an action brought by A for damage caused by the carelessness (a neutral word) of B, for example a fire caused by the careless spillage of oil. It may, of course, become relevant to know what duty B owed to A, but the only liability that is in question is the liability for damage by fire. It is vain to isolate the liability from its context and to say that B is or is not liable, and then to ask for what damage he is liable. For his liability is in respect of that damage and no other. If, as admittedly it is, B's liability (culpability) depends on the reasonable foreseeability of the consequent damage, how is that to be determined except by the foreseeability of the damage which in fact happened—the damage in suit? And, if that damage is unforeseeable so as to displace liability at large, how can the liability be restored so as to make compensation payable? But, it is said, a different position arises if B's careless act has been shown to be negligent and has caused some foreseeable damage to A. Their Lordships have already observed that to hold B liable for consequences, however unforeseeable, of a careless act, if, but only if, he is at the same time liable for some other damage, however trivial, appears to be neither logical nor just. This becomes more clear if it is supposed that similar unforeseeable damage is suffered by A and C, but other foreseeable damage, for which B is liable, by A only. A system of law which would hold B liable to A but not to C for the similar damage suffered by each of them could not easily be defended. Fortunately, the attempt is not necessary. For the same fallacy is at the root of the proposition. It is irrelevant to the question whether B is liable for unforeseeable damage that he is liable for foreseeable damage, as irrelevant as would the fact that he had trespassed on Whiteacre be to the question whether he had trespassed on Blackacre. Again, suppose a claim by A for damage by fire by the careless act of B. Of what relevance is it to that claim that he has another claim arising out of the same careless act? It would surely not prejudice his claim if that other claim failed; it cannot assist it if it succeeds. Each of them rests on its own bottom and will fail if it can be established that the damage could not reasonably be foreseen. We have come back to the plain common sense stated by Lord Russell of Killowen in *Hay* (or *Bourhill*) *v Young*.[15] As Denning LJ said in *King v Phillips*[16] '...there can be no doubt since *Hay* (or *Bourhill*) *v Young*[16] that the

---

[14] [1920] AC 956 at 984. [The preceding words are 'What a defendant ought to have anticipated as a reasonable man is material when the question is whether or not he was guilty of negligence, that is, of want of due care according to the circumstances.']

[15] 16 [1943] AC 92, [1942] 2 All ER 396.   [16] 17 [1953] 1 QB 429 at 441, [1953] 1 All ER 617 at 623.

test of *liability for shock* is foreseeability of *injury by shock*. Their Lordships substitute the word 'fire' for 'shock' and indorse this statement of the law.[17]

Their Lordships conclude this part of the case with some general observations. They have been concerned primarily to displace the proposition that unforeseeability is irrelevant if damage is 'direct'. In doing so, they have inevitably insisted that the essential factor in determining liability is whether the damage is of such a kind as the reasonable man should have foreseen. This accords with the general view thus stated by Lord Atkin in *M'Alister* (or *Donoghue*) *v Stevenson*:[18]

'The liability for negligence, whether you style it such or treat it as in other systems as a species of "culpa," is no doubt based upon a general public sentiment of moral wrongdoing for which the offender must pay.'

It is a departure from this sovereign principle if liability is made to depend solely on the damage being the 'direct' or 'natural' consequence of the precedent act. Who knows or can be assumed to know all the processes of nature? But if it would be wrong that a man should be held liable for damage unpredictable by a reasonable man because it was 'direct' or 'natural', equally it would be wrong that he should escape liability, however 'indirect' the damage, if he foresaw or could reasonably foresee the intervening events which led to its being done; cf. *Woods v Duncan*.[19] Thus foreseeability becomes the effective test. In reasserting this principle, their Lordships conceive that they do not depart from, but follow and develop, the law of negligence as laid down by Alderson B, in *Blyth v Birmingham Waterworks Co*.[1]

It is proper to add that their Lordships have not found it necessary to consider the so-called rule of 'strict liability' exemplified in *Rylands v Fletcher*[2] and the cases that have followed or distinguished it. Nothing that they have said is intended to reflect on that rule....

[An alternative claim in nuisance was remitted to the Full Court to be dealt with as may be thought proper.]

Appeal allowed.

NOTES

1. For further litigation arising out of this incident, but with a different claimant, see *The Wagon Mound (No. 2)* [1967] 1 AC 617, [1966] 2 All ER 709 (p. 299, ante, and p. 802, post).
2. In terms of precedent, the Judicial Committee of the Privy Council does not bind other English courts. Therefore it was arguable that *Re Polemis* in strict theory should still have survived and been a binding precedent for certain courts. However, the decision has generally been treated as effectively overruled by *The Wagon Mound*, whatever the theoretical precedent position: see *Smith v Leech Brain & Co Ltd* (post).
3. For further discussion of *Re Polemis* and *The Wagon Mound*, see M. Davies (1982) 45 MLR 534, who, inter alia, describes the difficult financial situation facing the shipping industry at the time of the decision in *Re Polemis*. The decision would have been particularly welcomed by shipowners because of the protection it provided if their ships were damaged. Davies also points out that at the time *Re Polemis* was decided the effect of any wide-ranging remoteness rule was limited by a narrower conception of duty than has prevailed in more recent times; before *M'Alister* (or *Donoghue*) *v Stevenson* [1932] AC 562 (p. 30, ante) a duty of care only existed in certain relationships (e.g. bailment).

---

[17] On this point see now *Page v Smith* [1996] AC 155, [1995] 2 All ER 736 (p. 132, ante).

[18] [1932] AC 562 at 580, [1932] 1 All ER 617 at 623.   [19] [1946] AC at p. 442.

[1] (1856) 11 Exch 781, [1843–60] All ER Rep 478.

[2] (1868) LR 3 HL 330, [1861–73] All ER Rep 1.

It was the advent of a more general duty of care based on Lord Atkin's 'neighbour principle' which led to criticism of the results of the application of *Re Polemis*. Therefore, in assessing the merits of *Re Polemis at the time* this point should be borne in mind.

4.   The Privy Council in *The Wagon Mound (No. 1)* envisaged that reasonable foreseeability would become the sole criterion, not just for testing whether the type of damage suffered was too remote, but for answering all remoteness questions, including the impact of intervening causes. As already explained, it became clear that the two issues are separate: see *McKew v Holland and Hannen & Cubbitts (Scotland) Ltd* [1969] 3 All ER 1621 (p. 389, ante) and *Lamb v London Borough of Camden* [1981] 2 All ER 408, [1981] QB 625 (p. 401, ante), both cases being cited in the House of Lords in *Simmons v British Steel plc* [2004] ICR 585, [2004] UKHL 20 at [67] (and see also *The Sivand* [1998] 2 Lloyd's Rep 97).

5.   The interplay between duty of care and causation has already been mentioned (note 4, p. 406, ante). A further 'foreseeability requirement', which shares the same conceptual ambiguity is the notion that the *claimant* must be foreseeable. In *Bourhill v Young* [1943] AC 92, [1942] 2 All ER 396, the House of Lords regarded this issue as relevant to the existence of the duty of care. Here, the claimant had just alighted from a tramcar when a motorcyclist, who had just driven past the claimant, was killed as a result of a collision some distance away from where the claimant was standing. The claimant did not see the collision, but she did hear the sound of it and later saw blood on the road. She claimed damages for nervous shock from the estate of the motorcyclist, who was found to have been travelling excessively fast. The House of Lords rejected the claimant's appeal. Lord Wright explained that the duty of care is 'always relative to the individual affected. This raises a serious additional difficulty in the cases where it has to be determined not merely whether the act itself is negligent against someone but whether it is negligent vis-à-vis the [claimant].' His Lordship went on to conclude that, 'I cannot accept that [the motorcyclist] could reasonably have foreseen, or, more correctly, the reasonable hypothetical observer could reasonably have foreseen, the likelihood that anyone placed as the [claimant] was, could be affected in the manner in which she was.' Lord Porter was of the same view, regarding the issue as turning on the 'extent of the duty and not the remoteness of damages' and explaining that, 'The duty is not to the world at large.' See also the American case of *Palsgraf v Long Island Railroad Co* 162 NE 99 (1928). For an argument that the foreseeability of the claimant should be treated as a question of remoteness of damage, see A. J. E. Jaffey, *The Duty of Care* (1992), p. 8.

4 DEVELOPMENT OF *THE WAGON MOUND* DOCTRINE

(a) The extent of the harm and the 'thin skull rule'

■ Smith v Leech Brain & Co Ltd
Queen's Bench Division [1961] 3 All ER 1159

The plaintiff's husband was a labourer and galvaniser employed by the defendants at the Glaucus Iron Works, Poplar. The articles to be galvanised were lowered into a tank containing molten metallic zinc and flux. The method used depended on the size of the article. All articles were first dipped in hydrochloric acid and the larger articles were then lowered into the tank by means of an overhead crane, from a position behind a sheet of corrugated iron. On 15 August 1950, the plaintiff's husband was operating the overhead crane, using the corrugated iron sheet supplied, when a piece of molten metal or flux struck and burned his lower lip. The burn was treated at the time but he thought nothing of it. Ultimately the place where the burn had been began to ulcerate and get larger. He consulted his general practitioner, who sent him to hospital, where cancer was diagnosed. Treatment by radium needles enabled the lip to heal and destroy the primary growth. Subsequently, however, secondary growths were observed. Thereafter he had some six or seven operations, and he died of cancer on 14 October 1953.

Lord Parker CJ found that the defendants were negligent, that there had been no contributory negligence on the part of the plaintiff's husband, and that the burn was the promoting agency, promoting cancer in tissues which already had a premalignant condition as a result of his having worked at gas works, where he would have been in contact with tar or tar vapours from 1926 to 1935.

The case is reported only on the question of remoteness of damage.

LORD PARKER CJ:...
I am confronted with the recent decision of the Privy Council in *Overseas Tankship (UK) Ltd v Morts Dock and Engineering Co Ltd*. For convenience, that case is always referred to as *The Wagon Mound*. But for *The Wagon Mound*,[2] it seems to me perfectly clear that, assuming negligence proved, assuming that the burn caused in whole or in part the cancer and the death, this plaintiff would be entitled to recover. It is said on the one side by counsel for the defendants, that, although I am not strictly bound by *The Wagon Mound*[3] since it is a Privy Council case, I should treat myself as free, using the arguments to be derived from that case, to say that other cases in the Court of Appeal have been wrongly decided, and, particularly, that *Re Polemis and Furness, Withy & Co Ltd*[3] was wrongly decided, and that a further ground for taking that course is to be found in the various criticisms that have from time to time in the past been made by members of the House of Lords in regard to *Re Polemis*.[3] On the other hand, it is said by counsel for the plaintiff that I should hold that *Re Polemis*[3] was rightly decided and, secondly, that, even if that is not so, I must treat myself as completely bound by it. Thirdly, he said that in any event, whatever the true view is in regard to *Re Polemis*,[3] *The Wagon Mound*[3] has no relevance at all to this case.

For my part, I am quite satisfied that the Judicial Committee in *The Wagon Mound*[4] did not have what I may call, loosely, the 'thin skull' cases in mind. It has always been the law of this country that a tortfeasor takes his victim as he finds him. It is unnecessary to do more than refer to the short passage in the decision of Kennedy J in *Dulieu v White & Sons*,[4] where he said:

'If a man is negligently run over or otherwise negligently injured in his body, it is no answer to the sufferer's claim for damages that he would have suffered less injury, or no injury at all, if he had not had an unusually thin skull or an unusually weak heart.'

To the same effect is a passage in *The Arpad*.[5] But quite apart from those two references, as is well-known, the work of the courts for years and years has gone on on that basis. There is not a day that goes by where some trial judge does not adopt that principle, that the tortfeasor takes his victim as he finds him. If the Judicial Committee had any intention of making an inroad into that doctrine, I am quite satisfied that they would have said so.

It is true that, if one takes the wording in the advice given by Viscount Simonds in *The Wagon Mound*[3] and applies it strictly to such a case as this, it could be said that they were dealing with this

² [1961] AC 388, [1961] 1 All ER 404.   ³ [1921] 3 KB 560, [1921] All ER Rep 40.
⁴ [1901] 2 KB 669 at 679.   ⁵ [1934] P 189 at 202, 203, [1934] All ER Rep 326 at 331.

point. But, as I have said, it is, to my mind, quite impossible to conceive that they were, and, indeed, it has been pointed out that they disclose the distinction between such a case as this and the one which they were considering, when they comment on *Smith v London & South Western Rly* Co.[6] Lord Simonds, in dealing with that case in *The Wagon Mound*[3] said this:

> 'Three things may be noted about this case: the first, that, for the sweeping proposition laid down, no authority was cited; the second, that the point to which the court directed its mind was not unforeseeable damage of a different kind from that which was foreseen, but more extensive damage of the same kind . . .'

In other words, Lord Simonds is clearly there drawing a distinction between the question whether a man could reasonably anticipate a type of injury, and the question whether a man could reasonably anticipate the extent of injury of the type which could be foreseen. The Judicial Committee were, I think, disagreeing with the decision in *Re Polemis*[7] that a man is no longer liable for the type of damage which he could not reasonably anticipate. The Judicial Committee were not, I think, saying that a man is only liable for the extent of damage which he could anticipate, always assuming the type of injury could have been anticipated. The view is really supported by the way in which cases of this sort have been dealt with in Scotland. Scotland has never, as far as I know, adopted the principle laid down in *Re Polemis*,[7] and yet I am quite satisfied that they have throughout proceeded on the basis that the tortfeasor takes the victim as he finds him.

In those circumstances, it seems to me that this is plainly a case which comes within the old principle. The test is not whether these defendants could reasonably have foreseen that a burn would cause cancer and that Mr Smith would die. The question is whether these defendants could reasonably foresee the type of injury which he suffered, namely, the burn. What, in the particular case, is the amount of damage which he suffers as a result of that burn, depends on the characteristics and constitution of the victim. Accordingly, I find that the damages which the plaintiff claims are damages for which these defendants are liable. Before leaving that part of the case, I should say, in case the matter goes further, that I would follow, sitting as a trial judge, the decision in *The Wagon Mound*;[8] or rather, more accurately, I would treat myself, in the light of the arguments in that case, able to follow other decisions of the Court of Appeal, prior to *Re Polemis*,[7] rather than *Re Polemis*[7] itself. As I have said, *Re Polemis*[8] has been criticised by individual members of the House of Lords, although followed by the Court of Appeal in *Thurogood v Van Den Berghs and Jurgens Ltd*.[9] I should treat myself as at liberty to do that, and, for my part, I would do so the more readily, because I think that it is important that the common law, and the development of the common law, should be homogeneous in the various sections of the Commonwealth. It would be lamentable if a court sitting here had to say that, while the common law in the Commonwealth and Scotland has been developed in a particular way, yet we in this country, and sitting in these courts, are going to proceed in a different way. However, as I have said, that does not strictly arise in this case.

Judgment for the plaintiff.

QUESTION

Could Lord Parker CJ have classified the type of damage here as cancer? If so, what would have been the result of the case?

6 (1870) LR 6 CP 14.   7 [1921] 3 KB 560, [1921] All ER Rep 40.
8 [1961] AC 388, [1961] 1 All ER 404.   9 [1951] 2 KB 537, [1951] 1 All ER 682.

NOTES

1. The relationship of the 'thin skull' rule to *The Wagon Mound* doctrine is no easy one. This consideration was in evidence in the South African case of *Alston v Marine and Trade Insurance Co Ltd* 1964 (4) SA 112, noted by C. Turpin [1965] CLJ 34, where *The Wagon Mound* doctrine was not accepted; Hiemstra J spoke in the following terms (at p. 115):

   'This question, whether there can be a different criterion for determining culpability and compensation, so *The Wagon Mound* rightly says, "goes to the root of the matter". *The Wagon Mound* sweeps away all difference, and here it immediately becomes unconvincing. An accident and some injury can be foreseeable but the form and extent of the damage hardly ever. The escape from this truism is to say that the *type* of damage can be foreseen, namely, fire or bodily injury, and that the extent thereof was not meant to be included in the foreseeability test....

   The Wagon Mound has laid down a rule of thumb which will in most cases be easy to apply but is neither intellectually satisfying nor always just. It already breaks down upon the "eggshell skull" cases. Or, differently put, it has to be lovingly accommodated before it will harmonise with the well-established rule "You must take your victim as you find him". It is probably unforeseeable that you will run down a millionaire in a slum, but he is nevertheless entitled to his much higher compensation than the pauper. These considerations convince me that the dichotomy between culpability and compensation is not as fundamentally false as *The Wagon Mound* would make out.'

2. As *Smith v Leech Brain & Co Ltd* shows, the thin skull rule has been accommodated by English courts, however uneasily, with *The Wagon Mound* doctrine. See further *Wieland v Cyril Lord Carpets Ltd* [1969] 3 All ER 1006 and for discussion of the thin skull rule, see P. J. Rowe (1977) 40 MLR 377. Particular reference should also be made to *Robinson v Post Office* [1974] 2 All ER 737, [1974] 1 WLR 1176. The relevant facts for present purposes were that, as a result of an allergy, the claimant contracted encephalitis after he had been injected with an anti-tetanus serum. The injection had been given because the claimant had sustained an injury at work. The Court of Appeal was concerned with the liability of the Post Office (the claimant's employer) for the encephalitis, the Post Office's liability for the injury itself not being in dispute. In meeting the argument that the Post Office was not liable for the encephalitis as it was not reasonably foreseeable that the claimant would contract this illness, Orr LJ (delivering the judgment of the Court of Appeal) stated (at p. 750):

   In our judgment the principle that a defendant must take the [claimant] as he finds him involves that if a wrongdoer ought reasonably to foresee that as a result of his wrongful act the victim may require medical treatment he is, subject to the principle of novus actus interveniens, liable for the consequences of the treatment applied although he could not reasonably foresee those consequences or that they could be serious.

   Does this test require a kind of damage to be foreseen? (See further the note on this case by R. W. M. Dias [1975] CLJ 15.)

   Robinson's case was one where there was a pre-existing susceptibility. Unforeseeable damage following on from a foreseeable kind of damage may, of course, occur without any pre-existing susceptibility; the first injury may have *created* a new risk or susceptibility—e.g. where the foreseeable injury becomes infected and leads to more serious injury. In a New Zealand case, *Stephenson v Waite, Tileman Ltd* [1973] 1 NZLR 152, Richmond J (with Turner P concurring) discussed this last point (as well as the relationship of the thin skull cases with *The Wagon Mound*). At p. 168 he summarised his conclusions as follows:

'1 In cases of damage by physical injury to the person the principles imposing liability for consequences flowing from the pre-existing special susceptibility of the victim and/or from new risk or susceptibility created by the initial injury remain part of our law.

2 In such cases the question of foreseeability should be limited to the initial injury. The tribunal of fact must decide whether that injury is of a kind, type or character which the defendant ought reasonably to have foreseen as a real risk.

3 If the plaintiff establishes that the initial injury was within a reasonable foreseeable kind, type or character of injury, then the necessary link between the ultimate consequences of the initial injury and the negligence of the defendant can be forged simply as one of cause and effect—in other words by establishing an adequate relationship of cause and effect between the initial injury and the ultimate consequence.

If I am correct in the foregoing conclusions then juries will be left to deal with the question of foreseeability in an area which is readily comprehensible and in which the test of the ordinary reasonable man can be applied in an atmosphere of reality. They will not have to decide the ability of the ordinary man to foresee the risks of "kinds" of harm resulting from a "sub-compartmentalisation" of secondly consequences of an initial injury. Nor will it be necessary to decide whether a doctor driving a motor car is to be made liable for a greater field of injury than would the ordinary layman in similar circumstances.'

3.   The application of the 'thin skull' rule to 'nervous shock' cases was considered in *Page v Smith* [1996] AC 155, [1995] 2 All ER 736 (p. 132, ante). It will be recalled that in this case the House of Lords decided that a duty of care would be owed to a primary victim of a defendant's negligence who sustained nervous shock even though only physical injury and not nervous shock was reasonably foreseeable. In the case of primary victims this avoids the argument that there should be no duty because the claimant was not a 'reasonably strong-nerved person', and that nervous shock was not reasonably foreseeable; this argument can be raised in the case of secondary victims. Once a duty is owed, however, the defendant is not helped by pleading that the claimant was particularly susceptible to such illness or that the nervous shock which came about was rare in kind or more severe than might have been expected. The 'thin skull' rule applies. For earlier authority see *Brice v Brown* [1984] 1 All ER 997, though it should be read subject to the comments on it by Lord Lloyd in *Page v Smith* on the question of foresight of injury by shock.

■ Lagdon v O'Connor
House of Lords [2004] 1 All ER 277

This case raised the question what costs were recoverable in hiring a car to replace one that had been damaged in an accident. While the normal daily rate was deemed to be recoverable, the House of Lords in *Dimond v Lovell* [2002] 1 AC 384, [2000] 2 All ER 897 had denied recovery of the extra costs associated with hiring one from firms that did not require payment from the hirer but pursued the hirer's action against the other car driver. *Lagdon* differed from *Dimond v Lovell* in that the hirer in the former did not have the money to hire a car. This raised the question of the validity today of the much distinguished decision of the House of Lords in *The Liesbosch* [1933] AC 449. In *The Liesbosch* it had been held that the owners of a dredger, which had been sunk in an accident, could not claim for the extra losses associated with hiring a replacement dredger, as opposed to buying one which their lack of funds had prevented them from doing. For comment on that decision, see B. Coote [2001] CLJ 511.

LORD SLYNN OF HADLEY: . . .

[12] In *Alcoa Minerals of Jamaica Inc v Broderick* [2002] 1 AC 371, [2000] 3 WLR 23 the Judicial Committee of the Privy Council found it possible to distinguish the case from *Dredger Liesbosch (Owners) v SS Edison (Owners)* [1933] AC 449 . . . and accordingly thought it right to leave for consideration by your Lordships' House the question as to whether the *Liesbosch* case is still good law. In the light inter alia of the criticism and qualifications of that decision to which I refer in the Board's judgment, it seems to me with great respect that your Lordships should now say that the observations that a claimant's lack of means should not be taken into account when assessing his loss should no longer be followed . . .

LORD HOPE OF CRAIGHEAD: . . .

[61] The Judicial Committee did not go so far in the *Alcoa Minerals* case as to say that the *Liesbosch* case was wrongly decided. As it was a decision of the House of Lords, it was for the House and not the Board to decide whether the rule that was laid down in that case should now be departed from. The opportunity for the House to take that step has now come. It is not necessary for us to say that the *Liesbosch* case was wrongly decided. But it is clear that the law has moved on, and that the correct test of remoteness today is whether the loss was reasonably foreseeable. The wrongdoer must take his victim as he finds him: talem qualem, as Lord Collins said in *Clippens Oil Co Ltd v Edinburgh and District Water Trustees* [1907] AC 291 at 303. This rule applies to the economic state of the victim in the same way as it applies to his physical and mental vulnerability. It requires the wrongdoer to bear the consequences if it was reasonably foreseeable that the injured party would have to borrow money or incur some other kind of expenditure to mitigate his damages. . . .

[LORD NICHOLLS OF BIRKENHEAD, LORD SCOTT OF FOSCOTE, and LORD WALKER OF GESTINGTHORPE delivered speeches in which they agreed with LORD HOPE on this point.]

QUESTION

Is Lord Hope's approach in the above case actually consistent with the approach in the earlier 'thin skull' cases such as *Smith v Leech Brain*?

NOTE

In *Malcolm v Broadhurst* [1970] 3 All ER 508 a woman and her husband had been involved in a road accident caused by the defendant's negligent driving. She recovered damages for her injuries and for certain loss of wages in respect of her full-time job. However, she had also worked as a part-time secretary for her husband who had been injured in the accident. For about a year (until February 1968) her own injuries stopped her from working, but from that time onwards she lost this part-time employment purely because, as a result of his injuries, her husband had ceased to be self-employed, rendering the wife's secretarial services unnecessary. Although any other part-time employment was impractical in her circumstances, she was denied damages for her loss of wages after February 1968. Geoffrey Lane J refused to extend the rule that one takes one's victim as one finds him so as to cover a person's 'infirmities of employment', and this unforeseeable loss was irrecoverable. How does this stand after *Lagdon*?

(b) The type or kind of damage

■ Hughes v Lord Advocate
House of Lords [1963] 1 All ER 705

Some men employed by the Post Office were working on cables under a road and they reached the cables by means of a ladder in a manhole. There was a tent over the manhole and at the material time there were red warning paraffin lights around the site. Before going for their teabreak, the men took the ladder from the manhole and put it on the ground outside the tent and they pulled some tarpaulin over the entrance to the tent, leaving a gap of about two feet six inches between it and the ground. In their absence, the appellant and another ten year old boy (his uncle) took one of the lamps and the ladder into the tent and went down the manhole. After they had come out of the manhole, the appellant stumbled over the lamp which was knocked into the hole. There was a violent explosion and flames reached a height of thirty feet. The appellant fell into the hole and was badly burnt. On appeal to the House of Lords from the First Division of the Court of Session, 1961 SC 310, who, affirming the Lord Ordinary's decision, had held the respondent not liable:

LORD REID: . . .

My Lords, I have had an opportunity of reading the speech which my noble and learned friend Lord Guest is about to deliver. I agree with him that this appeal should be allowed and I shall only add some general observations. I am satisfied that the Post Office workmen were in fault in leaving this open manhole unattended and it is clear that if they had done as they ought to have done this accident would not have happened. It cannot be said that they owed no duty to the appellant. But it has been held that the appellant cannot recover damages.

It was argued that the appellant cannot recover because the damage which he suffered was of a kind which was not foreseeable. That was not the ground of judgment of the First Division or of the Lord Ordinary and the facts proved do not, in my judgment, support this argument. The appellant's injuries were mainly caused by burns, and it cannot be said that injuries from burns were unforeseeable. As a warning to traffic the workmen had set lighted red lamps around the tent which covered the manhole, and if boys did enter the dark tent it was very likely that they would take one of these lamps with them. If the lamp fell and broke it was not at all unlikely that the boy would be burned and the burns might well be serious. No doubt it was not to be expected that the injuries would be as serious as those which the appellant in fact sustained. But a defender is liable, although the damage may be a good deal greater in extent than was foreseeable. He can only escape liability if the damage can be regarded as differing in kind from what was foreseeable.

So we have (first) a duty owed by the workmen, (secondly) the fact that if they had done as they ought to have done there would have been no accident, and (thirdly) the fact that the injuries suffered by the appellant, though perhaps different in degree, did not differ in kind from injuries which might have resulted from an accident of a foreseeable nature. The ground on which this case has been decided against the appellant is that the accident was of an unforeseeable type. Of course the pursuer has to prove that the defender's fault caused the accident and there could be a case where the intrusion of a new and unexpected factor could be regarded as the cause of the accident rather than the fault of the defender. But that is not this case. The cause of this accident was a known source of danger, the lamp, but it behaved in an unpredictable way. The explanation of the accident which has been accepted, and which I would not seek to question, is that, when the lamp fell down the manhole and was broken, some paraffin escaped, and enough was vaporized to create an explosive mixture which was detonated by the naked light of the lamp. The experts agree that no one would have expected that to happen: it was so unlikely as to be unforeseeable. The explosion caused the boy to fall into the manhole: whether his injuries were directly caused by the explosion or aggravated by fire which started in the manhole is not at all clear....

...This accident was caused by a known source of danger, but caused in a way which could not have been foreseen, and in my judgment that affords no defence. I would therefore allow the appeal.

LORD JENKINS:...

It is true that the duty of care expected in cases of this sort is confined to reasonably foreseeable dangers, but it does not necessarily follow that liability is escaped because the danger actually materialising is not identical with the danger reasonably foreseen and guarded against. Each case must depend on its own particular facts. For example...in the present case the paraffin did the mischief by exploding, not burning, and it is said that, while a paraffin fire (caused, e.g. by the upsetting of the lighted lamp or otherwise allowing its contents to leak out) was a reasonably foreseeable risk so soon as the pursuer got access to the lamp, an explosion was not. To my mind the distinction drawn between burning and explosion is too fine to warrant acceptance....

LORD GUEST:...

In dismissing the appellant's claim the Lord Ordinary and the majority of the judges of the First Division reached the conclusion that the accident which happened was not reasonably foreseeable. In order to establish a coherent chain of causation it is not necessary that the precise details leading up to the accident should have been reasonably foreseeable: it is sufficient if the accident which occurred is of a type which should have been foreseeable by a reasonably careful person (*Miller v South of Scotland Electricity Board* per Lord Keith of Avonholm;[10] *Harvey v Singer Manufacturing Co Ltd* per Lord Patrick[11]); or as Lord Mackintosh,[12] expressed it in *Harvey*'s case[13] the precise concatenation of circumstances need not be envisaged. Concentration has been placed in the courts below on the explosion which it was said could not have been foreseen because it was caused in a unique fashion by the paraffin forming into vapour and being ignited by the naked flame of the wick. But this, in my opinion, is to concentrate on what is really a non-essential element in the dangerous situation created by the allurement. The test might better be put thus:– Was the igniting of paraffin outside the lamp by the flame a foreseeable consequence of the breach of duty? In the circumstances there was a combination of potentially dangerous circumstances against which the Post Office had to protect the appellant. If these formed an allurement to children it might have been foreseen that they would play with the lamp, that it might tip over, that it might be broken, and that when broken the paraffin might spill and be ignited by the flame. All these steps in the chain of causation seem to have been accepted by all the judges in the courts below as foreseeable. But because the explosion was the agent which caused the burning and was unforeseeable, therefore the accident, according to them, was not reasonably foreseeable. In my opinion this reasoning is fallacious. An explosion is only one way in which burning can be caused. Burning can also be caused by the contact between liquid paraffin and a naked flame. In the one case paraffin vapour and in the other case liquid paraffin is ignited by fire. I cannot see that these are two different types of accident. They are both burning accidents and in both cases the injuries would be burning injuries. On this view the explosion was an immaterial event in the chain of causation. It was simply one way in which burning might be caused by the potentially dangerous paraffin lamp....

I have therefore reached the conclusion that the accident which occurred and which caused burning injuries to the appellant was one which ought reasonably to have been foreseen by the Post Office employees and that they were at fault in failing to provide a protection against the appellant entering the shelter and going down the manhole.

I would allow the appeal.

LORD PEARCE:...

Did the explosion create an accident and damage of a different type from the misadventure and damage that could be foreseen? In my judgment it did not. The accident was but a variant of the foreseeable.

---

[10] 1958 S.C. (HL) at p. 34.   [11] 1960 S.C. at p. 168.
[12] 1960 S.C. at p. 172.   [13] 1960 S.C. at p. 155.

It was, to quote the words of Denning LJ in *Roe v Ministry of Health*[14] 'within the risk created by the negligence.' No unforeseeable extraneous, initial occurrence fired the train....

[LORD MORRIS OF BORTH-Y-GEST delivered a speech in favour of allowing the appeal.]

Appeal allowed.

NOTES

1.   *Hughes* represents a considerable relaxation of the strictures of the *Wagon Mound (No 1)* foreseeability hurdle for claimants. It adopts a broad view of the 'type' of damage which must have been foreseeable, and does not require that the 'precise concatenation of events' should have been foreseeable. Cases since *Hughes* have generally adopted a similarly broad view. So for example in *Bradford v Robinson Rentals Ltd* [1967] 1 All ER 267, [1967] 1 WLR 337, the claimant (a radio service engineer) was told by his employers to drive a considerable distance in freezing weather conditions to collect a new van. The van's heater was disconnected and the radiator had to be topped up frequently during the journey. The claimant took all reasonable precautions against the cold, but the lack of a heater meant that his breath formed ice on the windscreen, so that he had to keep a window open. The claimant suffered permanent injury to his hands and feet through frostbite, and sued his employers in negligence. Rees J decided that this was a reasonably foreseeable type of harm. Perhaps the broadest view of the foreseeable type of harm is found in *Page v Smith* [1996] AC 155, [1995] 2 All ER 736 (p. 132, ante), in which the House of Lords regarded the recurrence of myalgic encephalomyelitis as a foreseeable type of harm following a minor car accident, since all forms of personal injury, physical and psychiatric, were treated as harm of the same type. With a test of 'type' this broad, claimants will rarely fail on the basis of *Wagon Mound* foreseeability. Might the retention of a novus actus test not totally dependent on foreseeability have influenced this approach?

2.   In contrast, those isolated cases which have taken the message of *The Wagon Mound (No 1)* literally and adopted a narrow view of the foreseeable type of harm (mostly dated from shortly after the Privy Council's decision) have produced results which are difficult to justify. For example, in *Doughty v Turner Manufacturing Co Ltd* [1964] 1 QB 518, [1964] 1 All ER 98, a foundry worker accidentally knocked the asbestos cover of a cauldron into the molten metal in the cauldron. Shortly afterwards, an unforeseeable and violent chemical reaction took place between the metal and the asbestos, there was an explosion, and the claimant was showered with molten metal. The Court of Appeal, distinguishing *Hughes*, held that burning by being splashed with molten metal (which was foreseeable) was a different type of harm from being burned by a chemical explosion. Note, however, that in *Attorney General of the British Virgin Islands v Hartwell* [2004] 1 WLR 1273, [2004] UKPC 12, noted p. 1094, post, the Privy Council stated (at [29]) that it 'must be questionable whether a distinction of [the character in *Doughty*] would commend itself to the courts today'. Another restrictive approach to the foreseeable type of harm, albeit obiter, is found in *Tremain v Pike* [1969] 3 All ER 1303. Here, a herdsman employed on the defendant's farm contracted Weil's disease, a disease carried and spread via rats' urine. He sued the defendant, alleging that the defendant was negligent in failing to prevent him coming into contact with rats' urine. Payne J

---

[14]   [1954] 2 All ER 131 at p. 138, [1954] 2 QB 66 at p. 85.

concluded that the defendant was not at fault, since the extra precautions which would be needed to reduce the rat population on the farm 'would not be justified'. Obiter, Payne J went on to hold that, in any event, the risk of Weil's disease was not a reasonably foreseeable type of harm. In his words:

> The kind of damage suffered here was a disease contracted by contact with rats' urine. This, in my view, was entirely different in kind from the effect of a rat-bite, or food poisoning by the consumption of food and drink contaminated by rats. I do not accept that an illness or infection arising from an infestation of rats should be regarded as of the same kind.

See further *Crossley v Rawlinson* [1982] 1 WLR 369 and *Thompson v Bradford* [2005] EWCA Civ 1439.

3. For an example of different results arising from adopting a narrower or a wider view of the foreseeable type of harm, see the decisions of the Court of Appeal and House of Lords in *Jolley v Sutton London Borough Council* [2000] 3 All ER 409, [2000] 1 WLR 1082, noted by R. Williams (2001) 117 LQR 30. The case involved a rotten boat, which had been abandoned outside some flats owned by the defendant council. The council negligently failed to take steps to remove the boat. (For the duty imposed on occupiers under the Occupiers' Liability Act 1957, see p. 564, post.) Two teenage boys saw the abandoned boat and resolved to repair it, so that they might sail it to Cornwall to look for pirates. The boys borrowed a jack, jacked the boat up and crawled underneath it to repair it. One day, the boat slipped from the jack, crushing one of the boys and rendering him severely disabled. In the Court of Appeal, [1998] 3 All ER 559, [1998] 1 WLR 1546, Lord Woolf MR, distinguishing *Hughes*, rejected the claimant's action for damages, He held that 'it was not reasonably foreseeable that an accident could occur as a result of the boys deciding to work under a propped up boat' and '[n]or could any reasonably similar accident have been foreseen'. The House of Lords, however, allowed the appeal. Lord Steyn noted that the judge. at first instance had made a 'central finding...that an accident of the type which in fact occurred was reasonably foreseeable' and that therefore, 'the reasons given by the Court of Appeal are less than satisfactory'. Lord Hoffmann approved the trial judge's classification of the risk, which was that children would 'meddle with the boat at the risk of some physical injury', which was a foreseeable risk.

    In a case where physical injury is not reasonably foreseeable, but psychiatric injury is, and therefore where the doctrine in *Page v Smith* does not apply, it may still be necessary to draw distinctions as to ways in which the psychiatric injury comes about if that can be classified as a different type of damage. Distinctions between different types or methods of suffering psychiatric illness were suggested by *Pratley v Surrey County Council* [2004] ICR 159, [2003] EWCA Civ 1067, an employer/employee case. Although no negligence was found on the part of the employer, two members of the Court of Appeal (Mance and Buxton LJJ; cf. Ward LJ's judgment) drew a distinction (based on mechanism and timing) between a foreseeable risk of psychiatric illness in the future resulting from a continuation of too much work and the unforeseeable immediate psychiatric illness suffered by the claimant as a consequence of returning from holiday and discovering that a particular work practice, which had been talked about and agreed to prior to the holiday, had not been implemented. *Hughes v Lord Advocate* and *Jolley* were distinguished both by Mance LJ; and Buxton LJ distinguished *Jolley* and *Page v Smith* on the ground that they involved a foreseeable and direct injury from a specific source. Consider also *Corr v IBC Vehicles Ltd* [2008]

2 All ER 943, [2008] UKHL 13, noted p. 400, ante, where Lord Bingham, in dealing with foreseeability, stated (at [13]) that he 'could readily accept that some manifestations of severe depression could properly be held to be so unusual and unpredictable as to be outside the bounds of what is reasonably foreseeable, but suicide cannot be so regarded'. (Cf. the judgment of Sedley LJ in the Court of Appeal in *Corr* [2006] 2 All ER 929, [2006] EWCA Civ 331.)

CHAPTER SEVEN

DEFENCES: CONTRIBUTORY NEGLIGENCE, VOLENTI NON FIT INJURIA, EXCLUSION OF LIABILITY, AND ILLEGALITY AND PUBLIC POLICY

Although the question of causation has been considered in the previous chapter, it also plays an important role in the defence of contributory negligence, which, if successful, serves to reduce the claimant's damages. (See e.g. *Stapley v Gypsum Mines Ltd* [1953] AC 663, [1953] 2 All ER 478, p. 433, post.) As the phrase 'contributory negligence' would imply, before this defence will apply to reduce the claimant's damage award the claimant must not only have been negligent, but his negligence must have contributed to the damage which he has suffered: in the absence of this causal connection, the claimant's damages will not be reduced. On the other hand, in certain situations, the claimant's negligence, occurring after the defendant's negligent act, may not only have contributed to some item of damage for which he is claiming compensation, but may be held to have gone so far as to sever the chain of causation between the defendant's act and this damage: this will have the result that the claimant recovers nothing for this particular item. The result here is achieved not by virtue of the defence of contributory negligence, but because there is no sufficient causal connection between the defendant's act and the damage—see *McKew v Holland & Hannen & Cubitts (Scotland) Ltd* [1969] 3 All ER 1621 (p. 389, ante); *Winfield & Jolowicz*, p. 325; M. A. Millner (1971) 22 NILQ 168 at 176–179.

Whereas the phrase 'contributory negligence' gives some idea of the nature of that defence, the maxim volenti non fit injuria needs a greater amount of explanation. In the sphere of intentional interference this defence will be found described as 'consent', p. 754, post. The extent of the distinction, if any, between the scope of the defence of volenti in negligence and the defence of consent in cases of intentional interference with the person is not clear. In *Arthur v Anker* [1997] QB 564 at 572 Sir Thomas Bingham MR stated that 'the distinction 'does not appear to be crucial'. (However, for the uncertain position with regard to whether the defence of contributory negligence is available where intentional infliction of harm has occurred, compare *Murphy v Culhane* [1977] QB 94, [1976] 3 All ER 533, p. 751, post and p. 480 post with the approach adopted by the House of Lords in the deceit case of *Standard Chartered Bank v Pakistan National Shipping Corp* [2003] 1 All ER 173, [2002] UKHL 43, (p. 951, post): see in particular the comments of Lord Rodger at [42]–[45] of the latter decision.) In this chapter the volenti maxim is considered as a defence to the unintentional infliction of injuries and, in this context, writers (e.g. *Fleming*) use the term 'voluntary assumption of risk' to describe this defence.

Some uncertainty exists as to how the volenti maxim operates. *Salmond & Heuston* (at p. 472) mention one view—that there has been a breach of duty, which the claimant waives—but then state that 'the better view is that consent here means the agreement of the plaintiff, express or implied, to exempt the defendant from the duty of care which he would otherwise have owed'. This view was quoted by John Stephenson J in *Buckpitt v Oates* [1968] 1 All ER 11415 at 1148, and seemingly adopted obiter in the House of Lords in *Titchener v British Railways Board* [1983] 3 All ER 770 at 776 (although on the position in Scotland, cf. *Winnik v Dick* 1984 SLT 185). Compare the view adopted in *Freeman v Home Office (No 2)* [1984] QB 524, [1984] 1 All ER 1036. (See also R. W. M. Dias [1966] CLJ 75, esp. at 79.) Note that in *Dann v Hamilton* [1939] 1 KB 509 at 512, Asquith J appeared to combine both views, describing volenti as 'a denial of any duty at all, and, therefore, of any breach of duty'.

Contributory negligence and volenti non fit injuria are separate defences, but they can both be pleaded as defences in the same action. If the volenti defence fails, damages may still be reduced for contributory negligence, and there are important differences between the two defences. These should become apparent from a consideration of the nature of the defences through a study of the materials in this chapter. The most obvious is that the volenti maxim, if successful, provides a complete defence, but a successful plea of contributory negligence leads to a reduction of the damages by the court in accordance with the Law Reform (Contributory Negligence) Act 1945. Whether there can be a 100 per cent reduction for contributory negligence under the 1945 Act has been a matter of some debate, but now may not be available following the decision of the Court of Appeal in *Anderson v Newham College of Further Education* [2002] EWCA Civ 505: see p. 428, post.

The contributory negligence defence is today shaped by the provisions of the Law Reform (Contributory Negligence) Act 1945. Statute plays a less important role in the volenti or assumption of risk doctrine, but it can intervene so as to negate the defence where it might otherwise apply, e.g. s. 149 of the Road Traffic Act 1988 (p. 1144, post), and see also s. 2(3) of the Unfair Contract Terms 1977 (p. 462, post). In certain contexts, however, the volenti doctrine seems to have been enshrined in statutory form. Examples are provided by s. 2(5) of the Occupiers' Liability Act 1957 (p. 586, post) and by s. 5(2) of the Animals Act 1971 (p. 653, post), but see s. 6(5) of that Act (p. 654, post) and see also the views of Ormrod LJ in *Cummings v Granger* [1977] QB 397, at 408 (noted at p. 663, post).

Legislature provisions, in particular the Unfair Contract Terms Act 1977 (p. 462, post), have severely restricted the defendant's freedom to exclude liability in tort. The obvious method of attempting to exclude liability is by contract, but see also *White v Blackmore* [1972] 2 QB 651, [1972] 3 All ER 158 (p. 582, post). The student should consider the relationship between the volenti defence and exclusion of liability, a subject which will be mentioned later in the context of occupiers' liability (p. 582, post) but which is referred to initially in the third section of this chapter.

The final defence considered in this chapter has been variously termed illegality, public policy, or ex turpi causa non oritur actio. For the history of this Latin maxim and criticism of its use, see Windeyer J's judgment in *Smith v Jenkins* [1970] ALR 519 at 527–530. The essence of this defence is that, by virtue of his involvement in some illegal or other conduct, the claimant cannot recover damages for his loss. It should be noted that this defence has been given a very restrictive scope of application. However, in a given situation the defences of contributory negligence, volenti, and illegality or public policy can all be raised. The statutory restrictions on volenti do not rule out the 'illegality' defence, which may therefore prove attractive to defendants: see C. R. Symmons (1973) 123 NLJ 373 at 375; *Pitts v Hunt* [1990] 3 All ER 344 (p. 465, post).

1 CONTRIBUTORY NEGLIGENCE

(a) The defence in general

■ The Law Reform (Contributory Negligence) Act 1945

1. Apportionment of liability in case of contributory negligence.—(1) Where any person suffers damage as the result partly of his own fault and partly of the fault of any other person or persons, a claim in respect of that damage shall not be defeated by reason of the fault of the person suffering the damage, but the damages recoverable in respect thereof shall be reduced to such extent as the court thinks just and equitable having regard to the claimant's share in the responsibility for the damage:

Provided that—

(a) this subsection shall not operate to defeat any defence arising under a contract;

(b) where any contract or enactment providing for the limitation of liability is applicable to the claim, the amount of damages recoverable by the claimant by virtue of this subsection shall not exceed the maximum limit so applicable.

(2) Where damages are recoverable by any person by virtue of the foregoing subsection subject to such reduction as is therein mentioned, the court shall find and record the total damages which would have been recoverable if the claimant had not been at fault.

(5) Where, in any case to which subsection (1) of this section applies, one of the persons at fault avoids liability to any other such person or his personal representative by pleading the Limitation Act 1939[1], or any other enactment limiting the time within which proceedings may be taken, he shall not be entitled to recover any damages…from the other person or representative by virtue of the said subsection.

(6) Where any case to which subsection (1) of this section applies is tried with a jury, the jury shall determine the total damages which would have been recoverable if the claimant had not been at fault and the extent to which those damages are to be reduced.

4. Interpretation.—The following expressions have the meanings hereby respectively assigned to them, that is to say—

'court' means, in relation to any claim, the court or arbitrator by or before whom the claim falls to be determined;

'damage' includes loss of life and personal injury;

'fault' means negligence, breach of statutory duty or other act or omission which gives rise to a liability in tort or would, apart from this Act, give rise to the defence of contributory negligence;

NOTES

1.   On the question of the Act's applicability to:

   (i)   a contractual action, see G. H. Treitel, *The Law of Contract*, 12th edn by E. Peel (London, 2007), paras. 20–105 to 20–112, and note the Law Commission's report, *Contributory Negligence as a Defence in Contract* (Law Com No 219, 1993).

   (ii)   intentional infliction of harm to the person, see p. 751, post.

---

[1] This Act was repealed by the Limitation Act 1980, which was a consolidating measure.

(iii) deceit, see *Alliance and Leicester Building Society v Edgestop Ltd* [1994] 2 All ER 38, [1993] 1 WLR 1462 (p. 949, ante), approved by the House of Lords in *Standard Chartered Bank v Pakistan National Shipping Corpn* [2003] 1 All ER 173, [2002] UKHL 43, (p. 951, post), though note the criticism of the *Alliance and Leicester* case in *Howarth*, p. 661 and see p. 952, post.

2. For there to be contributory negligence under the Act, the claimant must have been at 'fault' according to the definition in s. 4. This definition has been the source of some difficulty because it can be read in a number of ways (see *Nationwide Building Society v Thimbleby* [1999] Lloyd's Rep PN 359). But the most important part of the definition is the final part: 'fault' under the Act includes anything that would have counted as 'fault' *apart* from the Act. This need not be the same as anything that counted as 'fault' *before* the Act, although anything that did so count would prima facie be a strong candidate for counting as fault under the Act. In *Standard Chartered Bank v Pakistan National Shipping Corpn*, Lord Hoffmann adopted the following interpretation of s. 4:

> 11. In my opinion, the definition of 'fault' is divided into two limbs, one of which is applicable to defendants and the other to plaintiffs. In the case of a defendant, fault means 'negligence, breach of statutory duty or other act or omission' which gives rise to a liability in tort. In the case of a plaintiff, it means 'negligence, breach of statutory duty or other act or omission' which gives rise (at common law) to a defence of contributory negligence. The authorities in support of this construction are discussed by Lord Hope of Craighead in *Reeves v Commissioner of Police of the Metropolis* [2000] 1 AC 360, 382. It was also the view of Professor Glanville Williams in *Joint Torts and Contributory Negligence* (1951) at p 318.

> 12. It follows that conduct by a plaintiff cannot be 'fault' within the meaning of the Act unless it gives rise to a defence of contributory negligence at common law. This appears to me in accordance with the purpose of the Act, which was to relieve plaintiffs whose actions would previously have failed and not to reduce the damages which previously would have been awarded against defendants. Section 1(1) makes this clear when it says that 'a claim in respect of that damage shall not be defeated by reason of the fault of the person suffering the damage, but [instead] the damages recoverable in respect thereof shall be reduced . . .'.

This approach obliges the court to consider the common law position as if the Act had never been passed: however, it also allows for development of the pre-Act law, not just for a formalistic recitation of it. Thus in *Reeves v Metropolitan Police Comr* [2000] 1 AC 360, [1999] 3 All ER 897, and *Corr v IBC Vehicles* [2008] UKHL 13 (p. 289, ante), the House of Lords considered that 'fault' could include deliberate self-harm by the claimant, even though there was no pre-Act authority to that effect.

Note that in *Reeves* the House of Lords surprisingly came to the conclusion that the claimant's suicide constituted 'fault' without any detailed consideration of the circumstances in which it occurred—can it be right to assume that self-harm is always unjustified? Consider claimants from cultures in which suicide is sometimes required by powerful codes of honour and where social taboos against suicide are less potent. Consider also the reality that many forms of self-harm stem from impairment of mental well-being which may effectively deny freedom of choice to the deceased.

Their Lordships adopted a more developed analysis of the psychological factors that may result in suicide in *Corr v IBC Vehicles* [2008] UKHL 13, where a majority of the House of Lords considered that there could be a reduction in damages awarded to the claimant for the loss attributable to the suicide of her husband under s. 5 of the Fatal Accidents Act 1976, which provides for awards made to the surviving dependents of a deceased person to be reduced if the deceased's fault contributed to his death and this fault would qualify as contributory negligence under the 1945 Act (see p. 289, post). (Note that only Lord Scott considered that a reduction in damages would be appropriate in this particular case, while Lord Mance and Lord Neuberger considered that such a reduction was possible in principle, but was not appropriate in the circumstances.) The defendant employer was held liable for causing the death of the husband, on the basis that the impairment to the mental well-being of the husband which resulted in his suicide resulted from a breach of a duty of care on the part of the defendant. However, Lords Scott, Mance, and Neuberger considered that it would be inconsistent with the principle of respect of personal autonomy for 100 per cent recovery to be awarded in such circumstances: Lord Mance emphasised at [51] that an 'impairment' should not be taken as wholly denying autonomy and freedom of choice to the deceased and reducing them to the status of an 'automaton' (see also Lord Scott at [31] and Lord Neuberger at [57]–[70]). In contrast, Lord Bingham and Lord Walker considered that in the circumstances no blame or element of 'fault' should be attached to the deceased and therefore no reduction in damages should be ordered, on the basis that the suicide was the result of the injury to his mental well-being which arose from the employer's breach of his duty to prevent causing this form of harm to the deceased. Lord Walker argued at [43] that this approach did not require denying the personal autonomy of the deceased: '[s]uicide was his decision, but it came from his feelings of worthlessness and hopelessness, which were the result of his depression, which was in turn the result of his accident'.

Common law 'fault' is a wide concept, and includes any failure by the claimant to take reasonable care for his or her own safety. It does not depend on any notion of the claimant owing a duty to anyone. Lord Hope in *Reeves* cited with approval the following statement of *Prosser & Keeton, Torts*, 5th edn (1984) section 65, p. 453:

Negligence as it is commonly understood is conduct which creates an undue risk of harm to others. Contributory negligence is conduct which involves an undue risk of harm to the actor himself. Negligence requires a duty, an obligation of conduct to another person. Contributory negligence involves no duty, unless we are to be so ingenuous as to say that the plaintiff is under an obligation to protect the defendant against liability for the consequences of the plaintiff's own negligence.

In an attempt, however, to ensure that the Act causes minimal change to the pre-Act law, the courts tend to interpret the other elements of the s. 4 definition narrowly. For example, contrary to their general view of fault apart from the Act, they tend to interpret 'negligence' in s. 4 as requiring the full tort (duty, breach, causation, and damage) rather than just the 'breach' element (see *Nationwide Building Society v Thimbleby*, [1999] Lloyd's Rep PN 359). It must be remembered, however, that, as applied to the claimant's conduct, the only function of the first three parts of the s. 4 definition (negligence, breach of statutory duty, or some other tort) is to *extend* the scope of contributory negligence beyond the original boundaries of the common law definition.

It should, however, be mentioned that there is a view that the drafting of the Act is an example of excessive elegance. To allow s. 1 to use the elegant parallel phrase 'partly of his own fault and partly of the fault of any other person or persons', s. 4's definition of 'fault' has to cover two very distinct concepts—what kinds of *liability* the defence applies to and what kind of *conduct* on the part of the claimant triggers the defence. The former explains the presence of the first three parts of the definition, the latter explains the presence of the fourth. The ambiguity of the language of s. 4 stems from this attempt to combine different elements within a single provision.

3.   The elegance of s. 1 is responsible for two other problems. First, what should happen where there is 'damage' for which the defendant is not responsible in tort in the first place but which has arisen from the 'fault' of the claimant? It has always been accepted that such damage is excluded from consideration. The court should calculate the total loss for which the defendant would otherwise be liable and then ask whether the claimant's fault contributed to that damage (see *Drinkwater v Kimber* [1952] 2 QB 281). But in *Platform Home Loans Ltd v Oyston Shipways Ltd* [2000] 2 AC 190, [1999] 1 All ER 833, Lord Hobhouse appears to endorse Morritt LJ's view, expressed in the same case in the Court of Appeal [1998] Ch 466, [1998] 4 All ER 265, that s. 1 is not restricted to damage caused both by the defendant's fault and by the claimant's fault (for the economic loss dimension to this case, see p. 277, ante). Such an interpretation would have extraordinary effects (see Howarth (2000) 8 Tort L Rev 85 at 87): for example, where the claimant's fault results in some damage for which the defendant is not liable (e.g. pure economic losses, mere emotional distress, or other non-recoverable forms of loss which are additional to the damage caused to the claimant by the defendant's breach of duty of care), the value of that damage under this approach would nevertheless be included in the total loss. Also, since s. 1 refers to 'other person or persons', presumably Morritt LJ's view means that harm caused by an intervening act that broke the chain of causation has to be counted against the defendant and, just as extraordinary, contributory negligence that only contributed to the damage caused by the intervention would count against the claimant for the whole loss. The *Drinkwater* view (endorsed by Lord Cooke in his dissenting opinion in *Platform*) is thus much to be preferred. Fortunately, the result in *Platform* can be justified on the alternative grounds put forward by Lord Millett (see p. 278, ante).

Second, there is the issue, mentioned in the introduction to this chapter, as to whether the Act allows 100 per cent contributory negligence. In *Pitts v Hunt* [1991] 1 QB 24 at 48 at 51 the Court of Appeal insisted that the word 'partly' in s. 1 means that 100 per cent reductions are impossible—if the claimant is 100 per cent responsible, it was claimed, the defendant could not be 'partly' responsible. See, however, *Howarth*, p. 658, who points out that such a finding has been approved in earlier cases and also that in any event, if the 1945 Act does not apply in situations where the claimant is 100 per cent responsible, then the claim will be in any case completely barred by the operation of the defence of contributory negligence at common law (see p. 430, post). In *Reeves v Metropolitan Police Comr* [1999] QB 169, [1998] 2 All ER 381, Morritt LJ pointed out that the Court of Appeal in *Pitts v Hunt* had not been referred to a previous Court of Appeal decision (*Jayes v IMI (Kynoch) Ltd* [1985] ICR 155) which had made an apportionment of 100 per cent: he considered that such an apportionment was appropriate in this case. However, in the same case, Lord Bingham LCJ thought that cases where a 100 per cent reduction had been made were perhaps 'properly to be understood as based on causation'.

When *Reeves* went to the House of Lords, [2000] 1 AC 360, [1999] 3 All ER 897, the question of the possibility of a 100 per cent reduction was not expressly discussed. However, in *Anderson v Newham College of Further Education* [2002] EWCA Civ 505, Sedley LJ questioned the authority of *Jayes v IMI (Kynoch) Ltd* as precedent, noting in particular that the decision of the House of Lords in *Boyle v Kodak* [1969] 2 All ER 439 on the scope of the employer's duty in question had not been referred to in *Jayes*. He proceeded to agree with Bedlam LJ in *Pitts v Hunt* that when a defendant establishes that the blame for the damage rests with the claimant, then there is no liability to be apportioned under s. 1 of the 1945 Act.

In sum, *Jayes* should, in my respectful view, not be followed by judges of first instance and should not be relied upon by advocates in argument. The relevant principles are straightforward. Whether the claim is in negligence or for breach of statutory duty, if the evidence, once it has been appraised as the law requires, shows the entire fault to lie with the claimant there is no liability on the defendant. If not, then the court will consider to what extent, if any, the claimant's share in the responsibility for the damage makes it just and equitable to reduce his damages. The phrase '100 per cent contributory negligence', while expressive, is unhelpful, because it invites the court to treat a statutory qualification of the measure of damages as if it were a secondary or surrogate approach to liability, which it is not. If there is liability, contributory negligence can reduce its monetary quantification, but it cannot legally or logically nullify it.

The Court of Appeal took a similar approach in *Buyukardicli v Hammerson UK Properties Plc* [2002] EWCA Civ 683, where Sedley LJ reiterated at para. 7 that 'conceptually, 100 per cent contributory negligence does not exist. It can only arise, putting it shortly, where there is primary fault; and, where there is primary fault, what the statute permits is an allocation of blame, not a negation of it.' See also the Australian case of *Wynbergen v Hoyts Corporation* (1997) 149 ALR 25.

■ Admiralty Comrs v SS Volute (Owners), The Volute

House of Lords [1922] All ER Rep 193

There was a collision between the *Volute* (an oil tank ship) and the *Radstock*, one of two destroyers in charge of a convoy of which the *Volute* was a member. The Court of Appeal had held the *Radstock* to be alone to blame. However, there was an appeal and the House of Lords held on the evidence that the *Volute* had been negligent in not giving a short blast on her whistle on altering her course. They also held the *Radstock* to blame for increasing her speed shortly before the collision.

VISCOUNT BIRKENHEAD LC:...
The matter, therefore rests in this way. On the one hand, if the *Volute* had signalled or had postponed her porting unless and until she signalled there would have been no collision. On the other hand, if the *Radstock* had not gone full speed ahead after the position of danger brought about by the action of the *Volute*, there would have been no collision...Contributory negligence certainly arises when the negligence is contemporaneous, but are the only cases of contributory negligence cases where the negligence is contemporaneous? Is it to be the rule in all cases if the tribunal can find a period at which A's negligence has ceased and after which B's negligence has begun that then the negligence of A is to be disregarded? If such should be the rule it will be found that the cases of contributory negligence would be few...

Upon the whole I think that this question of contributory negligence must be dealt with somewhat broadly and upon commonsense principles as a jury would probably dealt with it. While, no doubt, where a clear line can be drawn, the subsequent negligence is the only one to look to, there are cases in which the two acts come so closely together, and the second act of negligence is so much mixed up with the state of things brought about by the first act that the party secondly negligent, while not held free from blame...might, on the other hand, invoke the prior negligence as being part of the cause of the collision so as to make it a case of contribution....

Your Lordships have now to apply these considerations of law to the facts of the present case. As already stated, if the *Volute* had not neglected to give the appropriate whistle signal when she ported there would have been no collision. On the other hand, if the *Radstock*, in the position of danger brought about by the action of the *Volute* had not gone full speed ahead, there would have been no collision. The case seems to me to resemble somewhat closely that of *The Hero*.[2] In that case, as in this, notwithstanding the negligent navigation of the first ship, the collision could have been avoided if proper action had been taken by the second ship. Indeed, that case is remarkable because the proper order was actually given, but unfortunately countermanded. In that case this House held both vessels to blame, apparently considering the acts of navigation on the two ships as forming parts of one trans-action, and the second act of negligence as closely following upon and involved with the first. In the present case there does not seem to be a sufficient separation of time, place or circumstance between the negligent navigation of the *Radstock* and that of the *Volute* to make it right to treat the negligence on board the *Radstock* as the sole cause of the collision. The *Volute*, in the ordinary plain common sense of this business, having contributed to the accident, it would be right for your Lordships to hold both vessels to blame for the collision....

[VISCOUNT CAVE, VISCOUNT FINLAY, LORD SHAW, and LORD PHILLIMORE concurred.]

Appeal allowed.

NOTE

It will have been noticed that *The Volute* was decided before the enactment of the Law Reform (Contributory Negligence) Act. At common law the rule was that a claimant who was con-tributorily negligent failed in his action (see e.g. *Butterfield v Forrester* (1809) 11 East 60, but see the doctrine of 'last opportunity', p. 432, post). In contrast to the position at common law, the rule which developed in Admiralty was one of equal apportionment of the loss if a collision was caused by the negligence of both vessels (see *Glanville Williams*, pp. 341–342), but this was altered by the Maritime Conventions Act 1911. The relevant provisions of the 1911 Act were repealed and re-enacted by the Merchant Shipping Act 1995, s. 187(1), which states that '[w]here, by the fault of two or more ships, damage or loss is caused to one or more of those ships, to their cargoes or freight, or to any property on board, the liability to make good the damage or loss shall be in proportion to the degree in which each ship was in fault'. Liability is apportioned equally if, in a case to which s. 187(1) applies, it is not possible to establish different degrees of fault (s. 187(2)).

The *Volute* was concerned with Admiralty matters, but in *Marvin Sigurdson v British Columbia Electric Rly Co Ltd* [1953] AC 291, Lord Tucker, delivering judgment in the Privy Council, referred to certain of the passages quoted above in Viscount Birkenhead's judg-ment in *The Volute* and stated (at p. 299):

This was an Admiralty case, but now that common law courts have to apply the same principles to cases of collisions on land it seems to their Lordships that this language will be found particularly suited to the exposition to a jury of the principles which they have to apply in these cases, and is much to be preferred to attempts to classify acts in relation to one another with reference to time or with regard to the knowledge of one party at a particular moment of the negligence of the other party and his appreciation of the resulting danger, and by such tests to create categories in some of which one party is solely liable and others in which both parties are liable. Time and knowledge may often be decisive factors, but it is for the jury or other tribunal of fact to decide whether in any particular case the existence of one of these factors results or does not result in the ascertainment of that clear line to which Viscount Birkenhead referred—moreover, their Lordships do not read him as intending to lay down that the existence of "subsequent" negligence will alone enable that clear line to be found.

---

[2] [1912] AC 300.

■ Jones v Livox Quarries Ltd

Court of Appeal [1952] 2 QB 608

The plaintiff, an employee of the defendants, stood contrary to his instructions on the back of a traxcavator, a vehicle which travelled at about two and a half mph. The lunchtime whistle had gone, and the traxcavator was travelling along the route to the canteen. The driver gave evidence that he was not aware of the plaintiff's presence on the vehicle. Having driven the traxcavator round a stationary excavator and made a sharp left turn, the traxcavator was stopped (or nearly stopped) by the driver so that he could change gear. A dumper, travelling behind the traxcavator, collided with the back of that vehicle, injuring the plaintiff. Hallett J found that the dumper driver had been negligent, but that the plaintiff had been contributorily negligent, and reduced his damages by one-fifth. There was an appeal by the plaintiff, and a cross-appeal by the defendants (the employers of the dumper driver) to the Court of Appeal.

DENNING LJ: ...

The case of *Davies v Swan Motor Co (Swansea) Ltd*[3] has been much discussed before us. It has been said that the three judgments in that case do not proceed on precisely the same lines. That is true, but it is, I suggest, quite understandable, because the court was there feeling its way in difficult country. Since that time, however, the ground has been cleared considerably. It can now be safely asserted that the doctrine of last opportunity[4] is obsolete; and also that contributory negligence does not depend on the existence of a duty. But the troublesome problem of causation still remains to be solved.

Although contributory negligence does not depend on a duty of care, it does depend on foreseeability. Just as actionable negligence requires the foreseeability of harm to others, so contributory negligence requires the foreseeability of harm to oneself. A person is guilty of contributory negligence if he ought reasonably to have foreseen that, if he did not act as a reasonable, prudent man, he might be hurt himself; and in his reckonings he must take into account the possibility of others being careless.

Once negligence is proved, then no matter whether it is actionable negligence or contributory negligence, the person who is guilty of it must bear his proper share of responsibility for the consequences. The consequences do not depend on foreseeability, but on causation. The question in every case is: What faults were there which caused the damage? Was his fault one of them? The necessity of causation is shown by the word 'result' in s. 1(1) of the Act of 1945, and it was accepted by this court in *Davies v Swan Motor Co (Swansea) Ltd*.

There is no clear guidance to be found in the books about causation. All that can be said is that causes are different from the circumstances in which, or on which, they operate. The line between the two depends on the facts of each case. It is a matter of common sense more than anything else. In the present case, as the argument of Mr Arthian Davies proceeded, it seemed to me that he sought to make foreseeability the decisive test of causation. He relied on the trial judge's statement that a man who rode on the towbar of the traxcavator 'ran the risk of being thrown off and no other risk'. That is, I think, equivalent to saying that such a man could reasonably foresee that he might be thrown off the traxcavator, but not that he might be crushed between it and another vehicle.

In my opinion, however, foreseeability is not the decisive test of causation. It is often a relevant factor, but it is not decisive. Even though the plaintiff did not foresee the possibility of being crushed, nevertheless in the ordinary plain common sense of this business the injury suffered by the plaintiff was due in part to the fact that he chose to ride on the towbar to lunch instead of walking down on his feet. If he had been thrown off in the collision, Mr Arthian Davies admits that his injury would be partly due to his own negligence in riding on the towbar; but he says that, because he was crushed, and not thrown off, his injury is in no way due to it. That is too fine a distinction for me. I cannot believe that that purely fortuitous circumstance can make all the difference to the case. ...

---

[3] [1949] 2 KB 291, [1949] 1 All ER 620.   [4] See p. 432, post.

In order to illustrate this question of causation, I may say that if the plaintiff, whilst he was riding on the towbar, had been hit in the eye by a shot from a negligent sportsman, I should have thought that the plaintiff's negligence would in no way be a cause of his injury. It would only be the circumstance in which the cause operated. It would only be part of the history. But I cannot say that in the present case. The man's negligence here was so much mixed up with his injury that it cannot be dismissed as mere history. His dangerous position on the vehicle was one of the causes of his damage....

The present case is a good illustration of the practical effect of the Act of 1945. In the course of the argument my Lord suggested that before the Act of 1945 he would have regarded this case as one where the plaintiff should recover in full. That would be because the negligence of the dumper driver would then have been regarded as the predominant cause. Now, since the Act, we have regard to all the causes, and one of them undoubtedly was the plaintiff's negligence in riding on the towbar of the traxcavator. His share in the responsibility was not great—the trial judge assessed it at one-fifth—but, nevertheless, it was his share, and he must bear it himself....

It all comes to this: If a man carelessly rides on a vehicle in a dangerous position, and subsequently there is a collision in which his injuries are made worse by reason of his position than they otherwise would have been, then his damage is partly the result of his own fault, and the damages recoverable by him fall to be reduced accordingly.

[SINGLETON and HODSON LJJ delivered the judgments in favour of dismissing the appeal and cross-appeal.]

Appeal and cross-appeal dismissed.

NOTES

1.   For comment on Denning LJ's treatment of causation in *Jones v Livox Quarries Ltd*, see I. Fagelson (1979) 42 MLR 646 at 655–656.

2.   The effect of the complicated 'last opportunity' doctrine (which in Denning LJ's opinion is obsolete) is explained by the following passage from *Winfield & Jolowicz* (p. 318—footnotes omitted):

> If the claimant's injuries have been caused partly by the negligence of the defendant and partly by his own negligence, then, at common law, the claimant could recover nothing... The courts modified the defence of contributory negligence by the so-called rule of last opportunity. This enabled the plaintiff to recover notwithstanding his own negligence, if upon the occasion of the accident the defendant could have avoided the accident while the plaintiff could not. The authorities were confused, and confusion was made worse confounded by the extension of the rule, in *British Columbia Electric Ry Co v Loach* [1916] 1 AC 719, to cases of 'constructive last opportunity.' This meant that if the defendant would have had the last opportunity but for his own negligence, he was in the same position as if he had actually had it, and the plaintiff again recovered in full.

For further reading on this topic, see *Glanville Williams*, chap. 9 and §66; A. L. Goodhart (1949) 65 LQR 237; *Rouse v Squires* [1973] QB 889, [1973] 2 All ER 903. In *Lloyds Bank Ltd v Budd* [1982] RTR 80 Lord Denning MR reiterated his opinion about the 'last opportunity' rule, saying that it had 'gone forever'. If so, note that there are now cases in which damages are reduced under the Act but in which there would have been no contributory negligence at all before the Act.

3.   The Court of Appeal in *Sahib Foods Ltd v Paskin Kyriakides Sands (a firm)* [2003] EWCA Civ 1832 reiterated that a claimant's negligence could serve to reduce the damages arising from a breach of the defendant's duty towards the claimant, even where that duty was to protect the claimant against the consequences of any negligence on their part. Clarke LJ took the view that in such a situation, it would only be in a case where 'it could be seen that the whole of the responsibility for the damage was the defendants' failure

to protect the claimants' against their own negligence, that it would be appropriate to hold that the claimant was not guilty of contributory negligence (para. 68)'. See also *Reeves v Metropolitan Police Comr* [2000] 1 AC 360, [1999] 3 All ER 897, and *Calvert v William Hill Credit Ltd* [2008] EWHC 454, where despite the existence of a duty of care on a bookmaker to take steps to prevent the claimant, a pathological gambler, using their facilities for gambling, Briggs J took the view that the claimant would have been mainly responsible through his own conduct for the losses he had incurred, even if the bookmaker's breach of duty had in fact caused loss.

■ Stapley v Gypsum Mines Ltd
House of Lords [1953] 2 All ER 478

Appeal from an order of the Court of Appeal (Singleton, Birkett and Morris LJJ), dated 7 April 1952, and reported, [1952] 1 All ER 1092, reversing an order of Sellers J, dated 20 December 1951.

The appellant, the widow of a miner employed in the respondents' gypsum mine, claimed damages against the respondents ... in respect of the death of her husband which was caused by the fall of the roof of a stope in which he was working. The deceased and a fellow work-man had been charged by the respondents with the duty of bringing down the roof so as to make the stope safe to work in, but they had failed to do so, and the deceased had gone to work in the stope. The learned judge found in favour of the appellant on the ground that the respondents were liable for the negligence or breach of statutory duty of the workman who was working with the deceased, but he deducted one half of the award which he would otherwise have made, as he held that the deceased was partly to blame for the accident. On an appeal by the respondents and cross-appeal by the appellant, the Court of Appeal held that the deceased's own negligence and breach of statutory duty, and not that of the respond-ents, was the substantial cause of the deceased's death, and, accordingly, they allowed the appeal and dismissed the cross-appeal.

LORD REID: . . .
My Lords, in the respondents' mines the workings are driven at right angles away from the main haul-age way. The actual working place is the stope and the part between it and the haulage way is the twitten. The miners all work in pairs, one being the borer and the other the breaker. There is no sharp demarcation between their work and neither can give orders to the other, though the borer appears to be the senior man. Before the accident Stapley and Dale were working together, Stapley being the breaker. He was a steady workman with long experience, but rather slow. He had for a time been a borer but had reverted to being a breaker. A well recognised danger in the mine is a fall of part of the roof. The roof is not generally shored up as any weakness in it can be detected by tapping it. If it is 'drummy', giving a hollow sound, it is unsafe and must be taken down. There are three ways of doing this—with a pick, or with a pinch bar or crow bar, or by firing a shot. Whichever way is adopted, of course, men doing the necessary work must not stand immediately below the dangerous part of the roof. One morning when Stapley and Dale arrived at their stope they tested the roof and found it to be drummy. They saw the foreman, Church, about it and he ordered them to fetch it down. They all knew that that meant that no one was to work under the roof before it had come down. Church did not say which method was to be adopted. Both men were accustomed to this work and the method was properly left to their discretion. They used picks, but after half an hour had made no impression. The work was awkwardly placed as a fault ran across the mouth of the stope, the floor and roof inside being about eighteen inches higher than outside it. Probably they could not use a pinch bar, but they

could easily have prepared the place for firing a shot and sent for the shot-firer. Instead, according to Dale whose evidence was accepted, they agreed that the roof was safe enough for them to resume their ordinary work, and did so. There was a quantity of gypsum lying in the stope and if the roof had been safe their first task would have been to get this to the haulage way. To do that, Stapley had to enter the stope and break the gypsum into smaller pieces and Dale had to make preparations in the twitten. So they separated, and when Dale came back half an hour later he found Stapley lying dead in the stope under a large piece of the roof which had fallen on him.

There is no doubt that if these men had obeyed their orders the accident would not have happened. Both acted in breach of orders and in breach of safety regulations, and both ought to have known quite well that it was dangerous for Stapley to enter the stope. The present action against the respondents is chiefly based on Dale's fault having contributed to the accident, and on the respondents being responsible for it, the defence of common employment being no longer available. So it is necessary to consider what would have happened if Dale had done his duty. It was his duty either to try a pinch bar or to start boring holes for the shot-firer, and on the evidence I think that it is highly probable that, if he had insisted on doing that instead of agreeing with Stapley to neglect their orders and the regulations, Stapley would not have stood out against him or tried to resume his ordinary work. Stapley had nothing to gain from his disobedience, and, if he had not found Dale in agreement with him, it appears to me unlikely that he would have persisted. But if he had persisted and thereby prevented Dale from carrying out his orders—because Dale could not have worked at the roof if Stapley had persisted in going below it—then it was Dale's duty to go for the foreman, as he, Dale, could not give orders to Stapley. We do not know how soon the roof fell or how long it would have taken Dale to find and bring the foreman, but it is, at least, quite likely that the foreman would have arrived in time to prevent the accident. If Dale's failure to contribute to the accident, then I do not see on what ground the respondents can escape liability in respect of that failure.

In these circumstances it is necessary to determine what caused the death of Stapley. If it was caused solely by his own fault, then the appellant cannot succeed. But if it was caused partly by his own fault and partly by the fault of Dale, then the appellant can rely on the Law Reform (Contributory Negligence) Act 1945. To determine what caused an accident from the point of view of legal liability is a most difficult task. If there is any valid logical or scientific theory of causation, it is quite irrelevant to this connection. In a court of law, this question must be decided as a properly instructed and reasonable jury would decide it. . . . The question must be determined by applying common sense to the facts of each particular case. One may find that, as a matter of history, several people have been an fault and that if any one of them had acted properly the accident would not have happened, but that does not mean that the accident must be regarded as having been caused by the faults of all of them. One must discriminate between those faults which must be discarded as being too remote and those which must not. Sometimes it is proper to discard all but one and to regard that one as the sole cause, but in other cases it is proper to regard two or more as having jointly caused the accident. I doubt whether any test can be applied generally. It may often be dangerous to apply to this kind of case tests which have been used in traffic accidents by land or sea, but in this case I think it useful to adopt phrases from the speech of Viscount Birkenhead LC ([1922] 1 AC 129, pp. 144, 145) in *Admiralty Comrs v SS Volute*, and to ask: Was Dale's fault 'so much mixed up with the state of things brought about' by Stapley that 'in the ordinary plain common sense of this business' it must be regarded as having contributed to the accident? I can only say that I think it was and that there was no 'sufficient separation of time, place or circumstance' between them to justify its being excluded. Dale's fault was one of omission rather than commission and it may often be impossible to say that, if a man had done what he omitted to do, the accident would certainly have been prevented. It is enough, in my judgment, if there is a sufficiently high degree of probability that the accident would have been prevented. I have already stated my view of the probabilities in this case and I think that it must lead to the conclusion that Dale's fault ought to be regarded as having contributed to the accident.

Finally, it is necessary to apply the Law Reform (Contributory Negligence) Act 1945. Sellers J reduced the damages by one half holding both parties equally to blame. Normally one would not disturb such an award, but Sellers J does not appear to have taken into account the fact that Stapley deliberately and culpably entered the stope. By doing so, it appears to me that he contributed to the accident much more directly than Dale. Section 1(1) of the Act directs that the damages

> '... shall be reduced to such extent as the court thinks just and equitable having regard to the claimant's share in the responsibility for the damage.'

A court must deal broadly with the problem of apportionment, and, in considering what is just and equitable, must have regard to the blameworthiness of each party, but 'the claimant's share in the responsibility for the damage' cannot, I think, be assessed without considering the relative importance of his acts in causing the damage apart from his blameworthiness. It may be that in this case Dale was not much less to blame than Stapley, but Stapley's conduct in entering the stope contributed more immediately to the accident than anything that Dale did or failed to do. I agree with your Lordships that in all the circumstances it is proper in this case to reduce the damages by eighty per cent and to award twenty per cent of the damages to the appellant. I have not dealt with the question whether, at the time of the accident, the respondents were in breach of reg. 7(3) of the Metalliferous Mines General Regulations 1938, because, whichever way that question was decided, it would not in this case affect my view as to the amount by which the damages should be reduced.

[LORD TUCKER and LORD OAKSEY delivered speeches in favour of allowing the appeal. LORD PORTER and LORD ASQUITH OF BISHOPSTONE delivered speeches in favour of dismissing the appeal.]

Appeal allowed.

■ Froom v Butcher

Court of Appeal [1975] 3 All ER 520

Mr Froom was driving his car carefully along a road at a speed of between 30 and 35 mph with his wife sitting beside him in the front and his daughter in the back seat. The front seats of the car were fitted with seat belts but neither Mr nor Mrs Froom was wearing them. Unfortunately, Mr Froom's car was struck head on by a car travelling quickly in the opposite direction and on its wrong side of the road as it had pulled out to overtake a line of traffic. Nield J, [1974] 3 All ER 517, held that failure to wear a seat belt was not contributory negligence. There was an appeal to the Court of Appeal. It should be noted that at the time this case was decided, it was not compulsory to wear seat belts: see p. 439, post.

LORD DENNING MR: . . .
Mr Froom and his wife and daughter were all injured. Mr Froom was forced up against the steering column. He had a broken rib and bruises on his chest. He had abrasions on his head. He would probably have been saved from these injuries if he had worn a seat belt. He also had a broken finger, but the seat belt would not have saved that. These injuries were not at all severe. He was back at work next day. The judge assessed his general damages at £450. Mrs Froom was also injured but the seat belt would not have saved her from them. The question that arises is whether Mr Froom's damages are to be reduced because he was not wearing a seat belt. The judge held they were not. The defendant appeals to this court.

This is the first case to reach this court about seat belts. But there have been a dozen or more cases in the lower courts; and they have disclosed a remarkable conflict of opinion. Half the judges think that, if a person does not wear a seat belt, he is guilty of contributory negligence and his damages ought to be reduced. The other half think that it is not contributory negligence and they ought not to be reduced. . . .

The cause of the damage

In these seat belt cases, the injured plaintiff is in no way to blame for the accident itself. Sometimes he is an innocent passenger sitting beside a negligent driver who goes off the road. At other times he is an innocent driver of one car which is run into by the bad driving of another car which pulls out on to its wrong side of the road. It may well be asked: Why should the injured plaintiff have his damages reduced? The accident was solely caused by the negligent driving by the defendant. Sometimes outrageously bad driving. It should not lie in his mouth to say: 'You ought to have been wearing a seat belt.'...

I do not think that is the correct approach. The question is not what was the cause of the accident. It is rather what was the cause of the damage. In most accidents on the road the bad driving, which causes the accident, also causes the ensuing damage. But in seat belt cases the cause of the accident is one thing. The cause of the damage is another. The *accident* is caused by the bad driving. The *damage* is caused in part by the bad driving of the defendant, and in part by the failure of the plaintiff to wear a seat belt. If the plaintiff was to blame in not wearing a seat belt, the damage is in part the result of his own fault. He must bear some share in the responsibility for the damage and his damages fall to be reduced to such extent as the court thinks just and equitable....

The sensible practice

It is compulsory for every motor car to be fitted with seat belts for the front seats. The regulations[5] so provide. They apply to every motor car registered since [1 Jan] 1965. In the regulations seat belts are called, in cumbrous language, 'body-restraining seat belts.' A 'seat belt' is defined[6] as 'a belt intended to be worn by a person in a vehicle and designed to prevent or lessen injury to its wearer in the event of an accident to the vehicle...'

Seeing that it is compulsory to fit seat belts, Parliament must have thought it sensible to wear them. But it did not make it compulsory for anyone to wear a seat belt. Everyone is free to wear it or not, as he pleases.[7] Free in this sense, that if he does not wear it, he is free from any penalty by the magistrates. Free in the sense that everyone is free to run his head against a brick wall, if he pleases. He can do it if he likes without being punished by the law. But it is not a sensible thing to do. If he does it, it is his own fault; and he has only himself to thank for the consequences.

Much material has been put before us about the value of wearing a seat belt. It shows quite plainly that everyone in the front seats of a car should wear a seat belt. Not only on long trips, but also on short ones. Not only in the town, but also in the country. Not only when there is fog, but also when it is clear. Not only by fast drivers, but also by slow ones. Not only on motorways, but also on side roads....this material confirms the provision of the Highway Code which contains this advice: 'Fit seat belts in your car and make sure they are always used.' This advice has been in the Highway Code since 1968, and should have been known to Mr Froom at the time of his accident in November 1972.

The Road Traffic [Act] 1972 says that a failure to observe that provision does not render a person liable to criminal proceedings of any kind, but it can be relied on in civil proceedings as tending to establish or negative liability: see 37(5)[8]....

The effect of failure to wear a seat belt

(i) *Majority versus minority*

Quite a lot of people, however, think differently about seat belts. Some are like Mr Froom here. They think that they would be less likely to injured if they were thrown clear than if they were strapped in. They would be wrong. The chances of injury are four times as great. Yet they believe it honestly and firmly. On this account Nield J thought they should not bear any responsibility. He recognised that such

---

[5] Motor Vehicles (Construction and Use) Regulations 1973 (SI 1973/24).   [6] Regulation 17(9).
[7] But see now p. 439, post.   [8] See now s. 38(7) of the Road Traffic Act 1988.

persons are in a minority, but he thought that proper respect should be paid to the minority view. He said:[9]

> '...I do not feel that the courts are justified in invading the freedom of choice of the motorist by holding it to be negligence, lack of care or fault to act on an opinion firmly and honestly held and shared by many other sensible people.'

I am afraid I do not agree. In determining responsibility, the law eliminates the personal equation. It takes no notice of the views of the particular individual; or of others like him. It requires everyone to exercise all such precautions as a man of ordinary prudence would observe: see *Vaughan v Menlove*;[10] *Glasgow Corpn v Muir*[11] by Lord Macmillan. Nowadays, when we have no juries to help us, it is the duty of the judge to say what a man of ordinary prudence would do. He should make up his own mind, leaving it to the Court of Appeal to correct him if he is wrong.

(ii) *The high risk argument*
Other people take the view that the risk of an accident is so remote that it is not necessary to wear a seat belt on all occasions; but only when there are circumstances which carry a high risk, for example, driving on a motorway in conditions of fog, ice or snow; or engaging in road racing activities. . . . I cannot accept this view either. You never know when a risk may arise. It often happens suddenly and when least anticipated, when there is no time to fasten the seat belt. Besides, it is easy to forget when only done occasionally. But, done regularly, it becomes automatic. Every time a car goes out on the road there is the risk of an accident. Not that you yourself will be negligent. But that someone else will be. That is a possibility which a prudent man should, and will, guard against. He should always, if he is wise, wear a seat belt.

(iii) *Mere forgetfulness*
Lastly, there are many people who do not wear their seat belts, simply through forgetfulness or inadvertence or thoughtlessness. Their fault is far less serious than that of the negligent driver who causes an accident. Some judges have expressed themselves strongly about this . . . I am afraid I cannot share this view. The case for wearing seat belts is so strong that I do not think the law can admit forgetfulness as an excuse. If it were, everyone would say: 'Oh, I forgot.' In order to bring home the importance of wearing seat belts, the law should say that a person who fails to wear it must share some responsibility for the damages.

Thus far I have spoken only of the ordinary run of cases. There are, of course, exceptions. A man who is unduly fat or a woman who is pregnant may rightly be excused because, if there is an accident, the strap across the abdomen may do more harm than good. But, apart from such cases, in the ordinary way a person who fails to wear a seat belt should accept some share of responsibility for the damage—if it could have been prevented or lessened by wearing it.

The share of responsibility
Whenever there is an accident, the negligent driver must bear by far the greater share of responsibility. It was his negligence which caused the accident. It also was a prime cause of the whole of the damage. But insofar as the damage might have been avoided or lessened by wearing a seat belt, the injured person must bear some share. But how much should this be? Is it proper to enquire whether the driver was grossly negligent or only slightly negligent? or whether the failure to wear a seat belt was entirely inexcusable or almost forgivable? If such an enquiry could easily be undertaken, it might be as well to do it. In *Davies v Swan Motor Co*[11] we said that consideration should be given not only to the causative potency of a particular factor, but also its blameworthiness. But we live in a practical world. In most of these cases the liability of the driver is admitted; the failure to wear a seat belt is admitted; the only

---

[9] [1974] 3 All ER at p. 520, [1974] 1 WLR at p. 1302.
[10] (1837) 3 Bing NC 468, [1835–42] All ER Rep 156.
[11] [1943] AC 448 at 457, [1943] 2 All ER 44 at 48.

question is: what damages should be payable? This question should not be prolonged by an expensive enquiry into the degree of blame-worthiness on either side, which would be hotly disputed. Suffice it to assess a share of responsibility which will be just and equitable in the great majority of cases.

Sometimes the evidence will show that the failure made no difference. The damage would have been the same, even if a seat belt had been worn. In such cases the damages should not be reduced at all. At other times the evidence will show that the failure made all the difference. The damage would have been prevented altogether if a seat belt had been worn. In such cases I would suggest that the damages should be reduced by 25 per cent. But often enough the evidence will only show that the failure made a considerable difference. Some injuries to the head, for instance, would have been a good deal less severe if a seat belt had been worn, but there would still have been some injury to the head. In such a case I would suggest that the damages attributable to the failure to wear a seat belt should be reduced by 15 per cent.

Conclusion

Everyone knows, or ought to know, that when he goes out in a car he should fasten the seat belt. It is so well-known that it goes without saying, not only for the driver, but also the passenger. If either the driver or the passenger fails to wear it and an accident happens—and the injuries would have been prevented or lessened if he had worn it—then his damages should be reduced. Under the Highway Code a driver may have a duty to invite his passenger to fasten his seat belt, but adult passengers possessed of their faculties should not need telling what to do. If such passengers do not fasten their seat belts, their own lack of care for their own safety may be the cause of their injuries. In the present case the injuries to the head and chest would have been prevented by the wearing of a seat belt and the damages on that account might be reduced by 25 per cent. The figure would have been broken anyway and the damages for it not reduced at all. Overall the judge suggested 20 per cent and Mr Froom has made no objection to it. So I would not interfere.

I would allow the appeal and reduce the damages by £100.

[LAWTON and SCARMAN LJJ agreed.]

Appeal allowed.

QUESTIONS

1. Is it consistent with s. 1(1) of the Law Reform (Contributory Negligence) Act 1945 for Lord Denning to suggest fixed percentage reductions in certain types of cases? (See further J. R. Spencer [1976] CLJ 44, at 45.)

2. Do Lord Denning's suggested percentage reductions apply in the case of a driver who fails to wear a seat belt and who is also partly to blame for the occurrence of the accident?

3. Suppose a person injured in a car accident did not wear a seat belt because he or she found it unbearable to wear one as a result of the fear of being trapped in the car if an accident should occur. Is the position of a person with such a phobia analogous to that of fat men or pregnant women who, according to *Froom v Butcher*, are not contributorily negligent if they do not wear a seat belt? (Consider *Condon v Condon* [1978] RTR 483 (*sed quaere*).)

4. In a case where the injuries that did occur would have been avoided or lessened by the use of a seat belt, should the court take account of any different injuries that *might* have occurred if the claimant had been wearing a seat belt (e.g. by being crushed or burnt if he had been restrained in his seat, rather than being projected through the windscreen)? Compare the approach in *Patience v Andrews* [1983] RTR 447 with that in *Mackay v Borthwick* 1982 SLT 265.

5. Do you think this decision in fact encouraged people to wear seat belts? (See further note 2, post.)

NOTES

1. Compare with *Froom v Butcher* the discussion of the policy issues in an article written before the Court of Appeal's decision by J. C. Hicks (1974) 37 MLR 308 at 314–316. As Hicks makes clear, one point to appreciate is that a contributorily negligent claimant will have to bear part of the loss himself in this sort of case, whereas a negligent defendant will nearly always be insured. See *Atiyah*, pp. 49–50, for a similar point in a more general context. For the role of public health warnings in establishing what should be expected from a claimant, see *Badger v The Ministry of Defence* [2005] EWHC 2941 (QB), where Stanley Burnton J at [48] considered that the claimant's causative contribution via his heavy smoking to the lung cancer that killed him should result in a deduction of 20 per cent on the basis that 'a reasonably prudent man, warned that there is a substantial risk that smoking will seriously damage his health, would stop smoking'.

2. A few years before *Froom v Butcher* the Court of Appeal decided that it could be contributory negligence to ride a motor bike without wearing a crash helmet: *O'Connell v Jackson* [1972] 1 QB 270, [1971] 3 All ER 129. In 1973, as a result of subordinate legislation made under s. 32 of the Road Traffic Act 1972, it became compulsory to wear protective headgear whilst riding a motor bike: see now s. 16 of the Road Traffic Act 1988. Section 16(2), re-enacting the prior position under the Motor-Cycle Crash-Helmets (Religious Exemption) Act 1976, provides that any requirement imposed under the law-making powers granted by s. 16 'shall not apply to any follower of the Sikh religion while he is wearing a turban'. Does this mean that a follower of the Sikh religion who wears a turban whilst riding a motor bike and who suffers injury which a crash helmet would have avoided would not have his damages reduced for contributory negligence? Cf. s. 11 of the Employment Act 1989, dealing with the position of Sikhs wearing turbans on building sites.

    After more than one attempt to introduce it, the wearing of seat belts in the front seats of cars was made compulsory by s. 33A of the Road Traffic Act 1972 (enacted by s. 27 of the Transport Act 1981) and subordinate legislation made under that provision. There are some exceptions to the requirement that a seat belt be worn: see, for example, reg. 6 of SI 1993/176 (dealing with the wearing of seat belts by adults) which mentions, inter alia, drivers reversing; taxi drivers; persons in respect of whom a doctor has signed a certificate 'to the effect that it is inadvisable on medical grounds for him to wear a seat belt'.

    Breach of or compliance with the regulations could be introduced as evidence either for or against an allegation of contributory negligence. It would seem unlikely that a claimant possessing a certificate of exemption would be held to be contributorily negligent if a seat belt were not worn. What do you think the courts' attitude would be to (a) a pregnant woman who has not got a medical certificate; (b) a pregnant woman who had sought but been refused a medical certificate by a doctor? The fact that there was an exception for taxi drivers was reared as a 'not insignificant point' by Dyson J in *Jones (Kenneth) v Morgan (Jonathan)* [1994] CLY 3344 when considering an argument of contributory negligence; the case also considers the question of the risk of attack from passengers. See further *Pace v Cully* 1992 SLT 1073.

    In the first eleven months since the wearing of seat belts was made compulsory, there were over 7,000 fewer fatal and serious casualties in the front seats of cars than in the previous year (65 H.C. Debs (6th Series) col. 11). To what extent does this suggest that the criminal law is a more effective deterrent than the tort 'fine' involved in the application of contributory negligence?

3. In *Capps v Miller* [1989] 2 All ER 333, [1989] 1 WLR 839 it was accepted that Lord Denning MR's guidelines in *Froom v Butcher* should normally also be applied in cases where a crash helmet was not worn. However, Glidewell and May LJJ distinguished the case where the straps were not fastened or not properly fastened (albeit this is also a breach of statutory duty). In Glidewell LJ's opinion, the blame was less in such a case and this would be reflected in the percentage deduction that was made. May LJ, who agreed with Glidewell LJ's 10 per cent reduction in this case (cf. the approach of Croom-Johnson LJ), pointed out that he reached this conclusion on his 'best consideration' of the facts and circumstances of the case without embarking on what Lord Denning MR referred to in *Froom v Butcher* as an 'expensive enquiry into the degree of blameworthiness on either side which would be hotly disputed'.

4. In *Capps v Miller* Croom-Johnson LJ thought it was of great importance that Lord Denning MR's guidelines should be adhered to 'for the sake of the swift conduct, and it may be settlement, of litigation'. (As has been seen ante, he would have applied them more widely than his brethren in that case, but see May LJ's comment also referred to ante.) On the increase in uncertainty produced by the mere raising of contributory negligence in the settlement process and its effect in making claimants more likely to accept an offer (as well as justifying a lower offer), see H. Genn, *Hard Bargaining: Out of Court Settlement in Personal Injury Actions* (OUP, 1987) pp. 112–113. Adoption of Lord Denning MR's guidelines increases certainty. Do you think that this means that fewer cases are settled?

    In *Hitchens v Berks County Council*, Bingham's Motor Claims (11th edn) p. 236, the trial judge indicated that he was 'unhappily' bound by the reductions suggested in *Froome v Butcher*, suggesting that in an appropriate 'seat-belt' case he would prefer to apply a discount of 50 per cent or higher. The Court of Appeal approved a subsequent settlement in this case, where provision was made for a deduction of 50 per cent. However, in *Jones v Wilkins* [2001] PIQR P12, Keene LJ emphasised the importance of adhering in the main to the *Froom* guidelines, indicating that while first instance courts should not consider themselves 'bound' to follow the guidelines, they should only be departed from in 'very rare' circumstances. This approach was approved in *Elliott v Laverty* [2006] NIQB 97, and the general approach adopted in *Froom* and *Capps* was also applied by the Outer Court of Session in *McFarlane v Thain* [2007] CSOH 176.

5. The percentage reductions suggested in *Froom v Butcher* may be increased in suitable circumstances. For example, in *Gregory v Kelly* [1978] RTR 426 the claimant, who was suing the driver of the car in which he had been a passenger, would have suffered no injury if he had been wearing a seat belt. He also knew that the car had no operative footbrake and Kenneth Jones J reduced the damages by 40 per cent. Consider further *Ashton v Turner* [1981] QB 137, [1980] 3 All ER 870; *Salmon v Newland* (1983) *Times*, 16 May.

    Even if a seat belt is worn, it is surely normally still contributory negligence to ride in a car knowing that it has no operative footbrake. Similarly, knowledge on the claimant's part that the driver has been drinking may also mean that it is contributory negligence to ride in the car with him. In *Owens v Brimmell* [1977] QB 859, [1976] 3 All ER 765 Tasker Watkins J stated (at p. 771):

    …[I]t appears to me that there is widespread and weighty authority abroad for the proposition that a passenger may be guilty of contributory negligence if he rides with the driver of a car whom he knows has consumed alcohol in such quantity as is likely to impair to a dangerous degree that driver's capacity to driver properly and safely. So, also, may a passenger be guilty of contributory negligence if he, knowing that he is going to be driven in a car by his companion later, accompanies him on a bout of drinking which has the effect, eventually of robbing the passenger of clear thought and perception and diminishes the driver's capacity to drive properly and carefully. Whether this principle can be relied on successfully is a question of fact and degree to be determined in the circumstances out of which the issue is said to arise.

For comment on *Owens v Brimmell*, see C. R. Symmons (1977) 40 MLR 350, who points in particular to the difficulties of assessing the passenger's share in the responsibility in such a case. *Owens v Brimmell* is also discussed by N. P. Gravells (1977) 93 LQR 581, although the article ranges more widely. See further p. 445, post. See further *Meah v McCreamer* [1985] 1 All ER 367 and consider *Donelan v Donelan and General Accident Fire and Life Assurance* [1993] PIQR P205; cf. *Malone v Rowan* [1984] 3 All ER 402; and see further *Ashton v Turner* [1981] QB 137. However, in *Booth v White* [2003] EWCA Civ 1708, the Court of Appeal held a failure by a passenger to make positive inquiries about how much alcohol a driver had consumed would not necessarily qualify as contributory negligence, even when the passenger was aware that the driver had consumed some alcohol.

6. In *Parkinson v Dyfed Powys Police* [2004] EWCA Civ 802, the claimant walked out while under the influence of alcohol into the path of a police car being driven at excessive speed, where the driver should have anticipated the possibility of pedestrians being in the condition of the claimant in that vicinity. At first instance, it was concluded that both the claimant and the defendant bore responsibility for the accident and the judge apportioned responsibility for the consequential injuries as to 65 per cent against the defendant and 35 per cent against the claimant. Counsel for the defendant appealed this apportionment, arguing that the driver should not bear the majority of the responsibility, by analogy with the seat-belt cases and in particular *Froom v Butcher*. This ambitious argument was based on the finding by the trial judge that the accident was inevitable in the circumstances, even if the defendant had been travelling at a reasonable speed, but that the speed at which the car had been driven had considerably increased the severity of the injuries. Counsel for the defendant therefore contended that, as with the seat-belt cases, the claimant's contributory negligence had increased both the risk of the accident happening and the severity of the injuries suffered and therefore a further apportionment similar to that awarded in *Froom* should be applied. The Court of Appeal rejected this argument, taking the view that *Froom* and the other seat-belt cases are concerned with extent of liability of a claimant in relation to a precaution which he should have taken in order to avoid or reduce injury to himself. In contrast, the key issue here was the responsibility of the defendant to avoid causing injury to others while driving a car—which Latham LJ described as 'effectively a dangerous instrument for causing injury to others'—which was 'causatively more potent' in relation to the injuries than the claimant's failure to take more care. As a consequence, the *Froom* apportionment was not suitable to be applied here.

7. This emphasis on the defendant's responsibility for safe driving and how it should be accorded considerable weight when balanced against any negligent behaviour on the part of the claimant can also be seen in the Court of Appeal decision of *Eagle v Garth Maynard Chambers* [2003] EWCA Civ 1107. Hale LJ noted the 'destructive disparity' that existed between those driving and pedestrian claimants on the roads, and commented that '[t]hose who are befuddled by drink and who drive heavy machinery at or beyond 30 mph are not properly to be categorised as less culpable or less blameworthy

or less responsible than a 17 year old girl walking along a straight well lit road in the middle of a Norfolk resort'. See also *Russell v Smith* [2003] EWHC 2060.

(b) Emergencies

■ Jones v Boyce
Nisi Prius (1816) 1 Stark 493

It was an action on the case against the defendant, a coach proprietor, for so negligently conducting the coach, that the plaintiff, an outside passenger, was obliged to jump off the coach, in consequence of which his leg was broken.

It appeared that soon after the coach had set off from an inn, the coupling rein broke, and one of the leaders being ungovernable, whilst the coach was on a descent, the coachman drew the coach to one side of the road, where it came in contact with some piles, one of which it broke, and afterwards the wheel was stopped by a post. Evidence was adduced to shew that the coupling rein was defective, and that the breaking of the rein had rendered it necessary for the coachman to drive to the side of the road in order to stop the career of the horses. Some of the witnesses stated that the wheel was forced against the post with great violence; and one of the witnesses stated, that at that time the plaintiff, who had before been seated on the back part of the coach, was jerked forwards in consequence of the concussion, and that one of the wheels was elevated to the height of eighteen or twenty inches; but whether the plaintiff jumped off, or was jerked off, he could not say. A witness also said, I should have jumped down had I been in his (the plaintiff's) place, as the best means of avoiding the danger. The coach was not overturned, but the plaintiff was immediately afterwards seen lying on the road with his leg broken, the bone having been protruded through the boot.

Upon this evidence, Lord Ellenborough was of opinion, that there was a case to go to the jury, and a considerable mass of evidence was then adduced, tending to shew that there was no necessity for the plaintiff to jump off.

[LORD ELLENBOROUGH, in his address to the jury, said:] . . .
This case presents two questions for your consideration; first, whether the proprietor of the coach was guilty of any default in omitting to provide the safe and proper means of conveyance, and if you should be of that opinion, the second question for your consideration will be, whether that default was conducive to the inquiry which the plaintiff has sustained; for if it was not so far conducive as to create such a reasonable degree of alarm and apprehension in the mind of the plaintiff, as rendered it necessary for him to jump down from the coach in order to avoid immediate danger, the action is not maintainable. To enable the plaintiff to sustain the action, it is not necessary that he should have been thrown off the coach; it is sufficient if he was placed by the misconduct of the defendant in such a situation as obliged him to adopt the alternative of a dangerous leap, or to remain at certain peril; if that position was occasioned by the default of the defendant, the action may be supported. On the other hand, if the plaintiff's act resulted from a rash apprehension of danger, which did not exist, and the injury which he sustained is to be attributed to rashness and imprudence, he is not entitled to recover. The question is, whether he was placed in such a situation as to render what he did a prudent precaution, for the purpose of self-preservation.—His Lordship, after recapitulating the facts, and commenting upon them, and particularly on the circumstance of the rein being defective, added:– If the defect in the rein was not the constituent cause of the injury, the plaintiff will not be entitled to your verdict. Therefore it is for your consideration, whether the plaintiff's act was the measure of an unreasonably alarmed mind, or such as a reasonable and prudent mind would have adopted. If I place a man in such a situation that he must adopt a perilous alternative, I am responsible for the consequences; if, therefore, you should be of opinion, that the reins were defective,

did this circumstance create a necessity for what he did, and did he use proper caution and prudence in extricating himself from the apparently impending peril. If you are of that opinion, then, since the original fault was in the proprietor, he is liable to the plaintiff for the injury which his misconduct has occasioned. This is the first case of the kind which I recollect to have occurred. A coach proprietor certainly is not to be responsible for the rashness and imprudence of a passenger; it must appear that there existed a reasonable cause for alarm.

The jury found a verdict for the plaintiff. Damages £300.

NOTE

If the defendant's negligence results in an emergency, then the conduct of rescuers and others who respond to the emergency will be assessed with reference to the existence of an emergency situation. See *Baker v TE Hopkins & Son Ltd* [1959] 3 All ER 225, [1959] 1 WLR 966, noted at p. 451, post, where the defendant alleged that the claimant's husband, who had died coming to the defendant's rescue, contributed to his death through his own negligence, but Willmer LJ took the view that a rescuer in such a situation would have to show a 'wholly unreasonable disregard for his own safety'.

(c) Children

■ Gough v Thorne
Court of Appeal [1966] 3 All ER 398

LORD DENNING MR: . . .
On 13 June 1962, a group of children were crossing the New Kings Road, Chelsea, London. They were Malcolm Gough, who was seventeen; his brother John, who was ten; and his sister Elizabeth, the plaintiff, who was 13½. They were coming from the Wandsworth Bridge Road, crossing the New Kings Road, and going to a swimming pool on the other side. They waited on the pavement for some little time to see if it was safe to cross. Then a lorry came up, coming up the Wandsworth Bridge Road and turning left into the New Kings Road. The lorry driver had got pretty well half-way across the road, towards the bollards, and he stopped at about five feet from the bollards. He put his right hand out to warn the traffic which was coming up the road. He saw the children waiting; he beckoned to them to cross; and they did. They had got across just beyond the lorry when a 'bubble' car, driven by the defendant, came through the gap between the front of the lorry and the bollard, about five feet, just missed the eldest boy, and struck the young boy of ten, but ran into and seriously injured the plaintiff, Elizabeth, aged 13½. Now, on the plaintiff's behalf, there is a claim against the driver of the 'bubble' car for negligence.

The judge has found that the defendant driver was negligent. He said that the 'bubble' car was going too fast in the circumstances, and that the driver did not keep a proper look-out because he ought to have seen the lorry driver's signal and he did not see it. He found, therefore, that the defendant, the driver of the 'bubble' car, was to blame and negligent. Then there came the question whether the little girl, the plaintiff, was herself guilty of contributory negligence. As to that, the judge found that she was one-third to blame for this accident. I will read what the judge said about it. 'Was there contributory negligence?', he asked. He answered:

> 'I think that there was. I think that the plaintiff was careless in advancing past the lorry into the open road without pausing to see whether there was any traffic coming from her right. I do not think that her responsibility was very great. After all, the lorry driver had beckoned her on. She might have thought it unlikely that any traffic would try to come through the gap. She might have thought that if there were any traffic coming from that direction, it would wait until the lorry started to move

or gave the all clear. She was, after all, only thirteen years old. I assess her degree of responsibility at one-third.'

I am afraid that I cannot agree with the judge. A very young child cannot be guilty of contributory negligence. An older child may be; but it depends on the circumstances. A judge should only find a child guilty of contributory negligence if he or she is of such an age as reasonably to be expected to take precautions for his or her own safety: and then he or she is only to be found guilty if blame should be attached to him or her. A child has not the road sense or the experience of his or her elders. He or she is not to be found guilty unless he or she is blameworthy.

In this particular case I have no doubt that there was no blameworthiness to be attributed to the plaintiff at all. Here she was with her elder brother crossing a road. They had been beckoned on by the lorry driver. What more could you expect the child to do than to cross in pursuance of the beckoning? It is said by the judge that she ought to have leant forward and looked to see whether anything was coming. That indeed might be reasonably expected of a grown-up person with a fully developed road sense, but not of a child of 13½.

I am clearly of opinion that the judge was wrong in attributing any contributory negligence to the plaintiff, aged 13½; and I would allow the appeal accordingly.

SALMON LJ: . . .
The question as to whether the plaintiff can be said to have been guilty of contributory negligence depends on whether any ordinary child of 13½ could be expected to have done any more than this child did. I say, 'any ordinary child'. I do not mean a paragon of prudence; nor do I mean a scatter-brained child; but the ordinary girl of 13½. . . .

[DANCKWERTS LJ delivered a brief judgment in favour of allowing the appeal, and agreed in particular with LORD DENNING's observations on contributory negligence.]

Appeal allowed.

QUESTIONS

1.   If a young child, who wandered on to the road but who was found not to have been contributorily negligent because of his age, is injured by a negligent motorist, how might the motorist cut down the amount of damages he (or his insurance company) has to pay? (See D. J. Gibson-Watt (1972) 122 NLJ 280.)
2.   If a twelve-year-old claimant was found to have a mental age of fifteen years, by what standard should the child be judged in deciding whether he has been contributorily negligent?

NOTES

1.   On the position where an infant is the defendant, see p. 311, ante.
2.   The position in tort should not be confused with that in criminal law, where a child below the age of ten cannot be liable for a crime, whatever mental element that crime might require.
3.   Lord Denning MR stated in *Gough v Thorne* that a very young child cannot be contributorily negligent. Of course, in the case of extremely young children, it may seem obvious that this is so, but several of the leading textbooks take the view that there is no age below which it can be said, as a matter of law, that a finding of contributory negligence cannot be made against a child—*Clerk & Lindsell*, para. 355; *Winfield & Jolowicz*, p. 328. This view was accepted in *Speirs v Gorman* [1966] NZLR

897. Note also *Barnes v Flucker* 1985 SLT 142, where counsel conceded that as a matter of law the two five-year-olds hit by a car in that case could be contributorily negligent. See also *Morales v Ecclestone* [1991] RTR 151, where an eleven-year-old boy injured while running out onto a road without looking was deemed to be 75 per cent at fault for his ensuing injuries. Note also *Young v Kent County Council* [2005] EWCA 1342, and *Honnor v Lewis* [2005] EWHC 747. The Pearson Commission recommended that in cases of motor vehicle injury, contributory negligence should not be a defence if the claimant was less than twelve years old (vol. 1, para. 1077). In the Scottish case of *Galbraith's Curator ad litem v Stewart (No 2)* 1998 SLT 1305, Lord Nimmo Smith took the view that 'no hard and fast rule' could be derived from *Gough v Thorne* or the other cases, and much would depend on the nature of the particular danger and the particular child's capacity to appreciate that danger.

(d) Workers

In *Caswell v Powell Duffryn Associated Collieries Ltd* [1939] 3 All ER 722, the House of Lords took the view that in assessing whether employees had been contributarily negligent, the standard of care to which they would be expected to adhere should be adopted to reflect the actual conditions of work in question.

NOTE

The comments in the *Caswell* case on the position of workers in relation to contributory negligence were spoken in the context of the tort of breach of statutory duty and it is not certain whether they apply to a negligence action. See further I. Fagelson (1979) 42 MLR 646, at 651–652, who submits that they do so apply. In *Griffiths v Vauxhall Motors Ltd* [2003] EWCA Civ 412, *Caswell* was applied to an action brought both in negligence and in breach of statutory duty, but there was no discussion of this distinction.

(e) Apportionment of damages

■ Stapley v Gypsum Mines Ltd
p. 433, ante

■ Froom v Butcher
p. 435, ante

NOTES

1. See generally the standard textbooks on tort; D. Payne (1955) 18 MLR 344; N. Gravells (1977) 93 LQR 581, 594–609; Fagelson op cit., pp. 656–663. See also O. Howarth (1994) 14 LS 88.
2. For 'sub-apportionment', see *The Calliope* [1970] P 172, [1970] 1 All ER 624.
3. Apportionment of damages under the 1945 Act (contributory negligence) must be distinguished from apportionment of damages under the Civil Liability (Contribution) Act 1978 (p. 1122, post) (contribution between joint tortfeasors). The former task needs

to be kept distinct from the latter: see *Fitzgerald v Lane* [1989] AC 328, [1988] 2 All ER 961, noted by H. McLean [1989] CLJ 14 and see further p. 1125, post. According to this decision, in apportionment under the 1945 Act when there are joint tortfeasors, the claimant's actions are contrasted with the 'totality of the tortious conduct of the defendants': the responsibility of each individual tortfeasor is not decided in this exercise, but rather in any contribution proceedings between them.

2 VOLENTI NON FIT INJURIA

■ Dann v Hamilton
King's Bench Division [1939] 1 All ER 59

The plaintiff and her mother were driven by Hamilton to see the Coronation decorations, and during the evening Hamilton consumed a certain amount of drink. They met a man named Taunton, and he was given a lift in the car. However, he left the car shortly before it was involved in an accident in which the plaintiff was injured and Hamilton was killed. The action was against his widow who represented his estate. It was found by the learned judge (Asquith J) that as Taunton left the car a conversation took place along the following lines (although Asquith J conceded that it was not clear how seriously the words were spoken):—Taunton said to the plaintiff and her mother 'You two have more pluck than I have', to which the plaintiff answered 'You should be like me. If anything is going to happen, it will happen.' The defence relied upon the maxim volenti non fit injuria, negligence being admitted at the trial.

ASQUITH J: . . .

As a matter of strict pleading, it seems that the plea volenti is a denial of any duty at all, and, therefore, of any breach of duty, and an admission of negligence cannot strictly be combined with the plea. The plea volenti differs in this respect from the plea of contributory negligence, which is not raised in this case: see the observations of Bowen LJ in *Thomas v Quartermaine*.[12] This technicality, however, is of no consequence in the present case. . . .

. . . [I]t is common ground that the deceased, Hamilton, negligently caused the collision, and the evidence further satisfied me that his driving at the time of the collision was that of a man, not only negligent, but negligent through excess of drink. The question is whether, on those facts, the rule or maxim volenti non fit injuria applies so as to defeat the plaintiff's claim. It has often been pointed out that the maxim says volenti, not scienti. A complete knowledge of the danger is in any event necessary, but such knowledge does not necessarily import consent. It is evidence of consent, weak or strong according to circumstances. The question whether the plaintiff was volens is one of fact, to be determined on this amongst other evidence: see *Smith v Baker & Sons*,[13] and other authorities.

As to knowledge, I find as a fact that the plaintiff knew at 11.50 pm, when Taunton was set down, that Hamilton, while far from being dead drunk, was under the influence of drink to such an extent as substantially to increase the chances of a collision arising from his negligence, that with this knowledge she re-entered the car, and that, in so doing, she was not acting under the pressure of any legal or social duty, or through the absence of alternative and practicable forms of transport, since she could have gone home by bus for 2*d*. Is this enough to constitute her volens for the purposes of the maxim? Indeed, is it clear that the maxim applies at all to the present case? . . .

---

[12] (1887) 18 QBD 685.   [13] [1891] AC 325.

The maxim … undoubtedly applies in many cases of pure tort, but case law in this field is very scanty. This is not, perhaps, because its application is rare in this field, but because in a large class of cases its applicability is so obvious as not to be brought to the test of litigation. It is manifest, for instance, that the consent of the patient relieves the dentist who extracts a tooth, or the surgeon who extracts an appendix, of liability for assault, to which their action would otherwise amount. In these cases, the certainty of physical injury is consented to. In another class of cases, perhaps more numerous, a man is not courting injury, but wishes to avoid it, but he nevertheless consents to the risk of its occurrence—for example, when he voluntarily engages in a game of cricket, or a boxing-match (with adequately padded gloves), or a fencing bout (with adequately buttoned foils). In such cases, he impliedly consents to the risks ordinarily incident to those sports, and here again, in the absence of consent, the party who sustains injury would be entitled to sue for assault, or otherwise for trespass to the person. …

Those are cases of trespass to the person. How stands the matter with regard to the tort of negligence, as we may now venture to call it? Does the maxim apply to negligence at all? …

Some text-book writers of authority, notably *Beven on Negligence*, 4th edn, at p. 790, roundly deny that the maxim applies to cases of negligence at all. This is a hard saying, and must be read, I think, subject to some implied limitation. Where a dangerous physical condition has been brought about by the negligence of the defendant, and, after it has arisen, the plaintiff, fully appreciating its dangerous character, elects to assume the risk thereof, the maxim has often been held to apply, and to protect the defendant. Instances are *Torrance v Ilford UDC*[14] and the more recent *Cutler v United Dairies (London) Ltd*.[15] Where, however, the act of the plaintiff relied on as a consent precedes, and is claimed to license in advance, a possible subsequent act of negligence by the defendant (and this, I think, must be the case Beven had in mind), the case may well be different. Here, *Smith v Baker & Sons*[16] does not help as much as might be expected. In any case, it turned on contract, which is not in question here.

With some qualifications, *Pollock on Torts*, 13th edn, supports Beven's dictum, declaring, at p. 172:

> 'The whole law of negligence assumes the principle of volenti non fit injuria not to be applicable.'

He points out, quoting the observations of Lord Halsbury LC in *Smith v Baker & Sons*.[17] that anyone crossing a London street knows that a substantial percentage of drivers are negligent. If a man crosses deliberately, with the knowledge, and is negligently run down, he is certainly not volens, and is not, therefore, precluded from a remedy. Sir Frederick Pollock adds, at p. 173:

> 'A man is not bound at his peril to fly from a risk from which it is another's duty to protect him, merely because the risk is known.'

In *Woodley v Metropolitan District Rly Co*,[18] Mellish LJ carries this illustration a step further. He says, at p. 394:

> 'Suppose this case: a man is employed by a contractor for cleansing the street, to scrape a particular street, and for the space of a fortnight he has the opportunity of observing that a particular hansom cabman drives his cab with extremely little regard for the safety of the men who scrape the streets. At the end of a fortnight the man who scrapes the streets is negligently run over by the cabman. An action is brought in the county court, and the cabman says in his defence: "You know my style of driving, you had seen me drive for a fortnight, I was only driving in my usual style." '

The judgment of Mellish LJ in this particular case was a minority judgment, but seems to have been preferred to that of the majority [by] the House of Lords in the later case of *Membery v Great Western Rly Co*.[19]

Cannot a yet further step be safely taken? I find it difficult to believe, although I know of no authority directly in point, that a person who voluntarily travels as a passenger in a vehicle driven by a driver

---

[14] (1909) 73 JP 225. [15] [1933] 2 KB 297. [16] [1891] AC 325. [17] [1891] AC 325.
[18] (1877) 2 Ex D 384. [19] 19 (1889) 14 App Cas 179.

who is known by the passenger to have driven negligently in the past is volens as to future negligent acts of such driver, even though he could have chosen some other form of transport if he had wished. Then, to take the last step, suppose that such a driver is likely to drive negligently on the material occasion, not because he is known to the plaintiff to have driven negligently in the past, but because he is known to the plaintiff to be under the influence of drink. That is the present case. Ought the result to be any different? After much debate, I have come to the conclusion that it should not, and that the plaintiff, by embarking in the car, or re-entering it, with knowledge that through drink the driver had materially reduced his capacity for driving safely, did not impliedly consent to, or absolve the driver from liability for, any subsequent negligence on his part whereby the plaintiff might suffer harm.

There may be cases in which the drunkenness of the driver at the material time is so extreme and so glaring that to accept a lift from him is like engaging in an intrinsically and obviously dangerous occupation, inter-meddling with an unexploded bomb or walking on the edge of an unfenced cliff. It is not necessary to decide whether in such a case the maxim volenti non fit injuria would apply, for in the present case I find as a fact that the driver's degree of intoxication fell short of this degree. I therefore conclude that the defence fails, and the claim succeeds. . . .

Judgment for the plaintiff.

NOTES

1. For an example where it was thought that, if it had not been for s. 148(3) of the Road Traffic Act 1972 (see now s. 149 of the Road Traffic Act 1988, p. 1144, post), the volenti maxim would have precluded a passenger from recovering damages from a driver who had been drinking, see *Winnik v Dick* 1981 SLT 23 and 101 (Sh Ct); 1984 SLT 185. Reference to several earlier Commonwealth cases can be found in D. M. Gordon's article (1966) 82 LQR 62. As has just been indicated, the effect of s. 149 of the Road Traffic Act 1988 must be borne in mind today, on which see p. 1144, post.

2. The lack of any statutory equivalent to the Road Traffic Act in the case of aircraft was referred to in *Morris v Murray* [1991] 2 QB 6, [1990] 3 All ER 801, noted by C. A. Hopkins [1991] CLJ 27 at 28–29. *Dann v Hamilton* was also distinguished in this case, in which the claimant knowingly and willingly went on a flight in a light aircraft with a drunken pilot, and was injured when the plane crashed. The Court of Appeal allowed the defence of volenti. Rejecting a mere reduction for contributory negligence, Fox LJ stated that 'the wild irresponsibility of the venture is such that the law should not intervene to award damages and should leave the loss where it falls'. What rationale does this suggest for the defence? Cf. A. J. E. Jaffey [1985] CLJ 87 at 88.

3. In *Slater v Clay Cross Co Ltd* [1956] 2 QB 264, [1956] 2 All ER 625, Denning LJ (at 627–628) referring to *Dann v Hamilton*, spoke in the following terms:

   Asquith J held that the maxim volenti non fit injuria had no application to the case; and he gave judgment in favour of the injured passenger. I must say that I agree with him. I know that the decision has in some quarters been criticised, but I would point out that Lord Asquith himself wrote a note in the *Law Quarterly Review* for July 1953, vol. 69 at p. 317, which explains what he decided. He wrote:

   "The criticisms . . . were to the effect that even if the volenti doctrine did not apply, there was here a cast iron defence on the ground of contributory negligence. I have since had the pleadings and my notes exhumed, and they very clearly confirm my recollection that contributory negligence was not pleaded. Not merely so, but my notes show that I encouraged counsel for the defence to ask for leave to amend by adding this plea, but he would not be drawn: why, I have no idea. As the case has been a good deal canvassed on the opposite assumption, I hope you will not grudge the space for this not unimportant corrigendum."

In so far as he decided that the doctrine of volenti did not apply, I think the decision was quite correct. In so far as he suggested that the plea of contributory negligence might have been available, I agree with him.

See further *Owens v Brimmell* [1977] QB 859, [1976] 3 All ER 765, noted p. 440, ante, and see also *Fookes v Slaytor* [1979] 1 All ER 137, [1978] 1 WLR 1293, where this passage from Denning LJ's judgment was treated as impliedly stating that contributory negligence must be pleaded before it is available as a defence in any case.

4. For an example (obiter) of volenti (encapsulated in s. 2(3) of the Occupiers' Liability (Scotland) Act 1960), see *Titchener v British Railways Board* [1983] 3 All ER 770, [1983] 1 WLR 1427, and for comment on this and other cases see Jaffey, op cit. Volenti is also discussed by C. G. S. Tan (1995) 3 Tort L Rev 208.

■ Nettleship v Weston
Court of Appeal [1971] 3 All ER 581

The facts and part of the judgment have been set out on p. 307, ante.

LORD DENNING MR: . . .
This brings me to the defence of volenti non fit injuria. Does it apply to the instructor? In former times this defence was used almost as an alternative defence to contributory negligence. Either defence defeated the action. Now that contributory negligence is not a complete defence, but only a ground for reducing the damages, the defence of volenti non fit injuria has been closely considered, and, in consequence, it has been severely limited. Knowledge of the risk of injury is not enough. Nor is a willingness to take the risk of injury. Nothing will suffice short of an agreement to waive any claim for negligence. The plaintiff must agree, expressly or impliedly, to waive any claim for any injury that may befall him due to the lack of reasonable care by the defendant: or more accurately, due to the failure of the defendant to measure up to the standard of care that the law requires of him. That is shown in England by *Dann v Hamilton*[20] and *Slater v Clay Cross Co Ltd*,[1] and in Canada by *Lehnert v Stein*;[2] and in New Zealand by *Morrison v Union S S Co of New Zealand Ltd*.[3] The doctrine has been so severely curtailed that in the view of Diplock LJ: '. . . the maxim, in the absence of express contract, has no application to negligence simpliciter where the duty of care is based solely on proximity or "neighbourship" in the Atkinian sense': see *Wooldridge v Sumner*.[4]

Applying the doctrine in this case, it is clear that Mr Nettleship did not agree to waive any claim for injury that might befall him. Quite the contrary. he enquired about the insurance policy so as to make sure that he was covered. If and insofar as Mrs Weston fell short of the standard of care which the law required of her, he has a cause of action. But his claim may be reduced insofar as he was at fault himself—as in letting her take control too soon or in not being quick enough to correct her error.

I do not say that the professional instructor—who agrees to teach for reward—can likewise sue. There may well be implied in the contract an agreement by him to waive any claim for injury.[5] He ought to insure himself, and may do so, for aught I know. But the instructor who is just a friend helping to teach never does insure himself. He should, therefore, be allowed to sue. . . .

MEGAW LJ [referring to cases where passengers knew a driver was likely to drive unsafely because of drink or drugs, yet still accepted a lift:] . . .
There may in such cases sometimes be an element of aiding and abetting a criminal offence; or, if the facts fall short of aiding and abetting, the passenger's mere assent to benefit from the commission

---

[20] [1939] 1 KB 509, [1939] 1 All ER 59.
  [1] [1956] 2 QB 264, [1956] 2 All ER 625.   [2] (1963) 36 DLR (2d) 159.   [3] [1964] NZLR 468.
  [4] [1963] 2 QB 43 at 69, [1962] 2 All ER 978 at 990.
  [5] See now the Road Traffic Act 1988, s. 149, p. 1144, post.

of a criminal offence may involve questions of turpis causa. For myself, with great respect, I doubt the correctness on its facts of the decision in *Dann v Hamilton*.[6] But the present case involves no such problem....

[MEGAW LJ was not speaking of the volenti maxim here. However he went on to hold the volenti maxim inapplicable for, in his view, the facts did not show that the plaintiff had accepted the risk of injury through the defendant's inexperience. SALMON LJ rejected 'any possible defence' of volenti non fit injuria because of the assurance given about the position regarding insurance.]

NOTES

1. In *Reeves v Metropolitan Police Commissioner* [2000] 1 AC 360, [1999] 3 All ER 897, Lord Hobhouse endorsed Lord Denning's restrictive view of the availability of volenti in negligence. He remarked:

    In the law of negligence [volenti] means the acceptance variously of the risk created by the defendant's negligence or of the risk of the defendant's negligence. In such cases it is probably best confined to cases where it can be said that the plaintiff has expressly or impliedly agreed to exempt the defendant from the duty of care which he would otherwise have owed.

2. There have been several cases where the volenti defence has been pleaded against passengers in cars in which there were notices stating that passengers travelled at their own risk. (See *Buckpitt v Oates* [1968] 1 All ER 1145; *Bennett v Tugwell* [1971] 2 QB 267, [1971] 2 All ER 248; cf. *Birch v Thomas* [1972] 1 All ER 905, [1972] 1 WLR 294.) Section 149 of the Road Traffic Act 1988 (p. 1144, post) will today exclude the defence in this situation. *Nettleship*'s case must be read subject to this section.

3. On 'turpis causa', which was mentioned by Megaw LJ, see p. 465, post.

■ Bowater v The Mayor, Aldermen and Burgesses of the Borough of Rowley Regis
Court of Appeal [1944] 1 All ER 465

The plaintiff was employed by the defendants as a carter, and his job was to take away rubbish swept up by the road sweepers. The foreman told him to take out a horse which had tried to run away on more than one occasion when driven by one of the plaintiff's fellow employees. Both the plaintiff and the defendants' foreman were aware of the incidents. The plaintiff expressed his dislike of the proposed course of action, but was told that the borough surveyor had said that he was to take the horse out, and the plaintiff obeyed. About a month later the horse ran away, and the plaintiff was thrown out of the cart and injured. Singleton J upheld the plea of volenti non fit injuria. An appeal to the Court of Appeal was successful and a new trial was ordered on the question of damages.

GODDARD LJ:...
The maxim volenti non fit injuria is one which in the case of master and servant is to be applied with extreme caution. Indeed, I would say that it can hardly ever be applicable where the act to which the plaintiff is said to be 'volens' arises out of his ordinary duty, unless the work for which the plaintiff is engaged is one in which danger is necessarily involved. Thus a man in an explosives factory must take the risk of an explosion occurring in spite of the observance and provision of all statutory regulations and safeguards. A horse-breaker must take the risk of being thrown or injured by a restive or unbroken horse; it is an ordinary risk of his employment. But a man whose occupation is not one of a nature inherently dangerous but who is asked or required to undertake a risky operation is in a

---

[6] [1939] 1 KB 509, [1939] 1 All ER 59.

different position. To rely on this doctrine the master must show that the workman undertook that the risk should be on him. It is not enough that, whether under protest or not, he obeyed an order or complied with a request which he might have declined as one which he was not bound either to obey or to comply with. It must be shown that he agreed that what risk there was should like on him. I do not mean that it must necessarily be shown that he contracted to take the risk, as that would involve consideration, though a simple case of showing that a workman did take a risk upon himself would be that he was paid extra for so doing, and in some occupations 'danger money' is often paid.

This, in my opinion, is the result of *Yarmouth v France*,[7] *Smith v Baker*,[8] and *Monaghan v Rhodes*,[9] and the further citation of authority, in support of what I think is now a well-settled principle, is unnecessary. Though the question in the last resort is one of fact I find myself unable to agree with Singleton J on the evidence in this case. I venture to think he approached the case from a wrong angle. A corporation carter or dustman is not like a horse-breaker because he is also a horse-keeper. It is no part of his duty to break or tame the horse which draws the dust cart. Nor is it right to inquire into the mental processes that may lead him to do what he is told or to consider what degree of appreciation of the risk was apparent to him. As Lord Esher MR said in *Yarmouth v France*,[10] that would be to say that for the same accident an unintelligent man might recover while a more intelligent one would not. For this maxim or doctrine to apply it must be shown that a servant who is asked or required to use dangerous plant is a volunteer in the fullest sense, that, knowing of the danger, he expressly or impliedly said that he would do the job at his own risk and not at that of his master. The evidence in this case fell far short of that and, in my opinion, the plaintiff was entitled to recover.

The appeal is allowed with costs and the case must go down for a new trial on damages only, unless the parties will agree to this court assessing the damages....

[SCOTT and DU PARCQ LJJ delivered judgments in favour of allowing the appeal.]

NOTES

1. As this case clearly shows, mere knowledge of the risk by the claimant will not per se bring him within the scope of the maxim. Indeed, many years earlier, Bowen LJ had stressed that the maxim was volenti non fit injuria and not scienti non fit injuria (*Thomas v Quartermain* (1887) 18 QBD 685 at 696).
2. In employment cases, the workman who has knowledge of a danger is unlikely to have true freedom of choice, for this is an area in which economic pressures operate. See further comments of *Millner*, pp. 102–108. The volenti maxim has, in fact, been of little importance in master and servant cases since *Smith v Baker & Sons* [1891] AC 325. Compare *Burnett v British Waterways Board* [1973] 2 All ER 631, [1973] 1 WLR 700. It would however be a mistake to suppose that the volenti defence can never apply in this context, for the next case extract provides an example of its application, though in a rather restricted sphere.
3. Another category of claimant often taken to lack real freedom of choice is rescuers. In *Baker v TE Hopkins and Sons Ltd* [1959] 3 All ER 225, [1959] 1 WLR 966 two employees of the defendant company were overcome by carbon monoxide fumes in a well they were attempting to de-contaminate. A doctor, the claimant, was called to the scene. Despite warnings about the fumes and despite being told that the fire brigade was on its way, the claimant climbed down the well in an attempt to rescue the employees. The claimant also succumbed to the fumes and all three men died. In the subsequent action, the defendant said that Dr Baker had consented. The Court of Appeal said that the defendant's argument was 'ungracious' and it was neither 'rational' nor 'seemly'

---

[7] (1887) 19 QBD 647.   [8] [1891] AC 325.   [9] [1920] 1 KB 487.   [10] (1887) 19 QBD 647.

to say that a rescuer freely and voluntarily takes on the risks inherent in the rescue attempt. The principle, perhaps surprisingly, applies as much to 'professional' rescuers (such as fire fighters) as to amateurs—see *Ogwo v Taylor* [1988] AC 431, [1987] 3 All ER 961, approving *Salmon v Seafarer Restaurants Ltd* [1983] 3 All ER 729, [1983] 1 WLR 1264, and *White v Chief Constable of South Yorkshire Police* [1999] 2 AC 455, [1999] 1 All ER 1 (p. 137, ante).

4.   Volenti does not, it seems, apply at all when the defendant's duty exceptionally includes the prevention of the very act of the claimant alleged to constitute consent (e.g. the suicide of a prisoner, see *Reeves v Metropolitan Police Comr* p. 426, ante). In such a case, it does not matter whether the claimant was of sound mind or mentally ill. The House of Lords applied this 'scope of the duty' point to novus actus interveniens (see p. 426, ante). One puzzle, however, is why the same argument did not also exclude contributory negligence.

■ Imperial Chemical Industries Ltd v Shatwell
House of Lords [1964] 2 All ER 999

This was an appeal from the Court of Appeal who dismissed an appeal from a judgment of Elwes J. Elwes J had held the appellants vicariously liable to the respondent for his fellow servant's negligence and breach of statutory duty. He had further held that the volenti defence was not open to the appellants in the claim based on the breach of statutory duty, but reduced the damages by half because of the respondent's share of the blame for the accident. On the tort of breach of statutory duty which is also raised in the speeches in the House of Lords, see chap. 12.

LORD REID: . . .

My Lords, this case arises out of the accidental explosion of a charge at a quarry belonging to the appellants which caused injuries to the respondent George Shatwell and his brother James, who were both qualified shotfirers. On 8 June 1960, these two men and another shotfirer, Beswick, had bored and filled fifty shot holes and had inserted electric detonators and connected them up in series. Before firing it was necessary to test the circuit for continuity. This should have been done by connecting long wires so that the men could go to a shelter some eighty yards away and test from there. They had not sufficient wire with them and Beswick went off to get more. The testing ought not to have been done until signals had been given, so that other men could take shelter, and these signals were not due to be given for at least another hour. Soon after Beswick had left George said to his brother 'Must we test them', meaning shall we test them, and James said 'yes'. The testing is done by passing a weak current through the circuit in which a small galvanometer is included and if the needle of the instrument moves when a connexion is made the circuit is in order. So George got a galvanometer and James handed two short wires to him. Then George applied the wires to the galvanometer and the needle did not move. This showed that the circuit was defective so the two men went round inspecting the connections. They saw nothing wrong and George said that that meant there was a dud detonator somewhere, and decided to apply the galvanometer to each individual detonator. James handed two other wires to him and George used them to apply the galvanometer to the first detonator. The result was an explosion which injured both men.

This method had been regularly used without mishap until the previous year. Then some research done by the appellants showed that it might be unsafe and in October 1959, the appellants gave orders that testing must in future be done from a shelter and a lecture was given to all the shotfirers, including the Shatwells, explaining the position. Then in December 1959, new statutory regulations[11]

----

[11]   The Quarries (Explosives) Regulations 1959.

were made (S.I. 1959 No. 2259) probably because the Ministry had been informed of the results of the appellants' research. These regulations came into operation in February 1960, and the Shatwells were aware of them. But some of the shotfirers appeared to have gone on in the old way. An instance of this came to the notice of the management in May 1960, and the management took immediate action and revoked the shotfiring certificate of the disobedient man, and told the other shotfirers about this. George admitted in evidence that he knew all this. He admitted that they would only have had to wait ten minutes until Beswick returned with the long wires. When asked why he did not wait, his only excuse was that he could not be bothered to wait.

George now sues the appellants on the ground that he and his brother were equally to blame for this accident, and that the appellants are vicariously liable for his brother's conduct. He has been awarded £1,500, being half the agreed amount of his loss. There is no question of the appellants having been in breach of the regulations because the duty under the regulation is laid on the shotfirer personally. So counsel for George frankly and rightly admitted that if George had sued James personally instead of suing his employer the issue would have been the same. If this decision is right it means that if two men collaborate in doing what they know is dangerous and is forbidden and as a result both are injured, each has a cause of action against the other.

The appellants have two grounds of defence, first that James' conduct had no causal connexion with the accident the sole cause being George's own fault, and secondly volenti non fit injuria. I am of the opinion that they are entitled to succeed on the latter ground, but I must deal shortly with the former ground because it involves the decision of this House in *Stapley v Gypsum Mines Ltd*,[12] and I think that there has been some misunderstanding of that case.... The only issue before the House was whether the conduct of Dale had contributed to cause the accident, and the House decided by a majority that it had. There was little, if any, difference of opinion as to the principles to be applied; the difference was in their application to the facts of the case. The case gives authoritative guidance on the question of causation, but beyond that it decided nothing. It clearly appears from the argument of counsel[13] that the defence volenti non fit injuria was never taken and nothing about it was said by any of their lordships.

Applying the principles approved in *Stapley*'s case[12] I think that James' conduct did have a causal connexion with this accident. It is far from clear that George would have gone on with the test if James had not agreed with him; but, perhaps more important, James did collaborate with him in making the test in a forbidden and unlawful way. His collaboration may not have amounted to much, but it was not negligible.... So I do not think that the appellants could succeed entirely on this defence and I turn to consider their second submission.

The defence volenti non fit injuria has had a chequered history. At one time it was very strictly applied.... More recently it appears to have been thought in some quarters that, at least as between master and servant, volenti non fit injuria is a dead or dying defence. That, I think, is because in most cases where the defence would now be available it has become usual to base the decision on contributory negligence. Where the plaintiff's own disobedient act is the sole cause of his injury, it does not matter in the result whether one says 100 per cent contributory negligence[14] or volenti non fit injuria; but it does matter in a case like the present. If we adopt the inaccurate habit of using the word 'negligence' to denote a deliberate act done with full knowledge of the risk, it is not surprising that we sometimes get into difficulties. I think that most people would say, without stopping to think of the reason, that there is a world of difference between two fellow servants collaborating carelessly, so that the acts of both contribute to cause injury to one of them, and two fellow servants combining to disobey an order deliberately, though they know the risk involved. It seems reasonable that the injured man should recover some compensation in the former case, but not in the latter. If the law treats both as merely cases of negligence, it cannot draw a distinction. In my view the law does and should draw a distinction. In the first case only the partial defence of contributory negligence is available. In the

---

[12] [1953] AC 663, [1953] 2 All ER 478.   [13] See [1953] AC at p. 665.

[14] But see now *Pitts v Hunt* [1991] 1 QB 24 at 48 and 51, noted p. 465, post.

second volenti non fit injuria is a complete defence, if the employer is not himself at fault and is only liable vicariously for the acts of the fellow servant. If the plaintiff invited or freely aided and abetted his fellow servant's disobedience, then he was volens in the fullest sense. He cannot complain of the resulting injury either against the fellow servant or against the master on the ground of his vicarious responsibility for his fellow servant's conduct. I need not here consider the common case where the servant's disobedience puts the master in breach of a statutory obligation, and it would be wrong to decide in advance whether that would make any difference. There remain two other arguments for the respondent which I must dealt with.

It was argued that in this case it has not been shown that George had a full appreciation of the risk. In my view it must be held that he had. . . .

Finally the respondent argues that there is a general rule that the defence of volenti non fit injuria is not available where there has been a breach of statutory obligation. It would be odd if that were so. In the present case the prohibition of testing except from a shelter had been imposed by the appellants before the statutory prohibition was made. So it would mean that, if the respondent had deliberately done what he did in full knowledge of the risk the day before the statutory prohibition was made, this defence would have been open to the appellants, but if he had done the same thing the day after the regulation came into operation it would not. . . .

I entirely agree that an employer who is himself at fault in persistently refusing to comply with a statutory rule could not possibly be allowed to escape liability because the injured workman had agreed to waive the breach. If it is still permissible for a workman to make an express agreement with his employer to work under an unsafe system, perhaps in consideration of a higher wage—a matter on which I need express no opinion—then there would be a difference between breach of a statutory obligation by the employer and breach of his common law obligation to exercise due care: it would be possible to contract out of the latter, but not out of the former type of obligation. But all that is very far removed from the present case. . . .

I can find no reason at all why the fact that these two brothers agreed to commit an offence by contravening a statutory prohibition imposed on them as well as agreeing to defy their employer's orders should affect the application of the principle volenti non fit injuria either to an action by one of them against the other or to an action by one against their employer based on his vicarious responsibility for the conduct of the other. I would therefore allow this appeal.

LORD PEARCE: . . .

In *Wheeler v New Merton Board Mills Ltd*[15] the Court of Appeal laid down that the defence of volenti non fit injuria was no answer to a claim by a workman against his employer for injury caused through a breach by the employer of a duty imposed on him by statute. They so held (with some reluctance which I do not share) principally because the case of *Baddeley v Earl Granville*[16] had stood for some fifty years. But in those cases the defendants were themselves in breach of statutory duty (as were the defendants in *Stapley*'s case).[17] In the present case the defendants themselves were in breach of no statutory duty. The questions of public policy and fairness which reinforced those decisions do not help the plaintiff in the present case but rather tell the other way. In my opinion, the rule which the courts have rightly created disallowing the defence where the employer is in breach of statutory duty should not apply to a case such as the present. The defence should be available where the employer was not himself in breach of statutory duty and was not vicariously in breach of any statutory duty through the neglect of some person who was of superior rank to the plaintiff and whose commands the plaintiff was bound to obey (or who had some special and different duty of care, see, e.g. *National Coal Board v England*,[18] where a miner was injured by the shotfirer firing the charge) and where the plaintiff himself assented to and took part in the breaking of the statutory duty in question. If one does not allow some such exception one is plainly shutting out a defence which, when applied in the right circumstances, is fair and sensible.

---

[15] [1933] 2 KB 669, [1933] All ER Rep 28. [16] (1887) 19 QBD 423, [1886–90] All ER Rep 374.
[17] [1953] AC 663, [1953] 2 All ER 478. [18] [1954] AC 403, [1954] 1 All ER 546.

So far as concerns common law negligence, the defence of volenti non fit injuria is clearly applicable if there was a genuine full agreement, free from any kind of pressure, to assume the risk of loss....

In the present case it seems clear that as between George and James there was a voluntary assumption of risk. George was clearly acting without any constraint or persuasion; he was in fact inaugurating the enterprise. On the facts it was an implied term (to the benefit of which the employers are vicariously entitled) that George would not sue James for any injury that he might suffer, if an accident occurred. Had an officious bystander raised the possibility, can one doubt that George would have ridiculed it? ...

[VISCOUNT RADCLIFFE, LORD HODSON, and LORD DONOVAN delivered speeches in favour of allowing the appeal.]

Appeal allowed.

QUESTION

Would the result of this case have been any different if James, although employed as a shot-firer, had been George's supervisor?

■ Wooldridge v Sumner
Court of Appeal [1962] 2 All ER 978

The first defendant owned Work of Art, a horse taking part in a competition for heavyweight hunters at the National Horse Show. The horses were required to walk, trot, canter, and gallop, and this was a class of competition in which both the horse and its rider, Mr Holladay, were experienced. There was a line of tubs and benches two feet from the edge of the competition area, which was surrounded by a cinder running track. The plaintiff, a professional photographer, was standing at the end of one of those benches. The defendant's horse was kept close into the corner of the bandstand end of the arena so as to give the horse the best chance to show off its gallop in the straight. However, having rounded the corner, the horse apparently jumped two of the tubs, knocked over a third, and then moved from the line of tubs on to a course taking it several feet behind the bench at the end of which the plaintiff was standing. The plaintiff, who had become frightened by the horse's approach, tried to pull someone away from the bench, but stepped or fell back and was knocked down by the horse. Barry J, who dismissed the claim against the second defendants (the organisers of the show, who were occupiers of the stadium), found that the horse was being ridden too fast into and out of the corner, so that it was inevitable that it would come into contact with the tubs, and that Mr Holladay's conduct and control of the horse amounted to negligence for which the first defendant was liable. He also decided that if Mr Holladay had allowed it, the horse would have gone safely on to the cinder track. However, Barry J found that Mr Holladay tried to get the horse back on to the course and so carried along the line of tubs, and that Mr Holladay knew, or should have known, that the people sitting or standing along the line of benches and tubs were highly likely to be endangered by these efforts. The first defendant appealed:

SELLERS LJ: ...
In all the circumstances, in so far as the judgment found that Mr Holladay was going 'too fast' I would not hold this to be negligence; and in any case its effect had ceased when the horse was straightened up, as it was, some twenty-five yards before the accident, and with regard to the second

finding on which the judgment was based, I am unable to find fault in Mr Holladay amounting to negligence. It was, I think, the horse's course and not his which took them along the line of tubs instead of
to the right of that line and for this I do not think that he can be blamed....

In my opinion, a competitor or player cannot, at least, in the normal case of competition or game,
rely on the maxim volenti non fit injuria in answer to a spectator's claim, for there is no liability unless
there is negligence, and the spectator comes to witness skill and with the expectation that it will be
exercised. But, provided the competition or game is being performed within the rules and the requirement of the sport and by a person of adequate skill and competence, the spectator does not expect
his safety to be regarded by the participant. If the conduct is deliberately intended to injure someone
whose presence is known, or is reckless and in disregard of all safety of others so that it is a departure
from the standards which might reasonably be expected in anyone pursuing the competition or game,
then the performer might well be held liable for any injury his act caused. There would, I think, be a
difference, for instance, in assessing blame which is actionable between an injury caused by a tennis
ball hit or a racket accidentally thrown in the course of play into the spectators at Wimbledon and a
ball hit or a racket thrown into the stands in temper or annoyance when play was not in progress. The
relationship of spectator and competitor or player is a special one, as I see it, as the standard of conduct of the participant, as accepted and expected by the spectator, is that which the sport permits or
involves. The different relationship involves its own standard of care. There can be no better evidence
that Mr Holladay was riding within the rules than that he won, notwithstanding this unfortunate accident in the course of the event, and I do not think that it can be said that he was riding recklessly and
in disregard of all safety or even, on this evidence, without skill....

I would allow the appeal and enter judgment for the first defendant also.

DIPLOCK LJ:...
Accepting, then, the primary facts as found by the trial judge but not those inferences which he drew
from them and which, on analysis of the evidence, I think are unjustified, one is left with two acts or
omissions by Mr Holladay which were causative factors in the accident. The first was the speed at which
he caused Work of Art to negotiate the bend, the second was his omission at some moment before he
reached the line of tubs to let the horse run out on to the cinder track....

The matter has to be looked at from the point of view of the reasonable spectator as well as the reasonable participant; not because of the maxim volenti non fit injuria, but because what a reasonable
spectator would expect a participant to do without regarding it as blameworthy is as relevant to what
is reasonable care as what a reasonable participant would think was blameworthy conduct in himself.
The same idea was expressed by Scrutton LJ in *Hall v Brooklands Auto-Racing Club*:[19]

> 'What is reasonable care would depend on the perils which might be reasonably expected to occur,
> *and the extent to which the ordinary spectator might be expected to appreciate and take the risk*
> *of such perils.*'

A reasonable spectator attending voluntarily to witness any game or competition knows, and presumably desires, that a reasonable participant will concentrate his attention on winning, and if the
game or competition is a fast-moving one will have to exercise his judgment and attempt to exert his
skill in what, in the analogous context of contributory negligence, is sometimes called 'the agony of
the moment'. If the participant does so concentrate his attention and consequently does exercise his
judgment and attempt to exert his skill in circumstances of this kind which are inherent in the game
or competition in which he is taking part, the question whether any mistake he makes amounts to a
breach of duty to take reasonable care must take account of those circumstances.

The law of negligence has always recognised that the standard of care which a reasonable man will
exercise depends on the conditions under which the decision to avoid the act or omission relied on
as negligence has to be taken. The case of the workman engaged on repetitive work in the noise and

---

[19] [1933] 1 KB 205 at 214, [1932] All ER Rep 208 at 213.

bustle of the factory is a familiar example. More apposite for present purposes are the collision cases where a decision has to be made on the spur of the moment.

> '...A's negligence makes collision so threatening that, though by the appropriate measure B could avoid it, B has not really time to think and by mistake takes the wrong measure. B is not held to be guilty of any negligence and A wholly fails.'

(*Admiralty Comrs v SS Volute*).[20] A fails not because of his own negligence; there never has been any contributory negligence rule in Admiralty. He fails because B has exercised such care as is reasonable in circumstances in which he has not really time to think. No doubt, if he has got into those circumstances as a result of a breach of duty of care which he owes to A, A can succeed on this antecedent negligence; but a participant in a game or competition gets into the circumstances in which he has no time or very little time to think by his decision to take part in the game or competition at all. It cannot be suggested that the participant, at any rate if he has some modicum of skill, is by the mere act of participating in breach of his duty of care to a spectator who is present for the very purpose of watching him do so. If, therefore, in the course of the game or competition at a moment when he really has no time to think, a participant by mistake takes a wrong measure, he is not, in my view, to be held guilty of any negligence.

Furthermore, the duty which he owes is a duty of care, not a duty of skill. Save where a consensual relationship exists between a plaintiff and a defendant by which the defendant impliedly warrants his skill, a man owes no duty to his neighbour to exercise any special skill beyond that which an ordinary reasonable man would acquire before indulging in the activity in which he is engaged at the relevant time. It may well be that a participant in a game or competition would be guilty of negligence to a spectator if he took part in it when he knew or ought to have known that his lack of skill was such that, even if he exerted it to the utmost, he was likely to cause injury to a spectator watching him. No question of this arises in the present case. It was common ground that Mr Holladay was an exceptionally skilful and experienced horseman.

The practical result of this analysis of the application of the common law of negligence to participant and spectator would, I think, be expressed by the common man in some such terms as these: 'A person attending a game or competition takes the risk of any damage caused to him by any act of a participant done in the course of and for the purposes of the game or competition, notwithstanding that such act may involve an error of judgment or a lapse of skill, unless the participant's conduct is such as to evince a reckless disregard of the spectator's safety'. The spectator takes the risk because such an act involves no breach of the duty of care owed by the participant to him. He does not take the risk by virtue of the doctrine expressed or obscured by the maxim volenti non fit injuria. The maxim states a principle of estoppel by the maxim volenti non fit injuria. The maxim states a principle of estoppel applicable originally to a Roman citizen who consented to being sold as a slave. Although pleaded and argued below, it was only faintly relied on by counsel for the first defendant in this court. In my view, the maxim, in the absence of express contract, has no application to negligence simpliciter where the duty of care is based solely on proximity or 'neighbourship' in the Atkinian sense. The maxim in English law pre-supposes a tortious act by the defendant. The consent that is relevant is not consent to the risk of injury but consent to the lack of reasonable care that may produce that risk (see *Kelly v Tarrants Ltd*,[1] per Lord MacDermott), and requires on the part of the plaintiff at the time at which he gives his consent full knowledge of the nature and extent of the risk that he ran (*Osborne v London and North Western Rly Co*,[2] per Wills J approved in *Letang v Ottawa Electric Rly Co*[3]). In *Dann v Hamilton*[4] Asquith J expressed doubts whether the maxim ever could apply to license in advance a subsequent act of negligence, for, if the consent precedes the act of negligence, the plaintiff cannot at that time

---

[20] [1922] 1 AC 129 at 136, [1921] All ER Rep 193 at 197.
[1] [1954] NI 41 at 45.   [2] (1888) 21 QBD 220 at 223, 224.
[3] [1926] AC 725, [1926] All ER Rep 546.   [4] [1939] 1 KB 509, [1939] 1 All ER 59.

have full knowledge of the extent as well as the nature of the risk which he will run. Asquith J, however, suggested that the maxim might, nevertheless, be applicable to cases where a dangerous physical condition had been brought about by the negligence of the defendant, and the plaintiff with full knowledge of the existing danger elected to run the risk thereof. With the development of the law of negligence in the last twenty years, a more consistent explanation of this type of case is that the test of liability on the part of the person creating the dangerous physical condition is whether it was reasonably foreseeable by him that the defendant[5] would so act in relation to it as to endanger himself. This is the principle which has been applied in the rescue cases (see *Cutler v United Dairies (London) Ltd*[6] and contrast *Haynes v Harwood*[7]) and that part of Asquith J's judgment in *Dann v Hamilton*[8] dealing with the possible application of the maxim to the law of negligence was not approved by the Court of Appeal in *Ward v TE Hopkins & So Ltd, Baker v Same.*[9] In the type of case envisaged by Asquith J if I may adapt the words of Morris LJ in *Ward v Hopkins*,[10] the plaintiff could not have agreed to run the risk that the defendant might be negligent for the plaintiff would only play his part after the defendant had been negligent.

Since the maxim has, in my view, no application to this or any other case of negligence simpliciter, the fact that the plaintiff, owing to his ignorance of horses, did not fully appreciate the nature and extent of the risk he ran did not impose on Mr Holladay any higher duty of care towards him than that which he owed to any ordinary reasonable spectator with such knowledge of horses and vigilance for his own safety as might be reasonably expected to be possessed by a person who chooses to watch a heavyweight hunter class in the actual arena where the class is being judged.... Beyond saying that the question is one of degree, the learned judge has not expressly stated in his judgment anything which would indicate the considerations which he had in mind in determining that Mr Holladay was in breach of the duty of care owed by a participant in a competition of this character to a spectator who had chosen to watch the event in the arena in which it was taking place. There is, however, no reference in his judgment to the fact, which is, in my view, of the utmost relevance, that Mr Holladay's decisions what he should do once the signal for the gallop had been given had to be made in circumstances in which he had no time to exercise an unhurried judgment. It is, I think, clear that, if the trial judge gave any weight to this factor, he did not make proper allowance for it....

[Having stated that, in the circumstances of the case, Mr Holladay's 'conduct in taking the corner too fast could not in my view amount to negligence', he continued:] As regards the second respect in which the learned judge found Mr Holladay to be negligent, namely, in his attempt to bring back the horse into the arena after it had come into contact with the first shrub...I am unable to accept the judge's inference of fact that the course taken by the horse along the line of shrubs was due to Mr Holladay's attempt to bring it back into the arena instead of letting it run out on to the cinder track. But, even if the judge's inference of fact be accepted, here was a classic case where Mr Holladay's decision what to do had to be taken in the 'agony of the moment' when he had no time to think, and if he took the wrong decision that could not in law amount to negligence. The most that can be said against Mr Holladay is that, in the course of, and for the purposes of, the competition he was guilty of an error or errors of judgment or a lapse of skill. That is not enough to constitute a breach of the duty of reasonable care which a participant owes to a spectator. In such circumstances, something in the nature of a reckless disregard of the spectator's safety must be proved, and of this there is no suggestion in the evidence.

I, too, would allow this appeal.

[DANCKWERTS LJ delivered a judgment in favour of allowing the appeal.]

Appeal allowed.

---

[5] It would seem that this should be read as 'the plaintiff'.
[6] [1933] 2 KB 297, [1933] All ER Rep 594.   [7] [1935] 1 KB 146, [1934] All ER Rep 103.
[8] [1939] 1 KB 509, [1939] 1 All ER 59.   [9] [1959] 3 All ER 225.   [10] [1959] 3 All ER at p. 233.

QUESTIONS

1. Do you think the phrase 'reckless disregard of the spectator's safety' implies an object-ive or a subjective standard, i.e. must the competitor actually have foreseen the danger to the spectator?
2. If a policeman who was on duty at a sporting event was carelessly injured by a competi-tor, would the 'reckless disregard of safety' test apply?

NOTES

1. The criticism to which this decision was subjected by A. L. Goodhart (1962) 78 LQR 490, was referred to in *Wilks v Cheltenham Home Guard Motor Cycle and Light Car Club* [1971] 2 All ER 369, [1971] 1 WLR 668. Edmund-Davies LJ stated (at p. 374) that he 'would with deference adopt the view of Dr Goodhart (1962) 78 LQR at p. 496 that the proper test is whether injury to a spectator has been caused "by an error of judgment that a reasonable competitor, being the reasonable man of the sport-ing world, would not have made"'. Although accepting that spectators expected the competitor to be doing his best to win, his Lordship would still require the competitor to exercise reasonable care *in all the circumstances*. Lord Denning MR, however, was still prepared to apply the 'reckless disregard of safety' test to riders in *races* (cf. pp. 370–371). Phillimore LJ stressed that the test was one of negligence and that the circumstances might not warrant the application of the tests to be found in *Wooldridge v Sumner*. For an example of such circumstances consider *Harrison v Vincent* [1982] RTR 8, although note that the claimant here was not a spectator but one of the participants in a race for motor bikes with sidecars. In this case the normal standard of care in negligence was regarded as applicable to the maintenance and inspection of equipment before a race; on the other hand, the 'reckless disregard of safety' test was thought to be applicable to activity 'in the flurry and excitement of the sport'. It is submitted, however, that the test adopted by Edmund-Davies LJ in the *Wilks* case should be followed. It is sufficiently flexible to cater for the special factors which arise in the context of competitions, and, as Dr Goodhart pointed out, the test 'is more in accord with the general principles on which the law of negligence is based'. Cf. the view of Jaffey, op cit., pp. 108–109, who prefers the 'reckless disregard of safety' test.

   Consider also the preferred approach in *Condon v Basi* [1985] 2 All ER 453, [1985] 1 WLR 866, where both claimant and defendant were participants in a game of soccer in which, as a result of a tackle by the defendant, the claimant sustained a broken leg. Sir John Donaldson MR (with whose judgment Stephen Brown LJ and Glidewell J agreed) referred to the decision in *Rootes v Shelton* [1968] ALR 33 with approval and cited from the judgments in that case of Barwick CJ and Kitto J (at pp. 34 and 37, respectively). He then continued (at p. 454):

   > I have cited from those two judgments because they show two different approaches which, as I see it, produce precisely the same result. One is to take a more generalised duty of care and modify it on the basis that the participants in the sport or pastime impliedly consent to taking risks which otherwise would be a breach of the duty of care. That seems to be the approach of Barwick CJ. The other is exemplified by the judgment of Kitto J, where he is saying, in effect, that there is a general standard of care, namely the Lord Atkin approach that you are under a

duty to take all reasonable care taking account of the circumstances in which you are placed (see *Donoghue (or M'Alister) v Stevenson* [1932] AC 562 at 580, [1932] All ER Rep 1 at 11); which, in a game of football, are quite different from those which affect you when you are going for a walk in the countryside. For my part I would prefer the approach of Kitto J, but I do not think it makes the slightest difference in the end if it is found by the tribunal of fact that the defendant failed to exercise that degree of care which was appropriate in all the circumstances, or that he acted in a way to which the plaintiff cannot be expected to have consented. In either event, there is liability.

Note that *Wooldridge v Sumner* was not cited in *Condon v Basi*, and, as A. H. Hudson has pointed out in a note on *Condon v Basi* (1986) 102 LQR 11, support can be found in the obiter dictum of Sir John Arnold P in *Harrison v Vincent* (mentioned ante) for the application in the case of participants of the 'reckless disregard of safety' test to activity in the 'flurry and excitement of the sport'. For a reconciliation of the tests in *Wooldridge v Sumner* and *Condon v Basi*, see Hudson, op cit., pp. 12–13.

In *Blake v Galloway* [2004] 3 All ER 315, [2004] EWCA Civ 814, where the Court of Appeal applied *Wooldridge v Sumner* and *Condon v Basi* without differentiating the two cases to horseplay between a group of fifteen-year-old friends, which involving throwing bark and twigs at one another and resulted in the claimant being struck in the right eye, causing serious injury. Dyson LJ at [16] adopted a modified version of Diplock LJ's approach in *Blake*: 'in a case such as the present there is a breach of the duty of care owed by participant A to participant B only where A's conduct amounts to recklessness or a very high degree of carelessness'. The consent issue here was subsumed within the breach of duty analysis (see p. 310, ante), and was only dealt with directly in the context of the claim for battery which the claimant brought alongside the claim for negligence: Dyson LJ took the view at [24] that '[b]y participating in this game, the claimant must be taken to have impliedly consented to the risk of a blow on any part of his body, provided that the offending missile was thrown more or less in accordance with the tacit understandings or conventions of the game'. See also *Caldwell v Maguire* [2002] PIQR P45, [2001] EWCA Civ 1054.

Note further that the 'appropriate degree of care in all the circumstances' test to be found in *Condon v Basi* was adopted and modified in *Smolden v Whitworth and Nolan* [1996] PIQR P133 in the case of a referee who was sued by a rugby player. The position of a referee in relation to players was distinguished from that of a participant in relation to spectators, with Lord Bingham CJ finding that the claimant, an injured player, 'cannot possibly be said to have consented to a breach of duty on the part of an official whose duty it was to apply the rules...' See also *Vowles v Evans* [2003] 1 WLR 1607, [2003] EWCA Civ 318. For a similar approach being adopted in other cases where injured participants in sporting activities sought recovery for injury incurred as a result of the alleged negligence of the organisers of sporting activity (as distinct from participants in the activity, as in *Wooldridge v Sumner*), see *Harrison v Vincent* [1982] RTR 8 (discussed above), *Wattleworth v Goodwood Road Racing Co Ltd* [2004] EWHC 140; *Watson v British Board of Boxing Control* [2001] QB 1134, [2000] EWCA Civ 2116. See, in contrast, the Australian decision of *Agar v Hyde* (2000) 201 CLR 552.

Note however that in these cases, as with the other 'sporting injury' cases, the consent issue has been largely if not completely absorbed within the breach of duty analysis, in line with the second approach set out in the extract above from Sir John Donaldson MR's opinion in *Condon v Basi*. This has led to the suggestion that the volenti defence in the context of sporting injuries is now 'otiose': see D. McArdle and M. James (2005) Tort LR 193, 210.

2. On Diplock LJ's comments in *Wooldridge v Sumner* concerning the restricted availability of the volenti defence in negligence, see *Morris v Murray* [1991] 2 QB 6, [1990] 3 All ER 801, noted p. 448, ante, where both Fox and Stocker LJJ thought that volenti applied, Stocker LJ being of the view that Diplock LJ's comments were not meant to apply to a driver/passenger case.

3. If a spectator is injured by a competitor in a sporting event, he is not restricted to an action against that person, but may bring an action against the occupier of the place where the event was staged—see *Murray v Harringay Arena Ltd* [1951] 2 KB 529, [1951] 2 All ER 320n; cf. *White v Blackmore* [1972] 2 QB 651, [1972] 3 All ER 158 (p. 582, post).

■ The Road Traffic Act 1988

See s. 149, p. 1144, post.

NOTE

It has been argued—see C. R. Symmons (1973) 123 NLJ 373—that s. 148(3) of the Road Traffic Act 1972, which has been re-enacted as s. 149 of the 1988 Act, did not rule out the volenti defence in cases where implied consent is relied upon by the defendant (i.e. where there are no express terms): this is on the basis that the phrase 'a person so carried' means a person carried under the sort of 'antecedent agreement or understanding' referred to earlier in the subsection, which might not cover the implied consent cases. However, the Court of Appeal in *Pitts v Hunt* [1991] 1 QB 24, [1990] 3 All ER 344 has now decided that it does catch such cases (although it was also accepted in that case that the defence of 'illegality' (p. 465, post) was unaffected, on which see p. 470, post).

■ The Unfair Contract Terms Act 1977

See s. 2(3), p. 462, post.

QUESTION

What more do you think is required under the terms of s. 2(3) of this Act for the volenti defence to be successful in a case to which s. 2(3) applies? (For discussion of this point in the context of occupiers' liability, see J. Mesher [1979] Conv 58 at 61–62.)

NOTE

On the interpretation of s. 2(3), see B. Coote (1978) 41 MLR 312 at 316–317. It should also be noted that dicta in *Johnstone v Bloomsbury Health Authority* [1992] QB 333 at 345–346, suggest that volenti cases based on express terms are subject to s. 2(1) of the 1977 Act.

3 EXCLUSION OF LIABILITY

■ White v Blackmore,

p. 582, post

■ The Unfair Contract Terms Act 1977

PART 1. AMENDMENT OF LAW FOR ENGLAND AND WALES AND NORTHERN IRELAND

Introductory

1. Scope of Part 1.—(1) For the purposes of this Part of this Act, 'negligence' means the breach—

    (a) of any obligation, arising from the express or implied terms of a contract, to take reasonable care or exercise reasonable skill in the performance of the contract;

    (b) of any common law duty to take reasonable care or exercise reasonable skill (but not any stricter duty);

    (c) of the common duty of care imposed by the Occupiers' Liability Act 1957 or the Occupiers' Liability Act (Northern Ireland) 1957.

(3) In the case of both contract and tort, sections 2 to 7 apply...only to business liability, that is liability for breach of obligations or duties arising –

    (a) from things done or to be done by a person in the course of a business (whether his own business or another's); or

    (b) from the occupation of premises used for business purposes of the occupier;

and references to liability are to be read accordingly [but liability of an occupier of premises for breach of an obligation or duty towards a person obtaining access to the premises for recreational or educational purposes, being liability for loss or damage suffered by reason of the dangerous state of the premises, is not a business liability of the occupier unless granting that person such access for the purposes concerned falls within the business purposes of the occupier].[11]

(4) In relation to any breach of duty or obligation, it is immaterial for any purpose of this Part of this Act whether the breach was inadvertent or intentional, or whether liability for it arises directly or vicariously.

Avoidance of liability for negligence, breach of contract, etc.

2. Negligence liability.—(1) A person cannot by reference to any contract term or to a notice given to persons generally or to particular persons exclude or restrict his liability for death or personal injury resulting from negligence.

(2) In the case of other loss or damage, a person cannot so exclude or restrict his liability for negligence except in so far as the term or notice satisfies the requirement of reasonableness.

(3) Where a contract term or notice purports to exclude or restrict liability for negligence a person's agreement to or awareness of it is not of itself to be taken as indicating his voluntary acceptance of any risk.

---

[11] Inserted by s. 2 of the Occupiers' Liability Act 1984 and art. 4 of the Occupiers Liability (Northern Ireland) Order 1987, SI 1987/1280 (NI 15).

Explanatory provisions

11. The 'reasonableness' test.—(1) In relation to a contract term, the requirement of reasonableness for the purposes of this Part of this Act…is that the term shall have been a fair and reasonable one to be included having regard to the circumstances which were, or ought reasonably to have been, known to or in the contemplation of the parties when the contract was made.

(3) In relation to a notice (not being a notice having contractual effect), the requirement of reasonableness under this Act is that it should be fair and reasonable to allow reliance on it, having regard to all the circumstances obtaining when the liability arose or (but for the notice) would have arisen.

(4) Where by reference to a contract term or notice a person seeks to restrict liability to a specified sum of money, and the question arises (under this or any other Act) whether the term or notice satisfies the requirement of reasonableness, regard shall be had in particular…to—

    (a) the resources which he could expect to be available to him for the purpose of meeting the liability should it arise; and

    (b) how far it was open to him to cover himself by insurance.

(5) It is for those claiming that a contract term or notice satisfies the requirement of reasonableness to show that it does.

13. Varieties of exemption clause.—(1) To the extent that this Part of this Act prevents the exclusion or restriction of any liability it also prevents—

    (a) making the liability or its enforcement subject to restrictive or onerous conditions;

    (b) excluding or restricting any right or remedy in respect of the liability, or subjecting a person to any prejudice in consequence of his pursuing any such right or remedy;

    (c) excluding or restricting rules of evidence or procedure;

and (to that extent) sections 2 and 5…also prevent excluding or restricting liability by reference to terms and notices which exclude or restrict the relevant obligation or duty.

(2) But an agreement in writing to submit present or future differences to arbitration is not to be treated under this Part of this Act as excluding or restricting any liability.

14. Interpretation of Part 1—In this Part of this Act—

'business' includes a profession and the activities of any government department or local or public authority;

'goods' has the same meaning as in [the Sale of Goods Act 1979]

…

'negligence' has the meaning given by section 1(1);

'notice' includes an announcement, whether or not in writing, and any other communication or pretended communication; and

'personal injury' includes any disease and any impairment of physical or mental condition.

NOTES

1.   Exclusion of liability by contract or notice can be found in some textbooks discussed under the heading of volenti or assumption of risk: see e.g. *Fleming*, pp. 328–332. However, s. 2 of the Occupiers' Liability Act 1957 (p. 586, post), s. 149 of the Road Traffic Act 1988 (p. 1144, post) and s. 2 of the Unfair Contract Terms Act 1977 treat volenti and exclusion separately. In *White v Blackmore* [1972] 2 QB 651, [1972] 3 All ER 158 (p. 582, post) it will be seen that volenti failed as a defence but that exclusion of liability was successful, and that Buckley LJ regarded the two defences as 'somewhat analogous'. See further *Fowler v Tierney* 1974 SLT (Notes) 23; *Burnett v British Waterways Board* [1973] 2 All ER 631, [1973] 1 WLR 700. One question to consider is

whether the knowledge required on the claimant's part for exclusion by contract or notice is the same as that required for the volenti defence.

2.   On exclusion of liability and the Unfair Contract Terms Act in the context of occupiers' liability, see p. 585, post.

3.   The general topic of exclusion clauses must be left to courses on Contract. However, on the interpretation of the scope of the Act, see *Smith v Eric S Bush* [1990] 1 AC 831, [1989] 2 All ER 514. Lord Templeman's views were set out at p. 219, ante. The matter was also discussed by Lord Griffiths and Lord Jauncey. In rejecting the view that the Act does not apply if the disclaimer (or exclusion notice) stops a duty of care arising, Lord Griffiths stated that he regarded s. 11(3) and s. 13(1) as establishing a 'but for' test in relation to an exclusion notice. 'They indicate that the existence of the common law duty to take reasonable care, referred to in section 1(1)(b), is to be judged by considering whether it would exist "but-for" the notice excluding liability' ([1990] 1 AC at p. 857) (though see *First National Commercial Bank plc v Loxleys* [1997] PNLR 211 at 214–215). The House of Lords went on to hold that it would not be fair and reasonable to allow reliance on the disclaimers on the facts involved. See generally T. Kaye (1989) 52 MLR 841 at 845–848. Cf. *McCullogh v Lane Fox & Partners Ltd* [1996] PNLR 205.

4.   It has been held that a clause transferring liability from one person to another is caught by the words 'exclud[ing] or restrict[ing] liability' in s. 2 of the 1977 Act: *Phillips Products Ltd v Hyland* [1987] 2 All ER 620, [1987] 1 WLR 659n. However, this case was distinguished in *Thompson v T. Lohan (Plant Hire) Ltd* [1987] 2 All ER 631, [1987] 1 WLR 649. Here the same clause was held to be outside s. 2, where it operated not between the defendant and claimant as was the situation in the *Phillips* case, but between a defendant and the third party: the clause in this situation was not regarded as excluding or restricting the *liability* which had been established between that defendant and the claimant. For comment on these two cases, see L. S. Sealey [1988] CLJ 6.

5.   Other instances of statutory provision invalidating the exclusion of liability will be found in this book; see s. 1(3) of the Law Reform (Personal Injuries) Act 1948 (p. 1102, post); s. 1(2) of the Employers' Liability (Defective Equipment) Act 1969 (p. 1104, post); s. 149 of the Road Traffic Act 1988 (p. 1144, post); s. 6(3) of the Defective Premises Act 1972 (p. 606, post); s. 7 of the Consumer Protection Act 1987 (p. 633, post). To what extent do any of these provisions overlap with those to be found in the Unfair Contract Terms Act 1977?

6.   Alongside the Unfair Contract Terms Act 1977, there now exist the Unfair Terms in Consumer Contract Regulations 1999 (SI 1999/2083, replacing SI 1994/3159), implementing Council Directive 93/13/EEC (O.J. No. L95, 21.4.93, p. 29). These regulations apply to contractual terms between a seller or a supplier (both as defined) and an consumer (as defined), where the term has not been individually negotiated. The regulations provide that 'unfair terms' (again as defined) are not binding. An exclusion clause could come within the category of an 'unfair term' (see Sch. 2 to the Regulations). There are various points of difference between the Unfair Contract Terms Act 1977 and the 1999 Regulations, some of which have already been indicated, and further discussion of this matter and the 1999 Regulations must be left to courses on Contract. Nevertheless, it must be emphasised here that the 1999 Regulations may negate a defence to a tort claim based on an exclusion clause in a contract.

7.   The Law Commission in its consultation paper, *Unfair Terms in Contracts* (London: 2005), Law Com. No. 292, has proposed to introduce a single piece of legislation regulating unfair contract terms for the UK. As part of that legislation, the Commission

has proposed that exclusions or restrictions of business liability for death or personal injury caused by negligence should be automatically ineffective, that the existing controls on the exclusion of business liability in tort should be retained, and that the powers of the Office of Fair Trading and other regulators should be extended to include control over such notices and contract terms.

4 ILLEGALITY AND PUBLIC POLICY

■ Pitts v Hunt
Court of Appeal [1990] 3 All ER 344

The first defendant was killed and the plaintiff injured when the first defendant's motor bike, ridden by the first defendant with the plaintiff as a pillion passenger, collided with the second defendant's car. The plaintiff and the first defendant had been drinking prior to the journey on which the collision occurred. The trial judge (Judge Fallon QC, sitting as a Deputy High Court judge) found that the defendant had not been negligent. As stated by Beldam LJ in the Court of Appeal, the trial judge further 'found that the deceased had drunk so much that he was obviously unfit to drive and that if the plaintiff had been in a proper state he would have realised that. He found that the deceased, very much aided and abetted by the plaintiff, was deliberately trying to frighten others who were on the road. No doubt because they had drunk so much, they viewed it as a joke or a game but it was certainly reckless driving. He found that the plaintiff had supported or encouraged the deceased whom he knew was under age, drunk, and uninsured, and he added ([1990] 1 QB 302 at 312):

On my findings the deceased was riding this motor cycle recklessly and dangerously and at the very least the plaintiff was aiding and abetting that driving. He was not manipulating the controls of the machine but he was fully in agreement with and was encouraging the way in which the deceased was manipulating the controls. Indeed, the eye-witness accounts which I have accepted demonstrate that both the plaintiff and the deceased were actually enjoying their experience, partly if not largely as a result of the very large amount they had drunk that night.

The trial judge decided that the plaintiff's claim was barred by the operation of the ex turpi maxim, and there was an appeal to the Court of Appeal.

BALCOMBE LJ: . . .

(1) *The joint illegal enterprise*

  In a case of this kind I find the ritual incantation of the maxim ex turpi causa non oritur actio more likely to confuse than to illuminate. I prefer to adopt the approach of the majority of the High Court of Australia in the most recent of the several Australian cases to which we were referred, *Jackson v Harrison* (1978) 138 CLR 438. That is to consider what would have been the cause of action had there been no joint illegal enterprise, that is the tort of negligence based on the breach of a duty of care owed by the deceased to the plaintiff, and then to consider whether the circumstances of the particular case are such as to preclude the existence of that cause of action. I find myself in complete agreement with the following passage from the judgment of Mason J in *Jackson v Harrison* (at 455–456):

  'If a joint participant in an illegal enterprise is to be denied relief against a co-participant for injury sustained in that enterprise, the denial of relief should be related not to the illegal character of the activity but rather to the character and incidents of the enterprise and to the hazards which are necessarily inherent in its application—and for that reason fairer in its operation—is to say that the plaintiff must fail when the character of the enterprise in which the parties are engaged is such that it is impossible for the court to determine the standard of care which is appropriate to be observed. The detonation of an explosive device is a case of this kind. But the driving of a motor vehicle by an unlicensed and disqualified driver, so long as it does not entail an agreement to drive the car recklessly on the highway (see *Bondarenko v Sommers* (1968) 69 SR (NSW) 269), stands in a somewhat different position. In this case the evidence indicates that the participants contemplated that the vehicle would be driven carefully—an accident or untoward event might, as in fact it did, lead to discovery of their breach of the law. It is not suggested that either party lacked the experience or ability to drive carefully—that they were unlicensed was due to their having been disqualified as a result of earlier traffic offences... A plaintiff will fail when the joint illegal enterprise in which he and the defendant are engaged is such that the court cannot determine the particular standard of care to be observed. It matters not whether this in itself provides a complete answer to the plaintiff's claim or whether it leads in theory to the conclusion that the defendant owes no duty of care to the plaintiff because no standard of care can be determined in the particular case.'

The facts of the earlier case in the High Court of Australia, *Smith v Jenkins* (1970) 119 CLR 397, are set out in the judgment of Dillon LJ[12] and I need not repeat them. Of those facts Jacobs J said in *Jackson v Harrison* (1978) 138 CLR 438 at 460:

'It appears to me that these facts lie at the basis of the conclusion that there was a relevant joint criminal enterprise. It was a jaunt, an escapade, a joy-ride even though of a most serious kind from the beginning to the end. How could a standard of care be determined for such a course of criminal activity? I doubt that the decision would have been the same if the accident had occurred days, weeks or months later when the circumstances of the taking of the vehicle had ceased to have any significant relationship to the manner in which the vehicle was being used.'

This approach seems to me to enable the court to differentiate between those joint enterprises which, although involving a contravention of the criminal law and hence illegal, e.g. the use of a car by an unlicensed and disqualified driver as in *Jackson v Harrison*, are not such as to disable that court from determining the standard of care to be observed, and those, such as the use of a get-away car as in *Ashton v Turner* [1980] 3 All ER 870, [1981] QB 137, where it is impossible to determine the appropriate standard of care.

Counsel for the plaintiff submitted that, however reprehensible the plaintiff's conduct may have been, his culpability involved neither dishonesty nor violence nor any moral turpitude such as is inherent in crimes of dishonesty or violence. Although an assessment of the degree of moral turpitude becomes unnecessary if one adopts, as I do, the approach of the majority of the High Court of Australia in *Jackson v Harrison*, I would not wish it to be thought that I accept this submission. It was only by good fortune that no innocent third party was injured by this disgraceful piece of motor cycle riding, in which the judge found on the facts that the plaintiff was an active participant. If moral turpitude were relevant, here was moral turpitude of a high degree.

However, I prefer to found my judgment on the simple basis that the circumstances of this particular case were such as to preclude the court from finding that the deceased owed a duty of care to the plaintiff....

DILLON LJ:...

It so happens that the cases where a passenger has been injured by the 'negligence' of the driver when the vehicle in which the passenger was being carried was being used for an illegal purpose

---

[12] Dillon LJ stated ([1990] 3 All ER at pp. 363–364): 'In *Smith v Jenkins* (1970) 119 CLR 397 a group of four youths all about 16 years of age, who had been drinking, robbed a man, stole his car keys, and then, having found out where his car was, stole the car and drove it off on a joyride. The plaintiff was the first driver, but after a couple of changes of driver he was merely a passenger; a relatively few miles from the scene of the theft the car left the road at 80 or 90 mph and hit a tree. The plaintiff was seriously injured and sued the youth who had been the driver at the time of the accident; it was held that he could not recover anything.'

in which the passenger was an accomplice have come before the High Court of Australia more often than before the appellate courts in this country. The factual situations in which the Australian courts have held that a passenger injured by the 'negligence' of the driver in the course of a joint criminal enterprise cannot recover damages from the driver are clear. But the reasoning by which the Australian courts have reached their conclusions from common law principles is, to me, very much less clear, not least because of the extent to which the judgments in one particular decision of the High Court, *Smith v Jenkins* (1970) 119 CLR 397, have been reinterpreted in later decisions of the High Court. There is also the problem of how the Australian approach, purportedly based on common law principles, is reconcilable with certain recent developments in the English courts, also purportedly based on common law principles, in cases to which the judge below was not referred.

It is clear for a start that the fact that a plaintiff was engaged in an illegal activity which brought about his injury does not automatically bring it about that his claim for damages for personal injury as a result of the negligence of the defendant must be dismissed. (See e.g. *Baker v Market Harborough Industrial Co-op Society Ltd* [1953] 1 WLR 1472, where, as in many cases, the court apportioned liability for a road accident which had been caused by each driver, independently, driving negligently and without due care and attention...)...

So much is common ground between the parties, but it raises questions which have been the subject of discussion in English and Australian judgments whether a line can be drawn between different grades of illegality, and whether there is a distinction, and if so, on what ground, between the ordinary case of negligence, albeit involving a criminal act...and cases where a passenger sues the driver for injuries sustained by reckless driving at the time of the accident when they were both engaged in a joint criminal enterprise of which the reckless driving was an inherent part.

Counsel for the plaintiff founds on certain recent authorities in this country which he relied on as establishing a 'conscience test' to be applied in cases of illegality.

The starting point is the judgment of Hutchison J in *Thackwell v Barclays Bank plc* [1986] 1 All ER 676. In that case the plaintiff claimed damages from the bank for having paid a cheque drawn in favour of the plaintiff to a third party in reliance on a forgery of the plaintiff's signature on an indorsement of the cheque. The claim was rejected on the ground that the cheque represented the proceeds of a fraud on a fourth party, to which the plaintiff, the drawer of the cheque and the forger of the indorsement were all parties. Hutchison J treated the case as one in which public policy would prevent the plaintiff suing just as it would prevent a burglar from whom the stolen goods were snatched by a third party just as the burglar left the victim's house from maintaining an action in conversion against the third party. The judge in reaching that conclusion seems to have accepted a submission from counsel for the defendants that there were two distinct but related lines of authority running through the cases of illegality, the second of which laid down the 'conscience test'. That test was put as follows (at 678):

> 'That test, he suggested, involved the court looking at the quality of the illegality relied on by the defendant and all the surrounding circumstances, without fine distinctions and seeking to answer two questions: first, whether there had been illegality of which the court should take notice and, second, whether in all the circumstances it would be an affront to the public conscience if by affording him the relief sought the court was seen to be indirectly assisting or encouraging the plaintiff in his criminal act.'

The context in which that submission was put forward in *Thackwell v Barclays Bank plc* [1986] 1 All ER 676 seems to have been one of the proximity of the illegality to the matters of which complaint was made in the action. There is authority in *Sajan Singh v Sardara Ali* [1960] 1 All ER 269, [1960] AC 167 that a person who has acquired property under an illegal contract and has been using it without a permit can none the less maintain an action for damages for conversion against a person, even the vendor of the property, who subsequently, on the facts some three or four years later, wrongly deprives him of that property. The suggestion seems to have been in *Thackwell v Barclays Bank plc* that it would be an affront to the public conscience to allow one thief to maintain an action because a second of the thieves had stolen the first's share in the course of the division of the swag.

The conscience test was approved by this court in *Saunders v Edwards* [1987] 2 All ER 651, [1987] 1 WLR 1116. That was again a case of the proximity, or relevance, of the illegality to the matters of which the plaintiff was complaining. The plaintiff claimed damages for fraudulent misrepresentation, which had induced him to purchase a flat from the defendant. The defendant sought unsuccessfully to defend himself by asserting that the contract for the sale of the flat, and presumably also the conveyance, were tainted with illegality in that in the apportionment of the purchase price in the contract between chattels and the flat itself the amount attributable to the chattels had been fraudulently inflated, and the amount attributable to the flat had been correspondingly reduced, in order to reduce the stamp duty payable to the Revenue. This court applied Hutchison J's test, to which Nicholls LJ added to the end of the formulation the words 'or encouraging others in similar criminal acts' (see [1987] 2 All ER 651 at 664, [1987] 1 WLR 1116 at 1132).

Saunders v Edwards was, it seems to me, a case where the alleged illegality over the stamp duty apportionment was independent of, or unrelated to, the wrong in the way of fraudulent misrepresentation for which the plaintiff was suing. Kerr LJ decided the case, however, on the basis that the cases 'show that there are no rigid rules for or against the ex turpi causa defence' and that the cases 'show that the conduct and relative moral culpability of the parties may be relevant in determining whether or not the ex turpi causa defence falls to be applied as a matter of public policy (see [1987] 2 All ER 651 at 660, [1987] 1 WLR 1116 at 1127). Bingham LJ used rather different language where he said ([1987] 2 All ER 651 at 666, [1987] 1 WLR 1116 at 1134):

'...I think that on the whole the courts have tended to adopt a pragmatic approach to those problems, seeking where possible to see that genuine wrongs are righted so long as the court does not thereby promote or countenance a nefarious object or bargain which it is bound to condemn. Where the plaintiff's action in truth arises directly ex turpi causa, he is likely to fail...Where the plaintiff has suffered a genuine wrong, to which allegedly unlawful conduct is incidental, he is likely to succeed...'

That passage was adopted by Kerr LJ in giving the leading judgment of this court in *Euro-Diam Ltd v Bathurst* [1988] 2 All ER 23 at 29, [1990] 1 QB 1 at 36. The latter part of it is sufficient to cover the decision in *Saunders v Edwards* [1987] 2 All ER 651, [1987] 1 WLR 1116.

I find a test that depends on what would or would not be an affront to the public conscience very difficult to apply, since the public conscience may well be affected by factors of an emotional nature, e.g. that these boys by their reckless and criminal behaviour happened to do no harm to anyone but themselves. Moreover, if the public conscience happened to think that the plaintiff should be compensated for his injuries it might equally think that the deceased driver of the motor cycle, had he survived and merely been injured, ought to be compensated, and that leads into the much-debated question whether there ought to be a universal scheme for compensation for the victims of accidents without regard to fault.

Beyond that, appeal to the public conscience would be likely to lead to a graph of illegalities according to moral turpitude, and I am impressed by the comments of Mason J in *Jackson v Harrison* (1978) 138 CLR 438 at 455, where he said:

'...there arises the difficulty, which I regard as insoluble, of formulating a criterion which would separate cases of serious illegality from those which are not serious. Past distinctions drawn between felonies and misdemeanours, malum in se and malum prohibitum, offences punishable by imprisonment and those which are not, non-statutory and statutory offences offer no acceptable discrimen.'

Bingham LJ's dichotomy between cases where the plaintiff's action in truth arises directly ex turpi causa and cases where the plaintiff has suffered a genuine wrong to which allegedly unlawful conduct is incidental avoids this difficulty, in that it does not involve grading illegalities according to moral turpitude.

In the Australian courts it was held by the High Court of Australia in *Jackson v Harrison* that the maxim ex turpi causa is a maxim of the law of contract which cannot apply in the law of tort. This however is, as it seems to me, a matter of terminology and in the present case rather a red herring. The most commonly cited anglicisation of the maxim is that of Lord Mansfield CJ in *Holman v Johnson* (1775) 1 Cowp 341 at 343, [1775–1802] All ER Rep 98 at 99 that 'No Court will lend its aid to a man who found his cause of action upon an immoral or an illegal act'. Whether that is or is not (see per Windeyer J in *Smith v Jenkins* (1970) 119 CLR 397 at 412) a correct translation of the maxim is now beside the point since it has been applied continuously as the law of England for over 200 years. . . .

That a defence of illegality can be pleaded to a case founded in tort is, in my judgment, clear, whether or not the defence is correctly called ex turpi causa. *Thackwell v Barclays Bank plc* [1986] 1 All ER 676 is one instance. Another is *Murphy v Culhane* [1976] 3 All ER 533, [1977] QB 94 . . .

[His Lordship went on to examine various Australian authorities (*Smith v Jenkins* (1970) 119 CLR 397; *Bondarenko v Sommers* (1968) 69 SR (NSW) 269; *Jackson v Harrison* (1978) 138 CLR 438; and *Progress and Properties Ltd v Craft* (1976) 135 CLR 651) and continued:] The distillation of the law by the High Court of Australia rests . . . now on the judgment of Jacobs J, with which the other members of the majority of the court concurred, in *Progress and Properties Ltd v Craft* and in the judgments of Mason and Jacobs JJ with whom Aicken J concurred in *Jackson v Harrison* (1978) 138 CLR 438. For relieve to be derived[13] on the ground of the illegality, the circumstances of the joint illegal venture in the course of which the accident which caused the plaintiff's injuries occurred must be such as to negate, as between the two of them, any ordinary standard of care. Thus Mason J said in *Jackson v Harrison* (at 456):

'A plaintiff will fail when the joint illegal enterprise in which he and the defendant are engaged is such that the court cannot determine the particular standard of care to be observed,'

And Jacobs J said in *Progress and Properties Ltd v Craft* (1976) 135 CLR 651 at 668:

'Where there is a joint illegal activity the actual act of which the plaintiff in a civil action may be complaining as done without care may itself be a criminal act of a kind in respect of which a court is not prepared to hear evidence for the purpose of establishing the standard of care which was reasonable in the circumstances.'

This formulation would clearly cover . . . the reckless driving, to escape capture, of the getaway car after a robbery as in the English case of *Ashton v Turner* [1980] 3 All ER 870, [1981] QB 137. It was regarded in *Jackson v Harrison* as also covering the factual situations in *Bondarenko v Soomers* (1968) 69 SR (NSW) 269, where there was, in the words of Mason J in *Jackson v Harrison* 138 CLR 438 at 456, 'an agreement to drive the [stolen] car recklessly' for the purpose of racing on the highway, and the factual situation in *Smith v Jenkins*. In reference to *Smith v Jenkins*, Jacobs J said in *Jackson v Harrison* 138 CLR 438 at 460:

'It was a jaunt, an escapade, a joy-ride even though of a most serious kind from the beginning to the end. How could a standard of care be determined for such a course of criminal activity?'

I feel unable to draw any valid distinction between the reckless riding of the motor cycle in the present case by the deceased boy, Hunt, and the plaintiff under the influence of drink, and the reckless driving of the cars, albeit stolen, in *Smith v Jenkins* and *Bondarenko v Sommers*. The words of Barwick CJ in *Smith v Jenkins* (1970) 119 CLR 397 at 399–400:

'The driving of the car by the appellant, the manner of which is the basis of the respondent's complaint, was in the circumstances as much a use of the car by the respondent as it was a use by the appellant. That use was their joint enterprise of the moment.'

---

[13] This word should, it seems, be 'denied'—see [1991] 1 QB at p. 59.

apply with equal force to the riding of the motor cycle in the present case. This is a case in which, in Bingham LJ's words, the plaintiff's action in truth arises directly ex turpi causa....

[BELDAM LJ delivered a judgment in favour of dismissing the appeal.]

Appeal dismissed.

QUESTION

What purpose was served by denying the claimant a remedy in *Pitts v Hunt*? Was it deterrence, punishment, or some other purpose? (See T. Hervey (1981) 97 LQR 537 at 539, commenting on the earlier decision of *Ashton v Turner* [1981] QB 137, [1980] 3 All ER 870; and on the purpose of the ex turpi doctrine generally see R. Glofcheski (1999) 19 LS 6 at 18–19).

NOTES

1. In *Pitts v Hunt* the third member of the court (Beldam LJ) seemed to apply the 'public conscience' test, on which see the comments in the extract from *Pitts v Hunt* above and see p. 471, post. His primary source for public policy was legislation relating to the use of motor vehicles, supplemented by the reasoning of those decisions in which courts had refused to enforce rights in this sphere. If, for example, public policy would bar a claim by a driver to indemnity under a policy which he is obliged to take out for a passenger's benefit, then in his opinion a passenger, jointly guilty of the offence, was barred by public policy from recovering damages. Beldam LJ went on to rule that the claim was barred in the circumstances of this case, but he was not prepared to decide what degree of seriousness was required in an offence before recovery would be denied. For Beldam LJ decisions in other jurisdictions were merely secondary guidance for finding public policy.

2. *Pitts v Hunt* has already been mentioned in relation to volenti and the Road Traffic Act 1988: see p. 461, ante. In the present context it should also be said that the case decided that s. 148(3) of the Road Traffic Act 1972 (now re-enacted as s. 149 of the Road Traffic Act 1988) does not affect the defence of illegality. 'The words "agreement or understanding" in section 148(3) do not contemplate an illegal agreement, express or tacit, to carry out an illegal purpose...' [1990] 3 All ER at p. 366 per Dillon LJ, with whom Balcombe LJ agreed.

3. For argument as to the precise scope of the difference between the approach in *Smith v Jenkins* (1970) 44 ALJR 78 and *Jackson v Harrison* (1978) 138 CLR 438 (two of the High Court of Australia decisions which were considered in *Pitts v Hunt*), see J. Swanton (1981) 9 Sydney LR 304 at 317–322. Several of the cases referred to in *Pitts v Hunt* were decisions of the High Court of Australia. That court returned to the issue in *Gala v Preston* (1991) 100 ALR 29 and adapted its approach so as to fit in with the later emphasis in its case law on the requirement that there be a relationship of proximity between the parties for a duty of care to be established. Having stated that the relevant factors to consider will include policy considerations, the majority of the High Court continued (at p. 36) that '[w]here ... the parties are involved in a joint criminal activity, those factors will include the appropriateness and feasibility of seeking to define the content of a relevant duty of care'.

    The Supreme Court of Canada in *Hall v Hebert* (1993) 101 DLR (4th) 129 (noted by M. McInnes [1963] CLJ 379 and J. A. Epp (1994) 110 LQR 357) has preferred to view the ex turpi doctrine as a limited defence rather than an aspect of the decision whether or not a duty of care exists. The doctrine should on this view only apply to cases where the integrity of the justice system would be otherwise undermined because recovery would create inconsistency within the system, for example where the claimant were allowed to profit from an illegal or wrongful act or avoid a criminal sanction.

4.   What is the conduct which may bar an action? The commission of a tort appears to be insufficient: see the important case of *Revill v Newbery* [1996] 1 All ER 291, where a claimant sued the defendant in battery, negligence, and breach of occupier's liability for shooting him without warning while the claimant was breaking into his property: the defendant's attempt to raise the defence of ex turpi on the basis that the defendant was trespassing failed. On the other hand, it has been stated that the conduct in question does not necessarily have to be illegal: see *Kirkham v Chief Constable of the Greater Manchester Police* [1990] 2 QB 283, [1990] 3 All ER 246, where suicide was regarded as conduct potentially barring an action under the ex turpi defence; and see *Euro-Diam Ltd v Bathurst* [1990] 1 QB 1 at 35. In *Kirkham*, Lloyd LJ expressly relied for this view on *Thackwell v Barclays Bank Ltd* [1986] 1 All ER 676; *Saunders v Edwards* [1987] 2 All ER 651, [1987] 1 WLR 1116; and *Euro-Diam Ltd*. These cases support the 'public conscience test', on which see the extract from *Pitts v Hunt* ante. However, this test has fallen into disfavour: see post. This may limit the range of conduct which can trigger this defence: see *Gray v Thames Trains* [2008] EWCA Civ 713. However, fraudulent misrepresentation can still qualify: see *Hewison v Meridian Shipping Pte* [2002] EWCA Civ 1821.

Crimes are an obvious category to which the defence might apply, but not all crimes are sufficient to stop the claimant from recovering damages: see *Revill v Newberry*, where the claimant's conviction for the offences he had committed on the night in question did not result in his claim being barred. A breach of statutory duty by the claimant may or may not be a crime (see *R v Horseferry Road Justices, ex p Independent Broadcasting Authority* [1987] QB 54, [1986] 2 All ER 666); but, whether or not it is a crime, a breach of a statutory duty imposed for the claimant's safety has been held not to bar his claim (*National Coal Board v England* [1954] AC 403, [1954] 1 All ER 546). Note in particular that s. 4 of the Law Reform (Contributory Negligence) Act 1945 (p. 425, ante) includes breach of statutory duty in its definition of 'fault' and which therefore is merely a ground for reducing damages: this could suggest that Parliament did not intend breach of statutory duty to be an absolute bar to recovery.

5.   The judgments of Balcombe and Dillon WJ in *Pitts v Hunt* began a serious erosion of the status in English law of the 'public conscience' test (although see Glofcheski (op cit., pp. 10–11) as to how far either judgment can totally avoid the test)? The 'public conscience' test was applied in the Court of Appeal in *Tinsley v Milligan* [1992] Ch 310, [1992] 2 All ER 391 but, on appeal, [1994] 1 AC 340, [1993] 3 All ER 65, comments in the House of Lords raised serious doubts as status. The case concerned a claim by the defendant to an equitable interest in a property which was in the claimant's sole name, this having been done to help the defendant make false claims for benefits to the Department of Social Security. The view of the House was that a test as uncertain as the 'public conscience' one should not be used to determine the consequences of being a party to an illegal transaction. Having referred to the development of the doctrine from *Thackwell v Barclays Bank plc* [1986] 1 All ER 676 onwards, Lord Goff (with the agreement of his brethren) stated ([1993] 3 All ER at p. 77):

I feel driven to say that what appears to have happened is that a principle developed by counsel for the defendant bank in *Thackwell v Barclays Bank plc* . . . for a limited purpose in the context of a claim in tort, has been allowed to expand, both in its terms and in its range of application, so that it now suggested that it operates as a broad qualifying principle, modifying and indeed transforming the long-established principles applicable in cases of illegality…

Lord Browne-Wilkinson agreed with Lord Goff that 'the consequences of being a party to an illegal transaction cannot depend, as the majority in the Court of Appeal held, on such an imponderable factor as the extent to which the public conscience would be affronted by recognising rights created by illegal transactions' ([1993] 3 All ER 65 at 85). However, it was unnecessary for the House to decide in *Tinsley* whether the public conscience test should be applied in any way outside of the limited context in which it originally emerged before Hutchison J in *Thackwell*.'

Taken together with the approach taken to this test in *Pitts v Hunt*, these criticisms made in *Tinsley* cast doubt over the status of the 'public conscience' test. This test did shape the approach to the question of ex turpi taken by the Court of Appeal in *Reeves v Metropolitan Police Comr* [1999] QB 169, [1998] 2 All ER 381, where Buxton LJ thought that the exposition of the doctrine in the *Euro-Diam* case 'remains a valuable guide to the basis of the defence'. However, in *Clunis v Camden and Islington Health Authority* [1998] QB 978, [1998] 3 All ER 180, noted by C. A. Hopkins [1998] CLJ 448, the Court of Appeal rejected the application of the 'public conscience' test, referring to the criticism it received in *Tinsley v Milligan*. In *Moore Stephens v Stone & Rolls Ltd* [2008] EWCA Civ 644, the Court of Appeal confirmed the correction of the approach adopted in *Clunis*.

In *Clunis* the claimant, who had been discharged from a hospital in which he had been detained by virtue of an order under s. 3 of the Mental Health Act 1983, had killed a person and been convicted of manslaughter on the ground of diminished responsibility. He was endeavouring to sue the defendant, who he alleged had been negligent in failing to arrange for an assessment of him and if an assessment had taken place, the killing would not, he argued, have taken place. The Court of Appeal reverted to the approach, to be found in older authorities (e.g. *Holman v Johnson* (1834) 1 Cowp 341 at 343 per Lord Mansfield CJ), that the court will not help someone who founds his claim on an illegal or immoral act, and took the view that this approach was not confined to particular causes of action e.g. contract. It then rejected the claimant's claim as it was based essentially on his own illegal act and he must be taken to have known what he was doing and that it was wrong. (See also *Worrall v British Railways Board* [1999] EWCA Civ 1312; *Meah v McCreamer* [1985] 1 All ER 367, but note that the Law Commission in its Consultation Paper No 160, *The Illegality Defence in Tort* (London: HMSO, 2001), considered that this case was wrongly decided ([2.6 and 6.58]. Contrast the more nuanced approach adopted in *Gray v Thames Trains Ltd* [2008] EWCA Civ 713.). Note also that in *Clunis v United Kingdom*, Application No. 45049/98, judgment of 11 September 2001, the European Court of Human Rights held that the denial of the claim brought by Clunis did not violate the right to fair trial.

6.   The rejection in *Clunis* and *Tinsley* of the 'public conscience' test and its replacement with a focus on whether the action in question was wholly or primarily founded upon an illegal act has been very influential. In *Cross v Kirkby* (2000) Times, 5 April, the claimant, an anti-hunt protester, was injured by the defendant whom he had menaced and initially attacked with a baseball bat after his partner had become engaged in a scuffle with the defendant. The defendant succeeded in establishing a claim for self-defence and for illegality. The claimant unsuccessfully argued that illegality would only preclude his claim if he was forced to plead, give evidence of, or rely on

his own illegality to establish his cause of action. Beldam LJ noted the disapproval expressed about the 'pubic conscience' test in *Tinsley* and considered instead that the correct approach was to ask whether 'the claimant's claim is so closely connected or inextricably bound up with his own criminal or illegal conduct that the court could not permit him to recover without appearing to condone that conduct'. This passage was cited by Peter Gibson LJ in the sex discrimination case of *Hall v Woolston Hall Leisure Ltd*, [2001] 1 WLR 215, [2000] 4 All ER 787 to support his view that a defence of illegality should apply where 'the applicant's claim arises out of or is so clearly connected to or inextricably bound up or linked with the illegal conduct of the applicant that the court could not permit the applicant to recover compensation without appearing to condone that conduct'.

Mance LJ in *Hall v Woolston Hall* took a similar approach, however, emphasising at [79] that 'it requires quite extreme circumstances before the test will exclude a tort claim'. Nelson J took a similar view in *Flaviis v Pauley* [2002] EWHC 2886 (QB), considering that the ex turpi defence could only apply if the unlawful conduct was of a particularly grave nature and brought about the loss which was the subject matter of the claim. This emphasis on the grave nature of the conduct required has, however, not been so pronounced in the more recent case law.

■ Vellino v Chief Constable of Greater Manchester
Court of Appeal [2002] 3 All ER 78

The claimant lived in a second floor flat, where he was frequently arrested. Often, when the police came to arrest the claimant, he would seek to evade arrest by jumping from the windows of his flat to the ground floor below. His propensity for escaping by that method was very well known to the police. In September 1994 the claimant was arrested at the flat. Almost immediately afterwards, he jumped from a window of the flat and injured himself, fracturing his skull, and suffering severe brain damage and tetraplegia. He commenced proceedings for negligence against the defendant chief constable, claiming that the latter was vicariously liable for the acts of two police officers, who he alleged had stood idly by as he was making his escape. The judge dismissed the claim, holding that the police had not owed the claimant a duty of care. On his appeal, the claimant contended that the police had been under a duty to prevent him sustaining foreseeable injury whilst foreseeably attempting to escape from custody. The issue arose whether the circumstances gave rise to the operation of the principle ex turpi causa non oritur actio, and, if so, whether that precluded the existence of the duty of care contended for by the claimant.

SEDLEY LJ:...

[40] ...At the conclusion of the argument it appeared to me that on these facts this appeal had to fail, essentially for the reasons given by Sir Murray Stuart-Smith in his judgment...Putting it baldly, it appeared to be the law that if the claimant was engaged in criminal or immoral conduct (turpis means literally ugly and figuratively shameful) his claim is barred even if the defendant was also engaged in such conduct. But our decision has coincided with the publication of the Law Commission's consultation paper on *The Illegality Defence in Tort* (2001) (Law Com no 160); and even in the short interval between our reserving judgment and the publication of the working paper, my own research had led me to doubt whether we had had all the help we needed on the law. Now that we have the benefit of the Law Commission's research and, at the court's invitation, of counsel's further written submissions, I have reached the conclusion that this appeal ought to be allowed and that the claimant should have

judgment for the one-third of his damages to which the trial judge considered his own contributory conduct reduced his entitlement.

[41] It is well settled that the court will refuse its aid to a claimant who, for example, sues on a contract tainted by fraud, at least where the defendant too was implicated in the fraud. Here it is readily apparent that if it were to adjudicate the court would be compounding the litigants' misconduct and permitting one of them to profit by his own wrongdoing. Where the dishonesty is unilateral, it is in general only the dishonest party who will be prevented from suing, and for a similar reason. Applied to tort actions, the principle has been recently applied in undiluted and undifferentiated form in the recent decisions of this court in *Pitts v Hunt* [1990] 3 All ER 344, [1991] 1 QB 24 and *Sacco v Chief Constable of South Wales Constabulary* [1998] CA Transcript 1382. In the latter case Beldam LJ, who had also given the principal judgment in the former case, cited the rule in its early form as stated by Lord Mansfield CJ in *Holman v Johnson* (1775) 1 Cowp 341 at 342, [1775–1802] All ER Rep 98 at 99: 'No court will lend its aid to a man who founds his cause of action upon an immoral or illegal act.'

[42] He added Lord Lyndhurst CB's holding in *Colburn v Patmore* (1834) 1 Cr M & R 73 at 83, 149 ER 999 at 1003, that a person who is declared by law to be guilty of a crime cannot be allowed to recover damages against another person who has participated in its commission. *Sacco*'s case itself concerned a claimant who had jumped from a moving police van in which he was being conveyed in custody to the police station, and who accordingly lost his claim.

[43] While these three propositions appear in the present state of the law of tort to be parts of a single doctrine by which the court declines jurisdiction once it has found the claim to be tainted with illegality, reflection shows that they are not necessarily so. Even where the only illegal act is that of the claimant, it is a question of legal policy whether he should fail because (as was the case in *Sacco*'s case) he is the author of his own misfortune or because (as held by Lord Mansfield CJ and reiterated in *Sacco*'s case) his act was criminal, or whether he should necessarily fail at all. In most cases the doctrine of voluntary acceptance of risk will prevent a criminal from suing a fellow offender for, say, injuries negligently inflicted on him in the course of a robbery. But it cannot, as Andrew Edis QC for the defendant accepts, cover the case of a criminal who is wantonly shot, whether by armed police or by a fellow criminal, albeit while committing a crime.

[44] But why not? Because, it is argued, the cause of action will be assault rather than negligence. But that is not a relevant distinction in the turpitude doctrine: it applies across the board. The reason has to be that the tort is either unrelated or is out of proportion to the criminality. I do not accept the submission of Mr Edis that this reasoning applies only to offences so minor as to be on the fringe of true criminality. We know that, at least where the tort is trespass to the person, it may apply to claimants who are committing quite serious crimes.

[45] If this is right, the suicide cases such as *Reeves v Metropolitan Police Comr* [1999] 3 All ER 897, [2000] 1 AC 360 have a bearing despite the fact they are predicated on suicide no longer being a crime. (The criminality of suicide, at least as a secular offence, was no more than a legal fiction necessary to give a foundation to the crimes of attempting and abetting suicide.) They establish that the state owes a duty of care to those whom, against their will, it takes into its custody. Of course a ubiquitous duty of care does not imply a uniform standard of care. The standard is heavily affected in general by the circumstances and in particular by the custodians' knowledge or ignorance of the detainee's tendencies to self-harm.

[46] Arrest is different from prolonged detention in degree, but not in kind. The sometimes unbearable pressure of isolation which detention in custody can create is not present in the moments following a lawful arrest, and the appropriate standard of care is accordingly quite different. But this is not to say that the only duty owed by arresting officers is to the public, nor that the standard of care is so low that the duty cannot in practice be breached...

[47] The approach I have described was taken by the majority of the Court of Appeal (Evans and Millett LJJ) in *Revill v Newbery* [1996] 1 All ER 291, [1996] QB 567, in which an award of damages to a burglar who was shot by the occupier was upheld. Evans LJ considered that to deny the claimant

compensation for an assault which went beyond self-defence was a different thing from denying him the fruits of his crime and was akin to outlawing him. Millett LJ took the view that in such a case there was simply no room for the turpitude doctrine. It was only Neill LJ who, albeit concurring in the result, based himself on the Occupiers Liability Act 1984; but he too started from a common law position which excluded the turpitude doctrine...

[48] Equally significantly, in the field of what one can call ordinary personal injury litigation the turpitude doctrine has been consciously eliminated by the courts on policy grounds. In road accident cases, for example, it is common enough to find that the injured claimant has contributed to the accident by speeding or driving with faulty brakes; but I know of no decision that such a claimant cannot sue another driver who has negligently caused his injuries. Nor can I see any justice in so deciding when the criminal law is there to deal with his criminality and the power to apportion damages will deal with his own contribution to his injuries...

[54] ...The legal reality has become what Bingham LJ described in *Saunders v Edwards* [1987] 2 All ER 651 at 665–666, [1987] 1 WLR 1116 at 1134:

> 'Where issues of illegality are raised, the courts have...to steer a middle course between two unacceptable positions. On the one hand it is unacceptable that any court of law should aid or lend its authority to a party seeking to pursue or enforce an object or agreement which the law prohibits. On the other hand, it is unacceptable that the court should, on the first indication of unlawfulness affecting any aspect of a transaction, draw up its skirts and refuse all assistance to the plaintiff, no matter how serious his loss or how disproportionate his loss to the unlawfulness of his conduct.'

[55] If so, what test should fill the space? The authorities are in my view not reconcilable: in their present state, as the Law Commission says (para 1.5), 'it is difficult to predict an outcome or to explain the outcome in terms of the apparent rationale of the illegality defence'. It is clear that since the passage of the 1945 Act the power to apportion liability between claimant and defendant in tort actions of all kinds has afforded a far more appropriate tool for doing justice than the blunt instrument of turpitude. In many cases, classically where both parties have been involved in a single criminal enterprise, the outcome would be the same. But the present case is unusual in that the offences committed by claimant and defendant, while causally connected, were not joint. The claimant's offence was able to be committed only because the constables' had been committed first...I consider that arresting officers owe a prisoner a duty not to afford both a temptation to escape and an opportunity of doing so when there is a known risk that the prisoner will do himself real harm, even if much of the blame for hurting himself will ultimately come to rest on the prisoner himself. That duty was breached in this case, and I do not believe that a legal system which shuts its eyes to such things is doing justice, especially—but not only—where the officers' neglect is also a crime. To deny the claimant redress in such a situation because of his own offending is both to make him an outlaw and to reward the misconduct of his captors. To apportion responsibility, as Elias J would have done had he not considered his path to be blocked by doctrine, is in my view to do justice.

[56] While I respectfully accept that the exegesis of the present state of the law set out in the concluding passage of Sir Murray Stuart-Smith's judgment is the nearest one can come to a consistent account of it, for the reasons I have given I do not think that the authorities are consistent or, therefore, that it is an analysis that we are bound to adopt. The approach suggested in the preceding paragraph is not only open to us on existing authority but corresponds with the two most helpful pointers noted in the Law Commission's paper...

[59] ...[O]nce turpitude is understood, as I believe the modern common law understands it, not as an indiscriminate barrier to unworthy claimants but as a large-mesh filter for criminality in claims, the difference becomes critical. Once through it, as I consider this claim is entitled to go, the next and discrete questions are whether there was a duty of care; if there was, what standard of care it imported in the situation facing the court; whether in the light of the standard the duty was broken; and whether,

if it was, the claimant is nevertheless partly or wholly responsible for his own loss. The judge's and my own answers to these, set out above, entitle the claimant to an appropriate fraction of his damages.

[60] The House of Lords in *Tinsley v Milligan* [1993] 3 All ER 65, [1994] 1 AC 340 rejected the 'public conscience' test articulated by Hutchison J in *Thackwell v Barclays Bank plc* [1986] 1 All ER 676 as a filter on claims with a criminal dimension. We are not now required, in other words, to look over our shoulders at what we fear the press will make of our decisions in this already difficult field. The public conscience, an elusive thing, as often as not turns out to be an echo chamber inhabited by journalists and public moralists. To allow judicial policy to be dictated by it would be as inappropriate as to let judges dictate editorial policy...

[61] For the reasons I have given I would allow this appeal, remit the case for the assessment of damages and direct the entry of judgment for the claimant for one-third of the sum assessed.

SIR MURRAY STUART-SMITH: ...

[62] I agree that this appeal should be dismissed for the reasons given by Schiemann LJ. I will also state my own reasons since we are not all in agreement. It is common ground that if the facts are such that the maxim ex turpi causa non oritur actio is applicable, it does not matter whether the correct legal analysis is that the defendants owed no duty of care, because the third limb of the test in *Caparo Industries plc v Dickman* [1990] 1 All ER 568, [1990] 2 AC 605, namely that it is just fair and reasonable to impose a duty of care, is not satisfied, or that the maxim affords a free standing reason for holding that the cause of action does not arise or cannot be pursued. The question in this appeal therefore is whether the judge was correct in holding that the maxim did apply.

[63] There are many statements of the principle to be found in the reports. In *Pitts v Hunt* [1990] 3 All ER 344 at 351, [1991] 1 QB 24 at 41 Beldam LJ said, after reviewing the authorities:

'I have quoted at some length the considerations which have led courts to refuse on grounds of public policy to permit a person to enforce a claim to indemnity for they illustrate to my mind how the courts have adjusted the application of the maxim to changing social conditions and in particular to the policy underlying the Road Traffic Acts. They establish, I believe, that it is the conduct of the person seeking to base his claim on an unlawful act which is determinative of the application of the maxim.'

[64] In *Sacco v Chief Constable of South Wales Constabulary* [1998] CA Transcript 1382, a case where the claimant sustained injury when he escaped from police custody by jumping from the police van, Beldam LJ said (at p 10):

'Finally, I would reject Mr Rees's submission that the decision of this court in *Reeves v Metropolitan Police Comr* [1999] 3 All ER 897, [2000] 1 AC 360 renders the judge's conclusion on public policy untenable. The actions of the deceased in that case were not unlawful, nor were they criminal. In *Scott v Brown Dearing McNab & Co* [1892] 2 QB 724 at 728, [1891–4] All ER Rep 654 at 657, Lindley LJ said of the maxim ex turpi causa non oritur actio: "This old and well-known legal maxim is founded in good sense, and expresses a clear and well-recognised legal principle, which is not confined to indictable offences. No Court ought to enforce an illegal contract or allow itself to be made the instrument of enforcing obligations alleged to arise out of a contract or transaction which is illegal, if the illegality is duly brought to the notice of the Court, and if the person invoking the aid of the Court is himself implicated in the illegality. It matters not whether the defendant has pleaded the illegality or whether he has not. If the evidence adduced by the plaintiff proves the illegality the Court ought not to assist him." The rule was stated by Lord Mansfield CJ in *Holman v Johnson* (1775) 1 Cowp 341 at 342, [1775–1802] All ER Rep 98 at 99 to be a rule of public policy that: "No court will lend its aid to a man who founds his cause of action upon an immoral or illegal act." There are many other statements to the same effect. I point for example to the observations of Lord Lyndhurst CB in *Colburn v Patmore* (1834) 1 Cr M & R 73 at 83, 149 ER 999 at 1003 where he said that a person who is declared by law to be guilty of a crime cannot be allowed to recover damages against another who has participated in its commission. I can see no reason, for my part, why a defendant, who is not participating in a crime, should be in a less favourable position.'

[65] And Schiemann LJ, giving the second of three grounds upon which the claim failed, said:

'Second, he was engaged in a criminal act, namely attempting to escape from lawful custody. As a matter of legal policy, I see no reason to permit a man to recover damages against the police if he hurts himself as part of that illegal enterprise. The basis of such recovery must be either an allegation of a breach of a duty owed to him not to let him escape, or of a duty owed to him to take care that he does not hurt himself if he tries to escape. I see no reason to create such duties owed to him. It is common ground that the policy of the law is not to permit one criminal to recover damages from a fellow criminal who fails to take care of him whilst they are both engaged on a criminal enterprise. The reason for that rule is not the law's tenderness towards the criminal defendant, but the law's unwillingness to afford a criminal plaintiff a remedy in such circumstances. I see no reason why that unwillingness should be any the less because the defendant is a policeman and not engaged in any crime.'

[66] In *Tinsley v Milligan* [1993] 3 All ER 65 at 79–80, [1994] 1 AC 340 at 361 Lord Goff of Chieveley, in the part of his speech agreed by Lord Browne-Wilkinson ([1993] 3 All ER 65 at 84, [1994] 1 AC 340 at 369) reaffirmed the principle and decisively rejected the public conscience test which had originated in the judgment of Hutchison J in *Thackwell v Barclays Bank plc* [1986] 1 All ER 676 and approved by Nicholls LJ in the Court of Appeal in *Tinsley*'s case.

[67] In *Cross v Kirkby* (2000) Times, 5 April, [2000] CA Transcript 321 Judge LJ said (at para 103):

'In my judgment, where the claimant is behaving unlawfully, or criminally, on the occasion when his cause of action in tort arises, his claim is not liable to be defeated ex turpi causa unless it is also established that the facts which give rise to it are inextricably linked with his criminal conduct. I have deliberately expressed myself in language which goes well beyond questions of causation in the general sense.'

...

[70] From [the] authorities I derive the following propositions. (1) The operation of the principle arises where the claimant's claim is founded upon his own criminal or immoral act. The facts which give rise to the claim must be inextricably linked with the criminal activity. It is not sufficient if the criminal activity merely gives occasion for tortious conduct of the defendant. (2) The principle is one of public policy; it is not for the benefit of the defendant. Since if the principle applies, the cause of action does not arise, the defendant's conduct is irrelevant. There is no question of proportionality between the conduct of the claimant and defendant. (3) In the case of criminal conduct this has to be sufficiently serious to merit the application of the principle. Generally speaking a crime punishable with imprisonment could be expected to qualify. If the offence is criminal, but relatively trivial, it is in any event difficult to see how it could be integral to the claim. (4) The 1945 Act is not applicable where the claimant's action amounts to a common law crime which does not give rise to liability in tort.

[71] Applying these principles it is common ground that the claimant has to rely on his criminal conduct in escaping lawful custody to found his claim. It is integral to the claim. The crime of escape is a serious one; it is a common law offence for which the penalty is at large. It is almost invariably punished by a sentence of imprisonment, although the length of the sentence is usually measured in months rather than years. In my judgment it is plainly a sufficiently serious offence for the purpose of the application of the maxim. I would have reached this conclusion in any event; but it accords with the judgments of the Court of Appeal in *Sacco*'s case.

[SCHIEMANN LJ delivered a judgment in favour of dismissing the appeal.]

Appeal dismissed.

QUESTION

Both Sedley LJ and Sir Murray Stuart-Smith appear to agree on the key principles to be extracted from the case law as to the scope of the illegality defence. Where do their approaches diverge? Sedley LJ suggests that if the illegality defence did have a place in the common law, it should be treated as confined in scope to serving as a 'large mesh filter' to catch cases where there was reliance on an 'illegal or immoral act' to found the cause of action. Does Sir Murray Stuart-Smith disagree with this analysis?

NOTES

1. This case is noted by J. Morgan (2002) 118 LQR 527. Note that, in addition to the arguments set out in the extract above, Sedley LJ also cited the decision of the House of Lords in *National Coal Board v England* [1954] AC 403, [1954] 1 All ER 546. Here an employer attempted to use the illegality defence to answer the claim of a miner who had been injured in a premature detonation but who was himself one-quarter to blame for his injury, on the basis that he had breached safety regulations (and thereby had committed a criminal offence) by attaching the cable to the detonator himself instead of leaving it to the expert shotfirer. The House of Lords took the view that public policy, far from justifying the application of the ex turpi principle, required that the action be 'entertained on its merits'. Lord Reid also suggested that s. 1(1) of the Law Reform (Contributory Negligence) Act 1945, in making provision for apportionment of loss to be permissible for all forms of fault, including 'negligence, breach of statutory duty or other act or omission which gives rise to a liability in tort', precluded the operation of the illegality defence. While the stance of the other members of the House of Lords on this issue was not so clear, Sedley LJ nevertheless suggested that *National Coal Board v England* could constitute binding authority to the effect that the ex turpi principle had been abolished by the 1945 Act. However, Sir Murray Stuart-Smith and Schiemann LJ disagreed, with Sir Murray Stuart-Smith noting that subsequent decisions had clearly indicated that the ex turpi principle was firmly established in the common law. In any case, as Morgan notes, the 1945 Act makes provision for apportionment to reflect failure to take care for one own's safety: moral turpitude does not enter into the contributory negligence framework.

2. Schiemann LJ agreed that the ex turpi defence as set out in *Tinsley*, *Clunis* and *Cross* would apply in this case, but primarily based his conclusion not on the seriousness of the offence itself: instead he took the view that the 'illegal enterprise' of the claimant, who seriously injured himself attempting to escape from the police, negatived any duty that the arresting police officers may have owed him to bar his attempted escape via a dangerous route. (Schiemann LJ took a similar view in *Sacco v Chief Constable of South Wales Constabulary* [1998] CA Transcript 1382.) In contrast, Sedley LJ took the view that the arresting police officers were under a duty to take steps to prevent the claimant injuring himself.

3. Both Sedley LJ and Sir Murray Stuart-Smith followed *Tinsley* and *Clunis* in rejecting the application of the public conscience test. The Court of Appeal in *Hewison v Meridian Shipping Pte* [2003] ICR 776, [2002] EWCA Civ 1821 also considered that the public conscience test was defunct. However, in applying the alternative approach developed in *Clunis* and *Cross*, the Court gave the illegality defence a broad application: the claimant seaman, who was injured as a result of negligence for which his employer was responsible, was precluded from recovering some of his lost earnings

on the basis that he had fraudulently concealed his epilepsy (Ward LJ dissenting). Clarke LJ set out his preferred approach as follows:

26. …the courts have not adopted the suggestion that, at any rate in a case where the maxim *ex turpi causa non oritur actio* applies, the correct approach is to identify whether the public conscience would be affronted. We have been shown no case in which the courts have adopted such an approach to a case of this kind. In these circumstances I, for my part, do not think that it is appropriate to adopt it.

27. The correct principle seems to me to be substantially the same as that identified by Beldam LJ as being applicable to cases in which the maxim *ex turpi causa non oritur actio* applies. It is common ground that that maxim does not itself apply here because it is correctly agreed that there is no principle of public policy which prevents the appellant from pursuing his cause of action for damages for negligence or breach of duty against the respondents. The question is not whether he can recover at all but whether he is debarred from recovering part of his alleged loss.

28. However, as I see it, the principle is closely related. It is common ground that there are cases in which public policy will prevent a claimant from recovering the whole of the damages which, but for the rule of public policy, he would otherwise have recovered. The principle can perhaps be stated as a variation of the maxim so that it reads *ex turpi causa non oritur damnum*, where the *damnum* is the loss which would have been recovered but for the relevant illegal or immoral act. A classic example is the principle that a person who makes his living from burglary cannot have damages assessed on the basis of what he would have earned from burglary but for the defendant's negligence.

29. To my mind the authorities support that approach. They seem to me to support the proposition that where a claimant has to rely upon his or her own unlawful act in order to establish the whole or part of his or her claim the claim will fail either wholly or in part. In the present context the principle can be seen from the decision of this court in *Hunter v Butler* [1996] RTR 396, although it has to be said that the case does give rise to some difficulties of interpretation.

An analysis similar to that adopted by the majority in *Hewison* was also applied in *Marlwood Commercial Inc v Kozeny* [2006] EWHC 872 (Comm); *Donegal International Ltd v Zambia* [2007] EWHC 197 (Comm); and *Moore Stephens v Stone & Rolls Ltd* [2008] EWCA Civ 644. At first instance in the latter case Langley J at [43] summarised his understanding of when the defence of illegality should be applied:

The conclusion I draw from these authorities is that the ex turpi maxim requires a 'reliance test' to be satisfied. The claim must be 'founded on' or 'arise from' an illegal act of the claimant (Lord Mansfield) or the illegal act must necessarily be pleaded or relied upon to sustain the claim (*Tinsley v Milligan*) or to put forward the case (*Clunis*) or the facts which give rise to the claim are 'inextricably linked with' the illegality (*Cross v Kirby* per Judge LJ). The contrast is with a claim to which the illegality is only 'collateral' or 'insignificant' (*Hewison*) or 'incidental' (Bingham LJ). It is also acceptable that only part of a claim or a loss is defeated by the maxim (*Hewison*).

It therefore appears as if recovery will be denied where there is reliance upon unlawful or potentially even immoral conduct. However, substantial differences of view appear to exist as to the nature and extent of the unlawful conduct that will be required, with Sedley LJ in *Vellino* and Ward LJ in *Hewison* taking a much more restrictive approach than the majority in either case. See now also the important decision of *Gray v Thames Trains Ltd* [2008] EWCA Civ 713.

4. The approach of the courts in the wake of *Clunis*, *Vellino* and *Hewison* is potentially difficult to reconcile with *Revill v Newbery*, in which it will be remembered that the claimant, who was trying to break into a shed on the defendant's allotment in the early hours of the morning, was unintentionally wounded when the defendant, who had been sleeping in the shed to protect his property, fired a shotgun through a hole in

the door of the shed. The claim was held not to be barred by ex turpi. Perhaps one way of reconciling them might be to rely on the point made by Neill LJ in *Revill* that Parliament in its legislation in relation to trespassers (s. 1 of the Occupiers' Liability Act 1984, p. 587, post) had not ruled out liability to a burglar. See further Glofcheski, op cit., pp. 19–20, and the Law Commission Consultation Paper No. 160, *The Illegality Defence in Tort*, para. 2.58.

Another way of reconciling *Revill* and *Clunis* is that in *Revill* the harm to the burglar would have been inflicted whether or not he was guilty of a crime (what if, for example, he had turned out to be a bailiff?), whereas in *Clunis* the claimant suffers no harm at all unless he is convicted of a crime. The illegal conduct in *Clunis*, therefore, did not establish or found the cause of action. Can the same analysis be applied to distinguish *Revill* and *Hewison*? In *Gray v Thames Trains Ltd* [2008] EWCA Civ 713, emphasis was placed on whether the wrongful act of the claimant had caused the harm in question.

5.   The 'reliance' test is applied when a claimant relies upon his illegality to found or establish a cause of action. In cases such as *Pitts v Hunt*, where the claimant is suing the defendant as a result of negligence in the course of a joint illegal activity, the 'reliance' approach finds its counterpart in the refusal to set a standard of care, referred to in *Pitts v Hunt*, ante. (See also *Flaviis v Pauley* [2002] EWHC 2886, para. 24.) It seems that on the 'standard of care' approach the courts will not fix a standard of care even though it might be possible for them to do so (see J. Swanton (1981) 9 Sydney LR 304 at 320–321).

6.   This raises the question as to how different the 'standard of care' approach and the 'public conscience' test really are (cf. Swanton, op cit., p. 322 and see Glofcheski, op cit., p. 12). Is the reason for not fixing a standard of care anything other than that to fix the standard of care in these cases would offend the public conscience? The same question can be asked about the 'reliance' approach. Given the very different approaches adopted by different judges applying the same basic principles in both the *Vellino* and *Hewison* judgments, do the related 'standard of care' and 'reliance' approaches really improve on the indeterminacy and imprecision of the 'public conscience' test?

7.   Another point to consider is how far the apparently conjoined 'reliance' and 'standard of care' approaches can apply outside the tort of negligence. For an example of its potential use in a different tort see *Murphy v Culhane* [1977] QB 94, [1976] 3 All ER 533 (p. 75, post) and see the discussion of *Thackwell v Barclays Bank plc* [1986] 1 All ER 676 and *Saunders v Edwards* [1987] 2 All ER 651, [1987 1 WLR 1116 in *Pitts v Hunt* (pp. 467, ante). See also *Daido Asia Japan Company Ltd v. Rothen* [2001] EWHC 163 (Ch), where Collins J considered that an ex turpi defence could be available in an action for deceit, but applying the approach set out by Aldous LJ in *Tinsley v Milligan*, held that no such defence could be established on the facts.

See now however s. 329 of the Criminal Justice Act 2003, which provides that court permission must be obtained before an action can be brought in *trespass to the person* (but not negligence) where the alleged act occurred in the course of the claimant committing an imprisonable offence. Under s. 329(3), a court may only give permission for the claim to proceed if the defendant's act was grossly disproportionate and the defendant believed that the claimant was committing or about to commit the offence, and that the act in question was necessary in self-defence, to protect his property, or to prevent a crime taking place. This piece of legislation is in many ways a political gesture in response to the controversy surrounding the imprisonment of a farmer, Tony Martin, for fatally shooting a burglar in 1999. It is difficult to see how it will be implemented, given that it will require a court to form a view of the proportionality of the defendant's response before granting approval for a claim to proceed. In addition, as negligence claims are not covered, the legislation may not prove a very formidable obstacle to the *Revill v Newbery*-style claims it was presumably intended to discourage.

8. For an example of what might be thought to be the harsh effects the application of the ex turpi defence can have, see *Burns v Edman* [1970] 2 QB 541, [1970] 1 All ER 886. In this case, in which a person had been killed in a motor accident, Crichton J thought it was a 'fair inference' that the support given by the deceased to his family had come from the proceeds of crime. In this situation, the judge accepted an argument that in the Fatal Accidents Act claims the injury (i.e. loss of support) to each defendant, who included the deceased's children, was 'turpis causa' and hence irrecoverable. Could there have been an action if the deceased in *Burns v Edman* had stolen a bottle of ginger beer for consumption by his children and they had been injured by a decomposed snail in the bottle? (This question is suggested by D. E. C. Yale [1970] CLJ 17 in his comment on the case). Consider further *Hunter v Butler* [1996] RTR 396, noted, p. 284, ante, dealing with undeclared income.

For the recovery of goods seized illegally, see *Webb v Chief Constable of Merseyside Police* [2000] 1 All ER 209; *Costello v Derbyshire Constabulary* [2001] 3 All ER 150, [2001] EWCA Civ 381; *Gough v Chief Constable of the Midlands Police* [2004] EWCA Civ 206. See G. Battersby (2002) 65 MLR 603. Contrast *Marsh v Clare* [2003] EWCA Civ 284.

In *Kirkham v Chief Constable of the Greater Manchester Police* [1990] 2 QB 283, [1990] 3 All ER 246, Sir Denys Buckley was not satisfied that a dependant's claim under the Fatal Accidents Act would be barred by any 'turpitude' by the deceased. Is this view distinguishable from *Burns v Edman*? Can Sir Denys Buckley's view be squared with the point (see pp. 283 and 558, ante) that the dependants cannot sue if the deceased did not have an action at his death?

Note that notwithstanding the inadmissibility decision in *Clunis v United Kingdom* (noted at p. 472, ante), the Law Commission in its Consultation Paper No. 160, *The Illegality Defence in Tort*, noted that there is concern that a broad application of the illegality defence could result in a denial of the right to fair trial under Article 6 ECHR or a violation of the right to property (which can in certain circumstances include choses in action) protected in Article 1, First Protocol ECHR: see para. 1.8.

9. It has been held that ex turpi cannot be raised so as to defeat a claim for contribution under the Civil Liability (Contribution) Act 1978 (p. 1122, post): *K v P (J, Third Party)* [1993] Ch 140, [1993] 1 All ER 521, noted p. 1126, post).

10. For discussion of this area of the law, see N. H. Crago (1963–4) 4 Melb ULR 534; G. H. L. Fridman (1972) 18 McGill LJ 275; E. J. Weinrib (1976) 26 Univ Tor LJ 28; W. J. Ford (1977) 11 Melb ULR 33; Swanton, op cit.; C. Debattista (1984) 13 Anglo-American LR 15; B. MacDougall (1991) 55 Sask LR 1; R. Glofcheski, op cit.

See also the Law Commission Consultation Paper No. 160, which analysed the current state of the illegality defence in tort and expressed serious concern about the inherent uncertainty of the existing state of the law. (Note that the Commission at paras 4.41 and 4.53 considered that the claimant's barred claim in *Cross v Kirkby*, which has become an important precedent, could not be said to be founded upon his illegal act.) As a consequence, the consultation paper sought views on a proposal to introduce a form of statutory structured discretion, under which the court would be directed to consider whether a claim should be allowed or disallowed, in the light of the underlying rationales of the illegality defence and taking into account a number of guiding factors. The Commission's analysis of the illegality defence remains relevant and persuasive.

■ Law Commission, 'The Illegality Defence in Tort'

(Law com. No. 160, 2001)

1.19 We propose that the discretion should be structured around a number of factors, to help provide certainty and guidance in the exercise of the discretion, and, importantly, to reflect the policies that lie behind the existence of the doctrine of illegality. In Consultation Paper No 154, and in the context of contract and trusts, we proposed that those factors should be (i) the seriousness of the illegality; (ii) the knowledge and intention of the plaintiff or illegal trust beneficiary; (iii) whether refusing to allow the claim or whether invalidity of the trust would act as a deterrent; (iv) whether refusing the claim would further the purpose of the rule which renders the contract or trust illegal, and (v) whether denying relief would be proportionate to the illegality involved. We discuss in Part VI the factors that we think are relevant to a discretion in the context of tort; they are along similar lines to those mentioned above. However, we will also raise other factors including one that reflects an argument that we discuss later in this paper, the need for "consistency".

1.20 Our consideration of the law has led us to the conclusion that there are two problems with the current law. First, there is a lack of clarity in the way the illegality defence is to be applied in tort cases. Secondly, the law could be applied in a way which would produce outcomes that we think are undesirable, by including within its scope situations in which we believe the use of the illegality defence would be difficult to justify.

1.21 Our provisional proposals for reform do not seek to draw up a finite list of situations when illegality would impact on a claim and when it would not—this would be unjustifiably rigid and practically impossible—but we do seek to provide a policy-based, structured discretion to assist the court in deciding that question. Under these proposals, we envisage that cases where the claimant is seeking damages as compensation for the direct consequences of his or her illegal acts, or seeking to be indemnified against such consequences, will generally continue to be barred by the courts.

1.22 However, there are several situations in which we feel that, although there is an element of illegality involved in the circumstances surrounding the claim, and *dicta* in recent cases that the defence may be available, barring the claim cannot reasonably be justified on the policy rationales that underlie the doctrine of illegality. In such cases we find it difficult to argue that the claimant should still be denied what would be his or her 'normal' rights under the civil law. Barring a claim where it cannot be justified on grounds other than 'criminals shouldn't have rights' or on an unreasoned, 'gut-feeling' basis would be potentially disproportionate and wrong.

1.23 Although we can note at the outset of this paper that, with one exception, we do not regard any of the reported tort cases as being wrongly decided in terms of final *outcome*—and to this extent our provisionally proposed reforms would not produce significantly different results—we do have significant concerns as to the current and potential future operation of the illegality doctrine. Many of the cases can be explained on a basis independent to that of illegality. Despite the outcome, we do question the correctness of the decision on the illegality point in a number of cases...

1.24 As will be seen later in this paper, one of the possible consequences of our proposed reforms might be a reduction in the number of cases where the court relies on the illegality doctrine to bar claims for personal injuries. We recognise that some of the points we make in this paper may be controversial. Public opinion may not be in favour of any perceived increase in the ability of a criminal to sue for damages seemingly arising out of his or her criminal activity. This perception may be particularly acute where the tortfeasor is seen as the victim of the claimant's crime, such as the householder who uses excessive self-defence against the burglar, and who is then sued by that burglar for the injury caused.

1.25 However, we make the (perhaps) obvious point that the law does not allow even a criminal who has committed a serious offence to be deprived of all his or her rights under either the civil or criminal law. This would amount to outlawry, and this has quite clearly, and in our view rightly, been rejected by the courts. Despite this, however, the law does recognise that in certain situations illegal conduct will as a matter of policy operate so as to prevent a person suing to enforce his or her rights under the civil law. The question is where the boundary is to be drawn between illegal conduct that will have an effect on the offender's rights, and where it will not. To be just, that boundary must not be drawn arbitrarily. It should reflect the underlying policy rationales. We believe that the outcomes of the existing cases can be justified in terms of the policy rationales or of other doctrines, but we are not convinced that this is true of the statements of law contained in some of the cases.

1.26 Finally, we make the point that the decision to bar a claimant from recovering damages in tort is a very serious one. It may mean that a claimant who has been barred from recovering damages for serious personal injury following a negligently caused accident will lose a substantial sum of money. He or she may have to fall back onto State benefits in respect of, for example, an inability to work as a result of the injury. In such a case this would involve both a substantial reduction in the sums available and a transfer of the financial responsibility from the defendant tortfeasor (or his or her insurers) to the public purse, the Criminal Injuries Compensation Authority, or possibly the Motor Insurers' Bureau…Given these points, we have serious doubts as to the appropriateness of the illegality doctrine operating in the context of personal injury cases.

CHAPTER EIGHT
ASSESSMENT OF DAMAGES

1 THE AIMS OF AN AWARD OF DAMAGES

■ McConnel v Wright
Court of Appeal [1903] 1 Ch 546

COLLINS MR: . . .
It is not an action for breach of contract, and, therefore, no damages in respect of prospective gains which the person contracting was entitled by his contract to expect come in, but it is an action of tort—it is an action for a wrong done . . . and therefore, prima facie, the highest limit of his damages is the whole extent of his loss . . .

■ Indata Equipment Supplies Ltd (t/a Autofleet) v ACL Ltd
Court of Appeal [1998] 1 BCLC 412

OTTON LJ: . . .
In my view the correct measure of damages was undoubtedly on a tortious basis, ie such sum as would have put the plaintiff into the position it would have been in had it not been for the tort . . .

QUESTION

Is it so easy to distinguish between the claimant's prospective gains and what the claimant has lost by being put in a worse position by the tort? What if it is possible to sell the prospective rights to another person as if they were a type of property, for example the 'goodwill' of a business? And what if the claimant was expected to lose soon what he lost by the tort, for example, a job? Will not the value of what the claimant lost reflect its prospective value?

NOTE

Notice that the gains made by the defendant do not figure in the traditional view of the measure of damages in tort. See *Pasley v Freeman* (1789) 3 Term Rep 51 (p. 939, post). But such gains do become relevant in a number of circumstances, for example in claims for exemplary or punitive damages (see p. 493, post), where the tort also amounts to a breach of a fiduciary duty and in other cases in which the claimant can take advantage of a restitutionary claim.

■ Severn Trent Water Ltd v Barnes

Court of Appeal [2004] EWCA Civ 570

Water supply companies, as statutory undertakers, have a power to lay water mains under land belonging to other people, but only if they give reasonable notice to the owner under s. 159(4) of the Water Industry Act 1991. The defendant water company omitted to give such notice to the claimant landowner in respect of 20 metres of land, which was unmarked grazing land used by a third party, Gartside, under a license agreement. The defendant installed part of a new 28 km water main under the land. This trespass, characterised by the Court of Appeal as 'trivial, accidental and unintentional', only came to light later, at which point it was impossible to invoke the statutory procedure. The judge at first instance found that there was no loss or damage to the land either in respect of its suitability for grazing or in respect of any future, albeit very unlikely, use as development land. He nevertheless awarded the claimant the following sums: (1) £110, which the parties agreed would have been the amount the Lands Tribunal would have awarded as compensation under the procedures of the 1991 Act itself; (2) £500, in recognition of the fact that the defendant's actions had denied the claimant the opportunity to negotiate its own compensation, a sum arrived at in the light of the claimant's (false) beliefs about the development value of the land and the defendant's admitted willingness to pay a sum higher than the expected Lands Tribunal award to avoid the inconvenience of having to go to the Lands Tribunal; and (3) £1560 'restitutionary damages' to reflect a small part of the defendant's profits obtained by using the whole 28 km water mains over a three-year period—which was how long the defendant's trespass continued before the parties should reasonably have come to an agreement about it. The defendant appealed against the £500 'loss of opportunity to bargain' damages and against the £1,560 'restitutionary' damages. The Court of Appeal upheld the £500 award, but allowed the appeal in respect of the £1,560 'restitutionary' damages.

POTTER LJ: . . .

[17] So far as the 'loss of opportunity' award is concerned it is clear (and indeed it is not in dispute) that, despite the award being so described in the latter part of the judgment, it was in fact one made by way of damages to compensate Mr Barnes for the invasion of his rights, on the basis that it was the price which, prior to the laying of the main, he could reasonably have required or obtained for the rights gained by Severn Trent. Upon that basis, Severn Trent contend that, the test being objective, the only sum which could reasonably have been demanded was the amount which the Lands Tribunal would have awarded, namely the £110 already awarded by the judge.

[18] As to the award of £1560, it is submitted that the judge erred in principle in making an additional 'restitutionary' award at all, upon a basis which was rightly claimed only *in the alternative* to his compensatory claim. It is also submitted that such an award was logically inconsistent with the basis of calculation of loss earlier adopted by the judge. Having rightly found that the loss on a 'compensatory' basis was that sum which the parties (or reasonable parties) would have negotiated on the basis of a notice notionally given *prior to* trespass, which *ex hypothesi* related to the installation and future use of the main by Severn Trent, it was logically wrong (and effectively gives rise to double counting) for the judge to make an additional 'restitutionary' award based on the assumption of the parties' reaching a notional compromise agreement three years *after* the commencement of the trespass. . . .

[19] In resisting the appeal, Mr Yell who appears for Mr Barnes has not sought to challenge the judge's findings that there was no loss of a chance in respect of any development value of the land, nor any loss of agricultural use. He is thus obliged to accept that, on a purely compensatory basis (that is to say compensation for loss actually suffered), Mr Barnes failed to establish any claim above the agreed figure of £110. Nonetheless, he asserts that the judge had jurisdiction to award damages:

(1) as if in lieu of an injunction under Lord Cairns' Act even though no claim for an injunction had been made.
(2) as a species of 'restitutionary' damages long employed in the field of proprietary torts, and more recently in the field of contract, in a situation where the benefit to the defendant through his wrongful act has far outstripped any loss which the claimant has suffered....

Discussion

...

[22] As observed in *McGregor on Damages* (17th ed) at paras 12–002 to 12–006, use of the term 'restitutionary' damages as an appropriate extension of the basic rule that damages are compensation for loss actually suffered by the claimant has enjoyed a mixed judicial reception. Whereas, in *A-G v Blake* [1998] Ch 439, [1998] 1 All ER 833, (breach of a contractual obligation of confidence) Lord Woolf MR giving the judgment of the court was content at 456b-459b to adopt that term in respect of cases where the benefit to the wrongdoer far exceeds the loss (if any) to the person wronged, Lord Nicholls in the House of Lords preferred to avoid it as an 'unhappy' expression (see [2001] 1 AC 268 at 284H), while at the same time recognising that:

"Even when awarding damages, the law does not adhere slavishly to the concept of compensation for financially measurable loss. When the circumstances require, damages are measured by reference to the benefit obtained by the wrongdoer. This applies to interference with property rights. Recently the approach has been applied to breach of contract." (285B–C)

[23] Within the law of tort and interference with the use of land this method of measuring damages has been accommodated within the basic compensatory rule on the basis of the 'user' principle articulated by Nicholls LJ in *Stoke City Council v W & J Wass* [1988] 3 All ER 394, [1988] 1 WLR 1406 at 1416a–d:

"It is an established principle concerning the assessment of damages that a person who has wrongfully used another's property without causing the latter any pecuniary loss may still be liable to that other for more than nominal damages. In general, he is liable to pay, as damages, a reasonable sum for the wrongful use he has made of the other's property. The law has reached this conclusion by giving to the concept of loss or damage in such a case a wider meaning than merely financial loss calculated by comparing the property owner's financial position after the wrongdoing with what it would have been had the wrongdoing never occurred. Furthermore, in such a case it is no answer for the wrongdoer to show that the property owner would probably not have used the property himself had the wrongdoer not done so. In *The Mediana* [1900] AC 113, 117, Earl of Halsbury LC made the famous observation that a defendant who had deprived the plaintiff of one of the chairs in his room for 12 months could not diminish the damages by showing that the plaintiff did not usually sit upon that chair or that there were plenty of other chairs in the room."

[24] The principle has largely been developed in relation to trespass to land, beginning with the 19th century cases of unauthorised mining (the 'wayleave' cases): see for instance *Martin v Porter* (1839) 5 M & W 351 and *Jegon v Vivian* (1871) 6 Ch App 742; see also *Whitwham v Westminster Brymbo Coal Co* [1896] 2 Ch 538 (trespass by tipping of refuse).

[25] In *A-G v Blake*, in reviewing the position in relation to trespass to land, Lord Nicholls said at 278 F–C:

"A trespasser who enters another's land may cause the landowner no financial loss. In such a case damages are measured by the benefit received by the trespasser, namely, by his use of the land. The same principle is applied where the wrong consists of the use of another's land for depositing waste, or by using a path across the land or using passages in an underground mine. In this type of case the damages recoverable will be, in short, the price a reasonable person would pay for the right of user... "

[26] That principle has been applied in relation to wrongful interference involving easements. In *Bracewell v Appelby* [1975] Ch 408, [1975] 1 All ER 993, the defendant wrongly used and asserted a right of way over a private road to a house which he had built. The court (Graham J) refused an injunction on the grounds of the plaintiff's delay in commencing proceedings and, following the decision of Brightman J in *Wrotham Park Estate Co Ltd v Parkside Homes Ltd* [1974] 2 All ER 321, [1974] 1 WLR 798 (a restrictive covenant case—see further below), held the defendant

"...liable to pay an amount of damages which so far as it can be estimated is equivalent to a proper and fair price which would be payable for the acquisition of the right of way in question."

Graham J observed:

"The circumstances here are very different from those in the *Wrotham Park* case and I think that the proper approach is to endeavour to arrive at a fair figure which, on the assumption made, the parties would have arrived at as one which the plaintiffs would accept as compensating them for loss of amenity and increased user, and which at the same time, whilst making the blue land a viable building plot, would not be so high as to deter the defendant from building at all."

[27] In that case and in the subsequent case of *Carr-Saunders v Dick McNeil Associates* [1986] 2 All ER 888, [1986] 1 WLR 922 (interference with the plaintiff's right to light) the court made clear that, in deciding upon an appropriate award in relation to the notional 'reasonable sum' or 'fair figure' for the defendant to pay, regard was to be had to the bargaining position of the parties in order to arrive at a price which would have been likely to have been negotiated as the reasonable price of a licence for the action taken by the defendant which constituted the invasion of the claimant's rights.

[28] The relevance of that bargaining position is of course because, in most cases, without the approval of the claimant, the defendant is in no position to proceed: see the position as explained by Millett J in the *Carr-Saunders* case at 895. That was a case involving obstruction of a right enjoyed by virtue of a prescriptive easement. However, Millett J, by reference to *Bracewell v Appelby* and the *Wrotham Park* case, made clear that, as between claims in contract or in tort, there is no reason for any difference of approach when awarding damages in respect of wrongful interference by a defendant with the use and enjoyment of the claimant's land.

[29] In the *Wrotham Park* case, 55 houses had been built by the defendant in knowing breach of a restrictive covenant, in the face of objections by the claimant. Brightman J held that on its natural construction the covenant was a prohibition against development without obtaining prior approval from the claimant as estate owner. The claimant sought an injunction to restrain building on the land and a mandatory injunction for the demolition of buildings already erected in breach of covenant but did not apply for a interlocutory injunction and by trial the houses were complete. Acting under the jurisdiction which originated in Lord Cairns' Act, Brightman J made an award of damages in the sum which the plaintiff might reasonably have demanded as a *quid pro quo* for relaxing the covenant had the defendants first applied to them for relaxation. In the circumstances of the case he found that faced with a request from the developer which the plaintiff felt reluctantly obliged to grant, a sum would have been negotiated on the basis of the profit which the developer expected to make from his operations and would then reasonably have required a certain percentage of that anticipated profit as a price for the relaxation of the covenant. Upon that basis he made an award in a sum equal to 5% of the defendant's anticipated profit as being fair in all the circumstances.

[30] That decision was approved and applied in *Jaggard v Sawyer* [1995] 2 All ER 189, [1995] 1 WLR 269. In the latter case, Sir Thomas Bingham MR stated at 281:

"I cannot, however, accept that Brightman J's assessment of damages in the *Wrotham Park* case was based on other than compensatory principles. The defendants had committed a breach of covenant, the effects of which continued. The judge was not willing to order the defendants to undo the continuing effects of that breach. He had therefore to assess the damages necessary to compensate the plaintiffs for this continuing invasion of their right. He paid attention to the profits earned by the defendants, as it seemed to me, not in order to strip the defendants of their unjust gains, but because of the obvious relationship between the profits earned by the defendants and the sum which the defendants could reasonably have been willing to pay to secure a release from the covenant. I am reassured to find that this is the view taken of the *Wrotham Park* case by Sir Robert Megarry V-C in *Tito v Waddell (No 2)* [1977] Ch 106, 335 . . . "

[31] . . . Millett LJ [in *Jaggard*] went on to state:

"It is plain from his judgment in the *Wrotham Park* case that Brightman J's approach was compensatory, not restitutionary. He sought to measure the damages by a reference to what the plaintiff had lost, not by reference to what the defendant had gained. He did not award the plaintiff the profit which the defendant had made by the breach, but the amount which he judged the plaintiff might have obtained as the price of giving its consent. The amount of the profit which the defendant expected to make was a relevant factor in that assessment, but that was all."

His judgment concluded at 292d:

"In the present case the plaintiff brought proceedings at a time when her rights were still capable of being protected by injunction. She has accordingly been able to invoke the court's jurisdiction to award in substitution for an injunction damages which take account of the future as well as the past. In my view there is no reason why compensatory damages for future trespasses and continuing breaches of covenant should not reflect the value of the rights which she has lost, or why such damages should not be measured by the amount which she could reasonably have expected to receive for their release."

[32] In *A-G v Blake* Lord Nicholls stated at 281:

" . . . in the same way as damages at common law for violations of a property right may be measured by reference to the benefits wrongfully obtained by a defendant, so under Lord Cairns' Act damages may include damages measured by reference to the benefits likely to be obtained in future by the defendant. This approach has been adopted on many occasions. Recent examples are *Bracewell v Appelby* [1975] Ch 408 and *Jaggard v Sawyer* [1995] 1 WLR 269, both cases concerned with access to a newly-built house over another's land.

The measure of damages awarded in this type of case is often analysed as damages for loss of a bargaining opportunity or, which comes to the same, the price payable for the compulsory acquisition of a right. This analysis is correct."

[33] In this case, Mr Barnes did not claim damages in lieu of an injunction under the Lord Cairns' Act jurisdiction but simply damages for past injury at common law on the basis set out in the pleading ie loss of (development) value, alternatively damages which, though described as 'restitutionary', were expressly based on the 'fair price' principle assessed by reference to Thames Water's tariff charges for water passed through the main.

(a) The £110 element

[34] It is not in dispute between the parties that £110 was rightly awarded as the statutory compensation payable had notice been served. It clearly represented the minimum value of the right wrongfully obtained by Severn Trent by proceeding to lay the main without notice having been given.

(b) The £500 element

[35] In the circumstances of this case, as it seems to me, the judge was plainly correct not to limit the damages awarded to the sum of £110. No notice having been given before the works were carried out, the continuing trespass could not be reversed and the judge was right to approach matters on the basis succinctly described by Lord Nicholls as:

"loss of a bargaining opportunity or, which comes to the same, the price payable for the compulsory acquisition of a right."

In this case Severn Water had by its actions effectively compulsorily acquired the right to run its water main under Mr Barnes' land *without* complying with the statutory procedures which would have limited the compensation to £110. Accordingly, the judge was right to go through the exercise which he did in treating as the fair price the likely reasonable outcome of any negotiations which would have taken place had notice been served prior to the works being done. In this respect, however, he was equally right to have regard to the fact that, had notice been served, upon its expiry Mr Barnes would have had no power to prevent or hold up the doing of the works until compensation had been agreed or assessed . On that basis, Mr Barnes would have had some (but very limited) nuisance value to Severn Trent which the judge was entitled to quantify in the manner he did in the passage from his judgment quoted at para 14 above. I thus would not interfere with that aspect of his award.

(c) The additional element of £1560

[36] It appears to me however that the judge was in error when he went on to make the additional award of £1560. It seems…that the exercise the judge sought to perform by awarding the additional sum of £1560 was to compensate for the financial advantage to Severn Trent of using the main without having paid an appropriate sum by way of compensation during a period of 3 years up to the time (July 1995) when the judge considered that the matter would have been settled had Mr Barnes been properly advised. This reasoning is difficult to follow. The judge had held that £610 was the total sum which represented Mr Barnes' lost opportunity to negotiate compensation prior to the trespass. Because of Severn Trent's power to serve notice upon Mr Barnes had it been aware of his interest, the financial advantage to Severn Trent in proceeding without payment was no more than the mirror image of the financial disadvantage to Mr Barnes of being kept out of money properly payable to him as from the date when it fell due. In that respect the appropriate award was an award of interest on £610 (which was indeed made).

[37] By doing what he did the judge, having rightly applied the approach to compensation taken from the authorities and on which the parties based their argument, reached his figure of £610 as the fair price which would or could have been negotiated *prior* to trespass; however, he then 'topped up' his award with three years' notional rent charge of £520 per annum which he had already found that Mr Barnes would *not* have obtained either from the Lands Tribunal or in negotiation with Severn Trent….

[39] It may be that the judge was concerned that £610 was a low figure by way of damages. I do not think he need have felt so concerned. The reason why application of the 'fair price' principle was apt to produce substantial sums by way of compensation in the line of authority referred to above, but only an insubstantial sum in this case, is twofold. First, because in the cases cited the court was concerned to calculate a theoretical price or licence fee in a situation in which the parties, if negotiating prior to trespass, would have been constrained only by market forces, the defendant being unable to proceed at all in the absence of the claimant owner's permission. The position of Severn Trent on the other hand was that of a statutory undertaker entitled to enter onto the land and to do the work subject only to service of notice and (later) payment of compensation as assessed by the Lands Tribunal in the absence of agreement. This it would plainly have done, had it been aware of Mr Barnes' interest. The parties accepted that such assessment would have yielded no more than £110. Second, whether the damages were assessed on the basis of the loss or detriment to Mr Barnes, or on the basis of the 'benefits wrongly obtained' by Severn Trent (cf Lord Nicholls in *A-G v Blake* at para 32 above), they were insignificant.

[40] So far as Mr Barnes was concerned, he had by reason of Severn Trent's actions lost no opportunity to develop or exploit his land which was and remained at all material times let to Mr Gartside under a grazing licence which was in no way affected. Nor, if the parties had been aware of the position, with the result that notice was served by Severn Trent, did Mr Barnes have any power to prevent the works being done. The measure of Mr Barnes' loss was in reality not the loss of any valuable right to charge Severn Trent an annual charge in respect of the installation and use of the main, but simply loss of the right or opportunity to seek by negotiation to obtain a higher sum than that which could

be expected from the Lands Tribunal in the absence of agreement. That higher sum was assessed by the judge at £500.

[41] Finally, it is to be noted that the judge appears to have taken the view that some additional award was necessary on the basis that:

> "to reflect the fact that the defendants were liable, as trespassers…the claimant is *entitled* to damages for some barely appreciable percentage of the defendant's profits"

…In this respect I consider that he misunderstood the authorities. It is of course the position that in cases of trespass of this kind there is no right to a share in, or account of, profits in any conventional sense. The only relevance of the defendant's profits is that they are likely to be a helpful reference point for the court when seeking to fix upon a fair price for a notional licence. However, while it will generally be appropriate for the judge in such cases to 'pay attention' to the profits made by the defendants as a result of their trespass (see per Sir Thomas Bingham MR as quoted at para 30 above) he is not obliged to do so and there may well be cases where such an approach is inappropriate, for instance where the profits made are negligible or are impossible to assess…

Conclusion

[43] I would allow the appeal to the extent of reducing the sum awarded by £1560 and the amount of the interest awarded thereon.

[PARKER LJ and SIR SWINTON THOMAS agreed with POTTER LJ.]

Appeal allowed.

NOTES

1. On the point that damages for unlawfully using someone else's property should not be limited to compensation for damage to the property itself but should extend to compensation, in the form of a 'reasonable price', for failing to negotiate with the owner about what price should have been paid for the use of the property, see R.J. Sharpe and S.M. Waddams (1982) 2 Oxf JLS 290. The purpose of the principle is to reflect the law's determination to protect the right of property owners to exclude others from using their property, regardless of whether the owners have any intention or desire to use the property themselves, which is why there is no requirement for the claimant to show that the property would have been used by the claimant or rented out to a third party. The law protects the owner's power to use or not to use the property at the owner's discretion, not merely actual 'enjoyment' of the property.

    The more difficult question, however, is to decide what the reasonable price should be. The parties, if they came to an agreement about the price for use of the property, would presumably strike a bargain at a price somewhere between the owner's valuation and the defendant's valuation—which is why the court takes into account the defendant's profit as a guide to what the defendant might have been willing to pay—but that begs the question of whether the parties could have come to an agreement at all. What if the owner's minimum valuation was greater than the defendant's maximum value? Can there be a 'reasonable' price below the owner's minimum?

    In any case, what counts as 'reasonable' from the owner's point of view? The court in *Severn Trent* allowed the owner credit for the fact that he, falsely, believed that the land in question had prospects of becoming available for development. Is that correct? What limits should there be to a claimant's excessive optimism? Conversely, if the owner has moral or political reasons for limiting the price they would have required for permitting use (for example, a social landlord committed to providing housing at affordable rents), should the reasonable price be reduced—and what if the moral or political reasons would not have applied, or applied only in a limited way, to the specific defendant? See e.g. *Ministry of Defence v Ashman* (1993) 25 HLR 513.

On the other side of the case, should the defendant be able to point to the fact that its project was unprofitable, or even loss-making, as a way of reducing the court's estimate of a reasonable price? In *Lewisham London Borough Council v Masterson* [2000] 1 EGLR 134 the Court of Appeal did not think so. An award was made regardless of the fact that the defendant's enterprise failed. Moreover, in contrast to what happens in an action for an account of profits—such as in intellectual property cases—the Court of Appeal would not allow the defendant to make deductions for the defendant's own expenditure on the venture. (See further D. Howarth in S. Hedley and M. Halliwell, *Law of Restitution* (London, 2002), p. 253.)

Lewisham shows that the defendant's actual profits might not be the correct starting point. More relevant to the issue of the defendant's valuation of the violated right is the profit the defendant hoped to make from the tort in advance of committing it. The actual profit is only a very rough guide to the defendant's valuation of the right to use the property as it would have been at the time of committing the tort. But a parallel question arises in relation to the defendant that arises in relation to the claimant with regard to excessive optimism: what about (arguably) unreasonably pessimistic defendants who committed the tort even though they underestimated the profits they would obtain?

J. Edelman, in *Gain-based Damages* (2002), pp. 80–81 and at (2006) 122 LQR 391 (commenting on *Horsford v Bird (Jamaica)* [2006] 1 EGLR 75, [2006] UKPC 3), suggests that if the defendant has acted 'cynically' or 'willfully', the whole of the profit should be paid over to the claimant. With respect, that formulation mistakes the basis of the calculation of damages in these cases. There is no obvious connection between being prepared to violate the claimant's right deliberately and being willing to pay more for it. In fact, the opposite is more plausible, that cynicism would be related to a lower willingness to pay. The issue of cynicism or willfulness goes instead to exemplary or punitive damages, which is precisely how the Privy Council in *Horsford* itself approached the issue. (In addition, reference to 'cynical' breach would be incompatible with the approach the law takes to the parallel question of the availability of restitutionary damages in contract: see *Attorney-General v Blake* [2001] 1 AC 268, [2000] 4 All ER 385. For the latest position in contract, see *WWF—World Wide Fund for Nature v World Wrestling Federation Entertainment Inc* [2008] 1 All ER 74, [2007] EWCA Civ 286.)

On the other hand, since it seems to be inherently difficult to estimate what the parties would have decided (though perhaps less difficult to determine what 'reasonable' parties would have decided), it might be argued that any uncertainty arising from the inherently hidden nature of the required information should be decided against the interest of the party in breach, to correct for the risk that defendants might end up, after judgment, in a position better than they would have bargained for.

2. *Severn Trent* and *Lewisham* both suggest that one should approach with great caution the proposition advanced by Hoffmann LJ in the earlier Court of Appeal case, *Ministry of Defence v Ashman* (1993) 25 HLR 513 (see also *Gondal v Dillon Newsagents Ltd* (LEXIS Transcript 29 July 1998 and *Sinclair v Gavaghan* [2007] EWHC 2256 (Ch)) that claimants in trespass cases (and more generally in property tort cases) can elect either ordinary 'compensatory' damages or 'restitutionary' damages calculated on the

basis of the defendant's actual profit from the tort. The other members of the Court of Appeal in *Ashman* did not adopt Hoffmann LJ's reasoning, which, on its face, is incompatible with an important feature of the 'user principle' approach, namely that the defendant's profit is relevant only as a way of estimating the price the defendant, or a reasonable defendant, would have been prepared to pay, not as the defendant's direct entitlement.

3. There is a debate, the practical point of which might be called into question, about whether the adjective 'restitutionary' ought to be applied to the remedy available in these cases (see e.g. J. Edelman (2006) 122 LQR 391). In *Inverugie Investments Ltd v Hackett* [1995] 3 All ER 841, [1995] 1 WLR 713 the Privy Council said, 'The [user] principle need not be characterised as exclusively compensatory, or exclusively restitutionary; it combines elements of both.' One might add, however, that it stands apart from both. To the extent that 'restitutionary' is to be equated with the account of profits remedy from other parts of the law, the user principle is not 'restitutionary' at all, as the *Lewisham* case illustrates. But in so far as it does not require the claimant to show any interference with use or any real inclination to have bargained with the defendant, it is not 'compensatory' in any ordinary sense either. In *Attorney-General v Blake,* in the context of contract law, Lord Nicholls said that the phrase 'restitutionary damages' was an 'unhappy expression', and the same might well apply to tort law.

The terminological debate seems to be a rather indirect proxy for a deeper debate about the extent to which the law should be interested in shifting gains (or profits) from defendants to claimants as well as (or instead of) shifting losses—arguably a traditional function of tort law. That debate is itself connected to, although not necessarily identical with, a debate about the extent the law should recognise the principle that those who enrich themselves unjustly (or 'unjustifiably') at the expense of others should be obliged to hand over their ill-gotten gains. See, for example, in a voluminous literature, H. Dagan, *The Law and Ethics of Restitution* (Cambridge, 2004), J. Neyers, M. McInnes, and S. Pitel, *Understanding Unjust Enrichment* (Oxford, 2004), and S. Hedley (2002) 2 OUCLJ 181.

The existence of these debates explains why judges sometimes feel the need to point out that there is a difference between where some theorists would like the law to go and how it currently stands. See e.g. Lewison J in *Devenish Nutrition Ltd v Sanofi-Aventis SA (France)* [2008] 2 All ER 249, [2007] EWHC 2394. More encouraging for theorists, however, is the Law Commission's Report, Law Com. No. 247, *Aggravated, Exemplary and Restitutionary Damages* (1997), which proposed that restitutionary damages should additionally be available in any tort case in which the defendant has deliberately and outrageously disregarded the claimant's rights, the same test it proposes for punitive damages. For further discussion of restitutionary damages, see the recent Consultation Paper from the Department of Constitutional Affairs (DCA), *The Law of Damages* (CP 9/07), paras. 200–202: the Government is not minded to legislate.

4. For more general discussion of this area, see *Goff and Jones, The Law of Restitution* 7th edn (London, 2007), chap. 36; G. Virgo, *The Principles of the Law of Restitution* 2nd edn (Oxford, 2006), chaps. 15–17; A. Burrows, *Remedies for Tort and Breach of Contract* 3rd edn (London, 2004), pp. 375–395; J. Edelman, *Gain-based Damages* (2002), chap. 4; and D. Howarth in S. Hedley and M. Halliwell, *The Law of Restitution* (London, 2002), chaps. 11 and 12.

■ Rookes v Barnard

House of Lords [1964] 1 All ER 367

For the facts and discussion of the cause of action, see p. 917, post. On the issue of exemplary damages the other members of the House of Lords agreed with the speech from which this extract is taken.

LORD DEVLIN:...
It must be remembered that in many cases of tort damages are at large, that is to say, the award is not limited to the pecuniary loss that can be specifically proved. In the present case, for example, and leaving aside any question of exemplary or aggravated damages, the appellant's damages would not necessarily be confined to those which he would obtain in an action for wrongful dismissal. He can invite the jury to look at all the circumstances, the inconvenience caused to him by the change of job and the unhappiness maybe by a change of livelihood. In such a case as this, it is quite proper without any departure from the compensatory principle to award a round sum based on the pecuniary loss proved. Moreover, it is very well established that in cases where the damages are at large the jury (or the judge if the award is left to him) can take into account the motives and conduct of the defendant where they aggravate the injury done to the plaintiff. There may be malevolence or spite or the manner of committing the wrong may be such as to injure the plaintiff's proper feelings of dignity and pride. These are matters which the jury can take into account in assessing the appropriate compensation. Indeed, when one examines the cases in which large damages have been awarded for conduct of this sort, it is not at all easy to say whether the idea of compensation or the idea of punishment has prevailed.

There are also cases in the books where the awards given cannot be explained as compensatory, and I propose therefore to begin by examining the authorities in order to see how far and in what sort of cases the exemplary principle has been recognised. The history of exemplary damages is briefly and clearly stated by Professor Street in his recent work on the law of damages.[1] They originated just two hundred years ago in the cause celebre of John Wilkes and the North Briton in which the legality of a general warrant was successfully challenged. Mr. Wilkes' house had been searched under a general warrant and the action of trespass which he brought as a result of it is reported in *Wilkes v.Wood*.[2] SERJEANT GLYNN on his behalf asked[3] for "large and exemplary damages", since trifling damages, he submitted, would put no stop at all to such proceedings. PRATT, C.J., in his direction to the jury said:[4]

> "Damages are designed not only as a satisfaction to the injured person, but likewise as a punish-ment to the guilty, to deter from any such proceeding for the future, and as a proof of the detest-ation of the jury to the action itself."

The jury awarded £1,000....

In *Benson v. Frederick*[5] the plaintiff a common soldier, obtained damages of £150 against his col-onel who had ordered him to be flogged so as to vex a fellow officer. LORD MANSFIELD, L.C., said[6] that the damages "were very great, and beyond the proportion of what the man had suffered". But the sum awarded was upheld as damages in respect of an arbitrary and unjustifiable action and not more than the defendant was able to pay. These authorities clearly justified the use of the exemplary principle; and for my part I should not wish, even if I felt at liberty to do so, to diminish its use in this type of case where it serves a valuable purpose in restraining the arbitrary and outrageous use of executive power.

Some considerable time elapsed thereafter before the principle eo nomine was extended in other directions....

---

[1] *Principles of the Law of Damages* by H. Street at p. 28.   [2] (1763), Lofft. 1.
[3] (1763), Lofft. at p. 3   [4] (1763), Lofft. at p. 18.   [5] (1766), 3 Burr. 1845.
[6] (1766), 3 Burr. at p. 1847.

It is not until *Bell* v. *Midland Ry. Co.*,[7] that there is a clear dictum. The plaintiff brought an action against the railway company for wrongful obstruction of access from the railway to his wharf. It does not appear that at the trial exemplary damages were asked for, and it appears[8] that ERLE, C.J., at the trial told the jury to confine the damages to pecuniary loss proved. The jury appears to have gone beyond that and awarded £1,000. In the argument on the rule nisi ERLE, C.J., said[9] that when the company's conduct was looked at, careless whether they were doing right or wrong, they prevented all access to the plaintiff's wharf for the purpose of extinguishing his trade and advancing their own profit. He was therefore entitled to ample compensation and £1,000 was very temperate. WILLES, J., said:[10]

> "I must say, that, if ever there was a case in which the jury were warranted in awarding damages of an exemplary character, this is that case. The defendants have committed a grievous wrong with a high hand and in plain violation of an Act of Parliament; and persisted in it for the purpose of destroying the plaintiff's business and securing gain to themselves. If it were necessary to cite any authority for such a position, it will be found in the case of *Emblen* v. *Myers*[11] which I cite only for illustration."

In *Owen and Smith (Trading as Nuagin Car Service)* v. *Reo Motors (Britain), Ltd.*[12] the plaintiff, a motor dealer, had on his premises for display a chassis belonging to the defendants which they were at liberty to remove at any time except that it was specially provided that if the plaintiff had constructed a body on the vehicle he should be at liberty to dismantle it before removal. The defendants without notice to the plaintiff entered his garage, took the chassis and dismantled the body in the street, the process being observed by some members of the public including one of the plaintiff's creditors. It does not appear that any injury was done to the plaintiff's property but the Court of Appeal said it was a case for exemplary damages and awarded £100. *Loudon* v *Ryder*[13] was a case of trespass and assault. The plaintiff was a young girl and the defendant broke into her flat and tried to turn her out. Her injuries were comparatively trivial but his behaviour was outrageous. The jury awarded her £1,500 damages for trespass, and £1,000 for assault; and £3,000 as exemplary damages, making £5,500 in all. This award was upheld in the Court of Appeal. In *Williams* v. *Settle*[14] the defendant was a professional photographer who had taken photographs of the plaintiff's wedding, the copyright being vested in the plaintiff. Two years later, when an event had occurred which caused the plaintiff to be exposed to publicity, the defendant sold the photographs to two national newspapers and their publication caused the plaintiff great distress. The county court judge awarded the plaintiff £1,000 damages for breach of copyright. This award was upheld in the Court of Appeal and in both courts it was described as one of exemplary damages. The Court of Appeal considered that exemplary damages could have been awarded at common law, but they relied also on the Copyright Act, 1956, s. 17(3), which provides that the court may have regard to the flagrancy of the infringement and to any benefit shown to have accrued to the defendant by reason of the infringement and, if satisfied that effective relief would not otherwise be available to the plaintiff, may award such additional damages as it considers appropriate.

My lords, I express no view on whether the Copyright Act, 1956, authorises an award of exemplary, as distinct from aggravated damages. But there are certainly two other Acts of Parliament which mention exemplary damages by name.... These authorities convince me of two things. First, that your lordships could not without a complete disregard of precedent, and indeed of statute, now arrive at a determination that refused altogether to recognise the exemplary principle. Secondly, that there are certain categories of cases in which an award of exemplary damages can serve a useful purpose in vindicating the strength of the law, and thus affording a practical justification for admitting into the civil law a principle which ought logically to belong to the criminal. I propose to state what these two categories are; and I propose also to state three general considerations which, in my opinion, should

---

[7] (1861), 10 CBNS 287.   [8] (1861), 10 CBNS at p. 295.   [9] (1861), 10 CBNS at p. 304.
[10] (1861), 10 CBNS at p. 307.   [11] (1860), 6 H. & N. 54.   [12] [1934] All ER Rep. 734.
[13] [1953] 1 All ER 741, [1953] 2 QB 202.   [14] [1960] 2 All ER 806.

always be borne in mind when awards of exemplary damages are being made. I am well aware that what I am about to say will, if accepted, impose limits not hitherto expressed on such awards and that there is powerful, though not compelling, authority for allowing them a wider range. I shall not therefore conclude what I have to say on the general principles of law without returning to the authorities and making it clear to what extent I have rejected the guidance which they may be said to afford.

The first category is oppressive, arbitrary or unconstitutional action by the servants of the government. I should not extend this category—I say this with particular reference to the facts of this case—to oppressive action by private corporations or individuals. Where one man is more powerful than another, it is inevitable that he will try to use his power to gain his ends; and if his power is much greater than the other's, he might perhaps be said to be using it oppressively. If he uses his power illegally, he must of course pay for his illegality in the ordinary way; but he is not to be punished simply because he is the more powerful. In the case of the government it is different, for the servants of the government are also the servants of the people and the use of their power must always be subordinate to their duty of service. It is true that there is something repugnant about a big man bullying a small man and very likely the bullying will be a source of humiliation that makes the case one for aggravated damages, but it is not in my opinion punishable by damages.

Cases in the second category are those in which the defendant's conduct has been calculated by him to make a profit for himself which may well exceed the compensation payable to the plaintiff.... It is a factor also that is taken into account in damages for libel; one man should not be allowed to sell another man's reputation for profit. Where a defendant with a cynical disregard for a plaintiff's rights has calculated that the money to be made out of his wrongdoing will probably exceed the damages at risk, it is necessary for the law to show that it cannot be broken with impunity. This category is not confined to moneymaking in the strict sense. It extends to cases in which the defendant is seeking to gain at the expense of the plaintiff some object—perhaps some property which he covets—which either he could not obtain at all or not obtain except at a price greater than he wants to put down. Exemplary damages can properly be awarded whenever it is necessary to teach a wrongdoer that tort does not pay.

To these two categories, which are established as part of the common law, there must of course be added any category in which exemplary damages are expressly authorised by statute.

I wish now to express three considerations which I think should always be borne in mind when awards of exemplary damages are being considered. First, the plaintiff cannot recover exemplary damages unless he is the victim of the punishable behaviour. The anomaly inherent in exemplary damages would become an absurdity if a plaintiff totally unaffected by some oppressive conduct which the jury wished to punish obtained a windfall in consequence. Secondly, the power to award exemplary damages constitutes a weapon that, while it can be used in defence of liberty, as in the *Wilkes* case,[15] can also be used against liberty. Some of the awards that juries have made in the past seem to me to amount to a greater punishment than would be likely to be incurred if the conduct were criminal; and moreover a punishment imposed without the safeguard which the criminal law gives to an offender. I should not allow the respect which is traditionally paid to an assessment of damages by a jury to prevent me from seeing that the weapon is used with restraint. It may even be that the House may find it necessary to follow the precedent it set for itself in *Benham v. Gambling*,[16] and place some arbitrary limit on awards of damages that are made by way of punishment. Exhortations to be moderate may not be enough. Thirdly, the means of the parties, irrelevant in the assessment of compensation, are material in the assessment of exemplary damages. Everything which aggravates or mitigates the defendant's conduct is relevant.

Thus a case for exemplary damages must be presented quite differently from one for compensatory damages; and the judge should not allow it to be left to the jury unless he is satisfied that it can be brought within the categories which I have specified. But the fact that the two sorts of damage differ

---

[15] (1763), Lofft. 1. [16] [1941] 1 All ER 7, [1941] AC 157.

essentially does not necessarily mean that there should be two awards. In a case in which exemplary damages are appropriate, a jury should be directed that if, but only if, the sum which they have in mind to award as compensation (which may of course be a sum aggravated by the way in which the defendant has behaved to the plaintiff) is inadequate to punish him for his outrageous conduct, to mark their disapproval of such conduct and to deter him from repeating it, then they can award some larger sum. If a verdict given on such direction has to be reviewed on appeal, the appellate court will first consider whether the award can be justified as compensation, and, if it can, there is nothing further to be said. If it cannot, the court must consider whether or not the punishment is in all the circumstances excessive. There may be cases in which it is difficult for a judge to say whether or not he ought to leave to the jury a claim for exemplary damages. In such circumstances and in order to save the possible expense of a new trial, I see no objection to his inviting the jury to say what sum they would fix as compensation and what additional sum, if any, they would award if they were entitled to give exemplary damages. . . .

I must now return to the authorities I have already reviewed and make quite plain what it is that I have not accepted from them. As I have said, damages that are at large can always be fixed as a round sum. Some juries have in the past been very liberal in their ideas of what a round sum should be and the courts which have always been very reluctant to interfere with awards of damages by a jury, have allowed very liberal awards to stand. *Williams* v. *Currie*,[17] might on one view be regarded as a rather extreme example of this. It would not be right to take the language that judges have used on such occasions to justify their non-intervention and treat their words as a positive formulation of a type of case in which exemplary damages can be awarded. They have used numerous epithets—wilful, wanton, high-handed, oppressive, malicious, outrageous. But these sort of adjectives are used in the judgments by way of comment on the facts of a particular case. It would on any view be a mistake to suppose that any of them can be selected as definitive and a jury directed, for example, that it can award exemplary damages whenever it finds conduct that is wilful or wanton. When this has been said, there remains one class of case for which the authority is much more precise. It is the class of case in which the injury to the plaintiff has been aggravated by malice or by the manner of doing the injury, that is, the insolence or arrogance by which it is accompanied. There is clear authority that this can justify exemplary damages, though (except in *Loudon* v. *Ryder*[18]) it is not clear whether they are to be regarded as in addition to, or in substitution for, the aggravated damages that could certainly be awarded.

It is not, I think, authority of great antiquity. The older group of six cases which I have cited, beginning with *Tullidge* v. *Wade*[19] discloses no statement of principle. In my opinion, all these cases can best be explained in principle as cases of aggravated damage, though I am not saying that in all the cases the sums awarded can be taken as an example of what compensatory damages ought to be. The direct authority for exemplary damages in this category of case lies in the three modern decisions of the Court of Appeal. I think that your lordships, if you agree with my conclusion, are bound to express your dissent from most of the reasoning in all of them. *Owen* v. *Reo*[20] and *Williams* v. *Settle*,[1] even if the latter is considered apart from the Copyright Act, 1956, can be justified in the result as cases of aggravated damage; and indeed the sums awarded could, to my mind, more easily be justified on that ground than on the ground that they were exemplary. *Loudon* v. *Ryder* ought, I think, to be completely overruled. The sums awarded as compensation for the assault and trespass seem to me to be as high as, if not higher than, any jury could properly have awarded even in the outrageous circumstances of the case; and I can see no justification for the addition of an even larger sum as exemplary damages. The case was not one in which exemplary damages ought to have been given as such.

This conclusion will, I hope, remove from the law a source of confusion between aggravated and exemplary damages which has troubled the learned commentators on the subject. Otherwise, it will not, I think, make much difference to the substance of the law or rob the law of the strength which it ought to have. Aggravated damages in this type of case can do most, if not all, of the work that could

---

[17] (1845), 1 CB 841.　　[18] [1953] 1 All ER 741, [1953] 2 QB 202.　　[19] (1769), 3 Wils. 18.
[20] [1934] All ER Rep 734.　　[1] [1960] 2 All ER 806.

be done by exemplary damages. In so far as they do not, assaults and malicious injuries to property can generally be punished as crimes, whereas the objectionable conduct in the categories in which I have accepted the need for exemplary damages are not, generally speaking, within the criminal law and could not, even if the criminal law was to be amplified, conveniently be defined as crimes. I do not care for the idea that in matters criminal an aggrieved party should be given an option to inflict for his own benefit punishment by a method which denies to the offender the protection of the criminal law…

NOTES

1. *Rookes v Barnard* was generally seen as an attempt to restrict the availability of exemplary damages. In the United States, whether under common law or by statute, exemplary or punitive damages are still obtainable according to the pre-*Rookes* formula, that is when the defendant has acted in a way that can be characterised as malicious, oppressive, gross, wilful, wanton, or fraudulent. (See e.g. California Civil Code §3294: 'In an action for the breach of an obligation not arising from contract, where it is proven by clear and convincing evidence that the defendant has been guilty of oppression, fraud or malice, the plaintiff, in addition to the actual damages, may recover damages for the sake of example and by way of punishing the defendant.')

2. Lord Devlin distinguishes between 'aggravated' and 'exemplary' damages. The former are said to be compensatory, the latter not. But note that although 'aggravated' damages compensate the claimant's subjective feelings of injured dignity or pride, such injured feelings are not usually themselves a recognised form of loss sufficient to support a cause of action: see p. 118, ante.

3. Lord Devlin emphasises that the availability of punitive damages should normally coincide with the absence of criminal law provisions covering the same conduct. Might that explain why Lord Devlin makes oppressive behaviour by state officials his first category of case in which punitive damages should continue to be available? Is Lord Devlin making a realistic, if cynical, assumption that state officials might not be prosecuted for certain offences? False imprisonment and assault are, after all, crimes as well as torts.

4. What justifies punitive damages in Lord Devlin's second category? R. Cooter and T. Ulen, *Law & Economics*, 5th edn (2007), pp. 393–398 point out that even in negligence, if defendants can rely on the fact that some of their victims will not bring successful actions against them, they will take less than optimal care. D. Ellis (1983) 3 Int Rev Law and Econ 45 adds that punitive damages might be necessary to deter defendants who are 'malicious' in the sense of getting positive enjoyment out of their torts. Lord Devlin rules out punitive damages merely because of 'malice', but Lord Diplock points out in *Cassell & Co. Ltd v Broome* [1972] AC 1027, [1972] 1 All ER 801 that the second category need not be confined to cases of arithmetical calculation of pecuniary profit. S. Shavell and A. M. Polinsky in their comprehensive article at (1998) 111 Harv L Rev. 869 similarly argue for punitive damages where otherwise defendants will be under-deterred, but they add that the measure of punitive damages should relate to estimates of the degree of under-deterrence. Setting damages at the amount of the defendant's gain, they argue, risks going too far.

5. Lord Devlin's call that the amount of punitive damages might have to be limited arbitrarily faced procedural difficulties until s. 8 of the Courts and Legal Services Act 1990 and RSC Ord 59, r 11(4)—see now CPR 52.10(3)(c)—gave the Court of Appeal power 'to substitute for the sum awarded by the jury such sum as appears to the Court to be proper'. In the following case, the Court of Appeal laid down some guidance for cases

of malicious prosecution, false imprisonment and assault by the police. (Note that in such actions, jury trial is still common.) The Court of Appeal also took the opportunity to clarify the relationship between basic, aggravated, and exemplary damages in a way that is applicable to other types of case.

■ Thompson v Metropolitan Police Commissioner

Court of Appeal [1997] 2 All ER 762

LORD WOOLF MR [delivering the judgment of the court]:...
While there is no formula which is appropriate for all cases and the precise form of a summing up is very much a matter within the discretion of the trial judge, it is suggested that in many cases it will be convenient to include in a summing up on the issue of damages additional directions on the following lines. As we mention later in this judgment we think it may often be wise to take the jury's verdict on liability before they receive directions as to quantum.

[1] It should be explained to the jury that if they find in the plaintiff's favour the only remedy which they have power to grant is an award of damages. Save in exceptional situations such damages are only awarded as compensation and are intended to compensate the plaintiff for any injury or damage which he has suffered. They are not intended to punish the defendant.

[2] As the law stands at present compensatory damages are of two types. (a) ordinary damages which we would suggest should be described as basic, and (b) aggravated damages. Aggravated damages can only be awarded where they are claimed by the plaintiff and where there are aggravating features about the defendant's conduct which justify the award of aggravated damages. (We would add that in the rare case where special damages are claimed in respect of some specific pecuniary loss this claim should be explained separately.)

[3] The jury should be told that the basic damages will depend on the circumstances and the degree of harm suffered by the plaintiff. But they should be provided with an appropriate bracket to use as a starting point. The judge will be responsible for determining the bracket, and we envisage that in the ordinary way the judge will have heard submissions on the matter from counsel in the absence of the jury...

[4] In a straightforward case of wrongful arrest and imprisonment or malicious prosecution the jury should be informed of the approximate figure to be taken as the correct starting point for basic damages for the actual loss of liberty or for the wrongful prosecution, and also given an approximate ceiling figure. It should be explained that these are no more than guideline figures based on the judge's experience and on the awards in other cases and the actual figure is one on which they must decide.

[5] In a straightforward case of wrongful arrest and imprisonment the starting point is likely to be about £500 for the first hour during which the plaintiff has been deprived of his or her liberty. After the first hour an additional sum is to be awarded, but that sum should be on a reducing scale so as to keep the damages proportionate with those payable in personal injury cases and because the plaintiff is entitled to have a higher rate of compensation for the initial shock of being arrested. As a guideline we consider, for example, that a plaintiff who has been wrongly kept in custody for 24 hours should for this alone normally be regarded as entitled to an award of about £3,000. For subsequent days the daily rate will be on a progressively reducing scale....

[6] In the case of malicious prosecution the figure should start at about £2,000 and for prosecution continuing for as long as two years, the case being taken to the Crown Court, an award of about £10,000 could be appropriate. If a malicious prosecution results in a conviction which is only set aside on an appeal this will justify a larger award to reflect the longer period during which the plaintiff has been in peril and has been caused distress.

[7] The figures which we have identified so far are provided to assist the judge in determining the bracket within which the jury should be invited to place their award. We appreciate, however, that circumstances can vary dramatically from case to case and that these and the subsequent figures which we provide are not intended to be applied in a mechanistic manner.

[8] If the case is one in which aggravated damages are claimed and could be appropriately awarded, the nature of aggravated damages should be explained to the jury. Such damages can be awarded where there are aggravating features about the case which would result in the plaintiff not receiving sufficient compensation for the injury suffered if the award were restricted to a basic award. Aggravating features can include humiliating circumstances at the time of arrest or any conduct of those responsible for the arrest or the prosecution which shows that they had behaved in a high-handed, insulting, malicious or oppressive manner either in relation to the arrest or imprisonment or in conducting the prosecution. Aggravating features can also include the way the litigation and trial are conducted....

[9] The jury should then be told that if they consider the case is one for the award of damages other than basic damages then they should usually make a separate award for each category. (This is contrary to the present practice but in our view will result in greater transparency as to the make up of the award.)

[10] We consider that where it is appropriate to award aggravated damages the figure is unlikely to be less than £1,000. We do not think it is possible to indicate a precise arithmetical relationship between basic damages and aggravated damages because the circumstances will vary from case to case. In the ordinary way, however, we would not expect the aggravated damages to be as much as twice the basic damages except perhaps where, on the particular facts, the basic damages are modest.

[11] It should be strongly emphasised to the jury that the total figure for basic and aggravated damages should not exceed what they consider is fair compensation for the injury which the plaintiff has suffered. It should also be explained that if aggravated damages are awarded such damages, though compensatory and not intended as a punishment, will in fact contain a penal element as far as the defendant is concerned.

[12] Finally the jury should be told in a case where exemplary damages are claimed and the judge considers that there is evidence to support such a claim, that though it is not normally possible to award damages with the object of punishing the defendant, exceptionally this is possible where there has been conduct, including oppressive or arbitrary behaviour, by police officers which deserves the exceptional remedy of exemplary damages. It should be explained to the jury: (a) that if the jury are awarding aggravated damages these damages will have already provided compensation for the injury suffered by the plaintiff as a result of the oppressive and insulting behaviour of the police officer and, inevitably, a measure of punishment from the defendant's point of view; (b) that exemplary damages should be awarded if, but only if, they consider that the compensation awarded by way of basic and aggravated damages is in the circumstances an inadequate punishment for the defendants; (c) that an award of exemplary damages is in effect a windfall for the plaintiff and, where damages will be payable out of police funds, the sum awarded may not be available to be expended by the police in a way which would benefit the public (this guidance would not be appropriate if the claim were to be met by insurers); and (d) that the sum awarded by way of exemplary damages should be sufficient to mark the jury's disapproval of the oppressive or arbitrary behaviour but should be no more than is required for this purpose.

[13] Where exemplary damages are appropriate they are unlikely to be less than £5,000. Otherwise the case is probably not one which justifies an award of exemplary damages at all. In this class of action the conduct must be particularly deserving of condemnation for an award of as much as £25,000 to be justified and the figure of £50,000 should be regarded as the absolute maximum, involving directly officers of at least the rank of superintendent.

[14] In an appropriate case the jury should also be told that even though the plaintiff succeeds on liability any improper conduct of which they find him guilty can reduce or even eliminate any award of aggravated or exemplary damages if the jury consider that this conduct caused or contributed to the behaviour complained of.

The figures given will of course require adjusting in the future for inflation. We appreciate that the guideline figures depart from the figures frequently awarded by juries at the present time. However they are designed to establish some relationship between the figures awarded in this area and those

awarded for personal injuries. In giving guidance for aggravated damages we have attached importance to the fact that they are intended to be compensatory and not punitive although the same circumstances may justify punishment.

In the case of exemplary damages we have taken into account the fact that the action is normally
brought against the chief officer of police and the damages are paid out of police funds for what is
usually a vicarious liability for the acts of his officers in relation to which he is a joint tortfeasor (see now
s 88 of the Police Act 1996). In these circumstances it appears to us wholly inappropriate to take into
account the means of the individual officers except where the action is brought against the individual
tortfeasor. This would raise a complication in the event of the chief officer seeking an indemnity or
contribution as to his liability from a member of his force. It is our view if this situation does arise it
should be resolved by the court exercising its power under s 2(1) or (2) of the Civil Liability (Contribution)
Act 1978 to order that the exemplary damages should not be reimbursed in full or at all if they are
disproportionate to the officer's means.

In deciding upon what should be treated as the upper limits for exemplary damages we have
selected a figure which is sufficiently substantial to make it clear that there has been conduct of a
nature which warrants serious civil punishment and indicates the jury's vigorous disapproval of what
has occurred but at the same time recognises that the plaintiff is the recipient of a windfall in relation
to exemplary damages. As punishment is the primary objective in this class of case it is more difficult to
tie the amount of exemplary damages to the award of compensatory damages, including aggravated.
However, in many cases it could prove a useful check subject to the upper limits we have identified if
it is accepted that it will be unusual for the exemplary damages to produce a result of more than three
times the basic damages being awarded (as the total of the basic aggravated and exemplary damages)
except again where the basic damages are modest.

NOTES

1. Under the Civil Procedure Rules both exemplary and aggravated damages have to be
   pleaded (CPR 16.4(1)(c)).
2. In *Richardson v Howie* [2005] PIQR Q3, [2004] EWCA Civ 1127 the Court of Appeal
   thought that in a tort where injury to feelings can be compensated, the award of damages for that head should (apart possibly from the most exceptional of cases) be classed
   as general damages rather than aggravated damages. This point is noted in *Rowlands
   v Chief Constable of Merseyside Police* [2007] 1 WLR 1065, [2006] EWCA Civ 1773,
   where it is stated that, however classified (i.e. as general or aggravated), it is important
   to remember that as *Thompson* indicates the basic aim of 'aggravated' damages is compensation and not punishment. A court must be careful not to award damages twice
   for the same injury. Nevertheless, aggravated damages would still be important in their
   own right while recovery 'for intangible consequences such as humiliation, injury to
   pride and dignity as well as for the hurt caused by the spiteful, malicious insulting or
   arrogant conduct of the defendant attaches to some causes of actions and not others'.
   Consider further *Choudhary v Martins* [2008] 1 WLR 617, [2007] EWCA Civ 1379 at
   [20] (Smith LJ) and [28], where Sir Anthony Chadwick MR agrees with the general
   approach in *Richardson v Howie*.

   The approach in *Richardson* should be put alongside that of the Law Commission,
   which in Law Com. No. 247, *Aggravated, Exemplary and Restitutionary Damages*
   (1997) proposed that the phrase 'damages for mental distress' should displace 'aggravated damages' as the ordinary way of referring to this form of compensation and
   also recommends statutory confirmation of the point that aggravated damages are

compensation for mental distress, and are not punitive. The Government's view (in DCA Consultation Paper 9/07) is that the law is now sufficiently clear to render legislation unnecessary on this latter point. On aggravated damages and deceit, see the note, p. 949, post.

3.   On the question of vicarious liability in the case of exemplary damages, see note, p. 508, post.

■ Cassell & Co Ltd v Broome
House of Lords [1972] 1 All ER 801

The defendant publisher published a book solely for financial gain, knowing it to be libellous and not caring whether it was true. The appeal concerned damages alone.

LORD REID:...
Damages for any tort are or ought to be fixed at a sum which will compensate the plaintiff, so far as money can do it, for all the injury which he has suffered. Where the injury is material and has been ascertained it is generally possible to assess damages with some precision. But that is not so where he has been caused mental distress or when his reputation has been attacked where to use the traditional phrase he has been held up to hatred, ridicule or contempt. Not only is it impossible to ascertain how far other people's minds have been affected, it is almost impossible to equate the damage to a sum of money. Any one person trying to fix a sum as compensation will probably find in his mind a wide bracket within which any sum could be regarded by him as not unreasonable and different people will come to different conclusions. So in the end there will probably be a wide gap between the sum which on an objective view could be regarded as the least and the sum which could be regarded as the most to which the plaintiff is entitled as compensation.

It has long been recognised that in determining what sum within that bracket should be awarded, a jury, or other tribunal, is entitled to have regard to the conduct of the defendant. He may have behaved in a high-handed, malicious, insulting or oppressive manner in committing the tort or he or his counsel may at the trial have aggravated the injury by what they there said. That would justify going to the top of the bracket and awarding as damages the largest sum that could fairly be regarded as compensation.

Frequently in cases before *Rookes v Barnard*[2] when damages were increased in that way but were still within the limit of what could properly be regarded as compensation to the plaintiff, it was said that punitive, vindictive or exemplary damages were being awarded. As a mere matter of language that was true enough. The defendant was being punished or an example was being made of him by making him pay more than he would have had to pay if his conduct had not been outrageous. But the damages although called punitive were still truly compensatory; the plaintiff was not being given more than his due.

On the other hand when we came to examine the old cases we found a number which could not be explained in that way. The sums awarded as damages were more, sometimes much more, than could on any view be justified as compensatory and courts, perhaps without fully realising what they were doing, appeared to have permitted damages to be measured not by what the plaintiff was fairly entitled to receive but by what the defendant ought to be made to pay as punishment for his outrageous conduct. That meant that the plaintiff, by being given more than on any view could be justified as compensation, was being given a pure and undeserved windfall at the expense of the defendant, and that insofar as the defendant was being required to pay more than could possibly be regarded as compensation he was being subjected to pure punishment.

---

[2]   [1964] AC 1129, [1964] 1 All ER 367.

I thought and still think that that is highly anomalous. It is confusing the function of the civil law which is to compensate with the function of the criminal law which is to inflict deterrent and punitive penalties. Some objection has been taken to the use of the word 'fine' to denote the amount by which punitive or exemplary damages exceed anything justly due to the plaintiff. In my view the word 'fine' is an entirely accurate description of that part of any award which goes beyond anything justly due to the plaintiff and is purely punitive.

Those of us who sat in *Rookes v Barnard*[3] thought that the loose and confused use of words like 'punitive' and 'exemplary' and the failure to recognise the difference between damages which are compensatory and damages which go beyond that and are purely punitive had led to serious abuses, so we took what we thought was the best course open to us to limit those abuses. Theoretically we might have held that as purely punitive damages had never been sanctioned by any decision of this House (as to which I shall say more later) there was no right under English law to award them. But that would have been going beyond the proper function of this House. There are many well established doctrines of the law which have not been the subject of any decision by this House. We thought we had to recognise that it had become an established custom in certain classes of case to permit awards of damages which could not be justified as compensatory, and that that must remain the law. But we thought and I still think it well within the province of this House to say that that undesirable anomaly should not be permitted in any class of case where its use was not covered by authority. In order to determine the classes of case in which this anomaly had become established it was of little use to look merely at the words which had been used by the judges because, as I have said, words like 'punitive' and 'exemplary' were often used with regard to damages which were truly compensatory. We had to take a broad view of the whole circumstances.

I must now deal with those parts of Lord Devlin's speech which have given rise to difficulties. He set out two categories of cases which in our opinion comprised all or virtually all the reported cases in which it was clear that the court had approved of an award of a larger sum of damages than could be justified as compensatory. Critics appear to have thought that he was inventing something new. That was not my understanding. We were confronted with an undesirable anomaly. We could not abolish it. We had to choose between confining it strictly to classes of cases where it was firmly established, although that produced an illogical result, or permitting it to be extended so as to produce a logical result. In my view it is better in such cases to be content with an illogical result than to allow any extension.

It will be seen that I do not agree with Lord Devlin's view that in certain classes of case exemplary damages serve a useful purpose in vindicating the strength of the law. That view did not form an essential step in his argument. Concurrence with the speech of a colleague does not mean acceptance of every word which he has said. If it did there would be far fewer concurrences than there are. So I did not regard disagreement on this side issue as preventing me from giving my concurrence.

I think that the objections to allowing juries to go beyond compensatory damages are overwhelming. To allow pure punishment in this way contravenes almost every principle which has been evolved for the protection of offenders. There is no definition of the offence except that the conduct punished must be oppressive, high-handed, malicious, wanton or its like terms far too vague to be admitted to any criminal code worthy of the name. There is no limit to the punishment except that it must not be unreasonable. The punishment is not inflicted by a judge who has experience and at least tries not to be influenced by emotion; it is inflicted by a jury without experience of law or punishment and often swayed by considerations which every judge would put out of his mind. And there is no effective appeal against sentence. All that a reviewing court can do is to quash the jury's decision if it thinks the punishment awarded is more than any 12 reasonable men could award. The court cannot substitute its own award. The punishment must then be decided by another jury and if they too award heavy punishment the court is virtually powerless. It is no excuse to say that we need not waste sympathy on people who behave outrageously. Are we wasting sympathy on vicious criminals when we insist on proper

---

[3] [1964] AC 1129, [1964] 1 All ER 367.

legal safeguards for them? The right to give punitive damages in certain cases is so firmly embedded in our law that only Parliament can remove it. But I must say that I am surprised by the enthusiasm of Lord Devlin's critics in supporting this form of palm tree justice.

Lord Devlin's first category is set out in the passage where he said:[4]

> 'The first category is oppressive, arbitrary or unconstitutional action by the servants of the government. I should not extend this category. I say this with particular reference to the facts of this case to oppressive action by private corporations or individuals.'

This distinction has been attacked on two grounds: first, that it only includes Crown servants and excludes others like the police who exercise governmental functions but are not Crown servants and, secondly, that it is illogical since both the harm to the plaintiff and the blameworthiness of the defendant may be at least equally great where the offender is a powerful private individual. With regard to the first I think that the context shows that the category was never intended to be limited to Crown servants. The contrast is between 'the government' and private individuals. Local government is as much government as national government, and the police and many other persons are exercising governmental functions. It was unnecessary in *Rookes v Barnard*[5] to define the exact limits of the category. I should certainly read it as extending to all those who by common law or statute are exercising functions of a governmental character.

The second criticism is I think misconceived. I freely admit that the distinction is illogical. The real reason for the distinction was, in my view, that the cases showed that it was firmly established with regard to servants of 'the government' that damages could be awarded against them beyond any sum justified as compensation, whereas there was no case except one that was overruled where damages had been awarded against a private bully or oppressor to an amount that could not fairly be regarded as compensatory, giving to that word the meaning which I have already discussed. I thought that this House was therefore free to say that no more than that was to be awarded in future.

We are particularly concerned in the present case with the second category.[6] With the benefit of hindsight I think I can say without disrespect to Lord Devlin that it is not happily phrased. But I think the meaning is clear enough. An ill disposed person could not infrequently deliberately commit a tort in contumelious disregard of another's rights in order to obtain an advantage which would outweigh any compensatory damages likely to be obtained by his victim. Such a case is within this category. But then it is said, suppose he commits the tort not for gain but simply out of malice why should he not also be punished. Again I freely admit there is no logical reason. The reason for excluding such a case from the category is simply that firmly established authority required us to accept this category however little we might like it, but did not require us to go farther. If logic is to be preferred to the desirability of cutting down the scope for punitive damages to the greatest extent that will not conflict with established authority then this category must be widened. But as I have already said I would, logic or no logic, refuse to extend the right to inflict exemplary damages to any class of case which is not already clearly covered by authority. On that basis I support this category....

LORD WILBERFORCE [dissenting]:...

It cannot lightly be taken for granted, even as a matter of theory, that the purpose of the law of tort is compensation, still less that it ought to be, an issue of large social import, or that there is something inappropriate or illogical or anomalous (a question-begging word) in including a punitive element in civil damages, or, conversely, that the criminal law, rather than the civil law is in these cases the better instrument for conveying social disapproval, or for redressing a wrong to the social fabric; or that damages in any case can be broken down into two separate elements. As a matter of practice English law has not committed itself to either of these theories; it may have been wiser than it knew...

---

[4] [1964] AC at p. 1226, [1964] 1 All ER at p. 410.
[5] [1964] AC 1129, [1964] 1 All ER 367.   [6] See p. 495, ante.

NOTES

1. Viscount Dilhorne dissented, alongside Lord Wilberforce. Lord Diplock agreed with Lord Reid that exemplary damages were 'anomalous' and declared that he would not even have retained them for the 'state oppression' category, on the ground that they were a 'blunt instrument' in the age of judicial review. Moreover, Lord Kilbrandon, while purporting to give no view on the desirability of punitive damages, claimed that no one now writing a civil code would provide them. But Lord Hailsham LC did not dissent from Lord Devlin's view that punitive damages were justified by the need to vindicate the strength of the law, although he also thought that Lord Devlin had not intended in any way to expand the number of torts in which punitive damages were awardable. (On this point, however, see the next extract.) Lord Morris of Borth-y-Gest made no comment on the desirability of punitive damages and contented himself with asserting the authority of *Rookes v Barnard* against what the Law Lords saw as the insolence of the Court of Appeal in seeking to take the law back to its pre-*Rookes* state. Thus, there was no majority for Lord Reid's views. There was a majority, however, in favour of affirming Lord Devlin's approach.

2. Lord Wilberforce's view that it cannot be taken for granted that the purpose of the law of tort is compensation alone is surely correct. The purpose of injunctions in nuisance, the economic torts and other torts is to prevent harm, not to compensate for it. Is it so outrageous to suggest that another purpose of damages might also be to prevent future harm by acting as a deterrent? Note, furthermore, that in *The Gleaner Co Ltd v Abrahams* [2004] 1 AC 628, [2003] UKPC 55 (p. 1019, post) Lord Hoffmann (at [42]) stated that in any tort action 'liability to pay damages as compensation for loss or harm is capable of some deterrent or exemplary effect'. There may also be a vindicatory purpose: see *Ashley v Chief Constable of Sussex Police* [2008] 2 WLR 975, [2008] UKHL 25, noted p. 716, post.

■ Kuddus v Chief Constable of Leicestershire Constabulary
House of Lords [2001] 3 All ER 193

LORD SLYNN OF HADLEY: . . .

[1] My Lords, it seems to me that in this case the issues of law which have been raised could have been more satisfactorily dealt with after the facts had been found. Your Lordships, however, have to deal with the case on the basis that the recorder and the majority of the Court of Appeal (Auld LJ dissenting) in this case struck out a claim for exemplary damages on the basis that it disclosed no cause of action.

[2] The relevant pleaded facts are short. The appellant plaintiff told a police constable that he had come back to his flat where a friend had been staying to find that a lot of property was missing. The officer said that the matter would be investigated but some two months later he forged the plaintiff's signature on a written statement withdrawing the complaint of theft. Accordingly the police investigation ceased.

[3] The defendant Chief Constable admits the forgery and that the officer's conduct amounts to misfeasance in a public office. He successfully contended, however, that exemplary damages are not recoverable for the tort of misfeasance by a public officer so that that part of the claim should be struck out. He accepts that there is a viable claim for aggravated damages for such misfeasance.

[4] The parties agree that an award of exemplary damages may be made in appropriate cases in English law even though, being punitive in nature, such an award is inconsistent with the principle that

damages are intended to be compensatory. As the law now stands that agreement in my view is well founded....

[Having referred to Lord Devlin's speech *in Rookes v Barnard* [1964] AC 1129, [1964] 1 All ER 367 (p. 493, ante), LORD SLYNN continued:]

[7] Lord Devlin stressed that a judge should not allow a case for exemplary damages to be left to the jury unless he is satisfied that it can be brought within the categories he had specified and that a claimant can only recover exemplary damages if he is 'the victim of the punishable behaviour' ([1964] 1 All ER 367 at 411, [1964] AC 1129 at 1227). The means of the parties are material in the assessment of exemplary damages. 'Everything which aggravates or mitigates the defendant's conduct is relevant' ([1964] 1 All ER 367 at 411, [1964] AC 1129 at 1228).

[8] It seems to me that there is nothing in Lord Devlin's analysis which requires that in addition to a claim falling within one of the two categories it should also constitute a cause of action which had before 1964 been accepted as grounding a claim for exemplary damages.

[9] In *AB v South West Water Services Ltd* [1993] 1 All ER 609, [1993] QB 507, the court was concerned with claims for public nuisance and breach of statutory duty. Exemplary damages were claimed on the basis that servants or agents of the defendants as employees of a statutory body had acted in an arrogant and high-handed way and had deliberately misled their customers. It was contended that exemplary damages did not lie for nuisance and that the allegations in the case did not fall within either of Lord Devlin's 'categories'. But in addition it was said ([1993] 1 All ER 609 at 614, [1993] QB 507 at 517) that the combined effect of *Rookes v Barnard* and *Cassell & Co Ltd v Broome* [1972] 1 All ER 801, [1972] AC 1027 was that the claim must be 'in respect of a cause of action for which prior to 1964 such an award had been made'.

[10] Stuart-Smith LJ ([1993] 1 All ER 609 at 617, [1993] QB 507 at 519) accepted that this last limitation was not to be found in the speech of Lord Devlin in *Rookes v Barnard* but was to be deduced from the majority of speeches in *Cassell & Co Ltd v Broome*....

[Having examined the speeches in *Cassell & Co Ltd v Broome*, LORD SLYNN concluded:]

[21] My Lords, Lord Hailsham and Lord Kilbrandon appeared to attach importance to the existence of the pre-1964 cause of action test. It is arguable that Lord Reid and Lord Wilberforce took the same view. I am not, however, satisfied that it was their intention. Lord Reid lays much emphasis on 'principles' and 'categories' and 'class of case' rather than on specific or precise causes of action. It seems to me, despite his general agreement with Lord Hailsham, that Lord Wilberforce contemplated a wide interpretation of both 'government' and the excessive use of executive power. Accordingly, although I well understand the approach of the Court of Appeal in *AB v South West Water Services Ltd*, I do not consider that the House is bound by a clear or unequivocal decision in *Cassell & Co Ltd v Broome* to hold that the power to award exemplary damages is limited to cases where it can be shown that the cause of action had been recognised before 1964 as justifying an award of exemplary damages. It is certainly not bound by anything said by Lord Devlin in what is after all the basic statement of the law.

[22] I do not consider that in principle it should be so limited. In any event, like Auld LJ, I do not think that courts should be required to undertake a trawl of the authorities in order to decipher whether awards of damages for misfeasance pre-1964 might have included an award for exemplary damages. Such a task would be all the more difficult given the fact... that the distinction between exemplary and aggravated damages was not until *Rookes v Barnard* clearly articulated. To adopt such a rigid rule seems to me to limit the future development of the law even within the restrictive categories adopted by Lord Devlin in a way which is contrary to the normal practice of the courts as referred to by Lord Evershed in *Rookes v Barnard* [1964] 1 All ER 367 at 384, [1964] AC 1129 at 1185, and by Lord Diplock in *Cassell & Co Ltd v Broome* [1972] 1 All ER 801 at 871, [1972] AC 1027 at 1127. Such a restrictive approach also justifies the comments in *Winfield and Jolowicz on Tort* (15th edn, 1998) p 746 in relation to the pre-1964 test:

'In other words, that decision [*Rookes v Barnard*] was not a 'new start' for the law under two rationalised categories but a further restriction upon then existing authority. Whatever one's views on exemplary damages this is an unfortunate state of affairs because it commits the law to an irrational position in which the result depends not on principle but upon the accidents of litigation (or even of law reporting) before 1964, at a time, moreover, when the distinction between exemplary and aggravated damages was by no means so clearly drawn as it is now.'

[23] It is also to be borne in mind that the Law Commission in its report on *Aggravated, Exemplary and Restitutionary Damages* (Law Com No 247) (1997) para 5.49 recommended that the availability of punitive damages be extended for most torts, which would entail the rejection of 'the rationally indefensible position which the common law reached' in deciding claims on the basis of the existence or absence of pre-1964 precedents.

[24] I do not think that the government's view (Hansard (HC Debates), 9 November 1999, col 502) that it was right to defer a decision on further legislation on this issue coupled with the comment 'It may be that some further judicial development of the law in this area might help clarify the issues' should inspire your Lordships to the view that the whole matter should be reopened and the Law Commission's report revisited. It is no more than a comment that issues might become clearer as decisions on particular facts emerge.

[25] For my part I do not consider that it would be right in this case to consider reopening the whole question as to whether exemplary damages should be available at all. The House clearly refused in *Rookes v Barnard* and *Cassell & Co Ltd v Broome* to abolish the rule that exemplary damages are in some cases available and in *Cassell & Co Ltd v Broome* the House refused to reopen the basic decision in *Rookes v Barnard*.

[26] There are obviously strong views as to whether exemplary damages should or should not ever be awarded. It has not been contended in this case that your Lordships should hold that in principle they can never be awarded. In my view therefore the starting point is that the two decisions of the House already accept that exemplary damages may be awarded in some cases. The task of the House in the present appeal is to say whether it is arguable that they can, and if the facts are established should, be awarded in the present case for the tort of misfeasance in public office. In Lord Devlin's speech in *Rookes v Barnard* it seems to me that it is the features of the behaviour rather than the cause of action which must be looked at in order to decide whether the facts fall into the first category. In *Cassell & Co Ltd v Broome* Lord Diplock was also recognising that the task of the judge was to decide whether the facts brought the case into one of the categories.

[27] So on the present appeal the question is whether the exemplary damages claimed are on the basis of facts which if established fall within the first category. For the purpose of the strike-out application, it is accepted that they do so fall. The claim is not excluded because it is not shown that a case on the basis of misfeasance in a public office had been decided before 1964. I would therefore allow the appeal. The claim for exemplary damages should not have been struck out on the basis argued before the House. The question whether in principle the defendant can be vicariously liable has not been argued and I do not think it right to discuss or to rule on it in this case.

LORD NICHOLLS OF BIRKENHEAD: . . .

[63] The arguments for and against exemplary damages need no rehearsing. They are familiar enough, and they are set out clearly in the Law Commission's report. In the end, and in respectful agreement with the views expressed by Lord Wilberforce in *Cassell & Co Ltd v Broome*, the feature which I find most striking is the extent to which the principle of exemplary damages continues to have vitality. The availability of exemplary damages has played a significant role in buttressing civil liberties, in claims for false imprisonment and wrongful arrest. From time to time cases do arise where awards of compensatory damages are perceived as inadequate to achieve a just result between the parties. The nature of the defendant's conduct calls for a further response from the courts. On occasion conscious wrongdoing by a defendant is so outrageous, his disregard of the claimant's rights so contumelious, that something more is needed to show that the law will not tolerate such behaviour. Without an award of exemplary damages, justice will not have been done. Exemplary damages, as a remedy of last resort, fill what otherwise would be a regrettable lacuna.

[64] This experience has not been confined to this country. Exemplary damages continue to discharge a role, perceived to be useful and valuable, in other common law jurisdictions. Indeed, the restrictions on exemplary damages imposed by *Rookes v Barnard* and *Cassell & Co Ltd v Broome* did not strike a receptive chord, for instance, in Canada, Australia or New Zealand. Outside the United Kingdom *Rookes v Barnard* received a generally negative reception.

[65] If exemplary damages are to continue as a remedial tool, as recommended by the Law Commission after extensive consultation, the difficult question which arises concerns the circumstances in which this tool should be available for use. Stated in its broadest form, the relevant principle is tolerably clear: the availability of exemplary damages should be co-extensive with its rationale. As already indicated, the underlying rationale lies in the sense of outrage which a defendant's conduct sometimes evokes, a sense which is not always assuaged fully by a compensatory award of damages, even when the damages are increased to reflect emotional distress.

[66] In *Rookes v Barnard*, Lord Devlin drew a distinction between oppressive acts by government officials and similar acts by companies or individuals. He considered that exemplary damages should not be available in the case of non-governmental oppression or bullying. Whatever may have been the position 40 years ago, I am respectfully inclined to doubt the soundness of this distinction today. National and international companies can exercise enormous power. So do some individuals. I am not sure it would be right to draw a hard-and-fast line which would always exclude such companies and persons from the reach of exemplary damages. Indeed, the validity of the dividing line drawn by Lord Devlin when formulating his first category is somewhat undermined by his second category, where the defendants are not confined to, and normally would not be, government officials or the like.

[67] Nor, I may add, am I wholly persuaded by Lord Devlin's formulation of his second category (wrongful conduct expected to yield a benefit in excess of any compensatory award likely to be made). The law of unjust enrichment has developed apace in recent years. In so far as there may be a need to go further, the key here would seem to be the same as that already discussed: outrageous conduct on the part of the defendant. There is no obvious reason why, if exemplary damages are to be available, the profit motive should suffice but a malicious motive should not.

[68] As I have said, difficult questions arise here. In view of the limited scope of the submissions made by the parties on this appeal, this is not the occasion for attempting to state comprehensive conclusions on these matters. For the purposes of the present appeal it is sufficient, first, to express the view that the House should now depart from its decision in *Cassell & Co Ltd v Broome*, in so far as that decision confirmed the continuing existence of what has subsequently been described as the 'cause of action' condition and, secondly, to note that the essence of the conduct constituting the court's discretionary jurisdiction to award exemplary damages is conduct which was an outrageous disregard of the claimant's rights. Whether the conduct of PC Cavendish satisfies that test in this case is a matter to be resolved at trial. I would allow this appeal.

[LORD MACKAY OF CLASHFERN, LORD HUTTON, and LORD SCOTT OF FOSCOTE delivered speeches in favour of allowing the appeal.]

Appeal allowed.

QUESTION

Although Lord Nicholls had referred earlier in his speech to exemplary damages being intended to punish and deter, does the rationale for exemplary damages stated by Lord Nicholls (at [63] in the extract ante) add to this? (See J. Manning (2003) 119 LQR 24 at 26, commenting on *A v Botterill* [2003] 1 AC 449, [2002] UKPC 44.)

NOTES

1. Their Lordships were agreed that there should not be a 'cause of action' test. However, there was not total agreement on the merits of exemplary damages (although the House of Lords were not invited to consider their abolition). In the extract ante, Lord Nicholls might be thought to see some merit in them, but Lord Scott would have been 'receptive' to the argument that they should not be available. Lord Scott and Lord Hutton were not at one as to the potential deterrent effects of such an award. More generally, consider Stevens' rights-based approach to exemplary damages (*Stevens*, pp. 85–88).

2. Should an employer be vicariously liable for punitive damages? The means and blame-worthiness of the employer and the employee will differ, and in particular note that it is established that where there are joint tortfeasors the lowest of the figures against any one tortfeasor is the appropriate one against all the tortfeasors. The question of vicarious liability was referred to in *Thompson* (see p. 498, ante), but in *Kuddus* four of the Law Lords left the position open. Lord Scott would have rejected vicarious liability. For the Law Commission's view, see note 5, post. The matter re-arose in *Rowlands v Chief Constable of Merseyside Police* [2007] 1 WLR 1065, [2006] EWCA Civ 1773, where Moore-Bick LJ (with whose judgment Richards and Ward LJJ agreed) thought that a substantial award could be made even though the Chief Constable was only vicariously liable, and stated (at [47]):

   > However, since the power to award exemplary damages rests on policy rather than principle, it seems to me that the question whether awards can be made against persons whose liability is vicarious only must also be answered by resort to considerations of policy rather than strict principle. While the common law continues to recognise a power to award exemplary damages in respect of wrongdoing by servants of the government of a kind that has a direct effect on civil liberties, which for my own part I think it should, I think that it is desirable as a matter of policy that the courts should be able to make punitive awards against those who are vicariously liable for the conduct of their subordinates without being constrained by the financial means of those who committed the wrongful acts in question. Only by this means can awards of an adequate amount be made against those who bear public responsibility for the conduct of the officers concerned.

   Would this apply even if the police officer responsible were joined in the action?

3. It will have been seen that Lord Nicholls in *Kuddus* draws attention to the connection between Lord Devlin's second category and a restitutionary award of damages. Indeed, for Lord Scott the development of restitutionary awards was part of the reasoning for his view set out in note 1, ante. In *Borders (UK) Ltd v Commissioner of the Police of the Metropolis* [2005] EWCA Civ 197 both Sedley and Rix LJJ referred to this point and to the argument in *McGregor on Damages*, para 11.027–11.028 that the emergence of restitutionary damages may render the use of this second category of exemplary damages unnecessary (although Sedley LJ seemed the more enthusiastic of the two that this should come about). The *Borders* case is discussed by D. Campbell and J. Devenney [2006] CLJ 208.

4. Since the rejection of the 'cause of action test' by *Kuddus* there have been awards of punitive damages in, for example, cases of conversion (*Borders*) and breach of statutory duty (*Design Progression Ltd v Thurloe Properties Ltd* [2005] 1 WLR 1, [2004] EWHC 324 (Ch)). This last-mentioned situation is particularly interesting since it is regarded as the tort under which actions are brought for breach of European Community Law: see *Garden Cottage Foods Ltd v Milk Marketing Board* [1983] 2 All ER 770, [1984] AC 130 (p. 709, post). European Community law does not expressly require the award of exemplary damages, but leaves it up to the Member State's domestic law. The matter has been discussed recently in *Devenish Nutrition Ltd v Sonofi-Aventis SA* [2008] 2 All

ER 249, [2007] EWHC 2394 (Ch), where the view was taken that it was the principle of equivalence rather than the principle of effectiveness that may require an English court to award exemplary damages in such a case. A different 'European context' (here the European Convention on Human Rights) is raised by the Human Rights Act 1988, where damages may be awarded as a remedy under s. 8, though the Act is not a 'tort statute' (*R (Greenfield) v Secretary of State for the Home Department* [2005] 2 All ER 240, [2005] UKHL 14). However, the European Court of Human Rights, whose decisions English courts are required by s. 2 of the 1998 Act to take into account, has never awarded such damages and has specifically rejected the chance to do so: see para. 3.47 of the Law Commission's Report, Law Com. No. 266, *Damages under the Human Rights Act 1998*. The position under the Convention was acknowledged in *Watkins v Secretary of State for the Home Department* [2006] 2 All ER 353, [2006] UKHL 17, where a reluctance to extend the role of exemplary damages after the liberalisation in *Kuddus* can be found. One reason in favour of the decision that the tort of misfeasance in public office is not actionable without proof of damage was that if the position were otherwise, exemplary damages might be awarded in such a situation. In Lord Bingham's view (at [26])—and Lord Hope agreed with his speech—the 'policy of the law is not in general to encourage the award of exemplary damages'. Lord Carswell would wish the award of such damages to be very closely confined, and Lord Rodger did not think, in the light of the position under the European Convention, the common law should be developed so as to make them available when not available in an equivalent action under the 1998 Act. Whilst not disagreeing with the decision in the case, Lord Walker did state (at [75]) that such damages 'even if anomalous, have a part to play in discouraging abuses of power in a democratic society'.

5.   Contrast with Lord Bingham's recently stated view in *Watkins* the earlier Law Commission Report, Law Com. No. 247, *Aggravated, Exemplary and Restitutionary Damages* (1997), which proposed major reforms to the law of exemplary (or, as it prefers, 'punitive') damages. The report rejected Lord Reid's view that the only purpose of tort damages should be compensation and also rejected calls that punitive damages should be abolished. The Law Commission preferred the view that tort law has a role, albeit as a last resort, in deterring outrageous conduct, and considered that Lord Devlin's restriction of punitive damages in *Rookes v Barnard* went too far. Instead of the *Rookes* 'categories' approach, it suggested that punitive damages should be available whenever the defendant has 'deliberately and outrageously disregarded the [claimant's] rights', either in committing a wrong or in subsequent conduct.

The Law Commission, however, insisted that only judges, not juries, should award punitive damages and that a judge should only do so if satisfied that the use of other remedies available to the court would be insufficient to punish the defendant. A judge should not normally award punitive damages against a defendant who has already suffered punishment at the hands of the criminal courts, but should be able to take into account the possible deterrent effects of punitive damages, both on the defendant and on others. Moreover, the civil standard of proof, not the more onerous criminal burden, should continue to apply. For recent discussion of the idea of 'double jeopardy' in this context, see the *Devenish Nutrition* case, discussing *Borders* and supporting the idea that 'there should be no danger of...duplication of penalty'.

The Law Commission report also recommended that punitive damages should be set at the minimum amount needed to punish the defendant. The judge would have to take into account the defendant's state of mind, the nature of the rights disregarded, the extent of the intended harm, and any benefit the defendant might have obtained through the wrong. Defendants should be able to argue, however, that they do not have the means, without excessive hardship, to pay the full amount the judge is minded to impose, and that the judge should reduce the sum to avoid excessive hardship.

The Law Commission urged the retention of vicarious liability for punitive damages (but would allow a vicariously liable employer the argument of hardship which has just been mentioned): otherwise, it says that punitive damages should be treated on a several basis (each tortfeasor judged separately) rather than a joint basis (all tortfeasors liable for the full amount of the loss). (Shavell and Polinsky op cit., in contrast, believe that punitive damages should not be awarded against corporations, since such awards punish the corporation's owners and customers rather than the people who do wrong—but, as the Law Commission pointed out, are not employers in a very strong position to discourage outrageous behaviour by their employees?)

The Law Commission's proposals were reconsidered in the DCA's Consultation Paper (CP 9/07). The Government's view is that the categories set out by Lord Devlin in *Rookes v Barnard* should not be extended, and that the one case where by statute exemplary damages can be awarded (the Reserve and Auxiliary Forces (Protection of Civil Interests) Act 1951) should be altered so as to provide for the possibility of aggravated rather than exemplary damages. On the other hand, there was approval of the decision in *Kuddus*.

2 PERSONAL INJURIES

(a) In general

■ Todorovic v Waller
High Court of Australia (1981) 37 ALR 481

GIBBS CJ AND WILSON J [in a joint judgment]: . . .
In the first place, a plaintiff who has been injured by the negligence of the defendant should be awarded such a sum of money as will, as nearly as possible, put him in the same position as if he had not sustained the injuries. Secondly, damages for one cause of action must be recovered once and forever, and (in the absence of any statutory exception) must be awarded as a lump sum; the court cannot order a defendant to make periodic payments to the plaintiff. Thirdly, the court has no concern with the manner in which the plaintiff uses the sum awarded to him; the plaintiff is free to do what he likes with it. Fourthly, the burden lies on the plaintiff to prove the injury or loss for which he seeks damages.

Although the aim of the court in awarding damages is to make good to the plaintiff, so far as money can do, the loss which he has suffered, it is obvious that it is impossible to assess damages for pain and suffering and loss of amenities of life by any process of arithmetical calculation. It may be less obvious, but is no less certain, that the assessment of damages for future pecuniary loss resulting from personal injuries can never be a mere matter of mathematics. It is true that as the assessment of damages has become more sophisticated, calculations are made in an attempt to achieve greater precision. Such calculations may sometimes give a false appearance of accuracy. Some of the figures on which they are based are the result of estimate or speculation. In the case of loss of earning capacity it is necessary to compare what the plaintiff might have earned if he had not suffered the injury with what he is likely to earn in his injured condition. In many cases this means that the court has to engage in 'a double exercise in the art of prophesying': *Paul v Rendell* (1981) 55 ALJR 371 at 372; 34 ALR 569 at 571....

The difficulty inherent in the assessment of damages provides no reason for the courts to shirk the task of arriving at the estimate most likely to provide fair and reasonable compensation. But it may provide a reason for approaching with some caution a proposal to overturn an established method of assessment, in an attempt to achieve an accuracy which it is not humanly possible to attain....

NOTE

In recent years there has been the possibility that in certain cases periodical payments rather than a lump sum award may be ordered: see p. 548, post. This point should be borne in mind throughout this section.

■ Lim Poh Choo v Camden and Islington Area Health Authority
House of Lords [1979] 2 All ER 910

The plaintiff, Dr Lim Poh Choo, a psychiatrist then aged 36, was admitted to hospital for a minor operation. As the result of the negligence of some person for whom the area health authority was vicariously liable, the plaintiff experienced a cardiac arrest in the recovery room. She consequently suffered extensive and irremediable brain damage, which left her only intermittently, and then barely, sentient and totally dependent on others.

The defendants admitted liability. The issue at trial was the question of damages.

LORD SCARMAN:...
Lord Denning MR in the Court of Appeal declared that a radical reappraisal of the law is needed. I agree. But I part company with him on ways and means. Lord Denning MR believes it can be done by the judges, whereas I would suggest to your Lordships that such a reappraisal calls for social, finan-cial, economic and administrative decisions which only the legislature can take. The perplexities of the present case, following on the publication of the report of the Royal Commission on Civil Liability and Compensation for Personal Injury (the Pearson report),[7] emphasise the need for reform of the law.

The course of the litigation illustrates, with devastating clarity, the insuperable problems implicit in a system of compensation for personal injuries which (unless the parties agree otherwise) can yield only a lump sum assessed by the court at the time of judgment. Sooner or later, and too often later rather than sooner, if the parties do not settle, a court (once liability is admitted or proved) has to make an award of damages. The award, which covers past, present and future injury and loss, must, under our law, be of a lump sum assessed at the conclusion of the legal process. The award is final; it is not susceptible to review as the future unfolds, substituting fact for estimate. Knowledge of the future being denied to mankind, so much of the award as is to be attributed to future loss and suffering (in many cases the major part of the award) will almost surely be wrong. There is really only one certainty: the future will prove the award to be either too high or too low....

The judge awarded Dr Lim a total sum of £254,765. He apportioned it as follows:

(1)	Pain, suffering, loss of amenities	£20,000	
	Interest from date of writ	£5,930	£25,930
(2)	Out-of-pocket expenses, including £680 for cost of stay at Tang Tock Seng Hospital and Singapore Nursing Home	£3,596	
(3)	Cost of care to date of judgment: 40 months at £200 per month	£8,000	
(4)	Interest on (2) and (3) from date of accident (1 March 1973) to judgment	£2,482	£14,078

---

[7] March 1978, Cmnd. 7054.

(5) Loss of earnings to date of judgment	£14,213	
(6) Interest on (5) from date of accident to judgment	£3,044	£17,257
(7) Cost of future care:		
Malaysia, 7 years at £2,600 per annum discounted to:	£17,500	
England, 8 years at £8,000 per annum discounted to:	£88,000	£105,500
(8) Loss of future earnings:		
14 years at £6,000	£84,000	
Loss of pension	£8,000	£92,000

On appeal to the Court of Appeal, the defendants attacked the award in many respects....

(a) The total of damages (£254,765)
The submission that the total of the award was excessive was one of the broadest generality. Whether or not he can establish duplication or overlap or any other error in calculating the separate items of the award, counsel for the appellants submitted that an award of damages, being a 'jury question', must be fair to both sides, and that in a case such as the present a judge should bear in mind (a) comparable cases, (b) the effect of high awards on the level of insurance premiums or, if, as here, the taxpayer foots the bill, on the taxpayer, (c) the availability of care for the victim under the national health service and (d) public policy. Such generalities as that damages must be treated as a jury question and kept in line with public policy I do not find helpful. Their very breadth merely contributes to uncertainty and inconsistency in an area of the law, the history if not the present practice of which is notorious for both vices. Invoking the memory of the days when juries assessed damages for personal injuries does no more than remind us that the modern practice of reasoned awards by judges is a substantial advance on the inscrutable awards of juries. Of course, awards must be fair. But this means no more than that they must be a proper compensation for the injury suffered and the loss sustained. Nor in this case do I find helpful a comparison of one total award with another. In so far as an award consists of 'conventional' items, e.g. for pain and suffering, comparability with other awards is certainly of value in keeping the law consistent. But pecuniary loss depends on circumstances; and, where (as in the present case) such loss predominates, comparison with total awards in other cases does not help, and may be misleading.

The two specific matters counsel for the appellants mentioned, the burden on the public (through premiums or taxes) and the availability of national health service care, prove on examination to be for the legislator, not the judge. As to the first, the principle of the law is that compensation should as nearly as possible put the party who has suffered in the same position as he would have been in if he had not sustained the wrong (per Lord Blackburn in *Livingstone v Rawyards Coal Co*[8]). There is no room here for considering the consequences of a high award on the wrongdoer or those who finance him. And, if there were room for any such consideration, on what principle, or by what criterion, is the judge to determine the extent to which he is to diminish on this ground the compensation payable?

The second matter, though introduced by counsel for the appellants as part of his general submissions on the total award, is really one, as he recognised, which falls to be considered in assessing the cost of future care. It is convenient, however, to deal with it at this stage. Section 2(4) of the Law Reform (Personal Injuries) Act 1948 provides that in an action for damages for personal injuries there shall be disregarded, in determining the reasonableness of any expenses, the possibility of avoiding those expenses or part of them by taking advantage of facilities available in the national health service. In *Harris v Brights Asphalt Contractors Ltd*[9] Slade J said of the subsection:

> 'I think all [it] means is that, when an injured plaintiff in fact incurs expenses which are reasonable, that expenditure is not to be impeached on the ground that, if he had taken advantage of the facilities available under the National Health Service Act 1946, those reasonable expenses might

---

[8] (1880) 5 App Cas 25 at 39.   [9] [1953] 1 QB 617 at 635.

have been avoided. I do not understand section 2(4) to enact that a plaintiff shall be deemed to be entitled to recover expenses which in fact he will never incur.'

In *Cunningham v Harrison*[10] the Court of Appeal expressed the same view, Lawton LJ[11] saying that a defendant can, notwithstanding the statute, submit that the plaintiff will probably not incur such expenses because he will be unable to obtain outside the national health service the domestic and nursing help which he requires.

I agree with Slade J and the Court of Appeal. It has not been suggested that expenses so far incurred in the care and treatment of Dr Lim have been unreasonable. They are, therefore, protected by the subsection. But it is open to serious question whether for the rest of her life it will continue to be possible to obtain for Dr Lim, outside the national health service, the domestic and nursing help she will require. However, Lord Denning MR and Lawton LJ both of whom were parties to the decision in *Cunningham v Harrison*, have proceeded in the instant case on the basis, which the trial judge must also have accepted, that it will be possible and that the expense of doing so is reasonable, in the absence of any evidence to the contrary, I am not prepared to take a different view, though I recognise the force of the case developed in the Pearson report[12] for legislation repealing the subsection.

The attack, therefore, on the total of damages awarded as being excessive, merely by reason of its size, fails. If the appellants are to succeed, they must show that one or more of the component items of the award are wrong.

(b) The award for pain and suffering and loss of amenities

Counsel for the appellants recognised, at the outset of his argument, that, if *Wise v Kaye*[13] and *H West & Son Ltd v Shephard*[14] were correctly decided, his...submission (that the sum awarded should be comparable with the small conventional awards in fatal cases for loss of expectation of life) must fail.

My Lords, I think it would be wrong now to reverse by judicial decision the two rules which were laid down by the majority of the House in *H West & Son Ltd v Shephard*, namely (1) that the fact of unconsciousness does not eliminate the actuality of the deprivation of the ordinary experiences and amenities of life (see the formulation used by Lord Morris of Borth-y-Gest[15]) and (2) that, if damages are awarded on a correct basis, it is of no concern to the court to consider any question as to the use that will thereafter be made of the money awarded. The effect of the two cases (*Wise v Kaye* being specifically approved in *H West & Son Ltd v Shephard*) is twofold. First, they draw a clear distinction between damages for pain and suffering and damages for loss of amenities. The former depend on the plaintiff's personal awareness of pain, her capacity for suffering. But the latter are awarded for the fact of deprivation, a substantial loss, whether the plaintiff is aware of it or not. Secondly, they establish that the award in *Benham v Gambling*[16] (assessment in fatal cases of damages for loss of expectation of life) is not to be compared with, and has no application to, damages to be awarded to a living plaintiff for loss of amenities.

I do not underrate the formidable logic and good sense of the minority opinions expressed in *Wise v Kaye*[17] and *H West & Son Ltd v Shephard*.[18] The quality of the minority opinions was, however, matched by the equally formidable logic and good sense of the majority opinions. The question on which opinions differed was, in truth, as old and as obstinate as the philosopher's stone itself. A decision having been taken by this House in 1963 (the year *H West & Son Ltd v Shephard* was decided), its reversal would cause widespread injustice, unless it were to be part and parcel of a comprehensive reform of the law. For since 1962 settlements have proceeded on the basis that the rule adopted in *Wise v Kaye* was correct: and judges have had to assess damages on the same basis in contested cases. We are in the area of 'conventional' awards for non-pecuniary loss, where comparability matters. Justice requires

[10] [1973] QB 942, [1973] 3 All ER 463.   [11] [1973] QB 942 at 957, [1973] 3 All ER 463 at 473.
[12] Cmnd. 7054-I, paras. 340–342.   [13] [1962] 1 QB 638, [1962] 1 All ER 257.
[14] [1964] AC 326, [1963] 2 All ER 625.   [15] [1964] AC 326 at 349, [1963] 2 All ER 625 at 633.
[16] [1941] AC 157, [1941] 1 All ER 7.   [17] [1962] 1 QB 638, [1962] 1 All ER 257.
[18] [1964] AC 326, [1963] 2 All ER 625.

that such awards continue to be consistent with the general level accepted by the judges. If the law is to be changed by the reversal of *H West & Son Ltd v Shephard*, it should be done not judicially but legislatively within the context of a comprehensive enactment dealing with all aspects of damages for personal injury.

...I think the judge's award of £20,000 and interest for pain, suffering and loss of amenities should be upheld.

(c) Loss of earnings, and duplication (overlap)
The appellants' submission is brief and simple. In para. 8 of their case it was put in three short sentences:

> 'The Plaintiff ought not to have been awarded damages for loss of earnings as well as for loss of amenities and cost of care. The sum awarded for cost of care exceeded her estimated loss of earnings and *covered all her needs*. The additional award of damages for loss of earnings was duplicatory.'

As developed in argument, the submission was a twofold one. First, it was submitted that in catastrophic cases 'loss of earnings' does not reflect a real loss. Secondly, if damages are recoverable for loss of earnings, duplication with other heads of damage is to be avoided. The law must, therefore, ensure that no more is recovered for loss of earnings than what the plaintiff, if not injured, would have saved, or reserved for the support of his, or her, dependants. Since there was no evidence to suggest that Dr Lim would have accumulated any surplus income after meeting her working and living expenses, the trial judge's award for loss of earnings was wholly wrong.

The first submission is contrary to an established line of authority which, beginning with *Phillips v London and South Western Rly Co*,[19] has recently received the seal of this House's approval in *Pickett v British Rail Engineering Ltd*.[20] It is also contrary to the principle of the common law that a genuine deprivation (be it pecuniary or non-pecuniary in character) is a proper subject of compensation. The principle was recognised both in *Phillip's* case,[1] where the loss was pecuniary, and in *H West & Son Ltd v Shephard*,[2] where the loss was non-pecuniary.

The second submission is more formidable. Undoubtedly, the courts must be vigilant to avoid not only duplication of damages but the award of a surplus exceeding a true compensation for the plaintiff's deprivation or loss.

The separate items, which together constitute a total award of damages, are interrelated. They are the parts of a whole, which must be fair and reasonable. 'At the end', as Lord Denning MR said in *Taylor v Bristol Omnibus Co Ltd*,[3] 'the judges should look at the total figure in the round, so as to be able to cure any overlapping or other source of error'. In most cases the risk of overlap is not great, nor, where it occurs, is it substantial. Living expenses continue, or progressively increase, for most plaintiffs after injury as they would have done if there had been no injury. But where, as in *Pickett's* case, the plaintiff claims damages for the earnings of his 'lost years', or, as in the present case, the claim is in respect of a lifetime's earnings lost because, though she will live, she cannot earn her living, a real risk arises that the plaintiff may recover, not merely compensation for loss, which is the entitlement given by law, but a surplus greater than could have been achieved if there had been no death or incapacity. Two deductions, therefore, fall to be made from the damages to be awarded. First, as the cases have always recognised, the expenses of earning the income which has been lost. Counsel for the respondent conceded this much. Secondly, the plaintiff's living expenses. This is necessarily a hypothetical figure in the case of a 'lost years' claim, since the plaintiff does not survive to earn the money; and, since there is no cost of care claim (the plaintiff being assumed to be dead), it falls to be deducted from the loss of earnings

---

[19] (1879) 5 CPD 280, [1874–80] All ER Rep 1176.   [20] [1979] 1 All ER 774, [1978] 3 WLR 955.
[1] (1879) 5 CPD 280 at 292, [1874–80] All ER Rep 1176 at 1181 per Brett LJ.
[2] [1964] AC 326 at 349, [1963] 2 All ER 625 at 633 per Lord Morris.
[3] [1975] 2 All ER 1107 at 1111, [1979] 1 WLR 1054 at 1057.

award. But where, as in the present case, the expectancy of life is not shortened but incapacity exists, there will be a cost of care claim as well as a loss of earnings claim. How should living expenses be assessed and deducted in such a case? One approach, analogous to the method necessarily adopted in 'lost years' cases, would be to attempt an assessment of how much the plaintiff would have spent and on what, always a most speculative exercise. How, for instance, could anyone tell how Dr Lim would have ordered her standard of living, had she been able to pursue her career? Another approach is however, available in the case of a living plaintiff. In *Shearman v Folland*[4] the Court of Appeal deducted what has been described as the 'domestic element' from the cost of care. Inevitably, a surviving plaintiff has to meet her living expenses. This approach, being on the basis of a future actuality (subject to the uncertainties of life), is far less hypothetical than the former (which, faute de mieux, has to be adopted in 'lost years' cases). It is a simpler, more realistic, calculation and accords more closely with the general principle of the law that the courts in assessing compensation for loss are not concerned either with how the plaintiff would have used the moneys lost or how she (or he) will use the compensation received.

In the present case, my Lords, it is perfectly possible to estimate the domestic element in Dr Lim's cost of care. The estimated figure must, therefore, be deducted in the assessment of her damages for the cost of her care. In the result Dr Lim will recover in respect of her future loss a capital sum which, after all proper discounts, will represent her loss of earnings, net after allowing for working expenses, and her cost of care, net after deducting the domestic element. A capital sum so assessed will compensate for a genuine loss and for a genuine item of additional expenditure, both of which arise from the injury she has sustained. It will not contain any element of duplication or go beyond compensation into surplus.

A further argument was addressed to your Lordships in the context of duplication. It was urged that there was an overlap between the sum awarded for loss of amenities and that for loss of future earnings. The amenities which Dr Lim has lost, it was submitted, would have had to be provided out of her earnings. If, therefore, she is to be compensated for the former, she should suffer a deduction from her loss of earnings claim. Reliance was placed on the judgment of Diplock LJ in *Fletcher v Autocar and Transporters Ltd.*[5]

The question whether there can be any overlap between damages for non-pecuniary loss and for pecuniary loss does not arise for decision on the facts of this case. As the majority of the Court of Appeal said, the amount of damages awarded to Dr Lim for loss of amenities was a modest sum. It was not assessed by reference to any expensive pleasures or pursuits such as Diplock LJ postulated in *Fletcher's* case.[6] There was, indeed, no evidence to suggest that Dr Lim had, or was likely to develop, any such tastes or pursuits. There is, therefore, no duplication of damages between the two items in this case.

On the point of principle whether damages for non-pecuniary loss can properly be reduced to avoid an overlap with damages for pecuniary loss I express no final opinion. I confess, however, that I doubt the possibility of overlap; and I note that the Pearson Commission[7] considers it wrong in principle to reduce the one by reason of the size of the other.

(D) Cost of future care
Both parties were agreed that damages under this head are recoverable....

Conclusion
On the questions of principle argued before the House I find that the appellants have substantially failed in the appeal, but have succeeded on the cross-appeal. Nevertheless, for the reasons I have given

---

[4] [1950] 2 KB 43, [1950] 1 All ER 976.
[5] [1968] 2 QB 322 esp at 342, [1968] 1 All ER 726 esp at 737.
[6] [1968] 2 QB 322 at 342, [1968] 1 All ER 726 at 737.
[7] Report of the Royal Commission on Civil Liability and Compensation for Personal Injury (Cmnd. 7054-1) para. 759.

and because of the changed circumstances of Dr Lim and her family, the award is diminished, though to no very great extent. Excluding interest, which should be calculated and, if possible, agreed by the parties when the House makes its decision, the award should, I propose, be as follows:

Pain, suffering, loss of amenities	£20,000
Out-of-pocket expenses	£3,596
Cost of care to date of judgment in this House	
(a) Malaysia	£16,500
(b) travelling	£1,923
(c) (calculated from 4 September 1978 to an arbitrary date, 4 May 1979, it will require to be revised upwards to the actual date of judgment in the House)	£4,266.64
Loss of earnings to date of judgment at trial	£14,213
Cost of future care	£76,800
Loss of future earnings (including pension rights)	£92,000
Total	£229,298.64

to which the appropriate interest will have to be added.

My Lords, I would propose that, subject to the necessary variations to the amount of the award, the appeal be dismissed with costs and the cross-appeal dismissed with no order as to costs.

[LORD DIPLOCK, VISCOUNT DILHORNE, and LORD SIMON OF GLAISDALE agreed with the speech of LORD SCARMAN.]

Appeal and cross-appeal dismissed.

NOTES

1. Subsequently, Parliament passed the Administration of Justice Act, 1982, s. 5 of which reads:

   In an action under the law of England and Wales or the law of Northern Ireland for damages for personal injuries (including any such action arising out of a contract) any saving to the injured person which is attributable to his maintenance wholly or partly at public expense in a hospital, nursing home or other institution shall be set off against any income lost by him as a result of his injuries.

2. Section 1(1)(a) of the 1982 Act abolished the right to claim damages for loss of expectation of life, but provided that in assessing damages in respect of pain and suffering caused by the injuries, account must be taken of any suffering caused, or likely to be caused to the claimant by awareness that his expectation of life has been so reduced (s. 1(1)(b)). Parliament has recognised the feelings of mourners in the head of damages for bereavement (see p. 285, ante), and we have seen (p. 129, ante) that the courts have shown some flexibility in awarding damages in tort in respect of injured feelings, as well as lifting restrictions on damages for 'recognisable psychiatric illness' (p. 132, ante) at least in its 'non-secondary' form. In *The Mediana* [1900] AC 113 at 116–117, the Earl of Halsbury LC asked: 'What manly mind cares about pain and suffering that is past?', and critics have claimed that awards for pain and suffering tend to over-compensate the victim, particularly in less serious cases. The Pearson Commission, vol. I, paras. 382–389 proposed the abolition of damages for non-pecuniary loss during the first three months after the injury. In an equally restrictive vein, in one of the Hillsborough disaster cases, *Hicks v Chief Constable of South Yorkshire* [1992] 1 All ER 690 (confirmed by the House of Lords [1992] 1 AC 310, [1992] 2 All ER 65), the Court of Appeal held that the pain suffered by the victims of suffocation in the moments before they died was not actionable.

3.   'Loss of amenity' refers to the inability to continue in the lifestyle the claimant had before the accident and is based on the post-accident expectation of life. The amounts awarded are conventional in nature. The Courts are heavily influenced by the tariff laid down in a publication called, *Guidelines for the Assessment of General Damages in Personal Injury Cases*, published by the Judicial Studies Board.

Lord Scarman (p. 514, ante) said it would be wrong to reverse by judicial decision the rule that an unconscious claimant is entitled to damages for loss of amenity. The Pearson Commission, which said that damages for non-pecuniary loss serve the functions of a palliative, a means of purchasing alternative sources of satisfaction for those lost and for meeting hidden expenses caused by the injury (para. 360), recommended additionally the abolition of damages for non-pecuniary loss in the case of permanent unconsciousness (paras. 397–398). The Law Commission in its Consultation Paper No. 140 *Damages for Personal Injury: Non-Pecuniary Loss* said (pp. 87–88):

[W]e are attracted by the view that non-pecuniary loss should be rationalised in terms of the mental suffering and loss of happiness caused to the plaintiff. If the plaintiff is so badly injured that he or she is incapable of suffering, then we consider that, just as if the plaintiff had been instantly killed, the plaintiff should be regarded as incurring no non-pecuniary loss at all; that, in other words, all non-pecuniary loss should be assessed subjectively (through the plaintiff's awareness of it and not objectively) irrespective of the plaintiff's unawareness of it.

But both the present approach and the 'subjective' approach are open to the objection that they let tortfeasors off too lightly. One could say that victims who are killed suffer a kind of 100 per cent loss of amenity. Whatever they were getting out of life they have now lost. Although everyone must die at some point, it is surely a cost to die early or permanently to lose consciousness. Equally, one could say the abolition of damages for 'loss of expectation of life' (Administration of Justice Act 1982, s. 1) has produced an injustice because the loss of years to be lived is itself a loss, although the extent of the injustice is offset by the limited compensation available for lost earnings in the lost years (see p. 524, post) and by the small amounts paid in some circumstances to relatives for 'bereavement'. Note that tortfeasors in such cases do not face the costs of the consequences of their torts. A systematic underestimation of the value of being alive will, over time, feed into the decisions made by organisations whose activities tend to be dangerous. The present law produces the bizarre incentive that it is cheaper to invest in activities that kill other people than in activities that maim them. The subjective approach would mean that it is cheaper to put someone in a coma than injure them less severely.

But there is one advantage of the subjective theory over the present system. Under the subjective theory it would cost no more to put someone in a coma than to kill them. Under the present system, if the victim is in a coma, damages are piling up against the defendant for loss of amenity, damages that cease to accumulate as soon as the victim dies. Therefore, at least one can say that the subjective theory would remove an artificial incentive either to keep coma victims alive, or, in some circumstances, for example before the trial where the next-of-kin or the doctors are the tortfeasors, to end the victim's life.

4.   The Law Commission, in its report Law Com. No. 257, said that awards for pain and suffering and for loss of amenity (PSLA) had become far too low both in the view of victims and of public opinion generally. It recommended substantial increases, especially for the more serious cases. The issue came up for consideration in the next extract.

■ Heil v Rankin

Court of Appeal [2000] 3 All ER 138

LORD WOOLF MR [delivering the judgment of a five-member Court of Appeal]: ...

[23] [The] principle of 'full compensation' applies to pecuniary and non-pecuniary damage alike. But ... this statement immediately raises a problem in a situation where what is in issue is what the appropriate level of 'full compensation' for non-pecuniary injury is when the compensation has to be expressed in pecuniary terms. There is no simple formula for converting the pain and suffering, the loss of function, the loss of amenity and disability which an injured person has sustained, into monetary terms. Any process of conversion must be essentially artificial. Lord Pearce expressed it well in *H West & Son Ltd v Shephard* [1963] 2 All ER 625 at 642, [1964] AC 326 at 364 when he said:

> 'The court has to perform the difficult and artificial task of converting into monetary damages the physical injury and deprivation and pain and to give judgment for what it considers to be a reasonable sum. It does not look beyond the judgment to the spending of the damages.'

[24] The last part of this statement is undoubtedly right. The injured person may not even be in a position to enjoy the damages he receives because of the injury which he has sustained. Lord Clyde recognised this in *Wells v Wells* [1998] 3 All ER 481 at 512, [1999] 1 AC 345 at 394 when he said: 'One clear principle is that what the successful plaintiff will in the event actually do with the award is irrelevant.'

[25] In the case of pecuniary loss, the courts have progressively been prepared to adopt ever more sophisticated calculations in order to establish the extent of a claimant's loss. ... In the case of non-pecuniary damages, the scale of damages has remained a 'jury question'. This is the position notwithstanding s 6 of the Administration of Justice (Miscellaneous Provisions) Act 1933, as a result of which the use of a jury to try personal injuries cases became discretionary. In practice, since the 1960's the assessment of damages has been carried out primarily by the judiciary. The assessment requires the judge to make a value judgment. That value judgment has been increasingly constrained by the desire to achieve consistency between the decisions of different judges. Consistency is important, because it assists in achieving justice between one claimant and another and one defendant and another. It also assists to achieve justice by facilitating settlements. The courts have become increasingly aware that this is in the interests of the litigants and society as a whole, particularly in the personal injury field. Delay in resolving claims can be a source of great injustice as well as the cause of expense to the parties and the justice system. It is for this reason that the introduction of the guidelines by the Judicial Studies Board (JSB) in 1992 was such a welcome development. ...

[27] Excessive importance must not, however, be attached to consistency. Care must be exercised not to freeze the compensation for non-pecuniary loss at a level which the passage of time and changes in circumstances make inadequate. The compensation must remain fair, reasonable and just. Fair compensation for the injured person. The level must also not result in injustice to the defendant, and it must not be out of accord with what society as a whole would perceive as being reasonable.

[28] While recognising the dangers which can arise from too rigid an application of tariffs, it has been the continuous responsibility of the courts not only to set tariffs for damages for non-pecuniary loss in the case of personal injuries, but also, having done so, to keep the tariffs up to date. The courts sought to achieve this by deciding guideline cases and subsequently making allowance for inflation, that is the depreciation in the value of money, since the guideline was laid down. This usually involved doing no more than applying to the guideline decision the appropriate difference between the RPI at the date on which the guideline case was decided and the RPI at the date on which the guideline was applied.

[29] However, the changes which take place in society are not confined to changes in the RPI. Other changes in society can result in a level of damages which was previously acceptable no longer providing fair, reasonable and just compensation, taking into account the interests of the claimants, the

defendants and society as a whole. For this reason, it is clearly desirable for the courts at appropriate intervals to review the level of damages so as to consider whether what was previously acceptable remains appropriate....

[38] For reasons we will identify later, as the claimants submit, the change in economic circumstances can contribute to causing a tariff to be no longer appropriate. Similarly, in setting the tariff the court should not ignore the economic impact of the level of damages which it selects. The economic consequences of a level of damages will not dictate the decision, but they will inform the decision. They are part of the background facts against which the decision must be taken. The court is not interested in the detail but it is interested in the broad picture. A distinction exists here between the task of the court when determining the level of pecuniary loss and when determining the level of non-pecuniary loss. In the case of pecuniary loss, and issues such as that which engaged the House of Lords in *Wells v Wells*, the court is only required to make the correct calculation. Economic consequences are then irrelevant. When the question is the level of damages for non-pecuniary loss the court is engaged in a different exercise. As we have said, it is concerned with determining what is the fair, reasonable and just equivalent in monetary terms of an injury and the resultant PSLA. The decision has to be taken against the background of the society in which the court makes the award. The position is well illustrated by the decisions of the courts of Hong Kong. As the prosperity of Hong Kong expanded, the courts by stages increased their tariff for damages so that it approached the level in England. (See *Chan Pui Ki v Leung On* [1996] 2 HKLR 401 at 406–408.)...

[40] We accept as well that the question of what is an appropriate award for general damages for PSLA is always a difficult task, and that to attempt the task of altering the level of awards generally can involve the courts in highly controversial issues which it would be preferable for the courts to avoid if this is not inconsistent with the courts' responsibility. However, changing the current levels of damages, if they are no longer reflecting what should be the correct level of awards, is, as Mr King submitted, part of the courts' duty. A duty which the court should not shirk.

[41] The level of awards does involve questions of social policy. But the questions are ones with which the courts are accustomed to deal as part of their normal role. Parliament remains sovereign. It can still intervene after the court has given its decision. The task would be a novel one for Parliament. However, Parliament's intervention in this instance would not necessarily result in a loss of flexibility or interfere with the ability of the court to craft an award to the individual facts of a case, which is a virtue of the present system. The commission have provided a draft Bill in their report in case it is necessary to legislate. The terms of the proposed Bill would avoid the undesirable consequences of lack of flexibility. If legislation based on the proposed Bill were to be passed, the legislation could also, by statutory provision, avoid the retrospective effect of an intervention by a court. This we recognise is an undesirable consequence of an intervention by a court. We accept that it would be preferable if a court was also able to consider making its guidance only prospective. But the parties do not argue for this and to do so would create invidious distinctions....

[47] We...have no intention of seeking to involve ourselves with matters of policy-making which are more suited for Parliament than for the courts. We do have to concern ourselves with current standards within our society and economic conditions, but only so far as the performance of our duty to set the level of damages makes this necessary. We are not contravening the wise advice that the courts should seek, when possible, to avoid becoming involved in determining broad questions of social and economic policy which is contained in the administrative law cases cited by Mr Havers. (See eg *Nottinghamshire CC v Secretary of State for the Environment* [1986] 1 All ER 199, [1986] AC 240.)

[48] In summary, our conclusion is therefore that it is appropriate for the court to consider the commission's recommendation. What is involved is part of the traditional role of the courts. It is a role in which juries previously were involved. Now it is the established role of the judiciary. It is a role which, as a result of their accumulated experience, the judiciary is well qualified to perform. Parliament can still intervene. It has, however, shown no inclination that it intends to do so. If it should decide to do so then the fact that the courts have already considered the question will be of assistance to Parliament. Until

Parliament does so, the courts cannot avoid their responsibility. While a public debate on this subject would no doubt be salutary, the contribution which it could make to the actual decision of the court is limited. The court has the report of the commission. It also has the other material which the parties have placed before it. It is in as good a position as it is likely to be to make a decision in the context of the present appeals. We see no reason to accede to Mr Havers' submission that we should postpone doing so. To postpone would be to neglect our responsibility to provide certainty in this area as soon as it is practical to do so....

Conclusions of the court

[82] We have already indicated that it is our responsibility, having regard to the material which has been placed before us, to review the general levels of award for PSLA. The conclusion to which we have come makes it clear that the result of our decision will not radically alter the courts present approach to the assessment of damages. This is because we do not consider that it would be appropriate to increase the levels of awards to the substantial extent recommended by the commission. We are of the opinion that a modest increase is required to bring some awards up to the standard, on which both sides are agreed, namely to a sum which is fair, reasonable and just.

[83] We are satisfied that it is in the case of the most catastrophic injuries that the awards are most in need of adjustment and that the scale of adjustment which is required reduces as the level of existing awards decreases. At the highest level, we see a need for awards to be increased by a sum in the region of one third. We see no need for an increase in awards which are at present below £10,000. It is our view that between those awards at the highest level, which require an upwards adjustment of one third, and those awards where no adjustment is required, the extent of the adjustment should taper downwards, as illustrated by our decisions on the individual appeals which are before us....

NOTES

1. The increases in *Heil v Rankin* fell far short of the Law Commission's recommendations. In the guise of discussing public opinion, the Court of Appeal took into account what it perceived to be the likely effects of increases of the scale recommended by the Law Commission on insurance rates and National Health Service expenditure. But, perhaps puzzlingly, the effects of undercompensation on the deterrent effect of tort law, either directly or through insurance, and thus on the number and seriousness of accidents, were not taken into account.

2. On Lord Woolf's reference at [41] ante to the inability of the court to make prospective decisions, note now *In re Spectrum Plus* [2005] 4 All ER 209, [2005] UKHL 41, where the House of Lords decided that in the most exceptional of cases prospective overruling might be possible.

3. In his speech in *Lim Poh Choo* (p. 511, ante), Lord Scarman referred to s. 2(4) of the Law Reform (Personal Injuries) Act 1948. This section reads:

   In an action for damages for personal injuries...there shall be disregarded, in determining the reasonableness of any expenses the possibility of avoiding those expenses or part of them by taking advantage of facilities available under the National Health Service.

   The Law Commission in its Consultation Paper No. 144, *Damages for Personal Injury: Medical, Nursing and Other Expenses*, reported (at p. 8):

   The law on this issue should be seen in the context of the evidence provided by our empirical report. A sizeable proportion of those who took part in the survey—34% of those whose settlement had been between £5,000 and £19,999 ("band 1") and 44% of those whose settlement had been £20,000 or more ("bands 2 to 4")—had received some form of private medical treatment, including tests. However, the proportions of respondents whose treatment had been *exclusively* private was very small indeed: 4% and 2% respectively of the two groups. Therefore, the pattern, where private treatment has been used at all, seems to be one of recourse to both public and private sectors. Various reasons were cited for the use of private rather than NHS facilities, but the chief ones were the necessity of a private examination for the compensation claim to proceed (22% of band 1 and 30% of bands 2 to 4), and perceived differences in the speed (36% and 27%) and quality (22% and 20%) of private treatment as compared with the NHS. [footnotes omitted]

In *Thomas v Wignall* [1987] QB 1098, [1987] 1 All ER 1185, there was an award of £435,000 for the cost of the claimant's future medical care in the private sector, although during the nine years since the accident she had been in NHS institutions for seven years and in private care for only 18 months. In cases like this, based on predictions about the claimant's future care, no undertaking has to be given by the claimant that she will use the damages for private care. The claimant must, however, show on the balance of probabilities that the care in question will be privately provided. (See *Woodrup v Nicol* [1993] PIQR Q104.)

The Law Commission concluded in its final report on *Damages for Personal Injury: Medical, Nursing and Other Expenses; Collateral Benefits* (Law Com. No. 276) that s. 2(4) is still a reasonable way to deal with the point. The Commission interpreted the section as enacting that claimants are not to be taken as having failed to mitigate their loss merely by choosing, or showing on the balance of probabilities that they would choose in the future, to opt for private care. Given the wide latitude normally allowed claimants in showing that they acted reasonably in not mitigating their loss further the rule did not strike the Commission as onerous or anomalous. Compare with the position under s. 2(4) the reasonableness requirement in relation to future local authority care and accommodation: see *Sowden v Lodge* [2005] 1 All ER 581, [2004] EWCA Civ 1370 and *Crofton v National Health Service Litigation Authority* [2007] 1 WLR 923, [2007] EWCA Civ 923. Whether s. 2(4) should be repealed is one of the issues raised in the DCA Consultation Paper, CP 9/07, chap. 5, which contains a list of arguments for and against its repeal.

4. In *British Transport Commission v Gourley* [1956] AC 185, [1955] 3 All ER 796 the House of Lords decided that the claimant should be compensated for actual loss, that is, the amount left in his hands after *compulsory* deductions such as tax. This has been applied to national insurance contributions (*Cooper v Firth Brown Ltd* [1963] 2 All ER 31, [1963] 1 WLR 418, a wrongful dismissal case). In *Dews v National Coal Board* [1988] AC 1, [1987] 2 All ER 545 the principle was apparently extended to *voluntary* contributions, at least to pension contributions. On the other hand, if the accident results in a loss of pension rights, a separate claim can be made under that head. Note the following view in *Harris*, p. 345 (footnotes omitted):

    The *Gourley* principle has attracted much critical comment. Critics point to the difficult calculation the tribunal is called to make, the shortfall of revenue to the Treasury, the reduced deterrent of tort liability, the inconsistent treatment of damages, the unjust advantage derived by D from his reduced liability and the potential undercompensation that might result because damages are "reduced" when C would not otherwise have had a capital sum to invest and C will be taxed in any event upon the income produced from investing that sum. As a result *Gourley* has not always been popular in other jurisdictions.

5. In *Lim Poh Choo* Lord Scarman also discussed the issue of whether future inflation should be taken into account. His views did not, however, find favour with the House of Lords in the subsequent case *Wells v Wells* [1999] 1 AC 345, [1998] 3 All ER 481 (p. 525, post).

■ Pickett v British Rail Engineering Ltd

House of Lords [1979] 1 All ER 774

The plaintiff developed lung disease as a result of inhaling asbestos dust while working in the defendant's workshops. The defendant admitted liability. In 1975, when he was 52 years old, the plaintiff issued a writ and the action was tried in 1976, when the medical evidence put his expectation of life at one year, whereas if he had not been exposed to asbestos he could have looked forward to employment up to the age of 65. Stephen Brown J awarded damages under various heads, including £7,000 for pain and suffering and loss of amenities, together with interest from the date of service of the writ to the date of trial. He awarded only £1,508.88 in respect of loss of earnings, being the amount the plaintiff could have expected to earn during the survival period of one year. Following *Oliver v Ashman* [1962] 2 QB 210, [1961] 3 All ER 323, he decided that the plaintiff should recover nothing in respect of the years of which he had been deprived (the lost years). The plaintiff died five months after the trial and his widow as administratrix was substituted as plaintiff. The Court of Appeal increased the general damages to £10,000 but refused to allow any interest on the increased sum and left undisturbed the award in respect of future loss of earnings.

The House of Lords allowed the plaintiff's appeal against the refusal to award interest on the general damages, and also allowed a cross-appeal by the defendant against the increase in general damages. The plaintiff also appealed against the refusal to award any sum for loss of earnings during the lost years.

LORD WILBERFORCE: . . .

Oliver v Ashman[8] is part of a complex of law which has developed piecemeal and which is neither logical nor consistent. Judges do their best to make do with it but from time to time cases appear, like the present, which do not appeal to a sense of justice. I shall not review in any detail the state of the authorities for this was admirably done by Holroyd Pearce LJ in *Oliver v Ashman*. The main strands in the law as it then stood were: (1) the Law Reform (Miscellaneous Provisions) Act 1934 abolished the old rule actio personalis moritur cum persona and provided for the survival of causes of action in tort for the benefit of the victim's estate; (2) the decision of this House in *Rose v Ford*[9] that a claim for loss of expectation of life survived under the 1934 Act, and was not a claim for damages based on the death of a person and so barred at common law (cf. *Admiralty Comrs v SS Amerika (Owners)*[10]); (3) the decision of this House in *Benham v Gambling*[11] that damages for loss of expectation of life could only be given up to a conventional figure, then fixed at £200; (4) the Fatal Accidents Acts under which proceedings may be brought for the benefit of dependants to recover the loss caused to those dependants by the death of the breadwinner; the amount of this loss is related to the probable future earnings which would have been made by the deceased during 'lost years'.

This creates a difficulty. It is assumed in the present case, and the assumption is supported by authority, that if an action for damages is brought by the victim during his lifetime, and either proceeds to judgment or is settled, further proceedings cannot be brought after his death under the Fatal Accidents Acts. If this assumption is correct, it provides a basis, in logic and justice, for allowing the victim to recover for earnings lost during his lost years.

This assumption is based on the wording of s. 1 of the 1846 Act (now s. 1 of the Fatal Accidents Act 1976) and is not supported by any decision of this House. It cannot however be challenged in this appeal, since there is before us no claim under the Fatal Accidents Acts. I think, therefore, that we must for present purposes act on the basis that it is well founded, and that if the present claim, in respect

---

[8] [1962] 2 QB 210, [1961] 3 All ER 323.   [9] [1937] AC 826, [1937] 3 All ER 359.
[10] [1917] AC 38, [1916–17] All ER Rep 177.   [11] [1941] AC 157, [1941] 1 All ER 7.

of earnings during the lost years, fails it will not be possible for a fresh action to be brought by the deceased's dependants in relation to them....

[His Lordship considered the authorities and then continued]:

As to principle, the passage which best summarises the underlying reasons for the decision in *Oliver v Ashman*[12] is the following:

> '...what has been lost by the person assumed to be dead is the opportunity to enjoy what he would have earned, whether by spending it or saving it. Earnings themselves strike me as being of no significance without reference to the way in which they are used. To inquire what would have been the value to a person in the position of this plaintiff of any earnings which he might have made after the date when ex hypothesi he will be dead strikes me as a hopeless task.'

Or as Holroyd Pearce LJ put it:[13] 'What is lost is an expectation, not the thing itself.'

My Lords, I think that these are instinctual sentences, not logical propositions or syllogisms, none the worse for that because we are not in the field of pure logic. It may not be unfair to paraphrase them as saying: 'Nothing is of value except to a man who is there to spend or save it. The plaintiff will not be there when these earnings hypothetically accrue: so they have no value to him.' Perhaps there are additional strands, one which indeed Willmer LJ had earlier made explicit, that the whole process of assessment is too speculative for the courts to undertake; another that the only loss is a subjective one, an emotion of distress. But if so I would disagree with them. Assumptions, chances, hypotheses enter into most assessments, and juries had, we must suppose, no difficulties with them; the judicial approach, however less robust, can manage too. And to say that what calls for compensation is injured feelings does not provide an answer to the vital question which is whether, in addition to this subjective element, there is something objective which has been lost.

But is the main line of reasoning acceptable? Does it not ignore the fact that a particular man, in good health, and sound earning, has in these two things an asset of present value quite separate and distinct from the expectation of life which every man possesses? Compare him with a man in poor health and out of a job. Is he not, and not only in the immediate present, a richer man? Is he not entitled to say, at one moment I am a man with existing capability to earn well for 14 years, the next moment I can only earn less well for one year? And why should he be compensated only for the immediate reduction in his earnings and not for the loss of the whole period for which he has been deprived of his ability to earn them? To the argument that 'they are of no value because you will not be there to enjoy them' can he not reply, 'Yes they are; what is of value to me is not only my opportunity to spend them enjoyably, but to use such part of them as I do not need for my dependants, or for other persons or causes which I wish to support. If I cannot do this, I have been deprived of something on which a value, a present value, can be placed'?

I do not think that the problem can be solved by describing what has been lost as an 'opportunity' or a 'prospect' or an 'expectation'. Indeed these words are invoked both ways, by the Lords Justices as denying a right to recover (on grounds of remoteness, intangibility or speculation), by those supporting the appellant's argument as demonstrating the loss of some real asset of true value. The fact is that the law sometimes allows damages to be given for the loss of things so described (e.g. *Chaplin v Hicks*[14]), sometimes it does not. It always has to answer a question which in the end can hardly be more accurately framed than as: 'Is the loss of this something for which the claimant should and reasonably can be compensated?'

The defendant, in an impressive argument, urged on us that the real loss in such cases as the present was to the victim's dependants and that the right way in which to compensate them was to change the law (by statute; judicially it would be impossible) so as to enable the dependants to recover their loss independently of any action by the victim. There is much force in this, and no doubt the law could be

---

12 [1962] 2 QB 210 at 240, [1961] 3 All ER 323 at 338, per Willmer LJ.
13 [1962] 2 QB 210 at 230, [1961] 3 All ER 323 at 332.
14 [1911] 2 KB 786, [1911–13] All ER Rep 224.

changed in this way. But I think that the argument fails because it does not take account, as in an action for damages account must be taken, of the interest of the victim. Future earnings are of value to him in order that he may satisfy legitimate desires, but these may not correspond with the allocation which the law makes of money recovered by dependants on account of his loss. He may wish to benefit some dependants more than, or to the exclusion of, others; this (subject to family inheritance legislation) he is entitled to do. He may not have dependants, but he may have others, or causes, whom he would wish to benefit, for whom he might even regard himself as working. One cannot make a distinction, for the purposes of assessing damages, between men in different family situations.

There is another argument, in the opposite sense; that which appealed to Streatfield J in *Pope v D Murphy & Son Ltd*.[15] Why, he asked, should the tortfeasor benefit from the fact that as well as reducing his victim's earning capacity he has shortened his victim's life? Good advocacy but unsound principle, for damages are to compensate the victim not to reflect what the wrongdoer ought to pay.

My Lords, in the case of the adult wage earner with or without dependants who sues for damages during his lifetime, I am convinced that a rule which enables the 'lost years' to be taken account of comes closer to the ordinary man's expectations than one which limits his interest to his shortened span of life. The interest which such a man has in the earnings he might hope to make over a normal life, if not saleable in a market, has a value which can be assessed. A man who receives that assessed value would surely consider himself and be considered compensated; a man denied it would not. And I do not think that to act in this way creates insoluble problems of assessment in other cases. In that of a young child (cf. *Benham v Gambling*[16]) neither present nor future earnings could enter into the matter; in the more difficult case of adolescents just embarking on the process of earning (cf. *Skelton v Collins*[17]) the value of 'lost' earnings might be real but would probably be assessable as small . . . .

[LORD SALMON, LORD EDMUND-DAVIES, and LORD SCARMAN also delivered speeches in favour of allowing the appeal on this point. LORD RUSSELL OF KILLOWEN delivered a speech dissenting on this point.]

Appeal and cross-appeal allowed.

NOTES

1. The decision in the above case is along the lines of the rule proposed by the Law Commission (Law Com. No. 56, para. 87) and the Pearson Commission (vol. I, para. 335). As a result of s. 4 of the Administration of Justice Act 1982 the claim in respect of the 'lost years' does not survive for the benefit of the victim's estate (see p. 558, post). There has been some controversy as to the calculation of the living expenses to be deducted from the prospective earnings. In *Harris v Empress Motors Ltd* [1983] 3 All ER 561, [1984] 1 WLR 212 the Court of Appeal, overruling several first instance decisions, held that the sum to be deducted is what the claimant would have spent exclusively on himself to maintain his standard of life, but, unlike the position under the Fatal Accidents Act, sums spent on joint living expenses are divided by the number of people in the household and the claimant's share is deductible. The Court of Appeal followed *Harris* in *Phipps v Brooks Dry Cleaning Service Ltd* [1996] PIQR Q100. It is pointed out in *Thompson v Thompson* [2007] EWHC 1875 (QB) at [28] that a claimant who is aware that he is close to death and who wants his dependants to benefit from the more generous regime can either seek an interim award up to the amount of a lifetime award or seek an adjournment or, indeed, both. (On the problem in mesothelioma cases, see the DCA's Consultation Paper, chap.1, paras. 27–30.)

---

[15] [1961] 1 QB 222, [1960] 2 All ER 873.   [16] [1941] AC 157, [1941] 1 All ER 7.
[17] (1966) 115 CLR 94.

2.   In *Jamil bin Harun v Yang Kamsiah Bte Meor Rasdi* [1984] AC 529, [1984] 2 WLR 668 the passage from Lord Wilberforce's speech in *Pickett* (p. 524, ante) concerning the position of young children and adolescents was quoted in the Privy Council's judgment; but it was interpreted as 'not directed to a case…where the infant plaintiff is expected to live for her normal span or, at the very least, for a substantial number of years'. In the Privy Council's view, the court would just have to do its best in making this difficult calculation in relation to the years the child will live.

In the earlier case of *Croke (a minor) v Wiseman* [1981] 3 All ER 852, [1982] 1 WLR 71, noted by P. J. Davies (1982) 45 MLR 333—and see further *Joyce v Yeomans* [1981] 2 All ER 21, [1981] 1 WLR 549—a majority of the Court of Appeal accepted that damages could be awarded for such a period to the claimant, who was aged 21 months when he suffered catastrophic injury. The approach of the trial judge in this case had been to take the average national earnings for a young man as the basis of the award and this was regarded by the majority of the Court of Appeal as appropriate in the circumstances of the case (cf. *Mitchell v Liverpool Area Health Authority (Teaching)* (1985) *Times*, 17 June). In the case of the 'lost years', however, the court in *Croke v Wiseman* was not prepared to award damages for loss of earnings in a case where there would be no need for any such sum of money, since there would be no dependants. It was thought that there were no compelling social reasons to justify carrying out what would be a more speculative exercise, more speculative since living expenses would have to be assessed and deducted (but see Davies, op cit., p. 334). This decision was regarded in *Whipps Cross University NHS Trust v Iqbal* [2008] PIQR P9, [2007] EWCA Civ 1190 as inconsistent with *Pickett* and *Gammell v Wilson* [1981] 1 All ER 578, [1982] AC 27, but the Court of Appeal in *Whipps Cross* also regarded itself as bound by the doctrine of precedent to follow *Croke v Wiseman*.

(b) Multipliers

■ Wells v Wells
House of Lords [1998] 3 All ER 481

LORD LLOYD OF BERWICK:…
My Lords,

Introduction
There are before the House appeals in three actions for personal injuries, all raising the same question, namely, the correct method of calculating lump sum damages for the loss of future earnings and the cost of future care. Negligence was admitted in all three cases.

In *Wells v Wells* the plaintiff, a part-time nurse, aged nearly 58, was very severely injured in a traffic accident when she was travelling as a passenger in a car driven by her husband. She suffered serious brain damage. As a consequence she is no longer capable of working, or caring for herself or her family. She will require care for the rest of her life. Judge David Wilcox sitting as a judge of the High Court in the Queen's Bench Division ([1996] PIQR Q62) awarded her £120,000 for pain and suffering. The total award, including loss of future earnings and cost of future care on a life expectancy of 15 years, came to £1,619,332. The Court of Appeal ([1997] 1 All ER 673, [1997] 1 WLR 652) reduced the figure for pain and suffering to £100,000 and substituted a life expectancy of 10 years 3 months. They arrived at a total of £1,086,959. The main reason for the sharp reduction was that the Court of Appeal took a discount rate of 4.5% in calculating the lump sum for future loss, whereas the judge had taken 2.5%.

[His Lordship then referred to the two other cases (*Thomas v Brighton Health Authority* [1996] PIQR Q44, on appeal [1997] 1 All ER 673, [1997] 1 WLR 652 and *Page v Sheerness Steel Co Ltd* ([1996] PIQR Q26, on appeal [1997] 1 All ER 673, [1997] 1 WLR 652 and continued:].

A number of separate points arise in relation to the individual cases. They would not by themselves have justified leave to appeal. However, the point which is common to all three appeals is of considerable importance, both for the plaintiffs themselves and for the insurance industry in general. It is convenient to deal with that point first.

It was common ground between all parties that the task of the court in assessing damages for personal injuries is to arrive at a lump sum which represents as nearly as possible full compensation for the injury which the plaintiff has suffered. . . .

It is of the nature of a lump sum payment that it may, in respect of future pecuniary loss, prove to be either too little or too much. So far as the multiplier is concerned, the plaintiff may die the next day, or he may live beyond his normal expectation of life. So far as the multiplicand is concerned, the cost of future care may exceed everyone's best estimate. Or a new cure or less expensive form of treatment may be discovered. But these uncertainties do not affect the basic principle. The purpose of the award is to put the plaintiff in the same position, financially, as if he had not been injured. The sum should be calculated as accurately as possible, making just allowance, where this is appropriate, for contingencies. But once the calculation is done, there is no justification for imposing an artificial cap on the multiplier. There is no room for a judicial scaling down. Current awards in the most serious cases may seem high. The present appeals may be taken as examples. But there is no more reason to reduce the awards, if properly calculated, because they seem high than there is to increase the awards because the injuries are very severe.

The approach to the basic calculation of the lump sum has been explained in many cases, but never better than by Stephen J in the High Court of Australia in *Todorovic v Waller* (1981) 150 CLR 402 at 427 ff (see Kemp and Kemp *The Quantum of Damages* (looseleaf edn (1997)) vol 1, para 7–010), by Lord Pearson in *Taylor v O'Connor* [1970] 1 All ER 365 at 377, [1971] AC 115 at 140, and by Lord Oliver of Aylmerton in *Hodgson v Trapp* [1988] 3 All ER 870 at 879, [1989] AC 807 at 826.

The starting point is the multiplicand, that is to say the annual loss of earnings or the annual cost of care, as the case may be. (I put so-called *Smith v Manchester* damages (*Smith v Manchester Corp* (1974) 17 KIR 1) on one side.) The medical evidence may be that the need for care will increase or decrease as the years go by, in which case it may be necessary to take different multiplicands for different periods covered by the award. But to simplify the illustration, one can take an average annual cost of care of £10,000 on a life expectancy of 20 years. If one assumes a constant value for money, then if the court were to award 20 times £10,000 it is obvious that the plaintiff would be overcompensated. For the £10,000 needed to purchase care in the 20th year should have been earning interest for 19 years. The purpose of the discount is to eliminate this element of overcompensation. The objective is to arrive at a lump sum which by drawing down both interest and capital will provide exactly £10,000 a year for 20 years, and no more. This is known as the annuity approach. It is a simple enough matter to find the answer by reference to standard tables. The higher the assumed return on capital, net of tax, the lower the lump sum. If one assumes a net return of 5% the discounted figure would be £124,600 instead of £200,000. If one assumes a net return of 3% the figure would be £148,800.

The same point can be put the other way round. £200,000 invested at 5% will produce £10,000 a year for 20 years. But there would still be £200,000 left at the end. So far there is no problem. The difficulty arises because, contrary to the assumption made above, money does not retain its value. How is the court to ensure that the plaintiff receives the money he will need to purchase the care he needs as the years go by despite the impact of inflation? In the past the courts have solved this problem by assuming that the plaintiff can take care of future inflation in a rough and ready way by investing the lump sum sensibly in a mixed 'basket' of equities and gilts. But the advent of the index-linked government stock (they were first issued in 1981) has provided an alternative. The return of income and capital on index-linked government stock (ILGS) is fully protected against inflation. Thus the purchaser of £100 of ILGS with a maturity date of 2020 knows that his investment will then be worth £100 plus x % of £100, where x represents the percentage increase in the retail price index between the date of issue and the date of maturity (or, more accurately, eight months before the two dates). Of course if the plaintiff were to invest his £100 in equities it might then be worth much more. But it might also be worth less. The virtue of ILGS is that it provides a risk-free investment.

The first instance judges in these appeals have broken with the past. They have each assumed for the purpose of the calculation that the plaintiffs will go into the market, and purchase the required amount of ILGS so as to provide for his or her future needs with the minimum risk of their damages being eroded by inflation. How the plaintiffs will in fact invest their damages is, of course, irrelevant. That is a question for them. It cannot affect the calculation. The question for decision therefore is whether the judges were right to assume that the plaintiffs would invest in ILGS with a low average net return of 2.5%, instead of a mixed portfolio of equities and gilts. The Court of Appeal has held not. They have reverted to the traditional 4 to 5% with the consequential reduction in the sums awarded.

The argument

Mr Leighton Williams QC and Mr Coonan QC for the defendants pointed out that those who receive large awards are likely to be given professional investment advice. All but one of the accountants called as experts at the three trials gave as their opinion that lump sum awards should be invested in a mixed portfolio of 70% equities and 30% gilts. This is what the ordinary prudent investor would do. For experience shows that equities provide the best long-term security. Thus Mr Topping, the account- ant called on behalf of the defendant in *Wells v Wells*, produced a table which showed the real rate of return on equities to 31 December 1992 on an investment made on 1 January in each year from 1973 to 1992. In only two of those years has the return been less than 4.5% net of tax. If the ordinary prudent investor would invest substantially in equities, it was to be assumed that the plaintiffs would do the same....

Mr Leighton Williams went so far as to argue that it was the plaintiff's duty to invest in equities in order to mitigate his damage.

...Granted that a substantial proportion of equities is the best long term investment for the ordinary prudent investor, the question is whether the same is true for these plaintiffs. The ordinary investor may be presumed to have enough to live on. He can meet his day-to-day requirements. If the equity market suffers a catastrophic fall, as it did in 1972, he has no immediate need to sell. He can bide his time, and wait until the equity market eventually recovers.

The plaintiffs are not in the same happy position. They are not 'ordinary investors' in the sense that they can wait for long-term recovery, remembering that it was not until 1989 that equity prices regained their old pre-1972 level in real terms. For they need the income, and a portion of their capital, every year to meet their current cost of care. A plaintiff who invested the whole of his award in equities in 1972 would have found that their real value had fallen by 41% in 1973 and by a further 62% in 1974. The real value of the income on his equities had also fallen.

So it does not follow that a prudent investment for the ordinary investor is a prudent investment for the plaintiffs. Equities may well prove the best long-term investment. But their volatility over the short term creates a serious risk. This risk was well understood by the experts. Indeed Mr Coonan conceded that if you are investing so as to meet a plaintiff's needs over a period of five years, or even 10 years, it would be foolish to invest in equities. But that concession, properly made as it was on the evidence, is fatal to the defendants' case. For, as Mr Purchas pointed out in reply, every long period starts with a short period. If there is a substantial fall in equities in the first five or 10 years, during which the plaintiff will have had to call on part of his capital to meet his needs, and will have had to realise that part of his capital in a depressed market, the depleted fund may never recover.

While therefore I agree with the Court of Appeal that, in calculating the lump sum, courts are entitled to assume that the plaintiff will behave prudently, I do not agree that what is prudent for the ordinary investor is necessarily prudent for the plaintiff. Indeed the opposite may be the case. What the prudent plaintiff needs is an investment which will bring him the income he requires without the risks inherent in the equity market; which brings us back to ILGS. . . .

The Court of Protection
I have left to last the argument on which the defendants placed the greatest reliance, and which weighed heavily with the Court of Appeal. Two of the three plaintiffs are patients. Their affairs are being administered by the Court of Protection. One of the witnesses called for the defence was Mr Bruce Denman, who is in charge of the investment branch of the Public Trust Office dealing with Court of Protection cases. His evidence was that in the case of a long term investment for an individual patient the portfolio would consist of about 70% UK equities with the balance in gilts and cash. The Court of Appeal ([1997] 1 All ER 673 at 696, [1997] 1 WLR 652 at 677) said that they were 'strongly influenced' by the policy of the Court of Protection.

   But in the case of short term investment (five years or under) the policy of the Court of Protection is very different. The fact sheet published by the Court of Protection shows that in such a case 'very little risk is acceptable'. Equities should be excluded altogether. This corresponds with the expert evidence in the present case, and with Mr Coonan's concession. What is not explained in the policy statement is why risk is any more acceptable in the long term than in the short term. I can understand an argument that in the case of a long-term fund the equities will have had time to recover after a fall such as occurred in 1972 and October 1987. But as already explained it may by then be too late. The gilts may have been sold and the cash may all have been spent.

   In the end it comes back to the question of risk. Ex hypothesi equities are riskier than gilts. That is the very reason why the return on equities is likely to be greater. The plaintiffs say that they are not obliged to bear that extra risk for the benefit of the defendants. Others like them, with fixed outgoings at stated intervals, take the same view as to prudent investment policy. So the plaintiffs are not alone. Thus Mr Prevett's evidence [for the plaintiff in *Wells v Wells*] was that, since index-linked stocks have been available, it has become the general practice for closed pension funds to be invested in ILGS, so as to be sure of being able to meet their liabilities as they fall due. I would not be surprised to find others in the same position, but on a smaller scale, taking the same view, such as school governors investing a prepaid fees fund. The Court of Appeal rejected this part of Mr Prevett's evidence, but without giving any very satisfactory reason, other than the need for an investment which affords some flexibility in view of the inevitable uncertainty in estimating the multiplicand. I agree, of course, that there is bound to be some uncertainty in fixing the multiplicand. But that does not seem to me to be a good reason for introducing an unnecessary uncertainty in fixing the multiplier. Two wrongs may make a right. But they are just as likely to make a double wrong. . . .

[LORD LLOYD then referred to the views of commentators and textbook writers, and continued:]

The authorities
. . . Mr Leighton Williams rightly relied on *Lim Poh Choo v Camden and Islington Area Health Authority* [1979] 2 All ER 910, [1980] AC 174. It is the strongest authority in his favour. Lord Scarman ([1979] 2 All ER 910 at 923, [1980] AC 174 at 193) acknowledged the wisdom of Lord Reid's dictum in *Taylor v O'Connor* [1970] 1 All ER 365 at 368, [1971] AC 115 at 130 that it would be unrealistic to ignore inflation in calculating lump sum damages for future loss. He nevertheless held that it was 'the better course' to disregard inflation in the great majority of cases. Among the reasons he gave was that it was inherent in any lump sum system of compensation, and just, that the sum be calculated at current market values, leaving plaintiffs in the same position as others who have to rely on capital for their support. To attempt to protect them against inflation 'would be to put them into a privileged position at the expense of the tortfeasor, and so to impose upon him an excessive burden, which might go far beyond compensation for loss' ([1979] 2 All ER 910 at 923, [1980] AC 174 at 194).

   No doubt it was this passage which the Court of Appeal ([1997] 1 All ER 673 at 696, [1997] 1 WLR 652 at 677) had in mind when they said that it was necessary 'to hold the balance evenly between both sides'. I have to say that I do not find Lord Scarman's reasoning persuasive. If the object of an award of damages is to put the plaintiff in the same position as he would have been in if he had not been injured by the negligence of the defendant (as was common ground) then one ought, in principle, to get as near as one can to the wages which he would actually have earned but for the injury and the cost of the needs which he will actually incur. In other words, one ought so far as possible to take account of inflation, as Lord Reid had said.

What then did Lord Scarman mean by saying that this would put the plaintiff in a privileged position in comparison with others who have to rely on capital for their support? Once the lump sum has been calculated and paid, he is in exactly the same position as others, such as those who have saved or inherited a lump sum. But in calculating the sum his position is in no way comparable. For the plaintiff is entitled to be protected against future inflation at the expense of the tortfeasor; otherwise he does not receive full compensation. The others are not so entitled. It is only in that sense that the plaintiff is in a privileged position. I cannot for my part see anything unjust in requiring the defendant to compensate the plaintiff in full, however burdensome that may prove. Lord Scarman recognised this himself when he said ([1979] 2 All ER 910 at 917–918, [1980] AC 174 at 187):

'There is no room here for considering the consequences of a high award upon the wrongdoer or those who finance him. And, if there were room for any such consideration, upon what principle, or by what criterion, is the judge to determine the extent to which he is to diminish upon this ground the compensation payable?'

Conclusion

My conclusion is that the judges in these three cases were right to assume for the purpose of their calculations that the plaintiffs would invest their damages in ILGS for the following reasons.

(1) Investment in ILGS is the most accurate way of calculating the present value of the loss which the plaintiffs will actually suffer in real terms.

(2) Although this will result in a heavier burden on these defendants, and, if the principle is applied across the board, on the insurance industry in general, I can see nothing unjust. It is true that insurance premiums may have been fixed on the basis of the 4 to 5% discount rate indicated in *Cookson v Knowles* [1978] 2 All ER 604, [1979] AC 556 and the earlier authorities. But this was only because there was then no better way of allowing for future inflation. The objective was always the same. No doubt insurance premiums will have to increase in order to take account of the new lower rate of discount. Whether this is something which the country can afford is not a subject on which your Lordships were addressed. So we are not in a position to form any view as to the wider consequences.

(3) The search for a prudent investment will always depend on the circumstances of the particular investor. Some are able to take a measure of risk, others are not. For a plaintiff who is not in a position to take risks, and who wishes to protect himself against inflation in the short term of up to ten years, it is clearly prudent to invest in ILGS It cannot therefore be assumed that he will invest in equities and gilts. Still less is it his duty to invest in equities and gilts in order to mitigate his loss.

(4) Logically the same applies to a plaintiff investing for the long term. In any event it is desirable to have a single rate applying across the board, in order to facilitate settlements and to save the expense of expert evidence at the trial. I take this view even though it is open to the Lord Chancellor under s 1(3) of the 1996 Act to prescribe different rates of return for different classes of case. Mr Leighton Williams conceded that it is not desirable in practice to distinguish between different classes of plaintiff when assessing the multiplier.

(5) How the plaintiff, or the majority of plaintiffs, in fact invest their money is irrelevant. The research carried out by the Law Commission does not suggest that the majority of plaintiffs in fact invest in equities and gilts, but rather in a building society or a bank deposit.

(6) There was no agreement between the parties as to how much greater, if at all, the return on equities is likely to be in the short or long term. But it is at least clear that an investment in ILGS will save up to 1% per annum by obviating the need for continuing investment advice.

(7) The practice of the Court of Protection when investing for the long term affords little guidance. In any event the policy may change when lump sums are calculated at a lower rate of return.

(8) The views of the Ogden Working Party, the Law Commission and the author of *Kemp and Kemp* in favour of an investment in ILGS are entitled to great weight.

(9) There is nothing in the previous decisions of the House which inhibits a new approach. It is therefore unnecessary to have resort to the 1966 practice statement ([1966] 3 All ER 77, [1966] 1 WLR 1234).

Consequences

Once it is accepted that the lump sum should be calculated on the basis of the rate of return available on ILGS, then an assessment of the average rate of return at the relevant date presents no problem. . . .

. . . So far as the three appeals currently before the House are concerned I would regard 3% as the appropriate net return. It follows that the award in *Wells v Wells* will have to be recalculated on that basis.

Guidelines

Section 1 of the 1996 Act provides:

'(1) In determining the return to be expected from the investment of a sum awarded as damages for future pecuniary loss in an action for personal injury the court shall, subject to and in accordance with rules of court made for the purposes of this section, take into account such rate of return (if any) as may from time to time be prescribed by an order made by the Lord Chancellor . . . '

The section came into force on 24 September 1996, but no rate has yet been prescribed [but see now note 4, p. 532, post]. Lord Mackay of Clashfern, the previous Lord Chancellor, was said to be awaiting the decision of the Court of Appeal in the instant cases. It goes without saying that the sooner the Lord Chancellor sets the rate the better. The present uncertainty does not make the settling of claims any easier.

In the meantime it is for your Lordships to set guidelines to replace the old 4% to 5% bracket. There is something to be said for a bracket, since it allows some flexibility in exceptional cases, as where, for example, the impact of higher-rate tax would result in substantial under-compensation. Thus on an award of £2m higher rate tax payable over the first half of a 20-year period would alone amount to nearly £75,000. But the majority of your Lordships prefer a single figure. I do not disagree provided it is subject to the same flexibility as is to be found in s. 1(2) of the 1996 Act.

[LORD LLOYD then proceeded to decide upon a guideline rate of 3% and continued:]

Wells v Wells

I come now to the miscellaneous points. They do not call for extensive discussion, since they were argued only briefly. The underlying question is whether the defendants in each case succeeded in showing that damages awarded by the judges at first instance in respect of any particular head of damage (see *George v Pinnock* [1973] 1 All ER 926 at 934, [1973] 1 WLR 118 at 126 per Sachs LJ) are outside the appropriate bracket (see *Every v Miles* [1964] CA Transcript 261 per Diplock LJ; *Kemp and Kemp* vol 1, para 19–006), or else represented a 'wholly erroneous estimate', whether due to mistake of law or a misapprehension of the facts (see *Pickett v British Rail Engineering Ltd* [1979] 1 All ER 774 at 782, 799, [1980] AC 136, at 151, 172 per Lord Wilberforce and Lord Scarman respectively) . . .

[His Lordship agreed with the Court of Appeal's reduction of the award for pain and suffering to £100,000 from £120,000 but, criticising the Court of Appeal for substituting its own view of the witnesses' evidence for that of the judge, restored the judge's figure of 15 years as the estimation of loss of expectation of life and the judge's view of how much care the claimant required].

Thomas v Brighton Health Authority

The agreed medical evidence was that the plaintiff has a life expectancy to the age of 60. Collins J ([1996] PIQR Q44 at Q57) held, however, that he ought to reduce the arithmetical multiplier by about 20% 'to cater for the hazards of life in such cases'. In the result he took a multiplier of 23. The Court of Appeal agreed with the judge's approach but started from a different starting point. With a 4.5% discount rate the arithmetical multiplier came to 20. Reduced by 15%, rather than 20%, they arrived at a multiplier of 17.

Was it correct for the judge and the Court of Appeal to reduce the arithmetical multiplier, and therefore, in effect, override the expectation of life agreed by the doctors? Mr Owen submitted that there could be no rational basis for applying a further discount for 'contingencies', since the doctors had already taken account of all the contingencies that might affect the plaintiff, such as the increased risk of accident, chest infection, and so on. The only reason given by the judge was that the courts had 'tended to reduce multipliers by about 20%'. The Court of Appeal took the same line.

I can see no answer to Mr Owen's argument. The inevitable result of reducing the multiplier to 17, as Mr Havers pointed out, will be that the plaintiff's damages will run out when he is 39. He will have nothing to cover his needs for the remaining 21 years of his life.

Mr Havers conceded that there is room for a judicial discount when calculating the loss of future earnings, when contingencies may indeed affect the result. But there is no room for any discount in the case of a whole life multiplier with an agreed expectation of life. In the case of loss of earnings the contingencies can work in only one direction—in favour of the defendant. But in the case of life expectancy, the contingency can work in either direction. The plaintiff may exceed his normal expectation of life, or he may fall short of it.

There is no purpose in the courts making as accurate a prediction as they can of the plaintiff's future needs if the resulting sum is arbitrarily reduced for no better reason than that the prediction might be wrong. A prediction remains a prediction. Contingencies should be taken into account where they work in one direction, but not where they cancel out. There is no more logic or justice in reducing the whole life multiplier by 15% or 20% on an agreed expectation of life than there would be in increasing it by the same amount. . . .

In *Hunt v Severs* [1994] 2 All ER 385, [1994] 2 AC 350 the plaintiff had a life expectancy of 25 years. The appropriate multiplier by reference to a 4.5% discount rate was 14.821. But the judge reduced this figure to 14 because 14 seemed more in line with the multiplier applied in other comparable cases. The Court of Appeal, correctly in my view, substituted a multiplier of 15, as being the nearest round figure to 14.821. Bingham MR ([1993] 4 All ER 180 at 201, [1993] QB 815 at 841) observed that an allowance for contingencies may sometimes be appropriate. But he continued:

> 'Such an allowance is not appropriate in the present case, where the agreed life expectancy of the plaintiff is 25 years. That is a fact, or rather an agreed assumption, upon which the damages payable for future care must be based.'

But the House disagreed. Lord Bridge of Harwich said ([1994] 2 All ER 385 at 396–397, [1994] 2 AC 350 at 365):

> 'The passage I have cited from the judgment of the Court of Appeal appears to show the court as treating the circumstance that both doctors in evidence estimated the plaintiff's expectation of life at 25 years as establishing the "fact" or "assumption" that she would live for 25 years and thus converting the process of assessing future loss into "a simple arithmetical calculation". I cannot think that this was the correct approach to the evidence. A man or woman in normal health, at a given age, no doubt has an ascertainable statistical life expectancy. But in using such a figure as the basis for assessment of damages with respect to future losses, some discount in respect of life's manifold contingencies is invariably made.'

I have some difficulty with this passage. The plaintiff's life expectancy was not derived from any tables. It was the agreed life expectancy of this particular plaintiff, taking her individual characteristics into account. I cannot for my part see what further room there was for 'life's manifold contingencies'. The whole point of agreeing a life expectancy, if it can be done, is to exclude any further speculation. With respect therefore I prefer the approach of Bingham MR and the Court of Appeal.

The explanation for the different approach of the House in *Hunt v Severs* may be a continuing hesitation to embrace the actuarial tables. I do not suggest that the judge should be a slave to the tables. There may well be special factors in particular cases. But the tables should now be regarded as the starting point, rather than a check. A judge should be slow to depart from the relevant actuarial multiplier on impressionistic grounds, or by reference to 'a spread of multipliers in comparable cases' especially when the multipliers were fixed before actuarial tables were widely used. This may be the explanation for the relatively low multiplier chosen by the House in *Lim Poh Choo's* case.

For the reasons I have given, I consider that the Court of Appeal in the present case were wrong to substitute a multiplier of 17 for the judge's 23. But the judge himself was also too low. The appropriate multiplier derived from the tables on the agreed life expectancy was 26.58. . . .

[LORD LLOYD then dealt with *Page v Sheerness Steel Co plc* and concluded:]
. . . I would allow all three appeals.

[LORD STEYN, LORD HOPE OF CRAIGHEAD, LORD CLYDE, and LORD HUTTON delivered speeches in favour of allowing the appeals.]

Appeals allowed.

NOTES

1. *Wells v Wells* concerns only the traditional lump sum award. For discussion of the position in relation to structured settlements and periodic payments, see pp. 548–557, post.

2. In *Smith v Manchester Corpn* (1974) 17 KIR 1, to which Lord Lloyd referred, the Court of Appeal decided that even if the claimant's present employers undertake to keep the claimant in employment for the foreseeable future, the claimant was entitled to claim damages, for loss of earning capacity, for being in a weakened position in the job market if she were eventually to lose her job.

3. Lord Lloyd in *Wells v Wells* refers to the reluctance shown by some judges to admit actuarial evidence. See *Mitchell v Mulholland (No. 2)* [1972] 1 QB 65, [1971] 2 All ER 1205. Parliament sought to end this reluctance in the Civil Evidence Act 1995, which came into force in 1997 and s. 10 of which provides:

    '(1) The actuarial tables (together with explanatory notes) for use in personal injury and fatal accident cases issued from time to time by the Government Actuary's Department are admissible in evidence for the purpose of assessing, in an action for personal injury, the sum to be awarded as general damages for future pecuniary loss.

    (2) They may be proved by the production of a copy published by Her Majesty's Stationery Office.

    (3) For the purposes of this section—

        (a) 'personal injury' includes any disease and any impairment of a person's physical or mental condition; and

        (b) 'action for personal injury' includes an action brought by virtue of the Law Reform (Miscellaneous Provisions) Act 1934 or the Fatal Accidents Act 1976.'

4. Lord Lloyd also refers to s. 1 of the Damages Act 1996, which provides:

    '(1) In determining the return to be expected from the investment of a sum awarded as damages for future pecuniary loss in an action for personal injury the court shall, subject to and in accordance with rules of court made for the purposes of this section, take into account such rate of return (if any) as may from time to time be prescribed by an order made by the Lord Chancellor.

(2) Subsection (1) above shall not however prevent the court taking a different rate of return into account if any party to the proceedings shows that it is more appropriate in the case in question.

(3) An order under subsection (1) above may prescribe different rates of return for different classes of case.

(4) Before making an order under subsection (1) above the Lord Chancellor shall consult the Government Actuary and the Treasury; and any order under that subsection shall be made by statutory instrument subject to annulment in pursuance of a resolution of either House of Parliament.

In 2001 the Lord Chancellor fixed the rate at 2.5 per cent and issued a detailed statement of his reasons for so doing. It is of course possible to argue under s. 1(2) that a different rate should be used, but the Court of Appeal has made it clear that this will be no easy task for a claimant: see *Warriner v Warriner* [2003] 3 All ER 447, [2002] EWCA Civ 81; *Cooke v United Bristol Healthcare NHS Trust* [2004] 1 All ER 797, [2003] EWCA Civ 1370 (and for the position under *Wells* before the rate was fixed in 2001, see *Warren v Northern General Hospital NHS Trust (No. 2)* [2000] 1 WLR 1404). In *Warriner* the court noted the policy grounds in *Wells* for fixing the 'rough and ready' rate—certainty, facilitating settlements and saving on the cost of expert witnesses—and thought that these factors had influenced the Lord Chancellor to fix a single rate and had retained their importance. In deciding whether a different rate was 'more appropriate' within the wording of s. 1(2), the Lord Chancellor's reasons for fixing the rate must be considered by the court, and Dyson LJ (with whose judgment Latham and Mummery LJJ agreed) continued (at [33]):

If the case in question falls into a category that the Lord Chancellor did not take into account and/or there are special features of the case which (a) are material to the choice of rate of return and (b) are shown from an examination of the Lord Chancellor's reasons not to have been taken into account, then a different rate of return may be 'more appropriate'.

This view was followed in *Cooke*, which also decided that arguments about increase in the costs of care above the RPI index could not be used to increase the *multiplicand*, which is to be assessed on the relevant costs at the time of trial.

The position is different, however, in the case of periodic payments and this matter will be addressed at p. 557, post.

(c) Collateral benefits and costs

■ Law Commission Consultation Paper 147: Collateral Benefits

1. THE MEANING OF COLLATERAL BENEFITS AND MAIN ISSUES

1.1 In this paper we deal with the treatment of what lawyers term "collateral benefits" in the calculation of damages for personal injury. Using jargon-free language we can say that we are considering the extent to which an injured person may recover compensation from both the tort system and from another source. For example, should an injured plaintiff be entitled to recover full damages plus sick pay provided by his or her employer and/or a voluntary payment made by his or her trade union and/or the proceeds of a personal accident insurance policy? This problem of overlapping compensation frequently arises and has long perplexed the courts. It raises complex issues of policy.

1.2 We must also make clear the central strategic importance of this issue. If collateral benefits are deducted, the quantum of damages for personal injury is reduced. One argument that we shall consider is that such deduction is merited because while not unduly prejudicing plaintiffs, who will be fully compensated in any event, deduction reduces the costs of the tort system. The savings could instead be used to improve provision for the ill and injured. Indeed the savings could be used to fund provisional recommendations which will increase tort damages, that we have put forward in other aspects of this damages project.

1.3 A collateral benefit is a payment or benefit in kind (other than the tort damages being claimed) which the tort victim would not have received but for the tort. Although the term collateral benefit has the shortcoming that it may be taken to imply that the benefit is in some sense unrelated to the tort, when the opposite is true, in our view it may nevertheless usefully be employed as a term of art.

1.4 The central issues to be considered in this paper are: first, whether payments (or benefits in kind) received or to be received as a result of an injury should be deducted from damages or ignored; and secondly, whether the provider of the payment (or benefit in kind) should have the right to recover its value from the tortfeasor (or from the victim). Although we shall be focusing on payments the same law does, and should, apply to benefits in kind.

1.5 The key difficulty in this area of the law resides in the conflict between the fundamental principle that (leaving aside exceptional measures of damages) tort damages are designed to compensate but not to overcompensate, and a set of policy arguments favouring overcompensation. If tort damages are compensatory, recovery by the plaintiff of damages for a loss which has already been, or will be, met from elsewhere would, on the face of it, be wrong. Yet for some collateral benefits but not others the courts have found this to be acceptable....[Footnotes omitted]

NOTES

1. In the DCA's Consultation Paper (CP 9/07) the Government's general position on collateral benefits is that the claimant should only be compensated once and that the payment should come from the tortfeasor if it is practicable to do so. The preferred route to achieve this result is that the benefits should be disregarded in assessing damages.

2. Benefits accruing to the claimant as a result of the tort but only indirectly related to the tort so as to be coincidental to it are not deducted. See *British Westinghouse Electric & Manufacturing Co Ltd v Underground Electric Railways Co of London Ltd* [1912] AC 673; *Lavarack v Woods of Colchester Ltd* [1967] 1 QB 278, [1966] 3 All ER 683; *Bellingham v Dhillon* [1973] QB 304, [1973] 1 All ER 20; *Hussey v Eels* [1990] 2 QB 227, [1990] 1 All ER 449; *Gardner v Marsh & Parsons A Firm)* [1997] 3 All ER 871, [1997] 1 WLR 489. The Law Commission's Consultation Paper complained that it is difficult to determine what counts as 'indirect' and recommends confining the scope of the rule to obvious cases of coincidence, for example winning the lottery as a result of having more spare time to hang around shops that sell lottery tickets. The Commission's final report (Law Com. No. 262) did not, however, recommend any statutory change.

3. Even where the benefits are directly related to the tort, other arguments of justice, reasonableness, and public policy might justify not deducting them. In *Parry v Cleaver* [1970] AC 1, [1969] 1 All ER 555 the House of Lords decided that disablement pensions should be disregarded. More generally, Lord Reid said that benefits arising from the benevolence of others should be disregarded because it would be wrong for the tortfeasor to benefit from that benevolence and deduction would discourage benevolence. See also *Redpath v Belfast and County Down Railway* [1947] NI 167 (using remoteness reasoning) and *Hussain v New Taplow Mills* [1988] AC 514, [1988] 1 All ER 54. Ex gratia payments by the tortfeasor will not fall within the benevolence exception, even if

inspired by benevolence, unless (perhaps) they are explicitly stated to be additional to any damages that may be awarded: *Gaca v Pirelli General plc* [2004] 3 All ER 348, [2004] EWCA Civ 373. Benevolence is encouraged rather than discouraged by this rule.

In *Parry v Cleaver* Lord Reid also said that insurance obtained by the victim should be disregarded because the victim had already paid for it in the insurance premiums and because the tortfeasor should not benefit from the victim's foresight. *Bradburn v Great Western Railway* (1874) LR 10 Exch 1 had come to the same result by remoteness reasoning.

The House of Lords confirmed *Parry v Cleaver* in *Hussain v New Taplow Mills* and *Hodgson v Trapp* [1989] AC 807, [1988] 3 All ER 870. In the DCA's Consultation Paper (CP 9/07) the Government proposes no change to the position over charitable payments or insurance payments, other than that, in the case of the latter, it should not matter who has paid the premium (cf. *Gaca*).

4. Contractual sick pay is deducted from compensation for lost earnings for the reason that the courts consider sick pay to be wages in another guise, so that there is no loss in the first place. (See *Parry v Cleaver*.) What happens if the employer is paying for sick pay by taking out an insurance contract? In *Page v Sheerness Steel plc* [1996] PIQR Q26 (first instance), [1997] 1 All ER 673, CA, [1998] 3 All ER 481, HL the claimant was entitled to half pay for life under a permanent health insurance policy paid for by his employers but to whose benefits he was entitled only because he contributed 4.5 per cent of his income to the employers' pension scheme. Dyson J at first instance deducted the claimant's health insurance benefits from his compensation. The Court of Appeal affirmed and the House of Lords affirmed the Court of Appeal without giving further reasons. This approach was followed by the Court of Appeal (Dyson LJ (as he had become), Mummery and Brooke LJJ) in *Gaca*, which concerned disability insurance payments. In this case it was stated that for the insurance exception to apply the claimant must have contributed directly or indirectly to the payment of the premium. Mere employment with the benefit of insurance arranged by the employer was insufficient. Could it be argued that in a very general way wages might be higher if the employer was not paying the insurance? Cf. *Smoker v London Fire and Civil Defence Authority* [1991] 2 AC 502, [1991] 2 All ER 449, where a pension was paid by the employer/tortfeasor but was regarded as the fruit of the claimant's work. On the Government's preferred approach to collateral benefits (as stated in CP 9/07) the law would be changed so that sick pay is disregarded, but that the employer would have a claim for recompense.

5. The deductibility of retirement pensions is a complex matter. The courts generally say that contributory pensions should not be deductible, on the principle of *Parry v Cleaver* that the tortfeasor should not benefit from the claimant's prudence. See *Hewson v Downs* [1970] 1 QB 73, [1969] 3 All ER 193. On the other hand, one could argue that a pension is a method of deferring paying the claimant's salary, so that, as in the sick pay example, the position is that paying the pension reduces the claimant's loss in the same way as paying wages does. The question would then be whether the claimant was due to receive more under the pension than would otherwise have occurred in the normal course of events. In *Dews v National Coal Board* [1988] AC 1, [1987] 2 All ER 545 the House of Lords decided that where, because of the particular contractual arrangements, the claimant's entitlement to a pension was unchanged despite both his and the employer's missing several contributions, the right approach was to ask whether the claimant had suffered any loss. The claimant was not entitled to claim the

missing employer's contributions as damages. In *Longden v British Coal Corpn* [1998] AC 653, [1998] 1 All ER 289 the question before the court was how to deal with a case in which the claimant was entitled to a disablement pension, not deductible under *Parry*, but as a result lost his claim to a retirement pension. The defendant said that the sums paid under the disablement pension before retirement age should be counted against any loss suffered by the claimant after retirement age if the retirement pension would have been more generous than the disablement pension. The House of Lords decided that no such deduction should be made, except that a proportionate part of a lump sum received by the claimant at the start of his entitlement to the disablement pension could be offset. In the DCA's Consultation Paper, the Government does not propose any change in relation to the non-deductibility of pensions.

6.   According to the House of Lords in the Scottish case *Wilson v National Coal Board* [1981] SC (HL) 9, redundancy payments should normally not be deducted, since they were compensation for loss of a secure job, rather than compensation for lost income, which would be deductible. But where the tort caused the redundancy, there should be a deduction, because otherwise employers would be tempted to dismiss for ill-health, rather than redundancy. The Court of Appeal in *Colledge v Bass Mitchells & Butlers Ltd* [1988] 1 All ER 536 makes the point that 'loss of a secure job' is merely an aspect of loss of future earnings, namely it is a relevant consideration in estimating the risk that the job would have been lost anyway. The Law Commission's view is that this area of the law is somewhat confused (see Law Com. No. 262, p. 115). One possible way forward would be to notice that the claimant would have had a certain chance of being made redundant anyway, so that even though redundancy payments should be deducted from loss of earnings, the claimant should be able to put back in an amount representing the discounted amount of redundancy money he might have received anyway. In the DCA's Consultation Paper (CP 9/07), the Government has expressed the opinion that the courts are in the best position to develop the law in relation to these payments.

7.   On deducting collateral benefits, see further R. Lewis *Deducting Benefits from Damages for Personal Injury* (Oxford, 2000) and (1998) 18 LS 15.

■ Hunt v Severs
House of Lords [1994] 2 All ER 385

The plaintiff was paralysed as a result of a road accident when she was riding on the pillion of a motorcycle negligently driven by the defendant. The plaintiff spent long periods in various hospitals, but when she was not in hospital she and the defendant lived together and eventually married.

LORD BRIDGE OF HARWICH: . . .
My Lords, a plaintiff who establishes a claim for damages for personal injury is entitled in English law to recover as part of those damages the reasonable value of services rendered to him gratuitously by a relative or friend in the provision of nursing care or domestic assistance of the kind rendered necessary by the injuries the plaintiff has suffered. The major issue which arises for determination in this appeal is whether the law will sustain such a claim in respect of gratuitous services in the case where the voluntary carer is the tortfeasor himself. . . .

Included in the award of special damages was a sum of £4,429 representing the defendant's travelling expenses incurred in visiting the plaintiff while she was in hospital and a sum of £17,000 representing the value of the past services rendered by the defendant in caring for the plaintiff when she was at home. Included in the award for future loss was a sum of £60,000 representing the estimated value of the services which would be rendered by the defendant in caring for the plaintiff in future.

The defendant appealed against the inclusion in the award of the sums in respect of the defendant's travelling expenses and care for the plaintiff. The plaintiff cross-appealed on various grounds. The Court of Appeal (Sir Thomas Bingham MR, Staughton and Waite LJJ) ([1993] 4 All ER 180, [1993] QB 815)...dismissed the defendant's appeal...

The defendant now appeals by leave of the Court of Appeal to your Lordships' House. Three issues arise for decision. The first relates to the award in respect of the defendant's travelling expenses, the second to that in respect of his past and future care of the plaintiff, ...[18] The first two issues are theoretically distinct, but I propose to address them together. There is no dispute that the defendant's visits to the plaintiff in hospital made a valuable and important contribution to her general well-being and were calculated to assist her recovery from the devastating consequences of the accident. But for the fact that the defendant was himself the tortfeasor, the propriety of the award under this head would be no more open to question than the award for his services as a voluntary carer. Accordingly, it seems to me that both these issues must depend upon the same considerations of principle....

The trial judge said of the claims now in dispute:

'It is said that these sums are irrecoverable, that they represent in effect a benefit to the defendant himself, that in so far as they reflect a loss on the plaintiff's part it has been made good by the defendant so that there is in truth no loss, and that if the incidence of insurance is put on one side it can be seen that the claim is misconceived. However, in my judgment this ignores the basis upon which the claim is made. It is merely a notional monetary figure placed on the true nature of the loss for which she is entitled to compensation. This loss is the need she now has by reason of the accident for care and support which she did not have before. This follows from the analysis of the legal basis of such claims by Megaw LJ in *Donnelly v Joyce* [1973] 3 All ER 475 at 480, [1974] QB 454 at 462. The valuation of this need remains a difficult exercise. In *Housecroft v Burnett* [1986] 1 All ER 332 O'Connor LJ made it clear that when provided by unpaid carers there remains a value to be placed on it. In my view that remains so whether provided by the tortfeasor or not. He may give his care in response to the need, but that does not make good the loss, otherwise there will be no sustainable claim in any case where the need has apparently been "met" by unpaid carers.'

In the Court of Appeal the judgment of Megaw LJ in *Donnelly v Joyce* [1973] 3 All ER 475, [1974] QB 454 again provided the main foundation for the court's reasoning. Having examined this and other authorities, Sir Thomas Bingham MR, delivering the judgment of the court expressed their conclusion ([1993] 4 All ER 180 at 191–192, [1993] QB 815 at 831):

'Where services are voluntarily rendered by a tortfeasor in caring for the plaintiff from motives of affection or duty they should in our opinion be regarded as in the same category as services rendered voluntarily by a third party, or charitable gifts, or insurance payments. They are adventitious benefits, which for policy reasons are not to be regarded as diminishing the plaintiff's loss. On the facts of the present case the judge's decision was not in our view contrary to principle or authority and it was fortified by what we regard as compelling considerations of public policy. We consider that he reached the right conclusion and would accordingly dismiss the defendant's appeal.'

The starting point for any inquiry into the measure of damages which an injured plaintiff is entitled to recover is the recognition that damages in the tort of negligence are purely compensatory. He should recover from the tortfeasor no more and no less than he has lost. Difficult questions may arise when the plaintiff's injuries attract benefits from third parties. According to their nature these may or may not be taken into account as reducing the tortfeasor's liability. The two well-established categories of receipt which are to be ignored in assessing damages are the fruits of insurance which the plaintiff

---

[18] The third issue is not relevant here.

himself has provided against the contingency causing his injuries (which may or may not lead to a claim by the insurer as subrogated to the rights of the plaintiff) and the fruits of the benevolence of third parties motivated by sympathy for the plaintiff's misfortune. The policy considerations which underlie these two apparent exceptions to the rule against double recovery are, I think, well understood: see, for example, *Parry v Cleaver* [1969] 1 All ER 555 at 558, [1970] AC 1 at 14 and *Hussain v New Taplow Paper Mills Ltd* [1988] 1 All ER 541 at 545, [1988] AC 514 at 528. But I find it difficult to see what considerations of public policy can justify a requirement that the tortfeasor himself should compensate the plaintiff twice over for the self same loss. If the loss in question is a direct pecuniary loss (eg loss of wages) *Hussain's* case is clear authority that the defendant employer, as the tortfeasor who makes good the loss either voluntarily or contractually, thereby mitigates his liability in damages pro tanto. The Court of Appeal, in the judgment appealed from, readily accepted a number of examples advanced in argument for the defendant as showing that a tortfeasor may mitigate his liability by making good in kind the physical damage which his tort has caused to the plaintiff's property. In a wide-ranging argument before your Lordships, where many hypothetical examples were examined of gratuitous services rendered by a tortfeasor to an injured plaintiff in satisfaction of a need occasioned by his tort, Mr McGregor QC for the plaintiff was constrained to accept as a general rule that the tortfeasor, having provided those services, cannot also be held liable to the plaintiff in damages for their value. But he submitted that where the tortfeasor is a relative or close friend of the plaintiff and gratuitously provides services of an intimate personal or domestic character, he is required by law, as a narrow exception to the general rule, also to pay the plaintiff the value of those services.

The law with respect to the services of a third party who provides voluntary care for a tortiously injured plaintiff has developed somewhat erratically in England. The voluntary carer has no cause of action of his own against the tortfeasor. The justice of allowing the injured plaintiff to recover the value of the services so that he may recompense the voluntary carer has been generally recognised, but there has been difficulty in articulating a consistent juridical principle to justify this result.

[Having discussed *Roach v Yates*, [1938] 1 KB 256, [1937] 3 All ER 442, *Schneider v Eisovitch*, [1960] 2 QB 430, [1960] 1 All ER 169 and *Wattson v Port of London Authority* [1969] 1 Lloyd's Rep 95, LORD BRIDGE continued:]

In *Cunningham v Harrison* [1973] 3 All ER 463, [1973] QB 942 and *Donnelly v Joyce* [1973] 3 All ER 475, [1974] QB 454 judgments were delivered by different divisions of the Court of Appeal on successive days. In *Cunningham* the wife of a severely disabled plaintiff, who had initially looked after him, had died before the trial. Lord Denning MR said ([1973] 3 All ER 463 at 469–470, [1973] QB 942 at 951–952):

> 'Before dealing with [the claim for future nursing expenses] I would like to consider what the position would have been if the wife had not died and had continued to look after her husband, as she had been doing. The plaintiff's advisers seem to have thought that a husband could not claim for the nursing services rendered by a wife unless the husband was legally bound to pay her for them. So, on their advice on 11th July 1972 an agreement was signed whereby the husband agreed to pay his wife £2,000 per annum in respect of her nursing services. We were told that such advice is often given by counsel in such cases as these when advising on evidence. I know the reason why such advice is given. It is because it has been said in some cases that a plaintiff can only recover for services rendered to him when he was legally liable to pay for them: see for instance *Kirkham v Boughey* [1957] 3 All ER 153 at 156, [1958] 2 QB 338 at 342 and *Janney v Gentry* (1966) 110 SJ 408. But, I think that view is much too narrow. It seems to me that when a husband is grievously injured—and is entitled to damages—then it is only right and just that, if his wife renders service to him, instead of a nurse, he should recover compensation for the value of the services that his wife has rendered. It should not be necessary to draw up a legal agreement for them. On recovering such an amount, the husband should hold it on trust for her and pay it over to her. She cannot herself

sue the wrongdoer . . . but she has rendered services necessitated by the wrongdoing, and should be compensated for it. If she had given up paid work to look after him, he would clearly have been entitled to recover on her behalf, because the family income would have dropped by so much: see *Wattson v Port of London Authority* [1969] 1 Lloyd's Rep 95 at 102 per Megaw J. Even though she had not been doing paid work but only domestic duties in the house, nevertheless all extra attendance on him certainly calls for compensation.'

In *Donnelly v Joyce*, the injured plaintiff was a boy of six. His mother gave up her work for a period to provide necessary care for him and the disputed item in his claim related to the mother's loss of wages. The judgment of the court delivered by Megaw LJ contains a lengthy review of the authorities, but the key passage relied on by the trial judge and the Court of Appeal in the instant case reads ([1973] 3 All ER 475 at 479–480, [1974] QB 454 at 461–462):

'We do not agree with the proposition, inherent in counsel for the defendant's submission, that the plaintiff's claim, in circumstances such as the present, is properly to be regarded as being, to use his phrase, "in relation to someone else's loss", merely because someone else has provided to, or for the benefit of, the plaintiff—the injured person—the money, or the services to be valued as money, to provide for needs of the plaintiff directly caused by the defendant's wrongdoing. The loss is the plaintiff's loss. The question from what source the plaintiff's needs have been met, the question who has paid the money or given the services, the question whether or not the plaintiff is or is not under a legal or moral liability to repay, are, so far as the defendant and his liability are concerned, all irrelevant. The plaintiff's loss, to take this present case, is not the expenditure of money to buy the special boots or to pay for the nursing attention. His loss is the existence of the need for those special boots or for those nursing services, the value of which for purposes of damages—for the purpose of the ascertainment of the amount of his loss—is the proper and reasonable cost of supplying those needs. That, in our judgment, is the key to the problem. So far as the defendant is concerned, the loss is not someone else's loss. It is the plaintiff's loss. Hence it does not matter, so far as the defendant's liability to the plaintiff is concerned, whether the needs have been supplied by the plaintiff out of his own pocket or by a charitable contribution to him from some other person whom we shall call "the provider"; it does not matter, for that purpose, whether the plaintiff has a legal liability, absolute or conditional, to repay to the provider what he has received, because of the general law or because of some private agreement between himself and the provider; it does not matter whether he has a moral obligation, however ascertained or defined, so to do. The question of legal liability to reimburse the provider may be very relevant to the question of the legal right of the provider to recover from the plaintiff. That may depend on the nature of the liability imposed by the general law or the particular agreement. But it is not a matter which affects the right of the plaintiff against the wrongdoer.' . . .

With respect, I do not find this reasoning convincing. I accept that the basis of a plaintiff's claim for damages may consist in his need for services but I cannot accept that the question from what source that need has been met is irrelevant. If an injured plaintiff is treated in hospital as a private patient he is entitled to recover the cost of that treatment. But if he receives free treatment under the National Health Service, his need has been met without cost to him and he cannot claim the cost of the treatment from the tortfeasor. So it cannot, I think, be right to say that in all cases the plaintiff's loss is 'for the purpose of damages . . . the proper and reasonable cost of supplying [his] needs'.

In Scotland the law on this subject has developed differently. . . . The difference in this regard between Scottish and English law was examined by the Scottish Law Commission in 1978 (Scot Law Com No 51). In para 20 they adopted the view that 'the value of the services of persons who have assisted the injured person should be recoverable by the latter in his action against the wrongdoer' but considered that 'the principle should only apply as between members of the injured person's family group or circle'.

In para 22 they criticised the reasoning used in the judgment of Megaw LJ in *Donnelly v Joyce* in the following terms:

'...it is artificial to regard [the victim] as having suffered a net loss in the events which happened. The loss is in fact sustained by the person rendering the services, a point vividly illustrated in cases where he has lost earnings in the course of rendering those services. We suggest, therefore, that it is wrong in principle, in cases where services have been rendered gratuitously by another to an injured person, to regard the latter as having in fact suffered a net loss.'

They concluded (at para 23)—

'that it would be right to devise an approach which will enable the injured person to recover in his own action the value of services which have been rendered to him by relatives but which would, at the same time, enable the relative to recover, if he so wished, the value of these services from the injured person.'

The Commission's recommendations in this respect were implemented by Pt II of the Administration of Justice Act 1982, which applies to damages for personal injuries in Scotland...

Thus, in both England and Scotland the law now ensures that an injured plaintiff may recover the reasonable value of gratuitous services rendered to him by way of voluntary care by a member of his family. Differences between the English common law route and the Scottish statutory route to this conclusion are, I think, rarely likely to be of practical importance, since in most cases the sum recovered will simply go to swell the family income. But it is nevertheless important to recognise that the underlying rationale of the English law, as all the cases before *Donnelly v Joyce* demonstrate, is to enable the voluntary carer to receive proper recompense for his or her services and I would think it appropriate for the House to take the opportunity so far as possible to bring the law of the two countries into accord by adopting the view of Lord Denning MR in *Cunningham v Harrison* that in England the injured plaintiff who recovers damages under this head should hold them on trust for the voluntary carer.

By concentrating on the plaintiff's need and the plaintiff's loss as the basis of an award in respect of voluntary care received by the plaintiff, the reasoning in *Donnelly v Joyce* diverts attention from the award's central objective of compensating the voluntary carer. Once this is recognised it becomes evident that there can be no ground in public policy or otherwise for requiring the tortfeasor to pay to the plaintiff, in respect of the services which he himself has rendered, a sum of money which the plaintiff must then repay to him. If the present case had been brought in Scotland and the claim in respect of the tortfeasor's services made in reliance on s 8 of the Administration of Justice Act 1982, it would have been immediately obvious that such a claim was not sustainable.

The case for the plaintiff was argued in the Court of Appeal without reference to the circumstance that the defendant's liability was covered by insurance. But before your Lordships Mr McGregor, recognising the difficulty of formulating any principle of public policy which could justify recovery against the tortfeasor who has to pay out of his own pocket, advanced the bold proposition that such a policy could be founded on the liability of insurers to meet the claim. Exploration of the implications of this proposition in argument revealed the many difficulties which it encounters. But I do not think it necessary to examine these in detail. The short answer, in my judgment, to Mr McGregor's contention is that its acceptance would represent a novel and radical departure in the law of a kind which only the legislature may properly effect. At common law the circumstance that a defendant is contractually indemnified by a third party against a particular legal liability can have no relevance whatever to the measure of that liability....

I would allow the appeal, set aside the Court of Appeal's order and vary the trial judge's order by reducing the principal award by £81,429 and reducing the award of interest on special damages by so much as represents interest on the sum of £21,429 included in the principal award.

[LORD KEITH OF KINKEL, LORD JAUNCEY OF TULLICHETTLE, LORD BROWNE-WILKINSON, and LORD NOLAN agreed with the speech of LORD BRIDGE OF HARWICH.]

Appeal allowed.

■ Law Commission Consultation Paper No 144, 'Damages For Personal Injury: Medical, Nursing And Other Expenses'

2.19 There are three principal legal problems which have been addressed by the case law in relation to gratuitous nursing care. The first problem is that of who actually suffers loss where a victim receives free nursing care. The second relates to the particular situation where the person providing the care is the defendant. The third problem is that of the quantum of damages recoverable under this head.

2.20 The first two questions were the subject of the recent controversial decision of the House of Lords in *Hunt v Severs*.[19] . . .

(a) Who suffers the loss?
2.21 Where the plaintiff is receiving free nursing care, for example from a member of his or her family, one must ask who has incurred the loss that is being compensated by the award of damages for that care. If the loss is the plaintiff's, then, in the absence of any legal or equitable obligation to account to the carer for the expenses, the plaintiff, in receipt of both the care and the money intended to pay for it, experiences a "windfall" gain, unless he or she passes on the money out of a sense of moral obligation. On the other hand, if the loss is the carer's, then it seems that the plaintiff should not be able to recover the expenses, because he or she has not suffered a loss in this respect; but the carer cannot recover them either because he or she has no cause of action against the defendant.

2.22 In his speech in *Hunt* Lord Bridge of Harwich reviewed[20] a line of cases dealing with this problem, culminating in the decision of the Court of Appeal in *Donnelly v Joyce*.[1] . . .

2.28 However, the "trust" approach had, before its adoption by the House of Lords in *Hunt*, already been subject to criticism. For example, the Pearson Commission had indicated its practical difficulties:

> A requirement to set up a trust fund could present practical difficulties if several people were involved. The court would have to ascertain the amount expended and the value of the services rendered by each, so that the plaintiff could hold the right sum in trust for each of them.[2]

The Pearson Commission, accepting the reasoning of Megaw LJ in *Donnelly v Joyce*, thought that any formal provision for reimbursement was unnecessary for the reason that the loss would often be suffered in practice by a family income pool. . . .

(b) Care provided by defendant
2.30 The second of the three problems mentioned above is the special case where the person providing the gratuitous care is the defendant himself or herself. This situation typically occurs where the plaintiff is a member of the defendant's family, or has a similarly close relationship with the defendant, and the injury occurs when the plaintiff is a passenger in a car or, as in *Hunt v Severs*, on a motor cycle, driven by the defendant. In *Hunt*, the Court of Appeal had followed *Donnelly v Joyce*,[3] and supported this decision with an argument based on policy,[4] namely that, if plaintiffs were denied damages in these circumstances, there would be incentives to the plaintiff to obtain the care she needed by adopting other, comparatively less desirable, routes which would enable her to recover the cost. These means were: relying on paid help from third parties; relying on unpaid assistance from persons other than

---

[19] [1994] 2 AC 350.   [20] [1994] 2 AC 350, 358–361.   [1] [1974] QB 454.
[2] (1977) Cmnd 7054, vol 1 para 349.   [3] [1974] QB 454.
[4] [1993] QB 815, 831, *per* Sir Thomas Bingham MR.

the defendant; and entering into a contract under which the defendant would provide the services for payment.[5] ...

(c) The quantum of damages

2.33 The third problem is that of the quantum of damages. Before the House of Lords' decision in *Hunt v Severs* changed the approach which the law took to damages for gratuitous care, the leading case on this subject was *Housecroft v Burnett*.[6] In that case, the Court of Appeal was applying the now overruled approach of *Donnelly v Joyce* in regarding the loss as the plaintiff's rather than the carer's. O'Connor LJ referred to "two extreme solutions"[7] in resolving the problem of assessing the "proper and reasonable cost" of supplying the plaintiff's needs[8] where care is provided by a relative or friend gratuitously. The first was to assess the carer's contribution at the full commercial rate for the services provided by the carer. The second was to assess the cost as nil, just as it is where the plaintiff is treated under the NHS. O'Connor LJ concluded that neither of the extreme solutions was correct, and that any assessment should be somewhere between the two, depending on the facts of the case. The award would have to be:

> ...sufficient to enable the plaintiff, among other things, to make reasonable recompense to the relative. So, in cases where the relative has given up gainful employment to look after the plaintiff, I would regard it as natural that the plaintiff would not wish the relative to be the loser and the court would award sufficient to enable the plaintiff to achieve that result. The ceiling would be the commercial rate.[9] ...

2.34 ...In *Woodrup v Nicol*[10] the Court of Appeal cited the decision in *Housecroft v Burnett* and on this basis reduced the damages awarded by Wright J at first instance in relation to the care provided by the plaintiff's father. These damages consisted of the father's estimated loss of earnings for the period in question, amounting to twice the commercial cost of his services, although the sum awarded by the Court of Appeal still exceeded the commercial rate.[11] In at least one case[12] the court has expressly regarded the ceiling as a guideline rather than as a binding rule of law.

2.35 In cases where there has been no loss of earnings as such, courts have tended to calculate damages for care by relatives by taking the commercial rate for home helps and applying a discount to it.[13] The discount may be reduced if the plaintiff can show a likely future need for commercial care.[14] It may also be reduced if the quality of the care required from the carers is of a particularly high level.[15] In exceptional cases courts have refrained from making a discount at all,[16] and in one case, the Court of Appeal upheld an award based on one and a half times the earnings which the plaintiff's mother, a

---

[5]   Cf *Donnelly v Joyce* [1974] QB 454, 463–464, *per* Megaw LJ.

[6]   [1986] 1 All ER 332.   [7]   [1986] 1 All ER 332, 342.   [8]   *Donnelly v Joyce* [1974] QB 454, 462.

[9]   [1986] 1 All ER 332, 343. See also, eg, *Bell v Gateshead AHA* (1986) *Kemp & Kemp* A4-101, in which the claimant's mother had given up plans to return to work. Alliott J took her lost earnings as the starting point to value her services, past and future, but applied the commercial ceiling.

[10]   [1993] PIQR Q104.

[11]   The estimated cost, at commercial rates, was £2,400 for the period in question. Wright J had awarded £5,000, which was reduced to £3,500 on appeal.

[12]   *Lamey v Wirral HA* (1993) *Kemp & Kemp* A4-120 (Morland J).

[13]   See, eg, *Nash v Southmead HA* [1993] PIQR Q156, in which Alliott J applied a one-third discount to the commercial rates.

[14]   In *Maylen v Morris* (1988) *Kemp & Kemp* A3-105 it was anticipated that future care would be by the claimant's mother and two other relatives, but it was anticipated that the mother might later become unable to cope because of old age. The Court of Appeal refused the defendant's appeal against the 25 per cent discount set by Mann J.

[15]   Eg *Fairhurst v St Helens and Knowsley HA* [1995] PIQR Q1 (25 per cent discount).

[16]   See *Lamey v Wirral HA* (1993) *Kemp & Kemp* A4-120 (Morland J).

qualified nurse, would have earned, on the basis that the mother was doing the work of the two nurses who would otherwise have been needed to provide the care.[17]

2.36 It is too early as yet to gauge the effect which the decision in *Hunt v Severs*[18] (which views the provision of the care as a loss to the carer rather than a loss to the plaintiff) will have on the quantum of damages for gratuitous care.[19] It might, for example, result in an increase in the number of cases in which courts award damages beyond the "commercial ceiling". Where, however, a carer gives up well-paid employment to look after the plaintiff, and the income which he or she forgoes is far beyond the cost of obtaining the same care commercially, it may be that the general duty to mitigate will impose a control on the damages, even in the absence of a strict commercial ceiling. There are other reasons why the practical difference which *Hunt v Severs* makes to the quantum of awards may be limited. First, although the object of damages for gratuitous care before *Hunt v Severs* was to compensate the plaintiff rather than the carer, it was clear that the adequate compensation of the carer was an important, if not the most important, factor in deciding the level of damages.[20] Secondly, in many cases, where the carer is not forgoing an income, the only available starting point in calculating the damages will still be the commercial rate.

QUESTION

If a relative gives up a well-paid job to act as a carer, should the ceiling be the commercial rate for carers as stated in *Housecroft v Burnett* [1986] 1 All ER 332 (see para. 2.33 in the extract ante)? (Cf. *Evans v Pontypridd Roofing Ltd* [2002] PIQR Q5, [2001] EWCA Civ 1657 at [25].)

NOTES

1. For (mainly hostile) comment on *Hunt* see e.g. D. Kemp (1994) 110 LQR 526; L. C. H. Hoyano [1995] Tort L Rev 63 at p. 69; A. Reed (1995) 15 Oxf JLS 133, at pp. 137–138; P. Matthews and M. Lunney (1995) 58 MLR 395 at p. 399.

2. In its final report (Law Com. No. 262 at pp. 46–53) the Law Commission recommended that the damages should continue to be awarded for care gratuitously but reasonably provided by friends and relatives. It recommended that the claimant should have a statutory duty to pay over the damages in respect of past care to the carer, but that there should be no such duty in respect of future care. It rejected the proposal to give the carer a direct action against the tortfeasor but recommended the legislative reversal of the treatment in *Hunt v Severs* of care provided by the tortfeasor, concluding that 'the defendant's liability to pay damages to the claimant for nursing or other care should be unaffected by any liability of the claimant, on receipt of those damages, to pay them or a proportion of them back to the defendant as the person who has gratuitously provided (or will provide) such care'. The Law Commission criticised *Hunt*, principally on the ground that it tends to discourage the provision of voluntary care. In *Dimond v Lovell* [2002] 1 AC 384, [2000] 2 All ER 897, however, the House of Lords re-affirmed its commitment to *Hunt v Severs* on the ground that the source of a collateral benefit

---

[17] *Hogg v Doyle* (unreported, 6 March 1991). See *Kemp & Kemp* vol 1 para 5–024.

[18] [1994] 2 AC 350.

[19] In Australia, the loss is clearly regarded as the claimant's and the High Court has held that the carer's lost earnings are not an appropriate measure of damages for gratuitous care. See *Van Gervan v Fenton* (1992) 175 CLR 327.

[20] See, e.g., *Housecroft v Burnett* [1986] 1 All ER 332, 343. See also *Aboul-Hosn v Trustees of the Italian Hospital* (1987) *Kemp & Kemp* A4–104.

was highly relevant to whether it should be disregarded and that, because of insurance and other economic mechanisms which tend to spread the loss, the basic principle expressed in *Parry v Cleaver* (see p. 534, ante) should not be extended. In the DCA's Consultation Paper (CP 9/07) the Government's view is that the *Hunt v Severs* trust obligation should be replaced by a personal obligation to account to the carer and that it should cover past and future services actually rendered; in the case of services rendered by the tortfeasor, the proposal was to make an alteration to the *Hunt v Severs* position by providing that there should be a payment for future (though not past) services but with the obligation to account to the tortfeasor if in fact rendered by that person (which would avoid some uncertainty arising under the present position).

   Note, however, that services other than caring do not come within the principle. See *Hardwick v Hudson* [1999] 3 All ER 426, [1999] 1 WLR 1770, although the Government's view in CP 9/07 is that business services gratuitously provided should not be treated differently from caring. Furthermore, payments from local authorities to claimants to cover the costs of care and accommodation can be deducted from damages (*Sowden v Lodge* [2004] 1 All ER 581, [2004] EWCA Civ 1370; *Crofton v National Health Service Litigation Authority* [2007] 1 WLR 923, [2007] EWCA Civ 1, and the local authority cannot benefit from the *Hunt v Severs* principle: see *Islington London Borough Council v University College London Hospital NHS Trust* [2006] PIQR P3, [2005] EWCA Civ 596 at [3]. Note also that in any case no trust for the benefit of the third party can arise to remedy the third party's own failure to comply with a statutory requirement which has rendered an agreement between the third party and the claimant unenforceable. See *Dimond v Lovell* [2000] 1 QB 216, [1999] 3 All ER 1, CA, confirmed by the House of Lords [2002] 1 AC 384, [2000] 2 All ER 897.

3. Should the law equally recognise lost ability to carry out household services as a head of damage? In *Daly v General Steam Navigation Co Ltd* [1980] 3 All ER 696, [1981] 1 WLR 120, an award was made in respect of the lost ability to carry out housekeeping duties. The Law Commission in Consultative Paper 144 (para. 237) called the Court of Appeal's reasoning 'confusing' on the ground that whereas the court allows the claimant to recover for the future by looking at the commercial cost of having someone else do the work, regardless of whether the claimant actually intended to hire such a person, for the past no recovery is allowed unless the claimant had actually and reasonably hired someone else to do the work or unless someone else had given up paid employment to do it (although soldiering on alone could be taken into account as part of pain, suffering, and loss of amenity). In its final report (Law Com. No. 262 at p. 57) the Law Commission recommended that the law should be changed so that for the future, no award for pecuniary loss should be made unless claimants can establish that they will reasonably pay someone else to do the work. Awards would still be possible for where the future work was likely to be done gratuitously by a friend or relative, but without any duty on the part of the claimant to pay the sums over to the carer. It would still be possible to award extra sums under pain and suffering if the claimant chose to soldier on alone. Since the Law Commission's report, it has been held that the principle in *Daly* would cover a case where the injured person could no longer devote particular care to looking after a spouse, partner, or relative living in the same household: *Lowe v Guise* [2002] 3 All ER 454, [2002] EWCA Civ 197. In fact, Potter LJ in *Lowe* would like past and future loss to be assessed on the same basis, but precedent, in the shape of *Daly*, stood in the way.

4.   As stated in note 2, ante, payments from local authorities for the care of tortiously injured people can be deducted from the damages award, although the position can raise difficulty in practice: see paras. 164–172 of the DCA's Consultation Paper (CP 9/07). A direct claim against the tortfeasor would fall foul of the general non-recoverability for pure economic loss: see *Islington London Borough Council v University College London Hospital NHS Trust* [2006] PIQR P3, [2005] EWCA Civ 596, noted p. 256, ante. Under s. 157 of the Road Traffic Act 1988 and Part 3 of the Health and Social Care (Community Health and Standards) Act 2003 (the latter coming into force on 29 January 2007), various costs of medical treatment have been made recoverable by health service bodies: see notes 6 and 7, p. 1146, post. In *Crofton v National Health Service Litigation Authority* the Court of Appeal, noting that the tortfeasor may gain a benefit at the expense of the public, speculated (at [89]) whether the 2003 Act 'signals a general trend in the attitude of the legislature to the responsibilities of tortfeasors to pay for the costs presently imposed upon the public purse'. The matter was regarded as one for Parliament, and similar sentiments can be found in the slightly different context of the *Islington* case. In CP 9/07 the Government's view is that tortfeasors 'should pay for the costs of care, wherever possible' although they attached the caveat that 'those costs should be based on providing appropriate treatment in a cost-effective way'. Further consultation was promised after proposals emanating from this consultation had been formulated.

■ The Social Security (Recovery of Benefits) Act 1997

Introductory
1 Cases in which this Act applies
(1) This Act applies in cases where—

(a) a person makes a payment (whether on his own behalf or not) to or in respect of any other person in consequence of any accident, injury or disease suffered by the other, and

(b) any listed benefits have been, or are likely to be, paid to or for the other during the relevant period in respect of the accident, injury or disease.

(2) The reference above to a payment in consequence of any accident, injury or disease is to a payment made—

(a) by or on behalf of a person who is, or is alleged to be, liable to any extent in respect of the accident, injury or disease, or

(b) in pursuance of a compensation scheme for motor accidents;

but does not include a payment mentioned in Part I of Schedule 1.[1]

(3) Subsection (1)(a) applies to a payment made—

(a) voluntarily, or in pursuance of a court order or an agreement, or otherwise, and

(b) in the United Kingdom or elsewhere.

(4) In a case where this Act applies—

(a) the "injured person" is the person who suffered the accident, injury or disease,

(b) the "compensation payment" is the payment within subsection (1)(a), and

(c) "recoverable benefit" is any listed benefit which has been or is likely to be paid as mentioned in subsection (1)(b).

. . .

---

[1] Sch. 1 lists, inter alia, criminal court compensation payments, payments from certain trusts, and redundancy payments.

3 "The relevant period"

(1) In relation to a person ("the claimant") who has suffered any accident, injury or disease, "the relevant period" has the meaning given by the following subsections.

(2) Subject to subsection (4), if it is a case of accident or injury, the relevant period is the period of five years immediately following the day on which the accident or injury in question occurred.

(3) Subject to subsection (4), if it is a case of disease, the relevant period is the period of five years beginning with the date on which the claimant first claims a listed benefit in consequence of the disease.

(4) If at any time before the end of the period referred to in subsection (2) or (3)—

(a) a person makes a compensation payment in final discharge of any claim made by or in respect of the claimant and arising out of the accident, injury or disease, or

(b) an agreement is made under which an earlier compensation payment is treated as having been made in final discharge of any such claim,

the relevant period ends at that time.

Certificates of recoverable benefits

4 Applications for certificates of recoverable benefits

(1) Before a person ("the compensator") makes a compensation payment he must apply to the Secretary of State for a certificate of recoverable benefits.

(2) Where the compensator applies for a certificate of recoverable benefits, the Secretary of State must—

(a) send to him a written acknowledgement of receipt of his application, and

(b) [. . .], issue the certificate before the end of the following period.

(3) The period is—

(a) the prescribed period, or

(b) if there is no prescribed period, the period of four weeks,

which begins with the day following the day on which the application is received.

. . .

6 Liability to pay Secretary of State amount of benefits

(1) A person who makes a compensation payment in any case is liable to pay to the Secretary of State an amount equal to the total amount of the recoverable benefits.

(2) The liability referred to in subsection (1) arises immediately before the compensation payment or, if there is more than one, the first of them is made.

. . .

8 Reduction of compensation payment

(1) This section applies in a case where, in relation to any head of compensation listed in column 1 of Schedule 2—

(a) any of the compensation payment is attributable to that head, and

(b) any recoverable benefit is shown against that head in column 2 of the Schedule.

(2) In such a case, any claim of a person to receive the compensation payment is to be treated for all purposes as discharged if—

(a) he is paid the amount (if any) of the compensation payment calculated in accordance with this section, and

(b) if the amount of the compensation payment so calculated is nil, he is given a statement saying so by the person who (apart from this section) would have paid the gross amount of the compensation payment.

(3) For each head of compensation listed in column 1 of the Schedule for which paragraphs (a) and (b) of subsection (1) are met, so much of the gross amount of the compensation payment as is attributable

to that head is to be reduced (to nil, if necessary) by deducting the amount of the recoverable benefit or, as the case may be, the aggregate amount of the recoverable benefits shown against it.

(4) Subsection (3) is to have effect as if a requirement to reduce a payment by deducting an amount which exceeds that payment were a requirement to reduce that payment to nil.

(5) The amount of the compensation payment calculated in accordance with this section is—

(a) the gross amount of the compensation payment, less

(b) the sum of the reductions made under subsection (3),

(and, accordingly, the amount may be nil).

NOTES

1. It has long been controversial whether social security benefits should be offset against damages. The argument for deduction, voiced in the Beveridge Report, is that an injured person should not have the same need met twice. This was supported, in 1946, by a Departmental Committee on Alternative Remedies (the Monckton Committee) (Cmd. 6860), which recommended that 'the injured person or his dependants should not be permitted to recover by way of damages and benefits more than the maximum which he could recover from either source alone'. The argument against deduction, expressed by a minority of the Monckton Committee, is that the claimant earns many social security benefits by contributions in the same way as private insurance. In the result, a compromise was adopted. Section 2(1) of the Law Reform (Personal Injuries) Act 1948 provided that in assessing damages for loss of income due to personal injury, the court should take into account one half of the value of certain social security benefits for five years. Only awards made by the court, and not out-of-court settlements, were subject to this deduction and the deduction could be made only from the award for past and future loss of earnings. The Pearson Commission (chap. 13, paras. 487–488, and minority opinion, paras. 543–548) recommended that the full value of social security benefits should be deducted from damages, with the proviso that the set-off should only be against the like head of damages.

    The present legislation maintains the five year compromise, but has the effect of deducting the relevant benefits in full against the relevant head of damages. (On double recovery after the recoupment period, see the DCA Consultation paper (CP 9/07), para. 140.) The key innovation since 1948, originating in 1990, reformed in 1992, and again in 1997, is that the government, rather than the tortfeasor, benefits from the deduction. The government 'claws back' or 'recoups' from the tortfeasor the amounts paid or to be paid in benefits to the victim.

2. Schedule 2 to the 1997 Act provides that the five-year full deduction of social security benefits applies only to damages for earnings lost, cost of care, and loss of mobility. The schedule lists which benefits are to be deducted against which head of damages. Under the predecessor legislation to the 1997 Act, other heads of damages, for example pain and suffering, were liable to deduction.

3. What about benefits not mentioned by Sch. 2? Examples include housing benefit and council tax benefit. The pre-recoupment era case *Hodgson v Trapp* [1989] AC 807, [1988] 3 All ER 870 suggests that benefits that are relevant to losses the claimant has suffered should be deducted in full unless the legislation says otherwise, and it was decided in *Clenshaw v Tanner* [2002] EWCA Civ 1848 that housing benefit is so deductible. See further the discussion in *Ballantine v Newalls Insulation Co Ltd* [2001] ICR 25. The DCA Consultation Paper (CP 9/07) did not deal with State benefits, but contrast the

Government's general approach in that paper referred to at note 1, p. 534, ante. What answer would that suggest?

QUESTIONS

What is the justification for the recovery of benefits by the government from the tortfeasor? Is it simply a matter of reducing public spending? Or can it be justified economically on the ground that to allow tortfeasors to benefit from social security payments to victims would undermine the incentives provided by tort law to behave reasonably? Cf. R Cooter (1989) 75 Va. L. Rev. 383. Note that if the government is not able to recover benefit payments, the effect of the deductibility of benefits is that of an indiscriminate subsidy of tortfeasors, something commented on adversely by courts in recent years in the context of local authority payments for care and accommodation.

(d) Lump sums vs periodic payments

■ Report of the Royal Commission on Civil Liability and Compensation for Personal Injury
Cmnd. 7054. Vol. I

555 The main component of a claim for future pecuniary loss is, almost invariably, loss of income or, in fatal cases, lost dependency. The plaintiff's loss is therefore in periodic form, whether it is made up of weekly wages, a monthly salary, or regular contributions to a family budget. Any expenses included in a claim for future pecuniary loss also tend to be regular outgoings.

556 It seems to most of us that the lump sum is not the most natural form of compensation for losses of this sort, given the objective of tort of restoring the plaintiff as closely as possible to his position before the injury. Yet it is at present the only form of tort compensation. In assessing damages, the court must translate a periodic future loss into a capital sum.

557 This process is inevitably inexact. The court must compare the plaintiff's expected income with the income which he might have enjoyed if he had not been injured. Allowance must be made for the likely duration of incapacity, and for the chances of promotion or increase in earnings; and, on the other hand, for the chances of loss of earnings, unemployment, unconnected illness or death. The court must also make assumptions about future economic conditions. In particular, it must make some assumptions about future rates of inflation, tax, and return on invested capital.

558 None of these factors is certain. The plaintiff may live for a longer or shorter period than was assumed; his medical condition may improve or deteriorate unexpectedly; he may lose his job or fail to find another; or he may be unable to derive the hoped-for return on his investment. As a result, he may be extensively over compensated or under compensated.

560 The lump sum is said, however, to have a number of advantages. Among those urged upon us was finality in litigation. A lump sum completely disposes of a tort claim. This is said to be in the interest both of the parties and of the community, in that there is an end of legal dispute and an end of expense. The defendant can discharge his liability fully and then forget the matter. In practice, this means that his insurer can close his file without incurring the expenses (which would ultimately be reflected in higher premiums) of continued administration. The plaintiff, if he is not too badly injured, can concentrate his efforts on recovery and put his injury and his grievance behind him. Because people like to finish with their claims a final lump sum award is said to promote settlements, and thus to help to contain the cost of the tort system.

561 The lump sum is also said to give freedom of choice. Although the compensation is awarded for future pecuniary loss, the plaintiff may, if he wishes, spend all or a large part of it immediately. He may, for example, use it to buy a house or to pay off his existing mortgage; or to buy a business; or simply to purchase some luxury which he could not otherwise afford but which may give him pleasure that to some extent makes up for his loss.

564 In the less serious cases, we think, the arguments in favour of lump sums should normally prevail. There is no doubt that any system of periodic payments would require more elaborate and expensive administration than the present system of lump sum awards; and although … we would not rule out periodic payments otherwise than for serious and long term pecuniary losses, we would not expect such cases to be very common. It is in the interests of the community that most of the smaller tort claims, even for future pecuniary loss, should be finally, and so far as possible quickly, disposed of.

565 Most of us feel, however, that in cases of death or serious and lasting injury the arguments in favour of lump sums are not convincing. The finality of the lump sum may operate to the plaintiff's disadvantage if the forecast on which it is based proves erroneous for example by overstating his chances of physical recovery or underestimating the effect of inflation on income from his invested damages. Its relative immediacy may not be preferable to the provision of assured long term financial support, either from the point of view of the plaintiff or from the point of view of the community who have to support him if his damages prove inadequate. Indeed, the payment of supplementary benefit to a person whose damages were exhausted would be a form of double compensation paid for by taxpayers. Finally, the freedom of choice offered by the lump sum is something which the plaintiff would not have enjoyed if he had not been injured.

566 By contrast, periodic payments seem to us to offer important advantages in serious cases, although we recognise that it would not be practicable to eliminate all the uncertainties of awards of damages for future pecuniary loss.

QUESTION

The Pearson Commission in the extract ante referred to uncertainties remaining in a system of periodic payments for future pecuniary loss. What are they?

NOTE

The survey for the Oxford Centre for Socio-Legal Studies (*Harris* et al, pp. 122–125) found that many of those awarded lump sums used them to buy tangible, durable items; about half saved some for the future; a fifth put some towards a house or other improvements; but only a quarter used some for living expenses (although, of course, expenditure on durable items and houses presumably represents a saving on future living expenses). Claimants explained that they had accepted lower sums in out-of-court settlements than they had expected because of their urgent need for money, or their fear of further trouble or delay. H. Genn, *Hard Bargaining: Out of Court Settlement in Personal Injury Actions*, pp. 75–78, found that insurance claims inspectors, and lawyers, had the greatest difficulty in estimating the quantum of damages, especially in relation to future loss of earnings. This imprecision and uncertainty made it hard for claimants to argue convincingly against low offers of settlement.

■ The Supreme Court Act 1981

32A Orders for provisional damages for personal injuries
(1) This section applies to an action for damages for personal injuries in which there is proved or admitted to be a chance that at some definite or indefinite time in the future the injured person will, as a

result of the act or omission which gave rise to the cause of action, develop some serious disease or suffer some serious deterioration in his physical or mental condition.

(2) Subject to subsection (4) below, as regards any action for damages to which this section applies in which a judgment is given in the High Court, provision may be made by rules of court for enabling the court, in such circumstances as may be prescribed, to award the injured person—

(a) damages assessed on the assumption that the injured person will not develop the disease or suffer the deterioration in his condition; and

(b) further damages at a future date if he develops the disease or suffers the deterioration.

(3) Any rules made by virtue of this section may include such incidental, supplementary and consequential provisions as the rule-making authority may consider necessary or expedient.

(4) Nothing in this section shall be construed—

(a) as affecting the exercise of any power relating to costs, including any power to make rules of court relating to costs; or

(b) as prejudicing any duty of the court under any enactment or rule of law to reduce or limit the total damages which would have been recoverable apart from any such duty.

NOTE

For detail on the operation of this power, see CPR Rule 41 and the Practice Direction on Provisional Damages, and for the position concerning provisional damages and the Fatal Accidents Acts 1976, see note 2, p. 284, ante.

■ Tort Law in Practice: Appearance and Reality in Reforming Periodical Payments of Damages

Richard Lewis in *Emerging Issues in Tort Law*, edited by J.W. Neyers, E. Chamberlain, and S.G.A. Pitel (2007) pp. 487–492 (footnotes omitted)

Almost twenty years ago the concept of a structured settlement was imported from North America and first used in the UK in order to provide continuing lifetime payments for seriously injured claimants. However, the idea was slow to develop. Proposals for a structure were easily defeated if either of the parties objected. To counter this, legislation has now removed the veto: taking into account the needs of the claimant, a judge can make a periodical payments order even if it is against the wishes of either or even both of the parties; The court must consider making such an order in any case involving future financial loss. The lump sum award is thus under attack.

II. THE FIRST JUDICIALLY APPROVED STRUCTURE

Traditionally damages for personal injury in the UK were always paid by means of a lump sum, and never a pension. It did not matter that the compensation was for losses that might be suffered in the future: both the monthly wage that the accident victim may have lost, and the continuing costs of care that would have to be met, were compensated by one large payment. In recent years this once-and-for-all lump sum system has been subject to increasing criticism. In particular, it results in much uncertainty and imposes upon a claimant an enormous responsibility for safeguarding the future. Inflation and the vagaries of the returns on investment of the lump sum can result in rapid erosion of the compensation. As a result, a new form of payment via a structured settlement has made limited inroads into the use of lump sums. In effect, such a settlement usually converts the traditional lump sum into a series of payments derived from an annuity and these continue to be made no matter how long the claimant lives. In addition, these payments can he protected against price inflation and are free of tax.

These attractions of periodical payments were clearly illustrated in 1989 by the first judicially approved structure for a UK resident. *Kelly v Dawes* arose out of a tragic road accident which took place three years earlier. Catherine Kelly was then a 22-year-old nurse, and was a passenger in a car driven by her husband, Andrew, a stonemason. Not far from their home they were involved in a road accident caused entirely by the negligence of the driver of the other vehicle. Both drivers were killed. Catherine lost the husband she had recently married, and suffered catastrophic injuries herself. The judge described the effect upon her as follows:

> She was transformed from a lively young woman…into a bedridden invalid with grossly impaired neurological functions, almost totally unaware of her surroundings, totally dependent on skilled nursing care and the devoted attention of her loving parents and family. Her condition will not improve for the rest of her life, in respect of which her life expectancy has been reduced to some 20 years. That figure is the product of a compromise medical view between doctors whose best guesses are on either side of the figure agreed.

In seeking damages on her behalf, Catherine's father was keen to ensure that she would be looked after in a private nursing home for the rest of her life. Any money that might accrue to her estate upon her death was not an important consideration. Instead the major concern was that, given her uncertain life expectancy, the damages should be managed in order to ensure that, if she lived longer than the projected period, there would continue to be money to pay for her care. The best means of achieving this proved to be via a structure.

The settlement provided for most of Catherine's damages to be used to purchase an annuity from a life insurance company. The damages could be used in this way because there remained additional capital to provide a contingency fund for unexpected events. This reserve fund derived from the equity in Catherine's home, and from the estate she inherited from her husband, including the damages for his fatal accident. The annuity purchased with the damages was for an 'impaired life'. This meant that it provided a substantially higher annual return than a standard policy because the life insurer believed that the accident had reduced Catherine's life expectancy and the payments would therefore be made over a shorter period of time. In fact, for rating purposes the life office treated her as thirty-five years older than she actually was.

The major benefits of structuring the award were clearly revealed: the index-linked instalment payments were free of tax, and to last either for the rest of Catherine's life or for ten years, whichever proved longer. They would therefore ensure that she could continue to be kept at a private nursing home even if she lived beyond her projected span of years. Based on certain assumptions, the monies from a lump sum settlement invested in the conventional portfolio of fixed interest stocks and blue-chip shares would have been exhausted within twelve years, whereas the monthly payments under a structure would continue to be made. In addition, Catherine's father would not be subject to the stress of having to invest and be responsible for a lump sum greater than most people would encounter in their lifetime. Nor would the cost of obtaining investment advice have to be met. The financial advantages of the structure and the peace of mind it gave to the concerned relatives were clearly shown.

Ten years after the settlement Catherine's father spoke about his decision to seek periodical payments. He said:

> I wanted the certainty of knowing that money would be available for the rest of Cathy's life. Looking back, the medical experts' view on her life expectation ranged from 5–10 years to 10–20 years. Physically, Cathy is in better shape now and if they come back today, they would say that she could live another 20–30 years from now. They got it wrong…. I have absolute peace of mind in knowing that, even if I am no longer here, there will still be money available for Cathy's needs for the rest of her life.

III. THE NEED TO IMPOSE PERIODICAL PAYMENTS

Since *Kelly* there have been over 1,500 seriously-injured people who have received part of their compensation in the form of periodical payments. However, further expansion of structured settlements has been hindered in several ways. One difficulty has been the refusal by many lawyers to give proper consideration to the merits of the alternative form of payment, even though they might be liable for failing to do so. Their reluctance to investigate structures has partly been attributed to the innate conservatism of the legal profession, together with ignorance or misconception of what might be involved. Sometimes structures have been raised as a possibility only at a late stage in the proceedings, by which time the claimant and his or her advisors have become used to the idea of receiving a lump sum and are suspicious of the change in approach. As a result, in practice, structures have been examined only in a minority of the cases in which they could have been sought. For example, in 2001–02 the National Health Service (NHS) paid over 500 claims in excess of £100,000 and yet less than ten per cent involved a structured settlement.

The overall result has been that, largely through inertia, the lump sum has retained its dominance. A major factor in this has been the ability of either of the parties to object and thereby defeat with ease any proposed settlement based on periodical payments. It is this veto which is directly attacked by the new legislation. After lengthy consultation, the parties' veto was removed by the Courts Act 2003 with effect from 2005.

■ The Damages Act 1996[2]

2(1) A court awarding damages for future pecuniary loss in respect of personal injury—

(a) may order that the damages are wholly or partly to take the form of periodical payments, and
(b) shall consider whether to make that order.

(2) A court awarding other damages in respect of personal injury may, if the parties consent, order that the damages are wholly or partly to take the form of periodical payments.

(3) A court may not make an order for periodical payments unless satisfied that the continuity of payment under the order is reasonably secure.

(4) For the purpose of subsection (3) the continuity of payment under an order is reasonably secure if—

(a) it is protected by a guarantee given under section 6 of or the Schedule to this Act,
(b) it is protected by a scheme under section 213 of the Financial Services and Markets Act 2000 (compensation) (whether or not as modified by section 4 of this Act), or
(c) the source of payment is a government or health service body.

(5) An order for periodical payments may include provision—

(a) requiring the party responsible for the payments to use a method (selected or to be selected by him) under which the continuity of payment is reasonably secure by virtue of subsection (4);
(b) about how the payments are to be made, if not by a method under which the continuity of payment is reasonably secure by virtue of subsection (4);
(c) requiring the party responsible for the payments to take specified action to secure continuity of payment, where continuity is not reasonably secure by virtue of subsection (4);
(d) enabling a party to apply for a variation of provision included under paragraph (a), (b) or (c).

(6) Where a person has a right to receive payments under an order for periodical payments, or where an arrangement is entered into in satisfaction of an order which gives a person a right to receive periodical payments, that person's right under the order or arrangement may not be assigned or charged without the approval of the court which made the order; and—

(a) a court shall not approve an assignment or charge unless satisfied that special circumstances make it necessary, and
(b) a purported assignment or charge, or agreement to assign or charge, is void unless approved by the court.

(8) An order for periodical payments shall be treated as providing for the amount of payments to vary by reference to the retail prices index (within the meaning of section 833(2) of the Income and

---

[2] [Substituted or amended by ss. 100–101 of the Courts Act 2003.]

Corporation Taxes Act 1988) at such times, and in such a manner, as may be determined by or in accordance with Civil Procedure Rules.

(9) But an order for periodical payments may include provision—

(a) disapplying subsection (8), or

(b) modifying the effect of subsection (8).

2A Periodical payments: supplementary

(1) Civil Procedure Rules may require a court to take specified matters into account in considering—

(a) whether to order periodical payments;

(b) the security of the continuity of payment;

(c) whether to approve an assignment or charge.

(2) For the purposes of section 2(4)(c) . . . "government or health service body" means a body designated as a government body or a health service body by order made by the Lord Chancellor.

(5) In section 2 "damages" includes an interim payment which a court orders a defendant to make to a claimant.

(7) Section 2 is without prejudice to any power exercisable apart from that section.

2B Variation of orders and settlements

(1) The Lord Chancellor may by order enable a court which has made an order for periodical payments to vary the order in specified circumstances (otherwise than in accordance with section 2(5)(d)).

(2) The Lord Chancellor may by order enable a court in specified circumstances to vary the terms on which a claim or action for damages for personal injury is settled by agreement between the parties if the agreement—

(a) provides for periodical payments, and

(b) expressly permits a party to apply to a court for variation in those circumstances.

(4) An order under this section may apply (with or without modification) or amend an enactment about provisional or further damages.

4 Enhanced protection for periodical payments

(1) Subsection (2) applies where—

(a) a person has a right to receive periodical payments, and

(b) his right is protected by a scheme under section 213 of the Financial Services and Markets Act 2000 (compensation), but only as to part of the payments.

(2) The protection provided by the scheme shall extend by virtue of this section to the whole of the payments.

(3) Subsection (4) applies where—

(a) one person ("the claimant") has a right to receive periodical payments from another person ("the defendant"),

(b) a third person ("the insurer") is required by or in pursuance of an arrangement entered into with the defendant (whether or not together with other persons and whether before or after the creation of the claimant's right) to make payments in satisfaction of the claimant's right or for the purpose of enabling it to be satisfied, and

(c) the claimant's right to receive the payments would be wholly or partly protected by a scheme under section 213 of the Financial Services and Markets Act 2000 if it arose from an arrangement of the same kind as that mentioned in paragraph (b) but made between the claimant and the insurer.

(4) For the purposes of the scheme under section 213 of that Act—

(a) the claimant shall be treated as having a right to receive the payments from the insurer under an arrangement of the same kind as that mentioned in subsection (3)(b),

(b) the protection under the scheme in respect of those payments shall extend by virtue of this section to the whole of the payments, and

(c) no person other than the claimant shall be entitled to protection under the scheme in respect of the payments.

(5) In this section "periodical payments" means periodical payments made pursuant to—

(a) an order of a court in so far as it is made in reliance on section 2 above (including an order as varied), or

(b) an agreement in so far as it settles a claim or action for damages in respect of personal injury (including an agreement as varied).

(6) In subsection (5)(b) the reference to an agreement in so far as it settles a claim or action for damages in respect of personal injury includes a reference to an undertaking given by the Motor Insurers' Bureau (being the company of that name incorporated on 14th June 1946 under the Companies Act 1929), or an Article 75 insurer under the Bureau's Articles of Association, in relation to a claim or action in respect of personal injury.

6 Guarantees for public sector settlements

(1) This section applies where—

(a) a claim or action for damages for personal injury is settled on terms whereby the damages are to consist wholly or partly of periodical payments; or

(b) a court awarding damages for personal injury makes an order incorporating such terms.

(2) If it appears to a Minister of the Crown that the payments are to be made by a body in relation to which he has, by virtue of this section, power to do so, he may guarantee the payments to be made under the agreement or order.

(3) The bodies in relation to which a Minister may give such a guarantee shall, subject to subsection (4) below, be such bodies as are designated in relation to the relevant government department by guidelines agreed upon between that department and the Treasury.

(4) A guarantee purporting to be given by a Minister under this section shall not be invalidated by any failure on his part to act in accordance with such guidelines as are mentioned in subsection (3) above.

(5) A guarantee under this section shall be given on such terms as the Minister concerned may determine but those terms shall in every case require the body in question to reimburse the Minister, with interest, for any sums paid by him in fulfilment of the guarantee.

(8) In this section "government department" means any department of Her Majesty's government in the United Kingdom and for the purposes of this section a government department is a relevant department in relation to a Minister if he has responsibilities in respect of that department.

7 Interpretation

(1) …[I]n this Act "personal injury" includes any disease and any impairment of a person's physical or mental condition and references to a claim or action for personal injury include references to such a claim or action brought by virtue of the Law Reform (Miscellaneous Provisions) Act 1934 and to a claim or action brought by virtue of the Fatal Accidents Act 1976.

QUESTION

As the extract at p. 550, ante reveals, 'structured settlements' are based on an initial assessment of the lump sum. How do you think periodical payments under the 1996 Act are assessed (and see Lewis (2006) 69 MLR 418 at 427–430)?

NOTES

1. For comment on s. 2, see the article by Lewis from which the extract was taken at p. 550, ante and that mentioned in the Question, ante.
2. The version of s. 2 above was substituted by the Courts Act 2003 and came into force on 1 April 2005. Prior to the substitution, the Damages Act had only allowed periodical payments if both parties consented. In *Wells v Wells* [1999] 1 AC 345, [1998] 3 All ER 481 Lord Steyn referred to this and commented ([1998] 3 All ER at p. 502):

   Such agreement is never, or virtually never, forthcoming. The present power to order periodic payments is a dead letter. The solution is relatively straightforward. The court ought to be given the power of its own motion to make an award for periodic payments rather than a lump sum in appropriate cases. Such a power is perfectly consistent with the principle of full compensation for pecuniary loss. Except perhaps for the distaste of personal injury lawyers for change to a familiar system, I can think of no substantial argument to the contrary. But the judges cannot make the change. Only Parliament can solve the problem.

3. The power granted in s. 2A to make rules has been exercised: see CPR 41. There is also an accompanying Practice Direction on Periodical Payments. Under s. 1 of the Practice Direction, when the court is considering whether to make a periodical payments order, which by CPR 41.7 requires it to consider the type of award which 'best meets the claimant's needs', it should take into account the scale of the annual payments, the views of the claimant and the defendant as to the form of the award and, in the case of the claimant, the nature of his or her financial advice about the choice. The power to make rules concerning variation of periodical payments has also been exercised: see the Damages (Variation of Periodical Payments) Order 2005, SI 2005/841, which allows the court to order that the periodical payments may be altered if at the trial it is proved that there is a chance at some time in the future the claimant will as a result of the tort 'develop some serious disease or suffer some serious deterioration or that his physical or mental condition which has been adversely affected by the tort will significantly improve'.
4. Fatal Accidents Act claims are also covered by the periodical payments provisions: see *McGregor on Damages*, para. 36–004.
5. Note that periodical payment orders (PPOs) under the 1996 Act, as with payments made under structured settlements, are free of tax.

■ The Politics and Economics of Tort Law: Judicially Imposed Periodical Payments of Damages
R. Lewis (2006) 69 MLR 419 at 422–425 (footnotes omitted)

If a personal injury case comes to court and involves future pecuniary loss, the judge has no choice but to consider making a PPO. An order can be made even if not requested or wanted by the parties or where they envisaged alternative provision. The cases affected will usually be those involving serious injury where claims for future earnings or the cost of care are made. Although relatively few in number, these are much more likely to come before a court and be in the public eye. They are also where the claimant is likely to be in the most need and in the greatest danger of being under-compensated. Although the court's power to make a PPO is limited, the threat of its use affects the bargaining position of the parties in most major cases.

The power to make a PPO is limited in three particular respects. Firstly, it cannot be exercised in respect of damages for past pecuniary or non-pecuniary loss unless the parties agree. This means that only a minority of all claims in tort are in danger of having an order imposed because over ninety per cent involve only these two heads of damage and have no element of future loss. The typical claim is for a very small sum of money and it will continue to be disposed of by means of a lump sum. The preponderance of these small claims in the system is reflected in the fact that non-pecuniary loss accounts for about two thirds of the overall damages bill and past financial loss for about a further quarter. However, these percentages change considerably in serious injury cases when future loss becomes much more important. For example, it has been estimated that, on average, 83 per cent of a claim exceeding £250,000 against the NHS comprises future loss. In addition, it must be emphasised that these few serious injury cases are responsible for a substantial amount of the overall damages bill: in 2002 insurers estimated that although only one per cent of cases resulted in a payment of £100,000 or more, they accounted for 32 per cent of the total compensation received by claimants. It is in cases involving this level of damages, albeit a minority of all claims, where the new rules will have the greatest effect.

The second limitation upon the court's power is that these new orders can only be made if the continuity of payment is 'reasonably secure.' Legislation prescribes that the payments will be secure if either they are to be made by a Government or health service body, or if they are protected by a compensation scheme which guarantees payment in the event of an insurer's insolvency. In effect, this means that orders can be made in the overwhelming majority of personal injury claims. One exception is that the Motor Insurers Bureau is not covered, but it has already been able to demonstrate successfully to a court that it is sufficiently secure for a PPO to be made in cases in which it is involved. Those against whom questions of security will be raised include Lloyd's syndicates, the medical defence organisations, offshore insurance companies, and private self-insured defendants. Even in these cases, a PPO could still be made and the security requirement met if the payments were arranged via the purchase of an annuity from a life insurer which was covered by the scheme guaranteeing payment in the event of insolvency.

The third limitation on the power to impose periodical payments is more important in practice. It is that it can only be exercised if the case comes to court for the judge to make the order. Even though cases of serious injury are more likely to come to court, it remains the case that only a minority of them do so. It is true that the court will always be involved in cases involving children or patients unable to manage their affairs because then there must be formal approval of any settlement. However, in such cases the parties are effectively seeking an order by consent, and the legislative requirements of PPOs need not apply. This means, for example, that a wider range of annuities can be used. This is a tremendously important point, and one which hitherto many practitioners have failed to appreciate. Settlements out of court therefore can still take place in one of two ways. Firstly, there can still be private agreements to pay damages periodically. In effect, this means that much of the previous structured settlement regime survives, even though the use of that term has now been expunged from the legislation. Alternatively, if neither party wants periodic payments to be considered, there is every incentive to settle privately for a lump sum. No matter what the court might have considered to be the needs of the claimant, the parties will get their wish for such a deal if they keep their negotiations behind closed doors and avoid judicial involvement.

It would be a mistake to assume that because new legislation has been passed it will necessarily be used in the way intended by the draftsman. The legal rules provide a framework for bargaining between the parties, and the results can be very different from the picture of litigation envisaged by the black letter lawyer. Within the shadow of the new rules it is likely that a number of claimants will try to take advantage of the removal of the defendant's veto: they will threaten to take the case to court and burden the defendant with a PPO involving uncertain liabilities unless there is agreement to a higher lump sum than previously was on offer. Exactly the same tactic has been used to obtain higher lump sums instead of provisional damages awards...in relation to variation of payments. Somewhat less successfully, insurers may also use the threat of periodical payments to bargain harder with a claimant who is set on receiving a lump sum, or worried about whether the court's assessment of needs will correspond to his own. Can a judge be trusted to leave enough of a contingency lump sum fund to provide for unexpected events? Claimants may also be concerned that even an index-linked settlement may not be enough to pay for their future care costs. Because of these worries bargains will be struck to settle out of court. The experience of other countries is that these deals have undermined the power to make periodic awards to such an extent that 'lump-sum settlements have like termites reduced the rent system to but a hollow shell.' Because negotiations between the parties will water down the effect of the reform we can expect lump sums to be commonly used even in the majority of serious injury cases involving future financial losses. But the possibility of imposing a PPO substantially influences the bargaining position of the parties, and it is in that sense that all serious injury cases are affected.

NOTES

1. One factor that will affect the desirability or otherwise of periodical payments to claimants and defendants is the rate at which they are indexed: see s. 2(8) and (9) of the Act. Contrast the position in s. 1(1) and (2) of the Damages Act 1996, noted along with certain case law at pp. 532–533, ante (although, of course, the former provisions were substituted by the Courts Act 2003). It has been seen that it is very difficult to persuade a court to act under s. 1(2); however, the attitude is different in the case of s. 2(9). In *Flora v Wakom (Heathrow) Ltd* [2006] 4 All ER 492, [2006] EWCA Civ 1103 lump sums and periodical payments were regarded as 'entirely different in character…as…mechanism[s] for compensating for [future pecuniary] loss', and it was decided that it did not have to be an exceptional case before the court could depart from the RPI. In the later decision of *Tameside and Glossop Acute Services NHS Trust v Thompstone* [2008] 1 All ER 553, [2008] EWCA Civ 5, the Court of Appeal regarded itself as bound by *Flora,* but also clearly approved of it. There is a concern that the RPI will not accurately reflect wage rises. The issue in *Thompstone* concerned periodical payments in relation to the cost of future care (where wages will be an important element), and here the Court of Appeal approved of the use of an index (known as ASHE 6115) rather than the RPI. The court also gave general guidance as to the approach in periodical payment cases. An index might be the most suitable even though it was not perfect, and the suitability of a particular index should be assessed in accordance with the following criteria (see [75]): 'i) Accuracy of match of the particular data series to the loss or expenditure being compensated; ii) Authority of the collector of the data; iii) Statistical reliability; iv) Accessibility; v) Consistency over time; vi) Reproducibility in the future; vii) Simplicity and consistency in application'. The court envisaged that in a substantial case there would be evidence from the claimant's financial adviser as to the appropriate form of order which would best meet the claimant's needs, but was in general opposed to contrary evidence on this point being presented by the defendant. On the *Thompstone* case, see H Trusted [2008] JPIL 44.

2. For argument as to the extra costs that the new regime will impose on defendants, see Lewis, (2006) 69 MLR at 436–439. On the other hand, he also argues (pp. 439–441) that the 'catalyst for the reform lay within Government itself', and that bodies such as the NHS which can self-fund periodical payments, as opposed to having to buy annuities, will gain in the short term, though not in the long term.

3. The pressure on claimants to settle because of the delay in obtaining a court award of damages was referred to in the note, p. 549, ante. One way in which advance payments may be encouraged is through 'split' trials, in which the issue of liability can be dealt with early, leaving assessment of damages to a later hearing, pending which interim payments may be made. Since 1990, the court has had power to order a split trial of its own motion.

4.   The lapse of time between the injury and the payment of damages would leave the claimant seriously out of pocket, especially in times of inflation, if interest was not awarded on lump sum damages. Section 35A of the Supreme Court Act 1981 (inserted by the Administration of Justice Act 1982) provides that interest should be awarded unless the court is satisfied that there are special reasons for not doing so. In *Cookson v Knowles* [1979] AC 556, [1978] 2 All ER 604 the House of Lords held that claims for pecuniary loss up to the date of trial should bear interest at half the current short-term interest rates, but no interest should be awarded on future pecuniary loss since that has not yet been sustained. In *Wright v British Railways Board* [1983] 2 AC 773, [1983] 2 All ER 698 the House of Lords held that interest at the moderate rate of 2 per cent from the date of service of the writ to date of judgment should be made in respect of non-pecuniary loss. It is customary to calculate the multiplier at the date of trial. This has been criticised for leading to excessive awards and also for putting a premium on delay. In *Pritchard v J H Cobden Ltd* [1988] Fam 22, [1987] 1 All ER 300, the Court of Appeal rejected an attempt to reverse this practice. This case had taken nine years to come to trial; interest was disallowed for two years reflecting the period in which the claimant's solicitor had been guilty of unjustified delay. See further *Laurence v Chief Constable of Gloucestershire* [2000] PIQR Q349. In its 2004 report *Pre-judgment Interest on Debts and Damages* Law Com. No. 287, the Law Commission recommended that its proposals for compound interest should apply to awards of damages for past pecuniary losses, but not to awards for non-pecuniary losses in personal injury cases: see generally Part VII of the report.

(e) Effect of death on causes of action

■ The Law Reform (Miscellaneous Provisions) Act 1934

1. Effect of death on certain causes of action

(1) Subject to the provisions of this section, on the death of any person after the commencement of this Act all causes of action subsisting against or vested in him shall survive against, or, as the case may be, for the benefit of, his estate. Provided that this subsection shall not apply to causes of action for defamation....

(1A) The right of a person to claim under section 1A of the Fatal Accidents Act 1976 (bereavement) shall not survive for the benefit of his estate on his death.[3]

(2) Where a cause of action survives as aforesaid for the benefit of the estate of a deceased person, the damages recoverable for the benefit of the estate of that person:-

(a) shall not include
(ii) any exemplary damages;
(iii) any damages for loss of income in respect of any period after that person's death;[4]

. . .

(c) where the death of that person has been caused by the act or omission which gives rise to the cause of action, shall be calculated without reference to any loss or gain to his estate consequent on his death, except that a sum in respect of funeral expenses may be included.

(4) Where damage has been suffered by reason of any act or omission in respect of which a cause of action would have subsisted against any person if that person had not died before or at the same time

---

[3] Inserted by the Administration of Justice Act 1982, s. 4.   [4] Ibid.

as the damage was suffered, there shall be deemed, for the purposes of this Act, to have been subsisting against him before his death such cause of action in respect of that act or omission as would have subsisted if he had died after the damage was suffered.

(5) The rights conferred by this Act for the benefit of the estates of deceased persons shall be in addition to and not in derogation of any rights conferred on the dependants of deceased persons by the Fatal Accidents Acts 1846 to 1908,[5]...and so much of this Act as relates to causes of action against the estates of deceased persons shall apply in relation to causes of action under the said Acts as it applies in relation to other causes of action not expressly excepted from the operation of subsection (1) of this section.

NOTES

1. *Section 1(1).* This Act comes into play if either the claimant or the defendant dies before the commencement of proceedings. The Act enables the personal representatives of the deceased victim to recover such damages as he might have received had he lived, subject to certain exceptions. Likewise, if the tortfeasor dies there can be recovery against the estate. In *Ashley v Chief Constable of Sussex Police* [2008] 2 WLR 975, [2008] UKHL 25, noted p. 716, post, it was decided that an action being pursued for a vindicatory purpose would not be ruled out by the reference to 'the benefit of the estate' in s. 1(1) of the 1934 Act. Quite independently of the survival of the claimant's cause of action under this Act, the surviving dependants have their own cause of action for economic loss which they have suffered as a result of the death of their breadwinner (p. 280, ante) (s. 1(5)).

    Because of the exceptions, where the claimant dies instantaneously as the result of the accident that is the subject of the proceedings, the estate might find difficulty in establishing a cause of action in respect of any loss apart from funeral expenses. Section 1(2)(a)(ii) removes any right to sue for future lost earnings (see ante). Instantaneous death rules out any claim for past lost earnings, medical or other expenses and loss of amenity. As far as pain and suffering is concerned, *Hicks v Chief Constable of the South Yorkshire Police* [1992] 1 All ER 690, CA, [1992] 1 AC 310, [1992] 2 All ER 65, HL establishes that it is open to trial judges to hold that the pain suffered in the moments before death as a result of the injury that resulted in death do not count as 'physical injury' capable of supporting an action for damages. The House of Lords also said that fear of death occasioned by the fatal incident could not by itself constitute actionable injury.

2. *Section 1(1A).* The action for damages for bereavement is discussed p. 285, ante.

3. *Section 1(2)(a)*

    (i) Exemplary or punitive damages are discussed at p. 493, ante.

    (ii) The exclusion of 'loss of income in respect of any period after that person's death' gives effect to the substance of recommendations by the Law Commission (Law Com. No. 56, Draft Bill, cl. 16(3)), and the Pearson Commission vol. 1, paras. 433–437. The intention is to exclude the possibility of double recovery against the defendant. This possibility arose because in *Pickett v British Rail Engineering Ltd* [1980] AC 136, [1979] 1 All ER 774 (p. 552, ante), the House of Lords decided that a *living* claimant could claim damages in respect of the income which he would have earned during the years of his life which he expects to 'lose' as a result of the tort, and in *Gammell v Wilson* [1982] AC 27, [1981] 1 All ER 578, the House of

---

[5] This now includes a reference to the Fatal Accidents Act 1976.

Lords held that this applied as well to a person who had died when the action was commenced. 'Double' recovery could arise if either (a) the dependants were not the beneficiaries of the estate, so that the defendants would have to pay damages both to the estate for the 'lost years', and to the dependants for their loss of dependency in those years, or (b) the damages awarded to the estate for the 'lost years' were substantially larger than the damages for loss of dependency; in this case, if the dependants were the beneficiaries of the estate they would be entitled to the larger amount. P. Cane and D. Harris (1983) 46 MLR 478 criticise the new s. 1(2)(a)(ii) as a 'lesson in how not to reform the law' on a number of grounds. One of these is that the abolition of damages for the 'lost' years in *all* claims by estates, even where the dependants have no claim for loss of dependency (e.g. where the injury to the claimant caused a loss in his earnings but he died from some other non-tortious cause), leaves the dependants in some cases without provision. Note also that if the claimant dies as a result of an unrelated incident before recovering damages, the estate cannot claim for the lost years. On the other hand, the beneficiaries of the estate may still receive a windfall of damages for loss of amenity suffered by (even) an unconscious victim before he died (p. 511, ante). It is also worth nothing that s. 1(2)(a)(ii) refers only to loss of 'income'. This leaves open the possibility that the estate may claim for the loss of opportunity to inherit capital, which falls within the *Pickett* rule: see *Adsett v West* [1983] QB 826, [1983] 2 All ER 985. The Government, however, has no intention of changing the current position on the 'lost years': see the DCA's Consultation Paper (CP 9/07), chap. 1, para. 25.

4.   *Section 1(2)(c).* The damages recoverable are the same as would have been recovered by the victim subject to the exceptions mentioned. Apart from funeral expenses, this is true also where the death has been caused by the act or omission which gives rise to the cause of action, for example the loss of an annuity ceasing on death or the gain arising from a life insurance policy payable upon death are disregarded.

5.   *Section 1(4).* This deals with the situation where the tortfeasor dies.

3 PROPERTY DAMAGE

NOTE

Space precludes consideration of this topic, on which the student is referred to the standard works on Tort.

PART TWO

SPECIFIC DUTIES AND INTERESTS

CHAPTER NINE

LIABILITY FOR DEFECTIVE PREMISES

In earlier chapters we have examined the main elements of the tort of negligence, defences and the assessment of damages. We turn now to a consideration of liability for defective premises in which judge-made duties and immunities have been affected by statute. This area can be divided into (1) the occupier's liability, and (2) the non-occupier's liability in respect of premises. The materials in this chapter will reveal examples of different levels at which 'duty' may be formulated. The occupier's duty to 'visitors' is described as a 'common duty of care' by statute (p. 564, post). The non-occupier doing work on the premises owes a duty of care at common law, while the statutory duty to build dwellings properly (Defective Premises Act 1972, s. 1, p. 603, post) appears to be a high one. The occupier's duty to trespassers has historically been regarded as lower than the normal duty of care and the student will have to consider the extent to which the trespasser today, in the light of s. 1 of the Occupiers' Liability Act 1984 (p. 587, post) is still owed a lower duty.

1 OCCUPIERS' LIABILITY

(a) To 'visitors'

NOTE

A consideration of occupiers' liability at common law had to take into account particular categories of entrant on to the premises. The duty of care required of the occupier varied according to whether the lawful entrant was entering under a contract, or as a non-contractual invitee or licensee. The Occupiers' Liability Act 1957 ('a little gem of a statute' per Lord Hailsham, 443 H. L. Debs. (5th Series) col. 720) followed from the Third Report of the Law Reform Committee (Cmd. 9305) 1954 and it brings the invitee and the licensee together into the category of lawful visitors to whom the occupier owes the common duty of care (s. 1(2)). The Act overall was 'codification-plus', a mixture of restatement and amendment, according to Carnwath LJ in *Maguire v Sefton Metropolitan Borough Council* [2006] 1 WLR 2550, [2006] EWCA Civ 316, in which his Lordship also testifies as to the satisfactory way in which the Act has worked. Decisions under the Act have been said to be very 'fact sensitive' (*Jolley v Sutton London Borough Council* [2000] 3 All ER 409, [2000] 1 WLR 1082). Trespassers remain outside the scope of this Act, as section 1(b) of this chapter will show, and their position is regulated by more recent legislation.

Some doubt has arisen as to the scope of the Act. At common law, if the claimant was injured by the occupier's activities on the premises (e.g. driving a car) as opposed to their static condition, then liability could be based on a duty of care arising from those activities. The relevance of the category of lawful entrant in which the law placed the claimant was confined to the 'occupancy duty' rather than the 'activity duty'. (For these terms, see F. H. Newark (1954) 17 MLR 102 at 109; and see generally P. M. North, *Occupiers' Liability* (London, 1971), pp. 71–80.) Writers have disagreed whether the 1957 Act now governs the 'activity duty' as well as the 'occupancy duty', but today it seems to be accepted that the Act does not apply to the former, which will be governed by the tort of negligence. See e.g. *Ogwo v Taylor* [1988] AC 431, [1987] 3 All ER 961, where the House of Lords decided it as a common law negligence case, and see *Winfield & Jolowicz*, pp. 392–393. Consider further the views in *Ferguson v Welsh* [1987] 3 All ER 777, [1987] 1 WLR 1553 and see the discussion in *Fairchild v Glenhaven Funeral Services Ltd* [2002] 1 WLR 1052, [2003] EWCA Civ 1881, when that case was in the Court of Appeal (the matter did not arise on the appeal to the House of Lords). A linked facet of this issue is whether an injury truly arises from a danger due to the state of the premises: see *Tomlinson v Congleton Borough Council* [2003] 3 All ER 1122, [2003] UKHL 47 (p. 590, post). In any event, *Winfield & Jolowicz* state (at p. 393), the issue is rarely likely to be of very much practical significance for there 'will typically be little if any difference between the duty of care in negligence and the common duty of care as applied to current activities' (though consider note 5, p. 569, post). Following from this, it is interesting to note that the Act provides an example of a statutory duty of care in which Parliament has attempted to lay down certain factors for the courts' consideration (see s. 2(3)–(5)). The student should consider how far these factors would be relevant in the common law tort of negligence. The common law, nevertheless, is relevant in interpreting the Act: see s. 1(2), post.

■ The Occupiers' Liability Act 1957

LIABILITY IN TORT

1. Preliminary.—(1) The rules enacted by the two next following sections shall have effect, in place of the rules of the common law, to regulate the duty which an occupier of premises owes to his visitors in respect of dangers due to the state of the premises or to things done or omitted to be done on them.

(2) The rules so enacted shall regulate the nature of the duty imposed by law in consequence of a person's occupation or control of premises and of any invitation or permission he gives (or is to be treated as giving) to another to enter or use the premises, but they shall not alter the rules of the common law as to the persons on whom a duty is so imposed or to whom it is owed; and accordingly for the purpose of the rules so enacted the persons who are to be treated as an occupier and as his visitors are the same (subject to subsection (4) of this section) as the persons who would at common law be treated as an occupier and as his invitees or licensees.

(3) The rules so enacted in relation to an occupier of premises and his visitors shall also apply, in like manner and to the like extent as the principles applicable at common law to an occupier of premises and his invitees or licensees would apply, to regulate—

    (a) the obligations of a person occupying or having control over any fixed or moveable structure, including any vessel, vehicle or aircraft; and

(b) the obligations of a person occupying or having control over any premises or structure in respect of damage to property, including the property of persons who are not themselves his visitors.

[(4) A person entering any premises in exercise of rights conferred by virtue of –

(a) section 2 (1) of the Countryside and Rights of Way Act 2000 , or
(b) an access agreement or order under the National Parks and Access to the Countryside Act 1949,

is not, for the purposes of this Act, a visitor of the occupier of those premises.][1]

2. Extent of occupier's ordinary duty.—(1) An occupier of premises owes the same duty, the 'common duty of care', to all his visitors, except in so far as he is free to and does extend, restrict, modify or exclude his duty to any visitor or visitors by agreement or otherwise.

(2) The common duty of care is a duty to take such care as in all the circumstances of the case is reasonable to see that the visitor will be reasonably safe in using the premises for the purposes for which he is invited or permitted by the occupier to be there.

(3) The circumstances relevant for the present purpose include the degree of care, and of want of care, which would ordinarily be looked for in such a visitor, so that (for example) in proper cases—

(a) an occupier must be prepared for children to be less careful than adults; and
(b) an occupier may expect that a person, in the exercise of his calling, will appreciate and guard against any special risks ordinarily incident to it, so far as the occupier leaves him free to do so.

(4) In determining whether the occupier of premises has discharged the common duty of care to a visitor, regard is to be had to all the circumstances, so that (for example)—

(a) where damage is caused to a visitor by a danger of which he had been warned by the occupier, the warning is not to be treated without more as absolving the occupier from liability, unless in all the circumstances it was enough to enable the visitor to be reasonably safe; and
(b) where damage is caused to a visitor by a danger due to the faulty execution of any work of construction, maintenance or repair by an independent contractor employed by the occupier, the occupier is not to be treated without more as answerable for the danger if in all the circumstances he had acted reasonably in entrusting the work to an independent contractor and had taken such steps (if any) as he reasonably ought in order to satisfy himself that the contractor was competent and that the work had been properly done.

(5) The common duty of care does not impose on an occupier an obligation to a visitor in respect of risks willingly accepted as his by the visitor (the question whether a risk was so accepted to be decided on the same principles as in other cases in which one person owes a duty of care to another).

(6) For the purposes of this section, persons who enter premises for any purpose in the exercise of a right conferred by law are to be treated as permitted by the occupier to be there for that purpose, whether they in fact have his permission or not.

3. Effect of contract on occupier's liability to third party.—(1) Where an occupier of premises is bound by contract to permit persons who are strangers to the contract to enter or use the premises, the duty of care which he owes to them as his visitors cannot be restricted or excluded by that contract, but (subject to any provision of the contract to the contrary) shall include the duty to perform his obligations under the contract, whether undertaken for their protection or not, in so far as those obligations go beyond the obligations otherwise involved in that duty.

(2) A contract shall not by virtue of this section have the effect, unless it expressly so provides, of making an occupier who has taken all reasonable care answerable to strangers to the contract for dangers due to the faulty execution of any work of construction, maintenance or repair or other like operation by persons other than himself, his servants and persons acting under his direction and control.

[1] Amended by the countryside and Rights of Way Act 2000.

(3) In this section 'stranger to the contract' means a person not for the time being entitled to the benefit of the contract as a party to it or as the successor by assignment or otherwise of a party to it, and accordingly includes a party to the contract who has ceased to be so entitled.

(4) Where by the terms or conditions governing any tenancy (including a statutory tenancy which does not in law amount to a tenancy) either the landlord or the tenant is bound, though not by contract, to permit persons to enter or use premises of which he is the occupier, this section shall apply as if the tenancy were a contract between the landlord and the tenant.

...

LIABILITY IN CONTRACT

5. Implied term in contracts.—(1) Where persons enter or use, or bring or send goods to, any premises in exercise of a right conferred by contract with a person occupying or having control of the premises, the duty he owes them in respect of dangers due to the state of the premises or to things done or omitted to be done on them, in so far as the duty depends on a term to be implied in the contract by reason of its conferring that right, shall be the common duty of care.

(2) The foregoing subsection shall apply to fixed and moveable structures as it applies to premises.

(3) This section does not affect the obligations imposed on a person by or by virtue of any contract for the hire of, or for the carriage for reward of persons or goods in, any vehicle, vessel, aircraft or other means of transport, or by or by virtue of any contract of bailment.

...

GENERAL

6. Application to Crown.—This Act shall bind the Crown, but as regards the Crown's liability in tort shall not bind the Crown further than the Crown is made liable in tort by the Crown Proceedings Act 1947, and that Act and in particular section to of it shall apply in relation to duties under sections two to four of this Act as statutory duties.

NOTES

1. Section 4 of the above Act was repealed by s. 6(4) of the Defective Premises Act 1972, but see now s. 4 of that Act, p. 605, post.

2. Various provisions of the Unfair Contract Terms Act 1977 which affect the operation of s. 2(1) and s. 2(5) of the 1957 Act are set out pp. 462–463, ante.

3. The 1957 Act does not apply to non-visitors. Most non-visitors (see note 4, post for an exception) are now covered by the Occupiers' Liability Act 1984, discussed at p. 587, post. The most important category of non-visitors to whom the 1984 Act, rather than the 1957 Act, applies is trespassers. It is therefore often an important preliminary point in an occupiers' liability case to establish whether the claimant was a trespasser or not. For treatment of the law of trespass to land, see p. 778, post. Two specific points which arise most naturally in the context of occupiers' liability deserve mention at this point, however. Both relate to the point that the person who has the occupier's permission to be on the premises cannot be a trespasser.

    The first concerns the extent to which people have permission to be on the premises. Where the occupier invites the other person to enter the premises there is clearly express permission. But even express permission is usually taken to be subject to an implied limitation that the entrant will use the permission only for reasonable purposes (see e.g. *The Calgarth* [1927] P 93). Entrants who enter for one purpose and then switch to another, unreasonable, purpose may find that they count as non-visitors for the purposes of occupiers' liability (and consider *Tomlinson v Congleton Borough Council* [2003] 3 All ER 1122, [2003] UKHL 47 (p. 573, post).

There is also implied permission, for example, to walk up the drive to the front door of a house (*Dunster v Abbott* [1953] 2 All ER 1572, [1954] 1 WLR 58). Implied permission of a rather more artificial kind lies behind the doctrine, less invoked since the 1984 Act but still, apparently, good law (see the Court of Appeal in *Jolley v Sutton London Borough Council* [1998] 3 All ER 559, [1998] 1 WLR 1546) that children who are tempted to enter premises by 'allurements'—objects attractive to childish curiosity—do not count as trespassers. See e.g. *Glasgow Corpn v Taylor* [1922] 1 AC 44, *Lynch v Nurdin* (1841) 1 QB 29; *Holdman v Hamlyn* [1943] KB 664, [1943] 2 All ER 137. Cf. *Keown v Coventry Healthcare NHS Trust* [2006] 1 WLR 953, [2006] EWCA Civ 39 at [32].

The second point concerns the authority of non-occupiers to give permission to enter. Those whom the occupier has given actual authority to invite others in can confer permission, but the law extends that power beyond those with actual authority to those with 'ostensible' authority. 'Ostensible' authority means that the occupier has somehow given the impression to potential entrants that a person other than the occupier does have authority to give permission to enter. That person is then taken to have such authority even if there is no actual authority, as long as the invitee has no notice of the lack of actual authority. In *Ferguson v Welsh* [1987] 3 All ER 777, [1987] 1 WLR 1553, for example, the defendant hired a contractor to demolish a wall under a contract which said that the contractor was not to sub-contract the work. The contractor nevertheless hired the claimant as a sub-contractor. Although the defendant won the case on other grounds, the House of Lords said that he was not a trespasser because the contractor had 'ostensible' authority to invite him in. In the general law of agency, 'ostensible' authority is limited in scope to the 'ordinary' or 'normal' authority that a person in that position would have, so that, for example, where a bouncer does not have actual authority to allow persons of a particular type to enter a club, there might nevertheless be ostensible authority to give permission to that kind of person to enter the club, but there would not be ostensible authority to give permission to enter parts of the building that guests would not normally be permitted to enter by bouncers, the administrative offices, for example.

4. The category of 'visitor' does not include persons exercising private rights of way vis-à-vis the owner of the servient tenement (*Holden v White* [1982] QB 679, [1982] 2 All ER 328) since they were not his invitees or licensees at common law. Those exercising public rights of way were also not invitees or licensees at common law and therefore are not 'visitors' under the 1957 Act (*Greenhalgh v British Railways Board* [1969] 2 QB 286, [1969] 2 All ER 114). This was later confirmed by the House of Lords in *McGeown v Northern Ireland Housing Executive* [1995] 1 AC 233, [1994] 3 All ER 53. In the case of highways maintainable at the public expense the position is now governed by the Highways Act 1980, on which see *Winfield & Jolowicz*, pp. 689–692 and for the effect of the Occupiers' Liability Act 1984, see note 8, p. 589, post.

The traditional common law position in relation to public and private rights of way was that there could be liability for misfeasance (e.g. repairing badly, causing fresh danger) but not for non-feasance (e.g. not repairing) on the part of the owner of the land which was subject to the right of way. This limited liability to those exercising public rights of way was also confirmed in *McGeown*, where the claimant was injured when she tripped in a hole on a footpath which had become a public right of way. The path was part of a way to and from the house of which her husband, with whom she lived, was the tenant. If the path had not been subject to a public right of way, the claimant would have had an implied licence to use it and thus would have been a visitor to whom the common duty of care was owed; however, the House of Lords held that the creation of the public right of way extinguished the claimant's position as a licensee which she would otherwise have enjoyed and her claim failed.

Though agreeing with this, Lord Browne-Wilkinson, in a separate speech, reserved his opinion as to the position where, before the creation of the public right of way, the claimant would have been an invitee rather than a licensee: indeed, his understanding was that the rest of their Lordships were not deciding that it was impossible still to be an invitee in that situation. Lord Browne-Wilkinson saw a danger, if the position were otherwise, that an occupier of, for example, a shopping centre might allow the premises to become a public right of way so as to reduce the obligation owed in respect of entrants' safety. In his view where one was dealing with an invitee rather than a licensee, 'there is no logical inconsistency between the [claimant's] right to be on the premises in exercise of the right of way and his actual presence there in response to the express or implied invitation of the occupier. It is the invitation which gives rise to an occupier's duty of care to an invitee' ([1994] 3 All ER at p. 64).

One problem with Lord Browne-Wilkinson's view of the opinion of his brethren is to reconcile it with a passage in Lord Keith's speech with which the rest of their Lordships agreed and which seems to treat licensees and invitees in a similar fashion. His Lordship stated ([1994] 3 All ER at p. 62): 'The concept of licensee or visitor involves that the person in question has at least the permission of the relevant occupier to be in a particular place. Once a public right of way has been established, there is no question of permission being granted by the owner of the solum to those who choose to use it. They do so as of right and not by virtue of any licence *or invitation*' (emphasis added).

Another problem with Lord Browne-Wilkinson's reservation is that it involves the resurrection of a distinction between invitees and licensees which the 1957 Act did so much to eliminate and which courts might be reluctant to revive, albeit for a limited purpose.

Finally there is a fundamental objection to Lord Browne-Wilkinson's proposal. The response he envisages from shopping centres and malls is surely inherently unlikely. Shopping centres derive extensive benefits from being able to privatise public space, especially rights to control access to the centre and to exclude people whose presence might offend other potential customers. Indeed, these rights are potentially so powerful that some writers see them as a threat to human rights. See K. Gray and S. Gray [1999] European Human Rights Law Review 46 and consider further *Appleby v United Kingdom* (2003) 37 EHRR 38.

McGeown was an appeal to the House of Lords from Northern Ireland, and the Northern Ireland courts revisited the issue in *Campbell v Northern Ireland Housing Executive* [1995] NI 167. In this case the Northern Ireland Court of Appeal took the view that the distinction drawn for this purpose between invitees and licensees by Lord Browne-Wilkinson was not consistent with Lord Keith's speech, citing, inter alia, the passage quoted ante. Hutton LCJ also noted that the distinction between invitees and licensees had been expressly removed by the Occupiers' Liability Act 1957. Nevertheless, he did express the hope that there would be Parliamentary intervention in this area.

On *McGeown*'s case, see T. Sutton [1995] Conv. 57; F. R. Barker and N. D. Parry (1995) 15 LS 355; J. Murphy [1997] Conv. 362. *Howarth*, pp. 372–373 argues, in respect of Lord Keith's concern that liability for non-feasance would be too burdensome on landowners, that the expense and difficulty of maintenance of a right of way would be taken into account in the question of breach.

5. On the relation of s. 2(1) and s. 5(1) of this Act see *Sole v W J Hallt Ltd* [1973] QB 574, [1973] 1 All ER 1032. Swanwick J held that in general a person who came within the scope of s. 5(1) could also claim in tort as a visitor under s. 2(1). (For criticism see *Street*, p. 210, note 110, who regards the decision 'as almost certainly wrong since the Act specifically limits visitors (to whom . . . s. 2(1) refers) to those who were either invitees or licensees at common law'.) Swanwick J's decision that the claimant could sue in contract or in tort at his option was an important one since, having found a breach of the common duty of care, he also held that the claimant's contributory negligence broke the chain of causation in the contract action under s. 5 but not in the tort action under s. 2, where it merely led to a reduction in the damages. Are there any additional advantages or disadvantages which might lead a claimant to choose one of these actions rather than the other?

Section 5 may, in fact, provide an example where the distinction between 'occupancy' and 'activity' duties is important. *Maguire v Sefton Metropolitan Borough Council* [2006] 1 WLR 2550, [2006] EWCA Civ 316, which concerned an injury incurred on an exercise machine at a leisure centre, suggests that if an action is brought in relation to an activity, then the party permitting entry by contract may, as an implied term of the contract, warrant that an independent contractor has taken care; however, if the action is classed as relating to occupancy, then s. 5 of the 1957 Act will apply and that contracting party as occupier who has employed an independent contractor will only be liable if he or she has not taken reasonable care. On *Maguire*, see further *Stevens*, p. 120.

(i) Occupation

■ Wheat v E Lacon & Co Ltd
House of Lords [1966] 1 All ER 582

Winn J had dismissed the appellant's action. The majority of Court of Appeal (Harman and Diplock LJJ), [1965] 2 All ER 700, dismissed her appeal, holding that the respondents had not owed the common duty of care to the appellant's deceased husband. On appeal to the House of Lords:

LORD DENNING: . . .
My Lords, the 'Golfer's Arms' at Great Yarmouth is owned by the respondents, the brewery company, E. Lacon & Co Ltd. The ground floor was run as a public house by Mr Richardson as manager for the respondents. The first floor was used by Mr and Mrs Richardson as their private dwelling. In the summer Mrs Richardson took in guests for her private profit. Mr and Mrs Wheat and their family were summer guests of Mrs Richardson. About 9 pm one evening, when it was getting dark, Mr Wheat fell down the back staircase in the private portion and was killed. Winn J held that there were two causes: (i) the handrail was too short because it did not stretch to the foot of the stairs; (ii) someone had taken the bulb out of the light at the top of the stairs.

The case raises this point of law: did the respondents owe any duty to Mr Wheat to see that the handrail was safe to use or to see that the stairs were properly lighted? That depends on whether the respondents were 'an occupier' of the private portion of the 'Golfer's Arms', and Mr Wheat was their 'visitor' within the Occupiers' Liability Act 1957: for, if so, the respondents owed him the 'common duty of care'.

In order to determine this question we must have resort to the law before the Occupiers' Liability Act 1957: for it is expressly enacted by s. 1(2) that the Act of 1957

'shall not alter the rules of the common law as to the person on whom a duty is so imposed or to whom it is owed; and accordingly . . . the persons who are to be treated as an occupier and as his visitors are the same ... as the persons who would at common law be treated as an occupier and as his invitees or licensees ...'

At the outset, I would say that no guidance is to be obtained from the use of the word 'occupier' in other branches of the law: for its meaning varies according to the subject-matter.

In the Occupiers' Liability Act 1957, the word 'occupier' is used in the same sense as it was used in the common law cases on occupiers' liability for dangerous premises. It was simply a convenient word to denote a person who had a sufficient degree of control over premises to put him under a duty of care towards those who came lawfully on to the premises. [Having referred to Lord Atkin's general principle in *Donoghue v Stevenson* [1932] AC at 580, LORD DENNING continued:] Translating this general principle into its particular application to dangerous premises, it becomes simply this: wherever a person has a sufficient degree of control over premises that he ought to realise that any failure on his part to use care may result in injury to a person coming lawfully there, then he is an 'occupier'. ... In order to be an 'occupier' it is not necessary for a person to have entire control over the premises. He need not have exclusive occupation. Suffice it that he has some degree of control. He may share the control with others. Two or more may be 'occupiers'. And whenever this happens, each is under a duty to use care towards persons coming lawfully on to the premises, dependent on his degree of control. If each fails in his duty, each is liable to a visitor who is injured in consequence of his failure, but each may have a claim to contribution from the other.

In *Salmond on Torts* (14th edn, 1965) p. 372, it is said that an 'occupier' is 'he who has the immediate supervision and control and the power of permitting or prohibiting the entry of other persons'. This definition was adopted by Roxburgh J in *Hartwell v Grayson Rollo and Clover Docks Ltd*[2] and by Diplock LJ in the present case.[3] There is no doubt that a person who fulfils that test is an 'occupier'. He is the person who says 'come in'; but I think that that test is too narrow by far. There are other people who are 'occupiers', even though they do not say 'come in'. If a person has any degree of control, over the state of the premises it is enough. The position is best shown by examining the cases in four groups.

First, where a landlord let premises by demise to a tenant, he was regarded as parting with all control over them. He did not retain any degree of control, even though he had undertaken to repair the structure. Accordingly, he was held to be under no duty to any person coming lawfully on to the premises, save only to the tenant under the agreement to repair.

Secondly, where an owner let floors or flats in a building to tenants, but did not demise the common staircase or the roof or some other parts, he was regarded as having retained control of all parts not demised by him. Accordingly, he was held to be under a duty in respect of those retained parts to all persons coming lawfully on to the premises. So he was held liable for a defective staircase in *Miller v Hancock*,[4] for the gutters of the roof in *Hargroves, Aronson & Co v Hartopp*[5] and for the private balcony in *Sutcliffe v Clients Investment Co.*[6] ... [T]he old cases still apply so as to show that the landlord is responsible for all parts not demised by him, on the ground that he is regarded as being sufficiently in control of them to impose on him a duty of care to all persons coming lawfully on to the premises.

Thirdly, where an owner did not let premises to a tenant but only licensed a person to occupy them on terms which did not amount to a demise, the owner still having the right to do repairs, he was regarded as being sufficiently in control of the structure to impose on him a duty towards all persons coming lawfully on to the premises. So he was held liable for a visitor who fell on the defective step to the front door in *Hawkins v Coulsdon and Purley UDC*;[7] and to the occupier's wife for the defective ceiling which fell on her in *Greene v Chelsea Borough Council.*[8] The extent of the duty was that owed to a licensee, but since the Act of 1957 the duty is the common duty of care to see that the structure is reasonably safe.

---

[2] [1947] KB 901 at 917.   [3] [1965] 2 All ER at p. 711, letter E.
[4] [1893] 2 QB 177, [1891–94] All ER Rep 736.   [5] [1905] 1 KB 472.   [6] [1924] 2 KB 746.
[7] [1954] 1 QB 319, [1954] 1 All ER 97.   [8] [1954] 2 QB 127, [1954] 2 All ER 318.

Fourthly, where an owner employed an independent contractor to do work on premises or a structure, the owner was usually still regarded as sufficiently in control of the place as to be under a duty towards all those who might lawfully come there. In some cases he might fulfil that duty by entrusting the work to the independent contractor: see *Haseldine v Daw & Son Ltd*[9] and s. 2(4) of the Act of 1957. In other cases he might only be able to fulfil it by exercising proper supervision himself over the contractor's work, using due diligence himself to prevent damage from unusual danger (see *Thomson v Cremin*[10] as explained by Lord Reid in *Davie v New Merton Board Mills Ltd*[11]). But in addition to the owner, the courts regarded the independent contractor as himself being sufficiently in control of the place where he worked as to owe a duty of care towards all persons coming lawfully there. He was said to be an 'occupier' also (see *Hartwell v Grayson Rollo and Clover Docks Ltd*[12]), but this is only a particular instance of his general duty of care (see *A C Billings & Sons Ltd v Riden*[13] per Lord Reid).

In the light of these cases, I ask myself whether the respondents had a sufficient degree of control over the premises to put them under a duty to a visitor. Obviously they had complete control over the ground floor and were 'occupiers' of it. But I think that they had also sufficient control over the private portion. They had not let it out to Mr Richardson by a demise. They had only granted him a licence to occupy it, having a right themselves to do repairs. That left them with a residuary degree of control which was equivalent to that retained by the Chelsea Corporation in *Greene*'s case.[8] They were in my opinion 'an occupier' within the Act of 1957. Mr Richardson, who had a licence to occupy, had also a considerable degree of control. So had Mrs Richardson, who catered for summer guests. All three of them were, in my opinion, 'occupiers' of the private portion of the 'Golfer's Arms'. There is no difficulty in having more than one occupier at one and the same time, each of whom is under a duty of care to visitors. The Court of Appeal so held in the recent case of *Fisher v CHT Ltd*.[14]

What did the common duty of care demand of each of these occupiers towards their visitors? Each was under a duty to take such care as 'in all the circumstances of the case' was reasonable to see that the visitor would be reasonably safe. So far as the respondents were concerned, the circumstances demanded that on the ground floor they should, by their servants, take care not only of the structure of the building, but also the furniture, the state of the floors and lighting, and so forth, at all hours of day or night when the premises were open. In regard to the private portion, however, the circumstances did not demand so much of the respondents. They ought to have seen that the structure was reasonably safe, including the handrail, and that the system of lighting was efficient; but I doubt whether they were bound to see that the lights were properly switched on or the rugs laid safely on the floor. The respondents were entitled to leave those day-to-day matters to Mr and Mrs Richardson. They, too, were occupiers. The circumstances of the case demanded that Mr and Mrs Richardson should take care of those matters in the private portion of the house. And of other matters, too. If they had realised that the handrail was dangerous, they should have reported it to the respondents.

We are not concerned here with Mr and Mrs Richardson. The judge has absolved them from any negligence and there is no appeal. We are only concerned with the respondents. They were, in my opinion, occupiers and under a duty of care. In this respect I agree with Sellers LJ[15] and Winn J, but I come to a different conclusion on the facts. I can see no evidence of any breach of duty by the respondents. So far as the handrail was concerned, the evidence was overwhelming that no-one had any reason before this accident to suppose that it was in the least dangerous. So far as the light was concerned, the proper inference was that it was removed by some stranger shortly before Mr Wheat went down the staircase. Neither the respondents nor Mr and Mrs Richardson could be blamed for the act of a stranger.

I would, therefore, dismiss this appeal.

---

[9] [1941] 2 KB 343, [1941] 3 All ER 156.   [10] (1941) [1953] 2 All ER 1185.

[11] [1959] AC 604 at 642–645, [1959] 1 All ER 346 at 348, pt 365–367.

[12] [1947] KB 901 at 912, 913.   [13] [1958] AC 240 at 250, [1957] 3 All ER 1 at 5.

[14] [1966] 1 All ER 88.   [15] [1965] 2 All ER at p. 705, letter B.

LORD MORRIS OF BORTH-Y-GEST: . . .

Who, then, for this purpose is an occupier? I say 'for this purpose' because in other circumstances there may be different identification (e.g. in connexion with rating or in connexion with the franchise). Section 1(1) of the Act of 1957 speaks of 'an occupier of premises'. Section 1(2) refers to 'a person's occupation or control of premises': it goes on to refer to 'any invitation or permission he gives (or is to be treated as giving) to another to enter or use the premises'. This, I think, shows that exclusive occupation is not necessary to constitute a person an occupier. . . . [T]here may be someone who would ordinarily be regarded as the occupier of premises while at the same time there may be another occupier who has 'control so far as material'. . . . Questions of fact may arise as to the nature and extent of occupation and control. . . . It was said by Jenkins LJ, in *Pegler v Craven*,[16] that the conception of 'occupation' is not necessarily and in all circumstances confined to the actual personal occupation of the person termed the occupier himself, and that in certain contexts and for certain purposes it extends to vicarious occupation by a caretaker or other servant or by an agent.

[His Lordship referred to the service agreement between the respondents and Mr Richardson, under which, inter alia, the respondents retained the right of entry for certain purposes, including inspection of the state of repair of the property. He also referred to the arrangements allowing guests and continued:] . . . The general result of the agreement and of the arrangements to which I have referred was that the respondents through their servant were in occupation of the whole premises. Their servant was required to be there. The contemplation, it would appear, was that the respondents would see to the condition of the premises and would effect any necessary repairs. As the residential part would constitute the home of the manager and his family it was reasonable inference, and it would be mutually assumed, that his privacy in regard to it would be respected. It would be mutually assumed that the respondents could not as of right enter that part save for the defined purpose of viewing its condition and state of repair. There was freedom for the manager or his wife to make contracts with and to receive and entertain visitors for reward.

The conclusion which I reach is that as regards the premises as a whole both the respondents and the manager were occupiers but that by mutual arrangement the respondents would not (subject to certain over-riding considerations) exercise control over some parts. They gave freedom to their manager to live in his home in privacy. They gave him freedom to furnish it as and how he chose. They gave him freedom to receive personal guests and also to receive guests for reward. I think it follows that both the respondents and the Richardsons were 'occupiers' vis-à-vis Mr Wheat and his party. . . .

LORD PEARSON: . . .

It seems to me clear that Mr and Mrs Richardson had at least some occupational control of the upper part of the premises to which the appeal relates. . . . I think that the respondents, however, also had some occupational control of the upper part of the premises. The lower part, the licensed part, was occupied by the respondents through their servant Mr Richardson and their agent Mrs Richardson for the purpose of the liquor-selling business of the respondents. The agreement applied to the whole of the premises without distinguishing between the two parts. Mr Richardson as manager for the respondents was required as well as entitled to occupy the whole of the premises on their behalf. He was required to live in the upper part for the better performance of his duties as manager of the business of the respondents. His right to live there, and the permission to take in paying guests, were perquisites of the employment. The paying guests, though invited by the Richardsons, had the respondents' permission to come and were therefore visitors of the respondents as well as of the Richardsons. The fact that the respondents gave permission for the Richardsons to take in paying guests is important as showing that the respondents had some control over the admission of persons to the upper part of the premises. The respondents did not themselves say 'Come in', but they authorised the Richardsons to say 'Come in'. The respondents had, under cl. 5 of the agreement, an express right to enter the premises for viewing the state of repair, and, as was conceded (correctly in my opinion), an implied right to do the repairs found to be necessary. It is fair to attribute to the respondents some responsibility for the

[16] [1952] 2 QB 69 at 74, [1952] 1 All ER 685 at 687.

safety of the premises for those who would, in pursuance of the authority given by the respondents, be invited to enter as paying guests the upper part of the premises. In matters relating to the design and condition of the structure they would be in a position to perform the common duty of care.

For these reasons I agree that there was, for the purposes of occupiers' liability, dual occupation of the upper part of the premises; but as there was no proof of negligence on the part of the respondents I would dismiss the appeal.

[VISCOUNT DILHORNE and LORD PEARCE delivered speeches in favour of dismissing the appeal.]

Appeal dismissed.

QUESTION

What was the basis for the decision that the respondents were in occupation of the area in question? Cf. *Stone v Taffe* [1974] 3 All ER 1016, [1974] 1 WLR 1575.

NOTE

The four groups of cases to which Lord Denning referred in *Wheat v Lacon* were cited in *Harris v Birkenhead Corpn* [1976] 1 All ER 341, [1976] 1 WLR 279 in support of the view that a person does not need to have actual physical possession to be an occupier. In the *Harris* case a house owned by one person but let out to a tenant was to be compulsorily purchased by the defendant local authority which served notices of entry on the tenant and the owner. The notices stated that the local authority would enter and take possession of the property fourteen days after service; however, possession was not taken for several months and in fact did not occur until shortly after the relevant date for the purposes of this case. Before the relevant date, though some months after the service of the notices of entry, the tenant left the house which thereafter remained unoccupied. The local authority argued that before it could be an occupier in this case there had to be an actual or symbolic taking of possession on its behalf. This contention was rejected. Whilst the possibility that someone with an immediate right to enter premises might not be an occupier until he physically took possession was left open, the local authority was held by the Court of Appeal to be an occupier on the facts of this case; the facts which were stressed were (a) that the house was uninhabited, and (b) that the previous occupier had left because of the local authority's lawful assertion of an immediate right to enter and control which allowed it at any time to dispossess the owner and the person occupying the house at the time of the assertion of the right.

(ii) The common duty of care—relevant factors

■ Tomlinson v Congleton Borough Council
House of Lords [2003] 3 All ER 1122

This case also contains discussion of the Occupiers' Liability Act 1984, and an extract dealing with that issue will be found at p. 590, post

LORD HOFFMANN:

[2] My Lords, in rural south-east Cheshire the early May Bank Holiday weekend in 1995 was unseasonably hot. John Tomlinson, aged 18, had to work until midday on Saturday 6 May but then met some of his friends and drove them to Brereton Heath Country Park, between Holmes Chapel and Congleton. The park covers about 80 acres. In about 1980 Congleton Borough Council acquired the

land, surrounding what was then a derelict sand quarry, and laid it out as a country park. Paths now run through woods of silver birch and in summer bright yellow brimstone butterflies flutter in grassy meadows. But the attraction of the park for John Tomlinson and his young friends was a 14-acre lake which had been created by flooding the old sand quarry. The sandy banks provided some attractive beaches and in hot weather many people, including families with children, went there to play in the sand, sunbathe and paddle in the water. A beach at the far end of the lake from the car park was where in fine weather groups of teenagers like John Tomlinson would regularly hang out. He had been going there since he was a child.

[3] After sitting in the hot sun for a couple of hours, John Tomlinson decided that he wanted to cool off. So he ran out into the water and dived. He had done the same thing many times before. But this time the dive was badly executed because he struck his head hard on the sandy bottom. So hard that he broke his neck at the fifth vertebra. He is now a tetraplegic and unable to walk....

OCCUPIERS' LIABILITY

[5] In these proceedings Mr Tomlinson sues the Congleton Borough Council and the Cheshire County Council, claiming that as occupiers of the park they were in breach of their duties under the Occupiers' Liability Acts 1957 and 1984. If one had to decide which of the two councils was the occupier, it might not be easy. Although the park belongs to the borough council, it is managed on their behalf by the countryside management service of the county council. The borough council provides the funds to enable the countryside management service to maintain the park. It is the county which employs the rangers who look after it. But the two councils very sensibly agreed that one or other or both was the occupier. Unless it is necessary to distinguish between the county council and the borough council for the purpose of telling the story, I shall call them both the council....

[7] At first Mr Tomlinson claimed that the council was in breach of its common duty of care under s 2(2). His complaint was that the premises were not reasonably safe because diving into the water was dangerous and the council had not given adequate warning of this fact or taken sufficient steps to prevent or discourage him from doing it. But then a difficulty emerged. The county council, as manager of the park, had for many years pursued a policy of prohibiting swimming or the use of inflatable dinghies or mattresses. Canoeing and windsurfing were allowed in one area of the lake and angling in another. But not swimming; except, I suppose, by capsized canoeists or windsurfers. Notices had been erected at the entrance and elsewhere saying 'DANGEROUS WATER. NO SWIMMING'. The policy had not been altogether effective because many people, particularly rowdy teenagers, ignored the notices. They were sometimes rude to the rangers who tried to get them out of the water. Nevertheless, it was hard to say that swimming or diving was, in the language of s 2(2), one of the purposes 'for which [Mr Tomlinson was] invited or permitted by the occupier to be there'. The council went further and said that once he entered the lake to swim, he was no longer a 'visitor' at all. He became a trespasser, to whom no duty under the 1957 Act is owed. The council cited a famous bon mot of Scrutton LJ in *The Calgarth, The Otarama* [1927] P 93 at 110: 'When you invite a person into your house to use the staircase, you do not invite him to slide down the banisters ...' This quip was used by Lord Atkin in *Hillen v ICI (Alkali) Ltd* [1936] AC 65 at 69, [1935] All ER Rep 555 at 558 to explain why stevedores who were lawfully on a barge for the purpose of discharging it nevertheless became trespassers when they went onto an inadequately supported hatch cover in order to unload some of the cargo. They knew, said Lord Atkin ([1936] AC 65 at 69–70, [1935] All ER Rep 555 at 558) that they ought not to use the covered hatch for this purpose 'for them for such a purpose it was out of bounds; they were trespassers'. So the stevedores could not complain that the barge owners should have warned them that the hatch cover was not adequately supported. Similarly, says the council, Mr Tomlinson became a trespasser and took himself outside the 1957 Act when he entered the water to swim.

[8] Mr Tomlinson's advisers, having reflected on the matter, decided to concede that he was indeed a trespasser when he went into the water...

[13] ...I have...come to the conclusion that the concession was rightly made. The duty under the 1984 Act was intended to be a lesser duty, as to both incidence and scope, than the duty to a lawful

visitor under the 1957 Act. That was because Parliament recognised that it would often be unduly burdensome to require landowners to take steps to protect the safety of people who came upon their land without invitation or permission. They should not ordinarily be able to force duties upon unwilling hosts. In the application of that principle, I can see no difference between a person who comes upon land without permission and one who, having come with permission, does something which he has not been given permission to do. In both cases, the entrant would be imposing upon the landowner a duty of care which he has not expressly or impliedly accepted. The 1984 Act provides that even in such cases a duty may exist, based simply upon occupation of land and knowledge or foresight that unauthorised persons may come upon the land or authorised persons may use it for unauthorised purposes. But that duty is rarer and different in quality from the duty which arises from express or implied invitation or permission to come upon the land and use it.

[14] In addition, I think that the concession is supported by the high authority of Lord Atkin in *Hillen's* case. There too, it could be said that the stevedores' complaint was that they should have been warned not to go upon the hatch cover and that logically this duty was owed to them, if at all, when they were lawfully on the barge.

[15] I would certainly agree with Longmore LJ [in the Court of Appeal in *Tomlinson*] that the incidence and content of the duty should not depend on the precise moment at which Mr Tomlinson crossed the line between the status of lawful visitor and that of trespasser. But there is no dispute that the act in respect of which Mr Tomlinson says that he was owed a duty, namely, diving into the water, was to his knowledge prohibited by the terms upon which he had been admitted to the park. It is, I think, for this reason that the council owed him no duty under the 1957 Act and that the incidence and content of any duty they may have owed was governed by the 1984 Act. But I shall later return to the question of whether it would have made any difference if swimming had not been prohibited and the 1957 Act had applied....

[LORD HOFFMANN proceeded to consider the position under the 1984 Act (see p. 590, post) but his comments at [25]–[29] (p. 590, post) concerning whether the injury was due to the state of the premises should also be considered at this point as they are relevance to the 1957 Act. His Lordship continued:]

[34] My Lords, the majority of the Court of Appeal appear to have proceeded on the basis that if there was a foreseeable risk of serious injury, the council was under a duty to do what was necessary to prevent it. But this in my opinion is an oversimplification. Even in the case of the duty owed to a lawful visitor under s 2(2) of the 1957 Act and even if the risk had been attributable to the state of the premises rather than the acts of Mr Tomlinson, the question of what amounts to 'such care as in all the circumstances of the case is reasonable' depends upon assessing, as in the case of common law negligence, not only the likelihood that someone may be injured and the seriousness of the injury which may occur, but also the social value of the activity which gives rise to the risk and the cost of preventative measures. These factors have to be balanced against each other....

[37] This is the kind of balance which has to be struck even in a situation in which it is clearly fair, just and reasonable that there should in principle be a duty of care or in which Parliament, as in the 1957 Act, has decreed that there should be. And it may lead to the conclusion that even though injury is foreseeable, as it was in *Bolton v Stone* [[1951] AC 850, [1951] 1 All ER 1078 (p.296, ante)], it is still in all the circumstances reasonable to do nothing about it....

THE BALANCE UNDER THE 1957 ACT

[39] My Lords, it will in the circumstances be convenient to consider first the question of what the position would have been if Mr Tomlinson had been a lawful visitor owed a duty under s 2(2) of the 1957 Act. Assume, therefore, that there had been no prohibition on swimming. What was the risk of serious injury? To some extent this depends upon what one regards as the relevant risk. As I have mentioned, the judge thought it was the risk of injury through diving while the Court of Appeal thought it was any kind of injury which could happen to people in the water. Although, as I have said, I am inclined to agree with the judge, I do not want to put the basis of my decision too narrowly. So I accept that we are

concerned with the steps, if any, which should have been taken to prevent any kind of water accident. According to the Royal Society for the Prevention of Accidents, about 450 people drown while swimming in the United Kingdom every year (see *Darby v National Trust* [2001] PIQR P372 at 374). About 25–35 break their necks diving and no doubt others sustain less serious injuries. So there is obviously some degree of risk in swimming and diving, as there is in climbing, cycling, fell walking and many other such activities.

[40] I turn then to the cost of taking preventative measures. Ward LJ described it (£5,000) as 'not excessive'. Perhaps it was not, although the outlay has to be seen in the context of the other items (rated 'essential' and 'highly desirable') in the borough council budget which had taken precedence over the destruction of the beaches for the previous two years.

[41] I do not however regard the financial cost as a significant item in the balancing exercise which the court has to undertake. There are two other related considerations which are far more important. The first is the social value of the activities which would have to be prohibited in order to reduce or eliminate the risk from swimming. And the second is the question of whether the council should be entitled to allow people of full capacity to decide for themselves whether to take the risk.

[42] The Court of Appeal made no reference at all to the social value of the activities which were to be prohibited. The majority of people who went to the beaches to sunbathe, paddle and play with their children were enjoying themselves in a way which gave them pleasure and caused no risk to themselves or anyone else. This must be something to be taken into account in deciding whether it was reasonable to expect the council to destroy the beaches.

[43] I have the impression that the Court of Appeal felt able to brush these matters aside because the council had already decided to do the work. But they were held liable for having failed to do so before Mr Tomlinson's accident and the question is therefore whether they were under a legal duty to do so. Ward LJ placed much emphasis upon the fact that the council had decided to destroy the beaches and that its officers thought that this was necessary to avoid being held liable for an accident to a swimmer. But the fact that the council's safety officers thought that the work was necessary does not show that there was a legal duty to do it. In *Darby's* case the claimant's husband was tragically drowned while swimming in a pond on the National Trust estate at Hardwick Hall. Miss Rebecca Kirkwood, the water and leisure safety consultant to the Royal Society for the Prevention of Accidents, gave uncontradicted evidence, which the judge accepted, that the pond was unsuitable for swimming because it was deep in the middle and the edges were uneven. The National Trust should have made it clear that swimming in the pond was not allowed and taken steps to enforce the prohibition. But May LJ said robustly that it was for the court, not Miss Kirkwood, to decide whether the Trust was under a legal duty to take such steps. There was no duty because the risks from swimming in the pond were perfectly obvious.

FREE WILL

[44] The second consideration, namely the question of whether people should accept responsibility for the risks they choose to run, is the point made by Lord Phillips MR in *Donoghue v Folkestone Properties Ltd* [2003] 3 All ER 1101 at [53] and which I said was central to this appeal. Mr Tomlinson was freely and voluntarily undertaking an activity which inherently involved some risk....

[45] I think it will be extremely rare for an occupier of land to be under a duty to prevent people from taking risks which are inherent in the activities they freely choose to undertake upon the land. If people want to climb mountains, go hang gliding or swim or dive in ponds or lakes, that is their affair. Of course the landowner may for his own reasons wish to prohibit such activities. He may be think that they are a danger or inconvenience to himself or others. Or he may take a paternalist view and prefer people not to undertake risky activities on his land. He is entitled to impose such conditions, as the council did by prohibiting swimming. But the law does not require him to do so.

[46] My Lords, as will be clear from what I have just said, I think that there is an important question of freedom at stake. It is unjust that the harmless recreation of responsible parents and children with buckets and spades on the beaches should be prohibited in order to comply with what is thought to

be a legal duty to safeguard irresponsible visitors against dangers which are perfectly obvious. The fact that such people take no notice of warnings cannot create a duty to take other steps to protect them. I find it difficult to express with appropriate moderation my disagreement with the proposition of Sedley LJ ([2003] 3 All ER 1122 at [45]) that it is 'only where the risk is so obvious that the occupier can safely assume that nobody will take it that there will be no liability'. A duty to protect against obvious risks or self-inflicted harm exists only in cases in which there is no genuine and informed choice, or in the case of employees, or some lack of capacity, such as the inability of children to recognise danger (see *British Railways Board v Herrington* [1972] 1 All ER 749, [1972] AC 877) or the despair of prisoners which may lead them to inflict injury on themselves (see *Reeves v Metropolitan Police Comr* [1999] 3 All ER 897, [2000] 1 AC 360).

[47] It is of course understandable that organisations like the Royal Society for the Prevention of Accidents should favour policies which require people to be prevented from taking risks. Their function is to prevent accidents and that is one way of doing so. But they do not have to consider the cost, not only in money but also in deprivation of liberty, which such restrictions entail. The courts will naturally respect the technical expertise of such organisations in drawing attention to what can be done to prevent accidents. But the balance between risk on the one hand and individual autonomy on the other is not a matter of expert opinion. It is a judgment which the courts must make and which in England reflects the individualist values of the common law.

[48] As for the council officers, they were obviously motivated by the view that it was necessary to take defensive measures to prevent the council from being held liable to pay compensation. The borough leisure officer said that he regretted the need to destroy the beaches but saw no alternative if the council was not to be held liable for an accident to a swimmer. So this appeal gives your Lordships the opportunity to say clearly that local authorities and other occupiers of land are ordinarily under no duty to incur such social and financial costs to protect a minority (or even a majority) against obvious dangers. On the other hand, if the decision of the Court of Appeal were left standing, every such occupier would feel obliged to take similar defensive measures. Sedley LJ was able to say that if the logic of the Court of Appeal's decision was that other public lakes and ponds required similar precautions, 'so be it'. But I cannot view this prospect with the same equanimity. In my opinion it would damage the quality of many people's lives....

[50] My Lords, for these reasons I consider that even if swimming had not been prohibited and the council had owed a duty under s 2(2) of the 1957 Act, that duty would not have required them to take any steps to prevent Mr Tomlinson from diving or warning him against dangers which were perfectly obvious....

[LORD NICHOLLS OF BIRKENHEAD agreed with LORD HOFFMANN's speech. LORD HUTTON and LORD HOBHOUSE OF WOOD-BOROUGH delivered speeches in which they agreed that a claim under the 1957 Act would fail. LORD SCOTT OF FOSCOTE delivered a speech in which he agreed with LORD HOFFMANN's speech, except that he would have regarded the claimant as a visitor and not a trespasser.]

NOTES

1. For an earlier example of a case where an occupier was not liable for an obvious danger, see *Staples v West Dorset District Council* [1995] PIQR P439 (and see further *Cotton v Derbyshire Dales District Council* (1994) Times, 20 June; *Darby v National Trust* [2001] PIQR P27, [2001] EWCA Civ 189). In *Staples*, for example, there was no duty to warn of slipping on algae that had visibly collected on the surface of the harbour wall at Lyme Regis.

2. The speeches in *Tomlinson* can be related to the topic of the 'compensation culture': see pp. 28 and 293, ante. Lord Hobhouse stated at [81] that the 'pursuit of an unrestrained culture of blame and compensation has many evil consequences and one is certainly the interference with the liberty of the citizen'. (Cf. the views of Ward LJ in *Corr v IBC*

Vehicles Ltd, (when that case was in the Court of Appeal [2006] 2 All ER 929, [2006] EWCA Civ 331 at [63]) on this comment of Lord Hobhouse.)

3.   The individualistic spirit to be found in *Tomlinson* was reflected in a different context—here s.3 of the Health and Safety Act 1974—in *Hampstead Heath Winter Swimming Club v Corporation of London* [2005] EWHC 713 (Admin), where it was stated that the risk run by an adult when swimming unsupervised with knowledge of the risk resulted from that adult's decision to swim and not from the permission of another body which allowed him to swim.

■ Roles v Nathan

Court of Appeal [1963] 2 All ER 908

A central heating boiler produced a great deal of smoke when lit, and a boiler engineer advised that the flues should be cleaned. Two chimney sweeps were, therefore, engaged to clean the flues of the boiler, which burnt coke and gave off carbon monoxide gas. The engineer warned the sweeps of the danger presented by the fumes, but his warning was disregarded, and one of the sweeps crawled into one of the flues. The next day, after the fire had gone out, the flues were cleaned by the sweeps. However, when the boiler was relit, the fumes still caused problems. Mr Collingwood, an expert, was brought in, and, although he warned the sweeps of the dangers of the fumes, it was only with great difficulty that he could get them to leave the room. Their attitude, he said, was that they were experts. He also advised them, amongst others, that, before the boiler was relit, the vent holes (an inspection chamber in the horizontal flue and a sweep hole in the vertical flue) should be sealed, and he repeated the warning about the gases. Some time later the boiler was lit by an unknown person (it was thought it might have been the caretaker, who later disappeared). Whilst the fire was burning, the sweeps carried on with and nearly completed their work. Only the sweep hole in the vertical flue remained to be sealed when they told Mr Corner (the occupier's son-in-law and the man at that time in charge of the rooms where the boiler was situated) that they would finish the job the next day. In fact they came back that evening, but died when they were overcome by the fumes. The widows of the two sweeps sued the occupier of the rooms.

LORD DENNING MR: . . .

It is quite plain that these men died because they were overcome by fumes of carbon monoxide. It would appear to a layman that the fumes must have come from the sweep-hole, but the judge on the evidence thought that they probably came from the boiler. But I do not think that it matters. The fumes came from the boiler or the sweep-hole or both. The question is whether anyone was at fault. The judge found Mr Corney guilty of negligence because he 'failed to take such care as should have ensured that there was no fire until the sweep-hole had been sealed'. He said: '. . . unhappily, he did not tell the caretaker to draw the fire, or at any rate not to stoke it up'. On this account he held that Mr Corney was at fault, and the occupier liable. But he found the two sweeps guilty of contributory negligence, and halved the damages. The judge said:

> 'That negligence [of the chimney sweeps] consisted in the knowledge that there was gas about, or probably would be, the way they ignored explicit warnings, and showed complete indifference to the danger which was pointed out to them in plain language, and this strange indifference to the fact that the fire was alight, when Mr Collingwood had said it ought not to be, until the sweep-hole had been sealed.'

The occupier now appeals and says that it is not a case of negligence and contributory negligence, but that, on the true application of the Occupiers' Liability Act 1957, the occupier was not liable at all. This is the first time that we have had to consider that Act. It has been very beneficial. It has rid us of those two unpleasant characters, the invitee and the licensee, who haunted the courts for years, and it has replaced them by the attractive figure of a visitor, who has so far given no trouble at all. The Act has now been in force six years, and hardly any case has come before the courts in which its interpretation has had to be considered. The draftsman expressed the hope[17] that the Act would

> 'replace a principle of the common law with a new principle of *the common law*: instead of having the judgment of Willes J[18] construed as if it were a statute, one is to have a statute which can be construed as if it were a judgment of Willes J.'

It seems that his hopes are being fulfilled. All the fine distinctions about traps have been thrown aside and replaced by the common duty of care....

[Having cited s. 2(3) of the 1957 Act, he continued:] That subsection shows that *Christmas v General Cleaning Contractors Ltd*[19] is still good law under this new Act. There a window cleaner (who was employed by independent contractors) was sent to clean the windows of a club. One of the windows was defective; it had not been inspected and repaired as it should have been. In consequence, when the window cleaner was cleaning it, it ran down quickly and trapped his hand, thus causing him to fall. It was held that he had no cause of action against the club. If it had been a guest who had his fingers trapped by the defective window, the guest could have recovered damages from the club. But the window cleaner could not do so. The reason is this: The householder is concerned to see that the windows are safe for his guests to open and close, but he is not concerned to see that they are safe for a window cleaner to hold on to. The risk of a defective window is a special risk, but it is ordinarily incident to the calling of a window cleaner, and so he must take care for himself, and not expect the householder to do so. Likewise, in the case of a chimney sweep who comes to sweep the chimneys or to seal up a sweep-hole. The householder can reasonably expect the sweep to take care of himself so far as any dangers from the flues are concerned. These chimney sweeps ought to have known that there might be dangerous fumes about and ought to have taken steps to guard against them. They ought to have known that they should not attempt to seal up the sweep-hole whilst the fire was still alight. They ought to have had the fire withdrawn before they attempted to seal it up, or at any rate they ought not to have stayed in the alcove too long when there might be dangerous fumes about. All this was known to these two sweeps; they were repeatedly warned about it, and it was for them to guard against the danger. It was not for the occupier to do it, even though he was present and heard the warnings. When a householder calls in a specialist to deal with a defective installation on his premises, he can reasonably expect the specialist to appreciate and guard against the dangers arising from the defect. The householder is not bound to watch over him to see that he comes to no harm. I would hold, therefore, that the occupier here was under no duty of care to these sweeps, at any rate in regard to the dangers which caused their deaths. If it had been a different danger, as for instance if the stairs leading to the cellar gave way, the occupier might no doubt be responsible, but not for these dangers which were special risks ordinarily incidental to their calling.

Even if I am wrong about this point, and the occupier was under a duty of care to these chimney sweeps, the question arises whether the duty was discharged by the warning that was given to them. This brings us to s. 2(4)....We all know the reason for this subsection. It was inserted so as to clear up the unsatisfactory state of the law as it had been left by the decision of the House of Lords in *London Graving Dock Co Ltd v Horton*.[20] That case was commonly supposed to have decided that, when a person comes on to premises as an invitee, and is injured by the defective or dangerous condition of the premises (due to the default of the occupier), it is, nevertheless, a complete defence for the occupier to

[17] See *Salmond on Tort* (13th edn) at pp. 512, 513, note 51.

[18] In *Indermaur v Dames* (1866) LR 1 CP 274 at 288.

[19] [1952] 1 KB 141, [1952] 1 All ER 39; affd sub nom *General Cleaning Contractor Ltd v Christmas* [1953] AC 180, [1952] 2 All ER 1110.

[20] [1951] AC 737, [1951] 2 All ER 1.

prove that the invitee knew of the danger, or had been warned of it. Supposing, for instance that there was only one way of getting in and out of premises, and it was by a footbridge over a stream which was rotten and dangerous. According to *Horton*'s case,[20] the occupier could escape all liability to any visitor by putting up a notice: 'This bridge is dangerous', even though there was no other way by which the visitor could get in or out, and he had no option but to go over the bridge. In such a case, s. 2(4)(a) makes it clear that the occupier would not[1] be liable. But if there were two footbridges, one of which was rotten, and the other safe a hundred yards away, the occupier could still escape liability, even today, by putting up a notice: 'Do not use this footbridge. It is dangerous. There is a safe one further upstream'. Such a warning is sufficient because it does enable the visitor to be reasonably safe.

I think that the law would probably have developed on these lines in any case; see *Greene v Chelsea Borough Council*,[2] where I ventured to say:

> '... knowledge or notice of the danger is only a defence when the plaintiff is free to act on that knowledge or notice so as to avoid the danger.'

But the subsection has now made it clear. A warning does not absolve the occupier unless it is enough to enable the visitor to be reasonably safe. Apply s. 2(4) to this case. I am quite clear that the warnings which were given to the sweeps were enough to enable them to be reasonably safe. The sweeps would have been quite safe if they had heeded these warnings. They should not have come back that evening and attempted to seal up the sweep-hole while the fire was still alight. They ought to have waited till next morning, and then they should have seen that the fire was out before they attempted to seal up the sweep-hole. In any case they should not have stayed too long in the sweep-hole. In short, it was entirely their own fault. The judge held that it was contributory negligence. I would go further and say that, under the Act, the occupier has, by the warnings, discharged his duty.

I would, therefore, be in favour of allowing this appeal and entering judgment for the defendants.

[HARMAN LJ delivered a judgment in favour of allowing the appeal. PEARSON LJ delivered a judgment in favour of dismissing the appeal, but differing 'only as to the interpretation of the evidence, and not as to any question of law'.]

Appeal allowed.

QUESTION

Suppose a claimant was injured by a danger in which the normal occupier of premises would not have been aware. If the occupier was in fact aware of this danger, and put up a warning notice, but in the wrong place, could he be liable? (Cf. *Woollins v British Celanese Ltd* (1966) 1 KIR 438.)

NOTES

1. Firemen obviously have special skills in dealing with fires and on the position of firemen entering property, see *Ogwo v Taylor* [1988] AC 431, [1987] 3 All ER 961, where the claim by a fireman against the person who started the fire (who was the occupier) was decided as a common law negligence claim by the House of Lords. Cf. s. 2(3)(b) of the 1957 Act. Liability under that Act can be based on events after the commencement of the fire. An occupier might be liable to an injured fireman if, for example, he

---

[1] [The word should be 'nowadays'—[1963] 1 WLR 1117 at 1124.]
[2] [1954] 2 QB 127 at 139, [1954] 2 All ER 318 at 325.

negligently failed to warn him of an unexpected danger. Note, however, the view of the House of Lords in *Bermingham v Sher Bros* 1980 SC 67 (dealing with the Occupiers' Liability (Scotland) Act 1960) that there is no duty to provide a safe way of getting into and out of the premises throughout the duration of a fire.

2. *Roles v Nathan* discussed s. 2(3)(b) of the 1957 Act. The other limb of s. 2(3) (i.e. s. 2(3) (a)) requires an occupier to expect children to be less careful than adults. On the other hand, there is the balancing factor that parents have some responsibility for the safety of their children. An occupier is entitled to rely upon parents acting reasonably in protecting their offspring from danger, which is obvious to an adult: see *Simkiss v Rhondda Borough Council* (1982) 81 LGR 460 at 467 referring to the pre-1957 Act case of *Glasgow Corpn v Taylor* [1922] 1 AC 44. Consider further the pre-1957 Act case of *Phipps v Rochester Corpn* [1955] 1 QB 450, [1955] 1 All ER 129, which was also cited in *Simkiss* and where Devlin J stated ([1955] 1 All ER at p. 143):

> A licensor [occupier] who tacitly permits the public to use his land without discriminating between its members must assume that the public may include little children. But as a general rule he will have discharged his duty towards them if the dangers which they may encounter are only those which are obvious to a guardian or of which he has given a warning comprehensible by a guard-ian. To every general rule there are, of course, exceptions. A licensor cannot divest himself of the obligation of finding out something about the sort of people who are availing themselves of his permission and the sort of use they are making of it. He may have to take into account the social habits of the neighbourhood. No doubt, there are places where little children go to play unaccompanied. If the licensor knows or ought to anticipate that, he may have to take steps accordingly. But the responsibility for the safety of little children must rest primarily on the parents; it is their duty to see that such children are not allowed to wander about by themselves, or, at the least, to satisfy themselves that the places to which they do allow their children to go unaccompanied are safe for them to go to. It would not be socially desirable if parents were, as a matter of course, able to shift the burden of looking after their children from their own shoulders to those of persons who happen to have accessible bits of land. Different considerations may well apply to public parks or to recognised playing grounds where parents allow their children to go unaccompanied in the reasonable belief that they are safe.

3. Section 2(4)(b) deals with the occupier's liability for independent contractors. See *Ferguson v Welsh* [1987] 3 All ER 777, [1987] 1 WLR 1553. In recent years, there has been debate about the extent to which the occupier (or more generally the employer) of an independent contractor has any duty to check upon the insurance position/ financial viability of the contractor. See *Gwilliam v West Hertfordshire Hospitals NHS Trust* [2003] QB 443, [2002] EWCA Civ 1041; *Bottomley v Todmorden Cricket Club* [2004] PIQR P18, [2003] EWCA Civ 1575; *Naylor (t/a Mainstreet) v Payling* [2004] PIQR P36, [2004] EWCA Civ 560. The result of these cases (not all of which concerned the 1957 Act) seems to be that the employer of a contractor may, as part of discharging his duty of reasonable care, be obliged to check whether his contractor carries appropriate insurance as the attitude to this may be evidence of the contractor's ability to do the job properly. On the other hand, where reasonable steps (separate from any inquiry as to the insurance position) have been taken in the selection of the contractor, no inquiry into the insurance position is required. For discussion of this issue in a more general context, see note 2, p. 1100, post.

4. Breach of duty is, of course, not enough by itself. Remoteness considerations are as relevant under the 1957 Act as they are at common law—see e.g. *Jolley v Sutton London Borough Council* [2000] 3 All ER 409, [2000] 1 WLR 1082, noted p. 421, ante; *Morgan v*

Blunden (1986) Times, 1 February. See also *Cunningham v Reading Football Club Ltd* [1992] PIQR P141, in which the defendant football club was held liable under the 1957 Act and at common law for injuries sustained by police officers when they were attacked by supporters of the visiting team. Drake J said that the defendant club was negligent in not maintaining its stadium so that visiting supporters found it easy to tear lumps of concrete from the terraces and throw them at the police. Drake J met the obvious point that the club could not be held liable for the deliberate acts of third party intervenors by referring to the 'inevitability' test developed by Oliver LJ in *Lamb v Camden London Borough Council* [1981] QB 625, [1981] 2 All ER 408: see p. 403, ante. It is submitted, however, that a football club should not be held responsible for the deliberate wrongful acts of third parties who have merely exploited the situation created by the club's negligence unless there is some control relationship between the club and the wrongdoers, some additional element of wrongdoing by the club, or some assumption of responsibility for the wrongdoers' actions by the club to the victims (see p. 406, ante).

(iii) Exclusion of liability

■ White v Blackmore
Court of Appeal [1972] 3 All ER 158

On a Sunday morning, the plaintiff's husband entered as a competitor for some 'jalopy' races. Later that day, he returned with his wife (the plaintiff), baby, and mother-in-law to the course, and paid the entrance fee for his wife and mother-in-law. As he was a competitor, he entered free. Near to the entrance there was one of several notices headed 'Warning to the public, Motor Racing is Dangerous'. It stated that it was 'a condition of admission that all persons having any connection with the promotion and/or organisation and/or conduct of the meeting, including...the drivers...of the vehicles...are absolved from all liabilities arising out of accidents causing damage or personal injury (whether fatal or otherwise) howsoever caused to spectators or ticketholders'. In addition, p. 2 of the programme, of which he received three copies when he entered the course with his family, contained a substantially similar clause, although the cover of the programme made no reference to there being any conditions. At one point after a race, the plaintiff's husband went across to join his family, who were behind the spectators' rope some way from the track, although he did not cross the rope. After another race had started, a car's wheel became entangled in the safety ropes about 1/3 of a mile away with the result that it pulled up the stakes holding these ropes, and the master stake, which held several ropes, close to where the husband was standing. He was thrown through the air, badly injured, and later died. His widow claimed damages from several defendants, two of whom were the chairman of the jalopy club which was holding the races and the racing organiser. The meeting was being held to aid a charity. The widow's claim was rejected by the trial judge on the ground that the maxim volenti non fit injuria applied. The plaintiff appealed, but her appeal was dismissed.

BUCKLEY LJ: ...
The learned judge found the defendants, who are sued personally and as representing the members of the Severn Valley Jalopy Club, guilty of negligence as organisers of the jalopy race meeting on account of the way in which the ropes were attached to the post near which the deceased was standing when the accident happened. Counsel for the defendants has submitted that the judge applied too high a standard in arriving at this decision. There was, in my judgment, material before the learned judge on which he could properly arrive at this conclusion, which I think should not be disturbed.

The judge went on to hold that the defendants were nevertheless entitled to succeed in their defence on the ground of the doctrine enshrined in the maxim volenti non fit injuria. Strictly, I think that that doctrine is not applicable in the present case, but the somewhat analogous law relating to exclusion of liability.

The doctrine of volenti non fit injuria affords a shield of defence to a party who would otherwise be liable in tort to an opponent who has by his conduct voluntarily encountered a risk which was fully known to him at the time.... The learned judge expressed the view that it might not have been at all obvious to the deceased that he was standing in a particularly dangerous place when the accident occurred. Accepting this, I do not think it can be said in the present case that the deceased had full knowledge of the risk which he was running.

In my judgment the case must turn on the effect of the various warnings which the deceased saw or had ample opportunity to see. If these warnings were, or any of them was, sufficient to exclude any duty of care on the part of the organisers of the meeting towards the deceased, the defendants were not guilty of negligence and consequently they do not need the shield of the doctrine of volenti. The learned judge in fact based his decision on these warnings.

[Having rejected the contention of counsel for the plaintiff that a contract had been concluded with the defendant when the plaintiff signed in the morning, BUCKLEY LJ continued:]

When the deceased returned with his family in the afternoon, the notice[3]...was prominently displayed near the entrance to the ground. The learned judge found as a fact that the deceased saw that notice and appreciated that it was a notice governing the conditions under which people were to be admitted to watch the racing.

No argument was addressed to us based on the Occupiers' Liability Act 1957, s. 2(4). This, I think, was right. To the extent that the notice at the entrance was a warning of danger, I agree with Lord Denning MR[4] that it did not enable a visitor to be reasonably safe, but the notice was more than a warning of a danger: it was designed to subject visitors to a condition that the classes of persons mentioned in it should be exempt from liability arising out of accidents. Section 2(4) has, it seems to me, no application to this aspect of the notice.

In my opinion, when the deceased came on to the field in the afternoon, he did so as a gratuitous licensee. I have already said that, in my view, no contract was made in the morning. The deceased made no payment for entry in the afternoon. Nothing that occurred in the morning could afford consideration for any contract entered into in the afternoon. In my judgment, no contract between the promoters and the deceased was made in the afternoon. The deceased remained willing to take part in the races and the promoters remained willing to allow him to do so. On the evidence, he was not, in my judgment, either bound or entitled contractually to take part in the races. In this state of affairs he was allowed on to the field free of charge.

I think that when the deceased came on to the field in the afternoon he did so in a dual capacity, as a prospective competitor and as a spectator. ... In the circumstances of this case I think any licence granted to the deceased in the morning was revocable summarily subject only to his right to recover his jalopy. If it was revocable, it was to a like extent variable.

What then was the effect of the situation which arose when the deceased returned to the field in the afternoon? It is clear that the occupier of land, who permits someone else to enter on that land as his licensee, can by imposing suitable conditions limit his own liability to the licensee in respect of any risks which may arise while the licensee is on the land (*Ashdown v Samuel Williams & Sons Ltd*[5]). The Occupiers' Liability Act 1957, which in s. 2(1) refers to an occupier excluding his duty of care to any visitor 'by agreement or otherwise', has not altered the law in this respect. [BUCKLEY LJ then proceeded to decide that the 'notice was sufficiently explicit in its application to the deceased' and continued:] The organisers are, I think, shown to have taken all reasonable steps to draw the condition contained in the

---

³ See the statement of facts, ante. ⁴ His dissenting judgment has been omitted.
⁵ [1957] 1 QB 409, [1957] 1 All ER 35.

notice to the attention of the deceased. The learned judge found that warnings of this character were a common feature at jalopy races with which the deceased would have been familiar. He also found, as I have already said, that the deceased saw this particular notice and appreciated its character. He also found that the deceased saw a number of other notices in identical terms posted about the field and that he appreciated what these notices were intended to effect. I think that he came on to the field in the afternoon on the terms contained in the notice displayed at the entrance to the ground.

…At the time when the accident occurred the deceased was, in my opinion, a spectator. The limitation on the liability of the organisers in these circumstances is to be found in the notice. The condition set out in the notice was that they were to be absolved from all liabilities arising out of accidents causing damage or personal injury howsoever caused. The use of the words 'howsoever caused' makes clear that the absolution was intended to be of a general character. The effect of the condition must, in my judgment, amount to the exclusion of liability for accidents arising from the organisers' own negligence. For these reasons I consider that the learned judge was right in dismissing the action. This makes it unnecessary for me to consider the effect of the warning notice which was printed on the inner face of the programme.

I would dismiss this appeal.

[ROSKILL LJ delivered a judgment in favour of dismissing the appeal. LORD DENNING MR delivered a judgment in favour of allowing the appeal.]

QUESTION

If the deceased had been killed as a result of being run over by a negligently driven jalopy, would the notice in this case have protected the driver? (See generally *North*, pp. 126–130.)

NOTE

The question of exclusion of liability arose in an important case decided just before the 1957 Act—*Ashdown v Samuel Williams & Sons Ltd* [1957] 1 QB 409, [1957] 1 All ER 35. The claimant's place of work was on property leased by the first defendants to her employers, the second defendants, and to reach her place of employment the claimant used a short cut which lay across land retained by the first defendants. The short cut crossed several railway lines, and the claimant, when crossing one of these lines, was injured by a truck which was being shunted by the first defendants' employees. They were found to have been negligent. A notice erected by the first defendants could be seen by people using the short cut, and it stated that those on the property were there at their own risk, and that they should not have any claim against these defendants for any injury they received, however caused. The Court of Appeal held that the claimant entered the land as a licensee, and that the terms of the notice were effective to exclude the first defendants' liability. The defendants had 'taken all reasonable steps to bring the conditions to her notice' (per Parker LJ): it did not matter that she had only read part of the notice. It was mentioned above that *Ashdown v Samuel Williams & Sons Ltd* was a pre-Occupiers' Liability Act decision. In the light of s. 2(1) of that Act, it was thought that it was still valid after the Act was passed, and this view is supported by *White v Blackmore*. See also the comments on this decision in *Burnett v British Waterways Board* [1973] 2 All ER 631, [1973] 1 WLR 700. For further comment on *Ashdown*'s case, see notes by L. C. B. Gower (1956) 20 MLR 532 (dealing with the decision in the court below) and (1957) 20 MLR 181, and see F. J. Odgers [1957] CLJ 39 at 42–54. However, it should be noted that the actual decision on exclusion in *Ashdown*'s case would not be the same today because of the statutory provisions referred to post and set out at p. 462, ante.

■ The Unfair Contract Terms Act 1977

p. 462, ante

NOTES

1. For discussion of the position of the occupier before this Act was passed, see C. R. Symmons (1974) 38 Conv (NS) 253. Although the Unfair Contract Terms Act 1977 has curtailed the scope of the occupier's ability to exclude his liability, it has only brought about a curtailment and not a total ban in all circumstances. On the question of whether there is a minimum non-excludable duty, see note 8, p. 596, post.

    In the first place, by virtue of s. 1(3), the relevant part of the Act only applies to 'business liability'. Section 1(3) does tell us a little more about this phrase and s. 14 includes certain activities within the meaning of the word 'business'; apart from this, however, and apart from such guidance as can be obtained from judicial decisions interpreting the word 'business' in other contexts, we must await future case law for the precise scope of the word 'business' to be made clearer. For general discussion, see e.g. J. Mesher [1979] Conv 58 at 58–60; W. V. H. Rogers and M. G. Clarke, *The Unfair Contract Terms Act 1977*. The Act has obviously affected *Ashdown v Samuel Williams & Sons Ltd* [1957] 1 QB 409, [1957] 1 All ER 35, but *White v Blackmore* (p. 582, ante) is an example of a case in which liability was excluded, but which may not be caught by s. 2.

    The Occupiers' Liability Act 1957 applies to damage to property (though see *North*, pp. 94–112) and therefore the second point to note about s. 2 is that sub-s. (2) allows the occupier to exclude his liability for damage to property if the contract term or notice 'satisfies the requirement of reasonableness'. Thus, to apply this sub-section the student needs to know about the pre-Act position concerning the exclusion of liability, as well as the requirement of reasonableness under the Unfair Contract Terms Act 1977.

2. The purpose of the amendment to s. 1 of the Unfair Contract Terms Act 1977 by s. 2 of the Occupiers' Liability Act 1984 was to promote greater access to the countryside. It was thought that landowners would be more willing to allow access for the purposes laid down by the amendment if liability to such visitors could be excluded. However, during the debates in Parliament, some concern was expressed that the section needed to be amended so as to clarify the position where a charge is made for access. If too uncertain, of course, the section might fail to achieve its object. What is the position of a landowner who charges for entry to his premises purely to cover expenses and no more? Do you think this would take the case into the category of 'business liability'?

    Another point to notice is that the amendment to s. 1(3) of the 1977 Act only covers damage arising from the dangerous state of the premises. This raises the distinction between what has been termed the 'activity duty' and the 'occupancy duty' on which see p. 564, ante. Contrast the wording of s. 1(1) of the 1984 Act (p. 587, post). Do you think that activities associated with occupation (e.g. driving a tractor from one field to another, as opposed to driving a car on one's property while on the way to the shops) are or are not covered by this amendment to the 1977 Act? What about operating machinery fixed in one place on the land?

    In relation to the stated purpose of this amendment are there in any event reasons, other than fear of legal liability, which discourage landowners from permitting access and which are not of course affected by the amendment (e.g. fear of the damage the public might do)? See M. A. Jones (1984) 47 MLR 713 at 726. Generally on the interpretation of s. 2 of the 1984 Act, see R. J. Bragg and M. R. Brazier (1986) 130 SJ 251 and 274.

3. Section 2(3) of the Unfair Contract Terms Act 1977 is concerned with the defence of volenti non fit injuria, which in the Occupiers' Liability Act 1957 is enshrined in s. 2(5). This defence has already been discussed in chap. 7, but note at this stage that in *White v Blackmore* (p. 582, ante) Buckley LJ distinguished this defence from the law relating to exclusion of liability. Nevertheless, according to *Burnett v British Waterways Board* [1973] 2 All ER 631, [1973] 1 WLR 700, exclusion of liability may, as does volenti, require the claimant to have had a choice in the matter. (See the note on the *Burnett* case by J. R. M. Lowe (1974) 37 MLR 218, which discusses the point under consideration here.)

(b) To trespassers

NOTE

The Occupiers' Liability Act 1957 does not regulate the duty which is owed to trespassers. This used to depend on the common law, which, once a person had been classified as a trespasser, traditionally excluded him from the ambit of any duty of reasonable care. This is shown by *R Addie & Sons (Collieries) Ltd v Dumbreck* [1929] AC 358, [1929] All ER Rep 1, where Lord Hailsham LC put forward (at p. 4) the following celebrated proposition:

Towards the trespasser the occupier has no duty to take reasonable care for his protection or even to protect him from concealed danger. The trespasser comes on to the premises at his own risk. An occupier is in such a case liable only where the injury is due to some wilful act involving something more than the absence of reasonable care. There must be some act done with the deliberate intention of doing harm to the trespasser, or at least some act done with reckless disregard of the presence of the trespasser.

Whilst it might be said that a burglar deserves no better treatment, it was much more difficult to apply this remark to the case of an 'innocent' trespassing child. Nevertheless, the traditional approach asserted that this was the only duty owed to the 'innocent' child, once he was classified as a trespasser, and it equated the position of the adult and the child within this category. This was a rigid approach which could operate harshly, and yet if the magic tag 'occupier' was absent, then the contractor, who was carrying on activities on the land but who was not an occupier of that land, could be held liable for negligence to a person whom he injured, even though that person was a trespasser vis-à-vis the occupier.

It was not surprising, therefore, that ways were sought to mitigate the harshness of the law. This could be achieved if it were decided that the claimant had an implied licence and, therefore, was not a trespasser, a decision which could more readily be reached in the case of a child. A more drastic step was taken in *Videan v British Transport Commission* [1963] 2 QB 650, [1963] 2 All ER 860, in which the Court of Appeal made some progress towards the imposition of liability for negligence. Lord Denning MR took the view that, where the occupier was conducting activities on his land, a duty of care extended to a trespasser whose presence ought to be foreseen, and Harman LJ also based the occupier's liability to trespassers for activities he carried out on his land on the foreseeability doctrine (cf. Pearson LJ). However, it was not long before these views were criticised by the Privy Council in *Railways Comr v Quinlan* [1964] AC 1054, [1964] 1 All ER 897, which basically reaffirmed the *Addie* rule. Undeterred, the Court of Appeal in *Kingzett v British Railways Board* (1968) 112 Sol Jo 625 followed *Videan*, and this conflict of authority remained until, a few years later, the issue reached the House of Lords in *British Railways Board v Herrington* [1972] AC 877, [1972] 1 All ER 749. The House had an opportunity to restate the duty owed to trespassers, but unfortunately did not speak with one voice. Without purporting to give a comprehensive picture of the decision, three particular approaches in the speeches might perhaps be mentioned. In Lord Reid's opinion (at p. 758):

…[T]he question whether an occupier is liable in respect of an accident to a trespasser on his land would depend on whether a conscientious humane man with his knowledge, skill and resources could reasonably have been expected to have done or refrained from doing before the accident something which would have avoided it. If he knew before the accident that there was a substantial probability that trespassers would come, I think that most people would regard as culpable failure to give any thought to their safety.

On the other hand, Lord Pearson thought that if the occupier knew of or should reasonably have anticipated the presence of a trespasser, then he owed that trespasser a duty of humanity. Somewhere between these two views was that of Lord Diplock. The occupier must actually know of the trespasser's presence or of facts that make it likely; similarly, he must actually know of facts concerning his land or activities on it which are likely to cause injury to a trespasser. The reasonable man's perception of the likelihood of the trespasser's presence and the danger was then the yardstick, but it had to be based on facts actually known to the occupier. The duty was confined to 'taking reasonable steps to enable the trespasser to avoid the danger'; and for the duty to arise the degree of likelihood 'of the trespasser's presence at the actual time and place of danger to him [must be] such as would impel a man of ordinary humane feelings to take some steps to mitigate the risk of injury to the trespasser to which the particular danger exposes him' ([1972] 1 All ER at p. 796).

The duty owed to a trespasser (the duty of common humanity) was seen in *Herrington* as a lower duty than the common duty of care under the Occupiers' Liability Act 1957. Particularly noteworthy features of the decision were that a majority of the House of Lords favoured the view that the occupier's actual resources should be taken into account, and, as indicated ante, that there was support for some degree of subjectivity in relation to the occupier's knowledge. More detailed treatment of *Herrington* and discussion of the later case law will not be undertaken, however, because of the legislative activity in this field. The question of liability of trespassers was referred to the Law Commission after the *Herrington* decision and its report was published in 1976 (*Report on Liability for Damage or Injury to Trespassers and Related Questions of Occupiers' Liability*, Law Com. No. 75, Cmnd. 6428). The proposals contained in this report in relation to uninvited entrants were approved by the Pearson Commission (vol. 1, chap. 28) and were the basis for s. 1 of the Occupiers' Liability Act 1984, post, although there are differences.

■ The Occupiers' Liability Act 1984

1. **Duty of occupier to persons other than his visitors.**—(1) The rules enacted by this section shall have effect, in place of the rules of the common law, to determine—

    (a) whether any duty is owed by a person as occupier of premises to persons other than his visitors in respect of any risk of their suffering injury on the premises by reason of any danger due to the state of the premises or to things done or omitted to be done on them; and

    (b) if so, what that duty is.

(2) For the purposes of this section, the persons who are to be treated respectively as an occupier of any premises (which, for those purposes, include any fixed or movable structure) and as his visitors are—

    (a) any person who owes in relation to the premises the duty referred to in section 2 of the Occupiers' Liability Act 1957 (the common duty of care), and

    (b) those who are his visitors for the purposes of that duty.

(3) An occupier of premises owes a duty to another (not being his visitor) in respect of any such risk as is referred to in subsection (1) above if—

(a) he is aware of the danger or has reasonable grounds to believe that it exists;

(b) he knows or has reasonable grounds to believe that the other is in the vicinity of the danger concerned or that he may come into the vicinity of the danger (in either case, whether the other has lawful authority for being in that vicinity or not); and

(c) the risk is one against which, in all the circumstances of the case, he may reasonably be expected to offer the other some protection.

(4) Where, by virtue of this section, an occupier of premises owes a duty to another in respect of such a risk, the duty is to take such care as is reasonable in all the circumstances of the case to see that he does not suffer injury on the premises by reason of the danger concerned.

(5) Any duty owed by virtue of this section in respect of a risk may, in an appropriate case, be discharged by taking such steps as are reasonable in all the circumstances of the case to give warning of the danger concerned or to discourage persons from incurring the risk.

(6) No duty is owed by virtue of this section to any person in respect of risks willingly accepted as his by that person (the question whether a risk was so accepted to be decided on the same principles as in other cases in which one person owes a duty of care to another).

[(6A) At any time when the right conferred by section 2(1) of the Countryside and Rights of Way Act 2000 is exercisable in relation to land which is access land for the purposes of Part I of that Act, an occupier of the land owes (subject to subsection (6C) below) no duty by virtue of this section to any person in respect of—

(a) a risk resulting from the existence of any natural feature of the landscape, or any river, stream, ditch or pond whether or not a natural feature, or

(b) a risk of that person suffering injury when passing over, under or through any wall, fence or gate, except by proper use of the gate or of a stile.

(6B) For the purposes of subsection (6A) above, any plant, shrub or tree, of whatever origin, is to be regarded as a natural feature of the landscape.

(6C) Subsection (6A) does not prevent an occupier from owing a duty by virtue of this section in respect of any risk where the danger concerned is due to anything done by the occupier–

(a) with the intention of creating that risk, or

(b) being reckless as to whether that risk is created.][6]

(7) No duty is owed by virtue of this section to persons using the highway, and this section does not affect any duty owed to such persons.

(8) Where a person owes a duty by virtue of this section, he does not, by reason of any breach of the duty, incur any liability in respect of any loss of or damage to property.

(9) In this section—

'highway' means any part of a highway other than a ferry or waterway;

'injury' means anything resulting in death or personal injury, including any disease and any impairment of physical or mental condition; and

'movable structure' includes any vessel, vehicle or aircraft.

[1A Special considerations relating to access land

In determining whether any, and if so what, duty is owed by virtue of section 1 by an occupier of land at any time when the right conferred by section 2(1) of the Countryside and Rights of Way Act 2000 is exercisable in relation to the land, regard is to be had, in particular, to—

(a) the fact that the existence of that right ought not to place an undue burden (whether financial or otherwise) on the occupier,

---

[6] Inserted by s. 13(2) of the Countryside and Rights of Way Act 2000.

(b) the importance of maintaining the character of the countryside, including features of historic, traditional or archaeological interest, and

(c) any relevant guidance given under section 20 of that Act.][7]

3. Application to Crown.—Section 1 of this Act shall bind the Crown, but as regards the Crown's liability in tort shall not bind the Crown further than the Crown is made liable in tort by the Crown Proceedings Act 1947.

QUESTIONS

1. When introducing at its Second Reading in the House of Lords the provision which became (with some amendment) s. 1 of the 1984 Act, Lord Hailsham stated that it 'does not aim to destroy the existing law but follows the biblical injunction to fulfil it by combining in a single set of propositions the slightly different lines of argument by which the members of the Appellate Committee, who were concerned in *Herrington*'s case, arrived at the same general conclusion' (443 H. L. Debs. (5th Series) col. 720). Do you think that s. 1 has this effect?

2. The amendments introduced by the Countryside and Rights of Way Act 2000 govern the position of those exercising rights of way over 'access land'. Was it necessary to provide specifically for this situation or would the existing provisions of the 1984 Act have sufficed? (See *Winfield & Jolowicz*, p. 421). What does 'reckless' mean in s. 1(6C)(b)—is it subjective or objective?

NOTES

1. For comment on the Occupiers' Liability Act 1984 see M.A. Jones (1984) 47 MLR 713; R.A. Buckley [1984] Conv 413.

2. Section 1 of the Occupiers' Liability Act 1984 does not cover damage to property; cf. the Occupiers' Liability (Scotland) Act 1960. Any such liability will, therefore, have to be found at common law. It might be thought that the common law would be unlikely to review such a claim favourably (note e.g. the references to 'humanity' in *Herrington*) and thus that the trespasser whose clothes or car are damaged may well have no redress. On the other hand, consider the Law Commission's view, note 6 post and note also *Tutton v AD Walter Ltd* [1986] QB 61, [1985] 3 All ER 757, pp. 595–596 where (obiter) *Herrington* was regarded as applicable to property damage (bees).

3. The duty imposed by the 1984 Act is not only owed to trespassers but also applies to other entrants who are not 'visitors' for the purpose of the Occupiers' Liability Act 1957. As we have seen (note 4, p. 567, ante) this category includes persons exercising private rights of way vis-à-vis the owner of the servient tenement, and for another category of 'non-visitor' see s. 1(4) of the Occupiers' Liability Act 1957, as substituted by s. 13(1) of the Countryside and Rights of Way Act 2000 (p. 565, ante). Those exercising public rights of way were also not 'visitors' for the purpose of the 1957 Act, but by virtue of s. 1(7) of the 1984 Act they are not owed the duty set out in that section. In the case of highways maintainable at the public expense the position is now governed by the Highways Act 1980, on which see *Winfield & Jolowicz*, pp. 689–692. With respect to highways not so maintainable, the common law operates and, as has been

---

[7] Inserted by s. 13(2) of the Countryside and Rights of Way Act 2000.

mentioned, the traditional position is that there can be liability for misfeasance (e.g. repairing badly) but not for non-feasance (e.g. not repairing). However, it has been argued that users of such a highway are protected by the duty of humanity in *British Railways Board v Herrington* [1972] AC 877, [1972] 1 All ER 749, and that support for this can be found in *Thomas v British Railways Board* [1976] QB 912, [1976] 3 All ER 15: see Buckley, op cit., pp. 415–416; cf. *Brady v Department of the Environment* [1988] 1 NIJB 1 and on appeal [1990] 2 NILR 200. No mention was made of any such idea in the speeches in the House of Lords in *McGeown v Northern Ireland Housing Executive* [1995] 1 AC 233, [1994] 3 All ER 53, noted p. 567, ante, which re-affirmed the traditional position. For further discussion see F. R. Barker and N. D. M. Parry (1995) 15 LS 335 (but note that *Stovin v Wise* to which they refer subsequently went to the House of Lords, and see also the later case law on the question of negligence in relation the statutory powers and duties (pp. 110–117, ante)); J. Murphy [1997] Conv 362. Barker and Parry point out that those exercising public rights of way are covered by the Occupiers' Liability (Scotland) Act 1960.

■ Tomlinson v Congleton Borough Council

House of Lords [2003] 3 All ER 1122

For the facts, see p. 573, ante, where an extract from this case discussing the Occupiers' Liability Act 1957 will be found. The extract post primarily concerns the Occupiers' Liability Act 1984.

LORD HOFFMANN: . . .

The scope of the duty under the 1984 act

[25] The conditions in s 1(3) of the 1984 Act determine whether or not a duty is owed to 'another' in respect of 'any such risk as is referred to in subsection (1)'. Two conclusions follow from this language. First, the risks in respect of which the Act imposes a duty are limited to those mentioned in sub-s (1)(a)—risks of injury 'by reason of any danger due to the state of the premises or to things done or omitted to be done on them'. The Act is not concerned with risks due to anything else. Secondly, the conditions have to be satisfied in respect of the claimant as 'another'; that is to say, in respect of a class of persons which includes him and a description of risk which includes that which caused his injury.

A danger 'due to the state of the premises'

[26] The first question, therefore, is whether there was a risk within the scope of the statute; a danger 'due to the state of the premises or to things done or omitted to be done on them'. The judge found that there was 'nothing about the mere at Brereton Heath which made it any more dangerous than any other ordinary stretch of open water in England'. There was nothing special about its configuration; there were no hidden dangers. It was shallow in some places and deep in others, but that is the nature of lakes. Nor was the council doing or permitting anything to be done which created a danger to persons who came to the lake. No power boats or jet skis threatened the safety of either lawful windsurfers or unlawful swimmers. So the council submits that there was no danger attributable to the state of premises or things done or omitted on them. In *Donoghue v Folkestone Properties Ltd* [2003] 3 All ER 1101 at [53] Lord Phillips MR expressed the same opinion. He said that he had been unable to identify the 'state of the premises' which carried with it the risk of the injury suffered by Mr Tomlinson:

'It seems to me that Mr Tomlinson suffered his injury because he chose to indulge in an activity which had inherent dangers, not because the premises were in a dangerous state.'

[27] In making this comment, Lord Phillips MR was identifying a point which is in my opinion central to this appeal. It is relevant at a number of points in the analysis of the duties under the 1957 and 1984 Acts. Mr Tomlinson was a person of full capacity who voluntarily and without any pressure or inducement engaged in an activity which had inherent risk. The risk was that he might not execute his dive properly and so sustain injury. Likewise, a person who goes mountaineering incurs the risk that he might stumble or misjudge where to put his weight. In neither case can the risk be attributed to the state of the premises. Otherwise any premises can be said to be dangerous to someone who chooses to use them for some dangerous activity. In the present case, Mr Tomlinson knew the lake well and even if he had not, the judge's finding was that it contained no dangers which one would not have expected. So the only risk arose out of what he chose to do and not out of the state of the premises.

[28] Mr Braithwaite was inclined to accept the difficulty of establishing that the risk was due to the state of the premises. He therefore contended that it was due to 'things done or omitted to be done' on the premises. When asked what these might be, he said that they consisted in the attraction of the lake and the council's inadequate attempts to keep people out of the water. The council, he said, were 'luring people into a deathtrap'. Ward LJ ([2003] All ER 1122 at [31]) said that the water was 'a siren call strong enough to turn stout men's minds'. In my opinion this is gross hyperbole. The trouble with the island of the sirens was not the state of the premises. It was that the sirens held mariners spellbound until they died of hunger. The beach, give or take a fringe of human bones, was an ordinary mediterranean beach. If Odysseus had gone ashore and accidentally drowned himself having a swim, Penelope would have had no action against the sirens for luring him there with their songs. Likewise in this case, the water was perfectly safe for all normal activities. In my opinion 'things done or omitted to be done' means activities or the lack of precautions which cause risk, like allowing speedboats among the swimmers. It is a mere circularity to say that a failure to stop people getting into the water was an omission which gave rise to a duty to take steps to stop people from getting into the water.

[29] It follows that in my opinion, there was no risk to Mr Tomlinson due to the state of the premises or anything done or omitted upon the premises. That means that there was no risk of a kind which gave rise to a duty under the 1957 or 1984 Acts. I shall nevertheless go on to consider the matter on the assumption that there was.

The conditions for the existence of a duty

(i) Knowledge or foresight of the danger

[30] Section 1(3) of the 1984 Act has three conditions which must be satisfied. First, under para (a), the occupier must be aware of the danger or have reasonable grounds to believe that it exists. For this purpose, it is necessary to say what the relevant danger was. The judge thought it was the risk of suffering an injury through diving and said that the council was aware of this danger because two men had suffered minor head injuries from diving in May 1992. In the Court of Appeal, Ward LJ described the relevant risk much more broadly. He regarded all the swimming incidents as indicative of the council's knowledge that a danger existed. I am inclined to think that this is too wide a description. The risk of injury from diving off the beach was in my opinion different from the risk of drowning in the deep water. For example, the council might have fenced off the deep water or marked it with buoys and left people to paddle in the shallows. That would have reduced the risk of drowning but would not have prevented the injury to Mr Tomlinson. We know very little about the circumstances in which two men suffered minor cuts to their heads in 1992 and I am not sure that they really provide much support for an inference that there was knowledge, or reasonable grounds to believe, that the beach posed a risk of serious diving injury. Dr Penny, a consultant occupational health and safety physician with long experience of advising organisations involved in acquatic sports (and himself a diver) said that the Code of Safety for Beaches, published in 1993 by the Royal Life Saving Society and the Royal Society for the Prevention of Accidents, made no mention of diving risks, no doubt assuming that, because there was little possibility of high diving from a beach, the risk of serious diving injuries was very small compared with the risk of drowning. I accept that the council must have known that there was a possibility that some boisterous teenager

would injure himself by horseplay in the shallows and I would not disturb the concurrent findings that this was sufficient to satisfy para (a). But the chances of such an accident were small. I shall return later, in connection with para (c), to the relevance of where the risk comes on the scale of probability.

(ii) Knowledge or foresight of the presence of the trespasser
[31] Once it is found that the risk of a swimmer injuring himself by diving was something of which the council knew or which they had reasonable grounds to believe to exist, para (b) presents no difficulty. The council plainly knew that swimmers came to the lake and Mr Tomlinson fell within that class.

(iii) Reasonable to expect protection
[32] That leaves para (c). Was the risk one against which the council might reasonably be expected to offer Mr Tomlinson some protection? The judge found that 'the danger and risk of injury from diving in the lake where it was shallow were obvious'. In such a case the judge held, both as a matter of common sense and following consistent authority (*Staples v West Dorset DC* (1995) 93 LGR 536, *Ratcliff v McConnell* [1999] 1 WLR 670, *Darby v National Trust* [2001] PIQR P372), that there was no duty to warn against the danger. A warning would not tell a swimmer anything he did not already know. Nor was it necessary to do anything else. 'I do not think', said the judge, 'that the defendants' legal duty to the claimant in the circumstances required them to take the extreme measures which were completed after the accident'. Even if Mr Tomlinson had been owed a duty under the 1957 Act as a lawful visitor, the council would not have been obliged to do more than they did.

[33] The Court of Appeal disagreed. Ward LJ said that the council was obliged to do something more. The gravity of the risk, the number of people who regularly incurred it and the attractiveness of the beach created a duty. The prohibition on swimming was obviously ineffectual and therefore it was necessary to take additional steps to prevent or discourage people from getting into the water. Sedley LJ said ([2003] 3 All ER 1122 at [45]): '... it is only where the risk is so obvious that the occupier can safely assume that nobody will take it that there will be no liability.' Longmore LJ dissented. The majority reduced the damages by two-thirds to reflect Mr Tomlinson's contributory negligence, although Ward LJ said that he would have been inclined to reduce them only by half. The council appeals against the finding of liability and Mr Tomlinson appeals against the apportionment, which he says should have been in accordance with the view of Ward LJ.

The balance of risk, gravity of injury, cost and social value
[34] My Lords, the majority of the Court of Appeal appear to have proceeded on the basis that if there was a foreseeable risk of serious injury, the council was under a duty to do what was necessary to prevent it. But this in my opinion is an oversimplification. Even in the case of the duty owed to a lawful visitor under s 2(2) of the 1957 Act and even if the risk had been attributable to the state of the premises rather than the acts of Mr Tomlinson, the question of what amounts to 'such care as in all the circumstances of the case is reasonable' depends upon assessing, as in the case of common law negligence, not only the likelihood that someone may be injured and the seriousness of the injury which may occur, but also the social value of the activity which gives rise to the risk and the cost of preventative measures. These factors have to be balanced against each other....

[37] This is the kind of balance which has to be struck even in a situation in which it is clearly fair, just and reasonable that there should in principle be a duty of care or in which Parliament, as in the 1957 Act, has decreed that there should be. And it may lead to the conclusion that even though injury is foreseeable, as it was in *Bolton v Stone* [[1951] AC 850, [1951] All ER 1078 (p. 296, ante)], it is still in all the circumstances reasonable to do nothing about it.

The 1957 and 1984 Acts contrasted
[38] In the case of the 1984 Act, there is the additional consideration that unless in all the circumstances it is reasonable to expect the occupier to do something, that is to say, to 'offer the other some protection', there is no duty at all. One may ask what difference there is between the case in which the claimant is a lawful visitor and there is in principle a duty under the 1957 Act but on the particular facts

no duty to do anything, and the case in which he is a trespasser and there is on the particular facts no duty under the 1984 Act. Of course in such a case the result is the same. But Parliament has made it clear that in the case of a lawful visitor, one starts from the assumption that there is a duty whereas in the case of a trespasser one starts from the assumption that there is none.

[LORD HOFFMANN then proceeded to consider the balance under the 1957 Act—see p. 575, ante—and continued:]

[50] My Lords, for these reasons I consider that even if swimming had not been prohibited and the council had owed a duty under s 2(2) of the 1957 Act, that duty would not have required them to take any steps to prevent Mr Tomlinson from diving or warning him against dangers which were perfectly obvious. If that is the case, then plainly there can have been no duty under the 1984 Act. The risk was not one against which he was entitled under s 1(3)(c) to protection. I would therefore allow the appeal and restore the decision of Jack J. It follows that the cross-appeal against the apportionment of damages must be dismissed.

[LORD NICHOLLS OF BIRKENHEAD agreed with LORD HOFFMANN. LORD HUTTON delivered a speech in favour of allowing the appeal. LORD HOBHOUSE OF WOODBOROUGH and LORD SCOTT OF FOSCOTE delivered speeches in favour of allowing the appeal in which they agreed with the speech of LORD HOFFMANN, except that LORD SCOTT would have regarded the claimant as a visitor and not a trespasser.]

Appeal allowed.

QUESTION

How far should the age of the trespasser affect the question whether there is a danger 'due to the state of the premises' as opposed to the question of what steps should be taken thereafter? (Consider *Keown v Coventry Healthcare NHS Trust* [2006] 1 WLR 953, [2006] EWCA Civ 39, discussing the case of a toddler crawling into a derelict building.)

NOTES

1. *Ratcliff v McConnell* [1999] 1 WLR 670 was an important case decided before *Tomlinson*. The claimant, a 19-year-old student, went drinking with two friends, after which they decided to go swimming in his college's swimming pool. The claimant knew that the pool was closed for the winter and that swimming was prohibited during that period. In addition, there were signs at the pool which said that it was closed. The gate to the pool was locked, but the claimant gained access by climbing over it. The only lighting at the pool was a motion activated security light. The claimant dived into the pool, hit his head on the bottom and suffered very severe injuries. The judge held the defendant, the college, liable, subject to 40 per cent contributory negligence. The Court of Appeal, however, decided that there was no liability at all. Unfortunately, the Court of Appeal's reasoning is far from easy to follow since the court does not examine the case in the way the 1984 Act seems to require. Logically, the Act requires the court to decide first whether a duty arises at all (ss. 1(3)(a), 1(3)(b) and 1(3)(c)), secondly whether the defendant has acted reasonably in all the circumstances to see that injury did not occur by reason of the danger (that is, breach and causation) (s. 1(4)), thirdly whether any warnings or other measures to discourage people from taking the risk discharged the duty (s. 1(5)), and finally whether common law volenti applies (s. 1(6)). In *Ratcliff* the Court of Appeal decided the case on the basis on s. 1 (6), i.e. that the claimant should be taken to have accepted the risk. It was argued in the previous

edition of this work (at p. 579) that even if it is accepted the defendant fails the tests contained in ss. 1(3)(a) and 1(3)(b), it is far from clear that it would be reasonable to expect the defendant to provide the claimant with any protection against the relevant risk (s. 1(3)(c)); and even if it was reasonable to expect some protection, it is far from clear that the defendant acted unreasonably, either at large (s. 1(4)) or in the light of the measures it had taken to keep students out of the pool (s. 1(5)). In the light of the reasoning in *Tomlinson*, it is suggested that these questions would loom larger if a case like *Ratcliff* arose today (and note the context in which *Ratcliff* is cited in para. 32 of the extract ante).

2. The question of the extent to which s. 1(3)(a) and (b) involve a subjective or objective test was not discussed in *Tomlinson*. It had, however, previously arisen, in the context of s. 1(3)(b), in *Swain v Natui Ram Puri* [1996] PIQR P442, where the Court of Appeal opted for an approach like that of Lord Diplock in *Herrington* [1972] AC at 941, noted ante, whose view was regarded as the 'genesis' of s. 1. To establish 'reasonable grounds to believe' a claimant would have to show that the occupier actually knew certain facts from which reasonable grounds to believe could be inferred: it was not sufficient to show that a defendant ought to have known these facts (although wilful blindness would not excuse). This obviously has implications for the interpretation of s. 1(3)(a) as well. Furthermore, *Ratcliff*, noted ante, supports the application of Lord Diplock's speech in *Herrington* to s. 1(3)(a) and (b) and this was approved in *Donoghue v Folkstone Properties Ltd* [2003] 3 All ER 1101, [2003] EWCA Civ 231. In *White v St Albans City* (1990) Times, 12 March it was accepted that the mere fact of a defendant having taken measures to stop entry onto land containing some danger did not necessarily mean that the 'reasonable grounds to believe' element in s. 1(3)(b) had been satisfied. Note also *Higgs v W.H. Foster (t/a Avalon Coaches)* [2004] EWCA Civ 843 at [8], relying on *Donoghue v Folkstone Properties Ltd* for the proposition that 'although it may be sufficient for a claimant to show he was one of a class of trespassers whom the occupier had reason to believe may be in the vicinity of the danger, the existence of the duty had to be determined by reference to the likelihood of the individual claimant's presence in that vicinity at the actual time and place that gave rise to the danger to him'.

3. The Occupiers' Liability (Scotland) Act 1960 covers both lawful visitors and trespassers. Section 2(1) states:

The care which an occupier of premises is required, by reason of his occupation or control of the premises, to show towards a person entering thereon in respect of dangers which are due to the state of the premises or to anything done or omitted to be done on them and for which the occupier is in law responsible shall, except in so far as he is entitled to and does extend, restrict, modify or exclude by agreement his obligations towards that person, be such care as in all the circumstances of the case is reasonable to see that that person will not suffer injury or damage by reason of any such danger.

The Scottish Act contains no provision equivalent to s. 1(3) of the 1984 Act; yet it does not appear to have caused any problems in practice. What cases are excluded by s. 1(3)(c) that would otherwise have been successful under a straightforward 'reasonable care in all the circumstances' requirement? Compare para. 27 of the Law Commission's Report and consider the approach in *Tomlinson*. See generally M. A. Jones *Textbook on Torts* 8th edn (London, 2002) pp. 317–319.

4. It has been pointed out (p. 587, ante) that a majority of their Lordships in *Herrington* would have taken account of the occupier's actual resources. Should this happen under s. 1 of the 1984 Act? The answer would seem to be in the negative; and such a

consideration is certainly not specifically mentioned in s. 1. See Jones (1984) 47 MLR at p. 719. *Winfield & Jolowicz*, p. 418, point out that the Court of Appeal in *Ratcliff v McConnell* 'treated the Act as largely a restatement of what Lord Diplock had said in *Herrington*, citing a passage which had referred to the occupier's resources'. However, having set out the relevant passage from *Herrington* which appears at [1972] AC at pp. 941–942 as a 'convenient summary' of *Herrington*, when the Court of Appeal in *Ratcliff* later referred to the passage of Lord Diplock as 'still apposite' on the post-1984 Act law (albeit with one exception irrelevant for present purposes) the court intriguingly merely referred to the passage of Lord Diplock at [1972] AC at p. 941. The reason why this is intriguing is that it is the passage at p. 942 that contains Lord Diplock's reference to the occupier's resources. (The whole passage in *Ratcliff* was approved in *Donoghue v Folkstone Properties Ltd*.)

5. One point in *Tomlinson* concerned whether the injury was caused by a danger due to the state of the premises within the scope of the 1984 Act (or indeed the 1957 Act). On this point the House of Lords by a majority decided that it did not, but Lord Hutton inclined to the contrary opinion on the basis that the claimant could not in fact see the bottom of the lake on which he hit his head. Note also that in *Rhind v Astbury Water Park* Ltd [2004] EWCA Civ 756 the Court of Appeal distinguished *Tomlinson* where the claimant hit his head on a fibre glass container lying on the bottom of a lake and covered in silt: this was regarded as an injury due to the state of the premises within s. 1(1)(a) of the 1984 Act. (The claim in fact failed on the basis of s. 1(3)(a).) In the *Keown* case, s. 1(1)(a) was not met when an eleven-year-old boy, who knew that climbing on an external fire escape was dangerous, was injured in a fall during this activity. A flat roof of a building would also not fall within s. 1(1)(a), but it might be different if the injury was caused by falling through a brittle skylight: see the comments in *Keown* on *Young v Kent County Council* [2005] EWHC 1342 (QB). Note further *Donoghue v Folkstone Properties Ltd* and *Siddorn v Patel* [2007] EWHC 1248 (QB).

6. Linked to the discussion in the previous note, it should be remembered that the question whether the similarly worded Occupiers' Liability Act 1957 covered what has been termed the 'activity duty' as well as the 'occupancy duty'; but it may also be remembered that the issue was unlikely to be of practical importance. On the difficulties of this distinction in the pre-1957 law, see *North*, pp. 71–82. If the 1957 Act does not cover the 'activity duty', nevertheless it should be noted that the 'occupancy duty' that it does cover includes activities which affect the safety of the premises. The Law Commission, which took the view that the 1957 Act does not apply to the 'activity duty', thought the scope of its proposed legislation concerning the duty owed to uninvited entrants (which to an extent became the 1984 Act) should be similar. The Law Commission's view was referred to in *Revill v Newbery* [1996] QB 567, [1996] 1 All ER 291, noted by T. Weir [1996] CLJ 182, where the question of the scope of the 1984 Act arose. In this case the claimant, who was trying to break into a shed on the defendant's allotment in the early hours of the morning, was unintentionally wounded when the defendant, who had been sleeping in the shed to protect his property, fired a shotgun through a hole in the door of the shed. Neill LJ thought that the better view is that the duty under the 1984 Act is imposed on a defendant *qua* occupier and did not cover the case in hand (though see post for his view of the liability outside the Act). Evans LJ, however, whilst referring to the point, did not express any concluded view on the matter, and Millett LJ did not specifically refer to the question at all. Recent authority supporting the view that the 1957 Act only applies to occupancy duties (see the Court of Appeal's decision

in *Fairchild v Glenhaven Funeral Services Ltd* [2002] 1 WLR 1052, [2003] EWCA Civ 1881) backs up Neill LJ's view.

If the 1984 Act is given the more restricted scope, what duty is owed in relation to activities carried out by the occupier? One argument can be derived from *British Railways Board v Herrington* [1972] AC 877, [1972] 1 All ER 749. Whereas a distinction between the static condition of the land and the occupier's operations on it had been drawn in relation to trespassers in *Videan v British Transport Commission* [1963] 2 QB 650, [1963] 2 All ER 860 (though see *North*, pp. 76–78), this distinction was not accepted by the House of Lords in *Herrington*. If *Herrington* was interpreted as covering all activities by the occupier, even driving his car, then it would appear that the duty of humanity should prevail in the area unaffected by the 1984 Act. On the other hand, the Law Commission thought that the trespasser injured, for example, by the negligent driving of a car by a person who was the occupier would be left to bring a claim at common law for negligence: the fact that the claimant was trespassing would merely affect the foreseeability of his presence and thereby be relevant to the question of negligence liability.

The matter has now received some attention in *Revill v Newbery*. On the facts of that case both Neill and Evans LJJ thought that the approach at common law was along the same lines as that spelled out in s. 1 of the 1984 Act. This leaves open the position at common law in different circumstances to those they were dealing with; and further uncertainty is created, if and insofar as Neill and Evans LJJ might not be thought to have accepted the interpretation bestowed upon s. 1(3) in *Swain v Naturi Ram Puri* [1996] PIQR P442, noted ante. The defendant in *Revill v Newbery* was in fact held liable, but the damages were reduced by two-thirds on account of the claimant's contributory negligence. A defence of *ex turpi causa* was rejected, on which see p. 479, ante.

7. The Law Commission's view of the position of the trespasser in relation to the 'activity duty', as outlined in the previous note, is similar to what was thought to be the position of the trespasser vis-à-vis the contractor who was not an occupier of the land: see *Buckland v Guildford Gas, Light and Coke Co* [1949] 1 KB 410, [1948] 2 All ER 1086. There was an indication in *Herrington* that the position of the occupier and contractor might be equated: see [1972] AC at pp. 914 and 929 per Lords Wilberforce and Pearson, but see [1972] AC at p. 943 per Lord Diplock, and consider *Pannett v P McGuinness & Co Ltd* [1972] 2 QB 599, [1972] 3 All ER 137; M. H. Matthews [1972A] CLJ 214 at 217–218. Is this likely to pose any problems after the 1984 Act? See further Buckley, op cit., pp. 416–417.

8. Suppose a person (A), having permission under a licence to enter one part of the premises of another (B), in fact goes into a different part of the premises, becoming a trespasser there, and is injured. If the licence contains a term excluding liability for any injury to A occurring anywhere on B's property, howsoever caused, would this term be struck down by the Unfair Contract Terms Act 1977 (assuming that this is a case of 'business liability')? If not, note that there was an argument (before the 1984 Act was passed) that at common law as a matter of public policy the courts would not allow exclusion of the duty owed to a trespasser: see e.g. B. Coote (1975) 125 NLJ 752; Law Commission, op cit., para. 60; Mesher, op cit., pp. 63–64. Can this sort of argument now be applied to the 1984 Act? If the 1984 Act provides the minimum duty which an occupier can owe another (though see note 3, p. 589, ante), it might be assumed by the courts that Parliament did not intend to allow the duty to be derogated from; however, note that the 1984 Act specifically permits the volenti defence.

One point to bear in mind is that the Law Commission did expressly provide (in cl. 3 of its proposed legislation) for exclusion of the duty owed to uninvited entrants by a contract term or notice to the extent that reliance on such a term or notice would be fair or reasonable. (This clause in fact also dealt with the question of exclusion in relation to lawful entrants and its provisions on this matter are inconsistent with the Unfair Contract Terms Act 1977.) No such clause appears in the 1984 Act; cf. s. 2(1) of the 1957 Act. What inferences, if any, should be drawn from this? Should the Act be so interpreted as to permit exclusion of the duty there laid down, but not intentional or reckless conduct by the occupier (Jones, (1984) 47 MLR at p. 724) or perhaps not even a breach of the duty of humanity? (For the problems concerning the method of exclusion of liability to trespassers (assuming exclusion is possible), see the Law Commission, op cit., paras. 64–66; K. M. Stanton, *The Modern Law of Tort* (London, 1994), pp. 115–116.)

What of the visitor to whom the common duty of care has been excluded? It was arguable that a duty of humanity to him could not be excluded before the 1984 Act. If the duty in the 1984 Act is a non-excludable minimum duty to trespassers, which equally cannot be excluded in relation to a visitor, then it would meet the criticism that such a visitor may otherwise be in a worse position than a trespasser. On the other hand, as *Winfield & Jolowicz*, p. 413, point out, this would largely destroy the freedom to exclude that Parliament has conferred. Might the duty of humanity remain as an unexcludable minimum duty owed to such a visitor (see Buckley, op cit., p. 422); or might the minimum duty only be a duty not to injure intentionally or recklessly?

2. NON-OCCUPIERS' LIABILITY FOR PREMISES

■ Murphy v Brentwood District Council

p. 183, ante

NOTES

1. On recovery for economic loss in the tort of negligence in general, see chap. 4, ante. Here it is worth noting that a seven-member House of Lords found it necessary to overrule their own earlier decision in *Anns v Merton London Borough Council* [1978] AC 728, [1977] 2 All ER 492. The assumed facts in that case were that there was a threat to health and safety due to defective foundations, the defective foundations having caused cracks in the walls of the building. The damages which the occupiers were allowed to recover consisted in such sums as each of them had to expend to put his dwelling in a state in which it was no longer a danger to health and safety. P. Cane (1979) 95 LQR 117 described these as 'preventive damages'. The case was regarded as one of 'physical damage', although all that seemed to be needed was a 'present and imminent threat' of physical damage (see I. N. D. Wallace (1978) 94 LQR 60; P. Cane (1984) 10 Monash Univ LR 17 (at 45). The effect of *Murphy* is generally to rule out the possibility of recovery for preventive damages, subject to Lord Bridge's view concerning the building close to the boundary of the land, though see Lord Oliver's speech. Lord Bridge's view was

in fact followed in the High Court case of *Morse v Barratt (Leeds) Ltd* (1992) 9 Const LJ 158—and see *Payne v John Setchell Ltd* [2002] PNLR 146 at [41]—but regarded as inconsistent with the ratio of *Murphy* by Judge Hicks in *George Fischer Holdings Ltd v Multi Design Consultants Ltd (Roofdec Ltd, third parties)* (1998) 61 Con LR 85 at 110–111, and cf. *Losinjska Plovidba v Transco Overseas Ltd, The 'Orjula'* [1995] 2 Lloyd's Rep 395 at 402–403. P. Cane (1989) 52 MLR 200 at 207 argues that recovery for preventive damages may be 'economically justified in that prevention is often cheaper than cure'. Stevens suggests that recovery here could be justified on the basis that exempting the builder from liability could result in unjustified enrichment: see *Stevens*, pp. 30–32. See generally on the earlier law J. Stapleton (1988) 104 LQR 23, 389 and for discussion of *Murphy* in the context of liability for defective premises, see R. Cooke, (1991) 107 LQR 46; I. N. D. Wallace (1991) 107 LQR 228 and (1995) 111 LQR 285; M. Giles and E. Szyszczak (1991) 11 LS 85; A. Grubb and A. C. Mullis [1991] Conv 225. Grubb and Mullis refer (at pp. 240–241) to various policies underlying tort law, e.g. to deter dangerous conduct, and argue that the application of the policies should not depend on whether the item in question has yet caused any physical damage.

2. *Junior Books Ltd v Veitchi Co Ltd* [1983] 1 AC 520, [1982] 3 All ER 201, noted p. 240, ante, which is referred to but not overruled in *Murphy*, is a particularly difficult case allowing the recovery of pure economic loss in the buildings context. It is further considered at p. 600, post.

3. *Murphy's* main significance is its overruling of *Anns*. This has rendered a good deal of the previous case law redundant. Note, however, that the House of Lords left open the position of the local authority where personal injury or damage to other property is caused. Nevertheless, on personal injury, the courts have subsequently proven to be reluctant to create statutory torts out of environmental health legislation (see *Issa v Hackney London Borough Council* [1997] 1 All ER 999, [1997] 1 WLR 956, noted p. 679, post), and the current attitude of the courts towards common law negligence claims in the context of statutory powers or duties is hostile: see pp. 110–117, ante. On the question of damage to property see the view of Lord Keith in *Murphy* indicating that he would not be in favour of allowing recovery for this type of damage from a local authority in this context; cf. Lord Bridge's speech. In *Tesco Stores Ltd v Wards Construction (Industrial) Ltd* (1995) 76 BLR 94, which involved a local authority's powers under the Building Act 1984 and the Building Regulations, it was decided that no duty of care was owed in respect of damage to other property.

    Given that the liability of the local authority may not have disappeared totally, let us note two points from the earlier case law. First, could the local authority, in performing its duties in relation to the approval or non-approval of plans under the Public Health Act 1936 (see now the Building Act 1984), be liable where it has sought advice from an independent contractor and the latter has been negligent? (See generally p. 1095, post.) The Court of Appeal in *Murphy* [1991] 1 AC 398, [1990] 2 All ER 269 decided that the authority would be liable in such a situation, the common law duty not being discharged if the delegate is negligent. This aspect of the Court of Appeal's decision in *Murphy* (i.e. liability for a delegate) was another point that the House of Lords left open and it therefore remains of relevance if the courts decide that a local authority does owe the more limited duty of care referred to earlier in this note (though see Wallace op cit., p. 245). Second, in *Anns* Lord Wilberforce denied that the local authority owed any duty to a negligent building owner; and that case law decided that normally no duty was owed to a building owner who was in breach of the building regulations even if it was the act of an independent contractor, such as an architect or a builder, which had put him in breach and he was not personally negligent. For discussion see *Richardson v West Lindsey District Council* [1990] 1 All ER 296, [1990] 1 WLR 552, interpreting in particular *Governors of the Peabody Donation Fund v Sir Lindsay Parkinson & Co Ltd* [1985] AC 210, [1984] 3 All ER 529; *Investors in Industry Commercial Properties Ltd v South Bedfordshire District Council* [1986] QB 1034, [1986] 1 All ER 787 and *Dennis v Charnwood Borough Council* [1983] QB 409, [1982] 3 All ER 486. In special circumstances (see the *Dennis* case) the claimant could still sue. For more general discussion, see *Ingles v City of Toronto* (2000) 183 DLR (4th) 193. This will also need to be borne in mind if it transpires that a local authority can be liable in cases of personal injury or damage to other property.

4. The House of Lords was influenced in its decision as to whether to overrule *Anns* by its view of the relationship of the courts and the legislature in this field and in particular by the existence of the Defective Premises Act 1972. See also the approach in *D & F Estates Ltd v Church Comrs for England* [1989] AC 177 at 207–208 (when considering the position of a builder) and *McNerny v Lambeth London Borough Council* (1988) 21 HLR 188, noted p. 602, post (dealing with the position of a landlord). Generally on this point, however, consider the argument of P. Cane (1989) 52 MLR 200 at 211 (commenting on *D & F Estates Ltd*) which will be found p. 607, post after the Defective Premises Act 1972 has been set out. Note also vis-à-vis the Defective Premises Act that, as has been pointed out (Cooke, op cit., 68), s. 6(2) of the Act (p. 606, post) makes duties imposed by or enforceable by virtue of any provision of the Act, additional to any duty owed apart from that provision.

5. The Privy Council has held in *Invercargill City Council v Hamlin* [1996] AC 624, [1996] 1 All ER 756, noted by I. N. D. Wallace (1996) 112 LQR and R. Martin (1997) 60 MLR 94, that the New Zealand Court of Appeal, taking the view that conditions were different in New Zealand and this country, could, despite *Murphy*, hold a local authority liable for negligent inspection of defective foundations of a house causing economic loss. The Privy Council commented ([1996] 1 All ER at pp. 766–767) that in 'a succession of cases in New Zealand over the last 20 years it has been decided that community standards and expectations demand the imposition of a duty of care on local authorities and builders alike to ensure compliance with local byelaws' and that 'New Zealand judges are in a much better position to decide on such matters than the Board'. It was the perception of the differences between the two countries that was important. See, however, *Three Meade Street Ltd v Rotorua District Council* [2005] 1 NZLR 504, where it is stated that the duty of care may not be owed to industrial and/or commercial property owners.

■ Anns v London Borough of Merton
House of Lords [1977] 2 All ER 492

As will have been seen, *Anns* was a case in which a local authority was sued, and its current status on this point has been considered. However, Lord Wilberforce's speech (with which three of the other members of the House of Lords agreed) also contains some comments on the position of the builder.

LORD WILBERFORCE: . . .
The position of the builder. I agree with the majority in the Court of Appeal in thinking that it would be unreasonable to impose liability in respect of defective foundations on the council, if the builder,

whose primary fault it was, should be immune from liability. So it is necessary to consider this point, although it does not directly arise in the present appeal. If there was at one time a supposed rule that the doctrine of *Donoghue v Stevenson*[8] did not apply to realty, there is no doubt under modern authority that a builder of defective premises may be liable in negligence to persons who thereby suffer injury: see *Gallagher v N McDowell Ltd*,[9] per Lord MacDermott CJ, a case of personal injury. Similarly decisions have been given in regard to architects (*Clayton v Woodman & Son (Builders) Ltd*,[10] *Clay v A J Crump & Sons Ltd*.[11] *Gallagher*'s case[9] expressly leaves open the question whether the immunity against action of builder-owners, established by older authorities (e.g. *Bottomley v Bannister*[12]) still survives.

That immunity, as I understand it, rests partly on a distinction being made between chattels and real property, partly on the principle of 'caveat emptor' or, in the case where the owner leases the property, on the proposition that (fraud apart) there is no law against letting a 'tumbledown house' (*Robbins v Jones*,[13] per Erle CJ). But leaving aside such cases as arise between contracting parties, when the terms of the contract have to be considered (see *Voli v Inglewood Shire Council*,[14] per Windeyer J), I am unable to understand why this principle or proposition should prevent recovery in a suitable case by a person, who has subsequently acquired the house, on the principle of *Donoghue v Stevenson*:[8] the same rules should apply to all careless acts of a builder: whether he happens also to own the land or not. I agree generally with the conclusions of Lord Denning MR on this point (*Dutton*'s case[15]).

NOTES

1.   Apart from apparently confirming that builders have no immunity at common law (a point made in the extract from *Anns*; cf. note 5, post), *Murphy* provides guidance on the situations when they can be sued in negligence: see further pp. 194–198, ante. *Junior Books Ltd v Veitchi Co Ltd* [1983] 1 AC 520, [1982] 3 All ER 201, noted p. 240, ante) has been one of the most controversial cases in this area. The assumed facts were that the pursuers contracted with a firm of builders to construct a factory for them. The pursuers' architects nominated the defenders as specialist sub-contractors to lay the flooring. The defenders entered into a contract with the builders but not with the pursuers to carry out this work. Owing to the negligence of the defenders the floor became defective and developed cracks. It was not suggested that there was a threat to health and safety or threatened damage to any other property of the pursuers. The entire floor surface needed replacing. The House of Lords held (by a majority of 4–1) that the pursuers could recover from the flooring sub-contractors (a) the cost of replacement of the floor surface; and (b) consequential economic losses such as those arising from storing their books elsewhere. Lord Roskill (with whom Lord Fraser and Russell agreed, Lord Keith agreeing with the result on a narrower ground) rejected any distinction in principle between 'pure' economic loss and economic loss caused by physical damage, and he said that the requirement of 'proximity' 'must always involve, at least in most cases, some degree of reliance'. Both he and Lord Fraser emphasised that the relationship between the pursuers and the sub-contractors fell only just short of contract, and there was reliance on the skill and judgment of the sub-contractors (although on this point see A. Rodger in *The Frontiers of Liability*, edited by P. B. H. Birks (1994), pp. 66–67).

[8] [1932] AC 562, [1932] All ER Rep 1.   [9] [1961] NI 26.
[10] [1962] 2 All ER 33, [1962] 1 WLR 585.   [11] [1963] 3 All ER 687, [1964] 1 QB 533.
[12] [1932] 1 KB 458, [1931] All ER Rep 99.
[13] (1863) 15 CBNS 221, [1861–73] All ER Rep 544.   [14] (1863) 110 CLR 74 at 85.
[15] *Dutton v Bognor Regis UDC* [1972] 1 All ER 462 at 471, 472, [1972] 1 QB 373 at 392–394.

The decision provoked a good deal of discussion: see note 5, p. 240, ante. Of particular relevance to the present context is *Henderson v Merrett Syndicates Ltd* [1995] 2 AC 145, [1994] 3 All ER 506 (p. 232, ante), which, as will have been seen, laid down the broad assumption of responsibility and reliance principle from *Hedley Byrne* (extending beyond statements). The House of Lords in *Henderson* ruled out economic loss claims in tort by a building owner against a sub-contractor whose work did not meet the standard laid down in the sub-contract, even if the building owner had nominated that sub-contractor. This was because the parties had so arranged their relationship that it was inconsistent with an assumption of responsibility by the sub-contractor to the building owner. *Junior Books* was thought to cause 'some difficulty' in relation to this matter, but it was also thought to be unnecessary to reconsider it for purposes of the *Henderson* case. See further *Architype Projects Ltd v Dewhurst MacFarlane & Partners (A Firm)* [2004] PNLR 38, [2003] EWHC 3341.

The *Henderson v Merrett* approach has been applied in a building context by the Court of Appeal, here between a sub-sub-contractor and a sub-contractor, in *Barclays Bank Ltd v Fairclough Building Ltd (No 2)* (1995) 76 BLR 1, but note that, as has been pointed out, this allowed the court to reduce damages for contributory negligence in the concurrent contract claim: see on this point, and more generally on the case, J. Cartwright (1996) 12 Const LJ 157. However, in *Hamble Fisheries Ltd v L Gardner & Sons Ltd (The 'Rebecca Elaine')* [1999] 2 Lloyd's Rep 1 (p. 620, post), a product liability case, the Court of Appeal confirmed that, in general, sub-contractors, like manufacturers, are not taken to have assumed responsibility for the ultimate client's economic well-being, whereas they are usually taken to have assumed responsibility for the client's physical well-being and property. It should be noted though that it is possible to reach the same result as *Junior Books* by the difficult route of finding that a collateral contract was formed between the sub-contractor and the claimant—see *George Fischer Holding Ltd v Davis Langdon & Everest* (1998) 61 Con LR 85.

On the receipt of *Junior Books* in Scotland, from where the appeal in that case came, see J. M. Thomson (1994) 110 LQR 361, and the recent decision in *Realstone Ltd v J & E Shepherd* [2008] Scots CS CSOH 31, noted p. 240, ante; for some background to *Junior Books*, and on the case more generally, see A. Rodger, op cit., p. 64. For recent cases on the position of builders and economic loss in other jurisdictions, see note 10, p. 197, ante.

2. On the question of whether there may be a civil liability for a breach of the building byelaws or regulations see pp. 478–479 of the fourth edition of this work; *Emden's Construction Law*, IV, paras. 200–204. Note in particular that s. 38 of the Building Act 1984 provides that breach of a duty imposed by building regulations is to be actionable if it causes damage unless the regulations provide to the contrary, but note also that this provision was not in force at the time of writing.

3. On the liability of a non-occupying contractor carrying out work on premises to those coming lawfully there, see *A C Billings & Sons Ltd v Riden* [1958] AC 240, [1957] 3 All ER 1 (normal negligence principles). For the liability of surveyors, see *Jackson and Powell on Professional Negligence* sixth edn (London, 2007) chap. 10, and for argument that *Murphy* may increase the liability of surveyors (and also solicitors), see T. Dugdale (1991) 7 PN 91.

4. It might well be thought that the vendor or lessor of defective premises would have been liable to someone injured as a result of his negligence, if not before *M'Alister (or Donoghue) v Stevenson* [1932] AC 562, then certainly after that decision. However, for

a long time the authorities (e.g. *Cavalier v Pope* [1906] AC 428) indicated that a vendor or lessor was not liable in negligence for his acts (or failure to act) prior to the sale or letting where persons on the premises were injured after such sale or letting as a result of the premises' defective state. It was thought that this was an area of law which was unaffected by *M'Alister (or Donoghue) v Stevenson*. This was to be distinguished from the case of a builder who was not an owner (*Sharpe v E T Sweeting & Sons Ltd* [1963] 2 All ER 455, [1963] 1 WLR 665). It should be noted that the landlord's immunity was cut down by s. 4 of the Occupiers' Liability Act 1957 (now repealed by the Defective Premises Act 1972, but replaced in wider terms by s. 4 of that Act). In *Dutton v Bognor Regis UDC* [1972] 1 QB 373, [1972] 1 All ER 462 Lord Denning MR and Sachs LJ attacked this common law immunity, at least so far as hidden defects created on the premises were concerned (per Sachs LJ) and, as we have seen, in *Anns* the House of Lords rejected the supposed immunity of the builder/vendor, an aspect of *Anns* which was seemingly accepted in *Murphy*.

What is the position at common law of a landlord or vendor who merely omits to repair the floorboards or who omits to warn of a defect which is not of his own creation (although in the case of landlords see the wide terms of s. 4 of the Defective Premises Act 1972, p. 605, post)? In the light of *Anns* and *Murphy* would he now be liable in tort at common law to an injured person? Note *Bowen v Paramount Builders (Hamilton) Ltd* [1977] 1 NZLR 394 at 415, where Richmond P expressed the hope that in the case of a vendor who is not a builder 'the time has now arrived when the courts can recognise a duty in tort on the part of the vendor who has actual knowledge of a dangerous but latent defect to warn his purchaser of the existence of that defect'. In *Boldack v East Lindsey District Council* (1998) 31 HLR 41 at 49 it is reiterated that where *Cavalier v Pope* does apply, a landlord is not liable, short of fraud, for letting premises, even where he knows they are dilapidated. See further *Winfield & Jolowicz*, pp.429–430; J. H. Holyoak and D. K. Allen, *Civil Liability for Defective Premises* (London, 1982), paras. 6.40–6.60; J. Martin (1984) 37 Current LP 85.

In *Rimmer v Liverpool City Council* [1985] QB 1, [1984] 1 All ER 930 the Court of Appeal was not prepared to impose a duty of care on landlords to see that the premises were reasonably safe at the time of the letting. In the current state of the law the imposition of such a duty was thought to be a matter for the House of Lords, if not the legislature. On the other hand, the landlords in that particular case were held to owe a duty of care as they had designed and built the flat in which injury to the claimant had occurred; in that capacity they owed a duty of reasonable care, in relation to its design and construction, to see that the premises were reasonably safe on being let to a tenant (though see Martin, op cit., pp. 101–102 on the question whether in the Court of Appeal's view the duty would cover a case of a failure to act on information received by such a landlord before a particular letting but after a non-negligent design and construction). Consider further *Ryan v London Borough of Camden* (1982) 8 HLR 75, on which see Martin, op cit., pp. 99–101. Note also *McNerny v Lambeth London Borough Council* (1988) 21 HLR 188, where the Court of Appeal, regarding itself as bound by *Cavalier v Pope*, rejected the idea of a duty in negligence on a landlord (who was not liable as a builder) to take reasonable steps to ensure the premises are habitable. As was suggested in *Rimmer*, the courts are likely to regard legislation as necessary to overrule *Cavalier v Pope*. In *McNerny* Dillon LJ said that even if *Cavalier v Pope* was not binding, the task of creating the new duty (referred to ante) was for Parliament not the courts, since this was 'an area where Parliament has intervened to prescribe the duties for landlords that Parliament thinks appropriate' (e.g. s. 4 of the Defective Premises Act 1972, p. 605, post). Is this too great a self-denying ordinance? See further the approach of the House of Lords in *Murphy v Brentwood District Council* [1991] 1 AC 398, [1990] 2 All ER 908. Taylor LJ also expressed the view in *McNerny* that the question of the reform of *Cavalier v Pope* was a matter for Parliament because of the problems and uncertainty its demise would cause. On *Cavalier v Pope,* see further *Boldack v East Lindsey District Council* (1998) 31 HLR 41.

5. Even if a claimant is aware of the danger on the premises, the danger may not have been eliminated and physical damage may ensue. Does *Murphy* rule out liability in such a case? In *Targett v Torfaen Borough Council* [1992] 3 All ER 27 the claimant fell on a part of the steps leading to the house which he leased from the defendants. The steps had no handrail and the accident occurred in the dark, there being no effective artificial lighting. The claimant had in fact complained to the defendants about the absence of lighting before taking up his weekly tenancy. Although it was argued, based on *Murphy,* that the claimant knew of the potential danger and therefore could not sue for the physical damage, the Court of Appeal was not prepared to bar the claim. It was not unreasonable for the claimant to have taken the risk nor was it reasonable to have expected him to eliminate or avoid it, although on the facts his damages were reduced by 25 per cent for contributory negligence. *Rimmer v Liverpool City Council*, noted ante, which decided that knowledge of a danger did not necessarily prevent recovery of damages for physical damage emanating from it, was regarded as still good law after *Murphy.* (Consider further *Nitrigin Eireann Teoranta v Inco Alloys Ltd* [1992] 1 All ER 854, [1992] 1 WLR 498, noted p. 196, ante.)

6. Before the developments in the Court of Appeal and the House of Lords mentioned in the previous note, the Law Commission had given its attention to this area of the law in 1970 (*Civil Liability of Vendors and Lessors of Defective Premises*, Law Com. No. 40), and two years later the Defective Premises Act was passed. Section 3 of the Act must be read subject to the developments mentioned in the preceding note.

■ The Defective Premises Act 1972

1. Duty to build dwellings properly.—(1) A person taking on work for or in connection with the provision of a dwelling (whether the dwelling is provided by the erection or by the conversion or enlargement of a building) owes a duty—

(a) if the dwelling is provided to the order of any person, to that person; and

(b) without prejudice to paragraph (a) above, to every person who acquires an interest (whether legal or equitable) in the dwelling;

to see that the work which he takes on is done in a workmanlike or, as the case may be, professional manner, with proper materials and so that as regards that work the dwelling will be fit for habitation when completed.

(2) A person who takes on any such work for another on terms that he is to do it in accordance with instructions given by or on behalf of that other shall, to the extent to which he does it properly in accordance with those instructions, be treated for the purposes of this section as discharging the duty imposed on him by subsection (1) above except where he owes a duty to that other to warn him of any defects in the instructions and fails to discharge that duty.

(3) A person shall not be treated for the purposes of subsection (2) above as having given instructions for the doing of work merely because he has agreed to the work being done in a specified manner, with specified materials or to a specified design.

(4) A person who—
  (a) in the course of a business which consists of or includes providing or arranging for the provision of dwellings or installations in dwellings; or
  (b) in the exercise of a power of making such provision or arrangements conferred by or by virtue of any enactment;

arranges for another to take on work for or in connection with the provision of a dwelling shall be treated for the purposes of this section as included among the persons who have taken on the work.

(5) Any cause of action in respect of a breach of the duty imposed by this section shall be deemed, for the purposes of the Limitation Act 1939, the Law Reform (Limitation of Actions, &c) Act 1954 and the Limitation Act 1963,[16] to have accrued at the time when the dwelling was completed, but if after that time a person who has done work for or in connection with the provision of the dwelling does further work to rectify the work he has already done, any such cause of action in respect of that further work shall be deemed for those purposes to have accrued at the time when the further work was finished.

2. Cases excluded from the remedy under section 1.—(1) Where—
  (a) in connection with the provision of a dwelling or its first sale or letting for habitation any rights in respect of defects in the state of the dwelling are conferred by an approved scheme to which this section applies on a person having or acquiring an interest in the dwelling; and
  (b) it is stated in the document of a type approved for the purposes of this section that the requirements as to design or construction imposed by or under the scheme have, or appear to have, been substantially complied with in relation to the dwelling;

no action shall be brought by any person having or acquiring an interest in the dwelling for breach of the duty imposed by section 1 above in relation to the dwelling.

(2) A scheme to which this section applies—
  (a) may consist of any number of documents and any number of agreements or other transactions between any number of persons; but
  (b) must confer, by virtue of agreements entered into with persons having or acquiring an interest in the dwellings to which the scheme applies, rights on such persons in respect of the defects in the state of the dwellings....

(7) Where an interest in a dwelling is compulsorily acquired—
  (a) no action shall be brought by the acquiring authority for breach of the duty imposed by section 1 above in respect of the dwelling; and
  (b) if any work for or in connection with the provision of the dwelling was done otherwise than in the course of a business by the person in occupation of the dwelling at the time of the compulsory acquisition, the acquiring authority and not that person shall be treated as the person who took on the work and accordingly as owing that duty.

3. Duty of care with respect to work done on premises not abated by disposal of premises.—(1) Where work of construction, repair, maintenance or demolition or any other work is done on or in relation to premises, any duty of care owed, because of the doing of the work, to persons who might reasonably be expected to be affected by defects in the state of the premises created by the doing of the work shall not be abated by the subsequent disposal of the premises by the person who owed the duty.

(2) This section does not apply—
  (a) in the case of premises which are let, where the relevant tenancy of the premises commenced, or the relevant tenancy agreement of the premises was entered into, before the commencement of this Act [1 January, 1974];

---

[16] [And note the Limitation Act 1980, a consolidating statute.]

(b) in the case of premises disposed of in any other way, when the disposal of the premises was completed, or a contract for their disposal was entered into, before the commencement of this Act; or

(c) in either case, where the relevant transaction disposing of the premises is entered into in pursuance of an enforceable option by which the consideration for the disposal was fixed before the commencement of this Act.

4. Landlord's duty of care in virtue of obligation or right to repair premises demised.—(1) Where premises are let under a tenancy which puts on the landlord an obligation to the tenant for the maintenance or repair of the premises, the landlord owes to all persons who might reasonably be expected to be affected by defects in the state of the premises a duty to take such care as is reasonable in all the circumstances to see that they are reasonably safe from personal injury or from damage to their property caused by a relevant defect.

(2) The said duty is owed if the landlord knows (whether as a result of being notified by the tenant or otherwise) or if he ought in all the circumstances to have known of the relevant defect.

(3) In this section 'relevant defect' means a defect in the state of the premises existing at or after the material time and arising from, or continuing because of, an act or omission by the landlord which constitutes or would if he had had notice of the defect, have constituted a failure by him to carry out his obligation to the tenant for the maintenance or repair of the premises; and for the purposes of the foregoing provision 'the material time' means—

(a) where the tenancy commenced before this Act, the commencement of this Act; and

(b) in all other cases, the earliest of the following times, that is to say—

(i) the time when the tenancy commences;

(ii) the time when the tenancy agreement is entered into;

(iii) the time when possession is taken of the premises in contemplation of the letting.

(4) Where premises are let under a tenancy which expressly or impliedly gives the landlord the right to enter the premises to carry out any description of maintenance or repair of the premises, then, as from the time when he first is, or by notice or otherwise can put himself, in a position to exercise the right and so long as he is or can put himself in that position, he shall be treated for the purposes of subsections (1) to (3) above (but for no other purpose) as if he were under an obligation to the tenant for that description of maintenance or repair of the premises; but the landlord shall not owe the tenant any duty by virtue of this subsection in respect of any defect in the state of the premises arising from, or continuing because of, a failure to carry out an obligation expressly imposed on the tenant by the tenancy.

(5) For the purposes of this section obligations imposed or rights given by any enactment in virtue of a tenancy shall be treated as imposed or given by the tenancy.

(6) This section applies to a right of occupation given by contract or any enactment and not amounting to a tenancy as if the right were a tenancy, and 'tenancy' and cognate expressions shall be construed accordingly.

5. Application to Crown.—This Act shall bind the Crown, but as regards the Crown's liability in tort shall not bind the Crown further than the Crown is made liable in tort by the Crown Proceedings Act 1947.

6. Supplemental.—(1) In this Act—

'disposal', in relation to premises, includes a letting, and an assignment or surrender of a tenancy, of the premises and the creation by contract of any other right to occupy the premises, and 'dispose' shall be construed accordingly;

'personal injury' includes any disease and any impairment of a person's physical or mental condition;

'tenancy' means—

(a) a tenancy created either immediately or derivatively out of the freehold, whether by a lease or underlease, by an agreement for a lease or underlease or by a tenancy agreement, but not including a mortgage term or any interest arising in favour of a mortgagor by his attorning tenant to his mortgagee; or

(b) a tenancy at will or a tenancy on sufferance; or

(c) a tenancy, whether or not constituting a tenancy at common law, created by or in pursuance of any enactment;

and cognate expressions shall be construed accordingly.

(2) Any duty imposed by or enforceable by virtue of any provision of this Act is in addition to any duty a person may owe apart from that provision.

(3) Any term of an agreement which purports to exclude or restrict, or has the effect of excluding or restricting, the operation of any of the provisions of this Act, or any liability arising by virtue of any such provision, shall be void.

QUESTIONS

1. How does s. 1 alter the common law position? What is the level of the duty which is imposed? Could s. 1 cover economic loss? (Consider Lord Bridge's view in *Murphy v Brentwood District Council* [1990] 2 All ER 908 at 930, p. 188, ante.)

2. Could s. 1 of the Act cover the case of a local authority in the sort of situation discussed in *Anns v Merton London Borough Council* [1978] AC 728, [1977] 2 All ER 492 and *Murphy*? (Consider *Sparham-Souter v Town and Country Developments (Essex) Ltd* [1976] QB 858 at 869–870 and 877.) If it could, how important would this be after *Murphy*?

3. Would any of the sections of the Act be of assistance to a trespasser? (See P. M. North (1973) 36 MLR 628 at 636.)

NOTES

1. For discussion of s. 1 of the Act, see *Alexander v Mercouris* [1979] 3 All ER 305, [1979] 1 WLR 1270. Following views expressed in this case, it was decided in *Thompson v Clive Alexander & Partners Ltd* (1992) 59 BLR 81 that the last clause of s. 1(1) (i.e. from the words 'so that' to the end) do not create a separate obligation but rather qualify what has gone before: thus to be actionable the defect in question must render the dwelling unfit for habitation on completion. See also *Catlin Estates Ltd v Carter Jonas (a firm)* [2006] PNLR 15, [2005] EWHC 2315 (TCC) which, in addition, defines a dwelling as 'a building used or capable of being used as a dwelling house, not being a building which is used predominantly for commercial and industrial purposes'. On s. 1 of the 1972 Act see further *Andrews v Schooling* [1991] 3 All ER 723, [1991] 1 WLR 783 deciding that it applies to omissions as well as to positive acts, and *Alderson v Beetham Organisation Ltd* [2003] 1 WLR 1686, [2003] EWCA Civ 408: the latter case decides that the proviso in s. 1(5)—concerning further work to rectify work previously done—creates a fresh cause of action for breach of the s. 1 duty when the further work, albeit in itself done competently, does not correct the original work.

2. Under s. 2 of the Act, it is for the Secretary of State to approve schemes, which he is to do by order exercisable by statutory instrument. Various schemes established by the National House-Building Council (N.H.B.C.) have been approved for the purposes of s. 2. The last approval was given to a scheme in 1977, and more recently it has not been the practice of the N.H.B.C. to seek approval for its schemes.

3. Section 4 of the Act replaces in wider terms s. 4 of the Occupiers' Liability Act 1957, and on s. 4 and implying terms, see *McAuley v Bristol City Council* [1992] QB 134, [1992] 1 All ER 749. The 'relevant defect' in s. 4(3) is concerned with maintenance or repair; in *Alkar v Collingwood Housing Association* [2007] EWCA Civ 343 the Court of Appeal refused, in the case of a glass panel, to equate an argument about a duty to make safe with a duty of repair and/or maintenance. A landlord, of course, could be liable in contract to his tenant, on which see Holyoak and Allen, op cit., paras. 7.4–7.20. See further *Sykes v Harry* [2001] QB 1014, [2001] EWCA Civ 167, distinguishing between an action under s. 11 of the Landlord and Tenant Act 1985 and one under s. 4 of the 1972 Act.

4. For detailed consideration of the 1972 Act, see J. R. Spencer [1974] CLJ 307 and [1975] CLJ 48. In relation to his Addendum [1975] CLJ at p. 48 discussing the Health and Safety at Work etc Act 1974, note now s. 38 of the Building Act 1984.

5. Note the use made of the existence of the Defective Premises Act in *Murphy v Brentwood District Council* [1991] 1 AC 398, [1990] 2 All ER 908 (p. 183, ante). Consider, however, the following argument of P. Cane (1989) 52 MLR 200 at 211, commenting on the earlier decision in *D & F Estates Ltd v Church Comrs for England* [1989] AC 177, [1988] 2 All ER 992:

> Lord Bridge [in *D & F Estates Ltd*]... expressed the view that since the enactment of the Defective Premises Act 1972, it would not be right for the courts to impose liability for losses recoverable under that Act by means of a rule which might allow recovery in circumstances where the Act would not. In particular, the common law should not be used to impose liability for the cost of repairing premises other than dwellings, and it should not be used to evade the limitation period for claims under the Act. This argument seems to be based on the problematic idea that once the legislature has enacted legislation on a particular subject matter in this case, defective premises, the courts are precluded from developing the common law in that area. It also seems to be based on the misplaced faith that the legislature always does, and indeed did in the Defective Premises Act, lay down a set of rules which are much more precise and more carefully limited and crafted than the common law can achieve. Finally, Lord Bridge expressed the opinion that consumer protection is better left to the legislature. Does this mean that when it has the chance the House of Lords will also reverse *Hedley Byrne v Heller* [[1964] AC 465, [1963] 2 All ER 575] and all other rules and principles of the law of tort (including those based on *Donoghue v Stevenson* [[1932] AC 562]) which are intended to, or can be, or are used to protect the consumers of goods and services against producers?

> See further J. Stapleton in *The Frontiers of Liability*, edited by P. B. H. Birks, (Oxford, 1994), pp. 89–90.

■ Latent Damage Act 1986

Accrual of cause of action to successive owners in respect of latent damage to property

3 Accrual of cause of action to successive owners in respect of latent damage to property.—
(1) Subject to the following provisions of this section, where—

(a) a cause of action ("the original cause of action") has accrued to any person in respect of any negligence to which damage to any property in which he has an interest is attributable (in whole or in part); and

(b) another person acquires an interest in that property after the date on which the original cause of action accrued but before the material facts about the damage have become known to any person who, at the time when he first has knowledge of those facts, has any interest in the property;

a fresh cause of action in respect of that negligence shall accrue to that other person on the date on which he acquires his interest in the property.

(2) A cause of action accruing to any person by virtue of subsection (1) above—

(a) shall be treated as if based on breach of a duty of care at common law owed to the person to whom it accrues; and

(b) shall be treated for the purposes of section 14A of the 1980 Act[17] (special time limit for negligence actions where facts relevant to cause of action are not known at date of accrual) as having accrued on the date on which the original cause of action accrued.

(3) Section 28 of the 1980 Act (extension of limitation period in case of disability) shall not apply in relation to any such cause of action.

(4) Subsection (1) above shall not apply in any case where the person acquiring an interest in the damaged property is either—

(a) a person in whom the original cause of action vests by operation of law; or

(b) a person in whom the interest in that property vests by virtue of any order made by a court under section 538 of the Companies Act 1985 (vesting of company property in liquidator).

(5) For the purposes of subsection (1)(b) above, the material facts about the damage are such facts about the damage as would lead a reasonable person who has an interest in the damaged property at the time when those facts become known to him to consider it sufficiently serious to justify his instituting proceedings for damages against a defendant who did not dispute liability and was able to satisfy a judgment.

(6) For the purposes of this section a person's knowledge includes knowledge which he might reasonably have been expected to acquire—

(a) from facts observable or ascertainable by him; or

(b) from facts ascertainable by him with the help of appropriate expert advice which it is reasonable for him to seek;

but a person shall not be taken by virtue of this subsection to have knowledge of a fact ascertainable by him only with the help of expert advice so long as he has taken all reasonable steps to obtain (and, where appropriate, to act on) that advice.

(7) This section shall bind the Crown, but as regards the Crown's liability in tort shall not bind the Crown further than the Crown is made liable in tort by the Crown Proceedings Act 1947.

5 Citation, interpretation, commencement and extent....

(2) In this Act—

...

'action' includes any proceeding in a court of law, an arbitration and any new claim within the meaning of section 35 of the 1980 Act[18] (new claims in pending actions).

(3) This Act shall come into force at the end of the period of two months beginning with the date [18 July 1986] on which it is passed.

(4) This Act extends to England and Wales only.

NOTE

Limitation of actions is not generally dealt with in this book, and the Latent Damage Act 1996 is concerned with that topic. However, s. 3 of the act creates a new cause of action and should be dealt with at this point.

---

[17] [The Limitation Act 1980. Section 14A was inserted in the 1980 Act by s. 1 of the Latent Damage Act 1986.]

[18] [The Limitation Act 1980.]

In *Pirelli General Cable Works Ltd v Oscar Faber & Partners (A Firm)* [1983] 2 AC 1, [1983] 1 All ER 65 the House of Lords decided that as a general rule the cause of action accrued—and hence time started to run—when physical damage occurred (here cracks in a chimney). This was the case whether or not the damage had been discovered or was even capable of being discovered. The position concerning limitation has now been altered by the Latent Damage Act (and there is separate legislative provision dealing with cases of personal injuries). The decision in *Pirelli* had revealed a problem for the successors in title to the person who was the owner of the property when the physical damage occurred. This was because of the general rule that a claimant has to have a possessory or proprietary interest in the article which is physically damaged at the time when the damage occurs. (See generally p. 176, ante.) For comment on this point from *Pirelli* see G. Robertson (1983) 99 LQR 559; Hepple All ER Rev 1983, p. 332; M. A. Jones (1984) 100 LQR 413, which also discuss the opinion expressed in *Pirelli* by Lord Fraser, with whose speech the other members of the House of Lords agreed, that 'the true view is that the duty of the builder . . . is owed to owners of the property as a class, and that if time runs against one owner, it also runs against all his successors in title'. Section 3 of the Latent Damage Act now provides a legislative solution to the difficulty. Has its practical importance been reduced after *Murphy* in the light of the views in that case about the type of damage that is actionable? In *Payne v John Setchell Ltd* [2002 PNLR 146 at [44] it was stated that the Act was 'passed to prevent a mischief which does not or may not now exist'. Note furthermore how *Pirelli* was interpreted by Lord Keith in *Murphy v Brentwood District Council* [1990] 2 All ER 908 at 919 (p. 185, ante) and see *Invercargill City Council v Hamlin* [1996] AC 624, [1996] 1 All ER 756. In *Invercargill* the Privy Council treated an action in respect of defective foundations which had produced cracks in a house as one for economic loss (which had been acknowledged by post—*Pirelli* English case law). This had the consequence that the cause of action was not necessarily complete when the cracks occurred, but rather 'when the cracks become so bad, or the defects so obvious, that any reasonable homeowner would call in an expert'. The economic loss occurred at this point since this was when market value would be adversely affected. The Privy Council was careful not to rule whether *Pirelli* was still good law for England (as opposed to New Zealand), and in *Abbott v Will Gannon and Smith* [2005] PNLR 30, [2005] EWCA Civ 198 the Court of Appeal thought it was still bound by *Pirelli*. (See further the earlier cases of *New Islington and Hackney Housing Association Ltd v Pollard Thomas and Edwards* [2001] BLR 74 and *The Mayor and Burgesses of the London Borough of Lewisham v MR Ltd* [2003] BLR 504.)

An additional point to note about s. 3 is the argument (see E. Griew (1986) 136 NLJ 1201) that it could have a wider impact than might be anticipated and affect the position laid down in *Leigh and Sillivan Ltd v Aliakmon Shipping Co Ltd* [1986] AC 785, [1986] 2 All ER 145 (p. 176, ante).

CHAPTER TEN

LIABILITY FOR DAMAGE CAUSED BY THINGS

Those who keep or put into circulation *things* create special dangers. Not surprisingly, therefore, there have been attempts to create special rules, going beyond the tort of negligence, to place responsibility for resulting damage on those who create the risk, subject to certain defences. One situation where the attempt was successful at common law is provided by the rule in *Rylands v Fletcher* (1868) LR 3 HL 330 (p. 828, post) which imposes strict liability for the escape of dangerous things from land. Liability under this rule will be discussed in chap. 14, post because of its close connection with the factual circumstances which may give rise to an action in nuisance, and it will be seen at that point that there are restrictions upon its operation. The courts, it might be noted here, declined the opportunity to use this rule so as to impose strict liability on the part of those using motor vehicles on the road (see J. R. Spencer [1983] CLJ 65); and they also missed the opportunity (in *Phillips v Britannia Hygienic Laundry Co Ltd* [1923] 2 KB 832, p. 692, post) to develop, through statutory interpretation, a principle of strict liability for damage caused by motor vehicles. More generally, the courts did not follow the lead given by the courts in the United States in developing a principle of strict liability for defective products which built on the idea of extending contractual warranties to third parties (see Prosser and Keeton, *The Law of Torts* 5th edn (St. Paul, Minnesota, 1984), chap. 17). A stricter liability regime was, however, created by statute, the Consumer Protection Act 1987, in response to an initiative by the European Community (see p. 635, post). The precise nature of the liability regime created by the Act is still a matter of some uncertainty. In the meantime, following a barrage of academic criticism (see e.g. J. Henderson and A Twerski (1990) 65 NYU L Rev 265 and (1991) 66 NYU L Rev 1263) the fashion in the United States has turned away from strict liability towards a mixed regime in which liability without proof of fault remains for 'manufacturing' defects (where the product has departed from its 'intended design') but re-introduces fault-based liability for 'design' defects and for failures to warn. (See Restatement of the Law, 3d, Torts: Products Liability (1998) Chap 1, Topic 1, s. 2).

So far as the tort of negligence is concerned, the 'manufacturer's rule' in *M'Alister (or Donoghue) v Stevenson* [1932] AC 562, p. 30, ante) has been extended to a wide range of ultimate consumers and has on occasions almost reached the level of strict liability. However, the theory of the tort rests firmly upon the idea of negligence. At one time the classification of a chattel as dangerous or non-dangerous was considered important, and it is still of importance to the rule in *Rylands v Fletcher*; but today it is clear that this classification in the tort of negligence affects only the degree of care which will be required of a defendant in a particular situation.

A consumer does get some degree of protection from the criminal law and the possibility of an action in contract needs to be borne in mind when the materials in this chapter are studied. Recovery of damages on a strict liability basis may, of course, be available in contract, the scope of which has been extended by the Contracts (Rights of Third Parties) Act 1999 (see p. 256, ante). An action for breach of statutory duty (see chap. 12 post), which is a tort action, may also provide a stricter form of liability than negligence and here the student's attention is directed to s. 41 of the Consumer Protection Act 1987.

The common law negligence and contractual remedies continue to be important despite the introduction of stricter tort liability in the 1987 Act for a number of reasons. One is that the Act only applies to some types of damage (see pp. 631–632, post)—it is assumed, for example, that it does not cover pure economic loss; another is that the undoubted difficulties of interpretation the Act presents mean that claimants will dual-track their claims, using both the Act and the common law, unless and until it becomes clear that liability under the Act is in all relevant respects easier for claimants to establish than common law liability. On the subject of product liability generally, see J. Stapleton, *Product Liability* (London, 1994); C. J. Miller and R.S. Goldberg, *Product Liability* 2nd edn (Oxford, 2004); *The Law of Product Liability* (general editor G. Howells) 2nd edn (London, 2007).

1 NEGLIGENCE

(a) In general

■ M'Alister (or Donoghue) v Stevenson

p. 30, ante

(b) Development of the law

■ Grant v Australian Knitting Mills Ltd

Judicial Committee of the Privy Council [1935] All ER Rep 209

The appellant, Dr Grant, of Adelaide, South Australia, claimed damages on the ground that he had contracted dermatitis by reason of the improper condition of some underpants bought by him from the defendants, John Martin and Co Ltd, and manufactured by the defendants, Australian Knitting Mills Ltd.

The appellant bought the underwear on 3 June 1931. He put on one suit on the morning of 28 June 1931. By the evening of that date he felt itching, but no objective symptoms appeared until the next day, when a redness appeared in front of each ankle over an area of about 2½ in, by 1½ in. His condition got worse, the rash became generalised and very acute, and he was confined to bed for seventeen weeks. In November he became convalescent and went to New Zealand to recuperate. He returned in the following February, but soon had a relapse, and by March his condition was so serious that in April he went into hospital where he remained until July. In April he began this action.

The Supreme Court of South Australia (Murray CJ) gave judgment against both defendants, against the retailers on the contract of sale, and against the manufacturers in tort, following the decision of the House of Lords in *M'Alister (or Donoghue) v Stevenson*, but the decision of the Supreme Court was reversed by the High Court of Australia by a majority. On appeal to the Privy Council:

LORD WRIGHT: . . .

The appellant's claim was that the disease was caused by the presence in the cuffs or angle ends of the underpants which he purchased and wore, of an irritating chemical, namely, free sulphite, the presence of which was due to negligence in manufacture, and also involved on the part of the respondents, John Martin & Co Ltd, a breach of the relevant implied conditions under the Sale of Goods Act.

[Having held that the retailers were liable in contract and that there was negligence in the manufacture, he continued:] . . . According to the evidence, the method of manufacture was correct; the danger of excess sulphites being left was recognised and was guarded against; the process was intended to be foolproof. If excess sulphites were left in the garment, that could only be because someone was at fault. The appellant is not required to lay his finger on the exact person in all the chain who was responsible or to specify what he did wrong. Negligence is found as a matter of inference from the existence of the defects taken in connection with all the known circumstances; even if the manufacturers could by apt evidence have rebutted that inference they have not done so.

On this basis, the damage suffered by the appellant was caused in fact (because the interposition of the retailers may for this purpose in the circumstances of the case be disregarded) by the negligent or improper way in which the manufacturers made the garments. But this mere sequence of cause and effect is not enough in law to constitute a cause of action in negligence, which is a complex concept, involving a duty as between the parties to take care, as well as a breach of that duty and resulting damage. . . .

. . . Their Lordships, like the judges in the courts in Australia, will follow [*M'Alister* (or *Donoghue*) *v Stevenson*[1]], and the only question here can be what that authority decides and whether this case comes within its principles. . . .

Their Lordships think that the principle of the decision is summed up in the words of Lord Atkin ([1932] AC at p. 599):

> 'A manufacturer of products, which he sells in such a form as to show that he intends them to reach the ultimate consumer in the form in which they left him with no reasonable possibility of intermediate examination, and with the knowledge that the absence of reasonable care in the preparation or putting up of the products will result in an injury to the consumer's life or property, owes a duty to the consumer to take that reasonable care.'

This statement is in accord with the opinions expressed by Lord Thankerton and Lord Macmillan, who in principle agreed with Lord Atkin.

In order to ascertain whether the principle applies to the present case, it is necessary to define what the decision involves and consider the points of distinction relied upon before their Lordships.

It is clear that the decision treats negligence, where there is a duty to take care, as a specific tort in itself, and not simply as an element in some more complex relationship or in some specialised breach of duty, and still less as having any dependence on contract. All that is necessary as a step to establish the tort of actionable negligence is to define the precise relationship from which the duty to take care is to be deduced. It is, however, essential in English law that the duty should be established; . . . In *Donoghue*'s case,[1] the duty was deduced simply from the facts relied on, namely, that the injured party was one of a class for whose use, in the contemplation and intention of the makers, the article was issued to the world, and the article was used by that party in the state in which it was prepared and issued without it being changed in any way and without there being any warning of, or means of detecting, the hidden danger; there was, it is true, no personal intercourse between the maker and the user; but though the duty is personal, because it is inter partes, it needs no interchange of words,

---

[1] [1932] AC 562.

spoken or written, or signs of offer or assent; it is thus different in character from any contractual relationship; no question of consideration between the parties is relevant; for these reasons the use of the word 'privity' in this connection is apt to mislead because of the suggestion of some overt relationship like that in contract, and the word 'proximity' is open to the same objection; if the term proximity is to be applied at all, it can only be in the sense that the want of care and the injury are in essence directly and intimately connected; though there may be intervening transactions of sale and purchase and intervening handling between these two events, the events are themselves unaffected by what happened between them: proximity can only properly be used to exclude any element of remoteness, or of some interfering complication between the want of care and the injury, and, like 'privity' may mislead by introducing alien ideas. Equally also may the word 'control' embarrass, though it is conveniently used in the opinions in *Donoghue*'s case[2] to emphasise the essential factor that the consumer must use the article exactly as it left the maker, that is in all material features, and use it as it was intended to be used. In that sense the maker may be said to control the thing until it is used. But that again is an artificial use, because, in the natural sense of the word, the makers parted with all control when they sold the article and divested themselves of possession and property. An argument used in the present case based on the word 'control' will be noticed later.

It is obvious that the principles thus laid down involve a duty based on the simple facts detailed above, a duty quite unaffected by any contracts dealing with the thing, for instance, of sale by maker to retailer, and again by retailer to consumer or to the consumer's friend.

It may be said that the duty is difficult to define, because when the act of negligence in manufacture occurs there was no specific person towards whom the duty could be said to exist: the thing might never be used: it might be destroyed by accident or it might be scrapped, or in many ways fail to come into use in the normal way: in other words, the duty cannot at the time of manufacture be other than potential or contingent, and only can become vested by the fact of actual use by a particular person. But the same theoretical difficulty has been disregarded in cases like *Heaven v Pender*,[3] or in the case of things dangerous per se or known to be dangerous, where third parties have been held entitled to recover on the principles explained in *Dominion Natural Gas Co Ltd v Collins and Perkins*.[4] In *Donoghue*'s case[2] the thing was dangerous in fact, though the danger was hidden, and the thing was dangerous only because of want of care in making it; as Lord Atkin points out in *Donoghue*'s case[2] ([1932] AC at p. 595), the distinction between things inherently dangerous and things only dangerous because of negligent manufacture cannot be regarded as significant for the purpose of the questions here involved.

One further point may be noted. The principle of *Donoghue*'s case[2] can only be applied where the defect is hidden and unknown to the consumer, otherwise the directness of cause and effect is absent: the man who consumes or uses a thing which he knows to be noxious cannot complain in respect of whatever mischief follows because it follows from his own conscious volition in choosing to incur the risk or certainty of mischance.

If the foregoing are the essential features of *Donoghue*'s case[2] they are also to be found, in their Lordships' judgment, in the present case. The presence of the deleterious chemical in the pants, due to negligence in manufacture, was a hidden and latent defect, just as much as were the remains of the snail in the opaque bottle: it could not be detected by any examination that could reasonably be made. Nothing happened between the making of the garments and their being worn to change their condition. The garments were made by the manufacturers for the purpose of being worn exactly as they were worn in fact by the appellant: it was not contemplated that they should be first washed. It is immaterial that the appellant has a claim in contract against the retailers, because that is a quite independent cause of action, based on different considerations, even though the damage may be the same. Equally irrelevant is any question of liability between the retailers and the manufacturers on the contract of sale between them. The tort liability is independent of any question of contract. It was argued, but not perhaps very strongly, that *Donoghue*'s case[2] was a case of food or drink to

---

² [1932] AC 562.   ³ (1883) 11 QBD 503.   ⁴ [1909] AC 640.

be consumed internally, whereas the pants here were to be worn externally. No distinction, however, can be logically drawn for this purpose between a noxious thing taken internally and a noxious thing applied externally: the garments were made to be worn next to the skin: indeed Lord Atkin ([1932] AC at p. 583) specifically puts as examples of what is covered by the principle he is enunciating things operating externally, such as 'an ointment, a soap, a cleaning fluid, or cleaning powder'.

Counsel for the respondents, however, sought to distinguish *Donoghue*'s case[5] from the present on the ground that in the former the makers of the ginger beer had retained 'control' over it in the sense that they had placed it in stoppered and sealed bottles, so that it would not be tampered with until it was opened to be drunk, whereas the garments in question were merely put into paper packets, each containing six sets, which in ordinary course would be taken down by the shopkeeper and opened and the contents handled and disposed of separately so that they would be exposed to the air. He contended that, though there was no reason to think that the garments, when sold to the appellant were in any other condition, least of all as regards sulphur contents, then when sold to the retailers by the manufacturers, still the mere possibility and not the fact of their condition having been changed was sufficient to distinguish *Donoghue*'s case:[5] there was no 'control' because nothing was done by the manufacturers to exclude the possibility of any tampering while the goods were on their way to the user. Their Lordships do not accept that contention. The decision in *Donoghue*'s case[5] did not depend on the bottle being stoppered and sealed; the essential point in this regard was that the article should reach the consumer or user subject to the same defect as it had when it left the manufacturer. That this was true of the garment is in their Lordships' opinion beyond question. At most there might in other cases be a greater difficulty of proof of the fact.

...[T]heir Lordships hold the present case to come within the principle of *Donoghue*'s case[6] and they think that the judgment of the Chief Justice was right and should be restored as against both respondents, and that the appeal should be allowed with costs here and in the courts below, and that the appellant's petition for leave to adduce further evidence should be dismissed without costs. They will humbly so advise His Majesty.

Appeal allowed.

NOTE

The claim in contract against the retailers also succeeded in this case, and the possibility of such an action must always be borne in mind in the context of products liability. See generally Miller and Goldberg, op cit., chaps. 2–6. A particular advantage for the claimant, compared with the tort of negligence, is that liability can be stricter in contract (see e.g. *Christopher Hill Ltd v Ashington Piggeries Ltd* [1969] 1 Lloyd's Rep 425 and s. 14(2) of the Sale of Goods Act 1979 as amended by the Sale and Supply of Goods Act 1994); although strict liability in tort has now been introduced alongside negligence, the type of damage covered is not as wide-ranging as in negligence or contract. Another advantage for the claimant is that the difficulty over the recovery of economic loss in tort is avoided. The student should also consider the position relating to contributory negligence (see p. 425, ante) and remoteness of damage (see *H Parsons (Livestock) Ltd v Uttley Ingham & Co Ltd* [1978] QB 791, [1978] 1 All ER 525). Limitation periods may be more favourable in tort than contract.

If sued, the retailer can of course claim in contract from the person who sold him the product and in theory the cost can be laid at the manufacturer's door through the chain of contracts connecting him with the retailer. However, in practice this may not be so easy; for example, one party in the chain of distribution may have gone bankrupt or, as in *Lexmead (Basingstoke) Ltd v Lewis* [1982] AC 225, [1981] 2 All ER 1185 (see also *Dodd and Dodd v*

---

[5] [1932] AC 562.

Wilson and McWilliam [1946] 1 All ER 691), one party may be unable to identify the party from whom the product was obtained. In this situation the party who has been held liable for breach of contract could try to recover this loss from the manufacturer in tort, but, since the coming into force of the Civil Liability (Contribution) Act 1978 (p. 1122, post), there has been the possibility of a claim for contribution even though the party claiming contribution is liable in contract and the party from whom it is claimed is liable in tort if both are liable for the same damage to a third party. This could, therefore, avoid the difficulty of claiming for economic loss in tort if the damage caused by the product was personal injury or damage to property.

■ Evans v Triplex Safety Glass Co Ltd
King's Bench Division [1936] 1 All ER 283

In 1934, Mr Evans bought a Vauxhall car which had been fitted by the Vauxhall Motor Co with a windscreen made of 'Triplex Toughened Safety Glass'. In July 1935, he was driving the car, with his wife and son as passengers, when the windscreen cracked and disintegrated. Part of the windscreen fell on the boy, part on Mr Evans and a considerable portion fell on the wife, who suffered severe shock. The plaintiffs (Mr Evans and his wife) brought an action against the manufacturers of the windscreen.

PORTER J: . . .

In this case I do not think that I ought to infer negligence on the part of the defendants. . . . I cannot draw the inference that the cause of the disintegration was the faulty manufacture. It is true that the human element may fail and then the manufacturers would be liable for negligence of their employee, but then that was not proved in this case. The disintegration may have been caused by any accident. There was every opportunity for failure on the part of the human element in fastening the windscreen, and I think that the disintegration was due rather to the fitting of the windscreen than to faulty manufacture having regard to its use on the road and the damage done to a windscreen in the course of use.

It is true that, as Mr Macaskie[6] points out, in these cases he has not got to eliminate every possible element, but he has got to eliminate every probable element. He has not displaced sufficiently the balance of probabilities in this case. I think that this glass is reasonably safe and possibly more safe than other glasses. One cannot help seeing that in all these cases one has to look with considerable care. One has to consider the question of time. The plaintiff had had the windscreen for about a year. Then there is the possibility of examination. The suppliers of the car had every opportunity to examine the windscreen. I do not propose to lay down any rule of law; it is a question of degree and these elements must be taken into consideration. This article was put into a frame and screwed; one must consider that. As I have said there is the element of time, the opportunity of examination and the opportunity of damage from other causes. One must consider all these factors.

In *M'Alister* (or *Donoghue*) *v Stevenson*[7] there was a snail in the ginger beer bottle and there was no opportunity of seeing it as you could not see through the glass. In *Grant v Australian Knitting Mills Ltd*[8] the article passed on to the purchaser and it is quite clear that a reasonable examination of the garment would not have revealed the presence of the sulphite. That case is different from this. In that case there was found in some of the garments an excess of sulphites and that clearly was the cause of the injury. Here are a number of causes which might have caused disintegration. I do not find any negligence proved against the defendants and I give the defendants judgment with costs.

---

[6] Council for the plaintiffs.   [7] [1932] AC 562.   [8] [1936] AC 85.

■ Kubach v Hollands

King's Bench Division [1937] 3 All ER 907

A science teacher bought from the second defendants a powder labelled manganese dioxide, but which was in fact a mixture of that chemical and a much larger quantity of antimony sulphide. The second defendants had purchased the powder as manganese dioxide from a third party, but the invoice stated, inter alia, that the goods 'must be examined and tested by user before use'. The second defendants did not examine or test the powder, nor did they inform the teacher of the need for such examination or test. The use of manganese dioxide in a particular chemical experiment would have been safe but when this powder was used, there was an explosion and a schoolgirl was injured. The schoolgirl (and her father) unsuccessfully claimed damages against the first defendant (the proprietress of the school). However, the second defendants, who had notice of the powder's intended use, were held liable for negligence, and they claimed contribution or an indemnity from the third party.

LORD HEWART CJ: ...

After hearing and considering the very careful arguments of counsel on both sides, I have come, reluctantly enough, to the conclusion that the third party is entitled to succeed....

[Having quoted Lord Atkin's 'manufacturer principle',[9] he continued:] The case which is there contemplated is, I think, in essential respects the opposite of the present case. The manganese dioxide which the third party ought to have supplied here to the second defendants might have been resold for a variety of purposes or in innocuous compounds or mixtures. The use of it for school experiments was only one of the many possible uses, and the third party, unlike the second defendants, had no notice of the intended use. More than that, it was common ground that a very simple test, if it had been carried out, as the third party's invoice prescribed, and as the first defendant was not warned, would immediately have exhibited the fact that antimony sulphide had erroneously been made up and delivered as manganese dioxide. The second defendants had ample and repeated opportunity of intermediate examination, and, if they had taken the simple precaution which the invoice warned them to take, no mischief would have followed....

Finally, it was attempted, although faintly, to derive some assistance for the second defendants from the provisions of the Law Reform (Married Women and Tortfeasors) Act 1935[10]....In my opinion, there was no joint tort, nor could the plaintiff have sued the third party....

Judgment for the third party against the second defendants.

QUESTIONS

1.   What is the relevance of a warning to the question of intermediate examination?
2.   Do you think that there should be a duty to warn or take some action in relation to a defect in a product that the manufacturer discovers after the product has left his hands? (Consider *V and M Walton v British Leyland (UK) Ltd* [1980] PLI 156; *E Hobbs (Farms) Ltd v Baxenden Chemical Co Ltd* [1992] 1 Lloyd's Rep 54 at 65; cf. *Hamble Fisheries Ltd v L Gardner & Sons Ltd (The Rebecca Elaine)* [1999] 2 Lloyd's Rep 1 (p. 620, post) and *Carroll v Fearon* [1998] PIQR P416).

---

[9] [1932] AC 562 at 599.
[10] See now the Civil Liability (Contribution) Act 1978, p. 1122, post.

NOTES

1. Common law negligence draws no important distinction between manufacturing defects, design defects and failures to warn. Each is subject to a reasonableness test—see e.g. *Barnes v Irwell Valley Water Board* [1938] 2 All ER 650 (failure to correct departure from normal processing and failure to warn), *Barry v Black-Clawson International Ltd* (1966) 2 KIR 237 (design and manufacturing defects) and *Carroll v Fearon* (manufacturing defect and failure to warn).

    It should be emphasised that an unreasonable failure to warn can give rise to liability by itself, without having to be linked to negligence in manufacturing or design (*Castree v E R Squibb & Sons Ltd* [1980] 2 All ER 589, [1980] 1 WLR 1248). Note also that in judging the reasonableness of a failure to warn, courts are unlikely to be impressed by the argument that a warning, though accurate and likely to enhance safety, should not have been given because it would have caused people to be alarmed (see *Barnes v Irwell Valley Water Board*).

2. *Stennett v Hancock and Peters* [1939] 2 All ER 578, provides an illustration of an increase in the class of claimants (i.e. liability not being restricted to consumers) and also in the class of defendants. The claimant's leg was badly bruised when it was struck by a flange which had come off one of the wheels of the first defendant's lorry, the claimant being on the pavement of the highway along which the lorry was being driven. In fact, the wheel had earlier been in the possession of the second defendant whose servants had mended a puncture, re-assembled the wheel and on the day of the accident put it back on the lorry. The cause of the accident was found to be the careless re-assembly of the wheel by one of the second defendant's servants. Neither the first defendant himself nor his driver inspected the wheel to see that its re-assembly had been carried out correctly, but Branson J, relying on the decision in *Phillips v Britannia Hygienic Laundry Co Ltd* [1923] 1 KB 539, took the view that the first defendant could assume that the wheel had been properly assembled. The claim against the first defendant failed, but the second defendant (the repairer) was held liable on the principle of *M'Alister (or Donoghue) v Stevenson* [1932] AC 562. Each element which according to that decision had been necessary to impose liability on the manufacturer of a product to its ultimate user was, in Branson J's opinion, present in this case. On repairers and suppliers see further *Haseldine v CA Daw & Son Ltd* [1941] 2 KB 343, [1941] 3 All ER 156 and *Herschtal v Stewart and Ardern Ltd* [1939] 4 All ER 123. Note further that in *Kubach v Hollands* the second defendants were the owners of the shop from which the chemical had been bought.

3. Proof of fault and causation and the application of the maxim 'res ipsa loquitur' (see p. 337, ante) have been of particular importance in the field of common law products liability. In *Daniels and Daniels v R White & Sons Ltd and Tarbard* [1938] 4 All ER 258 Lewis J said that convincing evidence that the defendant had a 'foolproof system' of manufacture excluded the possibility of finding that the defendant had been careless. *Evans v Triplex Safety Glass Co Ltd* seems to say, moreover, that the claimant has to 'exclude' every other 'probable' sequence of events that might have caused the harm. However, in *Carroll v Fearon* the Court of Appeal said that it was not for the court to speculate about other sequences of events that might have caused the harm and that it was legitimate for a court to reason that if the parties had put to the court two theories of how the harm came about and the court was persuaded that one of the theories was wrong, the other theory was established as correct. Moreover in *Barnett v H & J*

Packer & Co Ltd [1940] 3 All ER 575 Singleton J said: 'In this case, I am faced with the fact that the defendants tell me: "We put on two people to examine. Those people would have seen this wire or nail if it had been present." If the matter is left in that state, and if I am satisfied, as I am, that the metal was in that sweet, how can I find that that was not negligence? It seems to me that I am bound to find that the defendants were negligent.' In other words, contrary to *Daniels v R White & Sons Ltd*, evidence of a system of checking combined with evidence that it had not worked was taken to show that the checking had been careless, rather than that it was foolproof. Similarly in *Herschthal v Stewart & Ardern Ltd* Tucker J said that the facts spoke for themselves and that there must have been carelessness where a wheel came off a vehicle at 7 am when it had been checked by the defendant the evening before. See also *Hill v James Crowe (Cases) Ltd* [1978] 1 All ER 812, which accepted the criticism of *Daniels* that it was inconsistent with *Grant v Australian Knitting Mills Ltd*. In *Carroll v Fearon*, the Court of Appeal declined to systematise these various decisions, but said that the application of 'res ipsa loquitur' was not a matter of detailed doctrine but an exercise in drawing inferences from the evidence in a commonsense way.

4.   It has been suggested that the words 'reasonable possibility' in Lord Atkin's reference (in *M'Alister (or Donoghue) v Stevenson*) to the opportunity for intermediate examination should be changed to 'probability' (Goddard LJ in *Haseldine v C A Daw & Son Ltd* [1941] 2 KB 343 at 376); but even in this situation *Fleming*, p. 542 argues that the probability of intermediate examination will only excuse 'if the defendant was justified in regarding the expected test as sufficient to defuse the danger prior to use and thus provide a safeguard to persons who might otherwise be harmed'. Note further *Murphy v Brentwood District Council* [1991] 1 AC 398 at 464, where Lord Keith referred to a 'reasonable prospect of intermediate examination' and Lord Jauncey (at p. 495—and consider also p. 492) mentioned that the duty laid down by Lord Atkin 'only extended to articles which were likely to be used before a reasonable opportunity of inspection had occurred'.

Lord Atkin's reference to intermediate examination was also considered in *Aswan Engineering Establishment Co v Lupdine Ltd* [1987] 1 All ER 135, [1987] 1 WLR 1. Lloyd LJ, with whose judgment Fox LJ agreed, accepted that this had on occasions been treated as an independent requirement for the claimant to meet; but, expressing the opinion that this phrase of Lord Atkin's 'take[s] colour from the preceding words', he preferred to see it as a factor to be considered on the question of reasonable foresight of damage to person or property. This approach in *Aswan* relates the issue to the question of the scope of the manufacturer's duty of care (and consider Lord Jauncey's view, ante). Compare the earlier case of *The Diamantis Pateras* [1966] 1 Lloyd's Rep 179 in which Lawrence J stated (at p. 188): 'A consideration of modern authorities leads me to the conclusion that the opportunity of intermediate examination is a matter which goes now rather to the question of causation than to the issue of whether or not a duty of care is imposed on the defendants.' This approach would find support in *Pearson Education Ltd v The Charter Partnership Ltd* [2007] EWCA Civ 130 at [44]–[45], albeit the case is concerned on its facts with a building, on which see note 7, p. 196, ante.

The claimant himself may have had a chance to inspect the article and have gained some knowledge of its dangerous nature. In *Denny v Supplies and Transport Co Ltd* [1950] 2 KB 374 the claimant, an employee of certain wharfingers, was injured in the course of unloading timber from a barge. The timber had earlier been loaded from a ship on to the barge by stevedores, who were found by the county court judge to have done the job very badly. The movement of the timber from the ship to the land was 'one continuous process'. At one time, before the accident occurred, the claimant had asked the wharf superintendent for danger money, complaining that the barge had been badly loaded, and was thus unsafe. However, in the Court of Appeal, Evershed MR would not assent to the proposition that an experienced man must have realised danger was *imminent*: further, in his Lordship's view, there was 'no practical alternative to the course of conduct adopted'. It was held that the chain of causation between the stevedores' acts and the claimant's injury remained intact, and that the claimant was still the stevedores' 'neighbour'. The stevedores' appeal from the county court judge's decision awarding the claimant £100 was dismissed. *Denny's* case was cited in *Rimmer v Liverpool City Council* [1985] QB 1, [1984] 1 All ER 930. In the latter case, which concerned liability for premises, *Denny's* case was used as one of the authorities to support the following view of the Court of Appeal (at 938):

...[W]e take the law to be that an opportunity for inspection of a dangerous defect, even if successfully taken by A who is injured by it, will not destroy his proximity to B who created the danger, or exonerate B from liability to A, unless A was free to remove or avoid the danger in the sense that it was reasonable to expect him to do so, and unreasonable for him to run the risk of being injured by the danger.

See also the view in *Fleming* set out ante. Compare *Farr v Butters Bros & Co* [1932] 2 KB 606 and see a note at (1955) 66 LQR 427. In *Murphy v Brentwood District Council* [1991] 1 AC 398, [1990] 2 All ER 908, Lord Keith emphasised that it is the 'latency of the defect which constitutes the mischief' and would disallow a claim if a claimant knew of the defect in the product (and see also Lord Jauncey [1991] 1 AC at p. 492). A question which often arose was the effect, if any, of *Murphy* on the passage quoted from *Rimmer* (and indeed *Fleming*), but it has been decided (*Targett v Torfaen Borough Council* [1992] 3 All ER 27, noted p. 603, ante, which, like *Rimmer*, was a case dealing with premises) that it has left that principle untouched. Cf. *Nitrigin Eireann Teoranta v Inco Alloys Ltd* [1992] 1 All ER 854, [1992] 1 WLR 498, noted p. 196, ante. Note also that negligent failure by those with an opportunity to inspect the product can itself give rise to liability to subsequent users (see *Barry v Black-Clawson International Ltd* and *Davie v New Merton Board Mills Ltd* [1959] AC 604, [1959] 1 All ER 346), even though acceptance by an intermediary that the goods have been tested and found to be free of defects does not necessarily break the chain of causation between the manufacturer and the end-user (see *Herschthal v Stewart & Ardern Ltd*).

5.   In *Kubach v Hollands* Lord Hewart CJ referred to the invoice which warned the second defendants to take a simple precaution. The question of warning by a vendor arose in *Hurley v Dyke* [1979] RTR 265, where the defendant had sold at an auction a car which was dangerously defective; some days later, the claimant, who was a passenger in the car and was not its owner, was injured in an accident due to the car's dangerous condition. According to the House of Lords, the highest at which the defendant's knowledge could be put was that he knew 'of the very real potential danger of driving the car without further examination' and without effecting any repairs which were shown to be necessary by that examination. On this finding it was conceded that the defendant had satisfied the duty of care he owed, as the car had been sold at the auction with the warning that it was sold 'As seen and with all its faults'. Furthermore, three of their Lordships subscribed to the view that even if it had been established that the defendant had known the car was dangerous, it should not be assumed that he would have been liable. If a similar case arose today and there was a claim in tort by the purchaser of the

car, would any legislative restriction on *exclusion of liability* (p. 462, ante) be relevant? Such provisions must, of course, be borne in mind when liability for defective products is under consideration. On the duty of a purchaser of a second-hand car and in particular on the relevance of an MOT certificate, consider *Rees v Saville* [1983] RTR 332 (which concerned injury to a third party's car).

6. Psychiatric injury caused by anticipation of personal injury arising out of the consumption of a defective product (for example, a pharmaceutical product) may also be actionable. See *Group B Plaintiffs v Medical Research Council* (1997) 41 BMLR 157, but consider also the general discussion of this sort of case in *Rothwell v Chemical & Insulating Co Ltd* [2007] 4 All ER 1047, [2008] UKHL 39, noted p. 129, ante.

7. On liability for products in the sphere of employment, see the Employer's Liability (Defective Equipment) Act 1969 (p. 1104, post).

(c) Economic loss

■ Hamble Fisheries Ltd v L Gardner & Sons Ltd (The 'Rebecca Elaine')
Court of Appeal [1999] 2 Lloyd's Rep 1

The appellant fishing company contracted with boatbuilders to build a fishing vessel, the Rebecca Elaine. The vessel was fitted with an engine made by a company whose business was later bought by the respondents. The engine came with a manufacturer's guarantee for one year against defects in workmanship or material and with a manual which said the engine's pistons would run for 20,000 hours or more without needing to be dismantled or replaced. There was a chain of contracts between the manufacturers and the boatbuilders.

A year after selling the engine fitted in the appellants' vessel, the defendants started to receive reports that pistons in similar engines were breaking down well before 20,000 hours' use. The defendants did nothing to warn anyone that the engines might fail.

The Rebecca Elaine's engine failed well before they had been used for 20,000 hours. At the time she was 4½ miles out at sea. Fortunately, no personal injury ensued as the vessel was promptly towed back to port, but the plaintiffs lost earnings during the time the vessel was out of commission and also had to pay for the repair of the engine. The appellants alleged negligence in the respondents' failure to warn them of the risk that their engine would fail. The trial judge rejected the claim and there was an appeal to the Court of Appeal.

TUCKEY LJ: . . .
1 In what circumstances is there a common law duty of care to warn where it is foreseeable that the failure to do so will cause economic loss? . . .

[15] As they were developed from the notice of appeal, their skeleton argument and orally by Mr Tugendhat, QC, I think the appellants' submissions can be summarized as follows.

(a) There is no reason in principle why a plaintiff should not recover for a negligent failure to warn causing economic loss. The House of Lords in *Murphy v Brentwood District Council*, [1990] 2 Lloyd's Rep. 467 at pp. 476, col. 1 and 485, cols. 1 and 2, [1991] 1 AC 398 at pp. 466G and 481D–E recognized that a relationship 'akin to contract' could give rise to a duty of care not to cause economic loss. In *Banque Keyser Ullmann S.A. v Skandia (U.K.) Insurance Co. Ltd.*, [1988] 2 Lloyd's Rep. 514 at p. 559, [1990] 1 QB 665 at p. 794 this Court held that a mere failure to speak could give rise to a liability under *Hedley Byrne* principles. The law in this field should be developed incrementally and not by too rigid an application of statements of principle in earlier cases. There should be a duty of care in the present case because the appellants selected the engine by its brand name relying on the manufacturer to ensure that its parts were adequate, the engine required maintenance of its moving parts and only the manufacturer would know what was required and the respondents actually knew that if the part failed there was a danger of economic loss or worse.

(b) The limitation of the duty of care in *Murphy* to a duty to safeguard from physical damage was not a reason why the same limitation should be applied in cases where the defendant does know of the danger. This principle can be derived by analogy from the principle in *Langridge v Levy*, (1837) 2 M. & W. 519 and was applied in similar circumstances by the Canadian Supreme Court in *Rivtow Marine Ltd v Washington Iron Works*, [1973] 40 DLR 530.

(c) The Judge misdirected himself on the question of reliance. It was not an essential element as cases such as *White v Jones*, [1995] 2 AC 207 show and in any event on the facts which he found the Judge ought to have held that there was reliance in the sense required to establish the duty.

(d) The respondents assumed responsibility by stepping into the manufacturers' shoes and by dealing with the complaints which were made about the defective pistons and the other matters referred to by the Judge.

[16] These are bold submissions as Mr Tugendhat recognized. To strengthen our resolve he reminded us that *Murphy* has been criticized extrajudicially and not followed in some other common law jurisdictions. The appellants have no remedy against anyone else and there are no policy reasons why we should not fill the gap and give them a remedy against the respondents.

[17] To see if Mr Tugendhat's submissions are well founded I must start with what was said in *Murphy*. The basis for the House's decision that the Council was not liable was that the claim was for pure economic loss. The decision had no claim in tort was reached by analogy with the position of a manufacturer who had no liability in tort for a defective chattel. At p. 481, cols. 1 and 2; p. 475 A–E Lord Bridge stated the principle quite clearly as follows:

> If a manufacturer negligently puts into circulation a chattel containing a latent defect which renders it dangerous to persons or property, the manufacturer, on the well known principles established by *Donoghue v Stevenson*, [1932] AC 562, will be liable in tort for injury to persons or damage to property which the chattel causes. but if a manufacturer produces and sells a chattel which is merely defective in quality, even to the extent that it is valueless for the purpose for which it is intended, the manufacturer's liability at common law arises only under and by reference to the terms of any contract to which he is a party in relation to the chattel, the common law does not impose on him any liability in tort to persons to whom he owes no duty in contract but who, having acquired the chattel, suffer economic loss because the chattel is defective in quality. If a dangerous defect in a chattel is discovered before it causes any personal injury or damage to property, because the danger is now known and the chattel cannot safely be used unless the defect is repaired, the defect becomes merely a defect in quality. The chattel is either capable of repair at economic cost or it is worthless and must be scrapped. In either case the loss sustained by the owner or hirer of the chattel is purely economic. It is recoverable against any party who owes the loser a relevant contractual duty. But it is not recoverable in tort in the absence of a special relationship of proximity imposing on the tortfeasor a duty of care to safeguard the plaintiff from economic loss. There is no such special relationship between the manufacturer of a chattel and a remote owner or hirer.

[18] So the general rule is that in a case such as this a manufacturer and a fortiori, someone who has purchased the manufacturer's business owes no duty. To see whether this case fell within the exception, the Judge asked himself the right question, that is: was there a special relationship of proximity imposing a duty on the respondents to safeguard the appellants from economic loss? Mr Tugendhat had to accept this although he would have preferred the Judge to ask simply whether there was a duty to warn. He also accepted that the Judge was right on this analysis to disregard the fact that there was a duty to safeguard against damage to person or property however difficult it might be to justify drawing

the line in this way. This may not seem the logical place to draw the line, but there can be no doubt that it has been drawn here by the English Courts. As Lord Oliver said in *Murphy*:

> The infliction of physical injury to the person or property of another universally requires to be justified. The causing of economic loss does not.

[19] So what is required to establish a special relationship of proximity? In *White v Jones* at p. 274 Lord Browne-Wilkinson said:

> Though the categories of cases in which such special relationship can be held to exist are not closed, as yet only two categories have been identified, viz. 1. where there is a fiduciary relationship and 2. where the defendant has voluntarily answered a question or tendered skilled advice or services in circumstances where he knows or ought to know that an identified plaintiff will rely on his answers or advice. In both these categories this special relationship is created by the defendant voluntarily assuming to act in the matter by involving himself in the plaintiff's affairs or by choosing to speak. If he does so assume to act or speak he is said to have assumed responsibility for carrying through the matter he has entered upon.

But for the absence of consideration there would have been a contract between the parties in *Hedley Byrne & Co v Heller & Partners*, [1963] 1 Lloyd's Rep. 485. In *White v Jones* there was no privity of contract between the solicitor and the beneficiary although the contract was intended to benefit the latter. This is now the accepted explanation for the decision in *Junior Books Ltd v Veitchi Co Ltd*, [1983] 1 AC 520 where the nominated specialist sub-contractor was to replace flooring for the benefit of the building owner. The emphasis in the recent cases is on the assumption of responsibility by the defendant. But this means assumption of responsibility to the plaintiff. Reliance by the plaintiff would obviously be relevant in considering whether there has been such an assumption of responsibility and of course to causation. 'Something akin to contract' was what Mr Tugendhat contended for in the present case. I am prepared to accept this as a working definition for what is required to establish a special relationship of proximity in a case of this kind.

[20] But what is one looking for in order to decide whether a defendant has assumed responsibility in a situation which is akin to contract? In *Williams v Natural Life Health Foods Ltd*, [1998] 1 WLR 830 the plaintiff sought to make a director of the defendant company personally liable for negligent misrepresentations made in the name of the company. Lord Steyn at p. 835 said:

> The touchstone of liability is not the state of mind of the defendant. An objective test means that the primary focus must be on things said or done by the defendant or on his behalf in dealings with the plaintiff. Obviously the impact of what a defendant says or does must be judged in the light of the relevant contextual scene. Subject to this qualification the primary focus must be on exchanges (in which term I include statements and conduct) which cross the line between the defendant and the plaintiff.

[21] So far I have not considered the significance of the fact that in this case the duty contended for is a duty to speak. In a case like *Hedley Byrne* where the defendant chooses to speak he is taken to have assumed responsibility from that fact alone. This is obviously not so where the defendant keeps silent. In *Skandia* the Court had to consider whether the underwriter of the defendant insurers who knew that a broker had issued a false cover note to the plaintiff bank owed a duty of care to warn the bank who lent large sums of money on the security of the cover. At p. 559; p. 794 Lord Justice Slade giving the judgment of the Court said:

> Can a mere failure to speak ever give rise to liability in negligence under *Hedley Byrne* principles? In our view it can, but subject to the all important proviso that there has been on the facts a voluntary assumption of responsibility in the relevant sense and reliance on that assumption. These features may be much more difficult to infer in the case of mere silence than in the case of misrepresentation.

Later he referred to the principle that the common law does not impose liability for what are called pure omissions and said at p. 561; p. 798:

> ...The reluctance of the Courts to give a remedy in tort for pure omission applies—perhaps even more so—when the omission is a failure to prevent economic harm.

In contract there was no obligation to speak in the context of negotiations for an ordinary commercial contract. Likewise the Court held that there was no legal obligation on the underwriter to disclose the broker's dishonesty merely because there was an established business relationship between the parties.

[22] So do we get any help from the Canadian case of *Rivtow*? There the plaintiffs were the charterers of a logging barge fitted with cranes manufactured and supplied by the defendants. The defendants became aware of dangerous defects in the cranes but did not warn the plaintiffs. If they had been warned the plaintiffs would have been able to carry out the necessary repairs in a slack period. As it was the barge had to be removed from service for repairs during one of the most profitable periods of the year. The Supreme Court upheld the award of loss of profits made by the trial Judge but by a majority rejected the claim for the cost of repairs to the cranes. The Court emphasized the fact that this was not a case of a negligent manufacturer whose defective or dangerous goods have caused damage to some unknown member of the public. The defendants knew that the cranes were going to be used by the plaintiffs and the exact use to which they were to be put. At pp. 536–537 Mr Justice Ritchie said that:

> Although there was no contractual relationship between the manufacturer and (the plaintiffs) (the defendants) knew (the plaintiffs) as one who was using the cranes for their intended purpose in reliance on their advice.

He drew a distinction between the liability of a manufacturer and liability for a failure to warn of a known danger. He derived the distinction from a passage in the judgment of Lord Thankerton in *Donoghue v Stevenson* who had said at p. 602:

> We are not dealing here with a case of what is called an article per se dangerous or one which was known by the defender to be dangerous, in which case a special duty of protection or adequate warning is placed upon the person who uses or distributes it.

Mr Justice Ritchie then continued at p. 543 saying:

> The circumstances of the present case give rise to a duty to warn...just as surely as such a duty arises in the case of the producer of a thing which is dangerous in itself.

Having found that there was a duty in this way he went on to consider the cases on economic loss including *Hedley Byrne* which he considered to be of no relevance other than to show that:

> ...where liability is based on negligence the recovery is not limited to physical damage but extends also to economical loss.

[23] Mr Tugendhat submitted that the House of Lords approved *Rivtow* in *Murphy*. It is referred to in the speeches of Lord Keith at p. 478, col. 1; pp. 469G–470C and Lord Oliver at p. 490, col. 1; pp. 488F–489A. However, it is quite clear from the context that the references are to those parts of the judgment in *Rivtow* which deal with the recovery of the cost of repairs to the cranes. There is no analysis or approval of the basis for finding that there was a duty of care.

[24] It is clear that the Court in *Rivtow* found that there was a duty by analogy to liability for a dangerous chattel. We were referred to *Langridge v Levy* which is a case of a dangerous chattel (a gun) but the plaintiff in that case succeeded on the grounds of deceit so that case has no relevance to the law of negligence. There is no doubt that in some of the earlier cases the Court sought to distinguish between chattels which were inherently dangerous and chattels which were not of themselves dangerous. However, in *Donoghue v Stevenson* Lord Atkin argued that the distinction was relevant to the

degree of care that might be expected but was not the basis for any logical differentiation between the rules applicable to each category and this seems to have been the English Courts' approach since that time. (See Clerk and Lindsell (17th ed.) par. 7–151).

[25] So under English law I do not think that there is any basis for putting failure to warn of a known danger into a category of its own. The distinction therefore which the Court made in *Rivtow* is not a valid one under English law. But there is a stronger reason for saying that *Rivtow* does not provide useful guidance for our decision in this case. This is that the Court attached no significance to the fact that the claim was a claim for economic loss. After the passage I have already cited at p. 543 in which the Judge held the duty to exist, he continued by saying:

> Neither the case of *Donoghue v Stevenson* nor that of *Grant v Australian Knitting Mills* contains any suggestion that the plaintiffs in those actions would have been precluded from recovery for economic loss if such had been claimed...

But those cases and the defective chattels cases only decide that a manufacturer has a duty of care to avoid physical damage to persons or property. Under English law one must look to *Hedley Byrne* and the cases which have followed to see whether there is a duty of care to avoid economic loss. In *Rivtow* the Court said in terms that they did not consider *Hedley Byrne* to be relevant. In any event even if they had approached the question of duty on *Hedley Byrne* principles it is possible on the facts of that case that they would have concluded that there was something akin to contract which gave rise to a duty to warn. This was the finding in the other Canadian case to which we were referred, *Can-Arc Helicopters v Textron*, 86 DLR 404. There the British Columbia Supreme Court found the manufacturers of a helicopter liable for economic loss for a failure to give an adequate warning of a defect in a service bulletin which they knew their customers relied on. The Court followed *Rivtow* but also cited *Murphy* and found that there was a special relationship of proximity on the basis that:

> It seems hard to conceive of a set of circumstances in which recoverability for economic loss of the kind claimed here could be more justified...

[26] So I do not think that *Rivtow* helps. My review of the authorities shows that the general rule is that a manufacturer in the position of the respondents owes no duty of care to avoid economic loss. Exceptionally he may be under such a duty if he assumes responsibility to his customers in a situation which is akin to contract. That duty may include a duty to warn but it would be much more difficult to infer in the case of mere silence than in the case of misrepresentation. Reliance by the customer is relevant to whether there has been an assumption of responsibility and essential as to causation.

[27] The central question in the present case is whether the respondents assumed a responsibility to warn the appellants. In answering this question the Judge considered that he should look at the matter subjectively and objectively. This approach was too favourable to the appellants. The test is an objective one so the focus of the inquiry must be on statements and conduct which cross the line between the parties. Here the appellants had no dealings with the respondents or the manufacturers at any time. The appellants were unknown to them as one of an unspecified number of customers who had purchased Gardner engines. Only the manual 'crossed the line' to the appellants and that had not been issued by the respondents. However, I think the respondents should be taken to have adopted it when they bought the business and continued to trade as if there had been no change of owner. In his evidence Mr Pallot did not say that he relied on the manual. However, I think it is safe to assume that a manufacturer who issues or takes responsibility for a manual of this kind will expect that users of his product will usually rely on any statements of fact and advice which it contains.

[28] Do these facts lead to the conclusion that the respondents assumed a responsibility to warn the appellants of the defective pistons? I think not. I cannot spell out of the facts something akin to contract. The parties simply had no dealings with one another. If subsequent discovery of an error in a manual of this kind gives rise to a duty to speak to avoid economic loss, I think the consequences would be far reaching. All manufacturers of machinery put to commercial use where the product is accompanied

by a fairly detailed manual would be within the ambit of such a duty. Despite Mr Tugendhat's submissions to the contrary, I think such a result enters Cardozo country: 'liability in an indeterminate amount to an indeterminate class'. But I would not decide this appeal as a matter of policy; rather as an application of established principles to the facts of this case. That is how the Judge decided it and I agree with his conclusion that there was no assumption of responsibility by the respondents in this case.

[29] In the course of this judgment I hope I have dealt with the main points raised by the appellants. I feel considerable sympathy for them. Mr Gee, QC, their Counsel did not dispute the view that the respondents had behaved badly. I think they did. But hard facts should not make bad law. There are situations where the law does not provide a remedy for economic loss caused by failure to take care. This is one of them.

For these reasons I would dismiss this appeal.

MUMMERY LJ: . . .
I agree.

The arguments of Mr Tugendhat, QC and Mr Gee, QC on the maze of the modern law of negligence revived memories of an early initiation into the mysteries of *Donoghue v Stevenson* in tutorials with the editor of Salmond on Torts nearly 40 years ago. (Mr R. E. V. Heuston once paid a visit to Minchella's Cafe in Paisley, out of academic curiosity, not for liquid refreshment.)

After such an excellent tutorial by the Bar a summary of the legal position in this case should at least be attempted.

[1] The defective design of piston No. 7 in the engine of *Rebecca Elaine* fortunately did not cause any physical damage to person or property. Hamble Fisheries' claim is confined to financial loss: the cost of repairing the engine (£25,972) and the loss of profits (£21,344) flowing from temporary loss of use of the boat.

[2] Hamble Fisheries had no contractual relationship or commercial contact with the respondent or its predecessors in business. The respondent did not build the boat or sell it to them or make the engine or the No. 7 piston for them or supply the operating manual or any maintenance, advisory or other services to them.

[3] There is no general duty in English law to take reasonable care to avoid inflicting financial loss on those whom it is reasonably foreseeable will suffer such loss in consequence of acts or omissions. In *Donoghue v Stevenson* the majority in the House of Lords recognized a duty of care on the part of the manufacturer of a defective product not to cause reasonably foreseeable physical damage to a person. It was observed by Mr Justice Ritchie in the Supreme Court of Canada in *Rivtow Marine Ltd v Washington Iron Works*, [1973] 40 DLR (3d) 520 at p. 544 that, although *Donoghue v Stevenson* did not contain any suggestion that the plaintiff would have been precluded from recovery for economic loss if such had been claimed, it was not authority for holding a manufacturer liable for damage to the defective product or for the loss which the consumer would have sustained if he had been properly warned by the manufacturer. In that case, cited and relied on by Mr Tugendhat, QC for Hamble Fisheries, the majority of the Court refused to award damages for the cost of repairing damage to the defective product itself (a decision approved by Lord Keith in *Murphy v Brentwood District Council*, [1990] 2 Lloyd's Rep. 467 at p. 478, [1991] 1 AC 398 at p. 469 and by Lord Oliver at p. 490; p. 488), but then proceeded (inconsistently, in my view) to award damages for loss of profit caused by the defective product, apparently on the basis of a duty on the part of the manufacturer of the defective crane to warn against the risk of *physical* damage. Under English law liability for pure economic loss has developed by the rather different route of the special relationship test formulated in *Hedley Bryne*.

[4] If a generalization can confidently be made about this controversial and difficult aspect of the law of negligence, it is that the recent decisions of the House of Lords cited by Lord Justice Tuckey affirm a general principle ruling out recovery for carelessly inflicted foreseeable financial loss in the absence of a contract or of a special relationship of proximity between the parties, giving rise to a voluntary assumption of responsibility for financial loss. It may not seem logical to draw a legal line between, on the one hand, awarding a sum of money for physical damage to person and property, including compensation for financial loss consequential on such damage and, on the other hand, rejecting totally

any liability for pure financial loss of similar extent suffered by the very same plaintiff in the absence of any physical damage to his person or property. But a boundary line has now been drawn by the House of Lords so as to bring more certainty to the law and to the affairs of those affected by it. The judicial line has not been drawn arbitrarily: it is explicable by rational and pragmatic considerations, some more potent than others, some more often articulated than others: the disproportionate burden of imposing indeterminate liability of the kind envisaged by Judge Cardozo in the *Ultramares* case; the evidential difficulties in establishing causation and delimiting remoteness; the relative cost and practicability of obtaining insurance cover for risks of pure financial loss suffered to an unlimited degree by an amorphous class of claimants; the apprehension of a deluge, in an already overstretched legal system, of litigation by an indefinite number of claimants with multiple claims arising out of a single incident (e.g. the businessman driver losing a profitable deal as a result a breakdown of his car caused by a defective engine part or as a result of delays in a traffic tailback caused by the breakdown of another's car for a similar reason); the dubious and lethal colonization by the tort of negligence of the conceptual territory of contract; the perception that financial loss occupies a significantly lower place than physical injury to person and property in the scale of contemporary social and ethical values; and the inevitability (and acceptability) of widespread and uncompensatable financial loss in a free market economy, in which even intentional infliction of substantial financial loss (e.g. by one trade competitor on another) does not normally attract legal liability. As comparisons with other jurisdictions (e.g. Canada) show, different legal systems draw the boundary line in different positions; and they do not all find the same force in the policy factors affecting the decisions of the English Courts. Economic loss is, however, universally recognized to be an area which presents exceptionally difficult problems in laying down the limits of legal liability to compensate for loss caused to another.

[5] If, as recent authorities have held, liability for purely financial loss is confined to cases of special relationships, involving a voluntary assumption of responsibility, there cannot be any liability on this case because, as Mr Gee put it, there has been no 'crossing of the line' between the parties so as to bring them into proximity with one another: no direct supply of goods, advice or services, no commercial contact, nothing 'akin to contract'.

[6] A relationship of proximity does not arise simply from the fact that the respondent knew of the defect in the piston and failed to warn those liable to be physically damaged as a result. As appears from the judgments in *Donoghue v Stevenson* knowledge of a dangerous defect in a product may provide a foundation for a case of fraud against a person who makes or circulates a dangerous product without warning of the danger of physical damage known to him: see *Langridge v Levy*, (1837) 4 M. & W. 337. But no dishonesty of any kind has ever been pleaded against the respondent. There is a great gulf in law, not always fully appreciated by an aggrieved plaintiff, between the duty not to be dishonest, which is almost universal, and the more circumscribed duty not to be careless.

[7] A voluntary assumption of responsibility to warn Hamble Fisheries of the risk of financial loss on the premature failure of the piston No. 7 did not arise from the two factors singled out by Mr Tugendhat, QC, in this case as 'special' and therefore apt to produce the necessary proximity: (a) Hamble Fisheries' nomination to the maker of the boat of the respondent's engine by brand name (a 'Gardner engine') and (b) the character of the piston as maintaining a complex moving structure. Those factors may well suffice to impose on the respondent a duty to warn against the risk of *physical* damage to person and property; but the duty to warn of the foreseeable risk of physical damage, which never in fact materialized, does not by itself constitute the requisite degree of proximity to give rise to a voluntary assumption of responsibility either (a) for the cost of repair to or replacement of the defective product itself or (b) for loss of profit or for any other kind of pure financial loss flowing from the failure of the defective product.

For all these reasons as well as those given by Lord Justice Tuckey I would dismiss this appeal.

[NOURSE LJ delivered a judgment in favour of dismissing the appeal.]

Appeal dismissed.

NOTES

1. The main message of this case is that pure economic loss in a products case is to be treated in exactly the same way as pure economic loss in other contexts. The basic rule is that pure economic loss is not recoverable, but there is an exception where there has been an 'assumption of responsibility' or where in special circumstances the test in *Caparo Industries plc v Dickman* [1990] 2 AC 605, [1990] 1 All ER 568 is met: see Chap. 4, ante. For cases reaching similar conclusions but using the older language of 'reliance' and 'proximity' see *Muirhead v Industrial Tank Specialities Ltd* [1986] QB 507, [1985] 3 All ER 705 and *Simaan General Contracting Co v Pilkington Glass Ltd (No 2)* [1988] QB 758, [1988] 1 All ER 791. The central question, however, is whether there was such an assumption of responsibility in this case, a question complicated by the need to find a similar assumption of responsibility to overcome another established rule that there is generally no duty to warn (see p. 66, ante). Is the Court of Appeal's emphasis on there having to be some 'dealings' between the parties consistent with the House of Lords decision in *White v Jones* [1995] 2 AC 207, [1995] 1 All ER 691 (p. 243, ante)? Is it even still true, after the Contracts (Rights of Third Parties) Act 1999 (see p. 256, ante) that there have to be 'dealings' between the parties before the relationship between the parties may be characterised as 'akin to contract'?

2. The Court of Appeal emphasised the Cardozo 'floodgates' argument about indeterminate liability. It is not clear how that concern is relevant in this case. How many vessels can use an engine at any one time? If liability is based solely on an assumption of responsibility derived from the fact that boatbuilders will pass the manual on to the eventual owner, the defendants will know precisely how many potential claimants there are because they know how many engines they have made. The assumption of responsibility would not go beyond the owner of the vessel because no one else will receive the manual in circumstances in which they might reasonably believe that the manufacturer was assuming responsibility towards them. The Court of Appeal's argument seems more appropriate to those who suffer economic loss because they or their customers relied on advertising, rather than on a manual. Cf *Lexmead (Basingstoke) Ltd v Lewis* [1981] 1 All ER 1185 in which the Court of Appeal in a passage (at p. 1003), on which the House of Lords made no comment, doubted whether there could be *Hedley Byrne* liability against advertisers for pure economic loss (see also P. Cane (1979) 95 LQR 117 at 139–140).

3. When *Amiri Flight Authority v BAE Systems Plc* [2003] 2 Lloyd's Rep 767, [2003] EWCA Civ 1447 was in the lower court, [2003] 1 Lloyd's Rep 59, [2002] EWHC 2481 (Comm), Tomlinson J (at [36]) referred to Mummery LJ's judgment in *The Rebecca Elaine* as containing 'a masterly and economical summary of the current state of English Law'.

4. Mummery LJ says that a duty to warn can arise out of the mere facts (a) that the claimants specified that they wanted an engine made by the particular manufacturer, and (b) that the piston maintained a complex moving structure, but that the duty to warn applied only to personal injury and property damage, not to pure economic loss. It is difficult to see why the fact that the claimant specified the defendant's product should give rise to the sort of special relationship that overcomes the rule against liability in negligence for pure omissions (see p. 66, ante)—surely there has to be something on the side of the defendant as well, and something beyond the complexity of the product, since otherwise how would defendants know when they were exposed to the risk of liability? But if we bring into play the element that does put the defendants on notice, the

manual the defendants themselves put into circulation, there seems to be no particular reason why any distinction should be drawn in these circumstances between purely economic loss and other types of loss. If the defendants are taken to have assumed responsibility for the accuracy of the manual, it seems arbitrary and legalistic to say the scope of that assumption of responsibility is limited to particular forms of loss. The question should be whether the claimants did anything to show that they were re-assuming responsibility for their own economic welfare despite their reasonable reliance on the manual.

5.   For further discussion of *Murphy v Brentwood District Council* [1991] 1 AC 398, [1990] 2 All ER 908 and *Junior Books Ltd v Veitchi Co Ltd* [1983] 1 AC 520, [1982] 3 All ER 201, see p. 194 and p. 240, ante. Both those decisions bring into focus the important problem, discussed in *The Rebecca Elaine* only indirectly in the context of rejecting the approach of the Canadian *Rivtow Marine* case, of distinguishing between pure economic loss and property damage. Why does *The Rebecca Elaine* not count as property damage—a case in which the failure of the engine has 'damaged' the vessel in the sense of temporarily rendering it commercially useless? In *Aswan Engineering Establishment Co v Lupdine Ltd* [1987] 1 All ER 135, [1987] 1 WLR 1, the claimants bought quantities of a waterproofing compound contained in pails. The compound and the pails were made by different companies. The pails disintegrated in the heat of Kuwait and the compound was lost. Lloyd LJ and Fox LJ thought that what happened to the compound should count as property damage, caused by the failure of the pails. Nicholls LJ was unhappy about this line of reasoning, although he accepted that 'in strict legal analysis' it was correct. This difference of opinion was acknowledged in *Bacardi-Martini Beverages Ltd v Thomas Hardy Packaging Ltd* [2002] 2 Lloyd's Rep 379, [2002] EWCA Civ 549, at [16], where it is also pointed out that the decision preceded *Murphy* and occurred at a time when 'the star of *Junior Books Ltd v Veitchi Co Ltd* [1983] AC 520 was still high in the sky'. In *Murphy* the House of Lords rejected what might be seen as a parallel argument, the 'complex structure' argument which had attracted their Lordships in *D&F Estates Ltd v Church Comrs for England* [1989] AC 177, [1988] 2 All ER 992 (see p. 194, ante). However, *Aswan* was not explicitly disapproved in *Murphy*, although Mance J in *Losinjska Plovidba v Transco Overseas Ltd, The Orjula* [1995] 2 Lloyd's Rep 395 thought that Nicholls LJ's view seemed to have gained 'further force' after *Murphy*. It could be argued that there is a difference between cases in which the failure of one product destroys another product (*Aswan*) and cases in which the failure of one product merely renders a valuable asset of which it forms part temporarily less valuable (as in *The Rebecca Elaine*, in which the repair of the engine would restore the value of the vessel). The position of the law on negligent damage to capital assets (i.e. assets whose value is the value of what they help to produce) is still, however, fundamentally confusing—see p. 203, ante.

Consider also in this context the *Bacardi* case, where carbon dioxide which had been contaminated with benzine was supplied to the defendant, who mixed it with water and with a drink concentrate (this concentrate being the property of the claimant throughout, as was the finished product). This process produced a drink which, although not hazardous to health, was on account of adverse publicity withdrawn from sale and destroyed by the claimant. The Court of Appeal regarded the drink that had been produced as a new, albeit defective, product, rather than as a damaged product. For comment see Miller and Goldberg, op cit., paras. 16.35–16.37, who suggest that the contractual context might have influenced the approach. In their view, if there were an action against the manufacturer of a defective control device which had allowed far too much of an ingredient or even the wrong ingredient to flow into the concentrate which made it useless, 'the concentrate should be seen as having been "damaged" just as it would have been if the rogue ingredient were broken glass'. Nevertheless, one could argue that in such cases, even if they are strictly property damage cases, there are such similarities with pure economic loss that the same requirement of an assumption of responsibility should apply. See pp. 206–207, ante for discussion of *Marc Rich & Co AG v Bishop Rock Marine Ltd, The Nicholas H* [1996] AC 211, [1995] 3 All ER 307. For cases discussing damage to property in the context of the Nuclear Installations Act 1965, see note 3, p. 667, post.

The product in *Bacardi* was not in fact dangerous. Should it make any difference if it were? Although directly concerned with defective buildings, *Murphy* is also relevant to this issue in the context of products, i.e. the claimant who, learning that the product is defective, takes preventive action to render it safe. *Murphy* says that expenditure on such preventive action is pure economic loss, so that it would not now generally be recoverable in negligence. The claimant is left to any remedy which might be available in contract. Nevertheless, the comments of Lord Bridge in *Murphy* about recovery of the costs of repair of a dangerous structure near to the boundary of the land on which it stands were cited in *The Orjula* [1995] 2 Lloyd's Rep 395 by Mance J as possibly supporting a claim for the cost of preventative measures taken on a ship (removing a positive source of danger—leaking containers).

According to the House of Lords in *Lexmead (Basingstoke) Ltd v Lewis* [1982] AC 225, [1981] 1 All ER 1185, contradicting the Court of Appeal's views in the same case, it is arguable that in a contractual chain case in which the ultimate victim suffers personal injury or property damage, if any of the intermediate claims for recourse against others in the chain are tort claims rather than contract claims, they should count as claims for personal injury or property damage, not pure economic loss. See also *The Kapetan Georgis* [1988] 1 Lloyd's Rep 352. The status of this argument must, however, be treated as doubtful in the light of *Murphy*'s rejection (see p. 183, ante) of the somewhat fictional position taken in *Anns* that potential harm to health and safety turns pure economic loss into something else (a point also rejected in *The Rebecca Elaine* in the context of *Rivtow Marine*). There is a strong argument that claims along the chain are inherently relational and thus core examples of pure economic losses (see p. 166, ante).

2 STATUTORY LIABILITY

■ Consumer Protection Act 1987

PART I PRODUCT LIABILITY

1 Purpose and construction of Part I.—(1) This part shall have effect for the purpose of making such provision as is necessary in order to comply with the product liability Directive and shall be construed accordingly.

(2) In this Part, except in so far as the context otherwise requires—

...

'dependent' and 'relative' have the same meaning as they have in, respectively, the Fatal Accidents Act 1976 and the Damages (Scotland) Act 1976;

'producer', in relation to a product, means—

(a) the person who manufactured it;

(b) in the case of a substance which has not been manufactured but has been won or abstracted, the person who won or abstracted it;

(c) in the case of a product which has not been manufactured, won or abstracted but essential characteristics of which are attributable to an industrial or other process having been carried out (for example, in relation to agricultural produce), the person who carried out that process;

'product' means any goods or electricity and (subject to subsection (3) below) includes a product which is comprised in another product, whether by virtue of being a component part or raw material or otherwise; and

'the product liability Directive' means the Directive of the Council of the European Communities, dated 25th July 1985, (No 85/374/EEC)[11] on the approximation of the laws, regulations and administrative provisions of the member States concerning liability for defective products.

(3) For the purposes of this Part a person who supplies any product in which products are comprised, whether by virtue of being component parts or raw materials or otherwise, shall not be treated by reason only of his supply of that product as supplying any of the products so comprised.

2 Liability for defective products.—(1) Subject to the following provisions of this Part, where any damage is caused wholly or partly by a defect in a product, every person to whom subsection (2) below applies shall be liable for the damage.

(2) This subsection applies to—

(a) the producer of the product;

(b) any person who, by putting his name on the product or using a trade mark[12] or other distinguishing mark in relation to the product, has held himself out to be the producer of the product;

(c) any person who has imported the product into a member State from a place outside the member States in order, in the course of any business of his, to supply it to another.

(3) Subject as aforesaid, where any damage is caused wholly or partly by a defect in a product, any person who supplied the product (whether to the person who suffered the damage, to the producer of any product in which the product in question is comprised or to any other person) shall be liable for the damage if—

(a) the person who suffered the damage requests the supplier to identify one or more of the persons (whether still in existence or not) to whom subsection (2) above applies in relation to the product;

(b) that request is made within a reasonable period after the damage occurs and at a time when it is not reasonably practicable for the person making the request to identify all those persons; and

(c) the supplier fails, within a reasonable period after receiving the request, either to comply with the request or to identify the person who supplied the product to him.

(5) Where two or more persons are liable by virtue of this Part for the same damage, their liability shall be joint and several.

(6) This section shall be without prejudice to any liability arising otherwise than by virtue of this Part.

3 Meaning of 'defect'.—(1) Subject to the following provisions of this section, there is a defect in a product for the purposes of this Part if the safety of the product is not such as persons generally are entitled to expect; and for those purposes 'safety', in relation to a product, shall include safety with respect to products comprised in that product and safety in the context of risks of damage to property, as well as in the context of risks of death or personal injury.

---

[11] See p. 635, post.

[12] This is to be construed as a reference to a trade mark within the meaning of the Trade Marks Act 1994: see s. 106(1) and Sch. 4, para. 1 of that Act.

(2) In determining for the purposes of subsection (1) above what persons generally are entitled to expect in relation to a product all the circumstances shall be taken into account, including—

(a) the manner in which, and purposes for which, the product has been marketed, its get-up, the use of any mark in relation to the product and any instructions for, or warnings with respect to, doing or refraining from doing anything with or in relation to the product;

(b) what might reasonably be expected to be done with or in relation to the product; and

(c) the time when the product was supplied by its producer to another;

and nothing in this section shall require a defect to be inferred from the fact alone that the safety of a product which is supplied after that time is greater than the safety of the product in question.

4. Defences.—(1) In any civil proceedings by virtue of this Part against any person ('the person proceeded against') in respect of a defect in a product it shall be a defence for him to show—

(a) that the defect is attributable to compliance with any requirement imposed by or under any enactment or with any Community obligation; or

(b) that the person proceeded against did not at any time supply the product to another; or

(c) that the following conditions are satisfied, that is to say—

(i) that the only supply of the product to another by the person proceeded against was otherwise than in the course of a business of that person's; and

(ii) that section 2(2) above does not apply to that person or applies to him by virtue only of things done otherwise than with a view to profit; or

(d) that the defect did not exist in the product at the relevant time; or

(e) that the state of scientific and technical knowledge at the relevant time was not such that a producer of products of the same description as the product in question might be expected to have discovered the defect if it had existed in his products while they were under his control; or

(f) that the defect—

(i) constituted a defect in a product ('the subsequent product') in which the product in question had been comprised; and

(ii) was wholly attributable to the design of the subsequent product or to compliance by the producer of the product in question with instructions given by the producer of the subsequent product.

(2) In this section 'the relevant time', in relation to electricity, means the time at which it was generated, being a time before it was transmitted or distributed, and in relation to any other product, means—

(a) if the person proceeded against is a person to whom subsection (2) of section 2 above applies in relation to the product, the time when he supplied the product to another;

(b) if that subsection does not apply to that person in relation to the product, the time when the product was last supplied by a person to whom that subsection does apply in relation to the product.

5 Damage giving rise to liability.—(1) Subject to the following provisions of this section, in this Part 'damage' means death or personal injury or any loss of or damage to any property (including land).

(2) A person shall not be liable under section 2 above in respect of any defect in a product for the loss of or any damage to the product itself or for the loss of or any damage to the whole or any part of any product which has been supplied with the product in question comprised in it.

(3) A person shall not be liable under section 2 above for any loss of or damage to any property which, at the time it is lost or damaged, is not—

(a) of a description of property ordinarily intended for private use, occupation or consumption; and

(b) intended by the person suffering the loss or damage mainly for his own private use, occupation or consumption.

(4) No damages shall be awarded to any person by virtue of this Part in respect of any loss of or damage to any property if the amount which would fall to be so awarded to that person, apart from this subsection and any liability for interests, does not exceed £275.

(5) In determining for the purposes of this Part who has suffered any loss of or damage to property and when any such loss or damage occurred, the loss or damage shall be regarded as having occurred at the earliest time at which a person with an interest in the property had knowledge of the material facts about the loss or damage.

(6) For the purposes of subsection (5) above the material facts about any loss of or damage to any property are such facts about the loss or damage as would lead a reasonable person with an interest in the property to consider the loss or damage sufficiently serious to justify his instituting proceedings for damages against a defendant who did not dispute liability and was able to satisfy a judgment.

(7) For the purposes of subsection (5) above a person's knowledge includes knowledge which he might reasonably have been expected to acquire—

(a) from facts observable or ascertainable by him; or
(b) from facts ascertainable by him with the help of appropriate expert advice which it is reasonable for him to seek;

but a person shall not be taken by virtue of this subsection to have knowledge of a fact ascertainable by him only with the help of expert advice unless he has failed to take all reasonable steps to obtain (and, where appropriate, to act on) that advice.

(8) Subsections (5) and (7) above shall not extend to Scotland.

6 Application of certain enactments.—(1) Any damage for which a person is liable under section 2 above shall be deemed to have been caused—

(a) for the purposes of the Fatal Accidents Act 1976, by that person's wrongful act, neglect or default;

. . .

(2) Where—

(a) a person's death is caused wholly or partly by a defect in a product, or a person dies after suffering damage which has been so caused;
(b) a request such as mentioned in paragraph (a) of subsection (3) of section 2 above is made to a supplier of the product by that person's personal representatives or, in the case of a person whose death is caused wholly or partly by the defect, by any dependant or relative of that person; and
(c) the conditions specified in paragraphs (b) and (c) of that subsection are satisfied in relation to that request,

this Part shall have effect for the purposes of the Law Reform (Miscellaneous Provisions) Act 1934, the Fatal Accidents Act 1976 and the Damages (Scotland) Act 1976 as if liability of the supplier to that person under that subsection did not depend on that person having requested the supplier to identify certain persons or on the said conditions having been satisfied in relation to a request made by that person.

(3) Section 1 of the Congenital Disabilities (Civil Liability) Act 1976 shall have effect for the purposes of this part as if—

(a) a person were answerable to a child in respect of an occurrence caused wholly or partly by a defect in a product if he is or has been liable under section 2 above in respect of any effect of the occurrence on a parent of the child, or would be so liable if the occurrence caused a parent of the child to suffer damage;
(b) the provisions of this Part relating to liability under section 2 above applied in relation to liability by virtue of paragraph (a) above under the said section 1; and (c) subsection (6) of the said section 1 (exclusion of liability) were omitted.

(4) Where any damage is caused partly by a defect in a product and partly by the fault of the person suffering the damage, the Law Reform (Contributory Negligence) Act 1945 and section 5 of the Fatal Accidents Act 1976 (contributory negligence) shall have effect as if the defect were the fault of every person liable by virtue of this Part for the damage caused by the defect.

(5) In subsection (4) above 'fault' has the same meaning as in the said Act of 1945.

(6) Schedule 1 to this Act shall have effect for the purpose of amending the Limitation Act 1980 and the Prescription and Limitation (Scotland) Act 1973 in their application in relation to the bringing of actions by virtue of this Part.

(7) It is hereby declared that liability by virtue of this Part is to be treated as liability in tort for the purposes of any enactment conferring jurisdiction on any court with respect to any matter.

(8) Nothing in this part shall prejudice the operation of section 12 of the Nuclear Installations Act 1965 (rights to compensation for certain breaches of duties confined to rights under that Act).

7 Prohibition on exclusions from liability.—The liability of a person by virtue of this Part to a person who has suffered damage caused wholly or partly by a defect in a product, or to a dependant or relative of such a person, shall not be limited or excluded by any contract term, by any notice or by any other provision.

8 Power to modify Part I.—(1) Her Majesty may by Order in council make such modifications of this Part and of any other enactment (including an enactment contained in the following Parts of this Act, or in an Act passed after this Act) as appear to Her Majesty in Council to be necessary or expedient in consequence of any modification of the product liability Directive which is made at any time after the passing of this Act.

(2) An Order in Council under subsection (1) above shall not be submitted to Her Majesty in Council unless a draft of the Order has been laid before, and approved by a resolution of, each House of Parliament.

9 Application of Part I to Crown.—(1) Subject to subsection (2) below, this Part shall bind the Crown.

(2) The Crown shall not, as regards the Crown's liability by virtue of this part, be bound by this Part further than the Crown is made liable in tort or in reparation under the Crown Proceedings Act 1947, as that Act has effect from time to time.

45 Interpretation.—(1) In this Act, except in so far as the context otherwise requires—

'aircraft' includes gliders, balloons and hovercraft;

'business' includes a trade or profession and the activities of a professional or trade association or of a local authority or other public authority;

'conditional sale agreement', 'credit-sale agreement' and 'hire-purchase agreement' have the same meanings as in the Consumer Credit Act 1974 but as if in the definition in that Act 'goods' had the same meaning as in this Act;

. . .

'gas' has the same meaning as in Part I of the Gas Act 1986;

'goods' includes substances, growing crops and things comprised in land by virtue of being attached to it and any ship, aircraft or vehicle;

. . .

'modifications' includes additions, alterations and omissions, and cognate expressions shall be construed accordingly;

'motor vehicle' has the same meaning as in [the Road Traffic Act 1988];[13]

. . .

----

[13] Substituted by the Road Traffic (Consequential Provisions) Act 1988, Sch. 3.

'personal injury' includes any disease and any other impairment of a person's physical or mental condition;

. . .

'ship' includes any boat and any other description of vessel used in navigation;

. . .

'substance' means any natural or artificial substance, whether in solid, liquid or gaseous form or in the form of a vapour, and includes substances that are comprised in or mixed with other goods;

'supply' and cognate expressions shall be construed in accordance with section 46 below;

46 Meaning of 'supply'.—(1) Subject to the following provisions of this section, references in this Act to supplying goods shall be construed as references to doing any of the following, whether as principal or agent, that is to say—

(a) selling, hiring out or lending the goods;

(b) entering into a hire-purchase agreement to furnish the goods;

(c) the performance of any contract for work and materials to furnish the goods;

(d) providing the goods in exchange for any consideration (including trading stamps) other than money;

(e) providing the goods in or in connection with the performance of any statutory function; or

(f) giving the goods as a prize or otherwise making a gift of the goods;

and, in relation to gas or water, those references shall be construed as including references to providing the service by which the gas or water is made available for use.

(2) For the purposes of any reference in this Act to supplying goods, where a person ('the ostensible supplier') supplies goods to another person ('the customer') under a hire-purchase agreement, conditional sale agreement or credit-sale agreement or under an agreement for the hiring of goods (other than a hire-purchase agreement) and the ostensible supplier—

(a) carries on the business of financing the provision of goods for others by means of such agreements; and

(b) in the course of that business acquired his interest in the goods supplied to the customer as a means of financing the provision of them for the customer by a further person ('the effective supplier'),

the effective supplier and not the ostensible supplier shall be treated as supplying the goods to the customer.

(3) Subject to subsection (4) below, the performance of any contract by the erection of any building or structure on any land or by the carrying out of any other building works shall be treated for the purposes of this Act as a supply of goods in so far as, but only in so far as, it involves the provision of any goods to any person by means of their incorporation into the building, structure or works.

(4) Except for the purposes of, and in relation to, notices to warn or any provision made by or under Part III of this Act, references in this Act to supplying goods shall not include references to supplying goods comprised in land where the supply is effected by the creation or disposal of an interest in the land.

(8) Where any goods have at any time been supplied by being hired out or lent to any person, neither a continuation or renewal of the hire or loan (whether on the same or different terms) nor any transaction for the transfer after that time of any interest in the goods to the person to whom they were hired or lent shall be treated for the purposes of this Act as a further supply of the goods to that person.

(9) A ship, aircraft or motor vehicle shall not be treated for the purposes of this Act as supplied to any person by reason only that services consisting in the carriage of goods or passengers in that ship, aircraft or vehicle, or in its use for any other purpose, are provided to that person in pursuance of an agreement relating to the use of the ship, aircraft or vehicle for a particular period or for particular voyages, flights or journeys.

50...(1) This Act may be cited as the Consumer Protection Act 1987.

(7) Nothing in this Act...shall make any person liable by virtue of Part I of this Act for any damage caused wholly or partly by a defect in a product which was supplied to any person by its producer before the coming into force of Part I of this Act.

...

NOTE

The Consumer Protection Act 1987 was passed to implement a European Community Directive on Product Liability. The preamble to this Directive, which does not appear in the 1987 Act, and various parts of this Directive which may be of particular use for comparison with the 1987 Act in discussing this area or which are referred to in the materials later in this chapter, are set out post.

■ Council Directive of 25 July 1985 on the approximation of the laws, regulations and administrative provisions of the Member States concerning liability for defective products (85/374/EEC)

THE COUNCIL OF THE EUROPEAN COMMUNITIES,

Having regard to the Treaty establishing the European Economic Community, and in particular Article 100 thereof,

Having regard to the proposal from the Commission,

Having regard to the opinion of the European Parliament,

Having regard to the opinion of the Economic and Social Committee,

Whereas approximation of the laws of the Member States concerning the liability of the producer for damage caused by the defectiveness of his products is necessary because the existing divergences may distort competition and affect the movement of goods within the common market and entail a differing degree of protection of the consumer against damage caused by a defective product to his health or property;

Whereas liability without fault on the part of the producer is the sole means of adequately solving the problem, peculiar to our age of increasing technicality, of a fair apportionment of the risks inherent in modern technological production;

Whereas liability without fault should apply only to movables which have been industrially produced; whereas, as a result, it is appropriate to exclude liability for agricultural products and game, except where they have undergone a processing of an industrial nature which could cause a defect in these products; whereas the liability provided for in this Directive should also apply to movables which are used in the construction of immovables or are installed in immovables;

Whereas protection of the consumer requires that all producers involved in the production process should be made liable, in so far as their finished product, component part or any raw material supplied by them was defective; whereas, for the same reason, liability should extend to importers of products into the Community and to persons who present themselves as producers by affixing their name, trade mark or other distinguishing feature or who supply a product the producer of which cannot be identified;

Whereas, in situations where several persons are liable for the same damage, the protection of the consumer requires that the injured person should be able to claim full compensation for the damage from any one of them;

Whereas, to protect the physical well-being and property of the consumer, the defectiveness of the product should be determined by reference not to its fitness for use but to the lack of the safety which the public at large is entitled to expect; whereas the safety is assessed by excluding any misuse of the product not reasonable under the circumstances;

Whereas a fair apportionment of risk between the injured person and the producer implies that the producer should be able to free himself from liability if he furnishes proof as to the existence of certain exonerating circumstances;

Whereas the protection of the consumer requires that the liability of the producer remains unaffected by acts or omissions of other persons having contributed to cause the damage; whereas, however, the contributory negligence of the injured person may be taken into account to reduce or disallow such liability;

Whereas the protection of the consumer requires compensation for death and personal injury as well as compensation for damage to property; whereas the latter should nevertheless be limited to goods for private use or consumption and be subject to a deduction of a lower threshold of a fixed amount in order to avoid litigation in an excessive number of cases; whereas this Directive should not prejudice compensation for pain and suffering and other non-material damages payable, where appropriate, under the law applicable to the case;

Whereas a uniform period of limitation for the bringing of action for compensation is in the interests both of the injured person and of the producer;

Whereas products age in the course of time, higher safety standards are developed and the state of science and technology progresses; whereas, therefore, it would not be reasonable to make the producer liable for an unlimited period of the defectiveness of his product; whereas, therefore, liability should expire after a reasonable length of time, without prejudice to claims pending at law;

Whereas, to achieve effective protection of consumers, no contractual derogation should be permitted as regards the liability of the producer in relation to the injured person;

Whereas under the legal systems of the Member States an injured party may have a claim for damages based on grounds of contractual liability or on grounds of non-contractual liability other than that provided for in this Directive; in so far as these provisions also serve to attain the objective of effective protection of consumers, they should remain unaffected by this Directive; whereas, in so far as effective protection of consumers in the sector of pharmaceutical products is already also attained in a Member State under a special liability system, claims based on this system should similarly remain possible;

Whereas, to the extent that liability for nuclear injury or damage is already covered in all Member States by adequate special rules, it has been possible to exclude damage of this type from the scope of this Directive;

Whereas, since the exclusion of primary agricultural products and game from the scope of this Directive may be felt, in certain Member States, in view of what is expected for the protection of consumers, to restrict unduly such protection, it should be possible for a Member State to extend liability to such products;

Whereas, for similar reasons, the possibility offered to a producer to free himself from liability if he proves that the state of scientific and technical knowledge at the time when he put the product into circulation was not such as to enable the existence of a defect to be discovered may be felt in certain Member States to restrict unduly the protection of the consumer; whereas it should therefore be possible for a Member State to maintain in its legislation or to provide by new legislation that this exonerating circumstance is not admitted; whereas, in the case of new legislation, making use of this derogation should, however, be subject to a Community stand-still procedure, in order to raise, if possible, the level of protection in a uniform manner throughout the Community;

Whereas, taking into account the legal traditions in most of the Member States, it is inappropriate to set any financial ceiling on the producer's liability without fault; whereas, in so far as there are, however, differing traditions, it seems possible to admit that a Member State may derogate from the principle of unlimited liability by providing a limit for the total liability of the producer for damage resulting from a death or personal injury and caused by identical items with the same defect, provided that this limit is established at a level sufficiently high to guarantee adequate protection of the consumer and the correct functioning of the common market;

Whereas the harmonisation resulting from this cannot be total at the present stage, but opens the way towards greater harmonisation; whereas it is therefore necessary that the Council receive at regular intervals, reports from the Commission on the application of this Directive, accompanied, as the case may be, by appropriate proposals;

Whereas it is particularly important in this respect that a re-examination be carried out of those parts of the Directive relating to the derogations open to the Member States, at the expiry of a period of sufficient length to gather practical experience on the effects of these derogations on the protection of consumers and on the functioning of the common market,

HAS ADOPTED THIS DIRECTIVE: . . .

Article 6

1. A product is defective when it does not provide the safety which a person is entitled to expect, taking all circumstances into account, including:

(a) the presentation of the product;

(b) the use to which it could reasonably be expected that the product would be put;

(c) the time when the product was put into circulation.

2. A product shall not be considered defective for the sole reason that a better product is subsequently put into circulation.

Article 7

The producer shall not be liable as a result of this Directive if he proves: . . .

(b) that, having regard to the circumstances, it is probable that the defect which caused the damage did not exist at the time when the product was put into circulation by him or that this defect came into being afterwards; or . . .

(e) that the state of scientific and technical knowledge at the time when he put the product into circulation was not such as to enable the existence of the defect to be discovered; . . .

Article 9

For the purpose of Article 1, 'damage' means:

(a) damage caused by death or by personal injuries;

(b) damage to, or destruction of, any item of property other than the defective product itself, with a lower threshold of 500 ECU, provided that the item of property:

(i) is of a type ordinarily intended for private use or consumption, and

(ii) was used by the injured person mainly for his own private use or consumption.

This Article shall be without prejudice to national provisions relating to non-material damage.

Article 12

The liability of the producer arising from this Directive may not, in relation to the injured person, be limited or excluded by a provision limiting his liability or exempting him from liability.

Article 13

This Directive shall not affect any rights which an injured person may have according to the rules of the law of contractual or non-contractual liability or a special liability system existing at the moment when this Directive is notified.

Article 15

1. Each Member State may:

(a) by way of derogation from Article 2, provide in its legislation that within the meaning of Article 1 of this Directive 'product' also means primary agricultural products and game;

(b) by way of derogation from Article 7(e), maintain or, subject to the procedure set out in paragraph 2 of this Article, provide in this legislation that the producer shall be liable even if he proves that the state of scientific and technical knowledge at the time when he put the product into circulation was not such as to enable the existence of a defect to be discovered.

2. A Member State wishing to introduce the measures specified in paragraph 1(*b*) shall communicate the text of the proposed measure to the Commission. The Commission shall inform the other Member States thereof.

The Member State concerned shall hold the proposed measure in abeyance for nine months after the Commission is informed and provided that in the meantime the Commission has not submitted to the Council a proposal amending this Directive on the relevant matter. However, if within three months of receiving the said information, the Commission does not advise the Member State concerned that it intends submitting such a proposal to the Council, the Member State may take the proposed measure immediately.

If the Commission does submit to the Council such a proposal amending this Directive within the aforementioned nine months, the Member State concerned shall hold the proposed measure in abeyance for a further period of 18 months from the date on which the proposal is submitted.

3. Ten years after the date of notification of this Directive, the Commission shall submit to the Council a report on the effect that rulings by the courts as to the application of Article 7(e) and of paragraph 1(*b*) of this Article have on consumer protection and the functioning of the common market. In the light of this report the Council, acting on a proposal from the Commission and pursuant to the terms of Article 100 of the Treaty, shall decide whether to repeal Article 7(e).

Article 16

1. Any Member State may provide that a producer's total liability for damage resulting from a death or personal injury and caused by identical items with the same defect shall be limited to an amount which may not be less than 70 million ECU.

2. Ten years after the date of notification of this Directive, the Commission shall submit to the Council a report on the effect on consumer protection and the functioning of the common market of the implementation of the financial limit on liability by those Member States which have used the option provided for in paragraph 1. In the light of this report the Council, acting on a proposal from the Commission and pursuant to the terms of Article 100 of the Treaty, shall decide whether to repeal paragraph 1.

...

Article 21

Every five years the Commission shall present a report to the Council on the application of this Directive and, if necessary, shall submit appropriate proposals to it.

QUESTIONS

1. What test of remoteness of damage do you think will be applied to liability under the Consumer Protection Act 1987? (See C. Newdick (1987) 103 LQR 288 at 297–300; S. Whittaker (1985) 5 YEL 233 at 253–254; *Howarth*, pp. 424–426; Miller and Goldberg, op cit., paras. 17.57–17.58)

2. In what ways might a claimant's misuse of a product affect a claim under the 1987 Act?

3. Are the conditions for the recovery of damages for nervous shock laid down in *Alcock v Chief Constable of the South Yorkshire Police* [1992] 1 AC 310, [1991] 4 All ER 907 (p. 120, ante) relevant under this Act? (Consider A. Bell (1991) 20 Anglo-American LR 340; Miller and Goldberg, op cit., paras. 16.11–16.12).

4. *Clerk & Lindsell*, para. 11–82 suggest that punitive damages should not be available under the Directive. Would this be a disadvantage compared with a negligence action?

NOTES

1. Liability for defective buildings was considered in the previous chapter. Does the Consumer Protection Act 1987 have any application to the case where a person suffers damage as a result of a defect in a building? Consider the definition of 'product' in s. 1(2), and of 'goods' in s. 45(1) and what is laid down about 'supply' in s. 4(1)(b) and s. 46(3) and (4) (and see *Winfield & Jolowicz*, pp. 455–456). Who might be liable if, for example, a tile on the roof cracks, due to a defect in its manufacture, and falls, thereby causing personal injury? (Consider generally Miller and Goldberg op cit., paras. 9.21–9.25.) Another point that has been raised is whether books are covered by the Act. See S. Whittaker (1989) 105 LQR 125 on this question and generally on the coverage of intellectual property and note the discussion, in the context of the Sale of Goods Act 1979, by Sir Iain Glidewell in *St Albans City and District Council v International Computers Ltd* [1996] 4 All ER 481 of the position of a computer disk containing a program. See further Stapleton, op cit., pp. 332–336, where this sort of issue is raised as part of the debate about the difficult distinction between defective products and services.

2. It will have been seen that s. 2(2) of the Act covers not only the producer (as defined by s. 1), but also the importer into a Member State of the European Community and the 'own brander'. In addition, s. 2(3) provides a potential liability for a supplier of the product unless certain information is given (in the circumstances there set out) to the person who has suffered damage. The advantage for the claimant is fairly obvious here and is particularly necessary in cases of 'anonymous' goods: see the Law Commission and the Scottish Law Commission, *Liability for Defective Products*, Law Com. No. 82, Scot Law Com. No. 45, paras. 100–101. However, J. R. Bradgate and N. Savage (1987) 137 NLJ 935 at 954 comment that the 'keeping and storage of the records needed to avoid liability under s. 2(3) may prove crippling to many small businesses; insurance against liability may be the easiest solution in such cases, but the insurer may want to inspect stock recording systems before fixing a premium, and in any case it is likely that the very businesses most at risk from s. 2(3) [small businesses supplying a large number of small products] are those least likely to know of its provisions'. More generally, what is the disadvantage of providing several potential defendants? Note also that the producer of a complete product is liable for a defect in a component part of the product. Should he be? An important feature of s. 2(2) and (3) to appreciate is the element of strict liability which is imposed: see Stapleton, op cit., pp. 242–244; cf. note 35, post. However, in *Skov AEg v Bilka Lanprisvarehus A/S* [2006] 2 CMLR 16, noted by C. Hodges (2006) 122 LQR 393, the European Court of Justice decided that a Member State could not in its national law make a supplier liable for a strictly liable producer beyond the terms laid down by the Directive, although it is otherwise in the case of any fault-based liability of a producer. This reflects the general position the ECJ has taken that the Directive leaves no discretion to a Member State to implement it in national law in a way more favourable to the claimant (*Gonzalez-Sanchez v Medicare Asturiana SA* [2002] ECR 1-3901).

3. To what extent does the Act introduce a standard of liability that is stricter than negligence? This raises the question of the interpretation of s. 3 of the Act. What test or tests may evolve? The phrase 'such as persons generally are entitled to expect' in s. 3 appears, by its use of the word 'entitled', to be different from the 'consumer expectation', one of the tests that had been deployed in the United States of America in the context of strict liability for defective products.

The difficulty with the inclusion of the word 'entitled' is that it introduces an element of circularity. How are we to judge whether consumers are 'entitled' to expect a certain level of safety, as opposed to the level of safety consumers did in fact expect? Presumably the point of the 'entitled' test is to allow the court to say that actual consumer expectations were too high, although technically it also allows the court to say that actual expectations were too low. Consumers might be said to be entitled to expect various levels of safety, including: the level of safety that a reasonable producer would provide (i.e. the same as negligence); the level of safety a producer would provide who was concerned with the balance of risks and benefits of the product for the public but who was not concerned with its own profitability (i.e. negligence but disallowing the rule in *Latimer v AEC Ltd* [1953] AC 643, [1953] 2 All ER 449 (p. 320, ante) that the costs to the defendant of preventing the accident may be taken into account); and, the level of safety a producer would provide if it had to bear all the costs of accidents arising out of the use of the product (i.e. 'strict' liability in the sense of requiring the full internalisation of the risks by the producer). There are objections to all these tests. If the Act imposes a negligence standard, how does it fulfil the aim of the Directive to achieve a 'fair apportionment of the risks inherent in modern technological production' by means of 'liability without fault'? The second rule, the public interest standard, can be criticised for being economically inefficient—it requires producers to use more resources in preventing injury than the resources which would be used up if the accidents happen. The third rule, 'risk internalisation' strict liability, might have dramatic and undesirable effects for industries whose products have benefits for society as a whole beyond their benefits for individual consumers, for example the manufacturers of vaccines. Every time a person uses a vaccine against a contagious disease, the risk of other people contracting the disease goes down because there will be fewer infected people overall. Under the risk internalisation standard, a private manufacturer will be influenced by the risk that some people might have an allergic reaction to the vaccine, but not by the benefits to non-vaccine takers of people taking the vaccine. The result will be under-production of the vaccine, or, in extreme conditions, no vaccine production at all.

Any test in which the risks and benefits of the product are balanced, at least in cases based on an allegation of defective design, raises the question as to which risks are to be taken into account. In negligence it is the risks which were or which should have been known to the defendant, but a stricter rule would include all the risks that in fact existed, whether discoverable or not, and it is on this issue that the development risks defence becomes significant: see p. 647, ante. When considering this point, bear in mind, however, that, as Stapleton points out, op cit., pp. 244–247, the notion of 'benefits' involves a consideration of the relative benefits of the product in the light of feasible alternatives at the time of supply, i.e. developments in this respect since that time will not be taken into account: see the last part of s. 3(2) of the 1987 Act. For early discussion of the test for what is defective, see A. M. Clark, *Product Liability* (London, 1989), chaps. 2 and 4; Stapleton, op cit., chap. 10; Lord Griffiths, P. De Val and R. J. Donner (1988) 62 Tulane LR 353 at 375–384; A. Stoppa (1992) 12 LS 210. Case law began to emerge (albeit slowly). *Abouzaid v Mothercare (UK) Ltd* [2000] All ER (D) 2436 provided one example of strict liability under the Act. A twelve-year-old boy was injured when pulling an elastic strap used to attach a sleeping bag (for the use of his younger brother) to a pushchair. The strap slipped out of his grip and the metal buckle on the end of the strap ricocheted back and hit the claimant in his eye. The Court of

Appeal decided that negligence was not proved given the state of knowledge at the time of manufacture, but that there was a defect in that the safety of the product was below what could be expected. The question of defectiveness received detailed consideration in the following case.

■ A v National Blood Authority

Queen's Bench Division [2001] 3 All ER 289

The claimants were suing for damages for suffering from Hepatitis C from infected blood or blood products via blood transfusions. The blood had been supplied by the defendants, but had been infected prior to being taken from the donors. It was known that there was a very small risk that any one bag of blood could contain the infection but it was impossible at the relevant time to detect infection in any particular bag. In the extract Burton J refers to the articles of the EC directive, rather than the Consumer Protection Act.

BURTON J: . . .

[36] . . . [A] *standard* product is one which is and performs as the producer intends. A *non-standard* product is one which is different, obviously because it is deficient or inferior in terms of safety, from the standard product: and where it is the harmful characteristic or characteristics present in the non-standard product, but not in the standard product, which has or have caused the material injury or damage. . . .

[39] United States tort law has developed a difference between manufacturing defects, design defects and instruction defects (the last category being irrelevant for our purposes). This was worked through in case law, though it did not appear in the Second Restatement, published in 1965, but it has been expressly incorporated into the Third Restatement, published in 1998 (s 2(a)(b)(c): Categories of Product Defects). There is almost a separate jurisprudence for manufacturing defects as opposed to design defects. A manufacturing defect is defined as being 'when the product departs from its intended design even though all possible care was exercised in the preparation and marketing of the product' and a design defect as—

> 'when the foreseeable risks of harm imposed by the product could have been reduced or avoided by the adoption of a reasonable alternative design by the seller or other distributor, or a predecessor in the commercial chain of distribution, and the omission of the alternative design renders the product not reasonably safe.'

The claimants say that, in terms of that dichotomy, the infected blood here is a manufacturing defect—an error in production has led to a one-off. The defendants say that, if a defect at all, it is a design defect, because the process as designed leads inevitably to the occasional failure as a result of an inherent defect in the raw material. . . . . However, notwithstanding that there was some use of these American terms in the travaux préparatoires, there is no place for them in the directive. . . .

[40] The significance to my mind only arose at all in our discussions because, by virtue of the fact that many European experts in product liability, both academics and practitioners, have been steeped in the US jurisprudence, 'rogue products', or rather what I now call 'non-standard products', have been almost automatically defined by them as manufacturing defects. Given that there is a dispute between the parties in this case as to what is meant by a manufacturing defect, it seems to me sensible to concentrate simply on the concept of a standard or non-standard product. . . .

[41] If the distinction is between a standard and non-standard product, the critique of a non-standard product will be the same, namely by virtue of its difference from a standard product, whether it is treated as a one-off manufacturing defect or as a design defect resulting from a way in which the producer's system was designed, which led to all the producer's product being subject to

the same risk. The approach to whether non-standard and standard products are defective may, however, be different, primarily because non-standard products fall to be compared principally with the standard product, while standard products, if compared at all, will be compared with other products on the market.…

Conclusions on Article 6

[55] I do not consider it to be arguable that the consumer had an actual expectation that blood being supplied to him was not 100% clean, nor do I conclude that he had knowledge that it was, or was likely to be, infected with Hepatitis C. It is not seriously argued by the defendants, notwithstanding some few newspaper cuttings which were referred to, that there was any public understanding or acceptance of the infection of transfused blood by Hepatitis C. Doctors and surgeons knew, but did not tell their patients unless asked, and were very rarely asked. It was certainly, in my judgment, not known and accepted by society that there was such a risk, which was thus not 'sozialadaquat' (socially acceptable), as Professor Taschner and Count von Westphalen would describe such risks: Taschner and Riesch *Produkthaftungsgesetz und EG Produkthaftungsrichtlinie* (1990) at p 291 and von Westphalen *Produkthaftungshandbuch* at 27. Thus blood was not, in my judgment, the kind of product referred to in the Flesch/Davenant question and answer in the European Parliament ie 'a product which by its very nature carries a risk and which has been presented as such (instructions for use, labelling, publicity, etc.)', 'risks which are…inherent in [a] product and generally known': nor as referred to by Professor Howells…as being risks which 'consumers can be taken to have chosen to expose themselves to in order to benefit from the product'.

[56] I do not consider that the legitimate expectation of the public at large is that legitimately expectable tests will have been carried out or precautions adopted. Their legitimate expectation is as to the safeness of the product (or not). The court will act as what Dr Bartl called the *appointed representative of the public at large*, but in my judgment it is impossible to inject into the consumer's legitimate expectation matters which would not by any stretch of the imagination be in his actual expectation. He will assume perhaps that there are tests, but his expectations will be as to the safeness of the blood. In my judgment it is as inappropriate to propose that the public should not 'expect the unattainable'-in the sense of tests or precautions which are impossible—at least unless it is informed as to what is unattainable or impossible, as it is to reformulate the expectation as one that the producer will not have been negligent or will have taken all reasonable steps.

[57] In this context I turn to consider what is intended to be included within 'all circumstances' in art 6. I am satisfied that this means all *relevant* circumstances. It is quite plain to me that (albeit that Professor Stapleton has been pessimistic about its success) the directive was intended to eliminate proof of fault or negligence. I am satisfied that this was not simply a legal consequence, but that it was also intended to make it easier for claimants to prove their case, such that not only would a consumer not have to prove that the producer did not take reasonable steps, or all reasonable steps, to comply with his duty of care, but also that the producer did not take all legitimately expectable steps either.…

[58] The Court of Justice in its judgment [in *European Commission v UK* Case C–300/95 [1997] All ER (EC) 481] perhaps refers implicitly to this when it states (at 494 (para 24)): 'In order for a producer to incur liability for defective products under…the directive, the victim must prove the damage, the defect and the causal relationship between defect and damage, but not that the producer was at fault.' It seems to me clear that, even without the full panoply of allegations of negligence, the adoption of tests of avoidability or of legitimately expectable safety precautions must inevitably involve a substantial investigation. What safety precautions or tests were available or reasonably available? Were they tests that would have been excessively expensive? Tests which would have been more expensive than justified the extra safety achieved? Are economic or political circumstances or restrictions to be taken into account in legitimate expectability? Once it is asserted that it is legitimately expectable that a certain safety precaution should have been taken, then the producer must surely be able to explain why such was not possible or why he did not do it; in which case it will then be explored as to whether such tests would or could have been carried out, or were or would have been too expensive or impracticable

to carry out. If risk and benefit should be considered, then it might be said that, the more beneficial the product, the lower the tolerable level of safety; but this could not be arrived at without consideration as to whether, beneficial or not, there would have nevertheless been a safer way of setting about production or design. As Mr Brown pointed out, even if an alleged impracticability is put forward by a producer, it would still be possible to go back further, and see why it was impracticable, and whether earlier or different research and expenditure could not have resolved the problem.

[59] Mr Underhill submitted that he accepted that liability was irrespective of fault and that investigation of negligence was inappropriate, and that that was not the exercise he submitted the court was involved in. No criticisms were being made of the defendants on the basis that they were negligent. The investigation that was being carried out was not, as it would have been in a negligence action, as to what steps actually taken by these defendants were negligent, so that their individual acts and omissions were not being investigated. However, many of Mr Underhill's submissions were indistinguishable from those that he would have made had a breach of a duty of care—albeit one with a high standard of care, so that breach of it might not carry any stigma or criticism—been alleged against him. Did the defendants act reasonably in doing, or not doing, may often have been carefully replaced by 'can it be legitimately expected that . . . ?': but often the language of reasonableness . . . . crept in. . . .

[63] I conclude . . . that *avoidability* is not one of the *circumstances* to be taken into account within art 6. I am satisfied that it is not a *relevant* circumstance, because it is outwith the purpose of the directive, and indeed that, had it been intended that it would be included as a derogation from, or at any rate a palliation of, its purpose, then it would certainly have been mentioned; for it would have been an important circumstance, and I am clear that, irrespective of the absence of any word such as 'notamment' in the English-language version of the directive, it was intended that the most significant circumstances were those listed.

[64] This brings me to a consideration of art 7(e) in the context of consideration of art 6. Article 7(e) provides a very restricted escape route, and producers are, as emphasised in *European Commission v UK*, unable to take advantage of it, unless they come within its very restricted conditions, whereby a producer who has taken all possible precautions (certainly all legitimately expectable precautions, if the terms of art 6, as construed by Mr Underhill, are to be cross-referred) remains liable unless that producer can show that 'the state of scientific and technical knowledge [anywhere and anyone's in the world, provided reasonably accessible] was not such as to enable the existence of the defect to be discovered'. The significance seems to be as follows. Article 7(e) is the escape route (if available at all) for the producer who has done all he could reasonably be expected to do (and more); and yet that route is emphatically very restricted, because of the purpose and effect of the directive (see particularly [1997] All ER (EC) 481 at 494–495, 495, 496 (paras 26, 36 and 38)). This must suggest a similarly restricted view of art 6, indeed one that is even more restricted, given the availability of the (restricted) art 7(e) escape route. If that were not the case, then if the art 7(e) defence were excluded, an option permitted (and indeed taken up, in the case of Luxembourg and Finland) for those member states who wish to delete this 'exonerating circumstance' as 'unduly restricting the protection of the consumer' (Recital 16 and art 15), then, on the defendants' case, an even less restrictive 'exonerating circumstance', and one available even in the case of risks known to the producer, would remain in art 6; and indeed one where the onus does not even rest on the defendant, but firmly on the claimant.

[65] Further, in my judgment, the infected bags of blood were non-standard products. . . . [I]t does not seem to me to matter whether they would be categorised in US tort law as manufacturing or design defects. They were in any event different from the norm which the producer intended for use by the public. (i) I do not accept that all the blood products were equally defective because all of them carried the risk. That is a very philosophical approach. It is one which would, as Mr Forrester pointed out, be equally apt to a situation in which one tyre in one million was defective because of an inherent occasional blip in the strength of the rubber's raw material. The answer is that the test relates to the use of the blood bag. For, and as a result of, the intended use, 99 out of 100 bags would cause no injury and would not be infected, unlike the 100th. (ii) Even in the case of standard products such as drugs,

side-effects are to my mind only capable of being 'socially acceptable' if they are made known.... I am satisfied...that the problem was not known to the consumer. However, in any event, I do not accept that the consumer expected, or was entitled to expect, that his bag of blood was defective even if (which I have concluded was not the case) he had any knowledge of any problem. I do not consider, as Mr Forrester put it, that he was expecting or entitled to expect a form of Russian roulette. That would only arise if, contrary to my conclusion, the public took that as socially acceptable (sozialadaquat). For such knowledge and acceptance there would need to be at the very least publicity and probably express warnings, and even that might not, in the light of the no-waiver provision in art 12 [of the Directive]...be sufficient.

[66] Accordingly I am quite clear that the infected blood products in this case were non-standard products (whether on the basis of being manufacturing or design defects does not appear to me to matter). Where, as here, there is a harmful characteristic in a *non-standard* product, a decision that it is defective is likely to be straightforward, and I can make my decision accordingly. However, the consequence of my conclusion is that 'avoidability' is also not in the basket of circumstances, even in respect of a harmful characteristic in a *standard* product. So I shall set out what I consider to be the structure for consideration under art 6. It must be emphasised that safety and intended, or foreseeable, use are the lynchpins: and, leading on from these, what legitimate expectations there are of safety in relation to foreseeable use. (i) I see no difficulty, on that basis, in an analysis which is akin to contract or warranty. Recital 6 ('the defectiveness of the product should be determined by reference not to its fitness for use but to the lack of the safety which the public at large are entitled to expect') does not in my judgment counter-indicate an approach analogous to contract, but is concerned to emphasise that it is safety which is paramount. (ii) In the circumstances, there may in a simple case be a straightforward answer to the art 6 question, and the facts may be sufficiently clear. But an expert may be needed...For art 6 purposes, the function of such expert would be, in my judgment, to describe the composition or construction of the product and its effect and consequence in use: not to consider what could or should have been done, whether in respect of its design or manufacture, to avoid the problem (that may be relevant in relation to art 7(e), if that arises). (iii) In the following analysis I ignore questions that may obviously arise, either by way of 'exoneration' in respect of other heads of art 7 or in respect of misuse or contributory negligence (art 8...).

[67] The first step must be to identify the harmful characteristic which caused the injury (art 4). In order to establish that there is a defect in art 6, the next step will be to conclude whether the product is standard or non-standard. This will be done (in the absence of admission by the producer) most easily by comparing the offending product with other products of the same type or series produced by that producer. If the respect in which it differs from the series includes the harmful characteristic, then it is, for the purpose of art 6, non-standard. If it does not differ, or if the respect in which it differs does not include the harmful characteristic, but all the other products, albeit different, share the harmful characteristic, then it is to be treated as a standard product.

Non-standard products

[68] The *circumstances* specified in art 6 may obviously be relevant—the product may be a second—as well as the circumstances of the supply. But it seems to me that the primary issue in relation to a non-standard product may be whether the public at large accepted the non-standard nature of the product, ie they accept that a proportion of the products is defective (as I have concluded they do not in this case). That, as discussed, is not of course the end of it, because the question is of legitimate expectation, and the court may conclude that the expectation of the public is too high or too low. But manifestly questions such as warnings and presentations will be in the forefront. However, I conclude that the following are not relevant: (i) avoidability of the harmful characteristic, ie impossibility or unavoidability in relation to precautionary measures; (ii) the impracticality, cost or difficulty of taking such measures; and (iii) the benefit to society or utility of the product (except in the context of whether—with *full information* and *proper knowledge*—the public does and ought to accept the risk).

[69] Lord Griffiths et al in their 1988 article appear to accept (62 Tulane LR 353 at 382) that an overt approach by English judges to consider these latter factors would not be likely, but I do not conclude that they enter into the exercise at all. This is obviously a tough decision for any common lawyer to make. But I am entirely clear that this was the purpose of the directive, and that without the exclusion of such matters (subject only to the limited defence of art 7(e)) it would not only be toothless but pointless. . . .

Standard products

[71] If a standard product is unsafe, it is likely to be so as a result of alleged error in design, or at any rate as a result of an allegedly flawed system. The harmful characteristic must be identified, if necessary with the assistance of experts. The question of presentation/time/circumstances of supply/social acceptability etc will arise as above. The sole question will be safety for the foreseeable use. If there are any comparable products on the market, then it will obviously be relevant to compare the offending product with those other products, so as to identify, compare and contrast the relevant features. There will obviously need to be a full understanding of how the product works—particularly if it is a new product . . . so as to assess its safety for such use. Price is obviously a significant factor in legitimate expectation, and may well be material in the comparative process. But again it seems to me there is no room in the basket for: (i) what the producer could have done differently; and (ii) whether the producer could or could not have done the same as the others did.

[72] . . . [T]here are areas of anomaly . . . . . [One] area arises out of art 6(2), which I repeat for convenience: 'A product shall not be considered defective for the sole reason that a better product is subsequently put into circulation.' In the comparative process, the claimant may point to a product which is safer, but which the producer shows to be produced five years later. Particularly if no other contemporary product had these features, this is likely to be capable of being established, and insofar as such product has improved safety features which have only evolved later in time, they should be ignored, as a result of art 6(2). The claimant might, however, want to allege that the later safety features could have been developed earlier by the producer. That would obviously amount to the claimant running the evidence of 'should have done', to which the producer would no doubt respond 'could not have done'. This would, however, once again go to the issue of *avoidability*, which I have concluded to be outside the ambit of art 6, and so once again if the claimant really wanted to do so he could run the point, but only in negligence.

[73] I can accept that resolution of the problem of the defective standard product will be more complex than in the case of a non-standard product. This trial has been in respect of what I am satisfied to be a non-standard product, and I see, after a three-month hearing, no difficulty in eliminating evidence of avoidability from art 6. It may be that, if I am right in my analysis, and if it is followed in other cases, problems may arise in the consideration of a standard product on such basis, but I do not consider any such problems will be insurmountable if safety, use and the identified *circumstances* are kept in the forefront of consideration. Negligence, fault and the conduct of the producer or designer can be left to the (limited) ambit of art 7(e) to which I now turn [see p .648, post]. . . . .

QUESTIONS

1. To what extent did Burton J adopt a 'consumer expectation' test for 'defectiveness'?
2. Does Burton J give sufficient weight to the fact that doctors and surgeons knew of the risk? (See Miller and Goldberg, op cit., paras. 10.87–10.88.)
3. Is the failure to meet legitimate expectations evidence of the defect or the defect? (See the argument of G. Howells in chap. 8 in *Product Liability in Comparative Perspective*, edited by D. Fairgrieve (Cambridge, 2005); cf. G. Howells and M. Mildred (2002) 65 MLR 95 at 99.)

4. Consider Burton J's views about warnings and exclusion of liability in [65] ante. In the light of the approach to warnings and exclusions in the Occupiers' Liability Act 1957 (s. 2(1) and s. 2(4)(a)) revealed by a case such as *White v Blackmore* [1972] 2 QB 651, [1972] 3 All ER 158 (p. 582, ante), would Article 12 of the Directive (s. 7 of the Consumer Protection Act 1987) affect the situation he envisages there?

NOTES

1. For background to the case, see M. Brooke and I. Forrester, chap. 2 in *Product Liability in Comparative Perspective*. The *A* case is noted by C. Hodges (2001) 117 LQR 528 and Howells and Mildred op cit., and discussed in an article by R. Goldberg [2002] Med L Rev 165. See further J. Stapleton (2002) 53 SC L Rev 1226 at 1249–1251, who points out that Article 6 refers to 'all the relevant circumstances', and argues that Burton J was too selective in the circumstances he took into account under Article 6, reading this as meaning circumstances relevant to the Directive's purposes and focusing only on its pro-consumer goals; cf. Hodges op cit., p. 530. Consider also S. Whittaker, *Liability for Products* (Oxford, 2005), pp. 489–491.

2. In *Bogle v McDonalds Restaurants Ltd* [2002] EWHC 490 there was an unsuccessful attempt to establish strict liability in the case of a cup of coffee spilling and scalding the claimant. Here Field J thought at [12] that people's expectation was that the drink would be hot, that precautions would be taken to guard against the risk of spilling the liquid, 'but not to the point that they are denied the basic utility of being able to buy hot drinks to be consumed on the premises from a cup with the lid off'. Although Field J adopted the analysis in the *A* case, the European Commission in its *Third Report* on the application of the Directive (COM (2006) 496), p. 10, contrast this decision with the *A* case because Field J considered relevant the defendants' steps to train their staff in respect of safe service. Compare also with the *A* case the decision of the Court of Appeal in *Tesco Stores Ltd v Pollard* [2006] EWCA Civ 393, which involved a 13-month-old child consuming some dishwasher powder. The issue concerned the cap (meant to be child-resistant) on the bottle and the appropriate expectation to be associated with it. It was decided that it should not be expected that it would meet its design standard, as had been argued. The design standard was not stated on the product, and, on the facts of this case, the appropriate expectation was that the bottle would be 'more difficult to open than if it had an ordinary screwtop'. For comment, see M. Mildred [2007] JPIL 141 at 145–146 and Howells, op cit., para. 4.151, who regards it as a 'relatively weak interpretation of consumer expectations' and who also (at para 4.148) points out that *Pollard* (as opposed to the *A* case) concerns a design defect.

3. As mentioned in the extract ante, different classification to the standard/non-standard product dichotomy adopted in the *A* case has been used in the United States of America. Types of defect can be classified as 'manufacturing defects', 'design defects' and 'failures to warn'. See e.g. Newdick, op cit., though for difficulty, see Howells and Mildred (2006) 65 MLR at pp. 98–99. Should the same test apply to all? The latest US Restatement (Restatement of the Law, (3d), Torts: Products Liability (1998)) differentiates between these forms of defect. It imposes liability without fault for manufacturing defects (defined as where the product has departed from its 'intended design') but re-introduces a fault-based regime for design defects and failures to warn (see J. Henderson and A. Twerski (1991) 66 NYU L Rev 1263). For an instructive comparison of the Restatement and the European Directive, see G. Howells and M. Mildred (1998) 65 Tennessee. L. Rev. 985. For Hodges (2001) 117 LQR at p. 530, Burton J's classification is

'little more than renaming as a non-standard product one which has traditionally been described as one with a manufacturing defect': for Stapleton (2002) 53 SC L Rev at 1251, it is adding cases of products with premanufacture infections to those with manu-facturing defects. On the other hand, Howells and Mildred (2002) 65 MLR at p. 98 approve of the judge's rejection of a distinction between manufacturing and design defects, arguing that in some cases it can be difficult to decide on the appropriate classi-fication. For further discussion, see Miller and Goldberg, op cit., paras. 10.91–10.100.

4. Section 4 sets out various defences to the strict liability introduced by the Act. On s. 4(1)(c) note that a non-profit-making public service supplier does not come within its terms as the *A* case shows (and see *Veedfald v Arhus Amtskommune* [2001] ECR 1-3569). Section 4(1)(e) has been controversial. Compare its wording with Art. 7(e) of the Directive. Are the two compatible? In *European Commission v United Kingdom* [1997] All ER (EC) 481, the European Court of Justice decided that the two were, at least potentially, compatible. The ECJ decided that despite the absence of any explicit word-ing in the Directive about the question, it was implicit in the Directive that the relevant scientific knowledge must have been 'accessible' at the time when the product was put into circulation, although the exact details of what amounted to accessibility would have to be left to national courts to work out. The 'Manchurian' example given by the Advocate-General in his opinion in this case is often cited, namely that a European product manufacturer would not lose the defence just because at the moment of the product's circulation the defect had been discovered and its discovery published in Chinese in a local scientific journal in Manchuria. In the ECJ's opinion the British rule, with its apparent requirement that the relevant scientific knowledge must be accessible to producers of 'products of the same description', is not necessarily in contravention of the Directive. Furthermore, the ECJ decided that the fact that the British version of the defence did not allow the producer to escape liability on the purely subject-ive ground that the producer did not know about the relevant scientific research (but instead judged the producer against an 'objective' standard of what other people might be expected to have done) meant that the British rule was within the Directive because the Directive also imposes an 'objective' test. The ECJ also took account of the fact that s. 1(1) of the Act requires the Act to be construed so that it complies with the Directive (though see Clark, op cit., p. 154; cf. Miller and Goldberg, op cit., para. 13.58). It is inter-esting to note that although the accident in *Abouzaid v Mothercare (UK) Ltd* [2000] All ER (D) 2436 was not reasonably foreseeable, the strict liability claim was not ruled out by s. 4(1)(e), even though no similar accident was recorded on the DTI's database when the product was supplied; in fact, Pill LJ doubted whether such a record fell within the meaning of scientific and technical knowledge in this context.

As was mentioned ante, the development risks defence was one of the optional facets of the Directive, and only two of the Member States have not availed themselves of this option (totally or partially). Generally on the development risks defence, see Newdick op cit. and [1988] CLJ 455; Stapleton, *Product Liability*, pp. 236–242, Clark, op cit., chap. 6; Miller and Goldberg, op cit., paras. 13.25–13.105; Griffiths, De Val and Donner, op cit., pp. 384–391; M. Mildred, chap. 10 in *Product Liability in Comparative Perspective*; and the 2004 report for the European Commission of the Fondazione Roselli Foundation which concluded that its findings 'seem to support the argument that the [defence] is a significant factor in achieving the Directive's balance between the need to preserve incentives to innovation and the consumers' interests'. The Foundation also concluded that development risks might be uninsurable. The defence was considered in the *A* case from which the next extract is taken.

■ A v National Blood Authority

Queen's Bench Division [2001] 3 All ER 289

For the facts and an extract concerning the question whether the product was defective, see p. 641, ante.

BURTON J: ...

Conclusions on Article 7(e)

[74] As to construction: (i) I note (without resolving the question) the force of the argument that the defect in art 7(b) falls to be construed as the defect in the particular product; but I do not consider that to be determinative of the construction of art 7(e), and indeed I am firmly of the view that such is not the case in art 7(e); (ii) the analysis of art 7(e), with the guidance of *European Commission v UK*, seems to me to be entirely clear. If there is a known risk, ie the existence of the defect is known or should have been known in the light of non-Manchurianly accessible information, then the producer continues to produce and supply at his own risk. It would, in my judgment, be inconsistent with the purpose of the directive if a producer, in the case of a known risk, continues to supply products simply because, and despite the fact that, he is unable to identify in which if any of his products that defect will occur or recur, or, more relevantly in a case such as this, where the producer is obliged to supply, continues to supply without accepting the responsibility for any injuries resulting, by insurance or otherwise; and (iii) the existence of the defect is in my judgment clearly generic. Once the existence of the defect is known, then there is then the risk of that defect materialising in any particular product.

[75] The purpose of the directive, from which art 7(e) should obviously not derogate more than is necessary (see Recital 16) is to prevent injury, and facilitate compensation for injury. The defendants submit that this means that art 7(e) must be construed so as to give the opportunity to the producer to do all he can in order to avoid injury: thus concentrating on what can be done in relation to the particular product. The claimants submit that this will rather be achieved by imposing obligation in respect of a known risk irrespective of the chances of finding the defect in the particular product, and I agree.

[76] The purpose of art 7(e) was plainly not to discourage innovation, and to exclude development risks from the directive, and it succeeds in its objective, subject to the very considerable restrictions that are clarified by *European Commission v UK*: namely that the risk ceases to be a development risk and becomes a known risk not if and when the producer in question (or, as the CPA inappropriately sought to enact in s 4(1)(e) 'a producer of products of the same description as the product in question') had the requisite knowledge, but if and when such knowledge were accessible anywhere in the world outside Manchuria. Hence it protects the producer in respect of the unknown (inconnu). But the consequence of acceptance of the defendants' submissions would be that protection would also be given in respect of the known.

[77] The effect is, it seems to me, not ... that non-standard products are incapable of coming within art 7(e). Non-standard products may qualify once, ie if the problem which leads to an occasional defective product is (unlike the present case) not known: this may perhaps be more unusual than in relation to a problem with a standard product, but does not seem to me to be an impossible scenario. However, once the problem is known by virtue of accessible information, then the non-standard product can no longer qualify for protection under art 7(e).

QUESTION

Does Burton J use the notion of defect in the same way for Article 6 and Article 7(e)? (See J. Stapleton (2007) 26 Rev Litigation 991 at 1006, note 35.)

NOTES

1. Compare with the *A* case the decision on HIV infected blood in the 1999 Dutch case of *Scholten v Foundation Sanquin of Blood Supply*, where although the product was regarded as defective, the state of the art defence succeeded. Compare the German decision on the case of an exploding mineral water bottle discussed by Mildred, p. 171 in *Product Liability in Comparative Perspective*.

2. Contributory negligence can also be applicable to a suit under the 1987 Act (s. 6(4)). Should it be? See J. A. Jolowicz in *Accident Compensation after Pearson*, edited by D. K. Allen, C. J. Bourn and J. Holyoak (London, 1979), pp. 59–61 and cf. P. J. Sherman at p. 133. In purely economic terms, the answer depends on the nature of the producer's liability. To the extent that the producer's liability is strict, the absence of a contributory negligence defence will be inefficient, since potential victims will not have proper incentives to look after their own property and, to a lesser extent, themselves. Under strict liability, potential victims can assume that their losses will be compensated whatever the producer has done. Under fault, however, the existence of contributory negligence is less important. Potential victims, knowing that the effect of a fault rule is that it is far more expensive for producers to behave unreasonably than to behave reasonably, so that producers have both the opportunity to escape liability and a powerful incentive to do so, will see that there is a high probability that if they are injured, the producer will be found to have acted reasonably and therefore will not have to pay compensation. That in turn means that potential victims will have an incentive to look after their own property (and, less powerfully, themselves). See R. Cooter and T. Ulen, *Law and Economics* 5th edn (2007), pp. 339, 344–347 and 365–366.

3. The range of recoverable damage is limited under s. 5, and recovery for damage not covered by the Act (e.g. damage to a factory) will have to be sought under other torts or in contract. (It has also been pointed out that negligence may be of practical importance even in relation to types of damage covered by the Act because of limitation periods: note that Sch. 1 to the 1987 Act contains the limitation period for individual cases but also a ten-year 'long stop' from the 'relevant time' within the meaning of s. 4.) The Act covers death and personal injuries. Damage to certain property is compensatable under the Act, provided the monetary threshold of £275 is met, and Member States have no discretion to remove the threshold (*European Commission v France* [2002] ECR 1-3827; *European Commission v Greece* [2002] ECR 1-3879; and more generally *Gonzalez-Sanchez v Medicare Asturiana SA* [2002] ECR 1-3901). In some Member States—but not in others—the threshold figure is deducted from the sum awarded: see p. 11 of the European Commission's *Third Report* (COM (2006) 496) on the application of the Directive. However, should such loss be covered by a strict liability scheme? This question is related to the incidence of first party insurance in respect of such damage and what might be thought to be the desirable goal of encouraging it. (See Whittaker (1985) 5 YEL at pp. 274–275.) Damage to the product itself is not covered. What if one part of a car (e.g. the brakes), which is supplied by a component manufacturer, is defective and causes an accident in which the rest of the car is damaged? (Cf. the position in negligence, p. 628, ante). Are Article 9 of the Directive and s. 5(2) of the Act consistent on this point? (See C. J. Miller and M. Mildred, *Product Liability and Safety Encyclopaedia*, III, para. 140.2; *Clerk & Lindsell*, para. 11–81, note 25.)

4. From the outset, a striking feature of the Act has been that it has not produced many decided cases, and that phenomenon has appeared to be a pan-European one. One

point that might have had some influence is that in cases in which the victims claim to have suffered harm after using the product for many years, tobacco smokers for example, using the Act rather than merely suing in common law negligence leads to the unwanted complication of having to prove that liability arose solely out of events subsequent to the Act having come into force. In addition, it needs to be borne in mind that the Act does nothing to make any easier what is often the claimant's most difficult task, namely to prove causation. It has also been pointed out that a number of cases have been brought and then settled, and that the pressures on litigants to settle in the English legal system are very strong (see M. Mildred in *Directive 85/374/EEC on Product Liability: Ten Years After*, edited by M. Goyens (1996)). Note further the same author's opinion ([2007] JPIL 141 at 149) that while earlier speculation for the lack of case law referred to 'lawyers' conservatism and familiarity with negligence', in more recent times experience 'suggests that the lack of clarity of the defectiveness concept has been a disincentive to claimants'.

There have been three reports from the European Commission on the working of the Directive: see *First Report*, COM(95) 617 (1995), *Second Report*, COM(2000) 893 and *Third Report*, COM(2006) 496, and for comment on this most recent report, see D. Fairgrieve and G. Howells (2007) 70 MLR 962. In its most recent report, the Commission did not think that there was any need for it to propose amendments and that the goal of harmonisation could be promoted by the European Court of Justice's decisions, certain powers available to the Commission and the continuing operation of its working groups. One of the reports carried out for the Commission was that by the Rosselli Foundation referred to in note 4, p. 647, ante; another report was carried out by Lovells, *Product Liability in the European Union*, A report for the European Commission, MARKT/2001/11/D, and was published in 2003. The next extract is taken from this latter report.

■ Lovells Report on Product Liability in the European Union, *A report for the European Commission*, MARKT/2001/11/D

5.1 Principal findings

The differences in product liability risks as between the Member States

1. The prospects of product liability claims being brought, and their likely outcome, do differ as between the Member States. There is no single cause of these differences. They result from:

- the optional provisions in the Product Liability Directive
- discrepancies in implementation and interpretation of the Product Liability Directive
- differences in the national liability systems that exist alongside the Product Liability Directive
- differing approaches to the assessment of damages
- differing procedural rules and levels of access to justice
- variations in consumer attitudes from Member State to Member State.

The impact of the Directive on product liability risks

2. The Product Liability Directive has moderately increased the prospects of product liability claims being brought, and of their success.

3. The Product Liability Directive has contributed a little to increasing the level of safety of products marketed in the EU.

The effect of differences in product liability risks as between the Member States

4. There is little evidence that disparities as between Member States in the practical functioning of product liability regimes create significant barriers to trade or distortions to competition in the EU. A few Producers indicated that their businesses are affected in some ways by such disparities.

5. There is some evidence that disparities as between Member States in the practical functioning of product liability regimes may affect the basis on which insurance coverage is offered in different Member States. There is no evidence however, that such disparities restrict the availability of insurance in any Member State. As to the Product Liability Directive itself, some Producers and Insurers reported that insurance premiums increased somewhat as a result of the Directive.

The experience of product liability claims in the EU

6. There has been a noticeable increase in the number of product liability claims in the EU in the last 10 years.

7. Whilst the Product Liability Directive has contributed to the increase in product liability claims, more important factors have been increased consumer awareness of rights, increased consumer access to information, and media activity.

8. There is evidence that product liability claims in the EU have become more successful in the past 10 years. The Product Liability Directive has contributed to this increase. Other important factors have been greater access to legal assistance/advice and changes in judicial attitudes to claims.

9. There is evidence that claims by consumers are generally more likely to be successful if brought under the Product Liability Directive rather than under other national laws. This is more so in some Member States than in others.

10. In the last 10 years, the incidence of out-of-court settlements has increased somewhat. The main factors responsible for the increase appear to be media activity, greater access to legal assistance and the Product Liability Directive.

CHAPTER ELEVEN

LIABILITY FOR ANIMALS

We have seen in chap. 10, ante that liability for defective products is a blend of common law and statute. This is also the case when damage is caused by animals. In this sphere, however, strict liability at common law was more prevalent than in the case of products (see p. 610, ante), but legislation has taken over and attention now has to be paid to the Animals Act 1971 (post). This Act was based on a report of the Law Commission in 1967 (*Civil Liability for Animals*, Law Com. No. 13), although it should be noted that it departs in some respects from the provisions of the Draft Bill to be found in that report. Liability for damage caused by animals can still be grounded on torts such as negligence, nuisance or *Rylands v Fletcher* (1868) LR 3 HL 330. Nevertheless, it should not be forgotten that liability in negligence is affected by the 1971 Act, for s. 8 alters the common law position concerning liability for negligence where animals stray onto a highway. For discussion of this area of the law, in addition to the standard textbooks, see P. M. North, *The Modern Law of Animals* (London, 1972).

■ The Animals Act 1971

STRICT LIABILITY FOR DAMAGE DONE BY ANIMALS

1. **New provisions as to strict liability for damage done by animals.**—(1) The provisions of sections 2 to 5 of this Act replace—
    (a) the rules of the common law imposing a strict liability in tort for damage done by an animal on the ground that the animal is regarded as ferae naturae or that its vicious or mischievous propensities are known or presumed to be known;
    (b) subsections (1) and (2) of section 1 of the Dogs Act 1906 as amended by the Dogs (Amendment) Act 1928 (injury to cattle or poultry); and
    (c) the rules of the common law imposing a liability for cattle trespass.

    (2) Expressions used in those sections shall be interpreted in accordance with the provisions of section 6 (as well as those of section 11) of this Act.

2. **Liability for damage done by dangerous animals.**—(1) Where any damage is caused by an animal which belongs to a dangerous species, any person who is a keeper of the animal is liable for the damage, except as otherwise provided by this Act.

    (2) Where damage is caused by an animal which does not belong to a dangerous species, a keeper of the animal is liable for the damage, except as otherwise provided by this Act, if—
    (a) the damage is of a kind which the animal, unless restrained, was likely to cause or which, if caused by the animal, was likely to be severe; and

(b) the likelihood of the damage or of its being severe was due to characteristics of the animal which are not normally found in animals of the same species or are not normally so found except at particular times or in particular circumstances; and

(c) those characteristics were known to that keeper or were at any time known to a person who at that time had charge of the animal as that keeper's servant or, where that keeper is the head of a household, were known to another keeper of the animal who is a member of that household and under the age of sixteen.

3. Liability for injury done by dogs to livestock.—Where a dog causes damage by killing or injuring livestock, any person who is a keeper of the dog is liable for the damage, except as otherwise provided by this Act.

4. Liability for damage and expenses due to trespassing livestock.—(1) Where livestock belonging to any person strays on to land in the ownership or occupation of another and—

(a) damage is done by the livestock to the land or to any property on it which is in the ownership or possession of the other person; or

(b) any expenses are reasonably incurred by that other person in keeping the livestock while it cannot be restored to the person to whom it belongs or while it is detained in pursuance of section 7 of this Act, or in ascertaining to whom it belongs;

the person to whom the livestock belongs is liable for the damage or expenses, except as otherwise provided by this Act.

(2) For the purposes of this section any livestock belongs to the person in whose possession it is.

5. Exceptions from liability under sections 2 to 4.—(1) A person is not liable under section 2 to 4 of this Act for any damage which is due wholly to the fault of the person suffering it.

(2) A person is not liable under section 2 of this Act for any damage suffered by a person who has voluntarily accepted the risk thereof.

(3) A person is not liable under section 2 of this Act for any damage caused by an animal kept on any premises or structure to a person trespassing there, if it is proved either—

(a) that the animal was not kept there for the protection of persons or property; or

(b) (if the animal was kept there for the protection of persons or property) that keeping it there for that purpose was not unreasonable.

(4) A person is not liable under section 3 of this Act if the livestock was killed or injured on land on to which it had strayed and either the dog belonged to the occupier or its presence on the land was authorised by the occupier.

(5) A person is not liable under section 4 of this Act where the livestock strayed from a highway and its presence there was a lawful use of the highway.

(6) In determining whether any liability for damage under section 4 of this Act is excluded by subsection (1) of this section the damage shall not be treated as due to the fault of the person suffering it by reason only that he could have prevented it by fencing; but a person is not liable under that section where it is proved that the straying of the livestock on to the land would not have occurred but for a breach by any other person, being a person having an interest in the land, of a duty to fence.

6. Interpretation of certain expressions used in sections 2 to 5.—(1) The following provisions apply to the interpretation of sections 2 to 5 of this Act.

(2) A dangerous species is a species—

(a) which is not commonly domesticated in the British Islands; and

(b) whose fully grown animals normally have such characteristics that they are likely, unless restrained, to cause severe damage or that any damage they may cause is likely to be severe.

(3) Subject to subsection (4) of this section, a person is a keeper of an animal if—

(a) he owns the animal or has it in his possession; or

(b) he is the head of a household of which a member under the age of sixteen owns the animal or has it in his possession;

and if at any time an animal ceases to be owned by or to be in the possession of a person, any person who immediately before that time was a keeper thereof by virtue of the preceding provisions of this subsection continues to be a keeper of the animal until another person becomes a keeper thereof by virtue of those provisions.

(4) Where an animal is taken into and kept in possession for the purpose of preventing it from causing damage or of restoring it to its owner, a person is not a keeper of it by virtue only of that possession.

(5) Where a person employed as a servant by a keeper of an animal incurs a risk incidental to his employment he shall not be treated as accepting it voluntarily.

DETENTION AND SALE OF TRESPASSING LIVESTOCK

7. Detention and sale of trespassing livestock.—(1) The right to seize and detain any animal by way of distress damage feasant is hereby abolished.

(2) Where any livestock strays on to any land and is not then under the control of any person the occupier of the land may detain it, subject to subsection (3) of this section, unless ordered to return it by a court.

(3) Where any livestock is detained in pursuance of this section the right to detain it ceases—

(a) at the end of a period of forty-eight hours, unless within that period notice of the detention has been given to the officer in charge of a police station and also, if the person detaining the livestock knows to whom it belongs, to that person; or

(b) when such amount is tendered to the person detaining the livestock as is sufficient to satisfy any claim he may have under section 4 of this Act in respect of the livestock; or

(c) if he has no such claim, when the livestock is claimed by a person entitled to its possession.

(4) Where livestock has been detained in pursuance of this section for a period of not less than fourteen days the person detaining it may sell it at a market or by public auction, unless proceedings are then pending for the return of the livestock or for any claim under section 4 of this Act in respect of it.

(5) Where any livestock is sold in the exercise of the right conferred by this section and the proceeds of the sale, less the costs thereof and any costs incurred in connection with it, exceed the amount of any claim under section 4 of this Act which the vendor had in respect of the livestock, the excess shall be recoverable from him by the person who would be entitled to the possession of the livestock but for the sale.

(6) A person detaining any livestock in pursuance of this section is liable for any damage caused to it by a failure to treat it with reasonable care and supply it with adequate food and water while it is so detained.

(7) References in this section to a claim under section 4 of this Act in respect of any livestock do not include any claim under that section for damage done by or expenses incurred in respect of the livestock before the straying in connection with which it is detained under this section.

ANIMALS STRAYING ON TO HIGHWAY

8. Duty to take care to prevent damage from animals straying on to the highway.—(1) So much of the rules of the common law relating to liability for negligence as excludes or restricts the duty which a person might owe to others to take such care as is reasonable to see that damage is not caused by animals straying on to a highway is hereby abolished.

(2) Where damage is caused by animals straying from unfenced land to a highway a person who placed them on the land shall not be regarded as having committed a breach of the duty to take care by reason only of placing them there if—

   (a) the land is common land, or is land situated in an area where fencing is not customary, or is a town or village green; and

   (b) he had a right to place the animals on that land.

PROTECTION OF LIVESTOCK AGAINST DOGS

9. Killing of or injury to dogs worrying livestock.—(1) In any civil proceedings against a person (in this section referred to as the defendant) for killing or causing injury to a dog it shall be a defence to prove—

   (a) that the defendant acted for the protection of any livestock and was a person entitled to act for the protection of that livestock; and

   (b) that within forty-eight hours of the killing or injury notice thereof was given by the defendant to the officer in charge of a police station.

   (2) For the purposes of this section a person is entitled to act for the protection of any livestock if, and only if—

   (a) the livestock or the land on which it is belongs to him or to any person under whose express or implied authority he is acting; and

   (b) the circumstances are not such that liability for killing or causing injury to the livestock would be excluded by section 5(4) of this Act.

   (3) Subject to subsection (4) of this section, a person killing or causing injury to a dog shall be deemed for the purposes of this section to act for the protection of any livestock if, and only if, either—

   (a) the dog is worrying or is about to worry the livestock and there are no other reasonable means of ending or preventing the worrying; or

   (b) the dog has been worrying livestock, has not left the vicinity and is not under the control of any person and there are no practicable means of ascertaining to whom it belongs.

   (4) For the purposes of this section the condition stated in either of the paragraphs of the preceding subsection shall be deemed to have been satisfied if the defendant believed that it was satisfied and had reasonable ground for that belief.

   (5) For the purposes of this section—

   (a) an animal belongs to any person if he owns it or has it in his possession; and

   (b) land belongs to any person if he is the occupier thereof.

SUPPLEMENTAL

10. Application of certain enactments to liability under sections 2 to 4.—For the purposes of the Fatal Accidents Acts 1846 to 1959,[1] the Law Reform (Contributory Negligence) Act 1945 and [the Limitation Act 1980][2] any damage for which a person is liable under sections 2 to 4 of this Act shall be treated as due to his fault.

11. General interpretation.—In this Act—

'common land', and 'town or village green' have the same meanings as in the Commons Registration Act 1965[3];

   'damage' includes the death of, or injury to, any person (including any disease and any impairment of physical or mental condition);

   'fault' has the same meaning as in the Law Reform (Contributory Negligence) Act 1945;

---

  [1] This now includes a reference to the Fatal Accidents Act 1976. The Fatal Accidents Acts 1846 and 1959 have been repealed.

  [2] Substituted by the Limitation Act 1980, s. 40(2) and Sch. 3.

  [3] This will be altered by para 5 of Schedule 2 to the Common Act 2006 when it comes into force.

'fencing' includes the construction of any obstacle designed to prevent animals from straying;

'livestock' means cattle, horses, asses, mules, hinnies, sheep, pigs, goats and poultry, and also deer not in the wild state and, in sections 3 and 9, also, while in captivity, pheasants, partridges and grouse;

'poultry' means the domestic varieties of the following, that is to say, fowls, turkeys, geese, ducks, guinea-fowls, pigeons, peacocks and quails; and

'species' includes sub-species and variety.

12. Application to Crown.—(1) This Act binds the Crown, but nothing in this section shall authorise proceedings to be brought against Her Majesty in her private capacity.

(2) Section 38(3) of the Crown Proceedings Act 1947 (interpretation of references to Her Majesty in her private capacity) shall apply as if this section were contained in that Act.

■ Mirvahedy v Henley

House of Lords [2003] 2 All ER 401

LORD NICHOLLS OF BIRKENHEAD: . . .

[1] My Lords, shortly after midnight on the night of 28–29 August 1996 Hossein Mirvahedy was driving home from his work as manager of a hotel in Devon. He was driving along a dual carriageway stretch of the A380 from Torquay to Exeter. His car came into collision with a horse when it ran across the road and crashed into the car. He suffered serious personal injuries.

[2] The horse belonged to Andrew and Susan Henley. It had escaped from the field where it was kept. Dr and Mrs Henley lived about a mile from where the accident occurred. In an adjacent field they kept three horses, of which the horse involved in the accident was one. On the night of the accident all three horses stampeded out of a corner of their field. They pushed over an electric wire fence and a surrounding wooden fence, and then trampled through a strip of tall bracken and vegetation. Something seems to have frightened them very badly, but nobody knows what it was. The horses fled 300 yards up a track and then for a distance of almost a mile along a minor road before reaching the busy A380 road.

[3] Such behaviour is usual in horses when sufficiently alarmed by a threat. They attempt to flee, ignoring obstacles in their way, and are apt to continue in their flight for a considerable distance, even beyond the point where the perceived threat was detectable.

[4] Mr Mirvahedy brought a claim against Dr and Mrs Henley as keepers of the horse. He based his claim in negligence. He said Dr and Mrs Henley had not fenced the field properly. The judge, Judge O'Malley sitting in the Exeter County Court, rejected this claim. No appeal was pursued from this decision. Mr Mirvahedy also advanced a claim under s 2 of the Animals Act 1971. He asserted that, even if they were not at fault, Dr and Mrs Henley were liable for the damage caused by their runaway horse. Under the 1971 Act they were strictly liable. They were liable independently of fault. That claim, too, failed before the judge. It succeeded on appeal to the Court of Appeal ([2001] EWCA Civ 1749, [2002] QB 769, [2002] 2 WLR 566). The court comprised Dame Elizabeth Butler-Sloss P and Hale and Keene LJJ. Dr and Mrs Henley then appealed to your Lordships' House.

[5] The appeal raises one question: is the keeper of an animal such as a horse strictly liable for damage caused by the animal when the animal's behaviour in the circumstances was in no way abnormal for an animal of the species in those circumstances? . . .

[7] . . . [T]he answer to the question I have posed lies in interpreting the provisions of this Act, and in particular s2(2), in accordance with established principles of statutory interpretation.

THE 1971 ACT

[Having pointed out that a horse did not fall within the category of a 'dangerous species' under s.6(2) of the 1971 Act, his Lordship continued:]

[14] Section 2(2) established a different regime where damage is caused by an animal not belonging to a dangerous species. This subsection applies, therefore, to all species of animals commonly domesticated here. It includes horses. The material part of s 2(2) provides:

'Where damage is caused by an animal which does not belong to a dangerous species, a keeper of the animal is liable for the damage, except as otherwise provided by this Act, if—(a) the damage is of a kind which the animal, unless restrained, was likely to cause or which, if caused by the animal, was likely to be severe; and (b) the likelihood of the damage or of its being severe was due to characteristics of the animal which are not normally found in animals of the same species or are not normally so found except at particular times or in particular circumstances; and (c) those characteristics were known to that keeper ...'

[15] In the present case nothing turns on requirement (a). It is accepted that this precondition of liability is satisfied. Similarly with requirement (c): the judge found that this requirement was satisfied in this case, and his finding has not been challenged.

[16] The crucial requirement is requirement (b). Requirement (b) is concerned, in short, with the source of the animal's dangerousness. If requirement (b) is to be met, the dangerousness of the animal, as described in requirement (a), must be attributable to the animal having characteristics falling within one or other of two classes. The first limb of para (b) identifies one class. The animal must have characteristics 'which are not normally found in animals of the same species'. The second limb of para (b) identifies the other class of qualifying characteristics. The animal must have characteristics which are not normally found in animals of the same species 'except at particular times or in particular circumstances'.

[17] Both these classes, it can be noticed at once, are described in terms of abnormality. The first class is that the particular animal has characteristics not normally found in animals of the same species. Unless the relevant characteristic of the animal which caused the damage satisfies this test of abnormality, the case does not fall within the first class. Likewise, the case does not fall within the second class unless the relevant characteristic of the animal is one which, except at particular times or in particular circumstances, is abnormal. The characteristic of the particular animal must be a characteristic which, save on particular occasions, is not a characteristic of animals of the same species.

[18] Thus, the first class embraces a case where animals of the species are normally docile but the particular animal is not. In such a case requirement (b) is met. However, there are many species of animals which are normally docile but which, in certain circumstances or at particular times, behave differently, even dangerously. Dogs are not normally prone to bite all and sundry. But a dog guarding its territory, or a bitch with a litter whose pups are being threatened, may well be vicious. The second class is directed at this type of case. A dog which is prone to bite is likely to fall within the second class. A dog with a general propensity to bite has a characteristic which, save in particular circumstances, is not normally found in dogs. Such a dog has an abnormal characteristic. In such a case requirement (b) is satisfied.

[19] Thus far there is no difficulty. But what of the case where the dog which attacks and bites is at the time acting as a guard dog or is a bitch with pups? Such an animal is behaving dangerously but it is doing so in a manner characteristic of its species *in the circumstances*. Does such a case also fall within the second class of cases? On this there has been a difference of judicial opinion. This difference of view exists also in your Lordships' House on the instant appeal.

[20] Some judges have held that such a case is within the second class of cases. It falls within the literal language of the statute. The likelihood that the guard dog or the bitch with pups will bite is due to a characteristic of the particular animal which is not normally found in members of the species except in the particular circumstances of guarding territory or protecting pups. To that extent the animal's behaviour was a departure from the normal behaviour of animals of the same species.

[21] I shall call this interpretation of the second limb of s 2(2)(b) 'the *Cummings* interpretation'. This interpretation was adopted in *Cummings v Granger (sued as Grainger)* [1977] 1 All ER 104, [1977]

QB 397. On this interpretation, Mr Mirvahedy's claim succeeds. Horses do not normally behave as did the horses of Dr and Mrs Henley during the night of 28 August 1996. They do so only in particular circumstances, namely, when seriously frightened.

[22] Other judges have said that this type of case is outside the second class of cases identified in para (b). The second limb of s 2(2)(b) does not treat as abnormal behaviour which is characteristic of the species in the circumstances in which it occurred. The object of the second limb is to provide that characteristics not normally found in the species do not cease to be abnormal because, in certain circumstances or at certain times, all animals of the species behave in that way. A dog prone to attack all strangers has an abnormal characteristic. It is an abnormal characteristic even though in *some* circumstances all dogs are liable to attack strangers.

[23] I shall call this 'the *Breeden* interpretation'. This interpretation was favoured in the unreported decision of the Court of Appeal in *Breeden v Lampard* [1985] CA Transcript 1035. On this construction of the second limb of s 2(2)(b), Mr Mirvahedy's claim fails. The horse which escaped from the field and collided with his car was not behaving differently from the way any normal horse would have behaved in the circumstances.

THE AUTHORITIES

[24] I turn to the court decisions where this point has been considered. There are four relevant decisions, each of the Court of Appeal. Two [*Cummings v Granger* and *Curtis v Betts* [1990] 1 All ER 769, [1990] 1 WLR 459] adopted one interpretation, two [*Breeden v Lampard* and *Gloster v Chief Constable of Greater Manchester Police* [2000] PIQR P114] favoured the other.

[Having discussed these four cases, LORD NICHOLLS continued:]

[32] The starting point is to seek to identify the purpose of requirement (b). Stated in general terms the function of requirement (b) is not in doubt. The purpose of this paragraph is to limit the circumstances in which there will be strict liability for damage caused by an animal having the dangerous characteristics described in requirement (a). Possession of such characteristics by an animal (requirement (a)), together with the keeper's awareness that the animal has these characteristics (requirement (c)), is not enough. Meeting requirements (a) and (c) will not suffice. Something more is needed before strict liability arises.

[33] That this is the purpose of requirement (b) is self-evident. Requirement (b) is a precondition of liability additional to requirements (a) and (c). That this is the purpose of para (b) is also confirmed by the background to the legislation.

[His Lordship then discussed the Law Commission's report which had preceded the legislation in 1971 and the Parliamentary history of the legislation and continued:]

[41] . . . As drafted, requirement (b) is apt to exclude cases where an animal has a dangerous characteristic as described in requirement (a) but that characteristic is normally found at all times in animals of that species. This is the heart of the problem. The difficulty lies in identifying the type of dangerous characteristic which will satisfy this formula, and thus exclude the keeper from strict liability under s 2(2). Section 2(2)(b) was intended to have some content. The problem is to identify that content.

[42] Neither the *Cummings* interpretation nor the *Breeden* interpretation provides a compellingly clear solution to this problem. The principal difficulty with the *Cummings* interpretation is that it seems to leave s 2(2)(b) with very limited content. This point was well summarised by Judge O'Malley in the present case:

> 'It is very hard to contemplate or define the characteristics that are not normally found in animals "except at particular times or in particular circumstances". I am concerned at the generalness of words which are expressed as a limitation as to time and circumstance but which can be applied to any case and are therefore no limitation at all . . . If the [*Cummings*] construction . . . is correct the claimant must succeed in establishing this particular criterion in every case. Either the animal is proved to be an abnormal animal or to have abnormal characteristics or it has normal characteristics upon which the claimant can rely in the particular circumstances of the instant case. For as it seems

to me all times and all circumstances can be said to be "particular". One can always find particularity attaching to any time or to any circumstance.'

[43] In other words, if the tendency of a horse to bolt when sufficiently alarmed is to be regarded as a normal characteristic of horses 'in particular circumstances' and, hence, a horse with this characteristic will meet requirement (b), it is not easy to conceive of circumstances where dangerous behaviour which is characteristic of a species will not satisfy requirement (b). A normal but dangerous characteristic of a species will usually be identifiable by reference to particular times or particular circumstances. Thus the *Cummings* interpretation means that requirement (b) will be met in most cases where damage was caused by dangerous behaviour as described in requirement (a). Requirement (b) will be satisfied whenever the animal's conduct was *not* characteristic of the species in the particular circumstances. Requirement (b) will also be satisfied when the animal's behaviour *was* characteristic of the species in those circumstances.

[44] This is a cogent argument. Ultimately, despite this argument, on balance I prefer the *Cummings* interpretation of s 2(2)(b), for a combination of reasons. First, this interpretation accords more easily and naturally with the statutory language. Damage caused by an attack by a newly-calved cow or a dog on guard duty fits readily into the description of damage due to characteristics of a cow or a dog which are not normally found in cows or dogs except in particular circumstances. That is not so with the *Breeden* interpretation. The *Breeden* interpretation has the effect that these examples would fall outside both limbs of para (b). This result makes sense only on the supposition that, by the references to abnormal characteristics in s 2(2)(b) (characteristics 'not normally found'), Parliament intended that strict liability should never arise if the animal's conduct was normal for the species in the circumstances in which it occurred. But the language of the paragraph provides no substantial support for this supposition.

[45] Secondly, the *Breeden* interpretation would depart radically from the legislative scheme recommended by the Law Commission. There is no evidence that any such departure was intended. Indeed, far from such a departure being intended, the wording of cl 2(2)(b) of the reformulated Animals Bill, subsequently enacted as s 2(2)(b) of the 1971 Act, was plainly drawn from, and closely followed, the language of paras 18(ii) and 91(iv) of the Law Commission's report.

[46] Thirdly, the 'lack of content' argument levelled against the *Cummings* interpretation cannot be pressed too far. The *Cummings* interpretation does not empty requirement (b) of all content. Some forms of accidental damage are instances where this requirement could operate. Take a large and heavy domestic animal such as a mature cow. There is a real risk that if a cow happens to stumble and fall onto someone, any damage suffered will be severe. This would satisfy requirement (a). But a cow's dangerousness in this regard may not fall within requirement (b). This dangerousness is due to a characteristic normally found in all cows at all times. The dangerousness results from their very size and weight. It is not due to a characteristic not normally found in cows 'except at particular times or in particular circumstances'.

[47] For these reasons I agree with the interpretation of s 2(2)(b) adopted in *Cummings v Granger (sued as Grainger)* [1977] 1 All ER 104, [1977] QB 397 and *Curtis v Betts* [1990] 1 All ER 769, [1990] 1 WLR 459 and by the Court of Appeal in the instant case. The fact that an animal's behaviour, although not normal behaviour for animals of that species, was nevertheless normal behaviour for the species in the particular circumstances does not take the case outside s 2(2)(b).

[48] I also agree with the decision of the Court of Appeal on the facts in the present case. Horses are large and heavy animals. But it was not this innate physical characteristic of the defendants' horses which caused the road accident. The horses escaped because they were terrified. They were still not behaving ordinarily when they careered over the main road, crashing into vehicles rather than the other way about. Hale LJ concluded that it was precisely because they were behaving in this unusual way caused by their panic that the road accident took place: see [2002] QB 769 at [16]. That conclusion, on the evidence, seems to me irrefutable and to be fatal to the case of Dr and Mrs Henley. I would dismiss this appeal.

LORD HOBHOUSE OF WOODBOROUGH: . . .

[61] My Lords, in agreement with my noble and learned friends Lord Nicholls of Birkenhead and Lord Walker of Gestingthorpe, I would dismiss this appeal. . . .

[71] . . . It is true that there is an implicit assumption of fact in s 2(2) that domesticated animals are not normally dangerous. But the purpose of para (b) is to make provision for those that are. It deals with two specific categories where that assumption of fact is falsified. The first is that of an animal which is possessed of a characteristic, not normally found in animals of the same species, which makes it dangerous. The second is an animal which, although belonging to a species which does not normally have dangerous characteristics, nevertheless has dangerous characteristics at particular times or in particular circumstances. The essence of these provisions is the falsification of the assumption, in the first because of the departure of the individual from the norm for its species, in the second because of the introduction of special factors. Criticisms can be, and have been, made of the drafting of paras (a) and (b) of s 2(2); but they should not be made, and are not justified, in this respect of the drafting of para (b). It does not lack coherence.

[72] The statute, in this respect following the recommendation of the Law Commission, had to reflect a choice as to the division of risk between the keeper of an animal and members of the general public. Neither is blameworthy but it is the member of the public who suffers the injury or damage and it is the keeper who knows of the characteristics of the animal which make it dangerous and liable to cause such injury or damage. The element of knowledge makes the choice a coherent one but it, in any event, was a choice which it was for the legislature to make.

[73] For these reasons, which accord in most respects with those given by my noble and learned friend Lord Nicholls of Birkenhead and to be given by my noble and learned friend Lord Walker of Gestingthorpe, I would dismiss the appeal.

LORD WALKER OF GESTINGTHORPE: . . .

[155] In my view the crux of the matter is this. Both sides agree that Parliament intended to impose strict liability only for animals which are (in some sense) dangerous. Subsections (1) and (2) of s 2 mark the first subdivision which Parliament has made in identifying one (very limited) class of dangerous animals. This rather crude subdivision has contributed to the difficulties which have arisen, since it implies (but does not clearly spell out) that *entirely* normal behaviour of an animal of a non-dangerous species can never give rise to strict liability. . . . Domesticated animals are to be the subject of strict liability only if their behavioural characteristics are (in some sense) abnormal (and so dangerous). Did Parliament contemplate that the generality of animals in a domesticated species might in some circumstances show dangerous behavioural characteristics so as to be liable to be treated, in those circumstances, as dangerous? Or is there a presumption underlying the 1971 Act (and providing guidance as to the correct construction of s 2) that an animal of a domesticated species behaving in a way that is (in particular circumstances) normal and natural for its species cannot be treated as dangerous?

[156] In my view the scheme and language of the 1971 Act do not yield any such underlying presumption. I consider that the respondent's [i.e. claimant's] proposed construction of the second limb of s 2(2)(b) is more natural as a matter of language, and that it is not inconsistent with Parliament's general intention to impose strict liability only for animals known to present special dangers. . . . Moreover the respondent's proposed construction is in my view closer to what [leading counsel for the Henleys] (echoing the Law Commission) referred to as the common experience of everyday life.

[157] It is common knowledge (and was known to the appellants in this case) that horses, if exposed to a very frightening stimulus, will panic and stampede, knocking down obstacles in their path (in this case an electric fence, a post and barbed wire fence behind that, and then high undergrowth) and may continue their flight for a considerable distance. Horses loose in that state, either by day or by night, are an obvious danger on a road carrying fast-moving traffic. The appellants knew these facts; they could decide whether to run the unavoidable risks involved in keeping horses; they could decide whether or not to insure against those risks. Although I feel sympathy for the appellants, who were held not to have been negligent in the fencing of the field, I see nothing unjust or unreasonable in the appellants

having to bear the loss resulting from their horses' escape rather than the respondent (who suffered very serious and painful injuries in the accident, although he was wearing a seatbelt and slowed down as soon as he saw the first horse in his headlights). . . .

[LORD SLYNN OF HADLEY and LORD SCOTT OF FOSCOTE delivered speeches in favour of allowing the appeal.]

Appeal dismissed.

NOTES

1. *Mirvahedy v Henley* is noted by K. Amirthalingam (2003) 119 LQR 563 and by D. Howarth [2003] CLJ 548.

2. For an example of an animal falling within s. 2(1) of the Act, see *Tutin v M Chipperfield Promotions Ltd* (1980) 130 NLJ 807 (camel); cf. the pre-1971 Act law, as shown by *McQuaker v Goddard* [1940] 1 KB 687, [1940] 1 All ER 471.

3. As Sedley LJ stated in *Clark v Bowlt*, [2007] PIQR P12, [2007] EWCA Civ 978 at [22], the 1971 Act was passed to replace 'over-complex common law rules' with 'the apparently clear and simple formula in section 2(2)', but he also stated that '[l]ike many such lamps its flame has since flickered in the winds of reality'. In addition to the debate concerning s. 2(2)(b) (with which *Mirvahedy v Henley* was primarily concerned), the interpretation of s. 2(2)(a) has also troubled the courts:

   i) In *Curtis v Betts* [1990] 1 All ER 769, [1990] 1 WLR 459 the Court of Appeal insisted that the three elements of s. 2(2) had to be taken separately, so that there is no need to show, for the purposes of s. 2(2)(a), that the animal had unusual characteristics which rendered it likely to cause severe damage. It was enough for the animal to be of a type that was likely to cause severe damage. Abnormal characteristics are relevant only to s. 2(2)(b) and (c). On the other hand, a link between s. 2(2)(a) and s.2(2)(b) is shown in *Clark v Bowlt,* which underlines that it is the particular limb of s. 2(2)(a) into which it has been decided that the case falls (ie 'likely to cause' or 'likely to be severe') which must be due to the relevant characteristics in s. 2(2)(b).

   ii) 'Likely' in s. 2(2)(a) has been said (in *Smith v Ainger* (1990) Times, 5 June) to include events that merely *might* happen, not just those which are more likely than not. However, in *Mirvahedy* Lord Scott (at [97]) disagreed with this view. His Lordship rejected the idea that a mere possibility was sufficient, preferring the phrase 'reasonably to be expected' as an explanation of the word 'likely' in this context. (Lord Scott was dissenting, but the other speeches did not touch on this point—it was conceded that s. 2(2)(a) had been satisfied.)

   iii) 'Kind of damage' in s. 2(2)(a) is reminiscent of the term of art used in judging *Wagon Mound* remoteness (see p. 408, ante). In *Smith v Ainger* Neill LJ decided that there was no difference between being bitten and being knocked down by a dog, both being 'personal injury . . . caused by the direct application of force'. Nevertheless, in *Mirvahedy* Lord Scott (at [101]) thought that the meaning of this phrase was not 'entirely clear'.

4. Section 2(2)(b) has given rise to particular difficulties in the case law, the extract from *Mirvahedy* being but one example.

   i) As can be seen in the reference to *Clark v Bowlt* in note 3(i), ante, s. 2(2)(b) requires some kind of causation to be shown involving the 'characteristics' and the damage, but the exact nature of this connection is obscure. In *Curtis v Betts* Stuart-Smith LJ and Nourse LJ state that, despite the wording of the sub-section, the requirement is for causation between the characteristics and the damage (and see *McKenny v Foster T/A Foster Partnership* [2008] EWCA Civ 173 at [33]). The sub-section itself seems to require a causal link between the characteristics and the *likelihood* of damage or the *likelihood* of its being severe. Stuart-Smith LJ said that if taken over-literally this would mean a foreseeability test rather than a causation test, but this is not necessarily so, since likelihood can be judged either *ex ante* (the way it would have seemed before the event) or *ex post* (the way it seems now). Compare the approach of Slade LJ who thought the difficulty could be avoided by reading the words 'due to' not as 'caused by' but as 'attributable to'. Do you think the Lord Justices are referring to factual causation or to (at least in part) legal causation as well? In *Jaundrill v Gillett* (1996) Times, 30 January the claimant ran into one of the defendant's horses, which had been let out onto the road at night by a malicious third party. The abnormal characteristic—although the Court of Appeal doubted whether it did in fact so qualify, and see *Clark v Bowlt* post—was that the horses galloped about aimlessly, something they do not normally do, when let out into the road. The Court of Appeal accepted the defendant's argument that the 'real and effective' cause of the accident was that the horses had been let out at all. The 'abnormal characteristic' of galloping about aimlessly was said to have made no difference because the horses could just as easily have galloped in a safer direction as in a more dangerous one. Is this a reference to factual or legal causation? However, although the decision in *Jaundrill* was cited by the trial judge in *Mirvahedy* in rejecting the claim on causation grounds, this was reversed by the Court of Appeal [2002] QB 769, [2001] EWCA Civ 1749, a view which was approved when the case reached the House of Lords. The causation point in *Jaundrill*, would, it seems, be decided differently today.

ii) Section 2(2)(b) requires a comparison to be drawn between the animal in question and other animals of the same species (defined to include sub-species and variety). In *Hunt v Wallis* [1994] PIQR P128, Pill J decided that with regard to dogs of an identifiable breed, the comparison should be with other dogs of the same breed, not with dogs generally, but, puzzlingly, only as long as 'it is a breed whose qualities are recognised as beneficial to man', a condition apparently without justification in the words of the Act. In *Gloster v Chief Constable of Greater Manchester Police* [2000] PIQR P114 the Court of Appeal, in reviewing the cases, did not mention Pill J's additional qualification of the statute.

iii) A particular difficulty comes in interpreting the two forms of 'characteristic'—the so-called 'permanent' limb, that of characteristics not normally found in animals of the same kind, and the so-called 'temporary' limb, that of characteristics not normally found 'except at particular times or in particular circumstances'. (This 'permanent/temporary' terminology can be found in Stuart-Smith's judgment in *Curtis v Betts*.) In his dissenting speech in *Mirvahedy* Lord Scott (at [111]) doubted that this distinction was helpful, but in the same case (at [138]) Lord Walker, who was one of the majority, found it useful, albeit to be treated with 'some caution'.

The 'permanent' limb gives slightly less trouble (see, for example, *Kite v Napp* (1982) Times, 1 June for a fairly straightforward example—a dog which attacked people who carried bags), but it is often unclear exactly what should count as a 'characteristic'. See also, for example, *Clark v Bowlt* (albeit in the context of the second limb of s. 2(2)(b)) where the Court of Appeal doubted that the 'propensity [of a horse] occasionally to move otherwise than as directed' could be a characteristic under the Act. In particular, it is usually the case that among any group of animals the likelihood of the animals' behaving in a particular way is distributed around an average. What degree of deviation from the mean counts as abnormal? In *Fox v Kohn* (2 November 1995, unreported), for example, it was recognised that all horses are difficult to stop, and the fact that some are more difficult to stop than others did not in itself create a category of abnormality. In *McKenny v Foster (t/a Foster Partnership)* [2008] EWCA Civ 173, in which a cow had escaped onto a highway, where, when stationary, a car ran into it, the relevant characteristic was agitation when separated from its recently weaned calf. The claim failed as this was neither dangerous nor causative in the case; being exceptionally agitated in this situation (as the cow must have been to have reached the highway) was not normal and, indeed, was not in itself a characteristic.

In *Gloster v Chief Constable of Greater Manchester Police* the point arose as to whether a dog which had been trained to bite in certain circumstances came within the 'permanent' limb of s. 2(2)(b). Pill LJ thought that the crucial question was whether the dog was unusual in its capacity for being trained, rather than whether the dog had been trained to do something unusual, and so held that the case fell outside the subsection. Hale LJ, however, preferred to decide the case on the ground that s. 2(2)(a) had not been satisfied.

iv) The word 'normally' in s. 2(2)(b) has recently been interpreted in *Welsh v Stokes* [2008] 1 All ER 921, [2007] EWCA Civ 796 as meaning 'conforming to type', rather than 'usually'.

v) Satisfaction of s. 2(2)(c) was conceded in *Mirvahedy*, but that decision on s. 2(2)(b) was cited by the Court of Appeal in *Welsh v Stokes* (at [71]) to support its view that it was sufficient in relation to the characteristic under the temporary limb of s.2(2)(b) for the keeper to know that the species in general had the characteristic in question.

vi) Having seen the difficulty to which the interpretation of s. 2(2)(b) has given rise, consider the view of Howarth who concludes (op cit., 551):

> One cannot see, however, how any interpretation of 2(2)(*b*) can be entirely satisfactory. As Lord Walker said [in *Mirvahedy*], section 2(2) deals with too many different types of accident —traffic accidents, dog bites, the spread of diseases and so on. It may well be that strict liability is better for cases of horse-owners versus car drivers, since, one might surmise, the number of such accidents is likely to be more sensitive to the number of horses near roads than to the number of car trips drivers make in the countryside. But that result might not hold for dog-owners and door-to-door sellers. The Act over-generalises, a problem that the courts will always find it difficult to overcome.

5. *Cummings v Granger* [1977] QB 397, [1977] 1 All ER 104, which was cited in *Mirvahedy* on the question of the interpretation of s. 2(2)(b), also dealt with some of the defences in the 1971 Act. The claimant was bitten one night by the defendant's Alsatian, which was used as a guard-dog in a scrapyard occupied by the defendant. The dog was allowed to run loose at night in the yard. In large letters on the gates of the yard there appeared the warning 'Beware of the Dog'. Next to these gates was a wicket gate which the claimant's companion used a key to open. It was found that the claimant was a trespasser in the yard. This, therefore, raised the issue of the defence in s. 5(3) which was thought to be available: at that time it was not unreasonable to use a guard dog to protect the scrapyard, although Lord Denning pointed out that the case might be affected by the passing of the Guard Dogs Act 1975, which had not existed at the relevant time. Could the Occupiers Liability Act 1984 (p. 587, ante) help a claimant barred from suing under s. 2 of the 1971 Act by s. 5(3)? The other defence which succeeded in *Cummings v Granger*

was that set out in s. 5(2) of the 1971 Act. This consent defence is well established at common law (see pp. 446–461, ante), but Ormrod LJ expressed the following opinion ([1977] 1 All ER 104 at 111):

> I would like to read [the words of s.5(2)] in their ordinary English meaning and not to complicate the question too much with the old, long history of the doctrine of volenti. That doctrine was developed in quite different conditions. It has nothing to do with strict liability; and I would not, for my part, like to see that defence whittled down by too fine distinctions as to what 'voluntarily accepted the risk' means.

Bridge LJ agreed with Ormrod LJ's judgment but he also agreed with Lord Denning's judgment, and the latter did refer to the position at common law in a similar situation to the one under consideration. Do you agree with Ormrod LJ's view, or do you think Parliament intended the history of the doctrine to be more relevant than Ormrod LJ was prepared to accept?

For an example where the s. 5(2) defence failed on the facts, see *Flack v Hudson* [2002] QB 698 (which, incidentally, also decided that one keeper could sue another keeper under s. 2). On s. 5(2) see further *Dhesi v Chief Constable of West Midlands Police* (2000) Times, 9 May, a case that also deals with the defence in s. 5(1).

6. Under the Dangerous Wild Animals Act 1976 a person keeping a dangerous wild animal (as specified in the Act, as amended) must in general have a licence from a local authority. One of the conditions which s. 1 of that Act lays down must be attached to the licence is that the licensee should be insured against liability for any damage caused by the animal in question. Note further the Riding Establishments Acts 1964 and 1970, and on the position of zoos see the Zoo Licensing Act 1981, which may require their operation to be licensed by a local authority. A condition relating to insurance against liability for damage caused by the animals is something the local authority *may* impose in granting a licence (s. 5); cf. the Dangerous Wild Animals Act 1976.

7. The report of the Scottish Law Commission (*Obligations: Report on Civil Liability in Relation to Animals*, Scot Law Com. No. 97) led to the Animals (Scotland) Act in 1987. Note the consideration, in Part V of the report, of the question of compulsory insurance and no fault liability in the context of liability for animals.

8. As was mentioned in the introduction to this chapter, liability for animals is not only governed by the Animals Act 1971. There can be liability in torts such as negligence, nuisance or the rule in *Rylands v Fletcher* (1868) LR 3 HL 330, on which see North, *Animals*, chap. 6.

9. The Pearson Commission (in vol. 1 chap. 30 of its 1970 Report) discussed the question of liability for injuries caused by animals and did not see any need to change English law in this area (para. 1626). There were calls for reform after the decision in *Mirvahedy* and more than one attempt was made to amend the Animals Act. For the most recent, see the Animals (Amendment) Bill 2008, but at the time of writing the future of legislative reform is uncertain. During the debate in the House of Commons on this Bill (473 H.C. Debs (6th Series) cots 514–588, concern was expressed about a rise in insurance premiums since the decision in *Mirvahedy*.

CHAPTER TWELVE

NON-INTENTIONAL STATUTORY TORTS

We have already considered two ways in which statutes may affect tortious duties: (a) statutory reform of pre-existing common law (e.g. the Occupiers' Liability Acts of 1957 and 1984, p. 564 and p. 587, ante, the Defective Premises Act 1972, p. 603, ante and the Animals Act 1971, p. 652, ante); and (b) negligence by bodies established by statute the cause of statutory powers or the carrying out of statutory duties (see p. 88, ante).

The cases and materials collected in this chapter concern a third question, namely when do statutes themselves create liabilities for non-intentional harm separate from and possibly in addition to duties in common law negligence? Put another way, the question is about when statutory provisions themselves create private rights of action for aggrieved individuals.

The starting point for analysis is the statute itself. Some statutes expressly create new private rights of action. Some of these are collected in the first section of the chapter. Other statutes expressly deny that they create private rights of action. The second section collects together some examples of this kind of statute. The main legal problems arise, however, where the statute omits to say whether it creates or denies a private right of action. The tangled judicial treatment of this situation is contained in the third and fourth sections of the chapter: the third concentrates on the creation or denial of duties, the fourth on questions of causation and remoteness.

Note that a fourth aspect of the role of statutes in tort, that of the intentional common law torts of inducing a breach of statutory duty and interference in trade or business by the unlawful means of breaching a statute are dealt with in Chap. 15, ante.

Many statutory duties concern the duties of employers towards their employees. This is a specialist field much influenced by European legislation. The chapter ends with a note on the basic principles of this area of the law, but for details the reader is referred to general works on employment law, e.g. S. Deakin and G. Morris, *Labour Law* 4th edn (Oxford, 2005) and specialist works on health and safety at work, e.g. M. Ford and J. Clarke, *Redgrave's Health and Safety* 5th edn (London, 2007). For a comprehensive analysis of statutory torts in general, see K. Stanton, P. Skidmore, M. Harris, and J. Wright, *Statutory Torts* (London, 2003). In its comultation paper, Administrative Redress (Law Com. 187), the Law Commission has proposed far-reaching reforms in this tangled area of law, see the Appendix.

1 EXPRESS CREATION OF NEW TORTS

■ The Nuclear Installations Act 1965

7. Duty of licensee of licensed site. (1) … [w]here a nuclear site licence has been granted in respect of any site, it shall be the duty of the licensee to secure that

(a) no such occurrence involving nuclear matter as is mentioned in subsection (2) of this section causes injury to any person or damage to any property of any person other than the licensee, being injury or damage arising out of or resulting from the radioactive properties, or a combination of those and any toxic, explosive or other hazardous properties, of that nuclear matter; and

(b) no ionising radiations emitted during the period of the licensee's responsibility

(i) from anything caused or suffered by the licensee to be on the site which is not nuclear matter; or

(ii) from any waste discharged (in whatever form) on or from the site,

cause injury to any person or damage to any property of any person other than the licensee.

(2) The occurrences referred to in subsection (1)(a) of this section are

(a) any occurrence on the licensed site during the period of the licensee's responsibility, being an occurrence involving nuclear matter;

(b) any occurrence elsewhere than on the licensed site involving nuclear matter which is not excepted matter and which at the time of the occurrence—

(i) is in the course of carriage on behalf of the licensee as licensee of that site; or

(ii) is in the course of carriage to that site with the agreement of the licensee from a place outside the relevant territories; and

(iii) in either case, is not on any other relevant site in the United Kingdom;

(c) any occurrence elsewhere than on the licensed site involving nuclear matter which is not excepted matter and which

(i) having been on the licensed site at any time during the period of the licensee's responsibility; or

(ii) having been in the course of carriage on behalf of the licensee as licensee of that site,

has not subsequently been on any relevant site, or in the course of any relevant carriage, or (except in the course of relevant carriage) within the territorial limits of a country which is not a relevant territory.…

13. Exclusion, extension or reduction of compensation in certain cases.
(4) The duty imposed by section 7, 8, 9, 10 or 11 of this Act—

(a) shall not impose any liability on the person subject to that duty with respect to injury or damage caused by an occurrence which constitutes a breach of that duty if the occurrence, or the causing thereby of the injury or damage, is attributable to hostile action in the course of any armed conflict, including any armed conflict within the United Kingdom; but

(b) shall impose such a liability where the occurrence, or the causing thereby of the injury or damage, is attributable to a natural disaster, notwithstanding that the disaster is of such an exceptional character that it could not reasonably have been foreseen.

NOTES

1. Consider the defences in s. 13(4) of the Act. How do these compare with the defences available in an action for negligence, nuisance or under the *Rylands v Fletcher* rule? (See chap. 14.)

2. Section 13(6) provides that damages may be reduced by reason of the fault of the claimant only if he has intentionally caused harm or had reckless disregard for the consequences of his act.

3. 'Injury' is defined as personal injury including loss of life (s. 26(1)). In *Merlin v British Nuclear Fuels plc* [1990] 2 QB 557, [1990] 3 All ER 711, the claimants' house was contaminated by radioactive dust from the Sellafield nuclear power station. They decided to move so as not to expose their children to the health risk they believed would result from longterm occupation of the house. They claimed compensation for the diminution in the value of their house, which they alleged was due to contamination in contravention of s. 7(1) of the Act. Gatehouse J held that the increased risk to the occupants of developing cancer did not amount to 'injury' and that 'damage to property' did not include economic loss or damage to property rights. (For commentary, see R. Macrory (1991) 3 Journal of Environmental Law 122.)

    However, the Court of Appeal distinguished *Merlin* in *Blue Circle Industries plc v Ministry of Defence* 1999] Ch 289, [1998] 3 All ER 385. Radioactive water stored on the defendant's land overflowed into the claimant's marshland, contaminating the topsoil and causing negotiations for the sale of the claimant's large estate containing the marshland to fall through. The Court of Appeal held that the damage was 'damage to property' under the Act since plutonium had 'intermingled' with the soil. They also decided that damages could be awarded for the lost chance of the sale of the land, following *Allied Maples Group Ltd v Simmons and Simmons (a firm)* [1995] 4 All ER 907, [1995] 1 WLR 1602, noted p. 374, ante. Aldous LJ said:

    > In *Merlin*'s case the dust was in the house and the judge did not hold that the house and the radioactive material were so intermingled as to mean that the characteristics of the house had in any way altered. It was therefore possible on those facts for the judge to hold that the cause of the reduction in the value of the plaintiffs' house resulted from stigma, not from damage to the house itself. There is no need to decide whether Merlin's case was rightly decided as this case is distinguishable on the facts.
    >
    > The present case is more analogous to *Losinjska Plovidba v Transco Overseas Ltd, The Orjula* [1995] 2 Lloyd's Rep 395, where a vessel was held to be damaged because it had to be decontaminated and *Hunter v Canary Wharf Ltd* [1997] 2 All ER 426 where the Court of Appeal held that dust could in certain circumstances cause damage to property, eg where it was trampled into a carpet in such a way as to lessen the value of the fabric. The damage in the present case was not mere economic damage . . .

    This distinction is not particularly satisfactory. There are two ways of putting it. One is that the claimant in *Blue Circle* owned the topsoil but the claimants in *Merlin* did not own the air inside the house. The second is that the loss in value in *Blue Circle* was restricted by the court to the consequences of past contamination, that is the cost of decontaminating the land and the fear that such decontamination was not complete, whereas in *Merlin* it came entirely from potential buyers' fears that contamination would happen again in the future. The former is closer to what Gatehouse J said in *Merlin*, but it sounds odd to talk about owning a house with no air inside it. The latter fits better with Aldous LJ's judgment in *Blue Circle*, and is more consonant with *Murphy v Brentwood District Council* [1991] 1 AC 398, [1990] 2 All ER 908 (p. 183, ante), but it distorts what happened in *Merlin*. The dust was physically present in the house in *Merlin* and its presence was the main reason the house could not be sold. All one might say is that in *Merlin* the claimants did not try very hard to remove the radioactive dust because they knew that it would quickly be replaced by the wind and brought back in on people's shoes and clothes. But it seems capricious to distinguish between contamination that is difficult to deal with because it is 'intermingled' with something else and contamination that is difficult to deal with because it quickly builds up again. (For further discussion, see M. Lee (2000) 12 Journal of Environmental Law 317).

See also the Scottish case of *Magnohard Ltd v UKAEA* [2003] SLT 1083, [2004] Env LR 19, where petitioners brought judicial review proceedings against UKAEA, seeking a declaration that UKAEA was not complying with s. 7 of the 1965 Act on the basis that particles of nuclear matter originating from the power station had been found on an adjacent private beach. In her judgment, Lady Paton took the view that the word 'occurrence' in s. 7 was broad enough to cover both the arrival of the particles on the beach and the subsequent deposit of particles remaining on the beach until subsequent clean-up operations took place. Section 7 was also interpreted as requiring the petitioners to show either personal injury or damage to property: one or the other was held to be sufficient to result in liability, but, as in *Merlin*, Lady Paton considered that no recovery was available for risk of future injury or current stress and emotional distress falling short of psychiatric loss. However, the beach was held to have suffered property damage in the form of a 'physical change', caused by the radioactive properties of the material, which had rendered the property less useful, less frequently used, and less valuable. While quick particle removal was possible and was being implemented in this case, *Merlin* was nevertheless again distinguished, on the arguably tenuous grounds that in *Merlin* no special measures had been required to remove the dust and therefore no damage had taken place. Lady Paton granted a declaration to the effect that UKAEA had failed, and was continuing to fail in its duty under s. 7 of the 1965 Act. However, the petitioners failed to receive an order for specific performance requiring UKAEA to implement additional monitoring and clean-up measures, as s. 7 was interpreted as not requiring the imposition of any specific statutory duty to monitor or to clean up any damage to or contamination of property caused by an occurrence involving nuclear matter.

4. An exposure to nuclear matter or ionising radiations may affect the unborn. Section 3 of the Congenital Disabilities (Civil Liability) Act 1976 clarifies the above Act by stating that anything which affects the ability of parents to have a normal healthy child is an 'injury' for the purposes of the Nuclear Installations Act 1965. Disabilities sustained by the child of those parents as a result of the exposure give rise to a claim for compensation under the 1965 Act any time within thirty years of the exposure. For the difficulties of showing causation in this context, see *Reay v British Nuclear Fuels plc* [1994] 5 Med L Rev 1.

5. The new tort was created as part of a carefully worked out scheme between the Government and the insurance companies. Under s. 16 of the Act, as amended by the Energy Act 1983 and SI 1994/909, the operator's liability is limited to an aggregate of £140 million per incident (or £10 million for some prescribed small operators). Under s. 19 of the Act, as amended by the Energy Act 1983 and the Atomic Energy Act 1989, licensed operators must make arrangements to have available sufficient funds to satisfy claims regulated by s. 16. For amounts over these limits, under s. 18 of the Act, as amended by both the 1983 and 1989 Acts, Parliament guarantees about another 300 million IMF special drawing rights worth of compensation (about £250 million at April 2008 exchange rates). For commentary on the general legal implications of the policy shift back towards greater use of nuclear power announced in the Energy Review

conducted in 2006 by the Department of Trade and Industry, *The Energy Challenge* (London: 2006) see P. Cameron (2007) 19 Journal of Environmental Law 71.

6. Another example of the express creation of an action is s. 11 of the Mineral Workings (Offshore Installations) Act 1971, which provides that breach of any provision of the Act, or of regulations made thereunder, shall be actionable so far as it causes personal injury. This Act, like most other safety legislation in England, was passed in response to a particular tragedy, in this case the loss of thirteen lives when the drilling rig *Sea Gem* collapsed, capsized, and sank. A committee of inquiry (Cmnd. 3409) found that there had been several important breaches of the Institute of Petroleum's voluntary Code of Safe Practice (although these failures were not the direct cause of the loss of life). Compliance with this Code had been a condition of the grant of a drilling licence to the owners of the rig. The committee said nothing about the creation of civil liability for breach of statutory duty. It should be noted that (a) civil liability under the Act is co-existent with common law duties; and (b) certain defences available in criminal proceedings (i.e. under s. 9(3) of the 1971 Act) are not available in civil proceedings. See also the Offshore Installations and Pipeline Works (Management and Administration) Regulations 1995, SI 1995/738 and subsequent amending regulations.

7. Examples of other Acts which expressly create a civil remedy are the Misrepresentation Act 1967, s. 2(1), the Consumer Protection Act 1987, s. 41, the Control of Pollution Act 1974, s. 88; the Data Protection Act 1998, s. 13 (replacing the Data Protection Act 1984, s. 22 and 23); the Telecommunications Act 1984, s. 18; the Electricity Act 1989, s. 39(3); the Protection from Harassment Act 1997 s. 3; the Petroleum Act 1998, s. 23; and the Financial Services and Markets Act 2000, s. 150. See also ss. 62–66 of the Sex Discrimination Act 1975, and equivalent provisions in other anti-discrimination legislation. See also s. 47(1)(a) of the Health and Safety at Work Act 1974, but note that the general duty in s. 2(1) of the Act does not give rise to a private action for damages (see p. 714, ante). Note that the Human Rights Act 1998 itself could be regarded as creating a civil remedy for breach of statutory duty. However, the 1998 Act has been described as 'not a tort statute': see *R (Greenfield) v Secretary of State for the Home Department* [2005] 2 All ER 240, [2005] UKHL 14 at [19].

2 EXPRESS EXCLUSION OF CIVIL REMEDY

■ The Medicines Act 1968

133. General provisions as to operation of Act.—(2) Except in so far as this Act otherwise expressly provides, and subject to the provisions of section [18 of the Interpretation Act 1978] (which relates to offences under two or more laws), the provisions of this Act shall not be construed as

(a) conferring a right of action in any civil proceedings (other than proceedings for the recovery of a fine) in respect of any contravention of this Act or of any regulations or order made under this Act, or

(b) affecting any restrictions imposed by or under any other enactment, whether contained in a public general Act or in a local or private Act, or

(c) derogating from any right of action or other remedy (whether civil or criminal) in proceedings instituted otherwise than under this Act.

NOTE

The Medicines Act creates various offences in relation to the adulteration of medicinal products and requires compliance with certain standards. But Parliament apparently thought that enforcement could best be left to the criminal law. Do you agree?

Examples of other statutes which expressly exclude a civil remedy for breach of statutory duty are s. 13 of the Safety of Sports Grounds Act 1975, s. 12 of the Fire Safety and Safety of Places of Sport Act 1987, and s. 5 of the Guard Dogs Act 1975.

3 CREATION OF NEW TORTS BY JUDICIAL INTERPRETATION OF STATUTES

■ London Passenger Transport Board v Upson
House of Lords [1949] 1 All ER 60

LORD WRIGHT:....
I think that the authorities such as *Caswell's case*,[1] *Lewis v Denye*[2] and *Sparks v Edward Ash Ltd*[3] show clearly that a claim for damages for breach of a statutory duty intended to protect a person in the position of the particular plaintiff is a special common law right which is not to be confused in essence with a claim for negligence. The statutory right has its origin in the statute, but the particular remedy of an action for damages is given by the common law in order to make effective for the benefit of the injured plaintiff his right to the performance by the defendant of the defendant's statutory duty. It is an effective sanction. It is not a claim in negligence in the strict or ordinary sense. As I said ([1939] 3 All ER 739) in *Caswell's case*:

> 'I do not think that an action for breach of a statutory duty such as that in question is completely or accurately described as an action in negligence. It is a common law action based on the purpose of the statute to protect the workman, and belongs to the category often described as that of strict or absolute liability. At the same time it resembles actions in negligence in that the claim is based on a breach of a duty to take care for the safety of the workman.'

But, whatever the resemblances, it is essential to keep in mind the fundamental differences of the two classes of claim. Here I shall, perhaps, be guilty of hypercriticism if I were to quarrel with the expression of Asquith LJ in the Court of Appeal ([1947] 2 All ER 516) that the common law duty is enhanced by the duty contained in the regulations. One duty does not, in truth, enhance the other, though the same damage may be caused by action which might equally be characterised as ordinary negligence at common law or as breach of the statutory duty. On the other hand, the damage may be due either to negligence or to breach of the statutory duty. In the present case Asquith LJ decided, as I understand, in favour of the respondent, not on the ground of negligence, which he did not find, but specifically on the ground of breach of statutory duty. There is, I think, a logical distinction which accords with what I regard as the correct view that the causes of action are different. It follows that the correct pleading would be to allege each cause of action separately so as to avoid the confusion which seems to me to have crept in at certain points of these proceedings. I have desired before I deal specifically with the regulations to make it clear how, in my judgment, they should be approached, and also to make it clear that a claim for their breach may stand or fall independently of a claim for negligence. There is always

---

[1] [1940] AC 152, [1939] 3 All ER 722.   [2] [1940] AC 921, [1940] 3 All ER 299.
[3] [1943] 1 KB 223, [1943] 1 All ER 1.

a danger, if the claim is not sufficiently specific, that the due consideration of the claim for breach of statutory duty may be prejudiced if it is confused with the claim in negligence . . . .

NOTES

1. In *Morris v National Coal Board* [1963] 3 All ER 644, [1963] 1 WLR 1382 it was held that a claimant who presents his case exclusively as one of breach of statutory duty cannot on appeal seek to support the decision on grounds that there was common law negligence, even though there is a considerable amount of evidence of breach of a common law duty. Is the result satisfactory in view of the abolition of the forms of action and the fact that the claimant does not have to plead matters of law (see e.g. *G L Baker Ltd v Medway Building and Supplies Ltd* [1958] 3 All ER 540, [1958] 1 WLR 1216)?

2. The independence of the action for breach of statutory duty from common law negligence is illustrated by *Bux v Slough Metals Ltd* [1974] 1 All ER 262, [1973] 1 WLR 1358, in which the claimant failed to establish a breach of statutory duty by his employer, who had provided safety goggles which the claimant had not worn. The claimant succeeded, however, in an action for damages for negligence because the evidence showed that the claimant would have worn the goggles had he been instructed to do so in a reasonable and firm manner followed up by supervision. This was a breach of the employer's duty to provide a safe system of work (see p. 714, post). The claimant's damages were reduced by 40 per cent on grounds of his contributory negligence.

3. In most jurisdictions, breaches of statutes are not treated separately from general liability in tort. In most common law jurisdictions, for example, breaches of a statute are dealt with from within the tort of negligence. For discussion, see below p. 674.

4. The relationship between common law liability in negligence and liability for breach of statutory duties in the context of the wide range of statutory duties imposed upon public authorities was analysed by the House of Lords in *Gorringe v Calderdale Metropolitan Borough Council* [2004] 2 All ER 326, [2004] UKHL 15 (p. 111, ante). Lord Steyn at [3] noted that:

   '. . . there is a principled distinction which is not always in the forefront of discussions. It is this: in a case founded on breach of statutory duty the central question is whether from the provisions and structure of the statute an intention can be gathered to create a private law remedy? In contradistinction in a case framed in negligence, against the background of a statutory duty or power, a basic question is whether the statute excludes a private law remedy? An assimilation of the two inquiries will sometimes produce wrong results.'

   All of their Lordships agreed that the existence of a statutory duty upon public authorities to undertake a particular task would not by itself be sufficient to generate a common law duty of care (see p. 114, post). Lord Hoffmann also stated at [23] that '[i]f the statute does not create a private right of action, it would be, to say the least, unusual if the mere existence of the statutory duty could generate a common law duty of care'. Lord Scott took a similar, but perhaps even tougher, approach at [71]. (Whether Lord Hoffmann's speech gave sufficient weight to the distinction Lord Steyn drew is a question that was raised at p. 114, ante.) However, these statements were made in the context of an attempt by counsel for the claimant to establish the existence of a common law duty of care solely on the basis of the existence of non-actionable statutory duties, in this case to ensure provision of warning signs and other steps to improve road safety. Lord Hoffmann's suggestion that the absence of a remedy for breach of statutory duty would therefore establish a presumption against the imposition of a common law duty of care should therefore be confined to this particular context, where reliance was completely placed on the statutory duties themselves in the absence of any meaningful 'special relationship' between the local authority and the injured driver. Dyson LJ in *Carty v Croydon London Borough Council* [2005] 2 All ER 517, [2005] EWCA Civ 19 adopted this interpretation of the judgments in *Gorringe* at [40]–[41] of his judgment, taking the view that 'the question whether there can be a common law duty of care where there is no private law right to claim damages for breach of statutory duty does not admit of a blanket answer', while recognising that Parliamentary intent may be relevant. (See further p. 108, ante.)

■ 'The Effect of Penal Legislation in the Law of Tort'
Glanville Williams (1960) 23 MLR 233

I'm the Parliamentary Draftsman,
I compose the country's laws,
And of half the litigation
I'm undoubtedly the cause.
J. p. C., Poetic Justice (1947).

It is a favourite charge; and yet (if we may breathe it) others than the draftsman are sometimes account-able for the trouble in interpreting statutes. Good rules of interpretation, consistently applied, could do much to reduce the area of doubt. It is the absence of such rules, or the failure to apply existing rules with sufficient regularity to preserve their character as rules, that has brought about the situation in which it is almost impossible to predict when statutory standards of behaviour will be imported into the law of tort.

The present position of penal legislation in the civil law—and it is only of penal legislation that we are speaking, since a study of other legislation would extend the discussion too much—the position of penal legislation may be oversimplified into two generalisations. When it concerns industrial welfare, such legislation results in absolute liability in tort. In all other cases it is ignored. There are exceptions both ways, but, broadly speaking, that is how the law appears from the current decisions. One may make bold to say that both propositions are the result of a wrong approach to the problem of assimi-lating statutory rules into the civil law.

■ Law Commission, 'The Interpretation of Statutes' (Law Com. No. 21, 1969)

Appendix A
DRAFT CLAUSES
Presumption as to enforcement of statutory duty
4. Where any Act passed after this Act imposes or authorises the imposition of a duty, whether posi-tive or negative and whether with or without a special remedy for its enforcement, it shall be presumed, unless express provision to the contrary is made, that a breach of the duty is intended to be actionable (subject to the defences and other incidents applying to actions for breach of statutory duty) at the suit of any person who sustains damage in consequence of the breach.

QUESTIONS

1. R. Pound (1908) 21 Harv LR 383 at 406–407 preferred legislation above judicial decision as 'the more truly democratic form of law-making'. He thought it followed from this

that judicial analogies from the social policies expressed in statutes should be encouraged. Will this draft clause, if enacted, help or hinder this kind of judicial legislation?

2.   If Parliament has said that a certain activity should be unlawful, whom does it benefit to say that those who engage in that activity cannot be sued? Is it only the defendant? Or is it also the state? (See *Howarth*, pp. 336–338.) For example, does a criminal law statute create duties in citizens to comply with its requirements, or does it simply create a power in the police or prosecution authorities to enforce it if they wish?

3.   In *Cutler v. Wandsworth Stadium* [1949] AC 398, [1949] 1 All ER 544, Lord du Parq commented that:

> To a person unversed in the science or art of legislation it may well seem strange that Parliament has not by now made it a rule to state explicitly what its intention is in a matter which is often of no little importance, instead of leaving it to the courts to discover, by a careful examination and analysis of what is expressly said, what that intention may be supposed probably to be. There are no doubt reasons which inhibit the legislature from revealing its intention in plain words. I do not know, and must not speculate, what those reasons may be. I trust, however, that it will not be thought impertinent, in any sense of that word, to suggest respectfully that those who are responsible for framing legislation might consider whether the traditional practice, which obscures, if it does not conceal, the intention which Parliament has, or must be presumed to have, might not safely be abandoned.

Note in the light of this comment that the presumption as to the enforceability of statutory duties recommended by the Law Commission above has not been implemented through legislation or via judicial development of the common law. The draft clause proposed by the Commission above was inserted into an Interpretation of Legislation Bill put before Parliament in 1980, but the Bill never became law.

■ X (minors) v Bedfordshire County Council
House of Lords [1995] 3 All ER 353

For the facts and the other issues, see p. 89, ante.

LORD BROWNE-WILKINSON: . . .

(a) A breach of statutory duty simpliciter
This category comprises those cases where the statement of claim alleges simply (i) the statutory duty, (ii) a breach of that duty, causing (iii) damage to the plaintiff. The cause of action depends neither on proof of any breach of the plaintiffs' common law rights nor on any allegation of carelessness by the defendant.

   The principles applicable in determining whether such statutory cause of action exists are now well established, although the application of those principles in any particular case remains difficult. The basic proposition is that in the ordinary case a breach of statutory duty does not, by itself, give rise to any private law cause of action. However, a private law cause of action will arise if it can be shown, as a matter of construction of the statute, that the statutory duty was imposed for the protection of a limited class of the public and that Parliament intended to confer on members of that class a private right of action for breach of the duty. There is no general rule by reference to which it can be decided whether a statute does create such a right of action but there are a number of indicators. If the statute provides no other remedy for its breach and the Parliamentary intention to protect a limited class is shown, that indicates that there may be a private right of action since otherwise there is no method of securing the protection the statute was intended to confer. If the statute does provide some other means of enforcing the duty that will normally indicate that the statutory right was intended to be enforceable by those means and not by private right of action: see *Cutler v Wandsworth Stadium Ltd* [1949] 1 All ER 544, [1949] AC 398 and *Lonrho Ltd v Shell Petroleum Co Ltd (No 2)* [1981] 2 All ER 456, [1982] AC 173. However, the mere existence of some other statutory remedy is not necessarily decisive. It is still possible to show that on the true construction of the statute the protected class was intended by Parliament to have a private remedy. Thus the specific duties imposed on employers in relation to factory premises are enforceable by an action for damages, notwithstanding the imposition by the statutes of criminal penalties for any breach: see *Groves v Lord Wimborne* [1898]2 QB 402, [1895–9] All ER Rep 147.

Although the question is one of statutory construction and therefore each case turns on the provisions in the relevant statute, it is significant that your Lordships were not referred to any case where it had been held that statutory provisions establishing a regulatory system or a scheme of social welfare for the benefit of the public at large had been held to give rise to a private right of action for damages for breach of statutory duty. Although regulatory or welfare legislation affecting a particular area of activity does in fact provide protection to those individuals particularly affected by that activity, the legislation is not to be treated as being passed for the benefit of those individuals but for the benefit of society in general. Thus legislation regulating the conduct of betting or prisons did not give rise to a statutory right of action vested in those adversely affected by the breach of the statutory provisions, ie bookmakers and prisoners: see *Cutler v Wandsworth Stadium Ltd* and *Hague v Deputy Governor of Parkhurst Prison* [1991] 3 All ER 733, [1992] 1 AC 58. The cases where a private right of action for breach of statutory duty have been held to arise are all cases in which the statutory duty has been very limited and specific as opposed to general administrative functions imposed on public bodies and involving the exercise of administrative discretions.

NOTES

1. Although this passage expresses the accepted judicial orthodoxy, the fact that the Law Commission has recommended a very different approach should perhaps have given the judiciary pause for thought. The Canadian Supreme Court in *The Queen in Right of Canada v Saskatchewan Wheat Pool* (1983) 143 DLR (3d) 9 rejected the English judicial approach, calling it 'painful' and agreeing with Glanville Williams that it produces arbitrary results. The existence of another method of enforcement, including criminal fines, was no bar to recovery in tort, not only in *Groves v Lord Wimborne* [1898] 2 QB 402, [1895–9] All ER Rep 147 and many other Factories Acts cases, but also in *London Passenger Transport Board v Upson* [1949] AC 155, [1949] 1 All ER 60 (road accident: see p. 670, ante); *Monk v Warbey* [1935] 1 KB 75, [1934] All ER Rep 373 (lack of motor insurance) (p. 680, post); and *Rickless v United Artists Corpn* [1988] QB 40, [1987] 1 All ER 679 (breach of copyright by 'bootlegging'). The 'protected class' approach was attacked as 'strange' and 'too narrow' by Atkin LJ in *Phillips v Britannia Hygienic Laundry Co Ltd* [1923] 2 KB 832, [1923] All ER Rep 127. Lord Browne-Wilkinson offers no exposition of the conditions under which it is plausible to say that the 'true construction' of the statute is that there is an intention to create a private right of action when there is a protected class. He also offers no explanation of what a 'protected class' is. For further discussion see p. 694, post.

2. Other possible approaches to this issue are (a) to say that the existence of a statutory duty settles both that there is a duty of care in negligence and what the standard of care is; (b) to say that the statute settles that there is a duty of care but that breach of the statute is only evidence that there has been a breach of duty; and (c) to say that the statute settles that there is a duty of care but whether there has been breach depends on the ordinary principles of common law negligence. The first approach, often called

'negligence per se', is adopted by several US states. The second approach, 'evidence of negligence', is also used in the USA and was adopted by Canada in the *Saskatchewan Wheat Pool* case. The third approach is that used in Germany under BGB Art 828 II: see B. Markesinis and H. Unberath, *The German Law of Torts*, 4th edn (Oxford, 2002), pp. 885–888. For general discussion, see Howarth, pp. 332–338, K. M. Stanton, *Breach of Statutory Duty in Tort* (London, 1986) esp. p. 54 (suggesting, contrary to the Law Commission, a presumption of non-actionability unless the statute in question expressly provides the contrary, on the grounds that this would discourage new forms of liability, based on legislation, in the absence of express authority); E. Thayer, (1914) 27 Harv. L. Rev. 317; C. Morris (1949) 49 Col LR 21; J. R. S. Prichard and A. Brudner in *Justice, Rights and Tort Law*, edited by M. D. Bales and B. Chapman (Dordrecht/ Boston, 1983), pp. 149–177; M. H. Matthews (1984) 4 Oxf JLS 429 and R. A. Buckley (1984) 100 LQR at pp. 206–210. See also K. Stanton (2004) 120 LQR 324, and in particular 333–334 for a defence of the English position.

3.   Stanton has described the process of determining whether a civil action exists for breach of statutory duty as 'one of ad hoc decisions which will exceptionally lead to the recognition of a remedy': see (2004) 120 LQR 324, at pp. 325–326. He also suggests that in the wake of the restrictive approach adopted by the House of Lords in cases such as *X (minors) v Bedfordshire County Council* and *O'Rourke v Camden London Borough Council* [1988] AC 188, [1997] 3 All ER 23, 'it is difficult to mourn the decline of the traditional form of the tort' as exemplified by cases such as *Groves v Lord Wimborne* [1898] 2 QB 402 (p. 688, post) and *Cutler v Wandsworth Stadium Ltd* [1949] AC 398, [1949] 1 All ER 544. Considering the case extracts that follow, would you agree with this assessment? Note that Stanton also draws attention to the constant introduction of new forms of expressly created forms of statutory liability through the intervention of Parliament, and suggests that the approaches developed in the case law should not unduly constrain the interpretation of these new forms of action, each based on specific Parliamentary decisions to impose liability in response to specific problems.

■ O'Rourke v Camden London Borough Council
House of Lords [1997] 3 All ER 23

LORD HOFFMANN: . . .
My Lords, Mr. O'Rourke is suing the London Borough of Camden ('Camden') for damages for breaches of various statutory duties which he says were owed to him under Pt III of the Housing Act 1985. His Honour Judge Tibber, sitting in the Central London County Court, struck out all his claims as disclosing no cause of action. But the Court of Appeal reinstated one of them and against that decision Camden appeals to your Lordships' House.

Mr. O'Rourke says in his particulars of claim that, when he was released from prison in February 1991, he had nowhere to go. He applied to Camden as housing authority for accommodation. By s. 62 of the 1985 Act, if the authority:

'. . . have reason to believe that he may be homeless . . . they shall make such inquiries as are necessary to satisfy themselves as to whether he is homeless. . . .'

By s. 63(1), if the authority:

'. . . have reason to believe that an applicant may be homeless and have a priority need, they shall secure that accommodation is made available for his occupation pending a decision as a result of their inquiries under section 62.'

Persons who have a priority need include those who are 'vulnerable as a result of...physical disability or other special reason' and Mr O'Rourke says he falls within this category.

The particulars of claim allege that after an initial refusal, Camden agreed to make inquiries pursuant to s. 62 and on 12 April 1991 provided temporary accommodation pursuant to s. 63(1) at the Northumberland Hotel. Mr. O'Rourke says that Camden thereby acknowledged that it owed him a duty under s. 63(1) to secure that accommodation was made available. But he alleges that, in breach of that duty, on 24 April Camden wrongfully evicted him from the hotel and did not offer him any other accommodation. He claims damages.

The question is whether s. 63(1) creates a duty to Mr O'Rourke which is actionable in tort. There is no doubt that, like several other provisions in Pt III, it creates a duty which is enforceable by proceedings for judicial review. But whether it gives rise to a cause of action sounding in damages depends upon whether the Act shows a legislative intention to create such a remedy. In *X and ors (minors) v Bedfordshire CC, M (a minor) v Newham London BC, E (a minor) v Dorset CC* [1995] 3 All ER 353 at 363, [1995] 2 AC 633 at 731, the principles were analysed by Lord Browne-Wilkinson in a speech with which the other members of the House agreed. He said that although there was no general rule by reference to which it could be decided that a statute created a private right of action, there were a number of 'indicators'. The indicator upon which Mr Drabble QC, who appeared for Mr. O'Rourke, placed most reliance was the common sense proposition that a statute which appears intended for the protection of a limited class of people but provides no other remedy for breach should ordinarily be construed as intended to create a private right of action. Otherwise, as Lord Simonds said in *Cutler v Wandsworth Stadium Ltd* [1949] 1 All ER 544 at 548, [1949] AC 398 at 407, 'the statute would be but a pious aspiration'.

Camden, on the other hand, says that although Pt III does not expressly enact any remedy for breach, that does not mean that it would be toothless without an action for damages or an injunction in private law. It is enforceable in public law by individual homeless persons who have locus standi to bring proceedings for judicial review. Furthermore, there are certain contra-indications which make it unlikely that Parliament intended to create private law rights of action.

The first is that the Act is a scheme of social welfare, intended to confer benefits at the public expense on grounds of public policy. Public money is spent on housing the homeless not merely for the private benefit of people who find themselves homeless but on grounds of general public interest: because, for example, proper housing means that people will be less likely to suffer illness, turn to crime or require the attention of other social services. The expenditure interacts with expenditure on other public services such as education, the National Health Service and even the police. It is not simply a private matter between the claimant and the housing authority. Accordingly, the fact that Parliament has provided for the expenditure of public money on benefits in kind such as housing the homeless does not necessarily mean that it intended cash payments to be made by way of damages to persons who, in breach of the housing authority's statutory duty, have unfortunately not received the benefits which they should have done. This was the view forcibly expressed by Geoffrey Lane LJ in *Wyatt v Hillingdon London Borough Council* (1978) 76 LGR 727 at 733 when the plaintiff claimed damages from his local authority for failure to provide benefits under the Chronically Sick and Disabled Persons Act 1970:

> 'It seems to me that a statute such as this, which is dealing with the distribution of benefits—or, to put it perhaps more accurately, comforts to the sick and disabled—does not in its very nature give rise to an action by the disappointed sick person. It seems to me quite extraordinary that if the local authority, as is alleged here, provided, for example, two hours less home help than the sick person considered herself entitled to, that that can amount to a breach of statutory duty which will permit the sick person to claim a sum of monetary damages by way of breach of statutory duty.'

This was an unreserved judgment and I think that on reflection Lord Lane would have been willing to substitute 'was' for 'considered herself'. With that amendment, I would associate myself with these remarks. In *X and ors (minors) v Bedfordshire CC* [1995] 3 All ER 353 at 364, [1995] 2 AC 633 at

731–732, Lord Browne-Wilkinson likewise said:

'Although regulatory or welfare legislation affecting a particular area of activity does in fact provide protection to those individuals particularly affected by that activity, the legislation is not to be treated as being passed for the benefit of those individuals but for the benefit of society in general.'

A second contra-indication is that Pt III of the 1985 Act makes the existence of the duty to provide accommodation dependent upon a good deal of judgment on the part of the housing authority. The duty to inquire under s. 62(1) arises if the housing authority 'have reason to believe' that the applicant may be homeless and the inquiries must be such as are 'necessary to satisfy themselves' as to whether he is homeless, whether he has a priority need and whether he became homeless intentionally. When the investigations are complete, the various duties under s. 65 arise only if the authority are 'satisfied' that the applicant is homeless and the extent of those duties depends upon whether or not they are 'satisfied' as to two other matters, namely that he has a priority need and that he became homeless intentionally. If a duty does arise, the authority has a wide discretion in deciding how to provide accommodation and what kind of accommodation it will provide. The existence of all these discretions makes it unlikely that Parliament intended errors of judgment to give rise to an obligation to make financial reparation. Control by public law remedies would appear much more appropriate: *X and ors (minors) v Bedfordshire CC* [1995] 3 All ER 353 at 378–379, [1995] 2 AC 633 at 747–748 per Lord Browne-Wilkinson.

[LORD HOFFMANN then examined whether the state of public law remedies at the time of the original enactment of the legislation meant that in the absence of a remedy in damages, it would at the time it was enacted have been no more than a 'pious aspiration'. He concluded that this would not have been the case. His Lordship then continued:]

. . . The question of the appropriate remedy for breach of the duties owed under the 1977 Act was considered by this House in *Cocks v Thanet District Council* [1983] 2 AC 286, which was decided on the same day as *O'Reilly v Mackman* [1983] 2 AC 237. Mr. Cocks brought an action in the Thanet County Court, alleging that he was homeless and in priority need but that in breach of duty, the housing authority, Thanet District Council, had refused to house him. He claimed a declaration that the council was in breach of duty, a mandatory injunction and damages. The action was transferred to the Queen's Bench Division and a preliminary issue ordered as to 'whether the proceedings were properly brought by action or could only be brought by application for judicial review.' In his judgment, Lord Bridge of Harwich . . . (with whom the other members of the House agreed) decided that no duty in private law could arise until the housing authority had made its inquiries and decided whether or not it was satisfied as to the various matters upon which the existence of the duty depended. Until the authority had declared itself so satisfied, its decision could be challenged only by judicial review. This was sufficient to dispose of the appeal. The House made a declaration that the plaintiff was not entitled to continue his proceedings 'otherwise than by application for judicial review'.

Lord Bridge went on, however, to say that a duty in private law would arise once the housing authority had made a decision in the applicant's favour. He said ([1982] 3 All ER 1135 at 1138, [1983] 2 AC 286 at 292–293):

'On the other hand, the housing authority are charged with executive functions. Once a decision has been reached by the housing authority which gives rise to the temporary, the limited or the full housing duty, rights and obligations are immediately created in the field of private law. Each of the duties referred to, once established, is capable of being enforced by injunction and the breach of it will give rise to a liability in damages. But it is inherent in the scheme of the Act that an appropriate public law decision of the housing authority is a condition precedent to the establishment of the private law duty.'

My Lords, I must say with all respect that I cannot accept this reasoning. There is no examination of the legislative intent, the various considerations which I have discussed earlier as indicating whether or not a statute was intended to create a duty in private law sounding in damages. The fact that the housing authority is 'charged with executive functions' is treated as sufficient to establish a private law duty. No doubt because the question did not have to be decided, Lord Bridge did not undertake a careful examination of the statutory intent such as he afterwards made in *Hague v Deputy Governor of Parkhurst Prison, Weldon v Home Office* [1991] 3 All ER 733 at 739–742, [1992] 1 AC 58 at 157–161. I feel sure that if he had, he would have expressed a different opinion.

The concept of a duty in private law which arises only when it has been acknowledged to exist is anomalous. It means that a housing authority which accepts that it has a duty to house the applicant but does so inadequately will be liable in damages but an authority which perversely refuses to accept that it has any such duty will not. This seems to me wrong. Of course a private law relationship may arise from the implementation of the housing authority's duty. The applicant may become the authority's tenant or licensee and so brought into a contractual relationship. But there seems to me no need to interpose a statutory duty actionable in tort merely to bridge the gap between the acknowledgement of the duty and its implementation.

In his speech in *Cocks v Thanet DC* [1982] 3 All ER 1135 at 1139, [1983] 2 AC 286 at 294, Lord Bridge cited a passage from his own earlier judgment in *De Falco v Crawley BC* [1980] 1 All ER 913 at 923, [1980] QB 460 at 480:

> 'If an ordinary action lies in respect of an alleged breach of duty, it must follow, it seems to me, that in such an action the plaintiff as well as claiming damages or an injunction as his remedy for the breach of duty can claim any declaration necessary to establish that there was a relevant breach of duty, and, in particular, a declaration that a local authority's decision adverse to him under the Act was not validly made.'

On reflection, Lord Bridge said that he thought that passage was a non sequitur. It seems to me, however, that the conclusion necessarily follows from the premise. The decision of the House that the plaintiff could not claim a declaration that the local authority's decision was not validly made means that the premise must be wrong and that the plaintiff has no private law action for breach of duty at all. It follows that in my view *Thornton v Kirklees Metropolitan BC* [1979] 2 All ER 349, [1979] QB 626, which held that he did have such a cause of action, was wrongly decided.

Mr. Drabble did not attempt to support the proposition that a private law duty which had not previously existed could arise when the housing authority had made a decision in the applicant's favour. He accepted *Cocks v Thanet District Council* as authority for the proposition that the Pt III duties which depended upon the housing authority being satisfied or not being satisfied as to various matters gave rise to no private cause of action in tort. But he said that the temporary duty under s. 63(1) was different. It did not depend upon the authority being subjectively satisfied. It was framed in objective terms and arose if the authority 'had reason to believe' that the applicant was homeless and had a priority need.

My Lords, I recognise the difference in language, although I would observe that despite its objective form, the nature of the subject-matter might incline a court to allow a housing authority some latitude in deciding whether it has 'reason to believe' the facts giving rise to the duty. The question of what kind of accommodation should be provided also involves a considerable degree of discretion. But the main difficulty I have with this argument is that it requires the court to suppose that, in an Act imposing a number of important duties which are accepted as enforceable only in public law, Parliament intended to embed one temporary duty enforceable by a private action in tort. There seems to me no rational explanation for such a scheme.

Both in principle and on the authority of the actual decision of this House in *Cocks v Thanet DC* [1982] 3 All ER 1135, [1983] 2 AC 286 I would therefore hold that the breach of statutory duty of which the plaintiff complains gives rise to no cause of action in private law and I would allow the appeal and restore the order of Judge Tibber striking out the action.

[LORD GOFF OF CHIEVELEY, LORD MUSTILL, LORD NICHOLLS OF BIRKENHEAD, and LORD STEYN agreed with LORD HOFFMANN.]

Appeal allowed.

NOTES

1. Note that the European Court of Human Rights subsequently declared inadmissible an attempt by the claimant in *O'Rourke* to claim that his right to private life, home life, and family life under Article 8 of the ECHR had been violated by the failure of the defendant to provide him with accommodation: see *O'Rourke v United Kingdom*, Application No. 39022/97, 26 June 2001.

2. The argument that no private right of action arises whenever a statute benefits the public at large as well as a specific group seems to have no rational limit. Would Parliament accept the implication that it sometimes passes statutes that benefit specific groups but which have no merit for the public at large? In any case, the primary purpose of the Housing (Homeless Persons) Act 1977 was certainly to benefit homeless people. The benefits to the public at large were incidental—useful as arguments in favour of the bill but not the reasons the bill was brought forward. The defects of the previous law were that it failed to protect the interests of homeless people. See 926 H.C. Debs (5th series) col. 896ff for the remarks of the bill's sponsor, Stephen Ross MP and R. Carnwath, *A Guide to the Housing (Homeless Persons) Act 1977* (London, 1978) pp. 9–10 for the views of the relevant minister, Mr E. Armstrong MP.

3. Mr O'Rourke's counsel did not try to argue that a private right arose as soon as the Council decided that O'Rourke qualified under the Act. Why not? Surely the argument would be that until that point the applicant's entitlement is for the application to be considered fairly, whereas after that point the applicant is entitled to be housed. The former is the kind of entitlement that only public law can deal with. The latter is no more inherently a public law matter than whether a local council has to comply with the terms of its commercial leases. The only discretion the local authority has apparently left after it is satisfied that the applicant qualifies is how to comply with its duty. However, the courts have tended to preserve a considerable scope for discretionary decision-making by local authorities in this context: see e.g. *Ali v Tower Hamlets London Borough Council* [1993] QB 407, [1992] 3 All ER 512 (what counts as 'suitable' accommodation is a matter of public law discretion challengeable only by way of judicial review).

   Furthermore, Lord Hoffmann says that a private law duty that exists only when it is acknowledged to exist would be an anomaly. How does this square with the concept of 'assumption of responsibility' now so prominent in the general law of negligence? (See pp. 37–71, ante). In any case, does Parliament never intend to create anomalies?

4. Lord Hoffmann says that there has to be a parliamentary intention to create a remedy 'sounding in damages'. The emphasis on the nature of the remedy seems to be a new departure, and might be related to judicial concerns about the public expenditure consequences of tort actions. If Parliament imposes duties on local authorities that they cannot fulfil because of Parliament's own financial restrictions on local government, should the courts rescue Parliament from its own folly by lightening the burden of those duties? Or is taking the reality of resource constraints into account simply common-sense decision-making? See *R v Gloucestershire County Council, ex p Barry* [1997] AC 584, [1997] 2 All ER 1, especially the dissent of Lord Lloyd. See also *R v East Sussex County Council, ex p Tandy* [1998] AC 714, [1998] 2 All ER 769; *R v London Borough of Barnet, ex p W* [2004] 1 All ER 97, [2003] UKHL 57.

5. Housing seems to be a particularly unhappy area for claimants with breach of statutory duty claims: see e.g. *Issa v Hackney London Borough Council* [1997] 1 All ER 999, [1997] 1 WLR 956, where the claimant children claimed that they had suffered

ill-health as a result of the defendant local authority's admitted breach of a statutory duty not to create a nuisance contrary to the Public Health Act 1936 (see now Part III of the Environmental Protection Act 1990). The defendants were the landlords of the claimants' parents' flat. The flat was plagued by damp to the extent that it was unfit for human habitation and constituted a statutory nuisance contrary to the 1936 Act. The claimants' parents successfully prosecuted the defendants in the Magistrates' Court. The defendants were fined and required to pay compensation to the parents. But the claimants' ill-health caused by the damp was not covered by the criminal compensation. The claimants therefore attempted to sue the defendants. Their difficulty was that their obvious route, s. 4 of the Defective Premises Act 1972 (p. 603, ante) was not open to them because the landlord was, apparently, not in breach of any relevant covenant in the lease or rental agreement. The claimants therefore attempted to build a private right of action on the Public Health Act itself. The Court of Appeal, reversing the first instance judge, dismissed the claim on the basis that since, in 1936, remedies in common law would have been available to the claimants' parents and other tenants in similar circumstances: it therefore would be unlikely that Parliament intended to create a private right of action solely for those claimants who had no rights at common law. However, is it so unlikely for Parliament to have created a new set of rights without regard at all to the common law position? A worrying aspect of *Issa* is its extremely static theory of parliamentary intention, apparently conceded by counsel for both parties. Is it not possible for Parliament to intend that an Act should change its meaning in the light of other legal developments? Should there be such close consideration of what would have been understood to be the legal position in 1936?

6. For further discussion of *O'Rourke*, see Sir R. Carnwath [1998] PL 407. Note that the Human Rights Act 1998 may require in certain circumstances public health and housing legislation to be interpreted so as to ensure adequate respect for the right to home life protected in Article 8 of the ECHR: see e.g. *Lee v Leeds City Council* [2002] EWCA Civ 6.

7. Note that in general there appears to be some reluctance to recognise liability for breach of statutory duty in the context of social welfare, health, prison-related, or educational duties imposed upon public authorities. See e.g. *Phelps v London Borough of Hillingdon* [2001] 2 AC 619, [2000] 4 All ER 504 (p. 99, ante), where duties cast on local authorities in relation to the special educational needs of children with such needs living within the area of the authority were not held to generate liability for breach of statutory duty. See also e.g. *R v Deputy Governor of Parkhurst Prison, ex p. Hague* [1992] 1 AC 58, [1991] 3 All ER 733. In the wider context of statutory duties imposed upon public authorities, much depend on the extent to which legislation can be identified as intended to benefit a particular class of persons in a particular way, and the nature and extent of other alternative remedies: see e.g. *Cutler v Wandsworth Stadium Ltd* [1949] AC 498, [1949] 1 All ER 544, and the Privy Council decision in *Kirvek Management and Consulting Services Ltd v Attorney General of Trinidad and Tobago* [2002] 1 WLR 2792, [2002] UKPC 43.

■ Monk v Warbey

Court of Appeal [1934] All ER Rep 373

GREER LJ: . . .

The facts can be stated quite shortly. Warbey, the defendant to the action in the court below and the appellant in this court, was the owner of a motor car which he had insured under a Lloyd's policy in which the liability was described under the head of 'Liability to the public' as 'liability at law for compensation for death or bodily injury caused by the use of the car'. The question whether or not the events which happened in this case were within the terms of the policy has not been presented for argument either in the court below or in this court. It was conceded by the parties when this came before the court that the policy did not cover the events that happened, and the action which was brought by the plaintiff was an action on the ground that there had been a breach of the statutory duty imposed by s. 35 of the Road Traffic Act 1930, and the damages which he sought to recover were alleged to be the result of that breach of the statute.

In his clear-cut argument counsel for the defendant takes three points. First, he submits to this court that the learned judge was wrong in deciding that a breach of s. 35 was available for the benefit of the plaintiff, who alleged that he had been injured by the negligent driving of the motor car by the servant of an uninsured person, and his contention is—and the matter is capable of considerable argument—that, having regard to the fact that a very serious penalty is imposed by the statute for the breach of s. 35, it cannot be concluded that that section was intended to create any right on the part of a member of the public who was injured by reason of the breach. Numbers of cases have been cited. In my judgment, this is a stronger case in favour of the plaintiff than *Groves v Lord Wimborne* [1898] 2 QB 402 and the cases which relate to breaches of statutory duties towards minors, such as *Britannic Merthyr Coal Co Ltd v David* [1910] AC 74.

The Road Traffic Act 1930, was passed in these circumstances. It had become apparent that people who were injured by the negligence of drivers of motor cars on the roads were in a parlous situation if they happened to be injured by somebody who was unable to pay damages for the injuries which they had suffered, and, accordingly, two Acts were passed. One was for the purpose of enabling persons who were so injured to recover, in the case of the bankruptcy of the insured person, the money which would be payable to him by the insurance company—that is the Third Parties (Rights Against Insurers) Act 1930. It was thought right by Parliament that in such a case the insurers' money should not go to the general creditors of the bankrupt, but should be available for the purpose of compensating the injured person, and it was provided that in the case of bankruptcy proceedings being taken against a defendant who could not pay the amount of the damage, but was insured, then in the course of the bankruptcy the person injured could make the insurance company liable for the damage caused to him although he was not a party to the contract of insurance. But that did not meet the whole difficulty because the owners of motor cars sometimes lent their motor cars to uninsured persons, and if the person causing the injury was an uninsured person then the remedy provided by that Act to which I have just referred was unavailable for the injured person. Provision, therefore, was made in the Road Traffic Act 1930, for the protection of third persons against the risks arising out of the negligent driving of a motor vehicle by an uninsured person to whom an insured owner had lent his car and, in connection with such protection, to amend the Assurance Companies Act 1909. How could Parliament make provision for the protection of third parties against such risks if it did not enable an injured third person to recover for a breach of s. 35 of the Road Traffic Act 1930? That section is to be found in Part II of the Act, which is headed 'Provision against third party risks arising out of the use of motor vehicles'. It would be a very poor protection of the person injured by the negligence of an uninsured person to whom a car had been lent by an insured person if the person injured had no civil remedy for a breach of the section....

The power to prosecute for a penalty is no protection whatever to the injured person except in the sense that it affords a strong incentive for people not to break the provisions of the statute. But the power to prosecute is a poor consolation to the man who has been damaged by reason of a breach of the provisions of s. 35....

[MAUGHAM and ROCHE LJJ delivered judgments in favour of dismissing the appeal.]

Appeal dismissed.

■ Richardson v Pitt-Stanley
Court of Appeal [1995] 1 All ER 460

RUSSELL LJ: . . .

On 1 July 1989 the plaintiff suffered a serious mutilating injury to his hand in an accident that occurred during the course of his employment by Bridge Metals (Basildon) Ltd in their factory at Basildon. It seems that there was a clear breach of s. 14(1) of the Factories Act 1961 which resulted in the injury. In due course the plaintiff obtained judgment against the company with damages to be assessed. Thereafter the company went into liquidation, there being no assets to satisfy any judgment. Furthermore it emerged that the company had not taken out any insurance cover in respect of their liability to their employees injured as was the plaintiff.

. . . [The plaintiff] asserted that all five defendants had committed an offence under s. 5 of the Employers Liability (Compulsory Insurance) Act 1969 and that consequently the plaintiff had suffered 'loss in an amount equal to the sum which he would have recovered inclusive of damages, interest and costs against the said company had it been properly insured'.

Master Hodson struck out . . . the statement of claim as disclosing no reasonable cause of action. The plaintiff appealed and . . . Mr William Crowther QC (sitting as a deputy judge of the High Court in the Queen's Bench Division) allowed the appeal . . . . It is from that order that the defendants appeal to this court, the fundamental question being whether the 1969 Act creates civil as well as criminal liability on the part of the defendants. If it does then plainly the plaintiff is a legitimate party to the proceedings.

Section 1 of the Act reads, so far as material, as follows:

'(1) Except as otherwise provided by this Act, every employer carrying on any business in Great Britain shall insure, and maintain insurance, under one or more approved policies with an authorised insurer or insurers against liability for bodily injury or disease sustained by his employees, and arising out of and in the course of their employment in Great Britain in that business . . .

(2) Regulations may provide that the amount for which an employer is required by this Act to insure and maintain insurance shall, either generally or in such cases or classes of cases as may be prescribed by the regulations, be limited in such manner as may be so prescribed . . .'

Section 2 gives a broad definition of the term 'employee' and plainly includes the plaintiff. . . . Section 5 is the crucial section and reads:

'An employer who on any day is not insured in accordance with this Act when required to be so shall be guilty of an offence and shall be liable on summary conviction to a fine not exceeding level 4 on the standard scale; and where an offence under this section committed by a corporation has been committed with the consent or connivance of, or facilitated by any neglect on the part of, any director, manager, secretary or other officer of the corporation, he, as well as the corporation shall be deemed to be guilty of that offence and shall be liable to be proceeded against and punished accordingly.'

The fine, therefore, is £1,000 for each day that an offence is committed.

The ratio of the judgment of the judge was that this case is on all fours with *Monk v Warbey* [1935] 1 KB 75, [1934] All ER Rep 373, and that consequently civil liability attaches to the employers who are in breach of s. 1 of the Act. Having referred to s. 5 the judge continued:

'So the mechanism of the Act is that where—to use a shorthand term—the requisite mens rea has been established on behalf of the director then he is equated to the corporation in so far as guilt of the offence, and the penalty, is concerned.'

Having considered what he described as the 'social purpose' of the Act the judge continued:

'So it seems to me that the social reasons and the policy reasons for saying that there is a cause of action for breach of s. 5 against the directors are very strong. As I have said, the argument for the defendants is that there is no duty imposed in terms...So it seems to me that in reality s. 5 is creating a duty on the directors and other officers of the company not to consent or connive. Once one reaches that conclusion as a matter of construction then, as I have said, it is common ground that *Monk v Warbey* [1935] 1 KB 75, [1934] All ER Rep 373 must apply and that there must be a cause of action on behalf of the plaintiff against directors who are guilty under s. 5.'

...Mr Foyon on behalf of the respondent plaintiff...emphasised that the merits were all one way and that if the appeal were to be allowed the plaintiff would be left grievously injured through no fault of his own despite the fact that the statute was designed to protect him and despite the fact that it created obligations on the part of the employers and directors which, had they been complied with, would have resulted in the plaintiff being properly compensated. Whilst I have much sympathy for the plaintiff I do not consider that this approach is the right one. The task of the court is to ascertain as best it can the intention of Parliament in passing the legislation by a proper construction of the statute.

As to the intention of Parliament we were referred, with the consent of both counsel, to the report of proceedings in both Houses as recorded in Hansard. I have to say that I have derived little assistance from the reports save that, inter alia, it was emphasised in both Houses that the Act would remedy, if its provisions were complied with, not only the injustice of the uncompensated workman but also the small employer who might be bankrupted by a claim unless insured against it. But in the House of Lords, Lord Pargiter in the committee stage of the Bill did observe:

> 'May I say at the outset that there is nothing in this Bill, so far as I am concerned, or the sponsor in another place is concerned, to alter the Common Law regarding liability in the relationship between an employer and an employee.' (See 304 HL Official Report (5th series) col 1496, 14 October 1969.)

This brings me to consider the relationship between an employer and his employee. Duties are owed by the employer both at common law and by statute whereby the employee is protected against the negligence or breach of statutory duty of the employer. If such a duty is breached and it causes personal injury to the employee he has the right to claim damages against the employer. The breach of statutory duty owed to the employee may also involve the employer in criminal proceedings, for example under the Factory Acts, but the converse does not apply unless it can be shown that the particular statute creating the criminal offence, either by virtue of its express provisions or by necessary implication, creates civil liability.

In the instant case there is no express provision in the 1969 statute creating civil liability on the part of the employers. Nor is there any such express provision relating to directors. Indeed it would be anomalous if the directors were to bear civil liability whilst the company of which they were directors was subject to no such liability...

In my judgment the 1969 Act is and was intended to be a statute within the confines of our criminal law. I say this in regard not only to employers but a fortiori in regard to directors. The plaintiff's remedy against the company subsisted at common law and under the 1961 Act. The failure to insure did not deprive the plaintiff of his remedy as such, but rather the enforcement of that remedy by way of the recovery of damages.

In the past, criminal statutes have created civil liability in the field of personal injury litigation but generally the breach of the statute has resulted in direct physical injury to the plaintiff. Not so in this case. The breach of the 1969 statute in this case does no more than involve the plaintiff in economic loss, namely the inability to recover damages. So far as the company is concerned the failure to insure does not provide an effective remedy to the injured workman. He can recover his damages from the assets of the company if there are any; if there are none the absence of insurance does not avail him.

All these considerations, in my judgment, tend to establish that the statute was not intended to create civil liability on the part of the employer. Without the creation of that liability, I cannot believe that directors of a corporate employer could be liable.

Finally, I must deal with *Monk v Warbey*, upon which so much reliance was placed by the judge. Section 35 of the Road Traffic Act 1930 provides:

'(1) Subject to the provisions of this Part of this Act, it shall not be lawful for any person to use, or to cause or permit any other person to use, a motor vehicle on a road unless there is in force in relation to the user of the vehicle by that person or that other person, as the case may be, such a policy of insurance or such a security in respect of third-party risks as complies with the requirements of this Part of this Act.'

Subsection (2) provides for criminal penalties if a person acts in contravention of the section. Those provisions of s. 35(1) and (2) are now consolidated in identical terms in s. 143(1) of the Road Traffic Act 1972.[4]

In my judgment there are a number of distinguishing features between *Monk v Warbey* and the instant case. The owner of the motor vehicle, unlike the employer, has no direct liability to the injured party in a road traffic accident occasioned by the negligence of the driver to whom the vehicle has been lent. Secondly, the wording of s. 143 of the 1972 Act is different to the wording of the 1969 Act. In the former the words used are 'it shall not be lawful' whereas those words do not appear in the 1969 statute. Thirdly, the position of anyone other than the owner of the vehicle is not dealt with by the 1972 Act, and if a director of a company which owns a vehicle has been involved in the failure to insure, the 1972 Act does not create direct criminal responsibility on the part of the director. In all these circumstances I have come to the conclusion that the judge fell into error.... I would allow the appeal and restore the order of the master.

STUART-SMITH LJ: Whether or not a breach of statutory duty gives rise to a civil cause of action is a question of construction of the relevant statutory provision in the context of the act or statutory instrument as a whole.

The general rule was stated by Lord Diplock in *Lonrho Ltd v Shell Petroleum Co Ltd* [1981] 2 All ER 456 at 461, [1982] AC 173 at 185:

'So one starts with the presumption laid down originally by Lord Tenterden CJ in *Doe d Bishop of Rochester v Bridges* (1831) 1 B & Ad 847 at 859, [1824–34] All ER Rep 167 at 170, where he spoke of the "general rule" that "where an Act creates an obligation, and enforces the performance in a specified manner...that performance cannot be enforced in any other manner", a statement that has frequently been cited with approval ever since, including on several occasions in speeches in this House. Where the only manner of enforcing performance for which the Act provides is prosecution for the criminal offence of failure to perform the statutory obligation or for contravening the statutory provision which the Act creates, there are two classes of exception to this general rule. The first is where on the true construction of the Act it is apparent that the obligation or prohibition was imposed for the benefit or protection of a particular class of individuals, as in the case of the Factories Acts and similar legislation.'

It is accepted in this case by Mr Haycroft, on behalf of the appellants, that one of the purposes of the Employers' Liability (Compulsory Insurance) Act 1969 is to secure that an injured employee does not obtain a barren judgment against his employer. The deputy judge appears to have thought that this was the primary, if not the sole social purpose of the Act, and thus it would be frustrated if there was no right of action against a director of a corporate employer who was guilty of an offence under s. 5 of the Act.

If this was the sole purpose of the 1969 Act there might be more force to the respondent's argument, which is based very largely upon it. But, in my judgment, it is not the sole purpose. Insurance is normally taken out for the protection of the insured, so that by paying a relatively small premium he may be protected against a heavy claim or loss. A small, or even medium sized, employer may be faced

---

[4] See now s. 143 of the Road Traffic Act 1988.

with disastrous consequences for his business, with adverse consequences for his other employees, if he is faced with a large claim by an injured workman, which will make large inroads into his resources. Although these consequences may not be so catastrophic as they are for a seriously injured employee who cannot enforce his judgment, they are likely to be serious, more widespread and more frequent, since it is only in those cases where the assets of the employer are insufficient to meet the claim, that the employee is affected.

In my opinion, there are a number of features about this Act, and ss. 1 and 5 in particular, which point against a director who is guilty of an offence under s. 5 being civilly liable.

(1) Section 1 of the Act does not, in my judgment, impose any civil liability on the employer at the suit of the injured employee. This is because no new liability is created by the section for the benefit of the employee; the liability already exists for breach of the common law duty of care or breach of statutory duty, for example under the Factories Acts; there is therefore no need or purpose in creating any civil liability for failure to insure against these liabilities. Mr Foy submitted that though in practice it would not be used, nevertheless the cause of action against the employer exists. I cannot accept this. It seems to me to be strange that civil liability should be imposed on a director, who consents to, connives at or facilitates by neglect a breach of criminal law by the company of which he is a director, and thus becomes both civilly and criminally liable, when the company itself is not civilly liable.

(2) Where civil statutory duty is created where the only penalty prescribed is a criminal one, the activity involved is usually declared unlawful per se with a penalty imposed for contravention of that activity, rather than the activity merely being classified as a criminal offence. An example of this is Monk v Warbey . . . .

Although logically it may be thought that there is no difference between declaring an activity to be unlawful and imposing a criminal penalty, and simply imposing a criminal penalty if the activity is proved, I do not see why this should not be regarded as some indication of the intention of Parliament.

(3) In my opinion, the court will more readily construe a statutory provision so as to provide a civil cause of action where the provision relates to the safety and health of a class of persons rather than where they have merely suffered economic loss. Certainly, the line of authority which has developed into the modern law seems to have stemmed from such cases as *Groves v Lord Wimborne* [1898] 2 QB 402, [1895–9] All ER Rep 147 a case under the Factory and Workshop Act 1878, where duties are imposed for the protection of workmen which involve a higher standard of duty than the common law duty of care.

This point clearly cannot be taken too far because *Monk v Warbey* itself is a case of protecting the injured claimant against economic loss.

(4) Very substantial penalties are imposed by the 1969 Act on the employer in default; and similar penalties are imposed on the delinquent director. This is not limited to £1,000, as the deputy judge appears to have thought, but is a maximum of £1,000 per day, which could amount to a very large fine. Moreover, the fact that that is a daily penalty shows that it is to some extent a special penalty, a feature which militates against civil liability. It differs from a fine for a single offence, for example, breach of s. 14 of the Factories Act 1961 for having unfenced machinery.

(5) At common law a director of a corporate employer to whom the duty of organising employer's liability insurance has been delegated, could not, in my view, be liable in negligence to an employee of the company who suffered economic loss through failure to effect insurance. It seems to me that it would be surprising if Parliament intended to impose an unlimited civil liability on such a director, who may have done no more than overlook the need to renew a policy. Such a person may well have had no personal responsibility for causing the injury, and indeed the employer's liability itself may arise from the negligence of a fellow employee for which the employer is vicariously liable, but for which none of the directors is personally culpable. As Mr Haycroft points out, this would be a case of piercing the corporate veil with a vengeance.

(6) Although I am doubtful whether the considerations laid down in *Pepper (Inspector of Taxes) v Hart* [1993] 1 All ER 42, [1993] AC 593 are satisfied so that the court can derive any real assistance from the Parliamentary debates, what can be said is that in the debate on cl 5 of the Bill, there is no

suggestion that any civil liability is imposed on directors (786 HC Official Report (5th series) col 1805ff, 11 July 1969) and in the House of Lords (304 HL Official Report (5th series) col 1396, 14 October 1969). Lord Pargiter, who sponsored the Bill in the House, said that 'there is nothing in this Bill . . . to alter the Common Law regarding liability in the relationship between an employer and an employee'.

I do not think this could have been said if it was the intention to impose a wholly new civil liability on the director of a corporate employer.

(7) The deputy judge considered that the case was indistinguishable from *Monk v Warbey*. I do not agree. I have already drawn attention to one distinction in para (2). I agree with Mr Haycroft that there is another. The owner of a motor car who causes or permits another to drive his vehicle puts into the hands of that person a potentially lethal object, which, if it is not driven with proper care, may cause injury to members of the public on the road. There is nothing similar in the action or inaction of a director who commits an offence under s. 5 of this Act.

(8) Although the words 'facilitate by any neglect' in s. 5 suggest breach of a duty to do something, it is clear to my mind that the duty in question is owed to the company/employer, and not the employee.

Although it may well be that none of these reasons are compelling in themselves, cumulatively in my judgment they point very strongly against the creation of any civil liability on the part of a director who has committed an offence under s. 5.

For these reasons, I would allow the appeal.

SIR JOHN MEGAW [dissenting]: . . .

The question is: what principle is to be applied in deciding whether a civil liability—a liability to be sued in the civil courts—is created where a statute imposes a duty to do something and provides that a breach of the duty shall be an offence, involving a criminal penalty; but the statute does not expressly impose any civil liability for a breach of the duty. . . .

The principle, as I understand it to be, is that which was clearly and specifically expressed by Lord Diplock, albeit in a passage of his speech which may have been technically obiter dictum, in *Lonrho Ltd v Shell Petroleum Co Ltd* [1981] 2 All ER 456 at 461, [1982] AC 173 at 185. The passage has been cited in the judgment of Stuart-Smith LJ. Lord Diplock expressed 'the general rule' to be that—

> 'where an Act creates an obligation, and enforces the performance in a specified manner . . . that performance cannot be enforced in any other manner.'

Lord Diplock then goes on to say, however, that—

> 'there are two classes of exception to this general rule. The first is where on the true construction of the Act it is apparent that the obligation . . . was imposed for the benefit or protection of a particular class of individuals, as in the case of the Factories Acts and similar legislation.'

In my opinion, that 'first exception' undoubtedly applies in this case. The obligation to insure against bodily injury or disease sustained by employees was imposed by Parliament for one purpose, and one purpose only. The purpose was to give protection to a particular class of individuals, the employees, to eliminate, or, at least, reduce, the risk to an injured employee of finding that he was deprived of his lawful compensation because of the financial position of the employer. I am confident that it was no part of the purpose or intention of Parliament in enacting this legislation to confer a benefit or protection on the employer. It might or might not be in the employer's interest, on its own account, to have insurance against this risk. But that would depend on various factors, such as the relationship of the amount of the premium, as compared with its assessment of the risk. The purpose of Parliament's enactment was the protection of the employees.

Hence the statutory requirement of compulsory insurance comes clearly and specifically within Lord Diplock's 'first exception'. Failure to perform the obligation gives rise to civil liability.

With great respect, I find it difficult to believe that the Parliamentary draftsman would have intended to make provision that there should be no civil right or remedy by using the formula of s. 1 of the 1969 Act, 'shall insure', followed by s. 5, 'shall be guilty of an offence'; as contrasted with the formula of declaring an act or omission to be unlawful and then separately providing a criminal penalty for the breach. Why should such subtle wording be used to indicate that the breach of duty which it contemplates is not actionable when that intention can be expressed in clear and precise words? (See eg s. 13 of Safety of Sports Grounds Act 1975 and s. 5(1) of Guard Dogs Act 1975.)

It is important to consider the possible consequences of the legislation, if it were to provide for a criminal penalty, but not a civil remedy. An employee, one of the class of individuals for whose protection the duty was imposed, has a claim against the employer which ought to have been, but was not, covered by insurance. The injured employee or his representatives fear that the employer may be in, or heading for, financial difficulties, and discover that there is no insurance. The employee applies to the civil court for an injunction to require the employer to take out a policy forthwith. If there is no civil action, the injunction will be refused for lack of jurisdiction. The employee is left with no remedy. Indeed, his position may be made worse by the legislation, with its provision for a criminal penalty. If the person or body which has the responsibility of initiating criminal proceedings decides to bring those proceedings, they may ultimately result in a conviction and a fine, which may be up to £1,000 a day for the duration of the failure to insure. So, far from being of any benefit to the employee for whose benefit the statutory obligation was intended, the unhappy employee may find that the imposition of the fine on the employer may have destroyed his last remaining chance of obtaining the compensation due to him.

That, as I see it, points to one excellent reason for the existence and importance of Lord Diplock's 'first exception'. In contrast with cases where the statutory obligation is an entirely general one, owed to the world at large, the fact that the intention of the statutory provision is for the benefit or protection of individuals of a particular, definable, class would make it very surprising if the only remedy for the breach of the duty was one which in no way compensated the individual but which might prevent his being compensated.

The 'first exception' applies with equal force to the liability imposed on the directors etc by the second part of s. 5 of the Act. It is equally imposed for the benefit or protection of the employees. There might be an argument to the contrary, involving what might be described as an exception to the first exception, if the liability imposed on the directors was an absolute liability, as is the liability of the employer itself under the first part of s. 5. But in order that the liability should exist, for the purpose of civil proceedings under the second part of s. 5, it is necessary for the employee to establish that the director in question consented to or connived at the failure to insure, or facilitated that failure by any neglect: in other words, there has to be shown a relevant fault on the part of the individual, other than the mere fact that he has general responsibilities as a director.

For my part, I would dismiss the appeal.

Appeal allowed.

NOTES

1. *Richardson v Pitt-Stanley* is noted by J. O'Sullivan [1995] CLJ 241.
2. Both the judges in the majority in *Richardson v Pitt-Stanley* mention that the claimant was claiming for pure economic loss. A certain reluctance can at times be detected on the part of the courts to find that statutes create rights to claim pure economic loss. See e.g. *Cutler v Wandsworth Stadium Ltd* [1949] AC 398, [1949] 1 All ER 544 and *Governors of the Peabody Donation Fund v Sir Lindsay Parkinson & Co Ltd* [1985] AC 210, [1984] 3 All ER 529. *Monk v Warbey* is an exception, as is the Privy Council decision in *Kirvek Management and Consulting Services Ltd v Attorney General of Trinidad and Tobago* [2002] UKPC 43, [2002] 1 WLR 2792. However, Stanton appears correct when he suggests that there is no 'invariable rule that the tort cannot permit the recovery of economic losses': (2004) 120 LQR 324, at 333–334. More generally, the courts are reluctant to create private rights of action on statutes where to do so would

be to allow recovery for forms of loss that are not allowed in negligence. See *Pickering v Liverpool Daily Post* [1991] 2 AC 58, [1991] 1 All ER 622 (no statutory duty protecting privacy); *Cullen v Chief Constable of the Royal Ulster Constabulary* [2004] 2 All ER 237, [2003] UKHL 39 (p. 699, post). However, is it appropriate to carry over approaches developed in negligence to the breach of statutory duty context? Given that the intention of Parliament is presumed to be the determining consideration in whether a breach of statutory duty should result in liability, does the introduction of 'external' criteria from other private law contexts risk distorting the approach of the courts to ascertaining this presumed intention? (See K. Stanton (2004) 120 LQR 324.)

3.   Since English law works by creating separate torts on statutes rather than by incorporating breaches of statutes into common law negligence, Lord Pargiter's remarks during the parliamentary debates on the bill, cited in *Richardson* above, that it was not intended to change common law liability relating to the relationship between employer and employee, can be read either way.

4.   Sir John Megaw's powerful dissent deserves careful scrutiny, especially on the questions of the intention to protect employees and reliance on the absence of an 'it shall be unlawful' provision. One point Sir John does not deal with directly is whether the court should distinguish *Monk v Warbey*. Is Russell LJ's judgment convincing on this point? On the liability of car owners for the torts of other drivers, see pp. 1140, post. Which direction does it cut that the Road Traffic Act 1972 did not create criminal liability in company directors? Is Stuart-Smith LJ any more convincing when he says that there should be liability in *Monk* but not in *Richardson* because in *Monk* the defendant put a lethal object into the hands of another person? Many factories are presumably also potentially lethal and directors do not usually operate factories entirely by themselves. Moreover, does the existence of insurance in either case make the potential claimant any safer?

5.   Lord Diplock's judgment in *Lonrho Ltd v Shell Petroleum Co Ltd* [1982] AC 173, [1981] 2 All ER 456 is discussed at p. 695, post.

■ Groves v Lord Wimborne

Court of Appeal [1898] 2 QB 402

A. L. SMITH LJ: . . .

This is an action brought against the occupier of the Dowlais ironworks, founded upon a breach of the defendant's statutory duty to fence certain machinery at the works, by reason of which breach of duty the plaintiff, in the course of his employment there, suffered personal injuries. At the trial of the action Grantham J gave judgment for the defendant upon the ground that no action would lie for the breach of the statutory duty alleged by the plaintiff.

By the Factory and Workshop Act 1878, certain duties as to fencing machinery are cast upon the occupiers of factories. In imposing these duties that Act has followed the principles of many previous Acts relating to factories and workshops. It is a public Act passed to compel the occupiers of factories to take certain precautions on behalf of their workmen. It is not, as the learned judge at the trial thought it was, in the nature of a private legislative bargain between masters and men, but a legislative enactment in compulsion of the masters. Let us now consider what are the duties imposed by this Act upon occupiers of factories with regard to fencing machinery. Section 5 makes certain provisions 'with respect to the fencing of machinery in a factory', and by sub-s. (3) as amended by the Factory and Workshop Act, 1891, s. 6(2):

'All dangerous parts of the machinery and every part of the mill-gearing shall either be securely fenced or be in such position or of such construction as to be equally safe to every person employed in the factory as it would be if it were securely fenced.'

By sub-s. (4):

'All fencing shall be constantly maintained in an efficient state while the parts required to be fenced are in motion.'

In the present case it is conceded that the machinery which caused the injury to the plaintiff was not fenced as required by the Act. Proof that there has been a breach of the statutory duty to fence imposed on the defendant, and that the plaintiff had been thereby injured would prima facie establish the plaintiff's cause of action.

Assuming that the matter depended on s. 5 alone, and that ss. 81, 82, and 86 had formed no part of the Act, could it be doubted that a person injured as the plaintiff has been could sue for the damage caused to him by the breach of the statutory duty imposed on the defendant? Clearly not. Therefore, unless it can be found from the whole purview of the Act that the legislature intended that the only remedy for a breach of the duty created by the Act should be the infliction of a fine upon the master, it seems clear to me that upon proof of such a breach of duty and of an injury done to the workman, a cause of action is given to the workman against the master.

That brings me to the question whether the cause of action which would prima facie be given by the Act has been taken away by any of the provisions enacted in the statute. Reliance has been placed upon ss. 81, 82, and 86, and it has been argued that, under these sections, the only remedy provided in a case where a workman has been injured by a breach of a duty imposed upon the master by the Act is an application to a court of summary jurisdiction for the infliction of a fine. In considering this question, I ask myself in whose favour was the Act passed? As was pointed out by Kelly CB in *Gorris v Scott*[5] the purposes which the legislature had in view in passing the Act are very material. I feel no doubt that the Act was passed for the benefit of workmen in factories, by compelling the masters to do certain things for their protection. I do not think that ss. 81, 82 and 86 can be interpreted so as to take away from an injured workman the remedy which otherwise he would have under the statute against his master. Not one penny of a fine imposed under these sections need ever go into the pocket of the person injured. It is only when a Secretary of State so determines that any part of the fine is to be applied for the benefit of the injured workman. I cannot think that such an enactment was intended to deprive the workman of his right of action. Moreover, upon what grounds are the magistrates to whom application has been made under these sections to estimate the amount of the fine to be imposed? Suppose that a workman has been killed in consequence of a breach of the master's statutory duty to fence his machinery, should the fine be of the same amount whether the breach of duty was a flagrant one or not? It is contended that the magistrates ought to take into consideration the nature of the injury which the workman has suffered, but I do not feel at all clear that that is what the legislature intended by these sections. I am inclined to think that the object of these provisions is the infliction of punishment on the master who has neglected his duty, and that the fine should be in proportion to his offence. The consideration of these points leads me to the conclusion that it was not the intention of the legislature to take away by means of these sections the right which the workman would otherwise have to be properly compensated for any injury caused to him by his master's neglect of duty.

There is also another ground which I should have mentioned which supports me in arriving at that conclusion. It is this. There is no necessity that the fine inflicted under these sections should be payable by the master, who would presumably be a man of some means. Under ss. 86 and 87 the fine may be imposed upon the actual offender, and it is provided that the master may then obtain exemption from the penalty. The actual offender may be a workman earning weekly wages, and yet it is said that the infliction of a fine on him is to be the only remedy that the injured person is to have. I cannot read this statute in the way in which the defendant seeks to read it. In my opinion, s. 5 gives to a workman a right of action upon the statute, when he has been injured through a breach of the duties created by the statute, and his rights of compensation are not limited by the provisions of the Act with regard to a fine that may be imposed by a court of a summary jurisdiction....

[5] (1874) LR 9 Exch 125.

But another point was taken for the defendant. It was said that the doctrine of common employment afforded a defence to the action. The general doctrine of law is that the master is responsible for the negligent act of his servant, acting within the scope of his employment…but the case of *Priestly v Fowler* [3 M&W 1] imposed a limitation on this doctrine in favour of the master. It was decided that the master is not responsible in respect of injuries occasioned to his servant by the negligence of a fellow servant, and the ground of that exception…is that the servant, when contracting with the master, is supposed to undertake the risk of injury to himself by the negligence of his fellow-servant. But in my judgment the defence of common employment only applies where the action is by a servant against his master and is founded upon the negligence or misconduct of his fellow servant….In the present case, which is an action founded upon the statute, there is no resort to negligence on the part of a fellow-servant or of anyone else. There being an unqualified statutory obligation imposed upon the defendant, what answer can it be to an action for breach of that duty that his servant was guilty of negligence, and therefore he was not liable? The defendant cannot shift his responsibility for the performance of the statutory duty onto the shoulders of another person…. I think the doctrine of common employment has no application to this case….

In my opinion the appeal must be allowed, and the judgment entered for the £150 damages assessed by the jury.

[RIGBY and VAUGHAN WILLIAMS LJJ delivered judgments agreeing that the appeal should be allowed.]

NOTES

1. The common employment doctrine, the evasion of which played such an important part in *Groves*, was further undermined by the invention of the employers' 'personal and non-delegable' common law duties (see p. 1098 and p. 1101, post) and was finally abolished by statute in 1948.

2. It is not every piece of industrial safety legislation that is so interpreted: e.g. *Biddle v Truvox Engineering Co Ltd* [1952] 1 KB 101, [1951] 2 All ER 835, in which it was held that a person who sells or lets defective factory machinery contrary to the provisions of s. 17(2) of the Factories Act 1961 is not civilly liable to a workman injured by reason of the defect. The worker's only remedy is at common law. The fact that this case post-dates the 1948 Act abolishing the common employment defence is, perhaps, not coincidental.

3. The Health and Safety at Work Act 1974 now imposes a range of obligations upon employers and specifies which obligations, if breached, will generate liability for breach of statutory duty: see p. 713, post. However, *Groves* remains authority in respect of duties that predate or fall outside the scope of the provisions of the 1974 Act. In *Todd v Adams* [2002] 2 All ER (Comm) 97, a much more restrictive approach to determining whether a breach of statutory duty existed than that applied in *Groves* was adopted in the context of regulations made under s. 121(1) of the Merchant Shipping Act 1995. However, *Todd v Adams* was distinguished and *Groves* applied in the subsequent Court of Appeal decision in *Ziemniak v ETPM Deep Sea Ltd* [2003] 2 All ER (Comm) 283, [2003] EWCA Civ 636.

4. In *Atkinson v Newcastle and Gateshead Waterworks Co* (1877) 2 Ex D 441, [1874–80] All ER Rep 757 the Court of Appeal said that the fact that the penalty of £10 could not be applied to the benefit of the claimant was an argument against the imposition of a civil remedy. In *London Passenger Transport Board v Upson* [1949] AC 155, [1949] 1 All ER 60, (p. 670, ante) there was a £2 penalty for breach of a regulation not in any way recoverable by the claimant. The House of Lords said that nevertheless there was a civil remedy under the regulation. In *Glover*, AL Smith LJ considered that the absence

of a fine or penalty was a strong argument in favour of imposing liability, conferring what he described as a 'prima facie' entitlement to recover on the claimant. In *Cutler v Wandsworth Stadium Ltd* [1949] AC 498, [1949] 1 All ER 544, Viscount Simonds considered that the absence of a penalty was not a decisive factor in precluding liability and indeed took the view that such an absence could result in an assumption that a right of civil action would accrue to the claimant. Do these distinctions based on penalties make any sense at all?

5.   In *Atkinson*, the claimant's premises caught fire and, owing to the pressure in the defendants' pipes being insufficient, the fire could not be extinguished and the premises were burnt down. The claimant brought an action for damages against the defendants, alleging that they were in breach of the statutory duty imposed on them by s. 42 of the Waterworks Clauses Act 1847. The section provided:

The undertakers shall, at all times, keep charged with water under [sufficient] pressure…all their pipes to which fire-plugs shall be fixed, unless prevented by frost, unusual drought or other unavoidable cause or accident, or during necessary repairs, and shall allow all persons at all times to take and use such water for extinguishing fire without making compensation for the same.

The Court of Appeal decided that no private right of action arose on the statute.

In *Dawson v Bingley Urban District Council* [1911] 2 KB 149, however, a local authority negligently put up a plate with a misleading direction in that it did not correctly denote the position of a fire-plug, as the authority was required to do under s. 66 of the Public Health Act 1875. The fire-plug became covered in dirt and ashes with the result that a fire-brigade coming to a fire was delayed for fifteen or twenty minutes in finding it. The claimant's property consequently suffered additional damage in the fire. The local authority was held liable to compensate him.

Kennedy LJ distinguished *Atkinson* on the ground that (a) the defendants there were not a public body but a private company; and (b) the Act in that case imposed remedies in the form of penalties, while s. 66 of the Public Health Act 1875 contained no specific remedy for infringement. Is there any other ground for distinction? Note that the jury in *Dawson* found that the defendant had been negligent on two counts, a finding not made in *Atkinson*. (See *Howarth*, pp. 341–342).

6.   In *Read v Croydon Corpn* [1938] 4 All ER 631 the corporation supplied impure drinking water, as a result of which the infant claimant contracted typhoid. The corporation had negligently failed to take certain precautions during work at the wells which were the source of the water supply. It was held that (a) they were liable for common law negligence; and (b) they were guilty of breach of statutory duty under the Waterworks Clauses Act 1847, s. 35, but that this conferred a right of action upon ratepayers only (and so not the infant claimant, but her father who claimed certain special damages he had suffered as a result of her illness). Stable J said (at p. 654) that 'in *Atkinson*'s case, in the absence of the statute, or of any contractual obligation, there could not have been any common law remedy at the suit of a person whose shop was burnt down because the pressure of water in a particular pipe was insufficient to enable the fire engines to put out the fire'. Compare *McCall v Abelesz* [1976] QB 585, [1976] 1 All ER 727, in which it was held that the harassment of a tenant contrary to s. 30(2) of the Rent Act 1965 did not give rise to a right to damages, one point being that the tenant already had a possible action for breach of the covenant of quiet enjoyment.

7.   Modern legislation, such as the Water Industry Act 1991 and the Electricity Act 1989, has placed express duties on privatised public utilities to pay compensation or damages to consumers for loss or damage suffered from failure or defects in the supply of their

services in certain circumstances. It has been argued that the approach in *Atkinson v Newcastle and Gateshead Waterworks Co* had the underlying purpose of protecting the discretionary decisions of public bodies from attack by way of an action for damages (R. A. Buckley (1984) 100 LQR 204). *Dawson* and *Read* point in the opposite direction, of course. The restrictive approach in *Atkinson* raises the wider question of the avail-ability of damages in this tort as a remedy in administrative law. See generally Stanton, *Breach of Statutory Duty in Tort*, pp. 73–84 and 148–152.

8. Is the approach adopted in *Groves*, which continues to be applied as good authority (see *Ziemniak v ETPM Deep Sea Ltd* [2003] 2 All ER (Comm) 283, [2003] EWCA Civ 636), compatible with that adopted by the House of Lords in *X v Bedforshire* (p. 673, ante)? Does a distinction exist between the health and safety context and other contexts? Should such a distinction exist?

■ Phillips v Britannia Hygienic Laundry Co Ltd
Court of Appeal [1923] All ER Rep 127

The Motor Cars (Use and Construction) Order 1904, provided: 'the motor car and all fittings thereof shall be in such a condition as not to cause, or to be likely to cause, danger to any per-son in the motor car or on the highway'. The defendants' vehicle was in a defective condition not due to any negligence on their part but because of the negligence of repairers to whom they had sent the vehicle for overhaul. As a result of the defective condition of the vehicle, there was a collision with a van belonging to the plaintiff. The plaintiff claimed damages on the ground of a breach of the statutory duty imposed by the Use and Construction regulations. A criminal penalty was provided for the breach of any one of those regulations. The Divisional Court held that the action must be dismissed. An appeal to the Court of Appeal was unsuccessful.

BANKES LJ: . . .

We have not here to consider the case of a person injured on the highway. The injury was done to the plaintiff's van, and the plaintiff, as a member of the public, claims a right of action as being a member of a class for whose benefit cl. 6 was enacted. He contends that the public using the highway is the class so favoured. I do not agree. In my view, the public using the highway is not a class; it is the public itself and not a class of the public. I think this clause does not apply to individual members or sections of the pub-lic, but to the public generally, and it is included in a batch of regulations for breach of which it cannot have been intended that a person aggrieved should have a civil remedy by way of action in addition to the more appropriate statutory remedy already provided. In my opinion, the plaintiff has failed to show that this case is an exception to the general rule. The appeal, therefore, fails and must be dismissed.

ATKIN LJ: . . .

I am of the same opinion. This is an important and a difficult question. I was much impressed by the argument of counsel for the plaintiff when dealing with these regulations, because there can be little doubt that the scope of the regulations was to promote the safety of the public using the highway. The question is whether they were intended to be enforced only by the special penalty attached to them in the Act. I conceive the rule to be that when a statute imposes a duty of commission or omission upon an individual, the question whether a person aggrieved by a breach of the duty has a right of action depends upon the intention of the statute. Was it intended that a duty should be owed to the individ-ual aggrieved as well as to the State, or is it a public duty only? That depends upon the construction of the statute as a whole, and the circumstances in which it was made and to which it relates. One of the matters to be taken into consideration is this: Does the statute on the face of it contain a refer-ence to a remedy for the breach of it? If so, it would, prima facie, be the only remedy, but that is not conclusive. One must still look to the intention of the legislature to be derived from the words used, and one may come to the conclusion that, although the statute creates a duty and imposes a penalty for the breach of that duty, it may still intend that the duty should be owed to individuals. Instances of this are *Groves v Lord Wimborne*[6] and *Britannic Merthyr Coal Co v David*.[7] To my mind, and on this point I differ from McCardie J, the question is not to be determined solely by the test whether or not the person aggrieved can fall within some special class of the community, or whether he is some designated individual. It would, I think, be strange if it were so. The duty imposed may be of such paramount importance that it is owed to every member of the public. It would be strange if a less important duty which is owed to a section of the public may be enforced by an action, while a more important duty which is owed to the public at large cannot be so enforced. The right of action does not depend upon whether a statutory enactment or prohibition is proclaimed for the benefit of the public as a whole or for the benefit of a particular class. It may well be enforced by an individual who cannot be otherwise specified than as a member of the public who passed along the highway. Therefore I think McCardie J is applying too narrow a test when he says ([1923] 1 KB at p. 547):

> 'In my view, the Motor Car Acts and regulations were not enacted for the benefit of any particular class of folk. They are provisions for the benefit of the whole public, whether pedestrians or vehicle users, whether aliens or British citizens, and whether working or walking or standing upon the highway.'

In stating the argument of the defendant in *Gorris v Scott*,[8] Kelly CB refers to the obligation imposed upon railway companies by s. 47 of the Railways Clauses Consolidation Act 1845, to erect gates across public carriage roads crossed by the railway on the level and to keep the gates closed except when the crossing is being actually and properly used, under the penalty of 40s for every default. It has never been doubted that if a member of the public crossing the railway were injured by the railway company's breach of duty, either in not erecting a gate or in not keeping it closed, he would have a right of action. Therefore, the question is whether these regulations, having regard to the circumstances in which they were made and to which they relate, were intended to impose a duty, which is a public duty, or whether they were intended also to impose a duty, enforceable by an individual aggrieved. Upon the whole, I have come to the conclusion that it was not intended to impose a duty enforceable by individuals aggrieved, but only a public duty, the sole remedy for breach of which is the remedy provided by way of a fine. The regulations impose obligations of varying degrees of importance; some of them are more concerned with the maintenance of the highway than with the protection of the public. Yet there is one penalty imposed for the breach of any one of them. Upon the whole, I think the true inference is that the legislature did not permit the Department which had been empowered to make regulations for the use and construction of motor vehicles to impose new duties in favour of individuals and new causes of action for breach of them. That seems to me to be the more reasonable conclusion when it is realised that the obligations of those who bring vehicles upon highways have been already well provided for and regulated by the common law. It is not likely that the legislature intended by these regulations to impose upon the owners of vehicles an absolute obligation to make them roadworthy in all events, even in the absence of negligence. For these reasons I am of opinion that the conclusion arrived at by the Divisional Court was correct, and that the appeal should therefore be dismissed.

[YOUNGER LJ agreed.]

QUESTIONS

1.   Can Atkin LJ's reasoning be reconciled with that of A. L. Smith LJ in *Groves v Lord Wimborne* (p. 688, ante)? Do you agree with Atkin LJ that 'It is not likely that the legislature intended by these regulations to impose upon the owners of vehicles an absolute

---

[6] [1898] 2 QB 402.   [7] [1910] AC 74.   [8] (1874) LR 9 Exch 125.

obligation to make them roadworthy in all events, even in the absence of negligence'? Compare also *Scott v Green & Sons* [1969] 1 All ER 849, [1969] 1 WLR 301, in which the claimant fell through the pavement into the defendant's cellar. The claimant said the defendant should be liable under a section of the Highways Act which said that owners of cellars had to keep the openings of such cellars in good repair, even though they were on the street. Lord Denning MR said that the section did not itself give rise to a cause of action, but it did mean that the defendant was in control of the pavement and could be sued at common law if fault could be proved.

2. Atkin LJ disapproves of McCardie J's narrow approach of asking whether the statute was passed for the benefit of a particular class. Is Atkin LJ also disapproving of Bankes LJ's approach? If so, would it be legitimate to join these approaches together, saying that they are two parts of the same test, or are they fundamentally different ways of thinking about the question? The modern law assumes the former (see *Lonrho Ltd v Shell Petroleum Co Ltd (No 2)* [1982] AC 173, [1981] 2 All ER 456, p. 695 post). But one suspects that Atkin LJ might be surprised by such a conclusion.

NOTES

1. In general the courts have refused to create civil remedies out of road traffic legislation. See e.g. *Tan Chye Choo v Chong Kew Moi* [1970] 1 All ER 266, [1970] 1 WLR 147; *Coote v Stone* [1971] 1 All ER 657, [1971] 1 WLR 279. One important exception is that the House of Lords held that there was a civil action for breach of the Pedestrian Crossing Places (Traffic) Regulations in *London Passenger Transport Board v Upson* [1949] AC 155, [1949] 1 All ER 60 (p. 670, ante). But note that in that case, a majority of the Law Lords thought that the defendant had been negligent and that the regulation did not set up a strict liability offence, in the sense of creating liability for a result regardless of the nature of the conduct causing the result. Rather, it said that it counted as driving too fast to proceed through a crossing at such speed that the driver could not stop in favour of a pedestrian.

2. *Atiyah*, p. 135 comments on the *Phillips* case:

   Perhaps the court was influenced—consciously or unconsciously—by the fact that in 1923 it was still not compulsory to insure against third party liability, and the court may have shrunk from imposing a form of liability without fault on individual motorists who might not have had the resources to meet a judgment for damages. Had this problem arisen after compulsory insurance was introduced in 1930 the result might conceivably have been different.

3. Public authorities are subject to a variety of specific duties in relation to the maintenance of transport systems. The duty imposed upon public authorities to 'maintain the highway' by s. 1(1) of the Highways (Miscellaneous Provisions) Act 1961, now contained in s. 41 of the Highways Act 1980, is particularly important. This duty will generate liability in tort for its breach by a public authority and has been interpreted as requiring public authorities to put and keep the highway in repair: see *Burnside v Emerson* [1968] 3 All ER 741, [1968] 1 WLR 1490; *Skilton v Epson & Ewell Urban District Council* [1937] 1 KB 112, [1936] 2 All ER 50; *Department for Transport, Environment and the Regions v McDonald Ltd* [2006] EWCA Civ. 1089; and *Roe v Sheffield City Council* [2003] EWCA Civ 1 (note that in the latter case, provisions of the Tramways Act 1870 were also interpreted as imposing private law liability). However, this duty does not extend beyond keeping the fabric of the road surface in sufficient repair as to render its physical condition safe for ordinary traffic. In *Goodes v East Sussex County Council* [2000] 3 All ER

603, [2000] 1 WLR 1356, the House of Lords decided that the duty did not require the highway authority to remove ice or snow from the road or to grit the road surfaces: the presence of ice and snow did not mean that the highway was out of repair. As a result, no liability was imposed for damage arising from an accident allegedly caused by the failure to grit the surfaces. Section 111 of the Railways and Transport Safety Act 2003 subsequently imposed a new duty on local authorities 'to ensure, so far as reasonably practicable, that safe passage along a highway is not endangered by snow or ice': breach of this duty would generate liability. However, the basic s. 41 duty continues to be interpreted in a restrictive manner, with the House of Lords in *Gorringe v Calderdale Metropolitan Borough Council* [2004] 2 All ER 326, [2004] UKHL 15 (p. 111, ante) taking the view that a failure to provide adequate warning signs on a dangerous stretch of road did not constitute a breach of the s. 41 duty, and therefore no liability would be imposed for breach of statutory duty. Alleged breaches of other relevant duties, such as the duty contained in s. 39 of the Road Traffic Act 1988 to carry out a programme of road safety measures, were held not to be actionable either per se or indirectly by the generation of a parallel common law duty of care. For a similar approach to the scope of this duty, see *Thompson v Hampshire County Council* [2004] EWCA Civ 1016, but compare the approach adopted by Carnwath LJ in *Department for Transport, Environment and the Regions v McDonald Ltd* [2006] EWCA Civ 1089.

■ Lonrho Ltd v Shell Petroleum Co Ltd
House of Lords [1981] 2 All ER 456

This appeal arose out of an arbitration between the appellants (Lonrho) and the respondents (Shell and BP). Lonrho were the claimants in the arbitration. They owned a crude oil pipeline running from the ocean port of Beira in Mozambique to a refinery near Umtali in what was then called Southern Rhodesia, now Zimbabwe. The refinery was owned and operated by a Rhodesian company controlled by Shell and BP and other oil companies. The pipeline was operated under an agreement between Lonrho and the oil companies, including Shell and BP. On 11 November 1965 the government of Southern Rhodesia unilaterally declared independence (UDI). Five days later the United Kingdom Parliament passed the Southern Rhodesia Act 1965 and pursuant to that Act the Southern Rhodesia (Petroleum) Order 1965, SI 1965/2140 was made (replaced in 1968 by a more comprehensive Order in Council), prohibiting any unauthorised person from supplying or delivering crude oil or petroleum products to Southern Rhodesia on a penalty of a fine or imprisonment. As a result, from December 1965 no oil was shipped to the Beira terminal and Lonrho's revenue from operating the pipeline ceased. Lonrho claimed damages in excess of £100 million against Shell and BP, alleging that before the making of the sanctions order Shell and BP assured the illegal regime in Rhodesia that an adequate supply of petroleum products would reach that country after UDI and thereby influenced the regime to declare UDI. Lonrho also alleged that after the sanctions order was made Shell and BP supplied petroleum products to Rhodesia by other means and thereby prolonged the period during which the sanctions order prevented the pipeline from operating. The arbitrators, before deciding the facts in issue, decided that Lonrho's points of claim disclosed no cause of action against Shell and BP. This finding was upheld by both the judge at first instance and the Court of Appeal. Lonrho appealed to the House of Lords on the grounds, inter alia, that contravention of the sanctions order, if proved, would amount to an actionable breach of statutory duty by Shell and by BP, or a conspiracy by Shell and BP jointly. For Lord Diplock's remarks on the conspiracy issue, see p. 877, post.

LORD DIPLOCK:...

My Lords, it is well settled by authority of this House in *Cutler v Wandsworth Stadium Ltd* [1949] 1 All ER 544, [1949] AC 398 that the question whether legislation which makes the doing or omitting to do a particular act a criminal offence renders the person guilty of such offence liable also in a civil action for damages at the suit of any person who thereby suffers loss or damage is a question of construction of the legislation.

[His Lordship set out the legislation and continued:]...The sanctions order thus creates a statutory prohibition on the doing of certain classes of acts and provides the means of enforcing the prohibition by prosecution for a criminal offence which is subject to heavy penalties including imprisonment. So one starts with the presumption laid down originally by Lord Tenterden CJ in *Doe d Bishop of Rochester v Bridges* (1831) 1 B & Ad 847 at 859, [1824-34] All ER Rep 167 at 170, where he spoke of the 'general rule' that 'where an Act creates an obligation, and enforces the performance in a specified manner...that performance cannot be enforced in any other manner', a statement that has frequently been cited with approval ever since, including on several occasions in speeches in this House. Where the only manner of enforcing performance for which the Act provides is prosecution for the criminal offence of failure to perform the statutory obligation or for contravening the statutory prohibition which the Act creates, there are two classes of exception to this general rule.

The first is where on the true construction of the Act it is apparent that the obligation or prohibition was imposed for the benefit or protection of a particular class of individuals, as in the case of the Factories Acts and similar legislation. As Lord Kinnear put it in *Black v Fife Coal Co Ltd* [1912] AC 149 at 165, in the case of such a statute:

'There is no reasonable ground for maintaining that a proceeding by way of penalty is the only remedy allowed by the statute...We are to consider the scope and purpose of the statute and in particular for whose benefit it is intended. Now the object of the present statute is plain. It was intended to compel mine owners to make due provision for the safety of the men working in their mines, and the persons for whose benefit all these rules are to be enforced are the persons exposed to danger. But when a duty of this kind is imposed for the benefit of particular persons there arises at common law a correlative right in those persons who may be injured by its contravention.'

The second exception is where the statute creates a public right (i. e. a right to be enjoyed by all those of Her Majesty's subjects who wish to avail themselves of it) and a particular member of the public suffers what Brett J in *Benjamin v Storr* (1874) LR 9 CP 400 at 407 described as 'particular, direct and substantial' damage 'other and different from that which was common to all the rest of the public'. Most of the authorities about this second exception deal not with public rights created by statute but with public rights existing at common law, particularly in respect of use of highways. *Boyce v Paddington Borough Council* [1903] 1 Ch 109 is one of the comparatively few cases about a right conferred on the general public by statute. It is in relation to that class of statute only that Buckley J's oft-cited statement (at 114) as to the two cases in which a plaintiff, without joining the Attorney General, could himself sue in private law for interference with that public right must be understood. The two cases he said were:

'first, where the interference with the public right is such as that some private right of his is at the same time interfered with...and, secondly, where no private right is interfered with, but the plaintiff, in respect of his public right, suffers special damage peculiar to himself from the interference with the public right.'

The first case would not appear to depend on the existence of a public right in addition to the private one: while to come within the second case at all it has first to be shown that the statute, having regard to its scope and language, does fall within that class of statutes which create a legal right to be enjoyed by all of Her Majesty's subjects who wish to avail themselves of it. A mere prohibition on members of the public generally from doing what it would otherwise be lawful for them to do is not enough.

My Lords, it has been the unanimous opinion of the arbitrators . . . , of Parker J and of each of the three members of the Court of Appeal that the sanctions orders made pursuant to the Southern Rhodesia Act 1965 fell within neither of these two exceptions. Clearly they were not within the first category of exception. They were not imposed for the benefit or protection of a particular class of individuals who were engaged in supplying or delivering crude oil or petroleum products to Southern Rhodesia. They were intended to put an end to such transactions. Equally plainly they did not create any public right to be enjoyed by all those of Her Majesty's subjects who wished to avail themselves of it. On the contrary, what they did was to withdraw a previously existing right of citizens of, and companies incorporated in, the United Kingdom to trade with Southern Rhodesia in crude oil and petroleum products. Their purpose was, perhaps, most aptly stated by Fox LJ. He said:

'I cannot think that they were concerned with conferring rights either on individuals or the public at large. Their purpose was the destruction, by economic pressure, of the UDI regime in Southern Rhodesia; they were instruments of state policy in an international matter.'

Until the United Nations called on its members to impose sanctions on the illegal regime in Southern Rhodesia it may not be strictly accurate to speak of it as an international matter, but from the outset it was certainly state policy in affairs external to the United Kingdom.

In agreement with all those present and former members of the judiciary who have considered the matter I can see no ground on which contraventions by Shell and BP of the sanctions orders, though not amounting to any breach of their contract with Lonrho, nevertheless constituted a tort for which Lonrho could recover in a civil suit any loss caused to them by such contraventions.

. . . I should mention briefly two cases, one in the Court of Appeal of England, *Ex p Island Records Ltd* [1978] 3 All ER 824, [1978] Ch 122, and one in the High Court of Australia, *Beaudesert Shire Council v Smith* (1966) 120 CLR 145, which counsel for Lonrho, as a last resort, relied on as showing that some broader principle has of recent years replaced those long-established principles that I have just stated for determining whether a contravention of a particular statutory prohibition by one private individual makes him liable in tort to another private individual who can prove that he has suffered damage as a result of the contravention.

Ex p Island Records Ltd was an unopposed application for an Anton Piller order against a defendant who, without the consent of the performers, had made records of musical performances for the purposes of trade. This was an offence, punishable by a relatively small penalty under the Dramatic and Musical Performers' Protection Act 1958. The application for the Anton Piller order was made by performers whose performances had been 'bootlegged' by the defendant without their consent and also by record companies with whom the performers had entered into exclusive contracts. So far as the application by performers was concerned, it could have been granted for entirely orthodox reasons. The Act was passed for the protection of a particular class of individuals, dramatic and musical performers; even the short title said so. Whether the record companies would have been entitled to obtain the order in a civil action to which the performers whose performances had been bootlegged were not parties is a matter which for present purposes it is not necessary to decide. Lord Denning MR, however, with whom Waller LJ agreed (Shaw LJ dissenting) appears to enunciate a wider general rule, which does not depend on the scope and language of the statute by which a criminal offence is committed, that whenever a lawful business carried on by one individual in fact suffers damages as the consequence of a contravention by another individual of any statutory prohibition the former has a civil right of action against the latter for such damage.

My Lords, with respect, I am unable to accept that this is the law; and I observe that in his judgment rejecting a similar argument by the appellants in the instant appeal Lord Denning MR accepts that the question whether a breach of sanctions orders gives rise to a civil action depends on the object and intent of those orders, and refers to *Ex p Island Records Ltd* as an example of a statute passed for the protection of private rights and interests, viz those of the performers.

Beaudesert Shire Council v Smith is a decision of the High Court of Australia. It appeared to recognise the existence of a novel innominate tort of the nature of an 'action for damages upon the case' available to 'a person who suffers harm or loss as the inevitable consequence of the unlawful, intentional and positive acts of another'. The decision, although now 15 years old, has never been followed in any Australian or other common law jurisdiction. In subsequent Australian cases it has invariably been distinguished, most recently by the Privy Council in *Dunlop v Woollahra Municipal Council* [1981] 1 All ER 1202, [1981] 2 WLR 693, on appeal from the Supreme Court of New South Wales. It is clear now from a later decision of the Australian High Court in *Kitano v Commonwealth of Australia* (1974) 129 CLR 151 that the adjective 'unlawful' in the definition of acts which give rise to this new action for damages on the case does not include every breach of statutory duty which in fact causes damage to the plaintiff. It remains uncertain whether it was intended to include acts done in contravention of a wider range of statutory obligations or prohibitions than those which under the principles that I have discussed above would give rise to a civil action at common law in England if they are contravened. If the tort described in *Beaudesert* was really intended to extend that range, I would invite your Lordships to declare that it forms no part of the law of England.[9]

I would therefore answer [the] question . . . No.

[LORD EDMUND-DAVIES, LORD KEITH OF KINKEL, LORD SCARMAN, and LORD BRIDGE OF HARWICH agreed with the speech of LORD DIPLOCK in favour of dismissing the appeal.]

Appeal dismissed.

NOTES

1. The broad principle, stated by Lord Denning MR in *Ex p Island Records Ltd* [1978] Ch 122, [1978] 3 All ER 824, that wherever the violation of a statute causes interference with a lawful trade or calling there is a civil right of action, was treated as wrong by the Court of Appeal in *Rickless v United Artists Corpn* [1988] QB 40 at 54, in view of the ratio decidendi of *Lonrho*. The *Rickless* case was concerned with s. 2 of the Dramatic and Musical Performers' Protection Act 1958 (now repealed by the Copyright, Designs and Patents Act 1988), which made it a criminal offence to make unauthorised recording of dramatic and musical performances without the performer's consent. The Court of Appeal held that despite strong indications in the wording of the Act and its history that the Act did not create private rights of action, the Act was in its terms expressly made for the protection of performers, in accordance with an international convention to which Parliament was giving effect, and so fell within Lord Diplock's first exceptional case. However, in *RCA Corpn v Pollard* [1983] Ch 135, [1982] 3 All ER 771 it was held that the Act gave no civil right of action in favour of the recording companies against defendants who were marketing 'bootlegged' Elvis Presley records. The protection of the business interests of those companies was not regarded as being within the scope of the Act. Part II of the Copyright, Designs and Patents Act 1988 now protects those with recording rights, as well as performers.

2. The notion put forward by Lord Diplock in *Lonrho* that an action for breach of statutory duty can only arise where i) the obligation or prohibition has been imposed for the benefit or protection of a particular class of persons; or where ii) a 'public right' has been created and a particular member of the public suffers what 'particular, direct and substantial' damage 'other and different from that which was common to all the rest of the public' cannot be reconciled with the view of Atkin LJ in the *Phillips* case: 'It would be strange if a less important duty, which is owed to a section of the public, may

---

[9] Note that the High Court of Australia subsequently overruled *Beaudesert*: see *Northern Territory v Mengel* (1995) 129 ALR 1, [1995] 69 ALJR 527.

be enforced by action, while a more important duty owed to the public at large cannot'
([1923] 2 KB at pp. 841–842). Furthermore, judicial decisions about what counts as a
protected class are notoriously difficult to justify. In *Issa v Hackney London Borough
Council* [1997] 1 All ER 999, [1997] 1 WLR 956, for example, the Court of Appeal said
that people whose health might be affected by a breach of statutory duties not to commit nuisances was 'too nebulous' to constitute a protected class, whereas 'workmen
in factories' did count as a protected class in *Groves v Lord Wimborne* (p. 688, ante).
In *Phillips* itself, Bankes LJ thought that road-users could not constitute a protected
class, but that did not prevent a road-user from winning in *Upson* (see p. 670, ante). In
Coote v Stone [1971] 1 WLR 279, Davies LJ explained *Upson* on the ground that those
regulations were 'designed for the safety of pedestrians', suggesting that statutes which
protect specific sub-groups of road-users give rise to liability but not those that protect
all road users—a remarkable rule, if true.

3. In *Issa v Hackney London Borough Council*, noted p. 679, ante, the Court of Appeal
    appeared to accept counsel's view that Lord Diplock's approach only applies where
    the statute lays down one and only one method of enforcement (or, more strictly still,
    lays down enforcement by criminal penalty alone). The argument seems to be that if
    Parliament only makes provision for one method of enforcement, a presumption must
    exist that there should be no civil right of action: however, if an obligation is imposed
    for the benefit of a particular class or particular persons suffer particular damage
    'other and different' from general damage to the public, then this presumption may be
    rebutted. Note that this approach does not appear to place much emphasis on ascer-
    taining the will of Parliament where these conditions are satisfied. Note also that Lord
    Diplock's second set of circumstances where breach of statutory duty can be imposed,
    namely where a particular member of the public suffers what 'particular, direct and
    substantial' damage 'other and different from that which was common to all the rest
    of the public', appears to be difficult to reconcile with other approaches adopted in the
    case law. If applied, it would have the potential to expand greatly the range of circum-
    stances where a breach of statutory duty would result in liability. However, few if any
    existing cases where a breach of statutory duty was recognised fit within this category.

4. For the political background to *Lonrho v Shell*, see *Howarth*, pp. 337–338. The under-
    lying issue in *Lonrho v Shell* was whether a private citizen could challenge a political
    decision by the government not to prosecute politically favoured wrongdoers. Compare
    Gouriet v Union of Post Office Workers [1978] AC 435, [1977] 3 All ER 70. Should it make
    any difference when such cases concern foreign policy as opposed to domestic policy?

■ Cullen v Chief Constable of the Royal Ulster Constabulary
House of Lords [2004] 2 All ER 237

The claimant was arrested in Northern Ireland on suspicion of having been concerned in
acts of terrorism. He was taken to a police station and held in custody. Under s 15(1)(a) of
the Northern Ireland (Emergency Provisions) Act 1987, a person detained under terrorism
provisions and held in custody was entitled, if he so requested, to consult a solicitor privately.
During his detention the claimant received only one unsupervised visit from his solicitor,
the police thereafter unlawfully delaying access. The claimant subsequently commenced an
action for damages against the defendant chief constable, claiming, inter alia, infringement
of his right of access to a solicitor under s. 15 of the 1987 Act. At first instance, the judge held

that procedural breaches of s. 15 conferred no right of action for damages upon the appellant, that he had suffered no damage and that no loss had been proved. The Court of Appeal of Northern Ireland ([1999] NI 237) dismissed the claimant's appeal and he appealed to the House of Lords.

LORD BINGHAM OF CORNHILL and LORD STEYN [Joint opinion]:...

[9] It is necessary to consider why Carswell LCJ (with the agreement of Nicholson and Campbell LJJ) held that there was no private law claim for damages. Carswell LCJ thought that the statute was 'silent' on the question ([1999] NI 237 at 245) and there was no sufficient basis to 'infer' that Parliament intended to allow a claim for damages (at 251). Secondly, given this hypothesis, Carswell LCJ found guidance in *R v Deputy Governor of Parkhurst Prison, ex p Hague* [1991] 3 All ER 733, [1992] 1 AC 58, which turned on the interpretation of the Prison Rules. In *Hague's* case the House characterised the Prison Rules as regulatory in character, namely dealing with the management, treatment and control of prisoners. Carswell LCJ accepted that s 58 of the 1984 Act, and s 15 of the 1987 Act, were also regulatory or 'control' provisions: [1999] NI 237 at 249–250. Thirdly, Carswell LCJ found assistance in decisions on social welfare legislation, where the statutes contained no language conferring rights and when the House considered that judicial review was the appropriate remedy: *X and ors (minors) v Bedfordshire CC, M (a minor) v Newham LBC, E (a minor) v Dorset CC* [1995] 3 All ER 353, [1995] 2 AC 633. Fourthly, Carswell LCJ stated that 'the fact that it is unlikely that personal injury, injury to property or economic loss could be proved tends to show that the breach was not intended to be actionable': [1999] NI 237 at 257. Fifthly, at one stage Carswell LCJ described a breach of s 15 as 'a mistake in procedure' (at 255). And counsel for the respondent invoked this point on several occasions. These are the principal planks of the reasoning of the Court of Appeal on the issue of the recoverability of damages for breach of s 15. It will be necessary to examine them in some detail...

(i) The language of the statute and its context

[10] In respectful but firm disagreement with Carswell LCJ we would reject the idea that the statute is silent on the issue. The long title, the heading of Pt II, and the substantive provisions of ss 14 and 15 make clear that Parliament was passing a new and remedial provision for the conferment on detainees of a statutory right of access to solicitors. The statutory language is entirely apt to create private law rights. And on ordinary principles of statutory construction the language must be interpreted so as to give the effective protection which Parliament envisaged.

[11] This interpretation is reinforced by the fact, already explained, that before the enactment of s 58 of the 1984 Act the common law already recognised a legal principle entitling a detainee to legal advice: see *Ex p Begley* [1997] 4 All ER 833 at 837, [1997] 1 WLR 1475 at 1479. It could be the basis of judicial review proceedings. In enacting s 58 of the 1984 Act, and s 15 of the 1987 Act, the legislature clearly intended to confer further protection on detainees. The only or virtually only way of doing so was to confer private law rights on them. While *Ex p Begley* was cited in the Court of Appeal, the significance of this point emerging from it may not have been placed squarely before the Court of Appeal.

[12] An even more important aid to construction is the report of the Royal Commission [on Criminal Procedure (The Investigation and Prosecution of Criminal Offences in England and Wales: The Law and Procedure (1981) (Cmnd 8092)] which formed the background to the enactment of s 58 of the 1984 Act. It reveals, as already explained, a clear view in favour of a right of access enforced by a private claim for damages. This contextual factor explains the purpose of s 58 of the 1984 Act on which s 15 of the 1987 Act was modelled. Unfortunately, this material was not placed before the Court of Appeal. It was also not drawn to the attention of the House by counsel. Having now examined the Report of the Royal Commission, we question whether the Court of Appeal would have reached a decision that Parliament did not intend to create a right to civil damages if it had been alerted to it.

(ii) The Hague *decision*

[13] It is true, of course, that in the Hague case prisoners were denied a right to claim damages for breach of the Prison Rules on the ground that the rules were not intended to create private rights: the

rules were regarded as concerned only with the management, treatment and control of prisoners. Section 58 of the 1984 Act, and s 15 of the 1987 Act, are quite differently worded and structured. They are specifically designed to protect individual rights of detained persons. This part of the reasoning of the Court of Appeal cannot be supported.

(iii) The decisions in X v Bedfordshire *and* O'Rourke

[14] In *X v Bedfordshire*, Lord Browne-Wilkinson observed ([1995] 3 All ER 353 at 365, [1995] 2 AC 633 at 732):

> 'The cases where a private right of action for breach of statutory duty have been held to arise are all cases in which the statutory duty has been very limited and specific as opposed to general administrative functions imposed on public bodies and involving the exercise of administrative discretions.'

While Carswell LCJ's quotation from this decision extended to this passage, he did not say that the rights conferred by s 15 do not come within this category. Counsel did, however, so submit. We would reject this argument. Section 15 protects the rights of a limited and specific class, i e detained persons.

[15] On a broader basis it is difficult to compare the social welfare legislation in *X v Bedfordshire* and *O'Rourke*, with no express provision for individual rights, with s 58 of the 1984 Act and s 15 of the 1987 Act, which are redolent with the expression of individual rights. Those decisions do, of course, support the proposition that, where the statute is silent, the existence of an alternative remedy, such as judicial review, may be a relevant factor to take into account when considering what is the best interpretation: see, however, *Barrett v Enfield LBC* [1999] 3 All ER 193 at 228, [2001] 2 AC 550 at 589 per Lord Hutton. For Carswell LCJ this was the significance of these decisions. In the present context, however, such arguments are ruled out by a contextual interpretation of s 15. The Royal Commission did not treat judicial review as a sufficient and effective protection for detained persons. In England and Wales cross-examination on an application for judicial review is only permitted in exceptional cases. In any event, it has to be said that the more serious a breach of refusing access to a solicitor under s 15 the more difficult it will be for a detained person to launch judicial review proceedings. There will be cases in which it is not an effective remedy as envisaged by the Royal Commission.

(iv) No personal injury, property damage or financial loss

[16] Carswell LCJ regarded the fact that a breach of s 15 was unlikely to result in personal injury, injury to property or economic loss as pointing against a legislative intent to treat a breach of s 15 as giving rise to an action in damages: [1999] NI 237 at 257. We cannot accept this proposition. In the context of a breach of a right of access to a solicitor the natural and obvious solution is that the breach is actionable per se, ie without proof of special damage. That is what the Royal Commission contemplated and what Parliament must have intended. In any event Carswell LCJ ([1999] NI 237 at 257) rightly accepted and counsel for the chief constable conceded that, if a breach of duty under s 15 is indeed actionable, it would give rise to damages without proof of loss: [1999] NI 237 at 257.

(v) A Mistake in procedure

[17] To refer to a breach of s 15 as a mistake in procedure suggests that it is not of great importance. Such a view is understandable in respect of the anticipatory breaches but not warranted in respect of a total failure to give reasons. It is a sufficient answer to quote the observation of Frankfurter J in *McNabb v US* (1943) 318 US 332 at 347, that 'The history of liberty has largely been the history of observance of procedural safeguards'...

[21] We would hold that a breach of the right under s 15 is actionable per se. But, applying the test enunciated by the Court of Justice of the European Communities, we would be inclined to hold that proof of a serious breach is required for a damages action.

LORD HUTTON: ...

(ii) The need to prove harm

[41] In my opinion damages are awarded for a breach of statutory duty in order to compensate a person for loss or damage suffered by him by reason of the breach of that duty. This principle was stated by

Lord Bridge of Harwich (with whose speech the other members of the House concurred) in *Pickering v Liverpool Daily Post and Echo Newspapers plc* [1991] 1 All ER 622 at 632, [1991] 2 AC 370 at 420 where he said that in order to award damages for breach of statutory duty—

> 'it must, in my opinion, appear upon the true construction of the legislation in question that the intention was to confer on members of the protected class a cause of action sounding in damages occasioned by the breach. In the well-known passage in the speech of Lord Simonds in *Cutler v Wandsworth Stadium Ltd (in liq)* [1949] 1 All ER 544 at 547–548, [1949] AC 398 at 407–409, in which he discusses the problem of determining whether a statutory obligation imposed on A should be construed as giving a right of action to B, the whole discussion proceeds upon the premise that B will be damnified by A's breach of the obligation. I know of no authority where a statute has been held, in the application of Lord Diplock's principle, to give a cause of action for breach of statutory duty when the nature of the statutory obligation or prohibition was not such that a breach of it would be likely to cause to a member of the class for whose benefit or protection it was imposed either personal injury, injury to property or economic loss. But publication of unauthorised information about proceedings on a patient's application for discharge to a mental health review tribunal, though it may in one sense be adverse to the patient's interest, is incapable of causing him loss or injury of a kind for which the law awards damages.'

[42] Therefore in the present case where, not only did the appellant suffer no personal injury, injury to property or economic loss, but there was no evidence of any harm sustained by him and where judicial review would have afforded an effective and speedy remedy, I consider that the law should not award him nominal damages for the breaches of the duties imposed by s 15 . . .

[43] In their judgment the Court of Appeal considered that the application of the principle stated by the House in Pickering's case led to the conclusion that there should be no award of damages for breach of the statutory duties imposed by s 15 unless the claimant had suffered personal injury, injury to property or economic loss. However, the right expressly given to a person held in police custody by s 15 was given to him for his protection and the Royal Commission considered that a person who suffered substantial inconvenience, distress or other disadvantage as a result of a breach of such a right should be able to obtain damages. The decisions of the House in *Ex p Hague* and *X v Bedfordshire CC* are, in my respectful opinion, distinguishable as applying to statutory provisions which are regulatory as opposed to s 15 which is intended to give an express and specific right to a person in police custody. Therefore I am of opinion that in relation to a breach of s 15 it would be right to extend the principle stated by Lord Bridge and to regard harm, as I have defined it, as 'loss or injury of a kind for which the law awards damages'. But I consider that to award damages for an infringement of a statutory right which has resulted in no harm to the claimant and for which judicial review would have constituted an effective remedy would be an unjustifiable extension of the principle stated in *Pickering*'s case. Moreover if damages were to be awarded when the claimant had suffered no harm, it is difficult to discern a principle which would enable a court to distinguish between a trivial breach for which no damages should be awarded and a breach of sufficient seriousness to call for an award of nominal or virtually nominal damages . . .

LORD MILLETT: . . .

[62] . . . In *X and ors (minors) v Bedfordshire CC, M (a minor) v Newham LBC, E (a minor) v Dorset CC* [1995] 3 All ER 353 at 363, [1995] 2 AC 633 at 730 Lord Browne-Wilkinson emphasised that an action for breach of statutory duty is a private law action . . .

[63] Accordingly the question is whether the statutory right of person in custody to be afforded access to a solicitor (or to be informed of the reasons why such access is being denied or delayed) is a private law right enforceable by an action for damages. If it is, then damages are not discretionary; if loss is established, damages are as of right. But if it is a public law right, it is not enforceable by an action for damages, though it may be enforceable by other means which, prior to the 1998 Act, did not lead to an award of damages.

[64] Lord Browne-Wilkinson summarised the principles which are applicable in determining whether a cause of action for breach of statutory duty exists. He said ([1995] 3 All ER 353 at 364, [1995] 2 AC 633 at 731):

'The principles applicable in determining whether such statutory cause of action exists are now well established, although the application of those principles in any particular case remains difficult. The basic proposition is that in the ordinary case a breach of statutory duty does not, by itself, give rise to any private law cause of action. However a private law cause of action will arise if it can be shown, as a matter of construction of the statute, that the statutory duty was imposed for the protection of a limited class of the public and that Parliament intended to confer on members of that class a private right of action for breach of the duty. There is no general rule by reference to which it can be decided whether a statute does create such a right of action but there are a number of indicators. If the statute provides no other remedy for its breach and the Parliamentary intention to protect a limited class is shown, that indicates that there may be a private right of action since otherwise there is no method of securing the protection the statute was intended to confer.'

[65] In that case Lord Browne-Wilkinson was considering the effect of statutory provisions establishing a regulatory system or a scheme of social welfare for the benefit of the public at large. He observed that the House had not been referred to any case where a statute of this kind had been held to give rise to a private right of action for damages for breach of statutory duty. He acknowledged the fact that regulatory or welfare legislation affecting a particular area of activity did in fact give protection to individuals particularly affected by that activity, but said that such legislation was not to be treated as being passed for the benefit of those individuals but for the benefit of society in general. Such legislation may be contrasted with the kind referred to by Lord Diplock in *Lonrho Ltd v Shell Petroleum Co Ltd (No 2)* [1981] 2 All ER 456 at 461, [1982] AC 173 at 185:

'where upon the true construction of the Act it is apparent that the obligation or prohibition was imposed for the benefit or protection of a particular class of individuals, as in the case of the Factories Acts and similar legislation.'

[66] Although not referred to by Lord Browne-Wilkinson, the cases show that there is a further aspect to be considered before a cause of action for breach of statutory duty can arise. It is not enough that Parliament shall have imposed the duty for the protection of a limited class of the public. It must also be shown that breach of the duty is calculated to occasion loss of a kind for which the law normally awards damages...

[67] In my opinion Mr Cullen's claim does not satisfy these tests. The right of access to a solicitor affords a vital protection for persons in custody, but I do not think that such persons constitute a limited class of the public in the sense in which that expression is used in the present context. It is a quasi-constitutional right of fundamental importance in a free society—indeed its existence may be said to be one of the tests of a free society—and like habeas corpus and the right to a fair trial it is available to everyone. It is for the benefit of the public at large...

[69] These considerations alone persuade me that Mr Cullen's right of access to a lawyer was a public law right incapable of forming the basis of a private law action for breach of statutory duty. But they are reinforced by the reflection that denial of the right by itself (that is to say where it does not cause or prolong unlawful detention) is incapable of causing loss or injury of a kind for which the law normally awards damages. I agree with my noble and learned friend Lord Hutton that this may be wider than the formulation adopted by the Court of Appeal that the claimant must have suffered personal injury, injury to property or economic loss. But even on the wider formulation Mr Cullen suffered no damage. He was constrained to argue that an action for breach of statutory duty is actionable per se, that is to say without proof of damage. I do not think that the submission can stand with Lord Bridge's statement of principle in Pickering's case...

[LORD RODGER OF EARLSFERRY delivered a speech in which he agreed with LORD HUTTON and LORD MILLETT that the appeal should be dismissed.]

Appeal dismissed.

QUESTION

Lord Millett cites the fact that the statutory duty in question was a 'quasi-constitutional right of fundamental importance' as a reason for considering the claimant not to be in a sufficiently limited class of the public. However, could it not be equally argued that the statutory duty is imposed to benefit a very specific group, i.e. those arrested and held under suspicion of involvement in terrorism-related offences?

NOTES

1. This is another decision that turns on questionable definitions of how constitutes a 'limited class' of the public at large. Does the approach adopted by Lord Millett serve to narrow the scope of the *X v Bedfordshire* test even further, by appearing to preclude any statute passed to benefit the public at large from generating private law liability?

2. The Court of Appeal took the view that recovery was confined to where a claimant suffered personal injury, injury to property, or economic loss. Lord Millett and Lord Hutton take the slightly wider view that a claimant must have suffered some 'harm'. Could it be argued that a delay in having access to a solicitor in itself does constitute 'harm', as it involves a denial of what Lord Millett described as a 'quasi-constitutional right'? Note that Stanton has questioned whether there is any general rule that recovery for breach of statutory duty should be limited to certain categories of loss, and notes that many statutory duties make express provision for private law liability to be imposed when alternative forms of loss have occurred, such as s. 3(1) of the Protection from Harassment Act 1997: see (2004) 120 LQR 324 at 335.

3. Lord Bingham and Lord Steyn in their joint dissent adopt a very different approach to interpreting the will of Parliament to that adopted by the majority. Which approach in your opinion best reflects the interpretative approach adopted in previous cases such as *O'Rourke*? Which approach do you consider to be preferable, given the greater emphasis on human rights in the post-Human Rights Act era? (Note that the facts of this case pre-dated the coming into force of the HRA 1998.)

4. Note that Lords Bingham and Steyn in their joint opinion at [21] suggest that 'applying the test enunciated by the Court of Justice of the European Communities, we would be inclined to hold that proof of a serious breach is required for a damages action'. The European Court of Justice in *Francovich v Italy*, Joined cases C-6/90 and C-9/90 [1991] I-ECR 5357, established at [37] that 'it is a principle of Community law that the Member States are obliged to make good loss and damage caused to individuals by breaches of Community law for which they can be held responsible'. In its developing case law on when damages caused to individuals by breaches of Community law attributable to the state will be recoverable, the Court of Justice has established that the breach in question must be 'sufficiently serious' and there must be a 'direct causal link between the breach and the damage sustained by the individuals'. (See e.g. *Brasserie du Pêcheur SA v Germany, R v Secretary of State for Transport, ex p Factortame Ltd*, Joined cases C-46 and 48/93 [1996] ECR I-1029, (*Factortame No 3*), at [101].) For an application of this

test by the House of Lords, see *R v Secretary of State for Transport, ex p Factortame Ltd* [2000] 1 AC 524, [1999] 4 All ER 906 (*Factortame No 5*), where the existence of a 'manifest and grave' breach was sought before liability under *Francovich* would be imposed upon the United Kingdom. See now Spencer v Secretary of State for Work and Pensions [2008] EWCA Civ. 750.

The introduction into English tort law of a similar requirement that a 'sufficiently serious' breach must be shown to have occurred before liability will be imposed for breach of statutory duty might have a considerable impact. The use of such a test could limit the availability of recovery in some circumstances. However, it might also expand the impact and scope of the breach of statutory duty action by opening the door for liability to be imposed in circumstances where the current 'parliamentary intention' analysis would not ordinarily permit recovery. Such a test would perhaps have the advantage of linking liability to the existence of serious breaches of statutory duties. This could be a more satisfactory and defensible approach than the current practice of relying upon nebulous and often unconvincing exegesis of what Parliament might or might not have intended. However, the use of such a test would require judicial interpretation of what would constitute a 'sufficiently serious breach' of a statutory duty. How would *O'Rourke v London Borough of Camden* (p. 675, ante) or *Lonrho Ltd v Shell Petroleum Co Ltd* (p. 695, ante) be decided using such a test? In both cases, the breaches of duty in question could readily be descried as 'serious', depending upon one's perspective. Similarly, might a failure to place adequate warning signs on dangerous stretches of road constitute a 'serious' breach of road safety requirements in some circumstances? (Consider for example the facts of *Gorringe*, p. 111, ante.)

The use of such a 'sufficiently serious breach' was advocated by R. Carnwath [1998] PL 407 at 422. However, for now, the dissenting opinion of Lord Bingham and Lord Steyn in *Cullen* remains the most significant sighting of this test in the case law. The Law Commission's Discussion Paper, *Monetary Remedies in Public Law* (London, 2004) discusses their Lordships' dictum in *Cullen* at [4.27]:

This is the first explicit judicial endorsement of the adoption into domestic law of the sufficiently serious breach test. Any such adoption was, however, not supported by the majority. The majority held that, construing the statute, there was no cause of action for breach of statutory duty. It is not unusual for judges to disagree on the interpretation of a statute. However, it is arguable that the majority were influenced against finding a cause of action because they feared excessively wide liability. In this regard, they may have failed to see the useful role which could be played by the EC law sufficiently serious breach test.

The Law Commission has now proposed a wide-ranging reform of the remedies available against public bodies: see the Appendix.

4 THE SCOPE OF PROTECTION

■ Gorris v Scott
Court of Exchequer (1874) 30 LT 431, LR 9 Exch 125

The facts of this case, as they appear in the Law Times report, were as follows:

'The plaintiffs in this action were cattle dealers at Hamburgh and the defendant was the owner of the screw steam ship Hastings, which, on the 6th March 1873 was lying at Hamburgh. On that day the plaintiffs shipped on board the Hastings a number of sheep for delivery at Newcastle, under the following bill of lading.

> Shipped in good order and well conditioned by Gorris... 100 sheep... to be delivered in the like good order and condition at... Newcastle, all and every dangers and accidents of the sea, fire, machinery, boilers, steam, and steam navigation of what nature or kind soever excepted...
>
> On deck at shipper's risk. Not answerable for washing or throwing overboard...
>
> The defendant's vessel was not fitted with proper pens nor provided with proper battens or footholds as prescribed by [the Animals Order of 1871 as authorised by the Contagious Diseases (Animals) Act 1869, s. 75, which provided that regulations might be made 'for protecting... animals from unnecessary suffering during... passage and on landing'].... [I]n consequence... a large number of the plaintiffs' sheep were washed overboard by the sea in a gale which the vessel encountered on the passage from Hamburgh to Newcastle, and were drowned. Thereupon the plaintiffs commenced an action against the defendant as owner of the said vessel, to recover damages from him for the loss of their sheep through his breach of the statutory duty in that respect imposed upon him by the Act...
>
> The defendant pleaded... that the said sheep were washed and swept away... by dangers and accidents of the seas, and steam navigation, within the true intent and meaning of the said [contractual] terms.'

KELLY CB:[10]...

[The 1869] Act was passed merely for sanitary purposes, in order to prevent animals in a state of infectious disease from communicating it to other animals with which they might come in contact. Under the authority of that Act, certain orders were made; amongst others, an order by which any ship bringing sheep or cattle from any foreign port to ports in Great Britain is to have the place occupied by such animals divided into pens of certain dimensions, and the floor of such pens furnished with battens or foot-holds. The object of this order is to prevent animals from being overcrowded, and so brought into a condition in which the disease guarded against would be likely to be developed. This regulation has been neglected, and the question is, whether the loss, which we must assume to have been caused by that neglect, entitles the plaintiffs to maintain an action.

The argument of the defendant is, that the Act has imposed penalties to secure the observance of its provisions, and that, according to the general rule, the remedy prescribed by the statute must be pursued; that although, when penalties are imposed for the violation of a statutory duty a person aggrieved by its violation may sometimes maintain an action for the damage so caused, that must be in cases where the object of the statute is to confer a benefit on individuals, and to protect them against the evil consequences which the statute was designed to prevent, and which have in fact ensued; but that if the object is not to protect individuals against the consequences which have in fact ensued, it is otherwise; that if, therefore, by reason of the precautions in question not having been taken, the plaintiffs had sustained that damage against which it was intended to secure them, an action would lie, but that when the damage is of such a nature as was not contemplated at all by the statute, and as to which it was not intended to confer any benefit on the plaintiffs, they cannot maintain an action founded on the neglect. The principle may be well illustrated by the case put in argument of a breach by a railway company of its duty to erect a gate on a level crossing, and to keep the gate closed except when the crossing is being actually and properly used. The object of the precaution is to prevent injury from being sustained through animals or vehicles being upon the line at unseasonable times; and if by reason of such a breach of duty, either in not erecting the gate, or in not keeping it closed, a person attempts to cross with a carriage at an improper time, and injury ensues to a passenger, no doubt an action would lie against the railway company, because the intention of the legislature was that, by the erection of the gates and by their being kept closed individuals should be protected against accidents of this description. And if we could see that it was the object, or among the objects of this Act, that the owners of sheep and cattle coming from a foreign port should be protected by the means described

---

[10] According to the LR Exch report.

against the danger of their property being washed overboard, or lost by the perils of the sea, the present action would be within the principle.

But, looking at the Act, it is perfectly clear that its provisions were all enacted with a totally different view; there was no purpose, direct or indirect, to protect against such dangers; but, as is recited in the preamble, the Act is directed against the possibility of sheep or cattle being exposed to disease on their way to this country. The preamble recites that 'it is expedient to confer on Her Majesty's most honourable Privy Council power to take such measures as may appear from time to time necessary to prevent the introduction into Great Britain of contagious or infectious diseases among cattle, sheep, or other animals, by prohibiting or regulating the importation of foreign animals,' and also to provide against the 'spreading' of such diseases in Great Britain. Then follow numerous sections directed entirely to this object. Then comes s. 75, which enacts that 'the Privy Council may from time to time make such orders as they think expedient for all or any of the following purposes.' What, then, are these purposes? They are 'for securing for animals brought by sea to ports in Great Britain a proper supply of food and water during the passage and on landing,' 'for protecting such animals from unnecessary suffering during the passage and on landing,' and so forth; all the purposes enumerated being calculated and directed to the prevention of disease, and none of them having any relation whatever to the danger of loss by the perils of the sea. That being so, if by reason of the default in question the plaintiff's sheep had been overcrowded, or had been caused unnecessary suffering, and so had arrived in this country in a state of disease, I do not say that they might not have maintained this action. But the damage complained of here is something totally apart from the object of the Act of Parliament, and it is in accordance with all the authorities to say that the action is not maintainable.

PIGOTT B:[11] ...

[The Act of 1869] was never for a moment contemplated to effect any alteration in the relation between the cattle owner and the carrier, except in so far as the special and particular purpose of the Act is concerned. No power is given...to provide something for the purpose of preventing animals from being washed overboard...

POLLOCK B:[12] ...

I also think that this declaration is bad on demurrer. I am inclined to agree with Mr Hershell [for the plaintiffs] with respect to the fact of the present action being founded on contract, or brought by a person with whom there was a contract, and that that distinction removes it from the cases of *Stevens v Jeacocke*,[13] and *Atkinson v The Newcastle and Gateshead Waterworks Company*[14] ... Now it must be taken, in the present case, that the animals were washed away by reason of the want of certain statutory requirements, but that gives the plaintiffs no cause of action, because the Act was passed *alio intuitu* [with another thing in mind]. ...

[AMPHLETT B agreed that the declaration disclosed no cause of action, and judgment was given for the defendant.]

QUESTIONS

1. Would the claimants' action have succeeded had their sheep died from an infectious disease communicated by other animals due to the absence of the required pens? What if the contract had excluded that risk as well? (See *Howarth*, p. 353.)

2. It is sometimes argued that an action upon the statute is an aid to law enforcement, because it encourages the victim to set the law in motion (C. Morris (1933) 46 Harv LR 453 at 458). Can this rationale be reconciled with the decision in *Gorris v Scott*?

[11] According to the LT report.   [12] According to the LT report.
[13] (1848) 11 QB 731, 17 LJQB 163.   [14] (1877) 2 Ex D 441, [1874–80] All ER Rep 757.

NOTES

1.   *Gorris v Scott* is authority for the proposition that for certain forms of breach of statutory duty, the loss or damage sought to be recovered must be the kind of loss or damage, and have must have occurred in the manner, that the statute intended to prevent. For a further application of this principle, see *Close v Steel Company of Wales* [1962] AC 367, [1962] 2 All ER 953; *Vibixa Ltd v Komori UK Ltd and others; Polestar Jowetts Ltd v Komori UK Ltd* [2006] 4 All ER 294, [2006] EWCA Civ 536, where regulations providing for civil liability for breach of certain of the duties under the Health and Safety at Work Act 1974 were interpreted as not giving rise to claims for injury to property or economic loss which was not consequent upon personal injury to the employee.

2.   Deakin, Johnston, and Markesinis have argued for the application of a more flexible approach than that set out in *Gorris v Smith* when personal injury is at issue, in particular in respect of the requirement that the statute must have intended to prevent the manner of the injury: see *Markesinis and Deakin*, pp. 392–393. See also *Donaghy v Boulton & Paul Ltd* [1968] AC 1, [1963] 2 All ER 1014, where the House of Lords distinguished *Gorris* on the basis that the damage in this case was the type contemplated by the regulations in question, even if the exact manner of its occurrence was not necessarily contemplated by the maker of the regulations.

3.   The claimant must also come within the class of person intended to be benefited by the statute in question. See *Knapp v Railway Executive* [1949] 2 All ER 508; *Hartley v Mayoh & Co* [1954] 1 QB 383, [1954 1 All ER 375. Once again, a broader approach to defining the class of protected persons can be detected in the context of health and safety legislation: see e.g. *Stanton Iron Works v Skipper* [1956] 1 QB 255. See, however, *Fytche v Wincanton Logistics plc* [2004] 4 All ER 221, [2004] UKHL 31 (p. 1106, post).

4.   The appropriate standard of care to which the defendant will be held will also be derived from interpretation of the statute in question. In certain cases, statutory provisions have been interpreted as imposing strict liability upon defendants: the occurrence of the injury the statue intended to prevent may be sufficient to result in the imposition of liability. See e.g. s. 14(1) of the Factories Ac 1961, as applied in *John Summers & Sons Ltd v Frost* [1955] AC 740, [1955] 1 All ER 870 (the effect of which was subsequently reversed by the Abrasive Wheels Regulations 1970 (SI 1970/535, reg. 3.). See also *Cherry Tree Machine Co Ltd and Shell Tankers (UK) Ltd v Dawson* [2001] PIQR P19, [2001] EWCA Civ 101. In other cases, the language of the statute will be construed as making provision for a standard of care closer to or equivalent to the standard negligence requirement of 'reasonableness': see s. 29 of the Factories Act 1961, as applied in *Nimmo v Alexander Cowan & Sons* [1968] AC 107, [1967] 3 All ER 187.

5.   The law on causation applies as much to breach of statutory duties as it does to breach of common law duties (see chap. 6, ante). However, the scope of the statutory duty and the nature of the requirements it imposes play an important role in how causation analysis is applied. In *Boyle v Kodak Ltd* [1969] 2 All ER 439, [1969] 1 WLR 661, the claimant was injured by falling off a ladder that should have been lashed to a rail. Regulation 29(4) of the Building (Health, Safety and Welfare) Regulations 1948 imposed obligations on both the defendant employer and the claimant to secure ladders appropriately. Both parties were at fault for not complying with the regulation. However, the House of Lords held that the employer's duty was of a different nature than that of the employee and required the employer to instruct the employee to take care, in particular in situations such as were at issue in this case, where the danger that the regulation was intended to advert appeared remote. As a result, their Lordships considered that

the employer was partially responsible for causing the accident. For a similar causation analysis, see *Robb v Salamis (M & I) Ltd* [2007] 2 All ER 97, [2006] UKHL 56, where again the nature of the statutory duty imposed upon the employer meant that the failure to discharge this duty could be said to have caused the accident.

6. In *Boyle v Kodak Ltd* [1969] 2 All ER 439, [1969] 1 WLR 661, the Court of Appeal had considered that even if the employer had warned the claimant, he would nevertheless have proceeded without lashing the ladder, which would have served the chain of causation leading back to the employer: however, the House of Lords considered that this finding was not available for the Court of Appeal to make on the facts. However, see also *Cummings (or McWilliams) v Sir William Arrol & Co* [1962] 1 All ER 623, [1962] 1 WLR 295, where a steel erector was killed when he fell from a steel tower in circumstances where had he been wearing a safety belt he would not have been killed. It was held that his widow could not recover reparation in respect of the breach of statutory duty to provide belts because even had he been provided with a belt he would not have worn one. Compare *Bux v Slough Metals Ltd* [1974] 1 All ER 262, [1973] 1 WLR 1358. See too *Ross v Associated Portland Cement Manufacturers Ltd* [1964] 2 All ER 452, [1964] 1 WLR 768 and *Nelhams v Sandells Maintenance Ltd* (1995) 46 Con LR 40 (where employer sub-contracts supervision, the employer will still be liable but may be able to recover a 100 per cent contribution from the sub-contractor).

7. Causation is particularly difficult to establish where the statutory provision breached is a requirement to obtain a licence to carry on an activity during the course of which the damage occurred. The problem is that often very different answers result if one asks the causation question first in terms of what would have happened had the defendant obtained a licence, and secondly, in terms of what would have happened if the defendant had refrained completely from the carrying on the activity. In *The Empire Jamaica* [1957] AC 386, [1956] 3 All ER 144, the court took the view that the relevant question was what would have happened if the defendant had obtained a licence, and consequently found in favour of the defendant. But what if obtaining the licence would have been very difficult, especially if the defendant could not have obtained a licence without undergoing training, which would probably have prevented the accident?

8. The standard defences to a negligence action appear to be available in actions for breach of statutory duty. However, in *ICI v Shatwell* [1965] AC 656, [1964] 2 All ER 999, the House of Lords adopted a cautious approach in applying the volenti defence, considering that this defence would not usually be available where an employer directly or through its management and supervision of its employees breached a statutory duty. Also note that many statutes may exclude the application of exclusion and limitation clauses: see *Stanton*, op cit., pp. 123–124.

5 THE 'EUROTORT'

■ Garden Cottage Foods Ltd v Milk Marketing Board
House of Lords [1983] 2 All ER 770

LORD DIPLOCK: . . .

The company, which started business in May 1980, operates from the residence of Mr Bunch at Crowborough in East Sussex. Mr Bunch and his wife are its only employees. In effect, it is

Mr and Mrs Bunch with limited liability. The only part of its business that is dealt with in the evidence is its purchase and resale of bulk butter. Between May 1980 and the commencement of the action in April 1982 this accounted for 80% of the company's turnover. Of its purchases during that period 90% were from the board, and of its resales 95% were for export to a single purchaser in the Netherlands, J Wijffels BV (the Dutch company). Save that the company purchased bulk butter from the board ex creamery or ex cold store, there is no evidence as to the terms on which it was sold on to the Dutch company or whether the company or the Dutch company itself was responsible for making arrangements for the transport of consignments from creamery or cold store to the Netherlands. Your Lordships may take judicial notice that under the common agricultural policy (CAP) mountainous surpluses of butter are produced in the EEC, for which there is no market for human consumption as such within the member states of the EEC. Some of this surplus, it would appear, goes into the 'bulk butter' market where it is dealt in by private traders as distinct from being purchased by the intervention agency at intervention prices under the CAP but how this bulk butter market operates and whether it bears any resemblance to other international commodity markets your Lordships can find no inkling in the evidence.

The board is a statutory authority established by the Milk Marketing Scheme 1933, as subsequently amended. The scheme is made under legislation that is now contained in the Agricultural Marketing Act 1958. The board is also subject to the EEC Council Regulation 804/68 on the common organisation of the market in milk and milk products and to a further EEC Council Regulation 1422/78 which authorises the grant to the board, and to other milk marketing boards in Scotland and Northern Ireland, of exclusive rights to purchase milk in those three parts of the United Kingdom respectively, and contains other provisions which on the face of them appear to permit the imposition of restrictions on free competition in milk products. At this stage of the proceedings in the instant case, however, your Lordships are not concerned with any of the detailed EEC regulations relating to the organisation of the market in milk products under the CAP as they affect the operations of the board. It is sufficient to draw attention to the fact that the market is subject to a special regime and the application of the EEC's rules on competition to this regime may well give rise to questions of EEC law of considerable complexity. Factually, the evidence does disclose that the board produces some 75% of the butter produced in England and Wales (not the United Kingdom) and it is reasonable to infer that it is the largest, and maybe by far the largest, producer of bulk butter exported from the United Kingdom for trading in the bulk butter market. The board started to accept tenders from the company for the purchase of bulk butter in August 1980. It continued to do so roughly once or twice a month until May 1981, after which there was a gap until it made a tender that was accepted in August 1981. Thereafter no further tenders were accepted although delivery was continued under earlier forward contracts until the end of 1981. There was, however, no express refusal by the board to do further business in bulk butter with the company until, by letter dated 24 March 1982, it informed Mr Bunch that it had decided to revise its sales and marketing strategy and to appoint four independent distributors (whose names and addresses were given) to handle the sales of its bulk butter for export, with effect from 1 April 1982. Mr Bunch was advised that he should contact those distributors to discuss availability of supplies if the company should require the board's bulk butter for export. This letter was followed by a meeting between Mr Bunch and a representative of the board at which the latter said that the board was not prepared to reconsider its decision. This refusal triggered off the present action....

The cause of action alleged by the company in its writ issued on 14 April 1982 was contravention by the board of art 86 of the EEC Treaty by withholding supplies of butter from the company or otherwise refusing to maintain normal business relations with it. Article 86 is in the following terms:

'Any abuse by one or more undertakings of a dominant position within the common market or in a substantial part of it shall be prohibited as incompatible with the common market in so far as it may affect trade between Member States. Such abuse may, in particular, consist in: (a) directly or indirectly imposing unfair purchase or selling prices or other unfair trading conditions; (b) limiting production, markets or technical development to the prejudice of consumers; (c) applying dissimilar conditions to equivalent transactions with other trading parties, thereby placing them at a competitive disadvantage; (d) making the conclusion of contracts subject to acceptance by the other parties of supplementary obligations which, by their nature or according to commercial usage, have no connection with the subject of such contracts.'

This article of the EEC Treaty was held by the Court of Justice of the European Communities in *Belgische Radio en Televisie v SV SABAM* Case 127/73[1974] ECR 51 at 62 to produce direct effects in relations between individuals and to create direct rights in respect of the individuals concerned which the national courts must protect. This decision of the Court of Justice as to the effect of art 86 is one which s. 3(1) of the European Communities Act 1972 requires your Lordships to follow. The rights which the article confers on citizens in the United Kingdom accordingly fall within s. 2(1) of the 1972 Act. They are without further enactment to be given legal effect in the United Kingdom and enforced accordingly. A breach of the duty imposed by art 86 not to abuse a dominant position in the Common Market or in a substantial part of it can thus be categorised in English law as a breach of a statutory duty that is imposed not only for the purpose of promoting the general economic prosperity of the Common Market but also for the benefit of private individuals to whom loss or damage is caused by a breach of that duty.

If this categorisation be correct, and I can see none other that would be capable of giving rise to a civil cause of action in English private law on the part of a private individual who sustained loss or damage by reason of a breach of a directly applicable provision of the EEC Treaty, the nature of the cause of action cannot, in my view, be affected by the fact that the legislative provision by which the duty is imposed takes the negative form of a prohibition of particular kinds of conduct rather than the positive form of an obligation to do particular acts. Of the many statutory duties imposed on employers under successive Factories Acts and regulations made thereunder, which have provided far and away the commonest cases of this kind of action, some take the form of prohibitions, others positive obligations to do something, yet it has never been suggested that it makes any difference to the cause of action whether the breach relied on was a failure to perform a positive duty or the doing of a prohibited act.

My Lords, when faced with the company's application for an interlocutory injunction, the first task of the judge was to make up his mind whether there was a serious question to be tried. Plainly a number of difficult and doubtful questions would be involved in any trial of the action. The jurisprudence of the Court of Justice of the European Communities, which in this field of law is well settled, indicates that there are three matters that must be proved to constitute a contravention of art 86. First, the contravenor must be in a dominant position in a substantial part of the Common Market, and this involves as a preliminary question the identification of the 'relevant market' not necessarily an easy task as *Europemballage Corp and Continental Can Co Inc v EC Commission* Case 6/72 [1973] ECR 215 shows. Second, there must be shown an 'abuse' of that dominant position. The particular examples in paras (b) and (c) of art 86 on which the company principally relies may constitute an abuse but do not necessarily do so, and in this connection it may be necessary to take into account the interaction between the EEC rules on competition and the CAP. Third, it must be shown that the abuse affects trade between member states. My Lords, I express no view as to what is likely to be the answer to any of those questions, save to observe that it would be quite impossible at this stage, and probably at any stage until after a reference under art 177 of the treaty to the Court of Justice of the European Communities, to say on the one hand that the board's behaviour that forms the subject matter of the action is clearly not capable of having any appreciable effect on competition or on trade between member states, or, on the other hand, that there is no doubt of the incompatibility of that behaviour with art 86....

My Lords, Parker J, having rightly, indeed inevitably, decided that there were serious questions to be tried, next turned, as directed by *American Cyanamid Co v Ethicon Ltd*, to consider whether if the company were to succeed at the trial in establishing its right to a permanent injunction (if a permanent injunction in some appropriate form could be devised) it would be adequately compensated by an award of damages for the loss it would have sustained as a result of the board's continuing to do what was sought to be enjoined between the time of the application for the interim injunction and the time of the trial.

[His Lordship, supported by three other members of the court, decided that no interlocutory injunction should issue because damages at trial would be an adequate remedy:]

NOTES

1. This case illustrates that private rights of action can be created out of European legislation as much as out of domestic legislation. But note that the same restrictive principles appear to apply. In *Bourgoin SA v Ministry of Agriculture, Fisheries and Food* [1986] QB 716, [1985] 3 All ER 585, the Court of Appeal decided that no private rights of action arose out of the then Article 30 of the Treaty of Rome, forbidding quantitative restrictions on imports, because its purpose was to protect the interests of the public as a whole rather than to protect the interests of individual traders. Further complications arose because of considerations concerning the propriety of awarding damages against the state using European Community law which, however, would not appear now to be relevant given the recognition of the possibility of state liability for breach of EC law by the European Court of Justice in Case 6/90, *Francovich v Italy* [1991] ECR I-5357. (See the doubts cast on elements of the reasoning adopted in Bourgoin by Lord Goff in *Kirklees Metropolitan Borough Council v Wickes Building Supplies Ltd* [1993] AC 227 at 281.) Nevertheless, the same approach is apparently adopted to breaches of statutory duty arising out of EC law as is applied to breaches of domestic statutory duties. For example, in *R v Secretary of State for Transport, ex p Factortame (No 7)* [2001] 1 WLR 942, [2000] EWHC (TCC) 179 the approach adopted in *Garden Cottage Foods* was applied by Judge John Toulmin QC in determining that an action in an English court seeking compensation from a member state for infringement of rights conferred by EC law constituted an 'action founded on tort' and therefore was subject to the limitation period established by s. 2 of the Limitation Act 1980. The state's alleged breach of duty was treated for the purposes of English law as equivalent to a standard domestic action for breach of statutory duty and was therefore subject to normal domestic limitation periods.

2. These cases give rise to an interesting classification issue. In *Garden Cottage Foods*, Lord Diplock's use of the phrase 'breach of statutory duty' could be interpreted in a wide descriptive sense as simply indicating that the cause of action in question stemmed from a statute, in this case the European Communities Act 1972 and the relevant EC legislation. Alternatively, this reference could be taken as implying that this form of action is yet another aspect of the traditional 'breach of statutory duty' category of case recognised in English law. It would appear preferable to recognise this form of liability as a separate species of tort liability, which commentators have described as a 'Eurotort'. See K. Stanton (2004) 120 LQR 324, at 329–30. In particular, it should be noted that this form of tort liability is ultimately controlled by the dictates of EC law, in particular by the requirement that domestic law must provides adequate and effective protection for rights recognised by EC law (Case C-213/89, *R v Secretary of State for Transport, ex p. Factortame Ltd* [1990] ECR I-2433) and that domestic legislation must be interpreted where necessary and possible to avoid a breach of the EC Treaty (see Case C-264/96, *ICI v Colmar* [1998] ECR I-4695. Note too that states may be liable for failure to implement EC law: see Case 6/90, *Francovich v Italy* [1991] ECR I-5357. For the 'sufficiently serious' test applied by the European Court of Justice to determine whether a breach of duty should give rise to liability, see *Brasserie du Pêcheur SA v Germany, R v Secretary of State for Transport, ex p Factortame Ltd*, Joined cases C-46 and 48/93 [1996] All ER

(EC) 301 at 365, (*Factortame No 3*) (p. 704, ante). For an application of this test by the House of Lords, see *R v Secretary of State for Transport, ex p Factortame Ltd* [2000] 1 AC 524, [1999] 4 All ER 906 (*Factortame No 5*).

3. In *Three Rivers District Council v Bank of England* [2003] 2 AC 1, [2000] 3 All ER 1 Council Directive (EEC) 77/780 was interpreted by the House of Lords as not conferring rights upon individuals to maintain an action for breach of the Directive's provisions. In his leading judgment, Lord Hope considered that the Directive did not prescribe specific supervision duties to be undertaken by national banking regulators and, taking its purpose into account, should therefore be interpreted as not conferring rights in EC law on the claimants to bring claims in respect of alleged failures in banking supervision duties by the claimants. It could be argued that the narrow approach adopted by the English courts towards actions for breach of statutory duty is reflected in this interpretation of EC law.

4. An action under this 'Eurotort' may entitle a claimant to be compensated for a broader spectrum of loss than would be awarded under an equivalent domestic statute, on the basis of the existence of the *Factortame* principle of effectiveness: nevertheless, it is a matter for the national courts to determine the appropriate measure of damages. See *Devenish Nutrition Ltd v Sanofi-Aventis SA (France)* [2008] 2 All ER 249, [2007] EWHC 2394 (Ch) at [18]; *Crehan v Inntrepreneur Pub Co (CPC)* [2004] 3 EGLR 128, 144 (this point was unaffected by the subsequent reversal of this decision by the House of Lords in *Inntrepreneur Pub Company (CPC) v Crehan* [2006] 4 All ER 465, [2006] UKHL 38). See now *Spencer v Secretary of State for Work and Pensions* [2008] EWCA Civ. 750.

6 HEALTH AND SAFETY LEGISLATION: A NOTE ON THE 'EUROPEAN REVOLUTION'

The action for breach of statutory duty, when applied to some industrial health and safety legislation, was a useful way around the doctrine of common employment (*Groves v Lord Wimborne*, p. 688, ante). Despite the abolition of that doctrine by s. 1 of the Law Reform (Personal Injuries) Act 1948 the action has survived.

As we have seen, as a general rule an action lies for the breach of a statute passed for the protection of workers, notwithstanding the existence of parallel penal sanctions. Given the existence of a right of action, the claimant must prove: (a) that he or she belongs to the class of persons whom the statute is designed to protect; (b) that the defendant was in breach of the duty; and (c) that the breach caused the damage. We have seen (section 4, ante) that this third question, the relationship between the breach and the resultant damage, raises questions of fault. The first two questions, particularly the second, may also do so. It all depends on the wording of the statutory duty or, where the meaning is not clear, upon judicial interpretations of those words.

Unfortunately, health and safety legislation has grown up in a piecemeal fashion. Surveying the legal scene, an official Committee of Inquiry (under the Chairmanship of Lord Robens, Cmnd. 5034) reported in 1972 that there were nine main groups of statutes (controlling respectively factories, commercial premises, mining and quarrying, agriculture, explosives, petroleum, nuclear installations, radioactive substances, and alkali etc. works) supported by nearly 500 subordinate statutory instruments, which were added to each year. The mass of statute law comprised—in the words of the Committee—an 'haphazard mass of ill-assorted and intricate detail'. The various Acts showed neither internal logic nor consistency with one another. The rate of technological change meant that they were often out of date; and they were far from comprehensive because, according to a Department of Employment estimate, something like 5 million of the 23 million workers in Britain were not covered by any kind of occupational health and safety legislation. In relation to those who were covered it was found that some duties were strict (the word 'absolute' is a misnomer), while other duties were based on a requirement of some degree of fault. The random distribution of duties between strict and not-so-strict duties depended upon the 'accident of language' (see G. Williams (1960) 23 MLR 233 at 243—a seminal article).

As a result of the recommendations of the Committee, the comprehensive Health and Safety at Work Act 1974 (in force since 1975) was enacted. The general duties in the Act to safeguard health and safety covers all persons at work and others against risks to health and safety arising out of or in connection with work activities. These general duties confer no right of action in civil proceedings (s. 47(1)(a)).

The aim was to replace the large body of existing regulations with a comprehensive, simplified, harmonious, and orderly set of revised regulations and by non-statutory codes of practice, with the emphasis on the latter. Section 47(2) of the 1974 Act provides that 'breach of a duty imposed by health and safety regulations....shall, so far as it causes damage, be actionable except in so far as the regulations provide otherwise'.

Unfortunately, twenty-five years after the Act, the major pre-1974 Acts are still in force and the laudable goal of harmonising and extending their provisions has not been achieved. However, those provisions are now of limited significance because of another development—described by J. Hendy and M. Ford in *Munkman*, 12th edn (1996) as a 'European revolution'.

The impetus for producing a comprehensive and orderly set of revised provisions has come not from the 1974 Act, but from Directives adopted by the European Community which are binding on Member States. The first and most important of these is the Framework Directive 89/391/EC, which has been followed by a number of 'daughter' Directives on specific risks. These are now implemented in the UK by the Management of Health and Safety at Work Regulations, SI 1999/3242, the Workplace (Health, Safety and Welfare) Regulations, 1992 SI 1992/3004, and a series of other regulations, Approved Codes of Practices (ACOPS) and Guidance Notes issued by the Health and Safety Executive (HSE), under the provisions of ss. 15 and 16 of the 1974 Act.

The basic feature of the new European approach is that general duties are imposed on all employers but, unlike the general duties in the 1974 Act, these are accompanied by specific procedures to eliminate or reduce risks. Employers are given duties of avoiding risks to safety and health; evaluating risks which cannot be avoided; combating risks at source; adapting the work to the individual; adapting to technical progress; replacing the dangerous by the less dangerous or by the non-dangerous; developing an overall protection policy; giving collective protective measures priority over individual measures; and giving appropriate instructions to workers.

The regulations have to be interpreted purposively so as to give effect to the results envisaged in the Directives, under the 'indirect effect' doctrine of EC law. So, for example, in order to determine whether an action could be maintained for breach of reg. 4(1)(a) of the Provision and Use of Work Equipment Regulations 1998, the House of Lords in *Robb v*

Salamis (M & I) Ltd [2007] 2 All ER 97, [2006] UKHL 56 referred to the provisions of the relevant EC Directives to which the regulations had been introduced to give effect. See also *Vibixa Ltd v Komori UK Ltd; Polestar Jowetts Ltd v Komori UK Ltd* [2006] 4 All ER 294, [2006] EWCA Civ 536.

Where regulations cannot be so construed, a claimant may nevertheless rely directly on a Directive against an organ of the state if certain conditions are fulfilled. (For the wide definition of an 'organ of the state' in EC law, see e.g. Case 188/90, *Foster v British Gas* [1990] ECR I-3133.) In addition, if direct enforcement of the Directive is not possible, there may be an action for damages against the Government for a deliberate failure to implement the Directive: see Case 6/90, *Francovich v Italy* [1991] ECR I-5357 (p. 704 and p. 712, *ante*).

CHAPTER THIRTEEN

INTENTIONAL INTERFERENCE WITH THE PERSON

This chapter includes not only the torts traditionally known as assault, battery, and false imprisonment, which can be grouped under the heading trespass to the person, but also covers the additional circumstances where liability may be imposed for wrongful interference with the person in situations where an action under any of the first three torts may be inappropriate but where the requisite element of intention is nevertheless present on the part of the defendant. This requirement that a defendant must have the relevant intention is often presented as the unifying factor underlying these separate and distinct causes of action. It should be noted, however, that whether a claim under trespass to the person is still actionable where the defendant has acted negligently rather than intentionally remains a disputed question. In relation to this point, the first section of this chapter (admittedly 'trespassing' to some extent from its title) deals with the interrelationship of the trespass action and an action in the tort of negligence, although the history of these two actions cannot really be explored here.

Whereas an action in the tort of negligence requires proof of damage, trespass to the person is actionable per se. The rationale for this was stated in *John Lewis & Co Ltd v Tims* [1952] 1 All ER 1203, 1204, where Lord Porter stated (in the context of false imprisonment) that when 'the liberty of the subject is at stake questions as to the damage sustained become of little importance': see also *Murray v Ministry of Defence* [1988] 2 All ER 521 at 529 (p. 732, post). Indeed, the trespass action can be a particularly important weapon in safeguarding the freedom of the individual. Substantial sums of money have been awarded in the past to vindicate this freedom, but such awards are less likely now in the light of *Thompson v Metropolitan Police Comr* [1998] QB 498, [1997] 2 All ER 762 (p. 498, ante). Exemplary damages (see p. 493, ante) can be awarded against the police for infringing this freedom, but once again this will be a relatively rare occurrence. Often, claimants will seek a declaration that their person has been unlawfully interfered with. In *Ashley v Chief Constable of Sussex Police* [2008] 2 WLR 975, [2008] UKHL 25, the House of Lords permitted a claim for assault and battery brought against the police to proceed to trial, even though the defendant had admitted liability in negligence and false imprisonment, and the claim for assault and battery would not result in any increase of the damages that the claimants could obtain. (The claimants wished to obtain a finding via the action for assault and battery that the police action in question, which had resulted in the shooting and killing of a family member, was unlawful.) The majority of their Lordships considered that the claimants were seeking a vindication of their claim that an unlawful killing had taken place through the action for assault and battery, and that this was a form of declaratory relief which the claimants were entitled to pursue. It is also important to bear in mind that the protection offered to personal autonomy by these torts overlaps with and is increasingly influenced by the requirements of the European Convention on Human Rights: this is an area where Convention standards and the common law are closely intertwined.

The three torts of assault, battery, and false imprisonment are also crimes, and acts giving rise to tortious liability may, therefore, involve criminal liability as well. Criminal cases are used as precedents in determining the scope of these torts, but, since the policy of the law in the two spheres may differ, some caution must be exercised when this is done. Apart from the possibility of the same act giving rise to both civil and criminal liability, a particular factual situation may also involve liability under more than one of the various torts which come within the category of trespass to the person. A battery will usually, but not always, be preceded by an assault, although each can exist independently of the other, and acts amounting to false imprisonment could, in addition, involve liability for assault or battery. The student should be warned, however, that the word 'assault' is often used loosely to cover both the technical assault and the battery.

The wrongful interference principle derived from *Wilkinson v Downton* [1897] 2 QB 57 has the potential to develop a wide area of liability. The wrongful interference principle is distinct from the trespass action: while proof of damage must be shown, in contrast to trespass, the *Wilkinson v Downton* principle does not appear to require that the harm in question be a direct consequence of the defendant's act. However, while this principle still may have some limited role to play, its scope has been circumscribed by the decisions of *Wainwright v Home Office* [2003] 4 All ER 969, [2003] UKHL 53 and *Wong v Parkside Authority* [2003] 3 All ER 932, [2001] EWCA Civ. 1721. The *lacunae* in the law that the *Wilkinson v Downton* principle at one point was deployed to redress has been partially filled by the Protection from Harassment Act 1997, which is also considered in this chapter.

1 TRESPASS, INTENTION, AND NEGLIGENCE

■ Fowler v Lanning

Queen's Bench Division [1959] 1 All ER 290

DIPLOCK J: . . .

The writ in this case claims damages for trespass to the person committed by the defendant at Corfe Castle, in the county of Dorset, on 19 November 1957. The statement of claim alleges laconically that at that place and on that date 'the defendant shot the plaintiff', and that by reason thereof the plaintiff sustained personal injuries and has suffered loss and damage. By his defence the defendant, in addition to traversing the allegations of fact, raises the objection

> 'that the statement of claim is bad in law and discloses no cause of action against him on the ground that the plaintiff does not allege that the said shooting was intentional or negligent.'

An order has been made that this point of law be disposed of before the trial of the issues of fact in the action. That order is binding on me, and, in disposing of it, I can look no further than the pleadings. I must confess that at first glance at the pleadings I felt some anxiety lest I was being invited to decide a point which has long puzzled the professors (see the article by Professors Goodhart and Winfield (1933) 49 Law Quarterly Review 359; *Pollock on Torts* (15th edn) p. 129; *Salmond on Torts* (12th edn) p. 311; *Winfield on Tort* (5th edn) p. 213), only to learn ultimately that, just as in *M'Alister* (or *Donoghue*) v *Stevenson* ([1932] AC 562), there was in fact no snail in the ginger beer bottle, so in this case there was in fact no pellet in the defendant's gun.

The point of law is not, however, a mere academic one even at the present stage of the action. The alleged injuries were, I am told, sustained at a shooting party; it is not suggested that the shooting was intentional. The practical issue is whether, if the plaintiff was in fact injured by a shot from a gun fired by the defendant, the onus lies on the plaintiff to prove that the defendant was negligent, in which case, under the modern system of pleading, he must so plead and give particulars of negligence... or whether it lies on the defendant to prove that the plaintiff's injuries were not caused by the defendant's negligence, in which case the plaintiff's statement of claim is sufficient and discloses a cause of action.... The issue is thus a neat one of onus of proof.

[Having surveyed the history of this area of the law, DIPLOCK J continued:] I can summarise the law as I understand it from my examination of the cases as follows:

(1) Trespass to the person does not lie if the injury to the plaintiff, although the direct consequence of the act of the defendant, was caused unintentionally and without negligence on the defendant's part.

(2) Trespass to the person on the highway does not differ in this respect from trespass to the person committed in any other place.

(3) If it were right to say with Blackburn J in 1865[1] that negligence is a necessary ingredient of unintentional trespass only where the circumstances are such as to show that the plaintiff had taken on himself the risk of inevitable injury (i.e. injury which is the result of neither intention nor carelessness on the part of the defendant), the plaintiff must today in this crowded world be considered as taking on himself the risk of inevitable injury from any acts of his neighbour which, in the absence of damage to the plaintiff, would not in themselves be unlawful—of which discharging a gun at a shooting party in 1957...[is an] obvious [example]. For Blackburn J in...*Fletcher v Rylands* ((1866) LR 1 Exch at p. 286) was in truth doing no more than stating the converse of the principle referred to by Lord Macmillan in *Read v J Lyons & Co Ltd* ([1946] 2 All ER at p. 476), that a man's freedom of action is subject only to the obligation not to infringe any duty of care which he owes to others.

(4) The onus of proving negligence, where the trespass is not intentional, lies on the plaintiff, whether the action be framed in trespass or in negligence. This has been unquestioned law in highway cases ever since *Holmes v Mather* ((1875) LR 10 Exch 261), and there is no reason in principle, nor any suggestion in the decided authorities, why it should be any different in other cases. It is, indeed, but an illustration of the rule that he who affirms must prove, which lies at the root of our law of evidence....

If, as I have held, the onus of proof of intention or negligence on the part of the defendant lies on the plaintiff, then, under the modern rules of pleading, he must allege either intention on the part of the defendant, or, if he relies on negligence, he must state the facts which he alleges constitute negligence. Without either of such allegations the bald statement that the defendant shot the plaintiff in unspecified circumstances with an unspecified weapon in my view discloses no cause of action....

[In relation to] negligent trespass to the person, there is here the bare allegation that on a particular day at a particular place 'the defendant shot the plaintiff'. In what circumstances, indeed with what weapon, from bow and arrow to atomic warhead, is not stated. So bare an allegation is consistent with the defendant's having exercised reasonable care. It may be—I know not—that, had the circumstances been set out with greater particularity, there would have been disclosed facts which themselves shouted negligence, so that the doctrine of res ipsa loquitur would have applied. In such a form the statement of claim might have disclosed a cause of action even although the word 'negligence' itself had not been used, and the plaintiff in that event would have been limited to relying for proof of

---

[1] See *Fletcher v Rylands* (1866) LR 1 Exch 265.

negligence on the facts which he had alleged. But I have today to deal with the pleading as it stands. As it stands, it neither alleges negligence in terms nor alleges facts which, if true, would of themselves constitute negligence; nor, if counsel for the plaintiff is right, would he be bound at any time before the trial to disclose to the defendant what facts he relies on as constituting negligence.

I do not see how the plaintiff will be harmed by alleging now the facts on which he ultimately intends to rely. On the contrary, for him to do so, will serve to secure justice between the parties. It offends the underlying purpose of the modern system of pleading that a plaintiff, by calling his grievance 'trespass to the person' instead of 'negligence', should force a defendant to come to trial blindfold; and I am glad to find nothing in the authorities which compels the court in this case to refrain from stripping the bandage from his eyes.

I hold that the statement of claim in its present form discloses no cause of action.

Order accordingly. Leave to make immediate amendments to statement of claim granted; consequential amendments to defence to be made within fourteen days.

NOTE

At the ultimate trial of the action, the claimant failed because he was unable to prove whose shot had caused the injury; see *The Times*, 21 and 22 May, 1959; G. Dworkin (1959) 22 MLR 538. Diplock J's approach has much to commend it, especially from the point of view of procedural justice, requiring as it does the claimant to state the exact nature of the claim against the defendant. However, see the general comment by Glanville Williams at [1959] CLJ 33.

■ Letang v Cooper
Court of Appeal [1964] 2 All ER 929

LORD DENNING MR:...
On 10 July 1957, Mrs Letang, the plaintiff, was on holiday in Cornwall. She was staying at a hotel and thought she would sunbathe on a piece of grass where cars were parked. While she was lying there, Mr Cooper, the defendant, came into the car park driving his Jaguar motor car. He did not see her. The car went over her legs and she was injured. On 2 February 1961, more than three years after the accident, the plaintiff brought this action against the defendant for damages for loss and injury caused by (i) the negligence of the defendant in driving a motor car and (ii) the commission by the defendant of a trespass to the person. The sole question is whether the action is statute barred. The plaintiff admits that the action for negligence is barred after three years, but she claims that the action for trespass to the person is not barred until six years have elapsed. The judge has so held and awarded her £575 damages for trespass to the person.

Under the Limitation Act 1939, the period of limitation was six years in all actions founded 'on tort'; but in 1954 Parliament reduced it to three years in actions for damages for personal injuries, provided that the actions come within these words of s. 2(1) of the Law Reform (Limitation of Actions, &c.) Act 1954:

> '...in the case of actions for damages for negligence, nuisance or breach of duty (whether the duty exists by virtue of a contract or of a provision made by or under a statute or independently of any contract or any such provision) where the damages claimed by the plaintiff for the negligence, nuisance or breach of duty consist of or include damages in respect of personal injuries to any person...'[2]

The plaintiff says that these words do not cover an action for trespass to the person, and that, therefore, the time bar is not the new period of three years, but the old period of six years.

---

[2] [See now s. 11 of the Limitation Act 1980.]

The argument, as it was developed before us, became a direct invitation to this court to go back to the old forms of action and to decide this case by reference to them. The statute bars *an action on the case*, it is said, after three years, whereas *trespass to the person* is not barred for six years. The argument was supported by reference to text-writers, such as *Salmond on Torts* (13th edn) p. 790. I must say that if we are, at this distance of time, to revive the distinction between trespass and case, we should get into the most utter confusion. The old common lawyers tied themselves in knots over it, and we should find ourselves doing the same. Let me tell you some of their contortions. Under the old law, whenever one man injured another by the *direct* and immediate application of force, the plaintiff could sue the defendant in *trespass* to the person, without alleging negligence (see *Leame v Bray*),[3] whereas if the injury was only *consequential*, he had to sue in *case*. You will remember the illustration given by Fortescue J in *Reynolds v Clarke*, in 1752:[4]

> 'If a man throws a log into the highway and in that act it hits me, I may maintain trespass because it is an immediate wrong; but if, as it lies there, I tumble over it and receive an injury, I must bring an action upon the case because it is only prejudicial in consequence.'

Nowadays, if a man carelessly throws a piece of wood from a house into a roadway, then whether it hits the plaintiff or he tumbles over it the next moment, the action would not be *trespass* or *case*, but simply negligence. Another distinction which the old lawyers drew was this: If the driver of a horse and gig negligently ran down a passer-by, the plaintiff could sue the driver either in *trespass* or in *case* (see *Williams v Holland*, in 1833);[5] but if the driver was a servant, the plaintiff could not sue the master in trespass, but only in case (see *Sharrod v London and North Western Rly Co* in 1849).[6] In either case today, the action would not be *trespass* or *case*, but only negligence.

If we were to bring back these subtleties into the law of limitation, we should produce the most absurd anomalies; and all the more so when you bear in mind that under the Fatal Accidents Acts the period of limitation is three years from the death.[7] The decision of Elwes J, if correct, would produce these results. It would mean that if a motorist ran down two people, killing one and injuring another, the widow would have to bring her action within three years, but the injured person would have six years. It would mean also that if a lorry driver was in collision at a cross-roads with an owner-driver, an injured passenger would have to bring his action against the employer of the lorry driver within three years, but he would have six years in which to sue the owner-driver. Not least of all the absurdities in a case like the present. It would mean that the plaintiff could get out of the three-year limitation by suing in trespass instead of in negligence.

I must decline, therefore, to go back to the old forms of action in order to construe this statute. I know that in the last century Maitland said 'the forms of action we have buried but they still rule us from their graves'. But we have in this century shaken off their trammels. These forms of action have served their day. They did at one time form a guide to substantive rights; but they do so no longer. Lord Atkin told us what to do about them:

> 'When these ghosts of the past stand in the path of justice, clanking their mediaeval chains, the proper course for the judge is to pass through them undeterred',

see *United Australia Ltd v Barclays Bank Ltd*.[8]

The truth is that the distinction between trespass and case is obsolete. We have a different sub-division altogether. Instead of dividing actions for personal injuries into *trespass* (direct damage) or *case* (consequential damage), we divide the causes of action now according as the defendant did the injury intentionally or unintentionally. If one man intentionally applies force directly to another, the plaintiff has a cause of action in assault and battery, or, if you so please to describe it, in trespass to the person.

---

[3] (1803) 3 East 593.   [4] (1725) 1 Stra 634 at 636.   [5] (1833) 10 Bing 112.
[6] (1849) 4 Exch 580.   [7] [See now ss. 12–14 and 33 of the Limitation Act 1980.]
[8] [1941] AC 1 at 29, [1940] 4 All ER 20 at 37.

'The least touching of another in anger is a battery.' If he does not inflict injury intentionally, but only unintentionally, the plaintiff has no cause of action today in trespass. His only cause of action is in negligence, and then only on proof of want of reasonable care. If the plaintiff cannot prove want of reasonable care, he may have no cause of action at all. Thus, it is not enough nowadays for the plaintiff to plead that 'the defendant shot the plaintiff'.[9] He must also allege that he did it intentionally or negligently. If intentional, it is the tort of assault and battery. If negligent and causing damage, it is the tort of negligence.

The modern law on this subject was well expounded by my brother Diplock J in *Fowler v Lanning*[10] with which I fully agree. But I would go this one step further: when the injury is not inflicted intentionally, but negligently, I would say that the only cause of action is negligence and not trespass. If it were trespass, it would be actionable without proof of damage; and that is not the law today.

In my judgment, therefore, the only cause of action in the present case (where the injury was unintentional) is negligence and is barred by reason of the express provision of the statute.

[LORD DENNING then went on to deal with the position if, contrary to his view, the plaintiff had a cause of action in trespass, and decided that the phrase 'breach of duty' in the relevant legislation covered a cause of action in trespass. This was later disapproved by the House of Lords in *Stubbings v Webb* [1993] AC 498, [1993] 1 All ER 322, but *Stubbings v Webb* was in its turn deemed to be wrongly decided by the House of Lords in *A v Hoare* [2008] UKHL 6, [2008] 2 WLR 311, where the term 'breach of duty' in the Limitation Act 1980 was once again read as extending to causes of action in trespass against the person. LORD DENNING continued:]

I come, therefore, to the clear conclusion that the plaintiff's cause of action here is barred by the statute of limitation. Her only cause of action here, in my judgment (where the damage was unintentional), was negligence and not trespass to the person. It is therefore barred by the word 'negligence' in the statute...

I would allow the appeal accordingly.

DIPLOCK LJ:...

A cause of action is simply a factual situation the existence of which entitles one person to obtain from the court a remedy against another person. Historically the means by which the remedy was obtained varied with the nature of the factual situation and causes of action were divided into categories according to the 'form of action' by which the remedy was obtained in the particular kind of factual situation which constituted the cause of action; but that is legal history, not current law. If A, by failing to exercise reasonable care, inflicts direct personal injury on B, those facts constitute a cause of action on the part of B against A for damages in respect of such personal injuries. The remedy for this cause of action could, before 1873, have been obtained by alternative forms of action, namely, originally either trespass vi et armis or trespass on the case, later either trespass to the person or negligence. (See Bullen and Leake's *Precedents of Pleadings*, 3rd edn.) Certain procedural consequences, the importance of which diminished considerably after the Common Law Procedure Act 1852, flowed from the plaintiff's pleader's choice of the form of action used. The Supreme Court of Judicature Act 1873, abolished forms of action. It did not affect causes of action; so it was convenient for lawyers and legislators to continue to use, to describe the various categories of factual situations which entitled one person to obtain from the court a remedy against another, the names of the various 'forms of action' by which formerly the remedy appropriate to the particular category of factual situation was obtained. But it is essential to realise that when, since 1873, the name of a form of action is used to identify a cause of action, it is used as a convenient and succinct description of a particular category of factual situation which entitles one person to obtain from the court a remedy against another person. To forget this will indeed encourage the old forms of action to rule us from their graves.

If A, by failing to exercise reasonable care, inflicts direct personal injuries on B, it is permissible today to describe this factual situation indifferently, either as a cause of action in negligence or as a cause of

[9] See *Fowler v Lanning* [1959] 1 QB 426, [1959] 1 All ER 290.
[10] [1959] 1 QB 426, [1959] 1 All ER 290.

action in trespass, and the action brought to obtain a remedy for this factual situation as an action for negligence or an action for trespass to the person—though I agree with Lord Denning MR that today 'negligence' is the expression to be preferred. But no procedural consequences flow from the choice of description by the pleader (see *Fowler v Lannng*).[11] They are simply alternative ways of describing the same factual situation.

In the judgment under appeal, Elwes J[12] has held that the Law Reform (Limitation of Actions, &c.) Act 1954, has, by s. 2(1) created an important difference in the remedy to which B is entitled in the factual situation postulated according to whether he chooses to describe it as negligence or as trespass to the person. If he selects the former description, the limitation period is three years; if he selects the latter, the limitation period is six years. The terms of the subsection have already been cited, and I need not repeat them.

The factual situation on which the plaintiff's action was founded is set out in the statement of claim. It was that the defendant, by failing to exercise reasonable care (of which failure particulars were given), drove his motor car over the plaintiff's legs and so inflicted on her direct personal injuries in respect of which the plaintiff claimed damages. That factual situation was the plaintiff's cause of action. It was the cause of action 'for' which the plaintiff claimed damages in respect of the personal injuries which she sustained. That cause of action or factual situation falls within the description of the tort of 'negligence' and an action founded on it, that is, brought to obtain the remedy to which the existence of that factual situation entitles the plaintiff, falls within the description of an 'action for negligence'. The description 'negligence' was in fact used by the plaintiff's pleader; but this cannot be decisive, for we are concerned not with the description applied by the pleader to the factual situation and the action founded on it, but with the description applied to it by Parliament in the enactment to be construed. It is true that that factual situation also falls within the description of the tort of 'trespass to the person'. But that, as I have endeavoured to show, does not mean that there are two causes of action. It merely means that there are two apt descriptions of the same cause of action. It does not cease to be the tort of 'negligence', because it can also be called by another name. An action founded on it is none the less an 'action for negligence' because it can also be called an 'action for trespass to the person'.

It is not, I think, necessary to consider whether there is today any respect in which a cause of action for unintentional as distinct from intentional 'trespass to the person' is not equally aptly described as a cause of action for 'negligence'. The difference stressed by Elwes J[12] that actual damage caused by failure to exercise reasonable care forms an essential element in the cause of action for 'negligence', but does not in the cause of action in 'trespass to the person', is, I think, more apparent than real when the trespass is unintentional; for, since the duty of care, whether in negligence or in unintentional trespass to the person, is to take reasonable care to avoid causing actual damage to one's neighbour, there is no breach of the duty unless actual damage is caused. Actual damage is thus a necessary ingredient in unintentional as distinct from intentional trespass to the person. Whether this be so or not, the subsection which falls to be construed is concerned only with actions in which actual damage in the form of personal injuries has in fact been sustained by the plaintiff. Where this factor is present, every factual situation which falls within the description 'trespass to the person' is, where the trespass is unintentional, equally aptly described as negligence.

I am, therefore, of opinion that the facts pleaded in the present action make it an 'action for negligence...where the damages claimed by the plaintiff for the negligence...consist of or include damaged in respect of personal injuries to' the plaintiff, within the meaning of the subsection, and that the limitation period was three years....

[DANCKWERTS LJ agreed with LORD DENNING MR.]

Appeal allowed.

---

[11] [1959] 1 QB 426, [1959] 1 All ER 290.   [12] [1964] 1 All ER 669 at 673.

QUESTIONS

1. What do you understand by the 'forms of action'?
2. Shepherd threw a lighted squib into a crowded market house where it landed on the stall of Yates, a gingerbread seller. Willis, to prevent injury to himself and Yates' wares, instantly took up the squib and threw it across the market house, where it fell upon the stall of Ryal, who, to save his own goods, in turn picked it up and threw it away. It struck the claimant in the face and burst, putting out one of his eyes. In *Scott v Shepherd* (1773) 2 Wm Bl 892, the majority of the Court of King's Bench held that an action of trespass was properly brought against Shepherd. Blackstone J (dissenting) was of the opinion that Willis and Ryal, being free agents, were not 'instruments' in the hands of Shepherd, and so the damage was not sufficiently 'direct' for trespass to be maintainable. How would this case be pleaded today?
3. Does an action for trespass lie if the injury, though direct, was caused neither intentionally nor by negligence?
4. D accidentally parked his car on P's foot but refused to remove it when asked several times to do so. He then relented and moved the car. How would you plead this as a civil case, assuming alternatively that (a) P's foot was injured; (b) P suffered only momentary distress but no physical injury? (Cf. *Fagan v Metropolitan Police Comr* [1969] 1 QB 439, [1968] 3 All ER 442.)

NOTES

1. Those interested in exploring the history of trespass and case will derive pleasure from the research of S. F. C. Milsom, *Historical Foundations of the Common Law* 2nd edn (London, 1981), chap. 11, and his earlier articles (1958) 74 LQR 195, 407 and 561; (1965) 81 LQR 396, [1954] CLJ 105. See also D. J. Ibbetson, *A Historical Introduction to the Law of Obligations* (Oxford, 1999), chaps. 3, 4, 6, 8, 9 and 10. M. J. Prichard [1964] CLJ 234 provides an illuminating account of the line of cases which decided that the action upon the case for negligence overlapped trespass; more generally, see also the same author's Selden Society Lecture (published in 1976) entitled '*Scott v Shepherd* (1773) and the Emergence of the Tort of Negligence'.
2. A number of technical distinctions between negligent trespass to the person and the tort of negligence are suggested by F. A. Trindade (1971) 20 ICLQ 706, but recognising these distinctions in the common law may require the English courts to depart from *Fowler v Lanning* and *Letang v Cooper*, where negligent trespass is essentially treated as assimilated within and indistinguishable from the tort of negligence: see further A. J. Harding and K. F. Tan (1980) 22 Mal LR 29 at 32–33 (though see note 4, post). In *Miller v Jackson* [1977] QB 966, [1977] 3 All ER 338, Lord Denning MR reiterated his view (described as 'judicial legislation' by Bray CJ in *Venning v Chin* (1974–75) 10 SASR 299 at 307) that where injury is inflicted unintentionally, an action would not lie in trespass but only in negligence; and in *Wilson v Pringle* [1987] QB 237, [1986] 2 All ER 440 the idea that an action in trespass cannot be brought if the defendant has acted negligently met with support in the Court of Appeal. Note that Diplock LJ was less categorical in his judgment in *Letang*: his judgment leaves open the possibility that an action for unintentional trespass to the person may still be recognised in the common law, but took the approach that, in the context of construing the relevant provisions of

the Statute of Limitations, 'every factual situation which falls within the description "trespass to the person" is, where the trespass is unintentional, equally aptly described as negligence'. In other words, if careless or unintentional interference with the person can also be classified as 'negligence', then it should be treated as an act of negligence and not be simultaneously described as also constituting another form of action.

3.   In *Williams v Humphrey* (1975) Times, 20 February the defendant pushed the claimant into a swimming pool, with the result that the latter was injured when his foot struck the side of the pool. The defendant did not intend to cause any harm, but Talbot J found that the reasonable man would have foreseen the likelihood of harm to the claimant and the claimant succeeded in negligence. However, Talbot J went on to say that he could also succeed in trespass on proof that the defendant acted intentionally. Is this duality of action consistent with Lord Denning's judgment in *Letang v Cooper*? (Note also that in *Wilson v Pringle* the reasoning in *Williams v Humphrey* was said not to have gone far enough in that it did not require the claimant to establish that the defendant acted with an element of 'hostility'. However, this requirement is questionable: see p. 728, post.)

   Jolowicz has criticised the apparent assumption that appears to underlie the judgments in *Letang v Cooper* that in general only one description of the factual situation at issue is appropriate, i.e. that a claim based upon a specific set of facts should either be classified as negligence or trespass, but not as both, or that two separate but overlapping claims in negligence and trespass should not be capable of arising from the one set of facts: see [1964] CLJ 200 at 202. It would certainly be an unusual anomaly within the framework of the common law if a claimant was always obliged to fit the facts of their claim within the framework of either trespass or negligence, but not both. It is common across tort law for a number of causes of action to be based upon the same set of facts, and for claimants successfully to sustain a claim under one cause of action while failing in respect of others: see e.g. *Kaye v Robertson* [1991] FSR 92. The assumption underlying *Williams v Humphrey* appears to be that it is possible for separate trespass and negligence claims to be founded on the same set of facts: the same assumption appears to underlie the decision in *Ashley v Chief Constable of Sussex Police* [2008] 2 WLR 975, [2008] UKHL 25.

   This approach seems also to have also been implicitly endorsed in *Bici v Ministry of Defence* [2004] EWHC 786, [2004] The Times, 11 June, where Elias J treated the shooting of civilians in a car in Kosovo by British soldiers on peace-keeping duties as a factual event capable of giving rise to claims for both negligence and trespass to the person. The soldiers were held to have breached a duty of care and thereby were negligent: but Elias J also was of the view that the soldiers could be liable in trespass on the basis of the doctrine of 'transferred intent', whereby if a person performs an act with the intention of striking another, but accidentally strikes another person instead, the intent is 'transferred' and the defendant will be liable to the struck person (see below at p. 725). Following the approach taken by Hutton J in *Livingstone v Ministry of Defence* [1984] NILR 356, Elias J in *Bici* specifically rejected the contention by counsel for the Ministry that the judgments in *Letang v Cooper* precluded the possibility that an intention to strike can be 'transferred'.

   See further Trindade (1982) 2 Oxf JLS 211, at 212–213; cf. *Paterson Zochonis & Co Ltd v Merfarken Packaging Ltd* [1986] 3 All ER 522 at 541.

4.   In *Wilson v Pringle* [1987] QB 237, [1986] 2 All ER 440, the important question arose as to whether the necessary intention for a trespass action to be available had to relate to

the contact with the claimant or to the infliction of the injury. Counsel for the defendant argued that it was both, citing passages from *Fowler v Lanning* (Diplock J's first proposition, p. 718, ante) and *Letang v Cooper*. It will have been seen that in *Letang v Cooper* Lord Denning does distinguish between trespass and negligence in terms of the *injury* being inflicted intentionally or unintentionally (see p. 721, ante). However, in the Court of Appeal's view, in *Wilson v Pringle* it was only the defendant's *act* which had to be intentional in a trespass action and neither Lord Denning's judgment nor Diplock J's first proposition in *Fowler v Lanning* were intended to support a requirement of intention to *injure* in such a case (see [1987] QB at p. 249). For support for this view, see F. A. Trindade (1982) 2 Oxf JLS 211, at 219–220 (and note ibid pp. 220–225 for discussion of the nature of intention in this context). In *Bici v Ministry of Defence*, as discussed ante, Elias J followed the approach taken by Hutton J in *Livingstone v Ministry of Defence* [1984] NILR 356 and held that if a person performs an act with the intention of striking another, but accidentally strikes another person instead, the intent is 'transferred' and the defendant will be liable to the struck person. This concept of 'transferred intent' strongly supports the concept that the required intention must relate to the performance of the act, not to the injury that occurs.

5. Persistent uncertainty has surrounded the issue of whether a reckless act by the defendant, either in the form of an act involving gross negligence or an act done with subjective disregard for its consequences, which results in contact will be sufficient to satisfy the requirement for intention to be present before a claim in trespass can be brought. At first glance, reckless acts might be viewed as falling on the negligence side of the line drawn in *Fowler* and *Letang*. However, given the importance of the interest in personal freedom and autonomy that underpins the torts that comprise the generic category of trespass to the person, an argument could be made that recklessness as to the consequences of the act in question should be capable of satisfying the intention requirement.

6. This argument could apply with particular force to false imprisonment, which the House of Lords described in *R v Governor of Brockhill Prison, ex p Evans (No 2)* [2001] 2 AC 19, [2000] 4 All ER 15 as a 'tort of strict liability'. What apparently was meant by this reference was that if a defendant intentionally performed an act which led to the confinement of the claimant, then liability would arise even if the defendant was unaware that the act would result in false imprisonment. This well-established position stems from the value the common law places on the freedom of the individual. Given this, a case could even be made that negligence may be a sufficient state of mind for the tort of false imprisonment in particular. The issue was raised in Ralph Gibson LJ's judgment in *Weldon v Home Office* [1992] 1 AC 58 at 135 (when that case was in the Court of Appeal), but his Lordship found it unnecessary to consider the point. However, if *Letang v Cooper* is followed without deviation, what is the position today of someone who is negligently falsely imprisoned?

One related issue that might be raised (and which would become very important if deprivation of liberty resulting from negligence could not give rise to an action for false imprisonment) is whether a deprivation of liberty for a short time period will constitute actionable damage for the purposes of the tort of negligence, given that such an imprisonment will often not produce tangible losses to the claimant (see Harding and Tan, op cit., and P. G. Heffey (1983) 14 Melb ULR 53, at 57–64). As is pointed out by U. Burnham (1998) 61 MLR 573, the Court of Appeal in *W v Home Office* [1997] Imm AR 302 regarded detention as damage for the purposes of a negligence action, although this was obiter as the Court of Appeal first rejected a duty of care on the part of the immigration officers in the case. (Note that the House of Lords in *Watkins v Home Office* [2006] 2 All ER 353, [2006] UKHL 17 took the view that the tort of misfeasance in public office, which also touches upon fundamental pubic interests, was not actionable per se in the absence of damages, unlike the trespass to the person torts. However, the Court of Appeal has subsequently determined that loss of liberty counts as special damage for the purpose of a misfeasance suit: *Karagozlu v Metropolitan Police Commissioner* [2007] 2 All ER 1055, [2006] EWCA Civ 1691.)

In the light of the difficulty of suing public bodies in the tort of negligence, and the importance of the interest in personal freedom at stake here, Burnham op cit. argues for a re-assessment of the views in *Letang v Cooper* and for the right to sue for negligent false imprisonment to be recognised as part of trespass to the person. In general, the strict demarcation lines used in *Letang v Cooper* to distinguish between trespass and negligence may be open to the criticism of being too rigid.

2 ASSAULT AND BATTERY

■ Stephens v Myers
Nisi Prius (1830) 4 C & P 349

Assault. The declaration stated, that the defendant threatened and attempted to assault the plaintiff. Plea—Not guilty.

It appeared, that the plaintiff was acting as chairman, at a parish meeting, and sat at the head of a table, at which table the defendant also sat, there being about six or seven persons between him and the plaintiff. The defendant having, in the course of some angry discussion, which took place, been very vociferous, and interrupted the proceedings of the meeting, a motion was made, that he should be turned out, which was carried by a very large majority. Upon this, the defendant said, he would rather pull the chairman out of the chair, than be turned out of the room; and immediately advanced with his fist clenched towards the chairman, but was stopt by the churchwarden, who sat next but one to the chairman, at a time when he was not near enough for any blow he might have meditated to have reached the chairman; but the witnesses said, that it seemed to them that he was advancing with an intention to strike the chairman.

Spankie, Serjt., for the defendant, upon this evidence, contended, that no assault had been committed, as there was no power in the defendant, from the situation of the parties, to execute his threat—there was not a present ability—he had not the means of executing his intention at the time he was stopt.

TINDAL CJ in his summing up, said: . . .
It is not every threat, when there is no actual personal violence, that constitutes an assault, there must, in all cases, be the means of carrying the threat into effect. The question I shall leave to you will be, whether the defendant was advancing at the time, in a threatening attitude, to strike the chairman, so that his blow would almost immediately have reached the chairman, if he had not been stopt; then, though he was not near enough at the time to have struck him, yet if he was advancing with that intent, I think it amounts to an assault in law. If he was so advancing, that, within a second or two of time, he would have reached the plaintiff, it seems to me it is an assault in

law. If you think he was not advancing to strike the plaintiff, then only can you find your verdict for the defendant; otherwise you must find it for the plaintiff, and give him such damages, as you think the nature of the case requires.

Verdict for the plaintiff—Damages, 1s.

QUESTIONS

1. Would there have been an assault in this case if the defendant 'was not advancing to strike the claimant', but the claimant reasonably believed that he was?
2. Would there be sufficient immediacy for an assault if the defendant, having entered an enclosed garden in the evening, intentionally frightened the claimant by looking through a closed window at her? (Consider *Smith v Chief Superintendent, Woking Police Station* (1983) 76 Cr App Rep 234.) What if the window had bars on it?

NOTES

1. It was said in *Thomas v National Union of Mineworkers* [1986] Ch 20, [1985] 2 All ER 1 that there had to be the ability to carry out the immediate intention to commit the battery at the time the act (accompanied by the intention) occurred. But note that this comment was made in the context of a situation in which the inability so to act would have been apparent. A particular problem which has arisen in this area is whether it is an assault to point an unloaded gun at a person. In *R v St George* (1840) 9 C & P 483, Parke B stated in the course of argument (at p. 490), that 'it is an assault to point a weapon at a person, though not loaded, but so near, that if loaded, it might do injury' (see also p. 493). The view of Lord Abinger CB in *Blake v Barnard* (1840) 9 C & P 626 is in conflict with that of Parke B, but in neither case is the ratio of the decision entirely clear. However, Parke B's view is difficult to reconcile with the later view in *R v Ireland* [1998] AC 147, [1997] 4 All ER 225, noted by J. Herring [1998] CLJ 10 and S. Gardner (1998) 114 LQR 33, where the House of Lords accepted that a silent telephone call could, depending on the circumstances, constitute an assault. Lord Steyn stated that the recipient of a call might apprehend the imminent arrival at the door of the caller and might fear the possibility of immediate personal violence. As Herring points out (op cit., p. 12), the requirement of immediacy is being relaxed, since 'the fear of violence need not be of immediate violence—fear that violence may occur in a few minutes time was sufficient; and the victim need only fear that violence *might* occur'. However, see *Mbasago v Logo Ltd* [2006] EWCH Civ. 1370, [71]–[82].
2. There has been uncertainty as to the intention required to commit assault. In *Read v Coker* (1853) 13 CB 850, it was suggested that intent to put the claimant in fear of an immediate battery was required, but in *Bici v Ministry of Defence* [2004] EWHC 786, Elias J required that a defendant must have intended to put the claimant in fear of immediate violence. The distinction appears abstract: however, in *Bici*, Elias J considered that while there was intent on the part of the soldiers to commit a battery which was 'transferred' to the ultimate victim, there was no intention to put any of the claimants in fear of violence, and so the claim in assault failed. Also, the victim was shot from behind, and therefore in Elias J's view would not have been put in immediate fear. This approach, while generating some rather abstract reasoning in *Bici*, appears in line with the definition of assault given by Lord Hope in *R v Ireland* at [1997] 4 All ER 225

at 239 as 'any act by which the defendant, intentionally or recklessly, causes the claimant to apprehend immediate and unlawful personal violence'.

■ Tuberville v Savage
Court of King's Bench (1669) 1 Mod Rep 3

Action of *assault*, *battery* and *wounding*. The evidence to prove a provocation was, that the plaintiff put his hand upon his sword and said, *'If it were not assize-time, I would not take such language from you.'*—The question was, If that were an assault?—The Court agreed that it was not; for the declaration of the plaintiff was, that he would not assault him, the Judges being in town; and *the intention* as well as *the act* makes an assault. Therefore if one strike another upon the hand, or arm, or breast in discourse, it is no assault, there being no *intention* to assault; but if one, intending to assault, strike *at* another and miss him, this is an assault: so if he hold up his hand against another in a threatening manner and say nothing, it is an assault.—In the principal case the plaintiff had judgment.

QUESTION

Would there have been an assault if the assizes were ending that day?

NOTE

As *Tuberville v Savage* shows, words accompanying an act may lead the court to deny that there has been any assault. In contrast, it has also been accepted for some time that words accompanied by threatening actions could constitute an assault: see *Read v Coker* (1853) 13 CB 850. However, there has been a conflict of authority on the question of whether words alone can amount to an assault. For general discussion, see G. Williams [1957] Crim LR 219; P. R. Handford (1976) 54 Can Bar Rev 563 at 568–573; Trindade (1982) 2 Oxf JLS at pp. 231–233. *R v Ireland* [1998] AC 147, [1997] 4 All ER 225 has now established that words can constitute an assault (as can silent telephone calls: see note 1, p. 727, ante).

■ Cole v Turner
Nisi Prius (1704) 6 Mod Rep 149

HOLT CJ: Upon evidence in trespass for assault and battery, declared,

First, that the least touching of another in anger is a battery.

Secondly, if two or more meet in a narrow passage, and without any violence or design of harm, the one touches the other gently, it will be no battery.

Thirdly, if any of them use violence against the other, to force his way in a rude inordinate manner, it will be a battery; or any struggle about the passage to that degree as may do hurt, will be a battery....

NOTE

It will have been seen that Holt CJ refers to the touching of another 'in anger' as being a battery. In *Wilson v Pringle* [1987] QB 237, [1986] 2 All ER 440 the Court of Appeal, relying, amongst other authorities, on *Cole v Turner*, asserted that for the touching of another to be a battery it has to be 'hostile'; they did not think it 'practicable to define a battery as "physical contact which is not generally acceptable in the ordinary conduct of daily life"'. This latter view had been expressed by Robert Goff LJ when discussing the defences in this area of the law in the Divisional Court in *Collins v Wilcock* [1984] 3 All ER 374, [1984] 1 WLR 1172, part of which is set out at p. 756, post.

Having asserted the 'hostility' requirement, the Court of Appeal in *Wilson v Pringle* continued (at pp. 447–448):

Hostility cannot be equated with ill-will or malevolence. It cannot be governed by the obvious intention shown in acts like punching, stabbing or shooting. It cannot be solely governed by an expressed intention, although that may be strong evidence. But the element of hostility, in the sense in which it is now to be considered, must be a question of fact for the tribunal of fact. It may be imported from the circumstances. Take the example of the police officer in *Collins v Wilcock*. She touched the woman deliberately, but without an intention to do more than restrain her temporarily. Nevertheless, she was acting unlawfully and in that way was acting with hostility. She was acting contrary to the woman's legal right not to be physically restrained.

This example shows that in this context 'hostility' can take on a meaning rather wider than its everyday sense. Is the penultimate sentence of this passage from *Wilson v Pringle* an example of circular reasoning?

Collins v Wilcock and *Wilson v Pringle* were discussed in *T v T* [1988] Fam 52, [1988] 1 All ER 613, where Robert Goff LJ's analysis was found by Wood J to be of greater assistance than the analysis in *Wilson v Pringle*. In *Re F* [1990] 2 AC 1, sub nom *F v West Berkshire Health Authority (Mental Health Act Commission intervening)* [1989] 2 All ER 545 (p. 757, post), Lord Goff reiterated his approach in *Collins v Wilcock* and expressed doubt about the 'hostility' requirement.

In *R v Brown* [1994] 1 AC 212, [1993] 2 All ER 75, the House of Lords adopted the language of 'hostility', but essentially defined a 'hostile' act as an unlawful interference: see e.g. Lord Slynn's speech (at p. 280), where the hostility requirement is regarded as met if what is done is done intentionally and against the wishes of the recipient. However, subsequent decisions have indicated a preference for Lord Goff's approach in *Collins v Wilcock* and *Re F*. In *Wainwright v Home Office* [2003] 4 All ER 969 at 973, Lord Hoffmann defined battery as involving 'a touching of the person with what is sometimes called hostile intent (as opposed to a friendly pat on the back) but which Robert Goff LJ in *Collins v Wilcock* [1984] 3 All ER 374 at 378, [1984] 1 WLR 1172 at 1177 redefined as meaning any intentional physical contact which was not "generally acceptable in the ordinary conduct of daily life"'. Lord Hoffman then also cited *Wilson v Pringle*, muddying the waters a little. Nevertheless, the use in *Wainwright* of Lord Goff's formulation has resulted in its further application by Tugendhat J in *KD v Chief Constable of Hampshire* [2005] EWHC 2550 (QB), who also approved Lord Denning's remark in *R v Chief Constable of Devon and Cornwall, ex p CEGB* [1982] QB 458, at 471, that 'an unwanted kiss may be a battery', which is difficult to reconcile with the concept of 'hostility'. Lord Goff's formulation appears to have the advantage of being more precise than the vague and potentially highly misleading use of 'hostility', and now appears to be largely accepted following its adoption in *Wainwright*.

■ Innes v Wylie

Nisi Pruis (1844) 1 Car & Kir 257

The plaintiff belonged to a Society which purported to expel him, and a policeman, acting under the defendants' orders, stopped the plaintiff from entering a room to attend a dinner of the Society. For reasons which need not be mentioned here, Lord Denman CJ took the view that the expulsion was invalid, but his summing up to the jury also dealt with the question of assault.

LORD DENMAN CJ: . . .
You will say, whether, on the evidence, you think that the policeman committed an assault on the plaintiff, or was merely passive. If the policeman was entirely passive like a door or a wall put to prevent the plaintiff from entering the room, and simply obstructing the entrance of the plaintiff, no assault has been committed on the plaintiff, and your verdict will be for the defendant. The question is, did the policeman take any active measures to prevent the plaintiff from entering the room, or did he stand in the door-way passive, and not move at all.

Verdict for the plaintiff, damages 40s.

[A motion for a new trial was later made, but without success.]

NOTES

As *Innes v Wylie* shows, a positive act will be usually required for an action to lie in battery, but see *Fagan v Metropolitan Police Comr* [1969] 1 QB 439, [1968] 3 All ER 442. Also, the contact required for a claim in battery to be made out must be direct. This requirement, originally the product of the distinctions between the historical forms of action, still plays an important role, as can be seen in the extracts from *Letang v Cooper*, above. The requirement of 'directness' can be satisfied if an intermediary object is used, such as the bullets in *Bici v Ministry of Defence* (noted p. 724, ante), or even if body-to-body contact does not occur: spitting has been held to constitute a battery (see *R v Cotesworth* (1704) 3 Mod 172, 87 ER 928).

■ The Offences Against the Person Act 1861

44.[13] **If the magistrates shall dismiss any complaint of assault or battery, they shall make out a certificate to that effect.**—If the justices, upon the hearing of any case of assault or battery upon the merits, where the complaint[14] was preferred by or on behalf of the party aggrieved, shall deem the offence not to be proved, or shall find the assault or battery to have been justified, or so trifling as not to merit any punishment, and shall accordingly dismiss the complaint,[14] they shall forthwith make out a certificate under their hands stating the fact of such dismissal, and shall deliver such certificate to the party against whom the complaint[14] was preferred.

45. Certificate or conviction shall be a bar to any other proceedings.—if any person against whom any such complaint[14] as [is mentioned in section 44 of this Act][15] shall have been preferred by or on the behalf of the party aggrieved shall have obtained such certificate, or, having been convicted, shall have paid the whole amount adjudged to be paid, or shall have suffered the imprisonment or imprisonment with hard labour[16] awarded, in every such case he shall be released from all further or other proceedings, civil or criminal, for the same cause.

NOTES

1.   The problem of interpretation of these provisions are considered by P. M. North (1966) 29 MLR 16, who points out, incidentally, that the rule which bars later civil proceedings

---

[13] Law Reform (Limitation of Actions, &c.) Act 1954, s. 2(1).
[14] As amended by the Criminal Justice Act 1988, s. 170, Sch. 15 and Sch. 16.
[15] The word should now be read as 'information'—Magistrates' Courts Act 1980, s 50.
[16] Added by the Criminal Justice Act 1988, s. 170 and Sch. 15.

'can easily be evaded by the simple expedient of suing first and making a complaint later'. He concludes (at p. 31): 'The moral is: sue first. This does not detract from the conclusion that section 45 does appear to be based upon the fallacious assumption that the rules of civil and criminal liability for assault and battery are identical.' In *Wong v Parkside Health NHS Trust* [2003] 3 All ER 932, [2001] EWCA Civ 1721, the Court of Appeal confirmed that s. 45 of the 1861 Act precluded a claimant who had brought a private prosecution against a defendant for assault from subsequently bringing any other claim under any other cause of action in respect of that assault: the prosecution 'destroyed' any right to bring another claim on the same facts. Hale LJ acknowledged the 'anomalous' situation the Act produced, given the different standards of proof for civil and criminal actions, but concluded that the courts had no choice but to apply the provisions of s. 45.

2. In 1980 the Criminal Law Revision Committee's Fourteenth Report (*Offences Against the Person*, Cmnd. 7844) recommended repeal (without replacement) of ss. 44 and 45 of the 1861 Act (paras. 163–164); but no such legislative activity occurred.

3. Under s. 130(1)(a) and (b) of the Powers of Criminal Courts (Sentencing) Act 2000, where a person is convicted of an offence, the court may 'make an order…requiring him to pay compensation for any personal injury, loss or damage resulting from that offence or any other offence which is taken into consideration by the court in determining sentence or to make payments for funeral expenses or bereavement in respect of a death resulting from any such offence, other than a death due to an accident arising out of the presence of a motor vehicle on a road'. (Previously, provision for these powers had been made in s. 35 of the Powers of Criminal Courts Act 1973, as amended by s. 67 of the Criminal Justice Act 1982 and s. 104 of the Criminal Justice Act 1988.) Furthermore, under s. 130(3), a court is obliged to give reasons if it does not make an order when it could do so under this section. Section 130(6) contains provisions limiting the situations in which compensation orders can be made in relation to injury, loss or damage resulting from road accidents involving a motor vehicle. Section 130(10) also limits compensation orders in relation to bereavement: such an order can only be made for the benefit of anyone entitled to claim such damages under the Fatal Accidents Act 1976 (p. 280, ante) and the amount awarded may not exceed the amount fixed under that legislation. The means of the offender must be considered by the court (s. 130(11), but see s. 130(12)). Where later civil proceedings are brought, no attention should be paid to an earlier compensation order in *assessing* the damages 'but the claimant may only recover an amount equal to the aggregate of the following—(a) any amount by which they exceed the compensation; and (b) a sum equal to any portion of the compensation which he fails to recover' (s. 134). (Enforcement of the judgment, so far as it relates to this latter sum, requires the leave of the court.) See further s. 133 dealing with the review of an order. Note also that there is a limit imposed on the amount magistrates' courts can award under a compensation order (s. 131), which at present stands at £5,000. P. S. Atiyah [1979] Crim LR 503 pointed to the uncertainty surrounding the question whether a compensation order could be made in a case in which there could be no civil liability, but it was later held in *R v Chappell* (1985) 80 Cr App Rep 31 that civil liability is not a pre-condition to the making of a compensation order.

4. A person who has been intentionally injured may recover compensation from the Criminal Injuries Compensation Scheme, discussed in more detail p. 1158, post. Note also that if a confiscation order is made against the defendant under the Proceeds of Crime Act 2002, victims can be compensated using money derived from the confiscated

sum. If it is clear that there would otherwise be insufficient means to compensate the victim, the court must order the shortfall to be paid from the confiscated sum.

5. Note the provisions of s. 329 of the Criminal Justice Act 2003, discussed at p. 480, ante.

3 FALSE IMPRISONMENT

■ Murray v Ministry of Defence
House of Lords [1988] 2 All ER 521

For the purposes of this extract it is sufficient to say that one issue raised in the case concerned an unsuccessful claim for damages for false imprisonment for a period for 7 a.m. to 7.30 a.m., that the House of Lords held that the plaintiff had been under arrest (under s. 14 of the Northern Ireland (Emergency Provisions) Act 1978) during this period, and that the House rejected the challenge to the legality of the arrest. (In later proceedings before the European Court of Human Rights (1994) 19 EHRR 193, no breach of the European Convention on Human Rights was found.)

LORD GRIFFITHS: . . .

Although on the facts of this case I am sure that the plaintiff was aware of the restraint on her liberty from 7.00 am, I cannot agree with the [Northern Ireland] Court of Appeal that it is an essential element of the tort of false imprisonment that the victim should be aware of the fact of denial of liberty. The Court of Appeal relied on *Herring v Boyle* (1834) 1 Cr M & R 377, 149 ER 1126 for this proposition which they preferred to the view of Atkin LJ to the opposite effect in *Meering v Grahame-White Aviation Co Ltd* (1919) 122 LT 44. *Herring v Boyle* is an extraordinary decision of the Court of Exchequer: a mother went to fetch her 10-year-old son from school on 24 December 1833 to take him home for the Christmas holidays. The headmaster refused to allow her to take her son home because she had not paid the last term's fees, and he kept the boy at school over the holidays. An action for false imprisonment brought on behalf of the boy failed. In giving judgment Bolland B said (1 Cr M & R 366 at 381, 149 ER 1126 at 1127):

> '. . . as far as we know, the boy may have been willing to stay; he does not appear to have been cognizant of any restraint, and there was no evidence of any act whatsoever done by the defendant in his presence. I think that we cannot construe the refusal to the mother in the boy's absence, and without his being cognizant of any restraint, to be an imprisonment of him against his will . . .'

I suppose it is possible that there are schoolboys who prefer to stay at school rather than go home for the holidays but it is not an inference that I would draw, and I cannot believe that on the same facts the case would be similarly decided today. In *Meering v Grahame-White Aviation Co Ltd* the plaintiff's employers, who suspected him of theft, sent two of the works police to bring him in for questioning at the company's offices. He was taken to a waiting-room where he said that if he was not told why he was there he would leave. He was told he was wanted for the purpose of making inquiries about things that had been stolen and he was wanted to give evidence; he then agreed to stay. Unknown to the plaintiff, the works police had been instructed not to let him leave the waiting-room until the Metropolitan Police arrived. The works police therefore remained outside the waiting-room and would not have allowed the plaintiff to leave until he was handed over to the Metropolitan Police, who subsequently arrested him. The question for the Court of Appeal was whether on this evidence the plaintiff was falsely imprisoned during the hour he was in the waiting-room, or whether there could be no 'imprisonment' sufficient to found a civil action unless the plaintiff was aware of the restraint on his liberty.

ATKIN LJ said (122 LY 44 at 53–54): . . .

> 'It appears to me that a person could be imprisoned without his knowing it. I think a person can be imprisoned while he is asleep, while he is in a state of drunkenness, while he is unconscious, and while he is a lunatic. Those are cases where it seems to me that the person might properly complain if he were imprisoned, though the imprisonment began and ceased while he was in that state. Of course, the damages might be diminished and would be affected by the question whether he was conscious of it or not. So a man might in fact, to my mind, be imprisoned by having the key of a door turned against him so that he is imprisoned in a room in fact although he does not know that the key has been turned. It may be that he is being detained in that room by persons who are anxious to make him believe that he is not in fact being imprisoned, and at the same time his captors outside that room may be boasting to persons that he is imprisoned, and it seems to me that if we were to take this case as an instance supposing it could be proved that Prudence had said while the plaintiff was waiting: "I have got him detained there waiting for the detective to come in and take him to prison"—it appears to me that that would be evidence of imprisonment. It is quite unnecessary to go on to show that in fact the man knew that he was imprisoned. If a man can be imprisoned by having the key turned upon him without his knowledge, so he can be imprisoned if, instead of a lock and key or bolts and bars, he is prevented from, in fact, exercising his liberty by guards and warders or policemen. They serve the same purpose. Therefore it appears to me to be a question of fact. It is true that in all cases of imprisonment so far as the law of civil liberty is concerned that "stone walls do not a prison make," in the sense that they are not the only form of imprisonment, but any restraint within defined bounds which is a restraint in fact may be an imprisonment.'

I agree with this passage. In the first place it is not difficult to envisage cases in which harm may result from unlawful imprisonment even though the victim is unaware of it. Dean William L Prosser gave two examples in 'False Imprisonment: Consciousness of Confinement' (1955) 55 Col LR 847, in which he attacked § 42 of the American Law Institute's Restatement of the Law of Torts, which at that time stated the rule that 'there is no liability for intentionally confining another unless the person physically restrained knows of the confinement'. Dean Prosser wrote (at 849):

> 'Let us consider several illustrations. A locks B, a child two days old, in the vault of a bank. B is, of course, unconscious of the confinement, but the bank vault cannot be opened for two days. In the meantime, B suffers from hunger and thirst, and his health is seriously impaired; or it may be that he even dies. Is this no tort? Or suppose that A abducts B, a wealthy lunatic, and holds him for ransom for a week. B is unaware of his confinement, but vaguely understands that he is in unfamiliar surroundings, and that something is wrong. He undergoes mental suffering affecting his health. At the end of the week, he is discovered by the police and released without ever having known that he has been imprisoned. Has he no action against B? . . . If a child of two is kidnapped, confined, and deprived of the care of its mother for a month, is the kidnapping and the confinement in itself so minor a matter as to call for no redress in tort at all?'

The Restatement of the Law of Torts has now been changed and requires that the person confined 'is conscious of the confinement or is harmed by it' (see Restatement of the Law, Second, Torts 2nd (1965) § 35, p. 52).

If a person is unaware that he has been falsely imprisoned and has suffered no harm, he can normally expect to recover no more than nominal damages, and it is tempting, to redefine the tort in the terms of the present rule in the American Law Institute's Restatement of the Law of Torts. On reflection, however, I would not do so. The law attaches supreme importance to the liberty of the individual and if he suffers a wrongful interference with that liberty it should remain actionable even without proof of special damage. . . .

[LORD KEIGH OF KINKEL, LORD TEMPLEMAN, LORD OLIVER OF AYLMERTON, and LORD JAUNCEY OF TULLICHETTLE agreed with LORD GRIFFITHS' speech.]

NOTES

1. A person who loses their liberty as a result of being falsely imprisoned is entitled to general damages: see *Roberts v Chief Constable of the Cheshire Constabulary* [1999] 2 All ER 326 [1999] 1 WLR 662, and *Thompson v Metropolitan Police Commissioner* [1998] QB 498, [1997] 2 All ER 762 (p. 498, ante). As with the other trespass to the person torts, a claimant need not show any special damage: the loss of liberty itself entitles the claimant to damages and other forms of relief. Note however that, as mentioned by Lord Griffiths in *Murray v Ministry of Defence*, in the absence of knowledge of the imprisonment and of any harm, the claimant can normally only expect to be awarded nominal damages. However, it should be noted that in appropriate circumstances—see p. 493, ante—exemplary damages would be available to such a person.

2. Atkin LJ's views in *Meering v Grahame-White Aviation Co Ltd* (1919) 122 LT 44 at 53–54 were approved in *Murray* and also in *R v Deputy Governor of Parkhurst Prison, ex p Hague* [1992] 1 AC 58 at 134 by Ralph Gibson LJ (whose judgment met with agreement from Parker and Fox LJJ) when one of the two consolidated appeals in *Hague* was in the Court of Appeal (sub nom *Weldon v Home Office*) and seemingly also in *Hague* at p. 174 by Lord Jauncey in the House of Lords. The importance which the courts place on protecting a person's liberty was emphasised by Ralph Gibson LJ in the judgment just mentioned, when he said that it appears that if someone was falsely imprisoned in a room, liability would not be affected by the fact that the person would not have had occasion to leave the room in the relevant period, whilst acknowledging that this might affect damages. However, for criticism of *Murray*, see G. Williams (1991) 54 MLR 408 at 411–412, who makes the point that the passage extracted ante from *Murray* is obiter.

3. One issue facing the House of Lords in *R v Deputy Governor of Parkhurst Prison, ex p Hague* [1992] 1 AC 58, [1991] 3 All ER 733 was whether a prisoner could be falsely imprisoned by the prison governor, or prison officers acting under his authority, by being confined in an area within the prison. The House's answer was in the negative, even if the confinement in question was in breach of the Prison Rules 1964. (On the question of any action for the tort of breach of statutory duty in this case, see p. 680, ante.) The reason for this lay in s. 12(1) of the Prison Act 1952, which provides that a 'prisoner…may be lawfully confined in any prison' and the lack, under the prison regime, of any 'residual liberty' on the part of the prisoner in relation to the prison governor which the law would protect. In other words, the *detention itself* was lawful, even if the *conditions* of detention were in breach of the Prison Rules, and therefore the claimant could not succeed in his claim for false imprisonment.

4. Note that some criticisms can be made of the *Hague* decision. The decision ensures that a prisoner has minimal 'residual liberty' once held in lawful detention. The concern present in some of their Lordships' judgments that the existence of a common law remedy in false imprisonment would be incompatible with the absence of a remedy for breach of statutory duty under the Prison Rules is not wholly convincing: both causes of action are separate and distinct, and whether each applies should arguably be considered separately. Nevertheless, in *Cullen v Chief Constable of the RUC* [2004] 2 All ER 237, [2003] UKHL 39 (p. 699, ante), the House of Lords confirmed that a claim for false imprisonment would not succeed where the right to access to a solicitor provided for in s. 15(1)(a) of the Northern Ireland (Emergency Provisions) Act 1987 had been violated: the denial of access did not render the detention unlawful.

5. It should be noted that alternative remedies may be available to a prisoner for unlawful conditions of detention. In *Karagozlu v Metropolitan Police Commissioner* [2007] 2

All ER 1055, [2006] EWCA Civ 1691, a prisoner who was moved from open conditions as a category D prisoner to closed conditions in a category B prison as a result of false information passed maliciously to the prison authorities by a police officer was able to recover damages for his loss of liberty under the tort of misfeasance in public office: the Court of Appeal considered that deprivation of liberty constituted actionable loss for the purposes of misfeance in public office (see also p. 726, ante). Where imprisonment is by a 'public authority' as defined by s. 6 of the Human Rights Act, damages and additional relief may also be available, as Article 5 of the ECHR provides that '[n]o one shall be deprived of his liberty save in the following cases and in accordance with a procedure prescribed by law'. However, the English courts have taken the view that a defence of lawful imprisonment that is sufficient for the purposes of an action for false imprisonment will usually also suffice to satisfy Article 5: see e.g. *R v Leeds Crown Court, ex p Wardle* [2001] 2 All ER 1. However, see the important decision of the European Court of Human Rights in *HL v United Kingdom* (2005) 40 EHRR 32 (p. 739, post).

6. The House of Lords in *R v Deputy Governor of Parkhurst Prison, ex p Hague* did indicate that the position in respect of the availability of a claim in false imprisonment is different if the more restricted confinement is imposed by a prison official acting in bad faith or by a fellow-prisoner. Lord Ackner would allow an action against a fellow-prisoner in this situation. Lord Jauncey (with whom Lord Lowry agreed) also suggested that the case of the fellow-prisoner could be distinguished from that of the governor, but did not need to decide the matter. Nevertheless, he did go on to indicate (as did Lord Ackner) that in general there could be liability for confining to a more restricted area someone who was already subject to a measure of restriction. Thus, for example, a miner who had contracted to stay down a mine during his shift could be falsely imprisoned if locked in the lift at the bottom of the mine shaft. On the position of prison officers, see now *Toumia v Evans* (1999) Times, 1 April. In this case the Court of Appeal regarded it as arguable having regard to the comments of Lord Jauncey and others in *Hague* that it was false imprisonment for a prison officer to lock a prisoner in his cell contrary to the governor's orders and also to fail to unlock a cell contrary to the normal working duties.

7. Another point canvassed in the *Hague* case concerned the question whether an imprisonment was rendered unlawful if the conditions of imprisonment became intolerable. There had been support for this idea in the Court of Appeal in both *Middleweek v Chief Constable of the Merseyside Police (Note)* [1992] 1 AC 179, [1990] 3 All ER 662 and the two cases (*Weldon v Home Office* and *Hague*) which were consolidated in the appeal to the House of Lords in *Hague*. An example given in *Middleweek* was where a cell became and remained badly flooded, thereby seriously prejudicing the health of the prisoner. However, in the House of Lords in *Hague* the possibility of suing for damages for false imprisonment where the conditions of imprisonment became intolerable was rejected. The House was not prepared to read this limit into the authority for imprisonment contained in s. 12(1) of the Prison Act 1952 (and it would seem the same would apply to other statutory or contractual authority justifying imprisonment). The solution to the problem in the House's opinion lay in the availability of other remedies, a particular one being a negligence action based on the 'custodian' duty of care to the prisoner. On one aspect of this action, however, there seemed to be some difference of opinion amongst their Lordships. Lord Bridge would allow an action for pain and intolerable discomfort even though there was no physical injury or damage to health; but Lords Ackner and Jauncey only referred to injury to health being actionable in this tort, and

Lord Goff required the damage in question to be an accepted type of damage in the tort of negligence (which pain and discomfort in the absence of physical injury or damage to health (including psychiatric illness) would not be). The Human Rights Act may provide a remedy where detention conditions violated the prohibition on inhuman and degrading treatment contained in Article 3 of the ECHR: see e.g. *Napier v Scottish Ministers* [2005] SC 307, IH (prison 'slopping out' regime held to violate Article 3 of the ECHR).

8. Another aspect of the prison regime to raise issues of false imprisonment was considered by the House of Lords in *R v Governor of Brockhill Prison, ex p Evans (No 2)* [2001] 2 AC 19, [2000] 4 All ER 15. Here, Evans was sentenced to four concurrent terms of two years imprisonment but, as she had spent time in custody before sentence, she was entitled to a reduction in the actual period to be served. The prison governor, acting in accordance with Home Office guidelines, calculated that her release date would be 18 November 1996. However, subsequent judicial review proceedings established that the guidelines were wrong and her release date should have been 17 September 1996. Evans brought proceedings for false imprisonment for the period between the two dates and succeeded before the House of Lords, recovering £5,000 in damages. Their Lordships held that false imprisonment can be seen as a tort of strict liability, whereby if the prison governor intended the act of continued imprisonment but the continued detention was unlawful, then the elements of the cause of action were made out. As a consequence, the action for false imprisonment could not be escaped even by showing that a defendant had acted in accordance with a view of the law which was accepted as correct at the time. For comment and criticism, see P. Cane (2001) 117 LQR 5. Note that in *Quinland v Governor of Swaleside Prison* [2003] 1 All ER 1173, [2002] EWCA Civ 174, the (pre-*Evans*) case of *Olutu v Home Office* [1997] 1 All ER 385, [1997] 1 WLR 328 was applied by the Court of Appeal in finding that, as the mistaken detention in question was the result of a mistaken calculation by the judge at trial rather than the prison governor (unlike the case in *Evans*), the continued detention was 'lawful'.

9. The question of when detention is lawful also arises where police detain individuals under their powers of arrest and detention. This is discussed further below (see p. 774)—for now, it is sufficient to note that justification is viewed in the main as a defence to a claim for false imprisonment and therefore the onus appears to be on the defendant to establish the lawfulness of detention. This appears consistent with the approach adopted by the House of Lords in *R (on the application of Laporte) v Chief Constable of Gloucestershire Constabulary* [2007] 2 All ER 529, [2006] UKHL 55 and the Court of Appeal in *Austin v Metropolitan Police Comr* [2008] 1 All ER 564, [2007] EWCA Civ 989.

10. The requirement that the acts leading to false imprisonment (as with the other torts within the generic trespass to the person category) be 'direct' was important in *Davidson v Chief Constable of North Wales* [1994] 2 All ER 597, where the Court of Appeal held that a store detective who gave incorrect information to the police which lead to the claimant's imprisonment could not be held liable for false imprisonment, as the arrest had not been caused 'directly' by the defendant. The police had an independent discretion whether to arrest, meaning that the link between the actions of the defendant and the eventual arrest was too indirect to generate liability. (The police had a lawful authorisation for the arrest under s. 24 of the Police and Criminal Evidence Act 1984.)

■ Bird v Jones

Court of Queen's Bench (1845) 7 QB 742

The following statement of facts is taken from the judgment of Patteson J: 'A part of Hammersmith Bridge which is ordinarily used as a public footway was appropriated for seats to view a regatta on the river, and separated for that purpose from the carriage way by a temporary fence. The plaintiff insisted on passing along the part so appropriated, and attempted to climb over the fence. The defendant, being clerk of the Bridge Company, seized his coat, and tried to pull him back: the plaintiff, however, succeeded in climbing over the fence. The defendant then stationed two policemen to prevent, and they did prevent, the plaintiff from proceeding forwards along the footway; but he was told that he might go back into the carriage way, and proceed to the other side of the bridge, if he pleased. The plaintiff would not do so, but remained where he was above half an hour: and then, on the defendant still refusing to suffer him to go forwards along the footway, he endeavoured to force his way, and, in so doing, assaulted the defendant: whereupon he was taken into custody.' By virtue of the pleadings in the case, the question arose whether there had been an imprisonment of the plaintiff before he committed the assault. At the trial the Lord Chief Justice told the jury that there had, and a rule nisi for a new trial was obtained on the ground of misdirection:

COLERIDGE J: . . .

And I am of opinion that there was no imprisonment. To call it so appears to me to confound partial obstruction and disturbance with total obstruction and detention. A prison may have its boundary large or narrow, visible and tangible, or, though real, still in the conception only; it may itself be moveable or fixed: but a boundary it must have; and that boundary the party imprisoned must be prevented from passing; he must be prevented from leaving that place, within the ambit of which the party imprisoning would confine him, except by prison-breach. Some confusion seems to me to arise from confounding imprisonment of the body with mere loss of freedom: it is one part of the definition of freedom to be able to go whithersoever one pleases; but imprisonment is something more than the mere loss of this power; it includes the notion of restraint within some limits defined by a will or power exterior to our own.

. . . If, in the course of a night, both ends of a street were walled up, and there was no egress from the house but into the street, I should have no difficulty in saying that the inhabitants were thereby imprisoned; but, if only one end were walled up, and an armed force stationed outside to prevent any scaling of the wall or passage that way, I should feel equally clear that there was no imprisonment. If there were, the street would obviously be the prison; and yet, as obviously, none would be confined to it.

Knowing that my Lord has entertained strongly an opinion directly contrary to this, I am under serious apprehension that I overlook some difficulty in forming my own: but, if it exists, I have not been able to discover it, and am therefore bound to state that, according to my view of the case, the rule should be absolute for a new trial.

PATTESON J: . . .

But imprisonment is, as I apprehend, a total restraint of the liberty of the person, for however short a time, and not a partial obstruction of his will, whatever inconvenience it may bring on him. . . .

LORD DENMAN CJ [dissenting]: . . .

I had no idea that any person in these times supposed any particular boundary to be necessary to constitute imprisonment, or that the restraint of a man's person from doing what he desires ceases to be an imprisonment because he may find some means of escape.

It is said that the party here was at liberty to go in another direction. I am not sure that in fact he was, because the same unlawful power which prevented him from taking one course might, in case of acquiescence, have refused him any other. But this liberty to do something else does not appear to me to affect the question of imprisonment. As long as I am prevented from doing what I have a right to do, of what importance is it that I am permitted to do something else? How does the imposition of an unlawful condition shew that I am not restrained? If I am locked in a room, am I not imprisoned because I might effect my escape through a window, or because I might find an exit dangerous or inconvenient to myself, as by wading through water or by taking a route so circuitous that my necessary affairs would suffer by delay?

It appears to me that this is a total deprivation of liberty with reference to the purpose for which he lawfully wished to employ his liberty: and, being effected by force, it is not the mere obstruction of a way, but a restraint of the person. . . .

[WILLIAMS J also delivered a judgment to the effect that there was no imprisonment on these facts.]

Rule made absolute.

NOTE

At one point in *Bird v Jones* Coleridge J referred to imprisonment, including the 'notion of restraint within some limits defined by a will or power exterior to our own'. Consider in this connection the case of *Pritchard v Ministry of Defence* (1995) Times, 27 January, which concerned service in the Army, where there are restrictions on the movement of soldiers. Even if the powers of compulsion over soldiers, which are enforceable by military law, were not exercised, the view was taken that their existence meant that there had been an imprisonment. On the facts, though, it was held that the claimant had been lawfully required to serve in the Army during the disputed period.

Compare *Bird v Jones* with *Austin v Metropolitan Police Comr* [2008] 1 All ER 564, [2007] EWCA Civ 989, where confinement was held to exist where several hundred people were held within a police cordon for up to seven hours in Oxford Circus in order to prevent a breach of the peace.

Bird v Jones should also be compared with *R v Bournewood Community and Mental Health NHS Trust, ex p L* [1999] AC 458, [1998] 3 All ER 289, noted by J. Dawson (1999) 115 LQR 40. Here, a severely disturbed man was admitted to a mental hospital as a voluntary patient. It was decided that he did not need to be formally detained under the Mental Health Act 1983, as he appeared compliant and did not resist admission, so he was admitted informally. The House of Lords had to consider whether the patient in these circumstances had been unlawfully detained. A majority held that he was not restrained, even though, had he attempted to leave, he would have been restrained, since the deprivation of liberty must be actual, not potential. Lord Goff referred to the distinction drawn in *Meering v Grahame-White Aviation Co* (1919) 122 LT 44 at 54–55 between 'restraint upon the claimant's liberty which is conditional upon his seeking to exercise his freedom (which would not amount to false imprisonment), and an actual restraint upon his liberty, as where the defendant decided to restrain the claimant within a room and placed a policeman outside the door to stop him leaving (which would amount to false imprisonment)'. Dissenting on this issue (with Lord Nolan), Lord Steyn regarded the defendant's argument that the patient was always free to leave the hospital as one which 'stretches credulity to breaking point', although he agreed with the rest of their Lordships that the NHS Trust's appeal should nonetheless be allowed, since the detention was justified by the principle of necessity, preserved in the relevant provisions of the Mental Health Act 1983. (See further on this point p. 763, post.) Is the thrust of the majority decision in *Bournewood* reconcilable with *Murray v Ministry of Defence* [1988] 2 All ER 521 (p. 732, ante), given that the requirement for actual restraint would appear to require the claimant in this situation to have actual knowledge of their imprisonment?

Subsequently, the European Court of Human Rights in *HL v United Kingdom* (2005) 40 EHRR 32 held that the claimant in *Bournewood* had been detained in a manner that violated his right to liberty under Article 5 of the ECHR, and that the UK government had failed to make out a defence under Article 5(1)(e) of the ECHR on the basis that there were insufficient safeguards in UK law to protect against arbitrary deprivation of liberty. (Also, the Strasbourg court found a violation of Article 5(4), on the grounds that the applicant had inadequate means available to challenge the legality of his detention.) The Strasbourg Court took the view that the scope of the common law's concept of false imprisonment as adopted by the majority in *Bournewood* was insufficiently narrow and formalistic to accord with the Convention concept of 'deprivation of liberty' under Article 5.

■ HL v United Kingdom
European Court of Human Rights (2005) 40 EHRR 32

[89] It is not disputed that in order to determine whether there has been a deprivation of liberty, the starting-point must be the concrete situation of the individual concerned and account must be taken of a whole range of factors arising in a particular case such as the type, duration, effects and manner of implementation of the measure in question. The distinction between a deprivation of, and a restriction upon, liberty is merely one of degree or intensity and not one of nature or substance (see *Guzzardi v. Italy*, judgment of 6 November 1980, Series A no. 39, p. 33, § 92...).

[90] The Court observes that the High Court and the majority of the House of Lords found that the applicant had not been detained during this period, while the Court of Appeal and a minority of the House of Lords found that he had. Although this Court will have regard to the domestic courts' related findings of fact, it does not consider itself bound by their legal conclusions as to whether the applicant was detained or not, not least because the House of Lords considered the question from the point of view of the tort of false imprisonment (see paragraph 39 above) rather than the Convention concept of "deprivation of liberty" in Article 5 § 1, the criteria for assessing those domestic and Convention issues being different.

In this latter respect, considerable emphasis was placed by the domestic courts, and by the Government, on the fact that the applicant was compliant and never attempted, or expressed the wish, to leave. The majority of the House of Lords specifically distinguished actual restraint of a person (which would amount to false imprisonment) and restraint which was conditional upon his seeking to leave (which would not constitute false imprisonment). The Court does not consider such a distinction to be of central importance under the Convention. Nor, for the same reason, can the Court accept as determinative the fact relied on by the Government that the regime applied to the applicant (as a compliant incapacitated patient) did not materially differ from that applied to a person who had the capacity to consent to hospital treatment, neither objecting to their admission to hospital. The Court reiterates that the right to liberty is too important in a democratic society for a person to lose the benefit of Convention protection for the single reason that he may have given himself up to be taken into detention (see *De Wilde, Ooms and Versyp v. Belgium*, judgment of 18 June 1971, Series A no. 12, p. 36, §§ 64–65), especially when it is not disputed that that person is legally incapable of consenting to, or disagreeing with, the proposed action.

[91] ...Accordingly, the concrete situation was that the applicant was under continuous supervision and control and was not free to leave. Any suggestion to the contrary is, in the Court's view, fairly described by Lord Steyn as "stretching credulity to breaking point" and as a "fairy tale" (see paragraph 46 above)...

[The Court therefore considered that the applicant had been deprived of his liberty within the meaning of Article 5(1) of the Convention. The Court then held that the UK government had failed to show that the detention was "in accordance with a procedure prescribed by law" and "lawful" within the meaning of Article 5(1) (e): see p. 774, post.]

NOTE

The decision in *HL* indicates that the English courts will have to adopt a broader concept of deprivation of liberty when the ECHR is in play than the standard adopted in *Bournewood*. However, the Court of Appeal in *Austin v Metropolitan Police Comr* [2008] 1 All ER 564, [2007] EWCA Civ 989 considered that the detention of a large group of individuals at Oxford Circus for an extended time did constitute confinement for the purposes of false imprisonment, but not a deprivation of liberty for the purposes of Article 5 of the ECHR. It appears doubtful that *Austin* is reconcilable with *HL v United Kingdom*.

■ Robinson v Balmain New Ferry Co Ltd
Judicial Committee of the Privy Council [1910] AC 295

The plaintiff, who intended to cross a harbour on the defendant company's ferry, paid one penny to enter the company's wharf. Between the wharf and the street there was a barrier with two turnstiles, and a notice board (above the turnstiles and on each side of the barrier) stated that a penny must be paid on entering or leaving the wharf, whether or not the passenger had used the ferry. The practice of the company was to collect fares on one side of the harbour only. The plaintiff, who had gone through the entry turnstile, discovered that there would be a twenty minute wait before the next steamer left, and, wishing to leave the wharf, he approached the exit turnstile. He refused to pay a penny, however, and was prevented from forcing his way out for some time by two of the company's officers. On appeal from a decision of the High Court of Australia by the plaintiff who claimed damages for assault and false imprisonment:

LORD LOREBURN LC [delivering the judgment of their Lordships]: . . .
There was no complaint, at all events there was no question left to the jury by the plaintiff's request, of any excessive violence, and in the circumstances admitted it is clear to their Lordships that there was no false imprisonment at all. The plaintiff was merely called upon to leave the wharf in the way in which he contracted to leave it. There is no law requiring the defendants to make the exit from their premises gratuitous to people who come there upon a definite contract which involves their leaving the wharf by another way; and the defendants were entitled to resist a forcible passage through their turnstile.

The question whether the notice which was affixed to these premises was brought home to the knowledge of the plaintiff is immaterial, because the notice itself is immaterial.

When the plaintiff entered the defendants' premises there was nothing agreed as to the terms on which he might go back, because neither party contemplated his going back. When he desired to do so the defendants were entitled to impose a reasonable condition before allowing him to pass through their turnstile from a place to which he had gone of his own free will. The payment of a penny was a quite fair condition, and if he did not choose to comply with it the defendants were not bound to let him through. He could proceed on the journey he had contracted for. . . .

Their Lordships will humbly advise His Majesty that this appeal should be dismissed with costs.

QUESTION

Why was the notice immaterial?

■ Herd v Weardale Steel, Coal and Coke Co Ltd

House of Lords [1915] AC 67

The appellant (and his fellow workers) descended the respondent company's mine at 9.30 am and he would have been entitled to be raised to the surface at the end of his shift (about 4 pm) by a cage which was used at other times to carry coal. The cage was, in fact, the only way out of the mine. The appellant, whose verbal contract of service provided for fourteen days' notice on either side, refused to do certain work which he had been told to do on the grounds that it was unsafe, and also that the instruction was in breach of an oral agreement between the men's representative and the colliery manager. At about 11 am he asked to be allowed to use the cage, but this request was refused. The appellant was not allowed to use the cage until approximately 1.30 pm, although it had been standing at the bottom of the mine shaft since 1.10 pm and could have been used to carry him to the surface. He was employed subject to the provisions of the Coal Mines Regulation Acts 1887–1908, certain rules established under the 1887 Act and an agreement between the Durham Coal Owners' Association and the Durham Miners' Association. One of the terms of his contract was that he should be raised from the mine at the end of his shift, and a notice containing the times of raising and lowering, which had been fixed under the 1887 Act and the agreement, was posted at the pit head. In an earlier action the company were awarded 5s. damages for the appellant's breach of contract. The appellant sued for damages for false imprisonment, but Pickford J's judgment in his favour was reversed by the Court of Appeal, [1913] 3 KB 771. An appeal to the House of Lords was dismissed.

VISCOUNT HALDANE LC:...

My Lords, by the law of this country no man can be restrained of his liberty without authority in law. That is a proposition the maintenance of which is of great importance; but at the same time it is a proposition which must be read in relation to other propositions which are equally important. If a man chooses to go into a dangerous place at the bottom of a quarry or the bottom of a mine, from which by the nature of physical circumstances he cannot escape, it does not follow from the proposition I have enunciated about liberty that he can compel the owner to bring him up out of it. The owner may or may not be under a duty arising from circumstances, on broad grounds the neglect of which may possibly involve him in a criminal charge or a civil liability. It is unnecessary to discuss the conditions and circumstances which might bring about such a result, because they have, in the view I take, nothing to do with false imprisonment.

My Lords, there is another proposition which has to be borne in mind and that is the application of the maxim volenti non fit injuria. If a man gets into an express train and the doors are locked pending its arrival at its destination, he is not entitled, merely because the train has been stopped by signal, to call for the doors to be opened to let him out. He has entered the train on the terms that he is to be conveyed to a certain station without the opportunity of getting out before that, and he must abide by the terms on which he has entered the train. So when a man goes down a mine, from which access to the surface does not exist in the absence of special facilities given on the part of the owner of the mine, he is only entitled to the use of these facilities (subject possibly to the exceptional circumstances to which I have alluded) on the terms on which he has entered. I think it results from what was laid down by the Judicial Committee of the Privy Council in *Robinson v Balmain New Ferry Co.*[17] that that is so. There was a pier, and by the regulations a penny was to be paid by those who entered and a penny on getting out. The manner of the exit gate refused to allow a man who had gone in, having paid his penny, but having changed his mind about embarking on a steamer, and wishing to return, to come out without paying his penny. It was held that that was not false imprisonment; volenti non fit injuria. The man had gone in upon the pier knowing that those were the terms and conditions as to exit, and

[17] The courts may no longer sentence to imprisonment with hard labour: Criminal Justice Act 1948, s. 1(2).

it was not false imprisonment to hold him to conditions which he had accepted. So, my Lords, it is not false imprisonment to hold a man to the conditions he has accepted when he goes down a mine.

My Lords, I do not wish to be understood as saying that no other question than that of contract comes into this case, for the Coal Mines Regulation Act 1887 lays down a statutory obligation on the owner of mines to provide access to the surface, and it lays down conditions as regards the availability of that access. but the material point is this: that on considering the provisions of that statute I find nothing which entitles a miner to claim to use the winding-up cage at any moment he pleases. It may be that the cage is full of coal; it may be that it is employed in drawing other people up; it may be that it is very inconvenient for other reasons to use it at the moment. It is enough that no right is given by statute which enables the workman to claim to use the cage at any moment he pleases.

Now, my Lords, in the present case what happened was this. The usage of the mine—a usage which I think must be taken to have been notified—was that the workman was to be brought up at the end of his shift. In this case the workman refused to work; it may have been for good reasons or it may have been for bad,—I do not think that question concerns us. He said that the work he had been ordered to do was of a kind that was dangerous, and he threw down his tools and claimed to come up to the surface. The manager, or at any rate the person responsible for the control of the cage, said: 'No, you have chosen to come at a time which is not your proper time, and although there is the cage standing empty we will not bring you up in it,' and the workman was in consequence under the necessity of remaining at the bottom of the shaft for about twenty minutes. There was no refusal to bring him up at the ordinary time which was in his bargain; but there was a refusal,—and I am quite ready to assume that the motive of it was to punish him, I will assume it for the sake of argument, for having refused to go on with his work—by refusing to bring him up at the moment when he claimed to come. Did that amount to false imprisonment? In my opinion it did not. No statutory right under the Coal Mines Regulation Act 1887 avails him, for the reason which I have already spoken of. Nor had he any right in contract. His right in contract was to come up at the end of his shift. Was he then falsely imprisoned? There were facilities, but they were facilities which, in accordance with the conditions that he had accepted by going down, were not available to him until the end of his shift, at any rate as of right.

My Lords, under these circumstances I find it wholly impossible to come to the conclusion that the principle to which I have alluded, and on which the doctrine of false imprisonment is based, has any application to the case. Volenti non fit injuria. The man chose to go to the bottom of the mine under these conditions,—conditions which he accepted. He had no right to call upon the employers to make use of special machinery put there at their cost, and involving cost in its working, to bring him to the surface just when he pleased. . . .

[LORD SHAW OF DUNFERMLINE and LORD MOULTON delivered speeches in favour of dismissing the appeal.]

QUESTIONS

1. Does Viscount Haldane's explanation of *Robinson's* case accord with what is stated in that case? (See M. S. Amos (1928) 44 LQR 464, at 465–466.)
2. Once the miners got to the surface would it have been false imprisonment for the respondent to have stopped them leaving the colliery before the end of their shift by (a) refusing to unlock the gates of the pit yard, or (b) locking those gates? (See *Burns v Johnston* [1916] 2 IR 444; affd [1917] 2 IR 137 cited by G. Williams, 'Two Cases on False Imprisonment', in Holland and Schwarzenberger (eds.) *Law, Justice and Equity* (1967), chap. 5, an essay which discusses both *Herd*'s case and *Robinson*'s case.)
3. Could it be argued that the employer in *Herd* had not performed a positive act and therefore had not directly interfered with the claimants? Or is it more accurate to describe the employer as refusing permission to the employees to ascend as a punishment, and

therefore committing a direct interference (see the dissenting opinion of Vaughan Williams LJ in the Court of Appeal)?

NOTE

In his essay entitled 'Two Cases on False Imprisonment' (loc cit), Glanville Williams concludes that '*Robinson*'s case is of small general interest because it is confined to a situation that is not likely to occur frequently. A condition may be attached to exit, but only when the claimant has a choice of two exits, A and B, the condition being attached to A. Further, no condition may be attached when exit B is extremely onerous.... Nor does the decision apply when the condition attached to exit A is unreasonable, unless exit B gives practically immediate freedom. If exit B is in an intermediate position, neither being extremely onerous nor giving practically immediate freedom, the reasonableness of the condition attached to exit A becomes relevant; and this is the only case where it is relevant.' For further discussion of *Herd*'s case and *Robinson*'s case, see K. F. Tan (1981) 44 MLR 166.

4 WRONGFUL INTERFERENCE

■ Wilkinson v Downton

Queen's Bench Division [1895–99] All ER Rep 267

WRIGHT J:...
read a judgment in which he referred to the plaintiff's allegations, in the statement of claim, and continued: The defendant, in the execution of what he seems to have regarded as a practical joke, represented to the female plaintiff that he was charged by her husband with a message to her to the effect that the husband had been smashed up in an accident, and was lying at the Elms public-house at Leytonstone with both legs broken, and that she was to go at once in a cab to fetch him home. All this was false. The effect of this statement on the female plaintiff was a violent shock to the nervous system producing vomiting and other more serious and permanent physical consequences, at one time threatening her reason and entailing weeks of suffering and incapacity to her as well as expense to her husband for medical treatment of her. These consequences were not in any way the result of previous ill-health or weakness of constitution, nor was there any evidence of predisposition to nervous shock or of any other idiosyncrasy. In addition to these matters of substance there is a small claim for 1s 10½d for the cost of railway fares of persons sent by the female plaintiff to Leytonstone in obedience to the pretended message. As to this 1s 10½d expended in railway fares on the faith of the defendant's statement, it is clearly within the scope of the decision in *Pasley v Freeman*.[18] It was a misrepresentation intended to be acted on to the damage of the plaintiff.

The real question is as to the £100, the greatest part of which is given as compensation for the female plaintiff's illness and suffering. It was argued for her that she is entitled to recover this as being damage caused by fraud, and, therefore, within the doctrine established by *Pasley v Freeman*[18] and *Langridge v Levy*.[19] I am not sure that this would not be an extension of that doctrine, the real ground of which appears to be that a person who makes a false statement, intending it to be acted on, must make good the damage naturally resulting from its being acted on. Here is no injuria of that kind. I think, however, that the verdict may be supported on another ground. The defendant has, as I assume for the moment,

---

[18] [1910] AC 295.   [19] (1789) 3 Term Rep 51.

wilfully done an act calculated to cause physical harm to the female plaintiff, i.e., to infringe her legal right to personal safety, and has thereby in fact caused physical harm to her. That proposition, without more, appears to me to state a good cause of action, there being no justification alleged for the act. This wilful injuria is in law malicious, although no malicious purpose to cause the harm which was caused, nor any motive of spite, is imputed to the defendant.

It remains to consider whether the assumptions involved in the proposition are made out. One question is whether the defendant's act was so plainly calculated to produce some effect of the kind which was produced, that an intention to produce it ought to be imputed to the defendant regard being had to the fact that the effect was produced on a person proved to be in an ordinary state of health and mind. I think that it was. It is difficult to imagine that such a statement, made suddenly and with apparent seriousness, could fail to produce grave effects under the circumstances upon any but an exceptionally indifferent person, and therefore an intention to produce such an effect must be imputed, and it is no answer in law to say that more harm was done than was anticipated, for that is commonly the case with all wrongs. The other question is whether the effect was, to use the ordinary phrase, too remote to be in law regarded as a consequence for which the defendant is answerable. Apart from authority I should give the same answer, and on the same grounds, as to the last question, and say that it was not too remote. Whether, as the majority of the Lords thought in *Lynch v Knight*,[20] the criterion is in asking what would be the natural effect on reasonable persons, or whether, as Lord Wensleydale thought, the possible infirmities of human nature ought to be recognised, it seems to me that the connection between the cause and the effect is sufficiently close and complete....

Judgment for plaintiffs.

NOTE

For the present position where nervous shock is *negligently* inflicted, see chap. 3, ante.

■ Janvier v Sweeney

Court of Appeal [1918–19] All ER Rep 1056

This was an appeal by Sweeney, a private detective and Barker, his assistant from a judgment for the plaintiff for £250 entered by Avory J sitting with a jury.

BANKES LJ:...

The case for the plaintiff was that she was employed by a lady in whose house she resided, and that, on 16 July 1917, a man called at the house and told her that he was a detective inspector from Scotland Yard representing the military authorities and that she was the woman they wanted as she had been corresponding with a German spy. The plaintiff said that she was extremely frightened, with the result that she suffered from a severe nervous shock, and she attributed a long period of nervous illness to the shock she received from the language used to her on that occasion. If she could establish the truth of that story and satisfy the jury that her illness was the direct result of the shock, she was entitled to maintain this action. At the trial the defendants disputed the plaintiff's story altogether....These matters were entirely for the jury. The court cannot interfere with their findings merely because it might think the opposite inference preferable. It is clear that the learned judge would not have arrived at the same conclusion as the jury. The defendants cannot complain of the summing-up. But in spite of that summing-up in favour of the defendants, the jury accepted the plaintiff's story, and their findings as to the words used by Barker is not challenged in this court. We must take it then that Barker went to this house and deliberately threatened the plaintiff in order to induce or compel her to commit a gross breach of the duty[1] she owed to her employer.

---

[20] (1861) 9 HL Cas 577.

[1] I.e. to allow him to see some letters in the possession of a resident in the house.

It is no longer contended that this was not a wrongful act which would amount to an actionable wrong if damage which the law recognises can be shown to have flowed directly from that act. But counsel for the defendant, Barker, contended that no action would lie for words followed by such damage as the plaintiff alleges here. In order to sustain that contention it would be necessary to overrule *Wilkinson v Downton*.[3] In my opinion, that judgment was right. It has been approved in subsequent cases. It did not create any new rule of law, though it may be said to have extended existing principles over an area wider than that which they had been recognised as covering, because the court there accepted the view that the damage there relied on was not in the circumstances too remote in the eye of the law....

DUKE LJ:...
I am anxious not to overlay or weaken the force of the judgment which has just been delivered, with every word of which I agree. My observations will, therefore, be brief. This is a much stronger case than *Wilkinson v Downton*.[2] In that case there was no intention to commit a wrongful act; the defendant merely intended to play a joke upon the plaintiff. In the present case there was an intention to terrify the plaintiff for the purpose of attaining an unlawful object in which both the defendants were jointly concerned....

[A. T. LAWRENCE J delivered a judgment in favour of dismissing the appeal.]

Appeal dismissed.

■ Protection from Harassment Act 1997

1 Prohibition of harassment
(1) A person must not pursue a course of conduct—

(a) which amounts to harassment of another, and

(b) which he knows or ought to know amounts to harassment of the other.

(2) For the purposes of this section, the person whose course of conduct is in question ought to know that it amounts to harassment of another if a reasonable person in possession of the same information would think the course of conduct amounted to harassment of the other.

(3) Subsection (1) does not apply to a course of conduct if the person who pursued it shows—

(a) that it was pursued for the purpose of preventing or detecting crime,

(b) that it was pursued under any enactment or rule of law or to comply with any condition or requirement imposed by any person under any enactment, or

(c) that in the particular circumstances the pursuit of the course of conduct was reasonable.

2 Offence of harassment
(1) A person who pursues a course of conduct in breach of section 1 is guilty of an offence.

(2) A person guilty of an offence under this section is liable on summary conviction to imprisonment for a term not exceeding six months, or a fine not exceeding level 5 on the standard scale, or both.

3 Civil remedy
(1) An actual or apprehended breach of section 1 may be the subject of a claim in civil proceedings by the person who is or may be the victim of the course of conduct in question.

(2) On such a claim, damages may be awarded for (among other things) any anxiety caused by the harassment and any financial loss resulting from the harassment.

(3) Where—

(a) in such proceedings the High Court or a county court grants an injunction for the purpose of restraining the defendant from pursuing any conduct which amounts to harassment, and

[2] [1897] 2 QB 57.

(b) the plaintiff considers that the defendant has done anything which he is prohibited from doing by the injunction,

the plaintiff may apply for the issue of a warrant for the arrest of the defendant.

(4) An application under subsection (3) may be made—

(a) where the injunction was granted by the High Court, to a judge of that court, and

(b) where the injunction was granted by a county court, to a judge or district judge of that or any other county court.

(5) The judge or district judge to whom an application under subsection (3) is made may only issue a warrant if—

(a) the application is substantiated on oath, and

(b) the judge or district judge has reasonable grounds for believing that the defendant has done anything which he is prohibited from doing by the injunction.

(6) Where—

(a) the High Court or a county court grants an injunction for the purpose mentioned in subsection (3)(a), and

(b) without reasonable excuse the defendant does anything which he is prohibited from doing by the injunction,

he is guilty of an offence.

(7) Where a person is convicted of an offence under subsection (6) in respect of any conduct, that conduct is not punishable as a contempt of court.

(8) A person cannot be convicted of an offence under subsection (6) in respect of any conduct which has been punished as a contempt of court.

(9) A person guilty of an offence under subsection (6) is liable—

(a) on conviction on indictment, to imprisonment for a term not exceeding five years, or a fine, or both, or

(b) on summary conviction, to imprisonment for a term not exceeding six months, or a fine not exceeding the statutory maximum, or both.

4 Putting people in fear of violence

(1) A person whose course of conduct causes another to fear, on at least two occasions, that violence will be used against him is guilty of an offence if he knows or ought to know that his course of conduct will cause the other so to fear on each of those occasions.

(2) For the purposes of this section, the person whose course of conduct is in question ought to know that it will cause another to fear that violence will be used against him on any occasion if a reasonable person in possession of the same information would think the course of conduct would cause the other so to fear on that occasion.

(3) It is a defence for a person charged with an offence under this section to show that—

(a) his course of conduct was pursued for the purpose of preventing or detecting crime,

(b) his course of conduct was pursued under any enactment or rule of law or to comply with any condition or requirement imposed by any person under any enactment, or

(c) the pursuit of his course of conduct was reasonable for the protection of himself or another or for the protection of his or another's property.

(4) A person guilty of an offence under this section is liable—

(a) on conviction on indictment, to imprisonment for a term not exceeding five years, or a fine, or both, or

(b) on summary conviction, to imprisonment for a term not exceeding six months, or a fine not exceeding the statutory maximum, or both.

(5) If on the trial on indictment of a person charged with an offence under this section the jury find him not guilty of the offence charged, they may find him guilty of an offence under section 2.

(6) The Crown Court has the same powers and duties in relation to a person who is by virtue of subsection (5) convicted before it of an offence under section 2 as a magistrates' court would have not convicting him of the offence.

5 Restraining orders

(1) A court sentencing or otherwise dealing with a person ('the defendant') convicted of an offence under section 2 or 4 may (as well as sentencing him or dealing with him in any other way) make an order under this section.

(2) The order may, for the purpose of protecting the victim of the offence, or any other person mentioned in the order, from further conduct which—

(a) amounts to harassment, or

(b) will cause a fear of violence,

prohibit the defendant from doing anything described in the order.

(3) The order may have effect for a specified period or until further order.

(4) The prosecutor, the defendant or any other person mentioned in the order may apply to the court which made the order for it to be varied or discharged by a further order.

(5) If without reasonable excuse the defendant does anything which he is prohibited from doing by an order under this section, he is guilty of an offence.

(6) A person guilty of an offence under this section is liable—

(a) on conviction on indictment, to imprisonment for a term not exceeding five years, or a fine, or both, or

(b) on summary conviction, to imprisonment for a term not exceeding six months, or a fine not exceeding the statutory maximum, or both.

6 Limitation

In section 11 of the Limitation Act 1980 (special time limit for actions in respect of personal injuries), after subsection (1) there is inserted—

'(1A) This section does not apply to any action brought for damages under section 3 of the Protection from Harassment Act 1997.'

7 Interpretation of this group of sections

(1) This section applies for the interpretation of sections 1 to 5.

(2) References to harassing a person include alarming the person or causing the person distress.

(3) A 'course of conduct' must involve conduct on at least two occasions.

(3A) A person's conduct on any occasion shall be taken, if aided, abetted, counselled or procured by another

(a) to be conduct on that occasion of the other (as well as conduct of the person whose conduct it is); and

(b) to be conduct in relation to which the other's knowledge and purpose, and what he ought to have known, are the same as they were in relation to what was contemplated or reasonably foreseeable at the time of the aiding, abetting, counselling or procuring summary conviction, to imprisonment for a term not exceeding six months, or a fine not exceeding the statutory maximum, or both.

(4) 'Conduct' includes speech.

NOTES

1.   This statute makes harassment a criminal offence and provides for civil remedies as well. In many respects, the ambit of the statute is far wider than the common law

principle derived from *Wilkinson v Downton*. For example, s. 1(2) sets an objective standard for defining a course of conduct which amounts to harassment, so that it appears to be irrelevant whether or not the defendant intended to cause harassment or realised that in fact they were so doing. Under ss. 3(1), (2), compensation can include relief for anxiety and distress, but these forms of harm are not a requirement for liability to arise under the Act: all that suffices is that harassment has taken place. So far as civil remedies are concerned, the courts can order both damages and injunctions (s. 3). The remedies are available even where the harassment does not cause the claimant to fear that violence will be used.

2.   The scope of what constitutes harassment is potentially very wide: in *Thomas v News Group* [2002] EMLR 4, [2001] EWCA Civ 1233, a series of newspaper stories focusing on a particular individual was treated as capable of constituting harassment. However, the Court of Appeal considered that the provisions of the 1997 Act had to be interpreted in light of the Article 10 right to freedom of expression contained in the ECHR. In assessing whether a proposed series of publications which was likely to cause distress to an individual constituted harassment, courts were required to take into account the Convention right to freedom of expression and the proportionality of any restriction on this right. However, in *KD v Chief Constable of Hampshire* [2005] EWHC 2550 (QB), Tugendhat J also considered that the right to privacy contained in Article 8 of the Convention had to be taken into account in interpreting the Act, and in particular the scope of the exemptions contained in s. 1(3). This may be all the more important given the extent of the positive obligation imposed upon states by the Convention to protect the privacy rights of individuals in *Von Hannover v Germany* [2005] 40 EHRR 1 (see p. 1040, post). In *KD*, Tugendhat J also considered that the burden to establish the existence of harassment as defined in s. 1(1) lay with the claimant, while the obligation to establish the existence of a defence under s. 1(3) rested on the defendant. In *Daiichi v Stop Huntingdon Animal Cruelty* [2004] 1 WLR 2503, [2003] EWHC 2337 (QB), Owen J considered that s. 1 of the Act could not be interpreted as extending protection to a corporate entity. However, in *Majrowski v Guy's and St Thomas's NHS Trust* [2006] 4 All ER 395, [2006] UKHL 34, (p. 1103, post), the House of Lords interpreted the Act as permitting an employer to be held vicariously liable in damages under s. 3 of the 1997 Act for harassment. For the limits to this vicarious liability, see *Daniels v Comr for the Metropolitan Police* [2006] EWHC 1622.

3.   Before the Act was passed, the common law had gone some way towards developing a common law tort of harassment. So for example in *Thomas v National Union of Mineworkers (South Wales Area)* [1986] Ch 20, [1985] 2 All ER 1, Scott J stated that unreasonable interference with the rights of others was actionable in tort and more specifically was prepared to recognise unreasonable harassment in the exercise of a person's right to use the highway as actionable in tort. The most significant judicial innovation came in *Khorasandjian v Bush* [1999] QB 727, [1993] 3 All ER 669 (see also *Patel v Patel* [1988] 2 FLR 179, and *Burris v Azadani* [1995] 4 All ER 802, [1005] 1 WLR 1372). Here, the teenage claimant complained of harassment by her former boyfriend, including assaults, threats of violence, and pestering telephone calls made to her parents' home. The Court of Appeal approved the interlocutory injunction made by the county court judge, relying on authorities including *Janvier v Sweeney*. However, the precise cause of action relied on by the Court of Appeal in *Khorasandjian v Bush* was the tort of private nuisance, despite the fact that the teenage claimant had no proprietary interest in her parents' home, a traditional requirement for standing to sue

in nuisance. For this reason *Khorasandjian v Bush* was subsequently overruled by the House of Lords in *Hunter v Canary Wharf Ltd* [1997] AC 655, [1997] 2 All ER 426. (For more detail on the nuisance issues involved, see chap. 14, post.) For this purpose, it is worth noting the House of Lords' comments on tort liability for harassment in *Hunter*, observing that, since the enactment of the Protection from Harassment Act, there is no longer any need for the common law to be distorted to provide a remedy in deserving cases. For example, Lord Goff emphasized:

If a plaintiff, such as the daughter of the householder in *Khorasandjian v Bush*, is harassed by abusive telephone calls, the gravaman of the complaint lies in the harassment which is just as much an abuse, or indeed an invasion of her privacy, whether she is pestered in this way in her mother's or her husband's house, or she is staying with a friend, or is at her place of work, or even in her car with a mobile phone. In truth, what the Court of Appeal appears to have been doing was to exploit the law of private nuisance in order to create by the back door a tort of harassment which was only partially effective in that it was artificially limited to harassment which takes place in her home. . . . In any event, a tort of harassment has now received statutory recognition (see the Protection from Harassment Act 1997). We are therefore no longer troubled with the question whether the common law should be developed to provide such a remedy.

4.   One significant limitation on the scope of the statutory regime is that it only catches a course of conduct amounting to harassment, so that there is no remedy for a one-off incident. In such a case, the principle derived from *Wilkinson v Downton* and *Janvier v Sweeney* may continue to provide a useful remedy. However, the potential scope of the *Wilkinson v Downton* principle has been cut back by a number of recent decisions, which may have reduced the principle to a vestigial role. It appears as if Lord Goff's comments cited above, to the effect that judicial intervention to extend the protection offered by the common law was not required in the wake of the 1997 Act, largely reflect prevailing currents of judicial opinion. One significant question which remained uncertain for some time is whether a defendant could be liable under the *Wilkinson v Downton* principle for the infliction of purely mental distress, falling short of a recognised physical or psychiatric injury. See in particular the arguments of F. A. Trindade (1986) 6 Oxf JLS 211, at 219; Bridgemen and Jones (1994) 14 LS 180. Lord Hoffmann's *obiter* comments in *Hunter* gave some support to the argument that recovery could be available in such circumstances. He said at [1997] AC 655, at 707:

The perceived gap in *Khorasandjian's* case was the absence of a tort of intentional harassment causing distress without actual bodily or psychiatric illness. This limitation is thought to arise out of cases like *Wilkinson v Downton* . . . and *Janvier v Sweeney* . . . The law of harassment has now been put on a statutory basis (see the Protection from Harassment Act 1997) and it is unnecessary to consider how the common law might have developed. But as at present advised, I see no reason why a tort of intention should be subject to the rule which excludes compensation for mere distress, inconvenience or discomfort in actions based on negligence (see *Hicks v Chief Constable of Yorkshire Police* [1992] 1 AC 310, [1992] 2 All ER 65). The policy considerations are quite different.

However, in *Wong v Parkside Health NHS Trust* [2003] 3 All ER 932, [2001] EWCA Civ 1721 the Court of Appeal took the view that actual damage in the form of physical damage or recognised psychiatric illness was required for liability to be imposed under *Wilkinson v Downton*. Also, the defendant was required to have intended to cause this type of harm: rudeness and bad behaviour causing emotional distress was not sufficient to give rise to liability. In her judgment, Hale LJ emphasised that the *Wilkinson v*

Downton principle could not be stretched to become a wider tort of harassment or of causing emotional harm ([2003] 3 All ER 932 at 938):

> For the tort to be committed, as with any other action on the case, there has to be actual damage. The damage is physical harm or recognised psychiatric illness. The defendant must have intended to violate the claimant's interest in his freedom from such harm. The conduct complained of has to be such that that degree of harm is sufficiently likely to result that the defendant cannot be heard to say that he did not 'mean' it to do so. He is taken to have meant it to do so by the combination of the likelihood of such harm being suffered as the result of his behaviour and his deliberately engaging in that behaviour.

■ Wainwright v Home Office

House of Lords [2003] 4 All ER 969

For the facts, see p. 1033, post.

LORD HOFFMANN: . . .

By the time of *Janvier*'s case, therefore, the law was able comfortably to accommodate the facts of *Wilkinson v Downton* in the law of nervous shock caused by negligence. It was unnecessary to fashion a tort of intention or to discuss what the requisite intention, actual or imputed, should be. Indeed, the remark of Duke LJ to which I have referred suggests that he did not take seriously the idea that Downton had in any sense intended to cause injury.

Commentators and counsel have nevertheless been unwilling to allow *Wilkinson v Downton* to disappear beneath the surface of the law of negligence. Although, in cases of actual psychiatric injury, there is no point in arguing about whether the injury was in some sense intentional if negligence will do just as well, it has been suggested (as the claimants submit in this case) that damages for distress falling short of psychiatric injury can be recovered if there was an intention to cause it. This submission was squarely put to the Court of Appeal in *Wong v Parkside Health NHS Trust* [2001] EWCA Civ 1721, [2003] 3 All ER 932 and rejected. Hale LJ said that before the passing of the Protection from Harassment Act 1997 there was no tort of intentional harassment which gave a remedy for anything less than physical or psychiatric injury. That leaves *Wilkinson v Downton* with no leading role in the modern law . . .

I do not resile from the proposition that the policy considerations which limit the heads of recoverable damage in negligence do not apply equally to torts of intention. If someone actually intends to cause harm by a wrongful act and does so, there is ordinarily no reason why he should not have to pay compensation. But I think that if you adopt such a principle, you have to be very careful about what you mean by intend. In *Wilkinson v Downton* Wright J wanted to water down the concept of intention as much as possible. He clearly thought, as the Court of Appeal did afterwards in *Janvier*'s case, that the plaintiff should succeed whether the conduct of the defendant was intentional or negligent. But the *Victorian Railway Comrs* case prevented him from saying so. So he devised a concept of imputed intention which sailed as close to negligence as he felt he could go.

If, on the other hand, one is going to draw a principled distinction which justifies abandoning the rule that damages for mere distress are not recoverable, imputed intention will not do. The defendant must actually have acted in a way which he knew to be unjustifiable and either intended to cause harm or at least acted without caring whether he caused harm or not . . .

Even on the basis of a genuine intention to cause distress, I would wish . . . to reserve my opinion on whether compensation should be recoverable. In institutions and workplaces all over the country, people constantly do and say things with the intention of causing distress and humiliation to others. This shows lack of consideration and appalling manners but I am not sure that the right way to deal with it is always by litigation. The Protection from Harassment Act 1997 defines harassment in s 1(1) as a 'course of conduct' amounting to harassment and provides by s 7(3) that a course of conduct must involve conduct on at least two occasions. If these requirements are satisfied, the claimant may pursue a civil remedy for damages for anxiety: see s 3(2). The requirement of a course of conduct shows that Parliament was conscious that it might not be in the public interest to allow the law to be set in motion for one boorish incident. It may be that any development of the common law should show similar caution.

In my opinion, therefore, the claimants can build nothing on *Wilkinson v Downton* [1897] 2 QB 57, [1895–9] All ER Rep 267. It does not provide a remedy...'

[LORD BINGHAM OF CORNHILL, LORD HOPE OF CRAIGHEAD, and LORD HUTTON agreed with LORD HOFFMANN. LORD SCOTT OF FOSCOTE delivered a speech in favour of dismissing the appeal and in which he also agreed with LORD HOFFMANN.]

Appeal dismissed.

NOTES

1. Lord Hoffmann adopts the view that *Wilkinson v Downton* had been decided at a time when damages for psychiatric harm were not recoverable in negligence and the decision in that case was essentially an attempt to circumvent that limitation. Given the subsequent developments in the law of negligence, which opened up the possibility of recovery for psychiatric loss under that tort, *Wilkinson v Downton* in his view now had little role to play in contemporary law. However, given the limits that exist to the recovery of psychiatric loss within negligence (see pp. 117–149, ante), is it valid to dismiss the usefulness of the *Wilkinson v Downton* principle in this manner?

2. While referring approvingly to Hale LJ's decision in *Wong*, Lord Hoffmann appeared to leave open the question of whether the tort was available for compensating mere distress falling short of psychiatric injury, or whether intention to cause distress falling short of physical or psychiatric harm was sufficient. However, see now the views of the Court of Appeal in *Mbasago v Logo Ltd*, [2006] EWCA Civ 1370, [87]–[99].

3. Illustrating that this cause of action still has a role to play, the *Wilkinson* principle was subsequently to the decision in *Wainwright* applied in *C v D* [2006] EWHC 166, where a headmaster was held liable for psychiatric injury caused by an intentional act of sexual abuse against a pupil.

5 DEFENCES

The scope and extent of the defences available to claims of intentional interference with the person are of considerable importance. Four are particularly important—lawful authority, consent, necessity, and self-defence, although others—such as contributory negligence and provocation—may also be relevant, as the following decision illustrates.

■ Murphy v Culhane
Court of Appeal [1976] 3 All ER 533

LORD DENNING MR:...

Timothy Murphy's widow...brings an action against John Culhane for damages under the Fatal Accidents Acts, claiming damages on behalf of herself and her baby daughter.... The question is whether or not Mrs Murphy is entitled to judgment on the pleadings without any trial. The statement of claim says:

'On or about the nineteenth day of September 1974, near Grove Place, in the area of Greater London, the Defendant assaulted and beat the Deceased by striking him on the head with a plank.

The said assault was unlawful. The Plaintiff intends to adduce evidence pursuant to section 11 of the Civil Evidence Act 1968, that the Defendant was on the 25th day of April 1975, convicted on his own plea of guilty before the Central Criminal Court of manslaughter of the Deceased.'

The defence admits those allegations and further admits that, by reason of the assault, Mr Murphy was killed. It then says:

'The said assault occurred during and as part of a criminal affray which was initiated by the Deceased and others who had together come to 20 Grove Place on the occasion in question with the joint criminal intent to assaulting and beating the Defendant.'

That is followed by legal contentions of ex turpi causa non oritur actio, volenti non fir injuria, and that the deceased's said death was caused in part by his own aforesaid fault.

... There are two cases which seem to show that, in a civil action for damages for assault, damages are not to be reduced because the plaintiff was himself guilty of provocation. Provocation, it was said, can be used to wipe out the element of exemplary damages but not to reduce the actual figure of pecuniary damages. It was so said by the High Court of Australia in 1962 in *Fontin v Katapodis*[3] and followed by this court in 1967 in *Lane v Holloway.*[4] But those were cases where the conduct of the injured man was trivial—and the conduct of the defendant was savage—entirely out of proportion to the occasion. So much so that the defendant could fairly be regarded as solely responsible for the damage done. I do not think they can or should be applied where the injured man, by his own conduct, can fairly be regarded as partly responsible for the damage he suffered. So far as general principle is concerned. I would like to repeat what I said in the later case of *Gray v Barr:*[5]

'In an action for assault, in awarding damages, the judge or jury can take into account, not only circumstances which go to aggravate damages, but also those which go to mitigate them.'

That is the principle I prefer rather than the earlier cases. Apart altogether from damages, however, I think there may well be a defence on liability. If Murphy was one of a gang which set out to beat up Culhane, it may well be that he could not sue for damages if he got more than he bargained for. A man who takes part in a criminal affray may well be said to have been guilty of such a wicked act as to deprive himself of a cause of action or, alternatively, to have taken on himself the risk....

There is another point, too, even if Mrs Murphy were entitled to damages under the Fatal Accidents Acts, they fall to be reduced under the Law Reform (Contributory Negligence) Act 1945 because the death of her husband might be the result partly of his own fault and partly of the default of the defendant: see s. 1(1) and (4) of the 1945 Act. On this point I must explain a sentence in *Gray v Barr*[5] where the widow of the dead man was held to be entitled to full compensation without any reduction. Her husband had not been guilty of any 'fault' within s. 4 of the 1945 Act because his conduct had not been such as to make him liable in an action of tort or, alternatively, was not such that he should be regarded as responsible in any degree for the damage. So also in *Lane v Holloway,*[6] as Winn LJ pointed out. But in the present case the conduct of Mr Murphy may well have been such as to make him liable in tort.

It seems to me that this is clearly a case where the facts should be investigated before any judgment is given. It should be open to Mr Culhane to be able to put forward his defences so as to see whether or not and to what extent he is liable in damages.

I would therefore allow the appeal. The judgment[7] should be set aside and the case go for trial accordingly.

[ORR and WALLER LJJ agreed.]

Appeal allowed.

[3] (1962) 108 CLR 177.   [4] [1968] 1 QB 379, [1967] 3 All ER 129.
[5] [1971] 2 QB 554 at 569, [1971] 2 All ER 949 at 957.
[6] [1968] 1 QB 379 at 393, [1967] 3 All ER 129 at 135.
[7] In Mrs Murphy's favour.

NOTES

1. There is a conflict of authority in relation to the question of whether any provocation on the claimant's part can mitigate compensatory, as opposed to exemplary, damages for trespass to the person. *Murphy v Culhane* represents one side of the argument, but in *Barnes v Nayer* (1986) Times, 19 December, it was said in the Court of Appeal that the better view is that provocation does not have this effect and serves only to reduce exemplary damages: see also *Lane v Holloway* [1968] 1 QB 379, [1967] 3 All ER 129.

2. On the Law Reform (Contributory Negligence) Act 1945 and contributory negligence in general, see p. 425, ante and see also *Glanville Williams*, pp. 197–202 and p. 318, note 3; and for an article which involves discussion of later case law, see Hudson (1984) 4 LS 332. See esp. Hudson, op cit., pp. 337–338 for criticism of Lord Denning MR's approach to this issue in *Murphy v Culhane*. However, Hutton J also accepted in *Wasson v Chief Constable of the Royal Ulster Constabulary* [1987] 8 NIJB 34 that contributory negligence could apply in actions for trespass to the person, reducing the claimant's damages by half in that particular case after he had been struck by a plastic baton while participating in a riot: see also *Tumelty v Ministry of Defence* [1988] 3 NIJB 51. See, nevertheless, the concerns expressed by B. Childs, (1993) 44 NILQ 34, that permitting contributory negligence to apply in such cases could have a deleterious effect on the crucial role of the trespass action as an important mechanism for vindicating civil liberties.

3. Note further that not all 'contributory negligence' may count. In *Alliance and Leicester Building Society v Edgestop Ltd* [1994] 2 All ER 38, [1993] 1 WLR 1462 (see p. 949, post), which deals with the tort of deceit, *Murphy v Culhane* was distinguished as a case in which the deceased's conduct could have been actionable in tort. In addition, even where contributory negligence has been recognised as capable of being applied in trespass actions, there has been a distinct tendency for the courts to treat any contribution by the claimant as being 'dwarfed' by the intentional act committed by the defendant. For example, the Court of Appeal in *Barnes v Nayer* accepted that the 1945 Act could apply to assault cases, although in that case the view was taken that it—and indeed the defences of volenti (the voluntary assumption of a risk) and ex turpi (illegality) as well—would not succeed on the ground of the strong disparity on the alleged facts between the deceased's acts and the defendant's response. In other words, the response of the defendant 'overwhelmed' the contributory acts of the claimant. See also the decision of the Court of Appeal in *Malcolm v Walsh* [1997] EWCA Civ 1679 and the treatment to similar effect of *Murphy, Barnes v Nayer* and *Walsh* in *Nationwide Building Society v Thimbleby* [1999] PNLR 733 at 757–760. In *Bici v Ministry of Defence* [2004] EWHC 786, Elias J described as 'persuasive' Hutton J's view in *Wasson v Chief Constable of the Royal Ulster Constabulary* that contributory negligence could be available in trespass to the person cases, but proceeded to find that the contribution of the claimants had again been 'dwarfed' by the intentional act of the defendants. He also noted, at [111]:

    …even allowing that contributory negligence can be raised as a defence, it would in my view be a very rare case where damages should be reduced in circumstances where the defendant's conduct is intentional and unjustified and the claimant's is merely negligent. Moreover, in my view this feature should in most cases at least defeat a claim to contributory negligence, whether the cause of action is framed in trespass or negligence. In my opinion, even assuming that the claimants' imprudence could fairly justify the epithet 'negligent', this would not be one of the exceptional cases where contributory fault should be found.

The House of Lords in *Standard Chartered Bank v Pakistan National Shipping Corpn* [2003] 1 All ER 173, [2002] UKHL 43 (p. 951, post); took the view that contributory negligence would not apply in cases of deceit. Lord Rodger even suggested at [42]–[45] that contributory negligence may not be available in any case where harm is intentionally caused, expressly reserving his opinion on whether Lord Denning's views to the contrary in *Murphy v Culhane* were correct. Therefore, it appears that contributory negligence will play a limited role at best in claims based upon intentional interference with the person.

4. On the defence of ex turpi causa non oritur actio (illegality) to which Lord Denning MR referred, see p. 465, ante. Again, its role in the context of intentional interference with the person will be limited.

5. Consent—here a form of implied consent—was raised in *Murphy v Culhane* under the guise of volenti non fit injuria or assumption of risk. In criminal law, consent will in general serve as a complete defence to a criminal prosecution for assault. However, a different approach appears to exist in civil law. Compare the criminal law approach to that taken in *Murphy v Culhane* and *Barnes v Nayer*. Why might the civil law take a different line? Note Hudson, op cit., p. 333, who argues that volenti might not provide a defence in circumstances similar to those in *Murphy v Culhane* and consider now *Re F* [1990] 2 AC 1, sub nom *F v West Berkshire Health Authority (Mental Health Commission intervening)* [1989] 2 All ER 545 (p. 757, post). When that case was in the Court of Appeal, support can be found (see [1989] 2 WLR at pp. 1038, 1049, and 1058) for the view that public policy can invalidate consent in both criminal *and* civil law, something which was indeed expressly stated by Neill LJ. One example given was a prize fight, where public policy might strongly support the invalidation of consent. When *F v West Berkshire Health Authority* reached the House of Lords, Lord Goff (p. 758, post) acknowledged that the public interest might negate the effect of consent 'in certain limited circumstances' and Lord Griffiths ([1989] 2 All ER at p. 562) in his dissent referred to consent not being available in the case of a bare knuckle prize fight to fighting which might result in actual bodily harm.

6. However, consent does clearly exist as a defence for trespass to the person: see *Blake v Galloway* [2004] 3 All ER 315 at 323, where a child's consent to participate in a game featuring the throwing of various objects at the body meant, in the words of Dyson LJ, that he was presumed to have 'impliedly consented to the risk of a blow on any part of his body, provided that the offending missile was thrown more or less in accordance with the tacit understandings or conventions of the game'. In other words, consent to the general nature of the activity in question was sufficient to constitute consent to the risks inherent in the activity. A similar analysis was adopted in the following case.

■ Chatterton v Gerson

Queen's Bench Division [1981] 1 All ER 257

This case was concerned with the extent to which a doctor must inform a patient of the nature of, and risks involved in, a particular course of treatment. At this point the relevant issue is the unsuccessful claim in trespass to the person and the question of consent.

BRISTOW J: . . . *Trespass to the person and consent*

It is clear law that in any context in which consent of the injured party is a defence to what would otherwise be a crime or a civil wrong, the consent must be real. Where, for example, a woman's consent to sexual intercourse is obtained by fraud, her apparent consent is no defence to a charge of rape. It is not difficult to state the principle or to appreciate its good sense. As so often, the problem lies in its application.

No English authority was cited before me of the application of the principle in the context of consent to the interference with bodily integrity by medical or surgical treatment. . . .

In my judgment what the court has to do in each case is to look at all the circumstances and say, 'Was there a real consent?' I think justice requires that in order to vitiate the reality of consent there must be a greater failure of communication between doctor and patient than that involved in a breach of duty if the claim is based on negligence. When the claim is based on negligence the plaintiff must prove not only the breach of duty to inform but that had the duty not been broken she would not have chosen to have the operation. Where the claim is based on trespass to the person, once it is shown that the consent is unreal, then what the plaintiff would have decided if she had been given the information which would have prevented vitiation of the reality of her consent is irrelevant.

In my judgment once the patient is informed in broad terms of the nature of the procedure which is intended, and gives her consent, that consent is real, and the cause of the action on which to base a claim for failure to go into risks and implications is negligence, not trespass. Of course, if information is withheld in bad faith, the consent will be vitiated by fraud. Of course, if by some accident, as in a case in the 1940s in the Salford Hundred Court, where a boy was admitted to hospital for tonsillectomy and due to administrative error was circumcised instead, trespass would be the appropriate cause of action against the doctor, though he was as much the victim of the error as the boy. But in my judgment it would be very much against the interests of justice if actions which are really based on a failure by the doctor to perform his duty adequately to inform were pleaded in trespass. . . . I should add that getting the patient to sign a pro forma expressing consent to undergo the operation 'the effect and nature of which have been explained to me' . . . should be a valuable reminder to everyone of the need for explanation and consent. But it would be no defence to an action based on trespass to the person if no explanation had in fact been given. The consent would have been expressed in form only, not in reality. . . .

NOTES

1. Bristow J's view in the final sentence of the penultimate paragraph of the extract ante was approved in *Hills v Potter* [1983] 3 All ER 716, [1984] 1 WLR 641n: see also *Sidaway v Board of Governors of the Bethlem Royal Hospital and the Maudsley Hospital* [1985] AC 871 at 883 and 894 (p. 329, ante). See further *Freeman v Home Office (No 2)* [1984] QB 524, [1983] 3 All ER 589 (per McCowan J), where it is pointed out that, in addition to consent obtained by fraud being inoperative, consent induced by misrepresentation (as to the nature of the treatment) is also not 'real consent'. (This last point was not specifically mentioned in *Chatterton v Gerson*.) See also *Appleton v Garrett* [1997] 8 Med LR 75, where a dishonest dentist carried out unnecessary dental treatment on his patients, so as to defraud the NHS. Dyson J held him liable, on the basis that the patients' apparent consent was vitiated by fraud. A similar approach is adopted in the criminal law: see *R v Williams* [1923] 1 KB 340.

2. For comment on the use of the distinction between failure of advice relating to the *nature* of the treatment and that relating to the *risks* involved in it as a key basis for deciding whether the action is trespass or negligence, see K. F. Tan (1987) 7 LS 149 (though note that the references to the 'hostility' standard established in *Wilson v Pringle* [1987] QB 237, [1986] 2 All ER 440, but see now p. 728, ante and note 6, post). In *Sidaway v Board of Governors of the Bethlem Royal Hospital and the Maudsley Hospital*, the House of Lords concluded, following *Chatterton*, that claims based on inadequate medical advice or a lack of informed consent as to the risks inherent in a medical

procedure could only be addressed via negligence, not through trespass to the person. For the difficulties this generates, see *Chester v Afshar* [2004] 4 All ER 587, [2004] UKHL 41 (p. 383, ante), noted by K. Amirthalingam [2005] CLJ 32.

3.   In *Freeman v Home Office (No. 2)* when dealing with an unsuccessful claim for damages for trespass to the person (based on the administration of drugs to the claimant prisoner), Sir John Donaldson MR stated ([1984] 1 All ER at pp. 1044–1045):

> The maxim volenti non fit injuria can be roughly translated as "You cannot claim damages if you have asked for it", and "it" is something which is and remains a tort. The maxim, where it applies, provides a bar to enforcing a cause of action. It does not negative the cause of action itself. This is a wholly different concept from consent which, in this context, deprives the act of its tortious character. Volenti would be a defence in the unlikely scenario of a patient being held not to have in fact consented to treatment, but having by his conduct caused the doctor to believe that he had consented.

4.   On the question of consent by children to medical treatment and the role of parents, see *Gillick v West Norfolk and Wisbech Area Health Authority* [1986] AC 112, [1985] 3 All ER 402; *Re P(A Minor)* (1981) 80 LGR 301.

5.   For discussion of where the burden of proof lies in relation to the issue of consent, see Trindade op cit., pp. 228–229, who submits that the onus of establishing consent should rest upon the defendant. Trindade finds support for his view in Bristow J's reference in the judgment in *Chatterton v Gerson* to consent being a defence: the onus lies on the defendant to establish his defence. (See further note 6, post.) However, in the later case of *Freeman v Home Office (No. 2)*, McCowan J construed Bristow J's judgment in *Chatterton v Gerson* as favouring the view that the burden of proof lay on the claimant to show absence of consent, and he went on to rule to that effect. Do you agree with his interpretation of *Chatterton v Gerson*? A passage from Sir John Donaldson MR's judgment in the Court of Appeal (when *Freeman v Home Office (No. 2)* went on appeal) has been set out ante (and note that Fox LJ agreed with his reasons for dismissing the appeal). Does this passage support the view that the burden of proof is on the claimant? Does it suggest that consent in this area should not properly be regarded as a 'defence'? Whatever the answer to this question, treating consent as a matter to be shown to exist by the defendant would appear to be more consistent with how similar forms of justification such as necessity and lawful justification are treated: the House of Lords in *Ashley v Chief Constable of Sussex Police* [2008] 2 WLR 975, [2000] UKHL 25 appeared to take the view that the obligation to establish a justification of self-defence rested on the defendant.

6.   As has been said, consent can be implied. Such consent was discussed in *Collins v Wilcock* [1984] 3 All ER 374, [1984] 1 WLR 1172, in which the Divisional Court stated (at p. 378):

> Generally speaking, consent is a defence to battery; and most of the physical contacts of ordinary life are not actionable because they are impliedly consented to by all who move in society and so expose themselves to the risk of bodily contact. So nobody can complain of the jostling which is inevitable from his presence in, for example, a supermarket, an underground station or a busy street; nor can a person who attends a party complain if his hand is seized in friendship, or even if his back is (within reason) slapped. . . . Although such cases are regarded as examples of implied consent, it is more common nowadays to treat them as falling within a general exception [to the rule that touching another is a battery] embracing all physical contact which is generally acceptable in the ordinary conduct of daily life.

For comment (in *Wilson v Pringle* [1987] QB 237, [1986] 2 All ER 440) on Robert Goff LJ's judgment in *Collins v Wilcock*, see p. 729, ante. Note, however, that as previously discussed, in *F v West Berkshire Health Authority*, post Lord Goff reiterated his approach in *Collins v Wilcock* and expressed doubt about the 'hostility' requirement which was referred to in *Wilson v Pringle*, with his formulation being applied by Lord Hoffmann in *Wainwright v Home Office* (see p. 729, ante).

In some situations a patient cannot consent to physical contact, e.g. because of unconsciousness. In *Wilson v Pringle*, an urgent operation in such a situation was thought to come within the exception referred to in the passage from *Collins v Wilcock* ante, but this view has not met with approval in later cases (*T v T* [1988] Fam 52, [1988] 1 All ER 613; *F v West Berkshire Health Authority* post and also when that case was in the Court of Appeal [1990] 2 AC 1). As will be seen from the next extract, this question takes the discussion beyond the issue of consent and onto the defence of necessity (although questions of consent and necessity can be closely linked: see notes 1 and 2, p. 763, post).

■ F v West Berkshire Health Authority (Mental Health Act Commission Intervening)
House of Lords [1989] 2 All ER 545

The House of Lords in this case had to consider the legality of a sterilisation operation which it was proposed to carry out on F, an adult woman whose mental capacity was such that she was unable to consent to the operation. The view of the trial judge (Scott Baker J) and of the Court of Appeal, [1990] 2 AC 1, that such an operation was in F's best interests was not challenged in this appeal to the House of Lords. Scott Baker J had granted a declaration that the sterilisation of F would not be an unlawful act by reason only of the absence of F's consent. An appeal to the Court of Appeal was unsuccessful and a further appeal to the House of Lords was dismissed. The House of Lords did, however, amend the declaration so that it read 'the operation of sterilisation proposed to be performed on the plaintiff being in the existing circumstances in her best interests can lawfully be performed on her despite her inability to consent to it'. (It was also ordered that if there was a material change in the existing circumstances before the operation took place, any party could apply to the court for such further or other declaration or order as might be just.) The House of Lords (with Lord Griffiths dissenting on this point) did not think that it was legally mandatory in the case of such a sterilisation operation to obtain a declaration from the court that the operation was lawful, but nevertheless thought that as a matter of practice such a declaration should be sought. (See now *Practice Note* [1993] 3 All ER 222.)

LORD BRANDON OF OAK BROOK: . . .

At common law a doctor cannot lawfully operate on adult patients of sound mind, or give them any other treatment involving the application of physical force however small (which I shall refer to as 'other treatment'), without their consent. If a doctor were to operate on such patients, or give them other treatment, without their consent, he would commit the actionable tort of trespass to the person. There are, however, cases where adult patients cannot give or refuse their consent to an operation or other treatment. One case is where, as a result of an accident or otherwise, an adult patient is unconscious and an operation or other treatment cannot be safely delayed until he or she recovers consciousness. Another case is where a patient, though adult, cannot by reason of mental disability understand the nature or purpose of an operation or other treatment. The common law would be seriously defective if it failed to provide a solution to the problem created by such inability to consent. In my opinion, however, the common law does not fail. In my opinion, the solution to the problem which the common law provides is that a doctor can lawfully operate on, or give other treatment to, adult patients who are incapable, for one reason or another, of consenting to his doing so, provided that the operation or other treatment concerned is in the best interests of such patients. The operation or other treatment will be in their best interests of such patients. The operation or other treatment will be in their best interests if, but only if, it is carried out in order either to save their lives or to ensure improvement or prevent deterioration in their physical or mental health.

Different views have been put forward with regard to the principle which makes it lawful for a doctor to operate on or give other treatment to adult patients without their consent in the two cases to which I have referred above. The Court of Appeal in the present case regarded the matter as depending on the public interest. I would not disagree with that as a broad proposition, but I think that it is helpful to consider the principle in accordance with which the public interest leads to this result. In my opinion, the principle is that, when persons lack the capacity, for whatever reason, to take decisions about the performance of operations on them, or the giving of other medical treatment to them, it is necessary that some other person or persons, with the appropriate qualifications, should take such decisions for them. Otherwise they would be deprived of medical care which they need and to which they are entitled.

In many cases, however, it will not only be lawful for doctors, on the ground of necessity, to operate on or give other medical treatment to adult patients disabled from giving their consent: it will also be their common law duty to do so....

LORD GRIFFITHS: ...
I have had the advantage of reading the speeches of my noble and learned friends Lord Brandon and Lord Goff and there is much therein with which I agree. I agree that those charged with the care of the mentally incompetent are protected from any criminal or tortious action based on lack of consent. Whether one arrives at this conclusion by applying a principle of 'necessity' as do Lord Brandon and Lord Goff or by saying that it is in the public interest as did Neil LJ in the Court of Appeal, appear to me to be inextricably interrelated conceptual justifications for the humane development of the common law. Why is it necessary that the mentally incompetent should be given treatment to which they lack the capacity to consent? The answer must surely be because it is in the public interest that it should be so.

In a civilised society the mentally incompetent must be provided with medical and nursing care and those who look after them must do their best for them. Stated in legal terms the doctor who undertakes responsibility for the treatment of a mental patient who is incapable of giving consent to treatment must give the treatment that he considers to be in the best interests of his patient, and the standard of care required of the doctor will be that laid down in *Bolam v Friern Hospital Management Committee* [1957] 2 All ER 118, [1957] 1 WLR 582. The doctor will however be subject to the specific statutory constraints on treatment for mental disorder provided by Pt IV of the Mental Health Act 1983....

LORD GOFF OF CHIEVELEY: ...
My Lords, the question in this case is concerned with the lawfulness of a proposed operation of sterilisation on the plaintiff, F, a woman of 36 years of age, who by reason of her mental incapacity is disabled from giving her consent to the operation. It is well established that, as a general rule, the performance of a medical operation on a person without his or her consent is unlawful, as constituting both the crime of battery and the tort of trespass to the person. Furthermore, before Scott Baker J and the Court of Appeal, it was common ground between the parties that there was no power in the court to give consent on behalf of F to the proposed operation of sterilisation, or to dispense with the need for such consent. This was because it was common ground that the parens patriae jurisdiction in respect of persons suffering from mental incapacity, formerly vested in the courts by royal warrant under the sign manual, had ceased to be so vested by revocation of the last warrant on 1 November 1960, and further that there was no statutory provision which could be invoked in its place.... [W]ith

the assistance of counsel, I for my part have become satisfied that the concessions made below on these points were rightly made.

It follows that, as was recognised in the courts below, if the operation on F is to be justified, it can only be justified on the applicable principles of common law. The argument of counsel revealed the startling fact that there is no English authority on the question whether as a matter of common law (and if so in what circumstances) medical treatment can lawfully be given to a person who is disabled by mental incapacity from consenting to it. Indeed, the matter goes further, for a comparable problem can arise in relation to persons of sound mind who are, for example, rendered unconscious in an accident or rendered speechless by a catastrophic stroke. All such persons may require medical treatment and, in some cases, surgical operations. All may require nursing care. In the case of mentally disordered persons, they may require care of a more basic kind, dressing, feeding and so on, to assist them in their daily life, as well as routine treatment by doctors and dentists. It follows that, in my opinion, it is not possible to consider in isolation the lawfulness of the proposed operation of sterilisation in the present case. It is necessary first to ascertain the applicable common law principles and then to consider the question of sterilisation against the background of those principles.

Counsel for the Official Solicitor advanced the extreme argument that, in the absence of a parens patriae or statutory jurisdiction, no such treatment or care of the kind I have described can lawfully be given to a mentally disordered person who is unable to consent to it. This is indeed a startling proposition, which must also exclude treatment or care to persons rendered unconscious or unable to speak by accident or illness. For centuries, treatment and care must have been given to such persons, without any suggestion that it was unlawful to do so. I find it very difficult to believe that the common law is so deficient as to be incapable of providing for so obvious a need. Even so, it is necessary to examine the point as a matter of principle.

I start with the fundamental principle, now long established, that every person's body is inviolate. As to this, I do not wish to depart from what I myself said in the judgment of the Divisional Court in *Collins v Wilcock* [1984] 3 All ER 374, [1984] 1 WLR 1172, and in particular from the statement that the effect of this principle is that everybody is protected not only against physical injury but against any form of physical molestation (see [1984] 3 All ER 274 at 378, [1984] 1 WLR 1172 at 1177).

Of course, as a general rule physical interference with another person's body is lawful if he consents to it; though in certain limited circumstances the public interest may require that his consent is not capable of rendering the act lawful. There are also specific cases where physical interference without consent may not be unlawful: chastisement of children, lawful arrest, self-defence, the prevention of crime and so on. As I pointed out in *Collins v Wilcock* [1984] 3 All ER 374 at 378, [1984] 1 WLR 1172 at 1177, a broader exception has been created to allow for the exigencies of everyday life: jostling in a street or some other crowded place, social contact at parties and such like. This exception has been said to be founded on implied consent, since those who go about in public places, or go to parties, may be taken to have impliedly consented to bodily contact of this kind. Today this rationalisation can be regarded as artificial: and, in particular, it is difficult to impute consent to those who, by reason of their youth or mental disorder, are unable to give their consent. For this reason, I consider it more appropriate to regard such cases as falling within a general exception embracing all physical contact which is generally acceptable in the ordinary conduct of everyday life.

In the old days it used to be said that, for a touching of another's persons to amount to a battery, it had to be a touching 'in anger' (see *Cole v Turner* (1704) Holt KB 108, 90 ER 958 per Holt CJ); and it has recently been said that the touching must be 'hostile' to have that effect (see *Wilson v Pringle* [1986] 2 All ER 440 at 447, [1987] QB 237 at 253). I respectfully doubt whether that is correct. A prank that gets out of hand, an over-friendly slap on the back, surgical treatment by a surgeon who mistakenly thinks that the patient has consented to it, all these things may transcend the bounds of lawfulness, without being characterised as hostile. Indeed, the suggested qualification is difficult to reconcile with the principle that any touching of another's body is, in the absence of lawful excuse, capable of amounting to a battery and a trespass. Furthermore, in the case of medical treatment, we have to bear well in mind the libertarian principle of self-determination which, to adopt the words of Cardozo J (in *Schloendorff v Society of New York Hospital* (1914) 211 NY 125 at 126), recognises that—

> 'Every human being of adult years and sound mind has a right to determine what shall be done with his own body; and a surgeon who performs an operation without his patient's consent, commits an assault...'

This principle has been reiterated in more recent years by Lord Reid in *S v S, W v Official Solicitor* [1970] 3 All ER 107 at 111, [1972] AC 24 at 43.

It is against this background that I turn to consider the question whether, and if so when, medical treatment or care of a mentally disordered person who is, by reason of his incapacity, incapable of giving his consent can be regarded as lawful. As is recognised in Cardozo J's statement of principle, and elsewhere (see eg *Sidaway v Bethlem Royal Hospital Governors* [1985] 1 All ER 643 at 649, [1985] AC 871 at 882 per Lord Scarman), some relaxation of the law is required to accommodate persons of unsound mind. In *Wilson v Pringle* the Court of Appeal considered that treatment of care of such persons may be regarded as lawful, as falling within the exception relating to physical contact which is generally acceptable in the ordinary conduct of everyday life. Again, I am with respect unable to agree. That exception is concerned with the ordinary events of everyday life, jostling in public places and such like, and affects all persons, whether or not they are capable of giving their consent. Medical treatment, even treatment for minor ailments, does not fall within that category of events. The general rule is that consent is necessary to render such treatment lawful. If such treatment administered without consent is not to be unlawful, it has to be justified on some other principle.

On what principle can medical treatment be justified when given without consent? We are searching for a principle on which, in limited circumstances, recognition may be given to a need, in the interests of the patient, that treatment should be given to him in circumstances where he is (temporarily or permanently) disabled from consenting to it. It is this criterion of a need which points to the principle of necessity as providing justification.

That there exists in the common law a principle of necessity which may justify action which would otherwise be unlawful is not in doubt. But historically the principle has been seen to be restricted to two groups of cases, which have been called cases of public necessity and cases of private necessity. The former occurred when a man interfered with another man's property in the public interest, for example (in the days before we could dial 999 for the fire brigade) the destruction of another man's house to prevent the spread of a catastrophic fire, as indeed occurred in the Great Fire of London in 1666. The latter cases occurred when a man interfered with another's property to save his own person or property from imminent danger, for example when he entered on his neighbour's land without his consent in order to prevent the spread of fire onto his own land.

There is, however, a third group of cases, which is also properly described as founded on the principle of necessity and which is more pertinent to the resolution of the problem in the present case. These cases are concerned with action taken as a matter of necessity to assist another person with his consent. To give a simple example, a man who seizes another and forcibly drags him from the path of an oncoming vehicle, thereby saving him from injury or even death, commits no wrong. But there are many emanations of this principle, to be found scattered through the books. These are concerned not only with the preservation of the life or health of the assisted person, but also with the preservation of his property (sometimes an animal, sometimes an ordinary chattel) and even to certain conduct on his behalf in the administration of his affairs. Where there is a pre-existing relationship between the parties, the intervener is usually said to act as an agent of necessity on behalf of the principal in whose interests he acts, and his action can often, with not too much artificiality, be referred to the pre-existing relationship between them. Whether the intervener may be entitled either to reimbursement or to remuneration raises separate questions which are not relevant to the present case.

We are concerned here with action taken to preserve the life, health or well-being of another who is unable to consent to it. Such action is sometimes to be justified as arising from an emergency; ...

In truth, the relevance of an emergency is that it may give rise to a necessity to act in the interests of the assisted person without first obtaining his consent. Emergency is however not the criterion or even a prerequisite; it is simply a frequent origin of the necessity which impels intervention. The principle is one of necessity, not of emergency.

We can derive some guidance as to the nature of the principle of necessity from the cases on agency of necessity in mercantile law. When reading those cases, however, we have to bear in mind that it was there considered that (since there was a pre-existing relationship between the parties) there was a duty on the part of the agent to act on his principal's behalf in an emergency. [His Lordship then referred to statements in *Prager v Blatspiel, Stamp and Heacock Ltd* [1924] 1 KB 566 at 572 and in *Australasian Steam Navigation Co v Morse* (1872) LR 4 PC 222 at 230 and continued:]...[From these statements] can be derived the basic requirements, applicable in these cases of necessity, that, to fall within the principle, not only (1) must there be a necessity to act when it is not practicable to communicate with the assisted person, but also (2) the action taken must be such as a reasonable person would in all the circumstances take, acting in the best interests of the assisted person.

On this statement of principle, I wish to observe that officious intervention cannot be justified by the principle of necessity. So intervention cannot be justified when another more appropriate person is available and willing to act; nor can it be justified when it is contrary to the known wishes of the assisted person, to the extent that he is capable of rationally forming such a wish. On the second limb of the principle, the introduction of the standard of a reasonable man should not in the present context be regarded as materially different from that of Sir Montague Smith's 'wise and prudent man',[8] because a reasonable man would, in the time available to him, proceed with wisdom and prudence before taking action in relation to another man's person or property without his consent. I shall have more to say on this point later. Subject to that, I hesitate at present to indulge in any greater refinement of the principle, being well aware of many problems which may arise in its application, problems which it is not necessary, for present purposes, to examine. But as a general rule, if the above criteria are fulfilled, interference with the assisted person's person or property (as the case may be) will not be unlawful. Take the example of a railway accident, in which injured passengers are trapped in the wreckage. It is this principle which may render lawful the actions of other citizens, railway staff, passengers or outsiders, who rush to give aid and comfort to the victims: the surgeon who amputates the limb of an unconscious passenger to free him from the wreckage; the ambulance man who conveys him to hospital; the doctors and nurses who treat him and care for him while he is still unconscious. Take the example of an elderly person who suffers a stroke which renders him incapable of speech or movement. It is by virtue of this principle that the doctor who treats him, the nurse who cares for him, even the relative or friend or neighbour who comes in to look after him will commit no wrong when he or she touches his body.

The two examples I have given illustrate, in the one case, an emergency and, in the other, a permanent or semi-permanent state of affairs. Another example of the latter kind is that of a mentally disordered person who is disabled from giving consent. I can see no good reason why the principle of necessity should not be applicable in his case as it is in the case of the victim of a stroke. Furthermore, in the case of a mentally disordered person, as in the case of a stroke victim, the permanent state of affairs calls for a wider range of care than may be requisite in an emergency which arises from accidental injury. When the state of affairs is permanent, or semi-permanent, action properly taken to preserve the life, health or well-being of the assisted person may well transcend such measures as surgical operation or substantial medical treatment and may extend to include such humdrum matters as routine medical or dental treatment, even simple care such as dressing and undressing and putting to bed.

The distinction I have drawn between cases of emergency and cases where the state of affairs is (more or less) permanent is relevant in another respect. We are here concerned with medical treatment, and I limit myself to cases of that kind. Where, for example, a surgeon performs an operation without his consent on a patient temporarily rendered unconscious in an accident, he should do no more than

---

[8] In *Australasian Steam Navigation Co v Morse* (1872) LR 4 PC 222, at 230.

is reasonably required, in the best interests of the patient, before he recovers consciousness. I can see no practical difficulty arising from this requirement, which derives from the fact that the patient is expected before long to regain consciousness and can then be consulted about longer term measures. The point has however arisen in a more acute form where a surgeon, in the course of an operation, discovers some other condition which, in his opinion, requires operative treatment for which he has not received the patient's consent. In what circumstances he should operate forthwith, and in what circumstances he should postpone the further treatment until he has received the patient's consent, is a difficult matter which has troubled the Canadian courts (see *Marshall v Curry* [1933] 3 DLR 260 and *Murray v McMurchy* [1949] 2 DLR 442), but which it is not necessary for your Lordships to consider in the present case.

But where the state of affairs is permanent or semi-permanent, as may be so in the case of a mentally disordered person, there is no point in waiting to obtain the patient's consent. The need to care for him is obvious; and the doctor must then act in the best interests of his patient, just as if he had received his patient's consent so to do. Were this not so, much useful treatment and care could, in theory at least, be denied to the unfortunate. It follows that, on this point, I am unable to accept the view expressed by Neill LJ in the Court of Appeal, that the treatment must be shown to have been necessary. Moreover, in such a case, as my noble and learned friend Lord Brandon has pointed out, a doctor who has assumed responsibility for the care of a patient may not only be treated as having the patient's consent to act, but also be under a duty so to act. I find myself to be respectfully in agreement with Lord Donaldson MR when he said:

'I see nothing incongruous in doctors and others who have a caring responsibility being required, when acting in relation to an adult who is incompetent, to exercise a right of choice in exactly the same way as would the court or reasonable parents in relation to a child, making due allowance, of course, for the fact that the patient is not a child, and I am satisfied that that is what the law does in fact require.'

In these circumstances, it is natural to treat the deemed authority and the duty as interrelated. But I feel bound to express my opinion that, in principle, the lawfulness of the doctor's action is, at least in its origin, to be found in the principle of necessity. This can perhaps be seen most clearly in cases where there is no continuing relationship between doctor and patient. The 'doctor in the house' who volunteers to assist a lady in the audience who, overcome by the drama or by the heat in the theatre, has fainted away is impelled to act by no greater duty than that imposed by his own Hippocratic oath. Furthermore, intervention can be justified in the case of a non-professional, as well as a professional, man or woman who has no pre-existing relationship with the assisted person, as in the case of a stranger who rushes to assist an injured man after an accident. In my opinion, it is the necessity itself which provides the justification for the intervention.

I have said that the doctor has to act in the best interests of the assisted person. In the case of routine treatment of mentally disordered persons, there should be little difficulty in applying this principle. In the case of more serious treatment, I recognise that its application may create problems for the medical profession; however, in making decisions about treatment, the doctor must act in accordance with a responsible and competent body of relevant professional opinion, on the principles set down in *Bolam v Friern Hospital Management Committee* [1957] 2 All ER 118, [1957] 1 WLR 582. No doubt, in practice, a decision may involve others besides the doctor. It must surely be good practice to consult relatives and others who are concerned with the care of the patient. Sometimes, of course, consultation with a specialist or specialists will be required; and in others, especially where the decision involves more than a purely medical opinion, an inter-disciplinary team will in practice participate in the decision. It is very difficult, and would be unwise, for a court to do more than to stress that, for those who are involved in these important and sometimes difficult decisions, the overriding consideration is that they should act in the best interests of the person who suffers from the misfortune of being prevented by incapacity from deciding for himself what should be done to his own body in his own best interests.

In the present case, your Lordships have to consider whether the foregoing principles apply in the case of a proposed operation of sterilisation on an adult woman of unsound mind, or whether sterilisation is (perhaps with one or two other cases) to be placed in a separate category to which special principles apply.

[LORD GOFF went on to decide that the 'foregoing principles' did apply to the case he had outlined.]

[LORD BRIDGE OF HARWICH and LORD JAUNCEY OF TULLICHETTLE delivered speeches in which they concurred with the reasons given for dismissing the appeal by LORD BRANDON and LORD GOFF.]

QUESTIONS

1. How would you answer the surgeon's dilemma posed by Lord Goff (p. 762, ante)?
2. If an unconscious person who needed urgent medical treatment had to the knowledge of the defendant previously expressed the view that he did not wish to have the type of treatment in question (e.g. a Jehovah's Witness carrying a card stating that they did not wish to have a blood transfusion), would the necessity principle justify the use of this treatment? (See S. Y. S. Lam (1989) 5 PN 118, discussing the Canadian case of *Malette v Shulman* (1987) 47 DLR (4th) 18.)

NOTES

1. Sections 214–226 of the Mental Capacity Act 2005 when in force will govern advance decisions to refuse medical treatment. For a discussion of the position where, despite an apparent refusal of consent, the necessity principle can apply to justify treatment, see *Re T (Consent to Medical Treatment) (Adult Patient)* [1992] 4 All ER 649, [1992] 2 FLR 458. See further *Re L (Medical Treatment: Gillick Competency)* [1998] 2 FLR 810, discussed by C. Bridge (1999) 62 MLR 585.
2. In relation to the question of consent and the provision of medical treatment concerned with *mental disorder* where Part IV of the Mental Health Act 1983 needs to be considered, see *Reid v Secretary of State for Scotland* [1999] 2 AC 512, [1999] 1 All ER 481.
3. The concept of 'best interests' as developed in *Re F* has been applied to authorise the treatment of patients suffering from vCJD with new drugs: see *Simms v Simms* [2002] EWHC 2734 (Fam). See also *Re Y (Mental Incapacity: Bone Marrow Transplant)* [1996] 2 FLR 7. For criticism of the 'best interests' test and an alternative formulation based upon the question whether treatment has any therapeutic benefit and whether withholding treatment would adequately respect the 'sanctity of life', see J. Keown (1997) 113 LQR 482–503. For responses, see O. Price (2001) 21 LS 618; A. McGee (2005) 13 Med. L.R. 357; J. Keown (2006) 26 LS 109.
4. In *Re A (Children) (Conjoined Twins: Surgical Separation)* [2001] Fam 147, [2000] 4 All ER 961, the courts were called upon to exercise their wardship jurisdiction where two conjoined twins had a life expectancy of a few months if they were not separated, but the separation operation would inevitably result in the death of one of the twins. The parents refused to give their approval. The Court of Appeal held that the 'balance of interests' of the twins lay in granting permission for the operation to proceed. The operation was also held not to be a violation of the criminal law: Ward LJ took the approach that the doctors in performing the operation would be coming to the aid of the survivor twin and therefore the intervention was justified; Brooke LJ considered that the defence of necessity was available. Does Keown's analysis, above, have

more potential to better resolve the dilemmas inherent in this case than the Court of Appeal's balancing of the best interests of both twins?

5. The *Bolam* test may exceptionally be used, as the following case shows, to justify the withdrawal of treatment when it is no longer of any benefit to the patient.

■ Airedale NHS Trust v Bland

House of Lords [1993] 1 All ER 821

Anthony Bland, was seriously injured at the Hillsborough football disaster when aged 17. As a result of his injuries he sustained catastrophic and irreversible brain damage, which had left him in a persistent vegetative state (P.V.S.) with no prospect of improvement or recovery. With the agreement of his family, the doctors responsible for his care sought declarations that they might lawfully discontinue all life-sustaining treatment and medical support measures, including the termination of ventilation, nutrition, and hydration by artificial means, and that they need not provide any medical treatment to the patient except with the sole purpose of enabling him to die peacefully with the greatest dignity and the least of pain, suffering, and distress. The President of the Family Division granted the declaration sought and this was approved on appeal to the Court of Appeal. The Official Solicitor, representing the patient, appealed to the House of Lords.

LORD GOFF OF CHIEVELLEY: . . .

[His Lordship stated the facts. He then discussed the abolition of the court's inherent parens patriae jurisdiction to grant consent on behalf of incapable adults, which meant that the only appropriate form of proceedings in a case of the present kind was an application for declaratory relief. LORD GOFF continued:]

I start with the simple fact that, in law, Anthony is still alive. It is true that his condition is such that it can be described as a living death; but he is nevertheless still alive. This is because, as a result of developments in modern medical technology, doctors no longer associate death exclusively with breathing and heart beat, and it has come to be accepted that death occurs when the brain, and in particular the brain stem, has been destroyed: see Professor Ian Kennedy's paper entitled 'Switching off Life Support Machines: The Legal Implications,' reprinted in *Treat Me Right, Essays in Medical Law and Ethics*, (1988), especially at pp. 351–352, and the material there cited. There has been no dispute on this point in the present case, and it is unnecessary for me to consider it further. The evidence is that Anthony's brain stem is still alive and functioning and it follows that, in the present state of medical science, he is still alive and should be so regarded as a matter of law.

It is on this basis that I turn to the applicable principles of law. Here, the fundamental principle is the principle of the sanctity of human life—a principle long recognised not only in our own society but also in most, if not all, civilised societies throughout the modern world, as is indeed evidenced by its recognition both in article 2 of the European Convention for the Protection of Human Rights and Fundamental Freedoms (1953) (Cmd. 8969), and in article 6 of the International Covenant of Civil and Political Rights 1966.

But this principle, fundamental though it is, is not absolute. Indeed there are circumstances in which it is lawful to take another man's life, for example by a lawful act of self-defence, or (in the days when capital punishment was acceptable in our society) by lawful execution. We are not however concerned with cases such as these. We are concerned with circumstances in which it may be lawful to withhold from a patient medical treatment or care by means of which his life may be prolonged. But here too there is no absolute rule that the patient's life must be prolonged by such treatment or care, if available, regardless of the circumstances.

First, it is established that the principle of self-determination requires that respect must be given to the wishes of the patient, so that if an adult patient of sound mind refuses, however unreasonably, to consent to treatment or care by which his life would or might be prolonged, the doctors responsible for his care must give effect to his wishes, even though they do not consider it to be in his best interests to do so: see *Schloendorff v Society of New York Hospital* (1914) 105 N.E. 92, 93, *per* Cardozo J.; *S. v McC. (orse S.) and M. (D.S. Intervener); W. v W.* [1972] AC 24, 43, *per* Lord Reid; and *Sidaway v Board of Governors of the Bethlem Royal Hospital and the Maudsley Hospital* [1985] AC 871, 882, *per* Lord Scarman. To this extent, the principle of the sanctity of human life must yield to the principle of self-determination...and, for present purposes perhaps more important, the doctors' duty to act in the best interests of his patient must likewise be qualified. On this basis, it has been held that a patient of sound mind may, if properly informed, require that life support should be discontinued: see *Nancy B. v Hôtel-Dieu de Québec* (1992) 86 DLR (4th) 385. Moreover the same principle applies where the patient's refusal to give his consent has been expressed at an earlier date, before he became unconscious or otherwise incapable of communicating it; though in such circumstances especial care may be necessary to ensure that the prior refusal of consent is still properly to be regarded as applicable in the circumstances which have subsequently occurred: see, e.g., *In re T. (Adult: Refusal of Treatment)* [1993] Fam 95. I wish to add that, in cases of this kind, there is no question of the patient having committed suicide, nor therefore of the doctor having aided or abetted him in doing so. It is simply that the patient has, as he is entitled to do, declined to consent to treatment which might or would have the effect of prolonging his life, and the doctor has, in accordance with his duty complied with his patient's wishes.

But in many cases not only may the patient be in no condition to be able to say whether or not he consents to the relevant treatment or care, but also he may have given no prior indication of his wishes with regard to it. In the case of a child who is a ward of court, the court itself will decide whether medical treatment should be provided in the child's best interests, taking into account medical opinion. But the court cannot give its consent on behalf of an adult patient who is incapable of himself deciding whether or not to consent to treatment. I am of the opinion that there is nevertheless no absolute obligation upon the doctor who has the patient in his care to prolong his life, regardless of the circumstances. Indeed, it would be most startling, and could lead to the most adverse and cruel effects upon the patient, if any such absolute rule were held to exist. It is scarcely consistent with the primacy given to the principle of self-determination in those cases in which the patient of sound mind has declined to give his consent, that the law should provide no means of enabling treatment to be withheld in appropriate circumstances where the patient is in no condition to indicate, if that was his wish, that he did not consent to it. The point was put forcibly in the judgment of the Supreme Judicial Court of Massachusetts in *Superintendent of Belchertown State School v Saikewicz* (1977) 370 NE 2d 417, 428, as follows:

> 'To presume that the incompetent person must always be subjected to what many rational and intelligent persons may decline is to downgrade the status of the incompetent person by placing a lesser value on his intrinsic human worth and vitality.'

I must however stress, at this point, that the law draws a crucial distinction between cases in which a doctor decides not to provide, or to continue to provide, for his patient treatment or care which could or might prolong his life, and those in which he decides, for example by administering a lethal drug, actively to bring his patient's life to an end. As I have already indicated, the former may be lawful, either because the doctor is giving effect to his patient's wishes by withholding the treatment or care, or even in certain circumstances in which (on principles which I shall describe) the patient is incapacitated from stating whether or not he gives his consent. But it is not lawful for a doctor to administer a drug to his patient to bring about his death, even though that course is prompted by a humanitarian desire to end his suffering, however great that suffering may be: see *Reg. v Cox* (unreported), 18 September 1992...

At the heart of this distinction lies a theoretical question. Why is it that the doctor who gives his patient a lethal injection which kills him commits an unlawful act and indeed is guilty of murder, whereas a doctor who, by discontinuing life support, allows his patient to die, may not act unlawfully—and will not do so, if he commits no breach of duty to his patient? Professor Glanville Williams has suggested (see his *Textbook of Criminal Law*, 2nd ed. (1983), p. 282) that the reason is that what the doctor does when he switches off a life support machine 'is in substance not an act but an omission to struggle,' and that 'the omission is not a breach of duty by the doctor, because he is not obliged to continue in a hopeless case.'

I agree that the doctor's conduct in discontinuing life support can properly be categorised as an omission. It is true that it may be difficult to describe what the doctor actually does as an omission, for example where he takes some positive step to bring the life support to an end. But discontinuation of life support is, for present purposes, no different from not initiating life support in the first place. In each case, the doctor is simply allowing his patient to die in the sense that he is desisting from taking a step which might, in certain circumstances, prevent his patient from dying as a result of his pre-existing condition; and as a matter of general principle an omission such as this will not be unlawful unless it constitutes a breach of duty to the patient. I also agree that the doctor's conduct is to be differentiated from that of, for example, an interloper who maliciously switches off a life support machine because, although the interloper may perform exactly the same act as the doctor who discontinues life support, his doing so constitutes interference with the life-prolonging treatment then being administered by the doctor. Accordingly, whereas the doctor, in discontinuing life support, is simply allowing his patient to die of his pre-existing condition, the interloper is actively intervening to stop the doctor from prolonging the patient's life, and such conduct cannot possibly be categorised as an omission.

The distinction appears, therefore, to be useful in the present context in that it can be invoked to explain how discontinuance of life support can be differentiated from ending a patient's life by a lethal injection. But in the end the reason for that difference is that, whereas the law considers that discontinuance of life support may be consistent with the doctor's duty to care for his patient, it does not, for reasons of policy, consider that it forms any part of his duty to give his patient a lethal injection to put him out of his agony.

I return to the patient who, because for example he is of unsound mind or has been rendered unconscious by accident or by illness, is incapable of stating whether or not he consents to treatment or care. In such circumstances, it is now established that a doctor may lawfully treat such a patient if he acts in his best interests, and indeed that, if the patient is already in his care, he is under a duty so to treat him: see *In re F. (Mental Patient: Sterilisation)* [1990] 2 AC 1, in which the legal principles governing treatment in such circumstances were stated by this House. For my part I can see no reason why, as a matter of principle, a decision by a doctor whether or not to initiate, or to continue to provide, treatment or care which could or might have the effect of prolonging such a patient's life, should not be governed by the same fundamental principle. Of course, in the great majority of cases, the best interests of the patient are likely to require that treatment of this kind, if available, should be given to a patient. But this may not always be so. To take a simple example given by Thomas J. in *Auckland Area Health Board v Attorney-General* [1993] 1 NZLR 235, 253, to whose judgment in that case I wish to pay tribute, it cannot be right that a doctor, who has under his care a patient suffering painfully from terminal cancer, should be under an absolute obligation to perform upon him major surgery to abate another condition which, if unabated, would or might shorten his life still further. The doctor who is caring for such a patient cannot, in my opinion, be under an absolute obligation to prolong his life by any means available to him, regardless of the quality of the patient's life. Common humanity requires otherwise, as do medical ethics and good medical practice accepted in this country and overseas. As I see it, the doctor's decision whether or not to take any such step must (subject to his patient's ability to give or withhold his consent) be made in the best interests of the patient. It is this principle too which, in my opinion, underlies the established rule that a doctor may, when caring for a patient who is, for example, dying of cancer, lawfully administer painkilling drugs despite the fact that he knows that an incidental effect of that application will be to abbreviate the patient's life. Such a decision may properly be made as part of the care of the living patient, in his best interests; and, on this basis, the treatment will be lawful.

Moreover, where the doctor's treatment of his patient is lawful, the patient's death will be regarded in law as exclusively caused by the injury or disease to which his condition is attributable . . .

The question which lies at the heart of the present case is, as I see it, whether on that principle the doctors responsible for the treatment and care of Anthony Bland can justifiably discontinue the process of artificial feeding upon which the prolongation of his life depends.

It is crucial for the understanding of this question that the question itself should be correctly formulated. The question is not whether the doctor should take a course which will kill his patient, or even take a course which has the effect of accelerating his death. The question is whether the doctor should or should not continue to provide his patient with medical treatment or care which, if continued, will prolong his patient's life. The question is sometimes put in striking or emotional terms, which can be misleading. For example, in the case of a life support system, it is sometimes asked: should a doctor be entitled to switch it off, or to pull the plug? And then it is asked: can it be in the best interests of the patient that a doctor should be able to switch the life support system off, when this will inevitably result in the patient's death? Such an approach has rightly been criticised as misleading, for example by Professor Ian Kennedy in his paper in *Treat Me Right, Essays in Medical Law and Ethics* and by Thomas J. in *Auckland Area Health Board v Attorney-General* [1993] 1 NZLR 235, 247. This is because the question is not whether it is in the best interests of the patient that he should die. The question is whether it is in the best interests of the patient that his life should be prolonged by the continuance of this form of medical treatment or care.

The correct formulation of the question is of particular importance in a case such as the present, where the patient is totally unconscious and where there is no hope whatsoever of any amelioration of his condition. In circumstances such as these, it may be difficult to say that it is in his best interests that the treatment should be ended. But if the question is asked, as in my opinion it should be, whether it is in his best interests that treatment which has the effect of artificially prolonging his life should be continued, that question can sensibly be answered to the effect that his best interests no longer require that it should be.

Even so, a distinction may be drawn between (1) cases in which, having regard to all the circumstances (including, for example, the intrusive nature of the treatment, the hazards involved in it, and the very poor quality of the life which may be prolonged for the patient if the treatment is successful), it may be judged not to be in the best interests of the patient to initiate or continue life-prolonging treatment, and (2) cases such as the present in which, so far as the living patient is concerned, the treatment is of no benefit to him because he is totally unconscious and there is no prospect of any improvement in his condition. In both classes of case, the decision whether or not to withhold treatment must be made in the best interests of the patient. In the first class, however, the decision has to be made by weighting the relevant considerations. For example, in *In re J. (A Minor) (Wardship: Medical Treatment)* [1991] Fam 33, the approach to be adopted in that case was stated by Taylor LJ as follows, at p. 55:

> 'I consider the correct approach is for the court to judge the quality of life the child would have to endure if given the treatment and decide whether in all the circumstances such a life would be so afflicted as to be intolerable to that child.'

With this class of case, however, your Lordships are not directly concerned in the present case; and though I do not wish to be understood to be casting any doubt upon any of the reported cases on the subject, nevertheless I must record that argument was not directed specifically towards these cases, and for that reason I do not intend to express any opinion about the precise principles applicable in relation to them.

By contrast, in the latter class of case, of which the present case provides an example, there is in reality no weighing operation to be performed. Here the condition of the patient, who is totally unconscious and in whose condition there is no prospect of any improvement, is such that life-prolonging treatment is properly regarded as being, in medical terms, useless. As Sir Thomas Bingham MR pointed out . . . in the present case, medical treatment or care may be provided for a number of different purposes. It may be provided, for example, as an aid to diagnosis; for the treatment of physical or mental injury or illness; to alleviate pain or distress, or to make the patient's condition more tolerable. Such purposes may include prolonging the patient's life, for example to enable him to survive during diagnosis and treatment. But for my part I cannot see that medical treatment is appropriate or requisite simply to prolong a patient's life, when such treatment has no therapeutic purpose of any kind, as where it is futile because the patient is unconscious and there is no prospect of any improvement in his condition. It is reasonable also that account should be taken of the invasiveness of the treatment and of the indignity to which, as the present case shows, a person has to be subjected if his life is prolonged by artificial means, which must cause considerable distress to his family—a distress which reflects not only their own feelings but their perception of the situation of their relative who is being kept alive. But in the end, in a case such as the present, it is the futility of the treatment which justifies its termination. I do not consider that, in circumstances such as these, a doctor is required to initiate or to continue life-prolonging treatment or care in the best interests of his patient. It follows that no such duty rests upon the respondents, or upon Dr Howe, in the case of Anthony Bland, whose condition is in reality no more than a living death, and for whom such treatment or care would, in medical terms, be futile . . .

In *In re F.* [1990] 2 AC 1 it was stated that, where a doctor provides treatment for a person who is incapacitated from saying whether or not he consents to it, the doctor must, when deciding on the form of treatment, act in accordance with a responsible and competent body of treatment, act in accordance with a responsible and competent body of relevant professional opinion, on the principles set down in *Bolam v Friern Hospital Management Committee* [1957] 1 WLR 582. In my opinion, this principle must equally be applicable to decisions to initiate, or to discontinue, life support, as it is to other forms of treatment. However, in a matter of such importance and sensitivity as discontinuance of life support, it is to be expected that guidance will be provided for the profession; and, on the evidence in the present case, such guidance is for a case such as the present to be found in a Discussion Paper on Treatment of Patients in Persistent Vegetative State, issued in September 1992 by the Medical Ethics Committee of the British Medical Association. Anybody reading this substantial paper will discover for himself the great care with which this topic is being considered by the profession. Mr Francis, for the respondents, drew to the attention of the Appellate Committee four safeguards in particular which, in the committee's opinion, should be observed before discontinuing life support for such patients. They are: (1) every effort should be made at rehabilitation for at least six months after the injury; (2) the diagnosis of irreversible P.V.S. should not be considered confirmed until at least 12 months after the injury, with the effect that any decision to withhold life-prolonging treatment will be delayed for that period; (3) the diagnosis should be agreed by two other independent doctors; and (4) generally, the wishes of the patient's immediate family will be given great weight . . .

Study of this document left me in no doubt that, if a doctor treating a P.V.S. patient acts in accordance with the medical practice now being evolved by the Medical Ethics Committee of the B.M.A., he will be acting with the benefit of guidance from a responsible and competent body of relevant professional opinion, as required by the *Bolam* test [1957] 1 WLR 582. I also feel that those who are concerned that a matter of life and death, such as is involved in a decision to withhold life support in case of this kind, should be left to the doctors, would do well to study this paper. . . . To me, the crucial point in which I found myself differing from Mr Munby [on behalf of the Official Solicitor] was that I was unable to accept his treating the discontinuance of artificial feeding in the present case as equivalent to cutting a mountaineer's rope, or severing the air pipe of a deep sea diver. Once it is recognised, as I believe it must be, that the true question is not whether the doctor should take a course in which he will actively kill his patient, but rather whether he should continue to provide his patient with medical treatment or care which, if continued, will prolong his life, then, as I see it, the essential basis of Mr Munby's submissions disappears. I wish to add that I was unable to accept his suggestion that recent decisions show that the law is proceeding down a 'slippery slope,' in the sense that the courts are becoming more and more ready to allow doctors to take steps which will result in the ending of life. On the contrary, as I have attempted to demonstrate, the courts are acting within a structure of legal principle, under which in particular they continue to draw a clear distinction between the bounds of lawful treatment of a living patient, and unlawful euthanasia.

[LORD KEITH OF KINKEL, LORD LOWRY, LORD BROWNE-WILKINSON, and LORD MUSTILL delivered speeches in favour of dismissing the appeal.]

QUESTION

In the light of this and the previous case, does the *Bolam* test give too much latitude to doctors in making decisions about the treatment of their patients? On the *Bolam* test, see p. 326, ante, and note its interpretation in *Bolitho v City and Hackney Health Authority* [1998] AC 232, [1997] 4 All ER 771 (p. 326, ante).

NOTES

1. In *NHS Trust A v M* [2001] 2 FLR 367, the approach taken in *Bland* was challenged as being incompatible with Article 2 of the ECHR, which guarantees the right to life, and Article 3 of the ECHR, which guarantees freedom from inhuman and degrading treatment which would allegedly take place between withdrawal of feeding and death. Butler-Sloss P held that a responsible decision by medical staff in line with *Bland* would not amount to intentional deprivation of life contrary to Article 2, or to a violation of Article 3, if it satisfied the 'best interests' requirement.
2. On necessity, see further p. 773, post. See also M. A. Jones (1989) 5 PN 178; J. Shaw (1990) 53 MLR 91, at 102–106 (both writing before *Bolitho*).
3. The Law Commission recommended in 1995 that there should be a new jurisdiction, on a statutory footing, to enable the courts to deal with adult patients who lack capacity to make their own decisions (*Mental Incapacity*, Law Com. No. 231). The Mental Capacity Act 2005 now makes provision for this.
4. A further dilemma arises where a pregnant mother refuses consent to treatment, which refusal risks both her own life and that of her unborn child, as seen in the following case.

■ St George's Healthcare NHS Trust v S
Court of Appeal [1998] 3 All ER 673

S, who was 36 weeks pregnant, was diagnosed with pre-eclampsia, a condition which is potentially life-threatening for both mother and unborn child. S was advised that she needed to be admitted to hospital immediately for an induced delivery but she refused, stating that she wanted nature to take its course. S was depressed, but competent to refuse consent. Against her will, S was detained in a mental hospital (under s. 2 of the Mental Health Act 1983) and was then transferred to another hospital, which applied for an emergency declaration dispensing with her consent to treatment. The declaration was granted by a judge and S was delivered of a baby girl by Caesarean section. S subsequently appealed to the Court of Appeal.

JUDGE LJ (giving the judgment of the Court of Appeal) [after summarising the facts and course of the litigation so far, JUDGE LJ continued] . . .

Autonomy

Even when his or her own life depends on receiving medical treatment, an adult of sound mind is entitled to refuse it. This reflects the autonomy of each individual and the right of self-determination.

[JUDGE LJ cited passages from *Airedale NHS Trust v Bland* (see p. 764, ante) and continued...]

The speeches in *Airedale NHS Trust v Bland* did not establish the law, but rather underlined the principle found in a series of authoritative decisions. With the exception of one short passage from the observations of Lord Reid in *S v S, W v Official Solicitor* [1970] 3 All ER 107, (1972) AC 24 no further citation is necessary.

In that case the House of Lords considered whether it was right to order blood tests on two infants to help establish whether or not they were legitimate. Lord Reid examined the legal position and said ([1970] 3 All ER 107 at 111, [1972] AC 24 at 43):

'There is no doubt that a person of full age and capacity cannot be ordered to undergo a blood test against his will...The real reason is that English law goes to great lengths to protect a person of full age and capacity from interference with his personal liberty. We have too often seen freedom disappear in other countries not only by coups d'état but by gradual erosion; and often it is the first step that counts. So it would be unwise to make even minor concessions.'

The importance of this salutary warning remains undiminished.

There are occasions when an individual lacks the capacity to make decisions about whether or not to consent to treatment. This may arise when he is unconscious or suffering from mental disability. This question will have to be examined more closely in due course, but dealing with it generally for the moment, where the adult patient is disabled from giving consent the medical practitioners must act in his best interests and if appropriate, may carry out major invasive surgery without express consent.

The status of the foetus

Ignoring those occasions when consent may be implied or dispensed with on the ground of incapacity, each woman is entitled to refuse treatment for herself. It does not follow without any further analysis that this entitles her to put at risk the healthy viable foetus which she is carrying. Concern for the sanctity of human life led Lord Donaldson MR in *Re T* (*adult: refusal of medical treatment*) [1992] 4 All ER 649 at 653, [1993] Fam 95 at 102 to express a degree of hesitation against making any such assumption.

'An adult patient who...suffers from no mental incapacity has an absolute right to choose...one rather than another of the treatments being offered. The only possible qualification is a case in which the choice may lead to the death of a viable foetus. That is not this case and, if and when it arises, the courts will be faced with a novel problem of considerable legal and ethical complexity.'

(See also *Re S* (*adult: refusal of medical treatment*) [1992] 4 All ER 671, [1993] Fam 123, where Sir Stephen Brown P granted a declaration that, notwithstanding her refusal of consent on religious grounds, a Caesarean section could be performed on a mother to save her life and that of her unborn child.)

Whatever else it may be, a 36-week foetus is not nothing; if viable, it is not lifeless and it is certainly human. In *A-G's Reference (No 3 of 1994)* [1997] 3 All ER 936, [1998] AC 245 the House of Lords considered the status of the foetus before birth in the context of an allegation of murder arising when a pregnant woman was stabbed and, following premature labour, gave birth to a child who survived for 121 days before dying as a result of the stabbing. The conclusion of the Court of Appeal was that the foetus should be treated as an integral part of the mother in the same way as any other part of her body, such as her foot or her arm. This view was rejected in the House of Lords...

Accordingly, the interests of the foetus cannot be disregarded on the basis that in refusing treatment which would benefit the foetus, a mother is simply refusing treatment for herself.

In the present case there was no conflict between the interests of the mother and the foetus; no one was faced with the awful dilemma of deciding on one form of treatment which risked one of their lives in order to save the other. Medically, the procedures to be adopted to preserve the mother and her unborn child did not involve a preference for one rather than the other. The crucial issue can be identified by expressing the problem in different ways. If human life is sacred why is a mother entitled to refuse to undergo treatment if this would preserve the life of the foetus without damaging her own? In the United States, where such treatment has on occasion been forced on an unwilling mother, this question has been described as 'the unborn child's right to live' and 'the State's compelling interest in preserving the life of the foetus' (*Jefferson v Griffin Spalding County Hospital Authority* (1981) 274 SE 2d 457) or 'the potentiality of human life' (in *Re Madyyun* (1986) 573 A 2d 1259). In *Winnipeg Child and Family Services (Northwest Area) v G* (1997) 3 BHRC 611, a decision which will need further examination, in his dissenting judgment Major J commented (at 645): 'Where the harm is so great and the temporary remedy so slight, the law is compelled to act…Someone must speak for those who cannot speak for themselves.' That said however, how can a forced invasion of a competent adult's body against her will even for the most laudable of motives (the preservation of life) be ordered without irremediably damaging the principle of self-determination? When human life is at stake the pressure to provide an affirmative answer authorising unwanted medical intervention is very powerful. Nevertheless, the autonomy of each individual requires continuing protection even, perhaps particularly, when the motive for interfering with it is readily understandable, and indeed to many would appear commendable; hence the importance of remembering Lord Reid's warning against making 'even minor concessions'. If it has not already done so, medical science will no doubt one day advance to the stage when a very minor procedure undergone by an adult would save the life of his or her child, or perhaps the life of a child of a complete stranger. The refusal would rightly be described as unreasonable, the benefit to another human life would be beyond value, and the motives of the doctors admirable. If however the adult were compelled to agree, or rendered helpless to resist, the principle of autonomy would be extinguished…

In the particular context of the mother's right to self-determination and the interests of her foetus, this tension was considered in *Re MB (an adult: medical treatment)* [1997] 2 FCR 541, 38 BMLR 175. In this most difficult area of the law, practical decisions affecting the rights of a mother and her unborn child and the position of those responsible for their care, frequently require urgent resolution without the luxury of time to analyse the complex ethical problems which invariably arise. Accordingly, with the advantage of detailed skeleton arguments, the relevant statutory provisions and authorities were closely studied.

Giving the judgment of the court, Butler-Sloss LJ said ([1997] 2 FCR 541 at 561):

'…a competent woman who has the capacity to decide may, for religious reasons, other reasons, or no reasons at all, choose not to have medical intervention even though…the consequence may be the death or serious handicap of the child she bears or her own death. She may refuse to consent to the anaesthesia injection in the full knowledge that her decision may significantly reduce the chance of her unborn child being born alive. The foetus up to the moment of birth does not have any separate interests capable of being taken into account when a court has to consider an application for a declaration in respect of a Caesarean section operation. The court does not have the jurisdiction to declare that such medical intervention is lawful to protect the interests of the unborn child even at the point of birth.

As the mother in *Re MB* was found not to have been competent, strictly speaking this question did not arise for decision and, as Butler-Sloss LJ herself recognised, the observation was obiter.

It was however consistent with the reasoning in a line of authorities where a husband had made an unsuccessful application to prevent an abortion being performed on his wife: see *Paton v Trustees of BPAS* [1978] 2 All ER 987, [1979] QB 276 and *C v S* [1987] 1 All ER 1230, [1988] QB 135 and with *Re F (in utero)* [1988] 2 All ER 193 at 200, [1988] Fam 122 at 143…

In our judgment while pregnancy increases the personal responsibilities of a woman it does not diminish her entitlement to decide whether or not to undergo medical treatment. Although human, and protected by the law in a number of different ways set out in the judgment in *Re MB*, an unborn child is not a separate person from its mother. Its need for medical assistance does not prevail over her rights. She is entitled not to be forced to submit to an invasion of her body against her will, whether her own life or that of her unborn child depends on it. Her right is not reduced or diminished merely because her decision to exercise it may appear morally repugnant. The declaration in this case involved the removal of the baby from within the body of her mother under physical compulsion. Unless lawfully justified, this constituted an infringement of the mother's autonomy. Of themselves, the perceived needs of the foetus did not provide the necessary justification.

The Mental Health Act 1983

The Act cannot be deployed to achieve the detention of an individual against her will merely because her thinking process is unusual, even apparently bizarre and irrational, and contrary to the views of the overwhelming majority of the community at large. The prohibited reasoning is readily identified and easily understood. Here is an intelligent woman. She knows perfectly well that if she persists with this course against medical advice she is likely to cause serious harm, and possibly death, to her baby and to herself. No normal mother-to-be could possibly think like that. Although this mother would not dream of taking any positive steps to cause injury to herself or her baby, her refusal is likely to lead to such a result. Her bizarre thinking represents a danger to their safety and health. It therefore follows that she *must* be mentally disordered and detained in hospital in her own interests and those of her baby. The short answer is that she may be perfectly rational and quite outside the ambit of the Act, and will remain so notwithstanding her eccentric thought process.

Even when used by well-intentioned individuals for what they believe to be genuine and powerful reasons, perhaps shared by a large section of the community, unless the individual case falls within the prescribed conditions, the Act cannot be used to justify detention for mental disorder:

> '...no adult citizen of the United Kingdom is liable to be confined in any institution against his will, save by the authority of the law. That is a fundamental constitutional principle, traceable back to Ch 29 of Magna Carta 1297 (25 Edw 1 c 1) and before that to Ch 39 of Magna Carta (1215)...Powers therefore exist to ensure that those who suffer from mental illness may, in appropriate circumstances, be involuntarily admitted to mental hospitals and detained. But, and it is a very important but, the circumstances in which the mentally ill may be detained are very carefully prescribed by statute.' (*See Re S-C (mental patient: habeas corpus)* [1996] 1 All ER 532 at 534–535, [1996] QB 599 at 603 per Bingham MR.)

[JUDGE LJ considered the conditions for lawful detention under s 2 of the Mental Health Act and concluded]...

...The contemporaneous documents themselves demonstrate that those involved in the decision to make an application for admission failed to maintain the distinction between the urgent need of S for treatment arising from her pregnancy, and the separate question whether her mental disorder (in the form of depression) warranted her detention in hospital. From the reasoning to be found in them, the conclusion that the detention was believed to be warranted in order that adequate provision could be made to deal with S's pregnancy and the safety of her unborn child is unavoidable. The reasoning process emerges most strongly from [the social worker's] assessment. She expressly acknowledged that a psychiatric ward was not 'the best place' for S (a judgment confirmed by the very brief period S remained in Springfield Hospital before being transferred to St George's). She believed, rightly, that S's condition was threatened by her very severe pre-eclampsia. At the time when she reached her conclusion she did not suggest that detention was required for the purpose of assessing S's mental condition or treating her depression. Put another way, if S had not been suffering from severe pre-eclampsia there is nothing in the contemporaneous documents to suggest that an application for her detention would have been considered, let alone justified.

We are satisfied that, notwithstanding our view that the requirements of s 2(2)(b) might well have been fulfilled, the cumulative grounds prescribed in s 2(2)(a) were not established. Therefore the application for admission was unlawful. Appropriate declaratory relief will be ordered....

[JUDGE LJ went on to conclude that the admission of S to both hospitals was unlawful, and that there were serious deficiencies in the procedure which led to the granting by HOGG J of emergency declaratory relief.]

Appeal allowed.

QUESTION

Should an expectant mother be under a duty to act in the best interests of her unborn child?

NOTE

1. The decision in *St George's Healthcare NHS Trust v S* is noted by J. Herring [1998] CLJ 438. Herring points out that the Court of Appeal regards an individual's right of autonomy and bodily integrity as outweighing other principles, such as the sanctity of life, but queries ([1998] CLJ 438, at 440):

    Is it really true, as the Court of Appeal suggests, that there are no circumstances when it is permissible to infringe an individual's bodily integrity however great the harm caused to other people and however small the invasion of bodily integrity? No doubt if S's child had been born alive and needed a kidney transplant few would approve of the forcible taking of a kidney from S to save the child's life. However if a fearful epidemic threatened a State's population, would it not be permissible to take by force a blood sample from a citizen who appeared to have developed an immunity to the disease?

    How, if at all, could you distinguish between these two examples of forcible invasion of an individual's bodily integrity?

2. Note that in *R. Pretty v DPP* [2002] 1 All ER 1, [2001] UKHL 61, the House of Lords held that the claimant's right to life under Article 2 of the ECHR did not extend to encompass a right to assistance in ending her own life. This was upheld by the European Court of Human Rights in *Pretty v UK* (2002) 35 EHRR 1. For commentary, see D. Morris (2003) 1 EHRLR 65. Compare *Re B (adult: refusal of treatment)* [2002] 2 All ER 449, [2002] EWHC 429 (form), where a tetraplegic patient obtained a declaration that her life-support ventilator should be turned off.

3. Compare and contrast the decision in *Leigh v Gladstone* (1909) 26 TLR 139, where the force-feeding of a hunger-striking suffragette was deemed lawful, with *Secretary of State for the Home Department v Robb* [1995] Fam 12, where a declaration was obtained by prison officers that it was lawful to refrain from providing nutrition to a prisoner on hunger strike as long as he retained the capacity to refuse consent to that nutrition: in the latter case, Thorpe J accepted that the prisoner's right to autonomy and self-determination entitled him to refuse nutrition. Is *Robb* compatible with the decision in *Pretty*?

4. In *St George's Healthcare NHS Trust v S*, the detention of S was deemed to be unlawful. As already discussed above in respect of false imprisonment (p. 738, *ante*), the arrest and detention of a person can be lawful if authorised by statute or the residual common law powers of arrest. In the absence of such lawful authority, then arrest and detention will constitute false imprisonment, and the 'laying on of hands' necessary to

facilitate arrest may constitute battery. Absent any statutory or common law authorisation, there is no general lawful authority to detain for non-payment of debt: see *Sunbolf
v Alford* (1838) 3 M&W 247, 150 ER 1135. However, is this reconcilable with *Herd v
Weardale Steel Coal and Coke Co Ltd* (p. 741, ante), or with *Robertson v Balmain New
Ferry Company* (p. 740, ante)?

5.   Police powers of arrest and detention are set out in the Police and Criminal Evidence
Act 1984 (which are supplemented by additional powers contained in the Terrorism
Act 2000 and in other statutes). The powers of detention of prison authorities are set
out in the Prisons Act 1952, and those of mental health authorities are set out in the
Mental Health Act 1983. If these powers are exceeded or wrongfully invoked, then
a cause of action for trespass to the person exists: see *Murray v Ministry of Defence*
(p. 732, ante), and the discussion above of *Hague v Deputy Governor of Parkhurst Prison*
noted at p. 734, ante. This is one of the ways in which trespass to the person functions
as an essential guarantor of civil liberties and individual freedom in a rule of law-based
system: the tort remedies provide the sanction for failure to conform to the lawful use
of state power.

6.   The importance of ensuring adherence to the limits of lawful authority were confirmed in the significant House of Lords decision in *R (Laporte) v Chief Constable of
Gloucestershire Constabulary* [2007] 2 All ER 529, [2006] UKHL 55, where the House
of Lords held that the police power to take preventive action to prevent a breach of the
peace could only be exercised when a breach of the peace was imminent. As no such
breach of the peace had been imminent in the circumstances of this case, the police had
acted outside the scope of their powers in preventing a coach-load of demonstrators
from proceeding to protest at an RAF airbase against the war on Iraq. Note that their
Lordships differed as to when the police could be said to have acted outside the scope of
their powers: Lord Bingham and Lord Mance applied an objective test and considered
that on the facts of the case the police could not have regarded a breach of the peace
as imminent; Lord Rodger and Lord Carswell took the view that the police had not in
fact considered that a breach of the peace was imminent; while Lord Brown considered
that the view that a breach of the peace was imminent was not open to the police in the
circumstances, either as a matter of fact or of law. Note also that this case involved an
application for judicial review and was decided to a considerable degree by reference to
the European Convention on Human Rights, and in particular the rights to expression
and freedom of association protected in Articles 10 and 11 of the Convention, respectively. No claim for false imprisonment was made in this case, but such an action would
have been available: *Laporte* shows how the protection of the Convention is paralleling
and even at times standing in for the role traditionally performed by trespass to the
person. Note, however, that in *Austin v Metropolitan Police Comr* [2008] 1 All ER 564,
[2007] EWCA Civ 989, the Court of Appeal viewed the concept of confinement under
the tort of false imprisonment as capable of applying in a situation where the ECHR
concept of deprivation of liberty did not, indicating that there may be circumstances
where the common law provides greater protection than the Convention. Note too that
only 'public authorities' as defined under s. 6 HRA are subject to the requirement to
adhere to the Convention rights, although there is no doubt that the Convention standards may 'seep' into the common law.

7.   In *Thames Valley Police v Hepburn* [2002] EWCA Civ 1841, Sedley LJ commented that
'[i]t is a bedrock of our civil liberties that a citizen's freedom of person and movement
is inviolable except where the law unequivocally gives the state power to restrict it...'.

However, the Court of Appeal in *Austin v Metropolitan Police Comr* considered that the confinement of the protestors was lawfully justified, on the basis that it was necessary to prevent a breach of the peace. Is the defence of necessity stretched too far here, especially given the far-reaching nature of the confinement in question? See also *Connor v Chief Constable of Merseyside Police* [2006] EWCA Civ 1549, and contrast the approach taken in *Thames Valley Police v Hepburn*. Also, contrast how necessity is applied in both *Austin* and *Connor* with how this concept is applied in *St George's Healthcare NHS Trust v S* [1999] Fam 26, [1998] 3 All ER 673 (p. 769, ante).

■ Cockcroft v Smith
Court of Queen's Bench (1705) 11 Mod Rep 43

Cockcroft in a scuffle ran his finger towards Smith's eyes, who bit a joint off from the plaintiff's finger.

The question was, whether this was a proper defence for the defendant to justify in an action of *mayhem*.

HOLT CJ: . . .
said, if a man strike another, who does not immediately after resent it, but takes his opportunity, and then some time after falls upon him and beats him, in this case, *son assault* is no good plea; neither ought a man, in case of a small assault, give a violent or an unsuitable return; but in such case plead what is necessary for a man's defence, and not who struck first; though this, he said, has been the common practice, but this he wished was altered; for hitting a man a little blow with a little stick on the shoulder, is not a reason for him to draw a sword and cut and hew the other, &c.

NOTE

The conduct of the *claimant* which is involved in this section may be a crime and in his situation the student should note s. 3 of the Criminal Law Act 1967 (replacing the common law), which provides that the 'person may use such force as is reasonable in the circumstances in the prevention of crime....'. See further *Farrell v Secretary of State for Defence* [1980] 1 All ER 166, [1980] 1 WLR 172.

■ Green v Goddard
Court of Queen's Bench (1702) 2 Salk 641

. . . *Et per Cur.* There is a force *in law*, as in every trespass *quare clausum fregit*: as if one enters into my ground, in that case the owner must request him to depart before he can lay hands on him to turn him out; for every *impositio manuum* is an assault and battery, which cannot be justified upon the account of breaking the close in law, without a request. The other is an *actual force*, as in burglary, as breaking open a door or gate; and in that case it is lawful to oppose force to force; and if one breaks down the gate, or comes into my close *vi & armis*, I need not request him to be gone, but may lay hands on him immediately, for it is but returning violence with violence: so if one comes forcibly and takes away my goods, I may oppose him without any more ado, for there is no time to make a request. . . .

NOTES

1. In *Lane v Holloway* [1968] 1 QB 379, [1967] 3 All ER 129, the Court of Appeal held that a blow struck in retaliation for an initial blow by the claimant was out of all proportion to the original act, so self-defence was not available as a justification.

2.   In *Ashley v Chief Constable of Sussex Police* [2008] 2 WLR 975, [2008] UKHL 25, the House of Lords took the position that, in order to establish self-defence in civil proceedings for battery, the defendant had to show not only that the action taken in self-defence must be reasonable, but also that the belief that it was necessary to act in self-defence was both honestly and reasonably held. This varies from the criminal law standard, where honest belief will be sufficient. However, their Lordships considered that the differing functions of the criminal and civil law, and the need to strike a balance between the different rights of different individuals in the latter, justified imposing a requirement that the belief in question was reasonably held and thus departing from the criminal standard. Lord Scott even suggested at [20] that a defendant may have to show that there was in fact an imminent and real risk of attack before self-defence could be established. Lord Neuberger at [89] and Lord Carswell at [76] were of the opinion that this was not necessary, as was Sir Anthony Clarke MR in the Court of Appeal. However, as this was not argued before their Lordships, this discussion remained obiter.

CHAPTER FOURTEEN

INTERFERENCE WITH LAND

It was pointed out in the Introduction (p. 1, ante) that to a lawyer from a civil law system the arrangement of English law seems faulty because the possession of land is protected in English law through trespass, an action in tort. The law regulating some aspects of the conduct of neighbouring landowners is also dealt with in tort, through the action in respect of nuisance, rather than as a part of the law of property.

It has been seen (chap. 13, ante) that fault is now an essential ingredient in trespass to the person, and this is also the position in the case of trespass to goods (*National Coal Board v Evans* [1951] 2 KB 861, [1951] 2 All ER 310): whether fault (in the sense of intention or negligence) in respect of the entry is essential in all cases of actions for trespass to land is less clear; but in an action for trespass by hounds (*League Against Cruel Sports Ltd v Scott* [1986] QB 240, [1986] 2 All ER 489) it was decided that the master of hounds was only liable if he had intended their entry or was negligent in failing to stop it. Whatever the position on that point, one common characteristic of all these trespass actions is that they are actionable without proof of damage. Nevertheless, it should be noted that a claimant who has not suffered any damage risks having a 'frivolous action' disapproved of by the awarding of 'contemptuous damages', and is likely to have to pay his own costs. A further point to note about actions for trespass to land is that they can be used not simply to settle questions of title to land, but again in common with other trespass actions (in particular false imprisonment), they can be important in the constitutional sphere, protecting the Englishman's castle/home against unlawful intrusions: *Entick v Carrington* (1765) 19 State Trials 1029.

The tort of nuisance takes two forms, the one called public nuisance, the other private nuisance, but the same conduct may amount to both. Public nuisance has been said to 'cover a multitude of sins, great and small' (per Denning LJ in *Southport Corpn v Esso Petroleum Co Ltd* [1954] 2 QB 182 at 196), and a definition will be found in the judgment of Lawton J in *British Celanese Ltd v A H Hunt (Capacitors) Ltd* [1969] 2 All ER 1252, [1969] 1 WLR 959 (p. 798, post). A public nuisance is primarily a crime, but can give rise to a civil action by an individual where he suffers some particular damage greater than that suffered by the public. Public nuisances share with private nuisances the element of annoyance or inconvenience; more broadly, private nuisance is described (by *Winfield & Jolowicz*, p. 646) as 'unlawful interference with a person's use or enjoyment of land, or some right over, or in connection with it'.

Nuisance differs from trespass in that an action will lie for nuisance, but not trespass, if the damage is merely consequential upon the defendant's act and not 'direct'; moreover, nuisance is in general actionable only on proof of actual damage. The rule in *Rylands v Fletcher* (1868) LR 3 HL 330 (p. 828, post), which is concerned with the escape of dangerous things from land, may also have to be distinguished from trespass, since in *Rigby v Chief Constable of Northamptonshire* [1985] 2 All ER 985, [1985] 1 WLR 1242 Taylor J was inclined to agree with the argument that *Rylands v Fletcher* is only concerned with indirect damage, and that it does not apply in cases of intentional or voluntary release of dangerous things (which would have to be remedied in trespass). On the other hand, in *Crown River Cruises Ltd v Kimbolton Fireworks Ltd* [1996] 2 Lloyd's Rep 533 at 547, Potter J would not limit liability to accidental escapes 'at least where the release (though not intentional) is not deliberately aimed in the direction of the plaintiff or with the intention of impinging upon his property'.

Rylands v Fletcher is now, it seems, to be treated as a particular sub-species of nuisance, following the House of Lords' decisions in *Cambridge Water Co Ltd v Eastern Countries Leather plc* [1994] AC 264, [1994] 1 All ER 53 (p. 834, post) and *Transco plc v Stockport Metropolitan Borough Council* [2004] 1 All ER 589, [2003] UKHL 61 (p. 843, post), although for critical commentary on *Transco* see D. Nolan (2005) 121 LQR 421 and J. Murphy (2004) 24 OJLS 643. Nuisance was firmly restated as a tort protecting property rights, and not any broader interest in occupation, in *Hunter v Canary Wharf* [1997] AC 655, [1997] 2 All ER 426 (p. 790, post), although for a challenge to this on Human Rights Act grounds, cf. *McKenna v British Aluminium*, noted p. 853, post. A very difficult problem is the role of fault in this tort (or torts). In *The Wagon Mound (No. 2)* [1967] 1 AC 617, [1966] 2 All ER 709 (p. 802, post), Lord Reid remarked enigmatically that although 'negligence in the narrow sense is not essential', in much of what is called the tort of nuisance, 'fault of some kind is almost always necessary'. The process of assimilation between nuisance and negligence seems to have proceeded apace in recent years: see e.g. Lord Cooke's remarks in *Delaware Mansions v Westminster City Council* [2001] 4 All ER 737, [2001] UKHL 55, noted p. 807, post. However, in *Transco* the House of Lords refused an invitation to follow the Australian absorption of *Rylands v Fletcher* into negligence. A distinction (however indistinct!) thus remains.

The final section of this chapter deals with liability for fire, which has often been considered to be within the rule in *Rylands v Fletcher*, although liability for fire at common law has its own separate history. In *H & N Emanuel Ltd v Greater London Council* [1971] 2 All ER 835 (p. 856, post) the old common law action for damage by fire received judicial attention. A more modern hazard, nuclear installations, has been subject to special legislation, and liability for such installations should be studied in the light of that legislation, p. 666, ante. For further legislative activity relevant to 'dangerous things', see the Environment Protection Act 1990, which can, in certain circumstances, entail civil liability.

1 TRESPASS TO LAND

■ Salmond and Heuston on the Law of Torts (21st edn, p. 40)

The tort of trespass to land (trespass *quare clausum fregit*) consists in the act of (1) entering upon land in the possession of the plaintiff, or (2) remaining upon such land, or (3) placing or projecting any object upon it—in each case without lawful justification.

(a) Special situations

(i) The highway

■ Director of Public Prosecutions v Jones
House of Lords [1999] 2 All ER 257

The appellants and the members of their group, who had been on the grass verge of the A344 near to Stonehenge, were found by the Salisbury Crown Court to have acted peacefully and to have been making a reasonable user of the highway, and thus not to have committed an offence under s.14B(2) of the Public Order Act 1986. The Divisional Court restored their convictions [1997] 2 All ER 119, and there was a further appeal to the House of Lords. The certified point of law of general public importance was whether a peaceful, non-obstructive assembly of 20 or more persons on the public highway, within the area and time covered by an order made under s. 14A(2) of the Public Order Act 1986 prohibiting the holding of trespassory assemblies, exceeded the public's right of access to the highway so as to constitute a trespass.

LORD IRVINE OF LAIRG LC:...
The central issue in the case...turns on two interrelated questions: (i) what are the 'limits' of the public's right of access to the public highway at common law? and (ii) what is the 'particular purpose' for which the public has a right to use the public highway?...

The position at common law
The Divisional Court's decision is founded principally on three authorities.

[Having referred to *Ex p Lewis* (1888) 21 QBD 191, LORD IRVINE continued:]
In *Harrison v Duke of Rutland* [1893] 1 QB 142, [1891–4] All ER Rep 514 the plaintiff had used the public highway, which crossed the defendant's land, for the sole and deliberate purpose of disrupting grouse shooting upon the defendant's land, and was forcibly restrained by the defendant's servants from doing so. The plaintiff sued the defendant for assault; and the defendant pleaded justification on the basis that the plaintiff had been trespassing upon the highway. Lord Esher MR held ([1893] 1 QB 142 at 146, [1891–4] All ER Rep 514 at 516–517):

> '...on the ground that the plaintiff was on the highway, the soil of which belonged to the Duke of Rutland, not for the purpose of using it in order to pass and repass, *or for any reasonable or usual mode of using the highway as a highway*, I think he was a trespasser.' (My emphasis.)

Plainly Lord Esher MR contemplated that there may be 'reasonable or usual' uses of the highway beyond passing and repassing. He continued ([1893] 1 QB 142 at 146–147, [1891–4] All ER Rep 514 at 517):

> 'Highways are, no doubt, dedicated prima facie for the purpose of passage; but things are done upon them by everybody which are recognised as being rightly done, and as constituting a reasonable and usual mode of using a highway as such. If a person on a highway does not transgress such reasonable and usual mode of using it, I do not think that he will be a trespasser.'

[His Lordship then referred to the judgments of Lopes and Kay LJJ in this case which stated that the right of the public on the highway was only to pass and repass, and continued:]
The question to which this appeal gives rise is whether the law today should recognise that the public highway is a public place, on which all manner of reasonable activities may go on. For the reasons I set out below in my judgment it should. Provided these activities are reasonable, do not involve the commission of a public or private nuisance, and do not amount to an obstruction of the highway unreasonably impeding the primary right of the general public to pass and repass, they should not constitute a

trespass. Subject to these qualifications, therefore, there would be a public right of peaceful assembly on the public highway....

To commence from a premise, that the right of passage is the only right which members of the public are entitled to exercise on a highway, is circular: the very question in this appeal is whether the public's right is confined to the right of passage. I conclude that the judgments of Lord Esher MR and Collins LJ [in *Hickman v Maisey* [1900] 1 QB 752 at 757–758] are authority for the proposition that the public have the right to use the public highway for such reasonable and usual activities as are consistent with the general public's primary right to use the highway for purposes of passage and repassage.

Nor can I attribute any hard core of meaning to a test which would limit lawful use of the highway to what is incidental or ancillary to the right of passage. In truth very little activity could accurately be described as 'ancillary' to passing along the highway; perhaps stopping to tie one's shoe lace, consulting a street-map, or pausing to catch one's breath. But I do not think that such ordinary and usual activities as making a sketch, taking a photograph, handing out leaflets, collecting money for charity, singing carols, playing in a Salvation Army band, children playing a game on the pavement, having a picnic, or reading a book, would qualify. These examples illustrate that to limit lawful use of the highway to that which is literally 'incidental or ancillary' to the right of passage would be to place an unrealistic and unwarranted restriction on commonplace day-to-day activities. The law should not make unlawful what is commonplace and well accepted.

Nor do I accept that the broader modern test which I favour materially realigns the interests of the general public and landowners. It is no more than an exposition of the test Lord Esher MR proposed in 1892. It would not permit unreasonable use of the highway, nor use which was obstructive. It would not, therefore, afford carte blanche to squatters or other uninvited visitors. Their activities would almost certainly be unreasonable or obstructive or both. Moreover the test of reasonableness would be strictly applied where narrow highways across private land are concerned, for example, narrow footpaths or bridle paths, where even a small gathering would be likely to create an obstruction or a nuisance....

I conclude therefore the law to be that the public highway is a public place which the public may enjoy for any reasonable purpose, provided the activity in question does not amount to a public or private nuisance and does not obstruct the highway by unreasonably impeding the primary right of the public to pass and repass; within these qualifications there is a public right of peaceful assembly on the highway....

LORD HUTTON:...

[T]he issue which arises in the present appeal is whether the right of the public to use the highway, as stated by Lopes LJ in *Harrison v Duke of Rutland*,[1] should be extended and should include the right to hold a peaceful public assembly on a highway...which causes no obstruction to persons passing along the highway and which the Crown Court found to be a reasonable user of the highway.

In my opinion your Lordships' House should so hold for three main reasons which are as follows. First, the common law recognises that there is a right for members of the public to assemble together to express views on matters of public concern and I consider that the common law should now recognise that this right, which is one of the fundamental rights of citizens in a democracy, is unduly restricted unless it can be exercised in some circumstances on the public highway. Secondly, the law as to trespass on the highway should be in conformity with the law relating to proceedings for wilful obstruction of the highway under s. 137 of the Highways Act 1980 that a peaceful assembly on the highway may be a reasonable use of the highway. Thirdly, there is a recognition in the authorities that it may be appropriate that the public's right to use the highway should be extended, in the words of Collins LJ in *Hickman v Maisey* [1900] 1 QB 752 at 758:

> '...in accordance with the enlarged notions of people in a country becoming more populous and highly civilised, but they must be such as are not inconsistent with the maintenance of the paramount idea that the right of the public is that of passage.

[1] [1893] 1 QB 142 at 54—this was to pass and repass at their pleasure for the purpose of legitimate travel.

[LORD HUTTON then proceeded to expand on these reasons. When elaborating on the first reason, he referred to the judgment of Lord Denning MR in *Hubbard v Pitt* [1976] 1 QB 142 at 178–179 and to that of Otton LJ in *Hirst v Chief Constable of West Yorkshire* (1987) 85 Cr App Rep 143 at 151, both of which refer to a right to protest and to demonstrate, and continued:]

If, as in my opinion it does, the common law recognises the right of public assembly, I consider that the common law should also recognise that in some circumstances this right can be exercised on the highway, provided that it does not obstruct the passage of other citizens, because otherwise the value of the right is greatly diminished....

Therefore, for the reasons which I have given, I am of opinion that the holding of a public assembly on a highway can constitute a reasonable user of the highway and accordingly will not constitute a trespass and I would allow the appeal. But I desire to emphasise that my opinion that this appeal should be allowed is based on the finding of the Crown Court that the assembly in which the defendants took place on this particular highway, the A344, at this particular time, constituted a reasonable use of the highway. I would not hold that a peaceful and non-obstructive public assembly on a highway is always a reasonable user and is therefore not a trespass.

It is for the tribunal of fact to decide whether the user was reasonable. In *Hirst*'s case (1987) 85 Cr App R 143 at 150 Glidewell LJ makes it clear that a reasonable activity in the street may become unreasonable by reason of the space occupied or the duration of time for which it goes on, 'but it is a matter on the facts for the magistrates, in my view'.

If members of the public took part in an assembly on a highway but the highway was, for example, a small, quiet country road or was a bridleway or a footpath, and the assembly interfered with the landowner's enjoyment of the land across which the highway ran or which is bordered, I think it would be open to the justices to hold that, notwithstanding the importance of the democratic right to hold a public assembly, nevertheless in the particular circumstances of the case the assembly was an unreasonable user of the highway and therefore constituted a trespass....

For the reasons which I have given I would allow the appeal and would answer the certified question before your Lordships' House as follows: 'No, if the tribunal of fact finds that the assembly was a reasonable user of the highway'.

[LORD CLYDE delivered a speech in favour of allowing the appeal. LORD SLYNN OF HADLEY and LORD HOPE OF CRAIGHEAD delivered speeches in favour of dismissing the appeal.]

Appealed allowed.

NOTES

1. In his dissenting speech in *DPP v Jones* Lord Slynn would have restricted the public's right on the highway to passing and repassing and 'reasonably incidental uses associated with passage'; and Lord Hope, also dissenting, emphasised that the highway is for passage and any other use of it by the public must be 'a reasonable and usual mode of using it as such' to fall within the public right. *DPP v Jones* has a constitutional dimension; this cannot be explored here (cf. I. Hare [1999] CLJ 265). Furthermore, as Lord Hope pointed out, the decision affects private landowners and no-one had been heard to defend their interests. A point of contrast between the majority and minority opinions is that the focus of the former is on the compatibility of the activity in question with the *passage of others* on the highway (although this is not the only test); the focus of the latter is on the link between the activity in question and the use of the highway for *passage by the person carrying out the activity*.

2. If a defendant obstructs the highway, he may commit not only a trespass but also a public nuisance. Furthermore, he may involve himself in criminal liability: see s. 137 of the Highways Act 1980 and *Hirst v Chief Constable of West Yorkshire* (1987) 85 Cr App Rep 143, discussed in Lord Hutton's speech, ante.

(ii) Air Space

NOTES

1. In *Lord Bernstein of Leigh v Skyviews and General Ltd* [1978] QB 479, [1977] 2 All ER 902 the defendants flew over the claimant's house, photographed it, and offered to sell him the image. The claimant brought an action alleging invasion of privacy. Griffiths J held that there had been no trespass to the claimant's land. He commented that while it might be sensible to regard buildings or structures overhanging a claimant's land as a trespass, 'wholly different considerations arise when considering the passage of aircraft at a height which in no way affects the user of the land'. The learned judge referred to the maxim *'cujus est solum ejus est usque ad coelum et ad inferos'* as 'a colourful phrase often on the lips of lawyers since it was first coined by Accursius in Bologna in the 13th century'. He warned, however, that 'if applied literally it is a fanciful notion leading to the absurdity of a trespass at common law being committed by a satellite every time it passes over a suburban garden. The academic writers speak with one voice in rejecting the uncritical and literal application of the maxim.' Applying the test to the facts, Griffiths J stated that the defendants' aircraft was 'on any view of the evidence flying many hundreds of feet above the ground and it is not suggested that by its mere presence in the air space it caused any interference with any use to which the [claimant] put or might wish to put his land'. Thus, there was no trespass.

2. In *Bernstein*, Griffiths J commented that the real basis of the claimant's complaint was the aerial photograph, but there was 'no law against taking a photograph, and the mere taking of a photograph cannot turn an act which is not a trespass into the plaintiff's air space into one that is a trespass'. On invasion of privacy, which in suitable circumstances the tort of trespass may remedy (but not, as this case shows, in all cases), see further chapter 17, post. See also the note on *Bernstein* by R. Wacks (1977) 93 LQR 491.

3. On aircraft, see further the Civil Aviation Act 1982, s. 76, which provides that no action in nuisance or trespass shall lie against an aircraft flying over land at a height which is reasonable in the circumstances, provided that the provisions of any Air Navigation Order etc. have been complied with. Section 76(2) provides, however, that the owner of an aircraft shall be strictly liable for material loss or damage to 'any person or property on land or water' caused by an aircraft in flight (unless the damage 'was caused or contributed to by the negligence of the person by whom it was suffered'). The provisions survived a challenge in the European Court of Human Rights: see *Powell and Rayner v United Kingdom* (1990) 12 EHRR 355. For a further case of noise nuisance from aircraft see *Hatton v United Kingdom* [2003] All ER (D) 122 (Jul), relied upon by the House of Lords in *Marcic v Thames Water Utilities* [2004] 1 All ER 135, [2003] UKHL 66 (p. 821, post).

4. In *Anchor Brewhouse Developments Ltd v Berkely House Docklands Developments Ltd* [1987] 2 EGLR 173 the question arose whether there could be a trespass action in respect of tower cranes which stood on the defendant's property, but of which part would swing into the air space over the plaintiff's property. Reference was made by counsel for the defendant to dicta of Griffiths J in the *Bernstein* case concerning the need to balance the owner's rights against those of the public. However, Scott J in *Anchor Brewhouse* thought it would be wrong to apply that approach, which in his view related

to the question of aircraft, to the general problem of invasion of the air space. In his opinion 'if somebody erects on his own land a structure, part of which invades the air space above the land of another, the invasion is trespass'. (Scott J in *Anchor Brewhouse* also rejected the argument that the test should be one of interference with the ordinary use and enjoyment.) On the question of injunctive relief for trespass, see further *Jaggard v Sawyer* [1995] 2 All ER 189, [1995] 1 WLR 269.

(b) The claimant

NOTES

1. In *Graham v Peate* (1801) 1 East 244, the claimant was able to maintain an action in trespass despite defects in his title (owing to a statute concerning leases of ecclesiastical lands). Lord Kenyon CJ said:

    Any possession is a legal possession against a wrongdoer. Suppose a burglary committed in the dwelling-house of such an one, must it not be laid to be his dwelling-house notwithstanding the defect of his title under that statute.

    This case shows that the saying that possession is nine tenths of the law is not without truth. (On the concept of possession, see further F. Pollock and R. S. Wright, *An Essay on Possession in the Common Law* (Oxford, 1888).)

2. A person with possession of property will not always succeed in a trespass action. In *Delaney v T P Smith Ltd* [1946] KB 393, [1946] 2 All ER 23 the claimant made an oral agreement with an agent of the defendants for the tenancy of a house which was being repaired. Before the house was ready, the defendants decided that they would sell the house (along with several others), and wrote to the claimant to that effect. Some time later the claimant obtained a key and took possession of the premises, but nine days later was forcibly ejected by the defendants, from whom he claimed damages for trespass. He alleged that he was the tenant of the house and protected by the provisions of the Rent and Mortgage Interest Restrictions Acts 1923–1939, but was faced by an argument from the defendants, based on s. 40 of the Law of Property Act 1925, that no note or memorandum existed relating to the alleged tenancy. (Section 40 of the Law of Property Act 1925 has subsequently been replaced by s. 2 of the Law of Property (Miscellaneous Provision) Act 1989.) It was pointed out in the Court of Appeal that in an action for trespass to land, an allegation of possession by a claimant would suffice against a wrongdoer, but not against the lawful owner. Against the freeholder here, the claimant had to rely on the oral agreement, to which s. 40 provided an answer. (Cf. *Lane v Dixon* (1847) 3 CB 776.) *Delaney v T P Smith Ltd* was cited in *Portland Managements Ltd v Harte* [1977] QB 306, [1976] 1 All ER 225, where the position of an owner bringing a trespass action against someone alleged to be in possession of his property was considered. In this situation it was accepted that once the court is satisfied that the claimant in a trespass action is the owner of the property in question and intending to regain possession, then the burden is on the defendant to establish some right to possession which is consistent with the claimant being the owner.

    On the question of who may sue in trespass, see further *Winfield & Jolowicz*, pp. 474–476; *Street*, pp. 77–79; *Clerk & Lindsell*, paras. 17-09–17-23.

(c) The nature of the defendant's act

■ Smith v Stone
Court of King's Bench (1647) Sty 65

Smith brought an action of trespasse against Stone pedibus ambulando, the defendant pleads this special plea in justification, viz. that he was carryed upon the land of the plaintiff by force, and violence of others, and was not there voluntarily, which is the same trespasse, for which the plaintiff brings his action. The plaintiff demurs to this plea: in this case Roll Iustice said, that it is the trespasse of the party that carryed the defendant upon the land, and not the trespasse of the defendant: as he that drives my cattel into another mans land is the trespassor against him, and not I who am owner of the cattell.

■ Gilbert v Stone
Court of King's Bench (1647) Sty 72

Gilbert brought an action of trespasse quare clausum fregit, and taking of a gelding, against Stone. The defendant pleads that he for fear of his life, and wounding of twelve armed men, who threatened to kill him if he did not the fact, went into the house of the plaintiff, and took the gelding. The plaintiff demurred to this plea; Roll Iustice. This is no plea to justifie and defendant; for I may not do a trespasse to one for fear of threatnings of another, for by this means the party injured shall have no satisfaction, for he cannot have it of the party that threatened. Therefore let the plaintiff have his judgment.

QUESTION

What duty does an occupier of land owe to someone who has involuntarily gone on to his property?

(d) Necessity

NOTES

1. This defence, which has been mentioned in the context of intentional interference with the person (see p. 763, ante), might also be raised as a defence to trespass to land. However, in *London Borough of Southwark v Williams* [1971] Ch 734, [1971] 2 All ER 175, a case concerning squatters, the Court of Appeal seemed determined to keep the defence within fairly limited bounds. Lord Denning MR stated (at p. 179):

    If homelessness were once admitted as a defence to trespass, no one's house could be safe. Necessity would open a door which no man could shut. It would not only be those in extreme need who would enter. There would be others who would imagine that they were in need, or would invent a need, so as to gain entry. Each man would say his need was greater than the next man's. The plea would be an excuse for all sorts of wrongdoing. So the courts must, for the sake of law and order, take a firm stand. They must refuse to admit the plea of necessity to the hungry and the homeless; and trust that their distress will be relieved by the charitable and the good.

Edmund Davies LJ took the view that 'all the cases where a plea of necessity has succeeded are cases which deal with an urgent situation of imminent peril', though on the need for an 'emergency' in relation to this defence in general, see now *F v West Berkshire Health Authority (Mental Health Act Commission intervening)* [1989] 2 All ER 545 at 565 (p. 757, ante). On the defence of necessity consider further the position in cases such as *Cope v Sharpe (No 2)* [1912] 1 KB 496, and see *Monsanto plc v Tilly* [2000] Env LR 313 (no defence of public interest or necessity to protect third parties available to campaigners against genetically modified crops).

Compare the Access to Neighbouring Land Act 1992. Under this statute the court is required to grant a person an access order authorising entry onto one piece of land (the servient land) to allow them to carry out work which is reasonably necessary for the preservation of all or part of another piece of land (the dominant land) and, where, in the absence of such entry, it would not be possible to carry out the work at all or without substantially more difficulty. No order should be made, however, if the court thinks it unreasonable so to do in the light of the interference with anyone's use or enjoyment of the servient land or the hardship to its occupier(s) caused by such an order.

2. The necessity defence did succeed in *Rigby v Chief Constable of Northamptonshire* [1985] 2 All ER 985, [1855] 1 WLR 1242, but it was emphasised that for the plea to be successful the necessity for taking measures must not have been caused or contributed to by any negligence on the defendant's part. Negligence is used here in the sense of the standard required by the tort of negligence, rather than any stricter standard (see [1985] 2 All ER at pp. 944–945), and once the issue of negligence is raised, the burden is on the defendant to disprove it.

2 NUISANCE

(a) In general

■ St Helen's Smelting Co v Tipping
House of Lords (1865) 11 HL Cas 642

The Lord Chancellor (Lord Westbury) stated the following facts: 'Now, in the present case, it appears that the Plaintiff purchased a very valuable estate, which lies within a mile and a half from certain large smelting works. What the occupation of these copper smelting premises was anterior to the year 1860 does not clearly appear. The Plaintiff became the proprietor of an estate of great value in the month of June 1860. In the month of September 1860 very extensive smelting operations began on the property of the present Appellants [defendants] in their works at St Helen's. Of the effect of the vapours exhaling from whose works upon the Plaintiff's property, and the injury done to his trees and shrubs, there is abundance of evidence in the case.' The report sets out the direction which was given to the jury by Mellor J:

The learned Judge told the jury that an actionable injury was one producing sensible discomfort; that every man, unless enjoying rights obtained by prescription or agreement, was bound to use his own property in such a manner as not to injure the property of his neighbours; that there was no prescriptive right in this case; that the law did not regard trifling inconveniences; that everything must be looked at from a reasonable point of view; and therefore, in an action for nuisance to property, arising from noxious vapours, the injury to be actionable must be such as visibly to diminish the value of the property and the comfort and enjoyment of it. That when the jurors came to consider the facts, all the circumstances, including those of time and locality, ought to be taken into consideration; and that with respect to the latter it was clear that in counties where great works had been erected and carried on, persons must not stand on their extreme rights and bring actions in respect of every matter of annoyance, for if so, the business of the whole country would be seriously interfered with.

The Defendants' counsel submitted that the three questions which ought to be left to the jury were, 'whether it was a necessary trade, whether the place was a suitable place for such a trade, and whether it was carried on in a reasonable manner.' The learned judge did not put the questions in this form, but did ask the jury whether the enjoyment of the Plaintiff's property was sensibly diminished, and the answer was in the affirmative. Whether the business there carried on was an ordinary business for smelting copper, and the answer was, 'We consider it an ordinary business, and conducted in a proper manner, in as good a manner as possible.' But to the question whether the jurors thought that it was carried on in a proper place, the answer was, 'We do not.' The verdict was therefore entered for the Plaintiff, and the damages were assessed at £361 18s 4½d. A motion was made for a new trial, on the ground of misdirection, but the rule was refused (4 Best and Sm 608). Leave was however given to appeal, and the case was carried to the Exchequer Chamber, where the judgment was affirmed, Lord Chief Baron Pollock there observing, 'My opinion has not always been that which it is now. Acting upon what has been decided *in this Court* my brother Mellor's direction is not open to a bill of exception' (4 Best and Sm 616). This appeal was then brought.

[The direction to the jury was approved by the House of Lords, and by the judges who were summoned. LORD WESTBURY LC continued:]...My Lords, in matters of this description it appears to me that it is a very desirable thing to mark the difference between an action brought for a nuisance upon the ground that the alleged nuisance produces material injury to the property, and an action brought for a nuisance on the ground that the thing alleged to be a nuisance is productive of sensible personal discomfort. With regard to the latter, namely, the personal inconvenience and interference with one's enjoyment, one's quiet, one's personal freedom, anything that discomposes or injuriously affects the senses or the nerves, whether that may or may not be denominated a nuisance, must undoubtedly depend greatly on the circumstances of the place where the thing complained of actually occurs. If a man lives in a town, it is necessary that he should subject himself to the consequences of those operations of trade which may be carried on in his immediate locality, which are actually necessary for trade and commerce, and also for the enjoyment of property, and for the benefit of the inhabitants of the town and of the public at large. If a man lives in a street where there are numerous shops, and a shop is opened next door to him, which is carried on in a fair and reasonable way, he has no ground for complaint, because to himself individually there may arise much discomfort from the trade carried on in that shop. But when an occupation is carried on by one person in the neighbourhood of another, and the result of that trade, or occupation, or business, is a material injury to property, then there unquestionably arises a very different consideration. I think, my Lords, that in a case of that description, the submission which is required from persons living in society to that amount of discomfort which may be necessary for the legitimate and free exercise of the trade of their neighbours, would not apply to circumstances the immediate result of which is sensible injury to the value of the property....

[Having stated the facts as above, he continued:] My Lords, the action has been brought upon that, and the jurors have found the existence of the injury; and the only ground upon which your Lordships are asked to set aside that verdict, and to direct a new trial, is this, that the whole neighbourhood where these copper smelting works were carried on, is a neighbourhood more or less devoted to manufacturing purposes of a similar kind, and therefore it is said, that inasmuch as this copper smelting is carried on in what the Appellant contends is a fit place, it may be carried on with impunity, although the result may be the utter destruction, or the very considerable diminution, of the value of the Plaintiff's property. My Lords, I apprehend that that is not the meaning of the word 'suitable', or the meaning of the word 'convenient', which has been used as applicable to the subject. The word 'suitable' unquestionably cannot carry with it this consequence, that a trade may be carried on in a particular locality, the consequence of which trade may be injury and destruction to the neighbouring property. Of course, my Lords, I except cases where any prescriptive right has been acquired by a lengthened user of the place.

On these grounds, therefore, shortly, without dilating farther upon them…I advise your Lordships to affirm the decision of the Court below, and to refuse the new trial, and to dismiss the appeal with costs.

[LORD CRANWORTH delivered a brief speech, in which he concurred with the LORD CHANCELLOR. LORD WENSLEYDALE agreed with both their Lordships.]

Judgment of the Exchequer Chamber affirming the judgment of the Court of Queen's Bench affirmed. Appeal dismissed.

NOTES

1. On the background to this case, see A. W. B Simpson, *Leading Cases in the Common Law* (Oxford, 1995), chap. 7. Simpson points out that Tipping later obtained an injunction to stop the defendants using the works in such a way that vapour or smoke from the works damaged the timber, plantations, gardens, pleasure grounds, and crops on his estate. He argues that the practical effect of the House of Lords' decision was very small because of the expense of bringing a nuisance action and the discretion given to juries under Mellor J's direction, whilst also noting McLaren's study ((1983) 3 OJLS 155), which shows how institutional and other factors greatly reduced the importance of the nuisance action in pollution cases.

2. Note further Lord Hoffmann's discussion in *Hunter v Canary Wharf Ltd* [1997] AC 655, [1997] 2 All ER 426 (p. 790, post) of the distinction drawn in the *St Helen's* case between 'material injury to property' and 'sensible personal discomfort'.

3. For criticism of the 'locality' principle in the *St Helen's* case, see R. A. Buckley, *The Law of Nuisance* 2nd edn (London, 1996), pp. 8–10; A. I. Ogus and G. M. Richardson [1977] CLJ 284 at 299.

4. As the *St Helen's* case shows, the nuisance action may play some part in the protection of the environment. Attention might also be paid to *Halsey v Esso Petroleum Co Ltd* [1961] 2 All ER 145, [1961] 1 WLR 683 where the defendants, who operated an oil-distributing depot near to the claimant's house, were held liable for: (a) damage caused by acid smuts escaping from the depot on to laundry hung out to dry (liability in nuisance and under *Rylands v Fletcher*); (b) damage similarly caused to the claimant's motor car on the highway (whether or not there could be a claim in private nuisance, there was liability under *Rylands v Fletcher* and in public nuisance); (c) nuisance caused by a 'nauseating smell' escaping from the depot; (d) nuisance at night caused by noise from the plant at the depot; (e) nuisance during the night shift caused by noise from tankers arriving at and leaving the depot (liability here was based either on private nuisance or in the alternative on public nuisance by virtue of their use of the highway). The character of the neighbourhood was relevant to the question of nuisance by smell and by noise. On the role of the tort of nuisance in environmental protection, see J. Steele, (1995) 15 LS 236. For statutory aspects of environmental protection, see e.g. *Winfield & Jolowicz*, pp. 640–643.

5. For an application of economic analysis to the action in private nuisance, see Ogus and Richardson op cit.; *Howarth*, pp. 497–499.

6.   Many circumstances may be taken into account in deciding whether there has been a nuisance. It is in this context that malice is relevant, although this statement must be read in the light of *Bradford Corpn v Pickles* [1895] AC 587. In that case, the defendant's excavations on his land interfered with percolating water under his land, and resulted in the claimants' water supply being diminished and occasionally discoloured. The claimants sought an injunction but were unsuccessful. The defendant had a right to act in this way (see *Chasemore v Richards* (1859) 7 HL Cas 349), and to the allegation that the defendant was acting maliciously, Lord Halsbury LC answered (at p. 594) that 'if it was a lawful act, however ill the motive might be, he had a right to do it'. In fact, Lord Macnaghten stated that it could be taken that Pickles' objective was to compel the Corporation to purchase his property at a price which suited him, but his Lordship drew attention to the lack of spite and ill-will on Pickles' part. *Salmond & Heuston* (21st edn, at p. 20) suggest that the common law did not regard his motive as improper.

    This decision, and particularly Lord Halsbury LC's dictum on the irrelevance of motive, must be compared with *Hollywood Silver Fox Farm Ltd v Emmett* [1936] 2 KB 468, [1936] 1 All ER 825. The claimant company was engaged in breeding silver foxes. There had been a disagreement between the defendant (an adjoining landowner) and the managing director of the claimant company about a notice on the claimant's land, and some months later the defendant sent his son out to the boundary of his land which was closest to the vixens' pens to fire a gun: the shooting was repeated for the next three evenings. The noise affected the vixens and caused the claimant loss, for there was evidence that the number of cubs reared was less than could have been expected. Some vixens did not mate and one ate her cubs. On the defendant's side, there was evidence that his son was shooting there to cut down the number of rabbits, but in fact the learned judge found that the son was sent to shoot there to frighten the vixens. Taking the view that *Bradford Corpn v Pickles* did not govern the case, and that the defendant's intention was relevant, Macnaghten J gave judgment for the claimant in his action for nuisance. (See also *Christie v Davey* [1893] 1 Ch 316.) The explanation of *Emmett*'s case would appear to lie in the following reasoning. Noise can be an interference with a person's use and enjoyment of land. However, the law of nuisance is concerned with balancing the interests of neighbouring landowners, and to be actionable as nuisance, it appears that there has to be an 'unreasonable' use of land by the defendant. Therefore, the purpose behind the creation of the 'nuisance' becomes a relevant factor, and the presence of malice may mean that a given amount of noise constitutes an actionable nuisance, where, in the absence of malice, it would not do so. As was pointed out in a note on *Emmett*'s case, the presence of malice destroys the 'qualified privilege to act in a reasonable manner' (1936) 52 LQR 460 at 461 (but see (1937) 53 LQR 1–4).

    The results in *Pickles*' case and *Emmett*'s case can be reconciled on the basis that a landowner has absolutely no right to the percolating water beneath his land: unlike noise, it is entirely unprotected by the law of nuisance. See also the discussion of the absence of any right to a pleasant view in *Hunter v Canary Wharf Ltd* [1997] AC 655, [1997] 2 All ER 426, p. 790, post. However, even on this basis, Lord Halsbury LC's dictum, cited above, is too wide. On the position in negligence concerning percolating water, see *Stephens v Anglian Water Authority* [1987] 3 All ER 379, [1987] 1 WLR 1381, noted p. 35, ante. Malice is relevant in the tort of conspiracy but is not in itself a cause of action—see *Allen v Flood* [1898] AC 1 (p. 865, post). On the question of 'reasonable user', see further the reference in note 4, p. 843, post, discussing Lord Goff's comments in *Cambridge Water Co Ltd v Eastern Counties Leather plc* [1994] 2 AC 264, [1994] 1 All ER 53 (p. 834, post).

7. It was pointed out in note 6, ante, that noise could constitute a nuisance, but also that the law of nuisance involved a balancing of the respective parties' interests. Following on from this, note the consolidated appeals in *Southwark London Borough Council v Mills* and *Baxter v Camden London Borough Council* [2001] 1 AC 1, [1999] 4 All ER 449, noted by by J. O'Sullivan [2000] CLJ 11 at 16–18, which concerned residents in flats and in which the House of Lords held that noise consequent upon normal occupation of property could not be a nuisance, even where it substantially interfered with the enjoyment of another's property. The problem lay in the inadequacy of the sound insulation.

8. Another factor to consider is the use to which the claimant is putting his land, and *Robinson v Kilvert* (1889) 41 Ch D 88 is often cited in this context. There, the defendants, who had let the ground floor of a warehouse to the claimant, started making paper boxes, for which heat and dry air were necessary. The heat passed into the claimant's room and dried his stocks of brown paper. Far from gaining any weight (which would happen if this paper was kept at a 'proper temperature' in an atmosphere with a normal moisture content), the paper lost weight and became brittle. In fact the paper was sold by weight, and the claimant suffered a loss of profit. Ordinary paper would not have been affected by the heat, nor was the heat such as to 'incommode' the claimant's workers, and the action failed. Doing something which was non-noxious was not a nuisance merely because it affected a particularly sensitive trade. On the other hand, a person suffering an interference with a sensitive use of land is not barred from recovery in nuisance if there would still have been a nuisance by normal standards. Both propositions are consistent with the orthodox understanding of private nuisance, now reaffirmed by *Hunter v Canary Wharf Ltd* [1997] AC 655, [1997] 2 All ER 426, p. 790, post, that it is a tort protecting land values.

    What sort of loss did the claimant sustain in *Robinson v Kilvert*—was it economic or physical loss? On recovery for economic loss in nuisance, see Buckley, op cit., pp. 75–77 (public nuisance) and pp. 126–127 (private nuisance).

    Robinson v Kilvert was considered by the Court of Appeal in *Network Rail Infrastructure Ltd v Morris (t/a Soundstar Studio)* [2004] EWCA Civ 172. Buxton LJ commented (relying upon *Delaware Mansions v Westminster City Council* [2001] 4 All ER 737, [2001] UKHL 55, noted p. 807, post) that a broad and unstructured balancing test based upon 'reasonableness' has come to replace the more detailed and particular rules found in earlier nuisance authorities such as *Robinson*. Buxton LJ commented at [35] that the development of nuisance in this regard was 'not dissimilar' to the tort of negligence, 'in which the generalisation of the law . . . initiated by *Donoghue v Stevenson* [p. 30, ante] has rendered obsolete the previous categories of dangerous chattels; duties of occupiers of land; duties attaching to specific trades; and the like'. However, since inordinate sensitivity of the claimant's land use must be relevant when considering 'reasonableness' of the defendant's activity (even when such sensitivity is foreseeable, as required by *Delaware Mansions*), it is suggested that the change will make little difference in practice.

■ Hunter v Canary Wharf Ltd

House of Lords [1997] 2 All ER 426

This case involved two actions brought by residents living in the area around Canary Wharf. In one action, brought in nuisance and negligence (although the latter head was later abandoned), damages were sought for a period of time when there was interference with television reception caused by the building of the Canary Wharf Tower on land Canary Wharf Ltd had developed; in the other action, also based on these two torts but with the addition of a claim (later abandoned) under *Rylands v Fletcher* (1868) LR 3 HL 330 (p. 828, post), damages were sought against the London Docklands Development Corporation for dust arising from their construction of a road in the area. A trial of various preliminary issues of law was ordered, and by the time the cases reached the House of Lords two remained. The first concerned whether interference with television reception could be an actionable nuisance and is not dealt with in this extract: it is, however, considered in note 5, p. 798, post. The second issue, which was raised in relation to both actions, concerned whether a plaintiff in private nuisance had to have an interest in land to be able to sue, and, if so, the nature of that interest.

LORD GOFF OF CHIEVELEY:...

Right to sue in private nuisance

...In the two cases now under appeal before your Lordships' House, one of which relates to interference with television signals and the other to the generation of dust from the construction of a road, the plaintiffs consist in each case of a substantial group of local people. Moreover, they are not restricted to householders who have the exclusive right to possess the places where they live, whether as freeholders or tenants, or even as licensees. They include people with whom householders share their homes, for example as wives or husbands or partners, or as children or other relatives. All of these people are claiming damages in private nuisance, by reason of interference with their television viewing or by reason of excessive dust.

Judge Havery [(1994) 42 Con LR 22 and 53] held that the right to sue in private nuisance did not extend to include so wide a class of plaintiffs, but was limited to those with a right to exclusive possession of the relevant property. His decision on this point was, however, reversed by the Court of Appeal, who, in the judgment delivered by Pill LJ, held (]1996] 1 All ER 482 at 498, [1996] 2 WLR 348 at 365):

> 'A substantial link between the person enjoying the use and the land on which he or she is enjoying it is essential but, in my judgment, occupation of property, as a home, does confer upon the occupant a capacity to sue in private nuisance.'

Against that decision, the defendants in both actions now appeal to your Lordships' House.

The basic position is, in my opinion, most clearly expressed in Professor Newark's classic article on 'The Boundaries of Nuisance' (1949) 65 LQR 480 at 482 when he stated that the essence of nuisance was that 'it was a tort to land. Or to be more accurate it was a tort directed against the plaintiff's enjoyment of rights over land'....

There are many authoritative statements which bear out this thesis of Professor Newark. I refer in particular to *Sedleigh-Denfield v O'Callaghan* [1940] 3 All ER 349 at 364, [1940] AC 880 at 902–903 per Lord Wright, *Read v J Lyons & Co Ltd* [1946] 2 All ER 471 at 482, [1947] AC 156 at 183 per Lord Simonds, *Tate & Lyle Food and Distribution Ltd v Greater London Council* [1983] 1 All ER 1159 at 1170, [1983] 2 AC 509 at 536–537 per Lord Templeman and Fleming *The Law of Torts* (8th edn, 1992) p. 416.

Since the tort of nuisance is a tort directed against the plaintiff's enjoyment of his rights over land, an action of private nuisance will usually be brought by the person in actual possession of the land affected, either as the freeholder or tenant of the land in question, or even as a licensee with exclusive possession of the land (see *Newcatle-under-Lyme Corp v Wolstanton Ltd* [1946] 2 All ER 447 at

455–456, [1947] Ch 92 at 106–108 per Evershed J); though a reversioner may sue in respect of a nuisance of a sufficiently permanent character to damage his reversion. It was however established, in *Foster v Warblington UDC* [1906] 1 KB 648, [1904–7] All ER Rep 366 that, since jus tertii is not a defence to an action of nuisance, a person who is in exclusive possession of land may sue even though he cannot prove title to it....

Subject to this exception, however, it has for many years been regarded as settled law that a person who has no right in the land cannot sue in private nuisance. For this proposition, it is usual to cite the decision of the Court of Appeal in *Malone v Laskey* [1907] 2 KB 141, [1904–7] All ER Rep 304....

The decision in *Malone v Laskey* on nuisance has since been followed in many cases, of which notable examples are *Cunard v Antifyre Ltd* [1933] 1 KB 551, [1932] All ER Rep 558 and *Oldham v Lawson (No 1)* [1976] VR 654. Recently, however, the Court of Appeal departed from this line of authority in *Khorasandjian v Bush* [1993] 3 All ER 669, [1993] QB 727, a case which I must examine with some care.

The plaintiff, a young girl who at the time of the appeal was 18, had formed a friendship with the defendant, then a man of 28. After a time the friendship broke down and the plaintiff decided that she would have no more to do with the defendant, but the defendant found this impossible to accept. There followed a catalogue of complaints against the defendant, including assaults, threats of violence, and pestering the plaintiff at her parents' home where she lived. As a result of the defendant's threats and abusive behaviour he spent some time in prison. An injunction was granted restraining the defendant from various forms of activity directed at the plaintiff, and this included an order restraining him from 'harassing, pestering or communicating with' the plaintiff. The question before the Court of Appeal was whether the judge had jurisdiction to grant such an injunction, in relation to telephone calls made to the plaintiff at her parents' home. The home was the property of the plaintiff's mother, and it was recognised that her mother could complain of persistent and unwanted telephone calls made to her; but it was submitted that the plaintiff, as a mere licensee in her mother's house, could not invoke the tort of private nuisance to complain of unwanted and harassing telephone calls made to her in her mother's home. The majority of the Court of Appeal (Peter Gibson J dissenting) rejected this submission, relying on the decision of the Appellate Division of the Alberta Supreme Court in *Motherwell v Motherwell* (1976) 73 DLR (3d) 62. In that case, the Appellate Division not only recognised that the legal owner of property could obtain an injunction, on the ground of private nuisance, to restrain persistent harassment by unwanted telephone calls to his home, but also that the same remedy was open to his wife who had no interest in the property. In the Court of Appeal Peter Gibson J dissented on the ground that it was wrong in principle that a mere licensee or someone without any interest in, or right to occupy, the relevant land should be able to sue in private nuisance.

It is necessary therefore to consider the basis of the decision in *Motherwell v Motherwell* that a wife, who has no interest in the matrimonial home where she lives, is nevertheless able to sue in private nuisance in respect of interference with her enjoyment of that home. The case was concerned with a claim for an injunction against the defendant, who was the daughter of one of the plaintiffs, the other two plaintiffs being her brother and sister-in-law. The main ground of the complaint against the defendant was that, as a result of a paranoid condition from which she suffered which produced in her the conviction that her sister-in-law and her father's housekeeper were inflaming her brother and her father against her, she persistently made a very large number of telephone calls to her brother's and her father's homes, in which she abused her sister-in-law and the housekeeper. The Appellate Division of the Alberta Supreme Court, in a judgment delivered by Clement JA, held that not only could her father and brother, as householders, obtain an injunction against the defendant to restrain this activity as a private nuisance, but so also could her sister-in-law although she had no interest in her husband's property. Clement JA said (at 78):

'Here we have a wife harassed in the matrimonial home. She has a status, a right to live there with her husband and children. I find it absurd to say that her occupancy of the matrimonial home is insufficient to found an action in nuisance. In my opinion she is entitled to the same relief as is her husband, the brother.'

This conclusion was very largely based on the decision of the Court of Appeal in *Foster v Warblington UDC* [1906] 1 KB 648, [1904–7] All ER Rep 366, which Clement JA understood to establish a distinction between 'one who is "merely present"' and 'occupancy of a substantial nature', and that in the latter case the occupier was entitled to sue in private nuisance. However, *Foster v Warblington UDC* does not, in my opinion, provide authority for the proposition that a person in the position of a mere licensee, such as a wife or husband in her or his spouse's house, is entitled to sue in that action. This misunderstanding must, I fear, undermine the authority of *Motherwell v Motherwell* on this point; and in so far as the decision of the Court of Appeal in *Khorasandjian v Bush* is founded upon *Motherwell v Motherwell* it is likewise undermined.

But I must go further. If a plaintiff, such as the daughter of the householder in *Khorasandjian v Bush*, is harassed by abusive telephone calls, the gravamen of the complaint lies in the harassment which is just as much an abuse, or indeed an invasion of her privacy, whether she is pestered in this way in her mother's or her husband's house, or she is staying with a friend, or is at her place of work, or even in her car with a mobile phone. In truth, what the Court of Appeal appears to have been doing was to exploit the law of private nuisance in order to create by the back door a tort of harassment which was only partially effective in that it was artificially limited to harassment which takes place in her home. I myself do not consider that this is a satisfactory manner in which to develop the law, especially when, as in the case in question, the step so taken was inconsistent with another decision of the Court of Appeal, viz *Malone v Laskey* [1907] 2 KB 141, [1904–7] All ER Rep 304, by which the court was bound. In any event, a tort of harassment has now received statutory recognition (see the Protection from Harassment Act 1997). We are therefore no longer troubled with the question whether the common law should be developed to provide such a remedy. For these reasons, I do not consider that any assistance can be derived from *Khorasandjian v Bush* by the plaintiffs in the present appeals.

It follows that, on the authorities as they stand, an action in private nuisance will only lie at the suit of a person who has a right to the land affected. Ordinarily, such a person can only sue if he has the right to exclusive possession of the land, such as a freeholder or tenant in possession, or even a licensee with exclusive possession. Exceptionally however, as *Foster v Warblington UDC* shows, this category may include a person in actual possession who has no right to be there; and in any event a reversioner can sue in so far his reversionary interest is affected. But a mere licensee on the land has no right to sue.

The question therefore arises whether your Lordships should be persuaded to depart from established principle, and recognise such a right in others who are no more than mere licensees on the land. At the heart of this question lies a more fundamental question, which relates to the scope of the law of private nuisance. Here, I wish to draw attention to the fact that although, in the past, damages for personal injury have been recovered at least in actions of public nuisance, there is now developing a school of thought that the appropriate remedy for such claims as these should lie in our now fully developed law of negligence, and that personal injury claims should be altogether excluded from the domain of nuisance. The most forthright proponent of this approach has been Professor Newark in his article 'The Boundaries of Nuisance' (1949) 65 LQR 480.... Furthermore, it is now being suggested that claims in respect of physical damage to the land should also be excluded from private nuisance (see eg the article by Mr Conor Gearty The Place of Private Nuisance in a Modern Law of Torts' [1989] CLJ 214). In any event, it is right for present purposes to regard the typical cases of private nuisance as being those concerned with interference with the enjoyment of land and, as such, generally actionable only by a person with a right in the land. Characteristic examples of cases of this kind are those concerned with noise, vibrations, noxious smells and the like. The two appeals with which your Lordships are here concerned arise from actions of this character.

For private nuisances of this kind, the primary remedy is in most cases an injunction, which is sought to bring the nuisance to an end, and in most cases should swiftly achieve that objective. The right to bring such proceedings is, as the law stands, ordinarily vested in the person who has exclusive possession of the land. He or she is the person who will sue, if it is necessary to do so. Moreover he or she can, if thought appropriate, reach an agreement with the person creating the nuisance, either that it may continue for a certain period of time, possibly on the payment of a sum of money, or that it shall cease, again perhaps on certain terms including the time within which the cessation will take place. The former may well occur when an agreement is reached between neighbours about the circumstances in which one of them may carry out major repairs to his house which may affect the other's enjoyment of his property. An agreement of this kind was expressly contemplated by Fletcher Moulton LJ in his judgment in *Malone v Laskey* [1907] 2 KB 141 at 153, [1904–7] All ER Rep 304 at 306. But the efficacy of arrangements such as these depends upon the existence of an identifiable person with whom the creator of the nuisance can deal for this purpose. If anybody who lived in the relevant property as a home had the right to sue, sensible arrangements such as these might in some cases no longer be practicable.

Moreover, any such departure from the established law on this subject, such as that adopted by the Court of Appeal in the present case, faces the problem of defining the category of persons who would have the right to sue. The Court of Appeal adopted the not easily identifiable category of those who have a 'substantial link' with the land, regarding a person who occupied the premises 'as a home' as having a sufficient link for this purpose. But who is to be included in this category? It was plainly intended to include husbands and wives, or partners, and their children, and even other relatives living with them. But is the category also to include the lodger upstairs, or the au pair girl or resident nurse caring for an invalid who makes her home in the house while she works there? If the latter, it seems strange that the category should not extend to include places where people work as well as places where they live, where nuisances such as noise can be just as unpleasant or distracting. In any event, the extension of the tort in this way would transform it from a tort to land into a tort to the person, in which damages could be recovered in respect of something less serious than personal injury and the criteria for liability were founded not upon negligence but upon striking a balance between the interests of neighbours in the use of their land. This is, in my opinion, not an acceptable way in which to develop the law.

It was suggested in the course of argument that at least the spouse of a husband or wife who, for example as freeholder or tenant, had exclusive possession of the matrimonial home should be entitled to sue in private nuisance. For the purposes of this submission, your Lordships were referred to the relevant legislation, notably the Matrimonial Homes Act 1983 and the Family Law Act 1996. I do not, however, consider it necessary to go through the statutory provisions. As I understand the position, it is as follows. If under the relevant legislation a spouse becomes entitled to possession of the matrimonial home or part of it, there is no reason why he or she should not be able to sue in private nuisance in the ordinary way. But I do not see how a spouse who has no interest in the matrimonial home has, simply by virtue of his or her cohabiting in the matrimonial home with his or her wife or husband whose freehold or leasehold property it is, a right to sue. No distinction can sensibly be drawn between such spouses and other cohabitees in the home, such as children, or grandparents. Nor do I see any great disadvantage flowing from this state of affairs. If a nuisance should occur, then the spouse who has an interest in the property can bring the necessary proceedings to bring the nuisance to an end, and can recover any damages in respect of the discomfort or inconvenience caused by the nuisance. Even if he or she is away from home, nowadays the necessary authority to commence proceedings for an injunction can usually be obtained by telephone. Moreover, if the other spouse suffers personal injury, including injury to health, he or she may, like anybody else, be able to recover damages in negligence. The only disadvantage is that the other spouse cannot bring an independent action in private nuisance for damages for discomfort or inconvenience. . . .

For all these reasons, I can see no good reason to depart from the law on this topic as established in the authorities. I would therefore hold that *Khorasandjian v Bush* must be overruled in so far as it holds that a mere licensee can sue in private nuisance, and I would allow the appeal or cross-appeal of the defendants in both actions and restore the order of Judge Havery on this issue.

LORD HOFFMANN:....

The right to sue

In the dust action it is not disputed that, in principle, activities which cause dust to be deposited on the plaintiff's property can constitute an actionable nuisance. The question raised by the preliminary issue is who can sue? In order to answer this question, it is necessary to decide what exactly he is suing for. Since these questions are fundamental to the scope of the tort of nuisance, I shall deal with them first.

Up to about 20 years ago, no one would have had the slightest doubt about who could sue. Nuisance is a tort against land including interests in land such as easements and profits. A plaintiff must therefore have an interest in the land affected by the nuisance.

[Having quoted a passage from Lord Wright's speech in *Sedleigh-Denfield v O'Callaghan* [1940] AC 880 at 902–903 in which Lord Wright concluded that '[w]ith possibly certain anomalous exceptions, not here material, possession or occupation is still the test', LORD HOFFMANN continued:]

In speaking of 'possession or occupation' Lord Wright was, in my view, intending to refer both to a right to possession based upon (or derived through) title and to de facto occupation. In each case the person in possession is entitled to sue in trespass and in nuisance. An example of an action for nuisance by a de facto possessor is *Foster v Warblington UDC* [1906] 1 KB 648, [1904–7] All ER Rep 366, in which the plaintiff sued the council for excharging sewage so as to pollute his oyster ponds on the foreshore. He had some difficulty in proving any title to the soil, but Vaughan Williams LJ said ([1906] 1 KB 648 at 659–660, [1904–7] All ER Rep 366 at 370):

> 'But, even if title could not be proved in my judgment there has been such an occupation of these beds for such a length of time—not that the length of time is really material for this purpose—as would entitle the plaintiff as against the defendants, who have no interest in the foreshore, to sustain this action for the injury which it is alleged has been done by the sewage to his oysters so kept in those beds.'

Thus, even a possession which is wrongful against the true owner can found an action for trespass or nuisance against someone else (see *Asher v Whitlock* (1865) LR 1 QB 1). In each case, however, the plaintiff (or joint plaintiffs) must be enjoying or asserting exclusive possession of the land (see *Allan v Liverpool Overseers* (1874) LR 9 QB 180 per Blackburn J). Exclusive possession distinguishes an occupier who may in due course acquire title under the Limitation Act 1980 from a mere trespasser. It distinguishes a tenant holding a leasehold estate from a mere licensee. Exclusive possession de jure or de facto, now or in the future, is the bedrock of English land law....

The leading case on the need for exclusive possession to found an action in nuisance is *Malone v Laskey* [1907] 2 KB 141, 1914–7] All ER Rep 304....

Dillon LJ brushed *Malone*'s case aside. He said ([1993] 3 All ER 669 at 675, [1993] QB 727 at 734):

> 'To my mind, it is ridiculous if in this present age the law is that the making of deliberately harassing and pestering telephone calls to a person is only actionable in the civil courts if the recipient of the calls happens to have the freehold or a leasehold proprietary interest in the premises in which he or she has received the calls.'

This reasoning, which is echoed in some academic writing and the Canadian case of *Motherwell v Motherwell* (1976) 73 DLR (3d) 62, which the Court of Appeal followed, is based upon a fundamental mistake about the remedy which the tort of nuisance provides. It arises, I think out of a misapplication of an important distinction drawn by Lord Westbury LC in *St Helen's Smelting Co v Tipping* (1865) 11 HL Cas 642 at 650, 11 ER 1483 at 1486.

[His Lordship went on to quote a passage from Lord Westbury's speech in the *St Helen's* case which has been set out as the first paragraph of the extract from that speech on p. 784, ante, and continued:]

St Helen's Smelting Co v Tipping was a landmark case. It drew the line beyond which rural and landed England did not have to accept external costs imposed upon it by industrial pollution. But there has been, I think, some inclination to treat it as having divided nuisance into two torts, one of causing 'material injury to the property', such as flooding or depositing poisonous substances on crops, and the other of causing 'sensible personal discomfort', such as excessive noise or smells. In cases in the first category, there has never been any doubt that the remedy, whether by way of injunction or damages, is for causing damage to the land. It is plain that in such a case only a person with an interest in the land can sue. But there has been a tendency to regard cases in the second category as actions in respect of the discomfort or even personal injury which the plaintiff has suffered or is likely to suffer. On this view, the plaintiff's interest in the land becomes no more than a qualifying condition or springboard which entitles him to sue for injury to himself.

If this were the case, the need for the plaintiff to have an interest in land would indeed be hard to justify. The passage I have quoted from Dillon LJ in *Khorasandjian v Bush* [1993] 3 All ER 669 at 675, [1993] QB 727 at 734 is an eloquent statement of the reasons. but the premise is quite mistaken. In the case of nuisances 'productive of sensible personal discomfort', the action is not for causing discomfort to the person but, as in the case of the first category, for causing injury to the land. True it is that the land has not suffered 'sensible' injury, but its utility has been diminished by the existence of the nuisance. It is for an unlawful threat to the utility of his land that the possessor or occupier is entitled to an injunction and it is for the diminution in such utility that he is entitled to compensation.

I cannot therefore agree with Stephenson LJ in *Bone v Seale* [1975] 1 All ER 787 at 793–794, [1975] 1 WLR 797 at 803–804, when he said that damages in an action for nuisance caused by smells from a pigsty should be fixed by analogy with damages for loss of amenity in an action for personal injury. In that case it was said that 'efforts to prove diminution in the value of the property as a result of this persistent smell over the years failed' (see [1975] 1 All ER 787 at 793, [1975] 1 WLR 797 at 803). I take this to mean that it had not been shown that the property would sell for less. But diminution in capital value is not the only measure of loss. It seems to me that the value of the right to occupy a house which smells of pigs must be less than the value of the occupation of an equivalent house which does not. In the case of a transitory nuisance, the capital value of the property will seldom be reduced. But the owner or occupier is entitled to compensation for the diminution in the amenity value of the property during the period for which the nuisance persisted. To some extent this involves placing a value on intangibles. But estate agents do this all the time. The law of damages is sufficiently flexible to be able to do justice in such a case (cf *Ruxley Electronics and Construction Ltd v Forsyth, Laddington Enclosures Ltd v Forsyth* [1995] 3 All ER 268, [1996] AC 344).

There may of course be cases in which, in addition to damages for injury to his land, the owner or occupier is able to recover damages for consequential loss. He will, for example, be entitled to loss of profits which are the result of inability to use the land for the purposes of his business. Or if the land is flooded, he may also be able to recover damages for chattels or livestock lost as a result. But inconvenience, annoyance or even illness suffered by persons on land as a result of smells or dust are not damage consequential upon the injury to the land. It is rather the other way about: the injury to the amenity of the land consists in the fact that the persons on it are liable to suffer inconvenience, annoyance or illness.

It follows that damages for nuisance recoverable by the possessor or occupier may be affected by the size, commodiousness and value of his property but cannot be increased merely because more people are in occupation and therefore suffer greater collective discomfort. If more than one person has an interest in the property, the damages will have to be divided among them. If there are joint owners, they will be jointly entitled to the damages. If there is a reversioner and the nuisance has caused damage of a permanent character which affects the reversion, he will be entitled to damages according to his interest. But the damages cannot be increased by the fact that the interests in the land are divided; still less according to the number of persons residing on the premises. As Cotton LJ said in *Rust v Victoria Graving Dock Co* (1887) 36 Ch D 113 at 130:

> '...where there are divided interests in land the amount of damages to be paid by the Defendants must not be increased in consequence of that subdivision of interests.'

Once it is understood that nuisances 'productive of sensible personal discomfort' do not constitute a separate of causing discomfort to people but are merely part of a single tort of causing injury to land, the rule that the plaintiff must have an interest in the land falls into place as logical and, indeed, inevitable (see *St Helen's Smelting Co v Tipping* (1865) 11 HL Cas 642 at 650, 11 ER 1483 at 1486).

Is there any reason of policy why the rule should be abandoned? Once nuisance has escaped the bounds of being a tort against land, there seems no logic in compromise limitations, such as that proposed by the Court of Appeal in this case, requiring the plaintiff to have been residing on land as his or her home. This was recognised by the Court of Appeal in *Khorasandjian*'s case, where the injunction applied whether the plaintiff was at home or not. There is a good deal in this case and other writings about the need for the law to adapt to modern social conditions. But the development of the common law should be rational and coherent. It should not distort its principles and create anomalies merely as an expedient to fill a gap.

The perceived gap in *Khorasandjian*'s case was the absence of a tort of intentional harassment causing distress without actual bodily or psychiatric illness. This limitation is thought to arise out of cases like *Wilkinson v Downton* [1897] 2 QB 57, [1895–9] All ER Rep 267 and *Janvier v Sweeney* [1919] 2 KB 316, [1918–19] All ER Rep 1056. The law of harassment has now been put on a statutory basis (see the Protection from Harassment Act 1997) and it is unnecessary to consider how the common law might have developed. But as at present advised, I see no reason why a tort of intention should be subject to the rule which excludes compensation for mere distress, inconvenience or discomfort in actions based on negligence (see *Hicks v Chief Constable of the South Yorkshire Police* [1992] 2 All ER 65). The policy considerations are quite different. I do not therefore say that *Khorasandjian*'s case was wrongly decided. But it must be seen as a case on intentional harassment, not nuisance.

So far as the claim is for personal injury, it seems to me that the only appropriate cause of action is negligence. It would be anomalous if the rules for recovery of damages under this head were different according as to whether, for example, the plaintiff was at home or at work. It is true, as I have said, that the law of negligence gives no remedy for discomfort or distress which does not result in bodily or psychiatric illness. But this is a matter of general policy and I can see no logic in making an exception for cases in which the discomfort or distress was suffered at home rather than somewhere else.

Finally, there is the position of spouses. It is said to be contrary to modern ways of thinking that a wife should not be able to sue for interference with the enjoyment of the matrimonial home merely because she has no proprietary right in the property. To some extent, this argument is based upon the fallacy which I have already discussed, namely that the action in nuisance lies for inconvenience or annoyance caused to people who happen to be in possession or occupation of land. But so far as it is thought desirable that the wife should be able to sue for injury to a proprietary or possessory interest in the home, the answer, in my view, lies in the law of property, not the law of tort. The courts today will readily assume that a wife has acquired a beneficial interest in the matrimonial home. If so she will be entitled to sue for damage to that interest. On the other hand, if she has no such interest, I think it would be wrong to create a quasi-proprietary interest only for the purposes of giving her locus standi to sue for nuisance. What would she be suing for? Mr Brennan QC, who appeared for the plaintiffs, drew our attention to the rights conferred on a wife with no proprietary interest by the Matrimonial Homes Act 1983. The effect of these provisions is that a spouse may, by virtue of an order of the court upon a break-up of the marriage, become entitled to exclusive possession of the home. If so, she will become entitled to sue for nuisance. Until then, her interest is analogous to a contingent reversion. It cannot be affected by a nuisance which merely damages the amenity of the property while she has no right to possession.

I would therefore allow the appeal of the defendants in the dust case and their cross-appeal in the television case and restore the declaration made on this point by the judge.

[LORD LLOYD OF BERWICK delivered a speech in favour of allowing the appeal on the issue concerning title to sue, and LORD HOPE OF CRAIGHEAD delivered a speech in which he agreed with the speeches of LORD GOFF OF CHIEVELEY and LORD HOFFMANN on this point. LORD COOKE OF THORNDON delivered a dissenting speech on this issue.]

QUESTIONS

1. It had previously been thought that a claimant could sue for damage to chattels in a private nuisance action: see, for example, *Halsey v Esso Petroleum Co Ltd* [1961] 2 All ER 145, [1961] 1 WLR 683, noted p. 787, ante. Is this still the case?

2. Explain why a claimant cannot recover for personal injuries in private nuisance, given that he can recover for 'sensible personal discomfort'.

NOTES

1. The *Hunter* case is noted by J. O'Sullivan [1997] CLJ 483, p. Cane (1997) 113 LQR 515 and J. Wightman (1997) 61 MLR 870.

2. On the question of harassment and the Protection from Harassment Act 1997, to which reference is made in *Hunter*, see p. 745, ante.

3. Before the decision in *Hunter* it had been assumed (eg in *Malone v Laskey* [1907] 2 KB 141) that there could be recovery for personal injuries in private nuisance, but in *Hunter* Lord Hoffmann, with whose speech Lord Hope agreed, rejected this. Lord Lloyd took a similar view to Lord Hoffmann, whereas Lord Cooke in his dissent would allow recovery for such injury. It should be noted that, as Lord Cooke pointed out, damages can be recovered for personal injuries in public nuisance. This has been confirmed by the Court of Appeal (distinguishing dicta to the contrary in *Hunter* and also *Transco*, p. 843, post) in *Corby Group Litigation v Corby Borough Council* [2008] EWCA Civ 463. But of course, this is not the only difference between the torts: see further note 3, p. 801, post.

4. In his dissenting judgment Lord Cooke stated ([1997] 2 All ER at pp. 461–462):

> Although hitherto the law of England on the point has not been settled by your Lordship's House, it is agreed on all hands that some link with the land is necessary for standing to sue in private nuisance. The precise nature of that link remains to be defined, partly because of the ambiguity of "occupy" and its derivatives. In ordinary usage the verb can certainly include "reside in", which is indeed the first meaning given in the *Concise Oxford Dictionary*. In logic more than one answer can be given. Logically it is possible to say that the right to sue for interference with the amenities of a home should be confined to those with proprietary interests and licensees with exclusive possession. No less logically, the right can be accorded to all who live in the home. Which test should be adopted, that is to say which should be the governing principle, is a question of the policy of the law. It is a question not capable of being answered by analysis alone. All that analysis can do is expose the alternatives. Decisions such as *Malone*'s case do not attempt that kind of analysis, and in refraining from recognising that value judgments are involved they compare less favourably with the approach of the present-day Court of Appeal in *Khorasandjian*'s case and this case. The reason why I prefer the alternative…is that it gives better effect to widespread conceptions concerning the home and family.

Lord Cooke went on to acknowledge that there might be difficult borderline cases, but did not think this was a sufficient reason for not laying down what he saw as a just rule for spouses and children. His answer to Lord Goff's practical argument (p. 793, ante) about the efficacy of arrangements with the creator of the nuisance was that the householder is impliedly authorised by the other members of the household to represent them.

Remedies for a non-proprietary occupant in a Human Rights Act 1998 claim (for interferences with the right to private and family life under Article 8 of the ECHR) were considered in *Dobson v Thames Water Utilities* [2008] 2 All ER 362, [2007] EWHC 2021 (TCC). Ramsey J observed that the question under s. 8(3) of the 1998 Act is whether damages (etc.) must be awarded to provide 'just satisfaction to the injured party'. He held that where damages have been recovered in nuisance by the householder, these must be taken into account in a claim by a family member, and that (at [209]) 'when the court awards damages for nuisance to those with a legal interest that will usually afford just satisfaction to partners and children but that there might be circumstances where they will not'. The judge also considered (at [226]) that damages awarded to a proprietor for breach of Article 8 must include 'damages for inconvenience, mental distress and physical suffering', in contrast with *Hunter*, ante. Thus, the court might potentially need to award such damages in a Human Rights Act claim to 'top up' damages for nuisance, although Ramsey J commented (at [234]) that nuisance damages are assessed 'on principles that are sufficiently flexible to do justice as between the parties' and therefore it was 'unlikely' that such further damages would be necessary to give 'just satisfaction' under the Human Rights Act.

5. The other main point discussed in *Hunter* was the question of whether interference with television reception could be a nuisance. The adverse impact on television reception was said to be caused by the existence of the Canary Wharf Tower, and on these facts the House of Lords held that there was no actionable nuisance. This was based on the freedom of an owner of land at common law, in the absence of a restrictive covenant or easement of light or air, to build as he pleased. For example, the loss of view is not generally actionable. The safeguard mentioned in the House of Lords for a person adversely affected by a building was that person's ability to raise such matters in the process involved in the application for the grant of planning permission. (It was acknowledged, however, that this was designated as an enterprise zone and consequently planning permission did not have to be sought.) It is important to note that the House of Lords did not rule out the possibility of an interference with television reception being actionable in nuisance: indeed, Lord Hoffmann expressly stated that he could see no reason in principle why it should not be actionable in an appropriate case and Lord Cooke thought it would be so actionable.

Lord Cooke based his agreement on the non-actionability of television interference by the presence of a building on the principle of reasonable user in nuisance. Thus, for his Lordship if a building breached the terms of the planning permission, the television interference would become actionable in nuisance, as the planning permission mapped out the acceptable standard in the area. The other members of the House of Lords did not directly address this question (though cf. Lord Hope's speech at p. 469), but it is suggested that their approach would appear to go against this idea. Lord Cooke also took the view that the malicious erection of a building for the purpose of interfering with television reception would be actionable. Again, this is not expressly dealt with by Lord Cooke's brethren (though there is a possible inference to be drawn from Lord Hope's speech at p. 469), but their reasoning suggests a similar approach to that adopted in *Bradford Corpn v Pickles* [1895] AC 587 (see note 6, p. 788, ante).

■ British Celanese Ltd v A H Hunt (Capacitors) Ltd
Queen's Bench Division [1969] 2 All ER 1252

This was the trial of a preliminary issue whether the defendants were liable in law for the damage claimed on the alleged facts which were as follows: The defendants, who made electrical components, occupied a site on the trading estate where the plaintiffs carried on their business. For their business purposes the defendants had collected on their site strips of metal foil, which could be blown about in the wind. An electricity supply sub-station, owned by the local Electricity Board, provided power to both the plaintiffs' and the defendants' factories. The sub-station was 120 yards away from the defendants' premises, and if the foil made contact with more than one of the 'bus-bars' which stood in the open air at the sub-station, there could be a 'flash-over', which could in turn lead to a power failure. The defendants knew this was likely to happen, and that damage would be caused to those with premises in the area through interruption of the light and power supply, because, on an earlier occasion, foil had blown into the overhead conductors, causing an interruption of supply, and the district engineer of the Electricity Board had written to the defendants and told them what had happened and of the danger of interruption of supplies. Three-and-a-half years after this incident, some foil which was lying about in the open air on or near the defendants' premises, blew away and came into contact with the bus-bars. This led to interruption in the light and power supply at the plaintiffs' factory, and their machinery came to a halt. Certain machines, in which materials had solidified, had to be cleaned: materials and time were wasted and production and profit were lost. The plaintiffs claimed that if they proved these allegations, the defendants would be liable under *Rylands v Fletcher* (1868) LR 3 HL 330 (p. 828, post), and in negligence, nuisance and public nuisance. Only the last two heads are dealt with in the extract below, but it should be noted that, in considering the claim under *Rylands v Fletcher*, Lawton J took the view that the averments 'amount to an allegation of damage, including injury to property, flowing directly from the escape of the metal foil from the defendants' premises'. When considering remoteness of damage (in the context of the negligence claim), he took the view that there was an 'averment that the defendants at the very least ought reasonably to have foreseen that their conduct was likely to cause injury to the plaintiffs' property and that it in fact did so'.

LAWTON J: . . .

I turn now to the plaintiffs' contention that the re-amended statement of claim discloses a cause of action both in private and public nuisance. As to private nuisance they say that the defendants' alleged method of storing metal foil resulted, as the defendants knew it would, in an interference with the beneficial enjoyment of their own premises whereby they suffered damage; and as to public nuisance their case is that the nuisance was one which affected a class of persons, namely, those members of the public supplied with electricity from the sub-station, and that as members of that class they suffered special damage.

The defendants made three answers to these contentions: first, that an isolated happening such as the plaintiffs relied on was not enough to found an action in nuisance since this tort can only arise out of a continuing condition: secondly, that if there was a nuisance on the defendants' premises, it did not affect the plaintiffs' premises directly; and thirdly that the re-amended statement of claim did not disclose enough facts to justify a ruling that a class of the public had been injuriously affected by the alleged nuisance.

In my judgment, all three answers are misconceived. Most nuisances do arise from a long continuing condition; and many isolated happenings do not constitute a nuisance. It is, however, clear from the authorities that an isolated happening by itself can create an actionable nuisance. Such an authority is *Midwood & Co Ltd v Manchester Corpn*,[2] where an electric main installed by the defendants fused. This caused an explosion and a fire whereby the plaintiffs' goods were damaged. The Court of Appeal

---

[2] [1905] 2 KB 597.

held that the defendants were liable, all the Lord Justices being of the opinion that they had caused a nuisance. The explosion in that case arose out of the condition of the electric main: the 'flash-over' in this case was caused by the way in which the defendants stored their metal foil whereby those in the neighbourhood were exposed to the risk of having their electric power cut off. I am satisfied that the law is correctly stated in *Winfield on Tort* (8th edn) at p. 364:

> 'Where the nuisance is the escape of tangible things which damage the plaintiff in the enjoyment of his property, there is no rule that he cannot sue for the first escape.'

Anyway, in this case, the alleged happening of 7 December 1964 was not the first escape; there is said to have been one in 1961.

The second of the defendants' answers is a repetition of the argument which was addressed to me on remoteness of damage. I accept that those who are only indirectly affected by a nuisance cannot sue for any damage which they may suffer: but...I adjudge that the plaintiffs were directly and fore-seeably affected.

Finally, I come to the last of the defendants' answers. Paragraph 6 of the re-amended statement of claim alleges that the defendants knew and foresaw that a 'flash-over' caused by pieces of metal foil blowing about was likely to cause an interruption of power—

> '...to the premises of members of the public in the said area supplied [with electricity] from the said sub-station including the plaintiffs' said premises...'

This averment identifies the class of persons said to have been affected by the nuisance and alleges that the plaintiffs were members of that class. Whether this class was big enough to attract the description 'public' to the nuisance must await the evidence at the trial. In *A-G v PYA Quarries Ltd*[3] Romer LJ, after a learned examination of the authorities, summarised the law as follows:

> '...any nuisance is "public" which materially affects the reasonable comfort and convenience of life of a class of Her Majesty's subjects. The sphere of the nuisance may be described generally as "the neighbourhood"; but the question whether the local community within that sphere comprises a sufficient number of persons to constitute a class of the public is a question of fact in every case.'

For the reasons given and to the extent specified, I adjudge that on the facts set out in the re-amended statement of claim the defendants are liable in law for the damage claimed.

Order accordingly.

NOTES

1.   Apart from the claim in nuisance, Lawton J held that the *Rylands v Fletcher* claim failed, and this point is noted, p. 843, post, but he did not rule out the negligence claim if the allegations could be proved: cf. *Spartan Steel and Alloys Ltd v Martin & Co (Contractors) Ltd* [1973] QB 27, [1972] 3 All ER 557 (p. 199, *ante*).

2.   For discussion of the question whether an isolated escaped is actionable, see *Winfield & Jolowicz*, pp. 656–657. (It is, of course, actionable under the *Rylands v Fletcher* principle, on which see F. H. Newark (1949) 65 LQR 480 at 488.) The quotation from *Winfield on Tort* (8th edn) in the extract above is not to be found in those terms in the current edition of *Winfield & Jolowicz*. They do quote the following statement of Thesiger J in *SCM (United Kingdom) Ltd v W J Whittall & Son Ltd* [1970] 2 All ER 417 at 430 that 'while there is no doubt that a single isolated escape may cause the damage that entitles a plaintiff to sue for nuisance, yet it must be proved that the nuisance arose from the

---

³ [1957] 2 QB 169 at 184, [1957] 1 All ER 894 at 902.

condition of the defendant's land or premises or property or activities thereon that constituted a nuisance'. He denied that one negligent act causing damage to an electric cable was *thereby* a nuisance. In this context, note the distinction drawn by Potter J in *Crown Rivers Cruises Ltd v Kimbolton Fireworks Ltd* [1996] 2 Lloyd's Rep 533 at 545 where he stated:

It seems to me that those authorities which have held that a particular type of interference has not amounted to a nuisance by reason of its short duration, have generally been concerned with complaints relating to nuisance, noise, vibration, dust etc. which are to an extent to be regarded as a normal incident of urban living, in respect of which a degree of give and take is to be expected, unless by undue length or repetition they become intolerable. Where an activity creates a state of affairs which gives rise to risk of escape of physically dangerous or damaging material, such as water, gas or fire, then the law of nuisance is, and should be, available to give a remedy in respect of that state of affairs, albeit brief in duration. In my opinion, the holding of a firework display in a situation where it is inevitable that for 15–20 minutes debris, some of it hot and burning, will fall upon nearby property of a potentially flammable nature creates a nuisance actionable at the suit of a property owner who suffers damage as a result.

Is this approach consistent with the decision of the House of Lords in *Hunter v Canary Wharf Ltd*, p. 790, ante? With no risk of repetition, has the claimant's land value been reduced?

3.   The claimants in the *British Celanese* case argued that they had a cause of action in both public and private nuisance. A common example of public nuisance, which is also a crime, is causing an obstruction on the highway. (For recent discussion of the scope of the offence, rejecting the argument that its definition was too uncertain and unpredictable to satisfy the European Convention on Human Rights, see *R v Goldstein; R v Rimmington* [2006] 2 All ER 257, [2005] UKHL 63.) Public nuisance is only actionable as a tort by a private individual where he suffers some particular damage greater than that suffered by the public. See G. Kodilyne (1986) 6 LS 182 and esp. 189–191 on the question whether the damage suffered must be greater in kind or merely greater in degree than that suffered by the public in general. On public nuisance generally (both as a crime and as a tort), see J. R. Spencer [1989] CLJ 55 and see *R v Shorrock* [1994] QB 279, [1993] 3 All ER 917 (applied in *R v Rimmington*)—requisite knowledge or means of knowledge the same whether dealing with public nuisance as a crime or as a tort, and was the same as in private nuisance, on which see *Sedleigh-Denfield v O'Callaghan* [1940] AC 880, [1940] 3 All ER 349, p. 807, post. It should be noted that the similarities between the two nuisance actions only go so far—see *Street*, 458–462; Lord Wright in *Sedleigh-Denfield v O'Callaghan* [1940] AC at 905; cf. the observations of Lord Romer in that case at p. 913, and see Lord Porter at p. 918. See also *Corby Group Litigation v Corby Borough Council* [2008] EWCA Civ 463.

4.   In relation to nuisance and the highway, the Court of Appeal held in *Hubbard v Pitt* [1976] QB 142, [1975] 3 All ER 1 that the defendants' actions in picketing the highway outside the office of the claimant estate agents arguably amounted to a private nuisance, which should be restrained by interlocutory injunction. However, Lord Denning MR dissented, opined that the defendants' peaceful demonstration which involved 'no obstruction, no violence, no intimidation, no molestation, no noise, no smells' did not amount to a nuisance. In *Church of Jesus Christ of Latter Day Saints v Price* [2004] EWHC 3245 (QB), the defendant repeatedly mounted vociferous demonstrations against the Mormon system of beliefs, in the streets outside Mormon churches belonging to the claimants. Granting an injunction, the court held that this amounted

to private nuisance (and harassment contrary to s.1 of the Protection from Harassment Act 1997, noted p. 745, ante). Beatson J at [168] rejected the defendant's submissions that Lord Irvine LC's opinion in *Jones v DPP* (see p. 779, ante) meant that there was a right to use the highway for 'any reasonable purpose': Lord Irvine's formulation expressly excluded conduct which amounts to nuisance from the category of reasonable and lawful activity.

5.   Consider further *Thomas v National Union of Mineworkers (South Wales Area)* [1986] Ch 20, [1985] 2 All ER 1. In this case, which was concerned with picketing during the 1984–5 miners' strike, Scott J stated at one point that unreasonable interference with the rights of others was actionable in tort and, more specifically, was prepared to recognise a case as actionable in tort if there had been unreasonable interference with a person's right to use the highway. This could, in his opinion, be described 'as a species of private nuisance', though his Lordship did not think that the label mattered. The case has attracted a good deal of comment: see H. Carty [1985] PL 542; K. D. Ewing [1985] CLJ 374; S. Lee and S. Whittaker (1986) 102 LQR 35; B. A. Hepple, All ER Ann Rev 1982, p. 305; R. Benedictus (1985) 14 ILJ 176 at 181–185. The two last-named authors make the point, inter alia, that Scott J's view circumvents the requirements of an interest in land in the case of private nuisance and of special damage in the case of public nuisance. Note further *News Group Newspapers Ltd v SOGAT '82 (No 2)* [1987] ICR 181 at 206, where Stuart-Smith J saw force in the defendants' criticism of Scott J's judgment, but did not need to express a final view. On the *Thomas* case as an aspect of protection from harassment, see note 2, p. 748, ante.

(b) Foreseeability, fault and nuisance

■ Sedleigh-Denfield v O'Callaghan (Trustees for St. Joseph's Society for Foreign Missions)
p. 807, post

■ The Wagon Mound (No 2), Overseas Tankship (UK) Ltd v The Miller Steamship Co Pty Ltd
Judicial Committee of the Privy Council [1966] 2 All ER 709

The facts are set out, p. 408, ante.
LORD REID: . . .
Having made these findings Walsh J[4] went on to consider the case in nuisance. There is no doubt that the carelessness of the appellant's servants in letting this oil overflow did create a public nuisance by polluting the waters of Sydney Harbour. Also there can be no doubt that anyone who suffered special damage from that pollution would have had an action against the appellants; but the special damage sustained by the respondents was caused not by pollution but by fire. So, having held in finding (v) that risk of fire was not reasonably foreseeable, Walsh J had to consider whether foreseeability has any place in the determination of liability for damage caused by nuisance. He made an extensive survey of the case law and said that the principles which he found there[4]

'suggest that a plaintiff may set up a case depending on the following steps. The defendant has committed a "wrongful" act in that it has created a public nuisance by polluting the harbour waters

---

[4] [1963] 1 Lloyd's Rep 402 at 426.

with oil. As a result of the presence of that "nuisance" (i.e., of the oil) the plaintiff has suffered damage over and above that suffered by others. This gives the plaintiff an action, subject only to proof that there is the requisite relationship between the presence of that nuisance and the injury, so that it can be said that the injury suffered was direct. It matters not that the injury was different in kind from a fouling of the ship by the polluted waters.'

Then, coming to the words used by the judges in numerous cases of nuisance, he said that[5]

'...by and large, the judgments are not expressed in terms of the concept of foreseeability. The term used again and again is "direct". It is true that other expressions are also used, but one does not find in express terms any testing of the matter by what the defendant might have contemplated or might have foreseen.'

And later he added[6]

'I do not find in the case law on nuisance until the time of the [*Wagon Mound*] decision,[7] any authority for the view that liability depends on foreseeability.'

Their lordships must now make their own examination of the case law. They find the most striking feature to be the variety of words used: and that is not very surprising because in the great majority of cases the facts were such that it made no difference whether the damage was said to be the direct or the natural or probable or foreseeable result of the nuisance. The word 'natural' is found very often, and it is peculiarly ambiguous. It can and often does mean a result which one would naturally expect, i.e., which would not be surprising: or it can mean the result at the end of a chain of causation unbroken by any conscious act, the result produced by so-called natural laws however surprising or even unforeseeable in the particular case. Another word frequently used is 'probable'. It is used with various shades of meaning. Sometimes it appears to mean more probable than not, sometimes it appears to include events likely but not very likely to occur, sometimes it has a still wider meaning and refers to events the chance of which is anything more than a bare possibility, and sometimes, when used in conjunction with other adjectives, it appears to serve no purpose beyond rounding off a phrase.

Their lordships must first refer to a number of cases on which Walsh J relied because they require that the damage suffered by the plaintiff must be the direct or immediate result of the nuisance (generally obstruction of a highway), and they make no reference to foreseeability or probability. But that is because they were dealing with quite a different matter from measure of damages.

'...by the common law of England, a person guilty of a public nuisance might be indicted; but, if injury resulted to a private individual, other and greater than that which was common to all the Queen's subjects, the person injured has his remedy by action'

(per Brett J in *Benjamin v Storr*[8]). So the first step is to decide whether the plaintiff has suffered what may for brevity be called special damage. The authorities on this matter are numerous and exceedingly difficult to reconcile; but one thing is clear. There have been excluded from the category of special damage many cases where the damage suffered by the plaintiff was clearly caused by the nuisance; it was not only foreseeable but probable, and was indeed the inevitable result of the nuisance—the obstruction by the defendant of a highway giving access to the plaintiffs' premises. The words direct and immediate have often been used in determining whether the damage caused by the nuisance is special damage....

Such cases have nothing to do with measure of damages: they are dealing with the entirely different question whether the damage caused to the plaintiff by the nuisance was other and different from the damage caused by the nuisance to the rest of the public. When the word direct is used in determining that question, its meaning or connotation appears to be narrower than when it is used in determining

---

[5] [1963] 1 Lloyd's Rep at p. 42.   [6] [1963] 1 Lloyd's Rep at p. 433.
[7] [1961] AC 388, [1961] 1 All ER 404.   [8] (1874) LR 9 CP 400 at 406.

whether damage is too remote, so their lordships do not propose to deal further with cases determining what is and what is not special damage. No one denies that the respondents have suffered special damage in this case within the meaning of these authorities. The question is whether they can recover notwithstanding the finding that it was not foreseeable.

Of the large number of cases cited in argument there were few in which there was separate consideration of the proper measure of damages for nuisance. Many of the cases cited deal with the measure of damages for breach of contract, and their lordships will later explain why they do not propose to examine these cases. Moreover a larger number were cases based purely on negligence in which there was no element of nuisance. Their lordships do not intend to examine these cases in detail.... The respondents can only succeed on this branch of the case by distinguishing nuisance from negligence, either because the authorities indicate that foreseeability is irrelevant in nuisance or because on principle it ought to be held to be irrelevant....

[Having discussed several authorities he continued:] In their lordships' judgment the cases point strongly to there being no difference as to the measure of damages between nuisance and negligence, but they are not conclusive. So it is desirable to consider the question of principle.

The appellant's first argument was that damages depend on the same principles throughout the law of tort and contract. This was stated emphatically by Sir Baliol Brett MR in *The Notting Hill*[9] and by Lord Esher MR in *The Argentino*,[10] and it has often been repeated. But the matter has not been fully investigated recently.[11] There has in recent times been much development of the law of torts, and developments in the law of contract may not have proceeded on parallel lines. To give but one example, it is not obvious that the grounds of decision of the House of Lords in *Hughes v Lord Advocate*[12] are consistent with the first rule in *Hadley v Baxendale*[13] as that rule is commonly interpreted. It is unnecessary, however, to pursue this question in this case, and therefore their lordships do not intend to examine cases arising out of breach of contract.

The next argument was that at all events the measure of damages is the same throughout the law of tort; but there are many special features in various kinds of tort, and again their lordships do not find it necessary to make the extensive investigations which would be required before reaching a conclusion on this matter.

Comparing nuisance with negligence the main argument for the respondent was that in negligence foreseeability is an essential element in determining liability, and therefore it is logical that foreseeability should also be an essential element in determining the amount of damages; but negligence is not an essential element in determining liability for nuisance, and therefore it is illogical to bring in foreseeability when determining the amount of damages. It is quite true that negligence is not an essential element in nuisance. Nuisance is a term used to cover a wide variety of tortious acts or omissions, and in many negligence in the narrow sense is not essential. An occupier may incur liability for the emission of noxious fumes or noise, although he has used the utmost care in building and using his premises. The amount of fumes or noise which he can lawfully emit is a question of degree, and he or his advisers may have miscalculated what can be justified. Or he may deliberately obstruct the highway adjoining his premises to a greater degree than is permissible hoping that no one will object. On the other hand the emission of fumes or noise or the obstruction of the adjoining highway may often be the result of pure negligence on his part. There are many cases (e.g., *Dollman v Hillman*)[14] where precisely the same facts will establish liability both in nuisance and in negligence. And although negligence may not be necessary, fault of some kind is almost always necessary and fault generally involves foreseeability, e.g., in cases like *Sedleigh-Denfield v O'Callaghan*[15] the fault is in failing to abate a nuisance of the existence of

---

[9] (1884) 9 PD 105 at 113.   [10] (1888) 13 PD 191 at 197.
[11] [See now *H. Parsons (Livestock) Ltd v Uttley Ingham & Co Ltd* [1978] QB 791, [1978] 1 All ER 525.]
[12] [1963] AC 837, [1963] 1 All ER 705.   [13] (1854) 9 Exch 341, [1843–60] All ER Rep 461.
[14] [1941] 1 All ER 355.   [15] [1940] AC 880, [1940] 3 All ER 349.

which the defender is or ought to be aware as likely to cause damage to his neighbour. (Their lordships express no opinion about cases like *Wringe v Cohen*[16] on which neither counsel relied.) The present case is one of creating a danger to persons or property in navigable waters (equivalent to a highway) and there it is admitted that fault is essential—in this case the negligent discharge of the oil.

> 'But how are we to determine whether a state of affairs in or near a highway is [a] danger? This depends, I think, on whether injury may reasonably be foreseen. If you take all the cases in the books you will find that if the state of affairs is such that injury may reasonably be anticipated to persons using the highway it is a public nuisance'

(per Denning LJ in *Morton v Wheeler*).[17] So in the class of nuisance which includes this case foreseeability is an essential element in determining liability.

It could not be right to discriminate between different cases of nuisance so as to make foreseeability a necessary element in determining damages in those cases where it is a necessary element in determining liability, but not in others. So the choice is between it being a necessary element in all cases of nuisance or in none. In their lordships' judgment the similarities between nuisance and other forms of tort to which the *Wagon Mound*[18] applies far outweigh any differences, and they must therefore hold that the judgment appealed from is wrong on this branch of the case. It is not sufficient that the injury suffered by the respondents' vessels was the direct result of the nuisance, if that injury was in the relevant sense unforeseeable....

Appeal against the verdict for the respondents on the nuisance claim allowed, but the judgment for the respondents was affirmed, because their cross-appeal against the verdict for the appellants on the negligence claim was allowed.

QUESTIONS

1. In discussing the relationship of negligence and nuisance, Lord Reid used the term 'negligence in the narrow sense'. What do you think he meant by this?
2. If one applies the Privy Council's view on the foreseeability of damage and the law they laid down relating to nuisance, to the actual nuisance claim in the case, why was the appeal from the verdict in favour of the respondents on the nuisance claim allowed? (See R. J. Buxton (1966) 29 MLR 676 at 681 and L. H. Hoffmann (1967) 83 LQR 13.)

■ Cambridge Water Co Ltd v Eastern Counties Leather Plc

p. 834, post

NOTES

1. The passage in the *Cambridge Water* case to consider at this point is that to be found at pp. 837–838, post under the heading '*Foreseeability of damage in nuisance*'.
2. The use of the term 'measure of damages' by Lord Reid in *The Wagon Mound (No 2)* should, it is submitted, be read as remoteness of damage, or at least so read for analytical purposes.
3. For argument on the application of the reasonable foreseeability test in nuisance in the light of the *Cambridge Water* case, see G. Cross (1995) 111 LQR 445 at 458–473, who

---

[16] [1940] 1 KB 229, [1939] 4 All ER 241.
[17] (1956) unreported.   [18] [1961] AC 388, [1961] 1 All ER 404.

favours the view that the type of damage must be a reasonably foreseeable consequence given that the event that brings it about has happened, not that it must be a reasonably foreseeable consequence of the activity in question. See further T. Weir [1994] CLJ 216 at 217. (A similar point will be addressed when liability under *Rylands v Fletcher* is considered in note 2, p. 842, post). Other commentators do not agree: see for example A. Ogus [1984] JEL 151 at 152.

As has been pointed out, this is linked to the question of fault and of how strict liability in nuisance is. The role of negligence in the tort of nuisance, discussed by Lord Reid in *The Wagon Mound (No 2)* and by Lord Goff in *Cambridge Water*, is difficult. Cross, op. cit., pp. 446–468, argues that Lord Goff's speech in *Cambridge Water* allows *The Wagon Mound (No 2)* to be restricted in its effects to the question of remoteness of damage and not to affect the question of liability. Do you agree? It is undoubtedly true that the creator of a nuisance may be liable in the tort of private nuisance even if he took all reasonable care to minimise the interference to his neighbour: the relevant control mechanism is instead the requirement of reasonable user. On the other hand, as will be seen, persons other than the creator of the nuisance (such as those from whose land a nuisance created by a trespasser or by natural forces emanates) will only be liable in nuisance if they are at fault, in a sense very close to that used in the tort of negligence.

Generally on the issues in this note, see (in addition to the standard textbooks on tort) R. M. W. Dias [1967] CLJ 62; J. M. Eekelaar (1973) 8 Ir Jur (NS) 191; Cross, op. cit.; J. Steele (1995) 15 LS 236 at 252–257. On the interrelationship of the torts of private nuisance and negligence, see C. Gearty [1989] CLJ 214. Gearty argues that claims for damages in relation to physical damage to land should only be allowed in the tort of negligence, on proof of fault, and not in private nuisance. This view was referred to by Lord Goff in *Hunter v Canary Wharf Ltd* [1997] 2 All ER 426 at 439 and by Hirst LJ in *Hussain v Lancaster City Council* [1999] 4 All ER 125 at 146 (see further p. 809, post), who thought that the law was moving strongly towards Gearty's desired position, but did not need to decide whether it had yet reached that destination. Does *Hunter v Canary Wharf Ltd* accept the recovery of damages for physical damage to land under the tort of private nuisance? A more recent consideration of these issues is M. Lee (2003) 119 LQR 298.

4.   The Privy Council in *The Wagon Mound (No 2)* expressed no opinion on cases such as *Wringe v Cohen* [1940] 1 KB 229, [1939] 4 All ER 241. This was understandable for they relate to an area where liability need not be based on fault. In *Wringe v Cohen* the claimant's shop stood next to the defendant's premises, which he let to a tenant. There was evidence that the wall which formed the gable end of the house above this shop had been in a defective state for three years, and one day it fell, damaging the roof of the shop. In the Court of Appeal it was admitted that there was evidence on which the judge in the court below could find an agreement by the defendant with the tenant that the former would keep the premises in repair, and on which he could hold that the gable end wall had become a nuisance because of the lack of repair. Nevertheless, it was argued that the defendant could only be held liable if he knew or should have known of the want of repair. Atkinson J's reply for the Court of Appeal (at p. 243) was that:

…[I]f, owing to want of repair, premises upon a highway become dangerous, and, therefore, a nuisance, and a passer-by or adjoining owner suffers damage by their collapse, the occupier, or the owner, if he has undertaken the duty of repair, is answerable, whether or not he knew, or ought to have known, of the danger. The undertaking to repair gives the owner control of the premises, and a right of access thereto for the purpose of maintaining them in a safe condition.

On the other hand, if the nuisance is created, not by want of repair, but, for example, by the act of a trespasser, or by a secret and unobservable operation of nature, such as a subsidence under or near the foundations of the premises, neither an occupier nor an owner responsible for repair is answerable, unless with knowledge or means of knowledge he allows the danger to continue. In such a case, he has in no sense caused the nuisance by any act or breach of duty. I think that every case decided in the English courts is consistent with this view.

It should be noted that today an owner can be liable if he has an express or implied right to enter to do repairs, rather than an obligation to repair (*Mint v Good* [1951] 1 KB 517, [1950] 2 All ER 1159). The collapse in *Wringe v Cohen*, of course, was not onto the highway, but onto a neighbour's property. If the strict duty can be justified on the grounds of danger to the public on the highway, should it also apply for the benefit of the neighbour? Would the neighbour's action be in public or private nuisance? What, in any case, are premises upon a highway? Does this phrase include a case where the grounds stretch to the highway, and the house is 100 yards away at the end of a private drive but close to the neighbour's house? For comment on *Wringe v Cohen*, see W. Friedmann (1943) 59 LQR 63 at 67–69. Consider further Buckley, op cit., pp. 81–84 and p. 94, note 5, who argues that the judgment in *Wringe v Cohen* does not represent the law on the question of the standard of liability imposed.

5.   On the role of fault in nuisance, see further the ensuing sections of this chapter on liability for acts of third parties and for naturally occurring nuisances. In *Delaware Mansions v Westminster City Council* [2001] 4 All ER 737, [2001] UKHL 55, a case of soil dehydration by encroaching tree roots, Lord Cooke of Thorndon held at [29] that 'the answer to the issue falls to be found by applying the concepts of reasonableness between neighbours (real or figurative) and reasonable foreseeability which underlie much modern tort law and, more particularly, the law of nuisance'. Thus, a landowner would be liable for such tree-root damage only when he had notice of its occurrence: i.e. the dehydration must be reasonably foreseeable. This decision has been criticised for complicating the previously straightforward situation of strict liability for damage by trees: T. Weir, *A Casebook on Tort* 10th edn (London, 2004) pp. 441–442. For an application of Lord Cooke's approach see *Network Rail Infrastructure Ltd v Morris* [2004] EWCA Civ 172, see note 8, p. 789, ante.

6.   On the colonisation of nuisance (and other torts) by fault-based ideas see also, more generally (but equally critically), T. Weir, 'The Staggering March of Negligence', in *The Law of Obligations: Essays in Celebration of John Fleming* (Oxford, 1998), edited by P. Cane and J. Stapleton.

(c) Act of trespasser

■ Sedleigh-Denfield v O'Callagan (Trustees for St. Joseph's Society for Foreign Missions)
House of Lords [1940] 3 All ER 349

The appellant (plaintiff) owned land on the north side of which there was a ditch which, it was held, belonged to the respondents (defendants), the owners of adjoining property. A pipe (or culvert) was laid in the ditch by a trespasser, and the workmen involved did not place a grid near the mouth of the pipe so as to intercept any refuse: in fact, they laid it on top of the pipe where it served no useful purpose. When the pipe was being laid, Brother Dekker, who was then responsible for cleaning the ditch, saw the work being carried out. Further, the ditch was cleaned out twice a year on behalf of the respondents by the person in charge of it. After a heavy rainstorm the pipe became blocked with refuse and the appellant's land was flooded. In the House of Lords, Viscount Maugham expressed the view, with which all their Lordships agreed, that before the flooding 'the respondents must be taken to have had knowledge of the existence of the unguarded culvert'. Branson J, [1938] 3 All ER 321, had dismissed the plaintiff's action, and that decision had been affirmed by the Court of Appeal, [1939] 1 All ER 725. On further appeal to the House of Lords:

VISCOUNT MAUGHAM: . . .

The statement that an occupier of land is liable for the continuance of a nuisance created by others, e.g., by trespassers, if he continues or adopts it—which seems to be agreed—throws little light on the matter, unless the words 'continues or adopts' are defined. In my opinion, an occupier of land 'continues' a nuisance if, with knowledge or presumed knowledge of its existence, he fails to take any reasonable means to bring it to an end, though with ample time to do so. He 'adopts' it if he makes any use of the erection, building, bank or artificial contrivance which constitutes the nuisance. In these sentences, I am not attempting exclusive definitions. . . .

My Lords, in the present case, I am of opinion that the respondents both continued and adopted the nuisance. After the lapse of nearly 3 years, they must be taken to have suffered the nuisance to continue, for they neglected to take the very simple step of placing a grid in the proper place, which would have removed the danger to their neighbour's land. They adopted the nuisance, for they continued during all that time to use the artificial contrivance of the conduit for the purpose of getting rid of water from their property without taking the proper means for rendering it safe. For these reasons, I am of opinion that this appeal should be allowed for damages to be assessed. . . .

LORD ATKIN: . . .

I treat it as established that the entrance to the offending pipe, when it was laid, was on the defendants' land, abutting on the premises occupied by the plaintiff. I agree with the finding of the judge, accepted by the Court of Appeal, that the laying of a 15-inch pipe with an unprotected orifice was, in the circumstances, the creation of a nuisance, or of that which would be likely to result in a nuisance. It created a state of things from which, when the ditch was flowing in full stream, an obstruction might reasonably be expected in the pipe, from which obstruction flooding of the plaintiff's ground might reasonably be expected to result, though I am not satisfied that, granted this reasonable expectation of obstruction, it would be necessary for the plaintiff to prove that the particular injury was such as reasonably to be expected to result from the obstruction. If the defendants had themselves laid the pipe in the manner described, I have no hesitation in saying that, once the plaintiff had suffered damage from flooding so caused, he would have had a good cause of action against them for nuisance. It is probably strictly correct to say that, as long as the offending condition is confined to the defendants' own land without causing damage, it is not a nuisance, though it may threaten to become a nuisance. Where damage has accrued, however, the nuisance has been caused. I should regard the case on this hypothesis as having the same legal consequences as if the defendants, instead of laying a pipe, had placed an obvious obstruction in the course of the ditch. The question here is what the legal position is if such an obstruction is placed by a trespasser. In the present case, I consider it established that the defendants by their responsible agents had knowledge of the erection of the pipe, of the reasonable expectation that it might be obstructed, of the result of such obstruction, and of its continued existence in the condition complained of since it was first placed in position. Brother Dekker, a member of the community, was in charge of the defendants' farming operations, and obviously represented the defendants in this matter, so far as is relevant. He had doubtless no authority to consent to a trespass, and probably no authority to incur any appreciable expense in remedying it, but the defendants obviously had to rely upon him to report to them what was found on the farm likely to be injurious to them or their neighbours.

In this state of the facts, the legal position is not, I think, difficult to discover. For the purpose of ascertaining whether, as here, the plaintiff can establish a private nuisance, I think that nuisance is sufficiently defined as a wrongful interference with another's enjoyment of his land or premises by the use of land or premises either occupied—or, in some cases, owned—by oneself. The occupier or owner is not an insurer. There must be something more than the mere harm done to the neighbour's property to make the party responsible. Deliberate act or negligence is not an essential ingredient, but some degree of personal responsibility is required, which is connoted in my definition by the word 'use'. This conception is implicit in all the decisions which impose liability only where the defendant has 'caused or continued' the nuisance. We may eliminate, in this case, 'caused.' What is the meaning of 'continued'? In the context in which it is used, 'continued' must indicate mere passive continuance. If a man uses on premises something which he finds there, and which itself causes a nuisance by noise, vibration, smell or fumes, he is himself, in continuing to bring into existence the noise, vibration, smell of fumes, causing a nuisance. Continuing in this sense, and causing are the same thing. It seems to me clear that, if a man permits an offensive thing on his premises to continue to offend—that is, if he knows that it is operating offensively, is able to prevent it, and omits to prevent it—he is permitting the nuisance to continue. In other words, he is continuing it. . . .

   In the present case . . . there is, as I have said, sufficient proof of the knowledge of the defendants both of the cause and of its probable effect. What is the legal result of the original cause being due to the act of a trespasser? In my opinion, the defendants clearly continued the nuisance, for they come clearly within the terms I have mentioned above. They knew the danger, they were able to prevent it, and they omitted to prevent it. In this respect, at least, there seems to me to be no difference between the case of a public nuisance and that of a private nuisance, and *A-G v Tod Heatley*[19] is conclusive to show that, where the occupier has knowledge of a public nuisance, has the means of remedying it, and fails to do so, he may be enjoined from allowing it to continue. I cannot think that the obligation not to 'continue' can have a different meaning in 'public' and in 'private' nuisance. . . . I think, therefore, that, in the present case, the plaintiff established the liability of the defendants to him, and that the appeal should be allowed. The orders of the judge and the Court of Appeal should be set aside and judgment entered for the plaintiff for damages to be assessed. . . .

LORD PORTER: . . .

[T]he true view is that the occupier of land is liable for a nuisance existing on his property to the extent that he can reasonably abate it, even though he neither created it nor received any benefit from it. It is enough if he permitted it to continue after he knew, or ought to have known, of its existence. To this extent, but to no greater extent, he must be proved to have adopted the act of the creator of the nuisance. . . .

[LORD WRIGHT and LORD ROMER delivered speeches in favour of allowing the appeal.]

Appeal allowed.

NOTES

1. The case above is an example where an occupier was held liable in nuisance. Several textbooks take the view that the person who by some positive act creates the nuisance may be liable, even though he is not an occupier of the land: see for example Buckley, op cit., pp. 4–5.

2. However, in *Hussain v Lancaster City Council* [2000] QB 1, [1999] 4 All ER 125 the Court of Appeal indicated that nuisance did require the use by the defendant of his land. In *Hussain*, the claimants were the victims of appalling racial harassment and attacks committed by council tenants and others, who assembled on the public highway outside the claimants' property (situated within a council estate). The claimants brought proceedings in negligence and nuisance against the council for failing to take

[19] [1897] 1 Ch 560.

steps to prevent the harassment and attacks, but the claim was struck out as disclosing no reasonable cause of action. One reason given by Hirst LJ at [1999] 4 All ER 125, at 144 was, 'In the present case the acts complained of unquestionably interfered persistently and intolerably with the [claimants'] enjoyment of the [claimants'] land, but they did not involve the tenants' use of the tenants' land and therefore fell outside the scope of the tort [of private nuisance].' He reached this view in reliance on Lord Goff's general approval in *Hunter v Canary Wharf Ltd* of the article by F. H. Newark (1949) 65 LQR 480, and on certain views expressed by Lord Wright in *Sedleigh-Denfield* [1940] 3 All ER 349 at 365 and 375.

But it is difficult to find support for this proposition in Newark's article (as opposed to the requirement of the claimant having an interest in the land affected). Furthermore, *Sedleigh-Denfield* was dealing with the liability of the owner/occupier of the property, and in this context references such as those to the defendants' 'use of their land' (Lord Wright) are not unexpected, but do not necessarily support this as an essential requirement for the tort. See also *Lippiatt v South Gloucestershire Council* [2000] QB 51, [1999] 4 All ER 149, in which *Hussain* is distinguished by the Court of Appeal on this point, in tones of some scepticism, discussed by J. O'Sullivan [2000] CLJ 11. See generally *Street*, p. 445, *Winfield & Jolowicz*, p. 668, n. 91.

3.   In *L E Jones (Insurance Brokers) Ltd v Portsmouth City Council* [2003] 1 WLR 427, [2002] EWCA Civ 1723 the claimants' building was damaged by roots encroaching from the highway. The defendant council objected that the relevant highway authority was the occupier of the highway, and thus liable for the nuisance. But this argument was rejected. The basis for liability of an occupier was not occupation as such, 'Rather, it is that, by virtue of his occupation, an occupier usually has it in his power to take the measures that are necessary to prevent or eliminate the nuisance. He has sufficient control over the hazard which constitutes the nuisance for it to be reasonable to make him liable for the foreseeable consequences of his failure to exercise that control so as to remove the hazard' (per Dyson LJ at [11]). Thus, it was immaterial whether Portsmouth City Council or the highway authority was truly 'the occupier', since Portsmouth undoubtedly had the right and duty to maintain the trees (including limiting their height and root growth), pursuant to an agreement with the highway authority. This factual degree of control was sufficient to affix Portsmouth with liability for the tree-root nuisance.

(On tree roots, see also *Delaware Mansions v Westminster City Council* [2001] 4 All ER 737, [2001] UKHL 55, discussed at note 5, p. 807, ante.)

4.   For the position where an independent contractor creates the nuisance, see p. 1097, post. On the liabilities of landlord and tenant, see *Winfield & Jolowicz*, pp. 674–677 and see also *Hussain v Lancaster City Council* [2000] 1 QB 1, [1999] 4 All ER 125 and *Southwark London Borough Council v Mills* [2001] 1 AC 1, [1999] 4 All ER 449. On licensees, see the discussion in *Lippiatt v South Gloucestershire Council* [2000] QB 51, [1999] 4 All ER 149, in which *Hussain* was distinguished. Note also the earlier case of *A-G v Corke* [1933] Ch 89, as explained in *Smith v Scott* [1973] Ch 314 at 321–322. See further J. Morgan [2001] CLJ 382.

5.   Compare the *Sedleigh-Denfield* case with *Wringe v Cohen* [1940] 1 KB 229, [1939] 4 All ER 241, noted p. 806, ante, and consider *Salmond & Heuston*, pp. 66–67.

(d) Natural hazards

■ Leakey v National Trust for Places of Historic Interest or Natural Beauty
Court of Appeal [1980] 1 All ER 17

The plaintiffs owned houses lying at the base of Burrow Mump, a steep conical hill, which at the point where it met the plaintiffs' property took the form of a bank. The defendants admitted in their pleadings that Burrow Mump was owned and occupied by them. As a result of the operation of natural agencies, from time to time there had been slides of soil, rocks, tree roots and the like from this bank on to the plaintiffs' land, and, since 1968 at least, the defendants appreciated that the bank was a part of their property and that it was a threat to the houses below because of the real possibility of falls of material from it. In 1976 there was a large fall of the bank and shortly thereafter the plaintiffs brought an action in nuisance against the defendants. At the trial of the action O'Connor J, [1978] 3 All ER 234 held that a nuisance had been established and the defendants appealed to the Court of Appeal. The extract from the judgment contains several references to *Rylands v Fletcher* (1868) LR 3 HL 330, which can be found set out at p. 828, post.

MEGAW LJ: . . .
O'Connor J . . . based his decision on the judgment of the Judicial Committee of the Privy Council in *Goldman v Hargrave*[20]. The main issue in this appeal is whether *Goldman v Hargrave*[20] accurately states the law of England. If it does, the appeal fails, and the defendants are liable. . . .

For the defendants in this appeal, the fundamental proposition was formulated by counsel as follows: in English law, neither the owner nor the occupier of land from which, solely as the result of natural causes, natural mineral material encroaches onto, or threatens to encroach onto, adjoining land, causing damage, is under any liability to the adjoining land owner.

. . . [T]he opening words, 'In English law', are properly and deliberately included so as to emphasise that, even if the proposition has to be treated as being inconsistent with the ratio decidendi of *Goldman v Hargrave*[1], that case, however persuasive, does not have the status of a binding authority as to English law. . . .

The defendants' second proposition, which I propose to consider in the course of considering the first proposition, is that, if the first proposition be wrong, so that *Goldman v Hargrave*[1] does represent the law of England, nevertheless the liability which is imposed under the *Goldman v Hargrave*[1] principle is a liability in negligence and not in nuisance. The present claim was pleaded, and pleaded only, in nuisance. Hence, it is said, it must fail. . . .

The relevant facts of *Goldman v Hargrave*[1] were simple. A redgum tree, 100 feet high, on the defendant's land was struck by lightning and caught fire. The defendant caused the land around the burning tree to be cleared and the tree was then cut down and sawn into sections. So far there could be no complaint that the defendant had done anything which he ought not to have done or left undone anything which he ought to have done, so as in any way to increase the risk which had been caused by this act of natural forces setting fire to the tree. Thereafter the defendant (this was the state of the facts on which the Judicial Committee based their decision) did not do anything which he ought not to have done. He took no positive action which increased the risk of the fire spreading. But he failed to do something which he could have done without any substantial trouble or expense, which would, if done, have eliminated or rendered unlikely the spreading of the fire, that is, to have doused with water the burning or smouldering sections of the tree as they lay on the ground. Instead, the defendant chose

---

[20] [1967] 1 AC 645, [1966] 2 All ER 989.   [1] [1967] 1 AC 645, [1966] 2 All ER 989.

to allow or encourage the fire to burn itself out. Foreseeably (again it was the forces of nature and not human action), the weather became even hotter and a strong wind sprang up. The flames from the tree spread rapidly through the defendant's land to the land of neighbours where it did extensive damage to their properties.

The judgment of the Board was delivered by Lord Wilberforce. It was held that the risk of the consequence which in fact happened was foreseeable. This, it is said, 'was not really disputed'. The legal issue was then defined[2]:

> '...the case is not one where a person has brought a source of danger on to his land, nor one where an occupier has so used his property as to cause a danger to his neighbour. It is one where an occupier, faced with a hazard accidentally arising on his land, fails to act with reasonable prudence so as to remove the hazard. The issue is therefore whether in such a case the occupier is guilty of legal negligence, which involves the issue whether he is under a duty of care, and, if so, what is the scope of that duty.'

It is to my mind clear, from this passage and other passages in the judgment, that the duty which is being considered, and which later in the judgment held to exist, does not involve any distinction of principle between what, in another sphere of the law, used to be known as misfeasance and nonfeasance may have a bearing on the question whether the duty has been broken. It is to my mind clear, also, that no distinction is suggested in, or can properly be inferred from, the judgment as between a hazard accidentally arising on the defendant's land which, on the one hand, gives rise to a risk of damage to a neighbour's property by the encroachment of fire and, on the other hand, gives rise to such a risk by the encroachment of the soil itself, falling from the bank onto the neighbour's land. There is no valid distinction, to my mind, between an encroachment which consists, on the one hand, of the spread of fire from a tree on fire on the land, and, on the other hand, of a slip of soil or rock resulting from the instability of the land itself, in each case, the danger of encroachment, and the actual encroachment, being brought about by the forces of nature.

If any such distinctions as I have referred to in the previous paragraph were sought to be made, I should have thought that their acceptance as being material, as leading to different conclusions of principle in law, would make the law on this topic incoherent, artificial, uncertain and unpredictable. In other words, they would lead to bad law.

At the point in the Board's judgment immediately following the passage which I have quoted above, the judgment goes on to deal briefly with the question of the appropriate description of the cause of action. Their Lordships in that case found it unnecessary to decide[3]—

> 'whether if responsibility is established it should be brought under the heading of nuisance or placed in a separate category...The present case is one where liability, if it exists, rests on negligence and nothing else; whether it falls within or overlaps the boundaries of nuisance is a question of classification which need not here be resolved.'

It is convenient at this stage to deal with the second proposition put forward by the defendants in the present appeal. The plaintiffs' claim is expressed in the pleadings to be founded in nuisance. There is no express references to negligence in the statement of claim. But there is an allegation of a breach of duty, and the duty asserted is, in effect, a duty to take reasonable care to prevent part of the defendants' land from falling onto the plaintiffs' property. I should, for myself, regard that as being properly described as a claim in nuisance. But even if that were, technically, wrong, I do not think that the point could or should avail the defendants in this case. If it were to do so, it would be a regrettable modern instance of the forms of action successfully clanking their spectral chains; for there would be no conceivable prejudice to the defendants in this case that the word 'negligence' had not been expressly set out in the statement of claim....

---

[2] [1967] 1 AC 645 at 656, [1966] 2 All ER 989 at 991.
[3] [1967] 1 AC 645 at 656, [1966] 2 All ER 989 at 992.

If the defendants' first and main proposition is wrong. I do not see that they can succeed on their second proposition.

I return to the judgment in *Goldman v Hargrave*.[4] The law of England as it used to be is set out in the following passage:

'... It is only in comparatively recent times that the law has recognised an occupier's duty as one of a more positive character than merely to abstain from creating, or adding to, a source of danger or annoyance. It was for long satisfied with the conception of separate or autonomous proprietors, each of which was entitled to exploit his territory in a "natural" manner and none of whom was obliged to restrain or direct the operations of nature in the interest of avoiding harm to his neighbours.'

The judgment of the Board then goes on to review the development of the law which, as the board held,[5] had changed the law so that there now exists 'a general duty on occupiers in relation to hazards occurring on their land, whether natural or man-made'....

The approval by the House of Lords in [*Sedleigh-Denfield v O'Callagan*[6] of Scrutton LJ's judgment in [*Job Edwards Ltd v Birmingham Navigation*[7]] meant, at any rate unless it could properly be said that it was a decision inconsistent with an earlier decision of the House of Lords, that it was thereafter the law of England that a duty existed under which the occupier of land might be liable to his neighbour for damage to his neighbour's property as a result of a nuisance spreading from his land to his neighbour's land, even though the existence and the operative effect of the nuisance were not caused by any 'non-natural' use by the defendant of his own land. But the liability was not a strict liability such as that which was postulated by the House of Lords in *Rylands v Fletcher*[8] as arising where damage was caused to another by an 'unnatural' user of land. The obligation postulated in the *Sedleigh-Denfield* case[6], in conformity with the development of the law in *Donoghue v Stevenson*,[9] was an obligation to use reasonable care. A defendant was not to be liable as a result of a risk of which he neither was aware nor ought, as a reasonable careful landowner, to have been aware.

The decision in the *Sedleigh-Denfield* case[6] was in a case where, on the facts, something which might be described as 'not natural' had been introduced onto the defendant's land in the building of the culvert, but not by the defendant. It had been done by a trespasser without the defendant's knowledge or consent. It was not a case in which the potential damage to the neighbour's land had been brought about by natural causes. Therefore it may be said that the *Sedleigh-Denfield* case[6] did not decide, so as to bind lower courts in England, that an owner or occupier of land was under a duty to exercise reasonable care where natural causes, as distinct from the act of a trespasser, brought about the dangerous condition of the land, of which he, the owner or occupier, knew or which he should have realised. If I had taken the view that the *Sedleigh-Denfield* case[6] does not bear on the question raised by the present appeal (and therefore also ought not to have influenced the decision in *Goldman v Hargrave*[10]), I should have reached a different conclusion on this appeal. I do not, however, accept the suggested distinction.

My first comment is that the whole tenor of the speeches in the *Sedleigh-Denfield* case[6] suggests that the view of their Lordships, if not their decision, was that the same duty arose....

My second comment on the suggested distinction is that it involves a fallacy. I cite a passage from the judgment in *Goldman v Hargrave*[11] which, I respectfully suggest, makes this clear beyond dispute:

'It was suggested as a logical basis for the distinction that in the case of a hazard originating in an act of man, an occupier who fails to deal with it can be said to be using his land in a manner

---

  [4] [1967] 1 AC 645 at 657, [1966] 2 All ER 989 at 992.
  [5] [1967] 1 AC 645 at 661–663, [1966] 2 All ER 989 at 995.
  [6] [1940] AC 880, [1940] 3 All ER 349.   [7] [1924] 1 KB 341.
  [8] (1868) LR 3 HL 330, [1861–73] All ER Rep 1.   [9] [1932] AC 562, [1932] All ER Rep 1.
  [10] [1967] 1 AC 645, [1966] 2 All ER 989.   [11] [1967] 1 AC 645 at 661, [1966] 2 All ER 989 at 995.

detrimental to his neighbour and so to be within the classical field of responsibility in nuisance, whereas this cannot be said when the hazard originates without human action so long at least as the occupier merely abstains. The fallacy of this argument is that, as already explained, the basis of the occupier's liability lies not in the use of his land: in the absence of "adoption" there is no such use; but in the neglect of action in the face of something which may damage his neighbour. To this, the suggested distinction is irrelevant.'

...Is there, then, anything in the ratio decidendi of *Rylands v Fletcher*,[12] or in any subsequent authority binding on this court, which requires or entitles us to disregard the decision in the *Sedleigh-Denfield* case[13] or to prevent us from accepting the logical extension of it (so far as it is an extension) which was regarded as proper in *Goldman v Hargrave*?[14]

...It was no part of the decision, as distinct from dicta, in *Rylands v Fletcher*[12] that one who has not himself brought something of an unusual nature on his land, or used his land in an unnatural way (whatever that may mean or include), is in no circumstances liable if something from his land encroaches on his neighbour's land....

Rylands v Fletcher[12] does not impose strict liability except where there has been some non-natural use of the land. But it does not hold, by way of binding authority, that there can be no duty where there has not been a 'non-natural' use of the land....

So I find nothing in *Rylands v Fletcher*,[12] or at least in its ratio decidendi, which could properly be used to justify the suggestion that the House of Lords in 1940 in the *Sedleigh-Denfield* case[13] departed, consciously or unconsciously, from the law as laid down in *Rylands v Fletcher*,[12] or which was inconsistent with the extension, if it be an extension, of the *Sedleigh-Denfield*[13] decision to defects naturally arising on land which constitute nuisances and give rise to damage to the land of neighbours. The House of Lords was not in 1940 precluded by earlier decisions of the House from following the *Donoghue v Stevenson*[15] approach or from holding that the neighbour in Lord Atkin's speech in *Donoghue v Stevenson*[16] included one who was a neighbour in the literal sense as being the owner of adjoining land.

Is there, then, any subsequent authority binding on this court which prevents it, by the doctrine of precedent, from holding that the law of England, as laid down in the *Sedleigh-Denfield* case[13], is extended by what the Judicial Committee of the Privy Council regarded as inevitable logic?

[MEGAW LJ found no such authority. In particular, he thought that the Divisional Court's decision in *Giles v Walker*[17] should be overruled, and disapproved of Eve J's reasoning in *Pontardawe RDC v Moore-Gwyn*:[18] Both were cases on which the defendants had placed 'much reliance'. He continued:]...Suppose that we are not bound by *Rylands v Fletcher*[12] or any other authority to hold in favour of the defendants where the nuisance arises solely from natural forces; but suppose also that we are not bound by the decision in *Sedleigh-Denfield*[19] or other binding authority to hold that there is a duty on the defendants in a case such as the present. Ought we as a matter of policy to develop the law by holding that there is a duty in a case such as the present?

If, as a result of the working of the forces of nature, there is, poised above my land, or above my house, a boulder or a rotten tree, which is liable to fall at any moment of the day or night, perhaps destroying my house, and perhaps killing or injuring me or members of my family, am I without remedy? (Of course the standard of care required may be much higher where there is risk to life or limb as contrasted with mere risk to property, but can it be said that the duty exists in the one case and not in the other?) Must I, in such a case, if my protests to my neighbour go unheeded, sit and wait and hope that the worst will not befall?....

---

[12] (1868) LR 3 HL 330, [1861–73] All ER Rep 1.   [13] [1940] AC 880, [1940] 3 All ER 349.
[14] [1967] 1 AC 645, [1966] 2 All ER 989.   [15] [1932] AC 562, [1932] All ER Rep 1.
[16] [1932] AC 562 at 580, [1932] All ER Rep 1 at 11.
[17] (1890) 24 QBD 656, [1886–90] All ER Rep 501.   [18] [1929] 1 Ch 656.
[19] [1940] AC 880, [1940] 3 All ER 349.

In the example which I have given above, I believe that few people would regard it as anything other than a grievous blot on the law if the law recognises the existence of no duty on the part of the owner or occupier. But take another example, at the other end of the scale, where it might be thought that there is, potentially, an equally serious injustice the other way. If a stream flows through A's land, A being a small farmer, and there is a known danger that in times of heavy rainfall, because of the configuration of A's land and the nature of the stream's course and flow, there may be an overflow, which will pass beyond A's land and damage the property of A's neighbours: perhaps much wealthier neighbours. It may require expensive works, far beyond A's means, to prevent or even diminish the risk of such flooding. Is A to be liable for all the loss that occurs when the flood comes, if he has not done the impossible and carried out these works at his own expense?

In my judgment, there is, in the scope of the duty as explained in *Goldman v Hargrave*,[20] a removal, or at least a powerful amelioration, of the injustice which might otherwise be caused in such a case by the recognition of the duty of care. Because of that limitation on the scope of the duty, I would say that, as a matter of policy, the law ought to recognise such a duty of care.

This leads on to the question of the scope of the duty. This is discussed, and the nature and extent of the duty is explained, in the judgment in *Goldman v Hargrave*.[1] The duty is a duty to do that which is reasonable in all the circumstances, and no more than what, if anything, is reasonable, to prevent or minimise the known risk of damage or injury to one's neighbour or to his property. The considerations with which the law is familiar are all to be taken into account in deciding whether there has been a breach of duty, and, if so, what that breach is, and whether it is causative of the damage in respect of which the claim is made. Thus, there will fall to be considered the extent of the risk. What, so far as reasonably can be foreseen, are the chances that anything untoward will happen or that any damage will be caused? What is to be foreseen as to the possible extent of the damage if the risk becomes a reality? Is it practicable to prevent, or to minimise, the happening of any damage? If it is practicable, how simple or how difficult are the measures which could be taken, how much and how lengthy work do they involve, and what is the probable cost of such works? Was there sufficient time for preventive action to have been taken, by persons acting reasonably in relation to the known risk, between the time when it became known to, or should have been realised by, the defendant, and the time when the damage occurred? Factors such as these, so far as they apply in a particular case, fall to be weighed in deciding whether the defendant's duty of care requires, or required, him to do anything, and, if so, what.

There is a passage in this part of the judgment in *Goldman v Hargrave*[2] defining the scope of the duty, which, on the one hand, is said to be likely, if accepted, to give rise to insuperable difficulties in its practical working, and, on the other hand, is said to provide a sensible and just limitation on the scope of the duty, avoiding the danger of substantial injustice being caused, even in exceptional cases, by the existence of the duty. The passage in question reads as follows:

> '...the owner of a small property where a hazard arises which threatens a neighbour with substantial interests should not have to do so much as one with larger interests of his own at stake and greater resources to protect them: if the small owner does what he can and promptly calls on this neighbour to provide additional resources, he may be held to have done his duty: he should not be liable unless it is clearly proved that he could, and reasonably in his individual circumstances should, have done more.'

...The difficulties which are foreseen, arising out of the passage which I have quoted, include unpredictability of the outcome of litigation, delay in reaching decisions (which in everyone's interests ought to be made promptly) as to protective measures to prevent damage, and the increased complexity, length and expense of litigation, if litigation is necessary. All this, and other disadvantages, would arise, it is suggested, because the parties and their advisers, before they could form a fair and confident view

---

[20] [1967] 1 AC 645, [1966] 2 All ER 989.
[1] [1967] 1 AC 645 at 663, 664, [1966] 2 All ER 989 at 996.
[2] [1967] 1 AC 645 at 663, [1966] 2 All ER 989 at 996.

of their respective rights and liabilities, and before they could safely ask the court to decide these matters, whether finally or at an interlocutory hearing, would find it necessary, or at least desirable, to put themselves in a position to ascertain and compare the respective financial resources of the parties. This might involve detailed, embarrassing and prolonged investigation, even before the stage of discovery in an action.

If I thought that that sort of result would be likely to follow, or to follow in a substantial number or proportion of cases where this duty comes in question, I should, at least, hesitate long before accepting that this factor could be regarded as a proper factor in deciding whether the duty had or had not been broken in a particular case. but I do not think that anything of that sort is contemplated by *Goldman v Hargrave*[3]....

...The defendant's duty is to do that which it is reasonable for him to do. The criteria of reasonableness include, in respect of a duty of this nature, the factor of what the particular man, not the average man, can be expected to do, having regard, amongst other things, where a serious expenditure of money is required to eliminate or reduce the danger, to his means. Just as, where physical effort is required to avert an immediate danger, the defendant's age and physical condition may be relevant in deciding what is reasonable, so also logic and good sense require that, where the expenditure of money is required, the defendant's capacity to find the money is relevant. But this can only be in the way of a broad, and not a detailed, assessment; and, in arriving at a judgment on reasonableness, a similar broad assessment may be relevant in some cases as to the neighbour's capacity to protect himself from damage, whether by way of some form of barrier on his own land or by way of providing funds for expenditure on agreed works on the land of the defendant.

...It may be that in some cases the introduction of this factor may give rise to difficulties to litigants and to their advisers and to the courts. But I believe that the difficulties are likely to turn out to be more theoretical than practical.... If and when problems do arise, they will have to be solved. I do not think that the existence of such potential difficulties justifies a refusal to accept as a part of the law of England the duty as laid down in *Goldman v Hargrave*,[4] including the whole of the exposition as to the scope of the duty. As I have said, no difficulty now[5] arises in this present appeal as regards the application of the *Goldman v Hargrave*[4] scope of the duty, once it is held that the duty exists.

I would dismiss the appeal.

[SHAW LJ delivered a judgment in favour of dismissing the appeal. CUMMING-BRUCE LJ agreed with MEGAW LJ.]

Appeal dismissed.

QUESTIONS

1. Is the standard of care adopted in this case the same as that adopted in the materials to be found in the chapter on breach of duty (p. 291, ante)?

?   If the damage had been held to be reasonably foreseeable in *Smith v Littlewoods Organisation Ltd* [1987] AC 241, [1987] 1 All ER 710 (p. 78, ante) could there have been liability in nuisance? (Consider the comments of A. Tettenborn [1984] CLJ 19 at 20–21 and M. A. Jones (1984) 47 MLR 223 at 226–227 on *P Perl (Exporters) Ltd v Camden London Borough Council* [1984] QB 342, [1983] 3 All ER 161, noted p. 86, ante.)

---

[3] [1967] 1 AC 645, [1966] 2 All ER 989.   [4] [1967] 1 AC 645, [1966] 2 All ER 989.

[5] [During the proceedings in the Court of Appeal it transpired that the defendants did not challenge the judgment against them if there was a duty laid on them and its scope was that set out in *Goldman v Hargrave* [1967] 1 AC 645, [1966] 2 All ER 989.]

NOTES

1.   In *Green v Lord Somerleyton* [2003] EWCA Civ 198 at [81] Jonathan Parker LJ observed that 'in the English landscape...what at first glance may appear as a wholly "natural" feature of the landscape may, on further examination, turn out to owe something to the intervention of man. To my mind, therefore, in the context of the English landscape a distinction between "natural" and "artificial" features is an inherently uncertain foundation on which to rest a decision as to the existence of liability in nuisance.' See further O. Rackham, *The History of the Countryside* (London, 1997).

2.   The principles derived from *Goldman v Hargrave* and *Leakey v National Trust* were considered by the Court of Appeal in *Holbeck Hall Hotel Ltd v Scarborough Borough Council* [2000] QB 836, [2000] 2 All ER 705. Here, the claimants owned a hotel which stood on a cliff which was owned and occupied by the defendant local authority. The cliff was inherently unstable because of maritime erosion, and eventually a massive land slip occurred and the hotel collapsed into the sea. The claimants brought proceedings against the defendant, alleging that it was in breach of the modified duty of care imposed on landowners under *Goldman v Hargrave* and *Leakey v National Trust*. The Court of Appeal held that, in theory, the same principles apply to natural nuisances caused by erosion of support as to any other naturally occurring nuisance, so that the applicable principle was whether the defendant had adopted or continued the nuisance. In all such cases, liability was based on the modified negligence standard. However, on the facts the authority was not liable. The defect was not obvious and the risk of a massive land slip had not been foreseeable. The Court of Appeal applied the *Caparo* 'fair, just and reasonable' limitation on liability. Stuart Smith LJ held (at [2000] 2 All ER 705 at 724), 'I do not think it is just and reasonable in a case like the present to impose liability for damage which is greater in extent than anything that was foreseen or foreseeable (without further geological investigation), especially where the defect and danger existed as much on the claimants' land as the defendants.'

3.   *Leakey* was also relied upon in *Rees v Skerrett* [2001] 1 WLR 1541, [2001] EWCA Civ 760, where the court held that a landowner who demolishes a terraced house owes a duty to the neighbouring householder to make reasonable efforts to weatherproof the dividing wall thereby exposed to the elements. Waller LJ recorded the Court of Appeal's anxiety that its decision was inconsistent with *Phipps v Pears* [1965] 1 QB 76, [1964] 2 All ER 35, which laid down (in similar factual circumstances) that there was no such easement known to the law as one to be protected from the weather. However, Waller LJ argued at [42] that if a landowner may be liable to his neighbours in respect of naturally occurring nuisances (*Leakey*) or nuisances created by third parties (*Sedleigh-Denfield*), 'it would seem strange that he should not owe some duty when he pulls down the house which he appreciates protects the wall of the neighbouring house'. Consistent with *Leakey*, this was a duty to weatherproof only to the extent 'reasonable having regard to the position and resources of the two house owners'.

4.   It was argued after *Leakey* that the subjective approach in that case also applied to cases where it was sought to hold the defendant liable for a nuisance brought about by the act of a third party (e.g. *Sedleigh-Denfield*), and this view is supported by *Page Motors Ltd v Epsom and Ewell Borough Council* (1982) 80 LGR 337. In *Anthony v Coal Authority* [2005] EWHC 1654 (QB), Pitchford J held that the 'measured duty of care' also applied when a landowner created a state of affairs on its land (spoil heaps) which was not initially dangerous, but 'which subsequently-acquired experience demonstrated carried

a foreseeable risk of damage' (on the facts, of spontaneous combustion) [133]. As the landowner was initially innocent of any wrongdoing, he was morally (and legally) to be equiparated with a landowner required to cope with the forces of nature, as in *Leakey* and *Holbeck Hall*, discussed ante.

5. The actual circumstances of the defendant which are to be taken into account are not restricted to his physical or financial resources. Thus in the *Page Motors* case, which concerned nuisance arising from the activities of gypsies who were camped on the defendant's land, the defendant's position as a local authority had to be considered, which involved factors such as the need to satisfy the 'democratic process of consultation'. There can be situations, therefore, in which a public authority might not be liable for a nuisance when a private citizen could be so liable. Contrast, however, the rejection in *Page Motors* of the 'intra vires' protection for public authorities enshrined in *Anns v Merton London Borough Council* [1978] AC 728, [1977] 2 All ER 492 (but see now pp. 88–117, ante): the defendant was sued in its capacity as landowner and was not exercising a statutory power. In *Winch v Mid Bedfordshire District Council* (Unreported, QBD, 2002), another case of nuisance committed by licensees (gypsies on a local authority campsite), Astill J rejected an argument that because of their protection against eviction under the Caravan Sites Act 1968 the licensees were, in effect, in the same relation to the landowner as if they had been tenants (for the distinction, see note 4, p. 810, ante). While controlling the licensees (and ultimately, securing their eviction) was undoubtedly difficult, the problems thus required more rather than less care from the local authority, which was not to be allowed to 'abandon attempts to control anti-social activities emanating from [the caravan] site'.

6. For comment on Megaw LJ's view in *Leakey* on the defence of volenti, see Buckley, op cit., pp. 118–119. In this passage Megaw LJ also mentioned that it is no defence for a claimant to come to a nuisance. *Sturges v Bridgman* (1879) 11 Ch D 852 provides support for this proposition, although the position is different between landlord and tenant: *Baxter v Camden London Borough Council* [2001] 1 QB 1, [1999] 1 All ER 237. When this case went on appeal to the House of Lords, this point was not mentioned ([2001] 1 AC 1, [1999] 4 All ER 449). The position in *Sturgess v Bridgman* was followed, albeit with some reluctance, by a majority of the Court of Appeal in *Miller v Jackson* [1977] QB 966, [1977] 3 All ER 338.

The facts of *Miller v Jackson* were given at p. 299, ante, when the question of the claimants' action in negligence was under consideration; however, the claimants also sought damages and an injunction on the basis of nuisance. The majority of the Court of Appeal thought that an actionable nuisance had been established, but one of the majority (Cumming-Bruce LJ) then sided with Lord Denning MR in refusing to grant an injunction. In Lord Denning's opinion, the injunction should be refused, as the private interest in the privacy of home and garden should be subordinated to the public interest in preserving playing fields, but in any event the Master of the Rolls did not think that a nuisance had been committed. Cumming-Bruce LJ felt that on the facts of the case the interest of the inhabitants of the village in question in not losing their facilities for enjoying the game of cricket should be given priority. In exercising this discretion to refuse an injunction, he made the point that the claimants must or ought to have realised before completing the purchase of the house that cricket balls would be hit into their property: thus, in Cumming-Bruce LJ's judgment, the idea of coming to the nuisance was relevant at this stage and militated against the grant of an injunction, though not the initial establishment of the nuisance. The claimants had to be content with damages.

7.   Damages in lieu of an injunction can be awarded under jurisdiction originally conferred by Lord Cairns's Act (s. 2 of the Chancery Amendment Act 1858), on which see generally J. A. Jolowicz [1975] CLJ 224, and see now s. 50 of the Supreme Court Act 1981 and *Jaggard v Sawyer* [1995] 2 All ER 189, [1995] 1 WLR 269. Unless the damage to the claimants' interests was trivial, the general line adopted by the courts has been that the public interest in the continuation of the activity causing the nuisance should not be allowed to override the claimant's claim for injunctive relief, once the nuisance has been established: see e.g. *Shelfer v City of London Electric Lighting Co* [1895] 1 Ch 287; Buckley, op cit., pp. 140–143.

Three years after *Miller v Jackson*, ante, the question of the relevance of the public interest in this area arose before a differently composed Court of Appeal in *Kennaway v Thompson* [1981] QB 88, [1980] 3 All ER 329: the nuisance in this case was constituted by noise from the activities of a motor boat racing club and the effect of an injunction on those watching or participating in the racing was put forward as an argument against the grant of such a remedy. The court was not prepared to give priority to the public interest; in particular, Lawton LJ, delivering the judgment of the Court of Appeal, expressed the view that Lord Denning's statement in *Miller v Jackson* 'that the public interest should prevail over the private interest runs counter to the principles enunciated in *Shelfer*'s case' ([1981] QB 88 at p. 93). For a criticism of the approach in *Kennaway v Thompson* to *Shelfer* see Buckley, op cit., p. 151. Cf. Harris, *Remedies*, p. 483, noting that the injunction in *Kennaway v Thompson* 'was formulated in terms which amounted to a compromise which was obviously influenced by the public interest: motor-boat racing was permitted to continue on a lake, subject to restrictions as to the number and duration of the club, national and international events to be held there each season, and as to the noise level of boats using the lake at any other time'. However, it might be argued that the terms of the injunction were merely fixing what would or would not be a nuisance and were not specifically taking account of the public interest: consider R. A. Buckley (1981) 44 MLR 212 at 215 and *Rosling v Pinnegar* (1986) 54 P & CR 124. The public interest can be brought into account to a certain extent on the question of *liability* (see e.g. *Winfield & Jolowicz*, pp. 651–652), although in *Kennaway v Thompson* it was not expressly mentioned on this issue.

The dilemma was raised again, in acute form, in *Dennis v Ministry of Defence* [2003] Env LR 34, [2003] EWHC 793 (QB), noted by R. Bagshaw (2004) 120 LQR 37. The claimant's estate suffered severe noise from the training flights of jet aircraft based at nearby Royal Air Force stations. Buckley J held that there had been a nuisance, but awarded damages instead of specific relief (a declaration had been sought 'rather than debate the niceties of claiming injunctions against the Crown' [80]). Buckley J described the facts of the case as 'extreme', and held that the public interest in the continued operation of the RAF stations was unusually strong (defence of the realm; 'the enormous inconvenience and cost of uprooting RAF Wittering and RAF Cottesmore to another location' [48]–[49]). However, the public interest must be weighed at the stage of *remedies*, rather than in considering the initial question of *liability*. If it was held that there was no nuisance at all, so that the MoD did not have to pay damages, this would not only be unjust ([46]) but, moreover, would result in a breach of the rights to private life and peaceful enjoyment of possessions (Article 8 of the ECHR, and Article 1 of the 1st Protocol to the Convention), as given effect by the Human Rights Act 1998: [61]–[63]. (On human rights, see further *Marcic v Thames Water Utilities* [2004] 1 All ER 135, [2003] UKHL 66, p. 821 post.)

In *Goode v Four Ashes Golf Centre Ltd* [2001] EWCA Civ 2101, golf balls emanating from the defendant's land 'contaminated' part of the claimant farmer's fields, rendering the hay produced in them unsuitable for fodder. Although this constituted a nuisance, the Court of Appeal (overruling the trial judge) refused to order the defendants to erect a fence to stop the balls at the cost of £60,000: 'The possible and partial sterilisation of the area of one and a half acres [of grazing land] cannot justify a requirement to erect and maintain a large and expensive fence', [27] Pill LJ. But in *Regan v Paul Properties Ltd* [2007] 4 All ER 48, [2006] EWCA Civ 1319 (noted by D.M. Fox [2007] CLJ 267), reasserting the primacy of *Shelfer's* case (ante), the Court of Appeal issued an injunction to limit the height of a building being erected on the defendants' land, which would have reduced light levels in the claimant's living room. The trial judge had been wrong 'in denying [the claimant] an injunction and effectively forcing him to accept compensation from the defendants for losing the light in respect of his home', ([75] per Mummery LJ). The Court of Appeal was unmoved by the argument that this would be 'oppressive' of the defendants, given that the diminution in value of the claimant's land from loss of light would be at most £5,500, whereas the restrictions placed upon the defendants' development by the injunction meant an estimated loss of £175,000.

To grant damages in lieu of an injunction once a nuisance has been established could be seen as a form of expropriation of the claimant's rights, albeit with compensation (see Lindley LJ in *Shelfer's* case [1895] 1 Ch at p. 316). In what situations, if any, do you think *courts* should bring about this result? See G. Calabresi and D. Melamed (1972) 85 Harvard LR 1089; L. Kaplow and S. Shavell (1996) 109 Harvard LR 713; I. Ayres and J. Balkin (1996) 106 Yale LJ 703. (Consider further Lord Denning's 'new principle' (in the context of statutory authority) in *Allen v Gulf Oil Refining Ltd* [1980] QB 156 at 168–169, but note that it was not adopted when that case reached the House of Lords, [1981] AC 1001, [1981] 1 All ER 353.) On damages in lieu of an injunction, see further S. Tromans [1982] CLJ 87 and on nuisance and remedies generally, see Harris, *Remedies*, chap. 25.

8.   For defences to nuisance, see the standard textbooks on tort; statutory authority, for example, may provide a defence. This defence will not be discussed here, but it might be noted that Cumming-Bruce LJ highlighted (in *Allen v Gulf Oil Refining Ltd* [1979] 3 All ER 1008) one particular way in which the existence of a statute may affect certain actions in nuisance. He stated (at p. 1018):

> …[I]n the instant case, if as a matter of interpretation of the Act it is clear that the intention of Parliament was to change the immediate environment of the village of Waterston by the construction on the specified site immediately beside the village of a great oil refinery with jetties appropriate to the berthing of large tankers bringing in vast quantities of crude oil, and a railway to carry the products of the refinery away overland, it would follow that Parliament has authorised a dramatic change in the neighbourhood of the village. Thereafter a complaint of nuisance by interference with the enjoyment of life in the village would on any view have to show such a degree of interference with enjoyment as exceeded such levels of noise and impurity of air as are inevitable in a neighbourhood in which oil refinery business is to be regarded as the norm.

This point met with approval when the case reached the House of Lords [1981] AC 1001, [1981] 1 All ER 353; see Lord Wilberforce [1981] AC 1001 at pp. 1013–1014, with whose speech Lord Diplock and Lord Roskill expressly agreed.

The grant of planning permission, which takes place under delegated statutory powers, is to be distinguished from the defence of statutory authority (*Wheeler v J J Saunders Ltd* [1996] Ch 19, [1995] 2 All ER 697, noted by S. Tromans [1995] CLJ 494, commenting on *Gillingham Borough Council v Medway (Chatham) Dock Co Ltd* [1993]

QB 343, [1992] 1 All ER 923, noted by J. Steele and T. Jewell (1993) 53 MLR 568) and see *Hunter v Canary Wharf Ltd* [1996] 1 All ER 482 (when that case was in the Court of Appeal); the fact that a nuisance is the inevitable result of such a grant will not per se provide a defence as it would in the case of statutory authority. In *Allen v Gulf Oil Refining Ltd* Cumming-Bruce LJ had referred to planning permission when he said (in a later part of his judgment—[1979] 3 All ER 1008 at 1020) that 'the planning authority has no jurisdiction to authorise nuisance save (if at all) in so far as it has statutory power to permit the change of the character of a neighbourhood in relation to the comfort and convenience of the inhabitants'. This comment was noted in the *Gillingham* case by Buckley J, who went on to state that where planning permission had been obtained, then it was the neighbourhood with the permitted development in it that had to be taken into account. That the change in character of the neighbourhood *could* mean that what might otherwise be a nuisance would not be actionable seems to be approved in *Wheeler* (but note Staughton LJ's caveat [1996] Ch 19 at 30) and see also *Hunter*. It had not, however, done so on the facts of *Wheeler*.

9. The interplay of a public utility's statutory authority with the Human Rights Act 1998 was considered in the next case.

■ Marcic v Thames Water Utilities Ltd
House of Lords [2004] 1 All ER 135

The claimant's garden suffered regular flooding because, after heavy rain, the drains and sewers of the defendant sewerage undertaker were inadequate to cope with the volume of rainwater produced, and regularly overflowed. The sewers, when first built, had been adequate to cope with the demands placed upon them, but their capacity had been exceeded owing to the number of new buildings subsequently erected in the locality (all having a statutory right to connect to the defendant's sewers). The claimant argued that the defendant undertaker had a duty to enlarge the capacity of its sewers to prevent the flooding, and claimed for damages and an injunction in the tort of private nuisance, and under the Human Rights Act 1998.

Under the Water Industry Act 1991, a sewerage undertaker such as the defendant has a duty 'to ensure that [its] area is and continues to be effectually drained' (s. 94(1)). That duty is enforceable by the procedure in s. 18 (s. 94(3)). The Director General of Water Services (the regulator of the water industry under Part I of the Act) shall order a sewerage undertaker to comply with a statutory duty which it is failing to perform: s. 18(1). However, the Director General is, in certain circumstances, given a discretion whether or not to make an order, including when the sewerage undertaker makes satisfactory undertakings regarding its performance of the duty, or when the undertaker would not be able to finance the performance of the duty given the levels of existing sewerage charges: s. 19. However, s. 18(8) provides a saving for actions 'available in respect of [an] act or omission otherwise than by virtue of its constituting such a contravention [of a statutory requirement enforceable under this section]'.

Judge Richard Havery QC [2001] 3 All ER 698 held, following a line of cases beginning with *Glossop v Heston and Isleworth Local Board* (1879) 12 Ch D 102, that no common law nuisance action lay against a sewerage authority for failing to enlarge the capacity of their sewers. However, he upheld the human rights claim, deciding that the flooding had infringed the claimant's rights to private and family life (Article 8, ECHR) and to the peaceful enjoyment of his possessions (Article 1 of the 1st Protocol to ECHR), and that the defendant had failed to show that its system of priorities for flooding alleviation justified that infringement of rights as a matter of public interest.

The Court of Appeal [2002] EWCA Civ 64, [2002] 2 All ER 55 held that the *Glossop* line of authority had been superseded by *Sedleigh-Denfield v O'Callaghan* and *Leakey v National Trust* (see p. 807, ante), and dismissed the defendant's appeal against Human Rights Act liability.

The House of Lords, reversing the Court of Appeal, held that the defendant was not liable either in nuisance or under the Human Rights Act.

LORD HOFFMANN: . . .

[54] Until the decision of the Court of Appeal in this case, there was a line of authority which laid down that the failure of a sewage authority to construct new sewers did not constitute an actionable nuisance. The only remedy was by way of enforcement of the statutory duty now contained in s 94(1) of the 1991 Act, previously contained in s 14 of the Public Health Act 1936 and before that in s 15 of the Public Health Act 1875. The earlier acts also had a special procedure for enforcement which the courts held to be exhaustive: see *Robinson v Workington Corp* [1897] 1 QB 619. The existence of this procedure for the enforcement of statutory duties did not (any more than s 18(8) of the 1991 Act) exclude common law remedies for common law torts, such as a nuisance arising from failure to keep a sewer properly cleaned: see *Baron v Portslade UDC* [1900] 2 QB 588. But the courts consistently held that failure to construct new sewers was not such a nuisance.

[55] The principal authorities for this last proposition were three cases in the late nineteenth century: *Glossop v Heston and Isleworth Local Board* (1879) 12 Ch D 102, [1874–80] All ER Rep 836, *A-G v Guardians of the Poor of Union of Dorking* (1881) 20 Ch D 595, [1881–5] All ER Rep 320 and *Robinson's* case, to which I have already referred, to which may be added *Hesketh v Birmingham Corp* [1924] 1 KB 260, [1922] All ER Rep 243 which followed *Robinson's* case. . . .

[57] Mr Marcic can therefore have a cause of action in nuisance only if these authorities are no longer good law. The Court of Appeal decided that they should no longer be followed. They said that the earlier cases had been overtaken by developments in the concept of 'adopting' or 'continuing' a nuisance which enabled one to say, in appropriate circumstances, that a sewerage undertaker had a common law duty to lay new sewers in order to prevent overloaded old ones from flooding neighbouring properties.

[60] The Court of Appeal said that since the four cases were decided, the law of nuisance had been 'radically extended' by *Sedleigh-Denfield's* case. . . . *Goldman's* case and *Leakey's* case were said to have made a 'significant extension' to the law. It is true that they rejected a distinction between acts of third parties and natural events which Lord Wilberforce said ([1966] 2 All ER 989 at 994, [1967] 1 AC 645 at 661) was 'well designed to introduce confusion into the law' and lacked 'any logical foundation'. Both cases also discussed in greater detail the extent of the duty to remedy a potential nuisance. Otherwise, however, they were applications of the *Sedleigh-Denfield* principle.

[61] Why should sewers be different? If Sedleigh-Denfield's case lays down a general principle that an owner of land has a duty to take reasonable steps to prevent a nuisance arising from a known source of hazard, even though he did not himself create it, why should that not require him to construct new sewers if the court thinks it would have been reasonable to do so?

[62] The difference in my opinion is that *Sedleigh-Denfield's* case, *Goldman's* case and *Leakey's* case were dealing with disputes between neighbouring land owners simply in their capacity as individual landowners. In such cases it is fair and efficient to impose reciprocal duties upon each landowner to take whatever steps are reasonable to prevent his land becoming a source of injury to his neighbour. Even then, the question of what measures should reasonably have been taken may not be uncomplicated. As Lord Wilberforce said in *Goldman's* case ([1966] 2 All ER 989 at 996, [1967] 1 AC 645 at 663), the court must (unusually) have regard to the individual circumstances of the defendant. In *Leakey's* case ([1980] 1 All ER 17 at 37, [1980] QB 485 at 527) Megaw LJ recoiled from the prospect of a detailed examination of the defendant's financial resources and said it should be done 'on a broad basis'.

[63] Nevertheless, whatever the difficulties, the court in such cases is performing its usual function of deciding what is reasonable as between the two parties to the action. But the exercise becomes very different when one is dealing with the capital expenditure of a statutory undertaking providing public utilities on a large scale. The matter is no longer confined to the parties to the action. If one customer is given a certain level of services, everyone in the same circumstances should receive the same level of services. So the effect of a decision about what it would be reasonable to expect a sewerage undertaker to do for the plaintiff is extrapolated across the country. This in turn raises questions of public interest. Capital expenditure on new sewers has to be financed; interest must be paid on borrowings and privatised undertakers must earn a reasonable return. This expenditure can be met only by charges paid by consumers. Is it in the public interest that they should have to pay more? And does expenditure on the particular improvements with which the plaintiff is concerned represent the best order of priorities?

[64] These are decisions which courts are not equipped to make in ordinary litigation. It is therefore not surprising that for more than a century the question of whether more or better sewers should be constructed has been entrusted by Parliament to administrators rather than judges....

[LORD HOFFMANN referred to the provisions of the Public Health Acts of 1875 and 1936, and continued:]

[65] The enforcement procedure under the [Water Industry Act 1991] is much more elaborate. The Director has a duty under s 30(4) to consider a complaint and take such steps as he considers appropriate. He has a prima facie duty under s 18(1) to make an enforcement order if he is satisfied that the company is contravening its statutory duty. But that duty is qualified by s 19(1), which provides that he is not required to make an order if satisfied, among other things, that the company is willing to give suitable undertakings or that the duties imposed upon him by Pt I of the Act preclude the making of such an order. His duties under Pt I require him to exercise his powers in the manner best calculated to achieve certain objectives. The overriding objectives (see s 2(2)) are to secure that the functions of a sewerage undertaker are properly carried out and that the undertakers are able '(in particular, by securing reasonable returns on their capital)' to finance the proper carrying out of their functions. More particular objectives are to protect the interests of customers liable to pay charges and promote economy and efficiency on the part of the company.

[66] Pursuant to these duties, the Director has addressed himself to the question of flooding and formulated policies which the statutory undertakers should follow. Undertakers are required to submit a quinquennial strategic business plan which includes a statement of the capital expenditure required to achieve a reasonable level of alleviation of flooding. If the Director accepts such expenditure as reasonable, it is taken into account in assessing the charges which will give the undertaker a reasonable return on capital. Otherwise it is not. During the three quinquennia starting in 1990, the Director was willing to allow expenditure on work in relation to properties classified as at risk of internal flooding. But no allowance was made for properties, like that of Mr Marcic, which were only at risk of external flooding.

[67] After the widespread floods of October 2000, the Director commissioned further studies of the flooding problem. In March 2002 he issued a consultation paper proposing a policy revision for the 2005–2010 quinquennium by which remedial work for properties only at risk of external flooding should also be included. He also made an interim agreement with Thames by which he approved additional investment before 2005 to free 250 properties (including that of Mr Marcic) from risk of external flooding. Your Lordships were told that this work has been done.

[68] It is plain that the Court of Appeal, in deciding that better sewers should have been laid to serve Mr Marcic's property, was in no position to take into account the wider issues which Parliament requires the Director to consider. [Judge Havery QC], who heard fairly detailed evidence about what the cost of such improvements would be, confessed himself unable to decide whether the priorities laid down by the Director were fair or not ([2001] 3 All ER 698 at [102], [2002] QB 929 at [102]):

'The system of priorities used by the defendant may be entirely fair, and I have no reason to doubt that it is intended to be. But its fairness in balancing the competing interests of the defendant's various customers must depend in part on the numbers in each class, the total costs involved in relation to each class, and the resources of the defendant. The answers to the questions raised above as matters for consideration might depend on the figures. If the exercise of assessing the fairness of the system were carried out, it might lead to the conclusion that for all its apparent faults, the system fell within the wide margin of discretion open to the defendant and the director. But on the limited evidence available to me, it is not possible to carry out such an exercise.'

[69] As a result, the judge had to resort to deciding the matter upon the burden of proof: he said that the burden was upon Thames to satisfy him that it had done what was reasonable and that it had not done so. The judge said this in the context of whether Thames was in breach of its duty under s 6 of the Human Rights Act 1998, having previously decided that there was no cause of action in nuisance. But the Court of Appeal (at [87]) treated it as a finding that Thames Water had not taken reasonable steps to abate the nuisance emanating from its sewers: '…Thames failed to persuade the judge that their system of priorities was a fair one.'

[70] My Lords, I think that this remark, together with the judge's frank admission that the fairness of the priorities adopted by Thames Water was not justiciable, provides the most powerful argument for rejecting the existence of a common law duty to build new sewers. The 1991 Act makes it even clearer than the earlier legislation that Parliament did not intend the fairness of priorities to be decided by a judge. It intended the decision to rest with the Director, subject only to judicial review. It would subvert the scheme of the 1991 Act if the courts were to impose upon the sewerage undertakers, on a case-by-case basis, a system of priorities which is different from that which the Director considers appropriate.

[71] That leaves only the question of whether the remedies provided under the 1991 Act do not adequately safeguard Mr Marcic's rights under the European Convention for the Protection of Human Rights and Fundamental Freedoms 1950 (as set out in Sch 1 to the 1998 Act) to the privacy of his home and the protection of his property. The judge, who found for Mr Marcic on this ground, did not have the benefit of the decision of the Grand Chamber of the European Court of Human Rights in Hatton v UK [2003] All ER (D) 122 (Jul). That decision makes it clear that the convention does not accord absolute protection to property or even to residential premises. It requires a fair balance to be struck between the interests of persons whose homes and property are affected and the interests of other people, such as customers and the general public. National institutions, and particularly the national legislature, are accorded a broad discretion in choosing the solution appropriate to their own society or creating the machinery for doing so. There is no reason why Parliament should not entrust such decisions to an independent regulator such as the Director. He is a public authority within the meaning of the 1998 Act and has a duty to act in accordance with convention rights. If (which there is no reason to suppose) he has exceeded the broad margin of discretion allowed by the convention, Mr Marcic will have a remedy under s 6 of the 1998 Act. But that question is not before your Lordships. His case is that he has a convention right to have the decision as to whether new sewers should be constructed made by a court in a private action for nuisance rather than by the Director in the exercise of his powers under the 1991 Act. In my opinion there is no such right.

[72] I would therefore allow the appeal and dismiss the action.

LORD NICHOLLS OF BIRKENHEAD [having set out his reasons, similar to those of LORD HOFFMANN, as to why the claim in nuisance should fail, continued:]…

[37] I turn to Mr Marcic's claim under the 1998 Act. His claim is that as a public authority within the meaning of s 6 of the 1998 Act Thames Water has acted unlawfully. Thames Water has conducted itself in a way which is incompatible with Mr Marcic's convention rights under art 8 of the convention and art 1 of the First Protocol to the convention. His submission was to the following effect. The flooding of Mr Marcic's property falls within the first paragraph of art 8 and also within art 1 of the First Protocol. That was common ground between the parties. Direct and serious interference of this nature with a person's home is prima facie a violation of a person's right to respect for his private and family life

(art 8) and of his entitlement to the peaceful enjoyment of his possessions (art 1 of the First Protocol). The burden of justifying this interference rests on Thames Water. At the trial of the preliminary issues Thames Water failed to discharge this burden. The trial judge found that the system of priorities used by Thames Water in deciding whether to carry out flood alleviation works might be entirely fair. The judge also said that on the limited evidence before him it was not possible to decide this issue, or to decide whether for all its apparent faults the system fell within the wide margin of discretion open to Thames Water and the Director: [2001] 3 All ER 698 at [102].

[38] To my mind the fatal weakness in this submission is the same as that afflicting Mr Marcic's claim in nuisance: it does not take sufficient account of the statutory scheme under which Thames Water is operating the offending sewers. The need to adopt some system of priorities for building more sewers is self-evident. So is the need for the system to be fair. A fair system of priorities necessarily involves balancing many intangible factors. Whether the system adopted by a sewerage undertaker is fair is a matter inherently more suited for decision by the industry regulator than by a court. And the statutory scheme so provides. Moreover, the statutory scheme provides a remedy where a system of priorities is not fair. An unfair system of priorities means that a sewerage undertaker is not properly discharging its statutory drainage obligation so far as those who are being treated unfairly are concerned. The statute provides what should happen in these circumstances. The director is charged with deciding whether to make an enforcement order in respect of a sewerage undertaker's failure to drain property properly. Parliament entrusted this decision to the director, not the courts.

[39] What happens in practice accords with this statutory scheme. When people affected by sewer flooding complain to the Director he considers whether he should require the sewerage undertaker to take remedial action. Before doing so he considers, among other matters, the severity and history of the problem in the context of that undertaker's sewer flooding relief programme, as allowed for in its current price limits. In many cases the company agrees to take action, but sometimes he accepts that a solution is not possible in the short term.

[40] So the claim based on the 1998 Act raises a broader issue: is the statutory scheme as a whole, of which this enforcement procedure is part, convention-compliant? Stated more specifically and at the risk of over-simplification, is the statutory scheme unreasonable in its impact on Mr Marcic and other householders whose properties are periodically subjected to sewer flooding?

[41] The recent decision of the European Court of Human Rights, sitting as a Grand Chamber, in *Hatton v UK* [2003] All ER (D) 122 (Jul) confirms how courts should approach questions such as these. In Hatton's case the applicants lived near Heathrow airport. They claimed that the government's policy on night flights at Heathrow violated their rights under art 8. The court emphasised 'the fundamentally subsidiary nature' of the convention. National authorities have 'direct democratic legitimation' and are in principle better placed than an international court to evaluate local needs and conditions. In matters of general policy, on which opinions within a democratic society may reasonably differ widely, 'the role of the domestic policy maker should be given special weight'. A fair balance must be struck between the interests of the individual and of the community as a whole.

[42] In the present case the interests Parliament had to balance included, on the one hand, the interests of customers of a company whose properties are prone to sewer flooding and, on the other hand, all the other customers of the company whose properties are drained through the company's sewers. The interests of the first group conflict with the interests of the company's customers as a whole in that only a minority of customers suffer sewer flooding but the company's customers as a whole meet the cost of building more sewers. As already noted, the balance struck by the statutory scheme is to impose a general drainage obligation on a sewerage undertaker but to entrust enforcement of this obligation to an independent regulator who has regard to all the different interests involved. Decisions of the Director are of course subject to an appropriately penetrating degree of judicial review by the courts.

[43] In principle this scheme seems to me to strike a reasonable balance. Parliament acted well within its bounds as policy maker. In Mr Marcic's case matters plainly went awry. It cannot be acceptable that in 2001, several years after Thames Water knew of Mr Marcic's serious problems, there was

still no prospect of the necessary work being carried out for the foreseeable future. At times Thames Water handled Mr Marcic's complaint in a tardy and insensitive fashion. But the malfunctioning of the statutory scheme on this occasion does not cast doubt on its overall fairness as a scheme. A complaint by an individual about his particular case can, and should, be pursued with the Director pursuant to the statutory scheme, with the long stop availability of judicial review. That remedial avenue was not taken in this case.

[46] For these reasons I consider the claim under the 1998 Act is ill-founded. The scheme set up by the 1991 Act is convention-compliant. The scheme provides a remedy for persons in Mr Marcic's unhappy position, but Mr Marcic chose not to avail himself of this remedy.

[47] Accordingly this appeal should be allowed....

[LORD STEYN and LORD SCOTT OF FOSCOTE concurred with the speeches of LORD NICHOLLS OF BIRKENHEAD and LORD HOFFMANN. LORD HOPE OF CRAIGHEAD agreed with LORD NICHOLLS, and delivered a speech rejecting the Human Rights Act claim.]

Appeal allowed.

QUESTION

The Court of Appeal [2002] 2 All ER 55, [2002] EWCA Civ 64 at [111]-[118] raised (without finally answering) the following question: in a case where carrying out remedial action could not be cost-justified (e.g. a single property at risk of flooding once in five years, where the cost of eliminating the risk was prohibitive), does it necessarily follow that the householder should receive no compensation for the damage done? Lord Phillips MR at [113] stated that it was 'at least arguable that to strike a fair balance between the individual and the general community, those who pay to make use of a sewerage system should be charged sufficient to cover the cost of paying compensation to the minority who suffer damage as a consequence of the operation of the system'. Do you agree?

Note that Lord Nicholls in the House of Lords [2004] 1 All ER 135 registered his 'concern' at [44]-[45] about the lack of compensation for those in Mr Marcic's position in similar terms, urging that 'the director and others should reconsider [this matter] in the light of the facts in the present case'. Compare also *Dennis v Ministry of Defence*, noted p. 819, ante.

The Law Commission is currently undertaking a wide-ranging inquiry into the whole issue of compensation for losses caused by public authorities, through both their lawful and unlawful actions. In its Discussion Paper of 2004, *Monetary Remedies in Public Law*, the Commission notes the existence of statutes such as the Land Compensation Act 1973 (requiring compensation for losses caused by public works), but stresses that these are only isolated examples, few in number, and no attempt has been made to co-ordinate or system-atize them (para. 2.84). (For discussion of *Marcic* see ibid. paras. 5.25–5.28.) See further the Appendix, post.

NOTES

1. *Marcic* is noted by H. Wilberg (2004) 120 LQR 574 and J. O'Sullivan [2004] CLJ 552.
2. The House of Lords' decision shows that although *Sedleigh-Denfield* and *Leakey* have led to a considerable expansion of liability for non-feasance in nuisance (consider, e.g. *Rees v Skerrett* [2001] 1 WLR 1541, [2001] EWCA Civ 760, noted p. 817, ante), there are still some remaining islands of no-liability.
3. For the relationship between public authorities' statutory duties and common law liability for non-feasance, consider further *Stovin v Wise* [1996] AC 923, [1996] 3 All

ER 801 and *Gorringe v Calderdale Metropolitan Borough Council* [2004] 2 All ER 326, [2004] UKHL 15 (p. 111, ante).

4. Crucial to the decision of the House of Lords was the distinction between the situation in *Marcic*, requiring a complicated allocation of expenditure priorities, engaging the public interest, and ordinary nuisance disputes 'between neighbouring land owners simply in their capacity as individual land owners', per Lord Hoffmann at [62]. Contrast *Bybrook Barn Garden Centre Ltd v Kent County Council* [2001] Env LR 30, where the defendant highway authority was held liable when a culvert it had laid under a road proved inadequate to cope with the rising volume of water in the relevant watercourse, leading to flooding of the claimant's property. Once the culvert had foreseeably become inadequate, the authority had a duty to take reasonable steps to eliminate the danger. The Court of Appeal relied upon *Leakey* and *Sedleigh-Denfield* as superseding *Radstock Co-operative and Industrial Society Ltd v Norton-Radstock Urban District Council* [1968] Ch 605, [1968] 2 All ER 59. Waller LJ commented at [46] that it was not a case of 'an inadequate sewage system and a plaintiff ratepayer seeking to get the local authority to do its public duty.... It is not a case where it would be right to conduct a general inquiry as to the budget available to the highway authority or as to its backlog.'

    Dobson v Thames Water Utilities [2008] 2 All ER 362, [2007] EWHC 2021 (TCC) considers the boundaries of the '*Marcic* principle'. Ramsey J held that while a *nuisance* claim was ruled out by *Marcic* in a case about smells and insects emanating from a sewage works, a *negligence* action was not necessarily precluded. The question was whether, in a particular situation, the enforcement mechanisms in the Water Industry Act 1991 were intended to exclude an action at common law. The judge admitted at [140] that the 'boundary may be difficult to draw and may depend on such uncertain phrases as matters or decisions relating to "policy" or "capital expenditure" matters or decisions as contrasted with "operational" or "current expenditure" matters or decisions. In *Marcic* the boundary fell between building new sewers and cleaning and maintaining the existing sewers.' Ultimately, he held at [143]: 'If there is fault in the form of negligence and if there is a different cause of action which is not inconsistent and does not conflict [with the statutory scheme] then I consider there is nothing to preclude a claim being made on that basis. 'Policy matters are likely to lead to such inconsistency and conflict whilst operational matters are less likely to do so. It must be a question of fact and degree.'

5. A landowner is permitted to defend his land from rising floodwater, even though this diverts the floods onto the land of his neighbour. In *R v Commissioners of Sewers for Pagham* (1828) 8 B & C 355, Lord Tenterden CJ held that 'each land-owner for himself... may erect such defences for the land under [his] care as the necessity of the case requires, leaving it to others, in like manner, to protect themselves against the common enemy'.

6. In *Arscott v Coal Authority* [2004] EWCA Civ 892 this 'common enemy' rule was challenged as breaching the right to peaceful enjoyment of possessions under Article 1, 1st Protocol to the ECHR. The Court of Appeal held that the Human Rights Act 1998 had not been in force at the relevant time, but Laws LJ indicated his view that the rule anyway did not breach the human rights of a landowner who is flooded by his neighbour's defensive measures. Laws LJ pointed out that Convention rights are not absolute, but require balancing against other individuals' rights, and balancing between such rights and the general public interest. Yet this is precisely what traditional common

law nuisance also seeks to do: see per Lord Wright in *Sedleigh-Denfield v O'Callaghan* [1940] AC 880 at 903: 'A balance has to be maintained between the right of the occupier to do what he likes with his own, and the right of his neighbour not to be interfered with.' The 'common enemy' rule, like the law of nuisance generally, seeks to maintain such a balance. There are well-established limits on its applicability. First, the flood defences cannot be built within the 'alveus' (i.e. within an established watercourse), as by raising the banks of a river: *Rex v Trafford* (1831) 1 B & Ad 874. Secondly, the landowner is entitled to defend his land from approaching waters, but not to discharge onto his neighbour's land floodwater which has already come onto his land: *Hurdman v North Eastern Railway* (1878) 3 CPD 168. As Laws LJ observed at [39], [40], and [46], these distinctions might seem 'fragile', but they represent a 'pragmatic drawing of the line' to achieve the balance required both by the tort of nuisance, and now by the Human Rights Act.

7.   For further Human Rights Act challenges, see *Dobson v Thames Water Utilities*, noted p. 798, ante and *McKenna v British Aluminium Ltd* [2002] Env LR 30, noted p. 853, post.

3 ESCAPE OF DANGEROUS THINGS FROM LAND

■ Rylands v Fletcher

Court of Exchequer Chamber and House of Lords [1861–73] All ER Rep 1

Appeal from a decision of the Court of Exchequer ... by the defendants in an action brought against them by the plaintiff for damage done to his mines through the escape of water from a reservoir on the defendants' land.

The plaintiff was a tenant of Lord Wilton. The defendants, who were proprietors of a mill, made upon land of Lord Wilton's, in pursuance of an arrangement made with him for that purpose, a reservoir, employing competent persons to construct the same. It turned out that beneath the site of the reservoir were old shafts running down into coal workings long disused which communicated with other old workings situate under the land of one Whitehead. The plaintiff's colliery, called the Red House Colliery, adjoined Whitehead's land, and the plaintiff, soon after he had commenced working the Red House Colliery, made arrangements with Whitehead to get, by means of the Red House pit, the coal lying under Whitehead's land. In pursuance of those arrangements the plaintiff had worked through from the Red House Colliery into the coal lying under Whitehead's land, and so into the old workings situated under Whitehead's land. As a result the workings of the plaintiff's colliery were made to communicate with the old workings under the reservoir. These underground works were effected several years before the defendants commenced making their reservoir, but the fact of their existence was not known to the defendants or any agent of theirs, or any person employed by them, until the reservoir burst, as is hereinafter mentioned. In the course of constructing the reservoir the shafts were perceived, but it was not known or suspected that they had been made for the purpose of getting coal beneath the site of the reservoir. The Special Case stated in the action contained a finding that there was no personal negligence or default on the part of the defendants themselves in relation to the selection of the site or the construction of the reservoir, but reasonable and proper care was not used by the persons employed with reference to the shafts so met with to provide for the sufficiency of the reservoir to bear the pressure which, when filled, it would have to bear. The reservoir in consequence burst downwards into the shafts, and the water found its way into the plaintiff's mine. The majority of the Court of Exchequer held that the non-exercise of sufficient care upon the part of the persons employed to construct the reservoir did not, in the absence of any notice to the defendants of the underground communication, affect the defendants with any liability, there being in the absence of such notice no duty cast upon the defendants to use any particular amount of care in the construction of a reservoir upon their own land. Bramwell B was of opinion that the question of knowledge was immaterial, and that the defendants were, therefore, liable. The plaintiff appealed to the Court of Exchequer Chamber.

BLACKBURN J (reading the judgment of the Court): . . .

The plaintiff, though free from all blame on his part, must bear the loss, unless he can establish that it was the consequence of some default for which the defendants are responsible.

The question of law, therefore, arises: What is the liability which the law casts upon a person who, like the defendants, lawfully brings on his land something which, though harmless while it remains there, will naturally do mischief if it escape out of his land? It is agreed on all hands that he must take care to keep in that which he has brought on the land, and keep it there in order that it may not escape and damage his neighbour, but the question arises whether the duty which the law casts upon him under such circumstances is an absolute duty to keep it in at his peril, or is, as the majority of the Court of Exchequer have thought, merely a duty to take all reasonable and prudent precautions in order to keep it in, but no more. If the first be the law, the person who has brought on his land and kept there something dangerous, and failed to keep it in, is responsible for all the natural consequences of its escape. If the second be the limit of his duty, he would not be answerable except on proof of negligence, and consequently would not be answerable for escape arising from any latent defect which ordinary prudence and skill could not detect. Supposing the second to be the correct view of the law, a further question arises subsidiary to the first, namely, whether the defendants are not so far identified with the contractors whom they employed as to be responsible for the consequences of their want of skill in making the reservoir in fact insufficient with reference to the old shafts, of the existence of which they were aware, though they had not ascertained where the shafts went to.

We think that the true rule of law is that the person who, for his own purposes, brings on his land, and collects and keeps there anything likely to do mischief if it escapes, must keep it in at his peril, and, if he does not do so, he is prima facie answerable for all the damage which is the natural consequence of its escape. He can excuse himself by showing that the escape was owing to the plaintiff's default, or, perhaps, that the escape was the consequence of *vis major*, or the act of God; but, as nothing of this sort exists here, it is unnecessary to inquire what excuse would be sufficient. The general rule, as above stated, seems on principle just. The person whose grass or corn is eaten down by the escaped cattle of his neighbour, or whose mine is flooded by the water from his neighbour's reservoir, or whose cellar is invaded by the filth of his neighbour's privy, or whose habitation is made unhealthy by the fumes and noisome vapours of his neighbour's alkali works, is damnified without any fault of his own; and it seems but reasonable and just that the neighbour who has brought something on his own property which was not naturally there, harmless to others so long as it is confined to his own property, but which he knows will be mischievous if it gets on his neighbour's, should be obliged to make good the damage which ensues if he does not succeed in confining it to his own property. But for his act in bringing it there no mischief could have accrued, and it seems but just that he should at his peril keep it there, so that no mischief may accrue, or answer for the natural and anticipated consequences. On authority this, we think, is established to be the law, whether the thing so brought be beasts or water, or filth or stenches. . . .

The view which we take of the first point renders it unnecessary to consider whether the defendants would or would not be responsible for the want of care and skill in the persons employed by them. We are of opinion that the plaintiff is entitled to recover....

[On appeal by the defendants to the House of Lords:]

LORD CAIRNS LC: ...

The principles on which this case must be determined appear to me to be extremely simple. The defendants, treating them as the owners or occupiers of the close on which the reservoir was constructed, might lawfully have used that close for any purpose for which it might, in the ordinary course of the enjoyment of land, be used, and if, in what I may term the natural user of that land, there had been any accumulation of water, either on the surface or underground, and if by the operation of the laws of nature that accumulation of water had passed off into the close occupied by the plaintiff, the plaintiff could not have complained that that result had taken place. If he had desired to guard himself against it, it would have lain on him to have done so by leaving or by interposing some barrier between his close and the close of the defendants in order to have prevented that operation of the laws of nature.

As an illustration of that principle, I may refer to a case which was cited in the argument before your Lordships, *Smith v Kendrick*[6] in the Court of Common Pleas. On the other hand, if the defendants, not stopping at the natural use of their close, had desired to use it for any purpose which I may term a non-natural use, for the purpose of introducing into the close that which, in its natural condition, was not in or upon it—for the purpose of introducing water, either above or below ground, in quantities and in a manner not the result of any work or operation on or under the land, and if in consequence of their doing so, or in consequence of any imperfection in the mode of their doing so, the water came to escape and to pass off into the close of the plaintiff, then it appears to me that that which the defendants were doing they were doing at their own peril; and if in the course of their doing it the evil arose to which I have referred—the evil, namely, of the escape of the water, and its passing away to the close of the plaintiff and injuring the plaintiff—then for the consequence of that, in my opinion, the defendants would be liable....

These simple principles, if they are well founded, as it appears to me they are, really dispose of this case. The same result is arrived at on the principles referred to by Blackburn J in his judgment in the Court of Exchequer Chamber....

In that opinion, I must say, I entirely concur. Therefore, I have to move your Lordships that the judgment of the Court of Exchequer Chamber be affirmed, and that the present appeal be dismissed with costs.

LORD CRANWORTH:

I concur with my noble and learned friend in thinking that the rule of law was correctly stated by Blackburn J in delivering the opinion of the Exchequer chamber....

Appeal dismissed.

NOTES

1   For an account of the background to this decision concerning the problem of legal liability for damage caused by burst reservoirs and argument as to the influence of such an historical context, see A.W.B. Simpson *Leading Cases in the Common Law* (Oxford, 1995), chap. 8. See also G. T. S. Schwartz in *The Law of Obligations*, P. Cane and J. Stapleton (eds.) (Oxford, 1998); K.S. Abraham in *Torts Stories*, R. Rabin and S. Sugarman (eds.) (West Law School, 2003).

2.   One particular mystery which surrounds this decision is neatly stated in the title of a note by R. F. V. Heuston—'Who was the Third Lord in *Rylands v Fletcher*?' (1970) 86 LQR 160. See D. E. C. Yale (1970) 86 LQR 311 for a further contribution on this question.

[6] (1849) 7 CB 515.

3.   The decision in *Rylands v Fletcher* has 'no place in Scots law': *R H M Bakeries (Scotland) Ltd v Strathclyde Regional Council* 1985 SLT 214, noted by K. Miller (1985) 101 LQR 472, and the High Court of Australia has decided that in that country the rule in *Rylands v Fletcher* should, with one qualification in relation to the law of nuisance or trespass, be seen as absorbed by the tort of negligence, albeit cases within the rule would involve a non-delegable duty thereby involving liability for independent contractors (*Burnie Port Authority v General Jones Pty Ltd* (1994) 120 ALR 42, discussed by the House of Lords in the *Transco* case, p. 893, post).

■ Read v J Lyons & Co Ltd
House of Lords [1946] 2 All ER 471

VISCOUNT SIMON LC: My Lords, in fulfilment of an agreement dated 26 January 1942, and made between the Ministry of Supply and the respondents, the latter undertook the operation, management and control of the Elstow Ordnance Factory as agents for the Ministry. The respondents carried on in the factory the business of filling shell cases with high explosives. The appellant was an employee of the Ministry, with the duty of inspecting this filling of shell cases, and her work required her (although she would have preferred and had applied for other employment) to be present in the shell filling shop. On 31 August 1942, while the appellant was lawfully in the shell filling shop in discharge of her duty, an explosion occurred which killed a man and injured the appellant and others. No negligence was averred or proved against the respondents. The plea of volenti non fit injuria, for whatever it might be worth, has been expressly withdrawn before this House by the Attorney-General on behalf of the respondents, and thus the simple question for decision is whether in these circumstances the respondents are liable, without any proof or inference that they were negligent, to the appellant in damages, which have been assessed at £575 2s 8d, for her injuries.

Cassels J, who tried the case, considered that it was governed by *Rylands v Fletcher*,[7] and held that the respondents were liable, on the ground that they were carrying on an ultra-hazardous activity and so were under what is called a 'strict liability' to take successful care to avoid causing harm to persons whether on or off the premises. The Court of Appeal (Scott, MacKinnon and du Parcq LJJ) reversed this decision, Scot LJ, in an elaborately reasoned judgment, holding that a person on the premises had, in the absence of any proof of negligence, no cause of action, and that there must be an escape of the damage-causing thing from the premises and damage caused outside before the doctrine customarily associated with the case of *Rylands v Fletcher*[7] can apply.

I agree that the action fails. . . .

Blackburn J, in delivering the judgment of the Court of Exchequer Chamber in *Fletcher v Rylands*[8] (LR 1 Exch 265 at 279), laid down the proposition that:

> '. . . the person who, for his own purposes brings on his lands and collects and keeps there, anything likely to do mischief if it escapes, must keep it in at his peril, and, if he does not do so, is prima facie answerable for all the damage which is the natural consequence of its escape.'

It has not always been sufficiently observed that in the House of Lords, when the appeal from *Fletcher v Rylands*[8] was dismissed and Blackburn J's pronouncement was expressly approved, Lord Cairns LC emphasized another condition which must be satisfied before liability attaches without proof of negligence. This is that the use to which the defendant is putting his land is a 'non-natural' use (LR 3 HL 330 at 338–339). Blackburn J had made a parenthetic reference to this sort of test when he said (LR 1 Exch 265 at 280):

> '. . . it seems but reasonable and just that the neighbour, who has brought something on his own property, *which was not naturally there*, harmless to others so long as it is confined to his own

---

[7] (1868) LR 3 HL 330.   [8] (1866) LR 1 Exch 265.

property, but which he knows to be mischievous if it gets on his neighbour's, should be obliged to make good the damage which ensues if he does not succeed in confining it to his own property.'

I confess to finding this test of 'non-natural' user (or of bringing on the land what was not 'naturally there,' which is not the same test) difficult to apply. . . .

The classic judgment of Blackburn J besides deciding the issue before the court and laying down the principle of duty between neighbouring occupiers of land on which the decision was based, sought to group under a single and wider proposition other instances in which liability is independent of negligence. . . . There are instances, no doubt, in our law in which liability for damage may be established apart from proof of negligence, but it appears to me logically unnecessary and historically incorrect to refer to all these instances as deduced from one common principle. The conditions under which such a liability arises are not necessarily the same in each class of case. Lindley LJ issued a valuable warning in *Green v Chelsea Waterworks Co*[9] (70 LT 547 at 549), when he said of *Rylands v Fletcher*[10] that that decision:

'. . . is not to be extended beyond the legitimate principle on which the House of Lords decided it. If it were extended as far as strict logic might require, it would be a very oppressive decision.'

It seems better, therefore, when a plaintiff relies on *Rylands v Fletcher*[10] to take the conditions declared by this House to be essential for liability in that case and to ascertain whether these conditions exist in the actual case.

Now, the strict liability recognised by this House to exist in *Rylands v Fletcher*[10] is conditioned by two elements which I may call the condition of 'escape' from the land of something likely to do mischief if it escapes, and the condition of 'non-natural use' of the land. This second condition has in some later cases, which did not reach this House, been otherwise expressed, e.g. as 'exceptional' user, when such user is not regarded as 'natural' and at the same time is likely to produce mischief if there is an 'escape'. . . . It is not necessary to analyse this second condition on the present occasion, for in the case now before us the first essential condition of 'escape' does not seem to me to be present at all. 'Escape', for the purpose of applying the proposition in *Rylands v Fletcher*[10] means escape from a place which the defendant has occupation of, or control over, to a place which is outside his occupation or control. Blackburn J several times refers to the defendant's duty as being the duty of 'keeping a thing in' at the defendant's peril and by 'keeping in' he means, not preventing an explosive substance from exploding, but preventing a thing which may inflict mischief from escaping from the area which the defendant occupies or controls. . . .

In these circumstances it becomes unnecessary to consider other objections that have been raised, such as the question whether the doctrine of *Rylands v Fletcher*[11] applies where the claim is for damages for personal injury as distinguished from damages to property. It may be noted, in passing, that Blackburn J himself when referring to the doctrine of *Rylands v Fletcher*[11] in the later case of *Cattle v Stockton Waterworks*[12] leaves this undealt with. He treats damages under the *Rylands v Fletcher*[11] principle as covering damages to property, such as workmen's clothes or tools, but says nothing about liability for personal injuries.

[His Lordship then left open the question whether there would have been a non-natural user of land in this case, and continued:]

In this appeal the question is immaterial, as I hold that the appellant fails for the reason that there was no 'escape' from the respondents' factory. I move that the appeal be dismissed with costs.

LORD MACMILLAN: . . .

The action is one of damages for personal injuries. Whatever may have been the law of England in early times I am of opinion that, as the law now stands an allegation of negligence is in general essential

---

[9] (1894) 70 LT 547.   [10] (1868) LR 3 HL 330.   [11] (1868) LR 3 HL 330.
[12] (1875) LR 10 QB 453.

to the relevancy of an action of reparation for personal injuries. The gradual development of the law in the matter of civil liability is discussed and traced with ample learning and lucidity in Holdsworth's *History of English Law*, Vol. 8, pp. 446 et seq., and need not here be rehearsed. Suffice it to say that the process of evolution has been from the principle that every man acts at his peril and is liable for all the consequences of his acts to the principle that a man's freedom of action is subject only to the obligation not to infringe any duty of care which he owes to others. The emphasis formerly was on the injury sustained and the question was whether the case fell within one of the accepted classes of common law actions; the emphasis now is on the conduct of the person whose act has occasioned the injury and the question is whether it can be characterised as negligent. I do not overlook the fact that there is at least one instance in the present law in which the primitive rule survives, namely, in the case of animals *ferae naturae* or animals *mansuetae naturae* which have shown dangerous proclivities.[13] . . . But such an exceptional case as this affords no justification for its extension by anology.

The appellant in her printed case in this House thus poses the question to be determined:

> 'Whether the manufacturer of high explosive shells is under strict liability to prevent such shells from exploding and causing harm to persons on the premises where such manufacture is carried on as well as to persons outside such premises.'

Two points arise on this statement of the question. In the first place, the expression 'strict liability', though borrowed from authority, is ambiguous. If it means the absolute liability of an insurer irrespective of negligence, then the answer, in my opinion, must be in the negative. If it means that an exacting standard of care is incumbent on manufacturers of explosive shells to prevent the occurrence of accidents causing personal injuries I should answer the question in the affirmative, but this will not avail the plaintiff. In the next place, the question as stated would seem to assume that liability would exist in the present case to persons injured outside the defendants' premises without any proof of negligence on the part of the defendants. Indeed, Cassels J in his judgment ([1944] 2 All ER 98 at 101) records that:

> 'It was not denied that if a person outside the premises had been injured in the explosion the defendants would have been liable without proof of negligence.'

I do not agree with this view. In my opinion, persons injured by the explosion inside or outside the defendant'' premises would alike require to aver and prove negligence to render the defendants liable. . . . The doctrine of *Rylands v Fletcher*,[14] as I understand it, derives from a conception of the mutual duties of adjoining or neighbouring landowners and its congeners are trespass and nuisance. If its foundation is to be found in the injunction *sic utere tuo ut alienum non laedas*, then it is manifest that it has nothing to do with personal injuries. The duty is to refrain from injuring not *alium* but *alienum*. The two prerequisites of the doctrine are that there must be the escape of something from one man's close to another man's close and that that which escapes must have been brought on the land from which it escapes in consequences of some non-natural use of that land whatever precisely that may mean. Neither of these features exists in the present case . . . [N]othing escaped from the defendants' premises, and, were it necessary to decide the point, I should hesitate to hold that in these days and in an industrial community it was a non-natural use of land to build a factory on it and conduct there the manufacture of explosives. I could conceive it being said that to carry on the manufacture of explosives in a crowded urban area was evidence of negligence, but there is no such case here and I offer no opinion on the point. . . .

It is noteworthy in *Rylands v Fletcher*[14] that all the counts in the declaration alleged negligence and that on the same page of the report on which his famous dictum is recorded (LR 1 Exch 265 at 279), Blackburn J states that:

> 'the plaintiff . . . must bear the loss, unless he can establish that it was the consequence of some default for which the defendants are responsible.'

---

[13] [See now the Animals Act 1971, p. 652, ante.]   [14] (1868) LR 3 HL 330.

His decision for the plaintiff would thus logically seem to imply that he found some default on the part of the defendants in bringing on their land and failing to confine there an exceptional quantity of water. Notwithstanding the width of some of the pronouncements...I think that the doctrine of *Rylands v Fletcher*,[14] when studied in its setting, is truly a case on the mutual obligations of the owners or occupiers of neighbouring closes and is entirely inapplicable to the present case, which is quite outside its ambit....

LORD PORTER:...

Normally at the present time in an action of tort for personal injuries if there is no negligence there is no liability. To this rule, however, the appellant contends that there are certain exceptions, one of the best known of which is to be found under the principle laid down in *Rylands v Fletcher*.[15] The appellant's counsel relied on that case and naturally put it in the forefront of his argument. To make the rules applicable, it is at least necessary for the person whom it is sought to hold liable to have brought on to his premises, or, at any rate, to some place over which he has a measure of control, something which is dangerous in the sense that, if it escapes, it will do damage. Possibly a further requisite is that to bring the thing to the position in which it is found is to make a non-natural use of that place. Such, at any rate, appears to have been the opinion of Lord Cairns, and this limitation has more than once been repeated and approved: see *Rickards v Lothian* ([1913] AC 263 at 280, per Lord Moulton). Manifestly, these requirements must give rise to difficulty in applying the rule in individual cases and necessitate at least a decision as to what can be dangerous and what is a non-natural use. Indeed, there is a considerable body of case law dealing with these questions and a series of findings or assumptions as to what is sufficient to establish their existence. Among dangerous objects have been held to be included gas, explosive substances, electricity, oil, fumes, rusty wire, poisonous vegetation, vibrations, a flag-pole, and even dwellers in caravans....

I do not, however, think that it is necessary for Your Lordships to decide these matters now, inasmuch as the defence admits that high explosive shells are dangerous things, and, whatever view may be formed whether the filling of them is or is not a non-natural use of land, the present case can, in my opinion, be determined upon a narrower ground. In all cases which have been decided, it has been held necessary, to establish liability, that there should have been some form of escape from the place in which the dangerous object has been retained by the defendant to some other place not subject to his control....

It was urged on Your Lordships that it would be a strange result to hold the respondents liable if the injured person was just outside their premises but not liable if she was just within them. There is force in the objection, but the liability is itself an extension of the general rule, and, in my view, it is undesirable to extend it further....

[LORD UTHWATT and LORD SIMONDS delivered speeches in favour of dismissing the appeal.]

Appeal dismissed.

■ Cambridge Water Co Ltd v Eastern Counties Leather plc

House of Lords [1994] 1 All ER 53

LORD GOFF OF CHIEVELEY....

My Lords, this appeal is concerned with the question whether the appellant company, Eastern Counties Leather plc (ECL), is liable to the respondent company, Cambridge Water Co (CWC), in damages in respect of damage suffered by reason of the contamination of water available for abstraction at CWC's borehole at Sawston Mill near Cambridge. The contamination was caused by a solvent known as perchloroethene (PCE), used by ECL in the process of degreasing pelts at its tanning works in Sawston, about 1.3 miles away from CWC's borehole, the PCE having seeped into the ground beneath ECL's works and thence having been conveyed in percolating water in the direction of the

---

[15] (1868) LR 3 HL 330.

borehole. CWC's claim against ECL was based on three alternative grounds, viz negligence, nuisance and the rule in *Rylands v Fletcher* (see *Rylands v Fletcher* (1868) LR 3 HL 330, [1861–73] All ER Rep 1; *affd Fletcher v Rylands* (1866) LR 1 Ex 265). The judge, Ian Kennedy J, dismissed CWC's claim on all three grounds—on the first two grounds, because . . . he held that ECL could not reasonably have foreseen that such damage would occur, and on the third ground because he held that the use of a solvent such as PCE in ECL's tanning business constituted, in the circumstances, a natural use of ECL's land. The Court of Appeal, however, allowed CWC's appeal from the decision of the judge, on the ground that ECL was strictly liable for the contamination of the water percolating under CWC's land, on the authority of *Ballard v Tomlinson* (1885) 29 Ch D 115, and awarded damages against ECL in the sum assessed by the judge, viz £1,064,886 together with interest totalling £642,885, and costs. It is against that decision that ECL now appeals to your Lordships' House, with leave of this House.

. . . [T]he following relevant facts may be selected as being of particular relevance.

(1) The spillage of PCE, and its seepage into the ground beneath the floor of the tannery at ECL's works, occurred during the period which ended in 1976, as a result of regular spillages of small quantities of PCE onto the floor of ECL's tannery.

(2) The escape of dissolved phase PCE[16] from the pools of neat PCE which collected at or towards the base of the chalk aquifers beneath ECL's works, into the chalk aquifers under the adjoining land and thence in the direction of Sawston Mill, must have begun at some unspecified date well before 1976 and be still continuing to the present day.

(3) As held by the judge, the seepage of the PCE beneath the floor of ECL's works down into the chalk aquifers below was not foreseeable by a reasonable supervisor employed by ECL, nor was if foreseeable by him that detectable quantities of PCE would be found down-catchment, so that he could not have foreseen, in or before 1976, that the repeated spillages would lead to any environmental hazard or damage. The only foreseeable damage from a spillage of PCE was that somebody might be overcome by fumes from a substantial spillage of PCE on the surface of the ground.

(4) The water so contaminated at Sawston Mill has never been held to be dangerous to health. But under criteria laid down in the UK Regulations, issued in response to the EEC Directive,[17] the water so contaminated was not 'wholesome' and, since 1985, could not lawfully be supplied in this country as drinking water.

Nuisance and the rule in Rylands v Fletcher

. . . [T]here was no appeal by CWC to the Court of Appeal against the judge's conclusion in nuisance. The question of ECL's liability in nuisance has really only arisen again because the Court of Appeal allowed CWC's appeal on the ground that ECL was liable on the basis of strict liability in nuisance on the principle laid down, as they saw it, in *Ballard v Tomlinson*. Since, for the reasons I have given[18], that case does not give rise to any principle of law independent of the ordinary law of nuisance or the rule in *Rylands v Fletcher*, the strict position now is that CWC, having abandoned its claim in nuisance, can only uphold the decision of the Court of Appeal on the basis of the rule in *Rylands v Fletcher*. However, one important submission advanced by ECL before the Appellate Committee was that strict liability for an escape only arises under that rule where the defendant knows or reasonably ought to have foreseen, when collecting the relevant things on his land, that those things might, if they escaped, cause damage of the relevant kind. Since there is a close relationship between nuisance and the rule in *Rylands v Fletcher*, I myself find it very difficult to form an opinion as to the validity of that submission without first considering whether foreseeability of such damage is an essential element in the law of nuisance. For that reason, therefore, I do not feel able altogether to ignore the latter question simply because it was no longer pursued by CWC before the Court of Appeal.

---

[16] I.e. the PCE dissolved in ground water in the aquifers.

[17] The EEC Directive relating to the Quality of Water intended for Human Consumption (80/778 (EEC)).

[18] This part of Lord Goff's speech has been omitted.

In order to consider the question in the present case in its proper legal context, it is desirable to look at the nature of liability in a case such as the present in relation both to the law of nuisance and the rule in *Rylands v Fletcher*, and for that purpose to consider the relationship between the two heads of liability.

I begin with the law of nuisance. Our modern understanding of the nature and scope of the law of nuisance was much enhanced by Professor Newark's seminal article 'The boundaries of nuisance' (1949) 65 LQR 480. The article is avowedly a historical analysis, in that it traces the nature of the tort of nuisance to its origins, and demonstrates how the original view of nuisance as a tort to land (or more accurately, to accommodate interference with servitudes, a tort directed against the plaintiff's enjoyment of rights over land) became distorted as the tort was extended to embrace claims for personal injuries, even where the plaintiff's injury did not occur while using land in his occupation. In Professor Newark's opinion (at p. 487), this development produced adverse effects, viz. that liability which should have arisen only under the law of negligence was allowed under the law of nuisance which historically was a tort of strict liability; and that there was a tendency for 'cross-infection to take place, and notions of negligence began to make an appearance in the realm of nuisance proper'. But in addition, Professor Newark considered (at pp. 487–488), it contributed to a misappreciation of the decision in *Rylands v Fletcher*:

> 'This case is generally regarded as an important landmark, indeed a turning point—in the law of tort; but an examination of the judgments shows that those who decided it were quite unconscious of any revolutionary or reactionary principles in the decision. They thought of it as calling for no more than a restatement of settled principles, and Lord Cairns went so far as to describe those principles as "extremely simple". And in fact the main principle involved was extremely simple, being no more than the principle that negligence is not an element in the tort of nuisance. It is true that Blackburn J in his great judgment in the Exchequer Chamber never once used the word "nuisance", but three times he cited the case of fumes escaping from an alkali works—a clear case of nuisance—as an instance of liability, under the rule which he was laying down. Equally it is true that in 1866 there were a number of cases in the reports suggesting that persons who controlled dangerous things were under a strict duty to take care, but as none of these cases had anything to do with nuisance Blackburn J. did not refer to them. But the profession as a whole, whose conceptions of the boundaries of nuisance were now becoming fogged, failed to see in *Rylands v Fletcher* a simple case of nuisance. They regarded it as an exceptional case—and the rule in *Rylands v Fletcher* as a generalisation of exceptional cases, where liability was to be strict on account of 'the magnitude of danger, coupled with the difficulty of proving negligence' [*Pollock on Torts* (14th edn, 1939) p. 386] rather than on account of the nature of the plaintiff's interest which was invaded. They therefore jumped rashly to two conclusions: firstly, that the rule in *Rylands v Fletcher* could be extended beyond the case of neighbouring occupiers; and secondly, that the rule could be used to afford a remedy in cases of personal injury. Both these conclusions were stoutly denied by Lord Macmillan in *Read v J. Lyons & Co Ltd* ([1946] 2 All ER 471, [1947] AC 156), but it remains to be seen whether the House of Lords will support his opinion when the precise point comes up for decision.'

We are not concerned in the present case with the problem of personal injuries, but we are concerned with the scope of liability in nuisance and in *Rylands v Fletcher*. In my opinion it is right to take as our starting point the fact that, as Professor Newark considered, *Rylands v Fletcher* was indeed not regarded by Blackburn J as a revolutionary decision: see e.g. his observations in *Ross v Fedden* (1872) 26 LT 966 at 968. He believed himself not to be creating new law, but to be stating existing law, on the basis of existing authority; and, as is apparent from his judgment, he was concerned in particular with the situation where the defendant collects things upon his land which are likely to do mischief if they escape, in which event the defendant will be strictly liable for damage resulting from any such escape. It follows that the essential basis of liability was the collection by the defendant of such things upon his land; and the consequence was a strict liability in the event of damage caused by their escape, even if the escape was an isolated event. Seen in its context, there is no reason to suppose that Blackburn J intended to create a liability any more strict than that created by the law of nuisance; but even so he must have intended that, in the circumstances specified by him, there should be liability for damage resulting from an isolated escape.

Of course, although liability for nuisance has generally been regarded as strict, at least in the case of a defendant who has been responsible for the creation of a nuisance, even so that liability has been kept under control by the principle of reasonable user—the principle of give and take as between neighbouring occupiers of land, under which 'those acts necessary for the common and ordinary use and occupation of land and houses may be done, if conveniently done, without subjecting those who do them to an action': see *Bamford v Turnley* (1862) 3 B & S 62 at 83, [1861–73] All ER Rep 706 at 712 per Bramwell B. The effect is that, if the user is reasonable, the defendant will not be liable for consequent harm to his neighbour's enjoyment of his land; but if the user is not reasonable, the defendant will be liable, even though he may have exercised reasonable care and skill to avoid it. Strikingly, a comparable principle has developed which limits liability under the rule in *Rylands v Fletcher*. This is the principle of natural use of the land. I shall have to consider the principle at a later stage in this judgment. The most authoritative statement of the principle is now to be found in the advice of the Privy Council delivered by Lord Moulton in *Rickards v Lothian* [1913] AC 263 at 280, [1911–13] All ER Rep 71 at 80 when he said of the rule in *Rylands v Fletcher*:

> 'It is not every use to which land is put that brings into play that principle. It must be some special use bringing with it increased danger to others, and must not merely be the ordinary use of the land or such a use as is proper for the general benefit of the community.'

It is not necessary for me to identify precise differences which may be drawn between this principle, and the principle of reasonable user as applied in the law of nuisance. It is enough for present purposes that I should draw attention to a similarity of function. The effect of this principle is that, where it applies, there will be no liability under the rule in *Rylands v Fletcher*; but that where it does not apply, i.e. where there is a non-natural use, the defendant will be liable for harm caused to the plaintiff by the escape, notwithstanding that he has exercised all reasonable care and skill to prevent the escape from occurring.

Foreseeability of damage in nuisance

It is against this background that it is necessary to consider the question whether foreseeability of harm of the relevant type is an essential element of liability either in nuisance or under the rule in *Rylands v Fletcher*. I shall take first the case of nuisance. In the present case, as I have said, this is not strictly speaking a live issue. Even so, I propose briefly to address it, as part of the analysis of the background to the present case.

It is, of course, axiomatic that in this field we must be on our guard, when considering liability for damages in nuisance, not to draw inapposite conclusions from cases concerned only with a claim for an injunction. This is because, where an injunction is claimed, its purpose is to restrain further action by the defendant which may interfere with the plaintiff's enjoyment of his land, and ex hypothesi the defendant must be aware, if and when an injunction is granted, that such interference may be caused by the act which he is restrained from committing. It follows that these cases provide no guidance on the question whether foreseeability of harm of the relevant type is a prerequisite of the recovery of damages for causing such harm to the plaintiff. In the present case, we are not concerned with liability in damages in respect of a nuisance which has arisen through natural causes, or by the act of a person for whose actions the defendant is not responsible, in which cases the applicable principles in nuisance have become closely associated with those applicable in negligence: see *Sedleigh-Denfield v O'Callaghan* [1940] 3 All ER 349, [1940] AC 880 and *Goldman v Hargrave* [1966] 2 All ER 989, [1967] 1 AC 645. We are concerned with the liability of a person where a nuisance has been created by one for whose actions he is responsible. Here, as I have said, it is still the law that the fact that the defendant has taken all reasonable care will not of itself exonerate him from liability, the relevant control mechanism being found within the principle of reasonable user. But it by no means follows that the defendant should be held liable for damage of a type which he could not reasonably foresee; and the development of the law of negligence in the past sixty years points strongly towards a requirement that such foreseeability should be a prerequisite of liability in damages for nuisance, as it is of liability in negligence. For if a plaintiff is in ordinary circumstances only able to claim damages in respect of personal injuries where he can prove such foreseeability on the part of the defendant, it is difficult to see why, in common justice, he should be in a stronger position to claim damages for interference with the enjoyment of his land where the defendant was unable to foresee such damage. Moreover, this appears to have been the conclusion of the Privy Council in *The Wagon Mound (No 2), Overseas Tankship (UK) Ltd v Miller Steamship Co Pty Ltd* [1966] 2 All ER 709, [1967] 1 AC 617.

[Having quoted the passage from *The Wagon Mound (No 2)* which appears as the last paragraph in the extract from that case, p. 805, ante, LORD GOFF continued:]

It is widely accepted that this conclusion, although not essential to the decision of the particular case, has nevertheless settled the law to the effect that foreseeability of harm is indeed a prerequisite of the recovery of damages in private nuisance, as in the case of public nuisance. I refer in particular to the opinion expressed by Professor Fleming in his book on *Torts* (8th edn, 1992) pp. 443–444. It is unnecessary in the present case to consider the precise nature of this principle; but it appears from Lord Reid's statement of the law that he regarded it essentially as one relating to remoteness of damage.

Foreseeability of damage under the rule in Rylands v Fletcher
It is against this background that I turn to the submission advanced by ECL before your Lordships that there is a similar prerequisite of recovery of damages under the rule in *Rylands v Fletcher* (1866) LR 1 Exch 265.

I start with the judgment of Blackburn J in *Fletcher v Rylands* itself.…

[LORD GOFF quoted a passage from that case which is set out p. 829, ante, and continued:]

…Blackburn J spoke of 'anything *likely* to do mischief if it escapes'; and later he spoke of something 'which he *knows* to be mischievous if it gets on to his neighbour's [property]', and the liability to 'answer for the natural *and anticipated* consequences'. Furthermore, time and again he spoke of the strict liability imposed upon the defendant as being that he must keep the thing in at his peril; and, when referring to liability in actions for damage occasioned by animals, he referred (at 282) to the established principle 'that it is quite immaterial whether the escape is by negligence or not'. The general tenor of his statement of principle is therefore that knowledge, or at least foreseeability of the risk, is a prerequisite of the recovery of damages under the principle; but that the principle is one of strict liability in the sense that the defendant may be held liable notwithstanding that he had exercised all due care to prevent the escape from occurring.

…In my opinion, the matter is open for consideration by your Lordships in the present case, and, despite recent dicta to the contrary (see e.g. *Leakey v National Trust for Places of Historic Interest or Natural Beauty* [1980] 1 All ER 17 at 30, [1980] QB 485 at 519 per Megaw LJ), should be considered as a matter of principle.…

The point is one on which academic opinion appears to be divided: cf *Salmond and Heuston on Torts* (20th edn, 1992) pp. 324–325, which favours the prerequisite of foreseeability, and *Clerk and Lindsell on Torts* (16th edn, 1989) para 25.09, which takes a different view. However, quite apart from the indications to be derived from the judgment of Blackburn J in *Fletcher v Rylands* LR 1 Exch 265 itself, to which I have already referred, the historical connection with the law of nuisance must now be regarded as pointing towards the conclusion that foreseeability of damage is a prerequisite of the recovery of damages under the rule. I have already referred to the fact that Blackburn J himself did not regard his statement of principle as having broken new ground; furthermore, Professor Newark has convincingly shown that the rule in *Rylands v Fletcher* was essentially concerned with an extension of the law of nuisance to cases of isolated escape. Accordingly since, following the observations of Lord Reid when delivering the advice of the Privy Council in *The Wagon Mound (No 2)* [1966] 2 All ER 709 at 717, [1967] 1 AC 617 at 640, the recovery of damages in private nuisance depends on foreseeability by the defendant of the relevant type of damage, it would appear logical to extend the same requirement to liability under the rule in *Rylands v Fletcher*.

Even so, the question cannot be considered solely as a matter of history. It can be argued that the rule in *Rylands v Fletcher* should not be regarded simply as an extension of the law of nuisance, but should rather be treated as a developing principle of strict liability from which can be derived a general rule of strict liability for damage caused by ultra-hazardous operations, on the basis of which persons conducting such operations may properly be held strictly liable for the extraordinary risk to others involved in such operations. As is pointed out in *Fleming on Torts* (8th edn, 1992) pp. 327–328, this would lead to the practical result that the cost of damage resulting from such operations would have to be absorbed as part of the overheads of the relevant business rather than be borne (where there is no negligence) by the injured person or his insurers, or even by the community at large. Such a development appears to have been taking place in the United States, as can be seen from § 519 of the *Restatement of Torts* (2d) vol 3 (1977). The extent to which it has done so is not altogether clear; and I infer from para 519, and the comment on that paragraph, that the abnormally dangerous activities there referred to are such that their ability to cause harm would be obvious to any reasonable person who carried them on.

I have to say, however, that there are serious obstacles in the way of the development of the rule in *Rylands v Fletcher* in this way. First of all, if it was so to develop, it should logically apply to liability to all persons suffering injury by reason of the ultra-hazardous operations; but the decision of this House in *Read v J Lyons & Co Ltd* [1946] 2 All ER 471, [1947] AC 156, which establishes that there can be no liability under the rule except in circumstances where the injury has been caused by an escape from land under the control of the defendant, has effectively precluded any such development. Professor Fleming has observed that 'the most damaging effect of the decision in *Read v Lyons* is that it prematurely stunted the development of a general theory of strict liability for ultra-hazardous activities; (see *Fleming on Torts* (8th edn, 1992) p. 341). Even so, there is much to be said for the view that the courts should not be proceeding down the path of developing such a general theory. In this connection, I refer in particular to the Report of the Law Commission on *Civil Liability for Dangerous Things and Activities* (Law Com no 32) 1970. In paras 14–16 of the report the Law Commission expressed serious misgivings about the adoption of any test for the application of strict liability involving a general concept of 'especially dangerous' or 'ultra-hazardous' activity, having regard to the uncertainties and practical difficulties of its application. If the Law Commission is unwilling to consider statutory reform on this basis, it must follow that judges should if anything be even more reluctant to proceed down that path.

Like the judge in the present case, I incline to the opinion that, as a general rule, it is more appropriate for strict liability in respect of operations of high risk to be imposed by Parliament, than by the courts. If such liability is imposed by statute, the relevant activities can be identified, and those concerned can know where they stand. Furthermore, statute can where appropriate lay down precise criteria establishing the incidence and scope of such liability.

It is of particular relevance that the present case is concerned with environmental pollution. The protection and preservation of the environment is now perceived as being of crucial importance to the future of mankind; and public bodies, both national and international, are taking significant steps towards the establishment of legislation which will promote the protection of the environment, and make the polluter pay for damage to the environment for which he is responsible—as can be seen from the WHO, EEC and national regulations to which I have previously referred. But it does not follow from these developments that a common law principle, such as the rule in *Rylands v Fletcher*, should be developed or rendered more strict to provide for liability in respect of such pollution. On the contrary, given that so much well-informed and carefully structured legislation is now being put in place for this purpose, there is less need for the courts to develop a common law principle to achieve the same end, and indeed it may well be undesirable that they should do so.

Having regard to these considerations, and in particular to the step which this House has already taken in *Read v Lyons* to contain the scope of liability under the rule in *Rylands v Fletcher*, it appears to me to be appropriate now to take the view that foreseeability of damage of the relevant type should be regarded as a prerequisite of liability in damages under the rule. Such a conclusion can, as I have already stated, be derived from Blackburn J's original statement of the law; and I can see no good reason why this prerequisite should not be recognised under the rule, as it has been in the case of private nuisance. In particular, I do not regard the two authorities cited to your Lordships, *West v Bristol Tramways Co* [1908] 2 KB 14, [1908–10] All ER Rep 215 and *Rainham Chemical Works Ltd v Belvedere Fish Guano Co Ltd* [1921] 2 AC 465, [1921] All ER Rep 48, as providing any strong pointer towards a contrary conclusion. It would moreover lead to a more coherent body of common law principles if the rule were to be regarded essentially as an extension of the law of nuisance to cases of isolated escapes from land, even though the rule as established is not limited to escapes which are in fact isolated. I wish to point out, however, that in truth the escape of the PCE from ECL's land, in the form of trace elements carried in percolating water, has not been an isolated escape, but a continuing escape resulting from a state of affairs which has come into existence at the base of the chalk aquifer underneath ECL's premises. Classically, this would have been regarded as a case of nuisance; and it would seem strange if, by characterising the case as one falling under the rule in *Rylands v Fletcher*, the liability should thereby be rendered more strict in the circumstances of the present case.

The facts of the present case
Turning to the facts of the present case, it is plain that, at the time when the PCE was brought onto ECL's land, and indeed when it was used in the tanning process there, nobody at ECL could reasonably have foreseen the resultant damage which occured at CWC's borehole at Sawston.

However, there remains for consideration a point adumbrated in the course of argument, which is relevant to liability in nuisance as well as under the rule in *Rylands v Fletcher*. It appears that, in the present case, pools of neat PCE are still in existence at the base of the chalk aquifer beneath ECL's premises, and the escape of dissolved phase PCE from ECL's land is continuing to the present day. On this basis it can be argued that, since it has become known that PCE, if it escapes, is capable of causing damage by rendering water available at boreholes unsaleable for domestic purposes, ECL could be held liable, in nuisance or under the rule in *Rylands v Fletcher*, in respect of damage caused by the continuing escape of PCE from its land occurring at any time after such damage had become foreseeable by ECL.

For my part, I do not consider that such an argument is well founded. Here we are faced with a situation where the substance in question, PCE, has so travelled down through the drift and the chalk aquifer beneath ECL's premises that it has passed beyond the control of ECL. To impose strict liability on ECL in these circumstances, either as the creator of a nuisance or under the rule in *Rylands v Fletcher*, on the ground that it has subsequently become reasonably foreseeable that the PCE may, if it escapes, cause damage, appears to me to go beyond the scope of the regimes imposed under either of these two related heads of liability. This is because when ECL created the conditions which have ultimately led to the present state of affairs—whether by bringing the PCE in question onto its land, or by retaining it there, or by using it in its tanning process—it could not possibly have foreseen that damage of the type now complained of might be caused thereby. Indeed, long before the relevant legislation came into force, the PCE had become irretrievably lost in the ground below. In such circumstances, I do not consider that ECL should be under any greater liability than that imposed for negligence. At best, if the case is regarded as one of nuisance, it should be treated no differently from, for example, the case of the landslip in *Leakey v National Trust for Places of Historic Interest or Natural Beauty* [1980] 1 All ER 17, [1980] QB 485.

I wish to add that the present case may be regarded as one of what is nowadays called historic pollution, in the sense that the relevant occurrence (the seepage of PCE through the floor of ECL's premises) took place before the relevant legislation came into force; and it appears that, under the current philosophy, it is not envisaged that statutory liability should be imposed for historic pollution (see e.g. the Council of Europe's Draft Convention on Civil Liability for Damages Resulting from Activities Dangerous to the Environment (Strasbourg, 29 January 1993) art 5.1, and para 48 of the Explanatory Report). If so, it would be strange if liability for such pollution were to arise under a principle of common law.

In the result, since those responsible at ECL could not at the relevant time reasonably have foreseen that the damage in question might occur, the claim of CWC for damages under the rule in *Rylands v Fletcher* must fail.

Natural use of land

I turn to the question whether the use by ECL of its land in the present case constituted a natural use, with the result that ECL cannot be held liable under the rule in *Rylands v Fletcher*. In view of my conclusion on the issue of foreseeability, I can deal with this point shortly.

The judge held that it was a natural use....

It is a commonplace that this particular exception to liability under the rule has developed and changed over the years. It seems clear that in *Fletcher v Rylands* (1866) LR 1 Ex 265 itself Blackburn J's statement of the law was limited to things which are brought by the defendant onto his land, and so did not apply to things that were naturally upon the land. Furthermore, it is doubtful whether in the House of Lords in the same case Lord Cairns, to whom we owe the expression 'non-natural use' of the land, was intending to expand the concept of natural use beyond that envisaged by Blackburn J. Even so, the law has long since departed from any such simple idea, redolent of a different age; and, at least since the advice of the Privy Council delivered by Lord Moulton in *Rickards v Lothian* [1913] AC 263 at 280, [1911–13] All ER Rep 71 at 80, natural use has been extended to embrace the ordinary use of land. I ask to be forgiven if I again quote Lord Moulton's statement of the law, which has lain at the heart of the subsequent development of this exception:

> 'It is not every use to which land is put that brings into play at that principle. It must be some special use bringing with it increased danger to others, and must not merely be the ordinary use of the land or such a use as is proper for the general benefit of the community.'

Rickards v Lothian itself was concerned with a use of a domestic kind, viz. the overflow of water from a basin whose runaway had become blocked. But over the years the concept of natural use, in the sense of ordinary use, has been extended to embrace a wide variety of uses, including not only domestic uses but also recreational uses and even some industrial uses.

It is obvious that the expression 'ordinary use of the land' in Lord Moulton's statement of the law is one which is lacking in precision. There are some writers who welcome the flexibility which has thus been introduced into this branch of the law, on the ground that it enables judges to mould and adapt the principle of strict liability to the changing needs of society; whereas others regret the perceived absence of principle in so vague a concept, and fear that the whole idea of strict liability may as a result be undermined. A particular doubt is introduced by Lord Moulton's alternative criterion 'or such a use as is proper for the general benefit of the community'. If these words are understood to refer to a local community, they can be given some content as intended to refer to such matters as, for example, the provision of services; indeed the same idea can, without too much difficulty, be extended to, for example, the provision of services to industrial premises, as in a business park or an industrial estate. But if the words are extended to embrace the wider interests of the local community or the general benefit of the community at large, it is difficult to see how the exception can be kept within reasonable bounds. A notable extension was considered in your Lordships' House in *Read v J Lyons & Co Ltd* [1946] 2 All ER 471 at 475, 478, [1947] AC 156 at 169–170, 174 per Viscount Simon and Lord Macmillan, where it was suggested that, in time of war, the manufacture of explosives might be held to constitute a natural use of land, apparently on the basis that, in a country in which the greater part of the population was involved in the war effort, many otherwise exceptional uses might become 'ordinary' for the duration of the war. It is however unnecessary to consider so wide an extension as that in a case such as the present. Even so, we can see the introduction of another extension in the present case, when the judge invoked the creation of employment as clearly for the benefit of the local community, viz. 'the industrial village' at Sawston. I myself, however, do not feel able to accept that the creation of employment as such, even in a small industrial complex, is sufficient of itself to establish a particular use as constituting a natural or ordinary use of land.

Fortunately, I do not think it is necessary for the purposes of the present case to attempt any redefinition of the concept of natural or ordinary use. This is because I am satisfied that the storage of chemicals in substantial quantities, and their use in the manner employed at ECL's premises, cannot fall within the exception. For the purpose of testing the point, let it be assumed that ECL was well aware of the possibility that PCE, if it escaped, could indeed cause damage, for example by contaminating any water with which it became mixed so as to render that water undrinkable by human beings. I cannot think that it would be right in such circumstances to exempt ECL from liability under the rule in *Rylands v Fletcher* on the ground that the use was natural or ordinary. The mere fact that the use is common in the tanning industry cannot, in my opinion, be enough to bring the use within the exception, nor the fact that Sawston contains a small industrial community which is worthy of encouragement or support. Indeed I feel bound to say that the storage of substantial quantities of chemicals on industrial premises should be regarded as an almost classic case of non-natural use; and I find it very difficult to think that it should be thought objectionable to impose strict liability for damage caused in the event of their escape. It may well be that, now that it is recognised that foreseeability of harm of the relevant type is a prerequisite of liability in damages under the rule, the courts may feel less pressure to extend the concept of natural use to circumstances such as those in the present case; and in due course it may become easier to control this exception, and to ensure that it has a more recognisable basis of principle. For these reasons, I would not hold that ECL should be exempt from liability on the basis of the exception of natural use.

However, for the reasons I have already given, I would allow ECL's appeal with costs before our Lordships' House and in the courts below.

[LORD TEMPLEMAN, LORD JAUNCEY OF TULLICHETTLE, LORD LOWRY, and LORD WOOLF agreed with LORD GOFF's speech.]

Appeal allowed.   No   R + F.   due to lack of foreseeability.

main control/
mechanism,

QUESTIONS

1.   Putting aside the question of non-natural user, do you agree with Lord Goff that ECL should not be liable under *Rylands v Fletcher* for damage due to the escape of PCE from their land, albeit not under their control, once the damage it could cause was reasonably foreseeable? (See D. Wilkinson (1994) 57 MLR 799 at 807–809.)

2.   What sort of damage did CWC suffer in this case?

3.   To what extent does the *Cambridge Water* case support the principle that 'the polluter pays'? (See G. Cross, (1995) 111 LQR 445 at 473; Lord Goff, p. 839, ante.)

NOTES

1.   For notes on the *Cambridge Water* case, see R. F. V. Heuston (1994) 110 LQR 185; A. Ogus [1994] JEL 151; T. Weir [1994] CLJ 216; D. Wilkinson op cit., and see the general discussion by G. Cross, op cit.; J. Steele (1995) 15 LS 236.

2.   One difficult question thrown up by the case is how the foresight test is applied. One view is that it is to be applied given that the reasonable man knows of the escape. An alternative opinion is that the case requires the escape to be foreseeable, as well as the type of damage which ensues. See generally on this question of interpretation and on the passages in *Cambridge Water* which support the particular views, Wilkinson, op cit., pp. 803–807 and consider Cross, op cit., pp. 467–468; *Winfield & Jolowicz*, pp. 661–662: see further the notes referred to ante, which do not speak with one voice on the matter. As Wilkinson points out, if the latter view were adopted, it would undermine

strict liability under *Rylands v Fletcher*. But it might be argued that there is still an important difference from negligence liability, since a negligence suit can fail even where the damage is foreseeable if the reasonable man would have acted as the defendant did (e.g. if a small but foreseeable risk was outweighed by social utility): and see the discussion in the context of nuisance by Cross, op cit., pp. 460–464.

3.   Lord Moulton's analysis of non-natural user in *Rickards v Lothian* [1913] AC 263 at 280, which was quoted and commented upon by Lord Goff, had previously been described by Viscount Simon in *Read v J Lyons & Co Ltd* [1947] AC 156 at 169 as 'of the first importance'. It has been quoted, for example, in *British Celanese Ltd v A H Hunt (Capacitors) Ltd* [1969] 2 All ER 1252, [1969] 1 WLR 959. The facts were given on p. 799, ante in detail. The statement of claim alleged, inter alia that the defendants had collected strips of metal foil (the 'things' which had escaped) on their land for the purposes of their business (the manufacture of electrical and electronic parts) and that the premises they occupied were on a trading estate. It was held that to use these premises for manufacturing purposes was an ordinary use, that neither the manufacturing of these components nor the storing of the foil was a special use, that no special risks were created by the mere use of the premises to store foil, and that the manufacture of the products, in the course of which the foil was used, was beneficial to the community. Thus the claimants did not bring their case within the *Rylands v Fletcher* principle. Has this decision been affected by Lord Goff's comments in the *Cambridge Water* case?

     The question of non-natural user has proved to be a difficult one over the years. See further *Burnie Port Authority v General Jones Pty Ltd* (1994) 120 ALR 42 at 54, and especially now the discussion in *Transco*.

4.   Lord Goff referred to the similarity of function between the idea of reasonable user in nuisance and that of non-natural user under *Rylands v Fletcher*, while finding it unnecessary to identify precise differences between the two concepts. There are certainly differences. For example, the locality is relevant in the decision whether a use is non-natural or not, whereas in nuisance it is only of relevance in cases of amenity damage (*St Helen's Smelting Co v Tipping* 1865) 11 HL Cas 642, p. 785, ante). The question of the role of social utility in each case also needs to be considered. It might, in addition, be noted that the passage in Lord Goff's speech has been used to argue that reasonable user is a factor to be considered in all nuisance cases and not just in cases of amenity damage: see J. Steele, op cit., pp. 251–253. For further argument on Lord Goff's treatment of reasonable user, see G. Cross, op cit., pp. 445–458. One concern of Cross is that it opens up the possibility of subverting the strict liability nature of nuisance.

5.   On reform in this area, to which Lord Goff referred, see note 6, p. 854, post. On Lord Goff's view of the relationship between judicial development and legislative development of the law in this context, cf. Weir op cit., p. 218, who supports Lord Goff's approach. Consider further Ogus op cit., pp. 154–155 and Atkin LJ in *Phillips v Britannia Hygienic Laundry Co Ltd* [1923] All ER Rep 127 (p. 692, ante).

■ Transco Plc v Stockport Metropolitan Borough Council

House of Lords [2004] 1 All ER 589

The defendant council owned a high-rise block of flats. The main water-pipe supplying the flats fractured, leading to the underground escape of large quantities of water. This water saturated a nearby disused railway embankment, causing it to collapse and leaving exposed a buried gas main belonging to the claimants. Having been compelled to make emergency repairs, the claimants brought an action for damages. The trial judge held the council liable in *Rylands v Fletcher*, but his decision was reversed by the Court of Appeal [2001] Env LR 44, [2001] EWCA Civ 212, on the basis that the rule did not apply to the provision of water to a block of flats. The claimants appealed unsuccessfully to the House of Lords.

LORD BINGHAM OF CORNHILL: ...

The future development of Rylands v Fletcher

[4] In the course of his excellent argument for the council, Mr Mark Turner QC canvassed various ways in which the rule in *Rylands v Fletcher* might be applied and developed in future, without however judging it necessary to press the House to accept any one of them. The boldest of these courses was to follow the trail blazed by a majority of the High Court of Australia in *Burnie Port Authority v General Jones Pty Ltd* [1996] 4 LRC 605, (1994) 120 ALR 42 by treating the rule in *Rylands v Fletcher* as absorbed by the principles of ordinary negligence. In reaching this decision the majority were influenced by the difficulties of interpretation and application to which the rule has undoubtedly given rise ([1996] 4 LRC 605 at 622–625, 120 ALR 42 at 52–55), by the progressive weakening of the rule by judicial decision ([1996] 4 LRC 605 at 625, 120 ALR 42 at 54–55), by recognition that the law of negligence has been very greatly developed and expanded since *Rylands v Fletcher* was decided ([1996] 4 LRC 605 at 625–636, 120 ALR 42 at 55–65) and by a belief that most claimants entitled to succeed under the rule would succeed in a claim for negligence anyway (see [1996] 4 LRC 605 at 636–638, 120 ALR 42 at 65–67).

[5] Coming from such a quarter these comments of course command respect, and they are matched by expressions of opinion here. Megaw LJ observed in *Leakey v National Trust for Places of Historic Interest or Natural Beauty* [1980] 1 All ER 17 at 30, [1980] QB 485 at 519 that application of the decision and of the dicta in *Rylands v Fletcher* had given rise to continual trouble in the law of England. In its report on Civil Liability for Dangerous Things and Activities (Law Com no 32) (1970) p 12, para 20(a) the Law Commission described the relevant law as 'complex, uncertain and inconsistent in principle'. There is a theoretical attraction in bringing this somewhat anomalous ground of liability within the broad and familiar rules governing liability in negligence. This would have the incidental advantage of bringing the law of England and Wales more closely into line with what I understand to be the law of Scotland (see *RHM Bakeries (Scotland) Ltd v Strathclyde Regional Council* 1985 SC (HL) 17 at 41, 1985 SLT 214 at 217, where Lord Fraser of Tullybelton described the suggestion that the decision in *Rylands v Fletcher* had any place in Scots law as 'a heresy which ought to be extirpated'). Consideration of the reported English case law over the past 60 years suggests that few if any claimants have succeeded in reliance on the rule in *Rylands v Fletcher* alone.

[6] I would be willing to suppress an instinctive resistance to treating a nuisance-based tort as if it were governed by the law of negligence if I were persuaded that it would serve the interests of justice to discard the rule in Rylands v Fletcher and treat the cases in which it might have been relied on as governed by the ordinary rules of negligence. But I hesitate to adopt that solution for four main reasons. First, there is in my opinion a category of case, however small it may be, in which it seems just to impose liability even in the absence of fault. In the context of then recent catastrophes *Rylands v Fletcher* itself was understandably seen as such a case. With memories of the tragedy at Aberfan still green, the same view might now be taken of *Attorney General v Cory Bros & Co Ltd, Kennard v Cory Bros & Co Ltd* [1921] 1 AC 521 even if the claimants had failed to prove negligence, as on the facts they were able to do. I would regard *Rainham Chemical Works Ltd (in liq) v Belvedere Fish Guano Co Ltd* [1921] 2 AC 465, [1921] All ER Rep 48, and *Cambridge Water Co Ltd v Eastern Counties Leather plc* [1994] 1 All ER 53, [1994] 2 AC 264 (had there been foreseeability of damage), as similarly falling within that category. Second, it must be remembered that common law rules do not exist in a vacuum, least of all rules which have stood for over a century during which there has been detailed statutory regulation of matters to which they might potentially relate. With reference to water, s 209 of the Water Industry Act 1991 imposes strict liability (subject to certain exemptions) on water undertakers and Sch 2 to the Reservoirs Act 1975 appears to assume that on facts such as those of *Rylands v Fletcher* strict liability

would attach. If the law were changed so as to require proof of negligence by those previously thought to be entitled to recover under the rule in *Rylands v Fletcher* without proving negligence, the effect might be (one does not know) to falsify the assumption on which Parliament has legislated, by significantly modifying rights which Parliament may have assumed would continue to exist. Third, although in the *Cambridge Water case* [1994] 2 AC 264 at 283–285 the possibility was ventilated that the House might depart from *Rylands v Fletcher* in its entirety, it is plain that this suggestion was not accepted. Instead, the House looked forward to a more principled and better controlled application of the existing rule (see, for example, [1994] 1 All ER 53 at 79–80, [1994] 2 AC 264 at 309). While this is not a conclusive bar to acceptance of the detailed argument presented to the House on this occasion, 'stop-go' is in general as bad an approach to legal development as to economic management. Fourth, while replacement of strict *Rylands v Fletcher* liability by a fault-based rule would tend to assimilate the law of England and Wales with that of Scotland, it would tend to increase the disparity between it and the laws of France and Germany. Having reviewed comparable provisions of French and German law, van Gerven, Lever and Larouche (Cases, Materials and Text on National, Supranational and International Tort Law (2000) p 205) observe:

> 'Even if the contours of the respective regimes may differ, all systems studied here therefore afford a form of strict liability protection in disputes between neighbouring landowners.'

The authors indeed suggest that the English rule as laid down in Rylands v Fletcher is 'the most developed of these regimes.'

[7] Should, then, the rule be generously applied and the scope of strict liability extended? There are certainly respected commentators who favour such a course and regret judicial restrictions on the operation of the rule (see Fleming The Law of Torts (9th edn, 1998) p 377; Markesinis and Deakin Tort Law (5th edn, 2003) p 544). But there is to my mind a compelling objection to such a course, articulated by Lord Goff of Chieveley in the *Cambridge Water* case [1994] 1 All ER 53 at 76, [1994] 2 AC 264 at 305:

> 'Like the judge in the present case, I incline to the opinion that, as a general rule, it is more appropriate for strict liability in respect of operations of high risk to be imposed by Parliament, than by the courts. If such liability is imposed by statute, the relevant activities can be identified, and those concerned can know where they stand. Furthermore, statute can where appropriate lay down precise criteria establishing the incidence and scope of such liability.'

It may be added that statutory regulation, particularly when informed by the work of the Law Commission, may take such account as is judged appropriate of the comparative law considerations on which I have briefly touched.

[8] There remains a third option, which I would myself favour: to retain the rule, while insisting upon its essential nature and purpose; and to restate it so as to achieve as much certainty and clarity as is attainable, recognising that new factual situations are bound to arise posing difficult questions on the boundary of the rule, wherever that is drawn.

[9] The rule in *Rylands v Fletcher* is a sub-species of nuisance, which is itself a tort based on the interference by one occupier of land with the right in or enjoyment of land by another occupier of land as such. From this simple proposition two consequences at once flow. First, as very clearly decided by the House in *Read v J Lyons & Co Ltd* [1946] 2 All ER 471, [1947] AC 156, no claim in nuisance or under the rule can arise if the events complained of take place wholly on the land of a single occupier. There must, in other words, be an escape from one tenement to another. Second, the claim cannot include a claim for death or personal injury, since such a claim does not relate to any right in or enjoyment of land. This proposition has not been authoritatively affirmed by any decision at the highest level. It was left open by Parker LJ in *Perry v Kendricks Transport Ltd* [1956] 1 All ER 154 at 160–161, [1956] 1 WLR 85 at 92, and is inconsistent with decisions such as *Shiffman v Venerable Order of the Hospital of St John of Jerusalem* [1936] 1 All ER 557 and *Miles v Forest Rock Granite Co (Leicestershire) Ltd* (1918) 34 TLR 500. It is however clear from Lord Macmillan's opinion in *Read's* case [1946] 2 All ER 471 at 476,

[1947] AC 156 at 170–171 that he regarded a personal injury claim as outside the scope of the rule, and his approach is in my opinion strongly fortified by the decisions of the House in the *Cambridge Water* case [1994] 1 All ER 53, [1994] 2 AC 264 and *Hunter v Canary Wharf Ltd, Hunter v London Docklands Development Corp* [1997] 2 All ER 426, [1997] AC 655, in each of which nuisance was identified as a tort directed, and directed only, to the protection of interests in land.

[10] It has from the beginning been a necessary condition of liability under the rule in *Rylands v Fletcher* that the thing which the defendant has brought on his land should be 'something which . . . will naturally do mischief if it escape out of his land', 'something dangerous . . .', 'anything likely to do mischief if it escapes . . .' (see (1866) LR 1 Exch 265 at 279 per Blackburn J) . . . The practical problem is of course to decide whether in any given case the thing which has escaped satisfies this mischief or danger test, a problem exacerbated by the fact that many things not ordinarily regarded as sources of mischief or danger may none the less be capable of proving to be such if they escape. I do not think this condition can be viewed in complete isolation from the non-natural user condition to which I shall shortly turn, but I think the cases decided by the House give a valuable pointer. In *Rylands v Fletcher* itself the courts were dealing with what Lord Cranworth called 'a large accumulated mass of water' stored up in a reservoir . . . *Rainham Chemical Works Ltd (in liq) v Belvedere Fish Guano Co Ltd* [1921] 2 AC 465 at 471, [1921] All ER Rep 48 at 50, involved the storage of chemicals, for the purpose of making munitions, which 'exploded with terrific violence'. In *Attorney General v Cory Bros & Co Ltd, Kennard v Cory Bros & Co Ltd* [1921] 1 AC 521 at 525, 530, 534, 536, the landslide in question was of what counsel described as an 'enormous mass of rubbish', some 500,000 tons of mineral waste tipped on a steep hillside. In the *Cambridge Water* case [1994] 1 All ER 53, [1994] 2 AC 264 the industrial solvents being used by the tannery were bound to cause mischief in the event, unforeseen on the facts, that they percolated down to the water table. These cases are in sharp contrast with those arising out of escape from a domestic water supply (such as *Carstairs v Taylor* (1871) LR 6 Exch 217, *Ross v Fedden* (1872) 26 LT 966 or *Anderson v Oppenheimer* (1880) 5 QBD 602) which, although decided on other grounds, would seem to me to fail the mischief or danger test. Bearing in mind the historical origin of the rule, and also that its effect is to impose liability in the absence of negligence for an isolated occurrence, I do not think the mischief or danger test should be at all easily satisfied. It must be shown that the defendant has done something which he recognised, or judged by the standards appropriate at the relevant place and time, he ought reasonably to have recognised, as giving rise to an exceptionally high risk of danger or mischief if there should be an escape, however unlikely an escape may have been thought to be.

[11] No ingredient of *Rylands v Fletcher* liability has provoked more discussion than the requirement of Blackburn J ((1866) LR 1 Exch 265 at 280) that the thing brought on to the defendant's land should be something 'not naturally there' . . . Read literally, the expressions used by Blackburn J and Lord Cairns might be thought to exclude nothing which has reached the land otherwise than through operation of the laws of nature. But such an interpretation has been fairly described as 'redolent of a different age' (see the *Cambridge Water* case [1994] 1 All ER 53 at 78, [1994] 2 AC 264 at 308), and in *Read v J Lyons & Co Ltd* [1946] 2 All ER 471 at 475, 478, 484, [1947] AC 156 at 169, 176, 187 and the *Cambridge Water* case [1994] 1 All ER 53 at 78, [1994] 2 AC 264 at 308 the House gave its imprimatur to Lord Moulton's statement, giving the advice of the Privy Council in *Rickards v Lothian* [1913] AC 263 at 280, [1911–13] All ER Rep 71 at 80:

> 'It is not every use to which land is put that brings into play that principle. It must be some special use bringing with it increased danger to others, and must not merely be the ordinary use of the land or such a use as is proper for the general benefit of the community.'

I think it clear that ordinary user is a preferable test to natural user, making it clear that the rule in *Rylands v Fletcher* is engaged only where the defendant's use is shown to be extraordinary and unusual. This is not a test to be inflexibly applied: a use may be extraordinary and unusual at one time or in one place but not so at another time or in another place (although I would question whether, even in wartime, the manufacture of explosives could ever be regarded as an ordinary user of land, as contemplated by Viscount Simon, Lord Macmillan, Lord Porter and Lord Uthwatt in *Read v J Lyons & Co Ltd* [1946] 2 All ER 471 at 476, 477, 479, 484, [1947] AC 156 at 169–170, 174, 176–177, 186–187). I also doubt whether a test of reasonable user is helpful, since a user may well be quite out of the ordinary but not unreasonable, as was that of *Rylands v Fletcher*, the *Rainham Chemical Works* case or the tannery in the *Cambridge Water* case. Again, as it seems to me, the question is whether the defendant has done something which he recognises, or ought to recognise, as being quite out of the ordinary in the place and at the time when he does it. In answering that question, I respectfully think that little help is gained (and unnecessary confusion perhaps caused) by considering whether the use is proper for the general benefit of the community. In *Rickards v Lothian* itself, the claim arose because the outflow from a washbasin on the top floor of premises was maliciously blocked and the tap left running, with the result that damage was caused to stock on a floor below: not surprisingly, the provision of a domestic water supply to the premises was held to be a wholly ordinary use of the land. An occupier of land who can show that another occupier of land has brought or kept on his land an exceptionally dangerous or mischievous thing in extraordinary or unusual circumstances is in my opinion entitled to recover compensation from that occupier for any damage caused to his property interest by the escape of that thing, subject to defences of act of God or of a stranger, without the need to prove negligence.

The present appeal

[13] It is of course true that water in quantity is almost always capable of causing damage if it escapes. But the piping of a water supply from the mains to the storage tanks in the block was a routine function which would not have struck anyone as raising any special hazard. In truth, the council did not accumulate any water, it merely arranged a supply adequate to meet the residents' needs. The situation cannot stand comparison with the making by Mr Rylands of a substantial reservoir. Nor can the use by the council of its land be seen as in any way extraordinary or unusual. It was entirely normal and routine. Despite the attractive argument of Mr Ian Leeming QC for Transco, I am satisfied that the conditions to be met before strict liability could be imposed on the council were far from being met on the facts here.

[14] I would accordingly dismiss the appeal with costs.

LORD HOFFMANN [having reviewed the facts of the case and the legal background to the decision in *Rylands v Fletcher*, continued:] . . .

[27] *Rylands v Fletcher* was therefore an innovation in being the first clear imposition of liability for damage caused by an escape which was not alleged to be either intended or reasonably foreseeable. I think that this is what Professor Newark meant when he said in his celebrated article, 'The Boundaries of Nuisance' (1949) 65 LQR 480 at 488, that the novelty in *Rylands v Fletcher* was the decision that 'an isolated escape is actionable'. That is not because a single deluge is less of a nuisance than a steady trickle, but because repeated escapes such as the discharge of water in the mining cases and the discharge of chemicals in the factory cases do not raise any question about whether the escape was reasonably foreseeable. If the defendant does not know what he is doing, the plaintiff will certainly tell him. It is the single escape which raises the question of whether or not it was reasonably foreseeable and, if not, whether the defendant should nevertheless be liable. *Rylands v Fletcher* decided that he should.

The social background to the rule

[28] Although the judgment of Blackburn J is constructed in the traditional common law style of deducing principle from precedent, without reference to questions of social policy, Professor Brian Simpson has demonstrated in his article 'Legal Liability for Bursting Reservoirs: The Historical Context of *Rylands v Fletcher*' (1984) 13 JLS 209 that the background to the case was public anxiety about the safety of reservoirs, caused in particular by the bursting of the Bradfield Reservoir near Sheffield on 12 March 1864, with the loss of about 250 lives. The judicial response was to impose strict liability upon the proprietors of reservoirs. But, since the common law deals in principles rather than ad hoc solutions, the rule had to be more widely formulated.

[29] It is tempting to see, beneath the surface of the rule, a policy of requiring the costs of a commercial enterprise to be internalised; to require the entrepreneur to provide, by insurance or otherwise, for the risks to others which his enterprise creates. That was certainly the opinion of Bramwell B, who was in favour of liability when the case was before the Court of Exchequer ((1865) 3 H & C 774). He had a clear and consistent view on the matter: see *Bamford v Turnley* (1862) 3 B & S 62 at 84–85, [1861–73] All ER Rep 706 at 712–713 and *Hammersmith and City Rly Co v Brand* (1867) LR 2 QB 223 at 230–231. But others thought differently. They considered that the public interest in promoting economic development made it unreasonable to hold an entrepreneur liable when he had not been negligent: see *Wildtree Hotels Ltd v Harrow London BC* [2000] 3 All ER 289 at 295–296, [2001] 2 AC 1 at 8–9 for a discussion of this debate in the context of compensation for disturbance caused by the construction and operation of works authorised by statutory powers. On the whole, it was the latter view—no liability without fault—which gained the ascendancy. With hindsight, *Rylands v Fletcher* can be seen as an isolated victory for the internalisers. The following century saw a steady refusal to treat it as laying down any broad principle of liability. I shall briefly trace the various restrictions imposed on its scope.

Restrictions on the rule
[LORD HOFFMANN considered the defence of statutory authority (where negligence must be shown to establish liability); the defences of Acts of God and of third parties; the requirement that the damage must be a foreseeable consequence of an escape; the requirement that the dangerous thing must escape from the defendant's land; and that the land was used for "non-natural" purposes; and further stated his view that *Cambridge Water Co Ltd v Eastern Counties Leather plc* [1994] 1 All ER 53 and *Hunter v Canary Wharf Ltd* [1997] 2 All ER 426 showed that no action for personal injuries may be brought in *Rylands v Fletcher*. His Lordship continued:]

Where stands the rule today?
[39] I pause at this point to summarise the very limited circumstances to which the rule has been confined. First, it is a remedy for damage to land or interests in land. As there can be few properties in the country, commercial or domestic, which are not insured against damage by flood and the like, this means that disputes over the application of the rule will tend to be between property insurers and liability insurers. Secondly, it does not apply to works or enterprises authorised by statute. That means that it will usually have no application to really high-risk activities. As Professor Simpson points out ([1984] 13 JLS 225) the Bradfield Reservoir was built under statutory powers. In the absence of negligence, the occupiers whose lands had been inundated would have had no remedy. Thirdly, it is not particularly strict because it excludes liability when the escape is for the most common reasons, namely vandalism or unusual natural events. Fourthly, the cases in which there is an escape which is not attributable to an unusual natural event or the act of a third party will, by the same token, usually give rise to an inference of negligence. Fifthly, there is a broad and ill-defined exception for 'natural' uses of land. It is perhaps not surprising that counsel could not find a reported case since the 1939–45 war in which anyone had succeeded in a claim under the rule. It is hard to escape the conclusion that the intellectual effort devoted to the rule by judges and writers over many years has brought forth a mouse.

Is it worth keeping?
[40] In *Burnie Port Authority v General Jones Pty Ltd* [1996] 4 LRC 605, (1994) 179 CLR 520 a majority of the High Court of Australia lost patience with the pretensions and uncertainties of the rule and decided that it had been 'absorbed' into the law of negligence. Your Lordships have been invited by the respondents to kill off the rule in England in similar fashion. It is said, first, that in its present attenuated form it serves little practical purpose; secondly, that its application is unacceptably vague ('an essentially unprincipled and ad hoc subjective determination' said the High Court in the *Burnie* case [1996] 4 LRC 605 at 625, (1994) 120 ALR 42 at 54) and thirdly, that strict liability on social grounds is better left to statutory intervention.

[41] There is considerable force in each of these points. It is hard to find any rational principle which explains the rule and its exceptions. In *Read v J Lyons & Co Ltd* [1946] 2 All ER 471 at 478, [1947] AC 156

at 175 Lord Macmillan said with Scottish detachment, 'your Lordships are not called on to rationalise the law of England'...And the proposition that strict liability is best left to statute receives support from the speech of Lord Goff of Chieveley in the *Cambridge Water* case [1994] 1 All ER 53 at 76, [1994] 2 AC 264 at 305...

[42] An example of statutory strict liability close to home is s 209 of the [Water Industry Act 1991]:

'(1) Where an escape of water, however caused, from a pipe vested in a water undertaker causes loss or damage, the undertaker shall be liable, except as otherwise provided in this section, for the loss or damage...

(3) A water undertaker shall not incur any liability under subsection (1) above in respect of any loss or damage for which the undertaker would not be liable apart from that subsection and which is sustained...(b) by any public gas supplier within the meaning of Part I of the Gas Act 1986...'

This provision is designed to avoid all argument over which insurers should bear the loss. Liability is far stricter than under the rule in *Rylands v Fletcher*. There is no exception for acts of third parties or natural events. The undertaker is liable for an escape 'however caused' and must insure accordingly. On the other hand, certain potential claimants like public gas suppliers (now called public gas transporters) must insure themselves. The irony of the present case is that if the leak had been from a high pressure water main, belonging to the North West Water Authority, a much more plausible high-risk activity, there could have been no dispute. Section 209(3)(b) would have excluded a statutory claim and the authority's statutory powers would have excluded the rule in *Rylands v Fletcher*.

[43] But despite the strength of these arguments, I do not think it would be consistent with the judicial function of your Lordships' House to abolish the rule. It has been part of English law for nearly 150 years and despite a searching examination by Lord Goff of Chieveley in the *Cambridge Water* case [1994] 1 All ER 53 at 78, [1994] 2 AC 264 at 308, there was no suggestion in his speech that it could or should be abolished. I think that would be too radical a step to take.

[44] It remains, however, if not to rationalise the law of England, at least to introduce greater certainty into the concept of natural user which is in issue in this case....Whatever Blackburn J and Lord Cairns may have meant by 'natural', the law was set on a different course by the opinion of Lord Moulton in *Rickards v Lothian* [1913] AC 263, [1911–13] All ER Rep 71 and the question of what is a natural use of land or, (the converse) a use creating an increased risk, must be judged by contemporary standards.

[45] Two features of contemporary society seem to me to be relevant. First, the extension of statutory regulation to a number of activities, such as discharge of water (s 209 of the 1991 Act), pollution by the escape of waste (s 73(6) of the Environmental Protection Act 1990) and radio-active matter (s 7 of the Nuclear Installations Act 1965). It may have to be considered whether these and similar provisions create an exhaustive code of liability for a particular form of escape which excludes the rule in Rylands v Fletcher.

[LORD HOFFMANN then referred to the possibility of potential claimants insuring themselves against property damage, and continued:]

[47] In the present case, I am willing to assume that if the risk arose from a 'non-natural user' of the council's land, all the other elements of the tort were satisfied. Transco complains of expense having to be undertaken to avoid damage to its gas pipe; I am willing to assume that if damage to the pipe would have been actionable, the expense incurred in avoiding that damage would have been recoverable. I also willing to assume that Transco's easement which entitled it to maintain its pipe in the embankment and receive support from the soil was a sufficient proprietary interest to enable it to sue in nuisance and therefore, by analogy, under the rule in *Rylands v Fletcher*. Although the council, as owner of Hollow End Towers, was no doubt under a statutory duty to provide its occupiers with water, it had no statutory duty or authority to build that particular tower block and it is therefore not suggested that the pipe was laid pursuant to statutory powers so as to exclude the rule. So the question is whether the risk came within the rule.

[48] The damage which eventuated was subsidence beneath a gas main: a form of risk against which no rational owner of a gas main would fail to insure. The casualty was caused by the escape of water from the council's land. But the source was a perfectly normal item of plumbing. The pipe was, it is true, considerably larger than the ordinary domestic size. But it was smaller than a water main. It was installed to serve the occupiers of the council's high rise flats; not strictly speaking a commercial purpose, but not a private one either.

[49] In my opinion the Court of Appeal was right to say that it was not a 'non-natural' user of land. I am influenced by two matters. First, there is no evidence that it created a greater risk than is normally associated with domestic or commercial plumbing. True, the pipe was larger. But whether that involved greater risk depends upon its specification. One cannot simply assume that the larger the pipe, the greater the risk of fracture or the greater the quantity of water likely to be discharged. I agree with my noble and learned friend Lord Bingham of Cornhill that the criterion of exceptional risk must be taken seriously and creates a high threshold for a claimant to surmount. Secondly, I think that the risk of damage to property caused by leaking water is one against which most people can and do commonly insure. This is, as I have said, particularly true of Transco, which can be expected to have insured against any form of damage to its pipe. It would be a very strange result if Transco were entitled to recover against the council when it would not have been entitled to recover against the Water Authority for similar damage emanating from its high pressure main.

LORD HOBHOUSE OF WOODBOROUGH [delivered an opinion in favour of dismissing the appeal, including the following remarks:] . . .

[55] The principle which the rule [in *Rylands v Fletcher*] reflects is also easily apparent. It is that the law of private nuisance recognises that the risk must be born by the person responsible for creating it and failing to control it. It reflects a social and economic utility. The user of one piece of land is always liable to affect the users or owners of other pieces of land. An escape of water originating on the former, or an explosion, may devastate not only the land on which it originates but also adjoining and more distant properties. The damage caused may be very serious indeed both in physical and financial terms. There may be a serious risk that if the user of the land, the use of which creates the risk, does not take active and adequate steps to prevent escape, an escape may occur. The situation is entirely under his control: other landowners have no control. In such a situation, two types of solution might be adopted. One would be to restrict the liberty of the user of the land, the source of the risk, to make such use of his land as he chooses. The other is to impose a strict liability on the landowner for the consequences of his exercising that liberty. The rule adopts the second type of solution as is clear from the language used by Blackburn J and on appeal and was explicit in the statements of Bramwell B at first instance (sic utere tuo . . .) . . . It is a coherent principle which accords with justice and with the existing legal theory at the time.

[56] This approach was entirely in keeping with the economic and political culture of the nineteenth century, laissez-faire and an understanding of the concept of risk. During the twentieth century and particularly during the second half, the culture has changed. Government has increasingly intervened to limit the freedom of a landowner to use his land as he chooses, eg through the planning laws, and has regulated or forbidden certain dangerous or anti-social uses of land such as the manufacture or storage of explosives or the emission of noxious effluents. Thus the present state of the law is that some of the situations where the rule in *Rylands v Fletcher* applies are now also addressed by the first type of solution. But this does not deprive the rule of its utility. The area of regulation is not exhaustive; it does not necessarily give the third party affected an adequate or, even, any say; the government decision may give priority to some national or military need which it considers must override legitimate individual interests; it will not normally deal with civil liability for damage to property; it does not provide the third party with adequate knowledge and control to evaluate and protect himself from the consequent risk and insurance cost. As Lord Goff pointed out in the *Cambridge Water* case, the occasions where *Rylands v Fletcher* may have to be invoked by a claimant may be reducing but that is not to say that it has ceased to be a valid part of English law. The only way it could be rendered obsolete is by a compulsory

strict public liability insurance scheme for all persons using their land for dangerous purposes. However this would simply be to re-enact Rylands v Fletcher in another guise.

Conclusions

[66] I consider that the rule in *Rylands v Fletcher* should not be abrogated. The rationale for it was and remains valid. The content of the rule has been clearly spelled out by Blackburn J and the relevant constituent elements can be easily stated as I have done at [54], above. The academic and judicial criticisms of the rule are largely the result of later confusions. The rule itself and the laws of private nuisance already in existence in the mid-nineteenth century and still in existence today provide appropriate defences or, to adopt the current jargon, sufficient control mechanisms.

LORD WALKER [having considered the development of the tort of nuisance, and criticisms of the requirements of the 'dangerous' and 'non-natural' user of land in the *Burnie Port* case (1994) 120 ALR 42 at 54 continued:]...

[103] There is obvious force in this criticism. A proliferation of adjectival paraphrase may not succeed in giving a full explanation of the twin requirements, but some explanation is called for, since 'non-natural use' (the expression used by Lord Cairns LC in *Rylands v Fletcher* itself) is, as Lord Goff said in the *Cambridge Water* case [1994] 1 All ER 53 at 78, [1994] 2 AC 264 at 308, 'redolent of a different age'. In my opinion the twin requirements are best understood if they are taken together, as is implicit in Lord Moulton's reference to danger: '...some special use bringing with it increased danger to others'. It is the extraordinary risk to neighbouring property, if an escape occurs, which makes the land use 'special' for the purposes of the principle in *Rylands v Fletcher*.

[104] This point is brought out vividly in an interesting and scholarly article by Professor AWB Simpson, 'Legal Liability for Bursting Reservoirs: The Historical Context of *Rylands v Fletcher*' (1984) 13 JLS 209 at 219:

> '...In 19th century Britain there occurred two sensational reservoir disasters, and to appreciate the significance of these incidents it is important to appreciate the menacing character of a large dam once anxiety as to its security becomes current. Those who live or work in the area thought to be endangered by failure can conceive of themselves as permanently and continuously threatened; and depending on the state of the law, they may be, or at least think themselves to be, impotent in the face of the ever present threat. Nuclear power stations possess this menacing character for many people today, and it is not a product of the frequency of accidents at all.'

The same may be said of industrial complexes producing or processing explosive or volatile substances. During the first half of the twentieth century the terrible explosion at Rainham in Essex found its way into the law reports (*Rainham Chemical Works Ltd (in liq) v Belvedere Fish Guano Co Ltd* [1921] 2 AC 465, [1921] All ER Rep 48). During the second half of the twentieth century, the explosion at Flixborough in Humberside did not end in contested litigation. But no one who owned a house in the close vicinity of those disasters would readily have accepted that Lord Moulton's proposition was devoid of objective content.

[105] Where Lord Moulton's formulation becomes questionable is, as Lord Goff pointed out in the *Cambridge Water* case [1994] 1 All ER 53 at 79, [1994] 2 AC 264 at 308, his reference to land use 'for the general benefit of the community'. It is understandable that any court might be inclined to deal more strictly with a defendant who has profited from a dangerous activity conducted on his own land, and less strictly with persons conducting similar activities for the general public good. But in this area (which is some way removed from the 'give and take' of minor nuisances) the court cannot sensibly determine what is an ordinary or special (that is, specially dangerous) use of land by undertaking some utilitarian balancing of general good against individual risk. The court must beware of what David Campbell has called 'unsustainably ambitious claims to be able to identify the social welfare function' (see 'Of Coase & Corn: A (Sort of) Defence of Private Nuisance' (2000) 63 MLR 197 at 204)...The temptation to make a utilitarian judgment even led Viscount Simon and Lord Macmillan in *Read v J Lyons &*

Co Ltd [1946] 2 All ER 471 at 475, 478, [1947] AC 156 at 169–170, 174 to contemplate that in wartime the manufacture of explosive munitions might be regarded as an ordinary use of land. Regardless of any national emergency that sort of activity is (in Lord Goff's words in the *Cambridge Water* case [1994] 1 All ER 53 at 79, [1994] 2 AC 264 at 309) 'an almost classic case of non-natural use'.

[106] My Lords, it is most desirable, after Burnie, that this House should state, with as much precision as the subject matter allows, the way in which Lord Moulton's test, now 90 years old, should be understood and applied in the twenty-first century. I have had the great advantage of reading in draft the speeches of my noble and learned friends Lord Bingham of Cornhill and Lord Hoffmann. I respectfully agree with their observations on this topic, and in particular on what should now be understood by the 'non-natural' or 'special' use of land. I refrain from saying any more on the topic for fear of obscuring or qualifying in any way the clarity of my Lords' exposition.

[109] There has, as already noted, been some assimilation of the principles of nuisance and negligence in the limited area where the law imposes, in respect of an adventitious hazard, a measured duty of care (the phrase first used in England, I think, by Lord Wilberforce in *Goldman v Hargrave* [1966] 2 All ER 989 at 995, [1967] 1 AC 645 at 662). Your Lordships' House has in the *Delaware Mansions* case shown some readiness to extend the process of assimilation. But the principle in *Rylands v Fletcher* is the area of nuisance least open to that sort of assimilation. I am not persuaded that it would assist the development of the law to recast the *Rylands v Fletcher* principle as a 'non-delegable duty of care' (see *Burnie* [1996] 4 LRC 605 at 632–636, (1994) 120 ALR 42 at 61–65) especially if the end result were to stretch the principles of negligence so far that (in the words of Lord Macmillan in *Donoghue v Stevenson* [1932] AC 562 at 612, [1932] All ER Rep 1 at 26, cited in *Burnie* [1996] 4 LRC 605 at 636, (1994) 120 ALR 42 at 65): 'the law exacts a degree of diligence so stringent as to amount practically to a guarantee of safety.'

[116] For these reasons, and for the further reasons given by my noble and learned friends, Lord Bingham of Cornhill and Lord Hoffmann, I would dismiss this appeal.

[Lord Scott of Foscote delivered a speech in favour of dismissing the appeal on the basis that there had been no escape from the land, and agreeing with the reasons of Lord Bingham, Lord Hoffmann, and Lord Walker of Gestinthorpe.]

Appeal dismissed.

QUESTIONS

1. To what extent does *Rylands v Fletcher* remain a tort of 'strict liability'? Do you agree with Lord Hoffmann's withering remark at [39] that 'the intellectual effort devoted to the rule by judges and writers over many years has brought forth a mouse'? [Cf Horace, *Ars Poetica*: '*Parturient montes, nascetur ridiculus mus*' ('The mountains will go into labour, and give birth to a ridiculous mouse').] See further Nolan, note 1, post.

2. Is Lord Walker correct to say at [109] that *Rylands v Fletcher* is the area of nuisance least suitable for assimilation with the law of negligence? What, after *Cambridge Water* and *Transco*, is the precise relationship between nuisance and *Rylands v Fletcher*?

3. Should English tort law preferably develop in parallel with delict in (a) Scotland, or (b) France and Germany? Cf. the comparative study cited by Lord Bingham at [6].

4. In *Pride of Derby and Derbyshire Angling Association Ltd v British Celanese Ltd* [1953] Ch 149 at 189 Denning LJ suggested that a sewerage undertaker would not be liable for overflowing drains in *Rylands v Fletcher*, 'for the simple reason that the use of land for drainage purposes by the [undertaker] is "such a use as is proper for the general benefit of the community" [quoting *Rickards v Lothian* [1913] AC 263, 280]'. In *Marcic v*

Thames Water Utilities (p. 821, ante) the Court of Appeal shared Denning LJ's doubts about the applicability of *Rylands v Fletcher*, for the same reasons: [2002] EWCA Civ 64 at [46]. Does *Transco* require any reconsideration of Denning LJ's approach?

NOTES

1. For full analysis of *Rylands v Fletcher* after *Transco* see D. Nolan (2005) 121 LQR 421 and J. Murphy (2004) 24 OJLS 643. Murphy argues that *Rylands v Fletcher* developed quite separately from private nuisance, and thus suggests that notwithstanding the powerful dicta in *Read v Lyons* and now *Transco*, 'a brave judge' might still in the future decide that personal injuries fall within the rule (commending the judgment of Parker LJ in *Perry v Kendricks Transport Ltd* [1956] 1 All ER 154 at 160–161).

    Nolan also defends 'the distinctiveness of *Rylands v Fletcher*' on both historical and policy grounds (for instance, that assimilating *Rylands* with nuisance will be 'bad for nuisance' by obstructing the rationalisation of that tort proposed by C. Gearty [1989] CLJ 214). Both Murphy and Nolan reject the 'Australian solution' of absorption into negligence. Nolan, however, regrets that the House of Lords in *Transco* did not take the opportunity to kill off the tort altogether: 'sometimes it is better simply to extinguish the flickering flame that remains when legal developments leave past doctrines behind'.

    Other notes of *Transco* are by R. Bagshaw (2004) 120 LQR 388 and K. Amirthalingam [2004] CLJ 273.

2. For discussion of the 'non-delegable duty' (liability for torts of independent contractors) see further p. 1095 et seq, post.

3. For further comments on Lord Hoffmann's views about the relevance of insurance of damage to property (with which Lord Hobhouse vehemently disagreed), see further p. 1139, post.

4. Regarding Lord Hoffmann's remark at [39] that 'counsel could not find a reported case since the 1939–45 war in which anyone had succeeded in a claim under the rule', cf. *LMS International Ltd v Styrene Packaging & Insulation Ltd* [2005] EWHC 2065 (TCC) at [26]: 'there have in fact been quite a few cases since the Second World War where the rule in *Rylands v Fletcher* has been successfully relied on. A number of those cases were concerned with the escape of fire, and they were not all cited to the House of Lords', per Judge Peter Coulson QC.

5. In *McKenna v British Aluminium Ltd* [2002] Env LR 30 Neuberger J held that for a claim to be brought in *Rylands v Fletcher*, the claimant must have an interest in the land such as would be sufficient to maintain an action in private nuisance (on which see *Hunter v Canary Wharf*, p. 790, ante). However, it was argued for the claimants that Article 8 of the ECHR required that the common law should be extended in this respect, since an individual's right to protection of his home under Article 8 does not require him to have a property interest in the land. All members of a family should be able to bring a claim, not only the householder. The defendant submitted that it would nevertheless be inappropriate to extend torts based on the protection of *property rights* (like nuisance, or *Rylands v Fletcher*) to provide such protection. Neuberger J agreed that that argument was 'powerful' and 'may very well turn out to be right', but nevertheless refused to strike the case out given that the courts were still in the early days of the Human Rights Act, and 'bearing in mind in particular the way in which the case is pleaded, namely to include a common law tort analogous to nuisance'. For the assessment of damages

under the Human Rights Act for non-proprietary occupants, see *Dobson v Thames Water Utilities* [2008] 2 All ER 362, [2008] EWHC 2021 (TCC), noted p. 798, ante.

6.   Before leaving this section on the rule in *Rylands v Fletcher*, mention should be made of the question of reform of the law relating to dangerous things and activities. This matter was referred to by Lord Goff in the *Cambridge Water* case, where he inclined to the view that in general it was more appropriate for strict liability for high-risk activities to be imposed by Parliament (see also Lord Bingham at [7] in *Transco*). Consider alongside Lord Goff's reasons for preferring legislative intervention the view (in 1978) of the Pearson Commission, in vol. 1, chap. 31 of its Report, where the question of liability for exceptional risks was being considered. The Commission recommended that:

strict liability should be imposed on the controllers of things or operations in each of two categories—first, those which by their unusually hazardous nature require close, careful and skilled supervision, the failure of which may cause death or personal injury; and, secondly, those which, although normally by their nature perfectly safe, are likely, if they do go wrong, to cause serious and extensive casualties (para. 1643).

This second category includes things such as major stores and stadiums.

The favoured method for implementing this strict liability was for a statute to be passed containing general provisions which should be applied by statutory instruments (along with any other special provisions thought necessary) to certain listed dangerous things and activities (para. 1651). The Commission thought that contributory negligence and voluntary assumption of risk should be permitted as defences, although with a qualification in the case of the latter where an employee is injured (para. 1654). Statutory authority was not to provide a defence (para. 1653), nor in general was the fact that the claimant was a trespasser, though here it was proposed that the maker of a statutory instrument should have the power to permit it as a defence (para. 1656). Any other defences (a majority thought) should be set out in the statute and stated to be applicable to all listed things and activities (para. 1659); however, by a majority the Commission wished to exclude the defence of act of a third party (para. 1660).

For comment see J. G. Fleming (1979) 42 MLR 249 at 265–267; *Accident Compensation After Pearson*, edited by Allen, Bourn and Holyoak, pp. 46–49 and 55–61 (J. A. Jolowicz) and pp. 234–238 (P. S. Atiyah); K. M. Stanton in *Torts Tomorrow: A Tribute to John Fleming* (Sydney, 1998), edited by N. Mullany and A. M. Linden, chap. 6. See further *Winfield & Jolowicz*, p. 699, who point out that 'power already exists [under the Health and Safety at Work etc. Act 1974] to utilise delegated legislation to go a good way along the road to statutory strict liability'. Stanton, op cit., p. 96, is sympathetic to the refusal in *Cambridge Water* to introduce 'a vague general principle of strict liability for ultra-hazardous activities', but continues that 'it is far from clear that the legislature could frame legislation designed to apply generally to dangerous activities in a way which would do a significantly better job'. Cf. the debates concerning products liability, pp. 610 et seq, ante.

In 1970 the rule in *Rylands v Fletcher* was considered by the Law Commission (*Civil Liability for Dangerous Things and Activities*, Law Com. No. 32), but, because of the scope of the inquiry which the Law Commission was invited to undertake, that body refrained from making any recommendations to change the law (see paras. 2, 11 and 18 of the Report).

4 FIRE

■ The Fires Prevention (Metropolis) Act 1774

86. No action to lie against a person where the fire accidentally begins.—And…no action, suit or process whatever shall be had, maintained or prosecuted against any person in whose house, chamber, stable, barn or other building, or on whose estate any fire shall…accidentally begin, nor shall any recompense be made by such person for any damage suffered thereby, any law, usage or custom to the contrary notwithstanding:…provided that no contract or agreement made between landlord and tenant shall be hereby defeated or made void.

NOTES

1. Despite the title of this statute, this section is not restricted to the 'Metropolis' but applies generally: *Filliter v Phippard* (1847) 11 QB 347. That case also decided that the section does not give any protection where the fire has been caused by the defendant's negligence, nor where the defendant intentionally lit the fire.

2. Further consideration was given to the 1774 Act in *Musgrove v Pandelis* [1919] 2 KB 43. In that case, a fire occurred in a garage at the back of a house of which the claimant was the lessee. The garage had living rooms above. Part of the garage had been let to the defendant, who kept his car there, and on one occasion when his servant started the car, the petrol in the carburettor caught fire. If the servant had turned off the petrol tap straightaway the fire would have been rendered harmless, but when he did attempt to do this, the fire, which by then was burning more fiercely, thwarted his efforts. The fire spread and burnt the car, the garage, the claimant's rooms above and some of his furniture. The defendant relied on s. 86 of the 1774 Act, and the Court of Appeal resolved two questions relating to its construction. The word 'fire' in the Act, was interpreted to mean 'the fire which causes the damage'. This was held to be the fire, fed by petrol from the tank, which spread and burnt the car, and was to be distinguished from the original fire in the carburettor, which would have burnt itself out if the petrol tap had been turned off. Thus the Act would not protect the defendant since the later fire did not 'accidentally begin', but was a result of the servant's negligence. Is this a sensible distinction? (Note, however, that this approach was accepted by the Privy Council in *Goldman v Hargrave* [1967] 1 AC 645, [1966] 2 All ER 989.) It was also held in *Musgrove v Pandelis* that the Act did not provide a defence where liability for fire could be based on the principle of *Rylands v Fletcher*, a principle which Bankes LJ thought had existed in the law 'long before' that decision. For criticism, see A. I. Ogus [1969] CLJ 104 at 113–116.

3. The view that the 1774 Act is inapplicable where the *Rylands v Fletcher* principle is invoked was doubted, but followed, by MacKenna J in *Mason v Levy Auto Parts of England Ltd* [1967] 2 QB 530, [1967] 2 All ER 62. Having discussed *Musgrove v Pandelis*, he went on to say (at pp. 69–70):

   What then is the principle? As Romer LJ pointed out in *Collingwood v Home and Colonial Stores Ltd* [1936] 3 All ER 200 at 208–209, it cannot be exactly that of *Rylands v Fletcher* (1868) LR 3 HL 330. A defendant is not held liable under *Rylands v Fletcher* unless two conditions are satisfied: (i) that he has brought something on to his land likely to do mischief if it escapes, which has in fact escaped, and (ii) that these things happened in the course of some non-natural user of the land. However, in *Musgrove*'s case, [1919] 2 KB 43, the car had not escaped from the land, neither had the petrol in its tank. The principle must be, Romer LJ said, [1936] 3 All ER at p. 209, the wider one on which *Rylands v Fletcher* itself was based, *Sic utere tuo ut alienum non laedas*. If, for the rule in *Musgrove*'s case to apply, there need be no escape of anything brought on to the defendant's land, what must be proved against him? There is, it seems to me, a choice of two alternatives. The first would require the plaintiff to prove (a) that the defendant had brought something on to his land likely to do mischief if it escaped, (b) that he had done so in the course of a non-natural user of the land, and (c) that the thing had ignited and that the fire had spread. The alternative would be to hold the defendant liable if (a) he brought on to his land things likely to catch fire, and kept them there in such conditions that, if they did ignite, the fire would be likely to spread to the plaintiff's land, (b) he did so in the course of some non-natural use, and (c) the thing ignited and the fire spread.

'The second test is, I think, the more reasonable one, since to make the likelihood of damage if the thing escapes a criterion of liability, when the thing has not in fact escaped but has caught fire, would not be very sensible. I propose, therefore, to apply the second test....'

4.   *Mason v Levy Auto Parts* was recently followed in *LMS International Ltd v Styrene Packaging & Insulation Ltd* [2005] EWHC 2065 (TCC), where the defendants were liable in negligence, nuisance, and *Rylands v Fletcher*.

■ Alcock v Wraith
p. 1095, post

■ H and N Emanuel Ltd v Greater London Council
Court of Appeal [1971] 2 All ER 835

The London County Council (LCC—the predecessor of the Greater London Council, GLC) managed two prefabricated bungalows for the government, who had put them up on land owned by the Council. In 1962 there was a request by the LCC to the Ministry of Housing for the bungalows to be removed, and their removal was approved by that Ministry: in the meantime, the LCC kept control and their district foreman held the keys. The Ministry of Housing asked the Ministry of Works to remove the bungalows, and the method adopted by the latter Ministry was to sell the bungalows to Mr King, a contractor. The contract specified that no rubbish was to be burnt on the site, that work was not to be started until the contractor had received written notice of the bungalows' release (which the Ministry of Works issued) and that the local authority, from whom the keys were to be obtained, must be told of the date of the commencement of the dismantling work. After the contractor obtained the written notice of release from the foreman, his men went to the site. However, they lit a bonfire, and sparks set fire to property on the plaintiff's adjoining premises. There was evidence that the burning of rubbish by the contractor was a regular practice, which was known to the Ministry of Works, and it was 'reasonable to assume' (per Lord Denning MR) that the practice and the term in the contract against it were also known by the LCC's foreman. James J held both the Council and Mr King liable and the Council appealed.

LORD DENNING MR: ...
After considering the cases, it is my opinion that the occupier of a house or land is liable for the escape of fire which is due to the negligence not only of his servants, but also of his independent contractors

and of his guests, and of anyone who is there with his leave or licence. The only circumstances when the occupier is not liable for the negligence is when it is the negligence of a stranger. It was so held in a case in the Year Books 570 years ago, *Beaulieu v Finglam*,[19] which is well translated by Mr Fifoot in his book on the *History and Sources of the Common Law*.[20] The occupier is, therefore, liable for the negligence of an independent contractor, such as the man who comes in to repair the pipes and uses a blowlamp: see *Balfour v Barty-King*[1]; and of a guest who negligently drops a lighted match: see *Boulcott Golf Club Inc v Engelbrecht*.[2] The occupier is liable because he is the occupier and responsible in that capacity for those who come by his leave and licence: see *Sturges v Hackett*.[3]

But the occupier is not liable for the escape of fire which is not due to the negligence of anyone. Sir John Holt himself said in *Tuberville v Stampe*[4] that if a man is properly burning up weeds or stubble and, owing to an unforeseen windstorm, without negligence, the fire is carried into his neighbour's ground, he is not liable. Again, if a haystack is properly built at a safe distance, and yet bursts into flames by spontaneous combustion, without negligence, the occupier is not liable. That is to be inferred from *Vaughan v Menlove*.[5] So also if a fire starts without negligence owing to an unknown defect in the electric wiring: *Collingwood v Home and Colonial Stores Ltd*[6]; or a spark leaps out of the fireplace without negligence: *Sochacki v Sas*.[7] All those cases are covered, if not by the common law, at any rate by the Fires Prevention (Metropolis) Act 1774, which covers all cases where a fire begins or spreads by accident without negligence. But that Act does not cover a fire which begins or is spread by negligence: see *Filliter v Phippard*,[8] *Musgrove v Pandelis*[9] and *Goldman v Hargrave*.[10]

Nevertheless, as I have said earlier, the occupier is not liable if the outbreak of fire is due to the negligence of a 'stranger'. But who is a 'stranger' for this purpose?…I think a 'stranger' is anyone who in lighting a fire or allowing it to escape acts contrary to anything which the occupier could anticipate that he would do: such as the person in *Rickards v Lothian*.[11] Even if it is a man whom you have allowed or invited into your house, nevertheless, if his conduct in lighting a fire is so alien to your invitation that he should *qua* the fire be regarded as a trespasser, he is a 'stranger'. Such as the man in Scrutton LJ's well-known illustration[12]:

> 'When you invite a person into your house to use the staircase you do not invite him to slide down the bannisters…'

which was quoted by Lord Atkin in *Hillen and Pettigrew v ICI (Alkali) Ltd*[13]…

There has been much discussion about the exact legal basis of liability for fire. The liability of the occupier can be said to be a strict liability in this sense that he is liable for the negligence not only of his servants but also of independent contractors and, indeed, of anyone except a 'stranger'. By the same token it can be said to be a 'vicarious liability', because he is liable for the defaults of others as well as his own. It can also be said to be a liability under the principle of *Rylands v Fletcher*,[14] because fire is undoubtedly a dangerous thing which is likely to do damage if it escapes. But I do not think it necessary to put it into any one of these three categories. It goes back to the time when no such categories were thought of. Suffice it to say that the extent of the liability is now well defined as I have stated it. The occupier is liable for the escape of fire which is due to the negligence of anyone other than a stranger.

Seeing that in this case the contractors were negligent both in lighting the fire in that place and in allowing it to spread, the only question is whether the LCC were 'occupiers' of the land and whether the contractors were 'strangers' to them.…I am clear that the LCC were occupiers of this site. They were the owners of it. Their foreman had the keys of the prefabs. Anyone who wanted to do anything

---

[19] (1401) YB 2 Hen 4, fo. 18, pl. 6. [20] 1949 p. 166. [1] [1957] 1 QB 496, [1957] 1 All ER 156.
[2] [1945] NZLR 556. [3] [1962] 3 All ER 166, [1962] 1 WLR 1257.
[4] (1697) 1 Ld Raym 264. [5] (1837) 3 Bing NC 468. [6] [1936] 3 All ER 200.
[7] [1947] 1 All ER 344. [8] (1847) 11 QB 347. [9] [1919] 2 KB 43. [10] [1966] 2 All ER 989.
[11] [1913] AC 263. [12] *The Carlgarth* [1927] P 93 at 110.
[13] [1936] AC 65 at 69, [1935] All ER Rep 555 at 558.
[14] (1868) LR 3 HL 330, [1861–73] All ER Rep 1.

with them had to get permission from him. On behalf of the LCC he could clearly say to anyone: 'You are not to light a fire on the site'; or: 'If you do light a fire, it must be well away from the road', or as the case may be. It may be that the Ministry of Housing and the Ministry of Works were also 'occupiers' because, as I pointed out in *Wheat v Lacon*,[15] there are often many 'occupiers' who have a sufficient degree of control to be responsible. But the position of the Ministry does not arise here.

The question: who is a 'stranger'? is more difficult. But I am quite clear that the contractors' men were not strangers. They were present on the site with the leave and with the knowledge of the LCC; true it is that they were prohibited from burning rubbish, but, nevertheless, it was their regular practice to burn it. The LCC ought to have taken better steps to prevent them. Not having done so, they cannot disclaim responsibility for the fire. The LCC could reasonably have anticipated that these men might start a fire; and that is enough, just as in the case in 1401[16] the householder might reasonably have anticipated that his guest might light a candle.

I think the judge was quite right. I would dismiss this appeal.

PHILLIMORE LJ: . . .
The LCC were undoubtedly occupiers of this land. They were sued in that capacity and they did not call any evidence to suggest otherwise. As such they owed a duty to their neighbours which is best described in the old latin maxim: *sic utere tuo ut alienum non laedas*. As Markham J put it in *Beaulieu v Fingham*:[17]

> 'I shall answer to my neighbour for him who enters my house by my leave or knowledge whether he is guest to me or my servant, if either of them acts in such a way with a candle or other things that my neighbour's house is burned.'

Since the Fires Prevention (Metropolis) Act 1774 it is I think necessary to insert the word 'negligently' after the word 'acts'.

. . . Now, it seems to me that if an occupier owes a duty, he cannot, by handing over the performance of the work on his land to somebody else refrain from any sort or kind of supervision, say: 'Well, I have delegated my responsibilities to the Ministry.' I think the LCC and consequently the GLC are liable for what was in effect the negligence of the Ministry of Works in failing to supervise the activities of the contractor. The Ministry of Works was on the site with leave and licence and indeed at the request of the LCC, and the LCC cannot escape liability for their act or omission any more than could the owner of the house in *Beaulieu v Fingham*.[10] Accordingly I would agree that this appeal must be dismissed.

[EDMUND DAVIES LJ delivered a judgment agreeing that the appeal should be dismissed.]

Appeal dismissed.

NOTES

1.   In *H and N Emanuel Ltd v Greater London Council*, Lord Denning MR referred to *Sochacki v Sas* [1947] 1 All ER 344, where a lodger was held not liable for damage caused by a fire which spread from his room, and which was probably caused by a spark from the fire in the fireplace setting light to the floorboards. It would appear that the lodger had lit the original fire, but he had not been negligent. Liability under *Rylands v Fletcher* was denied in particular on the ground that this was an ordinary user of the room. Lord Denning MR thought that, whatever the common law position, the case would

---

[15] [1966] AC at p. 578, [1966] 1 All ER at p. 594.
[16] *Beaulieu v Fingham* (1401) YB 2 Hen 4, fo. 18, pl. 6.
[17] (1401) YB 2 Hen 4, fo. 18, pl. 6.

be covered by the 1774 Act. Although *Fillite v Phippard* (1847) 11 QB 347 appears to exclude from the Act's protection the intentional fire (on which see F. H. Newark (1944) 6 NILQ 134 at 137–140), Lord Denning's view can be supported on the type of analysis adopted in *Musgrove v Pandelis* [1919] 2 KB 43—that the fire with which the Act is concerned started when the floorboards were set alight, and this fire did 'accidentally begin'. (See, however, *Musgrove v Pandelis* [1919] 2 KB at p. 51; cf. *Job Edwards Ltd v Birmingham Navigations* [1924] 1 KB 341 at 361.) *Salmond & Heuston* take the view that the Act almost certainly applies to fires intentionally lit which spread accidentally, but see the contrary view expressed in *New Zealand Forest Products Ltd v O'Sullivan* [1974] 2 NZLR 80 at 84.

2. Compare with Lord Denning's judgment in *H and N Emanuel Ltd v Greater London Council* the view of Mahon J in *New Zealand Forest Products Ltd v O'Sullivan,* and also in *Holderness v Goslin* [1975] 2 NZLR 46. In the former case Mahon J referred to the rule in *Rylands v Fletcher* as an accepted basis for strict liability for the escape of fire; this, he thought, was inconsistent with Lord Denning's opinion in *H and N Emanuel Ltd v Greater London Council* in so far as that opinion 'may be thought to have substituted negligence as the only basis of liability for escape of fire' ([1974] 2 NZLR at p. 88). Mahon J's dislike of the importation of negligence into liability for the escape of fire was also expressed in *Holderness v Goslin*; it was the reason why, in considering who was a stranger for whose fire a defendant would not be liable, he rejected the test (to be found in Lord Denning's judgment in *H and N Emanuel Ltd v Greater London Council*) of what the occupier could anticipate. In Mahon J's view, when the occupier has a power to control the activities of the visitor, then that person is not a stranger.

3. In *Ribee v Norrie* (2001) 33 HLR 69 the Court of Appeal applied Lord Denning's test, holding that the defendant landlord could reasonably have anticipated that his licensees or tenants, or their guests, might smoke in the common parts of the building, and 'could reasonably have anticipated that the cigarettes would not always be extinguished as they should be and that they could be left to smoulder and cause a fire', per Ward LJ at [23]. Thus, those who started the fire had not been strangers vis-à-vis the landlord. Ward LJ expressly refused at [30] to enter the 'academic debate' on whether damages for personal injuries (as suffered by the claimant *in casu*) could be recovered in nuisance or *Rylands v Fletcher*; for the instant purpose it was 'sufficient to repeat that the fire was negligently caused, the defendant is responsible for it and Miss Ribee entitled to her damages in respect of both her property and her health'. On this see further p. 853, ante.

4. In *Johnson (t/a Johnson Butchers) v BJW Property Developments* [2002] 3 All ER 574, [2002] EWHC 1131 (TCC), a fire in a domestic grate set fire to neighbouring premises because the contractor who installed the fireplace had negligently failed to provide a fire-proof lining. Judge Thornton QC followed *Sochacki v Sas* [1947] 1 All ER 344, holding that strict liability does not apply to a domestic fire. However, he further held that *H & N Emanuel Ltd v Greater London Council* recognised an exception to the doctrine that prevented an occupier being liable for an independent contractor's acts (on which see further p. 1100, post), and accordingly held the defendants liable for their contractor's negligence. On the general issue of liability for fire, Judge Thornton at [17] noted that he had to consider no fewer than four distinct causes of action, being the old Year Book liability for the escape of *ignis suus* (discussed by Lord Denning in

Emanuel v GLC), the escape of fire resulting from a dangerous use of land (*Rylands v Fletcher*), negligence, and nuisance. These areas of law, he pointedly commented, remain 'distinct' and yet are interrelated in a 'complex' fashion: 'The complexity of this area of law arises because each cause of action has moved slowly towards the others yet it remains unclear what is the extent to which all four causes of action have been assimilated, particularly as regards a defence of an occupier based on the negligence of an independent contractor.'

CHAPTER FIFTEEN

DELIBERATE INTERFERENCE WITH INTERESTS IN TRADE OR BUSINESS

The courts are reluctant to protect relational economic interests from *negligent* interference (see chap. 4, ante). Pragmatic objections, based on the fear of crushing liability, do not, however, apply to conduct which is specifically *aimed* at the claimant. Indeed, it was at one time suggested that intentionally inflicted harm is always tortious, unless justified. But this is not the rule of modern English law. Broadly speaking, liability in these so-called 'economic torts' is limited to the following circumstances, in all of which there must be proof of damage.

(1) The combination of two or more persons in a 'conspiracy' (a) whose predominant purpose is to inflict damage on the claimant rather than to serve their own bona fide and legitimate interests—variously described as 'lawful means conspiracy' or 'conspiracy to injure'—or (b) who use unlawful means intentionally to harm the claimant, regardless of their predominant purpose, often described as an 'unlawful means' or 'wrongful means' conspiracy' (p. 865, post).

(2) The intentional interference by A with a contract between B and C with knowledge of, or recklessness as to, its terms, by inducing B to break his contract with C (p. 891, post): the scope of this tort of 'inducement of breach of contract' was recently narrowed and redefined considerably in the seminal House of Lords decision in the combined cases of *OBG Ltd v Allan* [2007] 4 All ER 545, [2007] UKHL 21, which has substantially reshaped this area of the law.

(3) The intentional use by A of unlawful means (or threats by A to use such unlawful means), with the intention of causing economic loss to B, which (a) interfere with the freedom of action of B—described by Lord Hoffmann in *OBG Ltd v Allan* as 'two party' interference with trade by unlawful means (p. 917, post); or (b) interfere with the freedom of a third party ('C') in a way which was unlawful as against C and which was intended to cause loss to B, but only where the unlawful acts directed towards C were independently actionable by C, or would have been so actionable had C suffered loss—described by the House of Lords in *OBG Ltd v Allan* as 'third party' interference with trade by unlawful means' (p. 923, post).

(4) Representations by a trader that the claimant is in some way associated with his business, goods or services, where the representation is calculated to deceive, described as 'passing off' (p. 934, post).

(5) The making of a false statement of existing fact by the defendant with knowledge of its falsity and with the intention the claimant should rely upon it, where the claimant does rely upon it—known as the tort of 'deceit' (p. 939, post).

The wide tort of interference by unlawful means, which developed in the wake of cases such as *Rookes v Barnard* [1964] AC 1129, [1964] 1 All ER 367 (p. 917, post) brought together a variety of different forms of action that had previously often been classified as separate torts, such as the hitherto distinct causes of action for intimidation and unlawful interference with trade. This tort was regarded by some commentators as capable of being extended further than situations (3)(a) and (b) above to cover a wide range of forms of interference using unlawful means, and thereby of becoming a 'genus' tort of interference by unlawful means that would give a degree of unity to this chaotic area of the law. However, the majority of the House of Lords in *OBG Ltd v Allan* gave the tort of causing economic loss by unlawful means a much narrower and circumscribed range. The decision in *OBG* also appears to have introduced a distinction between 'two party' and 'third party' interference by unlawful means, i.e. between (3)(a) and (3)(b) above, with 'third party' interference having a narrower scope. However, the extent of the distinction between (3)(a) and (3)(b) remains unclear, for now.

In general, classifying these causes of action within a coherent framework can be difficult. Torts (1)–(3) are often described as torts involving 'wrongful actions', while torts (4) and (5) are described as involving misrepresentation. However, this form of classification can mislead as much as enlighten. In general, these torts require some element of intention to cause harm on the part of the defendant, but the nature of the intention required to establish liability can vary: in addition, in the case of passing-off, a 'misrepresentation' which 'deceives' the public at large is required, but not intention *per se*. For example, intention to induce a breach of contract is required for (2) above, but intention to cause economic harm to the defendant is required for (3). Even grouping these causes of action under a generic category of 'economic torts', as is sometimes done, is problematic: passing-off (action (4) above) primarily protects goodwill, not economic interests *per se*.

All these torts have to be considered against the background of the still authoritative decision of the House of Lords in *Allen v Flood* [1898] AC 1 (customarily described as the 'great' case of *Allen v Flood*, p. 865, post) that conduct which is not otherwise tortious does not become so simply because it was carried out with the deliberate purpose of harming the economic interests of another. In a market economy based upon competition and with an important role still assigned to trade union activities, making conduct tortious which deliberately caused economic loss to another would be unsustainable. However, note that this general principle is subject to the anomalous exception of conspiracy to injure ((1)(a), ante), but that tort is itself now strictly limited to conduct the predominant purpose of which is to harm the claimant (p. 878, post).

Although the 'unlawful means' torts ((1)(b)–(3) above) do not require a 'predominant purpose' to injure, the extent to which there should be a requirement within each of these different torts that defendants must somehow have 'aimed' their conduct at the defendant is a matter of lively debate. One view is that there should be sufficient intention where the defendant knew that harm to the claimant was an inevitable consequence of the defendant's act. Another view is that, although there is no need to prove that the defendant's predominant purpose was to harm the claimant, it is necessary to show that the act was directed at the claimant and that the harm was more than an incidental side-effect or a foreseeable or inevitable consequence of one's actions. The point of such 'aiming' requirements is to protect purely competitive behaviour and to limit the scope of these torts. A defence of justification is also available for some of these torts, which again acts as a control device in certain circumstances.

This desire to restrain the scope of the economic torts played a major role in the recent House of Lords decision in *OBG v Allan*; their Lordships adopted a narrow definition of torts (2) and 3(b) above, on the basis that the scope of liability under the economic torts should be confined and clearly defined. The scope of the tort of inducing a breach of contract ((2) above) was confined to where a breach of contract had actually taken place, in contrast to earlier decisions, which had accepted that liability could exist for interference with the performance of a contract. In addition, the majority of their Lordships considered that the 'unlawful means' required for the tort of causing loss by unlawful means had to be independently actionable by the third party affected, or else have been actionable by that third party had they suffered loss (with Lord Nicholls dissenting on this point). However, the subsequent decision of the House of Lords in *Revenue and Customs Commissioners v Total Network SL* [2008] 2 All ER 413, [2008] UKHL 19 (p. 883, post) established in contrast that where an action was brought in respect of an unlawful means conspiracy (tort 1(b) above), the required 'unlawful means' needed to establish liability on the part of the defendants could include conduct not in itself independently actionable by the claimants. In so doing, their Lordships consciously adopted a different approach to conspiracy than they had previously to interference by unlawful means.

The different approaches taken in *OBG* and *Total Network* demonstrate the underlying complexity and uncertainty that afflicts this area of law. Lord Wedderburn commented three decades ago that the economic torts have been at best 'a ramshackle construction for decades' ((1983) 46 MLR 224): it could be argued that little has changed. There has been no Lord Atkin ready to formulate a general principle, parallel to the duty of care, to unify these ramshackle torts, which collectively have been described by Lord Hoffmann as an 'extremely obscure' area of tort law (*OBG v Allan* [2007] 4 All ER 545 at 573). Concepts such as 'contract', 'right', 'property', and 'trade' have been used to delimit the scope of the torts (although there seems to be no reason why some of them should not protect other intangible interests, such as the alienation of affection). Vague words such as 'malice', 'inducement', 'interference', and 'unlawful means' have been used, with little consistency, to describe the conduct outlawed in the various torts. Loose terminology, casual *obiter dicta*, and imprecise analysis of leading precedent have tended to disfigure many of the key decisions in this area.

P. Sales and D. Stilitz (1999) 115 LQR 411 attempted a unification of this area of the law (with passing off and deceit exempted as *sui generis* torts) based on the proposition that there should be a presumption that it is a tort to cause harm intentionally by unlawful means, a proposal reminiscent of German law, which declares actionable all harm caused intentionally and against good morals. *Allen v Flood* (p. 865, post) stands in the way of a general tort of intentionally causing harm, which is why Sales and Stilitz required 'unlawful means'. In their unification theory, the argument was made that arguing that actions which involved a civil wrong against another person or breach of a criminal statute and perhaps even a statutory duty ('any act that the defendant is not at liberty to commit': (1999) 115 LQR 411, at 436) should be sufficient to ground liability. Sales and Stilitz argued that the potentially very wide scope of this unified approach could be kept in bounds by the imposition of a requirement that a defendant would have to have a specific intention to 'target' the claimant.

However, the problem with this unification attempt is that the definition of 'unlawful means' used included types of harm not presently recognised in other torts, including breaches of the criminal law or breaches of statutory duty which, under current English doctrine, would not create private rights of action (see chap. 12, ante). If we take seriously the central argument deployed against the creation of torts based on particular statutory duties, namely that Parliament did not intend to create private rights of action, it is difficult to see how adding the element of intentionality changes the situation, and justifies turning breaches of the criminal law and statutory regulation into springboards for private causes of action. In *OBG v Allen*, the majority of the House of Lords rejected this unification approach, clearly differentiated the torts of inducement to breach a contract and causing loss by unlawful means, while substantially narrowing the scope of both. (However, note Lord Nicholls's support for Sales and Stilitz's views in his minority opinion in *OBG v Allan* [2007] 4 All ER 545, at [173] (p. 912 post).) The subsequent decision of the House of Lords in *Revenue and Customs Commissioners v Total Network SL* has further widened the distinctions that exist between the different economic torts.

It may be a mistake to lament the absence of a single unifying framework in this area. The apparently divergent decisions in *OBG* and *Total Network* reflect broad agreement amongst their Lordships that the economic torts should not and cannot be herded within a single comprehensive framework. In different ways, both *OBG* and *Total Network* vindicate the suggestion made in the previous edition of this book that the central issues involved in the application of the economic torts concern 'not the scope of what counts as tortious conduct but who can sue and who can be sued in situations in which some well-established tort or other form of actionable wrong has been committed' (p. 851, previous edition). However, the complex framework of the economic torts continues to generate inconsistencies and uncertainties.

The difficulties presented to the student by these torts are compounded by the fact that many of the reported cases arise from applications for interlocutory injunctions to prevent the commission of *alleged* torts or their continuance pending the trial of the action, and so are concerned only with the question of whether or not there is a serious issue to be tried, without full investigation of the facts or of the legal principles.

Note however that in contrast with torts (1)–(4) above, both passing-off and deceit have clear and well-established definitions, a distinct role in regulating conduct in society, and have undergone little if any judicial reconstruction in recent times. It is also worth emphasising that the economic torts in general play a residual but nevertheless important role in the regulation of competition between traders, which may include the extremely important 'Eurotort' of breach of EU law where this has direct effect (see H. Carty (1988) 104 LQR 250, at 255, and see also p. 709, ante). There is also a growing awareness of the relevance of the economic torts in the context of commercial disputes, and a willingness to make use of these torts in new and creative ways in litigation. Sometimes depicted as residual, vestigial, or largely redundant, the economic torts in reality retain considerable significance.

Finally, it should be remembered that the economic torts (with again the exception of passing-off and deceit) largely developed in the sphere of industrial conflict, in which the fundamental problem has always been the incompatibility of collective industrial action with the individualist notions underpinning much of the nineteenth-century common law. When parliamentary policy favoured collective bargaining without legal restraint (broadly speaking, between 1906–1971 and 1974–1979), legislation limited the operation of specific economic torts committed by persons acting 'in contemplation or furtherance of a trade dispute'. At times (e.g. *Rookes v Barnard* [1964] AC 1129, [1964] 1 All ER 367, p. 917, post) the courts bypassed the statutory immunities by developing new torts, leading Parliament to restore and even to extend the immunities. By contrast, the policy of the Employment Acts 1980, and 1982, 1988 and 1990 and the Trade Union Act 1984 was to place severe restrictions on industrial action by withdrawing the immunities in a number of circumstances which are defined with great complexity. The study of these changing policies and the immunities belongs to labour law. However, the formative impact of this background upon the development of these torts should not be underestimated, as it continues to shape judicial attitudes towards these forms of action. It has in recent years encouraged the tendency amongst judges and academic commentators to rein in the scope of the economic torts, which has been described by Carty as an 'abstentionist' approach (*Carty*, p 6). This is exemplified by the following comments made by Baroness Hale in her judgment in *OBG v Allan*, at [306]:

It is also consistent with legal policy to limit rather than to encourage the expansion of liability in this area. In the modern age, Parliament has shown itself more than ready to legislate to draw the line between fair and unfair trade competition or between fair and unfair trade union activity. This can involve major economic and social questions which are often politically sensitive and require more complicated answers than the courts can devise. Such things are better left to Parliament. The common law need do no more than draw the lines that it might be expected to draw: procuring an actionable wrong between the third party and the target or committing an actionable... wrong against the third party inhibiting his freedom to trade with the target.

A similar reluctance to expand the existing parameters of these torts can be seen in *L'Oreal SA v Bellure NV* [2007] RPC 14, [2007] EWCA Civ 968, where the Court of Appeal refused to extend passing-off into a general tort of unfair competition.

1 CONSPIRACY

■ Allen v Flood
House of Lords [1895–9] All ER Rep 52

The plaintiffs, Flood and Taylor, were shipwrights employed to repair the woodwork on a ship. Members of the Boilermakers' Society, who worked with iron, discovered that the plaintiffs had previously repaired ironwork on another ship. Allen, the district secretary of the Boilermakers' Society, told the employers that the boilermakers would not work if the plaintiffs were allowed to do so. As a result the plaintiffs were dismissed that same day. All the men were free to leave their employment at the end of each day and they had no right to re-engagement on the following day.

Kennedy J ruled that there was no evidence of conspiracy or of intimidation or of coercion or of breach of contract. The jury found that Allen maliciously induced the employers to discharge the plaintiffs from their employment and not to re-engage them. He gave judgment for the plaintiffs for £20 each: [1895] 2 QB 21.

The Court of Appeal affirmed that decision: [1895] 2 QB 21. Allen appealed to the House of Lords. The case was argued for four days before seven Law Lords. Eight judges were then summoned to attend and the case was re-argued before all of them and, in addition, Lord Ashbourne and Lord James. The judges were asked the question: 'Assuming the evidence given by the [respondent's] witnesses to be correct, was there any evidence of a cause of

action fit to be left to the jury?' By a majority of 6–2 the judges answered this in the affirmative. However, the House of Lords allowed the appeal by a majority of 6–3.

LORD WATSON:...
Although the rule may be otherwise with regard to crimes, the law of England does not...take into
account motive as constituting an element of civil wrong. Any invasion of the civil rights of another person is in itself a legal wrong, carrying with it liability to repair its necessary and natural consequences, in
so far as these are injurious to the person whose right is infringed, whether the motive which prompted
it be good, bad, or indifferent. But the existence of a bad motive, in the case of an act which is not in
itself illegal, will not convert that act into a civil wrong, for which reparation is due. A wrongful act,
done knowingly, and with a view to its injurious consequences, may, in the sense of law, be malicious;
but such malice derives its essential character from the circumstance that the act done constitutes a
violation of the law.... The root of the principle is that, in any legal question, malice depends not upon
evil motive which influenced the mind of the actor, but upon the illegal character of the act which he
contemplated and committed. In my opinion, it is alike consistent with reason and common sense that
when the act done is, apart from the feelings which prompted it, legal, the civil law ought to take no
cognisance of its motive....

There are, in my opinion, two grounds only upon which a person who procures the act of another
can be made legally responsible for its consequences. In the first place, he will incur liability if he knowingly, and for his own ends, induces that other person to commit an actionable wrong. In the second
place, when the act induced is within the right of the immediate actor, and is, therefore, not wrongful
in so far as he is concerned, it may yet be to the detriment of a third party, and, in that case, according
to the law laid down by the majority in *Lumley* v. *Gye*,[1] the inducer may be held liable if he can be shown
to have procured his object by the use of illegal means directed against that third party....

The doctrine laid down by the Court of Appeal in this case and in *Temperton* v. *Russell*,[2] with regard
to the efficacy of evil motives in making to use the words of LORD ESHER 'that unlawful which would
otherwise be lawful,' is stated in wide and comprehensive terms; but the majority of the consulted
judges who approve of the doctrine have only dealt with it as applying to cases of interference with
a man's trade or employment. Even in that more limited application, it would lead, in some cases, to
singular results. One who committed an act not in itself illegal, but attended with consequences detrimental to several other persons, would incur liability to those of them whom it was proved that he
intended to injure, and the rest of them would have no remedy. A master who dismissed a servant
engaged from day to day, or whose contract of service had expired, and declined to give him further
employment because he disliked the man, and desired to punish him, would be liable in an action for
tort. And ex pari ratione, a servant would be liable in damages to a master whom he disliked, if he left
his situation at the expiry of his engagement and declined to be re-engaged, in the knowledge and
with the intent that the master would be put to considerable inconvenience, expense, and loss before
he could provide a substitute....

LORD HERSCHELL:...
It is to be observed, in the first place, that the company in declining to employ the plaintiffs were violat-
ing no contract; they were doing nothing wrongful in the eye of the law. The course which they took
was dictated by self-interest; they were anxious to avoid the inconvenience to their business which
would ensue from a cessation of work on the part of the ironworkers. It was not contended at the Bar
that merely to induce them to take this course would constitute a legal wrong, but it was said to do
so because the person inducing them acted maliciously. Lord Esher MR declined in the present case
to define what was meant by 'maliciously'; he considered this a question to be determined by a jury.
But if acts are, or are not, unlawful and actionable, according as this element of malice be present or
absent, I think it essential to determine what is meant by it. I can imagine no greater danger to the

---

[1] (1853) 2 E & B 216, [1843–60] All ER Rep 208.   [2] [1893] 1 QB 715, [1891–4] All ER Rep 724.

community than that a jury should be at liberty to impose the penalty of paying damages for acts which are otherwise lawful because they choose, without any legal definition of the term, to say that they are malicious. No one would know what his rights were. The result would be to put all our actions at the mercy of a particular tribunal whose view of their propriety might differ from our own.

However malice may be defined, if motive be an ingredient of it, my sense of the danger would not be diminished. The danger is, I think, emphasised by the opinions of some of the learned judges. In a case to which I shall refer immediately, LORD ESHER MR included within his definition of malicious acts persuasion used for the purpose 'of benefiting the defendant at the expense of the plaintiff'. Wills J thinks this 'going a great deal too far,' and that whether the act complained of was malicious depends upon whether the defendant has, in pursuing his own interests, 'done so by such means and with such a disregard to his neighbour as no honest and fair-minded man ought to resort to'. Here it will be seen that malice is not made dependent on motive. The assumed motive is a legitimate one, the pursuit of one's own interests. The malice depends on the means used and the disregard of one's neighbour, and the test of its existence is whether these are such as no honest and fair-minded man ought to resort to. There is here room for infinite differences of opinion. Some, I dare say, applying this test, would consider that a strike by workmen at a time damaging to the employer or a 'lockout' by an employer at a time of special hardship to the workmen were such means and exhibited such a disregard of his neighbour as an honest and fair-minded man ought not to resort to. Others would be of the contrary opinion. The truth is that this suggested test makes men's responsibility for their actions depend on the fluctuating opinions of the tribunal before whom the case may chance to come as to what a right-minded man ought or ought not to do in pursuing his own interests.....

In *Temperton* v. *Russell*,[3] the further step was taken by the majority of the court—AL SMITH LJ reserving his opinion on the point—of asserting that it was immaterial that the act induced was not the breach of a contract, but only the not entering into a contract, provided that the motive of desiring to injure the plaintiff, or to benefit the defendant at the expense of the plaintiff, was present. It seems to have been regarded as only a small step from the one decision to the other, and it was said that there seemed to be no good reason why, if an action lay for maliciously inducing a breach of contract, it should not equally lie for maliciously inducing a person not to enter into a contract. So far from thinking it a small step from the one decision to the other, I think there is a chasm between them. The reason for a distinction between the two cases appears to me to be this: that in the one case the act procured was the violation of a legal right, for which the person doing the act which injured the plaintiff could be sued, as well as the person who procured it, while in the other case, as no legal right was violated by the person who did the act from which the plaintiff suffered, he would not be liable to be sued in respect of the act done, while the person who induced him to do the act would be liable to an action. I think this was an entirely new departure....

It has recently been held in this House in *Bradford Corpn* v. *Pickles*[4] that acts done by the defendant upon his own land were not actionable when they were within his legal rights, even though his motive were to prejudice his neighbour. The language of the noble and learned Lords was distinct. LORD HALSBURY said ([1895] AC at 594):

'This is not a case where the state of mind of the person doing the act can affect the right. If it was a lawful act, however ill the motive be, he had a right to do it. If it was an unlawful act, however good the motive might be, he would have no right to do it.'

The statement was confined to the class of case then before the House, but I apprehend that what was said is not applicable only to rights of property, but is equally applicable to the exercise by an individual of his other rights....

I think these considerations (subject to a point which I will presently discuss) sufficient to show that the present action cannot be maintained. It is said that the statement that the defendant would call

---

[3] [1893] 1 QB 715, [1891–4] All ER Rep 724.   [4] [1895] 1 Ch 145, affd. [1895] AC 587.

men out, if made, was a threat. It is this aspect of the case which has obviously greatly influenced some of the learned judges. HAWKINS J says that the defendant without excuse or justification

'wilfully, unlawfully, unjustly, and tyrannically invaded the plaintiffs' right by intimidating and coercing their employers to deprive them of their present and future employment,'

and that the plaintiffs are, therefore, entitled to maintain this action. But 'excuse or justification' is only needed where an act is prima facie wrongful. Whether the defendant's act was so is the matter to be determined. To say that the defendant acted 'unlawfully', is, with all respect, to beg the question which is whether he did so or not? To describe his acts as unjust and tyrannical proves nothing, for these epithets may be, and are, in popular language constantly applied to acts which are within a man's rights, and unquestionably lawful. . . .

The proposition is, therefore, reduced to this, that the appellant invaded the plaintiffs' right by intimidating and coercing their employers. In another passage, in his opinion, the learned judge says that there is no authority for the proposition that to render threats, menaces, intimidation, or coercion available as elements in a cause of action, they must be of such a character as to create fear of personal violence. I quite agree with this. The threat of violence to property is equally a threat in the eye of the law. And many other instances might be given. On the other hand, it is undeniable that the terms 'threat', 'coercion', and even 'intimidation' are often applied in popular language to utterances which are quite lawful and give rise to no liability either civil or criminal. They mean no more than this, that the so-called threat puts pressure, perhaps extreme pressure, on the person to whom it is addressed, to take a particular course. Of this again, numberless instances might be given. Even then, if it can be said without abuse of language that the employers were 'intimidated and coerced' by the appellant, even if this be in a certain sense true, it by no means follows that he committed a wrong or is under any legal liability for his act. Everything depends on the nature of the representation or statement by which the pressure was exercised. The law cannot regard the act differently because you choose to call it a threat or coercion instead of an intimation or warning. . . .

The object which the appellant and the iron workers had in view was that they should be freed from the presence of men with whom they disliked working, or to prevent what they deemed an unfair interference with their rights by men who did not belong to their craft doing the work to which they had been trained. Whether we approve or disapprove of such attempted trade restrictions, it was entirely within the right of the iron workers to take any steps, not unlawful, to prevent any of the work which they regarded as legitimately theirs being intrusted to other hands.

. . . In the present case it was admitted that the defendant had no personal spite against the plaintiffs. His object was, at the utmost, to prevent them in the future from doing work which he thought was not within their province, but within that of the iron workers. If he had acted in exactly the same manner as he did at a time when the plaintiffs were engaged upon iron work, his motive would have been precisely the same as it was in the present case, and the result to the plaintiffs would have been in nowise different. I am unable to see, then, that there is any difference either in point of ethics or law between the two cases. The iron workers were no more bound to work with those whose presence was disagreeable to them than the plaintiffs were bound to refuse to work because they found that this was the case. The object which the defendant and those whom he represented had in view throughout was what they believed to be the interest of the class to which they belonged. The step taken was a means to that end. The act which caused the damage to the plaintiffs was that of the iron company in refusing to employ them. The company would not subordinate their own interests to the plaintiffs. It is conceded that they could take this course with impunity. Why, then, should the defendant be liable because he did not subordinate the interests of those he represented to the plaintiffs? Self-interest dictated alike the act of those who caused the damage and the act which is found to have induced them to cause it. . . .

[LORD MACNAGHTEN, LORD SHAND, LORD DAVEY, and LORD JAMES OF HEREFORD delivered speeches in favour of reversing the Court of Appeal's decision and dismissing the action. LORD HALSBURY LC, LORD ASHBOURNE, and LORD MORRIS delivered speeches in favour of dismissing the appeal.]

Appeal allowed.

NOTES

1. This case, and *Bradford Corporation v Pickles* [1895] AC 587, noted p. 788, ante, are often cited as authority for the proposition that the concept of abuse of rights has no place in English law (unlike the case in civil law systems). However, malicious and improper motives can be a source of liability for abuse of governmental power or can be evidence of unreasonable conduct, as in nuisance (p. 788, ante) or can act as a limitation on certain defences in defamation (pp. 986 and 999, post). But B. Napier, VII *Estratto da M Rotondi; Inchieste di Diritto Comparato* (Padua, 1979) 267, at 282, is correct when he explains that 'in British law . . . , in general, one cannot hope to object successfully to the exercise of a legal right, simply by pointing out that the actor's motivation is morally objectionable, and of little social utility'. In contrast, note the famous American case of *Tuttle v Buck* (1909) 119 NW 946, where a rich banker was held liable for spitefully driving the claimant barber out of business by opening a rival barber's shop and undercutting him, even though this activity was not unlawful as such. Do you consider that the absence of such a concept of abuse of rights based upon malice is a weakness or strength of the English common law? See the comments of Lord Hoffmann in *OBG v Allan* [2007] 4 All ER 545, at [14]; see also the comments of Lord Nicholls in the same case at [145]–[148].

2. Despite *Allen v Flood*, is there a *tort* of unjustifiable interference in restraint of trade? The point was raised but left open by Lord Denning MR in *Hadmor Productions Ltd v Hamilton* [1981] 2 All ER 724 at 734 (a point not considered in the subsequent appeal to the House of Lords). This tort could be relevant in situations where a body with monopoly control of a trade arbitrarily or capriciously prevents access to that trade, whether by rejecting from membership or refusing a licence. In *Nagle v Feilden* [1966] 2 QB 633, [1966] 1 All ER 689 a declaration, but not damages, was awarded for alleged sex discrimination by stewards of the Jockey Club (which controls horseracing on the flat) in the exercise of their discretion to grant a trainer's licence. The cause of action was not contractual, and the decision has been criticised by J.A. Weir [1966] CLJ 165, because adhering to an unlawful restraint of trade had not previously been recognised as a legal wrong. See also *Weinberger v Inglis (No 2)* [1919] AC 606, where the Stock Exchange was allowed to refuse a broker readmission on grounds of his German origin. (However, note the contrasting approach taken in *Constantine v Imperial Hotels* [1944] 1 KB 693.) In *Board of Governors of Seneca College of Applied Arts and Technology v Bhaudaria* (1981) 124 DLR (3d) 193, the Supreme Court of Canada decided that there was no common law tort of racial discrimination (cf. I.B. McKenna (1981) 1 LS 296). The supposed absence of such a tort led the legislature in Britain to introduce the statutory civil wrongs of unlawful discrimination on racial grounds and on grounds of sex and marital status (now contained in the Race Relations Act 1976 and the Sex Discrimination Act 1975), which have been subsequently extended under the influence of EU law to cover discrimination on the grounds of disability, religious or religious belief, sexual orientation and age. See N. Bamforth, M. Malik and C. O'Cinneide, *Discrimination Law: Theory and Context* (London, 2008).

3. Do you agree with J.D. Heydon, *Economic Torts*, 2nd edn (London, 1978), p. 28, that 'a legal system which lacks [a doctrine that malevolent action by one alone is tortious] seems deficient'? Note that inroads were made on *Allan v Flood* by developments in the torts of inducement of breach of contract (p. 891, post), and interference with trade by unlawful means (p. 917, post), which however were mainly (but not completely) reversed by the decision of the House of Lords in *OBG v Allan* [2007] 4 All ER 545,

[2007] UKHL 21. Consider why a 'lawful means conspiracy' is tortious if the real purpose is to inflict damage on the claimant, rather than to serve the legitimate interests of those who combine (post). But note also that in *Crédit Lyonnais Bank v Export Credits Guarantee Department* [2000] 1 AC 486, [1999] 1 All ER 929, the House of Lords refused to countenance the invention of a tort of assisting another to commit a tort, even with the requirement of an intention to harm.

■ Crofter Hand Woven Harris Tweed Co Ltd v Veitch
House of Lords [1942] 1 All ER 142

The pursuers marketed cloth woven by crofters on the Isle of Lewis, using yarn imported from the mainland. Yarn was also produced in spinning mills on the island and this was woven by the crofters into cloth and sold under the Harris Tweed mark. Most of the spinners belonged to the Transport & General Workers' Union. Officials of the union asked for higher wages for mill workers, but this was refused on the ground that an increase in costs would prevent the mill owners from competing with the pursuers and other firms on the island, who were importing yarn. To overcome this objection the defenders, officials of the union, instructed their members, who were dockers at the principal port on the island, not to handle yarn consigned to the pursuers or unfinished cloth despatched by them to the mainland. The embargo on the cloth was subsequently lifted. The pursuers sought an interdict (i.e. injunction) to prevent the continuing embargo on the yarn.

The Lord Ordinary recalled the interim interdict, and the Court of Session, Second Division (Lord Mackay dissenting) affirmed the decision: 1940 SC 141. On appeal by the pursuers to the House of Lords:

LORD WRIGHT: . . .
The cause of action set out in the appellants' claim is for a conspiracy to injure, which is a tort. The classical definition of conspiracy is that given by WILLES J. in advising the House of Lords in *Mulcahy* v. *R*,[5] at p. 317:

A conspiracy consists not merely in the intention of two or more, but in the agreement of two or more to do an unlawful act, or to do a lawful act by unlawful means.

This must be supplemented by observing that, though the crime is constituted by the agreement, the civil right of action is not complete unless the conspirators do acts in pursuance of their agreement to the damage of the plaintiffs.

The question is, then, what the unlawful acts were with which the respondents were charged, or what the unlawful means were which they employed to do acts otherwise lawful. In other words, what is the legal right of the appellants which is infringed, or what is the legal wrong committed by the respondents? The concept of a civil conspiracy to injure has been in the main developed in the course of the last half-century, particularly since *Mogul SS Co* v. *McGregor, Gow & Co*.[6] Its essential character is described by LORD MACNAGHTEN in *Quinn* v. *Leathem*,[7] at p. 510, basing himself on the words of LORD WATSON in *Allen* v. *Flood*,[8] at p. 108:

. . . a conspiracy to injure might give rise to civil liability even though the end were brought about by conduct and acts which by themselves and apart from the element of combination or concerted action could not be regarded as a legal wrong.

In this sense, the conspiracy is the gist of the wrong, though damage is necessary to complete the cause of action. . . . The rule may seem anomalous, so far as it holds that conduct by two may be actionable

---

[5] (1868) LR 3 HL 306.   [6] [1892] AC 25.   [7] [1901] AC 495.   [8] [1898] AC 1.

if it causes damage, whereas the same conduct done by one, causing the same damage, would give no redress. In effect, the plaintiff's right is that he should not be damnified by a conspiracy to injure him, and it is in the fact of the conspiracy that the unlawfulness resides. It is a different matter if the conspiracy is to do acts in themselves wrongful, as to deceive or defraud, [or] to commit violence…A conspiracy to injure, however, is a tort which requires careful definition, in order to hold the balance between the defendant's right to exercise his lawful rights and the plaintiff's right not to be injured by an injurious conspiracy. As I read the authorities, there is a clear and definite distinction which runs through them all between what LORD DUNEDIN in *Sorrell* v. *Smith*,[9] at p. 730, calls 'a conspiracy to injure' and 'a set of acts dictated by business interests'. I should qualify 'business' by adding 'or other legitimate interests', using the convenient adjective not very precisely. It may be a difficult task in some cases to apply this distinction. It depends largely on matters of fact, but also on a legal conception of what is meant by 'intention to injure'. The appellants contend that there was here an intention to injure, even though it is negatived that the respondents were actuated by malice or malevolence. In substance, what the appellants say is that the issue between the mill-owners and the yarn importers was one between two sets of employers, in which the men were not directly concerned, that the union's action was an unjustifiable and meddlesome interference with the appellants' right to conduct their own businesses as they pleased, and that the union were pushing into matters which did not concern them. The appellants further say, as I understand their case, that this unjustifiable intrusion was due to the union's desire to secure the assistance of the mill-owners towards the union's object, which was to get 100 per cent. membership in the textile workers, and thus there was no common object among the two main parties to the combination. Each set had its own selfish object. In effect, it was said, the union were bribed by the mill-owners to victimise the appellants in their trade by the promise of help in the matter of the union membership, which was entirely foreign to the question of the importation of yarn. These considerations, it was said, constituted 'malice' in law, even if there was no malevolence, and prevented the respondents from justifying the injury which they wilfully did to the appellants' trade, because they could not assert any legitimate interest of their union which was relevant to the action taken. Actual malevolence or spite was, it was said, not essential. There was no genuine intention to promote union interests by the stoppage of importation. The interference with the appellants' trade by stopping import of yarn was wilful and ultroneous action on the part of the union, supported by no relevant union interest. It was malicious or wrongful because it was intentionally and unjustifiably mischievous, even though not malevolent.

Before I refer to the authorities, there are some preliminary observations which I desire to make. I shall avoid the use of what BOWEN LJ in the *Mogul* case[10] described as the 'slippery' word 'malice' except in quotations. When I want to express spite or ill will, I shall use the word 'malevolence'. When I want to express merely intentional tortious conduct, I shall use the word 'wrongful'. As the claim is for a tort, it is necessary to ascertain what constitutes the tort alleged. It cannot be merely that the appellants' right to freedom in conducting their trade has been interfered with. That right is not absolute or unconditional. It is only a particular aspect of the citizen's right to personal freedom, and, like other aspects of that right, is qualified by various legal limitations, either by statute or by common law. Such limitations are inevitable in organised societies, where the rights of individuals may clash. In commercial affairs, each trader's rights are qualified by the right of others to compete. Where the rights of labour are concerned, the rights of the employer are conditioned by the rights of the men to give or withhold their services. The right of workmen to strike is an essential element in the principle of collective bargaining….

It is thus clear that employers of workmen, or those who, like the appellants, depend in part on the services of workmen, have in the conduct of their affairs to reckon with this freedom of the men, and to realise that the exercise of the men's rights may involve some limitation on their own freedom in the management of their business. Such interference with a person's business, so long as the limitations enforced by law are not contravened, involves no legal wrong against the person. In the present case,

---

[9] [1925] AC 700.   [10] [1892] AC 25.

the respondents are sued for imposing the 'embargo', which corresponds to calling out the men on strike. The dockers were free to obey or not to obey the call to refuse to handle the appellants' goods. In refusing to handle the goods, they did not commit any breach of contract with anyone. They were merely exercising their own rights. However, there might be circumstances which rendered the action wrongful. The men might be called out in breach of their contracts with their employer, and that would be clearly a wrongful act as against the employer, and an interference with his contractual right, for which damages could be claimed, not only as against the contract-breaker, but also against the person who counselled or procured or advised the breach. This is the principle laid down in *Lumley v. Gye*[11] which LORD MACNAGHTEN in *Quinn v. Leathem*,[12] defined to be that [p. 510]:

> . . . a violation of legal right committed knowingly is a cause of action and . . . it is a violation of legal right to interfere with contractual relations recognised by law if there be no sufficient justification for the interference.

That is something substantially different from a mere interference with a person's qualified right to exercise his free will in conducting his trade. A legal right was violated and needed justification, if it could be justified. This distinction was drawn by the majority of the Lords in *Allen v. Flood*,[13] who disapproved of the dicta in *Bowen v. Hall*[14] and *Temperton v. Russell*[15] that every person who persuades another not to enter into a contract with a third person may be sued by the third person, if the object is to benefit himself at the expense of such person. However, in *Allen v. Flood*,[16] this House was considering a case of an individual actor, where the element of combination was absent. In that case, it was held, the motive of the defendant is immaterial. Damage done intentionally, and even malevolently, to another thus, it was held, gives no cause of action so long as no legal right of the other is infringed.

That I take to be the English rule laid down by this House in *Bradford Corpn v. Pickles*[17] and in *Allen v. Flood*,[18] though in *Sorrell v. Smith*,[19] at p. 713, LORD CAVE LC doubts the proposition, and says that in general what is unlawful in two is not lawful in one. This, however, seems to be inconsistent with the express rulings in *Allen v. Flood*.[20] Though eminent authorities have protested against the principle, it must, I think, be accepted at present as the law in England. The precise issue does not arise in this case, which is concerned with combination or conspiracy. I need not consider whether any qualification may hereafter be found admissible.

Thus, for the purposes of the present case, we reach the position that, apart from combination, no wrong would have been committed. There was no coercion of the dockers. There were no threats to them. They were legally free to choose the alternative course which they preferred. In *Quinn v. Leathem*,[1] a wide meaning was given to words like 'threats', 'intimidation' or 'coercion', especially by LORD LINDLEY, but that was not the ratio decidendi adopted by the House. These words, as pointed out in *Wright on Criminal Conspiracy*, are not terms of art and are consistent with either legality or illegality. They are not correctly used in the circumstances of a case like this. In *Allen v. Flood*,[2] *Ware and De Freville Ltd v. Motor Trade Association*[3] and *Sorrell v. Smith*,[4] a more accurate definition was given . . . . There is nothing unlawful in giving a warning or intimation that, if the party addressed pursues a certain line of conduct, others may act in a manner which he will not like and which will be prejudicial to his interests, so long as nothing unlawful is threatened or done. In the words of LORD BUCKMASTER in *Sorrell v. Smith*,[5] at p. 747:

> A threat to do an act which is lawful cannot, in my opinion, create a cause of action whether the act threatened is to be done by many or by one.

No doubt the use of illegal threats or the exercise of unlawful coercion would create by itself a cause of action, but there was nothing of the sort in this case.

---

[11] (1853) 2 E & B 216.   [12] [1901] AC 495.   [13] [1898] AC 1.   [14] (1881) 6 QBD 333.
[15] [1893] 1 QB 715.   [16] [1898] AC 1.   [17] [1895] AC 587.   [18] [1898] AC 1.
[19] [1925] AC 700.   [20] [1898] AC 1.   [1] [1901] AC 495.   [2] [1898] AC 1.
[3] [1921] 3 KB 40.   [4] [1925] AC 700.   [5] [1925] AC 700.

The only way in this case in which the appellants can establish a cause of action in tort is by establishing that there was a conspiracy to injure, which would take the case out of the general ruling in *Allen* v. *Flood*[6] and bring it within the exception there reserved by LORD HERSCHELL, at pp. 123, 124:

> It is certainly a general rule of our law that an act prima facie lawful is not unlawful and actionable on account of the motive which dictated it. I put aside the case of conspiracy which is anomalous in more than one respect.

In the same case, LORD WATSON made a similar reservation, at p. 108. LORD MACNAGHTEN, at p. 153, said that the decision in *Allen* v. *Flood*[7] could have no bearing on any case which involved the element of oppressive combination. These reservations were acted upon in *Quinn* v. *Leathem*,[8] to which I shall refer later. That the decision in that case turned on conspiracy cannot now be doubted, especially after *Ware and De Freville Ltd* v. *Motor Trade Association*[9] and *Sorrell* v. *Smith*.[10]

The distinction between conduct by one man and conduct by two or more may be difficult to justify. LORD SUMNER in *Sorrell* v. *Smith*[11] puts the very artificial case of the owner of a large business who gave a small share to a partner and 'conspired' with him. For practical purposes, the position there is the same as if he had remained a sole trader. The fact that the sole trader employed servants or agents in the conduct of his business would not, in my opinion, make these others co-conspirators with him. The special rule relating to the effect of a combination has been explained on the ground that it is easier to resist one than two. That may appear to be true if a crude illustration is taken, such as the case of two men attacking another, but even there it would not always be true—for instance, if the one man was very strong and the two were very weak—and the power of a big corporation or trader may be greater than that of a large number of smaller fry in the trade. This explanation of the rule is not very satisfactory. The rule has been explained on grounds of public policy. The common law may have taken the view that there is always the danger that any combination may be oppressive, and may have thought that a general rule against injurious combinations was desirable on broad grounds of policy. Again, any combination to injure involves an element of deliberate concert between individuals to do harm. Whatever the moral or logical or sociological justification, the rule is as well established in English Law as I here take to be the rule that motive is immaterial in regard to the lawful act of an individual, a rule which has been strongly criticised by some high legal authorities, who would solve the apparent antinomy by holding that deliberate action causing injury is actionable whether done by one or by several.

A conspiracy to injure involves *ex vi termini* an intention to injure, or, more accurately, a common intention and agreement to injure. Both 'intention' and 'injure' need definition. The word 'injure' is here used in its correct meaning of 'wrongful harm', *damnum cum injuria*, not *damnum absque injuria*. That obviously raises the question of when the harm is wrongful. 'Intention' is generally determined by reference to overt acts and to the circumstances in which they are done....

...On principle, I am of the opinion that malevolence is no more essential to the intent to injure, the mens rea, than it is to the intent to deceive. On practical grounds, also I prefer that view. To leave to a jury to decide on the basis of an internal mental state, rather than on the facts from which intent is to be inferred, may be to leave the issue in the hands of the jury as clay to mould at their will. After all, the plaintiff has to prove actual damage, which can only result from things done. Mere malevolence does not damage anyone. I cannot see how the pursuit of a legitimate practical object can be vitiated by glee at the adversary's expected discomfiture. Such glee, however deplorable, cannot affect the practical result. I may add that a desire to injure does not necessarily involve malevolence. It may be motivated by wantonness or some object not justifiable.

As to the authorities, the balance, in my opinion, is in favour of the view that malevolence as a mental state is not the test. I accordingly agree with the appellants' contention that they are not concluded by the finding that the respondents were not malevolent. It thus becomes necessary to consider the

---

[6] [1898] AC 1.   [7] [1898] AC 1.   [8] [1901] AC 495.
[9] [1921] 3 KB 40.   [10] [1925] AC 700.   [11] [1925] AC 700.

further arguments on which the appellants base their claim to succeed. I approach the question on the assumption that the appellants have to prove that they have been damnified by tortious action. They do not prove that by showing that they have been harmed by acts done by the respondents in combination, these acts being, apart from any question of combination, otherwise within the respondents' rights. It is not, then, for the respondents to justify these acts. The appellants must establish that they have been damnified by a conspiracy to injure that is, that there was a wilful and concerted intention to injure without just cause and consequent damage. That was the view accepted by LORD DUNEDIN and LORD BUCKMASTER in *Sorrell's* case.[12] . . . It is not a question of onus of proof. It depends on the cause of action. The plaintiff has to prove the wrongfulness of the defendant's object. Of course, malevolence may be evidence tending to exclude a legitimate object or to establish a wrongful object.

The respondents had no quarrel with the yarn importers. Their sole object . . . was to promote their union's interests by promoting the interest of the industry on which the men's wages depended. On these findings . . . it could not be said that their combination was without sufficient justification. Nor would this conclusion be vitiated, even though their motives may have been mixed, so long as the real or predominant object, if they had more than one object, was not wrongful. Nor is the objection tenable that the respondents' real or predominant object was to secure the employers' help to get 100 per cent. membership of the union among the textile workers. Cases of mixed motives, or, as I should prefer to say, of the presence of more than one object, are not uncommon. If so, it is for the jury or judge of fact to decide which is the predominant object, as it may be assumed the jury did in *Quinn's* case,[13] when they decided on the basis that the object of the combiners was vindictive punishment, and not their own practical advantage. . . .

I may here note that the doctrine of civil conspiracy to injure extends beyond trade competition and labour disputes. *Thompson* v. *British Medical Association (NSW Branch)*[14] shows that it may extend to the affairs of a profession, . . . By way of contrast, *Gregory* v. *Duke of Brunswick*[15] may be regarded as a striking illustration of what might be held to constitute a conspiracy to injure. What was alleged was a conspiracy to hiss an actor off the stage in order to ruin him. To what legitimate interests other than those mentioned the general doctrine may extend I do not here seek to define, since beyond question it extends to the present case, whether the object of the action were the prosperity of the industry or the obtaining of 100 per cent. membership. The objects or purposes for which combinations may be formed, however, are clearly of great variety. It must be left to the future to decide, on the facts of the particular case, subject to the general doctrine, whether any combination is such as to give rise to a claim for a conspiracy to injure.

If, however, the object of object of securing 100 per cent. union membership were operative in inducing the respondents to combine with the employers, it was relied on by the appellants on other grounds as vitiating the combination. It was objected that there could be no combination between the employers and the union, because their respective interests were necessarily opposed. I think that that is a fallacious contention. It is true that employers and workmen are often at variance because the special interest of each side conflicts in the material respect, as, for instance, in questions of wages, conditions of hours of work, exclusion of non-union labour, but, apart from these differences in interest, both employers and workmen have a common interest in the prosperity of their industry, though the interest of one side may be in profits and of the other in wages. Hence a wider and truer view is that there is a community of interest. That view was acted upon in the present case in regard to the essential matter of yarn importation. As to the separate matter of the union membership, while that was something regarded as important by the respondents, it was probably regarded by the employers as a matter of indifference to them. It was, in any case, a side issue in the combination, even from the respondents' point of view. I may add that I do not accept as a general proposition that there must be complete identity of interest between parties to a combination. There must, however, be sufficient identity of object though the advantage to be derived from that same object may not be the same.

---

¹² [1925] AC 700.   ¹³ [1901] AC 495.   ¹⁴ [1924] AC 764.   ¹⁵ (1844) 6 Man & G 953.

.... I need merely add a few words on the objection that the embargo was the act of the dockers for the benefit, not of themselves, but of the textile workers. It is enough to say that both sections were members of the union, and there was, in my opinion, a sufficient community of interest, even if the matter is regarded from the standpoint of the men, as individuals, and not from the standpoint of the respondents, who were the only parties sued. Their interest, however, was to promote the advantage of the union as a whole. In my opinion, the judgment appealed from should be affirmed and the appeal dismissed.

[VISCOUNT SIMON LC, VISCOUNT MAUGHAM, LORD THANKERTON, and LORD PORTER delivered speeches in favour of dismissing the appeal.]

Appeal dismissed.

NOTES

1. 'Why should an act which causes economic loss to A but is not actionable at his suit if done by B alone become actionable because B did it pursuant to an agreement between B and C?' (per Lord Diplock in *Lonrho Ltd v Shell Petroleum Co Ltd* [1981] 2 All ER 456 at 464, p. 863, post.) The reply given in the first 'modern' case, *Mogul SS Co Ltd v McGregor, Gow & Co* (1889) 23 QBD 598 at 616; affd [1892] AC 25, by Bowen LJ was that 'a combination may make oppressive or dangerous that which if it proceeded only from a single person would be otherwise, and the very fact of the combination may shew that the object is to do harm, and not to exercise one's own just rights'. This argument partially lost its force once English law accepted the doctrine of separate corporate personality (*Salomon v Salomon & Co* [1897] AC 22), with the possibility of great economic power being concentrated in a single corporation, as Lord Diplock recognised in the *Lonrho* case (p. 877, post), but the 'anomalous' tort of civil conspiracy to injure is now 'too well-established to be discarded'. Note that Lord Walker in *Revenue and Customs Commissioners v Total Network SL* [2008] 2 All ER 413, [2008] UKHL 19, at [78], suggested that the common law's especial distrust of combinations also had a distinct historical root: 'I suspect that the judges at the end of the 19th century also had a third reason, largely unarticulated [for their disapproval of combinations designed to cause economic harm] ... That was the deep suspicion which the governing class had, in Georgian and Victorian England, of collective action in the political and economic spheres, as potential threats to the constitution and the framework of society.'

2. The historical link between the crime of conspiracy and the action for damages has been severed by s. 5(1) of the Criminal Law Act 1977, which abolishes the offence of conspiracy at common law subject to certain exceptions. The Act has no direct effect on civil proceedings. Note that husband and wife cannot be charged with a criminal conspiracy with each other (and see now s. 2(2)(a) of the 1977 Act), but they can conspire together for the purposes of the law of tort: *Midland Bank Trust Co Ltd v Green (No 3)* [1982] Ch 529, [1981] 3 All ER 744. Where the act complained of is a crime, or a conspiracy to commit a crime, and not also a tort against him, then no private person can bring an action to restrain a threatened breach of the law, unless the breach would infringe his private rights or would inflict special damage on him: *Gouriet v Union of Post Office Workers* [1978] AC 435, [1977] 3 All ER 70.

3. The pursuit of economic self-interest by traders (*Mogul SS Co Ltd v McGregor, Gow & Co* [1892] AC 25) and by trade unionists in combination with employers in the *Crofter* case have been held to be 'legitimate objects'. But a combination is unlawful if the real

object is to injure. For example, in *Huntley v Thornton* [1957] 1 All ER 234, [1957] 1 WLR 321, the claimant had been prevented from obtaining work by a district committee of the Amalgamated Engineering Union because he had failed to participate in an official union strike, and had shown an 'arrogant attitude' to the committee at a disciplinary meeting, by describing the committee as a 'shower'. The Executive Committee of the union refused to countenance his expulsion, but the local boycott continued. Harman J held that the claimant was entitled to damages of £500, and he was granted leave to apply for an injunction in the event of renewed victimisation, because 'the district committee had entirely lost sight of what the interests of the union demanded and thought only of their own ruffled dignity.... It had become a question of the committee's prestige...'. It was also held that they were not entitled to the benefit of the statutory immunity against tort liability in trade disputes because they had not acted in *furtherance* of such a dispute. Two officials who had helped to implement the boycott were not liable because, being ignorant of the background to the dispute between the claimant and the committee, they had acted in what they sincerely believed to be the best interests of the union.

4.   In *Scala Ballroom (Wolverhampton) Ltd v Ratcliffe* [1958] 3 All ER 220, [1958] 1 WLR 1057 the defendants were officials of the Musicians' Union who had organised a boycott of the claimants' ballroom in protest against a 'colour bar' (a ban on the employment of people from racial minorities) operated there. The claimants were refused an interlocutory injunction on the ground that no cause of action had been made out. The Court of Appeal held that the objects of the combination were legitimate, particularly in the light of an affidavit by one official in which he referred to the 'insidious effects' of a colour bar imposed on the audience because 'it is impossible for musicians to insulate themselves from their audience'. Hodson LJ said that legitimate interests were not to be confused with those which can be exchanged for cash. Morris LJ said that so long as the defendants honestly believed a certain policy to be desirable, even though it could not be translated into financial terms, there was no conspiracy to injure.

O. Kahn-Freund (1959) 22 MLR 69 comments: 'The line which separates lawful from unlawful action does not run between the markets of commodities or services and the labour market, but between a "policy of interest" and a "policy of prestige".' Compare *Sweeney v Coote* [1907] AC 221 (for a fuller exposition of the facts, see [1906] IR 51–126), in which an action alleging conspiracy by Protestant parents who withdrew their children from the school of a Catholic schoolmistress, with the alleged purpose of having her dismissed from her post, failed. Earl Halsbury LC (at p. 223) said: 'If the object [was]...to cause her to be dismissed, not upon any ground of personal objection to her, or any spite or ill-will to her, but upon the ground that in the view of the parents...it was an undesirable thing for a Roman Catholic to be put into that position, I am of opinion that there would be no ground of action.' Does this decision mean that a boycott against members of a particular religion would not be tortious? In contrast, in the *Crofter* case Lord Maugham ([1942] 1 All ER at p. 152) said that if 'the object of the combination [is] a dislike of the religious views or the politics or the race or the colour of the plaintiff, or a mere demonstration of power by busybodies...[t]here is, I think, no authority to be found which justifies the view that [such] a combination...would be lawful.' (See B. Hepple, *Race, Jobs and the Law in Britain*, 2nd edn (Harmondsworth, 1970), p. 246).

■ Lonrho Ltd v Shell Petroleum Co Ltd
House of Lords [1981] 2 All ER 456

For the facts and other aspects of this case see p. 695, ante.

LORD DIPLOCK [dealing with the question whether the contravention of the sanctions order, if proved, would amount to the tort of civil conspiracy by the respondents jointly]: . . .

Your Lordships are invited to answer it on the assumption that the purpose of Shell and BP in entering into the agreement to do the various things that it must be assumed they did in contravention of the sanctions order was to forward their own commercial interests, *not* to injure those of Lonrho. So the question of law to be determined is whether an intent by the defendants to injure the plaintiff is an essential element in the civil wrong of conspiracy, even where the acts agreed to be done by the conspirators amount to criminal offences under a penal statute. It is conceded that there is no direct authority either way on this question to be found in the decided cases; so if this House were to answer it in the affirmative, your Lordships would be making new law.

My Lords, conspiracy as a criminal offence has a long history. It consists of 'the agreement of two or more persons to effect any unlawful purpose, whether as their ultimate aim, or only as a means to it, and the crime is complete if there is such agreement, even though nothing is done in pursuance of it'. I cite from Viscount Simon LC's now classic speech in *Crofter Hand Woven Harris Tweed Co Ltd v Veitch* [1942] AC 435 at 439, [1942] 1 All ER 142 at 146. Regarded as a civil tort, however, conspiracy is a highly anomalous cause of action. The gist of the cause of action is damage to the plaintiff; so long as it remains unexecuted, the agreement, which alone constitutes the crime of conspiracy, causes no damage; it is only acts done in execution of the agreement that are capable of doing that. So the tort, unlike the crime, consists not of agreement but of concerted action taken pursuant to agreement . . .

[D]uring its chequered history between Lord Coleridge CJ's judgment at first instance in *Mogul Steamship Co v McGregor, Gow & Co* (1888) 21 QBD 544 and the *Crofter* case, the civil tort of conspiracy attracted more academic controversy than success in practical application. Why should an act which causes economic loss to A but is not actionable at his suit if done by B alone become actionable because B did it pursuant to an agreement between B and C? An explanation given at the close of the nineteenth century by Bowen LJ in the *Mogul* case 23 QBD 598 at 616 when it was before the Court of Appeal was: 'The distinction is based on sound reason, for a combination may make oppressive or dangerous that which if it proceeded only from a single person would be otherwise . . .' But to suggest today that acts done by one street-corner grocer in concert with a second are more oppressive and dangerous to a competitor than the same acts done by a string of supermarkets under a single ownership or that a multinational conglomerate such as Lonrho or oil company such as Shell or BP does not exercise greater economic power than any combination of small businesses is to shut one's eyes to what has been happening in the business and industrial world since the turn of the century and, in particular, since the end of the 1939–45 war. The civil tort of conspiracy to injure the plaintiff's commercial interests where that is the predominant purpose of the agreement between the defendants and of the acts done in execution of it which caused damage to the plaintiff must I think be accepted by this House as too well-established to be discarded, however anomalous it may seem today. It was applied by this House eighty years ago in *Quinn v Leathem* [1901] AC 495, [1900–3] All ER Rep 1, and accepted as good law in the *Crofter* case in 1942, where it was made clear that injury to the plaintiff and not the self-interest of the defendants must be the predominant purpose of the agreement in execution of which the damage-causing acts were done.

My Lords, in none of the judgments in decided cases in civil actions for damages for conspiracy does it appear that the mind of the author of the judgment was directed to a case where the damage-causing acts, although neither done for the purpose of injuring the plaintiff nor actionable at his suit if they had been done by one person alone, were nevertheless a contravention of some penal law. I will not recite the statements in those judgments to which your Lordships have been referred by Lonrho as amounting to dicta in favour of the view that a civil action for conspiracy does lie in such a case.

Even if the authors' minds had been directed to the point, which they were not, I should still find them indecisive. This House, in my view, has an unfettered choice whether to confine the civil action of conspiracy to the narrow field to which alone it has an established claim or whether to extend this already anomalous tort beyond those narrow limits that are all that common sense and the application of the legal logic of the decided cases require.

My Lords, my choice is unhesitatingly the same as that of Parker J and all three members of the Court of Appeal. I am against extending the scope of the civil tort of conspiracy beyond acts done in execution of an agreement entered into by two or more persons for the purpose not of protecting their own interests but of injuring the interests of the plaintiff. . . .

[LORD EDMUND-DAVIES, LORD KEITH OF KINKEL, LORD SCARMAN, and LORD BRIDGE OF HARWICH agreed with the speech of LORD DIPLOCK in favour of dismissing the appeal.]

Appeal dismissed.

■ Lonrho plc v Fayed
House of Lords [1991] 3 All ER 303

LORD BRIDGE OF HARWICH: . . .
Lonrho's pleaded case, in very short summary, is as follows. Lonrho at all material times intended to acquire control of HoF [House of Fraser plc (HoF), the company which owns, inter alia, Harrods department store]. The [Fayed brothers and House of Fraser Holdings plc (Holdings), a company owned and controlled by the Fayed brothers] induced the Secretary of State [for Trade and Industry] to abstain from referring their proposed acquisition of HoF to the [Monopolies and Mergers Commission (the MMC)] by false and fraudulent representations about themselves, their commercial background and the source of the finance available to them for the acquisition of HoF. If the Secretary of State had known the truth, he would have made a reference either before or after Holdings had acquired control. If the reference had been made before Holdings had acquired control, this would have left Lonrho, when released from its undertaking, in a position to bid for control of HoF without competition from the Fayeds or Holdings. If the reference had been made after Holdings acquired control, this would probably have led to an order under the 1973 Act requiring Holdings to divest itself of its controlling interest, which again Lonrho would have had the opportunity to acquire. . . .

As against all the defendants, Lonrho's statement of claim pleads that their intention was both to benefit the Fayeds and Holdings by furthering their interest in the acquisition of HoF and to injure Lonrho by preventing them from acquiring HoF. Lonrho claims to have lost the opportunity to acquire HoF by bidding for the shares without competition from the Fayeds or Holdings and thereby to have suffered damage. Lonrho asserts that these facts are sufficient to establish a cause of action for the common law tort of interfering with business by unlawful means. But the statement of claim also relied additionally or alternatively on the same allegations of fact as establishing the tort of conspiracy to injure . . .

The defendants applied by summons to strike out the statement of claim . . . . Master Topley dismissed the application, but an appeal against his decision was allowed by Pill J (see [1988] 3 All ER 464, [1990] 1 QB 490). . . . [On a further appeal i]t was . . . accepted in the Court of Appeal that the statement of claim had not alleged that the *predominant* purpose of the alleged conspiracy was to injure Lonrho and that accordingly the Court of Appeal were bound by their own decision in *Metall und Rohstoff AG v Donaldson Lufkin & Jenrette Inc* [1989] 3 All ER 14, [1990] 1 QB 391 to hold that the pleaded cause of action in conspiracy could not succeed. The Court of Appeal (Dillon, Ralph Gibson and Woolf LJJ) allowed the appeal in relation to the cause of action founded on the tort of interfering with business by unlawful means: see [1989] 2 All ER 65, [1990] 2 QB 479. The defendants now appeal and Lonrho cross-appeals in relation to the cause of action in conspiracy by leave of your Lordship's House.

It will be convenient to consider first the clear-cut issue of law which arises on the cross-appeal. In the *Metall* case the Court of Appeal interpreted the decision of this House in *Lonrho Ltd v Shell Petroleum Co Ltd* [1981] 2 All ER 456, [1982] AC 173 as holding it to be an essential ingredient in the civil tort of conspiracy to establish that the predominant purpose of the conspirators was to injure the plaintiff irrespective of whether the means they used to effect that purpose were lawful or unlawful. In inviting us to overrule the *Metall* case, Mr Kentridge QC submits that the true position in law is that the tort of conspiracy to injure, whilst requiring an intention to injure the plaintiff, may be established *either* by showing that this intention was the predominant purpose of the conspirators, even though the means used were lawful, *or* by showing that unlawful means were used. Where the primary or predominant purpose of the conspirators is to further or protect some legitimate interest of their own, but they also have the intention of injuring the plaintiff, it is sufficient to make their action tortious that they used unlawful means. This, Mr Kentridge, submits, is the law as it was always understood before the decision in [*Lonrho v Shell*] and it is inconceivable that this House should have intended to overturn that understanding in a case where no issue arose with respect to predominant purpose and the point was never argued.

In *Rookes v Barnard* [1964] 1 All ER 367 at 397, [1964] AC 1129 at 1204 Lord Devlin said:

> 'There are, as is well known, two sorts of conspiracies, the *Quinn v Leathem* ([1901] AC 495, [1901–3] All ER Rep 1) type which employs only lawful means but aims at an unlawful end, and the type which employs unlawful means.'

Of these two types of tortious conspiracy the *Quinn v Leathem* type, where no unlawful means are used, is now regarded as an anomaly for the reasons so clearly explained by Lord Diplock in *Lonrho Ltd v Shell Petroleum Ltd* [1981] 2 All ER 456 at 464, [1982] AC 173 at 188–189...

But this reasoning has no relevance to the second type of conspiracy which employs unlawful means. Of this type Lord Devlin said in his speech in *Rookes v Barnard* immediately following the passage I have just cited:

> 'In the latter type...the element of conspiracy is usually of only secondary importance, since the unlawful means are actionable by themselves.'

It is no doubt for the reason mentioned by Lord Devlin that there is no direct authority, unless it be *Rookes v Barnard* [1964] 1 All ER 367, [1964] AC 1129 itself, establishing the negative proposition that the tort of conspiracy to injure by unlawful means may be established without proof that the intention to injure the plaintiff was the predominant purpose of the conspirators. But in the many cases where plaintiffs have asserted a conspiracy to injure, but have been unable to prove that any unlawful means were used, judgments in the Court of Appeal and speeches in your Lordships' House emphasising the requirement of a predominant purpose to injure have repeatedly included dicta indicating that this requirement does not apply where the means used to effect the conspirator's purpose are unlawful. I need do no more than cite some outstanding examples.

[His Lordship cited *Ware & De Freville Ltd v Motor Trade Association* [1921] 3 KB 40 at 67, [1920] All ER Rep 387 at 397 per Scrutton LJ, *Sorrell v Smith* [1925] AC 700 at 712, [1925] All ER Rep 1 at 5 per Viscount Cave LC, and *Crofter Hand Woven Harris Tweed Co Ltd v Veitch* [1942] AC 435 at 445, [1942] 1 All ER 142 at 149 per Viscount Simon LC and per Lord Wright ([1942] 1 All ER 142 at 157–158, [1942] AC 435 at 461–462)]

The reasoning in these passages is both clear and cogent. Where conspirators act with the predominant purpose of injuring the plaintiff and in fact inflict damage on him, but do nothing which would have been actionable if done by an individual acting alone, it is in the fact of their concerted action for that illegitimate purpose that the law, however anomalous it may now seem, finds a sufficient ground to condemn their action as illegal and tortious. But when conspirators intentionally injure the plaintiff and use unlawful means to do so, it is no defence for them to show that their primary purpose was to further or protect their own interests; it is sufficient to make their action tortious that the means used were unlawful.

Did the House in *Lonrho Ltd v Shell Petroleum Co Ltd* [1981] 2 All ER 456, [1982] AC 173 depart from this reasoning and lay down for the first time a new principle that a plaintiff, seeking to establish the tort of conspiracy to injure, must in every case prove that the intention to injure him was the predominant purpose of the defendants, whether the means used were lawful or unlawful?...

The only questions considered in detail when the case came before this House were, first, whether breach of the sanctions order gave rise to a right of action for breach of statutory duty and, secondly, in a question referred to in the consultative case as question 5(b): 'whether the claimants have a cause of action for damage alleged to have been caused by such breaches by virtue only of the allegation that there was an agreement to effect them.' Both questions had been answered in the negative by Parker J at first instance (see [1981] Com LR 6) and by Lord Denning MR, Eveleigh and Fox LJJ in the Court of Appeal (see [1981] Com LR 74). They were similarly answered by the unanimous judgment of the House in which Lord Diplock delivered the only speech.

As the judgments in both courts below and the speech of Lord Diplock make clear, the fact dictating a negative answer to the second question was the absence of any intention to injure Lonrho....

In the *Metall* case [1989] 3 All ER 14, [1990] 1 QB 391 Slade LJ, delivering the judgment of the court, whilst expressly disclaiming any intention to construe Lord Diplock's speech as if it were a statute, nevertheless subjected it to a detailed textual analysis leading to the conclusion that it laid down a rule of law that the tort of conspiracy to injure required proof in every case not merely of an intention to injure the plaintiff but also that injury to the plaintiff was the predominant purpose of the conspiracy.

My Lords, I am quite unable to accept that Lord Diplock or the other members of the Appellate Committee concurring with him, of whom I was one, intended the decision in *Lonrho Ltd v Shell Petroleum Co Ltd* to effect, sub silentio, such a significant change in the law as it had been previously understood. The House, as is clear from the parties' printed cases, which we have been shown, had never been invited to take such a step. Moreover, to do so would have been directly contrary to the view of Lord Denning MR expressed in the judgment which the House was affirming and inconsistent with the dicta in what Lord Diplock described as 'Viscount Simon LC's now classic speech in *Crofter Hand Woven Harris Tweed Co Ltd v Veitch* [1942] 1 All ER 142 at 146, [1942] AC 435 at 439' (see [1981] 2 All ER 456 at 463, [1982] AC 173 at 188). I would overrule the *Metall* case in this respect.

It follows from this conclusion that Lonrho's acceptance that the pleaded intention on the part of the defendants to cause injury to Lonrho was not the predominant purpose of their alleged unlawful action is not necessarily fatal to the pleaded cause of action in conspiracy and therefore affords no separate ground for striking out that part of the pleading.

I would dismiss the appeal [and] allow the cross-appeal....

[LORD TEMPLEMAN, LORD BRANDON OF OAKBROOK, LORD GOFF OF CHIEVELEY, and LORD JAUNCEY OF TULLICHETTLE agreed with the speeches of LORD BRIDGE and LORD TEMPLEMAN.]

NOTES

1. Be clear about the distinction that Lord Bridge makes clear between 'lawful means' conspiracy (often termed 'conspiracy to injure') and 'unlawful means' conspiracy. See also Stuart-Smith LJ in *Powell v Boldaz* (1997) 39 BMLR 35 at 48–49:

    [A]lthough in an unlawful act conspiracy it is not necessary to prove that the predominant purpose is to injure, it is necessary to prove that the conspiracy was 'aimed or directed at the plaintiffs and it can reasonably be foreseen that it may injure him, and does in fact injure him' (per Lord Denning MR in *Lonrho Ltd v Shell Petroleum Co Ltd* [1981] 2 All ER 456, [1982] AC 173, cited with approval by Lord Bridge of Harwich in *Lonrho plc v Fayed* [1991] 3 All ER 303 at 307–308, [1992] 1 AC 448 at 467)

    or, as Woolf LJ said in *Lonrho v Fayed* in the Court of Appeal ([1989] 2 All ER 65 at 73):

    If a defendant has deliberately embarked on a course of conduct, the probable consequence of which on the plaintiff he appreciated, I do not see why the plaintiff should not be compensated.

Compare the approach to 'intention' in this context with that in the 'genus' tort of interference with trade by unlawful means (p. 917, post). In *Meretz Investments NV v ACP Ltd* [2008] 2 WLR 904, [2007] EWCA Civ 1303, Arden LJ suggested at [146] that no difference existed between the required intention for unlawful means conspiracy and that required for interference by unlawful means, as defined by the House of Lords in *OBG v Allan* (p. 924, post). She described the required intention to ground an unlawful means conspiracy action as follows: 'it is not enough that there is an intention to do an act which in fact causes loss. That act must be done with the intention that it will cause loss.'

2. Note that Stuart-Smith LJ in *Powell v Boldaz* took the view that the unlawful means relied upon by the conspirators in an unlawful means conspiracy in question had to be independently actionable by the claimant, i.e. that the claimant would have to show that they could sustain a cause of action in respect of the act or acts that caused them harm. However, the House of Lords in *Revenue and Customs Commissioners v Total Network SL* [2008] 2 All ER 413, [2008] UKHL 19 overruled *Powell v Boldaz* on this point and established that where an action was brought in respect of an unlawful means conspiracy, the required 'unlawful means' could include conduct such as breach of criminal law or statutory duties which was not in itself independently actionable by the claimants, see p. 883, post.

3. Unlawful means conspiracy can operate to widen the category of defendants and catch individuals who have not themselves acted unlawfully: see *Rookes v Barnard* [1964] AC 1129, [1964] 1 All ER 367, (p. 917, post), where a trade union official who participated in the threat of strike action but was not employed by BOAC and could not therefore have unlawfully threatened to break his contract was nevertheless held liable in conspiracy. This makes the question of what control devices apply to limit the width of this tort of particular importance.

4. Before the Court of Appeal decision in *Metall und Rohstoff AG v Donaldson Lufkin & Jenrette Inc* [1990] 1 QB 391, 1989] 3 All ER 14, the rule appeared to be that there was no defence of justification to an unlawful means conspiracy. The Court of Appeal in *Metall* appeared to set up a choice between the 'predominant purpose' rule and the 'no justification' rule as desirable devices which could control the scope of liability under this potentially very wide tort, and to opt for the 'predominant purpose' rule. The abrogation of the 'predominant purpose' rule in *Lonrho v Fayed* therefore potentially opens up the scope of this tort. (For an analysis of the flaws of the Court of Appeal's adoption of the 'predominant intention' test in *Metall* which was by and large subsequently confirmed by the House of Lords in *Lonrho v Fayed*, see p. Sales [1990] CLJ 491.)

5. It remains very doubtful whether a defence of justification could apply to involvement in a conspiracy to harm the claimant, if it is possible to 'justify' the alleged unlawful means themselves, then the alleged 'unlawful means' thereupon cease to be unlawful and the conspiracy reverts to being a conspiracy to injure in which, of course, predominant purpose to injure must be proved and in which a broad version of justification is available. In *Meretz Investments NV v ACP Ltd* [2008] 2WLR 904, [2007] EWCA Civ 1303, the Court of Appeal considered that where inducement to breach a contact could be justified on the basis that the defendant in question acted to further his own interests and had a genuine belief that he had a lawful right to do so, then this justification would prevent the claimant relying on the alleged act of inducement to make out a cause of action for unlawful means conspiracy. Note that Toulson LJ at [174] of *Meretz* appears to suggest that a defence of justification is available for conspiracy, but Arden

LJ's reasoning at [127] is more precise in regarding the justification question as relevant in establishing whether unlawful means were used, not to the actual participation in the combination in question.

6. In *Lonrho plc v Fayed (No 5)* [1994] 1 All ER 188, [1993] 1 WLR 1489, the Court of Appeal held that damages for lost reputation are not recoverable in conspiracy, but only in defamation.

7. There is a statutory immunity in s. 20 of the Trade Union and Labour Relations (Consolidation) Act 1992, where the agreement is to commit an act which would not be actionable in tort if committed by an individual and the act is 'in contemplation or furtherance of a trade dispute'. The precise limits of this defence are debatable, but the modern judicial acceptance of most trade union objectives as 'legitimate' (*Crofter's* case) and the requirement of some form of 'intention' to injure even when unlawful means are employed means that the immunity is of less importance than when it was first introduced as s. 1 of the Trade Disputes Act 1906 to counteract *Quinn v Leathem* [1901] AC 495.

8. Both types of conspiracy remain less than satisfactory. 'Lawful means' conspiracy permits a combination of persons to be sued even when they have not deployed unlawful means against their target, even if it the scope of the justification defence to this action and the requirement that harm be the 'predominant' intention of the combination serve to limit its use. In an era of EU and national competition legislation, does this tort still serve a useful purpose? 'Unlawful means' conspiracy is also controversial, as it permits liability to attach to participants in a conspiracy even if individual participants have themselves not used unlawful means.

    There is an argument that unlawful means conspiracy should be reclassified as a form of secondary liability, whereby liability would be imposed if participants in a combination come within the definition of joint tortfeasors (see pp. 1108, post): see Sales and Stilitz (1999) 115 LQR 411, H. Carty (1988) 104 *LQR* 250; *Stevens* pp. 248–250. See also Laddie J's judgment in *Michaels v Taylor Woodrow Developments Plc* [2001] Ch 493, [2000] 4 All ER 645. The attraction of this analysis is that it may provide a better justification for imposing liability on members of a combination: their 'wrong' could be defined as their common participation in the 'joint enterprise' of deploying the unlawful means in question to cause loss to the claimant. This reconceptualisation of the tort would limit its scope: participants in the combination would only be liable if they satisfied the requirements for joint liability to be imposed (see p. 1108, post), and the unlawful means in question were independently actionable by the claimant, i.e. were sufficient to give rise to a cause of action which the claimant could maintain. This would exclude breaches of criminal law or statutory duty from qualifying as 'unlawful means' for this tort, unless the claimant could maintain a legal action for breach of statutory duty (see chap. 12, ante). Refining unlawful means conspiracy in this way might render the tort redundant, as it would be absorbed within the requirements for secondary liability: see T. Weir (2002) 118 LQR 164, at 166. Whether this is considered a good or bad outcome will depend on the view one adopts of the tort's usefulness.

9. However, in *Revenue and Customs Commissioners v Total Network SL* [2008] 2 All ER 413, [2008] UKHL 19, the House of Lords rejected the argument that liability for unlawful means conspiracy could only be established where the unlawful means were actionable at the suit of the claimant. In so doing, their Lordships distinguished unlawful means conspiracy from the tort of causing loss by unlawful means, which the majority of the House of Lords in *OBG v Allan* had treated as requiring the use of independently

actionable unlawful loss, at least where the unlawful means in question were directed at a 'third party' (see p. 924, ante). Lord Walker and Lord Neuberger also disagreed with the view that unlawful means conspiracy was a form of secondary liability.

■ Revenue and Customs Commissioners v Total Network SL
House of Lords [2008] 2 All ER 413

The Revenue and Customs Commissioners claimed that Total Network SL was liable to it in damages at common law for unlawful means conspiracy for sums equivalent to the amounts of value added tax (VAT) which the commissioners said they had lost as a result of 'carousel frauds' in which Total had participated. The unlawful means on which the commissioners relied were, inter alia, the commission by two other companies alleged to be involved with Total Network in the conspiracy of the common law offence of cheating the public revenue. On the trial of a preliminary issue, the judge held that they had a cause of action in conspiracy where the unlawful means alleged was the common law offence of cheating the public revenue. The Court of Appeal ([2007] EWCA Civ 39, [2007] 2 WLR 1156) allowed Total's appeal against that decision, holding that it was bound by the authority of the Court of Appeal decision in *Powell v Boldaz* (1997) 39 BMLR 35 to the effect that the unlawful act relied on had to be actionable at the suit of the claimant, and that it was not sufficient that the unlawful means alleged in this case amounted to a crime or a breach of contract with a third party. It therefore struck out the commissioner's claim. The commissioners appealed against that decision, and Total Network cross-appealed, arguing that it was not open to the commissioners to maintain a cause of action in damages at common law as a means of recovering VAT from a person who had not been made accountable or otherwise liable for that tax by Parliament.

LORD HOPE OF CRAIGHEAD:...

[41]...As Lord Wright put it in [*Veitch*], it is in the fact of the conspiracy that the unlawfulness resides: [1942] AC 435, p 462. That is the essence of the lawful means conspiracy. It is for the claimant to show that to harm his economic interests was the predominant purpose of the conspiracy. The situation that was contemplated in that case was one where the combination had more than one purpose, which Viscount Simon LC described (... at 445) as 'the quagmire of mixed motives'. In a case of that kind the issue has to be resolved by ascertaining the predominant intention. If the predominant intention of the combination is to injure, what is done is actionable even though the means used were lawful. Harm caused by a conspiracy where the means used were unlawful would seem no less in need of a remedy...

[43] In *OBG Ltd v Allan* [2007] UKHL 21 at [56]..., para 56 Lord Hoffmann said that the courts should be cautious in extending the tort of causing loss by unlawful means beyond the description given by Lord Watson in *Allen v Flood* [1898] AC 1, 96 and Lord Lindley in *Quinn v Leathem* [1901] AC 495, 535, which was designed only to enforce standards of civilised behaviour in economic competition between traders or between employers and labour. I entirely appreciate the point that he makes that caution is needed where the unlawful act is directed against a third party at whose instance it is not actionable because he suffers no loss. There the claimant's cause of action is, as Hazel Carty, An Analysis of the Economic Torts (2001), p 274 puts it, parasitic on the unlawful means used by the defendant against another party. As to that situation I would prefer to reserve my opinion. But in this case there was no third party. The means used by the conspirators were directed at the claimants themselves. This is a case where the claimants were persuaded by the unlawful means to act to their own detriment which, in the *OBG* case [2007] 4 AUE R 545 at [61], Lord Hoffmann said raises altogether different issues. One has to ask why, in this situation, the law should not provide a remedy.

[44] The situation that is contemplated is that of loss caused by an unlawful act directed at the claimants themselves. The conspirators cannot, on the Commissioners' primary contention, be sued as joint tortfeasors because there was no independent tort actionable by the Commissioners. This is a gap which needs to be filled. For reasons that I have already explained, I do not accept that the Commissioners suffered economic harm in this case. But assuming that they did, they suffered that harm as a result of a conspiracy which was entered into with an intention of injuring them by the means that were deliberately selected by the conspirators. If, as Lord Wright said in *Crofter Hand Woven Harris Tweed Co v Veitch* [1942] 1 AUE R 142 at 158, [1942] AC 435 at 462, it is in the fact of the conspiracy that the unlawfulness resides, why should that principle not apply here? As a subspecies of the tort of unlawful means conspiracy, the case is virtually indistinguishable from the tort of conspiracy to injure. The fact that the unlawful means were not in themselves actionable does not seem, in this context at least, to be significant. As Professor Joe Thomson put it in Carey, Miller and Meyers (eds): *An island legacy—The delict of conspiracy, Comparative and Historical Essays in Scots Law*, ed Carey Miller and Meyers (1992), p 148, the rationale of the tort is conspiracy to injure. These factors indicate that a conspiracy is tortious if an intention of the conspirators was to harm the claimant by using unlawful means to persuade him to act to his own detriment, even if those means were not in themselves tortious.

[45] I would hold that the decision of the Court of Appeal in *Powell v Boladz* was erroneous and that it should be overruled. I would also hold, in agreement with all your Lordships' that criminal conduct at common law or by statute can constitute unlawful means in unlawful means conspiracy. Had it been open to the Commissioners to maintain a civil claim of damages the tort of unlawful means would have been available to them, even though the unlawful means relied upon were not in themselves actionable.

LORD WALKER OF GESTINGTHORPE: . . .

[89] My Lords, faced with this confusion in the recent case-law, the House must, I suggest, go back to the general principles to be derived from the older cases in which the economic torts have been developed. It is however necessary to bear in mind that their development has been a long and difficult process, and may not yet be complete, as Lord Templeman observed (with the concurrence of the majority) in *Lonrho v Fayed* [1992] 1 AC 448, 471, [1991] 3 AUE R 303 at 314. A particular difficulty is that it has been generally assumed, throughout the 20th-century cases, that 'unlawful means' should have the same meaning in the intentional harm tort and in the tort of conspiracy. A good deal of legal reasoning in the speeches and judgments (as to the ingredients of one or other of these torts) has been based on the assumption that the meaning must be the same in both. That assumption is however challenged, if the Commissioners are correct, by the speech of Lord Hoffmann in *OBG* (with which the majority concurred). I shall have to come back to that difficulty.

[90] In searching for general principle I start with a very simple, even naïve point. The man in the street, if asked what an unlawful act was, would probably answer 'a crime.' He might give as an example theft, obtaining money by false pretences, or assault occasioning actual bodily harm. He might or might not know that each of these was also a civil wrong (or tort) but it is unlikely that civil liability would be in the forefront of his mind.

[91] The reaction of a lawyer would be more informed but it would not, I suggest, be essentially different. In its ordinary legal meaning 'unlawful' certainly covers crimes and torts (especially intentional torts). Beyond that its scope may sometimes extend to breach of contract, breach of fiduciary duty, and perhaps even matters which merely make a contract unenforceable, but the word's appropriateness becomes increasingly debatable and dependent on the legal context. In the very important criminal case of *R v Clarence* (1888) 22 QBD 23 (in which a question of law on ss 20 and 47 of the Offences against the Person Act 1861 was argued before a court of 13 judges, several of whom later gave their opinions to the House in *Allen v Flood*) Stephen J (at p 40) expressed the view that:

> 'The word "unlawfully" must here be construed to mean "unlawfully" in the wide general sense in which the word is used with reference to acts which if done by conspirators are indictable, though

not if they are done by individuals. This general sense may, I think, be said to be "immoral and mischievous to the public". I do not agree with the doctrine that the word "unlawfully" is used here in this wide sense. The use of the word in relation to conspiracy appears to me to be exceptional.'

What was exceptional about it was its extension downwards in the scale of blameworthy conduct. The unlawfulness of criminal conduct was at the top end of the scale, and too obvious to call for mention.

[92] The enquiry how far downwards to go seems to me to be a feature common to all the leading cases in which the tort of unlawful means conspiracy has been developed. Until Lord Diplock's speech in *Lonrho v Shell* there was never a clear issue as to whether the alleged unlawful means must be actionable (as a separate tort) at the suit of the plaintiff. Lord Diplock himself acknowledged this [1981] 2 AUE R 456 at 464, [1982] AC 173, 189. His attention may have been drawn to the point by his earlier disapproval (at p187) of some wide observations made by Lord Denning MR in an interlocutory appeal in *Ex parte Island Records Ltd* [1978] 3 AUE R 824, [1978] Ch 122.

[93] In the long period during which this issue did not arise for decision there is, unsurprisingly, little discussion of it in the authorities. They concentrate on the issue of intention (which was also at the heart of question 5(b) in *Lonrho...*). But all the statements of general principle in the classic cases seem to me to be consistent with the proposition that unlawful means, both in the intentional harm tort and in the tort of conspiracy, include both crimes and torts (whether or not they include conduct lower on the scale of blameworthiness) provided that they are indeed the means by which harm is intentionally inflicted on the claimant (rather than being merely incidental to it)...

[94] From these and other authorities I derive a general assumption, too obvious to need discussion, that criminal conduct engaged in by conspirators as a means of inflicting harm on the claimant is actionable as the tort of conspiracy, whether or not that conduct, on the part of a single individual, would be actionable as some other tort. To hold otherwise would, as has often been pointed out, deprive the tort of conspiracy of any real content, since the conspirators would be joint tortfeasors in any event (and there are cases discussing the notion of conspiracy 'merging' into some other tort, but I need not go far into those: *Surzur Overseas Ltd v Koros* [1999] 2 LLR 611; *Kuwait Oil Tanker Co. SAK v Al Bader* [2000] 2 All ER (Comm) 271).

[95] In my opinion your Lordships should clarify the law by holding that criminal conduct (at common law or by statute) can constitute unlawful means, provided that it is indeed the means (what Lord Nicholls of Birkenhead in *OBG* at para 159 called 'instrumentality') of intentionally inflicting harm...

[96] Having said that I would accept that the sort of considerations relevant to determining whether a breach of statutory duty is actionable in a civil suit (*Cutler v Wandsworth Stadium Ltd* [1949] AC 398) may well overlap, or even occasionally coincide with, the issue of unlawful means in the tort of conspiracy. But the range of possible breaches of statutory duty, and the range of possible conspiracies, are both so wide and varied that it would be unwise to attempt to lay down any general rule. What is important, to my mind, is that in the phrase 'unlawful means' each word has an important part to play. It is not enough that there is an element of unlawfulness somewhere in the story.

[97] I must now come back to *OBG* [2007] 4 AUE R 545 [2007] 2 WLR 920...[In that case] Lord Hoffmann observed in relation to the intentional harm tort (at [49]):

'In my opinion, and subject to one qualification, acts against a third party count as unlawful means only if they are actionable by that third party. The qualification is that they will also be unlawful means if the only reason why they are not actionable is because the third party has suffered no loss.'

Lord Nicholls of Birkenhead took a different view (at [149]–[163]).

[98] LORD HOFFMANN stated at [56]:

'Your Lordships were not referred to any authority in which the tort of causing loss by unlawful means has been extended beyond the description given by Lord Watson in *Allen v Flood* [1898] AC1, 96 and Lord Lindley in *Quinn v Leathem* [1901] AC 495, 535. Nor do I think it should be.'

He added at [57] (on which I have already commented):

'Likewise, as it seems to me, in a case like [*Lonrho v Shell*], it is not for the courts to create a cause of action out of a regulatory or criminal statute which Parliament did not intend to be actionable in private law.'

And at [60]:

'I do not think that the width of the concept of 'unlawful means' can be counteracted by insisting upon a highly specific intention, which 'targets' the plaintiff. That, as it seems to me, places too much of a strain on the concept of intention.'

[99] These passages (on which [counsel for Total Network] relied in his printed case and his oral submissions) prompted me to mention, near the beginning of this opinion, the risk of a new layer of anomaly being added to the tort of conspiracy (that is, that "unlawful means" would have a meaning for the purposes of a conspiracy claim different from its meaning for the purposes of a claim based on the intentional harm tort). But as Lord Hoffmann develops his reasoning in [51]–[58] of his opinion it becomes apparent that he is concerned, not only with the legal quality of the unlawful means (tort or crime?) but also with their effect in interfering with a third party's freedom of economic action. Cases like *RCA Corporation v Pollard* [1983] Ch 135 and *Isaac Oren v Red Box Toy Factory* [1999] FSR 785, show that a trader may suffer economic loss as the result of a civil wrong by a bootlegger actionable by the proprietor (or sometimes, an exclusive licensee) of intellectual property rights, without the trader having a remedy. The breach of the intellectual property rights is a statutory tort, but it is actionable only by those with a sufficient title to them. As I understand his opinion, Lord Hoffmann was concerned to limit the intentional harm tort to cases where the claimant has been 'intentionally struck at through others' (in the words of Lord Lindley in *Quinn v Leathem* [1901] AC 495, 535, quoted by Lord Hoffmann at [46]). He made clear (at [61]) that 'two party intimidation' raises quite different issues. This point is developed at [43] of the opinion of my noble and learned friend Lord Hope of Craighead, and at [124] of the opinion of my noble and learned friend Lord Mance, and I respectfully agree with their observations.

[100] The intentional harm tort and the 'unlawful means' variety of conspiracy share the ingredients of the intentional infliction of harm on the claimant. But that variety of conspiracy is not simply the intentional harm tort committed by joint tortfeasors. The gist of the intentional harm tort (apart from exceptional 'two party' cases) is striking at the claimant through a third party, and doing so by interfering with his freedom of economic activity. The gist of conspiracy is damage intentionally inflicted by persons who combine for that purpose (Viscount Simon LC in *Crofter* at p 444) and the claimant need not be a trader who is injured in his trade, though that is the most common case. In my opinion your Lordships are driven to the conclusion that, as the economic torts have developed, 'unlawful means' has a wider meaning in the tort of conspiracy than it has in the intentional harm tort.

[101] Some scholars have classified the tort of unlawful means conspiracy as a form of secondary liability (notably Hazel Carty, *An Analysis of the Economic Torts* (2001) p 22, agreeing with Philip Sales, 'The Tort of Conspiracy and Civil Secondary Liability' [1990] CLJ 491). They would not apply this classification to a conspiracy to injure by lawful means. If an unlawful means conspiracy is indeed a form of secondary liability for a civil wrong then the need for the unlawful means to be actionable as a civil wrong would be self-evident.

[102] However the premise is in my opinion mistaken...

[LORD WALKER cited passages in the judgment of Lord Wright in *Crofter* [1942] 1 AUE R 142 at 157–158 and Lord Bridge in *Lonrho v Fayed* [1991] 3 AUE R 303 at 310 in support of his conclusion. He also noted that, in the context of *Lonrho v Shell*, the emphasis was on the absence of an intention to injure, and not on the need for an independently actionable wrong. As a result, Lord Diplock's judgment in *Lonrho v Shell* could not be read as supporting a requirement of independent actionability. LORD WALKER then continued:]

[104] In short, and with great respect to those who take a different view, any suggestion that the unlawful means conspiracy is a form of secondary liability, and must therefore have an actionable wrong as an essential ingredient, seems to me to be a circular argument which assumes what it sets out to prove.

LORD MANCE:...

[122] Assuming that cheating the public revenue is not, even apart from the statutory scheme of the VAT and other taxing statutes, itself tortious in the absence of some other recognised tort such as deceit, the fact of conspiracy in my opinion offers a sufficient justification for recognising tortious responsibility in the present context, as it does in cases of predominant purpose to injury. The present appeal illustrates the extent to which cheating the revenue is a crime likely to be facilitated by a combination of conspirators. A devious individual or entity might—possibly—achieve the same result by himself or itself, but would be a great deal less likely to try or succeed.

[123] Heavy reliance was placed by Total on the *OBG* case. In that case, the House considered and distinguished the accessory or secondary liability which exists under the principle in *Lumley v. Gye* (1853) 2 E & B 216, where C induces B to break B's contract with A, and the primary liability which exists under the tort of causing loss to a person (A) by unlawful means where C commits acts (including the threat to do acts) against B which are actionable by B or would be if B had suffered loss and which affect B's freedom to deal with A (see [2007] 4 AUE R 545 at [49], [51], [129], and [136], per Lord Hoffmann). The majority of the House in *OBG* held the actionability (or potential actionability) of C's acts against B to be a pre-requisite to A having a claim in tort against C for causing loss by unlawful means. The submission made to the House on this appeal is that the House should adopt the same view of unlawful means in the context of the tort of conspiracy to injure. The submission has on its face attraction, as I have myself said in *Grupo Torras SA v Al-Sabah* [1999] CLC 1469 at 1649 (though in support of an analysis according to which actionability at the suit of the plaintiff was not necessary). But another view has been suggested at the highest level (*Rookes v Barnard* [1964] AC 1129, 1210–1211 per Lord Devlin), and, on reflection, there can be danger in what Lord Goff of Chieveley called "the temptation of elegance" (*Henderson v. Merrett Syndicates Ltd* [1995] 2 AC 145, 186B-C). The two torts are different in their nature, and the interests of justice may require their development on somewhat different bases.

[124] Lord Hope (at [43]) and Lord Neuberger (at [223]) note that Lord Hoffmann in the *OBG* case [2007] 4 AUE R 545 at [61], in 'defining the tort of causing loss by unlawful means as a tort which requires interference with the actions of a third party in relation to the plaintiff', made clear that 'a case of "two party intimidation" raises altogether different issues'. In relation to the three-party tort of causing loss by unlawful means, Lord Hoffmann's criticism of the Court of Appeal's reasoning in *OBG* was that it first expanded the concept of 'unlawful means', and then sought to counteract the width of the concept 'by insisting upon a highly specific intention, which "targets" the plaintiff'; this, he considered, 'places too much strain on the concept of intention' (see [60] and [135]). That problem does not to my mind arise with anything like the same force in the present context. I accept that conspiracy can be categorised as a three- rather than two-party tort, in that liability depends on at least two persons joining together to injure another: see also Hazel Carty in *An Analysis of the Economic Torts* at e.g. pp.271 and 278. Nevertheless, there is in my view a distinction between the infliction of harm through the intermediary of a third party (as in the case of the tort of causing harm by unlawful means under consideration in *OBG Ltd. v. Allan*) and the present situation where two wrongdoers join and act together to inflict injury directly upon another person or body; and to do so, moreover, by committing an offence integrally related to the Revenue and recognised specifically to protect it from such injury. This in turn assists to delimit the liability for conspiracy by unlawful means which the House is recognising by its present decision.

LORD NEUBERGER OF ABBOTSBURY:...

[220] In *OBG Ltd v Allan* [2007] UKHL 21 at [57] Lord Hoffmann (expressing the majority view in this House) said that the fact that the means involve a crime, without also involving a civilly actionable

wrong, was insufficient to establish a claim for loss caused by unlawful means. Given the obvious desirability of consistency and coherence as between the economic torts, it can fairly be said that the same rule should apply to a claim in unlawful means conspiracy. Further, the point made by Lord Hoffmann at para [57] of the *OBG* case that 'it is not for the courts to create a cause of action out of a...criminal statute which Parliament did not intend to be actionable in private law' can fairly be said to be as applicable to unlawful means conspiracy as to causing loss by unlawful means.

[221] On the other hand, it appears that the law of tort takes a particularly censorious view where conspiracy is involved. Thus, a claim based on conspiracy to injure can be established even where no unlawful means, let alone any other actionable tort, is involved. That tort is therefore frequently described as anomalous; yet its existence is very well established. Its centrally important feature is that the conspiracy must have as its primary purpose injury to the claimant. In my judgment, given the existence of that tort, it would be anomalous if an unlawful means conspiracy could not found a cause of action where, as here, the means 'merely' involved a crime, where the loss to the claimant was the obvious and inevitable, indeed in many ways the intended, result of the sole purpose of the conspiracy, and where the crime involved, cheating the revenue, has as its purpose the protection of the victim of the conspiracy. The difference between intending to make a profit at the claimant's expense and intending to cause injury to the claimant is pretty fine and, in economic terms, artificial: that point emerges most clearly from the discussion at [130]–[134] in Lord Hoffmann's opinion in *OBG*...

[223] Further, in the *OBG* case at [61], Lord Hoffmann made it clear that his 'discussion of unlawful means' was limited to cases involving 'interference with the actions of a third party in relation to the plaintiff', and did not necessarily apply to 'a case of "two party intimidation"', which, he said, 'raises altogether different issues'. In this case, as Lord Hope and Lord Mance have explained, the tort is of a 'two party' nature, in that the conspiracy could be said to have been directed against the Commissioners. After all, it was directly intended (albeit for the purpose of enriching the conspirators) to deprive the Commissioners of money to which they were entitled, and, if successful, it was inevitably and foreseeably going to do so, and no tort, harm or crime as against any party other than the Commissioners was involved. As Lord Hoffmann implicitly recognised, it may therefore not be inappropriate to hold that the Commissioners have a cause of action in such circumstances, even though they might not have had a claim if they had suffered loss (particularly if it was as an incidental result) as a result of a crime directed at a third party.

[224] Thus the notion that the Commissioners have a claim here is not, in my view inconsistent with the reasoning of the majority in *OBG*, upon which Total relies. In any event, the notion of a single consistent approach as to what constitutes unlawfulness in relation to all the economic torts can be said to be inconsistent with what Clerk & Lindsell refer to as the 'ramshackle' nature of the economic torts (para 25–001) and with the statement in Stevens, on *Torts and Rights* (2007) at p 297 that the economic torts 'have no inherent unity' and that it is 'a mistake to group these "torts" together'. I would in any event, at least in a case such as this, where injury to the claimant is the direct, inevitable and foreseeable result of the conspiracy succeeding, and where the crime can be said to exist for the protection of the victim, I would find it far less offensive to hold that unlawfulness can extend to a 'mere' crime in unlawful means conspiracy, when it cannot do so in causing loss by unlawful means, than to hold that a "mere" crime cannot in any circumstances constitute unlawfulness in unlawful means conspiracy, when there is a tort of conspiracy to injure by means which are neither tortious nor criminal.

[225] In this connection, I should record my agreement with Lord Walker and Lord Mance that, for the reasons they give, the tort of unlawful means conspiracy is not a form of secondary liability. Furthermore, although it involves an element of pulling oneself up by one's own bootstraps, it is hard to see what role the tort of unlawful means conspiracy, whose existence is accepted by Total, could have if it did not apply in a case such as this. This is well illustrated by Stevens's suggestion, at p 249, that there is no need for the tort of unlawful means conspiracy. This is on the basis that there are three well-established tortious principles which, between them, effectively 'catch' almost all who would be caught by a claim in unlawful means conspiracy. First, there is the tort of causing loss by unlawful

means, the tort considered in *OBG*. Secondly, there is the tort of conspiracy to injure, where injury to the claimant has to be the principle purpose of the conspiracy. Thirdly, there is the well-established principle that, where two or more parties join together in some way with a view to assisting or enabling one or more of them to commit a tort, all are liable for the tort as joint tortfeasors.

[226] On this basis, Stevens suggests that there is really no role for an additional tort of conspiring to injure by unlawful means. However, if a criminal act is sufficient unlawful means, at least in some circumstances (which Stevens challenges), the present case is an example of a claim which can (at least on the basis that the case has been argued by both parties) only succeed in unlawful means conspiracy. Conspiracy to injure cannot be relied on as injury to the Commissioners was not, it is apparently accepted by the Commissioners, the primary aim of the carousel fraud. Total could not be a joint tortfeasor if there is no claim in unlawful means conspiracy, because unlawful means conspiracy is the only tort relied on. There can be no claim in causing loss by unlawful means, as if the means involve a crime which is not civilly actionable, it does not count as unlawful means for that purpose (see the *OBG* case [2007] 4 AUE R 545 at [57]).

[227] Accordingly, in my view, on the basis of the arguments before your Lordships, a claim in unlawful means conspiracy could have been maintained... That is because, at least where the conspiracy has loss or damage to the claimant as the direct, foreseeable and inevitable consequence of its success, the fact that the means "only" involve a crime, at least where that is other than incidentally, appears to me to give rise to sufficient unlawfulness to establish a claim in unlawful means conspiracy.

[228] However, it seems to me that, although this argument was abandoned by the Commissioners, it may be that the better route to this conclusion is that this is a case of conspiracy to injure, and that, as Stevens suggests, there is no need for the tort of unlawful means conspiracy. I referred earlier to the point that the reasoning in paras 130 to 134 of *OBG* supports the view that, in this case, there is little, if any, difference between the conspirators' intention to make money and their intention to deprive the Commissioners of money: each is the obverse of the other. On that basis, it may well be that it could be said that the predominant purpose of Total and the other conspirators was indeed to inflict loss on the Commissioners just as much as it was to profit the conspirators, and hence the claim in tort is made out in conspiracy to injure.

[LORD SCOTT OF FOSCOTE delivered a judgment concurring that the unlawful means at issue did not have to be actionable at the suit of the claimant for the purposes of the tort of unlawful means conspiracy. LORD MANCE, LORD SCOTT OF FOSCOTE, and LORD WALKER OF GESTINGTHORPE concluded that there was nothing in the scheme of the 1994 Act or the Bill of Rights to preclude the Commissioners pursuing a common law action against the defendant. LORD HOPE OF CRAIGHEAD AND LORD NEUBERGER OF ABBOTSBURY dissented on this point.]

Appeal allowed.

QUESTIONS

How was the reasoning of the majority in *OBG v Allan* distinguished in the speeches set out above? What reasons were given for treating conspiracy by unlawful means as separate from other economic torts?

NOTES

1. The approach to unlawful means conspiracy adopted by all five of their Lordships in *Total Network* appears to make this tort even more anomalous. The scope of 'unlawful means' that can trigger liability under this cause of action is now wider than is the case for the tort of causing loss by unlawful means when 'third party' interference is

at issue (see p. 932 below, where this is further discussed). However, a new distinction appears to be emerging in the case law between situations where A directly interferes with B using unlawful means to inflict loss on B, or conspires to cause B loss through the use of unlawful means, and circumstances in which A interferes with C using unlawful means in order to cause loss to B. In the case of 'two-party' interference (when A directly interferes with B), or conspiracy (A joins with others to interfere with B), a broad concept of unlawful means will be adopted. In contrast, in the case of 'third party' interference, where A interferes with C to cause loss to B, a much more restrictive definition of unlawful means has been adopted in *OBG v Allan*. In other words, a key distinction is being made between situations where the claimant is being interfered with, whether by conspiracy or by the defendant acting alone, and when others are being interfered with to the detriment of the claimant: see in particular [99] in Lord Walker's judgment and [124] in Lord Mance's judgment. (We will return to this at p. 931, post).

2. How developed do you think is the reasoning of their Lordships that the nature of unlawful means conspiracy requires that a wider concept of unlawful means be adopted? Lord Neuberger suggests at [221] that the common law adopts a 'particularly censorious' approach to acts by combinations intended to cause harm to individuals. But this again gives rise to the recurring question as to why the fact of combination should matter so much. Note that Total Network had managed in this case to obtain VAT refunds by acting with other companies who had behaved illegally: the combination made possible the tax avoidance. Therefore, the facts of this case could serve as an example of why a combination can cause more harm than individuals acting singly. However, does this justify giving a wide scope to the unlawful means conspiracy? If Total Network successfully manipulated the tax system and did not violate any law themselves in so doing, should liability nevertheless be imposed upon them? Lord Hope asks at [43] above '[o]ne has to ask why, in this situation, the law should not provide a remedy?': at [44], he states that there is a 'gap' that should be filled. See also the use of similar logic by Lord Neuberger at [226] above, and note that Lord Scott at [57] (not extracted above) stated that 'any coherent law of tortious liability for conspiracy must hold Total liable in tort if the facts of the conspiracies pleaded in this case can be proved'. But this reasoning is based upon the presumption that a remedy should be available in such circumstances, which is to beg the question.

3. Lord Walker at [95]–[96] above suggests that the 'unlawful means' used to ground a claim in conspiracy for unlawful means must be the means or vehicle whereby intentionally inflicted harm was caused to the claimant. This approach might result in certain forms of unlawful activity on the part of the defendant being deemed to be insufficiently linked to the harm actually caused for liability to be established. It remains to be seen whether Lord Walker's dictum will become a substantial control device on the scope of liability under conspiracy. (Note that Lord Nicholls adopted a similar approach in his dissenting opinion in *OBG v Allan* in the context of the tort of causing loss by unlawful means.)

4. In *Meretz Investments NV v ACP Ltd* [2008] 2 WLR 904, [2007] EWCA Civ 1303, the Court of Appeal took a similarly nuanced approach to determining whether sufficient 'unlawful means' existed to sustain an action for unlawful means conspiracy. Arden LJ took the view at [148] that 'where a party does something which he is entitled to do because of his contractual right conferred by A, the fact that it results in a breach of B's contract with A cannot in my judgment constitute unlawful means of which A can complain in an action for damages for unlawful means conspiracy. The court has to

look at the whole of the means used by the alleged tortfeasor and not simply its effect on the party rendered in breach.'

5.   In *Total Network*, Lord Neuberger at [228] above suggests that the Revenue Commissioners could have successfully sustained an action for conspiracy to injure, otherwise known as 'lawful means' conspiracy. He suggests that 'there is little, if any, difference between the conspirators' intention to make money and their intention to deprive the Commissioners of money: each is the obverse of the other'. As discussed above, a 'predominant' intention to harm the claimant is required for a cause of action for conspiracy to injure to be established. Can a scheme designed to obtain VAT refunds from the Revenue Commissioners really be described as driven by a 'predominant intention' to harm the Commissioners? Was counsel for the Commissioners correct not to argue this point?

2 INDUCING BREACH OF CONTRACT

■ Lumley v Gye
Court of Queen's Bench [1843–60] All ER Rep 208

Miss Wagner, an opera singer, contracted with the plaintiff, a theatre proprietor, to perform at his theatre for three months. The defendant, the proprietor of a rival theatre, 'knowing the premises and with a malicious intention', before the end of the three 'wrongfully and maliciously enticed and procured Miss Wagner to refuse to sing or perform at the theatre' thus breaching her contract and causing the plaintiff loss.

CROMPTON J: . . .
It was laid down broadly, as a general proposition of law, that no action will lie for procuring a person to break a contract, although such procuring is with a malicious intention and causes great and immediate injury. The law as to enticing servants was said to be contrary to the general rule and principle of law, to be anomalous, and probably to have had its origin from the state of society when serfdom existed and to be founded upon, or upon the equity of, the Statute of Labourers. It was said that it would be dangerous to hold that an action was maintainable for persuading a third party to break a contract unless some boundary or limits could be pointed out; that the remedy for enticing away servants was confined to cases where the relation of master and servant, in a strict sense, subsisted between the parties; and that, in all other cases of contract, the only remedy was against the party breaking the contract.

    Whatever may have been the origin or foundation of the law as to enticing of servants, and whether it be, as contended by the plaintiff, an instance and branch of a wider rule, or, as contended by the defendant, an anomaly and an exception from the general rule of law on such subjects, it must now be considered clear law that a person who wrongfully and maliciously, or, which is the same thing, with notice, interrupts the relation subsisting between master and servant by procuring the servant to depart from the master's service, or by harbouring and keeping him as servant after he has quitted it and during the time stipulated for as the period of service, whereby the master is injured, commits a wrongful act for which he is responsible at law. I think that the rule applies wherever the wrongful interruption operates to prevent the service during the time for which the parties have contracted that the service shall continue, and I think that the relation of master and servant subsists, sufficiently for the purpose of such action, during the time for which there is in existence a binding contract of hiring and service between the parties. I think that it is a fanciful and technical and unjust distinction to say that the not having actually entered into the service, or that the service is not actually continuing, can make any difference. The wrong and injury are surely the same whether the wrongdoer entices away the gardener, who has hired himself for a year, the night before he is to go to his work, or after he has planted the first cabbage on the first morning of his service. I should be sorry to support a distinction so unjust, and so repugnant to common sense, unless bound to do so by some rule or authority of law plainly showing that such distinction exists....

The objection as to the actual employment not having commenced would not apply in the present case to the third count, which states that Miss Wagner had become the artiste of the plaintiff and that the defendant had induced her to depart from the employment. But it was further said that the engagement, employment, or service, in the present case was not of such a nature as to constitute the relation of master and servant, so as to warrant the application of the usual rule of law giving a remedy in case of enticing away servants. The nature of the injury and of the damage being the same, and the supposed right of action being in strict analogy to the ordinary case of master and servant, I see no reason for confining the case to services or engagements under contracts for services of any particular description; and I think that the remedy, in the absence of any legal reason to the contrary, may well apply to all cases where there is an unlawful and malicious enticing away of any person employed to give his personal labour or service for a given time under the direction of a master or employer who is injured by the wrongful act, more especially when the party is bound to give such personal services exclusively to the master or employer though I by no means say that the service need be exclusive....

In deciding this case on the narrower ground, I wish by no means to be considered as deciding that the larger ground taken by counsel for the plaintiff is not tenable, or as saying that in no case except that of master and servant is an action maintainable for maliciously inducing another to break a contract to the injury of the person with whom such contract has been made. It does not appear to me to be a sound answer to say that the [actionable] act in such cases is the act of the party who breaks the contract, for that reason would apply in the acknowledged case of master and servant. Nor is it an answer to say that there is a remedy against the contractor and that the party relies on the contract, for, besides that reason also applying to the case of master and servant, the action on the contract and the action against the malicious wrongdoer may be for a different matter, and the damages payable for such malicious injury might be calculated on a very different principle from the amount of the debt which might be the only sum recoverable on the contract. Suppose a trader, with a malicious intent to ruin a rival trader, goes to a banker or other party who owes money to his rival, and begs him not to pay the money which he owes him, and by that means ruins or greatly prejudices the party. I am by no means prepared to say that an action could not be maintained, and that damages, beyond the amount of the debt if the injury were great, or much less than such amount if the injury were less serious, might not be recovered. Where two or more parties were concerned in inflicting such injury, an indictment, or a writ of conspiracy at common law, might, perhaps, have been maintainable. Where a writ of conspiracy would lie for an injury inflicted by two, an action on the case in the nature of conspiracy will generally lie, and in such an action on the case the plaintiff is entitled to recover against one defendant without proof of any conspiracy, the malicious injury and not the conspiracy being the gist of the action: see note (4) to *Skinner v Gunton* (1669) 1 Saund at p. 230. In this class of cases it must be assumed that it is the malicious act of the defendant, and that malicious act only, which causes the servant or contractor not to perform the work or contract which he would otherwise have done. The servant or contractor may be utterly unable to pay for anything like the amount of the damage sustained entirely from the wrongful act of the defendant, and it would seem unjust, and contrary to the general principles of law, if such a wrongdoer were not responsible for the damage caused by his wrongful and malicious act....

ERLE J:...

It is clear that the procurement of the violation of a right is a cause of action in all instances where the violation is an actionable wrong, as in violations of a right to property, whether real or personal, or to personal security. He who procures the wrong is a joint wrongdoer, and may be sued, either alone or jointly with the agent, in the appropriate action for the wrong complained of. Where a right to the performance of a contract has been violated by a breach thereof, the remedy is upon the contract against the contracting party. If he is made to indemnify for such breach, no further recourse is allowed, and, as in case of the procurement of a breach of contract the action is for a wrong and cannot be joined with the action on the contract, and as the act itself is not likely to be of frequent occurrence nor easy of proof, therefore, the action for this wrong, in respect of other contracts than those of hiring, are not numerous, but still they seem to me sufficient to show that the principle has been recognised....

This principle is supported by good reason. He who maliciously procures a damage to another by violation of his right ought to be made to indemnify, and that whether he procures an actionable wrong or a breach of contract. He who procures the non-delivery of goods according to contract may inflict an injury, the same as he who procures the abstraction of goods after delivery, and both ought on the same ground to be made responsible. The remedy on the contract may be inadequate, as where the measure of damages is restricted; or in the case of non-payment of a debt where the damage may be bankruptcy to the creditor who is disappointed, but the measure of damages against the debtor is interest only; or, in the case of the non-delivery of the goods, the disappointment may lead to a heavy forfeiture under a contract to complete a work within a time, but the measure of damages against the vendor of the goods for non-delivery may be only the difference between the contract price and the market value of the goods in question at the time of the breach. In such cases, he who procures the damage maliciously might justly be made responsible beyond the liability of the contractor....

[WIGHTMAN J delivered a judgment agreeing with CROMPTON J. COLERIDGE J dissented.]

NOTES

1. Note that the claimant failed to establish his case at the trial of the action. *Bowen v Hall* (1881) 6 QBD 333 was the next case of inducing breach of contract to reach an appellate court. An expert bricklayer had been induced to leave his employer's service by a rival firm. As in *Lumley v Gye*, the relationship of master and servant, in the strict sense, did not exist. The Court of Appeal (Lord Selborne LC and Brett LJ; Lord Coleridge CJ dissenting) allowed the claimant employer an action. The majority took the view that *Lumley v Gye* had been correctly decided on the wide ground stated by Erle J, i.e. the *malicious* violation of contractual rights. However, in *Quinn v Leathem* [1901] AC 495 at 510, Lord Macnaghten said: 'I think the decision [in *Lumley v Gye*] was right, not on the ground of malicious intention that was not, I think the gist of the action, but on the ground that a violation of a legal right committed knowingly is a cause of action, and that it is a violation of a legal right to interfere with contractual relations recognised by law if there be no sufficient justification for the interference.'

2. Not everyone agrees that *Lumley v Gye* was rightly decided. See F. Sayre (1923) 36 Harv LR 663 and D. Howarth (2005) 68 MLR 195. Waddams has suggested that the approach adopted in *Lumley* has been unnecessarily elevated to the status of a general principle: see S. Waddams (2001) 117 LQR 431. In contrast, see T. Weir, *Economic Torts* (Oxford, 1997), R. Bagshaw (1998) 18 Oxf JLS 729 and A. Simester and W. Chan [2004] CLJ 132. The fundamental question is why, where D induces X to breach a contract between P and X, P should have a right of action against D when P already has contractual rights against X. Any difficulties P is in will be P's own doing: why is D made liable for a breach of contract between P and X where contract law offers remedies to P? P voluntarily entered into the relationship with X and agreed to the specific terms of that relationship. *Lumley v Gye* liability is often justified on the basis that P's remedies against X will often be inadequate, especially if the contract is a contract of

employment—injunctions and specific performance are generally not available against employees, the method of calculating damages favours employees, and even if damages are adequate in particular cases, employees would often not be able to pay, or employers will be slow to sue them and therefore wreck any future relationship. But the counterargument to this justificatory argument is that the problems of contract damages should prompt changes to the law of contract, not an extension of tort law, which constantly threatens ordinary commercial competition and which has made organising strikes prima facie unlawful, thus requiring the introduction of the statutory trade disputes immunity. The facts that employees are often not worth suing and legal action would undermine the relationship between employer and employee are normal commercial risks. Howarth has developed this argument and suggested that while it may be too late to remove *Lumley v Gye* liability from the common law, the scope of the justification defence that exists for this action should be expanded to compensate for the inherent flaws of this form of tort liability.

■ 'Against Lumley v Gye'
D. Howarth (2005) 68 Modern Law Review 195, 231–2

The case against *Lumley* is that it assumes that there is something inherently wrong with persuading someone to breach a contract, whereas such persuasion can often be morally justified, as well as being economically desirable. We have hinted at two different options for the future of *Lumley*. One is that it should be over-ruled and not replaced. The other is that it should be modified so that it becomes easier to justify procuring a breach of contract. There are grounds for believing that both options are better than the existing law. The next question is which of these two options is preferable.

The case for opting for the simple over-ruling *of Lumley* is that it would reduce the need for the courts to make substantive moral judgments. It would restrict their role to ensuring that economic efficiency is maintained through the plaintiff's option to claim sufficient expectation damages. In arguably the most important context in which *Lumley* is relevant, namely strike law, this point amounts to saying that the courts should not have to decide about the substantive merits of strikes.

The case against opting for the simple over-ruling of *Lumley* is, first, that it is unrealistic to expect it to happen: *Lumley* is well-established in English law and overruling it would raise the prospect of a complicated untangling of the law that could take a long time, cause uncertainty and not necessarily end up with the law in a satisfactory state. Secondly, the abrogation of *Lumley* would amount to the exclusion of all grounds of judgment about the parties apart from the economic efficiency of the breach. That would tend to give the impression that the courts believed that economic efficiency is a substitute for morality.

Lumley should be seen primarily in its industrial relations context, as the foundation of the law on strikes. Although it is important in other commercial contexts, none of them compare in historical importance with strike law. If *Lumley* is unsatisfactory in its industrial relations context, as it appears to be, we should consider reforming it. But reform that merely exempted industrial relations cases from the scope of *Lumley* is itself unsatisfactory because it gives rise to the false appearance that trade unions would be obtaining 'special' treatment. We need to look for a wider reform of *Lumley* that takes its non-industrial relations uses into account, but which gives priority, if necessary, to its industrial relations uses.

One objection to the radical reform of *Lumley* is that one can infer *Lumley* liability from the very existence of contract law. But, as we have seen, justifying *Lumley* involves imposing contract law on parties, such as trade unions, who are unwilling participants in state contract law. The justifications for imposing contract law on the unwilling do not reach Lumley as it applies to strikes, and possibly not as it applies in other circumstances as well.

Another objection to radical reform is the argument that *Lumley* liability is justified because it adds to our certainty that contracts will be performed. The main problem with that argument is that it assumes that it is always worthwhile to add to certainty, a position that ignores the costs of producing such extra certainty. Although we cannot be sure that we have reached the point at which the costs of extra certainty outweigh its benefits, we have reasons, particularly in industrial relations cases, to be sceptical about whether, if the parties had to construct their own law by agreement, they would opt for a *Lumley* rule, at least in its present form.

The argument from certainty also ignores the point, inherent in efficient breach analysis, that additional certainty that a bad deal will be fulfilled should be counted as a bad thing, not as a good thing. That point, of course, raises the status of efficient breach analysis, but those who criticise efficient breach analysis on moral grounds miss the point that it is also immoral for one party to a contract to insist on performance where the contract would not have been agreed had the parties known at the time what they know now.

The possibility of immoral insistence on contractual performance, and its confluence with efficient breach analysis, suggests that there should be a wider defence to *Lumley* that would allow the court to take such moral and economic points into account. Although there are arguments for the abolition of *Lumley*, a more plausible way forward is to extend the justification defence so that *Lumley* has no effect where it would not be fair, just and reasonable that it should apply. Hints of such a wider defence already exist in the case law, especially in commercial cases outside the employment context.

The advantages of a wider justification defence in industrial relations law, combined with the lack of any clear detriment in the rest of the law, generate at least a good arguable case for reform. Although it might be too late to correct what was done in *Lumley*, and more especially what was done in *Bowen v Hall*, one of the beauties of the common law is that it allows us to reflect on our experience and to use it to point ourselves in a new direction.

QUESTIONS

An 'efficient contractual breach' occurs when a party intentionally breaches a contract and pays the ensuing damages on the basis that they would incur greater economic loss by performing under the contract. See R. Birmingham (1970) 24 Rutgers L. Rev. 273: C. Goetz and R. Scott (1970) 77 Colum L. Rev. 554. Do you agree with Howarth's argument that there may be circumstances where both moral and economic efficiency arguments justify contractual breach, which the *Lumley* action should accommodate by making provision for a wider justification defence? If such a wider justification defence was introduced what, if anything, would be left of the *Lumley* tort?

■ South Wales Miners' Federation v Glamorgan Coal Co Ltd
House of Lords [1904–7] All ER Rep 211

The Miners' Federation had ordered a number of stopdays. Bigham J, [1903] 1 KB 118, held that in doing so the Federation and the members of its executive had been actuated by an honest desire to forward the interests of the men without any prospect of personal gain to themselves and without any intention, malicious or otherwise, to injure the plaintiffs, who were colliery owners. The object had been to restrict output so as to keep up coal prices because, under the sliding scale agreement between the colliery owners and the miners, wages depended upon the selling price of coal. It was not disputed that the Federation had induced and procured workmen who were employed by the plaintiffs to break their contracts of service, so inflicting loss on the plaintiffs. It was argued, however, that the wrong was justifiable. The Court of Appeal held that it was not, [1903] 2 KB 545. On appeal to the House of Lords:

LORD MACNAGHTEN: . . .

That there may be a justification for that which in itself is an actionable wrong I do not for a moment doubt; and I do not think that it would be difficult to give instances, putting aside altogether cases complicated by the introduction of moral considerations. But what is the alleged justification in the present case? It was said that the council, the executive of the federation, had a duty cast upon them to protect the interests of the members of the union, and that they could not be made legally responsible for the consequences of their action if they acted honestly in good faith and without any sinister or indirect motive. The case was argued with equal candour and ability. But it seems to me that the argument may be disposed of by two simple questions. How was the duty created? What in fact was the alleged duty? The alleged duty was created by the members of the union themselves, who elected or appointed the officials of the union to guide and direct their action; and then it was contended that the body to whom the members of the union have thus committed their individual freedom of action are not responsible for what they do, if they act according to their honest judgment in furtherance of what they consider to be the interest of their constituents. It seems to me that if that plea were admitted there would be an end of all responsibility. It would be idle to sue the workmen, the individual wrongdoers, even if it were practicable to do so. Their counsellors and protectors, the real authors of the mischief, would be safe from legal proceedings. The only other question is, What is the alleged duty set up by the federation? I do not think that it can be better described than it was by counsel for the plaintiffs. It comes to this: it is the duty on all proper occasions, of which the federation or their officials are to be the sole judges, to counsel and procure a breach of duty. . . .

LORD JAMES OF HEREFORD: . . .

It yet remains to deal with the words 'wrongfully and maliciously' as averred in the statement of claim.

As to the word 'wrongfully', I think that no difficulty arises. If the breach of the contract of service by the workmen was an unlawful act, any one who induces and procures the workmen, without just cause and excuse, to break such contract also acts unlawfully, and thus the allegation that the act done was wrongfully done is established. But the word 'maliciously' has also to be dealt with. The judgment of Bigham J [[1903] 1 KB at p. 133], proceeds on the ground that:

'to support an action for procuring a breach of contract it is essential to prove actual malice.'

I cannot concur in this view of the law. The word 'maliciously' is often employed in criminal and civil pleadings without proof of actual malice, apart from the commission of the act complained of, being required. If A. utters a slander of B., even if he be a stranger to him, the averment that A. maliciously spoke such words of B. is established by simply proving the uttering of words taken to be false until the contrary be proved. In such an action the word 'maliciously' may be treated either as an unnecessary averment or as being proved by inference drawn from the proof of the act being wrongfully committed. . . .

LORD LINDLEY: . . .

The constitution of the union may have rendered it the duty of the officials to advise the men what could be legally done to protect their own interests, but a legal duty to do what is illegal and known so to be is a contradiction in terms. A similar argument was urged without success in *Read v. Friendly Society of Stonemasons*. . . .[16]

Then your Lordships were invited to say that there was a moral or social duty on the part of the officials to do what they did, and that, as they acted bona fide in the interests of the men and without any ill-will to the employers, their conduct was justifiable; and your Lordships were asked to treat this case as if it were like a case of libel or slander on a privileged occasion. This contention was not based

[16] [1902] 2 KB 732.

on authority, and its only merits are its novelty and ingenuity. The analogy is, in my opinion, misleading; and to give effect to this contention would be to legislate and introduce an entirely new law and not to expound the law as it is at present. It would be to render many acts lawful which, as the law stands, are clearly unlawful.

...I have purposely abstained from using the word 'malice'. Bearing in mind that malice may or may not be used to denote ill-will, and that in legal language presumptive or implied malice is distinguished from express malice, it conduces to clearness in discussing such cases as these to drop the word 'malice' altogether and to substitute for it the meaning which is really intended to be conveyed by it. Its use may be necessary in drawing indictments; but when all that is meant by malice is an intention to commit an unlawful act, and to exclude all spite or ill-feeling, it is better to drop the word and so avoid all misunderstanding. The appeal ought to be dismissed with costs.

[EARL HALSBURY LCdelivered a speech in favour of dismissing the appeal.]

Appeal dismissed.

■ Edwin Hill & Partners (a firm) v First National Finance Corpn plc
Court of Appeal [1988] 3 All ER 801

The defendants were a finance company who had made a substantial loan to a property developer, secured by a legal charge. The developer was unable to start the development and to repay the loan. Instead of exercising their powers of sale as mortgagees, the finance company agreed to make further advances to the developer, but on terms that the developer's contract with the plaintiff architects be terminated and that new architects be appointed in their place. The developer complied with this requirement. The plaintiffs thereupon sued the defendants for inducing breach of contract. Rose J held that all the elements of the tort were made out, but that the defendants had established the defence of justification because the right of the mortgagees to receive payment of their loan and interest constituted an equal or superior right to that of the plaintiffs. The question of justification was the main issue on appeal.

STUART-SMITH LJ: ...
Counsel for the defendants submitted that the judge's approach was correct. He contended that where the interferer's conduct is within the ambit or compass of his legal rights he is justified. By this phrase he means that if the defendants, instead of exercising their full legal rights of calling for repayment of the loan and exercising their powers of sale or appointment of a receiver, reach some accommodation with the mortgagor, which is more beneficial both to themselves and the mortgagor, they should not be held to lose the justification which they would have had if they had exercised the remedies available to them in the strict sense.

Alternatively he submits that the question of justification should be approached by what he called the 'broad brush' approach adumbrated by Romer LJ in *Glamorgan Coal Co Ltd v South Wales Miners' Federation* [1903] 2 KB 545. This is a convenient starting point for a consideration of the authorities. Romer LJ said (at 574):

'I respectfully agree with what Bowen L.J. said in [*Mogul Steamship Co Ltd v McGregor Gow & Co* (1889) 23 QBD 598 at 618, [1891–4] All ER Rep 263 at 281], when considering the difficulty that might arise whether there was sufficient justification or not: "The good sense of the tribunal which had to decide would have to analyze the circumstances and to discover on which side of the line each case fell." I will only add that, in analyzing or considering the circumstances, I think that regard might be had to the nature of the contract broken; the position of the parties to the contract; the grounds for the breach; the means employed to procure the breach; the relation of the person procuring the breach to the person who breaks the contract; and I think also to the object of the person in procuring the breach. But, though I deprecate the attempt to define justification, I think it right to express my opinion on certain points in connection with breaches of contract procured where the contract is one of master and servant. In my opinion, a defendant sued for knowingly procuring such a breach is not justified of necessity merely by his shewing that he had no personal animus against the employer, or that it was to the advantage or interest of both the defendant and the workman that the contract should be broken.'

Stirling LJ's judgment is to the same effect (at 577).

When the case reached the House of Lords ([1905] AC 239, [19047] All ER Rep 211) nothing was said by any members of the House to suggest that this was the wrong approach. Lord Lindley expressed entire agreement with the judgments of Romer and Stirling LJJ (see [1905] AC 239 at 252, [1904–7] All ER Rep 211 at 218). The other members of the House contented themselves with saying that the alleged justification did not amount to such in law. In my judgment it matters not that some of their Lordships treated the case as both conspiracy and wrongful interference with contracts (see for example [1905] AC 239 at 244, [19047] All ER Rep 211 at 244 per the Earl of Halsbury LC).

Counsel for the plaintiffs submitted that in the *Glamorgan* case the supposed justification was a duty to act in what was conceived to be the interests of both parties to the contract and that accordingly Romer LJ's test or approach should be confined to such cases, and should not extend to cases where the interferer's conduct is sought to be justified by reference to some equal or superior legal right. But I cannot see that the proposition should be so limited; in my judgment the courts have over the years worked on this principle, holding that some cases fall on one side of the line, others on the other....

Thus the following matters have been held not to amount to justification. (1) Absence of malice or ill-will or intention to injure the person whose contract is broken: *Smithies v National Association of Operative Plasterers* [1909] 1 KB 310, [1908–10] All ER Rep 455 and *South Wales Miners' Federation v Glamorgan Coal Co Ltd* [1905] AC 239, [1904–7] All ER Rep 211. (2) The commercial or other best interests of the interferer or the contract breaker: *Read v Friendly Society of Operative Stonemasons of England Ireland and Wales* [1902] 2 KB 88 at 97, [1902] 2 KB 732 at 737 per Darling J and Collins MR, the *Glamorgan* case [1905] AC 239 at 252, [1904–7] All ER Rep 211 at 217–218 per Lord James, *Pratt v British Medical Association* [1919] 1 KB 244 at 266, [1918–19] All ER Rep 104 at 115 per McCardie J and *De Jetley Marks v Lord Greenwood* [1936] 1 All ER 863 at 873 per Porter J. (3) The fact that A has broken his contract with X does not of itself justify X in revenge procuring a breach of an independent contract between A and B: *Smithies v National Association of Operative Plasterers* [1909] 1 KB 310 esp at 337, [1908–10] All ER Rep 455 esp at 467 per Buckley LJ.

On the other side of the line justification has been said to exist where (1) there is a moral duty to intervene, as for example in *Brimelow v Casson* [1924] 1 Ch 302, [1923] All ER Rep 40, where it was held that the defendants were justified in their actions since they owed a duty to their calling and its members to take all necessary steps to compel the plaintiff to pay his chorus girls a living wage so that they were not driven to supplement their earnings through prostitution, (2) where the contract interfered with is inconsistent with a previous contract with the interferer: see per Buckley LJ in *Smithies's* case [1909] 1 KB 310 at 337, [1908–10] All ER Rep 455 at 467....

This leads one to a consideration of the important case of *Read v Friendly Society of Operative Stonemasons of England Ireland and Wales* [1902] 2 KB 88. Darling J said (at 96–97):

'I think their sufficient justification for interference with plaintiff's right must be an equal or superior right in themselves, and that no one can legally excuse himself to a man, of whose contract he has procured the breach, on the ground that he acted on a wrong understanding of his own rights, or without malice, or bona fide, or in the best interests of himself, nor even that he acted as an altruist, seeking only the good of another and careless of his own advantage.'

Rose J adopted this test, namely whether the defendants had an equal or superior right in themselves. And much of the argument before us has been directed to the question whether he was right to hold that they did....

The submission of counsel for the plaintiffs to us is to the effect that the words 'sufficient justification for interference with plaintiff's right must be an equal or superior right in themselves' must be confined to the exercise of that right by the defendant. But I can find no warrant for his proposition and in my judgment it confuses right with the remedies available to protect the right. The defendants had the rights of a secured creditor, that is to say the right to be repaid their loan together with interest; in support of that right they had the remedies or rights granted by the legal charge and the law, namely to sell the land or appoint a receiver. They were not bound to exercise these remedies in defence of their rights, but they could do so. Had they done so, it is common ground, at least in so far as the power of sale and I think probably also on the appointment of a receiver, that the plaintiffs' contract would have come to an end. If instead of exercising these remedies in their full rigour, they reach an accommodation with the mortgagor in defence and protection of their rights as secured creditor, which has the same result of putting an end to the plaintiffs' contract, it would in my judgment be anomalous and illogical if they were justified in the one case but not in the other . . .

Justification for interference with the plaintiff's contractual right based on an equal or superior right in the defendant must clearly be a legal right. Such right may derive from property real or personal or from contractual rights. Property rights may simply involve the use and enjoyment of land or personal property. To give an example put in argument by Sir Nicolas Browne-Wilkinson V-C, if X carries on building operations on his land, they may to the knowledge of X interfere with a contract between A and B to carry out recording work on adjoining land occupied by A. But, unless X's activity amounts to a nuisance, he is justified in doing what he did. Alternatively, the law may grant legal remedies to the owner of property to act in defence or protection of his property; if in the exercise of these remedies he interferes with a contract between A and B of which he knows, he will be justified. If instead of exercising those remedies he reaches an accommodation with A, which has a similar effect of interfering with A's contract with B, he is still justified notwithstanding that the accommodation may be to the commercial advantage of himself or A or both. The position is the same if the defendant's right is to a contractual as opposed to a property right, provided it is equal or superior to the plaintiff's right.

In my judgment that is the position in this case; I therefore agree with the judge's conclusion and would dismiss the appeal. . . .

[NOURSE LJ delivered a judgment, in which he agreed with STUART-SMITH LJ, in favour of dismissing the appeal. SIR NICOLAS BROWNE-WILKINSON V-C agreed with both judgments.]

Appeal dismissed.

QUESTION

Would the defence of justification have succeeded had it been shown that the defendants could have secured further advances by other means? This and other issues are considered by R. O'Dair (1991) 11 Oxf JLS 227.

NOTES

1. The general approach to justification adopted in *Edwin* Hill has been approved by Lord Nicholls in *OBG v Allan* [2007] 4 All ER 545 at 598, and by the Court of Appeal in *Meretz Investments NV v ACP Ltd* [2008] 2 WLR 904, [2007] EWCA Civ 1303. Justification must be proved as against the *claimant*, irrespective of the rights and wrongs between the defendant and the intermediary. In *Greig v Insole* [1978] 3 All ER 449, [1978] 1 WLR 302 the international and English cricketing authorities had directly induced breaches of contract by imposing retrospective bans on playing first-class cricket against cricketers who had entered into contracts with Mr Kerry Packer's World Series Cricket Pty

Ltd (WSC). Slade J held that whatever the actions of the players might have been, the authorities had not given much thought to the possibility that they might be infringing WSC's rights and despite, their disinterested motives, the defence of justification against WSC could not succeed. One may ask whether the result would have been different had the authorities gone no further than was necessary to protect their legitimate interests of ensuring that first-class cricket is properly organised and administered ([1978] 3 All ER at p. 497). It seems that they could have done this by limiting the ban to those who contracted with WSC *after* the ban was announced (cf. ibid. p. 501). One may note that in an American case (*Knapp v Penfield* 5 NYS 41 (1932)) the promoter of a play (an 'angel') who induced the dismissal of an actress to protect his investment in the play, succeeded in the defence of justification; and in *Posluns v Toronto Stock Exchange and Gardiner* (1964) 46 DLR (2d) 210, on appeal (1966) 53 DLR (2d) 193, inducing breach of the employment contract of a broker's man to promote financial probity on the stock exchange was held to be justifiable.

2. Justification is judged at the time of the interference, not at the time of trial. Thus in *SOS Kinderdorf International v Ebrima B Bittaye* [1996] 1 WLR 987 the Privy Council decided that it would be no justification of the defendants' interference in an employment contract between the claimant and an employee that information later came to light that might have warranted the employee's dismissal.

3. Why were the combinations of shipping companies in *Mogul SS Co Ltd v McGregor, Gow & Co* [1892] AC 25 and of employers and trade union in the *Crofter* case (p. 876, ante) allowed to justify their actions, but not the South Wales Miners' Federation? For general discussion of the defence of justification see J.D. Heydon (1970) 6 Univ Tor LJ 139 at 161–171; and *Heydon*, pp. 38–47. An earlier but still useful discussion of principle is to be found in C.E. Carpenter (1928) 41 Harv LR 728 at 745 et seq; see too J. Nockleby (1980) 93 Harv LR 540.

4. Why should the burden of showing that the interference was 'justified' lie on the defendant? Compare what would happen if the question were whether the defendant's conduct counted as 'reasonable' in negligence, which to some degree reflects the position in French law: cf. D. Howarth, in *The Classfication of Obligations*, edited by P. Birks (Oxford, 1997), p. 233.

5. The absence of any common law defence of justification in respect of many trade union activities resulted in the enactment of a statutory immunity for inducing breach of contract. The Trade Union and Labour Relations Acts 1974 and 1976, s. 13 extended this to the breach or interference with the performance of any contract provided the act is done 'in contemplation or furtherance of a trade dispute' but this has now been modified by subsequent legislation. In New Zealand, in *Pete's Towing Services Ltd v Northern Industrial Union of Workers* [1970] NZLR 32, the common law defence of justification was allowed where a trade union defendant was found to be putting forward 'fair conditions' and the inducement was 'not being used as a sword to procure financial betterment but as a shield to avoid involvement in industrial discord' (Speight J at p. 51). C. Grunfeld (1971) 34 MLR 181 at 185 submits, in the light of this decision, that while the defence of justification is barred in economic disputes (*South Wales Miners' Federation* case, p. 895, ante) it is not in labour disputes of 'principle' (e.g. about recognition of a union, bona fide compliance with an agreed disputes procedure, or tolerating a breakaway union). See further *Morgan v Fry* [1968] 2 QB 710, [1968] 3 All ER 452 (similar considerations in the tort of intimidation, p. 921, post) and B.G. Hansen (1975) 38 MLR 217.

6. The gist of the *Lumley* action for inducing breach of contract was described as the 'violation of a legal right' and something that is 'in itself an actionable wrong' (Lord Macnaghten, in *Quinn v Leathem* [1901] AC 495 at 510, [1900–3] All ER Rep 1 at 9). As discussed below, this conceptual approach to the tort has been subsequently modified by the House of Lords in *OBG v Allen*, with considerable consequences for its scope. However, prior to this recent shift in how the *Lumley* tort is analysed, Lord Macnaghten's view that inducing a breach of a contractual agreement that was in itself an inherently actionable wrong has been very influential, and contributed to the extension of the tort to cover other instances of inducing breaches of legal obligations. Case law has recognised the existence of a cause of action for inducing a breach of statutory duty (*Meade v London Borough of Haringey* [1979] 2 All ER 1016, [1979] 1 WLR 637; *Associated British Ports v Transport and General Workers' Union* [1989] ICR 557, [1989] 3 All ER 796, reversed on a different point [1989] ICR 557, [1989] 3 All ER 822) and inducing breach of an equitable obligation (*Prudential Assurance Co Ltd v Lorenz* (1971) 11 KIR 78). However, it seems that it is not a tort to procure a breach of trust (*Metall und Rohstoff AG v Donaldson Lufkin & Jenrette Inc* [1989] 3 All ER 14 at 58–59). It also seems not to be a tort to induce unfair dismissal (*Wilson v Housing Corpn* [1998] ICR 151). The reasons for differentiating between these different forms of inducing a breach of pre-existing legal obligation are not wholly clear. Why should inducing a breach of an equitable obligation be treated as more blameworthy than inducing a breach of unfair dismissal law? As with much of the case law relating to the economic torts, one senses that a certain degree of *ad hoc* decision-making is guiding the evolution of these causes of action. Note as well that in *Law Debenture Trust Corpn plc v Ural Caspian Oil Corpn Ltd* [1995] Ch 152, [1995] 1 All ER 157, the Court of Appeal decided that there was a tort of interfering with the claimant's rights to remedies for breach of contract (as distinct from the claimant's 'primary' rights under the contract). But the court went on to say that remedies that are technically 'discretionary', such as injunctions and specific performance, will not normally attract the protection of the tort because the claimant has no right to them. On one view, such remedies give rise to no 'secondary' rights at all. On another view they give rise to rights only when the court makes an order, but not before. Either way, there are no pre-existing rights for an inducement to violate.

7. In *OBG v Allan* [2007] 4 All ER 545, [2007] UKHL 21, the House of Lords has redefined the conceptual basis of the *Lumley* cause of action, classifying it as a form of accessory liability: the inducement is not treated as a primary wrong in itself, but rather as a secondary form of wrong dependent upon the defendant's involvement with the contracting party's primary and actionable wrong of breach of contract. Presumably, if the derivative torts of inducing breach of statutory and equitable duties, as well as the tort of interference with rights to contractual remedies, are deemed to have survived the cull of authority carried out in *OBG v Allan*, the same analysis as adopted in that case in respect of inducing a breach of contract will be applied to them. It remains to be seen what impact this will have on their future application, but it is only logical that the same requirements that the House of Lords in *OBG* viewed as necessary for a cause of action for inducing a breach of contract to exist would also be applied here, i.e. that there be an actual breach of the duty or right in question, and that the defendant intended to cause the breach of duty or equitable right (see p. 907, post). For the action of inducement to breach a statutory duty, it would also appear that consistency with *OBG* would require that the breach of statutory duty be independently actionable by

the claimant against the induced party (see *Cutler v Wandsworth Stadium Ltd* [1949] AC 398, [1949] 1 All ER 544, noted p. 673, ante, and in general chap. 12 ante).

8. However, it should be noted that a passage in Lord Hoffmann's judgment in *OBG v Allan*, at [93], can be seen as casting some doubt over the continuing existence of inducement torts beyond the contractual context. In the Court of Appeal decision in *OBG v Allan* [2005] 2 All ER 602, [2005] EWCA Civ 106, Mance LJ suggested that the tort of inducing a breach of contract could be extended to covering the situation where an unauthorised agent takes over the handling of a contract in manner that causes loss to the 'principal'. Lord Hoffmann disagreed, stating that 'there is in my opinion no such liability outside contract' and suggesting that room for such a cause of action could only exist under the tort of causing loss by unlawful means. While the passage is ambiguous, Lord Hoffmann's comment does suggest that *Lumley* liability should be seen as confined to inducing breaches of contract, and where breaches of other legal arrangements exist, then the appropriate remedy may have to lie in the unlawful means tort.

9. However, before we turn to a close analysis of their Lordships judgments in *OBG v Allan*, which have reshaped the contours of the *Lumley* tort, it is necessary to examine how the scope of this tort was initially expanded in a controversial series of decisions stemming from the conceptual approach adopted by the House of Lords in *Quinn v Leathem* [1901] AC 495, [1900–3] All ER Rep 1 and Lord Hewart CJ in *GWK Ltd v Dunlop Rubber Co Ltd* (1926) 42 TLR 376, and subsequently given doctrinal shape in the Court of Appeal decision in *DC Thomson & Co Ltd v Deakin* [1952] Ch 646, [1952] 2 All ER 361. The approach that developed via these judgments treated 'indirect interference' with the performance of contractual obligations, i.e. when a person intentionally procured or attempted to procure a breach of contract by creating a situation or state of affairs where it was impossible for a third party to perform their contract with the claimant, as actionable if 'unlawful means' were used.

10. This extension of *Lumley* had several consequences. First, it blurred the distinction between the tort of inducing a breach on contract and the tort of intentional interference with trade by unlawful means, as 'indirect interference' imposed liability when the defendant had used unlawful means to achieve their goal. This blurring of the distinction between the torts not only caused some conceptual confusion, it also extended the scope of potential liability: as discussed below, an intention to 'target' or 'aim at' the claimant was required for the tort of interference with trade by unlawful means, but this control device was not available for indirect inducement, where mere intention to induce a breach of contract was sufficient. Furthermore, this extension of *Lumley* provided the springboard for another extension of the tort, with liability being imposed for 'bare' interference with the performance of a contract that fell short of a technical breach in *Torquay Co Ltd v Cousins* [1969] 2 Ch 106, [1969] 1 All ER 522 and *Merkur Island Shipping Corp v Laughton* [1983] 2 AC 570, [1983] 2 All ER 189. Combined with the 'looser' intention requirement that existed for the *Lumley* tort, its extension in these cases was criticised as potentially undermining the principle established in *Allen v Flood*, that causing economic loss in the absence of unlawful means was not actionable in English law: imposing liability for impeding the performance of a contract without inducing an actual breach appeared to be eating into this principle.

11. The House of Lords in *OBG v Allan* has dramatically reshaped this tort, reinterpreting several decades' worth of precedent and either explicitly or implicitly overruling two House of Lords decisions in the process. Inducing breach of contract has, in effect, been cut back to its original form, redefining as a form of accessory liability arising when

a defendant intentionally induced a breach of contract. Many of the 'indirect induce-ment' cases such as *DC Thomson & Co Ltd v Deakin* [1952] Ch 646, [1952] 2 All ER 361 and *GWK Ltd v Dunlop Rubber Co Ltd* (1926) 42 TLR 376 have been reinterpreted as involving the intentional infliction of loss by unlawful means. The key 'bare interfer-ence' cases have either been similarly reinterpreted or overruled. However, to under-stand the extensive surgery carried out in *OBG v Allan*, it is worth briefly discussing the earlier cases that caused the perceived problem in a little more detail.

12.   In *Quinn v Leathem* [1901] AC 495, [1900–3] All ER Rep 1, Lord Macnaghten, in the passage already quoted above ([1901] AC 495 at 510, [1900–3] All ER Rep 1 at 9), stated that 'a violation of a legal right committed knowingly is a cause of action, and that it is a violation of legal right to interfere with contractual relations recognised by law if there be no sufficient justification for the interference'. Described by Lord Hoffmann in *OBG* as 'sowing the seeds of confusion', this passage influenced the later decision in *GWK Ltd v Dunlop Rubber Co Ltd* (1926) 42 TLR 376, and then the important Court of Appeal decision in *DC Thompson*.

■ DC Thomson & Co Ltd v Deakin
Court of Appeal [1952] 2 All ER 361

The plaintiffs, a firm of printers and publishers, maintained a non-union shop. They dis-missed a man belonging to a union, whereupon a number of unions organised a boycott. Drivers and loaders employed by Bowaters, who supplied paper to the plaintiffs, expressed reluctance to load or deliver paper to the plaintiffs. Bowaters, not wishing to become involved in the dispute, refrained from ordering any of their employees to do so. The result was that no further supplies were taken to the plaintiffs' premises. Bowaters wrote to the plaintiffs informing them that they had been prevented from performing their contract to supply paper by union action. The plaintiffs issued a writ and sought an interlocutory injunction to restrain the defendant union officials from procuring any breach of Bowaters' contract with the plain-tiffs. Upjohn J refused to grant an injunction on the ground that there never was any direct action by the defendants with the object of persuading Bowaters to break an existing contract with the plaintiffs. An appeal to the Court of Appeal was dismissed on other grounds.

JENKINS LJ: . . .
The breach of contract complained of must be brought about by some act of a third party (whether alone or in concert with the contract breaker), which is in itself unlawful, but that act need not nec-essarily take the form of persuasion or procurement or inducement of the contract breaker, in the sense above indicated. Direct persuasion or procurement or inducement applied by the third party to the contract breaker, with knowledge of the contract and the intention of bringing about its breach, is clearly to be regarded as a wrongful act in itself, and where this is shown a case of actionable interference in its primary form is made out: *Lumley* v. *Gye*.[17] But the contract breaker may himself be a willing party to the breach, without any persuasion by the third party, and there seems to be no doubt that if a third party, with knowledge of a contract between the contract breaker and another, has dealings with the contract breaker which the third party knows to be inconsistent with the con-tract, he has committed an actionable interference: see, for example, *British Industrial Plastics Ltd* v. *Ferguson*,[18] where the necessary knowledge was held not to have been brought home to the third party; and *British Motor Trade Association* v. *Salvadori*.[19] The inconsistent dealing between the

---

[17] [(1853) 2 E & B 216; 22 LJQB 463.   [18] [1938] 4 All ER 504, [1940] 1 All ER 479.
[19] [1949] 1 All ER 208, [1949] Ch 556.

third party and the contract breaker may, indeed, be commenced without knowledge by the third party of the contract thus broken, but, if it is continued after the third party has notice of the contract, an actionable interference has been committed by him: see, for example, *De Francesco v. Barnum*.[20] Again, so far from persuading or inducing or procuring one of the parties to the contract to break it, the third party may commit an actionable interference with the contract, against the will of both and without the knowledge of either, if, with knowledge of the contract, he does an act which, if done by one of the parties to it, would have been a breach. Of this type of interference the case of *G.W.K. Ltd v. Dunlop Rubber Co., Ltd*[1] affords a striking example. Further, I apprehend that an actionable interference would, undoubtedly, be committed if a third party, with knowledge of a contract and intent to bring about its breach, placed physical restraint on one of the parties to the contract, so as to prevent him from carrying it out.

It is to be observed that in all these cases there is something amounting to a direct invasion by the third party of the rights of one of the parties to the contract, by prevailing on the other party to do, or doing in concert with him, or doing without reference to either party, that which is inconsistent with the contract, or by preventing, by means of actual physical restraint one of the parties from being where he should be or doing what he should do under the contract. But here the acts complained of as constituting the actionable interference do not amount to a direct invasion of the plaintiffs' contractual rights...

Nevertheless, I think that in principle an actionable interference with contractual relations may be committed by a third party who, with knowledge of a contract between two other persons and with the intention of causing its breach, or of preventing its performance, persuades, induces or procures the servants of one of those parties, on whose services he relies for the performance of his contract, to break their contracts of employment with him, either by leaving him without notice or by refusing to do what is necessary for the performance of his contract, provided that the breach of the contract between the two other persons intended to be brought about by the third party does in fact ensue as a necessary consequence of the third party's wrongful interference with the contracts of employment. I take this view because I see no distinction in principle for the present purpose between persuading a man to break his contract with another, preventing him by physical restraint from performing it, making his performance of it impossible by taking away or damaging his tools or machinery, and making his performance of it impossible by depriving him, in breach of their contracts, of the services of his employees. All these are wrongful acts, and, if done with knowledge and an intention to bring about a breach of a contract to which the person directly wronged is a party, and if in fact producing that result, I fail to see why they should not all alike fall within the sphere of actionable interference with contractual relations delimited by LORD MACNAGHTEN and LORD LINDLEY in *Quinn* v. *Leathem*.[2] But, while admitting this form of actionable interference in principle, I would hold it strictly confined to cases where it is clearly shown, first, that the person charged with actionable interference knew of the existence of the contract and intended to procure its breach; secondly, that the person so charged did definitely and unequivocally persuade, induce or procure the employees concerned to break their contracts of employment with the intent I have mentioned; thirdly, that the employees so persuaded, induced or procured did in fact break their contracts of employment; and, fourthly, that breach of the contract forming the alleged subject of interference ensued as a necessary consequence of the breaches by the employees concerned of their contracts of employment....

[RAYMOND EVERSHED MR and MORRIS LJ delivered judgments in favour of dismissing the appeal.]

NOTES

1. This case established the distinction between the 'direct' and 'indirect' forms of the *Lumley v Gye* tort, subsequently described by Lord Hoffmann in *OBG v Allan* [2007]

---

[20] (1890) 45 Ch D 430, 60 LJ Ch 63.   [1] (1926) 42 TLR 376.   [2] [1901] AC 495; 70 LJPC 76.

4 All ER 545, at [39], as 'unsatisfactory'. In *Greig v Insole* [1978] 3 All ER 449, [1978] 1 WLR 302, Slade J (at p. 486) offered the following definition of this distinction:

The phrase 'direct interference' covers the case where the intervener, either by himself or his agents, speaks, writes or publishes words or does other acts which communicate pressure or persuasion to the mind or person of one of the contracting parties themselves, while 'indirect interference' refers to the case where, without actually doing any of these things, the intervener nevertheless procures or attempts to procure a situation which will result or may result in a breach of the contract.

Note that *Greig v Insole* was described as constituting a clear case of 'accessory liability' by Lord Hoffmann in *OBG v Allan* [2007] 4 All ER 545, at [70]. The resolutions of the cricketing authorities which contained a threat of a ban directed at players who had contracted with a private promoter, coupled with a suggestion that they could escape from its operation by terminating their contracts with that promoter, were deemed in that case to be 'direct interference': now, as one of the 'saved' precedents in the wake of the *OBG v Allan* clearing of the Augean stables, it would be treated as a straightforward case of inducing breach of contract. In contrast, in *JT Stratford & Son Ltd v Lindley* [1965] AC 269, [1964] 3 All ER 102, a letter to an employers' association 'informing' them of an embargo placed on the movement of goods by a trade union could be described as an indirect inducement of the association's members not to deal with the person aimed at by the embargo, using the unlawful means of the threat of breach of employment contracts. (Lord Hoffmann appeared in *OBG v Allan* to view *JT Stratford & Son Ltd v Lindley* as a case of the infliction of harm by unlawful means: [2007] 4 All ER 545, at [32] and [47].)

2. Subsequently, this expanded tort was stretched further in *Torquay Co Ltd v Cousins* [1969] 2 Ch 106, [1969] 1 All ER 522, where industrial action involving interference with the performance of a contract that did not extend to in fact causing a breach of contract was treated as actionable, with Lord Denning MR stating that '[t]here must be interference in the execution of a contract. The interference is not confined to the procurement of a breach of contract. It extends to a case where a third person *prevents* or *hinders* one party from performing his contract, even though it not be a breach' ([1969] 2 Ch 106, at 138. The House of Lords confirmed the extension of the tort to 'interference with performance' in *Merkur Island Shipping Corpn v Laughton* [1983] 2 AC 570, [1983] 2 All ER 189, in which the defendant union organisers persuaded employees to breach their employment contracts to prevent the performance of a commercial contract between a shipowner and a charterer, neither of whom employed the employees in question. Technically there was no breach of the commercial contract because it included terms which dealt with precisely the circumstances that had arisen. The House of Lords declared that the lack of a breach was immaterial because 'interference with performance' could take its place.

3. Did the judgment of Jenkins LJ in *DC Thomson & Co Ltd v Deakin* (p. 903, ante) envisage such an extended liability? How could this expanded tort be reconciled with *Allen v Flood*? (See the trenchant comments by Wedderburn (1983) 46 MLR 632 on the threat which the new, extended version of *Lumley* could pose to commercial competition.) The expansive nature of 'interference' was illustrated in *Dimbleby & Sons Ltd v National Union of Journalists* [1984] 1 All ER 117, [1984] 1 WLR 67. Journalists employed by the claimants, publishers of local newspapers, who were members of the defendant union refused to supply copy to the claimants for printing by TBF (Printers) Ltd in response to a call by their union. One of the torts alleged against the union was

unlawful interference with the performance by the claimants of their contract with TBF (Printers). The Court of Appeal rejected the argument that, because the newspapers continued to be published, there was no interference. Sir John Donaldson MR affirmed (at 126) that 'interference' means 'hindrance as well as prevention and the loss of the services of staff journalists was quite clearly a hindrance to the performance by the plaintiffs of their contractual obligations towards TBF (Printers) Ltd....'

4.   Lord Diplock in the *Merkur Island* case went so far as to suggest that there might be liability for 'prevention of due performance of a primary obligation' short of breach of contract without the use of unlawfulness. The unchecked potential scope of this suggestion should be obvious. However, even without this further extension becoming embedded in the law, the potential dangers to industrial activism and freedom of speech posed by the lack of clarity and certain limits to *Lumley* liability potential dangers of this extension were illustrated by the case of *Middlebrook Mushrooms Ltd v Transport and General Workers' Union* [1993] ICR 612. The claimant in *Middlebrook* dismissed 89 employees following a dispute about new working practices and the defendant union launched a campaign to have the 89 employees reinstated. As part of that campaign it had leaflets printed and distributed at supermarkets calling on shoppers not to buy mushrooms supplied by the claimant. The claimant asked Blofeld J for an interlocutory injunction, which he granted, forbidding the defendants' distribution of the leaflet, on the basis that the defendant had committed the direct version of the *Lumley v Gye* tort. On appeal, the Court of Appeal distinguished *Merkur Island* on the ground that it was far from inevitable that a supermarket would have long-term supply contracts with Middlebrook that would be breached if customers declined to buy its mushrooms. There was therefore not sufficient evidence of direct interference with existing contracts to justify the grant of an injunction, and, as the defendant had used no unlawful means, there was no case for indirect interference. The fact, however, that the claimants had managed to succeed at first instance clearly shows how uncertain the scope of the tort of inducement had become.

5.   This uncertainty was compounded by a lack of clarity as to the required intention necessary to impose liability under *Lumley*. By making the use of unlawful means in cases of 'indirect inducement', the expansion of *Lumley* as already noted had closed much of the gap between the tort of inducing breach of contract and the tort of causing economic loss by unlawful means: however, while the latter tort required the defendant to have 'aimed' his unlawful conduct at the claimant so as to cause him loss, liability under *Lumley* only appeared to require that the defendant intended to induce the breach or interference.

6.   This left open a wide scope of liability, best illustrated by the case of *Millar v Bassey* [1994] EMLR 44. The singer Shirley Bassey was sued by the claimants on the basis that by refusing to perform her contract with a recording company, she had made it impossible for that recording company to honour the contracts it had agreed with the claimants, who were backing musicians who had been hired to play on the record she was to have made with the recording company. The claimants alleged that Bassey was aware of the existence of their contracts and knew they would be broken by her breach of contract. The trial judge struck out the claimants' claims on the ground that 'they had failed to allege or to establish that the respondent had acted with an intention to cause loss or damage to them or that her actions were directed at them'. However, the Court of Appeal (Peter Gibson LJ dissenting) upheld the claimants' appeal against the strike-out decision. While two of the three judges hearing the case took the view that

more than mere knowledge of the breached contracts was required, Bedlam LJ considered that a deliberate refusal to perform a contractual obligation in the knowledge that it would result in the breach of other contracts was sufficient to justify the imposition of liability. Bedlam LJ's approach is, in effect, dispensing with any requirement for an active intention to 'target' or 'aim at' the breach, potentially opening up considerable reservoirs of liability. Under this approach, the *Lumley* tort becomes concerned with the effects of the defendant's conduct rather than with the nature of the conduct itself (whether it was wrongful with regard to the victim, for example). If Beldam LJ is correct, people who are well-informed about the business practices of those with whom they transact are in danger of being held liable in circumstances in which ill-informed people will escape liability. See also *Stocznia Gdanska S.A. v Latvian Shipping Co., Latreefer Inc* [2002] 2 Lloyd's Rep 436, [2002] EWCA Civ 899.

7. The apparent uncertainty underlying the spread of *Lumley* liability and the blurred boundaries between this tort and causing loss by unlawful means generated a considerable degree of rigorous academic criticism. In the *Merkur Island* case [1983] 2 AC 570 at 609–610, when dealing with the statutory immunities, Lord Diplock appears to suggest that indirect interference with contract by unlawful means is a species of a 'genus' tort of interference with trade by unlawful means (p. 916, post). (See the comment by H. Carty (1983) 12 ILJ 166.) Weir has taken a similar view, while emphasising that 'targeted' economic harm should be required for all manifestations of this generic tort: see the general analysis in T. Weir, *Economic Torts* (OUP, 1997). In contrast, Sales and Stilitz, in making the case for the existence of an overarching 'unifying' tort structure based around the central concept of interference by unlawful means, took the view that directly inducing breach of contract should be regarded as separate from this structure and should be treated as a species of secondary civil liability (P. Sales and D. Shilitz (1999) 115 LQR 411, at 435). Indirect interference, on the other hand, is treated by Sales and Stilitz as part of the broader unified structure. Carty has also made the case that the *Lumley* tort should be seen as a matter of secondary or accessory liability, and has also suggested that this tort needs to be kept in 'strict bounds': 'the tort requires a 'targeted' breach of the claimant's contract and the presence of inducement/procurement of that breach (rather than prevention per se)' (see *Carty*, 85). Despite differences, however, virtually all commentators were united in expressing concern about the doctrinal vagueness and conceptual uncertainty underlying the expansion of *Lumley* liability.

8. Drawing extensively upon the work of Carty in particular, in *OBG v Allan* [2007] 4 All ER 545, [2007] UKHL 21, the House of Lords redefined the underlying nature of the *Lumley* action.

■ OBG Ltd v Allan; Douglas v Hello! Ltd (No 3); Mainstream Properties Ltd v Young
House of Lords [2007] 4 All ER 545

This case involved three separate appeals.

In the first appeal, *OBG v Allan*, the defendants were company receivers who were appointed under a floating charge, which subsequently was admitted to have been invalid. However, while acting in that capacity, the defendants took control of the claimant company's assets and undertakings. The claimant brought proceedings contending, inter alia, that that was an unlawful interference with its contractual relations and thereby a breach of the

Lumley v Gye tort. At first instance, the claim was upheld, but the Court of Appeal allowed the defendants' appeal: [2005] EWCA Civ 106, [2005] 2 All ER 602.

The second appeal, *Douglas v Hello! Ltd (No 3)*, was the latest instalment in the long-running legal battle resulting from the marriage of Michael Douglas and Catherine Zeta-Jones (for the important ramifications for privacy rights of this litigation, see p. 1031, post). A magazine, OK!, had contracted for the exclusive right to publish photographs of this celebrity wedding. A rival magazine, Hello!, published photographs of the wedding which it knew were surreptitiously taken at the event by an unauthorised photographer. OK! contended, inter alia, that Hello!'s publication of these photographs constituted interference by unlawful means with its contractual or business relations. At first instance, the judge, whilst allowing damages for loss of profit, rejected the claim for interference by unlawful means. On appeal, the Court of Appeal dismissed OK!'s cross-appeal on the ground that Hello! did not had the requisite subjective intention to cause harm: ([2005] EWCA Civ 595, [2005] 4 All ER 128). The primary issue at stake here therefore concerned the tort of causing loss by unlawful means, and the outcome of this case will be discussed in detail in that context (see p. 924, post). However, counsel for OK! also presented arguments that Hello! had interfered with the performance of the contract agreed between the celebrity couple and OK!

In the third appeal, *Mainstream Properties Ltd v Young*, two employees of a property company, in breach of their contracts, diverted a development opportunity to a joint venture in which they were interested. The defendant, knowing of their duties but wrongly thinking that they would not be in breach, facilitated the acquisition by providing finance. The company claimed that he was liable for the tort of wrongfully inducing breach of contract. The judge found that whilst the employees had been in breach of contract, the defendant had not intended to procure such a breach, and therefore dismissed the claim. That finding was upheld by the Court of Appeal: ([2005] EWCA Civ 861, [2005] IRLR 964).

The following extracts from the key speeches of Lord Hoffmann and Lord Nicholls concern the tort of inducing breach of contract: the elements of the judgment that analyse the tort of causing loss by unlawful means are examined later (see p. 924, post). Both judgments were structured in a similar manner, with both Lord Hoffmann and Lord Nicholls setting out the general approach to be adopted to inducement of breach of contract, and then applying this approach to the facts of each case. The extracts below mirror this approach.

LORD HOFFMANN:....

Inducing breach of contract

[5]....the important point to bear in mind about *Lumley v Gye* is that the person procuring the breach of contract was held liable as accessory to the liability of the contracting party. Liability depended upon the contracting party having committed an actionable wrong. Wightman J made this clear when he said ((1853) 2 E & B 216 at 238, 118 ER 749 at 757): 'It was undoubtedly primâ facie an unlawful act on the part of Miss Wagner to break her contract, and therefore a tortious act of the defendant maliciously to procure her to do so...'

[8] The tort of causing loss by unlawful means differs from the *Lumley v Gye* principle, as originally formulated, in at least four respects. First, unlawful means is a tort of primary liability, not requiring a wrongful act by anyone else, while *Lumley v Gye* created accessory liability, dependent upon the primary wrongful act of the contracting party. Secondly, unlawful means requires the use of means which are unlawful under some other rule ('independently unlawful') whereas liability under *Lumley v Gye* requires only the degree of participation in the breach of contract which satisfies the general requirements of accessory liability for the wrongful act of another person: for the relevant principles see *CBS Songs Ltd v Amstrad Consumer Electronics plc* [1988] 2 All ER 484, [1988] AC 1013 and *Unilever v Chefaro* [1994] FSR 135. Thirdly, liability for unlawful means does not depend upon the existence

of contractual relations. It is sufficient that the intended consequence of the wrongful act is damage in any form; for example, to the claimant's economic expectations. If the African canoeists had been delivering palm oil under a concluded contract of which notice had been given to the master of the Othello, Lord Kenyon would no doubt have considered that an a fortiori reason for granting relief but not as making a difference of principle. Under *Lumley v Gye*, on the other hand, the breach of contract is of the essence. If there is no primary liability, there can be no accessory liability. Fourthly, although both are described as torts of intention (the pleader in *Lumley v Gye* used the word 'maliciously', but the court construed this as meaning only that the defendant intended to procure a breach of contract), the *results* which the defendant must have intended are different. In unlawful means the defendant must have intended to cause damage to the claimant (although usually this will be, as in *Tarleton v M'Gawley* (1790) 1 Peake NPC 270, 170 ER 153, a means of enhancing his own economic position). Because damage to economic expectations is sufficient to found a claim, there need not have been any intention to cause a breach of contract or interfere with contractual rights. Under *Lumley v Gye*, on the other hand, an intention to cause a breach of contract is both necessary and sufficient. Necessary, because this is essential for liability as accessory to the breach. Sufficient, because the fact that the defendant did not intend to cause damage, or even thought that the breach of contract would make the claimant better off, is irrelevant. In *South Wales Miners' Federation v Glamorgan Coal Co Ltd* [1905] AC 239, [1904–7] All ER Rep 211 the miners' union said that their intention in calling a strike (inducing miners to break their contracts of employment) was, OPEC-like, to restrict production of coal and thereby raise its price. So far from wishing to cause the mine owners loss, they intended to make both owners and miners better off. The House of Lords said that this made no difference. It was sufficient that the union intended the employment contracts to be broken. It was no defence, as Lord Macnaghten put it ([1905] AC 239 at 246, [1904–7] All ER Rep 211 at 214), that 'if the masters had only known their own interest they would have welcomed the interference of the federation'...

Allen v Flood: *the torts kept separate*

[13] Thus the facts of *Allen v Flood* did not fall within *Lumley v Gye* because no breach of contract or other unlawful act had been procured and did not fall within the unlawful means tort because no unlawful means had been used. The majority did not accept that there was any other basis for liability. In particular, the fact that the defendant deliberately caused damage 'maliciously' in the sense of having a bad or improper motive was rejected as a ground for imposing liability. As Lord Watson (whose views, said Lord Macnaghten in *Quinn v Leathem* [1901] AC 495 at 509, [1900–3] All ER Rep 1 at 9 'represent the views of the majority better far than any other single judgment delivered in the case') summed up ([1898] AC 1 at 96, [1895–9] All ER Rep 52 at 69):

> 'There are, in my opinion, two grounds only upon which a person who procures the act of another can be made legally responsible for its consequences. In the first place, he will incur liability if he knowingly and for his own ends induces that other person to commit an actionable wrong. In the second place, when the act induced is within the right of the immediate actor, and is therefore not wrongful in so far as he is concerned, it may yet be to the detriment of a third party; and in that case, according to the law laid down by the majority in [*Lumley v Gye*], the inducer may be held liable if he can be shewn to have procured his object by the use of illegal means directed against that third party.'

[14] ...Some writers regret the failure of English law to accept bad motive as a ground for liability, as it is in the United States and Germany: see for example Dyson Heydon Economic Torts (2nd edn, 1978) p 28. But I agree with Tony Weir's opinion, forcibly expressed in his Clarendon Law Lectures on Economic Torts (1997) that we are better off without it. It seems to have created a good deal of uncertainty in the countries which have adopted such a principle. Furthermore, the rarity of actions for conspiracy (in which a bad motive can, exceptionally, found liability) suggests that it would not have made much practical difference.

Adoption of the unified theory: DC Thomson & Co Ltd v Deakin

[LORD HOFFMANN then analysed the judgments in *Quinn v Leathem* and *GWK Dunlop*, which he described as 'muddying the water' by opening the door to the imposition of liability for interference without actual breach. Then he examined the approach adopted by the Court of Appeal in *DC Thomson & Co Ltd v Deakin* [1952] 2 All ER 361, [1952] Ch 646 (see p. 903, ante), which he considered to have adopted what he describes as the 'unified theory', whereby the procurement of breach of contract, the old *Lumley v Gye* tort, was treated as 'one species of a more general tort of actionable interference with contractual rights'. His Lordship then continued:]

[31] Is there something to be said in principle for a unified theory? Tony Weir, in the Clarendon Law Lectures to which I have referred, makes a bravura case for one. Not, it is true, the version adopted in *DC Thomson v Deakin*, which he thinks paid too much attention to the contractual nature of the claimant's rights. Weir would prefer *Lumley v Gye* to be swallowed up by the tort of intentionally causing loss by unlawful means, treating the 'seduction' of the contracting party as a species of unlawful means and not distinguishing between interference with contractual rights and damage to economic expectations. The example of what Lord Atkin achieved for negligence in *Donoghue v Stevenson* [1932] AC 562, [1932] All ER Rep 1 always beckons (see Weir, *Economic Torts* (1997) p 25). But this too is a form of seduction which may lure writers onto the rocks.

[32] In my opinion the principle of accessory liability for breach of contract, the first of Lord Watson's principles of liability for the act of another in *Allen v Flood*, cannot be subsumed in the tort of causing loss by unlawful means (the second of Lord Watson's principles in *Allen v Flood*) simply by classifying 'seduction' as unlawful means. That only adds a pejorative description to a circular argument: see [18], above. To induce a breach of contract is unlawful means when the breach is used to cause loss to a third party, as in *JT Stratford & Son Ltd v Lindley* [1964] 3 All ER 102, [1965] AC 269, but it makes no sense to say that the breach of contract itself has been caused by unlawful means. Philip Sales and Daniel Stilitz, in their illuminating article 'Intentional Infliction of Harm by Unlawful Means' (1999) 115 LQR 411, make it clear (p 433) that *Lumley v Gye* was 'founded on a different principle of liability than the intentional harm tort'. It treats contractual rights as a species of property which deserve special protection, not only by giving a right of action against the party who breaks his contract but by imposing secondary liability on a person who procures him to do so. In this respect it is quite distinct from the unlawful means principle, which is concerned only with intention and wrongfulness and is indifferent as to the nature of the interest which is damaged. I therefore do not think that the two causes of action can be brought within a unified theory and agree with Professor Peter Cane ('Mens Rea in Tort Law' (2000) 20 OJLS 533, 552, that—

> '[t]he search for "general principles of liability" based on types of conduct is at best a waste of time and at worst a potential source of serious confusion; and the broader the principle, the more is this so. Tort law is a complex interaction between protected interests, sanctioned conduct, and sanctions; and although there are what might be called "principles of tort liability", by and large, they are not very "general". More importantly, they cannot be stated solely in terms of the sorts of conduct which will attract tort liability. Each principle must refer, as well, to some interest protected by tort law and some sanction provided by tort law.'

[33] That said, I would not expect your Lordships to reject the unified theory adopted in *DC Thomson & Co Ltd v Deakin* [1953] 2 All ER 361, [1952] Ch 646 unless it had serious practical disadvantages...To these problems created by the unified theory I now turn...

Direct and indirect interference

[34] The distinction between the original *Lumley v Gye* tort and its extension in *DC Thomson & Co Ltd v Deakin* has been described in later cases as a distinction between 'direct' and 'indirect' interference. The latter species requires the use of independently unlawful means while the former requires no more than inducement or persuasion. But the use of these terms seems to me to distract attention from the true questions which have to be asked in each case...

[LORD HOFFMANN then expressed the view that the decision in *Torquay Hotel Co Ltd v Cousins* [1969] 2 Ch 106, [1969] 1 All ER 522 was based on the distinction between direct and indirect interference which was 'irrelevant and misleading'. His Lordship then continued:]

[36]…This treats the distinction as turning simply upon whether there was communication, directly or through an agent, between the defendant and the contract-breaker. But, like Lord Denning MR in the *Daily Mirror* case, I cannot see why this should make a difference. If that is what the distinction between 'direct' and 'indirect' means, it conceals the real question which has to be asked in relation to *Lumley v Gye*: did the defendant's acts of encouragement, threat, persuasion and so forth have a sufficient causal connection with the breach by the contracting party to attract accessory liability?…

[38]…In my opinion, therefore, the distinction between direct and indirect interference is unsatisfactory and it is time for the unnatural union between the *Lumley v Gye* tort and the tort of causing loss by unlawful means to be dissolved. They should be restored to the independence which they enjoyed at the time of *Allen v Flood*. I shall therefore proceed to discuss separately the essential elements of each.

Inducing breach of contract: elements of the Lumley v Gye *tort*

[39] To be liable for inducing breach of contract, you must know that you are inducing a breach of contract. It is not enough that you know that you are procuring an act which, as a matter of law or construction of the contract, is a breach. You must actually realise that it will have this effect. Nor does it matter that you ought reasonably to have done so. This proposition is most strikingly illustrated by the decision of this House in *British Industrial Plastics Ltd v Ferguson* [1940] 1 All ER 479, in which the claimant's former employee offered the defendant information about one of the claimant's secret processes which he, as an employee, had invented. The defendant knew that the employee had a contractual obligation not to reveal trade secrets but held the eccentric opinion that if the process was patentable, it would be the exclusive property of the employee. He took the information in the honest belief that the employee would not be in breach of contract. In the Court of Appeal McKinnon LJ observed tartly (see [1938] 4 All ER 504 at 513) that in accepting this evidence the judge had 'vindicated [his] honesty…at the expense of his intelligence' but he and the House of Lords agreed that he could not be held liable for inducing a breach of contract.

[40] The question of what counts as knowledge for the purposes of liability for inducing a breach of contract has also been the subject of a consistent line of decisions. In *Emerald Construction Co Ltd v Lowthian* [1966] 1 All ER 1013, [1966] 1 WLR 691, union officials threatened a building contractor with a strike unless he terminated a sub-contract for the supply of labour. The defendants obviously knew that there was a contract—they wanted it terminated—but the court found that they did not know its terms and, in particular, how soon it could be terminated. Lord Denning MR said ([1966] 1 All ER 1013 at 1017, [1966] 1 WLR 691 at 700–701):

> 'Even if they did not know of the actual terms of the contract, but had the means of knowledge— which they deliberately disregarded—that would be enough. Like the man who turns a blind eye. So here, if the officers deliberately sought to get this contract terminated, heedless of its terms, regardless whether it was terminated by breach or not, they would do wrong. For it is unlawful for a third person to procure a breach of contract knowingly, or recklessly, indifferent whether it is a breach or not.'

[41] This statement of the law has since been followed in many cases and, so far as I am aware, has not given rise to any difficulty. It is in accordance with the general principle of law that a conscious decision not to inquire into the existence of a fact is in many cases treated as equivalent to knowledge of that fact (see *Manifest Shipping Co Ltd v Uni-Polaris Insurance Co Ltd* [2001] UKHL 1, [2001] 1 All ER 743, [2003] 1 AC 469). It is not the same as negligence or even gross negligence: in *British Industrial Plastics Ltd v Ferguson*, for example, Mr Ferguson did not deliberately abstain from inquiry into whether disclosure of the secret process would be a breach of contract. He negligently made the wrong inquiry, but that is an altogether different state of mind.

[42] The next question is what counts as an intention to procure a breach of contract. It is necessary for this purpose to distinguish between ends, means and consequences. If someone knowingly causes a breach of contract, it does not normally matter that it is the means by which he intends to achieve some further end or even that he would rather have been able to achieve that end without causing a breach. Mr Gye would very likely have preferred to be able to obtain Miss Wagner's services without her having to break her contract. But that did not matter. Again, people seldom knowingly cause loss by unlawful means out of simple disinterested malice. It is usually to achieve the further end of securing an economic advantage to themselves. As I said earlier, the Dunlop employees who took off the tyres in *GWK Ltd v Dunlop Rubber Co Ltd* (1926) 42 TLR 376 intended to advance the interests of the Dunlop company.

[43] On the other hand, if the breach of contract is neither an end in itself nor a means to an end, but merely a foreseeable consequence, then in my opinion it cannot for this purpose be said to have been intended. That, I think, is what judges and writers mean when they say that the claimant must have been 'targeted' or 'aimed at'. In my opinion the majority of the Court of Appeal was wrong to have allowed the action in *Miller v Bassey* [1994] EMLR 44 to proceed. Miss Bassey had broken her contract to perform for the recording company and it was a foreseeable consequence that the recording company would have to break its contracts with the accompanying musicians, but those breaches of contract were neither an end desired by Miss Bassey nor a means of achieving that end.

[44] Finally, what counts as a breach of contract? In *Torquay Hotel Co Ltd v Cousins* [1969] 1 All ER 522, [1969] 2 Ch 106 Lord Denning said that there could be liability for preventing or hindering performance of the contract on the same principle as liability for procuring a breach. This dictum was approved by Lord Diplock in *Merkur Island Shipping Corp v Laughton* [1983] 2 All ER 189, [1983] AC 570. One could therefore have liability for interference with contractual relations even though the contracting party committed no breach. But these remarks were made in the context of the unified theory which treated procuring a breach as part of the same tort as causing loss by unlawful means. If the torts are to be separated, then I think that one cannot be liable for inducing a breach unless there has been a breach. No secondary liability without primary liability. Cases in which interference with contractual relations has been treated as coming within the *Lumley v Gye* tort (like *Dimbleby & Sons v National Union of Journalists* [1984] 1 All ER 117, [1984] 1 WLR 67) are really cases of causing loss by unlawful means.

LORD NICHOLLS OF BIRKENHEAD: . . .

The tort of inducing a breach of contract

[172] . . . the rationale and the ingredients of the 'inducement' tort differ from those of the 'unlawful interference' tort. With the inducement tort the defendant is responsible for the third party's breach of contract which he procured. In that circumstance this tort provides a claimant with an additional cause of action. The third party who breached his contract is liable for breach of contract. The person who persuaded him to break his contract is also liable, in his case in tort. Hence this tort is an example of civil liability which is secondary in the sense that it is secondary, or supplemental, to that of the third party who committed a breach of his contract. It is a form of accessory liability.

[173] This form of liability is to be contrasted with the tort of unlawful interference. This is a 'stand-alone' tort of wide scope, imposing primary liability on a defendant for his own conduct, irrespective of whether on the facts anyone else may also be liable, either in contract or in tort. On this I agree with Philip Sales and Daniel Stilitz in their stimulating article 'Intentional Infliction of Harm by Unlawful Means' (1999) 115 LQR 411, 433 . . .

Preventing performance of a contract: 'interfering with contractual relations'

[178] With hindsight it is evident that application of the *Lumley v Gye* tort to a 'prevention' case was unfortunate. There is a crucial difference between cases where the defendant induces a contracting party not to perform his contractual obligations and cases where the defendant prevents a contracting

party from carrying out his contractual obligations. In inducement cases the very act of joining with the contracting party and inducing him to break his contract is sufficient to found liability as an accessory. In prevention cases the defendant does not join with the contracting party in a wrong (breach of contract) committed by the latter. There is no question of accessory liability. In prevention cases the defendant acts independently of the contracting party. The defendant's liability is a 'stand-alone' liability. Consistently with this, tortious liability does not arise in prevention cases unless, as was the position in the *GWK* case, the preventative means used were independently unlawful...

[180] Given this difference between prevention and inducement, it is confusing and misleading to treat prevention cases as part and parcel of the same tort as inducement cases. The rationale is not the same, nor are the ingredients. But the rationale and ingredients of liability in prevention cases are the same as those of the tort of interference with a business by unlawful means. Prevention cases should be recognised for what they are: straightforward examples of the latter tort, rather than as exemplifying a wider version of *Lumley v Gye* labelled 'interference with contractual relations'...

[LORD NICHOLLS then gave his opinion that *Torquay Hotels v Cousins* [1969] All ER 522 was wrongfully decided. His Lordship then continued:]

[185] With the very greatest respect I have difficulty with Lord Denning's extension of *Lumley v Gye*. The effect of this extension is that a person who directly prevents performance of a contract by wholly lawful means, and thereby intentionally inflicts damage on the claimant, is liable to the claimant. No reason was given, and none is discernible, for this fundamental extension of the law. Why should a defendant, acting wholly *lawfully*, be liable in such a case, although the use of *unlawful* means is a prerequisite of liability if he intentionally inflicts damage in any other way?

[186] Nor is the basis of the distinction between direct and indirect interference apparent. One would suppose the outcome on liability would be the same whether a person sought to achieve his end by direct or indirect means. It would be remarkable if this were not so.

[187] This extension of the *Lumley v Gye* tort must be going too far. To hold a defendant liable where the intentional harm is inflicted by lawful means runs counter to the limit on liability long established in English law. So long as this general limit is maintained in respect of other forms of interference with a claimant's business, and Lord Denning did not suggest this should be changed, the extension in liability proposed by him and seemingly approved by Lord Diplock is irrational. Despite the high authority of these cases, I have to say that on this occasion these distinguished judges fell into error. They were led astray by the width of Lord Macnaghten's observations made in 1901, long before the unlawful interference tort became shaped. The jurisprudence of the economic torts had not then been thought through.

[188] For these reasons this extension of the inducement tort of *Lumley v Gye* cannot stand consistently with the economic torts having a coherent framework. This extension is productive of obscurity and, hence, uncertainty. This, in turn, as Lord Diplock himself once said, is destructive of the rule of law: see *Merkur Island Shipping Corp v Laughton*.

[189] I feel bound to say therefore that the ambit of the *Lumley v Gye* tort should properly be confined to inducing a breach of contract. The unlawful interference tort requires intentional harm effected by unlawful means, and there is no in-between hybrid tort of 'interfering with contractual relations'. In so far as authorities suggest or decide otherwise they should not now be followed. I leave open the question of how far the *Lumley v Gye* principle applies equally to inducing a breach of other actionable obligations such as statutory duties or equitable or fiduciary obligations...

Inducing a breach of contract: the mental element

[191] I turn next to the mental ingredient of the *Lumley v Gye* tort. The mental ingredient is an intention by the defendant to procure or persuade ('induce') the third party to break his contract with the claimant. The defendant is made responsible for the third party's breach because of his intentional causative participation in that breach. Causative participation is not enough. A stranger to a contract may know nothing of the contract. Quite unknowingly and unintentionally he may procure a breach of the contract by offering an inconsistent deal to a contracting party which persuades the latter to default on his

contractual obligations. The stranger is not liable in such a case. Nor is he liable if he acts carelessly. He owes no duty of care to the victim of the breach of contract. Negligent interference is not actionable.

[192] The additional, necessary factor is the defendant's intent. He is liable if he intended to persuade the contracting party to breach the contract. Intentional interference presupposes knowledge of the contract. With that knowledge the defendant proceeded to induce the other contracting party to act in a way the defendant knew was a breach of that party's obligations under the contract. If the defendant deliberately turned a blind eye and proceeded regardless he may be treated as having intended the consequence he brought about. A desire to injure the claimant is not an essential ingredient of this tort.

[193] For completeness I mention, but without elaboration, that a defence of justification may be available to a defendant in inducement tort cases. A defendant may, for instance, interfere with another's contract in order to protect an equal or superior right of his own, as in *Edwin Hill & Partners (a firm) v First National Finance Corp plc* [1988] 3 All ER 801, [1989] 1 WLR 225.

A bird's-eye view

[194] It may be helpful to pause and take an overall look at where this leaves the law. The effect of the views expressed above is to draw a sharp distinction between two economic torts. One tort imposes primary liability for intentional and unlawful interference with economic interests. The other tort imposes accessory liability for inducing a third party to commit an actionable wrong, notably a breach of contract, but possibly some other actionable civil wrongs as well.

[195] This overall framework, it is to be hoped, should assist in the more coherent development of the economic torts. On this I am comforted by noting that this two-fold structure substantially accords with the views of at least some commentators, including Hazel Carty *An Analysis of the Economic Torts* (2001) pp 271–276, and Ken Oliphant (1999) 62 MLR 320, 322.

[Turning to the three cases on appeal, Lords Hoffmann and Nicholls separately applied their reformulation of the tort of inducement of breach of contract to each case. In *OBG v Allan* itself, both of their Lordships considered that there was no breach or non-performance of any contract and therefore no wrong to which accessory liability could attach. Both also considered that there was no intention on the part of the erroneously appointed receivers to induce OBG to breach any of its contracts.]

LORD HOFFMANN: . . .

[86] The present case amply illustrates the dangers of a broad reading of Lord Macnaghten's reference to 'interference' in *Lumley v Gye* and the promiscuous application of cases on accessory liability (such as *Greig v Insole*) to a case which, on any view, can only be a case of primary liability. There are only two possible causes of action: procuring a breach of contract in a way which creates accessory liability under *Lumley v Gye* or causing loss by unlawful means. It is, I think, plain and obvious that the requirements for liability under neither of these torts were satisfied. There was no breach or non-performance of any contract and therefore no wrong to which accessory liability could attach. And the receivers neither employed unlawful means nor intended to cause OBG any loss.

[In *Douglas v Hello! (No. 3)*, both of their Lordships considered that there was no inducement to breach a contract and that had been no breach or non-performance of the contract between the celebrity couple and OK! in any case. In *Mainstream v Young*, both of their Lordships agreed that the defendant had not intended to cause a breach of contract and the conditions for accessory liability under the *Lumley v Gye* tort were therefore not satisfied.]

LORD NICHOLLS OF BIRKENHEAD: . . .

[202] An honest belief by the defendant that the outcome sought by him will not involve a breach of contract is inconsistent with him intending to induce a breach of contract. He is not to be held responsible for the third party's breach of contract in such a case. It matters not that his belief is mistaken in law. Nor does it matter that his belief is muddle-headed and illogical, as was the position in *British Industrial Plastics Ltd v Ferguson* [1940] 1 All ER 479. As Lord Devlin said in *Rookes v Barnard* [1964] 1 All ER 367 at 401, [1964] AC 1129 at 1212, the defendant must know of the contract 'and of the fact

that the act induced will be a breach of it'. Counsel referred the House to several authorities where a contrary view seems to have been expressed; for instance, *Metropolitan Borough of Solihull v National Union of Teachers* [1985] IRLR 211 at 213 (paras 7–10), and *Welsh Development Agency v Export Finance Co Ltd* [1992] BCLC 148. If and in so far as observations in those cases depart from the principle outlined above they were wrong.

[LORD WALKER OF GESTINGTHORPE, LORD BROWN OF EATON-UNDER-HEYWOOD, and LADY HALE OF RICHMOND delivered judgments in which they expressed agreement with the analysis of the tort of inducing breach of contract offered by LORD HOFFMANN and LORD NICHOLLS OF BIRKENHEAD, with LORD WALKER noting that on this topic, 'Lord Nicholls and Lord Hoffmann are at one': [2007] 4 All ER 545, at 609.]

The appeals from the Court of Appeal decisions in OBG v Allan *and* Mainstream v Young *were dismissed. The appeal from the Court of Appeal decision in* Douglas v Hello (No. 3) *was allowed.*

QUESTIONS

Do you think the reasoning offered by Lords Hoffman and Nicholls to support their reinterpretation of the scope of the *Lumley* tort is convincing? What reasons do they give for departing from the approach adopted in cases such as *Merkur Shipping, Torquay Hotel v Cousins and DC Thompson v Deakin*? In the wake of *OBG v Allan*, what is the necessary degree of intention required to establish liability for inducement of a breach of contract? See Lord Hoffmann's judgment, [42]–[43], and that of Lord Nicholls, [192]. What is the state of knowledge of the contract required on the part of the defendant to give rise to liability? See Lord Hoffmann at [40], and Lord Nicholls at [191]. Why did Lord Hoffmann consider that the Court of Appeal was wrong to let the action in *Miller v Bassey* proceed?

NOTES

1. Their Lordships agreed in *OBG v Allan* that the receivers had neither employed unlawful means nor intended to cause the claimant any loss, so no liability existed under the tort of causing loss by unlawful means: see p. 924, post. The majority also held that the defendants were not liable in the tort of conversion for the appropriation of the company's choses in action. Lord Nicholls and Baroness Hale dissented on this point. In *Douglas v Hello (No 3)*, the majority concluded that OK! could sustain an action for breach of confidence in respect of the photographs: Lord Nicholls and Lord Walker dissented on this point (see p. 1043, post.) In *Mainstream v Young*, their Lordships agreed that there was also no liability under the tort of causing loss by unlawful means.

2. Few cases have involved such a radical departure from existing precedent as *OBG v Allan*. Lord Nicholls noted (correctly) that the questions at issue in this decision were 'much vexed subjects'. He proceeded to note at [139] that '[n]early 350 reported decisions and academic writings were placed before the House. There are many areas of uncertainty. Judicial observations are not always consistent, and academic consensus is noticeably absent. In the words of one commentator, the law is in a "terrible mess".'

3. The judgments of their Lordships in *OBG v Allan* can be seen as an attempt to clear away much of the confusion. This decision is notable in that it involved the implicit overruling of opinions expressed in two recent decisions of the House of Lords (*Merkur Shipping* [1983] 2 AC 570, [1983] 2 All ER 189 and *Dimbleby v & Sons Ltd v National Union of Journalists* [1984] 1 All ER 117, [1984] 1 WLR 427) and several decisions of the Court of Appeal (in particular *Torquay Hotel v Cousins* [1969] 1 All ER 522 and

DC Thomson & Co Ltd v Deakin [1952] 00 QB 000, [1952] 2 All ER 361). Many of these cases have been reclassified as involving the tort of causing loss by unlawful means, in respect of which the decision in *OBG v Allan* is also of great importance. Others, such as *Torquay Hotel* appear unsalvageable.

4.   It can be argued that in many ways *OBG v Allan* generates its own complexities and obscurities, but there was essential agreement between the key judgments of Lord Hoffmann and Lord Nicholls in respect of inducement of contract, with the other Law Lords signalled their agreement with this shared approach. Lord Hoffmann and Lord Nicholls describe the tort of inducing a breach of contract as a form of 'accessory liability'. Lord Hoffmann described liability under *Lumley* at [8] as 'dependent upon the primary wrongful act of the contracting party, referring back to the first of Lord Watson's principles of liability for the act of another set out in his judgment in *Allen v Flood*: '[a defendant] will incur liability if he knowingly, and for his own ends, induces that other person to commit an actionable wrong' (see *Allen v Flood*, p. 865, ante). Lord Nicholls took the same view at [178]: 'in inducement cases, the very act of joining with the contracting party and inducing him to break his contract is sufficient to found liability as an accessory'. As a consequence of this view of the nature of this tort, which sees liability as stemming from the wrongful act of the contract-breaker, this meant that interference alone with the performance of contracts would not be sufficient to establish liability under *Lumley v Gye*: a breach of contract or non-performance of contractual obligations is required to supply the primary liability onto which the secondary liability of the defendant is attached.

5.   This considerable narrowing of the scope of *Lumley* liability is very significant. Decisions such as *Torquay Hotel* that treat interference with contract performance which falls short of a breach of contract as actionable appear to be incompatible with the requirement for breach of contract that both Lord Hoffmann and Lord Nicholls require for liability to be imposed. This control device therefore substantially limits the scope of the tort and sharply reins in its gradual widening of scope since the decision in *DC Thompson v Deakin*. How would you now apply the judgments of Lord Hoffmann and Lord Nicholls to the facts at issue in *Deakin* (see p. 903, ante). Note that Lord Hoffmann at [36] criticises the distinction between direct and indirect interference as unhelpful and confusing and suggest that this conceals the real question which has to be asked in relation to *Lumley v Gye*: 'Did the defendant's acts of encouragement, threat, persuasion and so forth have a sufficient causal connection with the breach by the contracting party to attract accessory liability?'

6.   In *Meretz Investments NV v ACP Ltd* [2008] 2 WLR 904, [2007] EWCA Civ 1303, the Court of Appeal regarded Lord Nicholls at [180] above as having drawn a distinction between preventing performance of a contract, which would not qualify as an 'inducement', and persuading a party to a contract to breach that contract, which could constitute an inducement. However, this approach to defining what constituted an inducement was not treated as varying from that of Lord Hoffmann set out in [36].

7.   Note that Stevens has argued that the tort of inducement of breach of contract cannot logically be treated as a form of accessory liability: see *Stevens*, pp. 275–279. He argues that *Lumley* liability should be seen as a distinct form of wrongful act rather than as a form of secondary liability, principally on the basis that the liability in contract of the party in breach of contract cannot be consistently carried over into a form of tort liability.

8.   The decision in *OBG* represents a rejection of arguments that the economic torts can be brought together under a common framework whereby the intentional infliction of harm by unlawful means is prohibited. Instead, the *Lumley* tort is confined to its specific

contours, with a distinct intention requirement which varies from that required for the tort of causing harm by unlawful means. Returning to Howarth's arguments at p. 894, ante, given that the tort of inducing breach of contract is now narrow in scope, should it continue to exist? Might there be an argument to confine this tort even further to distinguishing between coercive and non-coercive interference in contractual obligations? Note that Simester and Chan argue that there is an interest in encouraging the keeping of promises, which serves as a justification for imposing liability for breach of contract: see A. Simester and W. Chan [2004] CLJ 132. Is this sufficient justification to retain the current (if shrunken) scope of *Lumley* liability?

3 CAUSING LOSS BY UNLAWFUL MEANS— 'TWO PARTY' AND 'THIRD PARTY' INTERFERENCE WITH ECONOMIC LOSS BY UNLAWFUL MEANS

■ **Rookes v Barnard**
House of Lords [1964] 1 All ER 367

The plaintiff was employed by BOAC at London airport. He left his union, the Association of Engineering and Shipbuilding Tradesman, because of disagreements about its policies. The union had an informal '100 per cent union membership' agreement with BOAC. Barnard and Fistal, two fellow draughtsmen who were local unpaid union officials, and Silverthorne (a district official of the union not employed by BOAC) conveyed to BOAC the substance of a resolution passed at a members' meeting that if the plaintiff was not removed from the design office within three days, all labour would be withdrawn. As a result, BOAC at first suspended and then dismissed the plaintiff with the (long) lawful period of notice. There was a clause in another (formal) collective agreement between BOAC and the union that there would be no strike or lockout. It was *conceded* by counsel for the defendants that this clause was incorporated into each individual contract of employment with BOAC. The threat by Barnard and Fistal and other employees to withdraw their labour was, in consequence, a threat to break their contracts. The plaintiff sued Barnard, Fistal and Silverthorne for conspiracy.

At the trial before Sachs J and a jury, [1961] 2 All ER 825, the plaintiff was awarded £7,500 damages, after an instruction that the jury were entitled to award exemplary damages. The Court of Appeal, [1962] 2 All ER 579, reversed this decision, unanimously taking the view that the tort of intimidation was confined to threats of violence. The House of Lords allowed the plaintiff's appeal on the question of liability (by this stage Silverthorne had died) but held that this was not a suitable case for the award of exemplary damages and sent the case for retrial on the question of damages (on this aspect of the case see chap. 8, p. 493, ante). The case was later settled for £4,000, plus costs estimated at £30,000: [1966] 1 QB 176, [1965] 3 All ER 549.

LORD REID: . . .

The question in this case is whether it was unlawful for them to use a threat to break their contracts with their employer as a weapon to make him do something which he was legally entitled to do, but which they knew would cause loss to the appellant.

The first contention of the respondents is very far reaching. They say there is no such tort as intimidation. That would mean that, short of committing a crime, an individual could with impunity virtually compel a third person to do something damaging to the plaintiff, which he does not want to do but can lawfully do: the wrongdoer could use every kind of threat to commit violence, libel or any other tort, and the plaintiff would have no remedy. And a combination of individuals could do the same, at least if they acted solely to promote their own interests. It is true that there is no decision of this House which negatives that argument. But there are many speeches in this House and judgments of eminent judges where it is assumed that that is not the law and I have found none where there is any real support for this argument. . . . It has often been stated that if people combine to do acts which they know will cause loss to the plaintiff, he can sue if either the object of their conspiracy is unlawful or they use unlawful means to achieve it. In my judgment, to cause such loss by threat to commit a tort against a third person if he does not comply with their demands is to use unlawful means to achieve their object.

. . . I can see no difference in principle between a threat to break a contract and a threat to commit a tort. If a third party could not sue for damage caused to him by the former I can see no reason why he should be entitled to sue for damage caused to him by the latter. A person is no more entitled to sue in respect of loss which he suffers by reason of a tort committed against someone else, than he is entitled to sue in respect of loss which he suffers by reason of breach of a contract to which he is not a party. What he sues for in each case is loss caused to him by the use of an unlawful weapon against him . . . intimidation of another person by unlawful means. So long as the defendant only threatens to do what he has a legal right to do he is on safe ground. At least if there is no conspiracy he would not be liable to anyone for doing the act, whatever his motive might be, and it would be absurd to make him liable for threatening to do it but not for doing it. But I agree with LORD HERSCHELL (*Allen v Flood*)[3] that there is a chasm between doing what you have a legal right to do and doing what you have no legal right to do, and there seems to me to be the same chasm between threatening to do what you have a legal right to do and threatening to do what you have no legal right to do. It must follow from *Allen v Flood*[4] that to intimidate by threatening to do what you have a legal right to do is to intimidate by lawful means. But I see no good reason for extending that doctrine. Threatening a breach of contract may be a much more coercive weapon than threatening a tort, particularly when the threat is directed against a company or corporation, and, if there is no technical reason requiring a distinction between different kinds of threats, I can see no other ground for making any such distinction . . . .

LORD DEVLIN: . . .
My lords, in my opinion there is a tort of intimidation of the nature described in chap. 18 of *Salmond on the Law of Torts* (13th edn), p. 697. The tort can take one of two forms which are set out in Salmond as follows:

'(1) Intimidation of the plaintiff himself.
    'Although there seems to be no authority on the point, it cannot be doubted that it is an actionable wrong intentionally to compel a person, by means of a threat of an illegal act, to do some act whereby loss accrues to him: for example, an action will doubtless lie at the suit of a trader who has been compelled to discontinue his business by means of threats of personal violence made against him by the defendant with that intention.
    '(2) Intimidation of other persons to the injury of the plaintiff.
    'In certain cases it is an actionable wrong to intimidate other persons with the intent and effect of compelling them to act in a manner or to do acts which they themselves have a legal right to do which cause loss to the plaintiff: for example, the intimidation of the plaintiff's customers whereby they are compelled to withdraw their custom from him, or the intimidation of an employer whereby he is compelled to discharge his servant, the plaintiff. Intimidation of this sort is actionable, as we have said, in certain classes of cases; for it does not follow that, because a plaintiff's customers have a right to cease to deal with him if they please, other persons have a right as against the plaintiff

---

[3] [1895–99] All ER Rep 52 at 79, [1898] AC 1 at 121.   [4] [1895–99] All ER Rep 52, [1898] AC 1.

to compel his customers to do so. There are at least two cases in which such intimidation may constitute a cause of action: (i) When the intimidation consists in a threat to do or procure an illegal act; (ii) When the intimidation is the act, not of a single person, but of two or more persons acting together, in pursuance of a common intention.'

…I note that no issue on justification was raised at the time and there is no finding of fact on it. Your lordships have not to consider what part, if any, justification plays in the tort of intimidation.

Your lordships are here concerned with the sort of intimidation which Salmond puts into the second category, and with the first of Salmond's two cases. The second case is, so Salmond later observed, 'one form of the tort of conspiracy.'[5] That form is the *Quinn* v. *Leathem*[6] type, so that it is no use to the appellant here. He relies on 'a threat to do or procure an illegal act', namely, a breach of contract. Doubtless it would suit him better if he could rely on the procuring of a breach of contract, for that is a tort; but immunity from that is guaranteed in terms by s. 3. So he complains only of the threat to break the service contracts, and the breach would undoubtedly be an act actionable by B.O.A.C., though it is neither tortious nor criminal. He does not have to contend that in the tort of intimidation, as in the tort of conspiracy, there can be, if the object is injurious, an unlawful threat to use lawful means. I do not think that there can be. The line must be drawn according to the law. It cannot be said that to use a threat of any sort is per se unlawful; and I do not see how, except in relation to the nature of the act threatened, i.e. whether it is lawful or unlawful, one could satisfactorily distinguish between a lawful and an unlawful threat.

This conclusion, while not directly in point, assists me in my approach to the matter to be determined here. It is not, of course, disputed that if the act threatened is a crime, the threat is unlawful. But otherwise is it enough to say that the act threatened is actionable as a breach of contract or must it be actionable as a tort? My lords, I see no good ground for the latter limitation. I find the reasoning on this point of Professor Hamson[7].… The essence of the offence is coercion. It cannot be said that every form of coercion is wrong. A dividing line must be drawn and the natural line runs between what is lawful and unlawful as against the party threatened. If the defendant threatens something that that party cannot legally resist, the plaintiff likewise cannot be allowed to resist the consequences; both must put up with the coercion and its results. But if the intermediate party is threatened with an illegal injury, the plaintiff who suffers by the aversion of the act threatened can fairly claim that he is illegally injured.

Accordingly, I reach the conclusion that the respondents' second point fails and on the facts of this case the tort of intimidation was committed. I do not share the difficulties which the lords justices felt about the idea of admitting breach of contract into the tort of intimidation. Out of respect to them I must state what those difficulties are and how in my opinion they can be satisfactorily resolved. I think that in one form or another they all stem from the error that any cause of action by the third party, that is the appellant, must in some way be supplemental to or dependent on a cause of action by B.O.A.C.. Thus, it is said to be anomalous that on the facts of this case the appellant should be able to sue the respondents when B.O.A.C. could not. The best way of answering that is to grant that B.O.A.C. would not be able to sue and to assert, as I shall seek to show, that there is nothing anomalous about it. But there was introduced into the argument a suggestion that B.O.A.C. could in fact have sued because although there was no actual breach of contract, one was threatened and therefore there was an anticipatory breach. Against that, it was said that B.O.A.C. could not have sued for an anticipatory breach unless they first elected to rescind, which they never did. I dare say that is right, but I do not think it matters at all whether B.O.A.C. could sue or not. The two causes of action B.O.A.C.'s and the appellant's are in law quite independent; and in fact they are virtually alternative because it is difficult to visualise (except in one case) a set of facts on which both could sue.

This last statement is best examined in relation to a threat of physical violence which would unquestionably constitute intimidation. If A threatens B with physical violence unless he harms C, B can either

⁵ (13th edn) p 699.   ⁶ [1900–03] All ER Rep 1, [1901] AC 495.
⁷ Cambridge Law Journal, November 1961, p 189 at 191, 192.

resist or comply. If he resists, B might obtain an injunction against A (as he could also in the case of a threatened breach of contract if the contract were of a kind that permitted that remedy); or if A carries out his threat, B can sue for assault and obtain damages. In neither case can C sue because he has suffered no harm. If B complies with the threat, B cannot sue for damages because ex hypothesi there has been no assault; and he is not likely to obtain an injunction against the execution of a threat which he has already taken other means to avoid. But C will be able to sue because through B's compliance he has been injured. There is no anomaly about this; and if one substitutes 'breach of contract' for 'physical violence', the position is the same. The only case in which B and C are both likely to sue is if they both sue for the tort of intimidation in a case in which B has harmed himself by also harming C. Then it is said that to give C a cause of action offends against the rule that one man cannot sue on another's contract. I cannot understand this. In no circumstances does C sue on B's contract. The cause of action arises not because B's contract is broken but because it is not broken; it arises because of the action which B has taken to avert a breach.

Then it is asked how it can be that C can sue when there is a threat to break B's contract but cannot sue if it is broken without a threat. This means, it is argued, that if A threatens first, C has a cause of action; but if he strikes without threatening, C has no cause of action. I think that this also is fallacious. What is material to C's cause of action is the threat and B's submission to it. Whether the threat is executed or not is *in law* quite immaterial. *In fact* it is no doubt material because if it is executed (whether it be an assault or a breach of contract) it presumably means that B has not complied with it; and if B has not complied with it, C is not injured; and if C is not injured, he has no cause of action. thus the reason why C can sue in one case and not in the other is because in one case he is injured and in the other he is not. The suggestion that it might pay A to strike without threatening negatives the hypothesis on which A is supposed to be acting. It must be proved that A's object is to injure C through the instrumentality of B. (That is why in the case of an 'innocent' breach of contract, ... that is, one into which A was forced by circumstances beyond his control, there could never be the basis of an actionable threat.) If A hits B without telling him why, he can hardly hope to achieve his object. Of course A might think it more effective to hit B first and tell him why afterwards. But if then B injures C, it would not be because B had been hit but because he feared that he might be hit again. So if in the present case A.E.S.D. went on strike without threatening, they would not achieve their object unless they made it plain why they were doing so. If they did that and B.O.A.C. then got rid of the appellant, his cause of action would be just the same as if B.O.A.C. had been threatened first, because the cause of the injury to the appellant would have been A.E.S.D.'s threat, express or implied, to continue on strike until the appellant was got rid of.

Finally, it is said that if a threat of breach of contract constitutes intimidation, one party to a contract could be sued for intimidation if he threatened reprisals. Suppose, for example, A has agreed to deliver goods to B in monthly instalments but has not made payment for the first a condition precedent to delivery of the second. If he threatens to withhold the second until payment has been made for the first, is he intimidating B? I doubt it. But the case introduces questions not in issue here whether a threat in such circumstances would be justifiable and whether it is intimidation to try to force a man into doing what the law, if invoked, would compel him to do. I find therefore nothing to differentiate a threat of a breach of contract from a threat of physical violence or any other illegal threat. The nature of the threat is immaterial, because, as Professor Hamson points out,[8] its nature is irrelevant to the plaintiff's cause of action. All that matters to the plaintiff is that, metaphorically speaking, a club has been used. It does not matter to the plaintiff what the club is made of whether it is a physical club or an economic club, a tortious club or an otherwise illegal club. If an intermediate party is improperly coerced, it does not matter to the plaintiff how he is coerced.

I think therefore that at common law there is a tort of intimidation and that on the facts of this case each of the respondents has committed it, both individually (since the jury has found that each took an overt and active part) and in combination with others. I must add that I have obtained no assistance

[8] *Cambridge Law Journal*, November 1961, at pp 191, 192.

from the numerous dicta cited to show what constitutes 'unlawful means' in the action of conspiracy. In some of the dicta the language suggest that the means must be criminal or tortious and in others that breach of contract would do; but in no case was the point in issue. Moreover, while a decision on that point might have been most illuminating, it is not the point that I have been considering. I have not been considering what amounts to unlawful means in the tort of conspiracy. I am not saying that a conspiracy to commit a breach of contract amounts to the tort of conspiracy; that point remains to be decided. I am saying that in the tort of intimidation a threat to break a contract would be a threat of an illegal act. It follows from that that a combination to intimidate by means of a threat of a breach of contract would be an unlawful conspiracy; but it does not necessarily follow that a combination to commit a breach of contract simpliciter would be an unlawful conspiracy....

[LORD EVERSHED, LORD HODSON, and LORD PEARCE delivered speeches in favour of allowing the appeal.]

NOTES

1. The immediate repercussion of this decision was the enactment of a specific immunity for those committing the tort of intimidation in circumstances similar to *Rookes v Barnard* by the Trade Disputes Act 1965. The immunity in extended form (covering additional forms of interfering with an employer's business by unlawful means) is now contained in s. 20 of the Trade Union and Labour Relations (Consolidation) Act 1992.

2. Why was Silverthorne, who had no contract to threaten to break, treated as a conspirator? (See the discussion of the two conspiracy causes of action, at p. 875 ante.) In *Morgan v Fry* [1968] 2 QB 710, [1968] 3 All ER 452 the only reason Lord Denning MR could find for Silverthorne not being protected from liability (by the then applicable provision, Trade Disputes Act 1906, s. 3) for inducing breach of contract was that he was a conspirator.

3. In *Morgan v Fry* Russell LJ suggested that not every threat to breach a contract of employment is sufficient to constitute intimidation. So where workers could have exerted equivalent or greater pressure on their employer by giving notice lawfully to terminate their contracts, Russell LJ said that the threat of a minor breach was not intimidatory. Perhaps the explanation for this is absence of proof that the threat of a minor breach would cause damage, proof of damage being an essential element of the tort. But in interlocutory proceedings the nature of the breach is unlikely to be investigated, meaning that this limit on the application of this tort may have a limited impact. See for example *Hadmor Productions Ltd v Hamilton* [1983] 1 AC 191, [1982] 1 All ER 1042.

4. The 'species' tort of intimidation, whose existence became firmly established in the wake of *Rookes v Barnard*, can constitute 'unlawful means' for purposes of the wider tort of interference with trade by unlawful means, which has been subsequently developed by the courts and encompasses a range of different circumstances where causing loss by unlawful means is actionable. Note that the recent decision of the House of Lords in *OBG v Allan* has had a considerable impact on this wider tort of causing loss by unlawful means by narrowing its scope, just as it has impacted upon the tort of inducing breach of contract by also limiting the scope of that cause of action (see p. 924, post).

■ Lonrho plc v Fayed

Court of Appeal [1989] 2 All ER 65

DILLON LJ:...
The...cause of action alleged...is...wrongful interference with trade or business. The existence of such a tort is conceded by the defendants...

It is submitted to us that, even with this tort, it must, as with the tort of conspiracy, have been the predominant purpose of the tortfeasor to injure the victim rather than to further the tortfeasor's own financial ends. I do not accept that. It would be inconsistent with the way Lord Diplock treated this tort and the tort of conspiracy differently in his speech in *Lonrho Ltd v Shell Petroleum Co Ltd* and in *Hadmor Productions Ltd v Hamilton* [1982] 1 All ER 1042 at 1052–1053, [1983] 1 AC 191 at 228–229. No predominant purpose to injure is required where the tortious act relied on is injury by wrongful interference with a third party's contract with the victim or by intimidation of a third party to the detriment of the victim, nor should it in my view be required where the wrongful interference has been by the practice of fraud on a third party, aimed specifically at the plaintiff, as it was put by Oliver LJ in *RCA Corp v Pollard* [1982] 3 All ER 771 at 780, [1983] Ch 135 at 151 ...

It also has to be proved by a plaintiff who seeks to rely on this tort, as counsel conceded for Lonrho, that the unlawful act was in some sense directed against the plaintiff or intended to harm the plaintiff. The origin of those phrases is the oft-quoted passage in the speech of Lord Watson in *Allen v Flood* [1898] AC 1 at 96, [1895–9] All ER Rep 52 at 69, which was applied by the majority of this court (Buckley and Kennedy LJJ) in *National Phonograph Co Ltd v Edison-Bell Consolidated Phonograph Co Ltd*. In that case the fraud was clearly directed against the plaintiff.

RALPH GIBSON LJ: ...

I agree that the appeal should be allowed to the extent indicated by Dillon LJ and for the reasons which he has given....

... This is a comparatively new tort of which the precise boundaries must be established from case to case. Those points include, first, the nature of the intention which is required to satisfy the requirement that the conduct be 'directed against' the plaintiffs, in particular where the fraudulent misstatement is made by A to B about A himself in order to cause B to act in such a way that A obtains or retains a commercial advantage over C or deprives C of a commercial advantage; second, the nature of the business interest by reference to which the plaintiff must prove that he has been damaged; third, whether there is sufficient nexus or directness of impact and consequence between the unlawful means employed and the alleged loss causing effect on the plaintiffs; and, fourth, whether the damage alleged is sufficient to support the existence of a cause of action....

[WOOLF LJ delivered a judgment agreeing with both judgments.]

Appeal allowed.

NOTES

1.   On a further appeal in this case to the House of Lords, ([1992] 1 AC 448, [1991] 3 All ER 303) the House of Lords rejected the Court of Appeal's views on whether there was a requirement for a predominant purpose to injure in unlawful means conspiracies (see p. 878, ante), but at the same time the House of Lords agreed with the Court of Appeal that the pleadings on interference with trade or business by unlawful means should be allowed to stand (which was the issue on appeal). There was no indication of the existence of any disagreement on their Lordships' part with the approach taken by the Court of Appeal to the scope of this tort.

2.   If A breaks his contract with B, this usually gives no remedy to C who is not a party. Why then, if A merely threatens to break his contract, should C have a cause of action? See L. H. Hoffmann (1965) 81 LQR 116 esp. at 126; K. W. Wedderburn (1964) 27 MLR 257; J. A. Weir [1964] CLJ 225. See also J. Neyers (2008) LS Online, 12 February 2008, who suggests that 'the tort of unlawful interference with economic relations is radically under-theorised and that it, and the other economic torts, could benefit tremendously from more intense academic examination'.

3.   The Court of Appeal in *Lonrho plc v Fayed*, uncontradicted by the House of Lords, says that there is no need to prove a 'predominant purpose to injure' in the interference

by unlawful means tort, unlike the case with 'lawful means' conspiracy, but there is a requirement to show that the defendant 'aimed at' the claimant through his use of unlawful means. This also brings this tort into line with unlawful means conspiracy. But it is far from clear what counts as 'aiming at' the claimant. Guidance on what will count as intention for the purposes of this tort have been provided by their Lordships in *OBG v Allan* (see p. 984 below), but as with the economic torts in general, defining the requirement degree of intention remains difficult.

4. Lord Devlin in *Rookes v Barnard* (p. 918, ante) recognised that 'an action [for intimidation] will doubtless lie at the suit of a trader who has been compelled to discontinue his business by means of threats of personal violence against him by the defendant with that intention' (see also *Godwin v Uzoigwe* [1993] Fam Law 65). Is this tort of 'two-party intimidation' appropriate in cases where the only threat is to break a contract to which the claimant is a party? Where A threatens B that he will break his contract with B so causing B damage, B may have other remedies: (a) he may be able to bring an action for anticipatory breach of contract, or await the breach and then sue for damages; or (b) he may be able to rely on the doctrine of economic duress defined by Lord Scarman in *Pao On v Lau Yiu Long* [1980] AC 614 at 635 as 'a coercion of the will so as to vitiate consent', so as to have a contract made under duress avoided or to recover money paid under duress. In *Universe Tankships Inc of Monrovia v International Transport Workers Federation* [1983] 1 AC 366 at 385, Lord Diplock said:

> The use of economic duress to induce another person to part with property or money is not a tort per se; the form that duress takes may, or may not, be tortious. The remedy to which economic duress gives rise is not an action for damages but an action for restitution of property or money exacted under any such duress and the avoidance of any contract that has been induced by it; but where the particular form taken by the economic duress used is itself a tort, the restitutional remedy for money had and received by the defendant to the plaintiff's use is one which the plaintiff is entitled to pursue as an alternative remedy to an action for damages in tort.

(Cf. Lord Scarman at p. 400.) Duress may be slightly wider than the tort of intimidation because it can, at least exceptionally, include a threat of coercive *lawful* action (see *CTN Cash and Carry Ltd v Gallaher Ltd* [1994] 4 All ER 714—economic duress by lawful action possible, though not likely in a commercial context); moreover, it seems that the 'threat' for the purposes of duress may amount to no more than an implied threat of non-performance of the contract: see *B & S Contracts and Design Ltd v Victor Green Publications Ltd* [1984] ICR 419 and the comments by N. E. Palmer and L. Catchpole (1985) 48 MLR 102. Note that the development of this doctrine reduces the importance of the tort of intimidation in a contractual context. However, also note that the potential for coercive lawful action to count as economic duress could come into tension with the *Allen v Flood* principle that liability will in general not be imposed in the absence of unlawful conduct. Nevertheless, this tension may only come into play in the exceptional circumstances where coercive lawful action will count as duress.

5. The distinction between 'two party' interference—where intimidation by A of B or the use by A of other forms of interference by unlawful means against B causes loss to B—and 'third party' interference—intimidation by A of C or the use by A of other forms of interference by unlawful means against C with the intention of interfering with C's freedom of action to cause loss to B—has not loomed large in case-law. However, the recent decision of the House of Lords in *OBG Ltd v Allan* has indicated that different rules may apply in these different circumstances: see p. 924, post.

■ OBG Ltd v Allan; Douglas v Hello! Ltd (No 3); Mainstream Properties Ltd v Young
House of Lords [2007] 4 All ER 545

This case involved three separate appeals: the facts of each and the relevant extracts from the decision that concern the tort of inducing breach of contract are set out at p. 907, ante.

LORD HOFFMANN:

Causing loss by unlawful means: elements of the tort

[45] The most important question concerning this tort is what should count as unlawful means. It will be recalled that in *Allen v Flood* [1898] AC 1 at 96, [1895–9] All ER Rep 52 at 69, Lord Watson described the tort thus:

> 'when the act induced is within the right of the immediate actor, and is therefore not wrongful in so far as he is concerned, it may yet be to the detriment of a third party; and in that case... the inducer may be held liable if he can be shewn to have procured his object by the use of illegal means directed against that third party.'

[46] The rationale of the tort was described by Lord Lindley in *Quinn v Leathem* [1901] AC 495 at 534–535, [1900–3] All ER Rep 1 at 10:

> 'a person's liberty or right to deal with others is nugatory, unless they are at liberty to deal with him if they choose to do so. Any interference with their liberty to deal with him affects him. If such interference is justifiable in point of law, he has no redress. Again, if such interference is wrongful, the only person who can sue in respect of it is, as a rule, the person immediately affected by it; another who suffers by it has usually no redress; the damage to him is too remote, and it would be obviously practically impossible and highly inconvenient to give legal redress to all who suffered from such wrongs. But if the interference is wrongful and is intended to damage a third person, and he is damaged in fact—in other words, if he is wrongfully and intentionally struck at through others, and is thereby damnified—the whole aspect of the case is changed: the wrong done to others reaches him, his rights are infringed although indirectly, and damage to him is not remote or unforeseen, but is the direct consequence of what has been done.'

[47] The essence of the tort therefore appears to be (a) a wrongful interference with the actions of a third party in which the claimant has an economic interest and (b) an intention thereby to cause loss to the claimant. The old cases of interference with potential customers by threats of unlawful acts clearly fell within this description. So, for the reasons I have given, did *GWK Ltd v Dunlop Rubber Co Ltd* (1926) 42 TLR 376. Recent cases in which the tort has been discussed have also concerned wrongful threats or actions against employers with the intention of causing loss to an employee (as in *Rookes v Barnard* [1964] AC 1129) or another employer (as *JT Stratford & Son Ltd v Lindley* [1964] 3 All ER 102, [1965] AC 269)... In the former case, the defendants conspired to threaten the employer that unless the employee was dismissed, there would be an unlawful strike. In the latter, the union committed the *Lumley v Gye* tort of inducing breaches of the contracts of the employees of barge hirers to prevent them from hiring the plaintiff's barges...

[49] In my opinion, and subject to one qualification, acts against a third party count as unlawful means only if they are actionable by that third party. The qualification is that they will also be unlawful means if the only reason why they are not actionable is because the third party has suffered no loss. In the case of intimidation, for example, the threat will usually give rise to no cause of action by the third party because he will have suffered no loss. If he submits to the threat, then, as the defendant intended, the claimant will have suffered loss instead. It is nevertheless unlawful means. But the threat must be to do something which *would* have been actionable if the third party had suffered loss. Likewise, in

National Phonograph Co Ltd v Edison-Bell Consolidated Phonograph Co Ltd [1908] 1 Ch 335, [1904–7] All ER Rep 116 the defendant intentionally caused loss to the plaintiff by fraudulently inducing a third party to act to the plaintiff's detriment. The fraud was unlawful means because it would have been actionable if the third party had suffered any loss, even though in the event it was the plaintiff who suffered. In this respect, procuring the actions of a third party by fraud (dolus) is obviously very similar to procuring them by intimidation (metus).

[50] *Lonrho plc v Fayed* [1989] 2 All ER 65, [1990] 2 QB 479 was arguably within the same principle as the *National Phonograph Co* case. The plaintiff said that the defendant had intentionally caused it loss by making fraudulent statements to the directors of the company which owned Harrods, and to the Secretary of State for Trade and Industry, which induced the directors to accept his bid for Harrods and the Secretary of State not to refer the bid to the Monopolies Commission. The defendant was thereby able to gain control of Harrods to the detriment of the plaintiff, who wanted to buy it instead. In the Court of Appeal, Dillon LJ ([1989] 2 All ER 65 at 69, [1990] 2 QB 479 at 489) referred to the *National Phonograph* case as authority for rejecting an argument that the means used to cause loss to the plaintiff could not be unlawful because neither the directors nor the Secretary of State had suffered any loss. That seems to me correct. The allegations were of fraudulent representations made to third parties, which would have been actionable by them if they had suffered loss, but which were intended to induce the third parties to act in a way which caused loss to the plaintiff. The Court of Appeal therefore refused to strike out the claim as unarguable and their decision was upheld by the House of Lords (see [1991] 3 All ER 303, [1992] 1 AC 448).

[51] Unlawful means therefore consists of acts intended to cause loss to the claimant by interfering with the freedom of a third party in a way which is unlawful as against that third party and which is intended to cause loss to the claimant. It does not in my opinion include acts which may be unlawful against a third party but which do not affect his freedom to deal with the claimant.

[52] Thus in *RCA Corp v Pollard* [1982] 3 All ER 771, [1983] Ch 135 the plaintiff had the exclusive right to exploit records made by Elvis Presley. The defendant was selling bootleg records made at Elvis Presley concerts without his consent. This was an infringement of s 1 of the Dramatic and Musical Performers' Protection Act 1958, which made bootlegging a criminal offence and, being enacted for the protection of performers, would have given Elvis Presley a cause of action: see Lord Diplock in *Lonrho Ltd v Shell Petroleum Co Ltd (No 2)* [1981] 2 All ER 456 at 462, [1982] AC 173 at 187. The Court of Appeal held that the infringement of the 1958 Act did not give RCA a cause of action. The defendant was not interfering with the liberty of the Presley estate to perform the exclusive recording contract which, as Oliver LJ noted ([1982] 3 All ER 771 at 779, [1983] Ch 135 at 149) was 'no more than an undertaking that he will not give consent to a recording by anyone else'. Nor did it prevent the Presley estate from doing any other act affecting the plaintiffs. The bootlegger's conduct, said Oliver LJ ([1982] 3 All ER 771 at 782, [1983] Ch 135 at 153): 'merely potentially reduces the profits which [the plaintiffs] make as the result of the performance by Mr Presley's executors of their contractual obligations.'

[53] It is true that there was no allegation that the defendant intended to cause loss to the plaintiff, although, given that the defendant was selling records in competition with the plaintiff, such an allegation would have been easy to make. But I do not think that it would have made any difference. The wrongful act did not interfere with the estate's liberty of action in relation to the plaintiff.

[54] Likewise in *Oren v Red Box Toy Factory Ltd* [1999] FSR 785, one of the claimants was the exclusive licensee of a registered design. The defendant sold articles alleged to infringe the design right. The registered owner had a statutory right to sue for infringement. But the question was whether the licensee could sue. In the case of some intellectual property rights, an exclusive licensee has a statutory right of action: see, for example, s 67(1) of the Patents Act 1977. But the exclusive licensee of a registered design has no such right. So the licensee claimed that the defendant was intentionally causing him loss by the unlawful means of infringing the rights of the registered owner. Jacob J rejected the claim on the principle of *RCA Corp v Pollard*. The defendant was doing nothing which affected the relations between the owner and licensee. The exclusive licence meant that the licensee was entitled

to exploit the design and that the owner contracted not to authorise anyone else to do so. As Jacob J said (at 798 (para 33)):

'It is true that the exploitation of the licence may not have been so successful commercially by reason of the infringement, but the contractual relations and their performance remain completely unaffected.'

[55] *Lonrho Ltd v Shell Petroleum Co Ltd (No 2)* was an attempt to found a cause of action simply on the fact that the conduct alleged to have caused loss was contrary to law. The defendant's conduct was alleged to be a criminal offence but not actionable by anyone. In this respect it was unlike *RCA Corp v Pollard* and *Oren v Red Box Toy Factory Ltd*, in which it could at least be said that the conduct was a wrong against someone in contractual relations with the claimant. Lonrho owned and operated a refinery in Rhodesia supplied by a pipeline from the port of Beira. When Rhodesia declared independence in 1965, the United Kingdom imposed sanctions which made it unlawful for anyone to supply the country with oil. As a result, the refinery and pipeline stood idle until the independence regime came to an end. Lonrho alleged that Shell had prolonged the regime by unlawfully supplying Rhodesia with oil through other routes and thereby caused it loss. The House of Lords decided that the alleged illegality gave rise to no cause of action on which Lonrho could rely. Again, there was no allegation that Shell had intended to cause loss to Lonrho, but I cannot see how that would have made any difference. Shell did not interfere with any third party's dealings with Lonrho and even if it had done so, its acts were not wrongful in the sense of being actionable by such third party.

[56] Your Lordships were not referred to any authority in which the tort of causing loss by unlawful means has been extended beyond the description given by Lord Watson in *Allen v Flood* and Lord Lindley in *Quinn v Leathem*. Nor do I think it should be. The common law has traditionally been reluctant to become involved in devising rules of fair competition, as is vividly illustrated by *Mogul Steamship Co Ltd v McGregor, Gow & Co* (1889) 23 QBD 598. It has largely left such rules to be laid down by Parliament. In my opinion the courts should be similarly cautious in extending a tort which was designed only to enforce basic standards of civilised behaviour in economic competition, between traders or between employers and labour. Otherwise there is a danger that it will provide a cause of action based on acts which are wrongful only in the irrelevant sense that a third party has a right to complain if he chooses to do so. As Jacob J said in *Oren v Red Box Toy Factory Ltd* [1999] FSR 785 at 800 (para 42):

'the right to sue under intellectual property rights created and governed by statute [is] inherently governed by the statute concerned. Parliament in various intellectual property statutes has, in some cases, created a right to sue, and in others not. In the case of the [Copyright, Designs and Patents Act 1988] it expressly re-conferred the right on a copyright exclusive licensee, conferred the right on an exclusive licensee under the new form of property called an unregistered design right (see section 234) but did not create an independent right to sue on a registered design exclusive licensee. It is not for the courts to invent that which Parliament did not create.'

[57] Likewise, as it seems to me, in a case like *Lonrho Ltd v Shell Petroleum Co Ltd (No 2)*, it is not for the courts to create a cause of action out of a regulatory or criminal statute which Parliament did not intend to be actionable in private law.

[58] It is not, I think, sufficient to say that there must be a causal connection between the wrongful nature of the conduct and the loss which has been caused. If a trader secures a competitive advantage over another trader by marketing a product which infringes someone else's patent, there is a causal relationship between the wrongful act and the loss which the rival has suffered. But there is surely no doubt that such conduct is actionable only by the patentee.

[59] Sales and Stilitz, 'Intentional Infliction of Harm by Unlawful Means' (1999) 115 LQR 411, take a very wide view of what can count as unlawful means, arguing that any action which involves a civil wrong against another person or breach of a criminal statute ('any act that the defendant is not at

liberty to commit') should be sufficient. In their opinion, a requirement of a specific intention to 'target' the claimant should keep the tort within reasonable bounds. Tony Weir in the Clarendon Law Lectures *Economic Torts* (1997) is of much the same opinion. But other writers consider that it would be arbitrary and illogical to make liability depend upon whether the defendant has done something which is wrongful for reasons which have nothing to do with the damage inflicted on the claimant: see Roderick Bagshaw's review of Weir in (1998) 18 OJLS 729, 732. I agree.

[60] I do not think that the width of the concept of 'unlawful means' can be counteracted by insisting upon a highly specific intention, which 'targets' the plaintiff. That, as it seems to me, places too much of a strain on the concept of intention. In cases in which there is obviously no reason why a claimant should be entitled to rely on the infringement of a third party's rights, courts are driven to refusing relief on the basis of an artificially narrow meaning of intention which causes trouble in later cases in which the defendant really has used unlawful means. This, as I shall in due course explain, is what may have happened in the *Douglas v Hello! Ltd* case.

[61] I would only add one footnote to this discussion of unlawful means. In defining the tort of causing loss by unlawful means as a tort which requires interference with the actions of a third party in relation to the plaintiff, I do not intend to say anything about the question of whether a claimant who has been compelled by unlawful intimidation to act to his own detriment, can sue for his loss. Such a case of 'two party intimidation' raises altogether different issues.

[62] Finally, there is the question of intention. In the *Lumley v Gye* tort, there must be an intention to procure a breach of contract. In the unlawful means tort, there must be an intention to cause loss. The ends which must have been intended are different. *South Wales Miners' Federation v Glamorgan Coal Co Ltd* [1905] AC 239, [1904–7] All ER Rep 211 shows that one may intend to procure a breach of contract without intending to cause loss. Likewise, one may intend to cause loss without intending to procure a breach of contract. But the concept of intention is in both cases the same. In both cases it is necessary to distinguish between ends, means and consequences. One intends to cause loss even though it is the means by which one achieved the end of enriching oneself. On the other hand, one is not liable for loss which is neither a desired end nor a means of attaining it but merely a foreseeable consequence of one's actions.

LORD NICHOLLS OF BIRKENHEAD: . . .

Unlawful means

[144] . . . In *Allen v Flood* [1898] AC 1 at 164, [1895–9] All ER Rep 52 at 97, Lord Shand likened the labour dispute in that case to one of 'competition in labour', which he said 'is in all essentials analogous to competition in trade, and to which the same principles must apply'. Lord Lindley adopted the same stance in another trade union case, *Quinn v Leathem* [1901] AC 495, [1900–3] All ER Rep 1. Lord Lindley approved Bowen LJ's observations quoted above (see [1901] AC 495 at 535, [1900–3] All ER Rep 1 at 16). He said the underlying principles are that an act 'otherwise lawful', although harmful, does not become actionable because it is done simply with intent to annoy or harm. But 'all wrongful acts' done intentionally to damage a particular individual and actually damaging him are remediable.

[145] Since then the common law of England has adhered to the view that 'unlawful' conduct is a prerequisite of liability under the tort of unlawful interference with trade. In the American case of *Tuttle v Buck* (1909) 119 NW 946 the court held a rich banker liable for spitefully driving the claimant barber out of business by opening a rival barber's shop and undercutting him. That is not the law in England. In this country intentionally causing damage without using unlawful means is not of itself actionable.

[146] The English approach has not lacked critics. On the 'unlawful conduct' approach the tort is parasitic on conduct defined as unlawful otherwise than because it amounts to a wrong to the claimant. This, it is said, is inherently unsatisfactory. It is inherently unsatisfactory because it means that a tort concerned with the regulation of trade is geared to commission of illegalities which were created for altogether different reasons: see JD Heydon *Economic Torts* (2nd edn, 1978) p 124. A wrong designed for some other purpose is being used as the criterion for deciding whether an act done with

an intention to harm is acceptable. This ingredient 'imposes an arbitrary and illogical limit on the development of a rational principle to explain this part of the law': *Salmond & Heuston on the Law of Torts* (21st edn, 1996) p 346. It 'can produce capricious results in which the distinction between permissible and impermissible...comes to turn on fictitious and, from a practical viewpoint, even irrelevant factors': Professor Fleming *The Law of Torts* (9th edn, 1998) p 761. In *JT Stratford & Son Ltd v Lindley* [1964] 3 All ER 102 at 110, [1965] AC 269 at 330, Viscount Radcliffe expressed unhappiness about this aspect of English law. He said the trade dispute in that case should be resolved 'according to its substance, without the comparatively accidental issue whether breaches of contract are looked for and involved'.

[147] These criticisms have force. The contrary, pragmatic view is that in this difficult and uncertain area of the law there is perhaps something to be said for having an objective element of unlawfulness as the boundary of liability. A defendant is not liable under this tort unless he has resorted to 'unlawful' means to achieve his end. Tony Weir, a staunch supporter of this approach, says this requirement is 'entirely correct, sensible and practical': *Economic Torts* (1997) p 3.

[148] I do not propose to enter upon the pros and cons of this particular debate. Your Lordships are not writing on a clean slate. English courts have long recognised they are not best equipped to regulate competitive practices at large. Parliament is better placed to decide what interests need protection and by what means. Fry LJ said that 'to draw a line between fair and unfair competition, between what is reasonable and unreasonable, passes the powers of the courts' (see *Mogul Steamship Co Ltd v McGregor, Gow & Co* (1889) 23 QBD 598 at 625–626). Since then Parliament has intervened on many occasions. The courts have taken, as their foothold, conduct which is unlawful. In English law it is now well established that 'unlawful means' is an essential ingredient of this tort.

[149] Although the need for 'unlawful means' is well established, the same cannot be said about the content of this expression. There is some controversy about the scope of this expression in this context.

[150] One view is that this concept comprises, quite simply, all acts which a person is not permitted to do. The distinction is between 'doing what you have a legal right to do and doing what you have no legal right to do' (see Lord Reid in *Rookes v Barnard* [1964] 1 All ER 367 at 374, [1964] AC 1129 at 1168–1169). So understood, the concept of 'unlawful means' stretches far and wide. It covers common law torts, statutory torts, crimes, breaches of contract, breaches of trust and equitable obligations, breaches of confidence, and so on.

[151] Another view is that in this context 'unlawful means' comprise only civil wrongs. Thus in *Allen v Flood* itself Lord Watson described illegal means as 'means which in themselves are in the nature of civil wrongs' (see [1898] AC at 97–98, [1895–9] All ER Rep 52 at 69). A variant on this view is even more restricted in its scope: 'unlawful means' are limited to torts and breaches of contract.

[152] The principal criticism of the first, wider view is that it 'tortifies' criminal conduct. The principal criticism of the second, narrower view is that it would be surprising if criminal conduct were excluded from the category of 'unlawful' means in this context. In the classical 'three-party' form of this tort the defendant seeks to injure the claimant's business through the instrumentality of a third party. By this means, as Lord Lindley said, the claimant is 'wrongfully and intentionally struck at through others, and is thereby damnified' (see *Quinn v Leathem* [1901] AC 495 at 535, [1900–3] All ER Rep 1 at 10). It would be very odd if in such a case the law were to afford the claimant a remedy where the defendant committed or threatened to commit a tort or breach of contract against the third party but not if he committed or threatened to commit a crime against him. In seeking to distinguish between acceptable and unacceptable conduct it would be passing strange that a breach of contract should be proscribed but not a crime...

[153] These different views are founded on different perceptions of the rationale underlying the unlawful interference tort. On the wider interpretation of 'unlawful means' the rationale is that by this tort the law seeks to curb clearly excessive conduct. The law seeks to provide a remedy for intentional economic harm caused by unacceptable means. The law regards all unlawful means as unacceptable in this context.

Lord Nicholls

[handwritten: Lord Hoffmann]

[154] On the narrower interpretation this tort has a much more limited role. On this interpretation the function of the tort of unlawful interference is a modest one. Its function is to provide a claimant with a remedy where intentional harm is inflicted indirectly as distinct from directly.

[155] In my view the former is the true rationale of this tort. The second interpretation represents a radical departure from the purpose for which this tort has been developed. If adopted, this interpretation would bring about an unjustified and unfortunate curtailment of the scope of this tort.

[156] On either interpretation complications may arise in the application of this tort in certain types of cases, notably where the civil rights of a third party infringed by the defendant are statute-based. The existence of these perceived complications is not a pointer in favour of either interpretation.

[157] Take the case of a patent. A manufacturer seeks to steal a march on his rival by employing a novel, patented process. In order to sell his product more cheaply, he does so without paying any licence fee to the owner of the patent. By means of this patent infringement he undercuts his law-abiding rival. He has damaged his rival's business by an unlawful means. But this conduct, however reprehensible, cannot afford the rival manufacturer a cause of action for damages for interference with trade by unlawful means. Parliament has specified the nature and extent of the remedies available for infringement of patents. Remedial relief for infringement of a patent is available to patentees and exclusive licensees. It would be inconsistent with the statutory scheme if the common law tort were to afford a remedy more widely . . .

[159] The difficulties here are more apparent than real. The answer lies in keeping firmly in mind that, in these three-party situations, the function of the tort is to provide a remedy where the claimant is harmed through the *instrumentality* of a third party. That would not be so in the patent example.

[160] Similarly with the oft quoted instance of a courier service gaining an unfair and illicit advantage over its rival by offering a speedier service because its motorcyclists frequently exceed speed limits and ignore traffic lights. The unlawful interference tort would not apply in such a case. The couriers' criminal conduct is not an offence committed against the rival company in any realistic sense of that expression.

[161] Nor am I persuaded that the effect of the broader interpretation of 'unlawful means' is to impose civil liability on a defendant simply because he reached his victim through an agent rather than directly. I am far from satisfied that, in a two-party situation, the courts would decline to give relief to a claimant whose economic interests had been deliberately injured by a crime committed against him by the defendant.

[162] For these reasons I accept the approach of Lord Reid and Lord Devlin and prefer the wider interpretation of 'unlawful means'. In this context the expression 'unlawful means' embraces all acts a defendant is not permitted to do, whether by the civil law or the criminal law . . .

Intent to injure

[164] . . . A defendant may intend to harm the claimant's business either as an end in itself or as a means to an end. A defendant may intend to harm the claimant as an end in itself where, for instance, he has a grudge against the claimant. More usually a defendant intentionally inflicts harm on a claimant's business as a means to an end. He inflicts damage as the means whereby to protect or promote his own economic interests.

[165] Intentional harm inflicted against a claimant in either of these circumstances satisfies the mental ingredient of this tort. This is so even if the defendant does not wish to harm the claimant, in the sense that he would prefer that the claimant were not standing in his way.

[166] Lesser states of mind do not suffice. A high degree of blameworthiness is called for, because intention serves as the factor which justifies imposing liability on the defendant for loss caused by a wrong otherwise not actionable by the claimant against the defendant. The defendant's conduct in relation to the loss must be deliberate. In particular, a defendant's foresight that his unlawful conduct may or will probably damage the claimant cannot be equated with intention for this purpose. The defendant must *intend* to injure *the claimant* . . .

[167] I add one explanatory gloss to the above. Take a case where a defendant seeks to advance his own business by pursuing a course of conduct which he knows will, in the very nature of things, necessarily be injurious to the claimant. In other words, a case where loss to the claimant is the obverse side of the coin from gain to the defendant. The defendant's gain and the claimant's loss are, to the defendant's knowledge, inseparably linked. The defendant cannot obtain the one without bringing about the other. If the defendant goes ahead in such a case in order to obtain the gain he seeks, his state of mind will satisfy the mental ingredient of the unlawful interference tort. This accords with the approach adopted by Lord Sumner in *Sorrell v Smith* [1925] AC 700 at 742, [1925] All ER Rep 1 at 20 . . .

LORD WALKER OF GESTINGTHORPE: . . .

[263] My Lords, I have had the privilege of reading in draft the opinions of my noble and learned friends Lord Nicholls of Birkenhead and Lord Hoffmann, both of which cast welcome light on the obscurities of the so-called economic torts. In relation to these torts there is (as I see it) a large measure of agreement between my noble and learned friends, though with some differences in emphasis, and some more substantial differences.

[264] Both my noble and learned friends agree that the 'unified theory' of the economic torts, attractive though it is, must be rejected. The tort of intentionally inducing a breach of contract is essentially different from inflicting harm by unlawful means, although in some factual situations they may overlap . . . . On these points Lord Nicholls and Lord Hoffmann are at one, and I respectfully concur in their reasoning and conclusions.

[265] I must however set out briefly my views on those points on the economic torts on which my noble and learned friends seem to differ . . .

[266] On the economic torts, the most important difference is in the identification of the control mechanism needed in order to stop the notion of unlawful means getting out of hand—for example, a pizza delivery business which obtains more business, to the detriment of its competitors, because its drivers regularly exceed the speed limit and jump red lights. Lord Hoffmann sees the rationale of the unlawful means tort as encapsulated in Lord Lindley's reference (in *Quinn v Leathem* [1901] AC 495 at 534, [1900–3] All ER Rep 1 at 10) to interference with 'a person's liberty or right to deal with others.' In his view acts against a third party count as unlawful means only if they are (or would be if they caused loss) actionable at the suit of the third party.

[267] Lord Hoffmann does not question the correctness of the decisions of the Court of Appeal in *RCA Corp v Pollard* [1982] 3 All ER 771, [1983] Ch 135 or of Jacob J in *Oren v Red Box Toy Factory Ltd* [1999] FSR 785, which show that a bootlegger's activities, although actionable by the owner of the intellectual property rights in question, are not actionable (by statute or at common law) by a contractual licensee entitled to exploit those rights, even if the licensee's profits are demonstrably reduced by the unlawful activities . . .

[268] Lord Nicholls also accepts the correctness of *Oren v Red Box Toy Factory Ltd* (and also, I infer, the correctness of *RCA Corp v Pollard*). He proposes a wider test of unlawful means relying on the notion of instrumentality as the appropriate control mechanism.

[269] Faced with these alternative views I am naturally hesitant. I would respectfully suggest that neither is likely to be the last word on this difficult and important area of the law. The test of instrumentality does not fit happily with cases like *RCA Corp v Pollard,* since there is no doubt that the bootlegger's acts were the direct cause of the plaintiff's economic loss. The control mechanism must be found, it seems to me, in the nature of the disruption caused, as between the third party and the claimant, by the defendant's wrong (and not in the closeness of the causal connection between the defendant's wrong and the claimant's loss).

[270] I do not, for my part, see Lord Hoffmann's proposed test as a narrow or rigid one. On the contrary, that test (set out in [51] of his opinion, above) of whether the defendant's wrong interferes with the freedom of a third party to deal with the claimant, if taken out of context, might be regarded as so flexible as to be of limited utility. But in practice it does not lack context. The authorities demonstrate its application in relation to a wide variety of economic relationships. I would favour a fairly cautious incremental approach to its extension to any category not found in the existing authorities.

[LORD BROWN OF EATON-UNDER-HEYWOOD and BARONESS HALE OF RICHMOND delivered judgments in which they expressed agreement with the approach taken by LORD HOFFMANN.]

The appeals from the Court of Appeal decisions in OBG v Allan *and* Mainstream v Young *were dismissed. The appeal from the Court of Appeal decision in* Douglas v Hello (No. 3) *was allowed.*

QUESTIONS

1. Identify the points on which Lord Hoffmann and Lord Nicholls are in agreement, and where they disagree. Note in particular Lord Hoffmann's views at [51]–[61], and those of Lord Nicholls at [152]–[161]. In your opinion, should breaches of the criminal law qualify as 'unlawful means' for the purposes of this tort? How do Lord Nicholls and Lord Walker deal with the example of the speeding pizza delivery service, which was extensively discussed with counsel during the course of the proceedings? Why would Lord Hoffmann permit a claimant to bring an action where unlawful means are used which would have been independently actionable by a third party if that third party had suffered loss? Does this permit liability to be imposed for intimidation of a third party?

2. Do Lord Hoffmann and Lord Nicholls share a similar view as to the intention required to establish a cause of action under this tort? If a defendant proceeds on the basis that he does not care about whether his activities will cause loss, will that be sufficient for liability to be imposed? What about a case where a defendant knows that loss will result to the claimant from his activities and nevertheless proceeds, on the basis that he is merely going about his own business?

NOTES

1. In the case of *OBG v Allan* itself, their Lordships agreed that the wrongly appointed receivers neither employed unlawful means nor intended to cause OBG any loss. Lord Nicholls and Baroness Hale dissented on the basis that the receivers had committed the tort of conversion. In the third case, *Mainstream v Young*, no intention to cause harm to the defendant existed, nor did the defendant use any unlawful means.

    In *Douglas v Hello! Ltd (No 3)*, the Court of Appeal dismissed OK!'s cross-appeal on the ground that Hello! did not have the requisite subjective intention to cause harm. The majority of their Lordships considered that OK! was entitled to bring proceedings for breach of an obligation of confidentiality to OK! itself. The information in question, namely the photographs, was deemed to be capable of being protected through the confidence action because it was information of commercial value over which the celebrity couple with whom OK! had contracted had sufficient control to enable them to impose an obligation of confidence. Lord Nicholls and Lord Walker dissented on this matter. Lord Hoffmann at [134]–[135] made clear that he considered that this claim would also succeed on the grounds that loss had been intentionally caused to the claimants by the use of unlawful means by the defendant, contrary to the position taken by Lindsay J at first instance and the Court of Appeal:

    [134] …the position of Senor Sanchez Junco [the controlling shareholder of Hello!, who had authorized the decision to publish the photograhs in question] was that he wished to defend his publication against the damage it might suffer on account of having lost the exclusive. But that, it seems to me, is precisely the position of every competitor who steps over the line and uses unlawful means. The injury which he inflicted on *OK!* in order to achieve the end of keeping up his sales

was simply the other side of the same coin . . . The injury to *OK!* was the means of attaining Senor Sanchez Junco's desired end and not merely a foreseeable consequence of having done so.

[135]. The analysis of intention by the Court of Appeal in my opinion illustrates the danger of giving a wide meaning to the concept of unlawful means and then attempting to restrict the ambit of the tort by giving a narrow meaning to the concept of intention. The effect is to enable virtually anyone who really has used unlawful means against a third party in order to injure the plaintiff to say that he intended only to enrich himself, or protect himself from loss. The way to keep the tort within reasonable bounds is to restrict the concept of unlawful means to what was contemplated in *Allen v Flood*; not to give an artificially narrow meaning to the concept of intention.

Lord Nicholls and Lord Walker disagreed on this point on the basis that Hello! had not made use of any unlawful means, following their rejection of the argument that OK! could bring an action in breach of confidence.

2. Lord Hoffmann places considerable emphasis on controlling the scope of the tort of causing loss by unlawful means: this is the rationale offered for confining the scope of unlawful means to acts independently actionable by third parties, where 'third party' interference is at issue. However, is this approach compatible with the emphasis placed by the House of Lords in *Rookes v Barnard* [1964] AC 1219, [1964] 1 All ER 367 on what Lord Reid described as the 'chasm between doing what you have a legal right to do and doing what you have no legal right to do' (see p. 918 ante)?

3. In contemporary society, statutory regulation and the criminal law are the primary means of shaping the rights and duties of individuals. Why therefore should liability for intentionally inflicting economic harm upon another via a third party only be actionable if the third party could sustain civil action against the defendant, or would have been so able had loss been sustained? Why should liability depend on the potential availability of a private law remedy only? Note that commentators have been in general supportive of the concept of 'unlawful means' being defined as including at least breaches of the criminal law: see H. Carty (1988) 104 LQR 250; P. Sales and D. Stilitz (1999) 115 LQR 41. See in particular the view adopted by p. Elias and A. Tettenborn [1981] CLJ 230, at 232: 'a criminal provision should ground liability in tort for causing loss by unlawful means unless there are clear reasons of policy or in its interpretation why it should not'.

4. In *Revenue and Customs Commissioners v Total Network SL* [2008] 2 All ER 413, [2008] UKHL 19, the House of Lords subsequently declined to impose a requirement of independent actionability when it came to the tort of unlawful means conspiracy: see p. 883, ante. The majority approach in *OBG v Allan* was distinguished in *Total Network* on the basis that it was confined to cases of third party interference, where A interferes with C to cause loss to B. In contrast, unlawful means conspiracy was treated as similar to 'two party' interference, where A directly interferes with B using unlawful means to inflict loss on B. Lord Hoffmann in *OBG v Allan* left open the question of what would constitute unlawful means in the context of two party interference, and Lord Nicholls suggested that a wider definition of unlawful loss could apply in cases of two party interference than would in the case of third party interference. Therefore, a distinction appears to have opened up in the case law between two party interference and third party interference, the former being apparently regarded as more immediate, direct and suitable for a wider definition of unlawful means to be applied. But how much weight should be placed on this distinction? Why should a wider definition of 'unlawful means' apply in the context of direct interference with the claimant, when an indirect interference via a third party may be as damaging?

5. Note that Lord Walker in *Total Network*, makes the following argument as to why criminal conduct should come within the scope of 'unlawful means' for the purposes of unlawful means conspiracy:

> 90. In searching for general principle I start with a very simple, even naïve point. The man in the street, if asked what an unlawful act was, would probably answer 'a crime.' He might give as an example theft, obtaining money by false pretences, or assault occasioning actual bodily harm. He might or might not know that each of these was also a civil wrong (or tort) but it is unlikely that civil liability would be in the forefront of his mind.
>
> 91. The reaction of a lawyer would be more informed but it would not, I suggest, be essentially different. In its ordinary legal meaning "unlawful" certainly covers crimes and torts (especially intentional torts). Beyond that its scope may sometimes extend to breach of contract, breach of fiduciary duty, and perhaps even matters which merely make a contract unenforceable, but the word's appropriateness becomes increasingly debatable and dependent on the legal context…

Why should these arguments not also apply in the context of causing loss by unlawful means by third party intervention? If a defendant commits a substantial breach of the criminal law or of statutory duties in order to interfere with the freedom of action of a third party with the intention of causing loss to the claimant, why should the claimant be precluded from seeking a remedy on the basis that the third party had no actionable claim?

6. In *Acrow (Automation) Ltd v Rex Chainbelt Inc* [1971] 3 All ER 1175, [1971] 1 WLR 1676, a refusal to continue deliveries to which the claimant had no contractual right was held by the Court of Appeal to be unlawful means and hence was actionable in tort because the defendants were aiding and abetting the breach of an injunction, in contempt of court at common law. Earlier, however, in *Chapman v Honig* [1963] 2 QB 502, [1963] 2 All ER 513 where a landlord gave a tenant notice to quit (in accordance with the lease) to punish him for giving evidence in an action brought by other tenants against the landlord, the Court of Appeal (Lord Denning MR dissenting) held that even if this amounted to a contempt of court, no tort had been committed. Applying Lord Hoffmann's analysis in *OBG v Allan*, how should this conflict of authority be resolved?

7. Should a breach of contract which is accompanied by the requisite intention generate a cause of action under this tort of causing loss by unlawful means? See J.A. Weir [1964] CLJ 225 and H. Carty (1988) 104 LQR 250 at 271–272 for contrasting views. In *Barretts & Baird (Wholesale) Ltd v Institution of Professional Civil Servants* [1987] IRLR 3 at [54], Henry J observed that the results of treating breach of contract as unlawful means in the law of tort were 'surprising' because they lead to 'large inroads into the doctrine of privity of contract': see S. Fredman (1987) 103 LQR 176; B. Simpson (1987) 50 MLR 506; K. Ewing [1987] CLJ 222. The main objection to defining a breach of contract as constituting 'unlawful means' is that it further complicates and constrains the position of trade unions and others acting in the course of industrial disputes. However, the approach taken in *OBG v Allan* means that an action can be sustained for breach of contract that confers a cause of action on a third party, but not for a crime. Is this justifiable? Is there a case for the opposite state of affairs to apply? See Lord Nicholl's judgment at [152], ante.

8. Note that in his dissent Lord Nicholls suggests at [159] that the scope of 'unlawful means' could be adequately limited by a requirement that the unlawful action at issue is used as a means to interfere with the third party and therefore to inflict harm intentionally on the claimant: 'the function of the tort is to provide a remedy where the

claimant is harmed through the *instrumentality* of a third party'. Lord Walker adopted a similar approach in defining the scope of 'unlawful means' in the context of unlawful means conspiracy in *Total Network*, at [95]–[96]: see p. 884, ante. Might this be a more efficient and flexible control device for reining in the potential scope of the tort of causing unlawful means than the 'independent actionability' requirement adopted by Lord Hoffmann and the majority in *OBG*?

4 PASSING-OFF AND OTHER FORMS OF UNLAWFUL COMPETITION

■ Erven Warnink BV v J Townend & Sons (Hull) Ltd
House of Lords [1979] 2 All ER 927

The plaintiffs ('Warnink') manufactured a drink known as 'advocaat' made out of a mixture of eggs and spirits. The defendants ('Keeling') produced an alcoholic drink from a mixture of dried eggs and sherry and marketed it as 'Keeling's Old English Advocaat'. They could undersell Warnink because the rate of excise duty was lower on fortified wine than on spirits. Keeling had not passed off their product as that of Warnink and it was unlikely that any purchaser would suppose Keeling's drink to be Warnink's product. Warnink applied for an injunction restraining Keeling from selling or distributing under the name 'advocaat' any product not made out of eggs and spirits without the addition of wine. They relied on the principle, first recognised by Danckwerts J in the Champagne case (*Bollinger v Costa Brava Wine Co Ltd* [1960] Ch 262, [1959] 3 All ER 800), and followed in the Sherry case (*Vine Products Ltd v Mackenzie & Co Ltd* [1969] RPC 1) and the Scotch Whisky case (*John Walker & Sons Ltd v Henry Ost & Co Ltd* [1970] 2 All ER 106, [1970] 1 WLR 917), that although they did not have an exclusive right to the use of the trade name 'advocaat', they were members of a class consisting of all those who had a right to use the name and as such were entitled to protect it. The judge granted the injunction. On appeal the Court of Appeal discharged the injunction and dismissed the action on the ground that the name 'advocaat' was purely descriptive and not distinctive. On appeal to the House of Lords:

LORD DIPLOCK:...
Unfair trading as a wrong actionable at the suit of other traders who thereby suffer loss of business or goodwill may take a variety of forms, to some of which separate labels have become attached in English law. Conspiracy to injure a person in his trade or business is one, slander of goods another, but most protean is that which is generally and nowadays, perhaps misleadingly, described as 'passing off'. The forms that unfair trading takes will alter with the ways in which trade is carried on and business reputation and goodwill acquired....

   The action for what has become known as 'passing off' arose in the 19th century out of the use in connection with his own goods by one trader of the trade name or trade mark of a rival trader so as to induce in potential purchasers the belief that his goods were those of the rival trader....

   My Lords, *A G Spalding & Bros v A W Gamage Ltd*[9] and the later cases make it possible to identify five characteristics which must be present in order to create a valid cause of action for passing off: (1) a misrepresentation, (2) made by a trader in the course of trade, (3) to prospective customers of his or

[9] (1915) 32 RPC 273.

ultimate consumers of goods or services supplied by him, (4) which is calculated to injure the business or goodwill of another trader (in the sense that this is a reasonably foreseeable consequence) and (5) which causes actual damage to a business or goodwill of the trader by whom the action is brought or (in a quia timet action) will probably do so.

In seeking to formulate general propositions of English law, however, one must be particularly careful to beware of the logical fallacy of the undistributed middle. It does not follow that because all passing-off actions can be shown to present these characteristics, all factual situations which present these characteristics give rise to a cause of action for passing off. True it is that their presence indicates what a moral code would censure as dishonest trading, based as it is on deception of customers and consumers of a trader's wares, but in an economic system which has relied on competition to keep down prices and to improve products there may be practical reasons why it should have been the policy of the common law not to run the risk of hampering competition by providing civil remedies to everyone competing in the market who has suffered damage to his business or goodwill in consequence of inaccurate statements of whatever kind that may be made by rival traders about their own wares. The market in which the action for passing off originated was no place for the mealy mouthed: advertisements are not on affidavit; exaggerated claims by a trader about the quality of his wares, assertions that they are better than those of his rivals, even though he knows this to be untrue, have been permitted by the common law as venial 'puffing' which gives no cause of action to a competitor even though he can show that he has suffered actual damage in his business as a result.

Parliament, however, beginning in the 19th century has progressively intervened in the interests of consumers to impose on traders a higher standard of commercial candour than the legal maxim caveat emptor calls for, by prohibiting under penal sanctions misleading descriptions of the character or quality of goods; but since the class of persons for whose protection the Merchandise Marks Acts 1887 to 1953 and even more rigorous later statutes are designed are not competing traders but those consumers who are likely to be deceived, the Acts do not themselves give rise to any civil action for breach of statutory duty on the part of a competing trader even though he sustains actual damage as a result: *Cutler v Wandsworth Stadium Ltd*;[10] and see *London Armoury Co Ltd v Ever Ready Co (Great Britain) Ltd*.[11] Nevertheless the increasing recognition by Parliament of the need for more rigorous standards of commercial honesty is a factor which should not be overlooked by a judge confronted by the choice whether or not to extend by analogy to circumstances in which it has not previously been applied a principle which has been applied in previous cases where the circumstances although different had some features in common with those of the case which he has to decide. Where over a period of years there can be discerned a steady trend in legislation which reflects the view of successive Parliaments as to what the public interest demands in a particular field of law, development of the common law in that part of the same field which has been left to it ought to proceed on a parallel rather than a diverging course.

The Champagne case came before Danckwerts J in two stages: the first[12] on a preliminary point of law, the second[13] on the trial of the action. The assumptions of fact on which the legal argument at the first stage was based were stated by the judge to be:[14]

'(1) The plaintiffs carry on business in a geographical area in France known as Champagne; (2) the plaintiffs' wine is produced in Champagne and from grapes grown in Champagne; (3) the plaintiffs' wine has been known in the trade for a long time as "Champagne" with a high reputation; (4) members of the public or in the trade ordering or seeing wine advertised as "Champagne" would expect to get wine produced in Champagne from grapes grown there and (5) the defendants are producing a wine not produced in that geographical area and are selling it under the name of "Spanish Champagne".'

---

[10] [1949] AC 398.   [11] [1941] 1 All ER 364, [1941] 1 KB 742.
[12] [1959] 3 All ER 800, [1960] Ch 262.   [13] [1961] 1 WLR 277, [1961] 1 All ER 561.
[14] [1959] 3 All ER 800 at 804, [1960] Ch 262 at 273.

These findings disclose a factual situation (assuming that damage was thereby caused to the plaintiff's business) which contains each of the five characteristics which I have suggested must be present in order to create a valid cause of action for passing off. The features that distinguished it from all previous cases were (a) that the element in the goodwill of each of the individual plaintiffs that was represented by his ability to use without deception (in addition to his individual house mark) the word 'champagne' to distinguish his wines from sparkling wines not made by the champenois process from grapes produced in the Champagne district of France was not exclusive to himself but was shared with every other shipper of sparkling wine to England whose wines could satisfy the same condition and (b) that the class of traders entitled to a proprietary right in 'the attractive force that brings in custom' represented by the ability without deception to call one's wines 'champagne' was capable of continuing expansion, since it might be joined by any future shipper of wine who was able to satisfy that condition....

...[T]he familiar argument that to extend the ambit of an actionable wrong beyond that to which effect has demonstrably been given in the previous cases would open the floodgates or, more ominously, a Pandora's box of litigation leaves me unmoved when it is sought to be applied to the actionable wrong of passing off.

I would hold the Champagne case to have been rightly decided and in doing so would adopt the words of Danckwerts J where he said:[15]

> 'There seems to be no reason why such licence [sc. to do a deliberate act which causes damage to the property of another person] should be given to a person, competing in trade, who seeks to attach to his product a name or description with which it has no natural association so as to make use of the reputation and goodwill which has been gained by a product genuinely indicated by the name or description. In my view, it ought not to matter that the persons truly entitled to describe their goods by the name and description are a class producing goods in a certain locality, and not merely one individual. The description is part of their goodwill and a right of property. I do not believe that the law of passing off, which arose to prevent unfair trading, is so limited in scope.'

In the Champagne case the descriptive term referred to the geographical provenance of the goods, and the class entitled to the goodwill in the term was accordingly restricted to those supplying on the English market goods produced in the locality indicated by it. Something similar was true in the Sherry case where the word 'sherry' as descriptive of a type of wine unless it was accompanied by some qualifying geographical adjective was held to denote wine produced by the solera method in the province of Jerez de la Frontera in Spain and the class entitled to the goodwill in the word was restricted to suppliers on the English market of wine produced in that province. In the Scotch Whisky case the product with which the case was primarily concerned was blended Whisky and the class entitled to the goodwill in the descriptive term 'Scotch whisky' was not restricted to traders who dealt in whisky that had been blended in Scotland but extended to suppliers of blended whisky wherever the blending process took place provided that the ingredients of their product consisted exclusively of whiskies that had been distilled in Scotland. But the fact that in each of these first three cases the descriptive name under which goods of a particular type or composition were marketed by the plaintiffs among others happened to have geographical connotations is in my view without significance. If a product of a particular character or composition has been marketed under a descriptive name and under that name has gained a public reputation which distinguishes it from competing products of different composition, I can see no reason in principle or logic why the goodwill in the name of those entitled to make use of it should be protected by the law against deceptive use of the name by competitors, if it denotes a product of which the ingredients come from a particular locality, but should lose that protection if the ingredients of the product, however narrowly identified, are not restricted as to their geographical provenance....

[O]n the findings of fact by Goulding J to which I referred at the beginning of this speech, the type of product that has gained for the name 'advocaat' on the English market the reputation and goodwill of

---

[15] [1960] Ch 262 at 284, [1959] 3 All ER 800 at 810–811.

which Keelings are seeking to take advantage by misrepresenting that their own product is of that type is defined by reference to the nature of its ingredients irrespective of their origin. The class of traders of whose respective businesses the right to describe their products as advocaat forms a valuable part of their goodwill are those who have supplied and are supplying on the English market an egg and spirit drink in broad conformity with an identifiable recipe. The members of that class are easily identified and very much fewer in number than in the Champagne, Sherry or Scotch Whisky cases. Warnink with 75 per cent of the trade have a very substantial stake in the goodwill of the name 'advocaat' and their business has been showed to have suffered serious injury as a result of Keelings putting on the English market in competition with Warnink and at a cheaper price an egg and wine based drink which they miscall advocaat instead of eggflip which is its proper name.

My Lords, all the five characteristics that I have earlier suggested must be present to create a valid cause of action in passing off today were present in the instant case. Prima facie, as the law stands today, I think the presence of those characteristics is enough, unless there is also present in the case some exceptional feature which justifies, on grounds of public policy, withholding from a person who has suffered injury in consequence of the deception practised on prospective customers or consumers of his product a remedy in law against the deceiver. On the facts found by the judge, and I stress their importance, I can find no such exceptional feature in the instant case.

I would allow this appeal and restore the injunction granted by Goulding J.

[LORD FRASER OF TULLYBELTON delivered a speech in favour of allowing the appeal and restoring the order made by Goulding J. VISCOUNT DILHORNE, LORD SALMON and LORD SCARMAN, agreed with both speeches.]

Appeal allowed.

■ Reckitt and Colman Products Ltd v Borden Inc
House of Lords [1990] 1 All ER 873

LORD OLIVER: . . .
Although your Lordships were referred in the course of the argument to a large number of reported cases, this is not a branch of the law in which reference to other cases is of any real assistance except analogically. It has been observed more than once that the questions which arise are, in general, questions of fact. Neither the appellants nor the respondents contend that the principles of law are in any doubt. The law of passing off can be summarised in one short general proposition, no man may pass off his goods as those of another. More specifically, it may be expressed in terms of the elements which the plaintiff in such an action has to prove in order to succeed. These are three in number. First, he must establish a goodwill or reputation attached to the goods or services which he supplies in the mind of the purchasing public by association with the identifying 'get-up' (whether it consists simply of a brand name or a trade description, or the individual features of labelling or packaging) under which his particular goods or services are offered to the public, such that the get-up is recognised by the public as distinctive specifically of the plaintiff's goods or services. Second, he must demonstrate a misrepresentation by the defendant to the public (whether or not intentional) leading or likely to lead the public to believe that goods or services offered by him are the goods or services of the plaintiff. Whether the public is aware of the plaintiff's identity as the manufacturer or supplier of the goods or services is immaterial, as long as they are identified with a particular source which is in fact the plaintiff. For example, if the public is accustomed to rely on a particular brand name in purchasing goods of a particular description, it matters not at all that there is little or no public awareness of the identity of the proprietor of the brand name. Third, he must demonstrate that he suffers or, in a quia timet action, that he is likely to suffer damage by reason of the erroneous belief engendered by the defendant's misrepresentation that the source of the defendant's goods or services is the same as the source of those offered by the plaintiff.

NOTES

1. Following his description of the three key elements of passing-off (often referred to by practitioners in this field as the 'classic trinity') in the above extract from *Reckitt & Colman Products Ltd v Borden Inc,* Lord Oliver said that 'the essence of the action for passing off is a deceit practised on the public and it can be no answer, in a case where it is demonstrable that the public has been or will be deceived, that they would not have been if they had been more careful, more literate or more perspicacious': [1990] 1 All ER 873, at 888. On the other hand, if the only people likely to buy the goods were not likely to be deceived, it does not matter that others might have been deceived. (See also *Hodgkinson & Corby Ltd v Wards Mobility Services* [1994] 1 WLR 1564.) The first requirement in *E Warnink v J Townend*—misrepresentation—need not be intentional but the public has to have been deceived, not just confused: see *Barnsley Brewery Co Ltd v RBNB* [1997] FSR 462). See also *L'Oreal SA v Bellure NV* [2008] RPC 9, [2007] EWCA Civ 968.

2. In his five-point test in *E Warnink v J Townend* Lord Diplock refers several times to 'business' and 'goodwill'. Passing-off is essentially a tort that protects commercial interests. More precisely it protects 'the goodwill and reputation of [the claimant's] business which is likely to be harmed by the defendant's misrepresentation', as noted by Millett LJ in *Harrods Ltd v Harrodian School Ltd* [1996] RPC 697 at 711. These basic principles have been refined over the years to protect appellations of origin, such as Swiss chocolate in *Chocosuisse Union Des Fabricants Suisses De Chocolat & Ors v Cadbury Ltd* [1999] RPC 826, [1999] EWCA Civ 856.

    But passing-off has also been held to extend its protection to the interest of charities in their capacity to raise funds (*British Diabetic Association v Diabetic Society Ltd* [1995] 4 All ER 812). It can also protect an author against the attribution to him of writings in fact produced by others. In *Clark v Associated Newspapers Ltd* [1998] 1 All ER 959, [1998] 1 WLR 1558 the rule was applied even to a parody. Lightman J explained (at 968 and 1568), 'A parody which occasions only a momentary and inconsequential deception is both successful and permissible; but a parody which occasions an enduring deception is neither.'

3. In addition to the common law tort of passing-off, it is possible by registering a trade mark in respect of any specification of goods or services, under the Trade Marks Act 1994 (which replaced existing UK legislation as well as implementing the Trade Mark Directive (89/104/EEC), to prevent the infringement of the right to use that trade mark within the specification. The registered proprietor may prevent its use by others even in ways that involve no passing-off. For the relationship between the tort of passing-off and trademark legislation, see *Inter Lotto (UK) Ltd. v Camelot Group Plc* [2003] 4 All ER 575, [2003] EWCA Civ 1132. Note also that certain forms of misrepresentation may constitute a criminal offence under the Trade Descriptions Act 1968.

4. The study of this subject and the related fields of patents and copyright belongs to specialist works on intellectual property. But a point of general interest is the relationship between this tort and the tort of negligence. Proof of an intention to deceive is not essential and, as Lord Diplock's definition (p. 934, ante) shows, the damage must be a reasonably foreseeable consequence of the misrepresentation. Is this different from a duty of care? There may even be circumstances in which a third person, such as a printer of labels, who facilitates a passing-off without actual knowledge, is liable in negligence. This would be rare because 'if a person approaches a printer and asks him to carry out certain work, there must be some limit to the extent to which the printer should be expected to, so to speak, look over his shoulder and consider whether or not

the material when printed might be used by the customer for passing-off his goods as another's': per Robert Goff LJ in *Paterson Zochonis & Co Ltd v Merfarken Packaging Ltd* [1986] 3 All ER 522 at 542.

5. A more generalised tort of unfair competition has not developed in England. In *Cadbury-Schweppes Pty Ltd v Pub Squash Co Pty Ltd* [1981] 1 All ER 213, [1981] 1 WLR 193, noted by G. Dworkin (1981) 44 MLR 564, a claim of unfair competition was raised but not pursued before the Privy Council where the defendant was alleged to have deliberately exploited the claimants' advertising campaign so as to secure a share of a market created by the claimants. In *Associated Newspapers Group plc v Insert Media Ltd* [1988] 2 All ER 420, [1988] 1 WLR 509, the defendants were inserting leaflets into the claimants' newspapers without the latter's approval. An interlocutory injunction pending trial was granted on grounds that there was a serious issue to be tried as to passing-off, a decision confirmed at trial by Mummery J [1990] 1 WLR 900 and in the Court of Appeal [1991] 3 All ER 535, [1991] 1 WLR 571. However, Hoffmann J held, as a matter of law, that an allegation of unfair competition by debasing or devaluing the claimants' goods was not actionable.

On the other hand, in *Bristol Conservatories Ltd v Conservatories Custom Built Ltd* [1989] RPC 455 the Court of Appeal held that it could amount to passing-off for the defendant to give potential customers the impression that he had been responsible for work which was really the work of the claimant. This is 'reverse' or 'inverse' passing-off—the deception is not about the work itself, which is genuine, but about who did it. The harm suffered by the claimant is said still to be damage to its business goodwill, in the broad sense that the defendant has appropriated to itself part of what makes the claimant's business attractive to customers. See also *ScanSafe Ltd v MessageLabs Ltd* [2006] EWHC 2015. But this explanation is somewhat artificial. The real damage to the claimant is not to its goodwill—there is no need to show, for example, that the defendant's customers had heard of the claimant—but to its market share. Laddie J has drawn a parallel between *Bristol Conservatories Ltd v Conservatories Custom Built Ltd* and the actions for unfair competition to be found in some other European legal systems (*Zino Davidoff SA v A & G Imports Ltd* [1999] 3 All ER 711). Aldous LJ suggested in *Arsenal v Reed* [2003] RPC 39 that a common law cause of action could exist for 'unfair trading' or 'unfair competition'. However, the Court of Appeal in *L'Oreal SA v Bellure NV* [2008] IPET 526, [2007] EWCA Civ 968 held that the tort of passing-off could not be extended into a general tort of unfair competition. Note that European competition law has become the primary vehicle for the regulation of unfair competition: see R. Whish, *Competition Law* 5th edn (Oxford, 2003).

5 THE TORT OF DECEIT

(a) Basics of liability

■ Pasley v Freeman
Court of King's Bench [1775–1802] All ER Rep 31 (1789)

Pasley and one Edward alleged that the defendant Freeman had 'falsely, deceitfully and fraudulently' told them that a certain John Falch was good for credit of over £2,634 for the purchase of 16 bags of cochineal. Falch defaulted. The plaintiffs obtained a verdict at a jury trial. The defendant moved to have the verdict set aside on the ground that it was not enough for the plaintiffs to have proved that he knew that Falch was not good for the credit at the time he induced the plaintiffs to extend it. Freeman said that the plaintiffs should also have alleged and proved either that he would benefit from misleading them, or that he had colluded with Falch. The Court of King's Bench decided by a majority of 3–1 that the verdict should stand.

GROSE, J. [dissenting]: ...

On the face of this count in the declaration, no privity of contract is stated between the parties. No consideration arises to the defendant, and he is in no situation in which the law considers him in any trust, or in which it demands from him any account of the credit of Falch. He appears not to be interested in any transaction between the plaintiffs and Falch, nor to have colluded with the latter, but he knowingly asserted a falsehood by saying that Falch might be safely entrusted with the goods and given credit to, for the purpose of inducing the plaintiffs to trust him with them, by which the plaintiffs lost the value of the goods. This, then, is an action against the defendant for making a false affirmation, or telling a lie respecting the credit of a third person, with intent to deceive, by which the plaintiffs were damnified; ...

On what principle is this act said to be an injury? The plaintiffs say on the ground that, when the question was asked, the defendant was bound to tell the truth. There are cases, I admit, where a man is bound not to misrepresent, but to tell the truth, but no such case has been cited except in the case of contracts.... So far from a person being bound in a case like the present to tell the truth, the books supply me with a variety of cases in which even the contracting party is not liable for a misrepresentation. There are cases of two sorts, in which, though a man is deceived, he can maintain no action. The first class of cases (though not analogous to the present) is where the affirmation is that the thing sold has not a defect which is a visible one. There the imposition, the fraudulent intent, is admitted, but it is no tort. The second head of cases is where the affirmation is (what is called in some of the books) a nude assertion, such as the party deceived may exercise his own judgment upon, as where it is matter of opinion where he may make inquiries into the truth of the assertion, and it becomes his own fault from laches that he is deceived ... The misrepresentation stated in the declaration is respecting the credit of Falch. The defendant asserted that the plaintiffs might safely give him credit, but credit to which a man is entitled is matter of judgment and opinion on which different men might form different opinions, and on which the plaintiffs might form their own.... [I]t is not an assertion of a fact peculiarly in the knowledge of the defendants. Whether Falch deserved credit depended on the opinion of many; for credit exists on the good opinion of many. Respecting this, the plaintiffs might have inquired of others, who knew as much as the defendant; it was their fault that they did not, and they have suffered damage by their own laches. It was owing to their own gross negligence that they gave credence to the assertion of the defendant without taking pains to satisfy themselves that that assertion was founded in fact, as in the case of *Bayly v. Merrel*.[14] I am, therefore, of opinion, that this action is as novel in principle as it is in precedent, that it is against the principles to be collected from analogous cases, and consequently that it cannot be maintained.

BULLER, J: ...

The foundation of this action is fraud and deceit in the defendant, and damage to the plaintiffs. The question is whether an action thus founded can be sustained in a court of law? Fraud without damage or damage without fraud gives no cause of action, but where these two concur, an action lies.... But it is contended, that this was a bare naked lie, that, as no collusion with Falch is charged, it does not amount to a fraud, and, if there were any fraud, the nature of it is not stated. It was supposed by the counsel who originally made the motion that no action could be maintained unless the defendant, who made this false assertion, had an interest in so doing. I agree that an action cannot be supported for telling a bare naked lie; that I define to be, saying a thing which is false knowing or not knowing it to be so, and without any design to injure, cheat, or deceive, another person. Every deceit comprehends a lie; but a deceit is more than a lie on account of the view with which it is practised, its being coupled with some dealing, and the injury which it is calculated to occasion, and does occasion, to another person.... Collusion is not necessary to constitute fraud.... The gist of the action is fraud and deceit, and if that fraud and deceit can be fixed by evidence on one who had no interest in his iniquity, it proves his malice to be the greater. It was objected to this declaration that, if there were any fraud, the nature of it is not stated. To this the declaration itself is so direct an answer, that the case admits of no other. The fraud is that the defendant procured the plaintiffs to sell goods on credit to one whom they would not otherwise have trusted, by asserting that which he knew to be false. Here then is the fraud, and the means by which it was committed, and it was done with a view to enrich Falch by impoverishing the plaintiffs, or, in other words, by cheating the plaintiffs out of their goods.... Some general arguments were urged at the Bar to show that mischiefs and inconveniences would arise if this action were sustained, for, if a man, who is asked a question respecting another's responsibility, hesitate or is silent he blasts the character of the tradesman, and if he say that he is insolvent he may not be able to prove it. Let us see what is contended for it is nothing less than that a man may assert that which he knows to be false and thereby do an everlasting injury to his neighbour, and yet not be answerable for it. This is as repugnant to law as it is to morality.

ASHHURST, J: ...

It is admitted that a fraudulent affirmation, when the party making it has an interest, is a ground of action, as in *Risney v Selby* [Salk. 211], which was a false affirmation made to purchaser as to the rent of a farm which the defendant was in treaty to sell to him. But it was argued that the action lies not unless where the party making it has an interest, or colludes with one who has. I do not recollect that any case was cited which proves such a proposition; but, if there were any such to be found, I should not hesitate to say that it could not be law, for I have so great a veneration for the law as to suppose that nothing can be law which is not founded in common sense or common honesty. For the gist of the action is the injury done to the plaintiff, not whether the defendant meant to be a gainer by it. What is it to the plaintiff whether the defendant was or was not to gain by it? The injury to him is the same. It should seem that it ought more emphatically to lie against him as the malice is more diabolical if he had not the temptation of gain. For the same reason, it cannot be necessary that the defendant should collude with one who has an interest. But if collusion were necessary there seems all the reason in the world to suppose both interest and collusion from the nature of the act, for it is to be hoped that there is not to be found a disposition so diabolical as to prompt any man to injure another without benefiting himself.

But it is said that, if this be determined to be law, any man may have an action brought against him for telling a lie by the crediting of which another happens eventually to be injured. This consequence by no means follows, for in order to make it actionable it must be accompanied with the circumstances averred in this count, namely, that the defendant,

> 'intending to deceive and defraud the plaintiffs, did deceitfully encourage and persuade them to do the act, and for that purpose made the false affirmation, in consequence of which they did the act.'

Any lie accompanied with those circumstances I should clearly hold to be the subject of an action, but not a mere lie thrown out at random without any intention of hurting anybody which some person was foolish enough to act upon....

LORD KENYON, CJ: ...

Undoubtedly where the common prudence and caution of man are sufficient to guard him, the law will not protect him in his negligence... How does the principle of that case apply to the present? There are many situations in life, and particularly in the commercial world, where a man cannot by any diligence inform himself of the degree of credit which ought to be given to the persons with whom he deals, in which case he must apply to those whose sources of intelligence enable them to give that information. The law of prudence leads him to apply to them, and the law of morality ought to induce them to give the information required...

Rule discharged.

NOTES

1.   What modern arguments can you see foreshadowed in *Pasley*? For example, the idea that the claimant will have double security if there is liability for deceit in these circumstances certainly foreshadows points made in the economic loss case of *White v Jones* [1995] 2 AC 207, 1995] 1 All ER 691(p. 243, ante). Also, the judges in *Pasley* say that there can be no liability for acting on information which the claimant was in just as good a position to check or information gained in unreliable circumstances. This idea has continued to operate in the guise of the 'reasonable reliance' requirement that exists in the context of economic loss. (See *South Australia Asset Management Corpn v York Montague Ltd* [1997] AC 191, [1996] 3 All ER 365, p. 271, ante.)

2.   The idea that telling someone a lie when one has no expectation of gain from the lie is even worse, morally, than telling a lie for gain perhaps explains the otherwise difficult rule in some economic torts that it is sometimes a defence to prove that one acted according to one's economic self-interest, such as the justification defence that operates in the context of inducing a breach of contract and lawful means conspiracy (see p. 881, post).

3.   Students of restitution might ponder Ashhurst J's remark that 'the gist of the action is the injury done to the plaintiff, and not whether the defendant meant to be a gainer by it. What is it to the plaintiff whether the defendant was or was not to gain by it? The injury to him is the same.'

■ Derry v Peek

House of Lords [1886-90] All ER Rep 1

For the facts and further extracts from the speeches in this case, see p. 172, ante.

LORD HERSCHELL: ...

This action is one which is commonly called an action of deceit, a mere common law action.' This is the description of it given by COTTON LJ in delivering judgment. I think it important that it should be borne in mind that such an action differs essentially from one brought to obtain rescission of the contract on the ground of misrepresentation of a material fact. The principles which govern the two actions differ widely. Where rescission is claimed it is only necessary to prove that there was misrepresentation. Then, however honestly it may have been made, however free from blame the person who made it, the contract, having been obtained by misrepresentation, cannot stand. In an action of deceit, on the contrary, it is not enough to establish misrepresentation alone; it is conceded on all hands that something more must be proved to cast liability upon the defendant, though it has been a matter of controversy what additional elements are requisite....

    To make a statement careless whether it be true or false, and, therefore, without any real belief in its truth, appears to me to be an essentially different thing from making, through want of care, a false statement which is nevertheless honestly believed to be true. And it is surely conceivable that a man may believe that what he states is the fact, though he has been so wanting in care that the court may think that there were no sufficient grounds to warrant his belief...

    I think there is here some confusion between that which is evidence of fraud, and that which constitutes it. A consideration of the grounds of belief is no doubt an important aid in ascertaining whether the belief was really entertained. A man's mere assertion that he believed the statement he made to be true is not accepted as conclusive proof that he did so. There may be such an absence of reasonable ground for his belief as, in spite of his assertion, to carry conviction to the mind that he had not really the belief which he alleges. If the learned Lord[6] intended to go further, as apparently he did, and to say that, though the belief was really entertained, yet, if there were no reasonable ground for it, the person making the statement was guilty of fraud in the same way as if he had known what he stated to be false, I say, with all respect, that the previous authorities afford no warrant for the view that an action of deceit would lie under such circumstances. A man who forms his belief carelessly, or is unreasonably credulous, may be blameworthy when he makes a representation on which another is to act, but he is not, in my opinion, fraudulent in the sense in which that word was used in all the cases from *Pasley v Freeman* down to that with which I am now dealing. Even when the expression 'fraud in law' has been employed, there has always been present, and regarded as an essential element, that the deception was wilful either because the untrue statement was known to be untrue, or because belief in it was asserted without such belief existing....

I think the authorities establish the following propositions: First, in order to sustain an action of deceit, there must be proof of fraud, and nothing short of that will suffice. Secondly, fraud is proved when it is shown that a false representation has been made (i) knowingly, or (ii) without belief in its truth, or (iii) recklessly, careless whether it be true or false. Although I have treated the second and third as distinct cases, I think the third is but an instance of the second, for one who makes a statement under such circumstances can have no real belief in the truth of what he states. To prevent a false statement being fraudulent, there must, I think, always be an honest belief in its truth. And this probably covers the whole ground, for one who knowingly alleges that which is false has obviously no such belief. Thirdly, if fraud be proved, the motive of the person guilty of it is immaterial. It matters not that there was no intention to cheat or injure the person to whom the statement was made....

NOTES

1. To establish liability for deceit 'there must ... be some active misstatement of fact, or, at all events, such a partial and fragmentary statement of fact as that the withholding of that which is not stated makes that which is stated absolutely false': per Lord Cairns in *Peek v Gurney* (1873) LR 6 HL 377 at 403. The reference to 'statements of fact' should not be read too literally. Statements of opinion may be actionable in the tort of deceit where some implicit dishonest misrepresentation of fact can be derived from the statement of opinion (see *AIC Ltd v ITS Testing Services (UK) Ltd 'The Kriti Palm'* [2007] 1 All ER (Comm) 667, at [255]), or the statement imports some information not equally available to the representee, such as an expert's opinion based on his background knowledge. Cf. *Bisset v Wilkinson* [1927] AC 177 (statement that land would support 2,000 sheep held to be opinion and not actionable since both parties had no knowledge of facts and no special expertise). Statements of present intention may also be a representation of an existing fact. '[T]he state of a man's mind is as much a fact as the state of his digestion': per Bowen LJ in *Edgington v Fitzmaurice* (1885) 29 Ch D 459, at 483. '[W]here a ... customer orders a meal in a restaurant, he must be held to make an implied representation that he can and will pay for it before he leaves': *DPP v Ray* [1974] AC 370, at 379. However, in *Wales v Wadham* [1977] 2 All ER 125, a wife's statement that she did not intend to remarry following divorce was not held to be a statement of existing fact. An ambiguous statement may constitute a statement of fact, but in such a case it is essential that the representor should have intended the statement to be understood in the sense in which it is understood by the claimant or deliberately used the ambiguity for the purpose of deceiving him: see *'The Kriti Palm'* [2007] 1 All ER (Comm) 667, at [253]). For the requirement of intention in general, see *Abu Dhabi* [2008] EWCA Civ 699.
2. Although deceit is mainly relevant to the protection of economic interests, it may also be utilised where there has been physical harm: *Langridge v Levy* (1837) 2 M & W 519

(liability for fraudulent misrepresentation as to condition of a gun which burst and injured claimant). (Compare *Wilkinson v Downton* [1897] 2 QB 57, p. 743, post.)

■ The Statute of Frauds Amendment Act 1828 (Lord Tenterden's Act)

6. Action not maintainable on representations of character, etc., unless they be in writing signed by the party chargeable.—No action shall be brought whereby to charge any person upon or by reason of any representation or assurance made or given concerning or relating to the character, conduct, credit, ability, trade, or dealings of any other person, to the intent or purpose that such other person may obtain credit, money, or goods upon, unless such representation or assurance be made in writing signed by the party to be charged therewith.

NOTE

The purpose of this section (relating to representations as to credit or credit worthiness) was to prevent evasion of the requirement in the Statute of Frauds that guarantees be in writing, by suing in tort instead of contract. For this reason the courts have held that the section does not apply to actions for breach of contract. Moreover it is limited to fraudulent representations, or those which are alleged to give rise to liability under s. 2(1) of the Misrepresentation Act 1967 (*UBAF Ltd v European American Banking Corpn* [1984] QB 713, [1984] 2 All ER 226) and does not extend to representations giving rise to a common law duty of care in negligence (*W B Anderson & Sons Ltd v Rhodes (Liverpool) Ltd* [1967] 2 All ER 850). This appears to be the only situation in which there is liability for a negligent act where there would not be liability if it were done intentionally.

(b) Detailed Points

(i) Inducement

■ Downs v Chappell
Court of Appeal [1996] 3 All ER 344

HOBHOUSE LJ: . . .
For a plaintiff to succeed in the tort of deceit it is necessary for him to prove that: (1) the representation was fraudulent; (2) it was material; and (3) it induced the plaintiff to act (to his detriment).

A representation is material when its tendency, or its natural and probable result, is to induce the representee to act on the faith of it in the kind of way in which he is proved to have in fact acted. The test is objective. In the present case it is clear that the test of materiality was satisfied and the contrary has not been suggested.

As regards inducement, this is a question of fact. The judge has found that the representations made did induce the plaintiffs to enter into the relevant transaction, that is to say, the contract with Mr Chappell to purchase his business and shop. The plaintiffs were induced to act to their detriment. The word 'reliance' used by the judge has a similar meaning, but is not the correct criterion.

The plaintiffs have proved what they need to prove by way of the commission of the tort of deceit and causation. They have proved that they were induced to enter into the contract with Mr Chappell by his fraudulent representations. The judge was wrong to ask how they would have acted if they had been told the truth. They were never told the truth. They were told lies in order to induce them to enter into the contract. The lies were material and successful; they induced the plaintiffs to act to their detriment and contract with Mr Chappell. The judge should have concluded that the plaintiffs had proved their case on causation and that the only remaining question was what loss the plaintiffs had suffered as a result of entering into the contract with Mr Chappell to buy his business and shop.

NOTE

Another common formulation of the tort of deceit is: 'making a wilfully false statement with the intention that the plaintiff should act in reliance upon it with the result that the plaintiff does so act and suffers damage in consequence' (see e.g. Fox LJ in *Steed v Neal* (30 July 1986, unreported), CA). But Hobhouse LJ says that 'reliance' is not quite right. Why? How can one be 'induced' to do something by a representation without also 'relying' on it? If someone has more than one reason for acting, including the false statement, is that person 'induced' to act by the false statement? Or does the person 'rely' on the false statement?

(ii) Silence and dishonesty

■ Thomas Witter Ltd v TBP Industries Ltd

Chancery Division [1996] 2 All ER 573

The defendants, a large conglomerate, acquired a business which included the plaintiff company, a carpet manufacturing business. After absorbing some parts of the business, it decided to sell the carpet business. Mr Puri expressed interest in purchasing the carpet business and after various negotiations bought it for £4m. The plaintiff company alleged, inter alia, that Mr Puri had made his offer on the basis of the management accounts supplied by the defendants, which were misleading because they (i) stated that they included a special one-off expense of £120,000 when the actual amount of that expense was no more than £50,000, and (ii) failed to disclose that they included deferred expenditure.

JACOB J: . . .
First then deceit. Mr Mann QC [for the plaintiff] relied upon part of the classic speech of Lord Herschell in *Derry v Peek* (1889) 14 App Cas 337 at 375–376, [1886–90] All ER Rep 1 at 22–23:

> 'The ground upon which an alleged belief was founded is a most important test of its reality. I can conceive many cases where the fact that an alleged belief was destitute of all reasonable foundation would suffice of itself to convince the Court that it was not really entertained, and that the representation was a fraudulent one. So, too . . . if I thought that a person making a false statement had shut his eyes to the facts, or purposely abstained from inquiring into them, I should hold that honest belief was absent, and that he was just as fraudulent as if he had knowingly stated that which was false.'

He further submitted that where a person has made a representation of fact and, before the contract is concluded, comes to learn of its falseness, that person comes under a duty to correct the representation and, if he fails to do so, then is taken to be fraudulent. Mr Mann relied upon the speech of Lord Blackburn in *Brownlie v Campbell* (1880) 5 App Cas 925 at 950:

> 'I quite agree in this, that whenever a man in order to induce a contract says that which is in his knowledge untrue with the intention to mislead the other side, and induce them to enter into the contract, that is downright fraud; in plain English, and Scotch also, it is a downright lie told to induce the other party to act upon it, and it should of course be treated as such. I further agree in this: that when a statement or representation has been made in the bona fide belief that it is true, and the party who has made it afterwards comes to find out that it is untrue, and discovers what he should

have said, he can no longer honestly keep up that silence on the subject after that has come to his knowledge, thereby allowing the other party to go on, and still more, inducing him to go on, upon a statement which was honestly made at the time when it was made, but which he has not now retracted when he has become aware that it can be no longer honestly persevered in. That would be fraud too, I should say, as at present advised.'

This argument related to the changed basis of profit forecast point. It was argued that Mr Simpson, having given to Mr Puri profit forecasts on one basis of pattern book expenditure, knew his later forecast was on a different basis and should be taken as fraudulent for not disclosing that fact.

In my judgment Mr Mann's argument is wrong in law. He takes the reference to 'recklessness' out of context—divorcing it from the heart of the tort of deceit, namely dishonesty. One only has to read earlier in the speech of Lord Herschell to see that this is so:

'... there has always been present, and regarded as an essential element, that the deception was wilful either because the untrue statement was known to be untrue, or because belief in it was asserted without such belief existing ... I cannot assent to the doctrine that a false statement made through carelessness, and which ought to have been known to be untrue, of itself renders the person who makes it liable to an action for deceit.' (See (1889) 14 App Cas 337 at 369, 373, [1886–90] All ER Rep 1 at 19, 21.)

(iii) Measure of Damages, Remoteness and Mitigation of Loss

■ South Australia Asset Management Corpn v York Montague Ltd
House of Lords [1996] 3 All ER 365

For the facts and further extracts from this case, see p. 271, ante.

LORD HOFFMANN: ...
The question of liability for fraud does not arise in this case and I therefore confine myself to two observations. The first is that although I have said that fraud is commonly thought to be an exception [to the rule that liability extends only to losses that would not have occurred if the information supplied had, contrary to the facts, been correct], Hobhouse LJ seems to have expressed a contrary view in the recent case of *Downs v Chappell* [1996] 3 All ER 344 at 362, when he said that the damages recoverable for fraudulent misrepresentation should not be greater than the loss which would have been suffered 'had the represented, or supposed, state of affairs actually existed'. In other words, the defendant should not be liable for loss which would have been a consequence of the transaction even if the representation had been true. This, as I have said, is what I conceive to be in accordance with the normal principle of liability for wrongful acts. But liability for fraud, or under s 2(1) of the Misrepresentation Act 1967, for a negligent misrepresentation inducing a contract with the representor, has usually been thought to extend to all loss suffered in consequence of having entered into the transaction. We have received written representations on *Downs v Chappell*, which was decided after the conclusion of the oral argument, but since the issue in that case is not before the House, I prefer not to express any concluded view.

My second observation is that, even if the maker of the fraudulent misrepresentation is liable for all the consequences of the plaintiff having entered into the transaction, the identification of those consequences may involve difficult questions of causation. The defendant is clearly not liable for losses which the plaintiff would have suffered even if he had not entered into the transaction or for losses attributable to causes which negative the causal effect of the misrepresentation. ...

NOTE

Downs v Chappell did not, in the event, reach the House of Lords, but their Lordships returned to these issues in the following case.

■ Smith New Court Securities Ltd v Scrimgeour Vickers (Asset Management) Ltd

House of Lords [1996] 4 All ER 769

The plaintiffs alleged that they were induced to buy a parcel of shares in Ferranti Inc at a particular price on the strength of fraudulent misrepresentations by the defendants that there were other bidders for the shares. The value of Ferranti shares subsequently collapsed when it was disclosed that Ferranti had itself at an earlier time been the victim of a separate large-scale fraud.

LORD STEYN [having dealt with the issues of liability continued]: . . .

DAMAGES
The issue
Given the fact that the subsequent dramatic fall in the value of Ferranti shares was caused by the disclosure of an earlier fraud practised on Ferranti by a third party the question is whether Smith is entitled to recover against Citibank the entire loss arising from the fraudulently induced transaction. Smith submits that the Court of Appeal adopted the wrong measure. Smith seeks to recover damages calculated on the basis of the price paid less the aggregate of subsequent realisations. Citibank contends that the loss attributable to the subsequent disclosure of the fraud by a third party is a misfortune risk and is irrecoverable. Citibank argues that the Court of Appeal adopted the correct measure.

Horses and shares
The fraud perpetrated by Mr Roberts on Smith related to shares quoted on the Stock Exchange. Undoubtedly, the legal measure of damages in an action in deceit when applied to transactions in shares may throw up special problems. It is not simply a matter of the perception of the market as to the value of the shares. If loss is to be determined by way of the price paid less a valuation of the shares at a given date, the determination of the real or true value of the shares, absent the deceit forming the basis of the claim, may give rise to difficult hypothetical problems. Even more difficult problems arise if it is alleged that for extrinsic reasons there has been a false market, e.g. because investors have been misled by widespread false statements about the value of the stock of the company. None of these practical considerations justify the adoption of a special rule in respect of share transactions. The same legal principle must govern sales of shares, goods, a business or land. It is therefore possible to simplify the problem. The example given by Cockburn CJ in *Twycross v Grant* (1877) 2 CPD 469 is instructive. He said (at 544–545):

> 'If a man buys a horse, as a racehorse, on the false representation that it has won some great race, while in reality it is a horse of very inferior speed, and he pays ten or twenty times as much as the horse is worth, and after the buyer has got the animal home it dies of some latent disease inherent in its system at the time he bought it, he may claim the entire price he gave; the horse was by reason of the latent mischief worthless when he bought; but if it catches some disease and dies, the buyer cannot claim the entire value of the horse, which he is no longer in a condition to restore, but only the difference between the price he gave and the real value at the time he bought.'

Counsel for Citibank argued that Cockburn CJ erred in saying that if the horse had some latent disease at the time of the transaction the buyer may claim the entire price he paid. He argued that in such a case there was no sufficient causal link between the latent disease and the eventual death of the horse. Counsel for Smith argued that the transaction, which was induced by deceit, directly led to the loss of the entire value of the horse. On any view it is clear that, if Cockburn CJ is right, the law imposes liability in an action for deceit for some consequences that were unforeseen and unforeseeable when the tortfeasor committed the wrong. And if that is right it may tell us something about the correct disposal of the present case.

The justification for distinguishing between deceit and negligence

That brings me to the question of policy whether there is a justification for differentiating between the extent of liability for civil wrongs depending on where in the sliding scale from strict liability to intentional wrongdoing the particular civil wrong fits in. It may be said that logical symmetry and a policy of not punishing intentional wrongdoers by civil remedies favour a uniform rule. On the other hand, it is a rational and defensible strategy to impose wider liability on an intentional wrongdoer. As Hart and *Honoré Causation in the Law* (2nd edn, 1985) p 304 observed: 'an innocent plaintiff may, not without reason, call on a morally reprehensible defendant to pay the whole of the loss he has caused'. The exclusion of heads of loss in the law of negligence, which reflects considerations of legal policy, does not necessarily avail the intentional wrongdoer. Such a policy of imposing more stringent remedies on an intentional wrongdoer serves two purposes. First it serves a deterrent purpose in discouraging fraud. Counsel for Citibank argued that the sole purpose of the law of tort generally, and the tort of deceit in particular, should be to compensate the victims of civil wrongs. That is far too narrow a view. Professor Glanville Williams identified four possible purposes of an action for damages in tort: appeasement, justice, deterrence and compensation (see 'The Aims of the Law of Tort' (1951) 4 CLP 137). He concluded (p 172):

'Where possible the law seems to like to ride two or three horses at once; but occasionally a situation occurs where one must be selected. The tendency is then to choose the deterrent purpose for tort of intention, and the compensatory purpose for other torts.'

And in the battle against fraud civil remedies can play a useful and beneficial role. Secondly, as between the fraudster and the innocent party, moral considerations militate in favour of requiring the fraudster to bear the risk of misfortunes directly caused by his fraud. I make no apology for referring to moral considerations. The law and morality are inextricably interwoven. To a large extent the law is simply formulated and declared morality. And, as Oliver Wendell Holmes, *The Common Law* (1968) p 106 observed, the very notion of deceit with its overtones of wickedness is drawn from the moral world.

[His Lordship considered the nineteenth-century cases and *Doyle v Olby (Ironmongers) Ltd* [1969] 2 QB 158, [1969] 2 All ER 119 and continued:] The logic of the decision in *Doyle v Olby (Ironmongers) Ltd* justifies the following propositions.

(1) The plaintiff in an action for deceit is not entitled to be compensated in accordance with the contractual measure of damage, ie the benefit of the bargain measure. He is not entitled to be protected in respect of his positive interest in the bargain.

(2) The plaintiff in an action for deceit is, however, entitled to be compensated in respect of his negative interest. The aim is to put the plaintiff into the position he would have been in if no false representation had been made.

(3) The practical difference between the two measures was lucidly explained in a contemporary case note on *Doyle* v Olby (Ironmongers) Ltd (see Treitel 'Damages for Deceit' (1969) 32 MLR 558–559). The author said:

'If the plaintiff's bargain would have been a bad one, even on the assumption that the representation was true, he will do best under the tortious measure. If, on the assumption that the representation was true, his bargain would have been a good one, he will do best under the first contractual measure (under which he may recover something even if the actual value of what he has recovered is greater than the price).'

(4) Concentrating on the tort measure, the remoteness test whether the loss was reasonably foreseeable had been authoritatively laid down in *The Wagon Mound* in respect of the tort of negligence a few years before *Doyle v Olby (Ironmongers) Ltd* was decided: *Overseas Tankship (UK) Ltd v Morts Dock and Engineering Co Ltd, The Wagon Mound* [1961] 1 All ER 404, [1961] AC 388. *Doyle v Olby (Ironmongers) Ltd* settled that a wider test applies in an action for deceit.

(5) The dicta in all three judgments, as well as the actual calculation of damages in *Doyle v Olby (Ironmongers) Ltd*, make it clear that the victim of the fraud is entitled to compensation for all the

actual loss directly flowing from the transaction induced by the wrongdoer. That includes heads of consequential loss.

(6) Significantly in the present context the rule in the previous paragraph is not tied to any process of valuation at the date of the transaction. It is squarely based on the overriding compensatory principle, widened in view of the fraud to cover all direct consequences. The legal measure is to compare the position of the plaintiff as it was before the fraudulent statement was made to him with his position as it became as a result of his reliance on the fraudulent statement...

Causation

So far I have discussed in general terms the scope of a fraudster's liability in accordance with the rule identified with *Doyle v Olby (Ironmongers) Ltd* [1969] 2 All ER 119, [1969] 2 QB 158. It is now necessary to consider separately the three limiting principles which, even in a case of deceit, serve to keep wrongdoers' liability within practical and sensible limits. The three concepts are causation, remoteness and mitigation. In practice the inquiries under these headings overlap. But they are distinct legal concepts. For present purposes causation is the most important. The major issue in the present case is whether there is a causal link between the fraud and the loss arising by reason of the pre-existing fraud perpetrated on Ferranti. How should this matter be approached? The development of a single satisfactory theory of causation has taxed great academic minds (see Hart and Honoré Causation in the Law (2nd edn, 1985) and Honoré '*Necessary and Sufficient Conditions in Tort Law*' in Owen *Philosophical Foundations of Tort Law* (1995) p 363). But, as yet, it seems to me that no satisfactory theory capable of solving the infinite variety of practical problems has been found. Our case law yields few secure footholds. But it is settled that at any rate in the law of obligations causation is to be categorised as an issue of fact... While acknowledging that this hardly amounts to an intellectually satisfying theory of causation, that is how I must approach the question of causation.

Remoteness and mitigation

The second limiting principle is remoteness. I have already discussed the special rule of remoteness developed by the courts in the context of deceit. This requirement is in issue in the present case: if there is a sufficient causal link it must still be shown that the entire loss suffered by Smith is a direct consequence of the fraudulently induced transaction. The third limiting principle is the duty to mitigate. The plaintiff is not entitled to damages in respect of loss which he could reasonably have avoided. This limiting principle has no special features in the context of deceit. There is no issue under this heading and I need say no more about it....

[LORD BROWNE-WILKINSON delivered a speech in favour of allowing the appeal, with which LORD MUSTILL agreed. LORD KEITH OF KINKEL and LORD SLYNN OF HADLEY agreed with the speeches of both LORD STEYN and LORD BROWNE-WILKINSON.]

Appeal allowed.

NOTES

See now *Eng Ltd v Harper* [2008] EWHC 915 (Ch). Aggravated damages for injured feelings and inconvenience may also be awarded in this tort: see *Archer v Brown* [1985] QB 401, [1984] 2 All ER 267, where a 'moderate' award of £500 was made to a claimant who had been induced by deceit to buy shares from a defendant who did not own them. In this case it was left open whether exemplary damages are recoverable (cf. Purchas LJ in *Metall und Rohstoff AG v ACLI Metals (London) Ltd* [1984] 1 Lloyds Rep 598 at 612, who said obiter that they are not).

(iv) Contributory negligence

■ **Alliance and Leicester Building Society v Edgestop Ltd**

Chancery Division [1994] 2 All ER 38

MUMMERY J: . . .

There is no decision precisely on the point whether contributory negligence could be a defence to a claim for deceit. In principle, however, the position before and apart from the [Law Reform (Contributory Negligence) Act 1945] is clear. The contributory negligence of a plaintiff suing in deceit could not be pleaded as a defence. There are at least three reasons for this. (1) At common law contributory negligence of a plaintiff is no defence in the case of an intentional tort. As Lord Lindley said in *Quinn v Leathem* [1901] AC 495 at 537 [1900–3] All ER Rep 1 at 17, 'The intention to injure the plaintiff negatives all excuses . . .' See also *Clerk and Lindsell on Tort*, 16th edn (1989) paras 1–115, 1–139, pp 79, 98. Deceit is a tort intentionally committed. (2) At common law a successful plea of contributory negligence would have startling consequences in the context of deceit. Before and apart from the Act, contributory negligence of a plaintiff would defeat the plaintiff's entire claim.. (3) That result would also have offended against the general principle stated by Jessel MR in *Redgrave v Hurd* (1881) 20 Ch D 1. He laid down general principles applicable in misrepresentation cases. Although that case was decided in the context of the equitable remedies of specific performance and rescission, his statements have been treated for over a century as applicable to claims for damages for misrepresentation. He said (at 13–14):

> 'Nothing can be plainer, I take it, on the authorities in equity than that the effect of false representation is not got rid of on the ground that the person to whom it was made has been guilty of negligence.'

He said of a person who had made a material representation to another inducing him to enter into a contract (at 21):

> ' If it is a material representation calculated to induce him to enter into the contract, it is an inference of law that he was induced by the representation to enter into it, and in order to take away his title to be relieved from the contract on the ground that the representation was untrue, it must be shewn either that he had knowledge of the facts contrary to the representation, or that he stated in terms, or shewed clearly by his conduct, that he did not rely on the representation.'

. . . That, in my view, was the position before 1945. Has it been changed by the Act of 1945? Mr Slater QC, on behalf of Hamptons, submitted that it has. The statute confers on the court in wide terms a power to reduce damages for tort to such extent as the court thinks just and equitable having regard to the claimant's share in the responsibility for the damage . . .

He submitted that the position had been altered from the common law position by the terms of the 1945 Act and that this is recognised in the following authorities.

First, the defence of contributory fault had been allowed since the Act in a case where the plaintiff's claim was for damages for a tort intentionally committed. *Murphy v Culhane* [1976] 3 All ER 533, [1977] QB 94 is a decision of the Court of Appeal. In that case, the deceased's widow claimed damages for the death of her husband. She alleged unlawful assault and manslaughter against the defendant. The defence pleaded that the assault occurred during a criminal affray in which the deceased had participated. Lord Denning MR said that the widow's claim for damages might fall to be reduced under the 1945 Act because 'the conduct of [the deceased man] may well have been such as to make him liable in tort.' (see [1976] 3 All ER 533 at 536, [1977] QB 94 at 99).

Lord Denning MR regarded the case as potentially falling within the first limb of the definition of 'fault' in section 4 of the 1945 Act.

The case is not on all fours with the present case for two reasons. First, it is not a case of deceit, to which different considerations applied before the Act and may well continue to apply. Secondly, the conduct of the plaintiff against whom contributory negligence was pleaded might have made him liable in tort and, therefore, liable to a counterclaim or action for damages. That is not the case here. It is no part of [the defendants'] case that the society is liable to it for damages in negligence or for breach of duty. The society's conduct, if it amounts to fault at all, is only within the second limb of s. 4 which requires the court to look at the position apart from the Act....

In my judgment, neither the 1945 Act nor any decision on it affects the general principles laid down by Jessel MR on the unavailability of the defence of negligence to an action for deceit....In brief, a person liable for deceit, whether personally or vicariously, is not entitled as a matter of law to deny by a plea of contributory negligence, that his deceit was the sole effective cause of the damage suffered by his victim. Nothing in the Act in principle or on authority entitles a person liable for deceit to plead contributory negligence.

■ Standard Chartered Bank v Pakistan National Shipping Corp (No 2)
House of Lords [2003] 1 All ER 173

LORD HOFFMANN:...
[12] conduct by a plaintiff cannot be 'fault' within the meaning of the [Law Reform (Contributory Negligence) Act 1945] unless it gives rise to a defence of contributory negligence at common law. This appears to me in accordance with the purpose of the 1945 Act, which was to relieve plaintiffs whose actions would previously have failed and not to reduce the damages which previously would have been awarded against defendants. Section 1(1) makes this clear when it says that 'a claim in respect of that damage shall not be defeated by reason of the fault of the person suffering the damage, but [instead] the damages recoverable in respect thereof shall be reduced'.

[14] the real question is whether the conduct of SCB would at common law be a defence to a claim in deceit. Sir Anthony Evans said that the only rule supported by the authorities was that if someone makes a false representation which was intended to be relied upon and the other party relies upon it, it is no answer to a claim for rescission or damages that the claimant could with reasonable diligence have discovered that the representation was untrue...But in my opinion there are other cases which can be explained only on the basis of a wider rule. In *Edgington v Fitzmaurice* (1885) 29 Ch D 459, [1881–5] All ER Rep 856 the plaintiff invested £1,500 in debentures issued by a company formed to run a provision market in Regent Street. Five months later the company was wound up and he lost nearly all his money. He sued the directors who had issued the prospectus, alleging that they had fraudulently or recklessly represented that the debenture issue was to raise money for the expansion of the company's business ('develop the arrangements ... for the direct supply of cheap fish from the coast') when in fact it was to pay off pressing liabilities. The judge found the allegation proved and that the representation played a part in inducing the plaintiff to take the debentures. But another reason for his taking the debentures was that he thought, without any reasonable grounds, that the debentures were secured upon the company's land. Cotton LJ said that this did not matter:

> 'It is true that if he had not supposed he would have a charge he would not have taken the debentures; but if he also relied on the misstatement in the prospectus, his loss none the less resulted from that misstatement. It is not necessary to shew that the misstatement was the sole cause of his acting as he did. If he acted on that misstatement, though he was also influenced by an erroneous supposition, the Defendants will still be liable.' (See (1885) 29 Ch D 459 at 481, [1881–5] All ER Rep 856 at 860.)

Bowen and Fry LJJ gave judgments to the same effect.

[15] his case seems to me to show that if a fraudulent representation is relied upon, in the sense that the claimant would not have parted with his money if he had known it was false, it does not matter that he also held some other negligent or irrational belief about another matter and, but for that belief, would not have parted with his money either. The law simply ignores the other reasons why he paid...

[18] In the case of fraudulent misrepresentation...I agree with Mummery J in *Alliance and Leicester Building Society v Edgestop Ltd* [1994] 2 All ER 38, [1993] 1 WLR 1462 that there is no common law defence of contributory negligence. It follows that, in agreement with the majority in the Court of Appeal, I think that no apportionment under the 1945 Act is possible.

Appeal allowed.

NOTE

Mummery J's conclusion that the defence of contributory negligence has no application to deceit was thus approved and endorsed by the House of Lords in *Standard Chartered Bank v Pakistan National Shipping Corpn* [2003] 1 All ER 173, [2002] UKHL 43. Nevertheless, some objections may be made to it. The contention by Mummery LJ that contributory negligence had no applicability to deceit before the 1945 Act seems incompatible with much of the reasoning in *Pasley v Freeman* (1789) 4 Term Rep 51 (p. 939, ante). Central to *Pasley* was the contention that most of the previous case law could be explained by recognising that the law will not give relief against a 'foolish credulity' (Ashhurst J). As Kenyon CJ said, 'Undoubtedly where the common prudence and caution of man are sufficient to guard him, the law will not protect him in his negligence.' But if, as appears from *Pasley*, negligence on the part of the claimant meant that the claimant had no action, it would not have been necessary to plead contributory negligence as a specific defence. That is presumably why counsel in *Alliance & Leicester* could find no cases on contributory negligence in deceit to cite to Mummery J.

CHAPTER SIXTEEN

INTERESTS IN REPUTATION—DEFAMATION

The tort of defamation protects interests in reputation. It consists in the *publication* to a third person of matter 'containing an untrue imputation against the *reputation* of another' (*Gatley on Libel and Slander*, 9th edn (London, 1998), para. 1.3). Since reputation is one's estimation in the eyes of others, publication to others is essential. Pride, self-respect, and dignity may be affronted by a communication to the person defamed, but without publication to a third person there is no hurt to reputation and hence no defamation. This distinguishes defamation from the Roman law of *injuria*, which, in modified form, exists in most civil law countries, and which protects *dignitas*. It also distinguishes the tort of defamation from criminal libel, for which there may be a prosecution without proof of publication to a third person.

Reputation may include a business reputation; but defamation is distinct from the tort of malicious falsehood (p. 876, post) because the latter is committed even if reputation is not besmirched (see *Duncan and Neill on Defamation*, 2nd edn (London, 1983), p. 3). To succeed in defamation the claimant must prove: (1) that the statement was defamatory; (2) that it referred to him (p. 974, post); (3) that the defendant published it to a third person (p. 979, post); and (4) (in a few cases) that damage resulted to him. Damage is presumed to flow from the publication of defamatory matter in permanent form or by broadcast (this is called libel); but if it is in the transitory form (called slander) damage must be proved, unless it falls within certain specified categories (p. 1027, post).

Defamation limits freedom of speech, notably the freedom of the press. Thus, Article 10 of the European Convention on Human Rights (incorporated into English law by the Human Rights Act 1998) has been relied upon by the defendant in numerous defamation cases in the last decade. But such arguments have frequently failed since the common law tort already contained many safeguards on freedom of expression, both procedural and substantive.

The first safeguard is trial by jury, although this right is gradually being eroded. The defendant's statutory right to a jury may be taken away if the trial requires 'any prolonged examination of documents or accounts or any scientific or local investigation which cannot conveniently be made with a jury', or the probable length of the trial makes the action one which cannot conveniently be tried with a jury (Supreme Court Act 1981, s. 69), or if the case is disposed of using the summary procedure under ss. 8–10 of the Defamation Act 1996.

Secondly, the courts will not restrain the threatened publication of a defamatory statement by interlocutory injunction if there is any doubt as to whether the words are defamatory, or if the defendant swears that he intends to justify the words, or if the occasion is a privileged one (see p. 1024, post).

Finally the defendant may, at the trial, prove any of a number of defences: (1) justification, i.e. truth (p. 984, post); (2) honest comment on a matter of public interest (p. 986, post); and (3) privilege, which may be (a) absolute, or (b) qualified (p. 991, post). The claimant may defeat the defences of comment or qualified privilege by proving 'malice', a concept which here includes dishonesty, the introduction of extraneous matter, and ulterior purposes. Apology is no defence at common law, although it may reduce the damages. The Defamation Act 1996 (ss. 2–4) provides for a new 'amends' procedure (p. 1011, post). Section 1 of the Defamation Act 1996 also provides for a defence of innocent publication. The conduct of the parties will affect damages: if the claimant has a bad reputation his damages may be reduced even down to the 'smallest coin in the realm' (p. 1024, post); if the defendant's conduct has been calculated to make a profit for himself which might well exceed the compensation payable to the claimant as damages, then exemplary damages may be awarded (p. 1015, post). An action for libel or slander must be commenced within one year from the date on which the cause of action accrued.

The publication of untruths is sometimes treated as an invasion of 'privacy', although most invasions of privacy do not involve any publication of false, defamatory facts about the victim. Privacy is therefore considered in the next chapter.

1 WHO CAN SUE? WHO CAN BE SUED?

■ Derbyshire County Council v Times Newspapers Ltd
House of Lords [1993] 1 All ER 1011

The defendant published two newspaper articles which questioned the propriety of investments made by the claimant, a local authority. The defendants applied to strike out the claim claiming that a local authority could not sue for libel. The judge held that a local authority could sue for libel in respect of its governmental and administrative functions. The Court of Appeal allowed an appeal, a decision upheld by the House of Lords.

LORD KEITH OF KINKEL: . . .
The authorities cited . . . clearly establish that a trading corporation is entitled to sue in respect of defamatory matters which can be seen as having a tendency to damage it in the way of its business. Examples are those that go to credit such as might deter banks from lending to it, or to the conditions experienced by its employees, which might impede the recruitment of the best qualified workers, or make people reluctant to deal with it. . . .

There are, however, features of a local authority which may be regarded as distinguishing it from other types of corporation, whether trading or non-trading. The most important of these features is that it is a governmental body. Further, it is a democratically elected body, the electoral process nowadays being conducted almost exclusively on party political lines. It is of the highest public importance that a democratically elected governmental body, or indeed any governmental body, should be open to uninhibited public criticism. The threat of a civil action for defamation must inevitably have an inhibiting effect on freedom of speech. In *City of Chicago v Tribune Co* (1923) 307 Ill 595 the Supreme Court of Illinois held that the city could not maintain an action of damages for libel. Thompson CJ said (at 606–607):

'The fundamental right of freedom of speech is involved in this litigation and not merely the right of liberty of the press. If this action can be maintained against a newspaper it can be maintained against every private citizen who ventures to criticise the ministers who are temporarily conducting the affairs of his government. Where any person by speech or writing seeks to persuade others to violate existing law or to overthrow by force or other unlawful means the existing government he may be punished...but all other utterances or publications against the government must be considered absolutely privileged. While in the early history of the struggle for freedom of speech the restrictions were enforced by criminal prosecutions, it is clear that a civil action is as great, if not a greater, restriction than a criminal prosecution. If the right to criticise the government is a privilege which, with the exceptions above enumerated, cannot be restricted, then all civil as well as criminal actions are forbidden. A despotic or corrupt government can more easily stifle opposition by a series of civil actions than by criminal prosecutions...'

After giving a number of reasons for this, he said (at 607–608):

'It follows, therefore, that every citizen has a right to criticise an inefficient or corrupt government without fear of civil as well as criminal prosecution. This absolute privilege is founded on the principle that it is advantageous for the public interest that the citizen should not be in any way fettered in his statements, and where the public service or due administration of justice is involved he shall have the right to speak his mind freely.'

These propositions were endorsed by the Supreme Court of the United States in *New York Times Co v Sullivan* (1964) 376 US 254 at 277. While these decisions were related most directly to the provisions of the American Constitution concerned with securing freedom of speech, the public interest considerations which underlaid them are no less valid in this country. What has been described as "the chilling effect" induced by the threat of civil actions for libel is very important. Quite often the facts which would justify a defamatory publication are known to be true, but admissible evidence capable of proving those facts is not available. This may prevent the publication of matters which it is very desirable to make public. In *Hector v Attorney-General of Antigua and Barbuda* [1990] 2 All ER 103, [1990] 2 AC 312 the Judicial Committee of the Privy Council held that a statutory provision which made the printing or distribution of any false statement likely to undermine public confidence in the conduct of public affairs a criminal offence contravened the provisions of the constitution protecting freedom of speech. Lord Bridge of Harwich said ([1990] 2 All ER 103 at 106, [1990] 2 AC 312 at 318):

'In a free democratic society it is almost too obvious to need stating that those who hold office in government and who are responsible for public administration must always be open to criticism. Any attempt to stifle or fetter such criticism amounts to political censorship of the most insidious and objectionable kind. At the same time it is no less obvious that the very purpose of criticism levelled at those who have the conduct of public affairs by their political opponents is to undermine public confidence in their stewardship and to persuade the electorate that the opponents would make a better job of it than those presently holding office. In the light of these considerations their Lordships cannot help viewing a statutory provision which criminalises statements likely to undermine public confidence in the conduct of public affairs with the utmost suspicion.'

It is of some significance to observe that a number of departments of central government in the United Kingdom are statutorily created corporations, including the Secretaries of State for Defence, Education and Science, Energy, Environment and Social Services. If a local authority can sue for libel there would appear to be no reason in logic for holding that any of these departments (apart from two which are made corporations only for the purpose of holding land) were not also entitled to sue. But as is shown by the decision in *A-G v Guardian Newspapers Ltd (No 2)* [1988] 3 All ER 545, [1990] 1 AC 109, a case concerned with confidentiality, there are rights available to private citizens which institutions of central government are not in a position to exercise unless they can show that it is the public interest to do so. The same applies, in my opinion, to local authorities. In both cases I regard it as right for this House to lay down that not only is there no public interest favouring the right of organs of government, whether central or local, to sue for libel, but that it is contrary to the public interest that they should have it. It is contrary to the public interest because to admit such actions would place an undesirable fetter on freedom of speech....

In *Die Spoorbond v South African Railways*, [1946] AD 999] Watermeyer CJ observed that the reputation of the Crown might fairly be regarded as distinct from that of the group of individuals temporarily responsible for the management of the railways on its behalf (at 1009). In the case of a local authority temporarily under the control of one political party or another it is difficult to say that the local authority as such has any reputation of its own. Reputation in the eyes of the public is more likely to attach itself to the controlling political party, and with a change in that party the reputation itself will change. A publication attacking the activities of the authority will necessarily be an attack on the body of councillors which represents the controlling party, or on the executives who carry on the day-to-day management of its affairs. If the individual reputation of any of these is wrongly impaired by the publication any of these can himself bring proceedings for defamation. Further, it is open to the controlling body to defend itself by public utterances and in debate in the council chamber.

The conclusion must be, in my opinion, that under the common law of England a local authority does not have the right to maintain an action of damages for defamation. That was the conclusion reached by the Court of Appeal, which did so principally by reference to art 10 of the European Convention on Human Rights (Convention for the Protection of Human Rights and Fundamental Freedoms (Rome, 4 November 1950; TS 71 (1953); Cmd 8969), to which the United Kingdom has adhered but which has not been enacted into domestic law.[1] Article 10 is in these terms:

> '(1) Everyone has the right to freedom of expression. This right shall include freedom to hold opinions and to receive and impart information and ideas without interference by public authority and regardless of frontiers...'(2) The exercise of these freedoms, since it carries with it duties and responsibilities, may be subject to such formalities, conditions, restrictions or penalties as are prescribed by law and are necessary in a democratic society, in the interests of national security, territorial integrity or public safety, for the prevention of disorder or crime, for the protection of health or morals, for the protection of the reputation or rights of others, for preventing the disclosure of information received in confidence, or for maintaining the authority and impartiality of the judiciary.'

As regards the words 'necessary in a democratic society' in connection with the restrictions on the right to freedom of expression which may properly be prescribed by law, the jurisprudence of the European Court of Human Rights has established that 'necessary' requires the existence of a pressing social need, and that the restrictions should be no more than is proportionate to the legitimate aim pursued. The domestic courts have 'a margin of appreciation' based upon local knowledge of the needs of the society to which they belong (see *Sunday Times v UK* (1979) 2 EHRR 245; *Barthold v Germany* (1985) 7 EHRR 383 and *Lingens v Austria* (1986) 8 EHRR 407 at 418....

My Lords, I have reached my conclusion upon the common law of England without finding any need to rely upon the European convention. My noble and learned friend, Lord Goff of Chieveley, in *Attorney-General v Guardian Newspapers Ltd (No 2)* [1988] 3 All ER 545 at 660, [1990] 1 AC 109 at 283-284, expressed the opinion that in the field of freedom of speech there was no difference in principle between English law on the subject and article 10 of the convention. I agree, and can only add that I find it satisfactory to be able to conclude that the common law of England is consistent with the obligations assumed by the Crown under the treaty in this particular field.

For these reasons I would dismiss the appeal.

[LORD GRIFFITHS, LORD GOFF OF CHIEVELEY, LORD BROWNE-WILKINSON, and LORD WOOLF agreed with LORD KEITH.]

NOTES

1.   Political parties are also excluded from suing for libel, see *Goldsmith v Bhoyrul* [1998] QB 459, [1997] 4 All ER 268. To the claimant political party's argument that 'because

---

[1] [But see now the Human Rights Act 1998.]

a party was only seeking power at an election and could not abuse what it had not got, it could not be equated with a government body that had that power' Buckley J responded, 'So far as it goes, that must be right; but it seems to me that the public interest in free speech and criticism in respect of those bodies putting themselves forward for office or to govern is also sufficiently strong to justify withholding the right to sue. Defamation actions or the threat of them would constitute a fetter on free speech at a time and on a topic when it is clearly in the public interest that there should be none.'

2.   The Human Rights Act 1998 incorporates the European Convention on Human Rights into English law and came into force in October 2000. For another important case antedating the Act but emphasising the importance of free speech see *Reynolds v Times Newspapers Ltd* (p. 999, post). Similarly, in *McCartan Turkington Breen v Times Newspapers Ltd* [2001] 2 AC 277, [2000] 4 All ER 913 the House of Lords emphasised that the phrase 'public meeting' (in s. 7 of the Defamation Act (Northern Ireland) 1955) must be construed broadly to encompass a press conference, so as to privilege a newspaper report of the meeting (for the defence of qualified privilege see pp. 993 et seq, post). Lord Steyn declared that 'Even before the coming into operation of the Human Rights Act 1998 the principle of freedom of expression attained the status of a constitutional right with attendant high normative force.'

3.   In another context, Lord Slynn of Hadley has said of the impact of the Human Rights Act that 'long or well entrenched ideas may have to be put aside, sacred cows culled' (*R v Lambert* [2002] 2 AC 545, [2001] 3 All ER 577, at [6]). However, in *Berezovsky v Forbes Inc (No 2)* [2001] EMLR 45, [2001] EWCA Civ 1251 the court rejected a submission by Mr Geoffrey Robertson QC that a newspaper article 'written ethically and honestly is now to be judged not by making nice distinctions of pleaded meaning but according to a broad judgment whether, having regard to those true facts and fair comments which the article contains, it is necessary in a democratic society to restrict the journal's freedom of expression by making its publisher and editor liable for its inaccuracies' (see [8]). Sedley LJ stated that while the courts should not 'rest on the laurels' of statements such as Lord Keith's in *Derbyshire County Council* and must be prepared 'to cull sacred jurisprudential cows', freedom of speech under Article 10 was not absolute, and to require a newspaper to prove the truth of the 'sting' of a libel (as determined in the normal common law way: see pp. 984–985 post) was 'not in our judgment a disproportionate invasion of the right of free expression. It meets the legitimate purpose, recognised by Article 10(2), of protecting people from the publication of damaging and unjustified falsehoods': see [10]–[12]. Eady J said at first instance in the same case: 'I should resist any temptation to become unduly intoxicated by the heady atmosphere engendered by the Human Rights Act. I ask myself to what extent, if any, English law fails to accommodate the policy considerations expounded in the Strasbourg jurisprudence. Having thought about it, I am not persuaded that there would be any incompatibility between it and the well known tests that an English judge has hitherto been required to apply on applications of this kind' (quoted by the Court of Appeal at [9]).

■ Jameel v Wall Street Journal Europe Sprl

House of Lords [2006] 4 All ER 1279

The claimants were a Saudi Arabian businessman and the company (incorporated in Saudi Arabia) of which he was president and general manager. They complained of a newspaper article published by the defendants linking the company to terrorist activities. The company, which did not trade within the United Kingdom, but which had an established trade reputation there, did not plead any special damage but relied on the common law presumption of damage in libel. The jury held the defendants liable and awarded damages to the claimants. On appeal, the defendants argued that the irrebutable presumption of damage was an unjustified restriction on freedom of speech, because it inhibits legitimate press criticism of trading corporations. The House of Lords, by a majority, rejected that argument.

LORD BINGHAM OF CORNHILL: . . .

[24] The tort of defamation exists to afford redress for unjustified injury to reputation. By a successful action the injured reputation is vindicated. The ordinary means of vindication is by the verdict of a judge or jury and an award of damages. Most plaintiffs are individuals, who are not required to prove that they have suffered financial loss or even that any particular person has thought the worse of them as a result of the publication complained of. I do not understand this rule to be criticised. Thus the question arises whether a corporation with a commercial reputation within the jurisdiction should be subject to a different rule.

[25] There are of course many defamatory things which can be said about individuals (for example, about their sexual proclivities) which could not be said about corporations. But it is not at all hard to think of statements seriously injurious to the general commercial reputation of trading and charitable corporations: that an arms company has routinely bribed officials of foreign governments to secure contracts; that an oil company has wilfully and unnecessarily damaged the environment; that an international humanitarian agency has wrongfully succumbed to government pressure; that a retailer has knowingly exploited child labour; and so on. The leading figures in such corporations may be understood to be personally implicated, but not, in my opinion, necessarily so. Should the corporation be entitled to sue in its own right only if it can prove financial loss? I do not think so, for two main reasons.

[26] First, the good name of a company, as that of an individual, is a thing of value. A damaging libel may lower its standing in the eyes of the public and even its own staff, make people less ready to deal with it, less willing or less proud to work for it. If this were not so, corporations would not go to the lengths they do to protect and burnish their corporate images. I find nothing repugnant in the notion that this is a value which the law should protect. Nor do I think it an adequate answer that the corporation can itself seek to answer the defamatory statement by press release or public statement, since protestations of innocence by the impugned party necessarily carry less weight with the public than the prompt issue of proceedings which culminate in a favourable verdict by judge or jury. Secondly, I do not accept that a publication, if truly damaging to a corporation's commercial reputation, will result in provable financial loss, since the more prompt and public a company's issue of proceedings, and the more diligent its pursuit of a claim, the less the chance that financial loss will actually accrue.

LORD HOPE OF CRAIGHEAD: . . .

[102] . . . As the European court recognised in *Steel v UK* (at 435 (para 94)), one of the main functions which the right of action for libel seeks to serve is to enable the claimant to challenge the truth, and limit the damage, of allegations which risk harming its reputation. It is to enable it to nail the lie, as it was put in argument. A requirement that special damage had to be proved in every case would deprive the trading company of that opportunity. It would have to wait until it was in a position to show that some damage had actually been done to its business which was capable of being proved. In its case proof of a risk of harm to its reputation—of a tendency to damage it in the way if its business, as Lord Keith put it in the *Derbyshire CC* case [1993] 1 All ER 1011 at 1017, [1993] AC 534 at 547—would not be enough. The effect would be to undermine the right of action and to leave trading companies whose reputation was put at risk without a means of averting the damage that might result from the libel. This could be incalculable.

LORD HOFFMANN [dissenting]:...

[91] In the case of an individual, his reputation is a part of his personality, the 'immortal part' of himself and it is right that he should be entitled to vindicate his reputation and receive compensation for a slur upon it without proof of financial loss. But a commercial company has no soul and its reputation is no more than a commercial asset, something attached to its trading name which brings in customers. I see no reason why the rule which requires proof of damage to commercial assets in other torts, such as malicious falsehood, should not also apply to defamation.

BARONESS HALE OF RICHMOND [dissenting]:...

[154] It seems, therefore, that while the retention of the rule that a company does not have to show that it has in fact been harmed in any way may be within our margin of appreciation, we should scrutinise its impact with some care to see whether it may have a disproportionately chilling effect upon freedom of speech. The earliest critical comment upon the rule in the United Kingdom to which we have been referred came again from Tony Weir, in a case note on *Bognor Regis UDC v Campion* [1972] 2 All ER 61, [1972] 2 QB 169: see 'Local Authority v Critical Ratepayer—A Suit in Defamation' [1972A] CLJ 238, pp 239–240 (but see also 'Libel and the Corporate Plaintiff ' (1969) 69 Columbia Law Review 1496):

> 'There is still some justification, however, for the rule that the human plaintiff need not prove any harm. If the statement is defamatory, he will feel bad and others will think badly of him; the first need not be proved and the second cannot be. Indeed, this duality of harm can be presumed precisely because it is required: you get damages only if the defendant has been rude *about you to someone else.*'

But it was absurd to give substantial damages to a trading company:

> 'It was absurd because [the company] had no feelings which might have been hurt and no social relations which might have been impaired. The two kinds of presumptive harm could not be presumed because they could not have occurred...the reasons for which we absolve the human plaintiff from the usual requirement of proving loss cannot and do not apply to the inhuman plaintiff...To prefer the interest in maintaining the corporate image to the right of the citizen to say what he reasonably believes to be true is a grim perversion of values.'

[158] My Lords, in my view such a requirement would achieve a proper balance between the right of a company to protect its reputation and the right of the press and public to be critical of it. These days, the dividing line between governmental and non-governmental organisations is increasingly difficult to draw. The power wielded by the major multi-national corporations is enormous and growing. The freedom to criticise them may be at least as important in a democratic society as the freedom to criticise the government.

[LORD SCOTT OF FOSCOTE delivered a speech rejecting the defendants' submissions.]

NOTES

1. The defendants' further appeal on *Reynolds* privilege, however, was successful. See p. 1006 post.
2. In *Jameel v Dow Jones & Co Inc* [2005] QB 946, [2005] EWCA Civ 75 the court rejected a similar challenge to the presumption of damage in a libel claim by an individual (the brother of the first claimant in the Wall Street Journal action, ante). The Court of Appeal applied the rule in *Duke of Brunswick v Harmer* (1849) 14 QB 185, that even a single publication suffices for a claim in libel without proof of special damage. There were 'strong pragmatic reasons for proceeding on the premise that a defamatory publication

will have caused the victim some damage rather than opening the door to the claimant and the defendant each marshalling witnesses to say that, respectively, they did or did not consider that the article damaged the claimant's reputation' per Lord Phillips MR at [31]. The jury must, however, assess the actual loss caused by the statement when calculating damages. Only in rare cases might free speech be disproportionately curtailed, i.e. when 'a claimant launches defamation proceedings in respect of a limited circulation which has caused his reputation no actual damage'. These exceptional situations were to be met by challenging the claimant's resort to English jurisdiction, or alleging abuse of process. On the facts, the court indeed went on to strike out the claim as an abuse of process, since publication within the jurisdiction was minimal and the damage to the claimant's reputation insignificant. Thus, there had been no 'real and substantial tort', and to hear the claim would be disproportionate, contrary to both the ECHR and the philosophy of the Civil Procedure Rules.

3. In *Collins Stewart Ltd v Financial Times Ltd* [2005] EWHC 262 (QB) Gray J held that aggravated damages could not be awarded in a libel action by a corporate claimant, which has no feelings to hurt and cannot suffer distress (for which aggravated damages are awarded).

2 WORDS OR MATTER DEFAMATORY OF THE CLAIMANT

■ Berkoff v Burchill
Court of Appeal [1996] 4 All ER 1008

The first defendant was a journalist who wrote for a newspaper published by the second defendant. The claimant, a well-known actor, director, and writer, brought an action for damages for libel against the defendants, claiming that in two articles they had made statements to the effect that he was hideously ugly. The claimant said these statements were defamatory since they would tend to expose him to ridicule or would tend to cause other people to shun or avoid him. The judge held that the meaning of the words pleaded by the claimant was capable of being defamatory. The defendants appealed, contending that the characteristic of the tort of defamation was injury to reputation and the fact that a statement might injure feelings or cause annoyance was irrelevant to whether it was defamatory. By a majority, the Court of Appeal dismissed the appeal.

NEILL LJ: . . .
The scope of the present application
. . . The question of fact: libel or no libel, is a matter for the jury. But the court has jurisdiction to rule that as a matter of law words are incapable of being defamatory. . . .

Definitions of 'defamatory'
I am not aware of any entirely satisfactory definition of the word 'defamatory'. It may be convenient, however, to collect together some of the definitions which have been used and approved in the past.

(1) The classic definition is that given by Lord Wensleydale (then Parke B) in *Parmiter v Coupland* (1840) 6 M & W 105 at 108. He said that in cases of libel it was for the judge to give a legal definition of the offence which he defined as being:

'A publication, without justification or lawful excuse, which is calculated to injure the reputation of another, by exposing him to hatred, contempt, or ridicule…'

It is to be noted that in *Tournier v National Provincial Union Bank of England Ltd* [1924] 1 KB 461 at 477, [1923] All ER Rep 550 at 557 Scrutton LJ said that he did not think that this 'ancient formula' was sufficient in all cases, because words might damage the reputation of a man as a business man which no one would connect with hatred, ridicule or contempt. Atkin LJ expressed a similar opinion ([1924] 1 KB 461 at 486–487, [1923] All ER Rep 550 at 561):

'I do not think that it is a sufficient direction to a jury on what is meant by "defamatory" to say, without more, that it means: Were the words calculated to expose the plaintiff to hatred, ridicule or contempt, in the mind of a reasonable man? The formula is well known to lawyers, but it is obvious that suggestions might be made very injurious to a man's character in business which would not, in the ordinary sense, excite either hate, ridicule, or contempt—for example, an imputation of a clever fraud which, however much to be condemned morally and legally, might yet not excite what a member of a jury might understand as hatred, or contempt.'

(2) In *Scott v Sampson* (1882) 8 QBD 491, [1881–5] All ER Rep 628 the Divisional Court was concerned with the question as to the evidence which might be called by a defendant relating to the character of the claimant. Cave J explained the nature of the right which is concerned in an action for defamation (8 QBD 491 at 503, [1881–5] All ER Rep 628 at 634):

'Speaking generally the law recognizes in every man a right to have the estimation in which he stands in the opinion of others unaffected by false statements to his discredit; and if such false statements are made without lawful excuse, and damage results to the person of whom they are made, he has a right of action.'

But, as was pointed out in the Faulks Committee *Report of the Committee on Defamation* (Cmnd 5909) para 62, the word 'discredit' is itself incapable of precise explication. Nevertheless, in *Youssoupoff v Metro-Goldwyn-Mayer Pictures Ltd* (1934) 50 TLR 581 Scrutton LJ said that he thought that it was difficult to improve upon the language of this definition.

(3) In *Sim v Stretch* [1936] 2 All ER 1237 at 1240 Lord Atkin expressed the view that the definition in *Parmiter v Coupland* was probably too narrow and that the question was complicated by having to consider the person or class of persons whose reaction to the publication provided the relevant test. He concluded this passage in his speech:

'…after collating the opinions of many authorities I propose in the present case the test: would the words tend to lower the plaintiff in the estimation of right-thinking members of society generally?'

(4) As I have already observed, both Scrutton and Atkin LJJ in *Tournier's* case drew attention to words which damage the reputation of a man as a business man. In *Drummond-Jackson v British Medical Association* [1970] 1 All ER 1094, [1970] 1 WLR 688 the Court of Appeal was concerned with an article in a medical journal which, it was suggested, impugned the claimant's reputation as a dentist. Lord Pearson said:

'…words may be defamatory of a trader or business man or professional man, although they do not impute any moral fault or defect of personal character. They [can] be defamatory of him if they impute lack of qualification, knowledge, skill, capacity, judgment or efficiency in the conduct of his trade or business or professional activity…' (See [1970] 1 All ER 1094 at 1104, [1970] 1 WLR 688 at 698–699.)

It is therefore necessary in some cases to consider the occupation of the claimant.

(5) In *Youssoupoff v Metro-Goldwyn-Mayer Pictures Ltd* (1934) 50 TLR 581 at 587 Slesser LJ expanded the *Parmiter v Coupland* definition to include words which cause a person to be shunned or avoided. He said:

'…not only is the matter defamatory if it brings the plaintiff into hatred, ridicule, or contempt by reason of some moral discredit on [the claimant's] part, but also if it tends to make the plaintiff be shunned and avoided and that without any moral discredit on [the claimant's] part. It is for that reason that persons who have been alleged to have been insane, or to be suffering from certain diseases, and other cases where no direct moral responsibility could be placed upon them, have been held to be entitled to bring an action to protect their reputation and their honour.'

Slesser LJ added, in relation to the facts in that case:

'One may, I think, take judicial notice of the fact that a lady of whom it has been said that she has been ravished, albeit against her will, has suffered in social reputation and in opportunities of receiving respectable consideration from the world.'

(6) The Faulks Committee in their report recommended that for the purpose of civil cases the following definition of defamation should be adopted (para 65):

'Defamation shall consist of the publication to a third party of matter which in all the circumstances would be likely to affect a person adversely in the estimation of reasonable people generally.'

(7) In the American Law Institute's *Restatement of the Law of Torts* (2nd edn, 1977) para 559 the following definition is given:

'A communication is defamatory if it tends so to harm the reputation of another as to lower him in the estimation of the community or to deter third persons from associating or dealing with him.'

(8) In some of the Australian states a definition of 'defamatory matter' is contained in the Code. In the Queensland Criminal Code para 366, the following definition is given:

'Any imputation concerning any person, or any member of his family, whether living or dead, by which the reputation of that person is likely to be injured, or by which he is likely to be injured in his profession or trade, or by which other persons are likely to be induced to shun or avoid or ridicule or despise him…'

It will be seen from this collection of definitions that words may be defamatory, even though they neither impute disgraceful conduct to the claimant nor any lack of skill or efficiency in the conduct of his trade or business or professional activity, if they hold him up to contempt, scorn or ridicule or tend to exclude him from society. On the other hand, insults which do not diminish a man's standing among other people do not found an action for libel or slander. The exact borderline may often be difficult to define.

The case for Mr Berkoff is that the charge that he is 'hideously ugly' exposes him to ridicule, and/ or alternatively, will cause him to be shunned or avoided. I turn therefore to such guidance as can be found in any of the decided cases to which we were either referred by counsel or to which my own limited researches have led me.

Guidance from decided cases…

(3) In *Dunlop Rubber Co Ltd v Dunlop* [1921] 1 AC 367, [1920] All ER Rep 745 the claimant, who was the inventor of a pneumatic tyre, had assigned his interest in the invention to the defendant company. The claimant lived in Ireland. In 1891 the claimant had presented the defendants' predecessors in title with a portrait bust of himself and his signature to be used as a trade mark. Later, however, the defendants, without his permission, exhibited advertisements containing pictures intended to represent him, but the features, which were adapted from the portrait bust, were placed upon the body of a very tall man dressed in an exaggeratedly foppish manner, wearing a tall white hat, a white waistcoat, and carrying a cane and eyeglass. The claimant had obtained an injunction against the defendant company in the Chancery Division in Ireland and the injunction was upheld by the Court of Appeal in Ireland. On

appeal to the House of Lords it was argued that leave should not have been given in Ireland to serve a writ in London.

But in the course of his speech dismissing the appeal Lord Birkenhead LC said ([1921] 1 AC 367 at 372, [1920] All ER Rep 745 at 747):

'...it was said in the Court below, and it has been said in other cases which were cited to us as authorities, that such an injunction would not be granted, and ought not to be granted, unless the Court was satisfied of the existence of a serious libel, unless indeed it was prepared confidently and completely to anticipate what the view of a jury would be when it tried the case. I am not sure that in some of the passages cited the case was not in this particular put rather too high. It is sufficient for me to say that the judges who tried this case have reached the conclusion (and I agree with them) that the exhibition of these pictures constituted a circumstance in which that which was done was at least capable of a defamatory meaning.'

It is to be noted that the claim in the writ for an injunction was to restrain the defendant from publishing any advertisements etc which contained pictures representing the claimant 'in absurd or unsuitable costumes or attitudes, or caricatures of him, or otherwise calculated to expose him to public ridicule or contempt by misrepresenting his appearance or costume'.

(4) In *Zbyszko v New York American Inc* (1930) 228 App Div 277 the claimant, who was a wrestler, complained of references to him in an article published by the defendant on the theory of evolution. The article called attention to the structural resemblance between man and the gorilla. Near the top of the page appeared a photograph of the claimant in a wrestling pose and under it the words: 'Stanislaus Zbyszko, the Wrestler, not Fundamentally Different from the Gorilla in Physique.' In close proximity to the photograph of the claimant was a photograph of a gorilla (described in the law report as 'hideous looking') which was stated to be a mounted specimen of the Great Kivu gorilla in Lord Rothschild's museum in England.

The claimant's action, in which it was pleaded that 'the claimant enjoyed an international reputation for dignity...kindliness, intelligence and culture', was struck out by the Supreme Court for New York County but the case was reinstated by the Appellate Division. It was held that the tendency of the article was to disgrace him and bring him into ridicule and contempt. Judge McAvoy said (at 413):

'Any written article is actionable...if it tends to expose the plaintiff to public contempt, ridicule, aversion, or disgrace, or induce an evil opinion of him in the minds of others and deprives him of their society. It is not necessary that words impute disgraceful conduct to the plaintiff. If they render him contemptible or ridiculous, he is equally entitled to redress.'

The court therefore held that the case could not be struck out before trial.

(5) In *Youssoupoff v Metro-Goldwyn-Mayer Pictures Ltd* (1934) 50 TLR 581 the claimant complained that she could be identified with the character Princess Natasha in the film 'Rasputin, the Mad Monk'. The princess claimed damages on the basis that the film suggested that, by reason of her identification with 'Princess Natasha', she had been seduced by Rasputin. The princess was awarded £25,000 damages. In the Court of Appeal it was contended that if the film indicated any relations between Rasputin and 'Natasha' it indicated a rape of Natasha and not a seduction. Slesser LJ considered the defamatory nature of the film (at 587):

'I, for myself, cannot see that from the plaintiff's point of view it matters in the least whether this libel suggests that she has been seduced or ravished. The question whether she is or is not the more or the less moral seems to me immaterial in considering this question whether she has been defamed, and for this reason, that, as has been frequently pointed out in libel, not only is the matter defamatory if it brings the plaintiff into hatred, ridicule, or contempt by reason of some moral discredit on her part, but also if tends to make the plaintiff be shunned and avoided and that without any moral discredit on her part. It is for that reason that persons who have been alleged to have been insane, or to be suffering from certain diseases, and other cases where no direct moral responsibility could be placed upon them, have been held to be entitled to bring an action to protect their reputation and their honour.'

Later he added (at 588):

'When this woman is defamed in her sexual purity I do not think that the precise manner in which she has been despoiled of her innocence and virginity is a matter which a jury can properly be asked to consider.'

(6) In *Winyard v Tatler Publishing Co Ltd* (1991) Independent, 16 August the Tatler magazine published an article which contained a reference to a residential health spa of which Mr Stephen Winyard and Mrs Winyard, his mother, were directors. Mrs Winyard complained of a sentence which was in these terms:

'His mother, Gaynor Winyard, is an internationally renowned beauty therapist (known more familiarly on the beautician circuit as "the international boot").'

One of the meanings of 'boot' relied on by Mrs Winyard was that it meant 'an ugly harridan'. At the trial the judge considered a submission that in this meaning the word 'boot' was not capable of being defamatory. He said:

'In their context, applied to a lady who is in the alleged libel itself described as "a beauty therapist" and "someone on the beautician circuit" to call such a person "an ugly harridan" is in my view something beyond mere ridicule. It is ridicule, no doubt. But it is ridicule which the jury, if it thought right, would be entitled, within the well-known definition (which I am not going to repeat here but I shall state to the jury) of finding to be defamatory.'

It seems that the 'well-known definition' was that of Lord Atkin in *Sim v Stretch* [1936] 2 All ER 1237 at 1240: '...would the words tend to lower the plaintiff in the estimation of right-thinking members of society generally?'

In his judgment in the Court of Appeal, Staughton LJ referred to the judge's ruling:

'It may well be that in some cases to say that a woman is old and ugly, or haggard, would do no more than cause injury to her feelings, and would not affect her character or reputation. But the judge evidently felt that a different view might be taken if she was a beauty therapist. It is not, apparently, that she would have failed to exercise her skills in preserving her own appearance, but that others might not wish her to be in charge of their treatment. I entirely agree with the judge's ruling on this point; it was open for the jury, if they thought fit, to find that this meaning of the word "boot" lowered Mrs Winyard's character or reputation. Whether they did reach that conclusion we do not know. It may be that their verdict was entirely based on the innuendo meaning of a promiscuous slut, which (if established) was far more serious.'

...

It was argued by counsel on behalf of the defendants that the defining characteristic of the tort of defamation is injury to reputation. The fact that a statement may injure feelings or cause annoyance is irrelevant to the question whether it is defamatory. He reminded us of Lord Atkin's words in *Sim v Stretch* [1936] 2 All ER 1237 at 1242 that though the freedom of juries to award damages for injury to reputation was one of the safeguards of liberty, the protection was undermined 'when exhibitions of bad manners or discourtesy are placed on the same level as attacks on character, and are treated as actionable wrongs'.

Counsel accepted that it was also defamatory to say of a man that he was suffering from certain diseases. But he submitted that a distinction had to be drawn between an allegation that someone was physically unwholesome and an allegation that someone was physically aesthetically unpleasing. It could not be defamatory to say that an individual had a streaming cold or influenza, so the test of being 'shunned or avoided' cannot be applied without qualification. It was also to be noted that it was not suggested in *Youssoupoff's* case that there was no evidence on which it could be found that the passages complained of were defamatory of the princess (see (1934) 50 TLR 581 at 586 per Greer LJ).

Counsel for Mr Berkoff on the other hand, contended that the present case fell into the residual class where words may be defamatory even though they do not involve an attack on a plaintiff's reputation in the conventional sense. Mr Berkoff, it was said, is an actor and a person in the public eye. It was submitted that it was necessary to look at all the circumstances. If this were done it was a matter for the jury to decide whether the words complained of had passed beyond mere abuse and had become defamatory by exposing Mr Berkoff to ridicule or by causing him to be shunned or avoided. It was suggested that these two passages would reduce the respect with which he was regarded. The words complained of might affect Mr Berkoff's standing among the public, particularly theatre-goers, and among casting directors.

In his helpful submissions on behalf of the defendants, Mr Price QC rightly underlined the central characteristic of an action for defamation as being a remedy for publications which damage a person's reputation. But the word 'reputation', by its association with phrases such as 'business reputation', 'professional reputation' or 'reputation for honesty', may obscure the fact that in this context the word is to be interpreted in a broad sense as comprehending all aspects of a person's standing in the community. A man who is held up as a figure of fun may be defeated in his claim for damages by, for example, a plea of fair comment, or, if he succeeds on liability, the compensation which he receives from a jury may be very small. But nevertheless, the publication of which he complains may be defamatory of him because it affects in an adverse manner the attitude of other people towards him. . . .

It is trite law that the meaning of words in a libel action is determined by the reaction of the ordinary reader and not by the intention of the publisher, but the perceived intention of the publisher may colour the meaning. In the present case it would, in my view, be open to a jury to conclude that in the context the remarks about Mr Berkoff gave the impression that he was not merely physically unattractive in appearance but actually repulsive. It seems to me that to say this of someone in the public eye who makes his living, in part at least, as an actor, is capable of lowering his standing in the estimation of the public and of making him an object of ridicule.

I confess that I have found this to be a far from easy case, but in the end I am satisfied that it would be wrong to decide this preliminary issue in a way which would withdraw the matter completely from the consideration of a jury.

I would dismiss the appeal.

MILLETT LJ [dissenting]: . . .

Many a true word is spoken in jest. Many a false one too. But chaff and banter are not defamatory, and even serious imputations are not actionable if no one would take them to be meant seriously. The question, however, is how the words would be understood, not how they were meant, and that issue is pre-eminently one for the jury. So, however difficult it may be, we must assume that Miss Julie Burchill might be taken seriously. The question then is: is it defamatory to say of a man that he is 'hideously ugly'?

Mr Berkoff is a director, actor and writer. Physical beauty is not a qualification for a director or writer. Mr Berkoff does not plead that he plays romantic leads or that the words complained of impugn his professional ability. In any case, I do not think that it can be defamatory to say of an actor that he is unsuitable to play particular roles.

How then can the words complained of injure Mr Berkoff's reputation? They are an attack on his appearance, not on his reputation. It is submitted on his behalf that they would cause people 'to shun and avoid him' and would 'bring him into ridicule'. Ridicule, it will be recalled, is the second member of a well-known trinity.

The submission illustrates the danger of trusting to verbal formulae. Defamation has never been satisfactorily defined. All attempted definitions are illustrative. None of them is exhaustive. All can be misleading if they cause one to forget that defamation is an attack on reputation, that is on a man's standing in the world.

The cases in which words have been held to be defamatory because they would cause the plaintiff to be shunned or avoided, or 'cut off from society', have hitherto been confined to allegations that he suffers from leprosy or the plague or the itch or is noisome and smelly (see *Villers v Monsley* (1769) 2 Wils 403). I agree with Phillips LJ and for the reasons which he gives that an allegation of ugliness is not of that character. It is a common experience that ugly people have satisfactory social lives—Boris Karloff is not known to have been a recluse—and it is a popular belief for the truth of which I am unable to vouch that ugly men are particularly attractive to women.

I have no doubt that the words complained of were intended to ridicule Mr Berkoff, but I do not think that they made him look ridiculous or lowered his reputation in the eyes of ordinary people. There are only two cases which have been cited to us which are at all comparable. In *Winyard v Tatler Publishing Co Ltd* (1991) Independent, 16 August it was held to be defamatory to call a professional beautician 'an ugly harridan', not because it reflected on her professional ability, but because some of her customers might not wish to be attended by an ugly beautician. I find the decision difficult to understand, since the reasoning suggests that the cause of action would more properly be classified as malicious falsehood rather than defamation, so that actual loss of custom would have to be proved.

The other case is *Zbyszko v New York American Inc* (1930) 228 App Div 277. A newspaper published a photograph of a particularly repulsive gorilla. Next to it appeared a photograph of the plaintiff above the caption: 'Stanislaus Zbyszko, the Wrestler, Not Fundamentally Different from the Gorilla in Physique.' The statement of claim alleged that this had caused the plaintiff to be shunned and avoided by his wife (who presumably had not noticed her husband's physique until it was pointed out to her by the newspaper), his relatives, neighbours, friends and business associates, and had injured him in his professional calling. The Appellate Division of the New York Supreme Court held that the caption was capable of being defamatory. The case was presumably cited to us as persuasive authority. I find it singularly unpersuasive except as a demonstration of the lengths of absurdity to which an enthusiastic New York lawyer will go in pleading his case.

The line between mockery and defamation may sometimes be difficult to draw. When it is, it should be left to the jury to draw. Despite the respect which is due to the opinion of Neill LJ, whose experience in this field is unrivalled, I am not persuaded that the present case could properly be put on the wrong side of the line. A decision that it is an actionable wrong to describe a man as 'hideously ugly' would be an unwarranted restriction on free speech. And if a bald statement to this effect would not be capable of being defamatory, I do not see how a humorously exaggerated observation to the like effect could be. People must be allowed to poke fun at one another without fear of litigation. It is one thing to ridicule a man; it is another to expose him to ridicule. Miss Burchill made a cheap joke at Mr Berkoff's expense; she may thereby have demeaned herself, but I do not believe that she defamed Mr Berkoff.

If I have appeared to treat Mr Berkoff's claim with unjudicial levity it is because I find it impossible to take it seriously. Despite the views of my brethren, who are both far more experienced than I am, I remain of the opinion that the proceedings are as frivolous as Miss Burchill's article. The time of the court ought not to be taken up with either of them. I would allow the appeal and dismiss the action.

[PHILLIPS LJ delivered a judgment in favour of dismissing the appeal.]

Appeal dismissed.

NOTES

1. In *Norman v Future Publishing* [1999] EMLR 325, Hirst LJ claimed that in *Berkoff v Burchill* the Court of Appeal was unanimous in distinguishing between mere mockery and defamation. According to Hirst LJ, the only difference between Millett LJ and Neill LJ was that Millett LJ thought that the words so clearly fell into the first category that it was not necessary to trouble a jury. Is this correct?

2. *Berkoff v Burchill* never came before a jury. The attitude of juries to such actions is probably best illustrated by a 1985 case in which a High Court jury decided that it was

not defamatory to compare someone, in a humorous sketch about politics, with Sue-Ellen, a promiscuous alcoholic character of the television soap opera *Dallas*: *The Times*, 2 February 1985, p. 1.

3. On discrimination against the ugly, see S. Stevenage and Y. McKay (1999) 90 Brit. Jo. Psychology 221. Note that there is discrimination even against those merely described by others as ugly—M. Snyder, E. Tanke, and E. Berscheid (1977) 35 Jo of Personality and Social Psychology 656. See generally Nancy Etcoff, *The Survival of the Prettiest: The Science of Beauty* (1999).

■ Byrne v Deane

Court of Appeal [1937] 2 All ER 204

Automatic gambling machines, popularly known as 'diddler' machines, were kept, unlawfully, by the defendants on golf club premises for the use of club members. Someone told the police about the existence of the machines, leading the police to require their removal. The next day the following lampoon appeared on the wall against which the machines had stood:

'For many years upon this spot
You heard the sound of a merry bell
Those who were rash and those who were not
Lost and made a spot of cash
But he who gave the game away
May he byrnne in hell and rue the day'

Diddleramus

The claimant brought an action for libel, alleging that the defendants meant and were understood to mean that the claimant had reported the machines' presence to the police, that he was guilty of disloyalty, and that he was a person unfit for other members of the club to associate with. Hilbery J held that the words were defamatory and awarded 40 shillings damages and costs. On appeal, all members of the court held that it was not defamatory to say that a person has informed the police of a crime. Slesser and Greene LJJ held that the words in this case were not defamatory, but Greer LJ held that they were defamatory because they meant something more than that the police had been informed of a crime, namely that the claimant had been guilty of disloyalty.

SLESSER LJ: . . .

In my view, to allege of a man—and for this purpose it does not matter whether the allegation is true or is not true—that he has reported certain acts, wrongful in law, to the police, cannot possibly be said to be defamatory of him in the minds of the general public. We have to consider in this connection the *arbitrium boni*, the view which would be taken by the ordinary good and worthy subject of the King (to quote the matter which appears in the old declarations), and I have assigned to myself no other criterion than what a good and worthy subject of the King would think of some person of whom it had been said that he had put the law into motion against wrongdoers, in thinking that such a good and worthy subject would not consider such an allegation in itself to be defamatory. That is the view taken by McCardie J in *Myroft v Sleight*[2] at p. 884, where he quotes with approval a judgment of the Irish

---

[2] (1921) 90 LJKB 883.   [3] (1869) IR 4 CL 54.

court in *Mawe v Piggot*[3] at p. 62, where Lawson J giving the judgment of the court says:

'[Counsel for the claimant], however, argued that amongst certain classes who were either themselves criminal, or who sympathised with crime, it would expose a person to great odium to represent him as an informer or a prosecutor, or otherwise aiding in the detection of crime; that is quite true, but we cannot be called upon to adopt that standard. The very circumstances which will make a person be regarded with disfavour by the criminal classes will raise his character in the estimation of right-thinking men. We can only regard the estimation in which a man is held by society generally . . .'

NOTES

1. The views of the 'ordinary good and worthy subject of the King' are obviously subject to change. At the time of Charles II it was defamatory to call a person a Papist (*Row v Clargis* (1683) T Raym 482); during the First World War it was defamatory to describe a firm as German (*Slazengers Ltd v Gibbs & Co* (1916) 33 TLR 35); in 1964 it was thought, by Lord Denning MR, to be defamatory to call a man with an English name a Czech, if that implied communist sympathies which made him disloyal (*Linklater v Daily Telegraph Ltd* (1964) 108 Sol Jo 992). In consequence, great care should be taken in interpreting past cases on what counts as defamatory. Note also that a statement made now about the claimant's conduct in the past is judged according to whether it is defamatory now, although the mores of the time when the conduct is alleged to have taken place are relevant to what the statement means now. It is not necessarily defamatory to say of someone that they shared the values of the time, even if those values are ones right-thinking people would now find extremely offensive (see *Mitchell v Book Sales Ltd* (1994) Independent, 25 March).

2. Is it still defamatory to say that someone is homosexual? In 1992 the singer and actor Jason Donovan sued 'The Face' magazine for publishing a picture allegedly doctored to suggest that he was homosexual. There is no proper report of the case, but a Press Association journalist was present at Drake J's summing up. The journalist reported as follows:

   The judge told the jury that it was 'very debatable' whether it would be defamatory simply to call a man a homosexual. For many years, grown-up males had been permitted to carry on homosexual activities in private. 'If you say someone is a homosexual and do not add that they have done it in circumstances which are illegal, it may not be defamatory,' he said. 'Whether it would make people think the less of them would probably depend on the circumstances.' If the article did call Mr Donovan a liar or a hypocrite, that would clearly be defamatory and would be calculated to lower him in people's estimation. (Press Association Newsfile 2 April 1992).

   Jason Donovan won the case.

3. It is usually thought that an imputation of heresy or an allegation concerning conduct thought inappropriate only within a small group is probably not defamatory unless it carries with it an allegation of hypocrisy. 'Would it be libellous to write of a lady of fashion that she had been seen on the top of an omnibus?' Even when Pollock CB asked this question in *Clay v Roberts* (1863) 8 LT 397 at 398 the answer given was in the negative. But is this fair? Should the law not protect any legitimate reputation, even if it is a reputation within a small group? Most people do not have reputations with the general public, to whom they are entirely unknown. Their reputation is with the few people who know them. Should one see *Byrne v Dean* as a case about reputations within small groups, or as a case about illegitimate reputations, that is reputations the law refuses to protect because, for example, they are reputations for breaking the law itself?

■ Tolley v Fry & Sons Ltd
House of Lords [1931] All ER Rep 131

The claimant was a well-known amateur golfer. The defendants manufactured chocolate. The defendants published in two mass circulation newspapers an advertisement which included a drawing depicting the claimant in his golfing costume accompanied by a caddie. A packet of the defendants' chocolate protruded from the claimant's pocket. Below the drawing was a limerick in the following terms:

'The caddie to Tolley said: "Oh, Sir!
Good shot, Sir! That ball, see it go, Sir.
My word, how it flies,
Like a Cartet of Fry's.
They're handy, they're good, and priced low, Sir." '

The claimant sued for libel, complaining not about the drawing or the limerick in themselves but alleging that the advertisement made it appear that he had agreed to endorse the product for money, something which, as an amateur, he was not supposed to do. The defendant appealed against an award of £1,000 damages, claiming that the judge should not have allowed the case to go to the jury. The Court of Appeal allowed the appeal, but the House of Lords reversed.

LORD DUNEDIN:
The sole question raised by this appeal is whether the case ought to have been withdrawn from the jury by the judge, and judgment entered for the defendants. It has been stated again and again, and is not in dispute, that the question for the judge is whether the writing or publication complained of is capable of a libellous meaning. It is for the jury, if the judge so rules, to say whether it has that meaning.

... I find that the caricature of the plaintiff, innocent itself as a caricature, is so to speak embedded in an advertisement. It is held out as part of an advertisement so that its presence there gives rise to speculation as to how it got there, or in other words provokes in the mind of the public an inference as to how and why the plaintiff's picture, caricatured as it was, became associated with a commercial advertisement. The inference that is suggested is that the consent was given, either gratuitously or for a consideration, to its appearance. Then it is said, and evidence on that point was given and not cross-examined to, that, if that were so, the status of the plaintiff as an amateur golfer would be called in question. It seems to me that all this is within the province of a jury to determine. The idea of the inference in the circumstances is not so extravagant as to compel a judge to say it was so beside the mark that no jury ought to be allowed to consider it.

[LORD HAILSHAM, LORD BUCKMASTER, and LORD TOMLIN delivered speeches in favour of allowing the appeal. LORD BLANESBURGH delivered a speech in favour of dismissing the appeal.]

NOTES

1. See further *Williams v Reason* [1988] 1 All ER 262, [1988] 1 WLR 96, in which an amateur Welsh international rugby player was awarded £20,000 damages for an allegation of 'shamateurism' (although a new trial was then ordered on procedural grounds.)

2. In *Re Elvis Presley Trade Marks* [1999] RPC 567, Robert Walker LJ commented 'It was an essential part of Mr Tolley's case that he was an amateur in days when the distinction between amateur and professional sportsmen was still very important. That brings out one of many paradoxical features of this case, that some celebrities wish to prevent "appropriation of personality" as a means of defending their privacy; others wish to

prevent unauthorised appropriation so as to secure a monopoly of commercial exploitation of their names, images and fame.' The British Code of Advertising Practice evidently managed to cover both extremes: see Frazer (1983) 99 LQR 281 at 282.

Tolley v Fry has been said to be 'the nearest the law of defamation ever came to protecting "privacy" as such' (*Report of the Committee on Privacy*, Cmnd. 5012, 1972, App. 1, para. 5; cf. S. Stoljar (1984) 4 LS 67 at 85).

In the United States, a tort of putting a person in a 'false light' has long been recognised. It is often actionable falsely to attribute to the claimant some opinion or utterance, or to include well-known persons, without their consent, in popularity contests or to use their photograph in books or articles with which they have no connection (see *Restatment of the Law, Second, Torts* §652E). It is also tortious in many US jurisdictions to '[appropriate] to [one's] own use or benefit the name or likeness of another' (see §652C).

For claims in the tort of passing-off in such situations in England, see *McCulloch v Lewis A May (Produce Distributors) Ltd* [1947] 2 All ER 845 and *Irvine v Talksport Ltd* [2002] 2 All ER 414, [2002] EWHC 367 (Ch).

3.   Statutory protection exists, in the Copyright, Designs and Patents Act 1988, s. 80, for the author of a copyright literary, dramatic, musical, or artistic work and for the director of a copyright film not to have his work subjected to 'derogatory treatment'. This is defined to cover the distortion or mutilation of the work or other treatment which is prejudicial to the honour or reputation of the author or director. Section 84 of the Act gives protection against false attribution of authorship (a right which, unlike defamation, survives 20 years after death). There is also the possibility of an action for passing-off (see *Clark v Associated Newspapers Ltd* [1998] 1 All ER 959, [1998] 1 WLR 1558).

■ Lewis v Associated Newspapers Ltd
House of Lords [1963] 2 All ER 151

The Daily Telegraph published a paragraph headed 'Inquiry on firm by City Police' and the Daily Mail one headed 'Fraud Squad probe Firm', the gist of both paragraphs being that the City Fraud Squad was inquiring into the firm's affairs, and identifying the firm and its chairman, Mr Lewis. In actions for libel by Mr Lewis and the firm, the defendants admitted that the words were defamatory in their ordinary meaning, but they said that the meaning was merely that the police were carrying out an inquiry and they sought to justify that this as true. The claimants, however, contended that the ordinary meaning was that they were guilty of, or suspected by the police of, fraud or dishonesty. The trial judge directed the juries so that it was open to them to accept the claimants' contention. From the amounts of damages awarded by them (£25,000 to Mr Lewis and £75,000 to the firm, in the case of the Daily Telegraph, and, the next day, by a different jury £7,000 and £100,000 against the Daily Mail), It was clear that the juries must have done this.

On appeal to the House of Lords, a majority held that the judge's failure to direct the juries whether the words were capable of imputing guilt of fraud as distinct from suspicion was a misdirection sufficient to warrant a new trial.

LORD REID: . . .
The leading case is *Capital and Counties Bank v. George Henty & Sons* [(1882), 7 App. Cas. 741]. In that case Lord Selborne, L.C., said [at p. 745]:

> 'The test according to the authorities is whether, under the circumstances in which the writing was published, reasonable men to whom the publication was made would be likely to understand it in a libellous sense.' . . .

In this case it is, I think, sufficient to put the test in this way. Ordinary men and women have different temperaments and outlooks. Some are unusually suspicious and some are unusually naive. One must try to envisage people between these two extremes and see what is the most damaging meaning that they would put on the words in question. So let me suppose a number of ordinary people discussing one of these paragraphs which they had read in the newspaper. No doubt one of them might say—"Oh, if the fraud squad are after these people you can take it they are guilty". But I would expect the others to turn on him, if he did say that, with such remarks as—"Be fair. This is not a police state. No doubt their affairs are in a mess or the police would not be interested. But that could be because Lewis or the cashier has been very stupid or careless. We really must not jump to conclusions. The police are fair and know their job and we shall know soon enough if there is anything in it. Wait till we see if they charge him. I wouldn't trust him until this is cleared up, but it is another thing to condemn him unheard".

What the ordinary man, not avid for scandal, would read into the words complained of must be a matter of impression. I can only say that I do not think that he would infer guilt of fraud merely because an inquiry is on foot. And if that is so then it is the duty of the trial judge to direct the jury that it is for them to determine the meaning of the paragraph but that they must not hold it to impute guilt of fraud because as a matter of law the paragraph is not capable of having that meaning. . . .

LORD DEVLIN: . . .

If it is said of a man—"I do not believe that he is guilty of fraud but I cannot deny that he has given grounds for suspicion", it seems to me to be wrong to say that in no circumstances can they be justified except by the speaker proving the truth of that which he has expressly said that he did not believe. It must depend on whether the impression conveyed by the speaker is one of frankness or one of insinuation. Equally in my opinion it is wrong to say that, if in truth the person spoken of never gave any cause for suspicion at all, he has no remedy because he was expressly exonerated of fraud. A man's reputation can suffer if it can truly be said of him that although innocent he behaved in a suspicious way; but it will suffer much more if it is said that he is not innocent.

It is not therefore correct to say as a matter of law that a statement of suspicion imputes guilt. It can be said as a matter of practice that it very often does so, because although suspicion of guilt is something different from proof of guilt, it is the broad impression conveyed by the libel that has to be considered and not the meaning of each word under analysis. A man who wants to talk at large about smoke may have to pick his words very carefully, if he wants to exclude the suggestion that there is also a fire; but it can be done. One always gets back to the fundamental question: what is the meaning that the words convey to the ordinary man; a rule cannot be made about that. They can convey a meaning of suspicion short of guilt; but loose talk about suspicion can very easily convey the impression that it is a suspicion that is well founded.

In the libel that the House has to consider there is, however, no mention of suspicion at all. What is said is simply that the plaintiff's affairs are being inquired into. That is defamatory, as is admitted, because a man's reputation may in fact be injured by such a statement even though it is quite consistent with innocence. I daresay that it would not be injured if everybody bore in mind, as they ought to, that no man is guilty until he is proved so, but unfortunately they do not. It can be defamatory without it being necessary to suggest that the words contained a hidden allegation that there were good grounds for inquiry. A statement that a woman has been raped can affect her reputation, although logically it means that she is innocent of any impurity: *Youssoupoff v Metro-Goldwyn-Mayer Pictures Ltd.*[4] So a statement that a man has been acquitted of a crime with which in fact he was never charged might lower his reputation. Logic is not the test. But a statement that an inquiry is on foot may go further and may positively convey the impression that there are grounds for the inquiry, i.e. that there is something to suspect. Just as a bare statement of suspicion may convey the impression that there are grounds for belief in guilt, so a bare statement of the fact of an inquiry may convey the impression that there are grounds for suspicion. I do not say that in this case it does; but I think that the words in their context and in the circumstances of publication are capable of conveying that impression. But can they convey an

---

[4] (1934) 50 TLR 581.

impression of guilt? Let it be supposed, first, that a statement that there is an inquiry conveys an impression of suspicion; and, secondly, that a statement of suspicion conveys an impression of guilt. It does not follow from these two suppositions that a statement that there is an inquiry conveys an impression of guilt. For that, two fences have to be taken instead of one. While, as I have said, I am prepared to accept that the jury could take the first I do not think that in a case like the present, where there is only the bare statement that a police inquiry is being made, it could take the second in the same stride. If the ordinary sensible man was capable of thinking that wherever there was a police inquiry there was guilt, it would be almost impossible to give accurate information about anything: but in my opinion he is not. I agree with the view of the Court of Appeal.

There is on this branch of the case a final point to be considered. It is undoubtedly the law that the judge should not leave the question "libel or no libel" to the jury unless the words are reasonably capable of a defamatory meaning. But if several defamatory meanings are pleaded or suggested, can the judge direct the jury that the words are capable of one meaning but not of another? The point is important here, because the defendants admit that the words are defamatory in one sense but dispute that they are defamatory in the senses pleaded in the statements of claim, and contend that the judge should have so directed the jury. Both counsel for the appellants appear at one time to have argued in the Court of Appeal that the function of the judge was exhausted when he ruled that the words were capable of being defamatory; and that it was not for him to inquire whether they were or were not capable of any particular defamatory meaning. But later they abandoned the point; and, therefore, did not initiate the discussion of it here. Nevertheless there was considerable discussion of it, because some of your lordships at one time felt that it was a point which ought to be considered. In the result I think that all your lordships are now clearly of the opinion that the judge must rule whether the words are capable of bearing each of the defamatory meanings, if there be more than one, put forward by the plaintiff. This supports indirectly my view on the desirability of pleading different meanings. If the plaintiff can get before the jury only those meanings which the judge rules as capable of being defamatory, there is good reason for having the meanings alleged set out precisely as part of the record.

For the reasons that I have given earlier, I agree that there must be a new trial on the ground of misdirection: but I should in any event have considered that there should be a new trial on the issue of damages as they are, in my opinion, ridiculously out of proportion to the injury suffered.

[LORD TUCKER agreed with LORD REID. LORD HODSON delivered a speech in favour of dismissing the appeal. LORD MORRIS OF BORTH-Y-GEST delivered a speech in favour of allowing the appeal, on the ground that the judge's direction to the jury was adequate in terms of the test proposed.]

NOTES

1. It is crucial to grasp the interconnection between the issue of what meanings the words are capable of bearing and the defence of justification or truth (see p. 984, post). If the court rules that the words are not capable of bearing a meaning the defence can justify, the defence will fail and the trial will proceed on the basis of the other meanings. But it will still be up to the jury to decide whether the words did bear a defamatory meaning on the occasion in question. The job of the court is to delimit the range of meanings and to rule out meanings outside the range (see eg *Mapp v News Group Newspapers Ltd* [1998] QB 520).

2. In *Skuse v Granada Television Ltd* [1996] EMLR 278 Sir Thomas Bingham MR, quoting Neill LJ in the unreported case *Hartt v Newspaper Publishing plc*, extracted from the various views in *Lewis* a now frequently cited formulation: that the court 'should give to the material complained of the natural and ordinary meaning which it would have conveyed to the ordinary reasonable reader ... [and that] the hypothetical reasonable reader ... is not unduly naïve but he is not unduly suspicious. He can read between the lines. He can read in an implication more readily than a lawyer, and may indulge in

a certain amount of loose thinking. But that he must be treated as being a man who is not avid for scandal and someone who does not ... select one bad meaning where other non-defamatory meanings are available.'

3. *Lewis* also establishes that different meanings only give rise to separate causes of action where there is a 'true innuendo', that is, where a defamatory meaning can only be extracted by people with special knowledge. This contrasts with 'false' or 'popular' innuendo, which is simply a possible meaning of or inference from the words themselves. Where a claimant relies on a 'true' innuendo meaning he must plead and prove that the words were published to specific persons and that they knew of specific facts which would enable them to understand the words in the innuendo meaning: *Fullam v Newcastle Chronicle and Journal Ltd* [1977] 3 All ER 32, [1977] 1 WLR 651. Moreover, since the cause of action arises as soon as the words complained of are published, any extrinsic facts relied on to support an innuendo have to be known at the time of publication by the person to whom the words were published. Inferences put on the words complained of as a result of facts coming to light after publication cannot make the words defamatory: *Grappelli v Derek Block (Holdings) Ltd* [1981] 2 All ER 272, [1981] 1 WLR 822; cf. *Hayward v Thompson* [1982] QB 47, [1981] 3 All ER 450. But there is no limitation in true innuendo that the article has to contain a 'pointer' to the claimant. It is sufficient that those with the special knowledge would reasonably understand the words as defaming the claimant (see *Morgans v Odhams Press Ltd* [1971] 2 All ER 1156, [1971] 1 WLR 1239).

4. Fox's Libel Act 1792 made the question of 'libel or no libel' essentially one for the jury. Although the Act applied to criminal proceedings only, it has been regarded as declaratory of the common law. The judge must, however, be satisfied that there is sufficient evidence to go to the jury, i.e. the statement must be 'capable' of the meaning alleged. If it is not, it must be withdrawn from the jury. Section 7 of the Defamation Act 1996 makes clear that the question is always whether the words are 'capable' of the meaning concerned, not merely 'arguably capable'.

5. At least in the absence of a true innuendo, judges ultimately ask juries to decide what the words 'meant' on the basis that only one meaning is the right one (see Diplock LJ in *Slim v Daily Telegraph Ltd* [1968] 1 All ER 497 at 504–505), an extraordinarily unrealistic assumption both as a matter of linguistic and philosophical theory and as a matter of everyday experience. Studied ambiguity, irony, and offering deliberately contradictory messages are the stock-in-trade of literature, journalism, and political rhetoric. It might be better to adopt the view that 'libel [should not be] a question of majority vote' per Holmes J in *Peck v Chicago Tribune* (1909) 214 US 185, so that the jury should be asked not what the words 'really' meant, but whether they would have been understood in the defamatory sense by a substantial proportion of the population, reasonable or otherwise. In *Charleston v News Group Newspapers Ltd* [1995] 2 AC 65, [1995] 2 All ER 313, however, the House of Lords insisted on the 'one meaning' approach to deny a remedy to victims of a spoof newspaper article in which the defamatory effect of the sensational headline, photograph, and picture caption were offset by the rather mundane text. There could be only one 'ordinary, reasonable reader' and thus only one 'meaning' of such an article. The argument that it is reasonable to read newspapers in different ways (including skimming headlines and pictures while ignoring the text) gave way to the doctrine that in such 'bane and antidote' cases, the defendant is entitled to have the material considered as a whole.

But for the relationship between the 'single meaning rule' and qualified privilege cf. *Bonnick v Morris* [2003] 1 AC 300, [2002] UKPC 31 noted p. 1005, post.

■ E Hulton & Co v Jones

House of Lords [1908–10] All ER Rep 29

The claimant, Thomas Artemus Jones, a barrister, brought an action for libel against the publishers of the Sunday Chronicle newspaper. The libel was said to be contained in an article purportedly describing a motor festival in Dieppe. The material parts were as follows: '"Whist! there is Artemus Jones with a woman who is not his wife, who must be—you know—the other thing!" whispers a fair neighbour of mine, into her bosom friend's ear. "Really; is it not surprising how certain of our fellow countrymen behave when they come abroad? Would you suppose by his goings-on, that he was a churchwarden at Peckham." No one, indeed, would assume that Jones in the atmosphere of London would take on so austere a job as the duties of a churchwarden. Here, in the atmosphere of Dieppe, on the French side of the Channel, he is the life and soul of a gay little band that haunts the Casino and turns night into day, besides betraying a most unholy delight in the society of female butterflies.'

The evidence of the writer of the article and the editor of the paper, which was that they knew nothing of the claimant, and that the article was not intended by them to refer to him, was accepted as true. At the trial, witnesses were called for the claimant, who said that they had read the article and thought that it referred to the claimant. The jury returned a verdict for the claimant with £1,750 damages, and Channell J gave judgment for the claimant. The defendants appealed unsuccessfully to the Court of Appeal (Fletcher Moulton LJ dissenting). On further appeal to the House of Lords:

LORD SHAW: . . .

In the publication of matter of a libellous character—that is, matter which would be libellous if applying to an actual person—the responsibility is as follows. In the first place, there is responsibility for the words used being taken to signify that which readers would reasonably understand by them; in the second place, there is responsibility also for the names used being taken to signify those whom the readers would reasonably understand by those names; and, in the third place, the same principle is applicable to persons unnamed, but sufficiently indicated by designation or description. I demur to the observation so frequently made in the argument that these principles are novel. Sufficient expression is given to the same principles by Abbott CJ in *Bourke v Warren*, in which that learned judge said ((1826) 2 C & P 307 at pp 309, 310):

> 'The question for your consideration is, whether you think that the libel designates the plaintiff in such a way as to let those who knew him understand that he was the person meant? It is not necessary that all the world should understand the libel; it is sufficient if those who know the plaintiff can make out that he is the person meant.'

I think that it is out of the question to suggest that that means "meant in the mind of the writer" or of the publisher: it must mean "meant by the words employed". . . .

[LORD LOREBURN LC (with whom LORD ATKINSON and LORD GORRELL concurred) delivered a speech in favour of dismissing the appeal.]

Appeal dismissed.

NOTES

1. *Salmond & Heuston*, p. 144, n. 63 claim that '[t]here is evidence that the [jury's] decision may have been based on the recklessness or even spite of the defendants. . . . The plaintiff had been a contributor to the defendants' paper for twelve years and his name was well known in their office, although not to the actual writer of the article. The

managing director admitted in cross-examination that he had read the article in proof and thought at first reading that it referred to the plaintiff.'

2. In dissent, Fletcher Moulton LJ had argued vigorously against strict liability: [1908–10] All ER Rep 29, [1909] 2 KB 444. He lamented ([1909] 2 KB 444 at 471 and 472):

The learned judge directs that it is immaterial whether the defendant intended the words to refer to the plaintiff or not, and that if persons who know of the existence of the plaintiff might reasonably think they referred to him, the plaintiff is entitled to succeed. He holds that you may accidentally libel a man of whose very existence you do not know. In my opinion, an unintentional libel in this sense is as impossible in English law as an honest fraud. . . . [E]ven the harmless domestic announcement that Mrs. A. B. had just had a baby might make a man liable to a grave charge of having accused a person of want of chastity if readers are at liberty from the similarity of name to apply it to a lady who was at the time a widow. It would indeed be a calamity if our English law of defamation burdened ordinary speech or writing with such a chaos of responsibilities.

3. But such responsibilities have been imposed: cf. *Newstead v London Express Newspaper Ltd* [1940] 1 KB 322, [1939] 4 All ER 319, in which the defendant newspaper published an account of the trial for bigamy of 'Harold Newstead, thirty-year old Camberwell man'. Unfortunately, there were two men of that name and age in Camberwell, and the other Harold Newstead sued the newspaper for libel. The judge instructed the jury that the question was, 'Would reasonable persons understand the words complained of to refer to the plaintiff?' The Court of Appeal dismissed the defendant's appeal, Sir Wilfred Greene MR commenting that 'If there is a risk of coincidence, it ought, I think, in reason to be borne, not by the innocent party to whom the words are held to refer, but by the party who puts them into circulation.'

The Faulks Committee, para. 123, thought that the principle in *Hulton v Jones* should stand. Lord Denning, however, in *What Next in the Law?* (London, 1982), p. 213 commented: 'I would like to see the House of Lords take *Hulton v Jones* by the scruff of the neck and throw it out of the courts, and start afresh.' Does the 'amends' defence in the 1996 Act (p. 1011, post) achieve a compromise between these two views?

4. The Human Rights Act 1998 may now have mitigated the stringency of *Hulton v Jones*. In *O'Shea v MGN Ltd* [2001] EMLR 40 a photograph used to advertise a pornographic website was alleged to bear such a strong resemblance to the claimant ('a respectable young woman') that members of her family had believed the image to be hers. Morland J held, striking the claim out, that strict liability would in the circumstances amount to 'an unjustifiable interference with the vital right of freedom of expression disproportionate to the legitimate aim of protecting the reputations of "look-alikes" and contrary to Article 10 of the [ECHR]'. 'It would impose an impossible burden on a publisher if he were required to check if the true picture of someone resembled someone else who because of the context of the picture was defamed. . . . Whereas theoretically the existence of the real Artemus Jones and the second Harold Newstead, a 30-year-old Camberwell man, could have been discovered, it would be impossible to discover whether a "look-alike" or "spit and image" of the photograph of a real person existed': see [33]–[34].

5. 'All lawyers are thieves' (an example given in *Eastwood v Holmes* (1858) 1 F & F 347 at 349) is group defamation and not actionable. 'The reason why a libel published of a large or indeterminate number of persons described by some general name generally fails to be actionable is the difficulty of establishing that the plaintiff was in fact included in the defamatory statement. . . .' (per Lord Atkin in *Knupffer v London Express Newspaper Ltd* [1944] 1 All ER 495 at 498). Whether or not the claimant succeeds will depend upon

'the size of the class, the generality of the charge and the extravagance of the accusation' (per Lord Porter at p. 499).

QUESTION

Does it make any difference in defamation to place a notice at the start of a film or in the preface of a book to the effect that 'All the characters in this book are fictitious. Any resemblance between them and real persons, living or dead, is purely coincidental'?

3 THE DISTINCTION BETWEEN DEFAMATION AND MALICIOUS FALSEHOODS

■ Joyce v Sengupta
Court of Appeal [1993] 1 All ER 897

The defendants, a newspaper and a journalist, published an article which falsely accused the plaintiff of having stolen letters from her former employer, the Princess Royal. Legal aid was not available for defamation, but was available for the different tort, malicious falsehood. The plaintiff therefore framed a claim in malicious falsehood but not in defamation. The judge struck out the claim because it was essentially a claim for libel and should have been framed as such. The plaintiff appealed successfully to the Court of Appeal.

SIR DONALD NICHOLLS V-C: . . .
Before turning to the issues raised by the appeal I should comment briefly on the difference between defamation and malicious falsehood. The remedy provided by the law for words which injure a person's reputation is defamation. Words may also injure a person without damaging his reputation. An example would be a claim that the seller of goods or land is not the true owner. Another example would be a false assertion that a person has closed down his business. Such claims would not necessarily damage the reputation of those concerned. The remedy provided for this is malicious falsehood, sometimes called injurious falsehood or trade libel. This cause of action embraces particular types of malicious falsehood such as slander of title and slander of goods, but it is not confined to those headings.

Falsity is an essential ingredient of this tort. The plaintiff must establish the untruth of the statement of which he complains. Malice is another essential ingredient. A genuine dispute about the ownership of goods or land should not of itself be actionable. So a person who acted in good faith is not liable. Further, since the object of this cause of action is to provide a person with a remedy for a false statement made maliciously which has caused him damage, at common law proof of financial loss was another essential ingredient. The rigour of this requirement was relaxed by statute. I shall have to refer to the question of damages at a later stage. For present purposes it is sufficient to note that if a plaintiff establishes that the defendant maliciously made a false statement which has caused him financial damage, or in respect of which he is relieved from proving damage by the Defamation Act 1952, the law gives him a remedy. The false statement may also be defamatory, or it may not. As already mentioned, it need not be defamatory. Conversely, the fact that the statement is defamatory does not exclude a cause of action for malicious falsehood although the law will ensure that a plaintiff does not recover damages twice over for the same loss. . . .

NOTE

'A bona fide assertion of title, however mistaken, if made for the protection of one's own interest or for some other proper purpose, is not malicious,' (*Balden v Shorter* [1932] Ch 427 at 430 per Maugham J). 'Malice' in malicious falsehood is often taken to mean a belief that the statement was false or recklessness as to its truth. But in *Balden v Shorter* Maugham J also says that lack of belief in the truth of the statement is evidence of malice, rather than malice itself. Malice itself is 'having some dishonest or otherwise improper motive'.

■ White v Mellin

House of Lords [1895] AC 154

The defendant sold the plaintiff's 'Infants' Food', affixing to plaintiff's wrappers a label stating that defendant's own 'food for infants and invalids' was far more nutritious and healthful than any other. It was not proved that this statement was untrue or had caused any damage to the plaintiff. Romer J dismissed an action for an injunction restraining publication and for damages. The Court of Appeal reversed this judgment. On appeal to the House of Lords:

LORD HERSCHELL LC: . . .

If an action will not lie because a man says that his goods are better than his neighbour's, it seems to me impossible to say that it will lie because he says that they are better in this or that or the other respect. Just consider what a door would be opened if this were permitted. That this sort of puffing advertisement is in use is notorious; and we see rival cures advertised for particular ailments. The Court would then be bound to inquire, in an action brought, whether this ointment or this pill better cured the disease which it was alleged to cure—whether a particular article of food was in this respect or that better than another. Indeed, the courts of law would be turned into a machinery for advertising rival productions by obtaining a judicial determination which of the two was the better. . . .

LORD WATSON: . . .

In the first place, I do not think the representation conveyed by the defendant's label is, in any legal sense, a representation of and concerning the infants' food of the plaintiff. It is a highly coloured laudation of Dr Vance's food and nothing else. It makes no reference to the plaintiff's goods beyond what might be implied in the case of every kind of food which is recommended and sold as being suitable for consumption by infant children. Nor, in my opinion, is the circumstance that the label was sometimes put upon the plaintiff's wrappers, however distressing it might be to him, sufficient to convert it into a disparagement of the contents of the wrapper. An advertisement in the window of a bootmaker, to the effect that he makes the best boots in the world, may be more offensive to his next neighbour in the same trade than to a bootmaker at a distance; but the disparagement in kind and degree is identical in both cases.

[LORD MORRIS concurred. LORD MACNAGHTEN and LORD SHAND delivered speeches in favour of allowing the appeal.]

Appeal allowed.

NOTES

1. In *Ciba-Geigy plc v Parke Davis & Co Ltd* [1994] FSR 8 Aldous J distinguished between comparative advertising, in which the defendant seeks to persuade readers that its product is as good as the claimant's product, and knocking advertising, in which the

defendant seeks to persuade readers that the claimant's product is a bad product. The former is perfectly proper, the latter not. If an advertisement seeks to persuade that one product is better than another, it does not necessarily mean that the other product is a bad product.

2. In *Schulke & Mayr UK Ltd v Alkapharm UK Ltd* [1999] FSR 161 Jacob J refused to allow an action to proceed on the basis merely that the defendant had made false statements in praise of his own goods 'without just cause or excuse', which threatened the claimant's sales of a rival product. Jacob J said that *White v Mellin* stood for the proposition that there had to be 'disparagement' in the sense of disparaging and untrue representations about the claimant or the claimant's goods. In *DSG Retail Ltd v Comet Group Plc* [2002] EWHC 116 (QB) however, Owen J held that where the defendant asserted that its prices were lower than the claimant's, this was disparagement of the claimant's goods or services (and therefore actionable if false and made maliciously).

3. In *De Beers Abrasive Products Ltd v International General Electric Co of New York Ltd* [1975] 2 All ER 599, [1975] 2 WLR 972, after a review of the authorities, Walton J suggested that where a trader chooses to denigrate the goods of a rival, the test to be applied is whether a reasonable man would take the claim being made as a serious claim or not. One indication that the disparagement is intended to be taken seriously could be a claim that the rival's goods had been subjected to a proper scientific test. The claimant must also prove 'malice'.

4. Comparative advertising may often make use of a competitor's trade mark. A defence to trade mark infringement is available when it a mark is used to identify the product of the competitor, unless 'otherwise than in accordance with honest practices in industrial or commercial matters' the use 'takes unfair advantage of, or is detrimental to, the distinctive character or repute of the trade mark': Trade Marks Act 1994, s. 10(6). See also Control of Misleading Advertisements Regulations 1988 (as amended: Control of Misleading Advertisements (Amendment) Regulations 2000), implementing EU harmonisation directives on the subject. A detailed consideration of trade mark law would be out of place here: see e.g. W.R. Cornish and D. Llewellyn, *Intellectual Property* 6th edn (London, 2007). However note that in *Boehringer Ingelheim Ltd v Vetplus Ltd* [2007] EWCA Civ 583 it was held that the *Bonnard v Perryman* rule on interlocutory injunctions in libel and malicious falsehood (see *Greene v Associated Newspapers Ltd* [2005] 1 All ER 30, [2004] EWCA Civ 1462, p. 1024, post) does not apply to a trade mark infringement (or passing-off) claim in a comparative advertising case.

5. The *Code of Advertising* (etc.), under the supervision of the Advertising Standards Authority (11th edn, 2003), says that comparative advertising is permissible 'in the interests of vigorous competition and public information' provided it is not likely to mislead (s. 18.1). Comparative claims must 'objectively compare one or more material, relevant, verifiable and representative features' of the products (s. 18.3). Other kinds of comparisons must be 'clear and fair' and 'not be selected in a way that gives the marketers an artificial advantage' (s. 19.1). Comparative claims must not 'discredit or denigrate' competitors' products or trade marks, and no marketing communications should 'unfairly attack or discredit businesses or their products' (s. 20.1). A complaint to the Code of Advertising Practice Committee may often succeed where a claim for malicious falsehood would have little prospect of success.

4 PUBLICATION

■ Theaker v Richardson
Court of Appeal [1962] 1 All ER 229

The defendant wrote a defamatory letter to the plaintiff, a fellow member of the local district council. The letter was placed in a sealed manilla envelope similar to the kind used for distributing election addresses. The envelope was addressed to the plaintiff. The plaintiff's husband, seeing the envelope on the mat, opened it thinking it was an election address. The jury found that it was a natural and probable consequence of the defendant's writing and delivery of the letter that the plaintiff's husband would open and read it.

PEARSON LJ: . . .

The question arising can be put in this form. The plaintiff's husband, acting carelessly and thoughtlessly but meaning no harm, picked up and opened and began to read the letter. Was his conduct something unusual, out of the ordinary and not reasonably to be anticipated, or was it something which could quite easily and naturally happen in the ordinary course of events? In my judgment that is a fair formulation of the question, and, when so formulated, it is seen to be a question of fact which in a trial with a jury can and should be left to and decided by the jury, who have observed the witnesses giving evidence and have and are expected to use their own common sense and general knowledge of the world and perhaps some particular knowledge (if they have it) of the locality concerned and the ways of its inhabitants. In my judgment, it would not be right to substitute the opinion of this court for the opinion of the jury on such a question arising in the course of a trial with a jury . . . .

[HARMAN LJ delivered a judgment in favour of dismissing the appeal. ORMEROD LJ delivered a judgment in favour of allowing the appeal.]

Appeal dismissed.

QUESTION

A writes a defamatory statement and locks it in his desk. A thief steals it and makes its contents known. Is there publication by A? (The example is given in *Pullman v Walter Hill & Co* [1891] 1 QB 524 at 527.)

NOTES

1. In *Huth v Huth* [1915] 3 KB 32, [1914–15] All ER Rep 242 the defendant sent a letter to his wife in an unsealed envelope suggesting that they were not married and that their children were illegitimate. The wife could not sue her husband in tort (but see now the Law Reform (Husband and Wife) Act 1962, s. 1). To circumvent this, his children brought an action for libel. To prove publication the family butler was called to give evidence that he had looked at the contents of the envelope before placing it on the breakfast table. The Court of Appeal, upholding the judge, decided that there was no publication to the butler because it was no part of his duties to read mail addressed to his employers, whether the envelope was sealed or not. There was also no argument based on publication to the Post Office. Although the courts will assume that postcards

are read by postal workers, they do not presume that postal workers habitually open envelopes, even unsealed ones.

2.   Dictation by managers to their secretaries is a publication and unless the communication is protected by some defence such as qualified privilege managers will be liable and so will their employer on the principle of vicarious liability (*Riddick v Thames Board Mills Ltd* [1977] QB 881 per Waller LJ at 906–907 and Stephenson LJ at p. 900; cf. Lord Denning MR, at 893–894, who resuscitated the doctrine of common employment (p. 1102, post).

3.   The law relating to responsibility for the republication by other people of defamatory statements was described by Stocker LJ in *Slipper v BBC* [1991] 1 QB 283, [1991] 1 All ER 165 as 'but an example of the rules of *novus actus interveniens*' (on which see pp. 388 et seq, ante). In *McManus v Beckham* [2002] 4 All ER 497, [2002] EWCA Civ 939 the court held that the test was whether there was a 'significant risk' of republication (or per Laws LJ, whether the defendant should have foreseen that 'further publication would probably take place' at [43]). Merely asking the jury whether republication was 'reasonably foreseeable' would lead to liability that was too wide. Laws LJ emphasised the 'value-laden' rather than 'factual' nature of all inquiries about causation and remoteness. He commented that the *novus actus interveniens* approach was misleading insofar as it suggested a 'decisive objective test of causation' if only the court looked 'hard enough and long enough' (at [38]–[39] referring to his own judgment in *Rahman v Arearose Ltd* [2001] QB 351, noted p. 387, ante).

■ Bunt v Tilley

Queen's Bench Division [2006] 3 All ER 336

The claimant alleged that defamatory statements had been posted by the first to third defendants, on websites provided by the fourth to sixth defendant internet service providers (ISPs). The ISPs successfully argued that the claims against them should be struck out, since they were not the publishers of the statements at common law.

EADY J: . . .

[9] When considering the internet, it is so often necessary to resort to analogies which, in the nature of things, are unlikely to be complete. That is because the internet is a new phenomenon. Nevertheless, an analogy has been drawn in this case with the postal services. That is to say, ISPs do not participate in the process of publication as such, but merely act as facilitators in a similar way to the postal services. They provide a means of transmitting communications without in any way participating in that process.

[15] Publication is a question of fact, and it must depend on the circumstances of each case whether or not publication has taken place: see eg *Byrne v Deane* [1937] 2 All ER 204 at 212, [1937] 1 KB 818 at 837–838 per Greene LJ. . . . As Dr Collins observes [in *The Law of Defamation and the Internet* (2nd edn, 2005)] (p 201 (para 15.43)):

'Mere conduit intermediaries who carry particular Internet communications from one computer to another . . . are analogous to postal services and telephone carriers in the sense that they facilitate communications, without playing any part in the creation or preparation of their content, and almost always without actual knowledge of the content.'

Such an approach would tend to suggest that at common law such intermediaries should not be regarded as responsible for publication. . . .

[23] Of course, to be liable for a defamatory publication it is not always necessary to be aware of the defamatory content, still less of its legal significance. Editors and publishers are often fixed with responsibility notwithstanding such lack of knowledge. On the other hand, for a person to be held responsible there must be knowing involvement in the process of publication of *the relevant words*. It is not enough that a person merely plays a passive instrumental role in the process. . . .

[24] . . . A submission was made to me that public policy requires that an ISP who merely facilitates internet publications *should* not be held responsible as a 'publisher', and that it would be desirable for ISPs to be protected in the same way that statutory immunity has been provided for, in respect of all proceedings in tort, by the Postal Services Act 2000. I am concerned here not with questions of public policy so much as whether or not any of the relevant defendants in this case could be said to have been liable for publication in accordance with established common law principles. Nonetheless, in seeking to determine that question, I should have regard to the European Convention for the Protection of Human Rights and Fundamental Freedoms 1950 (as set out in Sch 1 to the Human Rights Act 1998) and relevant Strasbourg jurisprudence, especially that relating to arts 8 and 10.

[37] I would not, in the absence of any binding authority, attribute liability at common law to a telephone company or other passive medium of communication, such as an ISP. It is not analogous to someone in the position of a distributor, who might at common law need to prove the absence of negligence: see *Gatley on Libel and Slander* (10th edn, 2004) pp 157–159 (para 6–18). There a defence is needed because the person is regarded as having 'published'. By contrast, persons who truly fulfil no more than the role of a passive medium for communication cannot be characterised as publishers: thus they do not need a defence.

■ The Defamation Act 1996

1. Responsibility for publication.—(1) In defamation proceedings a person has a defence if he shows that—

(a) he was not the author, editor or publisher of the statement complained of

(b) he took reasonable care in relation to its publication, and

(c) he did not know, and had no reason to believe, that what he did caused or contributed to the publication of a defamatory statement.

(2) For this purpose "author", "editor" and "publisher" have the following meanings, which are further explained in subsection (3)—

"author" means the originator of the statement, but does not include a person who did not intend that his statement be published at all;

"editor" means a person having editorial or equivalent responsibility for the content of the statement or the decision to publish it; and

"publisher" means a commercial publisher, that is, a person whose business is issuing material to the public, or a section of the public, who issues material containing the statement in the course of that business.

(3) A person shall not be considered the author, editor or publisher of a statement if he is only involved—

(a) in printing, producing, distributing or selling printed material containing the statement;

(b) in processing, making copies of, distributing, exhibiting or selling a film or sound recording (as defined in Part I of the Copyright, Designs and Patents Act 1988) containing the statement;

(c) in processing, making copies of, distributing or selling any electronic medium in or on which the statement is recorded, or in operating or providing any equipment, system or service by means of which the statement is retrieved, copied, distributed or made available in electronic form;

(d) as the broadcaster of a live programme containing the statement in circumstances in which he has no effective control over the maker of the statement;

(e) as the operator of or provider of access to a communications system by means of which the state-ment is transmitted, or made available, by a person over whom he has no effective control.

In a case not within paragraphs (a) to (e) the court may have regard to those provisions by way of ana-logy in deciding whether a person is to be considered the author, editor or publisher of a statement.

(4) Employees or agents of an author, editor or publisher are in the same position as their employer or principal to the extent that they are responsible for the content of the statement or the decision to publish it.

(5) In determining for the purposes of this section whether a person took reasonable care, or had reason to believe that what he did caused or contributed to the publication of a defamatory statement, regard shall be had to—

(a) the extent of his responsibility for the content of the statement or the decision to publish it,
(b) the nature or circumstances of the publication, and
(c) the previous conduct or character of the author, editor or publisher. . . .

■ Godfrey v Demon Internet Limited
Queen's Bench Division [1999] 4 All ER 342

An unknown malefactor sent an obscene message to an internet usenet newsgroup purport-ing to come from Dr Godfrey, thus defaming him. The defendant was an internet service provider which carried the relevant newsgroup. Dr Godfrey faxed the defendants, telling them that the message was a forgery and asking them to remove it. The defendant failed to remove the message. Dr Godfrey claimed damages for libel from the defendant from the time he told it the notice was defamatory.

MORLAND J: . . .
The plaintiff . . . seeks to strike out parts of the defence as disclosing no sustainable defence. In short, the defendants' contention is that they were not at common law the publishers of the Internet post-ing defamatory of the plaintiff and that even if they were there is material upon which they can avail themselves of the defence provided by s 1 of the Defamation Act 1996, 'a modern equivalent of the common law defence of innocent dissemination' (see 571 HL Official Report (5th series) col 214 (1996) per Lord Mackay LC). . . .

[His Lordship recited s. 1 of the 1996 Act (ante), remarking in passing that the three requirements of s. 1(1) are for the claimant to show.]

In my judgment the defendant was clearly not the publisher of the posting defamatory of the plaintiff within the meaning of section 1(2) and 1(3) and incontrovertibly can avail themselves of section 1(1)(a).

However the difficulty facing the Defendants is section 1(1)(b) and 1(1)(c). After 17 January 1997 after receipt of the plaintiff's fax the defendant knew of the defamatory posting but chose not to remove it from its Usenet news servers. In my judgment this places the defendant in an insuperable difficulty so that they cannot avail themselves of the defence provided by s 1

NOTES

1. See further the Electronic Commerce (EC Directive) Regulations 2002, implementing Directive 2000/31/EC, which harmonises the position of ISPs in different states of the EU. The Regulations provide defences for ISPs which passively transmit information (reg. 17), or store information (in a web cache, etc) without actual knowledge of its content (regs. 18, 19 and 22).

2. *Bunt v Tilley* makes the statutory defences in the 1996 Act and the 2002 Regulations less important (although Eady J proceeded to consider the legislation 'for the sake of completeness' at [38] et seq).

3. In *Godfrey*, Morland J held that Demon Internet had been a publisher at common law (and thus could only escape liability if it could bring itself within the Defamation Act 1996 defence, the 2002 Regulations not then being in force). He drew an analogy with cases holding a bookseller or lending library liable for publishing a defamatory book. Eady J in *Bunt v Tilley* distinguished *Godfrey* as a case where the ISP 'was not merely a passive owner of an electronic device through which postings were transmitted. It had actively chosen to receive and store the newsgroup exchanges containing the posting, and it could be accessed by its subscribers. It was within its power to obliterate the posting, as indeed later happened,' at [12]. Thus, *Godfrey* had left open for decision a situation where 'an ISP had truly fulfilled no more than a passive role as owner of an electronic device through which defamatory postings were transmitted,' at [14].

4. *Bunt v Tilley* aligns English law with the position in the USA: see e.g. *Lunney v Prodigy Services* [1998] AD 2d 230. In *Godfrey*, Morland J had distinguished the US case law thus: 'The impact of the First Amendment has resulted in a substantial divergence of approach between American and English defamation law.' It may be that the Human Rights Act 1998 has been responsible for the subsequent liberalisation in England, although in *Bunt v Tilley* (apart from the reference in passing at [24]) Eady J placed no obvious reliance on the ECHR or the Strasbourg jurisprudence.

■ The Defamation Act 1952

11 An agreement for indemnifying any person against civil liability for libel in respect of the publication of any matter shall not be unlawful unless at the time of the publication that person knows that the matter is defamatory, and does not reasonably believe there is a good defence to any action brought upon it.

NOTE

Publishers and printers usually protect themselves against the publication doctrine by an indemnity clause in the contract with the author. The following is a specimen clause:

The author warrants to the Publishers that the Work will in no way whatever be a violation of any existing copyright and that it will contain nothing of a libellous or scandalous character.

Section 11 means that such a clause is valid only if the defamation is unintentional on the part of the publishing company. Otherwise it is invalid on the basis that people should not benefit from their own wrong (see *Gardner v Moore* [1984] AC 548, [1984] 1 All ER 1100).

Insurance policies are also covered by s. 11. Intentional defamation cannot be insured against. A specimen insurance policy provides:

The insured shall at all times exercise diligence, care and restraint in an endeavour to avoid the printed publication of matter which would reasonably be expected to cause offence such as to incur a complaint or legal proceedings which would give rise to a claim under this Policy.

It is usual for the insured to bear some portion of the loss (e.g. the first ten per cent). A usual condition is that the insurer is to have full control of the defence of any claim for indemnity or damages and full discretion in the conduct of any negotiations or settlement proceedings. (Clauses reproduced from specimen policy of Guardian Royal Exchange Assurance. GREA ceased to be an insure, when the relevent businesses were consolidated with AXA, following AXA's acquisition of GREA in 1999. We are grateful to AXA for continued permission to use the historic clauses).

5 DEFENCES

(a) Justification

■ The Defamation Act 1952

5 Justification.—In an action for libel or slander in respect of words containing two or more distinct charges against the plaintiff, a defence of justification shall not fail by reason only that the truth of every charge is not proved if the words not proved to be true do not materially injure the plaintiff's reputation having regard to the truth of the remaining charges.

■ The Civil Evidence Act 1968

13 Conclusiveness of convictions for purposes of defamation actions.—(1) In an action for libel or slander in which the question whether [the claimant] did or did not commit a criminal offence is relevant to an issue arising in the action, proof that, at the time when that issue falls to be determined, [he] stands convicted of that offence shall be conclusive evidence that he committed that offence; and his conviction thereof shall be admissible in evidence accordingly.

NOTES

1. The defendant must 'justify' (i.e. *prove the truth of*) the 'sting' of the libel: '[I]t is sufficient if the substance of the libellous statement be justified . . . As much must be justified as meets the sting of the charge, and if anything be contained in a charge which does not add to the sting of it, that need not be justified' (*Edwards v Bell* (1824) 1 Bing 403 at 409, per Burrough J). The defendant cannot protect himself with a statement like: 'There is a rumour that . . .'. He must prove that the rumour is true: *Truth (NZ) Ltd v Holloway* [1960] 1 WLR 997 at 1002. This 'repetition rule' remains unaffected by the Human Rights Act for the defence of justification, but for the 'reportage' defence, an aspect of qualified privilege (and its relation to the repetition rule) see *Roberts v Gable* [2007] EWCA Civ 721, noted at p. 1010, post.

2. In *Turcu v News Group Newspapers* [2005] EWHC 799 (QB) Eady J stated at [109] that a defamatory allegation need only be proved 'on a balance of probabilities, to be substantially true. The court should not be too literal in its approach or insist upon proof of every detail where it is not essential to the sting of the article.' His Lordship also observed at [108] that: 'It is necessary to remember what has been said more than once in the European Court of Human Rights to the effect that journalists, in the exercise of their rights to freedom of expression, need to be permitted a degree of exaggeration even in the context of factual assertions.' If the substance of the libel could be justified it was 'no part of the court's function to penalise a defendant for sloppy journalism—still less for tastelessness of style,' at [111].

3. '[S]uppose a publication stated truthfully that the plaintiff was a murderer, but falsely that he had a conviction for speeding. It would be open to the plaintiff under the present law to ignore the very grave true allegation and to bring a libel action only on the trivial and false one. Although it is likely that a tribunal of fact would award no more

than contemptuous damages for the latter allegation in such circumstances, the plaintiff would be entitled technically to succeed' (Faulks Committee, para. 132).

However, the claimant is not entirely free to pick and choose those matters which he believes the defendant will be unable to justify. He can do so only when the two libels are severable and distinct. In *Polly Peck (Holdings) plc v Trelford* [1986] QB 1000, [1986] 2 All ER 84, the Court of Appeal held that when several defamatory statements have a 'common sting', then the defendant is entitled to justify that sting and it is fortuitous if some or all of the facts so pleaded are culled from parts of the publication of which the claimant has chosen not to complain. This does not mean that the defendant can plead as justification various suspicious matters without making it clear what meaning of the defamatory words he is seeking to justify. In *Lucas-Box v News Group Newspapers Ltd* [1986] 1 All ER 177, [1986] 1 WLR 147 the Court of Appeal held that the defendant must make clear in his pleadings the fact situation which he says justifies his words. The jury is not fettered by the pleadings, but can determine a meaning of the defamatory words as it sees fit; it then applies the facts of justification, as confined by the particulars given by the defendant, to that meaning in order to decide whether the defence is made out. The defendant may, however, only justify a meaning which the words are reasonably capable of bearing and may not seek to justify a distinct meaning of which the claimant does not complain. So, for example, in *Bookbinder v Tebbit* [1989] 1 All ER 1169, [1989] 1 WLR 640, the claimant leader of a Labour-controlled council complained only of a specific charge by the defendant, the chairman of the Conservative Party, that the council under the claimant's leadership had squandered public funds by overprinting school stationery with the caption 'Support Nuclear Free zones'. A defence of justification based on the alleged general squandering of public funds on other occasions by the council under the claimant's leadership was struck out by the Court of Appeal.

4.   The defendant is, however, entitled to rely in mitigation of damages on evidence of specific acts of misconduct adduced in support of an unsuccessful plea of partial justification (*Pamplin v Express Newspapers Ltd (No 2)* [1988] 1 All ER 282, [1988] 1 WLR 116n). See further pp. 1021–1024, post.

5.   There is nothing to prevent a defendant from relying on the fact of a criminal conviction which is 'spent' for the defence of justification or fair comment. A 'spent' conviction is one which s. 5 of the Rehabilitation of Offenders Act 1974 so classifies and this generally excludes sentences of imprisonment exceeding thirty months. However, s. 8(5) of the Act provides, in effect, that if the claimant proves that the defendant *maliciously* published details of a 'spent' conviction, the defence of justification is defeated. An interlocutory injunction to restrain publication of a 'spent' conviction will be granted only if the evidence of an irrelevant, spiteful, or improper motive is overwhelming: *Herbage v Pressdram Ltd* [1984] 2 All ER 769, [1984] 1 WLR 1160.

QUESTIONS

1.   A writes of B: 'B has stolen bicycles from X, Y and Z.' B has in fact stolen bicycles from X and Y, but not from Z. In his statement of claim he relies only on A's allegation that he has stolen Z's bicycle. May A plead and prove the thefts from X and Y by way of justification?

2.   Does it make any difference to preface a defamatory remark with the word 'allegedly'?

(b) Honest comment on a matter of public interest (formerly called 'fair comment')

■ **Tse Wai Chun v Cheng**

Court of Final Appeal of Hong Kong (2000) 10 BHRC 525

LORD NICHOLLS OF BIRKENHEAD: . . .

This is an appeal in a defamation action. It raises an important point on the defence of fair comment. The title of this defence is misleading. Comment, or honest comment, would be a more satisfactory name. In this judgment I adhere, reluctantly, to the traditional terminology.

Fair comment: the objective limits

In order to identify the point in issue I must first set out some non-controversial matters about the ingredients of this defence. These are well established. They are fivefold. First, the comment must be on a matter of public interest. Public interest is not to be confined within narrow limits today: see Lord Denning in *London Artists Ltd v Littler* [1969] 2 All ER 193 at 198.

Second, the comment must be recognisable as comment, as distinct from an imputation of fact. If the imputation is one of fact, a ground of defence must be sought elsewhere, for example, justification or privilege. Much learning has grown up around the distinction between fact and comment. For present purposes it is sufficient to note that a statement may be one or the other, depending on the context. Ferguson J gave a simple example in the New South Wales case of *Myerson v Smith's Weekly* (1923) 24 SR (NSW) 20 at 26:

> 'To say that a man's conduct was dishonourable is not comment, it is a statement of fact. To say that he did certain specific things and that his conduct was dishonourable is a statement of fact coupled with a comment.'

Third, the comment must be based on facts which are true or protected by privilege: see, for instance, *London Artists Ltd v Littler* [1969] 2 All ER 193 at 201. If the facts on which the comment purports to be founded are not proved to be true or published on a privilege occasion, the defence of fair comment is not available.

Next, the comment must explicitly or implicitly indicate, at least in general terms, what are the facts on which the comment is being made. The reader or hearer should be in a position to judge for himself how far the comment was well founded.

Finally, the comment must be one which could have been made by an honest person, however prejudiced he might be, and however exaggerated or obstinate his views: see Lord Porter in *Turner v Metro-Goldwyn-Mayer Pictures Ltd* [1950] 1 All ER 449 at 461, commenting on an observation of Lord Esher MR in *Merivale v Carson* (1888) 20 QBD 275 at 281. It must be germane to the subject matter criticised. Dislike of an artist's style would not justify an attack upon his morals or manners. But a critic need not be mealy-mouthed in denouncing what he disagrees with. He is entitled to dip his pen in gall for the purposes of legitimate criticism: see Jordan CJ in *Gardiner v Fairfax* (1942) 42 SR (NSW) 171 at 174.

These are the outer limits of the defence. The burden of establishing that a comment falls within these limits, and hence within the scope of the defence, lies upon the defendant who wishes to rely upon the defence.

Malice

That is not the end of the matter. Even when a defendant has brought his case within these limits, he will not necessarily succeed. The plaintiff may still defeat (rebut) the defence by proving that when he made his comment the defendant was, in the time-hallowed expression, 'actuated by malice'.

It is here that the storm clouds begin to appear. In ordinary usage malice carries connotations of spite and ill-will. This is not always so in legal usage. In legal usage malice sometimes bears its popular meaning, sometimes not. It is an imprecise term. Historically, even within the bounds of the law of defamation, malice has borne more than one meaning. Historically, defamation lay in publishing the words complained of 'falsely and maliciously'. In this context malice meant merely that publication had been a wrongful act, done intentionally and without lawful excuse: see Bayley J in *Bromage v Prosser* (1825) 4 B & C 247 at 255. This was sometimes called malice in law, as distinct from malice in fact. But even malice 'in fact', otherwise known as express malice or actual malice, may cover states of mind which are not malicious in the ordinary sense of the word. This is so in the context of the defence of qualified privilege. It is no wonder that Lord Bramwell described malice as 'that unfortunate word': see *Abrath v North Eastern Railway Co* (1886) 11 App Cas 247 at 253.

The question raised by this appeal concerns the meaning of malice in the context of the defence of fair comment. On this, two matters are clear. First, unlike the outer limits (as I have called them) of the defence of fair comment, which are objective, malice is subjective. It looks to the defendant's state of mind. Second, malice covers the case of the defendant who does not genuinely hold the view he expressed. In other words, when making the defamatory comment the defendant acted dishonestly. He put forward as his view something which, in truth, was not his view. It was a pretence. The law does not protect such statements. Within the objective limits mentioned above, the law protects the freedom to express opinions, not vituperative make-believe.

The legal issue on this appeal

The point of principle raised by this appeal, crucial to the outcome of the action, is whether, in contemplation of law, malice may exist in this context even when the defendant positively believed in the soundness of his comment. More specifically, the issue is whether the *purpose* for which a defendant stated an honestly held opinion may deprive him of the protection of the defence of fair comment; for instance, if his purpose was to inflict injury, as when a politician seeks to damage his political opponent, or if he was simply acting out of spite.

One would have expected that this basic issue in respect of the much-used defence of fair comment would have been settled long ago. This is not so. The meaning of malice has been comprehensively analysed in relation to the defence of qualified privilege, most notably in the speech of Lord Diplock in *Horrocks v Lowe* [1974] 1 All ER 662. But no similar exposition has been undertaken regarding fair comment. Indeed, there has been surprisingly little judicial discussion of this subject over the last 150 years. Most textbooks incline to the view that, as with qualified privilege, so with fair comment, the defence of an honest defendant may be vitiated by the motive with which the words were published. The (English) *Report of the Committee on Defamation*, published in 1975, stated that under the present state of the law a person was acting maliciously where he was dishonest or reckless 'or actuated by spite, ill-will, or any other indirect or improper motive': see para 153. On this appeal the defendants challenged this view of the law.

Motive

…Before turning to the authorities I shall go back to first principles. Proof of malice is the means whereby a plaintiff can defeat a defence of fair comment where a defendant is abusing the defence. Abuse consists of using the defence for a purpose other than that for which it exists. The purpose for which the defence of fair comment exists is to facilitate freedom of expression by commenting on matters of public interest. This accords with the constitutional guarantee of freedom of expression. And it is in the public interest that everyone should be free to express his own, honestly held views on such matters, subject always to the safeguards provided by the objective limits mentioned above. These safeguards ensure that defamatory comments can be seen for what they are, namely, comments as distinct from statements of fact. They also ensure that those reading the comments have the material enabling them to make up their own minds on whether they agree or disagree.

The public interest in freedom to make comments within these limits is of particular importance in the social and political fields. Professor Fleming stated the matter thus in his invaluable book on *The Law of Torts* (9th edn, 1998) p 648:

'...untrammelled discussion of public affairs and of those participating in them is a basic safeguard against irresponsible political power. The unfettered preservation of the right of fair comment is, therefore, one of the foundations supporting our standards of personal liberty.'

The purpose and importance of the defence of fair comment are inconsistent with its scope being restricted to comments made for particular reasons or particular purposes, some being regarded as proper, others not. Especially in the social and political fields, those who make public comments usually have some objective of their own in mind, even if it is only to publicise and advance themselves. They often have what may be described as an 'ulterior' object. Frequently their object is apparent, but not always so. They may hope to achieve some result, such as promoting one cause or defeating another, elevating one person or denigrating another. In making their comments they do not act dispassionately, they do not intend merely to convey information. They have other motives.

The presence of these motives, and this is of crucial importance for present purposes, is not a reason for excluding the defence of fair comment. The existence of motives such as these when expressing an opinion does not mean that the defence of fair comment is being misused. It would make no sense, for instance, if a motive relating to the very feature which causes the matter to be one of public interest were regarded as defeating the defence.

On the contrary, this defence is intended to protect and promote comments such as these. Liberty to make such comments, genuinely held, on matters of public interest lies at the heart of the defence of fair comment. That is the very object for which the defence exists. Commentators, of all shades of opinion, are entitled to 'have their own agenda'. Politicians, social reformers, busybodies, those with political or other ambitions and those with none, all can grind their axes. The defence of fair comment envisages that everyone is at liberty to conduct social and political campaigns by expressing his own views, subject always, and I repeat the refrain, to the objective safeguards which mark the limits of the defence.

Nor is it for the courts to choose between 'public' and 'private' purposes, or between purposes they regard as morally or socially or politically desirable and those they regard as undesirable. That would be a highly dangerous course. That way lies censorship. That would defeat the purpose for which the law accords the defence of freedom to make comments on matters of public interest. The objective safeguards, coupled with the need to have a genuine belief in what is said, are adequate to keep the ambit of permissible comment within reasonable bounds.

[His Lordship considered comments motivated by spite or ill-will, and doubted whether these would lose the protection of the defence, and continued:]

Horrocks v Lowe

I now turn to the authorities. As already indicated, there is no decision directly on the point now under consideration. It is no doubt for this reason that textbook writers have sought to fill the gap by resorting to the decision of the House of Lords in *Horrocks v Lowe* [1974] 1 All ER 662, even though that case related to a different defence, the defence of qualified privilege. In the absence of any clear guidance, it is temptingly easy to assume that malice must bear the same meaning in all respects for both defences. It is essential, therefore, to consider the reasoning which underlies Lord Diplock's authoritative analysis of malice for the purposes of the defence of qualified privilege, with a view to seeing how far it is applicable to the defence of fair comment. As will appear, I believe that misapplication of this analysis is largely responsible for the erroneous statements of the law in some of the textbooks.

In a much-quoted passage, Lord Diplock said this ([1974] 1 All ER 662 at 669–670):

'Even a positive belief in the truth of what is published on a privileged occasion...may not suffice to negative express malice if it can be proved that the defendant misused the occasion for some purpose other that that for which the privilege is accorded by the law. The commonest case is where the dominant motive which actuates the defendant is not a desire to perform the relevant duty or to protect the relevant interest, but to give vent to his personal spite or ill will towards the person he defames.'

Lord Diplock continued by noting that there may be other improper motives which destroy the privilege. He instanced the case where a defendant's dominant motive may have been to obtain 'some private advantage unconnected with the duty or the interest which constitutes the reason for the privilege'.

Lord Diplock's observations are in point to the extent that they enunciate the principle that express malice is to be equated with use of a privileged occasion for some purpose other than that for which the privilege is accorded by the law. The same approach is applicable to the defence of fair comment. Beyond that his observations do not assist in the present case, because the purposes for which the law has accorded the defence of qualified privilege and the defence of fair comment are not the same. So his examples of misuse of qualified privilege cannot be carried across to fair comment without more ado. Instances of misuse of qualified privilege may not be instances of misuse of fair comment. What amounts to misuse of fair comment depends upon the purposes for which that defence exists.

I must make good my statement that the purposes for which the two defences exist are not the same. The rationale of the defence of qualified privilege is the law's recognition that there are circumstances when there is a need, in the public interest, for a particular recipient to receive frank and uninhibited communication of particular information from a particular source: see *Reynolds v Times Newspapers Ltd* (1999) 7 BHRC 289 at 296. Traditionally, these occasions have been described in terms of persons having a duty to perform or an interest to protect in providing the information. If, adopting the traditional formulation for convenience, a person's dominant motive is not to perform this duty or protect this interest, he is outside the ambit of the defence. For instance, if a former employer includes defamatory statements in an employment reference with the dominant purpose of injuring the former employee, the former employer is misusing the privileged occasion and this will vitiate his defence of qualified privilege.

The rationale of the defence of fair comment is different, and is different in a material respect. It is not based on any notion of performance of a duty or protection of an interest. As already noted, its basis is the high importance of protecting and promoting the freedom of comment by everyone at all times on matters of public interest, irrespective of their particular motives. In the nature of things the instances of misuse of privilege highlighted by Lord Diplock (for example, 'some private advantage unconnected with the duty or interest which constitutes the reason for the privilege') are not necessarily applicable to fair comment. A failure to appreciate this has, I fear, led some textbook writers into the error of suggesting that parts of Lord Diplock's observations are equally applicable to the defence of fair comment even though they lack the rationale on which the observations were founded. . . .

Conclusion on the law

My conclusion on the authorities is that, for the most part, the relevant judicial statements are consistent with the views which I have expressed as a matter of principle. To summarise, in my view a comment which falls within the objective limits of the defence of fair comment can lose its immunity only by proof that the defendant did not genuinely hold the view he expressed. Honesty of belief is the touchstone. Actuation by spite, animosity, intent to injure, intent to arouse controversy or other motivation, whatever it may be, even if it is the dominant or sole motive, does not *of itself* defeat the defence. However, proof of such motivation may be evidence, sometimes compelling evidence, from which lack of genuine belief in the view expressed may be inferred. Proof of motivation may also be relevant on other issues in the action, such as damages.

It is said that this view of the law would have the undesirable consequence that malice would bear different meanings in the defences of fair comment and qualified privilege, and that this would inevitably cause difficulty for juries. I agree that if the term 'malice' were used, there might be a risk of confusion. The answer lies in shunning that word altogether. Juries can be instructed, regarding fair comment, that the defence is defeated by proof that the defendant did not genuinely believe the opinion he expressed. Regarding qualified privilege, juries can be directed that the defence is defeated by proof that the defendant used the occasion for some purpose other than that for which the occasion was privileged. This direction can be elaborated in a manner appropriate to the facts and issues in the case.

[LORD NICHOLLS found that the trial judge had misdirected the jury in requiring them to consider the defendant's motives for making the comments in question. The other members of the Court of Final Appeal agreed with LORD NICHOLLS.]

Appeal allowed.

NOTES

1.   In *Branson v Bower (No 2)* [2002] QB 737, the High Court 'gratefully adopted and followed' Lord Nicholls's exposition. Eady J rejected any 'objective limits' on permissible comments, observing that 'the law permits the language to be rude and offensive' and that public debate must not be 'hobbled by the constraints of conventional good manners—still less of deference. The law of fair comment must allow for healthy scepticism,' at [6] and [25]. Therefore, 'the touchstone is honesty', which has the benefit of being easy for a jury to apply: [26]. See also Girvan LJ's comment in *Convery v Irish News Ltd* [2008] NICA 14 at [51], and for further discussion see e.g. *Clerk and Lindsell*, paras. 23–168 & 23–171 to 23–172.

2.   The European Court of Human Rights draws a distinction between *value-judgements* and *statements of fact* and considers there to be a breach of Article 10 if the law forces the defendant to prove the truth of a value-judgement (see e.g. *Lingens v Austria* (1986) 8 EHRR 407 and *De Haes v Belgium* (1997) 25 EHRR 1).

3.   The distinction between fact and comment, although fundamental, is difficult to pin down. There is a dearth of case law, largely because the normal practice has been to leave the question to the jury. Defendants are in danger of having the defence struck out if they fail to make clear which parts of their statement they say are fact and which are comment. This has led some commentators to make the extraordinary claim that statements such as 'A is a disgrace to human nature' are statements of *fact*. It would be more accurate to say that such a statement might fail to meet the requirements for the comment defence if the basis of fact on which the defendant is relying is insufficiently clear. Where the negative connotations of a statement are a matter of general consensus, for example 'A is a thief', the statement can be taken as 'fact' rather than 'comment'. 'Comment' is where people might disagree on the evaluation of the facts (see *Howarth*, p. 572).

4.   In *Branson v Bower (No 1)* [2001] EMLR 800, [2001] EWCA Civ 791 Latham LJ approved the test of what amounts to comment set out by Cussen J in *Clarke v Norton* [1910] VLR 494 at 499: 'something which is or can reasonably be inferred to be a deduction, inference, conclusion, criticism, remark, observation, etc'. The jurisprudence of the European Court of Human Rights did not require any change to the English distinction between fact and comment, including the 'axiomatic' rule that in deciding this question, 'the article in which the words complained of appear must be read in its entirety': see at [16] per Sir Phillip Otton.

For further recent discussion of this 'difficult' and 'fairly subtle' distinction (per Kerr LCJ), see *Convery v Irish News Ltd* [2008] NICA 14. The Northern Ireland Court of Appeal considered that the jury had been improperly directed as to whether statements in the defendant's restaurant review column about the claimant's restaurant constituted fact or comment, and ordered a new trial. For example, Girvan LJ at [53] considered that the statement that cola served in the restaurant had been 'warm and watery' was not a statement of physical fact, but the reviewer's 'evaluative, subjective assessment' of the drink she had consumed. Campbell LJ at [49] stated: 'Once it was established that the various dishes and the cola on which the reviewer commented were served to her there was a sufficient substratum of fact for any comment on them that followed.' The decision has been warmly welcomed by restaurant critics nationwide.

5. A statement may be a comment, although no facts on which that opinion is based appear in the statement. Although Lord Nicholls says the statement must 'explicitly or implicitly indicate, at least in general terms, what are the facts on which the comment is being made' (see *Tse Wai Chun* at [19] ante), in *Lowe v Associated Newspapers Ltd* [2006] 3 All ER 357, [2006] EWHC 320 (QB), it was held enough that the facts are sufficiently well-known to readers to allow them to recognise the comments as comment. So if a matter was already before the public, it might safely be commented upon without first reciting the facts, provided the subject matter was clearly indicated. Having considered Article 10 of the ECHR Eady J was 'left in no doubt that the right to comment freely on matters of public interest would be far too circumscribed if it were a necessary ingredient of the English common law's defence of fair comment that the commentator should be confined to pleading facts stated in the words complained of', at [42].

■ The Defamation Act 1952

6 Fair comment.—In an action for libel or slander in respect of words consisting partly of allegations of fact and partly of expression of opinion, a defence of fair comment shall not fail by reason only that the truth of every allegation of fact is not proved if the expression of opinion is fair comment having regard to such of the facts alleged or referred to in the words complained of as are proved.

QUESTION

D writes and publishes the following statement: 'P is an undischarged bankrupt and a drug addict. He is not fit to be a councillor.' D proves the truth of the allegation that P is a drug addict, but was mistaken about him being an undischarged bankrupt. Does P have any remedy? What difference would it make if D had omitted the comment?

(c) Privilege

(i) Absolute privilege

■ Chatterton v Secretary of State for India
Court of Appeal [1895–9] All ER Rep 1035

The claimant claimed that the defendant Secretary of State had libelled him in communications to a junior minister, made to enable the junior minister to answer a question in the House of Commons.

LORD ESHER MR: ...

The Queen's Bench Division has held that the action cannot be maintained, on the ground that such an act as that which is the subject of the action cannot be inquired into by a civil court of law. It is beyond the powers of a civil court to hold any inquiry upon the matter. In all the reported cases upon the subject it has been laid down that a judge should stop the case, if such an action came before him for trial, because he would have no jurisdiction even to entertain the question. ...

What is the reason for the existence of this law? It does not exist for the benefit of the official. All judges have said that the ground of its existence is the injury to the public good which would result if such an inquiry were allowed as would be necessary if the action were maintainable. An inquiry would take away from the public official his freedom of action in a matter concerning the public welfare, because he would have to appear before a jury and be cross-examined as to his conduct. That would be contrary to the interest of the public, and the privilege is, therefore, absolute in regard to the contents of such a document as that upon which this action is founded. I shall not go through the reported cases since they are all to the same effect. The result of them is summed up thus by Mr Fraser in his book on *Libel and Slander* (1st edn) p. 95:

> 'For reasons of public policy the same protection would no doubt be given to anything in the nature of an act of State for example, to every communication relating to State matters made by one Minister to another, or to the Crown.'

I adopt that paragraph, which seems to me to be an exact statement of the law. ...

[KAY and A L SMITH LJJ delivered judgments in favour of dismissing the appeal.]

Appeal dismissed.

NOTES

1. In *Fayed v Al-Tajir* [1988] QB 712, [1987] 2 All ER 396, the Court of Appeal held that an internal memorandum of a foreign embassy in London was protected by absolute privilege in libel proceedings. This privilege was derived not from cases such as *Chatterton v Secretary of State for India*, but was said to rest upon the public policy of not meddling in the affairs of foreign states and on the law of diplomatic relations.

2. At common law, statements in Parliament are absolutely privileged. According to Lord Bingham, this reflects both the 'paramount need to protect freedom of speech in Parliament' and the 'important principle that the legislature and the courts should not intrude into the spheres reserved to another': *Buchanan v Jennings* [2005] 2 All ER 273 at [17]–[18]. (For parliamentary privilege and freedom of speech, see Article 9 of the Bill of Rights 1689, the Parliamentary Papers Act 1840 and A. Bradley and K. Ewing, *Constitutional and Administrative Law* 14th edn (London, 2007), pp. 224–229 and 567–569.) However, the Privy Council in *Buchanan v Jennings* held that the defence does not avail an MP who later adopts and confirms outside Parliament a statement made in the House.

3. 'Absolute' privilege means that the statement cannot give rise to liability in defamation, even if the speaker was actuated by 'malice' (on which see pp. 997–999, post).

■ The Defamation Act 1996

14 Reports of court proceedings absolutely privileged.—(1) A fair and accurate report of proceedings in public before a court to which this section applies, if published contemporaneously with proceedings, is absolutely privileged.

(2) A report of proceedings which by an order of the court, or as a consequence of any statutory provision, is required to be postponed shall be treated as published contemporaneously if it is published as soon as practicable after publication is permitted.

(3) This section applies to—

(a) any court in the United Kingdom,

(b) the European Court of Justice or any court attached to that court,

(c) the European Court of Human Rights, and

(d) any international criminal tribunal established by the Security Council of the United Nations or by an international agreement to which the United Kingdom is a party.

In paragraph (a) "court" includes any tribunal or body exercising the judicial power of the State.

NOTES

1. Some decisions say that a report can be 'fair and accurate' even if the reporter selects parts of a trial to report, e.g. counsel's opening speech in a libel case: *Burnett and Hallamshire Fuel Ltd v Sheffield Telegraph and Star Ltd* [1960] 2 All ER 157, [1960] 1 WLR 502. But in *Reynolds v Times Newspapers Ltd* [2001] 2 AC 127, [1999] 4 All ER 609 (p. 999, post) the House of Lords confirms that a report of parliamentary proceedings (in this case in Ireland) could not be fair and accurate if it omitted the reply of the very politician whose conduct was under attack.

2. Statements made in the course of proceedings in a court of law or other tribunal with attributes sufficiently similar to a court of law are absolutely privileged at common law: *Trapp v Mackie* [1979] 1 All ER 489, [1979] 1 WLR 377. There needs, however, to be some kind of dispute between identifiable parties. Regulatory licensing functions will therefore often not be sufficiently judicial (see *Mahon v Rahn (No 2)* [2000] 4 All ER 41). In *Buckley v Dalziel* [2007] EWHC 1025 (QB) it was held that absolute privilege extends to statements made by a witness or complainant in the course of a police investigation. Absolute privilege does not, however, attach to private conciliation proceedings: *Tadd v Eastwood* [1985] ICR 132.

(ii) Qualified privilege

■ The Defamation Act 1952

9 Extension of certain defences to broadcasting.—(1) Section three of the Parliamentary Papers Act 1840 (which confers protection in respect of proceedings for printing extracts from or abstracts of parliamentary papers) shall have effect as if the reference to printing included a reference to broadcasting by means of wireless telegraphy.

■ The Defamation Act 1996

15 Reports, etc protected by qualified privilege

(1) The publication of any report or other statement mentioned in Schedule 1 to this Act is privileged unless the publication is shown to be made with malice, subject as follows.

(2) In defamation proceedings in respect of the publication of a report or other statement mentioned in Part II of that Schedule, there is no defence under this section if the plaintiff shows that the defendant—

(a) was requested by him to publish in a suitable manner a reasonable letter or statement by way of explanation or contradiction, and

(b) refused or neglected to do so.

For this purpose "in a suitable manner" means in the same manner as the publication complained of or in a manner that is adequate and reasonable in the circumstances.

(3) This section does not apply to the publication to the public, or a section of the public, of matter which is not of public concern and the publication of which is not for the public benefit.

(4) Nothing in this section shall be construed—

(a) as protecting the publication of matter the publication of which is prohibited by law, or

(b) as limiting or abridging any privilege subsisting apart from this section.

Schedule 1

Qualified Privilege

PART I: STATEMENTS HAVING QUALIFIED PRIVILEGE WITHOUT EXPLANATION OR CONTRADICTION

1. A fair and accurate report of proceedings in public of a legislature anywhere in the world.
2. A fair and accurate report of proceedings in public before a court anywhere in the world.
3. A fair and accurate report of proceedings in public of a person appointed to hold a public inquiry by a government or legislature anywhere in the world.
4. A fair and accurate report of proceedings in public anywhere in the world of an international organisation or an international conference.
5. A fair and accurate copy of or extract from any register or other document required by law to be open to public inspection.
6. A notice or advertisement published by or on the authority of a court, or of a judge or officer of a court, anywhere in the world.
7. A fair and accurate copy of or extract from matter published by or on the authority of a government or legislature anywhere in the world.
8. A fair and accurate copy of or extract from matter published anywhere in the world by an international organisation or an international conference.

PART II: STATEMENTS PRIVILEGED SUBJECT TO EXPLANATION OR CONTRADICTION

9.—(1) A fair and accurate copy of or extract from a notice or other matter issued for the information of the public by or on behalf of—

(a) legislature in any member State or the European Parliament;

(b) the government of any member State, or any authority performing governmental functions in any member State or part of a member State, or the European Commission;

(c) an international organisation or international conference.

(2) In this paragraph "governmental" functions includes police functions.

10. A fair and accurate copy of or extract from a document made available by a court in any member State or the European Court of Justice (or any court attached to that court), or by a judge or officer of any such court.

11.—(1) A fair and accurate report of proceedings at any public meeting or sitting in the United Kingdom of—

(a) a local authority or local authority committee;

(b) a justice or justices of the peace acting otherwise than as a court exercising judicial authority;

(c) a commission, tribunal, committee or person appointed for the purposes of any inquiry by any statutory provision, by Her Majesty or by a Minister of the Crown or a Northern Ireland Department;

(d) a person appointed by a local authority to hold a local inquiry in pursuance of any statutory provision;

(e) any other tribunal, board, committee or body constituted by or under, and exercising functions under, any statutory provision.

(2) In sub-paragraph (1)(a)—

"local authority" means—

(a) in relation to England and Wales, a principal council within the meaning of the Local Government Act 1972, any body falling within any paragraph of section 100J(1) of that Act or an authority or body to which the Public Bodies (Admission to Meetings) Act 1960 applies,

(b) in relation to Scotland, a council constituted under section 2 of the Local Government etc (Scotland) Act 1994 or an authority or body to which the Public Bodies (Admission to Meetings) Act 1960 applies,

(c) in relation to Northern Ireland, any authority or body to which sections 23 to 27 of the Local Government Act (Northern Ireland) 1972 apply; and

"local authority committee" means any committee of a local authority or of local authorities, and includes—

(a) any committee or sub-committee in relation to which sections 100A to 100D of the Local Government Act 1972 apply by virtue of section 100E of that Act (whether or not also by virtue of section 100J of that Act), and

(b) any committee or sub-committee in relation to which sections 50A to 50D of the Local Government (Scotland) Act 1973 apply by virtue of section 50E of that Act.

(3) A fair and accurate report of any corresponding proceedings in any of the Channel Islands or the Isle of Man or in another member State.

12.—(1) A fair and accurate report of proceedings at any public meeting held in a member State.

(2) In this paragraph a "public meeting" means a meeting bona fide and lawfully held for a lawful purpose and for the furtherance or discussion of a matter of public concern, whether admission to the meeting is general or restricted.

13.—(1) A fair and accurate report of proceedings at a general meeting of a UK public company.

(2) A fair and accurate copy of or extract from any document circulated to members of a UK public company—

(a) by or with the authority of the board of directors of the company,

(b) by the auditors of the company, or

(c) by any member of the company in pursuance of a right conferred by any statutory provision.

(3) A fair and accurate copy of or extract from any document circulated to members of a UK public company which relates to the appointment, resignation, retirement or dismissal of directors of the company.

(4) In this paragraph "UK public company" means—

(a) a public company within the meaning of section 1(3) of the Companies Act 1985 or Article 12(3) of the Companies (Northern Ireland) Order 1986, or

(b) a body corporate incorporated by or registered under any other statutory provision, or by Royal Charter, or formed in pursuance of letters patent.

(5) A fair and accurate report of proceedings at any corresponding meeting of, or copy of or extract from any corresponding document circulated to members of, a public company formed under the law of any of the Channel Islands or the Isle of Man or of another member State.

14. A fair and accurate report of any finding or decision of any of the following descriptions of association, formed in the United Kingdom or another member State, or of any committee or governing body of such an association—

(a) an association formed for the purpose of promoting or encouraging the exercise of or interest in any art, science, religion or learning, and empowered by its constitution to exercise control over or adjudicate on matters of interest or concern to the association, or the actions or conduct of any person subject to such control or adjudication;

(b) an association formed for the purpose of promoting or safeguarding the interests of any trade, business, industry or profession, or of the persons carrying on or engaged in any trade, business, industry or profession, and empowered by its constitution to exercise control over or adjudicate upon matters connected with that trade, business, industry or profession, or the actions or conduct of those persons;

(c) an association formed for the purpose of promoting or safeguarding the interests of a game, sport or pastime to the playing or exercise of which members of the public are invited or admitted, and empowered by its constitution to exercise control over or adjudicate upon persons connected with or taking part in the game, sport or pastime;

(d) an association formed for the purpose of promoting charitable objects or other objects beneficial to the community and empowered by its constitution to exercise control over or to adjudicate on matters of interest or concern to the association, or the actions or conduct of any person subject to such control or adjudication.

15.—(1) A fair and accurate report of, or copy of or extract from, any adjudication, report, statement or notice issued by a body, officer or other person designated for the purposes of this paragraph—

(a) for England and Wales or Northern Ireland, by order of the Lord Chancellor, and
(b) for Scotland, by order of the Secretary of State.

(2) An order under this paragraph shall be made by statutory instrument which shall be subject to annulment in pursuance of a resolution of either House of Parliament.

PART III SUPPLEMENTARY PROVISIONS
16.—(1) In this Schedule—

"court" includes any tribunal or body exercising the judicial power of the State;
"international conference" means a conference attended by representatives of two or more governments;
"international organisation" means an organisation of which two or more governments are members, and includes any committee or other subordinate body of such an organisation; and
"legislature" includes a local legislature.

(2) References in this Schedule to a member State include any European dependent territory of a member State.

(3) In paragraphs 2 and 6 "court" includes—

(a) the European Court of Justice (or any court attached to that court) and the Court of Auditors of the European Communities,
(b) the European Court of Human Rights,
(c) any international criminal tribunal established by the Security Council of the United Nations or by an international agreement to which the United Kingdom is a party, and
(d) the International Court of Justice and any other judicial or arbitral tribunal deciding matters in dispute between States.

(4) In paragraphs 1, 3 and 7 "legislature" includes the European Parliament.

17.—(1) Provision may be made by order identifying—

(a) for the purposes of paragraph 11, the corresponding proceedings referred to in sub-paragraph (3);
(b) for the purposes of paragraph 13, the corresponding meetings and documents referred to in sub-paragraph (5).

(2) An order under this paragraph may be made—

(a) for England and Wales or Northern Ireland, by the Lord Chancellor, and
(b) for Scotland, by the Secretary of State.

(3) An order under this paragraph shall be made by statutory instrument which shall be subject to annulment in pursuance of a resolution of either House of Parliament.

NOTES

1.   In *Tsikata v Newspaper Publishing plc* [1997] 1 All ER 655, the Court of Appeal, considering these sections' predecessor provisions in the Defamation Act 1952, said that

they had to be given a wide, purposive interpretation and that, consequently, a 'report' of proceedings did not have to be a contemporary report or a report into recent events, that in judging the fairness of such a report, events subsequent to the matters reported did not have to be taken into account, and that 'proceedings in public' included an unpublished final report following a public inquiry. The Court also held that what counts as 'not of public concern and the publication of which is not for the public benefit' is a question of fact for the jury. See similarly *McCartan Turkington Breen v Times Newspapers Ltd* [2001] 2 AC 277, [2000] 4 All ER 913, noted p. 957, ante.

2. Even at common law a fair and accurate report of parliamentary proceedings is protected by qualified privilege: *Wason v Walter* (1868) LR 4 QB 73. Furthermore, in *Cook v Alexander* [1974] QB 279, [1973] 3 All ER 1037 it was held by the Court of Appeal that a reporter writing a sketch of parliamentary proceedings is entitled to select that part of the proceedings which he considers to be of genuine public interest. But *Curistan v Times Newspapers Ltd* [2008] EWCA Civ 432 confirms that a report will not be 'fair' if it 'intermingles' extraneous, non-privileged matters with the parliamentary statements. As Lord Denning said in *Dingle v Associated Newspapers Ltd* [1964] AC 371 at 411, where the publisher 'adds its own spice and prints a story to the same effect as the parliamentary paper, and garnishes and embellishes it with circumstantial detail, it goes beyond the privilege and becomes subject to the general law. None of its story on that occasion is privileged. It has "put the meat on the bones" and must answer for the whole joint.' On the facts of *Curistan* however, the court held at [48] that the parliamentary report was 'recognisably distinct' from the rest of the newspaper article, and thus (since it was otherwise accurate) privileged.

■ Horrocks v Lowe

House of Lords [1974] 1 All ER 662

The claimant, a Conservative councillor, complained that the defendant, a Labour councillor, slandered him at a council meeting. The judge decided that the occasion was privileged but that the defendant was guilty of express malice.

LORD DIPLOCK: . . . .
'Express malice' is the term of art. . . . Broadly speaking, it means malice in the popular sense of a desire to injure the person who is defamed and this is generally the motive which the plaintiff sets out to prove. But to destroy the privilege the desire to injure must be the dominant motive for the defamatory publication; knowledge that it will have that effect is not enough if the defendant is nevertheless acting in accordance with a sense of duty or in bona fide protection of his own legitimate interests.

The motive with which a person published defamatory matter can only be inferred from what he did or said or knew. If it be proved that he did not believe that what he published was true this is generally conclusive evidence of express malice, for no sense of duty or desire to protect his own legitimate interests can justify a man in telling deliberate and injurious falsehoods about another, save in the exceptional case where a person may be under a duty to pass on, without endorsing, defamatory reports made by some other person. . . .

Apart from those exceptional cases, what is required on the part of the defamer to entitle him to the protection of the privilege is positive belief in the truth of what he published or, as it is generally though tautologously termed, 'honest belief.' If he publishes untrue defamatory matter recklessly, without considering or caring whether it be true or not, he is in this, as in other branches of the law, treated as if he knew it to be false. But indifference to the truth of what he publishes is not to be equated with carelessness, impulsiveness or irrationality in arriving at a positive belief that it is true. The freedom of speech protected by the law of qualified privilege may be availed of by all sorts and conditions of men. In affording to them immunity from suit if they have acted in good faith in compliance with a legal or moral duty or in protection of a legitimate interest the law must take them as it finds them. In ordinary life it is rare indeed for people to form their beliefs by a process of logical deduction from facts ascertained by a rigorous search for all available evidence and a judicious assessment of its probative value. In greater or in less degree according to their temperaments, their training, their intelligence, they are swayed by prejudice, rely on intuition instead of reasoning, leap to conclusions on inadequate evidence and fail to recognise the cogency of material which might cast doubt on the validity of the conclusions they reach. But despite the imperfection of the mental process by which the belief is arrived at it may still be 'honest,' that is, a positive belief that the conclusions they have reached are true. The law demands no more.

Even a positive belief in the truth of what is published on a privileged occasion—which is presumed unless the contrary is proved—may not be sufficient to negative express malice if it can be proved that the defendant misused the occasion for some purpose other than that for which the privilege is accorded by the law. The commonest case is where the dominant motive which actuates the defendant is not a desire to perform the relevant duty or to protect the relevant interest, but to give vent to his personal spite or ill will towards the person he defames. If this be proved, then even positive belief in the truth of what is published will not enable the defamer to avail himself of the protection of the privilege to which he would otherwise have been entitled. There may be instances of improper motives which destroy the privilege apart from personal spite. A defendant's dominant motive may have been to obtain some private advantage unconnected with the duty or the interest which constitutes the reason for the privilege. If so, he loses the benefit of the privilege despite his positive belief that what he said or wrote was true.

Judges and juries should, however, be very slow to draw the inference that a defendant was so far actuated by improper motives as to deprive him of the protection of the privilege unless they are satisfied that he did not believe that what he said or wrote was true or that he was indifferent to its truth or falsity. The motives with which human beings act are mixed. They find it difficult to hate the sin but love the sinner. Qualified privilege would be illusory, and the public interest that it is meant to serve defeated, if the protection which it affords were lost merely because a person, although acting in compliance with a duty or in protection of a legitimate interest, disliked the person whom he defamed or was indignant at what he believed to be that person's conduct and welcomed the opportunity of exposing it. It is only where his desire to comply with the relevant duty or to protect the relevant interest plays no significant part in his motives for publishing what he believes to be true that 'express malice' can properly be found.

[His Lordship found there had been no evidence on which the judge could have found that the defendant lacked an honest belief in the truth of his statement, and confirmed the Court of Appeal's decision to overrule the finding of liability.]

[LORD WILBERFORCE, LORD HODSON, and LORD KILBRANDON agreed with LORD DIPLOCK. VISCOUNT DILHORNE delivered a speech in favour of dismissing the appeal.]

Appeal dismissed.

NOTES

1. Lord Diplock's views on statements believed to be true but made with an ulterior motive have been confined to privilege and rejected for the 'fair comment' defence: see pp. 986–990, ante.

2. It is often asserted that it is not malice, but rather the defence of a legitimate interest, for the defendant to have defended his or her reputation against hostile criticism. But in *Fraser-Armstrong v Hadow & Nelson* [1995] EMLR 140 the Court of Appeal said that it could not be legitimate to defend oneself against allegations one knew to be true.

3. In *Egger v Viscount Chelmsford* [1965] 1 QB 248, [1964] 3 All ER 406 the Court of Appeal, overruling previous cases to the contrary, decided that, in the words of Lord Denning MR, 'It is a mistake to suppose that, on a joint publication, the malice of one defendant infects his co-defendant. Each defendant is answerable severally, as well as jointly, for the joint publication: and each is entitled to his several defence, whether he be sued jointly or separately from the others. If the plaintiff seeks to rely on malice to aggravate damages, or to rebut a defence of qualified privilege, or to cause a comment, otherwise fair, to become unfair, then he must prove malice against each person whom he charges with it. A defendant is only affected by express malice if he himself was actuated by it: or if his servant or agent concerned in the publication was actuated by malice in the course of his employment.' However, the ordinary rules of vicarious liability apply so that an employer or principal is liable if his employee or agent was actuated by malice in making a defamatory statement in the scope of his employment: *Riddick v Thames Board Mills Ltd* [1977] QB 881 at 900.

4. In *Bryanston Finance Ltd v De Vries* [1975] QB 703, [1975] 2 All ER 609 the members of the Court of Appeal differed as to the exact scope of any original privilege in the situation where a letter is dictated to a typist, but it was said that if the communication ultimately was the subject of qualified privilege, then the dictation, too, was protected by a derivative privilege, if done in the normal course of business practice.

■ Reynolds v Times Newspapers Ltd

House of Lords [1999] 4 All ER 609

The plaintiff became Prime Minister of Ireland in 1992, heading a coalition that did much to promote the Northern Ireland peace process. The future of the coalition was thus a matter of public interest in Britain. The defendants published an article in the British edition of their Sunday newspaper about the plaintiff's resignation as Prime Minister in 1994, and the political crisis which led to it. The plaintiff claimed that the article said that the plaintiff had deliberately and dishonestly misled Parliament and his cabinet colleagues. The defendants claimed qualified privilege at common law. At the end of the trial the plaintiff was awarded one penny in damages, and was ordered to pay the defendant's costs as from the date of a payment into court. The plaintiff appealed, seeking a new trial. The defendants cross-appealed against the judge's ruling that they could not rely on qualified privilege. The Court of Appeal allowed the appeal, finding that the judge had made errors in his summing up of the facts, and ordered a new trial. The cross-appeal on qualified privilege failed. A further appeal to the House of Lords ensued solely against the Court of Appeal's decision on qualified privilege. The issue before the House of Lords was whether the new trial should be allowed to consider the qualified privilege defence.

LORD NICHOLLS OF BIRKENHEAD: . . .

[T]here are circumstances, in the famous words of Parke B in *Toogood v. Spyring* (1834) 1 Cr M & R 181 at 193, [1824–43] All ER Rep 735 at 738 when the 'common convenience and welfare of society' call for frank communication on questions of fact. In *Davies v. Snead* (1870) LR 5 QB 608 at 611, Blackburn J spoke of circumstances where a person is so situated that it 'becomes right in the interests of society' that he should tell certain facts to another. There are occasions when the person to whom a statement is made has a special interest in learning the honestly held views of another person, even if those views are defamatory of someone else and cannot be proved to be true. When the interest is of sufficient importance to outweigh the need to protect reputation, the occasion is regarded as privileged.

Sometimes the need for uninhibited expression is of such a high order that the occasion attracts absolute privilege, as with statements made by judges or advocates or witnesses in the course of judicial proceedings. More usually, the privilege is qualified in that it can be defeated if the plaintiff proves the defendant was actuated by malice....

Over the years the courts have held that many common form situations are privileged. Classic instances are employment references, and complaints made or information given to the police or appropriate authorities regarding suspected crimes. The courts have always emphasised that the categories established by the authorities are not exhaustive. The list is not closed. The established categories are no more than applications, in particular circumstances, of the underlying principle of public policy. The underlying principle is conventionally stated in words to the effect that there must exist between the maker of the statement and the recipient some duty or interest in the making of the communication. Lord Atkinson's dictum, in *Adam v. Ward* [1917] AC 309 at 334, [1916–17] All ER Rep 157 at 170, is much quoted:

> '...a privileged occasion is...an occasion where the person who makes a communication has an interest or a duty, legal, social, or moral, to make it to the person to whom it is made, and the person to whom it is so made has a corresponding interest or duty to receive it. This reciprocity is essential'.

The requirement that both the maker of the statement and the recipient must have an interest or duty draws attention to the need to have regard to the position of both parties when deciding whether an occasion is privileged. But this should not be allowed to obscure the rationale of the underlying public interest on which privilege is founded. The essence of this defence lies in the law's recognition of the need, in the public interest, for a particular recipient to receive frank and uninhibited communication of particular information from a particular source. That is the end the law is concerned to attain. The protection afforded to the maker of the statement is the means by which the law seeks to achieve that end. Thus the court has to assess whether, in the public interest, the publication should be protected in the absence of malice.

In determining whether an occasion is regarded as privileged the court has regard to all the circumstances: see, for example, the explicit statement of Lord Buckmaster LC in *London Association for Protection of Trade v. Greenlands Ltd* [1916] 2 AC 15 at 23, [1916–17] All ER Rep 452 at 456 ('every circumstance associated with the origin and publication of the defamatory matter'). And circumstances must be viewed with today's eyes. The circumstances in which the public interest requires a communication to be protected in the absence of malice depend upon current social conditions. The requirements at the close of the twentieth century may not be the same as those of earlier centuries or earlier decades of this century.

Privilege and publication to the world at large
Frequently a privileged occasion encompasses publication to one person only or to a limited group of people. Publication more widely, to persons who lack the requisite interest in receiving the information, is not privileged. But the common law has recognised there are occasions when the public interest requires that publication to the world at large should be privileged. In *Cox v. Feeney* (1863) 4 F & F 13 at 19 Cockburn CJ approved an earlier statement by Lord Tenterden CJ that 'a man has a right to publish, for the purpose of giving the public information, that which it is proper for the public to know'. Whether the public interest so requires depends upon an evaluation of the particular information in the circumstances of its publication. Through the cases runs the strain that, when determining whether the public at large had a right to know the particular information, the court has regard to all the circumstances. The court is concerned to assess whether the information was of sufficient value to the public that, in the public interest, it should be protected by privilege in the absence of malice.

This issue has arisen several times in the context of newspapers discharging their important function of reporting matters of public importance....

...[I]n *Blackshaw v. Lord* [1983] 2 All ER 311, [1984] 1 QB 1 the Court of Appeal rejected a claim to generic protection for a widely stated category: 'fair information on a matter of public interest' (see [1984] QB 1 at 6). A claim to privilege must be more precisely focused. In order to be privileged publication must be in the public interest. Whether a publication is in the public interest or, in the conventional phraseology, whether there is a duty to publish to the intended recipients, there the readers of the Daily Telegraph, depends upon the circumstances, including the nature of the matter published and its source or status. ...

In its valuable and forward-looking analysis of the common law, the Court of Appeal in the present case highlighted that in deciding whether an occasion is privileged the court considers, among other matters, the nature, status and source of the material published and the circumstances of the publication. In stressing the importance of these particular factors, the court treated them as matters going to a question (the circumstantial test) separate from, and additional to, the conventional duty-interest questions (see [1998] 3 All ER 961 at 994–995). With all respect to the Court of Appeal, this formulation of three questions gives rise to conceptual and practical difficulties and is better avoided. There is no separate or additional question. These factors are to be taken into account in determining whether the duty-interest test is satisfied or, as I would prefer to say in a simpler and more direct way, whether the public was entitled to know the particular information. The duty-interest test, or the right to know test, cannot be carried out in isolation from these factors and without regard to them. A claim to privilege stands or falls according to whether the claim passes or fails this test. There is no further requirement. ...

The newspaper seeks the incremental development of the common law by the creation of a new category of occasion when privilege derives from the subject matter alone: political information. Political information can be broadly defined, borrowing the language used by the High Court of Australia in *Lange*'s case,[5] as information, opinion and arguments concerning government and political matters that affect the people of the United Kingdom. Malice apart, publication of political information should be privileged regardless of the status and source of the material and the circumstances of the publication. The newspaper submitted that the contrary view requires the court to assess the public interest value of a publication, taking these matters into account. Such an approach would involve an unpredictable outcome. Moreover, it would put the judge in a position which in a free society ought to be occupied by the editor. Such paternalism would effectively give the court an undesirable and invidious role as a censor or licensing body.

These are powerful arguments, but I do not accept the conclusion for which the newspaper contended. ...

My starting point is freedom of expression. The high importance of freedom to impart and receive information and ideas has been stated so often and so eloquently that this point calls for no elaboration in this case. At a pragmatic level, freedom to disseminate and receive information on political matters is essential to the proper functioning of the system of parliamentary democracy cherished in this country. This freedom enables those who elect representatives to Parliament to make an informed choice, regarding individuals as well as policies, and those elected to make informed decisions. ...

Likewise, there is no need to elaborate on the importance of the role discharged by the media in the expression and communication of information and comment on political matters. It is through the mass media that most people today obtain their information on political matters. Without freedom of expression by the media, freedom of expression would be a hollow concept. The interest of a democratic society in ensuring a free press weighs heavily in the balance in deciding whether any curtailment of this freedom bears a reasonable relationship to the purpose of the curtailment. In this regard it should be kept in mind that one of the contemporary functions of the media is investigative journalism. This activity, as much as the traditional activities of reporting and commenting, is part of the vital role of the press and the media generally.

[5] (1997) 145 ALR 96.

Reputation is an integral and important part of the dignity of the individual. It also forms the basis of many decisions in a democratic society which are fundamental to its well-being: whom to employ or work for, whom to promote, whom to do business with or to vote for. Once besmirched by an unfounded allegation in a national newspaper, a reputation can be damaged for ever, especially if there is no opportunity to vindicate one's reputation. When this happens, society as well as the individual is the loser. For it should not be supposed that protection of reputation is a matter of importance only to the affected individual and his family. Protection of reputation is conducive to the public good. It is in the public interest that the reputation of public figures should not be debased falsely. In the political field, in order to make an informed choice, the electorate needs to be able to identify the good as well as the bad. Consistently with these considerations, human rights conventions recognise that freedom of expression is not an absolute right. Its exercise may be subject to such restrictions as are prescribed by law and are necessary in a democratic society for the protection of the reputations of others.

The crux of this appeal, therefore, lies in identifying the restrictions which are fairly and reasonably necessary for the protection of reputation. Leaving aside the exceptional cases which attract absolute privilege, the common law denies protection to defamatory statements, whether of comment or fact, proved to be actuated by malice, in the *Horrocks v Lowe* sense. This common law limitation on freedom of speech passes the 'necessary' test with flying colours. This is an acceptable limitation. Freedom of speech does not embrace freedom to make defamatory statements out of personal spite or without having a positive belief in their truth.

In the case of statements of opinion on matters of public interest, that is the limit of what is necessary for protection of reputation. Readers and viewers and listeners can make up their own minds on whether they agree or disagree with defamatory statements which are recognisable as comment and which, expressly or implicitly, indicate in general terms the facts on which they are based.

With defamatory imputations of fact the position is different and more difficult. Those who read or hear such allegations are unlikely to have any means of knowing whether they are true or not. In respect of such imputations, a plaintiff's ability to obtain a remedy if he can prove malice is not normally a sufficient safeguard. Malice is notoriously difficult to prove. If a newspaper is understandably unwilling to disclose its sources, a plaintiff can be deprived of the material necessary to prove, or even allege, that the newspaper acted recklessly in publishing as it did without further verification. Thus, in the absence of any additional safeguard for reputation, a newspaper, anxious to be first with a 'scoop', would in practice be free to publish seriously defamatory misstatements of fact based on the slenderest of materials. Unless the paper chose later to withdraw the allegations, the politician thus defamed would have no means of clearing his name, and the public would have no means of knowing where the truth lay. Some further protection for reputation is needed if this can be achieved without a disproportionate incursion into freedom of expression.

This is a difficult problem. No answer is perfect. Every solution has its own advantages and disadvantages. Depending on local conditions, such as legal procedures and the traditions and power of the press, the solution preferred in one country may not be best suited to another country. The appellant newspaper commends reliance upon the ethics of professional journalism. The decision should be left to the editor of the newspaper. Unfortunately, in the United Kingdom this would not generally be thought to provide a sufficient safeguard. In saying this I am not referring to mistaken decisions. From time to time mistakes are bound to occur, even in the best regulated circles. Making every allowance for this, the sad reality is that the overall handling of these matters by the national press, with its own commercial interests to serve, does not always command general confidence. . . .

For the newspaper, Lord Lester of Herne Hill QC's fall-back position was that qualified privilege should be available for political discussion unless the plaintiff proved the newspaper failed to exercise reasonable care. One difficulty with this suggestion is that it would seem to leave a newspaper open to publish a serious allegation which it had been wholly unable to verify. Depending on the circumstances, that might be most unsatisfactory. This difficulty would be removed if, as also canvassed by Lord Lester, the suggested limitation was stated more broadly, and qualified privilege was excluded if the plaintiff proved that the newspaper's conduct in making the publication was unreasonable. Whether this test would differ substantially from the common law test is a moot point. There seems to be no significant practical difference between looking at all the circumstances to decide if a publication attracts privilege, and looking at all the circumstances to see if an acknowledged privilege is defeated.

I have been more troubled by Lord Lester's suggested shift in the burden of proof. Placing the burden of proof on the plaintiff would be a reminder that the starting point today is freedom of expression and limitations on this freedom are exceptions. That has attraction. But if this shift of the onus were applied generally, it would turn the law of qualified privilege upside down. The repercussions of such a far-reaching change were not canvassed before your Lordships. If this change were applied only to political information, the distinction would lack a coherent rationale. There are other subjects of serious public concern. On balance I favour leaving the onus in its traditional place, on him who asserts the privilege, for two practical reasons. A newspaper will know much more of the facts leading up to publication. The burden of proof will seldom, if ever, be decisive on this issue....

My conclusion is that the established common law approach to misstatements of fact remains essentially sound. The common law should not develop 'political information' as a new 'subject matter' category of qualified privilege, whereby the publication of all such information would attract qualified privilege, whatever the circumstances. That would not provide adequate protection for reputation. Moreover, it would be unsound in principle to distinguish political discussion from discussion of other matters of serious public concern. The elasticity of the common law principle enables interference with freedom of speech to be confined to what is necessary in the circumstances of the case. This elasticity enables the court to give appropriate weight, in today's conditions, to the importance of freedom of expression by the media on all matters of public concern.

Depending on the circumstances, the matters to be taken into account include the following. The comments are illustrative only. (1) The seriousness of the allegation. The more serious the charge, the more the public is misinformed and the individual harmed, if the allegation is not true. (2) The nature of the information, and the extent to which the subject matter is a matter of public concern. (3) The source of the information. Some informants have no direct knowledge of the events. Some have their own axes to grind, or are being paid for their stories. (4) The steps taken to verify the information. (5) The status of the information. The allegation may have already been the subject of an investigation which commands respect. (6) The urgency of the matter. News is often a perishable commodity. (7) Whether comment was sought from the plaintiff. He may have information others do not possess or have not disclosed. An approach to the plaintiff will not always be necessary. (8) Whether the article contained the gist of the plaintiff's side of the story. (9) The tone of the article. A newspaper can raise queries or call for an investigation. It need not adopt allegations as statements of fact. (10) The circumstances of the publication, including the timing.

This list is not exhaustive. The weight to be given to these and any other relevant factors will vary from case to case. Any disputes of primary fact will be a matter for the jury, if there is one. The decision on whether, having regard to the admitted or proved facts, the publication was subject to qualified privilege is a matter for the judge. This is the established practice and seems sound. A balancing operation is better carried out by a judge in a reasoned judgment than by a jury. Over time, a valuable corpus of case law will be built up.

In general, a newspaper's unwillingness to disclose the identity of its sources should not weigh against it. Further, it should always be remembered that journalists act without the benefit of the clear light of hindsight. Matters which are obvious in retrospect may have been far from clear in the heat of the moment. Above all, the court should have particular regard to the importance of freedom of expression. The press discharges vital functions as a bloodhound as well as a watchdog. The court should be slow to conclude that a publication was not in the public interest and, therefore, the public had no right to know, especially when the information is in the field of political discussion. Any lingering doubts should be resolved in favour of publication....

LORD STEYN: ...

It is...necessary to explain what is meant by a generic qualified privilege. It is to be contrasted with each case being considered in the light of its own particular circumstances, that is, in an *ad hoc* manner, in the light of the concrete facts of the case, and balancing in each case the gravity of the damage to the plaintiff's reputation against the value of publication on the particular occasion. A generic privilege, on the other hand, uses the technique of applying the privilege to a category or categories of cases. An example is the rule in *New York Times Co v Sullivan*,[6] which requires proof of malice in all defamation actions by public officials and public figures. In the present case counsel for the newspaper argues for a generic test not applicable to a category of victim (such as public figures) but dependent on the subject matter (political speech).

On balance two particular factors have persuaded me to reject the generic test. First, the rule and practice in England is not to compel a newspaper to reveal its sources: see s 10 of the Contempt of Court Act 1981 ... and *Goodwin v. UK* (1996) 22 EHRR 123 at 143 (para 39). By contrast a plaintiff in the United States is entitled to a pre-trial enquiry into the sources of the story and editorial decision-making: *Herbert v Lando* (1979) 441 US 153. Without such information a plaintiff suing for defamation in England will be substantially handicapped [in trying to prove malice to rebut the privilege].... Secondly, a test expressed in terms of a category of cases, such as political speech, is at variance with the jurisprudence of the European Court of Human Rights which in cases of competing rights and interests requires a balancing exercise in the light of the concrete facts of each case. While there is as yet no decision directly in point, it seems to me that Professor John Fleming is right in saying that the basic approach of the European Court of Human Rights has been close to the German approach by insisting on individual evaluation of each case rather than categories: 'Libel and Constitutional Free Speech,' in *Essays for Patrick Atiyah*, Cane and Stapleton (1991), p 333 at pp 337 and 345. Our inclination ought to be towards the approach that prevails in the jurisprudence on the convention....

It was said by counsel for the newspaper that the English courts have not yet recognised that the press has a general duty to inform the public of political matters and that the public has a right to be so informed. If there is any doubt on the point, this is the occasion for the House to settle the matter. It is an open space in the law which can be filled by the courts....

In *De Haes v. Belgium* (1997) 25 EHRR 1 the European Court of Human Rights again emphasised that the press plays an essential role in a democratic society. The court trenchantly observed (at 53 (para 39)): 'It is incumbent on the press to impart information and ideas of public interest. Not only does the press have the task of imparting such information and ideas: the public also has a right to receive them.' This principle must be the foundation of our law on qualified privilege of political speech....

[LORD COOKE OF THORNDON and LORD HOBHOUSE OF WOODBOROUGH delivered speeches agreeing with LORD NICHOLLS's speech. LORD HOPE OF CRAIGHEAD delivered a speech in favour of allowing the appeal.]

Appeal dismissed.

NOTES

1. *Reynolds* is noted by I. Loveland [2000] PL 351 and (in comparative setting) F.A. Trindade (2000) 116 LQR 185.

2. Three members of the House thought that their decision on the scope of qualified privilege did not entitle the defendant to raise the privilege issue again at the new trial. They held that there was no prospect of the defence succeeding, largely because the defendants had not given the claimant any opportunity to respond to the allegations in the article. Lord Steyn and Lord Hope dissented. Lord Steyn said that fairness required the new trial to consider the defence anew because the House of Lords had fundamentally changed the defence. He also argued that since failure to give the defendant an opportunity to reply was only one factor to be considered, it could not as a matter of law decide the issue in favour of the claimant.

[6] (1964) 376 US 254.

3.   Although human rights concerns dominate several of the speeches, the House of Lords did not go so far along the road of protecting freedom of speech and of the press as, for example, the US Supreme Court has done in the light of its 'chilling effect' doctrine. The central point of that doctrine, that free speech requires extensive tolerance of the making of untrue statements because any other rule will cause the press to be cautious even about speaking the truth, is taken into account but not entirely accepted in *Reynolds*. There are dicta in the speeches of Lord Cooke, Lord Hope and Lord Hobhouse (who, however, puts forward pragmatic reasons for adopting a more libertarian stance) to the effect that there is no civil liberties interest in the dissemination of untruths and that the 'chilling effect' is not unacceptable in itself.

4.   A very extensive case law has grown up around '*Reynolds* privilege', in particular the House of Lords' decision in *Jameel v Wall Street Journal* [2006] 4 All ER 1279, [2006] UKHL 44, post.

5.   In *Bonnick v Morris* [2003] 1 AC 300, [2002] UKPC 31 the Privy Council considered whether 'responsible journalism' should be considered on the basis that the statement had the one meaning attributed to it for the purpose of deciding whether it was defamatory: see p. 973, ante. The court decided that it should not. It would be a mistake to apply a rule about the *meaning* of words to the question of the defendant's *conduct*. The *Reynolds* test of 'responsible journalism' must be applied in a 'flexible manner' having regard to 'practical realities', per Lord Nicholls at [24]. It would be unnecessarily rigid and legalistic to penalise a journalist 'for making a wrong decision on a question of meaning on which different people might reasonably take different views. . . . If the words are ambiguous to such an extent that they may readily convey a different meaning to an ordinary reasonable reader, a court may properly take this other meaning into account when considering whether *Reynolds* privilege is available as a defence.' Thus, it was open to a newspaper to argue that it had understood the words published to have a meaning other than their defamatory 'single meaning', although 'a responsible journalist will not disregard a defamatory meaning which is obviously one possible meaning of the article in question. Questions of degree arise here. The more obvious the defamatory meaning, and the more serious the defamation, the less weight will a court attach to other possible meanings when considering the conduct to be expected of a responsible journalist in the circumstances', at [25].

6.   In *Kearns v General Council of the Bar* [2003] 2 All ER 534, [2003] EWCA Civ 331 the defendant governing body wrote to all barristers to convey its suspicions that the claimants, who had been instructing counsel, were not bona fide qualified solicitors. The information turned out to be false, but the court held that publication had been privileged, applying the established test of reciprocal duty and interest ('legal, social, or moral') derived from *Adam v Ward* [1917] AC 309 at 334 (discussed by Lord Nicholls in *Reynolds*, p. 1000, ante). The Court of Appeal noted that such 'traditional' qualified privilege could only be rebutted by the claimant proving malice; the defendant did not have to show it had acted 'responsibly'. On the facts, the court commented that there would not have been '*Reynolds* privilege' had traditional privilege failed, because the Bar Council had failed to take any steps to verify the information before publishing it.

Note that in *Spring v Guardian Assurance* [1995] 2 AC 296, [1994] 3 All ER 129, p. 58, ante, the House of Lords held that an action for negligently inflicted economic loss was not precluded because the misstatement had been made on an occasion of qualified privilege, so that malice would need to be proved for an action in libel.

Similarly in *W v Westminster City Council* [2005] 4 All ER 96 (Note), Tugendhat J held (relying upon *Spring*) that the existence of qualified privilege in libel did not preclude a separate action for damages under s. 7 of the Human Rights Act 1998, where a statement by a public authority violated the claimant's right to private and family life (Article 8 of the ECHR).

■ Jameel v Wall Street Journal Europe Sprl

House of Lords [2006] 4 All ER 1279

The defendant newspaper published a list of companies whose bank accounts were being monitored by the central bank of Saudi Arabia (at the request of the US government), to prevent their use for channelling funds to terrorist organisations. The list included the claimants, who sued for libel. The newspaper appealed against the decision of the Court of Appeal [2005] 4 All ER 356, [2005] EWCA Civ 74 (affirming that of the trial judge, Eady J ([2004] 2 All ER 92, [2003] EWHC 2945 (QB)) that no '*Reynolds* privilege' attached to the article.

LORD BINGHAM OF CORNHILL: ...

[28] The decision of the House in *Reynolds v Times Newspapers Ltd* [1999] 4 All ER 609, [2001] 2 AC 127 built on the traditional foundations of qualified privilege but carried the law forward in a way which gave much greater weight than the earlier law had done to the value of informed public debate of significant public issues. Both these aspects are, I think, important in understanding the decision.

[32] Qualified privilege as a live issue only arises where a statement is defamatory and untrue. It was in this context, and assuming the matter to be one of public interest, that Lord Nicholls proposed ([1999] 4 All ER 609 at 623, [2001] 2 AC 127 at 202) a test of responsible journalism, a test repeated in *Bonnick v Morris* [2002] UKPC 31 at [22]–[24], (2002) 12 BHRC 558 at [22]–[24], [2003] 1 AC 300. The rationale of this test is, as I understand, that there is no duty to publish and the public have no interest to read material which the publisher has not taken reasonable steps to verify. As Lord Hobhouse observed with characteristic pungency ([1999] 4 All ER 609 at 657, [2001] 2 AC 127 at 238), 'No public interest is served by publishing or communicating misinformation'. But the publisher is protected if he has taken such steps as a responsible journalist would take to try and ensure that what is published is accurate and fit for publication.

[33] Lord Nicholls ([1999] 4 All ER 609 at 626, [2001] 2 AC 127 at 205) listed certain matters which might be taken into account in deciding whether the test of responsible journalism was satisfied. He intended these as pointers which might be more or less indicative, depending on the circumstances of a particular case, and not, I feel sure, as a series of hurdles to be negotiated by a publisher before he could successfully rely on qualified privilege. Lord Nicholls recognised ([1999] 4 All ER 609 at 623–624, [2001] 2 AC 127 at 202–203), inevitably as I think, that it had to be a body other than the publisher, namely the court, which decided whether a publication was protected by qualified privilege. But this does not mean that the editorial decisions and judgments made at the time, without the knowledge of falsity which is a benefit of hindsight, are irrelevant. Weight should ordinarily be given to the professional judgment of an editor or journalist in the absence of some indication that it was made in a casual, cavalier, slipshod or careless manner.

[35] These principles must be applied to the present case. [The] Court of Appeal upheld the judge's denial of *Reynolds* privilege on a single ground ... : that the newspaper had failed to delay publication of the [claimants'] names without waiting long enough for the [claimants] to comment. This seems to me, with respect, to be a very narrow ground on which to deny the privilege, and the ruling subverts the liberalising intention of the *Reynolds* decision. The subject matter was of great public interest, in the strictest sense. The article was written by an experienced specialist reporter and approved by senior staff on the newspaper and "Wall Street Journal" who themselves sought to verify its contents. The

article was unsensational in tone and (apparently) factual in content. The [claimants'] response was sought, although at a late stage, and the newspaper's inability to obtain a comment recorded. It is very unlikely that a comment, if obtained, would have been revealing, since even if the respondents' accounts were being monitored it was unlikely that they would know. It might be thought that this was the sort of neutral, investigative journalism which *Reynolds* privilege exists to protect. I would accordingly allow the appeal and set aside the Court of Appeal judgment.

LORD HOFFMANN: . . .

[38] Until very recently, the law of defamation was weighted in favour of claimants and the law of privacy weighted against them. True but trivial intrusions into private life were safe. Reports of investigations by the newspaper into matters of public concern which could be construed as reflecting badly on public figures domestic or foreign were risky. The House attempted to redress the balance in favour of privacy in *Campbell v MGN Ltd* [2004] UKHL 22, [2004] 2 All ER 995, [2004] 2 AC 457 and in favour of greater freedom for the press to publish stories of genuine public interest in *Reynolds*. But this case suggests that *Reynolds* has had little impact upon the way the law is applied at first instance. It is therefore necessary to restate the principles.

[43] The newspaper's principal defence was based on *Reynolds v Times Newspapers Ltd* [1999] 4 All ER 609, [2001] 2 AC 127. It is called in the trade '*Reynolds* privilege' but the use of the term privilege, although historically accurate, may be misleading. A defence of privilege in the usual sense is available when the defamatory statement was published on a privileged occasion and can be defeated only by showing that the privilege was abused. . . .

[46] Although Lord Nicholls uses the word 'privilege', it is clearly not being used in the old sense. It is the material which is privileged, not the occasion on which it is published. There is no question of the privilege being defeated by proof of malice because the propriety of the conduct of the defendant is built into the conditions under which the material is privileged. The burden is upon the defendant to prove that those conditions are satisfied. I therefore agree with the opinion of the Court of Appeal in *Loutchansky v Times Newspapers Ltd (No 2)* [2001] EWCA Civ 1805 at [35], [2002] 1 All ER 652 at [35], sub nom *Loutchansky v Times Newspapers Ltd (Nos 4 and 5)*, *Loutchansky v Times Newspapers Ltd (Nos 2, 3 and 5)* [2002] QB 783 that '*Reynolds* privilege' is 'a different jurisprudential creature from the traditional form of privilege from which it sprang'. It might more appropriately be called the *Reynolds* public interest defence rather than privilege.

[50] In answering the question of public interest, I do not think it helpful to apply the classic test for the existence of a privileged occasion and ask whether there was a duty to communicate the information and an interest in receiving it. The *Reynolds* defence was developed from the traditional form of privilege by a generalisation that in matters of public interest, there can be said to be a professional duty on the part of journalists to impart the information and an interest in the public in receiving it. The House having made this generalisation, it should in my opinion be regarded as a proposition of law and not decided each time as a question of fact. If the publication is in the public interest, the duty and interest are taken to exist. The *Reynolds* defence is very different from the privilege discussed by the Court of Appeal in *Blackshaw v Lord* [1983] 2 All ER 311, [1984] QB 1, where it was contemplated that in exceptional circumstances there could be a privileged occasion in the classic sense, arising out of a duty to communicate information to the public generally and a corresponding interest in receiving it. The Court of Appeal there contemplated a traditional privilege, liable to be defeated only by proof of malice. But the *Reynolds* defence does not employ this two-stage process. It is not as narrow as traditional privilege nor is there a burden upon the claimant to show malice to defeat it. . . .

Responsible journalism

[53] If the publication, including the defamatory statement, passes the public interest test, the inquiry then shifts to whether the steps taken to gather and publish the information were responsible and fair. As Lord Nicholls said in *Bonnick v Morris* [2002] UKPC 31 at [23], (2002) 12 BHRC 558 at [23], [2003] 1 AC 300:

'Stated shortly, the *Reynolds* privilege is concerned to provide a proper degree of protection for responsible journalism when reporting matters of public concern. Responsible journalism is the point at which a fair balance is held between freedom of expression on matters of public concern and the reputations of individuals. Maintenance of this standard is in the public interest and in the interests of those whose reputations are involved. It can be regarded as the price journalists pay in return for the privilege.'

[54] Lord Nicholls was speaking in the context of a publication in a newspaper but the defence is of course available to anyone who publishes material of public interest in any medium. The question in each case is whether the defendant behaved fairly and responsibly in gathering and publishing the information. But I shall for convenience continue to describe this as 'responsible journalism'.

[55] In this case, Eady J ([2004] EWHC 37, [2004] EMLR 196) said that the concept of 'responsible journalism' was too vague. It was, he said, 'subjective'. I am not certain what this means, except that it is obviously a term of disapproval. (In the jargon of the old Soviet Union, 'objective' meant correct and in accordance with the Party line, while 'subjective' meant deviationist and wrong.) But the standard of responsible journalism is as objective and no more vague than standards such as 'reasonable care' which are regularly used in other branches of law. Greater certainty in its application is attained in two ways. First, as Lord Nicholls said, a body of illustrative case law builds up. Secondly, just as the standard of reasonable care in particular areas, such as driving a vehicle, is made more concrete by extra-statutory codes of behaviour like the Highway Code, so the standard of responsible journalism is made more specific by the code of practice which has been adopted by the newspapers and ratified by the Press Complaints Commission. This too, while not binding upon the courts, can provide valuable guidance.

[56] In *Reynolds*, Lord Nicholls gave his well-known non-exhaustive list of ten matters which should in suitable cases be taken into account. They are not tests which the publication has to pass. In the hands of a judge hostile to the spirit of *Reynolds*, they can become ten hurdles at any of which the defence may fail. That is how Eady J treated them. The defence, he said (at [32]), can be sustained only after 'the closest and most rigorous scrutiny' by the application of what he called 'Lord Nicholls' ten tests'. But that, in my opinion, is not what Lord Nicholls meant. As he said in *Bonnick*'s case (2002) 12 BHRC 558 at [24] the standard of conduct required of the newspaper must be applied in a practical and flexible manner. It must have regard to practical realities.

[His Lordship found that the test of responsible journalism had been satisfied and allowed the appeal.]

BARONESS HALE OF RICHMOND [agreed with LORD HOFFMANN, and stated:] . . .

[146] It should by now be entirely clear that the *Reynolds* defence is a 'different jurisprudential creature' (*Loutchansky v Times Newspapers Ltd (No 2)* [2001] EWCA Civ 1805 at [35], [2002] 1 All ER 652 at [35], sub nom *Loutchansky v Times Newspapers Ltd (Nos 4 and 5)*, *Loutchansky v Times Newspapers Ltd (Nos 2, 3 and 5)* [2002] QB 783) from the law of privilege, although it is a natural development of that law. It springs from the general obligation of the press, media and other publishers to communicate important information upon matters of general public interest and the general right of the public to receive such information. It is not helpful to analyse the particular case in terms of a specific duty and a specific right to know. That can, as experience since *Reynolds* has shown, very easily lead to a narrow and rigid approach which defeats its object. In truth, it is a defence of publication in the public interest.

[147] This does not mean a free-for-all to publish without being damned. The public only have a right to be told if two conditions are fulfilled. First, there must [be] a real public interest in communicating and receiving the information. This is, as we all know, very different from saying that it is information which interests the public—the most vapid tittle-tattle about the activities of footballers' wives and girlfriends interests large sections of the public but no-one could claim any real public interest in our being told all about it. It is also different from the test suggested by Mr Robertson QC, on behalf of the Wall Street Journal Europe, of whether the information is 'newsworthy'. That is too subjective a test, based on the target audience, inclinations and interests of the particular publication. There must be

some real public interest in having this information in the public domain. But this is less than a test that the public 'need to know', which would be far too limited.

[148] If ever there was a story which met the test, it must be this one. In the immediate aftermath of 9/11, it was in the interests of the whole world that the sources of funds for such atrocities be identified and if possible stopped. There was and should have been a lively public debate about this....

[149] Secondly, the publisher must have taken the care that a responsible publisher would take to verify the information published. The actual steps taken will vary with the nature and sources of the information. But one would normally expect that the source or sources were ones which the publisher had good reason to think reliable, that the publisher himself believed the information to be true, and that he had done what he could to check it. We are frequently told that 'fact checking' has gone out of fashion with the media. But a publisher who is to avoid the risk of liability if the information cannot later be proved to be true would be well advised to do it. Part of this is, of course, taking reasonable steps to contact the people named for their comments. The requirements in 'reportage' cases, where the publisher is simply reporting what others have said, may be rather different, but if the publisher does not himself believe the information to be true, he would be well advised to make this clear. In any case, the tone in which the information is conveyed will be relevant to whether or not the publisher has behaved responsibly in passing it on.

[150] Once again, as my noble and learned friend Lord Hoffmann has demonstrated, the publication of this story passed this test. We have to judge the steps which are known to have been taken against the background of the style and tone of the publication in general and the article in particular. This is not a newspaper with an interest in publishing any sensational information however inaccurate (or even in some cases invented). It is, as the journalist quoted by my noble and learned friend said, 'gravely serious' (indeed some might find it seriously dull). We need more such serious journalism in this country and our defamation law should encourage rather than discourage it.

[151] In short, my Lords, if the public interest defence does not succeed on the known facts of this case, it is hard to see it ever succeeding.

[LORD HOPE OF CRAIGHEAD agreed with LORD BINGHAM, and delivered a speech in favour of allowing the appeal. LORD SCOTT OF FOSCOTE delivered a speech in favour of allowing the appeal.]

Appeal allowed.

NOTES

1. *Jameel* is noted by K. Beattie [2007] EHRLR 81 and J. Rowbottom [2007] CLJ 8.

2. On the jurisprudential nature of '*Reynolds* privilege' (see Lord Hoffmann at [43], [46], ante) contrast Lord Scott, who commented at [135] that *Reynolds* is simply the expression of the traditional duty-interest approach to qualified privilege 'in a particular journalistic context'.

3. Their Lordships in *Jameel* clearly believed that judges had been failing to take *Reynolds* to heart, and in particular Lord Nicholls's conclusion that: 'Any lingering doubts should be resolved in favour of publication.' In *Charman v Orion Publishing Group Ltd* [2008] 1 All ER 750, [2007] EWCA Civ 972 Ward LJ referred at [84] to the House of Lords' 'rebuke of the lower courts for their failure to appreciate how "liberalising" an opinion *Reynolds* was intended to be'.

4. *Seaga v Harper* [2008] 1 All ER 965, [2008] UKPC 9 confirms that *Reynolds* is not limited to journalistic situations (cf. Lord Hoffmann at [54], ante), but extends to publication of information in the public interest in any medium (*in casu* at a public meeting, although on the facts the defendant had failed to take sufficient care to check his facts and could not rely upon the defence).

5.   In *Loutchansky v Times Newspapers Ltd (Nos 4 and 5)* [2002] QB 783, [2002] 1 All ER 652 the Court of Appeal held that Gray J had misapplied *Reynolds* by asking whether the newspaper could legitimately have been criticised for failing to publish the statement in question (as the test for the existence of a duty to publish). This was 'too stringent' since a journalist might publish a statement wholly responsibly, even though he could not have been criticized for not publishing it.

On remission of the case, Gray J (applying the correct test) again found that the statement had not been privileged. The defendant argued in the European Court of Human Rights that this decision amounted to a breach of its right to freedom of speech under Article 10 of the ECHR (*Times Newspapers v United Kingdom*, 11 October 2005, unreported). The ECtHR held, however, that the High Court's reasons for denying privilege had been sufficient, and that the protection of Mr Loutchansky's reputation had not imposed a disproportionate restriction on the newspaper's freedom of speech. See R. Dunlop [2006] EHRLR 327. There are limits both to *Reynolds* and to Article 10.

6.   *Roberts v Gable* [2008] EWCA Civ 721 considers the 'reportage' defence (mentioned by Baroness Hale in *Jameel* [149], ante). This is a 'species' of qualified privilege which protects 'the neutral reporting without adoption or embellishment or subscribing to any belief in its truth of attributed allegations of both sides of a political and possibly some other kind of dispute,' per Ward LJ at [53]. The information must be in the public interest, and the other *Reynolds* indicia of 'responsible journalism' must be considered. However, the defendant need not take steps to verify the information: he is reporting not the truth of the statements, but the fact they were made.

Note that if a reported statement does not satisfy this test and thus is not privileged, the truth of the defamatory words (and not simply the fact that they were spoken) must be proved, i.e. the usual 'repetition rule' for the purposes of justification still applies: see p. 984, ante.

7.   In *Galloway v Telegraph Group Ltd* [2006] EMLR 11, [2006] EWCA Civ 17 the *Reynolds* defence failed when the newspaper published a story accusing the claimant MP of being in the pay of Iraqi dictator Saddam Hussein, based on documents which had been found in ruined government offices in occupied Baghdad. The information in those documents turned out to be false. The story was undoubtedly a matter of public interest. However, the Court of Appeal agreed with the trial judge (Eady J) that there had been no need for especial urgency in publishing it, and so the newspaper had been at fault in not making further inquiries about the allegations, especially of Mr Galloway himself. Moreover, the defendant could not rely on the *Reynolds* defence when it had 'embraced the allegations with relish and fervour' and indeed 'embellished' them, [73].

It may be that Eady J and the Court of Appeal were guilty in *Galloway* of the narrow approach to privilege for which they were about to be castigated by the House of Lords in *Jameel*. But note their Lordships' rather similar emphasis on the serious 'style and tone' of the Wall Street Journal in *Jameel* (e.g. Baroness Hale at [150], ante). It may be that graveness in reporting would be wise, whenever the media might have to rely on *Reynolds* privilege. On the other hand. Sedley LJ in *Roberts v Gable* (ante) at [74] stated that even in 'reportage' cases, the law does not prohibit a defendant from 'taking a perceptible pleasure in reporting the controversy'. Considering Baroness Hale's statement in *Jameel*, Sedley LJ said 'I do not imagine that she means the reportage defence to be a prize for bland journalism', ibid.

(d) Amends

■ Defamation Act 1996

2 Offer to make amends

(1) A person who has published a statement alleged to be defamatory of another may offer to make amends under this section.

(2) The offer may be in relation to the statement generally or in relation to a specific defamatory meaning which the person making the offer accepts that the statement conveys ("a qualified offer").

(3) An offer to make amends—

(a) must be in writing,

(b) must be expressed to be an offer to make amends under section 2 of the Defamation Act 1996, and

(c) must state whether it is a qualified offer and, if so, set out the defamatory meaning in relation to which it is made.

(4) An offer to make amends under this section is an offer—

(a) to make a suitable correction of the statement complained of and a sufficient apology to the aggrieved party,

(b) to publish the correction and apology in a manner that is reasonable and practicable in the circumstances, and

(c) to pay to the aggrieved party such compensation (if any), and such costs, as may be agreed or determined to be payable.

The fact that the offer is accompanied by an offer to take specific steps does not affect the fact that an offer to make amends under this section is an offer to do all the things mentioned in paragraphs (a) to (c).

(5) An offer to make amends under this section may not be made by a person after serving a defence in defamation proceedings brought against him by the aggrieved party in respect of the publication in question.

(6) An offer to make amends under this section may be withdrawn before it is accepted; and a renewal of an offer which has been withdrawn shall be treated as a new offer.

3 Accepting an offer to make amends

(1) If an offer to make amends under section 2 is accepted by the aggrieved party, the following provisions apply.

(2) The party accepting the offer may not bring or continue defamation proceedings in respect of the publication concerned against the person making the offer, but he is entitled to enforce the offer to make amends, as follows.

(3) If the parties agree on the steps to be taken in fulfilment of the offer, the aggrieved party may apply to the court for an order that the other party fulfil his offer by taking the steps agreed.

(4) If the parties do not agree on the steps to be taken by way of correction, apology and publication, the party who made the offer may take such steps as he thinks appropriate, and may in particular—

(a) make the correction and apology by a statement in open court in terms approved by the court, and

(b) give an undertaking to the court as to the manner of their publication.

(5) If the parties do not agree on the amount to be paid by way of compensation, it shall be determined by the court on the same principles as damages in defamation proceedings. The court shall take

account of any steps taken in fulfilment of the offer and (so far as not agreed between the parties) of the suitability of the correction, the sufficiency of the apology and whether the manner of their publication was reasonable in the circumstances, and may reduce or increase the amount of compensation accordingly.

(6) If the parties do not agree on the amount to be paid by way of costs, it shall be determined by the court on the same principles as costs awarded in court proceedings.

(7) The acceptance of an offer by one person to make amends does not affect any cause of action against another person in respect of the same publication, subject as follows.

(8) In England and Wales or Northern Ireland, for the purposes of the Civil Liability (Contribution) Act 1978—

(a) the amount of compensation paid under the offer shall be treated as paid in bona fide settlement or compromise of the claim; and

(b) where another person is liable in respect of the same damage (whether jointly or otherwise), the person whose offer to make amends was accepted is not required to pay by virtue of any contribution under section 1 of that Act a greater amount than the amount of the compensation payable in pursuance of the offer. . . .

(10) Proceedings under this section shall be heard and determined without a jury.

4 Failure to accept offer to make amends

(1) If an offer to make amends under section 2, duly made and not withdrawn, is not accepted by the aggrieved party, the following provisions apply.

(2) The fact that the offer was made is a defence (subject to subsection (3)) to defamation proceedings in respect of the publication in question by that party against the person making the offer.

A qualified offer is only a defence in respect of the meaning to which the offer related.

(3) There is no such defence if the person by whom the offer was made knew or had reason to believe that the statement complained of—

(a) referred to the aggrieved party or was likely to be understood as referring to him, and

(b) was both false and defamatory of that party;

but it shall be presumed until the contrary is shown that he did not know and had no reason to believe that was the case.

(4) The person who made the offer need not rely on it by way of defence, but if he does he may not rely on any other defence. If the offer was a qualified offer, this applies only in respect of the meaning to which the offer related.

(5) The offer may be relied on in mitigation of damages whether or not it was relied on as a defence.

NOTES

1. The requirement that the defendant has to renounce any other defences to invoke the amends procedure is one of the controversial aspects of this defence. D. Vick and L. Macpherson (1997) 49 Federal Communications L.J. 621 comment:

    While the new offer of amends procedure is a marked improvement over section 4 of the 1952 Act, several shortcomings may diminish its effectiveness. For example, an offer must be made before a defense has been served in defamation proceedings brought against the offeror. The Parliamentary Secretary to the Lord Chancellor's Department argued that the machinery created by sections 2–4 of the new Act is 'designed to provide immediate amends, avoiding all the trouble and expense of conventional proceedings' by encouraging a potential defendant to 'come[ ] forward at once,' and that allowing a defendant to invoke the procedure after serving defenses would render the process 'cluttered and confused.' The problem is that defendants may be unwilling to submit to the procedure (which entails a tacit admission of wrong-doing) on such short notice.

Vick and Macpherson also claim that the Act might have encouraged defendants to use the procedure more if it had capped the damages available when it is invoked.

2. The original draft of s. 3(4) allowed the court to impose methods of publishing the correction and apology on the parties when they could not agree. Media interests successfully lobbied to have the present draft inserted instead, fearing judicial control over the detailed presentation of news broadcasts and the layout of newspapers. But is the final version very different in its effect? In considering whether to approve the terms of a correction and apology under s. 3(4)(a), may not the court take into account the defendant's proposals for publishing the correction under s. 3(4)(b)? If it may, the defendant will eventually have to publish the correction and apology in the way the court wants.

3. In *Milne v Express Newspapers* [2005] 1 All ER 1021, [2004] EWCA Civ 664 the Court of Appeal held that where a claimant rejects an offer of amends, the defendant loses the defence only if he was in bad faith; the phrase that the defendant 'knew or had reason to believe' in s. 4(3) was construed to mean knowledge of the relevant facts, or recklessness, not caring whether they were true or not. It was not sufficient that the defendant would have known the facts if he had taken reasonable steps to find out.

4. It has always been open for the defendant to offer an apology as part of settlement negotiations, which may of course reduce the damages should the claim succeed, without providing a formal defence as such. The Libel Acts of 1843 and 1845 provide a defence for non-malicious newspapers who make both an apology and a payment into court, but they have been wholly superseded by the general provisions on payments into court applicable to all actions for damages (see *Duncan and Neill on Defamation* 2nd edn, para. 16.09).

6 REMEDIES

■ John v MGN Ltd
Court of Appeal [1996] 2 All ER 35

An article in the defendant newspaper alleged that the plaintiff, the singer Elton John, was on a bizarre diet which involved his chewing food then spitting it out without swallowing, and that he had been observed at a party spitting chewed food into a napkin. The plaintiff sued for libel, seeking exemplary damages. The defendant had made no effort to verify the accuracy of the story. The judge ruled that there was sufficient evidence of recklessness to refer to the question of exemplary damages to the jury. The jury awarded £350,000: £75,000 compensatory damages and £275,000 exemplary damages. The defendants appealed against the assessment of damages.

SIR THOMAS BINGHAM MR (for the Court): . . .

Compensatory damages
The successful plaintiff in a defamation action is entitled to recover, as general compensatory damages, such sum as will compensate him for the wrong he has suffered. That sum must compensate him for the damage to his reputation; vindicate his good name; and take account of the distress, hurt and humiliation which the defamatory publication has caused. In assessing the appropriate damages for injury to reputation the most important factor is the gravity of the libel; the more closely it touches the

plaintiff's personal integrity, professional reputation, honour, courage, loyalty and the core attributes of his personality, the more serious it is likely to be. The extent of publication is also very relevant: a libel published to millions has a greater potential to cause damage than a libel published to a handful of people. A successful plaintiff may properly look to an award of damages to vindicate his reputation: but the significance of this is much greater in a case where the defendant asserts the truth of the libel and refuses any retraction or apology than in a case where the defendant acknowledges the falsity of what was published and publicly expresses regret that the libellous publication took place. It is well established that compensatory damages may and should compensate for additional injury caused to the plaintiff's feelings by the defendant's conduct of the action, as when he persists in an unfounded assertion that the publication was true, or refuses to apologise, or cross-examines the plaintiff in a wounding or insulting way . . .

Respect for the constitutional role of the jury in such actions, and judicial reluctance to intrude into the area of decision-making reserved to the jury, have traditionally led judges presiding over defamation trials with juries to confine their jury directions to a statement of general principles, eschewing any specific guidance on the appropriate level of general damages in the particular case. . . .

Whatever the theoretical attractions of this approach, its practical disadvantages have become ever more manifest. A series of jury awards in sums wildly disproportionate to any damage conceivably suffered by the plaintiff has given rise to serious and justified criticism of the procedures leading to such awards. This has not been the fault of the juries. Judges, as they were bound to do, confined themselves to broad directions of general principle, coupled with injunctions to the jury to be reasonable. But they gave no guidance on what might be thought reasonable or unreasonable, and it is not altogether surprising that juries lacked an instinctive sense of where to pitch their awards. They were in the position of sheep loosed on an unfenced common, with no shepherd. . . .

Following the enactment of s 8(2) of the Courts and Legal Services Act 1990 . . . the Court of Appeal was for the first time empowered, on allowing an appeal against a jury's award of damages, to substitute for the sum awarded by the jury such sum as might appear to the court to be proper. . . .

Any legal process should yield a successful plaintiff appropriate compensation, that is, compensation which is neither too much nor too little. That is so whether the award is made by judge or jury. No other result can be accepted as just. But there is continuing evidence of libel awards in sums which appear so large as to bear no relation to the ordinary values of life. This is most obviously unjust to defendants. But it serves no public purpose to encourage plaintiffs to regard a successful libel action, risky though the process undoubtedly is, as a road to untaxed riches. Nor is it healthy if any legal process fails to command the respect of lawyer and layman alike, as is regrettably true of the assessment of damages by libel juries. We are persuaded by the arguments we have heard that the subject should be reconsidered. . . .

Other awards in actions for defamation
We wholly agree with the ruling in *Rantzen v Mirror Group Newspapers (1986) Ltd* [1993] 4 All ER 975 that juries should not at present be reminded of previous libel awards by juries. Those awards will have been made in the absence of specific guidance by the judge and may themselves be very unreliable markers. . . .

Awards approved or substituted by the Court of Appeal
We agree with the ruling in *Rantzen* that reference may be made to awards approved or made by the Court of Appeal. As and when a framework of awards is established this will provide a valuable pointer to the appropriate level of award in the particular case . . .

Reference to damages in actions for personal injuries
In *Cassell & Co Ltd v Broome* [1972] 1 All ER 801 at 824, Lord Hailsham LC gave his reason for rejecting comparison with awards of damages for personal injuries. He said:

'In actions of defamation and in any other actions where damages for loss of reputation are involved, the principle of *restitutio in integrum* has necessarily an even more highly subjective element. Such actions involve a money award which may put the plaintiff in a purely financial sense in a much stronger position than he was before the wrong. Not merely can he recover the estimated sum of his past and future losses, but, in case the libel, driven underground, emerges from its lurking place at some future date, he must be able to point to a sum awarded by a jury sufficient to convince a bystander of the baselessness of the charge....This is why it is not necessarily fair to compare awards of damages in this field with damages for personal injuries....What is awarded is...a figure which cannot be arrived at by any purely objective computation. This is what is meant when the damages in defamation are described as being "at large". In a sense, too, these damages are of their nature punitive or exemplary in the loose sense in which the terms were used before 1964, because they inflict an added burden on the defendant proportionate to his conduct, just as they can be reduced if the defendant has behaved well—as for instance by a handsome apology—or the plaintiff badly, as for instance by provoking the defendant, or defaming him in return....'

This reasoning would weigh strongly against any attempt to equiparate damages for personal injuries and damages for defamation. It would not weigh so heavily, if at all, against reference to conventional levels of award for personal injuries as a check on the reasonableness of a proposed award of damages for defamation....

It has often, and rightly, been said that there can be no precise correlation between a personal injury and a sum of money. The same is true, perhaps even more true, of injury to reputation. There is force in the argument that to permit reference in libel cases to conventional levels of award in personal injury cases is simply to admit yet another incommensurable into the field of consideration. There is also weight in the argument, often heard, that conventional levels of award in personal injury cases are too low and therefore provide an uncertain guide. But these awards would not be relied on as any exact guide, and of course there can be no precise correlation between loss of a limb, or of sight, or quadriplegia, and damage to reputation. But if these personal injuries respectively command conventional awards of, at most, about £52,000, £90,000 and £125,000 for pain and suffering and loss of amenity (of course excluding claims based on loss of earnings, the cost of care and other specific financial claims), juries may properly be asked to consider whether the injury to his reputation of which the plaintiff complains should fairly justify any greater compensation. The conventional compensatory scales in personal injury cases must be taken to represent fair compensation in such cases unless and until those scales are amended by the courts or by Parliament. It is in our view offensive to public opinion, and rightly so, that a defamation plaintiff should recover damages for injury to reputation greater, perhaps by a significant factor, than if that same plaintiff had been rendered a helpless cripple or an insensate vegetable. The time has in our view come when judges, and counsel, should be free to draw the attention of juries to these comparisons.

[The Master of the Rolls held, departing from the traditional practice, that counsel and the judge could in future suggest to the jury what would constitute an appropriate award of damages: 'far from developing into an auction (and we do not see how it could), the process of mentioning figures would, in our view, induce a mood of realism on both sides'. His Lordship continued:]

Exemplary damages
...The passage [in *Duncan and Neill on Defamation* (2nd edn, 1983) para 18.27] remains a correct summary of the relevant law. So far as relevant to this case, and omitting footnotes and references, the passage reads:

'(a) Exemplary damages can only be awarded if the plaintiff proves that the defendant when he made the publication knew that he was committing a tort or was reckless whether his action was tortious or not, and decided to publish because the prospects of material advantage outweighed the prospects of material loss. "What is necessary is that the tortious act must be done with guilty knowledge for the motive that the chances of economic advantage outweigh the chances of economic, or perhaps physical, penalty". (b) The mere fact that a libel is committed in the course of a business carried on for profit, for example the business of a newspaper publisher, is not by itself sufficient to justify an award of exemplary damages. (c) If the case is one where exemplary damages *can* be awarded the court or jury should consider whether the sum which it proposes to award by way of compensatory damages is sufficient not only for the purpose of compensating the plaintiff but also for the purpose of punishing the defendant. It is only if the sum proposed by way of compensatory damages (which may include an element of aggravated damages) is insufficient that the court or jury should add to it enough "to bring it up to a sum sufficient as punishment". (d) The sum awarded as damages should be a single sum which will include, where appropriate, any elements of aggravated or exemplary damages…(f) A jury should be warned of the danger of an excessive award. (g) The means of the parties, though irrelevant to the issue of compensatory damages, can be taken into account in awarding exemplary damages…'

…Since art 10 of the ECHR requires any restriction on freedom of expression to be prescribed by law and necessary in a democratic society for the protection of reputation, it was argued that the conditions for making an exemplary award should be closely scrutinised and rigorously applied. Our attention was accordingly drawn to certain aspects of the conditions established by authority.

First, the state of mind of the defendant publisher. Little difficulty arises in the straightforward but relatively rare case in which it can be shown that the defendant actually knew that he was committing a tort when he published. The alternative state of mind—recklessness—is not so easy. [His Lordship stressed the distinction between recklenssness and mere carelessness drawn in *Derry v Peek* (1889) 14 App Cas 337, [1886–90] All ER Rep 1, and continued:]

Secondly, the publisher must have acted in the hope or expectation of material gain. It is well established that a publisher need not be shown to have made any precise or arithmetical calculation. But his unlawful conduct must have been motivated by mercenary considerations: the belief that he would be better off financially if he violated the plaintiff's rights than if he did not. Mere publication of a newspaper for profit is not enough.

We do not accept, as was argued, that in seeking to establish that the conditions for awarding exemplary damages have been met the plaintiff must satisfy the criminal, rather than the civil, standard of proof. But a jury should in our judgment be told that as the charge is grave, so should the proof be clear. An inference of reprehensible conduct and cynical calculation of mercenary advantage should not be lightly drawn….

It is plain on the authorities that it is only where the conditions for making an exemplary award are satisfied, and only when the sum awarded to the plaintiff as compensatory damages is not itself sufficient to punish the defendant, show that tort does not pay and deter others from acting similarly, that an award of exemplary damages should be added to the award of compensatory damages….It is clear that the means of the defendant are relevant to the assessment of damages. Also relevant are his degree of fault and the amount of any profit he may be shown actually to have made from his unlawful conduct….

The amount awarded

The jury awarded exemplary damages of £275,000, making a grand total of £350,000. Mr. Browne supports that figure as reasonable, but in our judgment Mr. Gray is right in his submission that this sum is manifestly excessive, and goes well beyond the minimum sum needed to meet the two relevant requirements. We think that those requirements will be fully met by an award of £50,000 exemplary damages, making a grand total of damages under both headings of £75,000, which will ensure that justice is done to both sides, and will also fully secure the public interest involved.

Appeal allowed in part.

■ Kiam v MGN Ltd

Court of Appeal [2002] 2 All ER 219

The defendant was found to have maliciously published a baseless libel about the claimant, and to have conducted its defence of the action in a way that aggravated the damage. The judge, directing the jury, explained that general damages in a personal injury case were unlikely to exceed £150,000, and suggested a bracket of £40,000 to £80,000 damages. The jury assessed damages at £105,000. The Court of Appeal (Sedley LJ dissenting) dismissed the defendant's appeal against the level of damages.

WALLER LJ: . . .

[59] Naturally a comparison between the general damages awarded for serious personal injuries with those awarded in libel actions gives cause for anxiety. Furthermore at first sight the award seems a very high one. But what weighs with me on the critical question whether this court should interfere are the following factors. (i) The jury in this case were made aware (as is now the practice) of the sort of damages that would be awarded in personal injury cases. (ii) In an impeccable summing up they were given a bracket of £40,000 to £75,000–£80,000, but told 'I have to stress that the decision is yours and yours alone'. (iii) 'If the jury make an award outside any bracket indicated real weight must be given to the possibility that their judgment is to be preferred to that of the judge.' (See the passage quoted from the judgment of Bingham MR in *John v MGN Ltd* [1996] 2 All ER 35, [1997] QB 586 quoted at [27], above.) (iv) For the Court of Appeal to interfere, the award must be one which no jury properly directed could have arrived at or as the notes in the former annual practice continued and without citing the authorities there referred to:

> 'The matter may be otherwise expressed by saying that the verdict must be an "impossible" verdict . . . or represent an entirely erroneous estimate . . . or show no reasonable proportion between the amount awarded and the amount sustained . . .'

(v) The judge who had provided the bracket and presided over the five-day trial with the opportunity of getting a full 'feel' of the case which this court is simply not in a position to do, in refusing permission to appeal said: '. . . this was an award by the jury which, although higher than I suggested would be appropriate, was not clearly extravagant.'

[60] I have read the draft judgment of Sedley LJ and although I understand the strength of his views, it seems to me that whilst it remains the tradition for damages in defamation to be assessed by the jury, one must be careful in assuming that there should be the close analogy with personal injury awards which he assumes. We simply do not know precisely what views juries hold on such things. The verdict of a jury properly directed should not lightly be overturned in the court of appeal. For reasons which I do not understand to differ from Simon Brown LJ in my view this court should not interfere with the jury's award in this case.

SEDLEY LJ: . . .

[61] The law governing general damages depends upon the fiction that suffering can be translated into money. Because it is a fiction, damages as a whole are arbitrary. But as between damages for one kind of injury and another, both legal certainty and elementary justice require careful regard to be had to relativities.

[62] It was because of the vagaries of jury verdicts and awards in personal injury cases that the courts were given power, initially in 1854 (see *Ford v Blurton, Ford v Sauber* (1922) 38 TLR 801); then by s 6 of the Administration of Justice (Miscellaneous Provisions) Act 1933, and presently by s 69(3) of the Supreme Court Act 1981, to grant or refuse jury trial in such actions. In the exercise of this power the courts have since the decision of this court in *Ward v James* [1965] 1 All ER 563, [1966] 1 QB 273 adopted a uniform policy of having both liability and quantum tried by judge alone.

[63] One intended consequence of this development has been a reasonably coherent tariff of awards for personal injuries, which since 1992 has enabled the Judicial Studies Board to publish a booklet, *Guidelines for the Assessment of General Damages in Personal Injury Cases*, now in its fifth edition (2000). A second consequence has been that the traditional inhibition on the citation of comparables to trial courts has gone.

[64] It was the repeated contrast between the elevated sums awarded by juries in libel actions and the modest sums awarded by judges for personal injuries which led first to adverse public comment

(though its main source, the media, could not be said to have been disinterested) and then to judicial intervention. The critical decision was *John v MGN Ltd* [1996] 2 All ER 35, [1997] QB 586....

[66] But it is apparent that the decision in *John's* case has not succeeded in its avowed purpose. Counsel have helpfully prepared for us a table of recent indications given by trial judges to juries of suggested upper limits to any awards they make for defamation. In three recent high-profile cases the figure has been £150,000. For a disabled claimant that is a sum which represents both grave trauma and lifelong suffering. In others, indicating an upper end of £50,000 or £75,000, judges have told libel juries that in personal injury terms this represents the loss of a limb or paraplegia. Generally, though not always, jury awards have stayed within the figures suggested by the judge. But looking at these figures, it seems to me that the train has left the station again and is now accelerating.

[67] It may be that the re-escalation of libel damages is due in part to the fact that it began from a high base. This court replaced the enormous award in *John's* case with a sum of £25,000 general damages and £50,000 exemplary damages. Since I am dissenting, it will not be disruptive of precedent if I respectfully remark that in 1993, £25,000 was more than a claimant would get for the loss of sight in one eye, or for any but the gravest facial scarring. It was the sort of sum awarded to a person so psychiatrically traumatised as to face many years, possibly a lifetime, of inability to cope with relationships and of vulnerability to further trauma. In a case in which, as the court pointed out, the libel had neither attacked the plaintiff's personal integrity nor damaged his artistic reputation, how a figure of £25,000 articulated with the personal injury tariff is not immediately apparent and is not explained in the judgment of the court.

[68] Restarting from this already generous base, there has been a perceptible process of what Americans might call compensation creep, pushing up not only the brackets given by judges to juries but the base from which this court is now invited to start its reconsideration of arguably excessive awards.

[69] Even in this inflationary situation I do not consider that the award of £105,000 to Mr Kiam can be regarded as anything but excessive. It is some 30% above the top of the bracket proposed by the judge, a bracket which in itself—for the reasons I have been considering—is unrealistically high, and no less so for being commensurate with other recent judicial directions.....

[71] In this situation, it is relevant to ask what has gone so fundamentally wrong. The answer is not very far to seek. A fair analogy with personal injury damages would require judges to point out to juries that the compensation for the sometimes unspeakable grief of a bereavement is set at present by law at £7,500 (see s 1A(3), (5) of the Fatal Accidents Act 1976), and that the humiliation and wretchedness of being traduced in public with no chance to reply, bad as that is, is unlikely to be worse than this....

[74] ...[J]uries in these cases probably consider that they are dealing with wealthy media organisations for whom a four or five-figure sum is little more than petty cash. They ask themselves, and judges and lawyers too ask themselves, what is the use of setting damages at a level which makes libel cheap at the price.

[75] The law's answer, which has its own anomalies, is that in a case where the evidence reaches a sufficiently cogent level to attract an award of exemplary damages such a defendant can be taught that libel does not pay. The principal anomaly is that the penalty goes into the claimant's pocket as a pure windfall. But in a great many cases proof of a cold-blooded cost-benefit calculation that it was worth publishing a known libel is not there, and the ineffectiveness of a moderate award in deterring future libels is painfully apparent. It is this, I believe, that is leading both judges and juries once more to lift the level of general damages for libel into a different league from personal injury damages, at least in cases like the present where the newspaper has not simply got its facts wrong but has behaved outrageously from start to finish. Although this was a predictable by-product of any serious restriction of compensatory damages for libel, it is strangely enough a factor which, so far as counsel have been able to show us, is not addressed in any of the appellate decisions on the limitation of libel damages. Judges, juries and the public face the conundrum that compensation proportioned to personal injury damages is insufficient to deter, and that deterrent awards make a mockery of the principle of compensation.

[76] I do not, even so, believe that there is any necessary incompatibility between the moderation of compensatory awards for libel and the punitive and deterrent purposes which exemplary damages serve. Punishment in a modern society is not the business of private individuals: it is a matter for the state. If a motorist drives recklessly he will have to compensate any victim for the injury he inflicts, but it is to the state that he answers by way of punishment for his abuse of the right to drive a vehicle. Where it is appropriate that the victim should be fully compensated for his injury and loss, it is inappropriate that he should pocket the proceeds of punishment. If, comparably, the enormous power of the news media to misinform and to injure is to be matched with legal responsibility going beyond simple compensation and involving punitive measures, it is likewise to the state that the media ought to answer. A defendant who so conducts himself as to deserve punishment by law can and should be tried with the full safeguards of due process and proof beyond reasonable doubt. He should also be prepared to face the consequences of being convicted.

[77] It is Parliament who alone can decide whether this should happen. What needs unravelling is the single proceeding in which compensation and punishment have for centuries have been rolled together, and which is not appropriately adapted, either in its process or in its outcome, to the increasingly fundamental distinctions between the two. No doubt, as Lord Denning MR said in *Ward v James* [1965] 1 All ER 563, [1966] 1 QB 273, jury trial has no equal when honour or integrity are at stake. But when it comes to damages, the three virtues which he went on to enumerate—assessability, uniformity and predictability—also matter a great deal. Something needs to be done about the conflict between the need for fair but balanced compensation for victims of libel and the equal and opposite need to prevent libel from paying. It is possible within the present law for damages to be assessed by judges; but the underlying tension between compensation and deterrence is something, as it seems to me, that Parliament alone can resolve. So far as the courts are concerned it is now apparent that attempting to reduce the bracket produces an understandable but impermissible reaction against the effects of making libel cheap to commit.

[78] For my part, therefore, I would allow this appeal on the narrow ground that even by comparison with other libel awards, but especially by comparison with personal injury awards, the figure awarded by the jury as compensatory damages is wholly excessive. Although I have given £60,000 as the highest figure which I believe to be defensible in the present state of law and practice, the general level of compensatory libel damages which it represents is also in my view indefensible.

[SIMON BROWN LJ delivered a judgment in favour of dismissing the appeal.]

Appeal dismissed.

■ Gleaner Co Ltd v Abrahams

Judicial Committee of the Privy Council [2004] 1 AC 628

The defendant appealed to the Privy Council against the damages awarded in a libel case on the basis that the trial judge and the Court of Appeal of Jamaica had refused to refer juries to awards of general damages in personal injury cases.

LORD HOFFMANN: . . .

[50] Their Lordships express no view on the current practice in England. But the matter is clearly one on which different opinions may be held. The arguments in favour of comparison tend to stress the moral unacceptability of treating damage to reputation as having a higher 'value' than catastrophic damage to the person. It is however arguable that the assessment of general damages in both personal injury and libel cases is far more complicated than trying to 'value' the damage; an exercise which everyone agrees to be impossible on account of the incommensurability of the subject matter. Other factors enter into the calculation. Personal injury awards are almost always made in actions based on

negligence or breach of statutory duty rather than intentional wrongdoing. Furthermore, the damages are almost always paid out of public funds or by insurers under policies which are not very sensitive to the claims records of individual defendants. The cost is therefore borne by the public at large or large sections of the public such as motorists or consumers. The exemplary and deterrent elements in personal injury awards are minimal or non-existent. On the other hand, the total sums of compensation paid for personal injury are very large. They have an effect on the economy which libel damages do not. The amounts of the awards in personal injury actions therefore depend to some extent upon what society can afford to pay victims of accidents over and above compensation for the actual financial loss they have suffered. As Lord Woolf MR said of general damages in personal injury cases in *Heil v Rankin* [2001] QB 272, 297, para 36: 'Awards must be proportionate and take into account the consequences of increases in the awards of damages on defendants as a group and society as a whole.'

[51] Once it is appreciated that the awards are not paid by individual defendants but by society as a whole or large sections of society, there are also considerations of equity between victims of personal injury which influence the level of general damages. Compensation, both for financial loss and general damages, goes only to those who can prove negligence and causation. Those unable to do so are left to social security: no general damages and meagre compensation for loss of earnings. The unfairness might be more readily understandable if the successful tort plaintiffs recovered their damages from the defendants themselves but makes less sense when both social security and negligence damages come out of public funds. So any increase in general damages for personal injury awarded by the courts only widens the gap between those victims who can sue and those who cannot.

[52] In addition, as Sedley LJ pointed out in *Kiam's* case [2003] QB 281, 303, para 71, once one treats awards of general damages as simply an unsophisticated attempt to place a value upon misfortune, all kinds of anomalies appear. He drew attention to the maximum of £7,500 for a claim for bereavement set by section 1A(3) of the English Fatal Accidents Act 1976, which not infrequently constitutes the sole claim for the death of a child and provokes outraged headlines deploring a law which places so low a 'value' upon a child's life.

[53] Few of these considerations of equity and policy apply to awards in defamation cases. On the other hand, defamation cases have important features not shared by personal injury claims. The damages often serve not only as compensation but also as an effective and necessary deterrent. The deterrent is effective because the damages are paid either by the defendant himself or under a policy of insurance which is likely to be sensitive to the incidence of such claims. Indeed, the effectiveness of the deterrent is the whole basis of Lord Lester's argument that high awards will have a "chilling effect" on future publications. Awards in an adequate amount may also be necessary to deter the media from riding roughshod over the rights of other citizens....

[His Lordship referred to Sedley LJ's distaste for punitive damages in *Kiam*, [75]-[77], ante, and continued:]

[54] The remedy suggested by Sedley LJ to preserve the purity of the distinction between compensation and punishment was a revival of the prosecution for criminal libel. But some might feel that so drastic an intervention by the state in regulating the conduct of the media had other disadvantages. They might prefer instead to compromise the purity of the distinction and see practical wisdom in what Lord Wilberforce said in *Broome v Cassell & Co Ltd* [1972] AC 1027, 1114:

> 'It cannot lightly be taken for granted, even as a matter of theory, that the purpose of the law of tort is compensation, still less that it ought to be, an issue of large social import, or that there is something inappropriate or illogical or anomalous (a question-begging word) in including a punitive element in civil damages, or, conversely, that the criminal law, rather than the civil law, is in these cases the better instrument for conveying social disapproval, or for redressing a wrong in the social fabric, or that damages in any case can be broken down into two separate elements. As a matter of practice English law has not committed itself to any of these theories: it may have been wiser than it knew.'

Oil and vinegar may not mix in solution but they combine to make an acceptable salad dressing. [Cf. Lord Hailsham of St Marylebone LC on exemplary and compensatory damages in *Broome v Cassell* [1972] AC 1027, 1077, cited at [42].]

[55] In addition, as this case amply illustrates, there are other differences between general damages in personal injury cases and general damages in defamation actions. One is that the damages must be sufficient to demonstrate to the public that the plaintiff's reputation has been vindicated. Particularly if the defendant has not apologised and withdrawn the defamatory allegations, the award must show that they have been publicly proclaimed to have inflicted a serious injury. As Lord Hailsham of St Marylebone LC said in *Broome v Cassell & Co Ltd* [1972] AC 1027, 1071, the plaintiff 'must be able to point to a sum awarded by a jury sufficient to convince a bystander of the baselessness of the charge'.

[62] The appellants submit that the rejection of guidance from personal injury awards was an error of law. As will be apparent from the earlier discussion, their Lordships consider that this is a matter open to legitimate differences of opinion. They do not think that any question of legal principle is involved. Whether a link should be established between defamation awards and personal injury awards is a question of policy....

[63] ...Their Lordships are not willing to say that the Court of Appeal was wrong in considering that in Jamaica no change was desirable. They were entitled to hold the opinion that a conventional figure established for an award performing one social function [i.e. general damages for personal injury] was no guide to what should be the conventional figure for an award performing a different social function [i.e. damages for libel].

Appeal dismissed.

■ Burstein v Times Newspapers Ltd
Court of Appeal [2001] 1 WLR 579

The defendant newspaper alleged that the claimant, a composer, organised groups of hecklers to disrupt performances of modern atonal music. The claimant sued for libel. The defendant wished to rely upon evidence that the claimant had, in the past, associated with a group who booed concertedly at performances of such musical works. The judge held that such evidence was not admissible in mitigation of damages. The jury awarded the claimant £8,000 damages, and the defendant appealed.

MAY LJ: . . .

[19] *Gatley on Libel and Slander*, p 842, para 33.26, characterises evidence which is admissible in reduction of damages under six headings. These include (1) the claimant's bad reputation, (2) evidence properly before the court on some other issue, and (4) the claimant's own conduct.

[21] The admissibility of evidence properly before the court on some other issue may be illustrated by referring to the judgment of Neill LJ in *Pamplin v Express Newspapers Ltd (Note)* [1988] 1 WLR 116, 120, where he said:

> 'But a defendant is also entitled to rely in mitigation of damages on any other evidence which is properly before the court and jury. This other evidence can include evidence which has been primarily directed to, for example, a plea of justification or fair comment. [. . .] There may be many cases, however, where a defendant who puts forward a defence of justification will be unable to prove sufficient facts to establish the defence at common law and will also be unable to bring himself within the statutory extension of the defence contained in section 5 of the Defamation Act 1952. Nevertheless the defendant may be able to rely on such facts as he has proved to reduce the damages, perhaps almost to vanishing point. Thus a defence of partial justification, though it may not prevent the plaintiff from succeeding on the issue of liability, may be of great importance on the issue of damages.'

[28] In *Scott v Sampson* (1881) 8 QBD 491 the publication complained of was to the effect that the plaintiff, a theatrical critic, had tried to extort money by threatening to publish defamatory matter concerning a deceased actress. There was a defence of justification. The plaintiff himself did not give evidence in support of his own case. The defendant wanted to cross-examine witnesses, including the plaintiff (whom the defendant, surprisingly, himself called for that purpose), to show that the plaintiff's general conduct of his magazine was discreditable. The questions were objected to and the trial judge upheld the objections....

[29] In *Speidel v Plato Films Ltd* [1961] AC 1090, an attempt was made to persuade the House of Lords to modify the decision in *Scott v Sampson*...

[30] Viscount Simonds considered emphatically that *Scott v Sampson* was correctly decided....He said, at pp 1124–1125:

'It is, no doubt, true that in practice it may be difficult to define exactly either the borderline between evidence of general bad reputation and that of specific conduct which has led to it or the area of conduct which the general bad reputation is to cover. That is only to say that a libel action is an imperfect instrument for doing justice in every case. There may, in the result, be cases in which a rogue survives both evidence of general bad reputation and, where he has gone into the witness-box, a severe cross-examination nominally directed to credit, and recovers more damages than he should. But I would rather have it so than that the law should permit the injustice and, indeed, the cruelty of an attack upon a plaintiff for offences real or imaginary which, if they ever were committed, may have been known to few and by them have been forgotten. I say nothing more of the inconvenience of having one or more trials within the original trial. The main issue has to be determined when the defendant has failed in his plea of justification. How many other trials of the offences pleaded in mitigation are to be permitted?'

Viscount Simonds was thus concerned with the injustice of a plaintiff having to deal with a wide ranging attack on his general reputation by reference to specific conduct which has led to it. There was thus again a case management element in the consideration. The material which was objectionable was specific conduct leading to alleged general bad reputation, and not particular facts directly relevant to the context in which the defamatory publication came to be made.

...

[35] I have quoted at length from the speeches in *Speidel v Plato Films Ltd* to show that a main concern was to prevent libel trials from becoming roving inquiries into the plaintiff's reputation, character or disposition; that what was held to be inadmissible was particular facts said to be relevant to the plaintiff's general reputation or disposition; and that the case does not decide that particular facts directly relevant to the context in which a defamatory publication came to be made are inadmissible. Indeed, two of the speeches by inference accept that evidence of the circumstances surrounding the publication are admissible.

[37] In July 1991, a working group of the Supreme Court Procedure Committee, chaired by Neill LJ, made a report on Practice and Procedure in Defamation. They considered *Scott v Sampson*....They pointed out the injustice of a plaintiff who has misconducted himself in the same sector of his life as that to which the libel relates recovering damages on exactly the same generous basis as one who truly has an unblemished record in the relevant area of activity. They considered that there would be a significant improvement if it were possible for defendants to rely upon specific instances of misconduct on the part of the plaintiff for the purpose of reducing damages, provided that the allegations related to the same sector of the plaintiff's life as the defamatory publication.... They were concerned with the reputation to which the plaintiff is entitled rather than that which he might have enjoyed. They noted that the Porter Committee in 1948 and the Faulks Committee in 1975 had recommended that the rule *Scott v Sampson* should simply be abrogated.

[38] The Neill Committee's recommendations led to what became the Defamation Act 1996. Clause 13 of the Defamation Bill was drafted to implement the committee's recommendations with regard to

Scott v Sampson. The clause did not survive into the Act, we are told for want of parliamentary time. Various views were expressed in committee in support of and in opposition to the clause. In the circumstances, I do not think that any particular parliamentary intention can be discovered from the introduction of the clause and for its failure to survive into the Act. We are simply left with the law as it was.

[39] That, however, is to be seen in the light of the Civil Procedure Act 1997 and the Civil Procedure Rules 1998. These are a new procedural code with the overriding objective of enabling the court to deal with cases justly (rule 1.1(1))....

[40] The questions which the judge had to consider in the present case were essentially procedural case management questions. Although questions relating to the admissibility of evidence may raise issues properly characterised as issues of law, not only is the admissibility of evidence essentially procedural, but the authorities to which I have referred show that the admissibility or otherwise of evidence of reputation in reduction of libel damages is heavily affected, if not determined, by questions of procedural fairness and of case management. It will, generally speaking, normally be both unfair and irrelevant if a claimant complaining of a specific defamatory publication is subjected to a roving inquiry into aspects of his or her life unconnected with the subject matter of the defamatory publication. It is also in accordance with the overriding objective that evidence should be properly confined, both in its subject matter and its duration, to that which is directly relevant to the subject matter of the publication. Thus under the Civil Procedure Rules, the court now has ample power to deal justly with the problems which, in the main, gave rise to the first and third limbs of the decision in *Scott v Sampson*.

[47] ...[I]t is not permissible to advance an unsustainable defence of justification and thereby, under the guise of particulars of justification, seek to rely on particulars which *Scott v Sampson* 8 QBD 491 and *Speidel v Plato Films Ltd* [1961] AC 1090 would not permit. That, however, does not prevent a defendant from frankly accepting that there is no proper plea of justification, but seeking to rely in reduction of damages on particulars which *Scott v Sampson* and *Speidel v Plato Films Ltd* do not exclude. If this were not so, there is a danger that the jury would be required to assess damages in blinkers, in ignorance of background context directly relevant to the damage which the claimant claims has been caused by the defamatory publication. This is consistent with the sense of what Lord Denning said in *Speidel v Plato Films Ltd*, where his conclusion was that it was permissible to adduce the evidence in question. Thus, in my view, a defendant is not prevented from taking the sensible course of accepting that the publication means what it says and that it is not on the facts justified, and yet putting in evidence directly relevant facts which in other circumstances might have been ingredients of a defence of justification. It would, I think, be illogical and unfair if this were not so. Evidence in support of a plea of justification which fails is admissible in reduction of damages. But the very same evidence would not be admissible to a sensible defendant who acknowledges that it will not support a plea of justification. What is not permissible is to plead a defence of partial justification which in truth is no defence at all.

[His Lordship considered that the judge should not have ruled the evidence inadmissible, but dismissed the appeal on the grounds that he was not satisfied that the jury's award would have been any smaller.]

[Aldous LJ and Sir Christopher Slade agreed.]

Appeal dismissed.

NOTES

1. In *Turner v News Group Newspapers Ltd* [2006] 4 All ER 613, [2006] EWCA Civ 540 the court held that a '*Burstein* plea' was admissible in mitigation of damages assessed following an offer of amends under s. 3 of the Defamation Act 1996 (see p. 1011, ante). The court rejected the argument that *Burstein* was *per incuriam*, on the basis that Clause 13 of the Defamation Bill had been dropped because of difficulties in framing an alternative rule, rather than through lack of parliamentary time, as May LJ had believed

(see para [38], ante). May LJ had correctly placed no weight on the reasons why the opportunity for reform had not been taken in 1996. Moreover, *Burstein* was reconcilable with *Speidel v Plato Films Ltd* [1961] AC 1090, [1961] 1 All ER 876, which had never stated an absolute exclusionary rule (see e.g. *Pamplin v Express Newspapers Ltd* [1988] 1 All ER 282, [1988] 1 WLR 116, referred to in *Burstein* at [21], ante). Thus, 'directly relevant background facts' may be pled in mitigation, i.e. 'evidence which is so clearly relevant to the subject matter of the libel or to the claimant's reputation or sensitivity in that part of his life that there would be a real risk of the jury assessing damages on a false basis if they were kept in ignorance of the facts to which the evidence relates' (per Keene LJ at [56]).

As Moses LJ said at [85] applying the test to the facts: 'The sensitivities of one who is accused of pressurising, not forcing, his wife to have sex with men are bound to be less refined if he was prepared to encourage his wife in public displays of sexual exposure.' Thus, evidence of the latter 'encouragement' was admissible in mitigation.

Turner is noted by N. Hatzis (2007) 123 LQR 39.

2.   Another exception to the rule that specific acts of misconduct cannot be pled is that criminal convictions may be relied upon as evidence in mitigation: *Goody v Odhams Press Ltd* [1967] 1 QB 333, [1966] 3 All ER 369. For 'spent' convictions, see p. 985, ante.

3.   At the other end of the scale from exemplary damages are 'contemptuous' damages: awarding the smallest coin in the realm used to express the fact that although the claimant has technically been libelled, he has such a bad character that the libel was very nearly justified. It is always at the discretion of the judge whether to order that either party shall pay the other's costs and where the claimant has only gained the pyrrhic victory of contemptuous damages the judge will be very likely to exercise his discretion to refuse to make an order for costs in the claimant's favour (e.g. *Dering v Uris* [1964] 2 All ER 660n).

■ Greene v Associated Newspapers Ltd

Court of Appeal [2005] 1 All ER 30

Knowing that the defendant newspaper was planning to publish a story about her, the claimant sought an injunction to restrain publication. The newspaper maintained that the story was true and that it would plead justification at any trial. Applying the rule in *Bonnard v Perryman* [1891] 2 Ch 269, [1891–4] All ER Rep 965, the judge refused her application for an injunction. The claimant appealed.

BROOKE LJ (giving the reasons of the court): . . .

[1] In this country we have a free press. Our press is free to get things right and it is free to get things wrong. It is free to write after the manner of Milton, and it is free to write in a manner that would make Milton turn in his grave. Blackstone wrote in 1769 that the liberty of the press is essential in a free state, and this liberty consists in laying no previous restraints on publication. 'Every freeman', he said, 'has an undoubted right to lay what sentiments he pleases before the public: to forbid this, is to destroy the freedom of the press' (see *Commentaries on the Laws of England* (15th edn, 1809) vol IV, pp 151–152. It is this freedom which is under challenge in this appeal. Mr Richard Spearman QC has argued before us that the enactment of the Human Rights Act 1998 has significantly weakened the inhibitions that judges should feel before imposing prior restraint on the press. This was a surprising proposition, but it deserves careful analysis.

      . . .

[46] The rule in *Bonnard v Perryman* was laid down by five judges, including the Lord Chief Justice and the Master of the Rolls, who constituted the majority of the full Court of Appeal in that case. The libel in issue was a very damaging one. North J at first instance said ([1891] 2 Ch 269 at 274) that unless it could be justified at the trial it was one in which a jury would give the plaintiff 'very serious damages'. He went on to say ([1891] 2 Ch 269 at 277–278):

'...I have this to bear in mind, that, if in such a case as this an interlocutory injunction is not granted, I cannot imagine any case in which an interlocutory injunction to restrain a libel could be granted, whereas it is clear on the authorities that there are cases in which it would be proper to grant it. [...] I am perfectly satisfied there is not any jury in *England* who would say there should be a verdict for the Defendant in such a case, and, what is more, if they did, I am quite satisfied it is a case in which a new trial would be directed. This, of course, does not touch what may be the case when the action comes to be tried. There may be evidence before the Court then which would satisfy a jury who tries it that the Defendant has made out a justification. I am merely referring to the materials before me, which are all I can look to now in considering what I am to do in the matter. In these circumstances I have come to the conclusion that an injunction must be granted in the terms which I have mentioned.'

[47] In overruling that decision Lord Coleridge CJ quoted with approval what Lord Esher MR had said four years earlier in *William Coulson & Sons v James Coulson & Co* (1887) 3 TLR 846:

'...the question of libel or no libel was for the jury. It was for the jury and not for the Court to construe the document, and to say whether it was a libel or not. To justify the Court in granting an interim injunction it must come to a decision upon the question of libel or no libel, before the jury decided whether it was a libel or not. Therefore the jurisdiction was of a delicate nature. It ought only to be exercised in the clearest cases, where any jury would say that the matter complained of was libellous, and where if the jury did not so find the Court would set aside the verdict as unreasonable. The Court must also be satisfied that in all probability the alleged libel was untrue, and if written on a privileged occasion that there was malice on the part of the defendant. It followed from those three rules that the Court could only on the rarest occasions exercise their jurisdiction.'

[50] In *Bonnard v Perryman* [1891] 2 Ch 269 at 285, [1891–4] All ER Rep 965 at 969 Lord Coleridge CJ resolved North J's dilemma by saying that although the courts undoubtedly possessed the requisite jurisdiction, 'in all but exceptional cases' they should not issue an interlocutory injunction to restrain the publication of a libel which the defence sought to justify except where it was clear that that defence would fail. He based his approach on the particular need not to restrict the right of free speech in libel cases by interfering before the final determination of the matter by a jury otherwise than in a clear case of an untrue libel. He said ([1891] 2 Ch 269 at 284, [1891–4] All ER Rep 965 at 968):

'...the subject-matter of an action for defamation is so special as to require exceptional caution in exercising the jurisdiction to interfere by injunction before the trial of an action to prevent an anticipated wrong. The right of free speech is one which it is for the public interest that individuals should possess, and, indeed, that they should exercise without impediment, so long as no wrongful act is done; and, unless an alleged libel is untrue, there is no wrong committed; but, on the contrary, often a very wholesome act is performed in the publication and repetition of an alleged libel. Until it is clear that an alleged libel is untrue, it is not clear that any right at all has been infringed; and the importance of leaving free speech unfettered is a strong reason in cases of libel for dealing most cautiously and warily with the granting of interim injunctions...In the particular case before us, indeed, the libellous character of the publication is beyond dispute, but the effect of it upon the Defendant can be finally disposed of only by a jury, and we cannot feel sure that the defence of justification is one which, on the facts which may be before them, the jury may find to be wholly unfounded; nor can we tell what may be the damages recoverable.'

[52] In *Herbage v Pressdram Ltd* [1984] 2 All ER 769 at 771, [1984] 1 WLR 1160 at 1162 Griffiths LJ restated the effect of the rule and then said:

'These principles have evolved because of the value the court has placed on freedom of speech and I think also on the freedom of the press, when balancing it against the reputation of a single individual who, if wrong, can be compensated in damages.'

[53] He refused to water the principles down....

[57] This survey of the case law shows that in an action for defamation a court will not impose a prior restraint on publication unless it is clear that no defence will succeed at the trial. This is partly due to the importance the court attaches to freedom of speech. It is partly because a judge must not usurp the constitutional function of the jury unless he is satisfied that there is no case to go to a jury. The rule is also partly founded on the pragmatic grounds that until there has been disclosure of documents and cross-examination at the trial a court cannot safely proceed on the basis that what the defendants wish to say is not true. And if it is or might be true the court has no business to stop them saying it....

[59] ...Section 12 of the [Human Rights Act 1998] is entitled 'Freedom of expression' and sub-s (1) makes it clear that it applies 'if a court is considering whether to grant any relief which, if granted, might affect the exercise of the Convention right to freedom of expression'. This language does not suggest that Parliament intended within this very section to whittle down a defendant's right to freedom of expression in a case like this, but Mr Spearman told us that this was the effect of s 12(3) which provides:

'No such relief is to be granted so as to restrain publication before trial unless the court is satisfied that the applicant is likely to establish that publication should not be allowed.'

[61] ...In a section of an Act of Parliament which is expressly concerned with the protection of freedom of expression and not with undermining it, Parliament cannot be interpreted as having abrogated the rule in *Bonnard v Perryman* by a side wind. In any event the very language of s 12(3) does not require such an interpretation....

[70] ...[I]n *Reynolds v Times Newspapers Ltd* [1999] 4 All ER 609 at 612, [2001] 2 AC 127 at 190 Lord Nicholls said: 'My Lords, this appeal concerns the interaction between two fundamental rights: freedom of expression and protection of reputation.'

[71] Mr Spearman argued that a rights-based approach requires a careful balancing at every stage of every case between the competing rights....

[75] Scoops, as Mr Caldecott observed, are the lifeblood of the newspaper industry. He might have added that stale news is no news at all. If Mr Spearman was correct, people with a fair reputation they do not deserve could stifle public criticism by obtaining injunctions simply because on necessarily incomplete information a court thought it more likely than not that they would defeat a defence of justification at the trial.

[76] In our judgment Mr Caldecott's submissions are well founded.

....

[78] In cases involving confidential documents, the confidentiality of the documents will be lost completely if an injunction against disclosure is not granted when appropriate. In cases involving national security, great damage may similarly be done if an injunction is not granted when appropriate. In a defamation action, on the other hand, while some damage may be done by permitting the publication of what may later turn out to be false, everyone knows that it is at the trial that truth or falsehood will be tested and the claimant vindicated if the defendant cannot prove that the sting of the libel is justified or that he has some other defence the law will recognise. The damage that may on occasion be done by refusing an injunction where a less strict rule would facilitate its grant pales into insignificance compared with the damage which would be done to freedom of expression and the freedom of the press if the rule in *Bonnard v Perryman* was relaxed.

Appeal dismissed.

7 THE DISTINCTION BETWEEN LIBEL AND SLANDER

■ Youssoupoff v Metro-Goldwyn-Mayer Pictures Ltd
Court of Appeal (1934) 50 TLR 581

The claimant said that she had been defamed in a film (for the details of the allegation see p. 963, ante). The 'talkies', films with sound, were a recent invention. The question arose as to whether defamation in a 'talkie' was slander or libel.

SLESSER LJ: . . .

This action is one of libel and raises at the outset an interesting and difficult problem which, I believe, to be a novel problem, whether the product of the combined photographic and talking instrument which produces these modern films does, if it throws upon the screen and impresses upon the ear defamatory matter, produce that which can be complained of as libel or as slander.

In my view, this action, as I have said, was properly framed in libel. There can be no doubt that, so far as the photographic part of the exhibition is concerned, that is a permanent matter to be seen by the eye, and is the proper subject of an action for libel, if defamatory. I regard the speech which is synchronized with the photographic reproduction and forms part of one complex, common exhibition as an ancillary circumstance, part of the surroundings explaining that which is to be seen. . . .

QUESTION

Does Slesser LJ's reasoning mean that the *vision* constituted the libel? If so, does this imply that a gramophone record or other sound recording would only be a slander? Is skywriting by an aeroplane, or flag signals at sea, capable of giving rise to a libel?

NOTES

1. For the fascinating background to this case see H. Montgomery Hyde, *Sir Patrick Hastings* (London, 1960) pp. 274–283 and L.K. Treiger-Bar-Am (2000) 20 LS 291.
2. In *Monson v Tussauds Ltd* [1894] 1 QB 671, [1891–4] All ER Rep 1051, in which the claimant complained that a wax museum exhibition impliedly accused him of murder, Lopes LJ said, 'Libels are generally in writing or printing, but this is not necessary; the defamatory matter may be conveyed in some other permanent form. For instance, a statue, a caricature, an effigy, chalk marks on a wall, signs, or pictures may constitute a libel.'
3. For the history of the distinction between libel and slander (generally believed to be an historical accident) see J. M. Kaye (1975) 91 LQR 524 and R. Helmholz (1987) 103 LQR 624; see generally the Report of the Faulks Committee, Cmnd. 5909, 1975, Appendix VI.

■ The Broadcasting Act 1990

166 **Defamatory material.**—(1) For the purposes of the law of libel and slander (including the law of criminal libel so far as it relates to the publication of defamatory matter) the publication of words

in the course of any programme included in a programme service[7] shall be treated as publication in permanent form.

■ The Theatres Act 1968

4 Amendment of law of defamation.—(1) For the purposes of the law of libel and slander (including the law of criminal libel so far as it relates to the publication of defamatory matter) the publication of words in the course of a performance of a play shall, subject to section 7 of this Act, be treated as publication in permanent form.

...

(3) In this section 'words' includes pictures, visual images, gestures and other methods of signifying meaning....

■ Gray v Jones

King's Bench Division [1939] 1 All ER 798

The claimant brought an action for slander, alleging that the defendant had said of him: 'You are a convicted person. I will not have you here. You have a conviction.'

The defendant submitted that the words were not capable of being actionable without proof of special damage. It was held that the words were actionable per se and judgment was given for the claimant.

ATKINSON J: ...

The argument for the defendant is that the true view is that the reason why words imputing a crime are actionable is that the plaintiff is put in jeopardy of a criminal prosecution, and, therefore, if the words merely imply that the plaintiff has been guilty of a criminal offence, and has been convicted, and it is a thing of the past, then it is not actionable without proof of special damage, because the plaintiff is not put in jeopardy. That raises the question as to the real basis of the action. What is the real ground upon which a plaintiff may bring an action for such defamation without proof of special damage? Is it because the misconduct alleged is of so serious a character that the law visits it with punishment, and is therefore so likely to cause other people to shun the person defamed, and to exclude him from society, that damage is presumed? Or is the basis the fact he is put in jeopardy? In my opinion, the former view is the sound one....

NOTES

1. *Gray v Jones* illustrates one of the four categories of slander actionable per se. The other three are:
    (a) words imputing that the claimant is suffering from a contagious or infectious disease (e.g. *Bloodworth v Gray* (1844) 7 Man & G 334: 'He has got that damned pox (meaning the French pox otherwise known as venereal disease) from going to that woman on the Derby Road.' £50 damages awarded without proof of special damage).
    (b) words imputing unchastity or adultery to any woman or girl (Slander of Women Act 1891, post); in *Youssoupoff v Metro-Goldwyn-Mayer Pictures Ltd* Avory J, with whom Scrutton LJ agreed, said, obiter, that an allegation that a woman had been raped would fall into this category.
    (c) words calculated to disparage the claimant in any office, profession, calling, trade or business, held or carried on by him at the time of publication (Defamation Act 1952, s. 2, post).

[7] [Defined in s 201.]

2. A committee of the House of Lords in 1843 and the Faulks Committee on Defamation, para. 91, in 1975, recommended the abolition of the distinction between libel and slander.

■ The Slander of Women Act 1891

1 Amendment of law.—Words spoken and published . . . which impute unchastity or adultery to any woman or girl shall not require special damage to render them actionable.

Provided always, that in any action for words spoken and made actionable by this Act, a plaintiff shall not recover more costs than damages, unless the judge shall certify that there was reasonable ground for bringing the action.

■ The Defamation Act 1952

2 Slander affecting official, professional or business reputation.—In an action for slander in respect of words calculated to disparage the plaintiff in any office, profession, calling, trade or business held or carried on by him at the time of the publication, it shall not be necessary to allege or prove special damage, whether or not the words are spoken of the plaintiff in the way of his office, profession, calling, trade or business.

CHAPTER SEVENTEEN

INVASION OF PRIVACY

To date, English law has not recognised a general tort of invasion of privacy. A number of well-established torts may be pressed into action to protect particular aspects of private life: see Lord Hoffmann's summary in *Wainwright v Home Office* [2003] 4 All ER 969, [2003] UKHL 53, at [18] (p. 1033 post). However, in *Wainwright* the House of Lords confirmed that there is no privacy tort at common law. The lacunae illuminated by *Kaye v Robertson* [1991] FSR 62 (see *Wainwright* at [25]–[27]) might still leave the courts powerless to protect individuals against egregious intrusion into their private lives.

A development of vital importance has been the Human Rights Act 1998, which gives effect in English law to Article 8 of the European Convention on Human Rights (the right to private and family life). Sections 6–8 of the Act expressly grant a remedy when private life is violated by a public authority. More controversially, the courts have given some effect to Article 8 when privacy has been invaded by a private individual or organisation (typically a media corporation). Unwilling (so far) to apply Convention rights directly in such situations, the courts have 'developed' existing actions, above all (in the present context) the action for breach of confidence, to provide a remedy.

This chapter considers these early stages of the recognition of privacy as a human right in English law. It deals mostly with the expansion (or arguably, the subversion) of breach of confidence. The case law is already voluminous, and the issues complex, ranging far beyond the usual scope of a torts syllabus. The Human Rights Act 1998 (especially its 'horizontal effect') and the European Court of Human Rights jurisprudence on Articles 8 and 10 (freedom of speech), and the balance between them, are central issues in the modern law on privacy, but a lengthy consideration of them would be out of place here. Even breach of confidence would not usually be dealt with in a work such as this since, for historical reasons, it has usually been classified as an 'equitable wrong' rather than a (common law) tort. For further discussion, the reader is referred to specialist works on privacy, human rights, and media law, such as Part IV of H. Fenwick and G. Phillipson, *Media Freedom under the Human Rights Act* (Oxford, 2006) or M. Tugendhat and I. Christie, *The Law of Privacy and the Media* (Oxford, 2002).

■ **Douglas and others v Hello! Ltd**
Court of Appeal [2001] 2 All ER 289

The first and second claimants, celebrity couple Michael Douglas and Catherine Zeta-Jones, granted exclusive rights to the photographs taken at their wedding to 'OK!' magazine (published by the third claimants, Northern & Shell plc). At the ceremony and reception, unauthorised photography was forbidden. However, a freelance photographer managed to infiltrate the occasion, and sold the resulting images to 'Hello!' magazine. The claimants obtained an interlocutory injunction to prevent the publication of the unauthorised wedding pictures. Hello! appealed, and the Court of Appeal held that although the claimants had a strong case, this could sufficiently be protected by a later award of damages, and discharged the injunction.

SEDLEY LJ:...

[113] Lawyers in this country have learned to accept that English law recognises no right of privacy. It was for this express reason that counsel for the actor Gordon Kaye instead put his case against the Sunday Sport, whose reporter and photographer had shamefully invaded the hospital room where Mr Kaye was recovering from serious head injuries, not as a breach of privacy, which it plainly was, but as a case of libel, malicious falsehood, trespass to the person and passing off. He managed only to hold an injunction to stop the paper claiming, by way of malicious falsehood, that Mr Kaye had voluntarily given an interview. But this court in *Kaye v Robertson* [1991] FSR 62 did not affirmatively consider and decide whether there is a right of privacy in English law. The court adopted—for it plainly shared—counsel's assumption that there was none....

[116] Nobody supposes that the members of the court which expressed this view were unfamiliar with the body of cases of which the best-known is *Prince Albert v Strange* (1849) 1 Mac & G 25, 41 ER 1171 or therefore that their assent to counsel's concession was per incuriam. But it is unhelpful now to speculate whether they would have maintained their view had the point been argued before them. The legal landscape has altered.

[117] The argument would not have been that a right of privacy had been spelt out by the courts: plainly it had not. It would have been, as it has been in Mr Tugendhat's condensed but convincing submission, that the tort of breach of confidence contains all that is necessary for the fair protection of personal privacy, and that it is now a relatively small step to articulate it in that way—as was done four years after *Kaye v Robertson* by Laws J in *Hellewell v Chief Constable of Derbyshire* [1995] 4 All ER 473 at 476, [1995] 1 WLR 804 at 807:

> 'I entertain no doubt that disclosure of a photograph may, in some circumstances, be actionable as a breach of confidence... If someone with a telephoto lens were to take from a distance and with no authority a picture of another engaged in some private act, his subsequent disclosure of the photograph would, in my judgment, as surely amount to a breach of confidence as if he had found or stolen a letter or diary in which the act was recounted and proceeded to publish it. In such a case, the law would protect what might reasonably be called a right of privacy, although the name accorded to the cause of action would be breach of confidence.'

[125] I would conclude, at lowest, that Mr Tugendhat has a powerfully arguable case to advance at trial that his two first-named clients have a right of privacy which English law will today recognise and, where appropriate, protect. To say this is in my belief to say little, save by way of a label, that our courts have not said already over the years....

[126] What a concept of privacy does, however, is accord recognition to the fact that the law has to protect not only those people whose trust has been abused but those who simply find themselves subjected to an unwanted intrusion into their personal lives. The law no longer needs to construct an artificial relationship of confidentiality between intruder and victim: it can recognise privacy itself as a legal principle drawn from the fundamental value of personal autonomy.

KEENE LJ:...

[166] Since the coming into force of the Human Rights Act, the courts as a public authority cannot act in a way which is incompatible with a convention right: s 6(1). That arguably includes their activity in interpreting and developing the common law, even where no public authority is a party to the

litigation. Whether this extends to creating a new cause of action between private persons and bodies is more controversial, since to do so would appear to circumvent the restrictions on proceedings contained in s 7(1) of the Act and on remedies in s 8(1). But it is unnecessary to determine that issue in these proceedings, where reliance is placed on breach of confidence, an established cause of action, the scope of which may now need to be approached in the light of the obligation on this court arising under s 6(1) of the Act. Already before the coming into force of the Act there have been persuasive dicta...to the effect that a pre-existing confidential relationship between the parties is not required for a breach of confidence suit. The nature of the subject matter or the circumstances of the defendant's activities may suffice in some instances to give rise to liability for breach of confidence. That approach must now be informed by the jurisprudence of the convention in respect of art 8. Whether the resulting liability is described as being for breach of confidence or for breach of a right to privacy may be little more than deciding what label is to be attached to the cause of action, but there would seem to be merit in recognising that the original concept of breach of confidence has in this particular category of cases now developed into something different from the commercial and employment relationships with which confidentiality is mainly concerned.

NOTES

1. When the action came to trial, Lindsay J found for the first and second claimants in breach of confidence: [2003] 3 All ER 996, [2003] EWHC 786 (Ch). He subsequently awarded £3,750 to each, for the distress caused by the publication: [2003] EWHC 2629 (Ch). An extract from the Court of Appeal's decision on this aspect of the case [2005] 4 All ER 128, [2005] EWCA Civ 595 is at p. 1041, post. It might be noted that the court considered that it had earlier been wrong to discharge the interlocutory injunction, since the damages awarded could not be said to have adequately protected the claimants' rights, whereas the defendant's interest was essentially financial and could have been protected by a cross-undertaking in damages on granting the injunction, at [251]–[259].

2. Keene LJ at [166], ante alludes to the vexed question of the 'horizontal effect' of the Human Rights Act 1998 (which has particular importance for privacy claims which are mostly against non-state media organisations). A detailed consideration is out of place here. Suffice to note that the basic positions were staked out in influential articles by M. Hunt [1998] PL 423; R. Buxton (2000) 116 LQR 48; and H.W.R .Wade (2000) 116 LQR 217. The judicial consensus to date seems to be for the intermediate position, some but not full 'indirect' horizontal effect (see e.g. Lord Lester and D. Pannick (2000) 116 LQR 380). But as Mummery LJ warned in *X v Y* [2004] ICR 1634, [2004] EWCA Civ 662 at [45]: 'The academic debate continues. The general question of horizontality has not yet been resolved by a court. Indeed, it may never be resolved judicially at the same high level of abstraction on which the debate has been conducted for the most part in the law books and legal periodicals. The facts of particular cases and the legal contexts in which they fall to be decided tend to put very general propositions into a more limited and manageable perspective.' As Mummery LJ went on to point out at [57], courts (as public authorities within s. 6 of the Human Rights Act) must be particularly careful to protect Convention rights in contexts 'where the Strasbourg court has held that [the Convention] imposes a positive obligation on the state to secure the enjoyment of that right between private individuals'.

3. Another case decided shortly after the Human Rights Act came into force, *Venables v News Group Newspapers Ltd* [2001] Fam 430, [2001] 1 All ER 9081, has been described as 'perhaps the most dramatic use of the law of confidence to protect privacy' (*Douglas*

v Hello! (No 3) [2005] 4 All ER 128, [2005] EWCA Civ 595 at [68]). Butler-Sloss P granted injunctions against the whole world, to restrain publication of information which might lead to the identification of notorious child murderers, who had been released from prison under new identities. This certainly shows that 'a pre-existing confidential relationship between the parties is not required for a breach of confidence suit' as Keene LJ puts it, ante.

■ Wainwright v Home Office
House of Lords [2003] 4 All ER 969

The claimants visited a relative in prison. They were subjected to a humiliating strip-search by officers looking for drugs, who failed to follow the procedures laid down in the Prison Rules. The trial judge awarded damages for an extended tort of trespass to the person, namely 'causing a person to do something to himself which infringed his right to privacy'. The Court of Appeal [2003] 3 All ER 943, [2001] EWCA Civ 2081 held that the Human Rights Act 1998 did not apply since the facts arose before October 2000, and that there was no common law tort of invasion of privacy. The claimants appealed to the House of Lords.

LORD HOFFMANN: . . .

[15] My Lords, let us first consider the proposed tort of invasion of privacy. Since the famous article by Warren and Brandeis ('The Right to Privacy' (1890) 4 Harv LR 193) the question of whether such a tort exists, or should exist, has been much debated in common law jurisdictions. . . .

[18] The need in the United States to break down the concept of 'invasion of privacy' into a number of loosely-linked torts must cast doubt upon the value of any high-level generalisation which can perform a useful function in enabling one to deduce the rule to be applied in a concrete case. English law has so far been unwilling, perhaps unable, to formulate any such high-level principle. There are a number of common law and statutory remedies of which it may be said that one at least of the underlying values they protect is a right of privacy. Sir Brian Neill's well-known article 'Privacy: a challenge for the next century' in *Protecting Privacy* (ed B Markesinis) (1999) contains a survey. Common law torts include trespass, nuisance, defamation and malicious falsehood; there is the equitable action for breach of confidence and statutory remedies under the Protection from Harassment Act 1997 and the Data Protection Act 1998. There are also extra-legal remedies under codes of practice applicable to broadcasters and newspapers. But there are gaps; cases in which the courts have considered that an invasion of privacy deserves a remedy which the existing law does not offer. Sometimes the perceived gap can be filled by judicious development of an existing principle. The law of breach of confidence has in recent years undergone such a process: see in particular the judgment of Lord Phillips of Worth Matravers MR in *Campbell v MGN Ltd* [2002] EWCA Civ 1373, [2003] 1 All ER 224, [2003] QB 633. On the other hand, an attempt to create a tort of telephone harassment by a radical change in the basis of the action for private nuisance in *Khorasandjian v Bush* [1993] 3 All ER 669, [1993] QB 727 was held by the House of Lords in *Hunter v Canary Wharf Ltd, Hunter v London Docklands Development Corp* [1997] 2 All ER 426, [1997] AC 655 to be a step too far. The gap was filled by the 1997 Act.

[19] What the courts have so far refused to do is to formulate a general principle of 'invasion of privacy' (I use the quotation marks to signify doubt about what in such a context the expression would mean) from which the conditions of liability in the particular case can be deduced. . . .

[23] The absence of any general cause of action for invasion of privacy was again acknowledged by the Court of Appeal in *Kaye v Robertson* [1991] FSR 62, in which a newspaper reporter and photographer invaded the plaintiff's hospital bedroom, purported to interview him and took photographs. The law of trespass provided no remedy because the plaintiff was not owner or occupier of the room and his body had not been touched. Publication of the interview was restrained by interlocutory injunction

on the ground that it was arguably a malicious falsehood to represent that the plaintiff had consented to it. But no other remedy was available. At the time of the judgment (16 March 1990) a committee under the chairmanship of Sir David Calcutt QC (the Calcutt Committee) was considering whether individual privacy required statutory protection against intrusion by the press. Glidewell LJ said (at 66):

> 'The facts of the present case are a graphic illustration of the desirability of Parliament considering whether and in what circumstances statutory provision can be made to protect the privacy of individuals.'

[24] Bingham LJ likewise said (at 70):

> 'The problems of defining and limiting a tort of privacy are formidable, but the present case strengthens my hope that the review now in progress may prove fruitful.'

[25] Leggatt LJ (at 71) referred to Dean Prosser's analysis of the development of the law of privacy in the United States and said that similar rights could be created in England only by statute: '...it is to be hoped that the making good of this signal shortcoming in our law will not be long delayed.'

[26] All three judgments are flat against a judicial power to declare the existence of a high-level right to privacy and I do not think that they suggest that the courts should do so. The members of the Court of Appeal certainly thought that it would be desirable if there was legislation to confer a right to protect the privacy of a person in the position of Mr Kaye against the kind of intrusion which he suffered, but they did not advocate any wider principle. And when the Calcutt Committee reported in June 1990, they did indeed recommend that 'entering private property, without the consent of the lawful occupant, with intent to obtain personal information with a view to its publication' should be made a criminal offence: see *Report of the Committee on Privacy and Related Matters* (Cm 1102) para 6.33. The Calcutt Committee also recommended that certain other forms of intrusion, like the use of surveillance devices on private property and long-distance photography and sound recording, should be made offences.

[27] But the Calcutt Committee did not recommend, even within their terms of reference (which were confined to press intrusion) the creation of a generalised tort of infringement of privacy (para 12.5).... [T]hey considered that the problem could be tackled more effectively by a combination of the more sharply-focused remedies which they recommended (para 12.32). As for a 'general wrong of infringement of privacy', they accepted (para 12.12) that it would, even in statutory form, give rise to 'an unacceptable degree of uncertainty'....

[28] The claimants placed particular reliance upon the judgment of Sedley LJ in *Douglas v Hello! Ltd* [2001] 2 All ER 289, [2001] QB 967.... [His Lordship referred in particular to the dicta in para [126]–[127], ante, and continued:]

[30] I do not understand Sedley LJ to have been advocating the creation of a high-level principle of invasion of privacy. His observations are in my opinion no more (although certainly no less) than a plea for the extension and possibly renaming of the old action for breach of confidence. As Buxton LJ pointed out in this case in the Court of Appeal ([2003] 3 All ER 943 at [96]–[99], [2002] QB 1334 at [96]–[99]), such an extension would go further than any English court has yet gone and would be contrary to some cases (such as *Kaye v Robertson* [1991] FSR 62) in which it positively declined to do so. The question must wait for another day. But Sedley LJ's dictum does not support a principle of privacy so abstract as to include the circumstances of the present case.

[31] There seems to me a great difference between identifying privacy as a value which underlies the existence of a rule of law (and may point the direction in which the law should develop) and privacy as a principle of law in itself. The English common law is familiar with the notion of underlying values— principles only in the broadest sense—which direct its development. A famous example is *Derbyshire CC v Times Newspapers Ltd* [1993] 1 All ER 1011, [1993] AC 534, in which freedom of speech was the underlying value which supported the decision to lay down the specific rule that a local authority could not sue for libel. But no one has suggested that freedom of speech is in itself a legal principle which is

capable of sufficient definition to enable one to deduce specific rules to be applied in concrete cases. That is not the way the common law works.

[32] Nor is there anything in the jurisprudence of the European Court of Human Rights which suggests that the adoption of some high level principle of privacy is necessary to comply with art 8 of the convention. The European Court is concerned only with whether English law provides an adequate remedy in a specific case in which it considers that there has been an invasion of privacy contrary to art 8(1) and not justifiable under art 8(2). So in *Earl Spencer*'s case it was satisfied that the action for breach of confidence provided an adequate remedy for the Spencers' complaint and looked no further into the rest of the armoury of remedies available to the victims of other invasions of privacy. Likewise, in *Peck v UK* (2003) 13 BHRC 669 at 692 (para 103) the court expressed some impatience at being given a tour d'horizon of the remedies provided and to be provided by English law to deal with every imaginable kind of invasion of privacy. It was concerned with whether Mr Peck (who had been filmed in embarrassing circumstances by a CCTV camera) had an adequate remedy when the film was widely published by the media. It came to the conclusion that he did not.

[33] Counsel for the Wainwrights relied upon *Peck*'s case as demonstrating the need for a general tort of invasion of privacy. But in my opinion it shows no more than the need, in English law, for a system of control of the use of film from CCTV cameras which shows greater sensitivity to the feelings of people who happen to have been caught by the lens. For the reasons so cogently explained by Megarry V-C in *Malone v Comr of Police of the Metropolis* [1979] 2 All ER 620, [1979] Ch 344, this is an area which requires a detailed approach which can be achieved only by legislation rather than the broad brush of common law principle.

[34] Furthermore, the coming into force of the 1998 Act weakens the argument for saying that a general tort of invasion of privacy is needed to fill gaps in the existing remedies. Sections 6 and 7 of the Act are in themselves substantial gap fillers; if it is indeed the case that a person's rights under art 8 have been infringed by a public authority, he will have a statutory remedy. The creation of a general tort will, as Buxton LJ pointed out in the Court of Appeal ([2003] 3 All ER 943 at [92], [2003] QB 1334 at [92]) pre-empt the controversial question of the extent, if any, to which the convention requires the state to provide remedies for invasions of privacy by persons who are not public authorities.

[35] For these reasons I would reject the invitation to declare that since at the latest 1950 there has been a previously unknown tort of invasion of privacy.

[His Lordship then considered the tort in *Wilkinson v Downton*, on which see pp. 743, ante, and continued:]

[48] Counsel for the Wainwrights submit that unless the law is extended to create a tort which covers the facts of the present case, it is inevitable that the European Court of Human Rights will find that the United Kingdom was in breach of its convention obligation to provide a remedy for infringements of convention rights. In addition to a breach of art 8 [the right to private and family life], they say that the prison officers infringed their convention right under art 3 not to be subjected to degrading treatment.

[49] I have no doubt that there was no infringement of art 3. . . .

[51] Article 8 is more difficult. Buxton LJ thought ([2003] 3 All ER 943 at [62], [2002] QB 1334 at [62]), that the Wainwrights would have had a strong case for relief under s 7 if the 1998 Act had been in force. Speaking for myself, I am not so sure. Although art 8 guarantees a right of privacy, I do not think that it treats that right as having been invaded and requiring a remedy in damages, irrespective of whether the defendant acted intentionally, negligently or accidentally. It is one thing to wander carelessly into the wrong hotel bedroom and another to hide in the wardrobe to take photographs. Article 8 may justify a monetary remedy for an intentional invasion of privacy by a public authority, even if no damage is suffered other than distress for which damages are not ordinarily recoverable. It does not follow that a merely negligent act should, contrary to general principle, give rise to a claim for damages for distress because it affects privacy rather than some other interest like bodily safety: compare *Hicks v Chief Constable of the South Yorkshire Police* [1992] 2 All ER 65.

[52] Be that as it may, a finding that there was a breach of art 8 will only demonstrate that there was a gap in the English remedies for invasion of privacy which has since been filled by ss 6 and 7 of the 1998 Act. It does not require that the courts should provide an alternative remedy which distorts the principles of the common law.

[53] I would therefore dismiss the appeal.

[LORD BINGHAM OF CORNHILL, LORD HOPE OF CRAIGHEAD, and LORD HUTTON agreed with LORD HOFFMANN. LORD SCOTT OF FOSCOTE delivered a speech in favour of dismissing the appeal and agreed with LORD HOFFMANN.]

Appeal dismissed.

NOTES

1. *Wainwright* is noted by A. Johnston [2004] CLJ 15; M. Lester [2004] EHRLR 193; and J. Morgan (2004) 120 LQR 393.

2. In *Malone v Metropolitan Police Comr* [1979] Ch 344, [1979] 2 All ER 620, Megarry V-C held that there was no common law right in England to 'telephonic privacy' and refused to grant a declaration to the claimant that the police tapping of his telephone (on the authority of the Secretary of State) was unlawful. The Crown could profit from the maxim that everyone is free to do that which has not been specified as unlawful; one might compare the more robust attitude of judges to civil liberties in *Entick v Carrington* (1765) 19 State Tr 1029, and *Ashby v White* (1703) 2 Ld Raym 938 (see C. Harlow, *Compensation and Government Torts* (London, 1983), pp. 43–44; *Williams & Hepple*, pp. 61–66). The European Court of Human Rights subsequently ruled that the unregulated telephone tapping in the *Malone* case was contrary to Articles 8 and 13 of the European Convention on Human Rights and Fundamental Freedoms (*Malone v UK* (1984) 7 EHRR 14). Contrast now the Regulation of Investigatory Powers Act 2000.

3. *Wainwright* is in many ways a parallel decision to *Malone*; even though the officers were found to have breached the Prison Rules, this did not sound in damages unless a tort could be established. Since there was no tort of invasion of privacy and on the facts no *intentional* infliction of distress (see pp. 743–75, ante), no tort had been committed. Contrary to Lord Hoffmann's observations at [51], the European Court of Human Right subsequently found a violation of both Articles 8 and 13, and awarded damages to the claimants: *Wainwright v UK* (2007) 44 EHRR 40.

   Of course, as Lord Hoffmann points out at [34], since the Human Rights Act came into force in October 2000, there has been statutory redress for invasion of privacy by a public authority: ss. 6–8. These provisions cannot be relied upon in a case against a private individual or organisation, such as a newspaper, but in cases involving publication of private information, the action for breach of confidence has proved fruitful. As *Wainwright* itself shows, however, some invasions of privacy fall way outside the ambit of even the extended breach of confidence jurisdiction whose development is described in the cases that follow.

■ Campbell v Mirror Group Newspapers Ltd
House of Lords [2004] 2 All ER 995

The defendant newspaper published an article about the claimant celebrity's drug rehabilitation programme, accompanied by photographs of her in the public street, leaving a 'Narcotics Anonymous' group therapy meeting. Reversing the Court of Appeal [2003] 1 All

ER 224, [2002] EWCA Civ 1373 and restoring the judgment of Morland J [2002] EWHC 499 (QB), the House of Lords held (Lord Nicholls and Lord Hoffmann dissenting) that publishing the article and images was a breach of confidence, and the claimant's right to private life outweighed the newspaper's right to freedom of speech.

LORD NICHOLLS OF BIRKENHEAD: . . .

[12] The present case concerns one aspect of invasion of privacy: wrongful disclosure of private information. The case involves the familiar competition between freedom of expression and respect for an individual's privacy. Both are vitally important rights. Neither has precedence over the other. The importance of freedom of expression has been stressed often and eloquently, the importance of privacy less so. But it, too, lies at the heart of liberty in a modern state. A proper degree of privacy is essential for the well-being and development of an individual. And restraints imposed on government to pry into the lives of the citizen go to the essence of a democratic state: see La Forest J in *R v Dyment* [1988] 2 SCR 417 at 427–428.

[13] The common law or, more precisely, courts of equity have long afforded protection to the wrongful use of private information by means of the cause of action which became known as breach of confidence. A breach of confidence was restrained as a form of unconscionable conduct, akin to a breach of trust. Today this nomenclature is misleading. . . .

[14] This cause of action has now firmly shaken off the limiting constraint of the need for an initial confidential relationship. In doing so it has changed its nature. In this country this development was recognised clearly in the judgment of Lord Goff of Chieveley in *A-G v Guardian Newspapers Ltd (No 2)* [1988] 3 All ER 545 at 658–659, [1990] 1 AC 109 at 281. Now the law imposes a 'duty of confidence' whenever a person receives information he knows or ought to know is fairly and reasonably to be regarded as confidential. Even this formulation is awkward. The continuing use of the phrase 'duty of confidence' and the description of the information as 'confidential' is not altogether comfortable. Information about an individual's private life would not, in ordinary usage, be called 'confidential'. The more natural description today is that such information is private. The essence of the tort is better encapsulated now as misuse of private information.

[15] In the case of individuals this tort, however labelled, affords respect for one aspect of an individual's privacy. That is the value underlying this cause of action. An individual's privacy can be invaded in ways not involving publication of information. Strip searches are an example. The extent to which the common law as developed thus far in this country protects other forms of invasion of privacy is not a matter arising in the present case. . . .

[17] The time has come to recognise that the values enshrined in arts 8 and 10 are now part of the cause of action for breach of confidence. As Lord Woolf CJ has said, the courts have been able to achieve this result by absorbing the rights protected by arts 8 and 10 into this cause of action: see *A v B (a company)* [2002] EWCA Civ 337 at [4], [2002] 2 All ER 545 at [4], [2003] QB 195. Further, it should now be recognised that for this purpose these values are of general application. The values embodied in arts 8 and 10 are as much applicable in disputes between individuals or between an individual and a non-governmental body such as a newspaper as they are in disputes between individuals and a public authority.

LORD HOFFMANN: . . .

[36] My Lords, the House is divided as to the outcome of this appeal, but the difference of opinion relates to a very narrow point which arises on the unusual facts of this case. The facts are unusual because the plaintiff is a public figure who had made very public false statements about a matter in respect of which even a public figure would ordinarily be entitled to privacy, namely her use of drugs. It was these falsehoods which, as was conceded, made it justifiable, for a newspaper to report the fact that she was addicted. The division of opinion is whether in doing so the newspaper went too far in publishing associated facts about her private life. But the importance of this case lies in the statements of general principle on the way in which the law should strike a balance between the right to privacy

and the right to freedom of expression, on which the House is unanimous. The principles are expressed in varying language but speaking for myself I can see no significant differences.

[46] ... [T]here have been two [recent] developments of the law of confidence, typical of the capacity of the common law to adapt itself to the needs of contemporary life. One has been an acknowledgement of the artificiality of distinguishing between confidential information obtained through the violation of a confidential relationship and similar information obtained in some other way. The second has been the acceptance, under the influence of human rights instruments such as art 8 of the European Convention for the Protection of Human Rights and Fundamental Freedoms 1950 (Rome, 4 November 1950; TS 71 (1953); Cmd 8969), of the privacy of personal information as something worthy of protection in its own right.

[50] What human rights law has done is to identify private information as something worth protecting as an aspect of human autonomy and dignity. And this recognition has raised inescapably the question of why it should be worth protecting against the state but not against a private person. There may of course be justifications for the publication of private information by private persons which would not be available to the state—I have particularly in mind the position of the media, to which I shall return in a moment—but I can see no logical ground for saying that a person should have less protection against a private individual than he would have against the state for the publication of personal information for which there is no justification. Nor, it appears, have any of the other judges who have considered the matter.

[51] The result of these developments has been a shift in the centre of gravity of the action for breach of confidence when it is used as a remedy for the unjustified publication of personal information. It recognises that the incremental changes to which I have referred do not merely extend the duties arising traditionally from a relationship of trust and confidence to a wider range of people. As Sedley LJ observed in a perceptive passage in his judgment in *Douglas v Hello! Ltd* [2001] 2 All ER 289 at 320, [2001] QB 967 at 1001 (para 126), the new approach takes a different view of the underlying value which the law protects. Instead of the cause of action being based upon the duty of good faith applicable to confidential personal information and trade secrets alike, it focuses upon the protection of human autonomy and dignity—the right to control the dissemination of information about one's private life and the right to the esteem and respect of other people.

[52] These changes have implications for the future development of the law. They must influence the approach of the courts to the kind of information which is regarded as entitled to protection, the extent and form of publication which attracts a remedy and the circumstances in which publication can be justified.

[73] In the present case, the pictures were taken without Ms Campbell's consent. That in my opinion is not enough to amount to a wrongful invasion of privacy. The famous and even the not so famous who go out in public must accept that they may be photographed without their consent, just as they may be observed by others without their consent. As Gleeson CJ said in *Australian Broadcasting Corp v Lenah Game Meats Pty Ltd* (2001) 185 ALR 1 at 13 (para 41): 'Part of the price we pay for living in an organised society is that we are exposed to observation in a variety of ways by other people.'

[74] But the fact that we cannot avoid being photographed does not mean that anyone who takes or obtains such photographs can publish them to the world at large. ...

[75] In my opinion, therefore, the widespread publication of a photograph of someone which reveals him to be in a situation of humiliation or severe embarrassment, even if taken in a public place, may be an infringement of the privacy of his personal information. Likewise, the publication of a photograph taken by intrusion into a private place (for example, by a long distance lens) may in itself be such an infringement, even if there is nothing embarrassing about the picture itself: see *Hellewell v Chief Constable of Derbyshire* [1995] 4 All ER 473 at 476, [1995] 1 WLR 804 at 807. As Lord Mustill said in *R v Broadcasting Standards Commission, ex p BBC* [2000] 3 All ER 989 at 1002, [2001] QB 885 at 900 (para 48):

'An infringement of privacy is an affront to the personality, which is damaged both by the violation and by the demonstration that the personal space is not inviolate.'

[76] In the present case, however, there was nothing embarrassing about the picture, which showed Ms Campbell neatly dressed and smiling among a number of other people. Nor did the taking of the picture involve an intrusion into private space. Hundreds of such 'candid' pictures of Ms Campbell, taken perhaps on more glamorous occasions, must have been published in the past without objection....

LORD HOPE OF CRAIGHEAD: ...

[86] The language [of breach of confidence] has changed following the coming into operation of the 1998 Act and the incorporation into domestic law of arts 8 and 10 of the convention. We now talk about the right to respect for private life and the countervailing right to freedom of expression. The jurisprudence of the European Court of Human Rights offers important guidance as to how these competing rights ought to be approached and analysed. I doubt whether the result is that the centre of gravity, as my noble and learned friend Lord Hoffmann says, has shifted. It seems to me that the balancing exercise to which that guidance is directed is essentially the same exercise, although it is plainly now more carefully focussed and more penetrating. As Lord Woolf CJ said in *A v B* [2002] 2 All ER 545 at [4], new breadth and strength is given to the action for breach of confidence by these articles.

BARONESS HALE OF RICHMOND: ...

[126] My Lords, this case raises some big questions. How is the balance to be struck between everyone's right to respect for their private and family life under art 8 of the European Convention for the Protection of Human Rights and Fundamental Freedoms 1950 (as set out in Sch 1 to the Human Rights Act 1998) and everyone's right to freedom of expression, including the freedom to receive and impart information and ideas under art 10? How do those rights come into play in a dispute between two private persons? But the parties are largely agreed about the answers to these. They disagree about where that balance is to be struck in the individual case....

[132] Neither party to this appeal has challenged the basic principles which have emerged from the Court of Appeal in the wake of the 1998 Act. The 1998 Act does not create any new cause of action between private persons. But if there is a relevant cause of action applicable, the court as a public authority must act compatibly with both parties' convention rights. In a case such as this, the relevant vehicle will usually be the action for breach of confidence....

[133] The action for breach of confidence is not the only relevant cause of action: the inherent jurisdiction of the High Court to protect the children for whom it is responsible is another example: see *Re S (a child) (identification: restriction on publication)* [2003] EWCA Civ 963, [2003] 2 FCR 577, [2004] Fam 43. But the courts will not invent a new cause of action to cover types of activity which were not previously covered: see *Wainwright v Home Office* [2003] UKHL 53, [2003] 4 All ER 969, [2003] 3 WLR 1137....

[154] Publishing the photographs contributed both to the revelation and to the harm that it might do. By themselves, they are not objectionable. Unlike France and Quebec, in this country we do not recognise a right to one's own image: cf *Aubry v Editions Vice-Versa Inc* [1998] 1 SCR 591. We have not so far held that the mere fact of covert photography is sufficient to make the information contained in the photograph confidential. The activity photographed must be private. If this had been, and had been presented as, a picture of Naomi Campbell going about her business in a public street, there could have been no complaint. She makes a substantial part of her living out of being photographed looking stunning in designer clothing. Readers will obviously be interested to see how she looks if and when she pops out to the shops for a bottle of milk. There is nothing essentially private about that information nor can it be expected to damage her private life. It may not be a high order of freedom of speech but there is nothing to justify interfering with it....

[155] But here the accompanying text made it plain that these photographs were different. They showed her coming either to or from the [Narcotics Anonymous] meeting. They showed her in the company of others, some of whom were undoubtedly part of the group. They showed the place where the meeting was taking place, which will have been entirely recognisable to anyone who knew the locality. A picture is 'worth a thousand words' because it adds to the impact of what the words convey;

but it also adds to the information given in those words. If nothing else, it tells the reader what everyone looked like; in this case it also told the reader what the place looked like. In context, it also added to the potential harm, by making her think that she was being followed or betrayed, and deterring her from going back to the same place again.

[157] The weight to be attached to these various considerations is a matter of fact and degree....

[LORD CARSWELL delivered a speech in favour of allowing the appeal.]

Appeal allowed.

NOTES

1. *Campbell* is noted by N. Moreham [2004] CLJ 555 and J. Morgan (2004) 120 LQR 563.
2. *Campbell* raised two difficult issues which have recurred time and again in the developing privacy jurisprudence: when is information sufficiently 'private', and how is the balance between the claimant's privacy (Article 8) and the defendant's free speech (Article 10) to be struck?
3. The latter 'balancing' question is heavily fact-dependent. Lord Steyn has described the effect of *Campbell's* case in a much-cited summary in *In re S (A Child) (Identification: Restrictions on Publication)* [2004] 4 All ER 683, [2004] UKHL 47 at [17]:

   First, neither article has as such precedence over the other. Secondly, where the values under the two articles are in conflict, an intense focus on the comparative importance of the specific rights being claimed in the individual case is necessary. Thirdly, the justifications for interfering with or restricting each right must be taken into account. Finally, the proportionality test must be applied to each. For convenience I will call this the ultimate balancing test.

   It is difficult to state the approach any more precisely without descending into the facts of the numerous authorities: reference should be made to Fenwick and Phillipson, op cit., chap. 15. An example of the balancing test (assessing the level of legitimate public interest in the information being disseminated) is *McKennitt v Ash*, p. 1045, post.
4. Lord Nicholls in *Campbell* at [21] said that the 'the touchstone of private life is whether in respect of the disclosed facts the person in question had a reasonable expectation of privacy'. Lord Hoffmann explains at [73]–[75] that photographs taken in a public place may sometimes, but not always, violate that 'reasonable expectation'. On the facts of *Campbell*, his Lordship at [76] held that this was not satisfied but contrast the view of Baroness Hale (speaking for the majority) at [154]–[157], ante.

   In *Von Hannover v Germany* (2004) 40 EHRR 1 the European Court of Human Rights stated at [50] that 'Article 8 of the Convention is primarily intended to ensure the development, without outside interference, of the personality of each individual in his relations with other human beings. There is therefore a zone of interaction of a person with others, even in a public context, which may fall within the scope of "private life"' (citations omitted). Therefore photographs of Princess Caroline of Monaco going about her daily life in public places (e.g. shopping, playing tennis, leaving her flat) undoubtedly fell within the scope of her private life: [53].

   However, in *John v Associated Newspapers Ltd* [2006] EWHC 1611 (QB) Eady J held that photographs of Sir Elton John 'in the street abutting his London home' (published with a newspaper article likely to be 'dismissive and personally offensive') did not breach the pop-star's reasonable expectation of privacy. The learned judge held that the special features of *Campbell's* case (the proximity to the drug-rehabilitation clinic) were absent: the case was 'much more akin to "popping out for a pint of milk"' (cf. Baroness

Hale at [154], ante). *Von Hannover* was distinguished (perhaps questionably) on the grounds that press harassment had been an important factor in the European Court's reasoning: [16]. In *Murray v Express Newspapers plc* [2008] EWCA Civ 446 it was held at least arguable that the claimant, the infant son of a well-known author, had a reasonable expectation of privacy when in the public street that had been violated by the defendant's publication of photographs of him there (taken without his knowledge or consent). Clarke MR stated at [36] that the expectation of privacy, while ultimately a question of fact, required examination of all the circumstances including 'attributes of the claimant, the nature of the activity in which the claimant was engaged, the place at which it was happening, the nature and purpose of the intrusion, the absence of consent and whether it was known or could be inferred, the effect on the claimant and the circumstances in which and the purposes for which the information came into the hands of the publisher'. Carrying out this exercise on the facts of the case, the Court of Appeal stressed the claimant's infancy. At [56], Clarke MR disclaimed any 'predisposition' that 'routine acts such as a visit to a shop or a ride on a bus should not attract any reasonable expectation of privacy', emphasising that this must ultimately depend on the facts of the case. At [55] however, the Master of the Rolls commented that 'even after *Von Hannover*', ante, circumstances may still arise in which there is no reasonable expectation of privacy, but suggested that no bright-line rule could be laid down to exclude the so-called 'pint of milk' cases.

■ Douglas and others v Hello! Ltd (No 3)

Court of Appeal [2005] 4 All ER 128

For the facts see p. 1031, ante. At the trial of the action [2003] 3 All ER 996 Lindsay J decided in the claimants' favour. The defendant magazine appealed.

LORD PHILLIPS OF WORTH MATRAVERS MR (delivering the judgment of the court): . . .

[46] . . . The enactment of the [Human Rights Act 1998] provoked a lively discussion of the impact that it would have on the development of a law protecting privacy. The government has made it clear that it does not intend to introduce legislation in relation to this area of the law, but anticipates that the judges will develop the law appropriately, having regard to the requirements of the convention—see the comment of Lord Irvine LC in the course of the debate on the Human Rights Bill 583 HL Official Report (5th series) col 771 (24 November 1997) and the submissions of the United Kingdom in *Earl Spencer v UK* (1998) 25 EHRR CD 105. The courts have not accepted this role with whole-hearted enthusiasm. . . .

[53] We conclude that, in so far as private information is concerned, we are required to adopt, as the vehicle for performing such duty as falls on the courts in relation to convention rights, the cause of action formerly described as breach of confidence. As to the nature of that duty, it seems to us that ss 2, 3, 6 and 12 of the 1998 Act all point in the same direction. The court should, in so far as it can, develop the action for breach of confidence in such a manner as will give effect to both art 8 and art 10 rights. In considering the nature of those rights, account should be taken of the Strasbourg jurisprudence. In particular, when considering what information should be protected as private pursuant to art 8, it is right to have regard to the decisions of the European Court. We cannot pretend that we find it satisfactory to be required to shoe-horn within the cause of action of breach of confidence claims for publication of unauthorised photographs of a private occasion.

[The Court of Appeal held at [96] that in principle, 'photographs of the wedding plainly portrayed aspects of the Douglases' private life and fell within the protection of the law of confidentiality, as extended to cover private or personal information'.]

[103] Hello!'s argument, as advanced by Mr Price, is that, once the Douglases had committed themselves by the OK! contract to putting before the public photographs of their wedding, it was no longer possible for them to advance a claim that events at their wedding were private or confidential. Thereafter, publication of other photographs of that event could not possibly infringe art 8 of the convention or give rise to a claim for breach of confidence.

[104] We have seen that the first element of breach of confidence identified by Megarry J in *Coco v AN Clarke (Engineers) Ltd* was that the information had to be 'of a confidential nature', as opposed to being public property and public knowledge. The *Spycatcher* litigation concerned republication in English newspapers of extracts from a book, published without legal restraint in Australia and elsewhere, which had been written by a former member of the British secret service in breach of contract and confidence applicable under English law. In that litigation, which culminated in the decision of the House of Lords in *A-G v Guardian Newspapers Ltd (No 2)* [1988] 3 All ER 545, [1990] 1 AC 109, it was held, after much discussion, that the protection of the law of confidence had been lost as a result of the information coming into the public domain. Care must be exercised in applying that decision generally, for there is a special principle of law which precludes the state from asserting breach of confidence where it cannot be shown that this is in the public interest.

[105] In general, however, once information is in the public domain, it will no longer be confidential or entitled to the protection of the law of confidence, though this may not always be true: see *Gilbert v Star Newspaper Co Ltd* (1894) 51 TLR 4 and *Creation Records Ltd v News Group Newspapers Ltd* [1997] EMLR 444 at 456. The same may generally be true of private information of a personal nature. Once intimate personal information about a celebrity's private life has been widely published it may serve no useful purpose to prohibit further publication. The same will not necessarily be true of photographs. In so far as a photograph does more than convey information and intrudes on privacy by enabling the viewer to focus on intimate personal detail, there will be a fresh intrusion of privacy when each additional viewer sees the photograph and even when one who has seen a previous publication of the photograph, is confronted by a fresh publication of it. To take an example, if a film star were photographed, with the aid of a telephoto lens, lying naked by her private swimming pool, we question whether widespread publication of the photograph by a popular newspaper would provide a defence to a legal challenge to repeated publication on the ground that the information was in the public domain. There is thus a further important potential distinction between the law relating to private information and that relating to other types of confidential information.

[106] Nor is it right to treat a photograph simply as a means of conveying factual information. A photograph can certainly capture every detail of a momentary event in a way which words cannot, but a photograph can do more than that. A personal photograph can portray, not necessarily accurately, the personality and the mood of the subject of the photograph. It is quite wrong to suppose that a person who authorises publication of selected personal photographs taken on a private occasion, will not reasonably feel distress at the publication of unauthorised photographs taken on the same occasion.

[107] There is a further point. The objection to the publication of unauthorised photographs taken on a private occasion is not simply that the images that they disclose convey secret information, or impressions that are unflattering. It is that they disclose information that is private. The offence is caused because what the claimant could reasonably expect would remain private has been made public. The intrusion into the private domain is, of itself, objectionable. To the extent that an individual authorises photographs taken on a private occasion to be made public, the potential for distress at the publication of other, unauthorised, photographs, taken on the same occasion, will be reduced. This will be very relevant when considering the amount of any damages. The agreement that authorised photographs can be published will not, however, provide a defence to a claim, brought under the law of confidence, for the publication of unauthorised photographs. It follows that we do not accept Mr Price's submission that the effect of the OK! contract precluded the Douglases' right to contend that their wedding was a private occasion and, as such, protected by the law of confidence.

Appeal against decision in favour of the first and second claimants dismissed.

QUESTION

Why was the Court of Appeal unhappy about having to 'shoehorn' privacy cases into the action for breach of confidence?

NOTES

1. This stage of the *Douglas* litigation is noted by R. Bagshaw (2005) 121 LQR 550 and J. Morgan [2005] CLJ 549.
2. The Court of Appeal's apparent dislike of the 'breach of confidence' approach to privacy should be contrasted with the comments in *Campbell*, p. 1036, ante, defending the 'development' of the existing cause of action. For a note of *Campbell* contrasting the bolder approach of the New Zealand Court of Appeal in *Hosking v Runting* [2005] 1 NZLR 1, see J. Morgan (2004) 120 LQR 563.
3. In *Mosley v News Group Newspapers Ltd* [2008] EWHC 687 (QB) the claimant sought an injunction to remove from the defendant's website a video recording showing his sexual exploits with five prostitutes. Eady J held that while the footage was disproportionately intrusive upon the claimant's private life, an injunction would (reluctantly) be refused since the material had already been so extensively disseminated that 'the granting of an order against [the defendant] at the present juncture would merely be a futile gesture', [36]. The judge considered the Court of Appeal's observations about private photographs in *Douglas* at [105]–[107], ante, but held that the court could not ignore practical realities, must not act like King Canute, and that there came a point where, as in the case at hand, the information 'is so widely and generally accessible "in the public domain" that such an injunction would make no practical difference', [33]–[34]
4. Carefully limited dissemination of information may not put it into the public domain; it may retain the confidential nature necessary for a 'traditional' breach of confidence action (as well as the extended privacy sub-species). See *HRH Prince of Wales v Associated Newspapers Ltd* [2007] 2 All ER 139, [2006] EWCA Civ 1776, where extracts from the Prince's private diaries had been circulated to selected recipients (as many as 75 individuals) in envelopes marked 'private and confidential'. It was 'perfectly obvious' that the information was private; 'The journals were paradigm examples of confidential documents' at [35]. See also *Lord Browne of Madingley v Associated Newspapers Ltd* [2007] 3 WLR 289, [2007] EWCA Civ 295 at [61] and Lord Hoffmann's observations in *OBG/Mainstream/Douglas* [2007] 4 All ER 545, [2007] UKHL 21 (p. 907, ante) at [120]–[122].
5. In this chapter we have not dealt with the action of the third claimant (OK! Magazine) against Hello! The trial judge, Lindsay J, awarded OK! over £1m damages for breach of confidence. The Court of Appeal (ante) held that OK!'s exclusive licence to the wedding pictures 'did not carry with it any right to claim, through assignment or otherwise, the benefit of any other confidential information vested in the Douglases,' at [134], and allowed the appeal. The House of Lords [2007] 4 All ER 545, [2007] UKHL 21 (Lord Nicholls and Lord Walker dissenting) allowed the third claimant's further appeal and restored the judgment of Lindsay J. Lord Nicholls stated at [255] that breach of confidence 'now covers two distinct causes of action', protecting either privacy or secret information. Lord Hoffmann similarly said that the court should not be 'distracted by the concepts of privacy and personal information', which were irrelevant to OK!'s

claim. NB that the defendant did not cross-appeal against the Court of Appeal's decision, *ante*, in favour of the first and second claimants.

The economic torts aspects of OK!'s claim are considered at pp. 907–917, *ante*.

■ CC v AB

Queen's Bench Division [2007] EMLR 11

The claimant sought an injunction to prevent the defendant revealing the fact that the claimant had been carrying on a love affair with the defendant's wife. The defendant admitted that he sought media dissemination of the story out of revenge, and for payment.

EADY J: . . .

[25] Judges need to be wary about giving the impression that they are ventilating, while affording or refusing legal redress, some personal moral or social views, and especially at a time when society is far less homogeneous than in the past. At one time, when there was, or was perceived to be, a commonly accepted standard in such matters as sexual morality, it may have been acceptable for the courts to give effect to that standard in exercising discretion or in interpreting legal rights and obligations. Now, however, there is a strong argument for not holding forth about adultery, or attaching greater inherent worth to a relationship which has been formalised by marriage than to any other relationship.

[27] With such a wide range of differing views in society, perhaps more than for many generations, one must guard against allowing legal judgments to be coloured by personal attitudes. Even among judges, there is no doubt a wide range of opinion. It is all the more important, therefore, that the outcome of a particular case should not be determined by the judge's personal views or, as it used to be said, by 'the length of Chancellor's foot'. There is a risk that with greater emphasis on applying an 'intense focus' to the particular facts, with the room this leaves for the making of individual judgments, differing outcomes on what may seem to be broadly comparable facts may be interpreted by onlookers as being explicable on the basis of arbitrary personal differences between the judges. That is plainly undesirable because it would undermine faith in the rule of law, but the danger has to be recognised as inherent in the 'new methodology' of balancing Convention rights.

[28] It is not for judges when applying the European Convention, which is a secular code applying to those of all religions and none, to give an appearance of sanctimony by damning adulterers or seeking, as I was invited to do by Mr Bartley Jones [counsel for the defendant], to 'vindicate' the state of matrimony. Indeed, if the defendant is pretending that his desire to 'spill the beans' to a tabloid newspaper has anything to do with 'vindicating' the institution of marriage, that would be remarkable hypocrisy in the light of his own evidence. He wishes to expose and humiliate not only the claimant but also incidentally his own wife and to do so, on his own ready admission, for revenge and for financial profit.

[30] I have come to the conclusion that there can be no rule of 'generality' that an adulterer can never obtain an injunction to restrain the publication of matters relating to his adulterous relationship; or, to put it another way, even an adulterous relationship may attract, at least in certain respects, a legitimate expectation of privacy. That being so, there is no rule which exempts a 'wronged' husband from restraint automatically, by virtue of his status, although in any given situation there may be particular respects in which his right to free speech should be accorded greater priority.

Injunction granted.

NOTE

For earlier decisions on the exposure of transitory or 'illicit' relationships, see *A v B plc* [2002] 2 All ER 545, [2002] EWCA Civ 337 (often known as the 'Flitcroft case' after the claimant's subsequent exposure) and *Theakston v MGN Ltd* [2002] EMLR 22, [2002] EWHC

137 (QB) (where Ouseley J enjoined publication of photographs of the claimant in a brothel, but not of the 'details of the sexual activity' which took place there).

■ McKennitt v Ash
Court of Appeal [2007] 3 WLR 194

The defendant, formerly a close friend of the claimant (a noted musician), wrote a book about the claimant revealing information about her personal life. Eady J held that the claimant's right to private life outweighed the defendant's freedom of expression, and enjoined publication of a significant portion of the book. The defendant appealed.

BUXTON LJ: . . .

A taxonomy of the law of privacy and confidence

[8] It will be necessary to refer to the underlying law at various stages of the argument, and it would be tedious to repeat such reference more than is necessary. Since the content of that law is in some respects a matter of controversy, I set out what I understand the present state of that law to be. I start with some straightforward matters, before going on to issues of more controversy. (i) There is no English domestic law tort of invasion of privacy. Previous suggestions in a contrary sense were dismissed by Lord Hoffmann, whose speech was agreed with in full by Lord Hope of Craighead and Lord Hutton, in *Wainwright v Home Office* [2004] 2 AC 406 , paras 28–35. (ii) Accordingly, in developing a right to protect private information, including the implementation in the English courts of articles 8 and 10 of the European Convention for the Protection of Human Rights and Fundamental Freedoms , as scheduled to the Human Rights Act 1998, the English courts have to proceed through the tort of breach of confidence, into which the jurisprudence of article 8 and 10 has to be "shoehorned": *Douglas v Hello! Ltd (No 3)* [2006] QB 125, para 53. (iii) That a feeling of discomfort arises from the action for breach of *confidence* being employed where there was no pre-existing relationship of confidence between the parties, but the "confidence" arose from the defendant having acquired by unlawful or surreptitious means information that he should have known he was not free to use: as was the case in *Douglas v Hello! Ltd (No 3)*, and also in *Campbell v MGN Ltd* [2004] 2 AC 457. Two further points should however be noted. (iv) At least the verbal difficulty referred to in (iii) above has been avoided by the rechristening of the tort as misuse of private information: per Lord Nicholls of Birkenhead in *Campbell's* case, para 14. (v) Of great importance in the present case, as will be explained further below, the complaint here is of what might be called old-fashioned breach of confidence by way of conduct inconsistent with a pre-existing relationship, rather than simply of the purloining of private information. Something more now needs to be said about the way in which the rules laid down by articles 8 and 10 enter English domestic law.

[9] Most of the articles of the Convention impose negative obligations on the state and on public bodies. That accordingly affects the content of the articles and the obligations that they create, which are obligations owed only by public bodies. . . . [M]ost of the articles, since their content is restricted to creating obligations on public bodies, do not and cannot create obligations owed by private parties in private law. Article 8 has, however, always been seen as different; as, in this regard . . . Not in its terms, but as extended by jurisprudence, article 8 imposes not merely negative but also positive obligations on the state: to respect, and therefore to promote, the interests of private and family life. That means that a citizen can complain against the state about breaches of his private and family life committed by other individuals. That has been Convention law at least since *Marckx v Belgium* (1979) 2 EHRR 330, and a particularly strong statement of the obligation is to be found in *X and Y v The Netherlands* (1985) 8 EHRR 235.

[10] More difficulty has been experienced in explaining how that state obligation is articulated and enforced in actions between private individuals. However, judges of the highest authority have

concluded that that follows from section 6(1) and (3) of the Human Rights Act 1998, placing on the courts the obligations appropriate to a public authority: see per Baroness Hale of Richmond in Campbell's case [2004] 2 AC 457 , para 132; per Lord Phillips of Worth Matravers MR in *Douglas's* case [2006] QB 125, para 53; and in particular per Lord Woolf CJ in *A v B plc* [2003] QB 195, para 4:

> "under section 6 of the 1998 Act, the court, as a public authority, is required not to act 'in a way which is incompatible with a Convention right'. The court is able to achieve this by absorbing the rights which articles 8 and 10 protect into the long-established action for breach of confidence. This involves giving a new strength and breadth to the action so that it accommodates the requirements of those articles."

[11] The effect of this guidance is, therefore, that in order to find the rules of the English law of breach of confidence we now have to look in the jurisprudence of articles 8 and 10. Those articles are now not merely of persuasive or parallel effect but, as Lord Woolf CJ says, are the very content of the domestic tort that the English court has to enforce. Accordingly, in a case such as the present, where the complaint is of the wrongful publication of private information, the court has to decide two things. First, is the information private in the sense that it is in principle protected by article 8. If "no", that is the end of the case. If "yes", the second question arises: in all the circumstances, must the interest of the owner of the private information yield to the right of freedom of expression conferred on the publisher by article 10. The latter inquiry is commonly referred to as the balancing exercise, and I will use that convenient expression....

A pre-existing relationship of confidence
[15] Recent leading cases in this area, such as *Campbell's* case, *Douglas's* case, and the most recent case in the European Court of Human Rights, *Von Hannover v Germany* (2004) 40 EHRR 1, have wrestled with the problem of identifying the basis for claiming privacy or confidence in respect of unauthorised or purloined information: see para 8(iii) above. There, the primary focus has to be on the nature of the information, because it is the recipient's perception of its confidential nature that imposes the obligation on him: see for instance per Lord Goff of Chieveley in *Attorney General v Guardian Newspapers Ltd (No 2)* ("Spycatcher") [1990] 1 AC 109 , 281A. But, as Lord Goff immediately goes on to say, in the vast majority of cases the duty of confidence will arise from a transaction or relationship between the parties. And that is our case, which accordingly reverts to a more elemental inquiry into breach of confidence in the traditional understanding of that expression. That does not of course exempt the court from considering whether the material obtained during such a relationship is indeed confidential; but to inquire into that latter question without paying any regard to the nature of the pre-existing relationship between the parties, as the argument for the first defendant in this court largely did, is unlikely to produce anything but a distorted outcome.

The public interest: and the first claimant as a public figure
[56] One might instinctively think that there was little legitimate public interest in the matters addressed by the book, and certainly no public interest sufficient to outweigh the first claimant's article 8 right to private life. That is what the judge thought and, as already pointed out, in the absence of error of principle his view will prevail. That conclusion was contested under this head in two respects, which it is necessary to keep separate. First, there was a legitimate public interest in the affairs of the first claimant because she was a public figure, *and for that reason alone*. Second, if a public figure had misbehaved, the allegation in the present case being of hypocrisy, the public had a right to have the record put straight. The parallel for that argument was the case of Ms Campbell, who could not retain privacy for the fact that she was a drug addict because she had lied publicly about her condition.

[57] The first of these arguments involves consideration of two recent authorities, already introduced, *Von Hannover v Germany* 40 EHRR 1 and *A v B plc* [2003] QB 195 , to which I must now return.

Von Hannover v Germany
[58] There is no doubt that the European Court of Human Rights has restated what were previously thought to be the rights and expectations of public figures with regard to their private lives. The court

recognised the important role of the press in dealing with matters of public interest, and the latitude in terms of mode of expression there provided: 40 EHRR 1 , para 58. But a distinction was then drawn between a watchdog role in the democratic process and the reporting of private information about people who, although of interest to the public, were not public figures. The European Court of Human Rights said, at paras 63–64:

> "[63] The court considers that a fundamental distinction needs to be made between reporting facts—even controversial ones—capable of contributing to a debate in a democratic society relating to politicians in the exercise of their functions, for example, and reporting details of the private life of an individual who, moreover, as in this case, does not exercise official functions. While in the former case the press exercises its vital role of 'watchdog' in a democracy by contributing to 'impart[ing] information and ideas on matters of public interest' it does not do so in the latter case.
>
> "[64] Similarly, although the public has a right to be informed, which is an essential right in a democratic society that, in certain special circumstances, can even extend to aspects of the private life of public figures, particularly where politicians are concerned, this is not the case here. The situation here does not come within the sphere of any political or public debate because the published photos and accompanying commentaries relate exclusively to details of the applicant's private life."

59 …If we follow in this case the guidance given by the English courts, that the content of the law of confidence is now to be found in articles 8 and 10 (see para 10 above), then it seems inevitable that the first defendant's case must fail. Even assuming that the first claimant is a public figure in the relevant sense (which proposition I suspect the European Court of Human Rights would find surprising), there are no "special circumstances" apart from the allegation of hypocrisy dealt with in the next section to justify or require the exposure of her private life. But the first defendant argued that English courts could not follow or apply *Von Hannover's* case to the facts of the present case because we were bound by the contrary English authority of *A v B plc* [2003] QB 195. That effectively required the first claimant's private affairs to be exposed to the world, hypocrite or not.

A v B plc

[60] …The judgment of this court is notable for the detailed guidance that it contains as to how a court should address complaints about invasion of privacy by public or allegedly public figures. The first defendant placed particular reliance on the court's para 11(xii):

> "Where an individual is a public figure he is entitled to have his privacy respected in the appropriate circumstances. A public figure is entitled to a private life. The individual, however, should recognise that because of his public position he must expect and accept that his actions will be more closely scrutinised by the media. Even trivial facts relating to a public figure can be of great interest to readers and other observers of the media. Conduct which in the case of a private individual would not be the appropriate subject of comment can be the proper subject of comment in the case of a public figure. The public figure may hold a position where higher standards of conduct can be rightly expected by the public. The public figure may be a role model whose conduct could well be emulated by others. He may set the fashion. The higher the profile of the individual concerned the more likely that this will be the position. Whether you have courted publicity or not you may be a legitimate subject of public attention. If you have courted public attention then you have less ground to object to the intrusion which follows. In many of these situations it would be overstating the position to say that there is a public interest in the information being published. It would be more accurate to say that the public have an understandable and so a legitimate interest in being told the information. If this is the situation then it can be appropriately taken into account by a court when deciding on which side of the line a case falls. The courts must not ignore the fact that if newspapers do not publish information which the public are interested in, there will be fewer newspapers published, which will not be in the public interest. The same is true in relation to other parts of the media."

[61] The first defendant relied on two parts of this account. First, that "role models", voluntary or not, have less expectation of privacy. That was reinforced by a later passage in the judgment, at para 43(vi):

> "Footballers are role models for young people and undesirable behaviour on their part can set an unfortunate example. While [the trial judge] was right to say on the evidence which was before him that A had not courted publicity, the fact is that someone holding his position was inevitably a figure in whom a section of the public and the media would be interested."

The first claimant, it was said, was inevitably a figure in whom a section of the public would be, and was, interested. Second, the general interest in supporting the "media" in the publication of the sort of material that sells newspapers should extend to biographies and literary works generally, such as the book was claimed to be.

[62] The width of the rights given to the media by *A v B plc* cannot be reconciled with *Von Hannover's* case. Mr Price said that whether that was right or wrong, we had to apply *A v B plc*, in the light of the rule of precedent laid down by the House of Lords in *Kay v Lambeth London Borough Council* [2006] 2 AC 465, in particular by Lord Bingham of Cornhill, at paras 43–45. Put shortly, the precedential rules of English domestic law apply to interpretations of Convention jurisprudence....

[63] ...If the court in *A v B plc* had indeed ruled definitively on the content and application of article 10 then the position would be different; but that is what the court did not do. Having made the important observation that the content of the domestic law was now to be found in the balance between articles 8 and 10, the court then addressed the balancing exercise effectively in the former English domestic terms of breach of confidence. No Convention authority of any sort was even mentioned....

[64] ...it seems clear that *A v B plc* cannot be read as any sort of binding authority on the content of articles 8 and 10. To find that content, therefore, we do have to look to *Von Hannover's* case. The terms of that judgment are very far away from the automatic limits placed on the privacy rights of public figures by *A v B plc*.

[BUXTON LJ further held that no 'hypocrisy' had been established on the claimant's part: as EADY J had held at trial, this was 'simply being used as an excuse by [the defendant] to enable her to escape her obligations of confidence'.]

[LATHAM and LONGMORE LJJ agreed.]

Appeal dismissed.

NOTES

1. *McKennitt v Ash* is noted by N. Moreham (2007) 123 LQR 373. *Von Hannover v Germany* is analysed by M. Sanderson [2004] EHRLR 631.

2. *HRH Prince of Wales v Associated Newspapers Ltd* [2007] 2 All ER 139, [2006] EWCA Civ 1776 was another case involving an obligation of confidence arising from the relationship between the parties (for the classic form of the action, see [15], ante): the diary extracts had been leaked to the press by an employee in the Prince's private office. The court at [67]–[68] referred to the importance of upholding relationships of confidence. See further *Lord Browne of Madingley v Associated Newspapers Ltd* [2007] 3 WLR 289, [2007] EWCA Civ 295.

3. As well as the discussion in Fenwick and Phillipson op cit., there is a large secondary literature on this rapidly developing area of tort (and human rights) law. Other recent works to which reference might be made include:

   B. Markesinis, C. O'Cinneide, J. Fedtke and M. Hunter-Henin, 'Concerns and ideas about the developing English law of privacy (and how knowledge of foreign law might help)' (2004) 52 American Jo Comparative Law 133.

N. Moreham, 'The Protection of Privacy in English Common Law: a doctrinal and theoretical analysis' (2005) 121 LQR 628.

N. Moreham, 'Privacy in Public Spaces' [2006] CLJ 606.

J. Morgan, 'Privacy, confidence and horizontal effect: "Hello" trouble' [2003] CLJ 444.

Sir Brian Neill, 'Privacy: A challenge for the new century' in B. Markesinis (ed) *Protecting Privacy* (Oxford, 1999).

G. Phillipson and H. Fenwick, 'Breach of confidence as a privacy remedy in the human rights era' (2000) 63 MLR 660.

G. Phillipson, 'Transforming breach of confidence?' (2003) 66 MLR 726.

J. Rozenberg, *Privacy and the Press* (Oxford, 2004).

PART THREE

LOSS DISTRIBUTION

CHAPTER EIGHTEEN

VICARIOUS LIABILITY

The individual defendant in a tort action is often a man of straw. The typical modern way of ensuring that claimants actually receive the compensation to which they are entitled is through the device of compulsory insurance (p. 1142, post). But there is also an older legal mechanism which enables the claimant to fix responsibility on someone other than the impecunious actor. This is the principle of vicarious liability. The actor and the person to whom responsibility is imputed are jointly liable to the claimant (see generally chap. 19, post). The person who actually pays may be able to recover that payment from the actor (see *Lister v Romford Ice and Cold Storage Co Ltd* [1957] AC 555, [1957] 1 All ER 125, p. 1128, post); but so far as his liability to the claimant is concerned, liability is imposed regardless of personal fault. The justification for this principle is controversial. The most widely accepted theory is that the person with the power of control and direction over the actor is usually the best fitted to absorb the loss: this is likely to be an enterprise which can pass on liability costs to consumers of its products in the form of higher prices, to shareholders in the form of reduced dividends, and to employees in the form of lower real wages. If all those who committed torts were adequately insured there would be no need for a doctrine of vicarious liability. So goes the theory. A counter-argument says that the first theory cannot explain why organisations with even greater resources, the banks, for example, or the government, are not fixed with liability instead. According to this theory, employers are liable because they are in the best position to determine the risk attaching to their use of particular employees. Employers are in the best position to find out about the characteristics of their employees and re-train, move to other duties or, ultimately, dismiss employees who are unreasonably risky. All the theories have their critics, and it is clear that there is no particular connection between present-day justifications for vicarious liability and the historical development of the doctrine (see G Schwartz (1996) 69 So Cal LR 1739).

It is clear, however, that an important underlying problem in this field is how to attribute legal responsibility to organisations, rather than to individual people. The adaptation of legal doctrines based on personal responsibility to a world dominated by impersonal organisations, and within which responsibility is dispersed, has been no easy task. The chapter therefore begins with a brief view of the attribution of direct responsibility to corporations and other associations. The claimant may have been injured through a failure of teamwork, in which case the corporation is sometimes treated as, in the odd terminology which is still sometimes used, 'personally' liable. There is an increasing tendency for the courts to impose such primary or direct liability on the employer, rather than to resort to the device of vicarious liability (see E. McKendrick (1990) 53 MLR 77). The most important direct liabilities in practice are the employers' common law duties to employees to keep them reasonably safe, and material on this topic is included at the end of the chapter.

The most important factor delimiting the scope of vicarious liability is not any theoretical principle, but simply judicial precedent. As a matter of law, the defendant (D) will be made vicariously liable to the claimant (C) in respect of the acts of another person (X) only if C shows that:

(1) X has committed a *wrong* to which C objects; and
(2) some *special relationship recognised by law* exists between D and X, for example a contract of employment, or the delegation of the task of driving a motor vehicle for the owner's purposes; and
(3) some *connection* exists between the act of X and his special relationship with D—in the traditional formula the act must be in 'the course of X's employment' or, what amounts to much the same thing, in 'the scope of X's actual or ostensible authority'.

Each of these points raises its own difficulties. In regard to the first, there has been some debate about whether X's act must constitute a *tort*, or is the real basis of this form of liability the attribution of X's *act* to D so as to make it D's tort? This point is usually only raised when it is sought to attribute X's knowledge to D, or to allow D to limit its liability by an express prohibition on certain conduct by X (e.g. giving unauthorised lifts in *Rose v Plenty* [1976] 1 All ER 97, [1976] 1 WLR 141, p. 1083, post). But other explanations, such as the employee's 'ostensible authority', are available in such cases, and the 'employee's completed tort' theory now has the support of the House of Lords (*Credit Lyonnais Nederland Bank NV v Export Credits Guarantee Department* [2000] 1 AC 486, [1999] 1 All ER 929).

The second point raises problems of definition. One special relationship almost invariably gives rise to vicarious liability—that between employer and employee ('master and servant' in the older terminology). It is therefore necessary to consider the various tests for the existence of a contract of employment (i.e. *of service*) as distinct from a contract with an independent contractor (i.e. *for services*) (pp. 1061 et seq, post). The many borderline cases which arise, particularly in the context of the growing practice of employment under forms other than the contract of employment, indicate the artificiality of the general rule. Another special relationship which may sometimes, but does not always, give rise to vicarious liability is that between 'principal' and 'agent'. These terms have a special connotation in the law of contract; in the law of tort they are a form of shorthand, simply descriptive of circumstances in which vicarious liability has been imposed.

The third point is a question of mixed law and fact. Factual issues such as 'Did D authorise X to drive his car?' are sometimes closely connected with legal issues, such as whether particular acts should be regarded as a custom or should be implied as terms in a contract. In dealing with this question precedent must be treated with caution, because the cases are so often simply concerned with applying a general test to particular facts. The House of Lords has restated the proper approach to such questions, with particular regard to deliberate wrongdoing on the part of X, in *Lister v Hesley Hall* [2001] 2 All ER 769, [2001] UKHL 22 (p. 1088, post).

There are also exceptional circumstances in which liability is imposed for the torts of independent contractors, contrary to the ordinary rule. This form of liability raises controversial conceptual problems, although instances of it are rare. Do they rest upon the breach of some personal 'non-delegable' duty by the employer? Or is the notion of 'non-delegable' duties simply a 'logical fraud' (in the words of G. L. Williams [1956] CLJ 180) disguising vicarious liability? Historically, the adoption of the concept of 'non-delegable' duties enabled the courts to avoid the hardships to employees caused by the doctrine of common employment: see *Wilsons and Clyde Coal Co Ltd v English* [1938] AC 57, [1937] 3 All ER 628 (p. 1101, post). But the continued use of this terminology, despite the statutory abolition of the doctrine of common employment, has led to curious results in regard to the employer's liability to his own employees in respect of the acts of an independent contractor, which have only partially been remedied by the Employers' Liability (Defective Equipment) Act 1969 (p. 1104, post).

1 ATTRIBUTION OF LIABILITY TO ORGANISATIONS

■ Meridian Global Funds Management Asia Ltd v Securities Commission

Judicial Committee of the Privy Council [1995] 3 All ER 918

The question before the Court was whether the knowledge of two of the company's officers, Mr Koo and Mr Ng—senior investment managers but not the chief executive or chief operating officers—could be attributed to the company for the purpose of s. 20(4)(e) of the New Zealand Securities Amendment Act 1988. Heron J held that it could. The Court of Appeal of New Zealand reversed. There was a further appeal to the Privy Council.

LORD HOFFMANN: . . .

[The Court of Appeal of New Zealand] decided that Koo's knowledge should be attributed to Meridian because he was the 'directing mind and will' of the company . . . The phrase 'directing mind and will' comes of course from the celebrated speech of Viscount Haldane LC in *Lennard's Carrying Co Ltd v Asiatic Petroleum Co Ltd* [1915] AC 705 at 713, [1914–15] All ER Rep 280 at 283. But their Lordships think that there has been some misunderstanding of the true principle upon which that case was decided. It may be helpful to start by stating the nature of the problem in a case like this and then come back to *Lennard*'s case later.

Any proposition about a company necessarily involves a reference to a set of rules. A company exists because there is a rule (usually in a statute) which says that a *persona ficta* shall be deemed to exist and to have certain of the powers, rights and duties of a natural person. But there would be little sense in deeming such a *persona ficta* to exist unless there were also rules to tell one what acts were to count as acts of the company. It is therefore a necessary part of corporate personality that there should be rules by which acts are attributed to the company. These may be called 'the rules of attribution'.

The company's primary rules of attribution will generally be found in its constitution, typically the articles of association, and will say things such as 'for the purpose of appointing members of the board, a majority vote of the shareholders shall be a decision of the company' or 'the decisions of the board in managing the company's business shall be the decisions of the company'. There are also primary rules of attribution which are not expressly stated in the articles but implied by company law, such as 'the unanimous decision of all the shareholders in a solvent company about anything which the company under its memorandum of association has power to do shall be the decision of the company': see *Multinational Gas and Petrochemical Co v Multinational Gas and Petrochemical Services Ltd* [1983] 2 All ER 563, [1983] Ch 258.

These primary rules of attribution are obviously not enough to enable a company to go out into the world and do business. Not every act on behalf of the company could be expected to be the subject of a resolution of the board or a unanimous decision of the shareholders. The company therefore builds upon the primary rules of attribution by using general rules of attribution which are equally available to natural persons, namely, the principles of agency. It will appoint servants and agents whose acts, by a combination of the general principles of agency and the company's primary rules of attribution, count as the acts of the company. And having done so, it will also make itself subject to the general rules by which liability for the acts of others can be attributed to natural persons, such as estoppel or ostensible authority in contract and vicarious liability in tort.

It is worth pausing at this stage to make what may seem an obvious point. Any statement about what a company has or has not done, or can or cannot do, is necessarily a reference to the rules of attribution (primary and general) as they apply to that company. Judges sometimes say that a company 'as such' cannot do anything; it must act by servants or agents. This may seem an unexceptionable, even banal remark. And of course the meaning is usually perfectly clear. But a reference to a company 'as such' might suggest that there is something out there called the company of which one can meaningfully say that it can or cannot do something. There is in fact no such thing as the company as such, no '[D]ing an sich', only the applicable rules. To say that a company cannot do something means only that there is no one whose doing of that act would, under the applicable rules of attribution, count as an act of the company.

The company's primary rules of attribution together with the general principles of agency, vicarious liability and so forth are usually sufficient to enable one to determine its rights and obligations. In exceptional cases, however, they will not provide an answer. This will be the case when a rule of law, either expressly or by implication, excludes attribution on the basis of the general principles of agency or vicarious liability. For example, a rule may be stated in language primarily applicable to a natural person and require some act or state of mind on the part of that person 'himself', as opposed to his servants or agents. This is generally true of rules of the criminal law, which ordinarily impose liability only for the *actus reus* and *mens rea* of the defendant himself. How is such a rule to be applied to a company?

One possibility is that the court may come to the conclusion that the rule was not intended to apply to companies at all; for example, a law which created an offence for which the only penalty was community service. Another possibility is that the court might interpret the law as meaning that it could apply to a company only on the basis of its primary rules of attribution, i.e. if the act giving rise to liability was specifically authorised by a resolution of the board or a unanimous agreement of the shareholders. But there will be many cases in which neither of these solutions is satisfactory; in which the court considers that the law was intended to apply to companies and that, although it excludes ordinary vicarious liability, insistence on the primary rules of attribution would in practice defeat that intention. In such a case, the court must fashion a special rule of attribution for the particular substantive rule. This is always a matter of interpretation: given that it was intended to apply to a company, how was it intended to apply? Whose act (or knowledge, or state of mind) was for this purpose intended to count as the act etc of the company? One finds the answer to this question by applying the usual canons of interpretation, taking into account the language of the rule (if it is a statute) and its content and policy. . . .

Against this background of general principle, their Lordships can return to Viscount Haldane. In the *Lennard's* case the substantive provision for which an attribution rule had to be devised was s 502 of the Merchant Shipping Act 1894, which provided a shipowner with a defence to a claim for the loss of cargo put on board his ship if he could show that the casualty happened 'without his actual fault or privity'. The cargo had been destroyed by a fire caused by the unseaworthy condition of the ship's boilers. The language of s 502 excludes vicarious liability; it is clear that in the case of an individual owner, only his own fault or privity can defeat the statutory protection. How is this rule to be applied to a company? Viscount Haldane rejected the possibility that it did not apply to companies at all or (which would have come to the same thing) that it required fault or privity attributable under the company's primary rules. Instead, guided by the language and purpose of the section, he looked for the person whose functions in the company, in relation to the cause of the casualty, were the same as those to be expected of the individual shipowner to whom the language primarily applied. Who in the company was responsible for monitoring the condition of the ship, receiving the reports of the master and ship's agents, authorising repairs etc? This person was Mr Lennard, whom Viscount Haldane described as the 'directing mind and will' of the company. It was therefore his fault or privity which s 502 attributed to the company.

Because Lennard's Carrying Co Ltd does not seem to have done anything except own ships, there was no need to distinguish between the person who fulfilled the function of running the company's business in general and the person whose functions corresponded, in relation to the cause of the casualty, to those of an individual owner of a ship. They were one and the same person. It was this coincidence which left Viscount Haldane's speech open to the interpretation that he was expounding a general metaphysic of companies. In *H L Bolton (Engineering) Co Ltd v T J Graham & Sons Ltd* [1956] 3 All ER 624 at 630, [1957] 1 QB 159 at 172 Denning LJ certainly regarded it as a generalisation about companies 'as such' when, in an equally well-known passage, he likened a company to a human body:

> 'They have a brain and a nerve centre which controls what they do. They also have hands which hold the tools and act in accordance with directions from the centre.'

But this anthropomorphism, by the very power of the image, distracts attention from the purpose for which Viscount Haldane said he was using the notion of directing mind and will, namely to apply the attribution rule derived from s 502 to the particular defendant in the case:

> 'For if Mr. Lennard was the directing mind of the company, then his action must, unless a corporation is not to be liable at all, have been an action which was the action of the company itself within the meaning of s. 502....'

...[Their Lordships think that] difficulty has been caused by concentration on that particular phrase rather than the purpose for which Viscount Haldane was using it. It will often be the most appropriate description of the person designated by the relevant attribution rule, but it might be better to acknowledge that not every such rule has to be forced into the same formula.

Once it is appreciated that the question is one of construction rather than metaphysics, the answer in this case seems to their Lordships to be as straightforward as it did to Heron J. The policy of s 20 of the 1988 Act is to compel, in fast-moving markets, the immediate disclosure of the identity of persons who become substantial security holders in public issuers. Notice must be given as soon as that person knows that he has become a substantial security holder. In the case of a corporate security holder, what rule should be implied as to the person whose knowledge for this purpose is to count as the knowledge of the company? Surely the person who, with the authority of the company, acquired the relevant interest. Otherwise the policy of the Act would be defeated. Companies would be able to allow employees to acquire interests on their behalf which made them substantial security holders but would not have to report them until the board or someone else in senior management got to know about it. This would put a premium on the board paying as little attention as possible to what its investment managers were doing. Their Lordships would therefore hold that upon the true construction of s 20(4)(e), the company knows that it has become a substantial security holder when that is known to the person who had authority to do the deal. It is then obliged to give notice under s 20(3). The fact that Koo did the deal for a corrupt purpose and did not give such notice because he did not want his employers to find out cannot in their Lordships' view affect the attribution of knowledge and the consequent duty to notify.

It was therefore not necessary in this case to inquire into whether Koo could have been described in some more general sense as the 'directing mind and will' of the company. But their Lordships would wish to guard themselves against being understood to mean that whenever a servant of a company has authority to do an act on its behalf, knowledge of that act will for all purposes be attributed to the company. It is a question of construction in each case as to whether the particular rule requires that the knowledge that an act has been done, or the state of mind with which it was done, should be attributed to the company....

Appeal allowed.

NOTES

1. In *Carmarthenshire County Council v Lewis* [1955] AC 549, [1955] 1 All ER 565, noted
    p. 78, ante, the Court of Appeal treated the Council as vicariously liable for the teach-
    er's negligence in allowing the boy to escape on to the highway, while the House of
    Lords treated the Council as 'personally' negligent in allowing such an easy method of
    escape. Which approach is preferable? Note, as well, the cases on hospital authorities
    (p. 1059, post). Note also the oddity of using the word 'personal' for the impersonal
    liability of an organisation.

2. Employers are said to have 'personal' or 'non-delegable' duty to their own employees
    to provide and operate a safe system of work (see p. 1101, post). In *McDermid v Nash
    Dredging and Reclamation Co Ltd* [1987] AC 906, [1987] 2 All ER 878 the claimant was
    instructed by his employer, the defendant company, to work as a deckhand on a tug,
    owned by the defendants' parent company. As a result of the negligence of the master of
    the tug, the claimant suffered injuries involving the amputation of his leg. Staughton J
    held that the tug master was to be regarded as the defendants' employee, because the
    claimant had been instructed to work under his control, and so the defendants were
    vicariously responsible. However, both the Court of Appeal and the House of Lords
    held that the defendant company was under a personal duty to provide a safe system of
    work and to operate it. It was no defence to show that they had delegated this duty to the
    tug master, whether or not an employee, who was reasonably believed to be competent
    to perform it. Despite the delegation the employer was liable for the non-performance
    of the duty. D. Fleming [1988] CLJ 11 comments: 'now we have unequivocal authority
    for a duty owed by employers to employees, the content of which is such that resort to
    claims based on vicarious liability look a poor second best. Why hunt for a tortfeasor
    for whom the defendant *may* be responsible, when you can make him liable even when
    he has carefully delegated?' Why should these common law 'personal' duties take pre-
    cedence over vicarious liability when, according to Lord Hoffmann in *Meriden Global
    Funds*, the attribution of knowledge to a company for the purpose of statutory liabil-
    ities should be considered only after vicarious liability has been examined and found
    wanting?

3. In *Wilsher v Essex Area Health Authority* [1987] QB 730, [1986] 3 All ER 801 (over-
    ruled on other grounds, [1988] AC 1074, [1988] 1 All ER 871) both Sir Nicolas Browne-
    Wilkinson V-C and Glidewell LJ accepted (obiter) that there might be primary or direct
    liability on the part of a health authority for failure to provide doctors of sufficient skill
    and experience to give the treatment offered at the hospital. Browne-Wilkinson V-C
    recognised that this duty could cause 'awkward problems'; for example, 'should the
    hospital be liable if it demonstrates that due to the financial stringency under which it
    operates, it cannot afford to fill the posts with those possessing the necessary experi-
    ence?' (at p. 778). The claimant has the burden of proving negligence, and although
    the National Health Service Act 1977 lays a duty on the Secretary of State to provide
    medical services (which he may direct area health authorities to carry out), the court
    may regard the authority's exercise of discretion as a 'policy' rather than an 'oper-
    ational' decision: cf. *R v Central Birmingham AHA, ex p Walker* (1987) Independent,
    26 November, and pp. 88–117, ante. Subsequently, in *Re R (a minor) (No 2)* (1996) 33
    BMLR 178, the Court of Appeal held that a health authority or hospital had a 'dir-
    ect' duty to establish a proper system of care and to provide a patient with a regime
    of care of a standard that could reasonably be expected of a hospital of the size and

type in question. If, for example, harm results not from the failure of individuals to avail themselves of established systems of communication, the liability will be vicarious; but if harm comes about because there is no system of communication at all, the authority, or now the hospital trust, might be liable 'directly'. The main advantage of alleging the 'direct' tort is that the claimant does not have to identify a particular person who has acted carelessly. Furthermore, causation can be judged on the basis of a cumulative effect rather than looking at each incident separately (see *Barrett v Enfield London Borough Council* [2001] 2 AC 550, [1999] 3 All ER 193, per Lord Slynn). Cases in Australia and Canada (*Ellis v Wallsend District Hospital* [1990] 2 Med LR 103 and *Yepremian v Scarborough General Hospital* (1980) 110 DLR (3d) 513)) raise the further possibility of using the 'direct' tort to avoid having to show that any of the individuals involved were 'employees' as opposed to 'independent contractors' (see pp. 1061–1065, post). The Court of Appeal in *Re R* said that it was making no decision on that possibility, although it did use the word 'non-delegable' to describe the liability. See further *A (a child) v Ministry of Defence* [2005] QB 183, [2004] EWCA Civ 641, p. 1098, post.

The use of 'direct' liability has also been approved in cases concerning local authorities (see e.g. *Barrett*) and the police (*Waters v Metropolitan Police Comr* [2000] 4 All ER 934, [2000] 1 WLR 1607). However, in other cases involving public authorities, difficult issues which might arise in such a direct claim (for example liability for 'non-justiciable' or 'discretionary' decisions, on which see pp. 88–117, ante) have been circumvented by framing the claim as one of ordinary vicarious liability for the negligence of a professional employee or agent of the authority. See for example *Phelps v Hillingdon London Borough Council* [2001] 2 AC 619, [2000] 4 All ER 504 (educational psychologist) and *Carty v Croydon London Borough Council* [2005] 2 All ER 517, [2005] EWCA Civ 19 (local authority education officer). See further pp. 84–85, ante, but see also note 2, p. 1061, post.

4. In the case of unincorporated members' clubs there is liability for acts expressly or impliedly authorised in accordance with the rules of the club: *Flemyng v Hector* (1836) 2 M & W 172; *Re St James Club* (1852) 2 De G M & G 383.

5. For the special case of the liability of trade unions for the acts of their members, see S. Deakin and G. Morris, *Labour Law* 4th edn (Oxford, 2005) pp. 990–1006.

2 VICARIOUS LIABILITY FOR EMPLOYEES

■ Cassidy v Ministry of Health
Court of Appeal [1951] 1 All ER 574

The plaintiff lost the use of his left hand and had severe pain and suffering as a result of negligent treatment following an operation on his hand. The evidence showed a prima facie case of negligence on the part of persons in whose care the plaintiff was, although it was not clear whether this was to be imputed to Dr Fahrni, the full-time assistant medical officer, or to the house surgeon, or to one of the nurses. The Court of Appeal held that the hospital authority was liable.

SOMERVELL LJ: . . .

The evidence as to Dr. Fahrni's position in the present case is that he was an assistant medical officer, that he received a sum in lieu of residential emoluments, which indicates that, if there had been accommodation, or, perhaps, if he had been a bachelor, he would have lived in, and that he was employed whole time. His engagement was subject to the standing orders of the council, but these are not before us. Dr. Ronaldson was a house surgeon working under Dr Fahrni. The first question is whether the principles as laid down in *Gold's*[1] case cover them. In considering this, it is important to bear in mind that nurses are qualified professional persons. It is also important to remember, and MACKINNON LJ emphasised this (ibid., 244), that the principle of *respondeat superior* is not ousted by the fact that a 'servant' has to do work of a skilful or technical character, for which the servant has special qualifications. He instanced the certified captain who navigates a ship. On the facts as I have stated them, I would have said that both Dr. Fahrni and Dr. Ronaldson had contracts of service. They were employed like the nurses as part of the permanent staff of the hospital. . . .

SINGLETON LJ: . . .

In *Hillyer v St Bartholomew's Hospital (Governors)*,[2] the plaintiff's arm was burned when he was on an operating table. The examination was conducted by a consulting surgeon attached to the hospital, and it was admitted that the relationship of master and servant did not exist between the defendants and the consulting surgeon. FARWELL LJ assumed that the nurses and carriers were servants of the defendants for general purposes, but added ([1909] 2 KB 826):

> '. . . as soon as the door of the theatre or operating room has closed on them for the purposes of an operation . . . they cease to be under the orders of the defendants, and are at the disposal and under the sole orders of the operating surgeon until the whole operation has been completely finished; the surgeon is for the time being supreme, and the defendants cannot interfere with or gainsay his orders.'

I do not think that the words of Farwell LJ to which I have referred, can be applied to the facts of this case. The plaintiff was in the care of the hospital authorities. Those responsible for the post-operational treatment were all full-time employees of the corporation and it seems to me that it is not necessary for the plaintiff to establish precisely which individual employee was negligent. . . .

DENNING LJ: . . .

If a man goes to a doctor because he is ill, no one doubts that the doctor must exercise reasonable care and skill in his treatment of him, and that is so whether the doctor is paid for his services or not. If, however, the doctor is unable to treat the man himself and sends him to hospital, are not the hospital authorities then under a duty of care in their treatment of him? I think they are. Clearly, if he is a paying patient, paying them directly for their treatment of him, they must take reasonable care of him, and why should it make any difference if he does not pay them directly, but only indirectly through the rates which he pays to the local authority or through insurance contributions which he makes in order to get the treatment? I see no difference at all. Even if he is so poor that he can pay nothing, and the hospital treats him out of charity, still the hospital authorities are under a duty to take reasonable care of him just as the doctor is who treats him without asking a fee. In my opinion, authorities who run a hospital, be they local authorities, government boards, or any other corporation, are in law under the selfsame duty as the humblest doctor. Whenever they accept a patient for treatment, they must use reasonable care and skill to cure him of his ailment. The hospital authorities cannot, of course, do it by themselves. They have no ears to listen through the stethoscope, and no hands to hold the knife. They must do it by the staff which they employ, and, if their staff are negligent in giving the treatment, they are just as liable for that negligence as is anyone else who employs others to do his duties for him. What possible difference in law, I ask, can there be between hospital authorities who accept a patient for treatment and railway or shipping authorities who accept a passenger for carriage? None whatever. Once they undertake the task, they come under a duty to use care in the doing of it, and that is so

---

[1] *Gold v Essex County Council* [1942] 2 All ER 237, [1942] 2 KB 293.   [2] [1909] 2 KB 820.

whether they do it for reward or not. It is no answer for them to say that their staff are professional men and women who do not tolerate any interference by their lay masters in the way they do their work.... The reason why the employers are liable in such cases is not because they can control the way in which the work is done they often have not sufficient knowledge to do so but because they employ the staff and have chosen them for the task and have in their hands the ultimate sanction for good conduct the power of dismissal....

I decline to enter into the question whether any of the surgeons were employed only under a contract for services, as distinct from a contract of service. The evidence is meagre enough in all conscience on that point, but the liability of the hospital authorities should not, and does not, depend on nice considerations of that sort. The plaintiff knew nothing of the terms on which they employed their staff. All he knew was that he was treated in the hospital by people whom the hospital authorities appointed, and the hospital authorities must be answerable for the way in which he was treated....

NOTES

1. In *Roe v Minister of Health* [1954] 2 QB 66, [1954] 2 All ER 131, if negligence had been established a hospital authority would have been held liable for the acts of an anaesthetist who provided a regular service for the hospital but was also engaged in private practice. Somervell LJ (at p. 79) regarded him as part of the permanent staff; Morris LJ (at p. 91) said that he was part of the 'organisation' of the hospital, and left open the question whether the hospital was under a personal non-delegable duty; Denning LJ (at p. 82) adhered to what he had said in *Cassidy's* case.

2. Vicarious liability for employees of statutory bodies can be excluded if such liability would interfere with the fulfilment of such a body's primary statutory purpose. See *X (minors) v Bedfordshire County Council* [1995] 2 AC 633, [1995] 3 All ER 353 (p. 88, ante) and *Phelps v Hillingdon London Borough Council* [2001] 2 AC 619, [2000] 4 All ER 504 (p. 99, ante). A question arising from this principle is whether, nevertheless, the employee is still liable. Since the immunity is for the benefit of the statutory body, not the individual, it might be argued that there is no equivalent immunity for the individual. But individual liability without the option of vicarious liability in itself might impair the body in the exercise of its statutory functions because it will make recruiting staff more difficult.

■ Servants and Independent Contractors
O. Kahn-Freund (1951) 14 MLR 504 at 505–506

The traditional test was that a person working for another was regarded as a servant if he was 'subject to the command of the master as to the manner in which he shall do his work',[3] but if the so-called 'master' was only in a position to determine the 'what' and not the 'how' of the services, the substance of the obligation but not the manner of its performance, then the person doing the work was said to be not a servant but an independent contractor, and his contract one for work and labour and not of employment. This distinction was based upon the social conditions of an earlier age: it assumed that the employer of labour was able to direct and instruct the labourer as to the technical methods he should use in performing his work. In a mainly agricultural society and even in the earlier stages of the Industrial Revolution the master could be expected to be superior to the servant in the knowledge, skill and experience which had to be brought to bear upon the choice and handling of the tools. The control

---

[3] Per Bramwell LJ in *Yewens v Noakes* (1880) 6 QBD 530.

test was well suited to govern relationships like those between a farmer and an agricultural labourer (prior to agricultural mechanisation), a craftsman and a journeyman, a householder and a domestic servant, and even a factory owner and an unskilled 'hand'. It reflects a state of society in which the ownership of the means of production coincided with the possession of technical knowledge and skill and in which that knowledge and skill was largely acquired by being handed down from one generation to the next by oral tradition and not by being systematically imparted in institutions of learning from universities down to technical schools. The control test postulates a combination of managerial and technical functions in the person of the employer, i.e. what to modern eyes appears as an imperfect division of labour. The technical and economic developments of all industrial societies have nullified these assumptions. The rule respondeat superior (and, one may add, the whole body of principles governing the contract of employment) 'applies even though the work which the servant is employed to do is of a skilful or technical character, as to the method of performing which the employer himself is ignorant'.[4] To say of the captain of a ship, the pilot of an aeroplane, the driver of a railway engine, of a motor vehicle, or of a crane,[5] that the employer 'controls' the performance of his work is unrealistic and almost grotesque. But one need not think of situations in which the employee is physically removed from his employer's premises: a skilled engineer or toolmaker, draftsman or accountant may as often as not have been engaged just because he possesses that technical knowledge which the employer lacks. If in such a case the employee relied on the employer's instructions 'how to do his work' he would be breaking his contract and possibly be liable to summary dismissal for having misrepresented his skill. No wonder that the Courts found it increasingly difficult to cope with the cases before them by using a legal rule which, as legal rules so often do, had survived the social conditions from which it had been an abstraction. The judgments in *Mersey Docks and Harbour Board v Coggins and Griffiths*,[6] show plainly enough that the control test had to be transformed if it was to remain a working rule and to be more than a mere verbal incantation.

NOTE

The relationship between social and economic conditions and the test for who counts as an 'employee' or a 'servant' is perhaps more complex than Kahn-Freund suggests. For example, in the case Kahn-Freund identifies as standing for the 'how not just what' version of the control test, *Yewens v Noakes* (1880) 6 QBD 530, Baggallay LJ decides the issue by saying that the person concerned could not have been a 'servant' because he was 'almost a gentleman', suggesting that prevailing ideas of social status were also important, not just the relations of production. Furthermore, it is a mistake to think of the late nineteenth century as an era devoid of highly skilled workers. Indeed, the later introduction of 'time and motion' methods suggests that employers still had a great deal of employee knowledge to capture. The creation of the National Health Service, however, with its integration of professionals, namely hospital doctors, into a very large organisation, did represent a great challenge to the previous categories. More recently, the growth of 'flexible' forms of work—not just arguably abusive devices such as the 'zero hours contract', but the growth of self-employment, agency

---

[4] Per MacKinnon LJ in *Gold v Essex County Council* [1942] 2 All ER at 244.

[5] See *Mersey Docks and Harbour Board v Coggins and Griffiths Liverpool Ltd* [1947] AC 1, [1946] 2 All ER 345. In this case the House of Lords was compelled to give a new meaning to the 'control' test, see per Lord Simon, [1946] 2 All ER at 348; per Lord Porter, at 351; per Lord Simonds at 352; per Lord Uthwatt at 353. See C. Grunfeld's Note in (1947) 10 MLR 203.

[6] Lord Simon's formula (at p. 348) comes very near to what one may call the 'subordination' or 'organisation' test. Where does the authority lie to direct, or to delegate to the workman the manner in which he should do the work? Who delegates the discretion the workman exercises? Here subordination to the employer's managerial power is made the criterion, and this, it is submitted, is the only possible way of dealing with the matter in the conditions of modern industry.

work, labour-only sub-contracting and 'portfolio' working (deriving income from various jobs, taking a variety of legal and organisational forms) and even the rise of flexi-time and telecommuting—has produced a new challenge to cherished preconceptions about what 'employment' typically entails. The following cases explore the legal consequences of some of these developments.

■ Market Investigations Ltd v Minister of Social Security
Queen's Bench Division [1968] 3 All ER 732

The question arose as to whether a particular person should count as an insured person under the national insurance legislation. The person worked as an interviewer on an occasional basis for a market research company, carrying out specific surveys as and when she was required but staying on a list of potential interviewers in between engagements. She would count as an insured person if each job counted as a contract of employment.

COOKE J:...
[T]he fundamental test to be applied is this: "Is the person who has engaged himself to perform these services performing them as a person in business on his own account?". If the answer to that question is "yes", then the contract is a contract for services. If the answer is "no" then the contract is a contract of service. No exhaustive list has been compiled and perhaps no exhaustive list can be compiled of the considerations which are relevant in determining that question, nor can strict rules be laid down as to the relative weight which the various considerations should carry in particular cases. The most that can be said is that control will no doubt always have to be considered, although it can no longer be regarded as the sole determining factor; and that factors, which may be of importance, are such matters as whether the man performing the services provides his own equipment, whether he hires his own helpers, what degree of financial risk he takes, what degree of responsibility for investment and management he has, and whether and how far he has an opportunity of profiting from sound management in the performance of his task.

■ Lee Ting Sang v Chung Chi-Keung
Judicial Committee of the Privy Council [1990] 2 AC 374

The applicant was a casual worker on a building site working for the respondent, a sub-contractor, when he was injured in an accident. He claimed that he was entitled to be compensated under the Employees' Compensation Ordinance of Hong Kong, which entitlement was limited to employees employed under a contract of employment. He worked from time to time for other contractors, but when the work of the respondent was urgent would give priority to him, telling any other employer for whom he was then working to engage someone else to finish the work. The applicant had been working on this particular job for 20 days before the accident had occurred.

LORD GRIFFITHS:...
All the tests, or perhaps it is better to call them indicia, mentioned by Cooke J. in *Market Investigations Ltd. v. Minister of Social Security* ([1968] 3 All ER 732 at 737–738) point towards the status of an employee rather than an independent contractor. The applicant did not provide his own equipment, the equipment was provided by his employer. He did not hire his own helpers; this emerged with clarity in his evidence when he explained that he gave priority to the first respondent's work and if asked by the first respondent to do an urgent job he would tell those he was working for that they would have to employ someone else: if he was an independent contractor in business on his own account, one would expect that he would attempt to keep both contracts by hiring others to

fulfil the contract he had to leave. He had no responsibility for investment in, or management of, the work on the construction site, he simply turned up for work and chipped off concrete to the required depth upon the beams indicated to him on a plan by the first respondent. There is no suggestion in the evidence that he priced the job which is normally a feature of the business approach of a subcontractor; he was paid either a piece-work rate or a daily rate according to the nature of the work he was doing. It is true that he was not supervised in his work, but this is not surprising, he was a skilled man and he had been told the beams upon which he was to work and the depth to which they were to be cut and his work was measured to see that he achieved that result. There was no question of his being called upon to exercise any skill or judgment as to which beams required chipping or as to the depths that they were to be cut. He was simply told what to do and left to get on with it as, for example, would a skilled turner on a lathe who was required to cut a piece of metal to certain dimensions. Taking all the foregoing considerations into account the picture emerges of a skilled artisan earning his living by working for more than one employer as an employee and not as a small businessman venturing into business on his own account as an independent contractor with all its attendant risks. The applicant ran no risk whatever save that of being unable to find employment which is, of course, a risk faced by casual employees who move from one job to another, and such casual employees are specifically covered by the Ordinance.

NOTES

1.   In *Hall v Lorimer* [1992] STC 599 at 612 Mummery J warned:

> In order to decide whether a person carries on business on his own account it is necessary to consider many different aspects of that person's work activity. This is not a mechanical exercise of running through items on a check list to see whether they are present in, or absent from, a given situation...It is a matter of evaluation of the overall effect of the detail, which is not necessarily the same as the sum total of the individual details.

The Court of Appeal [1994] 1 All ER 250, [1994] 1 WLR 209 approved this statement. Nolan LJ commented:

> [T]he question whether the individual is in business on his own account, though often helpful, may be of little assistance in the case of one carrying on a profession or vocation. A self-employed author working from home or an actor or a singer may earn his living without any of the normal trappings of a business....Cooke J [in *Market Investigations*] was not intending to lay down an all-purpose definition of employment.

2.   In *Lane v Shire Roofing* [1995] IRLR 493 the Court of Appeal faced a question similar to that in *Lee v Chung*, namely whether a building worker should count as an employee or an independent contractor for the purposes of employers' liability for accidents at work. The Court of Appeal said:

> [T]he element of control will be important: who lays down what is to be done, the way in which it is to be done, the means by which it is to be done, and the time when it is done? Who provides (i.e. hires and fires) the team by which it is done, and who provides the material, plant and machinery and tools used? But it is recognised that the control test may not be decisive—for instance, in the case of skilled employees, with discretion to decide how their work should be done. In such cases the question is broadened to whose business was it? Was the workman carrying on his own business, or was he carrying on that of his employers?

Is this a return to giving priority to the older 'control test'? Note that 'control' in *Lane* includes elements that (a) previously would not have been thought to be unique to control, e.g. who lays down what is to be done, and (b) elements that could also form part of the *Market Investigations* test, e.g. who provides the material, plant, and machinery.

Note also that the limitation of the control test to unskilled employees now confines the application of the control test to a fairly small section of the workforce.

3.   The Court of Appeal in *Lane* also mentioned with approval the test proposed by the US Supreme Court in *United States of America v Silk* (1946) 331 US 704, namely whether the persons concerned were employees 'as a matter of economic reality'. The Court of Appeal commented, 'The answer to this question may cover much of the same ground as the control test (such as whether he provides his own equipment and hires his own helpers) but may involve looking to see where the financial risk lies, and whether and how far he has an opportunity of profiting from sound management in the performance of his task'.

4.   It is sometimes said that there can be no legal guidance as to the relative weight to be given to the various factors. However, in *Express & Echo Publications Ltd v Tanton* [1999] ICR 693 the Court of Appeal said that if there were any terms of the contract which were 'inherently incompatible' with an employment relationship, for example that the alleged employee was entitled to send a substitute to perform the contract, there was no need to consider any other factors. Which other factors count as 'inherently incompatible' with the 'irreducible minimum' of a contract of employment the court left unexplored. Difficulties will surely arise if it suggested that the scope of the *Express & Echo* rule should extend beyond substitution. Are there payment methods which are 'inherently incompatible'? What about degrees of financial risk?

5.   The label the parties put on their relationship is a relevant factor but is not decisive. See *Ferguson v Dawson* [1976] 3 All ER 817, [1976] 1 WLR 1213 and *Catamaran Cruisers Ltd v Williams* [1994] IRLR 386. On the other hand, except where there is a 'sham', what matters are the parties' contractual obligations, not what the parties actually did under the contract—Express & Echo Publications Ltd v Tanton [1999] ICR 693.

6.   In employment law it is often an important issue whether the alleged employee and employer had any sort of contract at all. If the alleged employee works casually, working, that is, as and when requested, with no obligation on either side to offer or to accept particular jobs, there may be no contract covering the whole relationship. See e.g. *O'Kelly v Trusthouse Forte plc* [1983] IRLR 369 and *Clark v Oxfordshire Health Authority* [1998] IRLR 125.

7.   Deakin and Morris, op cit., p. 119 lament that the common law tests for identifying a contract of employment have become 'notorious for their complexity' (for analysis, see ibid, pp. 136–176).

8.   In *United States of America v Silk* (1946) 331 US 704, the Supreme Court decided that when faced with the need to decide who counts as an employee for the purposes of applying a specific legislative provision the court should not apply indiscriminately the test used in vicarious liability cases but should instead choose an interpretation that furthers the purposes of the statute in question. See for a similar argument E. McKendrick (1990) 53 MLR 77. The English courts, however, still prefer to use the same considerations and formulae in cases of vicarious liability, employment law and tax law alike (but cf. *Jones v Tower Boot Co Ltd* [1997] 2 All ER 406, [1997] ICR 254). See e.g. the employment rights case of *Dacas v Brook Street Bureau (UK) Ltd* [2004] ICR 1437, [2004] EWCA Civ 217, where Sedley LJ argued that an agency cleaner had been an employee of the agency's client (Wandsworth Council). A crucial step in Sedley LJ's reasoning at [72] was the 'near-certainty' that the council would have been vicariously liable had the cleaner carelessly injured someone.

9. A question distinct from who counts as an employee is how does one tell which of a number of possible employers counts as the employer of this employee? What happens, for example, when one employer 'lends' an employee to another employer? *Mersey Docks and Harbour Board v Coggins & Griffith* [1947] AC 1 decides that the test in these cases is a version of the control test. On the facts, the 'general permanent employer' (the harbour board) remained liable for the negligence of a crane driver 'loaned' to stevedores, since the board could tell the driver how to do his job, backed up by the ultimate sanction of dismissal. Lord Porter stated that 'amongst the many tests suggested I think that the most satisfactory, by which to ascertain who is the employer at any particular time, is to ask who is entitled to tell the employee the way in which he is to do the work upon which he is engaged'.

In *Viasystems (Tyneside) Ltd v Thermal Transfer (Northern) Ltd* [2005] 4 All ER 1181, [2005] EWCA Civ 1151, noted by R. Stevens (2006) 122 LQR 201, it was held that 'dual vicarious liability' was conceptually possible, despite a longstanding assumption to the contrary. The sensible solution to a 'borrowed employee' situation where two employers were *both* in a position to control the employee's actions is for both to be vicariously liable. Rix LJ stated at [77] that dual vicarious liability (combined with the Civil Liability (Contribution Act) 1978) provided the fairest outcome. Rix LJ went on to doubt whether even *Mersey Docks v Coggins* made the control test 'wholly determinative', especially as 'the right of control has not retained the critical significance it once did' in vicarious liability generally. He preferred to say that 'what one is looking for is a situation where the employee in question, at any rate for relevant purposes, is so much a part of the work, business or organisation of both employers that it is just to make both employers answer for his negligence', at [79]. Nevertheless, the student should note the concentration by May LJ at [18] and [49] upon the more traditional question of control (only two judges sat in this appeal).

However, in *Hawley v Luminar Leisure Ltd* [2006] IRLR 817, [2006] EWCA Civ 18, where the defendant nightclub had been supplied with doormen by a security services company, the court applied *Mersey Docks* and distinguished *Viasystems*: there had been an effective and substantial transfer of control over the doorman in question from the supplier to the defendant. Thus the defendant was the sole employer for the purposes of vicarious liability.

10. If *Viasystems* is correct to hold that an employee may have several employers simultaneously for the purposes of vicarious liability, might this not call into question the "unified" approach to the employment concept described in note 7, ante? Dual vicarious liability might be a desirable outcome, but simultaneous employment may be less suitable when considering (for example) an employee's statutory employment rights, employers' national insurance contributions, etc.

■ The Police Act 1996

88(1) The chief officer of police for a police area shall be liable in respect of torts committed by constables under his direction and control in the performance or purported performance of their functions in like manner as a master is liable in respect of torts committed by his servants in the course of their employment, and accordingly shall in respect of any such tort be treated for all purposes as a joint tortfeasor.

NOTE

At common law the Crown enjoyed immunity from proceedings in tort, but the Crown Proceedings Act 1947 subjects the Crown to civil liability as if it were a private person of full age and capacity in respect of torts committed by its servants or agents. A servant of the Crown is not responsible for the torts of those in the same employment as himself: e.g. the First Lord of the Admiralty is not responsible for false imprisonment by his subordinates (*Fraser v Balfour* (1918) 87 LJKB 1116). Public officers may, of course, be liable for their own torts, and exemplary damages may be available against such an officer for arbitrary and unconstitutional action (see Rookes v Barnard, p. 493, ante). Despite the dubious nature of vicarious punishment, a chief officer of police has been held vicariously liable to pay such exemplary damages: *Rowlands v Chief Constable of Merseyside Police* [2007] 1 WLR 1065, [2006] EWCA Civ 1773, noted at p. 508, ante.

3 LIABILITY FOR DELEGATED TASKS

(a) Driving a motor vehicle

■ Morgans v Launchbury

House of Lords [1972] 2 All ER 606

The three plaintiffs were injured while passengers in a car registered in the name of the defendant. The defendant, however, was not in the car at the time of the accident. The defendant's husband had driven the car to work and then had used it to go to several pubs with a friend, Mr Cawfield. Realising he was unfit to drive, at some point in the evening the husband handed the car keys to Mr Cawfield, who then drove to other pubs. At the last of these the pair offered lifts to the three plaintiffs, Mr Cawfield suggesting as they drove off that they all go for a meal. While the husband lay asleep on the back seat, Mr Cawfield drove the car at 90 mph into a bus. Both Mr Cawfield and the husband were killed. There was evidence that before they were married the defendant and her husband each owned cars, but that on marriage they had given up one of the cars, the husband's, and subsequently both used the wife's car freely. The husband normally used the car every day to drive to work. There was also evidence that the defendant had discussed with her husband the circumstances of his being incapable of driving because of drink and that there was an 'understanding' between them that in those circumstances the husband would get a friend to drive or would telephone the defendant to collect him. The defendant, however, had no knowledge that her husband had asked Mr Cawfield to drive on the night in question.

The plaintiffs sued the defendant, both personally and as administratrix for her husband, and obtained a judgment that the defendant personally and her husband vicariously were liable for Mr Cawfield's negligence. The defendant appealed in her personal capacity alone.

LORD WILBERFORCE: . . .

Who could [the plaintiffs] sue? In the first place, there was the estate of Mr Cawfield as the negligent driver; in the second, the estate of the husband who requested Mr Cawfield to drive, this resting on the normal principle of the law of agency. But the respondents seek to go further and to place vicarious liability on the appellant. As to this, apart from the special circumstances of the 'understanding' there would seem, on accepted principle, to be insuperable difficulties in their way. The car cannot by any fair process of analysis be considered to have been used for the appellant's purposes at the time of the accident. During the whole of the evening's progress it was as clearly used for the husband's purposes as any car should be; and if there was any doubt about this the separation from any possible purpose of the appellant's at the time of the accident can only be intensified by the fact that Mr Cawfield, the husband's agent, was taking the car away from the appellant's (and the husband's) home for some fresh purpose. It seems clear enough that this was the purpose of Mr Cawfield but even if one attributes this to her husband, I am unable to formulate an argument for attributing it to the wife.

It is said, against this, that there are authorities which warrant a wider and vaguer test of vicarious liability for the negligence of another; a test of 'interest or concern'. Skilled counsel for the respondents at the trial was indeed able to put the word 'concerned' and 'interest' into the wife's mouth and it was on these words that he mainly rested his case.

On the general law, no authority was cited to us which would test vicarious liability on so vague a test, but it was said that special principles applied to motor cars. I should be surprised if this were so, and I should wish to be convinced of the reason for a special rule. But in fact there is no authority for it. The decisions will be examined by others of your Lordships and I do not find it necessary to make my own review. For I regard it as clear that in order to fix vicarious liability on the owner of a car in such a case as the present, it must be shown that the driver was using it for the owner's purposes, under delegation of a task or duty. The substitution for this clear conception of a vague test based on 'interest' or 'concern' has nothing in reason or authority to commend it. Every man who gives permission for the use of his chattel may be said to have an interest or concern in its being carefully used, and, in most cases if it is a car, to have an interest or concern in the safety of the driver, but it has never been held that mere permission is enough to establish vicarious liability. And the appearance of the words in certain judgments (*Ormrod v Crosville Motor Services Ltd*[7] per Devlin J and per Denning LJ[8]) in a negative context (no interest or concern, therefore no agency) is no warrant whatever for transferring them into a positive test. I accept entirely that 'agency' in contexts such as these is merely a concept, the meaning and purpose of which is to say 'is vicariously liable' and that either expression reflects a judgment of value—respondeat superior is the law saying that the owner ought to pay. It is this imperative which the common law has endeavoured to work out through the cases. The owner ought to pay, it says, because he has authorised the act, or requested it, or because the actor is carrying out a task or duty delegated, or because he is in control of the actor's conduct. He ought not to pay (on accepted rules) if he has no control over the actor, has not authorised or requested the act, or if the actor is acting wholly for his own purposes. These rules have stood the test of time remarkably well. They provide, if there is nothing more, a complete answer to the respondents' claim against the appellant.

I must now consider the special circumstances on which the judge relied—the understanding between the appellant and her husband. What does it amount to? In my opinion, it is nothing more than the kind of assurance that any responsible citizen would give to his friends, any child would give to his parent, any responsible husband would give to his wife: that he intends to do what is his legal and moral duty, not to drive if in doubt as to his sobriety. The evidence is that this assurance originated from the husband and no doubt it was welcomed by the wife. But it falls far short of any authority by the wife to drive on her behalf or of any delegation by her of the task of driving. If the husband was, as he clearly was, using the car for his own purposes, I am unable to understand how his undertaking to delegate his right to drive to another can turn the driver into the wife's agent in any sense of the word. The husband remains the user, the purposes remain his. So if one applies accepted principles of the law, the case is clear...

I would allow the appeal and dismiss the action.

---

[7] [1953] 1 All ER 711, [1953] 1 WLR 409.   [8] [1953] 2 All ER 753, [1953] 1 WLR 1120.

[LORD PEARSON, VISCOUNT DILHORNE, LORD CROSS OF CHELSEA, and LORD SALMON delivered speeches in favour of allowing the appeal.]

Appeal allowed.

QUESTIONS

1. Would Mrs Morgans have been liable if Mr Morgans had taken the car to do the family shopping? (Note *Norwood v Navan* [1981] RTR 457, in which Ormrod LJ said (at p. 461): 'if we were to hold that the mere fact that some part of this trip which the wife was doing was for what was called "general shopping" made her the agent of her husband, we should be getting into the position where, in any of these cases, it would be necessary to examine the contents of the shopping basket to see what had been purchased that day. We would be pushed into the absurd position of saying that, if all the purchases had been for the wife personally, there was no agency, whereas if she bought some minor household article, she would be an agent for the husband a distinction which is really absurd.')

2. Mr Morgans was not the registered owner of the car. Why was he vicariously liable for Cawfield's negligence? (See *Nottingham v Aldridge* [1971] 2 QB 739, [1971] 2 All ER 751.)

3. Lord Denning MR in the Court of Appeal in this case ([1971] 1 All ER 642 at 647) said: 'The words principal and agent are not used here in the connotation which they have in the law of contract (which is one thing), or the connotation which they have in the business community (which is another thing). They are used as a shorthand to denote the circumstances in which vicarious liability is imposed.' Why is there no general principle in the law of tort that a 'principal' is liable for the acts of his 'agent'? (See Atiyah, *Vicarious Liability*, chap. 9.)

NOTES

1. For the House of Lords' rejection of Lord Denning's 'family car doctrine' see pp. 1140–1141, post.

2. M asked O to drive M's Austin Healey from Liverpool to Monte Carlo. O collided with a bus due, in part, to his own negligence and, in part, to the negligence of the bus driver. O's wife was injured and she sued the bus driver's employer, who, in turn, brought the owner of the car, M, into the proceedings. At this time (which was prior to the enactment of the Law Reform (Husband and Wife) Act 1962) they could not bring in O's husband because spouses could not sue each other in tort. But if M were held responsible for O's driving, his insurance policy would cover his liability. M was held to be vicariously liable because the car was being used on M's business and for M's purposes: *Ormrod v Crossville Motor Services Co Ltd* [1953] 2 All ER 753, [1953] 1 WLR 1120. The authority of this decision is apparently unaffected by *Morgans v Launchbury*. See e.g. *Candler v Thomas (t/a London Leisure Lines)* [1998] RTR 214.

3. Many pre-*Morgans v Launchbury* decisions on similar facts use the test of the defendant's 'right to control' the vehicle. See e.g. *Samsom v Aitchison* [1912] AC 844 (father sitting next to son who was driving father's car); *Parker v Miller* (1926) 42 TLR 408 ('right to control' not lost by driver parking defendant's car in another place); *Chowdhary v Gillot* [1947] 2 All ER 541 (bailment ends right to control, therefore no vicarious

liability). The authority of these cases in now in doubt, although, it is submitted, the *Morgans v Launchbury* test produces the same results in the first two cases, though perhaps not in the third.

4. Sometimes there may be a personal non-delegable duty to provide a vehicle which is reasonably safe. In *Rogers v Night Riders (a firm)* [1983] RTR 324 a firm running a minicab service hired radios to drivers who owned, maintained, and controlled their own vehicles. On receiving a telephone call from a customer they contacted a driver by radio and directed him to the customer. The claimant, who obtained a minicab in this way, was injured by a defective door because the driver had failed properly to maintain the vehicle. The Court of Appeal held that the minicab firm was under a personal non-delegable duty to provide a vehicle which was reasonably maintained and reasonably fit for the purpose.

5. In *Scott v Davis* (2000) 204 CLR 333 the High Court of Australia held that the owner of a light aircraft was not liable for the negligence of a pilot who he had asked to fly the plane during a party at which the pilot (and the injured claimant) had been guests. Gummow, Hayne and Callinan JJ took the view that if *Morgans v Launchbury* (and the earlier Australian case of *Soblusky v Egan* (1960) 103 CLR 215) remained good law at all, such liability must be confined to owners of motor cars. Callinan J at [348] ridiculed the suggestion of general liability attaching to the owners of chattels by considering the hypothetical case of someone lending a cricket bat to an ostensibly competent player, only for the player negligently to strike a fielder during play. However, cf. *Moynihan v Moynihan* [1975] IR 192 (householder liability upon 'delegating control' of a teapot to her guest).

(b) Joint enterprises

■ Brooke v Bool

King's Bench Division [1928] All ER Rep 155

The plaintiff was the tenant of certain premises and she requested her landlord, the defendant, to search for a suspected gas leak in her basement. The defendant procured the help of a third party, one Morris, who applied a naked light to the pipe they were examining, with the result that there was an explosion damaging the plaintiff's property. The county court judge gave judgment for the defendant (although stating that 'he had very grave doubts whether his opinion was correct'). On appeal:

SALTER J: . . .

In my opinion there are three grounds on which it was competent in law for the learned judge to find that the defendant was responsible for what was obviously a grossly reckless act on the part of Morris namely, holding a naked light near to a place where he suspected an escape of gas. First, I think that there was evidence of agency. The defendant desired to examine this pipe, and examined it himself so far as he could in a most reckless and dangerous way with a naked light. He then desired to examine the upper part of it. Now the defendant was an old man of nearly eighty years of age, and he had in his company a much younger man. I think that there was ample evidence that the defendant impliedly invited and instructed Morris to get up on to the counter and complete the examination, when it was not convenient for him to continue it himself, and that Morris did what he did on the instructions of the defendant. The maxim *Qui facit per alium facit per se* applies, and on that first ground I think that there was evidence on which the judge could have found the defendant responsible.

Secondly, he could have been held responsible on the score of the control which he exercised over the proceedings. It is necessary to bear in mind the difference between the position of the defendant and that of Morris. The defendant was on the premises lawfully, at the request of the plaintiff, whereas Morris was a trespasser, unless the defendant had a right to invite him there to help. There was ample evidence on which the judge could find that the invitation by the plaintiff to the defendant to keep a watch over the premises extended to the right to bring in someone to help him on an occasion of that kind. In my opinion, Morris was there by the permission and invitation of the defendant, since otherwise he would have been a trespasser, and the defendant was in control of the enterprise....

Thirdly, I think there was here a joint enterprise on the part of the defendant and Morris, and that the act which was the immediate cause of the explosion was their joint act done in pursuance of a concerted enterprise....

...Here the defendant and Morris went into the room, obviously proceeding by tacit agreement to examine this pipe and both employing the same negligent means. I think that what Morris did negligently was done by him in concert with the defendant and in pursuance of their common enterprise. In [a] passage to which I wish to refer, Scrutton LJ says:[9]

> 'I am of opinion that the definition in *Clerk and Lindsell on Torts* (7th edn) 59, is much nearer the correct view: "Persons are said to be joint tortfeasors when their respective shares in the commission of the tort are done in furtherance of a common design...but mere similarity of design on the part of independent actors, causing independent damage, is not enough: there must be concerted action to a common end." '

That appears to me precisely to describe this case, and on that third ground also I think that the county court court judge was fully entitled in law to find for the plaintiff....

[TALBOT J gave a judgment agreeing with SALTER J, but adding that the case could also be decided on the ground of a non-delegable duty (see pp. 1095–1100, post).]

Appeal allowed.

QUESTION

What do you understand by Salter J's use of the word 'agency'? Cf. p. 1069, ante.

NOTES

1. 'Brooke v Bool has engendered curiously little in the way of subsequent reported authority, but no doubt has been cast in the intervening 60 years on the proposition that participation in a common venture may cause someone to become directly liable as tortfeasor, together with the person who actually did the damage' (*Unilever Plc v Gillette (UK) Ltd* [1989] RPC 583, per Mustill LJ). One of the few English cases in which liability was imposed on the ground of joint enterprise is *Scarsbrook v Mason* [1961] 3 All ER 767, in which Glyn-Jones J held that a passenger who had agreed to contribute 4 shillings towards the cost of petrol for a pleasure trip by car to Southend, was liable for the driver's negligence. He said: 'They knew they were joining a party, all equally concerned in the trip to Southend, and that one member of the party was going to drive on behalf of the others, so that the party could get to Southend. The members of that party are jointly and severally liable for the manner in which that motor car was driven.'

[9] *The Koursk* [1924] P 140 at 156.

Atiyah, *Vicarious Liability*, p. 124, suggests that 'being a road traffic case [*Scarsbrook v Mason*] may well have been influenced by special policy considerations'. What are these policy considerations? How have they been affected by *Morgans v Launchbury*? Atiyah, loc. cit., discusses the American cases in which the tendency is to require something more than a mere common purpose in the journey. Note that in *S v Walsall Metropolitan Borough Council* [1985] 3 All ER 294, [1985] 1 WLR 1150 considerable reservations were expressed about *Scarsbrook v Mason*.

2. In *R v Salmon* (1880) 6 QBD 79, a criminal case, several persons shot at a target in a negligent manner so that a stranger was killed. It was held that there was no need to show who fired the fatal shot. They were all principals in manslaughter. Do you agree with G. L. Williams (1953) 31 Can BR 315 at 316 that 'had the marksmen been sued in tort they could well have been held joint tortfeasors'? Cf. *Cook v Lewis* [1951] SCR 830, criticised by T. B. Hogan (1961) 24 MLR 331 and *Summers v Tice* 33 Cal 2d 80; 199 P 2d 1 (1948). See now also *Fairchild v Glenhaven Funeral Services Ltd* [2002] 3 All ER 305, [2002] UKHL 22 (p. 348, ante) and *Barker v Corus UK Ltd* [2006] 3 All ER 785, [2006] UKHL 20 (p. 357, ante).

3. On joint liability, see further Ch. 19, post.

(c) Partners

■ The Partnership Act 1890

10. Liability of the firm for wrongs. Where, by any wrongful act or omission of any partner acting in the ordinary course of the business of the firm, or with the authority of his co-partners, loss or injury is caused to any person not being a partner in the firm, or any penalty is incurred, the firm is liable therefor to the same extent as the partner so acting or omitting to act.

■ Dubai Aluminium Co Ltd v Salaam
House of Lords [2003] 1 All ER 97

The proceedings arose out of an elaborate fraud committed upon the claimant, Dubai Aluminium Co. It was alleged that Mr Amhurst, a solicitor and the senior partner of the third and fourth defendant firms of solicitors, had dishonestly assisted in the perpetration of the fraud. A dispute arose over whether the other partners of the firms (treated together as the 'Amhurst firm'), who were wholly innocent of any personal dishonesty, were liable under s. 10 of the Partnership Act 1890 for Mr Amhurst's fraud. The Court of Appeal [2001] QB 113 held that since the firm's partners had not authorised Mr Amhurst to act as he did on their behalf and it was not in the ordinary course of the business of a solicitors' firm to produce sham agreements giving effect to a scheme known to be dishonest, the firm was not vicariously liable for Mr Amhurst's acts. There was a further appeal to the House of Lords.

LORD NICHOLLS OF BIRKENHEAD: . . .

[18] Partnership is the relationship which subsists between persons carrying on a business in common with a view of profit (s 1 of the 1890 Act). Partnership is rooted in agreement, express or tacit, between the partners. So is the conduct of the partnership business. Clearly, the nature and scope of

a business carried on by partners are questions of fact. Similarly, what the ordinary course of the business comprises, in the sense of what is the normal manner in which the business is carried on, is also a question of fact. So also is the scope of a partner's authority.

[19] Vicarious liability is concerned with the responsibility of the firm to other persons for wrongful acts done by a partner while acting in the ordinary course of the partnership business or with the authority of his co-partners. At first sight this might seem something of a contradiction in terms. Partners do not usually agree with each other to commit wrongful acts. Partners are not normally authorised to engage in wrongful conduct. Indeed, if vicarious liability of a firm for acts done by a partner acting in the ordinary course of the business of the firm were confined to acts authorised in every particular, the reach of vicarious liability would be short indeed. Especially would this be so with dishonesty and other intentional wrongdoing, as distinct from negligence. Similarly restricted would be the vicarious responsibility of employers for wrongful acts done by employees in the course of their employment. Like considerations apply to vicarious liability for employees.

[20] Take the present case. The essence of the claim advanced by Dubai Aluminium against Mr Amhurst is that he and Mr Salaam engaged in a criminal conspiracy to defraud Dubai Aluminium. Mr Amhurst drafted the consultancy agreement and other agreements in furtherance of this conspiracy. Needless to say, Mr Amhurst had no authority from his partners to conduct himself in this manner. Nor is there any question of conduct of this nature being part of the ordinary course of the business of the Amhurst firm. Mr Amhurst had authority to draft commercial agreements. He had no authority to draft a commercial agreement for the dishonest purpose of furthering a criminal conspiracy.

[21] However, this latter fact does not of itself mean that the firm is exempt from liability for his wrongful conduct. Whether an act or omission was done in the ordinary course of a firm's business cannot be decided simply by considering whether the partner was authorised by his co-partners to do the very act he did. The reason for this lies in the legal policy underlying vicarious liability. The underlying legal policy is based on the recognition that carrying on a business enterprise necessarily involves risks to others. It involves the risk that others will be harmed by wrongful acts committed by the agents through whom the business is carried on. When those risks ripen into loss, it is just that the business should be responsible for compensating the person who has been wronged.

[22] This policy reason dictates that liability for agents should not be strictly confined to acts done with the employer's authority. Negligence can be expected to occur from time to time. Everyone makes mistakes at times. Additionally, it is a fact of life, and therefore to be expected by those who carry on businesses, that sometimes their agents may exceed the bounds of their authority or even defy express instructions. It is fair to allocate risk of losses thus arising to the businesses rather than leave those wronged with the sole remedy, of doubtful value, against the individual employee who committed the wrong. To this end, the law has given the concept of 'ordinary course of employment' an extended scope.

[23] If, then, authority is not the touchstone, what is? Lord Denning MR once said that on this question the cases are baffling (see *Morris v CW Martin & Sons Ltd* [1965] 2 All ER 725 at 730, [1966] 1 QB 716 at 724). Perhaps the best general answer is that the wrongful conduct must be so closely connected with acts the partner or employee was authorised to do that, for the purpose of the liability of the firm or the employer to third parties, the wrongful conduct may fairly and properly be regarded as done by the partner while acting in the ordinary course of the firm's business or the employee's employment. Lord Millett said as much in *Lister v Hesley Hall Ltd* [2001] UKHL 22 at [69], [2001] 2 All ER 769 at [69], [2002] 1 AC 215. So did Lord Steyn (at [15], [28]). McLachlin J said in *Bazley v Curry* (1999) 174 DLR (4th) 45 at 62 (para 37):

> '... the policy purposes underlying the imposition of vicarious liability on employers are served only where the wrong is so connected with the employment that it *can be said* that the employer has introduced the risk of the wrong (and is thereby fairly and usefully charged with its management and minimization).' (My emphasis.)

To the same effect is Professor Atiyah's monograph *Vicarious Liability in the Law of Torts* (1967) p 171: 'The master ought to be liable for all those torts which *can fairly be regarded* as reasonably incidental risks to the type of business he carried on.' (My emphasis.)

[24] In these formulations the phrases 'may fairly and properly be regarded', 'can be said', and 'can fairly be regarded' betoken a value judgment by the court. The conclusion is a conclusion of law, based on primary facts, rather than a simple question of fact.

[25] This 'close connection' test focuses attention in the right direction. But it affords no guidance on the type or degree of connection which will normally be regarded as sufficiently close to prompt the legal conclusion that the risk of the wrongful act occurring, and any loss flowing from the wrongful act, should fall on the firm or employer rather than the third party who was wronged. It provides no clear assistance on when, to use Professor Fleming's phraseology, an incident is to be regarded as sufficiently work-related, as distinct from personal (see Fleming *The Law of Torts* (9th edn, 1998) p 427). Again, the well-known dictum of Lord Dunedin in *Plumb v Cobden Flour Mills Co Ltd* [1914] AC 62 at 67, draws a distinction between prohibitions which limit the sphere of employment and those which only deal with conduct within the sphere of employment. This leaves open how to recognise the one from the other.

[26] This lack of precision is inevitable, given the infinite range of circumstances where the issue arises. The crucial feature or features, either producing or negativing vicarious liability, vary widely from one case or type of case to the next. Essentially the court makes an evaluative judgment in each case, having regard to all the circumstances and, importantly, having regard also to the assistance provided by previous court decisions. In this field the latter form of assistance is particularly valuable.

[36] On this assumed factual basis, I consider the firm is liable for Mr Amhurst's dishonest assistance in the fraudulent scheme, the assistance taking the form of drafting the necessary agreements. Drafting agreements of this nature for a proper purpose would be within the ordinary course of the firm's business. Drafting these particular agreements is to be regarded as an act done within the ordinary course of the firm's business even though they were drafted for a dishonest purpose. These acts were so closely connected with the acts Mr Amhurst was authorised to do that for the purpose of the liability of the Amhurst firm they may fairly and properly be regarded as done by him while acting in the ordinary course of the firm's business.

[LORD MILLETT and LORD HOBHOUSE OF WOODBOROUGH delivered speeches in favour of allowing the appeal. LORD SLYNN OF HADLEY agreed with LORD NICHOLLS, and LORD HUTTON and LORD HOBHOUSE agreed with LORD NICHOLLS and LORD MILLETT.]

Appeal allowed.

NOTES

1.   For the important decision in *Lister v Hesley Hall Ltd* [2001] 2 All ER 769, [2001] UKHL 22 mentioned by Lord Nicholls, see further p. 1088, post.

2.   The House of Lords in *Dubai Aluminium* seems to incorporate liability for a partner's or agent's fraud into mainstream 'tort' reasoning on the course of employment (see next section, post), rather than relying upon the 'contractual-agency' concepts of actual and apparent authority. Contrast the earlier decision in *The Ocean Frost* [1986] AC 717, [1986] 2 All ER 385. The House of Lords held that a principal could not be vicariously liable in tort for his agent's fraudulent misstatements when the (defrauded) third party knew that the agent lacked the principal's authority to make such statements. Lord Keith of Kinkel said that liability for fraud was governed by 'a set of principles and a line of authority of peculiar application' and refused to consider vicarious liability for negligence, trespass or other torts. Furthermore, in *Kooragang Investments Pty Ltd v Richardson and Wrench Ltd* [1982] AC 462, [1981] 3 All ER 65 Lord Wilberforce had suggested that an employer cannot be vicariously liable even for *negligent* misstatements which his employee was neither actually nor ostensibly authorised to make.

Lord Nicholls' approach in *Dubai Aluminium* seems to be quite different, viewing the words 'in the ordinary course of the business of the firm' in s. 10 of the Partnership Act 1890, as extending liability beyond acts of a fellow partner which the firm had actually or ostensibly authorised. C. Mitchell, in his case-note (2003) 119 LQR 364, points out that it is unclear whether Lord Nicholls meant to confine, distinguish, or overrule the *Ocean Frost* line of authority, and rightly comments that this urgently needs judicial consideration.

3. S. Baughen [2007] LMCLQ 545 considers three juridically distinct ways of making secondary parties liable for fraud: vicarious liability; as joint tortfeasors; and the action for dishonest assistance in equity. He argues that the differences in outcome between the three routes are unjustifiable, and that the area is ripe for reconsideration by the courts.

4. At first instance in *Dubai Aluminium* [1999] 1 Lloyd's Rep 415, Rix J held that although the partners of the firm had been vicariously liable for Mr Amhurst's participation in the fraud, their share of responsibility in proceedings under the Civil Liability (Contribution) Act 1978 (p. 1122, post) should be reduced to take account of the fact that they were personally innocent of wrongdoing. This approach was condemned in the House of Lords as misconceiving the nature of vicarious liability. The firm was answerable for Mr Amhurst's wrongdoing, and its liability was coextensive with his liability. Vicarious liability is 'substitutional': one thus liable 'stands in the shoes of the wrongdoer', and personal innocence is beside the point. The firm's contribution was therefore to be assessed in exactly the same way as Mr Amhurst's. See Lord Nicholls at [44]–[49] and Lord Millett at [153]–[155].

     Note that an innocent employer can be vicariously liable to pay punitive damages: *Rowlands v Chief Constable of Merseyside Police* [2007] 1 WLR 1065, [2006] EWCA Civ 1773, noted p. 1067, ante.

4 THE COURSE OF EMPLOYMENT

■ Salmond & Heuston on Torts

(21st edn) p. 443

[I]t is clear that the master is responsible for acts actually authorised by him: for liability would exist in this case, even if the relation between the parties was merely one of agency, and not one of service at all. But a master, as opposed to an employer of an independent contractor, is liable even for acts which he has not authorised, provided that they are so connected with acts which he has authorised that they may rightly be regarded as modes—although improper modes—of doing them … On the other hand if the unauthorised and wrongful act of the servant is not so connected with the authorised act as to be a mode of doing it, but is an independent act, the master is not responsible; for in such a case the servant is not acting in the course of his employment, but has gone outside of it.

As is often the case, the principle is easy to state but difficult to apply.

NOTE

The *Salmond & Heuston* test has in the past been very influential. However, the 'course of employment' test has now undergone a fundamental restatement by the House of Lords, in *Lister v Hesley Hall*, p. 1088, post, particularly as regards deliberate wrongdoing. First, some of the earlier decisions in this vexed area are presented.

■ Smith v Stages

House of Lords [1989] 1 All ER 833

Mr Machin and Mr Stages (the first defendants) were employed by the Darlington Insulation Co Ltd (the second defendants) as peripatetic laggers to install insulation at power stations. In August 1977 they were taken off work on Drakelow power station in Staffordshire and instructed by their employers to go to do urgent work at Pembroke power station (in Wales). They were paid for an 8-hour day for the journey to Pembroke and for an 8-hour day for the journey back to Staffordshire, and were given the equivalent of rail fare as travelling expenses, but no stipulation was made as to their mode of travel. The two employees travelled to Wales in Stages' car. On the way back to Staffordshire the car, driven by Stages, left the road and crashed into a brick wall. Both men were seriously injured. Smith (for Machin's estate) brought proceedings against Stages for damages and later joined the second defendants, alleging that they were vicariously liable for Stages' negligence (Stages being uninsured). The trial judge held that the accident had been caused by Stages' negligence but that the second defendants were not liable because Stages had not been acting in the course of his employment. On appeal, the Court of Appeal, [1988] ICR 201, reversed the decision and held that the second defendants were vicariously liable.

The second defendants appealed to the House of Lords.

LORD GOFF OF CHIEVELEY: . . .

The present case can be seen as one of those cases, which have troubled the courts in the past, in which the question has arisen whether an employee, travelling to or from a place of work, is acting in the course of his employment. . . .

The fundamental principle is that an employee is acting in the course of his employment when he is doing what he is employed to do, to which it is sufficient for present purposes to add, or anything which is reasonably incidental to his employment. . . .

We can begin with the simple proposition that, in ordinary circumstances, when a man is travelling to or from his place of work, he is not acting in the course of his employment. So a bank clerk who commutes to the City of London every day from Sevenoaks is not acting in the course of his employment when he walks across London Bridge from the station to his bank in the City. This is because he is not employed to travel from his home to the bank: he is employed to work at the bank, his place of work, and so his duty is to arrive there in time for his working day. Nice points can arise about the precise time, or place, at which he may be held to have arrived at work; but these do not trouble us in the present case. Likewise, of course, he is not acting in the course of his employment when he is travelling home after his day's work is over. If, however, a man is obliged by his employer to travel to work by means of transport provided by his employer, he may be held to be acting in the course of his employment when so doing.

These are the normal cases. There are, however, circumstances in which, when a man is travelling to (or from) a place where he is doing a job for his employer, he will be held to be acting in the course of his employment. Some of these are listed by Lord Atkin in *Blee v London and North Eastern Rly Co* [1937] 4 All ER 270 at 273, [1938] AC 126 at 131–132. So, if a man is employed to do jobs for his employer at various places during the day, such as a man who goes from door to door canvassing for business, or who distributes goods to customers, or who services equipment like washing machines or dishwashers, he will ordinarily be held to be acting in the course of his employment when travelling from one destination to another, and may also be held to do so when travelling from his home to his first destination and home again after his last. Again, it has been held that, in certain circumstances, a man who is called out from his home at night to deal with an emergency may be acting in the course of his employment when travelling from his home to his place of work to deal with the emergency: see *Blee v London and North Eastern Rly Co*. There are many other cases.

But how do we distinguish the cases in this category in which a man is acting in the course of his employment from those in which he is not? The answer is, I fear, that everything depends on the circumstances. As Sir John Donaldson MR said in *Nancollas v Insurance Officer* [1985] 1 All ER 833 at 836, the authorities

> 'approve an approach which requires the court to have regard to and to weigh in the balance every factor which can be said in any way to point towards or away from a finding that the claimant was in the course of his employment. In the context of the present appeals, there are a number of such factors to which we must have regard, but none is of itself decisive.'

For example, the fact that a man is being paid by his employer in respect of the relevant period of time is often important, but cannot of itself be decisive....

[T]o me, the question is this. Was Mr Stages employed to travel to and from Pembroke? Or was the pay given to him simply in recognition of the fact that he had lost two days' work at Drakelow because, in order to work at the power station at Pembroke, he would have to make his own way to Pembroke and back again to the Midlands? If we can solve that problem, we can answer the question whether Mr Stages was acting in the course of his employment when, worn out, he crashed his car on the A40 near Liandeilo....

I approach the matter as follows. I do not regard this case as an ordinary case of travelling to work. It would be more accurate to describe it as a case where an employee, who has for a short time to work for his employers at a different place of work some distance away from his usual place of work, has to move from his ordinary base to a temporary base (here lodgings in Pembroke) from which he will travel to work at the temporary place of work each day. For the purpose of moving base, a normal working day was set aside for Mr Stages' journey, for which he was paid as for an eight hour day. In addition to his day's pay he was given a travel allowance for his journey, and an allowance for his lodgings at his temporary base in Pembroke. In my opinion, in all the circumstances of the case, Mr Stages was required by the employers to make this journey, so as to make himself available to do his work at the Pembroke power station, and it would be proper to describe him as having been employed to do so. The fact that he was not required by his employer to make the journey by any particular means, nor even required to make it on the particular working day made available to him, does not detract from the proposition that he was employed to make the journey. Had Mr Stages wished, he could have driven down on the afternoon of Sunday, 21 August, and have devoted the Monday to (for example) visiting friends near Pembroke. In such circumstances it could, I suppose, be said that Stages was not travelling 'in his employers' time'. But this would not matter; for the fact remains that the Monday, a normal working day, was made available for the journey, with full pay for that day to perform a task which he was required by the employers to perform.

I have it very much in mind that Mr Machin and Mr Stages were described by counsel for the employers as peripatetic laggers working at such sites as were available. This may well be an accurate description of their work. If so, their contracts of service may have provided at least an indication as to how far they would be acting in the course of their employment when changing from one power station to another. Indeed, accepting the description as correct, it is difficult to know how much weight to give to it in the absence of their contracts of service. However, the present case can in any event be differentiated on the basis that it was a departure from the norm in that it was concerned with a move to a temporary base to deal with an emergency, on the terms I have described.

I turn to Mr Stages' journey back. Another ordinary working day, Tuesday, 30 August, was made available for the journey, with the same pay, to enable him to return to his base in the Midlands to be ready to travel to work on the Wednesday morning. In my opinion, he was employed to make the journey back, just as he was employed to make the journey out to Pembroke. If he had chosen to go to sleep on the Monday morning and afternoon for eight hours or so, and then to drive home on the Monday evening so that he could have Tuesday free (as indeed Mr Pye[10] expected him to do), that

---

[10] [The employers' contract manager.]

would not have detracted from the proposition that his journey was in the course of his employment. For this purpose, it was irrelevant that Monday was a bank holiday. Of course, it was wrong for him to succumb to the temptation of driving home on the Monday morning, just after he had completed so long a spell of work; but once again that cannot alter the fact that his journey was made in the course of his employment.

For these reasons, I would dismiss the appeal.

LORD LOWRY: . . .

The paramount rule is that an employee travelling on the highway will be acting in the course of his employment if, and only if, he is at the material time going about his employer's business. One must not confuse the duty to turn up for one's work with the concept of already being 'on duty' while travelling to it.

It is impossible to provide for every eventuality and foolish, without the benefit of argument, to make the attempt, but some prima facie propositions may be stated with reasonable confidence. (1) An employee travelling from his ordinary residence to his regular place of work, whatever the means of transport and even if it is provided by the employer, is not on duty and is not acting in the course of his employment, but, if he is obliged by his contract of service to use the employer's transport, he will normally, in the absence of an express condition to the contrary, be regarded as acting in the course of his employment while doing so. (2) Travelling in the employer's time between workplaces (one of which may be the regular workplace) or in the course of a peripatetic occupation, whether accompanied by goods or tools or simply in order to reach a succession of workplaces (as an inpector of gas meters might do), will be in the course of the employment. (3) Receipt of wages (though not receipt of a travelling allowance) will indicate that the employee is travelling in the employer's time and for his benefit and is acting in the course of his employment, and in such a case the fact that the employee may have discretion as to the mode and time of travelling will not take the journey out of the course of his employment. (4) An employee travelling *in the employer's time* from his ordinary residence to a workplace other than this regular workplace or in the course of a peripatetic occupation or to the scene of an emergency (such as a fire, an accident or a mechanical breakdown of plant) will be acting in the course of his employment. (5) A deviation from or interruption of a journey undertaken in the course of employment (unless the deviation or interruption is merely incidental to the journey) will for the time being (which may include an overnight interruption) take the employee out of the course of his employment. (6) Return journeys are to be treated on the same footing as outward journeys.

All the foregoing propositions are subject to any express arrangements between the employer and the employee or those representing his interests. They are not, I would add, intended to define the position of salaried employees, with regard to whom the touchstone of payment made in the employer's time is not generally significant . . . .

[LORD KEITH OF KINKEL and LORD GRIFFITHS agreed with LORD LOWRY's speech. LORD BRANDON OF OAKBROOK agreed with the speeches of LORD GOFF and LORD LOWRY.]

Appeal dismissed.

NOTES

1. In *Harvey v R G O'Dell Ltd* [1958] 2 QB 78, [1958] 1 All ER 657, McNair J held that it was 'fairly incidental' to their work for employees to get a meal during working hours, so a journey for this purpose was held to be impliedly authorised. In *Hilton v Burton (Rhodes) Ltd* [1961] 1 All ER 74, however, Diplock J held that it was not within the course of their employment for a group of workmen to travel seven or eight miles from their work site for tea, immediately after finishing their lunch in a public-house. Does this mean (a) that a tea break immediately after lunch is not impliedly authorised, or (b) that, in the second case, the workmen had, in effect, finished off their work for the day? On 'skylarking' see, for example, *Harrison v Michelin Tyre Co Ltd* [1985] 1 All ER 918, cf. *Aldred v Nacanco* [1987] IRLR 292.

2. In *Kay v ITW Ltd* [1968] 1 QB 140, [1967] 3 All ER 22, the issue was whether an employee instructed to drive a forklift truck had implied authority to remove obstacles in his path and, if so, what kind of obstacle. The Court of Appeal held that the removal of a five-ton diesel lorry was within the course of his employment. Although agreeing with this result, Danckwerts LJ was moved to say (at p. 27): 'It would be a good deal safer to keep lions or other wild animals in a park than to engage in business involving the employment of labour. In fact the position comes close to that in *Rylands v Fletcher* (1868) LR 3 HL 330.'

■ Century Insurance Co Ltd v Northern Ireland Road Transport Board
House of Lords [1942] 1 All ER 491

The respondents' employee, Davison, was delivering petrol from a tanker into the storage tank of a garage. While the petrol was flowing into the tank, Davison lit a cigarette and threw away the lighted match, causing a conflagration in which the tanker, a motor vehicle belonging to the garage proprietor, and several houses in the street were damaged. The appellants had insured the respondents against liability to third parties and, in answer to the claims based on this policy, one of their contentions was that the tanker driver's negligence was not done in the course of his employment so as to make the respondents liable.

The Court of Appeal of Northern Ireland held that the respondents were liable for the driver's negligence and were entitled to claim under the policy. The appellants appealed to the House of Lords. The appeal was dismissed.

LORD WRIGHT: . . . .
The act of a workman in lighting his pipe or cigarette is an act done for his own comfort and convenience and at least, generally speaking, not for his employer's benefit. That last condition, however, is no longer essential to fix liability on the employer (*Lloyd v Grace, Smith & Co*).[11] Nor is such an act prima facie negligent. It is in itself both innocent and harmless. The negligence is to be found by considering the time when and the circumstances in which the match is struck and thrown down. The duty of the workman to his employer is so to conduct himself in doing his work as not negligently to cause damage either to the employer himself or his property or to third persons or their property, and thus to impose the same liability on the employer as if he had been doing the work himself and committed the negligent act. This may seem too obvious as a matter of common sense to require either argument or authority. I think that what plausibility the contrary argument might seem to possess results from treating the act of lighting the cigarette in abstraction from the circumstances as a separate act. This was the line taken by the majority judgment in *Williams v Jones*[12] from which Mellor and Blackburn JJ as I think, rightly dissented. . . .

[VISCOUNT SIMON LC, with whom LORD ROMER concurred, delivered a speech in favour of dismissing the appeal. LORD PORTER concurred.]

■ Morris v CW Martin & Sons Ltd
Court of Appeal [1965] 2 All ER 725

The plaintiff sent her mink stole to Mr Beder, a furrier, for cleaning. With her consent, he sent it to the defendants, one of the biggest cleaners in the country, who knew that it belonged to an unspecified customer of Mr Beder. The current trade conditions were that

---

[11] [1912] AC 716.   [12] (1865) 3 H & C 602.

'goods belonging to customers' on the defendants' premises were held at the customer's risk and the defendants would 'not be responsible for loss or damage however caused'. While the fur was with the defendants, it was stolen by one of their employees, Morrissey.

The plaintiff brought an action for damages for loss of the fur. The trial judge found that the defendants were not negligent in employing Morrissey, that they had taken all proper steps to safeguard the fur while on their premises, and that Morrissey's act was not done in the scope of his employment. He gave judgment for the defendants. The plaintiff appealed to the Court of Appeal.

LORD DENNING MR: . . .

The law on this subject has developed greatly over the years. During the nineteenth century it was accepted law that a master was liable for the dishonesty or fraud of his servant if it was done in the course of his employment and for his master's benefit. Dishonesty or fraud by the servant for his own benefit took the case out of the course of his employment. The judges took this simple view: no servant who turns thief and steals is acting in the course of his employment. He is acting outside it altogether. But in 1912 the law was revolutionised by the case of *Lloyd* v. *Grace, Smith & Co.*,[13] where it was held that a master was liable for the dishonesty or fraud of his servant if it was done within the course of his employment, no matter whether it was done for the benefit of the master or for the benefit of the servant. Nevertheless there still remains the question: What is meant by the phrase 'in the course of his employment'? When can it be said that the dishonesty or fraud of a servant, done for his *own* benefit, is in the course of his employment?

On this question the cases are baffling. In particular those cases, much discussed before us, where a bailee's servant dishonestly drives a vehicle for his own benefit. These stretch from *The Coupe Co* v. *Maddick*[14] to the present day. Let me take an illustration well fitted for a moot. Suppose the owner of a car takes it to a garage to be repaired. It is repaired by a garage hand who is then told to drive it back to the owner. But instead, he takes it out on a 'frolic of his own' (to use the nineteenth century phrase) or on a 'joy-ride' (to come into the twentieth century). He takes it out, let us say, on a drunken escapade or on a thieving expedition. Nay more, for it is all the same, let us suppose the garage hand steals the car himself and drives off at speed. He runs into a motorcyclist. Both the car and the motorcycle are damaged. Both owners sue the garage proprietor for the negligence of his servant. The motorcyclist clearly cannot recover against the garage proprietor for the simple reason that at the time of the accident the servant was not acting in the course of his employment; see *Storey* v. *Ashton.*[15] You might think also that the owner of the car could not recover, and for the self-same reason, namely, that the servant was not acting in the course of his employment. Before 1912 the courts would undoubtedly have so held; see *Sanderson* v. *Collins; Cheshire* v. *Bailey,*[16] as explained by LORD SHAW OF DUNFERMLINE in *Lloyd* v. *Grace, Smith & Co.*[17] itself. But since 1912 it seems fairly clear that the owner of the damaged car could recover from the garage proprietor; see *Central Motors (Glasgow), Ltd.* v. *Cessnock Garage and Motor Co.*[18] on the ground that, although the garage hand was using the car for his own private purposes, 'he should be regarded as still acting in the course of his employment' (see *Aitchison* v. *Page Motors, Ltd.*):[19] and even if he stole the car on the journey, it was a conversion 'in the course of the employment' (see *United Africa Co., Ltd.* v. *Saka Owoade*).[20] I ask myself, how can this be? How can the servant on one and the same journey, be acting both within and without the course of his employment? Within *qua* the car owner. Without *qua* the motorcyclist. It is time we got rid of this confusion. And the only way to do it, so far as I can see, is by reference to the duty laid by the law on the master. The duty of the garage proprietor to the owner of the car is very different from his duty to the motorcyclist. He owes to the

---

[13] [1912] AC 716, [1911–13] All ER Rep 51.
[14] [1904] 1 KB 628, [1904–7] All ER Rep 561.   [15] (1869) LR 4 QB 476.
[16] [1905] 1 KB 237, [1904–07] All ER Rep 882.
[17] [1912] AC at p. 741, [1911–13] All ER Rep at p. 62.   [18] 1925 SC 796.
[19] [1935] All ER Rep 594 at 596–598.   [20] [1955] AC 130 at 144, [1957] 3 All ER 216 at 247.

owner of the car the duty of a bailee for reward, whereas he owes no such duty to the motorcyclist on the road. He does not even owe him a duty to use care not to injure him.

If you go through the cases on this difficult subject, you will find that in the ultimate analysis, they depend on the nature of the duty owed by the master towards the person whose goods have been lost or damaged. If the master is under a duty to use due care to keep goods safely and protect them from theft and depredation, he cannot get rid of his responsibility by delegating his duty to another. If he entrusts that duty to his servant, he is answerable for the way in which the servant conducts himself therein. No matter whether the servant be negligent, fraudulent, or dishonest, the master is liable. But not when he is under no such duty. The cases show this: . . .

[His Lordship then considered a number of decided cases and continued:]

From all these instances we may deduce the general proposition that when a principal has in his charge the goods or belongings of another in such circumstances that he is under a duty to take all reasonable precautions to protect them from theft or depredation, then if he entrusts that duty to a servant or agent, he is answerable for the manner in which that servant or agent carries out his duty. If the servant or agent is careless so that they are stolen by a stranger, the master is liable. So also if the servant or agent himself steals them or makes away with them. . . .

So far I have been dealing with the cases where the owner himself has entrusted the goods to the defendant. But here it was not the owner, the plaintiff, who entrusted the fur to the cleaners. She handed it to Mr Beder, who was a bailee for reward. He in turn, with her authority, handed it to the cleaners who were sub-bailees for reward. Mr Beder could clearly himself sue the cleaners for loss of the fur and recover the whole value (see *The Winkfield*),[1] unless the cleaners were protected by some exempting conditions. But can the plaintiff sue the cleaners direct for the misappropriation by their servant? And if she does, can she ignore the exempting conditions? . . .

[A]n action does lie by the owner direct against the wrongdoer if he has the right to immediate possession; see *Kahler* v. *Midland Bank, Ltd.*[2] Even if he has no right to immediate possession, he can sue for any permanent injury to, or loss of, the goods by a wrongful act of the defendant; see *Mears* v. *London and South Western Rly Co.*[3] But what is a wrongful act as between the owner and the sub-bailee? What is the duty of the sub-bailee to the owner? Is the sub-bailee liable for misappropriation by his servant? There is very little authority on this point. *Pollock and Wright on Possession* say this (at p. 169):

'If the bailee of a thing sub-bails it by authority . . . and there is no direct privity of contract between the third person and the owner *it would seem that both the owner and the first bailee have concurrently the rights of a bailor against the third person according to the nature of the sub-bailment.*'

By which I take it that if the sub-bailment is for reward, the sub-bailee owes to the owner all the duties of a bailee for reward: and the owner can sue the sub-bailee direct for loss of or damage to the goods; and the sub-bailee (unless he is protected by any exempting conditions) is liable unless he can prove that the loss or damage occurred without his fault or that of his servants. So the plaintiff can sue the defendants direct for the loss of the goods by the misappropriation by their servant, and the cleaners are liable unless they are protected by the exempting conditions. . . .

[His Lordship went on to find that the exempting conditions did not protect the defendants since, as a matter of construction, the word 'customer' meant the furrier and not the plaintiff.]

DIPLOCK LJ: . . .

If the bailee in the present case had been a natural person and had converted the plaintiff's fur by stealing it himself, no one would have argued that he was not liable to her for its loss; but the defendant bailees are a corporate person. They could not perform their duties to the plaintiff to take reasonable care of the fur and not to convert it otherwise than vicariously by natural persons acting as their servants or agents. It was one of their servants, to whom they had entrusted the care and custody

---

[1] [1902] p. 42, [1900–03] All ER Rep 346.
[2] [1949] 2 All ER 621 at 627, 628, 641, [1950] AC 24 at 33, 56. [3] (1862) 11 C.B.N.S. 850.

of the fur for the purpose of doing work on it, who converted it by stealing it. Why should they not be vicariously liable for this breach of their duty by the vicar whom they had chosen to perform it? ...

If the principle laid down in *Lloyd* v. *Grace, Smith & Co.*[4] is applied to the facts of the present case, the defendants cannot in my view escape liability for the conversion of the plaintiff's fur by their servant Morrissey. They accepted the fur as bailees for reward in order to clean it. They put Morrissey as their agent in their place to clean the fur and to take charge of it while doing so. The manner in which he conducted himself in doing that work was to convert it. What he was doing, albeit dishonestly, he was doing in the scope or course of his employment in the technical sense of that infelicitous but time-honoured phrase. The defendants as his masters are responsible for his tortious act.

... [We are not concerned here] with what would have been the liability of the defendants if the fur had been stolen by another servant of theirs who was not employed by them to clean the fur or to have the care or custody of it. The mere fact that his employment by the defendants gave him the opportunity to steal it would not suffice. ...

I base my decision in this case on the ground that the fur was stolen by the very servant whom the defendants as bailees for reward had employed to take care of it and to clean it.

I agree that the appeal should be allowed.

SALMON LJ: ...

[I agree] with my lords that the appeal should be allowed. I am anxious, however, to make it plain that the conclusion which I have reached depends on Morrissey being the servant through whom the defendants chose to discharge their duty to take reasonable care of the plaintiff's fur. The words of Willes J, in *Barwick's* case[5] are entirely applicable to these facts. The defendants

'put [their] agent [Morrissey] in [the defendants'] place as to such a class of acts, and ... must be answerable for the manner in which the agent conducts himself in doing the business which is the business of the master.'

A bailee for reward is not answerable for a theft by any of his servants, but only for a theft by such of them as are deputed by him to discharge some part of his duty of taking reasonable care. A theft by any servant who is not employed to do anything in relation to the goods bailed is entirely outside the scope of his employment and cannot make the master liable. So in this case, if someone employed by the defendants in another depot had broken in and stolen the fur, the defendants would not have been liable. Similarly in my view if a clerk employed in the same depot had seized the opportunity of entering the room where the fur was kept and had stolen it, the defendants would not have been liable. The mere fact that the master, by employing a rogue, gives him the opportunity to steal or defraud does not make the master liable for his depredations. *Ruben and Ladenburg* v. *Great Fingall Consolidated.*[6] It might be otherwise if the master knew or ought to have known that his servant was dishonest, because then the master could be liable in negligence for employing him. ...

Appeal allowed.

QUESTION

Do you agree with Lord Denning MR that the solution to cases like this is to abandon the notion of vicarious liability in favour of that of a primary non-delegable duty of the bailee (cf *Winfield & Jolowicz*, pp. 905–906)?

---

[4] [1912] AC 716, [1911–13] All ER Rep 51.
[5] [1861–73] All ER at p. 198; (1867) L.R. 2 Exch. at p. 266.
[6] [1906] AC 439, [1904–07] All ER Rep 460.

NOTE

In *Lloyd v Grace Smith & Co* [1912] AC 716 a solicitor was held liable for the fraud of his managing clerk, who induced a client to transfer property to him and then disposed of the property for his own benefit. The basis of the decision was that the managing clerk had been authorised to transact business on behalf of the firm. Lord Loreburn LC said (at p. 725): 'If the agent commits the fraud purporting to act in the course of business such as he was authorised, or held out as authorised, to transact on account of his principal, then the latter may be held liable for it.'

This 'revolutionary' case is also discussed in *Lister v Hesley Hall*, p. 1088, post.

■ Rose v Plenty

Court of Appeal [1976] 1 All ER 97

Mr Plenty, the first defendant, was a milk roundsman, employed by the second defendants, Co-operative Retail Services Ltd. His duties were to drive his float on his round delivering milk and collecting payment. There were notices up at the depot making it clear that rounds-men were not allowed in any circumstances to employ children in the performance of their duties or to give lifts on the milk float. Contrary to these prohibitions, Plenty invited Leslie Rose, then aged 13, to help him with his milk round in return for payment. While riding on the float in the course of helping Plenty, Rose was injured when Plenty drove negligently. He brought an action for damages against Plenty and the Co-op. The judge found that Rose was 25 per cent to blame for the accident and gave judgment against Plenty for 75 per cent of the assessed damages of £800. He held that Plenty was acting outside the scope of his employment and that Rose was a trespasser on the float. On appeal, it was contended for Rose that the Co-op were liable for the acts of Plenty.

LORD DENNING MR: . . .

This raises a nice point on the liability of a master for his servant. I will first take the notices to the roundsmen saying they must not take the boys on. Those do not necessarily exempt the employers from liability. The leading case is *Limpus v London General Omnibus Co.*[7] The drivers of omnibuses were furnished with a card saying they 'must not on any account race with or obstruct another omnibus...' Nevertheless the driver of one of the defendants' omnibuses did obstruct a rival omnibus and caused an accident in which the plaintiff's horses were injured. Martin B[8] directed the jury that, if the defendants' driver did it for the purposes of his employer, the defendants were liable; but if it was an act of his own, and in order to effect a purpose of his own, the defendants were not responsible. The jury found for the plaintiff. The Court of Exchequer Chamber[9] held that the direction was correct. It was a very strong court which included Willes and Blackburn JJ. Despite the prohibition, the employer was held liable because the injury resulted from an act done by the driver in the course of his service and for his master's purposes. The decisive point was that it was not done by the servant for his own purposes, but for his master's purposes.

I will next take the point about a trespasser. The boy was a trespasser on the milk float so far as Co-operative Services were concerned. They had not given him any permission to be on the float and had expressly prohibited the milk roundsman from taking him on. There are two early cases where it was suggested that the employer of a driver is not liable to a person who is a trespasser on the vehicle. They are *Twine v Bean's Express Ltd*[10] and *Conway v George Wimpey & Co Ltd.*[11] But these cases are

---

[7] (1862) 1 H & C 526.   [8] 1 H & C at 529, 530.
[9] (1863) 9 Jur NS 333, [1861–73] All ER Rep 556.
[10] (1946) 175 LT 131.   [11] [1951] 1 All ER 363, [1951] 2 KB 266.

to be explained on other grounds; and the statements about a trespasser are no longer correct. Those statements were made at a time when it was commonly supposed that occupiers of premises were under no duty to use care in regard to a trespasser. But that stern rule has now been abandoned, especially when the trespasser is a child.... So far as vehicles are concerned, I venture to go back to my own judgment in *Young v Edward Box & Co Ltd*,[12] when I said:

> 'In every case where it is sought to make the master liable for the conduct of his servant the first question is to see whether the servant was liable. If the answer is Yes, the second question is to see whether the employer must shoulder the servant's liability.'

... Applying the first question in *Young v Box*,[13] it is quite clear that the driver, Mr Plenty, was liable to the boy, Leslie Rose, for his negligent driving of the milk float. He actually invited the boy to ride on it. So the second question arises, whether his employers, Co-operative Services, are liable for the driver's negligence. That does not depend on whether the boy was a trespasser. It depends, as I said in *Young v Box*, on whether the driver, in taking the boy on the milk float, was acting in the course of his employment.

In considering whether a prohibited act was within the course of the employment, it depends very much on the purpose for which it is done. If it is done for his employers' business, it is usually done in the course of his employment, even though it is a prohibited act. That is clear from *Limpus v London General Omnibus Co*;[14] *Young v Box* and *Ilkiw v Samuels*.[15] But if it is done for some purpose other than his master's business, as, for instance, giving a lift to a hitchhiker, such an act, if prohibited, may not be within the course of his employment. Both *Twine v Bean's Express Ltd*[16] and *Conway v George Wimpey & Co Ltd*[17] are to be explained on their own facts as cases where a driver had given a lift to someone else contrary to a prohibition and not for the purposes of the employers. *Iqbal v London Transport Executive*[18] seems to be out of line and should be regarded as decided on its own special circumstances. In the present case it seems to me that the course of Mr Plenty's employment was to distribute the milk, collect the money and to bring back the bottles to the van. He got or allowed this young boy, Leslie Rose, to do part of that business which was the employers' business. It seems to me that although prohibited, it was conduct which was within the course of the employment; and on this ground I think the judge was in error. I agree it is a nice point in these cases on which side of the line the case falls; but, as I understand the authorities, this case falls within those in which the prohibition affects only the conduct within the sphere of the employment and did not take the conduct outside the sphere altogether. I would hold this conduct of Christopher Plenty to be within the course of his employment and the master is liable accordingly, and I would allow the appeal.

In parting with the case, it may be interesting to notice that this type of case is unlikely to arise so much in the future, since a vehicle is not to be used on a road unless there is in force an insurance policy covering, inter alia, injury to passengers.

SCARMAN LJ: ...

I think it important to realise that the principle of vicarious liability is one of public policy. It is not a principle which derives from a critical or refined consideration of other concepts in the common law, e.g. the concept of trespass or indeed the concept of agency. No doubt in particular cases it may be relevant to consider whether a particular plaintiff was or was not a trespasser. Similarly, when, as I shall indicate, it is important that one should determine the course of employment of the servant, the law of agency may have some marginal relevance. But basically, as I understand it, the employer is made vicariously liable for the tort of his employee not because the plaintiff is an invitee, nor because of the authority possessed by the servant, but because it is a case in which the employer, having put matters into motion, should be liable if the motion that he has originated leads to damage to another. What is the approach which the cases identify as the correct approach in order to determine this question

---

[12] [1951] 1 TLR 789 at 793.   [13] [1951] 1 TLR 789.   [14] (1862) 1 H & C 526.
[15] [1963] 2 All ER 879; [1963] 1 WLR 991.   [16] (1946) 175 LT 131.
[17] [1951] 1 All ER 363; [1951] 2 KB 266.   [18] (1973) 16 KIR 329, CA.

of public policy? First, as Lord Denning MR has already said, one looks to see whether the servant has committed a tort on the plaintiff. In the present case it is clear that the first defendant, the servant of the dairy company, who are the second defendants, by the negligent driving of the milk float, caused injury to the plaintiff, a boy 13 1/2 years old, who was on the float at his invitation. There was therefore a tort committed by the servant. The next question, as Lord Denning MR has said, is whether the employer should shoulder the liability for compensating the person injured by the tort. With all respect to the points developed by Lawton LJ, it does appear to me to be clear, since the decision of *Limpus v London General Omnibus Co*,[19] that that question has to be answered by directing attention to what the first defendant was employed to do when he committed the tort that has caused damage to the plaintiff. The first defendant was, of course, employed at the time of the accident to do a whole number of operations. He was certainly not employed to give the plaintiff a lift, and if one confines one's analysis of the facts to the incident of injury to the plaintiff, then no doubt one would say that carrying the plaintiff on the float—giving him a lift—was not in the course of the first defendant's employment. But in *Ilkiw v Samuels*[20] Diplock LJ indicated that the proper approach to the nature of the servant's employment is a broad one. He said:

> 'As each of these nouns implies [he is referring to the nouns used to describe course of employment, sphere, scope and so forth] the matter must be looked at broadly, not dissecting the servant's task into its component activities—such as driving, loading, sheeting and the like—by asking: What was the job on which he was engaged for his employer? and answering that question as a jury would.'

Applying those words to the employment of the first defendant, I think it is clear from the evidence that he was employed as a roundsman to drive his float round his round and to deliver milk, to collect empties and to obtain payment. That was his job. He was under an express prohibition—a matter to which I shall refer later—not to enlist the help of anyone doing that work. And he was also under an express prohibition not to give lifts on the float to anyone. How did he choose to carry out the task which I have analysed? He chose to disregard the prohibition and to enlist the assistance of the plaintiff. As a matter of common sense, that does seem to me to be a mode, albeit a prohibited mode, of doing the job with which he was entrusted. Why was the plaintiff being carried on the float when the accident occurred? Because it was necessary to take him from point to point so that he could assist in delivering milk, collecting empties and, on occasions, obtaining payment. The plaintiff was there because it was necessary that he should be there in order that he could assist, albeit in a way prohibited by the employers, in the job entrusted to the first defendant by his employers.

. . . .In *Twine's case*,[1] at the very end of the judgment, Lord Greene MR said: 'The other thing that he [i.e. the servant] was doing simultaneously was something totally outside the scope of his employment, namely, giving a lift to a person who had no right whatsoever to be there.' In that case the conclusion of fact was that the express prohibition on giving lifts was not only a prohibition but was also a limiting factor on the scope of the employment; and, of course, once a prohibition is properly to be treated as a defining or limiting factor on the scope of employment certain results follow. In *Twine's* case[2] the driver was engaged to drive his employers' van, his employers having a contract with the Post Office. When so doing, he gave Mr Twine a lift from A to B. True A and B happened to be, both of them, offices of the Post Office. Yet I can well understand why the court reached the conclusion that in the circumstances of that case it was not possible to say that the driver in giving Mr Twine a lift was acting within the scope of his employment or doing improperly that which he was employed to do. Similarly when one looks at *Conway's case*,[3] one again sees that on the facts of that case the court considered it right so to define the scope of employment that what was done, namely giving somebody a lift, was outside it and was not a mode of doing that which the servant was employed to do. That also was a case of a lift:

---

[19] (1862) 1 H & C 526.   [20] [1963] 2 All ER at p. 889, [1963] 1 WLR at p. 1004.
[1] (1946) 175 LT at p. 132.   [2] (1946) 175 LT 131.
[3] [1951] 2 KB 266, [1951] 1 All ER 363.

the person lifted was not in any way engaged, in the course of the lift or indeed otherwise, in doing the master's business or in assisting the servant to do the master's business; and no doubt it was for that reason that Asquith LJ was able to say[4] that what was done—that is giving somebody else's employee a lift from the airport home—was not a mode of performing an act which the driver was employed to do, but was the performance of an act which he was not employed to perform. In the present case the first defendant, the servant, was employed to deliver milk, to collect empties, to obtain payment from customers. The plaintiff was there on the float in order to assist the first defendant to do those jobs. I would have thought therefore that whereas *Conway v George Wimpey & Co Ltd*[5] was absolutely correctly decided on its facts, the facts of the present case lead to a very different conclusion. The dividing factor between, for instance, the present case and the decisions in *Twine v Bean's Express Ltd*[6] and *Conway v George Wimpey & Co Ltd* is the category into which the court, on the study of the facts of the case, puts the express prohibition issued by the employers to their servant. In *Ilkiw v Samuels*[7] Diplock LJ, in a judgment to which I have already referred, dealt with this problem of the prohibition, and quoted a dictum of Lord Dunedin in *Plumb v Cobden Flour Mills Co Ltd*,[8] which itself has been approved in the Privy Council case of *Canadian Pacific Rly Co v Lockhart*.[9] Lord Dunedin said:[10] '...there are prohibitions which limit the sphere of employment, and prohibitions which only deal with conduct within the sphere of employment.'... [In *Iqbal v London Transport Executive*[11]] the Court of Appeal had to consider whether London Transport Executive was liable for the action of a bus conductor in driving, contrary to his express instructions, a motor bus a short distance in a garage. Of course, the court had no difficulty at all in distinguishing between the spheres of employment of a driver and a conductor in London Transport. Accordingly, it treated the prohibition on conductors acting as drivers of motor buses as a prohibition which defined his sphere of employment. Now there was nothing of that sort in the prohibition in this case. The prohibition is twofold: (1) that the first defendant was not to give lifts on his float; and (2) that he was not to employ others to help him in delivering the milk and so forth. There was nothing in those prohibitions which defined or limited the sphere of his employment. The sphere of his employment remained precisely the same after as before the prohibitions were brought to his notice. The sphere was as a roundsman to go round the rounds delivering milk, collecting empties and obtaining payment. Contrary to instructions, this roundsman chose to do what he was employed to do in an improper way. But the sphere of his employment was in no way affected by his express instructions.

Finally, I think one can see how careful one must be not to introduce into a study of this sort of problem ideas of trespass and agency. It is perfectly possible, on the principle that I am now considering, that an employer may authorise his servant, if the servant chooses to do it—'permit' is perhaps a better word—to give lifts. But the effect of that permission does not make the employer liable if in the course of recreational or off duty but permitted activity the servant drives the vehicle negligently and injures the passenger. *Hilton v Thomas Burton (Rhodes) Ltd*[12] is a case in which the plaintiff failed although the journey was a permitted journey, because he was not able to show that the journey on which he was being carried was a journey which occurred in the course of the servant's employment. Conversely one has the classic case of *Limpus v London General Omnibus Co*[13] when what the servant was doing was a defiance and disregard of the bus company's instructions.

Nevertheless the plaintiff who was injured by the defiant and disobedient acts was entitled to recover against the employer....

[LAWTON LJ gave a dissenting judgment.]

Appeal allowed.

[4] [1951] 2 KB at p. 276, [1951] 1 All ER at p. 367.   [5] [1951] 1 All ER 363, [1951] 2 KB 266.
[6] (1946) 175 LT 131.   [7] [1963] 2 All ER at p. 889, [1963] 1 WLR at p. 1004.
[8] [1914] AC 62 at 67.   [9] [1942] 2 All ER 464, [1942] AC 591.
[10] [1914] AC at 67.   [11] (1973) 16 KIR 329.
[12] [1961] 1 All ER 74, [1961] 1 WLR 705.   [13] (1862) 1 H & C 526.

QUESTION

It may seem unfair on an employer that he can be held vicariously liable for conduct of his employees even though he has expressly prohibited them from acting in that way, as in *Limpus v London General Omnibus Co* and *Rose v Plenty*. However, what would be the likely effect on vicarious liability if those cases were overruled? Consider what terms a well-advised employer would seek to insert into its contracts of employment, given such a regime.

NOTES

1. Lawton LJ's dissenting judgment claimed that it was a fatal objection to the claimant's case that the employers did not owe a duty of care to the claimant, a view based on Lord Greene MR's judgment in *Twine v Bean's Express Ltd* (1946) 175 LT 131. This view is incompatible with the vicarious nature of vicarious liability and was rejected by the Privy Council in *New Zealand Guardian Trust Co Ltd v Brooks* [1995] 1 WLR 96.

2. Is it relevant whether the person injured as a result of the employee's negligence is aware of the prohibition? In *Stone v Taffe* [1974] 3 All ER 1016 Stephenson LJ suggested, obiter (at p. 1022), that a claimant who knew of the prohibition and who had the chance to avoid the danger of injury from the prohibited act cannot hold the employer liable; furthermore, he thought it would be sufficient for the employer to prove that the prohibition was likely to be known to the injured person. Where the injured person is a fellow employee of the wrongdoer he is more likely to know of the prohibition (as in *Iqbal v London Transport Executive* (1973) 16 KIR 329). For comment see I. M. Yeats (1976) 39 MLR 94 at 95–96.

3. It appears to be easier to limit the scope of a delegated task than the scope of authority of an employee. In *Watkins v Birmingham City Council* (1975) Times, 1 August; (1976) 126 NLJ 442, the deputy headmistress of a school was injured when she fell over a tricycle which had been negligently placed near a classroom door by a ten-year-old boy in the course of carrying out his assigned task of distributing milk in classrooms. There was a strict rule, which the boy had disobeyed, that tricycles were not to be moved from their safe position in the middle of the assembly hall. The Court of Appeal held that the boy was not an employee of the authority, since it was part of his education to render the services. Buckley LJ is reported to have said that 'the boy might well have been acting as an agent of the school authority, but it has been conceded that if the relationship was that of principal and agent but not master and servant, the strict school rule...was effective to protect the school from vicarious liability for any breach of the rule...'. The court indicated that had the boy been an employee, the rule against moving the tricycle would not have restricted the scope of the employment.

4. In *General Engineering Services Ltd v Kingston and St Andrew Corpn* [1988] 3 All ER 867, [1989] 1 WLR 69 as part of industrial action against their employers, firemen operated a 'go-slow' policy. As a result it took them 17 minutes to cover the distance to the claimant's premises instead of the normal three and a half minutes. The delay caused the claimant's premises to be completely destroyed. The Privy Council (on appeal from the Court of Appeal of Jamaica) decided that the employers of the firemen were not vicariously liable. Lord Ackner, delivering the judgment of the Board, regarded the mode and manner in which the firemen went to the fire in order to put pressure on their employers in an industrial dispute as a wrongful repudiation by the firemen of their contracts of employment and not in furtherance of their employers' business. This

conduct was 'the very negation of carrying out some act authorised by the employer, albeit in a wrongful and unauthorised mode'. But note that the employers still allowed the firemen to put on their uniforms and drive their fire engines. Would not a member of the public reasonably assume that the employer was still holding the firemen out to have their authority to act as firemen?

■ Lister v Hesley Hall Ltd
House of Lords [2001] 2 All ER 769

The claimants had, in childhood, been sexually abused by the warden of a boarding house, owned and commercially operated by the defendant company. The judge found that the defendants had not been negligent in their selection and control of the warden. The Court of Appeal, following *Trotman v North Yorkshire County Council* [1999] LGR 584, held that the warden's acts could not be regarded as an unauthorised mode of carrying out the duties he was employed by the defendants to perform, and thus they were not vicariously liable for the abuse. The claimants appealed to the House of Lords.

LORD STEYN:...

[8] On 25 February 1999 the judge gave judgment. He dismissed the claim in negligence against the employers. That left the claim based on vicarious liability to be considered. This claim appeared to be ruled out by the *Salmond* test *(Salmond on Torts* (9th edn, 1936) p 95; *Salmond and Heuston on the Law of Torts* (21st edn, 1996) p 443) as interpreted and applied by the Court of Appeal in *Trotman v North Yorkshire CC* [1999] LGR 584. The following passage in the judgment of Butler-Sloss LJ (at 591) reveals the perceived difficulty:

'18. Having looked at some of the relevant decisions on each side of the line, it is useful to stand back and ask: applying general principles, in which category in the *Salmond* test would one expect these facts to fall? A deputy headmaster of a special school, charged with the responsibility of caring for a handicapped teenager on a foreign holiday, sexually assaults him. Is that in principle an improper mode of carrying out an authorised act on behalf of his employer, the council, or an independent act outside the course of his employment? His position of caring for the plaintiff by sharing a bedroom with him gave him the opportunity to carry out the sexual assaults. But availing himself of that opportunity seems to me to be far removed from an unauthorised mode of carrying out a teacher's duties on behalf of his employer. Rather it is a negation of the duty of the council to look after children for whom it was responsible. Acts of physical assault may not be so easy to categorise, since they may range, for instance, from a brutal and unprovoked assault by a teacher to forceful attempts to defend another pupil or the teacher himself. But in the field of serious sexual misconduct, I find it difficult to visualise circumstances in which an act of the teacher can be an unauthorised mode of carrying out an authorised act, although I would not wish to close the door on the possibility.'

Thorpe LJ agreed with this judgment and Chadwick LJ expressed himself in materially similar terms. Not surprisingly, the judge felt compelled to conclude that the employers could not be held vicariously liable for the torts of the warden....

[14] Vicarious liability is legal responsibility imposed on an employer, although he is himself free from blame, for a tort committed by his employee in the course of his employment. Fleming observed that this formula represented—

'a compromise between two conflicting policies: on the one end, the social interest in furnishing an innocent tort victim with recourse against a financially responsible defendant; on the other, a hesitation to foist any undue burden on business enterprise'. (See *The Law of Torts* (9th edn, 1998) pp 409–410.)

[16] It is not necessary to embark on a detailed examination of the development of the modern principle of vicarious liability. But it is necessary to face up to the way in which the law of vicarious liability sometimes may embrace intentional wrongdoing by an employee. If one mechanically applies *Salmond*'s test, the result might at first glance be thought to be that a bank is not liable to a customer where a bank employee defrauds a customer by giving him only half the foreign exchange which he paid for, the employee pocketing the difference. A preoccupation with conceptualistic reasoning may lead to the absurd conclusion that there can only be vicarious liability if the bank carries on business in defrauding its customers. Ideas divorced from reality have never held much attraction for judges steeped in the tradition that their task is to deliver principled but practical justice. How the courts set the law on a sensible course is a matter to which I now turn.

[17] It is easy to accept the idea that where an employee acts for the benefit of his employer, or intends to do so, that is strong evidence that he was acting in the course of his employment. But until the decision of the House of Lords in *Lloyd v Grace, Smith & Co* [1912] AC 716, [1911–13] All ER Rep 51 it was thought that vicarious liability could only be established if such requirements were satisfied. This was an overly restrictive view and hardly in tune with the needs of society. In *Lloyd*'s case it was laid to rest by the House of Lords. A firm of solicitors were held liable for the dishonesty of their managing clerk who persuaded a client to transfer property to him and then disposed of it for his own advantage. The decisive factor was that the client had been invited by the firm to deal with their managing clerk. This decision was a breakthrough: it finally established that vicarious liability is not necessarily defeated if the employee acted for his own benefit. On the other hand, an intense focus on the connection between the nature of the employment and the tort of the employee became necessary.

[19] The classic example of vicarious liability for intentional wrong doing is *Morris v C W Martin & Sons Ltd* [1965] 2 All ER 725, [1966] 1 QB 716. . . . *Morris*' case has consistently been regarded as high authority on the principles of vicarious liability. Atiyah *Vicarious Liability in the Law of Torts* (1967) p 271 described it as 'a striking and valuable extension of the law of vicarious liability'. Palmer *Bailment* (2nd edn, 1991) pp 424–425 treats *Morris*' case as an authority on vicarious liability beyond bailment. He states that 'if a television repairman steals a television set he is called in to repair, his employers would be liable, for the loss occurred whilst he was performing one of the class of acts in respect of which their duty lay'. And that does not involve bailment. Moreover, in *Port Swettenham Authority v T W Wu & Co (M) Sdn Bhd* [1978] 3 All ER 337, [1979] AC 580 the Privy Council expressly approved *Morris*' case in respect of vicarious liability as explained by Diplock and Salmon LJJ.

[20] Our law no longer struggles with the concept of vicarious liability for intentional wrongdoing. Thus the decision of the House of Lords in *Racz v Home Office* [1994] 1 All ER 97, [1994] 2 AC 45 is authority for the proposition that the Home Office may be vicariously liable for acts of police officers which amounted to misfeasance in public office—and hence for liability in tort involving bad faith. It remains, however, to consider how vicarious liability for intentional wrongdoing fits in with Salmond's formulation. The answer is that it does not cope ideally with such cases. It must, however, be remembered that the great tort writer did not attempt to enunciate precise propositions of law on vicarious liability. At most he propounded a broad test which deems as within the course of employment 'a wrongful and unauthorised mode of doing some *act* authorised by the master'. And he emphasised the connection between the authorised *acts* and the 'improper modes' of doing them. In reality it is simply a practical test serving as a dividing line between cases where it is or is not just to impose vicarious liability. . . .

[25] In my view the approach of the Court of Appeal in *Trotman*'s case was wrong. It resulted in the case being treated as one of the employment furnishing a mere opportunity to commit the sexual abuse. The reality was that the county council were responsible for the care of the vulnerable children and employed the deputy headmaster to carry out that duty on its behalf. And the sexual abuse

took place while the employee was engaged in duties at the very time and place demanded by his employment. The connection between the employment and the torts was very close. I would overrule *Trotman's* case.

[28] …The question is whether the warden's torts were so closely connected with his employment that it would be fair and just to hold the employers vicariously liable. On the facts of the case the answer is yes. After all, the sexual abuse was inextricably interwoven with the carrying out by the warden of his duties in Axeholme House. Matters of degree arise. But the present cases clearly fall on the side of vicarious liability.

LORD CLYDE:…

[34] It is not useful to explore the historical origins of the vicarious liability of an employer in the hope of finding guidance in the principles of its modern application. In *Kilboy v South Eastern Fire Area Joint Committee* 1952 SC 280 at 285 the Lord President (Cooper) said of the rule respondeat superior: 'What was once presented as a legal principle has degenerated into a rule of expediency, imperfectly defined, and changing its shape before our eyes under the impact of changing social and political conditions.' Holmes *(The Common Law* (1888) ch 1, p 5 in the 44th printing of 1951), noting how rules may survive the customs or beliefs or needs which established them, described the situation more generally:

> 'The reason which gave rise to the rule has been forgotten, and ingenious minds set themselves to inquire how it is to be accounted for. Some ground of policy is thought of, which seems to explain it and to reconcile it with the present state of things; and then the rule adapts itself to the new reasons which have been found for it, and enters on a new career.'

[35] A variety of theories have been put forward to explain the rule. The expression 'respondeat superior' and the maxim 'qui facit per alium facit per se', while they may be convenient, do not assist in any analysis. Lord Reid observed in *Staveley Iron and Chemcial Co Ltd v Jones* [1956] 1 All ER 403 at 409, [1956] AC 627 at 643: 'The former merely states the rule baldly in two words, and the latter merely gives a fictional explanation of it.' Lord Pearce stated in *Imperial Chemical Industries Ltd v Shatwell* [1964] 2 All ER 999 at 1011–1012, [1965] AC 656 at 685: 'The doctrine of vicarious liability has not grown from any very clear, logical or legal principle but from social convenience and rough justice.' I am not persuaded that there is any reason of principle or policy which can be of substantial guidance in the resolution of the problem of applying the rule in any particular case. Theory may well justify the existence of the concept, but it is hard to find guidance from any underlying principle which will weigh in the decision whether in a particular case a particular wrongful act by the employee should or should not be regarded as falling within the scope of the employment.

[50] I turn finally to the facts of the present case. It appears that the care and safekeeping of the boys had been entrusted to the respondents and they in turn had entrusted their care and safekeeping, so far as the running of the boarding house was concerned, to the warden. That gave him access to the premises, but the opportunity to be at the premises would not in itself constitute a sufficient connection between his wrongful actings and his employment. In addition to the opportunity which access gave him, his position as warden and the close contact with the boys which that work involved created a sufficient connection between the acts of abuse which he committed and the work which he had been employed to do. It appears that the respondents gave the warden a quite general authority in the supervision and running of the house as well as some particular responsibilities. His general duty was to look after and to care for, among others, the appellants. That function was one which the respondents had delegated to him. That he performed that function in a way which was an abuse of his position and an abnegation of his duty does not sever the connection with his employment. The particular acts which he carried out upon the boys have to be viewed not in isolation but in the context and the circumstances in which they occurred. Given that he had a general authority in the management of the house and in the care and supervision of the boys in it, the employers should be liable for the way in which he behaved towards them in his capacity as warden of the house. The respondents

should then be vicariously liable to the appellants for the injury and damage which they suffered at the hands of the warden.

LORD MILLETT: . . .

[65] Vicarious liability is a species of strict liability. It is not premised on any culpable act or omission on the part of the employer; an employer who is not personally at fault is made legally answerable for the fault of his employee. It is best understood as a loss-distribution device: see Cane's edition of *Atiyah's Accidents, Compensation and the Law* (6th edn, 1999) p 85 and the articles cited by Atiyah in his monograph on *Vicarious Liability in the Law of Torts* (1967) p 24. The theoretical underpinning of the doctrine is unclear. Glanville Williams wrote ('Vicarious Liability and the Master's Indemnity' (1957) 20 MLR 220 at 231):

> 'Vicarious liability is the creation of many judges who have had different ideas of its justification or social policy, or no idea at all. Some judges may have extended the rule more widely, or confined it more narrowly than its true rationale would allow; yet the rationale, if we can discover it, will remain valid so far as it extends.'

Fleming observed *(The Law of Torts* (9th edn, 1998) p 410) that the doctrine cannot parade as a deduction from legalistic premises. He indicated that it should be frankly recognised as having its basis in a combination of policy considerations, and continued:

> 'Most important of these is the belief that a person who employs others to advance his own economic interest should in fairness be placed under a corresponding liability for losses incurred in the course of the enterprise . . .'

Atiyah *Vicarious Liability in the Law of Torts* wrote to the same effect. He suggested (at p 171): 'The master ought to be liable for all those torts which can fairly be regarded as reasonably incidental risks to the type of business he carries on.' These passages are not to be read as confining the doctrine to cases where the employer is carrying on business for profit. They are based on the more general idea that a person who employs another for his own ends inevitably creates a risk that the employee will commit a legal wrong. If the employer's objectives cannot be achieved without a serious risk of the employee committing the kind of wrong which he has in fact committed, the employer ought to be liable. The fact that his employment gave the employee the opportunity to commit the wrong is not enough to make the employer liable. He is liable only if the risk is one which experience shows is inherent in the nature of the business.

[66] While this proposition has never, so far as I am aware, been adopted in so many words as a test of vicarious liability in any of the decided cases, it does I think form the unspoken rationale of the principle that the employer's liability is confined to torts committed by an employee *in the course of his employment*. The problem is that, as Townshend-Smith has observed ((2000) 8 Tort Law Review 108 at 111), none of the various tests which have been proposed to determine this essentially factual question is either intellectually satisfying or effective to enable the outcome of a particular case to be predicted. The danger is that in borderline situations, and especially in cases of intentional wrongdoing, recourse to a rigid and possibly inappropriate formula as a test of liability may lead the court to abandon the search for legal principle.

[67] In the very first edition of his book on *Torts* (1907) p 83 Sir John Salmond wrote:

> '1. A master is not responsible for a wrongful act done by his servant unless it is done in the course of his employment. It is deemed to be so done if it is either (a) a wrongful act authorised by the master, or (b) a wrongful and unauthorised *mode* of doing some act authorised by the master.' (Author's emphasis.)

This passage has stood the test of time. It has survived unchanged for 21 editions, and has probably been cited more often than any other single passage in a legal textbook. Yet it is not without blemish.

As has often been observed, the first of the two alternatives is not an example of vicarious liability at all. Its presence (and the word 'deemed') may be an echo of the discredited theory of implied authority. More pertinently, the second is not happily expressed if it is to serve as a test of vicarious liability for intentional wrongdoing.

[68] In the present case the warden was employed to look after the boys in his care and secure their welfare. It is stretching language to breaking-point to describe the series of deliberate sexual assaults on them on which he embarked as merely a wrongful and unauthorised mode of performing that duty....

[70] But the precise terminology is not critical. The *Salmond* test, in either formulation, is not a statutory definition of the circumstances which give rise to liability, but a guide to the principled application of the law to diverse factual situations. What is critical is that attention should be directed to the closeness of the connection between the employee's duties and his wrongdoing and not to verbal formulae....

[71] Cases of intentional wrongdoing have always proved troublesome. At one time it was thought that the employer could not be held vicariously liable for his employee's deliberate wrongdoing....

[72] The heresy was not exposed until *Lloyd*'s case, and despite this has proved remarkably resilient....[R]egrettable traces of it appear in *Trotman*'s case. If the employer is to be absolved from liability in that case (or this) it cannot be because the acts complained of were 'independent acts of self-indulgence or self-gratification'.

[73] In *Lloyd*'s case a solicitor's managing clerk defrauded a client of the firm by obtaining her instructions to realise her property. He induced her to hand over the title deeds and to execute conveyances in his favour which he did not read over or explain to her. They enabled him to sell the property and pocket the proceeds. The firm was held liable for the fraud even though it was committed for the clerk's own benefit. In the course of argument before your Lordships in the present case it was accepted that the firm would not have been liable if the clerk had stolen the contents of his client's handbag. That is true, for the clerk would merely have been taking advantage of an opportunity which his employment gave him. But there was a much closer connection between the clerk's duties and his wrongdoing than that. The firm's liability arose from the fact that throughout the transaction the fraudulent clerk acted as the representative of the firm, and he received the custody of the documents of title with the consent of the client given because he was acting in that capacity.

[74] ...An excessively literal application of the *Salmond* test must also be discarded. Stealing a client's property cannot sensibly be described as an unauthorised mode of dealing with it on her behalf. It is, as Butler-Sloss LJ put it in *Trotman v North Yorkshire CC* [1999] LGR 584 at 591, the negation of the employer's duty. Yet the employer may be liable none the less.

[79] So it is no answer to say that the employee was guilty of intentional wrongdoing, or that his act was not merely tortious but criminal, or that he was acting exclusively for his own benefit, or that he was acting contrary to express instructions, or that his conduct was the very negation of his employer's duty. The cases show that where an employer undertakes the care of a client's property and entrusts the task to an employee who steals the property, the employer is vicariously liable. This is not only in accordance with principle but with the underlying rationale if *Atiyah* has correctly identified it. Experience shows that the risk of theft by an employee is inherent in a business which involves entrusting the custody of a customer's property to employees. But the theft must be committed by the very employee to whom the custody of the property is entrusted. He does more than make the most of an opportunity presented by the fact of his employment. He takes advantage of the position in which the employer has placed him to enable the purposes of the employer's business to be achieved. If the boys in the present case had been sacks of potatoes and the defendant, having been engaged to take care of them, had entrusted their care to one of its employees, it would have been vicariously liable for any criminal damage done to them by the employee in question, though not by any other employee. Given that the employer's liability does not arise from the law of bailment, it is not immediately apparent that it should make any difference that the victims were boys, that the wrongdoing took the form of sexual abuse, and that it was committed for the personal gratification of the employee.

[82] In the present case the warden's duties provided him with the opportunity to commit indecent assaults on the boys for his own sexual gratification, but that in itself is not enough to make the school liable. The same would be true of the groundsman or the school porter. But there was far more to it than that. The school was responsible for the care and welfare of the boys. It entrusted that responsibility to the warden. He was employed to discharge the school's responsibility to the boys. For this purpose the school entrusted them to his care. He did not merely take advantage of the opportunity which employment at a residential school gave him. He abused the special position in which the school had placed him to enable it to discharge its own responsibilities, with the result that the assaults were committed by the very employee to whom the school had entrusted the care of the boys. It is not necessary to conduct the detailed dissection of the warden's duties of the kind on which the Supreme Court of Canada embarked in *Bazley*'s case and *Jacobi*'s case. I would hold the school liable.

[83] I would regard this as in accordance not only with ordinary principle deducible from the authorities but with the underlying rationale of vicarious liability. Experience shows that in the case of boarding schools, prisons, nursing homes, old people's homes, geriatric wards, and other residential homes for the young or vulnerable, there is an inherent risk that indecent assaults on the residents will be committed by those placed in authority over them, particularly if they are in close proximity to them and occupying a position of trust.

[85] I would overrule *Trotman*'s case and allow the appeal.

[LORD HOBHOUSE OF WOODBOROUGH made a speech in favour of allowing the appeal, and agreed with the reasons of LORD STEYN. LORD HUTTON concurred with LORD STEYN.]

Appeal allowed.

QUESTIONS

When considering the connection between the employee's tortious acts and the tasks he had been employed to perform, how close is 'sufficiently' close? Does Lord Steyn adequately explain this at [28], ante, by asking whether it would be 'fair and just' to make the employer liable? Does Lord Millett's reliance upon Atiyah's test of 'reasonably incidental risks' at [65], ante provide a better answer?

NOTES

1. *Lister* is noted by p. Giliker (2002) 65 MLR 269. For an interesting analysis alongside the similar Commonwealth cases of *Bazley v Curry* (1999) 174 DLR (4th) 45 and *New South Wales v Lepore* (2003) 195 ALR 412, see S. Deakin (2003) 32 ILJ 97. Another persuasive analysis of *Lister* and the Canadian 'enterprise liability' theory is D. Brodie (2007) 27 OJLS 493. *Lister* was applied by the House of Lords in *Dubai Aluminium Co Ltd v Salaam* [2003] 1 All ER 97, [2002] UKHL 48 (p. 1072, ante).

2. In a passage which according to Deakin (op cit., p. 110) comes 'dangerously close to eliding' the ideas of vicarious liability and non-delegable duty, Lord Hobhouse in *Lister* at [55] focuses upon the responsibility assumed by the *employer* towards the victim, as the key to vicarious liability. R. Weekes points out that a non-delegable duty approach is 'attractive' for claimants, in that it 'circumvents the central conundrum of vicarious liability; proving that the employee's conduct was within the course of employment or sufficiently closely connected to it' [2004] CLJ 53, at 57–58. See further Lord Denning's judgment in *Morris v CW Martin & Sons Ltd* [1966] 1 QB 716, [1965] 2 All ER 725 (p. 1078, ante).

3.   Cases of deliberate assault, especially by state officials, test the underlying justifications of vicarious liability to its limit. A Canadian court has remarked that there may be little an employer can do to deter an assault when the threat of a prison sentence did not work (*Jacobi v Griffiths* (1999) 174 DLR (4th) 71 at 104). But that criticism does not take into account the range of possibilities the employer might have other than threats to potential tortfeasant employees for keeping other employees or members of the public safe—improving the selection and training of employees and increasing the surveillance of the workplace, for example (cf. J. H. Verkerke, (1995) 81 Virginia LR 273). A particular criticism of public sector vicarious liability for intentional torts is that public authorities, unlike private enterprises, allegedly do not respond to financial incentives (see P. S. Atiyah, *The Damages Lottery* (1997) at e.g. p. 8 and p. 82). This criticism ignores the political realities of public sector budgeting—pressure to economise in the public sector comes from politicians who want to spend more on services or to reduce tax. Devoting public resources to law suits and compensation claims is unlikely to result in re-election.

4.   In *Bernard v Attorney General of Jamaica* [2004] UKPC 47, the claimant had been using a public telephone when an off-duty police officer shouted 'police' and demanded to use the telephone. When the claimant refused, the policeman shot him. The Privy Council held that although 'the principle of vicarious liability is not infinitely extendable' (per Lord Steyn at [23]), the officer's acts were sufficiently closely connected to his employment to render the Jamaican police force vicariously liable for the shooting. It was of 'prime importance' that the incident 'followed immediately upon the constable's announcement that he was a policeman' (at [25]). Also, by allowing officers to carry service revolvers when off duty, 'the risks created by the police authorities reinforce the conclusion that vicarious liability is established' (at [27]). Contrast *Attorney General of the British Virgin Islands v Hartwell* [2004] UKPC 12, where an off-duty policeman, enraged by jealousy, shot at a man he had seen with his girlfriend in a bar, missing him and seriously injuring the claimant, a bystander. The Royal Virgin Islands Police Force was not vicariously liable for the shooting. The officer's conduct 'had nothing whatever to do with any police duties, either actually or ostensibly'; he had 'put aside his role as a police constable' to embark on 'a personal vendetta': 'That conduct falls wholly within the classical phrase of a "frolic of his own",' (per Lord Nicholls at [17]). However, the police force had been in breach of its own duty of care: 'when entrusting a police officer with a gun the police authorities owe to the public at large a duty to take reasonable care to see the officer is a suitable person to be entrusted with such a dangerous weapon'. Although this was a far-reaching duty, the hazardous nature of loaded guns justified it, and required a high degree of care from the force which on the facts (given the officer's history of threatening behaviour) they had failed to demonstrate.

5.   In *Mattis v Pollock (t/a Flamingos Nightclub)* [2004] 4 All ER 85, [2003] EWCA Civ 887 a nightclub bouncer of known aggressive disposition had been beaten up by a group of patrons; having fled the scene, the bouncer returned with a knife and attacked the group, seriously injuring the claimant. The Court of Appeal held the owner of the nightclub vicariously liable. It was important that a bouncer could be anticipated to use violence in carrying out his duties; indeed, 'he was encouraged and expected to perform his duties in an aggressive and intimidatory manner', at [30]. Had it been necessary, the court would also have held the defendant personally liable for negligence, by his encouraging violent behaviour. The case is analysed by R. Weekes [2004] CLJ 53. An

earlier account of vicarious liability for an employee's assaults (considered in *Mattis v Pollock*) is by F. D. Rose (1977) 40 MLR 420.

6.   Some writers have tried to develop purely causation-based theories of vicarious liability (e.g. A. Sykes (1988) 101 Harvard LR 563). The fundamental objection to these theories is that they are trying to substitute factual causation for legal causation, for the attribution of responsibility. The point of the 'course of employment' rule is to set the boundaries of the organisation's responsibility, which is not a merely factual question. Note that the contract of employment requirement is another aspect of the same issue of the boundaries of the organisation's responsibility.

7.   On the question of vicarious liability for statutory torts, see *Majrowski v Guy's and St Thomas's NHS Trust* [2006] 4 All ER 395, [2006] UKHL 34, noted p. 1103, post.

5 LIABILITY FOR INDEPENDENT CONTRACTORS

■ Alcock v Wraith

Court of Appeal (1991) 59 BLR 16

The facts are not material.

NEILL LJ: . . .

[W]here someone employs an independent contractor to do work on his behalf he is not in the ordinary way responsible for any tort committed by the contractor in the course of the execution of the work. . . . .

The main exceptions to the principle fall into the following categories:

(a) Cases where the employer is under some statutory duty which he cannot delegate.

(b) Cases involving the withdrawal of support from neighbouring land.

(c) Cases involving the escape of fire.

(d) Cases involving the escape of substances, such as explosives, which have been brought on to the land and which are likely to do damage if they escape; liability will attach under the rule in *Rylands v Fletcher* (1868) LR 3 HL 330.

(e) Cases involving operations on the highway which may cause danger to persons using the highway.

(f) Cases involving non-delegable duties of an employer for the safety of his employees.

(g) Cases involving extra-hazardous acts.

In the present case the relevant categories for consideration are categories (b) and (g). In addition, I propose to examine whether there is a further exception which can be relied upon in cases of nuisance.

The withdrawal of support cases

In the course of his judgment Judge Hall [below] referred to the decision in *Bower v Peate* (1876) 1 QBD 321. In that case the defendant employed a contractor to pull down his house and rebuild it. The adjoining house, which belonged to the plaintiff, was damaged as a result of the work. The defendant was held liable. At page 326 Lord Cockburn CJ said:

" . . . a man who orders work to be executed, from which, in the natural course of things, injurious consequences to his neighbour must be expected to arise, unless means are adopted by which such consequences may be prevented, is bound to see to the doing of that which is necessary to prevent the mischief, and cannot relieve himself of his responsibility by employing someone else—whether it be the contractor employed to do the work from which the danger arises or some independent person—to do what is necessary to prevent the act he has ordered to be done from becoming wrongful."

The decision in *Bower v Peate* was approved by the House of Lords in *Dalton v Angus* (1881) 6 App Cas 740 and in *Hughes v Percival* (1883) 8 App Cas 443, though in the latter case Lord Blackburn considered that Lord Cockburn might have stated the exception to the general rule too broadly. Lord Blackburn limited the exception to work on a party-wall. He put the matter as follows at page 446:

" …I think that the duty went as far as to require him [the defendant] to see that reasonable skill and care were exercised in those operations which involved a use of the party-wall, exposing it to this risk. If such a duty was cast upon the defendant he could not get rid of responsibility by delegating the performance of it to a third person."

Cases involving extra-hazardous activities
A clear statement of the exception which applies in the case of extra-hazardous activities is to be found in the judgment of the Court of Appeal delivered by Slesser LJ in *Honeywell and Stein v Larkin Brothers Ltd* [1934] 1 KB 191. At page 196 Slesser LJ said:

"It is established as a general rule of English law that an employer is not liable for the acts of his independent contractor in the same way as he is for the acts of his servants or agents, even though these acts are done in carrying out the work for his benefit under the contract…But there are exceptions to this rule; it may be that, as in other cases of vicarious liability, the tendency of the English law, as it has developed…, has been rather to enlarge the scope of these exceptions, but the development has followed certain broad lines. It is clear that the ultimate employer is not responsible for the acts of an independent contractor merely because what is to be done will involve danger to others if negligently done. The incidence of this liability is limited to certain defined classes, and for the purpose of this case it is only necessary to consider that part of this rule of liability which has reference to extra-hazardous acts, that is, acts which, in their very nature, involve in the eyes of the law special danger to others; of such acts the causing of fire and explosion are obvious and established instances."

Slesser LJ then referred to some of the earlier cases and at page 199 approved the statement of principle by Talbot J in *Brooke v Bool* [1928] 2 KB 578 at 587:

"The principle is that if a man does work on or near another's property which involves danger to that property unless proper care is taken, he is liable to the owners of the property for damage resulting to it from the failure to take proper care, and is equally liable if, instead of doing the work himself, he procures another, whether agent, servant or otherwise, to do it for him."

A little later Slesser LJ continued:

"Even of [extra-hazardous and dangerous operations] it may be predicated that if carefully and skilfully performed, no harm will follow; as instances of such operations may be given those of removing support from adjoining houses, doing dangerous work on the highway, or creating fire or explosion: hence it may be said, in one sense, that such operations are not necessarily attended with risk. But the rule of liability for independent contractors' acts attaches to these operations, because they are inherently dangerous and hence are done at the principal employer's peril."

The exception relating to extra-hazardous activities was considered again by the Court of Appeal in *Salsbury v Woodland* [1970] 1 QB 324, where the plaintiff's injuries were due in part to the negligence of a contractor who, in the course of removing a large tree from a garden, broke some telephone wires which fell into the roadway and caused an obstruction. The judge held that the occupier of the house who had employed the tree-felling contractor was liable "because there was an inherent risk of injury to others when the tree was felled unless proper care was taken to get rid of the risk". This conclusion, however, was unanimously rejected by the Court of Appeal. At page 338 Widgery LJ said:

"The act commissioned in the present case, if done with ordinary elementary caution by skilled men, presented no hazard to anyone at all."

Later at page 345 Harman LJ expressed himself in similar terms:

"The act of felling the tree did involve danger to others because it was negligently done. But it was a perfectly simple job to remove this tree without causing any danger to anybody and it was not work which was inherently dangerous so as to come within that exception."

Cases of nuisance

I have already referred to the fact that a neighbour can make a claim for compensation if a party-wall is damaged by work on an adjoining property and that he can do so even though the work is carried out by an independent contractor. It is therefore necessary to consider whether this exception to the general rule extends to all cases where property is affected by a nuisance committed on adjoining land.

It seems clear, however, that the general rule applies to the tort of nuisance as well as to other torts. In *Matania v National Provincial Bank* [1936] 2 All ER 633 the Court of Appeal was concerned with a claim for damages for nuisance caused by dust and noise during building operations on premises of which Mr Matania occupied the second and third floors. At page 645 Slesser LJ stated the general rule:

"There is no doubt in this case that Messrs Adamson are independent contractors, and being independent contractors, save for exceptional circumstances, in the ordinary way those employing them would not be liable for their wrongful acts in negligence or in nuisance."

Later in his judgment, however, Slesser LJ, having examined the facts, concluded that the work did constitute a hazardous operation within the exception to the general rule. Romer LJ took the same view, regarding the work as "work which of its very nature involves a risk of damage being occasioned to a third party." Finlay J, who was the third member of the court, expressed his opinion as follows:

"...I have been convinced that when the facts here are carefully examined it does appear that this is not a case of mere ordinary building operation; it is a case where unless precautions were taken there was a great and obvious danger that nuisance would be caused, as indeed it was caused."

Accordingly it seems to me to be clear that both the general rule and the exceptions apply whether the action is framed in negligence or nuisance. Furthermore, I am not aware of any different approach being adopted in an action for trespass. Thus, as I understand the matter, there is a general rule, which applies to all three torts, that an employer is not liable for the torts of an independent contractor. But there is also an established exception where the contractor is employed to carry out a task which is extra-hazardous. It is not possible in my judgment to provide a list of activities which will be regarded as "extra-hazardous" so as to fall within this exception, but it is clear that the activity must involve some special risk of damage, or—to use the test approved by Atkin LJ in *Belvedere Fish Guano Co Ltd v Rainham Chemical Works Ltd* [1920] 2 KB 487 at page 504 and by Harman LJ in *Salsbury*'s case at page 345—the work must be work "which from its very nature is likely to cause danger." I would only add that in many cases it will be more appropriate to substitute "damage" for "danger" in Atkin LJ's test. What one looks for is to see whether there is some special risk or whether the works from its very nature is likely to cause danger or damage.

■ A (a child) v Ministry of Defence
Court of Appeal [2005] QB 183

The Ministry of Defence contracted with German hospitals to provide health care for military personnel serving in Germany, and their dependants. The claimant son of a British Army soldier suffered brain damage through the negligence of one of the German hospitals' obstetricians. The claimant accepted that the Ministry was not vicariously liable for the negligence of staff at the German hospitals, but argued that the Ministry had a non-delegable duty of care to ensure that A was provided with adequate medical treatment. Bell J [2003] PIQR P607 dismissed the claim, and the claimant appealed.

LORD PHILLIPS OF WORTH MATRAVERS MR: . . .

[29] The circumstances that give rise to the non-delegable duty of care that [the claimant] seeks to establish are not readily identifiable in English case law. They perplexed Professor Glanville Williams nearly 50 years ago (see 'Liability for Independent Contractors' [1956] CLJ 180, 183) and they have become little clearer since then. The general rule is that a defendant will be liable for the negligent act of a servant committed in the course of his employment but not for the negligent act of an independent contractor. . . .

[30] *Charlesworth & Percy on Negligence*, 10th ed (2003), paras 2-278–2-302, explores the situations in which the courts have held a defendant to have been under a personal duty to exercise reasonable care which he could not delegate. In most cases it is possible to identify considerations of policy which led to the imposition of the duty. Thus, if a person intends to carry out a dangerous activity, he will owe a personal duty to ensure that reasonable care is exercised in relation to it because public policy requires that, whether he carries out the activity himself or engages another to do so, he should see that proper precautions are taken. In the field of employment, the courts have held that an employer owes a personal duty to ensure that reasonable care is taken for the safety of his workmen which he cannot delegate: see *Wilsons and Clyde Coal Co Ltd v English* [1938] AC 57. This decision has been said to have been motivated by the desire to escape the injustice flowing from the doctrine of common employment. . . .

[32] Those responsible for the operation of a hospital offer a medical service to those whom they accept for treatment. Some of the authorities recognise that this acceptance for treatment carries with it personal positive duties to the patient which cannot be discharged by delegation. . . .

[50] Mr Tattersall [counsel for the claimant] argued that, as a matter of public policy, it was desirable that British servicemen and their dependants should be able to sue the MoD in this country in respect of medical negligence suffered in a foreign hospital rather than being constrained to bring proceedings in the foreign jurisdiction in question. He sought to buttress his argument by reference to a paper for the guidance of primary care and acute trusts published by in November 2002: see the Department of Health Guidance for Primary Care and Acute Trusts: 'Treating more patients and extending choice: Overseas treatment for NHS patients'. . . .

[51] Mr Tattersall points to the statement that it is the Government's policy preference that NHS patients should be able to sue the NHS in the English courts, rather than have to resort to litigation abroad. He submits that this public policy must be equally applicable in the case of foreign hospital treatment provided to service personnel and their dependants. More generally, he submits that it is plainly desirable that claims such as that of A should be brought against the MoD rather than the foreign hospital.

Conclusions

[52] Mr Tattersall's submissions seek to extend the law of negligence beyond any previous decision of the English court, subject to one exception. The exception is the finding of the existence of a non-delegable duty of care made by Judge Garner as one of the grounds of his decision in *M v Calderdale and*

Kirklees Health Authority [1998] Lloyd's Rep Med 157. This finding did not represent the current state of English law. It seems to have been based on the observations of Lord Greene MR in *Gold v Essex County Council* [1942] 2 KB 293 and of Denning LJ in *Cassidy v Ministry of Health* [1951] 2 KB 343, although in neither instance did these represent the reasons for the decision of the majority of the court.

[53] … Thus Mr Tattersall is realistic in accepting, as he did, that, if he is to succeed on his appeal, he must persuade us on policy grounds to expand this area of tortious liability.

[54] The guidance paper on which Mr Tattersall relies appears to be contemplating claims against an NHS trust for breach of an organisational duty rather than the type of duty that he seeks to establish in this case. Even if it were correct to hold that an NHS trust, which sends one of its patients abroad for treatment, owes a non-delegable duty to ensure that the patient receives careful treatment, it would not follow that the same was true of the MoD in this case.

[55] The MoD is no longer in the business of treating patients in hospital in Germany. Its sole role is that of arranging for such treatment to be provided by others. If there is merit in Mr Tattersall's argument of public policy, it can only lie in his basic proposition that it is plainly desirable that someone in the position of A and his parents should be able to bring proceedings against the MoD in England rather than against the hospital in Germany. Despite Mr Tattersall's submissions, I remain unpersuaded of this. …

[60] There is no suggestion here that there has been any fault on the part of the MoD. There is no suggestion that the imposition of the duty of care for which Mr Tattersall contends would or could impact on the care actually taken by [the designated German hospitals]. In these circumstances I can see no justification for imposing a non-delegable duty on the MoD to ensure that due skill and care is exercised in those hospitals. It seems to me that Germany is the appropriate forum for this litigation and that the [German hospital] is the appropriate defendant. …

[TUCKEY LJ agreed. WALL LJ gave a judgment in favour of dismissing the appeal in which he agreed with LORD PHILLIPS.]

Appeal dismissed.

NOTES

1.   The meaning of 'extra-hazardous' is far from clear. One approach, taken by *Salsbury v Woodland* [1970] 1 QB 324, [1969] 3 All ER 863, is that an activity is extra-hazardous when the risk of substantial harm cannot be eliminated by reasonable care. In other words, the activity is inherently dangerous and there is a question mark over whether it should be attempted at all. The other approach, taken by Slesser LJ in *Honeywell and Stein v Larkin Brothers Ltd* [1934] 1 KB 191, [1933] All ER Rep 77 is that even extra-hazardous activities can be safe 'if carefully and skilfully performed'—they are merely more risky than other activities. The difficulty with the latter suggestion is that it is difficult to say by how much the risk has to exceed ordinary risks. Indeed, *Honeywell v Larkin Bros* holds that using an old-fashioned magnesium photographer's flash was 'extra-hazardous', but it is surely no more dangerous than, for example, driving a car. See G. L. Williams [1956] CLJ 180 at p. 186. In *Bottomley v Todmorden Cricket Club* [2004] PIQR P18, [2003] EWCA Civ 1575 Brooke LJ decided that it was not necessary to consider the criticisms made of *Honeywell v Larkin Bros*, but commented at [50] that 'it may well be that the House of Lords today would prefer to avoid subtle distinctions between what is and is not "extra-hazardous" and would follow Mason J. when he said [in *Stevens v Brodribb Sawmilling Co Pty Ltd* (1986) 160 CLR 16, 30]: "[T]he traditional common law response to the creation of a special danger is not to impose strict liability but to insist on a higher standard of care in the performance of an existing duty".'

2.   In *Gwilliam v West Hertfordshire Hospitals NHS Trust* [2003] QB 443, [2002] EWCA Civ 1041 the defendant engaged contractors to provide a fairground attraction (a 'splat wall') at a fete. The contractors injured the claimant by their negligence, but proved both impecunious and to lack public liability insurance. Waller LJ at [38] suggested that 'logically there is no reason why, even though the activity is not so hazardous as to impose liability on the employer without more, it may be hazardous enough and the circumstances such as to impose the slightly lesser duty in relation to the quality of the independent contractor in the sense of the ability of that independent contractor to meet a claim'. Thus given the nature of the activities in the case at hand, 'which, if not extra-hazardous, were hazardous' (at [43]) Waller LJ would have held it fair, just, and reasonable to impose upon the defendant employer a duty to check that the contractor was insured against potential liability in tort. However, Lord Woolf CJ gave rather different reasons for reaching a similar conclusion, and Sedley LJ disagreed altogether.

      In *Payling v Naylor (t/a Mainstreet)* [2004] PIQR P36, [2004] EWCA Civ 560, it was held that *Gwilliam* ('a difficult case on any view' per Neuberger LJ at [37]) did not create a general duty to check the insurance status of independent contractors. 'To invent a third and intermediate category, where the task is hazardous but not extra hazardous, and where the employer can delegate but only if he satisfies himself that the independent contractor is insured or otherwise good for a claim, seems to me to be unnecessary and to introduce an undesirable degree of rigidity into the field . . . [and] is unwarranted by authority' (per Neuberger LJ at [37]–[38]).

      For the occupiers' liability aspects of these cases, see note 3, p. 581, ante.

3.   *Salsbury v Woodland* [1970] 1 QB 324, [1969] 3 All ER 863 also considered the 'highway' cases (category (e) in Neill LJ's list in *Alcock v Wraith*, ante). The Court of Appeal held that the contractor's work must actually be carried out on the highway for the employer to be liable, and the category did not extend to cases like *Salsbury* itself of 'work to be done near a highway in circumstances in which, if due care is not taken, injury to passers-by on the highway may be caused'.

4.   Many judges (see e.g. *Re R (a minor) (No 2)* (1996) 33 BMLR 178, noted p. 1058, ante) treat 'direct' duties and 'non-delegable' duties as the same thing. Another view is that the two concepts are distinct, on the ground that it is possible to fulfil a 'direct' duty by choosing competent people to carry out the task (see e.g. *Maguire v Sefton Metropolitan Borough Council* [2006] 1 WLR 2550, [2006] EWCA Civ 316, noted p. 569, ante), but it is not possible to fulfil a 'non-delegable' duty in that way. The objection to the latter view is that a 'direct' duty is not very direct if it can be delegated. But, it is submitted, a better approach would be to treat the 'direct' duties as asking the question: 'has the organisation chosen a reasonable method to deal with the relevant risk of harm?' The choice of competent people to deal with the risk would be one part of the method the organisation has chosen, but would not be the only relevant consideration. That would leave 'non-delegability' to deal simply with the question of vicarious liability for the torts of independent contractors (cf. *McDermid v Nash Dredging and Reclamation Co Ltd* [1987] AC 906, [1987] 2 All ER 878).

5.   As regards an occupier's liability for the acts of independent contractors, see s. 2(4)(b) of the Occupiers Liability Act 1957 (p. 565, ante); and for the liability of highway authorities see s. 58 of the Highways Act 1980.

6.   For analysis of the non-delegable duty concept in comparison with vicarious liability, see the essay by R. Stevens in *Emerging Issues in Tort Law*, edited by J. Neyers et al, (Oxford, 2007), chap. 13 and by J. Murphy, ibid, chap. 14.

6 EMPLOYER'S LIABILITY TO EMPLOYEES

Although largely a matter of contract law, and now much governed by statute at both national and European level (see pp. 1104–1107, ante), the duties of employers towards their employees are often highly relevant in the context of vicarious liability since the claimant is often a fellow employee who has been injured at work. For ease of reference we provide here some materials concerning employers' duties, but for detailed coverage readers are referred to the general works on employment law, e.g. Deakin and Morris, op cit. and specialist works on health and safety at work, e.g. M. Ford, *Redgrave's Health and Safety* 4th edn (2002).

(a) At common law

■ Wilsons and Clyde Coal Co Ltd v English
House of Lords [1937] 3 All ER 628

The pursuer claimed damages in respect of personal injuries sustained while employed at the defendant company's Glencraig Colliery, Fife. At the end of a day-shift, as he was proceeding to the pit-bottom, he was crushed when the haulage plant was set in motion. His case was that it was a necessary part of a safe system of working, and recognised mining practice, that during the time when day-shift men were being raised to the surface the haulage plant should be stopped. The defendants claimed that they had effectively discharged their duty of providing a safe system of work by appointing a qualified manager, and they relied upon s. 2(4) of the Coal Mines Act 1911 which provided that only a qualified manager could control the technical management of the mine. In an appeal against an interlocutor pronounced by a court of seven judges of the Court of Session the House of Lords unanimously rejected this defence, and dismissed the appeal.

LORD WRIGHT: . . .
I do not mean that employers warrant the adequacy of plant, or the competence of fellow-employees, or the propriety of the system of work. The obligation is fulfilled by the exercise of due care and skill. But it is not fulfilled by entrusting its fulfilment to employees, even though selected with due care and skill. The obligation is threefold, 'the provision of a competent staff of men, adequate material, and a proper system and effective supervision' . . . .

The well established, but illogical, doctrine of common employment is certainly one not to be extended, and indeed has never in its long career been pushed so far as the Court of Appeal[14] sought to push it. . . .

I think the whole course of authority consistently recognises a duty which rests on the employer, and which is personal to the employer, to take reasonable care for the safety of his workmen, whether the employer be an individual, a firm, or a company, and whether or not the employer takes any share in the conduct of the operations. The obligation is threefold, as I have explained. The obligation to provide and maintain proper plant and appliances is a continuing obligation. It is not, however, broken by a mere misuse of, or failure to use, proper plant and appliances, due to the negligence of a fellow-servant, or a merely temporary failure to keep in order or adjust plant and appliances, or a casual departure from the system of working, if these matters can be regarded as the casual negligence of the managers, foremen, or other employees. It may be difficult, in some cases, to distinguish, on the

---

[14] Inter alia, in *Fanton v Denville* [1932] 2 KB 309.

facts, between the employer's failure to provide and maintain and the fellow-servants' negligence in the respects indicated. . . .

[LORD THANKERTON, LORD MACMILLAN, and LORD MAUGHAM delivered speeches in favour of dismissing the appeal. LORD ATKIN agreed with all the speeches.]

NOTES

1. The main purpose of the creation of 'personal' duties was the evasion of the 'common employment' or 'fellow servant' rule, according to which no action lay at the suit of an employee against the employer for injuries caused by another employee. The rule was said to have arisen from *Priestley v Fowler* [1835–42] All ER Rep 449. It was finally abolished the Law Reform (Personal Injuries) Act 1948, s. 1.

2. In *Wilson v Tyneside Cleaning Co* [1958] 2 QB 110, [1958] 2 All ER 265, Pearce LJ pointed out that, whereas 'Lord Wright [in *Wilsons and Clyde Coal*] divided up the duty of a master into three main headings, for convenience of definition or argument; but all three are ultimately only manifestations of the same duty of the master to take reasonable care so as to carry out his operations as not to subject those employed by him to unnecessary risk.' The duty is often said to amount to a duty to provide a 'safe system of work'.

3. *McDermid v Nash Dredging and Reclamation Co Ltd* [1987] AC 906, [1987] 2 All ER 878 (noted p. 1058, ante) shows that these duties are 'non-delegable' in the sense that the employer is liable whether it uses an employee or an independent contractor in attempting to fulfil them. The employer is not released from them merely by requiring the employee to work under the direction of another employer. Moreover, it is irrelevant whether the other employer would count as the employer for the purposes of vicarious liability.

4. The duty to provide proper plant, equipment and premises, overlaps with the occupier's duty to visitors, and is stringently interpreted: see e.g. *General Cleaning Contractors Ltd v Christmas* [1953] AC 180, [1952] 2 All ER 1110 (safe system includes an adequate system of instruction and supply of necessary protective equipment); cf. *Wilson v Tyneside Window Cleaning Co* (duty extends to premises not in employer's occupation, but less will be required of an employer when the employee is on someone else's premises).

5. It is compulsory for employers to insure against their liability to employees: Employers' Liability (Compulsory Insurance) Act 1969, p. 1146, post.

6. The provisions of s. 1(3) of the Law Reform (Personal Injuries) Act 1948 prevent contracting-out only of the employer's vicarious liability to an employee. Section 2(1) of the Unfair Contract Terms Act 1977 (p. 462, ante) supplements this by rendering void any term of a contract or notice which excludes or restricts liability for death or personal injury resulting from negligence. Section 2(2) prohibits exclusions or restrictions for negligence in the case of other 'loss or damage' (e.g. to the employee's property) unless the terms of the notice are 'reasonable'. These provisions cover both personal and vicarious liability.

7. The employer's duty extends to preventing psychiatric harm. After *White v Chief Constable of South Yorkshire Police* [1999] 2 AC 455, [1999] 1 All ER 1 (p. 137, ante) it was initially unclear whether employees outside the zone of physical danger would be primary or secondary victims for the purpose of 'nervous shock' and the '*Alcock*

tests' (pp. 120–132, ante). However in *Hatton v Sutherland* [2002] 2 All ER 1, [2002] EWCA Civ 76 (p. 146, ante) (reversed on different grounds sub nom *Barber v Somerset County Council* [2004] 2 All ER 385, [2004] UKHL 13), it was held that *Walker v Northumberland County Council* [1995] 1 All ER 737 remained good law—an employer is liable for psychiatric harm to employees caused by negligently subjecting them to unreasonable stress. In *Hatton* at [43], Hale LJ set out 16 propositions as guidelines for courts deciding whether employers are in breach of their duty of care in this context. These have proved very influential in later stress-at-work cases: see e.g. *Hartman v South Essex Mental Health and Community Care NHS Trust* [2005] EWCA Civ 6. However, in *Daw v Intel Corpn (UK) Ltd* [2007] 2 All ER 126, [2007] EWCA Civ 70 the court rejected the submission that for consistency's sake, 'there should be close adherence to the principles set out in *Hatton*'. Thus, although Hale LJ's 'eleventh proposition' states that 'An employer who offers a confidential advice service, with referral to appropriate counselling or treatment services, is unlikely to be found in breach of duty', it had been open to the trial judge to find on the facts of the case that the employer had not performed its duty to an overworked employee by making counselling available. 'The reference to counselling services in *Hatton* does not make such services a panacea by which employers can discharge their duty of care in all cases,' stated Pill LJ at [45].

8. Stress in the workplace is an extremely important problem. In 2006–7 according to Health and Safety Executive statistics, 13.8 million working days were lost through work-related stress, depression, or anxiety in Great Britain (out of 35.7 million lost days from all illnesses and injuries). It was the single biggest cause (next came musculo-skeletal disorders, responsible for 10.7 million lost days). Accidental injuries at work accounted for 5.8 million lost days.

9. In *Majrowski v Guy's and St Thomas's NHS Trust* [2006] 4 All ER 395, [2006] UKHL 34 the House of Lords held an employer vicariously liable for one employee's harassment of another employee, a tort sounding in damages under s. 3 of the Protection from Harassment Act 1997 (on which see p. 745, ante). Lord Nicholls stated at [16] that as a general principle, an employer will be liable for his employees' tortious breach of statutory duty unless the relevant provisions expressly or impliedly exclude that liability. That was not the case with the 1997 Act, and the prospect of a multiplicity of claims for workplace harassment did not provide sufficient reason to exclude vicarious liability: [29]–[30]. However, Lord Hope, Baroness Hale, and Lord Brown concurred with reluctance, feeling compelled by s. 10 of the 1997 Act (which inserts a new section into the Prescription and Limitation (Scotland) Act 1973 envisaging that the employer of a person responsible for harassment may be the defender in an action). Lady Hale pointed out at [69] that the result of the decision would be to circumvent the 'sound policy' whereby 'our law does not generally award damages for anxiety and injury to feelings unless these are so severe as to amount to a recognised psychiatric illness' (see pp. 118–119, ante), making further reference to the 'compensation culture' and to what is now the Compensation Act 2006 (p. 323, ante). The case is noted by B. Barrett (2006) 35 ILJ 431.

10. For further examples of the standard of care owed by employers to employees, see *Withers v Perry Chain Co Ltd* [1961] 3 All ER 676, [1961] 1 WLR 1314 (noted p. 317, ante) and *Sussex Ambulance NHS Trust v King* [2002] ICR 1413, [2002] EWCA Civ 953 (p. 322, ante).

(b) Statutory supplementation of common law rights

■ The Employers' Liability (Defective Equipment) Act 1969

1. Extension of employer's liability for defective equipment

(1) Where after the commencement of this Act

   (a) an employee suffers personal injury in the course of his employment in consequence of a defect in equipment provided by his employer for the purposes of the employer's business; and

   (b) the defect is attributable wholly or partly to the fault of a third party (whether identified or not),

the injury shall be deemed to be also attributable to negligence on the part of the employer (whether or not he is liable in respect of the injury apart from this subsection), but without prejudice to the law relating to contributory negligence and to any remedy by way of contribution or in contract or otherwise which is available to the employer in respect of the injury.

(2) In so far as any agreement purports to exclude or limit any liability of an employer arising under subsection (1) of this section, the agreement shall be void.

(3) In this section

'business' includes the activities carried on by any public body;

'employee' means a person who is employed by another person under a contract of service or apprenticeship and is so employed for the purposes of a business carried on by that other person, and 'employer' shall be construed accordingly;

'equipment' includes any plant and machinery, vehicle, aircraft and clothing;

'fault' means negligence, breach of statutory duty or other act or omission which gives rise to liability in tort in England and Wales or which is wrongful and gives rise to liability in damages in Scotland;

'personal injury' includes loss of life, any impairment of a person's physical or mental condition and any disease.

(4) This section binds the Crown, and persons in the service of the Crown shall accordingly be treated for the purposes of this section as employees of the Crown if they would not be so treated apart from this subsection.

NOTES

1.   The purpose of this statute was to overcome the effects of the decision in *Davie v New Merton Board Mills Ltd* [1959] AC 604, [1959] 1 All ER 346. In that case the claimant employee was blinded when a particle of metal chipped off the tool with which he was working. The employer had purchased the tool from reputable suppliers who, in turn, had bought in from reputable manufacturers. There had been negligence in the course of manufacture which had caused the tool to become excessively hard, but outwardly the tool was in good condition. The manufacturers were liable under the *Donoghue v Stevenson* rule (p. 30, ante). Most people believed that in such circumstances the employer would be liable too, because in *Wilsons and Clyde Coal Co Ltd v English* [1938] AC 57, [1937] 3 All ER 628 (p. 1101, ante) the House of Lords had held that the employer's threefold duty (to provide (a) competent staff, (b) proper plant, premises, and material, and (c) a safe system of work) was *personal* and *non-delegable*. It was thought to follow from this that an employer cannot delegate to an 'independent contractor' his duty to provide proper tools. However, in *Davie's* case the House of Lords

held that an employer who buys a tool from a reputable supplier or manufacturer does not 'delegate' his duty: he 'discharges' it. This restriction on the 'non-delegation' doctrine was criticised on legal and social grounds. The practical effect of the decision was to leave the injured employee without compensation where the negligent manufacturer or supplier could not be identified or was bankrupt. The Employer's Liability (Defective Equipment) Act 1969 did not, however, entirely remedy the situation: see B.A. Hepple [1970] CLJ 25. The employee still has to prove 'fault' against the third party. But note that the one effect of the Consumer Protection Act 1987 might have been to improve the employee's position, since the definition of 'fault' in the 1969 Act includes 'breach of statutory duty or other act or omission which gives rise to liability in tort', which presumably covers the 1987 Act. See pp. 629–651, ante and *Howarth*, p. 439.

2.   In *Coltman v Bibby Tankers Ltd* [1988] AC 276, [1987] 3 All ER 1068, the House of Lords held that the word 'equipment' in s. 1(1) of the Act includes a ship provided by the employer for the purposes of his business. Although their Lordships could not find any rational basis for the failure to mention ships, alongside vehicles and transport, in the statutory definition, the width of that definition as well as the purpose of the Act led them to conclude that the Act covers defective plant of every sort with which the employee is compelled to work. In *Knowles v Liverpool City Council* [1993] 4 All ER 321, [1993] 1 WLR 1428, the House of Lords further held that a flagstone could be 'equipment', even though it was more naturally described as the 'material' used. The House of Lords said that the 1969 Act should be interpreted widely and that 'equipment' should include whatever the employer used for the purposes of the business.

■ The Health and Safety at Work Act 1974

2. General duties of employers to their employees

(1) It shall be the duty of every employer to ensure, so far as is reasonably practicable, the health, safety and welfare at work of all his employees.

15. Health and safety regulations

(1) …the Secretary of State shall have power to make regulations under this section for any of the general purposes of this Part…

47. Civil liability

(1) Nothing in this Part shall be construed—

   (a) as conferring a right of action in any civil proceedings in respect of any failure to comply with any duty imposed by sections 2 to 7 […]

(2) Breach of a duty imposed by health and safety regulations…shall, so far as it causes damage, be actionable except in so far as the regulations provide otherwise.

■ The Personal Protective Equipment at Work Regulations 1992

Interpretation

Reg. 2.—(1) In these Regulations, unless the context otherwise requires, 'personal protective equipment' means all equipment (including clothing affording protection against the weather) which is intended to be worn or held by a person at work and which protects him against one or more risks to his health or safety, and any addition or accessory designed to meet that objective.

Provision of personal protective equipment

Reg. 4.—(1) Every employer shall ensure that suitable personal protective equipment is provided to his employees who may be exposed to a risk to their health or safety while at work except where and to the extent that such risk has been adequately controlled by other means which are equally or more effective.

Maintenance and replacement of personal protective equipment

Reg. 7.—(1) Every employer shall ensure that any personal protective equipment provided to his employees is maintained (including replaced or cleaned as appropriate) in an efficient state, in efficient working order and in good repair.

■ Fytche v Wincanton Logistics plc

House of Lords [2004] 4 All ER 221

The claimant was employed by the defendant company to deliver milk, and supplied with steel-toecapped boots to protect his feet from injury. One day while on duty, his milk tanker became stuck in a snow-drift. He attempted to dig it out. He contracted frostbite in his toe, because of a small hole in one of the boots which allowed penetration of the freezing water. He claimed that the boots were personal protective equipment that his employers had failed to maintain in good repair, contrary to Reg. 7(1) of the Personal Protective Equipment at Work Regulations 1992 (ante), and that the defendants were therefore liable for his frost-bitten toe. The trial judge found that the boots were adequate for the claimant's ordinary conditions of work, and dismissed the claim. The Court of Appeal [2003] EWCA Civ 874, [2003] ICR 1582 dismissed the claimant's appeal and he appealed to the House of Lords.

LORD HOFFMANN: . . .

[6] . . . Mr Fytche says that the existence of the hole meant that the boots were out of repair. Liability under the regulations is strict and the company is therefore liable for damage caused by the want of repair.

[7] Before even looking at the regulations, I am bound to say that this would be a very strange and arbitrary result. Mr Fytche claims that because his boots were designed to protect him against a risk of his employment, his employers are liable in damages because they were inadequate to protect him against an injury which was not a risk of his employment. If there had been no risks from heavy objects and he had been issued with ordinary leather boots without steel toecaps, the boots would not have been PPE [personal protective equipment] and the existence of the hole would not have given rise to any liability. I suppose that legislation can sometimes have these ricochet consequences but one usually expects a more rational scheme.

[15] Mr Fytche was provided with steel toecaps on his boots because his employers considered that there was a sufficient risk of heavy things falling on his feet. The boots were therefore PPE and there is nothing to suggest that they failed any of the tests of suitability. They fitted, were appropriate for conditions in milk parlours and so on. Nor did the hole in one of the boots create a secondary risk or increase overall risk. The secondary risk or overall risk must be a risk in the course of employment. As Mr Fytche was not expected to do anything which required him to have waterproof boots, the hole created no such risk. If, as my noble and learned friend Baroness Hale of Richmond suggests, there had been a weather risk against which the boots should have protected Mr Fytche, then of course he would have been able to recover. PPE includes 'clothing affording protection against the weather'. But Mr Fytche does not suggest that he should have been given PPE to protect him against the weather. He was not expected to expose himself to severe weather conditions and for ordinary purposes the boots were adequate. His case depends entirely on the irrelevant fact that he needed boots with steel toecaps.

[18] In my opinion, however, 'efficient state, in efficient working order and in good repair' is not an absolute concept but must be construed in relation to what makes the equipment PPE. What counts as being in an efficient state? Efficient for what purpose? In my opinion, for the purpose of protecting against the relevant risk. Regulation 7 extends in time the duty to provide suitable PPE under reg 4. By virtue of reg 7, it is not enough just to provide it and then leave the employee to his own devices. The employer has a duty to maintain it so that it continues to be suitable PPE. But he does not have a duty to do repairs and maintenance which have nothing to do with its function as PPE.

[LORD WALKER OF GESTINGHORPE delivered a speech in favour of dismissing the appeal, and agreed with LORD HOFFMANN. LORD NICHOLLS OF BIRKENHEAD agreed with LORD HOFFMANN and LORD WALKER OF GESTINGTHORPE. LORD HOPE OF CRAIGHEAD and BARONESS HALE OF RICHMOND delivered speeches in favour of allowing the appeal.]

Appeal dismissed.

QUESTION

Baroness Hale in her dissenting speech at [62] stated:

There is nothing irrational in a legislative scheme which: (1) requires an employer to provide protective clothing in certain circumstances, (2) requires the employee to wear it, and (3) compensates the employee who is injured as a result of a defect in that clothing. The reason why the employee was provided with the clothing in the first place is a separate matter from the content of the duty. The legislation might decide to limit the employer's duty by reference to that reason or it might not.

Do you agree?

CHAPTER NINETEEN

JOINT LIABILITY

The problems with which the materials in this chapter are concerned arise where the *same* damage is attributable to the conduct of two or more tortfeasors. If the tortfeasors have all participated in the same act leading to that damage they are called *joint* tortfeasors. The main examples of joint tortfeasors are (a) the person who authorises, procures or instigates the commission of a tort and the person who carries out his instructions; (b) those who participate in a joint enterprise—e.g. *Brooke v Bool* [1928] 2 KB 578, [1928] All ER Rep 155 (p. 1070, ante)—or 'common design'—e.g. *Unilever plc v Gillette (UK) Ltd* [1989] RPC 583; (c) where a relationship of principal and agent exists between two persons—e.g. *Scarsbrook v Mason* [1961] 3 All ER 767; (d) where tortfeasors act in breach of a joint duty; and (e) employer and employee, where the employer is vicariously liable for the torts of his employee (p. 1059, ante). It appears from the case law that mere 'assistance' or 'facilitation' of tortious acts is *not* a sufficient participation link to justify the imposition of joint liability: it also appears that it is unlikely that there will be joint liability imposed for 'assisting' or 'inciting' the commission of a tort, without some element of procuring, authorisation or common design. See e.g. *CBS Songs v Amstrad Consumer Electronics plc* [1988] 1 AC 1013, at 1058, per Lord Templeman; *Credit Lyonnnis Bank Nederland NV v Export Credits Guarantee Dept* [2000] 1 AC 486, [1999] 1 All ER 929; *MCA Records Inc v Charly Records Ltd* [2002] FSR 401, [2001] EWCA Civ 1441; *Global Projects Management Ltd v Citigroup Inc* [2006] FSR 39, [2005] EWHC 2663. Joint liability has been described by Peter Birks as an 'obscure and under-theorised area of the law': P. Birks, *Butterworths Lectures 1990–1* (London, 1992), p. 100. However, for an excellent analysis of joint liability in tort, see H. Carty (1999) 29 LS 489. For the argument that the common law recognises a wider principle of secondary civil liability, see P. Sales [1990] CLJ 491: for discussion of attribution and accessory liability in the common law more generally, see *Stevens*, chaps 11–12.

In contrast to the position with joint tortfeasors, if there are several *independent* acts all leading to the same damage, then those liable for these acts are called *several concurrent* tortfeasors. An example would be an accident in which two cars collide due to the negligent driving of each driver, causing injury to a pedestrian. The drivers are *severally* liable, and they cannot be described as *joint* tortfeasors. (For an illustration from maritime law, see *The Koursk* [1924] P 140.)

The distinction between joint tortfeasors and several concurrent tortfeasors is of little practical significance, except in one situation. This is that the release by the claimant of one joint tortfeasor from his liability discharges all others liable with him, while the release of one of two or more several concurrent tortfeasors will not have this effect (*Cutler v McPhail* [1962] 2 QB 292, [1962] 2 All ER 474, p. 1110, post). This is an anachronism and the courts have mitigated the strict rules in two ways: (a) by deciding that a mere promise not to sue does not amount to a release; and (b) by allowing the claimant, when releasing one joint tortfeasor, to make an express reservation of rights against the other joint tortfeasors. Indeed, this reservation may even be implied: *Gardiner v Moore* [1969] 1 QB 55, [1966] 1 All ER 365.

In all other respects joint tortfeasors and several concurrent tortfeasors are alike. Each tortfeasor is liable in full for the whole of the damage caused to the claimant. Satisfaction by any one tortfeasor usually discharges the liability of the others to the claimant. Although two or more tortfeasors may be joined as co-defendants in the action, only one sum can be awarded as damages and that sum must be the *lowest* sum for which any of the individual defendants can be held liable (*Cassell & Co Ltd v Broome* [1972] AC 1027, [1972] 1 All ER 801). Accordingly, in the words of Lord Hope in *Jameson v Central Electricity Generating Board* [2000] 1 AC 455, [1999] 1 All ER 193 (p. 1114, post), 'As the law now stands, a claimant is barred from going on with a separate action against another tortfeasor if the judgment which he has obtained in the first action has been satisfied.' The question in *Jameson* was whether the same rule should apply where there had been a 'full and final settlement' with one concurrent tortfeasor. The House of Lords decided, controversially, that if the claimant should be taken as having admitted to having obtained full satisfaction of his claim via the settlement, then the claimant would be barred from proceeding against another tortfeasor. The decision in *Jameson* appeared to hand defendants a significant bargaining advantage, and may also have the unfortunate effect of making claimants less willing to settle. The scope of the *Jameson* decision was clarified in the subsequent House of Lords decision in *Heaton v Axa Equity and Law Life Assurance Society plc* [2002] 2 All ER 961, [2002] UKHL 15 (p. 1118, post), which lessens the potential negative consequences of the *Jameson* decision but may not eliminate them fully.

If a judgment is obtained against one tortfeasor but not satisfied, the judgment is not in itself, as it once was, a bar to later proceedings against the others (Civil Liability (Contribution) Act 1978, s. 3) but the claimant is not entitled to his costs in the second action (ibid, s. 4). There is a right of contribution between tortfeasors and it is with this right that the chapter is principally concerned. The Law Reform (Married Women and Tortfeasors) Act 1935 abolished the common law rule (*Merryweather v Nixan* (1799) 8 Term Rep 186) which denied this right. The relevant parts of this Act have been repealed and replaced (with effect from 1 January 1979) by the Civil Liability (Contribution) Act 1978 (p. 1122, post), which clarifies and reforms the earlier legislation and extends the principle of the 1935 Act to all wrongdoers, whether the basis of liability is tort, breach of contract, breach of trust or otherwise (s. 6(1)). The Act is based, with some important modifications, on the Law Commission's *Report on Contribution* (Law Com. No. 79).

The right to recover contribution under the 1978 Act supersedes any other right except (a) an express or implied contractual or other (e.g. statutory) right to an indemnity; or (b) an express contractual provision regulating or excluding contribution (s. 7(3)). An example of an implied contractual right will be found in *Lister v Romford Ice and Cold Storage Co Ltd* [1957] AC 555, [1957] 1 All ER 125 (p. 1128, post). It was held that there is an implied term which allows an employer to recover an indemnity from the employee for whose torts he is vicariously liable. The exact scope of this implied term, particularly where insurance by the employer is compulsory (either as vehicle owner or as employer), is a matter for debate. Insurers have tended not to insist on the enforcement of the indemnity, largely because of the industrial relations consequences for their clients of their doing so, but more recently there have been reports of employers enforcing the indemnity themselves as a way, for example, to recover from ex-employees' increases in the employers' insurance premiums caused by findings of negligence against them.

1 EFFECT OF RELEASE OF JOINT TORTFEASOR

■ Cutler v McPhail
Queen's Bench Division [1962] 2 All ER 474

SALMON J . . .

The points raised on release are extremely interesting and by no means easy. The principle is quite plain, that, if there is a release of one joint tortfeasor, the cause of action against all the tortfeasors is extinguished; on the other hand, if there is merely an agreement not to sue one of several joint tortfeasors, the cause of action does not die and the other tortfeasors can properly be sued. What I have to decide here in respect of the publication in "The Villager", is whether there has been a release of the plaintiffs' cause of action against the defendant. In the *Price v Barker*[1] line of cases, the court has had to consider a release by deed, where, in the body of the document, there is an express release followed by words purporting to retain the right to sue other joint tortfeasors—an express reservation of right. In such cases, it is clear from the authorities that there is no magic in the use of the word "release" in the deed. The deed has to be looked at as a whole, and, if it appears from the deed, looked at as a whole, that, although the parties have used the word "release", the deed is not intended to operate as a release but is merely an agreement or a promise not to sue, then it is merely a promise not to sue and not a release. But in the class of case to which I have referred, the decision, when it has been in favour of the view that the deed did not operate as a release, has always proceeded on the basis that the express reservation of rights in the document showed that it was not intended to operate as a release.

Here, one has to consider a release by accord and satisfaction, and the release with which I am particularly concerned is the release of the Pinner Association officers. They are the persons responsible for the publication in "The Villager", and they settled their case with the plaintiffs on the basis that they paid £250 damages and costs, and published an apology. As far as they are concerned, the matter starts with the letter written by the plaintiffs' solicitor to Messrs Wyld, Collins and Crosse, appearing for the Pinner Association and its officers. I need not read the whole of the letter, but the vital paragraph reads:

> "Upon the apologies being published and the sum mentioned paid over, then my client will, of course, release from any further liability in respect of the publication complained of, all officers and members of the committee including, of course, the editor of 'The Villager'."

Presumably that letter means what it says. One can guess what the probability is; no doubt, when the letter was written the plaintiffs hoped to go on with their action against the present defendant. But I cannot see that stated anywhere in the letter, and, when I look at the rest of the correspondence following that letter, between the plaintiffs' solicitor and the solicitors for the Pinner Association officers, I still cannot find anything to indicate that, when the plaintiffs' solicitor used the word "release" in his letter of 19 February, 1959, he did not mean precisely what he said; nor is there any evidence before me from which I can come to the conclusion that a contrary intention was ever expressed by the plaintiffs to the Pinner Association officers.

Counsel for the plaintiffs has sought to rely on a letter which was written by the plaintiffs' solicitor to the solicitors for the printers and publishers, the Pinner Press, Ltd.; that letter also uses these words:

> "Upon the publication of the apologies by your clients and payment by them of my costs, they will of course be released from all further liability in the matter,"

---

[1]   (1855) 4 E & B 760.

and adds:

> "As a matter of interest, it has not proved possible to effect a settlement of the matter with [the defendant] and I have instructed counsel to settle writ and statement of claim."

It is suggested that those last words amount to an express reservation of rights and an intimation that this letter was intended only as an agreement not to sue. In my judgment, the letter does not contain an express reservation of rights; it is at least as consistent with the view that the solicitor writing the letter intended to release without fully appreciating the legal consequences of a release, as it is with any other suggested interpretation. But, as far as the release to the Pinner Association officers is concerned, there are no such additional words in the relevant letter and, as I have already indicated, I have looked, and looked in vain, to find anything which expresses an intention, or from which an intention could properly be deduced, negativing what the letter of Feb. 19 says in the plainest terms.

It may be that the law relating to release might be re-considered with advantage; the difference between a release and an agreement not to sue is highly technical but very real in its effect, but, whilst the law remains as it is, I feel bound to hold in this case that there has been a release of the Pinner Association officers, and that that release in law extinguishes the claim in respect of the separate tort alleged to have been committed by the defendant in causing his letter to be published in "The Villager" . . . .

NOTES

1. Note that since under vicarious liability employer and employee are treated as joint tortfeasors, the release of one counts as the release of the other. See e.g. *New Zealand Guardian Trust Co Ltd v Brooks* [1995] 1 WLR 96.

2. In *Gardiner v Moore* [1969] 1 QB 55, [1966] 1 All ER 365, Thesiger J held that there was no material difference between an express and an implied covenant not to sue. Being satisfied, on the facts, that there had been no intention to release the author of a libel when a claim against the newspaper proprietors and printers was settled, he held that the author had not been discharged from liability.

3. In *Watts v Aldington* (1993) Times, 16 December; (1994) Independent, 25 January, Neill LJ rejected the proposition that it was necessary to classify an agreement either as a release or as an agreement not to sue. Neill LJ (in the *Independent* report) said, '[I]n trying to fit the agreement into a particular category one may lose sight of the true enquiry: what is the meaning and effect of the agreement having regard to the surrounding circumstances and taking into account not only the express words used in the document but also any terms which can be properly implied?' Neill LJ decided that the meaning and effect of the agreement in that case was that one defendant was released but that there was an implied reservation of the right to proceed against the other defendant. See also *Johnson v Davies* [1999] Ch 117, [1998] 2 All ER 649. For analysis of the general approach to be adopted in the interpretation of release agreements, see *BCCI v Ali* [2001] 1 All ER 961, [2001] UKHL 8. In *Connex South Eastern Railways Ltd v MJ Building Services Group plc* [2005] EWCA Civ 193, the Court of Appeal interpreted a release agreement against the wider context of business dealing between the parties in question to conclude that, even if the defendants had been joint tortfeasors, the release would not have extended to cover all the points in issue between the parties.

4. The common law rule of release by accord and satisfaction has been abolished in several jurisdictions and Lord Denning MR stated, obiter, in *Bryanston Finance Ltd v De Vries* [1975] QB 703 at 723 that it should be disregarded. In *Watts v Aldington*, Steyn LJ called the rule an 'absurdity', though too well established for a Court of Appeal judge to reform. An attempt to claim that s. 3 of Civil Liability (Contribution) Act 1978

(p. 1122, post) had the effect of precluding the rule was rejected by the Court of Appeal in *Morris v Wentworth-Stanley* [1999] QB 1004. The Court of Appeal referred to the Law Commission's *Report on Contribution* (Law Com. No. 79) to show that s. 3 was intended merely to replace and improve s. 6(1)(a) of the Law Reform (Married Women and Tortfeasors) Act 1935, which had imperfectly abolished the rule in contract that a judgment obtained against one or more, but not all, persons jointly liable for the same damage operated as a bar to a further action against those not sued. Section 3 did not, however, 'purport to deal with the effect of a grant of a release of joint debtors by an accord and satisfaction reached with one of them'.

In *Deanplan Ltd v Mahmoud* [1993] Ch 151, [1992] 3 All ER 945 Judge Baker QC reviewed the cases on release by accord and satisfaction in contract law and extracted three reasons for the rule. (1) Where there is only 'one obligation', as in a contract made by joint debtors with a single creditor, if the creditor releases one debtor, the 'obligation' itself should be considered at an end. (2) Where the obligation of each is to perform insofar as it had not been performed by any other party, the acceptance of some other performance in lieu of the promised performance relieves the others because the claimant cannot have both the promised performance and some other performance which the claimant has agreed to accept. (3) If the other defendants are not released, they will still have a right of contribution against the released defendant, so that an action against another defendant would lead to a breach of the release agreement itself. Only the third of these arguments seems to have any applicability to tort actions and it is open to the objection that it seems to prove too much, for it would apply equally to concurrent tortfeasors, for whom s. 1(3) of the Civil Liability (Contribution) Act 1978 seems to settle the point in favour of liability.

Has not the time come for the House of Lords to say that in view of the changes in the legal landscape since the rule was formulated, especially the statutory changes culminating in the Civil Liability (Contribution) Act 1978, the rule should be declared no longer to be good law? As Steyn LJ said in *Watts v Aldington*, '[F]or those who are aware of the problem it is a potential disincentive to entering into bona fide and reasonable compromises. The rule requires re-examination, notably in the light of the suspect logic on which it was founded and, in any event, on the basis that the rationale of the rule disappeared once the "one cause of action" theory was undermined by the statute which authorized successive actions against joint tortfeasors.'

The case in the next section, however, seems to indicate that the House of Lords is not at present in a reforming mood.

2 EFFECTS OF SETTLEMENT ON CONCURRENT TORTFEASORS

■ Jameson (executors of Jameson (decd) v Central Electricity Generating Board (Babcock Energy Ltd, third party)
House of Lords [1999] 1 All ER 193

Mr Jameson was employed by Babcock Energy Ltd (Babcock) and worked for them at two power stations owned and operated by the Central Electricity Generating Board (CEGB).

He contracted malignant mesothelioma because of exposure to asbestos dust while working at the power stations and brought proceedings against his employer. He agreed to accept £80,000 in 'full and final settlement and satisfaction' of his cause of action, but died before the money was paid over. The money fell to his estate and was inherited by his widow. His executors then commenced proceedings against CEGB on behalf of his widow under s. 1 of the Fatal Accidents Act 1976 for damages for her loss of dependency, which was agreed to be worth £142,000. CEGB joined Babcock as a third party. The judge held that the plaintiffs were entitled to maintain their action against CEGB and that CEGB was entitled to maintain contribution proceedings against Babcock. The Court of Appeal dismissed an appeal, on the grounds that where a claimant settled an action for damages against a tortfeasor the settlement did not release a concurrent tortfeasor from liability unless the settlement amounted to satisfaction of the full value of the plaintiff's claim, since the concurrent tortfeasor was the subject of a separate cause of action. CEGB appealed successfully to the House of Lords.

LORD HOPE OF CRAIGHEAD: . . .
The liability which is in issue in this case is that of concurrent tortfeasors, because the acts of negligence and breach of statutory duty which are alleged against Babcock and the defendant respectively are not the same. So the plaintiff has a separate cause of action against each of them for the same loss. But the existence of damage is an essential part of the cause of action in any claim for damages. It would seem to follow, as a matter of principle, that once the plaintiff's claim has been satisfied by any one of several tortfeasors, his cause of action for damages is extinguished against all of them. As Lord Atkin said in *Clark v Urquhart, Stracey v Urquhart* [1930] AC 28 at 66: '. . . damage is an essential part of the cause of action and if already satisfied by one of the alleged tortfeasors the cause of action is destroyed.' In that case the plaintiff had received in satisfaction of his claim against one defendant the full amount of damages which he could have received on any of the causes of action against the rest. It was held that his acceptance of the money paid into court was a satisfaction of all the claims in the action and that his damage, in a question with the other defendants, had been satisfied. In *Tang Man Sit (decd) (personal representative) v Capacious Investments Ltd* [1996] 1 All ER 193 at 199, [1996] AC 514 at 522 Lord Nicholls of Birkenhead discussed the limitations on a plaintiff's freedom to sue successively two or more persons who are liable to him concurrently. He explained the point in this way:

'A third limitation is that a plaintiff cannot recover in the aggregate from one or more defendants an amount in excess of his loss. Part satisfaction of a judgment against one person does not operate as a bar to the plaintiff thereafter bringing an action against another who is also liable, but it does operate to reduce the amount recoverable in the second action. However, once a plaintiff has fully recouped his loss, of necessity he cannot thereafter pursue any other remedy he might have and which he might have pursued earlier. Having recouped the whole of his loss, any further proceedings would lack a subject matter. The principle of full satisfaction prevents double recovery.'

So the first question which arises on the facts of this case is whether satisfaction for this purpose is achieved where the plaintiff agrees to accept a sum from one of the alleged concurrent tortfeasors which is expressed to be in full and final settlement of his claim against that tortfeasor, if that sum is less than the amount which a judge would have held to be the amount of the damages which were due to him if the case had gone to trial and the defendant had been found liable.

In the Court of Appeal ([1997] 4 All ER 38 at 52, [1998] QB 323 at 341–342) Auld LJ, in a careful and impressive judgment, said that he could—

'see no basis in law or common sense why an agreement expressed to be in "in full and final settlement and satisfaction" between a claimant and one tortfeasor should be regarded as full satisfaction in respect of any claims that he may have against a concurrent tortfeasor who was not a party to [the settlement].'

This was because the causes of action against each of the concurrent tortfeasors are separate, not single and indivisible as is the case with joint tortfeasors. He said that satisfaction, as between concurrent tortfeasors, must depend not upon an agreement with one of them but on whether or not the claim against the second tortfeasor has in fact been satisfied. So the judge in the second action was not bound to equate full satisfaction with a figure acceptable to both parties representing their assessment of the risks of litigation.

I follow that reasoning as far as it goes but I do not think, with great respect, that it goes quite far enough. The causes of action are indeed separate. And it is clear that an agreement reached between the plaintiff and one concurrent tortfeasor cannot extinguish the plaintiff's claim against the other concurrent tortfeasor if his claim for damages has still not been satisfied. The critical question, as Auld LJ ([1997] 4 All ER 38 at 52, [1998] QB 323 at 342) was right to point out, is whether the claim has in fact been satisfied. I think that the answer to it will be found by examining the terms of the agreement and comparing it with what has been claimed. The significance of the agreement is to be found in the effect which the parties intended to give to it. The fact that it has been entered into by way of a compromise in order to conclude a settlement forms part of the background. But the extent of the element of compromise will vary from case to case. The scope for litigation may have been reduced by agreement, for example on the question of liability. There may be little room for dispute as to the amount which a judge would award as damages. So one cannot assume that the figure which the parties are willing to accept is simply their assessment of the risks of litigation. The essential point is that the meaning which is to be given to the agreement will determine its effect.

...The law used to be that the judgment against one joint tortfeasor was itself, without satisfaction, a sufficient bar to an action against another joint tortfeasor for the same cause.... In the case of concurrent tortfeasors, a judgment recovered against one of them did not put an end to the cause of action against any of the other tortfeasors until it had been satisfied... Section 6(1)(a) of the Law Reform (Married Women and Tortfeasors) Act 1935, which was replaced and extended by s 6 of the 1978 Act, altered the common law on these matters. As the law now stands, a plaintiff is barred from going on with a separate action against another tortfeasor if the judgment which he has obtained in the first action has been satisfied.

What then is the effect if the amount of the claim is fixed by agreement? Is the figure which the plaintiff has agreed to accept in full and final satisfaction of his claim from one concurrent tortfeasor open to review by the judge in a second action against the other concurrent tortfeasor on the ground that, despite the terms of his agreement, he has not in fact received the full value of his claim? Or is the fact that that figure was agreed to as the amount to be paid in full and final settlement of the first action to be taken as having fixed the amount of the claim in just the same way as if it had been fixed by a judgment, so that the claim must be held to have been extinguished as against all other concurrent tortfeasors?

As I have said, a claim of damages is a claim for a sum of money, the amount of which must necessarily remain unliquidated until something has been done to fix the amount. Where the claim is adjudicated upon by the court, the amount of the damages is fixed by the judgment which the court makes as to the sum required to make good to the plaintiff the full value of his loss. But it is well known that many claims are settled without the amount due as damages having been adjudicated by the court. They are settled by agreement between the parties. Were it not for the fact that most claims of damages are settled in this way, the parties would be exposed to greater expense and uncertainty and the burden of work on the courts would be intolerable. There is a strong element of public interest in facilitating the disposal of cases in this way.

In the typical case the plaintiff agrees to accept the sum which the defendant is willing to pay in full and final settlement of his claim. Such a settlement normally involves an element of compromise on both sides. Each side will have made concessions of one kind or another to reflect its assessment of the prospects of success if the case were to go to trial. The plaintiff will normally have made a discount from the amount which he regards as full compensation for his loss. He may have withdrawn some elements of his claim, reduced the amounts sought in settlement of others or accepted an overall reduction in the amount claimed. But, whatever the nature and extent of the compromise, one thing is common to all these cases. This is that the agreement brings to an end the plaintiff's cause of action against the defendant for the payment of damages. The agreed sum is a liquidated amount which replaces the claim for an illiquid sum. The effect of the compromise is to fix the amount of his claim in just the same way as if the case had gone to trial and he had obtained judgment. Once the agreed sum has been paid, his claim against the defendant will have been satisfied. Satisfaction discharges the tort and is a bar to any further action in respect of it: *United Australia Ltd v Barclays Bank Ltd* [1940] 4 All ER 20 at 31, [1941] AC 1 at 21 per Viscount Simon LC and *Kohnke v Karger* [1951] 2 All ER 179 at 181, [1951] 2 KB 670 at 675 per Lynskey J. I think that it follows that, if the claim was for the whole amount of the loss for which the defendant as one of the concurrent tortfeasors is liable to him in damages, satisfaction of the claim against him will have the effect of extinguishing the claim against the other concurrent tortfeasors.

There may be cases where the terms of the settlement, or the extent of the claim made against the tortfeasor with whom the plaintiff has entered into the settlement, will show that the parties have not treated the settlement as satisfaction for the full amount of the claim of damages. In the same way a judge, in awarding damages to the plaintiff in his action against one concurrent tortfeasor, may make it clear that he has restricted his award to a part only of the full value of the claim....

What the judge [in a subsequent action against another concurrent tortfeasor] may not do is allow the plaintiff to open up the question whether the amount which he has agreed to accept from the first concurrent tortfeasor under the settlement represents full value for what has been claimed. That kind of inquiry, if it were to be permitted, could lead to endless litigation as one concurrent tortfeasor after another was sued on the basis that the sums received by the plaintiff in his settlements with those previously sued were open to review by a judge in order to see whether or not the plaintiff had yet received full satisfaction for his loss. Different judges might arrive at different assessments of the amount of the damages. The court would then have to decide which of them was to be preferred as the basis for the apportionment between the various tortfeasors. I do not think that this can be regarded as acceptable. The principle of finality requires that there must be an end to litigation.

The question therefore is, as Mr McLaren QC for the CEGB put it, not whether the plaintiff has received the full value of his claim but whether the sum which he has received in settlement of it was intended to be in full satisfaction of the tort. In this case the words used cannot be construed as meaning that the sum which the deceased agreed to accept was in partial satisfaction only of his claim of damages. It was expressly accepted in full and final settlement and satisfaction of all his causes of action in the statement of claim. I would hold that the terms of his settlement with Babcock extinguished his claim of damages against the other tortfeasors...

LORD LLOYD OF BERWICK (dissenting):...
[T]he starting point is to distinguish between joint torts and concurrent torts. It is agreed between the parties that we are here concerned with concurrent torts, and not joint torts; that is to say, the claim against Babcock and the claim against the CEGB give rise to separate causes of action, each contributing to the same damage.

On the face of it, it would seem strange and unjust that a plaintiff who settles a claim against A in respect of one cause of action should be unable to pursue a claim in respect of a separate cause of action against B. Of course if the plaintiff recovers the whole of his loss from A, then he will have nothing left to recover against B. The payment received from A will have 'satisfied' his loss, though I would for my part prefer not to use the term 'satisfy' in this context, in order to avoid confusion with the quite different concept of accord and satisfaction. In the present case Mr Jameson agreed to accept £80,000 plus costs in settlement of his claim against Babcock. If during his lifetime he had started a fresh action against Babcock he would have been met with the defence of accord and satisfaction, the satisfaction being the £80,000 which he agreed to accept in settlement of his claim against Babcock. But there would have been nothing whatever to stop him claiming against the CEGB during his lifetime, unless, of course, £80,000 had been the full amount of his loss. But it was not. On the agreed facts it was less than two-thirds of his loss.

It is a matter of everyday occurrence in personal injury litigation that a plaintiff will begin an action against two concurrent tortfeasors. He may have a strong case against the first defendant, and a weak case against the second. In those circumstances he may be well advised to accept a payment into court made by the second defendant, and continue against the first.

Thus in *Townsend v Stone Toms & Partners (a firm)* [1981] 2 All ER 690, [1981] 1 WLR 1153 (a case in contract, but the same principle applies) the plaintiffs brought proceedings against a builder for defective work, and against the architect for negligence in supervising the work. The builder made a payment into court of £30,000 'in satisfaction of all the causes of action in respect of which the plaintiffs claim'. It was argued that the claim against the architect should be stayed by virtue of RSC Ord 22, r 3(4). The argument was rejected. Eveleigh LJ said ([1981] 2 All ER 690 at 696, [1981] 1 WLR 1153 at 1161): '...where there are two separate causes of action, satisfaction of the one should not be a bar to proceedings on the other.' So the case against the architect continued.

But when the case came on for trial, it was found as a fact that the £30,000 paid into court was more than sufficient to cover the whole of the loss suffered by the plaintiffs in respect of the overlapping claims. So the plaintiffs' claim against the architect in respect of the overlapping claims was dismissed, and the judge's decision to that effect was upheld by the Court of Appeal in *Townsend v Stone Toms & Partners (a firm) (No 2)* (1984) 27 BLR 26.

So the acceptance by a plaintiff of payment into court by one concurrent tortfeasor does not operate as a bar to proceedings against other concurrent tortfeasors, unless the plaintiff has recovered the whole of his loss. Exactly the same applies where judgment has been entered in respect of the amount paid into court (as happened in *Townsend*'s case), or where a claim is settled without any payment into court; and exactly the same applies whether the claims against the other tortfeasors are made in the same set of proceedings or in subsequent proceedings.

It follows that Mr Jameson would in my opinion have been entitled to commence proceedings against the CEGB during his lifetime for the whole of his loss, but he would have had to give credit for the £80,000 recovered from Babcock.

It is said that if Mr Jameson had proceeded to judgment against Babcock and recovered £120,000, then he would not have been able to challenge that figure in other proceedings before another judge. The same ought to be true, so it is said, where Mr Jameson has accepted £80,000 'in full and final settlement and satisfaction of all the causes of action in respect of which the Plaintiff claims'. The agreement stands in place of the judgment. But with great respect, the two cases are entirely different. The £80,000 is not an agreed figure of the plaintiff's loss, corresponding to the judge's award of £120,000. It is a figure which reflects the plaintiff's chances of success in the action. By the time the judge comes to make his award, the action has, ex hypothesi, succeeded. So there is no room for any discount. Like Auld LJ I can see no basis in law or common sense why the settlement of a claim in respect of one cause of action at 50% of the plaintiff's loss, so as to reflect the chances of success against that defendant, should impose a ceiling on the damages recoverable in respect of a separate cause of action against a different defendant.

A part of the difficulty may lie in the use of the word 'value' in this connection. When it is said that a claim has an agreed value of £80,000 it may mean one of two things; it may mean that the plaintiff's loss is agreed at £80,000. Or it may mean that his claim is worth £80,000 after taking account of the chances of success. In personal injury cases it frequently happens that quantum is agreed subject to liability. But since very few claims are settled at 100%, I would take a great deal of persuading that in agreeing a figure of £80,000 the parties were agreeing a figure for Mr Jameson's loss, which would then somehow enure to the benefit of concurrent tortfeasors. Nor can I see any reason for implying a term in the settlement agreement that Mr Jameson would not proceed against other tortfeasors who might or might not bring contribution proceedings against Babcock. Babcock were professionally advised. If they had reason to fear contribution proceedings by a concurrent tortfeasor they could have protected themselves by an express term in the settlement agreement. But they did not. On the other hand if the appellants are right, it will mean that in every case plaintiffs will have to insist on an express term reserving the right to proceed against other concurrent tortfeasors, even though there might be no other tortfeasors in mind at the time. The requirement for such a term would be to reintroduce a trap of just the kind which Parliament and the courts have consistently tried to eradicate in the field of joint and several torts over many years: see the passage quoted in the court below from the judgment of Steyn LJ in *Watts v Aldington, Tolstoy v Aldington* (1993) Times, 16 December, [1993] CA Transcript 1578, and the illuminating judgment of Neill LJ in the same case.

It is said that policy favours finality. So it does. But I do not see how it can make the settlement agreement mean something which it does not say, and on one view could not say.

[LORD BROWNE-WILKINSON and LORD HOFFMANN agreed with LORD HOPE. LORD CLYDE delivered a speech in favour of allowing the appeal.]

Appeal allowed.

NOTES

1. The real source of the majority's concern in *Jameson* seems to be that, in certain circumstances, the Fatal Accidents Act 1976 appears to allow a form of double recovery by a dependant who also happens to be a beneficiary of the deceased's estate. Under s. 4 of the Act, amounts received under the deceased's will are to be disregarded, so that if the deceased settles a claim against one defendant and then dies, a dependant might be able to proceed for full dependency from another defendant without having to deduct any amount received under the will (see p. 288, ante). The problem arose originally because of the order in which the reform of the law with regard to the death of the victims of torts took place, with the creation of dependants' actions under the Fatal Accidents Acts pre-dating the reform of the rule that personal causes of action died with the person. But Parliament has chosen to leave the situation as it is, and not, for example, to take the logical step of abolishing either the relevant provisions of the Fatal Accidents Act or the survival of causes of action. Should not their Lordships have accepted the policy as it stood, despite the lack of appeal of some of its consequences?

2. As Lord Lloyd points out in his dissent, there is a danger in the majority view that claimants will need to protect themselves by inserting a clause into settlement agreements to the effect that they reserve the right to proceed against the other tortfeasors. Not only is this an unnecessary trap for the unwary, or rather a trap for the litigant who lacks expensive legal advice, it also gives the defendant a very useful bargaining counter. Claimants will, in effect, have to pay defendants for the right to preserve their causes of action against other tortfeasors. It is also possible that negotiations might break down on such a point, in which case the rule will have had the effect, which Steyn LJ in *Watts v Aldington* warned about in the context of accord and satisfaction, of reducing the proportion of cases which end in settlement rather than in trial.

3. Attempts were made to distinguish *Jameson* in its wake: see e.g. *John v Price Waterhouse* [2001] EWHC Ch 438. In *Heaton v Axa Equity & Law Life Assurance Society plc* [2002] 2 AC 329, [2000] 4 All ER 673, the Court of Appeal attempted to ameliorate the position. Chadwick LJ distinguished between the 'full satisfaction' aspect of the question and the 'full settlement' aspect. 'Full satisfaction', he said, was the only point at issue in *Jameson*. It concerns whether the claimant has agreed with the first defendant that the compensation recovered from the first defendant in the settlement represents full compensation for the wrong the claimant has suffered. If so, there is no further damage on which to base an action against a different defendant. But that is a different point from the 'full settlement' point, which, according to Chadwick LJ, was not at

issue in *Jameson*, at least in the minds of the majority who agreed around Lord Hope's speech. The 'full settlement' point is whether, regardless of the adequacy of the amount accepted in compensation, the claimant has agreed not to proceed in relation to the same matter not only against the first defendant but also against anyone else. Chadwick LJ argued that the 'full settlement' point is governed by *Watts v Aldington* and *Johnson v Davies* rather than by *Jameson*, namely by Neill LJ's method of 'having regard to the surrounding circumstances and taking into account not only the express words used in the document but also any terms which can properly be implied', to which Chadwick LJ adds that such a term should not be implied where it is unnecessary to do so. On appeal, the House of Lords took the opportunity to clarify their previous judgment in *Jameson*, adopting a related analysis to that put forward by Chadwick LJ.

■ Heaton and others v Axa Equity and Law Life Assurance Society plc
House of Lords [2002] 2 All ER 961

LORD BINGHAM OF CORNHILL: . . .

[1] My Lords, the issue in this appeal may be expressed in this way: if A, having sued B for damages for breach of contract, enters into a settlement with B expressed to be in full and final settlement of all its claims against B, is A thereafter precluded from pursuing against C a claim for damages for breach of another contract to the extent that this claim is for damages which formed part of A's claim against B? Expressed in another way, the issue is whether the majority decision of the House in *Jameson (exors of Jameson (decd)) v Central Electricity Generating Board (Babcock Energy Ltd, third party)* [1999] 1 All ER 193, [2000] 1 AC, properly understood, laid down any rule of law and, if so, whether that rule applies to successive contract-breakers as well as concurrent tortfeasors.

[2] . . . The issues in the appeal can, I think, be illuminated by resort to schematic examples.

[3] A brings an action against B claiming damages for negligence in tort. The claim goes to trial, and judgment is given for A for £x. There is no appeal and the judgment sum is paid by B to A. £x will there-after be taken, in the ordinary way, to represent the full value of A's claim against B. A cannot thereafter maintain an action for damages for negligence in tort against C as a concurrent tortfeasor liable in respect of the same damage for two reasons: first, such a claim will amount to a collateral attack on the judgment already given; and secondly, A will be unable to allege or prove any damage, and damage is a necessary ingredient for a cause of action based on tortious negligence. A cannot maintain an action against C in contract either, in respect of the same damage, for the first reason which bars his tortious claim. There is however no reason of principle, in either case, on the assumptions made in this example, why B should not recover a contribution from C under the Civil Liability (Contribution) Act 1978 as a party liable with him for the same damage suffered by A.

[4] In a second example the facts are varied. A brings an action against B claiming damages for negligence in tort. The action does not proceed to judgment because B compromises A's claim by an agreement providing that he will pay A damages of £x, which he duly does. If £x is agreed or taken to represent the full value of A's claim against B, A cannot thereafter maintain an action against C in tort in respect of the same damage for the second reason given in the last paragraph, and although he is not precluded from pursuing a claim against C in contract in respect of the same damage he cannot claim or recover more than nominal damages. There is again, in the ordinary way, no reason of principle in either case, on the assumptions made in this example, why B should not recover a contribution from C under the 1978 Act as a party liable with him for the damage suffered by A.

[5] There is, however, an obvious difference between the action which culminates in judgment and the action which culminates in compromise: that whereas, save in an exceptional case (such as *Crawford v Springfield Steel Co Ltd* (18 July 1958, unreported) Lord Cameron), a judgment will

conclusively decide the full measure of damage for which B is liable to A, a sum agreed to be paid under a compromise may or may not represent the full measure of B's liability to A. Where a sum is agreed which makes a discount for the risk of failure or for a possible finding of contributory negligence or for any other hazard of litigation, the compromise sum may nevertheless be regarded as the full measure of B's liability. But A may agree to settle with B for £x not because either party regards that sum as the full measure of A's loss but for many other reasons: it may be known that B is uninsured and £x represents the limit of his ability to pay; or A may wish to pocket a small sum in order to finance litigation against other parties; or it may be that A is old and ill and prefers to accept a small sum now rather than a larger sum years later; or it may be that there is a contractual or other limitation on B's liability to A. While it is just that A should be precluded from recovering substantial damages against C in a case where he has accepted a sum representing the full measure of his estimated loss, it is unjust that A should be so precluded where he has not.

[6] The majority decision of the House in *Jameson's* case appears to have been understood by some as laying down a rule of law that A, having accepted and received a sum from B in full and final settlement of his claims against B in tort, is thereafter precluded from pursuing against C any claim which formed part of his claim against B. I do not think that my noble and learned friend Lord Hope of Craighead, in giving the opinion of the majority of the House, is to be so understood...

[8] [The] conclusion [in *Jameson*] was reached by a number of steps which included the following. (1) Proof of damage is an essential step in establishing a claim in tortious negligence ([1999] 1 All ER 193 at 202, [2000] 1 AC 455 at 472). (2) Such a claim is a claim for unliquidated damages ([1999] 1 All ER 193 at 203, [2000] 1 AC 455 at 473, 474). (3) Such a claim is liquidated when either judgment is given for a specific sum or a specific sum is accepted in a compromise agreement ([1999] 1 All ER 193 at 203, 204, [2000] 1 AC 455 at 473, 474). (4) A judgment on such a claim will ordinarily be taken to fix the full measure of a claimant's loss ([1999] 1 All ER 193 at 203, 204 [2000] 1 AC 455 at 473, 474). (5) A sum accepted in settlement of such a claim may also fix the full measure of a claimant's loss ([1999] 1 All ER 193 at 203, 204, [2000] 1 AC 455 at 473, 474): whether it does so or not depends on the proper construction of the compromise agreement in its context ([1999] 1 All ER 193 at 203, 204, 206, [2000] 1 AC 455 at 473, 474, 476). (6) On the facts of A's case, the sum accepted from B in settlement was to be taken as representing the full measure of A's loss: it followed that A's claim in tortious negligence was extinguished and he had no claim which could be pursued against C ([1999] 1 All ER 193 at 206, [2000] 1 AC 455 at 476). I do not think the first four of these steps are controversial. The fifth proposition may perhaps have been stated a little too absolutely in *Jameson's* case, but as expressed above I do not think it can be challenged. There was clearly room for more than one view, as the division of judicial opinion in *Jameson's* case showed, whether the sum accepted in settlement by A was to be taken as representing the full measure of his loss, but if it did the conclusion followed: A could not have proved damage, an essential ingredient, in his action against C, and that was fatal to the widow's Fatal Accidents Act claim against C.

[9] In considering whether a sum accepted under a compromise agreement should be taken to fix the full measure of A's loss, so as to preclude action against C in tort in respect of the same damage, and so as to restrict any action against C in contract in respect of the same damage to a claim for nominal damages, the terms of the settlement agreement between A and B must be the primary focus of attention, and the agreement must be construed in its appropriate factual context. In construing it various significant points must in my opinion be borne clearly in mind. (1) The release of one concurrent tortfeasor does not have the effect in law of releasing another concurrent tortfeasor and the release of one contract-breaker does not have the effect in law of releasing a successive contract-breaker. (2) An agreement made between A and B will not affect A's rights against C unless either (a) A agrees to forgo or waive rights which he would otherwise enjoy against C, in which case his agreement is enforceable by B, or (b) the agreement falls within that limited class of contracts which either at common law or by virtue of the Contracts (Rights of Third Parties) Act 1999 is enforceable by C as a third party. (3) The use of clear and comprehensive language to preclude the pursuit of claims and cross-claims as between A

and B has little bearing on the question whether the agreement represents the full measure of A's loss. The more inadequate the compensation agreed to be paid by B, the greater the need for B to protect himself against any possibility of further action by A to obtain a full measure of redress. (4) While an express reservation by A of his right to sue C will fortify the inference that A is not treating the sum recovered from B as representing the full measure of his loss, the absence of such a reservation is of lesser and perhaps of no significance, since there is no need for A to reserve a right to do that which A is in the ordinary way fully entitled to do without any such reservation. (5) If B, on compromising A's claim, wishes to protect himself against any claim against him by C claiming contribution, he may achieve that end either (a) by obtaining an enforceable undertaking by A not to pursue any claim against C relating to the subject matter of the compromise, or (b) by obtaining an indemnity from A against any liability to which B may become subject relating to the subject matter of the compromise. In my consideration of this matter I have gained much assistance from the clear and illuminating judgments of the New Zealand Court of Appeal in *Allison v KPMG Peat Marwick* [2000] 1 NZLR 560 and from the perceptive critique of *Jameson*'s case in Foskett *The Law and Practice of Compromise* (5th edn, 2002) pp 119–125, paras 6-42–6-57.

[10] …I do not conclude, on construing the compromise agreement made in this case, that it is to be taken as representing the full measure of the respondents' loss agreed between the parties to the compromise…There was nothing in the terms of the compromise agreement or in the relevant sur-rounding circumstances to suggest that the respondents entered into that agreement in full and final satisfaction of all their claims not only against Target but against Equity & Law as well…

LORD RODGER OF EARLSFERRY: …

[63] The decision in *Jameson*'s case has been criticised—for example, in *Foskett, The Law and Practice of Compromise* (5th edn, 2002) p 122, para 6–49 and by the New Zealand Court of Appeal in *Allison v KPMG Peat Marwick* [2000] 1 NZLR 560. The respondents' written case foreshadowed a possible challenge to *Jameson*'s case on the basis of these criticisms. In the event, however, counsel did not argue that it had been wrongly decided. Both sides proceeded on the basis that *Jameson*'s case was correctly decided: inevitably, however, each had a different view as to its effect in the present circum-stances…In particular, as part of his argument, counsel for the respondents contended that the deci-sion in *Jameson*'s case applied only to concurrent tortfeasors and should not be extended so as to apply in the case of concurrent or overlapping contract-breakers causing the same loss.

[65] It is not only a judgment that can have the effect of extinguishing the relevant loss: if one tort-feasor settles the victim's claim by paying him a sum which fully satisfies his right to damages for loss and injury, the victim cannot then sue any concurrent tortfeasor for damages for the same loss and injury. In *Allison v KPMG Peat Marwick* [2000] 1 NZLR 560 at 589 (para 134) Thomas J put the point in this way:

> 'Satisfaction discharges the loss. It is in the nature of an executed judgment in its effect. The loss no longer exists. There is nothing left for anyone to sue on; the injury or loss has been satisfied. As between the parties there is no problem. Where the co-defendants are concurrent tortfeasors, however, concurrently liable on a different cause of action, the satisfaction of one obligation cannot in itself discharge the other obligation. The concurrent tortfeasor will be released only if the satis-faction satisfies the injury or loss which flows from his or her separate cause of action. Its extinction is then independent of the agreement between the plaintiff and the defendant. Simply put, no injury or loss exists on which to sue.'

[67] Two points emerge clearly from these passages from Lord Hope's speech [in *Jameson*].

[68] First, the reasoning proceeds on the basis that, in certain cases, a settlement between a claim-ant and one tortfeasor, even though for a lesser sum than would have been awarded on full liability, can have the same effect as a judgment between the claimant and the same tortfeasor in preventing the claimant from suing another tortfeasor for the same injury. Just as the claimant who has been paid the sum of damages awarded by the court for his injuries has everything which he is entitled to and

can ask for no more, so, the House held, a claimant who has been paid a sum which was intended to be in full satisfaction of his claim is to be treated as having got everything he is entitled to and cannot ask for any more.

[69] Secondly, the effect of any particular settlement agreement depends on what the parties intended. Since that can be determined only by interpreting the agreement in question, in the end the whole issue turns on the interpretation of the agreement in question. That approach is consistent with the wider picture.

[70] As the authorities make clear, where his claim has been satisfied, the limitation on a claimant's right to bring successive proceedings follows simply from the nature of actions for the recovery of damages in compensation of a claimant's loss. If he has been paid full compensation, he no longer has any loss that he can seek to recover. The rule does not, therefore, depend on estoppel by record, on res judicata or on any similar technical doctrine...

[81] In considering whether a settlement agreement has this effect, the proper question is whether, when construed against the appropriate matrix of fact, the terms of the settlement show that the parties intended that the agreed sum should be in full satisfaction of the wrong done to the claimant. In that connection, an indication in the agreement—whether express or implied—that the claimant envisages the possibility of further proceedings against another wrongdoer may, of course, be of significance—but only as a pointer to the conclusion that the parties did not intend that the agreed sum should be in full satisfaction of the harm suffered by the claimant. Equally an indication in the agreement to the opposite effect will be a pointer that the parties intended that the agreed sum should constitute full satisfaction. In either event, the court will draw the appropriate conclusion as to the effect of the agreement on any claims against another wrongdoer...

Appeal dismissed.

NOTE

The judgments in *Heaton* have clarified that *Jameson* did not establish that any settlement expressed to be a final settlement of a claim against the defendant would bar any subsequent action against other tortfeasors. The crucial question will be whether the settlement is interpreted as showing that the parties intended that the agreed sum constituted full and complete satisfaction of the wrong done to the claimant. However, while the approach adopted in *Heaton* may reduce some of the disincentives to settlement imposed by *Jameson*, it may put a premium on careful and technical drafting of settlement agreements.

3 A SINGLE AWARD

■ Cassell & Co Ltd v Broome
House of Lords [1972] 1 All ER 801

For the facts and other material aspects of the case see p. 501, ante, and p. 504 ante.

LORD HAILSHAM:...

Less meritorious, in my view, was the second criticism of the direction put before us. This was in effect that the judge did not correctly direct the jury as to the principles on which a joint award of exemplary damages can be made against two or more defendants guilty of the joint publication of a libel in respect of which their relevant guilt may be different, and their means of different amplitude.... I think the effect of the law is...that awards of punitive damages in respect of joint publications should reflect only the lowest figure for which any of them can be held liable. This seems to me to flow inexorably both from the principle that only one sum may be awarded in a single proceeding for a joint tort, and from the authorities which were cited to us by counsel for the appellants in detail in the course of his argument.... I think that the inescapable conclusion to be drawn from these authorities is that only one sum can be awarded by way of exemplary damages where the plaintiff elects to sue more than one defendant in the same action in respect of the same publication, and that this sum must represent the highest *common* factor, that is the *lowest* sum for which any of the defendants can be held liable on this score. Although we were concerned with exemplary damages, I would think that the same principle applies generally and in particular to aggravated damages, and that dicta or apparent dicta to the contrary can be disregarded. As counsel conceded, however, plaintiffs who wish to differentiate between the defendants can do so in various ways, for example, by electing to sue the more guilty only, by commencing separate proceedings against each and then consolidating, or, in the case of a book or newspaper article, by suing separately in the same proceedings for the publication of the manuscript to the publisher by the author. Defendants, of course, have their ordinary contractual or statutory remedies for contribution or indemnity so far as they may be applicable to the facts of a particular case. But these may be inapplicable to exemplary damages....

4 CONTRIBUTION BETWEEN TORTFEASORS

(a) By statute

■ The Civil Liability (Contribution) Act 1978

Proceedings for contribution

1 Entitlement to contribution. (1) Subject to the following provisions of this section, any person liable in respect of any damage suffered by another person may recover contribution from any other person liable in respect of the same damage (whether jointly with him or otherwise).

(2) A person shall be entitled to recover contribution by virtue of subsection (1) above notwithstanding that he has ceased to be liable in respect of the damage in question since the time when the damage occurred, provided that he was so liable immediately before he made or was ordered or agreed to make the payment in respect of which the contribution is sought.

(3) A person shall be liable to make contribution by virtue of subsection (1) above notwithstanding that he has ceased to be liable in respect of the damage in question since the time when the damage occurred, unless he ceased to be liable by virtue of the expiry of a period of limitation or prescription which extinguished the right on which the claim against him in respect of the damage was based.

(4) A person who has made or agreed to make any payment in bona fide settlement or compromise of any claim made against him in respect of any damage (including a payment into court which has been accepted) shall be entitled to recover contribution in accordance with this section without regard to whether or not he himself is or ever was liable in respect of the damage, provided, however, that he would have been liable assuming that the factual basis of the claim against him could be established.

(5) A judgment given in any action brought in any part of the United Kingdom by or on behalf of the person who suffered the damage in question against any person from whom contribution is sought under this section shall be conclusive in the proceedings for contribution as to any issue determined by that judgment in favour of the person from whom the contribution is sought.

(6) References in this section to a person's liability in respect of any damage are references to any such liability which has been or could be established in an action brought against him in England and Wales by or on behalf of the person who suffered the damage; but it is immaterial whether any issue arising in any such action was or would be determined (in accordance with the rules of private international law) by reference to the law of a country outside England and Wales.

2 Assessment of contribution. (1) Subject to subsection (3) below, in any proceedings for contribution under section 1 above the amount of the contribution recoverable from any person shall be such as may be found by the court to be just and equitable having regard to the extent of that person's responsibility for the damage in question.

(2) Subject to subsection (3) below, the court shall have power in any such proceedings to exempt any person from liability to make contribution, or to direct that the contribution to be recovered from any person shall amount to a complete indemnity.

(3) Where the amount of the damages which have or might have been awarded in respect of the damage in question in any action brought in England and Wales by or on behalf of the person who suffered it against the person from whom the contribution is sought was or would have been subject to—

(a) any limit imposed by or under any enactment or by any agreement made before the damage occurred;

(b) any reduction by virtue of section 1 of the Law Reform (Contributory Negligence) Act 1945 or section 5 of the Fatal Accidents Act 1976; or

(c) any corresponding limit or reduction under the law of a country outside England and Wales;

the person from whom the contribution is sought shall not by virtue of any contribution awarded under section 1 above be required to pay in respect of the damage a greater amount than the amount of those damages as so limited or reduced.

Proceedings for the same debt or damage

3 Proceedings against persons jointly liable for the same debt or damage. Judgment recovered against any person liable in respect of any debt or damage shall not be a bar to an action, or to the continuance of an action, against any other person who is (apart from any such bar) jointly liable with him in respect of the same debt or damage.

4 Successive actions against persons liable (jointly or otherwise) for the same damage. If more than one action is brought in respect of any damage by or on behalf of the person by whom it was suffered against persons liable in respect of the damage (whether jointly or otherwise) the plaintiff shall not be entitled to costs in any of those actions, other than that in which judgment is first given, unless the court is of the opinion that there was reasonable ground for bringing the action. . . .

6 Interpretation. (1) A person is liable in respect of any damage for the purposes of this Act if the person who suffered it (or anyone representing his estate or dependants) is entitled to recover compensation from him in respect of that damage (whatever the legal basis of his liability, whether tort, breach of contract, breach of trust or otherwise).

(2) References in this Act to an action brought by or on behalf of the person who suffered any damage include references to an action brought for the benefit of his estate or dependants.

(3) In this Act "dependants" has the same meaning as in the Fatal Accidents Act 1976.

(4) In this Act, except in section 1(5) above, "action" means an action brought in England and Wales.

7 Savings. (1) Nothing in this Act shall affect any case where the debt in question became due or (as the case may be) the damage in question occurred before the date on which it comes into force.

(2) A person shall not be entitled to recover contribution or liable to make contribution in accordance with section 1 above by reference to any liability based on breach of any obligation assumed by him before the date on which this Act comes into force.

(3) The right to recover contribution in accordance with section 1 above supersedes any right, other than an express contractual right, to recover contribution (as distinct from indemnity) otherwise than under this Act in corresponding circumstances; but nothing in this Act shall affect—

(a) any express or implied contractual or other right to indemnity; or

(b) any express contractual provision regulating or excluding contribution;

which would be enforceable apart from this Act (or render enforceable any agreement for indemnity or contribution which would not be enforceable apart from this Act).

NOTES

1.   *Scope of the right to contribution.* Section 1(1) is much wider in scope than s. 6(1)(c) of the Law Reform (Married Women and Tortfeasors) Act 1935, which merely provided that a tortfeasor liable in respect of damage suffered by any person as a result of tort could recover contribution from any other tortfeasor who was, or would if sued have been, liable in respect of the same damage. There were situations in which there was no right of contribution, for example between a person liable in contract and a tortfeasor, although both were liable in respect of the same damage, or between persons liable under separate contracts for breaches of different kinds causing the same damage. This has now been remedied. The courts initally adopted a broad view of the types of claim that qualify under s. 1(1) and s. 6. *Friends' Provident Life Office v Hillier Parker May & Rowden* [1997] QB 85, [1995] 4 All ER 260, for example, held that restitutionary claims come within the statute. But the reference in s. 1(1) to the 'the same damage' is to be taken as referring only to damage to the same person. Damage to other people does not count, even though it flows from the same events (see *Birse Construction Ltd v Haiste Ltd* [1996] 2 All ER 1, [1996] 1 WLR 675).

2.   The House of Lords in *Royal Brompton Hospital NHS Trust v Hammond (Taylor Woodrow Construction (Holdings) Ltd, Pt 20 defendant)* [2002] 2 All ER 801, [2002] UKHL 14 took the view that the phrase 'same damage' in s. 1 should not be construed as including substantially or materially similar damage. Their Lordships considered that the context of the 1978 Act did not justify adopting a broad interpretation of the 'same damage' requirement, which could permit a tortfeasor to seek contribution from others who might have similar but different liabilities to the same claimant. In his judgment, Lord Bingham emphasised that the requirement for contributors to be liable for the 'same damage' does not require that each tortfeasor be liable for the same 'damages': it is not necessary for the tortfeasors to be liable for the same quantum of damages; it is sufficient if they are liable for the same loss or damage. For analysis of where tortfeasors will be deemed to be liable for the same damage, as distinct from being liable for different or 'divisible' forms of damage, see e.g. *Dingle v Associated Newspapers* [1961] 2 QB 162, at 188–189; *Rahman v Arearose* [2001] QB 351. (For criticism of *Rahman*, see T. Weir [2001] CLJ 237.) This can be a complex process, involving tricky issues of causation: see *Holtby v Brigham & Cowan (Hull) Ltd.* [2000] 3 All ER 421, and *Barker v Corus UK Ltd.* [2006] 3 All ER 785, [2006] UKHL 20 (p. 357, ante). (Note that s. 3 of the Compensation Act 2006 has restored the 'normal' joint and several liability rule in mesothelioma cases in the wake of *Barker*: see p. 369, ante.)

3.   In his opinion in *Royal Brompton Hospital*, Lord Steyn suggested at [26]–[34] that, while a broad interpretation to the 1978 Act was in general a correct approach to take, a restitutionary claim could not be classified as a claim for 'damage suffered' and

therefore a claim for restitution could not be said to be a claim to recover 'compensation' within the meaning of the Act. He therefore questioned the approach taken by Auld LJ in *Friends' Provident Life Office v Hillier Parker May & Rowden*, where a restitutionary claim was considered as coming within the 1978 Act. However, the Court of Appeal in *Niru Battery Manufacturing Co v Milestone Trading Ltd (No 2)* [2004] 2 All ER (Comm) 289, [2004] EWCA Civ 487 considered that it remained bound by the authority of the earlier decision in *Friends' Provident*. Nevertheless, in *Charter plc v City Index Ltd* [2007] 1 All ER 1049, [2006] EWHC 2508 (Ch), the court considered that the requirement for 'common liability' emphasised by the House of Lords in *Royal Brompton Hospital* did not preclude a party who received money transferred in breach of trust and who was liable as a knowing recipient if he retained the money or paid it away in unconscionable circumstances from recovering contribution from any other person responsible for damage to the party defrauded. Sir Andrew Morritt C considered that this restitutionary claim was 'parasitic' upon the breach of trust and therefore could be classified for the purposes of the 1978 Act as coming within the 'same damage' requirement (see G. Virgo [2007] CLJ 265).

4. *Persons entitled to claim*. Sections 1(2) and 1(4) deal with the problem which arose under the 1935 Act, where one tortfeasor (D1) had settled with the claimant. In order to recover a contribution from the other tortfeasor (D2) D1 had to show that he was 'liable' (*Stott v West Yorkshire Road Car Co Ltd* [1971] 2 QB 651, [1971] 3 All ER 534). This could deter settlements where there were doubts about D1's liability because D1 would not wish to put his right to contribution at risk. Section 1(4) removes this obstacle. The proviso, that the person claiming a contribution 'would have been liable assuming the factual basis of the claim against him could be established', was added during the Committee stage in the belief that it would prevent settlements based solely on the requirements of foreign law. However, as A. M. Dugdale (1979) 42 MLR 182 at 184 points out, the proviso has the effect of excluding all settlements based on legal rather than factual doubts.

5. *Persons liable to contribute*. Section 1(3) clarifies a point on which there was much difference of opinion in the House of Lords in *George Wimpey & Co Ltd v BOAC* [1955] AC 169, [1954] 3 All ER 661. D1 can bring a contribution claim against D2 within two years of his own liability to P being determined, but by then the limitation period between P and D2 may have expired. *Wimpey*'s case was generally regarded as authority for the proposition that D2 was to be regarded as 'liable' unless he had actually been sued by P and found not liable because of the expiration of the limitation period. In other words, D2's obligation to make a contribution depended upon whether P had attempted to sue after the limitation period had expired. Following the Law Commission's proposals, s. 1(3) means that a wrongdoer who has been held not liable to P because of the expiry of the limitation period or the dismissal of the claim by P for want of prosecution can still be regarded as liable to make a contribution. However, if the expiry of a limitation or prescription period extinguished not merely the remedy but also the right on which the claim against him was based, then he is not liable to make a contribution.

6. *Effect of contributory negligence*. Where P and D1 and D2 are all to blame, both the Law Reform (Contributory Negligence) Act 1945 (p. 425, ante) and the 1978 Act are relevant. In *Fitzgerald v Lane* [1989] AC 328, [1988] 2 All ER 961, the House of Lords held that the essential principles in this situation are that (a) where P successfully sues D1 and D2 and there is a claim between D1 and D2 for contribution, the apportionment

between D1 and D2 is a separate issue which should be considered only after the issues of contributory negligence and apportionment between P on the one hand and D1 and D2 on the other hand have been decided; and (b) in determining the issue of contributory negligence between P and D1 and D2, P's conduct should be compared with the totality of D1 and D2's conduct, rather than the extent to which the conduct of D1 and D2 each contributed to the damage (per Lord Ackner, at pp. 338–339).

7.   *Assessment.* Sections 2(1) and 2(2) reproduce s. 6(2) of the 1935 Act. Section 2(3), which is new, limits the court's apparently wide discretion to determine what contribution is 'just and equitable'. For example, if P suffers a £1,200 loss due equally to a tort by D1 and a breach of contract by D2 but D2's contract limits the damages for which he can be liable to P to £400, the court should first apportion the loss between D1 and D2 at £600 each and then reduce D2's share to £400 leaving D1 to pay £800 (Dugdale, op cit.).

The exact basis on which the court calculates the percentage shares remains obscure (see D. Howarth, (1994) 14 LS 88), but 100 per cent shares are possible—*Nelhams v Sandells Maintenance Ltd* (1995) 46 Con LR 40. Note that costs cannot form part of the loss or damage in respect of which a party is entitled to contribution (*J Sainsbury plc v Broadway Malyan* (1998) 61 Con LR 31).

K v P (J, Third Party) [1993] Ch 140, [1993] 1 All ER 521 is authority that a claim for contribution should not be excluded on the ground that the defendant claiming contribution could be said to be relying on his own wrong, even if the wrong is intentional or fraudulent. Such an application of the *ex turpi* principle would undermine the purpose of the Act, which is to provide some admitted wrongdoers with some relief. The intentional or fraudulent nature of the conduct of a particular defendant may, however, be taken into account in setting the percentages.

The relative levels of culpability of the different tortfeasors may, however, be an important factor in apportioning liability, and need not only relate to the causation of the harm in question. In *Re-Source America v Platt Site Services* [2005] All ER (D) 99 (Feb), [2004] EWCA Civ 665, the Court of Appeal took the manner in which a defendant conducted its defence and its attempts to evade detection into account in apportioning liability as between tortfeasors. See also *McDonald v Coys of Kensington* [2004] EWCA Civ 47. In *Brian Warwicker Partnership v Hok International Ltd* [2005] All ER (D) 386 (Jul), [2005] EWCA Civ 962, the Court of Appeal confirmed that the relevant material that courts may take into account in determining what apportionment was 'just and equitable' for the purposes of s. 2 of the Act was not limited to causative factors. While the Court of Appeal emphasised that relative causative responsibility was likely to be the most important factor in the assessment of contribution, courts could have regard to both the potency of the fault of the claimant and also the blameworthiness of the claimant. However, Keene LJ at [51] suggested that there would need to be 'some close connection between any non-causative factors taken into account...and the acts or omissions which give rise to liability in the first place'. Arden LJ at [45] similarly emphasised that non-causative factors should play a 'limited role' and be given 'less weight' than material showing the extent of the relative responsibility for the damage in question when courts exercise their 'semi-structured discretion' available to courts under s. 2 of the 1978 Act.

In *Dubai Aluminium Co Ltd v Salaam* [2003] 1 All ER 97, [2002] UKHL 48 (p. 1072, ante), the partners of a law firm, one of whose number had knowingly assisted in a dishonest scheme without the knowledge of the other partners, sought contribution from two other parties to the dishonest scheme. The House of Lords considered that the retention by the two parties to the scheme of undisgorged profits linked to their wrongful conduct justified an award of a total indemnity to the innocent law firm partners, even if this factor was irrelevant as regards 'responsibility' for the damage in question. (Note that under s. 2(1) of the 1978 Act, the courts are required to 'have regard' to the extent of a person's responsibility for the damage, but this does not prevent other considerations being taken into account in apportioning liability in a just and equitable manner.) Lord Nicholls at [52] commented that 'of necessity, the extent to which it is just and equitable to redistribute [the financial burden of compensating the claimant] cannot be decided without seeing where the burden already lies'. Note that the House of Lords considered that the personal innocence of the partners was not a relevant factor to be taken into account in allocating contribution, as their vicarious liability for the wrongdoing for their delinquent partner meant that, in Lord Nicholls's phrase, they stood 'in his shoes for all relevant purposes': see p. 1075, ante. Note that in apportioning liability, the court may also take into account whether one of the parties is insolvent (*Fisher v CMT Ltd* [1996] 2 QB 475, [1966] 1 All ER 88) or the prospect of a future insolvency (*Dubai Aluminium v Salaam*, per Lord Millett at [167]). In general, appellate courts will give trial judges a wide margin of discretion in apportioning liability, but any such apportionment needs to have an 'intellectually respectable basis': see *Stimpson v Curran* [2004] All ER (D) 191 (Sep), [2004] EWCA Civ 1249.

8. *Successive actions.* Section 3, replacing s. 6(1)(a) of the 1935 Act, refers not only to tortfeasors but to 'any person liable in respect of any debt or damage' (see s. 6(1) of the 1978 Act). It also makes it clear that this provision applies not only to successive actions but also to a single action against two or more persons, thus adopting the view of Lord Denning MR on the old s. 6(1)(a) in *Bryanston Finance Co Ltd v De Vries* [1975] QB 703 at 722. See *Cutler v McPhail* (p. 1110, ante) regarding release. Section 4 is intended to replace s. 6(1)(b) of the 1935 Act, but differs from that section, first in covering not only tortfeasors but also 'persons liable in respect of the damage' (s. 6(1) of the 1978 Act), and secondly, in setting no limit on sums recoverable under judgments other than the judgment first given.

9. *Limitation.* Section 10 of the Limitation Act 1980 provides that the right to claim contribution becomes statute-barred after the end of the period of two years from the date when the right accrued. The relevant date is the date of judgment against the first tortfeasor, or, where he makes or agrees to make any payment to one or more persons in compensation for the damage, the earliest date on which the amount to be paid is agreed between him and the person to whom the payment is to be made. In *Knight v Rochdale Healthcare NHS Trust* [2003] 4 All ER 416, [2003] EWHC 1831, Crane J considered that where a firm agreement had been made, time started to run for the purposes of s. 10 of the 1980 Act at that moment, unless the agreement required the making of a consent order by a court before it took effect. In *Aer Lingus plc v Gildacroft Ltd* [2006] 2 All ER 290, [2006] EWCA Civ 4, the Court of Appeal held that the relevant date when time began to run for the purposes of s. 10 was that of the relevant judgment on quantum, not that on liability: the judgment in question therefore had to determine the amount as well as the existence of liability before the time began to run. (As regards the situation where the breach of duty occurred before the 1978 Act came into force, but the damage occurred after that date, see *Lampitt v Poole Borough Council* [1991] 2 QB 545, [1990] 2 All ER 887.)

(b) Under the contract of employment

■ Lister v Romford Ice & Cold Storage Co Ltd
House of Lords [1957] 1 All ER 125

The appellant, Lister, was employed as a lorry driver by the respondents. He negligently ran down his mate (his father) while backing his lorry in a yard. The father recovered damages against the respondents on grounds of their vicarious liability. The respondents' insurers, acting in their name by virtue of a term in the contract of insurance, brought an action against the appellant for damages for breach of an implied term in his contract of employment that he would exercise reasonable care and skill in his driving. The appellant pleaded that it was an implied term that he was entitled to the benefit of any insurance which his employer either had effected or as a reasonable and prudent person should have effected and consequently the respondents could not claim an indemnity or contribution from him.

The Court of Appeal [1956] 2 QB 180, [1955] 3 All ER 460, Denning LJ dissenting, held that the respondents' action succeeded both under the Act of 1935 and because of the appellant's breach of the implied term. In the House of Lords this judgment was affirmed on the point of the implied term by 3:2 (the dissentients being Lord Radcliffe and Lord Somervell). Although all five of their Lordships held that there was an implied term to use reasonable care, the dissentients took the view that the employee was protected by an implied term that the employer will not seek an indemnity where it is understood that the employer will take out a third-party liability policy. The majority (Viscount Simonds, Lord Morton and Lord Tucker) said that such a term could not be implied.

VISCOUNT SIMONDS: . . .

It is, in my opinion, clear that it was an implied term of the contract that the appellant would perform his duties with proper care. The proposition of law stated by Willes J in *Harmer v Cornelius* ((1858) 5 CBNS 236 at p. 246) has never been questioned:

> "When a skilled labourer, artisan, or artist is employed, there is on his part an implied warranty that he is of skill reasonably competent to the task he undertakes, Spondes peritiam artis. Thus, if an apothecary, a watchmaker, or an attorney be employed for reward, they each impliedly undertake to possess and exercise reasonable skill in their several arts. . . . An express promise or express representation in the particular case is not necessary."

I see no ground for excluding from, and every ground for including in, this category a servant who is employed to drive a lorry which, driven without care, may become an engine of destruction and involve his master in very grave liability. Nor can I see any valid reason for saying that a distinction is to be made between possessing skill and exercising it. No such distinction is made in the cited case; on the contrary, "possess" and "exercise" are there conjoined. Of what advantage to the employer is his servant's undertaking that he possesses skill unless he undertakes also to use it? I have spoken of using skill rather than using care, for "skill" is the word used in the cited case, but this embraces care. For even in so-called unskilled operations an exercise of care is necessary to the proper performance of duty.

I have already said that it does not appear to me to make any difference to the determination of any substantive issue in this case whether the respondents' cause of action lay in tort or breach of contract. But, in deference to Denning LJ, I think it right to say that I concur in what I understand to be the unanimous opinion of your Lordships that the servant owes a contractual duty of care to his master, and that the breach of that duty founds an action for damages for breach of contract, and that this (apart from any defence) is such a case. It is trite law that a single act of negligence may give rise to a claim either in tort or for breach of a term express or implied in a contract. Of this, the negligence of a servant in performance of his duty is a clear example.

I conclude, then, the first stage of the argument by saying that the appellant was under a contractual obligation of care in the performance of his duty, that he committed a breach of it, that the respondents thereby suffered damage and they are entitled to recover that damage from him, unless it is shown either that the damage is too remote or that there is some other intervening factor which precludes the recovery....

My Lords, undoubtedly there are formidable obstacles in the path of the appellant, and they were formidably presented by counsel for the respondents. First, it is urged that it must be irrelevant to the right of the master to sue his servant for breach of duty that the master is insured against its consequences. As a general proposition it has not, I think, been questioned for nearly two hundred years that, in determining the rights inter se of A and B, the fact that one or other of them is insured is to be disregarded: see, e.g. *Mason v Sainsbury* ((1782) 3 Doug KB 61). This general proposition, no doubt, applies if A is a master and B his man; but its application to a case or class of case must yield to an express or implied term to the contrary, and, as the question is whether that term should be implied, I am not constrained by an assertion of the general proposition to deny the possible exception. Yet I cannot wholly ignore a principle so widely applicable as that a man insures at his own expense for his own benefit and does not thereby suffer any derogation of his rights against another man.

Next—and here I recur to a difficulty already indicated—if it has become part of the common law of England that, as between the employer and driver of a motor vehicle, it is the duty of the former to look after the whole matter of insurance (an expression which I have used compendiously to describe the plea as finally submitted), must not that duty be more precisely defined? It may be answered that in other relationships duties are imposed by law which can only be stated in general terms. Partners owe a duty of faithfulness to each other; what that duty involves in any particular case can only be determined in the light of all its circumstances. Other examples in other branches of the law may occur to your Lordships where a general duty is presented and its scope falls to be determined partly by the general custom of the country which is the basis of the law and partly, perhaps, by equitable considerations; but even so, the determination must rest on evidence of the custom or on such broad equitable considerations as have from early times guided a court of equity.

In the area in which this appeal is brought, there is no evidence to guide your Lordships. The single fact that, since the Road Traffic Act 1930 came into force, a measure of insurance against third-party risk is compulsory affords no ground for an assumption that an employer will take out a policy which covers more than the Act requires, for instance, a risk of injury to third parties not on the road but in private premises. There is, in fact, no assumption that can legitimately be made what policy will be taken out and what its terms and qualifications may be. I am unable to satisfy myself that, with such a background, there can be implied in the relationship of employer and driver any such terms as I have indicated. And though, as I have said, I feel the force of the argument as presented by Denning LJ, I must point out that, at least in his view, the indemnity of the driver was conditional on a policy which covered the risk having in fact been taken out. It may be that this was because his mind was directed to a case where such a policy was taken out, and that he would have gone on to say that there was a further implication that the employer would take out a policy whether required by law to do so or not. But here we are in the realm of speculation. Is it certain that, if the imaginary driver had said to his employer: "Of course you will indemnify me against any damage that I may do however gross my negligence may be", the employer would have said: "Yes, of course"! For myself, I cannot answer confidently that he would have said so or ought to have said so. It may well be that, if such a discussion had taken place, it might have ended in some agreement between them or in the driver not entering the service of that employer. That I do not know. But I do not know that I am ever driven further from an assured certainty what is the term which the law imports into the contract of service between the employer and the driver of a motor vehicle.

Another argument was, at this stage, adduced which appeared to me to have some weight. For just as it was urged that a term could not be implied unless it could be defined with precision, so its existence was denied if it could not be shown when it came to birth. Here, it was said, was a duty alleged to arise out of the relation of master and servant in this special sphere of employment which was imposed by the common law. When, then, did it first arise? Not, surely, when the first country squire exchanged his carriage and horses for a motor car or the first haulage contractor bought a motor lorry. Was it when the practice of insurance against third-party risk became so common that it was to be expected of the reasonable man, or was it only when the Act of 1930 made compulsory and, therefore, universal what had previously been reasonable and usual?

Then, again, the familiar argument was heard asking where the line is to be drawn. The driver of a motor car is not the only man in charge of an engine which, if carelessly used, may endanger and injure third parties. The man in charge of a crane was given as an example. If he, by his negligence, injures a third party who then makes his employer vicariously liable, is he entitled to assume that his employer has covered himself by insurance and will indemnify him, however gross and reprehensible his negligence? And does this depend on the extent to which insurance against third-party risks prevails and is known to prevail in any particular form of employment? Does it depend on the fact that there are fewer cranes than cars and that the master is less likely to drive a crane than a car? . . .

NOTES

1. In *Gregory v Ford* [1951] 1 All ER 121 Byrne J held that it was an implied term of the contract of employment that the employer would not require the employee to do an unlawful act and, consequently, the employer had a contractual duty to the employee to comply with the compulsory insurance provisions of the Road Traffic Act in respect of vehicles the employee was required to drive. The validity of this decision was accepted by both sides in *Lister*'s case (although Lord Morton expressed some doubts). G. L. Williams (1957) 20 MLR 220 at 226 argues that *Gregory v Ford* cannot demonstrably be founded on the wording of the Road Traffic Act. The present Road Traffic Act 1988 (p. 1142, post) requires the person who uses or causes or permits a motor vehicle to be used on a road to be covered against third party risks. The Act, like its predecessors, does not require the employer to take out a policy which covers the personal liability of its employee. If this is so, how can the Act be said to create an implied contractual duty to insure the employee?

2. An employee does have a right to indemnity where a road traffic policy is taken out under the provisions of the Road Traffic Act 1988 (p. 1142, post). In *Lister*'s case the insurance was not compulsory (the accident did not occur on a 'road') and, in any event, the insurance company which claimed by subrogation was not the company which issued the road traffic policy, but another company which had issued an employer's liability policy. Since 1 January 1972, employers' liability insurance has been compulsory (p. 1146, post) but the Employers' Liability (Compulsory Insurance) Act 1969 contains no statutory right of indemnity for an employee analogous to that contained in the Road Traffic Act. It has been argued that since the Employers' Liability (Compulsory Insurance) Act requires employers to cover *their* liability to employees and not the personal liability of employees to fellow employees or others, the Act does not create an implied contractual duty to insure the employee (cf. *Gregory v Ford*, ante). But in *Bernadone v Pall Mall Services Group* [1999] IRLR 617 Blofeld J, in the context of

deciding whether the benefit of the insurance contract transferred to a new employer under the Transfer of Undertakings (Protection of Employment) Regulations 1981 considered that there is an implied term in the employee's contract of employment that the employee will be protected by an appropriate insurance policy taken out by the employer under the 1969 Act. The employee's protection by the insurance policy is said to be a duty or liability of an employer arising out of the contract of employment. This was confirmed by the Court of Appeal in *Martin v Lancashire County Council* [2000] 3 All ER 554.

3.   In a case concerning a hire of plant with a worker (*Thompson v T Lohan (Plant Hire) Ltd* [1987] 2 All ER 631, [1987] I WLR 649), a clause providing that the hirer was to be liable for the negligence of the owner's employee while operating hired plant was held not to be an exclusion of liability clause and hence not invalidated by s. 2(1) of the Unfair Contract Terms 1977 Act; cf. *Phillips Products Ltd v Hyland* [1987] 2 All ER 620, [1987] 1 WLR 659.

■ Jones v Manchester Corporation
Court of Appeal [1952] 2 All ER 125

In an action for damages by the widow of a patient who died under negligent hospital treatment, the hospital board claimed an indemnity from Dr Wilkes, an inexperienced physician who had administered the fatal anaesthetic under the instructions of Dr Sejrup, a house surgeon.

SINGLETON LJ: . . .

The employer cannot have a right of indemnity if he himself has contributed to the damage or if he bears some part of the responsibility therefor, and the same reasoning applies if some other and senior employee's negligence has contributed to the damage. On the facts of this case I feel bound to reject the claim of the hospital board to an indemnity against Dr. Wilkes. I mentioned in the course of the argument the desirability of pleadings and of discovery if a question such as this was to be raised. Without this it is not easy to determine the true terms of the contract between the parties. All that we know is that Dr. Wilkes was appointed a house surgeon at the hospital a short time after she had been qualified, and after an interview. There is no evidence to show that she was ever instructed, or advised, at the hospital as to the use of drugs . . . .

DENNING LJ: . . .

The hospital authorities cannot come down on every negligent member of the staff for a full indemnity. Such a course could only be justified if the hospital authorities could be regarded as innocent parties who have been made vicariously liable without any fault in them. But the law does not regard them as innocent. It says that they are themselves under a duty of care and skill, and, if that duty is not fulfilled, it regards them as tortfeasors and makes them liable as such, no matter whether the negligence be their personal negligence or the negligence of their staff.

In all these cases the important thing to remember is that when a master employs a servant to do something for him, he is responsible for the servant's conduct as if it were his own. If the servant commits a tort in the course of his employment, then the master is a tortfeasor as well as the servant. The master is never treated as an innocent party. This is well seen by taking a simple case where two cars are damaged in a collision by the fault of both drivers. One is driven by a servant, the other by an owner-driver. The owner-driver can obviously only recover a proportion of the damage to his own car from the owner of the other one, and likewise the owner of the chauffeur-driven car can only recover a proportion of the damage to his car. He cannot recover the whole damage from the owner-driver. He cannot claim as if he was an innocent person damaged by the negligence of the two drivers. He can only claim upon the footing that he himself is a tortfeasor and that the damage is partly the result of his own fault within the Law Reform (Contributory Negligence) Act, 1945. Now suppose that a third person was injured in the collision, so that the owners of both cars are liable in tort to the injured person for his full damages. The owner of the chauffeur-driven car obviously cannot recover a full indemnity from his servant or from the owner-driver. He cannot claim as if he were an innocent person who has suffered damage as the result of the negligence of the two drivers. He can only claim as a tortfeasor for contribution under the Act of 1935.

My conclusion, therefore, is that the hospital authorities in this case were themselves tortfeasors who have no right to indemnity or contribution from any member of their staff except in so far as the court thinks it just and equitable, having regard to the extent of that person's responsibility for the damage. In considering what is just and equitable, I think the court can have regard to extenuating circumstances which would not be available as against the injured person. Errors due to inexperience or lack of supervision are no defence as against the injured person, but they are available to reduce the amount of contribution which the hospital authorities can demand. It would be in the highest degree unjust that hospital authorities, by getting inexperienced doctors to perform their duties for them, without adequate supervision, should be able to throw all the responsibility on to those doctors as if they were fully experienced practitioners. Applying this principle to the present case, I find it very difficult to place much blame on Dr Wilkes....

[HODSON LJ delivered a dissenting judgment.]

■ Harvey v R G O'Dell Ltd (Galway, Third Party)
Queen's Bench Division [1958] 1 All ER 657

Galway was employed by the first defendants as a storekeeper. On their instructions he went from London to Hurley to do some repair work, taking the plaintiff, a fellow employee with him as a passenger in his motor cycle combination. While on a journey from fetching some tools and materials, there was an accident partly due to Galway's negligence in which he was killed and the plaintiff was injured. In an action by the plaintiff against the defendants as Galway's employers, the defendants served a third party notice on Galway's administratrix claiming a contribution against his estate under s. 6(1)(c) of the Law Reform (Maried Women and Tortfeasors) Act of 1935 or alternatively for breach of an implied term in Galway's contract of service that he would indemnify them for any liability arising out of his negligence. McNair J held that, as joint tortfeasors, the defendant employers were entitled to a 100 per cent contribution from Galway's estate. He also considered the alleged implied term.

MCNAIR J: ...

Mr Galway was engaged and employed by the first defendants as a storekeeper; as a concession to the first defendants he from time to time used his own motor cycle on their business and was so using it at the time of the accident. I find it difficult to see on what grounds of justice and reason I should hold that, by making his motor cycle combination available for his employers' business on a particular occasion, he should be held in law to have impliedly agreed to indemnify them if he committed a casual act of negligence. Suppose in a time of labour disturbance in the docks master stevedores, as sometimes happens, induce their office staff to man the cranes or to do stevedoring; if a third party is injured through the negligence of such staff, no doubt the master stevedores would be vicariously liable, as, indeed, they might be primarily liable, on the basis that they had employed unskilled persons. But it would surely be contrary to all reason and justice to hold that the willing office staff, by abandoning their ledgers and undertaking manual tasks, had impliedly agreed to indemnify their employers against liability arising from their negligence in performing work which they were not employed to do.

I should, therefore, dismiss the claim of the first defendants against the third party, in so far as it rests on an allegation of breach of the contract of employment....

QUESTION

Did McNair J pose the right question? Should it have been 'Did Galway agree to exercise reasonable care about his employer's business?' (See J. A. Jolowicz (1959) 22 MLR 171, 189.)

NOTES

1. The student who relied simply on the law reports for an understanding of the indemnity and contribution arrangements between employers and their employees would be seriously misled. *Lister*'s case produced an uproar, if for no other reason than that 'the friendliest relation between the employer and his staff can now be disrupted, and the employee impoverished, by the action of an insurance company, which finds itself in the happy position of having received premiums for a risk that it does not have to bear' (G. L. Williams (1957) 20 MLR 220 at 221). An interdepartmental committee was set up to investigate the position and suggested that trade unions might, by collective bargaining, seek insurance cover for their members. This does not seem to have happened on any significant scale and, in any event, has now been overtaken by the Employers' Liability (Compulsory Insurance) Act 1969 (p. 1146, post). Moreover, a so-called 'gentlemen's agreement' among the majority of insurers not to enforce their subrogation rights against employees except in cases of collusion or wilful misconduct, had, according to the interdepartmental committee, prevented any 'practical problem' arising out of *Lister*'s case. Mr (later Lord) Gardiner commented: 'It is not clear that the Committee realised that the "gentlemen's agreement" leaves it open to the insurers to say to a trade union, "If you go on with this action on behalf of your insured member, and we choose with the consent of the assured to claim over against the foreman whose negligence is alleged to have caused the injury, the foreman who is also one of your members, may have to sell up his home"' ((1959) 22 MLR 652 at 654).

    The 'agreement' was later extended to cover all members of the British Insurance Association, all Lloyd's underwriters concerned with this class of business and nearly all other insurance companies. See generally R. Lewis (1985) 4 SMLR 270. Nevertheless, perhaps as a result of the declining influence of the trades unions, cases of enforcement of the *Lister* indemnity do very occasionally arise (see e.g. *Bean (t/a Car & Commercial Services) v Rothery* (Court of Appeal transcript, 5 December 1994)). If these arguably unattractive claims reach the higher courts, they might well prompt a reconsideration of the whole doctrine.

2. In *Morris v Ford Motor Co Ltd* [1973] QB 792, [1973] 2 All ER 1084, the Court of Appeal sought to limit the application of *Lister*'s case. C was engaged by F to perform cleaning services at F's factory. M, an employee of C, was injured due to the negligent driving of a forklift truck by R, one of F's employees. F's insurers paid M's damages and then, in F's name, recovered the full amount from C, in terms of a clause in the contract for cleaning services which obliged C to indemnify F against all losses. C then claimed an indemnity from R, the negligent employee of F. The Court of Appeal acknowledged that C, as indemnitor, was entitled to every right of action of the person indemnified.

However, Lord Denning MR and James LJ (Stamp LJ dissenting) held that, in an industrial setting, subrogation was unacceptable and unrealistic and so there was an implied term that this right was excluded. Lord Denning MR also held that subrogation was an equitable right, and it was not just or equitable to compel F to lend its name to proceedings against R, because this might lead to a strike and, anyway, C had been imprudent in failing to heed advice to insure.

CHAPTER TWENTY

INSURANCE AND COMPENSATION

As a general proposition it has not, I think, been questioned for nearly two hundred years that in determining the rights *inter se* of A and B, the fact that one of them is insured is to be disregarded: per Viscount Simonds in *Lister v Romford Ice and Cold Storage Co Ltd* [1957] 1 All ER 125 at 133 (p. 1128, ante).

This observation reveals a fundamental judicial dilemma implicit in many of the cases collected together in this sourcebook. The common law method of determining liability rests upon the notion of *loss shifting*: either the claimant or the defendant, or sometimes both, must individually bear the loss. The predominant mechanism is fault. At the same time, the fact of insurance makes it possible for losses to be *distributed*. Some large enterprises are able to operate as self-insurers and absorb the cost of paying compensation from their own resources. Most organisations and individuals, however, have recourse to insurance. This spreads the risk among those engaged in the same kind of activity—such as manufacturers, motorists or employers—and paying premiums against similar risks. Once this loss distributing function of the law of tort is acknowledged, many of the old arguments in favour of the fault principle have to be modified: in particular the imposition of liability on the defendant will not be a crushing economic burden. Occasionally (e.g. the views of Lord Denning MR in cases of economic loss) the courts have denied the existence of a duty of care on the ground that the defendant is not a suitable loss distributor: or conversely have imposed a duty on a member of a profession who carries insurance (e.g. the views of Lord Griffiths in *Smith v Eric S. Bush* [1989] 2 All ER 514 at 531, p. 218, ante); or (as in *Ackworth v Kempe* (1778) 1 Doug KB 40 and *Lloyd v Grace, Smith & Co* [1912] AC 716) have allowed recovery against an employer for his employee's wrongdoing on the ground that he could protect himself by fidelity insurance. However, these are exceptional cases. The observations in *Morgans v Launchbury* [1973] AC 127, [1972] 2 All ER 606 (p. 1140, post) indicate that English judges are not willing to innovate any general principle of risk distribution, i.e. the imposition of liability upon those parties best placed to act as a conduit of distribution.

[I]nsurance is traditionally ignored by courts not because they want to pretend it does not exist, but they reject its alleged relevance to the issue whether liability should be imposed . . . (Jane Stapleton, 'Tort, Insurance and Ideology' (1995) 58 MLR 820 at 822).

This does not mean that the student can afford to ignore the fact of insurance. The materials gathered together in this chapter have been relevant in other chapters. It has been suggested that the legal rules have been 'invisibly' affected by the existence of insurance: examples are the development of the manufacturer's duty in negligence (p. 611, ante), the raising of the standard of care required from learner drivers (p. 307, ante), the conversion from 'fault' to 'negligence without fault' through the *res ipsa loquitur* doctrine (p. 337, ante), the imposition of strict liability for dangerous escapes (p. 828, ante). But there is considerable controversy over whether insurance has actually had an impact on tort liability, whatever the courts might outwardly admit. Some recent judicial observations on this matter, especially those of Lord Hoffmann, are considered in the first section of this chapter.

Also very important in practice is the power of the insurance companies, having obtained a decision in their favour, to 'buy off' an appeal by paying ample compensation to the appellant so that they will have a legal precedent on their side for use in settling later cases (per Lord Denning MR in *Davis v Johnson* [1979] AC 264 at 278). Legislative policy has also been affected by the insurance situation: examples are the abolition of the rule against actions between husband and wife (Law Reform (Husband and Wife) Act 1962), the removal of the protection afforded to highway authorities (Highways (Miscellaneous Provisions) Act 1961, s. 1(1), and see now the Highways Act 1980, s. 58), and the imposition of strict liability for nuclear incidents upon site licensees (Nuclear Installations Act 1965, p. 666, ante). W.R. Cornish and G. de N. Clark, *Law and Society in England 1750–1950* (London, 1989) p. 540 even suggest that the demands of the insurance industry drove the flight from jury uncertainty towards predictable judicial tariffs, for the assessment of damages in personal injury cases.

By far the most important reason for understanding the insurance background is that it enables one to examine how far tort law is coping with the social and economic problems of allocating accident losses. Those who criticise the legal rules often do so because they are seen to be deficient in the performance of this function. The materials in this chapter consider, in the second section, the attempts made by Parliament to remedy one obvious injustice, that created by the defendant who is unable to pay. The Road Traffic Act 1988 re-enacts, with later amendments, provisions first enacted in 1930 to compel insurance in respect of death or bodily injury arising from the use of a motor vehicle on a road. The Employers' Liability (Compulsory Insurance) Act 1969 adopts a similar policy in regard to an employer's liability to his employees. Parliament has also assisted the victims of bankrupt tortfeasors by means of the Third Parties (Rights Against Insurers) Act 1930 (p. 1149, post) and the Road Traffic Act 1988, s. 153 (p. 1144, post).

The courts attempted to create a remedy against the uninsured motorist in *Monk v Warbey* [1935] 1 KB 75 (p. 680, ante). But this obviously unsatisfactory device has now almost been supplanted by a fascinating instance of 'private legislation': the agreements between the insurance industry and the government which, ignoring the formal legal rules, promise compensation to the victims of uninsured and untraced motorists. Like the 'gentlemen's agreement' not to rely on *Lister v Romford Ice and Cold Storage Co Ltd* [1957] AC 555, [1957] 1 All ER 125 (p. 1128, ante), these agreements remind the student of law that 'black letter' legal rules sometimes bear little relation to social reality. The Motor Insurers' Bureau's 'notes', which explain these agreements, are printed in the third section of this chapter. There are no corresponding institutions to protect the victims of uninsured or 'fly-by-night' employers.

Insurance is a matter of contract between insurer and insured. The policy may be one of *liability* insurance (e.g. products, employers' or 'public' liability) by which the insurer agrees, in consideration of a premium, to cover specified types of legal liability which the insured may incur. Or it may be one of *loss* (sometimes called 'first-party' or 'personal accident') insurance (e.g. on the life of the insured, or his home or business), by which the insurer agrees, in consideration of a premium, to indemnity the insured in respect of particular losses. Or it may be a combination of liability and loss insurance (e.g. a comprehensive motor insurance policy). A particular risk may be covered by both types of insurance (e.g. the owner of a damaged motor vehicle may claim under his own *loss* insurance policy or make a tort claim against the negligent motorist whose insurer will pay under the latter's *liability* policy). The student of tort is not concerned with the many problems of contract interpretation which may arise under policies such as these. His or her questions ought primarily to be functional ones such as: (1) What limits are there on the various types of liability insurance? (2) What is the effect of the law of contributory negligence on liability insurance? (3) What risks are covered by loss insurance that are not covered by liability insurance? (4) What is the nature and likely effect of no-claims discount clauses? (5) What are the advantages of loss (first-party) insurance in comparison with liability insurance? These and related questions can best be answered by reading the policies in conjunction with *Atiyah*, especially chaps. 9 and 11.

The institution of insurance has an important effect on the conduct of litigation, in particular because of the insurer's right of subrogation (p. 1155, post) and its right to full control over the conduct of legal proceedings in the insured's name (the latter being a contractual condition). This gives the insured the advantage of expert assistance; but by the same token it means that the uninsured party may find himself without similar assistance. The factors which influence the nature and amount of settlements of tort claims are considered in the fourth section of this chapter: see further *Atiyah*, chap. 10.

Tort provides only about one-quarter of all the compensation for personal injury in Britain. The main burden falls on the highly developed and complicated social security system. A brief guide to the main benefits under that system is provided in the fifth section (p. 1156, post). One of the state benefits is criminal injuries compensation and the text of the current scheme is printed (p. 1158, post).

These other sources of compensation are important to the student of tort in respect of the assessment of tort damages (Chap. 8, ante). They also have to be understood if there is to be any intelligent discussion of the likely future of tort as a method of compensation for incapacity. The final section of this chapter directs attention to the main avenues of possible reform of accident compensation.

1 THE RELATIONSHIP BETWEEN INSURANCE AND TORT LIABILITY

NOTE

As stated in the introduction to this chapter, there has been considerable controversy between commentators over the impact that liability insurance has had on the development of tort law and the incidence of liability. The article by Jane Stapleton cited there should be contrasted with those by Davies, Lewis, and Morgan (references given pp. 1171–1172 post). Perhaps the best survey of the arguments is by M. A. Clarke, *Policies and Perceptions of Insurance Law in the Twenty-First Century* (Oxford, 2005), chap. 8.

The best-known judicial advocate of the relevance of insurance to tort liability was Lord Denning. Take his observations about the standard of care in *Nettleship v Weston* [1971] 2 QB 691 at 699–700: Parliament requires drivers to insure against third party risks, but those 'third parties', if injured on the road, can only recover damages if the driver is liable in tort. Thus claimed Lord Denning, 'the judges see to it that he is liable, unless he can prove care and skill of a high standard... Thus we are, in this branch of the law, moving away from the concept: "No liability without fault". We are beginning to apply the test: "On whom should the risk fall?".' See further Lord Denning MR.'s remarks about household insurance in *Lamb v Camden London Borough Council* [1981] QB 625, [1981] 2 All ER 408 (p. 401, ante). Clarke, op cit., indeed describes the view that insurance has led to the expansion of tort liability as the 'Denning perception' (p. 309). Lest it be thought that this is merely the singular viewpoint of a heterodox judge, it is worth collecting some more recent statements to like effect, in particular those by Lord Hoffmann, before returning to the problems with the 'Denning perception'.

■ Stovin v Wise

House of Lords [1996] 3 All ER 801

For the facts of the case and decision, see p. 66, ante.

LORD HOFFMANN [considering the test of 'general reliance' suggested as the basis on which statutory powers might give rise to a duty of care by Mason J in *Sutherland Shire Council v Heyman* (1985) 157 CLR 424 at 464:]...

[The] application [of the doctrine of general reliance] may require some very careful analysis of the role which the expected exercise of the statutory power plays in community behaviour. For example, in one sense it is true that the fire brigade is there to protect people in situations in which they could not be expected to be able to protect themselves. On the other hand, they can and do protect themselves by insurance against the risk of fire. It is not obvious that there should be a right to compensation from a negligent fire authority which will ordinarily enure by right of subrogation to an insurance company. The only reason would be to provide a general deterrent against inefficiency. But there must be better ways of doing this than by compensating insurance companies out of public funds. And while premiums no doubt take into account the existence of the fire brigade and the likelihood that it will arrive swiftly upon the scene, it is not clear that they would be very different merely because no compensation was paid in the rare cases in which the fire authority negligently failed to perform its public duty.

NOTES

1. In *Capital & Counties Plc v Hampshire County Council* [1997] 2 All ER 865 at 877 the Court of Appeal explained this passage as follows:

    Although the plaintiffs' counsel have criticised Lord Hoffmann's reference to the existence of insurance as being an invalid ground for saying that it is not just, fair and reasonable to impose a duty of care, we do not think that this is what Lord Hoffmann is saying in this passage. Rather he is suggesting that there is not a general expectation that fires will necessarily be extinguished by the fire brigade; there is no doubt a hope that they will; but they may arrive too late to be of practical use, or they may not arrive at all; instead, for the most part people rely upon insurance for indemnification in case of loss.

2. At first instance in one of the appeals heard together in *Capital & Counties*, the trial judge had decided that the fire brigade did not owe a duty of care inter alia because: 'It is for the individual to insure against fire risks.' The Court of Appeal held that this argument was not 'persuasive' (while ultimately denying liability on other grounds: see p. 116, ante). They recorded the criticisms of counsel (which the court found to have 'considerable force') as follows at p. 891:

[Fire insurance] premiums are calculated having regard to the existence and likely response of the fire brigade; very substantial reductions in premiums are granted where buildings are protected by sprinklers, there may be underinsurances and absence of insurance, particularly in the lower end of the property market. Further, it would be unusual for there to be effective insurance against personal injury. Finally, there is nothing to prevent fire brigades insuring against their liability. Indeed the London and West Yorkshire brigades are insured.

■ Transco Plc v Stockport Metropolitan Borough Council
House of Lords [2004] 1 All ER 589

For the facts of the case and decision, see p. 843 ante.

LORD HOFFMANN [considering the modern ambit of the *Rylands v Fletcher* tort:] . . .

[46] . . . [S]o far as the rule does have a residuary role to play, it must be borne in mind that it is concerned only with damage to property and that insurance against various forms of damage to property is extremely common. A useful guide in deciding whether the risk has been created by a 'non-natural' user of land is therefore to ask whether the damage which eventuated was something against which the occupier could reasonably be expected to have insured himself. Property insurance is relatively cheap and accessible; in my opinion people should be encouraged to insure their own property rather than seek to transfer the risk to others by means of litigation, with the heavy transactional costs which that involves. The present substantial litigation over £100,000 should be a warning to anyone seeking to rely on an esoteric cause of action to shift a commonplace insured risk.

[49] In my opinion the Court of Appeal was right to say that it was not a 'non-natural' user of land. I am influenced by two matters. First, there is no evidence that it created a greater risk than is normally associated with domestic or commercial plumbing. . . . Secondly, I think that the risk of damage to property caused by leaking water is one against which most people can and do commonly insure. This is, as I have said, particularly true of Transco, which can be expected to have insured against any form of damage to its pipe. . . .

LORD HOBHOUSE OF WOODBOROUGH: . . .

[60] . . . [I]t is argued that the risk of property damage is 'insurable', just as is public liability. It is then said that, since insurers are likely to be the real parties behind any litigation, the rule has become unnecessary. This is an unsound argument for a number of reasons. It is historically unsound: in the second half of the nineteenth century there already existed in England, as the common law judges were well aware, a developed insurance market. The existence of an insurance market does not mean that such insurance is available free of charge: premiums have to be paid. Some risks may only be insurable at prohibitive rates or at rates which for the proposer are not commercially viable and so make the risk, for him, commercially uninsurable. (Indeed, in recent times it has been the experience that some insurers will not cover certain risks at all, eg loss or damage caused by flooding.) The rationale, he who creates the risk must bear the risk, is not altered at all by the existence of an insurance market. It is an application of the same concept, an acknowledgment of risk. The economic burden of insuring against the risk must be borne by he who creates it and has the control of it. Further, the magnitude of the burden will depend upon who ultimately has to bear the loss: the rule provides the answer to this. The argument that insurance makes the rule unnecessary is no more valid than saying that, because some people can afford to and sensibly do take out comprehensive car insurance, no driver should be civilly liable for his negligent driving. It is unprincipled to abrogate for all citizens a legal rule merely because it may be unnecessary as between major corporations.

NOTE

In *LMS International Ltd v Styrene Packaging & Insulation Ltd* [2005] EWHC 2065 (TCC)
Judge Peter Coulson QC noted at [33] that the relevance of insurance was a matter over
which the House of Lords in *Transco* had 'emphatically disagreed'. In such a situation the
judge felt that it would be a mistake to attach significance to the insurance position, although
he recorded 'with great diffidence' his own view that Lord Hoffmann was wrong and 'the
existence or otherwise of insurance in favour of a claimant should not, of itself, be determinative of that party's right of action in law': see [228].

■ Morgans v Launchbury
House of Lords [1972] 2 All ER 606

For the facts of the case and decision, see p. 1067, ante.

LORD WILBERFORCE: . . .

The respondents submitted that we should depart from accepted principle and introduce a new
rule, or set of rules, applicable to the use of motor vehicles, which would make the appellant liable as
owner. Lord Denning MR in the Court of Appeal [1971] 1 All ER 642, 648 formulated one such rule,
based on the conception of a matrimonial car, a car used in common by husband and wife for the daily
purposes of both. All purposes, or at least the great majority of purposes, he would say are matrimonial
purposes: shopping, going to work, transporting children, all are purposes of the owner, the car was
bought and owned for them to be carried out. And, consequently (this is the critical step) the owner
is ipso jure liable whatever the other spouse is using the car for, unless, it seems, although the scope
of the exception is not defined, the latter is 'on a frolic of his own'. Indeed Lord Denning MR seems to
be willing to go even further and to hold the owner liable on the basis merely of permission to drive,
actual or assumed.

My Lords, I have no doubt that the multiplication of motor cars on our roads, their increasing speed,
the severity of the injuries they may cause, the rise in accidents involving innocent persons, give rise to
problems of increasing social difficulty with which the law finds it difficult to keep abreast. And I am
willing to assume (although I think that more evidence is needed than this one case) that traditional
concepts of vicarious liability, founded on agency as developed in relation to less dangerous vehicles,
may be proving inadequate. I think, too, although counsel for the appellant argued eloquently to the
contrary, that some adaptation of the common law rules to meet these new problems of degree is
capable of being made by judges. I do not have to depend on my own judgment for this for it can be
seen that in the United States, so long ago as 1913, the judges in the state of Washington developed,
without legislative aid, a new doctrine of the family car (*Birch v Abercrombie* (1913) 74 Wash 486) and
some other states have, with variations, followed the same road (see *Prosser on Torts* 3rd edn, 1964,
pp. 494 et seq).Other states have resorted to statute. To be similarly creative, even 70 years later, has
its attraction. But I have come to the clear conclusion that we cannot in this House embark on the suggested innovation. I endeavour to state some reasons.

   1. Assuming that the desideratum is to fix liability in cases of negligent driving on the owner of the
      car (an assumption which may be disputable), there are at least three different systems which may
      be adopted: (a) that apparently advocated by Lord Denning MR of a 'matrimonial' car, the theory
      being that all purposes for which it is used by either spouse are presumed to be matrimonial pur-
      poses; (b) that adopted in some American states of a 'family' car, the theory being that any user
      by any member of the family is the owner's 'business' (see *Prosser*); (c) that any owner (including
      hire-purchaser) who permits another to use his motor vehicle on the highway should be liable by
      the fact of permission. This principle has been adopted *by statute* in certain Australian states (e.g.

the Motor Vehicles Insurance Acts 1936–45 (Queensland), s. 3(2)). Yet another possibility would be to impose liability on the owner in all cases regardless of whether he had given permission or not. My Lords, I do not know on what principle your Lordships acting judicially can prefer one of these systems to the others or on what basis any one can be formulated with sufficient precision or its exceptions defined. The choice is one of social policy; there are arguments for and against each of them. . . .

2. Whatever may have been the situation in 1913 in the youth of the motor car, it is very difficult now, when millions of people of all ages drive for a vast variety of purposes and when there is in existence a complicated legislative structure as to insurance—who must take it out, what risks it must cover, who has the right to sue for the sum assured. Liability and insurance are so intermixed that judicially to alter the basis of liability without adequate knowledge (which we have not the means to obtain) as to the impact this might make on the insurance system would be dangerous, and, in my opinion, irresponsible.

3. To declare as from the date of the decision in this House that a new and greatly more extensive principle of liability was to be applied in substitution for well-known and certain rules might inflict great hardships on a number of people, and at least would greatly affect their assumed legal rights. We cannot, without yet further innovation, change the law prospectively only . . .

My Lords, we may be grateful to Lord Denning MR for turning our thoughts in a new direction, a direction perceived, if not with unity of vision, by courts beyond the seas so long ago; but I must invite your Lordships to state that his judgment does not state the law. Any new direction, and it may be one of many alternatives, must be set by Parliament.

NOTES

1. Lord Salmon similarly observed:

   It seems to me that before any change resembling that proposed by Lord Denning MR is made in our law it is most important that full and careful investigations into all aspects of the question should be carried out, and perhaps the arrangements with the Motor Insurers' Bureau considered, so that a new code may be devised which will be fair for all and ensure that everyone who has been damaged by negligent driving shall be paid the damages to which he should be entitled. This is a task which can hardly be undertaken by your Lordships' House sitting in its judicial capacity. In my view, this is essentially a matter for the legislature.

2. In *Scott v Davis* (2000) 204 CLR 333, noted p. 1070, ante, Gleeson CJ at [10] relied upon these statements of Lords Salmon and Wilberforce to show that *Morgans v Launchbury* could not be taken to lay down a special principle relating to motor cars only, since such a precise category could be created only by legislation and not at common lawn (cf. McHugh J at [120]). However, Gummow, Hayne, and Callinan JJ felt less inhibited, seeking to confine a line of precedents they viewed as an anomalous extension of vicarious liability beyond its rightful commercial context.

3. M. Clarke, op cit., pp. 321–333, makes a powerful argument in favour of the cautious approach of the House of Lords. He collects examples of erroneous judicial assertions (or assumptions) about the functioning of the insurance market, querying (for example) whether the House of Lords in cases like *Murphy v Brentwood DC* ([1991] 1 AC 398), [1990] 2 All ER 908, (see p. 183, ante) had been aware that cover for liability for economic loss was (and is) available in England. The cogency of 'floodgates' arguments in pure economic loss cases (p. 216, ante) is suspect, accordingly. Clarke stresses the difficulty of arguments about the most efficient way to spread losses, even for insurance industry professionals (so 'in the case of carriage by sea, the arguments between loss insurance and liability insurance has been going on for much of the last hundred

years, and is far from having been resolved'). The assumption that loss insurance is always better (an argument against tort liability, as per Lord Hoffmann in *Transco*, ante) is unsafe. Clarke's conclusion is that 'the debate has no clear winners' and that the courts certainly do not have sufficient information to decide the efficient allocation of loss in individual cases (approving the conclusion of W. Bishop (1982) 1 OJLS 1 at 13). This supports the orthodox rejection of the 'alleged relevance' of insurance (as Stapleton puts it, op cit.), as defended by Viscount Simonds in *Lister v Romford Ice* (see p. 1135, ante).

4.   For a more recent consideration of whether the courts might exceptionally, in Lord Wilberforce's words, 'change the law prospectively only' see *Re Spectrum Plus Ltd* [2005] 4 All ER 209, [2005] UKHL 41.

2 COMPULSORY INSURANCE PROVISIONS

■ The Road Traffic Act 1988

PART VI. THIRD-PARTY LIABILITIES

Compulsory insurance or security against third-party risks

143. Users of motor vehicles to be insured or secured against third-party risks—(1) Subject to the provisions of this Part of this Act—

(a) a person must not use a motor vehicle on a road [or other public place] unless there is in force a relation to the use of the vehicle by that person such a policy of insurance or such a security in respect of third party risks as complies with the requirement of this Part of this Act, and

(b) a person must not cause or permit any other person to use a motor vehicle on a road [or other public place] unless there is in force in relation to the use of the vehicle by that other person such a policy of insurance or such a security in respect of third party risks as complies with the requirements of this Part of this Act.

(2) If a person acts in contravention of subsection (1) above he is guilty of an offence.

(3) A person charged with using a motor vehicle in contravention of this section shall not be convicted if he proves—

(a) that the vehicle did not belong to him and was not in his possession under a contract of hiring or of loan,

(b) that he was using the vehicle in the course of his employment, and

(c) that he neither knew nor had reason to believe that there was not in force in relation to the vehicle such a policy of insurance or security as is mentioned in subsection (1) above.

(4) This Part of this Act does not apply to invalid carriages.

144. Exceptions from requirement of third-party insurance or security—(1) Section 143 of this Act does not apply to a vehicle owned by a person who has deposited and keeps deposited with the Accountant General of the Supreme Court the sum of [£500,000], at a time when the vehicle is being driven under the owner's control.

[Sub-s. (1A) allows the Secretary of State to vary the amount. Sub-s. (2) provides that s. 143 shall not apply to specified local and police and certain other authorities.]

145. Requirements in respect of policies of insurance—(1) In order to comply with the requirements of this Part of this Act, a policy of insurance must satisfy the following conditions.

(2) The policy must be issued by an authorised insurer.

(3) Subject to subsection (4) below, the policy—

(a) must insure such person, persons or classes of persons as may be specified in the policy in respect of any liability which may be incurred by him or them in respect of the death of or bodily injury to any person or damage to property caused by, or arising out of, the use of the vehicle on a road [or other public place] in Great Britain, and…

(b) must also insure him or them in respect of any liability which may be incurred by him or them under the provisions of this Part of this Act relating to payment for emergency treatment.

(4) The policy shall not, by virtue of subsection (3)(a) above, be required—

(a) to cover liability in respect of the death, arising out of and in the course of his employment, of a person in the employment of a person insured by the policy or of bodily injury sustained by such a person arising out of and in the course of his employment, or

(b) to provide insurance of more than £250,000 in respect of all such liabilities as may be incurred in respect of damage to property caused by, or arising out of, any one accident involving the vehicle, or

(c) to cover liability in respect of damage to the vehicle, or

(d) to cover liability in respect of damage to goods carried for hire or reward in or on the vehicle or in or on any trailer (whether or not coupled) drawn by the vehicle, or

(e) to cover any liability of a person in respect of damage to property in his custody or under his control, or

(f) to cover any contractual liability.

[(4A) In the case of a person—

(a) carried in or upon a vehicle, or

(b) entering or getting on to, or alighting from, a vehicle,

the provisions of paragraph (a) of subsection (4) above do not apply unless cover in respect of the liability referred to in that paragraph is in fact provided pursuant to a requirement of the Employers' Liability (Compulsory Insurance) Act 1969.]

[Subs (5) requires that an 'authorised insurer' referred to in subs (2) means a member of the Motor Insurers' Bureau, on which see pp. 1150, post.]

148. Avoidance of certain exceptions to policies or securities—(1) Where a certificate of insurance or certificate of security has been delivered under section 147 of this Act to the person by whom a policy has been effected or to whom a security has been given, so much of the policy or security as purports to restrict—

(a) the insurance of the persons insured by the policy, or

(b) the operation of the security,

(as the case may be) by reference to any of the matters mentioned in subsection (2) below shall, as respects such liabilities as are required to be covered by a policy under section 145 of this Act, be of no effect.

(2) Those matters are—

(a) the age of physical or mental condition of persons driving the vehicle,

(b) the condition of the vehicle,

(c) the number of persons that the vehicle carries,

(d) the weight or physical characteristics of the goods that the vehicle carries,

(e) the time at which or the areas within which the vehicle is used,

(f) the horsepower or cylinder capacity or value of the vehicle,

(g) the carrying on the vehicle of any particular apparatus, or

(h) the carrying on the vehicle of any particular means of identification other than any means of identification required to be carried by or under the [Vehicle Excise and Registration Act 1994].

…

149. Avoidance of certain agreements as to liability towards passengers—(1) This section applies where a person uses a motor vehicle in circumstances such that under section 143 of this Act there is required to be in force in relation to his use of it such a policy of insurance or such security in respect of third-party as complies with the requirements of this Part of this Act.

(2) If any other person is carried in or upon the vehicle while the user is so using it, any antecedent agreement or understanding between them (whether intended to be legally binding or not) shall be of no effect so far as it purports or might be held—

(a) to negative or restrict any such liability of the user in respect of persons carried in or upon the vehicle as is required by section 145 of this Act to be covered by a policy of insurance, or

(b) to impose any conditions with respect to the enforcement of any such liability of the user.

(3) The fact that a person so carried has willingly accepted as his the risk of negligence on the part of the user shall not be treated as negativing any such liability of the user.

(4) For the purposes of this section—

(a) reference to a person being carried in or upon a vehicle include references to a person entering or getting on to, or alighting from, the vehicle, and

(b) the reference to an antecedent agreement is to one made at any time before the liability arose.

151. Duty of insurers or persons giving security to satisfy judgment against persons insured or secured against third-party risks—(1) This section applies where, after a certificate of insurance or certificate of security has been delivered under section 147 of this Act to the person by whom a policy has been effected or to whom a security has been given, a judgment to which this subsection applies is obtained.

(2) Subsection (1) above applies to judgments relating to a liability with respect to any matter where liability with respect to that matter is required to be covered by a policy of insurance under section 145 of this Act...

(5) Notwithstanding that the insurer may be entitled to avoid or cancel, or may have avoided or cancelled, the policy or security, he must, subject to the provisions of this section, pay to the persons entitled to the benefit of the judgment—

(a) as regards liability in respect of death or bodily injury, any sum payable under the judgment in respect of the liability, together with any sum which, by virtue of any enactment relating to interest on judgments, is payable in respect of interest on that sum,

(b) as regards liability in respect of damage to property, any sum required to be paid under subsection (6) below, and

(c) any amount payable in respect of costs.

(d) ...

153. Bankruptcy, etc, of insured or secured persons not to affect claims by third parties—(1) Where, after a certificate of insurance or certificate of security has been delivered under section 147 of this Act to the person by whom a policy has been effected or to whom a security has been given, any of the events mentioned in subsection (2) below happens, the happening of that event shall, notwithstanding anything in the Third Parties (Rights Against Insurers) Act 1930,[1] not affect any such liability of that person as is required to be covered by a policy of insurance under section 145 of this Act.

(2) In the case of the person by whom the policy was effected or to whom the security was given, the events referred to in subsection (1) above are—

(a) that he becomes bankrupt or makes a composition or arrangement with his creditors or that his estate is sequestrated or he grants a trust deed for his creditors,

[1] See p. 1149, post for this Act.

(b) that he dies and—
   (i) his estate falls to be administered in accordance with an order under section 421 of the Insolvency Act 1986,
   (ii) an award of sequestration of his estate is made, or
   (iii) a judicial factor is appointed to administer his estate under section 11A of the Judicial Factors (Scotland) Act 1889,
(c) that if that person is a company—
   (i) a winding-up order…is made with respect to the company [or the company enters administration],
   (ii) a resolution for a voluntary winding-up is passed with respect to the company,
   (iii) a receiver or manager of the company's business or undertaking is duly appointed, or
   (iv) possession is taken, by or on behalf of the holders of any debentures secured by a floating charge, of any property comprised in or subject to the charge.

(3) Nothing in subsection (1) above affects any rights conferred by the Third Parties (Rights Against Insurers) Act 1930 on the person to whom the liability was incurred, being rights so conferred against the person by whom the policy was issued or the security was given.

[Section 154 provides for a duty to give information as to insurance or security where a claim is made.]

NOTES

1. The duty to insure rests upon the person who 'uses' or 'causes or permits any other person to use' the vehicle. Subject to s. 143(3), a person may breach this duty even though he does not know that there is no policy of insurance in force for the permitted use: *Houston v Buchanan* 1940 SC (HL) 17. In addition to a fine or imprisonment, the offender's driving licence must be endorsed and he may be disqualified from driving: Road Traffic Offenders Act 1988, Sch. 23. There may also be a civil action for breach of statutory duty: see post.

2. It is the *use* of the vehicle which must be covered by insurance and not the personal or vicarious liability of the owner. So a situation may arise in which the owner is responsible in law (limited in *Morgans v Launchbury* [1973] AC 127, [1972] 2 All ER 606, ante, to the delegation of driving for the owner's purposes) but the use is not insured. This can happen because, by contract with the insurer, the owner may stipulate that the insurance covers the use of the vehicle only when used by himself or particular named drivers. If he nevertheless permits someone other than those named to use the vehicle he commits a criminal offence and may be liable in damages for breach of statutory duty. This is cumbersome and of little value to the person who suffers loss by virtue of the owner's failure to insure because, *ex hypothesi*, the owner will be uninsured in such cases and probably without funds to pay. Some other countries arrange matters more sensibly by attaching the insurance to the *vehicle* and not its use by particular drivers.

3. The provisions of ss. 145(1) and 145(3)(a) of the Road Traffic Act 1988 do not require insurance against the death or personal injury of the person actually driving the vehicle but are only intended to cover the user's liability to third parties: *Cooper v Motor Insurers' Bureau* [1985] QB 575, [1985] 1 All ER 449.

4. Since 1 December 1972, it has been compulsory to insure against liability to passengers (now Road Traffic Act 1988, s. 145). Under s. 149(3) the user cannot restrict his liability, either through agreement or by operation of the defence of volenti non fit injuria, by a notice on the dashboard saying 'Passengers ride at their own risk and on the condition that no claim shall be made against the driver or owner'.

5. Liability to employees will not be covered by a road traffic policy (s. 145(4)(a), but by an employer's liability policy (post).

6. The Financial Services Compensation Scheme (set up by the Financial Services and Markets Act 2000) secures payment of the full amount that an insurance company in liquidation is liable to pay to a person entitled to judgment under s. 151 of the Road Traffic Act 1988. It is funded by levies on authorised financial services firms.

7. The Road Traffic (NHS Charges) Act 1999 introduced a new administrative scheme to recoup the costs to the National Health Service of treating road accident victims. The costs of NHS treatment were levied on liability insurers when such a victim made a successful claim for compensation. In 2005/6 the scheme (operated by the Government's Compensation Recovery Unit) distributed over £120 million to NHS Trusts which had treated road accidents.

8. From January 2007, the recoupment scheme has been extended to all kinds of accidents which result in NHS treatment (now including ambulance care), on the commencement of Part III of the Health and Social Care (Community Health and Standards) Act 2003, which repeals the 1999 Act. The extension will have greatest impact on accidents at work, which comprise the largest area of tortious claims apart from road accidents. The scheme does not extend to diseases, since the Government believed that the costs to the NHS of treating them would be too difficult to quantify. On these statutory schemes, see further p. 545, ante.

9. For an unsuccessful attempt by one public authority to recoup the cost of looking after a person injured by another public authority, through an action in negligence, cf. *Islington London Borough Council v UCL Hospital NHS Trust* [2006] PIQR P3, [2005] EWCA Civ 596, noted p. 256, ante.

■ Monk v Warbey

p. 680, ante.

NOTE

The claimant nowadays will give notice of the bringing of proceedings against an uninsured driver, within fourteen days after the commencement of the proceedings, to the Motor Insurers' Bureau. (See notes on the agreement between the Secretary of State for the Environment and the MIB, p. 1150, post.) Any unsatisfied judgment will be paid by the MIB. The practical importance of *Monk v Warbey* therefore seems to be limited to those situations in which there is a relatively wealthy owner who has permitted his or her vehicle to be used without compulsory insurance cover. But in law the existence of the MIB agreements does not affect the action for breach of statutory duty: *Corfield v Groves* [1950] 1 All ER 488.

■ The Employers' Liability (Compulsory Insurance) Act 1969

An Act to require employers to insure against their liability for personal injury to their employees; and for purposes in connection with the matter aforesaid

1. Insurance against liability for employees.—(1) Except as otherwise provided by this Act, every employer carrying on any business in Great Britain shall insure, and maintain insurance, under one or more approved policies with an authorised insurer or insurers against liability for bodily injury or disease sustained by his employees, and arising out of and in the course of their employment in Great Britain in that business, but except in so far as regulations otherwise provide not including injury or disease suffered or contracted outside Great Britain.

(2) Regulations may provide that the amount for which an employer is required by this Act to insure and maintain insurance shall, either generally or in such cases or classes of case as may be prescribed by the regulations, be limited in such manner as may be so prescribed.

(3) For the purposes of this Act—

(a) 'approved policy' means a policy of insurance not subject to any conditions or exceptions prohibited for those purposes by regulations;

[(b) 'authorised insurer' means—

(i) a person who has permission under Part 4 of the Financial Services and Markets Act 2000 to effect and carry out contracts of insurance of a kind required by this Act . . .]

2. Employees to be covered.—(1) For the purposes of this Act the term 'employee' means an individual who has entered into or works under a contract of service or apprenticeship with an employer whether by way of manual labour, clerical work or otherwise, whether such contract is expressed or implied, oral or in writing.

(2) This Act shall not require an employer to insure—

(a) in respect of an employee of whom the employer is the husband, wife, [civil partner,] father, mother, grandfather, grandmother, step-father, step-mother, son, daughter, grandson, grand-daughter, step-son, step-daughter, brother, sister, half-brother or half-sister; or

(b) except as otherwise provided by regulations, in respect of employees not ordinarily resident in Great Britain.

3. Employers exempted from insurance.—(1) This Act shall not require any insurance to be effected by—

(a) any such authority as is mentioned in subsection (2) below; or

(b) any body corporate established by or under any enactment for the carrying on of any industry or part of an industry, or of any undertaking, under national ownership or control; or

(c) in relation to any such cases as may be specified in the regulations, any employer exempted by regulations.

(2) The authorities referred to in subsection (1)(a) above

[(a) a health service body, as defined in section 60(7) of the National Health Service and Community Care Act 1990] . . . [and

(b)] are the common Council of the City of London, . . . , the council of a London borough, the council of a county, . . . or county district in England [the council of a county or county borough in Wales], [the Broads Authority,] [a National Park authority] . . . [. . . a joint authority established by Part IV of the Local Government Act 1985], [the London Fire and Emergency Planning Authority] and any police authority.

5. Penalty for failure to insure.—An employer who on any day is not insured in accordance with this Act when required to be so shall be guilty of an offence and shall be liable on summary conviction to a fine not exceeding [level 4 on the standard scale]; and where an offence under this section committed by a corporation has been committed with the consent or connivance of, or facilitated by any neglect on the part of, any director, manager, secretary or other officer of the corporation, he, as well as the corporation shall be deemed to be guilty of that offence and shall be liable to be proceeded against and punished accordingly.

■ The Employers' Liability (Compulsory Insurance) Regulations 1998 SI 1998/2573
Prohibition of certain conditions in policies of insurance

2.—(1) For the purposes of the 1969 Act, there is prohibited in any contract of insurance any condition which provides (in whatever terms) that no liability (either generally or in respect of a particular claim) shall arise under the policy, or that any such liability so arising shall cease, if—

(a) some specified thing is done or omitted to be done after the happening of the event giving rise to a claim under the policy;

(b) the policyholder does not take reasonable care to protect his employees against the risk of bodily injury or disease in the course of their employment;

(c) the policyholder fails to comply with the requirements of any enactment for the protection of employees against the risk of bodily injury or disease in the course of their employment; or

(d) the policyholder does not keep specified records or fails to provide the insurer with or make available to him information from such records.

(2) For the purposes of the 1969 Act there is also prohibited in a policy of insurance any condition which requires—

(a) a relevant employee to pay; or

(b) an insured employer to pay the relevant employee,

the first amount of any claim or any aggregation of claims.

(3) Paragraphs (1) and (2) above do not prohibit for the purposes of the 1969 Act a condition in a policy of insurance which requires the employer to pay or contribute any sum to the insurer in respect of the satisfaction of any claim made under the contract of insurance by a relevant employee or any costs and expenses incurred in relation to any such claim.

Limit of amount of compulsory insurance

3.—(1) Subject to paragraph (2) below, the amount for which an employer is required by the 1969 Act to insure and maintain insurance in respect of relevant employees under one or more policies of insurance shall be, or shall in aggregate be not less than £5 million in respect of—

(a) a claim relating to any one or more of those employees arising out of any one occurrence; and

(b) any costs and expenses incurred in relation to any such claim.

(2) Where an employer is a company with one or more subsidiaries, the requirements of paragraph (1) above shall be taken to apply to that company with any subsidiaries together, as if they were a single employer.

NOTES

1.   It will be observed that the employee is not given a statutory right, analogous to that given to a road traffic victim, to sue upon the contract of insurance. Moreover, in *Richardson v Pitt-Stanley* [1995] QB 123, [1995] 1 All ER 460 (p. 682, ante) the Court of Appeal, by a majority, held that the 1969 Act does not create a civil liability on the part of the employer for failure to insure. *Monk v Warbey* (p. 680, ante) was distinguished on the ground, among others, that the wording of the Road Traffic Act and the 1969 Act are different.

2.   There is no Employers' Liability Insurers' Bureau comparable to the Motor Insurers' Bureau (p. 1150, post) but the Financial Services Compensation Scheme (see note 6,

p. 1146, ante) extends to employers' liability insurance (claims in respect of compulsory insurance are compensated in full under the scheme).

■ The Third Parties (Rights Against Insurers) Act 1930

1. Rights of third parties against insurers on bankruptcy, etc, of the insured.—(1) Where under any contract of insurance a person (hereinafter referred to as the insured) is insured against liabilities to third parties which he may incur, then—

- (a) in the event of the insured becoming bankrupt or making a composition or arrangement with his creditors; or
- (b) in the case of the insured being a company, in the event of a winding-up order being made, or a resolution for a voluntary winding-up being passed, with respect to the company, [or of the company entering administration,] or of a receiver or manager of the company's business or undertaking being duly appointed, or of possession being taken, by or on behalf of the holders of any debentures secured by a floating charge, of any property comprised in or subject to the charge [or of [a voluntary arrangement proposed for the purposes of Part I of the Insolvency Act 1986 being approved under the Part]];

if, either before or after that event, any such liability as aforesaid is incurred by the insured, his rights against the insurer under the contract in respect of the liability shall, notwithstanding anything in any Act or rule of law to the contrary, be transferred to and vest in the third party to whom the liability was so incurred.

(2) Where [the estate of any person falls to be administered in accordance with an order under section [421 of the Insolvency Act 1986]], then, if any debt provable in bankruptcy...is owing by the deceased in respect of a liability against which he was insured under a contract of insurance as being a liability to a third party, the deceased debtor's rights against the insurer under the contract in respect of that liability shall, notwithstanding anything in [any such order], be transferred to and vest in the person to whom the debt is owing.

(3) In so far as any contract of insurance made after the commencement of this Act in respect of any liability of the insured to third parties purports, whether directly or indirectly, to avoid the contract or to alter the rights of the parties thereunder upon the happening to be insured of any of the events specified in paragraph (a) or paragraph (b) of subsection (1) of this section or upon the [estate of any person falling to be administered in accordance with an order under section [421 of the Insolvency Act 1986]], the contract shall be of no effect.

. . .

3. Settlement between insurers and insured persons.—Where the insured has become bankrupt or where is the case of the insured being a company, a winding-up order [or an administration order] has been made or a resolution for a voluntary winding-up has been passed, with respect to the company, no agreement made between the insurer and the insured after liability has been incurred to a third party and after the commencement of the bankruptcy or winding up [or the day of the making of the administration order], as the case may be, nor any waiver, assignment, or other disposition made by, or payment made to the insured after the commencement [or day] aforesaid shall be effective to defeat or affect the rights transferred to the third party under this Act, but those rights shall be the same as if no such agreement, waiver, assignment, disposition or payment had been made.

NOTES

1. This Act does not prevent the insurer from avoiding the policy, e.g. on grounds of material non-disclosure by the insured: *McCormick v National Motor and Accident Insurance Union Ltd* (1934) 49 Ll L Rep 361.

2. The liability of the assured has to be established before there can be any basis for an action against the liability insurers under the Act. In *Bradley v Eagle Star Insurance Co Ltd* [1989] AC 957, [1989] 1 All ER 961 the House of Lords, Lord Templeman dissenting, held that the dissolution of a company prevented it from being sued and thus prevented its liability to the claimant from being established. This decision affected a large number of pending cases involving claimants who did not realise that they had claims against the company which had employed them or their relatives, until after the company had been removed from the register of companies. Under s. 651 of the Companies Act 1985, application could be made to the court for the revival of a company to allow it to be sued, but this was of no use in *Bradley* because the application had to be made within two years of dissolution. As a result of amendments to s. 651, the two-year limitation has been removed in cases where the applicant is seeking damages in relation to death or personal injury (see now s. 1030 of the Companies Act 2006). Consequently, claims such as those in *Bradley* are now possible under the 1930 Act, provided that the claim against the company is not statute-barred and the claimant can prove that the company's negligence or breach of duty caused the loss.

3 MOTOR INSURERS' BUREAU

■ Frequently asked questions

(from the website www.mib.org.uk)

It is difficult to summarize a complex legal situation without being misleading.

There is no substitute for studying the relevant Uninsured Drivers' and the Untraced Drivers' Agreements, but these are some of the more common questions....

2. Why was MIB formed?

It was established in 1946 as a central fund to provide a means of compensating the victims of road accidents by negligent uninsured or untraced drivers.

3. How does MIB function and on what legal basis?

It functions under two separate agreements between Government and the motor insurance industry. One Agreement—The Uninsured Drivers' Agreement [1999]—requires the MIB to meet unsatisfied Civil Court Judgments against identified motorists who may not have been insured as required by the Road Traffic Act 1988. The other—The Untraced Drivers' Agreement [2003], requires MIB to consider applications for compensation from victims of 'Hit & Run' motorists.

The MIB's obligations are linked to the compulsory insurance requirements of the Road Traffic Act, so the protection provided is limited to where there is a legal requirement to insure.

4. Who pays for MIB?

The MIB is funded by all motor insurers. Motor insurers are only allowed to operate if they belong to the Bureau and pay a share of its costs.

The ultimate cost falls to law-abiding motorists via their insurance premiums.

5. What is the cost of the operation of these agreements to the individual motor policyholder?

At the present time, the cost varies between £15–£30 per policy. However, the cost continues to rise in the light of increasing levels of compensation, legal costs and changes in legislation.

7. Is there any limit to such compensation?

In the case of bodily injury, there is no financial limit to the level of compensation. In the case of property damage, MIB does not pay the first £300 of any claim under its current Agreements.

However, new agreements are being negotiated to take account of the 5th Directive on motor insurance as far at it relates to EU members. Once agreed no excess will be applied in the majority of cases. The Bureau is not liable beyond the limit (set by the Road Traffic Act 1988) of £1,000,000.

9. What is MIB's position where the victim has other sources of compensation available?

As a general principle the MIB is a fund of last resort and does not pay where the victim has already been compensated from another source.

13. What about damage or injury caused by 'hit & run' motorists?

The Untraced Drivers' Agreement provides for compensation to be paid in respect of personal injury and losses arising from that injury. Compensation for damage to property is limited to accidents on or after 14 February 2003 but only if the accident is reported to the police within 5 days, or as soon as reasonably possible and the identity of the vehicle can be established. Claims for property damage must be made within nine months of the accident.

Notes for the assistance of claimants

These notes appear in question and answer format and deal with those questions that are most often raised by claimants.

The notes...do not replace or modify the Agreement and claimants are recommended to read the text of the Agreement under which they are submitting a claim.

What are the Uninsured Drivers' Agreements?

These are agreements between the Secretary of State for the Environment, Transport and the Regions and MIB which set out the circumstances under which claims will be paid. Whilst the agreements require that judgment be obtained in a Civil Court against the uninsured motorist, MIB will, wherever possible, pay compensation by agreement as opposed to demanding that a judgment be obtained first....

When should I make a claim on Motor Insurers' Bureau?

A claim should be submitted as soon as it becomes clear that the offending motorist who has caused the injury or damage is uninsured. MIB expects that a claimant will have made enquiries to try to identify an insurer. Those enquiries will include but not necessarily be limited to:

— Contacting the motorist;
— Enquiring of the Driver and Vehicle Licensing Authority in Swansea as to the identity of the registered keeper of the vehicle. (The registered keeper of the vehicle is more likely to have insurance information than the driver);
— Making a formal complaint to the police under Section 154 of the Road Traffic Act 1988. (Section 154 makes it an offence for a person against whom a claim is made to withhold details of insurance.).

You should also ask your own motor insurer to enquire of the Motor Insurance Database to see if the vehicle owner can be identified.

How long will my claim take?

This is difficult to predict as many factors are involved:

If your claim is limited to property damage or minor injury it should be resolved in 4 or 5 months, or less.

If, on the other hand, your claim involves contested liability, evidentiary difficulties, or serious injury it may require the police report to be obtained, which can take some time, especially if its release is delayed by criminal prosecutions.

Injury claims can also be delayed if it is difficult for your doctors to agree on the effects, and you may be advised to wait until you have recovered fully, before agreeing any compensation.

MIB will make every effort to reach a decision on responsibility for the accident within three months and to keep you informed. Where there seems to be the prospect of a long delay, MIB will consider an interim payment.

NOTES

1. As P. Cane comments in *Atiyah* pp. 258–259, the MIB is, 'in many respects, an anomalous institution'. Since the schemes which it operates are not embodied in legislation, but rather in a series of contracts between the MIB and the Government, accident victims (who are not parties to those contracts) would classically have had no redress against the MIB, had it refused to pay (although cf. now the Contracts (Rights of Third Parties) Act 1999, and clauses 31 and 32 of the Untraced Drivers' Agreement of 2003, providing for judicial enforcement by victims). Nevertheless, as Cane observes (ibid), the MIB has never sought to shelter behind such contractual defences, for 'if it did so there is not much doubt that the whole scheme—or some alternative—would be put on a statutory footing'.

2. Member States of the European Union are now legally obliged to set up a body to provide compensation for the victims of untraced or uninsured drivers, by Council Directive (EEC) 84/5. There have been several legal challenges to detailed provisions of the MIB agreements, for failing properly to implement the Directive. Precisely how the agreements should be interpreted in this context seems to be in doubt. Schiemann LJ has held that ordinary principles of contractual construction apply, rather than the requirement to interpret national laws 'so far as possible' to be compatible with EU law: *Evans v MIB, White v White* [1999] 1 CMLR 1251. The House of Lords, however, views the Directive as (at least) a relevant aid to construction of the MIB agreements: *White v White* [2001] 2 All ER 43, [2001] UKHL 9. This did not go far enough for the Advocate General in *Evans v Secretary of State for Environment, Transport and the Regions* [2003] ECR I-14447, who declared that it would be 'totally unacceptable' for the rights conferred by the Directive to be watered down by the British government choosing implementation by contract with the MIB, rather than through legislation. However, the ECJ's judgment (ibid) was much less forthright. Even so, it is rather surprising that Schiemann LJ's restrictive approach to the Directive has recently been followed: *Byrne v MIB* [2007] 3 All ER 499, [2007] EWHC 1268 (QB) (affd [2008] EWCA Civ 574, although the interpretation of the agreement was not appealed by the defendants). It may be that EU law will ultimately necessitate a formal statutory basis for the MIB scheme. As the *Byrne* case indicates, the British Government may be held liable in damages under the EU's *Francovich* principle (see p. 704, ante), where the MIB scheme fails to secure the rights protected by Directive 84/5. See also *Spencer v Secretary of State for Works and Pensions* [2008] EWCA Civ 750.

4 THE SETTLEMENT PROCESS

■ Hard Bargaining: Out of Court Settlement in Personal Injury Actions

Hazel Genn (Clarendon Press: Oxford, 1987), pp. 13–15, 163–169

The Significance of settlement

Because claims are settled without any court formalities there is no official source of information about the claims settlement process. No records of settlements are publicly available, nor are there any official statistics relating to the volume of claims pursued and compromised, the level of settlements, or the costs involved in achieving settlements. The research conducted by the Pearson Commission (1978) and detailed evidence from the Oxford national survey do, however, shed some light on these questions. The Oxford study obtained information from plaintiffs and their solicitors about the administration and settlement of claims. It showed that only a small proportion of those people injured in accidents each year actually initiate claims for damages; that only 80 per cent of those claims initiated achieve any kind of settlement..., [that] the settlements reached are generally for relatively small amounts (Harris *et al.* (1984); and that in two-thirds of cases the settlement is concluded on the basis of the *first* offer made by the defendant's insurers (Harris *et al.* (1984), p. 94). On the other hand, the evidence from both the Pearson Commission and the Oxford study indicates that the total cost of achieving these settlements is very high. For example, the Oxford study found that average total legal expenses for damages under £1,000 were 29 per cent of damages (Harris *et al.* (1984), p. 131); for damages over £1,000, average legal expenses were 15 per cent of damages (Harris *et al.* (1984), Figures 3.5A and 3.5B). The Pearson Commission, on the basis of data collected in 1972, estimated that the total cost of operating the tort system was 87 per cent of the total damages paid out as compensation (Pearson (1978), Table 158).

Although these studies provide valuable statistical information not previously available about the volume of claims, the characteristics of personal injury plaintiffs, and the amounts of damages obtained, the effect of the data is to raise more questions than are answered about the settlement process itself. For example, the most simple-minded assumptions about bargaining strategies would anticipate rather fewer than two-thirds of plaintiffs capitulating on the basis of the first offer to be made by a defendant insurance company.

The system of out of court claims settlement is essentially 'unsupervised'. Without a court hearing, plaintiffs and defendants are largely free to reach whatever compromise they choose, except in the case of infant plaintiffs, where court approval is necessary for agreed settlements made on their behalf. A plaintiff may instruct a solicitor to press his claim for him and authorize him to reach a settlement with the defendant; or the plaintiff may negotiate personally with the defendant unrepresented. In either situation he may accept a figure in full and final settlement of his claim against the defendant with no interference from outside parties or bodies. It is essentially a private matter for the individual plaintiff.

If things go badly wrong a plaintiff may have grounds to sue his solicitor or have a contract of settlement (if negotiated personally with the defendant insurers) set aside by the courts if it was deemed to be an unconscionable bargain or if made as a result of undue influence (*Horry v Tate and Lyle* [1982] 2 Lloyd's Rep 416; *Beach v Eames* (1978) 82 DLR (3rd) 736). However, the value of these potential remedies is severely constrained. They will only be used if the plaintiff ever becomes aware, subsequent to the conclusion of the settlement, that some mistake has been made...

One of the distinguishing features of personal injury litigation, in contrast with other forms of litigation (e.g. actions for breach of contract between businessmen; breach of contract in sale of goods; employment law litigation), is the fact that the injured plaintiff rarely has any informed or realistic expectation of the amount of compensation to which he may be entitled. He may know that he has a cause of action and that he might get *some* money, but he will generally be guided by his legal advisers or, possibly more perilously, by the defendant insurer, as to the quantum of his potential damages.

The obvious danger for the plaintiff in this unsupervised system of claims settlement is that the damages paid by defendants are once and for all payments in respect of past and *any* possible future losses. On signing the settlement contract most defendants will ensure that the plaintiff relinquishes any future rights of action in respect of his injury and its consequences.

One is looking, then, at a system of claims settlement which is of crucial importance to injured plaintiffs. For many it represents the only opportunity to obtain restitution for financial losses suffered as a result of injury, and yet there is considerable imprecision in this area of law and there is no person or body independent of the parties or their representatives overseeing the process....

Conclusion...
Within [the] general climate of uncertainty surrounding the legal principles which form the basis of claims, the parties to personal injury actions do not meet on equal terms and their objectives are

diametrically opposed. It has been argued in [an earlier part of the book] that there are both structural and situational inequalities between the parties in personal injury litigation and...the effect of these inequalities is evident throughout negotiations and the final out of court settlement of a claim. The law requires the injured plaintiff to prove that the defendant was guilty of negligence. The plaintiff is in a disadvantaged position from the outset. He is the person who has been injured, and in the early stages after his accident is more likely to be concerned about his recovery than about collecting good, fresh evidence, which might be necessary to prove some future claim arising from his injuries. He is unlikely to have had experience of bringing a claim for damages, may delay in deciding to make a claim, has limited resources, and may have no obvious means of locating an expert in personal injury litigation.

Insurance companies, on the other hand, by virtue of their position as 'repeat players' in litigation, are themselves specialists in the field. They are experienced negotiators and litigators and have the informational and financial resources to obtain expert legal advice whenever it is needed. They also have the resources to collect or to construct, from expert witnesses, the information necessary to help them refute the plaintiff's allegations of negligence. In many cases, however, the exertion of insurance companies in this respect is rendered unnecessary because the plaintiff's solicitor fails to undertake the same degree of case preparation on behalf of his client. It has been argued that this failure is both a direct result of limited resources on the plaintiff's side, and also an indirect result of the remunerative basis of civil litigation which deters solicitors from devoting sufficient time to case investigation and preparation....

A common response to the problems of uncertainty, lack of expertise in personal injury work, and concern about legal costs is to adopt an approach to claims settlement based on co-operation with the opponent rather than confrontation: reasonable negotiation, without the commencement of proceedings, rather than litigation. The co-operative approach is universally welcome and encouraged by insurance companies, who regard it as the most sensible way of dealing with the claims settlement process....

...Co-operation in this context does not mean being pleasant or courteous in dealings with the opponent. It means that in order to avoid 'antagonizing' the defendant, or in order to establish or maintain good relations with insurance companies, solicitors will postpone, or fail even to consider, the issue of formal proceedings. This approach can be developed into an extreme form, as was displayed by the solicitor...who claimed that he would not use the threat of litigation as a weapon against an insurance company. The problem arising from this situation is that the nature of personal injury claims settlement is inherently adversarial. The plaintiff wants to maximize his damages, while the defendant wants to avoid or minimize payment. Despite the emphasis on co-operation, the language of the parties is couched in the terminology of warfare or competition: for example, 'Going for the big prize—no liability'....

When a plaintiff relinquishes his claim for damages out of court, the defendant insurance company is spared the increase in two sets of legal costs that a trial would involve, and the risk that, in addition, a judge might have awarded the plaintiff more than he has now accepted. But what benefits accrue to the plaintiff? The plaintiff, it is said, is spared the uncertainty, the delay, and the stress of costs considerations. It is on these grounds that he accepts a discounted offer. It was argued in [an earlier part of the book], however, that there is a self-serving circularity in this contention and that much of the uncertainty, delay, and costs pressures which plague plaintiffs and weaken their resolve is deliberately manufactured or exacerbated by defendants' manipulation of legal and procedural rules. It was further argued that such tactics by defendants are capable of containment by plaintiffs' solicitors if they are able and willing to pressurize defendants into action by pushing them toward trial...

The understandable reluctance of insurance companies to part with their money is strengthened by the effects of the inequalities between the parties which have been stressed. Evidence from claims inspectors of the influence of legal aid on bargaining strategy...and their admission that they adopt a different approach when faced with trade union specialist solicitors, leads to the conclusion that, when the imbalance between the parties is somewhat redressed, plaintiffs are more likely to obtain better settlements of their claims than otherwise.

Should these findings give cause for concern? Should the pervasive practice of settling claims in the absence of formal adjudication or supervision be greeted with less enthusiasm? The settlement of some 99 per cent for damages without a court hearing obviously serves the civil justice system by freeing congested courts for other business and the public interest in smoothing the administration of justice is widely acknowledged. But is there also a public interest in seeing that justice is being done when parties settle their claims out of court, or is it simply a private matter for the parties to resolve as they wish? . . .

If there is, indeed, a public interest in seeing that injured plaintiffs obtain 'fair' compensation for their injuries, then the analysis of out of court settlement processes contained in this study suggests that there is a strong argument for attempting to reduce some of the imbalance between the parties by improving the access of unknowledgeable plaintiffs to solicitors who genuinely specialize in personal injury litigation; for speeding-up personal injury litigation procedure, particularly for low-value claims; for providing incentives to defendants to settle claims quickly; and for providing a means by which out of court settlements become more visible or subject to scrutiny.

NOTES

1. When an insurance company has paid a claim under a policy it is subrogated to the rights of the insured against third parties. This means that the insurer can sue third parties to the same extent as the insured could have done. The insurer, who sues in the name of the insured, has full control of the proceedings. The effect of this may be seen from cases such as *Lister v Romford Ice and Cold Storage Co Ltd* [1957] AC 555, [1957] 1 All ER 125 (p. 1128, ante), *Morris v Ford Motor Co Ltd* [1973] QB 792, [1973] 2 All ER 1084 (p. 1133, ante) and *Esso Petroleum Co Ltd v Hall Russell & Co Ltd* [1989] AC 643, [1989] 1 All ER 37 noted p. 204, ante). In the case of property insurance, 'knock-for-knock' agreements between insurance companies mean that the insurers' rights of subrogation are not exercised. Suppose that P and D are each comprehensively insured by different insurers and that D negligently damages P's car. Under a 'knock-for-knock' agreement, P's insurer will settle his claim and will not claim from D's insurer. However, *Atiyah*, p. 238, notes that most knock-for-knock agreements have collapsed because companies offering only liability-only insurance (rather than comprehensive insurance) benefited disproportionately from them; insurance companies now mitigate the 'complexity and cost which such agreements were designed to avoid' by using 'agreed formulaic approaches to the apportionment of blame between the parties'. R. Hasson (1985) 5 OJLS 416 argues that subrogation leads to overlapping insurance coverage and wasteful litigation and that subrogated claims do not deter negligent behaviour.

2. There is a growing literature on the settlement process. Among the leading works (in addition to Genn, op cit.) are: H. L. Ross, *Settled Out of Court: The Social Process of Insurance Claims Adjustment* 2nd edn (Chicago, 1980); R. H. Mnookin and L. Kornhauser (1979) 88 Yale LJ 950; *Atiyah*, chap. 10; *Harris, Campbell and Halson*, pp. 427–453; J. Phillips and K. Hawkins (1976) 39 MLR 497; R. Korobkin and C. Guthrie (1994) 93 Mich. LR 107; J. N. Hughes and E. A. Snyder (1995) 38 Journal of Law and Economics 225; and J. G. Fleming, *The American Tort Process* (Oxford, 1988).

5 OTHER COMPENSATION SYSTEMS

Social security benefits

About half of the total amount of compensation for personal injury and death comes from social security and a quarter from the tort system (see pp. 17–19, ante). There was a dramatic growth of state provision in the period from 1945 to 1980 (traced in vol. 1, chap. 5 of the Pearson Report, with detailed statistics in vol. 2, chap. 4). However, since then there have been profound changes. Reductions have been made in the real value of many benefits, responsibility for income maintenance during short periods of sickness and injury has been transferred from the state to the employer, benefits have been restructured, 'tax credits' (credited through the payroll to low earners) introduced, and the right to single and urgent needs payments replaced by a discretionary social fund subject to cash limits. New conditions have been imposed upon benefits aimed at providing incentives to work and at encouraging labour mobility. The following is a brief guide to the principal benefits relevant to compensation for personal injury and death. (The reference to 'contributory' benefits means that certain national insurance contributions must have been made by or credited to the claimant.) For details, N. Wikeley, A. I. Ogus, and E. Barendt, *The Law of Social Security* 5th edn (London, 2002), and the annual *Disability Rights Handbook* (Disability Alliance) should be consulted.

Compensation for loss of income

Statutory sick pay (SSP). Employers are obliged to pay statutory sick pay to employees when sick for four days or more. SSP is paid at a flat rate for up to 28 weeks. Then the claimant is transferred to (state) incapacity benefit. Although SSP is non-contributory, employees earning less than the lower earnings limit for national insurance contributions are not eligible, nor are those over pensionable age. It is not means-tested, but it counts as income for means-tested benefits. SSP is taxable. (Note that in practice many employees have a contractual right to sickness pay from their employers, generally known as 'occupational sick pay'. It is usually at a higher rate than SSP, and commonly 100% of salary for higher-paid workers.) The SSP Review Working Group recommended administrative simplification of the scheme in 2007 (but decided that radical reform was inappropriate, if employee rights were to be preserved).

Incapacity benefit. This is a contributory state benefit for those unable to work because of illness or disability. The claimant must not be eligible for SSP (ante), must not be over pensionable age, and must have paid national insurance contributions. The benefit is not means-tested, so the amount does not depend on the claimant's income or savings.

Income support. This is a non-contributory 'topping-up' benefit intended to keep incomes up to a statutory minimum level for persons working less than 16 hours a week. It is payable to those who are lone parents, those who are too sick or disabled to work, including the registered blind, and those staying at home to look after a severely disabled person. The claimant's capital must not exceed a specified amount. Income support is made up of personal allowances and additional premiums which depend upon age and health. These include a family premium, a pensioner's premium, a carer's premium, and a disability premium.

Employment and support allowance. From 2008, employment and support allowance will replace incapacity benefit and income support for new claimants (Welfare Reform Act 2007, Part I). Persons limited in their capability to work may claim it, eligibility being based either on NI contributions (as for incapacity benefit) or their level of income (as for income support). Mandatory medical assessments (the 'Personal Capability Assessment') will determine whether or not it would be reasonable to require the claimant to engage in work-related activity. If so, he or she may be required to undergo work-related interviews (to draw up a 'plan of action'), or work-related activity (to increase the likelihood of gaining employment, e.g. training), and/or further work-related health assessments. Sanctions will be imposed if these steps are refused without 'good cause'.

Working Tax Credit. Despite the name, working tax credit is not really a tax-break, but rather an income support for the low-paid, administered by HM Revenue and Customs. The tax credit system is designed to 'reinforce the link between receipt of benefits and participation in the labour market' (*Atiyah*, p. 348). The intention is to encourage people to return to or take-up work by topping up low earnings. Additional payments are available for lone parents, disabled people, or people aged over 50 who are returning to work after a period on benefits. There is also a childcare element, in addition to the separate Child Tax Credit.

Jobseeker's allowance (JSA). This is for people who are unemployed, or working less than 16 hours a week, and are available for, and actively looking for work. Those who are aged over 60 or incapable of work are eligible for income support instead (ante). There are two forms of JSA. Contributions-based JSA is a personal flat-rate allowance based on national insurance contributions; it is payable for six months and is taxable. Income-based JSA is means-tested and taxable, payable to those who have no income or a low income, have no savings above a specified limit, and whose partner is not working or is working less than 24 hours a week.

Vaccine damage payments. These are available to those who were severely disabled as a result of routine vaccination for specified common diseases. Claims must be made within six years of the vaccination, which must have been done before the claimant was 18 (except vaccinations against polio, meningitis C, and rubella, or performed in an epidemic). The payment is a lump sum (currently £120,000) which is tax free, non-contributory, and not means-tested: Vaccine Damage Payments Act 1979, as amended.

Haemophilia/HIV payments. The Macfarlane Trust (1987) set up by the Government makes grants and regular payments on the basis of need to haemophiliacs with HIV infection as a result of receiving infected blood products (Factor 8). In addition, under the Special Payments Trust, all who qualify on medical grounds receive lump sums of £20,000 each.

Armed Forces Compensation Scheme. This compensates personnel for injuries or diseases resulting from service in HM Forces. A lump-sum is paid, according to a tariff graded by seriousness of injury. (For military injuries sustained before 2005, War Disablement Pensions are provided.)

Compensation for non-pecuniary loss

Industrial injuries disablement benefit. This is a pension payable to employed earners who suffer disablement caused by an accident 'arising out of and in the course of employment', or a prescribed industrial disease. The amount of benefit depends upon the degree of disablement as assessed by a medical board. There are prescribed degrees of disablement, e.g.

absolute deafness, 100 per cent; amputation of both feet, 90 per cent; loss of one eye, the other being normal, 40 per cent, etc. Payment is made even if the employee resumes work, for it is not intended to replace lost income. It is tax free, non-contributory, and not means-tested. It counts as income for the assessment of means-tested benefits.

Note that in 2004 the Industrial Injuries Advisory Council decided that work-related stress should *not* be prescribed as an industrial disease, given their concerns over its definition, attribution and verification. This of course makes the developing common law liability in this area of even greater importance (see pp. 1102–1103, ante).

Compensation for expenses

Disability living allowance. This is a tax-free, non-contributory, non-means tested benefit for people who need help in looking after themselves. It has a care component, for help with personal care needs; and a mobility component for help with walking difficulties.

Attendance allowance. This is a tax-free allowance for those disabled and aged over 65, who need help with personal care. There are two rates of allowance, a higher rate if care is needed day and night, and a lower rate if needed by day only. It is non-contributory, not means-tested, and does not count as income for means-tested benefits.

Constant attendance allowance. This is paid to those receiving disablement benefit (i.e. as the result of industrial or war injury, or prescribed disease) who are at least 95 per cent disabled and need daily care and attendance for the necessities of life.

Carer's allowance. This is a taxable allowance for people spending at least 35 hours a week looking after someone who is severely disabled. It is non-contributory and not means-tested but counts as income for means-tested benefits.

Independent living funds. These funds are a non-departmental public body, established to help severely disabled people under the age of 65 to pay for personal care or domestic help, so that they do not have to go into residential care.

Social fund. This makes grants and loans, mainly to those on income support, for some exceptional expenses which cannot be paid for out of regular income; for example, funeral payments, maternity grants, cold-weather payments, and crisis loans. Savings must be below specified limits. Disabled people receive priority for the discretionary community care grants which are paid to those who remain in or re-establish themselves in the community rather than being in residential care.

Family fund. This assists families of children with very severe disabilities and makes grants for items not covered by statutory schemes. It is a registered charity funded by the Government. The income and savings of families are taken into account.

■ The Criminal Injuries Compensation Scheme (2001)

1. This Scheme is made by the Secretary of State under the Criminal Injuries Compensation Act 1995....

Administration of the Scheme

2. Claims officers in the Criminal Injuries Compensation Authority ("the Authority") will determine claims for compensation in accordance with this Scheme. Appeals against decisions taken on reviews

under this Scheme will be determined by adjudicators. Persons appointed as adjudicators are appointed as members of the Criminal Injuries Compensation Appeals Panel ("the Panel"). The Secretary of State will appoint one of the adjudicators as Chairman of the Panel. The Secretary of State will also appoint persons as staff of the Panel to administer the provisions of this Scheme relating to the appeal system.

4. The general working of this Scheme will be kept under review by the Secretary of State....

5. The Panel will advise the Secretary of State on matters on which he seeks its advice, as well as on such other matters and at such times as it considers appropriate....

Eligibility to apply for compensation
7. No compensation will be paid under this Scheme in the following circumstances:

(a) where the applicant has previously lodged any claim for compensation in respect of the same criminal injury under this or any other scheme for the compensation of the victims of violent crime in operation in Great Britain; or

(b) where the criminal injury was sustained before 1 October 1979 and the victim and the assailant were living together at the time as members of the same family.

8. For the purposes of this Scheme, "criminal injury" means one or more personal injuries as described in the following paragraph, being an injury sustained in Great Britain . . . and directly attributable to:

(a) a crime of violence (including arson, fire-raising or an act of poisoning); or

(b) an offence of trespass on a railway; or

(c) the apprehension or attempted apprehension of an offender or a suspected offender, the prevention or attempted prevention of an offence, or the giving of help to any constable who is engaged in any such activity.

9. For the purposes of this Scheme, personal injury includes physical injury (including fatal injury), mental injury (that is temporary mental anxiety, medically verified, or a disabling mental illness confirmed by psychiatric diagnosis) and disease (that is a medically recognised illness or condition). Mental injury or disease may either result directly from the physical injury or from a sexual offence or may occur without any physical injury. Compensation will not be payable for mental injury or disease without physical injury, or in respect of a sexual offence, unless the applicant:

(a) was put in reasonable fear of immediate physical harm to his own person; or

(b) had a close relationship of love and affection with another person at the time when that person sustained physical and/or mental injury (including fatal injury) directly attributable to conduct within paragraph 8(a), (b) or (c), and

(i) that relationship still subsists (unless the victim has since died), and

(ii) the applicant either witnessed and was present on the occasion when the other person sustained the injury, or was closely involved in its immediate aftermath; or

(c) in a claim arising out of a sexual offence, was the non-consenting victim of that offence (which does not include a victim who consented in fact but was deemed in law not to have consented); or

(d) being a person employed in the business of a railway, either witnessed and was present on the occasion when another person sustained physical (including fatal) injury directly attributable to an offence of trespass on a railway, or was closely involved in its immediate aftermath. Paragraph 12 below does not apply where mental anxiety or mental illness is sustained as described in this sub-paragraph.

10. It is not necessary for the assailant to have been convicted of a criminal offence in connection with the injury. Moreover, even where the injury is attributable to conduct within paragraph 8 in respect of which the assailant cannot be convicted of an offence by reason of age, insanity or diplomatic immunity, the conduct may nevertheless be treated as constituting a criminal act.

11. A personal injury is not a criminal injury for the purposes of this Scheme where the injury is attributable to the use of a vehicle, except where the vehicle was used so as deliberately to inflict, or attempt to inflict, injury on any person.

12. Where an injury is sustained accidentally by a person who is engaged in:

(a) any of the law-enforcement activities described in paragraph 8(c), or

(b) any other activity directed to containing, limiting or remedying the consequences of a crime,

compensation will not be payable unless the person injured was, at the time he sustained the injury, taking an exceptional risk which was justified in all the circumstances.

Eligibility to receive compensation

13. A claims officer may withhold or reduce an award where he considers that:

(a) the applicant failed to take, without delay, all reasonable steps to inform the police, or other body or person considered by the Authority to be appropriate for the purpose, of the circumstances giving rise to the injury; or

(b) the applicant failed to co-operate with the police or other authority in attempting to bring the assailant to justice; or

(c) the applicant has failed to give all reasonable assistance to the Authority or other body or person in connection with the application; or

(d) the conduct of the applicant before, during or after the incident giving rise to the application makes it inappropriate that a full award or any award at all be made; or

(e) the applicant's character as shown by his criminal convictions (excluding convictions spent under the Rehabilitation of Offenders Act 1974 at the date of application or death) or by evidence available to the claims officer makes it inappropriate that a full award or any award at all be made.

14. In considering the issue of conduct under paragraph 13(d) above, a claims officer may withhold or reduce an award where he considers that excessive consumption of alcohol or use of illicit drugs by the applicant contributed to the circumstances which gave rise to the injury in such a way as to make it inappropriate that a full award, or any award at all, be made.

15. Where the victim has died since sustaining the injury (whether or not in consequence of it), paragraphs 13 and 14 will apply in relation both to the deceased and to any applicant for compensation under paragraphs 37–44 (fatal awards).

16. A claims officer will make an award only where he is satisfied:

(a) that there is no likelihood that an assailant would benefit if an award were made; or

(b) where the applicant is under 18 years of age when the application is determined, that it would not be against his interest for an award to be made.

17. Where a case is not ruled out under paragraph 7(b) (injury sustained before 1 October 1979) but at the time when the injury was sustained, the victim and any assailant (whether or not that assailant actually inflicted the injury) were living in the same household as members of the same family, an award will be withheld unless:

(a) the assailant has been prosecuted in connection with the offence, except where a claims officer considers that there are practical, technical or other good reasons why a prosecution has not been brought; and

(b) in the case of violence between adults in the family, a claims officer is satisfied that the applicant and the assailant stopped living in the same household before the application was made and are unlikely to share the same household again.

For the purposes of this paragraph, a man and woman living together as husband and wife will be treated as members of the same family.

Consideration of applications

18. An application for compensation under this Scheme in respect of a criminal injury ("injury" hereafter in this Scheme) must be made in writing on a form obtainable from the Authority. It should be made as soon as possible after the incident giving rise to the injury and must be received by the Authority within two years of the date of the incident.

A claims officer may waive this time limit where he considers that, by reason of the particular circumstances of the case, it is reasonable and in the interests of justice to do so.

19. It will be for the applicant to make out his case…

Where an applicant is represented, the costs of representation will not be met by the Authority.

20. A claims officer may make such directions and arrangements for the conduct of an application, including the imposition of conditions, as he considers appropriate in all the circumstances. The standard of proof to be applied by a claims officer in all matters before him will be the balance of probabilities….

22. A Guide to the operation of this Scheme will be published by the Authority….

Types and limits of compensation

23. Subject to the other provisions of this Scheme, the compensation payable under an award will be:

   (a) a standard amount of compensation determined by reference to the nature of the injury in accordance with paragraphs 26–29;
   (b) where the applicant has lost earnings or earning capacity for longer than 28 weeks as a direct consequence of the injury (other than injury leading to his death), an additional amount in respect of such loss of earnings, calculated in accordance with paragraphs 30–34;
   (c) where the applicant has lost earnings or earning capacity for longer than 28 weeks as a direct consequence of the injury (other than injury leading to his death) or, if not normally employed, is incapacitated to a similar extent, an additional amount in respect of any special expenses, calculated in accordance with paragraphs 35–36;
   (d) where the victim has died in consequence of the injury, the amount or amounts calculated in accordance with paragraphs 37–43;
   (e) where the victim has died otherwise than in consequence of the injury, a supplementary amount calculated in accordance with paragraph 44.

24. The maximum award that may be made (before any reduction under paragraphs 13–15 above) in respect of the same injury will not exceed £500,000. For these purposes, where the victim has died in consequence of the injury, any application made by the victim before his death and any application made by any qualifying claimant or claimants after his death will be regarded as being in respect of the same injury.

25. The injury, or any exacerbation of a pre-existing condition, must be sufficiently serious to qualify for compensation equal at least to the minimum award under this Scheme in accordance with paragraph 26, but lesser compensation may be paid if an award is reduced under paragraphs 13, 14, or 15 of the Scheme.

Standard amount of compensation

26. The standard amount of compensation will be the amount shown in respect of the relevant description of injury in the Tariff, which sets out:

   (a) a scale of fixed levels of compensation;
   (b) the level and corresponding amount of compensation for each description of injury; and
   (c) qualifying notes.

Level 1 represents the minimum award under this Scheme, and Level 25 represents the maximum award for any single description of injury. Where the injury has the effect of accelerating or exacerbating a pre-existing condition, the compensation awarded will reflect only the degree of acceleration or exacerbation.

27. Minor multiple injuries will be compensated in accordance with Note 12 [omitted] to the Tariff. The standard amount of compensation for more serious but separate multiple injuries will, unless expressly provided for otherwise in the Tariff, be calculated as: (a) the Tariff amount for the highest-rated description of injury; plus (b) 30 per cent of the Tariff amount for the second highest-rated

description of injury; plus, where there are three or more injuries, (c) 15 per cent of the Tariff amount for the third highest-rated description of injury.

28. Where the Authority considers that any description of injury for which no provision is made in the Tariff is sufficiently serious to qualify for at least the minimum award under this Scheme, it will, following consultation with the Panel, refer the injury to the Secretary of State. In doing so the Authority will recommend to the Secretary of State both the inclusion of that description of injury in the Tariff and also the amount of compensation for which it should qualify. Any such consultation with the Panel or reference to the Secretary of State must not refer to the circumstances of any individual application for compensation under this Scheme other than the relevant medical reports.

29. Where . . . the Authority decides to refer the injury to the Secretary of State under the preceding paragraph, an interim award may be made of up to half the amount of compensation for which it is recommended that such description of injury should qualify if subsequently included in the Tariff. . . .

Compensation for loss of earnings

30. Where the applicant has lost earnings or earning capacity for longer than 28 weeks as a direct consequence of the injury (other than injury leading to his death), no compensation in respect of loss of earnings or earning capacity will be payable for the first 28 weeks of loss. The period of loss for which compensation may be payable will begin after 28 weeks' incapacity for work and continue for such period as a claims officer may determine.

31. For a period of loss ending before or continuing to the time the claim is assessed, the net loss of earnings or earning capacity will be calculated on the basis of:

(a) the applicant's emoluments (being any profit or gain accruing from an office or employment) at the time of the injury and what those emoluments would have been during the period of loss; and

(b) any emoluments which have become payable to the applicant in respect of the whole or part of the period of loss, whether or not as a result of the injury; and

(c) any changes in the applicant's pension rights; and

(d) in accordance with paragraphs 45–47 (reductions to take account of other payments), any social security benefits, insurance payments and pension which have become payable to the applicant during the period of loss; and

(e) any other pension which has become payable to the applicant during the period of loss, whether or not as a result of the injury.

32. Where, at the time the claim is assessed, a claims officer considers that the applicant is likely to suffer continuing loss of earnings and/or earning capacity, an annual rate of net loss (the multiplicand) or, where appropriate, more than one such rate will be calculated on the basis of:

(a) the current rate of net loss calculated in accordance with the preceding paragraph; and

(b) such future rate or rates of net loss (including changes in the applicant's pension rights) as the claims officer may determine; and

(c) the claims officer's assessment of the applicant's future earning capacity; and

(d) in accordance with paragraphs 45–47 (reductions to take account of other payments), any social security benefits, insurance payments and pension which will become payable to the applicant in future; and

(e) any other pension which will become payable to the applicant in future, whether or not as a result of the injury.

The compensation payable in respect of each period of continuing loss will be a lump sum, which is the product of that multiplicand and an appropriate multiplier. . . . . . The tables in *Note 3* [omitted] set out the multipliers and (where applicable) discounts and life expectancies to be applied. . . .

33. Where a claims officer considers that the approach in the preceding paragraph is impracticable, the compensation payable in respect of continuing loss of earnings and/or earning capacity will be such other lump sum as he may determine.

34. Any rate of net loss of earnings or earning capacity (before any reduction in accordance with this Scheme) which is to be taken into account in calculating any compensation payable under paragraphs 30–33 must not exceed one and a half times the gross average industrial earnings at the time of assessment according to the latest figures published by the Office for National Statistics.

Compensation for special expenses

35. Where the applicant has lost earnings or earning capacity for longer than 28 weeks as a direct consequence of the injury (other than injury leading to his death), or, if not normally employed, is incapacitated to a similar extent, additional compensation may be payable in respect of any special expenses incurred by the applicant from the date of the injury for:

(a) loss of or damage to property or equipment belonging to the applicant on which he relied as a physical aid, where the loss or damage was a direct consequence of the injury;

(b) costs (other than by way of loss of earnings or earning capacity) associated with National Health Service treatment for the injury;

(c) the cost of private health treatment for the injury, but only where a claims officer considers that, in all the circumstances, both the private treatment and its cost are reasonable;

(d) the reasonable cost, to the extent that it falls to the applicant, of

   (i) special equipment, and/or

   (ii) adaptations to the applicant's accommodation, and/or

   (iii) care, whether in a residential establishment or at home, which are not provided or available free of charge from the National Health Service, local authorities or any other agency, provided that a claims officer considers such expense to be necessary as a direct consequence of the injury; and

   (iv) the cost of the Court of Protection or of the curator bonis.

In the case of (d)(iii), the expense of unpaid care provided at home by a relative or friend of the victim will be compensated by having regard to the level of care required, the cost of a carer, assessing the carer's loss of earnings or earning capacity and/or additional personal and living expenses, as calculated on such basis as a claims officer considers appropriate in all the circumstances. Where the foregoing method of assessment is considered by the claims officer not to be relevant in all the circumstances, the compensation payable will be such sum as he may determine having regard to the level of care provided.

Compensation in fatal cases

37. Where the victim has died in consequence of the injury, no compensation other than funeral expenses will be payable for the benefit of his estate. Such expenses will, subject to the application of paragraphs 13 and 14 in relation to the actions, conduct and character of the deceased, be payable up to an amount considered reasonable by a claims officer, even where the person bearing the cost of the funeral is otherwise ineligible to claim under this Scheme.

38. Where the victim has died since sustaining the injury, compensation may be payable, subject to paragraphs 13–15 (actions, conduct and character), to any claimant (a "qualifying claimant") who at the time of the deceased's death was:

(a) the partner of the deceased, being only, for these purposes:

   (i) a person who was living together with the deceased as husband and wife or as a same sex partner in the same household immediately before the date of death and who, unless formally married to him, had been so living throughout the two years before that date, or

   (ii) a spouse or former spouse of the deceased who was financially supported by him immediately before the date of death; or

(b) a natural parent of the deceased, or a person who was not the natural parent, provided that he was accepted by the deceased as a parent of his family; or

(c) a natural child of the deceased, or a person who was not the natural child, provided that he was accepted by the deceased as a child of his family or was dependent on him.

Where the victim has died in consequence of the injury, compensation may be payable to a qualifying claimant under paragraphs 39–42 (standard amount of compensation, dependency, and loss of parent). Where the victim has died otherwise than in consequence of the injury, and before title to the award has been vested in the victim (see paragraph 50), no standard amount or other compensation will be payable to the estate or to a qualifying claimant other than under paragraph 44 (supplementary compensation).

39. A person who was criminally responsible for the death of a victim may not be a qualifying claimant. . . .

40. Additional compensation calculated in accordance with the following paragraph may be payable to a qualifying claimant where a claims officer is satisfied that the claimant was financially or physically dependent on the deceased. A financial dependency will not be established where the deceased's only normal income was from:

(a) United Kingdom social security benefits; or

(b) social security benefits or similar payments from the funds of other countries.

41. The amount of compensation payable in respect of dependency will be calculated on a basis similar to paragraphs 31–34 (loss of earnings) and paragraph 35 (d) (iii) (cost of care). The period of loss will begin from the date of the deceased's death and continue for such period as a claims officer may determine, with no account being taken, where the qualifying claimant was formally married to the deceased, of remarriage or prospects of remarriage. In assessing the dependency, the claims officer will take account of the qualifying claimant's income and emoluments (being any profit or gain accruing from an office or employment), if any. . . .

42. Where a qualifying claimant was under 18 years of age at the time of the deceased's death and was dependent on him for parental services, the following additional compensation may also be payable:

(a) a payment for loss of that parent's services at an annual rate of Level 5 of the Tariff; and

(b) such other payments as a claims officer considers reasonable to meet other resultant losses.

Each of these payments will be multiplied by an appropriate multiplier selected by a claims officer in accordance with paragraph 32 (future loss of earnings), taking account of the period remaining before the qualifying claimant reaches age 18 and of any other factors and contingencies which appear to the claims officer to be relevant.

44. Where a victim who would have qualified for additional compensation under paragraph 23(b) (loss of earnings) and/or paragraph 23(c) (special expenses) has died, otherwise than in consequence of the injury, before such compensation was awarded, supplementary compensation under this paragraph may be payable to a qualifying claimant who was financially dependent on the deceased within the terms of paragraph 40 (dependency), whether or not a relevant application was made by the victim before his death. Payment may be made in accordance with paragraph 31 in respect of the victim's loss of earnings (except for the first 28 weeks of the victim's loss of earnings and/or earning capacity) and in accordance with paragraph 35 in respect of any special expenses incurred by the victim before his death. The amounts payable to the victim and the qualifying claimant or claimants will not in total exceed £500,000.

Effect on awards of other payments

45. All awards payable under this Scheme, except those payable under paragraphs 26, 27, 39 and 42(a) (Tariff-based amounts of compensation), will be subject to a reduction to take account of social security benefits (or other state benefits) or insurance payments made by way of compensation for the same contingency. The reduction will be applied to those categories or periods of loss or need for which additional or supplementary compensation is payable, including compensation calculated on the basis of a multiplicand or annual cost. The amount of the reduction will be the full value of any relevant payment which the applicant has received, or to which he has or may have any present or future entitlement, by way of:

(a) United Kingdom social security benefits (or other state benefits);

(b) social security benefits or similar payments from the funds of other countries;

(c) payments under insurance arrangements, including, where a claim is made under paragraphs 35(c) and (d) and 36 (special expenses), insurance personally effected, paid for and maintained by the personal income of the victim or, in the case of a person under 18 years of age, by his parent. Insurance so personally effected will otherwise be disregarded.

In assessing the value of any such benefits and payments, account may be taken of any income tax liability likely to reduce their value.

46. Where, in the opinion of a claims officer, an applicant may be or may become eligible for any of the benefits and payments mentioned in the preceding paragraph, an award may be withheld until the applicant has taken such steps as the claims officer considers reasonable to claim them.

47. Where the victim is alive, any compensation payable under paragraphs 30–34 (loss of earnings) will be reduced to take account of any pension accruing as a result of the injury. Where the victim has died in consequence of the injury, any compensation payable under paragraphs 40–41 (dependency) will similarly be reduced to take account of any pension payable, as a result of the victim's death, for the benefit of the applicant. Where such pensions are taxable, one half of their value will be deducted, but they will otherwise be deducted in full (where, for example, a lump sum payment not subject to income tax is made). . . .

48. An award payable under this Scheme will be reduced by the full value of any payment in respect of the same injury which the applicant has received by way of:

(a) . . . ;

(b) any compensation award or similar payment from the funds of other countries;

(c) any award where:

(i) a civil court has made an order for the payment of damages;

(ii) a claim for damages and/or compensation has been settled on terms providing for the payment of money;

(iii) payment of compensation has been ordered by a criminal court in respect of personal injuries.

. . .

49. Where a person in whose favour an award under this Scheme is made subsequently receives any other payment in respect of the same injury in any of the circumstances mentioned in the preceding paragraph, but the award made under this Scheme was not reduced accordingly, he will be required to repay the Authority in full up to the amount of the other payment.

[Provisions as to determination of applications, reviews and appeals omitted.]

[Some examples of the injury tariffs, which extend over 30 detailed pages:]

Injuries to head and neck: Nose
Deviated nasal septum:

– no operation £1,000
– requiring septoplasty £2,000

Fracture of nasal bones:

– undisplaced £1,000
– displaced £1,500
– requiring manipulation £2,000
– requiring rhinoplasty £2,000
– requiring turbinectomy £2,000

Loss of smell/taste:

– partial loss of smell and/or taste £5,500
– total loss of smell or taste £11,000

– total loss of smell and taste £16,500

Partial loss of nose (at least 10%) £4,400

Injuries to lower limbs: Fibula (slender bone from knee to ankle)
Fractured:

- one leg
- substantial recovery £2,500
- continuing significant disability £3,800
- both legs
- substantial recovery £3,300
- continuing significant disability £5,500

NOTE

The fixed tariffs for particular injuries in the CICS were first introduced in 1996; the previous system had been case-by-case assessment, as for damages at common law. The tariffs have been criticised for inflexibility and for failing to reflect victims' individual circumstances, but the Government has resisted such arguments as undermining the point of the reform, which was to speed up and simplify decision-making by the Criminal Injuries Compensation Authority (see *Atiyah*, p. 321). It may be interesting to contrast some of the tariffs given above with the range of awards in tort cases, as summarised by the Judicial Studies Board figures (March 2007 levels). The JSB gives the awards for total loss of smell and taste as in the region of £23,320, for leg fractures with incomplete recovery in the range £10,810–£16,780, and for simple fracture of the tibia with full recovery as the upper end of the 'leg fracture' bracket, with maximum award of £5,510. These quanta are rather higher than the comparable CICS tariffs. When the present scheme was introduced in 2001, it could be said that the highest level in the tariffs, £250,000 (awarded for quadriplegia or very serious brain damage) 'was very much higher then the highest awards for non-pecuniary loss at common law (then about £130,000)' (*Atiyah*, ibid). However, even at this upper end of the scale, the common law is fast catching up: the JSB guidelines give £170,000–£242,000 as the range for very severe brain damage and £194,000–£242,000 for quadriplegia. Consider also the effect of para. 27 of the Scheme on the award of damages. For the general uplift in damages for non-pecuniary losses at common law, see *Heil v Rankin* [2001] QB 272, [2000] 3 All ER 138 (p. 518, ante).

6 THE FUTURE OF COMPENSATION

The fundamental question facing reformers is the balance between tort and other sources of compensation, in particular social security. No modern society relies exclusively on tort. Since the late 1960s there have been many critiques of the tort system as a means of compensating personal injury and death (see Further Reading, p. 1171, post). The alternatives are either to replace the tort system with enlarged social security benefits, or to retain a 'mixed' system in which one form of compensation complements but does not duplicate the other.

(a) Comprehensive approaches

The former was the model adopted in New Zealand based on the Woodhouse Report on Compensation for Personal Injury (December 1967). The New Zealand Accident

Compensation Act 1972 replaced the previous mixed system of common law damages, workers' compensation legislation, criminal injuries compensation, third party insurance for motor vehicle accidents, and social security, with a comprehensive scheme of no-fault benefits for accidental injury or death, medical misadventure, occupational diseases, and criminal injuries, but not other sources of personal injury, illness, or disability. The scheme was criticised, from the political left, on the grounds that it made anomalous distinctions treating those who were covered more favourably than other social security claimants. On the political right, which gained the ascendancy in the 1980s and 1990s, it was argued that the scheme's funding rules meant that employers were subsidising recreational injuries, and were paying too much. The Accident Rehabilitation and Compensation Insurance Act 1992 abolished lump sum payments, reduced the scope of coverage, and reduced the levels of compensation. Some of the strengths and weaknesses are discussed by Sir Geoffrey Palmer, 'New Zealand's Accident Compensation Scheme: Twenty Years On' (1994) 44 University of Toronto LJ 223–73; see further Terence G. Ison, 'Changes to the Accident Compensation System: an International Perspective' (1993) 23 Victoria University of Wellington LR 25–43; J. F. Keeler, 'Social Insurance, Disability and Personal Injury: a Retrospective View' (1994) 44 University of Toronto LJ 275–352; J. Stapleton, 'Private Law and Institutional Competition' (1999) 9 Otago LR 519–33. In the UK the case for a comprehensive approach was forcefully made by Donald Harris and his colleagues at the Oxford Centre for Socio-Legal Studies following their extensive empirical research in the 1970s.

■ Compensation and Support for Illness and Injury
Donald Harris et al. Oxford Socio-Legal Studies (Clarendon Press: Oxford, 1984), pp. 327–328

We believe, in the light of the data presented in this [study], that the future policy-maker should plan to phase out all existing compensation systems which favour accident victims (or any category of them) over illness victims. This proposal obviously applies to the damages system, whose deficiencies as revealed by the survey [see the summary pp. 24–25, ante] are too deep-rooted to be removed by any modification of the system. Relatively few accident victims recover any damages at all; most amounts recovered are low and therefore can do little to 'compensate'; and the cost of administering the system is very high. Delay and uncertainty are inherent in the system; the adversarial game permits defendants to adopt negotiating strategies which exploit—quite legitimately under the present rules—each uncertainty to defeat a claim, or to reduce the amount paid. The advantages claimed for the system do not, in our opinion, outweigh the disadvantages. Deterrence of carelessness operates in a random way, and accident victims themselves perceive no clear concept of fault or blame underlying the attribution of liability to pay damages. Our data establish that the roles of sick pay and social security in providing income support following illness and injury are now, in the aggregate, of much greater importance than the damages system. Yet the illness/injury demarcation is ignored by sick pay schemes and by all social security benefits introduced since 1946: within social security, only the historically anomalous industrial injuries scheme continues the preference for accident victims. We believe that the damages system for death and personal injury should be abolished as soon as improvements in sick pay and social security provision produce a rational, coherent, and integrated system of compensation for illness and injury.

Our view that we should move towards the abolition of every compensation scheme which is based on a particular category of causation means that we oppose the implementation of many of the recommendations of the Pearson Royal Commission, 1978. The Commission recommended many improvements to the tort claim; a new, no-fault scheme for injuries caused by road accidents; a special benefit for severely handicapped children; and that the criminal injuries scheme should be placed on a statutory basis. In our opinion, these proposals are difficult to justify in social policy terms, and would only increase the complexity of the present web of compensation systems, which are based, not on the relative extent of disabilities, but on the circumstances which give rise to disabilities....

Our proposals...are designed to permit some of the advantages of the tort system to be retained in any new schemes to replace tort: the individualized assessment of damages to be replaced by better and more flexible types of social security benefits for long-term cases of disability; and deterrence of carelessness through some risk-relationship, by extension of sick pay entitlement, and by new types of risk-related social security contributions. Our proposals would also allow the policy-maker (contrary, however, to our own preference) to choose to implement risk-relationship by special, no-fault schemes as part of the overall scheme....

(b) Mixed approaches

It had been widely expected that the Royal Commission on Civil Liability and Compensation for Personal Injury (under the chairmanship of Lord Pearson), appointed in 1973, would propose a rationalisation of the many different statutory and common law compensation schemes. Instead, after deliberating for five years, the Commission made recommendations which, although amounting to 188 in number, were disappointingly modest in purpose. The New Zealand scheme was not regarded as transplantable to the UK. Instead, the Commission examined the case for extending particular categories of no-fault provision. It concluded that a considerable shift of emphasis from the tort to the social security system was desirable. The only area for which it proposed a non-tort scheme was road accidents, but this has not been implemented, nor has a proposal by the Lord Chancellor's Department in 1991 for a non-tort scheme for minor road accidents (*Compensation for Road Accidents: a Consultation Paper*, May 1991). Many of the Commission's proposals were aimed at avoiding the overlap between different sources of compensation.

Very little by way of reform has sprung from the Report. The Thalidomide tragedy, which sparked the appointment of the Pearson Commission, led to the enactment of the Congenital Disabilities (Civil Liability) Act 1976 (p. 149, ante) even before the Commission reported, although the Commission proposed some amendments to the Act. The Commission proposed strict product liability, but the need for this came not from the Report but from an EC directive as implemented in the Consumer Protection Act 1987. The pressure for a no-fault scheme for medical misadventure has not met a favourable response from successive governments. The NHS Redress Act 2006 empowers the Secretary of State to 'establish a scheme for the purpose of enabling redress to be provided without recourse to civil proceedings' (s. 1(1)), but only when the NHS would anyway be liable in tort. Thus, the Act does not inaugurate no-fault liability, and the usual tests of medical negligence will continue to apply (see pp. 304–305, above). Rather, the point of the Act is to avoid the costs and delays of litigation in less severe cases, and to place more emphasis upon apologies and openness (willingness to admit and learn from mistakes) when things go wrong. Litigation is said to promote defensiveness and secrecy in the NHS, as well as the obvious problems of its high cost. See *NHS Redress: Statement of Policy* (Department of Health, 2005). See further the consultation paper in 2003 from the Chief Medical Officer, *Making Amends*. The 2006 Act does not go as far as the CMO's paper had suggested; and for general comment see A.-M. Farrell and S. Devaney (2007) 27 LS 630.

In the 3rd edition of his path-breaking book *Accidents, Compensation and the Law*, Professor Patrick Atiyah argued for a single comprehensive social security system, and the gradual abolition of tort actions, and the editor of subsequent editions, Professor Cane, continues to argue for this solution (while admitting that the political climate is 'uncongenial to comprehensive reform'): see *Atiyah*, pp. 488–493. However, Professor Atiyah himself now advocates the spread of first-party insurance, starting with the abolition of the tort-liability insurance system and its replacement with compulsory first-party insurance paid for by owners of motor vehicles. The insurance would cover the owner, passengers, and pedestrians on a no-fault basis. Atiyah suggests that for all other injuries and diseases tort liability should be abolished and replaced by voluntary first-party insurance: see Atiyah, *The Damages Lottery* (1997), chap. 8 (for criticism, see e.g. Cane in *Atiyah*, pp. 493–495). Atiyah's vision of leaving protection for medical accidents and work-related injuries and disease to the marketplace would remove protection from the poor who cannot afford private insurance, but at present have some possibility of recovering tort damages.

Readers will want to study the Atiyah–Cane debate themselves, and to look at some of the other writings below. By way of background the next extract provides a useful analysis of different responses to misfortune, and emphasises the political nature of the choices which have to be made.

■ Tort, Insurance and Ideology
Jane Stapleton (1995) 58 MLR 820, pp. 821–823, 843–845 (footnotes omitted)

Two of the important responses to misfortune require a pooling or 'collectivisation' of risk. The first is *insurance*. Here risks are pooled by those exposed to the same likelihood of risk of the relevant misfortune, be it of loss (first party insurance) or legal liability (liability insurance). The selection of which misfortunes are insured and at what level of cover are both choices for the insured (save in areas of compulsory insurance). For example, a person taking out first party accident insurance may choose only to cover the risk of income disruption (and not the misfortune of disfigurement, pain and suffering, etc) and then only up to a certain level of pre-accident salary. A characteristic of insurance is that it is a closed system in the sense that the group of people who pay into the finance pool is identical to the group of people who are entitled to claim from it: no one pays in who is not also entitled to claim and it is only those who pay in who can claim. But the most fundamental characteristic of insurance, the characteristic Abraham calls 'the heart of any insurance system,' is its pursuit of homogeneous risk pools: that is, the aim of insurance is to categorise insureds into groups according to the insured's likelihood of suffering the relevant misfortune, and to require that each insured pay risk-related premiums into the insurance pool corresponding to that group. Thus, although mutual support is what underpins insurance, it is a mutual support which only extends to and is defined in terms of support between the insureds. Over the very long term (and ignoring the administrative costs and profit of the insurer), each member of a truly homogeneous risk pool would pay in the same as it pulled out. This not only means that no member would subsidise other members, but that the ultimate moral logic of insurance is one of 'insured pays'; that is, in terms of the misfortune (be it loss or liability) for which the cover exists, a logic of 'victim pays'. Finally, it should be noted that because the pool is internally self-financed, the insurance arrangement itself carries with it no potential for imposing financial incentives on outsiders whose behaviour affects the likelihood of the misfortune occurring. In other words, deterrence of misfortune cannot be accommodated as a direct goal of insurance: for example, in first party insurance the creator of the misfortune does not pay!

The second response to misfortune which involves collectivisation of risk is what I term *socialisation of risk*. Here the selection of which misfortunes are to be covered by the arrangement is a choice by the state, as is the level to which the victim is financially supported and neither need be linked to the question of what the victim would have chosen (and would have been able to afford) to insure against. The key characteristic of these arrangements is that the victim of the relevant misfortune is ensured of receiving financial support even though the pool covers heterogeneous risks, even though the victim has not contributed risk-related contributions to the pool and even if the party responsible for the misfortune is not identified or required to contribute to the pool in relation to the cost of its risk-taking. In the sense that the arrangement ensures help to victims covered by the scheme, it is like insurance; but there the similarity ends because, while homogeneity of risks is the aim of insurance, in schemes of socialised risk this is positively rejected and mutual support operates across a group, the membership of which is heterogeneous in terms of each member's risk rating. Indeed, the pooling of heterogeneous risks is the central moral aim of these arrangements because, although it results in the cross-subsidisation from low risks to high risks, it fosters the goal of ensuring that victims receive cover.…

In schemes of socialised risk, no attempt is made at coincidence between any contributions to the fund by potential beneficiaries and their risk of suffering the misfortune. This flexibility in the mode of funding ensures that, unlike the insurance response to misfortune, a scheme of socialised risk is not impervious to the incorporation of goals other than the central one of ensuring relevant victims receive support. For example, schemes of socialised risk are free to incorporate a redistributional strategy: the relation of any contributions by potential beneficiaries to the level of benefit can redistribute to the rich (flat-rate contributions but earnings-related benefits) or redistribute to the poor (earnings-related contributions, say by income tax, but flat-rate benefits). More importantly for the current discussion, it is possible to require those who create the risk of the relevant misfortune to contribute to the fund without compromising the central commitment of ensuring that all those covered receive support. This 'injurer pays' source of funding allows non-incentive goals such as moral vindication or incentive goals such as deterrence to be pursued. Contributions from identifiable sources of risk are sometimes used in social insurance (e.g. levies on vehicle users in New Zealand) and sometimes not (e.g. no levies on manufacturers in New Zealand), and sometimes used in social welfare arrangements (e.g. state claw-back provisions: form fathers for state support of children; from tortfeasors for state support of tort victims) and sometimes not…

A third response to misfortune is *restoration* of the victim, that is one which seeks to restore the victim to his pre-misfortune position so far as money is able. No state system of support provides this level of cover. Tort does, but also predicates this level of support on the party responsible for the misfortune being identified; and that party alone is required to make the payment to the victim. Clearly, tort is a form of the third response, but what is its relation to the other forms of response to misfortune? Can it also be seen as insurance of victims or the socialisation of risk to victims; and what follows if it can be? It may seem obvious at this stage that tort could not be seen as a form of either. For example, in tort the incidence and level of cover is neither decided by the victim (as in insurance) nor by the state (as in socialised risk schemes) but by judicial development of legal doctrine. Similarly, in tort, unlike the other two forms of response, the payment to the victim is predicated on the identification of the injurer and is made by that party.…, [h]owever, in the postwar period those keen to extend support for the victims of misfortune made loose comparisons between tort and these other forms of response to misfortune which allowed an unfocused view to arise that tort law was somehow 'about insurance.' This then led some to argue that the law's traditional rejection of the relevance of insurance to liability was naive and should be now replaced by an approach that somehow took 'the realities of insurance' into account. As already noted, there has grown up more recently, especially in the United States, the argument that really we should see 'tort as insurance' and that, viewed as such, tort should be savagely cut back.

…

Commentators and judges should think twice before making off-hand comments that insurance should be relevant to the scope of tort liability, that judges should take into account 'the realities of insurance' or that they should address the comparative insurability of parties. Such statements are dangerous. They are not only indeterminate criteria but can mislead us into suppressing any corrective justice or deterrence goals we may have for tort liability and this then opens the door for the more radical argument that tort is a surrogate for first party insurance. This latter tort-as-insurance criterion then inexorably points to the need for the retrenchment of tort entitlements. But, far from being a construction of tort law with which we all agree, it is one with little judicial support and one which is based on ideological assumptions about the weight to be given to concerns about autonomy and dependency. Of course, resort to ideological assumptions here is inescapable because whether we should deploy tort, with its full restorative measure, to help the victim of a specified misfortune is not a matter of legal logic but a debatable political question....

Even if we decide that the full restorative measure of tort is not justified generally or for a specific misfortune, this does not mean we are content to abandon the victim to the mere possibility of first party insurance with its dual characteristics of 'the pool of victims pay'/'the injurer goes scot-free.'...

To sum up: tort is not a surrogate for insurance; its full restorative measure and no set-off rule for the proceeds of first party insurance confirm this. (Nor is tort a surrogate for social insurance; its predication of support on the identification of and payment by the injurer show this.) The scope of tort liability is a political question and concerns about autonomy and dependency are valid factors to be weighed in that balance. If the pool of tort liability is now thought to be overflowing, there is nothing wrong in identifying all such countervailing factors more carefully than in the past. But this should be done openly, acknowledging that the weight given to each factor is a matter of personal political judgment. It should also be acknowledged that for many people the degree to which they find dependency, free-riding or inroads into autonomy objectionable is heavily coloured by the weight they give other pro-liability values and concerns for which the core of tort law has long stood.... Those who argue for the retrenchment of tort from the tort-as-insurance perspective should acknowledge their political emphasis on dependency and autonomy concerns and be required to justify the enrichment of injurers which such retrenchment would generate. What the tort-as-insurance idea teaches those who choose to defend the core of tort entitlements (and programmes of socialised risk) is that it is crucial to prevent certain ideas such as insurability, autonomy and dependency being asserted as apolitical trumps in the debate about how society should respond to misfortunes....

FURTHER READING

The literature on the future of compensation is vast, expanding and international. The following is a select bibliography.

Richard L. Abel, 'Torts' in D. Kairys (ed), *The Politics of Law: a Progressive critique*, 3rd edn (New York, 1998).

P. S. Atiyah, *The Damages Lottery* (Oxford, 1997).

P. S. Atiyah, 'Personal Injuries in the Twenty-First Century: Thinking the Unthinkable' in P. B. H. Birks (ed), *Wrongs and Remedies in the Twenty-First Century* (Oxford, 1996).

P. A. Bell, and J. O'Connell, *Accidental Justice: the Dilemmas of Tort Law* (New Haven and London, 1997).

A. Burrows, 'In defence of tort' in his *Understanding the Law of Obligations* (Oxford, 1998).

P. F. Cane, *Atiyah's Accidents, Compensation and the Law*, 7th edn (Cambridge, 2006).

J. Conaghan and W. Mansell, *The Wrongs of Tort*, 2nd edn (London, 1999).

M. Davies, 'The end of the affair: Duty of care and liability insurance' (1989) 9 Legal Studies 67.

D. N. Dewees, D. Duff, and M. J. Trebilcock, *Exploring the Domain of Accident Law: Taking the Facts Seriously* (New York and Oxford, 1996).

J. G. Fleming, *The American Tort Process* (Oxford, 1988).

R. E. Goodin, 'Theories of Compensation' in R. G. Frey and C. W. Morris (eds), *Liability and Responsibility: Essays in Law and Morals* (Cambridge, 1991).

D. Harris et al., *Compensation and Support for Illness and Injury* (Oxford, 1984).

D. Harris, 'Evaluating the Goals of Personal Injury Law: Some Empirical Evidence' in P. Cane and J. Stapleton (eds), *Essays for Patrick Atiyah* (Oxford, 1991).

D. Harris, D. Campbell, and R. Halson, *Remedies in Contract and Tort*, 2nd edn (London, 2002), chap. 24.

R. Lewis, 'Insurance and the Tort System' (2005) 25 Legal Studies 85.

J. Morgan, 'Tort, Insurance and Incoherence' (2004) 67 MLR 384.

A. Morris, 'Spiralling or Stabilising? The Compensation Culture and Our Propensity to Claim Damages for Personal Injury' (2007) 70 MLR 349.

V. E. Nolan and E. Ursin, *Understanding Enterprise Liability: Rethinking Tort Reform for the Twenty-First Century* (Philadelphia, 1995).

J. O'Connell, 'The role of compensation in personal injury tort law: A response to the opposite concerns of Gary Schwartz and Patrick Atiyah' (1999) 32 Connecticut LR 137.

J. Stapleton, *Disease and the Compensation Debate* (Oxford, 1987).

J. Stapleton, 'Tort, Insurance and Ideology' (1995) 58 MLR 820.

S. D. Sugarman, *Doing Away with Personal Injury Law* (New York, 1989).

APPENDIX

Following a Discussion Paper in 2004 (*Monetary Remedies in Public Law*) and a Scoping Paper in 2006 (*Remedies against Public Bodies*), in July 2008 the Law Commission published a Consultation Paper, extracts from which are set out post.

■ Law Commission Consultation Paper No 187, Administrative Redress: Public Bodies and the Citizen

PART 2
OVERVIEW

2.1　At the outset, we wish to emphasise that everything contained in this Consultation Paper is provisional and depends on the responses to consultation.

2.2　This project examines the mechanisms through which claimants can obtain redress from public bodies for substandard administrative action. In undertaking this project, we have been guided by two fundamental conclusions. The first is that, in principle, claimants should be entitled to obtain redress for loss caused by clearly substandard administrative action. The second is that special consideration should be given to the role played by public bodies when considering when and under what terms they should be liable for such losses.

2.3　Part 3 starts the discussion of redress by analysing the various mechanisms currently available for aggrieved citizens who are seeking redress for substandard administrative action. We divide these mechanisms into four broad pillars of administrative justice. The first pillar consists of internal mechanisms for redress, such as formal complaint procedures. The second pillar is composed of external non-court avenues of redress, such as public inquiries and tribunals. The third pillar consists of the public sector ombudsmen. Finally, the fourth pillar is formed by the remedies available in public and private law by way of a court action.

2.4　Our general view is that, while the vast majority of complaints are handled effectively in the first three pillars, there is a comparatively small number of 'residual' complaints where the involvement of the courts is necessary. Therefore it is vital to consider the appropriateness and effectiveness of court-based remedies.

2.5　The analysis of court-based remedies is divided between those available in judicial review and in private law. In private law, we focus on the torts of misfeasance in public office, breach of statutory duty and negligence.

2.6　Part 4 builds on the analysis in Part 3 to highlight certain defects in the current law relating to court-based remedies. In judicial review, we consider that it is incorrect that damages are available in situations covered by EU law and by the Human Rights Act 1998 but are not available in other situations solely covered by domestic law.

2.7　In private law, we consider that the current situation is unsustainable. The uncertain and unprincipled nature of negligence in relation to public bodies, coupled with the unpredictable expansion of liability over recent years, has led to a situation that serves neither claimants nor public bodies. Furthermore, we believe that recent developments in the torts of misfeasance in public office and breach of statutory duty render them unsuitable in relation to public bodies in the modern era.

2.8   In light of this, we suggest that there is a strong argument for the reform of court-based administrative redress in both public and private law. In developing the structure of potential reform, we have drawn heavily on the principle of modified corrective justice. By 'modified corrective justice' we mean a model of 'corrective justice' that properly reflects the special position of public bodies and affords them appropriate protection from unmeritorious claims.

2.9   Part 4 goes on to suggest specific reforms of court-based redress in both public and private law. This would involve the creation of a specific regime for public bodies based around a series of individual elements. At the core of these individual elements would be a requirement to show 'serious fault' on the part of the public body. We feel this would properly address the concerns of public bodies and the needs of claimants.

2.10   We provisionally suggest that damages should be available in judicial review if the claimant satisfies the elements of conferral of benefit, serious fault and causation. However, an award of damages would serve only as an ancillary remedy in judicial review and could only be claimed alongside the prerogative remedies. In keeping with other remedies available in judicial review, damages would be discretionary in the public law scheme.

2.11   Our suggested approach in private law is to place certain activities, which can be regarded as 'truly public', in a specialised scheme. Within this scheme, the claimant would have to satisfy the same requirements as the public law scheme in order to establish liability. The general . . . effect of these reforms would be to restrict liability in some areas and widen the potential for liability in others. This reflects our attempts to strike a balance between the following competing demands:

        (1) Setting the boundaries in which citizens may obtain redress where they are subject to serious substandard administrative action; and

        (2) Appreciating that public bodies are subject to a wide range of competing demands and are thus in a special position. This means that imposing general negligence liability may not be in the interests of justice as it could adversely affect the activities of the public body and therefore harm the general public.

2.12   Cases that do not satisfy the 'truly public' test would be determined by the ordinary rules of negligence.

2.13   The other significant reform we suggest in Part 4 is to modify the operation of the general rule of joint and several liability in private law as it applies to public bodies, since it can operate in a particularly unjust way. For example, a failure in a public body's regulatory oversight is often not the direct cause of the claimant's loss, which may be the wrongdoing of another, but the public body may have to bear the loss in its entirety.

2.14   Allowing for a relaxation of the rule where the respondent is a public body will allow for an equitable apportionment of damages. After the requirement to show serious fault on the part of the public body, this constitutes a further limitation of liability. In addition, the normal rules relating to contributory negligence would apply, which would allow for an award to be reduced if the claimant was partly to blame.

2.15   The object of these reforms is to improve the public and private law systems to ensure they appropriately reflect the special nature of public bodies and balance those considerations with the interests of claimants. However, improving the court-based system is only part of this project. The other significant part is to facilitate the resolution of cases through non-court mechanisms, consistent with the Government's commitment to alternative dispute resolution. . . .

2.18   We recognise that any changes to the liability regimes for public bodies have the potential to cause concern to both claimants and public bodies themselves. In Part 6 we address some of these concerns by considering the potential costs and benefits for public bodies. We also draw on research contained in Appendix B to address concerns that liability leads to defensive practices. Lastly, Part 6 notes the range of options available to government if there is particular concern relating to liability exposure in specific areas. These would include the possibility of statutory immunities, such as that which exists for the Financial Services Authority under section 102 of the Financial Services and Markets Act 2000, or statutory caps for individual claims.

2.19   Unfortunately, in the absence of reliable empirical data in this area, what Part 6 cannot do is to quantify the resource implications of our suggested reforms. The lack of empirical data in this area is of particular concern to the Law Commission and a specific request for information on the possible consequences of changes in liability is made in Part 6.

2.20   In summary, the substance of the reforms proposed by the Law Commission are found in Parts 4 and 5, with Part 3 providing the broader context of the project. . . .

PART 4
LIABILITY IN PUBLIC AND PRIVATE LAW

INTRODUCTION

4.1   Building on the work of Part 3, Part 4 considers some of the limitations inherent in the current system and suggests options for reform. This is done whilst recognising the special nature of public bodies, particularly the multifaceted burdens placed on them as providers of public services.

4.2   Part 4 draws on our analysis of the 'modified corrective justice' principle. This principle suggests that where an aggrieved citizen cannot obtain just redress for substandard administrative action through alternative, non-court based mechanisms, they should be able to access the courts to obtain redress, within certain parameters.

4.3   These parameters are expressed as a package that attempts to balance the interests of aggrieved claimants against the danger that liability might create an undue burden on resources. The consequence of this is to modify the availability of damages in judicial review and create more certainty and predictability in the tortious liability of public bodies.

4.4   In judicial review, it is suggested that damages should be available as a remedy alongside the prerogative remedies where the administrative decision involved 'serious fault' and where the claimant suffers loss. This would essentially harmonise the system with that which already exists for a 'sufficiently serious' breach of EU law.

4.5   In tort, a similar 'serious fault' scheme would apply to the sphere of public action that can be described as 'truly public'. Action undertaken by public bodies that is not 'truly public' would be subject to the ordinary law of tort. It is not proposed that our suggested scheme would replace the current regime in areas such as medical negligence. Within the 'truly public' sphere the tortious standard of negligence would be replaced by a higher standard of 'serious fault'.

4.6   Within both of these schemes, potential liability would only be imposed where it could be demonstrated that the relevant legal regime 'conferred' a benefit on the claimant. Furthermore, the package would entail modifying the blanket rule on joint and several liability in this area of public body liability.

4.7   Lastly, if any change is to simplify the area, then it may be necessary to abolish the action for misfeasance in public office and significantly limit the ambit of breach of statutory duty as it applies to public bodies.

4.8   This Consultation Paper puts forward these proposals in the context of encouraging a real debate on the issues. We invite responses on all aspects of our proposals as well as on the underlying factors to be considered in any proposed reform of this area.

UNDERLYING PRINCIPLES

4.9   In Appendix A, we outline a principle of 'modified corrective justice'. This is the principle on which to base the liability of public bodies in those residual cases that require the court's attention. To summarise our conclusions in Appendix A:

(1)   In general, the principle of corrective justice underpins the relationship between the state and individual claimants;

(2)   However, in certain circumstances the normal principle of corrective justice needs to be modified. This is in order to take into account certain features of the relationship between the state and potential claimants;

(3)   In relation to monetary compensation, the relationship between the state and an individual claimant has a different moral complexion to the relationship between private individual claimants;

(4)   An individual's relationship with and expectations of the state are such that they should look first to non-monetary remedies against the state;

(5)   However, where compensation is in issue, there is a moral case for limiting it to particularly serious conduct where the state is the respondent;

(6)   This modification only applies where the state is undertaking 'truly public' activity. Therefore, it does not apply where the impugned activity could equally have been carried out by a private individual.

4.10   We draw on these principles of 'modified corrective justice' throughout this Part, as they provide the backdrop to the development of the options for reform.

4.11   That said, there are many ways to justify changes to the system, especially in light of the current confusion and over-complication. We do not feel that our options for reform are solely defensible by reference to any particular theory of justice. What is clear is that, within the process of reform of public service delivery, there should be open debate on the system through which citizens can obtain redress for substandard administrative action.. . .

Overview of elements in the proposed scheme

4.101   As the elements suggested for the public and private law schemes are essentially the same, they are discussed together in this Part. The effect of this is that liability would be no wider in private law than in public law and *vice versa*. However, we are not proposing a merging of judicial review with private law actions against public bodies. Cases would still be brought either as an application for judicial review in the Administrative Court or as a private law action in the civil courts. Prerogative remedies would be available only through judicial review.

4.102   A slight difference between the two schemes comes with the nature of the court awards in public and private law. It is intended that damages in the public law scheme be discretionary, so as to 'fit' with the nature of other orders. However, in private law we envisage that, if the strict requirements of the scheme are fulfilled, then damages be awarded as of right.

4.103   Our suggested scheme for dealing with such cases is set out in detail [in the Consultation Paper]. By way of overview, the various elements of that scheme may be summarised as follows:

(1) **Identifying 'truly public' activities**: The proposed ambit of the scheme is when public bodies act in a manner which is 'truly public'. In the public law scheme, this will be satisfied by virtue of the body being amenable to judicial review. As such, the test of 'truly public' will only be applied in private law actions. In determining what constitutes 'truly public', we suggest a test based on whether the contested action was conducted in the exercise of a statutory power or the prerogative. If the action is not 'truly public', then it will be subject to the normal rules of negligence.

(2) **Operation of justiciability rule**: Within our new scheme, we propose a tightening of the definition of justiciability in private law in order to eliminate the grey area of non-justiciability that currently exists and move away from the application of notions of *Wednesbury* unreasonableness in the private law context. To this end, we suggest an interpretation of justiciability akin to that used in judicial review.

(3) **Conferral of a benefit test**: We suggest replacing the duty of care concept in private law with a test to determine whether the underlying legislative scheme confers rights or benefits on the individual claimant. This test would also apply in the public law context. We envisage that this test would be interpreted broadly, in line with the jurisprudence of the European Court of Justice, which has provided the inspiration for this test.

(4) **Serious fault**: The next step in our proposed scheme is to make liability contingent upon the claimant proving 'serious fault' on the part of the public body. The claimant would need to show that the conduct of the public body fell far below the standard expected in the circumstances.

(5) **Causation**: A claimant will be required to show that the loss suffered was caused by an action, omission or decision of the public body.

(6) **Joint and several liability**: The normal rule will be modified giving the courts a discretion to apportion liability when this would [be] equitable in a given situation.

(7) **General rules on damages**: The normal rules on assessing compensatory damages would apply. This would include the rules relating to contributory negligence.

(8) **Immunity**: In areas where Parliament considers it necessary, there would continue to be the opportunity to enact either a general or limited immunity clause, which could be modelled on those already in existence, such as the immunity of the Financial Services Authority provided by section 102 of the Financial Services and Markets Act 2000. The approach we adopt would endorse the legitimacy of government making the judgement that, in a particular policy context, immunity was the correct form of modification to the principles of corrective justice.

4.104   In provisionally proposing these options for reform, we have tried to present a balanced package. The options should not, therefore, be considered in isolation, but rather as a system for ensuring that the small number of deserving claimants who did not find redress through internal or external non-court mechanisms can obtain redress. Respondents may take quite a different view of the problems and solutions, but even within our provisional proposals, there is no doubt room for movement in relation to the individual elements of the scheme . . .

4.105   Included in the options for reform of private law could be the abolition of the torts of misfeasance and breach of statutory duty in most contexts. Whilst we appreciate that in certain contexts the tort of breach of statutory duty should be preserved,[1] the generally restrictive approach adopted by the courts coupled with the inherent inflexibility of the tort in assessing the level of fault on the part of the public body lead us to conclude that our proposed system would provide a more just remedy.

[1] For instance, there are actions under Health and Safety legislation where it would be desirable to retain the action. Additionally, in relation to certain private individuals, it would be advantageous to retain the action.

INDEX